Short Fiction
Classic and Contemporary

Sixth Edition

Charles Bohner
Late of the University of Delaware

Lyman Grant
Austin Community College

PEARSON
Prentice
Hall

Upper Saddle River, New Jersey 07458

Library of Congress Cataloging-in-Publication Data

Short fiction: classic and contemporary/[edited by] Charles Bohner, Lyman Grant.—6th ed.
  p. cm.
  Includes index.
  ISBN 0-13-191675-0
  1. Short stories.   I. Bohner, Charles H.   II. Grant, Lyman.

  PN6120.2.S46   2006
  808'.83'1—dc22

                                                              2005000601

Editorial Director: Leah Jewell
Acquisitions Editor: Vivian Garcia
Editorial Assistant: Melissa Casciano
Director of Marketing: Brandy Dawson
Marketing Assistant: Kara Pottle
Prepress and Manufacturing Buyer: Brian Mackey
Cover Art Director: Jayne Conte
Cover Design: Bruce Kenselaar
Cover Photo: John Wilkes/Getty Images, Inc.—Taxi
Interior Design: Kari Callaghan Mazzola
Composition/Full-Service Project Management: Kari Callaghan Mazzola and John P. Mazzola
Printer/Binder: Courier Companies, Inc.
Cover Printer: Courier Companies, Inc.

This book was set in 9/11 Palatino.

*Grateful acknowledgment is made to the copyright holders on pages 1413–1419, which are hereby
a continuation of this copyright page.*

Pearson Education LTD.
Pearson Education Singapore, Pte. Ltd
Pearson Education, Canada, Ltd
Pearson Education–Japan
Pearson Education Australia PTY, Limited

Pearson Education North Asia Ltd
Pearson Educación de Mexico, S.A. de C.V.
Pearson Education Malaysia, Pte. Ltd
Pearson Education, Upper Saddle River, NJ

10 9 8 7 6 5 4 3 2 1
ISBN 0-13-191675-0

For Will, my son,
a really great guy

—L. G.

Contents

III   SHORT FICTION

V   APPROACHING SHORT FICTION CRITICALLY   1326

Preface

I am very pleased to be editing this sixth edition of *Short Fiction: Classic and Contemporary*. I began work on this book in its fifth edition and tried to continue the breadth and depth that Charles Bohner brought to the first four editions before his death. I have designed this edition to build upon the many changes I brought to the previous edition. The number and variety of stories remains large. The balance between classic stories and more contemporary stories remains more or less the same. The fifth edition's new features, such as the table-of-contents features "A Writer in Depth," "Context," and "Hypertext Fiction," and the end-of-selection feature "Responses," all remain in this sixth edition.

Friends and colleagues from other colleges kindly responded to my requests for evaluation of the text, and I have responded to their suggestions. Though he remains in the anthology with one story, Tomás Rivera is no longer featured in an "A Writer in Depth" section, but Raymond Carver and Joyce Carol Oates are now featured in "A Writer in Depth" sections. Several writers have been removed from the anthology and replaced by a variety of relatively new writers and by some older writers whose work is gaining new audiences: T. Coraghessan Boyle, Alice Carey, Oscar Casares, Charles W. Chesnutt, Philip K. Dick, E. M Forster, William Gibson, Sarah Orne Jewett, Jonathan Nolan, Banana Yoshimoto, and Anzia Yezierska. I have expanded the "Context: Writers on Writing" section with nonfiction essays by Walter Benjamin, Raymond Carver, E. M. Forster, and Joyce Carol Oates, all great critics and theorists of narrative.

The most significant change for this sixth edition is the addition of the section "Approaching Short Fiction Through Film." In this section, I have tried to recognize that many college students have more experience with narrative art by viewing films than by reading fiction. I do not view this addition as acquiescing in any way to the belief that today's college students are poor or reluctant readers. I suppose many are; but I suppose many have always been so. Instead, my view is that college students have had great opportunities through film to "read" narrative; to understand the principles of character, conflict, setting, point of view, language, and tone; and to confront the political, social, psychological, and historical messages of narrative. Certainly many people read films poorly or superficially. But many also read films in very sophisticated ways. The section "Approaching Short Fiction Through Film" attempts to build upon the cinematic literacy of today's students. I hope it provides some means for students and teachers to begin considering how to translate the skills and knowledge of reading fictional film into reading prose fiction.

In addition to the new "Approaching Short Fiction Through Film" section, I have added after many of the stories a feature called "Focus on Film," which offers opportunities for consideration and for writing about a work of short fiction that has been made into a film. For this reason, I have replaced Joseph Conrad's "The Secret Sharer" with his much anthologized story "The Heart of Darkness." In addition, I have brought back James Joyce's "The Dead" from the second and third editions of this anthology. Similarly, some stories new to this edition have been made into films—those by Raymond Carver, Philip K. Dick, William Gibson, Jonathan Nolan, and Anzia Yezierska. I am aware that some of the films are hard to locate—for instance, Yezierska's silent film *Hungry Hearts* from the 1920s—still, I believe it is important to offer these opportunities for thoughtful consideration of narrative art in prose and film. Some people who use this text have large libraries nearby, and everyone has the Internet and a large network of sources for purchasing new and used DVDs and videotapes.

I would like to thank my editors at Prentice Hall/Pearson Education for their support of this project. I also thank the following reviewers for their helpful comments: William A. Davis, College of Notre Dame of Maryland; Angela M. Thompson, University of Oregon; Clay Reynolds, University of Texas at Dallas; Darlene Harbour Unrue, University of Nevada–Las Vegas; Cynthia Maxson, Rio Salado College; Russell Greer, Texas Women's University; Diane Williams, College of Lake County, Illinois; and Allison P. Boyle, Texas Tech University. I thank my colleagues at Austin Community College for directing me to stories. In addition to those I thanked in the previous edition, I thank, this time, Dori Wagner, Anne Marie Thomas, Lee Moore, and Michael Sirmons. My wife Colleen helps in thousands of ways every day.

Finally, my thanks always go to the students at Austin Community College and elsewhere, who are, really, the only reason this book exists. This is what I wrote in the preface to the fifth edition. It still stands: This volume is inspired by my students, past and present. Everyone—professional educators, parents, newspaper pundits—has a pet theory about, a generational nickname for, and an all-too-wise criticism of you students. But this is what I have seen and continue to see: many young adults, and some older ones, too, struggling in and with a culture that expects you to go to college and make the grades and at the same time requires you to meet all your expenses for rent, automobiles, insurance, books, tuition, medical care, and food. On top of that, we've raised you in a culture that entertains you with violence, entices you with erotic images, freely offers you illegal drugs and alcohol, and defines your success by the size of your paycheck. Then we harshly judge you if you happen to acquire a handgun, STD, drug and alcohol addiction, or a suspicion of the value of the liberal arts. Nor, in this land of liberty and individualism, do you have to live very long to find yourself demonized because you are somehow different. I dedicate my work here to you because I admire your hard work, your dedication to the long process of higher education, and your ability to shift through the stories our culture gives you and to create your own life, your own life story—one that nurtures and sustains you. I wish you happy and profitable reading and writing.

I welcome any comments and suggestions you may have about the book.

Lyman Grant

lgrant@austincc.edu
http://www2.austincc.edu/lgrant

Introduction to Short Fiction

Do you know this song?

> *Come 'n listen to my story 'bout a man named Jed,*
> *Poor mountaineer barely kept his family fed.*
> *An' then one day, he was shootin' at some food,*
> *An' up thru the ground came a bubblin' crude.*
> *Oil that is! Black gold! Texas tea!*
>
> *Well, the first thing ya know, Jed's a millionaire.*
> *Kin-folk said, "Jed, move away from there."*
> *Said" Californy is the place y' oughta be,"*
> *So they loaded up the truck, and they moved to Beverly,*
> *Hills that is! Swimmin' pools! Movie stars!*

It would be frightening to know how many people in the world can sing the theme song to "The Beverly Hillbillies." Whether they learned it in the 1960s, when the television show originally appeared, or whether they learned it in reruns and syndication in the decades since, millions of people, worldwide, are familiar with the basic outline of this one family's story. The strange thing is that this family never existed.

At one time in the United States, there were families like the Clampetts who lived in the backwoods, growing up poor and unsophisticated. But Jed, Granny, Jethro, and Daisy Mae are not living, breathing people; they are characters imagined by writers, actors, and directors, and finally by us viewers. However, the fact that this family isn't real and that they never experienced any of the events we see them experience does not change the other equally valid fact that we viewers enjoy watching them. Somehow all of us who live our lives in a very real world of jobs, taxes, families, traffic, and so on, find pleasure and even a little enlightenment in the story of these people who never lived. The pleasure we receive from their story is an example of the magic of fiction.

THE TRUTH OF FICTION

What is *fiction?* Well, the answer to that can be a bit hard to pin down. On one hand, fiction is simply made-up stories, in other words, lies. On the other, fiction is a kind of artistic enterprise that answers the question "What if?" What if, some Hollywood producer asks, a family of hillbillies strikes it rich and moves to Beverly Hills? In the short story "Chrysanthemums," John Steinbeck asks what if a lonely woman lived on an isolated ranch and a traveling salesman visited the ranch. In "Sonny's Blues," James Baldwin asks what if an algebra teacher in Harlem learned his brother, a jazz pianist, was addicted to heroin. Part of these "fictions" can be truthful and come from the writer's experience or education, and part of them can be made up.

Other forms of writing depend on the veracity and sincerity of the writer—tax codes, menus, magazine articles, business letters. Certainly these documents would lose their usefulness for the reader if the writer treated the writing of these as exercises in imagination. But there is another kind of truth that fiction attempts to capture and portray.

In his essay "The Storyteller," excerpted in the Context section of this anthology, Walter Benjamin writes that the story "does not aim to convey the pure essence of the things, like information or a report. It sinks the thing into the life of the storyteller in order to bring it out of him again."

Two stories in this anthology can guide us toward understanding what Benjamin means. Toward the end of "Storyteller," Leslie Marmon Silko writes, "The old man would not change the story even when he knew the end was approaching. Lies could not stop what was coming." With such statements as this one, Silko enriches her story about a young Native-American woman in a snow-covered land, the dying man she lives with, and the lies and injustices of the Anglo Americans there to exploit the people and the land. The man is weaving a story, half-deliriously, about a bear stalking a hunter. We know that, somehow, this story is the story of the old man's life, his life being stalked by death. It is also the story of the young woman, who is also stalked.

But their tale is also the story of all storytellers, of all writers, who have a story to tell and will tell it until the story ends where it must end. The best storytellers know that within each tale there is a logic and inevitability that must be honored. In Grace Paley's "A Conversation with My Father," the father tells his daughter, who is writing a story for him, "As a writer that's your main trouble. You don't want to recognize it. Tragedy! Plain tragedy! Historical tragedy!" Then he adds later, "Truth first."

"Truth first." In fiction, this truth isn't necessarily the factual truth we strive for in balancing our checkbooks; it isn't the ontological or metaphysical truths we search for in philosophy and theology. Instead, it is the kind of truth we say is "true to life." This kind of truth says, "This is the way life is. This is the truth about human beings. This is the truth of what it feels like to be human." It is a kind of truth that is experienced, not known. It is a kind of truth very different from "The meeting starts at 10:00 tomorrow morning."

Benjamin sums up these beliefs:

Seen this way, the storyteller joins the ranks of the teachers and sages. He has counsel—not for a few situations, as the proverb does, but for many, like the sage. For it is granted to him to reach back to a whole lifetime (a life, incidentally, that comprises not only his own experience but no little of the experience of others; what the storyteller knows from hearsay is added to his own). His gift is the ability to relate his life; his distinction, to be able to tell his entire life. The storyteller: he is the man who could let the wick of his life be consumed completely by the gentle flame of his story. This is the basis of the incomparable aura about the storyteller, in Leskov as in Hauff, in Poe as in Stevenson. The storyteller is the figure in which the righteous man encounters himself.

THE EXPERIENCE OF FICTION

This anthology focuses on one type of fiction, the short story. Other kinds of fictions include novels, plays, epic poems, monologues, fables, and fairy tales. But these represent only the forms of fiction that are read. Fiction also is the basis for movies, for television programs like situation comedies and police dramas, for many forms of advertisement, for jokes told in the office, for exaggerated tales of fishing successes, and for stories told by teenagers to their parents. How these kinds of fictions differ from one another is a matter of much discussion among writers, critics, and teachers. So it is probably not an expression of cynicism or laziness to say that a short story is a story that is short. What we mean by story can be described as a series of events with characters in conflict somewhere in time and place (setting). These events are communicated in prose (as opposed, say, to a narrative painting or poem or song), and the events are told from a point of view with an authorial perspective or attitude (point of view and tone). For a definition of *short*, we can rely on Edgar Allan Poe's definition that states the short story can be read in about an hour or two.

Understanding why people tell stories is one way to understand what fiction is and what it can do. What can creative fiction do that other means of communicating can't do? Rhetoricians sometimes look at the purposes of communication as being to express oneself, to entertain others, to inform others, and to persuade others. This is only one way to examine the purposes of communication. But perhaps it can be useful here. These critics then say the main purpose of literature is to *entertain* others. And when one looks at a world of communication—varying as it does from laundry lists, diaries, manifestoes, dictionaries, advertisements for floor wax—saying that writers of short stories desire to entertain does makes a certain amount of sense.

How we are entertained, of course, depends on who we are. Still, we have one thing in common. We want to be moved; we want a story to provoke emotions in us. In this basic way, a short story, like any work of art, like any entertainment—from carnival rides, to dinner parties, to computer games, to sports—must grab us on an emotional level. We will discuss later in this part of the book the specific techniques or elements that writers use to grab us emotionally: plots, characters, conflicts, settings, language, tone. All of these are ways that writers entertain us. They create intriguing plots; describe interesting, likeable, despicable, fun, horrible characters; place their stories in times and places that we care about, want to know more about, can immerse ourselves in; and use language that is beautiful, emotionally disturbing, challenging, simple, or rich. Certainly, the worst charge that can be made about an entertainment, including a short story, is that it is boring and forgettable. Having said that, we should think about what readers find compelling.

Here again we can learn something from the rhetoricians. Some of us are entertained by people's personal stories; we like stories when we think the writer and certainly the narrator want to *express* themselves, telling us who they are, what they have experienced, how they felt about that experience. In this text, examples of this kind of work abound—"A & P," "A Party down at the Square," "Rape Fantasies," "I Want to Know Why," "A Scrap of Time." In so many stories, the narrator entertains us because we feel that we identify with the character telling the story, the one who experiences the events in the story, and to a certain extent we identify the authors with their characters. We feel, like any good listener, that the character is personally talking to us.

Readers of short stories also enjoy learning how to make their lives better. Writers of short stories then sometimes attempt to *persuade*. The writer may tell us a story about how terribly someone is treated or about habits and beliefs that have bad consequences. Some of us like this kind of literature, literature that is political or sociological in nature. A famous example in literary history is Upton Sinclair's novel *The Jungle,* about meat packing plants. After publication of the novel, new health laws were passed to protect the public. But a writer of short stories doesn't necessarily aspire to effect so great a change in society, but perhaps simply wants to change the public one story, one reader, at a time. One might suspect at the end of "Tiny, Smiling Daddy" that Mary Gaitskill wants the reader to consider how he or she treats his or her children. It seems likely that in "The Man Who Was Almost a Man" Richard Wright wants to argue that African Americans in the South are mistreated and exploited and that society must change. In "The Death of Ivan Ilych," it is probably safe to believe that Leo Tolstoy wants his readers to change their lives, to abandon their love of status and money, and to live a naturally moral and simple Christian life.

Readers also find pleasure when writers attempt to *inform* them. Certainly this is one of the important reasons any one reads manuals, textbooks, travel books, and so on. In basic ways, short stories inform us how people can behave; they teach us something about human psychology. In reading a story, we can recognize ourselves and thus understand ourselves a bit better, or we recognize others and better understand them. In some stories we learn about places we have never been or moments in history we may not have experienced. Steinbeck gives us the experience of living in the Salinas Valley; Mary Lavin introduces us to the home life of the Irish working class; Bessie Head dramatizes the myths of rural South Africans; Hanif Kureishi portrays the lives of immigrant Pakistanis in England. Last, storytellers make us think about ideas that may not have occurred to us before; in other words, they inform us about the world of ideas. In "The Birthmark," Hawthorne illustrates how scientific values can go wrong. Leslie Marmon Silko reveals the personal side of cultural conflicts.

Ever since Edgar Allan Poe reviewed Nathaniel Hawthorne's *Twice-Told Tales* and helped define the short story, others have been trying to redefine it. Writers, being creative people who are always looking for new ways to imagine what already exists, attempt to alter what has occurred and to find new definitions, to shift, expand, and refocus their art. Still, a good starting place at understanding short fiction is to think of it as a prose work that seeks to express an understanding of the nature of life through, as Poe theorized, a focused unified effect. The number of characters involved is few; the number and kinds of conflicts the characters have are few; the point of view is usually constant and clear; the language is direct and crisp. This said, we must realize that stories are written often and to great effect that break each and perhaps every aspect of the definition. But often the effect those stories have depends on their *not* being what we have come to expect in a story. Like wrestlers bouncing off the ropes of the wrestling rings, writers of these stories often create power by stretching the boundaries of what we have come to think of as a story.

THE ELEMENTS OF FICTION

Stories come, so to speak, in many shapes and sizes. But, as noted earlier, they all seem to possess in varying degrees of importance the same elements. Luckily, the language that critics use to discuss these elements are common terms that we can understand, generally, without any special training. These elements are plot, character, conflict, point of view, setting, language, and tone. All of these elements combine to create the theme, or central idea of the story. The remaining pages of this "Introduction to Short Fiction" are devoted to examining each of these elements. As we define each of these elements, we will look at other related terms and concepts that help us understand the element more completely. In addition, we will take a passage from a short story in this anthology and examine how the author treats the element of fiction in that passage.

THEME

Have you ever had a "Life Saver Moment"? A few years ago, the company that makes Life Savers candy advertised its product by depicting a child having some kind of accident, making some kind of mistake, getting his or her feelings hurt. Then a father or grandfather would sit next to the crying child and offer a Life Savers candy and a comforting story. "Did I ever tell you about the time when your aunt Juanita . . ."

Writers of short stories are like our friends or relatives telling us stories to make us feel better or to teach us something we might not yet know. The writer's purpose is to entertain us by dramatizing his or her ideas about the nature of life and how we humans experience it. When we can in turn rephrase these ideas in a sentence or two, we have begun formulating what is called the *theme,* or the central idea, of the story.

How we think about theme in fiction can be illustrated by remembering a time when our roommate watched us listening on the phone to a grandparent. The grandparent tells us a long and confusing story about a time when someone tempted her to do something she normally would not have done. When we got off the phone our roommate asked, "What was all that about?" And we said, "I don't know, but I think she was trying to tell me to be careful about who my friends are." In this case, we have formulated a statement of the theme for the grandparent's story. The grandparent never told us to be careful, but by relating us the story she let us infer what the story meant.

Stories vary in how difficult it is to discern a theme for them. David Foster Wallace's story "Suicide as a Sort of Present," though unusual in presentation, is fairly straightforward thematically. The brief story is almost just a list of the various ways that a mother behaves toward her child. But by the end, we realize the story is a kind of warning about selfishness and cruelty and narcissism.

Some writers even directly guide us toward their themes. At the end of James Joyce's "Araby," the protagonist, who is looking back on a youthful obsession, states, "Gazing up into the darkness, I saw myself as a creature driven and derided by vanity; and my eyes burned with anguish and anger." While this is not a statement of the story's theme, it does guide us in understanding the story as a comment about youth and love and memory.

To develop a clear understanding of a story's theme or central idea, we consider all the elements of a short story—characters, conflict, setting, point of view, language, and tone. In some stories, like Jack London's "To Build a Fire," setting is very important; in others, like W. Somerset Maugham's "The Outstation," character and conflict are central to the theme. In a story like Jamaica Kincaid's "Girl," language and point of view stand out. As we read more stories, we will find it easier to see how writers highlight particular elements of fiction.

All the elements of fiction contribute to our understanding of the theme of a story. For the most part, they can work without our even recognizing their role in the story—just as we can enjoy a movie without noticing a particular use of camera angle or a repetition of a particular color. However, it is true for most people that the more they understand about the elements of fiction the better they understand and enjoy a story. By knowing what to look for in a short story, by knowing what tools writers have at their disposal, we will be better able to see how a story's construction guides us toward perceiving particular themes. Most writers have read many, many short stories; therefore, they know what others have done and they use and build upon that knowledge. Sometimes they construct a strong, traditional story; sometimes they experiment to make a story like no one else has made before. By becoming more familiar with the elements of fiction, we can recognize what writers' purposes might have been. Certainly, we can read more fully and more creatively what we see on the page.

PLOT

The plot of the story might be defined simply as what happens. But plot is much more than a mere listing of events. E. M. Forster is famous for saying, "'The king died and then the queen died,' is a story. 'The king died and then the queen died of heartbreak' is a plot." While some critics have disagreed with Forster's use of the word "story," he makes an important distinction.

For instance, you might read someone's daily planner, which records the following events. Do you think these events make a plot?

6:30	Wake up, shower, breakfast (cereal, fruit, coffee)
8:30	Meeting with Peterson
9:00	Work on contracts with MJD
10:00	Telephone conference with Johnson (New York Office) and McBride (Chicago Office)
11:00	Work on contracts with MJD
12:00	Gym
1:15	Lunch (sandwich and juice)
1:30	Meeting with Staff
2:00	Work Session Goals for next year
4:00	Meeting with HR re: Insurance/Contract Employees
5:00	Complete Contracts with MJD
7:00	Dinner/Castle Hill/w/Pat (swordfish, pilaf, wine, a Semillon)
10:00	Home

There is much that a reader can glean by looking at the above schedule, much to learn and much to infer about the person who keeps such a calendar. But the list of events remains just that—a list of events. And a plot is more than a retelling of events, more than one thing happening after another. All of us, every day, lead lives in which one event follows the next, but many of our days lack drama—that essence that says that today we are living a story.

In telling stories, then, writers look for and highlight the emotional and dramatic connection between the events. It is this drama that turns events, individual episodes, into a *plot*. One thing the list lacks that prevents it from becoming a plot is the character's motivation, his or her needs, desires, fears, and hopes. Another missing ingredient is conflict, the forces that prevent the character from being happy or successful, the forces that want the character to fail.

To turn the above list of events into a plot, all we need do is imagine the 8:30 appointment with Peterson is a meeting with the character's boss, and Peterson says that if the contract with MJD is not completed by the next morning then the character will be fired. However, Pat, with whom the character has dinner planned that night, is the character's estranged spouse, who has said this night is the last chance to discuss reconciliation and that one of the conditions of their reconciliation is that Pat wants the character to be more successful at work. Now the day's events begin to have a significance they didn't have before. Now each of these events contributes or detracts from the completion of that contract and the possible reconciliation.

The plot of a traditional story follows a predictable structure. The writer begins the story providing basic information about the story's characters and setting. The writer establishes the point of view and tone of the story. These early paragraphs are called the *exposition*.

Let's look at the first paragraph from Isabel Allende's story "And of Clay Are We Created."

The story begins with a startling image.

Basic information, like names, is provided.

The setting and an atmosphere is established.

Background establishes how the television news made the girl familiar to viewers throughout the country.

Second character introduced. Last sentence hints at, foreshadows, events that will follow.

They discovered the girl's head protruding from the mudpit, eyes wide open, calling soundlessly. She had a First Communion name, Azucena, Lily. In that vast cemetery where the odor of death was already attracting vultures from far away, and where the weeping of orphans and wails of the injured filled the air, the little girl obstinately clinging to life became the symbol of the tragedy. The television cameras transmitted so often the unbearable image of the head budding like a black squash from the clay where there was no one who did not recognize her and know her name. And every time we saw her on the screen, right behind her was Rolf Carlé, who had gone there on assignment, never suspecting that he would find a fragment of his past, lost thirty years before.

After this basic information is communicated, the writer sets the plot into action by establishing a *conflict*. Then the bulk of the story follows as the conflict propels various actions to occur. The characters will react to those actions, and more conflict develops in other ways. This section of the story, called the *development* or *complication*, is described as having rising action, meaning that the tension in the story is heightened.

In "And of Clay Are We Created," the plot develops, first, when we read in the second paragraph of the great disaster that strikes a small mountain town.

The towns in the valley went about their daily life, deaf to the moaning of the earth until that fateful Wednesday night in November when a prolonged roar announced the end of the world, and walls of snow broke loose, rolling an avalanche of clay, stones, and water that descended on the villages and buried them beneath unfathomable meters of telluric vomit.

The character Rolf Carlé, hearing of the avalanche, "stuffed his gear in the green canvas backpack he always carried." In fewer than two paragraphs, Carlé is by Azucena's side, trying to help her. For the next several pages, the plot progresses for three days with Carlé trying to help Azucena, but experiencing frustration as he tries to pull her out, find pumps, and appeal to the president of the country.

As the complication of the plot increases, writers sometimes increase the tension by including events that occur before the story begins. One technique, called *flashback*, introduces a character's memories of events that may have occurred long before the rest of the events of the story. Flashback is used in "And of Clay Are We Created."

> Wandering in the mist of his memories he found his sister Katharina, a sweet retarded child who spent her life hiding, with the hope that her father would forget the disgrace of her having been born. With Katharina, Rolf crawled beneath the dining room table, with her hid under the long white tablecloth, two children forever embraced, alert to footsteps and voices. . . . He understood then that all his exploits as a reporter, the feats that had won him such recognition and fame, were merely an attempt to keep his most ancient fears at bay. . . .

Another technique some writers use is to abandon chronological order completely. In films, *Pulp Fiction* and *Annie Hall* employ this technique, and force the viewer to reconstruct the chronological order after having seen the story. William Faulkner's short story "A Rose for Emily" is a noteworthy example in this anthology.

Other works in this anthology stretch the boundaries of plot development even further. The most radical examples are the hypertext stories. In a Context reading in this anthology, "Hypertext Fiction," Michael Joyce points out that fiction, as we most often experience it, has some "terminal node," some last event that the story works its way toward. Hypertext fiction, instead, destroys this "myth of emerging order" by deemphasizing the goal of finding an end to the plot. Presented most often on computers, hypertext fiction allows readers to freely navigate, more or less randomly, from one portion of a story to another via hypertext links. The various plot moments in a story, or the nodes, consequently can be read in any order that the reader chooses; therefore, the plot of the story develops differently for each reader.

A second work of fiction, "Memento Mori" by Jonathan Nolan, became the inspiration for the film *Memento*. While the short story does not radically alter plot development, the film does by presenting the plot moments in backward chronological order, moving from the scenes most recent in time to those further back in time. Interestingly, the film still maintains the traditional structure of exposition, conflict, complication, and climax.

After a certain amount of complication, the tension will reach its highest level and then begin to release. This section, called the *turning point* or *climax*, is the moment toward which the story has been building. Decisions are made or not made, actions taken or not taken, in a final major confrontation. The last portion of the story, called the *resolution* or *denouement*, pulls together whatever loose strands of the story that still need to be completed or tied together. We won't include the climax of "And of Clay Are We Created" here, but the resolution of the plot—the story of a man trying to save a young girl from danger—is seen in these last sentences addressed to Rolf,

> Your cameras lie forgotten in a closet; you do not write or sing; you sit long hours before the window, staring at the mountains. Beside you, I wait for you

to complete the voyage into yourself, for the old wounds to heal. I know that when you return from your nightmares, we shall again walk hand in hand, as before.

As noted earlier, the movement of a story from exposition to complication to climax to resolution is the arrangement of the traditional plot. Yet many stories in this volume complicate or modify that general structure. Some stories open with a clear conflict and dive immediately into the complication. Others may end at the turning point on the last sentence. Others may postpone the conflict to relatively late in the story. Some stories, usually those longer ones, develop a series of conflicts; other very brief tales may have only one major event that peaks very quickly.

Two factors that are part of our enjoyment of a plot are surprise and suspense. *Surprise* is a plot device very popular with late nineteenth century writers such as Guy de Maupassant, O'Henry, and Kate Chopin, though, of course, writers still employ it. Surprise is a sudden shift in the direction of the plot, often at the very end of the story. At its worst, it is merely a trick where the narrator withholds vital information from the reader. At its best, surprise in a story can be very enjoyable and can enhance the theme.

Suspense is a plot device used to create in the reader an anticipation of the outcome of events. In some stories, suspense is created by forcing the reader to ask the questions *who, what,* or *how.* Mysteries, such as those by Edgar Allan Poe, use this type of suspense. In other stories, the reader, knowing *who, what* and *how,* is made to ask the question *when.* Much of the power of Flannery O'Connor's "A Good Man Is Hard to Find" derives from this kind of suspense.

CHARACTER

In our daily lives one of the greatest joys is to meet people with whom we feel some connection. "You won't believe it," we will say to a friend, "but I met the most interesting person today at work." What did we like about this person? The way he looked, the way he spoke, the way he behaved in a certain situation, his experiences and attitudes toward life? All of these factors can be what makes us care about a person and care what happens to that person.

In a work of fiction, perhaps the most important element, as least as far as grabbing the interest of the general reader, is character. Often on a first reading of a story, the characters are what determine if we enjoy the experience of reading the story or not. Are there characters that we can identify with, that we can sympathize with, and, on another level, are there characters that we can dislike, disapprove of, root against? If the power of fiction resides in the emotional reactions it provokes in the readers, characters may well be the main ingredient in that power.

Generally, fairly early in the story, the reader becomes aware that the narrator is focusing on one or more characters. There may be many characters in the story, but the narrator devotes most of the description of actions and personality to very few of the characters. By the end of the story, we may have learned a great deal of information about those characters. Sometimes, the narrator may even be one of the characters. In the best short stories, as we read we begin to care about what happens to the characters. We understand why they do the things they do, and we notice if they behave consistently with how the narrator has described them.

Literary critics have created a few categories to help us understand how writers develop their characters. The first distinction is the main character. Sometimes this person is called the *protagonist.* Usually, this character is the focus of the story, like a lead actor in a movie, the lead singer in a band. In some stories a second main character might oppose the protagonist in some manner. This character is called the *antagonist.* A story may also have a number of *secondary characters;* they may even perform important acts in the story, but you would never say the story is about them. In the story "A & P" for instance, Sammy is the main character, the protagonist. Lengel is the antagonist. Secondary characters include Stokesie, Queenie and her friends, and even the customer who is watching for a mistake.

Another classification method defines characters as round, flat, and stereotypical. This distinction is described by E. M. Forster in the excerpt from "Plot," from *Aspects of the Novel,* included as a Context reading in this anthology. *Round* characters are those the narrator tells us a good deal about, characters that we see as complicated, that we know in various ways. These characters strike us as unique creations, not necessarily like anyone we have ever met before. *Flat* characters are those that we do not know much about, who seem one dimensional. Sometimes a writer chooses to make the protagonist of a story a flat character, and there is probably a thematic reason for doing so. At other times, flat characters often perform set functions in the story; they are doorkeepers, next door neighbors, co-workers. *Stereotypical* characters are those that the writer has put into the story to fill classic stock roles. They tend to be flat characters, and they resemble every other character who fills that role in other stories: the harping mother-in-law, the distant dad, the dumb blonde, the nosey reporter, the rude frat boy. In some cases, the writer may make the main character a stereotype, as did Susan Sontag in "The Dummy." Most often main characters will be a round, and secondary characters will be flat and stereotypical.

Characters are also classified as dynamic or static. A *dynamic* character is one who in the course of the story changes in some way. The character might begin the story happy and then near the end of the story become sad. A sad, lonely character might find happiness and love. A frightened character might perform an act of bravery. In all these cases, the character develops and alters as the story progresses. A wonderful example of a dynamic character is Katherine Mansfield's Miss Brill, who throughout the story views herself in a particular way, but who, because of comments made by some young people in the park, can no longer see herself in that way. A *static* character is one who does not change. For instance, in Eudora Welty's "A Worn Path," Phoenix Jackson goes through many experiences on her way to town, but it would seem that none of those experiences changes her in any way. She is strong and determined at the beginning of the story and remains so to the end.

Examining whether characters are static or dynamic is important not only for main characters, but for all characters, including the narrator. Sometimes different characters react to the same situation in different ways, as in Hemingway's "Hills Like White Elephants." Other times the narrator's attitude may change in ways unlike the other characters, as in Raymond Carver's "Cathedral."

It must be said, however, that these terms—protagonist, antagonist, round, flat, stereotypical, static, and dynamic—merely represent methods for helping us get at the most important aspects of fictional characters: who they are and what they do. What do their behaviors and attitudes tell us about life? As readers and critics, our jobs are to examine the text closely and to look for how the characters are described by the narrator and by other characters, how the characters describe themselves, and how the characters behave and think. Applying the correct term is less important than understanding who the characters are.

Below is a passage from D. H. Lawrence's "The Rocking-Horse Winner." In this passage notice how the conversation between a boy and his mother tell us many things about them and other members of the family.

Paul is polite.	"Mother," said the boy Paul one day, "why don't we keep a car of our own? Why do we always use uncle's or else a taxi?"
Mother thinks she is poor.	"Because we're the poor members of the family," said the mother.
	"But why *are* we, mother?"
Mother is bitter. *Mother blames father.* *Mother places more value in luck than in money.* *Paul is innocent in some ways.*	"Well—I suppose," she said slowly and bitterly, "it's because your father has no luck."
	The boy was silent for some time.
	"Is luck money, mother?" he said, rather timidly.
	"No, Paul. Not quite. It's what causes you to have money."
	"Oh!" said Paul vaguely. "I thought when Uncle Oscar said *filthy lucker,* it meant money."
	"*Filthy lucre* does mean money," said the mother. "But it's lucre, not luck."
	"Oh!" said the boy. "Then what *is* luck, mother?"
Idea that mother thinks luck is better than money is reinforced.	"It's what causes you to have money. If you're lucky you have money. That's why it's better to be born lucky than rich. If you're rich, you may lose your money. But if you're lucky, you will always get more money."
Paul is learning to view father as his mother does.	"Oh! Will you? And is father not lucky."
	"Very unlucky, I should say," she said bitterly.
Paul is becoming confused.	The boy watched with unsure eyes. "Why?" he asked.
Mother feels helpless.	"I don't know. Nobody ever knows why one person is lucky and another unlucky."
	"Don't they? Nobody at all? Does *nobody* know?"
Mother believes God is silent.	"Perhaps God. But He never tells."
	"He ought to then. And aren't you lucky either, mother?"
Mother restates helplessness and restates view of husband.	"I can't be, if I married an unlucky husband."

We read stories in much the same way that we react to our day-to-day lives. We watch and listen and make judgments about the things we see and hear. Often writers directly tell us what characters are like, as when Lawrence uses the word "bitterly" to describe the mother's speech. At other times, writers present material less directly, as in Lawrence's portrayal of Paul as innocent and polite. In this passage, he doesn't say Paul is innocent, but he shows us that Paul is when Paul confuses the meaning of *lucre* and *lucker*.

One thing we can learn from stage and screen actors is to look at the character's motivations. Actors ask what their characters *want* in the stories they are in. To develop a scene, actors examine what characters want in each scene that they are in. In the scene on page 11 from "The Rocking-Horse Winner," what does Paul want? Might he want to make his mother happy? Anything else? And what does the mother want? Does she want to be lucky? Does she want someone to save her? Does she want to be alone? Examining the motivations of a character is a step toward understanding conflict in a story.

The final and perhaps most important facet of understanding characters in a short story is determining their relevance to the story's theme. Part of this analysis may seem obvious. If the characters are all members of the same family, then perhaps the theme of the story concerns family. If some characters are religious, the theme might make a statement about faith or other such matters. Other clues derive from more specific aspects of characters, their gender, ethnicity, or economic status. Occasionally, writers use these aspects to develop a theme about what it means to be a man or woman, a Hispanic, or Anglo American, a member of the middle class. In some stories, such as Stephen Crane's "The Open Boat" or Jorge Luis Borges's "The Other Duel," no one character is indisputably the central character. Perhaps in these instances, the theme deals with a larger generality about human nature or a human's place in nature.

CONFLICT

Most of us would probably say that in life we seek peace, happiness, contentment, and tranquility. Many of us, in fact, spend a considerable effort avoiding conflict in our lives. Someone yells at us and we walk away. The IRS asks for more money, and we write a check, rather than call a lawyer. Interestingly, the last thing we want in an entertainment is peace and tranquility. "I hated that movie! Nothing happened!" we might say. Or after a football game that ends 64–0, we might confess that "I wish it would have been more of a contest. I felt like leaving at halftime."

As an element in fiction, *conflict* is inextricably linked to plot and character. Conflict, the tensions in and between characters, propels the actions of the characters, turning individual actions into a plot. Characters respond to conflicts, often forcing other characters to act; then they react to those other characters' actions. Conflict, then, becomes the force that creates the tennis match sensation in many stories. It is that tension that makes us sit on the edge of our chairs and ask "what next?"

Short stories, unlike novels, are noted for the sharp focus of the conflicts. Critics have described conflicts being of two types: external and internal. *External conflicts* are often the most obvious. One type of external conflict shows one character in conflict with another character, a father and son, a mother and daughter, a worker and boss, a cop and robber. Joyce Carol Oates's story "Shopping" explores the conflict between a mother and daughter. Another kind of external conflict occurs when a character must fight society or large institutions. Stories that deal with racism and sexism have these conflicts. Ralph Ellison's story "A Party down at the Square" illustrates conflict between Anglos and African Americans, specifically how racism affects Anglos. A third kind of external conflict exists when a character is in conflict with natural forces, such as cold, heat, rain, tornadoes, and the like. Jack London's "To Build a Fire" is a famous example of a man confronting terrible cold, but Tomás Rivera's ". . . And the Earth Did Not Devour Him" just as powerfully explores a family confronting scorching heat. A fourth kind of external conflict occurs when characters confront forces they might call God or Fate. The Biblical story *Job* is a well-known example, as is Sophocles' *Oedipus Rex*. Elements of this conflict appear in Isaac Bashevis Singer's "Gimpel the Fool."

Conflicts also occur within a character. These *internal conflicts* are conflicts of self-doubt, self-hatred, fear, or insecurity. Characters may have pasts they want to forget. They may have done something they have difficulty forgiving themselves for. Some characters may desire something they feel has been denied them. Very often an internal conflict evolves into an external one. For instance, a worker who feels insecure about job performance (internal conflict) may treat co-workers rudely, and they, in turn, begin plotting against the worker (external conflict). In the beginning of John Updike's "A & P," Sammy hates his job and the customers, but it is not until his boss Lengel enters the scene that the conflict becomes external.

The important question is not so much what kind of conflict exists in a story as what the conflict is over. In the long run, conflicts are about values, philosophies, views of what is good and what is evil. Two characters may have a conflict over money, but that really doesn't say what the conflict is about. Might not the conflict be over what to do with the money—save it, spend it, spend it on what? And this can lead us to understand that one character believes that anything can happen in the world and one needs to be prepared; the other character believes that one should have a good time when one can. So the conflict is really over issues of trust and safety, freedom and pleasure.

In interpreting a story, the key factor is how the conflict is resolved. A story's theme is indicated by how the conflict is resolved, if the writer resolves it. We ask ourselves which side of the conflict wins, if any? For instance, if the unhappy worker overcomes the insecurities and wins favor of the co-workers or if the worker is framed by the co-workers and fired, the theme of the story will be changed drastically.

The following excerpts from Mary Gaitskill's "Tiny, Smiling Daddy" present a portion of the developing conflict within Stew Thorne and between Stew and his daughter Kitty. We can begin simply by looking at Stew's name. He is someone who stews, whose conflicts are at a low boil. In addition, he is someone who is prickly; someone, like a thorn, who is pricks and stings those who try to get near.

In these sentences, the first two sentences of the story, we can see that the man has conflicts. He is unhappy and lonely. He seems to have few friends, And he has actually driven some old friends away.	He lay in his reclining chair, barely awake enough to feel the dream moving just under his thoughts. It felt like one of those pure, beautiful dreams in which he was young again, and filled with the realization that the friends who had died, or gone away, or decided that they didn't like him anymore, had really been there all along loving him.

In a couple of paragraphs Stew receives a telephone call from his friend, Norm, whose name may indicate that he is a "normal guy," the norm.

Here is the incident that precipitates the major conflict in the story. If this incident had not occurred the rest of the days events would not have followed. It begins to show both his inner conflict and his outer ones.

"My daughter's got a subscription to this magazine, *Self.* And they printed an article that Kitty wrote about fathers and daughters talking to each other, and she, well, she wrote about you. Laurel showed it to me.

"My God."

In a following passage, we learn more about Stew's inner conflicts. And at the end of the passage we learn the cause of his conflict with his daughter.

In this passage, we learn a great deal about the vulnerability that Stew feels. He suffers a great conflict between his own need to be private and others desires for their lives, including their relationships with him, to be public. There seems to be a conflict between privacy and openness.

He felt helplessness move through his body the way a swimmer feels a large sea creature pass beneath him. How could she have done this to him? She knew how he dreaded exposure of any kind, she knew the way he guarded himself against strangers, the way he carefully drew all the curtains when twilight approached so that no one could see them walking through the house. She knew how ashamed he had been when, at sixteen, she announced that she was lesbian.

Later, after Stew remembers various incidents in his relationships with Kitty and incidents of his own childhood, he returns home from the market. His conflicts this day begin to create conflicts with his wife.

His conflicts with Kitty opened a door to vast conflicts he feels he has with the world at large.

"No, nothing is all right. I'm a tired old man in a shitty world I don't want to be in. I go out there, it's like walking on knives. Everything is an attack—the ugliness, the cheapness, the rudeness, everything." He sensed her withdrawing from him into her world of disgruntlement.

The narrator continues to explore Stew's past, this time with his own brutal father. We begin to learn that Stew has no resources for dealing with his own conflicts with his father. Then finally he remembers an important moment of his own cruelty to Kitty.

In this passage, we see the depth, not only of his sense of shame, but of his sense of guilt. Stew has at last discovered that he has become the mean, cruel father, his own father had been.

"You're a lesbian? Fine," he said. "You mean nothing to me. You walk out that door, it doesn't matter. And if you come back in, I'm going to spit in your face. I don't care if I'm on my deathbed, I'll still have the energy to spit in your face."

The story ends with Stew, more or less, alone. His wife completes massaging his shoulders; then "Marsha's hand lingered on him for a moment. Then she moved and sat away from him on the couch." The conflict is unresolved. It is as if Stew's conflicts, his inability to find a way past his father's cruelty and into kindness and compassion, have left him totally isolated.

THE NARRATOR AND POINT OF VIEW

We've all had experiences listening to older couples tell stories from their early days together. One might say to you, "Did we ever tell you about our first trip to New York? That was some trip."

Then the other will add, "Oh, yes, that was a wonderful trip."

"Wonderful?" the first will shout. "What trip were you on? It was a disaster. You were too cheap to check into a good hotel."

Then the second will respond, "Cheap? That hotel was fine. Right off Broadway! It was romantic."

Then for twenty minutes we hear not one, but two stories about the trip. It was the same trip, but the couple tells the story as if it was two different trips. What we have experienced is the importance of *point of view*. In telling a story, who tells it is of paramount importance.

Choosing a narrative point of view is perhaps the most important and most difficult decision a writer of a story makes. Point of view—like plot, character, setting, and language—is a creative decision; however, it is also very much a technical decision. Someone has to tell the story. That someone is called the *narrator*. But the question is who will that narrator be and what does that narrator know.

One way to understand point of view is to think of movies. When making a movie, the director must think about where the camera stands and what the camera looks at in every scene. In a horror movie, for instance, sometimes the camera becomes the monster, stalking the prey. At other times in horror movies, the camera becomes the person, slowly moving forward into the dark unknown. In other scenes, the camera, in a distant panning shot like the one with the feather in *Forest Gump*, allows the viewer to see more than any character in the movie could see. Sometimes we hear a voiceover, as if one of the characters were telling the story. In the movie *Annie Hall*, Woody Allen shows us two characters talking with each other, and in subtitles he adds what the characters are thinking, but not saying. All these methods in movies are in some form employed in short stories.

Critics and teachers fundamentally agree on the basic kinds of point of view used in fiction. The terms used relate to the types of personal pronouns: first person (I, we), second person (you), and third person (he, she, it, they). A first-person narrative is told by "I," one of the characters in the story. That character may be the main character (as in Leslie Marmon Silko's "Yellow Woman"), a supporting character (as in

Conrad's "The Heart of Darkness"), a reliable narrator (as in Ida Fink's "A Scrap of Time"), or an unreliable narrator (as in Charlotte Perkins Gilman's "The Yellow Wallpaper"). A second-person narrative makes "you" a character in the story. A third-person narrative is told from outside the story, and the narrator never participates in the story. The narrator is omniscient (as in Jack London's "To Build a Fire"), partially omniscient (as in Kate Chopin's "The Story of an Hour"), or objective (as in Ernest Hemingway's "Hills Like White Elephants").

First-Person Point of View: Subjective Point of View   In a story told from first-person point of view, the narrator is one of the characters and tells us what he or she experiences and thinks about those experiences. First-person point of view is probably the most immediately obvious. All the actions are seen and reported by a character in the story. The implication of this technique is that the author has placed an interpreter of the events between the reader and the events. If the narrator says, "Bill walked into the room looking around the room like a nervous criminal," we must decide to trust the narrator's assessment or not. In other words, we have to ask ourselves if the narrator is trustworthy or not trustworthy.

Another aspect of first-person point of view that we should examine is the relationship between the main character and the narrator. Sometimes the narrator is the main character, as with Sammy in "A & P" or Estelle in "Rape Fantasies." Sometimes the narrator is not the main character. In novels, *The Great Gatsby* is an excellent example. Edgar Allan Poe's "The Purloined Letter" is an example among short stories.

Another facet of first-person point of view to consider is the relationship between the narrator and the time the events occurred. The story is affected if the narrator tells us about events relatively soon after the events take place, as does Sammy in Updike's "A & P." Likewise, we should be aware if the narrator is relating events that occurred many years earlier, as in with "half of a century" delay in Poe's "The Cask of Amontillado." This distinction can be quite important. For instance, Sammy is speaking of incidents relatively soon after they occur. So when he says, "Now here comes the sad part of the story, as least my family says it's sad, but I don't think it's so sad myself," we cannot say that the theme of the story is that sometimes rash adolescent actions pay off later in life. In developing the theme of "The Cask of Amontillado," we must take into consideration why Montresor must tell his story fifty years after the fact. He had vowed revenge, a strictly defined revenge. Did he achieve it? If so, why does he not go to his grave knowing he achieved it?

Second-Person Point of View: The Objective Subjective Point of View   Second-person point of view permits us to experience a story as if we were a character in that story. A relatively recent development in fiction, second-person point of view turns the reader into a character, usually the main character. The technique is easy to recognize: "You walk into a room. You put down your briefcase and open the refrigerator." The effect of second-person point of view seems to be simultaneously to close the gap between character and reader and to objectify the character at the same time. On the one hand, the reader, by the act of reading, voluntarily accepts the manipulation of the narrator and at the same time recognizes it as manipulation. The reading experience differs, say, from reading a story in first-person point of view where we accept our identification with the *I* in a story and then forget we are, in fact, reading not experiencing the actual experiences. A highly regarded example of second-person point of view is the novel *Bright Lights, Big City*. Lorrie Moore and Dagoberto Gilb, among others, have published stories employing second-person point of view.

Third-Person Points of View: Objective Point of View Third-person points of view focus on what the characters experience, not what the narrator experiences. In a story told in third-person point of view, the narrator stands outside the events of the story and, usually, presents the readers with an objective presentation of those events. There are three kinds of third-person points of view: omniscient, limited omniscient, and dramatic-objective. The difference in these three is determined by the amount of information that occurs inside the heads of the characters and outside the frame of the story.

Omniscient A narrator who is omniscient tells the reader what two or more of the characters know and feel. What characters know and feel is, of course, secret to third parties unless the characters communicate it to others—that is, unless the narrator can enter the mind or heart of the characters. For instance, only an omniscient narrator could write, "Harold plopped into the easy chair and thought about how much brussels sprouts disgusted him. Brussels sprouts, he believed but did not say so his mom could hear, were vegetables for old people."

In the same way, unless information is communicated to a character in some direct manner—say, a messenger appearing—only an omniscient narrator can tell of events that occur outside the sight and experience of the characters in the story. Such a phrase as "Little did Smith know that the ship had arrived at noon," can only be delivered by an omniscient narrator. An omniscient narrator is more able to present a complete and unbiased story. We can learn not only what a character does, but also what other characters do when the main character is not present.

Jack London's "To Build a Fire" employs the omniscient narrator in a unique way. Not only does the narrator tell us what the main character, the tenderfoot, thinks and feels, but also at important points in the story the narrator reports what the tenderfoot's companion, his dog, thinks and feels.

Limited Omniscient The narrator that is limited in omniscience presents the thoughts or feelings of only one of the characters, usually the main character. This method presents an appearance of objectivity. However, by focusing on only one character and on that character's inner life, the narrator can make readers more sympathetic to that character, or if needed, more skeptical toward that character.

Katherine Anne Porter's "The Grave" follows the afternoon adventures of a young girl named Miranda and her brother, Paul. At various points in the story, the narrator shows us what Miranda is thinking and how on that afternoon she begins to understand the questions of life and death, and perhaps a woman's place in those questions. Then in a special twist in the story, the narrator shows us Miranda twenty years later remembering that day. The tension between these two instances of limited omniscient narration is important in formulating a theme for the story.

Dramatic-Objective The narrator of a story with dramatic-objective point of view communicates only what someone outside the story could know by looking and listening. The inner lives of the characters are closed off, secreted. We readers know only what characters do and say. Unless a character says why he or she did a particular act, we must hypothesize for ourselves, looking for clues and consistency. We can think of a story that uses dramatic-objective as being a play, a play in which no character ever speaks directly to the audience in asides or monologues. This method is the closest to experiencing a story as one experiences life, for in life we know only what we see and hear and what other people tell us.

Several well-known examples of dramatic-objective point of view are included in this anthology: Ernest Hemingway's "Hills Like White Elephants," Shirley Jackson's "The Lottery," and John Steinbeck's "Chrysanthemums." In "The Lottery," the effect of the ending is built upon the fact that the reader doesn't know what is about to happen on this summer morning. All the town's people know, for they participate in the lottery every year. One glimpse into one character's mind would have altered our reaction to the events, and thus would have changed the theme of the story.

After we have identified the kind of point of view a writer uses, we are ready to examine how a story's point of view opens avenues for understanding the story. For example, point of view raises the question of narrative trust. As we know from real-life experiences, there are some people that we simply cannot trust. They tell us one thing and very often the opposite is true. Writers, seeing new possibilities for the effects their stories can have, will sometimes create a narrator who is crazy, psychotic, or just plain manipulative. The narrator in Charlotte Perkins Gilman's "The Yellow Wallpaper" presents readers with an interesting dilemma. On the one hand, we recognize that the narrator is certainly emotionally unstable; on the other, we suspect that others around her have contributed to her desperate situation.

The writer's choice of point of view controls not only what we know but also how we experience the events in the story. If we trust the narrator, and the narrator is scared, we will probably be scared. But if we don't trust the narrator and the narrator is scared, the writer has put the reader in a tough, but perhaps very rewarding, situation of reading the story on two levels. We experience the story as the narrator does, and we experience the story as a skeptical observer of the story.

Point of view thus raises questions about the narrator's purposes. Why does the narrator want us to know certain information at certain moments? For instance, in the story "The Man Who Was Almost a Man," the first few paragraphs are a masterful use of point of view as Richard Wright's narrator takes us in and out of the mind of the young man. In the example on the next page, notice how Wright shifts from Standard Written English to African-American English. Why does Wright do this? Is it merely to show us that the character has not been educated in Anglo schools? Probably not. He could have done that simply by showing us the young man talking. Instead, here and later he shows us the immaturity and sloppy thinking of the young man. But that is not all. Wright also allows us, no . . ., he forces us to experience the young man's life. But because Wright maintains an objective limited omniscient point of view, he makes us see that even though Dave is indeed immature, he is manipulated, perhaps even enslaved, by Southern society. Wright helps us develop the sympathy for the young man, so that when he hops the train, we can feel how hard it will be for him up North. We realize that Dave has almost no other choices, that he lives in an area of the country that, no matter what his age or education, will not allow him to be a man.

The narrator shows us Dave from a distance across the field.
Suddenly we know what Dave is thinking. Shift back, outside of Dave's mind, to mother putting supper on table.

An interesting choice here to give this information in narrator's voice. These are not Dave's thoughts, but a statement about what, indeed, will happen.
Notice what is communicated about Dave's character and situation in the community.

What is the narrator saying here?

Wright shows us Dave's immaturity.

Dave struck out across the fields, looking homeward through paling light. Whut's the use talkin wid em niggers in the field? Anyhow, his mother was putting supper on the table. Them niggers can't understan nothing. One of these days he was going to get a gun and practice shooting, they couldn't talk to him as though he was a little boy. He slowed, looking at the ground. Shucks, Ah ain scarda them even ef they are biggern me! Aw, Ah know whut Amha do. Ahm going by ol Joe's stor n get that Sears Roebuck catlog n look at them guns. Mebbe Ma will lemme buy one when she gits mah pay from ol man Hawkins. Ahma beg her t gimme some money. Ahm ol ernough to hava gun. Ahm seventeen. Almost a man. He strode, feeling his long loose-jointed limbs. Shucks, a man oughta hava little gun aftah he done worked hard all day.

SETTING AND ATMOSPHERE

Understanding the importance of setting for a story is easy. If you were to plan what might be the most romantic moment in your life—say, the moment you ask the person you love to marry you—where would you plan to be? Taking an evening stroll on a Caribbean beach? Seated at a candlelit table in a quiet, beautiful restaurant? Sweating in the front seat of a Chevy Nova in five o'clock traffic, the Beastie Boys in the tape deck? Holding a supersized Hefty bag full of empty beer cans the morning after the Super Bowl party? Most of us know which of these places we would choose because we know, even without considering how, that there is a link between the meaning of events and where and when those events occur.

Therefore, if characters in a story encounter each other, we know they must do so in some place and at some time. The place and time of the story is its *setting*. Writers are able to decide how important the setting is to their story and in what manner they will treat that setting. Some stories have very specific settings. For instance, F. Scott Fitzgerald's "Babylon Revisited" takes place in Paris, France, in the early 1930s. This specific setting is very important because Fitzgerald assumes we know about the lifestyle of the wealthy in Paris of the 1920s and that we know the devastation brought by the stock market crash of 1929 and the early years of the Great Depression.

The setting also indicates certain facts about socioeconomic status of the characters. In "Barbie-Q" by Sandra Cisneros, we are aware that these young girls are not wealthy because of the way Cisneros describes the warehouse. The setting of Margaret Atwood's "Rape Fantasies" is unclear at the beginning of the story, but by the end of the story, it becomes clear where Estelle is sitting as she tells her stories. Suddenly, the story takes on an entirely new meaning, telling much about Estelle and her lifestyle.

In addition, the setting creates an emotional response. In Poe's "The Fall of the House of Usher" and in Hawthorne's "The Birthmark," we are taken into places that scare most of us. However, the rooms and lawns of the colonial leaders described in W. Somerset Maugham's "The Outstation" can make us feel very comfortable and pampered, or depending on our politics, angry and jealous.

But sometimes a writer decides to place a story in an unspecified setting. We cannot tell when the story takes place, and we cannot tell where, other than perhaps in a city or in a house. But a general setting might tell us several things. First, it might say that the story and characters could occur anywhere and at anytime. The author may want us to think of the story as a universal experience. A story that illustrates this effect is Leslie Marmon Silko's "Yellow Woman," which obviously takes place beside a stream and in the mountains, but we don't know much more than that. It is also a story unbound by time, and this unboundedness is part of the theme, the inexplicable but totally normal "disappearance" of a woman from her family. Second, the writer may be telling us that the story's characters are just like us, and that we, too, could be unbound by time and place just like them. Susan Sontag's story "The Dummy," a story about an average person struggling with an average life takes place in an unspecified city at an unspecified time. Sontag is telling us that our lives are just as meaningless as her character's.

An idea related to setting is that of *atmosphere*. While setting can be considered the specific or general time and place of a story, along with any associated historical and sociological meanings, atmosphere might be considered the psychological impact of the setting. In the story "The Cask of Amontillado," for instance, the setting is a carnival and subterranean catacombs. These details are factual and relevant. But the atmosphere of the story is a slightly different thing; it is our emotional response to the setting, or the emotional aspect of the setting. The atmosphere of the "The Cask of Amontillado" is spooky, scary, and dark.

It is important to note that atmosphere is a slightly different idea from tone, which will be discussed later. Tone is the attitude of the narrator toward the story, the characters, and perhaps the reader. The atmosphere, rather than growing from the voice of the author, grows more from the situations in the story. Think of John Updike's "A & P," which takes place in a grocery store in the late 1950s. Updike's humorous tone is created by jokes Sammy tells, the images he uses to describe the customers and the store. But the atmosphere of the place is bright and cheerful, with certain qualities of rigidity and forced orderliness. In thinking about atmosphere, we can ask ourselves how our bodies might react in the place as described. We can notice how we feel—scared, happy and playful, constricted, confused. These emotional reactions to setting hint at the atmosphere the setting possesses—frightening, calm and safe, restricting, chaotic.

In attempting to understand the theme of a short story, we often look for changes in the setting. In "A & P," all of the story but the last paragraph takes place in the grocery store; then Sammy is free of it. James Joyce's "Araby" begins in and near a house on a cul de sac, but it ends at the bazaar, far from home. Leslie Marmon Silko's "Yellow Woman" begins on a riverbank, then moves to the mountains, then returns. In Kate Chopin's "The Story of an Hour," Mrs. Mallard is downstairs when she learns of her husband's death; then she goes upstairs and feels new emotions; then she returns downstairs. To understand a story's theme, we analyze these changes or the lack of changes. For instance, in "The Story of an Hour," as Mrs. Mallard returns, we ask if her old feelings come back to her, or if her new feelings stay with her? How settings shift, or remain static, tells us symbolically how the characters have reacted to the events they have just experienced.

The deserved popularity of Shirley Jackson's story "The Lottery" is due in large part to the expectations she creates in her depiction of the setting. The story begins with the narrator's description of a beautiful, peaceful, and, one would think, typical, early summer's day.

Jackson describes a specific day, but notice that the year is not specified.

The day is beautiful; the world is bountiful.

A typical small town: post office, bank, square.

The first mention of the lottery as if it were a normal part of a normal town.

The lottery seems to be an unemotional affair as people eat dinner right after it is completed.

The morning of June 27th was clear and sunny, with the fresh warmth of a full-summer day; the flowers were blossoming profusely and the grass was richly green. The people of the village began to gather in the square, between the post office and the bank, around ten o'clock; in some towns there were so many people that the lottery took two days and had to be started on June 26th, but in this village where there were only about three hundred people, the whole lottery took less than two hours, so it could begin at ten o'clock in the morning and still be through in time to allow the villagers to get home for noon dinner.

After reading the entire story, we return to this opening description of the setting and see how Jackson prepared us for the journey her story takes us on.

LANGUAGE

Some scholars and critics would tell us that a story is simply and only language. What they may mean by this is that a story, whether it is told orally or is written, whether it is factually verifiable or fiction, is not an object like a shovel or a table, but is something that exits only as words. Therefore, the plot is constructed of language, as are the characters and the setting, and so forth. Add a few words, they might say, and the character is changed; take away a few and the plot is altered.

While these critics, no doubt, make very important points about the nature of language in our lives, about how stories manifest themselves in our minds, we need not become quite so philosophical in considering how the language writers use shapes how a story is told. Instead, we can focus on such practical matters as sentence structure, word choice, imagery, symbolism, and irony. Then after we have identified various syntactic and semantic practices, we can look for patterns and connections between those practices. For instance, we might notice that a writer has used the word "squat" to describe a character. Then we also notice a house is "tiny." Later, we read a person's temper is "short." Suddenly, a pattern exists that may relate to a theme of the story. In another story a conflict might be portrayed as "a conversation ranging from stinging to explosive." Then somewhere else in the story, bees might be seen swarming or a car backfiring. Those places, then, might be places to look for more significant details about what the writer is trying to tell us.

Sentence Structure   One place to begin looking at a story's language is with the length and type of sentences. The length of sentences can affect how we react emotionally. A series of short sentences can seem like bursts of energy, shots of action, similar to quick cutting in movies. On the other hand, long sentences slow our reading down and often give the feeling of a more leisurely and thoughtful approach to the subject. As we read a story, we react to the pace of the language, and often the kinds of sentences the writer employs, especially where describing people and places and when coming to the climax, are directly related to the information conveyed.

Another aspect of sentences to examine is the manner in which they are structured. Three basic kinds of sentences are called periodic, loose, and balanced. A *periodic sentence* begins with various phrases and is not grammatically complete until the very end. The effect of such a sentence is to postpone information to the end, sometimes in a shocking or revelatory manner. The opening sentence of Kate Chopin's "The Story of an Hour" is a periodic sentence: "Knowing that Mrs. Mallard was afflicted with heart trouble, great care was taken to break to her as gently as possible the news of her husband's death." A *loose sentence* is one that presents its most important information early and continues with additional descriptive but less important phrases. The following sentence from Joyce Carol Oates's "Shopping" is a loose sentence: "From there they will move on to Young Collector, then to Act IV, then to Petite Corner, then one or another boutique and designer—Liz Claiborne, Christian Dior, Calvin Klein, Carlos Falchi, and the rest." A *balanced sentence* joins two ideas—sometimes contradictory, sometimes complementary—in parallel grammatical structures. The last paragraph of Isabel Allende's "And of Clay Are We Created," which draws distinctions between the protagonist before and after the events of the story, includes several balanced sentences: "You are back with me, but you are not the same man. I often accompany you to the station and we watch the videos of Azucena again; you study them intently, looking for something you could have done to save her, something you did not think of in time. . . . Your cameras lie forgotten in a closet; you do not write or sing; you sit long hours before the window, staring at the mountains. . . ."

Each of these kinds of sentences can have subtle effects on readers and how they experience the story. The focus of Kate Chopin's opening periodic sentence in "The Story of an Hour," for instance, on "her husband's death" is extremely important to the ending of the story and thus to the story's theme. Similarly, Joyce Carol Oates's list of shops is a reflection of the general experience of her story: shops and shops, things and things, occupying time and space, but hiding the most important parts of our lives. And Isabel Allende's balanced closing sentences perfectly reflect the conflict Rolfe Carlé is living with.

Word Choice   Readers become sensitive to the emotional texture of the language of any story they read. Many teachers and critics propose that writers intentionally choose individual words to create particular emotions in readers; others find no need to worry about what the writers' intentions were. However we approach this question of writers' intentions, we can all agree that writers' word choices provoke emotions in their readers. Therefore, as we read stories we should become attuned to how particular words affect us.

We can analyze words for two kinds of meaning: denotation and connotation. *Denotation* is usually described as a word's literal, dictionary meaning. *Connotation* is a word's emotional meaning. For instance, the narrator in "Hills Like White Elephants" refers to the two main characters the "girl" and the "man." Because of the connotations of these two words, we make all sorts of assumptions about the two characters and their relationship. In analyzing the importance of these words, we can ask how would the story have been changed if the characters were the "woman" and the "boy"? The answer to that question, while not directly important to the theme, does help us focus on the connotations of "man" and "girl," which are important to arriving at a statement of theme. The connotations of words communicate such ideas as class status, power relationships, sexual play and desire, gender and generational issues, religious practices, and personal habits and values.

Imagery   Writers use imagery throughout their stories to convey what a scene or character looks like. In examining imagery in stories, on one level we are simply focusing on the connotations and denotations of the description. Is the character standing, for instance, on a "slope," "hillside," or "rise"? Is a character "thin," "skinny," "waifish," "emaciated"? These kinds of images are called *literal imagery*.

Another kind of imagery is called *figurative imagery*. This kind of imagery is comprised of figures of speech. The most notable figures of speech are similes and metaphors, but others include oxymoron, personification, apostrophe, and paradox, to name a few that readers sooner or later become familiar with. Similes and metaphors describe a person, object, or idea by comparing it to another person, object, or idea. Most writers use similes and metaphors more or less routinely in their stories. For instance, in an early section of "A Good Man Is Hard to Find," Flannery O'Connor writes, "'Aren't you ashamed?' hissed the grandmother." Then, later in the story, O'Connor adds, "She reached out and touched him on the shoulder. The misfit sprang back as if a snake had bitten him. . . ." Seeing how O'Connor twice portrays the grandmother as a snake, we will probably find clues toward understanding the story in these images.

Symbolism   Symbols can be understood as extensions of images. Images, especially figurative images, attach meaning to an object by drawing attention to certain qualities it has. One layer of meaning is clear when a writer describes a character as fluttering in the wind. The images make us see the character walking, perhaps, like a bird flies or a flag waves. But if the writer says the character stood on the hill, a flag in the wind, we would see the image of fluttering, but we would also understand something else about the character because a flag is a symbol for a nation. Has the character, we would ask, become a symbol, representing a particular nation or nation's value system? A symbol, therefore, is a word that is not drawing comparisons but is actually standing in for the thing it refers to. Political and religious symbols are fairly easy to notice. Natural symbols—like water, fire, sun, moon— often occur in stories, as do images that seem universal in their meaning. Such symbols include a road for a life's path, a day for a life (as in Mahfouz's "Half a Day"), various animals, colors, and the like.

Sometimes writers create their own symbols. In the course of writing a story, writers may find that the usual array of symbols is not appropriate for the their particular purposes. Instead, they find the story requires its own symbolic artifact, act, or character. One very famous symbolic act is at the end of Edgar Allan Poe's "The Fall of the House of Usher." The house has come to symbolize the family and the house falls and splits apart. Poe's contemporary, Nathaniel Hawthorne, goes so far as to title his story "The Birthmark" after such a symbol. In contemporary writing, Sandra Cisneros gives a girl's Barbie doll a symbolic flaw in the story "Barbie-Q."

Irony   Irony is a method the author or narrator uses to point out a contradiction between appearance and reality. This contradiction may simply exist between what is said and what is meant. Or it may exist between what the readers of a story know and what the characters in the story know. Or it may exist between what the readers expect to happen in a story and what actually does happen. Because irony is such a varied and versatile rhetorical and structural device, it is also useful to remember it when we consider point of view (narrators may be ironic, or unaware of an ironic situation) and tone (the narrator may have an ironic tone toward the characters, conflict, or setting).

Although some people think of the modern age as an ironic one, as a literary device, irony has a long history and is an important part of Sophocles' *Oedipus Rex*, Plato's Socratic dialogues, Cervantes'*Don Quixote*, Swift's "A Modest Proposal," and Thomas Hardy's novels, among many, many other works. As one might expect, a literary device with such a long history is practiced in many forms, and each has a name to differentiate it from other kinds: Some types of irony include cosmic irony, Socratic irony, and structural irony.

The many kinds of irony are interesting and important, but three are most important: verbal irony, dramatic irony, and situational irony. *Verbal irony,* the most basic and perhaps the most prevalent, involves the contradiction between what is said and what is meant, and often is used with comic intent. At work, if something goes wrong, like that photocopying machine is broken, a person uses verbal irony, when obviously frustrated, he or she says, "I love this place!" The narrator of the story or characters in a story may use verbal irony. In the story "The Man Who Was Almost a Man," Richard Wright includes the following passage:

> All the crowd was laughing now. They stood on tiptoe and poked heads over one another's shoulders.
> "Well, boy, looks like yuh done bought a dead mule! Hahaha!"
> "Ain that ershame."

The last comment, spoken anonymously by a member of the crowd, was not spoken to sympathize with Dave, but to laugh at him.

Dramatic irony occurs when there is a contradiction between what a character believes or says is true and what the readers know is true. Much of the story "The Man Who Was Almost a Man" is based on this type of irony. When Dave thinks to himself, "Ahm ol ernough to hava gun. Ahm seventeen," we readers suspect, even in the first paragraph, where these words occur, that Dave is not old enough or responsible enough to have a gun. Even the very end of the story includes irony, as Dave believes there is a place where he can be a man, but the readers may suspect there are other reasons for Dave's difficulty in becoming a man.

Situational irony is a contradiction between what the characters and also the readers expect to happen in a story, or believe is true, and what actually does happen or is shown to be true. Often this type of irony is used in stories with surprise endings. The readers of "The Lottery," like the central character of "The Lottery," Tess, do not expect the events of the day to turn out as they do. Throughout the story, the readers assume many things. Not until the final ironic end of the story do the readers see how wrong they have been.

On the next page is an early paragraph from Katherine Anne Porter's "The Grave." Porter is a writer noted for her graceful style and use of symbolic references. In reading any writer's work, though, we can discover new levels of meaning by noticing the patterns of diction, imagery, and sentence structure placed in their stories.

Notice the "poetry" of Porter's style, the repetition of the p and s sounds.
Connotation of "pit."

The very long first sentence, taking in so much of the scene and "adventure" in one sentence.

Connotation of "spectacle."

Is this observation true: "When the coffin is gone, a grave is just a hole in the ground"?

Image of "scratching" and "animal."

Connotation of "lump."
What is significance of "pleasurably" and "pleasantly"?
Connotation of "corrupt."

Why did Porter use a fragmentary sentence?

Connotation of "fierce."
Image of dove, wings, hollow, whorls.
Symbolism of dove.

Notice the sequence of fairly short sentences.
Connotation of "treasures."

Image of ring. Symbolism of ring.
Connotation of "smitten."

Periodic sentence ending with "coffin."

They peered into the pits all shaped alike with such purposeful accuracy, and looking at each other with pleased adventurous eyes, they said in solemn tones: "These were graves!" trying by words to shape a special, suitable emotion in their minds, but they felt nothing except an agreeable thrill of wonder: they were seeing a new sight, doing something they had not done before. In them both there was also a small disappointment at the entire commonplaceness of the actual spectacle. Even if it had once contained a coffin for years upon years, when the coffin was gone a grave was just a hole in the ground. Miranda leaped into the pit that had held her grandfather's bones. Scratching around aimlessly and pleasurably as any young animal, she scooped up a lump of earth and weighted it in her palm. It had a pleasantly sweet, corrupt smell, being mixed with cedar needles and small leaves, and as the crumbs fell apart, she saw a silver dove no larger than a hazel nut. With spread wings and a neat fan-shaped tail. The breast had a deep round hollow in it. Turning it up to the fierce sunlight, she saw that the inside of the hollow was cut in little whorls. She scrambled out, over the pile of loose earth that had fallen back into one end of the grave, calling to Paul that she had found something, he must guess what . . . His head appeared smiling over the rim of another grave. He waved a closed hand at her. "I've got something too!" They ran to compare treasures, making palms. Paul had found a thin wide gold ring carved with intricate flowers and leaves. Miranda was smitten at sight of the ring and wished to have it. Paul seemed more impressed by the dove. They made a trade, with some little bickering. After he had got the dove in his hand, Paul said, "Don't you know what this is? This is a screw head for a *coffin!* . . . I'll bet nobody else in the world has one like this!"

One sentence almost every child hears from his or her parents is "Don't take that tone with me!" In growing up, we almost always regret this moment. For some reason, now beyond our memory, we spoke in such a way that showed our parents nothing of our love and respect for them. Instead, we were surly, disrespectful, impatient or self-righteous. Or as some people would say, we had an attitude.

In a short story, tone can be thought of as the narrator's attitude toward the events in the story, the characters, the setting, and sometimes even the reader. In this way, tone is closely related to both point of view and language. Tone is related to point of view in that it is the emotional, attitudinal element of point of view. A story may be told in first person, but what are the narrator's emotions as he or she tells the story? Identifying Sammy as the narrator of John Updike's "A & P" is an important, yet basic step. A more important step toward understanding the story may be identifying his tone. Most people immediately identify that Sammy is quite funny as a narrator, so certainly there is a humorous tone to the story. Some might also point out that his sense of humor has an adolescent quality to it. The image he uses of the two scoops of vanilla comes to mind. Yet in looking more closely at what Sammy says, you may also notice that he is quite sarcastic. Sammy does not like Mr. Lengel or the patrons of the A & P. Sammy feels himself to be better, in some way, than these people.

Tone is, therefore, very closely related to language, because one of the major methods the writer has of conveying the tone of the narrator is in the use of image, metaphor, and sentence style. The reader then can closely examine, in "A & P," for instance, the use of such metaphors as sheep and pigs and witches when describing the customers. These metaphors carry emotional power, in this case, sarcasm and disdain. The concept of distance might clarify the notion of tone. Critics such as Wayne C. Booth point out that, in all reading experiences, there is a kind of implied dialogue or relationship among the author, the narrator, the characters, and the readers. Each of these "people" have various levels of closeness with or distance from each of the others in terms of lifestyles, philosophies, political and religious views, class and ethnic background, and the like. In looking at tone, we would focus on the distance between the narrator and characters and between the narrator and readers. How distant in attitude, philosophies, and so on is the narrator from these others?

Flannery O'Connor's short story "A Good Man Is Hard to Find" is particularly interesting in regard to these relationships. In the first pages of the story, the narrator is absolutely scathing in attitude toward the members of this family. For instance, the narrator compares the mother's face to a cabbage. The narrator repeatedly refers to the grandmother as "old lady," and the children insult the grandmother without the narrator commenting in any way about the rudeness of the children. Importantly, the narrator does all this, we can only assume, knowing that the reader will understand the insults and sarcasms and agree with them. At the beginning of the story, therefore, the distance between the narrator and the characters is quite large, while the distance between the narrator and the reader is small. The tone, at least in the beginning of the story, is comic and ironic, even judgmental. As the story continues, this tone shifts with the misfortunes of the family. The distance between the narrator and characters closes. At the same time, as the narrator turns a family vacation into the apocalypse and thus a warning about human behavior and cosmic justice, the distance widens between the narrator and the reader, who, like the characters in the story, is also human and guilty of human weaknesses.

The American writer James Baldwin is noted for his intelligence and for his deliberately and carefully wrought moral stances on issues of race, religion, and personal identity. Below is the second to last paragraph of his story, "Sonny's Blues." In it, an older brother, an algebra teacher, listens to his younger brother, Sonny, playing piano in a jazz club.

The narrator, Sonny's brother, seems to be looking very carefully, observing his brother closely.

The narrator imagines what his brother feels. He puts himself in his brother's place.

Notice the words used: amen, life, beautiful, lament, burning, freedom. These are words for large and powerful ideas. These are serious subjects.

Brother continues sympathetically to find himself in Sonny's feelings.

Hearing and listening, brother remembers pain of his past.

Tears. Remembers more personal pain, but realizes that his brother's piano playing makes it understandable and bearable.

They all seemed gathered around Sonny and Sonny played. Every now and again one of them seemed to say, amen. Sonny's fingers filled the air with life, his life. But that life contained so many others. And Sonny went all the way back, he really began with the spare, flat statement of the opening phrase of the song. Then he began to make it his. It was very beautiful because it wasn't hurried and it was no longer a lament. I seemed to hear with what burning he had made it his, with what burning we had to make it ours, how we could cease lamenting. Freedom lurked around us and I understood, at last, that he could help us to be free if we would listen, that he would never be free until we did. Yet, there was no battle in his face now. I heard what he had gone through, and would continue to go through until he came to rest in earth. He had made it his: that long line, of which we knew only Mama and Daddy. And he was giving it back, as everything must be given back, so that, passing through death, it can live forever. I saw my mother's face again, and felt, for the first time, how the stones in the road she had walked on must have bruised her feet. I saw the moon lit road where my father's brother died. And it brought something else back to me, and carried me past it, I saw my little girl again and felt Isabel's tears again, and I felt my own tears begin to rise. And I was yet aware that this was only a moment, that the world waited outside, as hungry as a tiger, and that trouble stretched above us, longer than the sky.

The tone that Baldwin establishes in his story is illustrated in this passage. The narrator has lived a painful life, has suffered. One element of his suffering has been his brother's addictions and troubles with the law. Yet of all the emotions he might feel toward life and his brother—anger, frustration, fear, horror, self-righteousness, irony—he feels love and compassion, perhaps even respect and admiration. This tone is conveyed in the syntax of the passage—a movement from short, clear observations to longer, more complicated memories and thoughts. The language is semiformal and religious. In the end, the tone Baldwin creates helps us read this story of addiction and sorrow and racism as a story of hope and forgiveness.

THE INTERPRETATION OF FICTION

The previous section details "The Elements of Fiction"—plot, character, conflict, setting, point of view, language, and tone. These are categories into which we can place various kinds of information that we gather while reading a work of fiction. A single sentence, like the first sentence of Isabel Allende's "And of Clay Are We Created" provides information for each of these categories:

> They discovered the girl's head protruding from the mudpit, eyes wide open, calling soundlessly.

This one sentence supplies information about the plot of story; Azucena and her life; the source of conflict for Azuena and those who discovered her; the setting of a mudpit; the language techniques of alliteration ("protruding" and "mudpit"); image and connotation ("mudpit" and "eyes wide open"); and oxymoron ("calling soundlessly"), and the narrator's mixed tone of objectivity and compassion.

However, we have not discussed why we might read this story and what it tells us. Nor have we discussed what we do with the story and information once we do read it. Certainly the circumstances in which we read are important: why we read, when, and how. But we would hope that, whatever the circumstances, we would find some pleasure in the reading, a pleasure in the use of our imaginations and a pleasure in the use of our own interpretive skills.

In his book *The Practice of Reading,* the critic Denis Donahue writes, "I believe that the purpose of reading literature is to exercise or incite one's imagination; specifically, one's ability to imagine being different." Reading "should provoke me to imagine what it would mean to have a life different from my own." Donahue also adds that this act of imagination is pleasurable, writing "The pleasure of reading literature arises from the exercise of one's imagination, a going out from one's self toward other lives, other forms of life, present and perhaps future." This view of reading literature in general, and fiction specifically, is both common and common sensical.

This view is common in that almost all readers describe the pleasures of reading about people and places they have never known, about people and places they could not have imagined before. Whether it is reading of the frightful catacombs of Poe's "The Cask of Amontillado," of the lives of wealthy Americans in "Shopping," of unreflective violence in "The Lottery," or of a cyberpunk future in "Johnny Mnemonic," part of the attraction of such reading is learning, through the imagination, of how others live and what other places are like or could be like.

This view is also common sensical. Why else would we read fiction? We wouldn't turn to a short story to learn how to do our taxes or repair our automobiles. There are, of course, humorous (and frightful) instances of people reading fiction literally. Shirley Jackson discusses this phenomenon in her essay "Biography of a Story," included in the Context section of this anthology. Still, most readers of fiction understand that they are engaged in an act of the imagination.

After a work of fiction has brought pleasure to us by provoking the exercise of our imaginations, we then engage in attempting to understand that provocation. We might ask, "What is it in the work of fiction that claimed our attention?" This question leads to the act of interpretation. Donohue writes, "Interpretation begins when we have acknowledged that claim [on our attention] and set about fulfilling it. We try to understand the text as if its character were hidden and must be brought to light. We move along the interpretive process when we try to make our preliminary understanding of the text explicit to ourselves."

The term "explicit" is an important word. The first goal of interpretation is to make explicit the various facets of the story that claimed our attention and the various reactions we had to them. At first we might not understand these facets and our reactions. Interpretation is the process of taking all that which goes on inside of us as we read (often without our recognizing it) and stating it, outside of ourselves. The process often boils down to stating what the story means—what its theme is—and explaining how we arrived at that meaning. Understanding and utilizing the elements of fiction is the first, and perhaps most important, part of that process. But the process also includes learning what other readers say about the story, what critics and scholars have written. Sometimes the process includes placing the story in context with other stories, understanding when the story was written, what kind of story it is (genre), who the original readers of the story were. These facets of interpretation are discussed in Part II of this anthology, "Reading Short Fiction." At other times the process of interpretation requires that we conduct our own primary research into the writer's life and the history related to the setting and topic of the story. And still other times the process includes bringing other information from other disciplines—such as psychology, mythology, sociology, linguistics—and applying that information to our reading of the story. These facets of interpretation are discussed in Part V of this anthology, "Approaching Short Fiction Critically."

Something else occurs within readers of fiction beyond "exercising the imagination." According to Donahue, exercising the imagination "denotes its relationship to sympathy, fellowship, the spirituality and morality of being human." The effect of literature upon the reader leads to another step in interpretation. The first step in interpretation, we have seen, is to make the meaning of the text explicit for ourselves. The second step is to make the meaning explicit for others, to expand the "fellowship" that lies in the imaginative power of a work of literature.

One way to do this is to discuss the work with others. Almost all of us talk to our friends about the meaning of current pop songs and movies. Some of us have, or will, interpret works of art professionally, as journalists, critics, scholars, and teachers. Almost all of us will practice this method of human sharing, of building community in literature classrooms by writing essays of interpretation for our instructors and fellow students. It is an important step in turning the inward, implicit experience of reading literature into the outward, explicit experience of being human in a human community.

Reading Short Fiction

For a minute, let's think about the past five or so days and recall the different pieces of writing we have looked at. The list is very long: cereal boxes, bills, computer manuals, street signs, billboards, clothing labels, instructions for measuring detergent, newspapers, textbooks for sociology and chemistry, our own essays in English class, e-mails from friends, various Web sites, a self-help book on time management. Yes, the list is very long. And add to that list several short stories.

Now let's think about how we read each of those documents. Why did we read it? Where did we read each one? What else were we doing? How quickly did we read it? How quickly did we expect to read it? What did we expect to "get out" of reading it? How did that expectation affect the way we read it? Was anything enjoyable to read? Did the various things we read differ in the kinds of enjoyment they provided?

Finally let's ask, What did the writing require of us? What kind of attention was asked of us? What kinds of previous knowledge? What level vocabulary? What sensibility did the work seem to favor?

One thing about reading is certain. We do not read everything the same way. The reason is that all writing is not created equal. Some kinds can be read while we are doing other things. Other kinds of writing demand our full attention. Some require us to read slowly and carefully; others need only quick perusals. Some kinds demand particular background knowledge; others open up to all readers. Some satisfy our quest for information; others our quest for beauty or adventure.

It may be obvious to say so, but when we read a short story, we make the job easier by remembering that we are indeed reading a short story. If we bring to a story the wrong expectations, if we come without the educational background the story assumes, if we don't apply to the story our own imaginations, we cannot expect the story to bring us enjoyment or wisdom. So knowing who we are as readers and what kind of story we are reading aids our ability to understand how and why we react to a work of fiction.

WHO ARE WE AS READERS?

In any communication, from letters to short stories, there are three spheres of meaning, three places where meaning might be created. They are the writer, the text, and the reader. Although critics and scholars debate passionately about the relative importance of these three spheres, common sense tells us that the reader is very important. For instance, if a reader misreads the word "house" for "horse," a relatively simple sentence can become, "The cowboy sat on the house and looked at the sunset." It doesn't matter what the text says or what the writer intends, the reader, rightly or wrongly, has made meaning of the sentence.

But the reader is important beyond simple questions of reading comprehension. We only need to recall a time when an "off-color" joke was told in a crowd. Some people thought the joke was hilarious; others, hearing the same words, heard something silly or something offensive. The reader is also the interpreter of the words.

In reading short fiction, our goal is to be entertained and to learn something about life. And very often who we are and what we bring to the short story will be the factors that determine whether we are entertained and whether we learn something. If we don't want our reading experience to be confusing, infuriating, or boring, then we may want to get to know ourselves as readers.

For instance, do we know what kinds of themes, characters, conflicts, and settings grab our attention and what kinds don't? Can we explain why? What is our vocabulary level, and how does that affect how we read and what we read? What are our personal values, and when we read, do those values begin debating with the values contained in the story? Behind all these questions and many more is one large question: Can we understand a story until we understand ourselves?

This isn't as odd a question as it might seem at first. It can be rephrased in many ways. For instance, can we understand others until we understand ourselves? This is a question appropriate for psychologists, salespeople, politicians, and corporate managers. Therefore, it can be argued that the skills required to be an effective reader of short stories are also the skills required to be effective at many other activities, including many professions.

Next, we need to look at who we are at each particular reading. Are we in a hurry? Are we in the mood for something wildly imaginative and find ourselves reading a family drama. Are we angry at somebody? Won't our own emotions affect how we read the story tonight?

Also very helpful is remaining aware of our experience as readers. The more we read the more we can bring to the next thing we read. If we know a good deal about the Vietnam War, then our reading of "The Things They Carried" by Tim O'Brien is very different from someone's who knows very little. Similarly, if we have been avid fans of early twentieth-century short stories—those by James Joyce, Ernest Hemingway, Katherine Mansfield, and Katherine Anne Porter—and we stumble upon a postmodernist story like Susan Sontag's "The Dummy," we might find ourselves disoriented and uninterested until we notice that her theme concerning our anxiety about living meaningless lives has its roots in stories by these previous writers.

One of the best things we can do as readers is to list all the books and stories we have read. For some of us the list is short; for others it is very long, and we have forgotten much of what we have read. Then we can note the works that we have most enjoyed at different times of our lives. Now we can ask what kind of person we were then that we so much enjoyed those works. Have we changed? Have the kinds of stories we enjoy remained more or less the same? Why have the kinds of stories changed? Why have they not?

WHAT KIND OF STORY ARE WE READING?

One problem some people have understanding and appreciating particular stories is that they try to read every story in the same manner. This is sort of like listening to bluegrass music in the same way that we listen to classical music. Certainly, there are elements of classical music in bluegrass—for instance, remnants on the sonata form. And some in-struments, like the mandolin, are the same. However, it hardly seems wise to dislike bluegrass merely because it shuns the harpsichord and includes banjoes, because it "sounds" country and not "sophisticated." Perhaps if we learned something about bluegrass—if we understood, for instance, its rural roots or its connections to jazz—we would find ways to appreciate it, and even enjoy it.

Since all stories are not alike, critics and scholars for several centuries have been struggling to understand these differences. In the process, they have developed many ways to classify fictional narratives. One way is to notice the difference between real-istic and nonrealistic works. Another classification is based on levels of structural com-plications. Others are based on the subject matter of the story. We can also classify fiction based on historical time periods.

REALISTIC AND NONREALISTIC STORIES

The first and perhaps most important distinction that we can make in reading a work of fiction is how realistic it is. In *realistic* fiction, the characters look, think, speak, and act like people we know. The setting looks like ones we are familiar with. Of course, we have to allow for historical differences: A character who wears a sword and says "Adieu" is not "realistic" today, but in a story set in Renaissance England, he certain-ly is. Another feature of realistic writing is that the laws of nature are adhered to in the work. Religious stories and myths, therefore, are sometimes not realistic, and in that difference is where they derive much of their power; gods don't obey the laws of na-ture. Most of the stories in this book are realistic: Young boys feel foolish ("Araby" by James Joyce), mothers shop with daughters ("Shopping" by Joyce Carol Oates), es-tranged brothers become friends again ("Sonny's Blues" by James Baldwin), and we grieve when people die ("To Hell with Dying" by Alice Walker). Some critics argue that no story can truly be realistic, because people do not experience their lives as stories, which have beginnings, middles, and endings. Some writers, therefore, leave the end-ings of stories open to interpretation, as Ernest Hemingway does in "Hills Like White Elephants." One kind of realistic fiction tries to present the workings of the human mind by using *stream of consciousness,* a technique for recording of the rambling, asso-ciative nature of human thought. In this text, "The Yellow Wallpaper" by Charlotte Perkins Gilman and "Roselily" by Alice Walker employ stream of consciousness.

A concept related to realism is *verisimilitude,* which refers to how the work creates a semblance of truth. A work of fiction that possesses verisimilitude does not neces-sarily have to be realistic. As Edgar Allan Poe used the concept, verisimilitude is cre-ated when the nonrealistic is presented realistically. Verisimilitude, therefore, is related to the concept of believability. For example, is it believable that the House of Usher should collapse? In Poe's hands, it is.

Nonrealistic fiction can refer to several categories of writing discussed below: myth, fairy tale, fantasy, science fiction, romance, and magical realism. As a general catego-ry, nonrealistic is that kind of writing about which we might say, "That doesn't hap-pen in real life." In a nonrealistic story, grandmothers become wolves ("The Werewolf" by Angela Carter), one day becomes a lifetime ("Half a Day" by Maguib Mahfouz), peo-ple make clones of themselves ("The Dummy" by Susan Sontag), and ancient artifacts cause changes in climate ("Chac-Mool" by Carlos Fuentes). Writers chose to include nonrealistic elements for various reasons. As readers, we can remain aware of how we react to these elements. There are some readers who vastly prefer nonrealistic stories to realistic ones because of the emotions they experience and because of the kinds of themes nonrealistic fiction often presents. "Who wants to read about real life?" they might say, "You can experience that all the time." For them, reading is an escape into worlds unlike their day-to-day lives. As we read, we can ask ourselves why a writer would chose to write a story realistically or nonrealistically. Which kind of story do we prefer? Why?

MYTH, LEGEND, ALLEGORY, PARABLE, FABLE, TALE, FAIRY TALE, FOLK TALE, TALL TALE

Other distinctions about stories that will help our reading and understanding of fiction are those that describe different kinds of stories as they have been developed historically. Most critics and scholars believe that the first kinds of stories that humans told were myths. *Myths* are anonymous stories, usually of religious importance, that explain why the world is as it is cosmologically (such as, why there is night and day), metaphysically (where people go when they die), socially (how a ritual originated), and naturally (why the snake sheds its skin). Although certain kinds of myths (like creation stories) appear to be universal, individual myths are shared by distinct cultural groups and depict the workings of supernatural beings within that group. While popular use of the word "myth" implies that myths are not true historically, factuality is not necessarily an important consideration when calling them myths. The birth of Aphrodite, the fall of Adam and Eve, the origin of the peace pipe, the death of Osiris— we can enjoy and learn from each of these myths, without believing in their factual truth. Myths differ from *legends* in that legends are more grounded in historical fact and recount the exploits, perhaps with exaggeration, of a real human. The legends of King Arthur, Robin Hood, Annie Oakley, and Geronimo are examples.

An *allegory* is an elaborate metaphor grafted onto a narrative. In allegories, people, places, objects, and actions derive their meaning from outside the story itself. Various facets of the story, therefore, exist parallel to other people, actions, or ideas, be they political, social, religious, or otherwise. Nathaniel Hawthorne's "Young Goodman Brown" can be read as a religious allegory in which a "Goodman" loses "Faith" when tempted by evil on the road of life. Without knowledge of New England Puritans and the Christian religion, a reader might think "Young Goodman Brown" is simply a horror story. A *parable* is a kind of allegory, usually shorter and more direct in its presentation of the religious or moral lesson. Usually parables are closely related to the context in which they are told. In the Christian tradition, for instance, Jesus told parables to teach specific lessons as a particular moment called for them. A *fable,* on the other hand, is a kind of allegory used to teach a more general life lesson, and the lesson is not so directly connected to the moment of its telling. Often fables feature animals that personify various human qualities. Whether they include animals or not, fables include a lesson explicitly stated at the end in an epigram. The fables by the Greek slave Aesop and by the seventeenth century Frenchman La Fontaine are the most famous.

The word "tale" has sometimes been used as a synonym for "short story." But more often distinctions are made between the two terms. Although there are notable exceptions, a *tale* is a relatively brief story, either fiction or nonfiction, about strange and perhaps exotic places and events. Generally, tales are considered to have looser plots than modern short stories, and at the same time to be more plot-driven. The modern short story is generally considered to be character-driven. One very popular type of tale is the fairy tale. In the strictest terms, the *fairy tale* recounts the adventures of little spirits, who guide, aid, and trick human beings for good or ill. In a broader sense, the fairy tale can include stories in which humans deal with such creatures as dwarfs, witches, and giants. Often, fairy tales were passed orally from generation to generation and then collected by scholars, as those collected by the Grimm brothers. Still, original fairy tales have been created by such writers as Hans Christian Andersen and Oscar Wilde. While, broadly speaking, *folk tales* can be thought of as any tale that is passed on orally, they can also be considered distinct from other orally transmitted stories as not considering fairies and other magical creatures or gods. Instead, folk tales seem to focus on native, rural wisdom, and explain how things came to be, in a local way, not cosmologically, as in myth. Finally, the *tall tale,* which is a kind of folk tale, is a humorous story using folk idioms to recount amazing feats of strength or cunning. Mark Twain's "The Celebrated Jumping Frog of Calaveras County" is a tall tale.

ROMANCE, REALISM, LOCAL COLOR, NATURALISM, MODERNISM, POST-MODERNISM, MAGICAL REALISM, NEW REALISM, HYPERTEXT FICTION

Around the end of the eighteenth century and the beginning of the nineteenth century, writers began to develop the kind of narrative that today we call the short story. The roots of the short story begin in the myths and tales discussed in the previous section, but they also sink into the literary narrative forms of the Middle Ages, Renaissance, and Enlightenment. These works include Boccaccio's *The Decameron,* Chaucer's *Canterbury Tales,* Cervantes' picaresque novel *Don Quixote,* Addison's informal essays and sketches in the "Sir Roger de Coverley Papers," and Voltaire's philosophical narratives, such as *Candide.* The reason the short story developed can be attributed to several factors, including the rise of a middle-class reading public and the increase in the number of newspapers and other periodicals that needed material for their pages. How the short story developed can be seen as the work of a series of writers accepting or rejecting the topics, themes, and techniques of their predecessors. Critics and scholars have named several periods and schools of fiction from the past two hundred years; as we read a short story, it is helpful to know to which period or school the story may belong.

The short stories written in the nineteenth century generally fall into three types, which also represent historical periods. The *romance,* as a literary distinction, has many and quite varied meanings. On the one hand, it refers to medieval romances dealing with knights and courtly love; on the other, it is a name for contemporary pulp love stories. The romance also refers to a kind of story popular in the early nineteenth century that includes characters with extreme sensibilities, exotic locales, exciting plots, and mysterious forces. As a kind of short story, it is a natural product of the values of the Romantic Age. Nathaniel Hawthorne, one of the most important writers of romances, said that the form "sins unpardonably" in presentation of reality, but he felt there were truths he could not tell without its devices. By mid-century, writers were reacting to the excessive qualities of romance and writing stories that more accurately reflected real life.

Realism eschews excessively strong heroes, bizarre settings, and fantastic events and replaces them with people, places, and events that readers recognize as those from their own day-to-day life. Among the greatest realists are those included in this text, Leo Tolstoy, Henry James, and Edith Wharton. The techniques and themes of these realists continue to exert a tremendous influence on contemporary writers. One particular kind of realism, called local color, flourished in the period following the Civil War in the United States. *Local color* writers employed the techniques of realism and applied them to particular regions, depicting the speech, clothing, habits, and culture of these regions. Writers in this text who are sometimes referred to as local colorists include Samuel Clemens (Mark Twain), Mary Wilkins Freeman, and Kate Chopin.

By the end of the nineteenth century, writers began to react to a kind of sentimentality and politeness that often imbues realistic fiction. These writers—including

Stephen Crane and Jack London—applied the tenets of scientific determinism to their otherwise realistic fiction, creating a kind of fiction called *naturalism*. Some critics emphasize that, while realism focuses on individuals succeeding or failing in their lives based on their inner strengths and weaknesses, naturalism shows individuals at the mercy of forces that they cannot overcome, such as nature and natural laws, including economic and social structures.

Short stories of the twentieth century employ a large and greatly varied number of approaches and sensibilities. Among those are adaptations of the romance, and of realistic and naturalistic fiction. The first half of the century, particularly from the end of World War I to about 1965, is dominated by a group of beliefs and practices generally called *modernism*. Modernist writers, while often quite individually distinct, sought to sever whatever connection they might have had with the nineteenth century, particularly with Victorian middle-class values. Therefore, they endeavored to create new forms, subjects, and attitudes in literature. These new approaches include the use of ideas developed by psychologists, including Sigmund Freud and Carl Jung, to explore the inner workings of their characters' minds, including aspects the characters may have suppressed. Katherine Anne Porter's "The Grave" illustrates one writer's exploration of the power of the unconscious.

Other approaches include the fragmentation of point of view. While not as often seen in short stories as in novels, experiments in point of view provide altered, distorted experiences. Virginia Woolf's "Kew Gardens" and William Faulkner's "A Rose for Emily" illustrate the kinds of experiments these writers were also making in their novels. Another characteristic feature of some modern fiction is a transnational focus, as is seen in the works of Ernest Hemingway, Katherine Anne Porter, and W. Somerset Maugham, among others. And, of course, modernism is noted for its experimentation with form, subject, and style. Kafka writes of a man who becomes an insect and of a man who starves himself. Hemingway builds stories on what is not said. Some modernist writers strive for a greater objectivity; thus, the third-person narrator, as a personality (as the narrator might have appeared in Hawthorne or James), often disappears. A favorite phrase of some modernists was "Show, don't tell." Other modern short stories include a greater and conscious use of myth and symbols. Finally, because modernist fiction was developed in the wake of the horrors of World War I, its themes often focus on a sense of alienation and absurdity and are critical of traditional values and institutions.

Post-modernism might simply be described as what modernism developed into following World War II. In some ways, post-modernism takes the assumptions of modernism—alienation, fragmentation, the importance of the unconscious, skepticism of traditional values—and expresses them in more extreme and experimental ways. A comparison of D. H. Lawrence's "The Rocking-Horse Winner" and David Foster Wallace's "Suicide as a Sort of Present" illustrates how two writers—one a modernist, the other a post-modernist—treat the same subject, a mother who does not love her children and what becomes of the children. Some critics note that modernism is elitist, and post-modernism is not. Post-modernism, for instance, has been a primary force pushing for consideration of works by ethnic minorities, women, and gays and lesbians. Post-modernist writers have also employed often very nonliterary language in their works, such as the jargon of business or academia and the clichés of advertising and pop songs. Writers such as Donald Barthelme, by frequently employing traditionally nonliterary language as a prominent part of their style, continually undermine the realistic illusion of their stories. Other writers use such language to heighten the reality of the story, as does Joyce Carol Oates, in "Shopping," when she lists names of stores in a mall.

Two final techniques used in writing fiction in the second half of the twentieth century deserve to be mentioned. *Magical realism* in fiction is the inclusion of nonrealistic elements, such as those from dreams or myth, in an otherwise realistic story. Writers known for their use of this technique include Jorge Luis Borges, Gabriel García Márquez, Isabel Allende, and Salman Rushdie. The technique, in many ways, resembles a modern version of the romance. A recent development in realism has been called *new realism*. As seen in the works of Raymond Carver, Bobbie Ann Mason, and Ann Beattie, among others, new realism is distinguished by the writers' focus on lower- and working-class characters. The style of these writers is often based on directness and simplicity without the deliberate educated grace or irony of previous modernist writers. For instance, Raymond Carver's protagonist in "Cathedral" is not the middle-class character we expect in works by Hemingway or Cheever.

Fiction is, of course, influenced by the way it is communicated. Stories told orally and printed in books can differ in many ways. A story that a reader can return to and reread allows for a different method of storytelling. Often oral tales, such as fairy tales, follow conventions that help the listener keep track and remember the story. For instance, how many fairy tales do we know in which the hero faces three trials? Cinderella goes to the ball three times; Jack goes up the beanstalk three times; Goldilocks sleeps in three beds. A story meant to be read need not follow such conventions. However, a story is read from a page in habitual ways also. In English we read from top to bottom, from page one to the end. The reader, therefore, is still following the story in the manner that the writer presents it. The plot of the story that we read is the plot that the writer presents to us.

With the invention of the computer and the development of computer-literate readers, a different kind of story, *Hypertext Fiction,* is now possible, and, in fact, remains largely undeveloped. Still, there are several writers actively developing this new approach to fiction. Perhaps the most important feature of hypertext fiction is that narrative and plot, as experienced by the reader, are controlled less by the writer. Imagine a story written on note cards. In theory, the reader could shuffle the note cards and then read the story. The implication is that every reader "reads" a different story because different readers shuffle the cards differently. In hypertext fiction, the writer provides the links that the reader can click on with the computer's mouse, and the reader chooses which link to follow. Computer games, such as *Myst*, in which the viewer moves from one room or landscape to another provides an analogy.

The implications of hypertext fiction for readers and writers are vast. Reading may become a multimedia event filled with graphics and music; words can become active on the computer screen, making visual puns and metaphors an integral part of the reading experience. Reading becomes less an experience of taking in words, but in creating connections.

DETECTIVE FICTION, MYSTERY, GHOST STORY, HORROR, FANTASY, SCIENCE FICTION

Some of the most popular fiction is what is sometimes called "genre fiction" or "formula fiction." One of the reasons readers enjoy these kinds of stories is that they know what to expect. Often, but not always, these types of fiction follow certain established formulae and part of the pleasure in reading them is watching how the writer works within those limits. *Detective fiction* has its roots in the stories of Edgar Allan Poe in such stories as "The Purloined Letter" and "The Murders in the Rue Morgue." The formula that detective fiction generally adheres to is well established. The writer will open the story with a crime, often a murder. The identity of the criminal is unknown, but a detective solves the case, following logically the evidence until it leads to the revelation of who the criminal is. The reader of "The Purloined Letter" will realize that Poe was already using various methods still used today to tell a detective story. A *mystery* is a related form, not as strict in its formula, sometimes identifying the criminal early, sometimes not focusing on a detective at all.

A *ghost story*, similar to the mystery, explores unexplained phenomenon, but does so by assigning powers to a spirit, phantom, or poltergeist. The atmosphere of a ghost story is often, but not always, foreboding and frightening. A broader category of ghost story is *horror*, which is not limited to ghosts, per se. Horror can include frightening creatures from werewolves to vampires to menaces of undefined natures. Often horror and ghost stories are concerned with incarnations of evil.

Fantasies are stories that take place in nonexistent and nonrealistic worlds. As in ghost stories, in fantasies phenomena occur that do not follow scientific and natural laws. In addition, characters need not resemble humans or other earthly creatures. *Science fiction* is often regarded as a form of fantasy. But in science fiction, the writer's imagination is somewhat limited to scientific fact or a reasonable projection of what scientific fact will be in the future. Such features as time travel, rapid space travel, extra-terrestrial life forms, and new technology often form the basis of this genre. Other genre fictions include romance (as in love stories) and pornography, but neither has yet been recognized by critics and academia as genres demanding serious study as literary forms. As cultural expressions, they have been often studied. Nor have either genre been the primary genre of any writers who have become mainstream or popular with academic audiences.

Readers who are familiar with these genres, their histories and distinguishing characteristics, have expectations about how the story might be presented and developed. They recognize the formula, and they recognize when writers deviate from the formula, and such deviations often become part of the thematic content of the fiction. One example is the work of William Gibson whose works, such as "Johnny Mnemonic," are a form of science fiction called cyberpunk, because its vision of the future combines elements of computer science and elements of the punk rock sensibility.

THE SHORT STORY, THE SHORT SHORT STORY, THE LONG SHORT STORY

In this text, the stories vary in length from slightly under one page to over thirty pages, from about 600 words to 23,000 words. The typical short story is about 5,000 words. Common sense would tell us that there must be differences in stories of such varied lengths, and, of course, there are. Defining those differences is another matter. There are no strict guidelines defining what a short short story must contain and how it must be developed, nor are there guidelines for any length of story. Since writers are continually looking at the tradition of their art and attempting to make it new, short stories will continue to adapt and change and perhaps even improve.

Generally, the shorter the story, the less complication the conflict goes through. The *short short story* may focus on one incident, one setting, one or two characters. This, of course, doesn't suggest that there will never be a long short story that does not focus on one incident, one setting, and one or two characters. However, long short stories, such as Leo Tolstoy's "The Death of Ivan Ilych" or Herman Melville's "Bartleby the Scrivener," tend to include several characters, several scenes, several settings, and a conflict that mutates and develops.

One other factor related to a story's length is the pace of the story. *Long short stories* from the nineteenth century and early twentieth century are developed at a more leisurely pace, almost painstakingly slowly. Stories like London's "To Build a Fire" and Kafka's "The Metamorphosis" explore in great detail a character's smallest sensation. Generally, stories are no longer written with such paces. If a story is longer than average nowadays, it probably contains more plot, more actions, or more complications. An example may be Milan Kundera's "Let the Old Dead Make Room for the Young Dead," which takes the two characters through several changes.

ASKING QUESTIONS ABOUT THE STORY

In addition to knowing who we are as readers and knowing what kind of story we are reading, we ask questions about the stories we are reading. Active and engaged readers keep track of where they are in understanding a story and think about what they need to do to gain understanding. One important way to do this is by asking questions of the text and striving to discover the answers.

The questions we can ask come from several categories. There are questions about the story's background, which we can ask any time as we read the story. Some readers ask these questions before they read the story; some prefer to wait until they've read the story; some readers are content never to ask background questions. And then there are questions about the story itself, which explore the elements of fiction and the story's structure and themes.

QUESTIONS ABOUT THE STORY'S BACKGROUND

1. Who is the writer of the story? What else did the writer produce? Is this story typical of the writer's other work? Is there anything in the story that is derived directly from the writer's life? What are the writer's main concerns about life and literature?

2. When was the story written? Is it typical for its time period? In what ways, in what ways not? How does the story reflect the values and concerns of its time period? What values did the time period suppress? How does the work reflect or contradict that suppression?

3. Who is the story's primary audience? Is the audience general or specific? What are the values of the audience? Does the writer agree or disagree with those values?

QUESTIONS ABOUT THE STORY

1. Who is this story about? What is the character's personality like? What are his or her values? Who are the supporting characters? What are their personalities like? What are their values? Do you like or dislike these characters? If we could ask them questions about their lives and roles in the narrative, what would those questions be? What do we imagine the answers would be?

2. What do the characters want? Do they want to change? How? What motivates them? Discourages them? What's going to happen to them if they don't succeed?

3. Where and when does the story take place? Is this time and place very specific or is it more general? Can the events of the story occur in other places or must they occur in this setting? Must the events occur at this specific time, or

can they take place at other times? Is the setting presented accurately? Is the story a regional story, a national story, or a universal story?

4. How well do we know what is going on in the story? Is the narrator secretive with information or open? Do we know what the characters are thinking or are we denied that information? Does the narrator tell us information that occurs before the story takes place or in locales other than that of the story? Is the narrator trustworthy? Does the narrator have a particular philosophical or religious stance? Does the narrator like or dislike the characters?

5. Is the style of the narrator's language straightforward and clear? Is the style convoluted and ambiguous? What does that say about the narrator? Does the narrator's diction tell us anything about the setting or characters? Is the narrator's language literary, using symbols, metaphors, similes, and other figures of speech? What do those devices contribute to the meaning of the story? How are they related in any way? To what extent is irony used by the characters and narrator? Why is irony being used?

QUESTIONS ABOUT THE STORY'S DEEP STRUCTURES AND THEMES

1. Does the story concern money and economic and social classes? Does the story concern gender issues? How men behave? How women behave? Does the story raise ethical questions? Does the story offer solutions to the ethical problems it depicts or does it avoid suggesting solutions?

2. Does the story employ basic, physical dualities: up/down, white/black, inside/outside, old/young, strong/weak, right/left? Does it employ abstract dualities: reality/fantasy, truth/fiction, good/evil, life/death?

KEEPING A READING JOURNAL

Keeping a journal is always a personal endeavor and should serve personal needs. Many people use journals to record their impressions of daily events and people that they meet. Serious readers and students sometimes keep reading journals, or they record in their personal journal what they have been reading. Exactly what they record in these reading journals is determined by their needs. Will they be writing essays about the readings or taking tests? Do they merely want a record of what they read because they have a goal of reading all of one writer's mystery novels? Do they write their own stories and are studying the ways various writers handle plot or character, and so forth? Since everyone might have different reasons for keeping a reading journal, each person needs to decide how to make the practice personally profitable. One or all the following suggestions might be helpful.

You might also wish to visit the Web site for this book, which includes an on-line journal for your use.

RECORDING IMPRESSIONS

One practice is to record our personal impressions as we read the story. This can be as simple as recording at the end of the first paragraph, "This is dull" or "I am already asking what's going on here. I'm curious." One thing we may want to do is commit to writing something at the end of each paragraph, or every third paragraph, or at every shift in the plot. Otherwise, we might get caught up reading and forget to write. While getting involved in a story is a wonderful thing, doing so can make it difficult to reconstruct the development of our feelings.

As the story progresses, our comments might resemble, "I can't believe that she takes that from him," or "This character reminds me of my grandmother. My grandmother used to talk all the time and everyone would slowly leave the kitchen because she had absolutely nothing to say that was positive." At the end of the story, we might write, "Wow, I never thought this is how this story would end. This kid is definitely making a bad choice here" or "Way to go! Tell them to take that job and shove it. We all have better things to do but live by the rules of the fearful and joyless."

RECORDING FACTUAL DATA

Similar to our writing general impressions, how we record factual data will depend on our purposes. If we are keeping track of our reading for personal or bibliographic purposes, all we need to write is title, author, date of publication, kind of story, where it was published, number of pages, and other similar information. Or we may want to expand the entry to include basic information about the story: names of characters, the setting, general description of writing style, statement of subject and theme.

If we think we might be writing about the story and, therefore, will need more in-depth information, we might want to divide the page into grids. In one section, we might list characters and their traits; in another section we might describe the setting and any changes in it; in another we might record phrases and sentences that are striking for thematic or aesthetic reasons, and so on with information we think could be important.

GRAPHING PLOTS AND CONFLICTS

Sometimes transforming a story into a diagram allows us to see developments in the story that might have escaped us while reading. Since the traditional plot follows a regular pattern, we can use a full page of our journal to draw the rise and fall of a story. Then we can fill in this *plot diagram* with events from the story. What event signals the beginning of the conflict? What events signal a complication or rising tension? Does a second conflict appear? Where? How many times does the conflict increase? Once, twice, three times, more? What event becomes the climax? Sometimes just forcing ourselves to be meticulous helps us see events in new ways. Or sometimes, with complicated or unconventional stories like William Faulkner's "A Rose for Emily" or Tim O'Brien's "The Things They Carried," a diagram unlocks the narrator's secret map of the story.

A *conflict diagram* can be made by drawing a series of boxes down the middle of the page and arrows on both sides of the box pointing at the box. In the boxes, we can write a brief description of a scene where there is conflict. On the two sides of the arrows, we put who or what is in conflict. Then beneath the characters or entities that are in conflict, we write what they want the outcome to be at that moment in the conflict. Actors will ask the question "What's at stake for this character in this scene?" Creating this diagram allows us to see how conflicts shift and change throughout a story. For instance, in Flannery O'Connor's "A Good Man Is Hard to Find," the conflict begins with very minor squabbling about such things as whether to take the cat on the trip and which road to take. Then the conflicts develop into the large philosophical question about what effect Jesus' life and death has and the larger more immediate conflict between life and death, between victims and their murderers. Drawing a diagram of these developing conflicts might reveal many things, including a multidimensional description of the characters and a revelation about the shift in tone in the story.

The techniques suggested above are, for the most part, rational reactions to a story. Another way to treat a story is to practice our own creativity. If we are artists, we can draw, or just doodle, what characters look like. If the narrator's descriptions are detailed, we sketch out how the narrator describes the character. If the narrator leaves the specifics of a character's appearance up to the reader, we can have fun imagining the character. Perhaps we have other artistic skills, such as pottery. We can create a piece of pottery expressing our feelings about the story. Or if we love to dance, certainly one way to react to a story is to put aside the text and our journals and dance whatever we feel. Another method is to choreograph a dance, and write it out in our journal. If we play an instrument or sing, perhaps writing a song that uses the characters or imagery from the story would be appealing. Some people may not understand how this helps us understand and write about a story, but we know from past creative work how much we learn when we experience things with our full talents and skills. Creating a dance for "Rape Fantasies" might open interpretations we would not have thought of in the traditional analytical manner. Our journals can be where we record the feelings and impressions we had while dancing. Then later if we need to write an essay, or, for another class, create a dance routine, we have our notes.

ANNOTATING A STORY WITH PERSONAL IMPRESSIONS

Some people find keeping a journal difficult. It might be the large, blank pages that intimidate them. It might be the problem of just keeping up with yet another notebook. These people might find annotating the text of the story to be an easy and useful method of recording impressions. The method is simple. As we read a story, we pause fairly often and write in the margins of the story what we are thinking at that point. If we have a question, we can write it in the margin. If we have an observation about a character's behavior or have a strong reaction to the setting, we can write that, too. The earlier section on "Recording Impressions" in a journal suggests a few more questions, but the technique here is to write our impressions in the margins of the text.

ANNOTATING A STORY FOR THE ELEMENTS OF FICTION

When we annotate a story focusing on the elements of fiction, we read the story with an awareness about character, conflict, setting, point of view, language, and tone. As we read the story, we will underline important, stimulating passages. In the margins of the story, we can write any observation we have about how that passage displays the elements of fiction. This can be done in many ways. Two methods are to write "character" or "conflict" or "tone" next to the passage that illustrates it, or write out fuller, more specific observations. You might say, "the character is nervous," "note the internal conflict has become external," "narrator shows us what the dog is feeling and thinking," or "the coat is a symbol of their separation from one another." Several examples of annotated text are included in Part I, "Introduction to Short Fiction." No matter how we annotate the text, when we discuss the story in class or when we write an essay about the story, we will be able to find important passages more quickly.

CHINUA ACHEBE

Chinua Achebe (b. 1930) was born in Ogidi, Nigeria. After graduating from University College, Ibadan, in 1953, he became a broadcaster. During Nigeria's civil war (1967–1970) he worked for the Biafran government. His most influential works are *Girls at War and Other Stories* (1972) and his first novel, *Things Fall Apart* (1958), which counters the distorted European picture of Africa. *No Longer at Ease* (1960), *Arrow of God* (1964), *A Man of the People* (1966), and *Anthills of the Savannah* (1987) are later novels. He has written books for children, *Chike and the River* (1962) and *How the Leopard Got His Claws* (1973), published poetry and political and social commentary, and coedited *African Short Stories* (1985). He has taught at several Nigerian universities and in the United States (University of Massachusetts, University of Connecticut, Bard College). *Conversations with Chinua Achebe* was published in 1997, *Home and Exile* (essays) in 2000, and *Collected Poems* in 2004.

Dead Men's Path

Michael's Obi's hopes were fulfilled much earlier than he had expected. He was appointed headmaster of Ndume Central School in January 1949. It had always been an unprogressive school, so the Mission authorities decided to send a young and energetic man to run it. Obi accepted this responsibility with enthusiasm. He had many wonderful ideas and this was an opportunity to put them into practice. He had had sound secondary school education which designated him a "pivotal teacher" in the official records and set him apart from the other headmasters in the mission field. He was outspoken in his condemnation of the narrow views of these older and often less-educated ones.

"We shall make a good job of it, shan't we?" he asked his young wife when they first heard the joyful news of his promotion.

"We shall do our best," she replied. "We shall have such beautiful gardens and everything will be just *modern* and delightful. . . ." In their two years of married life she had become completely infected by his passion for "modern methods" and his denigration of "these old and superannuated people in the teaching field who would be better employed as traders in the Onitsha market." She began to see herself already as the admired wife of the young headmaster, the queen of the school.

The wives of the other teachers would envy her position. She would set the fashion in everything. . . . Then, suddenly, it occurred to her that there might not be other wives. Wavering between hope and fear, she asked her husband, looking anxiously at him.

"All our colleagues are young and unmarried," he said with enthusiasm which for once she did not share. "Which is a good thing," he continued.

"Why?"

"Why? They will give all their time and energy to the school."

Nancy was downcast. For a few minutes she became sceptical about the new school; but it was only for a few minutes. Her little personal misfortune could not blind her to her husband's happy prospects. She looked at him as he sat folded up in a chair. He was stoop-shouldered and looked frail. But he sometimes surprised people with sudden bursts of physical energy. In his present posture, however, all his bodily strength seemed to have retired behind his deep-set eyes, giving them an extraordinary power of penetration. He was only twenty-six, but looked thirty or more. On the whole, he was not unhandsome.

"A penny for your thoughts, Mike," said Nancy after a while, imitating the woman's magazine she read.

"I was thinking what a grand opportunity we've got at last to show these people how a school should be run."

Ndume School was backward in every sense of the word. Mr. Obi put his whole life into the work, and his wife hers too. He had two aims. A high standard of teaching was insisted upon, and the school compound was to be turned into a place of beauty. Nancy's dream-gardens came to life with the coming of the rains, and blossomed. Beautiful hibiscus and allamanda hedges in brilliant red and yellow marked out the carefully tended school compound from the rank neighbourhood bushes.

One evening as Obi was admiring his work he was scandalized to see an old woman from the village hobble right across the compound, through a marigold flower-bed and the hedges. On going up there he found faint signs of an almost disused path from the village across the school compound to the bush on the other side.

"It amazes me," said Obi to one of his teachers who had been three years in the school, "that you people allowed the villagers to make use of this footpath. It is simply incredible." He shook his head.

"The path," said the teacher apologetically, "appears to be very important to them. Although it is hardly used, it connects the village shrine with their place of burial."

"And what has that got to do with the school?" asked the headmaster.

"Well, I don't know," replied the other with a shrug of the shoulders. "But I remember there was a big row some time ago when we attempted to close it."

"That was some time ago. But it will not be used now," said Obi as he walked away. "What will the Government Education Officer think of this when he comes to inspect the school next week? The villagers might, for all I know, decide to use the school-room for a pagan ritual during the inspection."

Heavy sticks were planted closely across the path at the two places where it entered and left the school premises. These were further strengthened with barbed wire.

Three days later the village priest of *Ani* called on the headmaster. He was an old man and walked with a slight stoop. He carried a stout walking-stick which he usually tapped on the floor, by way of emphasis, each time he made a new point in his argument.

"I have heard," he said after the usual exchange of cordialities, "that our ancestral footpath has recently been closed. . . ."

"Yes," replied Mr. Obi. "We cannot allow people to make a highway of our school compound."

"Look here, my son," said the priest bringing down his walking-stick, "this path was here before you were born and before your father was born. The whole life of this village depends on it. Our dead relatives depart by it and our ancestors visit us by it. But most important, it is the path of children coming in to be born. . . ."

Mr. Obi listened with a satisfied smile on his face.

"The whole purpose of our school," he said finally, "is to eradicate just such beliefs as that. Dead men do not require footpaths. The whole idea is just fantastic. Our duty is to teach your children to laugh at such ideas."

25   "What you say may be true," replied the priest, "but we follow the practices of our fathers. If you re-open the path we shall have nothing to quarrel about. What I always say is: let the hawk perch and let the eagle perch." He rose to go.

"I am sorry," said the young headmaster. "But the school compound cannot be a thoroughfare. It is against our regulations. I would suggest your constructing another path, skirting our premises. We can even get our boys to help in building it. I don't suppose the ancestors will find the little detour too burdensome."

"I have no more words to say," said the old priest, already outside.

Two days later a young woman in the village died in childbed. A diviner was immediately consulted and he prescribed heavy sacrifices to propitiate ancestors insulted by the fence.

Obi woke up next morning among the ruins of his work. The beautiful hedges were torn up not just near the path but right round the school, the flowers trampled to death and one of the school buildings pulled down. . . . That day, the white Supervisor came to inspect the school and wrote a nasty report on the state of the premises but more seriously about the "tribal-war situation developing between the school and the village, arising in part from the misguided zeal of the new headmaster."   [1953]

QUESTIONS

1. Does the story's first sentence suggest that good or bad things will happen?
2. Reread the last sentence in the first paragraph. Have we been forewarned about the type of trouble Obi will have?
3. Are Obi's views of his "young and unmarried" colleagues realistic?
4. Could teachers and administrators learn any practical advice from this story?
5. Since "Dead Men's Path" was written during the period of British colonialism rather than after African independence, what might Achebe be saying about the views of Obi and his wife?

RESPONSES

1. Write an essay explaining how Michael Obi's character is central to the theme of the story.
2. Compare the explicit and implicit conflicts between traditional and modern cultures in Achebe's "Dead Men's Path" and Head's "Looking for a Rain God."
3. Explain how the authorities in your schools tried to "eradicate just such beliefs" that you or your family held dear.

IQBAL AHMAD

Iqbal Ahmad (b. 1921) received his doctorate from York University, Ontario, and has written a book on Northrup Frye. He has taught English literature in India and Pakistan, and in Waterloo and Ryerson, Canada. *The Atlantic Monthly*, *The Canadian Forum*, *The South Asian Review*, and *The Literary Review* have published his short fiction, which has been collected in *The Opium Eater and Other Stories* (1992).

A Bicycle

The engines throbbed violently and the ferry pushed off. It was a fine morning, and in the blue waters of the Ganga° the falling rays of the sun seemed to break and scatter.

'Move a bit, Kesho,' said an old worker, and Kesho shifted. The old man propped his bicycle against the ferry's wall and squeezed himself down next to the young man.

Once the hustle and bustle of the start was over the confusion of the workers' talk rose again on the air. There were about fifty of them, smoking and talking and spitting into the water, crossing over to the tannery on the opposite bank. The workers living in the eastern part of the city always used the company's ferry, the city bridge across the river being some five miles further up the stream.

Kesho was silent. He was thinking that there was one less mouth to feed now; his mother had died the previous week. He looked towards the burning-ghat in the distance; they had cremated her there. The foul smell of burning flesh seemed to fill his nostrils and he leaned forward and spat into the river. A tortoise rose to the surface and instantly dove down. His mother's illness and the funeral rites had left him badly off. In fact, he was in debt. But from now on he was determined to put by some money every month.

The thought infused a happy satisfaction in him. He listened to the steady chugging of the engines and watched the bicycle before him. How visibly the tremor of the ferry was passing through its frame! He turned to the old man next to him and said, '*Baba*,° when did you buy that bicycle?'

5

°*the Ganga*: The Ganges River.
°*Baba*: Term of respect, father.

'Oh, long ago, my boy, years back. Let me see. It's a little older than my youngest son and he is almost a man now.'

'Things were cheap in those days, weren't they?' Kesho asked.

'Oh, yes, they were,' the old man replied, 'very cheap. Those were the better days. You earned little, but it was enough. Money was worth something. I don't know what things are coming to, prices going through the ceiling. It will become impossible to live if things go on like this. This bicycle you see before you, how much do you think I paid for it? Only twenty-five rupees, mind you, tools and all. Now it must be double that price, I guess.'

'Double!' echoed Kesho. 'A Hercules costs well over a hundred rupees now.'

10 '*Hei Bhagwan!*'° the old man exclaimed. 'Over a hundred rupees? A bicycle costing over a hundred rupees? Who can afford to buy a bicycle now?'

Kesho was silent for a while. A light of happy desire began to shine in his eyes until they looked like the waters of the Ganga in the morning sun. Then, with a little hesitation and blushing, he said, '*Baba*, I will buy a bicycle one day.'

'At that price!' the old man exclaimed. 'Not at that price! A hundred rupees is a lot of money. I should walk if I were you.'

And Kesho did continue to walk, for years and years. Each single pie that he could save he put by like a miser; even then the money did not seem to grow, unlike the price of a bicycle which kept mounting up. He denied himself and the family as much as he could. Four flat cakes of maize, a few chillies done to paste with some salt and occasionally some *dal*° had been his midday and evening meal. He barely spent anything on his clothes. He had a raise or two, but with the prices going up and more children coming, he found it increasingly difficult to save even two or three rupees a month.

He had three children by now. He had resolved after each not to have any more. But after the day's work, when his limbs were tired and the children were asleep, his desire would wake up. Resolution had been so easy in the light of day, but in the quiet of the night it was different. 'It's my own weakness; it's my own fault,' he would chide himself. 'I will never be able to buy a bicycle like that. In ten years I have saved only two hundred rupees (by now the price of a bicycle had climbed to two hundred and fifty). I take a vow that I shall not touch Radha any more.' But he went on touching her, all the same.

15 'Kesho,' his wife said one day, 'you need only fifty rupees more, why don't you sell my bracelets? We can get them again.'

'Radha,' he said, becoming angry and genuinely so, 'don't talk to me like that. A bicycle is a toy to me. Am I to take away your ornaments for it? Besides, you brought them with you, your people gave to you. Who am I to take them away from you?'

So a bicycle, in the heat of an argument and in the fatigue of the night was a toy to him. But not in the daytime when he was by himself. What had been a dream had now become a passion. Truly, from his childhood he had wanted a bicycle. But then the mere thought of it gave him pleasure. Now he must touch it, feel it, possess it. Every bicycle that passed him he noticed. Outside cinema houses he saw hundreds of them. He would stand there a long time, watching them. A thought would sometimes turn in his mind like a worm: one less out of so many wouldn't matter. 'No, no,' he would say, and brush away the thought with a movement of his hand and go away.

°*Hei Bhagwan*: Oh, God!
°*dal (dhal)*: Dish made of peas, beans, or lentils.

Five more years passed. Grey hairs had begun to appear on his temples, when one day he pocketed all his savings and set out to buy a bicycle, walking with the long measured strides of one who had walked all his life. In the store he spoke a few words and a Hercules bicycle was pumped up and handed to him.

'That will be . . .' and before the dealer had concluded his sentence Kesho handed him the bills that he held in his perspiring palm. The dealer counted out three hundred and eleven rupees, looked up in surprise at the rustic figure before him and said, 'Why, it's the exact amount. How did you know?'

Kesho tried to answer, but his lips were trembling and he could not say a word.   20

'Why, what's wrong with the man?' said the dealer. Kesho hung down his head, quietly lifted the bicycle out of the shop and walked away without looking back. His cheeks were wet with tears of happiness.

When he reached home the whole impoverished colony came flocking round.

'Kesho has bought a bicycle,'

'It's new and shining,'

'Brother Kesho how much did it cost?'   25

There was such excitement. Kesho's heart was ready to burst with joy, yet he was ashamed as if he had done something wrong, something which made him different from the rest of them, living in the gutter.

He had experienced a similar feeling when he got his first pair of shoes. He had told his father of his intention and the old man had said, 'Look at him, he wants to buy a pair of shoes. Who ever has worn shoes in the family? He wants to waste money on shoes. Is the earth too hard for your tender feet?' His face had burned with shame. But still he was glad when he bought them. He wished that the old man were alive now.

Life for him became one unbroken round of pleasure. When he went out on his bike and the air streamed through his hair, the swift motion exhilarated him, and happiness would bubble up in him till he hardly knew how to contain it. Everything was the same—the roads, the trees, the people around—but from the bicycle they looked so different. He liked them all and they made him happy. He thought that if everybody had a bicycle how happy the world would be.

'Radha,' he said one day to his wife, 'I'll take you out on my bicycle.'

'Who, me?' she asked in wonder, 'but it would be so shameless. What will people   30
say?'

'I won't take you out in the daytime,' he said, as confusion spread over his face at the very thought of people looking at him and his wife on the bicycle, and he added, 'we'll go out at night.'

'Imagine me on a bicycle!' she said laughing, but she was pleased.

At night, when the children had gone to bed, they came out. Everything was quiet and still. The stars hung like lamps in the clear sky. The road lay straight before them, and the road lights looked like a line of stars strung out beside them. Occasionally a car passed. They found a little mound by the roadside and, resting one foot on it, Kesho sat on the bicycle and asked Radha to get up on the carrier behind him. Her weight unsteadied him. With a lunge on the pedal he started forward. The bicycle swerved dangerously to one side, then to the other, and Radha gave a squeak of fright.

'Sit still, you silly,' he said, controlling the bicycle.

'I almost fell off,' she cried.   35

'Hold me. Why don't you hold me?' he said. She hung on to him.

Now the bicycle was steady. A whir rose from its wheels in the stillness, and one electric-light pole after another swept by with astonishing rapidity.

'Not so fast, Kesho. I feel afraid.'

'This is not fast,' he said with pride, 'I can go much faster. You should see me flying to work in the morning.'

40 'Kesho,' she said after a pause, 'you should not go fast. If you fell you would hurt yourself.'

'You talk silly,' he said. 'Who wants to fall? I don't want to break my bicycle.'

In the silence of the night they went on like this, talking foolishly, happily and intimately. He took her to the Ganga, showed her the lights of his tannery on the other side, showed her his ferry that blotted the darkness a few shades deeper. The waves of the river washed softly on the shore and somewhere in a temple a bell was sounding dolefully.

When they returned, Radha said, 'It was very nice, Kesho,' and Kesho took her in his arms.

Six months went by and Kesho kept his bicycle as good as new. Then the rains set in. Almost every day there were clouds in the sky and the roads were wet and slushy, and in spite of his best care a couple of tiny rust stains appeared on one of the tire rims. He didn't like the rains.

45 The next morning as he set out for work the weather looked worse than usual. There was a blustering wind and thick black clouds were rolling in from the east like herds of wild elephants shaking their heads. He fought his way against the wind till he reached the river. He dismounted and wheeled his bicycle onto the ferry, rested it against its side and sat down.

'Hurry up, fellows,' shouted the Captain, 'we are already behind time and they don't like it over there if we are late.' A few workers were still standing on the shore. They came aboard.

The engines snorted and the shore receded. Kesho looked at the river and did not like its unfriendly swagger. It was turning and twisting too much and hit the boat like solid blocks rather than liquid waves. Within ten days, he thought, it would break its banks and spread over the countryside for miles and miles.

Suddenly, there was a terrific crash of thunder, followed by blinding rain, and the wind grew to gale force. The little ferry was in trouble; it rose and plunged, pitched and rolled. All eyes were now on the hostile current. Then there went up a howl of despair. The boat shipped a huge wave, spun violently and capsized. Some of the men jumped overboard; the others went down with the ferry. The swirling, seething mass of water swallowed them all. Then some rose to the surface, battling desperately with the raging waves. Twenty-two of the fifty or so workers fought successfully to the shore; the rest were lost.

A few feeble and ill-equipped attempts were made at rescue, but to no effect. The raging elements were too much for little row boats trying to go in. In an hour or so the storm blew over, the police arrived, and a regular search for the lost was started. The river was dragged for miles. After hours of hard work, fifteen bodies were reclaimed; the others had been swept away by the strong current. It was decided that no more useful purpose would be served by continuing the search; so it was abandoned.

50 The recovered bodies lay on the sand, below the tannery wall, and the police cordoned off that area from the general public, giving access only to the tannery people and, of course, later on to the relatives of the deceased.

Two workers came that way and stood for some time looking at the dead men. One of them recognized his friend and said in shocked tones, 'Oh, that's Kesho over there.' And sure enough, it was Kesho, lying fifth from the left. Lying by his side was his bicycle, and he was attached to it with grips of steel.   [1992]

QUESTIONS

1. How early is the nature of the ending foreshadowed?
2. Is it important that the tannery owns the ferry boat?
3. Which revelations about Kesho's daily life are likely to surprise the reader?
4. Is Kesho a loving husband?
5. Discuss the importance of the flashback in which Kesho gets "his first pair of shoes."

RESPONSES

1. Write an essay explaining how this story is an allegory of the effects of colonialism and industrialization.
2. Write a short story set in the contemporary United States. What object would serve as an appropriate symbol of our desires?

SHERMAN ALEXIE

Sherman Alexie (b. 1966) was born in Wellpinit, Washington, on the Spokane Indian Reservation. After a childhood complicated by illnesses, he attended colleges in Washington and graduated from Washington State. He is a prolific, popular, and critically acclaimed writer of poetry, short stories, novels, and film. Among his many works are *The Business of Fancydancing* (1991), *First Indian on the Moon* (1993), *The Lone Ranger and Tonto Fist Fight in Heaven* (1993), *Reservation Blues* (1995), *The Toughest Indian in the World* (2000), *One Stick Song* (2000), *Ten Little Indians* (2003) and the films *Smoke Signals* (1998) and *The Business of Fancy Dancing* (2003).

Because My Father Always Said He Was the Only Indian Who Saw Jimi Hendrix Play "The Star-Spangled Banner" at Woodstock

During the sixties, my father was the perfect hippie, since all the hippies were trying to be Indians. Because of that, how could anyone recognize that my father was trying to make a social statement?

But there is evidence, a photograph of my father demonstrating in Spokane, Washington, during the Vietnam war. The photograph made it onto the wire service and was reprinted in newspapers throughout the country. In fact, it was on the cover of *Time*.

In the photograph, my father is dressed in bell-bottoms and flowered shirt, his hair in braids, with red peace symbols splashed across his face like war paint. In his hands my father holds a rifle above his head, captured in that moment just before he proceeded to beat the shit out of the National Guard private lying prone on the ground. A fellow demonstrator holds a sign that is just barely visible over my father's left shoulder. It read MAKE LOVE NOT WAR.

The photographer won a Pulitzer Prize, and editors across the country had a lot of fun creating captions and headlines. I've read many of them collected in my father's scrapbook, and my favorite was run in the *Seattle Times*. The caption under the photograph read DEMONSTRATOR GOES TO WAR FOR PEACE. The editors capitalized on my father's Native American identity with other headlines like ONE WARRIOR AGAINST WAR and PEACEFUL GATHERING TURNS INTO NATIVE UPRISING.

Anyway, my father was arrested, charged with attempted murder, which was re-   5
duced to assault with a deadly weapon. It was a high-profile case so my father was used as an example. Convicted and sentenced quickly, he spent two years in Walla Walla State Penitentiary. Although his prison sentence effectively kept him out of the war, my father went through a different kind of war behind bars.

"There was Indian gangs and white gangs and black gangs and Mexican gangs," he told me once. "And there was somebody new killed every day. We'd hear about somebody getting it in the shower or wherever and the word would go down the line. Just one word. Just the color of his skin. Red, white, black, or brown. Then we'd chalk it up on the mental scoreboard and wait for the next broadcast."

My father made it through all that, never got into any serious trouble, somehow avoided rape, and got out of prison just in time to hitchhike to Woodstock to watch Jimi Hendrix play "The Star-Spangled Banner."

"After all the shit I'd been through," my father said, "I figured Jimi must have known I was there in the crowd to play something like that. It was exactly how I felt."

Twenty years later, my father played his Jimi Hendrix tape until it wore down. Over and over, the house filled with the rockets' red glare and the bombs bursting in air. He'd sit by the stereo with a cooler of beer beside him and cry, laugh, call me over and hold me tight in his arms, his bad breath and body odor covering me like a blanket.

Jimi Hendrix and my father became drinking buddies. Jimi Hendrix waited for my   10
father to come home after a long night of drinking. Here's how the ceremony worked:

1. I would lie awake all night and listen for the sounds of my father's pickup.
2. When I heard my father's pickup, I would run upstairs and throw Jimi's tape into the stereo.
3. Jimi would bend his guitar into the first note of "The Star-Spangled Banner" just as my father walked inside.
4. My father would weep, attempt to hum along with Jimi, and then pass out with his head on the kitchen table.
5. I would fall asleep under the table with my head near my father's feet.   15
6. We'd dream together until the sun came up.

The days after, my father would feel so guilty that he would tell me stories as a means of apology.

"I met your mother at a party in Spokane," my father told me once. "We were the only two Indians at the party. Maybe the only two Indians in the whole town. I thought she was so beautiful. I figured she was the kind of woman who could make buffalo walk on up to her and give up their lives. She wouldn't have needed to hunt. Every time we went walking, birds would follow us around. Hell, tumbleweeds would follow us around."

Somehow my father's memories of my mother grew more beautiful as their relationship became more hostile. By the time the divorce was final, my mother was quite possibly the most beautiful woman who ever lived.

"Your father was always half crazy," my mother told me more than once. "And the   20
other half was on medication."

But she loved him, too, with a ferocity that eventually forced her to leave him. They fought each other with the kind of graceful anger that only love can create. Still, their love was passionate, unpredictable, and selfish. My mother and father would get drunk and leave parties abruptly to go home and make love.

"Don't tell your father I told you this," my mother said. "But there must have been a hundred times he passed out on top of me. We'd be right in the middle of it, he'd say *I love you*, his eyes would roll backwards, and then out went his lights. It sounds strange, I know, but those were good times."

I was conceived during one of those drunken nights, half of me formed by my father's whiskey sperm, the other half formed by my mother's vodka egg. I was born a goofy reservation mixed drink, and my father needed me just as much as he needed every other kind of drink.

One night my father and I were driving home in a near-blizzard after a basketball game, listening to the radio. We didn't talk much. One, because my father didn't talk much when he was sober, and two, because Indians don't need to talk to communicate.

25   "Hello out there, folks, this is Big Bill Baggins, with the late-night classics show on KROC, 97.2 on your FM dial. We have a request from Betty in Tekoa. She wants to hear Jimi Hendrix's version of 'The Star-Spangled Banner' recorded live at Woodstock."

My father smiled, turned the volume up, and we rode down the highway while Jimi led the way like a snowplow. Until that night, I'd always been neutral about Jimi Hendrix. But, in that near-blizzard with my father at the wheel, with the nervous silence caused by the dangerous roads and Jimi's guitar, there seemed to be more to all that music. The reverberation came to mean something, took form and function.

That song made me want to learn to play guitar, not because I wanted to be Jimi Hendrix and not because I thought I'd ever play for anyone. I just wanted to touch the strings, to hold the guitar tight against my body, invent a chord, and come closer to what Jimi knew, to what my father knew.

"You know," I said to my father after the song was over, "my generation of Indian boys ain't ever had no real war to fight. The first Indians had Custer to fight. My great-grandfather had World War I, my grandfather had World War II, you had Vietnam. All I have is video games."

My father laughed for a long time, nearly drove off the road into the snowy fields.

30   "Shit," he said. "I don't know why you're feeling sorry for yourself because you ain't had to fight a war. You're lucky. Shit, all you had was that damn Desert Storm. Should have called it Dessert Storm because it just made the fat cats get fatter. It was all sugar and whipped cream with a cherry on top. And besides that, you didn't even have to fight it. All you lost during that war was sleep because you stayed up all night watching CNN."

We kept driving through the snow, talked about war and peace.

"That's all there is," my father said. "War and peace with nothing in between. It's always one or the other."

"You sound like a book," I said.

"Yeah, well, that's how it is. Just because it's in a book doesn't make it not true. And besides, why the hell would you want to fight a war for this country? It's been trying to kill Indians since the very beginning. Indians are pretty much born soldiers anyway. Don't need a uniform to prove it."

35   Those were the kinds of conversations that Jimi Hendrix forced us to have. I guess every song has a special meaning for someone somewhere. Elvis Presley is still showing up in 7-11 stores across the country, even though he's been dead for years, so I

figure music just might be the most important thing there is. Music turned my father into a reservation philosopher. Music had powerful medicine.

"I remember the first time your mother and I danced," my father told me once. "We were in this cowboy bar. We were the only real cowboys there despite the fact that we're Indians. We danced to a Hank Williams song. Danced to that real sad one, you know. 'I'm So Lonesome I Could Cry.' Except your mother and I weren't lonesome or crying. We just shuffled along and fell right goddamn down into love."

"Hank Williams and Jimi Hendrix don't have much in common," I said.

"Hell, yes, they do. They knew all about broken hearts," my father said.

"You sound like a bad movie."

"Yeah, well, that's how it is. You kids today don't know shit about romance. Don't   40
know shit about music either. Especially you Indian kids. You all have been spoiled by those drums. Been hearing them beat so long, you think that's all you need. Hell, son, even an Indian needs a piano or guitar or saxophone now and again."

My father played in a band in high school. He was the drummer. I guess he'd burned out on those. Now, he was like the universal defender of the guitar.

"I remember when your father would haul that old guitar out and play me songs," my mother said. "He couldn't play all that well but he tried. You could see him thinking about what chord he was going to play next. His eyes got all squeezed up and his face turned all red. He kind of looked that way when he kissed me, too. But don't tell him I said that."

Some nights I lay awake and listened to my parents' lovemaking. I know white people keep it quiet, pretend they don't ever make love. My white friends tell me they can't even imagine their own parents getting it on. I know exactly what it sounds like when my parents are touching each other. It makes up for knowing exactly what they sound like when they're fighting. Plus and minus. Add and subtract. It comes out just about even.

Some nights I would fall asleep to the sounds of my parents' lovemaking. I would dream Jimi Hendrix. I could see my father standing in the front row in the dark at Woodstock as Jimi Hendrix played "The Star-Spangled Banner." My mother was at home with me, both of us waiting for my father to find his way back home to the reservation. It's amazing to realize I was alive, breathing and wetting my bed, when Jimi was alive and breaking guitars.

I dreamed my father dancing with all these skinny hippie women, smoking a few   45
joints, dropping acid, laughing when the rain fell. And it did rain there. I've seen actual news footage. I've seen the documentaries. It rained. People had to share food. People got sick. People got married. People cried all kinds of tears.

But as much as I dream about it, I don't have any clue about what it meant for my father to be the only Indian who saw Jimi Hendrix play at Woodstock. And maybe he wasn't the only Indian there. Most likely there were hundreds but my father thought he was the only one. He told me that a million times when he was drunk and a couple hundred times when he was sober.

"I was there," he said. "You got to remember this was near the end and there weren't as many people as before. Not nearly as many. But I waited it out. I waited for Jimi."

A few years back, my father packed up the family and the three of us drove to Seattle to visit Jimi Hendrix's grave. We had our photograph taken lying down next to the grave. There isn't a gravestone there. Just one of those flat markers.

Jimi was twenty-eight when he died. That's younger than Jesus Christ when he died. Younger than my father as we stood over the grave.

"Only the good die young," my father said.   50

"No," my mother said. "Only the crazy people choke to death on their own vomit."

"Why you talking about my hero that way?" my father asked.

"Shit," my mother said. "Old Jesse WildShoe choked to death on his own vomit and he ain't anybody's hero."

I stood back and watched my parents argue. I was used to these battles. When an Indian marriage starts to fall apart, it's even more destructive and painful than usual. A hundred years ago, an Indian marriage was broken easily. The woman or man just packed up all their possessions and left the tipi. There were no arguments, no discussions. Now, Indians fight their way to the end, holding onto the last good thing, because our whole lives have to do with survival.

55 After a while, after too much fighting and too many angry words had been exchanged, my father went out and bought a motorcycle. A big bike. He left the house often to ride that thing for hours, sometimes for days. He even strapped an old cassette player to the gas tank so he could listen to music. With that bike, he learned something new about running away. He stopped talking as much, stopped drinking as much. He didn't do much of anything except ride that bike and listen to music.

Then one night my father wrecked his bike on Devil's Gap Road and ended up in the hospital for two months. He broke both his legs, cracked his ribs, and punctured a lung. He also lacerated his kidney. The doctors said he could have died easily. In fact, they were surprised he made it through surgery, let alone survived those first few hours when he lay on the road, bleeding. But I wasn't surprised. That's how my father was.

And even though my mother didn't want to be married to him anymore and his wreck didn't change her mind about that, she still came to see him every day. She sang Indian tunes under her breath, in time with the hum of the machines hooked into my father. Although my father could barely move, he tapped his finger in rhythm.

When he had the strength to finally sit up and talk, hold conversations, and tell stories, he called for me.

"Victor," he said. "Stick with four wheels."

60 After he began to recover, my mother stopped visiting as often. She helped him through the worst, though. When he didn't need her anymore, she went back to the life she had created. She traveled to powwows, started to dance again. She was a champion traditional dancer when she was younger.

"I remember your mother when she was the best traditional dancer in the world," my father said. "Everyone wanted to call her sweetheart. But she only danced for me. That's how it was. She told me that every other step was just for me."

"But that's only half of the dance," I said.

"Yeah," my father said. "She was keeping the rest for herself. Nobody can give everything away. It ain't healthy."

"You know," I said, "sometimes you sound like you ain't even real."

65 "What's real? I ain't interested in what's real. I'm interested in how things should be."

My father's mind always worked that way. If you don't like the things you remember, then all you have to do is change the memories. Instead of remembering the bad things, remember what happened immediately before. That's what I learned from my father. For me, I remember how good the first drink of that Diet Pepsi tasted instead of how my mouth felt when I swallowed a wasp with the second drink.

Because of all that, my father always remembered the second before my mother left him for good and took me with her. No. I remembered the second before my father left my mother and me. No. My mother remembered the second before my father left her to finish raising me all by herself.

But however memory actually worked, it was my father who climbed on his motorcycle, waved to me as I stood in the window, and rode away. He lived in Seattle, San Francisco, Los Angeles, before he finally ended up in Phoenix. For a while, I got postcards nearly every week. Then it was once a month. Then it was on Christmas and my birthday.

On a reservation, Indian men who abandon their children are treated worse than white fathers who do the same thing. It's because white men have been doing that forever and Indian men have just learned how. That's how assimilation can work.

My mother did her best to explain it all to me, although I understood most of what happened.   70

"Was it because of Jimi Hendrix?" I asked her.

"Part of it, yeah," she said. "This might be the only marriage broken up by a dead guitar player."

"There's a first time for everything, enit?"

"I guess. Your father just likes being alone more than he likes being with other people. Even me and you."

Sometimes I caught my mother digging through old photo albums or staring at the   75
wall or out the window. She'd get that look on her face that I knew meant she missed my father. Not enough to want him back. She missed him just enough for it to hurt.

On those nights I missed him most I listened to music. Not always Jimi Hendrix. Usually I listened to the blues. Robert Johnson mostly. The first time I heard Robert Johnson sing I knew he understood what it meant to be Indian on the edge of the twenty-first century, even if he was black at the beginning of the twentieth. That must have been how my father felt when he heard Jimi Hendrix. When he stood there in the rain at Woodstock.

Then on the night I missed my father most, when I lay in bed and cried, with that photograph of him beating that National Guard private in my hands, I imagined his motorcycle pulling up outside. I knew I was dreaming it all but I let it be real for a moment.

"Victor," my father yelled. "Let's go for a ride."

"I'll be right down. I need to get my coat on."

I rushed around the house, pulled my shoes and socks on, struggled into my coat,   80
and ran outside to find an empty driveway. It was so quiet, a reservation kind of quiet, where you can hear somebody drinking whiskey on the rocks three miles away. I stood on the porch and waited until my mother came outside.

"Come on back inside," she said. "It's cold."

"No," I said, "I know he's coming back tonight."

My mother didn't say anything. She just wrapped me in her favorite quilt and went back to sleep. I stood on the porch all night long and imagined I heard motorcycles and guitars, until the sun rose so bright that I knew it was time to go back inside to my mother. She made breakfast for both of us and we ate until we were full.   [1993]

QUESTIONS

1. Can the story be described as nostalgic?
2. How does the narrator indicate that being "an Indian" is an important part of his identity?
3. Why is it important to have the mother's thoughts about the narrator's father? What do those thoughts add?

4. How does the newspaper photograph of the father become symbolic for the narrator? Symbolic of what?
5. Did Jimi Hendrix really break up the marriage? If so, how?

RESPONSES

1. Research the effects of alcoholism on families. Does Alexie's story accurately portray the dynamics of alcoholism on families?
2. Research how mainstream culture in the 1960s and 1970s used Native-American culture. How is this story a reaction to this appropriation?

FOCUS ON FILM

1. View the film *Smoke Signals*. Explain this story's role in the film. How is the information in this story conveyed in the film?
2. What adaptations were made to this story for *Smoke Signals*? In particular, examine point of view.

Isabel Allende

Isabel Allende (b. 1942) was born in Lima, Peru. Her father, a diplomat for Chili, was the brother of Salvador Allende, who in 1970 was elected president of Chili. Isabel Allende traveled much of her childhood, attending schools in Bolivia and Beirut. Her early writing career was as a journalist for a variety of magazines and television programs. After her uncle's government was overthrown by a coup d'etat led by General Augusto Pinochet, Allende and her family moved to Venezuela for thirteen years where she worked as a journalist and as a school administrator. Her works include *The House of Spirits* (1982), *Of Love and Shadows* (1984), *Eva Luna* (1987), *The Stories of Eva Luna* (1990), *The Infinite Plan* (1993), *Paula* (1994), *Aphrodite* (1997), *Daughter of Fortune* (1999), *City of Beasts* (2002), *Kingdom of the Golden Dragon* (2004), and *Forests of Pigmies* (2005).

And of Clay Are We Created

They discovered the girl's head protruding from the mudpit, eyes wide open, calling soundlessly. She had a First Communion name, Azucena. Lily. In that vast cemetery where the odor of death was already attracting vultures from far away, and where the weeping of orphans and wails of the injured filled the air, the little girl obstinately clinging to life became the symbol of the tragedy. The television cameras transmitted so often the unbearable image of the head budding like a black squash from the clay that there was no one who did not recognize her and know her name. And every time we saw her on the screen, right behind her was Rolf Carlé, who had gone there on assignment, never suspecting that he would find a fragment of his past, lost thirty years before.

First a subterranean sob rocked the cotton fields, curling them like waves of foam. Geologists had set up their seismographs weeks before and knew that the mountain had awakened again. For some time they had predicted that the heat of the eruption could detach the eternal ice from the slopes of the volcano, but no one heeded their warnings; they sounded like the tales of frightened old women. The towns in the valley went about their daily life, deaf to the moaning of the earth, until that fateful Wednesday night in November when a prolonged roar announced the end of the world, and walls of snow broke loose, rolling in an avalanche of clay, stones, and water that descended on the villages and buried them beneath unfathomable meters of telluric vomit. As soon as the survivors emerged from the paralysis of that first awful terror, they could see that houses, plazas, churches, white cotton plantations, dark coffee forests, cattle pastures—all had disappeared. Much later, after soldiers and volunteers had arrived to rescue the living and try to assess the magnitude of the cataclysm, it was calculated that beneath the mud lay more than twenty thousand human beings and an indefinite number of animals putrefying in a viscous soup. Forests and rivers had also been swept away, and there was nothing to be seen but an immense desert of mire.

When the station called before dawn, Rolf Carlé and I were together. I crawled out of bed, dazed with sleep, and went to prepare coffee while he hurriedly dressed. He stuffed his gear in the green canvas backpack he always carried, and we said goodbye, as we had so many times before. I had no presentiments. I sat in the kitchen, sipping my coffee and planning the long hours without him, sure that he would be back the next day.

He was one of the first to reach the scene, because while other reporters were fighting their way to the edges of that morass in jeeps, bicycles, or on foot, each getting there however he could, Rolf Carlé had the advantage of the television helicopter, which flew him over the avalanche. We watched on our screens the footage captured by his assistant's camera, in which he was up to his knees in muck, a microphone in his hand, in the midst of a bedlam of lost children, wounded survivors, corpses, and devastation. The story came to us in his calm voice. For years he had been a familiar figure in newscasts, reporting live at the scene of battles and catastrophes with awesome tenacity. Nothing could stop him, and I was always amazed at his equanimity in the face of danger and suffering; it seemed as if nothing could shake his fortitude or deter his curiosity. Fear seemed never to touch him, although he had confessed to me that he was not a courageous man, far from it. I believe that the lens of the camera had a strange effect on him; it was as if it transported him to a different time from which he could watch events without actually participating in them. When I knew him better, I came to realize that this fictive distance seemed to protect him from his own emotions.

5   Rolf Carlé was in on the story of Azucena from the beginning. He filmed the volunteers who discovered her, and the first persons who tried to reach her; his camera zoomed in on the girl, her dark face, her large desolate eyes, the plastered-down tangle of her hair. The mud was like quicksand around her, and anyone attempting to reach her was in danger of sinking. They threw a rope to her that she made no effort to grasp until they shouted to her to catch it; then she pulled a hand from the mire and tried to move, but immediately sank a little deeper. Rolf threw down his knapsack and the rest of his equipment and waded into the quagmire, commenting for his assistant's microphone that it was cold and that one could begin to smell the stench of corpses.

"What's your name?" he asked the girl, and she told him her flower name. "Don't move, Azucena," Rolf Carlé directed, and kept talking to her, without a thought for what he was saying, just to distract her, while slowly he worked his way forward in mud up to his waist. The air around him seemed as murky as the mud.

It was impossible to reach her from the approach he was attempting, so he retreated and circled around where there seemed to be firmer footing. When finally he was close enough, he took the rope and tied it beneath her arms, so they could pull her out. He smiled at her with that smile that crinkles his eyes and makes him look like a little boy; he told her that everything was fine, that he was here with her now, that soon they would have her out. He signaled the others to pull, but as soon as the cord tensed, the girl screamed. They tried again, and her shoulders and arms appeared, but they could move her no farther; she was trapped. Someone suggested that her legs might be caught in the collapsed walls of her house, but she said it was not just rubble, that she was also held by the bodies of her brothers and sisters clinging to her legs.

"Don't worry, we'll get you out of here," Rolf promised. Despite the quality of the transmission, I could hear his voice break, and I loved him more than ever. Azucena looked at him, but said nothing.

During those first hours Rolf Carlé exhausted all the resources of his ingenuity to rescue her. He struggled with poles and ropes, but every tug was an intolerable torture for the imprisoned girl. It occurred to him to use one of the poles as a lever but got no result and had to abandon the idea. He talked a couple of soldiers into working with him for a while, but they had to leave because so many other victims were calling for help. The girl could not move, she barely could breathe, but she did not seem desperate, as if an ancestral resignation allowed her to accept her fate. The reporter, on the other hand, was determined to snatch her from death. Someone brought him a tire, which he placed beneath her arms like a life buoy, and then laid a plank near the hole to hold his weight and allow him to stay closer to her. As it was impossible to remove the rubble blindly, he tried once or twice to dive toward her feet, but emerged frustrated, covered with mud and spitting gravel. He concluded that he would have to have a pump to drain the water, and radioed a request for one, but received in return a message that there was no available transport and it could not be sent until the next morning.

"We can't wait that long!" Rolf Carlé shouted, but in the pandemonium no one   10
stopped to commiserate. Many more hours would go by before he accepted that time had stagnated and reality had been irreparably distorted.

A military doctor came to examine the girl, and observed that her heart was functioning well and that if she did not get too cold she could survive the night.

"Hang on, Azucena, we'll have the pump tomorrow," Rolf Carlé tried to console her.

"Don't leave me alone," she begged.

"No, of course I won't leave you."

Someone brought him coffee, and he helped the girl drink it, sip by sip. The   15
warm liquid revived her and she began telling him about her small life, about her family and her school, about how things were in that little bit of world before the volcano had erupted. She was thirteen, and she had never been outside her village. Rolf Carlé, buoyed by a premature optimism, was convinced that everything would end well: the pump would arrive, they would drain the water, move the rubble, and Azucena would be transported by helicopter to a hospital where she would recover rapidly and where he could visit her and bring her gifts. He thought, She's already too old for dolls, and I don't know what would please her; maybe a dress. I don't know much about women, he concluded, amused, reflecting that although he had known many women in his lifetime, none had taught him these details. To pass the hours he began to tell Azucena about his travels and adventures as a newshound, and when he exhausted his memory, he called upon imagination, inventing things he thought might entertain her. From time to time she dozed, but he kept talking in the darkness, to assure her that he was still there and to overcome the menace of uncertainty.

That was a long night.

Many miles away, I watched Rolf Carlé and the girl on a television screen. I could not bear the wait at home, so I went to National Television, where I often spent entire nights with Rolf editing programs. There, I was near his world, and I could at least get a feeling of what he lived through during those three decisive days. I called all the important people in the city, senators, commanders of the armed forces, the North American ambassador, and the president of National Petroleum, begging them for a pump to remove the silt, but obtained only vague promises. I began to ask for urgent help on radio and television, to see if there wasn't *someone* who could help us. Between calls I would run to the newsroom to monitor the satellite transmissions that periodically brought new details of the catastrophe. While reporters selected scenes with most impact for the news report, I searched for footage that featured Azucena's mudpit. The screen reduced the disaster to a single plane and accentuated the tremendous distance that separated me from Rolf Carlé; nonetheless, I was there with him. The child's every suffering hurt me as it did him; I felt his frustration, his impotence. Faced with the impossibility of communicating with him, the fantastic idea came to me that if I tried, I could reach him by force of mind and in that way give him encouragement. I concentrated until I was dizzy—a frenzied and futile activity. At times I would be overcome with compassion and burst out crying; at other times, I was so drained I felt as if I were staring through a telescope at the light of a star dead for a million years.

I watched that hell on the first morning broadcast, cadavers of people and animals awash in the current of new rivers formed overnight from the melted snow. Above the mud rose the tops of trees and the bell towers of a church where several people had taken refuge and were patiently awaiting rescue teams. Hundreds of soldiers and volunteers from the Civil Defense were clawing through rubble searching for survivors, while long rows of ragged specters awaited their turn for a cup of hot broth. Radio networks announced that their phones were jammed with calls from families offering shelter to orphaned children. Drinking water was in scarce supply, along with gasoline and food. Doctors, resigned to amputating arms and legs without anesthesia, pled that at least they be sent serum and painkillers and antibiotics; most of the roads, however, were impassable, and worse were the bureaucratic obstacles that stood in the way. To top it all, the clay contaminated by decomposing bodies threatened the living with an outbreak of epidemics.

Azucena was shivering inside the tire that held her above the surface. Immobility and tension had greatly weakened her, but she was conscious and could still be heard when a microphone was held out to her. Her tone was humble, as if apologizing for all the fuss. Rolf Carlé had a growth of beard, and dark circles beneath his eyes; he looked near exhaustion. Even from that enormous distance I could sense the quality of his weariness, so different from the fatigue of other adventures. He had completely forgotten the camera; he could not look at the girl through a lens any longer. The pictures we were receiving were not his assistant's but those of other reporters who had appropriated Azucena, bestowing on her the pathetic responsibility of embodying the horror of what had happened in that place. With the first light Rolf tried again to dislodge the obstacles that held the girl in her tomb, but he had only his hands to work with; he did not dare use a tool for fear of injuring her. He fed Azucena a cup of the cornmeal mush and bananas the Army was distributing, but she immediately vomited it up. A doctor stated that she had a fever, but added that there was little he could do: antibiotics were being reserved for cases of gangrene. A priest also passed by and blessed her, hanging a medal of the Virgin around her neck. By evening a gentle, persistent drizzle began to fall.

20   "The sky is weeping," Azucena murmured, and she, too, began to cry.

"Don't be afraid," Rolf begged. "You have to keep your strength up and be calm. Everything will be fine. I'm with you, and I'll get you out somehow."

Reporters returned to photograph Azucena and ask her the same questions, which she no longer tried to answer. In the meanwhile, more television and movie teams arrived with spools of cable, tapes, film, videos, precision lenses, recorders, sound consoles, lights, reflecting screens, auxiliary motors, cartons of supplies, electricians, sound technicians, and cameramen: Azucena's face was beamed to millions of screens around the world. And all the while Rolf Carlé kept pleading for a pump. The improved technical facilities bore results, and National Television began receiving sharper pictures and clearer sound; the distance seemed suddenly compressed, and I had the horrible sensation that Azucena and Rolf were by my side, separated from me by impenetrable glass. I was able to follow events hour by hour; I knew everything my love did to wrest the girl from her prison and help her endure her suffering; I overheard fragments of what they said to one another and could guess the rest; I was present when she taught Rolf to pray, and when he distracted her with the stories I had told him in a thousand and one nights beneath the white mosquito netting of our bed.

When darkness came on the second day, Rolf tried to sing Azucena to sleep with old Austrian folk songs he had learned from his mother, but she was far beyond sleep. They spent most of the night talking, each in a stupor of exhaustion and hunger, and shaking with cold. That night, imperceptibly, the unyielding floodgates that had contained Rolf Carlé's past for so many years began to open, and the torrent of all that had lain hidden in the deepest and most secret layers of memory poured out, leveling before it the obstacles that had blocked his consciousness for so long. He could not tell it all to Azucena; she perhaps did not know there was a world beyond the sea or time previous to her own; she was not capable of imagining Europe in the years of the war. So he could not tell her of defeat, nor of the afternoon the Russians had led them to the concentration camp to bury prisoners dead from starvation. Why should he describe to her how the naked bodies piled like a mountain of firewood resembled fragile china? How could he tell this dying child about ovens and gallows? Nor did he mention the night that he had seen his mother naked, shod in stiletto-heeled red boots, sobbing with humiliation. There was much he did not tell, but in those hours he relived for the first time all the things his mind had tried to erase. Azucena had surrendered her fear to him and so, without wishing it, had obliged Rolf to confront his own. There, beside that hellhole of mud, it was impossible for Rolf to flee from himself any longer, and the visceral terror he had lived as a boy suddenly invaded him. He reverted to the years when he was the age of Azucena, and younger, and, like her, found himself trapped in a pit without escape, buried in life, his head barely above ground; he saw before his eyes the boots and legs of his father, who had removed his belt and was whipping it in the air with the never-forgotten hiss of a viper coiled to strike. Sorrow flooded through him, intact and precise, as if it had lain always in his mind, waiting. He was once again in the armoire where his father locked him to punish him for imagined misbehavior, there where for eternal hours he had crouched with his eyes closed, not to see the darkness, with his hands over his ears, to shut out the beating of his heart, trembling, huddled like a cornered animal. Wandering in the mist of his memories he found his sister Katharina, a sweet, retarded child who spent her life hiding, with the hope that her father would forget the disgrace of her having been born. With Katharina, Rolf crawled beneath the dining room table, and with her hid there under the long white tablecloth, two children forever embraced, alert to footsteps and voices. Katharina's scent melded with his own sweat, with aromas of cooking, garlic, soup, freshly baked bread, and the unexpected odor of putrescent clay. His sister's hand in his, her frightened breathing, her silk hair against his cheek, the candid gaze of her eyes. Katharina . . . Katharina materialized before him, floating on the air like a flag, clothed in the white tablecloth, now a winding sheet, and at last he could weep for her death and for the guilt of having abandoned her. He understood then that all his exploits as a reporter, the feats that had won him such recognition and fame, were merely an attempt to keep his most ancient fears at bay, a stratagem for taking refuge behind a lens to test whether reality was more tolerable from that perspective. He took excessive risks as an exercise of courage, training by day to conquer the monsters that tormented him by night. But he had come face to face with the moment of truth; he could not continue to escape his past. He *was* Azucena; he was buried in the clayey mud; his terror was not the distant emotion of an almost forgotten childhood, it was a claw sunk in his throat. In the flush of his tears he saw his mother, dressed in black and clutching her imitation-crocodile pocketbook to her bosom, just as he had last seen her on the dock when she had come to put him on the boat to South America. She had not come to dry his tears, but to tell him to pick up a shovel: the war was over and now they must bury the dead.

"Don't cry. I don't hurt anymore. I'm fine," Azucena said when dawn came.

25   "I'm not crying for you," Rolf Carlé smiled. "I'm crying for myself. I hurt all over."

The third day in the valley of the cataclysm began with a pale light filtering through storm clouds. The President of the Republic visited the area in his tailored safari jacket to confirm that this was the worst catastrophe of the century; the country was in mourning; sister nations had offered aid; he had ordered a state of siege; the Armed Forces would be merciless, anyone caught stealing or committing other offenses would be shot on sight. He added that it was impossible to remove all the corpses or count the thousands who had disappeared; the entire valley would be declared holy ground, and bishops would come to celebrate a solemn mass for the souls of the victims. He went to the Army field tents to offer relief in the form of vague promises to crowds of the rescued, then to the improvised hospital to offer a word of encouragement to doctors and nurses worn down from so many hours of tribulations. Then he asked to be taken to see Azucena, the little girl the whole world had seen. He waved to her with a limp statesman's hand, and microphones recorded his emotional voice and paternal tone as he told her that her courage had served as an example to the nation. Rolf Carlé interrupted to ask for a pump, and the President assured him that he personally would attend to the matter. I caught a glimpse of Rolf for a few seconds kneeling beside the mudpit. On the evening news broadcast, he was still in the same position; and I, glued to the screen like a fortuneteller to her crystal ball, could tell that something fundamental had changed in him. I knew somehow that during the night his defenses had crumbled and he had given in to grief; finally he was vulnerable. The girl had touched a part of him that he himself had no access to, a part he had never shared with me. Rolf had wanted to console her, but it was Azucena who had given him consolation.

I recognized the precise moment at which Rolf gave up the fight and surrendered to the torture of watching the girl die. I was with them, three days and two nights, spying on them from the other side of life. I was there when she told him that in all her thirteen years no boy had ever loved her and that it was a pity to leave this world without knowing love. Rolf assured her that he loved her more than he could ever love anyone, more than he loved his mother, more than his sister, more than all the women who had slept in his arms, more than he loved me, his life companion, who would have given anything to be trapped in that well in her place, who would have exchanged her life for Azucena's, and I watched as he leaned down to kiss her poor forehead, consumed by a sweet, sad emotion he could not name. I felt how in that instant both were saved from despair, how they were freed from the clay, how they rose above the vultures and helicopters, how together they flew above the vast swamp of corruption and laments. How, finally, they were able to accept death. Rolf Carlé prayed in silence that she would die quickly, because such pain cannot be borne.

By then I had obtained a pump and was in touch with a general who had agreed to ship it the next morning on a military cargo plane. But on the night of that third day, beneath the unblinking focus of quartz lamps and the lens of a hundred cameras, Azucena gave up, her eyes locked with those of the friend who had sustained her to the end. Rolf Carlé removed the life buoy, closed her eyelids, held her to his chest for a few moments, and then let her go. She sank slowly, a flower in the mud.

You are back with me, but you are not the same man. I often accompany you to the station and we watch the videos of Azucena again; you study them intently, looking for something you could have done to save her, something you did not think of in time. Or maybe you study them to see yourself as if in a mirror, naked. Your cameras lie forgotten in a closet; you do not write or sing; you sit long hours before the window, staring at the mountains. Beside you, I wait for you to complete the voyage into yourself, for the old wounds to heal. I know that when you return from your nightmares, we shall again walk hand in hand, as before.   [1989]

QUESTIONS

1. How does the narrator's distant relationship to the events contribute to the story?
2. Why does Rolf Carlé become so attached to Azucena?
3. The last paragraph of the story is written in present tense, while everything before is written in past tense. Why isn't the entire story told in past tense?
4. What statement does the story make about the power of governments and of the power of the media?
5. What is the meaning of the title? Why is it phrased in such a formal manner?

RESPONSES

1. Examine this story through the psychological approach. Write an essay interpreting the psychological impact of the image of the girl's face in the mud, after an avalanche.
2. Examine the story through the sociological/Marxist approach. What does the story say about money, power, and prestige?

DOROTHY ALLISON

Dorothy Allison (b. 1949) was born in Greenville, South Carolina, completed her undergraduate work at Florida Presbyterian College, and received an M.A. in anthropology at the New School for Social Research, New York. *Trash*, a collection of short stories, was published in 1988. *Bastard out of Carolina* (1992), her first novel, won the National Book Award and was later filmed for television (1996). Her second novel is *Cavedweller* (1998). Her book of essays is *Skin: Talking about Sex, Class and Literature* (1994).

I'm Working on My Charm

I'm working on my charm.

It was one of those parties where everyone pretends to know everyone else. My borrowed silk blouse kept pulling out of my skirt, so I tried to stay with my back to the buffet and ignore the bartender who had a clear view of my problem. The woman who brushed my arm was a friend of the director of the organization where I worked, a woman who was known for her wardrobe and sudden acts of well-publicized generosity. She tossed her hair back when she saw me and laughed like an old familiar friend. "Southerners are so charming, I always say, giving their children such clever names."

She had a wine glass in one hand and a cherry tomato in the other, and she gestured with that tomato—a wide, witty, "charmed" gesture I do not remember ever seeing in the South. "I just love yours. There was a girl at school had a name like yours, two names said as one actually. Barbara-Jean, I think, or Ruth-Anne. I can't remember anymore, but she was the sweetest, most soft-spoken girl. I just loved her."

She smiled again, her eyes looking over my head at someone else. She leaned in close to me, "It's so wonderful that you can be with us, you know. Some of the people who have worked here, well . . . you know, well, we have so much to learn from you—gentility, you know, courtesy, manners, charm, all of that."

5   For a moment I was dizzy, overcome with the curious sensation of floating out of the top of my head. It was as if I looked down on all the other people in that crowded room, all of them sipping their wine and half of them eating cherry tomatoes. I watched the woman beside me click her teeth against the beveled edge of her wine glass and heard the sound of my mother's voice hissing in my left ear, *Yankeeeeeees!* It was all I could do not to nod.

When I was sixteen I worked counter with my mama back of a Moses Drugstore planted in the middle of a Highway 50 shopping mall. I was trying to save money to go to college, and ritually, every night, I'd pour my tips into a can on the back of my dresser. Sometimes my mama'd throw in a share of hers to encourage me, but mostly hers was spent even before we got home—at the Winn Dixie at the far end of the mall or the Maryland Fried Chicken right next to it.

Mama taught me the real skills of being a waitress—how to get an order right, get the drinks there first and the food as fast as possible so it would still be hot, and to do it all with an expression of relaxed good humor. "You don't have to smile," she explained, "but it does help." "Of course," she had to add, "don't go 'round like a grinning fool. Just smile like you know what you're doing, and never *look* like you're in a hurry." I found it difficult to keep from looking like I was in a hurry, especially when I got out of breath running from steam table to counter. Worse, moving at the speed I did, I tended to sway a little and occasionally lost control of a plate.

"Never," my mama told me, "serve food someone has seen fall to the floor. It's not only bad manners, it'll get us all in trouble. Take it in the back, clean it off, and return it to the steam table." After awhile I decided I could just run to the back, count to ten, and take it back out to the customer with an apology. Since I usually just dropped biscuits, cornbread, and baked potatoes—the kind of stuff that would roll on a plate—I figured brushing it off was sufficient. But once, in a real rush to an impatient customer, I watched a ten-ounce T-bone slip right off the plate, flip in the air, and smack the rubber floor mat. The customer's mouth flew open, and I saw my mama's eyes shoot fire. Hurriedly I picked it up by the bone and ran to the back with it. I was running water on it when Mama came in the back room.

"All right," she snapped, "you are not to run, you are not even to walk fast. And," she added, taking the meat out of my fingers and dropping it into the open waste can, "you are not, not ever to drop anything as expensive as that again." I watched smoky frost from the leaky cooler float up toward her blonde curls, and I promised her tearfully that I wouldn't.

The greater skills Mama taught me were less tangible than rules about speed and smiling. What I needed most from her had a lot to do with being as young as I was, as naive, and quick to believe the stories put across the counter by all those travelers heading North. Mama always said I was the smartest of her daughters and the most foolish. I believed everything I read in books, and most of the stuff I heard on the TV, and all of Mama's carefully framed warnings never seemed to quite slow down my capacity to take people as who they wanted me to think they were. I tried hard to be like my mama but, as she kept complaining, I was just too quick to trust—badly in need of a little practical experience.

My practical education began the day I started work. The first comment by the manager was cryptic but to the point. "Well, sixteen." Harriet smiled, looking me up and down, "At least you'll up the ante." Mama's friend, Mabel, came over and squeezed my arm. "Don't get nervous, young one. We'll keep moving you around. You'll never be left alone."

Mabel's voice was reassuring even if her words weren't, and I worked her station first. A family of four children, parents, and a grandmother took her biggest table. She took their order with a wide smile, but as she passed me going down to the ice drawer, her teeth were point on point. "Fifty cents," she snapped, and went on. Helping her clean the table thirty-five minutes later I watched her pick up two lone quarters and repeat "fifty cents," this time in a mournfully conclusive tone.

It was a game all the waitresses played. There was a butter bowl on the back counter where the difference was kept, the difference between what you guessed and what you got. No one had to play, but most of the women did. The rules were simple. You had to make your guess at the tip *before* the order was taken. Some of the women would cheat a little, bringing the menus with the water glasses and saying, "I want ya'll to just look this over carefully. We're serving one fine lunch today." Two lines of conversation and most of them could walk away with a guess within five cents.

However much the guess was off went into the bowl. If you said fifty cents and got seventy-five cents, then twenty-five cents went to the bowl. Even if you said seventy-five cents and got fifty cents instead, you had to throw in that quarter—guessing high was as bad as guessing short. "We used to just count the short guesses," Mabel explained, "but this makes it more interesting."

15 Once Mabel was sure she'd get a dollar and got stiffed instead. She was so mad she counted out that dollar in nickels and pennies, and poured it into the bowl from a foot in the air. It made a very satisfying angry noise, and when those people came back a few weeks later no one wanted to serve them. Mama stood back by the pharmacy sign smoking her Pall Mall cigarette and whispered in my direction, "Yankees." I was sure I knew just what she meant.

At the end of each week, the women playing split the butter bowl evenly.

Mama said I wasn't that good a waitress, but I made up for it in eagerness. Mabel said I made up for it in "tail." "Those salesmen sure do like how you run back to that steam table," she said with a laugh, but she didn't say it where Mama could hear. Mama said it was how I smiled.

"You got a heartbreaker's smile," she told me. "You make them think of when they were young." Behind her back, Mabel gave me her own smile, and a long slow shake of her head.

Whatever it was, by the end of the first week I'd earned four dollars more in tips than my mama. It was almost embarrassing. But then they turned over the butter bowl and divided it evenly between everyone but me. I stared and Mama explained. "Another week and you can start adding to the pot. Then you'll get a share. For now just write down two dollars on Mr. Aubrey's form."

20 "But I made a lot more than that," I told her.

"Honey, the tax people don't need to know that." Her voice was patient. "Then when you're in the pot, just report your share. That way we all report the same amount. They expect that."

"Yeah, they don't know nothing about initiative," Mabel added, rolling her hips in illustration of her point. It made her heavy bosom move dramatically, and I remembered times I'd seen her do that at the counter. It made me feel even more embarrassed and angry.

When we were alone I asked Mama if she didn't think Mr. Aubrey knew that everyone's reports on their tips were faked.

"He doesn't say what he knows," she replied, "and I don't imagine he's got a reason to care."

25 I dropped the subject and started the next week guessing on my tips.

Salesmen and truckers were always a high guess. Women who came with a group were low, while women alone were usually a fair twenty-five cents on a light lunch— if you were polite and brought them their coffee first. It was 1966, after all, and a hamburger cost sixty-five cents. Tourists were more difficult. I learned that noisy kids meant a small tip, which seemed the highest injustice. Maybe it was a kind of defensive arrogance that made the parents of those kids leave so little, as if they were saying, "Just because little Kevin gave you a headache and poured ketchup on the floor doesn't mean I owe you anything."

Early morning tourists who asked first for tomato juice, lemon, and coffee were a bonus. They were almost surely leaving the Jamaica Inn just up the road, which had a terrible restaurant but served the strongest drinks in the county. If you talked softly you never got less than a dollar, and sometimes for nothing more than juice, coffee, and aspirin.

I picked it up. In three weeks I started to really catch on and started making sucker bets like the old man who ordered egg salad. Before I even carried the water glass over, I snapped out my counter rag, turned all the way around, and said, "five." Then as I turned to the stove and the rack of menus, I mouthed, "dollars."

Mama frowned while Mabel rolled her shoulders and said, "An't we growing up fast!"

I just smiled my heartbreaker's smile and got the man his sandwich. When he left 30 I snapped that five dollar bill loudly five times before I put it in my apron pocket. "My mama didn't raise no fool," I told the other women, who laughed and slapped my behind like they were glad to see me cutting up.

But Mama took me with her on her break. We walked up toward the Winn Dixie where she could get her cigarettes cheaper than in the drugstore.

"How'd you know?" she asked.

"'Cause that's what he always leaves," I told her.

"What do you mean *always?*"

"Every Thursday evening when I close up." I said it knowing she was going to be 35 angry.

"He leaves you a five dollar bill every Thursday night!" Her voice sounded strange, not angry exactly but not at all pleased either.

"Always," I said, and I added, "and he pretty much always has egg salad."

Mama stopped to light her last cigarette. Then she just stood there for a moment, breathing deeply around the Pall Mall and watching me while my face got redder and redder.

"You think you can get along without it?" she asked finally.

"Why?" I asked her. "I don't think he's going to stop." 40

"Because," she said, dropping the cigarette and walking on, "you're not working any more Thursday nights."

On Sundays the counter didn't open until after church at one o'clock. But at one sharp, we started serving those big gravy lunches and went right on till four. People would come in prepared to sit and eat big—coffee, salad, country fried steak with potatoes and gravy, or ham with red-eye gravy and carrots and peas. You'd also get a side of hog's head biscuits and a choice of three pies for dessert.

Tips were as choice as the pies, but Sunday had its trials. Too often, some tight-browed couple would come in at two o'clock and order breakfast—fried eggs and hash browns. When you told them we didn't serve breakfast on Sundays, they'd get angry.

"Look girl," they might say, "just bring me some of that ham you're serving those people, only bring me eggs with it. You can do that," and the contempt in their voices clearly added, "even you."

45   It would make me mad as sin. "Sir, we don't cook on the grill on Sundays. We only have what's on the Sunday menu. When you make up your mind, let me know."

"Tourists," I'd mutter to Mama.

"No, *Yankees*," she'd say, and Mabel would nod.

Then she might go over with an offer of boiled eggs, that ham, and a biscuit. She'd talk nice, drawling like she never did with me or friends, while she moved slower than you'd think a wide-awake person could. "Uh huh," she'd say, and "shore-nuf," and offer them honey for their biscuits or tell them how red-eye gravy is made, or talk about how sorry it is that we don't serve grits on Sunday. That couple would grin wide and start slowing their words down, while the regulars would choke on their coffee. Mama never bet on the tip, just put it all into the pot, and it was usually enough to provoke a round of applause after the couple was safely out the door.

Mama said nothing about it except the first time when she told me, "Yankees eat boiled eggs for breakfast," which may not sound like much, but had the force of a powerful insult. It was a fact that the only people we knew who ate boiled eggs in the morning were those stray tourists and people on the TV set who we therefore assumed had to be Yankees.

50   Yankees ate boiled eggs, laughed at grits but ate them in big helpings, and had plenty of money to leave outrageous tips but might leave nothing for no reason that I could figure out. It wasn't the accent that marked Yankees. They talked different, but all kinds of different. There seemed to be a great many varieties of them, not just Northerners, but Westerners, Canadians, Black people who talked oddly enough to show they were foreign, and occasionally strangers who didn't even speak English. Some were friendly, some deliberately nasty. All of them were Yankees, strangers, unpredictable people with an enraging attitude of superiority who would say the rudest things as if they didn't know what an insult was.

"They're the ones the world was made for," Harriet told me late one night. "You and me, your mama, all of us, we just hold a place in the landscape for them. Far as they're concerned, once we're out of sight we just disappear."

Mabel plain hated them. Yankees didn't even look when she rolled her soft wide hips. "Son of a bitch," she'd say when some fish-eyed, clipped-tongue stranger would look right through her and leave her less than fifteen cents. "He must think we get fat on the honey of his smile." Which was even funnier when you'd seen that the man hadn't smiled at all.

"But give me an inch of edge and I can handle them," she'd tell me. "Sweets, you just stretch that drawl. Talk like you're from Mississippi, and they'll eat it up. For some reason, Yankees got strange sentimental notions about Mississippi."

"They're strange about other things too," Mama would throw in. "They think they can ask you personal questions just 'cause you served them a cup of coffee." Some salesman once asked her where she got her hose with the black thread sewed up the back and Mama hadn't forgiven him yet.

55   But the thing everyone told me and told me again was that you just couldn't trust yourself with them. Nobody bet on Yankee tips, they might leave anything. Once someone even left a New York City subway token. Mama thought it a curiosity but not the equivalent of real money. Another one ordered one cup of coffee to go and twenty packs of sugar.

"They made 'road-liquor' out of it," Mabel said. "Just add an ounce of vodka and set it down by the engine exhaust for a month or so. It'll cook up into a bitter poison that'll knock you cross-eyed."

It sounded dangerous to me, but Mabel didn't think so. "Not that I would drink it," she'd say, "but I wouldn't fault a man who did."

They stole napkins, not one or two but a boxful at a time. Before we switched to sugar packets, they'd come in, unfold two or three napkins, open them like diapers, and fill them up with sugar before they left. Then they might take the knife and spoon to go with it. Once I watched a man take out a stack of napkins I was sure he was going to walk off with. But instead he sat there for thirty minutes making notes on them, then balled them all up and threw them away when he left.

My mama was scandalized by that. "And right over there on the shelf is a note-book selling for ten cents. What's wrong with these people?"

"They're living in the movies," Mabel whispered, looking back toward the counter.   60

"Yeah, Bette Davis movies," I added.

"I don't know about the movies." Harriet put her hand on Mama's shoulder. "But they don't live in the real world with the rest of us."

"No," Mama said, "they don't."

I take a bite of cherry tomato and hear Mama's voice again. *No,* she says.

"No," I say. I tuck my blouse into my skirt and shift in my shoes. If I close my eyes,   65
I can see Mabel's brightly rouged cheekbones, Harriet's pitted skin, and my mama's shadowed brown eyes. When I go home tonight I'll write her about this party and imagine how she'll laugh about it all. The woman who was talking to me has gone off across the room to the other bar. People are giving up nibbling and going on to more serious eating. One of the men I work with every day comes over with a full plate and a wide grin.

"Boy," he drawls around a bite of the cornbread I contributed to the buffet, "I bet you sure can cook."

"Bet on it," I say, with my Mississippi accent. I swallow the rest of a cherry toma-to and give him my heartbreaker's smile.   [1980]

QUESTIONS

1. Why is the narrator's mother upset about the five-dollar tip her daughter has been receiving?

2. What does the narrator mean by the title? What sort of "charm" does she mean?

3. How many different words and phrases in the second paragraph show the narrator's discomfiture and/or disdain?

4. At the beginning of the second section, the narrator says that she was "naive." Why?

5. What lessons has the narrator learned as a waitress? Do they influence the way she now treats people?

RESPONSE

1. Read Allison's essay "Context." Explore how her personal history is or is not part of this story.

SHERWOOD ANDERSON

Sherwood Anderson (1876–1941) was born in Camden, Ohio. Dropping out of school at the age of fourteen to become a stable boy, he worked at a number of odd jobs before enlisting at nineteen in the Spanish-American War. After the war he achieved considerable success as an advertising writer and paint manufacturer. In 1912, following a nervous breakdown, he abandoned business to devote himself to writing. His fourth book, *Winesburg, Ohio* (1919), a collection of interrelated tales depicting characters stifled by the provincialism of Midwestern life, brought him fame. Later writers, notably Faulkner and Hemingway, recognized Anderson's influence upon their own work, especially in his use of native materials and his psychological realism.

I Want to Know Why

We got up at four in the morning, that first day in the east. On the evening before we had climbed off a freight train at the edge of town, and with the true instinct of Kentucky boys had found our way across town and to the racetrack and the stables at once. Then we knew we were all right. Hanley Turner right away found a nigger we knew. It was Bildad Johnson who in the winter works at Ed Becker's livery barn in our home town, Beckersville. Bildad is a good cook as almost all our niggers are and of course he, like everyone in our part of Kentucky who is anyone at all, likes the horses. In the spring Bildad begins to scratch around. A nigger from our country can flatter and wheedle anyone into letting him do most anything he wants. Bildad wheedles the stable men and the trainers from the horse farms in our country around Lexington. The trainers come into town in the evening to stand around and talk and maybe get into a poker game. Bildad gets in with them. He is always doing little favors and telling about things to eat, chicken browned in a pan, and how is the best way to cook sweet potatoes and corn bread. It makes your mouth water to hear him.

When the racing season comes on and the horses go to the races and there is all the talk on the streets in the evenings about the new colts, and everyone says when they are going over to Lexington or to the spring meeting at Churchill Downs or to Latonia, and the horsemen that have been down to New Orleans or maybe at the winter meeting at Havana in Cuba come home to spend a week before they start out again, at such a time when everything talked about in Beckersville is just horses and nothing else and the outfits start out and horse racing is in every breath of air you breathe, Bildad shows up with a job as cook for some outfit. Often when I think about it, his always going all season to the races and working in the livery barn in the winter where horses are and where men like to come and talk about horses, I wish I was a nigger. It's a foolish thing to say, but that's the way I am about being around horses, just crazy. I can't help it.

Well, I must tell you about what we did and let you in on what I'm talking about. Four of us boys from Beckersville, all whites and sons of men who live in Beckersville regular, made up our minds we were going to the races, not just to Lexington or Louisville, I don't mean, but to the big eastern track we were always hearing our Beckersville men talk about, to Saratoga. We were all pretty young then. I was just turned fifteen and I was the oldest of the four. It was my scheme. I admit that and I talked the others into trying it. There was Hanley Turner and Henry Rieback and Tom Tumberton and myself. I had thirty-seven dollars I had earned during the winter working nights and Saturdays in Enoch Myer's grocery. Henry Rieback had eleven dollars and the others, Hanley and Tom, had only a dollar or two each. We fixed it all up and laid low until the Kentucky spring meetings were over and some of our men, the sportiest ones, the ones we envied the most, had cut out—then we cut out too.

I won't tell you the trouble we had beating our way on freights and all. We went through Cleveland and Buffalo and other cities and saw Niagara Falls. We bought things there, souvenirs and spoons and cards and shells with pictures of the Falls on them for our sisters and mothers, but thought we had better not send any of the things home. We didn't want to put the folks on our trail and maybe be nabbed.

We got into Saratoga as I said at night and went to the track. Bildad fed us up. He showed us a place to sleep in hay over a shed and promised to keep still. Niggers are all right about things like that. They won't squeal on you. Often a white man you might meet, when you had run away from home like that, might appear to be all right and give you a quarter or a half dollar or something, and then go right and give you away. White men will do that, but not a nigger. You can trust them. They are squarer with kids. I don't know why.

At the Saratoga meeting that year there were a lot of men from home. Dave Williams and Arthur Mulford and Jerry Myers and others. Then there was a lot from Louisville and Lexington Henry Rieback knew but I didn't. They were professional gamblers and Henry Rieback's father is one too. He is what is called a sheet writer and goes away most of the year to tracks. In the winter when he is home in Beckersville he don't stay there much but goes away to cities and deals faro. He is a nice man and generous, is always sending Henry presents, a bicycle and a gold watch and a Boy Scout suit of clothes and things like that.

My own father is a lawyer. He's all right, but don't make much money and can't buy me things and anyway I'm getting so old now I don't expect it. He never said nothing to me against Henry, but Hanley Turner and Tom Tumberton's fathers did. They said to their boys that money so come by is no good and they didn't want their boys brought up to hear gamblers' talk and be thinking about such things and maybe embrace them.

That's all right and I guess the men know what they are talking about, but I don't see what it's got to do with Henry or horses either. That's what I'm writing this story about. I'm puzzled. I'm getting to be a man and want to think straight and be O.K., and there's something I saw at the race meeting at the eastern track I can't figure out.

I can't help it, I'm crazy about thoroughbred horses. I've always been that way. When I was ten years old and saw I was growing to be big and couldn't be a rider I was so sorry I nearly died. Harry Hellinfinger in Beckersville, whose father is Postmaster, is grown up and too lazy to work, but likes to stand around in the street and get up jokes on boys like sending them to a hardware store for a gimlet to bore square holes and other jokes like that. He played one on me. He told me that if I would eat a half a cigar I would be stunted and not grow any more and maybe could be a rider. I did it. When father wasn't looking I took a cigar out of his pocket and gagged it down some way. It made me awful sick and the doctor had to be sent for, and then it did no good. I kept right on growing. It was a joke. When I told what I had done and why most fathers would have whipped me but mine didn't.

10   Well, I didn't get stunted and didn't die. It serves Harry Hellinfinger right. Then I made up my mind I would like to be a stable boy, but had to give that up too. Mostly niggers do that work and I knew father wouldn't let me go into it. No use to ask him.

If you've never been crazy about thoroughbreds it's because you've never been around where they are much and don't know any better. They're beautiful. There isn't anything so lovely and clean and full of spunk and honest and everything as some race horses. On the big horse farms that are all around our town Beckersville there are tracks and the horses run in the early morning. More than a thousand times I've got out of bed before daylight and walked two or three miles to the tracks. Mother wouldn't of let me go but father always says, "Let him alone." So I got some bread out of the bread box and some butter and jam, gobbled it and lit out.

At the tracks you sit on the fence with men, whites and niggers, and they chew tobacco and talk, and then the colts are brought out. It's early and the grass is covered with shiny dew and in another field a man is plowing and they are frying things in a shed where the track niggers sleep, and you know how a nigger can giggle and laugh and say things that make you laugh. A white man can't do it and some niggers can't but a track nigger can every time.

And so the colts are brought out and some are just galloped by stable boys, but almost every morning on a big track owned by a rich man who lives maybe in New York, there are always, nearly every morning, a few colts and some of the old race horses and geldings and mares that are cut loose.

It brings a lump up into my throat when a horse runs. I don't mean all horses but some. I can pick them nearly every time. It's in my blood like in the blood of race-track niggers and trainers. Even when they just go slop-jogging along with a little nigger on their backs I can tell a winner. If my throat hurts and it's hard for me to swallow, that's him. He'll run like Sam Hill when you let him out. If he don't win every time it'll be a wonder and because they've got him in a pocket behind another or he was pulled or got off bad at the post or something. If I wanted to be a gambler like Henry Rieback's father I could get rich. I know I could and Henry says so too. All I would have to do is to wait 'til that hurt comes when I see a horse and then bet every cent. That's what I would do if I wanted to be a gambler, but I don't.

15   When you're at the tracks in the morning—not the race tracks but the training tracks around Beckersville—you don't see a horse, the kind I've been talking about, very often, but it's nice anyway. Any thoroughbred, that is sired right and out of a good mare and trained by a man that knows how, can run. If he couldn't what would he be there for and not pulling a plow?

Well, out of the stables they come and the boys are on their backs and it's lovely to be there. You hunch down on top of the fence and itch inside you. Over in the sheds the niggers giggle and sing. Bacon is being fried and coffee made. Everything smells lovely. Nothing smells better than coffee and manure and horses and niggers and bacon frying and pipes being smoked out of doors on a morning like that. It just gets you, that's what it does.

But about Saratoga. We was there six days and not a soul from home seen us and everything came off just as we wanted it to, fine weather and horses and races and all. We beat our way home and Bildad gave us a basket with fried chicken and bread and other eatables in, and I had eighteen dollars when we got back to Beckersville. Mother jawed and cried but Pop didn't say much. I told everything we done except one thing. I did and saw that alone. That's what I'm writing about. It got me upset. I think about it at night. Here it is.

At Saratoga we laid up nights in the hay in the shed Bildad had showed us and ate with the niggers early and at night when the race people had all gone away. The men from home stayed mostly in the grandstand and betting field, and didn't come out around the places where the horses are kept except to the paddocks just before a race when the horses are saddled. At Saratoga they don't have paddocks under an open shed as at Lexington and Churchill Downs and other tracks down in our country, but saddle the horses right out in an open place under trees on a lawn as smooth and nice as Banker Bohon's front yard here in Beckersville. It's lovely. The horses are sweaty and nervous and shine and the men come out and smoke cigars and look at them and the trainers are there and the owners, and your heart thumps so you can hardly breathe.

Then the bugle blows for post and the boys that ride come running out with their silk clothes on and you run to get a place by the fence with the niggers.

I always am wanting to be a trainer or owner, and at the risk of being seen and caught and sent home I went to the paddocks before every race. The other boys didn't but I did. 20

We got to Saratoga on a Friday and on Wednesday the next week the big Mullford Handicap was to be run. Middlestride was in it and Sunstreak. The weather was fine and the track fast. I couldn't sleep the night before.

What had happened was that both these horses are the kind it makes my throat hurt to see. Middlestride is long and looks awkward and is a gelding. He belongs to Joe Thompson, a little owner from home who only has a half-dozen horses. The Mullford Handicap is for a mile and Middlestride can't untrack fast. He goes away slow and is always way back at the half, then he begins to run and if the race is a mile and a quarter he'll just eat up everything and get there.

Sunstreak is different. He is a stallion and nervous and belongs on the biggest farm we've got in our country, the Van Riddle place that belongs to Mr. Van Riddle of New York. Sunstreak is like a girl you think about sometimes but never see. He is hard all over and lovely too. When you look at his head you want to kiss him. He is trained by Jerry Tillford who knows me and has been good to me lots of times, lets me walk into a horse's stall to look at him close and other things. There isn't anything as sweet as that horse. He stands at the post quiet and not letting on, but he is just burning up inside. Then when the barrier goes up he is off like his name, Sunstreak. It makes you ache to see him. It hurts you. He just lays down and runs like a bird dog. There can't be anything I ever see run like him except Middlestride when he gets untracked and stretches himself.

Gee! I ached to see that race and those two horses run, ached and dreaded it too. I didn't want to see either of our horses beaten. We had never sent a pair like that to the races before. Old men in Beckersville said so and the niggers said so. It was a fact.

25   Before the race I went over to the paddocks to see. I looked a last look at Middlestride, who isn't such a much standing in a paddock that way, then I went to see Sunstreak.

It was his day. I knew when I seen him. I forgot all about being seen myself and walked right up. All the men from Beckersville were there and no one noticed me except Jerry Tillford. He saw me and something happened. I'll tell you about that.

I was standing looking at that horse and aching. In some way, I can't tell how, I knew just how Sunstreak felt inside. He was quiet and letting the niggers rub his legs and Mr. Van Riddle himself put the saddle on, but he was just a raging torrent inside. He was like the water in the river at Niagara Falls just before it goes plunk down. That horse wasn't thinking about running. He don't have to think about that. He was just thinking about holding himself back 'til the time for the running came. I knew that. I could just in a way see right inside him. He was going to do some awful running and I knew it. He wasn't bragging or letting on much or prancing or making a fuss, but just waiting. I knew it and Jerry Tillford his trainer knew. I looked up and then that man and I looked into each other's eyes. Something happened to me. I guess I loved the man as much as I did the horse because he knew what I knew. Seemed to me there wasn't anything in the world but that man and the horse and me. I cried and Jerry Tillford had a shine in his eyes. Then I came away to the fence to wait for the race. The horse was better than me, more steadier, and now I know better than Jerry. He was the quietest and he had to do the running.

Sunstreak ran first of course and he busted the world's record for a mile. I've seen that if I never see anything more. Everything came out just as I expected. Middlestride got left at the post and was way back and closed up to be second, just as I knew he would. He'll get a world's record too some day. They can't skin the Beckersville country on horses.

I watched the race calm because I knew what would happen. I was sure. Hanley Turner and Henry Rieback and Tom Tumberton were all more excited than me.

30   A funny thing had happened to me. I was thinking about Jerry Tillford the trainer and how happy he was all through the race. I liked him that afternoon even more than I ever liked my own father. I almost forgot the horses thinking that way about him. It was because of what I had seen in his eyes as he stood in the paddocks beside Sunstreak before the race started. I knew he had been watching and working with Sunstreak since the horse was a baby colt, had taught him to run and be patient and when to let himself out and not to quit, never. I knew that for him it was like a mother seeing her child do something brave or wonderful. It was the first time I ever felt for a man like that.

After the race that night I cut out from Tom and Hanley and Henry. I wanted to be by myself and I wanted to be near Jerry Tillford if I could work it. Here is what happened.

The track in Saratoga is near the edge of town. It is all polished up and trees around, the evergreen kind, and grass and everything painted and nice. If you go past the track you get to a hard road made of asphalt for automobiles, and if you go along this for a few miles there is a road turns off to a little rummy-looking farmhouse set in a yard.

That night after the race I went along that road because I had seen Jerry and some other men go that way in an automobile. I didn't expect to find them. I walked for a ways and then sat down by a fence to think. It was the direction they went in. I wanted to be as near Jerry as I could. I felt close to him. Pretty soon I went up the side road—I don't know why—and came to the rummy farmhouse. I was just lonesome to see Jerry, like wanting to see your father at night when you are a young kid. Just then an automobile came along and turned in. Jerry was in it and Henry Rieback's father, and Arthur Bedford from home, and Dave Williams and two other men I didn't know. They got out of the car and went into the house, all but Henry Rieback's father who quarreled with them and said he wouldn't go. It was only about nine o'clock, but they were all drunk and the rummy-looking farmhouse was a place for bad women to stay in. That's what it was. I crept up along a fence and looked through a window and saw.

It's what give me the fantods. I can't make it out. The women in the house were all ugly mean-looking women, not nice to look at or be near. They were homely too, except one who was tall and looked a little like the gelding Middlestride, but not clean like him, but with a hard ugly mouth. She had red hair. I saw everything plain. I got up by an old rosebush by an open window and looked. The women had on loose dresses and sat around in chairs. The men came in and some sat on the women's laps. The place smelled rotten and there was rotten talk, the kind a kid hears around a livery stable in a town like Beckersville in the winter but don't ever expect to hear talked when there are women around. It was rotten. A nigger wouldn't go into such a place.

I looked at Jerry Tillford. I've told you how I had been feeling about him on account of his knowing what was going on inside of Sunstreak in the minute before he went to the post for the race in which he made a world's record.   35

Jerry bragged in that bad-woman house as I know Sunstreak wouldn't never have bragged. He said that he made that horse, that it was him that won the race and made the record. He lied and bragged like a fool. I never heard such silly talk.

And then, what do you suppose he did! He looked at the woman in there, the one that was lean and hard-mouthed and looked a little like the gelding Middlestride, but not clean like him, and his eyes began to shine just as they did when he looked at me and at Sunstreak in the paddocks at the track in the afternoon. I stood there by the window—gee!—but I wished I hadn't gone away from the tracks, but had stayed with the boys and the niggers and the horses. The tall rotten-looking woman was between us just as Sunstreak was in the paddocks in the afternoon.

Then, all of a sudden, I began to hate that man. I wanted to scream and rush in the room and kill him. I never had such a feeling before. I was so mad clean through that I cried and my fists were doubled up so my fingernails cut my hands.

And Jerry's eyes kept shining and he waved back and forth, and then he went and kissed that woman and I crept away and went back to the tracks and to bed and didn't sleep hardly any, and then next day I got the other kids to start home with me and never told them anything I seen.

I been thinking about it ever since. I can't make it out. Spring has come again and   40
I'm nearly sixteen and go to the tracks mornings same as always, and I see Sunstreak and Middlestride and a new colt named Strident I'll bet will lay them all out, but no one thinks so but me and two or three niggers.

But things are different. At the tracks the air don't taste as good or smell as good. It's because a man like Jerry Tillford, who knows what he does, could see a horse like Sunstreak run, and kiss a woman like that the same day. I can't make it out. Darn him, what did he want to do like that for? I keep thinking about it and it spoils looking at horses and smelling things and hearing niggers laugh and everything. Sometimes I'm so mad about it I want to fight someone. It gives me the fantods. What did he do it for? I want to know why.   [1921]

QUESTIONS

1. What is the importance of the narrator's sensitivity to nature? How is that sensitivity reflected in his language?
2. How do the narrator's questions about blacks and gamblers foreshadow his questions about the conduct of Jerry Tillford?
3. How are the narrator's goals for himself revealed in his discussion of horses?
4. Does Jerry Tillford behave irresponsibly?
5. Is an answer to the question of the title implied in the course of the narrative?

RESPONSES

1. Write an essay analyzing the narrator's feelings toward African Americans, fathers and father figures, and horses. How do these feelings change and how do they relate to the theme of the story?
2. Compare this coming-of-age story with Joyce's "Araby" and Updike's "A & P."

MARGARET ATWOOD

Margaret Atwood (b. 1939) was born in Ottawa, Canada, and was educated at the University of Toronto and at Harvard. She has published more than a dozen volumes of poetry, nine novels, and five collections of short stories, including *Bluebeard's Egg* (1983) and *Wilderness Tips* (1991). Atwood is a Fellow of the Royal Society of Canada, and her reputation is international; much of her work has been translated into many languages. She edited *The New Oxford Book of Canadian Verse* (1982) and coedited *The New Oxford Book of Canadian Short Stories* (1995). *The Handmaid's Tale* (1985), a novel set in the near future, was made into a feature film. Her most recent works are *The Blind Assassin* (2000), *Oryx and Crake* (2003), and *Rude Ramsay and the Roaring Radishes* (2004).

Rape Fantasies

The way they're going on about it in the magazines you'd think it was just invented, and not only that but it's something terrific, like a vaccine for cancer. They put it in capital letters on the front cover, and inside they have these questionnaires like the ones they used to have about whether you were a good enough wife or an endomorph or an ectomorph, remember that? with the scoring upside down on page 73, and then these numbered do-it-yourself dealies, you know? RAPE, TEN THINGS TO DO ABOUT IT, like it was ten new hairdos or something. I mean, what's so new about it?

So at work they all have to talk about it because no matter what magazine you open, there it is, staring you right between the eyes, and they're beginning to have it on the television, too. Personally I'd prefer a June Allyson movie anytime but they don't make them anymore and they don't even have them that much on the Late Show. For instance, day before yesterday, that would be Wednesday, thank god it's Friday as they say, we were sitting around in the women's lunch room—the *lunch* room, I mean you'd think you could get some peace and quiet in there—and Chrissy closes up the magazine she's been reading and says, "How about it, girls, do you have rape fantasies?"

The four of us were having our game of bridge the way we always do, and I had a bare twelve points counting the singleton with not that much of a bid in anything. So I said one club, hoping Sondra would remember about the one club convention, because the time before when I used that she thought I really meant clubs and she bid us up to three, and all I had was four little ones with nothing higher than a six, and we went down two and on top of that we were vulnerable. She is not the world's best bridge player. I mean, neither am I but there's a limit.

Darlene passed but the damage was done, Sondra's head went round like it was on ball bearings and she said, "*What* fantasies?"

5   "Rape fantasies," Chrissy said. She's a receptionist and she looks like one; she's pretty but cool as a cucumber, like she's been painted all over with nail polish, if you know what I mean. Varnished. "It says here all women have rape fantasies."

"For Chrissake, I'm eating an egg sandwich," I said, "and I bid one club and Darlene passed."

"You mean, like some guy jumping you in an alley or something," Sondra said. She was eating her lunch, we all eat our lunches during the game, and she bit into a piece of that celery she always brings and started to chew away on it with this thoughtful expression in her eyes and I knew we might as well pack it in as far as the game was concerned.

"Yeah, sort of like that," Chrissy said. She was blushing a little, you could see it even under her makeup.

"I don't think you should go out alone at night," Darlene said, "you put yourself in a position," and I may have been mistaken but she was looking at me. She's the oldest, she's forty-one though you wouldn't know it and neither does she, but I looked it up in the employees' file. I like to guess a person's age and then look it up to see if I'm right. I let myself have an extra pack of cigarettes if I am, though I'm trying to cut down. I figure it's harmless as long as you don't tell. I mean, not everyone has access to that file, it's more or less confidential. But it's all right if I tell you, I don't expect you'll ever meet her, though you never know, it's a small world. Anyway.

10   "For *heaven's* sake, it's only *Toronto*," Greta said. She worked in Detroit for three years and she never lets you forget it, it's like she thinks she's a war hero or something, we should all admire her just for the fact that she's still walking this earth, though she was really living in Windsor the whole time, she just worked in Detroit. Which for me doesn't really count. It's where you sleep, right?

"Well, do you?" Chrissy said. She was obviously trying to tell us about hers but she wasn't about to go first, she's cautious, that one.

"I certainly don't," Darlene said, and she wrinkled up her nose, like this, and I had to laugh. "I think it's disgusting." She's divorced, I read that in the file too, she never talks about it. It must've been years ago anyway. She got up and went over to the coffee machine and turned her back on us as though she wasn't going to have anything more to do with it.

"Well," Greta said. I could see it was going to be between her and Chrissy. They're both blondes, I don't mean that in a bitchy way but they do try to outdress each other. Greta would like to get out of Filing, she'd like to be a receptionist too so she could meet more people. You don't meet much of anyone in Filing except other people in Filing. Me, I don't mind it so much, I have outside interests.

"Well," Greta said, "I sometimes think about, you know my apartment? It's got this little balcony, I like to sit out there in the summer and I have a few plants out there. I never bother that much about locking the door to the balcony, it's one of those sliding glass ones, I'm on the eighteenth floor for heaven's sake, I've got a good view of the lake and the CN tower and all. But I'm sitting around one night in my housecoat, watching TV with my shoes off, you know how you do, and I see this guy's feet, coming

down past the window, and the next thing you know he's standing on the balcony, he's
let himself down by a rope with a hook on the end of it from the floor above, that's the
nineteenth, and before I can even get up off the chesterfield he's inside the apartment.
He's all dressed in black with black gloves on"—I knew right away what show she got
the black gloves off because I saw the same one—"and then he, well, you know."

"You know what?" Chrissy said, but Greta said, "And afterwards he tells me that   15
he goes all over the outside of the apartment building like that, from one floor to another, with his rope and his hook . . . and then he goes out to the balcony and tosses
his rope, and he climbs up it and disappears."

"Just like Tarzan," I said, but nobody laughed.

"Is that all?" Chrissy said. "Don't you ever think about, well, I think about being
in the bathtub, with no clothes on. . . ."

"So who takes a bath in their clothes?" I said, you have to admit it's stupid when
you come to think of it, but she just went on, ". . . with lots of bubbles, what I use is
Vitabath, it's more expensive but it's so relaxing, and my hair pinned up, and the door
opens and this fellow's standing there. . . ."

"How'd he get in?" Greta said.

"Oh, I don't know, through a window or something. Well, I can't very well get out   20
of the bathtub, the bathrooms' too small and besides he's blocking the doorway, so I
just *lie* there, and he starts to very slowly take his own clothes off, and then he gets into
the bathtub with me."

"Don't you scream or anything?" said Darlene. She'd come back with her cup of coffee, she was getting really interested. "I'd scream like bloody murder."

"Who'd hear me?" Chrissy said. "Besides, all the articles say it's better not to resist,
that way you don't get hurt."

"Anyway you might get bubbles up your nose," I said, "from the deep breathing,"
and I swear all four of them looked at me like I was in bad taste, like I'd insulted the
Virgin Mary or something. I mean, I don't see what's wrong with a little joke now and
then. Life's too short, right?

"Listen," I said, "those aren't *rape* fantasies. I mean, you aren't getting *raped,* it's
just some guy you haven't met formally who happens to be more attractive than Derek
Cummins"—he's the Assistant Manager, he wears elevator shoes or at any rate they
have these thick soles and he has this funny way of talking, we call him Derek Duck—
"and you have a good time. Rape is when they've got a knife or something and you
don't want to."

"So what about you, Estelle," Chrissy said, she was miffed because I laughed at her   25
fantasy, she thought I was putting her down. Sondra was miffed too, by this time she'd
finished her celery and she wanted to tell about hers, but she hadn't got in fast enough.

"All right, let me tell you one," I said. "I'm walking down this dark street at night
and this fellow comes up and grabs my arm. Now it so happens that I have a plastic
lemon in my purse, you know how it always says you should carry a plastic lemon
in your purse? I don't really do it, I tried it once but the darn thing leaked all over my
checkbook, but in this fantasy I have one, and I say to him, 'You're intending to rape
me, right?' and he nods, so I open my purse to get the plastic lemon, and I can't find
it! My purse if full of all this junk, Kleenex and cigarettes and my change purse and
my lipstick and my driver's license, you know the kind of stuff; so I ask him to hold
out his hands, like this, and I pile all this junk into them and down at the bottom
there's the plastic lemon, and I can't get the top off. So I hand it to him and he's very
obliging, he twists the top off and hands it back to me, and I squirt him in the eye."

I hope you don't think that's too vicious. Come to think of it, it is a bit mean, especially when he was so polite and all.

"*That's* your rape fantasy?" Chrissy says. "I don't believe it."

"She's a card," Darlene says, she and I are the ones that've been here the longest and she never will forget the time I got drunk at the office party and insisted I was going to dance under the table instead of on top of it, I did a sort of Cossack number but then I hit my head on the bottom of the table—actually it was a desk—when I went to get up, and I knocked myself out cold. She's decided that's the mark of an original mind and she tells everyone new about it and I'm not sure that's fair. Though I did do it.

30   "I'm being totally honest," I say. I always am and they know it. There's no point in being anything else, is the way I look at it, and sooner or later the truth will come out so you might as well not waste the time, right? "You should hear the one about the Easy-Off Oven Cleaner."

But that was the end of the lunch hour, with one bridge game shot to hell, and the next day we spent most of the time arguing over whether to start a new game or play out the hands we had left over from the day before, so Sondra never did get a chance to tell about her rape fantasy.

It started me thinking though, about my own rape fantasies. Maybe I'm abnormal or something, I mean I have fantasies about handsome strangers coming in through the window too, like Mr. Clean, I wish one would, please god somebody without flat feet and big sweat marks on his shirt, and over five feet five, believe me being tall is a handicap though it's getting better, tall guys are starting to like someone whose nose reaches higher than their belly button. But if you're being totally honest you can't count those as rape fantasies. In a real rape fantasy, what you should feel is this anxiety, like when you think about your apartment building catching on fire and whether you should use the elevator or the stairs or maybe just stick your head under a wet towel, and you try to remember everything you've read about what to do but you can't decide.

For instance, I'm walking along this dark street at night and this short, ugly fellow comes up and grabs my arm, and not only is he ugly, you know, with a sort of puffy nothing face, like those fellows you have to talk to in the bank when your account's overdrawn—of course I don't mean they're all like that—but he's absolutely covered in pimples. So he gets me pinned against the wall, he's short but he's heavy, and he starts to undo himself and the zipper gets stuck. I mean, one of the most significant moments in a girl's life, it's almost like getting married or having a baby or something, and he sticks the zipper.

So I say, kind of disgusted, "Oh for Chrissake," and he starts to cry. He tells me he's never been able to get anything right in his entire life, and this is the last straw, he's going to go jump off a bridge.

35   "Look," I say, I feel so sorry for him, in my rape fantasies I always end up feeling sorry for the guy, I mean there has to be something *wrong* with them, if it was Clint Eastwood it'd be different but worse luck it never is. I was the kind of little girl who buried dead robins, know what I mean? It used to drive my mother nuts, she didn't like me touching them, because of the germs I guess. So I say, "Listen, I know how you feel. You really should do something about those pimples, if you got rid of them you'd be quite good looking, honest; then you wouldn't have to go around doing stuff like this. I had them myself once," I say, to comfort him, but in fact I did, and it ends up I give him the name of my old dermatologist, the one I had in high school, that was back in

Leamington, except I used to go to St. Catharine's for the dermatologist. I'm telling you, I was really lonely when I first came here; I thought it was going to be such a big adventure and all, but it's a lot harder to meet people in a city. But I guess it's different for a guy.

Or I'm lying in bed with this terrible cold, my face is all swollen up, my eyes are red and my nose is dripping like a leaky tap, and this fellow comes in through the window and *he* has a terrible cold too, it's a new kind of flu that's been going around. So he says, "I'b goig do rabe you"—I hope you don't mind me holding my nose like this but that's the way I imagine it—and he lets out this terrific sneeze, which slows him down a bit, also I'm no object of beauty myself, you'd have to be some kind of pervert to want to rape someone with a cold like mine, it'd be like raping a bottle of LePage's mucilage the way my nose is running. He's looking wildly around the room, and I realize it's because he doesn't have a piece of Kleenex! "Id's ride here," I say, and I pass him the Kleenex, god knows why he even bothered to get out of bed, you'd think if you were going to go around climbing in windows you'd wait till you were healthier, right? I mean, that takes a certain amount of energy. So I ask him why doesn't he let me fix him a Neo-Citran and scotch, that's what I always take, you still have the cold but you don't feel it, so I do and we end up watching the Late Show together. I mean, they aren't all sex maniacs, the rest of the time they must lead a normal life. I figure they enjoy watching the Late Show just like anybody else.

I do have a scarier one though . . . where the fellow says he's hearing angel voices that're telling him he's got to kill me, you know, you read about things like that all the time in the papers. In this one I'm not in the apartment where I live now, I'm back in my mother's house in Leamington and the fellow's been hiding in the cellar, he grabs my arm when I go downstairs to get a jar of jam and he's got hold of the axe too, out of the garage, that one is really scary. I mean, what do you say to a nut like that?

So I start to shake but after a minute I get control of myself and I say, is he sure the angel voices have got the right person, because I hear the same angel voices and they've been telling me for some time that I'm going to give birth to the reincarnation of St. Anne who in turn has the Virgin Mary and right after that comes Jesus Christ and the end of the world, and he wouldn't want to interfere with that, would he? So he gets confused and listens some more, and then he asks for a sign and I show him my vaccination mark, you can see it's sort of an odd-shaped one, it got infected because I scratched the top off, and that does it, he apologizes and climbs out the coal chute again, which is how he got in in the first place, and I say to myself there's some advantage in having been brought up a Catholic even though I haven't been to church since they changed the service into English, it just isn't the same, you might as well be a Protestant. I must write to Mother and tell her to nail up that coal chute, it always has bothered me. Funny, I couldn't tell you at all what this man looks like but I know exactly what kind of shoes he's wearing, because that's the last I see of him, his shoes going up the coal chute, and they're the old-fashioned kind that lace up the ankles, even though he's a young fellow. That's strange, isn't it?

Let me tell you though I really sweat until I see him safely out of there and I go upstairs right away and make myself a cup of tea. I don't think about that one much. My mother always said you shouldn't dwell on unpleasant things and I generally agree with that, I mean, dwelling on them doesn't make them go away. Though not dwelling on them doesn't make them go away either, when you come to think of it.

Sometimes I have these short ones where the fellow grabs my arm but I'm really a Kung-Fu expert, can you believe it, in real life I'm sure it would just be a conk on the head and that's that, like getting your tonsils out, you'd wake up and it would be all over except for the sore places, and you'd be lucky if your neck wasn't broken or something, I could never even hit the volleyball in gym and a volleyball is fairly large, you know?—and I just go *zap* with my fingers into his eyes and that's it, he falls over, or I flip him against a wall or something. But I could never really stick my fingers in anyone's eyes, could you? It would feel like hot jello and I don't even like cold jello, just thinking about it gives me the creeps. I feel a bit guilty about that one, I mean how would you like walking around knowing someone's been blinded for life because of you?

But maybe it's different for a guy.

The most touching one I have is when the fellow grabs my arm and I say, sad and kind of dignified, "You'd be raping a corpse." That pulls him up short and I explain that I've just found out I have leukemia and the doctors have only given me a few months to live. That's why I'm out pacing the streets alone at night, I need to think, you know, come to terms with myself. I don't really have leukemia but in the fantasy I do, I guess I chose that particular disease because a girl in my grade four class died of it, the whole class sent her flowers when she was in the hospital. I didn't understand then that she was going to die and I wanted to have leukemia too so I could get flowers. Kids are funny, aren't they? Well, it turns out that he has leukemia himself, and *he* only has a few months to live, that's why he's going around raping people, he's very bitter because he's so young and his life is being taken from him before he's really lived it. So we walk along gently under the street lights, it's spring and sort of misty, and we end up going for coffee, we're happy we've found the only other person in the world who can understand what we're going through, it's almost like fate, and after a while we just sort of look at each other and our hands touch, and he comes back with me and moves into my apartment and we spend our last months together before we die, we just sort of don't wake up in the morning, though I've never decided which one of us gets to die first. If it's him I have to go on and fantasize about the funeral, if it's me I don't have to worry about that, so it just about depends on how tired I am at the time. You may not believe this but sometimes I even start crying. I cry at the ends of movies, even the ones that aren't all that sad, so I guess it's the same thing. My mother's like that too.

The funny thing about these fantasies is that the man is always someone I don't know, and the statistics in the magazines, well, most of them anyway, they say it's often someone you do know, at least a little bit, like your boss or something—I mean, it wouldn't be *my* boss, he's over sixty and I'm sure he couldn't rape his way out of a paper bag, poor old thing, but it might be someone like Derek Duck, in his elevator shoes, perish the thought—or someone you just met, who invites you up for a drink, it's getting so you can hardly be sociable anymore, and how are you supposed to meet people if you can't trust them even that basic amount? You can't spend your whole life in the Filing Department or cooped up in your own apartment with all the doors and windows locked and the shades down. I'm not what you would call a drinker but I like to go out now and then for a drink or two in a nice place, even if I am by myself, I'm with Women's Lib on that even though I can't agree with a lot of other things they say. Like here for instance, the waiters all know me and if anyone, you know, bothers me. . . . I don't know why I'm telling you all this, except I think it helps you get to know a person, especially at first, hearing some of the things they think about. At work they call me the office worry wart, but it isn't so much like worrying, it's more like figuring out what you should do in an emergency, like I said before.

Anyway, another thing about it is that there's a lot of conversation, in fact I spend most of my time, in the fantasy that is, wondering what I'm going to say and what he's going to say, I think it would be better if you could get a conversation going. Like, how could a fellow do that to a person he's just had a long conversation with, once you let them know you're human, you have a life too, I don't see how they could go ahead with it, right? I mean, I know it happens but I just don't understand it, that's the part I really don't understand.   [1977]

QUESTIONS

1. To whom is the narrator talking?
2. What are the sources of humor in the story?
3. Is there a pattern in the narrator's fantasies?
4. How does the narrator attempt to elicit the listener's sympathy in her behalf?
5. What does the narrator reveal about herself in the course of the story?

RESPONSES

1. Research articles in magazines directed at women readers from the mid-1970s. How accurate is Atwood's portrayal of women and their thoughts about the possibility of rape?
2. Write an essay exploring how different readers can respond to Estelle and her narrative. Or write an essay pretending that you were the person she said everything to.
3. Write a short story that explores men's fantasies and fears.

JAMES BALDWIN

James Baldwin (1924–1987) was born and raised in Harlem, the son of a revivalist minister. Disenchanted by the racial situation in the United States, he moved to Paris in 1948. His first novel, *Go Tell It on the Mountain* (1953), grapples with racial and sexual identity, problems that continued to preoccupy him throughout his career. Returning to the United States in 1957, he became deeply involved in the civil rights movement. He collected his essays on black-white relations under such titles as *Nobody Knows My Name* (1961) and *The Fire Next Time* (1963). His play *The Amen Corner* (1968) has been recently revived with considerable success.

Sonny's Blues

I read about it in the paper, in the subway, on my way to work. I read it, and I couldn't believe it, and I read it again. Then perhaps I just stared at it, at the newsprint spelling out his name, spelling out the story. I stared at it in the swinging lights of the subway car, and in the faces and bodies of the people, and in my own face, trapped in the darkness which roared outside.

It was not to be believed and I kept telling myself that, as I walked from the subway station to the high school. And at the same time I couldn't doubt it. I was scared, scared for Sonny. He became real to me again. A great block of ice got settled in my belly and kept melting there slowly all day long, while I taught my classes algebra. It was a special kind of ice. It kept melting, sending trickles of ice water all up and down my veins, but it never got less. Sometimes it hardened and seemed to expand until I felt my guts were going to come spilling out or that I was going to choke or scream. This would always be at a moment when I was remembering some specific thing Sonny had once said or done.

When he was about as old as the boys in my class his face had been bright and open, there was a lot of copper in it; and he'd had wonderfully direct brown eyes, and great gentleness and privacy. I wondered what he looked like now. He had been picked up, the evening before, in a raid on an apartment downtown, for peddling and using heroin.

I couldn't believe it: but what I mean by that is that I couldn't find any room for it anywhere inside me. I had kept it outside me for a long time. I hadn't wanted to know. I had had suspicions, but I didn't name them, I kept putting them away. I told myself that Sonny was wild, but he wasn't crazy. And he'd always been a good boy, he hadn't ever turned hard or evil or disrespectful, the way kids can, so quick, so quick, especially in Harlem. I didn't want to believe that I'd ever see my brother going down, coming to nothing, all that light in his face gone out, in the condition I'd already seen so many others. Yet it had happened and here I was, talking about algebra to a lot of boys who might, every one of them for all I knew, be popping off needles every time they went to the head. Maybe it did more for them than algebra could.

I was sure that the first time Sonny had ever had horse, he couldn't have been much   5 older than these boys were now. These boys, now, were living as we'd been living then, they were growing up with a rush and their heads bumped abruptly against the low ceiling of their actual possibilities. They were filled with rage. All they really knew were two darknesses, the darkness of their lives, which was now closing in on them, and the darkness of the movies, which had blinded them to that other darkness, and in which they now, vindictively, dreamed, at once more together than they were at any other time, and more alone.

When the last bell rang, the last class ended, I let out my breath. It seemed I'd been holding it for all that time. My clothes were wet—I may have looked as though I'd been sitting in a steam bath, all dressed up, all afternoon. I sat alone in the classroom a long time. I listened to the boys outside, downstairs, shouting and cursing and laughing. Their laughter struck me for perhaps the first time. It was not the joyous laughter which—God knows why—one associates with children. It was mocking and insular, its intent was to denigrate. It was disenchanted, and in this, also, lay the authority of their curses. Perhaps I was listening to them because I was thinking about my brother and in them I heard my brother. And myself.

One boy was whistling a tune, at once very complicated and very simple, it seemed to be pouring out of him as though he were a bird, and it sounded very cool and moving through all that harsh, bright air, only just holding its own through all those other sounds.

I stood up and walked over to the window and looked down into the courtyard. It was the beginning of the spring and the sap was rising in the boys. A teacher passed through them every now and again, quickly, as though he or she couldn't wait to get out of that courtyard, to get those boys out of their sight and off their minds. I started collecting my stuff. I thought I'd better get home and talk to Isabel.

The courtyard was almost deserted by the time I got downstairs. I saw this boy standing in the shadow of a doorway, looking just like Sonny. I almost called his name. Then I saw that it wasn't Sonny, but somebody we used to know, a boy from around our block. He'd been Sonny's friend. He'd never been mine, having been too young for me, and, anyway, I'd never liked him. And now, even though he was a grown-up man, he still hung around that block, still spent hours on the street corners, was always high and raggy. I used to run into him from time to time and he'd often work around to asking me for a quarter or fifty cents. He always had some real good excuse, too, and I always gave it to him, I don't know why.

But now, abruptly, I hated him. I couldn't stand the way he looked at me, partly like   10 a dog, partly like a cunning child. I wanted to ask him what the hell he was doing in the school courtyard.

He sort of shuffled over to me, and he said, "I see you got the papers. So you already know about it."

"You mean about Sonny? Yes, I already know about it. How come they didn't get you?"

He grinned. It made him repulsive and it also brought to mind what he'd looked like as a kid. "I wasn't there. I stay away from them people."

"Good for you." I offered him a cigarette and I watched him through the smoke. "You come all the way down here just to tell me about Sonny?"

15   "That's right." He was sort of shaking his head and his eyes looked strange, as though they were about to cross. The bright sun deadened his damp dark brown skin and it made his eyes look yellow and showed up the dirt in his kinked hair. He smelled funky. I moved a little away from him and I said, "Well, thanks. But I already know about it and I got to get home."

"I'll walk you a little ways," he said. We started walking. There were a couple of kids still loitering in the courtyard and one of them said goodnight to me and looked strangely at the boy beside me.

"What're you going to do?" he asked me. "I mean, about Sonny?"

"Look. I haven't seen Sonny for over a year, I'm not sure I'm going to do anything. Anyway, what the hell *can* I do?"

"That's right," he said quickly, "ain't nothing you can do. Can't much help old Sonny no more, I guess."

20   It was what I was thinking and so it seemed to me he had no right to say it.

"I'm surprised at Sonny, though," he went on—he had a funny way of talking, he looked straight ahead as though he were talking to himself—"I thought Sonny was a smart boy, I thought he was too smart to get hung."

"I guess he thought so too," I said sharply, "and that's how he got hung. And how about you? You're pretty goddamn smart, I bet."

Then he looked directly at me, just for a minute. "I ain't smart," he said. "If I was smart, I'd have reached for a pistol a long time ago."

"Look. Don't tell *me* your sad story, if it was up to me, I'd give you one." Then I felt guilty—guilty, probably, for never having supposed that the poor bastard *had* a story of his own, much less a sad one, and I asked, quickly, "What's going to happen to him now?"

25   He didn't answer this. He was off by himself some place. "Funny thing," he said, and from his tone we might have been discussing the quickest way to get to Brooklyn, "when I saw the papers this morning, the first thing I asked myself was if I had anything to do with it. I felt sort of responsible."

I began to listen more carefully. The subway station was on the corner, just before us, and I stopped. He stopped, too. We were in front of a bar and he ducked slightly, peering in, but whoever he was looking for didn't seem to be there. The juke box was blasting away with something black and bouncy and I half watched the barmaid as she danced her way from the juke box to her place behind the bar. And I watched her face as she laughingly responded to something someone said to her, still keeping time to the music. When she smiled one saw the little girl, one sensed the doomed, still-struggling woman beneath the battered face of the semiwhore.

"I never *give* Sonny nothing," the boy said finally, "but a long time ago I come to school high and Sonny asked me how it felt." He paused, I couldn't bear to watch him, I watched the barmaid, and I listened to the music which seemed to be causing the pavement to shake. "I told him it felt great." The music stopped, the barmaid paused and watched the juke box until the music began again. "It did."

All this way carrying me some place I didn't want to go. I certainly didn't want to know how it felt. It filled everything, the people, the houses, the music, the dark, quick-silver barmaid, with menace; and this menace was their reality.

"What's going to happen to him now?" I asked again.

"They'll send him away some place and they'll try to cure him." He shook his head.   30
"Maybe he'll even think he's kicked the habit. Then they'll let him loose"—he gestured, throwing his cigarette into the gutter. "That's all."

"What do you mean, that's *all?*"

But I knew what he meant.

"I *mean*, that's *all*." He turned his head and looked at me, pulling down the corners
of his mouth. "Don't you know what I mean?" he asked, softly.

"How the hell *would* I know what you mean?" I almost whispered it, I don't know
why.

"That's right," he said to the air, "how would *he* know what I mean?" He turned to-   35
ward me again, patient and calm, and yet I somehow felt him shaking, shaking as
though he were going to fall apart. I felt that ice in my guts again, the dread I'd felt all
afternoon; and again I watched the barmaid, moving about the bar, washing glasses,
and singing. "Listen. They'll let him out and then it'll just start all over again. That's
what I mean."

"You mean—they'll let him out. And then he'll just start working his way back in
again. You mean he'll never kick the habit. Is that what you mean?"

"That's right," he said, cheerfully. *"You* see what I mean."

"Tell me," I said at last, "why does he want to die? He must want to die, he's killing
himself, why does he want to die?"

He looked at me in surprise. He licked his lips. "He don't want to die. He wants to
live. Don't nobody want to die, ever."

Then I wanted to ask him—too many things. He could not have answered, or if he   40
had, I could not have borne the answers. I started walking. "Well, I guess it's none of
my business."

"It's going to be rough on old Sonny," he said. We reached the subway station.
"This is your station?" he asked. I nodded. I took one step down. "Damn!" he said, suddenly. I looked up at him. He grinned again. "Damn it if I didn't leave all my money
home. You ain't got a dollar on you, have you? Just for a couple of days, is all."

All at once something inside gave and threatened to come pouring out of me. I
didn't hate him any more. I felt that in another moment I'd start crying like a child.

"Sure," I said. "Don't swear." I looked in my wallet and didn't have a dollar, I only
had a five. "Here," I said. "That hold you?"

He didn't look at it—he didn't want to look at it. A terrible, closed look came over
his face, as though he were keeping the number on the bill a secret from him and me.
"Thanks," he said, and now he was dying to see me go. "Don't worry about Sonny.
Maybe I'll write him or something."

"Sure," I said. "You do that. So long."   45

"Be seeing you," he said. I went down the steps.

And I didn't write Sonny or send him anything for a long time. When I finally did,
it was just after my little girl died, he wrote me back a letter which made me feel like
a bastard.

Here's what he said:

Dear Brother,
    You don't know how much I needed to hear from you. I wanted to write you   50
many a time but I dug how much I must have hurt you and so I didn't write. But
now I feel like a man who's been trying to climb up out of some deep, real deep
and funky hole and just saw the sun up there, outside. I got to get outside.

I can't tell you much about how I got here. I mean I don't know how to tell you. I guess I was afraid of something or I was trying to escape from something and you know I have never been very strong in the head (smile). I'm glad Mama and Daddy are dead and can't see what's happened to their son and I swear if I'd known what I was doing I would never have hurt you so, you and a lot of other fine people who were nice to me and who believed in me.

I don't want you to think it had anything to do with me being a musician. It's more than that. Or maybe less than that. I can't get anything straight in my head down here and I try not to think about what's going to happen to me when I get outside again. Sometime I think I'm going to flip and *never* get outside and sometime I think I'll come straight back. I tell you one thing, though, I'd rather blow my brains out than go through this again. But that's what they all say, so they tell me. If I tell you when I'm coming to New York and if you could meet me, I sure would appreciate it. Give my love to Isabel and the kids and I was sure sorry to hear about little Gracie. I wish I could be like Mama and say the Lord's will be done, but I don't know it seems to me that trouble is the one thing that never does get stopped and I don't know what good it does to blame it on the Lord. But maybe it does some good if you believe it.

> Your brother,
> Sonny

55   Then I kept in constant touch with him and I sent him whatever I could and I went to meet him when he came back to New York. When I saw him many things I thought I had forgotten came flooding back to me. This was because I had begun, finally, to wonder about Sonny, about the life that Sonny lived inside. This life, whatever it was, had made him older and thinner and it had deepened the distant stillness in which he had always moved. He looked very unlike my baby brother. Yet, when he smiled, when we shook hands, the baby brother I'd never known looked out from the depths of his private life, like an animal waiting to be coaxed into the light.

"How you been keeping?" he asked me.

"All right. And you?"

"Just fine." He was smiling all over his face. "It's good to see you again."

"It's good to see you."

60   The seven years' difference in our ages lay between us like a chasm: I wondered if these years would ever operate between us as a bridge. I was remembering, and it made it hard to catch my breath, that I had been there when he was born; and I had heard the first words he had ever spoken. When he started to walk, he walked from our mother straight to me. I caught him just before he fell when he took the first steps he ever took in this world.

"How's Isabel?"

"Just fine. She's dying to see you."

"And the boys?"

"They're fine, too. They're anxious to see their uncle."

65   "Oh, come on. You know they don't remember me."

"Are you kidding? Of course they remember you."

He grinned again. We got into a taxi. We had a lot to say to each other, far too much to know how to begin.

As the taxi began to move, I asked, "You still want to go to India?"

He laughed. "You still remember that. Hell, no. This place is Indian enough for me."

70   "It used to belong to them," I said.

And he laughed again. "They damn sure knew what they were doing when they got rid of it."

Years ago, when he was around fourteen, he'd been all hipped on the idea of going to India. He read books about people sitting on rocks, naked, in all kinds of weather, but mostly bad, naturally, and walking barefoot through hot coals and arriving at wisdom. I used to say that it sounded to me as though they were getting away from wisdom as fast as they could. I think he sort of looked down on me for that.

"Do you mind," he asked, "if we have the driver drive alongside the park? On the west side—I haven't seen the city in so long."

"Of course not," I said. I was afraid that I might sound as though I were humoring him, but I hoped he wouldn't take it that way.

So we drove along, between the green of the park and the stony, lifeless elegance   75
of hotels and apartment buildings, toward the vivid, killing streets of our childhood. These streets hadn't changed, though housing projects jutted up out of them now like rocks in the middle of a boiling sea. Most of the houses in which we had grown up had vanished, as had the stores from which we had stolen, the basements in which we had first tried sex, the rooftops from which we had hurled tin cans and bricks. But houses exactly like the houses of our past yet dominated the landscape, boys exactly like the boys we once had been found themselves smothering in these houses, came down into the streets for light and air and found themselves encircled by disaster. Some escaped the trap, most didn't. Those who got out always left something of themselves behind, as some animals amputate a leg and leave it in the trap. It might be said, perhaps, that I had escaped, after all, I was a school teacher; or that Sonny had, he hadn't lived in Harlem for years. Yet, as the cab moved uptown through streets which seemed, with a rush, to darken with dark people, and as I covertly studied Sonny's face, it came to me that what we both were seeking through our separate cab windows was that part of ourselves which had been left behind. It's always at the hour of trouble and confrontation that the missing member aches.

We hit 110th Street and started rolling up Lenox Avenue. And I'd known this avenue all my life, but it seemed to me again, as it had seemed on the day I'd first heard about Sonny's trouble, filled with a hidden menace which was its very breath of life.

"We almost there," said Sonny.

"Almost." We were both too nervous to say anything more.

We lived in a housing project. It hasn't been up long. A few days after it was up it seemed uninhabitably new, now, of course, it's already rundown. It looks like a parody of the good, clean, faceless life—God knows the people who live in it do their best to make it a parody. The beat-looking grass lying around isn't enough to make their lives green, the hedges will never hold out the streets, and they know it. The big windows fool no one, they aren't big enough to make space out of no space. They don't bother with the windows, they watch the TV screen instead. The playground is most popular with the children who don't play at jacks, or skip rope, or roller skate, or swing, and they can be found in it after dark. We moved in partly because it's not too far from where I teach, and partly for the kids; but it's really just like the houses in which Sonny and I grew up. The same things happen, they'll have the same things to remember. The moment Sonny and I started into the house I had the feeling that I was simply bringing him back into the danger he had almost died trying to escape.

Sonny has never been talkative. So I don't know why I was sure he'd be dying to   80
talk to me when supper was over the first night. Everything went fine, the oldest boy remembered him, and the youngest boy liked him, and Sonny had remembered to bring something for each of them; and Isabel, who is really much nicer than I am, more

open and giving, had gone to a lot of trouble about dinner and was genuinely glad to see him. And she's always been able to tease Sonny in a way that I haven't. It was nice to see her face so vivid again and to hear her laugh and watch her make Sonny laugh. She wasn't, or, anyway, she didn't seem to be, at all uneasy or embarrassed. She chatted as though there were no subject which had to be avoided and she got Sonny past his first, faint stiffness. And thank God she was there, for I was filled with that icy dread again. Everything I did seemed awkward to me, and everything I said sounded freighted with hidden meaning. I was trying to remember everything I'd heard about dope addiction and I couldn't help watching Sonny for signs. I wasn't doing it out of malice. I was trying to find out something about my brother. I was dying to hear him tell me he was safe.

"Safe!" my father grunted, whenever Mama suggested trying to move to a neighborhood which might be safer for children. "Safe, hell! Ain't no place safe for kids, nor nobody."

He always went on like this, but he wasn't, ever, really as bad as he sounded, not even on weekends, when he got drunk. As a matter of fact, he was always on the lookout for "something a little better," but he died before he found it. He died suddenly, during a drunken weekend in the middle of the war, when Sonny was fifteen. He and Sonny hadn't ever got on too well. And this was partly because Sonny was the apple of his father's eye. It was because he loved Sonny so much and was frightened for him, that he was always fighting with him. It doesn't do any good to fight with Sonny. Sonny just moves back, inside himself, where he can't be reached. But the principal reason that they never hit it off is that they were so much alike. Daddy was big and rough and loud-talking, just the opposite of Sonny, but they both had—that same privacy.

Mama tried to tell me something about this, just after Daddy died. I was home on leave from the army.

This was the last time I ever saw my mother alive. Just the same, this picture gets all mixed up in my mind with pictures I had of her when she was younger. The way I always see her is the way she used to be on a Sunday afternoon, say, when the old folks were talking after the big Sunday dinner. I always see her wearing pale blue. She'd be sitting on the sofa. And my father would be sitting in the easy chair, not far from her. And the living room would be full of church folks and relatives. There they sit, in chairs all around the living room, and the night is creeping up outside, but nobody knows it yet. You can see the darkness growing against the windowpanes and you hear the street noises every now and again, or maybe the jangling beat of a tambourine from one of the churches close by, but it's real quiet in the room. For a moment nobody's talking, but every face looks darkening, like the sky outside. And my mother rocks a little from the waist, and my father's eyes are closed. Everyone is looking at something a child can't see. For a minute they've forgotten the children. Maybe a kid is lying on the rug, half asleep. Maybe somebody's got a kid in his lap and is absentmindedly stroking the kid's head. Maybe there's a kid, quiet and big-eyed, curled up in a big chair in the corner. The silence, the darkness coming, and the darkness in the faces frightens the child obscurely. He hopes that the hand which strokes his forehead will never stop—will never die. He hopes that there will never come a time when the old folks won't be sitting around the living room, talking about where they've come from, and what they've seen, and what's happened to them and their kinfolk.

85   But something deep and watchful in the child knows that this is bound to end, is already ending. In a moment someone will get up and turn on the light. Then the old folks will remember the children and they won't talk any more that day. And when light fills the room, the child is filled with darkness. He knows that every time this

happens he's moved just a little closer to that darkness outside. The darkness outside is what the old folks have been talking about. It's what they've come from. It's what they endure. The child knows that they won't talk any more because if he knows too much about what's happened to *them*, he'll know too much too soon, about what's going to happen to *him*.

The last time I talked to my mother, I remember I was restless. I wanted to get out and see Isabel. We weren't married then and we had a lot to straighten out between us.

There Mama sat, in black, by the window. She was humming an old church song, *Lord, you brought me from a long ways off*. Sonny was out somewhere. Mama kept watching the streets.

"I don't know," she said, "if I'll ever see you again, after you go off from here. But I hope you'll remember the things I tried to teach you."

"Don't talk like that," I said, and smiled. "You'll be here a long time yet."

She smiled, too, but she said nothing. She was quiet for a long time. And I said, "Mama, don't you worry about nothing. I'll be writing all the time, and you be getting the checks. . . ." 90

"I want to talk to you about your brother," she said, suddenly. "If anything happens to me he ain't going to have nobody to look out for him."

"Mama," I said, "ain't nothing going to happen to you *or* Sonny. Sonny's all right. He's a good boy and he's got good sense."

"It ain't a question of his being a good boy," Mama said, "nor of his having good sense. It ain't only the bad ones, nor yet the dumb ones that gets sucked under." She stopped, looking at me. "Your Daddy once had a brother," she said, and she smiled in a way that made me feel she was in pain. "You didn't never know that, did you?"

"No," I said, "I never knew that," and I watched her face.

"Oh, yes," she said, "your Daddy had a brother." She looked out of the window again. "I know you never saw your Daddy cry. But *I* did—many a time, through all these years." 95

I asked her, "What happened to his brother? How come nobody's ever talked about him?"

This was the first time I ever saw my mother look old.

"His brother got killed," she said, "when he was just a little younger than you are now. I knew him. He was a fine boy. He was maybe a little full of the devil, but he didn't mean nobody no harm."

Then she stopped and the room was silent, exactly as it had sometimes been on those Sunday afternoons. Mama kept looking out into the streets.

"He used to have a job in the mill," she said, "and, like all young folks, he just liked to perform on Saturday nights. Saturday nights, him and your father would drift around to different places, go to dances and things like that, or just sit around with people they knew, and your father's brother would sing, he had a fine voice, and play along with himself on his guitar. Well, this particular Saturday night, him and your father was coming home from some place, and they were both a little drunk and there was a moon that night, it was bright like day. Your father's brother was feeling kind of good, and he was whistling to himself, and he had his guitar slung over his shoulder. They was coming down a hill and beneath them was a road that turned off from the highway. Well, your father's brother, being always kind of frisky, decided to run down this hill, and he did, with that guitar banging and clanging behind him, and he ran across the road, and he was making water behind a tree. And your father was sort of amused at him and he was still coming down the hill, kind of slow. Then he heard a car motor and that same minute his brother stepped from behind the tree, into the 100 road, in the moonlight. And he started to cross the road. And your father started to run down the hill, he says he don't know why. This car was full of white men. They was all drunk, and when they seen your father's brother they let out a great whoop and holler and they aimed the car straight at him. They was having fun, they just wanted to scare him, the way they do sometimes, you know. But they was drunk. And I guess the boy, being drunk, too, and scared, kind of lost his head. By the time he jumped it was too late. Your father says he heard his brother scream when the car rolled over him, and he heard the wood of that guitar when it give, and he heard them strings go flying, and he heard them white men shouting, and the car kept on a-going and it ain't stopped till this day. And, time your father got down the hill, his brother weren't nothing but blood and pulp."

Tears were gleaming on my mother's face. There wasn't anything I could say.

"He never mentioned it," she said, "because I never let him mention it before you children. Your Daddy was like a crazy man that night and for many a night thereafter. He says he never in his life seen anything as dark as that road after the lights of that car had gone away. Weren't nothing; weren't nobody on that road, just your Daddy and his brother and that busted guitar. Oh, yes. Your Daddy never did really get right again. Till the day he died he weren't sure but that every white man he saw was the man that killed his brother."

She stopped and took out her handkerchief and dried her eyes and looked at me.

"I ain't telling you all this," she said, "to make you scared or bitter or to make you hate nobody. I'm telling you this because you got a brother. And the world ain't changed."

105   I guess I didn't want to believe this. I guess she saw this in my face. She turned away from me, toward the window again, searching those streets.

"But I praise my Redeemer," she said at last, "that He called your Daddy home before me. I ain't saying it to throw no flowers at myself, but, I declare, it keeps me from feeling too cast down to know I helped your father get safely through this world. Your father always acted like he was the roughest, strongest man on earth. And everybody took him to be like that. But if he hadn't had *me* there—to see his tears!"

She was crying again. Still, I couldn't move. I said, "Lord, Lord, Mama, I didn't know it was like that."

"Oh, honey," she said, "There's a lot that you don't know. But you are going to find out." She stood up from the window and came over to me. "You got to hold on to your brother," she said, "and don't let him fall, no matter what it looks like is happening to him and no matter how evil you gets with him. You going to be evil with him many a time. But don't you forget what I told you, you hear?"

"I won't forget," I said. "Don't you worry, I won't forget. I won't let nothing happen to Sonny."

110   My mother smiled as though she were amused at something she saw in my face. Then, "You may not be able to stop nothing from happening. But you got to let him know you's *there*."

Two days later I was married, and then I was gone. And I had a lot of things on my mind and I pretty well forgot my promise to Mama until I got shipped home on a special furlough for her funeral.

And, after the funeral, with just Sonny and me alone in the empty kitchen, I tried to find out something about him.

"What do you want to do?" I asked him.

"I'm going to be a musician," he said.

For he had graduated, in the time I had been away, from dancing to the juke box to 115
finding out who was playing what, and what they were doing with it, and he had
bought himself a set of drums.

"You mean, you want to be a drummer?" I somehow had the feeling that being a
drummer might be all right for other people but not for my brother Sonny.

"I don't think," he said, looking at me very gravely, "that I'll ever be a good drummer. But I think I can play a piano."

I frowned. I'd never played the role of the older brother quite so seriously before,
had scarcely ever, in fact, *asked* Sonny a damn thing. I sensed myself in the presence
of something I didn't really know how to handle, didn't understand. So I made my
frown a little deeper as I asked: "What kind of musician do you want to be?"

He grinned. "How many kinds do you think there are?"

"Be *serious*," I said.   120

He laughed, throwing his head back, and then looked at me. "I *am* serious."

"Well, then, for Christ's sake, stop kidding around and answer a serious question. I
mean, do you want to be a concert pianist, you want to play classical music and all that,
or—or what?" Long before I finished he was laughing again. "For Christ's *sake*, Sonny!"

He sobered, but with difficulty. "I'm sorry. But you sound so—*scared!*" and he was
off again.

"Well, you may think it's funny now, baby, but it's not going to be so funny when
you have to make your living at it, let me tell you *that*." I was furious because I knew
he was laughing at me and I didn't know why.

"No," he said, very sober now, and afraid, perhaps, that he'd hurt me, "I don't want 125
to be a classical pianist. That isn't what interests me. I mean"—he paused, looking
hard at me, as though his eyes would help me to understand, and then gestured helplessly, as though perhaps his hand would help—"I mean, I'll have a lot of studying to
do, and I'll have to study *everything*, but, I mean, I want to play *with*—jazz musicians."
He stopped. "I want to play jazz," he said.

Well, the word had never before sounded as heavy, as real, as it sounded that afternoon in Sonny's mouth. I just looked at him and I was probably frowning a real
frown by this time. I simply couldn't see why on earth he'd want to spend his time
hanging around nightclubs, clowning around on bandstands, while people pushed
each other around a dance floor. It seemed—beneath him, somehow. I had never
thought about it before, had never been forced to, but I suppose I had always put jazz
musicians in a class with what Daddy called "goodtime people."

"Are you *serious?*"

"Hell, *yes*, I'm serious."

He looked more helpless than ever, and annoyed, and deeply hurt.

I suggested, helpfully: "You mean—like Louis Armstrong?"   130

His face closed as though I'd struck him. "No. I'm not talking about none of that
old-time, down home crap."

"Well, look, Sonny, I'm sorry, don't get mad. I just don't altogether get it, that's all.
Name somebody—you know, a jazz musician you admire."

"Bird."

"Who?"

"Bird! Charlie Parker! Don't they teach you nothing in the goddamn army?"   135

I lit a cigarette. I was surprised and then a little amused to discover that I was trembling. "I've been out of touch," I said. "You'll have to be patient with me. Now. Who's
this Parker character?"

"He's just one of the greatest jazz musicians alive," said Sonny, sullenly, his hands in his pockets, his back to me. "Maybe *the* greatest," he added, bitterly, "that's probably why *you* never heard of him."

"All right," I said, "I'm ignorant. I'm sorry. I'll go out and buy all the cat's records right away, all right?"

"It don't," said Sonny, with dignity, "make any difference to me. I don't care what you listen to. Don't do me no favors."

140   I was beginning to realize that I'd never seen him so upset before. With another part of my mind I was thinking that this would probably turn out to be one of those things kids go through and that I shouldn't make it seem important by pushing it too hard. Still, I didn't think it would do any harm to ask: "Doesn't all this take a lot of time? Can you make a living at it?"

He turned back to me and half leaned, half sat, on the kitchen table. "Everything takes time," he said, "and—well, yes, sure, I can make a living at it. But what I don't seem to be able to make you understand is that it's the only thing I want to do."

"Well, Sonny," I said, gently, "you know people can't always do exactly what they *want* to do—"

"*No,* I don't know that," said Sonny, surprising me. "I think people *ought* to do what they want to do, what else are they alive for?"

"You getting to be a big boy," I said desperately, "it's time you started thinking about your future."

145   "I'm thinking about my future," said Sonny, grimly. "I think about it all the time."

I gave up. I decided, if he didn't change his mind, that we could always talk about it later. "In the meantime," I said, "you got to finish school." We had already decided that he'd have to move in with Isabel and her folks. I knew this wasn't the ideal arrangement because Isabel's folks are inclined to be dicty and they hadn't especially wanted Isabel to marry me. But I didn't know what else to do. "And we have to get you fixed up at Isabel's."

There was a long silence. He moved from the kitchen table to the window. "That's a terrible idea. You know it yourself."

"Do you have a *better* idea?"

He just walked up and down the kitchen for a minute. He was as tall as I was. He had started to shave. I suddenly had the feeling that I didn't know him at all.

150   He stopped at the kitchen table and picked up my cigarettes. Looking at me with a kind of mocking, amused defiance, he put one between his lips. "You mind?"

"You smoking already?"

He lit the cigarette and nodded, watching me through the smoke. "I just wanted to see if I'd have the courage to smoke in front of you." He grinned and blew a great cloud of smoke to the ceiling. "It was easy." He looked at my face. "Come on, now. I bet you was smoking at my age, tell the truth."

I didn't say anything but the truth was on my face, and he laughed. But now there was something very strained in his laugh. "Sure. And I bet that ain't all you was doing."

He was frightening me a little. "Cut the crap," I said. "We already decided that you was going to go and live at Isabel's. Now what's got into you all of a sudden?"

155   "*You* decided it," he pointed out. "*I* didn't decide nothing." He stopped in front of me, leaning against the stove, arms loosely folded. "Look, brother. I don't want to stay in Harlem no more, I really don't." He was very earnest. He looked at me, then over toward the kitchen window. There was something in his eyes I'd never seen before, some thoughtfulness, some worry all his own. He rubbed the muscle of one arm. "It's time I was getting out of here."

"Where do you want to *go,* Sonny?"

"I want to join the army. Or the navy, I don't care. If I say I'm old enough, they'll believe me."

Then I got mad. It was because I was so scared. "You must be crazy. You goddamn fool, what the hell do you want to go and join the *army* for?"

"I just told you. To get out of Harlem."

"Sonny, you haven't even finished *school.* And if you really want to be a musician, how do you expect to study if you're in the *army?*"   160

He looked at me, trapped, and in anguish. "There's ways. I might be able to work out some kind of deal. Anyway, I'll have the G.I. Bill when I come out."

"*If* you come out." We stared at each other. "Sonny, please. Be reasonable. I know the setup is far from perfect. But we got to do the best we can."

"I ain't learning nothing in school," he said. "Even when I go." He turned away from me and opened the window and threw his cigarette out into the narrow alley. I watched his back. "At least, I ain't learning nothing you'd want me to learn." He slammed the window so hard I thought the glass would fly out, and turned back to me. "And I'm sick of the stink of these garbage cans!"

"Sonny," I said, "I know how you feel. But if you don't finish school now, you're going to be sorry later that you didn't." I grabbed him by the shoulders. "And you only got another year. It ain't so bad. And I'll come back and I swear I'll help you do *whatever* you want to do. Just try to put up with it till I come back. Will you please do that? For me?"

He didn't answer and he wouldn't look at me.   165

"Sonny. You hear me?"

He pulled away. "I hear you. But you never hear anything *I* say."

I didn't know what to say to that. He looked out of the window and then back at me. "OK," he said, and sighed. "I'll try."

Then I said, trying to cheer him up a little, "They got a piano at Isabel's. You can practice on it."

And as a matter of fact, it did cheer him up for a minute. "That's right," he said to   170
himself. "I forgot that." His face relaxed a little. But the worry, the thoughtfulness, played on it still, the way shadows play on a face which is staring into the fire.

But I thought I'd never hear the end of that piano. At first, Isabel would write me, saying how nice it was that Sonny was so serious about his music and how, as soon as he came in from school, or wherever he had been when he was supposed to be at school, he went straight to that piano and stayed there until suppertime. And, after supper, he went back to that piano and stayed there until everybody went to bed. He was at the piano all day Saturday and all day Sunday. Then he bought a record player and started playing records. He'd play one record over and over again, all day long sometimes, and he'd improvise along with it on the piano. Or he'd play one section of the record, one chord, one change, one progression, then he'd do it on the piano. Then back to the record. Then back to the piano.

Well, I really don't know how they stood it. Isabel finally confessed that it wasn't like living with a person at all, it was like living with sound. And the sound didn't make any sense to her, didn't make any sense to any of them—naturally. They began, in a way, to be afflicted by this presence that was living in their home. It was as though Sonny were some sort of god, or monster. He moved in an atmosphere which wasn't like theirs at all. They fed him and he ate, he washed himself, he walked in and out of their door; he certainly wasn't nasty or unpleasant or rude, Sonny isn't any of those things; but it was as though he were all wrapped up in some cloud, some fire, some vision all his own; and there wasn't any way to reach him.

At the same time, he wasn't really a man yet, he was still a child, and they had to watch out for him in all kinds of ways. They certainly couldn't throw him out. Neither did they dare to make a great scene about that piano because even they dimly sensed, as I sensed, from so many thousands of miles away, that Sonny was at that piano playing for his life.

But he hadn't been going to school. One day a letter came from the school board and Isabel's mother got it—there had, apparently, been other letters but Sonny had torn them up. This day, when Sonny came in, Isabel's mother showed him the letter and asked where he'd been spending his time. And she finally got it out of him that he'd been down in Greenwich Village, with musicians and other characters, in a white girl's apartment. And this scared her and she started to scream at him and what came up, once she began—though she denies it to this day—was what sacrifices they were making to give Sonny a decent home and how little he appreciated it.

175 Sonny didn't play the piano that day. By evening, Isabel's mother had calmed down but then there was the old man to deal with, and Isabel herself. Isabel says she did her best to be calm but she broke down and started crying. She says she just watched Sonny's face. She could tell, by watching him, what was happening with him. And what was happening was that they penetrated his cloud, they had reached him. Even if their fingers had been a thousand times more gentle than human fingers ever are, he could hardly help feeling that they had stripped him naked and were spitting on that nakedness. For he also had to see that his presence, that music, which was life or death to him, had been torture for them and that they had endured it, not at all for his sake, but only for mine. And Sonny couldn't take that. He can take it a little better today than he could then but he's still not very good at it and, frankly, I don't know anybody who is.

The silence of the next few days must have been louder than the sound of all the music ever played since time began. One morning, before she went to work, Isabel was in his room for something and she suddenly realized that all of his records were gone. And she knew for certain that he was gone. And he was. He went as far as the navy would carry him. He finally sent me a postcard from some place in Greece and that was the first I knew that Sonny was still alive. I didn't see him any more until we were both back in New York and the war had long been over.

He was a man by then, of course, but I wasn't willing to see it. He came by the house from time to time, but we fought almost every time we met. I didn't like the way he carried himself, loose and dreamlike all the time, and I didn't like his friends, and his music seemed to be merely an excuse for the life he led. It sounded just that weird and disordered.

Then we had a fight, a pretty awful fight, and I didn't see him for months. By and by I looked him up, where he was living, in a furnished room in the Village, and I tried to make it up. But there were lots of other people in the room and Sonny just lay on his bed, and he wouldn't come downstairs with me, and he treated these other people as though they were his family and I weren't. So I got mad and then he got mad, and then I told him that he might just as well be dead as live the way he was living. Then he stood up and he told me not to worry about him any more in life, that he *was* dead as far as I was concerned. Then he pushed me to the door and the other people looked on as though nothing were happening, and he slammed the door behind me. I stood in the hallway, staring at the door. I heard somebody laugh in the room and then the tears came to my eyes. I started down the steps, whistling to keep from crying, I kept whistling to myself, *You going to need me, baby, one of these cold, rainy days.*

I read about Sonny's trouble in the spring. Little Grace died in the fall. She was a beautiful little girl. But she only lived a little over two years. She died of polio and she suffered. She had a slight fever for a couple of days, but it didn't seem like anything and we just kept her in bed. And we would certainly have called the doctor, but the fever dropped, she seemed to be all right. So we thought it had just been a cold. Then, one day, she was up, playing, Isabel was in the kitchen fixing lunch for the two boys when they'd come in from school, and she heard Grace fall down in the living room. When you have a lot of children you don't always start running when one of them falls, unless they start screaming or something. And, this time, Grace was quiet. Yet, Isabel says that when she heard that *thump* and then that silence, something happened in her to make her afraid. And she ran to the living room and there was little Grace on the floor, all twisted up, and the reason she hadn't screamed was that she couldn't get her breath. And when she did scream, it was the worst sound, Isabel says, that she'd ever heard in all her life, and she still hears it sometimes in her dreams. Isabel will sometimes wake me up with a low, moaning, strangled sound and I have to be quick to awaken her and hold her to me and where Isabel is weeping against me seems a mortal wound.

I think I may have written Sonny the very day that little Grace was buried. I was sitting in the living room in the dark, by myself, and I suddenly thought of Sonny. My trouble made his real. 180

One Saturday afternoon, when Sonny had been living with us, or, anyway, been in our house, for nearly two weeks, I found myself wandering aimlessly about the living room, drinking from a can of beer, and trying to work up the courage to search Sonny's room. He was out, he was usually out whenever I was home, and Isabel had taken the children to see their grandparents. Suddenly I was standing still in front of the living room window, watching Seventh Avenue. The idea of searching Sonny's room made me still. I scarcely dared to admit to myself what I'd be searching for. I didn't know what I'd do if I found it. Or if I didn't.

On the sidewalk across from me, near the entrance to a barbecue joint, some people were holding an old-fashioned revival meeting. The barbecue cook, wearing a dirty white apron, his conked hair reddish and metallic in the pale sun, and a cigarette between his lips, stood in the doorway, watching them. Kids and older people paused in their errands and stood there, along with some older men and a couple of very tough-looking women who watched everything that happened on the avenue, as though they owned it, or were maybe owned by it. Well, they were watching this, too. The revival was being carried on by three sisters in black, and a brother. All they had were their voices and their Bibles and a tambourine. The brother was testifying and while he testified two of the sisters stood together, seeming to say, amen, and the third sister walked around with the tambourine outstretched and a couple of people dropped coins into it. Then the brother's testimony ended and the sister who had been taking up the collection dumped the coins into her palm and transferred them to the pocket of her long black robe. Then she raised both hands, striking the tambourine against the air, and then against one hand, and she started to sing. And the two other sisters and the brother joined in.

It was strange, suddenly, to watch, though I had been seeing these street meetings all my life. So, of course, had everybody else down there. Yet, they paused and watched and listened and I stood still at the window. *"Tis the old ship of Zion,"* they sang, and the sister with the tambourine kept a steady, jangling beat, *"it has rescued many a thousand!"* Not a soul under the sound of their voices was hearing this song for the first time, not one of them had been rescued. Nor had they seen much in the way of rescue work being done around them. Neither did they especially believe in the holiness of the three sisters and the brother, they knew too much about them, knew where they lived, and how. The woman with the tambourine, whose voice dominated the air, whose face was bright with joy, was divided by very little from the woman who stood watching her, a cigarette between her heavy, chapped lips, her hair a cuckoo's nest, her face scarred and swollen from many beatings, and her black eyes glittering like coal. Perhaps they both knew this, which was why, when, as rarely, they addressed each other, they addressed each other as Sister. As the singing filled the air the watching, listening faces underwent a change, the eyes focusing on something within; the music seemed to soothe a poison out of them; and time seemed, nearly, to fall away from the sullen, belligerent, battered faces, as though they were fleeing back to their first condition, while dreaming of their last. The barbecue cook half shook his head and smiled, and dropped his cigarette and disappeared into his joint. A man fumbled in his pockets for change and stood holding it in his hand impatiently, as though he had just remembered a pressing appointment further up the avenue. He looked furious. Then I saw Sonny, standing on the edge of the crowd. He was carrying a wide, flat notebook with a green cover, and it made him look, from where I was standing, almost like a schoolboy. The coppery sun brought out the copper in his skin, he was very faintly smiling, standing very still. Then the singing stopped, the tambourine turned into a collection plate again. The furious man dropped in his coins and vanished, so did a couple of the women, and Sonny dropped some change in the plate, looking directly at the woman with a little smile. He started across the avenue, toward the house. He has a slow, loping walk, something like the way Harlem hipsters walk, only he's imposed on this his own half-beat. I had never really noticed it before.

I stayed at the window, both relieved and apprehensive. As Sonny disappeared from my sight, they began singing again. And they were still singing when his key turned in the lock.

185 "Hey," he said.

"Hey, yourself. You want some beer?"

"No. Well, maybe." But he came up to the window and stood beside me, looking out. "What a warm voice," he said.

They were singing *If I could only hear my mother pray again!*

"Yes," I said, "and she can sure beat that tambourine."

190 "But what a terrible song," he said, and laughed. He dropped his notebook on the sofa and disappeared into the kitchen. "Where's Isabel and the kids?"

"I think they went to see their grandparents. You hungry?"

"No." He came back into the living room with his can of beer. "You want to come some place with me tonight?"

I sensed, I don't know how, that I couldn't possibly say no. "Sure. Where?"

He sat down on the sofa and picked up his notebook and started leafing through it. "I'm going to sit in with some fellows in a joint in the Village."

195 "You mean, you're going to play, tonight?"

"That's right." He took a swallow of his beer and moved back to the window. He gave me a sidelong look. "If you can stand it."

"I'll try," I said.

He smiled to himself and we both watched as the meeting across the way broke up. The three sisters and the brother, heads bowed, were singing *God be with you till we meet again.* The faces around them were very quiet. Then the song ended. The small crowd dispersed. We watched the three women and the lone man walk slowly up the avenue.

"When she was singing before," said Sonny, abruptly, "her voice reminded me for a minute of what heroin feels like sometimes—when it's in your veins. It makes you feel sort of warm and cool at the same time. And distant. And—and sure." He sipped his beer, very deliberately not looking at me. I watched his face. "It makes you feel—in control. Sometimes you've got to have that feeling."

"Do you?" I sat down slowly in the easy chair.   200

"Sometimes." He went to the sofa and picked up his notebook again. "Some people do."

"In order," I asked, "to play?" And my voice was very ugly, full of contempt and anger.

"Well"—he looked at me with great, troubled eyes, as though, in fact, he hoped his eyes would tell me things he could never otherwise say—"they *think* so. And *if* they think so—!"

"And what do *you* think?" I asked.

He sat on the sofa and put his can of beer on the floor. "I don't know," he said, and   205
I couldn't be sure if he were answering my question or pursuing his thoughts. His face didn't tell me. "It's not so much to *play*. It's to *stand* it, to be able to make it at all. On any level." He frowned and smiled: "In order to keep from shaking to pieces."

"But these friends of yours," I said, "they seem to shake themselves to pieces pretty goddamn fast."

"Maybe." He played with the notebook. And something told me that I should curb my tongue, that Sonny was doing his best to talk, that I should listen. "But of course you only know the ones that've gone to pieces. Some don't—or at least they haven't *yet* and that's just about all *any* of us can say." He paused. "And then there are some who just live, really, in hell, and they know it and they see what's happening and they go right on. I don't know." He sighed, dropped the notebook, folded his arms. "Some guys, you can tell from the way they play, they on something *all* the time. And you can see that, well, it makes something real for them. But of course," he picked up his beer from the floor and sipped it and put the can down again, "they *want* to, too, you've got to see that. Even some of them that say they don't—*some*, not all."

"And what about you?" I asked—I couldn't help it. "What about you? Do *you* want to?"

He stood up and walked to the window and remained silent for a long time. Then he sighed. "Me," he said. Then: "While I was downstairs before, on my way here, listening to that woman sing, it struck me all of a sudden how much suffering she must have had to go through—to sing like that. It's *repulsive* to think you have to suffer that much."

I said: "But there's no way not to suffer—is there, Sonny?"   210

"I believe not," he said and smiled, "but that's never stopped anyone from trying." He looked at me. "Has it?" I realized, with this mocking look, that there stood between us, forever, beyond the power of time or forgiveness, the fact that I had held silence—so long!—when he had needed human speech to help him. He turned back to the window. "No, there's no way not to suffer. But you try all kinds of ways to keep from drowning in it, to keep on top of it, and to make it seem—well, like *you*. Like you did something, all right, and now you're suffering for it. You know?" I said nothing. "Well you know," he said, impatiently, "Why *do* people suffer? Maybe it's better to do something to give it a reason, *any* reason."

"But we just agreed," I said, "that there's no way not to suffer. Isn't it better, then, just to—take it?"

"But nobody just takes it," Sonny cried, "that's what I'm telling you! *Everybody* tries not to. You're just hung up on the *way* some people try—it's not *your* way!"

The hair on my face began to itch, my face felt wet. "That's not true," I said, "that's not true. I don't give a damn what other people do, I don't even care how they suffer. I just care how *you* suffer." And he looked at me. "Please believe me," I said, "I don't want to see you—die—trying not to suffer."

215   "I won't," he said, flatly, "die trying not to suffer. At least, not any faster than anybody else."

"But there's no need," I said, trying to laugh, "is there? in killing yourself."

I wanted to say more, but I couldn't. I wanted to talk about will power and how life could be—well, beautiful. I wanted to say that it was all within; but was it? or, rather, wasn't that exactly the trouble? And I wanted to promise that I would never fail him again. But it would all have sounded—empty words and lies.

So I made the promise to myself and prayed that I would keep it.

"It's terrible sometimes, inside," he said, "that's what's the trouble. You walk these streets, black and funky and cold, and there's not really a living ass to talk to, and there's nothing shaking, and there's no way of getting it out—that storm inside. You can't talk it and you can't make love with it, and when you finally try to get with it and play it, you realize *nobody's* listening. So *you've* got to listen. You got to find a way to listen."

220   And then he walked away from the window and sat on the sofa again, as though all the wind had suddenly been knocked out of him. "Sometimes you'll do *anything* to play, even cut your mother's throat." He laughed and looked at me. "Or your brother's." Then he sobered. "Or your own." Then: "Don't worry. I'm all right now and I think I'll *be* all right. But I can't forget—where I've been. I don't mean just the physical place I've been, I mean where I've *been*. And *what* I've been."

"What have you been, Sonny?" I asked.

He smiled—but sat sideways on the sofa, his elbow resting on the back, his fingers playing with his mouth and chin, not looking at me. "I've been something I didn't recognize, didn't know I could be. Didn't know anybody could be." He stopped, looking inward, looking helplessly young, looking old. "I'm not talking about it now because I feel *guilty* or anything like that—maybe it would be better if I did, I don't know. Anyway, I can't really talk about it. Not to you, not to anybody," and now he turned and faced me. "Sometimes, you know, and it was actually when I was most *out* of the world, I felt that I was in it, that I was *with* it, really, and I could play or I didn't really have to *play*, it just came out of me, it was there. And I don't know how I played, thinking about it now, but I know I did awful things, those times, sometimes, to people. Or it wasn't that I *did* anything to them—it was that they weren't real." He picked up the beer can; it was empty; he rolled it between his palms: "And other times—well, I needed a fix, I needed to find a place to lean, I needed to clear a space to *listen*—and I couldn't find it, and I—went crazy, I did terrible things to *me*, I was terrible *for* me." He began pressing the beer can between his hands, I watched the metal begin to give. It glittered, as he played with it, like a knife, and I was afraid he would cut himself, but I said nothing. "Oh well. I can never tell you. I was all by myself at the bottom of something, stinking and sweating and crying and shaking, and I smelled it, you know? *my* stink, and I thought I'd die if I couldn't get away from it and yet, all the same, I knew that everything I was doing was just locking me in with it. And I didn't know," he paused, still flattening the beer can, "I didn't know, I still *don't* know, something kept telling me that maybe it was good to smell your own stink, but I didn't think that *that* was what I'd been trying to do—and—who can stand it?" and he abruptly dropped the ruined beer can, looking at me with a small, still smile, and then rose, walking to the window as though it were the lodestone rock. I watched his face, he watched the avenue. "I couldn't tell you when Mama died—but the reason I wanted to leave Harlem so bad was to get away from drugs. And then, when I ran away, that's what I was running from—really. When I came back, nothing had changed, *I* hadn't changed, I was just—older." And he stopped, drumming with his fingers on the windowpane. The sun had vanished, soon darkness would fall. I watched his face. "It can come again," he said, almost as though speaking to himself. Then he turned to me. "It can come again," he repeated. "I just want you to know that."

"All right," I said, at last. "So it can come again. All right."

He smiled, but the smile was sorrowful. "I had to try to tell you," he said.

"Yes," I said. "I understand that."   225

"You're my brother," he said, looking straight at me, and not smiling at all.

"Yes," I repeated, "yes. I understand that."

He turned back to the window, looking out. "All that hatred down there," he said, "all that hatred and misery and love. It's a wonder it doesn't blow the avenue apart."

We went to the only nightclub on a short, dark street, downtown. We squeezed through the narrow, chattering, jam-packed bar to the entrance of the big room, where the bandstand was. And we stood there for a moment, for the lights were very dim in this room and we couldn't see. Then, "Hello, boy," said a voice and an enormous black man, much older than Sonny or myself, erupted out of all that atmospheric lighting and put an arm around Sonny's shoulder. "I been sitting right here," he said, "waiting for you."

He had a big voice, too, and heads in the darkness turned toward us.   230

Sonny grinned and pulled a little away, and said, "Creole, this is my brother. I told you about him."

Creole shook my hand. "I'm glad to meet you, son," he said, and it was clear that he was glad to meet me *there* for Sonny's sake. And he smiled, "You got a real musician in *your* family," and he took his arm from Sonny's shoulder and slapped him, lightly, affectionately, with the back of his hand.

"Well. Now I've heard it all," said a voice behind us. This was another musician, and a friend of Sonny's, a coal-black, cheerful-looking man, built close to the ground. He immediately began confiding to me, at the top of his lungs, the most terrible things about Sonny, his teeth gleaming like a lighthouse and his laugh coming up out of him like the beginning of an earthquake. And it turned out that everyone at the bar knew Sonny, or almost everyone; some were musicians, working there, or nearby, or not working, some were simply hangers-on, and some were there to hear Sonny play. I was introduced to all of them and they were all very polite to me. Yet, it was clear that, for them, I was only Sonny's brother. Here, I was in Sonny's world. Or, rather: his kingdom. Here, it was not even a question that his veins bore royal blood.

They were going to play soon and Creole installed me, by myself, at a table in a dark corner. Then I watched them, Creole, and the little black man, and Sonny, and the others, while they horsed around, standing just below the bandstand. The light from the bandstand spilled just a little short of them and, watching them laughing and gesturing and moving about, I had the feeling that they, nevertheless, were being most careful not to step into that circle of light too suddenly: that if they moved into the light too suddenly, without thinking, they would perish in flame. Then, while I watched, one of them, the small, black man, moved into the light and crossed the band-stand and started fooling around with his drums. Then—being funny and being, also, extremely ceremonious—Creole took Sonny by the arm and led him to the piano. A woman's voice called Sonny's name and a few hands started clapping. And Sonny, also being funny and being ceremonious, and so touched, I think, that he could have cried, but neither hiding it nor showing it, riding it like a man, grinned, and put both hands to his heart and bowed from the waist.

235   Creole then went to the bass fiddle and a lean, very bright-skinned brown man jumped up on the bandstand and picked up his horn. So there they were, and the at-mosphere on the bandstand and in the room began to change and tighten. Someone stepped up to the microphone and announced them. Then there were all kinds of mur-murs. Some people at the bar shushed others. The waitress ran around, frantically get-ting in the last orders, guys and chicks got closer to each other, and the lights on the bandstand, on the quartet, turned to a kind of indigo. Then they all looked different there. Creole looked about him for the last time, as though he were making certain that all his chickens were in the coop, and then he—jumped and struck the fiddle. And there they were.

All I know about music is that not many people ever really hear it. And even then, on the rare occasions when something opens within, and the music enters, what we mainly hear, or hear corroborated, are personal, private, vanishing evocations. But the man who creates the music is hearing something else, is dealing with the roar rising from the void and imposing order on it as it hits the air. What is evoked in him, then, is of another order, more terrible because it has no words, and triumphant, too, for that same reason. And his triumph, when he triumphs, is ours. I just watched Sonny's face. His face was troubled, he was working hard, but he wasn't with it. And I had the feeling that, in a way, everyone on the bandstand was waiting for him, both waiting for him and pushing him along. But as I began to watch Creole, I realized that it was Creole who held them all back. He had them on a short rein. Up there, keeping the beat with his whole body, wailing on the fiddle, with his eyes half closed, he was listening to everything, but he was listening to Sonny. He was having a dialogue with Sonny. He wanted Sonny to leave the shoreline and strike out for the deep water. He was Sonny's witness that deep water and drowning were not the same thing—he had been there, and he knew. And he wanted Sonny to know. He was waiting for Sonny to do the things on the keys which would let Creole know that Sonny was in the water.

And, while Creole listened, Sonny moved, deep within, exactly like someone in torment. I had never before thought of how awful the relationship must be between the musician and his instrument. He has to fill it, this instrument, with the breath of life, his own. He has to make it do what he wants it to do. And a piano is just a piano. It's made out of so much wood and wires and little hammers and big ones, and ivory. While there's only so much you can do with it, the only way to find this out is to try; to try and make it do everything.

And Sonny hadn't been near a piano for over a year. And he wasn't on much bet-ter terms with his life, not the life that stretched before him now. He and the piano stammered, started one way, got scared, stopped; started another way, panicked, marked time, started again; then seemed to have found a direction, panicked again, got stuck. And the face I saw on Sonny I'd never seen before. Everything had been burned out of it, and, at the same time, things usually hidden were being burned in, by the fire and fury of the battle which was occurring in him up there.

Yet, watching Creole's face as they neared the end of the first set, I had the feeling that something had happened, something I hadn't heard. Then they finished, there was scattered applause, and then, without an instant's warning, Creole started into something else, it was almost sardonic, it was *Am I Blue*. And, as though he commanded, Sonny began to play. Something began to happen. And Creole let out the reins. The dry, low, black man said something awful on the drums, Creole answered, and the drums talked back. Then the horn insisted, sweet and high, slightly detached perhaps, and Creole listened, commenting now and then, dry, and driving, beautiful and calm and old. Then they all came together again, and Sonny was part of the family again. I could tell this from his face. He seemed to have found, right there beneath his fingers, a damn brand-new piano. It seemed that he couldn't get over it. Then, for awhile, just being happy with Sonny, they seemed to be agreeing with him that brand-new pianos certainly were a gas.

Then Creole stepped forward to remind them that what they were playing was the blues. He hit something in all of them, he hit something in me, myself, and the music tightened and deepened, apprehension began to beat the air. Creole began to tell us what the blues were all about. They were not about anything very new. He and his boys up there were keeping it new, at the risk of ruin, destruction, madness, and death, in order to find new ways to make us listen. For, while the tale of how we suffer, and how we are delighted, and how we may triumph is never new, it always must be heard. There isn't any other tale to tell, it's the only light we've got in all this darkness. 240

And this tale, according to that face, that body, those strong hands on those strings, has another aspect in every country, and a new depth in every generation. Listen, Creole seemed to be saying, listen. Now these are Sonny's blues. He made the little black man on the drums know it, and the bright, brown man on the horn. Creole wasn't trying any longer to get Sonny in the water. He was wishing him God-speed. Then he stepped back, very slowly, filling the air with the immense suggestion that Sonny speak for himself.

Then they all gathered around Sonny and Sonny played. Every now and again one of them seemed to say, amen. Sonny's fingers filled the air with life, his life. But that life contained so many others. And Sonny went all the way back, he really began with the spare, flat statement of the opening phrase of the song. Then he began to make it his. It was very beautiful because it wasn't hurried and it was no longer a lament. I seemed to hear with what burning he had made it his, with what burning we had yet to make it ours, how we could cease lamenting. Freedom lurked around us and I understood, at last, that he could help us to be free if we would listen, that he would never be free until we did. Yet, there was no battle in his face now. I heard what he had gone through, and would continue to go through until he came to rest in earth. He had made it his: that long line, of which we knew only Mama and Daddy. And he was giving it back, as everything must be given back, so that, passing through death, it can live forever. I saw my mother's face again, and felt, for the first time, how the stones of the road she had walked on must have bruised her feet. I saw the moonlit road where my father's brother died. And it brought something else back to me, and carried me past it, I saw my little girl again and felt Isabel's tears again, and I felt my own tears begin to rise. And I was yet aware that this was only a moment, that the world waited outside, as hungry as a tiger, and that trouble stretched above us, longer than the sky.

Then it was over. Creole and Sonny let out their breath, both soaking wet, and grinning. There was a lot of applause and some of it was real. In the dark, the girl came by and I asked her to take drinks to the bandstand. There was a long pause, while they talked up there in the indigo light and after awhile I saw the girl put a Scotch and milk on top of the piano for Sonny. He didn't seem to notice it, but just before they started playing again, he sipped from it and looked toward me, and nodded. Then he put it back on top of the piano. For me, then, as they began to play again, it glowed and shook above my brother's head like the very cup of trembling.°   [1957]

QUESTIONS

1. Who is the protagonist?
2. Although the two brothers hold competing philosophies of life, what do they have in common?
3. Is it essential to the meaning of the story that Sonny be a musician? Would the theme be affected if he were a painter or a writer?
4. What does the story have to say about the relationship of art to religion?
5. Explore the implications of the allusion to the book of Isaiah 51:17–23 in the concluding sentence. What has the narrator learned as the result of his experience?

RESPONSES

1. Research the development of be-bop in the late 1940s and early 1950s. How has Baldwin caught that moment in musical history?
2. Compare this story to those by Richard Wright and Ralph Ellison. How is it similar? How different?

FOCUS ON FILM

1. The film *Round Midnight* is not based on "Sonny's Blues" but it does concern the troubled life of a jazz musician. Compare Sonny to the saxophonist played by real life saxophonist Dexter Gordon in *Round Midnight*.
2. Are there moments in *Round Midnight* that portray a musician leaving "the shoreline and [striking] out for deep water"? Explain.

°*cup of trembling:* See Isaiah 51:22.

HONORÉ DE BALZAC

Honoré de Balzac (1799–1850) was born in Tours, France. He was educated in schools in Vendome, Tours, and Paris, but was an indifferent student who read widely in works not assigned in school. Through most of his adult life, even though his works were quite popular, he struggled with finances due largely to poor investments. His list of published works, including 95 novels, is extensive. He is most noted for his novels organized under the general title *La comedie humaine*. In this project he hoped to portray the entirety of French life. Some of his works include *The Country Doctor* (1833), *Old Goriot* (1834), and *Droll Stories* (1837).

A Passion in the Desert

"The whole show is dreadful," she cried, coming out of the menagerie of M. Martin. She had just been looking at that daring speculator "working with his hyena"—to speak in the style of the program.

"By what means," she continued, "can he have tamed these animals to such a point as to be certain of their affection for—."

"What seems to you a problem," said I, interrupting, "is really quite natural."

"Oh!" she cried, letting an incredulous smile wander over her lips.

"You think that beasts are wholly without passions?" I asked her. "Quite the reverse; we can communicate to them all the vices arising in our own state of civilization." 5

She looked at me with an air of astonishment.

"Nevertheless," I continued, "the first time I saw M. Martin, I admit, like you, I did give vent to an exclamation of surprise. I found myself next to an old soldier with the right leg amputated, who had come in with me. His face had struck me. He had one of those intrepid heads, stamped with the seal of warfare, and on which the battles of Napoleon are written. Besides, he had that frank good-humored expression which always impresses me favorably. He was without doubt one of those troopers who are surprised at nothing, who find matter for laughter in the contortions of a dying comrade, who bury or plunder him quite lightheartedly, who stand intrepidly in the way of bullets; in fact, one of those men who waste no time in deliberation, and would not hesitate to make friends with the devil himself. After looking very attentively at the proprietor of the menagerie getting out of his box, my companion pursed up his lips with an air of mockery and contempt, with that peculiar and expressive twist which superior people assume to show they are not taken in. Then when I was expatiating on the courage of M. Martin, he smiled, shook his head knowingly, and said, "Well known."

"How 'well known'? I said. "If you would only explain to me the mystery I should be vastly obliged."

"After a few minutes, during which we made acquaintance, we went to dine at the first restaurateur's whose shop caught our eye. At dessert a bottle of champagne completely refreshed and brightened up the memories of this odd old soldier. He told me his story, and I said he had every reason to exclaim, 'Well known.'"

10   When she got home, she teased me to that extent and made so many promises that I consented to communicate to her the old soldier's confidences. Next day she received the following episode of an epic which one might call "The Frenchman in Egypt."

During the expedition in Upper Egypt under General Desaix, a Provençal soldier fell into the hands of the Maugrabins, and was taken by these Arabs into the deserts beyond the falls of the Nile.

In order to place a sufficient distance between themselves and the French army, the Maugrabins made forced marches, and only rested during the night. They camped round a well overshadowed by palm trees under which they had previously concealed a store of provisions. Not surmising that the notion of flight would occur to their prisoner, they contented themselves with binding his hands, and after eating a few dates, and giving provender to their horses, went to sleep.

When the brave Provençal saw that his enemies were no longer watching him, he made use of his teeth to steal a scimitar, fixed the blade between his knees, and cut the cords which prevented using his hands; in a moment he was free. He at once seized a rifle and dagger, then taking the precaution to provide himself with a sack of dried dates, oats, and powder and shot, and to fasten a scimitar to his waist he leaped onto a horse, and spurred on vigorously in the direction where he thought to find the French army. So impatient was he to see a bivouac again that he pressed on the already-tired courser at such speed that its flanks were lacerated with his spurs, and at last the poor animal died, leaving the Frenchman alone in the desert. After walking some time in the sand with all the courage of an escaped convict, the soldier was obliged to stop, as the day had already ended. In spite of the beauty of an Oriental sky at night, he felt he had not strength enough to go on. Fortunately he had been able to find a small hill, on the summit of which a few palm trees shot up into the air; it was their verdure seen from afar which had brought hope and consolation to his heart. His fatigue was so great that he lay down upon a rock of granite, capriciously cut out like a camp bed; there he fell asleep without taking any precaution to defend himself while he slept. He had made the sacrifice of his life. His last thought was one of regret. He repented having left the Maugrabins, whose nomad life seemed to smile on him now that he was afar from them and without help. He was awakened by the sun, whose pitiless rays fell with all their force on the granite and produced an intolerable heat, for he had had the stupidity to place himself inversely to the shadow thrown by the verdant majestic heads of the palm trees. He looked at the solitary trees and shuddered—they reminded him of the graceful shafts crowned with foliage which characterize the Saracen columns in the cathedral of Arles.

But when, after counting the palm trees, he cast his eye around him, the most horrible despair was infused into his soul. Before him stretched an ocean without limit. The dark sand of the desert spread farther than sight could reach in every direction, and glittered like steel struck with a bright light. It might have been a sea of looking glass, or lakes melted together in a mirror. A fiery vapor carried up in streaks made a perpetual whirlwind over the quivering land. The sky was lit with an Oriental splendor of insupportable purity, leaving naught for the imagination to desire. Heaven and earth were on fire.

The silence was awful in its wild and terrible majesty. Infinity, immensity, closed in 15 upon the soul from every side. Not a cloud in the sky, not a breath in the air, not a flaw on the bosom of the sand, ever moving in diminutive waves; the horizon ended as at sea on a clear day, with one line of light, definite as the cut of a sword.

The Provençal threw his arms around the trunk of one of the palm trees, as though it were the body of a friend, and then in the shelter of the thin straight shadow that the palm cast upon the granite, he wept. Then sitting down he remained as he was, contemplating with profound sadness the implacable scene, which was all he had to look upon. He cried aloud, to measure the solitude. His voice, lost in the hollows of the hill, sounded faintly, and aroused no echo—the echo was in his own heart. The Provençal was twenty-two years old; he loaded his carbine.

"There'll be time enough," he said to himself, laying on the ground the weapon which alone could bring him deliverance.

Looking by turns at the black expanse and the blue expanse, the soldier dreamed of France—he smelled with delight the gutters of Paris—he remembered the towns through which he had passed, the faces of his fellow soldiers, the most minute details of his life. His southern fancy soon showed him the stones of his beloved Provence, in the play of the heat which waved over the spread sheet of the desert. Fearing the danger of this cruel mirage, he went down the opposite side of the hill to that by which he had come up the day before. The remains of a rug showed that this place of refuge had at one time been inhabited; at a short distance he saw some palm trees full of dates. Then the instinct which binds us to life awoke again in his heart. He hoped to live long enough to await the passing of some Arabs, or perhaps he might hear the sound of cannon, for at this time Bonaparte was traversing Egypt.

This thought gave him new life. The palm tree seemed to bend with the weight of the ripe fruit. He shook some of it down. When he tasted this unhoped-for manna, he felt sure that the palms had been cultivated by a former inhabitant—the savory, fresh meat of the dates was proof of the care of his predecessor. He passed suddenly from dark despair to an almost insane joy. He went up again to the top of the hill, and spent the rest of the day in cutting down one of the sterile palm trees, which the night before had served him for shelter. A vague memory made him think of the animals of the desert; and in case they might come to drink at the spring, visible from the base of the rocks but lost farther down, he resolved to guard himself from their visits by placing a barrier at the entrance of his hermitage.

In spite of his diligence, and the strength which the fear of being devoured asleep 20 gave him, he was unable to cut the palm in pieces, though he succeeded in cutting it down. At eventide the king of the desert fell; the sound of its fall resounded far and wide, like a sigh of solitude; the soldier shuddered as though he had heard some voice predicting woe.

But like an heir who does not long bewail a deceased parent, he tore off from this beautiful tree the tall broad green leaves which are its poetic adornment, and used them to mend the mat on which he was to sleep.

Fatigued by the heat and his work, he fell asleep under the red curtains of his wet cave.

In the middle of the night his sleep was troubled by an extraordinary noise; he sat up, and the deep silence around him allowed him to distinguish the alternative accents of a respiration whose savage energy could not belong to a human creature.

A profound terror, increased still further by the darkness, the silence, and his waking images, froze his heart within him. He almost felt his hair stand on end, when by straining his eyes to their utmost he perceived through the shadows two faint yellow lights. At first he attributed these lights to the reflection of his own pupils, but soon the vivid brilliance of the night aided him gradually to distinguish the objects around him in the cave, and he beheld a huge animal lying but two steps from him. Was it a lion, a tiger, or a crocodile?

25   The Provençal was not sufficiently educated enough to know under what species his enemy ought to be classed; but his fright was all the greater, as his ignorance led him to imagine all terrors at once; he endured a cruel torture, noting every variation of the breathing close to him without daring to make the slightest movement. An odor, pungent like that of a fox, but more penetrating, profounder—so to speak—filled the cave, and when the Provençal became sensible of this, his terror reached its height, for he could not longer doubt the proximity of a terrible companion, whose royal dwelling served him for shelter.

Presently the reflection of the moon, descending on the horizon, lit up the den, rendering gradually visible and resplendent the spotted skin of a panther.

This lion of Egypt slept, curled up like a big dog, the peaceful possessor of a sumptuous niche at the gate of a hotel; its eyes opened for a moment and closed again; its face was turned toward the man. A thousand confused thoughts passed through the Frenchman's mind; first he thought of killing it with a bullet from his gun, but he saw there was not enough distance between them for him to take proper aim—the shot would miss the mark. And if it were to wake!—the thought made his limbs rigid. He listened to his own heart beating in the midst of the silence, and cursed the too violent pulsations which the flow of blood brought on, fearing to disturb that sleep which allowed him time to think of some means of escape.

Twice he placed his hand on his scimitar, intending to cut off the head of his enemy; but the difficulty of cutting stiff, short hair compelled him to abandon this daring project. To miss would be to die for *certain*, he thought; he preferred the chances of fair fight, and made up his mind to wait till morning; the morning did not leave him long to wait.

He could now examine the panther at ease; its muzzle was smeared with blood.

30   "She's had a good dinner," he thought, without troubling himself as to whether her feast might have been on human flesh. "She won't be hungry when she gets up."

It was a female. The fur on her belly and flanks was glistening white; many small marks like velvet formed beautiful bracelets round her feet; her sinuous tail was also white, ending with black rings; the overpart of her dress, yellow like unburnished gold, very lissome and soft, had the characteristic blotches in the form of rosettes which distinguish the panther from every other feline species.

This tranquil and formidable hostess snored in an attitude as graceful as that of a cat lying on a cushion. Her bloodstained paws, nervous and well armed, were stretched out before her face, which rested upon them, and from which radiated her straight, slender whiskers, like threads of silver.

If she had been like that in a cage, the Provençal would doubtless have admired the grace of the animal, and the vigorous contrasts of vivid color which gave her robe an imperial splendor; but just then his sight was troubled by her sinister appearance.

The presence of the panther, even asleep, could not fail to produce the effect which the magnetic eyes of the serpent are said to have on the nightingale.

For a moment the courage of the soldier began to fail before this danger, though no doubt it would have risen at the mouth of a cannon charged with shell. Nevertheless, a bold thought brought daylight in his soul and sealed up the source of the cold sweat which sprang forth on his brow. Like men driven to bay who defy death and offer their body to the smiter, so he, seeing in this merely a tragic episode, resolved to play his part with honor to the last.

"The day before yesterday the Arabs would have killed me perhaps," he said; so considering himself as good as dead already, he waited bravely, with excited curiosity his enemy's awakening.

When the sun appeared, the panther suddenly opened her eyes; then she put out her paws with energy, as if to stretch them and get rid of cramp. At last she yawned, showing the formidable apparatus of her teeth and pointed tongue, rough as a file.

"A regular petite maitresse," thought the Frenchman, seeing her roll herself about so softly and coquettishly. She licked off the blood which stained her paws and muzzle, and scratched her head with reiterated gestures full of prettiness. "All right, make a little toilet," the Frenchman said to himself, beginning to recover his gaiety with his courage; "we'll say good morning to each other presently," and he seized the small, short dagger which he had taken from the Maugrabins. At this moment the panther turned her head toward the man and looked at him fixed without moving.

The rigidity of her metallic eyes and their insupportable luster made him shudder, especially when the animal walked toward him. But he looked at her caressingly, staring into her eyes in order to magnetize her, and let her come quite close to him; then with a movement both gentle and amorous, as though he were caressing the most beautiful of women, he passed his hand over her whole body, from the head to the tail, scratching the flexible vertebrae which divided the panther's yellow back. The animal waved her tail voluptuously, and her eyes grew gentle; and when for the third time the Frenchman accomplished this interesting flattery, she gave forth one of those purrings by which our cats express their pleasure; but this murmur issued from a throat so powerful and so deep that it resounded through the cave like the last vibrations of an organ in a church. The man, understanding the importance of his caresses, redoubled them in such a way as to surprise and stupefy his imperious courtesan. When he felt sure of having extinguished the ferocity of his capricious companion, whose hunger had so fortunately been satisfied the day before, he got up to go out of the cave; the panther let him go out, but when he had reached the summit of the hill she sprang with the lightness of a sparrow hopping from twig to twig, and rubbed herself against his legs, putting up her back after the manner of all the race of cats. Then regarding her guest with eyes whose glare had softened a little, she gave vent to that wild cry which naturalists compare to the grating of a saw.

"She is exacting," said the Frenchman, smilingly.

He was bold enough to play with her ears; he caressed her belly and scratched her head as hard as he could.

When he saw that he was successful, he tickled her skull with the point of his dagger, watching for the right moment to kill her, but the hardness of her bones made him tremble for his success.

The sultana of the desert showed herself gracious to her slave; she lifted her head, stretched out her neck and manifested her delight by the tranquillity of her attitude.

35

40

It suddenly occurred to the soldier that to kill this savage princess with one blow he must poniard her in the throat.

He raised the blade, when the panther, satisfied no doubt, laid herself gracefully at his feet, and cast up at him glances in which, in spite of their natural fierceness, was mingled confusedly a kind of good will. The poor Provençal ate his dates, leaning against one of the palm trees, and casting his eyes alternately on the desert in quest of some liberator and on his terrible companion to watch her uncertain clemency.

45   The panther looked at the place where the date stones fell, and every time that he threw one down her eyes expressed an incredible mistrust.

She examined the man with an almost commercial prudence. However, this examination was favorable to him, for when he had finished his meager meal she licked his boots with her powerful rough tongue, brushing off with marvelous skill the dust gathered in the creases.

"Ah, but when she's really hungry!" thought the Frenchman. In spite of the shudder this thought caused him, the soldier began to measure curiously the proportions of the panther, certainly one of the most splendid specimens of its race. She was three feet high and four feet long without counting her tail; this powerful weapon, rounded like a cudgel, was nearly three feet long. The head, large as that of a lioness, was distinguished by a rare expression of refinement. The cold cruelty of a tiger was dominant, it was true, but there was also a vague resemblance to the face of a sensual woman. Indeed, the face of this solitary queen had something of the gaiety of a drunken Nero: she had satiated herself with blood, and she wanted to play.

The soldier tried if he might walk up and down, and the panther left him free, contenting herself with following him with her eyes, less like a faithful dog than a big Angora cat, observing everything and every movement of her master.

When he looked around, he saw, by the spring, the remains of his horse; the panther had dragged the carcass all that way; about two thirds of it had been devoured already. The sight reassured him.

50   It was easy to explain the panther's absence, and the respect she had had for him while he slept. The first piece of good luck emboldened him to tempt the future, and he conceived the wild hope of continuing on good terms with the panther during the entire day, neglecting no means of taming her, and remaining in her good graces.

He returned to her, and had the unspeakable joy of seeing her wag her tail with an almost imperceptible movement at his approach. He sat down then, without fear, by her side, and they began to play together; he took her paws and muzzle, pulled her ears, rolled her over on her back, stroked her warm, delicate flanks. She let him do whatever he liked, and when he began to stroke the hair on her feet she drew her claws in carefully.

The man, keeping the dagger in one hand, thought to plunge it into the belly of the too-confiding panther, but he was afraid that he would be immediately strangled in her last conclusive struggle; besides, he felt in his heart a sort of remorse which bid him respect a creature that had done him no harm. He seemed to have found a friend, in a boundless desert; half unconsciously he thought of his first sweetheart, whom he had nicknamed "Mignonne" by way of contrast, because she was so atrociously jealous that all the time of their love he was in fear of the knife with which she had always threatened him.

This memory of his early days suggested to him the idea of making the young panther answer to this name, now that he began to admire with less terror her swiftness, suppleness, and softness. Toward the end of the day he had familiarized himself with his perilous position; he now almost liked the painfulness of it. At last his companion had got into the habit of looking up at him whenever he cried in a falsetto voice, "Mignonne."

At the setting of the sun Mignonne gave, several times running, a profound melancholy cry. "She's been well brought up," said the lighthearted soldier; "she says her prayers." But this mental joke only occurred to him when he noticed what a pacific attitude his companion remained in. "Come, *ma petite blonde*, I'll let you go to bed first," he said to her, counting on the activity of his own legs to run away as quickly as possible, directly she was asleep, and seek another shelter for the night.

The soldier waited with impatience the hour of his flight, and when it had arrived he walked vigorously in the direction of the Nile; but hardly had he made a quarter of a league in the sand when he heard the panther bounding after him, crying with that sawlike cry more dreadful even than the sound of her leaping. 55

"Ah!" he said, "then she's taken a fancy to me, she has never met anyone before, and it is really quite flattering to have her first love."

That instant the man fell into one of those movable quicksands so terrible to travelers and from which it is impossible to save oneself. Feeling himself caught, he gave a shriek of alarm; the panther seized him with her teeth by the collar, and, springing vigorously backward, drew him as if by magic out of the whirling sand.

"Ah, Mignonne!" cried the soldier, caressing her enthusiastically; "we're bound together for life and death but no jokes, mind!" and he retraced his steps.

From that time the desert seemed inhabited. It contained a being to whom the man could talk, and whose ferocity was rendered gentle by him, though he could not explain to himself the reason for their strange friendship. Great as was the soldier's desire to stay upon guard, he slept.

On awakening he could not find Mignonne; he mounted the hill, and in the distance saw her springing toward him after the habit of these animals, who cannot run on account of the extreme flexibility of the vertebral column. Mignonne arrived, her jaws covered with blood; she received the wonted caress of her companion, showing with much purring how happy it made her. Her eyes, full of languor, turned still more gently than the day before toward the Provençal who talked to her as one would to a tame animal. 60

"Ah! Mademoiselle, you are a nice girl, aren't you? Just look at that! So we like to be made much of, don't we? Aren't you ashamed of yourself? So you have been eating some Arab or other, have you? That doesn't matter. They're animals just the same as you are; but don't you take to eating Frenchmen, or I shan't like you any longer."

She played like a dog with its master, letting herself be rolled over, knocked about, and stroked, alternately; sometimes she herself would provoke the soldier, putting up her paw with a soliciting gesture.

Some days passed in this manner. This companionship permitted the Provençal to appreciate the sublime beauty of the desert; now that he had a living thing to think about, alternations of fear and quiet, and plenty to eat, his mind became filled with contrast and his life began to be diversified.

Solitude revealed to him all her secrets, and enveloped him in her delights. He discovered in the rising and setting of the sun sights unknown to the world. He knew what it was to tremble when he heard over his head the hiss of a bird's wing, so rarely did they pass, or when he saw the clouds, changing and many-colored travelers, melt one into another. He studied in the night time the effect of the moon upon the ocean of sand, where the simoom made waves swift of movement and rapid in their change.

He lived the life of the Eastern day, marveling at its wonderful pomp; then, after having reveled in the sight of a hurricane over the plain where the whirling sands made red, dry mists and death-bearing clouds, he would welcome the night with joy, for then fell the healthful freshness of the stars, and he listened to imaginary music in the skies. Then solitude taught him to unroll the treasures of dreams. He passed whole hours in remembering mere nothings, and comparing his present life with his past.

65 At last he grew passionately fond of the panther; for some sort of affection was a necessity.

Whether it was that his will powerfully projected had modified the character of his companion, or whether, because she found abundant food in her predatory excursions in the desert, she respected the man's life, he began to fear for it no longer, seeing her so well tamed.

He devoted the greater part of his time to sleep, but he was obliged to watch like a spider in its web that the moment of his deliverance might not escape him, if anyone should pass the line marked by the horizon. He had sacrificed his shirt to make a flag with, which he hung at the top of a palm tree, whose foliage he had torn off. Taught by necessity, he found the means of keeping it spread out, by fastening it with little sticks; for the wind might not be blowing at the moment when the passing traveler was looking through the desert.

It was during the long hours, when he had abandoned hope, that he amused himself with the panther. He had come to learn the different inflections of her voice, the expressions of her eyes; he had studied the capricious patterns of all the rosettes which marked the gold of her robe. Mignonne was not even angry when he took hold of the tuft at the end of her tail to count her rings, those graceful ornaments which glittered in the sun like jewelry. It gave him pleasure to contemplate the supple, fine outlines of her form, the whiteness of her belly, the graceful pose of her head. But it was especially when she was playing that he felt most pleasure in looking at her; the agility and youthful lightness of her movements were a continual surprise to him; he wondered at the supple way in which she jumped and climbed, washed herself and arranged her fur, crouched down and prepared to spring. However rapid her spring might be, however slippery the stone she was on, she would always stop short at the word "Mignonne."

One day, in a bright midday sun, an enormous bird coursed through the air. The man left his panther to look at this new guest; but after waiting a moment the deserted sultana growled deeply.

70 "My goodness! I do believe she's jealous," he cried, seeing her eyes become hard again; "the soul of Virginie has passed into her body; that's certain."

The eagle disappeared into the air, while the soldier admired the curved contour of the panther.

But there was such youth and grace in her form! She was beautiful as a woman! The blond fur of her robe mingled well with the delicate tints of faint white which marked her flanks.

The profuse light cast down by the sun made this living gold, these russet markings, to burn in a way to give them an indefinable attraction.

The man and the panther looked at one another with a look full of meaning; the coquette quivered when she felt her friend stroke her head; her eyes flashed like lightning—then she shut them tightly.

75 "She has a soul," he said, looking at the stillness of this queen of the sands, golden like them, white like them, solitary and burning like them.

"Well," she said, "I have read your plea in favor of beasts; but how did two so well adapted to understand each other end?"

"Ah, well! you see, they ended as all great passions do end—by a misunderstanding. For some reason one suspects the other of treason; they don't come to an explanation through pride, and quarrel and part from sheer obstinacy."

"Yet sometimes at the best moments a single word or a look is enough—but anyhow go on with your story."

"It's horribly difficult, but you will understand, after what the old villain told me over his champagne.

"He said—'I don't know if I hurt her, but she turned round, as if enraged, and with her sharp teeth caught hold of my leg—gently, I daresay; but I, thinking she would devour me, plunged my dagger into her throat. She rolled over, giving a cry that froze my heart; and I saw her dying, still looking at me without anger. I would have given all the world—my cross even, which I had not got then—to have brought her to life again. It was as though I had murdered a real person; and the soldiers who had seen my flag, and were come to my assistance, found me in tears.'

"'Well sir,' he said, after a moment of silence, 'since then I have been in war in Germany, in Spain, in Russia, in France; I've certainly carried my carcass about a good deal, but never have I seen anything like the desert. Ah! yes, it is very beautiful!'

"'What did you feel there?' I asked him.

"'Oh! that can't be described, young man. Besides, I am not always regretting my palm trees and my panther. I should have to be very melancholy for that. In the desert, you see, there is everything and nothing.'

"Yes, but explain——'

"'Well,' he said, with an impatient gesture, 'it is God without mankind.'"   [1830]   85

QUESTIONS

1. What purpose does the frame story serve? How does it affect the central idea of the story?
2. This story is built upon an improbable "what if" premise. Is Balzac successful in convincing you of its possibility?
3. Describe the importance of the story's setting.
4. Explain how this story might be seen as reflecting an imperialist attitude toward non-European peoples and ideas.
5. What does the last phrase mean: "it is God without mankind"?

RESPONSES

1. Examine the courtship rituals and/or the masculine view of the feminine in this story and in Hawthorne's "The Birthmark."
2. Compare Balzac's view of animal nature with Jack London's view of animal nature in "To Build a Fire."

Focus on Film

1. Describe the focus of the film *Passion in the Desert*. Which elements of the story does it emphasize and which does it deemphasize?
2. How does the film portray the development of the relationship of the soldier and the cat? Did the actor and director take liberties with Balzac's story of the relationship?

TONI CADE BAMBARA

Toni Cade Bambara (1939–1996), born in New York City, was graduated from Queens College and received an M.A. from City College of New York. Trained as a dancer and actress, she worked with Katherine Dunham and Etienne Decrouz of Mime in New York and Paris. Her short stories have been collected in *Gorilla, My Love* (1972) and *The Sea Birds Are Still Alive* (1977). She has published two novels, *The Salt Eaters* (1980) and *If Blessing Comes* (1987), and has written several screenplays, including *Tar Baby,* based on Toni Morrison's novel.

The Lesson

Back in the days when everyone was old and stupid or young and foolish and me and Sugar were the only ones just right, this lady moved on our block with nappy hair and proper speech and no makeup. And quite naturally we laughed at her, laughed the way we did at the junk man who went about his business like he was some big-time president and his sorry-ass horse his secretary. And we kinda hated her too, hated the way we did the winos who cluttered up our parks and pissed on our handball walls and stank up our hallways and stairs so you couldn't halfway play hide-and-seek without a goddamn gas mask. Miss Moore was her name. The only woman on the block with no first name. And she was black as hell, cept for her feet, which were fish-white and spooky. And she was always planning these boring-ass things for us to do, us being my cousin, mostly, who lived on the block cause we all moved North the same time and to the same apartment then spread out gradual to breathe. And our parents would yank our heads into some kinda shape and crisp up our clothes so we'd be presentable for travel with Miss Moore, who always looked like she was going to church, though she never did. Which is just one of the things the grownups talked about when they talked behind her back like a dog. But when she came calling with some sachet she'd sewed up or some gingerbread she'd made or some book, why then they'd all be too embarrassed to turn her down and we'd get handed over all spruced up. She'd been to college and said it was only right that she should take responsibility for the young ones' education, and she not even related by marriage or blood. So they'd go for it. Specially Aunt Gretchen. She was the main gofer in the family. You got some ole dumb shit foolishness you want somebody to go for, you send for Aunt

Gretchen. She been screwed into the go-along for so long, it's a blood-deep natural thing with her. Which is how she got saddled with me and Sugar and Junior in the first place while our mothers were in a la-de-da apartment up the block having a good ole time.

So this one day Miss Moore rounds us all up at the mailbox and it's puredee hot and she's knockin herself out about arithmetic. And school suppose to let up in summer I heard, but she don't never let up. And the starch in my pinafore scratching the shit outta me and I'm really hating this nappy-head bitch and her goddamn college degree. I'd much rather go to the pool or to the show where it's cool. So me and Sugar leaning on the mailbox being surly, which is a Miss Moore word. And Flyboy checking out what everybody brought for lunch. And Fat Butt already wasting his peanut-butter-and-jelly sandwich like the pig he is. And Junebug punchin on Q.T.'s arm for potato chips. And Rosie Giraffe shifting from one hip to the other waiting for somebody to step on her foot or ask her if she from Georgia so she can kick ass, preferably Mercedes'. And Miss Moore asking us do we know what money is, like we a bunch of retards. I mean real money, she say, like it's only poker chips or monopoly papers we lay on the grocer. So right away I'm tired of this and say so. And would much rather snatch Sugar and go to the Sunset and terrorize the West Indian kids and take their hair ribbons and their money too. And Miss Moore files that remark away for next week's lesson on brotherhood, I can tell. And finally I say we oughta get to the subway cause it's cooler and besides we might meet some cute boys. Sugar done swiped her mama's lipstick, so we ready.

So we heading down the street and she's boring us silly about what things cost and what our parents make and how much goes for rent and how money ain't divided up right in this country. And then she gets to the part about we all poor and live in the slums, which I don't feature. And I'm ready to speak on that, but she steps out in the street and hails two cabs just like that. Then she hustles half the crew in with her and hands me a five-dollar bill and tells me to calculate 10 percent tip for the driver. And we're off. Me and Sugar and Junebug and Flyboy hangin out the window and hollering to everybody, putting lipstick on each other cause Flyboy a faggot anyway, and making farts with our sweaty armpits. But I'm mostly trying to figure how to spend this money. But they all fascinated with the meter ticking and Junebug starts laying bets as to how much it'll read when Flyboy can't hold his breath no more. Then Sugar lays bets as to how much it'll be when we get there. So I'm stuck. Don't nobody want to go for my plan, which is to jump out at the next light and run off to the first bar-b-que we can find. Then the driver tells us to get the hell out cause we there already. And the meter reads eighty-five cents. And I'm stalling to figure out the tip and Sugar say give him a dime. And I decide he don't need it bad as I do, so later for him. But then he tries to take off with Junebug's foot still in the door so we talk about his mama something ferocious. Then we check out that we on Fifth Avenue and everybody dressed up in stockings. One lady in a fur coat, hot as it is. White folks crazy.

"This is the place," Miss Moore say, presenting it to us in the voice she uses at the museum. "Let's look in the windows before we go in."

5   "Can we steal?" Sugar asks very serious like she's getting the ground rules squared away before she plays. "I beg your pardon," say Miss Moore, and we fall out. So she leads us around the windows of the toy store and me and Sugar screamin, "This is mine, that's mine, I gotta have that, that was made for me, I was born for that," till Big Butt drowns us out.

"Hey, I'm goin to buy that there."

"That there? You don't even know what it is, stupid."

"I do so," he say punchin on Rosie Giraffe. "It's a microscope."

"Whatcha gonna do with a microscope, fool?"

"Look at things."   10

"Like what, Ronald?" ask Miss Moore. And Big Butt ain't got the first notion. So here go Miss Moore gabbing about the thousands of bacteria in a drop of water and the somethinorother in a speck of blood and the million and one living things in the air around us is invisible to the naked eye. And what she say that for? Junebug go to town on that "naked" and we rolling. Then Miss Moore ask what it cost. So we all jam into the window smudgin it up and the price tag say $300. So then she ask how long'd take for Big Butt and Junebug to save up their allowances. "Too long," I say. "Yeh," adds Sugar, "outgrown it by that time." And Miss Moore say no, you never outgrow learning instruments. "Why, even medical students and interns and," blah, blah, blah. And we ready to choke Big Butt for bringing it up in the first damn place.

"This here costs four hundred eighty dollars," say Rosie Giraffe. So we pile up all over her to see what she pointin out. My eyes tell me it's a chunk of glass cracked with something heavy, and different-color inks dripped into the splits, then the whole thing put into a oven or something. But for $480 it don't make sense.

"That's a paperweight made of semi-precious stones fused together under tremendous pressure," she explains slowly, with her hands doing the mining and all the factory work.

"So what's a paperweight?" asks Rosie Giraffe.

"To weigh paper with, dumbbell," say Flyboy, the wise man from the East.   15

"Not exactly," say Miss Moore, which is what she say when you warm or way off too. "It's to weigh paper down so it won't scatter and make your desk untidy." So right away me and Sugar curtsy to each other and then to Mercedes who is more the tidy type.

"We don't keep paper on top of the desk in my class," say Junebug, figuring Miss Moore crazy or lyin one.

"At home, then," she say. "Don't you have a calendar and a pencil case and a blotter and a letter-opener on your desk at home where you do your homework?" And she know damn well what our homes look like cause she nosys around in them every chance she gets.

"I don't even have a desk," say Junebug. "Do we?"

"No. And I don't get no homework neither," says Big Butt.   20

"And I don't even have a home," say Flyboy like he do at school to keep the white folks off his back and sorry for him. Send this poor kid to camp posters, is his specialty.

"I do," says Mercedes. "I have a box of stationery on my desk and a picture of my cat. My godmother bought the stationery and the desk. There's a big rose on each sheet and the envelopes smell like roses."

"Who wants to know about your smelly-ass stationery," say Rosie Giraffe fore I can get my two cents in.

"It's important to have a work area all your own so that . . ."

"Will you look at this sailboat, please," say Flyboy, cuttin her off and pointin to the   25
thing like it was his. So once again we tumble all over each other to gaze at this magnificent thing in the toy store which is just big enough to maybe sail two kittens across the pond if you strap them to the posts tight. We all start reciting the price tag like we in assembly. "Handcrafted sailboat of fiberglass at one thousand one hundred ninety-five dollars."

"Unbelievable," I hear myself say and am really stunned. I read it again for myself just in case the group recitation put me in a trance. Same thing. For some reason this pisses me off. We look at Miss Moore and she lookin at us, waiting for I dunno what.

"Who'd pay all that when you can buy a sailboat set for a quarter at Pop's, a tube of glue for a dime, and a ball of string for eight cents? It must have a motor and a whole lot else besides," I say. "My sailboat cost me about fifty cents."

"But will it take water?" say Mercedes with her smart ass.

"Took mine to Alley Pond Park once," say Flyboy. "String broke. Lost it. Pity."

30   "Sailed mine in Central Park and it keeled over and sank. Had to ask my father for another dollar."

"And you got the strap," laugh Big Butt. "The jerk didn't even have a string on it. My old man wailed on his behind."

Little Q.T. was staring hard at the sailboat and you could see he wanted it bad. But he too little and somebody'd just take it from him. So what the hell. "This boat for kids, Miss Moore?"

"Parents silly to buy something like that just to get all broke up," say Rosie Giraffe.

"That much money it should last forever," I figure.

35   "My father'd buy it for me if I wanted it."

"Your father, my ass," say Rosie Giraffe getting a chance to finally push Mercedes.

"Must be rich people shop here," say Q.T.

"You are a very bright boy," say Flyboy. "What was your first clue?" And he rap him on the head with the back of his knuckles, since Q.T. the only one he could get away with. Though Q.T. liable to come up behind you years later and get his licks in when you half expect it.

"What I want to know is," I says to Miss Moore though I never talk to her, I wouldn't give the bitch that satisfaction, "is how much a real boat costs? I figure a thousand'd get you a yacht any day."

40   "Why don't you check that out," she says, "and report back to the group?" Which really pains my ass. If you gonna mess up a perfectly good swim day least you could do is have some answers. "Let's go in," she say like she got something up her sleeve. Only she don't lead the way. So me and Sugar turn the corner to where the entrance is, but when we get there I kinda hang back. Not that I'm scared, what's there to be afraid of, just a toy store. But I feel funny, shame. But what I got to be shamed about? Got as much right to go in as anybody. But somehow I can't seem to get hold of the door, so I step away from Sugar to lead. But she hangs back too. And I look at her and she looks at me and this is ridiculous. I mean, damn, I have never ever been shy about doing nothing or going nowhere. But then Mercedes steps up and then Rosie Giraffe and Big Butt crowd in behind and shove, and next thing we all stuffed into the doorway with only Mercedes squeezing past us, smoothing out her jumper and walking right down the aisle. Then the rest of us tumble in like a glued-together jigsaw done all wrong. And people lookin at us. And it's like the time me and Sugar crashed into the Catholic church on a dare. But once we got in there and everything so hushed and holy and the candles and the bowin and the handkerchiefs on all the drooping heads, I just couldn't go through with the plan. Which was for me to run up to the altar and do a tap dance while Sugar played the nose flute and messed around in the holy water. And Sugar kept givin me the elbow. Then later teased me so bad I tied her up in the shower and turned it on and locked her in. And she'd be there till this day if Aunt Gretchen hadn't finally figured I was lyin about the boarder takin a shower.

Same thing in the store. We all walkin on tiptoe and hardly touchin the games and puzzles and things. And I watched Miss Moore who is steady watchin us like she waitin for a sign. Like Mama Drewery watches the sky and sniffs the air and takes note of just how much slant is in the bird formation. Then me and Sugar bump smack into each other, so busy gazing at the toys, 'specially the sailboat. But we don't laugh and go into our fat-lady bump-stomach routine. We just stare at that price tag. Then Sugar run a finger over the whole boat. And I'm jealous and want to hit her. Maybe not her, but I sure want to punch somebody in the mouth.

"Watcha bring us here for, Miss Moore?"

"You sound angry, Sylvia. Are you mad about something?" Givin me one of them grins like she tellin a grown-up joke that never turns out to be funny. And she's lookin very closely at me like maybe she plannin to do my portrait from memory. I'm mad, but I won't give her that satisfaction. So I slouch around the store bein very bored and say, "Let's go."

Me and Sugar at the back of the train watchin the tracks whizzin by large then small then getting gobbled up in the dark. I'm thinkin about this tricky toy I saw in the store. A clown that somersaults on a bar then does chin-ups just cause you yank lightly at his leg. Cost $35. I could see me askin my mother for a $35 birthday clown. "You wanna who that costs what?" she'd say, cocking her head to the side to get a better view of the hole in my head. Thirty-five dollars could buy new bunk beds for Junior and Gretchen's boy. Thirty-five dollars and the whole household could go visit Granddaddy Nelson in the country. Thirty-five dollars would pay for the rent and the piano bill too. Who are these people that spend that much for performing clowns and $1000 for toy sailboats? What kinda work they do and how they live and how come we ain't in on it? Where we are is who we are, Miss Moore always pointin out. But it don't necessarily have to be that way, she always adds then waits for somebody to say that poor people have to wake up and demand their share of the pie and don't none of us know what kind of pie she talking about in the first damn place. But she ain't so smart cause I still got her four dollars from the taxi and she sure ain't gettin it. Messin up my day with this shit. Sugar nudges me in my pocket and winks.

Miss Moore lines us up in front of the mailbox where we started from, seem like [45] years ago, and I got a headache for thinkin so hard. And we lean all over each other so we can hold up under the draggy-ass lecture she always finishes us off with at the end before we thank her for borin us to tears. But she just looks at us like she readin tea leaves. Finally she say, "Well, what did you think of F.A.O. Schwarz?"

Rosie Giraffe mumbles, "White folks crazy."

"I'd like to go there again when I get my birthday money," says Mercedes, and we shove her out the pack so she has to lean on the mailbox by herself.

"I'd like a shower. Tiring day," say Flyboy.

Then Sugar surprises me by sayin, "You know, Miss Moore, I don't think all of us here put together eat in a year what that sailboat costs." And Miss Moore lights up like somebody goosed her. "And?" she say, urging Sugar on. Only I'm standin on her foot so she don't continue.

"Imagine for a minute what kind of society it is in which some people can spend [50] on a toy what it would cost to feed a family of six or seven. What do you think?"

"I think," say Sugar pushing me off her feet like she never done before, cause I whip her ass in a minute, "that this is not much of a democracy if you ask me. Equal chance to pursue happiness means an equal crack at the dough, don't it?" Miss Moore is besides herself and I am disgusted with Sugar's treachery. So I stand on her foot one more time to see if she'll shove me. She shuts up, and Miss Moore looks at me, sorrowfully I'm thinkin. And somethin weird is goin on, I can feel it in my chest.

"Anybody else learn anything today?" lookin dead at me. I walk away and Sugar has to run to catch up and don't even seem to notice when I shrug her arm off my shoulder.

"Well, we got four dollars anyway," she says.

"Uh hunh."

55   "We could go to Hascombs and get half a chocolate layer and then go to the Sunset and still have plenty money for potato chips and ice cream sodas."

"Uh hunh."

"Race you to Hascombs," she say.

We start down the block and she gets ahead which is O.K. by me cause I'm going to the West End and then over to the Drive to think this day through. She can run if she want to and even run faster. But ain't nobody gonna beat me at nuthin.   [1972]

QUESTIONS

1. How is the narrator characterized by the inventiveness of her language?
2. What do the names of the children contribute to the story? Are the children sufficiently individualized for the purposes of the story?
3. Why does Miss Moore choose a Fifth Avenue toy store for the outing?
4. What are Miss Moore's motives?
5. What is "the lesson" of the story?

RESPONSES

1. Write an essay analyzing how Bambara uses various aspects of language to portray her characters.
2. Write an essay comparing this story to Wright's "The Man Who Was Almost a Man."

DONALD BARTHELME

Donald Barthelme (1931–1989) was born in Philadelphia but grew up in Texas, where he attended the University of Houston. After a varied apprenticeship in literature and the visual arts, he moved to New York City, where he edited an arts and literary review. During the 1960s he began to contribute to the *New Yorker* the unconventional and often surreal stories that are his trademark. In addition to his many volumes of short stories, Barthelme published three novels and a book of nonfiction, *Guilty Pleasures* (1974).

A City of Churches

"Yes," Mr. Phillips said, "ours is a city of churches all right."

Cecelia nodded, following his pointing hand. Both sides of the street were solidly lined with churches, standing shoulder to shoulder in a variety of architectural styles. The Bethel Baptist stood next to the Holy Messiah Free Baptist, St. Paul's Episcopal next to Grace Evangelical Covenant. Then came the First Christian Science, the Church of God, All Souls, Our Lady of Victory, the Society of Friends, the Assembly of God, and the Church of the Holy Apostles. The spires and steeples of the traditional buildings were jammed in next to the broad imaginative flights of the "contemporary" designs.

"Everyone here takes a great interest in church matters," Mr. Phillips said.

Will I fit in? Cecelia wondered. She had come to Prester to open a branch office of a car-rental concern.

"I'm not especially religious," she said to Mr. Phillips, who was in the real-estate business.

"Not *now*," he answered. "Not *yet*. But we have many fine young people here. You'll get integrated into the community soon enough. The immediate problem is, where are you to live? Most people," he said, "live in the church of their choice. All of our churches have many extra rooms. I have a few belfry apartments that I can show you. What price range were you thinking of?"

They turned a corner and were confronted with more churches. They passed St. Luke's, the Church of the Epiphany, All Saints Ukrainian Orthodox, St. Clement's, Fountain Baptist, Union Congregational, St. Anargyri's, Temple Emanuel, the First Church of Christ Reformed. The mouths of all the churches were gaping open. Inside, lights could be seen dimly.

121

"I can go up to a hundred and ten," Cecelia said. "Do you have any buildings here that are *not* churches?"

"None," said Mr. Phillips. "Of course many of our fine church structures also do double duty as something else." He indicated a handsome Georgian façade. "That one," he said, "houses the United Methodist and the Board of Education. The one next to it, which is Antioch Pentecostal, has the barbershop."

10 It was true. A red-and-white striped barber pole was attached inconspicuously to the front of the Antioch Pentecostal.

"Do many people rent cars here?" Cecelia asked. "Or would they, if there was a handy place to rent them?"

"Oh, I don't know," said Mr. Phillips. "Renting a car implies that you want to go somewhere. Most people are pretty content right here. We have a lot of activities. I don't think I'd pick the car-rental business if I was just starting out in Prester. But you'll do fine." He showed her a small, extremely modern building with a severe brick, steel, and glass front. "That's St. Barnabas. Nice bunch of people over there. Wonderful spaghetti suppers."

Cecelia could see a number of heads looking out of the windows. But when they saw that she was staring at them, the heads disappeared.

"Do you think it's healthy for so many churches to be gathered together in one place?" she asked her guide. "It doesn't seem . . . *balanced*, if you know what I mean."

15 "We are famous for our churches," Mr. Phillips replied. "They are harmless. Here we are now."

He opened a door and they began climbing many flights of dusty stairs. At the end of the climb they entered a good-sized room, square, with windows on all four sides. There was a bed, a table, and two chairs, lamps, a rug. Four very large bronze bells hung in the exact center of the room.

"What a view!" Mr. Phillips exclaimed. "Come here and look."

"Do they actually ring these bells?" Cecelia asked.

"Three times a day," Mr. Phillips said, smiling. "Morning, noon, and night. Of course when they're rung you have to be pretty quick at getting out of the way. You get hit in the head by one of these babies and that's all she wrote."

20 "God Almighty," said Cecelia involuntarily. Then she said, "Nobody lives in the belfry apartments. That's why they're empty."

"You think so?" Mr. Phillips said.

"You can only rent them to new people in town," she said accusingly.

"I wouldn't do that," Mr. Phillips said. "It would go against the spirit of Christian fellowship."

"This town is a little creepy, you know that?"

25 "That may be, but it's not for you to say, is it? I mean, you're new here. You should walk cautiously, for a while. If you don't want an upper apartment I have a basement over at Central Presbyterian. You'd have to share it. There are two women in there now."

"I don't want to share," Cecelia said. "I want a place of my own."

"Why?" the real-estate man asked curiously. "For what purpose?"

"Purpose?" asked Cecelia. "There is no particular purpose. I just want—"

"That's not usual here. Most people live with other people. Husbands and wives. Sons with their mothers. People have roommates. That's the usual pattern."

30 "Still, I prefer a place of my own."

"It's very unusual."

"Do you have any such places? Besides bell towers, I mean?"

"I guess there are a few," Mr. Phillips said, with clear reluctance. "I can show you one or two, I suppose."

He paused for a moment.

"It's just that we have different values, maybe, from some of the surrounding communities," he explained. "We've been written up a lot. We had four minutes on the C.B.S. Evening News one time. Three or four years ago. 'A City of Churches,' it was called." 35

"Yes, a place of my own is essential," Cecelia said, "if I am to survive here."

"That's kind of a funny attitude to take," Mr. Phillips said. "What denomination are you?"

Cecelia was silent. The truth was, she wasn't anything.

"I said, what denomination are you?" Mr. Phillips repeated.

"I can will my dreams," Cecelia said. "I can dream whatever I want. If I want to dream that I'm having a good time, in Paris or some other city, all I have to do is go to sleep and I will dream that dream. I can dream whatever I want." 40

"What do you dream, then, mostly?" Mr. Phillips said, looking at her closely.

"Mostly sexual things," she said. She was not afraid of him.

"Prester is not that kind of a town," Mr. Phillips said, looking away.

They went back down the stairs.

The doors of the churches were opening, on both sides of the street. Small groups of people came out and stood there, in front of the churches, gazing at Cecelia and Mr. Phillips. 45

A young man stepped forward and shouted, *"Everyone in this town already has a car! There is no one in this town who doesn't have a car!"*

"Is that true?" Cecelia asked Mr. Phillips.

"Yes," he said. "It's true. No one would rent a car here. Not in a hundred years."

"Then I won't stay," she said. "I'll go somewhere else."

"You must stay," he said. "There is already a car-rental office for you. In Mount Moriah Baptist, on the lobby floor. There is a counter and a telephone and a rack of car keys. And a calendar." 50

"I won't stay," she said. "Not if there's not any sound business reason for staying."

"We want you," said Mr. Phillips. "We want you standing behind the counter of the car-rental agency, during regular business hours. It will make the town complete."

"I won't," she said. "Not me."

"You must. It's essential."

"I'll dream," she said. "Things you won't like." 55

"We are discontented," said Mr. Phillips. "Terribly, terribly discontented. Something is wrong."

"I'll dream the Secret," she said. "You'll be sorry."

"We are like other towns, except that we are perfect," he said. "Our discontent can only be held in check by perfection. We need a car-rental girl. Someone must stand behind that counter."

"I'll dream the life you are most afraid of," Cecelia threatened.

"You are ours," he said, gripping her arm. "Our car-rental girl. Be nice. There is nothing you can do." 60

"Wait and see," Cecelia said. [1972]

QUESTIONS

1. What effect is achieved by the coolly objective description of a bizarre, dream-like experience?
2. What are the implications of Mr. Phillips's statement that most people "live in the church of their choice"?
3. Is Mr. Phillips's description of the city of churches consistent?
4. Is there a sense in which churches "do double duty as something else"?
5. Cecelia can "will her dreams." Is there a suggestion that the story is a dream she has willed?

RESPONSES

1. Write an essay analyzing how the elements of fiction contribute to the story.
2. Compare the power of religion in this story and in Hawthorne's "Young Goodman Brown." Compare how the main characters react to that power.

ANN BEATTIE

Ann Beattie (b. 1947) was born in Washington, D.C., and educated at American University and the University of Connecticut. In the mid-1970s the *New Yorker* began to publish her stories, which often focus on the efforts of her generation to reconcile their youthful idealism with an increasingly troubled and complex society. Beattie's short story collections include *Secrets and Surprises* (1978), *What Was Mine* (1991), *Park City* (1998), *Perfect Recall* (2001), and *Where You'll Find Me, And Other Stories* (2002).

What Was Mine

I don't remember my father. I have only two photographs of him—one of two soldiers standing with their arms around each other's shoulders, their faces even paler than their caps, so that it's difficult to make out their features; the other of my father in profile, peering down at me in my crib. In that photograph, he has no discernible expression, though he does have a rather noble Roman nose and thick hair that would have been very impressive if it hadn't been clipped so short. On the back of the picture in profile is written, unaccountably, "Guam," while the back of the picture of the soldiers says, "Happy with baby: 5/28/49."

Until I was five or six I had no reason to believe that Herb was not my uncle. I might have believed it much longer if my mother had not blurted out the truth one night when I opened her bedroom door and saw Herb, naked from the waist down, crouched at the foot of the bed, holding out a bouquet of roses much the way teasing people shake a biscuit in front of a sleeping dog's nose. They had been to a wedding earlier that day, and my mother had caught the nosegay. Herb was tipsy, but I had no sense of that then. Because I was a clumsy boy, I didn't wonder about his occasionally knocking into a wall or stepping off a curb a bit too hard. He was not allowed to drive me anywhere, but I thought only that my mother was full of arbitrary rules she imposed on everyone: no more than one hour of TV a day; put Bosco in the glass first, then the milk.

One of the most distinct memories of my early years is of that night I opened my mother's door and saw Herb lose his balance and fall forward on the bouquet like a thief clutching bread under his shirt.

"Ethan," my mother said, "I don't know what you are doing in here at a time when you are supposed to be in bed—and without the manners to knock—but I think the

125

time has come to tell you that Herbert and I are very close, but not close in the way family members such as a brother and sister are. Herbert is not your uncle, but you must go on as if he were. Other people should not know this."

5   Herb had rolled onto his side. As he listened, he began laughing. He threw the crushed bouquet free, and I caught it by taking one step forward and waiting for it to land in my outstretched hand. It was the way Herb had taught me to catch a ball, because I had a tendency to overreact and rush too far forward, too fast. By the time I had caught the bouquet, exactly what my mother said had become a blur: manners, Herbert, not family, don't say anything.

Herb rolled off the bed, stood, and pulled on his pants. I had the clear impression that he was in worse trouble than I was. I think that what he said to me was that his affection for me was just what it always had been, even though he wasn't actually my uncle. I know that my mother threw a pillow at him and told him not to confuse me. Then she looked at me and said, emphatically, that Herb was not a part of our family. After saying that, she became quite flustered and got up and stomped out of the bedroom, slamming the door behind her. Herb gave the door a dismissive wave of the hand. Alone with him, I felt much better. I suppose I had thought that he might vanish—if he was not my uncle, he might suddenly disappear—so that his continued presence was very reassuring.

"Don't worry about it," he said. "The divorce rate is climbing, people are itching to change jobs every five minutes. You wait: Dwight Eisenhower is going to be reevaluated. He won't have the same position in history that he has today." He looked at me. He sat on the side of the bed. "I'm your mother's boyfriend," he said. "She doesn't want to marry me. It doesn't matter. I'm not going anywhere. Just keep it between us that I'm not Uncle Herb."

My mother was tall and blond, the oldest child of a German family that had immigrated to America in the 1920s. Herb was dark-haired, the only child of a Lebanese father and his much younger English bride, who had considered even on the eve of her wedding leaving the Church of England to convert to Catholicism and become a nun. In retrospect, I realize that my mother's shyness about her height and her having been indoctrinated to believe that the hope of the future lay in her accomplishing great things, and Herb's self-consciousness about his kinky hair, along with his attempt as a child to negotiate peace between his mother and father, resulted in an odd bond between Herb and my mother: she was drawn to his conciliatory nature, and he was drawn to her no-nonsense attitude. Or perhaps she was drawn to his unusual amber eyes, and he was taken in by her inadvertently sexy, self-conscious girlishness. Maybe he took great pleasure in shocking her, in playing to her secret, more sophisticated desires, and she was secretly amused and gratified that he took it as a given that she was highly competent and did not have to prove herself to him in any way whatsoever.

She worked in a bank. He worked in the automotive section at Sears, Roebuck, and on the weekend he played piano, harmonica, and sometimes tenor sax at a bar off Pennsylvania Avenue called the Merry Mariner. On Saturday nights my mother and I would sit side by side, dressed in our good clothes, in a booth upholstered in blue Naugahyde, behind which dangled nets that were nailed to the wall, studded with starfish, conch shells, sea horses, and clamshells with small painted scenes or decals inside them. I would have to turn sideways and look above my mother to see them. I had to work out a way of seeming to be looking in front of me and listening appreciatively to Uncle Herb while at the very same time rolling my eyes upward to take in those tiny depictions of sunsets, rainbows, and ships sailing through the moonlight. Uncle Herb played a slowish version of "Let Me Call You Sweetheart" on the harmonica as I sipped my cherry Coke with real cherries in it: three, because the waitress liked me. He played "As Time Goes By" on the piano, singing so quietly it seemed he was humming. My mother and I always split the fisherman's platter: four shrimp, one crab cake, and a lobster tail, or sometimes two if the owner wasn't in the kitchen, though my mother often wrapped up the lobster tails and saved them for our Sunday dinner. She would slice them and dish them up over rice, along with the tomato-and-lettuce salad she served almost every night.

Some of Uncle Herb's songs would go out to couples celebrating an anniversary, or 10 to birthday boys, or to women being courted by men who preferred to let Uncle Herb sing the romantic thoughts they hesitated to speak. Once during the evening Herb would dedicate a song to my mother, always referring to her as "my own special someone" and nodding—but never looking directly—toward our booth.

My mother kept the beat to faster tunes by tapping her fingers on the shiny varnished tabletop. During the slow numbers she would slide one finger back and forth against the edge of the table, moving her hand so delicately she might have been testing the blade of a knife. Above her blond curls I would see miniature versions of what I thought must be the most exotic places on earth—so exotic that any small reference to them would quicken the heart of anyone familiar with the mountains of Hawaii or the seas of Bora-Bora. My mother smoked cigarettes, so that sometimes I would see these places through fog. When the overhead lights were turned from blue to pink as Uncle Herb played the last set, they would be transformed to the most ideal possible versions of paradise. I was hypnotized by what seemed to me their romantic clarity, as Herb sang a bemused version of "Stormy Weather," then picked up the saxophone for "Green Eyes," and finished, always, with a Billie Holiday song he would play very simply on the piano, without singing. Then the lights went to a dusky red and gradually brightened to a golden light that seemed as stupefying to me as the cloud rising at Los Alamos must have seemed to the observers of Trinity. It allowed people enough light to judge their sobriety, pay the bill, or decide to postpone functioning until later and vanish into the darker reaches of the bar at the back. Uncle Herb never patted me on the shoulder or tousled my cowlick. He usually sank down next to my mother—still bowing slightly to acknowledge the applause—then reached over with the same automatic motion my mother used when she withdrew a cigarette from the pack to run his thumb quickly over my knuckles, as if he were testing a keyboard. If a thunderbolt had left his fingertips, it could not have been more clear: he wanted me to be a piano player.

That plan had to be abandoned when I was thirteen. Or perhaps it did not really have to be abandoned, but at the time I found a convenient excuse to let go of the idea. One day, as my mother rounded a curve in the rain, the car skidded into a telephone pole. As the windshield splattered into cubes of glass, my wrist was broken and my shoulder dislocated. My mother was not hurt at all, though when she called Herb at work she became so hysterical that she had to be given an injection in the emergency room before he arrived to take us both away.

I don't think she was ever really the same after the accident. Looking back, I realize that was when everything started to change—though there is every chance that my adolescence and her growing hatred of her job might have changed things anyway. My mother began to seem irrationally angry at Herb and so solicitous of me I felt smothered. I held her responsible, suddenly, for everything, and I had a maniac's ability to transform good things into something awful. The five cherries I began to get in my Cokes seemed an unwanted pollution, and I was sure that my mother had told the waitress to be extra kind. Her cigarette smoke made me cough. Long before the surgeon general warned against the dangers of smoking, I was sure that she meant to poison me. When she drove me to physical therapy, I misconstrued her positive attitude and was sure that she took secret delight in having me tortured. My wrist set wrong, and had to be put in a cast a second time. My mother cried constantly. I turned to Herb to help me with my homework. She relented, and he became the one who drove me everywhere.

When I started being skeptical of my mother, she began to be skeptical of Herb. I heard arguments about the way he arranged his sets. She said that he should end on a more upbeat note. She thought the lighting was too stagy. He began to play—and end—in a nondescript silver glow. I looked at the shells on the netting, not caring that she knew I wasn't concentrating on Herb's playing. She sank lower in the booth, and her attention also drifted: no puffs of smoke carefully exhaled in the pauses between sung phrases; no testing the edge of the table with her fingertip. One Saturday night we just stopped going.

15   By that time, she had become a loan officer at Riggs Bank. Herb had moved from Sears to Montgomery Ward, where he was in charge of the lawn and leisure-activities section—everything from picnic tables to electric hedge clippers. She served TV dinners. She complained that there wasn't enough money, though she bought expensive high heels that she wore to work. On Wednesday nights Herb played handball with friends who used to be musicians but who were suddenly working white-collar jobs to support growing families. He would come home and say, either with disbelief or with disorientation, that Sal, who used to play in a Latino band, had just had twins, or that Earl had sold his drums and bought an expensive barbecue grill. She read Perry Mason. He read magazine articles about the Second World War: articles, he said, shaking his head, that were clearly paving the way for a reassessment of the times in which we lived.

I didn't have a friend—a real friend—until I was fourteen. That year my soul mate was a boy named Ryuji Anderson, who shared my passion for soccer and introduced me to *Playboy.* He told me to buy Keds one size too large and stuff a sock in that toe so that I could kick hard and the ball would really fly. We both suffered because we sensed that you had to *look* like John F. Kennedy in order to *be* John F. Kennedy. Ryuji's mother had been a war bride, and my mother had lost her husband six years after the war in a freak accident: a painter on scaffolding had lost his footing high up and tumbled backward to the ground, releasing, as he fell, the can of paint that struck my father on the head and killed him. The painter faithfully sent my mother a Christmas card every year, informing her about his own slow recovery and apologizing for my father's death. Uncle Herb met my mother when his mother, dead of leukemia, lay in the room adjacent to my father's room in the funeral home. They had coffee together one time when they both were exiled to the streets, late at night.

It was not until a year later, when he looked her up in the phone book (the number was still listed under my father's name), that he saw her again. That time I went along, and was bought a paper cone filled with french fries. I played cowboy, circling with an imaginary lasso the bench on which they sat. We had stumbled on a carnival. Since it was downtown Washington, it wasn't really a carnival but a small area of the mall, taken over by dogs who would jump through burning hoops and clowns on roller skates. It became a standing refrain between my mother and Herb that some deliberate merriment had been orchestrated just for them, like the play put on in *A Midsummer Night's Dream*.

I, of course, had no idea what to make of the world on any given day. My constants were that I lived with my mother, who cried every night; that I could watch only two shows each day on TV; and that I would be put to bed earlier than I wanted, with a nightlight left burning. That day my mother and Herb sat on the bench, I'm sure I sensed that things were going to be different, as I inscribed two people destined to be together in an imaginary lassoed magic circle. From then on, we were a threesome.

He moved in as a boarder. He lived in the room that used to be the dining room, which my mother and I had never used, since we ate off TV trays. I remember his hanging a drapery rod over the arch—nailing the brackets in, then lifting up the bar, pushing onto it the brocade curtain my mother had sewn, then lowering the bar into place. They giggled behind it. Then they slid the curtain back and forth, as if testing to see that it would really work. It was like one of the games I had had as a baby: a board with a piece of wood that slid back and forth, exposing first the sun, then the moon.

Of course, late at night they cheated. He would simply push the curtain aside and   20
go to her bed. Since I would have accepted anything, it's a wonder they didn't just tell me. A father, an uncle, a saint, Howdy Doody, Lassie—I didn't have a very clear idea of how any of them truly behaved. I believed whatever I saw. Looking back, I can only assume that they were afraid not so much of what I would think as of what others might think, and that they were unwilling to draw me into their deception. Until I wandered into her bedroom, they simply were not going to blow their cover. They were just going to wait for me. Eventually, I was sure to stumble into their world.

"The secret about Uncle Herb doesn't go any farther than this house," my mother said that night after I found them together. She was quite ashen. We stood in the kitchen. I had followed her—not because I loved her so much, or because I trusted her, but because I was already sure of Herb. Sure because even if he had winked at me, he could not have been clearer about the silliness of the slammed door. She had on a beige nightgown and was backlit by the counter light. She cast a pondlike shadow on the floor. I would like to say that I asked her why she had lied to me, but I'm sure I wouldn't have dared. Imagine my surprise when she told me anyway: "You don't know what it's like to lose something forever," she said. "It will make you do anything—even lie to people you love—if you think you can reclaim even a fraction of that thing. You don't know what *fraction* means. It means a little bit. It means a thing that's been broken into pieces."

I knew she was talking about loss. All week, I had been worried that the bird at school, with its broken wing, might never fly again and would hop forever in the cardboard box. What my mother was thinking of, though, was that can of paint—a can of paint that she wished had missed my father's head and sailed into infinity.

We looked down at the sepia shadow. It was there in front of her, and in front of me. Of course it was behind us, too.

Many years later, the day Herb took me out for "a talk," we drove aimlessly for quite a while. I could almost feel Herb's moment of inspiration when it finally came, and he went around a traffic circle and headed down Pennsylvania Avenue. It was a

Saturday, and on Saturdays the Merry Mariner was open only for dinner, but he had a key, so we parked and went inside and turned on a light. It was not one of those lights that glowed when he played, but a strong, fluorescent light. Herb went to the bar and poured himself a drink. He opened a can of Coke and handed it to me. Then he told me that he was leaving us. He said that he himself found it unbelievable. Then, suddenly, he began to urge me to listen to Billie Holiday's original recordings, to pay close attention to the paintings of Vermeer, to look around me and to listen. To believe that what to some people might seem the silliest sort of place might be, to those truly observant, a temporary substitute for heaven.

25   I was a teenager, and I was too embarrassed to cry. I sat on a bar stool and simply looked at him. That day, neither of us knew how my life would turn out. Possibly he thought that so many unhappy moments would have damaged me forever. For all either of us knew, he had been the father figure to a potential hoodlum, or even to a drifter—that was what the game of pretense he and my mother had been involved in might have produced. He shook his head sadly when he poured another drink. Later, I found out that my mother had asked him to go, but that day I didn't even think to ask why I was being abandoned.

Before we left the restaurant he told me—as he had the night I found him naked in my mother's room—how much he cared for me. He also gave me practical advice about how to assemble a world.

He had been the one who suggested that the owner string netting on the walls. First he and the owner had painted the ocean: pale blue, more shine than paint at the bottom, everything larger than it appeared on land. Then gradually the color of the paint changed, rays of light streamed in, and things took on a truer size. Herb had added, on one of the walls, phosphorescence. He had touched the paintbrush to the wall delicately, repeatedly, meticulously. He was a very good amateur painter. Those who sat below it would never see it, though. Those who sat adjacent to it might see the glow in their peripheral vision. From across the room, where my mother and I sat, the highlights were too delicate, and too far away to see. The phosphorescence had never caught my eye when my thoughts drifted from the piano music, or when I blinked my eyes to clear them of the smoke.

The starfish had been bought in lots of a dozen from a store in Chinatown. The clamshells had been painted by a woman who lived in Arlington, in the suburbs, who had once strung them together as necklaces for church bazaars, until the demand dried up and macramé was all the rage. Then she sold them to the owner of the restaurant, who carried them away from her yard sale in two aluminum buckets years before he ever imagined he would open a restaurant. Before Herb and I left the Merry Mariner that day, there wasn't anything about how the place had been assembled that I didn't know.

Fifteen years after that I drove with my fiancée to Herb's cousin's house to get some things he left with her for safekeeping in case anything happened to him. His cousin was a short, unattractive woman who lifted weights. She had converted what had been her dining room into a training room, complete with Nautilus, rowing machine, and barbells. She lived alone, so there was no one to slide a curtain back for. There was no child, so she was not obliged to play at anything.

30   She served us iced tea with big slices of lemon. She brought out guacamole and a bowl of tortilla chips. She had called me several days before to say that Herb had had a heart attack and died. Though I would not find out formally until some time later,

she also told me that Herb had left me money in his will. He also asked that she pass on to me a large manila envelope. She handed it to me, and I was so curious that I opened it immediately, on the back porch of some muscle-bound woman named Frances in Cold Spring Harbor, New York.

There was sheet music inside: six Billie Holiday songs that I recognized immediately as Herb's favorites for ending the last set of the evening. There were several notes, which I suppose you could call love notes, from my mother. There was a tracing, on a food-stained Merry Mariner place mat, of a cherry, complete with stem, and a fancy pencil-drawn frame around it that I vaguely remembered Herb having drawn one night. There was also a white envelope that contained the two pictures: one of the soldiers on Guam; one of a handsome young man looking impassively at a sleeping young baby. I knew the second I saw it that he was my father.

I was fascinated, but the more I looked at it—the more remote and expressionless the man seemed—the more it began to dawn on me that Herb wanted me to see the picture of my father because he wanted me to see how different he had been from him. When I turned over the picture of my father in profile and read "Guam," I almost smiled. It certainly wasn't my mother's handwriting. It was Herb's, though he had tried to slope the letters so that it would resemble hers. What sweet revenge, he must have thought—to leave me with the impression that my mother had been such a preoccupied, scatterbrained woman that she could not even label two important pictures correctly.

My mother had died years before, of pneumonia. The girl I had been dating at the time had said to me, not unkindly, that although I was very sad about my mother's death, one of the advantages of time passing was sure to be that the past would truly become the past. Words would become suspect. People would seem to be only poor souls struggling to do their best. Images would fade.

Not the image of the wall painted to look like the ocean, though. She was wrong about that. Herb had painted it exactly the way it really looks. I found this out later when I went snorkeling and saw the world underwater for the first time, with all its spooky spots of overexposure and its shimmering irregularities. But how tempting— how reassuring—to offer people the possibility of climbing from deep water to the surface by moving upward on lovely white nets, gigantic ladders from which no one need ever topple.

On Frances's porch, as I stared at the photographs of my father, I saw him as a young man standing on a hot island, his closest friend a tall broomstick of a man whom he would probably never see again once the war was over. He was a hero. He had served his country. When he got off Guam, he would have a life. Things didn't turn out the way he expected, though. The child he left behind was raised by another man, though it is true that his wife missed him forever and remained faithful in her own strange way by never remarrying. As I continued to look at the photograph, though, it was not possible to keep thinking of him as a hero. He was an ordinary man, romantic in context—a sad young soldier on a tropical island that would soon become a forgotten land. When the war was over he would have a life, but a life that was much too brief, and the living would never really recover from that tragedy.

Herb must also have believed that he was not a hero. That must have been what he was thinking when he wrote, in wispy letters, brief, transposed captions for two pictures that did not truly constitute any legacy at all.

In Cold Spring Harbor, as I put the pictures back in the envelope, I realized that no one had spoken for quite some time. Frances tilted her glass, shaking the ice cubes. She hardly knew us. Soon we would be gone. It was just a quick drive to the city, and she would see us off, knowing that she had discharged her responsibility by passing on to me what Herb had said was mine.   [1991]

QUESTIONS

1. The narrator offers several reasons for the attraction between his mother and Herb. What do you believe holds them together? Why do they break up?

2. How does the pattern of maritime imagery reinforce the theme?

3. The narrator wishes to discover "what was mine." What *is* his?

4. Do you believe the author has been successful in her attempt to cover a long stretch of time within the brief confines of a short story? Discuss.

5. Is the narrator correct in believing that "the past would truly become the past"?

RESPONSE

1. Write an essay focusing on either the mother or on Herb. Analyze their role in the narrator's life. How do their life stories affect what they can and cannot give to Ethan?

AMBROSE BIERCE

Ambrose Bierce (1842–1914?) was born in rural Ohio, the son of a devout but impoverished farmer. Enlisting in the Union Army at the outbreak of the Civil War, Bierce rose through the ranks from private to major. His experience of combat left him deeply embittered but provided him with a great subject for his fiction. After the war he became a journalist, first in San Francisco and later, after his marriage, in London. He published *Tales of Soldiers and Civilians* in 1891 and followed it two years later with *Can Such Things Be?* Disillusioned by divorce and by the death of his two sons, he vanished while in Mexico, where he had evidently gone to report on the Mexican Revolution.

An Occurrence at Owl Creek Bridge

1

A man stood upon a railroad bridge in northern Alabama, looking down into the swift water twenty feet below. The man's hands were behind his back, the wrists bound with a cord. A rope closely encircled his neck. It was attached to a stout cross-timber above his head and the slack fell to the level of his knees. Some loose boards laid upon the sleepers supporting the metals of the railway supplied a footing for him and his executioners—two private soldiers of the Federal army, directed by a sergeant who in civil life may have been a deputy sheriff. At a short remove upon the same temporary platform was an officer in the uniform of his rank, armed. He was a captain. A sentinel at each end of the bridge stood with his rifle in the position known as "support," that is to say, vertical in front of the left shoulder, the hammer resting on the forearm thrown straight across the chest—a formal and unnatural position, enforcing an erect carriage of the body. It did not appear to be the duty of these two men to know what was occurring at the center of the bridge; they merely blockaded the two ends of the foot planking that traversed it.

Beyond one of the sentinels nobody was in sight; the railroad ran straight away into a forest for a hundred yards, then, curving, was lost to view. Doubtless there was an outpost farther along. The other bank of the stream was open ground—a gentle acclivity topped with a stockage of vertical tree trunks, loopholed for rifles, with a single embrasure through which protruded the muzzle of a brass cannon commanding the bridge. Midway of the slope between bridge and fort were the spectators—a single company of infantry in line, at "parade rest," the butts of the rifles on the ground, the barrels inclining slightly backward against the right shoulder, the hands crossed upon the stock. A lieutenant stood at the right of the line, the point of his sword upon the ground, his left hand resting upon his right. Excepting the group of four at the centre of the bridge, not a man moved. The company faced the bridge, staring stonily, motionless. The sentinels, facing the banks of the stream, might have been statues to adorn the bridge. The captain stood with folded arms, silent, observing the work of his subordinates, but making no sign. Death is a dignitary who when he comes announced is to be received with formal manifestations of respect, even by those most familiar with him. In the code of military etiquette silence and fixity are forms of deference.

The man who was engaged in being hanged was apparently about thirty-five years of age. He was a civilian, if one might judge from his habit, which was that of a planter. His features were good—a straight nose, firm mouth, broad forehead, from which his long, dark hair was combed straight back, falling behind his ears to the collar of his well-fitting frock-coat. He wore a mustache and pointed beard, but no whiskers; his eyes were large and dark gray, and had a kindly expression which one would hardly have expected in one whose neck was in the hemp. Evidently this was no vulgar assassin. The liberal military code makes provision for hanging many kinds of persons, and gentlemen are not excluded.

The preparations being complete, the two private soldiers stepped aside and each drew away the plank upon which he had been standing. The sergeant turned to the captain, saluted and placed himself immediately behind that officer, who in turn moved apart one pace. These movements left the condemned man and the sergeant standing on the two ends of the same plank, which spanned three of the cross-ties of the bridge. The end upon which the civilian stood almost, but not quite, reached a fourth. This plank had been held in place by the weight of the captain; it was now held by that of the sergeant. At a signal from the former the latter would step aside, the plank would tilt and the condemned man go down between two ties. The arrangement commended itself to his judgment as simple and effective. His face had not been covered nor his eyes bandaged. He looked a moment at his "unsteadfast footing," then let his gaze wander to the swirling water of the stream racing madly beneath his feet. A piece of dancing driftwood caught his attention and his eyes followed it down the current. How slowly it appeared to move! What a sluggish stream!

5　　He closed his eyes in order to fix his last thoughts upon his wife and children. The water, touched to gold by the early sun, the brooding mists under the banks at some distance down the stream, the fort, the soldiers, the piece of drift—all had distracted him. And now he became conscious of a new disturbance. Striking through the thought of his dear ones was a sound which he could neither ignore nor understand, a sharp, distinct, metallic percussion like the stroke of a blacksmith's hammer upon the anvil; it had the same ringing quality. He wondered what it was, and whether immeasurably distant or nearby—it seemed both. Its recurrence was regular, but as slow as the tolling of a death knell. He awaited each stroke with impatience and—he knew not why—apprehension. The intervals of silence grew progressively longer; the delays became maddening. With their greater infrequency the sounds increased in strength and sharpness. They hurt his ear like the thrust of a knife; he feared he would shriek. What he heard was the ticking of his watch.

He unclosed his eyes and saw again the water below him. "If I could free my hands," he thought, "I might throw off the noose and spring into the stream. By diving I could evade the bullets and, swimming vigorously, reach the bank, take to the woods and get away home. My home, thank God, is as yet outside their lines; my wife and little ones are still beyond the invader's farthest advance."

As these thoughts, which have here to be set down in words, were flashed into the doomed man's brain rather than evolved from it the captain nodded to the sergeant. The sergeant stepped aside.

2

Peyton Farquhar was a well-to-do planter, of an old and highly respected Alabama family. Being a slave owner and like other slave owners a politician he was naturally an original secessionist and ardently devoted to the Southern cause. Circumstances of an imperious nature, which it is unnecessary to relate here, had prevented him from taking service with the gallant army that had fought the disastrous campaigns ending with the fall of Corinth, and he chafed under the inglorious restraint, longing for the release of his energies, the larger life of the soldier, the opportunity for distinction. That opportunity, he felt, would come, as it comes to all in war time. Meanwhile he did what he could. No service was too humble for him to perform in aid of the South, no adventure too perilous for him to undertake if consistent with the character of a civilian who was at heart a soldier, and who in good faith and without too much qualification assented to at least a part of the frankly villainous dictum that all is fair in love and war.

One evening while Farquhar and his wife were sitting on a rustic bench near the entrance to his grounds, a gray-clad soldier rode up to the gate and asked for a drink of water. Mrs. Farquhar was only too happy to serve him with her own white hands. While she was fetching the water her husband approached the dusty horseman and inquired eagerly for news from the front.

"The Yanks are repairing the railroads," said the man, "and are getting ready for another advance. They have reached the Owl Creek bridge, put it in order and built a stockade on the north bank. The commandant has issued an order, which is posted everywhere, declaring that any civilian caught interfering with the railroad, its bridges, tunnels, or trains will be summarily hanged. I saw the order."   10

"How far is it to the Owl Creek bridge?" Farquhar asked.

"About thirty miles."

"Is there no force on this side of the creek?"

"Only a picket post half a mile out, on the railroad, and a single sentinel at this end of the bridge."

"Suppose a man—a civilian and student of hanging—should elude the picket post and perhaps get the better of the sentinel," said Farquhar, smiling, "what could he accomplish?"   15

The soldier reflected. "I was there a month ago," he replied. "I observed that the flood of last winter had lodged a great quantity of driftwood against the wooden pier at this end of the bridge. It is now dry and would burn like tow."

The lady had now brought the water, which the soldier drank. He thanked her ceremoniously, bowed to her husband and rode away. An hour later, after nightfall, he repassed the plantation, going northward in the direction from which he had come. He was a Federal scout.

3

As Peyton Farquhar fell straight downward through the bridge he lost consciousness and was as one already dead. From this state he was awakened—ages later, it seemed to him—by the pain of a sharp pressure upon his throat, followed by a sense of suffocation. Keen, poignant agonies seemed to shoot from his neck downward through every fibre of his body and limbs. These pains appeared to flash along well-defined lines of ramification and to beat with an inconceivably rapid periodicity. They seemed like streams of pulsating fire heating him to an intolerable temperature. As to his head, he was conscious of nothing but a feeling of fullness—of congestion. These sensations were unaccompanied by thought. The intellectual part of his nature was already effaced; he had power only to feel, and feeling was torment. He was conscious of motion. Encompassed in a luminous cloud, of which he was now merely the fiery heart, without material substance, he swung through unthinkable arcs of oscillation, like a vast pendulum. Then all at once, with terrible suddenness, the light about him shot upward with the noise of a loud plash; a frightful roaring was in his ears, and all was cold and dark. The power of thought was restored; he knew that the rope had broken and he had fallen into the stream. There was no additional strangulation; the noose about his neck was already suffocating him and kept the water from his lungs. To die of hanging at the bottom of a river!—the idea seemed to him ludicrous. He opened his eyes in the darkness and saw above him a gleam of light, but how distant, how inaccessible! He was still sinking, for the light became fainter and fainter until it was a mere glimmer. Then it began to grow and brighten, and he knew that he was rising toward the surface—knew it with reluctance, for he was now very comfortable. "To be hanged and drowned," he thought, "that is not so bad; but I do not wish to be shot. No; I will not be shot; that is not fair."

He was not conscious of an effort, but a sharp pain in his wrist apprised him that he was trying to free his hands. He gave the struggle his attention, as an idler might observe the feat of a juggler, without interest in the outcome. What splendid effort!— what magnificent, what superhuman strength! Ah, that was a fine endeavor! Bravo! The cord fell away; his arms parted and floated upward, the hands dimly seen on each side in the growing light. He watched them with a new interest as first one and then the other pounced upon the noose at his neck. They tore it away and thrust it fiercely aside, its undulations resembling those of a water-snake. "Put it back, put it back!" He thought he shouted these words to his hands, for the undoing of the noose had been succeeded by the direst pang that he had yet experienced. His neck ached horribly, his brain was on fire; his heart, which had been fluttering faintly, gave a great leap, trying to force itself out at his mouth. His whole body was racked and wrenched with an insupportable anguish! But his disobedient hands gave no heed to the command. They beat the water vigorously with quick, downward strokes, forcing him to the surface. He felt his head emerge; his eyes were blinded by the sunlight; his chest expanded convulsively, and with a supreme and crowning agony his lungs engulfed a great draught of air, which instantly he expelled in a shriek!

20   He was now in full possession of his physical senses. They were, indeed, preternaturally keen and alert. Something in the awful disturbance of his organic system had so exalted and refined them that they made record of things never before perceived. He felt the ripples upon his face and heard their separate sounds as they struck. He looked at the forest on the bank of the stream, saw the individual trees, the leaves and the veining of each leaf—saw the very insects upon them: the locusts,

the brilliant-bodied flies, the gray spiders stretching their webs from twig to twig. He noted the prismatic colors in all the dewdrops upon a million blades of grass. The humming of the gnats that danced above the eddies of the stream, the beating of the dragon-flies' wings, the strokes of the water-spiders' legs, like oars which had lifted their boat—all these made audible music. A fish slid along beneath his eyes and he heard the rush of its body parting the water.

He had come to the surface facing down the stream; in a moment the visible world seemed to wheel slowly round, himself the pivotal point, and he saw the bridge, the fort, the soldiers upon the bridge, the captain, the sergeant, the two privates, his executioners. They were in silhouette against the blue sky. They shouted and gesticulated, pointing at him. The captain had drawn his pistol, but did not fire; the others were unarmed. Their movements were grotesque and horrible, their forms gigantic.

Suddenly he hard a sharp report and something struck the water smartly within a few inches of his head, spattering his face with spray. He heard a second report, and saw one of the sentinels with his rifle at his shoulder, a light cloud of blue smoke rising from the muzzle. The man in the water saw the eye of the man on the bridge gazing into his own through the sights of the rifle. He observed that it was a gray eye and remembered having read that gray eyes were keenest, and that all famous marksmen had them. Nevertheless, this one had missed.

A counter-swirl had caught Farquhar and turned him half round; he was again looking into the forest on the bank opposite the fort. The sound of a clear, high voice in a monotonous singsong now rang out behind him and came across the water with a distinctness that pierced and subdued all other sounds, even the beating of the ripples in his ears. Although no soldier, he had frequented camps enough to know the dread significance of that deliberate, drawling, aspirated chant; the lieutenant on shore was taking a part in the morning's work. How coldly and pitilessly—with what an even, calm intonation, presaging, and enforcing tranquility in the men—with what accurately measured intervals fell those cruel words:

"Attention, company! . . . Shoulder arms! . . . Ready! . . . Aim! . . . Fire!"

Farquhar dived—dived as deeply as he could. The water roared in his ears like the voice of Niagara, yet he heard the dulled thunder of the volley and, rising again toward the surface, met shining bits of metal, singularly flattened, oscillating slowly downward. Some of them touched him on the face and hands, then fell away, continuing their descent. One lodged between his collar and neck; it was uncomfortably warm and he snatched it out.

As he rose to the surface, gasping for breath, he saw that he had been a long time under water; he was perceptibly farther down stream—nearer to safety. The soldiers had almost finished reloading; the metal ramrods flashed all at once in the sunshine as they were drawn from the barrels, turned in the air, and thrust into their sockets. The two sentinels fired again, independently and ineffectually.

The hunted man saw all this over his shoulder; he was now swimming vigorously with the current. His brain was as energetic as his arms and legs; he thought with the rapidity of lightning.

"The officer," he reasoned, "will not make that martinet's error a second time. It is as easy to dodge a volley as a single shot. He has probably already given the command to fire at will. God help me, I cannot dodge them all!"

An appalling splash within two yards of him was followed by a loud, rushing sound, *diminuendo,* which seemed to travel back through the air to the fort and died in an explosion which stirred the very river to its deeps! A rising sheet of water curved

25

over him, fell down upon him, blinded him, strangled him! The cannon had taken a hand in the game. As he shook his head free from the commotion of the smitten water he heard the deflected shot humming through the air ahead, and in an instant it was cracking and smashing the branches in the forest beyond.

30   "They will not do that again," he thought; "the next time they will use a charge of grape. I must keep my eye upon the gun; the smoke will apprise me—the report arrives too late; it lags behind the missile. That is a good gun."

Suddenly he felt himself whirled round and round—spinning like a top. The water, the banks, the forests, the now distant bridge, fort and men—all were commingled and blurred. Objects were represented by their colors only; circular horizontal streaks of color—that was all he saw. He had been caught in a vortex and was being whirled on with a velocity of advance and gyration that made him giddy and sick. In a few moments he was flung upon the gravel at the foot of the left bank of the stream—the southern bank—and behind a projecting point which concealed him from his enemies. The sudden arrest of his motion, the abrasion of one of his hands on the gravel, restored him, and he wept with delight. He dug his fingers into the sand, threw it over himself in handfuls and audibly blessed it. It looked like diamonds, rubies, emeralds; he could think of nothing beautiful which it did not resemble. The trees upon the bank were giant garden plants; he noted a definite order in their arrangement, inhaled the fragrance of their blooms. A strange, roseate light shone through the spaces among their trunks and the wind made in their branches the music of aeolian harps. He had no wish to perfect his escape—was content to remain in that enchanting spot until retaken.

A whiz and rattle of grapeshot among the branches high above his head roused him from his dream. The baffled cannoneer had fired him a random farewell. He sprang to his feet, rushed up the sloping bank, and plunged into the forest.

All that day he traveled, laying his course by the rounding sun. The forest seemed interminable; nowhere did he discover a break in it, not even a woodman's road. He had not known that he lived in so wild a region. There was something uncanny in the revelation.

By night fall he was fatigued, footsore, famishing. The thought of his wife and children urged him on. At last he found a road which led him in what he knew to be the right direction. It was as wide and straight as a city street, yet it seemed untraveled. No fields bordered it, no dwelling anywhere. Not so much as the barking of a dog suggested human habitation. The black bodies of the trees formed a straight wall on both sides, terminating on the horizon in a point, like a diagram in a lesson in perspective. Overhead, as he looked up through this rift in the wood, shone great golden stars looking unfamiliar and grouped in strange constellations. He was sure they were arranged in some order which had a secret and malign significance. The wood on either side was full of singular noises, among which—once, twice, and again, he distinctly heard whispers in an unknown tongue.

35   His neck was in pain and lifting his hand to it he found it horribly swollen. He knew that it had a circle of black where the rope had bruised it. His eyes felt congested; he could no longer close them. His tongue was swollen with thirst; he relieved its fever by thrusting it forward from between his teeth into the cold air. How softly the turf had carpeted the untraveled avenue—he could no longer feel the roadway beneath his feet!

Doubtless, despite his suffering, he had fallen asleep while walking, for now he sees another scene—perhaps he has merely recovered from a delirium. He stands at the gate of his own home. All is as he left it, and all bright and beautiful in the morning sunshine. He must have traveled the entire night. As he pushes open the gate and passes up the wide white walk, he sees a flutter of female garments; his wife, looking fresh and cool and sweet, steps down from the veranda to meet him. At the bottom of the steps she stands waiting, with a smile of ineffable joy, an attitude of matchless grace and dignity. Ah, how beautiful she is! He springs forward with extended arms. As he is about to clasp her he feels a stunning blow upon the back of the neck; a blinding white light blazes all about him with a sound like the shock of a cannon—then all is darkness and silence!

Peyton Farquhar was dead; his body, with a broken neck, swung gently from side to side beneath the timbers of the Owl Creek bridge.   [1891]

QUESTIONS

1. From what point of view is each of the three sections told? How does the tripartite structure reinforce the theme?
2. What elements in Farquhar's character fit him for the role he will play?
3. How has the author handled the passage of time?
4. What effect is intended by mingling realistic details with poetic imagery? Is it successful?
5. Explore the interplay of exposition and foreshadowing in the story. How does the author's presentation of background information prepare the reader for the final revelation?

RESPONSES

1. Reread the story. Write an essay comparing your reactions to the story the first time you read it to your reactions the second or third time.
2. Find a copy of Bierce's book *The Devil's Dictionary*. Write an essay analyzing which elements of Bierce's attitude toward humanity you see in both works.
3. Compare Peyton Farquhar and his thoughts about war and home to Tim O'Brien's Jimmy Cross and his thoughts about war and home.

FOCUS ON FILM

1. Evaluate the filmed adaptation of this story. In what ways is the film more effective than the story? In what ways less effective?
2. Compare the characterization in the film and in the print story. How do director and writer create their lead character?

JORGE LUIS BORGES

Jorge Luis Borges (1899–1986) was born in Buenos Aires, the son of a wealthy and cultured family. Educated in Switzerland, he traveled widely as a young man, responding to the intellectual currents of post–World War I Europe. Returning to Argentina in 1921, he began to develop a reputation as a poet, translator, essayist, and writer of short stories. Borges survived the repressive regime of the dictator Juan Perón and in 1955, after the collapse of that government, was appointed director of the National Library and professor of English and American literature at the University of Buenos Aires. Much of his work has been translated into English, including *Ficciones* (1944), *Labyrinths* (1962), and *The Book of Sand* (1977).

The Other Duel

One summer evening in Adrogué many years ago, this story was told to me by Carlos Reyles, the son of the Uruguayan novelist. In my memory this chronicle of a long-held hatred and its tragic end still calls up the medicinal fragrance of the eucalyptus trees and the singing of the birds.

We were talking, as we always did, about the interwoven history of our two countries. At one point he said I'd surely heard of Juan Patricio Nolan, who had earned a reputation as a brave man, a teller of tall tales, and a practical joker. Lying myself, I said I had. Nolan had died in '90 or thereabout, but people still thought of him as a friend. He had his detractors, too, of course, as we all do. Carlos told me one of the many little pranks that Nolan was said to have played. The incident had taken place a short while before the Battle of Manantiales; its protagonists were Manuel Cardoso and Carmen Silveira, two gauchos from Cerro Largo.

How and why had the hatred between those two men begun? How, a century or more later, can we recover the shadowy story of those two men whose only fame was earned in their final duel? There was a man named Laderecha—an overseer at Reyles' father's ranch, "with a mustache like a tiger's"—who had gleaned from "oral tradition" certain details that I shall recount; I set them down here for what they are worth and with no further assurances as to their veracity, since both forgetfulness and recollection are creative.

Manuel Cardoso's and Carmen Silveira's small ranches bordered one another. As with the origins of other passions, the origins of a hatred are always obscure, but there was talk of a dispute over some unmarked animals, or, alternately, of a bareback horse race during which Silveira, who was the stronger, had bumped Cardoso's horse off the track. Months later, in the town's general store, there had been a long game of two-handed *truco;* Silveira congratulated his opponent on his play to virtually every trick, but he left him at the end without a penny. As he was raking the money into his purse, he thanked Cardoso for the lesson he had given him. It was then, I think, that they almost came to blows. The game had been hard fought; the onlookers (there had been many) had to separate them. On that frontier and at that time, man stood up to man and blade to blade; an unusual feature of this story is, as we will see, that Manuel Cardoso and Carmen Silveira crossed paths up in the mountains twice a day, morning and evening, though they never actually fought until the end. Perhaps their only possession in their coarse primitive lives was their hatred, and therefore they saved it and stored it up. Without suspecting, each of the two became the other's slave.

I have no way of knowing whether the events I am about to narrate are effects or causes. 5

Cardoso, less out of love than for something to do, took a fancy to a girl who lived nearby, a girl everyone called La Serviliana, and he began to court her; no sooner had Silveira discovered this than he began to court the girl in his own way, and carried her off to his ranch. After a few months he threw her out; she got on his nerves. Indignant, the woman sought refuge at Cardoso's place; Cardoso spent one night with her and sent her off at noon. He didn't want the other man's left-overs.

It was at about the same time—a little before or after La Serviliana—that the incident with the sheepdog took place. Silveira was very fond of the dog, and had named it Thirty-three. It was found dead in a ditch; Silveira always thought he knew who'd poisoned the dog.

In the winter of '70, Aparicio's revolution caught Cardoso and Silveira drinking in that same general-store-and-bar where they'd played their game of *truco.* A Brazilian soldier with mulatto features, heading up a small band of *montoneros*, came through the door. He gave the men gathered there a rousing speech; their country needed them, he said—the government's oppression was intolerable. He passed out white badges to pin on, and at the end of that exordium, which they had not understood, he and his platoon impressed them into service—they were not even allowed to say good-bye to their families. Manuel Cardoso and Carmen Silveira accepted their fate; a soldier's life was no harder than a gaucho's. They were used to sleeping in the open with a horse blanket as a mattress and a saddle as a pillow, and for the hand accustomed to killing animals, killing a man was not a great deal different. Their lack of imagination freed them from fear and pity alike, though fear did touch them sometimes, just as the cavalry charged them. (The rattle of stirrups and weapons is one of the things you can always hear when the cavalry rides into the action.) But if a man isn't wounded right away, he thinks himself invulnerable. They did not miss the places they'd been born and raised in. The concept of patriotism was foreign to them; in spite of the insignia worn on the hats, one side was much the same as the other to them. They learned what can be done with the lance. In the course of advances and retreats, they at last came to feel that being comrades allowed them to go on being rivals. They fought shoulder to shoulder yet they never, so far as is known, exchanged a single word.

In the fall of '71, which was a hard time, the end came to the two men.

The engagement, which lasted less than an hour, occurred at a place whose name they never learned—historians assign the names later. On the eve of the battle, Cardoso crawled into the captain's tent and asked him, in a whisper, to save one of the Reds for 10 him if they won the next day—he had never cut anybody's throat, he said, and he wanted to know what it was like. The captain promised that if he conducted himself like a man, he'd grant him that favor.

The Whites outnumbered the Reds, but the Reds had better weaponry. From the top of a hill they commanded, they rained devastation on the Whites. After two charges that failed to reach the peak, the White captain, gravely wounded, surrendered. There on the field, at his request, his men ended his life.

Then they laid down their arms. Captain Juan Patricio Nolan, commander of the Reds, gave a long-winded and flowery order that all the captives' throats be cut. But he was from Cerro Largo, and not unfamiliar with Silveira and Cardoso's long-standing grudge, so he had them brought to him.

"I know you two can't bear the sight of each other," he said, "and that you've been waiting a long time for the chance to settle scores. So I've got good news for you. Before the sun goes down, you're going to get the chance to show which one of you is the toughest. I'm going to have your throats cut, and then you're going to run a race. Like they say—may the best man win."

The soldier who had brought them took them away.

15   The news spread quickly through the camp. Nolan had wanted the race to crown that evening's performance, but the prisoners sent a committee to ask him if they couldn't watch it, too, and make bets on the winner. Nolan, a reasonable man, let himself be convinced. The men bet money, riding gear, knives, and horses; their winnings would be turned over to their widows and next of kin when the time came. The day was hot; so everyone could have a siesta, the event was put off till four. (They had a hard time waking Silveira up.) Nolan, typically, kept them all waiting for an hour. He had no doubt been reliving the victory with the other officers; the orderly made the rounds with the *mate*.

On each side of the dusty road, against the tents, the ranks of prisoners sat on the ground and waited, hands tied behind their backs so they'd give nobody any trouble. One would occasionally unburden himself with an oath, another murmur the beginning of the Lord's Prayer; almost all were in a state verging on stupefaction. Naturally, they couldn't smoke. They no longer cared about the race, but they all watched.

"When they slit my throat, they're going to grab me by the hair and pull my head back, too," said one man, as though to ally himself with the centers of attention.

"Yeah, but you'll be along with the herd," replied another.

"Along with you," the first man spit.

20   A sergeant drew the line across the road with a saber. Silveira's and Cardoso's hands had been untied so they wouldn't have to run off-balance. They stood more than five yards apart. They put their toes against the line; some of the officers called out for them not to let them down—they were counting on them. A great deal of money was riding on each man.

Silveira drew Nigger Nolan, whose grandparents had doubtlessly been slaves of the captain's family, and so bore his name; Cardoso drew the regular executioner, an older man from Corrientes who always patted the condemned man on the back and told him: "Buck up, friend; women suffer more than this when they have a baby."

Their torsos straining forward, the two anxious men did not look at each other.

Nolan gave the signal.

The part Nigger Nolan had been given to play went to his head, and he overacted—he slashed Silveira's throat from ear to ear. The man from Corrientes made do with a neat slice. The blood gushed, though, from both men's throats; they stumbled a few steps and then fell headlong. As he fell, Cardoso stretched out his arms. He had won, but he likely never knew that.   [1970]

QUESTIONS

1. What is the effect of the narrator's confessions of uncertainty about the events described?
2. Characterize the narrator's tone. Is it appropriate to the theme?
3. What is the significance of the narrator's comment, "Lying myself, I said I had."
4. What expectations does the story arouse? Are they fulfilled by the subsequent narrative?
5. Is there an element of humor in Nolan's "prank"?

RESPONSE

1. Analyze Borges's story as a tall tale and compare it to Samuel Clemens's (Mark Twain's) "The Celebrated Jumping Frog of Calaveras County."

T. Coraghessan Boyle

T. Coraghessan Boyle (b. 1948) was born in Peeskill, New York. He has described his early childhood as typical, but in his teens, he says, he became "a punk," interested in girls, alcohol, and then drugs. He graduated from the State University of New York in Potsdam, and then studied writing and literature at the University of Iowa, receiving both an MFA and Ph.D. He is currently a professor of English at the University of Southern California. He has published many novels and volumes of short fiction, including *Descent of Man* (1979), *Greasy Lake* (1985), *World's End* (1987), *If the River Was Whiskey* (1989), *The Road to Wellville* (1993), *The Tortilla Curtain* (1995), *T. C. Boyle Stories* (1998), *Drop City* (2003), and *The Inner Circle* (2004).

Greasy Lake

It's about a mile down on the dark side of Route 8.
—Bruce Springsteen

There was a time when courtesy and winning ways went out of style, when it was good to be bad, when you cultivated decadence like a taste. We were all dangerous characters then. We wore torn-up leather jackets, slouched around with toothpicks in our mouths, sniffed glue and ether and what somebody claimed was cocaine. When we wheeled our parents' whining station wagons out onto the street we left a patch of rubber half a block long. We drank gin and grape juice, Tango, Thunderbird, and Bali Hai. We were nineteen. We were bad. We read André Gide and struck elaborate poses to show that we didn't give a shit about anything. At night, we went up to Greasy Lake.

Through the center of town, up the strip, past the housing developments and shopping malls, street lights giving way to the thin streaming illumination of the headlights, trees crowding the asphalt in a black unbroken wall: that was the way out to Greasy Lake. The Indians had called it Wakan, a reference to the clarity of its waters. Now it was fetid and murky, the mud banks glittering with broken glass and strewn with beer cans and the charred remains of bonfires. There was a single ravaged island a hundred yards from shore, so stripped of vegetation it looked as if the air force had strafed it. We went up to the lake because everyone went there, because we wanted to sniff the rich scent of possibility on the breeze, watch a girl take off her clothes and plunge into the festering murk, drink beer, smoke pot, howl at the stars, savor the incongruous full-throated roar of rock and roll against the primeval susurrus of frogs and crickets. This was nature.

I was there one night, late, in the company of two dangerous characters. Digby wore a gold star in his right ear and allowed his father to pay his tuition at Cornell; Jeff was thinking of quitting school to become a painter/musician/headshop proprietor. They were both expert in the social graces, quick with a sneer, able to manage a Ford with lousy shocks over a rutted and gutted blacktop road at eighty-five while rolling a joint as compact as a Tootsie Roll Pop stick. They could lounge against a bank of booming speakers and trade "man"s with the best of them or roll out across the dance floor as if their joints worked on bearings. They were slick and quick and they wore their mirror shades at breakfast and dinner, in the shower, in closets and caves. In short, they were bad.

I drove. Digby pounded the dashboard and shouted along with Toots & the Maytals while Jeff hung his head out the window and streaked the side of my mother's Bel Air with vomit. It was early June, the air soft as a hand on your cheek, the third night of summer vacation. The first two nights we'd been out till dawn, looking for something we never found. On this, the third night, we'd cruised the strip sixty-seven times, been in and out of every bar and club we could think of in a twenty-mile radius, stopped twice for bucket chicken and forty-cent hamburgers, debated going to a party at the house of a girl Jeff's sister knew, and chucked two dozen raw eggs at mailboxes and hitchhikers. It was 2:00 A.M.; the bars were closing. There was nothing to do but take a bottle of lemon-flavored gin up to Greasy Lake.

The taillights of a single car winked at us as we swung into the dirt lot with its tufts 5
of weed and washboard corrugations; '57 Chevy, mint, metallic blue. On the far side of the lot, like the exoskeleton of some gaunt chrome insect, a chopper leaned against its kickstand. And that was it for excitement: some junkie halfwit biker and a car freak pumping his girlfriend. Whatever it was we were looking for, we weren't about to find it at Greasy Lake. Not that night.

But then all of a sudden Digby was fighting for the wheel. "Hey, that's Tony Lovett's car! Hey!" he shouted, while I stabbed at the brake pedal and the Bel Air nosed up to the gleaming bumper of the parked Chevy. Digby leaned on the horn, laughing, and instructed me to put my brights on. I flicked on the brights. This was hilarious. A joke. Tony would experience premature withdrawal and expect to be confronted by grim-looking state troopers with flashlights. We hit the horn, strobed the lights, and then jumped out of the car to press our witty faces to Tony's windows; for all we knew we might even catch a glimpse of some little fox's tit, and then we could slap backs with red-faced Tony, roughhouse a little, and go on to new heights of adventure and daring.

The first mistake, the one that opened the whole floodgate, was losing my grip on the keys. In the excitement, leaping from the car with the gin in one hand and a roach clip in the other, I spilled them in the grass—in the dark, rank, mysterious nighttime grass of Greasy Lake. This was a tactical error, as damaging and irreversible in its way as Westmoreland's decision to dig in at Khe Sanh. I felt it like a jab of intuition, and I stopped there by the open door, peering vaguely into the night that puddled up round my feet.

The second mistake—and this was inextricably bound up with the first—was identifying the car as Tony Lovett's. Even before the very bad character in greasy jeans and engineer boots ripped out of the driver's door, I began to realize that this chrome blue was much lighter than the robin's egg of Tony's car, and that Tony's car didn't have

rear-mounted speakers. Judging from their expressions, Digby and Jeff were privately groping toward the same inevitable and unsettling conclusion as I was.

In any case, there was no reasoning with this bad greasy character—clearly he was
a man of action. The first lusty Rockette kick of his steel-toed boot caught me under
the chin, chipped my favorite tooth, and left me sprawled in the dirt. Like a fool, I'd
gone down on one knee to comb the stiff hacked grass for the keys, my mind making
connections in the most dragged-out, testudineous way, knowing that things had gone
wrong, that I was in a lot of trouble, and that the lost ignition key was my grail and
my salvation. The three or four succeeding blows were mainly absorbed by my right
buttock and the tough piece of bone at the base of my spine.

10   Meanwhile, Digby vaulted the kissing bumpers and delivered a savage kungfu
blow to the greasy character's collarbone. Digby had just finished a course in martial
arts for phys-ed credit and had spent the better part of the past two nights telling us
apocryphal tales of Bruce Lee types and of the raw power invested in lightning blows
shot from coiled wrists, ankles, and elbows. The greasy character was unimpressed. He
merely backed off a step, his face like a Toltec mask, and laid Digby out with a single
whistling roundhouse blow . . . but by now Jeff had got into the act, and I was beginning to extricate myself from the dirt, a tinny compound of shock, rage, and impotence wadded in my throat.

Jeff was on the guy's back, biting at his ear. Digby was on the ground, cursing. I went
for the tire iron I kept under the driver's seat. I kept it there because bad characters always keep tire irons under the driver's seat, for just such an occasion as this. Never
mind that I hadn't been involved in a fight since sixth grade, when a kid with a sleepy
eye and two streams of mucus descending from his nostrils hit me in the knee with a
Louisville slugger, never mind that I'd touched the tire iron exactly twice before, to
change tires: it was there. And I went for it.

I was terrified. Blood was beating in my ears, my hands were shaking, my heart
turning over like a dirtbike in the wrong gear. My antagonist was shirtless, and a single cord of muscle flashed across his chest as he bent forward to peel Jeff from his back
like a wet overcoat. "Motherfucker," he spat, over and over, and I was aware in that
instant that all four of us—Digby, Jeff, and myself included—were chanting "motherfucker, motherfucker," as if it were a battle cry. (What happened next? the detective asks
the murderer from beneath the turned-down brim of his porkpie hat. I don't know, the
murderer says, something came over me. Exactly.)

Digby poked the flat of his hand in the bad character's face and I came at him like
a kamikaze, mindless, raging, stung with humiliation—the whole thing, from the initial boot in the chin to this murderous primal instant involving no more than sixty hy-
perventilating, gland-flooding seconds—I came at him and brought the tire iron down
across his ear. The effect was instantaneous, astonishing. He was a stunt man and this
was Hollywood, he was a big grimacing toothy balloon and I was a man with a straight
pin. He collapsed. Wet his pants. Went loose in his boots.

A single second, big as a zeppelin, floated by. We were standing over him in a circle, gritting our teeth, jerking our necks, our limbs and hands and feet twitching with
glandular discharges. No one said anything. We just stared down at the guy, the car
freak, the lover, the bad greasy character laid low. Digby looked at me; so did Jeff. I was
still holding the tire iron, a tuft of hair clinging to the crook like dandelion fluff, like
down. Rattled, I dropped it in the dirt, already envisioning the headlines, the pitted
faces of the police inquisitors, the gleam of handcuffs, clank of bars, the big black shadows rising from the back of the cell . . . when suddenly a raw torn shriek cut through
me like all the juice in all the electric chairs in the country.

It was the fox. She was short, barefoot, dressed in panties and a man's shirt. "Ani-   15
mals!" she screamed, running at us with her fists clenched and wisps of blow-dried hair
in her face. There was a silver chain round her ankle, and her toenails flashed in the
glare of the headlights. I think it was the toenails that did it. Sure, the gin and the
cannabis and even the Kentucky Fried may have had a hand in it, but it was the sight
of those flaming toes that set us off—the toad emerging from the loaf in *Virgin Spring*,
lipstick smeared on a child; she was already tainted. We were on her like Bergman's
deranged brothers—see no evil, hear none, speak none—panting, wheezing, tearing
at her clothes, grabbing for flesh. We were bad characters, and we were scared and
hot and three steps over the line—anything could have happened.

It didn't.

Before we could pin her to the hood of the car, our eyes masked with lust and greed
and the purest primal badness, a pair of headlights swung into the lot. There we were,
dirty, bloody, guilty, dissociated from humanity and civilization, the first of the *Ur-*
crimes behind us, the second in progress, shreds of nylon panty and spandex brassiere
dangling from our fingers, our flies open, lips licked—there we were, caught in the
spotlight. Nailed.

We bolted. First for the car, and then, realizing we had no way of starting it, for the
woods. I thought nothing. I thought escape. The headlights came at me like accusing
fingers. I was gone.

Ram-bam-bam, across the parking lot, past the chopper and into the feculent undergrowth at the lake's edge, insects flying up in my face, weeds whipping, frogs and
snakes and red-eyed turtles splashing off into the night: I was already ankle-deep in
muck and tepid water and still going strong. Behind me, the girl's screams rose in intensity, disconsolate, incriminating, the screams of the Sabine women, the Christian
martyrs, Anne Frank dragged from the garret. I kept going, pursued by those cries,
imagining cops and bloodhounds. The water was up to my knees when I realized
what I was doing: I was going to swim for it. Swim the breadth of Greasy Lake and hide
myself in the thick clot of woods on the far side. They'd never find me there.

I was breathing in sobs, in gasps. The water lapped at my waist as I looked out   20
over the moon-burnished ripples, the mats of algae that clung to the surface like scabs.
Digby and Jeff had vanished. I paused. Listened. The girl was quieter now, screams tapering to sobs, but there were male voices, angry, excited, and the high-pitched ticking of the second car's engine. I waded deeper, stealthy, hunted, the ooze sucking at
my sneakers. As I was about to take the plunge—at the very instant I dropped my
shoulder for the first slashing stroke—I blundered into something. Something unspeakable, obscene, something soft, wet, moss-grown. A patch of weed? A log? When
I reached out to touch it, it gave like a rubber duck, it gave like flesh.

In one of those nasty little epiphanies for which we are prepared by films and TV
and childhood visits to the funeral home to ponder the shrunken painted forms of
dead grandparents, I understood what it was that bobbed there so inadmissibly in the
dark. Understood, and stumbled back in horror and revulsion, my mind yanked in
six different directions (I was nineteen, a mere child, an infant, and here in the space
of five minutes I'd struck down one greasy character and blundered into the water-
logged carcass of a second), thinking, the keys, the keys, why did I have to go and lose
the keys? I stumbled back, but the muck took hold of my feet—a sneaker snagged,
balance lost—and suddenly I was pitching face forward into the buoyant black mass,
throwing out my hands in desperation while simultaneously conjuring the image of
reeking frogs and muskrats revolving in slicks of their own deliquescing juices.
AAAAArrrgh! I shot from the water like a torpedo, the dead man rotating to expose

a mossy beard and eyes cold as the moon. I must have shouted out, thrashing around in the weeds, because the voices behind me suddenly became animated.

"What was that?"

"It's them, it's them: they tried to, tried to . . . *rape* me!" Sobs.

A man's voice, flat Midwestern accent. "You sons a bitches, we'll kill you!"

Frogs, crickets.

Then another voice, harsh, *r*-less, Lower East Side: "Motherfucker!" I recognized the verbal virtuosity of the bad greasy character in the engineer boots. Tooth chipped, sneakers gone, coated in mud and slime and worse, crouching breathless in the weeds waiting to have my ass thoroughly and definitively kicked and fresh from the hideous stinking embrace of a three-days-dead-corpse, I suddenly felt a rush of joy and vindication: the son of a bitch was alive! Just as quickly, my bowels turned to ice. "Come on out of there, you pansy mothers!" the bad greasy character was screaming. He shouted curses till he was out of breath.

The crickets started up again, then the frogs. I held my breath. All at once was a sound in the reeds, a swishing, a splash: thunk-a-thunk. They were throwing rocks. The frogs fell silent. I cradled my head. Swish, swish, thunk-a-thunk. A wedge of feldspar the size of a cue ball glanced off my knee. I bit my finger.

It was then that they turned to the car. I heard a door slam, a curse, and then the sound of the headlights shattering—almost a good-natured sound, celebratory, like corks popping from the necks of bottles. This was succeeded by the dull booming of the fenders, metal on metal, and then the icy crash of the windshield. I inched forward, elbows and knees, my belly pressed to the muck, thinking of guerrillas and commandos and *The Naked and the Dead*. I parted the weeds and squinted the length of the parking lot.

The second car—it was a Trans-Am—was still running, its high beams washing the scene in a lurid stagy light. Tire iron flailing, the greasy bad character was laying into the side of my mother's Bel Air like an avenging demon, his shadow riding up the trunks of the trees. Whomp. Whomp. Whomp-whomp. The other two guys—blond types, in fraternity jackets—were helping out with tree branches and skull-sized boulders. One of them was gathering up bottles, rocks, muck, candy wrappers, used condoms, poptops, and other refuse and pitching it through the window on the driver's side. I could see the fox, a white bulb behind the windshield of the '57 Chevy. "Bobbie," she whined over the thumping, "come on." The greasy character paused a moment, took one good swipe at the left taillight, and then heaved the tire iron halfway across the lake. Then he fired up the '57 and was gone.

Blond head nodded at blond head. One said something to the other, too low for me to catch. They were no doubt thinking that in helping to annihilate my mother's car they'd committed a fairly rash act, and thinking too that there were three bad characters connected with that very car watching them from the woods. Perhaps other possibilities occurred to them as well—police, jail cells, justices of the peace, reparations, lawyers, irate parents, fraternal censure. Whatever they were thinking, they suddenly dropped branches, bottles, and rocks and sprang for their car in unison, as if they'd choreographed it. Five seconds. That's all it took. The engine shrieked, the tires squealed, a cloud of dust rose from the rutted lot and then settled back on darkness.

I don't know how long I lay there, the bad breath of decay all around me, my jacket heavy as a bear, the primordial ooze subtly reconstituting itself to accommodate my upper thighs and testicles. My jaws ached, my knee throbbed, my coccyx was on fire. I contemplated suicide, wondered if I'd need bridgework, scraped the recesses of my brain for some sort of excuse to give my parents—a tree had fallen on the car, I was blinded by a bread truck, hit and run, vandals had got to it while we were playing chess at Digby's. Then I thought of the dead man. He was probably the only person on the planet worse off than I was. I thought about him, fog on the lake, insects chirring eerily, and felt the tug of fear, felt the darkness opening up inside me like a set of jaws. Who was he, I wondered, this victim of time and circumstance bobbing sorrowfully in the lake at my back. The owner of the chopper, no doubt, a bad older character come to this. Shot during a murky drug deal, drowned while drunkenly frolicking in the lake. Another headline. My car was wrecked; he was dead.

When the eastern half of the sky went from black to cobalt and the trees began to separate themselves from the shadows, I pushed myself up from the mud and stepped out into the open. By now the birds had begun to take over for the crickets, and dew lay slick on the leaves. There was a smell in the air, raw and sweet at the same time, the smell of the sun firing buds and opening blossoms. I contemplated the car. It lay there like a wreck along the highway, like a steel sculpture left over from a vanished civilization. Everything was still. This was nature.

I was circling the car, as dazed and bedraggled as the sole survivor of an air blitz, when Digby and Jeff emerged from the trees behind me. Digby's face was crosshatched with smears of dirt; Jeff's jacket was gone and his shirt was torn across the shoulder. They slouched across the lot, looking sheepish, and silently came up beside me to gape at the ravaged automobile. No one said a word. After a while Jeff swung open the driver's door and began to scoop the broken glass and garbage off the seat. I looked at Digby. He shrugged. "At least they didn't slash the tires," he said.

It was true: the tires were intact. There was no windshield, the headlights were staved in, and the body looked as if it had been sledge-hammered for a quarter a shot at the county fair, but the tires were inflated to regulation pressure. The car was drivable. In silence, all three of us bent to scrape the mud and shattered glass from the interior. I said nothing about the biker. When we were finished, I reached in my pocket for the keys, experienced a nasty stab of recollection, cursed myself, and turned to search the grass. I spotted them almost immediately, no more than five feet from the open door, glinting like jewels in the first tapering shaft of sunlight. There was no reason to get philosophical about it: I eased into the seat and turned the engine over.

It was at that precise moment that the silver Mustang with the flame decals rumbled into the lot. All three of us froze; then Digby and Jeff slid into the car and slammed the door. We watched as the Mustang rocked and bobbed across the ruts and finally jerked to a halt beside the forlorn chopper at the far end of the lot. "Let's go," Digby said. I hesitated, the Bel Air wheezing beneath me. 35

Two girls emerged from the Mustang. Tight jeans, stiletto heels, hair like frozen fur. They bent over the motorcycle, paced back and forth aimlessly, glanced once or twice at us, and then ambled over to where the reeds sprang up in a green fence round the perimeter of the lake. One of them cupped her hands to her mouth. "Al," she called. "Hey, Al!"

"Come on," Digby hissed. "Let's get out of here."

But it was too late. The second girl was picking her way across the lot, unsteady on her heels, looking up at us and then away. She was older—twenty-five or six—and as she came closer we could see there was something wrong with her: she was stoned or drunk, lurching now and waving her arms for balance. I gripped the steering wheel as if it were the ejection lever of a flaming jet, and Digby spat out my name, twice, terse and impatient.

"Hi," the girl said.

40   We looked at her like zombies, like war veterans, like deaf-and-dumb pencil peddlers.

She smiled, her lips cracked and dry. "Listen," she said, bending from the waist to look in the window, "you guys seen Al?" Her pupils were pinpoints, her eyes glass. She jerked her neck. "That's his bike over there—Al's. You seen him?"

Al. I didn't know what to say. I wanted to get out of the car and retch, I wanted to go home to my parents' house and crawl into bed. Digby poked me in the ribs. "We haven't seen anybody," I said.

The girl seemed to consider this, reaching out a slim veiny arm to brace herself against the car. "No matter," she said, slurring the *t*'s, "he'll turn up." And then, as if she'd just taken stock of the whole scene—the ravaged car and our battered faces, the desolation of the place—she said: "Hey, you guys look like some pretty bad characters—been fightin', huh?" We stared straight ahead, rigid as catatonics. She was fumbling in her pocket and muttering something. Finally she held out a handful of tablets in glassine wrappers: "Hey, you want to party, you want to do some of these with me and Sarah?"

I just looked at her. I thought I was going to cry. Digby broke the silence. "No, thanks," he said, leaning over me. "Some other time."

45   I put the car in gear and it inched forward with a groan, shaking off pellets of glass like an old dog shedding water after a bath, heaving over the ruts on its worn springs, creeping toward the highway. There was a sheen of sun on the lake. I looked back. The girl was still standing there, watching us, her shoulders slumped, hand outstretched.   [1985]

QUESTIONS

1. When does this story take place? Is the time period important to the theme or is it irrelevant?
2. How have the characters changed over the course of the story?
3. Why do the boys begin to rape the woman?
4. What effect does the dead man have on the narrator?
5. Why is it significant that the narrator is driving his mother's car?

RESPONSES

1. Compare this story to Joyce Carol Oates's "Where Are You Going, Where Have You Been?"
2. Research myths about Dionysian frenzies, spirit possessions, and "the dark side." In what ways do they provide basic structure for this story?

ALICE CAREY

Alice Carey (1820–1871) was born in Mount Heather, Ohio. She, along with her sister Phoebe, was a prolific writer of poetry and fiction. With the publication of their first volume of poems, the sisters moved to New York City. There they established themselves as hostesses of literary salons, meeting and entertaining many of the important writers of the day. Alice was the author of several novels and volumes of short fiction, mostly dealing with the lives of rural and small town folk in Ohio. As such, she was an early important voice in the development of American local color writing. Her short fiction is included in *Clovernook or Recollections of Our Neighborhood in the West* (1852) and *Clovernook's Children* (1855).

The Pride of Sarah Worthington

I took up one of the papers published in the city which is nearest to Clovernook, and turning, as is the habit of women, to that part which chronicles the main points in all domestic histories, I read, that Sarah Worthington was dead; "after a painful illness, aged nineteen years, three months, and eleven days." I read it more than once, to satisfy all questionings of my unwilling heart; but there could be no error; the street, the incidental revelations of the stricken family, every thing confirmed the first impression that had stolen through my eyes to my shrinking consciousness. The old truth was again asserted by some friend, in the often repeated verse which followed, that

> "The good die young,
> While they whose hearts are dry as summer dust
> Burn to the socket."

How like a peal of thunder awakening us from some pleasant dream, when the dashing of the rain at the window, the howling of the tempest on the hill, and the blank darkness about us, take the place of the soft voice that was in our ears, and the smile that warmed our hearts, leaving us for a moment startled and bewildered, comes intelligence of the death of a friend, whom we left a few weeks, or it may be a few days ago, in the enjoyment of vigorous health.

After the first burst of surprise and sorrow, we fall into a train of melancholy musing—when, and under what circumstances, was our last meeting with the dead— what did she say, and how did she look? was it morning or evening? and was our language and manner kind, or reserved and formal? How many instances we recall in which kind words might have been said that were not said, or kind actions performed that were not performed! If it be a near relation who is gone, how much of harshness and coldness and indifference we have to reproach ourselves for, and how we are tortured with exaggerations of our short comings, and idle regrets.

Who of us all cannot remember some pale lips from which we would give all the world to hear the blessed words, "You are forgiven." For myself, there is one darker memory than all the rest—one, perpetually recurring, and from which I shrink away, afraid to think. Mountains, and woods, and waters, darken between me and the solitary grave of one who was my dearest friend, yet against whom I sinned— not with any premeditated wrong—but from childish ignorance and sudden passion. My lost one! if your dying hands had been laid upon my head in forgiveness as well as in blessing, my irrepressible grief might long ago have been stilled—that blessing, meant for innocency, falling upon guilt, has been my curse.

5   All the long summer time I knew that she was dying, yet I put off the day of confession. Now she would be better and talk of the future, and, accustomed to rely on all she said, I would grow hopeful, and in its brightening the dreadful error was almost forgot; and when she grew too weak to take me in her arms, as she had always done before, and lay all the day looking from the open window at the clouds and the grass, and I knew instinctively that she must leave us before long, I was more than ever afraid to speak. I could not embitter her sufferings with a knowledge of my early injustice. Sometimes my sisters would go away from her chamber for an hour, or even for a day, for youth is apt to be inconsiderate; but I was there always, bringing the cup of water, wrapping doubly the chilly hands and feet, or smoothing the counterpane. A strong-fascination would not allow me to leave, but when she praised my devotion I would go aside and weep.

So the time went on, and I said not, I have done wrong, I have sinned against you, sweet friend, and against heaven; till at last the dull shadows of autumn swept across the face of the summer, and my watching was all done, and the smile which they said was so life-like and loving looked reproachful to me.

At night, I am lifted to "the litter of close-curtained sleep" by the phantoms that come up from the grave; waking, in the morning, I go down under the long years, full of pains and sorrows and disappointments, and folding back the shroud, cry out to the dust for forgiveness. In vain! There is no green hollow in the wilderness, no blank sands of the desert, that to me would not be haunted. God, will the tormentor cross the threshold of the grave, clouding the pure radiance of eternity with the curse that has spread mildew along the summer of my mortal existence! Shall the ashes of life's roses never be taken from my head, nor the sackcloth unbound from my bosom?

But I meant not this digression—I know not that she of whom my little story chiefly is, she who has gone down to death and up to judgment before me, may plead against me anything at all. I mean by this no argument for the better actions of my riper years. I have perhaps learned to check impatience of temper and impetuosity of speech, but I fear I am farther off from heaven now than when I used to think the slender treetops close against the skies.

> "The moonlight stealing o'er the scene
> Was blended with the gifts of eve."

It was the midst of the harvest—the fragrance of the newly cut hay made all the air 10
delicious, for the sythe had been busy all day in the wide meadows, and along their
flat smooth surfaces, and up and down the hills, lay the straight, thick swaths—paths
for the starlight and beds for the tired winds, for the stars were peeping, one after another, above the edges of the tree-tops, and the airs, scarcely awake, gave no murmur
to the thick and dusty foliage.

Resting on the summit of the eastern hill stood the full moon, looking very large,
and so pale that "the man with the bag of thorns" was distinctly visible, else my juvenile employment—for we were playing Hide and Seek—made my childish fancy
more sharp in apprehension than it was wont to be.

Let me see—there were half a dozen of us: Ward, my little nephew, nine years old then;
Robert, a distant cousin, a young man of unusual beauty of character; Sarah Worthington, and Ellie, and Hal, and I. A merry party we were, and our laughter called up the
echoes from the high hills away across the orchard and the pasture field and the thick
woods. Little green stacks were heaped all about the yard; how sweet they made the air,
and what nice hiding places they were, especially where the shadows of the peach trees
fall darkly over and about them. Ward enjoyed the frolic vastly, though he felt that he was
caught less often than cousin Robert. It seems to me but yesterday, so fresh is it all in my
memory—memory, that sometimes is so good an angel. Down in the past are scattered
fountains, sealed with dark rocks almost always, from which it is sweet to drink. The
game of hide and seek, the time, the place, our abandonment of care, and our taking up
for a moment childish actions, and in part, childish feelings, are pleasant to those who
have come up into the noon of the world. New grave-mounds, the grass creeping over
one, and the other fresh and new, darken to-day between me and that time. Away in the
west stands an old ruinous church; I have seen it once or twice, and it is one of those
things which, once seen, are never forgotten. It has stood there a long time, for I can remember it was in little better state of preservation than now as long ago as I can remember. The oaks and walnuts that grow there throw shadows over the graves of the
pioneers, whose piety prompted the rude skill, that, earlier than the Revolution,

"Hewed the shaft and laid the architrave,"

for the temple about which they are sleeping. The living have almost deserted it now;
the swallows go in at the broken windows and build their nests where they will; the
thousand nails in the strong double door are rusty and black; the woodwork, never
painted, discolored by time to a sort of pearly gray; the weatherboards, in places decaying and dropping off. There was never belfry nor spire, and the steep mossy roof
retains still one or two of those angular projections of framework, which are only seen
on very old houses in the country—placed there probably for the convenience of the
builders. Once in a long time some itinerant preacher—some wilderness-crying John,
girt about with zeal, pauses in the village for a Sabbath, and the children of the house,
where for a time he abides, bear to all the neighbors—all persons living within a circuit of four or five miles—the intelligence, that at eleven o'clock on Sunday there will
be a sermon in the old church. At the appointed time the congregation gather, slow and
calm. But Robert is not there. Nor loud denunciation, nor soft admonition, nor trembling hymn, provokes the sleeping dust.

And the lady of his love, she, who took off the white bridal crown for the muffling
mourning veil, does she go apart and on the simple headstone read his name, the shelter of whose love death has broken away? I know not—nor is it well perhaps to pause
and inquire.

Full of health and hope he was, the night of our gamesome frolic in the moonlight. He had passed the twilight with one dearer than any of us, and was in genial mood, for in loving one we learn to love all. Scarcely could any of us get home to the doorsteps, from our retreats under the lilacs or behind the stacks of hay, without being caught, and paying the penalty prescribed by the childish law. Even Sarah, usually so stately, unbent from her dignity that night, and, when Robert was to be overtaken, ran more nimbly than when he was to be the pursuer. She was a beautiful girl, and I have called her stately, dignified, but she was also silent, unsocial, selfish. I think there was nothing in the world she loved, unless it were her little dog—to this she was always kind, giving it all the caresses and endearing words she had for anything. Mother nor brother nor any human being seemed ever to have found the way to her heart, and she spoke of her kindred with more than the indifference she gave the veriest stranger. Sometimes she would put her arms about me, and seem to love me, but the warm gush of feeling, if, for the moment, it really were such, would be in a moment put down with an iron will, and between us there was a sea of ice.

15   For a long time I marvelled whether the milk which is naturally in human nature had been thinned by some untimely frost, or whether it had always been as now. She spoke of no past season of sunshine, of no future hope, and to the present, a stock or a stone was not more indifferent. Little children that may scarcely plead in vain to any one for love, were thrown upon her care in vain. What they really required she performed, indeed, but lower than duty there was no softer feeling.

I would have solved the problem of her nature. I could never learn that she even felt pride in anything, unless perhaps in the scorn she bestowed on her fellow creatures.

Her hair, thick and luxuriant, and black as night, hung, when she loosened it from the braids in which it was commonly confined, and shook it over her shoulders, as she often did, almost to her feet. With what a queen-like manner I have seen her toss the dark masses from her forehead, and folding her arms across her bosom, pace backward and forward through her chamber, with no word, but, as if musing on the destruction of empires, scaring away, often until after midnight,

"Magic sleep, that comfortable bird."

One night I remember well, late in December, still and intensely cold, we had been sitting an hour before the glowing grate, talking of this and that, and I perceived, silently, at the time, that Sarah had not once said during our conversation that she hated any person or thing, and it was rare that she talked without doing so. She was tall, straight as an arrow, and seemed to possess a constitution that would resist the chances and changes of many years. I speak again of her beauty, for I know not whether it was this or her indifference, for we reach for the inaccessible always, that gave her the power of fascination: all who knew her admired, many even loved her. But the heartstrings of her worshippers were ever destined to tremble with the torture of her careless hand. Of these worshippers we had been speaking that night; I, with intent of bringing out her feelings, she, because I talked to her. Amongst other things, I chanced to say, "There is one of your admirers, Sarah, whom you have not seen; to-morrow, if you will, I shall give myself the pleasure of making him known to you. Who knows but that he is destined to bear from a hundred lovers the prize?"

"It may be, indeed it's probable, very probable," she replied sarcastically, and placing her hand on her heart, added, laughingly, "I think I begin to feel susceptible—where is he? tell me this hour, this moment! I am all impatience."

"Calm yourself," I said, speaking in the same vein, "and I will tell you 'the color of   20
his hair, and the garment he doth wear, and the day of the month he's to marry unto
you,' as our spinning-girl, Sally, used to say when she charmed the moon."

"Delay is torture," she said with assumed earnestness, and suddenly throwing herself on her knees, exclaimed, "Where, O, where is this Endymion, that, like the pale
Phœbus, hunting in a grove, I may stoop and kiss my sweetest!"

"You know lawyer D——," said I, meaning to interrogate.

The playfulness was gone, and standing erect, she asked in a tone I shall never forget—"Who told you I did?"

I explained briefly what I meant to say, and seating herself majestically, a little way
from me, she replied sententiously and coldly, that she slightly knew him.

"Our young friend is reading with D——," I said; "we shall find him at the office   25
in Fourth-street, when we go to town—shall we call?"

"No," was all her answer, and presently making the fire, which was growing dim,
an excuse, I sought my pillow and seemed to sleep, for I felt that farther conversation
would be an annoyance.

Left alone, Sarah took the comb from her hair, one of the most elaborate and expensive of the then newest style, and throwing it on the floor at her feet, shook down
her black tresses, and in her thin night-dress began walking to and fro across the room.
In one of the turns the comb broke beneath her tread, but she stooped not nor seemed
in any way to heed it. The lamp burned low, and flickered, and went out; the ashes
gathered gray over the coal, and the frost whitened on the panes, so very cold it was,
but neither the darkness nor the freezing atmosphere seemed to trouble her at all. The
clock had struck twelve and one and two; and dropping on her knees, before the window, she scratched away the frost, and flattening her cheek against the cold glass,
looked earnestly forth into the street. The lights were all gone from the windows, and
only once in a long while sounded a step on the frozen ground below.

So still was she, and so strange had been her conduct, that I was half afraid. At last
I ventured to speak, not as though I had been conscious of her manner all the night,
but rather as if she were but then missed.

"Pray, don't disturb me," she said, "I am talking with the angels."

Satisfied that she was neither dead nor insane, for strange speech was habitual to her,   30
and exhausted with the mental oppression I had endured, I fell asleep, and though I
dreamed that a skeleton was in my bed with me, I did not wake till morning. When I did
so, I was half buried in the heavy tresses of Sarah, who, stooping over me, bade me awake,
adding, "You know we are to make that call which is perhaps to decide my destiny."

Before the appointed time arrived, however, she had framed some excuse, which I
received without a question, and the visit was not made, nor then nor ever.

I have since seen D——, much and often; talked with him of life and death, and love;
but of love he spoke calmly as of a client. He is forty, or nearly so, handsome, wealthy,
influential, grave in manner, but of an iron will that nor hope nor fear nor hate nor love
may stir from its bent. His deep blue eyes would look as coldly and steadily on dying
loveliness as on the veriest wretch that ever lived and fattened, if he so resolved. He
is unmarried and a universal favorite. But no matter what he is—I have solved the
problem that once baffled, me—

> "As the waters to the marble,
> So my heart fell with a moan"

as I did so. Poor Sarah! I had sometimes blamed, but I only pitied her now.

It was but this morning I read her obituary, and I cannot yet think of her as pale, or sick, or dead. What did she think of at the last? and what did she say? did her thoughts ever cross the wild mountains and search me out? Mine have gone back to her a thousand times. As she went down step by step into those silent palaces whither we all are going, did she lean more upon the love of kindred? did she see more clearly than in life, God's purposes in the great woe about her heart? I know not, I only know that her locks will never again fall about my bosom, nor her voice call me to wake.

I know not whether she sleeps beneath a stately monument in the dark vaults, or under the swelling mound; but I know that to her pillow the mockery of no smile may come, nor to her heart the delusive sweetness of hollow and unmeaning words.

35   "And to sleep, you must lie down in just such a bed!"

[1852]

QUESTIONS

1. How is the erratic development of the plot of this story a kind of narrative game of "hide and seek"?
2. What is the narrator's tone? How does she view herself and her actions toward Sarah Worthington?
3. Explain the conflicts between the narrator and Sarah Worthington and the conflict within the narrator.
4. What does setting the game of hide and seek in a cemetery contribute to the story?
5. Explain the symbolic meaning of Sarah Worthington's hair.

RESPONSES

1. This story was published in 1852. Using a feminist perspective, explore the lives and options available to women at this time. Are the lives of the narrator and Sarah Worthington much different from those of young women today?
2. Compare this story to stories by Sandra Cisneros, Jamaica Kincaid, and Perri Klass.

ANGELA CARTER

Angela Carter (1940–1992) was born in Sussex, England, and educated at the University of Bristol. She wrote in a variety of styles, and her influences include Gothic fantasy, magic realism, science fiction, and the fairy tale. *The Bloody Chamber* (1979) is a collection of retold fairy tales. *The Collected Short Fiction* was published posthumously in 1996.

The Werewolf

It is a northern country; they have cold weather, they have cold hearts.

Cold; tempest; wild beasts in the forest. It is a hard life. Their houses are built of logs, dark and smoky within. There will be a crude icon of the virgin behind a guttering candle, the leg of a pig hung up to cure, a string of drying mushrooms. A bed, a stool, a table. Harsh, brief, poor lives.

To these upland woodsmen, the Devil is as real as you or I. More so; they have not seen us nor even know that we exist, but the Devil they glimpse often in the graveyards, those bleak and touching townships of the dead where the graves are marked with portraits of the deceased in the naïf style and there are no flowers to put in front of them, no flowers grow there, so they put out small votive offerings, little loaves, sometimes a cake that the bears come lumbering from the margins of the forest to snatch away. At midnight, especially on Walpurgisnacht,° the Devil holds picnics in the graveyards and invites the witches; then they dig up fresh corpses, and eat them. Anyone will tell you that.

Wreaths of garlic on the doors keep out the vampires. A blue-eyed child born feet first on the night of Saint John's Eve° will have second sight. When they discover a witch—some old woman whose cheeses ripen when her neighbors' do not, another old woman whose black cat, oh, sinister! *follows her about all the time,*—they strip the crone, search for her marks, for the supernumerary nipple her familiar sucks. They soon find it. Then they stone her to death.

Winter and cold weather.

5

°*Walpurgisnacht*: Eve of May 1, the night when witches travel to their meeting place (coincides with the feast of St. Walburga, an English saint).

°*Saint John's Eve*: Pre-Christian fertility festival (coincides with saint's feast day; modern covens have suggested March 31 and June 23).

Go and visit grandmother, who has been sick. Take her the oat cakes I've baked for her on the hearthstone and a little pot of butter.

The good child does as her mother bids—five miles' trudge through the forest; do not leave the path because of the bears, the wild boar, the starving wolves. Here, take your father's hunting knife; you know how to use it.

The child had a scabby coat of sheepskin to keep out the cold; she knew the forest too well to fear it but she must always be on her guard. When she heard that freezing howl of a wolf, she dropped her gifts, seized her knife and turned on the beast.

It was a huge one, with red eyes and running, grizzled chops; any but a mountaineer's child would have died of fright at the sight of it. It went for her throat, as wolves do, but she made a great swipe at it with her father's knife and slashed off its right forepaw.

10   The wolf let out a gulp, almost a sob, when it saw what had happened to it; wolves are less brave than they seem. It went lolloping off disconsolately between the trees as well as it could on three legs, leaving a trail of blood behind it. The child wiped the blade of her knife clean on her apron, wrapped up the wolf's paw in the cloth in which her mother had packed the oat cakes and went on towards her grandmother's house. Soon it came on to snow so thickly that the path and any footsteps, track or spoor that might have been upon it were obscured.

She found her grandmother was so sick she had taken to her bed and fallen into a fretful sleep, moaning and shaking so that the child guessed she had a fever. She felt the forehead, it burned. She shook out the cloth from her basket, to use it to make the old woman a cold compress, and the wolf's paw fell to the floor.

But it was no longer a wolf's paw. It was a hand, chopped off at the wrist, a hand toughened with work and freckled with old age. There was a wedding ring on the third finger and a wart on the index finger. By the wart, she knew it for her grandmother's hand.

She pulled back the sheet, but the old woman woke up at that, and began to struggle, squawking and shrieking like a thing possessed. But the child was strong, and armed with her father's hunting knife; she managed to hold her grandmother down long enough to see the cause of her fever. There was a bloody stump where her right hand should have been, festering already.

The child crossed herself and cried out so loud the neighbors heard her and came rushing in. They knew the wart on the hand at once for a witch's nipple; they drove the old woman, in her shift as she was, out into the snow with sticks, beating her old carcass as far as the edge of the forest, and pelted her with stones until she fell down dead.

15   Now the child lived in her grandmother's house; she prospered.   [1977]

QUESTIONS

1. From the second paragraph, do you like Carter's use of the word "guttering"?
2. Look up the implications of "Walpurgisnacht." Why did Carter choose to place this barrier between her story and some readers' understanding?
3. Did the break between the exposition and the action of the story create a problem for you?

4. Carter knows that you know the story of "Little Red Riding Hood." How well do you think she layered in that story with the story of a werewolf?
5. What does Carter's story have in common with "The Lottery" by Shirley Jackson?

RESPONSES

1. How is this story a feminist retelling of "Little Red Riding Hood"? How is it not?
2. Look at the last line of the story, "Now the child lived in her grandmother's house. She prospered." How does this last line open a Marxist interpretation of the story?

FOCUS ON FILM

1. Angela Carter adapted this story and another into the film *The Company of Wolves*. What elements of this story did she keep? Which change?
2. Discuss the fairytale qualities and dreamlike qualities of this story in their presentation in the film.

RAYMOND CARVER

Raymond Carver (1939–1988) was born in Clatskanie, Oregon, and educated at Humboldt State College and the University of Iowa. In the early 1970s the *New Yorker*, *Esquire*, and the *Atlantic Monthly* began to publish his poetry and short fiction. His first collection of short stories, *Will You Please Be Quiet, Please?* (1976) was nominated for the National Book Award. Other collections include *Cathedral* (1983) and *Where I'm Calling From* (1988).

Cathedral

This blind man, an old friend of my wife's, he was on his way to spend the night. His wife had died. So he was visiting the dead wife's relatives in Connecticut. He called my wife from his in-laws'. Arrangements were made. He would come by train, a five-hour trip, and my wife would meet him at the station. She hadn't seen him since she worked for him one summer in Seattle ten years ago. But she and the blind man had kept in touch. They made tapes and mailed them back and forth. I wasn't enthusiastic about his visit. He was no one I knew. And his being blind bothered me. My idea of blindness came from the movies. In the movies, the blind moved slowly and never laughed. Sometimes they were led by seeing-eye dogs. A blind man in my house was not something I looked forward to.

That summer in Seattle she had needed a job. She didn't have any money. The man she was going to marry at the end of the summer was in officers' training school. He didn't have any money, either. But she was in love with the guy, and he was in love with her, etc. She'd seen something in the paper: HELP WANTED—*Reading to Blind Man*, and a telephone number. She phoned and went over, was hired on the spot. She'd worked with this blind man all summer. She read stuff to him, case studies, reports, that sort of thing. She helped him organize his little office in the county social-service department. They'd become good friends, my wife and the blind man. How do I know these things? She told me. And she told me something else. On her last day in the office, the blind man asked if he could touch her face. She agreed to this. She told me he touched his fingers to every part of her face, her nose—even her neck! She never forgot it. She even tried to write a poem about it. She was always trying to write a poem. She wrote a poem or two every year, usually after something really important had happened to her.

160

When we first started going out together, she showed me the poem. In the poem, she recalled his fingers and the way they had moved around over her face. In the poem, she talked about what she had felt at the time, about what went through her mind when the blind man touched her nose and lips. I can remember I didn't think much of the poem. Of course, I didn't tell her that. Maybe I just don't understand poetry. I admit it's not the first thing I reach for when I pick up something to read.

Anyway, this man who'd first enjoyed her favors, the officer-to-be, he'd been her childhood sweetheart. So okay. I'm saying that at the end of the summer she let the blind man run his hands over her face, said goodbye to him, married her childhood etc., who was now a commissioned officer, and she moved away from Seattle. But they'd kept in touch, she and the blind man. She made the first contact after a year or so. She called him up one night from an Air Force base in Alabama. She wanted to talk. They talked. He asked her to send him a tape and tell him about her life. She did this. She sent the tape. On the tape, she told the blind man about her husband and about their life together in the military. She told the blind man she loved her husband but she didn't like it where they lived and she didn't like it that he was a part of the military-industrial thing. She told the blind man she'd written a poem and he was in it. She told him that she was writing a poem about what it was like to be an Air Force officer's wife. The poem wasn't finished yet. She was still writing it. The blind man made a tape. He sent her the tape. She made a tape. This went on for years. My wife's officer was posted to one base and then another. She sent tapes from Moody AFB, McGuire, McConnell, and finally Travis, near Sacramento, where one night she got to feeling lonely and cut off from people she kept losing in that moving-around life. She got to feeling she couldn't go it another step. She went in and swallowed all the pills and capsules in the medicine chest and washed them down with a bottle of gin. Then she got into a hot bath and passed out.

But instead of dying, she got sick. She threw up. Her officer—why should he have   5
a name? he was the childhood sweetheart, and what more does he want?—came home from somewhere, found her, and called the ambulance. In time, she put it all on a tape and sent the tape to the blind man. Over the years, she put all kinds of stuff on tapes and sent the tapes off lickety-split. Next to writing a poem every year, I think it was her chief means of recreation. On one tape, she told the blind man she'd decided to live away from her officer for a time. On another tape, she told him about her divorce. She and I began going out, and of course she told her blind man about it. She told him everything, or so it seemed to me. Once she asked me if I'd like to hear the latest tape from the blind man. This was a year ago. I was on the tape, she said. So I said okay, I'd listen to it. I got us drinks and we settled down in the living room. We made ready to listen. First she inserted the tape into the player and adjusted a couple of dials. Then she pushed a lever. The tape squeaked and someone began to talk in this loud voice. She lowered the volume. After a few minutes of harmless chitchat, I heard my own name in the mouth of this stranger, this blind man I didn't even know! And then this: "From all you've said about him, I can only conclude————" But we were interrupted, a knock at the door, something, and we didn't ever get back to the tape. Maybe it was just as well. I'd heard all I wanted to.

Now this same blind man was coming to sleep in my house.

"Maybe I could take him bowling," I said to my wife. She was at the draining board doing scalloped potatoes. She put down the knife she was using and turned around.

"If you love me," she said, "you can do this for me. If you don't love me, okay. But if you had a friend, any friend, and the friend came to visit, I'd make him feel comfortable." She wiped her hands with the dish towel.

"I don't have any blind friends," I said.

"You don't have *any* friends," she said. "Period. Besides," she said, "goddamn it, his wife's just died! Don't you understand that? The man's lost his wife!"

I didn't answer. She'd told me a little about the blind man's wife. Her name was Beulah. Beulah! That's a name for a colored woman.

"Was his wife a Negro?" I asked.

"Are you crazy?" my wife said. "Have you just flipped or something?" She picked up a potato. I saw it hit the floor, then roll under the stove. "What's wrong with you?" she said. "Are you drunk?"

"I'm just asking," I said.

Right then my wife filled me in with more detail than I cared to know. I made a drink and sat at the kitchen table to listen. Pieces of the story began to fall into place.

Beulah had gone to work for the blind man the summer after my wife had stopped working for him. Pretty soon Beulah and the blind man had themselves a church wedding. It was a little wedding—who'd want to go to such a wedding in the first place?—just the two of them, plus the minister and the minister's wife. But it was a church wedding just the same. It was what Beulah had wanted, he'd said. But even then Beulah must have been carrying the cancer in her glands. After they had been inseparable for eight years—my wife's word, *inseparable*—Beulah's health went into a rapid decline. She died in a Seattle hospital room, the blind man sitting beside the bed and holding on to her hand. They'd married, lived and worked together, slept together—had sex, sure—and then the blind man had to bury her. All this without his having ever seen what the goddamned woman looked like. It was beyond my understanding. Hearing this, I felt sorry for the blind man for a little bit. And then I found myself thinking what a pitiful life this woman must have led. Imagine a woman who could never see herself as she was seen in the eyes of her loved one. A woman who could go on day after day and never receive the smallest compliment from her beloved. A woman whose husband could never read the expression on her face, be it misery or something better. Someone who could wear makeup or not—what difference to him? She could, if she wanted, wear green eyeshadow around one eye, a straight pin in her nostril, yellow slacks and purple shoes, no matter. And then to slip off into death, the blind man's hand on her hand, his blind eyes streaming tears—I'm imagining now—her last thought maybe this: that he never even knew what she looked like, and she on an express to the grave. Robert was left with a small insurance policy and half of a twenty-peso Mexican coin. The other half of the coin went into the box with her. Pathetic.

So when the time rolled around, my wife went to the depot to pick him up. With nothing to do but wait—sure, I blamed him for that—I was having a drink and watching the TV when I heard the car pull into the drive. I got up from the sofa with my drink and went to the window to have a look.

I saw my wife laughing as she parked the car. I saw her get out of the car and shut the door. She was still wearing a smile. Just amazing. She went around to the other side of the car to where the blind man was already starting to get out. This blind man, feature this, he was wearing a full beard! A beard on a blind man! Too much, I say. The blind man reached into the back seat and dragged out a suitcase. My wife took his arm, shut the car door, and, talking all the way, moved him down the drive and then up the steps to the front porch. I turned off the TV. I finished my drink, rinsed the glass, dried my hands. Then I went to the door.

My wife said, "I want you to meet Robert. Robert, this is my husband. I've told you all about him." She was beaming. She had this blind man by his coat sleeve.

The blind man let go of his suitcase and up came his hand. 20

I took it. He squeezed hard, held my hand, and then he let it go.

"I feel like we've already met," he boomed.

"Likewise," I said. I didn't know what else to say. Then I said, "Welcome. I've heard a lot about you." We began to move then, a little group, from the porch into the living room, my wife guiding him by the arm. The blind man was carrying his suitcase in his other hand. My wife said things like, "To your left here, Robert. That's right. Now watch it, there's a chair. That's it. Sit down right here. This is the sofa. We just bought this sofa two weeks ago."

I started to say something about the old sofa. I'd liked that old sofa. But I didn't say anything. Then I wanted to say something else, small-talk, about the scenic ride along the Hudson. How going *to* New York, you should sit on the right-hand side of the train, and coming *from* New York, the left-hand side.

"Did you have a good train ride?" I said. "Which side of the train did you sit on, 25 by the way?"

"What a question, which side!" my wife said. "What's it matter which side?" she said.

"I just asked," I said.

"Right side," the blind man said. "I hadn't been on a train in nearly forty years. Not since I was a kid. With my folks. That's been a long time. I'd nearly forgotten the sensation. I have winter in my beard now," he said. "So I've been told, anyway. Do I look distinguished, my dear?" the blind man said to my wife.

"You look distinguished, Robert," she said. "Robert," she said. "Robert, it's just so good to see you."

My wife finally took her eyes off the blind man and looked at me. I had the feel- 30 ing she didn't like what she saw. I shrugged.

I've never met, or personally known, anyone who was blind. This blind man was late forties, a heavy-set, balding man with stooped shoulders, as if he carried a great weight there. He wore brown slacks, brown shoes, a light-brown shirt, a tie, a sports coat. Spiffy. He also had this full beard. But he didn't use a cane and he didn't wear dark glasses. I'd always thought dark glasses were a must for the blind. Fact was, I wished he had a pair. At first glance, his eyes looked like anyone else's eyes. But if you looked close, there was something different about them. Too much white in the iris, for one thing, and the pupils seemed to move around in the sock- ets without his knowing it or being able to stop it. Creepy. As I stared at his face, I saw the left pupil turn in toward his nose while the other made an effort to keep in one place. But it was only an effort, for that eye was on the roam without his know- ing it or wanting it to be.

I said, "Let me get you a drink. What's your pleasure? We have a little of every- thing. It's one of our pastimes."

"Bub, I'm a Scotch man myself," he said fast enough in this big voice.

"Right," I said. Bub! "Sure you are. I knew it."

He let his fingers touch his suitcase, which was sitting alongside the sofa. He 35 was taking his bearings. I didn't blame him for that.

"I'll move that up to your room," my wife said.

"No, that's fine," the blind man said loudly. "It can go up when I go up."

"A little water with the Scotch?" I said.

"Very little," he said.

40   "I knew it," I said.

He said, "Just a tad. The Irish actor, Barry Fitzgerald? I'm like that fellow. When I drink water, Fitzgerald said, I drink water. When I drink whiskey, I drink whiskey." My wife laughed. The blind man brought his hand up under his beard. He lifted his beard slowly and let it drop.

I did the drinks, three big glasses of Scotch with a splash of water in each. Then we made ourselves comfortable and talked about Robert's travels. First the long flight from the West Coast to Connecticut, we covered that. Then from Connecticut up here by train. We had another drink concerning that leg of the trip.

I remembered having read somewhere that the blind didn't smoke because, as speculation had it, they couldn't see the smoke they exhaled. I thought I knew that much and that much only about blind people. But this blind man smoked his cigarette down to the nubbin and then lit another one. This blind man filled his ashtray and my wife emptied it.

When we sat down at the table for dinner, we had another drink. My wife heaped Robert's plate with cube steak, scalloped potatoes, green beans. I buttered him up two slices of bread. I said, "Here's bread and butter for you." I swallowed some of my drink. "Now let us pray," I said, and the blind man lowered his head. My wife looked at me, her mouth agape. "Pray the phone won't ring and the food doesn't get cold," I said.

45   We dug in. We ate everything there was to eat on the table. We ate like there was no tomorrow. We didn't talk. We ate. We scarfed. We grazed that table. We were into serious eating. The blind man had right away located his foods, he knew just where everything was on his plate. I watched with admiration as he used his knife and fork on the meat. He'd cut two pieces of meat, fork the meat into his mouth, and then go all out for the scalloped potatoes, the beans next, and then he'd tear off a hunk of buttered bread and eat that. He'd follow this up with a big drink of milk. It didn't seem to bother him to use his fingers once in a while, either.

We finished everything, including half a strawberry pie. For a few moments, we sat as if stunned. Sweat beaded on our faces. Finally, we got up from the table and left the dirty plates. We didn't look back. We took ourselves into the living room and sank into our places again. Robert and my wife sat on the sofa. I took the big chair. We had us two or three more drinks while they talked about the major things that had come to pass for them in the past ten years. For the most part, I just listened. Now and then I joined in. I didn't want him to think I'd left the room, and I didn't want her to think I was feeling left out. They talked of things that had happened to them—to them!— these past ten years. I waited in vain to hear my name on my wife's sweet lips: "And then my dear husband came into my life"—something like that. But I heard nothing of the sort. More talk of Robert. Robert had done a little of everything, it seemed, a regular blind jack-of-all-trades. But most recently he and his wife had had an Amway distributorship, from which, I gathered, they'd earned their living, such as it was. The blind man was also a ham radio operator. He talked in his loud voice about conversations he'd had with fellow operators in Guam, in the Philippines, in Alaska, and even in Tahiti. He said he'd have a lot of friends there if he ever wanted to go visit those places. From time to time, he'd turn his blind face toward me, put his hand under his beard, ask me something. How long had I been in my present position? (Three years.) Did I like my work? (I didn't.) Was I going to stay with it? (What were the options?) Finally, when I thought he was beginning to run down, I got up and turned on the TV.

My wife looked at me with irritation. She was heading toward a boil. Then she looked at the blind man and said, "Robert, do you have a TV?"

The blind man said, "My dear, I have two TVs. I have a color set and a black-and-white thing, an old relic. It's funny, but if I turn the TV on, and I'm always turning it on, I turn on the color set. It's funny, don't you think?"

I didn't know what to say to that. I had absolutely nothing to say to that. No opinion. So I watched the news program and tried to listen to what the announcer was saying.

"This is a color TV," the blind man said. "Don't ask me how, but I can tell."

"We traded up a while ago," I said.

The blind man had another taste of his drink. He lifted his beard, sniffed it, and let it fall. He leaned forward on the sofa. He positioned his ashtray on the coffee table, then put the lighter to his cigarette. He leaned back on the sofa and crossed his legs at the ankles.

My wife covered her mouth, and then she yawned. She stretched. She said, "I think I'll go upstairs and put on my robe. I think I'll change into something else. Robert, you make yourself comfortable," she said.

"I'm comfortable," the blind man said.

"I want you to feel comfortable in this house," she said.

"I am comfortable," the blind man said.

After she'd left the room, he and I listened to the weather report and then to the sports roundup. By that time, she'd been gone so long I didn't know if she was going to come back. I thought she might have gone to bed. I wished she'd come back downstairs. I didn't want to be left alone with a blind man. I asked him if he wanted another drink, and he said sure. Then I asked if he wanted to smoke some dope with me. I said I'd just rolled a number. I hadn't, but I planned to do so in about two shakes.

"I'll try some with you," he said.

"Damn right," I said. "That's the stuff."

I got our drinks and sat down on the sofa with him. Then I rolled us two fat numbers. I lit one and passed it. I brought it to his fingers. He took it and inhaled.

"Hold it as long as you can," I said. I could tell he didn't know the first thing.

My wife came back downstairs wearing her pink robe and her pink slippers.

"What do I smell?" she said.

"We thought we'd have us some cannabis," I said.

My wife gave me a savage look. Then she looked at the blind man and said, "Robert, I didn't know you smoked."

He said, "I do now, my dear. There's a first time for everything. But I don't feel anything yet."

"This stuff is pretty mellow," I said. "This stuff is mild. It's dope you can reason with," I said. "It doesn't mess you up."

"Not much it doesn't, bub," he said, and laughed.

My wife sat on the sofa between the blind man and me. I passed her the number. She took it and toked and then passed it back to me. "Which way is this going?" she said. Then she said, "I shouldn't be smoking this. I can hardly keep my eyes open as it is. That dinner did me in. I shouldn't have eaten so much."

"It was the strawberry pie," the blind man said. "That's what did it," he said, and he laughed his big laugh. Then he shook his head.

"There's more strawberry pie," I said.

"Do you want some more, Robert?" my wife said.

"Maybe in a little while," he said.

We gave our attention to the TV. My wife yawned again. She said, "Your bed is made up when you feel like going to bed, Robert. I know you must have had a long day. When you're ready to go to bed, say so." She pulled his arm. "Robert?"

75 He came to and said, "I've had a real nice time. This beats tapes, doesn't it?"

I said, "Coming at you," and I put the number between his fingers. He inhaled, held the smoke, and then let it go. It was like he'd been doing it since he was nine years old.

"Thanks, bub," he said. "But I think this is all for me. I think I'm beginning to feel it," he said. He held the burning roach out for my wife.

"Same here," she said. "Ditto. Me, too." She took the roach and passed it to me. "I may just sit here for a while between you two guys with my eyes closed. But don't let me bother you, okay? Either one of you. If it bothers you, say so. Otherwise, I may just sit here with my eyes closed until you're ready to go to bed," she said. "Your bed's made up, Robert, when you're ready. It's right next to our room at the top of the stairs. We'll show you up when you're ready. You wake me up now, you guys, if I fall asleep." She said that and then she closed her eyes and went to sleep.

The news program ended. I got up and changed the channel. I sat back down on the sofa. I wished my wife hadn't pooped out. Her head lay across the back of the sofa, her mouth open. She'd turned so that her robe had slipped away from her legs, exposing a juicy thigh. I reached to draw her robe back over her, and it was then that I glanced at the blind man. What the hell! I flipped the robe open again.

80 "You say when you want some strawberry pie," I said.

"I will," he said.

I said, "Are you tired? Do you want me to take you up to your bed? Are you ready to hit the hay?"

"Not yet," he said. "No, I'll stay up with you, bub. If that's all right. I'll stay up until you're ready to turn in. We haven't had a chance to talk. Know what I mean? I feel like me and her monopolized the evening." He lifted his beard and he let it fall. He picked up his cigarettes and his lighter.

"That's all right," I said. Then I said, "I'm glad for the company."

85 And I guess I was. Every night I smoked dope and stayed up as long as I could before I fell asleep. My wife and I hardly ever went to bed at the same time. When I did go to sleep, I had these dreams. Sometimes I'd wake up from one of them, my heart going crazy.

Something about the church and the Middle Ages was on the TV. Not your run-of-the-mill TV fare. I wanted to watch something else. I turned to the other channels. But there was nothing on them, either. So I turned back to the first channel and apologized.

"Bub, it's all right," the blind man said. "It's fine with me. Whatever you want to watch is okay. I'm always learning something. Learning never ends. It won't hurt me to learn something tonight. I got ears," he said.

We didn't say anything for a time. He was leaning forward with his head turned at me, his right ear aimed in the direction of the set. Very disconcerting. Now and then his eyelids drooped and then they snapped open again. Now and then he put his fingers into his beard and tugged, like he was thinking about something he was hearing on the television.

On the screen, a group of men wearing cowls was being set upon and tormented by men dressed in skeleton costumes and men dressed as devils. The men dressed as devils wore devil masks, horns, and long tails. This pageant was part of a procession. The Englishman who was narrating the thing said it took place in Spain once a year. I tried to explain to the blind man what was happening.

"Skeletons," he said. "I know about skeletons," he said, and he nodded.   90

The TV showed this one cathedral. Then there was a long, slow look at another one. Finally, the picture switched to the famous one in Paris, with its flying buttresses and its spires reaching up to the clouds. The camera pulled away to show the whole of the cathedral rising above the skyline.

There were times when the Englishman who was telling the thing would shut up, would simply let the camera move around over the cathedrals. Or else the camera would tour the countryside, men in fields walking behind oxen. I waited as long as I could. Then I felt I had to say something. I said, "They're showing the outside of this cathedral now. Gargoyles. Little statues carved to look like monsters. Now I guess they're in Italy. Yeah, they're in Italy. There's paintings on the walls of this one church."

"Are those fresco paintings, bub?" he asked, and he sipped from his drink.

I reached for my glass. But it was empty. I tried to remember what I could remember. "You're asking me are those frescoes?" I said. "That's a good question. I don't know."

The camera moved to a cathedral outside Lisbon. The differences in the Por-   95
tuguese cathedral compared with the French and Italian were not that great. But they were there. Mostly the interior stuff. Then something occurred to me, and I said, "Something has occurred to me. Do you have any idea what a cathedral is? What they look like, that is? Do you follow me? If somebody says cathedral to you, do you have any notion what they're talking about? Do you know the difference between that and a Baptist church, say?"

He let the smoke dribble from his mouth. "I know they took hundreds of workers fifty or a hundred years to build," he said. "I just heard the man say that, of course. I know generations of the same families worked on a cathedral. I heard him say that, too. The men who began their life's work on them, they never lived to see the completion of their work. In that wise, bub, they're no different from the rest of us, right?" He laughed. Then his eyelids drooped again. His head nodded. He seemed to be snoozing. Maybe he was imagining himself in Portugal. The TV was showing another cathedral now. This one was in Germany. The Englishman's voice droned on. "Cathedrals," the blind man said. He sat up and rolled his head back and forth. "If you want the truth, bub, that's about all I know. What I just said. What I heard him say. But maybe you could describe one to me? I wish you'd do it. I'd like that. If you want to know, I really don't have a good idea."

I stared hard at the shot of the cathedral on the TV. How could I even begin to describe it? But say my life depended on it. Say my life was being threatened by an insane guy who said I had to do it or else.

I stared some more at the cathedral before the picture flipped off into the countryside. There was no use. I turned to the blind man and said. "To begin with, they're very tall." I was looking around the room for clues. "They reach way up. Up and up. Toward the sky. They're so big, some of them, they have to have these supports. To help hold them up, so to speak. These supports are called buttresses. They remind me of viaducts, for some reason. But maybe you don't know viaducts, either?

Sometimes the cathedrals have devils and such carved into the front. Sometimes lords and ladies. Don't ask me why this is," I said.

He was nodding. The whole upper part of his body seemed to be moving back and forth.

100   "I'm not doing so good, am I?" I said.

He stopped nodding and leaned forward on the edge of the sofa. As he listened to me, he was running his fingers through his beard. I wasn't getting through to him, I could see that. But he waited for me to go on just the same. He nodded, like he was trying to encourage me. I tried to think what else to say. "They're really big," I said. "They're massive. They're built of stone. Marble, too, sometimes. In those olden days, when they built cathedrals, men wanted to be close to God. In those olden days, God was an important part of everyone's life. You could tell this from their cathedral-building. I'm sorry," I said, "but it looks like that's the best I can do for you. I'm just no good at it."

"That's all right, bub," the blind man said. "Hey, listen. I hope you don't mind my asking you. Can I ask you something? Let me ask you a simple question, yes or no. I'm just curious and there's no offense. You're my host. But let me ask if you are in any way religious? You don't mind my asking?"

I shook my head. He couldn't see that, though. A wink is the same as a nod to a blind man. "I guess I don't believe in it. In anything. Sometimes it's hard. You know what I'm saying?"

"Sure, I do," he said.

105   "Right," I said.

The Englishman was still holding forth. My wife sighed in her sleep. She drew a long breath and went on with her sleeping.

"You'll have to forgive me," I said. "But I can't tell you what a cathedral looks like. It just isn't in me to do it. I can't do any more than I've done."

The blind man sat very still, his head down, as he listened to me.

I said, "The truth is, cathedrals don't mean anything special to me. Nothing. Cathedrals. They're something to look at on late-night TV. That's all they are."

110   It was then that the blind man cleared his throat. He brought something up. He took a handkerchief from his back pocket. Then he said, "I get it, bub. It's okay. It happens. Don't worry about it," he said. "Hey, listen to me. Will you do me a favor? I got an idea. Why don't you find us some heavy paper? And a pen. We'll do something. We'll draw one together. Get us a pen and some heavy paper. Go on, bub, get the stuff," he said.

So I went upstairs. My legs felt like they didn't have any strength in them. They felt like they did after I'd done some running. In my wife's room, I looked around. I found some ballpoints in a little basket on her table. And then I tried to think where to look for the kind of paper he was talking about.

Downstairs, in the kitchen, I found a shopping bag with onion skins in the bottom of the bag. I emptied the bag and shook it. I brought it into the living room and sat down with it near his legs. I moved some things, smoothed the wrinkles from the bag, spread it out on the coffee table.

The blind man got down from the sofa and sat next to me on the carpet.

He ran his fingers over the paper. He went up and down the sides of the paper. The edges, even the edges. He fingered the corners.

115   "All right," he said. "All right, let's do her."

He found my hand, the hand with the pen. He closed his hand over my hand. "Go ahead, bub, draw," he said. "Draw. You'll see. I'll follow along with you. It'll be okay. Just begin now like I'm telling you. You'll see. Draw," the blind man said.

So I began. First I drew a box that looked like a house. It could have been the house I lived in. Then I put a roof on it. At either end of the roof, I drew spires. Crazy.

"Swell," he said. "Terrific. You're doing fine," he said. "Never thought anything like this could happen in your lifetime, did you, bub? Well, it's a strange life, we all know that. Go on now. Keep it up."

I put in windows with arches. I drew flying buttresses. I hung great doors. I couldn't stop. The TV station went off the air. I put down the pen and closed and opened my fingers. The blind man felt around over the paper. He moved the tips of his fingers over the paper, all over what I had drawn, and he nodded.

"Doing fine," the blind man said. 120

I took up the pen again, and he found my hand. I kept at it. I'm no artist. But I kept drawing just the same.

My wife opened up her eyes and gazed at us. She sat up on the sofa, her robe hanging open. She said, "What are you doing? Tell me, I want to know."

I didn't answer her.

The blind man said, "We're drawing a cathedral. Me and him are working on it. Press hard," he said to me. "That's right. That's good," he said. "Sure. You got it, bub. I can tell. You didn't think you could. But you can, can't you? You're cooking with gas now. You know what I'm saying? We're going to really have us something here in a minute. How's the old arm?" he said. "Put some people in there now. What's a cathedral without people?"

My wife said, "What's going on? Robert, what are you doing? What's going on?" 125

"It's all right," he said to her. "Close your eyes now," the blind man said to me. I did it. I closed them just like he said.

"Are they closed?" he said. "Don't fudge."

"They're closed," I said.

"Keep them that way," he said. He said, "Don't stop now. Draw." 130

So we kept on with it. His fingers rode my fingers as my hand went over the paper. It was like nothing else in my life up to now.

Then he said, "I think that's it. I think you got it," he said. "Take a look. What do you think?"

But I had my eyes closed. I thought I'd keep them that way for a little longer. I thought it was something I ought to do.

"Well?" he said. "Are you looking?"

My eyes were still closed. I was in my house. I knew that. But I didn't feel like 135 I was inside anything.

"It's really something," I said. [1981]

QUESTIONS

1. How does the narrator's style reveal his character?
2. What is the narrator's relationship to his wife? Is he jealous of the blind man? Has the narrator reason to be jealous?

3. Is there any special significance in the fact that the wife and the blind man correspond by tapes?
4. What is the blind man's motive for encouraging the narrator to draw a cathedral?
5. How has the narrator changed as a consequence of his experience?

RAYMOND CARVER

Errand

Chekhov. On the evening of March 22, 1897, he went to dinner in Moscow with his friend and confidant Alexei Suvorin. This Suvorin was a very rich newspaper and book publisher, a reactionary, a self-made man whose father was a private at the battle of Borodino. Like Chekhov, he was the grandson of a serf. They had that in common: each had peasant's blood in his veins. Otherwise, politically and temperamentally, they were miles apart. Nevertheless, Suvorin was one of Chekhov's few intimates, and Chekhov enjoyed his company.

Naturally, they went to the best restaurant in the city, a former town house called the Hermitage—a place where it could take hours, half the night even, to get through a ten-course meal that would, of course, include several wines, liqueurs, and coffee. Chekhov was impeccably dressed, as always—a dark suit and waistcoat, his usual pince-nez. He looked that night very much as he looks in the photographs taken of him during this period. He was relaxed, jovial. He shook hands with the maître d', and with a glance took in the large dining room. It was brilliantly illuminated by ornate chandeliers, the tables occupied by elegantly dressed men and women. Waiters came and went ceaselessly. He had just been seated across the table from Suvorin when suddenly, without warning, blood began gushing from his mouth. Suvorin and two waiters helped him to the gentlemen's room and tried to stanch the flow of blood with ice packs. Suvorin saw him back to his own hotel and had a bed prepared for Chekhov in one of the rooms of the suite. Later, after another hemorrhage, Chekhov allowed himself to be moved to a clinic that specialized in the treatment of tuberculosis and related respiratory infections. When Suvorin visited him there, Chekhov apologized for the "scandal" at the restaurant three nights earlier but continued to insist there was nothing seriously wrong. "He laughed and jested as usual," Suvorin noted in his diary, "while spitting blood into a large vessel."

Maria Chekhov, his younger sister, visited Chekhov in the clinic during the last days of March. The weather was miserable; a sleet storm was in progress, and frozen heaps of snow lay everywhere. It was hard for her to wave down a carriage to take her to the hospital. By the time she arrived she was filled with dread and anxiety.

"Anton Pavlovich lay on his back," Maria wrote in her *Memoirs*. "He was not allowed to speak. After greeting him, I went over to the table to hide my emotions." There, among bottles of champagne, jars of caviar, bouquets of flowers from well-wishers, she saw something that terrified her: a freehand drawing, obviously done by a specialist in these matters, of Chekhov's lungs. It was the kind of sketch a doctor often makes in order to show his patient what he thinks is taking place. The lungs were outlined in blue, but the upper parts were filled in with red. "I realized they were diseased," Maria wrote.

Leo Tolstoy was another visitor. The hospital staff were awed to find themselves in the presence of the country's greatest writer. The most famous man in Russia? Of course they had to let him in to see Chekhov, even though "nonessential" visitors were forbidden. With much obsequiousness on the part of the nurses and resident doctors, the bearded, fierce-looking old man was shown into Chekhov's room. Despite his low opinion of Chekhov's abilities as a playwright (Tolstoy felt the plays were static and lacking in any moral vision. "Where do your characters take you?" he once demanded of Chekhov. "From the sofa to the junk room and back."), Tolstoy liked Chekhov's short stories. Furthermore, and quite simply, he loved the man. He told Gorky, "What a beautiful, magnificent man: modest and quiet, like a girl. He even walks like a girl. He's simply wonderful." And Tolstoy wrote in his journal (everyone kept a journal or a diary in those days), "I am glad I love . . . Chekhov."

Tolstoy removed his woollen scarf and bearskin coat, then lowered himself into a chair next to Chekhov's bed. Never mind that Chekhov was taking medication and not permitted to talk, much less carry on a conversation. He had to listen, amazedly, as the Count began to discourse on his theories of the immortality of the soul. Concerning that visit, Chekhov later wrote, "Tolstoy assumes that all of us (humans and animals alike) will live on in a principle (such as reason or love) the essence and goals of which are a mystery to us. . . . I have no use for that kind of immortality. I don't understand it, and Lev Nikolayevich [Tolstoy] was astonished I didn't."

Nevertheless, Chekhov was impressed with the solicitude shown by Tolstoy's visit. But, unlike Tolstoy, Chekhov didn't believe in an afterlife and never had. He didn't believe in anything that couldn't be apprehended by one or more of his five senses. And as far as his outlook on life and writing went, he once told someone that he lacked "a political, religious, and philosophical world view. I change it every month, so I'll have to limit myself to the description of how my heroes love, marry, give birth, die, and how they speak."

Earlier, before his t.b. was diagnosed, Chekhov had remarked, "When a peasant has consumption, he says, 'There's nothing I can do. I'll go off in the spring with the melting of the snows.'" (Chekhov himself died in the summer, during a heat wave.) But once Chekhov's own tuberculosis was discovered he continually tried to minimize the seriousness of his condition. To all appearances, it was as if he felt, right up to the end, that he might be able to throw off the disease as he would a lingering catarrh. Well into his final days, he spoke with seeming conviction of the possibility of an improvement. In fact, in a letter written shortly before his end, he went so far as to tell his sister that he was "getting fat" and felt much better now that he was in Badenweiler.

Badenweiler is a spa and resort city in the western area of the Black Forest, not far from Basel. The Vosges are visible from nearly anywhere in the city, and in those days the air was pure and invigorating. Russians had been going there for years to soak in the hot mineral baths and promenade on the boulevards. In June, 1904, Chekhov went there to die.

Earlier that month, he'd made a difficult journey by train from Moscow to Berlin. He traveled with his wife, the actress Olga Knipper, a woman he'd met in 1898 during rehearsals for "The Seagull." Her contemporaries describe her as an excellent actress. She was talented, pretty, and almost ten years younger than the playwright. Chekhov had been immediately attracted to her, but was slow to act on his feelings. As always, he preferred a flirtation to marriage. Finally, after a three-year courtship involving many separations, letters, and the inevitable misunderstandings, they were at last married, in a private ceremony in Moscow, on May 25, 1901. Chekhov was enormously happy. He called Olga his "pony," and sometimes "dog" or "puppy." He was also fond of addressing her as "little turkey" or simply as "my joy."

In Berlin, Chekhov consulted with a renowned specialist in pulmonary disorders, a Dr. Karl Ewald. But, according to an eyewitness, after the doctor examined Chekhov he threw up his hands and left the room without a word. Chekhov was too far gone for help: this Dr. Ewald was furious with himself for not being able to work miracles, and with Chekhov for being so ill.

A Russian journalist happened to visit the Chekhovs at their hotel and sent back this dispatch to his editor: "Chekhov's days are numbered. He seems mortally ill, is terribly thin, coughs all the time, gasps for breath at the slightest movement, and is running a high temperature." This same journalist saw the Chekhovs off at Potsdam Station when they boarded their train for Badenweiler. According to his account, "Chekhov had trouble making his way up the small staircase at the station. He had to sit down for several minutes to catch his breath." In fact, it was painful for Chekhov to move: his legs ached continually and his insides hurt. The disease had attacked his intestines and spinal cord. At this point he had less than a month to live. When Chekhov spoke of his condition now, it was, according to Olga, "with an almost reckless indifference."

Dr. Schwöhrer was one of the many Badenweiler physicians who earned a good living by treating the well-to-do who came to the spa seeking relief from various maladies. Some of his patients were ill and infirm, others simply old and hypochondriacal. But Chekhov's was a special case: he was clearly beyond help and in his last days. He was also very famous. Even Dr. Schwöhrer knew his name: he'd read some of Chekhov's stories in a German magazine. When he examined the writer early in June, he voiced his appreciation of Chekhov's art but kept his medical opinions to himself. Instead, he prescribed a diet of cocoa, oatmeal drenched in butter, and strawberry tea. This last was supposed to help Chekhov sleep at night.

On June 13, less than three weeks before he died, Chekhov wrote a letter to his mother in which he told her his health was on the mend. In it he said, "It's likely that I'll be completely cured in a week." Who knows why he said this? What could he have been thinking? He was a doctor himself, and he knew better. He was dying, it was as simple and as unavoidable as that. Nevertheless, he sat out on the balcony of his hotel room and read railway timetables. He asked for information on sailings of boats bound for Odessa from Marseilles. But he *knew*. At this stage he had to have known. Yet in one of the last letters he ever wrote he told his sister he was growing stronger by the day.

He no longer had any appetite for literary work, and hadn't for a long time. In fact, he had very nearly failed to complete *The Cherry Orchard* the year before. Writing that play was the hardest thing he'd ever done in his life. Toward the end, he was able to manage only six or seven lines a day. "I've started losing heart," he wrote Olga. "I feel I'm finished as a writer, and every sentence strikes me as worthless and of no use whatever." But he didn't stop. He finished his play in October, 1903. It was the last thing he ever wrote, except for letters and a few entries in his notebook.

A little after midnight on July 2, 1904, Olga sent someone to fetch Dr. Schwöhrer. It was an emergency: Chekhov was delirious. Two young Russians on holiday happened to have the adjacent room, and Olga hurried next door to explain what was happening.

15

One of the youths was in his bed asleep, but the other was still awake, smoking and reading. He left the hotel at a run to find Dr. Schwöhrer. "I can still hear the sound of the gravel under his shoes in the silence of that stifling July night," Olga wrote later on in her memoirs. Chekhov was hallucinating, talking about sailors, and there were snatches of something about the Japanese. "You don't put ice on an empty stomach," he said when she tried to place an ice pack on his chest.

Dr. Schwöhrer arrived and unpacked his bag, all the while keeping his gaze fastened on Chekhov, who lay gasping in the bed. The sick man's pupils were dilated and his temples glistened with sweat. Dr. Schwöhrer's face didn't register anything. He was not an emotional man, but he knew Chekhov's end was near. Still, he was a doctor, sworn to do his utmost, and Chekhov held on to life, however tenuously. Dr. Schwöhrer prepared a hypodermic and administered an injection of camphor, something that was supposed to speed up the heart. But the injection didn't help—nothing, of course, could have helped. Nevertheless, the doctor made known to Olga his intention of sending for oxygen. Suddenly, Chekhov roused himself, became lucid, and said quietly, "What's the use? Before it arrives I'll be a corpse."

Dr. Schwöhrer pulled on his big moustache and stared at Chekhov. The writer's cheeks were sunken and gray, his complexion waxen; his breath was raspy. Dr. Schwöhrer knew the time could be reckoned in minutes. Without a word, without conferring with Olga, he went over to an alcove where there was a telephone on the wall. He read the instructions for using the device. If he activated it by holding his finger on a button and turning a handle on the side of the phone, he could reach the lower regions of the hotel—the kitchen. He picked up the receiver, held it to his ear, and did as the instructions told him. When someone finally answered, Dr. Schwöhrer ordered a bottle of the hotel's best champagne. "How many glasses?" he was asked. "Three glasses!" the doctor shouted into the mouthpiece. "And hurry, do you hear?" It was one of those rare moments of inspiration that can easily enough be overlooked later on, because the action is so entirely appropriate it seems inevitable.

The champagne was brought to the door by a tired-looking young man whose blond hair was standing up. The trousers of his uniform were wrinkled, the creases gone, and in his haste he'd missed a loop while buttoning his jacket. His appearance was that of someone who'd been resting (slumped in a chair, say, dozing a little), when off in the distance the phone had clamored in the early-morning hours—great God in Heaven!—and the next thing he knew he was being shaken awake by a superior and told to deliver a bottle of Moët to Room 211. "And hurry, do you hear?"

20   The young man entered the room carrying a silver ice bucket with the champagne in it and a silver tray with three cut-crystal glasses. He found a place on the table for the bucket and glasses, all the while craning his neck, trying to see into the other room, where someone panted ferociously for breath. It was a dreadful, harrowing sound, and the young man lowered his chin into his collar and turned away as the ratchety breathing worsened. Forgetting himself, he stared out the open window toward the darkened city. Then this big imposing man with a thick moustache pressed some coins into his hand—a large tip, by the feel of it—and suddenly the young man saw the door open. He took some steps and found himself on the landing, where he opened his hand and looked at the coins in amazement.

Methodically, the way he did everything, the doctor went about the business of working the cork out of the bottle. He did it in such a way as to minimize, as much as possible, the festive explosion. He poured three glasses and, out of habit, pushed the cork back into the neck of the bottle. He then took the glasses of champagne over to the bed. Olga momentarily released her grip on Chekhov's hand—a hand, she said later, that burned her fingers. She arranged another pillow behind his head. Then she put the cool glass of champagne against Chekhov's palm and made sure his fingers closed around the stem. They exchanged looks—Chekhov, Olga, Dr. Schwöhrer. They didn't touch glasses. There was no toast. What on earth was there to drink to? To death? Chekhov summoned his remaining strength and said, "It's been so long since I've had champagne." He brought the glass to his lips and drank. In a minute or two Olga took the empty glass from his hand and set it on the nightstand. Then Chekhov turned onto his side. He closed his eyes and sighed. A minute later, his breathing stopped.

Dr. Schwöhrer picked up Chekhov's hand from the bedsheet. He held his fingers to Chekhov's wrist and drew a gold watch from his vest pocket, opening the lid of the watch as he did so. The second hand on the watch moved slowly, very slowly. He let it move around the face of the watch three times while he waited for signs of a pulse. It was three o'clock in the morning and still sultry in the room. Badenweiler was in the grip of its worst heat wave in years. All the windows in both rooms stood open, but there was no sign of a breeze. A large, black-winged moth flew through a window and banged wildly against the electric lamp. Dr. Schwöhrer let go of Chekhov's wrist. "It's over," he said. He closed the lid of his watch and returned it to his vest pocket.

At once Olga dried her eyes and set about composing herself. She thanked the doctor for coming. He asked if she wanted some medication—laudanum, perhaps, or a few drops of valerian. She shook her head. She did have one request, though: before the authorities were notified and the newspapers found out, before the time came when Chekhov was no longer in her keeping, she wanted to be alone with him for a while. Could the doctor help with this? Could he withhold, for a while anyway, news of what had just occurred?

Dr. Schwöhrer stroked his moustache with the back of a finger. Why not? After all, what difference would it make to anyone whether this matter became known now or a few hours from now? The only detail that remained was to fill out a death certificate, and this could be done at his office later on in the morning, after he'd slept a few hours. Dr. Schwöhrer nodded his agreement and prepared to leave. He murmured a few words of condolence. Olga inclined her head. "An honor," Dr. Schwöhrer said. He picked up his bag and left the room and, for that matter, history.

It was at this moment that the cork popped out of the champagne bottle; foam spilled down onto the table. Olga went back to Chekhov's bedside. She sat on a footstool, holding his hand, from time to time stroking his face. "There were no human voices, no everyday sounds," she wrote. "There was only beauty, peace, and the grandeur of death." 25

She stayed with Chekhov until daybreak, when thrushes began to call from the garden below. Then came the sound of tables and chairs being moved about down there. Before long, voices carried up to her. It was then a knock sounded at the door. Of course she thought it must be an official of some sort—the medical examiner, say, or someone from the police who had questions to ask and forms for her to fill out, or maybe, just maybe, it could be Dr. Schwöhrer returning with a mortician to render assistance in embalming and transporting Chekhov's remains back to Russia.

But, instead, it was the same blond young man who'd brought the champagne a few hours earlier. This time, however, his uniform trousers were neatly pressed, with stiff creases in front, and every button on his snug green jacket was fastened. He seemed quite another person. Not only was he wide awake but his plump cheeks were smooth-shaven, his hair was in place, and he appeared anxious to please. He was holding a porcelain vase with three long-stemmed yellow roses. He presented these to Olga with a smart click of his heels. She stepped back and let him into the room. He was there, he said, to collect the glasses, ice bucket, and tray, yes. But he also wanted to say that, because of the extreme heat, breakfast would be served in the garden this morning. He hoped this weather wasn't too bothersome; he apologized for it.

The woman seemed distracted. While he talked, she turned her eyes away and looked down at something in the carpet. She crossed her arms and held her elbows. Meanwhile, still holding his vase, waiting for a sign, the young man took in the details of the room. Bright sunlight flooded through the open windows. The room was tidy and seemed undisturbed, almost untouched. No garments were flung over chairs, no shoes, stockings, braces, or stays were in evidence, no open suitcases. In short, there was no clutter, nothing but the usual heavy pieces of hotel-room furniture. Then, be-cause the woman was still looking down, he looked down, too, and at once spied a cork near the toe of his shoe. The woman did not see it—she was looking somewhere else. The young man wanted to bend over and pick up the cork, but he was still holding the roses and was afraid of seeming to intrude even more by drawing any further atten-tion to himself. Reluctantly, he left the cork where it was and raised his eyes. Every-thing was in order except for the uncorked, half-empty bottle of champagne that stood alongside two crystal glasses over on the little table. He cast his gaze about once more. Through an open door he saw that the third glass was in the bedroom, on the night-stand. But someone still occupied the bed! He couldn't see a face, but the figure under the covers lay perfectly motionless and quiet. He noted the figure and looked else-where. Then, for a reason he couldn't understand, a feeling of uneasiness took hold of him. He cleared his throat and moved his weight to the other leg. The woman still didn't look up or break her silence. The young man felt his cheeks grow warm. It oc-curred to him, quite without his having thought it through, that he should perhaps sug-gest an alternative to breakfast in the garden. He coughed, hoping to focus the woman's attention, but she didn't look at him. The distinguished foreign guests could, he said, take breakfast in their rooms this morning if they wished. The young man (his name hasn't survived, and it's likely he perished in the Great War) said he would be happy to bring up a tray. Two trays, he added, glancing uncertainly once again in the direc-tion of the bedroom.

He fell silent and ran a finger around the inside of his collar. He didn't understand. He wasn't even sure the woman had been listening. He didn't know what else to do now; he was still holding the vase. The sweet odor of the roses filled his nostrils and inexplicably caused a pang of regret. The entire time he'd been waiting, the woman had apparently been lost in thought. It was as if all the while he'd been standing there, talking, shifting his weight, holding his flowers, she had been someplace else, some-where far from Badenweiler. But now she came back to herself, and her face assumed another expression. She raised her eyes, looked at him, and then shook her head. She seemed to be struggling to understand what on earth this young man could be doing there in the room holding a vase with three yellow roses. Flowers? She hadn't ordered flowers.

30   The moment passed. She went over to her handbag and scooped up some coins. She drew out a number of banknotes as well. The young man touched his lips with his tongue; another large tip was forthcoming, but for what? What did she want him to do? He'd never before waited on such guests. He cleared his throat once more.

No breakfast, the woman said. Not yet, at any rate. Breakfast wasn't the important thing this morning. She required something else. She needed him to go out and bring back a mortician. Did he understand her? Herr Chekhov was dead, you see. *Comprenez-vous*? Young man? Anton Chekhov was dead. Now listen carefully to me, she said. She wanted him to go downstairs and ask someone at the front desk where he could go to find the most respected mortician in the city. Someone reliable, who took great pains in his work and whose manner was appropriately reserved. A mortician, in short, worthy of a great artist. Here, she said, and pressed the money on him. Tell them downstairs that I have specifically requested you to perform this duty for me. Are you listening? Do you understand what I'm saying to you?

The young man grappled to take in what she was saying. He chose not to look again in the direction of the other room. He had sensed that something was not right. He became aware of his heart beating rapidly under his jacket, and he felt perspiration break out on his forehead. He didn't know where he should turn his eyes. He wanted to put the vase down.

Please do this for me, the woman said. I'll remember you with gratitude. Tell them downstairs that I insist. Say that. But don't call any unnecessary attention to yourself or to the situation. Just say that this is necessary, that I request it—and that's all. Do you hear me? Nod if you understand. Above all, don't raise an alarm. Everything else, all the rest, the commotion—that'll come soon enough. The worst is over. Do we understand each other?

The young man's face had grown pale. He stood rigid, clasping the vase. He managed to nod his head.

After securing permission to leave the hotel he was to proceed quietly and resolutely, though without any unbecoming haste, to the mortician's. He was to behave exactly as if he were engaged on a very important errand, nothing more. He *was* engaged on an important errand, she said. And if it would help keep his movements purposeful he should imagine himself as someone moving down the busy sidewalk carrying in his arms a porcelain vase of roses that he had to deliver to an important man. (She spoke quietly, almost confidentially, as if to a relative or a friend.) He could even tell himself that the man he was going to see was expecting him, was perhaps impatient for him to arrive with his flowers. Nevertheless, the young man was not to become excited and run, or otherwise break his stride. Remember the vase he was carrying! He was to walk briskly, comporting himself at all times in as dignified a manner as possible. He should keep walking until he came to the mortician's house and stood before the door. He would then raise the brass knocker and let it fall, once, twice, three times. In a minute the mortician himself would answer.

This mortician would be in his forties, no doubt, or maybe early fifties—bald, solidly built, wearing steel-frame spectacles set very low on his nose. He would be modest, unassuming, a man who would ask only the most direct and necessary questions. An apron. Probably he would be wearing an apron. He might even be wiping his hands on a dark towel while he listened to what was being said. There'd be a faint whiff of formaldehyde on his clothes. But it was all right, and the young man shouldn't worry. He was nearly a grownup now and shouldn't be frightened or repelled by any of this. The mortician would hear him out. He was a man of restraint and bearing, this mortician, someone who could help allay people's fears in this situation, not increase them. Long ago he'd acquainted himself with death in all its various guises and forms; death held no surprises for him any longer, no hidden secrets. It was this man whose services were required this morning.

The mortician takes the vase of roses. Only once while the young man is speaking does the mortician betray the least flicker of interest, or indicate that he's heard anything out of the ordinary. But the one time the young man mentions the name of the deceased, the mortician's eyebrows rise just a little. Chekhov, you say? Just a minute, and I'll be with you.

Do you understand what I'm saying, Olga said to the young man. Leave the glasses. Don't worry about them. Forget about crystal wineglasses and such. Leave the room as it is. Everything is ready now. We're ready. Will you go?

But at that moment the young man was thinking of the cork still resting near the toe of his shoe. To retrieve it he would have to bend over, still gripping the vase. He would do this. He leaned over. Without looking down, he reached out and closed it into his hand.   [1987]

QUESTIONS

1. Who is the protagonist of the story? What purpose do the supporting characters serve?

2. This story seems to be built in two parts—the part before Chekhov's death and the part after his death. How do the two parts relate and form a unified story?

3. Has Carver made Chekhov a sympathetic character? Does he need to?

4. How do the widow's instructions to the waiter help us to feel the quiet she feels?

5. Why does the waiter pick up the cork?

RESPONSES

1. Carver was considered the best writer of short fiction of his generation, and he was ill with cancer when he wrote this story. See the Context essay "About the Story 'Errand.'" Research Carver's life and attempt a biographical/psychological approach to the story.

2. Compare this story to Chekhov's stories. How is Carver's subject and approach to the subject similar to Chekhov's? How is it different?

A Small, Good Thing

Saturday afternoon she drove to the bakery in the shopping center. After looking through a loose-leaf binder with photographs of cakes taped onto the pages, she ordered chocolate, the child's favorite. The cake she chose was decorated with a space ship and launching pad under a sprinkling of white stars, and a planet made of red frosting at the other end. His name, SCOTTY, would be in green letters beneath the planet. The baker, who was an older man with a thick neck, listened without saying anything when she told him the child would be eight years old next Monday. The baker wore a white apron that looked like a smock. Straps cut under his arms, went around in back and then to the front again, where they were secured under his heavy waist. He wiped his hands on his apron as he listened to her. He kept his eyes down on the photographs and let her talk. He let her take her time. He'd just come to work and he'd be there all night, baking, and he was in no real hurry.

She gave the baker her name, Ann Weiss, and her telephone number. The cake would be ready on Monday morning, just out of the oven, in plenty of time for the child's party that afternoon. The baker was not jolly. There were no pleasantries between them, just the minimum exchange of words, the necessary information. He made her feel uncomfortable, and she didn't like that. While he was bent over the counter with the pencil in his hand, she studied his coarse features and wondered if he'd ever done anything else with his life besides be a baker. She was a mother and thirty-three years old, and it seemed to her that everyone, especially someone the baker's age—a man old enough to be her father—must have children who'd gone through this special time of cakes and birthday parties. There must be that between them, she thought. But he was abrupt with her—not rude, just abrupt. She gave up trying to make friends with him. She looked into the back of the bakery and could see a long, heavy wooden table with aluminum pie pans stacked at one end; and beside the table a metal container filled with empty racks. There was an enormous oven. A radio was playing country-Western music.

The baker finished printing the information on the special order card and closed up the binder. He looked at her and said, "Monday morning." She thanked him and drove home.

On Monday morning, the birthday boy was walking to school with another boy. They were passing a bag of potato chips back and forth and the birthday boy was trying to find out what his friend intended to give him for his birthday that afternoon. Without looking, the birthday boy stepped off the curb at an intersection and was immediately knocked down by a car. He fell on his side with his head in the gutter and his legs out in the road. His eyes were closed, but his legs moved back and forth as if he were trying to climb over something. His friend dropped the potato chips and started to cry. The car had gone a hundred feet or so and stopped in the middle of the road. The man in the driver's seat looked back over his shoulder. He waited until the boy got unsteadily to his feet. The boy wobbled a little. He looked dazed, but okay. The driver put the car into gear and drove away.

5   The birthday boy didn't cry, but he didn't have anything to say about anything either. He wouldn't answer when his friend asked him what it felt like to be hit by a car. He walked home, and his friend went on to school. But after the birthday boy was inside his house and was telling his mother about it—she sitting beside him on the sofa, holding his hands in her lap, saying, "Scotty, honey, are you sure you feel all right, baby?" thinking she would call the doctor anyway—he suddenly lay back on the sofa, closed his eyes, and went limp. When she couldn't wake him up, she hurried to the telephone and called her husband at work. Howard told her to remain calm, remain calm, and then he called an ambulance for the child and left for the hospital himself.

Of course, the birthday party was canceled. The child was in the hospital with a mild concussion and suffering from shock. There'd been vomiting, and his lungs had taken in fluid which needed pumping out that afternoon. Now he simply seemed to be in a very deep sleep—but no coma, Dr. Francis had emphasized, no coma, when he saw the alarm in the parents' eyes. At eleven o'clock that night, when the boy seemed to be resting comfortably enough after the many X-rays and the lab work, and it was just a matter of his waking up and coming around, Howard left the hospital. He and Ann had been at the hospital with the child since that afternoon, and he was going home for a short while to bathe and change clothes. "I'll be back in an hour," he said. She nodded. "It's fine," she said. "I'll be right here." He kissed her on the forehead, and they touched hands. She sat in the chair beside the bed and looked at the child. She was waiting for him to wake up and be all right. Then she could begin to relax.

Howard drove home from the hospital. He took the wet, dark streets very fast, then caught himself and slowed down. Until now, his life had gone smoothly and to his satisfaction—college, marriage, another year of college for the advanced degree in business, a junior partnership in an investment firm. Fatherhood. He was happy and, so far, lucky—he knew that. His parents were still living, his brothers and his sister were established, his friends from college had gone out to take their places in the world. So far, he had kept away from any real harm, from those forces he knew existed and that could cripple or bring down a man if the luck went bad, if things suddenly turned. He pulled into the driveway and parked. His left leg began to tremble. He sat in the car for a minute and tried to deal with the present situation in a rational manner. Scotty had been hit by a car and was in the hospital, but he was going to be all right. Howard closed his eyes and ran his hand over his face. He got out of the car and went up to the front door. The dog was barking inside the house. The telephone rang and rang while he unlocked the door and fumbled for the light switch. He shouldn't have left the hospital, he shouldn't have. "Goddamn it!" he said. He picked up the receiver and said, "I just walked in the door!"

"There's a cake here that wasn't picked up," the voice on the other end of the line said.

"What are you saying?" Howard asked.

"A cake," the voice said. "A sixteen-dollar cake." 10

Howard held the receiver against his ear, trying to understand. "I don't know anything about a cake," he said. "Jesus, what are you talking about?"

"Don't hand me that," the voice said.

Howard hung up the telephone. He went into the kitchen and poured himself some whiskey. He called the hospital. But the child's condition remained the same; he was still sleeping and nothing had changed there. While water poured into the tub, Howard lathered his face and shaved. He'd just stretched out in the tub and closed his eyes when the telephone rang again. He hauled himself out, grabbed a towel, and hurried through the house, saying, "Stupid, stupid," for having left the hospital. But when he picked up the receiver and shouted, "Hello!" there was no sound at the other end of the line. Then the caller hung up.

He arrived back at the hospital a little after midnight. Ann still sat in the chair beside the bed. She looked up at Howard, and then she looked back at the child. The child's eyes stayed closed, the head was still wrapped in bandages. His breathing was quiet and regular. From an apparatus over the bed hung a bottle of glucose with a tube running from the bottle to the boy's arm.

"How is he?" Howard said. "What's all this?" waving at the glucose and the tube. 15

"Dr. Francis's orders," she said. "He needs nourishment. He needs to keep up his strength. Why doesn't he wake up, Howard? I don't understand, if he's all right."

Howard put his hand against the back of her head. He ran his fingers through her hair. "He's going to be all right. He'll wake up in a little while. Dr. Francis knows what's what."

After a time, he said, "Maybe you should go home and get some rest. I'll stay here. Just don't put up with this creep who keeps calling. Hang up right away."

"Who's calling?" she asked.

"I don't know who, just somebody with nothing better to do than call up people. 20 You go on now."

She shook her head. "No," she said, "I'm fine."

"Really," he said. "Go home for a while, and then come back and spell me in the morning. It'll be all right. What did Dr. Francis say? He said Scotty's going to be all right. We don't have to worry. He's just sleeping now, that's all."

A nurse pushed the door open. She nodded at them as she went to the bedside. She took the left arm out from under the covers and put her fingers on the wrist, found the pulse, then consulted her watch. In a little while, she put the arm back under the covers and moved to the foot of the bed, where she wrote something on a clipboard attached to the bed.

"How is he?" Ann said. Howard's hand was a weight on her shoulder. She was aware of the pressure from his fingers.

"He's stable," the nurse said. Then she said, "Doctor will be in again shortly. Doc- 25 tor's back in the hospital. He's making rounds right now."

"I was saying maybe she'd want to go home and get a little rest," Howard said. "After the doctor comes," he said.

"She could do that," the nurse said. "I think you should both feel free to do that, if you wish." The nurse was a big Scandinavian woman with blond hair. There was the trace of an accent in her speech.

"We'll see what the doctor says," Ann said. "I want to talk to the doctor. I don't think he should keep sleeping like this. I don't think that's a good sign." She brought her hand up to her eyes and let her head come forward a little. Howard's grip tightened on her shoulder, and then his hand moved up to her neck, where his fingers began to knead the muscles there.

"Dr. Francis will be here in a few minutes," the nurse said. Then she left the room.

30 Howard gazed at his son for a time, the small chest quietly rising and falling under the covers. For the first time since the terrible minutes after Ann's telephone call to him at his office, he felt a genuine fear starting in his limbs. He began shaking his head. Scotty was fine, but instead of sleeping at home in his own bed, he was in a hospital bed with bandages around his head and a tube in his arm. But this help was what he needed right now.

Dr. Francis came in and shook hands with Howard, though they'd just seen each other a few hours before. Ann got up from the chair. "Doctor?"

"Ann," he said and nodded. "Let's just first see how he's doing," the doctor said. He moved to the side of the bed and took the boy's pulse. He peeled back one eyelid and then the other. Howard and Ann stood beside the doctor and watched. Then the doctor turned back the covers and listened to the boy's heart and lungs with his stethoscope. He pressed his fingers here and there on the abdomen. When he was finished, he went to the end of the bed and studied the chart. He noted the time, scribbling something on the chart, and then looked at Howard and Ann.

"Doctor, how is he?" Howard said. "What's the matter with him exactly?"

"Why doesn't he wake up?" Ann said.

35 The doctor was a handsome, big-shouldered man with a tanned face. He wore a three-piece blue suit, a striped tie, and ivory cufflinks. His gray hair was combed along the sides of his head, and he looked as if he had just come from a concert. "He's all right," the doctor said. "Nothing to shout about, he could be better, I think. But he's all right. Still, I wish he'd wake up. He should wake up pretty soon." The doctor looked at the boy again. "We'll know some more in a couple of hours, after the results of a few more tests are in. But he's all right, believe me, except for the hairline fracture of the skull. He does have that."

"Oh, no," Ann said.

"And a bit of a concussion, as I said before. Of course, you know he's in shock," the doctor said. "Sometimes you see this in shock cases. This sleeping."

"But he's out of any real danger?" Howard said. "You said before he's not in a coma. You wouldn't call this a coma, then—would you, doctor?" Howard waited. He looked at the doctor.

"No, I don't want to call it a coma," the doctor said and glanced over at the boy once more. "He's just in a very deep sleep. It's a restorative measure the body is taking on its own. He's out of any real danger, I'd say that for certain, yes. But we'll know more when he wakes up and the other tests are in," the doctor said.

40 "It's a coma," Ann said. "Of sorts."

"It's not a coma yet, not exactly," the doctor said. "I wouldn't want to call it coma. Not yet, anyway. He's suffered shock. In shock cases, this kind of reaction is common enough; it's a temporary reaction to bodily trauma. Coma. Well, coma is a deep, prolonged unconsciousness, something that could go on for days, or weeks even. Scotty's not in that area, not as far as we can tell. I'm certain his condition will show improvement by morning. I'm betting that it will. We'll know more when he wakes up, which shouldn't be long now. Of course, you may do as you like, stay here or go home for a time. But by all means feel free to leave the hospital for a while if you want. This is not easy, I know." The doctor gazed at the boy again, watching him, and then he turned to Ann and said, "You try not to worry, little mother. Believe me, we're doing all that can be done. It's just a question of a little more time now." He nodded at her, shook hands with Howard again, and then he left the room.

Ann put her hands over the child's forehead. "At least he doesn't have a fever," she said. Then she said, "My God, he feels so cold, though. Howard? Is he supposed to feel like this? Feel his head."

Howard touched the child's temples. His own breathing had slowed. "I think he's supposed to feel this way right now," he said. "He's in shock, remember? That's what the doctor said. The doctor was just in here. He would have said something if Scotty wasn't okay."

Ann stood there a while longer, working her lip with her teeth. Then she moved over to her chair and sat down.

Howard sat in the chair next to her chair. They looked at each other. He wanted to say something else and reassure her, but he was afraid, too. He took her hand and put it in his lap, and this made him feel better, her hand being there. He picked up her hand and squeezed it. Then he just held her hand. They sat like that for a while, watching the boy and not talking. From time to time, he squeezed her hand. Finally, she took her hand away. 45

"I've been praying," she said.

He nodded.

She said, "I almost thought I'd forgotten how, but it came back to me. All I had to do was close my eyes and say, 'Please God, help us—help Scotty,' and the rest was easy. The words were right there. Maybe if you prayed, too," she said to him.

"I've already prayed," he said. "I prayed this afternoon—yesterday afternoon, I mean—after you called, while I was driving to the hospital. I've been praying," he said.

"That's good," she said. For the first time, she felt they were together in it, this trouble. She realized with a start that, until now, it had only been happening to her and to Scotty. She hadn't let Howard into it, though he was there and needed all along. She felt glad to be his wife. 50

The same nurse came in and took the boy's pulse again and checked the flow from the bottle hanging above the bed.

In an hour, another doctor came in. He said his name was Parsons, from Radiology. He had a bushy mustache. He was wearing loafers, a Western shirt, and a pair of jeans.

"We're going to take him downstairs for more pictures," he told them. "We need to do some more pictures, and we want to do a scan."

"What's that?" Ann said. "A scan?" She stood between this new doctor and the bed. "I thought you'd already taken all your X-rays."

"I'm afraid we need some more," he said. "Nothing to be alarmed about. We just need some more pictures, and we want to do a brain scan on him." 55

"My God," Ann said.

"It's perfectly normal procedure in cases like this," this new doctor said. "We just need to find out for sure why he isn't back awake yet. It's normal medical procedure, and nothing to be alarmed about. We'll be taking him down in a few minutes," this doctor said.

In a little while, two orderlies came into the room with a gurney. They were black-haired, dark-complexioned men in white uniforms, and they said a few words to each other in a foreign tongue as they unhooked the boy from the tube and moved him from his bed to the gurney. Then they wheeled him from the room. Howard and Ann got on the same elevator. Ann gazed at the child. She closed her eyes as the elevator began its descent. The orderlies stood at either end of the gurney without saying anything, though once one of the men made a comment to the other in their own language, and the other man nodded slowly in response.

Later that morning, just as the sun was beginning to lighten the windows in the waiting room outside the X-ray department, they brought the boy out and moved him back up to his room. Howard and Ann rode up on the elevator with him once more, and once more they took up their places beside the bed.

60   They waited all day, but still the boy did not wake up. Occasionally, one of them would leave the room to go downstairs to the cafeteria to drink coffee and then, as if suddenly remembering and feeling guilty, get up from the table and hurry back to the room. Dr. Francis came again that afternoon and examined the boy once more and then left after telling them he was coming along and could wake up at any minute now. Nurses, different nurses from the night before, came in from time to time. Then a young woman from the lab knocked and entered the room. She wore white slacks and a white blouse and carried a little tray of things which she put on the stand beside the bed. Without a word to them, she took blood from the boy's arm. Howard closed his eyes as the woman found the right place on the boy's arm and pushed the needle in.

"I don't understand this," Ann said to the woman.

"Doctor's orders," the young woman said. "I do what I'm told. They say draw that one, I draw. What's wrong with him, anyway?" she said. "He's a sweetie."

"He was hit by a car," Howard said. "A hit-and-run."

The young woman shook her head and looked again at the boy. Then she took her tray and left the room.

65   "Why won't he wake up?" Ann said. "Howard? I want some answers from these people."

Howard didn't say anything. He sat down again in the chair and crossed one leg over the other. He rubbed his face. He looked at his son and then he settled back in the chair, closed his eyes, and went to sleep.

Ann walked to the window and looked out at the parking lot. It was night, and cars were driving into and out of the parking lot with their lights on. She stood at the window with her hands gripping the sill, and knew in her heart that they were into something now, something hard. She was afraid, and her teeth began to chatter until she tightened her jaws. She saw a big car stop in front of the hospital and someone, a woman in a long coat, get into the car. She wished she were that woman and somebody, anybody, was driving her away from here to somewhere else, a place where she would find Scotty waiting for her when she stepped out of the car, ready to say *Mom* and let her gather him in her arms.

In a little while, Howard woke up. He looked at the boy again. Then he got up from the chair, stretched, and went over to stand beside her at the window. They both stared out at the parking lot. They didn't say anything. But they seemed to feel each other's insides now, as though the worry had made them transparent in a perfectly natural way.

The door opened and Dr. Francis came in. He was wearing a different suit and tie this time. His gray hair was combed along the sides of his head, and he looked as if he had just shaved. He went straight to the bed and examined the boy. "He ought to have come around by now. There's just no good reason for this," he said. "But I can tell you we're all convinced he's out of any danger. We'll just feel better when he wakes up. There's no reason, absolutely none, why he shouldn't come around. Very soon. Oh, he'll have himself a dilly of a headache when he does, you can count on that. But all of his signs are fine. They're as normal as can be."

"It is a coma, then?" Ann said.

The doctor rubbed his smooth cheek. "We'll call it that for the time being, until he wakes up. But you must be worn out. This is hard. I know this is hard. Feel free to go out for a bite," he said. "It would do you good. I'll put a nurse in here while you're gone if you'll feel better about going. Go and have yourselves something to eat."

"I couldn't eat anything," Ann said.

"Do what you need to do, of course," the doctor said. "Anyway, I wanted to tell you that all the signs are good, the tests are negative, nothing showed up at all, and just as soon as he wakes up he'll be over the hill."

"Thank you, doctor," Howard said. He shook hands with the doctor again. The doctor patted Howard's shoulder and went out.

"I suppose one of us should go home and check on things," Howard said. "Slug needs to be fed, for one thing."

"Call one of the neighbors," Ann said. "Call the Morgans. Anyone will feed a dog if you ask them to."

"All right," Howard said. After a while, he said, "Honey, why don't *you* do it? Why don't you go home and check on things, and then come back? It'll do you good. I'll be right here with him. Seriously," he said. "We need to keep up our strength on this. We'll want to be here for a while even after he wakes up."

"Why don't *you* go?" she said. "Feed Slug. Feed yourself."

"I already went," he said. "I was gone for exactly an hour and fifteen minutes. You go home for an hour and freshen up. Then come back."

She tried to think about it, but she was too tired. She closed her eyes and tried to think about it again. After a time, she said, "Maybe I *will* go home for a few minutes. Maybe if I'm not just sitting right here watching him every second, he'll wake up and be all right. You know? Maybe he'll wake up if I'm not here. I'll go home and take a bath and put on clean clothes. I'll feed Slug. Then I'll come back."

"I'll be right here," he said. "You go on home, honey. I'll keep an eye on things here." His eyes were bloodshot and small, as if he'd been drinking for a long time. His clothes were rumpled. His beard had come out again. She touched his face, and then she took her hand back. She understood he wanted to be by himself for a while, not have to talk or share his worry for a time. She picked her purse up from the night-stand, and he helped her into her coat.

"I won't be gone long," she said.

"Just sit and rest for a little while when you get home," he said. "Eat something. Take a bath. After you get out of the bath, just sit for a while and rest. It'll do you a world of good, you'll see. Then come back," he said. "Let's try not to worry. You heard what Dr. Francis said."

She stood in her coat for a minute trying to recall the doctor's exact words, looking for any nuances, any hint of something behind his words other than what he had said. She tried to remember if his expression had changed any when he bent over to examine the child. She remembered the way his features had composed themselves as he rolled back the child's eyelids and then listened to his breathing.

She went to the door, where she turned and looked back. She looked at the child, and then she looked at the father. Howard nodded. She stepped out of the room and pulled the door closed behind her.

She went past the nurses' station and down to the end of the corridor, looking for the elevator. At the end of the corridor, she turned to her right and entered a little waiting room where a Negro family sat in wicker chairs. There was a middle-aged man in a khaki shirt and pants, a baseball cap pushed back on his head. A large woman wearing a housedress and slippers was slumped in one of the chairs. A teenaged girl in jeans, hair done in dozens of little braids, lay stretched out in one of the chairs smoking a cigarette, her legs crossed at the ankles. The family swung their eyes to Ann as she entered the room. The little table was littered with hamburger wrappers and Styrofoam cups.

"Franklin," the large woman said as she roused herself. "Is it about Franklin?" Her eyes widened. "Tell me now, lady," the woman said. "Is it about Franklin?" She was trying to rise from her chair, but the man had closed his hand over her arm.

"Here, here," he said. "Evelyn."

"I'm sorry," Ann said. "I'm looking for the elevator. My son is in the hospital, and now I can't find the elevator."

90   "Elevator is down that way, turn left," the man said as he aimed a finger.

The girl drew on her cigarette and stared at Ann. Her eyes were narrowed to slits, and her broad lips parted slowly as she let the smoke escape. The Negro woman let her head fall on her shoulder and looked away from Ann, no longer interested.

"My son was hit by a car," Ann said to the man. She seemed to need to explain herself. "He has a concussion and a little skull fracture, but he's going to be all right. He's in shock now, but it might be some kind of coma, too. That's what really worries us, the coma part. I'm going out for a little while, but my husband is with him. Maybe he'll wake up while I'm gone."

"That's too bad," the man said and shifted in the chair. He shook his head. He looked down at the table, and then he looked back at Ann. She was still standing there. He said, "Our Franklin, he's on the operating table. Somebody cut him. Tried to kill him. There was a fight where he was at. At this party. They say he was just standing and watching. Not bothering nobody. But that don't mean nothing these days. Now he's on the operating table. We're just hoping and praying, that's all we can do now." He gazed at her steadily.

Ann looked at the girl again, who was still watching her, and at the older woman, who kept her head down, but whose eyes were now closed. Ann saw the lips moving silently, making words. She had an urge to ask what those words were. She wanted to talk more with these people who were in the same kind of waiting she was in. She was afraid, and they were afraid. They had that in common. She would have liked to have said something else about the accident, told them more about Scotty, that it had happened on the day of his birthday, Monday, and that he was still unconscious. Yet she didn't know how to begin. She stood looking at them without saying anything more.

95   She went down the corridor the man had indicated and found the elevator. She waited a minute in front of the closed doors, still wondering if she was doing the right thing. Then she put out her finger and touched the button.

She pulled into the driveway and cut the engine. She closed her eyes and leaned her head against the wheel for a minute. She listened to the ticking sounds the engine made as it began to cool. Then she got out of the car. She could hear the dog barking inside the house. She went to the front door, which was unlocked. She went inside and turned on lights and put on a kettle of water for tea. She opened some dog-food and fed Slug on the back porch. The dog ate in hungry little smacks. It kept running into the kitchen to see that she was going to stay. As she sat down on the sofa with her tea, the telephone rang.

"Yes!" she said as she answered. "Hello!"

"Mrs. Weiss," a man's voice said. It was five o'clock in the morning, and she thought she could hear machinery or equipment of some kind in the background.

"Yes, yes! What is it?" she said. "This is Mrs. Weiss. This is she. What is it please?" She listened to whatever it was in the background. "Is it Scotty, for Christ's sake?"

"Scotty," the man's voice said. "It's about Scotty, yes. It has to do with Scotty, that 100 problem. Have you forgotten about Scotty?" the man said. Then he hung up.

She dialed the hospital's number and asked for the third floor. She demanded information about her son from the nurse who answered the telephone. Then she asked to speak to her husband. It was, she said, an emergency.

She waited, turning the telephone cord in her fingers. She closed her eyes and felt sick at her stomach. She would have to make herself eat. Slug came in from the back porch and lay down near her feet. He wagged his tail. She pulled at his ear while he licked her fingers. Howard was on the line.

"Somebody just called here," she said. She twisted the telephone cord. "He said it was about Scotty," she cried.

"Scotty's fine," Howard told her. "I mean, he's still sleeping. There's been no change. The nurse has been in twice since you've been gone. A nurse or else a doctor. He's all right."

"This man called. He said it was about Scotty," she told him. 105

"Honey, you rest for a little while, you need the rest. It must be that same caller I had. Just forget it. Come back down here after you've rested. Then we'll have breakfast or something."

"Breakfast," she said. "I don't want any breakfast."

"You know what I mean," he said. "Juice, something. I don't know. I don't know anything, Ann. Jesus, I'm not hungry, either. Ann, it's hard to talk now. I'm standing here at the desk. Dr. Francis is coming again at eight o'clock this morning. He's going to have something to tell us then, something more definite. That's what one of the nurses said. She didn't know any more than that. Ann? Honey, maybe we'll know something more then. At eight o'clock. Come back here before eight. Meanwhile, I'm right here and Scotty's all right. He's still the same," he added.

"I was drinking a cup of tea," she said, "when the telephone rang. They said it was about Scotty. There was a noise in the background. Was there a noise in the background on that call you had, Howard?"

"I don't remember," he said. "Maybe the driver of the car, maybe he's a psychopath 110 and found out about Scotty somehow. But I'm here with him. Just rest like you were going to do. Take a bath and come back by seven or so, and we'll talk to the doctor together when he gets here. It's going to be all right, honey. I'm here, and there are doctors and nurses around. They say his condition is stable."

"I'm scared to death," she said.

She ran water, undressed, and got into the tub. She washed and dried quickly, not taking the time to wash her hair. She put on clean underwear, wool slacks, and a sweater. She went into the living room, where the dog looked up at her and let its tail thump once against the floor. It was just starting to get light outside when she went out to the car.

She drove into the parking lot of the hospital and found a space close to the front door. She felt she was in some obscure way responsible for what had happened to the child. She let her thoughts move to the Negro family. She remembered the name

Franklin and the table that was covered with hamburger papers, and the teenaged girl staring at her as she drew on her cigarette. "Don't have children," she told the girl's image as she entered the front door of the hospital. "For God's sake, don't."

She took the elevator up to the third floor with two nurses who were just going on duty. It was Wednesday morning, a few minutes before seven. There was a page for a Dr. Madison as the elevator doors slid open on the third floor. She got off behind the nurses, who turned in the other direction and continued the conversation she had interrupted when she'd gotten into the elevator. She walked down the corridor to the little alcove where the Negro family had been waiting. They were gone now, but the chairs were scattered in such a way that it looked as if people had just jumped up from them the minute before. The tabletop was cluttered with the same cups and papers, the ashtray was filled with cigarette butts.

115   She stopped at the nurses' station. A nurse was standing behind the counter, brushing her hair and yawning.

"There was a Negro boy in surgery last night," Ann said. "Franklin was his name. His family was in the waiting room. I'd like to inquire about his condition."

A nurse who was sitting at a desk behind the counter looked up from a chart in front of her. The telephone buzzed and she picked up the receiver, but she kept her eyes on Ann.

"He passed away," said the nurse at the counter. The nurse held the hairbrush and kept looking at her. "Are you a friend of the family or what?"

"I met the family last night," Ann said. "My own son is in the hospital. I guess he's in shock. We don't know for sure what's wrong. I just wondered about Franklin, that's all. Thank you." She moved down the corridor. Elevator doors the same color as the walls slid open and a gaunt, bald man in white pants and white canvas shoes pulled a heavy cart off the elevator. She hadn't noticed these doors last night. The man wheeled the cart out into the corridor and stopped in front of the room nearest the elevator and consulted a clipboard. Then he reached down and slid a tray out of the cart. He rapped lightly on the door and entered the room. She could smell the unpleasant odors of warm food as she passed the cart. She hurried on without looking at any of the nurses and pushed open the door to the child's room.

120   Howard was standing at the window with his hands behind his back. He turned around as she came in.

"How is he?" she said. She went over to the bed. She dropped her purse on the floor beside the nightstand. It seemed to her she had been gone a long time. She touched the child's face. "Howard?"

"Dr. Francis was here a little while ago," Howard said. She looked at him closely and thought his shoulders were bunched a little.

"I thought he wasn't coming until eight o'clock this morning," she said quickly.

"There was another doctor with him. A neurologist."

125   "A neurologist," she said.

Howard nodded. His shoulders were bunching, she could see that. "What'd they say, Howard? For Christ's sake, what'd they say? What is it?"

"They said they're going to take him down and run more tests on him, Ann. They think they're going to operate, honey. Honey, they *are* going to operate. They can't figure out why he won't wake up. It's more than just shock or concussion, they know that much now. It's in his skull, the fracture, it has something, something to do with that, they think. So they're going to operate. I tried to call you, but I guess you'd already left the house."

"Oh, God," she said. "Oh, please, Howard, please," she said, taking his arms.

"Look!" Howard said. "Scotty! Look, Ann!" He turned her toward the bed.

The boy had opened his eyes, then closed them. He opened them again now. The eyes stared straight ahead for a minute, then moved slowly in his head until they rested on Howard and Ann, then traveled away again.

"Scotty," his mother said, moving to the bed.

"Hey, Scott," his father said. "Hey, son."

They leaned over the bed. Howard took the child's hand in his hands and began to pat and squeeze the hand. Ann bent over the boy and kissed his forehead again and again. She put her hands on either side of his face. "Scotty, honey, it's Mommy and Daddy," she said. "Scotty?"

The boy looked at them, but without any sign of recognition. Then his mouth opened, his eyes scrunched closed, and he howled until he had no more air in his lungs. His face seemed to relax and soften then. His lips parted as his last breath was puffed through his throat and exhaled gently through the clenched teeth.

The doctors called it a hidden occlusion and said it was a one-in-a-million circumstance. Maybe if it could have been detected somehow and surgery undertaken immediately, they could have saved him. But more than likely not. In any case, what would they have been looking for? Nothing had shown up in the tests or in the X-rays.

Dr. Francis was shaken. "I can't tell you how badly I feel. I'm so very sorry, I can't tell you," he said as he led them into the doctors' lounge. There was a doctor sitting in a chair with his legs hooked over the back of another chair, watching an early-morning TV show. He was wearing a green delivery-room outfit, loose green pants and green blouse, and a green cap that covered his hair. He looked at Howard and Ann and then looked at Dr. Francis. He got to his feet and turned off the set and went out of the room. Dr. Francis guided Ann to the sofa, sat down beside her, and began to talk in a low, consoling voice. At one point, he leaned over and embraced her. She could feel his chest rising and falling evenly against her shoulder. She kept her eyes open and let him hold her. Howard went into the bathroom, but he left the door open. After a violent fit of weeping, he ran water and washed his face. Then he came out and sat down at the little table that held a telephone. He looked at the telephone as though deciding what to do first. He made some calls. After a time, Dr. Francis used the telephone.

"Is there anything else I can do for the moment?" he asked them.

Howard shook his head. Ann stared at Dr. Francis as if unable to comprehend his words.

The doctor walked them to the hospital's front door. People were entering and leaving the hospital. It was eleven o'clock in the morning. Ann was aware of how slowly, almost reluctantly, she moved her feet. It seemed to her that Dr. Francis was making them leave when she felt they should stay, when it would be more the right thing to do to stay. She gazed out into the parking lot and then turned around and looked back at the front of the hospital. She began shaking her head. "No, no," she said. "I can't leave him here, no." She heard herself say that and thought how unfair it was that the only words that came out were the sort of words used on TV shows where people were stunned by violent or sudden deaths. She wanted her words to be her own. "No," she said, and for some reason the memory of the Negro woman's head lolling on the woman's shoulder came to her. "No," she said again.

140 "I'll be talking to you later in the day," the doctor was saying to Howard. "There are still some things that have to be done, things that have to be cleared up to our satisfaction. Some things that need explaining."

"An autopsy," Howard said.

Dr. Francis nodded.

"I understand," Howard said. Then he said, "Oh, Jesus. No, I don't understand, doctor. I can't, I can't. I just can't."

Dr. Francis put his arm around Howard's shoulders. "I'm sorry. God, how I'm sorry." He let go of Howard's shoulders and held out his hand. Howard looked at the hand, and then he took it. Dr. Francis put his arms around Ann once more. He seemed full of some goodness she didn't understand. She let her head rest on his shoulder, but her eyes stayed open. She kept looking at the hospital. As they drove out of the parking lot, she looked back at the hospital.

145 At home, she sat on the sofa with her hands in her coat pockets. Howard closed the door to the child's room. He got the coffee-maker going and then he found an empty box. He had thought to pick up some of the child's things that were scattered around the living room. But instead he sat down beside her on the sofa, pushed the box to one side, and leaned forward, arms between his knees. He began to weep. She pulled his head over into her lap and patted his shoulder. "He's gone," she said. She kept patting his shoulder. Over his sobs, she could hear the coffee-maker hissing in the kitchen. "There, there," she said tenderly. "Howard, he's gone. He's gone and now we'll have to get used to that. To being alone."

In a little while, Howard got up and began moving aimlessly around the room with the box, not putting anything into it, but collecting some things together on the floor at one end of the sofa. She continued to sit with her hands in her coat pockets. Howard put the box down and brought coffee into the living room. Later, Ann made calls to relatives. After each call had been placed and the party had answered, Ann would blurt out a few words and cry for a minute. Then she would quietly explain, in a measured voice, what had happened and tell them about arrangements. Howard took the box out to the garage, where he saw the child's bicycle. He dropped the box and sat down on the pavement beside the bicycle. He took hold of the bicycle awkwardly so that it leaned against his chest. He held it, the rubber pedal sticking into his chest. He gave the wheel a turn.

Ann hung up the telephone after talking to her sister. She was looking up another number when the telephone rang. She picked it up on the first ring.

"Hello," she said, and she heard something in the background, a humming noise. "Hello!" she said. "For God's sake," she said. "Who is this? What is it you want?"

"Your Scotty, I got him ready for you," the man's voice said. "Did you forget him?"

150 "You evil bastard!" she shouted into the receiver. "How can you do this, you evil son of a bitch?"

"Scotty," the man said. "Have you forgotten about Scotty?" Then the man hung up on her.

Howard heard the shouting and came in to find her with her head on her arms over the table, weeping. He picked up the receiver and listened to the dial tone.

Much later, just before midnight, after they had dealt with many things, the telephone rang again.

"You answer it," she said. "Howard, it's him, I know." They were sitting at the kitchen table with coffee in front of them. Howard had a small glass of whiskey beside his cup. He answered on the third ring.

"Hello," he said. "Who is this? Hello! Hello!" The line went dead. "He hung up," 155
Howard said. "Whoever it was."

"It was him," she said. "That bastard. I'd like to kill him," she said. "I'd like to shoot him and watch him kick," she said.

"Ann, my God," he said.

"Could you hear anything?" she said. "In the background? A noise, machinery, something humming?"

"Nothing, really. Nothing like that," he said. "There wasn't much time. I think there was some radio music. Yes, there was a radio going, that's all I could tell. I don't know what in God's name is going on," he said.

She shook her head. "If I could, could get my hands on him." It came to her then. 160
She knew who it was. Scotty, the cake, the telephone number. She pushed the chair away from the table and got up. "Drive me down to the shopping center," she said. "Howard."

"What are you saying?"

"The shopping center. I know who it is who's calling. I know who it is. It's the baker, the son-of-a-bitching baker, Howard. I had him bake a cake for Scotty's birthday. That's who's calling. That's who has the number and keeps calling us. To harass us about that cake. The baker, that bastard."

They drove down to the shopping center. The sky was clear and stars were out. It was cold, and they ran the heater in the car. They parked in front of the bakery. All of the shops and stores were closed, but there were cars at the far end of the lot in front of the movie theater. The bakery windows were dark, but when they looked through the glass they could see a light in the back room and, now and then, a big man in an apron moving in and out of the white, even light. Through the glass, she could see the display cases and some little tables with chairs. She tried the door. She rapped on the glass. But if the baker heard them, he gave no sign. He didn't look in their direction.

They drove around behind the bakery and parked. They got out of the car. There was a lighted window too high up for them to see inside. A sign near the back door said THE PANTRY BAKERY, SPECIAL ORDERS. She could hear faintly a radio playing inside and something creak—an oven door as it was pulled down? She knocked on the door and waited. Then she knocked again, louder. The radio was turned down and there was a scraping sound now, the distinct sound of something, a drawer, being pulled open and then closed.

Someone unlocked the door and opened it. The baker stood in the light and peered 165
out at them: "I'm closed for business," he said. "What do you want at this hour? It's midnight. Are you drunk or something?"

She stepped into the light that fell through the open door. He blinked his heavy eyelids as he recognized her. "It's you," he said.

"It's me," she said. "Scotty's mother. This is Scotty's father. We'd like to come in."

The baker said, "I'm busy now. I have work to do."

She had stepped inside the doorway anyway. Howard came in behind her. The baker moved back. "It smells like a bakery in here. Doesn't it smell like a bakery in here, Howard?"

170   "What do you want?" the baker said. "Maybe you want your cake? That's it, you decided you want your cake. You ordered a cake, didn't you?"

"You're pretty smart for a baker," she said. "Howard, this is the man who's been calling us." She clenched her fists. She stared at him fiercely. There was a deep burning inside her, an anger that made her feel larger than herself, larger than either of these men.

"Just a minute here," the baker said. "You want to pick up your three-day-old cake? That it? I don't want to argue with you, lady. There it sits over there, getting stale. I'll give it to you for half of what I quoted you. No. You want it? You can have it. It's no good to me, no good to anyone now. It cost me time and money to make that cake. If you want it, okay, if you don't, that's okay, too. I have to get back to work." He looked at them and rolled his tongue behind his teeth.

"More cakes," she said. She knew she was in control of it, of what was increasing in her. She was calm.

"Lady, I work sixteen hours a day in this place to earn a living," the baker said. He wiped his hands on his apron. "I work night and day in here, trying to make ends meet." A look crossed Ann's face that made the baker move back and say, "No trouble, now." He reached to the counter and picked up a rolling pin with his right hand and began to tap it against the palm of his other hand. "You want the cake or not? I have to get back to work. Bakers work at night," he said again. His eyes were small, mean-looking, she thought, nearly lost in the bristly flesh around his cheeks. His neck was thick with fat.

175   "I know bakers work at night," Ann said. "They make phone calls at night, too. You bastard," she said.

The baker continued to tap the rolling pin against his hand. He glanced at Howard. "Careful, careful," he said to Howard.

"My son's dead," she said with a cold, even finality. "He was hit by a car Monday morning. We've been waiting with him until he died. But, of course, you couldn't be expected to know that, could you? Bakers can't know everything—can they, Mr. Baker? But he's dead. He's dead, you bastard!" Just as suddenly as it had welled in her, the anger dwindled, gave way to something else, a dizzy feeling of nausea. She leaned against the wooden table that was sprinkled with flour, put her hands over her face, and began to cry, her shoulders rocking back and forth. "It isn't fair," she said. "It isn't, isn't fair."

Howard put his hand at the small of her back and looked at the baker. "Shame on you," Howard said to him. "Shame."

The baker put the rolling pin back on the counter. He undid his apron and threw it on the counter. He looked at them, and then he shook his head slowly. He pulled a chair out from under the card table that held papers and receipts, an adding machine, and a telephone directory. "Please sit down," he said. "Let me get you a chair," he said to Howard. "Sit down now, please." The baker went into the front of the shop and returned with two little wrought-iron chairs. "Please sit down, you people."

180   Ann wiped her eyes and looked at the baker. "I wanted to kill you," she said. "I wanted you dead."

The baker had cleared a space for them at the table. He shoved the adding machine to one side, along with the stacks of notepaper and receipts. He pushed the telephone directory onto the floor, where it landed with a thud. Howard and Ann sat down and pulled their chairs up to the table. The baker sat down, too.

"Let me say how sorry I am," the baker said, putting his elbows on the table. "God alone knows how sorry. Listen to me. I'm just a baker. I don't claim to be anything else. Maybe once, maybe years ago, I was a different kind of human being. I've forgotten, I don't know for sure. But I'm not any longer, if I ever was. Now I'm just a baker. That don't excuse my doing what I did, I know. But I'm deeply sorry. I'm sorry for your son, and sorry for my part in this," the baker said. He spread his hands out on the table and turned them over to reveal his palms. "I don't have any children myself, so I can only imagine what you must be feeling. All I can say to you now is that I'm sorry. Forgive me, if you can," the baker said. "I'm not an evil man, I don't think. Not evil, like you said on the phone. You got to understand what it comes down to is I don't know how to act anymore, it would seem. Please," the man said, "let me ask you if you can find it in your hearts to forgive me?"

It was warm inside the bakery. Howard stood up from the table and took off his coat. He helped Ann from her coat. The baker looked at them for a minute and then nodded and got up from the table. He went to the oven and turned off some switches. He found cups and poured coffee from an electric coffee-maker. He put a carton of cream on the table, and a bowl of sugar.

"You probably need to eat something," the baker said. "I hope you'll eat some of my hot rolls. You have to eat and keep going. Eating is a small, good thing in a time like this," he said.

He served them warm cinnamon rolls just out of the oven, the icing still runny. He   185
put butter on the table and knives to spread the butter. Then the baker sat down at the table with them. He waited. He waited until they each took a roll from the platter and began to eat. "It's good to eat something," he said, watching them. "There's more. Eat up. Eat all you want. There's all the rolls in the world in here."

They ate rolls and drank coffee. Ann was suddenly hungry, and the rolls were warm and sweet. She ate three of them, which pleased the baker. Then he began to talk. They listened carefully. Although they were tired and in anguish, they listened to what the baker had to say. They nodded when the baker began to speak of loneliness, and of the sense of doubt and limitation that had come to him in his middle years. He told them what it was like to be childless all these years. To repeat the days with the ovens endlessly full and endlessly empty. The party food, the celebrations he'd worked over. Icing knuckle-deep. The tiny wedding couples stuck into cakes. Hundreds of them, no, thousands by now. Birthdays. Just imagine all those candles burning. He had a necessary trade. He was a baker. He was glad he wasn't a florist. It was better to be feeding people. This was a better smell anytime than flowers.

"Smell this," the baker said, breaking open a dark loaf. "It's a heavy bread, but rich." They smelled it, then he had them taste it. It had the taste of molasses and coarse grains. They listened to him. They ate what they could. They swallowed the dark bread. It was like daylight under the fluorescent trays of light. They talked on into the early morning, the high, pale cast of light in the windows, and they did not think of leaving.   [1981]

QUESTIONS

1. Discuss the importance of the secondary characters in this story—such as Dr. Francis, the nurses, Franklin's family, and the baker.

2. What does Ann mean when she says, ". . . now we have to get used to that. To being alone"?

3. What does the scene with the black family contribute to the story?

4. Why is it important that the narrator focus on both Howard and Ann?

5. Examine the narrator's reference to food throughout the story—cake, potato chips, hamburgers, rolls and bread, and more.

RESPONSES

1. Compare the concept of luck as presented in this story with the concept of luck presented in "The Rocking-Horse Winner."

2. Compare this story to Carver's "Cathedral." How do basic activities like eating together and conversing become the means of creating hope and sacredness?

FOCUS ON FILM

1. Compare this story to how it is adapted in *Short Cuts*, the film by Robert Altman. What changes did Altman make? What effect do those changes have on your reactions to the plot, characters and theme?

2. What is gained or lost by Altman's inclusion of other Carver stories in his film?

OSCAR CASARES

Oscar Casares (b. 1964) was born and raised in Brownsville, Texas. After graduating from the University of Texas, he worked in advertising in Minnesota and Texas. He began taking classes in creative writing, published a few stories, and then was accepted into the MFA program at the University of Iowa. His stories have been published in the *Iowa Review, Colorado Review, Northwest Review,* and *Threepenny Review,* and in the book *Brownsville* (2003).

Yolanda

When I can't sleep at night I think of Yolanda Castro. She was a woman who lived next door to us one summer when I was growing up. I've never told Maggie about her because it's not something she'd appreciate knowing. Trust me. Tonight, like most nights, she fell asleep before I was even done brushing my teeth. And now all I can hear are little snores. Sometimes she even talks to herself, shouts out other people's names, and then in the morning says she can't remember any of it. Either way, I let her go on sleeping. She's over on her side of the bed. It's right where she ought to be. This thing with Yolanda doesn't really concern her.

I was only twelve years old when Frank and Yolanda Castro moved into the beige house with green trim. Frank pulled up on our street in a U-Haul he'd driven all the way from California to Texas. I remember it being a different neighborhood back then. Everybody knew everybody, and people left their doors unlocked at night. You didn't worry about people stealing shit you didn't lock up. I'm talking about more than twenty years ago now. I'm talking about before some drunk spent all afternoon in one of the cantinas on Fourteenth Street, then drove his car straight into the Rivas front yard and ran over the Baby Jesus that was still lying in the manger because Lonny Rivas was too *flojo* to put it away a month after Christmas, and then the guy tried to run, but fell down, asleep, in our yard, and when the cops were handcuffing him all he could say was *ma-ri-juan-a*, which even then, at the age of fifteen, I knew wasn't a good thing to say when you were being arrested. This was before Pete Zuniga was riding his brand-new ten-speed from Western Auto and, next to the Friendship Garden, saw a white dude who'd been knifed a couple of dozen times and was floating in the green water of the resaca. Before some crazy woman hired a curandera to put a spell on her daughter's ex-boyfriend, which really meant hiring a couple of hit men from Matamoros to do a drive-by. Before the cops ever had to show up at El Disco de Oro Tortillería. Like holding up a 7-Eleven was getting old, right? You know, when you could sit at the Brownsville Coffee Shop #1 and not worry about getting it in the back while you ate your menudo. When you didn't have to put an alarm *and* the Club on your car so it wouldn't end up in Reynosa. Before my father had to put iron bars on the windows and doors because some future convict from the junior high was always breaking into the house. And before my father had to put a fence in the front because, in his words, I'm sick and tired of all those damn dogs making poo in my yard. I guess what I'm trying to say is, things were different back then.

Frank Castro was an older man, in his fifties by that point, and Yolanda couldn't have been more than thirty, if that. My mother got along with Yolanda okay and even helped her get a job at the HEB store where she had worked since before I was born. You could say that was where the problems started, because Frank Castro didn't want his wife working at HEB, or any other place for that matter. You have no business being in that grocery store, I heard him yell one night when I was trying to fall asleep. I could hear almost everything Frank yelled that summer. Our houses were only a few yards apart, and my window was the closest to the action. My father's bougainvillaeas were the dividing line between the two properties. I heard Yolanda beg Frank to please let her take the job. I heard Frank yell something in Spanish about how no woman in his family had ever worked behind a cosmetics counter, selling lipstick. I heard her promise she'd only work part-time, and she'd quit if they ever scheduled her on nights or weekends. I heard her tell him how much she loved him and how she'd never take a job that would keep them apart. Francisco, tú eres mi vida, she said to him. I heard him get real quiet. Then I heard Frank and Yolanda Castro making love. I didn't know what making love sounded like back then, but I can tell you now that's what it was.

If you saw what Yolanda looked like, you might not have blamed Frank for not wanting her to leave the house. It also wouldn't have been a big mystery to you how she went into the store applying for a job in the meat department and ended up getting one in cosmetics. The only girl I'd ever seen that even came close to being as beautiful as Yolanda was in a *Playboy* I found under my parents' bed the summer before. The girl in the magazine had the same long black hair, light brown skin, and green eyes that Yolanda did, only she was sitting bareback on an Appaloosa.

5   The thing I remember most about Frank was his huge forearms. They were like Popeye's, except with a lot more black and gray hair mixed in. But the hair on his arms was just the beginning. There wasn't a time I saw the guy that he didn't look like he could've used a good shave. And it didn't help that his thick eyebrows were connected into one long eyebrow that stretched across the bottom of his forehead like a piece of electrical tape. He was average size, but he looked short and squatty when he stood next to Yolanda. Frank was a mechanic at the airport and, according to my father, probably made good money. I was with my father the first time he met Frank. He always made it a point to meet any new neighbors and then come back to the house and give a full report to my mother, who would later meet the neighbors herself and say he was exaggerating about how shifty so-and-so's eyes were or how rich he thought another neighbor might be because he had one of those new foreign cars in the driveway, un carro extranjero, a Toyota or a Honda. Frank was beginning to mow his front yard when we walked up. My father introduced me as his boy, and I shook our neighbor's sweaty hand. I've lived thirty-six years on this earth and never shaken hands with a

bear, but I have a good idea that it wouldn't be much different from shaking Frank Castro's hand. Even his fingers needed a haircut. Frank stood there answering a couple of my father's questions about whether he liked the neighborhood (he liked it) and how long he had lived in California before moving back to Texas (ten years—he held up both hands to show us exactly how many). Suddenly, my father nodded and said we had to go. He turned around and walked off, then looked over his shoulder and yelled at me to hurry up. This whole time, Frank had not shut off his mower. My father was forced to stand there and shout over the sound of the engine. The report on Frank wasn't pretty when we got back to the house. From that point on, my father would only refer to him as El Burro.

It wasn't just my father. Nobody liked Frank. He had this thing about his yard where he didn't want anybody getting near it. We found this out one day when Lonny and I were throwing the football around in the street. Lonny was showing off and he threw the ball over my head, way over, and it landed in Frank's yard. When I was getting the ball, Frank opened the front door and yelled something about it being private property. Then he went over, turned on the hose, and started watering his yard and half the street in front of his yard. He did this every afternoon from that day on. The hose with a spray gun in his right hand, and a Schlitz tallboy in his left. Lonny thought we should steal the hose when Frank wasn't home, or maybe poke a few holes in it, just to teach the fucker a lesson. One Saturday morning we even saw him turn the hose on some Jehovahs who were walking up the street towards his house. A skinny man wearing a tie and short-sleeve shirt kept trying to give him a pamphlet, but Frank wasn't listening.

My mother gave Yolanda a ride to work every day. In the afternoons, Yolanda got off work early enough to be waiting for Frank to pull up in his car and drive her back to the house. My mother told us at home that Yolanda had asked Frank to teach her how to drive when they first got married but that Frank had said she was his princesa now and any place she needed to go, he'd take her. One morning, when both my mother and Yolanda had the day off, my mother asked her if she wanted to learn how to drive. They drove out by the port, and my mother pulled over so Yolanda could take the wheel. I was hanging out at the Jiffy-Mart, down the street, when I saw Yolanda driving my mother's car. Yolanda honked the horn, and they both waved at me as they turned the corner.

That night—like a lot of nights that summer—I listened to Frank and Yolanda Castro. What they said went something like this:

"I can show you."

"I don't wanna see."

"Why not?" 10

"Because you have *no* business driving a car around town."

"But this way you don't have to pick me up every day. You can come straight home, and I'll be here already, waiting."

"I don't care. I'm talking about you learning to drive."

"Frank, it's nothing." 15

"You don't even have a car. What do you want with a license?"

"I can buy one."

"With what?"

"I've been getting bonuses. The companies give us a little extra if we sell more of their makeup."

20   "Is that right?"

"It isn't that much, Frank."

"And then?"

"Well, maybe I can buy a used one."

"It's because of that store."

25   "What's wrong with the store?"

"It's putting ideas in your head."

"Frank, what ideas?"

"Ideas! Is there some place I haven't taken you?"

"No."

30   "Well, then?"

"Francisco."

"Don't 'Francisco' me."

"Baby . . ."

"¡Qué no!"

35   They were beginning to remind me of one of my mother's novelas, which she was probably watching in the living room at that very moment. Things like that usually made me want to laugh—and I did a little, into my pillow, but it was only because I couldn't believe I was actually hearing it, and I could see Frank Castro pounding me into the ground with his big forearms if he ever found out.

"No! I said."

"I'm not Trini."

"I never said . . ."

"Then stop treating me like her. ¿No sabes qué tanto te quiero, Francisco?"

40   It got quiet for a while after that. Then there was the sound of something hitting the floor, the sound of two bodies dropping on a bed with springs that had seen better days (and nights), the sound of Yolanda saying, *Ay, Diosito*, over and over and over again—just like my tía Hilda did the day her son, my cousin Rudy, almost drowned in the swimming pool at the Civic Center—then the sound of the bed springs making their own crazy music, and the sound of what I imagine a bear is like when he's trying to make little bears.

Yolanda kept getting a ride to work with my mother, and Frank kept bringing her home in the afternoons. My mother had offered to drive Yolanda to the DPS office and let her borrow our car for the driving part of the test, but Yolanda said she'd changed her mind and didn't want to talk about it. I heard my mother telling my father what she'd said, and they agreed it probably had something to do with Frank. El Burro, my father let out when they didn't have anything else to say.

It was the Fourth of July when I got sick that summer. I remember my mother wouldn't let me go outside with Lonny. He kept yelling at me from the street that night to stop being a baby and come out of the house so I could pop some firecrackers. We'd been talking all week about shooting some bottle rockets in the direction of Frank's house. It didn't feel like anything at first, just a fever, but the next morning we knew it was the chicken pox. My mother had to miss a few days of work, staying home with me until I got over the worst part. After that, Yolanda volunteered to come look in on me when she wasn't working. But I told my mother I didn't want her coming over when I still looked like those dead people in that *Night of the Living Dead* movie. My mother said Yolanda would understand I was sick, and if she didn't, that's what I'd get for watching those kinds of movies. So for about a week she came over in the mornings and we watched *The Price Is Right* together. Yolanda was great at guessing the prices of things, and she said it was from working in a grocery store and having a good memory. I told her I thought she should go on the show. She laughed and said she probably wouldn't win anything, since she'd be too nervous. What I meant to say was that she should go on the show and be one of the girls who stands next to the car, smiling. She was prettier than any of them, but I never told her that, because I got embarrassed whenever I thought about saying it.

If Yolanda came over in the afternoon, we'd watch *General Hospital* together. She said she'd been watching it for years. There wasn't anything else on at that hour, so I didn't really care. Once, she brought over some lime sherbet, and we played Chinese checkers in my room until she had to get home to Frank Castro. Each time she left she'd reach down and give me a little kiss on the cheek, and each time her hair smelled like a different fruit. Sometimes like a pear, sometimes like a strawberry, sometimes like an apple. The strawberry was my favorite.

This was about the time when Frank said that from now on, he would take Yolanda to work in the morning—no matter how out of the way it was for him, or the fact that he and my mother were always pulling out of the driveway at the same time. A week or two went by, and then my mother told my father that Frank had started showing up at the store in the middle of the day, usually during his lunch hour, but sometimes also at two or three in the afternoon. He wouldn't talk to Yolanda, but instead just hung out by the magazine rack, pretending to read a wrestling magazine. Yolanda tried to ignore him. My mother said she had talked to her in the break room, but Yolanda kept saying it was nothing, that Frank's hours had changed at the airport.

There was one Saturday when he was off from work, and as usual, he spent it in his front yard, sitting in a green lawn chair, drinking tallboys. He had turned on the sprinkler and was watching his grass and half the street get a good watering. Lonny and I were throwing the football around. Frank sat in that stupid chair all afternoon. He only went in to grab another beer and, I guess, take a piss. Each time he got up and turned around, we shot him the finger.

That night, I heard Frank's voice loud and clear. He wanted answers. Something about a phone number. Something about a customer he'd seen Yolanda talking to a couple of days earlier. Did she think he was blind? What the hell was so funny when the two of them were talking? How many times? he wanted to know. ¡Desgraciado! Where? Goddammit! he wanted to know. What game show? ¡El sanavabiche! Something shattered against the wall and then a few seconds later Yolanda screamed. I sat up. I didn't know if I could form words if I had to. What the hell were you doing listening anyway? they would ask me. There was another scream and then the sound of the back door slamming. I looked out my window and saw Frank Castro chase Yolanda into their backyard. She was wearing a nightgown that came down to her knees. Frank had on the same khakis and muscle shirt he'd worn that afternoon. He only ran a few feet down from the back steps before his head hit the clothesline, and he fell to the ground, hard. Yolanda didn't turn to look back and ran around the right side of their house. I thought she'd gone back inside to call the police. Then I heard footsteps and a tapping on my window. It was Yolanda whispering, Open it, open it.

I didn't say anything for a long time. Yolanda had climbed in and let down the blinds. We were lying on the bed, facing the window. She was behind me, holding me tight. I finally asked her if she wanted a glass of water or some Kool-Aid. I made it myself, I told her. It's the orange kind, I said. I didn't know what else to talk about.

45

She said no, and then she told me to be quiet. I kept thinking, This has to be a dream and any minute now my mother's going to walk in and tell me the barbacoa is sitting on the table and to come eat because we're going to eleven o'clock mass and don't even think about putting on those blue jeans with the patches in the knees ¿me entiendes? But that wasn't happening, and something told me then that no matter what happened after tonight, this was something I'd never forget. There would always be a time *before* Yolanda crawled into my bed and a time *after*. As she held me, I could feel her heart beating. Then I felt her chiches pressed against my back. And even though I couldn't see them, I knew they were perfect like the rest of her. I knew that they'd fit right in the palms of my hands, if only I had enough guts to turn around. Just turn around, that's all I had to do. I thought back to when she was tapping on the window, and I was sure she wasn't wearing a bra. I was sure there was nothing but Yolanda underneath her nightgown. I could have sworn I'd seen even more. I'd been close to a woman's body before. But this wasn't like when my tía Gloria came into town and couldn't believe how much I'd grown, and then she squeezed me so hard my head got lost in her huge and heavily perfumed chiches. And it wasn't anything like the Sears catalog where the girls had a tiny rose at the top of their panties. No, this was Yolanda and she was in my bed, pressed up against my back, like it was the only place in the world for us to be.

I could go on and tell you the rest of the details—how I never turned around and always regretted it, how we stayed there and listened to Frank crying in his backyard, how Lonny's dad finally called the cops on his ass, how Yolanda had a cousin pick her up the next morning, how she ended up leaving Frank for a man who worked for one of the shampoo companies, how it didn't matter because she'd also been seeing an assistant manager and would be having his baby soon enough, and how it really didn't matter because the assistant manager was already married and wasn't about to leave his wife and kids, and how, actually, none of it mattered because she'd been taking money out of the register and was about to be caught—but that's not the part of the story I like to remember.

In that bed of mine, the one with the Dallas Cowboy pillows and covers, Yolanda and I were safe. We were safe from Frank Castro and safe from anybody else that might try to hurt us. And it was safe for me to fall asleep in Yolanda's arms, with her warm, beautiful body pressed against mine, and dream that we were riding off to some faraway place on an Appaloosa.   [2003]

QUESTIONS

1. What contribution to the theme does the "present day" first paragraph make?
2. What kind of man is Frank Castro? What kind of a role model as a husband and man is he for the narrator as a young boy?
3. Compare the marriage of Frank and Yolanda to the narrator's parents' marriage. What conflicting lessons about relationships did the boy learn?
4. Why can the narrator be so forgiving about Yolanda's shortcomings?
5. The narrator says "Things were different back then." How does the experience of knowing Yolanda belong to "back then"? How is the past so different from the present? Why?

RESPONSES

1. Compare this story to other coming-of-age stories, such as "A Sunrise on the Veld," "Because My Father Always Said He Was the Only Indian . . .," "I Want to Know Why," "Araby," and "A & P."
2. Using the mythological approach, explain how Yolanda is a "goddess." Using the feminist approach, explore how the narrator objectifies Yolanda.

WILLA CATHER

Willa Cather (1873–1947) was born in Virginia. At the age of ten she was taken by her family to Red Cloud, Nebraska, and her life there is mirrored in such works as *O Pioneers!* (1913) and *My Ántonia* (1918). After graduation from the University of Nebraska, she backtrailed, first to Pittsburgh as a journalist and teacher and then to New York City as an editor of *McClure's Magazine*. Success enabled her to devote full time to writing, and in later life she produced such distinguished novels as *A Lost Lady* (1923) and *Death Comes for the Archbishop* (1927). Perhaps her best-known collection of short stories is *Youth and the Bright Medusa* (1932). A selection of her essays appeared under the title *Not Under Forty* (1936).

Paul's Case

It was Paul's afternoon to appear before the faculty of the Pittsburgh High School to account for his various misdemeanors. He had been suspended a week ago, and his father had called at the Principal's office and confessed his perplexity about his son. Paul entered the faculty room suave and smiling. His clothes were a trifle outgrown, and the tan velvet on the collar of his open overcoat was frayed and worn; but for all that there was something of a dandy about him, and he wore an opal pin in his neatly knotted black four-in-hand, and a red carnation in his buttonhole. This latter adornment the faculty somehow felt was not properly significant of the contrite spirit befitting a boy under the ban of suspension.

Paul was tall for his age and very thin, with high, cramped shoulders and a narrow chest. His eyes were remarkable for a certain hysterical brilliancy, and he continually used them in a conscious, theatrical sort of way, peculiarly offensive in a boy. The pupils were abnormally large, as though he were addicted to belladonna, but there was a glassy glitter about them which that drug does not produce.

When questioned by the Principal as to why he was there, Paul stated, politely enough, that he wanted to come back to school. This was a lie, but Paul was quite accustomed to lying; found it, indeed, indispensable for overcoming friction. His teachers were asked to state their respective charges against him, which they did with such a rancor and aggrievedness as evinced that this was not a usual case. Disorder and impertinence were among the offenses named, yet each of his instructors felt that it was scarcely possible to put into words the real cause of the trouble, which lay in a sort of hysterically defiant manner of the boy's; in the contempt which they all knew he felt for them, and which he seemingly made not the least effort to conceal. Once, when he had been making a synopsis of a paragraph at the blackboard, his English teacher had stepped to his side and attempted to guide his hand. Paul had started back with a shudder and thrust his hands violently behind him. The astonished woman could scarcely have been more hurt and embarrassed had he struck at her. The insult was so involuntary and definitely personal as to be unforgettable. In one way and another, he had made all his teachers, men and women alike, conscious of the same feeling of physical aversion. In one class he habitually sat with his hand shading his eyes; in another he always looked out of the window during the recitation; in another had made a running commentary on the lecture, with humorous intent.

His teachers felt this afternoon that his whole attitude was symbolized by his shrug and his flippantly red carnation flower, and they fell upon him without mercy, his English teacher leading the pack. He stood through it smiling, his pale lips parted over his white teeth. (His lips were continually twitching, and he had a habit of raising his eyebrows that was contemptuous and irritating to the last degree.) Older boys than Paul had broken down and shed tears under that ordeal, but his set smile did not once desert him, and his only sign of discomfort was the nervous trembling of the fingers that toyed with the buttons of his overcoat, and an occasional jerking of the other hand which held his hat. Paul was also smiling, always glancing about him, seeming to feel that people might be watching him and trying to detect something. This conscious expression, since it was as far as possible from boyish mirthfulness, was usually attributed to insolence or "smartness."

As the inquisition proceeded, one of his instructors repeated an impertinent remark   5
of the boy's, and the Principal asked him whether he thought that a courteous speech to make to a woman. Paul shrugged his shoulders slightly and his eyebrows twitched.

"I don't know," he replied. "I didn't mean to be polite or impolite, either. I guess it's a sort of way I have, of saying things regardless."

The Principal asked him whether he didn't think that a way it would be well to get rid of. Paul grinned and said he guessed so. When he was told that he could go, he bowed gracefully and went out. His bow was like a repetition of the scandalous red carnation.

His teachers were in despair, and his drawing-master voiced the feeling of them all when he declared there was something about the boy which none of them understood. He added: "I don't really believe that smile of his comes altogether from insolence; there's something sort of haunted about it. The boy is not strong for one thing. There is something wrong about the fellow."

The drawing-master had come to realize that, in looking at Paul, one saw only his white teeth and the forced animation of his eyes. One warm afternoon the boy had gone to sleep at his drawing-board, and his master had noted with amazement what a white, blue-veined face it was; drawn and wrinkled like an old man's about the eyes, the lips twitching even in his sleep.

His teachers left the building dissatisfied and unhappy; humiliated to have felt so   10
vindictive toward a mere boy, to have uttered this feeling in cutting terms, and to have set each other on, as it were, in the gruesome game of intemperate reproach. One of them remembered having seen a miserable street cat set at bay by a ring of tormentors.

As for Paul, he ran down the hill whistling the Soldiers' Chorus from *Faust*, looking behind him now and then to see whether some of his teachers were not there to witness his light-heartedness. As it was now late in the afternoon and Paul was on duty that evening as usher at Carnegie Hall, he decided that he would not go home to supper.

When he reached the concert hall, the doors were not yet open. It was chilly outside, and he decided to go up into the picture gallery—always deserted at this hour—where there were some of Raffelli's gay studies of Paris streets and an airy blue Venetian scene or two that always exhilarated him. He was delighted to find no one in the gallery but the old guard, who sat in the corner, a newspaper on his knee, a black patch over one eye and the other closed. Paul possessed himself of the place and walked confidently up and down, whistling under his breath. After a while he sat down before a blue Rico and lost himself. When he bethought him to look at his watch, it was after seven o'clock, and he rose with a start and ran downstairs, making a face at Augustus Caesar, peering out from the cast-room, and an evil gesture at the Venus of Milo as he passed her on the stairway.

When Paul reached the ushers' dressing-room, half a dozen boys were there already, and he began excitedly to tumble into his uniform. It was one of the few that at all approached fitting, and Paul thought it very becoming—though he knew the tight, straight coat accentuated his narrow chest, about which he was exceedingly sensitive. He was always excited while he dressed, twanging all over to the tuning of the strings and the preliminary flourishes of the horns in the music-room; but tonight he seemed quite beside himself, and he teased and plagued the boys until, telling him that he was crazy, they put him down on the floor and sat on him.

Somewhat calmed by his suppression, Paul dashed out to the front of the house to seat the early comers. He was a model usher. Gracious and smiling he ran up and down the aisles. Nothing was too much trouble for him; he carried messages and brought programs as though it were his greatest pleasure in life, and all the people in his section thought him a charming boy, feeling that he remembered and admired them. As the house filled, he grew more and more vivacious and animated, and the color came to his cheeks and lips. It was very much as though this were a great reception and Paul were the host. Just as the musicians came out to take their places, his English teacher arrived with checks for the seats which a prominent manufacturer had taken for the season. She betrayed some embarrassment when she handed Paul the tickets, and a *hauteur* which subsequently made her feel very foolish. Paul was startled for a moment, and had the feeling of wanting to put her out; what business had she here among all these fine people and gay colors? He looked her over and decided that she was not appropriately dressed and must be a fool to sit downstairs in such togs. The tickets had probably been sent her out of kindness, he reflected, as he put down a seat for her, and she had about as much right to sit there as he had.

15   When the symphony began, Paul sank into one of the rear seats with a long sigh of relief, and lost himself as he had done before the Rico. It was not that symphonies, as such, meant anything in particular to Paul, but the first sight of the instruments seemed to free some hilarious spirit within him; something that struggled there like the Genius in the bottle found by the Arab fisherman. He felt a sudden zest of life; the lights danced before his eyes and the concert hall blazed into unimaginable splendor. When the soprano soloist came on, Paul forgot even the nastiness of his teacher's being there, and gave himself up to the peculiar intoxication such personages always had for him. The soloist chanced to be a German woman, by no means in her first youth, and the mother of many children; but she wore a satin gown and a tiara, and she had that indefinable air of achievement, that world-shine upon her, which always blinded Paul to any possible defects.

After a concert was over, Paul was often irritable and wretched until he got to sleep—and tonight he was even more than usually restless. He had the feeling of not being able to let down; of its being impossible to give up his delicious excitement which was the only thing that could be called living at all. During the last number he withdrew and, after hastily changing his clothes in the dressing-room, slipped out to the side door where the singer's carriage stood. Here he began pacing rapidly up and down the walk, waiting to see her come out.

Over yonder the Schenley, in its vacant stretch, loomed big and square through the fine rain, the windows of its twelve stories glowing like those of a lighted cardboard house under a Christmas tree. All the actors and singers of any importance stayed there when they were in Pittsburgh, and a number of the big manufacturers of the place lived there in the winter. Paul had often hung about the hotel, watching the people go in and out, longing to enter and leave schoolmasters and dull care behind him forever.

At last the singer came out, accompanied by the conductor, who helped her into her carriage and closed the door with a cordial *auf wiedersehen*—which set Paul to wondering whether she were not an old sweetheart of his. Paul followed the carriage over to the hotel, walking so rapidly as not to be far from the entrance when the singer alighted and disappeared behind the swinging glass doors which were opened by a Negro in a tall hat and a long coat. In the moment that the door was ajar, it seemed to Paul that he, too, entered. He seemed to feel himself go after her up the steps, into the warm, lighted building, into an exotic, tropical world of shiny, glistening surfaces and basking ease. He reflected upon the mysterious dishes that were brought into the dining-room, the green bottles in buckets of ice, as he had seen them in the supper-party pictures of the Sunday supplement. A quick gust of wind brought the rain down with sudden vehemence, and Paul was startled to find that he was still outside in the slush of the gravel driveway; that his boots were letting in the water and his scanty overcoat was clinging wet about him; that the lights in front of the concert hall were out, and that the rain was driving in sheets between him and the orange glow of the windows above him. There it was, what he wanted—tangibly before him, like the fairy world of a Christmas pantomime; as the rain beat in his face, Paul wondered whether he were destined always to shiver in the black night outside, looking up at it.

He turned and walked reluctantly toward the car tracks. The end had to come sometime; his father in his night-clothes at the top of the stairs, explanations that did not explain, hastily improvised fictions that were forever tripping him up, his upstairs room and its horrible yellow wallpaper, the creaking bureau with the greasy plush collar-box, and over his painted wooden bed the pictures of George Washington and John Calvin, and the framed motto. "Feed my Lambs," which had been worked in red worsted by his mother, whom Paul could not remember.

Half an hour later, Paul alighted from the Negley Avenue car and went slowly down one of the side streets off the main thoroughfare. It was a highly respectable street, where all the houses were exactly alike, and where business men of moderate means begot and reared large families of children, all of whom went to Sabbath School and learned the shorter catechism, and were interested in arithmetic; all of whom were as exactly alike as their homes, and of a piece of the monotony in which they lived. Paul never went up Cordelia Street without a shudder of loathing. His home was next to the house of the Cumberland minister. He approached it tonight with the nerveless sense of defeat, the hopeless feeling of sinking back forever into ugliness and commonness that he had always had when he came home. The moment he turned into

20

Cordelia Street he felt the waters close above his head. After each of these orgies of living, he experienced all the physical depression which follows a debauch; the loathing of respectable beds, of common food, of a house permeated by kitchen odors; a shuddering repulsion for the flavorless, colorless mass of every-day existence; a morbid desire for cool things and soft lights and fresh flowers.

The nearer he approached the house, the more absolutely unequal Paul felt to the sight of it all: his ugly sleeping chamber; the old bathroom with the grimy zinc tub, the cracked mirror, the dripping spigots; his father, at the top of the stairs, his hairy legs sticking out from his nightshirt, his feet thrust into carpet slippers. He was so much later than usual that there would certainly be enquiries and reproaches. Paul stopped short before the door. He felt that he could not be accosted by his father tonight; that he could not toss again on that miserable bed. He would not go in. He would tell his father that he had no carfare, and it was raining so hard he had gone home with one of the boys and stayed all night.

Meanwhile, he was wet and cold. He went around to the back of the house and tried one of the basement windows, found it open, and raised it cautiously, and scrambled down the cellar wall to the floor. There he stood, holding his breath, terrified by the noise he had made; but the floor above him was silent, and there was no creak on the stairs. He found a soap-box, and carried it over to the soft ring of light that streamed from the furnace door, and sat down. He was horribly afraid of rats, so he did not try to sleep, but sat looking distrustfully at the dark, still terrified lest he might have awakened his father.

In such reactions, after one of the experiences which made days and nights out of the dreary blanks of the calendar, when his senses were deadened, Paul's head was always singularly clear. Suppose his father had heard him getting in at the window and had come down and shot him for a burglar? Then, again, suppose his father had come down, pistol in hand, and he had cried out in time to save himself, and his father had been horrified to think how nearly he had killed him? Then again, suppose a day should come when his father would remember that night, and wish there had been no warning cry to stay his hand? With this last supposition Paul entertained himself until daybreak.

The following Sunday was fine; the sodden November chill was broken by the last flash of autumnal summer. In the morning Paul had to go to church and Sabbath School, as always. On seasonable Sunday afternoons the burghers of Cordelia Street usually sat out on their front "stoops," and talked to their neighbors on the next stoop, or called to those across the street in neighborly fashion. The men sat placidly on gay cushions placed upon the steps that led down to the sidewalk, while the women, in their Sunday "waists," sat in rockers on the cramped porches, pretending to be greatly at their ease. The children played in the streets; there were so many of them that the place resembled the recreation grounds of a kindergarten. The men on the steps, all in their shirt-sleeves, their vests unbuttoned, sat with their legs well apart, their stomachs comfortably protruding, and talked of the prices of things, or told anecdotes of the sagacity of their various chiefs and overlords. They occasionally looked over the multitude of squabbling children, listened affectionately to their high-pitched, nasal voices, smiling to see their own proclivities reproduced in their offspring, and interspersed their legends of the iron kings with remarks about their sons' progress at school, their grades in arithmetic, and the amounts they had saved in their toy banks.

25   On this last Sunday of November, Paul sat all afternoon on the lowest step of his "stoop," staring into the street, while his sisters, in their rockers, were talking to the

minister's daughters next door about how many shirtwaists they had made in the last week, and how many waffles someone had eaten at the last church supper. When the weather was warm, and his father was in a particularly jovial frame of mind, the girls made lemonade, which was always brought out in a red-glass pitcher, ornamented with forget-me-nots in blue enamel. This the girls thought very fine, and the neighbors joked about the suspicious color of the pitcher.

Today Paul's father, on the top step, was talking to a young man who shifted a restless baby from knee to knee. He happened to be the young man who was daily held up to Paul as a model, and after whom it was his father's dearest hope that he would pattern. This young man was of a ruddy complexion, with a compressed, red mouth, and faded, nearsighted eyes, over which he wore thick spectacles, with gold bows that curved about his ears. He was clerk to one of the magnates of a great steel corporation, and was looked upon in Cordelia Street as a young man with a future. There was a story that, some five years ago—he was now barely twenty-six—he had been a trifle "dissipated," but in order to curb his appetites and save the loss of time and strength that a sowing of wild oats might have entailed, he had taken his chief's advice, oft reiterated to his employees, and at twenty-one had married the first woman whom he could persuade to share his fortunes. She happened to be an angular schoolmistress, much older than he, who also wore thick glasses, and who had now borne him four children, all nearsighted like herself.

The young man was relating how his chief, now cruising in the Mediterranean, kept in touch with all the details of the business, arranging his office hours on his yacht just as though he were at home, and "knocking off work enough to keep two stenographers busy." His father told, in turn, the plan his corporation was considering, of putting in an electric railway plant at Cairo. Paul snapped his teeth; he had an awful apprehension that they might spoil it all before he got there. Yet he rather liked to hear these legends of the iron kings, that were told and retold on Sundays and holidays; these stories of palaces in Venice, yachts on the Mediterranean, and high play at Monte Carlo appealed to his fancy, and he was interested in the triumphs of cash-boys who had become famous, though he had no mind for the cash-boy stage.

After supper was over, and he had helped to dry the dishes, Paul nervously asked his father whether he could go to George's to get some help in his geometry, and still more nervously asked for carfare. This latter request he had to repeat, as his father, on principle, did not like to hear requests for money, whether much or little. He asked Paul whether he could not go to some boy who lived nearer, and told him that he ought not to leave his school work until Sunday; but he gave him the dime. He was not a poor man, but he had a worthy ambition to come up in the world. His only reason for allowing Paul to usher was that he thought a boy ought to be earning a little.

Paul bounded upstairs, scrubbed the greasy odor of the dishwater from his hands with the ill-smelling soap he hated, and then shook over his fingers a few drops of violet water from the bottle he kept hidden in his drawer. He left the house with his geometry conspicuously under his arm, and the moment he got out of Cordelia Street and boarded a downtown car, he shook off the lethargy of two deadening days, and began to live again.

The leading juvenile of the permanent stock company which played at one of the downtown theaters was an acquaintance of Paul's, and the boy had been invited to drop in at the Sunday-night rehearsals whenever he could. For more than a year Paul had spent every available moment loitering about Charley Edward's dressing-room. He had won a place among Edward's following not only because the young actor, who could not afford to employ a dresser, often found him useful, but because he recognized in Paul something akin to what churchmen term "vocation."

It was at the theater and at Carnegie Hall that Paul really lived; the rest was but a sleep and a forgetting. This was Paul's fairy tale, and it had for him all the allurement of a secret love. The moment he inhaled the gassy, painty, dusty odor behind the scenes, he breathed like a prisoner set free, and felt within him the possibility of doing or saying splendid, brilliant things. The moment the cracked orchestra beat out the overture from *Martha,* or jerked at the serenade from *Rigoletto,* all stupid and ugly things slid from him, and his senses were deliciously, yet delicately fired.

Perhaps it was because, in Paul's world, the natural nearly always wore the guise of ugliness, that a certain element of artificiality seemed to him necessary in beauty. Perhaps it was because his experience of life elsewhere was so full of Sabbath-School picnics, petty economies, wholesome advice as to how to succeed in life, and the unescapable odors of cooking, that he found this existence so alluring, these smartly clad men and women so attractive, that he was so moved by these starry apple orchards that bloomed perennially under the limelight. It would be difficult to put it strongly enough how convincingly the stage entrance of the theater was for Paul the actual portal of Romance. Certainly none of the company ever suspected it, least of all Charley Edwards. It was very like the old stories that used to float about London of fabulously rich Jews, who had subterranean halls, with palms, and fountains, and soft lamps and richly appareled women who never saw the disenchanting light of London day. So, in the midst of that smoke-palled city, enamored of figures and grimy oil, Paul had his secret temple, his wishing-carpet, his bit of blue-and-white Mediterranean shore bathed in perpetual sunshine.

Several of Paul's teachers had a theory that his imagination had been perverted by garish fiction; but the truth was he scarcely ever read at all. The books at home were not such as would either tempt or corrupt a youthful mind, and as for reading the novels that some of his friends urged upon him—well, he got what he wanted much more quickly from music; any sort of music, from an orchestra to a barrel-organ. He needed only the spark, the indescribable thrill that made his imagination master of his senses, and he could make plots and pictures enough of his own. It was equally true that he was not stage-struck—not, at any rate, in the usual acceptation of the expression. He had no desire to become an actor, any more than he had to become a musician. He felt no necessity to do any of these things; what he wanted was to see, to be in the atmosphere, float on the wave of it, to be carried out, blue league after league, away from everything.

After a night behind the scenes, Paul found the schoolroom more than ever repulsive; the bare floors and naked walls; the prosy men who never wore frock coats, or violets in their buttonholes; the women with their dull gowns, shrill voices, and pitiful seriousness about prepositions that govern the dative. He could not bear to have the other pupils think, for a moment, that he took these people seriously; he must convey to them that he considered it all trivial, and was there only by way of a joke, anyway. He had autographed pictures of all the members of the stock company which he showed his classmates, telling them the most incredible stories of his familiarity with these people, of his acquaintance with the soloists who came to Carnegie Hall, his suppers with them and the flowers he sent them. When these stories lost their effect, and his audience grew listless, he would bid all the boys goodbye, announcing that he was going to travel for a while; going to Naples, to California, to Egypt. Then, next Monday, he would slip back, conscious and nervously smiling; his sister was ill, and he would have to defer his voyage until spring.

Matters went steadily worse with Paul at school. In the itch to let his instructors   35
know how heartily he despised them, and how thoroughly he was appreciated elsewhere, he mentioned once or twice that he had no time to fool with theorems, adding—
with a twitch of the eyebrows and a touch of that nervous bravado which so perplexed
them—that he was helping the people down at the stock company; they were old
friends of his.

The upshot of the matter was that the Principal went to Paul's father, and Paul was
taken out of school and put to work. The manager at Carnegie Hall was told to get another usher in his stead; the doorkeeper at the theater was warned not to admit him
to the house; and Charley Edwards remorsefully promised the boy's father not to see
him again.

The members of the stock company were vastly amused when some of Paul's stories reached them—especially the women. They were hard-working women, most of
them supporting indolent husbands or brothers, and they laughed rather bitterly at
having stirred the boy to such fervid and florid inventions. They agreed with the faculty and with his father, that Paul's was a bad case.

The east-bound train was plowing through a January snowstorm; the dull dawn
was beginning to show grey when the engine whistled a mile out of Newark. Paul
started up from the seat where he had lain curled in uneasy slumber, rubbed the
breath-misted window-glass with his hand, and peered out. The snow was whirling
in curling eddies above the white bottom lands, and the drifts lay already deep in the
fields and along the fences, while here and there the tall dead grass and dried weed
stalks protruded black above it. Lights shone from the scattered houses, and a gang of
laborers who stood beside the track waved their lanterns.

Paul had slept very little, and he felt grimy and uncomfortable. He had made the
all-night journey in a day coach because he was afraid if he took a Pullman he might
be seen by some Pittsburgh business man who had noticed him in Denny and Carson's
office. When the whistle woke him, he clutched quickly at his breast pocket, glancing
about him with an uncertain smile. But the little, clay-bespattered Italians were still
sleeping, the slatternly women across the aisle were in open-mouthed oblivion, and
even the crumby, crying babies were for the time stilled. Paul settled back to struggle
with his impatience as best he could.

When he arrived at the Jersey City station, he hurried through his breakfast,   40
manifestly ill at ease and keeping a sharp eye about him. After he reached the
Twenty-Third Street station, he consulted a cabman, and had himself driven to a
men's furnishing establishment which was just opening for the day. He spent upward of two hours there, buying with endless reconsidering and great care. His
new street suit he put on in the fitting-room; the frock coat and dress clothes clothes
he had bundled into the cab with his new shirts. Then he drove to a hatter's and a
shoe house. His next errand was at Tiffany's, where he selected silver-mounted
brushes and a scarf-pin. He would not wait to have his silver marked, he said. Lastly, he stopped at a trunk shop on Broadway, and had his purchases packed into various traveling-bags.

It was a little after one o'clock when he drove up to the Waldorf, and, after settling with the cabman, went into the office. He registered from Washington; said
his mother and father had been abroad, and that he had come down to await the
arrival of their steamer. He told his story plausibly and had no trouble, since he offered to pay for them in advance, in engaging his rooms; a sleeping-room, sitting-
room, and bath.

Not once, but a hundred times Paul had planned his entry into New York. He had gone over every detail of it with Charley Edwards, and in his scrapbook at home there were pages of description about New York hotels, cut from the Sunday papers.

When he was shown to his sitting-room on the eighth floor, he saw at a glance that everything was as it should be; there was but one detail in his mental picture that the place did not realize, so he rang for the bell-boy and sent him down for flowers. He moved about nervously until the boy returned, putting away his new linen and fingering it delightedly as he did so. When the flowers came, he put them hastily into water, and then tumbled into a hot bath. Presently he came out of his white bathroom, resplendent in his new silk underwear, and playing with the tassels of his red robe. The snow was whirling so fiercely outside his windows that he could scarcely see across the street; but within, the air was deliciously soft and fragrant. He put the violets and jonquils on the taboret beside the couch, and threw himself down with a long sigh, covering himself with a Roman blanket. He was thoroughly tired; he had been in such haste, he had stood up to such a strain, covered so much ground in the last twenty-four hours, that he wanted to think how it had all come about. Lulled by the sound of the wind, the warm air, and the cool fragrance of the flowers, he sank into deep, drowsy retrospection.

It had been wonderfully simple; when they had shut him out of the theater and concert hall, when they had taken away his bone, the whole thing was virtually determined. The rest was a mere matter of opportunity. The only thing that at all surprised him was his own courage—for he realized well enough that he had always been tormented by fear, a sort of apprehensive dread which, of late years, as the meshes of the lies he had told closed about him, had been pulling the muscles of his body tighter and tighter. Until now, he could not remember a time when he had not been dreading something. Even when he was a little boy, it was always there—behind him, or before, or on either side. There had always been the shadowed corner, the dark place into which he dared not look, but from which something seemed always to be watching him—and Paul had done things that were not pretty to watch, he knew.

45   But now he had a curious sense of relief, as though he had at last thrown down the gauntlet to the thing in the corner.

Yet it was but a day since he had been sulking in the traces; but yesterday afternoon that he had been sent to the bank with Denny and Carson's deposit, as usual—but this time he was instructed to leave the book to be balanced. There was above two thousand dollars in checks, and nearly a thousand in the banknotes which he had taken from the book and quietly transferred to his pocket. At the bank he had made out a new deposit slip. His nerves had been steady enough to permit of his returning to the office, where he had finished his work and asked for a full day's holiday tomorrow, Saturday, giving a perfectly reasonable pretext. The bank book, he knew, would not be returned before Monday or Tuesday, and his father would be out of town for the next week. From the time he slipped the banknotes into his pocket until he boarded the night train for New York, he had not known a moment's hesitation.

How astonishingly easy it had all been; here he was, the thing done; and this time there would be no awakening, no figure at the top of the stairs. He watched the snowflakes whirling by his window until he fell asleep.

When he awoke, it was four o'clock in the afternoon. He bounded up with a start; one of his precious days gone already! He spent nearly an hour in dressing, watching every stage of his toilet carefully in the mirror. Everything was quite perfect; he was exactly the kind of boy he had always wanted to be.

When he went downstairs, Paul took a carriage and drove up Fifth Avenue toward the Park. The snow had somewhat abated; carriages and tradesmen's wagons were hurrying soundlessly to and fro in the winter twilight; boys in woolen mufflers were shoveling off the doorsteps; the Avenue stages made fine spots of color against the white street. Here and there on the corners whole flower gardens blooming behind glass windows, against which the snowflakes stuck and melted; violets, roses, carnations, lilies-of-the-valley—somehow vastly more lovely and alluring that they blossomed thus unnaturally in the snow. The Park itself was a wonderful stage winter-piece.

When he returned, the pause of the twilight had ceased, and the tune of the streets had changed. The snow was falling faster, lights streamed from the hotels that reared their many stories fearlessly up into the storm, defying the raging Atlantic winds. A long, black stream of carriages poured down the Avenue, intersected here and there by other streams, tending horizontally. There were a score of cabs about the entrance of his hotel, and his driver had to wait. Boys in livery were running in and out of the awning stretched across the sidewalk, up and down the red velvet carpet laid from the door to the street. Above, about, within it all, was the rumble and roar, the hurry and toss of thousands of human beings as hot for pleasure as himself, and on every side of him towered the glaring affirmation of the omnipotence of wealth.

The boy set his teeth and drew his shoulders together in a spasm of realization; the plot of all dramas, the text of all romances, the nerve-stuff of all sensations was whirling about him like the snowflakes. He burnt like a fagot in a tempest.

When Paul came down to dinner, the music of the orchestra floated up the elevator shaft to greet him. As he stepped into the thronged corridor, he sank back into one of the chairs against the wall to get his breath. The lights, the chatter, the perfumes, the bewildering medley of color—he had, for a moment, the feeling of not being able to stand it. But only for a moment; these were his own people, he told himself. He went slowly about the corridors, through the writing-rooms, smoking-rooms, reception-rooms, as though he were exploring the chambers of an enchanted palace, built and peopled for him alone.

When he reached the dining-room he sat down at a table near a window. The flowers, the white linen, the many-colored wine-glasses, the gay toilettes of the women, the low popping of corks, the undulating repetitions of the "Blue Danube" from the orchestra, all flooded Paul's dream with bewildering radiance. When the roseate tinge of his champagne was added—that cold, precious, bubbling stuff that creamed and foamed in his glass—Paul wondered that there were honest men in the world at all. This was what all the world was fighting for, he reflected; this was what all the struggle was about. He doubted the reality of his past. Had he ever known a place called Cordelia Street, a place where fagged-looking business men boarded the early car? Mere rivets in a machine they seemed to Paul—sickening men, with combings of children's hair always hanging to their coats, and the smell of cooking in their clothes. Cordelia Street—Ah, that belonged to another time and country! Had he not always been thus, had he not sat here night after night, from as far back as he could remember, looking pensively over just such shimmering textures, and slowly twirling the stem of a glass like this one between his thumb and middle finger? He rather thought he had.

He was not in the least abashed or lonely. He had no especial desire to meet or to know any of these people; all he demanded was the right to look on and conjecture, to watch the pageant. The mere stage properties were all he contended for. Nor was he lonely later in the evening, in his loge at the Opera. He was entirely rid of his nervous misgivings, of his forced aggressiveness, of the imperative desire to show himself different from his surroundings. He felt now that his surroundings explained him. Nobody questioned the purple; he had only to wear it passively. He had only to glance down at his dress coat to reassure himself that here it would be impossible for anyone to humiliate him.

55   He found it hard to leave his beautiful sitting-room to go to bed that night, and sat long watching the raging storm from his turret window. When he went to sleep, it was with the lights turned on in his bedroom; partly because of his old timidity, and partly so that, if he should wake in the night, there would be no wretched moment of doubt, no horrible suspicion of yellow wallpaper, or of Washington and Calvin above his bed.

On Sunday morning the city was practically snowbound. Paul breakfasted late, and in the afternoon he fell in with a wild San Francisco boy, a freshman at Yale, who said he had run down for a "little flyer" over Sunday. The young man offered to show Paul the night side of the town, and the two boys went off together after dinner, not returning to the hotel until seven o'clock the next morning. They had started out in the confiding warmth of a champagne friendship, but their parting in the elevator was singularly cool. The freshman pulled himself together to make his train, and Paul went to bed. He awoke at two o'clock in the afternoon, very thirsty and dizzy, and rang for ice-water, coffee, and the Pittsburgh papers.

On the part of the hotel management, Paul excited no suspicion. There was this to be said for him, that he wore his spoils with dignity and in no way made himself conspicuous. His chief greediness lay in his ears and eyes, and his excesses were not offensive ones. His dearest pleasures were the grey winter twilights in his sitting-room; his quiet enjoyment of his flowers, his clothes, his wide divan, his cigarette, and his sense of power. He could not remember a time when he had felt so at peace with himself. The mere release from the necessity of petty lying, lying every day and every day, restored his self-respect. He had never lied for pleasure, even at school; but to make himself noticed and admired, to assert his difference from other Cordelia Street boys; and he felt a good deal more manly, more honest, even, now that he had no need for boastful pretensions, now that he could, as his actor friends used to say, "dress the part." It was characteristic that remorse did not occur to him. His golden days went by without a shadow, and he made each as perfect as he could.

On the eighth day after his arrival in New York, he found the whole affair exploited in the Pittsburgh papers, exploited with a wealth of detail which indicated that local news of a sensational nature was at a low ebb. The firm of Denny and Carson announced that the boy's father had refunded the full amount of his theft, and that they had no intention of prosecuting. The Cumberland minister had been interviewed, and expressed his hope of yet reclaiming the motherless lad, and Paul's Sabbath-School teacher declared that she would spare no effort to that end. The rumor had reached Pittsburgh that the boy had been seen in a New York hotel, and his father had gone East to find him and bring him home.

Paul had just come in to dress for dinner; he sank into the chair, weak in the knees, and clasped his head in his hands. It was to be worse than jail, even; the tepid waters of Cordelia Street were to close over him finally and forever. The grey monotony stretched before him in hopeless, unrelieved years—Sabbath School, Young People's Meeting, the yellow-papered room, the damp dish-towels; it all rushed back upon him with sickening vividness. He had the old feeling that the orchestra had suddenly stopped, the sinking sensation that the play was over. The sweat broke out on his face, and he sprang to his feet, looked about him with his white, conscious smile, and winked at himself in the mirror. With something of the childish belief in miracles with which he had so often gone to class, all his lessons unlearned, Paul dressed and dashed whistling down the corridor to the elevator.

He had no sooner entered the dining-room and caught the measure of the music than his remembrance was lightened by his old elastic power of claiming the moment, mounting with it, and finding it all-sufficient. The glare and glitter about him, the mere scenic accessories had again, and for the last time, their old potency. He would show himself that he was game, he would finish the thing splendidly. He doubted, more than ever, the existence of Cordelia Street, and for the first time he drank his wine recklessly. Was he not, after all, one of these fortunate beings? Was he not still himself, and in his own place? He drummed a nervous accompaniment to the music and looked about him, telling himself over and over that it had paid.

He reflected drowsily, to the swell of the violin and the chill sweetness of his wine, that he might have done it more wisely. He might have caught an outbound steamer and been well out of their clutches before now. But the other side of the world had seemed too far away and too uncertain then; he could not have waited for it; his need had been too sharp. If he had to choose over again, he would do the same thing to-morrow. He looked affectionately about the dining-room, now gilded with a soft mist. Ah, it had paid indeed!

Paul was awakened next morning by a painful throbbing in his head and feet. He had thrown himself across the bed without undressing, and had slept with his shoes on. His limbs and hands were lead-heavy, and his tongue and throat were parched. There came upon him one of those fateful attacks of clear-headedness that never occurred except when he was physically exhausted and his nerves hung loose. He lay still and closed his eyes and let the tide of realities wash over him.

His father was in New York, "stopping at some joint or other," he told himself. The memory of successive summers on the front stoop fell upon him like a weight of black water. He had not a hundred dollars left; and he knew now, more than ever, that money was everything, the wall that stood between all he loathed and all he wanted. The thing was winding itself up; he had thought of that on his first glorious day in New York, and had even provided a way to snap the thread. It lay on his dressing-table now; he had got it out last night when he came blindly up from dinner—but the shiny metal hurt his eyes, and he disliked the look of it, anyway.

He rose and moved about with a painful effort, succumbing now and again to attacks of nausea. It was the old depression exaggerated; all the world had become Cordelia Street. Yet somehow he was not afraid of anything, was absolutely calm; perhaps because he had looked into the dark corner at last, and knew. It was bad enough, what he saw there; but somehow not so bad as his long fear of it had been. He saw everything clearly now. He had a feeling that he had made the best of it, that he had lived the sort of life he was meant to live, and for half an hour he sat staring at the revolver. But he told himself that was not the way, so he went downstairs and took a cab to the ferry.

When Paul arrived at Newark, he got off the train and took another cab, directing the driver to follow the Pennsylvania tracks out of town. The snow lay heavy on the roadways and had drifted deep in the open fields. Only here and there the dead grass or dried weed stalks projected, singularly black, above it.

Once well into the country, Paul dismissed the carriage and walked, floundering along the tracks, his mind a medley of irrelevant things. He seemed to hold in his brain an actual picture of everything he had seen that morning. He remembered every feature of both his drivers, the toothless old woman from whom he had bought the red flowers in his coat, the agent from whom he had got his ticket, and all of his fellow-passengers on the ferry. His mind, unable to cope with vital matters near at hand, worked feverishly and deftly at sorting and grouping these images. They made for him a part of the ugliness of the world, of the ache in his head, and the bitter burning on his tongue. He stooped and put a handful of snow into his mouth as he walked, but that, too, seemed hot. When he reached a little hillside, where the tracks ran through a cut some twenty feet below him, he stopped and sat down.

The carnations in his coat were drooping with cold, he noticed; their red glory over. It occurred to him that all the flowers he had seen in the show windows that first night must have gone the same way, long before this. It was only one splendid breath they had, in spite of their brave mockery at the winter outside the glass. It was a losing game in the end, it seemed, this revolt against the homilies by which the world is run. Paul took one of the blossoms carefully from his coat and scooped a little hole in the snow, where he covered it up. Then he dozed awhile, from his weak condition, seeming insensible to the cold.

The sound of an approaching train woke him and he started to his feet, remembering only his resolution, and afraid lest he should be too late. He stood watching the approaching locomotive, his teeth chattering, his lips drawn away from them in a frightened smile; once or twice he glanced nervously sidewise, as though he were being watched. When the right moment came, he jumped. As he fell, the folly of his haste occurred to him with merciless clearness, the vastness of what he had left undone. There flashed through his brain, clearer than ever before, the blue of Adriatic water, the yellow of Algerian sands.

He felt something strike his chest—his body being thrown swiftly through the air, on and on, immeasurably far and fast, while his limbs gently relaxed. Then, because the picture-making mechanism was crushed, the disturbing visions flashed into black, and Paul dropped back into the immense design of things.   [1905]

QUESTIONS

1. In what sense is this story a study of Paul's *case?* How is Cather's treatment shaped by the omniscient point of view?

2. What reason might be advanced for the almost total lack of dialogue in the story?

3. How are the contrasting settings of the story related to its theme?

4. Carefully analyze the paragraph beginning "The following Sunday was fine; . . ." How do the descriptive details reveal the author's attitude toward her subject?

5. Can the story be said to illustrate that there is an "immense design of things"?

JOHN CHEEVER

John Cheever (1912–1982) was born in Quincy, Massachusetts. His parents intended him for Harvard, but in his junior year he was expelled from prep school. He promptly announced his own plan for his life by publishing a sketch in the *New Republic* entitled "Expelled." For the next half-century he devoted himself chiefly to the short story. Appearing usually in the *New Yorker*, his stories chronicle the manners and morals of urban and suburban Americans. His stories have been collected in *The Way Some People Live* (1943), *The Enormous Radio* (1953), *The Housebreaker of Shady Hill* (1958), *Some People, Some Places and Things That Will Not Appear in My Next Novel* (1961), *The Brigadier and the Golf Widow* (1964), *The World of Apples* (1973), and *The Stories of John Cheever* (1978), which won the Pulitzer Prize. In addition to his short stories, he wrote five novels.

The Swimmer

It was one of those midsummer Sundays when everyone sits around saying: "I *drank* too much last night." You might have heard it whispered by the parishioners leaving church, heard it from the lips of the priest himself, struggling with his cassock in the *vestiarium*, heard it from the golf links and the tennis courts, heard it from the wildlife preserve where the leader of the Audubon group was suffering from a terrible hangover. "I *drank* too much," said Donald Westerhazy. "We all *drank* too much," said Lucinda Merrill. "It must have been the wine," said Helen Westerhazy. "I *drank* too much of that claret."

This was at the edge of the Westerhazys' pool. The pool, fed by an artesian well with a high iron content, was a pale shade of green. It was a fine day. In the west there was a massive stand of cumulus cloud so like a city seen from a distance—from the bow of an approaching ship—that it might have had a name. Lisbon. Hackensack. The sun was hot. Neddy Merrill sat by the green water, one hand in it, one around a glass of gin. He was a slender man—he seemed to have the especial slenderness of youth—and while he was far from young he had slid down his banister that morning and given the bronze backside of Aphrodite on the hall table a smack, as he jogged toward the smell of coffee in his dining room. He might have been compared to a summer's day, particularly the last hours of one, and while he lacked a tennis racket or a sail bag the impression was definitely one of youth, sport, and clement weather. He had been swimming and now he was breathing deeply, stertorously as if he could gulp into his lungs the components of that moment, the heat of the sun, the intenseness of his pleasure. It all seemed to flow into his chest. His own house stood in Bullet Park, eight miles to the south, where his four beautiful daughters would have had their lunch and might be playing tennis. Then it occurred to him that by taking a dogleg to the southwest he could reach his home by water.

His life was not confining and the delight he took in this observation could not be explained by its suggestion of escape. He seemed to see, with a cartographer's eye, that string of swimming pools, that quasi-subterranean stream that curved across the county. He had made a discovery, a contribution to modern geography; he would name the stream Lucinda after his wife. He was not a practical joker nor was he a fool but he was determinedly original and had a vague and modest idea of himself as a legendary figure. The day was beautiful and it seemed to him that a long swim might enlarge and celebrate its beauty.

He took off a sweater that was hung over his shoulders and dove in. He had an inexplicable contempt for men who did not hurl themselves into pools. He swam a choppy crawl, breathing either with every stroke or every fourth stroke and counting somewhere well in the back of his mind the one-two one-two of a flutter kick. It was not a serviceable stroke for long distances but the domestication of swimming had saddled the sport with some customs and in his part of the world a crawl was customary. To be embraced and sustained by the light green water was less a pleasure, it seemed, than the resumption of a natural condition, and he would have liked to swim without trunks, but this was not possible, considering his project. He hoisted himself up on the far curb—he never used the ladder—and started across the lawn. When Lucinda asked where he was going he said he was going to swim home.

5   The only maps and charts he had to go by were remembered or imaginary but these were clear enough. First there were the Grahams, the Hammers, the Lears, the Howlands, and the Crosscups. He would cross Ditmar Street to the Bunkers and come, after a short portage, to the Levys, the Welchers, and the public pool in Lancaster. Then there were the Hallorans, the Sachses, the Biswangers, Shirley Adams, the Gilmartins, and the Clydes. The day was lovely, and that he lived in a world so generously supplied with water seemed like a clemency, a beneficence. His heart was high and he ran across the grass. Making his way home by an uncommon route gave him the feeling that he was a pilgrim, an explorer, a man with a destiny, and he knew that he would find friends all along the way; friends would line the banks of the Lucinda River.

He went through a hedge that separated the Westerhazys' land from the Grahams', walked under some flowering apple trees, passed the shed that housed their pump and filter, and came out at the Grahams' pool. "Why, Neddy," Mrs. Graham said, "what a marvelous surprise. I've been trying to get you on the phone all morning. Here, let me get you a drink." He saw then, like any explorer, that the hospitable customs and traditions of the natives would have to be handled with diplomacy if he was ever going to reach his destination. He did not want to mystify or seem rude to the Grahams nor did he have the time to linger there. He swam the length of their pool and joined them in the sun and was rescued, a few minutes later, by the arrival of two carloads of friends from Connecticut. During the uproarious reunions he was able to slip away. He went down by the front of the Grahams' house, stepped over a thorny hedge, and crossed a vacant lot to the Hammers'. Mrs. Hammer, looking up from her roses, saw him swim by although she wasn't quite sure who it was. The Lears heard him splashing past the open windows of their living room. The Howlands and the Crosscups were away. After leaving the Howlands' he crossed Ditmar Street and started for the Bunkers', where he could hear, even at that distance, the noise of a party.

The water refracted the sound of voices and laughter and seemed to suspend it in midair. The Bunkers' pool was on a rise and he climbed some stairs to a terrace where twenty-five or thirty men and women were drinking. The only person in the water was Rusty Towers, who floated there on a rubber raft. Oh how bonny and lush were the banks of the Lucinda River! Prosperous men and women gathered by the sapphire-colored waters while caterer's men in white coats passed them cold gin. Overhead a red Haviland trainer was circling around and around and around in the sky with something like the glee of a child in a swing. Ned felt a passing affection for the scene, a tenderness for the gathering, as if it was something he might touch. In the distance he heard thunder. As soon as Enid Bunker saw him she began to scream: "Oh look who's here! What a marvelous surprise! When Lucinda said that you couldn't come I thought I'd *die.*" She made her way to him through the crowd, and when they had finished kissing she led him to the bar, a progress that was slowed by the fact that he stopped to kiss eight or ten other women and shake the hands of as many men. A smiling bartender he had seen at a hundred parties gave him a gin and tonic and he stood by the bar for a moment, anxious not to get stuck in any conversation that would delay his voyage. When he seemed about to be surrounded he dove in and swam close to the side to avoid colliding with Rusty's raft. At the far end of the pool he bypassed the Tomlinsons with a broad smile and jogged up the garden path. The gravel cut his feet but this was the only unpleasantness. The party was confined to the pool, and as he went toward the house he heard the brilliant, watery sound of voices fade, heard the noise of a radio from the Bunkers' kitchen, where someone was listening to a ballgame. Sunday afternoon. He made his way through the parked cars and down the grassy border of their driveway to Alewives' Lane. He did not want to be seen on the road in his bathing trunks but there was no traffic and he made the short distance to the Levys' driveway, marked with a private property sign and a green tube for the *New York Times.* All the doors and windows of the big house were open but there were no signs of life; not even a dog barked. He went around the side of the house to the pool and saw that the Levys had only recently left. Glasses and bottles and dishes of nuts were on a table at the deep end, where there was a bathhouse or gazebo, hung with Japanese lanterns. After swimming the pool he got himself a glass and poured a drink. It was his fourth or fifth drink and he had swum nearly half the length of the Lucinda River. He felt tired, clean, and pleased at that moment to be alone; pleased with everything.

It would storm. The stand of cumulus cloud—that city—had risen and darkened, and while he sat there he heard the percussiveness of thunder again. The de Haviland trainer was still circling overhead and it seemed to Ned that he could almost hear the pilot laugh with pleasure in the afternoon; but when there was another peal of thunder he took off for home. A train whistle blew and he wondered what time it had gotten to be. Four? Five? He thought of the provincial station at that hour, where a waiter, his tuxedo concealed by a raincoat, a dwarf with some flowers wrapped in newspaper, and a woman who had been crying would be waiting for the local. It was suddenly growing dark; it was that moment when the pin-headed birds seem to organize their song into some acute and knowledgeable recognition of the storm's approach. Then there was a fine noise of rushing water from the crown of an oak at his back, as if a spigot there had been turned. Then the noise of fountains came from the crowns of all the tall trees. Why did he love storms, what was the meaning of his excitement when the door sprang open and the rain wind fled rudely up the stairs, why had the simple task of shutting the windows of an old house seemed fitting and urgent, why did the first watery notes of a storm wind have for him the unmistakable sound of good news, cheer, glad tidings? Then there was an explosion, a smell of cordite, and rain lashed the Japanese lanterns that Mrs. Levy had bought in Kyoto the year before last, or was it the year before that?

He stayed in the Levys' gazebo until the storm had passed. The rain had cooled the air and he shivered. The force of the wind had stripped a maple of its red and yellow leaves and scattered them over the grass and the water. Since it was midsummer the tree must be blighted, and yet he felt a peculiar sadness at this sign of autumn. He braced his shoulders, emptied his glass, and started for the Welchers' pool. This meant crossing the Lindleys' riding ring and he was surprised to find it overgrown with grass and all the jumps dismantled. He wondered if the Lindleys had sold their horses or gone away for the summer and put them out to board. He seemed to remember having heard something about the Lindleys and their horses but the memory was unclear. Oh he went, barefoot through the wet grass, to the Welchers', where he found their pool was dry.

10   This breach in his chain of water disappointed him absurdly, and he felt like some explorer who seeks a torrential headwater and finds a dead stream. He was disappointed and mystified. It was common enough to go away for the summer but no one ever drained his pool. The Welchers had definitely gone away. The pool furniture was folded, stacked, and covered with a tarpaulin. The bathhouse was locked. All the windows of the house were shut, and when he went around to the driveway in front he saw a for-sale sign nailed to a tree. When had he last heard from the Welchers—when, that is, had he and Lucinda last regretted an invitation to dine with them. It seemed only a week or so ago. Was his memory failing or had he so disciplined it in the repression of unpleasant facts that he had damaged his sense of the truth? Then in the distance he heard the sound of a tennis game. This cheered him, cleared away all his apprehensions and let him regard the overcast sky and the cold air with indifference. This was the day that Neddy Merrill swam across the county. That was the day! He started off then for his most difficult portage.

Had you gone for a Sunday afternoon ride that day you might have seen him, close to naked, standing on the shoulders of route 424, waiting for a chance to cross. You might have wondered if he was the victim of foul play, had his car broken down, or was he merely a fool. Standing barefoot in the deposits of the highway—beer cans, rags, and blowout patches—exposed to all kinds of ridicule, he seemed pitiful. He had known when he started that this was a part of his journey—it had been on his maps—but confronted with the lines of traffic, worming through the summery light, he found himself unprepared. He was laughed at, jeered at, a beer can was thrown at him, and he had no dignity or humor to bring to the situation. He could have gone back, back to the Westerhazys', where Lucinda would still be sitting in the sun. He had signed nothing, vowed nothing, pledged nothing not even to himself. Why, believing as he did, that all human obduracy was susceptible to common sense, was he unable to turn back? Why was he determined to complete his journey even if it meant putting his life in danger? At what point had this prank, this joke, this piece of horseplay become serious? He could not go back, he could not even recall with any clearness the green water at the Westerhazys', the sense of inhaling the day's components, the friendly and relaxed voices saying that they had *drunk* too much. In the space of an hour, more or less, he had covered a distance that made his return impossible.

An old man, tooling down the highway at fifteen miles an hour, let him get to the middle of the road, where there was a grass divider. Here he was exposed to the ridicule of the northbound traffic, but after ten or fifteen minutes he was able to cross. From here he had only a short walk to the Recreation Center at the edge of the Village of Lancaster, where there were some handball courts and a public pool.

The effect of the water on voices, the illusion of brilliance and suspense, was the same here as it had been at the Bunkers' but the sounds here were louder, harsher, and more shrill, and as soon as he entered the crowded enclosure he was confronted with regimentation. "ALL SWIMMERS MUST TAKE A SHOWER BEFORE USING THE POOL. ALL SWIMMERS MUST USE THE FOOTBATH. ALL SWIMMERS MUST WEAR THEIR IDENTIFICATION DISKS." He took a shower, washed his feet in a cloudy and bitter solution and made his way to the edge of the water. It stank of chlorine and looked to him like a sink. A pair of lifeguards in a pair of towers blew police whistles at what seemed to be regular intervals and abused the swimmers through a public address system. Neddy remembered the sapphire water at the Bunkers' with longing and thought that he might contaminate himself—damage his own prosperousness and charm—by swimming in this murk, but he reminded himself that he was an explorer, a pilgrim, and that this was merely a stagnant bend in the Lucinda River. He dove, scowling with distaste, into the chlorine and had to swim with his head above water to avoid collisions, but even so he was bumped into, splashed and jostled. When he got to the shallow end both lifeguards were shouting at him: "Hey, you, you without the identification disk, get outa the water." He did, but they had no way of pursuing him and he went through the reek of suntan oil and chlorine out through the hurricane fence and passed the handball courts. By crossing the road he entered the wooded part of the Halloran estate. The woods were not cleared and the footing was treacherous and difficult until he reached the lawn and the clipped beech hedge that encircled their pool.

The Hallorans were friends, an elderly couple of enormous wealth who seemed to bask in the suspicion that they might be Communists. They were zealous reformers but they were not Communists, and yet when they were accused, as they sometimes were, of subversion, it seemed to gratify and excite them. Their beech hedge was yellow and he guessed this had been blighted like the Levys' maple. He called hullo, hullo, to warn the Hallorans of his approach, to palliate his invasion of their privacy. The Hallorans, for reasons that had never been explained to him, did not wear bathing suits. No explanations were in order, really. Their nakedness was a detail in their uncompromising zeal for reform and he stepped politely out of his trunks before he went through the opening in the hedge.

Mrs. Halloran, a stout woman with white hair and a serene face, was reading the *Times*. Mr. Halloran was taking beech leaves out of the water with a scoop. They seemed not surprised or displeased to see him. Their pool was perhaps the oldest in the county, a fieldstone rectangle, fed by a brook. It had no filter or pump and its waters were the opaque gold of the stream.   15

"I'm swimming across the county," Ned said.

"Why, I didn't know one could," exclaimed Mrs. Halloran.

"Well, I've made it from the Westerhazys'," Ned said. "That must be about four miles."

He left his trunks at the deep end, walked to the shallow end, and swam this stretch. As he was pulling himself out of the water he heard Mrs. Halloran say: "We've been *terribly* sorry to hear about all your misfortunes, Neddy."

"My misfortunes?" Ned asked. "I don't know what you mean."   20

"Why, we heard that you'd sold the house and that your poor children. . . ."

"I don't recall having sold the house," Ned said, "and the girls are at home."

"Yes," Mrs. Halloran sighed. "Yes. . . ." Her voice filled the air with an unseasonable melancholy and Ned spoke briskly. "Thank you for the swim."

"Well, have a nice trip," said Mrs. Halloran.

25   Beyond the hedge he pulled on his trunks and fastened them. They were loose and he wondered if, during the space of an afternoon, he could have lost some weight. He was cold and he was tired and the naked Hallorans and their dark water had depressed him. The swim was too much for his strength but how could he have guessed this, sliding down the banister that morning and sitting in the Westerhazys' sun? His arms were lame. His legs felt rubbery and ached at the joints. The worst of it was the cold in his bones and the feeling that he might never be warm again. Leaves were falling down around him and he smelled woodsmoke on the wind. Who would be burning wood at this time of year?

He needed a drink. Whiskey would warm him, pick him up, carry him through the last of his journey, refresh his feeling that it was original and valorous to swim across the county. Channel swimmers took brandy. He needed a stimulant. He crossed the lawn in front of the Hallorans' house and went down a little path to where they had built a house for their only daughter Helen and her husband Eric Sachs. The Sachses' pool was small and he found Helen and her husband there.

"Oh, *Neddy*," Helen said. "Did you lunch at Mother's?"

"Not *really*," Ned said. "I *did* stop to see your parents." This seemed to be explanation enough. "I'm terribly sorry to break in on you like this but I've taken a chill and I wonder if you'd give me a drink."

"Why, I'd *love* to," Helen said, "but there hasn't been anything in this house to drink since Eric's operation. That was three years ago."

30   Was he losing his memory, had his gift for concealing painful facts let him forget that he had sold his house, that his children were in trouble, and that his friend had been ill? His eyes slipped from Eric's face to his abdomen, where he saw three pale, sutured scars, two of them at least a foot long. Gone was his navel, and what, Neddy thought, would the roving hand, bed-checking one's gifts at 3 A.M. make of a belly with no navel, no link to birth, this breach in the succession?

"I'm sure you can get a drink at the Biswangers'," Helen said. "They're having an enormous do. You can hear it from here. Listen!"

She raised her head and from across the road, the lawns, the gardens, the woods, the fields, he heard again the brilliant noise of voices over water. "Well, I'll get wet," he said, still feeling that he had no freedom of choice about his means of travel. He dove into the Sachses' cold water and, gasping, close to drowning, made his way from one end of the pool to the other. "Lucinda and I want *terribly* to see you," he said over his shoulder, his face set toward the Biswangers'. "We're sorry it's been so long and we'll call you *very* soon."

He crossed some fields to the Biswangers' and the sounds of revelry there. They would be honored to give him a drink, they would be happy to give him a drink, they would in fact be lucky to give him a drink. The Biswangers invited him and Lucinda for dinner four times a year, six weeks in advance. They were always rebuffed and yet they continued to send out their invitations, unwilling to comprehend the rigid and undemocratic realities of their society. They were the sort of people who discussed the price of things at cocktails, exchanged market tips during dinner, and after dinner told dirty stories to mixed company. They did not belong to Neddy's set—they were not even on Lucinda's Christmas card list. He went toward their pool with feelings of indifference, charity, and some unease, since it seemed to be getting dark and these were the longest days of the year. The party when he joined it was noisy and large. Grace Biswanger was the kind of hostess who asked the optometrist, the veterinarian; the real-estate dealer and the dentist. No one was swimming and the twilight, reflected on the water of the pool, had a wintry gleam. There was a bar and he started for this. When Grace Biswanger saw him she came toward him, not affectionately as he had every right to expect, but bellicosely.

"Why, this party has everything," she said loudly, "including a gate crasher."

She could not deal him a social blow—there was no question about this and he did 35
not flinch. "As a gate crasher," he asked politely, "do I rate a drink?"

"Suit yourself," she said. "You don't seem to pay much attention to invitations."

She turned her back on him and joined some guests, and he went to the bar and ordered a whiskey. The bartender served him but he served him rudely. His was a world in which the caterer's men kept the social score, and to be rebuffed by a part-time barkeep meant that he had suffered some loss of social esteem. Or perhaps the man was new and uninformed. Then he heard Grace at his back say: "They went for broke overnight—nothing but income—and he showed up drunk one Sunday and asked us to loan him five thousand dollars. . . ." She was always talking about money. It was worse than eating your peas off a knife. He dove into the pool, swam its length and went away.

The next pool on his list, the last but two, belonged to his old mistress, Shirley Adams. If he had suffered any injuries at the Biswangers' they would be cured here. Love—sexual roughhouse in fact—was the supreme elixir, the painkiller, the brightly colored pill that would put the spring back into his step, the joy of life in his heart. They had had an affair last week, last month, last year. He couldn't remember. It was he who had broken it off, his was the upper hand, and he stepped through the gate of the wall that surrounded her pool with nothing so considered as self-confidence. It seemed in a way to be his pool as the lover, particularly the illicit lover, enjoys the possessions of his mistress with an authority unknown to holy matrimony. She was there, her hair the color of brass, but her figure, at the edge of the lighted, cerulean water, excited in him no profound memories. It had been, he thought, a lighthearted affair, although she had wept when he broke it off. She seemed confused to see him and he wondered if she was still wounded. Would she, God forbid, weep again?

"What do you want?" she asked.

"I'm swimming across the county." 40

"Good Christ. Will you ever grow up?"

"What's the matter?"

"If you've come here for money," she said, "I won't give you another cent."

"You could give me a drink."

"I could but I won't. I'm not alone." 45

"Well, I'm on my way."

He dove in and swam the pool, but when he tried to haul himself up onto the curb he found that the strength in his arms and his shoulders had gone, and he paddled to the ladder and climbed out. Looking over his shoulder he saw, in the lighted bathhouse, a young man. Going out onto the dark lawn he smelled chrysanthemums or marigolds—some stubborn autumnal fragrance—on the night air, strong as gas. Looking overhead he saw that the stars had come out, but why should he seem to see Andromeda, Cepheus, and Cassiopeia? What had become of the constellations of midsummer? He began to cry.

It was probably the first time in his adult life that he had ever cried, certainly the first time in his life that he had ever felt so miserable, cold, tired, and bewildered. He could not understand the rudeness of the caterer's barkeep or the rudeness of a mistress who had come to him on her knees and showered his trousers with tears. He had swum too long, he had been immersed too long, and his nose and his throat were sore from the water. What he needed then was a drink, some company, and some clean dry clothes, and while he could have cut directly across the road to his home he went on to the Gilmartins' pool. Here, for the first time in his life, he did not dive but went down the steps into the icy water and swam a hobbled side stroke that he might have learned as a youth. He staggered with fatigue on his way to the Clydes' and paddled the length of their pool, stopping again and again with his hand on the curb to rest. He climbed up the ladder and wondered if he had the strength to get home. He had done what he wanted, he had swum the county, but he was so stupefied with exhaustion that his triumph seemed vague. Stooped, holding onto the gateposts for support, he turned up the driveway of his own house.

The place was dark. Was it so late that they had all gone to bed? Had Lucinda stayed at the Westerhazys' for supper? Had the girls joined her there or gone someplace else? Hadn't they agreed, as they usually did on Sunday, to regret all their invitations and stay at home? He tried the garage doors to see what cars were in but the doors were locked and rust came off the handles onto his hands. Going toward the house, he saw that the force of the thunderstorm had knocked one of the rain gutters loose. It hung down over the front door like an umbrella rib, but it could be fixed in the morning. The house was locked, and he thought that the stupid cook or the stupid maid must have locked the place up until he remembered that it had been some time since they had employed a maid or a cook. He shouted, pounded on the door, tried to force it with his shoulder, and then, looking in at the windows, saw that the place was empty.   [1964]

QUESTIONS

1. Trace and account for the shifts in point of view in the story.
2. What pattern of imagery does the author employ to characterize Neddy Merrill?
3. How is the setting related to the theme?
4. How does the storm mark a redirection in the story?
5. Why is the protagonist so intent on completing his journey? Interpret the concluding sentences.

RESPONSES

1. Analyze the story from the sociological/Marxist approach. How is wealth and status portrayed in the story? What affect does it have on the protagonist?
2. Write an essay exploring the metaphor of "a lifetime is a day" in this story and in Mahfouz's "Half a Day."

FOCUS ON FILM

1. Compare the story to the filmed adaptation, also called *The Swimmer*. How does the film handle the shifts in point of view?
2. Which is more effective in conveying the "lifetime is a day" metaphor, the short story or the film? Why?

ANTON CHEKHOV

Anton Chekhov (1860–1904) was born in Taganrog, Russia. He began writing stories while studying to be a physician at Moscow University, and he published his first collection of tales in 1884, the same year he received his medical degree. Although occasionally practicing medicine, he quickly established a literary reputation. At first he was a fluent and facile writer. Chekhov's output significantly slowed, but his later, more studied stories assured his reputation as one of the greatest practitioners of short fiction. In 1901 he married a young actress, and the plays of his last years, among them *Uncle Vanya* (1899) and *The Cherry Orchard* (1904), are recognized as masterpieces of world drama.

The Darling

Olenka, the daughter of the retired collegiate assessor,° Plemyanniakov, was sitting in her back porch, lost in thought. It was hot, the flies were persistent and teasing, and it was pleasant to reflect that it would soon be evening. Dark rainclouds were gathering from the east, and bringing from time to time a breath of moisture in the air.

Kukin, who was the manager of an open-air theater called the Tivoli, and who lived in the lodge, was standing in the middle of the garden looking at the sky.

"Again!" he observed despairingly. "It's going to rain again! Rain every day, as though to spite me. I might as well hang myself! It's ruin! Fearful losses every day."

He flung up his hands, and went on, addressing Olenka:

5   "There! That's the life we lead, Olga Semyonovna. It's enough to make one cry. One works and does one's utmost, one wears oneself out, getting no sleep at night, and racks one's brain what to do for the best. And then what happens? To begin with, one's public is ignorant, boorish. I give them the very best operetta, a dainty masque, first rate music-hall artists. But do you suppose that's what they want! They don't understand anything of that sort. They want a clown; what they ask for is vulgarity. And then look at the weather! Almost every evening it rains. It started on the tenth of May, and it's kept it up all May and June. It's simply awful! The public doesn't come, but I've to pay the rent just the same, and pay the artists."

°*collegiate assessor*: Minor academic administrator.

The next evening the clouds would gather again, and Kukin would say with an hysterical laugh:

"Well, rain away, then! Flood the garden, drown me! Damn my luck in this world and the next! Let the artists have me up! Send me to prison!—to Siberia!—the scaffold! Ha, ha, ha!"

And the next day the same thing.

Olenka listened to Kukin with silent gravity, and sometimes tears came into her eyes. In the end his misfortunes touched her; she grew to love him. He was a small thin man, with a yellow face, and curls combed forward on his forehead. He spoke in a thin tenor; as he talked his mouth worked on one side, and there was always an expression of despair on his face; yet he aroused a deep and genuine affection in her. She was always fond of someone, and could not exist without loving. In earlier days she had loved her papa, who now sat in a darkened room, breathing with difficulty; she had loved her aunt who used to come every other year from Bryansk; and before that, when she was at school, she had loved her French master. She was a gentle, soft-hearted, compassionate girl, with mild, tender eyes and very good health. At the sight of her full rosy cheeks, her soft white neck with a little dark mole on it, and the kind, naïve smile, which came into her face when she listened to anything pleasant, men thought, "Yes, not half bad," and smiled too, while lady visitors could not refrain from seizing her hand in the middle of a conversation, exclaiming in a gush of delight, "You darling!"

The house in which she had lived from her birth upwards, and which was left her   10
in her father's will, was at the extreme end of the town, not far from the Tivoli. In the evenings and at night she could hear the band playing, and the crackling and banging of fireworks, and it seemed to her that it was Kukin struggling with his destiny, storming the entrenchments of his chief foe, the indifferent public; there was a sweet thrill at her heart, she had no desire to sleep, and when he returned home at daybreak, she tapped softly at her bedroom window, and showing him only her face and one shoulder through the curtain, she gave him a friendly smile. . . .

He proposed to her, and they were married. And when he had a closer view of her neck and her plump, fine shoulders, he threw up his hands, and said:

"You darling!"

He was happy, but as it rained on the day and night of his wedding, his face still retained an expression of despair.

They got on very well together. She used to sit in his office, to look after things in the Tivoli, to put down the accounts and pay the wages. And her rosy cheeks, her sweet, naïve, radiant smile, were to be seen now at the office window, now in the refreshment bar or behind the scenes of the theater. And already she used to say to her acquaintances that the theater was the chief and most important thing in life, and that it was only through the drama that one could derive true enjoyment and become cultivated and humane.

"But do you suppose the public understands that?" she used to say. "What they   15
want is a clown. Yesterday we gave 'Faust Inside Out,' and almost all the boxes were empty; but if Vanitchka and I had been producing some vulgar thing, I assure you the theater would have been packed. Tomorrow Vanitchka and I are doing 'Orpheus in Hell.' Do come."

And what Kukin said about the theater and the actors she repeated. Like him she despised the public for their ignorance and their indifference to art; she took part in the rehearsals, she corrected the actors, she kept an eye on the behavior of the musicians, and when there was an unfavorable notice in the local paper, she shed tears, and then went to the editor's office to set things right.

The actors were fond of her and used to call her "Vanitchka and I," and "the darling"; she was sorry for them and used to lend them small sums of money, and if they deceived her, she used to shed a few tears in private, but did not complain to her husband.

They got on well in the winter too. They took the theater in the town for the whole winter, and let it for short terms to a Little Russian company, or to a conjurer, or to a local dramatic society. Olenka grew stouter, and was always beaming with satisfaction, while Kukin grew thinner and yellower, and continually complained of their terrible losses, although he had not done badly all the winter. He used to cough at night, and she used to give him hot raspberry tea or lime-flower water, to rub him with eau-de-Cologne and to wrap him in her warm shawls.

"You're such a sweet pet!" she used to say with perfect sincerity, stroking his hair. "You're such a pretty dear!"

20   Towards Lent he went to Moscow to collect a new troupe, and without him she could not sleep, but sat all night at her window, looking at the stars, and she compared herself with the hens, who are awake all night and uneasy when the cock is not in the hen-house. Kukin was detained in Moscow, and wrote that he would be back at Easter, adding some instructions about the Tivoli. But on the Sunday before Easter, late in the evening, came a sudden ominous knock at the gate; someone was hammering on the gate as though on a barrel—boom, boom, boom! The drowsy cook went flopping with her bare feet through the puddles, as she ran to open the gate.

"Please open," said someone outside in a thick bass. "There is a telegram for you."

Olenka had received telegrams from her husband before, but this time for some reason she felt numb with terror. With shaking hands she opened the telegram and read as follows:

"Ivan Petrovitch died suddenly today. Awaiting immate instructions fufuneral Tuesday."

That was how it was written in the telegram—"fufuneral," and the utterly incomprehensible word "immate." It was signed by the stage manager of the operatic company.

25   "My darling!" sobbed Olenka. "Vanitchka, my precious, my darling! Why did I ever meet you! Why did I know you and love you! Your poor heart-broken Olenka is all alone without you!"

Kukin's funeral took place on Tuesday in Moscow. Olenka returned home on Wednesday, and as soon as she got indoors she threw herself on her bed and sobbed so loudly that it could be heard next door, and in the street.

"Poor darling!" the neighbors said, as they crossed themselves. "Olga Semyonovna, poor darling! How she does take on!"

Three months later Olenka was coming home from mass, melancholy and in deep mourning. It happened that one of her neighbors, Vassily Andreitch Pustovalov, returning home from church, walked back beside her. He was the manager at Babakeyev's, the timber merchant's. He wore a straw hat, a white waistcoat, and a gold watch-chain, and looked more like a country gentleman than a man in trade.

"Everything happens as it is ordained, Olga Semyonovna," he said gravely, with a sympathetic note in his voice; "and if any of our dear ones die, it must be because it is the will of God, so we ought to have fortitude and bear it submissively."

After seeing Olenka to her gate, he said goodbye and went on. All day afterwards   30
she heard his sedately dignified voice, and whenever she shut her eyes she saw his dark
beard. She liked him very much. And apparently she had made an impression on him
too, for not long afterwards an elderly lady, with whom she was only slightly acquainted, came to drink coffee with her, and as soon as she was seated at table began
to talk about Pustovalov, saying that he was an excellent man whom one could thoroughly depend upon, and that any girl would be glad to marry him. Three days later
Pustovalov came himself. He did not stay long, only about ten minutes, and he did not
say much, but when he left, Olenka loved him—loved him so much that she lay awake
all night in a perfect fever, and in the morning she sent for the elderly lady. The match
was quickly arranged, and then came the wedding.

Pustovalov and Olenka got on very well together when they were married.

Usually he sat in the office till dinnertime, then he went out on business, while
Olenka took his place, and sat in the office till evening, making up accounts and booking orders.

"Timber gets dearer every year; the price rises twenty per cent," she would say to
her customers and friends. "Only fancy we used to sell local timber, and now Vassitchka always has to go for wood to the Mogilev district. And the freight!" she would
add, covering her cheeks with her hands in horror. "The freight!"

It seemed to her that she had been in the timber trade for ages and ages, and that
the most important and necessary thing in life was timber; and there was something
intimate and touching to her in the very sound of words such as "baulk," "post,"
"beam," "pole," "scantling," "batten," "lath," "plank," etc.

At night when she was asleep she dreamed of perfect mountains of planks and   35
boards, and long strings of wagons, carting timber somewhere far away. She dreamed
that a whole regiment of six-inch beams forty feet high, standing on end, was marching upon the timber-yard; that logs, beams, and boards knocked together with the resounding crash of dry wood, kept falling and getting up again, piling themselves on
each other. Olenka cried out in her sleep, and Pustovalov said to her tenderly: "Olenka, what's the matter, darling? Cross yourself!"

Her husband's ideas were hers. If he thought the room was too hot, or that business
was slack, she thought the same. Her husband did not care for entertainments, and on
holidays he stayed at home. She did likewise.

"You're always at home or in the office," her friends said to her. "You should go to
the theater, darling, or to the circus."

"Vassitchka and I have no time to go to theaters," she would answer sedately. "We
have no time for nonsense. What's the use of these theaters?"

On Saturdays Pustovalov and she used to go to the evening service; on holidays to
early mass, and they walked side by side with softened faces as they came home from
church. There was a pleasant fragrance about them both, and her silk dress rustled
agreeably. At home they drank tea, with fancy bread and jams of various kinds, and
afterwards they ate pie. Every day at twelve o'clock there was a savory smell of beetroot soup and of mutton or duck in their yard, and on fastdays of fish, and no one
could pass the gate without feeling hungry. In the office the samovar was always boiling, and customers were regaled with tea and cracknels. Once a week the couple went
to the baths and returned side by side, both red in the face.

"Yes, we have nothing to complain of, thank God," Olenka used to say to her ac-   40
quaintances. "I wish every one were as well off as Vassitchka and I."

When Pustovalov went away to buy wood in the Mogilev district, she missed him
dreadfully, lay awake and cried. A young veterinary surgeon in the army, called

Smirnin, to whom they had let their lodge, used sometimes to come in in the evening. He used to talk to her and play cards with her, and this entertained her in her husband's absence. She was particularly interested in what he told her of his home life. He was married and had a little boy, but was separated from his wife because she had been unfaithful to him, and now he hated her and used to send her forty roubles a month for the maintenance of their son. And hearing of all this, Olenka sighed and shook her head. She was sorry for him.

"Well, God keep you," she used to say to him at parting, as she lighted him down the stairs with a candle. "Thank you for coming to cheer me up, and may the Mother of God give you health."

And she always expressed herself with the same sedateness and dignity, the same reasonableness, in imitation of her husband. As the veterinary surgeon was disappearing behind the door below, she would say:

"You know, Vladimir Platonitch, you'd better make it up with your wife. You should forgive her for the sake of your son. You may be sure the little fellow understands."

45   And when Pustovalov came back, she told him in a low voice about the veterinary surgeon and his unhappy home life, and both sighed and shook their heads and talked about the boy, who, no doubt, missed his father, and by some strange connection of ideas, they went up to the holy icons, bowed to the ground before them and prayed that God would give them children.

And so the Pustovalovs lived for six years quietly and peaceably in love and complete harmony.

But behold! one winter day after drinking hot tea in the office, Vassily Andreitch went out into the yard without his cap on to see about sending off some timber, caught cold and was taken ill. He had the best doctors, but he grew worse and died after four months' illness. And Olenka was a widow once more.

"I've nobody, now you've left me, my darling," she sobbed, after her husband's funeral. "How can I live without you, in wretchedness and misery! Pity me, good people, all alone in the world!"

She went about dressed in black with long "weepers," and gave up wearing hat and gloves for good. She hardly ever went out, except to church, or to her husband's grave, and led the life of a nun. It was not till six months later that she took off the weepers and opened the shutters of the windows. She was sometimes seen in the mornings, going with her cook to market for provisions, but what went on in her house and how she lived now could only be surmised. People guessed, from seeing her drinking tea in her garden with the veterinary surgeon, who read the newspaper aloud to her, and from the fact that, meeting a lady she knew at the post-office, she said to her:

50   "There is no proper veterinary inspection in our town, and that's the cause of all sorts of epidemics. One is always hearing of people's getting infection from the milk supply, or catching diseases from horses and cows. The health of domestic animals ought to be as well cared for as the health of human beings."

She repeated the veterinary surgeon's words, and was of the same opinion as he about everything. It was evident that she could not live a year without some attachment, and had found new happiness in the lodge. In any one else this would have been censured, but no one could think ill of Olenka; everything she did was so natural. Neither she nor the veterinary surgeon said anything to other people of the change in their relations, and tried, indeed, to conceal it, but without success, for Olenka could not keep a secret. When he had visitors, men serving in his regiment, and she poured out tea or served the supper, she would begin talking of the cattle plague, of the foot and mouth disease, and of the municipal slaughterhouses. He was dreadfully embarrassed, and when the guests had gone, he would seize her by the hand and hiss angrily:

"I've asked you before not to talk about what you don't understand. When we veterinary surgeons are talking among ourselves, please don't put your word in. It's really annoying."

And she would look at him with astonishment and dismay, and ask him in alarm: "But Voloditchka, what *am* I to talk about?"

And with tears in her eyes she would embrace him, begging him not to be angry, and they were both happy.

But this happiness did not last long. The veterinary surgeon departed, departed for ever with his regiment, when it was transferred to a distant place—to Siberia, it may be. And Olenka was left alone. 55

Now she was absolutely alone. Her father had long been dead, and his armchair lay in the attic, covered with dust and lame of one leg. She got thinner and plainer, and when people met her in the street they did not look at her as they used to, and did not smile to her; evidently her best years were over and left behind, and now a new sort of life had begun for her, which did not bear thinking about. In the evening Olenka sat in the porch, and heard the band playing and the fireworks popping in the Tivoli, but now the sound stirred no response. She looked into her yard without interest, thought of nothing, wished for nothing, and afterwards, when night came on she went to bed and dreamed of her empty yard. She ate and drank as it were unwillingly.

And what was worst of all, she had no opinions of any sort. She saw the objects about her and understood what she saw, but could not form any opinion about them, and did not know what to talk about. And how awful it is not to have any opinions! One sees a bottle, for instance, or the rain, or a peasant driving in his cart, but what the bottle is for, or the rain, or the peasant, and what is the meaning of it, one can't say, and could not even for a thousand roubles. When she had Kukin, or Pustovalov, or the veterinary surgeon, Olenka could explain everything, and give her opinion about anything you like, but now there was the same emptiness in her brain and in her heart as there was in her yard outside. And it was as harsh and as bitter as wormwood in the mouth.

Little by little the town grew in all directions. The road became a street, and where the Tivoli and the timber-yard had been, there were new turnings and houses. How rapidly time passes! Olenka's house grew dingy, the roof got rusty, the shed sank on one side, and the whole yard was overgrown with docks and stinging-nettles. Olenka herself had grown plain and elderly; in summer she sat in the porch, and her soul, as before, was empty and dreary and full of bitterness. In winter she sat at her window and looked at the snow. When she caught the scent of spring, or heard the chime of the church bells, a sudden rush of memories from the past came over her, there was a tender ache in her heart, and her eyes brimmed over with tears; but this was only for a minute, and then came emptiness again and the sense of the futility of life. The black kitten, Briska, rubbed against her and purred softly, but Olenka was not touched by these feline caresses. That was not what she needed. She wanted a love that would absorb her whole being, her whole soul and reason—that would give her ideas and an object in life, and would warm her old blood. And she would shake the kitten off her skirt and say with vexation:

"Get along; I don't want you!"

And so it was, day after day and year after year, and no joy, and no opinions. Whatever Mavra, the cook, said she accepted. 60

One hot July day, towards evening, just as the cattle were being driven away, and the whole yard was full of dust, some one suddenly knocked at the gate. Olenka went to open it herself and was dumbfounded when she looked out: she saw Smirnin, the veterinary surgeon, gray-headed, and dressed as a civilian. She suddenly remembered everything. She could not help crying and letting her head fall on his breast without uttering a word, and in the violence of her feeling she did not notice how they both walked into the house and sat down to tea.

"My dear Vladimir Platonitch! What fate has brought you?" she muttered, trembling with joy.

"I want to settle here for good. Olga Semyonovna," he told her. "I have resigned my post, and have come to settle down and try my luck on my own account. Besides, it's time for my boy to go to school. He's a big boy. I am reconciled with my wife, you know."

"Where is she?" asked Olenka.

65   "She's at the hotel with the boy, and I'm looking for lodgings."

"Good gracious, my dear soul! Lodgings? Why not have my house? Why shouldn't that suit you? Why, my goodness, I wouldn't take any rent!" cried Olenka in a flutter, beginning to cry again. "You live here and the lodge will do nicely for me. Oh dear! How glad I am!"

Next day the roof was painted and the walls were whitewashed, and Olenka, with her arms akimbo, walked about the yard giving directions. Her face was beaming with her old smile, and she was brisk and alert as though she had waked from a long sleep. The veterinary's wife arrived—a thin, plain lady, with short hair and a peevish expression. With her was her little Sasha, a boy of ten, small for his age, blue-eyed, chubby, with dimples in his cheeks. And scarcely had the boy walked into the yard when he ran after the cat, and at once there was the sound of his gay, joyous laugh.

"Is that your puss, auntie?" he asked Olenka. "When she has little ones, do give us a kitten. Mamma is awfully afraid of mice."

Olenka talked to him, and gave him tea. Her heart warmed and there was a sweet ache in her bosom, as though the boy had been her own child. And when he sat at the table in the evening, going over his lessons, she looked at him with deep tenderness and pity as she murmured to herself:

70   "You pretty pet! . . . my precious! . . . Such a fair little thing, and so clever."

"'An island is a piece of land which is entirely surrounded by water,'" he read aloud.

"An island is a piece of land," she repeated, and this was the first opinion to which she gave utterance with positive conviction after so many years of silence and dearth of ideas.

Now she had opinions of her own, and at supper she talked to Sasha's parents, saying how difficult the lessons were at the high schools, but that yet the high school was better than a commercial one, since with a high-school education all careers were open to one, such as being a doctor or an engineer.

Sasha began going to the high school. His mother departed to Harkov to her sister's and did not return; his father used to go off every day to inspect cattle, and would often be away from home for three days together, and it seemed to Olenka as though Sasha was entirely abandoned, that he was not wanted at home, that he was being starved, and she carried him off to her lodge and gave him a little room there.

75   And for six months Sasha had lived in the lodge with her. Every morning Olenka came into his bedroom and found him fast asleep, sleeping noiselessly with his hand under his cheek. She was sorry to wake him.

"Sashenka," she would say mournfully, "get up, darling. It's time for school."

He would get up, dress and say his prayers, and then sit down to breakfast, drink three glasses of tea, and eat two large cracknels and a half a buttered roll. All this time he was hardly awake and a little ill-humored in consequence.

"You don't quite know your fable, Sashenka," Olenka would say, looking at him as though he were about to set off on a long journey. "What a lot of trouble I have with you! You must work and do your best, darling, and obey your teachers."

"Oh, do leave me alone!" Sasha would say.

Then he would go down the street to school, a little figure, wearing a big cap and carrying a satchel on his shoulder. Olenka would follow him noiselessly.

"Sashenka!" she would call after him, and she would pop into his hand a date or a caramel. When he reached the street where the school was, he would feel ashamed of being followed by a tall, stout woman; he would turn round and say:

"You'd better go home, auntie. I can go the rest of the way alone."

She would stand still and look after him fixedly till he had disappeared at the school-gate.

Ah, how she loved him! Of her former attachments not one had been so deep; never had her soul surrendered to any feeling so spontaneously, so disinterestedly, and so joyously as now that her maternal instincts were aroused. For this little boy with the dimple in his cheek and the big school cap, she would have given her whole life, she would have given it with joy and tears of tenderness. Why? Who can tell why?

When she had seen the last of Sasha, she returned home, contented and serene, brimming over with love; her face, which had grown younger during the last six months, smiled and beamed; people meeting her looked at her with pleasure.

"Good-morning, Olga Semyonovna, darling. How are you, darling?"

"The lessons at the high school are very difficult now," she would relate at the market. "It's too much; in the first class yesterday they gave him a fable to learn by heart, and a Latin translation and a problem. You know it's too much for a little chap."

And she would begin talking about the teachers, the lessons, and the school books, saying just what Sasha said.

At three o'clock they had dinner together; in the evening they learned their lessons together and cried. When she put him to bed, she would stay a long time making the Cross over him and murmuring a prayer; then she would go to bed and dream of that far-away misty future when Sasha would finish his studies and become a doctor or an engineer, would have a big house of his own with horses and a carriage, would get married and have children. . . . She would fall asleep still thinking of the same thing, and tears would run down her cheeks from her closed eyes, while the black cat lay purring beside her: "Mrr, mrr, mrr."

Suddenly there would come a loud knock at the gate.

Olenka would wake up breathless with alarm, her heart throbbing. Half a minute later would come another knock.

"It must be a telegram from Harkov," she would think, beginning to tremble from head to foot. "Sasha's mother is sending for him from Harkov. . . . Oh, mercy on us!"

She was in despair. Her head, her hands, and her feet would turn chill, and she would feel that she was the most unhappy woman in the world. But another minute would pass, voices would be heard: it would turn out to be the veterinary surgeon coming home from the club.

"Well, thank God!" she would think.

95   And gradually the load in her heart would pass off, and she would feel at ease. She
would go back to bed thinking of Sasha, who lay sound asleep in the next room, sometimes crying out in his sleep:

"I'll give it you! Get away! Shut up!"   [1899]

QUESTIONS

1. How is Olenka defined by the men in her life?
2. Trace the changing definitions of "darling" through the story.
3. What can the reader infer about the author's attitude toward Olenka? Is his
   tone satiric?
4. Speaking of Olenka's devotion to Sasha, the narrator exclaims, "Who can tell
   why?" Does the story provide an answer?
5. What is the significance of the words that Sasha cries out in his sleep?

RESPONSES

1. Write an essay exploring how aspects of the fairy tale are employed in this
   story.
2. Write an essay from the feminist approach, exploring the Darling's relationship with men and with society.
3. Discuss the elements of realism and the elements of naturalism in this
   Chekhov story, as well as in "Gooseberries" and "The Lady with the Dog."

ANTON CHEKHOV

Gooseberries

The sky had been overcast since early morning; it was a still day, not hot, but tedious, as it usually is when the weather is gray and dull, when clouds have been hanging over the fields for a long time, and you wait for the rain that does not come. Ivan Ivanych, a veterinary, and Burkin, a high school teacher, were already tired with walking, and the plain seemed endless to them. Far ahead were the scarcely visible windmills of the village of Mironositzkoe; to the right lay a range of hills that disappeared in the distance beyond the village, and both of them knew that over there were the river, and fields, green willows, homesteads, and if you stood on one of the hills, you could see from there another vast plain, telegraph poles, and a train that from afar looked like a caterpillar crawling, and in clear weather you could even see the town. Now, when it was still and when nature seemed mild and pensive, Ivan Ivanych and Burkin were filled with love for this plain, and both of them thought what a beautiful land it was.

"Last time when we were in Elder Prokofy's barn," said Burkin, "you were going to tell me a story."

"Yes; I wanted to tell you about my brother."

Ivan Ivanych heaved a slow sigh and lit his pipe before beginning his story, but just then it began to rain. And five minutes later there was a downpour, and it was hard to tell when it would be over. The two men halted, at a loss; the dogs, already wet, stood with their tails between their legs and looked at them feelingly.

"We must find shelter somewhere," said Burkin. "Let's go to Alyohin's; it's quite near." 5

"Let's."

They turned aside and walked across a mown meadow, now going straight ahead, now bearing to the right, until they reached the road. Soon poplars came into view, a garden, then the red roofs of barns; the river gleamed, and the view opened on a broad expanse of water with a mill and a white bathing-cabin. That was Sofyino, Alyohin's place.

The mill was going, drowning out the sound of the rain; the dam was shaking. Wet horses stood near the carts, their heads drooping, and men were walking about, their heads covered with sacks. It was damp, muddy, dreary; and the water looked cold and unkind. Ivan Ivanych and Burkin felt cold and messy and uncomfortable through and through; their feet were heavy with mud and when, having crossed the dam, they climbed up the barns, they were silent as though they were cross with each other.

The noise of a winnowing-machine came from one of the barns, the door was open, and clouds of dust were pouring from within. On the threshold stood Alyohin himself, a man of forty, tall and rotund, with long hair, looking more like a professor or an artist than a gentleman farmer. He was wearing a white blouse, badly in need of washing, that was belted with a rope, and drawers, and his high boots were plastered with mud and straw. His eyes and nose were black with dust. He recognized Ivan Ivanych and Burkin and was apparently very glad to see them.

10   "Please go up to the house, gentlemen," he said, smiling; "I'll be there directly, in a moment."

It was a large structure of two stories. Alyohin lived downstairs in what was formerly the stewards' quarters: two rooms that had arched ceilings and small windows; the furniture was plain, and the place smelled of rye bread, cheap vodka, and harness. He went into the showy rooms upstairs only rarely, when he had guests. Once in the house, the two visitors were met by a chambermaid, a young woman so beautiful that both of them stood still at the same moment and glanced at each other.

"You can't imagine how glad I am to see you, gentlemen," said Alyohin, joining them in the hall. "What a surprise! Pelageya," he said, turning to the chambermaid, "give the guests a change of clothes. And, come to think of it, I will change, too. But I must go and bathe first, I don't think I've had a wash since spring. Don't you want to go into the bathing-cabin? In the meanwhile things will be got ready here."

The beautiful Pelageya, with her soft, delicate air, brought them bath towels and soap, and Alyohin went to the bathing-cabin with his guests.

"Yes, it's a long time since I've bathed," he said, as he undressed. "I've an excellent bathing-cabin, as you see—it was put up by my father—but somehow I never find time to use it." He sat down on the steps and lathered his long hair and neck, and the water around him turned brown.

15   "I say——" observed Ivan Ivanych significantly, looking at his head.

"I haven't had a good wash for a long time," repeated Alyohin, embarrassed, and soaped himself once more; the water about him turned dark-blue, the color of ink.

Ivan Ivanych came out of the cabin, plunged into the water with a splash and swam in the rain, thrusting his arms out wide; he raised waves on which white lilies swayed. He swam out to the middle of the river and dived and a minute later came up in another spot and swam on and kept diving, trying to touch bottom. "By God!" he kept repeating delightedly, "by God!" He swam to the mill, spoke to the peasants there, and turned back and in the middle of the river lay floating, exposing his face to the rain. Burkin and Alyohin were already dressed and ready to leave, but he kept on swimming and diving. "By God!" he kept exclaiming. "Lord, have mercy on me."

"You've had enough!" Burkin shouted to him.

They returned to the house. And only when the lamp was lit in the big drawing room upstairs, and the two guests, in silk dressing-gowns and warm slippers, were lounging in armchairs, and Alyohin himself, washed and combed, wearing a new jacket, was walking about the room, evidently savoring the warmth, the cleanliness, the dry clothes and light footwear, and when pretty Pelageya, stepping noiselessly across the carpet and smiling softly, brought in a tray with tea and jam, only then did Ivan Ivanych begin his story, and it was as though not only Burkin and Alyohin were listening, but also the ladies, old and young, and the military men who looked down upon them, calmly and severely, from their gold frames.

20   "We are two brothers," he began, "I, Ivan Ivanych, and my brother, Nikolay Ivanych, who is two years my junior. I went in for a learned profession and became a veterinary;

Nikolay at nineteen began to clerk in a provincial branch of the Treasury. Our father was a *kantonist*,° but he rose to be an officer and so a nobleman, a rank that he bequeathed to us together with a small estate. After his death there was a lawsuit and we lost the estate to creditors, but be that as it may, we spent our childhood in the country. Just like peasant children we passed days and nights in the fields and the woods, herded horses, stripped bast from the trees, fished, and so on. And, you know, whoever even once in his life has caught a perch or seen thrushes migrate in the autumn, when on clear, cool days they sweep in flocks over the village, will never really be a townsman and to the day of his death will have a longing for the open. My brother was unhappy in the government office. Years passed, but he went on warming the same seat, scratching away at the same papers, and thinking of one and the same thing: how to get away to the country. And little by little this vague longing turned into a definite desire, into a dream of buying a little property somewhere on the banks of a river or a lake.

"He was a kind and gentle soul and I loved him, but I never sympathized with his desire to shut himself up for the rest of his life on a little property of his own. It is a common saying that a man needs only six feet of earth. But six feet is what a corpse needs, not a man. It is also asserted that if our educated class is drawn to the land and seeks to settle on farms, that's a good thing. But these farms amount to the same six feet of earth. To retire from the city, from the struggle, from the hubbub, to go off and hide on one's own farm—that's not life, it is selfishness, sloth, it is a kind of monasticism, but monasticism without works. Man needs not six feet of earth, not a farm, but the whole globe, all of Nature, where unhindered he can display all the capacities and peculiarities of his free spirit.

"My brother Nikolay, sitting in his office, dreamed of eating his own *shchi*,° which would fill the whole farmyard with a delicious aroma, of picnicking on the green grass, of sleeping in the sun, of sitting for hours on the seat by the gate gazing at field and forest. Books on agriculture and the farming items in almanacs were his joy, the delight of his soul. He liked newspapers too, but the only things he read in them were advertisements of land for sale, so many acres of tillable land and pasture, with house, garden, river, mill, and millpond. And he pictured to himself garden paths, flowers, fruit, birdhouses with starlings in them, crucians in the pond, and all that sort of thing, you know. These imaginary pictures varied with the advertisements he came upon, but somehow gooseberry bushes figured in every one of them. He could not picture to himself a single country-house, a single rustic nook, without gooseberries.

"'Country life has its advantages,' he used to say. 'You sit on the veranda having tea, and your ducks swim in the pond, and everything smells delicious and—the gooseberries are ripening.'

"He would draw a plan of his estate and invariably it would contain the following features: a) the master's house; b) servants' quarters; c) kitchen-garden; d) a gooseberry patch. He lived meagerly: he deprived himself of food and drink; he dressed God knows how, like a beggar, but he kept on saving and salting money away in the bank. He was terribly stingy. It was painful for me to see it, and I used to give him small sums and send him something on holidays, but he would put that away too. Once a man is possessed by an idea, there is no doing anything with him.

°*kantonist*: A soldier's son who, in return for an education and upbringing by the army, enters military service upon coming of age.
°*shchi*: A hearty regional soup.

25   "Years passed. He was transferred to another province, he was already past forty, yet he was still reading newspaper advertisements and saving up money. Then I heard that he was married. Still for the sake of buying a property with a gooseberry patch he married an elderly, homely widow, without a trace of affection for her, but simply because she had money. After marrying her, he went on living parsimoniously, keeping her half-starved, and he put her money in the bank in his own name. She had previously been the wife of a postmaster, who had got her used to pies and cordials. This second husband did not even give her enough black bread. She began to sicken, and some three years later gave up the ghost. And, of course, it never for a moment occurred to my brother that he was to blame for her death. Money, like vodka, can do queer things to a man. Once in our town a merchant lay on his deathbed; before he died, he ordered a plateful of honey and he ate up all his money and lottery tickets with the honey, so that no one should get it. One day when I was inspecting a drove of cattle at a railway station, a cattle dealer fell under a locomotive and it sliced off his leg. We carried him in to the infirmary, the blood was gushing from the wound—a terrible business, but he kept begging us to find his leg and was very anxious about it: he had twenty rubles in the boot that was on that leg, and he was afraid they would be lost."

"That's a tune from another opera," said Burkin.

Ivan Ivanych paused a moment and then continued:

"After his wife's death, my brother began to look around for a property. Of course, you may scout about for five years and in the end make a mistake, and buy something quite different from what you have been dreaming of. Through an agent my brother bought a mortgaged estate of three hundred acres with a house, servants' quarters, a park, but with no orchard, no gooseberry patch, no duck-pond. There was a stream, but the water in it was the color of coffee, for on one of its banks there was a brickyard and on the other a glue factory. But my brother was not at all disconcerted: he ordered a score of gooseberry bushes, planted them, and settled down to the life of a country gentleman.

"Last year I paid him a visit. I thought I would go and see how things were with him. In his letter to me my brother called his estate 'Chumbaroklov Waste, or Himalaiskoe' (our surname was Chimsha-Himalaisky). I reached the place in the afternoon. It was hot. Everywhere there were ditches, fences, hedges, rows of fir trees, and I was at a loss as to how to get to the yard and where to leave my horse. I made my way to the house and was met by a fat dog with reddish hair that looked like a pig. It wanted to bark, but was too lazy. The cook, a fat, barelegged woman, who also looked like a pig, came out of the kitchen and said that the master was resting after dinner. I went in to see my brother, and found him sitting up in bed, with a quilt over his knees. He had grown older, stouter, flabby; his cheeks, his nose, his lips jutted out: it looked as though he might grunt into the quilt at any moment.

30   "We embraced and dropped tears of joy and also of sadness at the thought that the two of us had once been young, but were now gray and nearing death. He got dressed and took me out to show me his estate.

"'Well, how are you getting on here?' I asked.

"'Oh, all right, thank God. I am doing very well.'

"He was no longer the poor, timid clerk he used to be but a real landowner, a gentleman. He had already grown used to his new manner of living and developed a taste for it. He ate a great deal, steamed himself in the bathhouse, was growing stout, was already having a lawsuit with the village commune and the two factories and was very much offended when the peasants failed to address him as 'Your Honor.' And he concerned himself with his soul's welfare too in a substantial, upper-class manner, and performed good deeds not simply, but pompously. And what good works! He dosed the peasants with bicarbonate and castor oil for all their ailments and on his name day he had a thanksgiving service celebrated in the center of the village, and then treated the villagers to a gallon of vodka, which he thought was the thing to do. Oh, those horrible gallons of vodka! One day a fat landowner hauls the peasants up before the rural police officer for trespassing, and the next, to mark a feast day, treats them to a gallon of vodka, and they drink and shout 'Hurrah' and when they are drunk bow down at his feet. A higher standard of living, overeating and idleness develop the most insolent self-conceit in a Russian. Nikolay Ivanych, who when he was a petty official was afraid to have opinions of his own even if he kept them to himself, now uttered nothing but incontrovertible truths and did so in the tone of a minister of state: 'Education is necessary, but the masses are not ready for it; corporal punishment is generally harmful, but in some cases it is useful and nothing else will serve.'

"'I know the common people, and I know how to deal with them,' he would say. 'They love me. I only have to raise my little finger, and they will do anything I want.'

"And all this, mark you, would be said with a smile that bespoke kindness and in-   35
telligence. Twenty times over he repeated: 'We, of the gentry,' 'I, as a member of the gentry.' Apparently he no longer remembered that our grandfather had been a peasant and our father just a private. Even our surname, 'Chimsha-Himalaisky,' which in reality is grotesque, seemed to him sonorous, distinguished, and delightful.

"But I am concerned now not with him, but with me. I want to tell you about the change that took place in me during the few hours that I spent on his estate. In the evening when we were having tea, the cook served a plateful of gooseberries. They were not bought, they were his own gooseberries, the first ones picked since the bushes were planted. My brother gave a laugh and for a minute looked at the gooseberries in silence, with tears in his eyes—he could not speak for excitement. Then he put one berry in his mouth, glanced at me with the triumph of a child who has at last been given a toy he was longing for and said: 'How tasty!' And he ate the gooseberries greedily, and kept repeating: 'Ah, how delicious! Do taste them!'

"They were hard and sour, but as Pushkin° has it,

> The falsehood that exalts we cherish more
> Than meaner truths that are a thousand strong.

I saw a happy man, one whose cherished dream had so obviously come true, who   40
had attained his goal in life, who had got what he wanted, who was satisfied with his lot and with himself. For some reason an element of sadness had always mingled with my thoughts of human happiness, and now at the sight of a happy man I was assailed by an oppressive feeling bordering on despair. It weighed on me particularly at night. A bed was made up for me in a room next to my brother's bedroom, and I could hear that he was wakeful, and that he would get up again and again, go to the plate of gooseberries and eat one after another. I said to myself: how many contented, happy people there really are! What an overwhelming force they are! Look at life: the insolence and idleness of the strong, the ignorance and brutishness of the weak, horrible poverty everywhere, overcrowding, degeneration, drunkenness, hypocrisy, lying—

°*Pushkin*: Pushkin (1799–1837), the father of modern Russian literature.

Yet in all the houses and on all the streets there is peace and quiet; of the fifty thousand people who live in our town there is not one who would cry out, who would vent his indignation aloud. We see the people who go to market, eat by day, sleep by night, who babble nonsense, marry, grow old, good-naturedly drag their dead to the cemetery, but we do not see or hear those who suffer, and what is terrible in life goes on somewhere behind the scenes. Everything is peaceful and quiet and only mute statistics protest: so many people gone out of their minds, so many gallons of vodka drunk, so many children dead from malnutrition—And such a state of things is evidently necessary; obviously the happy man is at ease only because the unhappy ones bear their burdens in silence, and if there were not this silence, happiness would be impossible. It is a general hypnosis. Behind the door of every contented, happy man there ought to be someone standing with a little hammer and continually reminding him with a knock that there are unhappy people, that however happy he may be, life will sooner or later show him its claws, and trouble will come to him—illness, poverty, losses, and then no one will see or hear him, just as now he neither sees nor hears others. But there is no man with a hammer. The happy man lives at his ease, faintly fluttered by small daily cares, like an aspen in the wind—and all is well.

"That night I came to understand that I too had been contented and happy," Ivan Ivanych continued, getting up. "I too over the dinner table or out hunting would hold forth on how to live, what to believe, the right way to govern the people. I too would say that learning was the enemy of darkness, that education was necessary but that for the common people the three R's were sufficient for the time being. Freedom is a boon, I used to say, it is as essential as air, but we must wait awhile. Yes, that's what I used to say, and now I ask: Why must we wait?" said Ivan Ivanych, looking wrathfully at Burkin. "Why must we wait, I ask you? For what reason? I am told that nothing can be done all at once, that every idea is realized gradually, in its own time. But who is it that says so? Where is the proof that it is just? You cite the natural order of things, the law governing all phenomena, but is there law, is there order in the fact that I, a living, thinking man, stand beside a ditch and wait for it to close up of itself or fill up with silt, when I could jump over it or throw a bridge across it? And again, why must we wait? Wait, until we have no strength to live, and yet we have to live and are eager to live!

"I left my brother's place early in the morning, and ever since then it has become intolerable for me to stay in town. I am oppressed by the peace and the quiet, I am afraid to look at the windows, for there is nothing that pains me more than the spectacle of a happy family sitting at table having tea. I am an old man now and unfit for combat, I am not even capable of hating. I can only grieve inwardly, get irritated, worked up, and at night my head is ablaze with the rush of ideas and I cannot sleep. Oh, if I were young!"

Ivan Ivanych paced up and down the room excitedly and repeated, "If I were young!"

He suddenly walked up to Alyohin and began to press now one of his hands, now the other.

45   "Pavel Konstantinych," he said imploringly, "don't quiet down, don't let yourself be lulled to sleep! As long as you are young, strong, alert, do not cease to do good! There is no happiness and there should be none, and if life has a meaning and a purpose, that meaning and purpose is not our happiness but something greater and more rational. Do good!"

All this Ivan Ivanych said with a pitiful, imploring smile, as though he were asking a personal favor.

Afterwards all three of them sat in armchairs in different corners of the drawing room and were silent. Ivan Ivanych's story satisfied neither Burkin nor Alyohin. With the ladies and generals looking down from the golden frames, seeming alive in the dim light, it was tedious to listen to the story of the poor devil of a clerk who ate gooseberries. One felt like talking about elegant people, about women. And the fact that they were sitting in a drawing room where everything—the chandelier under its cover, the armchairs, the carpets underfoot—testified that the very people who were now looking down from the frames had once moved about here, sat and had tea, and the fact that lovely Pelageya was noiselessly moving about—that was better than any story.

Alyohin was very sleepy; he had gotten up early, before three o'clock in the morning, to get some work done, and now he could hardly keep his eyes open, but he was afraid his visitors might tell an interesting story in his absence, and he would not leave. He did not trouble to ask himself if what Ivan Ivanych had just said was intelligent or right. The guests were not talking about groats, or hay, or tar, but about something that had no direct bearing on his life, and he was glad of it and wanted them to go on.

"However, it's bedtime," said Burkin, rising. "Allow me to wish you good night."

Alyohin took leave of his guests and went downstairs to his own quarters, while   50
they remained upstairs. They were installed for the night in a big room in which stood two old wooden beds decorated with carvings and in the corner was an ivory crucifix. The wide cool beds which had been made by the lovely Pelageya gave off a pleasant smell of clean linen.

Ivan Ivanych undressed silently and got into bed.

"Lord forgive us sinners!" he murmured, and drew the bedclothes over his head.

His pipe, which lay on the table, smelled strongly of burnt tobacco, and Burkin, who could not sleep for a long time, kept wondering where the unpleasant odor came from.

The rain beat against the window panes all night. [1898]

QUESTIONS

1. Why does the author use the method of the frame tale—the story within a story?
2. Who is the protagonist?
3. How is Aloyhin characterized by his attitude toward Pelegeya?
4. What effect does Ivan's story have upon Aloyhin and Burkin?
5. What do the gooseberries symbolize?

ANTON CHEKHOV

The Lady with the Dog

1

It was said that a new person had appeared on the sea-front: a lady with a little dog. Dmitri Dmitritch Gurov, who had by then been a fortnight at Yalta, and so was fairly at home there, had begun to take an interest in new arrivals. Sitting in Verney's pavilion, he saw, walking on the sea-front, a fair-haired young lady of medium height, wearing a *béret*; a white Pomeranian dog was running behind her.

And afterwards he met her in the public gardens and in the square several times a day. She was walking alone, always wearing the same *béret*, and always with the same white dog; no one knew who she was, and every one called her simply "the lady with the dog."

"If she is here alone without a husband or friends, it wouldn't be amiss to make her acquaintance," Gurov reflected.

He was under forty, but he had a daughter already twelve years old, and two sons at school. He had been married young, when he was a student in his second year, and by now his wife seemed half as old again as he. She was a tall, erect woman with dark eyebrows, staid and dignified, and, as she said of herself, intellectual. She read a great deal, used phonetic spelling, called her husband, not Dmitri, but Dimitri, and he secretly considered her unintelligent, narrow, inelegant, was afraid of her, and did not like to be at home. He had begun being unfaithful to her long ago— had been unfaithful to her often, and, probably on that account, almost always spoke ill of women, and when they were talked about in his presence, used to call them "the lower race."

5   It seemed to him that he had been so schooled by bitter experience that he might call them what he liked, and yet he could not get on for two days together without "the lower race." In the society of men he was bored and not himself, with them he was cold and uncommunicative; but when he was in the company of women he felt free, and knew what to say to them and how to behave; and he was at ease with them even when he was silent. In his appearance, in his character, in his whole nature, there was something attractive and elusive which allured women and disposed them in his favour; he knew that, and some force seemed to draw him, too, to them.

240

Experience often repeated, truly bitter experience, had taught him long ago that with decent people, especially Moscow people—always slow to move and irresolute—every intimacy, which at first so agreeably diversifies life and appears a light and charming adventure, inevitably grows into a regular problem of extreme intricacy, and in the long run the situation becomes unbearable. But at every fresh meeting with an interesting woman this experience seemed to slip out of his memory, and he was eager for life, and everything seemed simple and amusing.

One evening he was dining in the gardens, and the lady in the *béret* came up slowly to take the next table. Her expression, her gait, her dress, and the way she did her hair told him that she was a lady, that she was married, that she was in Yalta for the first time and alone, and that she was dull there. . . . The stories told of the immorality in such places as Yalta are to a great extent untrue; he despised them, and knew that such stories were for the most part made up by persons who would themselves have been glad to sin if they had been able; but when the lady sat down at the next table three paces from him, he remembered these tales of easy conquests, of trips to the mountains, and the tempting thought of a swift, fleeting love affair, a romance with an unknown woman, whose name he did not know, suddenly took possession of him.

He beckoned coaxingly to the Pomeranian, and when the dog came up to him he shook his finger at it. The Pomeranian growled: Gurov shook his finger at it again.

The lady looked at him and at once dropped her eyes.

"He doesn't bite," she said, and blushed.   10

"May I give him a bone?" he asked; and when she nodded he asked courteously, "Have you been long in Yalta?"

"Five days."

"And I have already dragged out a fortnight here."

There was a brief silence.

"Time goes fast, and yet it is so dull here!" she said, not looking at him.   15

"That's only the fashion to say it is dull here. A provincial will live in Belyov or Zhidra and not be dull, and when he comes here it's 'Oh, the dullness! Oh, the dust!' One would think he came from Grenada."

She laughed. Then both continued eating in silence, like strangers, but after dinner they walked side by side; and there sprang up between them the light jesting conversation of people who are free and satisfied, to whom it does not matter where they go or what they talk about. They walked and talked of the strange light on the sea: the water was of a soft warm lilac hue, and there was a golden streak from the moon upon it. They talked of how sultry it was after a hot day. Gurov told her that he came from Moscow, that he had taken his degree in Arts, but had a post in a bank; that he had trained as an opera-singer, but had given it up, that he owned two houses in Moscow. . . . And from her he learnt that she had grown up in Petersburg, but had lived in S——since her marriage two years before, that she was staying another month in Yalta, and that her husband, who needed a holiday too, might perhaps come and fetch her. She was not sure whether her husband had a post in a Crown Department or under the Provincial Council—and was amused by her own ignorance. And Gurov learnt, too, that she was called Anna Sergeyevna.

Afterwards he thought about her in his room at the hotel—thought she would certainly meet him next day; it would be sure to happen. As he got into bed he thought how lately she had been a girl at school, doing lessons like his own daughter; he recalled the diffidence, the angularity, that was still manifest in her laugh and her manner of talking with a stranger. This must have been the first time in her life she had been alone in surroundings in which she was followed, looked at, and spoken to merely from a secret motive which she could hardly fail to guess. He recalled her slender, delicate neck, her lovely grey eyes.

"There's something pathetic about her, anyway," he thought, and fell asleep.

2

A week had passed since they had made acquaintance. It was a holiday. It was sultry indoors, while in the street the wind whirled the dust round and round, and blew people's hats off. It was a thirsty day, and Gurov often went into the pavilion, and pressed Anna Sergeyevna to have syrup and water or an ice. One did not know what to do with oneself.

In the evening when the wind had dropped a little, they went out on the groyne to see the steamer come in. There were a great many people walking about the harbour; they had gathered to welcome some one, bringing bouquets. And two peculiarities of a well-dressed Yalta crowd were very conspicuous: the elderly ladies were dressed like young ones, and there were great numbers of generals.

Owing to the roughness of the sea, the steamer arrived late, after the sun had set, and it was a long time turning about before it reached the groyne. Anna Sergeyevna looked through her lorgnette at the steamer and the passengers as though looking for acquaintances, and when she turned to Gurov her eyes were shining. She talked a great deal and asked disconnected questions, forgetting next moment what she had asked; then she dropped her lorgnette in the crush.

The festive crowd began to disperse; it was too dark to see people's faces. The wind had completely dropped, but Gurov and Anna Sergeyevna still stood as though waiting to see some one else come from the steamer. Anna Sergeyevna was silent now, and sniffed the flowers without looking at Gurov.

"The weather is better this evening," he said. "Where shall we go now? Shall we drive somewhere?"

She made no answer.

Then he looked at her intently, and all at once put his arm round her and kissed her on the lips, and breathed in the moisture and the fragrance of the flowers; and he immediately looked round him, anxiously wondering whether any one had seen them.

"Let us go to your hotel," he said softly. And both walked quickly.

The room was close and smelt of the scent she had bought at the Japanese shop. Gurov looked at her and thought: "What different people one meets in the world!" From the past he preserved memories of careless, good-natured women, who loved cheerfully and were grateful to him for the happiness he gave them, however brief it might be; and of women like his wife who loved without any genuine feeling, with superfluous phrases, affectedly, hysterically, with an expression that suggested that it was not love nor passion, but something more significant; and of two or three others, very beautiful, cold women, on whose faces he had caught a glimpse of a rapacious expression—an obstinate desire to snatch from life more than it could give, and these were capricious, unreflecting, domineering, unintelligent women not in their first youth, and when Gurov grew cold to them their beauty excited his hatred, and the lace on their linen seemed to him like scales.

But in this case there was still the diffidence, the angularity of inexperienced youth, an awkward feeling; and there was a sense of consternation as though some one had suddenly knocked at the door. The attitude of Anna Sergeyevna—"the lady with the dog"—to what had happened was somehow peculiar, very grave, as though it were her fall—so it seemed, and it was strange and inappropriate. Her face dropped and faded, and on both sides of it her long hair hung down mournfully; she mused in a dejected attitude like "the woman who was a sinner" in an old-fashioned picture.

"It's wrong," she said. "You will be the first to despise me now." 30

There was a water-melon on the table. Gurov cut himself a slice and began eating it without haste. There followed at least half an hour of silence.

Anna Sergeyevna was touching; there was about her the purity of a good, simple woman who had seen little of life. The solitary candle burning on the table threw a faint light on her face, yet it was clear that she was very unhappy.

"How could I despise you?" asked Gurov. "You don't know what you are saying."

"God forgive me," she said, and her eyes filled with tears. "It's awful."

"You seem to feel you need to be forgiven." 35

"Forgiven? No. I am a bad, low woman; I despise myself and I don't attempt to justify myself. It's not my husband but myself I have deceived. And not only just now; I have been deceiving myself for a long time. My husband may be a good, honest man, but he is a flunkey! I don't know what he does there, what his work is, but I know he is a flunkey! I was twenty when I was married to him. I have been tormented by curiosity; I wanted something better. 'There must be a different sort of life,' I said to myself. I wanted to live! To live, to live! . . . I was fired by curiosity . . . you don't understand it, but, I swear to God, I could not control myself; something happened to me: I could not be restrained. I told my husband I was ill, and came here. . . . And here I have been walking about as though I were dazed, like a mad creature; . . . and now I have become a vulgar, contemptible woman whom any one may despise."

Gurov felt bored already, listening to her. He was irritated by the naïve tone, by this remorse, so unexpected and inopportune; but for the tears in her eyes, he might have thought she was jesting or playing a part.

"I don't understand," he said softly. "What is it you want?"

She hid her face on his breast and pressed close to him.

"Believe me, believe me, I beseech you . . ." she said. "I love a pure, honest life, and 40 sin is loathsome to me. I don't know what I am doing. Simple people say: 'The Evil One has beguiled me.' And I may say of myself now that the Evil One has beguiled me."

"Hush, hush! . . ." he muttered.

He looked at her fixed, scared eyes, kissed her, talked softly and affectionately, and by degrees she was comforted, and her gaiety returned; they both began laughing.

Afterwards when they went out there was not a soul on the sea-front. The town with its cypresses had quite a deathlike air, but the sea still broke noisily on the shore; a single barge was rocking on the waves, and a lantern was blinking sleepily on it.

They found a cab and drove to Oreanda.

"I found out your surname in the hall just now: it was written on the board—Von 45 Diderits," said Gurov. "Is your husband a German?"

"No, I believe his grandfather was a German, but he is an Orthodox Russian himself."

At Oreanda they sat on a seat not far from the church, looked down at the sea, and were silent. Yalta was hardly visible through the morning mist; white clouds stood motionless on the mountain-tops. The leaves did not stir on the trees, grasshoppers chirruped, and the monotonous hollow sound of the sea rising up from below, spoke of the peace, of the eternal sleep awaiting us. So it must have sounded when there was no Yalta, no Oreanda here; so it sounds now, and it will sound as indifferently and monotonously when we are all no more. And in this constancy, in this complete indifference to the life and death of each of us, there lies hid, perhaps, a pledge of our eternal salvation, of the unceasing movement of life upon earth, of unceasing progress towards perfection. Sitting beside a young woman who in the dawn seemed so lovely, soothed and spellbound in these magical surroundings—the sea, mountains, clouds, the open sky—Gurov thought how in reality everything is beautiful in this world when one reflects: everything except what we think or do ourselves when we forget our human dignity and the higher aims of our existence.

A man walked up to them—probably a keeper—looked at them and walked away. And this detail seemed mysterious and beautiful, too. They saw a steamer come from Theodosia, with its lights out in the glow of dawn.

"There is dew on the grass," said Anna Sergeyevna, after a silence.

50   "Yes. It's time to go home."

They went back to the town.

Then they met every day at twelve o'clock on the sea-front, lunched and dined together, went for walks, admired the sea. She complained that she slept badly, that her heart throbbed violently; asked the same questions, troubled by jealousy and now by the fear that he did not respect her sufficiently. And often in the square or gardens, when there was no one near them, he suddenly drew her to him and kissed her passionately. Complete idleness, these kisses in broad daylight while he looked round in dread of some one's seeing them, the heat, the smell of the sea, and the continual passing to and fro before him of idle, well-dressed, well-fed people, made a new man of him; he told Anna Sergeyevna how beautiful she was, how fascinating. He was impatiently passionate, he would not move a step away from her, while she was often pensive and continually urged him to confess that he did not respect her, did not love her in the least, and thought of her as nothing but a common woman. Rather late almost every evening they drove somewhere out of town, to Oreanda or to the waterfall; and the expedition was always a success, the scenery invariably impressed them as grand and beautiful.

They were expecting her husband to come, but a letter came from him, saying that there was something wrong with his eyes, and he entreated his wife to come home as quickly as possible. Anna Sergeyevna made haste go to.

"It's a good thing I am going away," she said to Gurov. "It's the finger of destiny!"

55   She went by coach and he went with her. They were driving the whole day. When she had got into a compartment of the express, and when the second bell had rung, she said:

"Let me look at you once more . . . look at you once again. That's right."

She did not shed tears, but was so sad that she seemed ill, and her face was quivering.

"I shall remember you . . . think of you," she said. "God be with you; be happy. Don't remember evil against me. We are parting forever—it must be so, for we ought never to have met. Well, God be with you."

The train moved off rapidly, its lights soon vanished from sight, and a minute later there was no sound of it, as though everything had conspired together to end as quickly as possible that sweet delirium, that madness. Left alone on the platform, and gazing into the dark distance, Gurov listened to the chirrup of the grasshoppers and the hum of the telegraph wires, feeling as though he had only just waked up. And he thought, musing, that there had been another episode or adventure in his life, and it, too, was at an end, and nothing was left of it but a memory. . . . He was moved, sad, and conscious of a slight remorse. This young woman whom he would never meet again had not been happy with him; he was genuinely warm and affectionate with her, but yet in his manner, his tone, and his caresses there had been a shade of light irony, the coarse condescension of a happy man who was, besides, almost twice her age. All the time she had called him kind, exceptional, lofty; obviously he had seemed to her different from what he really was, so he had unintentionally deceived her. . . .

Here at the station was already a scent of autumn; it was a cold evening. 60

"It's time for me to go north," thought Gurov as he left the platform. "High time!"

3

At home in Moscow everything was in its winter routine; the stoves were heated, and in the morning it was still dark when the children were having breakfast and getting ready for school, and the nurse would light the lamp for a short time. The frosts had begun already. When the first snow has fallen, on the first day of sledge-driving it is pleasant to see the white earth, the white roofs, to draw soft, delicious breath, and the season brings back the days of one's youth. The old limes and birches, white with hoar-frost, have a good-natured expression; they are nearer to one's heart than cypresses and palms, and near them one doesn't want to be thinking of the sea and the mountains.

Gurov was Moscow born; he arrived in Moscow on a fine frosty day, and when he put on his fur coat and warm gloves, and walked along Petrovka, and when on Saturday evening he heard the ringing of the bells, his recent trip and the places he had seen lost all charm for him. Little by little he became absorbed in Moscow life, greedily read three newspapers a day, and declared he did not read the Moscow papers on principle! He already felt a longing to go to restaurants, clubs, dinner-parties, anniversary celebrations and he felt flattered at entertaining distinguished lawyers and artists, and at playing cards with a professor at the doctor's club. He could already eat a whole plateful of salt fish and cabbage. . . .

In another month, he fancied, the image of Anna Sergeyevna would be shrouded in a mist in his memory, and only from time to time would visit him in his dreams with a touching smile as others did. But more than a month passed, real winter had come, and everything was still clear in his memory as though he had parted with Anna Sergeyevna only the day before. And his memories glowed more and more vividly. When in the evening stillness he heard from his study the voices of his children, preparing their lessons, or when he listened to a song or the organ at the restaurant, or the storm howled in the chimney, suddenly everything would rise up in his memory: what had happened on the groyne, and the early morning with the mist on the mountains, and the steamer coming from Theodosia and the kisses. He would pace a long time about his room, remembering it all and smiling; then his memories passed into dreams, and in his fancy the past was mingled with what was to come. Anna Sergeyevna did not visit him in dreams, but followed him about everywhere like a shadow and haunted him. When he shut his eyes he saw her as though she were living before him, and she seemed to him lovelier, younger, tenderer than she was; and he imagined himself finer than he had been in Yalta. In the evenings she peeped out at him from the bookcase, from the fireplace, from the corner—he heard her breathing, the caressing rustle of her dress. In the street he watched the women, looking for some one like her.

He was tormented by an intense desire to confide his memories to some one. But 65 in his home it was impossible to talk of his love, and he had no one outside; he could not talk to his tenants nor to any one at the bank. And what had he to talk of? Had he been in love, then? Had there been anything beautiful, poetical, or edifying or simply interesting in his relations with Anna Sergeyevna? And there was nothing for him but to talk vaguely of love, of woman, and no one guessed what it meant; only his wife twitched her black eyebrows, and said: "The part of a lady-killer does not suit you at all, Dimitri."

One evening, coming out of the doctors' club with an official with whom he had been playing cards, he could not resist saying:

"If only you knew what a fascinating woman I made the acquaintance of in Yalta!"

The official got into his sledge and was driving away, but turned suddenly and shouted:

"Dmitri Dmitritch!"

"What?"

"You were right this evening: the sturgeon was a bit too strong!"

These words, so ordinary, for some reason moved Gurov to indignation, and struck him as degrading and unclean. What savage manners, what people! What senseless nights, what uninteresting, uneventful days! The rage for card-playing, the gluttony, the drunkenness, the continual talk always about the same thing. Useless pursuits and conversations always about the same things absorb the better part of one's time, the better part of one's strength, and in the end there is left a life grovelling and curtailed, worthless and trivial, and there is no escaping or getting away from it—just as though one were in a madhouse or a prison.

Gurov did not sleep all night, and was filled with indignation. And he had a headache all next day. And the next night he slept badly; he sat up in bed, thinking, or paced up and down his room. He was sick of his children, sick of the bank; he had no desire to go anywhere or to talk of anything.

In the holidays in December he prepared for a journey, and told his wife he was going to Petersburg to do something in the interests of a young friend—and he set off for S——. What for? He did not very well know himself. He wanted to see Anna Sergeyevna and to talk with her—to arrange a meeting, if possible.

He reached S——in the morning, and took the best room at the hotel, in which the floor was covered with grey army cloth, and on the table was an inkstand, grey with dust and adorned with a figure on horseback, with its hat and its hand and its head broken off. The hotel porter gave him the necessary information; Von Diderits lived in a house of his own in Old Gontcharny Street—it was not far from the hotel: he was rich and lived in good style, and had his own horses; every one in the town knew him. The porter pronounced the name "Dridirits."

Gurov went without haste to Old Gontcharny Street and found the house. Just opposite the house stretched a long grey fence adorned with nails.

"One would run away from a fence like that," thought Gurov, looking from the fence to the windows of the house and back again.

He considered: to-day was a holiday, and the husband would probably be at home. And in any case it would be tactless to go into the house and upset her. If he were to send her a note it might fall into her husband's hands, and then it might ruin everything. The best thing was to trust to chance. And he kept walking up and down the street by the fence, waiting for the chance. He saw a beggar go in at the gate and dogs fly at him; then an hour later he heard a piano, and the sounds were faint and indistinct. Probably it was Anna Sergeyevna playing. The front door suddenly opened, and an old woman came out, followed by the familiar white Pomeranian. Gurov was on the point of calling to the dog, but his heart began beating violently, and in his excitement he could not remember the dog's name.

He walked up and down, and loathed the grey fence more and more, and by now he thought irritably that Anna Sergeyevna had forgotten him, and was perhaps already amusing herself with some one else, and that that was very natural in a young woman who had nothing to look at from morning till night but that confounded fence. He went back to his hotel room and sat for a long while on the sofa, not knowing what to do, then he had dinner and a long nap.

"How stupid and worrying it is!" he thought when he woke and looked at the dark windows: it was already evening. "Here I've had a good sleep for some reason. What shall I do in the night?"

He sat on the bed, which was covered by a cheap grey blanket, such as one sees in hospitals, and he taunted himself in his vexation:

"So much for the lady with the dog . . . so much for the adventure. . . . You're in a nice fix. . . ."

That morning at the station a poster in large letters had caught his eye. "The Geisha" was to be performed for the first time. He thought of this and went to the theater.

"It's quite possible she may go to the first performance," he thought.

The theatre was full. As in all provincial theatres, there was a fog above the chandelier, the gallery was noisy and restless; in the front row the local dandies were standing up before the beginning of the performance, with their hands behind them; in the Governor's box the Governor's daughter, wearing a boa, was sitting in the front seat, while the Governor himself lurked modestly behind the curtain with only his hands visible; the orchestra was a long time tuning up; the stage curtain swayed. All the time the audience were coming in and taking their seats Gurov looked at them eagerly.

Anna Sergeyevna, too, came in. She sat down in the third row, and when Gurov looked at her his heart contracted, and he understood clearly that for him there was in the whole world no creature so near, so precious, and so important to him; she, this little woman, in no way remarkable, lost in a provincial crowd, with a vulgar lorgnette in her hand, filled his whole life now, was his sorrow and his joy, the one happiness that he now desired for himself, and to the sounds of the inferior orchestra, of the wretched provincial violins, he thought how lovely she was. He thought and dreamed.

A young man with small side-whiskers, tall and stooping, came in with Anna Sergeyevna, and sat down beside her; he bent his head at every step and seemed to be continually bowing. Most likely this was the husband whom at Yalta, in a rush of bitter feeling, she had called a flunkey. And there really was in his long figure, his side-whiskers, and the small bald patch on his head, something of the flunkey's obsequiousness; his smile was sugary, and in his buttonhole there was some badge of distinction like the number on a waiter.

During the first interval the husband went away to smoke; she remained alone in her stall. Gurov, who was sitting in the stalls, too, went up to her and said in a trembling voice, with a forced smile:

"Good-evening."

She glanced at him and turned pale, then glanced again with horror, unable to believe her eyes, and tightly gripped her fan and the lorgnette in her hands, evidently struggling with herself not to faint. Both were silent. She was sitting, he was standing, frightened by her confusion and not venturing to sit down beside her. The violins and the flute began tuning up. He felt suddenly frightened; it seemed as though all the people in the boxes were looking at them. She got up and went quickly to the door; he followed her, and both walked senselessly along passages, and up and down stairs, and figures in legal, scholastic, and civil service uniforms, all wearing badges, flitted before their eyes. They caught glimpses of ladies, of fur coats hanging on pegs; the draughts blew on them, bringing a smell of stale tobacco. And Gurov, whose heart was beating violently, thought:

"Oh, heavens! Why are these people here and this orchestra! . . ."

And at that instant he recalled how when he had seen Anna Sergeyevna off at the station he had thought that everything was over and they would never meet again. But how far they were still from the end!

On the narrow, gloomy staircase over which was written "To the Amphitheatre," she stopped.

"How you have frightened me!" she said, breathing hard, still pale and overwhelmed. "Oh, how you have frightened me! I am half dead. Why have you come? Why?"

95 "But do understand, Anna, do understand . . ." he said hastily in a low voice. "I entreat you to understand. . . ."

She looked at him with dread, with entreaty, with love; she looked at him intently, to keep his features more distinctly in her memory.

"I am so unhappy," she went on, not heeding him. "I have thought of nothing but you all the time; I live only in the thought of you. And I wanted to forget, to forget you; but why, oh, why, have you come?"

On the landing above them two schoolboys were smoking and looking down, but that was nothing to Gurov; he drew Anna Sergeyevna to him, and began kissing her face, her cheeks, and her hands.

"What are you doing, what are you doing!" she cried in horror, pushing him away. "We are mad. Go away to-day; go away at once. . . . I beseech you by all that is sacred, I implore you. . . . There are people coming this way!"

100 Some one was coming up the stairs.

"You must go away," Anna Sergeyevna went on in a whisper. "Do you hear, Dmitri Dmitritch? I will come and see you in Moscow. I have never been happy; I am miserable now, and I never, never shall be happy, never! Don't make me suffer still more! I swear I'll come to Moscow. But now let us part. My precious, good, dear one, we must part!"

She pressed his hand and began rapidly going downstairs, looking round at him, and from her eyes he could see that she really was unhappy. Gurov stood for a little while, listened, then, when all sound had died away, he found his coat and left the theatre.

4

And Anna Sergeyevna began coming to see him in Moscow. Once in two or three months she left S——, telling her husband that she was going to consult a doctor about an internal complaint—and her husband believed her, and did not believe her. In Moscow she stayed at the Slaviansky Bazaar hotel, and at once sent a man in a red cap to Gurov. Gurov went to see her, and no one in Moscow knew of it.

Once he was going to see her in this way on a winter morning (the messenger had come the evening before when he was out). With him walked his daughter, whom he wanted to take to school: it was on the way. Snow was falling in big wet flakes.

"It's three degrees above freezing-point, and yet it is snowing," said Gurov to his   105
daughter. "The thaw is only on the surface of the earth; there is quite a different temperature at a greater height in the atmosphere."

"And why are there no thunderstorms in the winter, father?"

He explained that, too. He talked, thinking all the while that he was going to see *her*,
and no living soul knew of it, and probably never would know. He had two lives: one,
open, seen and known by all who cared to know, full of relative truth and of relative
falsehood, exactly like the lives of his friends and acquaintances; and another life running its course in secret. And through some strange, perhaps accidental, conjunction
of circumstances, everything that was essential, of interest and of value to him, everything in which he was sincere and did not deceive himself, everything that made the
kernel of his life, was hidden from other people; and all that was false in him, the
sheath in which he hid himself to conceal the truth—such, for instance, as his work in
the bank, his discussions at the club, his "lower race," his presence with his wife at anniversary festivities—all that was open. And he judged of others by himself, not believing in what he saw, and always believing that every man had his real, most
interesting life under the cover of secrecy and under the cover of night. All personal
life rested on secrecy, and possibly it was partly on that account that civilised man was
so nervously anxious that personal privacy should be respected.

After leaving his daughter at school, Gurov went on to the Slaviansky Bazaar. He
took off his fur coat below, went upstairs, and softly knocked at the door. Anna
Sergeyevna, wearing his favourite grey dress, exhausted by the journey and the suspense, had been expecting him since the evening before. She was pale; she looked at
him, and did not smile, and he had hardly come in when she fell on his breast. Their
kiss was slow and prolonged, as though they had not met for two years.

"Well, how are you getting on there?" he asked. "What news?"

"Wait; I'll tell you directly. . . . I can't talk."   110

She could not speak; she was crying. She turned away from him, and pressed her
handkerchief to her eyes.

"Let her have her cry out. I'll sit down and wait," he thought, and he sat down in
an arm-chair.

Then he rang and asked for tea to be brought him, and while he drank his tea she
remained standing at the window with her back to him. She was crying from emotion, from the miserable consciousness that their life was so hard for them; they could
only meet in secret, hiding themselves from people, like thieves! Was not their life
shattered?

"Come, do stop!" he said.

It was evident to him that this love of theirs would not soon be over, that he could   115
not see the end of it. Anna Sergeyevna grew more and more attached to him. She
adored him, and it was unthinkable to say to her that it was bound to have an end
some day; besides, she would not have believed it!

He went up to her and took her by the shoulders to say something affectionate and
cheering, and at that moment he saw himself in the looking-glass.

His hair was already beginning to turn grey. And it seemed strange to him that he
had grown so much older, so much plainer during the last few years. The shoulders
on which his hands rested were warm and quivering. He felt compassion for this life,
still so warm and lovely, but probably already not far from beginning to fade and wither like his own. Why did she love him so much? He always seemed to women different from what he was, and they loved in him not himself, but the man created by their

imagination, whom they had been eagerly seeking all their lives; and afterwards, when they noticed their mistake, they loved him all the same. And not one of them had been happy with him. Time passed, he had made their acquaintance, got on with them, parted, but he had never once loved; it was anything you like, but not love.

And only now when his head was grey he had fallen properly, really in love—for the first time in his life.

Anna Sergeyevna and he loved each other like people very close and akin, like husband and wife, like tender friends; it seemed to them that fate itself had meant them for one another, and they could not understand why he had a wife and she a husband; and it was as though they were a pair of birds of passage, caught and forced to live in different cages. They forgave each other for what they were ashamed of in their past, they forgave everything in the present, and felt that this love of theirs had changed them both.

120   In moments of depression in the past he had comforted himself with any arguments that came into his mind, but now he no longer cared for arguments; he felt profound compassion, he wanted to be sincere and tender. . . .

"Don't cry, my darling," he said. "You've had your cry; that's enough. . . . Let us talk now, let us think of some plan."

Then they spent a long while taking counsel together, talked of how to avoid the necessity for secrecy, for deception, for living in different towns and not seeing each other for long at a time. How could they be free from this intolerable bondage?

"How? How?" he asked, clutching his head. "How?"

And it seemed as though in a little while the solution would be found, and then a new and splendid life would begin; and it was clear to both of them that they had still a long, long road before them, and that the most complicated and difficult part of it was only just beginning.   [1899]

QUESTIONS

1. How does each of the four sections of the story contribute to the reader's understanding of the lovers?
2. How does the imagery emphasize the characters' isolation?
3. How is the action related to the changing settings—Yalta, S——, Moscow?
4. How are Gurov and Anna changed by their love affair?
5. What does the story say about the nature of love?

RESPONSES

1. Write an essay about the story's portrayal of man and woman. Does the narrator treat Anna and Gurov equally?
2. Using the Marxist approach, what does this story say about the lives of the wealthy?

FOCUS ON FILM

1. Examine the images used in the film *The Lady with a Dog*. What emotions are conveyed in these images? Do they have counterparts in the print story?

2. The film focuses a great deal on the boredom of the characters. To what extent is this theme present in the print story? To what extent is it a creation of the filmmakers?

CHARLES W. CHESNUTT

Charles W. Chesnutt (1858–1932) was born in Cleveland, Ohio. He was educated at Howard School in Oberlin, Ohio, a public school built with funds from free African Americans. In his late teens and early twenties, he read widely, worked as a teacher and principal in several schools, and as stenographer, and studied the law. In the late 1880s he began publishing short fiction and essays in various newspapers and magazines. After several novels were rejected, he published the short story collection *The Conjure Woman* in 1899. For the rest of his life, while managing a stenographic firm, he continued to write fiction and essays and to speak widely on racial issues. Although several works were rejected during his lifetime, he did publish *The Wife of His Youth and Other Stories of the Color Line* (1899), *The House Behind the Cedars* (1900), *The March of Tradition* (1901), and *The Colonel's Dream* (1905). The novels *Paul Marchand, F.M.C.*, and *The Quarry* were published in 1999.

The Doll

When Tom Taylor, proprietor of the Wyandot Hotel barber shop, was leaving home, after his noonday luncheon, to return to his work, his daughter, a sprightly, diminutive brown maid, with very bright black eyes and very curly, black hair, thrust into his coat pocket a little jointed doll somewhat the worse for wear.

"Now, don't forget, papa," she said, in her shrill childish treble, "what's to be done to her. Her arms won't work, and her legs won't work, and she can't hold her head up. Be sure and have her mended this afternoon, and bring her home when you come to supper; for she's afraid of the dark, and always sleeps with me. I'll meet you at the corner at half-past six—and don't forget, whatever you do."

"No, Daisy, I'll not forget," he replied, as he lifted her to the level of his lips and kissed her.

Upon reaching the shop he removed the doll from his pocket and hung it on one of the gilded spikes projecting above the wire netting surrounding the cashier's desk, where it would catch his eye. Some time during the afternoon he would send it to a toy shop around the corner for repairs. But the day was a busy one, and when the afternoon was well advanced he had not yet attended to it.

252

Colonel Forsyth had come up from the South to attend a conference of Democrat-   5
ic leaders to consider presidential candidates and platforms. He had put up at the
Wyandot Hotel, but had been mainly in the hands of Judge Beeman, chairman of the
local Jackson club, who was charged with the duty of seeing that the colonel was made
comfortable and given the freedom of the city. It was after a committee meeting, and
about 4 in the afternoon, that the two together entered the lobby of the Wyandot. They
were discussing the platforms to be put forward by the two great parties in the approaching campaign.

"I reckon, judge," the colonel was saying, "that the Republican party will make a
mistake if it injects the Negro question into its platform. The question is primarily a
local one, and if the North will only be considerate about the matter, and let us alone,
we can settle it to our entire satisfaction. The Negro's place is defined by nature, and
in the South he knows it and gives us no trouble."

"The Northern Negroes are different," returned the judge.

"They are just the same," rejoined the colonel. "It is you who are different. You
pamper them and they take liberties with you. But they are all from the South, and
when they meet a Southerner they act accordingly. They are born to serve and to submit. If they had been worthy of equality they would never have endured slavery. They
have no proper self-respect; they will neither resent an insult, nor defend a right, nor
avenge a wrong."

"Well, now, colonel, aren't you rather hard on them? Consider their past."

"Hard? Why, no, bless your heart! I've got nothing against the nigger. I like him—   10
in his place. But what I say is the truth. Are you in a hurry?"

"Not at all."

"Then come downstairs to the barber shop and I'll prove what I say."

The shop was the handsomest barber shop in the city. It was in the basement, and
the paneled ceiling glowed with electric lights. The floor was of white tile, the walls
lined with large mirrors. Behind ten chairs, of the latest and most comfortable design,
stood as many colored barbers, in immaculate white jackets, each at work upon a white
patron. An air of discipline and good order pervaded the establishment. There was
no loud talking by patrons, no unseemly garrulity on the part of the barbers. It was very
obviously a well-conducted barber shop, frequented by gentlemen who could afford
to pay liberally for superior service. As the judge and the colonel entered a customer
vacated the chair served by the proprietor.

"Next gentleman," said the barber.

The colonel removed his collar and took his seat in the vacant chair, remarking, as   15
he ran his hand over his neck, "I want a close shave, barber."

"Yes, sir; a close shave."

The barber was apparently about forty, with a brown complexion, clean-cut features and curly hair. Committed by circumstances to a career of personal service, he
had lifted it by intelligence, tact and industry to the dignity of a successful business.
The judge, a regular patron of the shop, knew him well and had often, while in his chair,
conversed with him concerning his race—a fruitful theme, much on the public tongue.

"As I was saying," said the colonel, while the barber adjusted a towel about his
neck, "the Negro question is a perfectly simple one."

The judge thought it hardly good taste in the colonel to continue in his former
strain. Northern men might speak slightingly of the Negro, but seldom in his presence. He tried a little diversion.

20   "The tariff," he observed, "is a difficult problem."

"Much more complicated, suh, than the Negro problem, which is perfectly simple. Let the white man once impress the Negro with his superiority; let the Negro see that there is no escape from the inevitable, and that ends it. The best thing about the Negro is that, with all his limitations, he can recognize a finality. It is the secret of his persistence among us. He has acquired the faculty of evolution, suh—by the law of the survival of the fittest. Long ago, when a young man, I killed a nigger to teach him his place. One who learns a lesson of that sort certainly never offends again, nor fathers any others of his breed."

The barber, having lathered the colonel's face, was stropping his razor with long, steady strokes. Every word uttered by the colonel was perfectly audible to him, but his impassive countenance betrayed no interest. The colonel seemed as unconscious of the barber's presence as the barber of the colonel's utterance. Surely, thought the judge, if such freedom of speech were the rule in the South the colonel's contention must be correct, and the Negroes thoroughly cowed. To a Northern man the situation was hardly comfortable.

"The iron and sugar interests of the South," persisted the judge, "will resist any reduction of the tariff."

The colonel was not to be swerved from the subject, nor from his purpose, whatever it might be.

25   "Quite likely they will; and we must argue with them, for they are white men and amenable to reason. The nigger, on the other hand, is the creature of instinct; you cannot argue with him; you must order him, and if he resists shoot him, as I did.

"Don't forget, barber," said the colonel, "that I want a close shave."

"No, sir," responded the barber, who, having sharpened his razor, now began to pass it, with firm and even hand, over the colonel's cheek.

"It must have been," said the judge, "an aggravated case, to justify so extreme a step."

"Extreme, suh? I beg yo' pardon, suh, but I can't say I had regarded my conduct in that light. But it was an extreme case so far as the nigger was concerned. I am not boasting about my course; it was simply a disagreeable necessity. I am naturally a kind-hearted man, and don't like to kill even a fly. It was after the war, suh, and just as the reconstruction period was drawing to a close. My mother employed a Negro girl, the child of a former servant of hers, to wait upon her."

30   The barber was studying the colonel's face as the razor passed over his cheek. The colonel's eyes were closed, or he might have observed the sudden gleam of interest that broke through the barber's mask of self-effacement, like a flash of lightning from a clouded sky. Involuntarily the razor remained poised in midair, but, in less time than it takes to say it, was moving again, swiftly and smoothly, over the colonel's face. To shave a talking man required a high degree of skill, but they were both adepts, each in his own trade—the barber at shaving, the colonel at talking.

"The girl was guilty of some misconduct, and my mother reprimanded her and sent her home. She complained to her father, and he came to see my mother about it. He was insolent, offensive and threatening. I came into the room and ordered him to leave it. Instead of obeying, he turned on me in a rage, suh, and threatened me. I drew my revolver and shot him. The result was unfortunate; but he and his people learned a lesson. We had no further trouble with bumptious niggers in our town."

"And did you have no trouble in the matter?" asked the judge.

"None, suh, to speak of. There were proceedings, but they were the merest formality. Upon my statement, confirmed by that of my mother, I was discharged by the examining magistrate, and the case was never even reported to the grand jury. It was a clear case of self-defense."

The barber had heard the same story, with some details ignored or forgotten by the colonel. It was the barber's father who had died at the colonel's hand, and for many long years the son had dreamed of this meeting.

He remembered the story in this wise: His father had been a slave. Freed by the   35
Civil War, he had entered upon the new life with the zeal and enthusiasm of his people at the dawn of liberty, which seem, in the light of later discouragements, so pathetic in the retrospect. The chattel aspired to own property; the slave, forbidden learning, to educate his children. He had worked early and late, had saved his money with a thrift equal to that of a German immigrant, and had sent his children regularly to school.

The girl—the barber remembered her very well—had been fair of feature, soft of speech and gentle of manner, a pearl among pebbles. One day her father's old mistress had met him on the street and, after a kindly inquiry about his family, had asked if she might hire his daughter during the summer, when there was no school. Her own married daughter would be visiting her, with a young child, and they wanted some neat and careful girl to nurse the infant.

"Why, yas ma'am," the barber's father had replied. "I reckon it might be a good thing fer Alice. I wants her ter be a teacher; but she kin l'arn things from you, ma'am, that no teacher kin teach her. She kin l'arn manners, ma'am, an' white folks' ways, and nowhere better than in yo' house."

So Alice had gone to the home of her father's former mistress to learn white folks' ways. The lady had been kind and gracious. But there are ways and ways among all people.

When she had been three weeks in her new employment her mistress's son—a younger brother of the colonel—came home from college. Some weeks later Alice went home to her father. Who was most at fault the barber never knew. A few hours afterward the father called upon the lady. There was a stormy interview. Things were said to which the ears of white ladies were unaccustomed from the lips of black men. The elder son had entered the room and interfered. The barber's father had turned to him and exclaimed angrily:

"Go 'way from here, boy, and don't talk ter me, or I'm liable ter harm you."   40

The young man stood his ground. The Negro advanced menacingly toward him. The young man drew his ready weapon and fatally wounded the Negro—he lived only long enough, after being taken home, to gasp out the facts to his wife and children.

The rest of the story had been much as the colonel had related it. As the barber recalled it, however, the lady had not been called to testify, but was ill at the time of the hearing, presumably from the nervous shock.

That she had secretly offered to help the family the barber knew, and that her help had been rejected with cold hostility. He knew that the murderer went unpunished, and that in later years he had gone into politics, and became the leader and mouthpiece of his party. All the world knew that he had ridden into power on his hostility to Negro rights.

The barber had been a mere boy at the time of his father's death, but not too young to appreciate the calamity that had befallen the household. The family was broken up. The sordid details of its misfortunes would not be interesting. Poverty, disease and death had followed them, until he alone was left. Many years had passed. The brown

boy who had wept beside his father's bier, and who had never forgotten nor forgiv-
en, was now the grave-faced, keen-eyed, deft-handed barber, who held a deadly
weapon at the throat of his father's slayer.

45   How often he had longed for this hour! In his dreams he had killed this man a hundred times, in a dozen ways. Once, when a young man, he had gone to meet him, with
the definite purpose of taking his life, but chance had kept them apart. He had imagined situations where they might come face to face; he would see the white man struggling in the water; he would have only to stretch forth his hand to save him; but he
would tell him of his hatred and let him drown. He would see him in a burning house,
from which he might rescue him; and he would call him murderer and let him burn!
He would see him in the dock for murder of a white man, and only his testimony
could save him, and he would let him suffer the fate that he doubly deserved! He saw
a vision of his father's form, only an hour before thrilling with hope and energy, now
stiff and cold in death; while under his keen razor lay the neck of his enemy, the enemy,
too, of his race, sworn to degrade them, to teach them, if need be, with the torch and
with the gun, that their place was at the white man's feet, his heel upon their neck; who
held them in such contempt that he could speak as he had spoken in the presence of
one of them. One stroke of the keen blade, a deflection of half an inch in its course, and
a murder would be avenged, an enemy destroyed!

For the next sixty seconds the barber heard every beat of his own pulse, and the
colonel, in serene unconsciousness, was nearer death than he had ever been in the
course of a long and eventful life. He was only a militia colonel, and had never been
under fire, but his turbulent political career had been passed in a community where
life was lightly valued, where hot words were often followed by rash deeds, and murder was tolerated as a means of private vengeance and political advancement. He went
on talking, but neither the judge not the barber listened, each being absorbed in his own
thoughts.

To the judge, who lived in a community where Negroes voted, the colonel's frankness was a curious revelation. His language was choice, though delivered with the
Southern intonation, his tone easy and conversational, and, in addressing the barber
directly, his manner had been courteous enough. The judge was interested, too, in
watching the barber, who, it was evident, was repressing some powerful emotion. It
seemed very probable to the judge that the barber might resent this cool recital of murder and outrage. He did not know what might be true of the Negroes in the South, but
he had been judge of a police court in one period of his upward career, and he had
found colored people prone to sudden rages, when under the influence of strong emotion, handy with edged tools, and apt to cut thick and deep, nor always careful about
the color of the cuticle. The barber's feelings were plainly stirred, and the judge, a student of human nature, was curious to see if he would be moved to utterance. It would
have been no novelty—patrons of the shop often discussed race questions with the
barber. It was evident that the colonel was trying an experiment to demonstrate his contention in the lobby above. But the judge could not know the barber's intimate relation to the story, nor did it occur to him that the barber might conceive any deadly
purpose because of a purely impersonal grievance. The barber's hand did not even
tremble.

In the barber's mind, however, the whirlwind of emotions had passed lightly over
the general and settled upon the particular injury. So strong, for the moment, was the
homicidal impulse that it would have prevailed already had not the noisy opening of
the door to admit a patron diverted the barber's attention and set in motion a current
of ideas which fought for the colonel's life. The barber's glance toward the door, from

force of habit, took in the whole shop. It was a handsome shop, and had been to the barber a matter of more than merely personal pride. Prominent among a struggling people, as yet scarcely beyond the threshold of citizenship, he had long been looked upon, and had become accustomed to regard himself, as a representative man, by whose failure or success his race would be tested. Should he slay this man now beneath his hand, this beautiful shop would be lost to his people. Years before the whole trade had been theirs. One by one the colored master barbers, trained in the slovenly old ways, had been forced to the wall by white competition, until his shop was one of the few good ones remaining in the hands of men of his race. Many an envious eye had been cast upon it. The lease had only a year to run. Strong pressure, he knew, had been exerted by a white rival to secure the reversion. The barber had the hotel proprietor's promise of a renewal; but he knew full well that should he lose the shop no colored man would succeed him: a center of industry, a medium of friendly contact with white men, would be lost to his people—many a good turn had the barber been able to do for them while he had the ear—literally had the ear—of some influential citizen, or held some aspirant for public office by the throat. Of the ten barbers in the shop all but one were married, with families dependent upon them for support. One was sending a son to college; another was buying a home. The unmarried one was in his spare hours studying a profession, with the hope of returning to practice it among his people in a Southern State. Their fates were all, in a measure, dependent upon the proprietor of the shop. Should he yield to the impulse which was swaying him their livelihood would be placed in jeopardy. For what white man, while the memory of this tragic event should last, would trust his throat again beneath a Negro's razor?

Such, however, was the strength of the impulse against which the barber was struggling that these considerations seemed likely not to prevail. Indeed, they had presented themselves to the barber's mind in a vague, remote, detached manner, while the dominant idea was present and compelling, clutching at his heart, drawing his arm, guiding his fingers. It was by their mass rather than by their clearness that these restraining forces held the barber's arm so long in check—it was society against self, civilization against the primitive instinct, typifying, more fully than the barber could realize, the great social problem involved in the future of his race.

He had now gone once over the colonel's face, subjecting that gentleman to less 50 discomfort than he had for a long time endured while undergoing a similar operation. Already he had retouched one cheek and had turned the colonel's head to finish the other. A few strokes more and the colonel could be released with a close shave—how close he would never know!—or, one stroke, properly directed, and he would never stand erect again! Only the day before the barber had read, in the newspapers, the account of a ghastly lynching in a Southern State, where, to avenge a single provoked murder, eight Negroes had bit the dust and a woman had been burned at the stake for no other crime than that she was her husband's wife. One stroke and there would be one less of those who thus wantonly played with human life!

The uplifted hand had begun the deadly downward movement—when one of the barbers dropped a shaving cup, which was smashed to pieces on the marble floor. Fate surely fought for the colonel—or was it for the barber? Involuntarily the latter stayed his hand—instinctively his glance went toward the scene of the accident. It was returning to the upraised steel, and its uncompleted task, when it was arrested by Daisy's doll, hanging upon the gilded spike where he had left it.

If the razor went to its goal he would not be able to fulfil his promise to Daisy! She would wait for him at the corner, and wait in vain! If he killed the colonel he himself could hardly escape, for he was black and not white, and this was North and not South, and personal vengeance was not accepted by the courts as a justification for murder. Whether he died or not, he would be lost to Daisy. His wife was dead, and there would be no one to take care of Daisy. His own father had died in defense of his daughter; he must live to protect his own. If there was a righteous God, who divided the evil from the good, the colonel would some time get his just deserts. Vengeance was God's; it must be left to Him to repay!

The jointed doll had saved the colonel's life. Whether society had conquered self or not may be an open question, but it had stayed the barber's hand until love could triumph over hate!

The barber laid aside the razor, sponged off the colonel's face, brought him, with a movement of the chair, to a sitting posture, brushed his hair, pulled away the cloths from around his neck, handed him a pasteboard check for the amount of his bill, and stood rigidly by his chair. The colonel adjusted his collar, threw down a coin equal to double the amount of his bill and, without waiting for the change, turned with the judge to leave the shop. They had scarcely reached the door leading into the hotel lobby when the barber, overwrought by the long strain, collapsed heavily into the nearest chair.

55   "Well, judge," said the colonel, as they entered the lobby, "that was a good shave. What a sin it would be to spoil such a barber by making him a postmaster! I didn't say anything to him, for it don't do to praise a nigger much—it's likely to give him the big head—but I never had," he went on, running his hand appreciatively over his cheek, "I never had a better shave in my life. And I proved my theory. The barber is the son of the nigger I shot."

The judge was not sure that the colonel had proved his theory, and was less so after he had talked, a week later, with the barber. And, although the colonel remained at the Wyandot for several days, he did not get shaved again in the hotel barber shop.   [1912]

QUESTIONS

1. What is the point of view of the story? How does Chesnutt use it to develop his theme?
2. What are the differences in Southern Whites and Northern Whites as portrayed in this story?
3. Where is conflict located in this story? How is it developed?
4. Describe Chesnutt's use of irony in the story.
5. What are the barber's reasons for acting as he does?

RESPONSES

1. Compare this story to "Battle Royale" by Ralph Ellison or compare it to "Dry September" by William Faulkner.
2. This story was written several decades before the racial equality movement of the late 1950s and 1960s. Examine the argument made in the story and how that argument changed over time.

KATE CHOPIN

Kate Chopin (1851–1904) was born in St. Louis, Missouri. Married and widowed by the age of thirty-two and the mother of six children, she began to write stories and novels that attracted a widening circle of readers. Her career was halted abruptly with the publication of her novel, *The Awakening* (1899), which treated the themes of mixed marriage and adultery with unaccustomed candor. Finding herself virtually boycotted by editors, she wrote little else during the remainder of her life. *The Awakening* is now considered a landmark in the development of feminist literature.

Regret

Mamzelle Aurélie possessed a good strong figure, ruddy cheeks, hair that was changing from brown to gray, and a determined eye. She wore a man's hat about the farm, and an old blue army overcoat when it was cold, and sometimes topboots.

Mamzelle Aurélie had never thought of marrying. She had never been in love. At the age of twenty she had received a proposal, which she had promptly declined, and at the age of fifty she had not yet lived to regret it.

So she was quite alone in the world, except for her dog Ponto, and the negroes who lived in her cabins and worked her crops, and the fowls, a few cows, a couple of mules, her gun (with which she shot chicken-hawks), and her religion.

One morning Mamzelle Aurélie stood upon her gallery, contemplating, with arms akimbo, a small band of very small children who, to all intents and purposes, might have fallen from the clouds, so unexpected and bewildering was their coming, and so unwelcome. They were the children of her nearest neighbor, Odile, who was not such a near neighbor, after all.

The young woman had appeared but five minutes before, accompanied by these four children. In her arms she carried little Elodie; she dragged Ti Nomme by an unwilling hand; while Marcéline and Marcélette followed with irresolute steps. 5

Her face was red and disfigured from tears and excitement. She had been summoned to a neighboring parish by the dangerous illness of her mother; her husband was away in Texas—it seemed to her a million miles away; and Valsin was waiting with the mule-cart to drive her to the station.

"It's no question, Mamzelle Aurélie; you jus' got to keep those youngsters fo' me tell I come back. Dieu sait,° I wouldn' botha you with 'em if it was any otha way to do! Make 'em mine you, Mamzelle Aurélie; don' spare 'em. Me, there, I'm half crazy between the chil'ren, an' Léon not home, an' maybe not even to fine po' maman alive encore!"°—a harrowing possibility which drove Odile to take a final hasty and convulsive leave of her disconsolate family.

She left them crowded into the narrow strip of shade on the porch of the long, low house; the white sunlight was beating in on the white old boards; some chickens were scratching in the grass at the foot of the steps, and one had boldly mounted, and was stepping heavily, solemnly, and aimlessly across the gallery. There was a pleasant odor of pinks in the air, and the sound of negroes' laughter was coming across the flowering cotton-field.

Mamzelle Aurélie stood contemplating the children. She looked with a critical eye upon Marcéline, who had been left staggering beneath the weight of the chubby Elodie. She surveyed with the same calculating air Marcélette mingling her silent tears with the audible grief and rebellion of Ti Nomme. During those few contemplative moments she was collecting herself, determining upon a line of action which should be identical with a line of duty. She began by feeding them.

10   If Mamzelle Aurélie's responsibilities might have begun and ended there, they could easily have been dismissed; for her larder was amply provided against an emergency of this nature. But little children are not little pigs; they require and demand attentions which were wholly unexpected by Mamzelle Aurélie, and which she was ill prepared to give.

She was, indeed, very inept in her management of Odile's children during the first few days. How could she know that Marcélette always wept when spoken to in a loud and commanding tone of voice? It was a peculiarity of Marcélette's. She became acquainted with Ti Nomme's passion for flowers only when he had plucked all the choicest gardenias and pinks for the apparent purpose of critically studying their botanical construction.

"'Tain't enough to tell 'im, Mamzelle Aurélie," Marcéline instructed her; "you got to tie 'im in a chair. It's w'at maman all time do w'en he's bad: she tie 'im in a chair." The chair in which Mamzelle Aurélie tied Ti Nomme was roomy and comfortable, and he seized the opportunity to take a nap in it, the afternoon being warm.

At night, when she ordered them one and all to bed as she would have shooed the chickens into the hen-house, they stayed uncomprehending before her. What about the little white nightgowns that had to be taken from the pillow-slip in which they were brought over, and shaken by some strong hand till they snapped like ox-whips? What about the tub of water which had to be brought and set in the middle of the floor, in which the little tired, dusty, sunbrowned feet had every one to be washed sweet and clean? And it made Marcéline and Marcélette laugh merrily—the idea that Mamzelle Aurélie should for a moment have believed that Ti Nomme could fall asleep without being told the story of *Croquemitaine*° or *Loup-garou,*° or both; or that Elodie could fall asleep at all without being rocked and sung to.

°*Dieu sait:* God knows.
°*encore:* Still, yet.
°*Croquemitaine:* bogey, bogeyman.
°*Loup-garou:* Werewolf.

"I tell you, Aunt Ruby," Mamzelle Aurélie informed her cook in confidence; "me, I'd rather manage a dozen plantation' than fo' chil'ren. It's terrassent!° Bonté!° Don't talk to me about chil'ren!"

"'Tain' ispected sich as you would know airy thing 'bout 'em, Mamzelle Aurélie. I see dat plainly yistiddy w'en I spy dat li'le chile playin' wid yo' basket o' keys. You don' know dat makes chillun grow up hard-headed, to play wid keys? Des like it make 'em teeth hard to look in a lookin'-glass. Them's the things you got to know in the raisin' an' manigement o'chillun." 15

Mamzelle Aurélie certainly did not pretend or aspire to such subtle and far-reaching knowledge on the subject as Aunt Ruby possessed, who had "raised five an' bared (buried) six" in her day. She was glad enough to learn a few little mother-tricks to serve the moment's need.

Ti Nomme's sticky fingers compelled her to unearth white aprons that she had not worn for years, and she had to accustom herself to his moist kisses—the expressions of an affectionate and exuberant nature. She got down her sewing-basket, which she seldom used, from the top shelf of the armoire, and placed it within the ready and easy reach which torn slips and buttonless waists demanded. It took her some days to become accustomed to the laughing, the crying, the chattering that echoed through the house and around it all day long. And it was not the first or the second night that she could sleep comfortably with little Elodie's hot, plump body pressed close against her, and the little one's warm breath beating her cheek like the fanning of a bird's wing.

But at the end of two weeks Mamzelle Aurélie had grown quite used to these things, and she no longer complained.

It was also at the end of two weeks that Mamzelle Aurélie, one evening, looking away toward the crib where the cattle were being fed, saw Valsin's blue cart turning the bend of the road. Odile sat beside the mulatto, upright and alert. As they drew near, the young woman's beaming face indicated that her homecoming was a happy one.

But this coming, unannounced and unexpected, threw Mamzelle Aurélie into a flutter that was almost agitation. The children had to be gathered. Where was Ti Nomme? Yonder in the shed, putting an edge on his knife at the grindstone. And Marcéline and Marcélette? Cutting and fashioning doll-rags in the corner of the gallery. As for Elodie, she was safe enough in Mamzelle Aurélie's arms; and she had screamed with delight at sight of the familiar blue cart which was bringing her mother back to her. 20

The excitement was all over, and they were gone. How still it was when they were gone! Mamzelle Aurélie stood upon the gallery, looking and listening. She could no longer see the cart; the red sunset and the blue-gray twilight had together flung a purple mist across the fields and road that hid it from her view. She could no longer hear the wheezing and creaking of its wheels. But she could still faintly hear the shrill, glad voices of the children.

She turned into the house. There was much work awaiting her, for the children had left a sad disorder behind them; but she did not at once set about the task of righting it. Mamzelle Aurélie seated herself beside the table. She gave one slow

---

°*terrassent*: Exhausting.
°*Bonté*: Goodness.

glance through the room, into which the evening shadows were creeping and deepening around her solitary figure. She let her head fall down upon her bended arm,
and began to cry. Oh, but she cried! Not softly, as women often do. She cried like a
man, with sobs that seemed to tear her very soul. She did not notice Ponto licking
her hand.   [1894]

QUESTIONS

1. Between the title and the last sentence in the second paragraph, has Chopin
   given the reader enough foreshadowing?
2. Given your knowledge of setting, is Odile's demand unreasonable?
3. Does Chopin's use of small details announce a growing affection for the children? Point out some of those details.
4. On your first reading, did you expect that "Mamzelle Aurélie" would become angry at some of the children's behavior?
5. In paragraph ten there is the word "attentions." Is that "s" important?

RESPONSES

1. Approaching the story from a feminist perspective, write an essay analyzing
   what this writer is saying about women and motherhood.
2. Compare the women and their lives in all three of Chopin's stories to Kundera's "Let the Old Dead Make Room for the Young Dead."
3. Write a short story about a man who never married, whose features resemble a woman's, and who at the end of the story cries like a woman. What
   does he regret?

KATE CHOPIN

A Respectable Woman

Mrs. Baroda was a little provoked to learn that her husband expected his friend, Gouvernail, up to spend a week or two on the plantation.

They had entertained a good deal during the winter; much of the time had also been passed in New Orleans in various forms of mild dissipation. She was looking forward to a period of unbroken rest, now, and undisturbed tête-à-tête with her husband, when he informed her that Gouvernail was coming up to stay a week or two.

This was a man she had heard much of but never seen. He had been her husband's college friend; was now a journalist, and in no sense a society man or "a man about town," which were, perhaps, some of the reasons she had never met him. But she had unconsciously formed an image of him in her mind. She pictured him tall, slim, cynical; with eye-glasses, and his hands in his pockets; and she did not like him. Gouvernail was slim enough, but he wasn't very tall nor very cynical; neither did he wear eye-glasses nor carry his hands in his pockets. And she rather liked him when he first presented himself.

But why she liked him she could not explain satisfactorily to herself when she partly attempted to do so. She could discover in him none of those brilliant and promising traits which Gaston, her husband, had often assured her that he possessed. On the contrary, he sat rather mute and receptive before her chatty eagerness to make him feel at home and in face of Gaston's frank and wordy hospitality. His manner was as courteous toward her as the most exacting woman could require; but he made no direct appeal to her approval or even esteem.

Once settled at the plantation he seemed to like to sit upon the wide portico in the shade of one of the big Corinthian pillars, smoking his cigar lazily and listening attentively to Gaston's experience as a sugar planter.   5

"This is what I call living," he would utter with deep satisfaction, as the air that swept across the sugar field caressed him with its warm and scented velvety touch. It pleased him also to get on familiar terms with the big dogs that came about him, rubbing themselves sociably against his legs. He did not care to fish, and displayed no eagerness to go out and kill grosbecs when Gaston proposed doing so.

Gouvernail's personality puzzled Mrs. Baroda, but she liked him. Indeed, he was a lovable, inoffensive fellow. After a few days, when she could understand him no better than at first, she gave over being puzzled and remained piqued. In this mood she left her husband and her guest, for the most part, alone together. Then finding that

Gouvernail took no manner of exception to her action, she imposed her society upon him, accompanying him in his idle strolls to the mill and walks along the batture.° She persistently sought to penetrate the reserve in which he had unconsciously enveloped himself.

"When is he going—your friend?" she one day asked her husband. "For my part, he tires me frightfully."

"Not for a week yet, dear. I can't understand; he gives you no trouble."

10 "No. I should like him better if he did; if he were more like others, and I had to plan somewhat for his comfort and enjoyment."

Gaston took his wife's pretty face between his hands and looked tenderly and laughingly into her troubled eyes. They were making a bit of toilet sociably together in Mrs. Baroda's dressing-room.

"You are full of surprises, ma belle," he said to her. "Even I can never count upon how you are going to act under given conditions." He kissed her and turned to fasten his cravat before the mirror.

"Here you are," he went on, "taking poor Gouvernail seriously and making a commotion over him, the last thing he would desire or expect."

"Commotion!" she hotly resented. "Nonsense! How can you say such a thing? Commotion, indeed! But, you know, you said he was clever."

15 "So he is. But the poor fellow is run down by overwork now. That's why I asked him here to take a rest."

"You used to say he was a man of ideas," she retorted, unconciliated. "I expected him to be interesting, at least. I'm going to the city in the morning to have my spring gowns fitted. Let me know when Mr. Gouvernail is gone; I shall be at my Aunt Octavie's."

That night she went and sat alone upon a bench that stood beneath a live oak tree at the edge of the gravel walk.

She had never known her thoughts or her intentions to be so confused. She could gather nothing from them but the feeling of a distinct necessity to quit her home in the morning.

Mrs. Baroda heard footsteps crunching the gravel; but could discern in the darkness only the approaching red point of a lighted cigar. She knew it was Gouvernail, for her husband did not smoke. She hoped to remain unnoticed, but her white gown revealed her to him. He threw away his cigar and seated himself upon the bench beside her; without a suspicion that she might object to his presence.

20 "Your husband told me to bring this to you, Mrs. Baroda," he said, handing her a filmy, white scarf with which she sometimes enveloped her head and shoulders. She accepted the scarf from him with a murmur of thanks, and let it lie in her lap.

He made some commonplace observation upon the baneful effect of the night air at that season. Then as his gaze reached out into the darkness, he murmured, half to himself:

"'Night of south winds—night of the large few stars!
Still nodding night—'"

°*batture*: Riverbank.

She made no reply to this apostrophe to the night, which indeed, was not addressed to her.

Gouvernail was in no sense a diffident man, for he was not a self-conscious one. His periods of reserve were not constitutional, but the result of moods. Sitting there beside Mrs. Baroda, his silence melted for the time.

He talked freely and intimately in a low, hesitating drawl that was not unpleasant to hear. He talked of the old college days when he and Gaston had been a good deal to each other; of the days of keen and blind ambitions and large intentions. Now there was left with him, at least, a philosophic acquiescence to the existing order—only a desire to be permitted to exist, with now and then a little whiff of genuine life, such as he was breathing now.

Her mind only vaguely grasped what he was saying. Her physical being was for the moment predominant. She was not thinking of his words, only drinking in the tones of his voice. She wanted to reach out her hand in the darkness and touch him with the sensitive tips of her fingers upon the face or the lips. She wanted to draw close to him and whisper against his cheek—she did not care what—as she might have done if she had not been a respectable woman. 25

The stronger the impulse grew to bring herself near him, the further, in fact, did she draw away from him. As soon as she could so do without an appearance of too great rudeness, she rose and left him there alone.

Before she reached the house, Gouvernail had lighted a fresh cigar and ended his apostrophe to the night.

Mrs. Baroda was greatly tempted that night to tell her husband—who was also her friend—of this folly that had seized her. But she did not yield to the temptation. Beside being a respectable woman she was a very sensible one; and she knew there are some battles in life which a human being must fight alone.

When Gaston arose in the morning, his wife had already departed. She had taken an early morning train to the city. She did not return till Gouvernail was gone from under her roof.

There was some talk of having him back during the summer that followed. That is, Gaston greatly desired it; but this desire yielded to his wife's strenuous opposition. 30

However, before the year ended, she proposed, wholly from herself, to have Gouvernail visit them again. Her husband was surprised and delighted with the suggestion coming from her.

"I am glad, chère amie, to know that you have finally overcome your dislike for him; truly he did not deserve it."

"Oh," she told him, laughingly, after pressing a long, tender kiss upon his lips, "I have overcome everything! you will see. This time I shall be very nice to him."   [1894]

QUESTIONS

1. What does Chopin mean by, "They were making a bit of toilet sociably together . . ."?
2. Why does Mrs. Baroda feel "a distinct necessity to quit her home"?
3. Is the last paragraph a good or bad thing for Gaston?
4. Why, early in their acquaintance, is Mrs. Baroda disappointed in Gouvernail?

5. For the feelings that Chopin allows Mrs. Baroda to have—while she sat listening to Gouvernail—the writer's career was destroyed. Why?

RESPONSE

1. Write an essay analyzing who you think the audience of this story is. Who would read this story and why?

KATE CHOPIN

The Story of an Hour

Knowing that Mrs. Mallard was afflicted with heart trouble, great care was taken to break to her as gently as possible the news of her husband's death.

It was her sister Josephine who told her, in broken sentences; veiled hints that revealed in half concealing. Her husband's friend Richards was there, too, near her. It was he who had been in the newspaper office when intelligence of the railroad disaster was received, with Brently Mallard's name leading the list of "killed." He had only taken the time to assure himself of its truth by a second telegram, and had hastened to forestall any less careful, less tender friend in bearing the sad message.

She did not hear the story as many women have heard the same, with a paralyzed inability to accept its significance. She wept at once, with sudden, wild abandonment, in her sister's arms. When the storm of grief had spent itself she went away to her room alone. She would have no one follow her.

There stood, facing the open window, a comfortable, roomy armchair. Into this she sank, pressed down by a physical exhaustion that haunted her body and seemed to reach into her soul.

She could see in the open square before her house the tops of trees that were all 5 aquiver with the new spring life. The delicious breath of rain was in the air. In the street below a peddler was crying his wares. The notes of a distant song which some one was singing reached her faintly, and countless sparrows were twittering in the eaves.

There were patches of blue sky showing here and there through the clouds that had met and piled one above the other in the west facing her window.

She sat with her head thrown back upon the cushion of the chair, quite motionless, except when a sob came up into her throat and shook her, as a child who has cried itself to sleep continues to sob in its dreams.

She was young, with a fair, calm face, whose lines bespoke repression and even a certain strength. But now there was a dull stare in her eyes, whose gaze was fixed away off yonder on one of those patches of blue sky. It was not a glance of reflection, but rather indicated a suspension of intelligent thought.

There was something coming to her and she was waiting for it, fearfully. What was it? She did not know; it was too subtle and elusive to name. But she felt it, creeping out of the sky, reaching toward her through the sounds, the scents, the color that filled the air.

10 Now her bosom rose and fell tumultuously. She was beginning to recognize this thing that was approaching to possess her, and she was striving to beat it back with her will—as powerless as her two white slender hands would have been.

When she abandoned herself a little whispered word escaped her slightly parted lips. She said it over and over under her breath: "free, free, free!" The vacant stare and the look of terror that had followed it went from her eyes. They stayed keen and bright. Her pulses beat fast, and the coursing blood warmed and relaxed every inch of her body.

She did not stop to ask if it were or were not a monstrous joy that held her. A clear and exalted perception enabled her to dismiss the suggestion as trivial.

She knew that she would weep again when she saw the kind, tender hands folded in death; the face that had never looked save with love upon her, fixed and gray and dead. But she saw beyond that bitter moment a long procession of years to come that would belong to her absolutely. And she opened and spread her arms out to them in welcome.

There would be no one to live for her during those coming years; she would live for herself. There would be no powerful will bending hers in that blind persistence with which men and women believe they have a right to impose a private will upon a fellow-creature. A kind intention or a cruel intention made the act seem no less a crime as she looked upon it in that brief moment of illumination.

15 And yet she had loved him—sometimes. Often she had not. What did it matter! What could love, the unsolved mystery, count for in face of this possession of self-assertion which she suddenly recognized as the strongest impulse of her being!

"Free! Body and soul free!" she kept whispering.

Josephine was kneeling before the closed door with her lips to the keyhole, imploring for admission. "Louise, open the door! I beg; open the door—you will make yourself ill. What are you doing, Louise? For heaven's sake open the door."

"Go away. I am not making myself ill." No; she was drinking in a very elixir of life through that open window.

Her fancy was running riot along those days ahead of her. Spring days, and summer days, and all sorts of days that would be her own. She breathed a quick prayer that life might be long. It was only yesterday she had thought with a shudder that life might be long.

20 She arose at length and opened the door to her sister's importunities. There was a feverish triumph in her eyes, and she carried herself unwittingly like a goddess of Victory. She clasped her sister's waist, and together they descended the stairs. Richards stood waiting for them at the bottom.

Some one was opening the front door with a latchkey. It was Brently Mallard who entered, a little travel-stained, composedly carrying his gripsack and umbrella. He had been far from the scene of accident, and did not even know there had been one. He stood amazed at Josephine's piercing cry; at Richards' quick motion to screen him from the view of his wife.

But Richards was too late.

When the doctors came they said she had died of heart disease—of joy that kills.   [1894]

QUESTIONS

1. What is the significance of the title?
2. List the major ironies on which the plot is constructed. Do they seem persuasive, or do they strain credibility?

3. How does the description of the setting reflect Mrs. Mallard's shifts in mood?
4. What is the attitude of the author toward those who would comfort Mrs. Mallard?
5. What does Richards's "quick motion" at the climax reveal?

RESPONSES

1. Using the structuralist approach, especially the dichotomy of high and low, compare this story to Leslie Marmon Silko's "Yellow Woman."
2. Write an essay that explains how Chopin viewed women's lives in this story, "A Respectable Woman," and "Regret."

FOCUS ON FILM

1. View the film *The Joy That Kills*. Detail the additions made to the story "The Story of an Hour" and explain what those additions contribute to the film.
2. Research the life of Kate Chopin. In what ways does the film rely on Chopin's life when making additions to the source story?

Sandra Cisneros (b. 1954) is a highly regarded writer of poetry and short fiction. She was born in Chicago, Illinois, and attended Loyola University (B.A.) and the University of Iowa (M.F.A.). She has worked as a teacher, writer in schools, and arts director. In 1995, she was named a MacArthur fellow. She now lives in San Antonio, Texas. Her works include *The House on Mango Street* (stories, 1984), *My Wicked, Wicked Ways* (poetry, 1987), *Woman Hollering Creek and Other Stories* (stories, 1991), *Loose Woman* (poetry, 1994), and *Caramelo* (novel, 2002).

Barbie-Q

Yours is the one with mean eyes and a ponytail. Striped swimsuit, stilettos, sunglasses, and gold hoop earrings. Mine is the one with bubble hair. Red swimsuit, stilettos, pearl earrings, and a wire stand. But that's all we can afford, besides one extra outfit apiece. Yours, "Red Flair," sophisticated A-line coatdress with Jackie Kennedy pillbox hat, white gloves, handbag, and heels included. Mine, "Solo in the Spotlight," evening elegance in black glitter strapless gown with a puffy skirt at the bottom like a mermaid tail, formal-length gloves, pink chiffon scarf, and mike included. From so much dressing and undressing, the black glitter wears off where her titties stick out. This and a dress invented from an old sock when we cut holes here and here and here, the cuff rolled over for the glamorous, fancy-free, off-the-shoulder look.

Every time the same story. Your Barbie is roommates with my Barbie, and my Barbie's boyfriend comes over and your Barbie steals him, okay? Kiss kiss kiss. Then the two Barbies fight. You dumbbell! He's mine. Oh no he's not, you stinky! Only Ken's invisible, right? Because we don't have money for a stupid-looking boy doll when we'd both rather ask for a new Barbie outfit next Christmas. We have to make do with your mean-eyed Barbie and my bubblehead Barbie and our one outfit apiece not including the sock dress.

Until next Sunday when we are walking through the flea market on Maxwell Street and *there!* Lying on the street next to some tool bits, and platform shoes with the heels all squashed, and a fluorescent green wicker wastebasket, and aluminum foil, and hubcaps, and a pink shag rug, and windshield wiper blades, and dusty mason jars, and a coffee can full of rusty nails. *There!* Where? Two Mattel boxes. One with the "Career

Gal" ensemble, snappy black-and-white business suit, three-quarter-length sleeve jacket with kick-pleat skirt, red sleeveless shell, gloves, pumps, and matching hat included. The other, "Sweet Dreams," dreamy pink-and-white plaid nightgown and matching robe, lace-trimmed slippers, hair-brush and hand mirror included. How much? Please, please, please, please, please, please, please, until they say okay.

On the outside you and me skipping and humming but inside we are doing loopity-loops and pirouetting. Until at the next vendor's stand, next to boxed pies, and bright orange toilet brushes, and rubber gloves, and wrench sets, and bouquets of feather flowers, and glass towel racks, and steel wool, and Alvin and the Chipmunks records, *there!* And *there!* And *there!* And *there!* and *there!* and *there!* and *there!* Bendable Legs Barbie with her new page-boy hairdo. Midge, Barbie's best friend. Ken, Barbie's boyfriend. Skipper, Barbie's little sister. Tutti and Todd, Barbie and Skipper's tiny twin sister and brother. Skipper's friends, Scooter and Ricky. Alan, Ken's buddy. And Francie, Barbie's MOD'ern cousin.

Everybody today selling toys, all of them damaged with water and smelling of smoke. Because a big toy warehouse on Halsted Street burned down yesterday—see there?—the smoke still rising and drifting across the Dan Ryan expressway. And now there is a big fire sale at Maxwell Street, today only.

So what if we didn't get our new Bendable Legs Barbie and Midge and Ken and Skipper and Tutti and Todd and Scooter and Ricky and Alan and Francie in nice clean boxes and had to buy them on Maxwell Street, all water-soaked and sooty. So what if our Barbies smell like smoke when you hold them up to your nose even after you wash and wash and wash them. And if the prettiest doll, Barbie's MOD'ern cousin Francie with real eyelashes, eyelash brush included, has a left foot that's melted a little—so? If you dress her in her new "Prom Pinks" outfit, satin splendor with matching coat, gold belt, clutch, and hair bow included, so long as you don't lift her dress, right?—who's to know. [1991]

QUESTIONS

1. Who is the narrator? What can we discern about her from the story?
2. Why are the doll's outfits described in the way they are? Whose language is employed in the descriptions?
3. What is the conflict in the story?
4. What does "so long as you don't lift her dress" mean?
5. Is this a story about gender or is it a story about social class?

RESPONSES

1. Compare this story to others that feature girls and young women, for instance, Kincaid's "Girl," Lavin's "My Vocation," Oates's "Shopping," Silko's "Storyteller," and Viramontes's "The Moths." How do each of these comparisons affect your reading of the story?
2. Write a parallel story about a boy and GI Joe toys.

SAMUEL CLEMENS (MARK TWAIN)

Samuel Clemens (Mark Twain) (1835–1910) was born in Florida, Missouri, but his family soon moved to Hannibal, a village on the Mississippi River that he immortalized in his two novels of childhood, *The Adventures of Tom Sawyer* (1876) and *The Adventures of Huckleberry Finn* (1884). In fact, Mark Twain was his own best subject, and the chief sources of his life are his own works: his years as a riverboat pilot described in *Life on the Mississippi* (1883) and his travels, described in *Innocents Abroad* (1869) and *Roughing It* (1871). His fame as an author and as a platform performer made him perhaps the best-known American of his time, but the dark side of this comic genius became widely known only after his death with the posthumous publication of such works as *The Mysterious Stranger* (1916). His *Autobiography* (1924) is partly fictional, as much of his fiction is partly autobiographical.

The Celebrated Jumping Frog of Calaveras County

In compliance with the request of a friend of mine, who wrote me from the East, I called on good-natured, garrulous old Simon Wheeler, and inquired about my friend's friend, Leonidas W. Smiley, as requested to do, and I hereunto append the result. I have a lurking suspicion that *Leonidas* W. Smiley is a myth; that my friend never knew such a personage; and that he only conjectured that if I asked old Wheeler about him, it would remind him of his infamous *Jim* Smiley, and he would go to work and bore me to death with some exasperating reminiscence of him as long and as tedious as it should be useless to me. If that was the design, it succeeded.

I found Simon Wheeler dozing comfortably by the bar-room stove of the dilapidated tavern in the decayed mining camp of Angel's, and I noticed that he was fat and bald-headed, and had an expression of winning gentleness and simplicity upon his tranquil countenance. He roused up, and gave me good day. I told him that a friend of mine had commissioned me to make some inquiries about a cherished companion of his boyhood named *Leonidas* W. Smiley—a young minister of the Gospel, who he had heard was at one time a resident of Angel's Camp. I added that if Mr. Wheeler could tell me anything about this Rev. Leonidas W. Smiley, I would feel under many obligations to him.

Simon Wheeler backed me into a corner and blockaded me there with his chair, and then sat down and reeled off the monotonous narrative which follows this paragraph. He never smiled, he never frowned, he never changed his voice from the gentle-flowing key to which he tuned his initial sentence, he never betrayed the slightest suspicion of enthusiasm; but all through the interminable narrative there ran a vein of impressive earnestness and sincerity, which showed me plainly that, so far from his imagining that there was anything ridiculous or funny about his story, he regarded it as a really important matter, and admired its two heroes as men of transcendent genius in *finesse*. I let him go on in his own way, and never interrupted him once.

"Rev. Leonidas W. H'm, Reverend Le——well, there was a feller here once by the name of *Jim* Smiley, in the winter of '49—or maybe it was the spring of '50—I don't recollect exactly, somehow, though what makes me think it was one or the other is because I remember the big flume warn't finished when he first came to the camp; but anyway, he was the curiousest man about always betting on anything that turned up you ever see, if he could get anybody to bet on the other side; and if he couldn't he'd change sides. Any way that suited the other man would suit *him*—any way just so's he got a bet, *he* was satisfied. But still he was lucky, uncommon lucky; he most always come out winner. He was always ready and laying for a chance; there couldn't be no solit'ry thing mentioned but that feller'd offer to bet on it, and take ary side you please, as I was just telling you. If there was a horse-race, you'd find him flush or you'd find him busted at the end of it; if there was a dog-fight, he'd bet on it; if there was a cat-fight, he'd bet on it; if there was a chicken fight, he'd bet on it; why, if there was two birds setting on a fence he would bet you which one would fly first; or if there was a camp meeting, he would be there reg'lar to bet on Parson Walker, which he judged to be the best exhorter about here, and so he was too, and a good man. If he even see a straddle-bug start to go anywhere, he would bet you how long it would take him to get to—to wherever he was going to, and if you took him up, he would foller that straddle-bug to Mexico but what he would find out where he was bound for and how long he was on the road. Lots of the boys here has seen that Smiley, and can tell you about him. Why, it never made no difference to *him*—he'd bet on *any* thing—the dangdest feller. Parson Walker's wife laid very sick once, for a good while and it seemed as if they warn't going to save her; but one morning he come in, and Smiley up and asked him how she was, and he said she was considerable better—thank the Lord for his inf'nite mercy—and coming on so smart that with the blessing of Prov'dence she'd get well yet; and Smiley, before he thought, says, 'Well, I'll resk two-and-a-half she don't anyway.'

"Thish-yer Smiley had a mare—the boys called her the fifteen-minute nag, but that was only in fun, you know, because of course she was faster than that—and he used to win money on that horse, for all she was slow and always had the asthma, or the distemper, or the consumption, or something of that kind. They used to give her two or three hundred yards' start, and then pass her under way; but always at the fag end of the race she'd get excited and desperate like, and come cavorting and straddling up, and scattering her legs around limber, sometimes in the air, and sometimes out to one side among the fences, and kicking up m-o-r-e dust and raising m-o-r-e racket with her coughing and sneezing and blowing her nose—and *always* fetch up at the stand just about a neck ahead, as near as you could cipher it down.

"And he had a little small bull-pup, that to look at him you'd think he warn't worth a cent but to set around and look ornery and lay for a chance to steal something. But as soon as money was up on him he was a different dog; his under-jaw'd begin to stick out like the fo'castle of a steamboat, and his teeth would uncover and shine like the furnaces. And a dog might tackle him and bully-rag him, and bite him, and throw him over his shoulder two or three times, and Andrew Jackson—which was the name of the pup—Andrew Jackson would never let on but what *he* was satisfied, and hadn't ex-pected nothing else—and the bets being doubled and doubled on the other side all the time, till the money was all up; and then all of a sudden he would grab that other dog jest by the j'int of his hind leg and freeze to it—not chaw, you understand, but only just grip and hang on till they throwed up the sponge, if it was a year. Smiley always come out winner on that pup, till he harnessed a dog once that didn't have no hind legs, be-cause they'd been sawed off in a circular saw, and when the thing had gone along far enough, and the money was all up, and he come to make a snatch for his pet holt, he see in a minute how he'd been imposed on, and how the other dog had him in the door, so to speak, and he 'peared surprised, and then he looked sorter discouraged-like, and didn't try no more to win the fight, and so he got shucked out bad. He give Smiley a look, as much as to say his heart was broke, and it was *his* fault, for putting up a dog that hadn't no hind legs for him to take holt of, which was his main dependence in a fight, and then he limped off a piece and laid down and died. It was a good pup, was that Andrew Jackson, and would have made a name for hisself if he'd lived, for the stuff was in him and he had genius—I know it, because he hadn't no opportunities to speak of, and it don't stand to reason that a dog could make such a fight as he could under them circumstances if he hadn't no talent. It always makes me feel sorry when I think of that last fight of his'n, and the way it turned out.

"Well, thish-yer Smiley had rat-tarriers, and chicken cocks, and tom-cats and all them kind of things, till you couldn't rest, and you couldn't fetch nothing for him to bet on but he'd match you. He ketched a frog one day, and took him home, and said he cal'lated to educate him; and so he never done nothing for three months but set in his back yard and learn that frog to jump. And you bet you he *did* learn him, too. He'd give him a little punch behind, and the next minute you'd see that frog whirling in the air like a doughnut—see him turn one summerset, or maybe a couple, if he got a good start, and come down flat-footed and all right, like a cat. He got him up so in the matter of ketching flies, and kep' him in practice so constant, that he'd nail a fly every time as fur as he could see him. Smiley said all a frog wanted was education, and he could do 'most anything—and I believe him. Why, I've seen him set Dan'l Webster down here on this floor—Dan'l Webster was the name of the frog—and sing out, "Flies, Dan'l, flies!" and quicker'n you could wink he'd spring straight up and snake a fly off'n the counter there, and flop down on the floor ag'in as solid as a gob of mud, and fall to scratching the side of his head with his hind foot as indifferent as if he hadn't no idea he'd been doin' any more'n any frog might do. You never see a frog so modest and straightfor'ard as he was, for all he was so gifted. And when it come to fair and square jumping on a dead level, he could get over more ground at one straddle than any animal of his breed you ever see. Jumping on a dead level was his strong suit, you understand; and when it come to that, Smiley would ante up money on him as long as he had a red. Smiley was monstrous proud of his frog, and well he might be, for fellers that had traveled and been everywheres, all said he laid over any frog that ever *they* see.

"Well, Smiley kep' the beast in a little lattice box, and he used to fetch him down-town sometimes and lay for a bet. One day a feller—a stranger in the camp, he was—come acrost him with his box, and says:

"'What might it be that you've got in the box?'

"And Smiley says, sorter indifferent-like, 'It might be a parrot, or it might be a ca-   10
nary, maybe, but it ain't—it's only just a frog.'

"And the feller took it, and looked at it careful, and turned it round this way and
that, and says, 'H'm—so 'tis. Well, what's *he* good for?'

"'Well,' Smiley says, easy and careless, 'he's good enough for *one* thing, I should
judge—he can outjump any frog in Calaveras County.'

"The feller took the box again, and took another long, particular look, and give it
back to Smiley, and says, very deliberate, 'Well,' he says, 'I don't see no p'ints about
that frog that's any better'n any other frog.'

"'Maybe you don't,' Smiley says. 'Maybe you understand frogs and maybe you
don't understand 'em; maybe you've had experience, and maybe you ain't only a am-
ature, as it were. Anyways, I've got *my* opinion, and I'll resk forty dollars that he can
outjump any frog in Calaveras County.'

"And the feller studied a minute, and then says, kinder sadlike, 'Well, I'm only a   15
stranger here, and I ain't got no frog; but if I had a frog, I'd bet you.'

"And then Smiley says, 'That's all right—that's all right—if you'll hold my box a
minute, I'll go and get you a frog.' And so the feller took the box, and put up his forty
dollars along with Smiley's, and set down to wait.

"So he set there a good while thinking and thinking to himself, and then he got the
frog out and prized his mouth open and took a teaspoon and filled him full of quail-
shot—filled him pretty near up to his chin—and set him on the floor. Smiley he went
to the swamp and slopped around in the mud for a long time, and finally he ketched
a frog, and fetched him in, and give him to this feller, and says:

"'Now, if you're ready, set him alongside of Dan'l, with his fore paws just even with
Dan'l's, and I'll give the word.' Then he says, 'One—two—three—*git!*' and him and
the feller touched up the frogs from behind, and the new frog hopped off lively, but
Dan'l give a heave, and hysted up his shoulders—so—like a Frenchman, but it warn't
no use—he couldn't budge; he was planted as solid as a church, and he couldn't no
more stir than if he was anchored out. Smiley was a good deal surprised, and he was
disgusted too, but he didn't have no idea what the matter was, of course.

"The feller took the money and started away; and when he was going out at the
door, he sorter jerked his thumb over his shoulder—so—at Dan'l, and says again, very
deliberate, 'Well,' he says, 'I don't see no p'ints about that frog that's any better'n any
other frog.'

"Smiley he stood scratching his head and looking down at Dan'l a long time, and   20
at last he says, "I do wonder what in the nation that frog throw'd off for—I wonder if
there ain't something the matter with him—he 'pears to look mighty baggy, somehow.' And he ketched Dan'l by the nape of the neck, and hefted him, and says, 'Why
blame my cats if he don't weigh five pound!' and turned him upside down and he
belched out a double handful of shot. And then he see how it was, and he was the
maddest man—he set the frog down and took out after that feller, but he never ketched
him. And—"

[Here Simon Wheeler heard his name called from the front yard, and got up to see
what was wanted.] And turning to me as he moved away, he said: "Just set where you
are, stranger, and rest easy—I ain't going to be gone a second."

But, by your leave, I did not think that a continuation of the history of the enterprising vagabond *Jim* Smiley would be likely to afford me much information concerning the Rev. *Leonidas* W. Smiley, and so I started away.

At the door I met the sociable Wheeler returning, and he buttonholed me and
recommenced:

"Well, thish-yer Smiley had a yaller one-eyed cow that didn't have no tail, only just a short stump like a bannanner, and—"

25   However, lacking both time and inclination, I did not wait to hear about the afflicted cow, but took my leave.   [1865]

QUESTIONS

1. How is the effectiveness of the story dependent on the handling of the point of view?
2. How does Simon Wheeler differ in character and background from the first narrator?
3. How do the anecdotes of the horse race and the pup prepare the way for the episode of the frog?
4. What characteristics of Jim Smiley cause him to be victimized by the stranger?
5. How is the comedy of the story a function of its language?
6. Does the reader's appreciation of the story depend in part on his knowledge of familiar American character types?

RESPONSES

1. Write an essay explaining how this story adheres to and/or breaks the typical narrative plot pattern.
2. Evaluate the quality of the story for a contemporary reader. By what criteria is the story still successful and entertaining and by what criteria is it not?

COLETTE

Colette (1873–1954) was born Sidonie-Gabrielle Colette in a French provincial village. Her first husband, fourteen years her senior, was a writer who published her first efforts at fiction under his pen name. The marriage ended in divorce and a second proved equally disastrous. She at last found happiness in a third marriage to a devoted man who was tireless in promoting her career. She published more than fifty novels in addition to dozens of short stories and several volumes of memoirs. Renowned as a stylist and as a student of the battle of the sexes, Colette in later life was made a member of the French Académie Goncourt and an officer of the Légion d'Honneur, honors to which women rarely accede in France.

The Other Wife

"Table for two? This way, Monsieur, Madame, there is still a table next to the window, if Madame and Monsieur would like a view of the bay."

Alice followed the maître d'.

"Oh, yes. Come on, Marc, it'll be like having lunch on a boat on the water . . ."

Her husband caught her by passing his arm under hers. "We'll be more comfortable over there."

"There? In the middle of all those people? I'd much rather . . ."   5

"Alice, please."

He tightened his grip in such a meaningful way that she turned around. "What's the matter?"

"Shh . . ." he said softly, looking at her intently, and led her toward the table in the middle.

"What is it, Marc?"

"I'll tell you, darling. Let me order lunch first. Would you like the shrimp? Or the   10 eggs in aspic?"

"Whatever you like, you know that."

They smiled at one another, wasting the precious time of an overworked maître d', stricken with a kind of nervous dance, who was standing next to them, perspiring.

"The shrimp," said Marc. "Then the eggs and bacon. And the cold chicken with a romaine salad. *Fromage blanc?*° The house specialty? We'll go with the specialty. Two strong coffees. My chauffeur will be having lunch also, we'll be leaving again at two o'clock. Some cider? No, I don't trust it . . . Dry champagne."

He sighed as if he had just moved an armoire, gazed at the colorless midday sea, at the pearly white sky, then at his wife, whom he found lovely in her little Mercury hat with its large, hanging veil.

15 "You're looking well, darling. And all this blue water makes your eyes look green, imagine that! And you've put on weight since you've been traveling . . . It's nice up to a point, but only up to a point!"

Her firm, round breasts rose proudly as she leaned over the table.

"Why did you keep me from taking that place next to the window?"

Marc Seguy never considered lying. "Because you were about to sit next to someone I know."

"Someone I don't know?"

20 "My ex-wife."

She couldn't think of anything to say and opened her blue eyes wider.

"So what, darling? It'll happen again. It's not important."

The words came back to Alice and she asked, in order, the inevitable questions. "Did she see you? Could she see that you saw her? Will you point her out to me?"

"Don't look now, please, she must be watching us . . . The lady with brown hair, no hat, she must be staying in this hotel. By herself, behind those children in red . . ."

25 "Yes. I see."

Hidden behind some broad-brimmed beach hats, Alice was able to look at the woman who, fifteen months ago, had still been her husband's wife.

"Incompatibility," Marc said. "Oh, I mean . . . total incompatibility! We divorced like well-bred people, almost like friends, quietly, quickly. And then I fell in love with you, and you really wanted to be happy with me. How lucky we are that our happiness doesn't involve any guilty parties or victims!"

The woman in white, whose smooth, lustrous hair reflected the light from the sea in azure patches, was smoking a cigarette with her eyes half closed. Alice turned back toward her husband, took some shrimp and butter, and ate calmly. After a moment's silence she asked: "Why didn't you ever tell me that she had blue eyes, too?"

"Well, I never thought about it!"

30 He kissed the hand she was extending toward the bread basket and she blushed with pleasure. Dusky and ample, she might have seemed somewhat coarse, but the changeable blue of her eyes and her wavy, golden hair made her look like a frail and sentimental blonde. She vowed overwhelming gratitude to her husband. Immodest without knowing it, everything about her bore the overly conspicuous marks of extreme happiness.

They ate and drank heartily, and each thought the other had forgotten the woman in white. Now and then, however, Alice laughed too loudly, and Marc was careful about his posture, holding his shoulders back, his head up. They waited quite a long time for their coffee, in silence. An incandescent river, the straggled reflection of the invisible sun overhead, shifted slowly across the sea and shone with a blinding brilliance.

"She's still there, you know," Alice whispered.

°*Fromage blanc*: Cottage cheese, or, if intended for dessert, cream cheese.

"Is she making you uncomfortable? Would you like to have coffee somewhere else?"

"No, not at all! She's the one who must be uncomfortable! Besides, she doesn't exactly seem to be having a wild time, if you could see her . . ."

"I don't have to. I know that look of hers."   35

"Oh, was she like that?"

He exhaled his cigarette smoke through his nostrils and knitted his eyebrows. "Like that? No. To tell you honestly, she wasn't happy with me."

"Oh, really now!"

"The way you indulge me is so charming, darling . . . It's crazy . . . You're an angel . . . You love me . . . I'm so proud when I see those eyes of yours. Yes, those eyes . . . She . . . I just didn't know how to make her happy, that's all. I didn't know how."

"She's just difficult!"   40

Alice fanned herself irritably, and cast brief glances at the woman in white, who was smoking, her head resting against the back of the cane chair, her eyes closed with an air of satisfied lassitude.

Marc shrugged his shoulders modestly.

"That's the right word," he admitted. "What can you do? You have to feel sorry for people who are never satisfied. But we're satisfied . . . Aren't we, darling?"

She did not answer. She was looking furtively, and closely, at her husband's face, ruddy and regular; at his thick hair, threaded here and there with white silk; at his short, well-cared-for hands; and doubtful for the first time, she asked herself, "What more did she want from him?"

And as they were leaving, while Marc was paying the bill and asking for the chauffeur and about the route, she kept looking, with envy and curiosity, at the woman in white, this dissatisfied, this difficult, this superior . . .   45

[1926]

QUESTIONS

1. How does Marc Seguy's choice of a table foreshadow the outcome of the story?
2. What does the lunch order tell the reader about this couple?
3. Do you think the reader can trust the omniscient narrator's assurance that Marc Seguy "never considered lying"?
4. If you were a marriage counselor, what advice would you give to this couple?
5. How may the story be said to hinge on the last word?

RESPONSES

1. Write an essay explaining the importance of setting in this story. For instance, to what extent is a restaurant both intimate and public? To what extent is a marriage so?
2. Research Colette's life. How is this story reflective of Colette's life and writings?
3. Write an essay exploring the last line of the story. Can you make an argument that the author and/or narrator is the true superior?

JOSEPH CONRAD

Joseph Conrad (Josef Korzeniowski) (1857–1924) was born in Berdyczew, Poland. Orphaned at eleven, Conrad went to sea at seventeen and for two decades lived the roving life of a sailor. In 1895, by now a captain in the British merchant fleet, he published a novel, *Almayer's Folly*. The publication of his second novel the following year, *An Outcast of the Islands*, and his marriage determined him to make his living by his pen. The subtle psychology, the tendency toward symbolism, and the rich prose style of his later works, notably *Lord Jim* (1900) and *Nostromo* (1904), mark Conrad as one of the first great modernist writers.

The Heart of Darkness

I

The *Nellie*, a cruising yawl, swung to her anchor without a flutter of the sails, and was at rest. The flood had made, the wind was nearly calm, and being bound down the river, the only thing for it was to come to and wait for the turn of the tide.

The sea-reach of the Thames stretched before us like the beginning of an interminable waterway. In the offing the sea and the sky were welded together without a joint, and in the luminous space the tanned sails of the barges drifting up with the tide seemed to stand still in red clusters of canvas sharply peaked, with gleams of varnished sprits. A haze rested on the low shores that ran out to sea in vanishing flatness. The air was dark above Gravesend, and farther back still seemed condensed into a mournful gloom, brooding motionless over the biggest, and the greatest, town on earth.

The Director of Companies was our captain and our host. We four affectionately watched his back as he stood in the bows looking to seaward. On the whole river there was nothing that looked half so nautical. He resembled a pilot, which to a seaman is trustworthiness personified. It was difficult to realize his work was not out there in the luminous estuary, but behind him, within the brooding gloom.

Between us there was, as I have already said somewhere, the bond of the sea. Besides holding our hearts together through long periods of separation, it had the effect of making us tolerant of each other's yarns—and even convictions. The Lawyer—the best of old fellows—had, because of his many years and many virtues, the only cushion on deck, and was lying on the only rug. The accountant had brought out already a box of dominoes, and was toying architecturally with the bones. Marlow sat cross-legged right aft, leaning against the mizzen-mast. He had sunken cheeks, a yellow complexion, a straight back, and ascetic aspect, and, with his arms dropped, the palms of hands outwards, resembled an idol. The director, satisfied the anchor had good hold, made his way aft and sat down amongst us. We exchanged a few words lazily. Afterwards there was silence on board the yacht. For some reason or other we did not begin that game of dominoes. We felt meditative, and fit for nothing but placid staring. The day was ending in a serenity of still and exquisite brilliance. The water shone pacifically; the sky, without a speck, was a benign immensity of unstained light; the very mist on the Essex marshes was like a gauzy and radiant fabric, hung from the wooded rises inland, and draping the low shores in diaphanous folds. Only the gloom to the west, brooding over the upper reaches, became more somber every minute, as if angered by the approach of the sun.

And at last, in its curved and imperceptible fall, the sun sank low, and from glowing white changed to a dull red without rays and without heat, as if about to go out suddenly, stricken to death by the touch of that gloom brooding over a crowd of men. 5

Forthwith a change came over the water, and the serenity became less brilliant but more profound. The old river in its broad reach rested unruffled at the decline of day, after ages of good service done to the race that peopled its banks, spread out in the tranquil dignity of a waterway leading to the uttermost ends of the earth. We looked at the venerable stream not in the vivid flush of a short day that comes and departs forever, but in the august light of abiding memories. And indeed nothing is easier for a man who has, as the phrase goes, "followed the sea" with reverence and affection, than to evoke the great spirit of the past upon the lower reaches of the Thames. The tidal current runs to and fro in its unceasing service, crowded with memories of men and ships it had borne to the rest of home or to the battles of the sea. It had known and served all the men of whom the nation is proud, from Sir Francis Drake° to Sir John Franklin,° knights all, titled and untitled—the knights-errant of the sea. It had borne all the ships whose names are like jewels flashing in the night of time, from the *Golden Hind* returning with her round flanks full of treasure, to be visited by the Queen's Highness and thus pass out of the gigantic tale, to the *Erebus* and *Terror*, bound on other conquests—and that never returned. It had known the ships and the men. They had sailed from Deptford, from Greenwich, from Erith—the adventurers and the settlers; kings' ships and the ships of men on 'Change, captains, admirals, the dark "interlopers" of the Eastern trade, and the commissioned "Generals" of East India fleets. Hunters for gold or pursuers of fame, they all had gone out on that stream, bearing the sword, and often the torch, messengers of the night within the land, bearers of a spark from the sacred fire. What greatness had not floated on the ebb of that river into the mystery of an unknown earth! . . . The dreams of men, the seed of commonwealths, the germs of empires.

The sun set; the dusk fell on the stream, and lights began to appear along the shore. The Chapman lighthouse, a three-legged thing erect on a mud-flat, shone strongly. Lights of ships moved in the fairway—a great stir of lights going up and

---

°*Sir Francis Drake*: English navigator and pirate. His ship was the *Golden Hind*.
°*Sir John Franklin*: English explorer of the Arctic. His ships were the *Erebus* and the *Terror*.

going down. And farther west on the upper reaches the place of the monstrous town was still marked ominously on the sky, a brooding gloom in sunshine, a lurid glare under the stars.

"And this also," said Marlow suddenly, "has been one of the dark places on the earth."

He was the only man of us who still "followed the sea." The worst that could be said of him was that he did not represent his class. He was a seaman, but he was a wanderer, too, while most seamen lead, if one may so express it, a sedentary life. Their minds are of the stay-at-home order, and their home is always with them—the ship; and so is their country—the sea. One ship is very much like another, and the sea is always the same. In the immutability of their surroundings the foreign shores, the foreign faces, the changing immensity of life, glide past, veiled not by a sense of mystery but by a slightly disdainful ignorance; for there is nothing mysterious to a seaman unless it be the sea itself, which is the mistress of his existence and as inscrutable as Destiny. For the rest, after his hours of work, a casual stroll or a casual spree on shore suffices to unfold for him the secret of a whole continent, and generally he finds the secret not worth knowing. The yarns of seamen have a direct simplicity, the whole meaning of which lies within the shell of a cracked nut. But Marlow was not typical (if his propensity to spin yarns be excepted), and to him the meaning of an episode was not inside like a kernel but outside, enveloping the tale which brought it out only as a glow brings out a haze, in the likeness of one of these misty halos that sometimes are made visible by the special illumination of moonshine.

10   His remark did not seem at all surprising. It was just like Marlow. It was accepted in silence. No one took the trouble to grunt even; and presently he said, very slow—

"I was thinking of very old times, when the Romans first came here, nineteen hundred years ago—the other day. . . . Light came out of this river since—you say Knights? Yes; but it is like a running blaze on a plain, like a flash of lightning in the clouds. We live in the flicker—may it last as long as the old earth keeps rolling! But darkness was here yesterday. Imagine the feelings of a commander of a fine—what d'ye call 'em?— trireme in the Mediterranean, ordered suddenly to the north; run overland across the Gauls in a hurry; put in charge of one of these craft the legionaries—a wonderful lot of handy men they must have been, too—used to build, apparently by the hundred, in a month or two, if we may believe what we read. Imagine him here—the very end of the world, a sea the color of lead, a sky the color of smoke, a kind of ship about as rigid as a concertina—and going up this river with stores, or orders, or what you like. Sandbanks, marshes, forests, savages—precious little to eat fit for a civilized man, nothing but Thames water to drink. No Falernian wine° here, no going ashore. Here and there a military camp lost in a wilderness, like a needle in a bundle of hay—cold, fog, tempests, disease, exile, and death—death skulking in the air, in the water, in the bush. They must have been dying like flies here. Oh, yes—he did it. Did it very well, too, no doubt, and without thinking much about it either, except afterwards to brag of what he had gone through in his time, perhaps. They were men enough to face the darkness. And perhaps he was cheered by keeping his eye on a chance of promotion to the fleet at Ravenna by and by, if he had good friends in Rome and survived the awful climate. Or think of a decent young citizen in a toga— perhaps too much dice, you know—coming out here in the train of some prefect, or taxgatherer, or trader even, to mend his fortunes. Land in a swamp, march through

---

°*Falerian*: Roman wine.

the woods, and in some inland post feel the savagery, the utter savagery, had closed round him—all that mysterious life of the wilderness that stirs in the forest, in the jungles, in the hearts of wild men. There's no initiation either into such mysteries. He has to live in the midst of the incomprehensible, which is also detestable. And it has a fascination, too, that goes to work upon him. The fascination of the abomination— you know, imagine the growing regrets, the longing to escape, the powerless disgust, the surrender, the hate."

He paused.

"Mind," he began again, lifting one arm from the elbow, the palm of the hand outwards, so that, with his legs folded before him, he had the pose of a Buddha preaching in European clothes and without a lotus-flower—"Mind, none of us would feel exactly like this. What saves us is efficiency—the devotion to efficiency. But these chaps were not much account, really. They were no colonists; their administration was merely a squeeze, and nothing more, I suspect. They were conquerors, and for that you want only brute force—nothing to boast of, when you have it, since your strength is just an accident arising from the weakness of others. They grabbed what they could get for the sake of what was to be got. It was just robbery with violence, aggravated murder on a great scale, and men going at it blind—as is very proper for those who tackle a darkness. The conquest of the earth, which mostly means the taking it away from those who have a different complexion or slightly flatter noses than ourselves, is not a pretty thing when you look into it too much. What redeems it is the idea only. An idea at the back of it; not a sentimental pretense but an idea; and an unselfish belief in the idea—something you can set up, and bow down before, and offer a sacrifice to. . . ."

He broke off. Flames glided in the river, small green flames, red flames, white flames, pursuing, overtaking, joining, crossing each other—then separating slowly or hastily. The traffic of the great city went on in the deepening night upon the sleepless river. We looked on, waiting patiently—there was nothing else to do till the end of the flood; but it was more after a long silence, when he said, in a hesitating voice, "I suppose you fellows remember I did once turn fresh-water sailor for a bit," that we knew we were fated, before the ebb began to run, to hear one of Marlow's inconclusive experiences.

"I don't want to bother you much with what happened to me personally," he   15 began, showing in this remark the weakness of many tellers of tales who seem so often unaware of what their audience would best like to hear; "yet to understand the effect of it on me you ought to know how I got out there, what I saw, how I went up that river to the place where I first met the poor chap. It was the farthest point of navigation and the culminating point of my experience. It seemed somehow to throw a kind of light on everything about me—and into my thoughts. It was somber enough, too—and pitiful—not extraordinary in any way—not very clear either. No, not very clear. And yet it seemed to throw a kind of light.

"I had then, as you remember, just returned to London after a lot of Indian Ocean, Pacific, China Seas—a regular dose of the East—six years or so, and I was loafing about, hindering you fellows in your work and invading your homes, just as though I had got a heavenly mission to civilize you. It was very fine for a time, but after a bit I did get tired of resting. Then I began to look for a ship—I should think the hardest work on earth. But the ships wouldn't even look at me. And I got tired of that game, too.

"Now when I was a little chap I had a passion for maps. I would look for hours at South America, or Africa, or Australia, and lose myself in all the glories of exploration.

At that time there were many blank spaces on the earth, and when I saw one that looked particularly inviting on a map (but they all look that) I would put my finger on it and say, When I grow up I will go there. The North Pole was one of these places, I remember. Well, I haven't been there yet, and shall not try now. The glamour's off. Other places were scattered about the Equator, and in every sort of latitude all over the two hemispheres. I have been in some of them, and . . . well, we won't talk about that. But there was one yet—the biggest, the most blank, so to speak—that I had a hankering after.

"True, by this time it was not a blank space any more. It had got filled since my childhood with rivers and lakes and names. It had ceased to be a blank space of delightful mystery—a white patch for a boy to dream gloriously over. It had become a place of darkness. But there was in it one river especially, a mighty big river, that you could see on the map, resembling an immense snake uncoiled, with its head in the sea, its body at rest curving afar over a vast country, and its tail lost in the depths of the land. And as I looked at the map of it in a shop-window, it fascinated me as a snake would a bird—a silly little bird. Then I remembered there was a big concern, a Company for trade on that river. Dash it all! I thought to myself, they can't trade without using some kind of craft on that lot of fresh water—steamboats! Why shouldn't I try to get charge of one? I went on along Fleet Street, but could not shake off the idea. The snake had charmed me.

"You understand it was a Continental concern, that Trading society; but I have a lot of relations living on the Continent, because it's cheap and not so nasty as it looks, they say.

20 "I am sorry to own I began to worry them. This was already a fresh departure for me. I was not used to getting things that way, you know. I always went my own road and on my own legs where I had a mind to go. I wouldn't have believed it of myself; but, then—you see—I felt somehow I must get there by hook or by crook. So I worried them. The men said 'My dear fellow,' and did nothing. Then—would you believe it?—I tried the women. I, Charlie Marlow, set the women to work—to get a job. Heavens! Well, you see, the notion drove me. I had an aunt, a dear enthusiastic soul. She wrote: 'It will be delightful. I am ready to do anything, anything for you. It is a glorious idea. I know the wife of a very high personage in the Administration, and also a man who has lots of influence with,' etc., etc. She was determined to make no end of fuss to get me appointed skipper of a river steamboat, if such was my fancy.

"I got my appointment—of course; and I got it very quick. It appears the Company had received news that one of their captains had been killed in a scuffle with the natives. This was my chance, and it made me the more anxious to go. It was only months and months afterwards, when I made the attempt to recover what was left of the body, that I heard the original quarrel arose from a misunderstanding about some hens. Yes, two black hens. Fresleven—that was the fellow's name, a Dane—thought himself wronged somehow in the bargain, so he went ashore and started to hammer the chief of the village with a stick. Oh, it didn't surprise me in the least to hear this, and at the same time to be told that Fresleven was the gentlest, quietest creature that ever walked on two legs. No doubt he was; but he had been a couple of years already out there engaged in the noble cause, you know, and he probably felt the need at last of asserting his self-respect in some way. Therefore he whacked the old nigger mercilessly, while a big crowd of his people watched him, thunderstruck, till some man— I was told the chief's son—in desperation at hearing the old chap yell, made a tentative jab with a spear at the white man—and of course it went quite easy between the shoulder blades. Then the whole population cleared into the forest, expecting all kinds of calamities to happen, while, on the other hand, the steamer Fresleven commanded left also in a bad panic, in charge of the engineer, I believe. Afterwards nobody seemed to trouble much about Fresleven's remains, till I got out and stepped into his shoes. I couldn't let it rest, though; but when an opportunity offered at last to meet my predecessor, the grass growing through his ribs was tall enough to hide his bones. They were all there. The supernatural being had not been touched after he fell. And the village was deserted, the huts gaped black, rotting, all askew within the fallen enclosures. A calamity had come to it, sure enough. The people had vanished. Mad terror had scattered them, men, women, and children, through the bush, and they had never returned. What became of the hens I don't know either. I should think the cause of progress got them, anyhow. However, through this glorious affair I got my appointment, before I had fairly begun to hope for it.

"I flew around like mad to get ready, and before forty-eight hours I was crossing the Channel to show myself to my employers, and sign the contract. In a very few hours I arrived in a city that always makes me think of a whited sepulcher. Prejudice no doubt. I had no difficulty in finding the Company's offices. It was the biggest thing in the town, and everybody I met was full of it. They were going to run an over-sea empire, and make no end of coin by trade.

"A narrow and deserted street in deep shadow, high houses, innumerable windows with venetian blinds, a dead silence, grass sprouting between the stones, imposing carriage archways right and left, immense double doors standing ponderously ajar. I slipped through one of these cracks, went up a swept and ungarnished staircase, as arid as a desert, and opened the first door I came to. Two women, one fat and the other slim, sat on straw-bottomed chairs, knitting black wool. The slim one got up and walked straight at me—still knitting with downcast eyes—and only just as I began to think of getting out of her way, as you would for a somnambulist, stood still, and looked up. Her dress was as plain as an umbrella-cover, and she turned round without a word and preceded me into a waiting-room. I gave my name, and looked about. Deal table in the middle, plain chairs all around the walls, on one end a large shining map, marked with all the colors of a rainbow. There was a vast amount of red—good to see at any time, because one knows that some real work is done in there, a deuce of a lot of blue, a little green, smears of orange, and, on the East Coast, a purple patch, to show where the jolly pioneers of progress drink the jolly lagerbeer. However, I wasn't going into any of these. I was going into the yellow. Dead in the center. And the river was there— fascinating—deadly—like a snake. Ough! A door opened, a white-haired secretarial head, but wearing a compassionate expression, appeared, and a skinny forefinger beckoned me into the sanctuary. Its light was dim, and a heavy writing-desk squatted in the middle. From behind that structure came out an impression of pale plumpness in a frock-coat. The great man himself. He was five feet six, I should judge, and had his grip on the handle-end of ever so many millions. He shook hands, I fancy, murmured vaguely, was satisfied with my French. *Bon voyage.*

"In about forty-five seconds I found myself again in the waiting-room with the compassionate secretary, who, full of desolation and sympathy, made me sign some document. I believe I undertook amongst other things not to disclose any trade secrets. Well, I am not going to.

"I began to feel slightly uneasy. You know I am not used to such ceremonies, and there was something ominous in the atmosphere. It was just as though I had been let into some conspiracy—I don't know—something not quite right; and I was glad to

25

get out. In the outer room the two women knitted black wool feverishly. People were arriving, and the younger one was walking back and forth introducing them. The old one sat on her chair. Her flat cloth slippers were propped up on a footwarmer, and a cat reposed on her lap. She wore a starched white affair on her head, had a wart on one cheek, and silver-rimmed spectacles hung on the tip of her nose. She glanced at me above the glasses. The swift and indifferent placidity of that look troubled me. Two youths with foolish and cheery countenances were being piloted over, and she threw at them the same quick glance of unconcerned wisdom. She seemed to know all about them and about me, too. An eerie feeling came over me. She seemed uncanny and fateful. Often far away there I thought of these two, guarding the door of Darkness, knitting black wool as for a warm pall, one introducing, introducing continuously to the unknown, the other scrutinizing the cheery and foolish faces with unconcerned old eyes. *Ave!* Old knitter of black wool. *Morituri te salutant.* Not many of those she looked at ever saw her again—not half, by a long way.

"There was yet a visit to the doctor. 'A simple formality,' assured me the secretary, with an air of taking an immense part in all my sorrows. Accordingly a young chap wearing his hat over the left eyebrow, some clerk I suppose—there must have been clerks in the business, though the house was as still as a house in a city of the dead— came from somewhere upstairs, and led me forth. He was shabby and careless, with inkstains on the sleeves of his jacket, and his cravat was large and billowy, under a chin shaped like the toe of an old boot. It was a little too early for the doctor, so I pro- posed a drink, and thereupon he developed a vein of joviality. As we sat over our ver- mouths he glorified the Company's business, and by and by I expressed casually my surprise at him not going out there. He became very cool and collected all at once. 'I am not such a fool as I look, quoth Plato to his disciples,' he said sententiously, emp- tied his glass with great resolution, and we rose.

"The old doctor felt my pulse, evidently thinking of something else the while. 'Good, good for there,' he mumbled, and then with a certain eagerness asked me whether I would let him measure my head. Rather surprised, I said Yes, when he produced a thing like calipers and got the dimensions back and front and every way, taking notes carefully. He was an unshaven little man in a threadbare coat like a gaberdine, with his feet in slippers, and I thought him a harmless fool. 'I al- ways ask leave, in the interests of science, to measure the crania of those going out there,' he said. 'And when they come back, too?' I asked, 'Oh, I never see them,' he remarked; 'and, moreover, the changes take place inside, you know.' He smiled, as if at some quiet joke. 'So you are going out there. Famous. Interesting, too.' He gave me a searching glance, and made another note. 'Ever any madness in your family?' he asked, in a matter-of-fact tone. I felt very annoyed. 'Is that question in the interests of science, too?' 'It would be,' he said, without taking notice of my ir- ritation, 'interesting for science to watch the mental changes of individuals, on the spot, but. . . .' 'Are you an alienist?' I interrupted. 'Every doctor should be—a lit- tle,' answered that original, imperturbably. 'I have a little theory which you Messieurs who go out there must help me to prove. This is my share in the ad- vantages my country shall reap from the possession of such a magnificent depen- dency. The mere wealth I leave to others. Pardon my questions, but you are the first Englishman coming under my observation. . . .' I hastened to assure him I was not in the least typical. 'If I were,' said I 'I wouldn't be talking like this with you.' 'What you say is rather profound, and probably erroneous,' he said, with a laugh. 'Avoid irritation more than exposure to the sun. Adieu. How do you English say, eh? Good-by. Ah! Good-by. Adieu. In the tropics one must before everything keep calm.'. . . He lifted a warning forefinger. . . . '*Du calme, du calme. Adieu.*'°

"One thing more remained to do—say good-by to my excellent aunt. I found her triumphant. I had a cup of tea—the last decent cup of tea for many days—and in a room that most soothingly looked just as you would expect a lady's drawing-room to look, we had a long quiet chat by the fireside. In the course of these confidences it became quite plain to me I had been represented to the wife of the high dignitary, and goodness knows to how many more people besides, as an exceptional and gift-ed creature—a piece of good fortune for the Company—a man you don't get hold of every day. Good heavens! and I was going to take charge of a two-penny-half-penny river-steamboat with a penny whistle attached! It appeared, however, I was also one of the Workers, with a capital—you know. Something like an emissary of light, some-thing like a lower sort of apostle. There had been a lot of such rot let loose in print and talk just about that time, and the excellent woman, living right in the rush of all that humbug, got carried off her feet. She talked about 'weaning those ignorant millions from their horrid ways,' till, upon my word, she made me quite uncomfortable. I ven-tured to hint that the Company was run for profit.

"'You forget, dear Charlie, that the laborer is worthy of his hire,' she said, brightly. It's queer how out of touch with truth women are. They live in a world of their own, and there has never been anything like it, and never can be. It is too beautiful alto-gether, and if they were to set it up it would go to pieces before the first sunset. Some confounded fact we men have been living contentedly with ever since the day of cre-ation would start up and knock the whole thing over.

"After this I got embraced, told to wear flannel, be sure to write often, and so on—   30 and I left. In the street—I don't know why—a queer feeling came to me that I was an impostor. Odd thing that I, who used to clear out for any part of the world at twenty-four hours' notice, with less thought than most men give to the crossing of a street, had a moment—I won't say of hesitation, but of startled pause, before this commonplace affair. The best way I can explain it to you is by saying that, for a second or two, I felt as though, instead of going to the center of a continent, I were about to set off for the center of the earth.

"I left in a French steamer, and she called in every blamed port they have out there, for, as far as I could see, the sole purpose of landing soldiers and custom-house offi-cers. I watched the coast. Watching a coast as it slips by the ship is like thinking about an enigma. There it is before you—smiling, frowning, inviting, grand, mean, insipid, or savage, and always mute with an air of whispering, Come and find out. This one was almost featureless, as if still in the making, with an aspect of monotonous grim-ness. The edge of a colossal jungle, so dark-green as to be almost black, fringed with white surf, ran straight, like a ruled line, far, far away along a blue sea whose glitter was blurred by a creeping mist. The sun was fierce, the land seemed to glisten and drip with steam. Here and there grayish-whitish specks showed up clustered inside the white surf, with a flag flying above them perhaps. Settlements some centuries old, and still no bigger than pinheads on the untouched expanse of their background. We pounded along, stopped, landed soldiers; went on, landed custom-house clerks to levy toll in what looked like a God-forsaken wilderness, with a tin shed and a flag-pole lost in it; landed more soldiers—to take care of the custom-house clerks, presumably. Some, I heard, got drowned in the surf; but whether they did or not, nobody seemed

---

°"*Du calme, du calme Adieu*": "Those who are about to die salute you" (Latin).

particularly to care. They were just flung out there, and on we went. Every day the coast looked the same, as though we had not moved; but we passed various places—trading places—with names like Gran' Bassam, Little Popo; names that seemed to belong to some sordid farce acted in front of a sinister backcloth. The idleness of a passenger, my isolation amongst all these men with whom I had no point of contact, the oily and languid sea, the uniform somberness of the coast, seemed to keep me away from the truth of things, within the toil of a mournful and senseless delusion. The voice of the surf heard now and then was a positive pleasure, like the speech of a brother. It was something natural, that had its reason, that had a meaning. Now and then a boat from the shore gave one a momentary contact with reality. It was paddled by black fellows. You could see from afar the white of their eyeballs glistening. They shouted, sang; their bodies streamed with perspiration; they had faces like grotesque masks—these chaps; but they had bone, muscle, a wild vitality, an intense energy of movement, that was as natural and true as the surf along their coast. They wanted no excuse for being there. They were a great comfort to look at. For a time I would feel I belonged still to a world of straightforward facts, but the feeling would not last long. Something would turn up to scare it away. Once, I remember, we came upon a man-of-war anchored off the coast. There wasn't even a shed there, and she was shelling the bush. It appears the French had one of their wars going on thereabouts. Her ensign dropped limp like a rag; the muzzles of the long six-inch guns stuck out all over the low hull; the greasy, slimy swell swung her up lazily and let her down, swaying her thin masts. In the empty immensity of earth, sky, and water, there she was, incomprehensible, firing into a continent. Pop, would go one of the six-inch guns; a small flame would dart and vanish, a little white smoke would disappear, a tiny projectile would give a feeble screech—and nothing happened. Nothing could happen. There was a touch of insanity in the proceeding, a sense of lugubrious drollery in the sight; and it was not dissipated by somebody on board assuring me earnestly there was a camp of natives—he called them enemies!—hidden out of sight somewhere.

"We gave her her letters (I heard the men in that lonely ship were dying of fever at the rate of three a day) and went on. We called at some more places with farcical names, where the merry dance of death and trade goes on in a still and earthy atmosphere as of an overheated catacomb; all along the formless coast bordered by dangerous surf, as if Nature herself had tried to ward off intruders; in and out of rivers, streams of death in life, whose banks were rotting into mud, whose waters, thickened into slime, invaded the contorted mangroves, that seemed to writhe at us in the extremity of an impotent despair. Nowhere did we stop long enough to get a particularized impression, but the general sense of vague and oppressive wonder grew upon me. It was like a weary pilgrimage amongst hints for nightmares.

"It was upward of thirty days before I saw the mouth of the big river. We anchored off the seat of the government. But my work would not begin till some two hundred miles farther on. So as soon as I could I made a start for a place thirty miles higher up.

"I had my passage on a little sea-going steamer. Her captain was a Swede, and knowing me for a seaman, invited me on the bridge. He was a young man, lean, fair, and morose, with lanky hair and a shuffling gait. As we left the miserable little wharf, he tossed his head contemptuously at the shore. 'Been living there?' he asked. I said, 'Yes.' 'Fine lot these government chaps—are they not?' he went on, speaking English with great precision and considerable bitterness. 'It is funny what some people will do for a few francs a month. I wonder what becomes of that kind when it goes upcountry?' I said to him I expected to see that soon. 'So-o-o!' he exclaimed. He shuffled athwart, keeping one eye ahead vigilantly. 'Don't be too sure,' he continued. 'The other day I took up a man who hanged himself on the road. He was a Swede, too.' 'Hanged himself! Why, in God's name?' I cried. I kept on looking out watchfully. 'Who knows? The sun was too much for him, or the country perhaps.'

"At last we opened a reach. A rocky cliff appeared, mounds of turned-up earth by the shore, houses on a hill, others with iron roofs, amongst a waste of excavations, or hanging to the declivity. A continuous noise of the rapids above hovered over this scene of inhabited devastation. A lot of people, mostly black and naked, moved about like ants. A jetty projected into the river. A blinding sunlight drowned all this at times in a sudden recrudescence of glare. 'There's your Company's station,' said the Swede, pointing to three wooden barrack-like structures on the rocky slope. 'I will send your things up. Four boxes did you say? So. Farewell.' 35

"I came upon a boiler wallowing in the grass, then found a path leading up the hill. It turned aside for the boulders, and also for an undersized railway-truck lying there on its back with its wheels in the air. One was off. The thing looked as dead as the carcass of some animal. I came upon more pieces of decaying machinery, a stack of rusty rails. To the left a clump of trees made a shady spot, where dark things seemed to stir feebly. I blinked, the path was steep. A horn tooted to the right, and I saw the black people run. A heavy and dull detonation shook the ground, a puff of smoke came out of the cliff, and that was all. No change appeared on the face of the rock. They were building a railway. The cliff was not in the way of anything; but the objectless blasting was all the work going on.

"A slight clinking behind me made me turn my head. Six black men advanced in a file, toiling up the path. They walked erect and slow, balancing small baskets full of earth on their heads, and the clink kept time with their footsteps. Black rags were wound round their loins, and the short ends behind waggled to and fro like tails. I could see every rib, the joints of their limbs were like knots in a rope; each had an iron collar on his neck, and all were connected together with a chain whose bights swung between them, rhythmically clinking. Another report from the cliff made me think suddenly of that ship of war I had seen firing into a continent. It was the same kind of ominous voice; but these men could by no stretch of imagination be called enemies. They were called criminals, and the outraged law, like the bursting shells, had come to them, an insoluble mystery from the sea. All their meager breasts panted together, the violently dilated nostrils quivered, the eyes stared stonily uphill. They passed me within six inches, without a glance, with that complete, deathlike indifference of unhappy savages. Behind this raw matter one of the reclaimed, the product of the new forces at work, strolled despondently, carrying a rifle by its middle. He had a uniform jacket with one button off, and seeing a white man on the path, hoisted his weapon to his shoulder with alacrity. This was simple prudence, white men being so much alike at a distance that he could not tell who I might be. He was speedily reassured, and with a large, white, rascally grin, and a glance at his charge, seemed to take me into partnership in his exalted trust. After that, I also was a part of the great cause of these high and just proceedings.

"Instead of going up, I turned and descended to the left. My idea was to let that chain-gang get out of sight before I climbed the hill. You know I am not particularly tender, I've had to strike and to fend off. I've had to resist and to attack sometimes—that's only one way of resisting—without counting the exact cost, according to the demands of such sort of life as I had blundered into. I've seen the devil of violence, and the devil of greed, and the devil of hot desire; but, by all the stars! these were strong, lusty, red-eyed devils, that swayed and drove men—men, I tell you. But as I stood on this hillside, I foresaw that in the blinding sunshine of that land I would become acquainted with a flabby, pretending, weak-eyed devil of a rapacious and pitiless folly. How insidious he could be, too, I was only to find out several months later and a thousand miles farther. For a moment I stood appalled, as though by a warning. Finally I descended the hill, obliquely, towards the trees I had seen.

"I avoided a vast artificial hole somebody had been digging on the slope, the purpose of which I found it impossible to divine. It wasn't a quarry or a sandpit, anyhow. It was just a hole. It might have been connected with the philanthropic desire of giving the criminals something to do. I don't know. Then I nearly fell into a very narrow ravine, almost no more than a scar in the hillside. I discovered that a lot of imported drainage-pipes for the settlement had been tumbled in there. There wasn't one that was not broken. It was a wanton smash-up. At last I got under the trees. My purpose was to stroll into the shade for a moment; but no sooner within than it seemed to me I had stepped into the gloomy circle of some Inferno. The rapids were near, and an uninterrupted, uniform, headlong, rushing noise filled the mournful stillness of the grove, where not a breath stirred, not a leaf moved, with a mysterious sound—as though the tearing pace of the launched earth had suddenly become audible.

40   "Black shapes crouched, lay, sat between the trees leaning against the trunks, clinging to the earth, half coming out, half effaced within the dim light, in all the attitudes of pain, abandonment, and despair. Another mine on the cliff went off, followed by a slight shudder of the soil under my feet. The work was going on. The work! and this was the place where some of the helpers had withdrawn to die.

"They were dying slowly—it was very clear. They were not enemies, they were not criminals, they were nothing earthly now—nothing but black shadows of disease and starvation, lying confusedly in the greenish gloom. Brought from all the recesses of the coast in all the legality of time contracts, lost in uncongenial surroundings, fed on unfamiliar food, they sickened, became inefficient, and were then allowed to crawl away and rest. These moribund shapes were free as air—and nearly as thin. I began to distinguish the gleam of the eyes under the trees. Then, glancing down, I saw a face near my hand. The black bones reclined at full length with one shoulder against the tree, and slowly the eyelids rose and the sunken eyes looked up at me, enormous and vacant, a kind of blind, white flicker in the depths of the orbs, which died out slowly. The man seemed young—almost a boy—but you know with them it's hard to tell. I found nothing else to do but to offer him one of my good Swede's ship's biscuits I had in my pocket. The fingers closed slowly on it and held—there was no other movement and no other glance. He had tied a bit of white worsted round his neck—Why? Where did he get it? Was it a badge—an ornament—a charm—a propitiatory act? Was there any idea at all connected with it? It looked startling round his black neck, this bit of white thread from beyond the seas.

"Near the same tree two more bundles of acute angles sat with their legs drawn up. One, with his chin propped on his knees, stared at nothing, in an intolerable and appalling manner: his brother phantom rested its forehead, as if overcome with a great weariness; and all about others were scattered in every pose of contorted collapse, as in some picture of a massacre or a pestilence. While I stood horror-struck, one of these creatures rose to his hands and knees, and went off on all-fours towards the river to drink. He lapped out of his hand, then sat up in the sunlight, crossing his shins in front of him, and after a time let his woolly head fall on his breastbone.

"I didn't want any more loitering in the shade, and I made haste towards the station. When near the buildings I met a white man, in such an unexpected elegance of get-up that in the first moment I took him for a sort of vision. I saw a high starched collar, white cuffs, a light alpaca jacket, snowy trousers, a clean necktie, and varnished boots. No hat. Hair parted, brushed, oiled, under a green-lined parasol held in a big white hand. He was amazing, and had a penholder behind his ear.

"I shook hands with this miracle, and I learned he was the Company's chief accountant, and that all the bookkeeping was done at this station. He had come out for a moment, he said, 'to get a breath of fresh air.' The expression sounded wonderfully odd, with its suggestion of sedentary desk life. I wouldn't have mentioned the fellow to you at all, only it was from his lips that I first heard the name of the man who is so indissolubly connected with the memories of that time. Moreover, I respected the fellow. Yes; I respected his collars, his vast cuffs, his brushed hair. His appearance was certainly that of a hairdresser's dummy; but in the great demoralization of the land he kept up his appearance. That's backbone. His starched collars and got-up shirt-fronts were achievements of character. He had been out nearly three years; and, later, I could not help asking him how he managed to sport such linen. He had just the faintest blush, and said modestly, 'I've been teaching one of the native women about the station. It was difficult. She had a distaste for the work.' Thus this man had verily accomplished something. And he was devoted to his books, which were in apple-pie order.

"Everything else in the station was in a muddle—heads, things, buildings. Strings of dusty niggers with splay feet arrived and departed; a stream of manufactured goods, rubbishy cottons, beads, and brass-wire sent into the depths of darkness, and in return came a precious trickle of ivory.

"I had to wait in the station for ten days—an eternity. I lived in a hut in the yard, but to be out of the chaos I would sometimes get into the accountant's office. It was built of horizontal planks, and so badly put together that, as he bent over his high desk, he was barred from neck to heels with narrow strips of sunlight. There was no need to open the big shutter to see. It was hot there, too; big flies buzzed fiendishly, and did not sting, but stabbed. I sat generally on the floor, while, of faultless appearance (and even slightly scented), perching on a high stool, he wrote, he wrote. Sometimes he stood up for exercise. When a trucklebed with a sick man (some invalid agent from up-country) was put in there, he exhibited a gentle annoyance. 'The groans of this sick person,' he said, 'distract my attention. And without that it is extremely difficult to guard against clerical errors in this climate.'

"One day he remarked, without lifting his head, 'In the interior you will no doubt meet Mr. Kurtz.' On my asking who Mr. Kurtz was, he said he was a first-class agent; and seeing my disappointment at this information, he added slowly, laying down his pen, 'He is a very remarkable person.' Further questions elicited from him that Mr. Kurtz was at present in charge of a trading-post, a very important one, in the true ivory-country, at 'the very bottom of there. Sends in as much ivory as all the others put together. . . .' He began to write again. The sick man was too ill to groan. The flies buzzed in a great peace.

"Suddenly there was a growing murmur of voices and a great tramping of feet. A caravan had come in. A violent babble of uncouth sounds burst out on the other side of the planks. All the carriers were speaking together, and in the midst of the uproar the lamentable voice of the chief agent was heard 'giving it up' tearfully for the twentieth time that day. . . . He rose slowly. 'What a frightful row,' he said. He crossed the room gently to look at the sick man, and returning, said to me, 'He does not hear.' 'What! Dead?' I asked, startled. 'No, not yet,' he answered, with great composure. Then, alluding with a toss of the head to the tumult in the station-yard, 'When one has got to make correct entries, one comes to hate those savages—hate them to the

45

death.' He remained thoughtful for a moment. 'When you see Mr. Kurtz,' he went on, 'tell him for me that everything here'—he glanced at the desk—'is very satisfactory. I don't like to write to him—with those messengers of ours you never know who may get hold of your letter—at that Central Station.' He stared at me for a moment with his mild, bulging eyes. 'Oh, he will go far, very far,' he began again. 'He will be a somebody in the Administration before long. They, above—the Council in Europe, you know—mean him to be.'

"He turned to his work. The noise outside had ceased, and presently in going out I stopped at the door. In the steady buzz of flies the homeward-bound agent was lying flushed and insensible; the other, bent over his books, was making correct entries of perfectly correct transactions; and fifty feet below the doorstep I could see the still tree-tops of the grove of death.

50   "Next day I left the station at last, with a caravan of sixty men, for a two-hundred-mile tramp.

"No use telling you much about that. Paths, paths, everywhere; a stamped-in network of paths spreading over the empty land, through long grass, through burnt grass, through thickets, down and up chilly ravines, up and down stony hills ablaze with heat; and a solitude, a solitude, nobody, not a hut. The population had cleared out a long time ago. Well, if a lot of mysterious niggers armed with all kinds of fearful weapons suddenly took to traveling on the road between Deal and Gravesend, catching the yokels right and left to carry heavy loads for them, I fancy every farm and cottage thereabouts would get empty very soon. Only here the dwellings were gone, too. Still I passed through several abandoned villages. There's something pathetically childish in the ruins of grass walls. Day after day, with the stamp and shuffle of sixty pair of bare feet behind me, each pair under a sixty-pound load. Camp, cook, sleep, strike camp, march. Now and then a carrier dead in harness, at rest in the long grass near the path, with an empty water-gourd and his long staff lying by his side. A great silence around and above. Perhaps on some quiet night the tremor of far-off drums, sinking, swelling, a tremor vast, faint; a sound weird, appealing, suggestive, and wild—and perhaps with as profound a meaning as the sound of bells in a Christian country. Once a white man in an unbuttoned uniform, camping on the path with an armed escort of lank Zanzibaris, very hospitable and festive—not to say drunk. Was looking after the upkeep of the road, he declared. Can't say I saw any road or any upkeep, unless the body of a middle-aged Negro, with a bullet-hole in the forehead, upon which I absolutely stumbled three miles farther on, may be considered as a permanent improvement. I had a white companion, too, not a bad chap, but rather too fleshy and with the exasperating habit of fainting on the hot hillsides, miles away from the least bit of shade and water. Annoying, you know, to hold your own coat like a parasol over a man's head while he is coming to. I couldn't help asking him once what he meant by coming there at all. 'To make money, of course. What do you think?' he said, scornfully. Then he got fever, and had to be carried in a hammock slung under a pole. As he weighed sixteen stone I had no end of rows with the carriers. They jibbed, ran away, sneaked off with their loads in the night—quite a mutiny. So, one evening, I made a speech in English with gestures, not one of which was lost to the sixty pairs of eyes before me, and the next morning I started the hammock off in front all right. An hour afterwards I came upon the whole concern wrecked in a bush—man, hammock, groans, blankets, horrors. The heavy pole had skinned his poor nose. He was very anxious for me to kill somebody, but there wasn't the shadow of a carrier near. I remember the old doctor— 'It would be interesting for science to watch the mental changes of individuals, on the spot.' I felt I was becoming scientifically interesting. However, all that is to no purpose. On the fifteenth day I came in sight of the big river again, and hobbled into the Central Station. It was a backwater surrounded by scrub and forest, with a pretty border of smelly mud on one side, and on the three others enclosed by a crazy fence of rushes. A neglected gap was all the gate it had, and the first glance at the place was enough to let you see the flabby devil was running that show. White men with long staves in their hands appeared languidly from amongst the buildings, strolling up to take a look at me, and then retired out of sight somewhere. One of them, a stout, excitable chap with black mustaches, informed me with great volubility and many digressions, as soon as I told him who I was, that my steamer was at the bottom of the river. I was thunderstruck. What, how, why? Oh, it was 'all right.' The 'manager himself' was there. All quite correct. 'Everybody had behaved splendidly! splendidly!'—'you must,' he said in agitation, 'go and see the general manager at once. He is waiting!'

"I did not see the real significance of that wreck at once. I fancy I see it now, but I am not sure—not at all. Certainly the affair was too stupid—when I think of it—to be altogether natural. Still. . . . But at the moment it presented itself simply as a confounded nuisance. The steamer was sunk. They had started two days before in a sudden hurry up the river with the manager on board, in charge of some volunteer skipper, and before they had been out three hours they tore the bottom out of her on stones, and she sank near the south bank. I asked myself what I was to do there, now my boat was lost. As a matter of fact, I had plenty to do in fishing my command out of the river. I had to set about it the very next day. That, and the repairs when I brought the pieces to the station, took some months.

"My first interview with the manager was curious. He did not ask me to sit down after my twenty-mile walk that morning. He was commonplace in complexion, in feature, in manners, and in voice. He was of middle size and of ordinary build. His eyes, of the usual blue, were perhaps remarkably cold, and he certainly could make his glance fall on one as trenchant and heavy as an ax. But even at these times the rest of his person seemed to disclaim the intention. Otherwise there was only an indefinable, faint expression of his lips, something stealthy—a smile—not a smile—I remember it, but I can't explain. It was unconscious, this smile was, though just after he had said something it got intensified for an instant. It came at the end of his speeches like a seal applied on the words to make the meaning of the commonest phrase appear absolutely inscrutable. He was a common trader, from his youth up employed in these parts—nothing more. He was obeyed, yet he inspired neither love nor fear, nor even respect. He inspired uneasiness. That was it! Uneasiness. Not a definite mistrust—just uneasiness—nothing more. You have no idea how effective such a . . . a . . . faculty can be. He had no genius for organizing, for initiative, or for order even. That was evident in such things as the deplorable state of the station. He had no learning, and no intelligence. His position had come to him—why? Perhaps because he was never ill. . . . He had served three terms of three years out there. . . . Because triumphant health in the general rout of constitutions is a kind of power in itself. When he went home on leave he rioted on a large scale—pompously. Jack ashore—with a difference—in externals only. This one could gather from his casual talk. He originated nothing, he could keep the routine going—that's all. But he was great. He was great by this little thing that it was impossible to tell what could control such a man. He never gave the secret away. Perhaps there was nothing within him. Such a suspicion made one pause—for out there there were no external checks. Once when various tropical diseases had laid low almost every 'agent' in the station, he was heard to say, 'Men who come out here should have no entrails.' He sealed the utterance with that smile of his, as though it had been a door opening into a darkness he had in his keeping. You fancied you had seen things—but the seal was on. When annoyed at meal-times by the constant quarrels of the white men about precedence, he ordered an immense round table to be made, for which a special house had to be built. This was the station's messroom. Where he sat was the first place—the rest were nowhere. One felt this to be his unalterable conviction. He was neither civil nor uncivil. He was quiet. He allowed his 'boy'—an overfed young Negro from the coast—to treat the white men, under his very eyes, with provoking insolence.

"He began to speak as soon as he saw me. I had been very long on the road. He could not wait. Had to start without me. The upriver stations had to be relieved. There had been so many delays already that he did not know who was dead and who was alive, and how they got on—and so on, and so on. He paid no attention to my explanations, and, playing with a stick of sealing-wax, repeated several times that the situation was 'very grave, very grave.' There were rumors that a very important station was in jeopardy, and its chief, Mr. Kurtz, was ill. Hoped it was not true. Mr. Kurtz was . . . . I felt weary and irritable. Hang Kurtz, I thought. I interrupted him by saying I had heard of Mr. Kurtz on the coast. 'Ah! So they talk of him down there,' he murmured to himself. Then he began again, assuring me Mr. Kurtz was the best agent he had, an exceptional man, of the greatest importance to the Company; therefore I could understand his anxiety. He was, he said, 'very, very uneasy.' Certainly he fidgeted on his chair a good deal, exclaimed, 'Ah, Mr. Kurtz!' broke the stick of sealing-wax and seemed dumfounded by the accident. Next thing he wanted to know 'how long it would take to. . . .' I interrupted him again. Being hungry, you know, and kept on my feet too, I was getting savage. 'How can I tell?' I said. 'I haven't even seen the wreck yet—some months, no doubt.' All this talk seemed to me so futile. 'Some months,' he said. 'Well, let us say three months before we can make a start. Yes. That ought to do the affair.' I flung out of his hut (he lived all alone in a clay hut with a sort of veranda) muttering to myself my opinion of him. He was a chattering idiot. Afterwards I took it back when it was borne in upon me startlingly with what extreme nicety he had estimated the time requisite for the 'affair.'

55   "I went to work the next day, turning, so to speak, my back on that station. In that way only it seemed to me I could keep my hold on the redeeming facts of life. Still, one must look about sometimes; and then I saw this station, these men strolling aimlessly about in the sunshine of the yard. I asked myself sometimes what it all meant. They wandered here and there with their absurd long staves in their hands, like a lot of faithless pilgrims bewitched inside a rotten fence. The word 'ivory' rang in the air, was whispered, was sighed. You would think they were praying to it. A taint of imbecile rapacity blew through it all, like a whiff from some corpse. By Jove! I've never seen anything so unreal in my life. And outside, the silent wilderness surrounding this cleared speck on the earth struck me as something great and invincible, like evil or truth, waiting patiently for the passing away of this fantastic invasion.

"Oh, these months! Well, never mind. Various things happened. One evening a grass shed full of calico, cotton prints, beads, and I don't know what else, burst into a blaze so suddenly that you would have thought the earth had opened to let an avenging fire consume all the trash. I was smoking my pipe quietly by my dismantled steamer, and saw them all cutting capers in the light, with their arms lifted high, when the stout man with mustaches came tearing down to the river, a tin pail in his hand, assured me that everybody was 'behaving splendidly, splendidly,' dipped about a quart of water, and tore back again. I noticed there was a hole in the bottom of his pail.

"I strolled up. There was no hurry. You see the thing had gone off like a box of matches. It had been hopeless from the very first. The flame had leaped high, driven everybody back, lighted up everything—and collapsed. The shed was already a heap of embers glowing fiercely. A nigger was being beaten near by. They said he had caused the fire in some way; be that as it may, he was screeching most horribly. I saw him, later, for several days, sitting in a bit of shade looking very sick and trying to recover himself: afterwards he arose and went out—and the wilderness without a sound took him into its bosom again. As I approached the glow from the dark I found myself at the back of two men, talking. I heard the name of Kurtz pronounced, then the words, 'take advantage of this unfortunate accident.' One of the men was the manager. I wished him a good evening. 'Did you ever see anything like it—eh? it is incredible,' he said, and walked off. The other man remained. He was a first-class agent, young, gentlemanly, a bit reserved, with a forked little beard and a hooked nose. He was standoffish with the other agents, and they on their side said he was the manager's spy among them. As to me, I had hardly ever spoken to him before. We got into talk, and by and by we strolled away from the hissing ruins. Then he asked me to his room, which was in the main building of the station. He struck a match, and I perceived that this young aristocrat had not only a silver-mounted dressing-case but also a whole candle all to himself. Just at that time the manager was the only man supposed to have any right to candles. Native mats covered the clay walls; a collection of spears, assegais, shields, knives was hung up in trophies. The business intrusted to this fellow was the making of bricks—so I had been informed; but there wasn't a fragment of a brick anywhere in the station, and he had been there more than a year—waiting. It seems he could not make bricks without something, I don't know what—straw, maybe. Anyways, it could not be found there, and as it was not likely to be sent from Europe, it did not appear clear to me what he was waiting for. An act of special creation perhaps. However, they were all waiting—all the sixteen or twenty pilgrims of them—for something; and upon my word it did not seem an uncongenial occupation, from the way they took it, though the only thing that ever came to them was disease—as far as I could see. They beguiled the time by backbiting and intriguing against each other in a foolish kind of way. There was an air of plotting about that station, but nothing came of it, of course. It was as unreal as everything else—as the philanthropic pretense of the whole concern, as their talk, as their government, as their show of work. The only real feeling was a desire to get appointed to a trading-post where ivory was to be had, so that they could earn percentages. They intrigued and slandered and hated each other only on that account—but as to effectually lifting a little finger—oh, no. By heavens! there is something after all in the world allowing one man to steal a horse while another must not look at the halter. Steal a horse straight out. Very well. He has done it. Perhaps he can ride. But there is a way of looking at a halter that would provoke the most charitable of saints into a kick.

"I had no idea why he wanted to be sociable, but as we chatted in there it suddenly occurred to me the fellow was trying to get at something—in fact, pumping me. He alluded constantly to Europe, to the people I was supposed to know there—putting leading questions as to my acquaintances in the sepulchral city, and so on. His little eyes glittered like mica discs—with curiosity—though he tried to keep up a bit of superciliousness. At first I was astonished, but very soon I became awfully curious to see what he would find out from me. I couldn't possibly imagine what I had in me to make it worth his while. It was very pretty to see how he baffled himself, for in truth my body was full only of chills, and my head had nothing in it but that wretched steamboat business. It was evident he took me for a perfectly shameless prevaricator.

At last he got angry, and, to conceal a movement of furious annoyance, he yawned. I rose. Then I noticed a small sketch in oils, on a panel, representing a woman, draped and blindfolded, carrying a lighted torch. The background was somber—almost black. The movement of the woman was stately, and the effect of the torchlight on the face was sinister.

"It arrested me, and he stood by civilly, holding an empty half-pint champagne bottle (medical comforts) with the candle stuck in it. To my question he said Mr. Kurtz had painted this—in this very station more than a year ago—while waiting for means to go to his trading-post. 'Tell me, pray,' said I, 'who is this Mr. Kurtz?'

"'The chief of the Inner Station,' he answered in a short tone, looking away. 'Much obliged,' I said, laughing. 'And you are the brickmaker of the Central Station. Everyone knows that.' He was silent for a while. 'He is a prodigy,' he said at last. 'He is an emissary of pity, and science, and progress, and devil knows what else. We want,' he began to declaim suddenly, 'for the guidance of the cause intrusted to us by Europe, so to speak, higher intelligence, wide sympathies, a singleness of purpose.' 'Who says that?' I asked. 'Lots of them,' he replied. 'Some even write that; and so *he* comes here, a special being, as you ought to know.' 'Why ought I to know?' I interrupted, really surprised. He paid no attention. 'Yes. Today he is chief of the best station, next year he will be assistant-manager, two years more and . . . but I daresay you know what he will be in two years' time. You are of the new gang—the gang of virtue. The same people who sent him specially also recommended you. Oh, don't say no. I've my own eyes to trust.' Light dawned upon me. My dear aunt's influential acquaintances were producing an unexpected effect upon that young man. I nearly burst into a laugh. 'Do you read the Company's confidential correspondence?' I asked. He hadn't a word to say. It was great fun. 'When Mr. Kurtz,' I continued, severely, 'is General Manager, you won't have the opportunity.'

"He blew the candle out suddenly, and we went outside. The moon had risen. Black figures strolled about listlessly, pouring water on the glow, whence proceeded a sound of hissing; steam ascended in the moonlight, the beaten nigger groaned somewhere. 'What a row the brute makes!' said the indefatigable man with the mustaches, appearing near us. 'Serves him right. Transgression—punishment—bang! Pitiless, pitiless. That's the only way. This will prevent all conflagrations for the future. I was just telling the manager. . . .' He noticed my companion, and became crestfallen all at once. 'Not in bed yet,' he said, with a kind of servile heartiness; 'it's so natural. Ha! Danger—agitation.' He vanished. I went on to the riverside, and the other followed me. I heard a scathing murmur at my ear, 'Heap of muffs—go to.' The pilgrims could be seen in knots gesticulating, discussing. Several had still their staves in their hands. I verily believe they took these sticks to bed with them. Beyond the fence the forest stood up spectrally in the moonlight, and through the dim stir, through the faint sounds of that lamentable courtyard, the silence of the land went home to one's very heart—its mystery, its greatness, the amazing reality of its concealed life. The hurt nigger moaned feebly somewhere near by, and then fetched a deep sigh that made me mend my pace away from there. I felt a hand introducing itself under my arm. 'My dear sir,' said the fellow, 'I don't want to be misunderstood, and especially by you, you will see Mr. Kurtz long before I can have that pleasure. I wouldn't like him to get a false idea of my disposition. . . .'

"I let him run on, this papier-mâché Mephistopheles, and it seemed to me that if I tried I could poke my forefinger through him, and would find nothing inside but a little loose dirt, maybe. He, don't you see, had been planning to be assistant-manager by and by under the present man, and I could see that the coming of that Kurtz had upset them both not a little. He talked precipitately, and I did not try to stop him. I had my shoulders against the wreck of my steamer, hauled up on the slope like a carcass of some big river animal. The smell of mud, of primeval mud, by Jove! was in my nostrils, the high stillness of primeval forest was before my eyes; there were shiny patches on the black creek. The moon had spread over everything a thin layer of silver—over the rank grass, over the mud, upon the wall of matted vegetation standing higher than the wall of a temple, over the great river I could see through a somber gap glittering, glittering, as it flowed broadly by without a murmur. All this was great, expectant, mute, while the man jabbered about himself. I wondered whether the stillness on the face of the immensity looking at us two were meant as an appeal or as a menace. What were we who had strayed in here? Could we handle that dumb thing, or would it handle us? I felt how big, how confoundedly big, was that thing that couldn't talk, and perhaps was deaf as well. What was in there? I could see a little ivory coming out from there, and I had heard Mr. Kurtz was in there. I had heard enough about it, too—God knows! Yet somehow it didn't bring any image with it—no more than if I had been told an angel or a fiend was in there. I believed it in the same way one of you might believe there are inhabitants in the planet Mars. I knew once a Scotch sailmaker who was certain, dead sure, there were people in Mars. If you asked him for some idea how they looked and behaved, he would get shy and mutter something about 'walking on all-fours.' If you as much as smiled, he would—though a man of sixty—offer to fight you. I would not have gone so far as to fight for Kurtz, but I went for him near enough to a lie. You know I hate, detest, and can't bear a lie, not because I am straighter than the rest of us, but simply because it appalls me. There is a taint of death, a flavor of mortality in lies—which is exactly what I hate and detest in the world—what I want to forget. It makes me miserable and sick, like biting something rotten would do. Temperament, I suppose. Well, I went near enough to it by letting the young fool there believe anything he liked to imagine as to my influence in Europe. I became in an instant as much of a pretense as the rest of the bewitched pilgrims. This simply because I had a notion it somehow would be of help to that Kurtz whom at the time I did not see— you understand. He was just a word for me. I did not see the man in the name any more than you do. Do you see him? Do you see the story? Do you see anything? It seems to me I am trying to tell you a dream—making a vain attempt, because no relation of a dream can convey the dream-sensation, that commingling of absurdity, surprise, and bewilderment in a tremor of struggling revolt, that notion of being captured by the incredible which is of the very essence of dreams. . . ."

He was silent for a while.

". . . No, it is impossible; it is impossible to convey the life-sensation of any given epoch of one's existence—that which makes its truth, its meaning—its subtle and penetrating essence. It is impossible. We live, as we dream—alone. . . ."

He paused again as if reflecting, then added—

"Of course in this you fellows see more than I could then. You see me, whom you know. . . ."

It had become so pitch dark that we listeners could hardly see one another. For a long time already he, sitting apart, had been no more to us than a voice. There was not a word from anybody. The others might have been asleep, but I was awake. I listened, I listened on the watch for the sentence, for the word, that would give me the clew of the faint uneasiness inspired by this narrative that seemed to shape itself without human lips in the heavy night-air of the river.

". . . Yes—I let him run on," Marlow began again," and think what he pleased about the powers that were behind me. I did! And there was nothing behind me! There was nothing but that wretched, old, mangled steamboat I was leaning against, while he talked fluently about 'the necessity for every man to get on.' 'And when one comes out here, you conceive, it is not to gaze at the moon.' Mr. Kurtz was a 'universal genius,' but even a genius would find it easier to work with 'adequate tools—intelligent men.' He did not make bricks—why, there was a physical impossibility in the way—as I was well aware; and if he did secretarial work for the manager, it was because 'no sensible man rejects wantonly the confidence of his superiors.' Did I see it? I saw it. What more did I want? What I really wanted was rivets, by heavens! Rivets. To get on with the work—to stop the hole. Rivets I wanted. There were cases of them down at the coast—cases—piled up—burst—split! You kicked a loose rivet at every second step in that station yard on the hillside. Rivets had rolled into the grove of death. You could fill your pockets with rivets for the trouble of stooping down—and there wasn't one rivet to be found where it was wanted. We had plates that would do, but nothing to fasten them with. And every week the messenger, a lone Negro, letter-bag on shoulder and staff in hand, left our station for the coast. And several times a week a coast caravan came in with trade goods—ghastly glazed calico that made you shudder only to look at it; glass beads, valued about a penny a quart, confounded spotted cotton handkerchiefs. And no rivets. Three carriers could have brought all that was wanted to set that steamboat afloat.

"He was becoming confidential now, but I fancy my unresponsive attitude must have exasperated him at last, for he judged it necessary to inform me he feared neither God nor devil, let alone any mere man. I said I could see that very well, but what I wanted was a certain quantity of rivets—and rivets were what really Mr. Kurtz wanted, if he had only known it. Now letters went to the coast every week. . . . 'My dear sir,' he cried, 'I write from dictation.' I demanded rivets. There was a way—for an intelligent man. He changed his manner; became very cold, and suddenly began to talk about a hippopotamus; wondered whether sleeping on board the steamer (I stuck to my salvage night and day) I wasn't disturbed. There was an old hippo that had the bad habit of getting out on the bank and roaming at night over the station grounds. The pilgrims used to turn out in a body and empty every rifle they could lay hands on at him. Some even had sat up o' nights for him. All this energy was wasted, though. 'That animal had a charmed life,' he said; 'but you can say this only of brutes in this country. No man—you apprehend me?—no man here bears a charmed life.' He stood there for a moment in the moonlight with his delicate hooked nose set a little askew, and his mica eyes glittering without a wink, then, with a curt good night, he strode off. I could see he was disturbed and considerably puzzled, which made me feel more hopeful than I had been for days. It was a great comfort to turn from that chap to my influential friend, the battered, twisted, ruined, tin-pot steamboat. I clambered on board. She rang under my feet like an empty Huntley & Palmer biscuit-tin kicked along a gutter; she was nothing so solid in make, and rather less pretty in shape, but I had expended enough hard work on her to make me love her. No influential friend would have served me better. She had given me a chance to come out a bit—to find out what I could do. No, I don't like work. I had rather laze about and think of all the fine things that can be done. I don't like work—no man does—but I like what is in the work—the chance to find yourself. Your own reality—for yourself, not for others—what no other man can ever know. They can only see the mere show, and never tell me what it really means.

70   "I was not surprised to see somebody sitting aft, on the deck, with his legs dangling over the mud. You see I rather chummed with the few mechanics there were in

that station, whom the other pilgrims naturally despised—on account of their imperfect manners, I suppose. This was the foreman—a boiler-maker by trade—a good worker. He was a lank, bony, yellow-faced man, with big intense eyes. His aspect was worried, and his head was as bald as the palm of my hand; but his hair in falling seemed to have stuck to his chin; and had prospered in the new locality, for his beard hung down to his waist. He was a widower with six young children (he had left them in charge of a sister of his to come out there), and the passion of his life was pigeon-flying. He was an enthusiast and a connoisseur. He would rave about pigeons. After work hours he used sometimes to come over from his hut for a talk about his children and his pigeons; at work, when he had to crawl in the mud under the bottom of the steamboat, he would tie up that beard of his in a kind of white serviette he brought for the purpose. It had loops to go over his ears. In the evening he could be seen squatted on the bank rinsing that wrapper in the creek with great care, then spreading it solemnly on a bush to dry.

"I slapped him on the back and shouted, 'We shall have rivets!' He scrambled to his feet exclaiming, 'No! Rivets!' as though he couldn't believe his ears. Then in a low voice, 'You . . . eh?' I don't know why we behaved like lunatics. I put my finger to the side of my nose and nodded mysteriously. 'Good for you!' he cried, snapped his fingers above his head, lifting one foot. I tried a jig. We capered on the iron deck. A frightful clatter came out of that hulk, and the virgin forest on the other bank of the creek sent it back in a thundering roll upon the sleeping station. It must have made some of the pilgrims sit up in their hovels. A dark figure obscured the lighted doorway of the manager's hut, vanished, then, a second or so after, the doorway itself vanished, too. We stopped, and the silence driven away by the stamping of our feet flowed back again from the recesses of the land. The great wall of vegetation, an exuberant and entangled mass of trunks, branches, leaves, boughs, festoons, motionless in the moonlight, was like a rioting invasion of soundless life, a rolling wave of plants, piled up, crested, ready to topple over the creek, to sweep every little man of us out of his little existence. And it moved not. A deadened burst of mighty splashes and snorts reached us from afar as though an ichthyosaurus had been taking a bath of glitter in the great river. 'After all,' said the boiler-maker in a reasonable tone, 'why shouldn't we get the rivets?' Why not, indeed! I did not know of any reason why we shouldn't. 'They'll come in three weeks,' I said confidently.

"But they didn't. Instead of rivets there came an invasion, an infliction, a visitation. It came in sections during the next three weeks, each section headed by a donkey carrying a white man in new clothes and tan shoes, bowing from that elevation right and left to the impressed pilgrims. A quarrelsome band of footsore sulky niggers trod on the heels of the donkeys; a lot of tents, campstools, tin boxes, white cases, brown bales would be shot down in the courtyard, and the air of mystery would deepen a little over the muddle of the station. Five such installments came, with their absurd air of disorderly flight with the loot of innumerable outfit shops and provision stores, that, one would think, they were lugging, after a raid, into the wilderness for equitable division. It was an extricable mess of things decent in themselves but that human folly made look like the spoils of thieving.

"This devoted band called itself the Eldorado Exploring Expedition, and I believe they were sworn to secrecy. Their talk, however, was the talk of sordid buccaneers: it was reckless without hardihood, greedy without audacity, and cruel without courage; there was not an atom of foresight or of serious intention in the whole batch of them, and they did not seem aware these things are wanted for the work of the world. To tear treasure out of the bowels of the land was their desire, with no more moral purpose at the back of it than there is in burglars breaking into a safe. Who paid the expenses of the noble enterprise I don't know; but the uncle of our manager was leader of that lot.

"In exterior he resembled a butcher in a poor neighborhood, and his eyes had a look of sleepy cunning. He carried his fat paunch with ostentation on his short legs, and during the time his gang infested the station spoke to no one but his nephew. You could see these two roaming about all day long with their heads close together in an everlasting confab.

75   "I had given up worrying myself about the rivets. One's capacity for that kind of folly is more limited than you would suppose. I said Hang!—and let things slide. I had plenty of time for meditation, and now and then I would give some thought to Kurtz. I wasn't very interested in him. No. Still, I was curious to see whether this man, who had come out equipped with moral ideas of some sort, would climb to the top after all and how he would set about his work when there."

II

"One evening as I was lying flat on the deck of my steamboat, I heard voices approaching—and there were the nephew and the uncle strolling along the bank. I laid my head on my arm again, and had nearly lost myself in a doze, when somebody said in my ear, as it were: 'I am as harmless as a little child, but I don't like to be dictated to. Am I the manager—or am I not? I was ordered to send him there. It's incredible.' . . . I became aware that the two were standing on the shore alongside the forepart of the steamboat, just below my head. I did not move; it did not occur to me to move: I was sleepy. 'It *is* unpleasant,' grunted the uncle. 'He has asked the Administration to be sent there,' said the other, 'with the idea of showing what he could do; and I was instructed accordingly. Look at the influence that man must have. Is it not frightful?' They both agreed it was frightful, then made several bizarre remarks: 'Make rain and fine weather—one man—the Council—by the nose'—bits of absurd sentences that got the better of my drowsiness, so that I had pretty near the whole of my wits about me when the uncle said, 'The climate may do away with this difficulty for you. Is he alone there?' 'Yes,' answered the manager; 'he sent his assistant down the river with a note to me in these terms: "Clear this poor devil out of the country, and don't bother sending more of that sort. I had rather be alone than have the kind of men you can dispose of with me." It was more than a year ago. Can you imagine such impudence!' 'Anything since then?' asked the other, hoarsely. 'Ivory,' jerked the nephew; 'lots of it—prime sort—lots—most annoying, from him.' 'And with that?' questioned the heavy rumble. 'Invoice,' was the reply fired out, so to speak. Then silence. They had been talking about Kurtz.

"I was broad awake by this time, but, lying perfectly at ease, remained still, having no inducement to change my position. 'How did that ivory come all this way?' growled the elder man, who seemed very vexed. The other explained that it had come with a fleet of canoes in charge of an English half-caste clerk Kurtz had with him; that Kurtz had apparently intended to return himself, the station being by that time bare of goods and stores, but after coming three hundred miles, he suddenly decided to go back, which he started to do alone in a small dugout with four paddlers, leaving the half-caste to continue down the river with the ivory. The two fellows there seemed astounded at anybody attempting such a thing. They were at a loss for an adequate motive. As to me, I seemed to see Kurtz for the first time. It was a distinct glimpse: the dugout, four paddling savages, and the lone white man turning his back suddenly on the headquarters, on relief, on thoughts of home—perhaps; setting his face towards the depths of the wilderness, towards his empty and desolate station. I did not know the motive. Perhaps he was just simply a fine fellow who stuck to his work for its own sake. His name, you understand, had not been pronounced once. He was 'that man.' The half-caste, who, as far as I could see, had conducted a difficult trip with great prudence and pluck, was invariably alluded to as 'that scoundrel.' The 'scoundrel' had reported that the 'man' had been very ill—had recovered imperfectly. . . . The two below me moved away then a few paces, and strolled back and forth at some little distance. I heard: 'Military post—doctor—two hundred miles—quite alone now—unavoidable delays—nine months—no news—strange rumors.' They approached again, just as the manager was saying, 'No one, as far as I know, unless a species of wandering trader—a pestilential fellow, snapping ivory from the natives.' Who was it they were talking about now? I gathered in snatches that this was some man supposed to be in Kurtz's district, and of whom the manager did not approve. 'We will not be free from unfair competition till one of these fellows is hanged for an example,' he said. 'Certainly,' grunted the other; 'get him hanged! Why not? Anything—anything can be done in this country. That's what I say; nobody here, you understand, *here*, can endanger your position. And why? You stand the climate—you outlast them all. The danger is in Europe; but there before I left I took care to—' They moved off and whispered, then their voices rose again. 'The extraordinary series of delays is not my fault. I did my best.' The fat man sighed. 'Very sad.' 'And the pestiferous absurdity of his talk,' continued the other; 'he bothered me enough when he was here. "Each station should be like a beacon on the road towards better things, a center for trade, of course, but also for humanizing, improving, instructing." Conceive you—that ass! And he wants to be manager! No it's—' Here he got choked by excessive indignation, and I lifted my head the least bit. I was surprised to see how near they were—right under me. I could have spat upon their hats. They were looking on the ground, absorbed in thought. The manager was switching his leg with a slender twig: his sagacious relative lifted his head. 'You have been well since you came out this time?' he asked. The other gave a start. 'Who? I? Oh! Like a charm—like a charm. But the rest—oh, my goodness! All sick. They die so quick, too, that I haven't the time to send them out of the country—it's incredible!' 'H'm. Just so,' grunted the uncle. 'Ah! my boy, trust to this—I say, trust to this.' I saw him extend his short flipper of an arm for a gesture that took in the forest, the creek, the mud, the river—seemed to beckon with a dishonoring flourish before the sunlit face of the land a treacherous appeal to the lurking death, to the hidden evil, to the profound darkness of its heart. It was so startling that I leaped to my feet and looked back at the edge of the forest, as though I had expected an answer of some sort to that black display of confidence. You know the foolish notions that come to one sometimes. The high stillness confronted these two figures with its ominous patience, waiting for the passing away of a fantastic invasion.

"They swore aloud together—out of sheer fright, I believe—then pretending not to know anything of my existence, turned back to the station. The sun was low; and leaning forward side by side, they seemed to be tugging painfully uphill their two ridiculous shadows of unequal length, that trailed behind them slowly over the tall grass without bending a single blade.

"In a few days the Eldorado Expedition went into the patient wilderness, that closed upon it as the sea closes over a diver. Long afterwards the news came that all the donkeys were dead. I know nothing as to the fate of the less valuable animals. They, no doubt, like the rest of us, found what they deserved. I did not inquire. I was then rather excited at the prospect of meeting Kurtz very soon. When I say very soon I mean it comparatively. It was just two months from the day we left the creek when we came to the bank below Kurtz's station.

80   "Going up that river was like traveling back to the earliest beginnings of the world, when vegetation rioted on the earth and the big trees were kings. An empty stream, a great silence, an impenetrable forest. The air was warm, thick, heavy, sluggish. There was no joy in the brilliance of sunshine. The long stretches of the waterway ran on, deserted, into the gloom of overshadowed distances. On silvery sandbanks hippos and alligators sunned themselves side by side. The broadening waters flowed through a mob of wooded islands; you lost your way on that river as you would in a desert, and butted all day long against shoals, trying to find the channel, till you thought yourself bewitched and cut off forever from everything you had known once—somewhere— far away—in another existence perhaps. There were moments when one's past came back to one, as it will sometimes when you have not a moment to spare to yourself; but it came in the shape of an unrestful and noisy dream, remembered with wonder amongst the overwhelming realities of this strange world of plants, and water, and silence. And this stillness of life did not in the least resemble a peace. It was the stillness of an implacable force brooding over an inscrutable intention. It looked at you with a vengeful aspect. I got used to it afterwards; I did not see it any more; I had no time. I had to keep guessing at the channel; I had to discern, mostly by inspiration, the signs of hidden banks; I watched for sunken stones; I was learning to clap my teeth smartly before my heart flew out, when I shaved by a fluke some infernal sly old snag that would have ripped the life out of the tin-pot steamboat and drowned all the pilgrims; I had to keep a lookout for the signs of dead wood we could cut up in the night for next day's steaming. When you have to attend to things of that sort, to the mere incidents of the surface, the reality—the reality, I tell you—fades. The inner truth is hidden—luckily, luckily. But I felt it all the same; I felt often its mysterious stillness watching me at my monkey tricks, just as it watches you fellows performing on your respective tightropes for—what is it? half-a-crown a tumble—"

"Try to be civil, Marlow," growled a voice, and I knew there was at least one listener awake besides myself.

"I beg your pardon. I forgot the heartache which makes up the rest of the price. And indeed what does the price matter, if the trick be well done? You do your tricks very well. And I didn't do badly either, since I managed not to sink that steamboat on my first trip. It's a wonder to me yet. Imagine a blindfolded man set to drive a van over a bad road. I sweated and shivered over the business considerably, I can tell you. After all, for a seaman, to scrape the bottom of the thing that's supposed to float all the time under his care is the unpardonable sin. No one may know of it, but you never forget the thump—eh? A blow on the very heart. You remember it, you dream of it, you wake up at night and think of it—years after—and go hot and cold all over. I don't pretend to say that steamboat floated all the time. More than once she had to wade for a bit, with twenty cannibals splashing around and pushing. We had enlisted some of these chaps on the way for a crew. Fine fellows—cannibals—in their place. They were men one could work with, and I am grateful to them. And, after all, they did not eat each other before my face: they had brought along a provision of hippo-meat which went rotten, and made the mystery of the wilderness stink in my nostrils. Phoo! I can sniff it now. I had the manager on board and three or four pilgrims with their staves—all complete. Sometimes we came upon a station close by the bank, clinging to the skirts of the unknown, and the white men rushing out of a tumbledown hovel, with great gestures of joy and surprise and welcome, seemed very strange—had the appearance of being held there captive by a spell. The word ivory would ring in the air for a while—and on we went again into the silence, along empty reaches, round the still bends, between the high walls of our winding way, reverberating in hollow claps the ponderous beat of the stern-wheel. Trees, trees, millions of trees, massive, immense, running up high; and at their foot, hugging the bank against the stream, crept the little begrimed steamboat, like a sluggish beetle crawling on the floor of a lofty portico. It made you feel very small, very lost, and yet it was not altogether depressing, that feeling. After all, if you were small, the grimy beetle crawled on—which was just what you wanted it to do. Where the pilgrims imagined it crawled to I don't know. To some place where they expected to get something, I bet! For me it crawled towards Kurtz—exclusively; but when the steam-pipes started leaking we crawled very slow. The reaches opened before us and closed behind, as if the forest had stepped leisurely across the water to bar the way for our return. We penetrated deeper and deeper into the heart of darkness. It was very quiet there. At night sometimes the roll of drums behind the curtain of trees would run up the river and remain sustained faintly, as if hovering in the air over our heads, till the first break of day. Whether it meant war, peace, or prayer we could not tell. The dawns were heralded by the descent of a chill stillness; the wood-cutters slept, their fires burned low; the snapping of a twig would make you start. We were wanderers on a prehistoric earth, on an earth that wore the aspect of an unknown planet. We could have fancied ourselves the first men taking possession of an accursed inheritance, to be subdued at the cost of profound anguish and of excessive toil. But suddenly, as we struggled round a bend, there would be a glimpse of rush walls, of peaked grass-roofs, a burst of yells, a whirl of black limbs, a mass of hands clapping, of feet stamping, of bodies swaying, of eyes rolling, under the droop of heavy and motionless foliage. The steamer toiled along slowly on the edge of a black and incomprehensible frenzy. The prehistoric man was cursing us, praying to us, welcoming us—who could tell? We were cut off from the comprehension of our surroundings; we glided past like phantoms, wondering and secretly appalled, as sane men would be before an enthusiastic outbreak in a madhouse. We could not understand because we were too far and could not remember, because we were traveling in the night of first ages, of those ages that are gone, leaving hardly a sign—and no memories.

"The earth seemed unearthly. We are accustomed to look upon the shackled form of a conquered monster, but there—there you could look at a thing monstrous and free. It was unearthly, and the men were—No, they were not inhuman. Well, you know, that was the worst of it—this suspicion of their not being inhuman. It would come slowly to one. They howled and leaped, and spun, and made horrid faces; but what thrilled you was just the thought of their humanity—like yours—the thought of your remote kinship with this wild and passionate uproar. Ugly. Yes, it was ugly enough; but if you were man enough you would admit to yourself that there was in you just the faintest trace of a response to the terrible frankness of that noise, a dim suspicion of there being a meaning in it which you—you so remote from the night of first ages—could comprehend. And why not? The mind of man is capable of anything—because everything is in it, all the past as well as all the future. What was there after all? Joy, fear, sorrow, devotion, valor, rage—who can tell?—but truth—truth stripped of its cloak of time. Let the fool gape and shudder—the man knows, and can look on without a wink. But he must at least be as much of a man as these on the shore. He must meet the truth with his own true stuff—with his own inborn strength. Principles won't do. Acquisitions, clothes, pretty rags—rags that would fly off at the first good shake.

No; you want a deliberate belief. An appeal to me in this fiendish row—is there? Very well; I hear; I admit, but I have a voice, too, and for good or evil mine is the speech that cannot be silenced. Of course, a fool, what with sheer fright and fine sentiments, is always safe. Who's that grunting? You wonder I didn't go ashore for a howl and a dance? Well, no—I didn't. Fine sentiments, you say? Fine sentiments, be hanged! I had no time. I had to mess about with white-lead and strips of woolen blanket helping to put bandages on those leaky steam-pipes—I tell you. I had to watch the steering, and circumvent those snags, and get the tin-pot along by hook or by crook. There was surface-truth enough in these things to save a wiser man. And between whiles I had to look after the savage who was fireman. He was an improved specimen; he could fire up a vertical boiler. He was there below me, and, upon my word, to look at him was as edifying as seeing a dog in a parody of breeches and a feather hat, walking on his hindlegs. A few months of training had done for that really fine chap. He squinted at the steam-gauge and at the water-gauge with an evident effort of intrepidity—and he had filed teeth, too, the poor devil, and the wool of his pate shaved into queer patterns, and three ornamental scars on each of his cheeks. He ought to have been clapping his hands and stamping his feet on the bank, instead of which he was hard at work, a thrall to strange witchcraft, full of improving knowledge. He was useful because he had been instructed; and what he knew was this—that should the water in that transparent thing disappear, the evil spirit inside the boiler would get angry through the greatness of his thirst, and take a terrible vengeance. So he sweated and fired up and watched the glass fearfully (with an impromptu charm, made of rags, tied to his arm, and a piece of polished bone, as big as a watch, stuck flatways through his lower lip), while the wooden banks slipped past us slowly, the short noise was left behind, the interminable miles of silence—and we crept on, towards Kurtz. But the snags were thick, the water was treacherous and shallow, the boiler seemed indeed to have a sulky devil in it, and thus neither that fireman nor I had any time to peer into our creepy thoughts.

"Some fifty miles below the Inner Station we came upon a hut of reeds, an inclined and melancholy pole, with the unrecognizable tatters of what had been a flag of some sort flying from it, and a neatly stacked woodpile. This was unexpected. We came to the bank, and on the stack of firewood found a flat piece of board with some faded pencil-writing on it. When deciphered it said: 'Wood for you. Hurry up. Approach cautiously.' There was a signature, but it was illegible—not Kurtz—a much longer word. 'Hurry up.' Where? Up the river? 'Approach cautiously.' We had not done so. But the warning could not have been meant for the place where it could be only found after approach. Something was wrong above. But what—and how much? That was the question. We commented adversely upon the imbecility of that telegraphic style. The bush around said nothing, and would not let us look very far, either. A torn curtain of red twill hung in the doorway of the hut, and flapped sadly in our faces. The dwelling was dismantled; but we could see a white man had lived there not very long ago. There remained a rude table—a plank on two posts; a heap of rubbish reposed in a dark corner, and by the door I picked up a book. It had lost its covers, and the pages had been thumbed into a state of extremely dirty softness; but the back had been lovingly stitched afresh with white cotton thread, which looked clean yet. It was an extraordinary find. Its title was, *An Inquiry into Some Points of Seamanship*, by a man Towser, Towson—some such name— Master in his Majesty's Navy. The matter looked dreary reading enough, with illustrative diagrams and repulsive tables of figures, and the copy was sixty years old. I handled this amazing antiquity with the greatest possible tenderness, lest it should dissolve in my hands. Within, Towson or Towser was inquiring earnestly into the breaking strain of ships' chains and tackle, and other such matters. Not a very enthralling book; but at the first glance you could see there a singleness of intention, an honest concern for the right way of going to work, which made these humble pages, thought out so many years ago, luminous with another than a professional light. The simple old sailor, with his talk of chains and purchases, made me forget the jungle and the pilgrims in a delicious sensation of having come upon something unmistakably real. Such a book being there was wonderful enough; but still more astounding were the notes penciled in the margin, and plainly referring to the text. I couldn't believe my eyes! They were in cipher! Yes, it looked like cipher. Fancy a man lugging with him a book of that description into this nowhere and studying it—and making notes—in cipher at that! It was an extravagant mystery.

"I had been dimly aware for some time of a worrying noise, and when I lifted my eyes I saw the woodpile was gone, and the manager, aided by all the pilgrims, was shouting at me from the riverside. I slipped the book into my pocket. I assure you to leave off reading was like tearing myself away from the shelter of an old and solid friendship. 85

"I started the lame engine ahead. 'It must be this miserable trader—this intruder,' exclaimed the manager, looking back malevolently at the place we had left. 'He must be English,' I said. 'It will not save him from getting into trouble if he is not careful,' muttered the manager darkly. I observed with assumed innocence that no man was safe from trouble in this world.

"The current was more rapid now, the steamer seemed at her last gasp, the stern-wheel flopped languidly, and I caught myself listening on tiptoe for the next beat of the float, for in sober truth I expected the wretched thing to give up every moment. It was like watching the last flickers of a life. But still we crawled. Sometimes I would pick out a tree a little way ahead to measure our progress towards Kurtz by, but I lost it invariably before we got abreast. To keep the eyes so long on one thing was too much for human patience. The manager displayed a beautiful resignation. I fretted and fumed and took to arguing with myself whether or not I would talk openly with Kurtz; but before I could come to any conclusion it occurred to me that my speech or my silence, indeed any action of mine, would be a mere futility. What did it matter what anyone knew or ignored? What did it matter who was manager? One gets sometimes such a flash of insight. The essentials of this affair lay deep under the surface, beyond my reach, and beyond my power of meddling.

"Towards the evening of the second day we judged ourselves about eight miles from Kurtz's station. I wanted to push on; but the manager looked grave, and told me the navigation up there was so dangerous that it would be advisable, the sun being very low already, to wait where we were till next morning. Moreover, he pointed out that if the warning to approach cautiously were to be followed, we must approach in daylight—not at dusk, or in the dark. This was sensible enough. Eight miles meant nearly three hours' steaming for us, and I could also see suspicious ripples at the upper end of the reach. Nevertheless, I was annoyed beyond expression at the delay, and most unreasonably, too, since one night more could not matter much after so many months. As we had plenty of wood, and caution was the word, I brought up in the middle of the stream. The reach was narrow, straight, with high sides like a railway cutting. The dusk came gliding into it long before the sun had set. The current ran smooth and swift, but a dumb immobility sat on the banks. The living trees, lashed together by the creepers and every living bush of the undergrowth, might have been changed into stone, even to the slenderest twig, to the lightest leaf. It was not sleep—it seemed unnatural, like a state of trance. Not the faintest sound of any kind could be heard. You looked on amazed, and began to suspect yourself of being deaf—then the night came suddenly, and struck you blind as well. About three in the morning some large fish leaped, and the loud splash made me jump as though a gun had been fired. When the sun rose there was a white fog, very warm and clammy, and more blinding than the night. It did not shift or drive; it was just there, standing all around you like something solid. At eight or nine, perhaps, it lifted as a shutter lifts. We had a glimpse of the towering multitude of trees, of the immense matted jungle, with the blazing little ball of the sun hanging over it—all perfectly still—and then the white shutter came down again, smoothly, as if sliding in greased grooves. I ordered the chain, which we had begun to heave in, to be paid out again. Before it stopped running with a muffled rattle, a cry, a very loud cry, as of infinite desolation, soared slowly in the opaque air. It ceased. A complaining clamor, modulated in savage discords, filled our ears. The sheer unexpectedness of it made my hair stir under my cap. I don't know how it struck the others: to me it seemed as though the mist itself had screamed, so suddenly, and apparently from all sides at once, did this tumultuous and mournful uproar arise. It culminated in a hurried outbreak of almost intolerably excessive shrieking, which stopped short, leaving us stiffened in a variety of silly attitudes, and obstinately listening to the nearly as appalling and excessive silence. 'Good God! What is the meaning—' stammered at my elbow one of the pilgrims—a little fat man, with sandy hair and red whiskers, who wore side-spring boots, and pink pajamas tucked into his socks. Two others remained open-mouthed a whole minute, then dashed into the little cabin, to rush out incontinently and stand darting scared glances, with Winchesters at 'ready' in their hands. What we could see was just the steamer we were on, her outlines blurred as though she had been on the point of dissolving, and a misty strip of water, perhaps two feet broad, around her—and that was all. The rest of the world was nowhere, as far as our eyes and ears were concerned. Just nowhere. Gone, disappeared; swept off without leaving a whisper or a shadow behind.

"I went forward, and ordered the chain to be hauled in short, so as to be ready to trip the anchor and move the steamboat at once if necessary. 'Will they attack?' whispered an awed voice. 'We will be all butchered in this fog,' murmured another. The faces twitched with the strain, the hands trembling slightly, the eyes forgot to wink. It was very curious to see the contrast of expressions of the white men and of the black fellows of our crew, who were as much strangers to that part of the river as we, though their homes were only eight hundred miles away. The whites, of course, greatly discomposed, had besides a curious look of being painfully shocked by such an outrageous row. The others had an alert, naturally interested expression; but their faces were essentially quiet, even those of the one or two who grinned as they hauled at the chain. Several exchanged short, grunting phrases, which seemed to settle the matter to their satisfaction. Their headman, a young, broad-chested black, severely draped in dark-blue fringed cloths, with fierce nostrils and his hair all done up artfully in oily ringlets, stood near me. 'Aha!' I said, just for good fellowship's sake. 'Catch 'em,' he snapped, with a bloodshot widening of his eyes and a flash of sharp teeth—'catch 'im. Give 'im to us.' 'To you, eh?' I asked; 'what would you do with them?' 'Eat 'em!' he said, curtly, and, leaning his elbow on the rail, looked out into the fog in a dignified and profoundly pensive attitude. I would no doubt have been properly horrified, had it not occurred to me that he and his chaps must be very hungry: that they must have been growing increasingly hungry for at least this month past. They had been engaged for six months (I don't think a single one of them had any clear idea of time, as we at the end of countless ages have. They still belonged to the beginnings of time—had no inherited experience to teach them as it were), and of course, as long as there was a piece of paper written over in accordance with some farcical law or other made down the river, it didn't enter anybody's head to trouble how they would live. Certainly they had brought with them some rotten hippo-meat, which couldn't have lasted very long, anyway, even if the pilgrims hadn't, in the midst of a shocking hullabaloo, thrown a considerable quantity of it overboard. It looked like a high-handed proceeding; but it was really a case of legitimate self-defense. You can't breathe dead hippo waking, sleeping, and eating, and at the same time keep your precarious grip on existence. Besides that, they had given them every week three pieces of brass wire, each about nine inches long; and the theory was they were to buy their provisions with that currency in riverside villages. You can see how *that* worked. There were either no villages, or the people were hostile, or the director, who like the rest of us fed out of tins, with an occasional old he-goat thrown in, didn't want to stop the steamer for some more or less recondite reason. So, unless they swallowed the wire itself, or made loops of it to snare the fishes with, I don't see what good their extravagant salary could be to them. I must say it was paid with a regularity worthy of a large and honorable trading company. For the rest, the only thing to eat—though it didn't look eatable in the least—I saw in their possession was a few lumps of some stuff like half-cooked dough, of a dirty lavender color, they kept wrapped in leaves, and now and then swallowed a piece of, but so small that it seemed done more for the looks of the thing than for any serious purpose of sustenance. Why in the name of all the gnawing devils of hunger they didn't go for us—they were thirty to five—and have a good tuck-in for once, amazes me now when I think of it. They were big powerful men, with not much capacity to weigh the consequences, with courage, with strength, even yet, though their skins were no longer glossy and their muscles no longer hard. And I saw that something restraining, one of those human secrets that baffle probability, had come into play there. I looked at them with a swift quickening of interest—not because it occurred to me I might be eaten by them before very long, though I own to you that just then I perceived—in a new light, as it were—how unwholesome the pilgrims looked, and I hoped, yes, I positively hoped, that my aspect was not so—what shall I say?—so—unappetizing: a touch of fantastic vanity which fitted well with the dream-sensation that pervaded all my days at that time. Perhaps I had a little fever, too. One can't live with one's finger everlastingly on one's pulse. I had often 'a little fever,' or a little touch of other things—the playful paw-strokes of the wilderness, the preliminary trifling before the more serious onslaught which came in due course. Yes; I looked at them as you would on any human being, with a curiosity of their impulses, motives, capacities, weaknesses, when brought to the test of an inexorable physical necessity. Restraint! What possible restraint! Was it superstition, disgust, patience, fear—or some kind of primitive honor? No fear can stand up to hunger, no patience can wear it out, disgust simply does not exist where hunger is; and as to superstition, beliefs, and what you may call principles, they are less than chaff in a breeze. Don't you know the devilry of lingering starvation, its exasperating torment, its black thoughts, its somber and brooding ferocity? Well, I do. It takes a man all his inborn strength to fight hunger properly. It's really easier to face bereavement, dishonor, and the perdition of one's soul—than this kind of prolonged hunger. Sad, but true. And these chaps, too, had no earthly reason for any kind of scruple. Restraint! I would just as soon have expected restraint from a hyena prowling amongst the corpses of a battlefield. But there was the fact facing me—the fact dazzling, to be seen, like the foam on the depths of the sea, like a ripple on an unfathomable enigma, a mystery greater—when I thought of it—than the curious, inexplicable note of desperate grief in this savage clamor that had swept by us on the riverbank, behind the blind whiteness of the fog.

90   "Two pilgrims were quarreling in hurried whispers as to which bank, 'Left.' 'No, no; how can you? Right, right, of course.' 'It is very serious,' said the manager's voice behind me; 'I would be desolated if anything should happen to Mr. Kurtz before we came up.' I looked at him, and had not the slightest doubt he was sincere. He was just the kind of man who would wish to preserve appearances. That was his restraint. But when he muttered something about going on at once, I did not even take the trouble to answer him. I knew, and he knew, that it was impossible. Were we to let go our hold of the bottom, we would be absolutely in the air—in space. We wouldn't be able to tell where we were going to—whether up or down stream, or across—till we fetched against one bank or the other—and then we wouldn't know at first which it was. Of course I made no move. I had no mind for a smash-up. You couldn't imagine a more deadly place for a shipwreck. Whether drowned at once or not, we were sure to perish speedily in one way or another. 'I authorize you to take all the risks,' he said, after a short silence. 'I refuse to take any,' I said, shortly; which was just the answer he expected, though its tone might have surprised him. 'Well, I must defer to your judgment. You are captain,' he said, with marked civility. I turned my shoulder to him in sign of my appreciation, and looked into the fog. How long would it last? It was the most hopeless lookout. The approach to this Kurtz grubbing for ivory in the wretched bush was beset by as many dangers as though he had been an enchanted princess sleeping in a fabulous castle. 'Will they attack, do you think?' asked the manager, in a confidential tone.

"I did not think they would attack, for several obvious reasons. The thick fog was one. If they left the bank in their canoes they would get lost in it, as we would be if we attempted to move. Still, I had also judged the jungle of both banks quite impenetrable—and yet eyes were in it, eyes that had seen us. The riverside bushes were certainly very thick; but the undergrowth behind was evidently penetrable. However, during the short lift I had seen no canoes anywhere in the reach—certainly not abreast of the steamer. But what made the idea of attack inconceivable to me was the nature of the noise—of the cries we had heard. They had not the fierce character boding immediate hostile intention. Unexpected, wild, and violent as they had been, they had given me an irresistible impression of sorrow. The glimpse of the steamboat had for some reason filled those savages with unrestrained grief. The danger, if any, I expounded, was from our proximity to a great human passion let loose. Even extreme grief may ultimately vent itself in violence—but more generally takes the form of apathy. . . .

"You should have seen the pilgrims stare! They had no heart to grin, or even to revile me: but I believe they thought me gone mad—with fright, maybe. I delivered a regular lecture. My dear boys, it was no good bothering. Keep a lookout? Well, you may guess I watched the fog for the signs of lifting as a cat watches a mouse; but for anything else our eyes were of no more use to us than if we had been buried miles deep in a heap of cotton-wool. It felt like it, too—choking, warm, stifling. Besides, all I said, though it sounded extravagant, was absolutely true to fact. What we afterwards alluded to as an attack was really an attempt at repulse. The action was very far from being aggressive—it was not even defensive, in the usual sense: it was undertaken under the stress of desperation, and in its essence was purely protective.

"It developed itself, I should say, two hours after the fog lifted, and its commencement was at a spot, roughly speaking, about a mile and a half below Kurtz's station. We had just floundered and flopped round a bend, when I saw an islet, a mere grassy hummock of bright green, in the middle of the stream. It was the only thing of the kind; but as we opened the reach more, I perceived it was the head of a long sand-bank, or rather of a chain of shallow patches stretching down the middle of the river. They were discolored, just awash, and the whole lot was seen just under the water, ex-actly as a man's backbone is seen running down the middle of his back under the skin. Now, as far as I did see, I could go to the right or to the left of this. I didn't know ei-ther channel, of course. The banks looked pretty well alike, the depth appeared the same; but as I had been informed the station was on the west side, I naturally headed for the western passage.

"No sooner had we fairly entered it than I became aware it was much narrower than I had supposed. To the left of us there was the long uninterrupted shoal, and to the right a high, steep bank heavily overgrown with bushes. Above the bush the trees stood in serried ranks. The twigs overhung the current thickly, and from distance to distance a large limb of some tree projected rigidly over the stream. It was then well on in the afternoon, the face of the forest was gloomy, and a broad strip of shadow had already fallen on the water. In this shadow we steamed up—very slowly, as you may imagine. I sheered her well inshore—the water being deepest near the bank, as the sounding-pole informed me.

"One of my hungry and forbearing friends was sounding in the bows just below me. 95 This steamboat was exactly like a decked scow. On the deck, there were two little teak-wood houses, with doors and windows. The boiler was in the fore-end, and the ma-chinery right astern. Over the whole there was a light roof, supported on stanchions. The funnel projected through that roof, and in front of the funnel a small cabin built of light planks served for a pilot-house. It contained a couch, two campstools, a loaded Martini-Henry leaning in one corner, a tiny table, and the steering-wheel. It had a wide door in front and a broad shutter at each side. All these were always thrown open, of course. I spent my days perched up there on the extreme fore-end of that roof, before the door. At night I slept, or tried to, on the couch. An athletic black belonging to some coast tribe, and educated by my poor predecessor, was the helmsman. He sported a pair of brass earrings, wore a blue cloth wrapper from the waist to the ankles, and thought all the world of himself. He was the most unstable kind of fool I had ever seen. He steered with no end to a swagger while you were by; but if he lost sight of you, he be-came instantly the prey of an abject funk, and would let that cripple of a steamboat get the upper hand of him in a minute.

"I was looking down at the sounding-pole, and feeling much annoyed to see at each try a little more of it stick out that river, when I saw my poleman give up the business suddenly, and stretch himself flat on the deck, without even taking the trouble to haul his pole in. He kept hold on it though, and it trailed in the water. At the same time the fireman, whom I could also see below me, sat down abruptly before his furnace and ducked his head. I was amazed. Then I had to look at the river mighty quick, because there was a snag in the fairway. Sticks, little sticks, were flying about—thick: they were whizzing before my nose, dropping below me, striking behind me against my pilot-house. All this time the river, the shore, the woods, were very quiet—perfectly quiet. I could only hear the heavy splashing thump of the stern-wheel and the patter of these things. We cleared the snag clumsily. Arrows, by Jove! We were being shot at! I stepped in quickly to close the shutter on the land-side. That fool-helmsman, his hands on the spokes, was lifting his knees high, stamping his feet, champing his mouth, like a reined-in horse. Confound him! And we were staggering within ten feet of the bank. I had to lean right out to swing the heavy shutter, and I saw a face amongst the leaves on the level with my own, looking at me very fierce and steady;

and then suddenly, as though a veil had been removed from my eyes, I made out, deep in the tangled gloom, naked breasts, arms, legs, glaring eyes—the bush was swarming with human limbs in movement, glistening, of bronze color. The twigs shook, swayed, and rustled, the arrows flew out of them, and then the shutter came to. 'Steer her straight,' I said to the helmsman. He held his head rigid, face forward; but his eyes rolled, he kept on lifting and setting down his feet gently, his mouth foamed a little. 'Keep quiet!' I said in a fury. I might just as well have ordered a tree not to sway in the wind. I darted out. Below me there was a great scuffle of feet on the iron deck; confused exclamations; a voice screamed, 'Can you turn back?' I caught sight of a V-shaped ripple on the water ahead. What? Another snag! A fusillade burst out under my feet. The pilgrims had opened with their Winchesters, and were simply squirting lead into that bush. A deuce of a lot of smoke came up and drove slowly forward. I swore at it. Now I couldn't see the ripple or the snag either. I stood in the doorway, peering, and the arrows came in swarms. They might have been poisoned, but they looked as though they wouldn't kill a cat. The bush began to howl. Our wood-cutters raised a war-like whoop; the report of a rifle just at my back deafened me. I glanced over my shoulder, and the pilot-house was yet full of noise and smoke when I made a dash at the wheel. The fool-nigger had dropped everything to throw the shutter open and let off that Martini-Henry. He stood before the wide opening, glaring, and I yelled at him to come back, while I straightened the sudden twist out of that steamboat. There was no room to turn even if I had wanted to, the snag was somewhere very near ahead in that confounded smoke, there was no time to lose, so I just crowded her into the bank— right into the bank, where I knew the water was deep.

"We tore slowly along the overhanging bushes in a whirl of broken twigs and flying leaves. The fusillade below stopped short, as I had foreseen it would when the squirts got empty. I threw my head back to a glinting whizz that traversed the pilot-house, in at one shutter-hole and out at the other. Looking past that mad helmsman, who was shaking the empty rifle and yelling at the shore, I saw vague forms of men running bent double, leaping, gliding, distinct, incomplete, evanescent. Something big appeared in the air before the shutter, the rifle went overboard, and the man stepped back swiftly, looked at me over his shoulder in an extraordinary, profound, familiar manner, and fell upon my feet. The side of his head hit the wheel twice, and the end of what appeared a long cane clattered round and knocked over a little campstool. It looked as though after wrenching that thing from somebody ashore he had lost his balance in the effort. The thin smoke had blown away, we were clear of the snag, and looking ahead I could see that in another hundred yards or so I would be free to sheer off, away from the bank; but my feet felt so very warm and wet that I had to look down. The man had rolled on his back and stared straight up at me; both his hands clutched that cane. It was the shaft of a spear that, either thrown or lunged through the opening, had caught him in the side just below the ribs; the blade had gone in out of sight, after making a frightful gash; my shoes were full; a pool of blood lay very still, gleaming dark-red under the wheel; his eyes shone with an amazing luster. The fusillade burst out again. He looked at me anxiously, gripping the spear like something precious, with an air of being afraid I would try to take it away from him. I had to make an effort to free my eyes from his gaze and attend to steering. With one hand I felt above my head for the line of the steam-whistle, and jerked out screech after screech hurriedly. The tumult of angry and warlike yells was checked instantly, and then from the depths of the woods went out such a tremulous and prolonged wail of mournful fear and utter despair as may be imagined to follow the flight of the last hope from the earth. There was a great commotion in the bush; the shower of arrows stopped, a few dropping shots rang out sharply—then silence, in which the languid beat of the stern-wheel came plainly to my ears. I put the helm hard a-starboard at the moment when the pilgrim in pink pajamas, very hot and agitated, appeared in the doorway. 'The manager sends me—' he began in an official tone, and stopped short. 'Good God!' he said, glaring at the wounded man.

"We two whites stood over him, and his lustrous and inquiring glance enveloped us both. I declare it looked as though he would presently put to us some question in an understandable language; but he died without uttering a sound, without moving a limb, without twitching a muscle. Only in the very last moment, as though in response to some sign we could not see, to some whisper we could not hear, he frowned heavily, and that frown gave to his black death-mask an inconceivably somber, brooding, and menacing expression. The luster of inquiring glance faded swiftly into vacant glassiness. 'Can you steer?' I asked the agent eagerly. He looked very dubious; but I made a grab at his arm, and he understood at once I meant him to steer whether or no. To tell you the truth, I was morbidly anxious to change my shoes and socks. 'He is dead,' murmured the fellow, immensely impressed. 'No doubt about it,' said I tugging like mad at the shoe-laces. 'And by the way, I suppose Mr. Kurtz is dead as well by this time.'

"For the moment that was the dominant thought. There was a sense of extreme disappointment, as though I had found out I had been striving after something altogether without a substance. I couldn't have been more disgusted if I had traveled all this way for the sole purpose of talking with Mr. Kurtz. Talking with. . . . I flung one shoe overboard, and became aware that that was exactly what I had been looking forward to—a talk with Kurtz. I made the strange discovery that I had never imagined him as doing, you know, but as discoursing. I didn't say to myself, 'Now I will never see him,' or 'Now I will never shake him by the hand,' but, 'Now I will never hear him.' The man presented himself as a voice. Not of course that I did not connect him with some sort of action. Hadn't I been told in all the tones of jealousy and admiration that he had collected, bartered, swindled, or stolen more ivory than all the other agents together? That was not the point. The point was in his being a gifted creature, and that of all his gifts the one that stood out preeminently, that carried with it a sense of real presence, was his ability to talk, his words—the gift of expression, the bewildering, the illuminating, the most exalted and the most contemptible, the pulsating stream of light, or the deceitful flow from the heart of an impenetrable darkness.

"The other shoe went flying unto the devil-god of that river. I thought, by Jove! it's all over. We are too late; he has vanished—the gift has vanished, by means of some spear, arrow, or club. I will never hear that chap speak after all—and my sorrow had a startling extravagance of emotion, even such as I had noticed in the howling sorrow of these savages in the bush. I couldn't have felt more lonely desolation somehow, had I been robbed of a belief or had missed my destiny in life. . . . Why do you sigh in this beastly way, somebody? Absurd? Well, absurd. Good Lord! mustn't a man ever—Here, give me some tobacco." . . .

There was a pause of profound stillness, then a match flared, and Marlow's lean face appeared, worn, hollow, with downward folds and drooped eyelids, with an aspect of concentrated attention; and as he took vigorous draws at his pipe, it seemed to retreat and advance out of the night in the regular flicker of the tiny flame. The match went out.

"Absurd!" he cried. "This is the worst of trying to tell. . . . Here you all are, each moored with two good addresses, like a hulk with two anchors, a butcher round one corner, a policeman round another, excellent appetites, and temperature normal—

100

you hear—normal from year's end to year's end. And you say, Absurd! Absurd be—exploded! Absurd! My dear boys, what can you expect from a man who out of sheer nervousness had just flung overboard a pair of new shoes! Now I think of it, it is amazing I did not shed tears. I am, upon the whole, proud of my fortitude. I was cut to the quick at the idea of having lost the inestimable privilege of listening to the gifted Kurtz. Of course I was wrong. The privilege was waiting for me. Oh, yes, I heard more than enough. And I was right, too. A voice. He was very little more than a voice. And I heard—him—it—this voice—other voices—all of them were so little more than voices—and the memory of that time itself lingers around me, impalpable, like a dying vibration of one immense jabber, silly, atrocious, sordid, savage, or simply mean, without any kind of sense. Voices, voices—even the girl herself—now—"

He was silent for a long time.

"I laid the ghost of his gifts at last with a lie," he began, suddenly. "Girl! What? Did I mention a girl? Oh, she is out of it—completely. They—the women I mean—are out of it—should be out of it. We must help them to stay in that beautiful world of their own, lest ours gets worse. Oh, she had to be out of it. You should have heard the disinterred body of Mr. Kurtz saying, 'My Intended.' You would have perceived directly then how completely she was out of it. And the lofty frontal bone of Mr. Kurtz! They say the hair goes on growing sometimes, but this—ah—specimen, was impressively bald. The wilderness had patted him on the head, and, behold, it was like a ball—an ivory ball; it had caressed him, and—lo!—he had withered; it had taken him, loved him, embraced him, got into his veins, consumed his flesh, and sealed his soul to its own by the inconceivable ceremonies of some devilish initiation. He was its spoiled and pampered favorite. Ivory? I should think so. Heaps of it, stacks of it. The old mud shanty was bursting with it. You would think there was not a single tusk left either above or below the ground in the whole country. 'Mostly fossil,' the manager had remarked, disparagingly. It was no more fossil than I am; but they call it fossil when it is dug up. It appears these niggers do bury the tusks sometimes—but evidently they couldn't bury this parcel deep enough to save the gifted Mr. Kurtz from his fate. We filled the steamboat with it, and had to pile a lot on the deck. Thus he could see and enjoy as long as he could see, because the appreciation of this favor had remained with him to the last. You should have heard him say, 'My ivory.' Oh, yes, I heard him. 'My Intended, my ivory, my station, my river, my—' everything belonged to him. It made me hold my breath in expectation of hearing the wilderness burst into a prodigious peal of laughter that would shake the fixed stars in their places. Everything belonged to him—but that was a trifle. The thing was to know what he belonged to, how many powers of darkness claimed him for their own. That was the reflection that made you creepy all over. It was impossible—it was not good for one either—trying to imagine. He had taken a high seat amongst the devils of the land— I mean literally. You can't understand. How could you?—with solid pavement under your feet, surrounded by kind neighbors ready to cheer you or to fall on you, stepping delicately between the butcher and the policeman, in the holy terror of scandal and gallows and lunatic asylums—how can you imagine what particular region of the first ages a man's untrammeled feet may take him into by the way of solitude— utter solitude without a policeman—by the way of silence—utter silence, where no warning voice of a kind neighbor can be heard whispering of public opinion? These little things make all the great difference. When they are gone you must fall back upon your own innate strength, upon your own capacity for faithfulness. Of course you may be too much of a fool to go wrong—too dull even to know you are being assaulted by the powers of darkness. I take it, no fool ever made a bargain for his soul with the devil: the fool is too much of a fool, or the devil too much of a devil—I don't know which. Or you may be such a thunderingly exalted creature as to be altogether deaf and blind to anything but heavenly sights and sounds. Then the earth for you is only a standing place—and whether to be like this is your loss or your gain I won't pretend to say. But most of us are neither one nor the other. The earth for us is a place to live in, where we must put up with sights, with sounds, with smells, too, by Jove!—breathe dead hippo, so to speak and not be contaminated. And there, don't you see? your strength comes in, the faith in your ability for the digging of unostentatious holes to bury the stuff in—your power of devotion, not to yourself, but to an obscure, back-breaking business. And that's difficult enough. Mind, I am not trying to excuse or even explain—I am trying to account to myself for—for—Mr. Kurtz—for the shade of Mr. Kurtz. This initiated wraith from the back of Nowhere honored me with its amazing confidence before it vanished altogether. This was because it could speak English to me. The original Kurtz had been educated partly in England, and—as he was good enough to say himself—his sympathies were in the right place. His mother was half-English, his father was half-French. All Europe contributed to the making of Kurtz; and by and by I learned that, most appropriately, the International Society for the Suppression of Savage Customs had intrusted him with the making of a report, for its future guidance. And he had written it, too. I've seen it. I've read it. It was eloquent, vibrating with eloquence, but too high-strung, I think. Seventeen pages of close writing he had found time for! But this must have been before his—let us say—nerves, went wrong, and caused him to preside at certain midnight dances ending with unspeakable rites, which—as far as I reluctantly gathered from what I heard at various times—were offered up to him—do you understand?—to Mr. Kurtz himself. But it was a beautiful piece of writing. The opening paragraph, however, in the light of later information, strikes me now as ominous. He began with the argument that we whites, from the point of development he had arrived at, 'must necessarily appear to them [savages] in the nature of supernatural beings—we approach them with the might as of a deity,' and so on, and so on. 'By the simple exercise of our will we can exert a power for good practically unbounded,' etc., etc. From that point he soared and took me with him. The peroration was magnificent, though difficult to remember, you know. It gave me the notion of an exotic Immensity ruled by an august Benevolence. It made me tingle with enthusiasm. This was the unbounded power of eloquence—of words— of burning noble words. There were no practical hints to interrupt the magic current of phrases, unless a kind of note at the foot of the last page, scrawled evidently much later, in an unsteady hand, may be regarded as the exposition of a method. It was very simple, and at the end of that moving appeal to every altruistic sentiment it blazed at you, luminous and terrifying, like a flash of lightning in a serene sky: 'Exterminate all the brutes!' The curious part was that he had apparently forgotten all about that valuable postscriptum, because, later on, when he in a sense came to himself, he repeatedly entreated me to take good care of 'my pamphlet' (he called it), as it was sure to have in the future a good influence upon his career. I had full information about all these things, and, besides, as it turned out, I was to have the care of his memory. I've done enough for it to give me the indisputable right to lay it, if I choose, for an everlasting rest in the dust-bin of progress, amongst all the sweepings and, figuratively speaking, all the dead cats of civilization. But then, you see, I can't choose. He won't be forgotten. Whatever he was, he was not common. He had the power to charm or frighten rudimentary souls into an aggravated witch-dance in his honor; he could also fill the small souls of the pilgrims with bitter misgivings: he had one devoted friend at least, and he had conquered one soul in the world that was neither rudimentary nor tainted with self-seeking. No; I can't forget him, though I am not prepared to affirm the fellow was exactly worth the life we lost in getting to him. I missed my late helmsman awfully—I missed him even while his body was still lying in the pilot-house. Perhaps you will think it passing strange this regret for a savage who was no more account than a grain of sand in a black Sahara. Well, don't you see, he had done something, he had steered; for months I had him at my back—a help—an instrument. It was a kind of partnership. He steered for me—I had to look after him, I worried about his deficiencies, and thus a subtle bond had been created, of which I only became aware when it was suddenly broken. And the intimate profundity of that look he gave me when he received his hurt remains to this day in my memory—like a claim of distant kinship affirmed in a supreme moment.

105   "Poor fool! If he had only left that shutter alone. He had no restraint, no restraint— just like Kurtz—a tree swayed by the wind. As soon as I had put on a dry pair of slippers, I dragged him out, after first jerking the spear out of his side, which operation I confess I performed with my eyes shut tight. His heels leaped together over the little door-step; his shoulders were pressed to my breast; I hugged him from behind desperately. Oh! he was heavy, heavy; heavier than any man on earth, I should imagine. Then without more ado I tipped him overboard. The current snatched him as though he had been a wisp of grass, and I saw the body roll over twice before I lost sight of it forever. All the pilgrims and the manager were then congregated on the awning-deck about the pilot-house, chattering at each other like a flock of excited magpies, and there was a scandalized murmur at my heartless promptitude. What they wanted to keep that body hanging about for I can't guess. Embalm it, maybe. But I had also heard another, and a very ominous, murmur on the deck below. My friends the woodcutters were likewise scandalized, and with a better show of reason—though I admit that the reason itself was quite inadmissible. Oh, quite! I had made up my mind that if my late helmsman was to be eaten, the fishes alone should have him. He had been a very second-rate helmsman while alive, but now he was dead he might have become a first-class temptation, and possibly cause some startling trouble. Besides, I was anxious to take the wheel, the man in pink pajamas showing himself a hopeless duffer at the business.

"This I did directly the simple funeral was over. We were going half-speed, keeping right in the middle of the stream, and I listened to the talk about me. They had given up Kurtz, they had given up the station; Kurtz was dead, and the station had been burnt—and so on—and so on. The red-haired pilgrim was beside himself with the thought that at least this poor Kurtz had been properly avenged. 'Say! We must have made a glorious slaughter of them in the bush. Eh? What do you think? Say?' He positively danced, the blood-thirsty little gingery beggar. And he had nearly fainted when he saw the wounded man! I could not help saying, 'You made a glorious lot of smoke, anyhow.' I had seen, from the way the tops of the bushes rustled and flew, that almost all the shots had gone too high. You can't hit anything unless you take aim and fire from the shoulder; but these chaps fired from the hip with their eyes shut. The retreat, I maintained—and I was right—was caused by the screeching of the steam-whistle. Upon this they forgot Kurtz, and began to howl at me with indignant protests.

"The manager stood by the wheel murmuring confidentially about the necessity of getting well away down the river before dark at all events, when I saw in the distance a clearing on the riverside and the outlines of some sort of building. 'What's this?' I asked. He clapped his hands in wonder. 'The station!' he cried. I edged in at once, still going half-speed.

"Through my glasses I saw the slope of a hill interspersed with rare trees and perfectly free from undergrowth. A long decaying building on the summit was half buried in the high grass; the large holes in the peaked roof gaped black from afar; the jungle and the woods made a background. There was no enclosure or fence of any kind; but there had been one apparently, for near the house half-a-dozen slim posts remained in a row, roughly trimmed, and with their upper ends ornamented with round carved balls. The rails, or whatever there had been between, had disappeared. Of course the forest surrounded all that. The riverbank was clear, and on the waterside I saw a white man under a hat like a cart-wheel beckoning persistently with his whole arm. Examining the edge of the forest above and below, I was almost certain I could see movements—human forms gliding here and there. I steamed past prudently, then stopped the engines and let her drift down. The man on the shore began to shout, urging us to land. 'We have been attacked,' screamed the manager. 'I know—I know. It's all right,' yelled back the other, as cheerful as you please. 'Come along. It's all right, I am glad.'

"His aspect reminded me of something I had seen—something funny I had seen somewhere. As I maneuvered to get alongside, I was asking myself, 'What does this fellow look like?' Suddenly I got it. He looked like a harlequin. His clothes had been made of some stuff that was brown holland probably, but it was covered with patches all over, with bright patches, blue, red, and yellow—patches on the back, patches on the front, patches on elbows, on knees; colored binding around his jacket, scarlet edging at the bottom of his trousers; and the sunshine made him look extremely gay and wonderfully neat withal, because you could see how beautifully all this patching had been done. A beardless, boyish face, very fair, no features to speak of, nose peeling, little blue eyes, smiles and frowns chasing each other over that open countenance like sunshine and shadow on a windswept plain. 'Look out, captain!' he cried; 'there's a snag lodged in here last night.' What! Another snag? I confess I swore shamefully. I had nearly holed my cripple, to finish off that charming trip. The harlequin on the bank turned his little pug-nose up to me. 'You English?' he asked, all smiles. 'Are you?' I shouted from the wheel. The smiles vanished, and he shook his head as if sorry for my disappointment. Then he brightened up. 'Never mind!' he cried, encouragingly. 'Are we in time?' I asked. 'He is up there,' he replied with a toss of the head up the hill, and becoming gloomy all of a sudden. His face was like the autumn sky, overcast one moment and bright the next.

"When the manager, escorted by the pilgrims, all of them armed to the teeth, had gone to the house this chap came on board. 'I say, I don't like this. These natives are in the bush,' I said. He assured me earnestly it was all right. 'They are simple people,' he added; 'well, I am glad you came. It took me all my time to keep them off.' 'But you said it was all right,' I cried. 'Oh, they meant no harm,' he said; and as I stared he corrected himself, 'Not exactly.' Then vivaciously, 'My faith, your pilot-house wants a clean-up!' In the next breath he advised me to keep enough steam on the boiler to blow the whistle in case of any trouble. 'One good screech will do more for you than all your rifles. They are simple people,' he repeated. He rattled away at such a rate he quite overwhelmed me. He seemed to be trying to make up for lots of silence, and actually hinted, laughing, that such was the case. 'Don't you talk with Mr. Kurtz?' I said. 'You don't talk with that man—you listen to him,' he exclaimed with severe exaltation. 'But now—' He waved his arm, and in the twinkling of an eye was in the uttermost depths of despondency. In a moment he came up again with a jump, possessed himself of both my hands, and

110

shook them continuously, while he gabbled: 'Brother sailor . . . honor . . . pleasure . . . delight . . . introduce myself . . . Russian . . . son of an archpriest . . . Government of Tambov . . . What? Tobacco! English tobacco; the excellent English tobacco! Now, that's brotherly. Smoke? Where's a sailor that does not smoke?'

"The pipe soothed him, and gradually I made out he had run away from school, had gone to sea in a Russian ship; ran away again; served some time in English ships; was now reconciled with the arch-priest. He made a point of that. 'But when one is young one must see things, gather experience, ideas; enlarge the mind.' 'Here!' I interrupted. 'You can never tell! Here I met Mr. Kurtz,' he said, youthfully solemn and reproachful. I held my tongue after that. It appears he had persuaded a Dutch trading-house on the coast to fit him out with stores and goods, and had started for the interior with a light heart, and no more idea of what would happen to him than a baby. He had been wandering about that river for nearly two years alone, cut off from everybody and everything. 'I am not so young as I look. I am twenty-five,' he said. 'At first old Van Shuyten would tell me to go to the devil,' he narrated with keen enjoyment; 'but I stuck to him, and talked and talked, till at last he got afraid I would talk the hind-leg off his favorite dog, so he gave me some cheap things and a few guns, and told me he hoped he would never see my face again. Good old Dutchman, Van Shuyten. I've sent him one small lot of ivory a year ago, so that he can't call me a little thief when I get back. I hope he got it. And for the rest I don't care. I had some wood stacked for you. That was my old house. Did you see?'

"I gave him Towson's book. He made as though he would kiss me, but restrained himself. 'The only book I had left, and I thought I had lost it,' he said, looking at it ecstatically. 'So many accidents happen to a man going about alone, you know. Canoes get upset sometimes—and sometimes you've got to clear out so quick when the people get angry.' He thumbed the pages. 'You made notes in Russian?' I asked. He nodded. 'I thought they were written in cipher,' I said. He laughed, then became serious. 'I had lots of trouble to keep these people off,' he said. 'Did they want to kill you?' I asked. 'Oh, no!' he cried, and checked himself. 'Why did they attack us?' I pursued. He hesitated, then said shamefacedly, 'They don't want him to go.' 'Don't they?' I said, curiously. He nodded a nod full of mystery and wisdom. 'I tell you,' he cried, 'this man has enlarged my mind.' He opened his arms wide, staring at me with his little blue eyes that were perfectly round."

III

"I looked at him, lost in astonishment. There he was before me, in motley, as though he had absconded from a troupe of mimes, enthusiastic, fabulous. His very existence was improbable, inexplicable, and altogether bewildering. He was an insoluble problem. It was inconceivable how he had existed, how he had succeeded in getting so far, how he had managed to remain—why he did not instantly disappear. 'I went a little farther,' he said, 'then still a little farther—till I had gone so far that I don't know how I'll ever get back. Never mind. Plenty time. I can manage. You take Kurtz away quick—quick—I tell you.' The glamour of youth enveloped his parti-colored rags, his destitution, his loneliness the essential desolation of his futile wanderings. For months—for years—his life hadn't been worth a day's purchase; and there he was gallantly, thoughtlessly alive, to all appearance indestructible solely by the virtue of his few years and of his unreflecting audacity. I was seduced into something like admiration—like envy.

Glamour urged him on, glamour kept him unscathed. He surely wanted nothing from the wilderness but space to breathe in and to push on through. His need was to exist, and to move onwards at the greatest possible risk, and with a maximum of privation. If the absolutely pure, uncalculating, unpractical spirit of adventure had ever ruled a human being, it ruled this be-patched youth. I almost envied him the possession of this modest and clear flame. It seemed to have consumed all thought of self so complete-ly, that even while he was talking to you, you forgot that it was he—the man before your eyes—who had gone through these things. I did not envy him his devotion to Kurtz, though. He had not meditated over it. It came to him and he accepted it with a sort of eager fatalism. I must say that to me it appeared about the most dangerous thing in every way he had come upon so far.

"They had come together unavoidably, like two ships becalmed near each other, and lay rubbing sides at last. I suppose Kurtz wanted an audience, because on a cer-tain occasion, when encamped in the forest, they had talked all night, or more proba-bly Kurtz had talked. 'We talked of everything,' he said, quite transported at the recollection. 'I forgot there was such a thing as sleep. The night did not seem to last an hour. Everything! Everything! . . . Of love, too.' 'Ah, he talked to you of love!' I said, much amused. 'It isn't what you think,' he cried, almost passionately. 'It was in gen-eral. He made me see things—things.'

"He threw his arms up. We were on deck at the time, and the head-man of my wood-cutters, lounging near by, turned upon him his heavy and glittering eyes. I looked around, and I don't know why, but I assure you that never, never before, did this land, this river, this jungle, the very arch of this blazing sky, appear to me so hope-less and so dark, so impenetrable to human thought, so pitiless to human weakness. 'And, ever since, you have been with him, of course?' I said. 115

"On the contrary. It appears their intercourse had been very much broken by vari-ous causes. He had, as he informed me proudly, managed to nurse Kurtz through two illnesses (he alluded to it as you would to some risky feat), but as a rule Kurtz wan-dered alone far in the depths of the forest. 'Very often coming to this station, I had to wait days and days before he would turn up,' he said. 'Ah, it was worth waiting for!— sometimes.' 'What was he doing? exploring or what?' I asked. 'Oh, yes, of course'; he had discovered lots of villages, a lake, too—he did not know exactly in what direc-tion; it was dangerous to inquire too much—but mostly his expeditions had been for ivory. 'But he had no goods to trade with by that time,' I objected. 'There's a good lot of cartridges left even yet,' he answered, looking away. 'To speak plainly, he raided the country,' I said. He nodded. 'Not alone, surely!' He muttered something about the vil-lages round that lake. 'Kurtz got the tribe to follow him, did he?' I suggested. He fid-geted a little. 'They adored him,' he said. The tone of these words was so extraordinary that I looked at him searchingly. It was curious to see his mingled eagerness and re-luctance to speak of Kurtz. The man filled his life, occupied his thoughts, swayed his emotions. 'What can you expect?' he burst out; 'he came to them with thunder and lightning, you know—and they had never seen anything like it—and very terrible. He could be very terrible. You can't judge Mr. Kurtz as you would an ordinary man. No, no, no! Now—just to give you an idea—I don't mind telling you, he wanted to shoot me, too, one day—but I don't judge him.' 'Shoot you!' I cried. 'What for?' 'Well, I had a small lot of ivory the chief of that village near my house gave me. You see I used to shoot game for them. Well, he wanted it, and wouldn't hear reason. He declared he would shoot me unless I gave him the ivory and then cleared out of the country, be-cause he could do so, and had a fancy for it, and there was nothing on earth to prevent him killing whom he jolly well pleased. And it was true, too. I gave him the ivory. What did I care! But I didn't clear out. No, no. I couldn't leave him. I had to be careful, of course, till we got friendly again for a time. He had his second illness then. Afterwards I had to keep out of the way; but I didn't mind. He was living for the most part in those villages on the lake. When he came down to the river, sometimes he would take to me, and sometimes it was better for me to be careful. This man suffered too much. He hated all this, and somehow he couldn't get away. When I had a chance I begged him to try and leave while there was time; I offered to go back with him. And he would say yes, and then he would remain; go off on another ivory hunt; disappear for weeks; forget himself amongst these people—forget himself—you know.' 'Why! he's mad,' I said. He protested indignantly. Mr. Kurtz couldn't be mad. If I had heard him talk, only two days ago, I wouldn't dare hint at such a thing. . . . I had taken up my binoculars while we talked, and was looking at the shore, sweeping the limit of the forest at each side and at the back of the house. The consciousness of there being people in that bush, so silent, so quiet—as silent and quiet as the ruined house on the hill—made me uneasy. There was no sign on the face of nature of this amazing tale that was not so much told as suggested to me in desolate exclamations, completed by shrugs, in interrupted phrases, in hints ending in deep sighs. The woods were unmoved, like a mask—heavy, like the closed door of a prison—they looked with their air of hidden knowledge, of patient expectation, of unapproachable silence. The Russian was explaining to me that it was only lately that Mr. Kurtz had come down to the river, bringing along with him all the fighting men of that lake tribe. He had been absent for several months—getting himself adored, I suppose—and had come down unexpectedly, with the intention to all appearance of making a raid either across the river or down stream. Evidently the appetite for more ivory had got the better of the—what shall I say?—less material aspirations. However he had got much worse suddenly. 'I heard he was lying helpless, and so I came up—took my chance,' said the Russian. 'Oh, he is bad, very bad.' I directed my glass to the house. There were no signs of life, but there was the ruined roof, the long mud wall peeping above the grass, with three little square window-holes, no two of the same size; all this brought within reach of my hand, as it were. And then I made a brusque movement, and one of the remaining posts of that vanished fence leaped up in the field of my glass. You remember I told you I had been struck at the distance by certain attempts at ornamentation, rather remarkable in the ruinous aspect of the place. Now I had suddenly a nearer view, and its first result was to make me throw my head back as if before a blow. Then I went carefully from post to post with my glass, and I saw my mistake. These round knobs were not ornamental but symbolic; they were expressive and puzzling, striking and disturbing—food for thought and also for vultures if there had been any looking down from the sky; but at all events for such ants as were industrious enough to ascend the pole. They would have been even more impressive, those heads on the stakes, if their faces had not been turned to the house. Only one, the first I had made out, was facing my way. I was not so shocked as you may think. The start back I had given was really nothing but a movement of surprise. I had expected to see a knob of wood there, you know. I returned deliberately to the first I had seen—and there it was, black, dried, sunken, with closed eyelids—a head that seemed to sleep at the top of that pole, and with the shrunken dry lips showing a narrow white line of the teeth, was smiling, too, smiling continuously at some endless and jocose dream of that eternal slumber.

"I am not disclosing any trade secrets. In fact, the manager said afterwards that Mr. Kurtz's methods had ruined the district. I have no opinion on that point, but I want you clearly to understand that there was nothing exactly profitable in these heads being there. They only showed that Mr. Kurtz lacked restraint in the gratification of his various lusts, that there was something wanting in him—some small matter which, when the pressing need arose, could not be found under his magnificent eloquence. Whether he knew of this deficiency himself I can't say. I think the knowledge came to him at last—only at the very last. But the wilderness had found him out early, and had taken on him a terrible vengeance for the fantastic invasion. I think it had whispered to him things about himself which he did not know, things of which he had no conception till he took counsel with this great solitude—and the whisper had proved irresistibly fascinating. It echoed loudly within him because he was hollow at the core. . . . I put down the glass, and the head that had appeared near enough to be spoken to seemed at once to have leaped away from me into inaccessible distance.

"The admirer of Mr. Kurtz was a bit crestfallen. In a hurried indistinct voice he began to assure me he had not dared to take these—say, symbols—down. He was not afraid of the natives; they would not stir till Mr. Kurtz gave the word. His ascendancy was extraordinary. The camps of these people surrounded the place, and the chiefs came every day to see him. They would crawl. . . . 'I don't want to know anything of the ceremonies used when approaching Mr. Kurtz,' I shouted. Curious, this feeling that came over me that such details would be more intolerable than those heads drying on the stakes under Mr. Kurtz's windows. After all, that was only a savage sight, while I seemed at one bound to have been transported into some lightless region of subtle horrors, where pure, uncomplicated savagery was a positive relief, being something that had a right to exist—obviously—in the sunshine. The young man looked at me with surprise. I suppose it did not occur to him that Mr. Kurtz was no idol of mine. He forgot I hadn't heard any of these splendid monologues on, what was it? on love, justice, conduct of life—or what not. If it had come to crawling before Mr. Kurtz, he crawled as much as the veriest savage of them all. I had no idea of the conditions, he said: these heads were the heads of rebels. I shocked him excessively by laughing. Rebels! What would be the next definition I was to hear? There had been enemies, criminals, workers—and these were rebels. Those rebellious heads looked very subdued to me on their sticks. 'You don't know how such a life tries a man like Kurtz,' cried Kurtz's last disciple. 'Well, and you?' I said. 'I! I! I am a simple man. I have no great thoughts. I want nothing from anybody. How can you compare me to . . .?' His feelings were too much for speech, and suddenly he broke down. 'I don't understand,' he groaned. 'I've been doing my best to keep him alive, and that's enough. I had no hand in all this. I have no abilities. There hasn't been a drop of medicine or a mouthful of invalid food for months here. He was shamefully abandoned. A man like this, with such ideas. Shamefully! Shamefully! I—I—haven't slept for the last ten nights. . . .

"His voice lost itself in the calm of the evening. The long shadows of the forest had slipped downhill while we talked, had gone far beyond the ruined hovel, beyond the symbolic row of stakes. All this was in the gloom, while we down there were yet in the sunshine, and the stretch of the river abreast of the clearing glittered in a still and dazzling splendor, with a murky and overshadowed bend above and below. Not a living soul was seen on the shore. The bushes did not rustle.

"Suddenly round the corner of the house a group of men appeared, as though they had come up from the ground. They waded waist-deep in the grass, in a compact body, bearing an improvised stretcher in their midst. Instantly, in the emptiness of the landscape, a cry arose while shrillness pierced the still air like a sharp arrow flying straight to the very heart of the land; and, as if by enchantment, streams of human beings—of naked human beings—with spears in their hands, with bows, with shields, with wild glances and savage movements, were poured into the clearing by the dark-faced and pensive forest. The bushes shook, the grass swayed for a time, and then everything stood still in attentive immobility.

"'Now, if he does not say the right thing to them we are all done for,' said the Russian at my elbow. The knot of men with the stretcher had stopped, too, halfway to the steamer, as if petrified. I saw the man on the stretcher sit up, lank and with an up-lifted arm, above the shoulders of the bearers. 'Let us hope that the man who can talk so well of love in general will find some particular reason to spare us this time,' I said. I resented bitterly the absurd danger of our situation, as if to be at the mercy of that atrocious phantom had been a dishonoring necessity. I could not hear a sound, but through my glasses I saw the thin arm extended commandingly, the lower jaw moving, the eyes of that apparition shining darkly far in its bony head that nodded with grotesque jerks. Kurtz—Kurtz—that means short in German—don't it? Well, the name was as true as everything else in his life—and death. He looked at least seven feet long. His covering had fallen off, and his body emerged from it pitiful and appalling as from a winding-sheet. I could see the cage of his ribs all astir, the bones of his arm waving. It was as though an animated image of death carved out of old ivory had been shaking its hand with menaces at a motionless crowd of men made of dark and glittering bronze. I saw him open his mouth wide—it gave him a weirdly voracious aspect, as though he had wanted to swallow all the air, all the earth, all the men before him. A deep voice reached me faintly. He must have been shouting. He fell back suddenly. The stretcher shook as the bearers staggered forward again, and almost at the same time I noticed that the crowd of savages was vanishing without any perceptible movement of retreat, as if the forest that had ejected these beings so suddenly had drawn them in again as the breath is drawn in a long aspiration.

"Some of the pilgrims behind the stretcher carried his arms—two shotguns, a heavy rifle, and a light revolver-carbine—the thunderbolts of that pitiful Jupiter. The manager bent over him murmuring as he walked beside his head. They laid him down in one of the little cabins—just a room for a bedplace and a campstool or two, you know. We had brought his belated correspondence, and a lot of torn envelopes and open letters littered his bed. His hand roamed feebly amongst these papers. I was struck by the fire in his eyes and the composed languor of his expression. It was not so much the exhaustion of disease. He did not seem in pain. This shadow looked satiated and calm, as though for the moment it had had its fill of all the emotions.

"He rustled one of the letters, and looking straight in my face said, 'I am glad.' Somebody had been writing to him about me. These special recommendations were turning up again. The volume of tone he emitted without effort, almost without the trouble of moving his lips, amazed me. A voice! a voice! It was grave, profound, vibrating, while the man did not seem capable of a whisper. However, he had enough strength in him—factitious no doubt—to very nearly make an end of us, as you shall hear directly.

"The manager appeared silently in the doorway; I stepped out at once and he drew the curtain after me. The Russian, eyed curiously by the pilgrims, was staring at the shore. I followed the direction of his glance.

125   "Dark human shapes could be made out in the distance, flitting indistinctly against the gloomy border of the forest, and near the river two bronze figures, leaning on tall spears, stood in the sunlight under fantastic headdresses of spotted skins, war-like and still in statuesque repose. And from right to left along the lighted shore moved a wild and gorgeous apparition of a woman.

"She walked with measured steps, draped in striped and fringed cloths, treading the earth proudly, with a slight jingle and flash of barbarous ornaments. She carried her head high; her hair was done in the shape of a helmet; she had brass leggings to the knee, brass wire gauntlets to the elbow, a crimson spot on her tawny cheek, innumerable necklaces of glass beads on her neck; bizarre things, charms, gifts of witchmen, that hung about her, glittered and trembled at every step. She must have had the value of several elephant tusks upon her. She was savage and superb, wild-eyed and magnificent; there was something ominous and stately in her deliberate progress. And in the hush that had fallen suddenly upon the whole sorrowful land, the immense wilderness, the colossal body of the fecund and mysterious life seemed to look at her, pensive, as though it had been looking at the image of its own tenebrous and passionate soul.

"She came abreast of the steamer, stood still, and faced us. Her long shadow fell to the water's edge. Her face had a tragic and fierce aspect of wild sorrow and of dumb pain mingled with the fear of some struggling, half-shaped resolve. She stood looking at us without a stir, and like the wilderness itself, with an air of brooding over an inscrutable purpose. A whole minute passed, and then she made a step forward. There was a low jingle, a glint of yellow metal, a sway of fringed draperies, and she stopped as if her heart had failed her. The young fellow by my side growled. The pilgrims murmured at my back. She looked at us all as if her life had depended upon the unswerving steadiness of her glance. Suddenly she opened her bared arms and threw them up rigid above her head, as though in an uncontrollable desire to touch the sky, and at the same time the swift shadows darted out on the earth, swept around on the river, gathering the steamer into a shadowy embrace. A formidable silence hung over the scene.

"She turned away slowly, walked on, followed the bank, and passed into the bushes to the left. Once only her eyes gleamed back at us in the dusk of the thickets before she disappeared.

"'If she had offered to come aboard I really think I would have tried to shoot her,' said the man of patches, nervously. 'I have been risking my life every day for the last fortnight to keep her out of the house. She got in one day and kicked up a row about those miserable rags I picked up in the storeroom to mend my clothes with. I wasn't decent. At least it must have been that, for she talked like a fury to Kurtz for an hour, pointing at me now and then. I don't understand the dialect of this tribe. Luckily for me, I fancy Kurtz felt too ill that day to care, or there would have been mischief. I don't understand. . . . No—it's too much for me. Ah, well, it's all over now.'

"At this moment I heard Kurtz's deep voice behind the curtain: 'Save me!—   130
save the ivory, you mean. Don't tell me. Save *me!* Why, I've had to save you. You are interrupting my plans now. Sick! Sick! Not so sick as you would like to believe. Never mind. I'll carry my ideas out yet—I will return. I'll show you what can be done. You with your little peddling notions—you are interfering with me. I will return. I . . .'

"The manager came out. He did me the honor to take me under the arm and lead me aside. 'He is very low, very low,' he said. He considered it necessary to sigh, but neglected to be consistently sorrowful. 'We have done all we could for him—haven't we? But there is no disguising the fact, Mr. Kurtz has done more harm than good to the Company. He did not see the time was not ripe for vigorous action. Cautiously, cautiously—that's my principle. We must be cautious yet. The district is closed to us for a time. Deplorable! Upon the whole, the trade will suffer. I don't deny there is a remarkable quantity of ivory—mostly fossil. We must save it, at all events—but look how precarious the position is—and why? Because the method is unsound.' 'Do you,' said I, looking at the shore, 'call it "unsound method"?' 'Without doubt,' he exclaimed, hotly. 'Don't you?' . . . 'No method at all,' I murmured after a while. 'Exactly,' he exulted. 'I anticipated this. Shows a complete want of judgment. It is my duty to point it out in the proper quarter.' 'Oh,' said I, 'that fellow—what's his name?—the brick-maker, will make a readable report for you. He appeared confounded for a moment. It seemed to me I had never breathed an atmosphere so vile, and I turned mentally to Kurtz for relief—positively for relief. 'Nevertheless I think Mr. Kurtz is a remarkable man,' I said with emphasis. He started, dropped on me a cold heavy glance, said very quietly, 'he *was*,' and turned his back on me. My hour of favor was over; I found myself lumped along with Kurtz as a partisan of methods for which the time was not ripe: I was unsound! Ah! but it was something to have at least a choice of nightmares.

"I had turned to the wilderness really, not to Mr. Kurtz, who, I was ready to admit, was as good as buried. And for a moment it seemed to me as if I also were buried in a vast grave full of unspeakable secrets. I felt an intolerable weight oppressing my breast, the smell of the damp earth, the unseen presence of victorious corruption, the darkness of an impenetrable night. . . . The Russian tapped me on the shoulder. I heard him mumbling and stammering something about 'brother seaman—couldn't conceal—knowledge of matters that would affect Mr. Kurtz's reputation.' I waited. For him evidently Mr. Kurtz was not in his grave; I suspect that for him Mr. Kurtz was one of the immortals. 'Well,' said I at last, 'speak out. As it happens, I am Mr. Kurtz's friend—in a way.'

"He stated with a good deal of formality that had we not been 'of the same profession,' he would have kept the matter to himself without regard to consequences. 'He suspected there was an active ill will towards him on the part of these white men that—' 'You are right,' I said, remembering a certain conversation I had overheard. 'The manager thinks you ought to be hanged.' He showed a concern at this intelligence which amused me at first. 'I had better get out of the way quietly,' he said, earnestly. 'I can do no more for Kurtz now, and they would soon find some excuse. What's to stop them? There's a military post three hundred miles from here.' 'Well, upon my word,' said I, 'perhaps you had better go if you have any friends amongst the savages near by.' 'Plenty,' he said. 'They are simple people—and I want nothing, you know.' He stood biting his lip, then: 'I don't want any harm to happen to these whites here, but of course I was thinking of Mr. Kurtz's reputation—but you are a brother seaman and—' 'All right,' said I, after a time. 'Mr. Kurtz's reputation is safe with me.' I did not know how truly I spoke.

"He informed me, lowering his voice, that it was Kurtz who had ordered the attack to be made on the steamer. 'He hated sometimes the idea of being taken away—and then again. . . . But I don't understand these matters. I am a simple man. He thought it would scare you away—that you would give it up, thinking him dead. I could not stop him. Oh, I had an awful time of it this last month.' 'Very well,' I said. 'He is all right now.' 'Ye-e-es,' he muttered, not very convinced apparently. 'Thanks,' said I; 'I shall keep my eyes open.' 'But quiet—eh?' he urged, anxiously. 'It would be awful for his reputation if anybody here—' I promised a complete discretion with great gravity. 'I have a canoe and three black fellows waiting not very far. I am off. Could you give me a few Martini-Henry cartridges?' I could, and did, with proper secrecy. He helped himself, with a wink at me, to a handful of my tobacco. 'Between sailors—you know—good English tobacco.' At the door of the pilot-house he turned round—'I say, haven't you a pair of shoes you could spare?' He raised one leg. 'Look.' The soles were tied with knotted strings sandal-wise under his bare feet. I rooted out an old pair, at which he looked with admiration before tucking them under his left arm. One of his pockets (bright red) was bulging with cartridges, from the other (dark blue) peeped 'Towson's Inquiry,' etc., etc. He seemed to think himself excellently well equipped for a renewed encounter with the wilderness. 'Ah! I'll never, never meet such a man again. You ought to have heard him recite poetry—his own, too, it was, he told me. Poetry!' He rolled his eyes at the recollection of these delights. 'Oh, he enlarged my mind!' 'Good-by,' said I. He shook hands and vanished in the night. Sometimes I ask myself whether I had ever really seen him—whether it was possible to meet such a phenomenon! . . .

"When I woke up shortly after midnight his warning came to my mind with its hint of danger that seemed, in the starred darkness, real enough to make me get up for the purpose of having a look around. On the hill a big fire burned, illuminating fitfully a crooked corner of the station-house. One of the agents with a picket of a few of our blacks, armed for the purpose, was keeping guard over the ivory; but deep within the forest, red gleams that wavered, that seemed to sink and rise from the ground amongst confused columnar shapes of intense blackness, showed the exact position of the camp where Mr. Kurtz's adorers were keeping their uneasy vigil. The monotonous beating of a big drum filled the air with muffled shocks and a lingering vibration. A steady droning sound of many men chanting each to himself some weird incantation came out from the black, flat wall of the wood as the humming of bees comes out of a hive, and had a strange narcotic effect upon my half-awake senses. I believe I dozed off leaning over the rail, till an abrupt burst of yells, an overwhelming outbreak of a pent-up and mysterious frenzy, woke me up in a bewildered wonder. It was cut short all at once, and the low droning went on with an effect of audible and soothing silence. I glanced casually into the little cabin. A light was burning within, but Mr. Kurtz was not there.

"I think I would have raised an outcry if I had believed my eyes. But I didn't believe them at first—the thing seemed so impossible. The fact is I was completely unnerved by a sheer blank fright, pure abstract terror, unconnected with any distinct shape of physical danger. What made this emotion so overpowering was—how shall I define it?—the moral shock I received, as if something altogether monstrous, intolerable to thought and odious to the soul, had been thrust upon me unexpectedly. This lasted of course the merest fraction of a second, and then the usual sense of commonplace, deadly danger, the possibility of a sudden onslaught and massacre, or something of the kind, which I saw impending, was positively welcome and composing. It pacified me, in fact, so much, that I did not raise an alarm.

"There was an agent buttoned up inside an ulster and sleeping on a chair on deck within three feet of me. The yells had not awakened him; he snored very slightly; I left him to his slumbers and leaped ashore. I did not betray Mr. Kurtz—it was ordered I should never betray him—it was written I should be loyal to the nightmare of my choice. I was anxious to deal with this shadow by myself alone—and to this day I don't know why I was so jealous of sharing with anyone the peculiar blackness of that experience.

"As soon as I got on the bank I saw a trail—a broad trail through the grass. I remember the exultation with which I said to myself, 'He can't walk—he is crawling on all-fours—I've got him.' The grass was wet with dew. I strode rapidly with clenched fists. I fancy I had some vague notion of falling upon him and giving him a drubbing. I don't know. I had some imbecile thoughts. The knitting old woman with the cat obtruded herself upon my memory as a most improper person to be sitting at the other end of such an affair. I saw a row of pilgrims squirting lead in the air out of Winchesters held to the hip. I thought I would never get back to the steamer, and imagined myself living alone and unarmed in the woods to an advanced age. Such silly things—you know. And I remember I confounded the beat of the drum with the beating of my heart, and was pleased at its calm regularity.

"I kept to the track though—then stopped to listen. The night was very clear; a dark blue space, sparkling with dew and starlight, in which black things stood very still. I thought I could see a kind of motion ahead of me. I was strangely cocksure of everything that night. I actually left the track and ran in a wide semicircle (I verily believe chuckling to myself) so as to get in front of that stir, of that motion I had seen—if indeed I had seen anything. I was circumventing Kurtz as though it had been a boyish game.

140   "I came upon him, and, if he had not heard me coming, I would have fallen over him, too, but he got up in time. He rose, unsteady, long, pale, indistinct, like a vapor exhaled by the earth, and swayed slightly, misty and silent before me; while at my back the fires loomed between the trees, and the murmur of many voices issued from the forest. I had cut him off cleverly; but when actually confronting him I seemed to come to my senses, I saw the danger in its right proportion. It was by no means over yet. Suppose he began to shout? Though he could hardly stand, there was still plenty of vigor in his voice. 'Go away—hide yourself,' he said, in that profound tone. It was very awful. I glanced back. We were within thirty yards from the nearest fire. A black figure stood up, strode on long black legs, waving long black arms, across the glow. It had horns—antelope horns, I think—on its head. Some sorcerer, some witchman, no doubt: it looked fiend-like enough. 'Do you know what you are doing?' I whispered. 'Perfectly,' he answered, raising his voice for that single word: it sounded to me far off and yet loud, like a hail through a speaking-trumpet. If he makes a row we are lost, I thought to myself. This clearly was not a case for fisticuffs, even apart from the very natural aversion I had to beat that Shadow—this wandering and tormented thing. 'You will be lost,' I said—'utterly lost.' One gets sometimes such a flash of inspiration, you know. I did say the right thing, though indeed he could not have been more irretrievably lost than he was at this very moment, when the foundations of our intimacy were being laid—to endure—to endure—even to the end—even beyond.

"'I had immense plans,' he muttered irresolutely. 'Yes,' said I; 'but if you try to shout I'll smash your head with—' There was not a stick or a stone near. 'I will throttle you for good,' I corrected myself. 'I was on the threshold of great things,' he pleaded, in a voice of longing, with a wistfulness of tone that made my blood run cold. 'And now for this stupid scoundrel—' 'Your success in Europe is assured in any case,' I affirmed, steadily. I did not want to have the throttling of him, you understand—and indeed it would have been very little use for any practical purpose. I tried to break the spell—the heavy, mute spell of the wilderness—that seemed to draw him to its pitiless breast by the awakening of forgotten and brutal instincts, by the memory of gratified and monstrous passions. This alone, I was convinced, had driven him out to the edge of the forest, to the bush, towards the gleam of fires, the throb of drums, the drone of weird incantations; this alone had beguiled his unlawful soul beyond the bounds of permitted aspirations. And, don't you see, the terror of the position was not in being knocked on the head—though I had a very lively sense of that danger, too— but in this, that I had to deal with a being to whom I could not appeal in the name of anything high or low. I had, even like the niggers, to invoke him—himself—his own exalted and incredible degradation. There was nothing either above or below him, and I knew it. He had kicked himself loose of the earth. Confound the man! he had kicked the very earth to pieces. He was alone, and I before him did not know whether I stood on the ground or floated in the air. I've been telling you what we said—repeating the phrases we pronounced—but what's the good? They were common everyday words—the familiar, vague sounds exchanged on every waking day of life. But what of that? They had behind them, to my mind, the terrific suggestiveness of words heard in dreams, of phrases spoken in nightmares. Soul! If anybody had ever struggled with a soul, I am the man. And I wasn't arguing with a lunatic either. Believe me or not, his intelligence was perfectly clear—concentrated, it is true, upon himself with horrible intensity, yet clear; and therein was my only chance—barring, of course, the killing him there and then, which wasn't so good, on account of unavoidable noise. But his soul was mad. Being alone in the wilderness, it had looked within itself, and, by heavens! I tell you, it had gone mad. I had—for my sins, I suppose—to go through the ordeal of looking into it myself. No eloquence could have been so withering to one's belief in mankind as his final burst of sincerity. He struggled with himself, too. I saw it—I heard it. I saw the inconceivable mystery of a soul that knew no restraint, no faith, and no fear, yet struggling blindly with itself. I kept my head pretty well; but when I had him at last stretched on the couch, I wiped my forehead, while my legs shook under me as though I had carried half a ton on my back down that hill. And yet I had only supported him, his bony arm clasped round my neck—and he was not much heavier than a child.

"When next day we left at noon, the crowd, of whose presence behind the curtain of trees I had been acutely conscious all the time, flowed out of the woods again, filled the clearing, covered the slope with a mass of naked, breathing, quivering, bronze bodies. I steamed up a bit, then swung downstream, and two thousand eyes followed the evolutions of the splashing, thumping, fierce river-demon beating the water with its terrible tail and breathing black smoke into the air. In front of the first rank, along the river, three men, plastered with bright red earth from head to foot, strutted to and fro restlessly. When we came abreast again, they faced the river, stamped their feet, nodded their horned heads, swayed their scarlet bodies; they shook towards the fierce river-demon a bunch of black feathers, a mangy skin with a pendant tail—something that looked like a dried gourd; they shouted periodically together strings of amazing words that resembled no sounds of human language; and the deep murmurs of the crowd, interrupted suddenly, were like the responses of some satanic litany.

"We had carried Kurtz into the pilot-house: there was more air there. Lying on the couch, he stared through the open shutter. There was an eddy in the mass of human bodies, and the woman with helmeted head and tawny cheeks rushed out to the very brink of the stream. She put out her hands, shouted something, and all that wild mob took up the shout in a roaring chorus of articulated, rapid, breathless utterance.

"'Do you understand this?' I asked.

"He kept on looking out past me with fiery, longing eyes, with a mingled expression of wistfulness and hate. He made no answer, but I saw a smile, a smile of indefinable meaning, appear on his colorless lips that a moment after twitched convulsively. 'Do I not?' he said slowly, gasping, as if the words had been torn out of him by a supernatural power.

"I pulled the string of the whistle, and I did this because I saw the pilgrims on deck getting out their rifles with an air of anticipating a jolly lark. At the sudden screech there was a movement of abject terror through that wedged mass of bodies. 'Don't! don't you frighten them away,' cried someone on deck disconsolately. I pulled the string time after time. They broke and ran, they leaped, they crouched, they swerved, they dodged the flying terror of the sound. The three red chaps had fallen flat, face down on the shore, as though they had been shot dead. Only the barbarous and superb woman did not so much as flinch, and stretched tragically her bare arms after us over the somber and glittering river.

"And then that imbecile crowd down on the deck started their little fun, and I could see nothing more for smoke.

"The brown current ran swiftly out of the heart of darkness, bearing us down towards the sea with twice the speed of our upward progress; and Kurtz's life was running swiftly, too, ebbing out of his heart into the sea of inexorable time. The manager was very placid, he had no vital anxieties now, he took us both in with a comprehensive and satisfied glance: the 'affair' had come off as well as could be wished. I saw the time approaching when I would be left alone of the party of 'unsound method.' The pilgrims looked upon me with disfavor. I was, so to speak, numbered with the dead. It is strange how I accepted this unforeseen partnership, this choice of nightmares forced upon me in the tenebrous land invaded by these mean and greedy phantoms.

"Kurtz discoursed. A voice! a voice! It rang deep to the very last. It survived his strength to hide in the magnificent folds of eloquence the barren darkness of his heart. Oh, he struggled! he struggled! The wastes of his weary brain were haunted by shadowy images now—images of wealth and fame revolving obsequiously round his unextinguishable gift of noble and lofty expression. My Intended, my station, my career, my ideas—these were the objects for the occasional utterances of elevated sentiments. The shade of the original Kurtz frequented the bedside of the hollow sham, whose fate it was to be buried presently in the mold of primeval earth. But both the diabolic love and the unearthly hate of the mysteries it had penetrated fought for the possession of that soul satiated with primitive emotions, avid of lying fame, of sham distinction, of all the appearances of success and power.

150 "Sometimes he was contemptibly childish. He desired to have kings meet him at railway stations on his return from some ghastly Nowhere, where he intended to accomplish great things. 'You show them you have in you something that is really profitable, and then there will be no limits to the recognition of your ability,' he would say. 'Of course you must take care of the motives—right motives—always.' The long reaches that were like one and the same reach, monotonous bends that were exactly alike, slipped past the steamer with their multitude of secular trees looking patiently after this grimy fragment of another world, the forerunner of change, of conquest, of trade, of massacres, of blessings. I looked ahead—piloting. 'Close the shutter,' said Kurtz suddenly one day; 'I can't bear to look at this.' I did so. There was a silence. 'Oh, but I will wring your heart yet!' he cried at the invisible wilderness.

"We broke down—as I had expected—and had to lie up for repairs at the head of an island. This delay was the first thing that shook Kurtz's confidence. One morning he gave me a packet of papers and a photograph—the lot tied together with a shoestring. 'Keep this for me,' he said, 'This noxious fool' (meaning the manager) 'is capable of prying into my boxes when I am not looking.' In the afternoon I saw him. He was lying on his back with closed eyes, and I withdrew quietly, but I heard him mutter, 'Live rightly, die, die. . . .' I listened. There was nothing more. Was he rehearsing some speech in his sleep, or was it a fragment of a phrase from some newspaper article? He had been writing for the papers and meant to do so again, 'for the furthering of my ideas. It's a duty.'

"His was an impenetrable darkness. I looked at him as you peer down at a man who is lying at the bottom of a precipice where the sun never shines. But I had not much time to give him, because I was helping the engine-driver to take to pieces the leaky cylinders, to straighten a bent connecting-rod, and in other such matters. I lived in an infernal mess of rust, filings, nuts, bolts, spanners, hammers, ratchet-drills—things I abominate, because I don't get on with them. I tended the little forge we fortunately had aboard; I toiled wearily in a wretched scrap-heap—unless I had the shakes too bad to stand.

"One evening coming in with a candle I was startled to hear him say a little tremulously, 'I am lying here in the dark waiting for death.' The light was within a foot of his eyes. I forced myself to murmur, 'Oh, nonsense!' and stood over him as if transfixed.

"Anything approaching the change that came over his features I have never seen before, and hope never to see again. Oh, I wasn't touched. I was fascinated. It was as though a veil had been rent. I saw on that ivory face the expression of somber pride, of ruthless power, of craven terror—of an intense and hopeless despair. Did he live his life again in every detail of desire, temptation, and surrender during that supreme moment of complete knowledge? He cried in a whisper at some image, at some vision—he cried out twice, a cry that was no more than a breath—

"'The horror! The horror!'   155

"I blew the candle out and left the cabin. The pilgrims were dining in the mess-room, and I took my place opposite the manager, who lifted his eyes to give me a questioning glance, which I successfully ignored. He leaned back, serene, with that peculiar smile of his sealing the unexpressed depths of his meanness. A continuous shower of small flies streamed upon the lamp, upon the cloth, upon our hands and faces. Suddenly the manager's boy put his insolent black head in the doorway, and said in a tone of scathing contempt—

"'Mistah Kurtz—he dead.'

"All the pilgrims rushed out to see. I remained, and went on with my dinner. I believe I was considered brutally callous. However, I did not eat much. There was a lamp in there—light, don't you know—and outside it was so beastly, beastly dark. I went no more near the remarkable man who had pronounced a judgment upon the adventures of his soul on this earth. The voice was gone. What else had been there? But I am of course aware that next day the pilgrims buried something in a muddy hole.

"And then they very nearly buried me.

"However, as you see, I did not go to join Kurtz there and then. I did not. I remained   160
to dream the nightmare out to the end, and to show my loyalty to Kurtz once more. Destiny. My destiny! Droll thing life is—that mysterious arrangement of merciless logic for a futile purpose. The most you can hope from it is some knowledge of yourself—that comes too late—a crop of unextinguishable regrets. I have wrestled with death. It is the most unexciting contest you can imagine. It takes place in an impalpable grayness, with nothing underfoot, with nothing around, without spectators, without clamor, without glory, without the great desire of victory, without the great fear of defeat, in a sickly atmosphere of tepid skepticism, without much belief in your own right, and still less in that of your adversary. If such is the form of ultimate wisdom, then life is a greater riddle than some of us think it to be. I was within a hair's breadth of the last opportunity for pronouncement, and I found with humiliation that probably I would have nothing to say. This is the reason why I affirm that Kurtz was a remarkable man. He had something to say. He said it. Since I had peeped over the edge myself, I understand better the meaning of his stare, that could not see the flame of the candle, but was wide enough to embrace the whole universe, piercing enough to penetrate all the hearts that beat in the darkness. He had summed up—he had judged. 'The horror!' He was a remarkable

man. After all, this was the expression of some sort of belief; it had candor, it had conviction, it had a vibrating note of revolt in its whisper, it had the appalling face of a glimpsed truth—the strange commingling of desire and hate. And it is not my own extremity I remember best—a vision of grayness without form filled with physical pain, and a careless contempt for the evanescence of all things—even of this pain itself. No! It is his extremity that I seem to have lived through. True, he had made that last stride, he had stepped over the edge, while I had been permitted to draw back my hesitating foot. And perhaps in this is the whole difference; perhaps all the wisdom, and all truth, and all sincerity, are just compressed into that inappreciable moment of time in which we step over the threshold of the invisible. Perhaps! I like to think my summing-up would not have been a word of careless contempt. Better his cry—much better. It was an affirmation, a moral victory paid for by innumerable defeats, by abominable terrors, by abominable satisfactions. But it was a victory! That is why I have remained loyal to Kurtz to the last, and even beyond, when a long time after I heard once more, not his own choice, but the echo of his magnificent eloquence thrown to me from a soul as translucently pure as a cliff of crystal.

"No, they did not bury me, though there is a period of time which I remember mistily, with a shuddering wonder, like a passage through some inconceivable world that had no hope in it and no desire. I found myself back in the sepulchral city resenting the sight of people hurrying through the streets to filch a little money from each other, to devour their infamous cookery, to gulp their unwholesome beer, to dream their insignificant and silly dreams. They trespassed upon my thoughts. They were intruders whose knowledge of life was to me an irritating pretense, because I felt so sure they could not possibly know the things I knew. Their bearing, which was simply the bearing of commonplace individuals going about their business in the assurance of perfect safety, was offensive to me like the outrageous flauntings of folly in the face of a danger it is unable to comprehend. I had no particular desire to enlighten them, but I had some difficulty in restraining myself from laughing in their faces, so full of stupid importance. I daresay I was not very well at that time. I tottered about the streets—there were various affairs to settle—grinning bitterly at perfectly respectable persons. I admit my behavior was inexcusable, but then my temperature was seldom normal in these days. My dear aunt's endeavors to 'nurse up my strength' seemed altogether beside the mark. It was not my strength that wanted nursing, it was my imagination that wanted soothing. I kept the bundle of papers given me by Kurtz, not knowing exactly what to do with it. His mother had died lately, watched over, as I was told, by his Intended. A clean-shaven man, with an official manner and wearing gold-rimmed spectacles, called on me one day and made inquiries, at first circuitous, afterwards suavely pressing, about what he was pleased to denominate certain 'documents.' I was not surprised, because I had had two rows with the manager on the subject out there. I had refused to give up the smallest scrap out of that package, and I took the same attitude with the spectacled man. He became darkly menacing at last, and with much heat argued that the Company had the right to every bit of information about its 'territories.' And he said, 'Mr. Kurtz's knowledge of unexplored regions must have been necessarily extensive and peculiar—owing to his great abilities and to the deplorable circumstances in which he had been placed: therefore—' I assured him Mr. Kurtz's knowledge, however extensive, did not bear upon the problems of commerce or administration. He invoked then the name of science. 'It would be an incalculable loss if,' etc., etc. I offered him the report on the 'Suppression of Savage Customs,' with the postscriptum torn off. He took it up eagerly, but ended by sniffing at it with an air of contempt. 'This is not what we had a right to expect,' he remarked. 'Expect nothing else,' I said. 'There are only private letters.' He withdrew upon some threat of legal proceedings, and I saw him no more; but another fellow, calling himself Kurtz's cousin, appeared two days later, and was anxious to hear all the details about his dear relative's last moments. Incidentally he gave me to understand that Kurtz had been essentially a great musician. 'There was the making of an immense success,' said the man, who was an organist, I believe, with lank gray hair flowing over a greasy coat-collar. I had no reason to doubt his statement; and to this day I am unable to say what was Kurtz's profession, whether he ever had any—which was the greatest of his talents. I had taken him for a painter who wrote for the papers, or else for a journalist who could paint—but even the cousin (who took snuff during the interview) could not tell me what he had been—exactly. He was a universal genius—on that point I agreed with the old chap, who thereupon blew his nose noisily into a large cotton handkerchief and withdrew in senile agitation, bearing off some family letters and memoranda without importance. Ultimately a journalist anxious to know something of the fate of his 'dear colleague' turned up. This visitor informed me Kurtz's proper sphere ought to have been politics 'on the popular side.' He had furry straight eyebrows, bristly hair cropped short, an eye-glass on a broad ribbon, and, becoming expansive, confessed his opinion that Kurtz really couldn't write a bit—'But heavens! how that man could talk. He electrified large meetings. He had faith—don't you see?—he had the faith. He could get himself to believe anything—anything. He would have been a splendid leader of an extreme party.' 'What party?' I asked. 'Any party,' answered the other. 'He was an—an—extremist.' Did I not think so? I assented. Did I know, he asked, with a sudden flash of curiosity, 'what it was that had induced him to go out there?' 'Yes,' said I, and forthwith handed him the famous Report for publication, if he thought fit. He glanced through it hurriedly, mumbling all the time, judged 'it would do,' and took himself off with this plunder.

"Thus I was left at last with a slim packet of letters and the girl's portrait. She struck me as beautiful—I mean she had a beautiful expression. I know that the sunlight can be made to lie, too, yet one felt that no manipulation of light and pose could have conveyed the delicate shade of truthfulness upon those features. She seemed ready to listen without mental reservation, without suspicion, without a thought for herself. I concluded I would go and give her back her portrait and those letters myself. Curiosity? Yes; and also some other feeling perhaps. All that had been Kurtz's had passed out of my hands: his soul, his body, his station, his plans, his ivory, his career. There remained only this memory and his Intended—and I wanted to give that up, too, to the past; in a way—to surrender personally all that remained of him with me to that oblivion which is the last word of our common fate. I don't defend myself. I had no clear perception of what it was I really wanted. Perhaps it was an impulse of unconscious loyalty, or the fulfillment of one of those ironic necessities, that lurk in the facts of human existence. I don't know. I can't tell. But I went.

"I thought his memory was like the other memories of the dead that accumulate in every man's life—a vague impress on the brain of shadows that had fallen on it in their swift and final passage; but before the high and ponderous door, between the tall houses of a street as still and decorous as a well-kept alley in a cemetery, I had a vision of him on the stretcher, opening his mouth voraciously, as if to devour all the earth with all its mankind. He lived then before me; he lived as much as he had ever lived—a shadow insatiable of splendid appearances, of frightful realities; a shadow darker than the shadow of the night, and draped nobly in the folds of a gorgeous eloquence. The vision seemed to enter the house with me—the stretcher, the phantom-bearers, the wild crowd of obedient worshipers, the gloom of the forests, the glitter of the reach between the murky bends, the beat of the drum, regular and muffled like the beating of a heart—the heart of a conquering darkness. It was a moment of triumph for the wilderness, an invading and vengeful rush which, it seemed to me, I would have to keep back alone for the salvation of another soul. And the memory of what I had heard him say afar there, with the honored shapes stirring at my back, in the glow of fires, within the patient woods, those broken phrases came back to me, were heard again in their ominous and terrifying simplicity. I remembered his abject pleading, his abject threats, the colossal scale of his vile desires, the meanness, the torment, the tempestuous anguish of his soul. And later on I seem to see his collected languid manner, when he said one day, 'This lot of ivory now is really mine. The Company did not pay for it. I collected it myself at a very great personal risk. I am afraid they will try to claim it as theirs though. H'm. It is a difficult case. What do you think I ought to do—resist? Eh? I want no more than justice.' . . . He wanted no more than justice—no more than justice. I rang the bell before a mahogany door on the first floor, and while I waited he seemed to stare at me out of the glassy panel—stare with that wide and immense stare embracing, condemning, loathing all the universe. I seemed to hear the whispered cry, 'The horror! The horror!'

"The dusk was falling. I had to wait in a lofty drawing-room with three long windows from floor to ceiling that were like three luminous and be-draped columns. The bent gilt legs and backs of the furniture shone in indistinct curves. The tall marble fireplace had a cold and monumental whiteness. A grand piano stood massively in a corner; with dark gleams on the flat surfaces like a somber and polished sarcophagus. A high door opened—closed. I rose.

165   "She came forward, all in black, with a pale head, floating towards me in the dusk. She was in mourning. It was more than a year since his death, more than a year since the news came; she seemed as though she would remember and mourn forever. She took both my hands in hers and murmured, 'I had heard you were coming.' I noticed she was not very young—I mean not girlish. She had a mature capacity for fidelity, for belief, for suffering. The room seemed to have grown darker, as if all the sad light of the cloudy evening had taken refuge on her forehead. This fair hair, this pale visage, this pure brow, seemed surrounded by an ashy halo from which the dark eyes looked out at me. Their glance was guileless, profound, confident, and trustful. She carried her sorrowful head as though she were proud of that sorrow, as though she would say, I—I alone know how to mourn him as he deserves. But while we were still shaking hands, such a look of awful desolation came upon her face that I perceived she was one of those creatures that are not the playthings of Time. For her he had died only yesterday. And, by Jove! the impression was so powerful that for me, too, he seemed to have died only yesterday—nay, this very minute. I saw her and him in the same instant of time—his death and her sorrow—I saw her sorrow in the very moment of his death. Do you understand? I saw them together—I heard them together. She had said, with a deep catch of the breath, 'I have survived' while my strained ears seemed to hear distinctly, mingled with her tone of despairing regret, the summing up whisper of his eternal condemnation. I asked myself what I was doing there, with a sensation of panic in my heart as though I had blundered into a place of cruel and absurd mysteries not fit for a human being to behold. She motioned me to a chair. We sat down. I laid the packet gently on the little table, and she put her hand over it. . . . 'You knew him well,' she murmured, after a moment of mourning silence.

"'Intimacy grows quickly out there,' I said. 'I knew him as well as it is possible for one man to know another.'

"'And you admired him,' she said. 'It was impossible to know him and not to admire him. Was it?'

"'He was a remarkable man,' I said, unsteadily. Then before the appealing fixity of her gaze, that seemed to watch for more words on my lips, I went on, 'It was impossible not to—

"'Love him,' she finished eagerly, silencing me into an appalled dumbness. 'How true! how true! But when you think that no one knew him so well as I! I had all his noble confidence. I knew him best.'

"'You knew him best,' I repeated. And perhaps she did. But with every word spoken the room was growing darker, and only her forehead, smooth and white, remained illumined by the unextinguishable light of belief and love.

"'You were his friend,' she went on. 'His friend,' she repeated, a little louder. 'You must have been, if he had given you this, and sent you to me. I feel I can speak to you—and oh! I must speak. I want you—you have heard his last words—to know I have been worthy of him. . . . It is not pride. . . . Yes! I am proud to know I understood him better than anyone on earth—he told me so himself. And since his mother died I have had no one—no one—to—to—

"I listened. The darkness deepened. I was not even sure he had given me the right bundle. I rather suspect he wanted me to take care of another batch of his papers which, after his death, I saw the manager examining under the lamp. And the girl talked, easing her pain in the certitude of my sympathy; she talked as thirsty men drink. I had heard that her engagement with Kurtz had been disapproved by her people. He wasn't rich enough or something. And indeed I don't know whether he had not been a pauper all his life. He had given me some reason to infer that it was his impatience of comparative poverty that drove him out there.

"'. . . Who was not his friend who had heard him speak once?' she was saying. 'He drew men towards him by what was best in them.' She looked at me with intensity. 'It is the gift of the great,' she went on, and the sound of her low voice seemed to have the accompaniment of all the other sounds, full of mystery, desolation, and sorrow, I had ever heard—the ripple of the river, the soughing of the trees swayed by the wind, the murmurs of the crowds, the faint ring of incomprehensible words cried from afar, the whisper of a voice speaking from beyond the threshold of an external darkness. 'But you have heard him! You know!' she cried.

"'Yes, I know,' I said with something like despair in my heart, but bowing my head before the faith that was in her, before that great and saving illusion that shone with an unearthly glow in the darkness, in the triumphant darkness from which I could not have defended her—from which I could not even defend myself.

"'What a loss to me—to us!'—she corrected herself with beautiful generosity; then added in a murmur, 'To the world.' By the last gleams of twilight I could see the glitter of her eyes, full of tears—of tears that would not fall.

"'I have been very happy—very fortunate—very proud,' she went on. 'Too fortunate. Too happy for a little while. And now I am unhappy for—for life.'

"She stood up; her fair hair seemed to catch all the remaining light in a glimmer of gold. I rose, too.

"'And of all this,' she went on, mournfully, 'of all his promise, and of all his greatness, of his generous mind, of his noble heart, nothing remains—nothing but a memory. You and I—

"'We shall always remember him,' I said, hastily.

180 "'No!' she cried. 'It is impossible that all this should be lost—that such a life should be sacrificed to leave nothing—but sorrow. You know what vast plans he had. I knew of them, too—I could not perhaps understand—but others knew of them. Something must remain. His words, at least, have not died.'

"'His words will remain,' I said.

"'And his example,' she whispered to herself. 'Men looked up to him—his goodness shone in every act. His example—

"'True,' I said; 'his example, too. Yes, his example. I forgot that.'

"'But I do not. I cannot—I cannot believe—not yet. I cannot believe that I shall never see him again, that nobody will see him again, never, never, never.'

185 "She put out her arms as if after a retreating figure, stretching them black and with clasped pale hands across the fading and narrow sheen of the window. Never see him! I saw him clearly enough then. I shall see this eloquent phantom as long as I live, and I shall see her, too, a tragic and familiar Shade, resembling in this gesture another one, tragic also, and bedecked with powerless charms, stretching bare brown arms over the glitter of the infernal stream, the stream of darkness. She said suddenly very low, 'He died as he lived.'

"'His end,' said I, with dull anger stirring in me, 'was in every way worthy of his life.'

"'And I was not with him,' she murmured. My anger subsided before a feeling of infinite pity.

"'Everything that could be done—' I mumbled.

"'Ah, but I believed in him more than anyone on earth—more than his own mother, more than—himself. He needed me! Me! I would have treasured every sigh, every word, every sign, every glance.'

190 "I felt like a chill grip on my chest. 'Don't,' I said, in a muffled voice.

"'Forgive me. I—I have mourned so long in silence—in silence. . . . You were with him—to the last? I think of his loneliness. Nobody near to understand him as I would have understood. Perhaps no one to hear. . . .'

"'To the very end,' I said shakily. 'I heard his very last words. . . .' I stopped in a fright.

"'Repeat them,' she murmured in a heart-broken tone. 'I want—I want—something—something—to—live with.'

"I was on the point of crying at her, 'Don't you hear them?' The dusk was repeating them in a persistent whisper all around us, in a whisper that seemed to swell menacingly like the first whisper of a rising wind. 'The horror! The horror!'

195 "'His last word—to live with,' she insisted. 'Don't you understand I loved him—I loved him—I loved him!'

"I pulled myself together and spoke slowly.

"'The last word he pronounced was—your name.'

"I heard a light sigh and then my heart stood still, stopped dead short by an exulting and terrible cry, by the cry of inconceivable triumph and of unspeakable pain. 'I knew it—I was sure!' . . . She knew. She was sure. I heard her weeping, she had hidden her face in her hands. It seemed to me that the house would collapse before I could escape, that the heavens would fall upon my head. But nothing happened. The heavens do not fall for such a trifle. Would they have fallen, I wonder, if I had rendered Kurtz that justice which was his due? Hadn't he said he wanted only justice? But I couldn't. I could not tell her. It would have been too dark—too dark altogether. . . ."

Marlow ceased, and sat apart, indistinct and silent, in the pose of a meditating Buddha. Nobody moved for a time. "We have lost the first of the ebb," said the Director, suddenly. I raised my head. The offing was barred by a black bank of clouds, and the tranquil waterway leading to the uttermost ends of the earth flowed somber under an overcast sky—seemed to lead into the heart of an immense darkness. [1902]

QUESTIONS

1. Discuss the importance of circumstances in which Marlow tells his story about Kurtz.
2. Explain the changes that Marlow's attitude toward Kurtz goes through.
3. Discuss Marlow's portrayal of the Congo. How is his view of it confirmed or contradicted by others on the journey?
4. What meaning does Kurtz's final words "The horror! The horror!" convey?
5. Why does Marlow lie to Kurtz's fiancé? Is it in keeping with what he has learned on his journey?

RESPONSES

1. What does this story say about white colonization? Use a Marxist approach to examine the idea of capital.
2. Use an ecocritical approach to the story and examine the meaning that Conrad and his character put upon nature. How is nature similar to and different from civilization?

FOCUS ON FILM

1. Choose a portion of the text and study how that portion was depicted in the film *The Heart of Darkness*.
2. Choose one character in the film and the print story. Evaluate the actor's portrayal of that character? If you were to direct the film what would you have asked the actor to do differently?
3. View the film *Apocalypse Now*. Choose one portion of the film and explain how the director Francis Ford Coppula adapted Conrad's story for the film.

Julio Cortázar

Julio Cortázar (1914–1984) was born in Brussels, Belgium, to Argentine parents. His family returned to Argentina when he was a child. He studied to be a teacher at Escuela Normal de Profesores Mariano Acosta, then continued his studies at the University of Buenos Aires. By 1944, he was a professor of French literature at the University of Cuyo, Mendoza. There he became involved with protest movements, and moved to France in 1951 where he remained, except for brief periods of teaching abroad, until his death. Among his projects was translating the stories of Edgar Allan Poe for UNESCO. Cortázar, like Borges, is considered one of the masters of the modern, fantastic short story. His most highly regarded work is the novel *Rayuela*, translated as *Hopscotch* (1966). Among his many other works are *All Fires the Fire and Other Stories* (1966), *A Manual for Manuel* (1973), *We Love Glenda So Much and Other Tales* (1981), and *End of the Game and Other Stories* (1967), which included the story that became the basis of the movie *Blow-Up*.

Axolotl

There was a time when I thought a great deal about the axolotls. I went to see them in the aquarium at the Jardin des Plantes and stayed for hours watching them, observing their immobility, their faint movements. Now I am an axolotl.

I got to them by chance one spring morning when Paris was spreading its peacock tail after a wintry Lent. I was heading down the boulevard Port-Royal, then I took Saint-Marcel and L'Hôpital and saw green among all that grey and remembered the lions. I was friend of the lions and panthers, but had never gone into the dark, humid building that was the aquarium. I left my bike against the gratings and went to look at the tulips. The lions were sad and ugly and my panther was asleep. I decided on the aquarium, looked obliquely at banal fish until, unexpectedly, I hit it off with the axolotls. I stayed watching them for an hour and left, unable to think of anything else.

In the library at Sainte-Geneviève, I consulted a dictionary and learned that axolotls are the larval stage (provided with gills) of a species of salamander of the genus Ambystoma. That they were Mexican I knew already by looking at them and their little pink Aztec faces and the placard at the top of the tank. I read that specimens of them had been found in Africa capable of living on dry land during the periods of drought, and continuing their life under water when the rainy season came. I found their Spanish name, *ajolote*, and the mention that they were edible, and that their oil was used (no longer used, it said) like cod-liver oil.

I didn't care to look up any of the specialized works, but the next day I went back to the Jardin des Plantes. I began to go every morning, morning and afternoon some days. The aquarium guard smiled perplexedly taking my ticket. I would lean up against the iron bar in front of the tanks and set to watching them. There's nothing strange in this, because after the first minute I knew that we were linked, that something infinitely lost and distant kept pulling us together. It had been enough to detain me that first morning in front of the sheet of glass where some bubbles rose through the water. The axolotls huddled on the wretched narrow (only I can know how narrow and wretched) floor of moss and stone in the tank. There were nine specimens, and the majority pressed their heads against the glass, looking with their eyes of gold at whoever came near them. Disconcerted, almost ashamed, I felt it a lewdness to be peering at these silent and immobile figures heaped at the bottom of the tank. Mentally I isolated one, situated on the right and somewhat apart from the others, to study it better. I saw a rosy little body, translucent (I thought of those Chinese figurines of milky glass), looking like a small lizard about six inches long, ending in a fish's tail of extraordinary delicacy, the most sensitive part of our body. Along the back ran a transparent fin which joined with the tail, but what obsessed me was the feet, of the slenderest nicety, ending in tiny fingers with minutely human nails. And then I discovered its eyes, its face. Inexpressive features, with no other trait save the eyes, two orifices, like brooches, wholly of transparent gold, lacking any life but looking, letting themselves be penetrated by my look, which seemed to travel past the golden level and lose itself in a diaphanous interior mystery. A very slender black halo ringed the eye and etched it onto the pink flesh, onto the rosy stone of the head, vaguely triangular, but with curved and irregular sides which gave it a total likeness to a statuette corroded by time. The mouth was masked by the triangular plane of the face, its considerable size would be guessed only in profile; in front a delicate crevice barely slit the lifeless stone. On both sides of the head where the ears should have been, there grew three tiny sprigs red as coral, a vegetal outgrowth, the gills, I suppose. And they were the only thing quick about it; every ten or fifteen seconds the sprigs pricked up stiffly and again subsided. Once in a while a foot would barely move, I saw the diminutive toes poise mildly on the moss. It's that we don't enjoy moving a lot, and the tank is so cramped—we barely move in any direction and we're hitting one of the others with our tail or our head—difficulties arise, fights, tiredness. The time feels like it's less if we stay quietly.

It was their quietness that made me lean toward them fascinated the first time I saw the axolotls. Obscurely I seemed to understand their secret will, to abolish space and time with an indifferent immobility. I knew better later; the gill contraction, the tentative reckoning of the delicate feet on the stones, the abrupt swimming (some of them swim with a simple undulation of the body) proved to me that they were capable of escaping that mineral lethargy in which they spent whole hours. Above all else, their eyes obsessed me. In the standing tanks on either side of them, different fishes showed me the simple stupidity of their handsome eyes so similar to our own. The eyes of the axolotls spoke to me of the presence of a different life, of another way of seeing. Gluing my face to the glass (the guard would cough fussily once in a while), I tried to see better those diminutive golden points, that entrance to the infinitely slow and remote world of these rosy creatures. It was useless to tap with one finger on the glass directly in front of their faces; they never gave the least reaction. The golden eyes continued burning with their soft, terrible light; they continued looking at me from an unfathomable depth which made me dizzy.

And nevertheless they were close. I knew it before this, before being an axolotl. I learned it the day I came near them for the first time. The anthropomorphic features of a monkey reveal the reverse of what most people believe, the distance that is traveled from them to us. The absolute lack of similarity between axolotls and human beings proved to me that my recognition was valid, that I was not propping myself up with easy analogies. Only the little hands . . . But an eft, the common newt, has such hands also, and we are not at all alike. I think it was the axolotls' heads, that triangular pink shape with the tiny eyes of gold. That looked and knew. That laid the claim. They were not *animals*.

It would seem easy, almost obvious, to fall into mythology. I began seeing in the axolotls a metamorphosis which did not succeed in revoking a mysterious humanity. I imagined them aware, slaves of their bodies, condemned infinitely to the silence of the abyss, to a hopeless meditation. Their blind gaze, the diminutive gold disc without expression and nonetheless terribly shining, went through me like a message: "Save us, save us." I caught myself mumbling words of advice, conveying childish hopes. They continued to look at me, immobile; from time to time the rosy branches of the gills stiffened. In that instant I felt a muted pain; perhaps they were seeing me, attracting my strength to penetrate into the impenetrable thing of their lives. They were not human beings, but I had found in no animal such a profound relation with myself. The axolotls were like witnesses of something, and at times like horrible judges. I felt ignoble in front of them; there was such a terrifying purity in those transparent eyes. They were larvas, but larva means disguise and also phantom. Behind those Aztec faces, without expression but of an implacable cruelty, what semblance was awaiting its hour?

I was afraid of them. I think that had it not been for feeling the proximity of other visitors and the guard, I would not have been bold enough to remain alone with them. "You eat them alive with your eyes, hey," the guard said, laughing; he likely thought I was a little cracked. What he didn't notice was that it was they devouring me slowly with their eyes, in a cannibalism of gold. At any distance from the aquarium, I had only to think of them, it was as though I were being affected from a distance. It got to the point that I was going every day, and at night I thought of them immobile in the darkness, slowly putting a hand out which immediately encountered another. Perhaps their eyes could see in the dead of night, and for them the day continued indefinitely. The eyes of axolotls have no lids.

I know now that there was nothing strange, that that had to occur. Leaning over in front of the tank each morning, the recognition was greater. They were suffering, every fiber of my body reached toward that stifled pain, that stiff torment at the bottom of the tank. They were lying in wait for something, a remote dominion destroyed, an age of liberty when the world had been that of the axolotls. Not possible that such a terrible expression which was attaining the overthrow of that forced blankness on their stone faces should carry any message other than one of pain, proof of that eternal sentence, of that liquid hell they were undergoing. Hopelessly, I wanted to prove to myself that my own sensibility was projecting a nonexistent consciousness upon the axolotls. They and I knew. So there was nothing strange in what happened. My face was pressed against the glass of the aquarium, my eyes were attempting once more to penetrate the mystery of those eyes of gold without iris, without pupil. I saw from very close up the face of an axolotl immobile next to the glass. No transition and no surprise, I saw my face against the glass, I saw it on the outside of the tank, I saw it on the other side of the glass. Then my face drew back and I understood.

Only one thing was strange: to go on thinking as usual, to know. To realize that was, for the first moment, like the horror of a man buried alive awaking to his fate. Outside, my face came close to the glass again, I saw my mouth, the lips compressed with the effort of understanding the axolotls. I was an axolotl and now I knew instantly that no understanding was possible. He was outside the aquarium, his thinking was a thinking outside the tank. Recognizing him, being him himself, I was an axolotl and in my world. The horror began—I learned in the same moment—of believing myself prisoner in the body of an axolotl, metamorphosed into him with my human mind intact, buried alive in an axolotl, condemned to move lucidly among unconscious creatures. But that stopped when a foot just grazed my face, when I moved just a little to one side and saw an axolotl next to me who was looking at me, and understood that he knew also, no communication possible, but very clearly. Or I was also in him, or all of us were thinking humanlike, incapable of expression, limited to the golden splendor of our eyes looking at the face of the man pressed against the aquarium.

He returned many times, but he comes less often now. Weeks pass without his showing up. I saw him yesterday, he looked at me for a long time and left briskly. It seemed to me that he was not so much interested in us any more, that he was coming out of habit. Since the only thing I do is think, I could think about him a lot. It occurs to me that at the beginning we continued to communicate, that he felt more than ever one with the mystery which was claiming him. But the bridges were broken between him and me, because what was his obsession is now an axolotl, alien to his human life. I think that at the beginning I was capable of returning to him in a certain way—ah, only in a certain way—and of keeping awake his desire to know us better. I am an axolotl for good now, and if I think like a man it's only because every axolotl thinks like a man inside his rosy stone semblance. I believe that all this succeeded in communicating something to him in those first days, when I was still he. And in this final solitude to which he no longer comes, I console myself by thinking that perhaps he is going to write a story about us, that, believing he's making up a story, he's going to write all this about axolotls. [1954]

QUESTIONS

1. What does the narrator want the reader to understand? Does the narrator's goal differ from what Cortázar's goal might be as the writer?

2. Are the axolotls characters in the story? What qualities of fictional characters do they possess? What qualities do they lack?

3. How important is it that the narrator finds that the faces of the axolotls resemble Aztec faces?

4. How does Cortázar prepare us for the shift in person from man to axolotl?

5. What is the conflict in the story? Is it resolved?

RESPONSES

1. Write a comparison of this story to Kafka's "The Metamorphosis" or Sontag's "The Dummy."
2. Using the psychological approach, discuss how the story comments upon
   ego formation.

STEPHEN CRANE

Stephen Crane (1871—1900) was born in Newark, New Jersey. After spending one term each at Lafayette College and Syracuse University, he turned to freelance journalism. In covering the Greco-Turkist and Spanish-American wars, he rather self-consciously cultivated the reputation of the swashbuckling international correspondent. His novel *Maggie: A Girl of the Streets* (1893) is a starkly realistic account of the dark underside of urban existence. *The Red Badge of Courage* (1895), his powerful account of a Civil War soldier, is the prototype for the modern war novel. His sardonic, experimental verse has been much admired and foreshadows the style and tone of much poetry of this century. His finest stories are collected in *The Open Boat and Other Tales of Adventure* (1898).

The Open Boat

1

None of them knew the colour of the sky. Their eyes glanced level, and were fastened upon the waves that swept toward them. These waves were of the hue of slate, save for the tops, which were of foaming white, and all of the men knew the colours of the sea. The horizon narrowed and widened, and dipped and rose, and at all times its edge was jagged with waves that seemed thrust up in points like rocks.

Many a man ought to have a bathtub larger than the boat which here rode upon the sea. These waves were most wrongfully and barbarously abrupt and tall, and each froth-top was a problem in small-boat navigation.

The cook squatted in the bottom, and looked with both eyes at the six inches of gunwale which separated him from the ocean. His sleeves were rolled over his fat forearms, and the two flaps of his unbuttoned vest dangled as he bent to bail out the boat. Often he said, "Gawd! that was a narrow clip." As he remarked it he invariably gazed eastward over the broken sea.

The oiler, steering with one of the two oars in the boat, sometimes raised himself suddenly to keep clear of water that swirled in over the stern. It was a thin little oar, and it seemed often ready to snap.

5   The correspondent, pulling at the other oar, watched the waves and wondered why he was there.

The injured captain, lying in the bow, was at this time buried in that profound dejection and indifference which comes, temporarily at least, to even the bravest and most enduring when, willy-nilly, the firm fails, the army loses, the ship goes down. The mind of the master of a vessel is rooted deep in the timbers of her, though he command for a day or a decade; and this captain had on him the stern impression of a scene in the greys of dawn of seven turned faces, and later a stump of a topmast with a white ball on it, that slashed to and fro at the waves, went low and lower, and down. Thereafter there was something strange in his voice. Although steady, it was deep with mourning, and of a quality beyond oration or tears.

"Keep 'er a little more south, Billie," said he.

"A little more south, sir," said the oiler in the stern.

A seat in this boat was not unlike a seat upon a bucking bronco, and by the same token a bronco is not much smaller. The craft pranced and reared and plunged like an animal. As each wave came, and she rose for it, she seemed like a horse making at a fence outrageously high. The manner of her scramble over these walls of water is a mystic thing, and, moreover, at the top of them were ordinarily these problems in white water, the foam racing down from the summit of each wave requiring a new leap, and a leap from the air. Then, after scornfully bumping a crest, she would slide and race and splash down a long incline, and arrive bobbing and nodding in front of the next menace.

10   A singular disadvantage of the sea lies in the fact that after successfully surmounting one wave you discover that there is another behind it just as important and just as nervously anxious to do something effective in the way of swamping boats. In a ten-foot dinghy one can get an idea of the resources of the sea in the line of waves that is not probable to the average experience which is never at sea in a dinghy. As each slaty wall of water approached, it shut all else from the view of the men in the boat, and it was not difficult to imagine that this particular wave was the final outburst of the ocean, the last effort of the grim water. There was a terrible grace in the move of the waves, and they came in silence, save for the snarling of the crests.

In the wan light the faces of the men must have been grey. Their eyes must have glinted in strange ways as they gazed steadily astern. Viewed from a balcony, the whole thing would doubtless have been weirdly picturesque. But the men in the boat had no time to see it, and if they had had leisure, there were other things to occupy their minds. The sun swung steadily up the sky, and they knew it was broad day because the colour of the sea changed from slate to emerald green streaked with amber lights, and the foam was like tumbling snow. The process of the breaking day was unknown to them. They were aware only of this effect upon the colour of the waves that rolled toward them.

In disjointed sentences the cook and the correspondent argued as to the difference between a life-saving station and a house of refuge. The cook had said: "There's a house of refuge just north of the Mosquito Inlet Light, and as soon as they see us they'll come off in their boat and pick us up."

"As soon as who see us?" said the correspondent.

"The crew," said the cook.

15   "Houses of refuge don't have crews," said the correspondent. "As I understand them, they are only places where clothes and grub are stored for the benefit of shipwrecked people. They don't carry crews."

"Oh, yes, they do," said the cook.

"No, they don't," said the correspondent.

"Well, we're not there yet, anyhow," said the oiler, in the stern.

"Well," said the cook, "perhaps it's not a house of refuge that I'm thinking of as being near Mosquito Inlet Light; perhaps it's a life-saving station."

"We're not there yet," said the oiler in the stern. 20

2

As the boat bounced from the top of each wave the wind tore through the hair of the hatless men, and as the craft plopped her stern down again the spray slashed past them. The crest of each of these waves was a hill, from the top of which the men surveyed for a moment a broad tumultuous expanse, shining and wind-riven. It was probably splendid, it was probably glorious, this play of the free sea, wild with lights of emerald and white and amber.

"Bully good thing it's an on-shore wind," said the cook. "If not, where would we be? Wouldn't have a show."

"That's right," said the correspondent.

The busy oiler nodded his assent.

Then the captain, in the bow, chuckled in a way that expressed humour, contempt, 25
tragedy, all in one. "Do you think we've got much of a show now, boys?" said he.

Whereupon the three were silent, save for a trifle of hemming and hawing. To express any particular optimism at this time they felt to be childish and stupid, but they all doubtless possessed this sense of the situation in their minds. A young man thinks doggedly at such times. On the other hand, the ethics of their condition was decidedly against any open suggestion of hopelessness. So they were silent.

"Oh well," said the captain, soothing his children, "we'll get ashore all right."

But there was that in his tone which made them think; so the oiler quoth, "Yes! if this wind holds."

The cook was bailing. "Yes! if we don't catch hell in the surf."

Canton-flannel gulls flew near and far. Sometimes they sat down on the sea, near 30
patches of brown seaweed that rolled over the waves with a movement like carpets on a line in a gale. The birds sat comfortably in groups, and they were envied by some in the dinghy, for the wrath of the sea was no more to them than it was to a covey of prairie chickens a thousand miles inland. Often they came very close and stared at the men with black bead-like eyes. At these times they were uncanny and sinister in their unblinking scrutiny, and the men hooted angrily at them, telling them to be gone. One came, and evidently decided to alight on the top of the captain's head. The bird flew parallel to the boat and did not circle, but made short sidelong jumps in the air in chicken-fashion. His black eyes were wistfully fixed upon the captain's head. "Ugly brute," said the oiler to the bird. "You look as if you were made with a jackknife." The cook and the correspondent swore darkly at the creature. The captain naturally wished to knock it away with the end of the heavy painter, but he did not dare do it, because anything resembling an emphatic gesture would have capsized this freighted boat; and so, with his open hand, the captain gently and carefully waved the gull away. After it had been discouraged from the pursuit the captain breathed easier on account of his hair, and others breathed easier because the bird struck their minds at this time as being somehow gruesome and ominous.

In the meantime the oiler and the correspondent rowed. And also they rowed. They sat together in the same seat, and each rowed an oar. Then the oiler took both oars; then the correspondent took both oars; then the oiler, then the correspondent. They rowed and they rowed. The very ticklish part of the business was when the time came for the reclining one in the stern to take his turn at the oars. By the very last star of truth, it is easier to steal eggs from under a hen than it was to change seats in the dinghy. First the man in the stern slid his hand along the thwart and moved with care, as if he were of Sèvres.° Then the man in the rowing-seat slid his hand along the other thwart. It was all done with the most extraordinary care. As the two sidled past each other, the whole party kept watchful eyes on the coming wave, and the captain cried: "Look out, now! Steady, there!"

The brown mats of seaweed that appeared from time to time were like islands, bits of earth. They were travelling, apparently, neither one way nor the other. They were, to all intents, stationary. They informed the men in the boat that it was making progress slowly toward the land.

The captain, rearing cautiously in the bow after the dinghy soared on a great swell, said that he had seen the lighthouse at Mosquito Inlet. Presently the cook remarked that he had seen it. The correspondent was at the oars then, and for some reason he too wished to look at the lighthouse; but his back was toward the far shore, and the waves were important, and for some time he could not seize an opportunity to turn his head. But at last there came a wave more gentle than the others, and when at the crest of it he swiftly scoured the western horizon.

"See it?" said the captain.

35   "No," said the correspondent, slowly; "I didn't see anything."

"Look again," said the captain. He pointed. "It's exactly in that direction."

At the top of another wave the correspondent did as he was bid, and this time his eyes chanced on a small, still thing on the edge of the swaying horizon. It was precisely like the point of a pin. It took an anxious eye to find a lighthouse so tiny.

"Think we'll make it, Captain?"

"If this wind holds and the boat don't swamp, we can't do much else," said the captain.

40   The little boat, lifted by each towering sea and splashed viciously by the crests, made progress that in the absence of seaweed was not apparent to those in her. She seemed just a wee thing wallowing, miraculously top up, at the mercy of five oceans. Occasionally a great spread of water, like white flames, swarmed into her.

"Bail her, cook," said the captain, serenely.

"All right, Captain," said the cheerful cook.

3

It would be difficult to describe the subtle brotherhood of men that was here established on the seas. No one said that it was so. No one mentioned it. But it dwelt in the boat, and each man felt it warm him. They were a captain, an oiler, a cook, and a correspondent, and they were friends—friends in a more curiously iron-bound degree than may be common. The hurt captain, lying against the water-jar in the bow, spoke always in a low voice and calmly; but he could never command a more ready and swiftly obedient crew than the motley three of the dinghy. It was more than a mere recognition

---

°*Sèvres*: Delicate French porcelain.

of what was best for the common safety. There was surely in it a quality that was personal and heart-felt. And after this devotion to the commander of the boat, there was this comradeship, that the correspondent, for instance, who had been taught to be cynical of men, knew even at the time was the best experience of his life. But no one said that it was so. No one mentioned it.

"I wish we had a sail," remarked the captain. "We might try my overcoat on the end of an oar, and give you two boys a chance to rest." So the cook and the correspondent held the mast and spread wide the overcoat; the oiler steered; and the little boat made good way with her new rig. Sometimes the oiler had to scull sharply to keep a sea from breaking into the boat, but otherwise sailing was a success.

Meanwhile the lighthouse had been growing slowly larger. It had now almost assumed colour, and appeared like a little grey shadow on the sky. The man at the oars could not be prevented from turning his head rather often to try for a glimpse of this little grey shadow.   45

At last, from the top of each wave, the men in the tossing boat could see land. Even as the lighthouse was an upright shadow on the sky, this land seemed but a long black shadow on the sea. It certainly was thinner than paper. "We must be about opposite New Smyrna," said the cook, who had coasted this shore often in schooners. "Captain, by the way, I believe they abandoned that life-saving station there about a year ago."

"Did they?" said the captain.

The wind slowly died away. The cook and the correspondent were not now obliged to slave in order to hold high the oar. But the waves continued their old impetuous swooping at the dinghy, and the little craft, no longer under way, struggled woundily over them. The oiler or the correspondent took the oars again.

Shipwrecks are apropos of nothing. If men could only train for them and have them occur when the men had reached pink condition, there would be less drowning at sea. Of the four in the dinghy none had slept any time worth mentioning for two days and two nights previous to embarking in the dinghy, and in the excitement of clambering about the deck of a foundering ship they had also forgotten to eat heartily.

For these reasons, and for others, neither the oiler nor the correspondent was fond   50
of rowing at this time. The correspondent wondered ingenuously how in the name of all that was sane could there be people who thought it amusing to row a boat. It was not an amusement; it was a diabolical punishment, and even a genius of mental aberrations could never conclude that it was anything but a horror to the muscles and a crime against the back. He mentioned to the boat in general how the amusement of rowing struck him, and the weary-faced oiler smiled in full sympathy. Previously to the foundering, by the way, the oiler had worked a double watch in the engine-room of the ship.

"Take her easy now, boys," said the captain. "Don't spend yourselves. If we have to run a surf you'll need all your strength, because we'll sure have to swim for it. Take your time."

Slowly the land arose from the sea. From a black line it became a line of black and a line of white—trees and sand. Finally the captain said that he could make out a house on the shore. "That's the house of refuge, sure," said the cook. "They'll see us before long, and come out after us."

The distant lighthouse reared high. "The keeper ought to be able to make us out now, if he's looking through a glass," said the captain. "He'll notify the life-saving people."

"None of those other boats could have got ashore to give word of this wreck," said the oiler, in a low voice, "else the life-boat would be out hunting us."

55   Slowly and beautifully the land loomed out of the sea. The wind came again. It had veered from the north-east to the south-east. Finally a new sound struck the ears of the men in the boat. It was the low thunder of the surf on the shore. "We'll never be able to make the lighthouse now," said the captain. "Swing her head a little more north, Billie."

"A little more north, sir," said the oiler.

Whereupon the little boat turned her nose once more down the wind, and all but the oarsman watched the shore grow. Under the influence of this expansion doubt and direful apprehension were leaving the minds of the men. The management of the boat was still most absorbing, but it could not prevent a quiet cheerfulness. In an hour, perhaps, they would be ashore.

Their backbones had become thoroughly used to balancing in the boat, and they now rode this wild colt of a dinghy like circus men. The correspondent thought that he had been drenched to the skin, but happening to feel in the top pocket of his coat, he found therein eight cigars. Four of them were soaked with sea-water; four were perfectly scatheless. After a search, somebody produced three dry matches; and thereupon the four waifs rode impudently in their little boat and, with an assurance of an impending rescue shining in their eyes, puffed at the big cigars, and judged well and ill of all men. Everybody took a drink of water.

4

"Cook," remarked the captain, "there don't seem to be any signs of life about your house of refuge."

60   "No," replied the cook. "Funny they don't see us!"

A broad stretch of lowly coast lay before the eyes of the men. It was of low dunes topped with dark vegetation. The roar of the surf was plain, and sometimes they could see the white lip of a wave as it spun up the beach. A tiny house was blocked out black upon the sky. Southward, the slim lighthouse lifted its little grey length.

Tide, wind, and waves were swinging the dinghy northward. "Funny they don't see us," said the men.

The surf's roar was here dulled, but its tone was nevertheless thunderous and mighty. As the boat swam over the great rollers the men sat listening to this roar. "We'll swamp sure," said everybody.

It is fair to say here that there was not a life-saving station within twenty miles in either direction; but the men did not know this fact, and in consequence they made dark and opprobrious remarks concerning the eyesight of the nation's life-savers. Four scowling men sat in the dinghy and surpassed records in the invention of epithets.

65   "Funny they don't see us."

The light-heartedness of a former time had completely faded. To their sharpened minds it was easy to conjure pictures of all kinds of incompetency and blindness and, indeed, cowardice. There was the shore of the populous land, and it was bitter and bitter to them that from it came no sign.

"Well," said the captain, ultimately, "I suppose we'll have to make a try for ourselves. If we stay out here too long, we'll none of us have strength left to swim after the boat swamps."

And so the oiler, who was at the oars, turned the boat straight for the shore. There was a sudden tightening of muscles. There was some thinking.

"If we don't all get ashore," said the captain—"if we don't all get ashore, I suppose you fellows know where to send news of my finish?"

They then briefly exchanged some addresses and admonitions. As for the reflections of the men, there was a great deal of rage in them. Perchance they might be formulated thus: "If I am going to be drowned—if I am going to be drowned—if I am going to be drowned, why, in the name of the seven mad gods who rule the sea, was I allowed to come thus far and contemplate sand and trees? Was I brought here merely to have my nose dragged away as I was about to nibble the sacred cheese of life? It is preposterous. If this old ninny-woman, Fate, cannot do better than this, she should be deprived of the management of men's fortunes. She is an old hen who knows not her intention. If she has decided to drown me, why did she not do it in the beginning and save me all this trouble? The whole affair is absurd.—But no; she cannot mean to drown me. She dare not drown me. Not after all this work." Afterward the man might have had an impulse to shake his fist at the clouds. "Just you drown me, now, and then hear what I call you!"

The billows that came at this time were more formidable. They seemed always just about to break and roll over the little boat in a turmoil of foam. There was a preparatory and long growl in the speech of them. No mind unused to the sea would have concluded that the dinghy could ascend these sheer heights in time. The shore was still afar. The oiler was a wily surfman. "Boys," he said swiftly, "she won't live three minutes more, and we're too far out to swim. Shall I take her to sea again, Captain?"

"Yes; go ahead!" said the captain.

This oiler, by a series of quick miracles and fast and steady oarsmanship, turned the boat in the middle of the surf and took her safely to sea again.

There was a considerable silence as the boat bumped over the furrowed sea to deeper water. Then somebody in gloom spoke: "Well, anyhow, they must have seen us from the shore by now."

The gulls went in slanting flight up the wind toward the grey, desolate east. A squall, marked by dingy clouds and clouds brick-red like smoke from a burning building, appeared from the south-east.

"What do you think of those life-saving people? Ain't they peaches?"

"Funny they haven't seen us."

"Maybe they think we're out here for sport! Maybe they think we're fishin'. Maybe they think we're damned fools."

It was a long afternoon. A changed tide tried to force them southward, but wind and wave said northward. Far ahead, where coast-line, sea, and sky formed their mighty angle, there were little dots which seemed to indicate a city on the shore.

"St. Augustine?"

The captain shook his head. "Too near Mosquito Inlet."

And the oiler rowed, and then the correspondent rowed; then the oiler rowed. It was a weary business. The human back can become the seat of more aches and pains than are registered in books for the composite anatomy of a regiment. It is a limited area, but it can become the theatre of innumerable muscular conflicts, tangles, wrenches, knots, and other comforts.

"Did you ever like to row, Billie?" said the correspondent.

"No," said the oiler; "hang it!"

When one exchanged the rowing-seat for a place in the bottom of the boat, he suffered a bodily depression that caused him to be careless of everything save an obligation to wiggle one finger. There was cold sea-water swashing to and fro in the boat, and he lay in it. His head, pillowed on a thwart, was within an inch of the swirl of a wave-crest, and sometimes a particularly obstreperous sea came inboard and drenched him once more. But these matters did not annoy him. It is almost certain that if the boat had capsized he would have tumbled comfortably out upon the ocean as if he felt sure that it was a great soft mattress.

"Look! There's a man on the shore!"

"Where?"

"There! See 'im? See 'im!"

"Yes, sure! He's walking along."

90 "Now he's stopped. Look! He's facing us!"

"He's waving at us!"

"So he is! By thunder!"

"Ah, now we're all right! Now we're all right! There'll be a boat out here for us in half an hour."

"He's going on. He's running. He's going up to that house there."

95 The remote beach seemed lower than the sea, and it required a searching glance to discern the little black figure. The captain saw a floating stick, and they rowed to it. A bath towel was by some weird chance in the boat, and, tying this on the stick, the captain waved it. The oarsman did not dare turn his head, so he was obliged to ask questions.

"What's he doing now?"

"He's standing still again. He's looking, I think.—There he goes again—toward the house.—Now he's stopped again."

"Is he waving at us?"

"No, not now; he was, though."

100 "Look! There comes another man!"

"He's running."

"Look at him go, would you!"

"Why, he's on a bicycle. Now he's met the other man. They're both waving at us. Look!"

"There comes something up the beach."

105 "What the devil is that thing?"

"Why, it looks like a boat."

"Why, certainly, it's a boat."

"No; it's on wheels."

"Yes, so it is. Well, that must be the life-boat. They drag them along shore on a wagon."

110 "That's the life-boat, sure."

"No, by God, it's—it's an omnibus."

"I tell you it's a life-boat."

"It is not! It's an omnibus. I can see it plain. See. One of these big hotel omnibuses."

"By thunder, you're right. It's an omnibus, sure as fate. What do you suppose they are doing with an omnibus? Maybe they are going around collecting the life-crew, hey?"

115 "That's it, likely. Look! There's a fellow waving a little black flag. He's standing on the steps of the omnibus. There come those other two fellows. Now they're all talking together. Look at the fellow with the flag. Maybe he ain't waving it!"

"That ain't a flag, is it? That's his coat. Why, certainly, that's his coat."

"So it is; it's his coat. He's taken it off and is waving it around his head. But would you look at him swing it!"

"Oh, say, there isn't any life-saving station there. That's just a winter-resort hotel omnibus that has brought over some of the boarders to see us drown."

"What's that idiot with the coat mean? What's he signalling, anyhow?"

"It looks as if he were trying to tell us to go north. There must be a life-saving station up there."

"No; he thinks we're fishing. Just giving us a merry hand. See? Ah, there, Willie!"

"Well, I wish I could make something out of those signals. What do you suppose he means?"

"He don't mean anything; he's just playing."

"Well, if he'd just signal us to try the surf again, or to go to sea and wait, or go north, or go south, or go to hell, there would be some reason in it. But look at him! He just stands there and keeps his coat revolving like a wheel. The ass!"

"There come more people."

"Now there's quite a mob. Look! Isn't that a boat?"

"Where? Oh, I see where you mean. No, that's no boat."

"That fellow is still waving his coat."

"He must think we like to see him do that. Why don't he quit it? It don't mean anything."

"I don't know. I think he is trying to make us go north. It must be that there's a life-saving station there somewhere."

"Say, he ain't tired yet. Look at 'im wave!"

"Wonder how long he can keep that up. He's been revolving his coat ever since he caught sight of us. He's an idiot. Why aren't they getting men to bring a boat out? A fishing boat—one of those big yawls—could come out here all right. Why don't he do something?"

"Oh, it's all right now."

"They'll have a boat out here for us in less than no time, now that they've seen us."

A faint yellow tone came into the sky over the low land. The shadows on the sea slowly deepened. The wind bore coldness with it, and the men began to shiver.

"Holy smoke!" said one, allowing his voice to express his impious mood, "if we keep on monkeying out here! If we've got to flounder out here all night!"

"Oh, we'll never have to stay here all night! Don't you worry. They've seen us now, and it won't be long before they'll come chasing out after us."

The shore grew dusky. The man waving a coat blended gradually into this gloom, and it swallowed in the same manner the omnibus and the group of people. The spray, when it dashed uproariously over the side, made the voyagers shrink and swear like men who were being branded.

"I'd like to catch the chump who waved the coat. I feel like socking him one, just for luck."

"Why? What did he do?"

"Oh, nothing, but then he seemed so damned cheerful."

In the meantime the oiler rowed, and then the correspondent rowed, and then the oiler rowed. Grey-faced and bowed forward, they mechanically, turn by turn, plied the leaden oars. The form of the lighthouse had vanished from the southern horizon, but finally a pale star appeared, just lifting from the sea. The streaked saffron in the west passed before the all-merging darkness, and the sea to the east was black. The land had vanished, and was expressed only by the low and drear thunder of the surf.

"If I am going to be drowned—if I am going to be drowned—if I am going to be drowned, why, in the name of the seven mad gods who rule the sea, was I allowed to come thus far and contemplate sand and trees? Was I brought here merely to have my nose dragged away as I was about to nibble the sacred cheese of life?"

The patient captain, drooped over the water-jar, was sometimes obliged to speak to the oarsman.

145   "Keep her head up! Keep her head up!"

"Keep her head up, sir." The voices were weary and low.

This was surely a quiet evening. All save the oarsman lay heavily and listlessly in the boat's bottom. As for him, his eyes were just capable of noting the tall black waves that swept forward in a most sinister silence, save for an occasional subdued growl of a crest.

The cook's head was on a thwart, and he looked without interest at the water under his nose. He was deep in other scenes. Finally he spoke. "Billie," he murmured, dreamfully, "what kind of pie do you like best?"

5

"Pie!" said the oiler and correspondent, agitatedly. "Don't talk about those things, blast you!"

150   "Well," said the cook, "I was just thinking about ham sandwiches, and—"

A night on the sea in an open boat is a long night. As darkness settled finally, the shine of the light, lifting from the sea in the south, changed to full gold. On the northern horizon a new light appeared, a small bluish gleam on the edge of the water. These two lights were the furniture of the world. Otherwise there was nothing but waves.

Two men huddled in the stern, and distances were so magnificent in the dinghy that the rower was enabled to keep his feet partly warm by thrusting them under his companions. Their legs indeed extended far under the rowing-seat until they touched the feet of the captain forward. Sometimes, despite the efforts of the tired oarsman, a wave came piling into the boat, an icy wave of the night, and the chilling water soaked them anew. They would twist their bodies for a moment and groan, and sleep the dead sleep once more, while the water in the boat gurgled about them as the craft rocked.

The plan of the oiler and the correspondent was for one to row until he lost the ability, and then arouse the other from his sea-water couch in the bottom of the boat.

The oiler plied the oars until his head drooped forward and the overpowering sleep blinded him; and he rowed yet afterward. Then he touched a man in the bottom of the boat, and called his name. "Will you spell me for a little while?" he said meekly.

155   "Sure, Billie," said the correspondent, awaking and dragging himself to a sitting position. They exchanged places carefully, and the oiler, cuddling down in the sea-water at the cook's side, seemed to go to sleep instantly.

The particular violence of the sea had ceased. The waves came without snarling. The obligation of the man at the oars was to keep the boat headed so that the tilt of the rollers would not capsize her, and to preserve her from filling when the crests rushed past. The black waves were silent and hard to be seen in the darkness. Often one was almost upon the boat before the oarsman was aware.

In a low voice the correspondent addressed the captain. He was not sure that the captain was awake, although this iron man seemed to be always awake. "Captain, shall I keep her making for that light north, sir?"

The same steady voice answered him. "Yes. Keep it about two points off the port bow."

The cook had tied a life-belt around himself in order to get even the warmth which this clumsy cork contrivance could donate, and he seemed almost stove-like when a rower, whose teeth invariably chattered wildly as soon as he ceased his labour, dropped down to sleep.

The correspondent, as he rowed, looked down at the two men sleeping underfoot. The cook's arm was around the oiler's shoulders, and, with their fragmentary clothing and haggard faces, they were the babes of the sea—a grotesque rendering of the old babes in the wood.

Later he must have grown stupid at his work, for suddenly there was a growling of water, and a crest came with a roar and a swash into the boat, and it was a wonder that it did not set the cook afloat in his life-belt. The cook continued to sleep, but the oiler sat up, blinking his eyes and shaking with the new cold.

"Oh, I'm awful sorry, Billie," said the correspondent contritely.

"That's all right, old boy," said the oiler, and lay down again and was asleep.

Presently it seemed that even the captain dozed, and the correspondent thought that he was the one man afloat on all the ocean. The wind had a voice as it came over the waves, and it was sadder than the end.

There was a long, loud swishing astern of the boat, and a gleaming trail of phosphorescence, like blue flame, was furrowed on the black waters. It might have been made by a monstrous knife.

Then there came a stillness, while the correspondent breathed with open mouth and looked at the sea.

Suddenly there was another swish and another long flash of bluish light, and this time it was alongside the boat, and might almost have been reached with an oar. The correspondent saw an enormous fin speed like a shadow through the water, hurling the crystalline spray, and leaving the long glowing trail.

The correspondent looked over his shoulder at the captain. His face was hidden, and he seemed to be asleep. He looked at the babes of the sea. They certainly were asleep. So, being bereft of sympathy, he leaned a little way to one side and swore softly into the sea.

But the thing did not then leave the vicinity of the boat. Ahead or astern, on one side or the other, at intervals long or short, fled the long sparkling streak, and there was to be heard the *whirroo* of the dark fin. The speed and power of the thing was greatly to be admired. It cut the water like a gigantic and keen projectile.

The presence of this biding thing did not affect the man with the same horror that it would if he had been a picnicker. He simply looked at the sea dully and swore in an undertone.

Nevertheless, it is true that he did not wish to be alone with the thing. He wished one of his companions to awake by chance and keep him company with it. But the captain hung motionless over the water-jar, and the oiler and the cook in the bottom of the boat were plunged in slumber.

6

"If I am going to be drowned—if I am going to be drowned—if I am going to be drowned, why, in the name of the seven mad gods who rule the sea, was I allowed to come thus far and contemplate sand and trees?"

During this dismal night, it may be remarked that a man would conclude that it was really the intention of the seven mad gods to drown him, despite the abominable injustice of it. For it was certainly an abominable injustice to drown a man who had worked so hard, so hard. The man felt it would be a crime most unnatural. Other people had drowned at sea since galleys swarmed with painted sails, but still—

When it occurs to a man that nature does not regard him as important, and that she feels she would not maim the universe by disposing of him, he at first wishes to throw bricks at the temple, and he hates deeply the fact that there are no bricks and no temples. Any visible expression of nature would surely be pelleted with his jeers.

175   Then, if there be no tangible thing to hoot, he feels, perhaps, the desire to confront a personification and indulge in pleas, bowed to one knee, and with hands supplicant, saying, "Yes, but I love myself."

A high cold star on a winter's night is the word he feels that she says to him. Thereafter he knows the pathos of his situation.

The men in the dinghy had not discussed these matters, but each had, no doubt, reflected upon them in silence and according to his mind. There was seldom any expression upon their faces save the general one of complete weariness. Speech was devoted to the business of the boat.

To chime the notes of his emotion, a verse mysteriously entered the correspondent's head. He had even forgotten that he had forgotten this verse, but it suddenly was in his mind.

> *A soldier of the Legion lay dying in Algiers;*
180 > *There was lack of woman's nursing, there was dearth of woman's tears;*
> *But a comrade stood beside him, and he took that comrade's hand,*
> *And he said, "I never more shall see my own, my native land."°*

In his childhood the correspondent had been made acquainted with the fact that a soldier of the Legion lay dying in Algiers, but he had never regarded the fact as important. Myriads of his school-fellows had informed him of the soldier's plight, but the dinning had naturally ended by making him perfectly indifferent. He had never considered it his affair that a soldier of the Legion lay dying in Algiers, nor had it appeared to him as a matter for sorrow. It was less to him than the breaking of a pencil's point.

Now, however, it quaintly came to him as a human, living thing. It was no longer merely a picture of a few throes in the breast of a poet, meanwhile drinking tea and warming his feet at the grate; it was an actuality—stern, mournful, and fine.

185   The correspondent plainly saw the soldier. He lay on the sand with his feet out straight and still. While his pale left hand was upon his chest in an attempt to thwart the going of his life, the blood came between his fingers. In the far Algerian distance, a city of low square forms was set against a sky that was faint with the last sunset hues. The correspondent, plying the oars and dreaming of the slow and slower movements of the lips of the soldier, was moved by a profound and perfectly impersonal comprehension. He was sorry for the soldier of the Legion who lay dying in Algiers.

The thing which had followed the boat and waited had evidently grown bored at the delay. There was no longer to be heard the slash of the cutwater, and there was no longer the flame of the long trail. The light in the north still glimmered, but it was apparently

---

°*". . . my native land.":* From "Bingen on the Rhine" by Caroline Norton (1808–1877).

no nearer to the boat. Sometimes the boom of the surf rang in the correspondent's ears, and he turned the craft seaward then and rowed harder. Southward, some one had evidently built a watch-fire on the beach. It was too low and too far to be seen, but it made a shimmering, roseate reflection upon the bluff in back of it, and this could be discerned from the boat. The wind came stronger, and sometimes a wave suddenly raged out like a mountain cat, and there was to be seen the sheen and sparkle of a broken crest.

The captain, in the bow, moved on his water-jar and sat erect. "Pretty long night," he observed to the correspondent. He looked at the shore. "Those life-saving people take their time."

"Did you see that shark playing around?"

"Yes, I saw him. He was a big fellow, all right."

"Wish I had known you were awake."   190

Later the correspondent spoke into the bottom of the boat. "Billie!" There was a slow and gradual disentanglement. "Billie, will you spell me?"

"Sure," said the oiler.

As soon as the correspondent touched the cold, comfortable sea-water in the bottom of the boat and had huddled close to the cook's life-belt he was deep in sleep, despite the fact that his teeth played all the popular airs. This sleep was so good to him that it was but a moment before he heard a voice call his name in a tone that demonstrated the last stages of exhaustion. "Will you spell me?"

"Sure Billie."

The light in the north had mysteriously vanished, but the correspondent took his   195
course from the wide-awake captain.

Later in the night they took the boat farther out to sea, and the captain directed the cook to take one oar at the stern and keep the boat facing the seas. He was to call out if he should hear the thunder of the surf. This plan enabled the oiler and the correspondent to get respite together. "We'll give those boys a chance to get into shape again," said the captain. They curled down and, after a few preliminary chatterings and trembles, slept once more the dead sleep. Neither knew they had bequeathed to the cook the company of another shark, or perhaps the same shark.

As the boat caroused on the waves, spray occasionally bumped over the side and gave them a fresh soaking, but this had no power to break their repose. The ominous slash of the wind and the water affected them as it would have affected mummies.

"Boys," said the cook, with the notes of every reluctance in his voice, "she's drifted in pretty close. I guess one of you had better take her to sea again." The correspondent, aroused, heard the crash of the toppled crests.

As he was rowing, the captain gave him some whiskey-and-water, and this steadied the chills out of him. "If I ever get ashore and anybody shows me even a photograph of an oar—"

At last there was a short conversation.   200

"Billie!—Billie, will you spell me?"

"Sure," said the oiler.

When the correspondent again opened his eyes, the sea and the sky were each of the grey hue of the dawning. Later, carmine and gold was painted upon the waters. The morning appeared finally, in its splendour, with a sky of pure blue, and the sunlight flamed on the tips of the waves.

On the distant dunes were set many little black cottages, and a tall white windmill reared above them. No man, nor dog, nor bicycle appeared on the beach. The cottages might have formed a deserted village.

205   The voyagers scanned the shore. A conference was held in the boat. "Well," said the captain, "if no help is coming, we might better try a run through the surf right away. If we stay out here much longer we will be too weak to do anything for ourselves at all." The others silently acquiesced in this reasoning. The boat was headed for the beach. The correspondent wondered if none ever ascended the tall wind-tower, and if then they never looked seaward. This tower was a giant, standing with its back to the plight of the ants. It represented in a degree, to the correspondent, the serenity of nature amid the struggles of the individual—nature in the wind, and nature in the vision of men. She did not seem cruel to him then, nor beneficent, nor treacherous, nor wise. But she was indifferent, flatly indifferent. It is, perhaps, plausible that a man in this situation, impressed with the unconcern of the universe, should see the innumerable flaws of his life, and have them taste wickedly in his mind, and wish for another chance. A distinction between right and wrong seems absurdly clear to him, then, in this new ignorance of the grave-edge, and he understands that if he were given another opportunity he would mend his conduct and his words, and be better and brighter during an introduction or at a tea.

        "Now, boys," said the captain, "she is going to swamp sure. All we can do is to work her in as far as possible, and then when she swamps, pile out and scramble for the beach. Keep cool now, and don't jump until she swamps sure."

        The oiler took the oars. Over his shoulders he scanned the surf. "Captain," he said, "I think I'd better bring her about and keep her head-on to the seas and back her in."

        "All right, Billie," said the captain. "Back her in." The oiler swung the boat then, and, seated in the stern, the cook and the correspondent were obliged to look over their shoulders to contemplate the lonely and indifferent shore.

        The monstrous inshore rollers heaved the boat high until the men were again enabled to see the white sheets of water scudding up the slanted beach. "We won't get in very close," said the captain. Each time a man could wrest his attention from the rollers, he turned his glance toward the shore, and in the expression of the eyes during this contemplation there was a singular quality. The correspondent, observing the others, knew that they were not afraid, but the full meaning of their glances was shrouded.

210   As for himself, he was too tired to grapple fundamentally with the fact. He tried to coerce his mind into thinking of it, but the mind was dominated at this time by the muscles, and they did not care. It merely occurred to him that if he should drown it would be a shame.

        There were no hurried words, no pallor, no plain agitation. The men simply looked at the shore. "Now, remember to get well clear of the boat when you jump," said the captain.

        Seaward the crest of a roller suddenly fell with a thunderous crash, and the long white comber came roaring down upon the boat.

        "Steady now," said the captain. The men were silent. They turned their eyes from the shore to the comber and waited. The boat slid up the incline, leaped at the furious top, bounced over it, and swung down the long back of the wave. Some water had been shipped, and the cook bailed it out.

        But the next crest crashed also. The tumbling, boiling flood of white water caught the boat and whirled it almost perpendicular. Water swarmed in from all sides. The correspondent had his hands on the gunwale at this time, and when the water entered at that place he swiftly withdrew his fingers, as if he objected to wetting them.

215   The little boat, drunken with this weight of water, reeled and snuggled deeper into the sea.

"Bail her out, cook! Bail her out!" said the captain.

"All right, Captain," said the cook.

"Now, boys, the next one will do for us sure," said the oiler. "Mind to jump clear of the boat."

The third wave moved forward, huge, furious, implacable. It fairly swallowed the dinghy, and almost simultaneously the men tumbled into the sea. A piece of life-belt had lain in the bottom of the boat, and as the correspondent went overboard he held this to his chest with his left hand.

The January water was icy, and he reflected immediately that it was colder than 220 he had expected to find it off the coast of Florida. This appeared to his dazed mind as a fact important enough to be noted at the time. The coldness of the water was sad; it was tragic. This fact was somehow mixed and confused with his opinion of his own situation, so that it seemed almost a proper reason for tears. The water was cold.

When he came to the surface he was conscious of little but the noisy water. Afterward he saw his companions in the sea. The oiler was ahead in the race. He was swimming strongly and rapidly. Off to the correspondent's left, the cook's great white and corked back bulged out of the water; and in the rear the captain was hanging with his one good hand to the keep of the overturned dinghy.

There is a certain immovable quality to a shore, and the correspondent wondered at it amid the confusion of the sea.

It seemed also very attractive; but the correspondent knew that it was a long journey, and he paddled leisurely. The piece of life-preserver lay under him, and sometimes he whirled down the incline of a wave as if he were on a hand-sled.

But finally he arrived at a place in the sea where travel was beset with difficulty. He did not pause swimming to inquire what manner of current had caught him, but there his progress ceased. The shore was set before him like a bit of scenery on a stage, and he looked at it and understood with his eyes each detail of it.

As the cook passed, much farther to the left, the captain was calling to him, "Turn 225 over on your back, cook! Turn over on your back and use the oar."

"All right, sir." The cook turned on his back, and paddling with an oar, went ahead as if he were a canoe.

Presently the boat also passed to the left of the correspondent, with the captain clinging with one hand to the keel. He would have appeared like a man raising himself to look over a board fence if it were not for the extraordinary gymnastics of the boat. The correspondent marvelled that the captain could still hold to it.

They passed on nearer to shore—the oiler, the cook, the captain—and following them went the water-jar, bouncing gaily over the seas.

The correspondent remained in the grip of this strange new enemy—a current. The shore, with its white slope of sand and its green bluff topped with little silent cottages, was spread like a picture before him. It was very near to him then, but he was impressed as one who, in a gallery, looks at a scene from Brittany or Algiers.

He thought: "I'm going to drown? Can it be possible? Can it be possible? Can it be 230 possible?" Perhaps an individual must consider his own death to be the final phenomenon of nature.

But later a wave perhaps whirled him out of this small deadly current, for he found suddenly that he could again make progress toward the shore. Later still he was aware that the captain, clinging with one hand to the keel of the dinghy, had his face turned away from the shore and toward him, and was calling his name. "Come to the boat! Come to the boat!"

In his struggle to reach the captain and the boat, he reflected that when one gets properly wearied drowning must really be a comfortable arrangement—a cessation of hostilities accompanied by a large degree of relief; and he was glad of it, for the main thing in his mind for some moments had been horror of the temporary agony. He did not wish to be hurt.

Presently he saw a man running along the shore. He was undressing with most remarkable speed. Coat, trousers, shirt, everything flew magically off him.

"Come to the boat!" called the captain.

235   "All right, Captain." As the correspondent paddled, he saw the captain let himself down to bottom and leave the boat. Then the correspondent performed his own little marvel of the voyage. A large wave caught him and flung him with ease and supreme speed completely over the boat and far beyond it. It struck him even then as an event in gymnastics and a true miracle of the sea. An overturned boat in the surf is not a plaything to a swimming man.

The correspondent arrived in water that reached only to his waist, but his condition did not enable him to stand for more than a moment. Each wave knocked him into a heap, and the undertow pulled at him.

Then he saw the man who had been running and undressing, and undressing and running, come bounding into the water. He dragged ashore the cook, and then waded toward the captain; but the captain waved him away and sent him to the correspondent. He was naked—naked as a tree in winter; but a halo was about his head, and he shone like a saint. He gave a strong pull, and a long drag, and a bully heave at the correspondent's hand. The correspondent, schooled in the minor formulæ, said, "Thanks, old man." But suddenly the man cried, "What's that?" He pointed a swift finger. The correspondent said, "Go."

In the shallows, face downward, lay the oiler. His forehead touched sand that was periodically, between each wave, clear of the sea.

The correspondent did not know all that transpired afterward. When he achieved safe ground he fell, striking the sand with each particular part of his body. It was as if he had dropped from a roof, but the thud was grateful to him.

240   It seems that instantly the beach was populated with men with blankets, clothes, and flasks, and women with coffee-pots and all the remedies sacred to their minds. The welcome of the land to the men from the sea was warm and generous; but a still and dripping shape was carried slowly up the beach, and the land's welcome for it could only be the different and sinister hospitality of the grave.

When it came night, the white waves paced to and fro in the moonlight, and the wind brought the sound of the great sea's voice to the men on the shore, and they felt that they could then be interpreters.   [1897]

QUESTIONS

1. Does the story have a single major conflict? Are there minor conflicts?
2. Why are individual speakers not always named in the dialogue?
3. What is the significance of the poem the correspondent recalls?
4. What does the death of the oiler contribute to the theme?
5. Trace the changing attitudes of the men toward one another as they undergo the experience. What have they learned as a result of the ordeal?

Philip K. Dick

Philip K. Dick (1928–1982) was born in Chicago, Illinois. When his parents divorced, he moved with his mother to Berkeley, California. At the age of twelve, he began reading science fiction, and by his early twenties he was publishing short fiction regularly in science fiction magazines. He is the author of over twenty novels and several volumes of short fiction, and the winner of prestigious awards such as the Hugo Award. His books include *The Man in the High Castle* (1962), *Martian Time-Slip* (1964), *The Three Stigmata of Palmer Eldritch* (1965), and *Do Androids Dream of Electric Sheep?* (1968). His novels and stories have been adapted into films including *Blade Runner*, *The Minority Report*, *Screamers*, and *Total Recall*.

We Can Remember It for You Wholesale

He awoke—and wanted Mars. The valleys, he thought. What would it be like to trudge among them? Great and greater yet: the dream grew as he became fully conscious, the dream and the yearning. He could almost feel the enveloping presence of the other world, which only Government agents and high officials had seen. A clerk like himself? Not likely.

"Are you getting up or not?" his wife Kirsten asked drowsily, with her usual hint of fierce crossness. "If you are, push the hot coffee button on the darn stove."

"Okay," Douglas Quail said, and made his way barefoot from the bedroom of their conapt to the kitchen. There; having dutifully pressed the hot coffee button, he seated himself at the kitchen table, brought out a yellow, small tin of fine Dean Swift snuff. He inhaled briskly, and the Beau Nash mixture stung his nose, burned the roof of his mouth. But still he inhaled; it woke him up and allowed his dreams, his nocturnal desires and random wishes, to condense into a semblance of rationality.

I will go, he said to himself. *Before I die I'll see Mars.*

It was, of course, impossible, and he knew this even as he dreamed. But the daylight, the mundane noise of his wife now brushing her hair before the bedroom mirror—everything conspired to remind him of what he was. *A miserable little salaried employee,* he said to himself with bitterness. Kirsten reminded him of this at least once a day and he did not blame her; it was a wife's job to bring her husband down to Earth. *Down to Earth,* he thought, and laughed. The figure of speech in this was literally apt.

5

"What are you sniggering about?" his wife asked as she swept into the kitchen, her long busy-pink robe wagging after her. "A dream, I bet. You're always full of them."

"Yes," he said, and gazed out the kitchen window at the hover-cars and traffic runnels, and all the little energetic people hurrying to work. In a little while he would be among them. As always.

"I'll bet it had to do with some woman," Kirsten said witheringly.

"No," he said. "A god. The god of war. He has wonderful craters with every kind of plant-life growing deep down in them."

10   "Listen." Kirsten crouched down beside him and spoke earnestly, the harsh quality momentarily gone from her voice. "The bottom of the ocean—*our* ocean is much more, an infinity of times more beautiful. You know that; everyone knows that. Rent an artificial gill-outfit for both of us, take a week off from work, and we can descend and live down there at one of those year-round aquatic resorts. And in addition—" She broke off. "You're not listening. You should be. Here is something a lot better than that compulsion, that obsession you have about Mars, and you don't even listen!" Her voice rose piercingly. "God in heaven, you're doomed, Doug! What's going to become of you?"

"I'm going to work," he said, rising to his feet, his breakfast forgotten. "That's what's going to become of me."

She eyed him. "You're getting worse. More fanatical every day. Where's it going to lead?"

"To Mars," he said, and opened the door to the closet to get down a fresh shirt to wear to work.

Having descended from the taxi Douglas Quail slowly walked across three densely populated foot runnels and to the modern, attractively inviting doorway. There he halted, impeding mid-morning traffic, and with caution read the shifting-color neon sign. He had, in the past, scrutinized this sign before . . . but never had he come so close. This was very different; what he did now was something else. Something which sooner or later had to happen.

15   Rekal, Incorporated

Was this the answer? After all, an illusion, no matter how convincing, remained nothing more than an illusion. At least objectively. But subjectively—quite the opposite entirely.

And anyhow he had an appointment. Within the next five minutes.

Taking a deep breath of mildly smog-infested Chicago air, he walked through the dazzling polychromatic shimmer of the doorway and up to the receptionist's counter.

The nicely-articulated blonde at the counter, bare-bosomed and tidy, said pleasantly, "Good morning, Mr. Quail."

20   "Yes," he said. "I'm here to see about a Rekal course. As I guess you know."

"Not 'rekal' but *recall*," the receptionist corrected him. She picked up the receiver of the vidphone by her smooth elbow and said into it, "Mr. Douglas Quail is here, Mr. McClane. May he come inside, now? Or is it too soon?"

"Giz wetwa wum-wum wamp," the phone mumbled.

"Yes, Mr. Quail," she said. "You may go in; Mr. McClane is expecting you." As he started off uncertainly she called after him, "Room D, Mr. Quail. To your right."

After a frustrating but brief moment of being lost he found the proper room. The door hung open and inside, at a big genuine walnut desk, sat a genial-looking man, middle-aged, wearing the latest Martian frog-pelt gray suit; his attire alone would have told Quail that he had come to the right person.

"Sit down, Douglas," McClane said, waving his plump hand toward a chair which   25
faced the desk. "So you want to have gone to Mars. Very good."

Quail seated himself, feeling tense. "I'm not so sure this is worth the fee," he said.
"It costs a lot and as far as I can see I really get nothing." *Costs almost as much as going,*
he thought.

"You get tangible proof of your trip," McClane disagreed emphatically. "All the proof
you'll need. Here; I'll show you." He dug within a drawer of his impressive desk. "Ticket stub." Reaching into a manila folder, he produced a small square of embossed cardboard. "It proves you went—and returned. Postcards." He laid out four framed picture 3-D
full-color postcards in a neatly-arranged row on the desk for Quail to see. "Film. Shots
you took of local sights on Mars with a rented moving camera." To Quail he displayed
those, too. "Plus the names of people you met, two hundred poscreds worth of souvenirs,
which will arrive—from Mars—within the following month. And passport, certificates
listing the shots you received. And more." He glanced up keenly at Quail. "You'll know
you went, all right," he said. "You won't remember us, won't remember me or ever having been here. It'll be a real trip in your mind; we guarantee that. A full two weeks of recall; every last piddling detail. Remember this: if at any time you doubt that you really
took an extensive trip to Mars you can return here and get a full refund. You see?"

"But I didn't go," Quail said. "I won't have gone, no matter what proofs you provide me with." He took a deep, unsteady breath. "And I never was a secret agent with
Interplan." It seemed impossible to him that Rekal, Incorporated's extra-factual memory implant would do its job—despite what he had heard people say.

"Mr. Quail," McClane said patiently. "As you explained in your letter to us, you
have no chance, no possibility in the slightest, of ever actually getting to Mars; you can't
afford it, and what is much more important, you could never qualify as an undercover agent for Interplan or anybody else. This is the only way you can achieve your,
ahem, life-long dream; am I not correct, sir? You can't be this; you can't actually do
this." He chuckled. "But you can *have been* and *have done.* We see to that. And our fee
is reasonable; no hidden charges." He smiled encouragingly.

"Is an extra-factual memory that convincing?" Quail asked.   30

"More than the real thing, sir. Had you really gone to Mars as an Interplan agent, you
would by now have forgotten a great deal; our analysis of true-mem systems—authentic
recollections of major events in a person's life—shows that a variety of details are very
quickly lost to the person. Forever. Part of the package we offer you is such deep implantation of recall that nothing is forgotten. The packet which is fed to you while you're co-
matose is the creation of trained experts, men who have spent years on Mars; in every
case we verify details down to the last iota. And you've picked a rather easy extra-factual
system; had you picked Pluto or wanted to be Emperor of the Inner Planet Alliance we'd
have much more difficulty . . . and the charges would be considerably greater."

Reaching into his coat for his wallet, Quail said, "Okay. It's been my life-long ambition and so I see I'll never really do it. So I guess I'll have to settle for this."

"Don't think of it that way," McClane said severely. "You're not accepting second-
best. The actual memory, with all its vagueness, omissions and ellipses, not to say
distortions—that's second-best." He accepted the money and pressed a button on his
desk. "All right, Mr. Quail," he said, as the door of his office opened and two burly men
swiftly entered. "You're on your way to Mars as a secret agent." He rose, came over
to shake Quail's nervous, moist hand. "Or rather, you have been on your way. This afternoon at four-thirty you will, um, arrive back here on Terra; a cab will leave you off
at your conapt and as I say you will never remember seeing me or coming here; you
won't, in fact, even remember having heard of our existence."

His mouth dry with nervousness, Quail followed the two technicians from the office; what happened next depended on them.

35   *Will I actually believe I've been on Mars?* he wondered. *That I managed to fulfill my lifetime ambition?* He had a strange, lingering intuition that something would go wrong. But just what—he did not know.

He would have to wait and find out.

The intercom on McClane's desk, which connected him with the work area of the firm, buzzed and a voice said, "Mr. Quail is under sedation now, sir. Do you want to supervise this one, or shall we go ahead?"

"It's routine," McClane observed. "You may go ahead, Lowe: I don't think you'll run into any trouble." Programming an artificial memory of a trip to another planet—with or without the added fillip of being a secret agent—showed up on the firm's work-schedule with monotonous regularity. *In one month,* he calculated wryly, *me must do twenty of these . . . ersatz interplanetary travel has become our bread and butter.*

"Whatever you say, Mr. McClane," Lowe's voice came, and thereupon the intercom shut off.

40   Going to the vault section in the chamber behind his office, McClane searched about for a Three packet—trip to Mars—and a Sixty-two packet: secret Interplan spy. Finding the two packets, he returned with them to his desk, seated himself comfortably, poured out the contents—merchandise which would be planted in Quail's conapt while the lab technicians busied themselves installing false memory.

A one-poscred sneaky-pete side arm, McClane reflected; *that's the largest item. Sets us back financially the most.* Then a pellet-sized transmitter, which could be swallowed if the agent were caught. Code book that astonishingly resembled the real thing . . . the firm's models were highly accurate: based, whenever possible, on actual U.S. military issue. Odd bits which made no intrinsic sense but which would be woven into the warp and woof of Quail's imaginary trip, would coincide with his memory: half an ancient silver fifty-cent piece, several quotations from John Donne's sermons written incorrectly, each on a separate piece of transparent tissue-thin paper, several match folders from bars on Mars, a stainless steel spoon engraved PROPERTY OF DOME-MARS NATIONALKIB-BUZIM, a wire tapping coil which—

The intercom buzzed. "Mr. McClane, I'm sorry to bother you but something rather ominous has come up. Maybe it would be better if you were in here after all. Quail is already under sedation; he reacted well to the narkidrine; he's completely unconscious and receptive. But—"

"I'll be in." Sensing trouble, McClane left his office; a moment later he emerged in the work area.

On a hygienic bed lay Douglas Quail, breathing slowly and regularly, his eyes virtually shut; he seemed dimly—but only dimly—aware of the two technicians and now McClane himself.

45   "There's no space to insert false memory-patterns?" McClane felt irritation. "Merely drop out two work weeks; he's employed as a clerk at the West Coast Emigration Bureau, which is a government agency, so he undoubtedly has or had two weeks' vacation within the last year. That ought to do it." Petty details annoyed him. And always would.

"Our problem," Lowe said sharply, "is something quite different." He bent over the bed, said to Quail, "Tell Mr. McClane what you told us." To McClane he said, "Listen closely."

The gray-green eyes of the man lying supine in the bed focussed on McClane's face. The eyes, he observed uneasily, had become hard; they had a polished, inorganic quality, like semi-precious tumbled stones. He was not sure that he liked what he saw; the brilliance was too cold. "What do you want now?" Quail said harshly. "You've broken my cover. Get out of here before I take you all apart." He studied McClane. "Especially you," he continued. "You're in charge of this counter-operation."

Lowe said, "How long were you on Mars?"

"One month," Quail said gratingly.

"And your purpose there?" Lowe demanded.

The meager lips twisted; Quail eyed him and did not speak. At last, drawling the words out so that they dripped with hostility, he said, "Agent for Interplan. As I already told you. Don't you record everything that's said? Play your vid-aud tape back for your boss and leave me alone." He shut his eyes, then; the hard brilliance ceased. Mc-Clane felt, instantly, a rushing splurge of relief.

Lowe said quietly, "This is a tough man, Mr. McClane."

"He won't be," McClane said, "after we arrange for him to lose his memory-chain again. He'll be as meek as before." To Quail he said, "So *this* is why you wanted to go to Mars so terribly bad."

Without opening his eyes Quail said, "I never wanted to go to Mars. I was assigned it—they handed it to me and there I was: stuck. Oh yeah, I admit I was curious about it; who wouldn't be?" Again he opened his eyes and surveyed the three of them, Mc-Clane in particular. "Quite a truth drug you've got here; it brought up things I had absolutely no memory of." He pondered. "I wonder about Kirsten," he said, half to himself. "Could she be in on it? An Interplan contact keeping an eye on me . . . to be certain I didn't regain my memory? No wonder she's been so derisive about my wanting to go there." Faintly, he smiled; the smile—one of understanding—disappeared almost at once.

McClane said, "Please believe me, Mr. Quail; we stumbled onto this entirely by accident. In the work we do—"

"I believe you," Quail said. He seemed tired, now; the drug was continuing to pull him under, deeper and deeper. "Where did I say I'd been?" he murmured. "Mars? Hard to remember—I know I'd like to see it; so would everybody else. But me—" His voice trailed off. "Just a clerk, a nothing clerk."

Straightening up, Lowe said to his superior. "He wants a false memory implanted that corresponds to a trip he actually took. And a false reason which is the real reason. He's telling the truth; he's a long way down in the narkidrine. The trip is very vivid in his mind—at least under sedation. But apparently he doesn't recall it otherwise. Someone, probably at a government military-sciences lab, erased his conscious memories; all he knew was that going to Mars meant something special to him, and so did being a secret agent. They couldn't erase that; it's not a memory but a desire, undoubtedly the same one that motivated him to volunteer for the assignment in the first place."

The other technician, Keeler, said to McClane, "What do we do? Graft a false memory-pattern over the real memory? There's no telling what the results would be; he might remember some of the genuine trip, and the confusion might bring on a psychotic interlude. He'd have to hold two opposite premises in his mind simultaneously: that he went to Mars and that he didn't. That he's a genuine agent for Interplan and he's not, that it's spurious. I think we ought to revive him without any false memory implantation and send him out of here; this is hot."

50

55

"Agreed," McClane said. A thought came to him. "Can you predict what he'll remember when he comes out of sedation?"

60   "Impossible to tell," Lowe said. "He probably will have some dim, diffuse memory of his actual trip, now. And he'd probably be in grave doubt as to its validity; he'd
probably decide our programming slipped a gear-tooth. And he'd remember coming
here; that wouldn't be erased—unless you want it erased."

"The less we mess with this man," McClane said, "the better I like it. This is nothing for us to fool around with; we've been foolish enough to—or unlucky enough to—
uncover a genuine Interplan spy who has a cover so perfect that up to now even he
didn't know what he was—or rather is." The sooner they washed their hands of the
man calling himself Douglas Quail the better.

"Are you going to plant packets Three and Sixty-two in his conapt?" Lowe said.

"No," McClane said. "And we're going to return half his fee."

"'Half'! Why half?"

65   McClane said lamely, "It seems to be a good compromise."

As the cab carried him back to his conapt at the residential end of Chicago, Douglas Quail said to himself, *It's sure good to be back on Terra.*

Already the month-long period on Mars had begun to waver in his memory; he
had only an image of profound gaping craters, an ever-present ancient erosion of hills,
of vitality, of motion itself. A world of dust where little happened, where a good part
of the day was spent checking and rechecking one's portable oxygen source. And then
the life forms, the unassuming and modest gray-brown cacti and maw-worms.

As a matter of fact he had brought back several moribund examples of Martian
fauna; he had smuggled them through customs. After all, they posed no menace; they
couldn't survive in Earth's heavy atmosphere.

Reaching into his coat pocket, he rummaged for the container of Martian maw-
worms—

70   And found an envelope instead.

Lifting it out, he discovered, to his perplexity, that it contained five hundred and seventy poscreds, in cred bills of low denomination.

Where'd I get this? he asked himself. *Didn't I spend every 'cred I had on my trip?*

With the money came a slip of paper marked: *One-half fee ret'd. By McClane.* And then
the date. Today's date.

"Recall," he said aloud.

75   "Recall what, sir or madam?" the robot driver of the cab inquired respectfully.

"Do you have a phone book?" Quail demanded.

"Certainly, sir or madam." A slot opened; from it slid a microtape phone book for
Cook County.

"It's spelled oddly," Quail said as he leafed through the pages of the yellow section.
He felt fear, then; abiding fear. "Here it is," he said. "Take me there, to Rekal, Incorporated. I've changed my mind; I don't want to go home."

"Yes, sir or madam, as the case may be," the driver said. A moment later the cab was
zipping back in the opposite direction.

80   "May I make use of your phone?" he asked.

"Be my guest," the robot driver said. And presented a shiny new emperor 3-D color
phone to him.

He dialed his own conapt. And after a pause found himself confronted by a miniature but chillingly realistic image of Kirsten on the small screen. "I've been to Mars,"
he said to her.

"You're drunk." Her lips writhed scornfully. "Or worse."

"'s God's truth."

"When?" she demanded.

"I don't know." He felt confused. "A simulated trip, I think. By means of one of those artificial or extra-factual or whatever it is memory places. It didn't take."

Kirsten said witheringly, "You *are* drunk." And broke the connection at her end. He hung up, then, feeling his face flush. *Always the same tone,* he said hotly to himself. *Always the retort, as if she knows everything and I know nothing. What a marriage. Keerist,* he thought dismally.

A moment later the cab stopped at the curb before a modern, very attractive little pink building, over which a shifting polychromatic neon sign read: REKAL, INCORPORATED.

The receptionist, chic and bare from the waist up, started in surprise, then gained masterful control of herself. "Oh, hello, Mr. Quail," she said nervously. "H-how are you? Did you forget something?"

"The rest of my fee back," he said.

More composed now, the receptionist said, "Fee? I think you are mistaken, Mr. Quail. You were here discussing the feasibility of an extra-factual trip for you, but—" She shrugged her smooth pale shoulders. "As I understand it, no trip was taken."

Quail said, "I remember everything, miss. My letter to Rekal, Incorporated, which started this whole business off. I remember my arrival here, my visit with Mr. McClane. Then the two lab technicians taking me in tow and administering a drug to put me out." No wonder the firm had returned half his fee. The false memory of his "trip to Mars" hadn't taken—at least not entirely, not as he had been assured.

"Mr. Quail," the girl said, "although you are a minor clerk you are a good-looking man and it spoils your features to become angry. If it would make you feel any better, I might, ahem, let you take me out . . ."

He felt furious, then. "I remember you," he said savagely. "For instance the fact that your breasts are sprayed blue; that stuck in my mind. And I remember Mr. McClane's promise that if I remembered my visit to Rekal, Incorporated I'd receive my money back in full. Where is Mr. McClane?"

After a delay—probably as long as they could manage—he found himself once more seated facing the imposing walnut desk, exactly as he had been an hour or so earlier in the day.

"Some technique you have," Quail said sardonically. His disappointment—and resentment—was enormous, by now. "My so-called 'memory' of a trip to Mars as an undercover agent for Interplan is hazy and vague and shot full of contradictions. And I clearly remember my dealings here with you people. I ought to take this to the Better Business Bureau." He was burning angry, at this point; his sense of being cheated had overwhelmed him, had destroyed his customary aversion to participating in a public squabble.

Looking morose, as well as cautious, McClane said, "We capitulate, Quail. We'll refund the balance of your fee. I fully concede the fact that we did absolutely nothing for you." His tone was resigned.

Quail said accusingly, "You didn't even provide me with the various artifacts that you claimed would 'prove' to me I had been on Mars. All that song-and-dance you went into—it hasn't materialized into a damn thing. Not even a ticket stub. Nor postcards. Nor passport. Nor proof of immunization shots. Nor—"

"Listen, Quail," McClane said. "Suppose I told you—" He broke off. "Let it go." He pressed a button on his intercom. "Shirley, will you disburse five hundred and seventy

more 'creds in the form of a cashier's check made out to Douglas Quail? Thank you."
He released the button, then glared at Quail.

Presently the check appeared; the receptionist placed it before McClane and once
more vanished out of sight, leaving the two men alone, still facing each other across
the surface of the massive walnut desk.

"Let me give you a word of advice," McClane said as he signed the check and
passed it over. "Don't discuss your, ahem, recent trip to Mars with anyone."

"What trip?"

"Well, that's the thing." Doggedly, McClane said, "The trip you partially remember.
Act as if you don't remember; pretend it never took place. Don't ask me why; just take
my advice: it'll be better for all of us." He had begun to perspire. Freely. "Now, Mr.
Quail, I have other business, other clients to see." He rose, showed Quail to the door.

Quail said, as he opened the door, "A firm that turns out such bad work shouldn't
have any clients at all." He shut the door behind him.

On the way home in the cab Quail pondered the wording of his letter of complaint to the Better Business Bureau, Terra Division. As soon as he could get to his
typewriter he'd get started; it was clearly his duty to warn other people away from
Rekal, Incorporated.

When he got back to his conapt he seated himself before his Hermes Rocket portable,
opened the drawers and rummaged for carbon paper—and noticed a small, familiar
box. A box which he had carefully filled on Mars with Martian fauna and later smuggled through customs.

Opening the box he saw, to his disbelief, six dead maw-worms and several varieties
of the unicellular life on which the Martian worms fed. The protozoa were dried-up,
dusty, but he recognized them; it had taken him an entire day picking among the vast
dark alien boulders to find them. A wonderful, illuminated journey of discovery.

But I didn't go to Mars, he realized.

Yet on the other hand—

Kirsten appeared at the doorway to the room, an armload of pale brown groceries
gripped. "Why are you home in the middle of the day?" Her voice, in an eternity of
sameness, was accusing.

"*Did I go to Mars?*" he asked her. "You would know."

"No, of course you didn't go to Mars; *you* would know that, I would think. Aren't
you always bleating about going?"

He said, "By God, I think I went." After a pause he added, "And simultaneously I
think I didn't go."

"Make up your mind."

"How can I?" He gestured. "I have both memory-tracks grafted inside my head; one
is real and one isn't but I can't tell which is which. Why can't I rely on you? They
haven't tinkered with you." She could do this much for him at least—even if she never
did anything else.

Kirsten said in a level, controlled voice, "Doug, if you don't pull yourself together,
we're through. I'm going to leave you."

"I'm in trouble." His voice came out husky and coarse. And shaking. "Probably
I'm heading into a psychotic episode; I hope not, but—maybe that's it. It would explain
everything, anyhow."

Setting down the bag of groceries, Kirsten stalked to the closet. "I was not kidding,"
she said to him quietly. She brought out a coat, got it on, walked back to the door of
the conapt. "I'll phone you one of these days soon," she said tonelessly. "This is good-
bye, Doug. I hope you pull out of this eventually; I really pray you do. For your sake."

"Wait," he said desperately. "Just tell me and make it absolute; I did go or I didn't— tell me which one." *But they may have altered your memory-track also*, he realized.

The door closed. His wife had left. Finally!

A voice behind him said, "Well, that's that. Now put up your hands, Quail. And also please turn around and face this way."

He turned, instinctively, without raising his hands.

The man who faced him wore the plum uniform of the Interplan Police Agency, and his gun appeared to be UN issue. And, for some odd reason, he seemed familiar to Quail; familiar in a blurred, distorted fashion which he could not pin down. So, jerkily, he raised his hands.

"You remember," the policeman said, "your trip to Mars. We know all your actions today and all your thoughts—in particular your very important thoughts on the trip home from Rekal, Incorporated." He explained, "We have a tele-transmitter wired within your skull; it keeps us constantly informed."

A telepathic transmitter; use of a living plasma that had been discovered on Luna. He shuddered with self-aversion. The thing lived inside him, within his own brain, feeding, listening, feeding. But the Interplan police used them; that had come out even in the homeopapes. So this was probably true, dismal as it was.

"Why me?" Quail said huskily. What had he done—or thought? And what did this have to do with Rekal, Incorporated?

"Fundamentally," the Interplan cop said, "this has nothing to do with Rekal; it's between you and us." He tapped his right ear. "I'm still picking up your mentational processes by way of your cephalic transmitter." In the man's ear Quail saw a small white-plastic plug. "So I have to warn you: anything you think may be held against you." He smiled. "Not that it matters now; you've already thought and spoken yourself into oblivion. What's annoying is the fact that under narkidrine at Rekal, Incorporated you told them, their technicians and the owner, Mr. McClane, about your trip—where you went, for whom, some of what you did. They're very frightened. They wish they had never laid eyes on you." He added reflectively, "They're right."

Quail said, "I never made any trip. It's a false memory-chain improperly planted in me by McClane's technicians." But then he thought of the box, in his desk drawer, containing the Martian life forms. And the trouble and hardship he had had gathering them. The memory seemed real. And the box of life forms; that certainly was real. Unless McClane had planted it. Perhaps this was one of the "proofs" which McClane had talked glibly about.

The memory of my trip to Mars, he thought, *doesn't convince me—but unfortunately it has convinced the Interplan Police Agency. They think I really went to Mars and they think I at least partially realize it.*

"We not only know you went to Mars," the Interplan cop agreed, in answer to his thoughts, "but we know that you now remember enough to be difficult for us. And there's no use expunging your conscious memory of all this, because if we do you'll simply show up at Rekal, Incorporated again and start over. And we can't do anything about McClane and his operation because we have no jurisdiction over anyone except our own people. Anyhow, McClane hasn't committed any crime." He eyed Quail, "Nor, technically, have you. You didn't go to Rekal, Incorporated with the idea of regaining your memory; you went, as we realize, for the usual reason people go there—a love by plain, dull people for adventure." He added, "Unfortunately you're not plain, not dull, and you've already had too much excitement; the last thing in the universe you needed was a course from Rekal, Incorporated. Nothing could have been more lethal for you or for us. And, for that matter, for McClane."

120

125

130

Quail said, "Why is it 'difficult' for you if I remember my trip—my alleged trip—and what I did there?"

"Because," the Interplan harness bull said, "what you did is not in accord with our great white all-protecting father public image. You did, for us, what we never do. As you'll presently remember—thanks to narkidrine. That box of dead worms and algae has been sitting in your desk drawer for six months, ever since you got back. And at no time have you shown the slightest curiosity about it. We didn't even know you had it until you remembered it on your way home from Rekal; then we came here on the double to look for it." He added, unnecessarily, "Without any luck; there wasn't enough time."

A second Interplan cop joined the first one; the two briefly conferred. Meanwhile, Quail thought rapidly. He did remember more, now; the cop had been right about narkidrine. They—Interplan—probably used it themselves. Probably? He knew darn well they did; he had seen them putting a prisoner on it. Where would *that* be? Somewhere on Terra? More likely on Luna, he decided, viewing the image rising from his highly defective—but rapidly less so—memory.

And he remembered something else. Their reason for sending him to Mars; the job he had done.

135   No wonder they had expunged his memory.

"Oh, God," the first of the two Interplan cops said, breaking off his conversation with his companion. Obviously, he had picked up Quail's thoughts. "Well, this is a far worse problem, now; as bad as it can get." He walked toward Quail, again covering him with his gun. "We've got to kill you," he said. "And right away."

Nervously, his fellow officer said, "Why right away? Can't we simply cart him off to Interplan New York and let them—"

"*He* knows why it has to be right away," the first cop said; he too looked nervous, now, but Quail realized that it was for an entirely different reason. His memory had been brought back almost entirely, now. And he fully understood the officer's tension.

"On Mars," Quail said hoarsely, "I killed a man. After getting past fifteen body-guards. Some armed with sneaky-pete guns, the way you are." He had been trained, by Interplan, over a five-year period to be an assassin. A professional killer. He knew ways to take out armed adversaries ... such as these two officers; and the one with the ear-receiver knew it, too.

140   If he moved swiftly enough—

The gun fired. But he had already moved to one side, and at the same time he chopped down the gun-carrying officer. In an instant he had possession of the gun and was covering the other, confused, officer.

"Picked my thoughts up," Quail said, panting for breath. "He knew what I was going to do, but I did it anyhow."

Half sitting up, the injured officer grated, "He won't use that gun on you, Sam; I pick that up, too. He knows he's finished, and he knows we know it, too. Come on, Quail." Laboriously, grunting with pain, he got shakily to his feet. He held out his hand. "The gun," he said to Quail. "You can't use it, and if you turn it over to me I'll guarantee not to kill you; you'll be given a hearing, and someone higher up in Interplan will decide, not me. Maybe they can erase your memory once more, I don't know. But you know the thing I was going to kill you for; I couldn't keep you from remembering it. So my reason for wanting to kill you is in a sense past."

Quail, clutching the gun, bolted from the conapt, sprinted for the elevator. *If you follow me*, he thought, *I'll kill you. So don't.* He jabbed at the elevator button and, a moment later, the doors slid back.

The police hadn't followed him. Obviously they had picked up his terse, tense   145
thoughts and had decided not to take the chance.

With him inside the elevator descended. He had gotten away—for a time. But what next? Where could he go?

The elevator reached the ground floor; a moment later Quail had joined the mob of peds hurrying along the runnels. His head ached and he felt sick. But at least he had evaded death; they had come very close to shooting him on the spot, back in his own conapt.

And they probably will again, he decided. *When they find me. And with this transmitter inside me, that won't take too long.*

Ironically, he had gotten exactly what he had asked Rekal, Incorporated for. Adventure, peril, Interplan police at work, a secret and dangerous trip to Mars in which his life was at stake—everything he had wanted as a false memory.

The advantages of it being a memory—and nothing more—could now be ap-   150
preciated.

On a park bench, alone, he sat dully watching a flock of perts: a semi-bird imported from Mars' two moons, capable of soaring flight, even against Earth's huge gravity.

Maybe I can find my way back to Mars, he pondered. But then what? It would be worse on Mars; the political organization whose leader he had assassinated would spot him the moment he stepped from the ship; he would have Interplan and *them* after him, there.

Can you hear me thinking? he wondered. Easy avenue to paranoia; sitting here alone he felt them tuning in on him, monitoring, recording, discussing. . . . He shivered, rose to his feet, walked aimlessly, his hands deep in his pockets. *No matter where I go*, he realized, *you'll always be with me. As long as I have this device inside my head.*

I'll make a deal with you, he thought to himself—and to them. *Can you imprint a false-memory template on me again, as you did before, that I lived an average, routine life, never went to Mars? Never saw an Interplan uniform up close and never handled a gun?*

A voice inside his brain answered, "As has been carefully explained to you: that   155
would not be enough."

Astonished, he halted.

"We formerly communicated with you in this manner," the voice continued. "When you were operating in the field, on Mars. It's been months since we've done it; we assumed, in fact, that we'd never have to do so again. Where are you?"

"Walking," Quail said, "to my death." *By your officers' guns*, he added as an afterthought. "How can you be sure it wouldn't be enough?" he demanded. "Don't the Rekal techniques work?"

"As we said. If you're given a set of standard, average memories you get—restless. You'd inevitably seek out Rekal or one of its competitors again. We can't go through this a second time."

"Suppose," Quail said, "once my authentic memories have been canceled, some-   160
thing more vital than standard memories are implanted. Something which would act to satisfy my craving," he said. "That's been proved; that's probably why you initially hired me. But you ought to be able to come up with something else—something equal. I was the richest man on Terra but I finally gave all my money to educational foundations. Or I was a famous deep-space explorer. Anything of that sort; wouldn't one of those do?"

Silence.

"Try it," he said desperately. "Get some of your top-notch military psychiatrists; explore my mind. Find out what my most expansive daydream is." He tried to think. "Women," he said. "Thousands of them, like Don Juan had. An interplanetary playboy—a mistress in every city on Earth, Luna and Mars. Only I gave that up, out of exhaustion. Please," he begged. "Try it."

"You'd voluntarily surrender, then?" the voice inside his head asked. "If we agreed, to arrange such a solution? *If it's possible?*"

After an interval of hesitation he said, "Yes." *I'll take the risk*, he said to himself, *that you don't simply kill me.*

165   "You make the first move," the voice said presently. "Turn yourself over to us. And we'll investigate that line of possibility. If we can't do it, however, if your authentic memories begin to crop up again as they've done at this time, then—" There was silence and then the voice finished, "We'll have to destroy you. As you must understand. Well, Quail, you still want to try?"

"Yes," he said. Because the alternative was death now—and for certain. At least this way he had a chance, slim as it was.

"You present yourself at our main barracks in New York," the voice of the Interplan cop resumed. "At 580 Fifth Avenue, floor twelve. Once you've surrendered yourself, we'll have our psychiatrists begin on you; we'll have personality-profile tests made. We'll attempt to determine your absolute, ultimate fantasy wish—then we'll bring you back to Rekal, Incorporated, here; get them in on it, fulfilling that wish in vicarious surrogate retrospection. And—good luck. We do owe you something; you acted as a capable instrument for us." The voice lacked malice; if anything, they—the organization—felt sympathy toward him.

"Thanks," Quail said. And began searching for a robot cab.

"Mr. Quail," the stern-faced, elderly Interplan psychiatrist said, "you possess a most interesting wish-fulfillment dream fantasy. Probably nothing such as you consciously entertain or suppose. This is commonly the way; I hope it won't upset you too much to hear about it."

170   The senior ranking Interplan officer present said briskly, "He better not be too much upset to hear about it, not if he expects not to get shot."

"Unlike the fantasy of wanting to be an Interplan undercover agent," the psychiatrist continued, "which, being relatively speaking a product of maturity, had a certain plausibility to it, this production is a grotesque dream of your childhood; it is no wonder you fail to recall it. Your fantasy is this: you are nine years old, walking alone down a rustic lane. An unfamiliar variety of space vessel from another star system lands directly in front of you. No one on Earth but you, Mr. Quail, sees it. The creatures within are very small and helpless, somewhat on the order of field mice, although they are attempting to invade Earth; tens of thousands of other ships will soon be on their way, when this advance party gives the go-ahead signal."

"And I suppose I stop them," Quail said, experiencing a mixture of amusement and disgust. "Single-handed I wipe them out. Probably by stepping on them with my foot."

"No," the psychiatrist said patiently. "You halt the invasion, but not by destroying them. Instead, you show them kindness and mercy, even though by telepathy—their mode of communication—you know why they have come. They have never seen such humane traits exhibited by any sentient organism, and to show their appreciation they make a covenant with you."

Quail said, "They won't invade Earth as long as I'm alive."

"Exactly." To the Interplan officer the psychiatrist said, "You can see it does fit his personality, despite his feigned scorn." 175

"So by merely existing," Quail said, feeling a growing pleasure, "by simply being alive, I keep Earth safe from alien rule. I'm in effect, then, the most important person on Terra. Without lifting a finger."

"Yes, indeed, sir," the psychiatrist said. "And this is bedrock in your psyche; this is a life-long childhood fantasy. Which, without depth and drug therapy, you never would have recalled. But it has always existed in you; it went underneath, but never ceased."

To McClane, who sat intently listening, the senior police official said, "Can you implant an extra-factual memory pattern that extreme in him?"

"We get handed every possible type of wish-fantasy there is," McClane said. "Frankly, I've heard a lot worse than this. Certainly we can handle it. Twenty-four hours from now he won't just *wish* he'd saved Earth; he'll devoutly believe it really happened."

The senior police official said, "You can start the job, then. In preparation we've already once again erased the memory in him of his trip to Mars." 180

Quail said, "What trip to Mars?"

No one answered him, so reluctantly, he shelved the question. And anyhow a police vehicle had now put in its appearance; he, McClane and the senior police officer crowded into it, and presently they were on their way to Chicago and Rekal, Incorporated.

"You had better make no errors this time," the police officer said to heavy-set, nervous-looking McClane.

"I can't see what could go wrong," McClane mumbled, perspiring. "This has nothing to do with Mars or Interplan. Single-handedly stopping an invasion of Earth from another star-system." He shook his head at that. "Wow, what a kid dreams up. And by pious virtue, too; not by force. It's sort of quaint." He dabbed at his forehead with a large linen pocket handkerchief.

Nobody said anything. 185

"In fact," McClane said, "it's touching."

"But arrogant," the police official said starkly. "Inasmuch as when he dies the invasion will resume. No wonder he doesn't recall it; it's the most grandiose fantasy I ever ran across." He eyed Quail with disapproval. "And to think we put this man on our payroll."

When they reached Rekal, Incorporated the receptionist, Shirley, met them breathlessly in the outer office. "Welcome back, Mr. Quail," she fluttered, her melon-shaped breasts—today painted an incandescent orange—bobbing with agitation. "I'm sorry everything worked out so badly before; I'm sure this time it'll go better."

Still repeatedly dabbing at his shiny forehead with his neatly folded Irish linen handkerchief, McClane said, "It better." Moving with rapidity he rounded up Lowe and Keeler, escorted them and Douglas Quail to the work area, and then, with Shirley and the senior police officer, returned to his familiar office. To wait.

"Do we have a packet made up for this, Mr. McClane?" Shirley asked, bumping against him in her agitation, then coloring modestly. 190

"I think we do." He tried to recall, then gave up and consulted the formal chart. "A combination," he decided aloud, "of packets Eighty-one, Twenty, and Six." From the vault section of the chamber behind his desk he fished out the appropriate packets, carried them to his desk for inspection. "From Eight-one," he explained, "a magic healing rod given him—the client in question, this time Mr. Quail—by the race of beings from another system. A token of their gratitude."

"Does it work?" the police officer asked curiously.

"It did once," McClane explained. "But he, ahem, you see, used it up years ago, healing right and left. Now it's only a memento. But he remembers it working spectacularly." He chuckled, then opened packet Twenty. "Document from the UN Secretary General thanking him for saving Earth; this isn't precisely appropriate, because part of Quail's fantasy is that no one knows of the invasion except himself, but for the sake of verisimilitude we'll throw it in." He inspected packet Six, then. What came from this? He couldn't recall; frowning, he dug into the plastic bag as Shirley and the Interplan police officer watched intently.

"Writing," Shirley said. "In a funny language."

195   "This tells who they were," McClane said, "and where they came from. Including a detailed star map logging their flight here and the system of origin. Of course it's in *their* script, so he can't read it. But he remembers them reading it to him in his own tongue." He placed the three artifacts in the center of the desk. "These should be taken to Quail's conapt," he said to the police officer. "So that when he gets home he'll find them. And it'll confirm his fantasy. SOP—standard operating procedure." He chuckled apprehensively, wondering how matters were going with Lowe and Keeler.

The intercom buzzed. "Mr. McClane, I'm sorry to bother you." It was Lowe's voice; he froze as he recognized it, froze and became mute. "But something's come up. Maybe it would be better if you came in here and supervised. Like before, Quail reacted well to the narkidrine; he's unconscious, relaxed and receptive. But—"

McClane sprinted for the work area.

On a hygienic bed Douglas Quail lay breathing slowly and regularly, eyes half-shut, dimly conscious of those around him.

"We started interrogating him," Lowe said, white-faced. "To find out exactly when to place the fantasy-memory of him single-handedly having saved Earth. And strangely enough—"

200   "They told me not to tell," Douglas Quail mumbled in a dull drug-saturated voice. "That was the agreement. I wasn't even supposed to remember. But how could I forget an event like that?"

I guess it would be hard, McClane reflected. *But you did—until now.*

"They even gave me a scroll," Quail mumbled, "of gratitude. I have it hidden in my conapt; I'll show it to you."

To the Interplan officer who had followed after him, McClane said, "Well, I offer the suggestion that you better not kill him. If you do they'll return."

"They also gave me a magic invisible destroying rod," Quail mumbled, eyes totally shut now. "That's how I killed that man on Mars you sent me to take out. It's in my drawer along with the box of Martian maw-worms and dried-up plant life."

205   Wordlessly, the Interplan officer turned and stalked from the work area.

I might as well put those packets of proof-artifacts away, McClane said to himself resignedly. He walked, step by step, back to his office. *Including the citation from the UN Secretary General. After all—*

The real one probably would not be long in coming.   [1966]

QUESTIONS

1. In the opening passages, how does Dick establish the everyday life of Douglas Quail?
2. In what ways is the setting similar to the contemporary modern world and in what ways is it different? How are these similarities and differences important to the themes of the story?
3. Explain the development of the conflict: how a personal conflict grows to include others and to include conflicts of greater importance.
4. McClane says "actual memory, with all its vagueness, omissions, and ellipses, not to say distortions" is not as good as an implanted memory. How is this idea supported and/or contradicted in the story?
5. Examine Dick's use of language. In what ways does he employ the techniques of literary fiction; in what ways does he not?

RESPONSES

1. What facets of the stories by Kafka and/or Poe do you find in this story? Argue that Dick's work is a descendant of the work of one or both of these writers.
2. Compare Dick's vision of the future, as shown in this story, to Gibson's, as shown in the story "Johnny Mnemonic."
3. Using Frank O'Connor's discussion about Gogol's use of "the little man," examine Dick's continuation and adaptation of that concept.

FOCUS ON FILM

1. The film *Total Recall* is an adaptation of this story. Write an essay discussing whether the plot developments on Mars follow logically from the implications of the printed story.
2. Discuss the sets of the film and how they create a sense of reality for the story. To what degree are the sets based on descriptions in the print story?

Isak Dinesen

Isak Dinesen (1885–1962) was born Karen Blixen in Rungsted, Denmark. She studied art in Paris and Rome, then married her cousin, Baron Bror Blixen-Finecke in 1914. They managed a coffee plantation in Kenya until they divorced in 1921. She continued to run it until the worldwide economic depression forced her to return to Denmark in 1931. In 1934 she published her first collection of stories, *Seven Gothic Tales*, followed in three years by her masterpiece, *Out of Africa*. She continued to publish stories almost until her death.

The Blue Jar

There was once an immensely rich old Englishman who had been a courtier and a councillor to the Queen and who now, in his old age, cared for nothing but collecting ancient blue china. To that end he travelled to Persia, Japan, and China, and he was everywhere accompanied by his daughter, the Lady Helena. It happened, as they sailed in the Chinese Sea, that the ship caught fire on a still night, and everybody went into the lifeboats and left her. In the dark and the confusion the old peer was separated from his daughter. Lady Helena got up on deck late, and found the ship quite deserted. In the last moment a young English sailor carried her down into a lifeboat that had been forgotten. To the two fugitives it seemed as if fire was following them from all sides, for the phosphorescence played in the dark sea, and, as they looked up, a falling star ran across the sky, as if it was going to drop into the boat. They sailed for nine days, till they were picked up by a Dutch merchantman, and came home to England.

The old lord had believed his daughter to be dead. He now wept with joy, and at once took her off to a fashionable watering-place so that she might recover from the hardships she had gone through. And as he thought it must be unpleasant to her that a young sailor, who made his bread in the merchant service, should tell the world that he had sailed for nine days alone with a peer's daughter, he paid the boy a fine sum, and made him promise to go shipping in the other hemisphere and never come back. "For what," said the old nobleman, "would be the good of that?"

When Lady Helena recovered, and they gave her the news of the Court and of her family, and in the end also told her how the young sailor had been sent away never to come back, they found that her mind had suffered from her trials, and that she cared for nothing in all the world. She would not go back to her father's castle in its park, nor go to Court, nor travel to any gay town of the continent. The only thing which she now wanted to do was to go, like her father before her, to collect rare blue china. So she began to sail, from one country to the other, and her father went with her.

In her search she told the people, with whom she dealt, that she was looking for a particular blue color, and would pay any price for it. But although she bought many hundred blue jars and bowls, she would always after a time put them aside and say: "Alas, alas, it is not the right blue." Her father, when they had sailed for many years, suggested to her that perhaps the color which she sought did not exist. "O God, Papa," said she, "how can you speak so wickedly? Surely there must be some of it left from the time when all the world was blue."

Her two old aunts in England implored her to come back, still to make a great   5
match. But she answered them: "Nay, I have got to sail. For you must know, dear aunts, that it is all nonsense when learned people tell you that the seas have got a bottom to them. On the contrary, the water, which is the noblest of the elements, does, of course, go all through the earth, so that our planet really floats in the ether, like a soapbubble. And there, on the other hemisphere, a ship sails, with which I have got to keep pace. We two are like the reflection of one another, in the deep sea, and the ship of which I speak is always exactly beneath my own ship, upon the opposite side of the globe. You have never seen a big fish swimming underneath a boat, following it like a dark-blue shade in the water. But in that way this ship goes, like the shadow of my ship, and I draw it to and fro wherever I go, as the moon draws the tides, all through the bulk of the earth. If I stopped sailing, what would these poor sailors who make their bread in the merchant service do? But I shall tell you a secret," she said. "In the end my ship will go down, to the center of the globe, and at the very same hour the other ship will sink as well—for people call it sinking, although I can assure you that there is no up and down in the sea—and there, in the midst of the world, we two shall meet."

Many years passed, the old lord died, and Lady Helena became old and deaf, but she still sailed. Then it happened, after the plunder of the summer palace of the Emperor of China, that a merchant brought her a very old blue jar. The moment she set eyes on it she gave a terrible shriek. "There it is!" she cried. "I have found it at last. This is the true blue. Oh, how light it makes one. Oh, it is as fresh as a breeze, as deep as a deep secret, as full as I say not what." With trembling hands she held the jar to her bosom, and sat for six hours sunk in contemplation of it. Then she said to her doctor and her lady-companion: "Now I can die. And when I am dead you will cut out my heart and lay it in the blue jar. For then everything will be as it was then. All shall be blue round me, and in the midst of the blue world my heart will be innocent and free, and will beat gently, like a wake that sings, like the drops that fall from an oar blade." A little later she asked them: "Is it not a sweet thing to think that, if only you have patience, all that has ever been, will come back to you?" Shortly afterwards the old lady died.   [1942]

QUESTIONS

1. What elements of the fairy tale does the author employ?
2. What function is served in the story by the father and the two aunts?

3. What does the color blue symbolize in Lady Helena's life?
4. Explore the image of the ship that parallels Lady Helena in the other hemisphere. Is it an allegory to which the reader is intended to assign a meaning?
5. How do the similes in the final paragraph help define the story's meaning?

RALPH ELLISON

Ralph Ellison (1914–1994) was born in Oklahoma City. After studying at the Tuskegee Institute, he moved to New York City, where he worked for the Federal Writers Project. In 1942 he became editor of *Negro Quarterly*. Influenced by Richard Wright, Ellison published his only novel, *Invisible Man* (1952), which won the National Book Award. A second novel, *Juneteenth*, was published posthumously (1999). His essays have been published in *The Collected Essays of Ralph Ellison* (1995).

Battle Royale

It goes a long way back, some twenty years. All my life I had been looking for something, and everywhere I turned someone tried to tell me what it was. I accepted their answers too, though they were often in contradiction and even self-contradictory. I was naïve. I was looking for myself and asking everyone except myself questions which I, and only I, could answer. It took me a long time and much painful boomeranging of my expectations to achieve a realization everyone else appears to have been born with: That I am nobody but myself. But first I had to discover that I am an invisible man!

And yet I am no freak of nature, nor of history. I was in the cards, other things having been equal (or unequal) eighty-five years ago. I am not ashamed of my grandparents for having been slaves. I am only ashamed of myself for having at one time been ashamed. About eighty-five years ago they were told they were free, united with others of our country in everything pertaining to the common good, and, in everything social, separate like the fingers of the hand. And they believed it. They exulted in it. They stayed in their place, worked hard, and brought up my father to do the same. But my grandfather is the one. He was an odd old guy, my grandfather, and I am told I take after him. It was he who caused the trouble. On his deathbed he called my father to him and said, "Son, after I'm gone I want you to keep up the good fight. I never told you, but our life is a war and I have been a traitor all my born days, a spy in the enemy's country ever since I give up my gun back in the Reconstruction. Live with your head in the lion's mouth. I want you to overcome 'em with yeses, undermine 'em with grins, agree 'em to death and destruction, let 'em swoller you till they vomit or bust wide open." They thought the old man had gone out of his mind. He had been the meekest of men. The younger children were rushed from the room, the shades drawn and the flame of the lamp turned so low that it sputtered on the wick like the old man's breathing. "Learn it to the younguns," he whispered fiercely; then he died.

But my folks were more alarmed over his last words than over his dying. It was as though he had not died at all, his words caused so much anxiety. I was warned emphatically to forget what he had said and, indeed, this is the first time it has been mentioned outside the family circle. It had a tremendous effect upon me, however. I could never be sure of what he meant. Grandfather had been a quiet old man who never made any trouble, yet on his deathbed he had called himself a traitor and a spy, and he had spoken of his meekness as a dangerous activity. It became a constant puzzle which lay unanswered in the back of my mind. And whenever things went well for me I remembered my grandfather and felt guilty and uncomfortable. It was as though I was carrying out his advice in spite of myself. And to make it worse, everyone loved me for it. I was praised by the most lily-white men in town. I was considered an example of desirable conduct—just as my grandfather had been. And what puzzled me was that the old man had defined it as *treachery*. When I was praised for my conduct I felt a guilt that in some way I was doing something that was really against the wishes of the white folks, that if they had understood they would have desired me to act just the opposite, that I should have been sulky and mean, and that that really would have been what they wanted, even though they were fooled and thought they wanted me to act as I did. It made me afraid that some day they would look upon me as a traitor and I would be lost. Still I was more afraid to act any other way because they didn't like that at all. The old man's words were like a curse. On my graduation day I delivered an oration in which I showed that humility was the secret, indeed, the very essence of progress. (Not that I believed this—how could I, remembering my grandfather?—I only believed that it worked.) It was a great success. Everyone praised me and I was invited to give the speech at a gathering of the town's leading white citizens. It was a triumph for the whole community.

It was in the main ballroom of the leading hotel. When I got there I discovered that it was on the occasion of a smoker, and I was told that since I was to be there anyway I might as well take part in the battle royale to be fought by some of my schoolmates as part of the entertainment. The battle royale came first.

5   All of the town's big shots were there in their tuxedoes, wolfing down the buffet foods, drinking beer and whiskey and smoking black cigars. It was a large room with a high ceiling. Chairs were arranged in neat rows around three sides of a portable boxing ring. The fourth side was clear, revealing a gleaming space of polished floor. I had some misgivings over the battle royale, by the way. Not from a distaste for fighting but because I didn't care too much for the other fellows who were to take part. They were tough guys who seemed to have no grandfather's curse worrying their minds. No one could mistake their toughness. And besides, I suspected that fighting a battle royale might distract from the dignity of my speech. In those preinvisible days I visualized myself as a potential Booker T. Washington. But the other fellows didn't care too much for me either, and there were nine of them. I felt superior to them in my way, and I didn't like the manner in which we were all crowded together in the servants' elevator. Nor did they like my being there. In fact, as the warmly lighted floors flashed past the elevator we had words over the fact that I, by taking part in the fight, had knocked one of their friends out of a night's work.

We were led out of the elevator through a rococo hall into an anteroom and told to get into our fighting togs. Each of us was issued a pair of boxing gloves and ushered out into the big mirrored hall, which we entered looking cautiously about us and whispering, lest we might accidentally be heard above the noise of the room. It was foggy with cigar smoke. And already the whiskey was taking effect. I was shocked to see some of the most important men of the town quite tipsy. They were all there—bankers, lawyers, judges, doctors, fire chiefs, teachers, merchants. Even one of the more fashionable pastors. Something we could not see was going on up front. A clarinet was vibrating sensuously and the men were standing up and moving eagerly forward. We were a small tight group, clustered together, our bare upper bodies touching and shining with anticipatory sweat; while up front the big shots were becoming increasingly excited over something we still could not see. Suddenly I heard the school superintendent, who had told me to come, yell, "Bring up the shines, gentlemen! Bring up the little shines!"

We were rushed up to the front of the ballroom, where it smelled even more strongly of tobacco and whiskey. Then we were pushed into place. I almost wet my pants. A sea of faces, some hostile, some amused, ringed around us, and in the center, facing us, stood a magnificent blonde—stark naked. There was dead silence. I felt a blast of cold air chill me. I tried to back away, but they were behind me and around me. Some of the boys stood with lowered heads, trembling. I felt a wave of irrational guilt and fear. My teeth chattered, my skin turned to goose flesh, my knees knocked. Yet I was strongly attracted and looked in spite of myself. Had the price of looking been blindness, I would have looked. The hair was yellow like that of a circus kewpie doll, the face heavily powdered and rouged, as though to form an abstract mask, the eyes hollow and smeared a cool blue, the color of a baboon's butt. I felt a desire to spit upon her as my eyes brushed slowly over her body. Her breasts were firm and round as the domes of East Indian temples, and I stood so close as to see the fine skin texture and beads of pearly perspiration glistening like dew around the pink and erected buds of her nipples. I wanted at one and the same time to run from the room, to sink through the floor, or go to her and cover her from my eyes and the eyes of the others with my body; to feel the soft thighs, to caress her and destroy her, to love her and to murder her, to hide from her, and yet to stroke where below the small American flag tattooed upon her belly her thighs formed a capital V. I had a notion that of all in the room she saw only me with her impersonal eyes.

And then she began to dance, a slow sensuous movement; the smoke of a hundred cigars clinging to her like the thinnest of veils. She seemed like a fair bird-girl girdled in veils calling to me from the angry surface of some gray and threatening sea. I was transported. Then I became aware of the clarinet playing and the big shots yelling at us. Some threatened us if we looked and others if we did not. On my right I saw one boy faint. And now a man grabbed a silver pitcher from a table and stepped close as he dashed ice water upon him and stood him up and forced two of us to support him as his head hung and moans issued from his thick bluish lips. Another boy began to plead to go home. He was the largest of the group, wearing dark red fighting trunks much too small to conceal the erection which projected from him as though in answer to the insinuating low-registered moaning of the clarinet. He tried to hide himself with his boxing gloves.

And all the while the blonde continued dancing, smiling faintly at the big shots who watched her with fascination, and faintly smiling at our fear. I noticed a certain merchant who followed her hungrily, his lips loose and drooling. He was a large man who wore diamond studs in a shirtfront which swelled with the ample paunch underneath, and each time the blonde swayed her undulating hips he ran his hand through the thin hair of his bald head and, with his arms upheld, his posture clumsy like that of an intoxicated panda, wound his belly in a slow and obscene grind. This creature was completely hypnotized. The music had quickened. As the dancer flung herself about with a detached expression on her face, the men began reaching out to touch her. I could see their beefy fingers sink into her soft flesh. Some of the others tried to stop them and she began to move around the floor in graceful circles, as they gave chase, slipping and sliding over the polished floor. It was mad. Chairs went crashing, drinks were spilt, as they ran laughing and howling after her. They caught her just as she reached a door, raised her from the floor, and tossed her as college boys are tossed at a hazing, and above her red, fixed-smiling lips I saw the terror and disgust in her eyes, almost like my own terror and that which I saw in some of the other boys. As I watched, they tossed her twice and her soft breasts seemed to flatten against the air and her legs flung wildly as she spun. Some of the more sober ones helped her to escape. And I started off the floor, heading for the anteroom with the rest of the boys.

10   Some were still crying and in hysteria. But as we tried to leave we were stopped and ordered to get into the ring. There was nothing to do but what we were told. All ten of us climbed under the ropes and allowed ourselves to be blindfolded with broad bands of white cloth. One of the men seemed to feel a bit sympathetic and tried to cheer us up as we stood with our backs against the ropes. Some of us tried to grin. "See that boy over there?" one of the men said. "I want you to run across at the bell and give it to him right in the belly. If you don't get him, I'm going to get you. I don't like his looks." Each of us was told the same. The blindfolds were put on. Yet even then I had been going over my speech. In my mind each word was as bright as a flame. I felt the cloth pressed into place, and frowned so that it would be loosened when I relaxed.

But now I felt a sudden fit of blind terror. I was unused to darkness. It was as though I had suddenly found myself in a dark room filled with poisonous cottonmouths. I could hear the bleary voices yelling insistently for the battle royale to begin.

"Get going in there!"

"Let me at that big nigger!"

I strained to pick up the school superintendent's voice, as though to squeeze some security out of that slightly more familiar sound.

15   "Let me at those black sonabitches!" someone yelled.

"No Jackson, no!" another voice yelled. "Here, somebody, help me hold Jack."

"I want to get at that ginger-colored nigger. Tear him limb from limb," the first voice yelled.

I stood against the ropes trembling. For in those days I was what they called ginger-colored, and he sounded as though he might crunch me between his teeth like a crisp ginger cookie.

Quite a struggle was going on. Chairs were being kicked about and I could hear voices grunting as with terrific effort. I wanted to see, to see more desperately than ever before. But the blindfold was as tight as a thick skin-puckering scab and when I raised my gloved hand to push the layers of white aside a voice yelled, "Oh, no you don't, black bastard! Leave that alone!"

20   "Ring the bell before Jackson kills him a coon!" someone boomed in the sudden silence. And I heard the bell clang and the sound of the feet scuffling forward.

A glove smacked against my head. I pivoted, striking out stiffly as someone went past, and felt the jar ripple along the length of my arm to my shoulder. Then it seemed as though all nine of the boys had turned upon me at once. Blows pounded me from all sides while I struck out as best I could. So many blows landed upon me that I wondered if I were not the only blindfolded fighter in the ring, or if the man called Jackson hadn't succeeded in getting me after all.

Blindfolded, I could no longer control my motions. I had no dignity. I stumbled about like a baby or a drunken man. The smoke had become thicker and with each new blow it seemed to sear and further restrict my lungs. My saliva became like hot bitter glue. A glove connected with my head, filling my mouth with warm blood. It was everywhere. I could not tell if the moisture I felt upon my body was sweat or blood. A blow landed hard against the nape of my neck. I felt myself going over, my head hitting the floor. Streaks of blue light filled the black world behind the blindfold. I lay prone, pretending that I was knocked out, but felt myself seized by hands and yanked to my feet. "Get going, black boy! Mix it up!" My arms were like lead, my head smarting from blows. I managed to feel my way to the ropes and held on, trying to catch my breath. A glove landed in my midsection and I went over again, feeling as though the smoke had become a knife jabbed into my guts. Pushed this way and that by the legs milling around me, I finally pulled erect and discovered that I could see the black, sweat-washed forms weaving in the smoky-blue atmosphere like drunken dancers weaving to the rapid drum-like thuds of blows.

Everyone fought hysterically. It was complete anarchy. Everybody fought everybody else. No group fought together for long. Two, three, four, fought one, then turned to fight each other, were themselves attacked. Blows landed below the belt and in the kidney, with the gloves open as well as closed, and with my eye partly opened now there was not so much terror. I moved carefully, avoiding blows, although not too many to attract attention, fighting group to group. The boys groped about like blind, cautious crabs crouching to protect their midsections, their heads pulled in short against their shoulders, their arms stretched nervously before them, with their fists testing the smoke-filled air like the knobbed feelers of hypersensitive snails. In one corner I glimpsed a boy violently punching the air and heard him scream in pain as he smashed his hand against a ring post. For a second I saw him bent over holding his hand, then going down as a blow caught his unprotected head. I played one group against the other, slipping in and throwing a punch then stepping out of range while pushing the others into the melee to take the blows blindly aimed at me. The smoke was agonizing and there were no rounds, no bells at three minute intervals to relieve our exhaustion. The room spun round me, a swirl of lights, smoke, sweating bodies surrounded by tense white faces. I bled from both nose and mouth, the blood spattering upon my chest.

The men kept yelling, "Slug him, black boy! Knock his guts out!"

"Uppercut him! Kill him! Kill that big boy!"

Taking a fake fall, I saw a boy going down heavily beside me as though we were felled by a single blow, saw a sneaker-clad foot shoot into his groin as the two who had knocked him down stumbled upon him. I rolled out of range, feeling a twinge of nausea.

The harder we fought the more threatening the men became. And yet, I had begun to worry about my speech again. How would it go? Would they recognize my ability? What would they give me?

I was fighting automatically when suddenly I noticed that one after another of the boys were leaving the ring. I was surprised, filled with panic, as though I had been left alone with an unknown danger. Then I understood. The boys had arranged it among themselves. It was the custom for the two men left in the ring to slug it out for the

25

winner's prize. I discovered this too late. When the bell sounded two men in tuxedoes leaped into the ring and removed the blindfold. I found myself facing Tatlock, the biggest of the gang. I felt sick at my stomach. Hardly had the bell stopped ringing in my ears than it clanged again and I saw him moving swiftly toward me. Thinking of nothing else to do I hit him smash on the nose. He kept coming, bringing the rank sharp violence of stale sweat. His face was a black blank of a face, only his eyes alive—with hate of me and aglow with a feverish terror from what had happened to us all. I became anxious. I wanted to deliver my speech and he came at me as though he meant to beat it out of me. I smashed him again and again, taking his blows as they came. Then on a sudden impulse I struck him lightly and we clinched. I whispered, "Fake like I knocked you out, you can have the prize."

"I'll break your behind," he whispered hoarsely.

30   "For *them*?"

"For *me*, sonofabitch!"

They were yelling for us to break it up and Tatlock spun me half around with a blow, and as a joggled camera sweeps in a reeling scene, I saw the howling red faces crouching tense beneath the cloud of blue-gray smoke. For a moment the world wavered, unraveled, flowed, then my head cleared and Tatlock bounced before me. That fluttering shadow before my eyes was his jabbing left hand. Then falling forward, my head against his damp shoulder, I whispered,

"I'll make it five dollars more."

"Go to hell!"

35   But his muscles relaxed a trifle beneath my pressure and I breathed, "Seven?"

"Give it to your ma," he said, ripping me beneath the heart.

And while I still held him I butted him and moved away. I felt myself bombarded with punches. I fought back with hopeless desperation. I wanted to deliver my speech more than anything else in the world, because I felt that only these men could judge truly my ability, and now this stupid clown was ruining my chances. I began fighting carefully now, moving in to punch him and out again with my greater speed. A lucky blow to his chin and I had him going too—until I heard a loud voice yell, "I got my money on the big boy."

Hearing this, I almost dropped my guard. I was confused: Should I try to win against the voice out there? Would not this go against my speech, and was not this a moment for humility, for nonresistance? A blow to my head as I danced about sent my right eye popping like a jack-in-the-box and settled my dilemma. The room went red as I fell. It was a dream fall, my body languid and fastidious as to where to land, until the floor became impatient and smashed up to meet me. A moment later I came to. An hypnotic voice said FIVE emphatically. And I lay there, hazily watching a dark red spot of my own blood shaping itself into a butterfly, glistening and soaking into the soiled gray world of the canvas.

When the voice drawled TEN I was lifted up and dragged to a chair. I sat dazed. My eye pained and swelled with each throb of my pounding heart and I wondered if now I would be allowed to speak. I was wringing wet, my mouth still bleeding. We were grouped along the wall now. The other boys ignored me as they congratulated Tatlock and speculated as to how much they would be paid. One boy whimpered over his smashed hand. Looking up front, I saw attendants in white jackets rolling the portable ring away and placing a small square rug in the vacant space surrounded by chairs. Perhaps, I thought, I will stand on the rug to deliver my speech.

40   Then the M.C. called to us, "Come on up here boys and get your money."

We ran forward to where the men laughed and talked in their chairs, waiting. Everyone seemed friendly now.

"There it is on the rug," the man said. I saw the rug covered with coins of all dimensions and a few crumpled bills. But what excited me, scattered here and there, were the gold pieces.

"Boys, it's all yours," the man said. "You get all you grab."

"That's right, Sambo," a blond man said, winking at me confidentially.

I trembled with excitement, forgetting my pain. I would get the gold and the bills,   45
I thought. I would use both hands. I would throw my body against the boys nearest me to block them from the gold.

"Get down around the rug now," the man commanded, "and don't anyone touch it until I give the signal."

"This ought to be good," I heard.

As told, we got around the square rug on our knees. Slowly the man raised his freckled hand as we followed it upward with our eyes.

I heard, "These niggers look like they're about to pray!"

Then, "Ready," the man said. "Go!"   50

I lunged for a yellow coin lying on the blue design of the carpet, touching it and sending a surprised shriek to join those around me. I tried frantically to remove my hand but could not let go. A hot, violent force tore through my body, shaking me like a wet rat. The rug was electrified. The hair bristled up on my head as I shook myself free. My muscles jumped, my nerves jangled, writhed. But I saw that this was not stopping the other boys. Laughing in fear and embarrassment, some were holding back and scooping up the coins knocked off by the painful contortions of others. The men roared above us as we struggled.

"Pick it up, goddamnit, pick it up!" someone called like a bass-voiced parrot. "Go on, get it!"

I crawled rapidly around the floor, picking up the coins, trying to avoid the coppers and to get greenbacks and the gold. Ignoring the shock by laughing, as I brushed the coins off quickly, I discovered that I could contain the electricity—a contradiction but it works. Then the men began to push us onto the rug. Laughing embarrassedly, we struggled out of their hands and kept after the coins. We were all wet and slippery and hard to hold. Suddenly I saw a boy lifted into the air, glistening with sweat like a circus seal, and dropped, his wet back landing flush upon the charged rug, heard him yell and saw him literally dance upon his back, his elbows beating frenzied tattoo upon the floor, his muscles twitching like the flesh of a horse stung by many flies. When he finally rolled off, his face was gray and no one stopped him when he ran from the floor amid booming laughter.

"Get the money," the M.C. called. "That's good hard American cash!"

And we snatched and grabbed, snatched and grabbed. I was careful not to come too   55
close to the rug now, and when I felt the hot whiskey breath descend upon me like a cloud of four air I reached out and grabbed the leg of a chair. It was occupied and I held on desperately.

"Leggo, nigger! Leggo!"

The huge face wavered down to mine as he tried to push me free. But my body was slippery and he was too drunk. It was Mr. Colcord, who owned a chain of movie houses and "entertainment palaces." Each time he grabbed me I slipped out of his hands. It became a real struggle. I feared the rug more than I did the drunk, so I held on, surprising myself for a moment by trying to *topple* him upon the rug. It was such an enormous idea that I found myself actually carrying it out. I tried not to be obvious, yet when I grabbed his leg, trying to tumble him out of the chair, he raised up roaring with laughter, and, looking at me with soberness dead in the eye, kicked me viciously in the chest. The chair leg flew out of my hand and I felt myself going and rolled. It was as though I had rolled through a bed of hot coals. It seemed a whole century would pass before I would roll free, a century in which I was seared through the deepest levels of my body to the fearful breath within me and the breath seared and heated to the point of explosion. It'll all be over in a flash, I thought as I rolled clear. It'll all be over in a flash.

But not yet, the men on the other side were waiting, red faces swollen as though from apoplexy as they bent forward in their chairs. Seeing their fingers coming toward me I rolled away as a fumbled football rolls off the receiver's fingertips, back into the coals. That time I luckily sent the rug sliding out of place and heard the coins ringing against the floor and the boys scuffling to pick them up and the M.C. calling, "All right, boys, that's all. Go get dressed and get your money."

I was limp as a dish rag. My back felt as though it had been beaten with wires.

60   When we had dressed the M.C. came in and gave us each five dollars, except Tatlock, who got ten for being the last in the ring. Then he told us to leave. I was not to get a chance to deliver my speech. I thought. I was going out into the dim alley in despair when I was stopped and told to go back. I returned to the ballroom, where the men were pushing back their chairs and gathering in small groups to talk.

The M.C knocked on a table for quiet. "Gentlemen," he said, "we almost forgot an important part of the program. A most serious part, gentlemen. This boy was brought here to deliver a speech which he made at his graduation yesterday. . . ."

"Bravo!"

"I'm told that he is the smartest boy we've got out there in Greenwood. I'm told that he knows more big words than a pocket-sized dictionary."

Much applause and laughter.

65   "So now, gentlemen, I want you to give him your attention."

There was still laughter as I faced them, my mouth dry, my eyes throbbing. I began slowly, but evidently my throat was tense, because they began shouting, "Louder! Louder!"

"We of the younger generation extol the wisdom of that great leader and educator," I shouted, "who first spoke these flaming words of wisdom: 'A ship lost at sea for many days suddenly sighted a friendly vessel. From the mast of the unfortunate vessel was seen a signal: "Water, water; we die of thirst!" The answer from the friendly vessel came back: "Cast down your bucket where you are." The captain of the distressed vessel, at last heeding the injunction, cast down his bucket, and it came up full of fresh sparkling water from the mouth of the Amazon River.' And like him I say, and in his words, 'To those of my race who depend upon bettering their condition in a foreign land, or who underestimate the importance of cultivating friendly relations with the Southern white man, who is his next-door neighbor, I would say: "Cast down your bucket where you are"—cast it down in making friends in every manly way of the people of all races by whom we are surrounded. . . .'"

I spoke automatically and with such fervor that I did not realize that the men were still talking and laughing until my dry mouth, filling up with blood from the cut, almost strangled me. I coughed, wanting to stop and go to one of the tall brass, sand-filled spittoons to relieve myself, but a few of the men, especially the superintendent, were listening and I was afraid. So I gulped it down, blood, saliva and all, and continued. (What power of endurance I had during those days! What enthusiasm! What a belief in the rightness of things!) I spoke even louder in spite of the pain. But still they talked and still they laughed, as though deaf with cotton in dirty ears. So I spoke with greater emotional emphasis. I closed my ears and swallowed blood until I was nauseated. The speech seemed a hundred times as long as before, but I could not leave out a single word. All had to be said, each memorized nuance considered, rendered. Nor was that all. Whenever I uttered a word of three or more syllables a group of voices would yell for me to repeat it. I used the phrase "social responsibility" and they yelled:

"What's the word you say, boy?"

"Social responsibility," I said.   70

"What?"

"Social . . ."

"Louder."

". . . responsibility."

"More!"   75

"Respon—"

"Repeat!"

"—sibility."

The room filled with the uproar of laughter until, no doubt, distracted by having to gulp down my blood, I made a mistake and yelled a phrase I had often seen denounced in newspaper editorials, heard debated in private.

"Social . . ."   80

"What?" they yelled.

". . . equality—"

The laughter hung smokelike in the sudden stillness. I opened my eyes, puzzled. Sounds of displeasure filled the room. The M.C. rushed forward. They shouted hostile phrases at me. But I did not understand.

A small dry mustached man in the front row blared out, "Say that slowly, son!"

"What, sir?"   85

"What you just said!"

"Social responsibility, sir," I said.

"You weren't being smart, were you boy?" he said, not unkindly.

"No, sir!"

"You sure that about 'equality' was a mistake?"   90

"Oh, yes, sir," I said. "I was swallowing blood."

"Well, you had better speak more slowly so we can understand. We mean to do right by you, but you've got to know your place at all times. All right, now, go on with your speech."

I was afraid. I wanted to leave but I wanted also to speak and I was afraid they'd snatch me down.

"Thank you sir," I said, beginning where I had left off, and having them ignore me as before.

Yet when I finished there was a thunderous applause. I was surprised to see the   95
superintendent come forth with a package wrapped in white tissue paper, and, gesturing for quiet, address the men.

"Gentlemen, you see that I did not overpraise the boy. He makes a good speech and some day he'll lead his people in the proper paths. And I don't have to tell you that this is important in these days and times. This is a good, smart boy, and so to encourage him in the right direction, in the name of the Board of Education I wish to present him a prize in the form of this . . ."

He paused, removing the tissue paper and revealing a gleaming calfskin briefcase. "... in the form of this first-class article from Shad Whitmore's shop."

"Boy," he said, addressing me, "take this prize and keep it well. Consider it a badge of office. Prize it. Keep developing as you are and some day it will be filled with important papers that will help shape the destiny of your people."

100 I was so moved that I could hardly express my thanks. A rope of bloody saliva forming a shape like an undiscovered continent drooled upon the leather and I wiped it quickly away. I felt an importance that I had never dreamed.

"Open it and see what's inside," I was told.

My fingers a-tremble, I complied, smelling fresh leather and finding an official-looking document inside. It was a scholarship to the state college for Negroes. My eyes filled with tears and I ran awkwardly off the floor.

I was overjoyed; I did not even mind when I discovered the gold pieces I had scrambled for were brass pocket tokens advertising a certain make of automobile.

When I reached home everyone was excited. Next day the neighbors came to congratulate me. I even felt safe from grandfather, whose deathbed curse usually spoiled my triumphs. I stood beneath his photograph with my briefcase in hand and smiled triumphantly into his stolid black peasant's face. It was a face that fascinated me. The eyes seemed to follow everywhere I went.

105 That night I dreamed I was at a circus with him and that he refused to laugh at the clowns no matter what they did. Then later he told me to open my briefcase and read what was inside and I did, finding an official envelope stamped with the state seal; and inside the envelope I found another and another, endlessly, and I thought I would fall of weariness. "Them's years," he said. "Now open that one." And I did and in it I found an engraved stamp containing a short message in letters of gold. "Read it," my grandfather said. "Out loud."

"To Whom It May Concern," I intoned. "Keep This Nigger-Boy Running."

I awoke with the old man's laughter ringing in my ears.   [1952]

QUESTIONS

1. The narrator is looking back twenty years on the events of the story. What effect does that fact have on the narrator and on the reader?
2. What does the scene with the naked woman tell us about the white men in the city? About the young African-American men?
3. How is the Battle Royale a metaphor for U.S. racial relations at the time?
4. How does the narrator want us to view his prize of the scholarship?
5. What message does the narrator finally learn from his grandfather?

RESPONSES

1. In some ways, Ellison's story is one of survival. Compare it to other stories such as Ida Fink's "A Scrap of Time," Tomás Rivera's "... and the Earth Did Not Devour Him," or Leslie Marmon Silko's "Storyteller."
2. Compare Ellison's use of point of view in this story and in "A Party down at the Square."

RALPH ELLISON

King of the Bingo Game

The woman in front of him was eating roasted peanuts that smelled so good that he could barely contain his hunger. He could not even sleep and wished they'd hurry and begin the bingo game. There, on his right, two fellows were drinking wine out of a bottle wrapped in a paper bag, and he could hear soft gurgling in the dark. His stomach gave a low, gnawing growl. "If this was down South," he thought, "all I'd have to do is lean over and say, 'Lady, gimme a few of those peanuts, please ma'am,' and she'd pass me the bag and never think nothing of it." Or he could ask the fellows for a drink in the same way. Folks down South stuck together that way; they didn't even have to know you. But up here it was different. Ask somebody for something, and they'd think you were crazy. Well, I ain't crazy. I'm just broke, 'cause I got no birth certificate to get a job, and Laura 'bout to die 'cause we got no money for a doctor. But I ain't crazy. And yet a pinpoint of doubt was focused in his mind as he glanced toward the screen and saw the hero stealthily entering a dark room and sending the beam of a flashlight along a wall of bookcases. This is where he finds the trapdoor, he remembered. The man would pass abruptly through the wall and find the girl tried to a bed, her legs and arms spread wide, and her clothing torn to rags. He laughed softly to himself. He had seen the picture three times, and this was one of the best scenes.

On his right the fellow whispered wide-eyed to his companion, "Man, look a-yonder!"

"Damn!"

"Wouldn't I like to have her tied up like that . . ."

"Hey! That fool's letting her loose!"

"Aw, man, he loves her."

"Love or no love!"

The man moved impatiently beside him, and he tried to involve himself in the scene. But Laura was on his mind. Tiring quickly of watching the picture he looked back to where the white beam filtered from the projection room above the balcony. It started small and grew large, specks of dust dancing in its whiteness as it reached the screen. It was strange how the beam always landed right on the screen and didn't mess up and fall somewhere else. But they had it all fixed. Everything was fixed. Now suppose when they showed that girl with her dress torn the girl started taking off the rest of her clothes, and when the guy came in he didn't untie her but kept her there and went to taking off his own clothes? *That* would be something to see. If a picture got out of hand like that those guys up there would go nuts. Yeah, and there'd be so many folks in here you couldn't find a seat for nine months! A strange sensation played over his skin. He shuddered. Yesterday he'd seen a bedbug on a woman's neck as they walked out into the bright street. But exploring his thigh through a hole in his pocket he found only goose pimples and old scars.

The bottle gurgled again. He closed his eyes. Now a dreamy music was accompanying the film and train whistles were sounding in the distance, and he was a boy again walking along a railroad trestle down South, and seeing the train coming, and running back as fast as he could go, and hearing the whistle blowing, and getting off the trestle to solid ground just in time, with the earth trembling beneath his feet, and feeling relieved as he ran down the cinder-strewn embankment onto the highway, and looking back and seeing with terror that the train had left the track and was following him right down the middle of the street, and all the white people laughing as he ran screaming . . .

10   "Wake up there, buddy! What the hell do you mean hollering like that? Can't you see we trying to enjoy this here picture?"

He started at the man with gratitude.

"I'm sorry, old man," he said. "I musta been dreaming."

"Well, here, have a drink. And don't be making no noise like that, damn!"

His hands trembled as he tilted his head. It was not wine, but whiskey. Cold rye whiskey. He took a deep swoller, decided it was better not to take another, and handed the bottle back to its owner.

15   "Thanks, old man," he said.

Now he felt the cold whiskey breaking a warm path straight through the middle of him, growing hotter and sharper as it moved. He had not eaten all day, and it made him light-headed. The smell of the peanuts stabbed him like a knife, and he got up and found a seat in the middle aisle. But no sooner did he sit than he saw a row of intense-faced young girls, and got up again, thinking, "You chicks musta been Lindy-hopping somewhere." He found a seat several rows ahead as the lights came on, and he saw the screen disappear behind a heavy red and gold curtain; then the curtain rising, and the man with the microphone and a uniformed attendant coming on the stage.

He felt for his bingo cards, smiling. The guy at the door wouldn't like it if he knew about his having *five* cards. Well, not everyone played the bingo game; and even with five cards he didn't have much of a chance. For Laura, though, he had to have faith. He studied the cards, each with its different numerals; punching the free center hole in each and spreading them neatly across his lap; and when the lights faded he sat slouched in his seat so that he could look from his cards to the bingo wheel with but a quick shifting of his eyes.

Ahead, at the end of the darkness, the man with the microphone was pressing a button attached to a long cord and spinning the bingo wheel and calling out the number each time the wheel came to rest. And each time the voice rang out his finger raced over the cards for the number. With five cards he had to move fast. He became nervous; there were too many cards, and the man went too fast with his grating voice. Perhaps he should just select one and throw the others away. But he was afraid. He became warm. Wonder how much Laura's doctor would cost? Damn that, watch the cards! And with despair he heard the man call three in a row which he missed on all five cards. This way he'd never win . . .

When he saw the row of holes punched across the third card, he sat paralyzed and heard the man call three more numbers before he stumbled forward, screaming,

20   "Bingo! Bingo!"

"Let that fool up there," someone called.

"Get up there, man!"

He stumbled down the aisle and up the steps to the stage into a light so sharp and bright that for a moment it blinded him, and he felt that he had moved into the spell of some strange, mysterious power. Yet it was as familiar as the sun, and he knew it was the perfectly familiar bingo.

The man with the microphone was saying something to the audience as he held out his card. A cold light flashed from the man's finger as the card left his hand. His knees trembled. The man stepped closer, checking the card against the numbers chalked on the board. Suppose he had made a mistake? The pomade on the man's hair made him feel faint, and he backed away. But the man was checking the card over the microphone now, and he had to stay. He stood tense, listening.

"Under the O, forty-four," the man chanted. "Under the I, seven. Under the G, three. Under the B, ninety-six. Under the N, thirteen!"   25

His breath came easier as the man smiled at the audience.

"Yessir, ladies and gentlemen, he's one of the chosen people!"

The audience rippled with laughter and applause.

"Step right up to the front of the stage."

He moved slowly forward, wishing that the light was not so bright.   30

"To win tonight's jackpot of $36.90 the wheel must stop between the double zero, understand?"

He nodded, knowing the ritual from the many days and nights he had watched the winners march across the stage to press the button that controlled the spinning wheel and receive the prizes. And now he followed the instructions as though he'd crossed the slippery stage a million prize-winning times.

The man was making some kind of a joke, and he nodded vacantly. So tense had he become that he felt a sudden desire to cry and shook it away. He felt vaguely that his whole life was determined by the bingo wheel; not only that which would happen now that he was at last before it, but all that had gone before, since his birth, and his mother's birth and the birth of his father. It had always been there, even though he had not been aware of it, handing out the unlucky cards and numbers of his days. The feeling persisted, and he started quickly away. I better get down from here before I make a fool of myself, he thought.

"Here, boy," the man called. "You haven't started yet."

Someone laughed as he went hesitantly back.   35

"Are you all reet?"

He grinned at the man's jive talk, but no words would come, and he knew it was not a convincing grin. For suddenly he knew that he stood on the slippery brink of some terrible embarrassment.

"Where you from, boy?" the man asked.

"Down South."

"He's from down South, ladies and gentleman," the man said. "Where from? Speak   40
right into the mike."

"Rocky Mont," he said. "Rock' Mont, North Car'lina."

"So you decided to come down off that mountain to the U.S.," the man laughed. He felt that the man was making a fool of him, but then something cold was placed in his hand, and the lights were no longer behind him.

Standing before the wheel he felt alone, but that was somehow right, and he remembered his plan. He would give the wheel a short quick twirl. Just a touch of the button. He had watched it many times, and always it came close to double zero when it was short and quick. He steeled himself; the fear had left, and he felt a profound sense of promise, as though he were about to be repaid for all the things he'd suffered all his life. Trembling, he pressed the button. There was a whirl of lights, and in a second he realized with finality that though he wanted to, he could not stop. It was as though he held a high-powered line in his naked hand. His nerves tightened. As the wheel increased its speed it seemed to draw him more and more into its power, as though it held his fate; and with it came a deep need to submit, to whirl, to lose himself in its swirl of color. He could not stop it now, he knew. So let it be.

The button rested snugly in his palm where the man had placed it. And now he became aware of the man beside him, advising him through the microphone, while behind the shadowy audience hummed with noisy voices. He shifted his feet. There was still that feeling of helplessness within him, making part of him desire to turn back, even now that the jackpot was right in his hand. He squeezed the button until his fist ached. Then, like the sudden shriek of a subway whistle, a doubt tore through his head. Suppose he did not spin the wheel long enough? What could he do, and how could he tell? And then he knew, even as he wondered, that as long as he pressed the button, he could control the jackpot. He and only he could determine whether or not it was to be his. Not even the man with the microphone could do anything about it now. He felt drunk. Then, as though he had come down from a high hill into a valley of people, he heard the audience yelling.

45   "Come down from there, you jerk!"

"Let somebody else have a chance . . ."

"Ole Jack thinks he done found the end of the rainbow . . ."

The last voice was not unfriendly, and he turned and smiled dreamily into the yelling mouths. Then he turned his back squarely on them.

"Don't take too long, boy," a voice said.

50   He nodded. They were yelling behind him. Those folks did not understand what had happened to him. They had been playing the bingo game day in and night for years, trying to win rent money or hamburger change. But not one of those wise guys had discovered this wonderful thing. He watched the wheel whirling past the numbers and experienced a burst of exaltation: This is God! This is the really truly God! He said it aloud, "This is God!"

He said it with such absolute conviction that he feared he would fall fainting into the footlights. But the crowd yelled so loud that they could not hear. These fools, he thought. I'm here trying to tell them the most wonderful secret in the world, and they're yelling like they gone crazy. A hand fell upon his shoulder.

"You'll have to make a choice now, boy. You've taken too long."

He brushed the hand violently away.

"Leave me alone, man. I know what I'm doing!"

55   The man looked surprised and held on to the microphone for support. And because he did not wish to hurt the man's feelings he smiled, realizing with a sudden pang that there was no way of explaining to the man just why he had to stand there pressing the button forever.

"Come here," he called tiredly.

The man approached, rolling the heavy microphone across the stage.

"Anybody can play this bingo game, right?" he said.

"Sure, but . . ."

60   He smiled, feeling inclined to be patient with this slick looking white man with his blue sport shirt and his sharp gabardine suit.

"That's what I thought," he said. "Anybody can win the jackpot as long as they get the lucky number, right?"

"That's the rule, but after all . . ."

"That's what I thought," he said. "And the big prize goes to the man who knows how to win it?"

The man nodded speechlessly.

"Well then, go on over there and watch me win like I want to. I ain't going to hurt   65 nobody," he said, "and I'll show you how to win. I mean to show the whole world how it's got to be done."

And because he understood, he smiled again to let the man know that he held nothing against him for being white and impatient. Then he refused to see the man any longer and stood pressing the button, the voices of the crowd reaching him like sounds in distant streets. Let them yell. All the Negroes down there were just ashamed because he was black like them. He smiled inwardly, knowing how it was. Most of the time he was ashamed of what Negroes did himself. Well, let them be ashamed for something this time. Like him. He was like a long thin black wire that was being stretched and wound upon the bingo wheel; wound until he wanted to scream; wound, but this time himself controlling the winding and the sadness and the shame, and because he did, Laura would be all right. Suddenly the lights flickered. He staggered backwards. Had something gone wrong? All this noise. Didn't they know that although he controlled the wheel, it also controlled him, and unless he pressed the button forever and forever and ever it would stop, leaving him high and dry, dry and high on this hard high slippery hill and Laura dead? There was only one chance; he had to do whatever the wheel demanded. And gripping the button in despair, he discovered with surprise that it imparted a nervous energy. His spine tingled. He felt a certain power.

Now he faced the raging crowd with defiance, its screams penetrating his eardrums like trumpets shrieking from a juke-box. The vague faces glowing in the bingo lights gave him a sense of himself that he had never known before. He was running the show, by God! They had to read to him, for he was their luck. This is *me*, he thought. Let the bastards yell. Then someone was laughing inside him, and he realized that somehow he had forgotten his own name. It was a sad, lost feeling to lose your name, and a crazy thing to do. That name had been given him by the white man who had owned his grandfather a long time ago down South. But maybe those wise guys knew his name.

"Who am I?" he screamed.

"Hurry up and bingo, you jerk!"

They didn't know either, he thought sadly. They didn't even know their own   70 names, they were all poor nameless bastards. Well, he didn't need that old name; he was reborn. For as long as he pressed the button he was The-man-who-pressed-the-button-who-held-the-prize-who-was-the-King-of-Bingo. That was the way it was, and he'd have to press the button even if nobody understood, even though Laura did not understand.

"Live!" he shouted.

The audience quieted like the dying of a huge fan.

"Live, Laura, baby. I got holt of it now, sugar. Live!"

He screamed it, tears streaming down his face. "I got nobody but you!"

The screams tore from his very guts. He felt as though the rush of blood to his head   75 would burst out in baseball seams of small red droplets, like a head beaten by police clubs. Bending over he saw a trickle of blood splashing the toe of his shoe. With his free hand he searched his head. It was his nose. God, suppose something has gone wrong? He felt that the whole audience had somehow entered him and was stamping its feet in his stomach and he was unable to throw them out. They wanted the prize, that was it. They wanted the secret for themselves. But they'd never get it; he would keep the bingo wheel whirling forever, and Laura would be safe in the wheel. But would she? It had to be, because if she were not safe the wheel would cease to turn; it could not go on. He had to get away, *vomit* all, and his mind formed an image of himself running with Laura in his arms down the tracks of the subway just ahead of an A train, running desperately *vomit* with people screaming for him to come out but knowing no way of leaving the tracks because to stop would bring the train crushing down upon him and to attempt to leave across the other tracks would mean to run into a hot third rail as high as his waist which threw blue sparks that blinded his eyes until he could hardly see.

He heard singing and the audience was clapping its hands.

> *Shoot the liquor to him, Jim, boy!*
> *Clap-clap-clap*
> *Well a-calla the cop*
> *He's blowing his top!*
> *Shoot the liquor to him, Jim, boy!*

80

Bitter anger grew within him at the singing. They think I'm crazy. Well let 'em laugh. I'll do what I got to do.

He was standing in an attitude of intense listening when he saw that they were watching something on the stage behind him. He felt weak. But when he turned he saw no one. If only his thumb did not ache so. Now they were applauding. And for a moment he thought that the wheel had stopped. But that was impossible, his thumb still pressed the button. Then he saw them. Two men in uniform beckoned from the end of the stage. They were coming toward him, walking in step, slowly, like a tap-dance team returning for a third encore. But their shoulders shot forward, and he backed away, looking wildly about. There was nothing to fight them with. He had only the long black cord which led to a plug somewhere back stage, and he couldn't use that because it operated the bingo wheel. He backed slowly, fixing the men with his eyes as his lips stretched over his teeth in a tight, fixed grin; moved toward the end of the stage and realizing that he couldn't go much further, for suddenly the cord became taut and he couldn't afford to break the cord. But he had to do something. The audience was howling. Suddenly he stopped dead, seeing the men halt, their legs lifted as in an interrupted step of a slow-motion dance. There was nothing to do but run in the other direction and he dashed forward, slipping and sliding. The men fell back, surprised. He struck out violently going past.

"Grab him!"

85

He ran, but all too quickly the cord tightened, resistingly, and he turned and ran back again. This time he slipped them, and discovered by running in a circle before the wheel he could keep the cord from tightening. But this way he had to flail his arms to keep the men away. Why couldn't they leave a man alone? He ran, circling.

"Ring down the curtain," someone yelled. But they couldn't do that. If they did the wheel flashing from the projection room would be cut off. But they had him before he could tell them so, trying to pry open his fist, and he was wrestling and trying to bring his knees into the fight and holding on to the button, for it was his life. And now he was down, seeing a foot coming down, crushing his wrist cruelly, down, as he saw the wheel whirling serenely above.

"I can't give it up," he screamed. Then quietly, in a confidential tone, "Boys, I really can't give it up."

It landed hard against his head. And in the blank moment they had it away from him, completely now. He fought them trying to pull him up from the stage as he watched the wheel spin slowly to a stop. Without surprise he saw it rest at double-zero.

"You see," he pointed bitterly.

"Sure, boy, sure, it's O.K.," one of the men said smiling.

And seeing the man bow his head to someone he could not see, he felt very, very happy; he would receive what all the winners received.

But as he warmed in the justice of the man's tight smile he did not see the man's slow wink, nor see the bow-legged man behind him step clear of the swiftly descending curtain and set himself for a blow. He only felt the dull pain exploding in his skull, and he knew even as it slipped out of him that his luck had run out on the stage.   [1944]

90

QUESTIONS

1. Why is it significant that the protagonist has no birth certificate? That he forgets his name?
2. Why is the movie house an appropriate setting for the action? How does the movie foreshadow the outcome of the story?
3. What does the bingo wheel represent to the protagonist?
4. What does the protagonist discover in the course of the action?
5. In what sense is the protagonist "king"?

RESPONSE

1. Compare the protagonist of this story to the protagonists in "Battle Royale" and "A Party down at the Square." Compare their sense of disorientation.

A Party down at the Square

I don't know what started it. A bunch of men came by my Uncle Ed's place and said there was going to be a party down at the Square, and my uncle hollered for me to come on and I ran with them through the dark and rain and there we were at the Square. When we got there everybody was mad and quiet and standing around looking at the nigger. Some of the men had guns, and one man kept goosing the nigger in his pants with the barrel of a shotgun, saying he ought to pull the trigger, but he never did. It was right in front of the courthouse, and the old clock in the tower was striking twelve. The rain was falling cold and freezing as it fell. Everybody was cold, and the nigger kept wrapping his arms around himself trying to stop the shivers.

Then one of the boys pushed through the circle and snatched off the nigger's shirt, and there he stood, with his black skin all shivering in the light from the fire, and looking at us with a scaired look on his face and putting his hands in his pants pockets. Folks started yelling to hurry up and kill the nigger. Somebody yelled: "Take your hands out of your pockets, nigger; we gonna have plenty heat in a minnit." But the nigger didn't hear him and kept his hands where they were.

I tell you the rain was cold. I had to stick my hands in my pockets they got so cold. The fire was pretty small, and they put some logs around the platform they had the nigger on and then threw on some gasoline, and you could see the flames light up the whole Square. It was late and the streetlights had been off for a long time. It was so bright that the bronze statue of the general standing there in the Square was like something alive. The shadows playing on his moldy green face made him seem to be smiling down at the nigger.

They threw on more gas, and it made the Square bright like it gets when the lights are turned on or when the sun is setting red. All the wagons and cars were standing around the curbs. Not like Saturday though—the niggers weren't there. Not a single nigger was there except this Bacote nigger and they dragged him there tied to the back of Jed Wilson's truck. On Saturday there's as many niggers as white folks.

5   Everybody was yelling crazy 'cause they were about to set fire to the nigger, and I got to the rear of the circle and looked around the Square to try to count the cars. The shadows of the folks was flickering on the trees in the middle of the Square. I saw some birds that the noise had woke up flying through the trees. I guess maybe they thought it was morning. The ice had started the cobblestones in the street to shine

where the rain was falling and freezing. I counted forty cars before I lost count. I knew folks must have been there from Phenix City by all the cars mixed in with the wagons.

God, it was a hell of a night. It was some night all right. When the noise died down I heard the nigger's voice from where I stood in the back, so I pushed my way up front. The nigger was bleeding from his nose and ears, and I could see him all red where the dark blood was running down his black skin. He kept lifting first one foot and then the other, like a chicken on a hot stove. I looked down to the platform they had him on, and they had pushed a ring of fire up close to his feet. It must have been hot to him with the flames almost touching his big black toes. Somebody yelled for the nigger to say his prayers, but the nigger wasn't saying anything now. He just kinda moaned with his eyes shut and kept moving up and down on his feet, first one foot and then the other.

I watched the flames burning the logs up closer and closer to the nigger's feet. They were burning good now, and the rain had stopped and the wind was rising, making the flames flare higher. I looked, and there must have been thirty-five women in the crowd, and I could hear their voices clear and shrill mixed in with those of the men. Then it happened. I heard the noise about the same time everyone else did. It was like the roar of a cyclone blowing up from the gulf, and everyone was looking up into the air to see what it was. Some of the faces looked surprised and scaired, all but the nigger. He didn't even hear the noise. He didn't even look up. Then the roar came closer, right above our heads and the wind was blowing higher and higher and the sound seemed to be going in circles.

Then I saw her. Through the clouds and fog I could see a red and green light on her wings. I could see them just for a second; then she rose up into the low clouds. I looked out for the beacon over the tops of the buildings in the direction of the airfield that's forty miles away, and it wasn't circling around. You usually could see it sweeping around the sky at night, but it wasn't there. Then, there she was again, like a big bird lost in the fog. I looked for the red and green lights, and they weren't there anymore. She was flying even closer to the tops of the buildings than before. The wind was blowing harder, and leaves started flying about, making funny shadows on the ground, and tree limbs were cracking and falling.

It was a storm all right. The pilot must have thought he was over the landing field. Maybe he thought the fire in the Square was put there for him to land by. Gosh, but it scaired the folks. I was scaired too. They started yelling: "He's going to land. He's going to land." And: "He's going to fall." A few started for their cars and wagons. I could hear the wagons creaking and chains jangling and cars spitting and missing as they started the engines up. Off to my right, a horse started pitching and striking his hooves against a car.

I didn't know what to do. I wanted to run, and I wanted to stay and see what was going to happen. The plane was close as hell. The pilot must have been trying to see where he was at, and her motors were drowning out all the sounds. I could even feel the vibration, and my hair felt like it was standing up under my hat. I happened to look over at the statue of the general standing with one leg before the other and leaning back on a sword, and I was fixing to run over and climb between his legs and sit there and watch when the roar stopped some, and I looked up and she was gliding just over the top of the trees in the middle of the Square.

Her motors stopped altogether and I could hear the sound of branches cracking and snapping off below her landing gear. I could see her plain now, all silver and shining in the light of the fire with T.W.A. in black letters under her wings. She was sailing

10

smoothly out of the Square when she hit the high power lines that follow the Birmingham highway through the town. It made a loud crash. It sounded like the wind blowing the door of a tin barn shut. She only hit with her landing gear, but I could see the sparks flying, and the wires knocked loose from the poles were spitting blue sparks and whipping around like a bunch of snakes and leaving circles of blue sparks in the darkness.

The plane had knocked five or six wires loose, and they were dangling and swinging, and every time they touched they threw off more sparks. The wind was making them swing, and when I got over there, there was a crackling and spitting screen of blue haze across the highway. I lost my hat running over, but I didn't stop to look for it. I was among the first and I could hear the others pounding behind me across the grass of the Square. They were yelling to beat all hell, and they came up fast, pushing and shoving, and someone got pushed against a swinging wire. It made a sound like when a blacksmith drops a red hot horseshoe into a barrel of water, and the steam comes up. I could smell the flesh burning. The first time I'd ever smelled it. I got up close and it was a woman. It must have killed her right off. She was lying in a puddle stiff as a board, with pieces of glass insulators that the plane had knocked off the poles lying all around her. Her white dress was torn, and I saw one of her tits hanging out in the water and her thighs. Some woman screamed and fainted and almost fell on a wire, but a man caught her. The sheriff and his men were yelling and driving folks back with guns shining in their hands, and everything was lit up blue by the sparks. The shock had turned the woman almost as black as the nigger. I was trying to see if she wasn't blue too, or if it was just the sparks, and the sheriff drove me away. As I backed off trying to see, I heard the motors of the plane start up again somewhere off to the right in the clouds.

The clouds were moving fast in the wind and the wind was blowing the smell of something burning over to me. I turned around, and the crowd was headed back to the nigger. I could see him standing there in the middle of the flames. The wind was making the flames brighter every minute. The crowd was running. I ran too. I ran back across the grass with the crowd. It wasn't so large now that so many had gone when the plane came. I tripped and fell over the limb of a tree lying in the grass and bit my lip. It ain't well yet I bit it so bad. I could taste the blood in my mouth as I ran over. I guess that's what made me sick. When I got there, the fire had caught the nigger's pants, and the folks were standing around watching, but not too close on account of the wind blowing the flames. Somebody hollered, "Well, nigger, it ain't so cold now, is it? You don't need to put your hands in your pockets now." And the nigger looked up with his great white eyes looking like they was 'bout to pop out of his head, and I had enough. I didn't want to see anymore. I wanted to run somewhere and puke, but I stayed. I stayed right there in the front of the crowd and looked.

The nigger tried to say something I couldn't hear for the roar of the wind in the fire, and I strained my ears. Jed Wilson hollered, "What you say there, nigger?" And it came back through the flames in his nigger voice: "Will one a you gentlemen please cut my throat?" he said. "Will somebody please cut my throat like a Christian?" And Jed hollered back, "Sorry, but ain't no Christians around tonight. Ain't no Jew-boys neither. We're just one hundred percent Americans."

15   Then the nigger was silent. Folks started laughing at Jed. Jed's right popular with the folks, and next year, my uncle says, they plan to run him for sheriff. The heat was too much for me, and the smoke was making my eyes to smart. I was trying to back away when Jed reached down and brought up a can of gasoline and threw it in the fire

on the nigger. I could see the flames catching the gas in a puff as it went in in a silver sheet and some of it reached the nigger, making spurts of blue fire all over his chest.

Well, that nigger was tough. I have to give it to that nigger; he was really tough. He had started to burn like a house afire and was making the smoke smell like burning hides. The fire was up around his head, and the smoke was so thick and black we couldn't see him. And him not moving—we thought he was dead. Then he started out. The fire had burned the ropes they had tied him with, and he started jumping and kicking about like he was blind, and you could smell his skin burning. He kicked so hard that the platform, which was burning too, fell in, and he rolled out of the fire at my feet. I jumped back so he wouldn't get on me. I'll never forget it. Every time I eat barbeque I'll remember that nigger. His back was just like a barbecued hog. I could see the prints of his ribs where they start around from his backbone and curve down and around. It was a sight to see, that nigger's back. He was right at my feet, and somebody behind pushed me and almost made me step on him, and he was still burning.

I didn't step on him though, and Jed and somebody else pushed him back into the burning planks and logs and poured on more gas. I wanted to leave, but the folks were yelling and I couldn't move except to look around and see the statue. A branch the wind had broken was resting on his hat. I tried to push out and get away because my guts were gone, and all I got was spit and hot breath in my face from the woman and two men standing directly behind me. So I had to turn back around. The nigger rolled out of the fire again. He wouldn't stay put. It was on the other side this time. I couldn't see him very well through the flames and smoke. They got some tree limbs and held him there this time and he stayed there till he was ashes. I guess he stayed there. I know he burned to ashes because I saw Jed a week later, and he laughed and showed me some white finger bones still held together with little pieces of the nigger's skin. Anyway, I left when somebody moved around to see the nigger. I pushed my way through the crowd, and a woman in the rear scratched my face as she yelled and fought to get up close.

I ran across the Square to the other side, where the sheriff and his deputies were guarding the wires that were still spitting and making a blue fog. My heart was pounding like I had been running a long ways, and I bent over and let my insides go. Everything came up and spilled in a big gush over the ground. I was sick, and tired, and weak, and cold. The wind was still high, and large drops of rain were beginning to fall. I headed down the street to my uncle's place past a store where the wind had broken a window, and glass lay over the sidewalk. I kicked it as I went by. I remember somebody's fool rooster crowing like it was morning in all that wind.

The next day I was too weak to go out, and my uncle kidded me and called me "the gutless wonder from Cincinnati." I didn't mind. He said you get used to it in time. He couldn't go out hisself. There was too much wind and rain. I got up and looked out of the window, and the rain was pouring down and dead sparrows and limbs of trees were scattered all over the yard. There had been a cyclone all right. It swept a path right through the country, and we were lucky we didn't get the full force of it.

It blew for three days steady, and put the town in a hell of a shape. The wind blew sparks and set fire to the white-and-green-rimmed house on Jackson Avenue that had the big concrete lions in the yard and burned it down to the ground. They had to kill another nigger who tried to run out of the county after they burned this Bacote nigger. My Uncle Ed said they always have to kill niggers in pairs to keep the

20

other niggers in place. I don't know though, the folks seem a little skittish of the nig-gers. They all came back, but they act pretty sullen. They look mean as hell when you pass them down at the store. The other day I was down to Brinkley's store, and a white cropper said it didn't do no good to kill the niggers 'cause things don't get no better. He looked hungry as hell. Most of the croppers look hungry. You'd be surprised how hun-gry white folks can look. Somebody said that he'd better shut his damn mouth, and he shut up. But from the look on his face he won't stay shut long. He went out of the store muttering to himself and spit a big chew of tobacco right down on Brinkley's floor. Brinkley said he was sore 'cause he wouldn't let him have credit. Anyway, it didn't seem to help things. First it was the nigger and the storm, then the plane, then the woman and the wires, and now I hear the airplane line is investigating to find who set the fire that almost wrecked their plane. All that in one night, and all of it but the storm over one nigger. It was some night all right. It was some party too. I was right there, see. I was right there watching it all. It was my first party and my last. God, but that nigger was tough. That Bacote nigger was some nigger!   [1996]

QUESTIONS

1. How many events such as this one has the narrator attended? What does this fact contribute to the story?

2. What does the episode with the airplane and the broken electrical wires con-tribute to the story?

3. Why does Ellison make it clear that the sheriff and his deputies and women are present at "the party"?

4. Does it affect our experience of the story knowing that Ellison, an African American, tells this story as an Anglo narrator?

5. What is the narrator's attitude toward the killed man? How does this affect your sympathies toward the narrator?

RESPONSE

1. Read Ellison's essay "What America Would Be Like Without Blacks." What does this essay add to your interpretation of the story?

WILLIAM FAULKNER

William Faulkner (1897–1962) was born in New Albany, Mississippi, but the family soon moved to Oxford, where his father was a business administrator at the University of Mississippi. After serving in the Royal Canadian Air Force during World War I, Faulkner returned to Oxford. He was occasionally drawn away for brief periods—to the literary community in New Orleans and to Hollywood for script writing—but Oxford remained for the rest of his life both his home and a source of inspiration for his greatest fiction. Beginning with the publication of *Sartoris* in 1929, he created in novel after novel an imaginary county, Yoknapatawpha, which closely resembles the world about Oxford. Among the works written during this remarkable period of sustained creative energy are *The Sound and the Fury* (1929), *As I Lay Dying* (1930), *Light in August* (1932), and *Absalom, Absalom!* (1936). Faulkner was awarded the Nobel Prize in 1950, and his short stories, collected into one volume that same year, won the National Book Award.

Dry September

1

Through the bloody September twilight, aftermath of sixty-two rainless days, it had gone like a fire in dry grass—the rumor, the story, whatever it was. Something about Miss Minnie Cooper and a Negro. Attacked, insulted, frightened: none of them, gathered in the barber shop on that Saturday evening where the ceiling fan stirred, without freshening it, the vitiated air, sending back upon them, in recurrent surges of stale pomade and lotion, their own stale breath and odors, knew exactly what had happened.

"Except it wasn't Will Mayes," a barber said. He was a man of middle age; a thin, sand-colored man with a mild face, who was shaving a client. "I know Will Mayes. He's a good nigger. And I know Miss Minnie Cooper, too."

"What do you know about her?" a second barber said.

"Who is she?" the client said. "A young girl?"

"No," the barber said. "She's about forty, I reckon. She ain't married. That's why I dont believe—"

"Believe, hell!" a hulking youth in a sweat-stained silk shirt said. "Wont you take a white woman's word before a nigger's?"

"I dont believe Will Mayes did it," the barber said. "I know Will Mayes."

"Maybe you know who did it, then. Maybe you already got him out of town, you damn niggerlover."

"I dont believe anybody did anything. I dont believe anything happened. I leave it to you fellows if them ladies that get old without getting married dont have notions that man cant—"

"Then you are a hell of a white man," the client said. He moved under the cloth. The youth had sprung to his feet.

"You dont?" he said. "Do you accuse a white woman of lying?"

The barber held the razor poised above the half-risen client. He did not look around.

"It's this durn weather," another said. "It's enough to make a man do anything. Even to her."

Nobody laughed. The barber said in his mild, stubborn tone: "I aint accusing nobody of nothing. I just know and you fellows know how a woman that never—"

"You damn niggerlover!" the youth said.

"Shut up, Butch," another said. "We'll get the facts in plenty of time to act."

"Who is? Who's getting them?" the youth said. "Facts, hell! I—"

"You're a fine white man," the client said. "Aint you?" In his frothy beard he looked like a desert rat in the moving pictures. "You tell them, Jack," he said to the youth. "If there aint any white men in this town, you can count on me, even if I aint only a drummer and a stranger."

"That's right, boys," the barber said. "Find out the truth first. I know Will Mayes."

"Well, by God!" the youth shouted. "To think that a white man in this town—"

"Shut up, Butch," the second speaker said. "We got plenty of time."

The client sat up. He looked at the speaker. "Do you claim that anything excuses a nigger attacking a white woman? Do you mean to tell me you are a white man and you'll stand for it? You better go back North where you came from. The South dont want your kind here."

"North what?" the second said. "I was born and raised in this town."

"Well, by God!" the youth said. He looked about with a strained, baffled gaze, as if he was trying to remember what it was he wanted to say or to do. He drew his sleeve across his sweating face. "Damn if I'm going to let a white woman—"

"You tell them, Jack," the drummer said. "By God, if they—"

The screen door crashed open. A man stood on the floor, his feet apart and his heavy-set body poised easily. His white shirt was open at the throat; he wore a felt hat. His hot, bold glance swept the group. His name was McLendon. He had commanded troops at the front in France and had been decorated for valor.

"Well," he said, "are you going to sit there and let a black son rape a white woman on the streets of Jefferson?"

Butch sprang up again. The silk of his shirt clung flat to his heavy shoulders. At each armpit was a dark halfmoon. "That's what I been telling them! That's what I—"

"Did it really happen?" a third said. "This aint the first man scare she ever had, like Hawkshaw says. Wasn't there something about a man on the kitchen roof, watching her undress, about a year ago?"

"What?" the client said. "What's that?" The barber had been slowly forcing him back   30
into the chair; he arrested himself reclining, his head lifted, the barber still pressing him
down.

McLendon whirled on the third speaker. "Happen? What the hell difference does
it make? Are you going to let the black sons get away with it until one really does it?"

"That's what I'm telling them!" Butch shouted. He cursed, long and steady, pointless.

"Here, here," a fourth said. "Not so loud. Dont talk so loud."

"Sure," McLendon said: "no talking necessary at all. I've done my talking. Who's
with me?" He poised on the balls of his feet, roving his gaze.

The barber held the drummer's face down, the razor poised. "Find out the facts   35
first, boys. I know Willy Mayes. It wasn't him. Let's get the sheriff and do this thing
right."

McLendon whirled upon him his furious, rigid face. The barber did not look away.
They looked like men of different races. The other barbers had ceased also above their
prone clients. "You mean to tell me," McLendon said, "that you'd take a nigger's word
before a white woman's? Why, you damn niggerloving—"

The third speaker rose and grasped McLendon's arm; he too had been a soldier.
"Now, now. Let's figure this thing out. Who knows anything about what really
happened?"

"Figure out hell!" McLendon jerked his arm free. "All that're with me get up from
there. The ones that aint—" He roved his gaze, dragging his sleeve across his face.

Three men rose. The drummer in the chair sat up. "Here," he said, jerking at the
cloth about his neck; "get this rag off me. I'm with him. I don't live here, but by God,
if our mothers and wives and sisters—" He smeared the cloth over his face and flung
it to the floor. McLendon stood in the floor and cursed the others. Another rose and
moved toward him. The remainder sat uncomfortable, not looking at one another, then
one by one they rose and joined him.

The barber picked the cloth from the floor. He began to fold it neatly. "Boys, don't   40
do that. Will Mayes never done it. I know."

"Come on," McLendon said. He whirled. From his hip pocket protruded the butt
of a heavy automatic pistol. They went out. The screen door crashed behind them re-
verberant in the dead air.

The barber wiped the razor carefully and swiftly, and put it away, and ran to the rear,
and took his hat from the wall. "I'll be back as soon as I can," he said to the other barbers. "I cant let—" He went out, running. The two other barbers followed him to the
door and caught it on the rebound, leaning out and looking up the street after him. The
air was flat and dead. It had a metallic taste at the base of the tongue.

"What can he do?" the first said. The second one was saying "Jees Christ" under his
breath. "I'd just as lief be Will Mayes as Hawk, if he gets McLendon riled."

"Jees Christ, Jees Christ," the second whispered.

"You reckon he really done it to her?" the first said.   45

2

She was thirty-eight or thirty-nine. She lived in a small frame house with her invalid
mother and a thin, sallow, unflagging aunt, where each morning between ten and
eleven she would appear on the porch in a lace-trimmed boudoir cap, to sit swinging

in the porch swing until noon. After dinner she lay down for a while, until the afternoon began to cool. Then, in one of the three or four new voile dresses which she had each summer, she would go downtown to spend the afternoon in the stores with the other ladies, where they would handle the goods and haggle over the prices in cold immediate voices, without any intention of buying.

She was of comfortable people—not the best in Jefferson, but good people enough— and she was still on the slender side of ordinary looking, with a bright, faintly haggard manner and dress. When she was young she had a slender, nervous body and a sort of hard vivacity which enabled her for a time to ride upon the crest of the town's social life as exemplified by the high school party and church social period of her contemporaries while still children enough to be unclassconscious.

She was the last to realize that she was losing ground; that those among whom she had been a little brighter and louder flame than any other were beginning to learn the pleasure of snobbery—male—and retaliation—female. That was when her face began to wear that bright, haggard look. She still carried it to parties on shadowy porticoes and summer lawns, like a mask or a flag, with the bafflement of furious repudiation of truth in her eyes. One evening at a party she heard a boy and two girls, all schoolmates, talking. She never accepted another invitation.

She watched the girls with whom she had grown up as they married and got homes and children, but no man ever called on her steadily until the children of the other girls had been calling her "aunty" for several years, the while their mothers told them in bright voices about how popular Aunt Minnie had been as a girl. Then the town began to see her driving on Sunday afternoons with the cashier in the bank. He was a widower of about forty—a high-colored man, smelling always faintly of the barber shop or of whisky. He owned the first automobile in town, a red runabout; Minnie had the first motoring bonnet and veil the town ever saw. Then the town began to say: "Poor Minnie." "But she is old enough to take care of herself," others said. That was when she began to ask her old schoolmates that their children call her "cousin" instead of "aunty."

50   It was twelve years now since she had been relegated into adultery by public opinion, and eight years since the cashier had gone to a Memphis bank, returning for one day each Christmas, which he spent at an annual bachelors' party at a hunting club on the river. From behind their curtains the neighbors would see the party pass, and during the over-the-way Christmas day visiting they would tell her about him, about how well he looked, and how they heard that he was prospering in the city, watching with bright, secret eyes her haggard, bright face. Usually by that hour there would be a scent of whisky on her breath. It was supplied her by a youth, a clerk at the soda fountain: "Sure; I buy it for the old gal. I reckon she's entitled to a little fun."

Her mother kept to her room altogether now; the gaunt aunt ran the house. Against that background Minnie's bright dresses, her idle and empty days, had a quality of furious unreality. She went out in the evenings only with women now, neighbors, to the moving pictures. Each afternoon she dressed in one of the new dresses and went downtown alone, where her young "cousins" were already strolling in the late afternoons with their delicate, silken heads and thin, awkward arms and conscious hips, clinging to one another or shrieking and giggling with paired boys in the soda fountain when she passed and went on along the serried store fronts, in the doors of which the sitting and lounging men did not even follow her with their eyes any more.

3

The barber went swiftly up the street where the sparse lights, insect-swirled, glared in rigid and violent suspension in the lifeless air. The day had died in a pall of dust; above the darkened square, shrouded by the spent dust, the sky was as clear as the inside of a brass bell. Below the east was a rumour of the twice-waxed moon.

When he overtook them McLendon and three others were getting into a car parked in an alley. McLendon stooped his thick head, peering out beneath the top. "Changed your mind, did you?" he said. "Damn good thing; by God, tomorrow when this town hears about how you talked tonight—"

"Now, now," the other ex-soldier said. "Hawkshaw's all right. Come on, Hawk; jump in."

"Will Mayes never done it, boys," the barber said. "If anybody done it. Why, you   55
all know well as I do there aint any town where they got better niggers than us. And you know how a lady will kind of think things about men when there aint any reason to, and Miss Minnie anyway—"

"Sure, sure," the soldier said. "We're just going to talk to him a little; that's all."

"Talk hell!" Butch said. "When we're through with the—"

"Shut up, for God's sake!" the soldier said. "Do you want everybody in town—"

"Tell them, by God!" McLendon said. "Tell every one of the sons that'll let a white woman—"

"Let's go; let's go: here's the other car." The second car slid squealing out of a cloud   60
of dust at the alley mouth. McLendon started his car and took the lead. Dust lay like fog in the street. The street lights hung nimbused as in water. They drove on out of town.

A rutted lane turned at right angles. Dust hung above it too, and above all the land. The dark bulk of the ice plant, where the Negro Mayes was night watchman, rose against the sky. "Better stop here, hadn't we?" the soldier said. McLendon did not reply. He hurled the car up and slammed to a stop, the headlights glaring on the blank wall.

"Listen here, boys," the barber said; "if he's here, don't that prove he never done it? Dont it? If it was him, he would run. Dont you see he would?" The second car came up and stopped. McLendon got down; Butch sprang down beside him. "Listen, boys," the barber said.

"Cut the lights off!" McLendon said. The breathless dark rushed down. There was no sound in it save their lungs as they sought air in the parched dust in which for two months they had lived; then the diminishing crunch of McLendon's and Butch's feet, and a moment later McLendon's voice:

"Will! . . . Will!"

Below the east the wan hemorrhage of the moon increased. It heaved above the   65
ridge, silvering the air, the dust, so that they seemed to breathe, live, in a bowl of molted lead. There was no sound of nightbird nor insect, no sound save their breathing and a faint ticking of contracting metal about the cars. When their bodies touched one another they seemed to sweat dryly, for no more moisture came. "Christ!" a voice said; "let's get out of here."

But they didn't move until vague noises began to grow out of the darkness ahead; then they got out and waited tensely in the breathless dark. There was another sound: a blow, a hissing expulsion of breath and McLendon cursing in undertone. They stood a moment longer, then they ran forward. They ran in a stumbling clump, as though they

were fleeing something. "Kill him, kill the son," a voice whispered. McLendon flung
them back.

"Not here," he said. "Get him into the car." "Kill him, kill the black son!" the voice
murmured. They dragged the Negro to the car. The barber had waited beside the car.
He could feel himself sweating and he knew he was going to be sick at the stomach.

"What is it, captains?" the Negro said. "I aint done nothing. 'Fore God, Mr. John."
Someone produced handcuffs. They worked busily about the Negro as though he were
a post, quiet, intent, getting in one another's way. He submitted to the handcuffs, looking swiftly and constantly from dim face to dim face. "Who's here, captains?" he said,
leaning to peer into the faces until they could feel his breath and smell his sweaty reek.
He spoke a name or two. "What you all say I done, Mr. John?"

McLendon jerked the car door open. "Get in!" he said.

70   The Negro did not move. "What you all going to do with me, Mr. John? I aint done
nothing. White folks, captains, I aint done nothing: I swear 'fore God." He called another name.

"Get in!" McLendon said. He struck the Negro. The others expelled their breath
in a dry hissing and struck him with random blows and he whirled and cursed
them, and swept back his manacled hands across their faces and slashed the barber
upon the mouth, and the barber struck him also. "Get him in there," McLendon
said. They pushed at him. He ceased struggling and got in and sat quietly as the others took their places. He sat between the barber and the soldier, drawing his limbs
in so as not to touch them, his eyes going swiftly and constantly from face to face.
Butch clung to the running board. The car moved on. The barber nursed his mouth
with his handkerchief.

"What's the matter, Hawk?" the soldier said.

"Nothing," the barber said. They regained the highroad and turned away from
town. The second car dropped back out of the dust. They went on gaining speed; the
final fringe of houses dropped behind.

"Goddamn, he stinks!" the soldier said.

75   "We'll fix that," the drummer in front beside McLendon said. On the running board
Butch cursed into the hot rush of air. The barber leaned suddenly forward and touched
McLendon's arm.

"Let me out, John," he said.

"Jump out, niggerlover," McLendon said without turning his head. He drove swiftly. Behind them the sourceless lights of the second car glared in the dust. Presently
McLendon turned into a narrow road. It was rutted with disuse. It led back to an abandoned brick kiln—a series of reddish mounds and weed- and vine-choked vats without bottom. It had been used for pasture once, until one day the owner missed one of
his mules. Although he prodded carefully in the vats with a long pole, he could not
even find the bottom of them.

"John," the barber said.

"Jump out, then," McLendon said, hurling the car along the ruts. Beside the barber
the Negro spoke:

80   "Mr. Henry."

The barber sat forward. The narrow tunnel of the road rushed up and past. Their
motion was like an extinct furnace blast: cooler, but utterly dead. The car bounded
from rut to rut.

"Mr. Henry," the Negro said.

The barber began to tug furiously at the door. "Look out, there!" the soldier said,
but the barber had already kicked the door open and swung onto the running board.

The soldier leaned across the Negro and grasped at him, but he had already jumped. The car went on without checking speed.

The impetus hurled him crashing through dust-sheathed weeds, into the ditch. Dust puffed about him, and in a thin vicious crackling of sapless stems he lay choking and retching until the second car passed and died away. Then he rose and limped on until he reached the highroad and turned toward town, brushing at his clothes with his hands. The moon was higher, riding high and clear of the dust at last, and after a while the town began to glare beneath the dust. He went on, limping. Presently he heard cars and the glow of them grew in the dust behind him and he left the road and crouched again in the weeds until they passed. McLendon's car came last now. There were four people in it and Butch was not on the running board.

They went on; the dust swallowed them; the glare and the sound died away. The dust of them hung for a while, but soon the eternal dust absorbed it again. The barber climbed back onto the road and limped on toward town.

4

As she dressed for supper on that Saturday evening, her own flesh felt like fever. Her hands trembled among the hooks and eyes, and her eyes had a feverish look, and her hair swirled crisp and crackling under the comb. While she was still dressing the friends called for her and sat while she donned her sheerest underthings and stockings and a new voile dress. "Do you feel strong enough to go out?" they said, their eyes bright too, with a dark glitter. "When you have had time to get over the shock, you must tell us what happened. What he said and did; everything."

In the leafed darkness, as they walked toward the square, she began to breathe deeply, something like a swimmer preparing to dive, until she ceased trembling, the four of them walking slowly because of the terrible heat and out of solicitude for her. But as they neared the square she began to tremble again, walking with her head up, her hands clenched at her sides, their voices about her murmurous, also with that feverish, glittering quality of their eyes.

They entered the square, she in the center of the group, fragile in her fresh dress. She was trembling worse. She walked slower and slower, as children eat ice cream, her head up and her eyes bright in the haggard banner of her face, passing the hotel and the coatless drummers in chairs along the curb looking around at her: "That's the one: see? The one in pink in the middle." "Is that her? What did they do with the nigger? Did they—" "Sure. He's all right." "All right, is he?" "Sure. He went on a little trip." Then the drug store, where even the young men lounging in the doorway tipped their hats and followed with their eyes the motion of her hips and legs when she passed.

They went on, passing the lifted hats of the gentlemen, the suddenly ceased voices, deferent, protective. "Do you see?" the friends said. Their voices sounded like long hovering sighs of hissing exultation. "There's not a Negro on the square. Not one."

They reached the picture show. It was like a miniature fairyland with its lighted lobby and colored lithographs of life caught in its terrible and beautiful mutations. Her lips began to tingle. In the dark, when the picture began, it would be all right; she could hold back the laughing so it would not waste away so fast and so soon. So she hurried on before the turning faces, the undertones of low astonishment, and they took their accustomed places where she could see the aisle against the silver glare and the young men and girls coming in two and two against it.

The lights flicked away; the screen glowed silver, and soon life began to unfold, beautiful and passionate and sad, while still the young men and girls entered, scented and sibilant in the half dark, their paired backs in silhouette delicate and sleek, their slim, quick bodies awkward, divinely young, while beyond them the silver dream accumulated, inevitably on and on. She began to laugh. In trying to suppress it, it made more noise than ever; heads began to turn. Still laughing, her friends raised her and led her out, and she stood at the curb, laughing on a high, sustained note, until the taxi came up and they helped her in.

They removed the pink voile and the sheer underthings and the stockings, and put her to bed, and cracked ice for her temples, and sent for the doctor. He was hard to locate, so they ministered to her with hushed ejaculations, renewing the ice and fanning her. While the ice was fresh and cold she stopped laughing and lay still for a time, moaning only a little. But soon the laughing welled again and her voice rose screaming.

"Shhhhhhhhhhh! Shhhhhhhhhhhhhhh!" they said, freshening the icepack, smoothing her hair, examining it for gray; "poor girl!" Then to one another: "Do you suppose anything really happened?" their eyes darkly aglitter, secret and passionate. "Shhhhhhhhhh! Poor girl! Poor Minnie!"

5

It was midnight when McLendon drove up to his neat new house. It was trim and fresh as a birdcage and almost as small, with its clean, green-and-white paint. He locked the car and mounted the porch and entered. His wife rose from a chair beside the reading lamp. McLendon stopped in the floor and stared at her until she looked down.

95 "Look at that clock," he said, lifting his arm, pointing. She stood before him, her face lowered, a magazine in her hands. Her face was pale, strained, and weary-looking. "Haven't I told you about sitting up like this, waiting to see when I come in?"

"John," she said. She laid the magazine down. Poised on the balls of his feet, he glared at her with his hot eyes, his sweating face.

"Didn't I tell you?" He went toward her. She looked up then. He caught her shoulder. She stood passive, looking at him.

"Don't, John. I couldn't sleep . . . The heat; something. Please, John. You're hurting me."

"Didn't I tell you?" He released her and half struck, half flung her across the chair, and she lay there and watched him quietly as he left the room.

100 He went on through the house, ripping off his shirt, and on the dark, screened porch at the rear he stood and mopped his head and shoulders with the shirt and flung it away. He took the pistol from his hip and laid it on the table beside the bed, and sat on the bed and removed his shoes, and rose and slipped his trousers off. He was sweating again already, and he stooped and hunted furiously for the shirt. At last he found it and wiped his body again, and, with his body pressed against the dusty screen, he stood panting. There was no movement, no sound, not even an insect. The dark world seemed to lie stricken beneath the cold moon and the lidless stars.   [1931]

QUESTIONS

1. What effect is achieved by the abrupt shifts of point of view among the five sections of the story?
2. Are the attitudes toward women in the story consistent or inherently contradictory?
3. How do the images drawn from nature reinforce the theme?
4. What purpose does Hawkshaw serve in the story?
5. How is McLendon's treatment of his wife in the final scene related to the earlier action?

RESPONSE

1. Compare Faulkner's treatment of African Americans and of women to Ellison's in "A Party down at the Square."

WILLIAM FAULKNER

A Rose for Emily

1

When Miss Emily Grierson died, our whole town went to her funeral: the men through a sort of respectful affection for a fallen monument, the women mostly out of curiosity to see the inside of her house, which no one save an old manservant—a combined gardener and cook—had seen in at least ten years.

It was a big, squarish frame house that had once been white, decorated with cupolas and spires and scrolled balconies in the heavily lightsome style of the seventies, set on what had once been our most select street. But garages and cotton gins had encroached and obliterated even the august names of that neighborhood; only Miss Emily's house was left, lifting its stubborn and coquettish decay above the cotton wagons and the gasoline pumps—an eyesore among eyesores. And now Miss Emily had gone to join the representatives of those august names where they lay in the cedar-bemused cemetery among the ranked and anonymous graves of Union and Confederate soldiers who fell at the battle of Jefferson.

Alive, Miss Emily had been a tradition, a duty, and a care; a sort of hereditary obligation upon the town, dating from that day in 1894 when Colonel Sartoris, the mayor—he who fathered the edict that no Negro woman should appear on the streets without an apron—remitted her taxes, the dispensation dating from the death of her father on into perpetuity. Not that Miss Emily would have accepted charity. Colonel Sartoris invented an involved tale to the effect that Miss Emily's father had loaned money to the town, which the town, as a matter of business, preferred this way of repaying. Only a man of Colonel Sartoris' generation and thought could have invented it, and only a woman could have believed it.

When the next generation, with its more modern ideas, became mayors and aldermen, this arrangement created some little dissatisfaction. On the first of the year they mailed her a tax notice. February came, and there was no reply. They wrote her a formal letter, asking her to call at the sheriff's office at her convenience. A week later the mayor wrote her himself, offering to call or to send his car for her, and received in reply a note on paper of an archaic shape, in a thin, flowing calligraphy in faded ink, to the effect that she no longer went out at all. The tax notice was also enclosed, without comment.

They called a special meeting of the Board of Aldermen. A deputation waited 5
upon her, knocked at the door through which no visitor had passed since she ceased
giving china-painting lessons eight or ten years earlier. They were admitted by the
old Negro into a dim hall from which a stairway mounted into still more shadow. It
smelled of dust and disuse—a close, dank smell. The Negro led them into the parlor. It was furnished in heavy, leather-covered furniture. When the Negro opened
the blinds of one window, they could see that the leather was cracked; and when
they sat down, a faint dust rose sluggishly about their thighs, spinning with slow motions in the single sun-ray. On a tarnished gilt easel before the fireplace stood a crayon portrait of Miss Emily's father.

They rose when she entered—a small, fat woman in black, with a thin gold chain
descending to her waist and vanishing into her belt, leaning on an ebony cane with
a tarnished gold head. Her skeleton was small and spare; perhaps that was why
what would have been merely plumpness in another was obesity in her. She looked
bloated, like a body long submerged in motionless water, and of that pallid hue. Her
eyes, lost in the fatty ridges of her face, looked like two small pieces of coal pressed
into a lump of dough as they moved from one face to another while the visitors stated their errand.

She did not ask them to sit. She just stood in the door and listened quietly until
the spokesman came to a stumbling halt. Then they could hear the invisible watch
ticking at the end of the gold chain.

Her voice was dry and cold. "I have no taxes in Jefferson. Colonel Sartoris explained it to me. Perhaps one of you can gain access to the city records and satisfy
yourselves."

"But we have. We are the city authorities, Miss Emily. Didn't you get a notice
from the sheriff, signed by him?"

"I received a paper, yes," Miss Emily said. "Perhaps he considers himself the 10
sheriff . . . I have no taxes in Jefferson."

"But there is nothing on the books to show that, you see. We must go by the—"

"See Colonel Sartoris." (Colonel Sartoris had been dead almost ten years.) "I have
no taxes in Jefferson. Tobe!" The Negro appeared. "Show these gentlemen out."

2

So she vanquished them, horse and foot, just as she had vanquished their fathers
thirty years before about the smell. That was two years after her father's death and
a short time after her sweetheart—the one we believed would marry her—had deserted her. After her father's death she went out very little; after her sweetheart went
away, people hardly saw her at all. A few of the ladies had the temerity to call, but
were not received, and the only sign of life about the place was the Negro man—a
young man then—going in and out with a market basket.

"Just as if a man—any man—could keep a kitchen properly," the ladies said; so
they were not surprised when the smell developed. It was another link between the
gross, teeming world and the high and mighty Griersons.

A neighbor, a woman, complained to the mayor, Judge Stevens, eighty years old. 15
"But what will you have me do about it, madam?" he said.

"Why, send her word to stop it," the woman said. "Isn't there a law?"

"I'm sure that won't be necessary," Judge Stevens said. "It's probably just a snake or a rat that nigger of hers killed in the yard. I'll speak to him about it."

The next day he received two more complaints, one from a man who came in diffident deprecation. "We really must do something about it, Judge. I'd be the last one in the world to bother Miss Emily, but we've got to do something." That night the Board of Aldermen met—three graybeards and one younger man, a member of the rising generation.

20 "It's simple enough," he said. "Send her word to have her place cleaned up. Give her a certain time to do it in, and if she don't . . ."

"Dammit, sir," Judge Stevens said, "will you accuse a lady to her face of smelling bad?"

So the next night, after midnight, four men crossed Miss Emily's lawn and slunk about the house like burglars, sniffing along the base of the brickwork and at the cellar openings while one of them performed a regular sowing motion with his hand out of a sack slung from his shoulder. They broke open the cellar door and sprinkled lime there, and in all the outbuildings. As they recrossed the lawn, a window that had been dark was lighted and Miss Emily sat in it, the light behind her, and her upright torso motionless as that of an idol. They crept quietly across the lawn and into the shadow of the locusts that lined the street. After a week or two the smell went away.

That was when people had begun to feel sorry for her. People in our town, remembering how old lady Wyatt, her great-aunt, had gone completely crazy at last, believed that the Griersons held themselves a little too high for what they really were. None of the young men were quite good enough for Miss Emily and such. We had long thought of them as a tableau, Miss Emily a slender figure in white in the background, her father a spraddled silhouette in the foreground, his back to her and clutching a horsewhip, the two of them framed by the back-flung front door. So when she got to be thirty and was still single, we were not pleased exactly, but vindicated; even with insanity in the family she wouldn't have turned down all of her chances if they had really materialized.

When her father died, it got about that the house was all that was left to her; and in a way, people were glad. At last they could pity Miss Emily. Being left alone, and a pauper, she had become humanized. Now she too would know the old thrill and the old despair of a penny more or less.

25 The day after his death all the ladies prepared to call at the house and offer condolence and aid, as is our custom. Miss Emily met them at the door, dressed as usual and with no trace of grief on her face. She told them that her father was not dead. She did that for three days, with the ministers calling on her, and the doctors, trying to persuade her to let them dispose of the body. Just as they were about to resort to law and force, she broke down, and they buried her father quickly.

We did not say she was crazy then. We believed she had to do that. We remembered all the young men her father had driven away, and we knew that with nothing left, she would have to cling to that which had robbed her, as people will.

3

She was sick for a long time. When we saw her again, her hair was cut short, making her look like a girl, with a vague resemblance to those angels in colored church windows—sort of tragic and serene.

The town had just let the contracts for paving the sidewalks, and in the summer after her father's death they began the work. The construction company came with niggers and mules and machinery, and a foreman named Homer Barron, a Yankee—a big, dark, ready man, with a big voice and eyes lighter than his face. The little boys would follow in groups to hear him cuss the niggers, and the niggers singing in time to the rise and fall of picks. Pretty soon he knew everybody in town. Whenever you heard a lot of laughing anywhere about the square, Homer Barron would be in the center of the group. Presently we began to see him and Miss Emily on Sunday afternoons driving in the yellow-wheeled buggy and the matched team of bays from the livery stable.

At first we were glad that Miss Emily would have an interest, because the ladies all said, "Of course a Grierson would not think seriously of a Northerner, a day laborer." But there were still others, older people, who said that even grief could not cause a real lady to forget *noblesse oblige*—without calling it *noblesse oblige*. They just said, "Poor Emily. Her kinsfolk should come to her." She had some kin in Alabama; but years ago her father had fallen out with them over the estate of old lady Wyatt, the crazy woman, and there was no communication between the two families. They had not even been represented at the funeral.

And as soon as the old people said, "Poor Emily," the whispering began. "Do you suppose it's really so?" they said to one another. "Of course it is. What else could . . ." This behind their hands; rustling of craned silk and satin behind jalousies closed upon the sun of Sunday afternoon as the thin, swift clop-clop-clop of the matched team passed: "Poor Emily."

She carried her head high enough—even when we believed that she was fallen. It was as if she demanded more than ever the recognition of her dignity as the last Grierson; as if it had wanted that touch of earthiness to reaffirm her imperviousness. Like when she bought the rat poison, the arsenic. That was over a year after they had begun to say "Poor Emily," and while the two female cousins were visiting her.

"I want some poison," she said to the druggist. She was over thirty then, still a slight woman, though thinner than usual, with cold, haughty black eyes in a face the flesh of which was stained across the temples and about the eye-sockets as you imagine a lighthouse-keeper's face ought to look. "I want some poison," she said.

"Yes, Miss Emily. What kind? For rats and such? I'd recom—"

"I want the best you have. I don't care what kind."

The druggist named several. "They'll kill anything up to an elephant. But what you want is—"

"Arsenic," Miss Emily said. "Is that a good one?"

"Is . . . arsenic? Yes, ma'am. But what you want—"

"I want arsenic."

The druggist looked down at her. She looked back at him, erect, her face like a strained flag. "Why, of course," the druggist said. "If that's what you want. But the law requires you to tell what you are going to use it for."

Miss Emily just stared at him, her head tilted back in order to look him eye for eye, until he looked away and went and got the arsenic and wrapped it up. The Negro delivery boy brought her the package; the druggist didn't come back. When she opened the package at home there was written on the box, under the skull and bones: "For rats."

4

So the next day we all said, "She will kill herself"; and we said it would be the best thing. When she had first begun to be seen with Homer Barron, we had said, "She will marry him." Then we said, "She will persuade him yet," because Homer himself had remarked—he liked men, and it was known that he drank with the younger men in the Elks' Club—that he was not a marrying man. Later we said, "Poor Emily" behind the jalousies as they passed on Sunday afternoon in the glittering buggy, Miss Emily with her head high and Homer Barron with his hat cocked and a cigar in his teeth, reins and whip in a yellow glove.

Then some of the ladies began to say that it was a disgrace to the town and a bad example to the young people. The men did not want to interfere, but at last the ladies forced the Baptist minister—Miss Emily's people were Episcopal—to call upon her. He would never divulge what happened during that interview, but he refused to go back again. The next Sunday they again drove about the streets, and the following day the minister's wife wrote to Miss Emily's relations in Alabama.

So she had blood-kin under her roof again and we sat back to watch developments. At first nothing happened. Then we were sure that they were to be married. We learned that Miss Emily had been to the jeweler's and ordered a man's toilet set in silver, with the letters H.B. on each piece. Two days later we learned that she had bought a complete outfit of men's clothing, including a nightshirt, and we said, "They are married." We were really glad. We were glad because the two female cousins were even more Grierson than Miss Emily had ever been.

So we were not surprised when Homer Barron—the streets had been finished some time since—was gone. We were a little disappointed that there was not a public blowing-off, but we believed that he had gone on to prepare for Miss Emily's coming, or to give her a chance to get rid of the cousins. (By that time it was a cabal, and we were all Miss Emily's allies to help circumvent the cousins.) Sure enough, after another week they departed. And, as we had expected all along, within three days Homer Barron was back in town. A neighbor saw the Negro man admit him at the kitchen door at dusk one evening.

45 And that was the last we saw of Homer Barron. And of Miss Emily for some time. The Negro man went in and out with the market basket, but the front door remained closed. Now and then we would see her at a window for a moment, as the men did that night when they sprinkled the lime, but for almost six months she did not appear on the streets. Then we knew that this was to be expected too; as if that quality of her father which had thwarted her woman's life so many times had been too virulent and too furious to die.

When we next saw Miss Emily, she had grown fat and her hair was turning gray. During the next few years it grew grayer and grayer until it attained an even pepper-and-salt iron-gray, when it ceased turning. Up to the day of her death at seventy-four it was still that vigorous iron-gray, like the hair of an active man.

From that time on her front door remained closed, save for a period of six or seven years, when she was about forty, during which she gave lessons in china-painting. She fitted up a studio in one of the downstairs rooms, where the daughters and granddaughters of Colonel Sartoris' contemporaries were sent to her with the same regularity and in the same spirit that they were sent to church on Sundays with a twenty-five-cent piece for the collection plate. Meanwhile her taxes had been remitted.

Then the newer generation became the backbone and the spirit of the town, and the painting pupils grew up and fell away and did not send their children to her with boxes of color and tedious brushes and pictures cut from the ladies' magazines. The front door closed upon the last one and remained closed for good. When the town got free postal delivery, Miss Emily alone refused to let them fasten the metal numbers above her door and attach a mailbox to it. She would not listen to them.

Daily, monthly, yearly we watched the Negro grow grayer and more stooped, going in and out with the market basket. Each December we sent her a tax notice, which would be returned by the post office a week later, unclaimed. Now and then we would see her in one of the downstairs windows—she had evidently shut up the top floor of the house—like the carven torso of an idol in a niche, looking or not looking at us, we could never tell which. Thus she passed from generation to generation—dear, inescapable, impervious, tranquil, and perverse.

And so she died. Fell ill in the house filled with dust and shadows, with only a doddering Negro man to wait on her. We did not even know she was sick; we had long since given up trying to get any information from the Negro. He talked to no one, probably not even to her, for his voice had grown harsh and rusty, as if from disuse.

She died in one of the downstairs rooms, in a heavy walnut bed with a curtain, her gray head propped on a pillow yellow and moldy with age and lack of sunlight.

50

5

The Negro met the first of the ladies at the front door and let them in, with their husbands, sibilant voices and their quick, curious glances, and then he disappeared. He walked right through the house and out the back and was not seen again.

The two female cousins came at once. They held the funeral on the second day, with the town coming to look at Miss Emily beneath a mass of bought flowers, with the crayon face of her father musing profoundly above the bier and the ladies sibilant and macabre; and the very old men—some in their brushed Confederate uniforms—on the porch and the lawn, talking of Miss Emily as if she had been a contemporary of theirs, believing that they had danced with her and courted her perhaps, confusing time with its mathematical progression, as the old do, to whom all the past is not a diminishing road but, instead, a huge meadow which no winter ever quite touches, divided from them now by the narrow bottle-neck of the most recent decade of years.

Already we knew that there was one room in that region above stairs which no one had seen in forty years, and which would have to be forced. They waited until Miss Emily was decently in the ground before they opened it.

The violence of breaking down the door seemed to fill this room with pervading dust. A thin, acrid pall as of the tomb seemed to lie everywhere upon this room decked and furnished as for a bridal: upon the valance curtains of faded rose color, upon the rose-shaded lights, upon the dressing table, upon the delicate array of crystal and the man's toilet things backed with tarnished silver, silver so tarnished that the monogram was obscured. Among them lay a collar and tie, as if they had just been removed, which, lifted, left upon the surface a pale crescent in the dust. Upon a chair hung the suit, carefully folded; beneath it the two mute shoes and the discarded socks.

55

The man himself lay in the bed.

For a long while we just stood there, looking down at the profound and fleshless grin. The body had apparently once lain in the attitude of an embrace, but now the long sleep that outlasts love, that conquers even the grimace of love, had cuckolded him.

What was left of him, rotted beneath what was left of the nightshirt, had become inextricable from the bed in which he lay; and upon him and upon the pillow beside him lay that even coating of the patient and biding dust.

Then we noticed that in the second pillow was the indentation of a head. One of us lifted something from it, and leaning forward, that faint and invisible dust dry and acrid in the nostrils, we saw a long strand of iron-gray hair.   [1930]

QUESTIONS

1. What is the attitude of the townspeople toward Emily? Does it change in the course of the narrative?
2. What are the implications of the use of the pronoun "we" throughout the story?
3. How is it possible that a woman of Emily's background and social position could marry Homer Barron? Or murder him?
4. What effects does Faulkner achieve by the sudden shifts of tone?
5. What is the significance of the title?

RESPONSES

1. Choose one scene from the story and explain how it is important to understanding the entire story.
2. Write an essay analyzing how "A Rose for Emily" is or is not a horror story.
3. Compare how women are treated by men in Faulkner's story and in Gilman's "The Yellow Wallpaper."
4. Write an essay defining the gender of the narrator and exploring how the story would or would not have been told differently by the other gender.

Ida Fink

Ida Fink (b. 1921) was born in Poland. She survived the Holocaust under precarious conditions and in 1957 moved to Israel. She has written a novel, *The Journey* (1992), and two collections of short stories, *A Scrap of Time* (1987) and *Traces* (1997). She has also written several plays, most remarkable among them *The Table*, whose themes include the distillation and mutability of memory and the grinding force of bureaucracy.

A Scrap of Time

I want to talk about a certain time not measured in months and years. For so long I have wanted to talk about this time, and not in the way I will talk about it now, not just about this one scrap of time. I wanted to, but I couldn't, I didn't know how. I was afraid, too, that this second time, which is measured in months and years, had buried the other time under a layer of years, that this second time had crushed the first and destroyed it within me. But no. Today, digging around in the ruins of memory, I found it fresh and untouched by forgetfulness. This time was measured not in months but in a word— we no longer said "in the beautiful month of May," but "after the first 'action,' or the second, or right before the third." We had different measures of time, we different ones, always different, always with that mark of difference that moved some of us to pride and others to humility. We, who because of our difference were condemned once again, as we had been before in our history, we were condemned once again during this time measured not in months nor by the rising and setting of the sun, but by a word—"action," a word signifying movement, a word you would use about a novel or a play.

I don't know who used the word first, those who acted or those who were the victims of their action; I don't know who created this technical term, who substituted it for the first term, "round-up"—a word that became devalued (or dignified?) as time passed, as new methods were developed, and "round-up" was distinguished from "action" by the borderline of race. Round-ups were for forced labor.

We called the first action—that scrap of time that I want to talk about—a round-up, although no one was rounding anyone up; on that beautiful, clear morning, each of us made our way, not willingly, to be sure, but under orders, to the marketplace in our little town, a rectangle enclosed by high, crooked buildings—a pharmacy, clothing stores, an ironmonger's shop—and framed by a sidewalk made of big square slabs that time

411

had fractured and broken. I have never again seen such huge slabs. In the middle of the marketplace stood the town hall, and it was right there, in front of the town hall, that we were ordered to form ranks.

I should not have written "we," for I was not standing in the ranks, although, obeying the order that had been posted the previous evening, I had left my house after eating a perfectly normal breakfast, at a table that was set in a normal way, in a room whose doors opened onto a garden veiled in morning mists, dry and golden in the rising sun.

5   Our transformation was not yet complete; we were still living out of habit in that old time that was measured in months and years, and on that lovely peaceful morning, filled with dry, golden mists, we took the words "conscription of labor" literally, and as mature people tend to read between the lines, our imaginations replaced the word "labor" with "labor camp," one of which, people said, was being built nearby. Apparently those who gave the order were perfectly aware of the poverty of our imaginations; that is why they saved themselves work by issuing a written order. This is how accurately they predicted our responses: after finishing a normal breakfast, at a normally set table, the older members of the family decided to disobey the order because they were afraid of the heavy physical labor, but they did not advise the young to do likewise—the young, who, if their disobedience were discovered, would not be able to plead old age. We were like infants.

This beautiful, clear morning that I am digging out of the ruins of my memory is still fresh; its colors and aromas have not faded: a grainy golden mist with red spheres of apples hanging in it, and the shadows above the river damp with the sharp odor of burdock, and the bright blue dress that I was wearing when I left the house and when I turned around at the gate. It was then, probably at that very moment, that I suddenly progressed, instinctively, from an infantile state to a still naive caution—instinctively, because I wasn't thinking about why I avoided the gate that led to the street and instead set off on a roundabout route, across the orchard, along the riverbank, down a road we called "the back way" because it wound through the outskirts of town. Instinctively, because at that moment I still did not know that I wouldn't stand in the marketplace in front of the town hall. Perhaps I wanted to delay that moment, or perhaps I simply liked the river.

Along the way, I stopped and carefully picked out flat stones, and skipped them across the water; I sat down for a while on the little bridge, beyond which one could see the town, and dangled my legs, looking at my reflection in the water and at the willows that grew on the bank. I was not yet afraid then, nor was my sister. (I forgot to say that my younger sister was with me, and she, too, skipped stones across the water and dangled her legs over the river, which is called the Gniezna—a pitiful little stream, some eight meters wide.) My sister, too, was not yet afraid; it was only when we went further along the street, beyond the bridge, and the view of the marketplace leapt out at us from behind the building on the corner, that we suddenly stopped in our tracks.

There was the square, thick with people as on a market day, only different, because a market-day crowd is colorful and loud, with chickens clucking, geese honking, and people talking and bargaining. This crowd was silent. In a way it resembled a rally—but it was different from that, too. I don't know what it was exactly. I only know that we suddenly stopped and my sister began to tremble, and then I caught the trembling, and she said, "Let's run away," and although no one was chasing us and the morning was still clear and peaceful, we ran back to the little bridge, but we no longer noticed the willows or the reflections of our running figures in the water; we ran for a long time until we were high up the steep slope known as Castle Hill—the ruins of an old castle stood on top of it—and on this hillside, the jewel of our town, we sat down in the bushes, out of breath and still shaking.

From this spot we could see our house and our garden—it was just as it always was, nothing had changed—and we could see our neighbor's house, from which our neighbor had emerged, ready to beat her carpets. We could hear the slap slap of her carpet beater.

We sat there for an hour, maybe two, I don't know, because it was then that time measured in the ordinary way stopped. Then we climbed down the steep slope to the river and returned to our house, where we heard what had happened in the marketplace, and that our cousin David had been taken, and how they took him, and what message he had left for his mother. After they were taken away, he wrote down again what he had asked people to tell her; he threw a note out of the truck and a peasant brought it to her that evening—but that happened later. First we learned that the women had been told to go home, that only the men were ordered to remain standing there, and that the path chosen by our cousin had been the opposite of ours. We had been horrified by the sight of the crowd in the marketplace, while he was drawn towards it by an enormous force, a force as strong as his nerves were weak, so that somehow or other he did violence to his own fate, he himself, himself, himself, and that was what he asked people to tell his mother, and then he wrote it down: "I myself am to blame, forgive me."

We would never have guessed that he belonged to the race of the Impatient Ones, doomed to destruction by their anxiety and their inability to remain still, never—because he was round-faced and chubby, not at all energetic, the sort of person who can't be pulled away from his book, who smiles timidly, girlishly. Only the end of the war brought us the truth about his last hours. The peasant who delivered the note did not dare to tell us what he saw, and although other people, too, muttered something about what they had seen, no one dared to believe it, especially since the Germans offered proofs of another truth that each of us grasped at greedily; they measured out doses of it sparingly, with restraint—a perfect cover-up. They went to such trouble, created so many phantoms, that only time, time measured not in months and years, opened our eyes and convinced us.

Our cousin David had left the house later than we did, and when he reached the marketplace it was already known—not by everyone, to be sure, but by the so-called Council, which in time became the *Judenrat*—that the words "conscription for labor" had nothing to do with a labor camp. One friend, a far-sighted older man, ordered the boy to hide just in case, and since it was too late to return home because the streets were blocked off, he led him to his own apartment in one of the houses facing the marketplace. Like us, not comprehending that the boy belonged to the race of the Impatient Ones, who find it difficult to cope with isolation and who act on impulse, he left David in a room that locked from inside. What our cousin experienced, locked up in that room, will remain forever a mystery. Much can be explained by the fact that the room had a view of the marketplace, of that silent crowd, of the faces of friends and relatives, and it may be that finally the isolation of his hiding place seemed to him more unbearable than the great and threatening unknown outside the window—an unknown shared by all who were gathered in the marketplace.

It was probably a thought that came in a flash: not to be alone, to be together with everyone. All that was needed was one movement of his hand.

I think it incorrect to assume that he left the hiding place because he was afraid that they would search the houses. That impatience of the heart, that trembling of the nerves, the burden of isolation, condemned him to extermination together with the first victims of our town.

15   He stood between a lawyer's apprentice and a student of architecture and to the question, "Profession?" he replied, "Teacher," although he had been a teacher for only a short time and quite by chance. His neighbor on the right also told the truth, but the architecture student lied, declaring himself a carpenter, and this lie saved his life—or, to be more precise, postponed the sentence of death for two years.

Seventy people were loaded into trucks; at the last moment the rabbi was dragged out of his house—he was the seventy-first. On the way to the trucks they marched past the ranks of all those who had not yet managed to inform the interrogators about the work they did. It was then that our cousin said out loud, "Tell my mother that it's my own fault and that I beg her forgiveness." Presumably, he had already stopped believing what all of us still believed later: that they were going to a camp. He had that horrifying clarity of vision that comes just before death.

The peasant who that evening brought us the note that said, "I myself am to blame, forgive me," was somber and didn't look us in the eye. He said he had found the note on the road to Lubianki and that he didn't know anything else about it; we knew that he knew, but we did not want to admit it. He left, but he came back after the war to tell us what he had seen.

A postcard from the rabbi arrived two days later, convincing everyone that those who had been taken away were in a labor camp. A month later, when the lack of any further news began to make us doubt the camp, another postcard arrived, this one written by someone else who had been deported—an accountant, I think. After the postcard scheme came the payment of contributions: the authorities let it be understood that kilos of coffee or tea—or gold—would provide a family with news of their dear ones. As a gesture of compassion they also allowed people to send food parcels to the prisoners, who, it was said, were working in a camp in the Reich. Once again, after the second action, a postcard turned up. It was written in pencil and almost indecipherable. After this postcard, we said, "They're done for." But rumors told a different story altogether—of soggy earth in the woods by the village of Lubianki, and of a blood-stained handkerchief that had been found. These rumors came from nowhere; no eyewitnesses stepped forward.

The peasant who had not dared to speak at the time came back after the war and told us everything. It happened just as rumor had it, in a dense, overgrown forest, eight kilometers outside of town, one hour after the trucks left the marketplace. The execution itself did not take long; more time was spent on the preparatory digging of the grave.

20   At the first shots, our chubby, round-faced cousin David, who was always clumsy at gymnastics and sports, climbed a tree and wrapped his arms around the trunk like a child hugging his mother, and that was the way he died.   [1987]

Questions

1. What effect is achieved by having the two girls seeing and hearing their neighbor beating carpets?

2. There is some gentle description of nature in this story. Why?

3. Why did calling himself a "carpenter" instead of an "architecture student" save one person's life ("for two years")?

4. Why do the "postcard" and "contributions" schemes work?

5. On rereading the story, do you think that the images in the description of the town square are suggestive?

F. Scott Fitzgerald

F. Scott Fitzgerald (1896–1940) was born in St. Paul, Minnesota. He interrupted his studies at Princeton University to accept a commission in the army, and while stationed at Camp Sheriden, Alabama, he met the Montgomery belle, Zelda Sayre, whom he married in 1920. That same year, while working in a New York advertising agency, he published *This Side of Paradise*. The success of that novel, and of a volume of short stories published the following year, *Flappers and Philosophers*, won Fitzgerald financial independence. First in America, and then in Europe, the Fitzgeralds, like characters in his fiction, seemed to personify the youthful hedonism of the 1920s. The publication in 1925 of *The Great Gatsby* brought him critical success, but the illness of Zelda and his recklessness and alcoholism led them both to personal disaster. During the 1930s he struggled unsuccessfully to regain his Midas touch. He died broke and largely forgotten in Hollywood, where he had gone to try to recoup his fortunes by writing screenplays.

Babylon Revisited

1

"And where's Mr. Campbell?" Charlie asked.

"Gone to Switzerland. Mr. Campbell's a pretty sick man, Mr. Wales."

"I'm sorry to hear that. And George Hardt?" Charlie inquired.

"Back in America, gone to work."

5 "And where is the Snow Bird?"

"He was in here last week. Anyway, his friend, Mr. Schaeffer, is in Paris."

Two familiar names from the long list of a year and a half ago. Charlie scribbled an address in his notebook and tore out the page.

"If you see Mr. Schaeffer, give him this," he said. "It's my brother-in-law's address. I haven't settled on a hotel yet."

He was not really disappointed to find Paris was so empty. But the stillness in the Ritz bar was strange and portentous. It was not an American bar any more—he felt polite in it, and not as if he owned it. It had gone back into France. He felt the stillness from the moment he got out of the taxi and saw the doorman, usually in a frenzy of activity at this hour, gossiping with a *chasseur*° by the servant's entrance.

Passing through the corridor, he heard only a single, bored voice in the once-clamorous women's room. When he turned into the bar he traveled the twenty feet of green carpet with his eyes fixed straight ahead by old habit; and then, with his foot firmly on the rail, he turned and surveyed the room, encountering only a single pair of eyes that fluttered up from a newspaper in the corner. Charlie asked for the head barman, Paul, who in the latter days of the bull market had come to work in his own custom-built car—disembarking, however, with due nicety at the nearest corner. But Paul was at his country house today and Alix giving him information.

"No, no more," Charlie said, "I'm going slow these days."

Alix congratulated him: "You were going pretty strong a couple of years ago."

"I'll stick to it all right," Charlie assured him. "I've stuck to it for over a year and a half now."

"How do you find conditions in America?"

"I haven't been to America for months. I'm in business in Prague, representing a couple of concerns there. They don't know about me down there."

Alix smiled.

"Remember the night of George Hardt's bachelor dinner here?" said Charlie. "By the way, what's become of Claude Fessenden?"

Alix lowered his voice confidentially: "He's in Paris, but he doesn't come here any more. Paul doesn't allow it. He ran up a bill of thirty thousand francs, charging all his drinks and his lunches, and usually his dinner, for more than a year. And when Paul finally told him he had to pay, he gave him a bad check."

Alix shook his head sadly.

"I don't understand it, such a dandy fellow. Now he's all bloated up—" He made a plump apple of his hands.

Charlie watched a group of strident queens installing themselves in a corner.

"Nothing affects them," he thought. "Stocks rise and fall, people loaf or work, but they go on forever." The place oppressed him. He called for the dice and shook with Alix for the drink.

"Here for long, Mr. Wales?"

"I'm here for four or five days to see my little girl."

"Oh-h! You have a little girl?"

Outside, the fire-red, gas-blue, ghost-green signs shone smokily through the tranquil rain. It was late afternoon and the streets were in movement; the bistros gleamed. At the corner of the Boulevard des Capucines he took a taxi. The Place de la Concorde moved by in pink majesty; they crossed the logical Seine, and Charlie felt the sudden provincial quality of the Left Bank.

Charlie directed his taxi to the Avenue de l'Opéra, which was out of his way. But he wanted to see the blue hour spread over the magnificent façade, and imagine that the cab horns, playing endlessly the first few bars of *Le Plus que Lent*,° were the trumpets of the Second Empire. They were closing the iron grill in front of Brentano's Bookstore, and people were already at dinner behind the trim little bourgeois hedge of Duval's. He had never eaten at a really cheap restaurant in Paris. Five-course dinner, four francs fifty, eighteen cents, wine included. For some odd reason he wished that he had.

°*chasseur*: Footman.
°*Le Plus que Lent*: "Slower than slow," from a composition by Claude Debussy (1862–1918).

As they rolled on to the Left Bank, and he felt its sudden provincialism, he thought, "I spoiled this city for myself. I didn't realize it, but the days came along one after another, and then two years were gone, and everything was gone, and I was gone."

He was thirty-five, and good to look at. The Irish mobility of his face was sobered by a deep wrinkle between his eyes. As he rang his brother-in-law's bell in the Rue Palatine, the wrinkle deepened till it pulled down his brows; he felt a cramping sensation in his belly. From behind the maid who opened the door darted a lovely little girl of nine who shrieked "Daddy!" and flew up, struggling like a fish, into his arms. She pulled his head around by one ear and set her cheek against his.

30   "My old pie," he said.

"Oh, daddy, daddy, daddy, daddy, dads, dads, dads!"

She drew him into the salon, where the family waited, a boy and a girl his daughter's age, his sister-in-law and her husband. He greeted Marion with his voice pitched carefully to avoid either feigned enthusiasm or dislike, but her response was more frankly tepid, though she minimized her expression of unalterable distrust by directing her regard toward his child. The two men clasped hands in a friendly way and Lincoln Peters rested his for a moment on Charlie's shoulder.

The room was warm and comfortably American. The three children moved intimately about, playing through the yellow oblongs that led to other rooms; the cheer of six o'clock spoke in the eager smacks of the fire and the sounds of French activity in the kitchen. But Charlie did not relax; his heart sat up rigidly in his body and he drew confidence from his daughter, who from time to time came close to him, holding in his arms the doll he had brought.

"Really extremely well," he declared in answer to Lincoln's question. "There's a lot of business there that isn't moving at all, but we're doing even better than ever. In fact, damn well. I'm bringing my sister over from America next month to keep house for me. My income last year was bigger than it was when I had money. You see, the Czechs—"

35   His boasting was for a specific purpose; but after a moment, seeing a faint restiveness in Lincoln's eye, he changed the subject:

"Those are fine children of yours, well brought up, good manners."

"We think Honoria's a great little girl too."

Marion Peters came back from the kitchen. She was a tall woman with worried eyes, who had once possessed a fresh American loveliness. Charlie had never been sensitive to it and was always surprised when people spoke of how pretty she had been. From the first there had been an instinctive antipathy between them.

"Well, how do you find Honoria?" she asked.

40   "Wonderful. I was astonished how much she's grown in ten months. All the children are looking well."

"We haven't had a doctor for a year. How do you like being back in Paris?"

"It seems very funny to see so few Americans around."

"I'm delighted," Marion said vehemently. "Now at least you can go into a store without their assuming you're a millionaire. We've suffered like everybody, but on the whole it's a good deal pleasanter."

"But it was nice while it lasted," Charlie said. "We were a sort of royalty, almost infallible, with a sort of magic around us. In the bar this afternoon"—he stumbled, seeing his mistake—"there wasn't a man I knew."

45   She looked at him keenly. "I should think you'd have had enough of bars."

"I only stayed a minute. I take one drink every afternoon, and no more."

"Don't you want a cocktail before dinner?" Lincoln asked.

"I take only one drink every afternoon, and I've had that."

"I hope you keep to it," said Marion.

Her dislike was evident in the coldness with which she spoke, but Charlie only   50
smiled; he had larger plans. Her very aggressiveness gave him an advantage, and he
knew enough to wait. He wanted them to initiate the discussion of what they knew had
brought him to Paris.

At dinner he couldn't decide whether Honoria was most like him or her mother. Fortunate if she didn't combine the traits of both that had brought them to disaster. A
great wave of protectiveness went over him. He thought he knew what to do for her.
He believed in character; he wanted to jump back a whole generation and trust in
character again as the eternally valuable element. Everything else wore out.

He left soon after dinner, but not to go home. He was curious to see Paris by night
with clearer and more judicious eyes than those of other days. He bought a *strapontin*°
for the Casino and watched Josephine Baker go through her chocolate arabesques.

After an hour he left and strolled toward Montmartre, up the Rue Pigalle into the
Place Blanche. The rain had stopped and there were a few people in evening clothes
disembarking from taxis in front of cabarets, and *cocottes*° prowling singly or in pairs,
and many Negroes. He passed a lighted door from which issued music, and stopped
with the sense of familiarity; it was Bricktop's, where he had parted with so many
hours and so much money. A few doors farther on he found another ancient ren-
dezvous and incautiously put his head inside. Immediately an eager orchestra burst
into sound, a pair of professional dancers leaped to their feet and a maître d'hôtel
swooped toward him, crying, "Crowd just arriving, sir!" But he withdrew quickly.

"You have to be damn drunk," he thought.

Zelli's was closed, the bleak and sinister cheap hotels surrounding it were dark; up   55
in the Rue Blanche there was more light and a local, colloquial French crowd. The
Poet's Cave had disappeared, but the two great mouths of the Café of Heaven and the
Café of Hell still yawned—even devoured, as he watched, the meager contents of a
tourist bus—a German, a Japanese, and an American couple who glanced at him with
frightened eyes.

So much for the effort and ingenuity of Montmartre. All the catering to vice and
waste was on an utterly childish scale, and he suddenly realized the meaning of the
word "dissipate"—to dissipate into thin air; to make nothing out of something. In the
little hours of the night every move from place to place was an enormous human jump,
an increase of paying for the privilege of slower and slower motion.

He remembered thousand-franc notes given to an orchestra for playing a single
number, hundred-franc notes tossed to a doorman for calling a cab.

But it hadn't been given for nothing.

It had been given, even the most wildly squandered sum, as an offering to destiny
that he might not remember the things most worth remembering, the things that now
he would always remember—his child taken from his control, his wife escaped to a
grave in Vermont.

In the glare of a *brasserie*° a woman spoke to him. He bought her some eggs and cof-   60
fee, and then, eluding her encouraging stare, gave her a twenty-franc note and took a
taxi to his hotel.

°*strapontin*: A folding seat in the aisle.

°*cocottes*: Prostitutes.

°*brasserie*: Small restaurant.

2

He woke upon a fine fall day—football weather. The depression of yesterday was gone and he liked the people on the streets. At noon he sat opposite Honoria at Le Grand Vatel, the only restaurant he could think of not reminiscent of champagne dinners and long luncheons that began at two and ended in a blurred and vague twilight.

"Now, how about vegetables? Oughtn't you to have some vegetables?"

"Well, yes."

"Here's *épinards* and *chou-fleur* and carrots and *haricots.*"°

65 "I'd like *chou-fleur.*"

"Wouldn't you like to have two vegetables?"

"I usually only have one at lunch."

The waiter was pretending to be inordinately fond of children. *"Qu'elle est mignonne la petite! Elle parle exactement comme une française."*°

"How about dessert? Shall we wait and see?"

70 The waiter disappeared. Honoria looked at her father expectantly.

"What are we going to do?"

"First, we're going to that toy store in the Rue Saint-Honoré and buy you anything you like. And then we're going to the vaudeville at the Empire."

She hesitated. "I like it about the vaudeville, but not the toy store."

"Why not?"

75 "Well, you brought me this doll." She had it with her. "And I've got lots of things. And we're not rich any more, are we?"

"We never were. But today you are to have anything you want."

"All right," she agreed resignedly.

When there had been her mother and a French nurse he had been inclined to be strict; now he extended himself, reached out for a new tolerance; he must be both parents to her and not shut any of her out of communication.

"I want to get to know you," he said gravely. "First let me introduce myself. My name is Charles J. Wales, of Prague."

80 "Oh, daddy!" her voice cracked with laughter.

"And who are you, please?" he persisted, and she accepted a role immediately: "Honoria Wales, Rue Palatine, Paris."

"Married or single?"

"No, not married. Single."

He indicated the doll. "But I see you have a child, madame."

85 Unwilling to disinherit it, she took it to her heart and thought quickly: "Yes, I've been married, but I'm not married now. My husband is dead."

He went on quickly, "And the child's name?"

"Simone. That's after my best friend at school."

"I'm very pleased that you're doing so well at school."

"I'm third this month," she boasted. "Elsie"—that was her cousin—"is only about eighteenth, and Richard is about at the bottom."

90 "You like Richard and Elsie, don't you?"

"Oh, yes. I like Richard quite well and I like her all right."

Cautiously and casually he asked: "And Aunt Marion and Uncle Lincoln—which do you like best?"

°*épinards, chou-fleur, haricots*: Spinach, cauliflower, beans.
°". . . *comme une française.*": "What a pretty little girl! She speaks exactly as if she were French!"

"Oh, Uncle Lincoln, I guess."

He was increasingly aware of her presence. As they came in, a murmur of ". . . adorable" followed them, and now the people at the next table bent all their silences upon her, staring as if she were something no more conscious than a flower.

"Why don't I live with you?" she asked suddenly. "Because mamma's dead?"

"You must stay here and learn more French. It would have been hard for daddy to take care of you so well."

"I don't really need much taking care of any more. I do everything for myself."

Going out of the restaurant, a man and a woman unexpectedly hailed him.

"Well, the old Wales!"

"Hello there, Lorraine. . . . Dunc."

Sudden ghosts out of the past: Duncan Schaeffer, a friend from college. Lorraine Quarrles, a lovely, pale blonde of thirty; one of a crowd who had helped him make months into days in the lavish times of three years ago.

"My husband couldn't come this year," she said, in answer to his question. "We're poor as hell. So he gave me two hundred a month and told me I could do my worst on that. . . . This your little girl?"

"What about coming back and sitting down?" Duncan asked.

"Can't do it." He was glad for an excuse. As always, he felt Lorraine's passionate, provocative attraction, but his own rhythm was different now.

"Well, how about dinner?" she asked.

"I'm not free. Give me your address and let me call you."

"Charlie, I believe you're sober," she said judicially. "I honestly believe he's sober, Dunc. Pinch him and see if he's sober."

Charlie indicated Honoria with his head. They both laughed.

"What's your address?" said Duncan skeptically.

He hesitated, unwilling to give the name of his hotel.

"I'm not settled yet. I'd better call you. We're going to see the vaudeville at the Empire."

"There! That's what I want to do," Lorraine said. "I want to see some clowns and acrobats and jugglers. That's just what we'll do, Dunc."

"We've got to do an errand first," said Charlie. "Perhaps we'll see you there."

"All right, you snob. . . . Good-by, beautiful little girl."

"Good-by."

Honoria bobbed politely.

Somehow, an unwelcome encounter. They liked him because he was functioning, because he was serious; they wanted to see him, because he was stronger than they were now, because they wanted to draw a certain sustenance from his strength.

At the Empire, Honoria proudly refused to sit upon her father's folded coat. She was already an individual with a code of her own, and Charlie was more and more absorbed by the desire of putting a little of himself into her before she crystallized utterly. It was hopeless to try to know her in so short a time.

Between the acts they came upon Duncan and Lorraine in the lobby where the band was playing.

"Have a drink?"

"All right, but not up at the bar. We'll take a table."

"The perfect father."

Listening abstractedly to Lorraine, Charlie watched Honoria's eyes leave their table, and he followed them wistfully about the room, wondering what they saw. He met her glance and she smiled.

"I liked that lemonade," she said.

125 What had she said? What had he expected? Going home in a taxi afterward, he pulled her over until her head rested against his chest.

"Darling, do you ever think about your mother?"

"Yes, sometimes," she answered vaguely.

"I don't want you to forget her. Have you got a picture of her?"

"Yes, I think so. Anyhow, Aunt Marion has. Why don't you want me to forget her?"

130 "She loved you very much."

"I loved her too."

They were silent for a moment.

"Daddy, I want to come and live with you," she said suddenly.

His heart leaped; he had wanted it to come like this.

135 "Aren't you perfectly happy?"

"Yes, but I love you better than anybody. And you love me better than anybody, don't you, now that mummy's dead?"

"Of course I do. But you won't always like me best, honey. You'll grow up and meet somebody your own age and go marry him and forget you ever had a daddy."

"Yes, that's true," she agreed tranquilly.

He didn't go in. He was coming back at nine o'clock and he wanted to keep himself fresh and new for the thing he must say then.

140 "When you're safe inside, just show yourself in that window."

"All right. Good-by, dads, dads, dads, dads."

He waited in the dark street until she appeared, all warm and glowing, in the window above and kissed her fingers out into the night.

3

They were waiting. Marion sat behind the coffee service in a dignified black dinner dress that just faintly suggested mourning. Lincoln was walking up and down with the animation of one who had already been talking. They were as anxious as he was to get into the question. He opened it almost immediately:

"I suppose you know what I want to see you about—why I really came to Paris."

145 Marion played with the black stars on her necklace and frowned.

"I'm awfully anxious to have a home," he continued. "And I'm awfully anxious to have Honoria in it. I appreciate your taking in Honoria for her mother's sake, but things have changed now"—he hesitated and then continued more forcibly—"changed radically with me, and I want to ask you to reconsider the matter. It would be silly for me to deny that about three years ago I was acting badly—"

Marion looked up at him with hard eyes.

"—but all that's over. As I told you, I haven't had more than a drink a day for over a year, and I take that drink deliberately, so that the idea of alcohol won't get too big in my imagination. You see the idea?"

"No," said Marion succinctly.

150 "It's a sort of stunt I set myself. It keeps the matter in proportion."

"I get you," said Lincoln. "You don't want to admit it's got any attraction for you."

"Something like that. Sometimes I forget and don't take it. But I try to take it. Anyhow, I couldn't afford to drink in my position. The people I represent are more than satisfied with what I've done, and I'm bringing my sister over from Burlington to keep house for me, and I want awfully to have Honoria too. You know that even when her mother and I weren't getting along well we never let anything that happened touch Honoria. I know she's fond of me and I know I'm able to take care of her and—well, there you are. How do you feel about it?"

He knew that now he would have to take a beating. It would last an hour or two hours, and it would be difficult, but if he modulated his inevitable resentment to the chastened attitude of the reformed sinner, he might win his point in the end.

Keep your temper, he told himself. You don't want to be justified. You want Honoria.

Lincoln spoke first: "We've been talking it over ever since we got your letter last month. We're happy to have Honoria here. She's a dear little thing, and we're glad to be able to help her, but of course that isn't the question—" 155

Marion interrupted suddenly. "How long are you going to stay sober, Charlie?" she asked.

"Permanently, I hope."

"How can anybody count on that?"

"You know I never did drink heavily until I gave up business and came over here with nothing to do. Then Helen and I began to run around with—"

"Please leave Helen out of it. I can't bear to hear you talk about her like that." 160

He stared at her grimly; he had never been certain how fond of each other the sisters were in life.

"My drinking only lasted about a year and a half—from the time we came over until I—collapsed."

"It was time enough."

"It was time enough," he agreed.

"My duty is entirely to Helen," she said. "I try to think what she would have wanted me to do. Frankly, from the night you did that terrible thing you haven't really existed for me. I can't help that. She was my sister." 165

"Yes."

"When she was dying she asked me to look out for Honoria. If you hadn't been in a sanitarium then, it might have helped matters."

He had no answer.

"I'll never in my life be able to forget the morning when Helen knocked at my door, soaked to the skin and shivering, and said you'd locked her out."

Charlie gripped the sides of the chair. This was more difficult than he expected; he wanted to launch out into a long expostulation and explanation, but he only said, "The night I locked her out—" and she interrupted, "I don't feel up to going over that again." 170

After a moment's silence Lincoln said: "We're getting off the subject. You want Marion to set aside her legal guardianship and give you Honoria. I think the main point for her is whether she has confidence in you or not."

"I don't blame Marion," Charlie said slowly, "but I think she can have entire confidence in me. I had a good record up to three years ago. Of course, it's within human possibilities I might go wrong any time. But if we wait much longer I'll lose Honoria's childhood and my chance for a home." He shook his head. "I'll simply lose her, don't you see?"

"Yes, I see," said Lincoln.

"Why didn't you think of all this before?" Marion asked.

"I suppose I did, from time to time, but Helen and I were getting along badly. When I consented to the guardianship, I was flat on my back in a sanitarium and the market had cleaned me out. I knew I'd acted badly, and I thought if it would bring any peace 175 to Helen, I'd agree to anything. But now it's different. I'm functioning, I'm behaving damn well, so far as—"

"Please don't swear at me," Marion said.

He looked at her, startled. With each remark the force of her dislike became more and more apparent. She had built up all her fear of life into one wall and faced it toward him. This trivial reproof was possibly the result of some trouble with the cook several hours before. Charlie became increasingly alarmed at leaving Honoria in this atmosphere of hostility against himself; sooner or later it would come out, in a word here, a shake of the head there, and some of that distrust would be irrevocably implanted in Honoria. But he pulled his temper down out of his face and shut it up inside him; he had won a point, for Lincoln realized the absurdity of Marion's remark and asked her lightly since when she had objected to the word "damn."

"Another thing," Charlie said: "I'm able to give her certain advantages now. I'm going to take a French governess to Prague with me. I've got a lease on a new apartment—"

He stopped, realizing that he was blundering. They couldn't be expected to accept with equanimity the fact that his income was again twice as large as their own.

180 "I suppose you can give her more luxuries than we can," said Marion. "When you were throwing away money we were living along watching every ten francs. . . . I suppose you'll start doing it again."

"Oh, no," he said. "I've learned. I worked hard for ten years, you know—until I got lucky in the market, like so many people. Terrible lucky. It won't happen again."

There was a long silence. All of them felt their nerves straining, and for the first time in a year Charlie wanted a drink. He was sure now that Lincoln Peters wanted him to have his child.

Marion shuddered suddenly; part of her saw that Charlie's feet were planted on the earth now, and her own maternal feeling recognized the naturalness of his desire; but she had lived for a long time with a prejudice—a prejudice founded on a curious disbelief in her sister's happiness, which, in the shock of one terrible night, had turned to hatred for him. It had all happened at a point in her life where the discouragement of ill health and adverse circumstances made it necessary for her to believe in tangible villainy and a tangible villain.

"I can't help what I think!" she cried out suddenly. "How much you were responsible for Helen's death, I don't know. It's something you'll have to square with your own conscience."

185 An electric current of agony surged through him; for a moment he was almost on his feet, an unuttered sound echoing in his throat. He hung on to himself for a moment, another moment.

"Hold on there," said Lincoln uncomfortably. "I never thought you were responsible for that."

"Helen died of heart trouble," Charlie said dully.

"Yes, heart trouble." Marion spoke as if the phrase had another meaning for her.

Then, in the flatness that followed her outburst, she saw him plainly and she knew he had somehow arrived at control over the situation. Glancing at her husband, she found no help from him, and as abruptly as if it were a matter of no importance, she threw up the sponge.

190 "Do what you like!" she cried, springing up from her chair. "She's your child. I'm not the person to stand in your way. I think if it were my child I'd rather see her—" She managed to check herself. "You two decide it. I can't stand this. I'm sick. I'm going to bed."

She hurried from the room; after a moment Lincoln said:

"This has been a hard day for her. You know how strongly she feels—" His voice was almost apologetic: "When a woman gets an idea in her head."

"Of course."

"It's going to be all right. I think she sees now that you—can provide for the child, and so we can't very well stand in your way or Honoria's way."

"Thank you, Lincoln."

"I'd better go along and see how she is."

"I'm going."

He was still trembling when he reached the street, but a walk down the Rue Bonaparte to the *quais*° set him up, and as he crossed the Seine, fresh and new by the *quais* lamps, he felt exultant. But back in his room he couldn't sleep. The image of Helen haunted him. Helen whom he had loved so until they had senselessly begun to abuse each other's love, tear it into shreds. On that terrible February night that Marion remembered so vividly, a slow quarrel had gone on for hours. There was a scene at the Florida, and then he attempted to take her home, and then she kissed young Webb at a table; after that there was what she had hysterically said. When he arrived home alone he turned the key in the lock in wild anger. How could he know she would arrive an hour later alone, that there would be a snow storm in which she wandered about in slippers, too confused to find a taxi? Then the aftermath, her escaping pneumonia by a miracle, and all the attendant horror. They were "reconciled," but that was the beginning of the end, and Marion, who had seen with her own eyes and who imagined it to be one of many scenes from her sister's martyrdom, never forgot.

Going over it again brought Helen nearer, and in the white, soft light that steals upon half sleep near morning he found himself talking to her again. She said that he was perfectly right about Honoria and that she wanted Honoria to be with him. She said she was glad he was being good and doing better. She said a lot of other things— very friendly things—but she was in a swing in a white dress, and swinging faster and faster all the time, so that at the end he could not hear clearly all that she said.

4

He woke up feeling happy. The door of the world was open again. He made plans, vistas, futures for Honoria and himself, but suddenly he grew sad, remembering all the plans he and Helen had made. She had not planned to die. The present was the thing— work to do and someone to love. But not to love too much, for he knew the injury that a father can do to a daughter or a mother to a son by attaching them too closely: afterward, out in the world, the child would seek in the marriage partner the same blind tenderness and, failing probably to find it, turn against love and life.

It was another bright, crisp day. He called Lincoln Peters at the bank where he worked and asked if he could count on taking Honoria when he left for Prague. Lincoln agreed that there was no reason for delay. One thing—the legal guardianship. Marion wanted to retain that a while longer. She was upset by the whole matter, and it would oil things if she felt that the situation was still in her control for another year. Charlie agreed, wanting only the tangible, visible child.

195

200

°*quais*: Paved riverbank.

Then the question of a governess. Charlie sat in a gloomy agency and talked to a cross Béarnaise and to a buxom Breton peasant, neither of whom he could have endured. There were others whom he would see tomorrow.

He lunched with Lincoln Peters at Griffons, trying to keep down his exultation.

"There's nothing quite like your own child," Lincoln said. "But you understand how Marion feels too."

205   "She's forgotten how hard I worked for seven years there," Charlie said. "She just remembers one night."

"There's another thing." Lincoln hesitated. "While you and Helen were tearing around Europe throwing money away, we were just getting along. I didn't touch any of the prosperity because I never got ahead enough to carry anything but my insurance. I think Marion felt there was some kind of injustice in it—you not even working toward the end, and getting richer and richer."

"It went just as quick as it came," said Charlie.

"Yes, a lot of it stayed in the hands of *chasseurs* and saxophone players and maîtres d'hôtel—well, the big party's over now. I just said that to explain Marion's feeling about those crazy years. If you drop in about six o'clock tonight before Marion's too tired, we'll settle the details on the spot."

Back at his hotel, Charlie found a *pneumatique*° that had been redirected from the Ritz bar, where Charlie had left his address for the purpose of finding a certain man.

210   Dear Charlie:

You were so strange when we saw you the other day that I wondered if I did something to offend you. If so, I'm not conscious of it. In fact, I have thought about you too much for the last year, and it's always been in the back of my mind that I might see you if I came over here. We *did* have such good times that crazy spring, like the night you and I stole the butcher's tricycle, and the time we tried to call on the president and you had the old derby rim and the wire cane. Everybody seems so old lately, but I don't feel old a bit. Couldn't we get together some time today for old time's sake? I've got a vile hangover for the moment, but will be feeling better this afternoon and will look for you about five in the sweatshop at the Ritz.

Always devotedly,
Lorraine

His first feeling was one of awe that he had actually, in his mature years, stolen a tricycle and pedaled Lorraine all over the Étoile between the small hours and dawn. In retrospect it was a nightmare. Locking out Helen didn't fit in with any other act of his life, but the tricycle incident did—it was one of many. How many weeks or months of dissipation to arrive at that condition of utter irresponsibility?

215   He tried to picture how Lorraine had appeared to him then—very attractive; Helen was unhappy about it, though she said nothing. Yesterday, in the restaurant, Lorraine had seemed trite, blurred, worn away. He emphatically did not want to see her, and he was glad Alix had not given away his hotel address. It was a relief to think, instead, of Honoria, to think of Sundays spent with her and of saying good morning to her and knowing she was there in his house at night, drawing her breath in the darkness.

At five he took a taxi and bought presents for all the Peterses—a piquant cloth doll, a box of Roman soldiers, flowers for Marion, big linen handkerchiefs for Lincoln.

°*pneumatique*: An express letter sent via a compressed air system.

He saw, when he arrived in the apartment, that Marion had accepted the inevitable. She greeted him now as though he were a recalcitrant member of the family, rather than a menacing outsider. Honoria had been told she was going; Charlie was glad to see that her tact made her conceal her excessive happiness. Only on his lap did she whisper her delight and the question "When?" before she slipped away with the other children.

He and Marion were alone for a minute in the room, and on an impulse he spoke out boldly:

"Family quarrels are bitter things. They don't go according to any rules. They're not like aches or wounds; they're more like splits in the skin that won't heal because there's not enough material. I wish you and I could be on better terms."

"Some things are hard to forget," she answered. "It's a question of confidence." There 220 was no answer to this and presently she asked, "When do you propose to take her?"

"As soon as I can get a governess. I hoped the day after tomorrow."

"That's impossible. I've got to get her things in shape. Not before Saturday."

He yielded. Coming back into the room, Lincoln offered him a drink.

"I'll take my daily whisky," he said.

It was warm here, it was a home, people together by a fire. The children felt very 225 safe and important; the mother and father were serious, watchful. They had things to do for the children more important than his visit here. A spoonful of medicine was, after all, more important than the strained relations between Marion and himself. They were not dull people, but they were very much in the grip of life and circumstances. He wondered if he couldn't do something to get Lincoln out of his rut at the bank.

A long peal at the doorbell; the *bonne à tout faire*° passed through and went down the corridor. The door opened upon another long ring, and then voices, and the three in the salon looked up expectantly; Richard moved to bring the corridor within his range of vision, and Marion rose. Then the maid came back along the corridor, closely followed by the voices, which developed under the light into Duncan Schaeffer and Lorraine Quarrles.

They were gay, they were hilarious, they were roaring with laughter. For a moment Charlie was astounded; unable to understand how they ferreted out the Peterses' address.

"Ah-h-h!" Duncan wagged his finger roguishly at Charlie, "Ah-h-h!"

They both slid down another cascade of laughter. Anxious and at a loss, Charlie shook hands with them quickly and presented them to Lincoln and Marion. Marion nodded, scarcely speaking. She had drawn back a step toward the fire; her little girl stood beside her, and Marion put an arm about her shoulder.

With growing annoyance at the intrusion, Charlie waited for them to explain them 230 selves. After some concentration Duncan said:

"We came to invite you out to dinner. Lorraine and I insist that all this shishi, cagy business 'bout your address got to stop."

Charlie came closer to them, as if to force them backward down the corridor.

"Sorry, but I can't. Tell me where you'll be and I'll phone you in half an hour."

This made no impression. Lorraine sat down suddenly on the side of a chair, and focusing her eyes on Richard, cried, "Oh, what a nice little boy! Come here, little boy." Richard glanced at his mother, but did not move. With a perceptible shrug of her shoulder, Lorraine turned back to Charlie:

"Come and dine. Sure your cousins won' mine. See you so sel'om. Or solemn." 235

"I can't," said Charlie sharply. "You two have dinner and I'll phone you."

°*bonne à tout faire:* The maid.

Her voice became suddenly unpleasant. "All right, we'll go. But I remember once when you hammered on my door at four A.M. I was enough of a good sport to give you a drink. Come on, Dunc."

Still in slow motion, with blurred, angry faces, with uncertain feet, they retired along the corridor.

"Good night," Charlie said.

240　　"Good night!" responded Lorraine emphatically.

When he went back into the salon Marion had not moved, only now her son was standing in the circle of her other arm. Lincoln was still swinging Honoria back and forth like a pendulum from side to side.

"What an outrage!" Charlie broke out. "What an absolute outrage!"

Neither of them answered. Charlie dropped into an armchair, picked up his drink, set it down again and said:

"People I haven't seen for two years having the colossal nerve—"

245　　He broke off. Marion had made the sound "Oh!" in one swift, furious breath, turned her body from him with a jerk and left the room.

Lincoln set down Honoria carefully.

"You children go in and start your soup," he said, and when they obeyed, he said to Charlie:

"Marion's not well and she can't stand shocks. That kind of people make her really physically sick."

"I didn't tell them to come here. They wormed your name out of somebody. They deliberately—"

250　　"Well, it's too bad. It doesn't help matters. Excuse me a minute."

Left alone, Charlie sat tense in his chair. In the next room he could hear the children eating, talking in monosyllables, already oblivious to the scene between their elders. He heard a murmur of conversation from a farther room and then the ticking bell of a telephone receiver picked up, and in a panic he moved to the other side of the room and out of earshot.

In a minute Lincoln came back. "Look here, Charlie. I think we'd better call off dinner for tonight. Marion's in bad shape."

"Is she angry with me?"

"Sort of," he said, almost roughly. "She's not strong and—"

255　　"You mean she's changed her mind about Honoria?"

"She's pretty bitter right now. I don't know. You phone me at the bank tomorrow."

"I wish you'd explain to her I never dreamed these people would come here. I'm just as sore as you are."

"I couldn't explain anything to her now."

Charlie got up. He took his coat and hat and started down the corridor. Then he opened the door of the dining room and said in a strange voice, "Good night, children."

260　　Honoria rose and ran around the table to hug him.

"Good night, sweetheart," he said vaguely, and then trying to make his voice more tender, trying to conciliate something, "Good night, dear children."

5

Charlie went directly to the Ritz bar with the furious idea of finding Lorraine and Duncan, but they were not there, and he realized that in any case there was nothing he could do. He had not touched his drink at the Peters, and now he ordered a whisky-and-soda. Paul came over to say hello.

"It's a great change," he said sadly. "We do about half the business we did. So many fellows I hear about back in the States lost everything, maybe not in the first crash, but then in the second. Your friend George Hardt lost every cent, I hear. Are you back in the States?"

"No, I'm in business in Prague."

"I heard that you lost a lot in the crash."

"I did, and he added grimly, "but I lost everything I wanted in the boom." 265

"Selling short."

"Something like that."

Again the memory of those days swept over him like a nightmare—the people they had met traveling; then people who couldn't add a row of figures or speak a coherent sentence. The little man Helen had consented to dance with at the ship's party, who had insulted her ten feet from the table; the women and girls carried screaming with drink or drugs out of public places—

The men who locked their wives out in the snow, because the snow of twenty-nine 270 wasn't real snow. If you didn't want it to be snow, you just paid some money.

He went to the phone and called the Peterses' apartment; Lincoln answered.

"I called up because this thing is on my mind. Has Marion said anything definite?"

"Marion's sick," Lincoln answered shortly. "I know this thing isn't altogether your fault, but I can't have her go to pieces about it. I'm afraid we'll have to let it slide for six months; I can't take the chance of working her up to this state again."

"I see."

"I'm sorry, Charlie." 275

He went back to his table. His whisky glass was empty, but he shook his head when Alix looked at it questioningly. There wasn't much he could do now except send Honoria some things; he would send her a lot of things tomorrow. He thought rather angrily that this was just money—he had given so many people money. . . .

"No, no more," he said to another waiter. "What do I owe you?"

He would come back some day; they couldn't make him pay forever. But he wanted this child, and nothing was much good now, beside that fact. He wasn't young any more, with a lot of nice thoughts and dreams to have by himself. He was absolutely sure Helen wouldn't have wanted him to be so alone. [1931]

QUESTIONS

1. What does the Paris setting contribute to the story? What is the meaning of the allusion to Babylon?
2. What effect is achieved by opening the story in the middle of a conversation in the Ritz bar?
3. Charlie is largely defined by the women in his life. How do Marion, Lorraine, and Honoria vary in their views of him?
4. Trace the references to money throughout the story. What do they tell the reader about Charlie's values and motives?
5. Has Charlie changed as much as he thinks he has? Is there justification for Marion's decision?

RESPONSES

1. Using autobiographical and biographical materials, discuss the relationship between Fitzgerald's life and his story.
2. Using a Marxist approach, what does this story say about the lives of the rich and the effect of money on families and society?
3. Compare this story to "The Rocking-Horse Winner" by D. H. Lawrence.

FOCUS ON FILM

1. The film *The Last Time I Saw Paris* changes the time period of "Babylon Revisited." Explain the differences and postulate why a Hollywood film from the 1950s would make such changes.
2. The film *The Last Time I Saw Paris* hints at frustrated love interest between Charles and Marion. Evaluate the addition. What does it add to the story? How does it detract from the story?

E. M. FORSTER

E. M. (Edward Morgan) Forster (1879–1970) was born in London, England.
He attended Cambridge University and there became close to those who
would later form the Bloomsbury Group, which included Virginia Woolf.
Following a few years of travel, Forster began publishing stories, essays,
and his first novel, *Where Angels Fear to Tread* (1905). Throughout his life,
Forster traveled a great deal, worked in various capacities as a private tutor,
private secretary for a maharajah in India, and officer of literary institutions. In 1927, he delivered the Clark lectures at Cambridge, which became
the basis for *Aspects of the Novel* (1927). He wrote travel books, biographies,
literary criticism, and a libretto for an opera. His volumes of short fiction
include *The Celestial Omnibus* (1914) and *The Eternal Moment and Other Stories* (1928). His novels, all of which have been adapted into film, are *Where
Angels Fear to Tread* (1905), *A Room with A View* (1908), *Howard's End* (1910),
and *A Passage to India* (1924). *Maurice* (1970), a novel dealing with homo-
sexuality, was not published until after his death.

Mr. Andrews

The souls of the dead were ascending towards the Judgement Seat and the Gate of
Heaven. The world soul pressed them on every side, just as the atmosphere presses
upon rising bubbles, striving to vanquish them, to break their thin envelope of personality, to mingle their virtue with its own. But they resisted, remembering their glorious individual life on earth, and hoping for an individual life to come.

Among them ascended the soul of a Mr. Andrews who, after a beneficent and honourable life, had recently deceased at his house in town. He knew himself to be kind,
upright and religious, and though he approached his trial with all humility, he could
not be doubtful of its result. God was not now a jealous God. He would not deny salvation merely because it was expected. A righteous soul may reasonably be conscious
of its own righteousness and Mr. Andrews was conscious of his.

'The way is long,' said a voice, 'but by pleasant converse the way becomes shorter.
Might I travel in your company?'

'Willingly,' said Mr. Andrews. He held out his hand, and the two souls floated upwards together.

'I was slain fighting the infidel,' said the other exultantly, 'and I go straight to those joys of which the Prophet speaks.'

'Are you not a Christian?' asked Mr. Andrews gravely.

'No, I am a Believer. But you are a Moslem, surely?'

'I am not,' said Mr. Andrews. 'I am a Believer.'

The two souls floated upwards in silence, but did not release each other's hands. 'I am broad church,' he added gently. The word 'broad' quavered strangely amid the interspaces.

'Relate to me your career,' said the Turk at last.

'I was born of a decent middle-class family, and had my education at Winchester and Oxford. I thought of becoming a missionary, but was offered a post in the Board of Trade, which I accepted. At thirty-two I married, and had four children, two of whom have died. My wife survives me. If I had lived a little longer I should have been knighted.'

'Now I will relate my career. I was never sure of my father, and my mother does not signify. I grew up in the slums of Salonika. Then I joined a band and we plundered the villages of the infidel. I prospered and had three wives, all of whom survive me. Had I lived a little longer I should have had a band of my own.'

'A son of mine was killed travelling in Macedonia. Perhaps you killed him.'

'It is very possible.'

The two souls floated upward, hand in hand. Mr. Andrews did not speak again, for he was filled with horror at the approaching tragedy. This man, so godless, so lawless, so cruel, so lustful, believed that he would be admitted into Heaven. And into what a heaven—a place full of the crude pleasures of a ruffian's life on earth! But Mr. Andrews felt neither disgust nor moral indignation. He was only conscious of an immense pity, and his own virtues comforted him not at all. He longed to save the man whose hand he held more tightly, who, he thought, was now holding more tightly on to him. And when he reached the Gate of Heaven, instead of saying, 'Can I enter?' as he had intended, he cried out, 'Cannot *he* enter?'

And at the same moment the Turk uttered the same cry. For the same spirit was working in each of them.

From the gateway a voice replied, 'Both can enter.' They were filled with joy and pressed forward together.

Then the voice said, 'In what clothes will you enter?'

'In my best clothes,' shouted the Turk, 'the ones I stole.' And he clad himself in a splendid turban and a waistcoat embroidered with silver, and baggy trousers, and a great belt in which were stuck pipes and pistols and knives.

'And in what clothes will you enter?' said the voice to Mr. Andrews.

Mr. Andrews thought of his best clothes, but he had no wish to wear them again. At last he remembered and said, 'Robes.'

'Of what colour and fashion?' asked the voice.

Mr. Andrews had never thought about the matter much. He replied, in hesitating tones, 'White, I suppose, of some flowing soft material', and he was immediately given a garment such as he had described. 'Do I wear it rightly?' he asked.

'Wear it as it pleases you,' replied the voice. 'What else do you desire?'

'A harp,' suggested Mr. Andrews. 'A small one.'

A small gold harp was placed in his hand.

'And a palm—no, I cannot have a palm, for it is the reward of martyrdom; my life has been tranquil and happy.'

'You can have a palm if you desire it.'

But Mr. Andrews refused the palm, and hurried in his white robes after the Turk, who had already entered Heaven. As he passed in at the open gate, a man, dressed like himself, passed out with gestures of despair.

'Why is he not happy?' he asked.   30

The voice did not reply.

'And who are all those figures, seated inside on thrones and mountains? Why are some of them terrible, and sad, and ugly?'

There was no answer. Mr. Andrews entered, and then he saw that those seated figures were all the gods who were then being worshipped on the earth. A group of souls stood round each, singing his praises. But the gods paid no heed, for they were listening to the prayers of living men, which alone brought them nourishment. Sometimes a faith would grow weak, and then the god of that faith also drooped and dwindled and fainted for his daily portion of incense. And sometimes, owing to a revivalist movement, or to a great commemoration, or to some other cause, a faith would grow strong, and the god of that faith grow strong also. And, more frequently still, a faith would alter, so that the features of its god altered and became contradictory, and passed from ecstasy to respectability, or from mildness and universal love to the ferocity of battle. And at times a god would divide into two gods, or three, or more, each with his own ritual and precarious supply of prayer.

Mr. Andrews saw Buddha, and Vishnu, and Allah, and Jehovah, and the Elohim. He saw little ugly determined gods who were worshipped by a few savages in the same way. He saw the vast shadowy outlines of the neo-Pagan Zeus. There were cruel gods, and coarse gods, and tortured gods, and, worse still, there were gods who were peevish, or deceitful, or vulgar. No aspiration of humanity was unfulfilled. There was even an intermediate state for those who wished it, and for the Christian Scientists a place where they could demonstrate that they had not died.

He did not play his harp for long, but hunted vainly for one of his dead friends. And   35
though souls were continually entering Heaven, it still seemed curiously empty. Though he had all that he expected, he was conscious of no great happiness, no mystic contemplation of beauty, no mystic union with good. There was nothing to compare with that moment outside the gate, when he prayed that the Turk might enter and heard the Turk uttering the same prayer for him. And when at last he saw his companion, he hailed him with a cry of human joy.

The Turk was seated in thought, and round him, by sevens, sat the virgins who are promised in the Koran.

'Oh, my dear friend!' he called out. 'Come here and we will never be parted, and such as my pleasures are, they shall be yours also. Where are my other friends? Where are the men whom I love, or whom I have killed?'

'I, too, have only found you,' said Mr. Andrews. He sat down by the Turk, and the virgins, who were all exactly alike, ogled them with coal black eyes.

'Though I have all that I expected,' said the Turk, 'I am conscious of no great happiness. There is nothing to compare with that moment outside the gate when I prayed that you might enter, and heard you uttering the same prayer for me. These virgins are as beautiful and good as I had fashioned, yet I could wish that they were better.'

As he wished, the forms of the virgins became more rounded, and their eyes grew   40
larger and blacker than before. And Mr. Andrews, by a wish similar in kind, increased the purity and softness of his garment and the glitter of his harp. For in that place their expectations were fulfilled, but not their hopes.

'I am going,' said Mr. Andrews at last. 'We desire infinity and we cannot imagine it. How can we expect it to be granted? I have never imagined anything infinitely good or beautiful excepting in my dreams.'

'I am going with you,' said the other.

Together they sought the entrance gate, and the Turk parted with his virgins and his best clothes, and Mr. Andrews cast away his robes and his harp.

'Can we depart?' they asked.

45   'You can both depart if you wish,' said the voice, 'but remember what lies outside.'

As soon as they passed the gate, they felt again the pressure of the world soul. For a moment they stood hand in hand resisting it. Then they suffered it to break in upon them, and they, and all the experience they had gained, and all the love and wisdom they had generated, passed into it, and made it better.   [1928]

QUESTIONS

1. Describe the two main characters. How are they different? How are they alike?

2. Why do you think Mr. Andrews chose a white robe and a golden harp?

3. What are the sources for the narrator's description of the setting? Where in other literature does one find Heaven described such?

4. Discuss the meaning of the line, "For in that place their expectations were fulfilled, but not their hopes?"

5. What is the narrator's attitude toward these two characters and their choices, especially their last choice?

RESPONSES

1. Write an essay explaining how this is a story in response to England's imperialist history.

2. Compare this story to Kureishi's "My Son the Fanatic."

MARY WILKINS FREEMAN

Mary Wilkins Freeman (1852–1930) was born in Randolph, Massachusetts, to a family of diminishing financial security. She attended one year of college at Mount Holyoke, but had to return home to help support her family. By the mid 1880s, with both parents deceased, she was able to devote herself to writing, which quickly earned her acclaim as a writer of realistic fiction about New England women. In 1925 she was awarded the William Dean Howells medal for fiction by the American Academy of Letters, and in 1926 she became the first woman elected as a member of the National Institute of Arts. Among her many works are *A Humble Romance and Other Stories* (1887), *A New England Nun and Other Stories* (1891), *Silence and Other Stories* (1899), *The Copy-cat & Other Stories* (1914), and *Edgewater People* (1918).

Old Woman Magoun

The hamlet of Barry's Ford is situated in a sort of high valley among the mountains. Below it the hills lie in moveless curves like a petrified ocean; above it they rise in green-cresting waves which never break. It is *Barry's* Ford because one time the Barry family was the most important in the place; and *Ford* because just at the beginning of the hamlet the little turbulent Barry River is fordable. There is, however, now a rude bridge across the river.

Old Woman Magoun was largely instrumental in bringing the bridge to pass. She haunted the miserable little grocery, wherein whisky and hands of tobacco were the most salient features of the stock in trade, and she talked much. She would elbow herself into the midst of a knot of idlers and talk.

"That bridge ought to be built this very summer," said Old Woman Magoun. She spread her strong arms like wings, and sent the loafers, half laughing, half angry, flying in every direction. "If I were a *man*," said she, "I'd go out this very minute and lay the fust log. If I were a passel of lazy men layin' round, I'd start up for once in my life, I would." The men cowered visibly—all except Nelson Barry; he swore under his breath and strode over to the counter.

Old Woman Magoun looked after him majestically. "You can cuss all you want to, Nelson Barry," said she; "I ain't afraid of you. I don't expect you to lay ary log of the bridge, but I'm goin' to have it built this very summer." She did. The weakness of the masculine element in Barry's Ford was laid low before such strenuous feminine assertion.

5   Old Woman Magoun and some other women planned a treat—two sucking pigs, and pies, and sweet cake—for a reward after the bridge should be finished. They even viewed leniently the increased consumption of ardent spirits.

"It seems queer to me," Old Woman Magoun said to Sally Jinks, "that men can't do nothing' without havin' to drink and chew to keep their spirits up. Lord! I've worked all my life and never done nuther."

"Men is different," said Sally Jinks.

"Yes, they be," assented Old Woman Magoun, with open contempt.

The two women sat on a bench in front of Old Woman Magoun's house, and little Lily Barry, her granddaughter, sat holding her doll on a small mossy stone near by. From where they sat they could see the men at work on the new bridge. It was the last day of the work.

10   Lily clasped her doll—a poor old rag thing—close to her childish bosom, like a little mother, and her face, round which curled her long yellow hair, was fixed upon the men at work. Little Lily had never been allowed to run with the other children at Barry's Ford. Her grandmother had taught her everything she knew—which was not much, but tending at least to a certain measure of spiritual growth—for she, as it were, poured the goodness of her own soul into this little receptive vase of another. Lily was firmly grounded in her knowledge that it was wrong to lie or steal or disobey her grandmother. She had also learned that one should be very industrious. It was seldom that Lily sat idly holding her doll baby, but this was a holiday because of the bridge. She looked only a child, although she was nearly fourteen; her mother had been married at sixteen. That is, Old Woman Magoun said that her daughter, Lily's mother, had married at sixteen; there had been rumors, but no one had dared openly gainsay the old woman. She said that her daughter had married Nelson Barry and he had deserted her. She had lived in her mother's house, and Lily had been born there, and she had died when the baby was only a week old.

Lily's father, Nelson Barry, was the fairly dangerous degenerate of a good old family. Nelson's father before him had been bad. He was now the last of the family, with the exception of a sister of feeble intellect, with whom he lived in the old Barry house. He was a middle-aged man, still handsome. The shiftless population of Barry's Ford looked up to him as to an evil deity. They wondered how Old Woman Magoun dared brave him as she did. But Old Woman Magoun had within her a mighty sense of reliance upon herself as being on the right track in the midst of a maze of evil, which gave her courage. Nelson Barry had manifested no interest whatever in his daughter. Lily seldom saw her father. She did not often go to the store which was his favorite haunt. Her grandmother took care that she should not do so.

However, that afternoon she departed from her usual custom and sent Lily to the store.

She came in from the kitchen, whither she had been to baste the roasting pig. "There's no use talkin'," said she, "I've got to have some more salt. I've jest used the very last I had to dredge over that pig. I've got to go to the store."

Sally Jinks looked at Lily. "Why don't you send her?" she asked.

15   Old Woman Magoun gazed irresolutely at the girl. She was herself very tired. It did not seem to her that she could drag herself up the dusty hill to the store. She glanced with covert resentment at Sally Jinks. She thought that she might offer to go. But Sally Jinks said again, "Why don't you let her go?" and looked with a languid eye at Lily holding her doll on the stone.

Lily was watching the men at work on the bridge, with her childish delight in a spectacle of any kind, when her grandmother addressed her.

"Guess I'll let you go down to the store an' git some salt, Lily," said she.

The girl turned uncomprehending eyes upon her grandmother at the sound of her voice. She had been filled with one of the innocent reveries of childhood. Lily had in her the making of an artist or a poet. Her prolonged childhood went to prove it, and also her retrospective eyes, as clear and blue as blue light itself, which seemed to see past all that she looked upon. She had not come of the old Barry family for nothing. The best of the strain was in her, along with the splendid stanchness in humble lines which she had acquired from her grandmother.

"Put on your hat," said Old Woman Magoun; "the sun is hot and you might git a headache." She called the girl to her, and put back the shower of fair curls under the rubber band which confined the hat. She gave Lily some money, and watched her knot it into a corner of her little cotton handkerchief. "Be careful you don't lose it," said she, "and don't stop to talk to anybody, for I am in a hurry for that salt. Of course, if anybody speaks to you answer them polite, and then come right along."

Lily started, her pocket handkerchief weighted with the small silver dangling from one hand, and her rag doll carried over her shoulder like a baby. The absurd travesty of a face peeped forth from Lily's yellow curls. Sally Jinks looked after her with a sniff.

"She ain't goin' to carry that rag doll to the store?" said she.

"She likes to," replied Old Woman Magoun, in a half-shamed yet defiantly extenuating voice.

"Some girls at her age is thinkin' about beaux instead of rag dolls," said Sally Jinks.

The grandmother bristled, "Lily ain't big nor old for her age," said she. "I ain't in any hurry to have her git married. She ain't none too strong."

"She's got a good color," said Sally Jinks. She was crocheting white cotton lace, making her thick fingers fly. She really knew how to do scarcely anything except to crochet that coarse lace; somehow her heavy brain of her fingers had mastered that.

"I know she's got a beautiful color," replied Old Woman Magoun, with an odd mixture of pride and anxiety, "but it comes an' goes."

"I've heard that was a bad sign," remarked Sally Jinks, loosening some thread from her spool.

"Yes, it is," said the grandmother. "She's nothin' but a baby, though she's quicker than most to learn."

Lily Barry went on her way to the store. She was clad in a scanty short frock of blue cotton; her hat was tipped back, forming an oval frame for her innocent face. She was very small, and walked like a child, with the clap-clap of little feet of babyhood. She might have been considered, from her looks, under ten.

Presently she heard footsteps behind her; she turned around a little timidly to see who was coming. When she saw a handsome well-dressed man, she felt reassured. The man came alongside and glanced down carelessly at first; then his look deepened. He smiled, and Lily saw he was very handsome indeed, and that his smile was not only reassuring but wonderfully sweet and compelling.

"Well, little one," said the man, "where are you bound, you and your dolly?"

"I am going to the store to buy some salt for grandma," replied Lily, in her sweet treble. She looked up in the man's face, and he fairly started at the revelation of its innocent beauty. He regulated his pace by hers, and the two went on together. The man did not speak again at once. Lily kept glancing timidly up at him, and every time that she did so the man smiled and her confidence increased. Presently when the man's hand grasped her little childish one hanging by her side, she felt a complete trust in him. Then she smiled up at him. She felt glad that this nice man had come along, for just here the road was lonely.

After a while the man spoke. "What is your name, little one?" he asked, caressingly.

"Lily Barry."

35   The man started. "What is your father's name?"

"Nelson Barry," replied Lily.

The man whistled. "Is your mother dead?"

"Yes, sir."

"How old are you, my dear?"

40   "Fourteen," replied Lily.

The man looked at her with surprise. "As old as that?"

Lily suddenly shrank from the man. She could not have told why. She pulled her little hand from his, and he let it go with no remonstrance. She clasped both her arms around her rag doll, in order that her hand should not be free for him to grasp again.

She walked a little farther away from the man, and he looked amused.

"You still play with your doll?" he said, in a soft voice.

45   "Yes, sir," replied Lily. She quickened her pace and reached the store.

When Lily entered the store, Hiram Gates, the owner, was behind the counter. The only man besides in the store was Nelson Barry. He sat tipping his chair back against the wall; he was half asleep, and his handsome face was bristling with a beard of several days' growth and darkly flushed. He opened his eyes when Lily entered, the strange man following. He brought his chair down on all fours, and he looked at the man—not noticing Lily at all—with a look compounded of defiance and uneasiness.

"Hullo, Jim!" he said.

"Hullo, old man!" returned the stranger.

Lily went over to the counter and asked for the salt, in her pretty little voice. When she had paid for it and was crossing the store, Nelson Barry was on his feet.

50   "Well, how are you, Lily? It is Lily, isn't it?" he said.

"Yes, sir," replied Lily, faintly.

Her father bent down and, for the first time in her life, kissed her, and the whisky odor of his breath came into her face.

Lily involuntarily started, and shrank away from him. Then she rubbed her mouth violently with her little cotton handkerchief, which she held gathered up with the rag doll.

"Damn it all! I believe she is afraid of me," said Nelson Barry, in a thick voice.

55   "Looks a little like it," said the other man, laughing.

"It's that damned old woman," said Nelson Barry. Then he smiled again at Lily. "I didn't know what a pretty little daughter I was blessed with," said he, and he softly stroked Lily's pink cheek under her hat.

Now Lily did not shrink from him. Heredity instincts and nature itself were asserting themselves in the child's innocent, receptive breast.

Nelson Barry looked curiously at Lily. "How old are you, anyway, child?" he asked.

"I'll be fourteen in September," replied Lily.

60   "But you still play with your doll?" said Barry, laughing kindly down at her.

Lily hugged her doll more tightly, in spite of her father's kind voice. "Yes, sir," she replied.

Nelson glanced across at some glass jars filled with sticks of candy. "See here, little Lily, do you like candy?" said he.

"Yes, sir."

"Wait a minute."

Lily waited while her father went over to the counter. Soon he returned with a pack-   65
age of the candy.

"I don't see how you are going to carry so much," he said, smiling. "Suppose you
throw away your doll?"

Lily gazed at her father and hugged the doll tightly, and there was all at once in the
child's expression something mature. It became the reproach of a woman. Nelson's
face sobered.

"Oh, it's all right, Lily," he said; "keep your doll. Here, I guess you can carry this
candy under your arm."

Lily could not resist the candy. She obeyed Nelson's instructions for carrying it,
and left the store laden. The two men also left, and walked in the opposite direction,
talking busily.

When Lily reached home, her grandmother, who was watching for her, spied at   70
once the package of candy.

"What's that?" she asked, sharply.

"My father gave it to me," answered Lily, in a faltering voice. Sally regarded her with
something like alertness.

"Your father?"

"Yes, ma'am."

"Where did you see him?"   75

"In the store."

"He gave you this candy?"

"Yes, ma'am."

"What did he say?"

"He asked me how old I was, and—"   80

"And what?"

"I don't know," replied Lily; and it really seemed to her that she did not know, she
was so frightened and bewildered by it all, and, more than anything else, by her grandmother's face as she questioned her.

Old Woman Magoun's face was that of one upon whom a long-anticipated blow had
fallen. Sally Jinks gazed at her with a sort of stupid alarm.

Old Woman Magoun continued to gaze at her grandchild with that look of terrible
solicitude, as if she saw the girl in the clutch of a tiger. "You can't remember what else
he said?" she asked, fiercely, and the child began to whimper softly.

"No, ma'am," she sobbed. "I—don't know, and—"   85

"And what? Answer me."

"There was another man there. A real handsome man."

"Did he speak to you?" asked Old Woman Magoun.

"Yes, ma'am; he walked along with me a piece," confessed Lily, with a sob of terror and bewilderment.

"What did *he* say to you?" asked Old Woman Magoun, with a sort of despair.   90

Lily told, in her little, faltering, frightened voice, all of the conversation which
she could recall. It sounded harmless enough, but the look of the realization of a
long-expected blow never left her grandmother's face.

The sun was getting low and the bridge was nearing completion. Soon the workmen would be crowding into the cabin for their promised supper. There became visible in the distance, far up the road, the heavily plodding figure of another woman
who had agreed to come and help. Old Woman Magoun turned again to Lily.

"You go right upstairs to your own chamber now," said she.

"Good land! ain't' you goin' to let that poor child stay up and see the fun?" said Sally Jinks.

"You jest mind your own business," said Old Woman Magoun, forcibly, and Sally Jinks shrank. "You go right up there now, Lily," said the grandmother, in a softer tone, "and grandma will bring you up a nice plate of supper."

"When be you goin' to let that girl grow up?" asked Sally Jinks when Lily had disappeared.

"She'll grow up in the Lord's good time," replied Old Woman Magoun, and there was in her voice something both sad and threatening. Sally Jinks again shrank a little.

Soon the workmen came flocking noisily into the house. Old Woman Magoun and her two helpers served the bountiful supper. Most of the men had drunk as much as, and more than, was good for them, and Old Woman Magoun had stipulated that there was to be no drinking of anything except coffee during supper.

"I'll git you as good a meal as I know how," she said, "but if I see ary one of you drinkin' a drop, I'll run you all out. If you want anything to drink, you can go up to the store afterward. That's the place for you to go to, if you've got to make hogs of yourselves. I ain't goin' to have no hogs in my house."

Old Woman Magoun was implicitly obeyed. She had a curious authority over most people when she chose to exercise it. When the supper was in full swing, she quietly stole upstairs and carried some food to Lily. She found the girl, with the rag doll in her arms, crouching by the window in her little rocking-chair—a relic of her infancy, which she still used.

"What a noise they are makin', grandma!" she said, in a terrified whisper, as her grandmother placed the plate before her on a chair.

"They've 'most all of 'em been drinkin'. They air a passel of hogs," replied the old woman.

"Is the man that was with—with my father down there?" asked Lily, in a timid fashion. Then she fairly cowered before the look in her grandmother's eyes.

"No, he ain't, and what's more, he never will be down there if I can help it," said Old Woman Magoun, in a fierce whisper. "I know who he is. They can't cheat me. He's one of them Willises—that family the Barrys married into. They're worse than the Barrys, ef they *have* got money. Eat your supper, and put him out of your mind, child."

It was after Lily was asleep, when Old Woman Magoun was alone, clearing away her supper dishes, that Lily's father came. The door was closed, and he knocked, and the old woman knew at once who was there. The sound of that knock meant as much to her as the whir of a bomb to the defender of a fortress. She opened the door, and Nelson Barry stood there.

"Good evening, Mrs. Magoun," he said.

Old Woman Magoun stood before him, filling up the doorway with her firm bulk.

"Good evening, Mrs. Magoun," said Nelson Barry again.

"I ain't got no time to waste," replied the old woman, harshly. "I've got my supper dishes to clean up after them men."

She stood there and looked at him as she might have looked at a rebellious animal which she was trying to tame. The man laughed.

"It's no use," said he. "You know me of old. No human being can turn me from my way when I am once started in it. You may as well let me come in."

Old Woman Magoun entered the house, and Barry followed her.

Barry began without any preface. "Where is the child?" asked he.

"Upstairs. She has gone to bed."

"She goes to bed early."

"Children ought to," returned the old woman, polishing a plate.

Barry laughed. "You are keeping her a child a long while," he remarked, in a soft voice which had a sting in it.

"She *is* a child," returned the old woman, defiantly.

"Her mother was only three years older when Lily was born."

The old woman made a sudden motion toward the man which seemed fairly menacing. Then she turned again to her dish washing.   120

"I want her," said Barry.

"You can't have her," replied the old woman, in a still stern voice.

"I don't see how you can help yourself. You have always acknowledged that she was my child."

The old woman continued her task, but her strong back heaved. Barry regarded her with an entirely pitiless expression.

"I am going to have the girl, that is the long and short of it," he said, "and it is for   125
her best good, too. You are a fool, or you would see it."

"Her best good?" muttered the old woman.

"Yes, her best good. What are you going to do with her, anyway? The girl is a beauty, and almost a woman grown, although you try to make out that she is a baby. You can't live forever."

"The Lord will take care of her," replied the old woman, and again she turned and faced him, and her expression was that of a prophetess.

"Very well, let Him," said Barry, easily. "All the same I'm going to have her, and I tell you it is for her best good. Jim Willis saw her this afternoon, and—"

Old Woman Magoun looked at him. "Jim Willis!" she fairly shrieked.   130

"Well, what of it?"

"One of them Willises!" repeated the old woman, and this time her voice was thick. It seemed almost as if she were stricken with paralysis. She did not enunciate clearly.

The man shrank a little. "Now what is the need of your making such a fuss?" he said. "I will take her, and Isabel will look out for her."

"Your half-witted sister?" said Old Woman Magoun.

"Yes, my half-witted sister. She knows more than you think."   135

"More wickedness."

"Perhaps. Well, a knowledge of evil is a useful thing. How are you going to avoid evil if you don't know what it is like? My sister and I will take care of my daughter."

The old woman continued to look at the man, but his eyes never fell. Suddenly her gaze grew inconceivably keen. It was as if she saw through all externals.

"I know what it is!" she cried. "You have been playing cards and you lost, and this is the way you will pay him."

Then the man's face reddened, and he swore under his breath.   140

"Oh, my God!" said the old woman; and she really spoke with her eyes aloft as if addressing something outside of them both. Then she turned again to her dish washing.

The man cast a dogged look at her back. "Well, there is no use talking. I have made up my mind," said he, "and you know me and what that means. I am going to have the girl."

"When?" said the old woman, without turning around.

"Well, I am willing to give you a week. Put her clothes in good order before she comes."

The old woman made no reply. She continued washing dishes. She even handled   145
them so carefully they did not rattle.

"You understand," said Barry. "Have her ready a week from today."

"Yes," said Old Woman Magoun, "I understand."

Nelson Barry, going up the mountain road, reflected that Old Woman Magoun had a strong character, that she understood much better than her sex in general the futility of withstanding the inevitable.

"Well," he said to Jim Willis when he reached home, "the old woman did not make such a fuss as I expected."

150   "Are you going to have the girl?"

"Yes; a week from today. Look here, Jim; you've got to stick to your promise."

"All right," said Willis. "Go you one better."

The two were playing at cards in the old parlor, once magnificent, now squalid, of the Barry house. Isabel, the half-witted sister, entered, bringing some glasses on a tray. She had learned with her feeble intellect some tricks, like a dog. One of them was the mixing of sundry drinks. She set the tray on a little stand near the two men, and watched them with her silly simper.

"Clear out now and go to bed," her brother said to her, and she obeyed.

155   Early the next morning Old Woman Magoun went up to Lily's little sleeping chamber, and watched her a second as she lay asleep, with her yellow locks spread over the pillow. Then she spoke. "Lily," said she—"Lily, wake up. I am going to Greenham across the new bridge, and you can go with me."

Lily immediately sat up in bed and smiled at her grandmother. Her eyes were still misty, but the light of awakening was in them.

"Get right up," said the old woman. "You can wear your new dress if you want to."

Lily gurgled with pleasure like a baby. "And my new hat?" said she.

"I don't care."

160   Old Woman Magoun and Lily started for Greenham before Barry's Ford, which kept late hours, was fairly awake. It was three miles to Greenham. The old woman said that, since the horse was a little lame, they would walk. It was a beautiful morning, with a diamond radiance of dew over everything. Her grandmother had curled Lily's hair more punctiliously than usual. The little face peeped like a rose out of two rows of golden spirals. Lily wore her new muslin dress with a pink sash, and her best hat of a fine white straw trimmed with a wreath of rosebuds; also the neatest black openwork stockings and pretty shoes. She even had white cotton gloves. When they set out, the old, heavily stepping woman, in her black gown and cape and bonnet, looked down at the little pink fluttering figure. Her face was full of the tenderest love and admiration, and yet there was something terrible about it. They crossed the new bridge—a primitive structure built of logs in a slovenly fashion. Old Woman Magoun pointed to a gap.

"Jest see that," said she. "That's the way men work."

"Men ain't very nice, be they?" said Lily, in her sweet little voice.

"No, they ain't, take them all together," replied her grandmother.

"That man that walked to the store with me was nicer than some, I guess," Lily said, in a wishful fashion. Her grandmother reached down and took the child's hand in its small cotton glove. "You hurt me, holding my hand so tight," Lily said presently, in a deprecatory little voice.

165   The old woman loosened her grasp. "Grandma didn't know how tight she was holding your hand," said she. "She wouldn't hurt you for nothin', except it was to save your life, or somethin' like that." She spoke with an undertone of tremendous meaning which the girl was too childish to grasp. They walked along the country road.

Just before they reached Greenham they passed a stone wall overgrown with blackberry vines, and, an unusual thing in that vicinity, a lusty spread of deadly nightshade full of berries.

"Those berries look good to eat, grandma," Lily said.

At that instant the old woman's face became something terrible to see. "You can't have any now," she said, and hurried Lily along.

"They look real nice," said Lily.

When they reached Greenham, Old Woman Magoun took her way straight to the most pretentious house there, the residence of the lawyer, whose name was Mason. Old Woman Magoun bade Lily wait in the yard for a few moments, and Lily ventured to seat herself on a bench beneath an oak tree; then she watched with some wonder her grandmother enter the lawyer's office door at the right of the house. Presently the lawyer's wife came out and spoke to Lily under the tree. She had in her hand a little tray containing a plate of cake, a glass of milk, and an early apple. She spoke very kindly to Lily; she even kissed her, and offered her the tray of refreshments, which Lily accepted gratefully. She sat eating, with Mrs. Mason watching her, when Old Woman Magoun came out of the lawyer's office with a ghastly face.

"What are you eatin'?" she asked Lily, sharply. "Is that a sour apple?" 170

"I thought she might be hungry," said the lawyer's wife, with loving, melancholy eyes upon the girl.

Lily had almost finished the apple. "It's real sour, but I like it; it's real nice, grandma," she said.

"You ain't been drinkin' milk with a sour apple?"

"It was real nice milk, grandma."

"You ought never to have drunk milk and eat a sour apple," said her grandmother. 175 "Your stomach was all out of order this mornin', an' sour apples and milk is always apt to hurt anybody."

"I don't know but they are," Mrs. Mason said, apologetically, as she stood on the green lawn with her lavender muslin sweeping around her. "I am real sorry, Mrs. Magoun. I ought to have thought. Let me get some soda for her."

"Soda never agrees with her," replied the old woman, in a harsh voice. "Come," she said to Lily, "it's time we were goin' home."

After Lily and her grandmother had disappeared down the road, Lawyer Mason came out of his office and joined his wife, who had seated herself on the bench beneath the tree. She was idle, and her face wore the expression of those who review joys forever past. She had lost a little girl, her only child, years ago, and her husband always knew when she was thinking about her. Lawyer Mason looked older than his wife; he had a dry, shrewd, slightly one-sided face.

"What do you think, Maria?" he said. "That old woman came to me with the most pressing entreaty to adopt that little girl."

"She is a beautiful little girl," said Mrs. Mason, in a slightly husky voice. 180

"Yes, she is a pretty child," assented the lawyer, looking pityingly at his wife; "but it is out of the question, my dear. Adopting a child is a serious measure, and in this case a child who comes from Barry's Ford!"

"But the grandmother seems a very good woman," said Mrs. Mason.

"I rather think she is. I never heard a word against her. But the father! No, Maria, we cannot take a child with Barry blood in her veins. The stock has run out; it is vitiated physically and morally. It won't do, my dear."

"Her grandmother had her dressed up as pretty as a little girl could be," said Mrs. Mason, and this time the tears welled into her faithful, wistful eyes.

185   "Well, we can't help that," said the lawyer, as he went back to his office.

Old Woman Magoun and Lily returned, going slowly along the road to Barry's Ford. When they came to the stone wall where the blackberry vines and the deadly nightshade grew, Lily said she was tired, and asked if she could not sit down for a few minutes. The strange look on her grandmother's face had deepened. Now and then Lily glanced at her and had a feeling as if she were looking at a stranger.

"Yes, you can set down if you want to," said Old Woman Magoun, deeply and harshly.

Lily started and looked at her, as if to make sure that it was her grandmother who spoke. Then she sat down on a stone which was comparatively free of the vines.

"Ain't you goin' to set down, grandma?" Lily asked, timidly.

190   "No; I don't want to get into that mess," replied her grandmother. "I ain't tired. I'll stand here."

Lily sat still; her delicate little face was flushed with heat. She extended her tiny feet in her best shoes and gazed at them. "My shoes are all over dust," said she.

"It will brush off," said her grandmother, still in that strange voice.

Lily looked around. An elm tree in the field behind her cast a spray of branches over her head; a little cool puff of wind came on her face. She gazed at the low mountains on the horizon, in the midst of which she lived, and she sighed, for no reason that she knew. She began idly picking at the blackberry vines; there were no berries on them; then she put her little fingers on the berries of the deadly nightshade. "These look like nice berries," she said.

Old Woman Magoun, standing stiff and straight in the road, said nothing.

195   "They look good to eat," said Lily.

Old Woman Magoun still said nothing, but she looked up into the ineffable blue of the sky, over which spread at intervals great white clouds shaped like wings.

Lily picked some of the deadly nightshade berries and ate them. "Why, they are real sweet," said she. "They are nice." She picked some more and ate them.

Presently her grandmother spoke. "Come," she said, "it is time we were going. I guess you have set long enough."

Lily was still eating the berries when she slipped down from the wall and followed her grandmother obediently up the road.

200   Before they reached home, Lily complained of being very thirsty. She stopped and made a little cup of a leaf and drank long at a mountain brook. "I am dreadful dry, but it hurts me to swallow," she said to her grandmother when she stopped drinking and joined the old woman waiting for her in the road. Her grandmother's face seemed strangely dim to her. She took hold of Lily's hand as they went on. "My stomach burns," said Lily, presently. "I want some more water."

"There is another brook a little farther on," said Old Woman Magoun, in a dull voice.

When they reached that brook, Lily stopped and drank again, but she whimpered a little over her difficulty in swallowing. "My stomach burns, too," she said, walking on, "and my throat is so dry, grandma." Old Woman Magoun held Lily's hand more tightly. "You hurt me, holding my hand so tight, grandma," said Lily, looking up at her grandmother, whose face she seemed to see through a mist, and the old woman loosened her grasp.

When at last they reached home, Lily was very ill. Old Woman Magoun put her on her own bed in the little bedroom out of the kitchen. Lily lay there and moaned, and Sally Jinks came in.

"Why, what ails her?" she asked. "She looks feverish."

Lily unexpectedly answered for herself. "I ate some sour apples and drank some milk," she moaned.

"Sour apples and milk are dreadful apt to hurt anybody," said Sally Jinks. She told several people on her way home that Old Woman Magoun was dreadful careless to let Lily eat such things.

Meanwhile Lily grew worse. She suffered cruelly from the burning in her stomach, the vertigo, and the deadly nausea. "I am so sick, I am so sick, grandma," she kept moaning. She could no longer see her grandmother as she bent over her, but she could hear her talk.

Old Woman Magoun talked as Lily had never heard her talk before, as nobody had ever heard her talk before. She spoke from the depths of her soul; her voice was as tender as the coo of a dove, and it was grand and exalted. "You'll feel better very soon, little Lily," said she.

"I am so sick, grandma."

"You will feel better very soon, and then—"

"I am sick."

"You shall go to a beautiful place."

Lily moaned.

"You shall go to a beautiful place," the old woman went on.

"Where?" asked Lily, groping feebly with her cold little hands. Then she moaned again.

"A beautiful place, where the flowers grow tall."

"What color? Oh, grandma, I am so sick."

"A blue color," replied the old woman. Blue was Lily's favorite color. "A beautiful blue color, and as tall as your knees, and the flowers always stay there, and they never fade."

"Not if you pick them, Grandma? Oh!"

"No, not if you pick them; they never fade, and they are so sweet you can smell them a mile off; and there are birds that sing, and all the roads have gold stones in them, and the stone walls are made of gold."

"Like the ring grandpa gave you? I am so sick, grandma."

"Yes, gold like that. And all the houses are built of silver and gold, and the people all have wings, so when they get tired walking they can fly, and—"

"I am so sick, grandma."

"And all the dolls are alive," said Old Woman Magoun. "Dolls like yours can run, and talk, and love you back again."

Lily had her poor old rag doll in bed with her, clasped close to her agonized little heart. She tried very hard with her eyes, whose pupils were so dilated that they looked black, to see her grandmother's face when she said that, but she could not. "It is dark," she moaned, feebly.

"There where you are going it is always light," said the grandmother, "and the commonest things shine like that breastpin Mrs. Lawyer Mason had on today."

Lily moaned pitifully, and said something incoherent. Delirium was commencing. Presently she sat straight up in bed and raved; but even then her grandmother's wonderful compelling voice had an influence over her.

"You will come to a gate with all the colors of the rainbow," said her grandmother; "and it will open, and you will go right in and walk up the gold street, and cross the field where the blue flowers come up to your knees, until you find your mother, and she will take you home where you are going to live. She has a little white room all ready for you, white curtains at the windows, and a little white looking-glass, and when you look in it you will see—"

"What will I see? I am so sick, grandma."

230   "You will see a face like yours, only it's an angel's; and there will be a little white bed, and you can lay down an' rest."

"Won't I be sick, grandma?" asked Lily. Then she moaned and babbled wildly, although she seemed to understand through it all what her grandmother said.

"No, you will never be sick any more. Talkin' about sickness won't mean anything to you."

It continued. Lily talked on wildly, and her grandmother's great voice of soothing never ceased, until the child fell into a deep sleep, or what resembled sleep; but she lay stiffly in that sleep, and a candle flashed before her eyes made no impression on them.

Then it was that Nelson Barry came. Jim Willis waited outside the door. When Nelson entered he found Old Woman Magoun on her knees beside the bed, weeping with dry eyes and a might of agony which fairly shook Nelson Barry, the degenerate of a fine old race.

235   "Is she sick?" he asked, in a hushed voice.

Old Woman Magoun gave another terrible sob, which sounded like the gasp of one dying.

"Sally Jinks said that Lily was sick from eating milk and sour apples," said Barry, in a tremulous voice. "I remember that her mother was very sick once from eating them."

Lily lay still, and her grandmother on her knees shook with her terrible sobs.

Suddenly Nelson Barry started. "I guess I had better go to Greenham for a doctor if she's as bad as that," he said. He went close to the bed and looked at the sick child. He gave a great start. Then he felt of her hands and reached down under the bedclothes for her little feet. "Her hands and feet are like ice," he cried out. "Good God! why didn't you send for some one—for me—before? Why, she's dying; she's almost gone!"

240   Barry rushed out and spoke to Jim Willis, who turned pale and came in and stood by the bedside.

"She's almost gone," he said, in a hushed whisper.

"There's no use going for the doctor; she'd be dead before he got here," said Nelson, and he stood regarding the passing child with a strange, sad face—unutterably sad, because of his incapability of the truest sadness.

"Poor little thing, she's past suffering, anyhow," said the other man, and his own face also was sad with a puzzled, mystified sadness.

Lily died that night. There was quite a commotion in Barry's Ford until after the funeral, it was all so sudden, and then everything went on as usual. Old Woman Magoun continued to live as she had done before. She supported herself by the produce of her tiny farm; she was very industrious, but people said that she was a trifle touched, since every time she went over the log bridge with her eggs or her garden vegetables to sell in Greenham, she carried with her, as one might have carried an infant, Lily's old rag doll.   [1905]

QUESTIONS

1. What motivates Old Woman Magoun that makes it possible for her to do all the things she does throughout the story?

2. What elements of the fairy tale does the story rely on?

3. To what extent is this a story about a region, about an economic class, about gender, or about individual people?

4. At what point in the story do you know what decisions the main character is making?

5. Are we supposed to revile or condone Old Woman Magoun's choices?

RESPONSES

1. Write an essay explicating the first two paragraphs of the story. What did Old Woman Magoun actually bridge?

2. Write an essay that compares this story to Angela Carter's "The Werewolf." Or compare the use of the image of the doll in this story and in Sandra Cisneros's "Barbie-Q."

CARLOS FUENTES

Carlos Fuentes (b. 1928) is the son of a Mexican diplomat and has been very involved in Mexico's cultural and political life. He was born in Panama City, and growing up he lived in the United States, Argentina, and Chile. In addition to being a writer of the highest international stature, he has served as Mexico's Ambassador to France and as professor at many universities, including Harvard. Having received several prominent literary awards, Fuentes's most important works include *Where the Air Is Clearer* (1958), *The Death of Antonio Cruz* (1962), *A Change of Skin* (1967), *Terra Nostra* (1975), *The Hydra Head* (1978), *Burnt Water* (1981), *The Old Gringo* (1985), *The Campaign* (1990), *Diana, the Goddess Who Hunts Alone* (1995), *Years with Laura Diaz* (2000), *Where the Air Is Clear* (2004), and *This I Believe: An A to Z of a Life* (2005).

Chac-Mool

It was only recently that Filiberto drowned in Acapulco. It happened during Easter Week. Even though he'd been fired from his government job, Filiberto couldn't resist the bureaucratic temptation to make his annual pilgrimage to the small German hotel, to eat sauerkraut sweetened by the sweat of the tropical cuisine, dance away Holy Saturday on La Quebrada, and feel he was one of the "beautiful people" in the dim anonymity of dusk on Hornos Beach. Of course we all knew he'd been a good swimmer when he was young, but now, at forty, and the shape he was in, to try to swim that distance, at midnight! Frau Müller wouldn't allow a wake in her hotel—steady client or not; just the opposite, she held a dance on her stifling little terrace while Filiberto, very pale in his coffin, awaited the departure of the first morning bus from the terminal, spending the first night of his new life surrounded by crates and parcels. When I arrived, early in the morning, to supervise the loading of the casket, I found Filiberto buried beneath a mound of coconuts; the driver wanted to get him in the luggage compartment as quickly as possible, covered with canvas in order not to upset the passengers and to avoid bad luck on the trip.

When we left Acapulco there was still a good breeze. Near Tierra Colorada it began to get hot and bright. As I was eating my breakfast eggs and sausage, I had opened Filiberto's satchel, collected the day before along with his other personal belongings from the Müllers' hotel. Two hundred pesos. An old newspaper; expired lottery tickets; a one-way ticket to Acapulco—one way?—and a cheap notebook with graph-paper pages and marbleized-paper binding.

On the bus I ventured to read it, in spite of the sharp curves, the stench of vomit, and a certain natural feeling of respect for the private life of a deceased friend. It should be a record—yes, it began that way—of our daily office routine; maybe I'd find out what caused him to neglect his duties, why he'd written memoranda without rhyme or reason or any authorization. The reasons, in short, for his being fired, his seniority ignored and his pension lost.

"Today I went to see about my pension. Lawyer extremely pleasant. I was so happy when I left that I decided to blow five pesos at a café. The same café we used to go to when we were young and where I never go now because it reminds me that I lived better at twenty than I do at forty. We were all equals then, energetically discouraging any unfavorable remarks about our classmates. In fact, we'd open fire on anyone in the house who so much as mentioned inferior background or lack of elegance. I knew that many of us (perhaps those of most humble origin) would go far, and that here in school we were forging lasting friendships; together we would brave the stormy seas of life. But it didn't work out that way. Someone didn't follow the rules. Many of the lowly were left behind, though some climbed higher even than we could have predicted in those high-spirited, affable get-togethers. Some who seemed to have the most promise got stuck somewhere along the way, cut down in some extracurricular activity, isolated by an invisible chasm from those who'd triumphed and those who'd gone nowhere at all. Today, after all this time, I again sat in the chairs—remodeled, as well as the soda fountain, a kind of barricade against invasion—and pretended to read some business papers. I saw many of the old faces, amnesiac, changed in the neon light, prosperous. Like the café, which I barely recognized, along with the city itself, they'd been chipping away at a pace different from my own. No, they didn't recognize me now, or didn't want to. At most, one or two clapped a quick, fat hand on my shoulder. So long, old friend, how's it been going? Between us stretched the eighteen holes of the Country Club. I buried myself in my papers. The years of my dreams, the optimistic predictions, filed before my eyes, along with the obstacles that had kept me from achieving them. I felt frustrated that I couldn't dig my fingers into the past and put together the pieces of some long-forgotten puzzle. But one's toy chest is a part of the past, and when all's said and done, who knows where his lead soldiers went, his helmets and wooden swords. The make-believe we loved so much was only that, make-believe. Still, I'd been diligent, disciplined, devoted to duty. Wasn't that enough? Was it too much? Often, I was assaulted by the recollection of Rilke: the great reward for the adventure of youth is death; we should die young, taking all our secrets with us. Today I wouldn't be looking back at a city of salt. Five pesos? Two pesos tip."

"In addition to his passion for corporation law, Pepe likes to theorize. He saw me coming out of the Cathedral, and we walked together toward the National Palace. He's not a believer, but he's not content to stop at that: within half a block he had to propose a theory. If I weren't a Mexican, I wouldn't worship Christ, and . . . No, look, it's obvious. The Spanish arrive and say, Adore this God who died a bloody death nailed to a cross with a bleeding wound in his side. Sacrificed. Made an offering. What could be more natural than to accept something so close to your own ritual, your own life . . .? Imagine, on the other hand, if Mexico had been conquered by Buddhists or

5

Moslems. It's not conceivable that our Indians would have worshipped some person who died of indigestion. But a God that's not only sacrificed for you but has his heart torn out, God Almighty, checkmate to Huitzilopochtli! Christianity, with its emotion, its bloody sacrifice and ritual, becomes a natural and novel extension of the native religion. The qualities of charity, love, and turn-the-other-cheek, however, are rejected. And that's what Mexico is all about: you have to kill a man in order to believe in him.

"Pepe knew that ever since I was young I've been mad for certain pieces of Mexican Indian art. I collect small statues, idols, pots. I spend my weekends in Tlaxcala, or in Teotihuacán. That may be why he likes to relate to indigenous themes all the theories he concocts for me. Pepe knows that I've been looking for a reasonable replica of the Chac-Mool for a long time, and today he told me about a little shop in the flea market of La Lagunilla where they're selling one, apparently at a good price. I'll go Sunday.

"A joker put red coloring in the office water cooler, naturally interrupting our duties. I had to report him to the director, who simply thought it was funny. So all day the bastard's been going around making fun of me, with cracks about water. Motherfu . . ."

"Today, Sunday, I had time to go out to La Lagunilla. I found the Chac-Mool in the cheap little shop Pepe had told me about. It's a marvelous piece, life-size, and though the dealer assures me it's an original, I question it. The stone is nothing out of the ordinary, but that doesn't diminish the elegance of the composition, or its massiveness. The rascal has smeared tomato ketchup on the belly to convince the tourists of its bloody authenticity.

"Moving the piece to my house cost more than the purchase price. But it's here now, temporarily in the cellar while I reorganize my collection to make room for it. These figures demand a vertical and burning-hot sun; that was their natural element. The effect is lost in the darkness of the cellar, where it's simply another lifeless mass and its grimace seems to reproach me for denying it light. The dealer had a spotlight focused directly on the sculpture, highlighting all the planes and lending a more amiable expression to my Chac-Mool. I must follow his example."

10   "I awoke to find the pipes had burst. Somehow, I'd carelessly left the water running in the kitchen; it flooded the floor and poured into the cellar before I'd noticed it. The dampness didn't damage the Chac-Mool, but my suitcases suffered; everything has to happen on a weekday. I was late to work."

"At last they came to fix the plumbing. Suitcases ruined. There's slime on the base of the Chac-Mool."

"I awakened at one; I'd heard a terrible moan. I thought it might be burglars. Purely imaginary."

"The moaning at night continues. I don't know where it's coming from, but it makes me nervous. To top it all off, the pipes burst again, and the rains have seeped through the foundation and flooded the cellar."

"Plumber still hasn't come; I'm desperate. As far as the City Water Department's concerned, the less said the better. This is the first time the runoff from the rains has drained into my cellar instead of the storm sewers. The moaning's stopped. An even trade?"

ease now, the knees more relaxed than before, the smile more benevolent. And yesterday, finally, I awakened with a start, with the frightening certainty that two creatures are breathing in the night, that in the darkness there beats a pulse in addition to one's own. Yes, I heard footsteps on the stairway. Nightmare. Go back to sleep. I don't know how long I feigned sleep. When I opened my eyes again, it still was not dawn. The room smelled of horror, of incense and blood. In the darkness, I gazed about the bedroom until my eyes found two points of flickering, cruel yellow light.

"Scarcely breathing, I turned on the light. There was the Chac-Mool, standing erect, smiling, ocher-colored except for the flesh-red belly. I was paralyzed by the two tiny, almost crossed eyes set close to the wedge-shaped nose. The lower teeth closed tightly on the upper lip; only the glimmer from the squarish helmet on the abnormally large head betrayed any sign of life. Chac-Mool moved toward my bed; then it began to rain."

I remember that it was at the end of August that Filiberto had been fired from his job, with a public condemnation by the director, amid rumors of madness and even theft. I didn't believe it. I did see some wild memoranda, one asking the Secretary of the Department whether water had an odor; another, offering his services to the Department of Water Resources to make it rain in the desert. I couldn't explain it. I thought the exceptionally heavy rains of that summer had affected him. Or that living in that ancient mansion with half the rooms locked and thick with dust, without any servants or family life, had finally deranged him. The following entries are for the end of September.

"Chac-Mool can be pleasant enough when he wishes . . . the gurgling of enchanted water . . . He knows wonderful stories about the monsoons, the equatorial rains, the scourge of the deserts; the genealogy of every plant engendered by his mythic paternity: the willow, his wayward daughter; the lotus, his favorite child; the cactus, his mother-in-law. What I can't bear is the odor, the nonhuman odor, emanating from flesh that isn't flesh, from sandals that shriek their antiquity. Laughing stridently, the Chac-Mool recounts how he was discovered by Le Plongeon and brought into physical contact with men of other gods. His spirit had survived quite peacefully in water vessels and storms; his stone was another matter, and to have dragged him from his hiding place was unnatural and cruel. I think the Chac-Mool will never forgive that. He savors the imminence of the aesthetic.

"I've had to provide him with pumice stone to clean the belly the dealer smeared with ketchup when he thought he was Aztec. He didn't seem to like my question about his relation to Tlaloc, and when he becomes angry his teeth, repulsive enough in themselves, glitter and grow pointed. The first days he slept in the cellar; since yesterday, in my bed."

25   "The dry season has begun. Last night, from the living room where I'm sleeping now, I heard the same hoarse moans I'd heard in the beginning, followed by a terrible racket. I went upstairs and peered into the bedroom: the Chac-Mool was breaking the lamps and furniture; he sprang toward the door with outstretched bleeding hands, and I was barely able to slam the door and run to hide in the bathroom. Later he came downstairs, panting and begging for water. He leaves the faucets running all day; there's not a dry spot in the house. I have to sleep wrapped in blankets, and I've asked him please to let the living room dry out."°

°Filiberto does not say in what language he communicated with the Chac-Mool.

"The Chac-Mool flooded the living room today. Exasperated, I told him I was going to return him to La Lagunilla. His laughter—so frighteningly different from the laugh of any man or animal—was as terrible as the blow from that heavily braceleted arm. I have to admit it: I am his prisoner. My original plan was quite different. I was going to play with the Chac-Mool the way you play with a toy; this may have been an extension of the security of childhood. But—who said it?—the fruit of childhood is consumed by the years, and I hadn't seen that. He's taken my clothes, and when the green moss begins to sprout, he covers himself in my bathrobes. The Chac-Mool is accustomed to obedience, always; I, who have never had cause to command, can only submit. Until it rains—what happened to his magic power?—he will be choleric and irritable."

"Today I discovered that the Chac-Mool leaves the house at night. Always, as it grows dark, he sings a shrill and ancient tune, older than song itself. Then everything is quiet. I knocked several times at the door, and when he didn't answer I dared enter. The bedroom, which I hadn't seen since the day the statue tried to attack me, is a ruin; the odor of incense and blood that permeates the entire house is particularly concentrated here. And I discovered bones behind the door, dog and rat and cat bones. This is what the Chac-Mool steals in the night for nourishment. This explains the hideous barking every morning."

"February, dry. Chac-Mool watches every move I make; he made me telephone a restaurant and ask them to deliver chicken and rice every day. But what I took from the office is about to run out. So the inevitable happened: on the first they cut off the water and lights for nonpayment. But Chac has discovered a public fountain two blocks from the house; I make ten or twelve trips a day for water while he watches me from the roof. He says that if I try to run away he will strike me dead in my tracks; he is also the God of Lightning. What he doesn't realize is that I know about his nighttime forays. Since we don't have any electricity, I have to go to bed about eight. I should be used to the Chac-Mool by now, but just a moment ago, when I ran into him on the stairway, I touched his icy arms, the scales of his renewed skin, and I wanted to scream.

"If it doesn't rain soon, the Chac-Mool will return to stone. I've noticed his recent difficulty in moving; sometimes he lies for hours, paralyzed, and almost seems an idol again. But this repose merely gives him new strength to abuse me, to claw at me as if he could extract liquid from my flesh. We don't have the amiable intervals any more, when he used to tell me old tales; instead, I seem to notice a heightened resentment. There have been other indications that set me thinking: my wine cellar is diminishing; he likes to stroke the silk of my bathrobes; he wants me to bring a servant girl to the house; he has made me teach him how to use soap and lotions. I believe the Chac-Mool is falling into human temptations; now I see in the face that once seemed eternal something that is merely old. This may be my salvation: if the Chac becomes human, it's possible that all the centuries of his life will accumulate in an instant and he will die in a flash of lightning. But this might also cause my death: the Chac won't want me to witness his downfall; he may decide to kill me.

"I plan to take advantage tonight of Chac's nightly excursion to flee. I will go to Acapulco; I'll see if I can't find a job, and await the death of the Chac-Mool. Yes, it will be soon; his hair is gray, his face bloated. I need to get some sun, to swim, to regain my strength. I have four hundred pesos left. I'll go to the Müllers' hotel, it's cheap and comfortable. Let Chac-Mool take over the whole place; we'll see how long he lasts without my pails of water." 30

Filiberto's diary ends here. I didn't want to think about what he'd written; I slept as far as Cuernavaca. From there to Mexico City I tried to make some sense out of the account, to attribute it to overwork, or some psychological disturbance. By the time we reached the terminal at nine in the evening, I still hadn't accepted the fact of my friend's madness. I hired a truck to carry the coffin to Filiberto's house, where I would arrange for his burial.

Before I could insert the key in the lock, the door opened. A yellow-skinned Indian in a smoking jacket and ascot stood in the doorway. He couldn't have been more repulsive; he smelled of cheap cologne; he'd tried to cover his wrinkles with thick powder, his mouth was clumsily smeared with lipstick, and his hair appeared to be dyed.

"I'm sorry . . . I didn't know that Filiberto had . . ."

"No, matter. I know all about it. Tell the men to carry the body down to the cellar."   [1973]

QUESTIONS

1. Does the fact that Chac-Mool is a mythological being make this story more than a horror story? Should it?

2. Of what importance are Filiberto's feelings of professional failure before the purchase of the Chac-Mool?

3. How do Pepe's remarks about Christianity and Mexico's native religion foreshadow the ending of the story?

4. Why is Filiberto susceptible to the Chac-Mool's power?

5. What is gained by employing two narrators, Filiberto and Filiberto's friend?

RESPONSES

1. Write an essay illustrating what Fuentes's story owes to the work of Edgar Allan Poe.

2. Research the mythology of pre-Christian Mexico. In an essay, explain the connection, if any, to Fuentes's story.

MARY GAITSKILL

Mary Gaitskill (b. 1954) was born in Lexington, Kentucky, and attended the University of Michigan. She has published two volumes of short fiction, *Bad Behavior* (1988) and *Because They Wanted To* (1997), and one novel, *Two Girls, Fat and Thin* (1991). Escaping from an abusive home, she worked in massage parlors and strip clubs. Since then she has taught in various universities, including San Francisco State and University of Houston.

Tiny, Smiling Daddy

He lay in his reclining chair, barely awake enough to feel the dream moving just under his thoughts. It felt like one of those pure, beautiful dreams in which he was young again, and filled with the realization that the friends who had died, or gone away, or decided that they didn't like him anymore, had really been there all along, loving him. A piece of the dream flickered, and he made out the lips and cheekbones of a tender woman, smiling as she leaned toward him. The phone rang, and the sound rippled through his pliant wakefulness, into the pending dream. But his wife had turned the answering machine up too loud again, and it attacked him with a garbled, furred roar that turned into the voice of his friend Norm.

Resentful at being waked and grateful that for once somebody had called him, he got up to answer. He picked up the phone, and the answering machine screeched at him through the receiver. He cursed as he fooled with it, hating his stiff fingers. Irritably, he exchanged greetings with his friend, and then Norm, his voice oddly weighted, said, "I saw the issue of *Self* with Kitty in it."

He waited for an explanation. None came, so he said, "What? Issue of *Self*? What's *Self*?"

"Good grief, Stew, I thought for sure you'd of seen it. Now I feel funny."

The dream pulsed forward and receded again. "Funny about what?"   5

"My daughter's got a subscription to this magazine, *Self*. And they printed an article that Kitty wrote about fathers and daughters talking to each other, and she, well, she wrote about you. Laurel showed it to me."

"My God."

"It's ridiculous that I'm the one to tell you. I just thought—"

"It was bad?"

10   "No, she didn't say anything bad. I just didn't understand the whole idea of it. And I wondered what you thought."

He got off the phone and walked back into the living room, now fully awake. His daughter, Kitty, was living in South Carolina, working in a used-record store and making animal statuettes, which she sold on commission. She had never written anything that he knew of, yet she'd apparently published an article in a national magazine about him. He lifted his arms and put them on the windowsill; the air from the open window cooled his underarms. Outside, the Starlings' tiny dog marched officiously up and down the pavement, looking for someone to bark at. Maybe she had written an article about how wonderful he was, and she was too shy to show him right away. This was doubtful. Kitty was quiet, but she wasn't shy. She was untactful and she could be aggressive. Uncertainty only made her doubly aggressive.

He turned the edge of one nostril over with his thumb and nervously stroked his nose hairs with one finger. He knew it was a nasty habit, but it soothed him. When Kitty was a little girl he would do it to make her laugh. "Well," he'd say, "do you think it's time we played with the hairs in our nose?" And she would giggle, holding her hands against her face, eyes sparkling over her knuckles.

Then she was fourteen, and as scornful and rejecting as any girl he had ever thrown a spitball at when he was that age. They didn't get along so well anymore. Once, they were sitting in the rec room watching TV, he on the couch, she on the footstool. There was a Charlie Chan movie on, but he was mostly watching her back and her long, thick brown hair, which she had just washed and was brushing. She dropped her head forward from the neck to let the hair fall between her spread legs and began slowly stroking it with a pink nylon brush.

"Say, don't you think it's time we played with the hairs in our nose?"

15   No reaction from bent back and hair.

"Who wants to play with the hairs in their nose?"

Nothing.

"Hairs in the nose, hairs in the nose," he sang.

She bolted violently up from the stool. "You are so gross you disgust me!" She stormed from the room, shoulders in a tailored jacket of indignation.

20   Sometimes he said it just to see her exasperation, to feel the adorable, futile outrage of her violated girl delicacy.

He wished that his wife would come home with the car, so that he could drive to the store and buy a copy of *Self*. His car was being repaired, and he could not walk to the little cluster of stores and parking lots that constituted "town" in this heat. It would take a good twenty minutes, and he would be completely worn out when he got there. He would find the magazine and stand there in the drugstore and read it, and if it was something bad, he might not have the strength to walk back.

He went into the kitchen, opened a beer, and brought it into the living room. His wife had been gone for over an hour, and God knew how much longer she would be. She could spend literally all day driving around the county, doing nothing but buying a jar of honey or a bag of apples. Of course, he could call Kitty, but he'd probably just get her answering machine, and besides, he didn't want to talk to her before he understood the situation. He felt helplessness move through his body the way a swimmer feels a large sea creature pass beneath him. How could she have done this to him? She knew how he dreaded exposure of any kind, she knew the way he guarded himself against strangers, the way he carefully drew all the curtains when twilight approached so that no one could see them walking through the house. She knew how ashamed he had been when, at sixteen, she announced that she was lesbian.

The Starling dog was now across the street, yapping at the heels of a bow-legged old lady in a blue dress who was trying to walk down the sidewalk. "Dammit," he said. He left the window and got the afternoon opera station on the radio. They were in the final act of *La Bohème*.

He did not remember precisely when it had happened, but Kitty, his beautiful, happy little girl, turned into a glum, weird teenager that other kids picked on. She got skinny and ugly. Her blue eyes, which had been so sensitive and bright, turned filmy, as if the real Kitty had retreated so far from the surface that her eyes existed to shield rather than reflect her. It was as if she deliberately held her beauty away from them, only showing glimpses of it during unavoidable lapses, like the time she sat before the TV, daydreaming and lazily brushing her hair. At moments like this, her dormant charm broke his heart. It also annoyed him. What did she have to retreat from? They had both loved her. When she was little and she couldn't sleep at night, Marsha would sit with her in bed for hours. She praised her stories and her drawings as if she were a genius. When Kitty was seven, she and her mother had special times, during which they went off together and talked about whatever Kitty wanted to talk about.

He tried to compare the sullen, morbid Kitty of sixteen with the slender, self-possessed twenty-eight-year-old lesbian who wrote articles for *Self*. He pictured himself in court, waving a copy of *Self* before a shocked jury. The case would be taken up by the press. He saw the headlines: Dad Sues Mag—Dyke Daughter Reveals . . . reveals what? What had Kitty found to say about him that was of interest to the entire country, that she didn't want him to know about?

Anger overrode his helplessness. Kitty could be vicious. He hadn't seen her vicious side in years, but he knew it was there. He remembered the time he'd stood behind the half-open front door when fifteen-year-old Kitty sat hunched on the front steps with one of her few friends, a homely blonde who wore white lipstick and a white leather jacket. He had come to the door to view the weather and say something to the girls, but they were muttering so intently that curiosity got the better of him, and he hung back a moment to listen. "Well, at least your mom's smart," said Kitty. "My mom's not only a bitch, she's stupid."

This after the lullabies and special times! It wasn't just an isolated incident, either; every time he'd come home from work, his wife had something bad to say about Kitty. She hadn't set the table until she had been asked four times. She'd gone to Lois's house instead of coming straight home like she'd been told to do. She'd worn a dress to school that was short enough to show the tops of her panty hose.

By the time Kitty came to dinner, looking as if she'd been doing slave labor all day, he would be mad at her. He couldn't help it. Here was his wife doing her damnedest to raise a family and cook dinner, and here was this awful kid looking ugly, acting mean, and not setting the table. It seemed unreasonable that she should turn out so badly after taking up so much of their time. Her afflicted expression made him angry too. What had anybody ever done to her?

He sat forward and gently gnawed the insides of his mouth as he listened to the dying girl in *La Bohème*. He saw his wife's car pull into the driveway. He walked to the back door, almost wringing his hands, and waited for her to come through the door. When she did, he snatched the grocery bag from her arms and said, "Give me the keys." She stood openmouthed in the stairwell, looking at him with idiotic consternation. "Give me the keys!"

"What is it, Stew? What's happened?"

"I'll tell you when I get back."

25

30

He got in the car and became part of it, this panting mobile case propelling him through the incredibly complex and fast-moving world of other people, their houses, their children, their dogs, their lives. He wasn't usually so aware of this unpleasant sense of disconnection between him and everyone else, but he had the feeling that it had been there all along, underneath what he thought about most of the time. It was ironic that it should rear up so visibly at a time when there was in fact a mundane yet invasive and horribly real connection between him and everyone else in Wayne County: the hundreds of copies of *Self* magazine sitting in countless drugstores, bookstores, groceries, and libraries. It was as if there were a tentacle plugged into the side of the car, linking him with the random humans who picked up the magazine, possibly his very neighbors. He stopped at a crowded intersection, feeling like an ant in an enemy swarm.

Kitty had projected herself out of the house and into this swarm very early, ostensibly because life with him and Marsha had been so awful. Well, it had been awful, but because of Kitty, not them. As if it weren't enough to be sullen and dull, she turned into a lesbian. Kids followed her down the street, jeering at her. Somebody dropped her books in a toilet. She got into a fistfight. Their neighbors gave them looks. This reaction seemed only to steel Kitty's grip on her new identity; it made her romanticize herself, like the kid she was. She wrote poems about heroic women warriors, she brought home strange books and magazines, which, among other things, seemed to glorify prostitutes. Marsha looked for them and threw them away. Kitty screamed at her, the tendons leaping out on her slender neck. He punched Kitty and knocked her down. Marsha tried to stop him, and he yelled at her. Kitty jumped up and leapt between them, as if to defend her mother. He grabbed her and shook her, but he could not shake the conviction off her face.

Most of the time, though, they continued as always, eating dinner together, watching TV, making jokes. That was the worst thing; he would look at Kitty and see his daughter, now familiar in her withdrawn sullenness, and feel comfort and affection. Then he would remember that she was a lesbian, and a morass of complication and wrongness would come down between them, making it impossible for him to see her. Then she would just be Kitty again. He hated it.

35   She ran away at sixteen, and the police found her in the apartment of an eighteen-year-old bodybuilder named Dolores, who had a naked woman tattooed on her sinister bicep. Marsha made them put her in a mental hospital so psychiatrists could observe her, but he hated the psychiatrists—mean, supercilious sons of bitches who delighted in the trick question—so he took her out. She finished school, and they told her if she wanted to leave it was all right with them. She didn't waste any time getting out of the house.

She moved into an apartment near Detroit with a girl named George and took a job at a home for retarded kids. She would appear for visits with a huge bag of laundry every few weeks. She was thin and neurotically muscular, her body having the look of a fighting dog on a leash. She cut her hair like a boy's and wore black sunglasses, black leather half-gloves, and leather belts. The only remnant of her beauty was her erect, martial carriage and her efficient movements; she walked through a room like the commander of a guerrilla force. She would sit at the dining room table with Marsha, drinking tea and having a laconic verbal conversation, her body speaking its precise martial language while the washing machine droned from the utility room, and he wandered in and out, trying to make sense of what she said. Sometimes she would stay into the evening, to eat dinner and watch *All in the Family*. Then Marsha would send her home with a jar of homemade tapioca pudding or a bag of apples and oranges.

One day, instead of a visit they got a letter postmarked San Francisco. She had left George, she said. She listed strange details about her current environment and was vague about how she was supporting herself. He had nightmares about Kitty, with her brave, proudly muscular little body, lost among big fleshy women who danced naked in go-go bars and took drugs with needles, terrible women whom his confused, romantic daughter invested with oppressed heroism and intensely female glamour. He got up at night and stumbled into the bathroom for stomach medicine, the familiar darkness of the house heavy with menacing images that pressed about him, images he saw reflected in his own expression when he turned on the bathroom light over the mirror.

Then one year she came home for Christmas. She came into the house with her luggage and a shopping bag of gifts for them, and he saw that she was beautiful again. It was a beauty that both offended and titillated his senses. Her short, spiky hair was streaked with purple, her dainty mouth was lipsticked, her nose and ears were pierced with amethyst and dangling silver. Her face had opened in thousands of petals. Her eyes shone with quick perception as she put down her bag, and he knew that she had seen him see her beauty. She moved toward him with fluid hips; she embraced him for the first time in years. He felt her live, little body against his, and his heart pulsed a message of blood and love. "Merry Christmas, Daddy," she said.

Her voice was husky and coarse; it reeked of knowledge and confidence. Her T-shirt said "Chicks With Balls." She was twenty-two years old.

She stayed for a week, discharging her strange jangling beauty into the house and changing the molecules of its air. She talked about the girls she shared an apartment with, her job at a coffee shop, how Californians were different from Michiganders. She talked about her friends: Lorraine, who was so pretty men fell off their bicycles as they twisted their bodies for a better look at her; Judy, a martial arts expert; and Meredith, who was raising a child with her husband, Angela. She talked of poetry readings, ceramics classes, workshops on piercing.

40

He realized, as he watched her, that she was now doing things that were as bad as or worse than the things that had made him angry at her five years before, yet they didn't quarrel. It seemed that a large white space existed between him and her, and that it was impossible to enter this space or to argue across it. Besides, she might never come back if he yelled at her.

Instead, he watched her, puzzling at the metamorphosis she had undergone. First she had been a beautiful, happy child turned homely, snotty, miserable adolescent. From there she had become a martinet girl with the eyes of a stifled pervert. Now she was a vibrant imp, living, it seemed, in a world constructed of topsy-turvy junk pasted with rhinestones. Where had these three different people come from? Not even Marsha, who had spent so much time with her as a child, could trace the genesis of the new Kitty from the old one. Sometimes he bitterly reflected that he and Marsha weren't even real parents anymore but bereft old people rattling around in a house, connected not to a real child who was going to college, or who at least had some kind of understandable life, but to a changeling who was the product of only their most obscure quirks, a being who came from recesses that neither of them suspected they'd had.

There were only a few cars in the parking lot. He wheeled through it with pointless deliberation before parking near the drugstore. He spent irritating seconds searching for *Self*, until he realized that its airbrushed cover girl was grinning right at him. He stormed the table of contents, then headed for the back of the magazine. "Speak Easy" was written sideways across the top of the page in round turquoise letters. At the bottom was his daughter's name in a little box. "Kitty Thorne is a ceramic artist living in South Carolina." His hands were trembling.

It was hard for him to rationally ingest the beginning paragraphs, which seemed, incredibly, to be about a phone conversation they'd had some time ago about the emptiness and selfishness of people who have sex but don't get married and have children. A few phrases stood out clearly: ". . . my father may love me but he doesn't love the way I live." ". . . even more complicated because I'm gay." ". . . because it still hurts me."

45   For reasons he didn't understand, he felt a nervous smile tremble under his skin. He suppressed it.

"This hurt has its roots deep in our relationship, starting, I think, when I was a teenager."

He was horribly aware of being in public, so he paid for the thing and took it out to the car. He drove slowly to another spot in the lot, as far away from the drugstore as possible, picked up the magazine, and began again. She described the "terrible difficulties" between him and her. She recounted, briefly and with hieroglyphic politeness, the fighting, the running away, the return, the tacit reconciliation.

"There is an emotional distance that we have both accepted and chosen to work around, hoping the occasional contact—love, anger, something—will get through."

He put the magazine down and looked out the window. It was near dusk; most of the stores in the little mall were closed. There were only two other cars in the parking lot, and a big, slow, frowning woman with two grocery bags was getting ready to drive one away. He was parked before a weedy piece of land at the edge of the lot. In it were rough, picky weeds spread out like big green tarantulas, young yellow dandelions, frail old dandelions, and bunches of tough blue chickweed. Even in his distress he vaguely appreciated the beauty of the blue weeds against the cool white-and-gray sky. For a moment the sound of insects comforted him. Images of Kitty passed through his memory with terrible speed: her nine-year-old forehead bent over her dish of ice cream, her tiny nightgowned form ran up the stairs, her ringed hand brushed her face, the keys on her belt jiggled as she walked her slow blue-jeaned walk away from the house. Gone, all gone.

50   The article went on to describe how Kitty hung up the phone feeling frustrated and then listed all the things she could've said to him to let him know how hurt she was, paving the way for "real communication"; it was all in ghastly talk-show language. He was unable to put these words together with the Kitty he had last seen lounging around the house. She was twenty-eight now, and she no longer dyed her hair or wore jewels in her nose. Her demeanor was serious, bookish, almost old-maidish. Once, he'd overheard her saying to Marsha, "So then this Italian girl gives me the once-over and says to Joanne, "'You 'ang around with too many Wasp.' And I said, 'I'm not a Wasp, I'm white trash.'"

"Speak for yourself," he'd said.

"If the worst occurred and my father was unable to respond to me in kind, I still would have done a good thing. I would have acknowledged my own needs and created the possibility to connect with what therapists call 'the good parent' in myself."

"Well, if that was the kind of thing she was going to say to him, he was relieved she hadn't said it. But if she hadn't said it to him, why was she saying it to the rest of the country?

He turned on the radio. It sang: "Try to remember, and if you remember, then follow, follow." He turned it off. The interrupted dream echoed faintly. He closed his eyes. When he was nine or ten, an uncle of his had told him, "Everybody makes his own world. You see what you want to see and hear what you want to hear. You can do it right now. If you blink ten times and then close your eyes real tight, you can see anything you want to see in front of you." He'd tried it, rather halfheartedly, and hadn't seen anything but the vague suggestion of a yellowish-white ball moving creepily through the dark. At the time, he'd thought it was perhaps because he hadn't tried hard enough.

He had told Kitty to do the same thing, or something like it, when she was eight or nine. They were sitting on the back porch in striped lawn chairs, holding hands and watching the fireflies turn on and off.

She closed her eyes for a long time. Then very seriously, she said, "I see big balls of color, like shaggy flowers. They're pink and red and turquoise. I see an island with palm trees and pink rocks. There's dolphins and mermaids swimming in the water around it." He'd been almost awed by her belief in this impossible vision. Then he was sad, because she would never see what she wanted to see. Then he thought she was sort of stupid, even for a kid.

His memory flashed back to his boyhood. He was walking down the middle of the street at dusk, sweating lightly after a basketball game. There were crickets and the muted barks of dogs and the low, affirming mumble of people on their front porches. Securely held by the warm night and its sounds, he felt an exquisite blend of happiness and sorrow that life could contain this perfect moment, and a sadness that he would soon arrive home, walk into bright light, and be on his way into the next day, with its loud noise and alarming possibility. He resolved to hold this evening walk in his mind forever, to imprint in a permanent place all the sensations that occurred to him as he walked by the Oatlanders' house, so that he could always take them out and look at them. He dimly recalled feeling that if he could successfully do that, he could stop time and hold it.

He knew he had to go home soon. He didn't want to talk about the article with Marsha, but the idea of sitting in the house with her and not talking about it was hard to bear. He imagined the conversation grinding into being, a future conversation with Kitty gestating within it. The conversation was a vast, complex machine like those that occasionally appeared in his dreams; if he could only pull the switch, everything would be all right, but he felt too stupefied by the weight and complexity of the thing to do so. Besides, in this case, everything might not be all right. He put the magazine under his seat and started the car.

Marsha was in her armchair, reading. She looked up, and the expression on her face seemed like the result of internal conflict as complicated and strong as his own, but cross-pulled in different directions, uncomprehending of him and what he knew. In his mind, he withdrew from her so quickly that for a moment the familiar room was fraught with the inexplicable horror of a banal nightmare. Then the ordinariness of the scene threw the extraordinary event of the day into relief, and he felt so angry and bewildered he could've howled.

"Everything all right, Stew?" asked Marsha.

"No, nothing is all right. I'm a tired old man in a shitty world I don't want to be in. I go out there, it's like walking on knives. Everything is an attack—the ugliness, the cheapness, the rudeness, everything." He sensed her withdrawing from him into her own world of disgruntlement, her lips drawn together in that look of exasperated perseverance she'd gotten from her mother. Like Kitty, like everyone else, she was leaving him. "I don't have a real daughter, and I don't have a real wife who's here with me, because she's too busy running around on some—"

"We've been through this before. We agreed I could—"

"That was different! That was when we had two cars!" His voice tore through his throat in a jagged whiplash and came out a cracked half scream. "I don't have a car, remember? That means I'm stranded, all alone for hours, and Norm Pisarro can call me up and casually tell me that my lesbian daughter has just betrayed me in a national magazine and what do I think about that?" He wanted to punch the wall until his hand was bloody. He wanted Kitty to see the blood. Marsha's expression broke into soft, openmouthed consternation. The helplessness of it made his anger seem huge and terrible, then impotent and helpless itself. He sat down on the couch and, instead of anger, felt pain.

"What did Kitty do? What happened? What does Norm have—"

65   "She wrote an article in *Self* magazine about being a lesbian and her problems and something to do with me. I don't know; I could barely read the crap."

Marsha looked down at her nails.

He looked at her and saw the aged beauty of her ivory skin, sagging under the weight of her years and her cockeyed bifocals, the emotional receptivity of her face, the dark down on her upper lip, the childish pearl buttons of her sweater, only the top button done.

"I'm surprised at Norm, that he would call you like that."

"Oh, who the hell knows what he thought." His heart was soothed and slowed by her words, even if they didn't address its real unhappiness.

70   "Here," she said. "Let me rub your shoulders."

He allowed her to approach him, and they sat sideways on the couch, his weight balanced on the edge by his awkwardly planted legs, she sitting primly on one hip with her legs tightly crossed. The discomfort of the position negated the practical value of the massage, but he welcomed her touch. Marsha had strong, intelligent hands that spoke to his muscles of deep safety and love and the delight of physical life. In her effort, she leaned close, and her sweatered breast touched him, releasing his tension almost against his will. Through half-closed eyes he observed her sneakers on the floor—he could not quite get over this phenomenon of adult women wearing what had been boys' shoes—in the dim light, one toe atop the other as though cuddling, their laces in pretty disorganization.

Poor Kitty. It hadn't really been so bad that she hadn't set the table on time. He couldn't remember why he and Marsha had been so angry over the table. Unless it was Kitty's coldness, her always turning away, her sarcastic voice. But she was a teenager, and that's what teenagers did. Well, it was too bad, but it couldn't be helped now.

He thought of his father. That was too bad too, and nobody was writing articles about that. There had been a distance between them, so great and so absolute that the word "distance" seemed inadequate to describe it. But that was probably because he had known his father only when he was a very young child; if his father had lived longer, perhaps they would've become closer. He could recall his father's face clearly only at the breakfast table, where it appeared silent and still except for lip and jaw motions, comforting in its constancy. His father ate his oatmeal with one hand working the spoon, one elbow on the table, eyes down, sometimes his other hand holding a cold rag to his head, which always hurt with what seemed to be a noble pain, willingly taken on with his duties as a husband and father. He had loved to stare at the big face with its deep lines and long earlobes, its thin lips and loose, loopily chewing jaws. Its almost godlike stillness and expressionlessness filled him with admiration and reassurance, until one day his father slowly looked up from his cereal, met his eyes, and said, "Stop staring at me, you little shit."

In the other memories, his father was a large, heavy body with a vague oblong face. He saw him sleeping in the armchair in the living room, his large, hairy-knuckled hands grazing the floor. He saw him walking up the front walk with the quick, clipped steps that he always used coming home from work, the straight-backed choppy gait that gave the big body an awesome mechanicalness. His shirt was wet under the arms, his head was down, the eyes were abstracted but alert, as though keeping careful watch on the outside world in case something nasty came at him while he attended to the more important business inside.

"The good parent in yourself." 75

What did the well-meaning idiots who thought of these phrases mean by them? When a father dies, he is gone; there is no tiny, smiling daddy who appears, waving happily, in a secret pocket in your chest. Some kinds of loss are absolute. And no amount of self-realization or self-expression will change that.

As if she had heard him, Marsha urgently pressed her weight into her hands and applied all her strength to relaxing his muscles. Her sweat and scented deodorant filtered through her sweater, which added its muted woolliness to her smell. "All righty!" She rubbed his shoulders and briskly patted him. He reached back and touched her hand in thanks.

Across from where they sat had once been a red chair, and in it had once sat Kitty, looking away from him, her fist hiding her face.

"You're a lesbian? Fine," he said. "You mean nothing to me. You walk out that door, it doesn't matter. And if you come back in, I'm going to spit in your face. I don't care if I'm on my deathbed, I'll still have the energy to spit in your face."

She did not move when he said that. Tears ran over her fist and down her arm, but 80 she didn't look at him.

Marsha's hands lingered on him for a moment. Then she moved and sat away from him on the couch. [1997]

QUESTIONS

1. Why does Gaitskill choose to introduce the main character as he is napping and dreaming?
2. What is the significance of Kitty Thorne's article being published in a magazine titled *Self*?
3. Why is the father ashamed of his daughter?
4. What does the main character's memory of his father contribute to the story?
5. What is the tone of the story? Does the narrator sympathize with Stew Thorne?

RESPONSES

1. Using a psychological approach, write an essay that explains what role a character plays in Stew's psyche, such as the wife or the friend who telephones.
2. Compare the parent-child relationships in this story and in Wallace's "Suicide as a Sort of Present."

GABRIEL GARCÍA MÁRQUEZ

Gabriel García Márquez (b. 1928) was born in Aracotoca, a remote village on the Columbian seacoast. He studied at the University of Bogotá until it was closed by civil war. He continued his studies at the University of Cartagena and contributed articles to a local newspaper. Subsequently, he traveled widely as a journalist and later moved to Mexico City. The publication of *One Hundred Years of Solitude* (1967) brought him worldwide fame. He received the Nobel Prize in 1982. His recent novels include *Love in the Time of Cholera* (1988) and *The General in His Labyrinth* (1990). *News of a Kidnapping* (1997) is the true story of ten victims of the Columbian Medellin drug cartel. *Living to Tell the Tale* (2003) is an autobiographical work, and *Leaf Storm, and Other Stories* and *No One Writes to the Colonies, and Other Stories* appeared in 2005.

Tuesday Siesta

The train emerged from the quivering tunnel of sandy rocks, began to cross the symmetrical, interminable banana plantations, and the air became humid and they couldn't feel the sea breeze any more. A stifling blast of smoke came in the car window. On the narrow road parallel to the railway there were oxcarts loaded with green bunches of bananas. Beyond the road, in uncultivated spaces set at odd intervals there were offices with electric fans, red-brick buildings, and residences with chairs and little white tables on the terraces among dusty palm trees and rosebushes. It was eleven in the morning, and the heat had not yet begun.

"You'd better close the window," the woman said. "Your hair will get full of soot."

The girl tried to, but the shade wouldn't move because of the rust.

They were the only passengers in the lone third-class car. Since the smoke of the locomotive kept coming through the window, the girl left her seat and put down the only things they had with them: a plastic sack with some things to eat and a bouquet of flowers wrapped in newspaper. She sat on the opposite seat, away from the window, facing her mother. They were both in severe and poor mourning clothes.

5   The girl was twelve years old, and it was the first time she'd ever been on a train. The woman seemed too old to be her mother, because of the blue veins on her eyelids and her small, soft, and shapeless body, in a dress cut like a cassock. She was riding

with her spinal column braced firmly against the back of the seat, and held a peeling patent-leather handbag in her lap with both hands. She bore the conscientious serenity of someone accustomed to poverty.

By twelve the heat had begun. The train stopped for ten minutes to take on water at a station where there was no town. Outside, in the mysterious silence of the plantations, the shadows seemed clean. But the still air inside the car smelled like untanned leather. The train did not pick up speed. It stopped at two identical towns with wooden houses painted bright colors. The woman's head nodded and she sank into sleep. The girl took off her shoes. Then she went to the washroom to put the bouquet of flowers in some water.

When she came back to her seat, her mother was waiting to eat. She gave her a piece of cheese, half a corn-meal pancake, and a cookie, and took an equal portion out of the plastic sack for herself. While they ate, the train crossed an iron bridge very slowly and passed a town just like the ones before, except that in this one there was a crowd in the plaza. A band was playing a lively tune under the oppressive sun. At the other side of town the plantations ended in a plain which was cracked from the drought.

The woman stopped eating.

"Put on your shoes," she said.

The girl looked outside. She saw nothing but the deserted plain, where the train   10
began to pick up speed again, but she put the last piece of cookie into the sack and quickly put on her shoes. The woman gave her a comb.

"Comb your hair," she said.

The train whistle began to blow while the girl was combing her hair. The woman dried the sweat from her neck and wiped the oil from her face with her fingers. When the girl stopped combing, the train was passing the outlying houses of a town larger but sadder than the earlier ones.

"If you feel like doing anything, do it now," said the woman. "Later, don't take a drink anywhere even if you're dying of thirst. Above all, no crying."

The girl nodded her head. A dry, burning wind came in the window, together with the locomotive's whistle and the clatter of the old cars. The woman folded the plastic bag with the rest of the food and put it in the handbag. For a moment a complete picture of the town, on that bright August Tuesday, shone in the window. The girl wrapped the flowers in the soaking-wet newspapers, moved a little farther away from the window, and stared at her mother. She received a pleasant expression in return. The train began to whistle and slowed down. A moment later it stopped.

There was no one at the station. On the other side of the street, on the sidewalk shaded by the almond trees, only the pool hall was open. The town was floating in the heat.   15
The woman and the girl got off the train and crossed the abandoned station—the tiles split apart by the grass growing up between—and over to the shady side of the street.

It was almost two. At that hour, weighted down by drowsiness, the town was taking a siesta. The stores, the town offices, the public school were closed at eleven, and didn't reopen until a little before four, when the train went back. Only the hotel across from the station, with its bar and pool hall, and the telegraph office at one side of the plaza stayed open. The houses, most of them built on the banana company's model, had their doors locked from inside and their blinds drawn. In some of them it was so hot that the residents ate lunch on the patio. Others leaned a chair against the wall, in the shade of the almond trees, and took their siesta right out in the street.

Keeping to the protective shade of the almond trees, the woman and the girl entered the town without disturbing the siesta. They went directly to the parish house. The

woman scratched the metal grating on the door with her fingernail, waited a moment, and scratched again. An electric fan was humming inside. They did not hear the
steps. They hardly heard the slight creaking of a door, and immediately a cautious
voice, right next to the metal grating: "Who is it?" The woman tried to see through
the grating.

"I need the priest," she said.

"He's sleeping now."

20   "It's an emergency," the woman insisted.

Her voice showed a calm determination.

The door was opened a little way, noiselessly, and a plump, older woman appeared,
with very pale skin and hair the color of iron. Her eyes seemed too small behind her
thick eyeglasses.

"Come in," she said, and opened the door all the way.

They entered a room permeated with an old smell of flowers. The woman of the
house led them to a wooden bench and signaled them to sit down. The girl did so, but
her mother remained standing, absent-mindedly, with both hands clutching the handbag. No noise could be heard above the electric fan.

25   The woman of the house reappeared at the door at the far end of the room. "He says
you should come back after three," she said in a very low voice. "He just lay down five
minutes ago."

"The train leaves at three-thirty," said the woman.

It was a brief and self-assured reply, but her voice remained pleasant, full of undertones. The woman of the house smiled for the first time.

"All right," she said.

When the far door closed again, the woman sat down next to her daughter. The
narrow waiting room was poor, neat, and clean. On the other side of the wooden railing which divided the room, there was a worktable, a plain one with an oilcloth cover,
and on top of the table a primitive typewriter next to a vase of flowers. The parish
records were beyond. You could see that it was an office kept in order by a spinster.

30   The far door opened and this time the priest appeared, cleaning his glasses with a
handkerchief. Only when he put them on was it evident that he was the brother of the
woman who had opened the door.

"How can I help you?" he asked.

"The keys to the cemetery," said the woman.

The girl was seated with the flowers in her lap and her feet crossed under the bench.
The priest looked at her, then looked at the woman, and then through the wire mesh
of the window at the bright, cloudless sky.

"In this heat," he said. "You could have waited until the sun went down."

35   The woman moved her head silently. The priest crossed to the other side of the railing, took out of the cabinet a notebook covered in oilcloth, a wooden penholder, and
an inkwell, and sat down at the table. There was more than enough hair on his hands
to account for what was missing on his head.

"Which grave are you going to visit?" he asked.

"Carlos Centeno's," said the woman.

"Who?"

"Carlos Centeno," the woman repeated.

40   "He's the thief who was killed here last week," said the woman in the same tone
of voice. "I am his mother."

The priest scrutinized her. She stared at him with quiet self-control, and the Father
blushed. He lowered his head and began to write. As he filled the page, he asked the

woman to identify herself, and she replied unhesitatingly, with precise details, as if she were reading them. The Father began to sweat. The girl unhooked the buckle of her left shoe, slipped her heel out of it, and rested it on the bench rail. She did the same with the right one.

It had all started the Monday of the previous week, at three in the morning, a few blocks from there. Rebecca, a lonely widow who lived in a house full of odds and ends, heard above the sound of the drizzling rain someone trying to force the front door from outside. She got up, rummaged around in her closet for an ancient revolver that no one had fired since the days of Colonel Aureliano Buendía, and went into the living room without turning on the lights. Orienting herself not so much by the noise at the lock as by a terror developed in her by twenty-eight years of loneliness, she fixed in her imagination not only the spot where the door was but also the exact height of the lock. She clutched the weapon with both hands, closed her eyes, and squeezed the trigger. It was the first time in her life that she had fired a gun. Immediately after the explosion, she could hear nothing except the murmur of the drizzle on the galvanized roof. Then she heard a little metallic bump on the cement porch, and a very low voice, pleasant but terribly exhausted: "Ah, Mother." The man they found dead in front of the house in the morning, his nose blown to bits, wore a flannel shirt with colored stripes, everyday pants with a rope for a belt, and was barefoot. No one in town knew him.

"So his name was Carlos Centeno," murmured the Father when he finished writing.

"Centeno Ayala," said the woman. "He was my only boy."

The priest went back to the cabinet. Two big rusty keys hung on the inside of the door; the girl imagined, as her mother had when she was a girl and as the priest himself must have imagined at some time, that they were Saint Peter's keys. He took them down, put them on the open notebook on the railing, and pointed with his forefinger to a place on the page he had just written, looking at the woman.

"Sign here."

The woman scribbled her name, holding the handbag under her arm. The girl picked up the flowers, came to the railing shuffling her feet, and watched her mother attentively.

The priest sighed.

"Didn't you ever try to get him on the right track?"

The woman answered when she finished signing.

"He was a very good man."

The priest looked first at the woman and then at the girl, and realized with a kind of pious amazement that they were not about to cry. The woman continued in the same tone:

"I told him never to steal anything that anyone needed to eat, and he minded me. On the other hand, before, when he used to box, he used to spend three days in bed, exhausted from being punched."

"All his teeth had to be pulled out," interrupted the girl.

"That's right," the woman agreed. "Every mouthful I ate those days tasted of the beatings my son got on Saturday nights."

"God's will is inscrutable," said the Father.

But he said it without much conviction, partly because experience had made him a little skeptical and partly because of the heat. He suggested that they cover their heads to guard against sunstroke. Yawning, and now almost completely asleep, he gave them instructions about how to find Carlos Centeno's grave. When they came back, they didn't have to knock. They should put the key under the door; and in the same place, if they could, they should put an offering for the Church. The woman listened to his directions with great attention, but thanked him without smiling.

The Father had noticed that there was someone looking inside, his nose pressed against the metal grating, even before he opened the door to the street. Outside was a group of children. When the door was opened wide, the children scattered. Ordinarily, at that hour there was no one in the street. Now there were not only children. There were groups of people under the almond trees. The Father scanned the street swimming in the heat and then he understood. Softly, he closed the door again.

"Wait a moment," he said without looking at the woman.

60   His sister appeared at the far door with a black jacket over her nightshirt and her hair down over her shoulders. She looked silently at the Father.

"What was it?" he asked.

"The people have noticed," murmured his sister.

"You'd better go out by the door to the patio," said the Father.

"It's the same there," said his sister. "Everybody is at the windows."

65   The woman seemed not to have understood until then. She tried to look into the street through the metal grating. Then she took the bouquet of flowers from the girl and began to move toward the door. The girl followed her.

"Wait until the sun goes down," said the Father.

"You'll melt," said his sister, motionless at the back of the room. "Wait and I'll lend you a parasol."

"Thank you," replied the woman. "We're all right this way."

She took the girl by the hand and went into the street.   [1972]

QUESTIONS

1. How does the natural setting reinforce the theme and meaning of the story?
2. How are the mother and daughter characterized by their demeanor on the train ride to the village?
3. How is the muted tone of the narrator suited to the action?
4. What does the conduct of the priest and his sister reveal about the village of which they are a part?
5. What is the meaning of the title?

RESPONSES

1. Write an essay exploring how there may be multiple interpretations of the story of Carlos Centeno's death.
2. Compare García Márquez's story to Eudora Welty's "A Worn Path."
3. Write your own story about bravery and loyalty to loved ones.

WILLIAM GIBSON

William Gibson (b. 1948) was born in South Carolina, but in his early years moved often, following his father, who worked as a manager of a construction firm. When Gibson was still young, his father died accidentally. Gibson was then educated in a private boys' boarding school in Arizona. He later graduated from the University of British Columbia. His first novel, *Neuromancer* (1984), won the Hugo Award, the Nebula Award, and the Philip K. Dick Award, and is considered one of the sources for the subgenre of science fiction called "cyberpunk." His other works include *Count Zero* (1986), *Idoru* (1996), *All Tomorrow's Parties* (1999), and *Pattern Recognition* (2003). His short stories are published in *Burning Chrome* (1986).

Johnny Mnemonic

I put the shotgun in an Adidas bag and padded it out with four pairs of tennis socks, not my style at all, but that was what I was aiming for: If they think you're crude, go technical; if they think you're technical, go crude. I'm a very technical boy. So I decided to get as crude as possible. These days, though, you have to be pretty technical before you can even aspire to crudeness. I'd had to turn both these twelve-gauge shells from brass stock, on a lathe, and then load them myself; I'd had to dig up an old microfiche with instructions for hand-loading cartridges; I'd had to build a lever-action press to seat the primers—all very tricky. But I knew they'd work.

The meet was set for the Drome at 2300, but I rode the tube three stops past the closest platform and walked back. Immaculate procedure.

I checked myself out in the chrome siding of a coffee kiosk, your basic sharp-faced Caucasoid with a ruff of stiff, dark hair. The girls at Under the Knife were big on Sony Mao, and it was getting harder to keep them from adding the chic suggestion of epicanthic folds. It probably wouldn't fool Ralfi Face, but it might get me next to his table.

The Drome is a single narrow space with a bar down one side and tables along the other, thick with pimps and handlers and an arcane array of dealers. The Magnetic Dog Sisters were on the door that night, and I didn't relish trying to get out past them if things didn't work out. They were two meters tall and thin as greyhounds. One was black and the other white, but aside from that they were as nearly identical as cosmetic surgery could make them. They'd been lovers for years and were bad news in a tussle. I was never quite sure which one had originally been male.

"They pumped out the cellar. The Chac-Mool is covered with slime. It makes him 15 look grotesque; the whole sculpture seems to be suffering from a kind of green erysipelas, with the exception of the eyes. I'll scrape off the moss Sunday. Pepe suggested I move to an apartment on an upper floor, to prevent any more of these aquatic tragedies. But I can't leave my house; it's obviously more than I need, a little gloomy in its turn-of-the-century style, but it's the only inheritance, the only memory, I have left of my parents. I don't know how I'd feel if I saw a soda fountain with a jukebox in the cellar and an interior decorator's shop on the ground floor."

"Used a trowel to scrape the Chac-Mool. The moss now seemed almost a part of the stone; it took more than an hour and it was six in the evening before I finished. I couldn't see anything in the darkness, but I ran my hand over the outlines of the stone. With every stroke, the stone seemed to become softer. I couldn't believe it; it felt like dough. That dealer in La Lagunilla has really swindled me. His 'preColumbian sculpture' is nothing but plaster, and the dampness is ruining it. I've covered it with some rags and will bring it upstairs tomorrow before it dissolves completely."

"The rags are on the floor. Incredible. Again I felt the Chac-Mool. It's firm, but not stone. I don't want to write this: the texture of the torso feels a little like flesh: I press it like rubber, and feel something coursing through that recumbent figure . . . I went down again later at night. No doubt about it: the Chac-Mool has hair on its arms."

"This kind of thing has never happened to me before. I fouled up my work in the office: I sent out a payment that hadn't been authorized, and the director had to call it to my attention. I think I may even have been rude to my coworkers. I'm going to have to see a doctor, find out whether it's my imagination, whether I'm delirious, or what . . . and get rid of that damned Chac-Mool."

Up to this point I recognized Filiberto's hand, the large, rounded letters I'd seen on so many memoranda and forms. The entry for August 25 seemed to have been written by a different person. At times it was the writing of a child, each letter laboriously separated; other times, nervous, trailing into illegibility. Three days are blank, and then the narrative continues:

"It's all so natural, though normally we believe only in what's real . . . but this is real, 20 more real than anything I've ever known. A water cooler is real, more than real, because we fully realize its existence, or being, when some joker puts something in the water to turn it red . . . An ephemeral smoke ring is real, a grotesque image in a funhouse mirror is real; aren't all deaths, present and forgotten, real . . .? If a man passes through paradise in a dream, and is handed a flower as proof of having been there, and if when he awakens he finds this flower in his hand . . . then . . .? Reality: one day it was shattered into a thousand pieces, its head rolled in one direction and its tail in another, and all we have is one of the pieces from the gigantic body. A free and fictitious ocean, real only when it is imprisoned in a seashell. Until three days ago, my reality was of such a degree it would be erased today; it was reflex action, routine, memory, carapace. And then, like the earth that one day trembles to remind us of its power, of the death to come, recriminating against me for having turned my back on life, an orphaned reality we always knew was there presents itself, jolting us in order to become living present. Again I believed it to be imagination: the Chac-Mool, soft and elegant, had changed color overnight; yellow, almost golden, it seemed to suggest it was a god, at

5   Ralfi was sitting at his usual table. Owing me a lot of money. I had hundreds of megabytes stashed in my head on an idiot/savant basis, information I had no conscious access to. Ralfi had left it there. He hadn't, however, come back for it. Only Ralfi could retrieve the data, with a code phrase of his own invention. I'm not cheap to begin with, but my overtime on storage is astronomical. And Ralfi had been very scarce.

     Then I'd heard that Ralfi Face wanted to put out a contract on me. So I'd arranged to meet him in the Drome, but I'd arranged it as Edward Bax, clandestine importer, late of Rio and Peking.

     The Drome stank of biz, a metallic tang of nervous tension. Muscle-boys scattered through the crowd were flexing stock parts at one another and trying on thin, cold grins, some of them so lost under superstructures of muscle graft that their outlines weren't really human.

     Pardon me. Pardon me, friends. Just Eddie Bax here, Fast Eddie the Importer, with his professionally nondescript gym bag, and please ignore this slit, just wide enough to admit his right hand.

     Ralfi wasn't alone. Eighty kilos of blond California beef perched alertly in the chair next to his, martial arts written all over him.

10   Fast Eddie Bax was in the chair opposite them before the beef's hands were off the table. "You black belt?" I asked eagerly. He nodded, blue eyes running an automatic scanning pattern between my eyes and my hands. "Me, too," I said. "Got mine here in the bag." And I shoved my hand through the slit and thumbed the safety off. Click. "Double twelve-gauge with the triggers wired together."

     "That's a gun," Ralfi said, putting a plump, restraining hand on his boy's taut blue nylon chest. "Johnny has an antique firearm in his bag." So much for Edward Bax.

     I guess he'd always been Ralfi Something or Other, but he owed his acquired surname to a singular vanity. Built something like an overripe pear, he'd worn the once-famous face of Christian White for twenty years—Christian White of the Aryan Reggae Band, Sony Mao to his generation, and final champion of race rock. I'm a whiz at trivia.

     Christian White: classic pop face with a singer's high-definition muscles, chiseled cheekbones. Angelic in one light, handsomely depraved in another. But Ralfi's eyes lived behind that face, and they were small and cold and black.

     "Please," he said, "let's work this out like businessmen." His voice was marked by a horrible prehensile sincerity, and the corners of his beautiful Christian White mouth were always wet. "Lewis here," nodding in the beefboy's direction, "is a meatball." Lewis took this impassively, looking like something built from a kit. "You aren't a meatball, Johnny."

15   "Sure I am, Ralfi, a nice meatball chock-full of implants where you can store your dirty laundry while you go off shopping for people to kill me. From my end of this bag, Ralfi, it looks like you've got some explaining to do."

     "It's this last batch of product, Johnny." He sighed deeply. "In my role as broker—"

     "Fence," I corrected.

     "As broker, I'm usually very careful as to sources."

     "You buy only from those who steal the best. Got it."

20   He sighed again. "I try," he said wearily, "not to buy from fools. This time, I'm afraid, I've done that." Third sigh was the cue for Lewis to trigger the neural disruptor they'd taped under my side of the table.

I put everything I had into curling the index finger of my right hand, but I no longer seemed to be connected to it. I could feel the metal of the gun and the foam-pad tape I'd wrapped around the stubby grip, but my hands were cool wax, distant and inert. I was hoping Lewis was a true meatball, thick enough to go for the gym bag and snag my rigid trigger finger, but he wasn't.

"We've been very worried about you, Johnny. Very worried. You see, that's Yakuza property you have there. A fool took it from them, Johnny. A dead fool."

Lewis giggled.

It all made sense then, an ugly kind of sense, like bags of wet sand settling around my head. Killing wasn't Ralfi's style. Lewis wasn't even Ralfi's style. But he'd got himself stuck between the Sons of the Neon Chrysanthemum and something that belonged to them—or, more likely, something of theirs that belonged to someone else. Ralfi, of course, could use the code phrase to throw me into idiot/savant, and I'd spill their hot program without remembering a single quarter tone. For a fence like Ralfi, that would ordinarily have been enough. But not for the Yakuza. The Yakuza would know about Squids, for one thing, and they wouldn't want to worry about one lifting those dim and permanent traces of their program out of my head. I didn't know very much about Squids, but I'd heard stories, and I made it a point never to repeat them to my clients. No, the Yakuza wouldn't like that; it looked too much like evidence. They hadn't got where they were by leaving evidence around. Or alive.

Lewis was grinning. I think he was visualizing a point just behind my forehead   25
and imagining how he could get there the hard way.

"Hey," said a low voice, feminine, from somewhere behind my right shoulder, "you cowboys sure aren't having too lively a time."

"Pack it, bitch," Lewis said, his tanned face very still. Ralfi looked blank.

"Lighten up. You want to buy some good free base?" She pulled up a chair and quickly sat before either of them could stop her. She was barely inside my fixed field of vision, a thin girl with mirrored glasses, her dark hair cut in a rough shag. She wore black leather, open over a T-shirt slashed diagonally with stripes of red and black. "Eight thou a gram weight."

Lewis snorted his exasperation and tried to slap her out of the chair. Somehow he didn't quite connect, and her hand came up and seemed to brush his wrist as it passed. Bright blood sprayed the table. He was clutching his wrist white-knuckle tight, blood trickling from between his fingers.

But hadn't her hand been empty?   30

He was going to need a tendon stapler. He stood up carefully, without bothering to push his chair back. The chair toppled backward, and he stepped out of my line of sight without a word.

"He better get a medic to look at that," she said. "That's a nasty cut."

"You have no idea," said Ralfi, suddenly sounding very tired, "the depths of shit you have just gotten yourself into."

"No kidding? Mystery. I get real excited by mysteries. Like why your friend here's so quiet. Frozen, like. Or what this thing here is for," and she held up the little control unit that she'd somehow taken from Lewis. Ralfi looked ill.

"You, ah, want maybe a quarter-million to give me that and take a walk?" A fat   35
hand came up to stroke his pale, lean face nervously.

"What I want," she said, snapping her fingers so that the unit spun and glittered, "is work. A job. Your boy hurt his wrist. But a quarter'll do for a retainer."

Ralfi let his breath out explosively and began to laugh, exposing teeth that hadn't been kept up to the Christian White standard. Then she turned the disruptor off.

"Two million," I said.

"My kind of man," she said, and laughed. "What's in the bag?"

40   "A shotgun."

"Crude." It might have been a compliment.

Ralfi said nothing at all.

"Name's Millions. Molly Millions. You want to get out of here, boss? People are starting to stare." She stood up. She was wearing leather jeans the color of dried blood.

And I saw for the first time that the mirrored lenses were surgical inlays, the silver rising smoothly from her high cheekbones, sealing her eyes in their sockets. I saw my new face twinned there.

45   "I'm Johnny," I said. "We're taking Mr. Face with us."

He was outside, waiting. Looking like your standard tourist tech, in plastic zoris and a silly Hawaiian shirt printed with blowups of his firm's most popular microprocessor; a mild little guy, the kind most likely to wind up drunk on sake in a bar that puts out miniature rice crackers with seaweed garnish. He looked like the kind who sing the corporate anthem and cry, who shake hands endlessly with the bartender. And the pimps and the dealers would leave him alone, pegging him as innately conservative. Not up for much, and careful with his credit when he was.

The way I figured it later, they must have amputated part of his left thumb, somewhere behind the first joint, replacing it with a prosthetic tip, and cored the stump, fitting it with a spool and socket molded from one of the Ono-Sendai diamond analogs. Then they'd carefully wound the spool with three meters of monomolecular filament.

Molly got into some kind of exchange with the Magnetic Dog Sisters, giving me a chance to usher Ralfi through the door with the gym bag pressed lightly against the base of his spine. She seemed to know them. I heard the black one laugh.

I glanced up, out of some passing reflex, maybe because I've never got used to it, to the soaring arcs of light and the shadows of the geodesics above them. Maybe that saved me.

50   Ralfi kept walking, but I don't think he was trying to escape. I think he'd already given up. Probably he already had an idea of what we were up against.

I looked back down in time to see him explode.

Playback on full recall shows Ralfi stepping forward as the little tech sidles out of nowhere, smiling. Just a suggestion of a bow, and his left thumb falls off. It's a conjuring trick. The thumb hangs suspended. Mirrors? Wires? And Ralfi stops, his back to us, dark crescents of sweat under the armpits of his pale summer suit. He knows. He must have known. And then the joke-shop thumbtip, heavy as lead, arcs out in a lightning yo-yo trick, and the invisible thread connecting it to the killer's hand passes laterally through Ralfi's skull, just above his eyebrows, whips up, and descends, slicing the pear-shaped torso diagonally from shoulder to rib cage. Cuts so fine that no blood flows until synapses misfire and the first tremors surrender the body to gravity.

Ralfi tumbled apart in a pink cloud of fluids, the three mismatched sections rolling forward onto the tiled pavement. In total silence.

I brought the gym bag up, and my hand convulsed. The recoil nearly broke my wrist.

55   It must have been raining; ribbons of water cascaded from a ruptured geodesic and spattered on the tile behind us. We crouched in the narrow gap between a surgical

boutique and an antique shop. She'd just edged one mirrored eye around the corner to report a single Volks module in front of the Drome, red lights flashing. They were sweeping Ralfi up. Asking questions.

I was covered in scorched white fluff. The tennis socks. The gym bag was a ragged plastic cuff around my wrist. "I don't see how the hell I missed him."

"'Cause he's fast, so fast." She hugged her knees and rocked back and forth on her bootheels. "His nervous system's jacked up. He's factory custom." She grinned and gave a little squeal of delight. "I'm gonna get that boy. Tonight. He's the best, number one, top dollar, state of the art."

"What you're going to get, for this boy's two million, is my ass out of here. Your boyfriend back there was mostly grown in a vat in Chiba City. He's a Yakuza assassin."

"Chiba. Yeah. See, Molly's been Chiba, too." And she showed me her hands, fingers slightly spread. Her fingers were slender, tapered, very white against the polished burgundy nails. Ten blades snicked straight out from their recesses beneath her nails, each one a narrow, double-edged scalpel in pale blue steel.

I'd never spent much time in Nighttown. Nobody there had anything to pay me to remember, and most of them had a lot they paid regularly to forget. Generations of sharpshooters had chipped away at the neon until the maintenance crews gave up. Even at noon the arcs were soot-black against faintest pearl.   60

Where do you go when the world's wealthiest criminal order is feeling for you with calm, distant fingers? Where do you hide from the Yakuza, so powerful that it owns comsats and at least three shuttles? The Yakuza is a true multinational, like ITT and Ono-Sendai. Fifty years before I was born the Yakuza had already absorbed the Triads, the Mafia, the Union Corse.

Molly had an answer: you hide in the Pit, in the lowest circle, where any outside influence generates swift, concentric ripples of raw menace. You hide in Nighttown. Better yet, you hide *above* Nighttown, because the Pit's inverted, and the bottom of its bowl touches the sky, the sky that Nighttown never sees, sweating under its own firmament of acrylic resin, up where the Lo Teks crouch in the dark like gargoyles, black-market cigarettes dangling from their lips.

She had another answer, too.

"So you're locked up good and tight, Johnny-san? No way to get that program without the password?" She led me into the shadows that waited beyond the bright tube platform. The concrete walls were overlaid with graffiti, years of them twisting into a single metascrawl of rage and frustration.

"The stored data are fed in through a modified series of microsurgical contraautism,   65 prostheses." I reeled off a numb version of my standard sales pitch. "Client's code is stored in a special chip; barring Squids, which we in the trade don't like to talk about, there's no way to recover your phrase. Can't drug it out, cut it out, torture it. I don't *know* it, never did."

"Squids? Crawly things with arms?" We emerged into a deserted street market. Shadowy figures watched us from across a makeshift square littered with fish heads and rotting fruit.

"Superconducting quantum interference detectors. Used them in the war to find submarines, suss out enemy cyber systems."

"Yeah? Navy stuff? From the war? Squid'll read that chip of yours?" She'd stopped walking, and I felt her eyes on me behind those twin mirrors.

"Even the primitive models could measure a magnetic field a billionth the strength of geomagnetic force; it's like pulling a whisper out of a cheering stadium."

70   "Cops can do that already, with parabolic microphones and lasers."

"But your data's still secure." Pride in profession. "No government'll let their cops have Squids, not even the security heavies. Too much chance of interdepartmental funnies; they're too likely to watergate you."

"Navy stuff," she said, and her grin gleamed in the shadows. "Navy stuff. I got a friend down here who was in the navy, name's Jones. I think you'd better meet him. He's a junkie, though. So we'll have to take him something."

"A junkie?"

"A dolphin."

75   He was more than a dolphin, but from another dolphin's point of view he might have seemed like something less. I watched him swirling sluggishly in his galvanized tank. Water slopped over the side, wetting my shoes. He was surplus from the last war. A cyborg.

He rose out of the water, showing us the crusted plates along his sides, a kind of visual pun, his grace nearly lost under articulated armor, clumsy and prehistoric. Twin deformities on either side of his skull had been engineered to house sensor units. Silver lesions gleamed on exposed sections of his gray-white hide.

Molly whistled. Jones thrashed his tail, and more water cascaded down the side of the tank.

"What is this place?" I peered at vague shapes in the dark, rusting chain link and things under tarps. Above the tank hung a clumsy wooden framework, crossed and recrossed by rows of dusty Christmas lights.

"Funland. Zoo and carnival rides. 'Talk with the War Whale.' All that. Some whale Jones is. . . ."

80   Jones reared again and fixed me with a sad and ancient eye.

"How's he talk?" Suddenly I was anxious to go.

"That's the catch. Say 'hi,' Jones."

And all the bulbs lit simultaneously. They were flashing red, white, and blue.

           *   *   *

85
         RWBRWBRWB
         RWBRWBRWB
         RWBRWBRWB
         RWBRWBRWB
         RWBRWBRWB

90   "Good with symbols, see, but the code's restricted. In the navy they had him wired into an audiovisual display." She drew the narrow package from a jacket pocket. "Pure shit, Jones. Want it?" He froze in the water and started to sink. I felt a strange panic, remembering that he wasn't a fish, that he could drown. "We want the key to Johnny's bank, Jones. We want it fast."

The lights flickered, died.

"Go for it, Jones!"

            B
        BBBBBBBBB
95
            B
            B
            B

Blue bulbs, cruciform.

Darkness.

"Pure! It's *clean*. Come on, Jones."

```
WWWWWWWWW
WWWWWWWWW
WWWWWWWWW
WWWWWWWWW
WWWWWWWWW
```

White sodium glare washed her features, stark monochrome, shadows cleaving from her cheekbones.

```
      *     *     *
      R     RRRRR
      R     R
      RRRRRRRRR
          R     R
      RRRRR     R
```

The arms of the red swastika were twisted in her silver glasses. "Give it to him," I said. "We've got it."

Ralfi Face. No imagination.

Jones heaved half his armored bulk over the edge of his tank, and I thought the metal would give way. Molly stabbed him overhand with the Syrette, driving the needle between two plates. Propellant hissed. Patterns of light exploded, spasming across the frame and then fading to black.

We left him drifting, rolling languorously in the dark water. Maybe he was dreaming of his war in the Pacific, of the cyber mines he'd swept, nosing gently into their circuitry with the Squid he'd used to pick Ralfi's pathetic password from the chip buried in my head.

"I can see them slipping up when he was demobbed, letting him out of the navy with that gear intact, but how does a cybernetic dolphin get wired to smack?"

"The war," she said. "They all were. Navy did it. How else you get 'em working for you?"

"I'm not sure this profiles as good business," the pirate said, angling for better money. "Target specs on a comsat that isn't in the book—"

"Waste my time and you won't profile at all," said Molly, leaning across his scarred plastic desk to prod him with her forefinger.

"So maybe you want to buy your microwaves somewhere else?" He was a tough kid, behind his Mao-job. A Nighttowner by birth, probably.

Her hand blurred down the front of his jacket, completely severing a lapel without even rumpling the fabric.

"So we got a deal or not?"

"Deal," he said, staring at his ruined lapel with what he must have hoped was only polite interest, "Deal."

While I checked the two recorders we'd bought, she extracted the slip of paper I'd given her from the zippered wrist pocket of her jacket. She unfolded it and read silently, moving her lips. She shrugged. "This is it?"

"Shoot," I said, punching the RECORD studs of the two decks simultaneously.

"Christian White," she recited, "and his Aryan Reggae Band."

Faithful Ralfi, a fan to his dying day.

Transition to idiot/savant mode is always less abrupt than I expect it to be. The pirate broadcaster's front was a failing travel agency in a pastel cube that boasted a desk, three chairs, and a faded poster of a Swiss orbital spa. A pair of toy birds with blown-glass bodies and tin legs were sipping monotonously from a Styrofoam cup of water on a ledge beside Molly's shoulder. As I phased into mode, they accelerated gradually until their Day-Glo-feathered crowns became solid arcs of color. The LEDs that told seconds on the plastic wall clock had become meaningless pulsing grids, and Molly and the Mao-faced boy grew hazy, their arms blurring occasionally in insect-quick ghosts of gesture. And then it all faded to cool gray static and an endless tone poem in an artificial language.

130   I sat and sang dead Ralfi's stolen program for three hours.

The mall runs forty kilometers from end to end, a ragged overlap of Fuller domes roofing what was once a suburban artery. If they turn off the arcs on a clear day, a gray approximation of sunlight filters through layers of acrylic, a view like the prison sketches of Giovanni Piranesi. The three southernmost kilometers roof Nighttown. Nighttown pays no taxes, no utilities. The neon arcs are dead, and the geodesics have been smoked black by decades of cooking fires. In the nearly total darkness of a Nighttown noon, who notices a few dozen mad children lost in the rafters?

We'd been climbing for two hours, up concrete stairs and steel ladders with perforated rungs, past abandoned gantries and dust-covered tools. We'd started in what looked like a disused maintenance yard, stacked with triangular roofing segments. Everything there had been covered with that same uniform layer of spraybomb graffiti: gang names, initials, dates back to the turn of the century. The graffiti followed us up, gradually thinning until a single name was repeated at intervals. LO TEK. In dripping black capitals.

"Who's Lo Tek?"

"Not us, boss." She climbed a shivering aluminum ladder and vanished through a hole in a sheet of corrugated plastic. "'Low technique, low technology.'" The plastic muffled her voice. I followed her up, nursing my aching wrist. "Lo Teks, they'd think that shotgun trick of yours was effete."

135   An hour later I dragged myself up through another hole, this one sawed crookedly in a sagging sheet of plywood, and met my first Lo Tek.

"'S okay," Molly said, her hand brushing my shoulder. "It's just Dog. Hey, Dog."

In the narrow beam of her taped flash, he regarded us with his one eye and slowly extruded a thick length of grayish tongue, licking huge canines. I wondered how they wrote off tooth-bud transplants from Dobermans as low technology. Immunosuppressives don't exactly grow on trees.

"Moll." Dental augmentation impeded his speech. A string of saliva dangled from his twisted lower lip. "Heard ya comin'. Long time." He might have been fifteen, but the fangs and a bright mosaic of scars combined with the gaping socket to present a mask of total bestiality. It had taken time and a certain kind of creativity to assemble that face, and his posture told me he enjoyed living behind it. He wore a pair of decaying jeans, black with grime and shiny along the creases. His chest and feet were bare. He did something with his mouth that approximated a grin. "Bein' followed, you."

Far off, down in Nighttown, a water vendor cried his trade.

140   "Strings jumping, Dog?" She swung her flash to the side, and I saw thin cords tied to eyebolts, cords that ran to the edge and vanished.

"Kill the fuckin' light!"

She snapped it off.

"How come the one who's followin' you's got no light?"

"Doesn't need it. That one's bad news, Dog. Your sentries give him a tumble, they'll come home in easy-to-carry sections."

"This a *friend* friend, Moll?" He sounded uneasy. I heard his feet shift on the worn 145 plywood.

"No. But he's mine. And this one," slapping my shoulder, "he's a friend. Got that?"

"Sure," he said, without much enthusiasm, padding to the platform's edge, where the eyebolts were. He began to pluck out some kind of message on the taut cords.

Nighttown spread beneath us like a toy village for rats; tiny windows showed candlelight, with only a few harsh, bright squares lit by battery lanterns and carbide lamps. I imagined the old men at their endless games of dominoes, under warm, fat drops of water that fell from wet wash hung out on poles between the plywood shanties. Then I tried to imagine him climbing patiently up through the darkness in his zoris and ugly tourist shirt, bland and unhurried. How was he tracking us?

"Good," said Molly. "He smells us."

"Smoke?" Dog dragged a crumpled pack from his pocket and prized out a flat- 150 tened cigarette. I squinted at the trademark while he lit it for me with a kitchen match. Yiheyuan filters. Beijing Cigarette Factory. I decided that the Lo Teks were black marketeers. Dog and Molly went back to their argument, which seemed to revolve around Molly's desire to use some particular piece of Lo Tek real estate.

"I've done you a lot of favors, man. I want that floor. And I want the music."

"You're not Lo Tek. . . ."

This must have been going on for the better part of a twisted kilometer. Dog leading us along swaying catwalks and up rope ladders. The Lo Teks leech their webs and huddling places to the city's fabric with thick gobs of epoxy and sleep above the abyss in mesh hammocks. Their country is so attenuated that in places it consists of little more than holds for hands and feet, sawed into geodesic struts.

The Killing Floor, she called it. Scrambling after her, my new Eddie Bax shoes slipping on worn metal and damp plywood, I wondered how it could be any more lethal than the rest of the territory. At the same time I sensed that Dog's protests were ritual and that she already expected to get whatever it was she wanted.

Somewhere beneath us, Jones would be circling his tank, feeling the first twinges 155 of junk sickness. The police would be boring the Drome regulars with questions about Ralfi. What did he do? Who was he with before he stepped outside? And the Yakuza would be settling its ghostly bulk over the city's data banks, probing for faint images of me reflected in numbered accounts, securities transactions, bills for utilities. We're an information economy. They teach you that in school. What they don't tell you is that it's impossible to move, to live, to operate at any level without leaving traces, bits, seemingly meaningless fragments of personal information. Fragments that can be retrieved, amplified . . .

But by now the pirate would have shuttled our message into line for blackbox transmission to the Yakuza comsat. A simple message: Call off the dogs or we wideband your program.

The program. I had no idea what it contained. I still don't. I only sing the song, with zero comprehension. It was probably research data, the Yakuza being given to advanced forms of industrial espionage. A genteel business, stealing from Ono-Sendai as a matter of course and politely holding their data for ransom, threatening to blunt the conglomerate's research edge by making the product public.

But why couldn't any number play? Wouldn't they be happier with something to sell back to Ono-Sendai, happier than they'd be with one dead Johnny from Memory Lane?

Their program was on its way to an address in Sydney, to a place that held letters for clients and didn't ask questions once you'd paid a small retainer. Fourth-class surface mail. I'd erased most of the other copy and recorded our message in the resulting gap, leaving just enough of the program to identify it as the real thing.

160   My wrist hurt. I wanted to stop, to lie down, to sleep. I knew that I'd lose my grip and fall soon, knew that the sharp black shoes I'd bought for my evening as Eddie Bax would lose their purchase and carry me down to Nighttown. But he rose in my mind like a cheap religious hologram, glowing, the enlarged chip on his Hawaiian shirt looming like a reconnaissance shot of some doomed urban nucleus.

So I followed Dog and Molly through Lo Tek heaven, jury-rigged and jerry-built from scraps that even Nighttown didn't want.

The Killing Floor was eight meters on a side. A giant had threaded steel cable back and forth through a junkyard and drawn it all taut. It creaked when it moved, and it moved constantly, swaying and bucking as the gathering Lo Teks arranged themselves on the shelf of plywood surrounding it. The wood was silver with age, polished with long use and deeply etched with initials, threats, declarations of passion. This was suspended from a separate set of cables, which lost themselves in darkness beyond the raw white glare of the two ancient floods suspended above the Floor.

A girl with teeth like Dog's hit the Floor on all fours. Her breasts were tattooed with indigo spirals. Then she was across the Floor, laughing, grappling with a boy who was drinking dark liquid from a liter flask.

Lo Tek fashion ran to scars and tattoos. And teeth. The electricity they were tapping to light the Killing Floor seemed to be an exception to their overall aesthetic, made in the name of . . . ritual, sport, art? I didn't know, but I could see that the Floor was something special. It had the look of having been assembled over generations.

165   I held the useless shotgun under my jacket. Its hardness and heft were comforting, even though I had no more shells. And it came to me that I had no idea at all of what was really happening, or of what was supposed to happen. And that was the nature of my game, because I'd spent most of my life as a blind receptacle to be filled with other people's knowledge and then drained, spouting synthetic languages I'd never understand. A very technical boy. Sure.

And then I noticed just how quiet the Lo Teks had become.

He was there, at the edge of the light, taking in the Killing Floor and the gallery of silent Lo Teks with a tourist's calm. And as our eyes met for the first time with mutual recognition, a memory clicked into place for me, of Paris, and the long Mercedes electrics gliding through the rain to Notre Dame; mobile greenhouses, Japanese faces behind the glass, and a hundred Nikons rising in blind phototropism, flowers of steel and crystal. Behind his eyes, as they found me, those same shutters whirring.

I looked for Molly Millions, but she was gone.

The Lo Teks parted to let him step up onto the bench. He bowed, smiling, and stepped smoothly out of his sandals, leaving them side by side, perfectly aligned, and then he stepped down onto the Killing Floor. He came for me, across that shifting trampoline of scrap, as easily as any tourist padding across synthetic pile in any featureless hotel.

170   Molly hit the Floor, moving.

The Floor screamed.

It was miked and amplified, with pickups riding the four fat coil springs at the corners and contact mikes taped at random to rusting machine fragments. Somewhere the Lo Teks had an amp and a synthesizer, and now I made out the shapes of speakers overhead, above the cruel white floods.

A drumbeat began, electronic, like an amplified heart, steady as a metronome.

She'd removed her leather jacket and boots; her T-shirt was sleeveless, faint telltales of Chiba City circuitry traced along her thin arms. Her leather jeans gleamed under the floods. She began to dance.

She flexed her knees, white feet tensed on a flattened gas tank, and the Killing Floor   175
began to heave in response. The sound it made was like a world ending, like the wires that hold heaven snapping and coiling across the sky.

He rode with it, for a few heartbeats, and then he moved, judging the movement of the Floor perfectly, like a man stepping from one flat stone to another in an ornamental garden.

He pulled the tip from his thumb with the grace of a man at ease with social gesture and flung it at her. Under the floods, the filament was a refracting thread of rainbow. She threw herself flat and rolled, jackknifing up as the molecule whipped past, steel claws snapping into the light in what must have been an automatic rictus of defense.

The drum pulse quickened, and she bounced with it, her dark hair wild around the blank silver lenses, her mouth thin, lips taut with concentration. The Killing Floor boomed and roared, and the Lo Teks were screaming their excitement.

He retracted the filament to a whirling meter-wide circle of ghostly polychrome and spun it in front of him, thumbless hand held level with his sternum. A shield.

And Molly seemed to let something go, something inside, and that was the real   180
start of her mad-dog dance. She jumped, twisting, lunging sideways, landing with both feet on an alloy engine block wired directly to one of the coil springs. I cupped my hands over my ears and knelt in a vertigo of sound, thinking Floor and benches were on their way down, down to Nighttown, and I saw us tearing through the shanties, the wet wash, exploding on the tiles like rotten fruit. But the cables held, and the Killing Floor rose and fell like a crazy metal sea. And Molly danced on it.

And at the end, just before he made his final cast with the filament, I saw something in his face, an expression that didn't seem to belong there. It wasn't fear and it wasn't anger. I think it was disbelief, stunned incomprehension mingled with pure aesthetic revulsion at what he was seeing, hearing—at what was happening to him. He retracted the whirling filament, the ghost disk shrinking to the size of a dinner plate as he whipped his arm above his head and brought it down, the thumbtip curving out for Molly like a live thing.

The Floor carried her down, the molecule passing just above her head; the Floor whiplashed, lifting him into the path of the taut molecule. It should have passed harmlessly over his head and been withdrawn into its diamond-hard socket. It took his hand off just behind the wrist. There was a gap in the Floor in front of him, and he went through it like a diver, with a strange deliberate grace, a defeated kamikaze on his way down to Nighttown. Partly, I think, he took the dive to buy himself a few seconds of the dignity of silence. She'd killed him with culture shock.

The Lo Teks roared, but someone shut the amplifier off, and Molly rode the Killing Floor into silence, hanging on now, her face white and blank, until the pitching slowed and there was only a faint pinging of tortured metal and the grating of rust on rust.

We searched the Floor for the severed hand, but we never found it. All we found was a graceful curve in one piece of rusted steel, where the molecule went through. Its edge was bright as new chrome.

185   We never learned whether the Yakuza had accepted our terms, or even whether they got our message. As far as I know, their program is still waiting for Eddie Bax on a shelf in the back room of a gift shop on the third level of Sydney Central-5. Probably they sold the original back to Ono-Sendai months ago. But maybe they did get the pirate's broadcast, because nobody's come looking for me yet, and it's been nearly a year. If they do come, they'll have a long climb up through the dark, past Dog's sentries, and I don't look much like Eddie Bax these days. I let Molly take care of that, with a local anesthetic. And my new teeth have almost grown in.

I decided to stay up here. When I looked out across the Killing Floor, before he came, I saw how hollow I was. And I knew I was sick of being a bucket. So now I climb down and visit Jones, almost every night.

We're partners now, Jones and I, and Molly Millions, too: Molly handles our business in the Drome. Jones is still in Funland, but he has a bigger tank, with fresh seawater trucked in once a week. And he has his junk, when he needs it. He still talks to the kids with his frame of lights, but he talks to me on a new display unit in a shed that I rent there, a better unit than the one he used in the navy.

And we're all making good money, better money than I made before, because Jones's Squid can read the traces of anything that anyone ever stored in me, and he gives it to me on the display unit in languages I can understand. So we're learning a lot about all my former clients. And one day I'll have a surgeon dig all the silicon out of my amygdalae, and I'll live with my own memories and nobody else's, the way other people do. But not for a while.

In the meantime it's really okay up here, way up in the dark, smoking a Chinese filtertip and listening to the condensation that drips from the geodesics. Real quiet up here—unless a pair of Lo Teks decide to dance on the Killing Floor.

190   It's educational, too. With Jones to help me figure things out, I'm getting to be the most technical boy in town.   [1986]

QUESTIONS

1. Discuss the many ways that Johnny is "a technical boy."

2. Describe the settings in the story—the Drome and Nighttown. What are their similarities and differences?

3. Examine the characters in the story. Who is more "human" and who is less "human"? In what ways? What meaning can be inferred from these characterizations?

4. What is Gibson saying about memory and its role and importance in our lives?

5. Think about the usual archetypal meanings of rising/falling, going down/going up, higher/lower worlds. In what ways does Gibson's story incorporate these meanings? In what ways does the story subvert them?

RESPONSES

1. "Johnny Mnemonic" is considered one of the founding stories in the "cyberpunk" school of science fiction. Do an internet search on "cyberpunk" and research what its features are. Which of these features do you see in the story and where?
2. Examine Gibson's use of Eastern/Western cultural dichotomies. In the end, do you think he destroys or reinforces that set of binaries?
3. Focusing on the themes of memory and the construction of self, compare this story to Dick's "We Can Remember It for You Wholesale" or Nolan's "Memento Mori."

FOCUS ON FILM

1. Choose one of the elements of fiction and write an essay examining what William Gibson did in adapting his own story into a screenplay. What changes does he make? What effect do these changes have on theme and tone?
2. Discuss the importance of set design and lighting in contrasting the atmosphere of the film.

DAGOBERTO GILB

Dagoberto Gilb (b. 1950) worked at a variety of jobs before becoming a teacher of creative writing at Southwest Texas State University. He has lived most of his life in the Southwest United States, from El Paso to Los Angeles. He has published two volumes of short stories, *The Magic of Blood* and *Woodcuts of Women*, and one novel, *The Last Known Residence of Mickey Acuna*. In addition, he has won several prestigious awards, including the Piasano Award, PEN's Ernest Hemingway Foundation Award, the National Endowment for the Arts Creative Writing Fellowship, the Whiting Writers' Award, and the John Simon Guggenheim Memorial Foundation Fellowship. *Gritos: Essays* was published in 2003.

Hollywood!

Santa Monica beach was clean and quiet. The sand was moist, the air cool, the ocean as gentle as a bay, and Luís was happy that he didn't have to pay for the parking.

"The sun's out," he said. "Just look what a pretty day it is."

"It's still cold," Marta told him, making sure he didn't get away with it. She was trying to wrap her sweater around their son Ramón, who wasn't about to cooperate and was about to cry because his mommy wouldn't leave him alone.

"He'll be all right," Luís said to ease her worry. "It's good for him just to get out."

5   "It's not good for him to catch a cold!" Marta was mad at Luís for insisting that Ramón wouldn't need any more than shorts and a T-shirt at the beach.

"He won't. Look at how happy he is." That was the kind of reasoning Luís liked to use.

Ramón was happy. His plastic grader tore through the sand, slicing out a smooth road for his matchbox-sized cars. He didn't seem the least bit cold.

Marta had learned long ago that she couldn't fight with Luís's logic. She lay down on the old blanket she'd never convinced him to replace, draped the sweater over herself, and looped her arm over her eyes. The sun was out. She felt pained.

Fishing boats bobbed on the near horizon. Helicopters battered the air. Joggers came and went along the wet part of the shore.

10   "If they worked like us they wouldn't have to run," Luís said of the joggers.

"At least they move to keep warm," Marta shot back.

"We've got the whole beach to ourselves. Think of what memories he'll have."

She scoffed. Ramón's cars vroomed and squealed and crashed into themselves and mounds of sand.

"The beach is so great," Marta shivered. "I can't wait to tell everybody at home what a great experience our first ever vacation was." It was Luís's idea to visit California in the winter because the motels were said to be cheaper and everyone said it was warm anyway.

"He's gonna remember this forever," Luís said. Just to make sure, he went over to his son. "You wanna go see the ocean up close?"

Ramón looked over to his mommy. He seemed to know, even at his very young age, that his daddy didn't always have the best ideas.

Luís picked Ramón up and carried him to the water's edge. "Now those boats out there—they look like the ones you have for your bath, don't they?" Luís felt pretty clever thinking of that. It was always better to describe things to a child in a way he could understand. "Those boats go around and catch fish so that people can eat. It's just like at home at the groves. Except instead of nuts it's fish, like sardines. You know, those fish from those cans your mommy puts in my lunch sometimes."

Ramón seemed to listen and Luís was sure he was getting through to him, and he was determined not to lose the momentum.

"And the seagulls, those birds that are flying around out there, see? See how big they are? Those are called seagulls and they go around and catch fish too, just like those boats, and that's how they live."

Ramón was listening. He was watching the birds.

"The ocean's just like the land. Animals live in it. Men make a living on it the same way I do working in the groves for Mr. Oakes." Luís thought this over and realized he didn't know how to explain himself any better. "The only important thing in life is hard work." That was somehow what he was getting at, and in any case he loved these kinds of statements, and he always sincerely believed them.

Ramón started fidgeting.

"You wanna get down? Okay. You should get your feet wet. These are nice waves . . ."

Now Ramón was crying. The water was very cold and the little waves scared him. He ran up the sand to his mommy.

"Why can't we go to Disneyland?" Marta implored Luís back at the blanket. "It can't cost that much. He would have such a good time, even if it is expensive. I could pay with that money I saved . . ."

"It's not the money."

". . . Or we could leave a day or two earlier, and with the money we save by leaving . . ."

"No."

Marta rolled her eyes and shook her head. It was no use. Even though every little boy and girl dreams of going to Disneyland at least once, Luís had his ideas and this was one of them: it was better for his son to learn the important things first. What would a place like Disneyland teach him besides cartoons? Of course Marta didn't believe him for a second. She knew he was just being cheap.

A couple came wearing bathing suits and left with warmer clothes on. They didn't stay long. A teenage couple came carting a portable stereo with a cassette player. They listened to a tape of Tierra turned up loud and felt each other up. Luís finally couldn't stand it and told them to turn it down and to make their sex private. They left, but once he got a safe distance away the boy yelled something about Luís's mother. Marta laughed. Ramón wanted a hot dog because Luís promised to buy him one the day before.

"They do too sell hot dogs up on the pier," Marta told him. "I saw that man coming down the stairs eating one."

"No they don't," Luís insisted. "Besides, we brought these sandwiches."

"You already told him you would!"

"Hey, look at all the birds landing around us," Luís said to his son, changing the subject.

35   Ramón stopped whining and looked. They were seagulls and pigeons. They waited in segregated clumps.

"Let's feed them! We can feed them some of the bread!" Luís pinched off chunks of the white bread from his sandwich and threw them at the birds. They squawked and flapped their wings and moved in closer. Ramón watched ecstatically. Seagulls hovered in the air and Luís tossed the balled-up crumbs so they'd catch them there. More gulls flew in from the ocean and more pigeons from the pier, and Ramón threw them pieces of his sandwich too.

Luís tried to show Ramón how to tear little pieces off the bread so he wouldn't go through the sandwiches too quickly, but the boy had already lost control. Pigeons were almost crawling on the blanket, and it seemed all the ocean's gulls waited by him while he talked and laughed, letting the pigeons eat from his hand and making sure each and every seagull got something.

Pleased as he was, Luís was also relieved when the last sandwiches were spared by three high-pitched beeps, and then music and song, which distracted Ramón from the feeding.

"Look!" Marta pointed. "They're making a movie over there on the pier. See the camera?"

40   Ramón went back to the birds. Luís looked at the filming area skeptically. Marta demanded that they go see it up close. Luís, watching his son take out another sandwich from a plastic bag, gave in to Marta's wish and waved the birds away.

It was a commercial for A&W root beer but Marta didn't care. This was Hollywood! There were film people standing by electronic machines and under wire cables. There was a fat director, dressed in a casual velour suit, shooting scenes with his noisy hands and arms. There was a cameraman, who wore a cowboy hat, sitting on a rolling lift. And there were handsome young actors and beautiful young actresses and a punk style woman dabbing them with makeup.

"They're all blonds," remarked Luís cynically.

"Those two men on the roller skates have dark hair," Marta corrected him. "And there's a black man."

"Boys. Those are all boys."

45   First came the beeps, then the music, and then the action: cute, barelegged actresses drank from a can of the soda and expressed amazement and pretended to sing the jingle that screamed out of a speaker in front of them. Other actresses jogged to a stop and one of the actors twirled on his roller skates. They all moved toward a park bench while the camera aimed down and away from the crowded park bench.

They watched the actors do this several times before Luís made the move to another area behind the rope. He didn't like standing near the shirtless blond longhairs with tattoos who, according to Luís, didn't do anything more than smoke marijuana and drink beer.

After a while Luís stopped paying attention. He watched a man below him driving a tractor across the sand. He watched a truck collect the trash from the barrels on the beach. Then a uniformed guard was standing next to him telling him something in English. Luís noticed that the fat director was glaring at him and when he looked to his side for a translation he realized that Marta and Ramón had left him alone. He stiffened until the guard put his hand on his shoulder and slowly drew out the word "move" and pushed Luís further down the rope.

"It's because you were in the picture," Marta explained to him.

Luís still felt like everyone was looking at him. "The boy should be playing on the beach. Maybe he'll want to get wet in the ocean."

Marta frowned. "I want to see this a few more times. He's hungry. Buy him a hot dog." 50

"There's still two sandwiches," he reminded her.

"He wants a *hot dog*."

Luís wanted to argue, but once Ramón had heard his mommy mention hot dogs, he started whining again. Luís knew it was hopeless. He took his son to the nearby stand.

"One hot dog," Luís told the fry cook.

"The long or the short?" the man said in a hoarse foreign accent. "The sauerkraut, 55 the chili, the cheese?"

Luís stared at him mystified. "I want one hot dog," he said in English.

The man stared back at Luís. "You wannit the long dog or the regular? You wannit the chili, or the sauerkraut, or the cheese? You wannit the plain or the mustard and relish?"

Luís looked down at Ramón in defeat. The fry cook, irritated, started to go over the options again, but before he finished, Ramón, in clear English, told him he would have a regular hot dog with ketchup only.

Luís returned to Marta with the news.

"He watches television, and a lot of his friends talk to him in English," she said, 60 unimpressed. "And when I babysit for Mr. and Mrs. Oakes, the children speak English to him. The Oakes speak Spanish to you, but not to their children."

Luís wished he could talk to either Ramón or Marta on the way back home, but a sore throat and fever kept his son whimpering the whole way and made Marta mad at him. So he drove fourteen straight hours, secretly not unhappy that they were getting back from expensive California two days earlier that they'd planned.

Late the next night, Ramón was tossing and turning on the bed between his mommy and daddy, who had been trying everything to get him to stop his crying.

"He used to go to sleep when you sang to him," Luís reminded Marta.

"Well you see it hasn't been working this time," she said, tired. "Maybe you should tell him one of your stories. Tell him how much money we saved not going to Disneyland."

Luís, as always, ignored her sarcasm. But he liked the idea. He liked to tell what 65 Marta called his stories, and he believed Ramón liked them too, because many times he did go to sleep hearing about the men Luís worked with or the animals they raised or the plants they grew. And, according to Luís, this was good for him since the stories would help him in the future, especially since he went to sleep with them. He considered talking about the wild burros he saw in the Mojave Desert, or those saguaros near Picacho Peak, or the piscadores in the chile fields near the Rio Grande. Any of these could have worked.

"Remember when we were at the ocean, where the waves ran up your legs? And the helicopters, and those fishing boats?"

Ramón stopped whimpering.

"Remember those birds that flew around those boats, and how they all flew onto the beach when you and I started feeding them bread?"

Ramón seemed to listen, was quiet. Already Luís felt a little like gloating to Marta, who'd rolled her head over to watch. "Those birds make their life there, mijo, and with their wings . . ."

70   But suddenly Ramón lost interest. He turned to his mommy and cried about the sore throat and how hot he was. Luís was truly disappointed.

Luís and Marta stared up at the darkness toward their small bedroom ceiling. There were crickets outside, and they could hear a hard breeze rustle the trees and bushes around their house and a tumbleweed scraping against the back door screen. A cat yowled louder than the boy and that was comforting to them both.

Marta hummed a few unmelodic notes. "How did that go?" she asked Luís softly. "A and double U . . ."

Luís didn't know the words, but he tried to remember the music to the jingle. They'd heard it a dozen times or more, but things like this didn't stay with him.

"A and double U root beer . . ." she whispered, hoping that maybe Ramón had finally fallen asleep because he wasn't crying.

75   Marta kept trying. Luís would tell her when she didn't have it, which was every time.

Then Ramón, with his eyes barely open, sang the first words just loud enough for them all to hear.

Luís couldn't believe it. Marta laughed. She sang: "A and double U tastes so fine, sends a thrill up my spine! Taste that frosty mug sen*sa*tion—uuu!" And she laughed again, hummed the rest of it, laughing still more, and Ramón fell asleep as she sang it over and over to taunt Luís, who this night was happy to lose the battle.   [1993]

QUESTIONS

1. How is the title ironic?
2. What is the source of conflict between Luís and Marta?
3. Why is it important to Luís to teach Ramón about hard work?
4. How does Gilb handle the fact that his characters are really speaking Spanish? Does the method strengthen or weaken the story?
5. How is the time of year important to the central idea of the story?

RESPONSE

1. Using a sociological/Marxist approach, write an essay that explores Luís's relationship with his family.

CHARLOTTE PERKINS GILMAN

Charlotte Perkins Gilman (1860–1935) was born in Hartford, Connecticut, and was raised in an atmosphere of genteel poverty. She married an artist, Charles Stetson, in 1884. After the birth of a daughter the following year, she suffered a nervous collapse, and her treatment, similar to that described in "The Yellow Wallpaper," exacerbated her condition. Ultimately she divorced Stetson, moved to California, and began life anew as a lecturer on feminism and socialism. In 1898 she published a plea for women's economic freedom, *Women and Economics*. In 1900 she married George Gilman, and during the following decade she published several volumes on the role of women in society. Toward the end of her life she worked for social change through political activism, several times standing for elective office on the Socialist ticket.

The Yellow Wallpaper

It is very seldom that mere ordinary people like John and myself secure ancestral halls for the summer.

A colonial mansion, a hereditary estate, I would say a haunted house and reach the height of romantic felicity—but that would be asking too much of fate!

Still I will proudly declare that there is something queer about it.

Else, why should it be let so cheaply? And why have stood so long untenanted?

John laughs at me, of course, but one expects that.   5

John is practical in the extreme. He has no patience with faith, an intense horror of superstition, and he scoffs openly at any talk of things not to be felt and seen and put down in figures.

John is a physician, and *perhaps*—(I would not say it to a living soul, of course, but this is dead paper and a great relief to my mind)—*perhaps* that is one reason I do not get well faster.

You see, he does not believe I am sick! And what can one do?

If a physician of high standing, and one's own husband, assures friends and relatives that there is really nothing the matter with one but temporary nervous depression—a slight hysterical tendency—what is one to do?

My brother is also a physician, and also of high standing, and he says the same thing.   10

So I take phosphates or phosphites—whichever it is—and tonics, and air and exercise, and journeys, and am absolutely forbidden to "work" until I am well again.

Personally, I disagree with their ideas.

Personally, I believe that congenial work, with excitement and change, would do me good.

But what is one to do?

15   I did write for a while in spite of them; but it *does* exhaust me a good deal—having to be so sly about it, or else meet with heavy opposition.

I sometimes fancy that in my condition, if I had less opposition and more society and stimulus—but John says the very worst thing I can do is to think about my condition, and I confess it always makes me feel bad.

So I will let it alone and talk about the house.

The most beautiful place! It is quite alone, standing well back from the road, quite three miles from the village. It makes me think of English places that you read about, for there are hedges and walls and gates that lock, and lots of separate little houses for the gardeners and people.

There is a *delicious* garden! I never saw such a garden—large and shady, full of box-bordered paths, and lined with long grape-covered arbors with seats under them.

20   There were greenhouses, but they are all broken now.

There was some legal trouble, I believe, something about the heirs and coheirs; anyhow, the place has been empty for years.

That spoils my ghostliness, I am afraid, but I don't care—there is something strange about the house—I can feel it.

I even said so to John one moonlight evening, but he said what I felt was a draught, and shut the window.

I get unreasonably angry with John sometimes. I'm sure I never used to be so sensitive. I think it is due to this nervous condition.

25   But John says if I feel so I shall neglect proper self-control; so I take pains to control myself—before him, at least, and that makes me very tired.

I don't like our room a bit. I wanted one downstairs that opened onto the piazza and had roses all over the window, and such pretty old-fashioned chintz hangings! But John would not hear of it.

He said there was only one window and not room for two beds, and no near room for him if he took another.

He is very careful and loving, and hardly lets me stir without special direction.

I have a schedule prescription for each hour in the day; he takes all care from me, and so I feel basely ungrateful not to value it more.

30   He said he came here solely on my account, that I was to have perfect rest and all the air I could get. "Your exercise depends on your strength, my dear," said he, "and your food somewhat on your appetite; but air you can absorb all the time." So we took the nursery at the top of the house.

It is a big, airy room, the whole floor nearly, with windows that look all ways, and air and sunshine galore. It was nursery first, and then playroom and gymnasium, I should judge, for the windows are barred for little children, and there are rings and things in the walls.

The paint and paper look as if a boys' school had used it. It is stripped off—the paper—in great patches all around the head of my bed, about as far as I can reach, and in a great place on the other side of the room low down. I never saw a worse paper in my life. One of those sprawling, flamboyant patterns committing every artistic sin.

It is dull enough to confuse the eye in following, pronounced enough constantly to irritate and provoke study, and when you follow the lame uncertain curves for a little distance they suddenly commit suicide—plunge off at outrageous angles, destroy themselves in unheard-of contradictions.

The color is repellent, almost revolting: a smouldering unclean yellow, strangely faded by the slow-turning sunlight. It is a dull yet lurid orange in some places, a sick-ly sulphur tint in others.

No wonder the children hated it! I should hate it myself if I had to live in this room long.   35

There comes John, and I must put this away—he hates to have me write a word.

We have been here two weeks, and I haven't felt like writing before, since that first day.

I am sitting by the window now, up in this atrocious nursery, and there is nothing to hinder my writing as much as I please, save lack of strength.

John is away all day, and even some nights when his cases are serious.

I am glad my case is not serious!   40

But these nervous troubles are dreadfully depressing.

John does not know how much I really suffer. He knows there is no reason to suf-fer, and that satisfies him.

Of course it is only nervousness. It does weigh on me so not to do my duty in any way!

I meant to be such a help to John, such a real rest and comfort, and here I am a com-parative burden already!

Nobody would believe what an effort it is to do what little I am able—to dress and   45
entertain, and order things.

It is fortunate Mary is so good with the baby. Such a dear baby!

And yet I *cannot* be with him, it makes me so nervous.

I suppose John never was nervous in his life. He laughs at me so about this wall-paper!

At first he meant to repaper the room, but afterward he said that I was letting it get the better of me, and that nothing was worse for a nervous patient than to give way to such fancies.

He said that after the wallpaper was changed it would be the heavy bedstead, and   50
then the barred windows, and then that gate at the head of the stairs, and so on.

"You know the place is doing you good," he said, "and really, dear, I don't care to renovate the house just for a three months' rental."

"Then do let us go downstairs," I said. "There are such pretty rooms there."

Then he took me in his arms and called me a blessed little goose, and said he would go down cellar, if I wished, and have it whitewashed into the bargain.

But he is right enough about the beds and windows and things.

It is as airy and comfortable a room as anyone need wish, and, of course, I would   55
not be so silly as to make him uncomfortable just for a whim.

I'm really getting fond of the big room, all but that horrid paper.

Out of one window I can see the garden—those mysterious deep-shaded arbors, the riotous old-fashioned flowers, and bushes and gnarly trees.

Out of another I get a lovely view of the bay and a little private wharf belonging to the estate. There is a beautiful shaded lane that runs down there from the house. I al-ways fancy I see people walking in these numerous paths and arbors, but John has cautioned me not to give way to fancy in the least. He says that with my imaginative power and habit of story-making, a nervous weakness like mine is sure to lead to all manner of excited fancies, and that I ought to use my will and good sense to check the tendency. So I try.

I think sometimes that if I were only well enough to write a little it would relieve the press of ideas and rest me.

60   But I find I get pretty tired when I try.

It is so discouraging not to have any advice and companionship about my work. When I get really well, John says we will ask Cousin Henry and Julia down for a long visit; but he says he would as soon put fireworks in my pillow-case as to let me have those stimulating people about now.

I wish I could get well faster.

But I must not think about that. This paper looks to me as if it *knew* what a vicious influence it had!

There is a recurrent spot where the pattern lolls like a broken neck and two bulbous eyes stare at you upside down.

65   I get positively angry with the impertinence of it and the everlastingness. Up and down and sideways they crawl, and those absurd unblinking eyes are everywhere. There is one place where two breadths didn't match, and the eyes go all up and down the line, one a little higher than the other.

I never saw so much expression in an inanimate thing before, and we all know how much expression they have! I used to lie awake as a child and get more entertainment and terror out of blank walls and plain furniture than most children could find in a toy-store.

I remember what a kindly wink the knobs of our big old bureau used to have, and there was one chair that always seemed like a strong friend.

I used to feel that if any of the other things looked too fierce I could always hop into that chair and be safe.

The furniture in this room is no worse than inharmonious, however, for we had to bring it all from downstairs. I suppose when this was used as a playroom they had to take the nursery things out, and no wonder! I never saw such ravages as the children have made here.

70   The wallpaper, as I said before, is torn off in spots, and it sticketh closer than a brother—they must have had perseverance as well as hatred.

Then the floor is scratched and gouged and splintered, the plaster itself is dug out here and there, and this great heavy bed, which is all we found in the room, looks as if it had been through the wars.

But I don't mind it a bit—only the paper.

There comes John's sister. Such a dear girl as she is, and so careful of me! I must not let her find me writing.

She is a perfect and enthusiastic housekeeper, and hopes for no better profession. I verily believe she thinks it is the writing which made me sick!

75   But I can write when she is out, and see her a long way off from these windows.

There is one that commands the road, a lovely shaded winding road, and one that just looks off over the country. A lovely country, too, full of great elms and velvet meadows.

This wallpaper has a kind of sub-pattern in a different shade, a particularly irritating one, for you can only see it in certain lights, and not clearly then.

But in the places where it isn't faded and where the sun is just so—I can see a strange, provoking, formless sort of figure that seems to skulk about behind that silly and conspicuous front design.

There's sister on the stairs!

Well, the Fourth of July is over! The people are all gone, and I am tired out. John 80
thought it might do me good to see a little company, so we just had Mother and Nellie and the children down for a week.

Of course I didn't do a thing. Jennie sees to everything now.

But it tired me all the same.

John says if I don't pick up faster he shall send me to Weir Mitchell in the fall.

But I don't want to go there at all. I had a friend who was in his hands once, and
she says he is just like John and my brother, only more so!

Besides, it is such an undertaking to go so far. 85

I don't feel as if it was worthwhile to turn my hand over for anything, and I'm getting dreadfully fretful and querulous.

I cry at nothing, and cry most of the time.

Of course I don't when John is here, or anybody else, but when I am alone.

And I am alone a good deal just now. John is kept in town very often by serious
cases, and Jennie is good and lets me alone when I want her to.

So I walk a little in the garden or down that lovely lane, sit on the porch under the 90
roses, and lie down up here a good deal.

I'm getting really fond of the room in spite of the wallpaper. Perhaps *because* of the
wallpaper.

It dwells in my mind so!

I lie here on this great immovable bed—it is nailed down, I believe—and follow
that pattern about by the hour. It is as good as gymnastics, I assure you. I start, we'll
say, at the bottom, down in the corner over there where it has not been touched, and
I determine for the thousandth time that I *will* follow that pointless pattern to some sort
of a conclusion.

I know a little of the principle of design, and I know this thing was not arranged
on any laws of radiation, or alternation, or repetition, or symmetry, or anything else
that I ever heard of.

It is repeated, of course, by the breadths, but not otherwise. 95

Looked at in one way, each breadth stands alone; the bloated curves and flourishes—
a kind of "debased Romanesque" with delirium tremens go waddling up and down
in isolated columns of fatuity.

But, on the other hand, they connect diagonally, and the sprawling outlines run off
in great slanting waves of optic horror, like a lot of wallowing sea-weeds in full chase.

The whole thing goes horizontally, too, at least it seems so, and I exhaust myself trying to distinguish the order of its going in that direction.

They have used a horizontal breadth for a freize, and that adds wonderfully to the
confusion.

There is one end of the room where it is almost intact, and there, when the crosslights 100
fade and the low sun shines directly upon it, I can almost fancy radiation after all—
the interminable grotesque seems to form around a common center and rush off in
headlong plunges of equal distraction.

It makes me tired to follow it. I will take a nap, I guess.

I don't know why I should write this.

I don't want to.

I don't feel able.

And I know John would think it absurd. But I *must* say what I feel and think in 105
some way—it is such a relief!

But the effort is getting to be greater than the relief.

Half the time now I am awfully lazy, and lie down ever so much. John says I mustn't lose my strength, and has me take cod liver oil and lots of tonics and things, to say nothing of ale and wine and rare meat.

Dear John! He loves me very dearly, and hates to have me sick. I tried to have a real earnest reasonable talk with him the other day, and tell him how I wish he would let me go and make a visit to Cousin Henry and Julia.

But he said I wasn't able to go, nor able to stand it after I got there; and I did not make out a very good case for myself, for I was crying before I had finished.

110   It is getting to be a great effort for me to think straight. Just this nervous weakness, I suppose.

And dear John gathered me up in his arms, and just carried me upstairs and laid me on the bed, and sat by me and read to me till it tired my head.

He said I was his darling and his comfort and all he had, and that I must take care of myself for his sake, and keep well.

He says no one but myself can help me out of it, that I must use my will and self-control and not let any silly fancies run away with me.

There's one comfort—the baby is well and happy, and does not have to occupy this nursery with the horrid wallpaper.

115   If we had not used it, that blessed child would have! What a fortunate escape! Why, I wouldn't have a child of mine, an impressionable little thing, live in such a room for worlds.

I never thought of it before, but it is lucky that John kept me here after all; I can stand it so much easier than a baby, you see.

Of course I never mention it to them any more—I am too wise—but I keep watch for it all the same.

There are things in that wallpaper that nobody knows about but me, or ever will.

Behind that outside pattern the dim shapes get clearer every day.

120   It is always the same shape, only very numerous.

And it is like a woman stooping down and creeping about behind that pattern. I don't like it a bit. I wonder—I begin to think—I wish John would take me away from here!

It is so hard to talk with John about my case, because he is so wise, and because he loves me so.

But I tried it last night.

It was moonlight. The moon shines in all around just as the sun does.

125   I hate to see it sometimes, it creeps so slowly, and always comes in by one window or another.

John was asleep and I hated to waken him, so I kept still and watched the moonlight on that undulating wallpaper till I felt creepy.

The faint figure behind seemed to shake the pattern, just as if she wanted to get out.

I got up softly and went to feel and see if the paper *did* move, and when I came back John was awake.

"What is it, little girl?" he said. "Don't go walking about like that—you'll get cold."

130   I thought it was a good time to talk, so I told him that I really was not gaining here, and that I wished he would take me away.

"Why, darling!" said he. "Our lease will be up in three weeks, and I can't see how to leave before.

"The repairs are not done at home, and I cannot possibly leave town just now. Of course, if you were in any danger, I could and would, but you really are better, dear, whether you can see it or not. I am a doctor, dear, and I know. You are gaining flesh and color, your appetite is better, I feel really much easier about you."

"I don't weigh a bit more," said I, "nor as much; and my appetite may be better in the evening when you are here but it is worse in the morning when you are away!"

"Bless her little heart!" said he with a big hug. "She shall be as sick as she pleases! But now let's improve the shining hours by going to sleep, and talk about it in the morning!"

"And you won't go away?" I asked gloomily.

"Why, how can I, dear? It is only three weeks more and then we will take a nice little trip of a few days while Jennie is getting the house ready. Really, dear, you are better!"

"Better in body perhaps—" I began, and stopped short, for he sat up straight and looked at me with such a stern, reproachful look that I could not say another word.

"My darling," said he, "I beg of you, for my sake and for our child's sake, as well as for your own, that you will never for one instant let that idea enter your mind! There is nothing so dangerous, so fascinating, to a temperament like yours. It is a false and foolish fancy. Can you not trust me as a physician when I tell you so?"

So of course I said no more on that score, and we went to sleep before long. He thought I was asleep first, but I wasn't, and lay there for hours trying to decide whether that front pattern and the back pattern really did move together or separately.

On a pattern like this, by daylight, there is a lack of sequence, a defiance of law, that is a constant irritant to a normal mind.

The color is hideous enough, and unreliable enough, and infuriating enough, but the pattern is torturing.

You think you have mastered it, but just as you get well under way in following, it turns a back-somersault and there you are. It slaps you in the face, knocks you down, and tramples upon you. It is like a bad dream.

The outside pattern is a florid arabesque, reminding one of a fungus. If you can imagine a toadstool in joints, an interminable string of toadstools, budding and sprouting in endless convolutions—why, that is something like it.

That is, sometimes!

There is one marked peculiarity about this paper, a thing nobody seems to notice but myself, and that is that it changes as the light changes.

When the sun shoots in through the east window—I always watch for that first long, strait ray—it changes so quickly that I never can quite believe it.

That is why I watch it always.

By moonlight—the moon shines in all night when there is a moon—I wouldn't know it was the same paper.

At night in any kind of light, in twilight, candlelight, lamplight, and worst of all by moonlight, it becomes bars! The outside pattern, I mean, and the woman behind it is as plain as can be.

I didn't realize for a long time what the thing was that showed behind, that dim sub-pattern, but now I am quite sure it is a woman.

By daylight she is subdued, quiet. I fancy it is the pattern that keeps her so still. It is so puzzling. It keeps me quiet by the hour.

I lie down ever so much now. John says it is good for me, and to sleep all I can.

Indeed he started the habit by making me lie down for an hour after each meal.

It is a very bad habit, I am convinced, for you see, I don't sleep.

155 And that cultivates deceit, for I don't tell them I'm awake—oh, no!

The fact is I am getting a little afraid of John.

He seems very queer sometimes, and even Jennie has an inexplicable look.

It strikes me occasionally, just as a scientific hypothesis, that perhaps it is the paper!

I have watched John when he did not know I was looking, and come into the room suddenly on the most innocent excuses, and I've caught him several times *looking at the paper!* And Jennie too. I caught Jennie with her hand on it once.

160 She didn't know I was in the room, and when I asked her in a quiet, a very quiet voice, with the most restrained manner possible, what she was doing with the paper, she turned around as if she had been caught stealing, and looked quite angry—asked me why I should frighten her so!

Then she said that the paper stained everything it touched, that she had found yellow smooches on all my clothes and John's and she wished we would be more careful!

Did not that sound innocent? But I know she was studying that pattern, and I am determined that nobody shall find it out but myself!

Life is very much more exciting now than it used to be. You see, I have something more to expect, to look forward to, to watch. I really do eat better, and am more quiet than I was.

John is so pleased to see me improve! He laughed a little the other day, and said I seemed to be flourishing in spite of my wallpaper.

165 I turned it off with a laugh. I had no intention of telling him it was *because* of the wallpaper—he would make fun of me. He might even want to take me away.

I don't want to leave now until I have found it out. There is a week more, and I think that will be enough.

I'm feeling so much better!

I don't sleep much at night, for it is so interesting to watch developments; but I sleep a good deal during the daytime.

In the daytime it is tiresome and perplexing.

170 There are always new shoots on the fungus, and new shades of yellow all over it. I cannot keep count of them, though I have tried conscientiously.

It is the strangest yellow, that wallpaper! It makes me think of all the yellow things I ever saw—not beautiful ones like buttercups, but old, foul, bad yellow things.

But there is something else about that paper—the smell! I noticed it the moment we came into the room, but with so much air and sun it was not bad. Now we have had a week of fog and rain, and whether the windows are open or not, the smell is here.

It creeps all over the house.

I find it hovering in the dining-room, skulking in the parlor, hiding in the hall, lying in wait for me on the stairs.

175 It gets into my hair.

Even when I go to ride, if I turn my head suddenly and surprise it—there is that smell!

Such a peculiar odor, too! I have spent hours in trying to analyze it, to find what it smelled like.

It is not bad—at first—and very gentle, but quite the subtlest, most enduring odor I ever met.

In the damp weather it is awful. I wake up in the night and find it hanging over me.

180 It used to disturb me at first. I thought seriously of burning the house—to reach the smell.

But now I am used to it. The only thing I can think of that it is like is the *color* of the paper! A yellow smell.

There is a very funny mark on this wall, low down, near the mopboard. A streak that runs round the room. It goes behind every piece of furniture, except the bed, a long, straight, even *smooch,* as if it had been rubbed over and over.

I wonder how it was done and who did it, and what they did it for. Round and round and round—round and round and round—it makes me dizzy!

I really have discovered something at last.

Through watching so much at night, when it changes so, I have finally found out. 185

The front pattern *does* move—and no wonder! The woman behind shakes it!

Sometimes I think there are a great many women behind, and sometimes only one, and she crawls around fast, and her crawling shakes it all over.

Then in the very bright spots she keeps still, and in the very shady spots she just takes hold of the bars and shakes them hard.

And she is all the time trying to climb through. But nobody could climb through that pattern—it strangles so; I think that is why it has so many heads.

They get through and then the pattern strangles them off and turns them upside 190 down, and makes their eyes white!

If those heads were covered or taken off it would not be half so bad.

I think that woman gets out in the daytime!

And I'll tell you why—privately—I've seen her!

I can see her out of every one of my windows!

It is the same woman, I know, for she is always creeping, and most women do not 195 creep by daylight.

I see her in that long shaded lane, creeping up and down. I see her in those dark grape arbors, creeping all around the garden.

I see her on that long road under the trees, creeping along, and when a carriage comes she hides under the blackberry vines.

I don't blame her a bit. It must be very humiliating to be caught creeping by daylight!

I always lock the door when I creep by daylight! I can't do it at night, for I know John would suspect something at once.

And John is so queer now that I don't want to irritate him. I wish he would take an- 200 other room! Besides, I don't want anybody to get that woman out at night but myself.

I often wonder if I could see her out of all the windows at once.

But, turn as fast as I can, I can only see out of one at one time.

And though I always see her, she *may* be able to creep faster than I can turn! I have watched her sometimes away off in the open country, creeping as fast as a cloud shadow in a wind.

If only that top pattern could be gotten off from the under one! I mean to try it, little by little.

I have found out another funny thing, but I shan't tell it this time! It does not do to 205 trust people too much.

There are only two more days to get this paper off, and I believe John is beginning to notice. I don't like the look in his eyes.

And I heard him ask Jennie a lot of professional questions about me. She had a very good report to give.

She said I slept a good deal in the daytime.

John knows I don't sleep very well at night, for all I'm so quiet!

He asked me all sorts of questions, too, and pretended to be very loving and kind. 210

As if I couldn't see through him!

Still, I don't wonder he acts so, sleeping under this paper for three months.

It only interests me, but I feel sure John and Jennie are affected by it.

Hurrah! This is the last day, but it is enough. John is to stay in town over night, and won't be out until this evening.

215 Jennie wanted to sleep with me—the sly thing; but I told her I should undoubtedly rest better for a night all alone.

That was clever, for really I wasn't alone a bit! As soon as it was moonlight and that poor thing began to crawl and shake the pattern, I got up and ran to help her.

I pulled and she shook. I shook and she pulled, and before morning we had peeled off yards of that paper.

A strip about as high as my head and half around the room.

And then when the sun came and that awful pattern began to laugh at me, I declared I would finish it today!

220 We go away tomorrow, and they are moving all my furniture down again to leave things as they were before.

Jennie looked at the wall in amazement, but I told her merrily that I did it out of pure spite at the vicious thing.

She laughed and said she wouldn't mind doing it herself, but I must not get tired.

How she betrayed herself that time!

But I am here, and no person touches this paper but Me—not *alive!*

225 She tried to get me out of the room—it was too patent! But I said it was so quiet and empty and clean now that I believed I would lie down again and sleep all I could, and not to wake me even for dinner—I would call when I woke.

So now she is gone, and the servants are gone, and the things are gone, and there is nothing left but that great bedstead nailed down, with the canvas mattress we found on it.

We shall sleep downstairs tonight, and take the boat home tomorrow.

I quite enjoy the room, now it is bare again.

How those children did tear about here!

230 This bedstead is fairly gnawed!

But I must get to work.

I have locked the door and thrown the key down into the front path.

I don't want to go out, and I don't want to have anybody come in, till John comes.

I want to astonish him.

235 I've got a rope up here that even Jennie did not find. If that woman does get out, and tries to get away, I can tie her!

But I forgot I could not reach far without anything to stand on!

This bed will *not* move!

I tried to lift and push it until I was lame, and then I got so angry I bit off a little piece at one corner—but it hurt my teeth.

Then I peeled off all the paper I could reach standing on the floor. It sticks horribly and the pattern just enjoys it! All those strangled heads and bulbous eyes and waddling fungus growths just shriek with derision!

240 I am getting angry enough to do something desperate. To jump out of the window would be admirable exercise, but the bars are too strong even to try.

Besides I wouldn't do it. Of course not. I know well enough that a step like that is improper and might be misconstrued.

I don't like to *look* out of the windows even—there are so many of those creeping women, and they creep so fast.

I wonder if they all come out of that wallpaper as I did?

But I am securely fastened now by my well-hidden rope—you don't get *me* out in the road there!

I suppose I shall have to get back behind the pattern when it comes night, and that is hard! 245

It is so pleasant to be out in this great room and creep around as I please!

I don't want to go outside. I won't, even if Jennie asks me to.

For outside you have to creep on the ground, and everything is green instead of yellow.

But here I can creep smoothly on the floor, and my shoulder just fits in that long smooch around the wall, so I cannot lose my way.

Why, there's John at the door! 250

It is no use, young man, you can't open it!

How he does call and pound!

Now he's crying to Jennie for an axe.

It would be a shame to break down that beautiful door!

"John, dear!" said I in the gentlest voice. "The key is down by the front steps, 255 under a plantain leaf!"

That silenced him for a few moments.

Then he said, very quietly indeed, "Open the door, my darling!"

"I can't," said I. "The key is down by the front door under a plantain leaf!" And then I said it again, several times, very gently and slowly, and said it so often that he had to go and see, and he got it of course, and came in. He stopped short by the door.

"What is the matter?" he cried. "For God's sake, what are you doing!"

I kept on creeping just the same, but I looked at him over my shoulder. 260

"I've got out at last," said I, "in spite of you and Jane. And I've pulled off most of the paper, so you can't put me back!"

Now why should that man have fainted? But he did, and right across my path by the wall, so that I had to creep over him every time! [1892]

QUESTIONS

1. How does each of the first seven sentences foreshadow a later development in the story?
2. Who or what is responsible for the plight of the protagonist?
3. How clearly does the narrator understand her husband's character?
4. How do the sentence patterns and rhythms relate to the theme?
5. How does the narrator's evolving attitude toward the yellow wallpaper mirror the successive stages of her condition? How does the wallpaper function as a metaphor for the narrator's mind?

RESPONSES

1. Write an essay examining the binary of day and night in this story.
2. Research the history of medical treatment for women in the late nineteenth century. Write an essay illustrating how this story is a contribution to that social discourse.

FOCUS ON FILM

1. What does the television film *The Yellow Wallpaper* (1989) add to its portrayal of the husband? Are these additions fair to the print story?
2. How does the film adapt the first-person point of view of the print story?

NIKOLAI GOGOL

Nikolai Gogol (1809–1852) was born in the Russian Ukraine. Educated at local schools, he went in 1828 to St. Petersburg, where he supported himself in various government departments while aspiring to a literary career. He came to prominence with his first collection of stories, *Evenings on a Farm Near Dikanka* (1832), which was followed three years later by his historical romance, *Taras Bulba*. His satiric play *The Inspector General* (1836) offended the authorities, and he was forced into exile in Rome where he wrote his novel *Dead Souls* (1842). "The Overcoat" has been much praised as a landmark in the shift in European sensibility from romanticism to realism.

The Overcoat

In the department of . . . but I had better not mention in what department. There is nothing in the world more readily moved to wrath than a department, a regiment, a government office, and in fact any sort of official body. Nowadays every private individual considers all society insulted in his person. I have been told that very lately a petition was handed in from a police-captain of what town I don't recollect, and that in this petition he set forth clearly that the institutions of the State were in danger and that its sacred name was being taken in vain; and, in proof thereof, he appended to his petition an enormously long volume of some work of romance in which a police-captain appeared on every tenth page, occasionally, indeed, in an intoxicated condition. And so, to avoid any unpleasantness, we had better call the department of which we are speaking a certain department.

And so, in a certain department there was a government clerk; a clerk of whom it cannot be said that he was very remarkable; he was short, somewhat pock-marked, with rather reddish hair and rather dim, bleary eyes, with a small bald patch on the top of his head, with wrinkles on both sides of his cheeks and the sort of complexion which is usually associated with hæmorrhoids . . . no help for that, it is the Petersburg climate. As for his grade in the service (for among us the grade is what must be put first), he was what is called a perpetual titular councillor, a class at which, as we all know, various writers who indulge in the praiseworthy habit of attacking those who cannot defend themselves jeer and jibe to their hearts' content. This clerk's surname was Bashmatchkin. From the very name it is clear that it must have been derived from a shoe (*bashmak*); but when and under what circumstances it was derived from a shoe, it is impossible to say. Both his father and his grandfather and even his brother-in-law, and all the Bashmatchkins without exception wore boots, which they simply re-soled two or three times a year. His name was Akaky Akakyevitch. Perhaps it may strike the reader as a rather strange and far-fetched name, but I can assure him that it was not far-fetched at all, that the circumstances were such that it was quite out of the question to give him any other name. Akaky Akakyevitch was born towards nightfall, if my memory does not deceive me, on the twenty-third of March. His mother, the wife of a government clerk, a very good woman, made arrangements in due course to christen the child. She was still lying in bed, facing the door, while on her right hand stood the godfather, an excellent man called Ivan Ivanovitch Yeroshkin, one of the head clerks in the Senate, and the godmother, the wife of a police official, and a woman of rare qualities, Arina Semyonovna Byelobryushkov. Three names were offered to the happy mother for selection—Moky, Sossy, or the name of the martyr Hozdazat. "No," thought the poor lady, "they are all such names!" To satisfy her, they opened the calendar at another place, and the names which turned up were: Trifily, Dula, Varahasy. "What an infliction!" said the mother. "What names they all are! I really never heard such names. Varadat or Varuh would be bad enough, but Trifily and Varahasy!" They turned over another page and the names were: Pavsikahy and Vahtisy. "Well, I see," said the mother, "it is clear that it is his fate. Since that is how it is, he had better be called after his father, his father is Akaky, let the son be Akaky, too." This was how he came to be Akaky Akakyevitch. The baby was christened and cried and made wry faces during the ceremony, as though he foresaw that he would be a titular councillor. So that was how it all came to pass. We have recalled it here so that the reader may see for himself that it happened quite inevitably and that to give him any other name was out of the question. No one has been able to remember when and how long ago he entered the department, nor who gave him the job. However many directors and higher officials of all sorts came and went, he was always seen in the same place, in the same position, at the very same duty, precisely the same copying clerk, so that they used to declare that he must have been born a copying clerk in uniform all complete and with a bald patch on his head. No respect at all was shown him in the department. The porters, far from getting up from their seats when he came in, took no more notice of him than if a simple fly had flown across the vestibule. His superiors treated him with a sort of domineering chilliness. The head clerk's assistant used to throw papers under his nose without even saying: "Copy this" or "Here is an interesting, nice little case" or some agreeable remark of the sort, as is usually done in well-behaved offices. And he would take it, gazing only at the paper without looking to see who had put it there and whether he had the right to do so; he would take it and at once set to work to copy it. The young clerks jeered and made jokes at him to the best of their clerkly wit, and told before his face all sorts of stories of their own invention about him; they would say of his landlady, an old woman of seventy, that she beat him, would enquire when the wedding was to take place, and would scatter bits of paper on his head, calling them snow. Akaky Akakyevitch never answered a word, however, but behaved as though there were no one there. It had no influence on his work even; in the midst of all this teasing, he never made a single mistake in his copying. Only when the jokes were too unbearable, when they jolted his arm and prevented him from going on with his work, he would bring out: "Leave me alone! Why do you insult me?" and there was something strange in the words and in the voice in which they were uttered. There was a note in it of something that aroused compassion, so that one young man, new to the office, who, following the example of the rest, had allowed himself to mock at him, suddenly stopped as though cut to the heart, and from that time forth everything was, as it were, changed and appeared in a different light to him. Some unnatural force seemed to thrust him away from the companions with whom he had become acquainted, accepting them as well-bred, polished people. And long afterwards, at moments of the greatest gaiety, the figure of the humble little clerk with a bald patch on his head rose before him with his heart-rending words: "Leave me alone! Why do you insult me?" and in those heart-rending words he heard others: "I am your brother." And the poor young man hid his face in his hands, and many times afterwards in his life he shuddered, seeing how much inhumanity there is in man, how much savage brutality lies hidden under refined, cultured politeness, and, my God! even in a man whom the world accepts as a gentleman and a man of honour. . . .

It would be hard to find a man who lived in his work as did Akaky Akakyevitch. To say that he was zealous in his work is not enough; no, he loved his work. In it, in that copying, he found a varied and agreeable world of his own. There was a look of enjoyment on his face; certain letters were favourites with him, and when he came to them he was delighted; he chuckled to himself and winked and moved his lips, so that it seemed as though every letter his pen was forming could be read in his face. If rewards had been given according to the measure of zeal in the service, he might to his amazement have even found himself a civil councillor; but all he gained in the service, as the wits, his fellow-clerks expressed it, was a buckle in his button-hole and a pain in his back. It cannot be said, however, that no notice had ever been taken of him. One director, being a good-natured man and anxious to reward him for his long service, sent him something a little more important than his ordinary copying; he was instructed from a finished document to make some sort of report for another office, the work consisted only of altering the headings and in places changing the first person into the third. This cost him such an effort that it threw him into a regular perspiration: he mopped his brow and said at last, "No, better let me copy something."

From that time forth they left him to go on copying for ever. It seemed as though nothing in the world existed for him outside his copying. He gave no thought at all to his clothes; his uniform was—well, not green but some sort of rusty, muddy colour. His collar was very short and narrow, so that, although his neck was not particularly long, yet, standing out of the collar, it looked as immensely long as those of the plaster kittens that wag their heads and are carried about on trays on the heads of dozens of foreigners living in Russia. And there were always things sticking to his uniform, either bits of hay or threads; moreover, he had a special art of passing under a window at the very moment when various rubbish was being flung out into the street, and so was continually carrying off bits of melon rind and similar litter on his hat. He had never once in his life noticed what was being done and going on in the street, all those things at which, as we all know, his colleagues, the young clerks, always stare, carrying their sharp sight so far even as to notice any one on the other side of the pavement with a trouser strap hanging loose—a detail which always calls forth a sly grin. Whatever Akaky Akakyevitch looked at, he saw nothing anywhere but his clear, evenly written lines, and only perhaps when a horse's head suddenly appeared from nowhere just on his shoulder, and its nostrils blew a perfect gale upon his cheek, did he notice that he was not in the middle of his writing, but rather in the middle of the street.

On reaching home, he would sit down at once to the table, hurriedly sup his soup and eat a piece of beef with an onion; he did not notice the taste at all, but ate it all up together with the flies and anything else that Providence chanced to send him. When he felt that his stomach was beginning to be full, he would rise up from the table, get out a bottle of ink and set to copying the papers he had brought home with him. When he had none to do, he would make a copy expressly for his own pleasure, particularly if the document were remarkable not for the beauty of its style but for the fact of its being addressed to some new or important personage.

Even at those hours when the grey Petersburg sky is completely overcast and the whole population of clerks have dined and eaten their fill, each as best as he can, according to the salary he receives and his personal tastes; when they are all resting after the scratching of pens and bustle of the office, their own necessary work and other people's, and all the tasks that an over-zealous man voluntarily sets himself even beyond what is necessary; when the clerks are hastening to devote what is left of their time to pleasure; some more enterprising are flying to the theatre, others to the street to spend their leisure, staring at women's hats, some to spend the evening paying compliments to some attractive girl, the star of a little official circle, while some—and this is the most frequent of all—go simply to a fellow-clerk's flat on the third or fourth storey, two little rooms with an entry or a kitchen, with some pretentions to style, with a lamp or some such article that has cost many sacrifices of dinners and excursions— at the time when all the clerks are scattered about the little flats of their friends, playing a tempestuous game of whist, sipping tea out of glasses to the accompaniment of farthing rusks, sucking in smoke from long pipes, telling, as the cards are dealt, some scandal that has floated down from higher circles, a pleasure which the Russian can never by any possibility deny himself, or, when there is nothing better to talk about, repeating the everlasting anecdote of the commanding officer who was told that the tail had been cut off the horse on the Falconet monument—in short, even when every one was eagerly seeking entertainment, Akaky Akakyevitch did not give himself up to any amusement. No one could say that they had ever seen him at an evening party. After working to his heart's content, he would go to bed, smiling at the thought of the next day and wondering what God would send him to copy! So flowed on the peaceful life of a man who knew how to be content with his fate on a salary of four hundred roubles, and so perhaps it would have flowed on to extreme old age, had it not been for the various calamities that bestrew the path through life, not only of titular, but even of privy, actual court and all other councillors, even those who neither give council to others nor accept it themselves.

There is in Petersburg a mighty foe of all who receive a salary of four hundred roubles or about that sum. That foe is none other than our northern frost, although it is said to be very good for the health. Between eight and nine in the morning, precisely at the hour when the streets are full of clerks going to their departments, the frost begins giving such sharp and stinging flips at all their noses indiscriminately that the poor fellows don't know what to do with them. At that time, when even those in the higher grade have a pain in their brows and tears in their eyes from the frost, the poor titular councillors are sometimes almost defenceless. Their only protection lies in running as fast as they can through five or six streets in a wretched, thin little overcoat and then warming their feet thoroughly in the porter's room, till all their faculties and qualifications for their various duties thaw again after being frozen on the way. Akaky Akakyevitch had for some time been feeling that his back and shoulders were particularly nipped by the cold, although he did try to run the regular distance as fast as he could. He wondered at last whether there were any defects in his overcoat. After examining it thoroughly in the privacy of his home, he discovered that in two or three places, to wit on the back and the shoulders, it had become a regular sieve; the cloth was so worn that you could see through it and the lining was coming out. I must observe that Akaky Akakyevitch's overcoat had also served as a butt for the jibes of the clerks. It had even been deprived of the honourable name of overcoat and had been referred to as the "dressing jacket." It was indeed of rather a strange make. Its collar had been growing smaller year by year as it served to patch the other parts. The patches were not good specimens of the tailor's art, and they certainly looked clumsy and ugly. On seeing what was wrong, Akaky Akakyevitch decided that he would have to take the overcoat to Petrovitch, a tailor who lived on a fourth storey up a back staircase, and, in spite of having only one eye and being pock-marked all over his face, was rather successful in repairing the trousers and coats of clerks and others—that is, when he was sober, be it understood, and had no other enterprise in his mind. Of this tailor I ought not, of course, to say much, but since it is now the rule that the character of every person in a novel must be completely drawn, well, there is no help for it, here is Petrovitch too. At first he was called simply Grigory, and was a serf belonging to some gentleman or other. He began to be called Petrovitch from the time that he got his freedom and began to drink rather heavily on every holiday, at first only on the chief holidays, but afterwards on all church holidays indiscriminately, wherever there is a cross in the calendar. On that side he was true to the customs of his forefathers, and when he quarrelled with his wife used to call her "a worldly woman and a German." Since we have now mentioned the wife, it will be necessary to say a few words about her too, but unfortunately not much is known about her, except indeed that Petrovitch had a wife and that she wore a cap and not a kerchief, but apparently she could not boast of beauty; anyway, none but soldiers of the Guards peeped under her cap when they met her, and they twitched their moustaches and gave vent to a rather peculiar sound.

As he climbed the stairs, leading to Petrovitch's—which, to do them justice, were all soaked with water and slops and saturated through and through with that smell of spirits which makes the eyes smart, and is, as we all know, inseparable from the backstairs of Petersburg houses—Akaky Akakyevitch was already wondering how much Petrovitch would ask for the job, and inwardly resolving not to give more than two roubles. The door was open, for Petrovitch's wife was frying some fish and had so filled the kitchen with smoke that you could not even see the black-beetles. Akaky Akakyevitch crossed the kitchen unnoticed by the good woman, and walked at last into a room where he saw Petrovitch sitting on a big, wooden, unpainted table with his legs tucked under him like a Turkish Pasha. The feet, as is usual with tailors when they sit at work, were bare; and the first object that caught Akaky Akakyevitch's eye was the big toe, with which he was already familiar, with a misshapen nail as thick and strong as the shell of a tortoise. Round Petrovitch's neck hung a skein of silk and another of thread and on his knees was a rag of some sort. He had for the last three minutes been trying to thread his needle, but could not get the thread into the eye and so was very angry with the darkness and indeed with the thread itself, muttering in an undertone: "It won't go in, the savage! You wear me out, you rascal." Akaky Akakyevitch was vexed that he had come just at the minute when Petrovitch was in a bad humour; he liked to give him an order when he was a little "elevated," or, as his wife expressed it, "had fortified himself on fizz, the one-eyed devil." In such circumstances Petrovitch was as a rule very ready to give way and agree, and invariably bowed and thanked him, indeed. Afterwards, it is true, his wife would come wailing that her husband had been drunk and so had asked too little, but adding a single ten-kopeck piece would settle that. But on this occasion Petrovitch was apparently sober and consequently curt, unwilling to bargain, and the devil knows what price he would be ready to lay on. Akaky Akakyevitch perceived this, and was, as the saying is, beating a retreat, but things had gone too far, for Petrovitch was screwing up his solitary eye very attentively at him and Akaky Akakyevitch involuntarily brought out: "Good day, Petrovitch!" "I wish you a good day, sir," said Petrovitch, and squinted at Akaky Akakyevitch's hands, trying to discover what sort of goods he had brought.

"Here I have come to you, Petrovitch, do you see . . .!"

10   It must be noticed that Akaky Akakyevitch for the most part explained himself by apologies, vague phrases, and particles which have absolutely no significance whatever. If the subject were a very difficult one, it was his habit indeed to leave his sentences quite unfinished, so that very often after a sentence had begun with the words, "It really is, don't you know . . ." nothing at all would follow and he himself would be quite oblivious, supposing he had said all that was necessary.

"What is it?" said Petrovitch, and at the same time with his solitary eye he scrutinized his whole uniform from the collar to the sleeves, the back, the skirts, the button-holes—with all of which he was very familiar, they were all his own work. Such scrutiny is habitual with tailors, it is the first thing they do on meeting one.

"It's like this, Petrovitch . . . the overcoat, the cloth . . . you see everywhere else it is quite strong; it's a little dusty and looks as though it were old, but it is new and it is only in one place just a little . . . on the back, and just a little worn on one shoulder and on this shoulder, too, a little . . . do you see? that's all, and it's not much work. . . ."

Petrovitch took the "dressing jacket," first spread it out over the table, examined it for a long time, shook his head and put his hand out to the window for a round snuffbox with a portrait on the lid of some general—which precisely I can't say, for a finger had been thrust through the spot where a face should have been, and the hole had been pasted up with a square piece of paper. After taking a pinch of snuff, Petrovitch held the "dressing jacket" up in his hands and looked at it against the light, and again he shook his head; then he turned it with the lining upwards and once more shook his head; again he took off the lid with the general pasted up with paper and stuffed a pinch into his nose, shut the box, put it away and at last said: "No, it can't be repaired; a wretched garment!" Akaky Akakyevitch's heart sank at those words.

"Why can't it, Petrovitch?" he said, almost in the imploring voice of a child. "Why, the only thing is it is a bit worn on the shoulders; why, you have got some little pieces. . . ."

15   "Yes, the pieces will be found all right," said Petrovitch, "but it can't be patched, the stuff is quite rotten; if you put a needle in it, it would give way."

"Let it give way, but you just put a patch on it."

"There is nothing to put a patch on. There is nothing for it to hold on to; there is a great strain on it, it is not worth calling cloth, it would fly away at a breath of wind."

"Well, then, strengthen it with something—upon my word, really, this is . . .!"

"No," said Petrovitch resolutely, "there is nothing to be done, the thing is no good at all. You had far better, when the cold winter weather comes, make yourself leg wrappings out of it, for there is no warmth in stockings, the Germans invented them just to make money." (Petrovitch was fond of a dig at the Germans occasionally.) "And as for the overcoat, it is clear that you will have to have a new one."

20   At the word "new" there was a mist before Akaky Akakyevitch's eyes, and everything in the room seemed blurred. He could see nothing clearly but the general with the piece of paper over his face on the lid of Petrovitch's snuff-box.

"A new one?" he said, still feeling as though he were in a dream; "why, I haven't the money for it."

"Yes, a new one," Petrovitch repeated with barbarous composure.

"Well, and if I did have a new one, how much would it . . .?"

"You mean what will it cost?"

"Yes."

"Well, three fifty-rouble notes or more," said Petrovitch, and he compressed his lips significantly. He was very fond of making an effect, he was fond of suddenly disconcerting a man completely and then squinting sideways to see what sort of a face he made.

"A hundred and fifty roubles for an overcoat," screamed poor Akaky Akakyevitch— it was perhaps the first time he had screamed in his life, for he was always distinguished by the softness of his voice.

"Yes," said Petrovitch, "and even then it's according to the coat. If I were to put marten on the collar, and add a hood with silk linings, it would come to two hundred."

"Petrovitch, please," said Akaky Akakyevitch in an imploring voice, not hearing and not trying to hear what Petrovitch said, and missing all his effects, "do repair it somehow, so that it will serve a little longer."

"No, that would be wasting work and spending money for nothing," said Petrovitch, and after that Akaky Akakyevitch went away completely crushed, and when he had gone Petrovitch remained standing for a long time with his lips pursed up significantly before he took up his work again, feeling pleased that he had not demeaned himself nor lowered the dignity of the tailor's art.

When he got into the street, Akaky Akakyevitch was as though in a dream. "So that is how it is," he said to himself. "I really did not think it would be so . . ." and then after a pause he added, "So there it is! so that's how it is at last! and I really could never have supposed it would have been so. And there . . ." There followed another long silence, after which he brought out: "So there it is! well, it really is so utterly unexpected . . . who would have thought . . . what a circumstance . . ." Saying this, instead of going home he walked off in quite the opposite direction without suspecting what he was doing. On the way a clumsy sweep brushed the whole of his sooty side against him and blackened all his shoulder; a regular hatful of plaster scattered upon him from the top of a house that was being built. He noticed nothing of this, and only after he had jostled against a sentry who had set his halberd down beside him and was shaking some snuff out of his horn into his rough fist, he came to himself a little and then only because the sentry said: "Why are you poking yourself right in one's face, haven't you the pavement to yourself?" This made him look round and turn homeward; only there he began to collect his thoughts, to see his position in a clear and true light and began talking to himself no longer incoherently but reasonably and openly as with a sensible friend with whom one can discuss the most intimate and vital matters. "No, indeed," said Akaky Akakyevitch, "it is no use talking to Petrovitch now; just now he really is . . . his wife must have been giving it to him. I had better go to him on Sunday morning; after the Saturday evening he will be squinting and sleepy, so he'll want a little drink to carry it off and his wife won't giver him a penny. I'll slip ten kopecks into his hand and then he will be more accommodating and maybe take the overcoat. . . ."

So reasoning with himself, Akaky Akakyevitch cheered up and waited until the next Sunday; then, seeing from a distance Petrovitch's wife leaving the house, he went straight in. Petrovitch certainly was very tipsy after the Saturday. He could hardly hold his head up and was very drowsy: but, for all that, as soon as he heard what he was speaking about, it seemed as though the devil had nudged him. "I can't," he said,

"You must kindly order a new one." Akaky Akakyevitch at once slipped a ten-kopeck piece into his hand. "I thank you, sir, I will have just a drop to your health, but don't trouble yourself about the overcoat; it is not a bit of good for anything. I'll make you a fine new coat, you can trust me for that."

Akaky Akakyevitch would have said more about repairs, but Petrovitch, without listening, said: "A new one now I'll make you without fail; you can rely upon that, I'll do my best. It could even be like the fashion that has come in with the collar to button with silver claws under appliqué."

Then Akaky Akakyevitch saw that there was no escape from a new overcoat and he was utterly depressed. How indeed, for what, with what money could he get it? Of course he could to some extent rely on the bonus for the coming holiday, but that money had long ago been appropriated and its use determined beforehand. It was needed for new trousers and to pay the cobbler an old debt for putting some new tops to some old boot-legs, and he had to order three shirts from a seamstress as well as two specimens of an undergarment which it is improper to mention in print; in short, all that money absolutely must be spent, and even if the director were to be so gracious as to assign him a gratuity of forty-five or even fifty, instead of forty roubles, there would be still left a mere trifle, which would be but as a drop in the ocean beside the fortune needed for an overcoat. Though, of course, he knew that Petrovitch had a strange craze for suddenly putting on the devil knows what enormous price, so that at times his own wife could not help crying out: "Why, you are out of your wits, you idiot! Another time he'll undertake a job for nothing, and here the devil has bewitched him to ask more than he is worth himself." Though, of course, he knew that Petrovitch would undertake to make it for eighty roubles, still where would he get those eighty roubles? He might manage half of that sum; half of it could be found, perhaps even a little more; but where could he get the other half? . . . But, first of all, the reader ought to know where that first half was to be found. Akaky Akakyevitch had the habit every time he spent a rouble of putting aside two kopecks in a little locked-up box with a slit in the lid for slipping the money in. At the end of every half-year he would inspect the pile of coppers there and change them for small silver. He had done this for a long time, and in the course of many years the sum had mounted up to forty roubles and so he had half the money in his hands, but where was he to get the other half, where was he to get another forty rubles? Akaky Akakyevitch pondered and pondered and decided at last that he would have to diminish his ordinary expenses, at least for a year; give up burning candles in the evening, and if he had to do anything he must go into the landlady's room and work by her candle; that as he walked along the streets he must walk as lightly and carefully as possible, almost on tiptoe, on the cobbles and flagstones, so that his soles might last a little longer than usual; that he must send his linen to the wash less frequently, and that, to preserve it from being worn, he must take it off every day when he came home and sit in a thin cotton-shoddy dressing-gown, a very ancient garment which Time itself had spared. To tell the truth, he found it at first rather hard to get used to these privations, but after a while it became a habit and went smoothly enough—he even became quite accustomed to being hungry in the evening; on the other hand, he had spiritual nourishment, for he carried ever in his thoughts the idea of his future overcoat. His whole existence had in a sense become fuller, as though he had married, as though some other person were present with him, as though he were no longer alone, but an agreeable companion had consented to walk the path of life hand in hand with him, and that companion was no other than the new overcoat with its thick wadding and its strong, durable lining. He became, as it were, more alive, even more strong-willed, like a man who has set before himself a definite aim. Uncertainty, indecision, in fact all the hesitating and vague characteristics vanished from his face and his manners. At times there was a gleam in his eyes, indeed, the most bold and audacious ideas flashed through his mind. Why not really have marten on the collar? Meditation on the subject always made him absentminded. On one occasion when he was copying a document, he very nearly made a mistake, so that he almost cried out "ough" aloud and crossed himself. At least once every month he went to Petrovitch to talk about the overcoat, where it would be best to buy the cloth, and what colour it should be, and what price, and, though he returned home a little anxious, he was always pleased at the thought that at last the time was at hand when everything would be bought and the overcoat would be made. Things moved even faster than he had anticipated. Contrary to all expectations, the director bestowed on Akaky Akakyevitch a gratuity of no less than sixty roubles. Whether it was that he had an inkling that Akaky Akakyevitch needed a greatcoat, or whether it happened so by chance, owing to this he found he had twenty roubles extra. This circumstance hastened the course of affairs. Another two or three months of partial fasting and Akaky Akakyevitch had actually saved up nearly eighty roubles. His heart, as a rule very tranquil, began to throb. The very first day he set off in company with Petrovitch to the shops. They bought some very good cloth, and no wonder, since they had been thinking of it for more than six months before, and scarcely a month had passed without their going to the shop to compare prices; now Petrovitch himself declared that there was no better cloth to be had. For the lining they chose calico, but of a stout quality, which in Petrovitch's words was even better than silk, and actually as strong and handsome to look at. Marten they did not buy, because it certainly was dear, but instead they chose cat fur, the best to be found in the shop— cat which in the distance might almost be taken for marten. Petrovitch was busy over the coat for a whole fortnight, because there were a great many button-holes, otherwise it would have been ready sooner. Petrovitch asked twelve roubles for the work; less than that it hardly could have been, everything was sewn with silk, with fine double seams, and Petrovitch went over every seam afterwards with his own teeth imprinting various figures with them. It was . . . it is hard to say precisely on what day, but probably on the most triumphant day of the life of Akaky Akakyevitch that Petrovitch at last brought the overcoat. He brought it in the morning, just before it was time to set off for the department. The overcoat could not have arrived more in the nick of time, for rather sharp frosts were just beginning and seemed threatening to be even more severe. Petrovitch brought the greatcoat himself as a good tailor should. There was an expression of importance on his face, such as Akaky Akakyevitch had never seen there before. He seemed fully conscious of having completed a work of no little moment and of having shown in his own person the gulf that separates tailors who only put in linings and do repairs from those who make up new materials. He took the greatcoat out of the pocket-handkerchief in which he had brought it (the pocket-handkerchief had just come home from the wash), he then folded it up and put it in his pocket for future use. After taking out the overcoat, he looked at it with much pride and, holding it in both hands, threw it very deftly over Akaky Akakyevitch's shoulders, then pulled it down and smoothed it out behind with his hands; then draped it about Akaky Akakyevitch with somewhat jaunty carelessness. The latter, as a man advanced in years, wished to try it with his arms in the sleeves. Petrovitch helped him to put it on, and it appeared that it looked splendid too with his arms in the sleeves. In fact it turned out that the overcoat was completely and entirely successful. Petrovitch did not let slip the occasion for observing that it was only because he lived in a small street and had no signboard, and because he had known Akaky Akakyevitch so long, that he had done it so cheaply, but on the Nevsky Prospect they would have asked him seventy-five roubles for the work alone. Akaky Akakyevitch had no inclination to discuss this with Petrovitch, besides he was frightened of the big sums that Petrovitch was fond of flinging airily about in conversation. He paid him, thanked him, and went off on the spot, with his new overcoat on, to the department. Petrovitch followed him out and stopped in the street, staring for a good time at the coat from a distance and then purposely turned off and, taking a short cut by a side street, came back into the street and got another view of the coat from the other side, that is, from the front.

35   Meanwhile Akaky Akakyevitch walked along with every emotion in its most holiday mood. He felt every second that he had a new overcoat on his shoulders, and several times he actually laughed from inward satisfaction. Indeed, it had two advantages, one that it was warm and the other that it was good. He did not notice the way at all and found himself all at once at the department; in the porter's room he took off the overcoat, looked it over and put it in the porter's special care. I cannot tell how it happened, but all at once every one in the department learned that Akaky Akakyevitch had a new overcoat and that the "dressing jacket" no longer existed. They all ran out at once into the porter's room to look at Akaky Akakyevitch's new overcoat, they began welcoming him and congratulating him so that at first he could do nothing but smile and afterwards felt positively abashed. When, coming up to him, they all began saying that he must "sprinkle" the new overcoat and that he ought at least to stand them all a supper, Akaky Akakyevitch lost his head completely and did not know what to do, how to get out of it, nor what to answer. A few minutes later, flushing crimson, he even began assuring them with great simplicity that it was not a new overcoat at all, that it was just nothing, that it was an old overcoat. At last one of the clerks, indeed the assistant of the head clerk of the room, probably in order to show that he was not proud and was able to get on with those beneath him, said: "So be it, I'll give a party instead of Akaky Akakyevitch and invite you all to tea with me this evening; as luck would have it, it is my nameday." The clerks naturally congratulated the assistant head clerk and eagerly accepted the invitation. Akaky Akakyevitch was beginning to make excuses, but they all declared that it was uncivil of him, that it was simply a shame and a disgrace and that he could not possibly refuse. However, he felt pleased about it afterwards when he remembered that through this he would have the opportunity of going out in the evening, too, in his new overcoat. That whole day was for Akaky Akakyevitch the most triumphant and festive day in his life. He returned home in the happiest frame of mind, took off the overcoat and hung it carefully on the wall, admiring the cloth and lining once more, and then pulled out his old "dressing jacket," now completely coming to pieces, on purpose to compare them. He glanced at it and positively laughed, the difference was so immense! And long afterwards he went on laughing at dinner, as the position in which the "dressing jacket" was placed recurred to his mind. He dined in excellent spirits and after dinner wrote nothing, no papers at all, but just took his ease for a little while on his bed, till it got dark, then, without putting things off, he dressed, put on his overcoat, and went out into the street. Where precisely the clerk who had invited him lived we regret to say that we cannot tell; our memory is beginning to fail sadly, and everything there is in Petersburg, all the streets and houses, are so blurred and muddled in our head that it is a very difficult business to put anything in orderly fashion. However that may have been, there is no doubt that the clerk lived in the better part of the town and consequently a very long distance from Akaky Akakyevitch. At first the latter had to walk through deserted streets, scantily lighted, but as he approached his destination the streets became more lively, more full of people, and more brightly lighted; passers-by began to be

more frequent, ladies began to appear, here and there, beautifully dressed, beaver collars were to be seen on the men. Cabmen with wooden trellis-work sledges, studded with gilt nails, were less frequently to be met; on the other hand, jaunty drivers in raspberry coloured velvet caps with varnished sledges and bear-skin rugs appeared, and carriages with decorated boxes dashed along the streets, their wheels crunching through the snow.

Akaky Akakyevitch looked at all this as a novelty; for several years he had not gone out into the streets in the evening. He stopped with curiosity before a lighted shop-window to look at a picture in which a beautiful woman was represented in the act of taking off her shoe and displaying as she did so the whole of a very shapely leg, while behind her back a gentleman with whiskers and a handsome imperial on his chin was putting his head in at the door. Akaky Akakyevitch shook his head and smiled and then went on his way. Why did he smile? Was it because he had come across something quite unfamiliar to him, though every man retains some instinctive feeling on the subject, or was it that he reflected, like many other clerks, as follows: "Well, upon my soul, those Frenchmen! it's beyond anything! if they try on anything of the sort, it really is . . .!" Though possibly he did not even think that; there is no creeping into a man's soul and finding out all that he thinks. At last he reached the house in which the assistant head clerk lived in fine style; there was a lamp burning on the stairs, and the flat was on the second floor. As he went into the entry Akaky Akakyevitch saw whole rows of goloshes. Amongst them in the middle of the room stood a samovar hissing and letting off clouds of steam. On the walls hung coats and cloaks, among which some actually had beaver collars or velvet revers. The other side of the wall there was noise and talk, which suddenly became clear and loud when the door opened and the footman came out with a tray full of empty glasses, a jug of cream, and a basket of biscuits. It was evident that the clerks had arrived long before and had already drunk their first glass of tea. Akaky Akakyevitch, after hanging up his coat with his own hands, went into the room, and at the same moment there flashed before his eyes a vision of candles, clerks, pipes, and card tables, together with the confused sounds of conversation rising up on all sides and the noise of moving chairs. He stopped very awkwardly in the middle of the room, looking about and trying to think what to do, but he was observed and received with a shout and they all went at once into the entry and again took a look at his overcoat. Though Akaky Akakyevitch was somewhat embarrassed, yet, being a simple-hearted man, he could not help being pleased at seeing how they all admired his coat. Then of course they all abandoned him and his coat, and turned their attention as usual to the tables set for whist. All this— the noise, the talk, and the crowd of people—was strange and wonderful to Akaky Akakyevitch. He simply did not know how to behave, what to do with his arms and legs and his whole figure; at last he sat down beside the players, looked at the cards, stared first at one and then at another of the faces, and in a little while began to yawn and felt that he was bored—especially as it was long past the time at which he usually went to bed. He tried to take leave of his hosts, but they would not let him go, saying that he absolutely must have a glass of champagne in honour of the new coat. An hour later supper was served, consisting of salad, cold veal, a pasty, pies, and tarts from the confectioner's, and champagne. They made Akaky Akakyevitch drink two glasses, after which he felt that things were much more cheerful, though he could not forget that it was twelve o'clock and that he ought to have been home long ago. That his host might not take it into his head to detain him, he slipped out of the room, hunted in the entry for his greatcoat, which he found, not without regret, lying on the floor, shook it, removed some fluff from it, put it on, and went down the stairs into the street.

It was still light in the streets. Some little general shops, those perpetual clubs for houseserfs and all sorts of people, were open; others which were closed showed, however, a long streak of light at every crack of the door, proving that they were not yet deserted, and probably maids and men-servants were still finishing their conversation and discussion, driving their masters to utter perplexity as to their whereabouts. Akaky Akakyevitch walked along in a cheerful state of mind; he was even on the point of running, goodness knows why, after a lady of some sort who passed by like lightning with every part of her frame in violent motion. He checked himself at once, however, and again walked along very gently, feeling positively surprised himself at the inexplicable impulse that had seized him. Soon the deserted streets, which are not particularly cheerful by day and even less so in the evening, stretched before him. Now they were still more dead and deserted; the light of street lamps was scantier, the oil was evidently running low; then came wooden houses and fences; not a soul anywhere; only the snow gleamed on the streets and the low-pitched slumbering hovels looked black and gloomy with their closed shutters. He approached the spot where the street was intersected by an endless square, which looked like a fearful desert with its houses scarcely visible on the further side.

In the distance, goodness knows where, there was a gleam of light from some sentry-box which seemed to be standing at the end of the world. Akaky Akakyevitch's light-heartedness grew somewhat sensibly less at this place. He stepped into the square, not without an involuntary uneasiness, as though his heart had a foreboding of evil. He looked behind him and to both sides—it was as though the sea were all round him. "No, better not look," he thought, and walked on, shutting his eyes, and when he opened them to see whether the end of the square were near, he suddenly saw standing before him, almost under his very nose, some men with moustaches; just what they were like he could not even distinguish. There was a mist before his eyes and a throbbing in his chest. "I say the overcoat is mine!" said one of them in a voice like a clap of thunder, seizing him by the collar. Akaky Akakyevitch was on the point of shouting "Help" when another put a fist the size of a clerk's head against his very lips, saying: "You just shout now." Akaky Akakyevitch felt only that they took the overcoat off, and gave him a kick with their knees, and he fell on his face in the snow and was conscious of nothing more. A few minutes later he came to himself and got on to his feet, but there was no one there. He felt that it was cold on the ground and that he had no overcoat, and began screaming, but it seemed as though his voice could not carry to the end of the square. Overwhelmed with despair and continuing to scream, he ran across the square straight to the sentry-box, beside which stood a sentry leaning on his halberd and, so it seemed, looking with curiosity to see who the devil the man was who was screaming and running towards him from the distance. As Akaky Akakyevitch reached him, he began breathlessly shouting that he was asleep and not looking after his duty not to see that a man was being robbed. The sentry answered that he had seen nothing, that he had only seen him stopped in the middle of the square by two men, and supposed that they were his friends, and that, instead of abusing him for nothing, he had better go the next day to the superintendent and that he would find out who had taken the overcoat. Akaky Akakyevitch ran home in a terrible state: his hair, which was still comparatively abundant on his temples and the back of his head, was completely dishevelled; his sides and chest and his trousers were all covered with snow. When his old landlady heard a fearful knock at the door she jumped hurriedly out of bed and, with only one slipper on, ran to open it, modestly holding her shift across her bosom; but when she opened it she stepped back, seeing what a state Akaky

Akakyevitch was in. When he told her what had happened, she clasped her hands in horror and said that he must go straight to the superintendent, that the police constable of the quarter would deceive him, make promises and lead him a dance; that it would be best of all to go to the superintendent, and that she knew him indeed, because Anna the Finnish girl who was once her cook was now in service as a nurse at the superintendent's; and that she often saw him himself when he passed by their house, and that he used to be every Sunday at church too, saying his prayers and at the same time looking good-humouredly at every one, and that therefore by every token he must be a kind-hearted man. After listening to this advice, Akaky Akakyevitch made his way very gloomily to his room, and how he spent that night I leave to the imagination of those who are in the least able to picture the position of others. Early in the morning he set off to the police superintendent's, but was told that he was asleep. He came at ten o'clock, he was told again that he was asleep; he came at eleven and was told that the superintendent was not at home; he came at dinner-time, but the clerks in the anteroom would not let him in, and insisted on knowing what was the matter and what business had brought him and exactly what had happened; so that at last Akaky Akakyevitch for the first time in his life tried to show the strength of his character and said curtly that he must see the superintendent himself, that they dare not refuse to admit him, that he had come from the department on government business, and that if he made complaint of them they would see. The clerks dared to say nothing to this, and one of them went to summon the superintendent. The latter received his story of being robbed of his overcoat in an extremely strange way. Instead of attending to the main point, he began asking Akaky Akakyevitch questions, why had he been coming home so late? wasn't he going, or hadn't he been, to some house of ill-fame? so that Akaky Akakyevitch was overwhelmed with confusion, and went away without knowing whether or not the proper measures would be taken in regard to his overcoat. He was absent from the office all that day (the only time that it had happened in his life). Next day he appeared with a pale face, wearing his old "dressing jacket" which had become a still more pitiful sight. The tidings of the theft of the overcoat—though there were clerks who did not let even this chance slip of jeering at Akaky Akakyevitch—touched many of them. They decided on the spot to get up a subscription for him, but collected only a very trifling sum, because the clerks had already spent a good deal on subscribing to the director's portrait and on the purchase of a book, at the suggestion of the head of their department, who was a friend of the author, and so the total realised was very insignificant. One of the clerks, moved by compassion, ventured at any rate to assist Akaky Akakyevitch with good advice, telling him not to go to the district police inspector, because though it might happen that the latter might be sufficiently zealous of gaining the approval of his superiors to succeed in finding the overcoat, it would remain in the possession of the police unless he presented legal proofs that it belonged to him; he urged that far the best thing would be to appeal to a Person of Consequence; that the Person of Consequence, by writing and getting into communication with the proper authorities, could push the matter through more successfully. There was nothing else for it. Akaky Akakyevitch made up his mind to go to the Person of Consequence. What precisely was the nature of the functions of the Person of Consequence has remained a matter of uncertainty. It must be noted that this Person of Consequence had only lately become a person of consequence, and until recently had been a person of no consequence. Though, indeed, his position even now was not reckoned of consequence in comparison with others of still greater consequence. But there is always to be found a circle of persons to whom a person of little consequence in the eyes of others is a person of consequence. It is true that he did his utmost to increase the consequence of his position in various ways, for instance by insisting that his subordinates should come out on to the stairs to meet him when he arrived at his office; that no one should venture to approach him directly but all proceedings should be by the strictest order of precedence, that a collegiate registration clerk should report the matter to the provincial secretary, and the provincial secretary to the titular councillor or whomsoever it might be, and that business should only reach him by this channel. Every one in Holy Russia has a craze for imitation, every one apes and mimics his superiors. I have actually been told that a titular councillor who was put in charge of a small separate office, immediately partitioned off a special room for himself, calling it the head office, and set special porters at the door with red collars and gold lace, who took hold of the handle of the door and opened it for every one who went in, though the "head office" was so tiny that it was with difficulty that an ordinary writing table could be put into it. The manners and habits of the Person of Consequence were dignified and majestic, but not complex. The chief foundation of his system was strictness, "strictness, strictness, and—strictness!" he used to say, and at the last word he would look very significantly at the person he was addressing, though, indeed, he had no reason to do so, for the dozen clerks who made up the whole administrative mechanism of his office stood in befitting awe of him; any clerk who saw him in the distance would leave his work and remain standing at attention till his superior had left the room. His conversation with his subordinates was usually marked by severity and almost confined to three phrases: "How dare you? Do you know to whom you are speaking? Do you understand who I am?" He was, however, at heart a good-natured man, pleasant and obliging with his colleagues; but the grade of general had completely turned his head. When he received it, he was perplexed, thrown off his balance, and quite at a loss how to behave. If he chanced to be with his equals, he was still quite a decent man, a very gentlemanly man, in fact, and in many ways even an intelligent man, but as soon as he was in company with men who were even one grade below him, there was simply no doing anything with him: he sat silent and his position excited compassion, the more so as he himself felt that he might have been spending his time to incomparably more advantage. At times there could be seen in his eyes an intense desire to join in some interesting conversation, but he was restrained by the doubt whether it would not be too much on his part, whether it would not be too great a familiarity and lowering of his dignity, and in consequence of these reflections he remained everlastingly in the same mute condition, only uttering from time to time monosyllabic sounds, and in this way he gained the reputation of being a very tiresome man.

So this was the Person of Consequence to whom our friend Akaky Akakyevitch appealed, and he appealed to him at a most unpropitious moment, very unfortunate for himself, though fortunate, indeed, for the Person of Consequence. The latter happened to be in his study, talking in the very best of spirits with an old friend of his childhood who had only just arrived and whom he had not seen for several years. It was at this moment that he was informed that a man called Bashmatchkin was asking to see him. He asked abruptly, "What sort of man is he?" and received the answer, "A government clerk." "Ah! he can wait, I haven't time now," said the Person of Consequence. Here I must observe that this was a complete lie on the part of the Person of Consequence: he had time; his friend and he had long ago said all they had to say to each other and their conversation had begun to be broken by very long pauses during which they merely slapped each other on the knee, saying, "So that's how things are, Ivan Abramovitch!"—"There it is, Stepan Varlamovitch!" but, for all that, he told the clerk to wait in order to show his friend, who had left the service years before and was living at home in the country how long clerks had to wait in his ante-room. At last after they had talked, or rather been silent to their heart's content and had smoked a cigar in very comfortable arm-chairs with sloping backs, he seemed suddenly to recollect, and said to the secretary, who was standing at the door with papers for his signature: "Oh, by the way, there is a clerk waiting, isn't there? tell him he can come in." When he saw Akaky Akakyevitch's meek appearance and old uniform, he turned to him at once and said: "What do you want?" in a firm and abrupt voice, which he had pur-posely practised in his own room in solitude before the looking-glass for a week be-fore receiving his present post and the grade of a general. Akaky Akakyevitch, who was overwhelmed with befitting awe beforehand, was somewhat confused and, as far as his tongue would allow him, explained to the best of his powers, with even more frequent "ers" than usual, that he had had a perfectly new overcoat and now he had been robbed of it in the most inhuman way, and that now he had come to beg him by his intervention either to correspond with his honour the head policemaster or any-body else, and find the overcoat. This mode of proceeding struck the general for some reason as taking a great liberty. "What next, sir," he went on as abruptly, "don't you know the way to proceed? To whom are you addressing yourself? Don't you know how things are done? You ought first to have handed in a petition to the office; it would have gone to the head clerk of the room, and to the head clerk of the section, then it would have been handed to the secretary and the secretary would have brought it to me. . . ."

"But, your Excellency," said Akaky Akakyevitch, trying to collect all the small al-lowance of presence of mind he possessed and feeling at the same time that he was get-ting into a terrible perspiration, "I ventured, your Excellency, to trouble you because secretaries . . . er . . . are people you can't depend on. . . ."

"What? what? what?" said the Person of Consequence, "where did you get hold of that spirit? where did you pick up such ideas? What insubordination is spreading among young men against their superiors and betters." The Person of Consequence did not apparently observe that Akaky Akakyevitch was well over fifty, and therefore if he could have been called a young man it would only have been in comparison with a man of seventy. "Do you know to whom you are speaking? do you understand who I am? do you understand that, I ask you?" At this point he stamped, and raised his voice to such a powerful note that Akaky Akakyevitch was not the only one to be terrified. Akaky Akakyevitch was positively petrified; he staggered, trembling all over, and could not stand; if the porters had not run up to support him, he would have flopped upon the floor; he was led out almost unconscious. The Person of Consequence, pleased that the effect had surpassed his expectations and enchanted at the idea that his words could even deprive a man of consciousness, stole a sideway glance at his friend to see how he was taking it, and perceived not without satisfaction, that his friend was feel-ing very uncertain and even beginning to be a little terrified himself.

How he got downstairs, how he went out into the street—of all that Akaky Akakye-vitch remembered nothing, he had no feeling in his arms or his legs. In all his life he had never been so severely reprimanded by a general, and this was by one of anoth-er department, too. He went out into the snowstorm, that was whistling through the streets, with his mouth open, and as he went he stumbled off the pavement; the wind, as its way is in Petersburg, blew upon him from all points of the compass and from every side street. In an instant it had blown a quinsy into his throat, and when he got home he was not able to utter a word; with a swollen face and throat he went to bed. So violent is sometimes the effect of a suitable reprimand!

40

Next day he was in a high fever. Thanks to the gracious assistance of the Petersburg climate, the disease made more rapid progress than could have been expected, and when the doctor came, after feeling his pulse he could find nothing to do but prescribe a fomentation, and that simply that the patient might not be left without the benefit of medical assistance; however, two days later he informed him that his end was at hand, after which he turned to his landlady and said: "And you had better lose no time, my good woman, but order him now a deal coffin, for an oak one will be too dear for him." Whether Akaky Akakyevitch heard these fateful words or not, whether they produced a shattering effect upon him, and whether he regretted his pitiful life, no one can tell, for he was all the time in delirium and fever. Apparitions, each stranger than the one before, were continually haunting him: first, he saw Petrovitch and was ordering him to make a greatcoat trimmed with some sort of traps for robbers, who were, he fancied, continually under the bed, and he was calling his landlady every minute to pull out a thief who had even got under the quilt; then he kept asking why his old "dressing jacket" was hanging before him when he had a new overcoat, then he fancied he was standing before the general listening to the appropriate reprimand and saying "I am sorry, your Excellency," then finally he became abusive, uttering the most awful language, so that his old landlady positively crossed herself, having never heard anything of the kind from him before, and the more horrified because these dreadful words followed immediately upon the phrase "your Excellency." Later on, his talk was a mere medley of nonsense, so that it was quite unintelligible; all that could be seen was that his incoherent words and thoughts were concerned with nothing but the overcoat. At last poor Akaky Akakyevitch gave up the ghost. No seal was put upon his room nor upon his things, because, in the first place, he had no heirs and, in the second, the property left was very small, to wit, a bundle of goose-feathers, a quire of white government paper, three pairs of socks, two or three buttons that had come off his trousers, and the "dressing jacket" with which the reader is already familiar. Who came into all this wealth God only knows, even I who tell the tale must own that I have not troubled to enquire. And Petersburg remained without Akaky Akakyevitch, as though, indeed, he had never been in the city. A creature had vanished and departed whose cause no one had championed, who was dear to no one, of interest to no one, who never even attracted the attention of the student of natural history, though the latter does not disdain to fix a common fly upon a pin and look at him under the microscope—a creature who bore patiently the jeers of the office and for no particular reason went to his grave, though even he at the very end of his life was visited by a gleam of brightness in the form of an overcoat that for one instant brought colour into his poor life—a creature on whom calamity broke as insufferably as it breaks upon the heads of the mighty ones of this world . . .!

Several days after his death, the porter from the department was sent to his lodgings with instructions that he should go at once to the office, for his chief was asking for him; but the porter was obliged to return without him, explaining that he could not come, and to the enquiry "Why?" he added, "Well, you see: the fact is he is dead, he was buried three days ago." This was how they learned at the office of the death of Akaky Akakyevitch, and the next day there was sitting in his seat a new clerk who was very much taller and who wrote not in the same upright hand but made his letters more slanting and crooked.

But who could have imagined that this was not all there was to tell about Akaky Akakyevitch, that he was destined for a few days to make a noise in the world after his death, as though to make up for his life having been unnoticed by any one? But so it happened, and our poor story unexpectedly finishes with a fantastic ending. Rumors were suddenly floating about Petersburg that in the neighbourhood of the Kalinkin Bridge and for a little distance beyond, a corpse had taken to appearing at night in the form of a clerk looking for a stolen overcoat, and stripping from the shoulders of all passers-by, regardless of grade and calling, overcoats of all descriptions— trimmed with cat fur, or beaver or wadded, lined with raccoon, fox and bear—made, in fact, of all sorts of skin which men have adapted for the covering of their own. One of the clerks of the department saw the corpse with his own eyes and at once recognized it as Akaky Akakyevitch; but it excited in him such terror, however, that he ran away as fast as his legs could carry him and so could not get a very clear view of him, and only saw him hold up his finger threateningly in the distance.

From all sides complaints were continually coming that backs and shoulders, not of mere titular councillors, but even of upper court councillors, had been exposed to taking chills, owing to being stripped of their greatcoats. Orders were given to the police to catch the corpse regardless of trouble or expense, alive or dead, and to punish him in the cruellest way, as an example to others, and, indeed, they very nearly succeeded in doing so. The sentry of one district police station in Kiryushkin Place snatched a corpse by the collar on the spot of the crime in the very act of attempting to snatch a frieze overcoat from a retired musician, who used in his day to play the flute. Having caught him by the collar, he shouted until he had brought two other comrades, whom he charged to hold him while he felt just a minute in his boot to get out a snuffbox in order to revive his nose which had six times in his life been frost-bitten, but the snuff was probably so strong that not even a dead man could stand it. The sentry had hardly had time to put his finger over his right nostril and draw up some snuff in the left when the corpse sneezed violently right into the eyes of all three. While they were putting their fists up to wipe them, the corpse completely vanished, so that they were not even sure whether he had actually been in their hands. From that time forward, the sentries conceived such a horror of the dead that they were even afraid to seize the living and confined themselves to shouting from the distance: "Hi, you there, be off!" and the dead clerk began to appear even on the other side of the Kalinkin Bridge, rousing no little terror in all timid people.

We have, however, quite deserted the Person of Consequence, who may in reality almost be said to be the cause of the fantastic ending of this perfectly true story. To begin with, my duty requires me to do justice to the Person of Consequence by recording that soon after poor Akaky Akakyevitch had gone away crushed to powder, he felt something not unlike regret. Sympathy was a feeling not unknown to him; his heart was open to many kindly impulses, although his exalted grade very often prevented them from being shown. As soon as his friend had gone out of his study, he even began brooding over poor Akaky Akakyevitch, and from that time forward, he was almost every day haunted by the image of the poor clerk who had succumbed so completely to the befitting reprimand. The thought of the man so worried him that a week later he actually decided to send a clerk to find out how he was and whether he really could help him in any way. And when they brought him word that Akaky Akakyevitch had died suddenly in delirium and fever, it made a great impression on him, his conscience reproached him and he was depressed all day. Anxious to distract his mind and to forget the unpleasant impression, he went to spend the evening with one of his friends, where he found a genteel company and, what was best of all, almost every one was of the same grade so that he was able to be quite free from restraint. This had a wonderful effect on his spirits, he expanded, became affable and genial—in short,

spent a very agreeable evening. At supper he drank a couple of glasses of champagne—
a proceeding which we all know has a happy effect in inducing good-humour. The
champagne made him inclined to do something unusual, and he decided not to go
home yet but to visit a lady of his acquaintance, one Karolina Ivanovna—a lady apparently of German extraction, for whom he entertained extremely friendly feelings.
It must be noted that the Person of Consequence was a man no longer young, an excellent husband, and the respectable father of a family. He had two sons, one already
serving in his office, and a nice-looking daughter of sixteen with a rather turned-up,
pretty little nose, who used to come every morning to kiss his hand, saying, "*Bon jour,
Papa.*" His wife, who was still blooming and decidedly good-looking, indeed, used
first to give him her hand to kiss and then would kiss his hand, turning it the other side
upwards. But though the Person of Consequence was perfectly satisfied with the kind
amenities of his domestic life, he thought it proper to have a lady friend in another
quarter of the town. This lady friend was not a bit better looking nor younger than his
wife, but these mysterious facts exist in the world and it is not our business to criticise
them. And so the Person of Consequence went downstairs, got into his sledge, and
said to his coachman, "To Karolina Ivanovna," while luxuriously wrapped in his warm
fur coat he remained in that agreeable frame of mind sweeter to a Russian than anything that could be invented, that is, when one thinks of nothing while thoughts come
into the mind of themselves, one pleasanter than the other, without the labour of following them or looking for them. Full of satisfaction, he recalled all the amusing moments of the evening he had spent, all the phrases that had set the little circle laughing;
many of them he repeated in an undertone and found them as amusing as before, and
so, very naturally, laughed very heartily at them again. From time to time, however,
he was disturbed by a gust of wind which, blowing suddenly, God knows whence
and wherefore, cut him in the face, pelting him with flakes of snow, puffing out his coat-
collar like a sack, or suddenly flinging it with unnatural force over his head and giving him endless trouble to extricate himself from it. All at once, the Person of
Consequence felt that some one had clutched him very tightly by the collar. Turning
round he saw a short man in a shabby old uniform, and not without horror recognized him as Akaky Akakyevitch. The clerk's face was white as snow and looked like
that of a corpse, but the horror of the Person of Consequence was beyond all bounds
when he saw the mouth of the corpse distorted into speech and, breathing upon him
the chill of the grave, it uttered the following words: "Ah, so here you are at last! At
last I've . . . er . . . caught you by the collar. It's your overcoat I want, you refused to
help me and abused me into the bargain! So now give me yours!" The poor Person of
Consequence very nearly died. Resolute and determined as he was in his office and before subordinates in general, and though any one looking at his manly air and figure
would have said: "Oh, what a man of character!" yet in this plight he felt, like very
many persons of athletic appearance, such terror that not without reason he began to
be afraid he would have some sort of fit. He actually flung his overcoat off his shoulders as fast as he could and shouted to his coachman in a voice unlike his own: "Drive
home and make haste!" The coachman, hearing the tone which he had only heard in
critical moments and then accompanied by something even more rousing, hunched his
shoulders up to his ears in case of worse following, swung his whip and flew on like
an arrow. In a little over six minutes the Person of Consequence was at the entrance
of his own house. Pale, panic-strickened, and without his overcoat, he arrived home
instead of at Karolina Ivanovna's, dragged himself to his own room and spent the
night in great pertubation, so that next morning his daughter said to him at breakfast,
"You look quite pale to-day, Papa": but her papa remained mute and said not a word

to any one of what happened to him, where he had been, and where he had been going. The incident made a great impression upon him. Indeed, it happened far more rarely that he said to his subordinates, "How dare you? do you understand who I am?" and he never uttered those words at all until he had first heard all the rights of the case.

What was even more remarkable is that from that time the apparition of the dead clerk ceased entirely: apparently the general's overcoat had fitted him perfectly, anyway nothing more was heard of overcoats being snatched from any one. Many restless and anxious people refused, however, to be pacified, and still maintained that in remote parts of the town the ghost of the dead clerk went on appearing. One sentry in Kolomna, for instance, saw with his own eyes a ghost appear from behind a house; but, being by natural constitution somewhat feeble—so much so that on one occasion an ordinary, well-grown pig, making a sudden dash out of some building, knocked him off his feet to the vast entertainment of the cabmen standing round, from whom he exacted two kopecks each for snuff for such rudeness—he did not dare to stop it, and so followed it in the dark until the ghost suddenly looked round and, stopping, asked him: "What do you want?" displaying a fist such as you never see among the living. The sentry said: "Nothing," and turned back on the spot. This ghost, however, was considerably taller and adorned with immense moustaches, and directing its steps apparently towards Obuhov Bridge, vanished into the darkness of the night.   [1842]

QUESTIONS

1. What qualities of the narrator are immediately established in the opening paragraph? How would you describe the tone of the story?
2. How is the reader affected by the narrator's occasional admission that his account of Akaky Akakyevitch is frankly a fiction?
3. How is the protagonist changed by his new overcoat?
4. Who or what is the antagonist in the story?
5. What does the overcoat symbolize?

RESPONSE

1. Using Frank O'Connor's Context essay "The Legacy of Gogol's 'Overcoat,'" choose any story written in the twentieth century and show how Akaky Akakyevitch is or is not the prototype.

FOCUS ON FILM

1. See if you can find some of the many filmed versions of "The Overcoat." These include *The Overcoat* (2001), *Il Cappoto* (1952), *Shinel* (1959), and *The Overcoat* (1965). Compare these versions with each other and with the print story.
2. Using one of the filmed versions, explain how the film chooses to portray "the little man" as discussed by Frank O'Connor in the Context essay "The Legacy of Gogol's 'Overcoat.'"

Nadine Gordimer

Nadine Gordimer (b. 1923) was born in Springs, South Africa. Educated at the University of Witwaterstrand, she began to write during the 1930s and published her first collection, *Face to Face*, in 1949. Since then she has published many novels and collections of stories, often taking for her subject the racial problems of South Africa. She has taught in several American universities and has received many literary honors and awards. A collection of her essays, *The Essential Genture*, appeared in 1988. In 1991 she became the first South African to win the Nobel Prize for Literature and the first woman in 25 years to be awarded that honor. She makes her home in Johannesburg. Recent works include *The House Fun* (1998), *Pickup* (2001), *Ultimate Safari* (2001), and *Lost, and Other Stories* (2003).

The Life of the Imagination

As a child she did not inhabit their world, a place where whether the so-and-sos would fit in at dinner, and whose business it was to see that the plumber was called, and whether the car should be traded in or overhauled were the daily entries in a ledger of living. The sum of it was the comfortable, orderly house, beds with turned-down sheets from which nightmares and dreams never overstepped the threshold of morning, goodnight kisses as routine as the cleaning of teeth, a woman stating her truth, "Charles would never eat a warmed-over meal," a man defining his creed, "One thing I was taught young, the value of money."

From the beginning, for her, it was the mystery and not the carefully knotted net with which they covered it, as the highwire performer is protected from the fall. Instead of dust under the beds there was (for her) that hand that Malte Laurids Brigge saw reaching out towards him in the dark beneath his mother's table. Only she was not afraid, as she read, later, he was; she recognized, and grasped it.

And she never let go.

She did not make the mistake of thinking that because of this she must inevitably be able to write or paint; that was just another of the axioms that did for them (Barbara has such a vivid imagination, she is so artistic). She knew it was one thing to have entry to the other world, and another entirely to bring something of it back with you. She studied biology at the university for a while (the subject, incising soft fur and skin to get at the complexities beneath, lured her, and they heard there were good positions going for girls with a B.Sc. degree) but then left and took a job in a municipal art gallery. She began by sorting sepia postcards and went on to dust Chinese ceramic roof-tiles and to learn how to clean paintings. The smell of turpentine, size, and coffee in the room where she and the director worked was her first intimacy. They wondered how she could be so happy there, cut off from the company of young people, and once her father remarked half-meaningfully that he hoped the director wouldn't get any ideas.

The director had many ideas, including the only one her father thought of. He was an oldish man—to her, at the time, anyway—with the proboscis-face that often goes with an inquiring mind, and a sudden nakedness of tortoiseshell-colored eyes when he took off his huge glasses. His wife said, "It's wonderful for Dan to have you working for him. He's always been one of those men who are at their best mentally only when they are more or less in love." He told his assistant the story of Wu Ch'eng-ên's characters, the monkey, the pilgrim Tripitaka, Sandy, Pigsy and the two horses she had dusted, as well as giving her a masterly analysis of the breakdown of feudalism in relation to the success of the Long March.° He had a collection of photographs he had taken of intricate machinery and microphotography of the cells of plants, and together, using her skill in dissecting rats and frogs and grasshoppers, they added blowups of animal tissue. He kissed her occasionally, but rather as if that were simply part of the order of the cosmos; his lips were thin, now, and he knew it. It was through him that she met and fell in love with the young architect whom she married, and with whom she went to Japan, where he had won a scholarship to the University of Tokyo. They wandered about the East and Europe together for a year or two (it was just as her parents expected; she had no proper home) and then came back to South Africa where he became a very successful architect indeed and made an excellent living.

It was as simple and confounding as that. Government administration as well as the great mining and industrial companies employed him to design one public building after another. He and Barbara had a serene, self-effacing house on a *kopje* outside Pretoria—the garden demonstrated how well the spare, indigenous thorn trees of the Middle Veld followed the Japanese architectural idiom. They had children. Barbara remained, in her late thirties, a thin, tall creature with a bony face darkened by freckles, good-looking and much given to her own company. Money changed her dress little, and her tastes not at all; she was able to indulge them rather more. She had a *pondokkie*° down in the Low Veld, on the Crocodile River, where she went sometimes in the winter to stay for a week or two on her own. Marriage was not possible, of course. Certainly not of true minds, because if one is ever going to find release from the mesmerism of appearances one is condemned to make the effort by oneself. And daily intimacy was an inevitable attempt to avoid this that left one sharing bed, bathroom, and table, solitary as in any crowd. She and Arthur, her husband, knew it; they got on almost wordlessly well, now and then turned instinctively to each other, and were alone, he with his work and she with her books and her *pondokkie*. They made their children happy. The school headmaster said they were the most "creative" children that had ever passed through his hands (Barbara's children are so artistic, Barbara's children are so imaginative).

They got measles and ran sudden fevers at awkward times, just like other children, however, and one evening when Barbara and Arthur were about to go out to dinner,

---

°*Long March*: The 5,000-mile march from Hunan to Shen-si Province in the north, led by Mao Tse-tung from October 1934 to December 1935, to escape the forces of Chiang Kai-shek.
°*pondokkie*: A country place.

Pete was discovered to have a high temperature. The dinner was for a visiting Danish architect who had particularly requested to meet Arthur, so he went on ahead while Barbara stayed to see what the doctor would say. She had not been particularly pleased to hear that the family doctor was away on holiday in Europe and his locum tenens would be coming instead. He was perhaps a little surprised to be met at the door by a woman in evening dress—the house itself was something that made unexpected demands on the attention of people who had not seen anything like it before. She felt the necessity to explain her appearance, partly to disguise the slight hostility she felt towards him for being a substitute for a reassuring face—"We were just going out when I noticed my son looked like a beetroot."

He smiled. "It's a change from curlers and dressing-gowns." And they stood there, she in her long dress, he with coat and brown bag, as if for a split second the situation of their confrontation was not clear; had they bumped into one another, stupidly both dodging in the same direction to avoid colliding in the street? Then the lapse closed and they proceeded to the bedroom where Pete and Bruce sat up in their beds expectantly. Pete said, "That's not our doctor."

"No, I know, this is Doctor Asher, he's looking after everybody while Doctor Dickson's away."

10   "You won't give me an injection?" said Pete.

"I don't think you've got the sort of sickness that's going to need an injection," the man said. "Anyway, I give injections so fast you don't even know they've happened. Really."

The little one, Bruce, giggled, flopped back in bed and pulled the sheet over his mouth.

The doctor said, "You mustn't laugh at me. You can ask my children. One, two—before you can count three—it's done."

Bruce said to him, "It's not nice to swank."

15   The doctor looked up over his open bag and appeared to flinch at this grown-up dictum. "I'm sorry. I won't do it any more."

When he had examined Pete he prescribed a mixture that Dr. Dickson had often given the children; Barbara went to look in the medicine chest, and there was an almost full bottle there. Pete had swollen glands at the base of his skull and under the jawline. "We'll watch it," the doctor said, as Barbara preceded him down the passage. "I've seen several cases of glandular fever since I've been here. Ring me in the morning if you're worried." Again they stood in the entrance, she with her hands hanging at the sides of her long skirt, he getting into his coat. He was no taller than she, and probably about the same age, but tired, with the travel-worn look of general practitioners, perpetually lugging a bag around with them. His hair was a modified version of the sort of Julius Caesar cut affected by architects, journalists and advertising men; doctors usually stuck to short back and sides. She thanked him, using his name, and he remarked, pausing at the door, "By the way, it's Usher—with a U."

"Oh, I'm sorry—I misheard, over the phone. Usher."

He was looking up and around the house. "Japanese style, isn't it? They grow those miniature trees—amazing. There was an article about them the other day, I can't remember where I . . . What d'you call it?"

She had kept from childhood an awkward gesture of jerking her chin when embarrassed. One look at the house and people racked their brains for something apposite to say and up came those horrible little stunted trees. "Oh yes. Bonsai. Thank you very much. Good night."

When he had gone she went at once to give Pete his medicine and the nanny the   20
telephone number of the hotel where the dinner was being held. Afterwards, she remembered with a detached clarity those few minutes before she left the house, when
she was in and out of her sons' room: the light that seemed reddish, with the stuffy
warmth of childhood coloring it, the stained rugs, the nursery-school daubs stuck
on the walls, Dora's cheerfully scornful African voice and the hoist of her big rump
as she bent about tidying up, the smell of fever on Pete's lips as she kissed him and
the encounter, under the hand she leaned on, with the comforting midden of a
child's bed—bits of raw potato he had been using as ammunition in a pea-shooter,
the hard shape of a piece of jigsaw puzzle, the wooden spatula the doctor had used
to flatten his tongue. And it seemed to her that even at the time, she had had a rare
momentary vision of herself (she was not a woman given to awareness of creating
effects). She had thought—moving between the small beds slowly because of the
long dress, perfumed and painted—this is the image of the mother that men have
often chosen to perpetuate, the autobiographers, the Prousts. This is what I may be
for one of these little boys when I have become an old woman with bristles on her
chin, dead.

Pete was better next day. The doctor came at about half past one, when the child was
asleep and she was eating her lunch off a tray in the sun. The servant led the doctor
out onto the terrace. He didn't want to disturb her; but she was simply having a snack,
as he could see. He sat down while she told him about the child. She had a glass of
white wine beside her plate of left-over fish salad—the wine was a left-over, too, but
still, what interest could that be to him, whether or not she habitually bibbed wine
alone at lunch? The man looked with real pleasure round the calm and sunny terrace
and she felt sorry for him because he thought bonsai trees were wonderful. "Have a
glass of wine—it's lovely and cold." Her bony feet were bare in the winter sun. He refused; of course, a doctor can't do as he likes. But he took out a pipe, and smoked that.
"The sun's so pleasant, I must say Pretoria has its points." They were both looking at
her toes, on each foot the second one was crooked; it was because the child was asleep,
of course, that he sat there. He told her that he came from Cape Town, where it rained
all winter. They went upstairs to look at the child; he was breathing evenly and soundlessly. "Leave him," the doctor said. Downstairs he added, "Another day or two in
bed, I'd say. I'd like to check those glands again."

He came just before two the following day. This time he accepted a cup of coffee.
It was just as it had been yesterday; it might have been yesterday. It was almost the
same time of day. The sun had exactly the same strength. They sat on the broad brick
seat with its thick cushion. His pipe smoke hung a little haze before their eyes. She
was telling him the child was so much better that it really was impossible to keep him
in bed, when he looked at her amusedly, as if he had found them both out—himself
and her—and his arm, with the hand curved to bring her to him, drew her in. They
kissed and without thinking at all whether she wanted to kiss him or not, she found
herself anxious to be skillful. She seemed to manage very well because the kissing
went on for minutes, their heads turning this way and that as their mouths slowly detached and met.

And so it began. When they drew back from each other the words flew to her: why
this man, for heaven's sake—why you? And because she was ashamed of the thought,
she said aloud instead, "Why me?"

He found this apparent unawareness of her own attractions so moving that he
kissed her fiercely, answering, for her, both questions, the spoken and unspoken.

25　　　While they were kissing she became aware of the slightest, quickest sideways movement of the one slate-colored eye she could see, a second before she herself heard the squeak of the servant's sandshoes approaching from within the house. They drew apart, she in jerky haste, he with composed swiftness so that the intimacy between them held good even while he put his pipe in his pocket, took out a prescription pad and was remarking, when the servant picked up the coffee tray, "It mightn't be a bad idea to keep some sort of mild antipyretic in the house, not as strong as that mixture he's been having, I mean, but . . ."

So it began. The love-making, the absurdities of concealment; even the acceptance of the knowledge that this hard-working doctor with the sickle-line of a smile cut down either side of his mouth, and the brown, coarse-grained forehead, had gone through it all before, perhaps many times. So it began, exactly as it was to be.

They made love the first time in the flat he was living in temporarily. It was a ravishing experience for both of them and when it was over—for the moment—they knew that they must turn their attention urgently and at once to the intensely practical business of how, when and where they were to continue to be together. After a month his wife came up from Cape Town and things were more difficult. He had taken a house for his family; the sublet flat with other people's books and sheets and bric-à-brac, in which he and Barbara were the only objects familiar to each other, became a paradise lost. They drove then, separately, all the way to Johannesburg to spend an afternoon together in a hotel (Pretoria was too small a place for one to expect to go unrecognized). He was tied to his endless working hours; they had nowhere to go. Their problem was passion but they could hope for only the most down-to-earth, realistic solutions. One could not flinch from them. After the last patient left the consulting rooms in the evening the building was deserted—an office block. He made little popping noises on his pipe as he decided they would be quite safe there. Deaf and blind with anticipation of the meeting, she would come from the side street where her car was parked, through the dark foyer, past the mops and bucket of the African cleaner, up in the lift with its glowing eye showing as it rose through successive levels, then along the corridors of closed doors and commercial nameplates until she was there: Dr. J. McDow Dickson, M.B.B.Ch. Edin. Consulting Hours, Mornings 11–1, Afternoons 4–6. On the old daybed in Dr. Dickson's anteroom they made love, among the medical insurance calendars and the desk accessories advertising antibiotics. Once the cleaner was heard turning his pass-key in the waiting-room door; once someone (a patient, no doubt) hammered at it for a while, and then went away. She had always been sure, without censure, that shabby love-affairs would be useless, for her. She learnt that shabbiness is the judgment of the outsider, the one left in the cold; there are no shabby love-affairs for those who are the lovers.

They met wherever and however and for whatever length of time they could, but still by far the greater part of their time was spent apart. Communications, movements, meeting-places—all this had to be settled as between two secret agents whom the world must not suspect to be in contact. In order to plan strategy, each had to brief the other about the normal pattern of his life: this was how they got to know, bit by bit, that yawning area of each other's lives that existed outside one another's arms. "On Thursday nights I'm always alone because Arthur takes a seminar at the university." "You can safely ring me any Sunday morning between eight and nine because Yvonne goes to Mass."

So his wife was a Catholic. Well, yes, but he was not. Of course that meant that his children were being brought up as Catholics. One evening when he and Barbara were putting on their clothes again in the consulting rooms she had seen the picture of the three little girls, under the transparent plastic slot in his wallet. White-blond hair, short and straight as a nylon toothbrush, ribbon sashes, net petticoats, white socks held by elastic—the children of one of those nice, neat pretty women who look after them just as carefully as they used to take care of their dolls. Barbara never met her. He said that the local doctors' wives were being very kind—she was playing tennis regularly at the house of one, and another had little girls the same age who had become inseparable from his girls. If he and Barbara met at the consulting rooms on Friday evenings, he had to keep an eye on his watch—"Bridge night," he said, doggedly, resignedly. Sometimes he said, "Blast bridge night."

Between embraces, confessions, questions came easily, up to a point. "You lead a   30
very different life," he said.

He meant "from mine." Or from hers, perhaps—his wife's.

Lying there, Barbara pulled a dismissing face.

"Oh yes." He did not want to be expected, indulged, out of love; he had his own regard for the truth. "What was wrong about the Japanese trees, that time—that first night I came to your house—what did I say? There was such a look on your face."

"Oh that. The bonsai business." The reproach was for herself; he didn't understand the shrinking in repugnance from "good taste"—well, wasn't the shrinking as daintily fastidious, in its way, as the "good taste" itself? You went whoring after one concept or the other of your own sensibility. "Not different at all,"—she returned to his original remark; she had this quality, he noticed, of keeping a series of remarks you had passed laid out before her, and then unhesitatingly turning to pick up this one or that— "It's like putting a net into the sea. You bring up small fish or big fish, weeds, muck, little bright bits of things. But the water, the element that's living—that's drained away."

"—So tonight it's bridge," she added, putting out her hand to caress his chest.   35

He took the pipe out of his mouth. "When you're down at the Crocodile," he said— they called her *pondokkie* that because it was on the Crocodile River—"What are you doing there, when you're alone?"

She lay under his gaze; she felt the quality she had for him, awkwardly, as if he had stuck a jewel on her forehead. She didn't answer.

"Reading, eh? Reading and thinking your own thoughts." For years he had barely had time to get through the medical journals.

She was seeing the still, dry stretch to the horizon, each thorn bush like every other thorn bush, the narrow cattle paths leading back on themselves through the clean, dry grass, the silence into which one seemed to fall, at midday, as if into an airpocket; the silence there would be one day when one's heart stopped, while everything went on as it did in that veld silence, the hard trees waiting for sap to rise, the dead grass waiting to be sloughed off the new under rain, the boulders cracking into new forms under frost and sun.

But alive under her hand was the hair of his breast, still damp and soft from con-   40
tact with her body, and she said, keeping her teeth together, "I wish we could go there. I wish we were in bed there now."

That winter she did not go once to the shack. It had become nothing but a shelter where they could have made love, whole nights and days. There were so many hours when they could not see each other. Could not even telephone; he was at home with his family, she with hers. Such slow stretches of mornings, thawing in the sun; such long afternoons when the interruption of her children was a monstrous breaking-in upon—what? She was doing nothing. She saw him as she had once watched him without his being aware of her, crossing the street and walking the length of a block to their meeting-place: a slight man with a pipe held between his teeth in a rather brutal way, a smiling curve of the mouth denied by the downward, inward lines of brow and eyelids as his head bobbed. In his hand the elegant pigskin bag she had given him because it was easy to explain away as the gift of some grateful patient. He sees nobody, only where he is going. Sitting at dinner-parties or reading at night, she saw him like this in broad daylight, crossing the street, bag in hand. It seemed she could follow him through all the hill-cupped small city, make out his back among all others, crossing the square past Dr. Dolittle in his top hat (that was what her little boys thought the statue of President Kruger was), doing the rounds in the suburbs, the car full of pipe-smoke and empty phials with their necks snapped off, the smile a grim habit, greeting no one.

Sometimes he materialized at her own door—he'd had a call in the neighborhood, or told the nurse so, anyway. It would be in the morning, when the boys were at school and Arthur was at the town studio. He always went straight to the telephone and rang up the consulting rooms, so that he'd be covered if his car happened to be seen: "Oh, Birdie, I'm around Muckleneuk—if there's anyone I ought to drop in on out this way? My next call will be the Wilson child, Waterkloof Road, so—". Then they would sit on the terrace again and have coffee. And he would give his expert glance round doors and windows before kissing her; he smelt of the hospital theatre he had been in, or the soap he had washed his hands with in other people's houses. He wore a pullover his mother had sent him, he had pigskin gloves Yvonne had bought him—he smiled, telling it—because she thought the smart new bag made his old ones look so shabby. For Barbara there was the bloom on him of the times when he was not with her.

She had never been in his house, of course, and she did not know the disposition of the rooms, or the sound of voices calling through it in the early morning rush to get to school and hospital rounds (she knew he got up very early, before she would even be awake), or the kind of conversation that came to life over drinks when friends were there, or the atmosphere, so strongly personal in every house, of the hour late at night when outsiders have gone and doors are being locked and lights switched off, one by one.

She had never been with him in the company of other people (unless one counted Pete and Bruce) and she did not know how he would appear in their eyes, or what his manner would be. She listened with careful detachment when he telephoned the nurse; he had a tired, humorous way with her—but that was just professional camaraderie, with a touch of the flirtatiousness that pleases old ladies. Once or twice he had had to phone his wife in Barbara's presence: it was the anonymous telecommunication of long marriage—"Yvonne? I'm on my way. Oh, twenty minutes or so. Well, if he does, say I'll be in any time after nine. Yes. No, I won't. See you."

45   When they were together after love-making they talked about their past lives and discussed his future. He intended, within the next year, to go to America to do what he had always wanted—biological research. They discussed in great detail the planning of his finances: he had sold his practice in Cape Town in order to be able to keep his family while studying on a grant he'd been promised. The six months' locum-tenancy was a stop-gap between selling the practice and taking up the grant in Boston. He had moments of deep uncertainty: he should have gone ten years ago,

young and single-minded—but, helplessly, even then there was a girl, marriage, babies. From the depths of his uncertainty, he and Barbara looked at each other like two prisoners who wake up and find themselves on the floor of the same cell. He said, as if for what it was worth, "I love you." They became absorbed again in the questions of how he should best use his opportunities in America, and under whom he should try to get the chance to work. And then it was time to get dressed, time up, time to go, time to be home to change for his bridge evening, time to be home to receive Arthur's friends. Standing in the lift together they were silent, weary, at one. They left the consulting-room building separately; as she walked away he became again that figure crossing streets, going in and out of houses and car, pigskin doctor's bag in hand, seeing nobody, only where he was going.

Her mind constructed snatches of dialogue, like remembered fragments of a play. She was following him home to the bridge table (she had never played card games) or the dinner-table—there was a roast, that would be the sort of thing, a brown leg of pork with apple sauce, and he was carving, knowing what cut each member of the little family liked best. The white-haired, white-socked little girls had washed their hands. The bridge players talked with the ease of colleagues, the wives were saying, "John wouldn't touch it," "I must say the only thing he always does remember is when to pay the insurance," "I can't get anyone to do shirt collars properly." She had the feeling his wife bought his clothes for him; but the haircut—that he chose for himself. As he chose her, Barbara, and other women. On Sundays she lay with an unread book on the terrace or laughed and talked without listening among Arthur's friends (they all seemed to be Arthur's friends, now) and he was running about some clean, hard tennis court, red in the face, agile, happy perhaps, in the mindless happiness of physical exercise. She was not jealous, only slightly excited by the thought of him with her completely out of mind. Or perhaps this Sunday they had taken the children on some outing. Once when she had visualized him all afternoon on that tennis court, he had happened to mention that Sunday afternoon had been swallowed up in a family outing—the children had heard about a game park in Krugersdorp. The plain, white-haired little girl clambered over him to see better; was he irritated? Or was he smoothing the hair behind the child's ears with that lover's gesture of his, also, perhaps, a father's gesture? She read over again a paragraph in the book lying between her elbows on the grass: ". . . the word *lolo* means both 'soul' and 'butterfly' . . . the dual meaning is due to the fact that the chrysalis resembles a shrouded corpse and that the butterfly emerges from it like the soul from the body of a sleeping man." But the idea had no meaning for her. The words floated on her mind; no, a moth, quite an ordinary-looking, protectively colored moth, not noticed going about the streets, quickly crossing the square in the early evening, coming softly along the corridor, touching softly. Fierily, making quick the sleeping body.

One night when she had the good luck to be alone for a few days (Arthur was in the Cape), he was able to slip away and come to her at home. This rare opportunity required careful planning, like every other arrangement between them. He said he was going to a meeting of the medical association; she had an early dinner, to be sure the servants would be out of the way. She saw to it that all the windows of the house except those of her bedroom should be in darkness, so that any unexpected caller would presume she had gone to bed and not disturb her. In fact, she did lie on her bed, fully dressed, waiting for him. She had given him the key of the side door, off the terrace, that afternoon. He came with a quiet, determined hesitancy, through another man's house. He had never been into the bedroom before but he knew where the children's rooms were. When she heard him reach the passage where a turn divided the parents' quarters from the children's, she got up and went softly to meet him. But the little boys were asleep, long ago. She took his two clean hands, dryly cold from the winter night, in hers, and then they crept along together. In the bedroom, when she had shut the door behind them, she was cold and trembling, as if she too had just found shelter.

He had to leave not long after the time the meeting would end; now, because this was her own bed, in her own home, she lay there naked, flung back under the disarray of bedclothes, and watched him dress alone. He took her brush and put it through his hair before the mirror, with a quick, knowing look at himself. He sat on the bed, like a doctor, to embrace her a last time. She watched him softly release the handle of the door, almost without a click, as he closed it on her, heard him going evenly, quietly down the corridor, listened to the faint creak and stir of him making his way through the big living room, and then, after a pause, heard the clip of his footsteps dying away across the terrace. The engine of the car started up: shadows from its lights flew across the bedroom windows.

She put up her hand to switch off the bed lamp but did not move her head or body. She lay in the dark for a long time just as he had left her; perhaps she slept. There seemed to be a dark wind blowing through her hollow mind; she was awake, and there was a night wind come up, the cold gale of the winter veld, pressing against the walls and windows like pressure in one's ears. A thorn branch scrabbled on the terrace wall. She heard dry leaves swirl and trail across the flagstones. And irregularly, at long intervals, a door banged without engaging its latch. She tried to sleep or to return to sleep, but some part of her mind waited for the impact of the door in the wind. And it came, again and again. Slowly, reasoned thought cohered round the sound: she identified the direction from which it came, her mind travelled through the house the way he had gone, and arrived at the terrace door. The door banged, with a swinging shudder, again.

50   He's left the door open. She saw it; saw the gaping door, and the wind bellying the long curtains and sending papers skimming about the room, the leaves sailing in and slithering across the floors. The whole house was filling up with the wind. There had been burglaries in the suburb lately. This was one of the few houses without an alarm system—she and Arthur had refused to imprison themselves in the white man's fear of attack on himself and his possessions. Yet now the door was open like the door of a deserted house and she found herself believing, like any other suburban matron, that someone must enter. They would come in unheard, with that wind, and approach through the house, black men with their knives in their hands. She, who had never submitted to this sort of fear ever in her life, could hear them coming, hear them breathe under their dirty rag masks and their *tsotsi* caps. They had killed an old man on a farm outside Pretoria last week; someone described in the papers as a mother of two had held them off, at her bedside, with a golf club. Multiple wounds, the old man had received, multiple wounds.

She was empty, unable to summon anything but this stale fantasy, shared with the whole town, the whole white population. She lay there possessed by it, and she thought, she violently longed—they will come straight into the room and stick a knife in me. No time to cry out. Quick. Deep. Over.

The light came instead. Her sons began to play the noisy whispering games of children, about the house in the very early morning.   [1968]

QUESTIONS

1. What is Barbara's attitude toward her childhood?
2. Characterize the marriage of Barbara and Arthur.
3. What is Barbara's motive for beginning the affair?
4. How do you interpret Barbara's "stale fantasy" of violence, which concludes the story?
5. In what sense is the life described in the story "the life of the imagination"?

Nathaniel Hawthorne

Nathaniel Hawthorne (1804–1864) was born in Salem, Massachusetts. After graduation from Bowdoin College in 1825, he returned to Salem, where he lived in seclusion while he perfected his craft. His first novel, *Fanshawe* (1828), was a failure, and his first collection of short stories, *Twice-Told Tales* (1837), received little attention. Hawthorne was employed at the Custom House in Boston, but when he was turned out by a change in parties, he tried an experiment in communal living that provided material for *The Blithedale Romance* (1852). In 1842 he married and settled in Concord, where he wrote his best-known works, including *Mosses from an Old Manse* (1846) and his masterpiece, *The Scarlet Letter* (1850). In 1853 Hawthorne accepted an appointment as consul to Liverpool. Following this assignment, he traveled to Italy for an extended stay. *The Marble Faun* (1860), written in and about Italy, was his last major novel.

The Birthmark

In the latter part of the last century there lived a man of science, an eminent proficient in every branch of natural philosophy, who not long before our story opens had made experience of a spiritual affinity more attractive than any chemical one. He had left his laboratory to the care of an assistant, cleared his fine countenance from the furnace smoke, washed the stain of acids from his fingers, and persuaded a beautiful woman to become his wife. In those days when the comparatively recent discovery of electricity and other kindred mysteries of Nature seemed to open paths into the region of miracle, it was not unusual for the love of science to rival the love of woman in its depth and absorbing energy. The higher intellect, the imagination, the spirit, and even the heart might all find their congenial aliment in pursuits which, as some of their ardent votaries believed, would ascend from one step of powerful intelligence to another, until the philosopher should lay his hand on the secret of creative force and perhaps make new worlds for himself. We know not whether Aylmer possessed this degree of faith in man's ultimate control over Nature. He had devoted himself, however, too unreservedly to scientific studies ever to be weaned from them by any second passion. His love for his young wife might prove the stronger of the two; but it could only be by intertwining itself with his love of science, and uniting the strength of the latter to his own.

Such a union accordingly took place, and was attended with truly remarkable consequences and a deeply impressive moral. One day, very soon after their marriage, Aylmer sat gazing at his wife with a trouble in his countenance that grew stronger until he spoke.

"Georgiana," said he, "has it never occurred to you that the mark upon your cheek might be removed?"

"No, indeed," said she, smiling; but perceiving the seriousness of his manner, she blushed deeply. "To tell you the truth it has been so often called a charm that I was simple enough to imagine it might be so."

"Ah, upon another face perhaps it might," replied her husband; "but never on 5 yours. No, dearest Georgiana, you came so nearly perfect from the hand of Nature that this slightest possible defect, which we hesitate whether to term a defect or a beauty, shocks me, as being the visible mark of earthly imperfection."

"Shocks you, my husband!" cried Georgiana, deeply hurt; at first reddening with momentary anger, but then bursting into tears. "Then why did you take me from my mother's side? You cannot love what shocks you!"

To explain this conversation it must be mentioned that in the centre of Georgiana's left cheek there was a singular mark, deeply interwoven, as it were, with the texture and substance of her face. In the usual state of her complexion—a healthy though delicate bloom—the mark wore a tint of deeper crimson, which imperfectly defined its shape amid the surrounding rosiness. When she blushed it gradually became more indistinct, and finally vanished amid the triumphant rush of blood that bathed the whole cheek with its brilliant glow. But if any shifting motion caused her to turn pale there was the mark again, a crimson stain upon the snow, in which Aylmer sometimes deemed an almost fearful distinctness. Its shape bore not a little similarity to the human hand, though of the smallest pygmy size. Georgiana's loves were wont to say that some fairy at her birth hour had laid her tiny hand upon the infant's cheek, and left this impress there in token of the magic endowments that were to give her such sway over all hearts. Many a desperate swain would have risked life for the privilege of pressing his lips to the mysterious hand. It must not be concealed, however, that the impression wrought by this fairy sign manual varied exceedingly, according to the difference of temperament in the beholders. Some fastidious persons—but they were exclusively of her own sex—affirmed that the bloody hand, as they chose to call it, quite destroyed the effect of Georgiana's beauty, and rendered her countenance even hideous. But it would be as reasonable to say that one of those small blue stains which sometimes occur in the purest statuary marble would convert the Eve of Powers to a monster. Masculine observers, if the birthmark did not heighten their admiration, contented themselves with wishing it away, that the world might possess one living specimen of ideal loveliness without the semblance of a flaw. After his marriage—for he thought little or nothing of the matter before—Aylmer discovered that this was the case with himself.

Had she been less beautiful—if Envy's self could have found aught else to sneer at—he might have felt his affection heightened by the prettiness of this mimic hand, now vaguely portrayed, now lost, now stealing forth again and glimmering to and fro with every pulse of emotion that throbbed within her heart; but seeing her otherwise so perfect, he found this one defect grow more and more intolerable with every moment of their united lives. It was the fatal flaw of humanity which Nature, in one shape or another, stamps ineffaceably on all her productions, either to imply that they are temporary and finite, or that their perfection must be wrought by toil and pain. The crimson hand expressed the ineludible gripe in which mortality clutches the highest and purest of earthly mould, degrading them into kindred with the lowest, and even with the very brutes, like whom their visible frames return to the dust. In this manner, selecting it as the symbol of his wife's liability to sin, sorrow, decay, and death, Aylmer's sombre imagination was not long in rendering the birthmark a frightful object, causing him more trouble and horror than ever Georgiana's beauty, whether of soul or sense, had given him delight.

At all the seasons which should have been their happiest, he invariably and without intending it, nay, in spite of a purpose to the contrary, reverted to this one disastrous topic. Trifling as it at first appeared, it so connected itself with innumerable trains of thought and modes of feeling that it became the central point of all. With the morning twilight Aylmer opened his eyes upon his wife's face and recognized the symbol of imperfection; and when they sat together at the evening hearth his eyes wandered stealthily to her cheek, and beheld, flickering with the blaze of the wood fire, the spectral hand that wrote mortality where he would fain have worshipped. Georgiana soon learned to shudder at his gaze. It needed but a glance with the peculiar expression that his face often wore to change the roses of her cheek into a deathlike paleness, amid which the crimson hand was brought strongly out, like bas-relief of ruby on the whitest marble.

10   Late one night when the lights were growing dim, so as hardly to betray the stain on the poor wife's cheek, she herself, for the first time, voluntarily took up the subject.

"Do you remember, my dear Aylmer," said she, with a feeble attempt at a smile, "have you any recollection of a dream last night about this odious hand?"

"None! none whatever!" replied Aylmer, starting; but then he added, in a dry, cold tone, affected for the sake of concealing the real depth of his emotion, "I might well dream of it; for before I fell asleep it had taken a pretty firm hold of my fancy."

"And you did dream of it?" continued Georgiana, hastily; for she dreaded lest a gush of tears should interrupt what she had to say. "A terrible dream! I wonder that you can forget it. Is it possible to forget this one expression?—'It is in her heart now; we must have it out!' Reflect, my husband; for by all means I would have you recall that dream."

The mind is in a sad state when Sleep, the all-involving, cannot confine her spectres within the dim region of her sway, but suffers them to break forth, affrighting this actual life with secrets that perchance belong to a deeper one. Aylmer now remembered his dream. He had fancied himself with his servant Aminadab, attempting an operation for the removal of the birthmark; but the deeper went the knife, the deeper sank the hand, until at length its tiny grasp appeared to have caught hold of Georgiana's heart; whence, however, her husband was inexorably resolved to cut or wrench it away.

15   When the dream had shaped itself perfectly in his memory, Aylmer sat in his wife's presence with a guilty feeling. Truth often finds its way to the mind close muffled in robes of sleep, and then speaks with uncompromising directness of matters in regard to which we practise an unconscious self-deception during our waking moments. Until now he had not been aware of the tyrannizing influence acquired by one idea over his mind, and of the lengths which he might find in his heart to go for the sake of giving himself peace.

"Aylmer," resumed Georgiana, solemnly, "I know not what may be the cost to both of us to rid me of this fatal birthmark. Perhaps its removal may cause cureless deformity; or it may be the stain goes as deep as life itself. Again: do we know that there is a possibility, on any terms, of unclasping the firm gripe of this little hand which was laid upon me before I came into the world?"

"Dearest Georgiana, I have spent much thought upon the subject," hastily interrupted Aylmer. "I am convinced of the perfect practicability of its removal."

"If there be the remotest possibility of it," continued Georgiana, "let the attempt be made at whatever risk. Danger is nothing to me; for life, while this hateful mark makes me the object of your horror and disgust—life is a burden which I would fling down with joy. Either remove this dreadful hand, or take my wretched life! You have deep science. All the world bears witness of it. You have achieved great wonders. Cannot you remove this little, little mark, which I cover with the tips of two small fingers? Is this beyond your power, for the sake of your own peace, and to save your poor wife from madness?"

"Noblest, dearest, tenderest wife," cried Aylmer, rapturously, "doubt not my power. I have already given this matter the deepest thought—thought which might almost have enlightened me to create a being less perfect than yourself. Georgiana, you have led deeper than ever into the heart of science. I feel myself fully competent to render this dear cheek as faultless as its fellow; and then, most beloved, what will be my triumph when I shall have corrected what Nature left imperfect in her fairest work! Even Pygmalion, when his sculptured woman assumed life, felt not greater ecstasy than mine will be."

"It is resolved, then," said Georgiana, faintly smiling. "And, Aylmer, spare me not, 20 though you should find the birthmark take refuge in my heart at last."

Her husband tenderly kissed her cheek—her right cheek—not that which bore the impress of the crimson hand.

The next day Aylmer apprised his wife of a plan that he had formed whereby he might have opportunity for the intense thought and constant watchfulness which the proposed operation would require; while Georgiana, likewise, would enjoy the perfect repose essential to its success. They were to seclude themselves in the extensive apartments occupied by Aylmer as a laboratory, and where, during his toilsome youth, he had made discoveries in the elemental powers of Nature that had roused the admiration of all the learned societies in Europe. Seated calmly in this laboratory, the pale philosopher had investigated the secrets of the highest cloud region and of the profoundest mines; he had satisfied himself of the causes that kindled and kept alive the fires of the volcano; and had explained the mystery of the fountains, and how it is that they gush forth, some so bright and pure, and others with such rich medicinal virtues, from the dark bosom of the earth. Here, too, at an earlier period, he had studied the wonders of the human frame, and attempted to fathom the very process by which Nature assimilates all her precious influences from earth and air, and from the spiritual world, to create and foster man, her masterpiece. The latter pursuit, however, Aylmer had long laid aside in unwilling recognition of the truth—against which all seekers sooner or later stumble—that our great creative Mother, while she amuses us with apparently working in the broadest sunshine, is yet severely careful to keep her own secrets, and, in spite of her pretended openness, shows us nothing but results. She permits us, indeed, to mar, but seldom to mend, and, like a jealous patentee, on no account to make. Now, however, Aylmer resumed these half-forgotten investigations; not, of course, with such hopes or wishes as first suggested them; but because they involved much physiological truth and lay in the path of his proposed scheme for the treatment of Georgiana.

As he led her over the threshold of the laboratory, Georgiana was cold and tremulous. Aylmer looked cheerfully into her face, with intent to reassure her, but was so startled with the intense glow of the birthmark upon the whiteness of her cheek that he could not restrain a strong convulsive shudder. His wife fainted.

"Aminadab! Aminadab!" shouted Aylmer, stamping violently on the floor.

25   Forthwith there issued from an inner apartment a man of low stature, but bulky frame, with shaggy hair hanging about his visage, which was grimed with the vapors of the furnace. This personage had been Aylmer's underworker during his whole scientific career, and was admirably fitted for that office by his great mechanical readiness, and the skill with which, while incapable of comprehending a single principle, he executed all the details of his master's experiments. With his vast strength, his shaggy hair, his smoky aspect, and the indescribable earthiness that incrusted him, he seemed to represent man's physical nature; while Aylmer's slender figure, and pale, intellectual face, were no less apt a type of the spiritual element.

"Throw open the door of the boudoir, Aminadab," said Aylmer, "and burn a pastil."

"Yes, master," answered Aminadab, looking intently at the lifeless form of Georgiana; and then he muttered to himself, "If she were my wife, I'd never part with that birthmark."

When Georgiana recovered consciousness she found herself breathing an atmosphere of penetrating fragrance, the gentle potency of which had recalled her from her deathlike faintness. The scene around her looked like enchantment. Aylmer had converted those smoky, dingy, sombre rooms, where he had spent his brightest years in recondite pursuits, into a series of beautiful apartments not unfit to be the secluded abode of a lovely woman. The walls were hung with gorgeous curtains, which imparted the combination of grandeur and grace that no other species of adornment can achieve; and as they fell from the ceiling to the floor, their rich and ponderous folds, concealing all angles and straight lines, appeared to shut in the scene from infinite space. For aught Georgiana knew, it might be a pavilion among the clouds. And Aylmer, excluding the sunshine, which would have interfered with his chemical processes, had supplied its place with perfumed lamps, emitting flames of various hue, but all uniting in a soft, impurpled radiance. He now knelt by his wife's side, watching her earnestly, but without alarm; for he was confident in his science, and felt that he could draw a magic circle round her within which no evil might intrude.

"Where am I? Ah, I remember," said Georgiana, faintly; and she placed her hand over her cheek to hide the terrible mark from her husband's eyes.

30   "Fear not, dearest!" exclaimed he. "Do not shrink from me! Believe me, Georgiana, I even rejoice in this single imperfection, since it will be such a rapture to remove it."

"Oh, spare me!" sadly replied his wife. "Pray do not look at it again. I never can forget that convulsive shudder."

In order to soothe Georgiana, and, as it were, to release her mind from the burden of actual things, Aylmer now put in practice some of the light and playful secrets which science had taught him among its profounder lore. Airy figures, absolutely bodiless ideas, and forms of unsubstantial beauty came and danced before her, imprinting their momentary footsteps on beams of light. Though she had some indistinct idea of the method of these optical phenomena, still the illusion was almost perfect enough to warrant the belief that her husband possessed sway over the spiritual world. Then again, when she felt a wish to look forth from her seclusion, immediately, as if her thoughts were answered, the procession of external existence flitted across a screen. The scenery and the figures of actual life were perfectly represented, but with that bewitching, yet indescribable difference which always makes a picture, an image, or a shadow so much more attractive than the original. When wearied of this Aylmer bade her cast her eyes upon a vessel containing a quantity of earth. She did so, with little interest at first; but was soon startled to perceive the germ of a plant shooting upward from the soil. Then came the slender stalk; the leaves gradually unfolded themselves; and amid them was a perfect and lovely flower.

"It is magical!" cried Georgiana. "I dare not touch it."

"Nay, pluck it," answered Aylmer—"pluck it, and inhale its brief perfume while you may. The flower will wither in a few moments and leave nothing save its brown seed vessels; but thence may be perpetuated a race as ephemeral as itself."

But Georgiana had no sooner touched the flower than the whole plant suffered a 35 blight, its leaves turning coal-black as if by the agency of fire.

"There was too powerful a stimulus," said Aylmer, thoughtfully.

To make up for this abortive experiment, he proposed to take her portrait by a scientific process of his own invention. It was to be effected by rays of light striking upon a polished plate of metal. Georgiana assented; but, on looking at the result, was affrighted to find the features of the portrait blurred and indefinable; while the minute figure of a hand appeared where the cheek should have been. Aylmer snatched the metallic plate and threw it into a jar of corrosive acid.

Soon, however, he forgot these mortifying failures. In the intervals of study and chemical experiment he came to her flushed and exhausted, but seemed invigorated by her presence, and spoke in glowing language of the resources of his art. He gave a history of the long dynasty of the alchemists, who spent so many ages in quest of the universal solvent by which the golden principle might be elicited from all things vile and base. Aylmer appeared to believe that, by the plainest scientific logic, it was altogether within the limits of possibility to discover this long-sought medium; "but," he added, "a philosopher who should go deep enough to acquire the power would attain too lofty a wisdom to stoop to the exercise of it." Not less singular were his opinions in regard to the elixir vitae. He more than intimated that it was at his option to concoct a liquid that should prolong life for years, perhaps interminably; but that it would produce a discord in Nature which all the world, and chiefly the quaffer of the immortal nostrum, would find cause to curse.

"Aylmer, are you in earnest?" asked Georgiana, looking at him with amazement and fear. "It is terrible to possess such power, or even to dream of possessing it."

"Oh, do not tremble, my love," said her husband. "I would not wrong either you 40 or myself by working such inharmonious effects upon our lives; but I would have you consider how trifling, in comparison, is the skill requisite to remove this little hand."

At the mention of the birthmark, Georgiana, as usual, shrank as if a redhot iron had touched her cheek.

Again Aylmer applied himself to his labors. She could hear his voice in the distant furnace room giving directions to Aminadab, whose harsh, uncouth, misshapen tones were audible in response, more like the grunt or growl of a brute than human speech. After hours of absence, Aylmer reappeared and proposed that she should now examine his cabinet of chemical products and natural treasures of the earth. Among the former he showed her a small vial, in which, he remarked, was contained a gentle yet most powerful fragrance, capable of impregnating all the breezes that blow across a kingdom. They were of inestimable value, the contents of that little vial; and, as he said so, he threw some of the perfume into the air and filled the room with piercing and invigorating delight.

"And what is this?" asked Georgiana, pointing to a small crystal globe containing a gold-colored liquid. "It is so beautiful to the eye that I could imagine it the elixir of life."

"In one sense it is," replied Aylmer; "or, rather, the elixir of immortality. It is the most precious poison that ever was concocted in this world. By its aid I could apportion the lifetime of any mortal at whom you might point your finger. The strength of the dose would determine whether he were to linger out years, or drop dead in the midst of a breath. No king on his guarded throne could keep his life if I, in my private station, should deem that the welfare of millions justified me in depriving him of it."

45   "Why do you keep such a terrific drug?" inquired Georgiana in horror.

"Do not mistrust me, dearest," said her husband, smiling; "its virtuous potency is yet greater than its harmful one. But see! here is a powerful cosmetic. With a few drops of this in a vase of water, freckles may be washed away as easily as the hands are cleansed. A stronger infusion would take the blood out of the cheek, and leave the rosiest beauty a pale ghost."

"Is it with this lotion that you intend to bathe my cheek?" asked Georgiana anxiously.

"Oh, no," hastily replied her husband; "this is merely superficial. Your case demands a remedy that shall go deeper."

In his interviews with Georgiana, Aylmer generally made minute inquiries as to her sensations and whether the confinement of the rooms and the temperature of the atmosphere agreed with her. These questions had such a particular drift that Georgiana began to conjecture that she was already subjected to certain physical influences, either breathed in with the fragrant air or taken with her food. She fancied likewise, but it might be altogether fancy, that there was a stirring up of her system—a strange, indefinite sensation creeping through her veins, and tingling, half painfully, half pleasurably, at her heart. Still, whenever she dared to look into the mirror, there she beheld herself pale as a white rose and with the crimson birthmark stamped upon her cheek. Not even Aylmer now hated it so much as she.

50   To dispel the tedium of the hours which her husband found it necessary to devote to the processes of combination and analysis, Georgiana turned over the volumes of his scientific library. In many dark old tomes she met with chapters full of romance and poetry. They were the works of philosophers of the middle ages, such as Albertus Magnus, Cornelius Agrippa, Paracelsus, and the famous friar who created the prophetic Brazen Head. All these antique naturalists stood in advance of their centuries, yet were imbued with some of their credulity, and therefore were believed, and perhaps imagined themselves to have acquired from the investigation of Nature a power above Nature, and from physics a sway over the spiritual world. Hardly less curious and imaginative were the early volumes of the Transactions of the Royal Society, in which the members, knowing little of the limits of natural possibility, were continually recording wonders or proposing methods whereby wonders might be wrought.

But to Georgiana the most engrossing volume was a large folio from her husband's own hand, in which he had recorded every experiment of his scientific career, its original aim, the methods adopted for its development, and its final success or failure, with the circumstances to which either event was attributable. The book, in truth, was both the history and emblem of his ardent, ambitious, imaginative, yet practical and laborious life. He handled physical details as if there were nothing beyond them; yet spiritualized them all, and redeemed himself from materialism by his strong and eager aspiration towards the infinite. In his grasp the veriest clod of earth assumed a soul. Georgiana, as she read, reverenced Aylmer and loved him more profoundly than ever, but with a less entire dependence on his judgment than heretofore. Much as he had accomplished, she could not but observe that his most splendid successes were almost invariably failures, if compared with the ideal at which he aimed. His brightest diamonds were the merest pebbles, and felt to be so by himself, in comparison with the inestimable gems which lay hidden beyond his reach. The volume, rich with achievements that had won renown for its author, was yet as melancholy a record as ever mortal hand had penned. It was the sad confession and continual exemplification of the shortcomings of the composite man, the spirit burdened with clay and working in matter, and of the despair that assails the higher nature at finding itself so miserably thwarted by the earthly part. Perhaps every man of genius in whatever sphere might recognize the image of his own experience in Aylmer's journal.

So deeply did these reflections affect Georgiana that she laid her face upon the open volume and burst into tears. In this situation she was found by her husband.

"It is dangerous to read in a sorcerer's books," said he with a smile, though his countenance was uneasy and displeased. "Georgiana, there are pages in that volume which I can scarcely glance over and keep my senses. Take heed lest it prove as detrimental to you."

"It has made me worship you more than ever," said she.

"Ah, wait for this one success," rejoined he, "then worship me if you will. I shall deem myself hardly unworthy of it. But come, I have sought you for the luxury of your voice. Sing to me, dearest."

So she poured out the liquid music of her voice to quench the thirst of his spirit. He then took his leave with a boyish exuberance of gayety, assuring her that her seclusion would endure but a little longer, and that the result was already certain. Scarcely had he departed when Georgiana felt irresistibly impelled to follow him. She had forgotten to inform Aylmer of a symptom which for two or three hours past had begun to excite her attention. It was a sensation in the fatal birthmark, not painful, but which induced a restlessness throughout her system. Hastening after her husband, she intruded for the first time into the laboratory.

The first thing that struck her eye was the furnace, that hot and feverish worker, with the intense glow of its fire, which by the quantities of soot clustered above it seemed to have been burning for ages. There was a distilling apparatus in full operation. Around the room were retorts, tubes, cylinders, crucibles, and other apparatus of chemical research. An electrical machine stood ready for immediate use. The atmosphere felt oppressively close, and was tainted with gaseous odors which had been tormented forth by the processes of science. The severe and homely simplicity of the apartment, with its naked walls and brick pavement, looked strange, accustomed as Georgiana had become to the fantastic elegance of her boudoir. But what chiefly, indeed almost solely, drew her attention, was the aspect of Aylmer himself.

He was pale as death, anxious and absorbed, and hung over the furnace as if it depended upon his utmost watchfulness whether the liquid which it was distilling should be the draught of immortal happiness or misery. How different from the sanguine and joyous mien that he had assumed for Georgiana's encouragement!

"Carefully now, Aminadab; carefully, thou human machine; carefully, thou man of clay!" muttered Aylmer, more to himself than his assistant. "Now if there be a thought too much or too little, it is all over."

"Ho! ho!" mumbled Aminadab. "Look, master! look!"

Aylmer raised his eyes hastily, and at first reddened, then grew paler than ever, on beholding Georgiana. He rushed towards her and seized her arm with a gripe that left the print of his fingers upon it.

"Why do you come hither? Have you no trust in your husband?" cried he, impetuously, "Would you throw the blight of that fatal birthmark over my labors? It is not well done. Go, prying woman, go!"

"Nay, Aylmer," said Georgiana with the firmness of which she possessed no stinted endowment, "it is not you that have a right to complain. You mistrust your wife; you have concealed the anxiety with which you watch the development of this experiment. Think not so unworthily of me, my husband. Tell me all the risk we run, and fear not that I shall shrink; for my share in it is less than your own."

"No, no, Georgiana!" said Aylmer, impatiently; "it must not be."

65   "I submit," replied she calmly. "And, Aylmer, I shall quaff whatever draught you bring me; but it will be on the same principle that would induce me to take a dose of poison if offered by your hand."

"My noble wife," said Aylmer, deeply moved, "I knew not the height and depth of your nature until now. Nothing shall be concealed. Know, then, that this crimson hand, superficial as it seems, has clutched its grasp into your being with a strength of which I had no previous conception. I have already administered agents powerful enough to do aught except to change your entire physical system. Only one thing remains to be tried. If that fails us we are ruined."

"Why did you hesitate to tell me this?" asked she.

"Because, Georgiana," said Aylmer, in a low voice, "there is danger."

"Danger? There is but one danger—that this horrible stigma shall be left upon my cheek!" cried Georgiana. "Remove it, remove it, whatever be the cost, or we shall both go mad!"

70   "Heaven knows your words are too true," said Aylmer, sadly. "And now, dearest, return to your boudoir. In a little while all will be tested."

He conducted her back and took leave of her with a solemn tenderness which spoke far more than his words how much was now at stake. After his departure, Georgiana became rapt in musings. She considered the character of Aylmer, and did it completer justice than at any previous moment. Her heart exulted, while it trembled, at his honorable love—so pure and lofty that it would accept nothing less than perfection nor miserably make itself contented with an earthlier nature than he had dreamed of. She felt how much more precious was such a sentiment than that meaner kind which would have borne with the imperfection for her sake, and have been guilty of treason to holy love by degrading its perfect idea to the level of the actual; and with her whole spirit she prayed that, for a single moment, she might satisfy his highest and deepest conception. Longer than one moment she well knew it could not be; for his spirit was ever on the march, ever ascending, and each instant required something that was beyond the scope of the instant before.

The sound of her husband's footsteps aroused her. He bore a crystal goblet containing a liquor colorless as water, but bright enough to be the draught of immortality. Aylmer was pale; but it seemed rather the consequence of a highly wrought state of mind and tension of spirit than of fear or doubt.

"The concoction of the draught has been perfect," said he, in answer to Georgiana's look. "Unless all my science have deceived me, it cannot fail."

"Save on your account, my dearest Aylmer," observed his wife, "I might wish to put off this birthmark of mortality by relinquishing mortality itself in preference to any other mode. Life is but a sad possession to those who have attained precisely the degree of moral advancement at which I stand. Were I weaker and blinder it might be happiness. Were I stronger, it might be endured hopefully. But being what I find myself, methinks I am of all mortals the most fit to die."

"You are fit for heaven without tasting death!" replied her husband. "But why do   75
we speak of dying? The draught cannot fail. Behold its effect upon this plant."

On the window seat there stood a geranium diseased with yellow blotches, which
had overspread all its leaves. Aylmer poured a small quantity of the liquid upon the
soil in which it grew. In a little time, when the roots of the plant had taken up the moisture, the unsightly blotches began to be extinguished in a living verdure.

"There needed no proof," said Georgiana, quietly. "Give me the goblet. I joyfully
stake all upon your word."

"Drink, then, thou lofty creature!" exclaimed Aylmer, with fervid admiration.
"There is no taint of imperfection on thy spirit. Thy sensible frame, too, shall soon
be all perfect."

She quaffed the liquid and returned the goblet to his hand.

"It is grateful," said she with a placid smile. "Methinks it is like water from a heav-   80
enly fountain; for it contains I know not what of unobtrusive fragrance and deli-
ciousness. It allays a feverish thirst that had parched me for many days. Now, dearest,
let me sleep. My earthly senses are closing over my spirit like the leaves around the
heart of a rose at sunset."

She spoke the last words with a gentle reluctance, as if it required almost more energy than she could command to pronounce the faint and lingering syllables. Scarcely had they loitered through her lips ere she was lost in slumber. Aylmer sat by her side,
watching her aspect with the emotions proper to a man the whole value of whose existence was involved in the process now to be tested. Mingled with this mood, however, was the philosophic investigation characteristic of the man of science. Not the
minutest symptom escaped him. A heightened flush of the cheek, a slight irregularity of breath, a quiver of the eyelid, a hardly perceptible tremor through the frame—
such were the details which, as the moments passed, he wrote down in his folio
volume. Intense thought had set its stamp upon every previous page of that volume,
but the thoughts of years were all concentrated upon the last.

While thus employed, he failed not to gaze often at the fatal hand, and not without
a shudder. Yet once, by a strange and unaccountable impulse, he pressed it with his lips.
His spirit recoiled, however, in the very act; and Georgiana, out of the midst of her
deep sleep, moved uneasily and murmured as if in remonstrance. Again Aylmer resumed his watch. Nor was it without avail. The crimson hand, which at first had been
strongly visible upon the marble paleness of Georgiana's cheek, now grew more faintly outlined. She remained not less pale than ever; but the birthmark, with every breath
that came and went, lost somewhat of its former distinctness. Its presence had been
awful; its departure was more awful still. Watch the stain of the rainbow fading out the
sky, and you will know how the mysterious symbol passed away.

"By Heaven! it is well-nigh gone!" said Aylmer to himself, in almost irrepressible
ecstasy. "I can scarcely trace it now. Success! success! And now it is like the faintest rose
color. The lightest flush of blood across her cheek would overcome it. But she is so
pale!"

He drew aside the window curtain and suffered the light of natural day to fall into
the room and rest upon her cheek. At the same time he heard a gross, hoarse chuckle,
which he had long known as his servant Aminadab's expression of delight.

"Ah, clod! ah, earthly mass!" cried Aylmer, laughing in a sort of frenzy, "you have   85
served me well! Matter and spirit—earth and heaven—have both done their part in
this! Laugh, thing of the senses! You have earned the right to laugh."

These exclamations broke Georgiana's sleep. She slowly unclosed her eyes and
gazed into the mirror which her husband had arranged for that purpose. A faint smile

flitted over her lips when she recognized how barely perceptible was now that crimson hand which had once blazed forth with such disastrous brilliancy as to scare away all their happiness. But then her eyes sought Aylmer's face with a trouble and anxiety that he could by no means account for.

"My poor Aylmer!" murmured she.

"Poor? Nay, richest, happiest, and most favored!" exclaimed he. "My peerless bride, it is successful! You are perfect!"

"My poor Aylmer," she repeated, with a more than human tenderness, "you have aimed loftily; you have done nobly. Do not repent that with so high and pure a feeling, you have rejected the best the earth could offer. Aylmer, dearest Aylmer, I am dying!"

90   Alas! it was too true! the fatal hand had grappled with the mystery of life, and was the bond by which an angelic spirit kept itself in union with a mortal frame. As the last crimson tint of the birthmark—that sole token of human imperfection—faded from her cheek, the parting breath of the now perfect woman passed into the atmosphere, and her soul, lingering a moment near her husband, took its heavenward flight. Then a hoarse, chuckling laugh was heard again! Thus ever does the gross fatality of earth exult in its invariable triumph over the immortal essence which, in this dim sphere of half development, demands the completeness of a higher state. Yet, had Aylmer reached a profounder wisdom, he need not thus have flung away the happiness which would have woven his mortal life of the selfsame texture with the celestial. The momentary circumstance was too strong for him; he failed to look beyond the shadowy scope of time, and, living once for all in eternity, to find the perfect future in the present.   [1846]

QUESTIONS

1. In what sense are the three major characters allegorical figures? How do they differ in their reaction to the birthmark?
2. How do Alymer's dream and his experiments foreshadow the outcome of the story?
3. Is Georgiana's analysis of her husband's character convincing?
4. Does the symbol of the birthmark take on new meanings as the story unfolds?
5. The author speaks of his tale as possessing a "deeply impressive moral." What is that moral? Does the substance of the tale in any way contradict the moral?

RESPONSES

1. Approach the story from the feminist perspective. What is Hawthorne saying about how men view women? Perhaps compare the story to Gilman's "The Yellow Wallpaper."
2. Write an essay exploring how science was viewed in the early nineteenth century.

NATHANIEL HAWTHORNE

Young Goodman Brown

Young Goodman° Brown came forth at sunset into the street at Salem village; but put his head back, after crossing the threshold, to exchange a parting kiss with his young wife. And Faith, as the wife was aptly named, thrust her own pretty head into the street, letting the wind play with the pink ribbons on her cap while she called to Goodman Brown.

"Dearest heart," whispered she, softly and rather sadly, when her lips were close to his ear, "prithee put off your journey until sunrise and sleep in your own bed to-night. A lone woman is troubled with such dreams and such thoughts that she's afeard of herself sometimes. Pray tarry with me this night, dear husband, of all nights in the year."

"My love and my Faith," replied young Goodman Brown, "of all nights in the year, this one night must I tarry away from thee. My journey, as thou callest it, forth and back again, must needs be done 'twixt now and sunrise. What, my sweet, pretty wife, dost thou doubt me already, and we but three months married?"

"Then God bless you!" said Faith, with the pink ribbons; "and may you find all well when you come back."

"Amen!" cried Goodman Brown. "Say thy prayers, dear Faith, and go to bed at   5
dusk, and no harm will come to thee."

So they parted; and the young man pursued his way until, being about to turn the corner by the meeting-house, he looked back and saw the head of Faith still peeping after him with a melancholy air, in spite of her pink ribbons.

"Poor little Faith!" thought he, for his heart smote him. "What a wretch am I to leave her on such an errand! She talks of dreams, too. Methought as she spoke there was trouble in her face, as if a dream had warned her what work is to be done to-night. But no, no; 'twould kill her to think it. Well, she's a blessed angel on earth; and after this one night I'll cling to her skirts and follow her to heaven."

With this excellent resolve for the future, Goodman Brown felt himself justified in making more haste on his present evil purpose. He had taken a dreary road, darkened by all the gloomiest trees of the forest, which barely stood aside to let the narrow path creep through, and closed immediately behind. It was all as lonely as could be; and

---

°*Goodman*: Title of respect for farmer or householder.

there is this peculiarity in such a solitude, that the traveller knows not who may be concealed by the innumerable trunks and the thick boughs overhead; so that with lonely footsteps he may yet be passing through an unseen multitude.

"There may be a devilish Indian behind every tree," said Goodman Brown to himself; and he glanced fearfully behind him as he added, "What if the devil himself should be at my very elbow!"

His head being turned back, he passed a crook of the road, and, looking forward again, beheld the figure of a man, in grave and decent attire, seated at the foot of an old tree. He arose at Goodman Brown's approach and walked onward side by side with him.

"You are late, Goodman Brown," said he. "The clock of the Old South was striking as I came through Boston, and that is full fifteen minutes agone."

"Faith kept me back a while," replied the young man, with a tremor in his voice, caused by the sudden appearance of his companion, though not wholly unexpected.

It was now deep dusk in the forest, and deepest in that part of it where these two were journeying. As nearly as could be discerned, the second traveller was about fifty years old, apparently in the same rank of life as Goodman Brown, and bearing a considerable resemblance to him, though perhaps more in expression than features. Still they might have been taken for father and son. And yet, though the elder person was as simply clad as the younger, and as simple in manner too, he had an indescribable air of one who knew the world, and who would not have felt abashed at the governor's dinner table or in King William's° court, were it possible that his affairs should call him thither. But the only thing about him that could be fixed upon as remarkable was his staff, which bore the likeness of a great black snake, so curiously wrought that it might almost be seen to twist and wriggle itself like a living serpent. This, of course, must have been an ocular deception, assisted by the uncertain light.

"Come, Goodman Brown," cried his fellow-traveller, "this is a dull pace for the beginning of a journey. Take my staff, if you are so soon weary."

"Friend," said the other, exchanging his slow pace for a full stop, "having kept covenant by meeting thee here, it is my purpose now to return whence I came. I have scruples touching the matter thou wot'st of."

"Sayest thou so?" replied he of the serpent, smiling apart. "Let us walk on, nevertheless, reasoning as we go; and if I convince thee not thou shalt turn back. We are but a little way in the forest yet."

"Too far! too far!" exclaimed the goodman, unconsciously resuming his walk. "My father never went into the woods on such an errand, nor his father before him. We have been a race of honest men and good Christians since the days of the martyrs; and shall I be the first of the name of Brown that ever took this path and kept"—

"Such company, thou wouldst say," observed the elder person, interpreting his pause. "Well said, Goodman Brown! I have been as well acquainted with your family as with ever a one among the Puritans; and that's no trifle to say. I helped your grandfather, the constable, when he lashed the Quaker woman so smartly through the streets of Salem; and it was I that brought your father a pitch-pine knot, kindled at my own hearth, to set fire to an Indian village, in King Philip's war. They were my good friends, both; and many a pleasant walk have we had along this path, and returned merrily after midnight. I would fain be friends with you for their sake."

"If it be as thou sayest," replied Goodman Brown, "I marvel they never spoke of these matters; or, verily, I marvel not, seeing that the least rumor of the sort would

---

°*King William*: William III, King of England, reigned 1689–1702.

have driven them from New England. We are a people of prayer, and good works to boot, and abide no such wickedness."

"Wickedness or not," said the traveller with the twisted staff, "I have a very gen-   20
eral acquaintance here in New England. The deacons of many a church have drunk the communion wine with me; the selectmen of divers towns make me their chairman; and a majority of the Great and General Court° are firm supporters of my interest. The governor and I, too—But these are state secrets."

"Can this be so?" cried Goodman Brown, with a stare of amazement at his undisturbed companion. "Howbeit, I have nothing to do with the governor and council; they have their own ways, and are no rule for a simple husbandman like me. But, were I to go with thee, how should I meet the eye of that good old man, our minister, at Salem village? Oh, his voice would make me tremble both Sabbath day and lecture day."

Thus far the elder traveller had listened with due gravity; but now burst into a fit of irrepressible mirth, shaking himself so violently that his snake-like staff actually seemed to wriggle in sympathy.

"Ha! ha! ha!" shouted he again and again; then composing himself, "Well, go on, Goodman Brown, go on; but, prithee, don't kill me with laughing."

"Well, then, to end the matter at once," said Goodman Brown, considerably nettled, "there is my wife, Faith. It would break her dear little heart; and I'd rather break my own."

"Nay, if that be the case," answered the other, "e'en go thy ways, Goodman Brown.   25
I would not for twenty old women like the one hobbling before us that Faith should come to any harm."

As he spoke he pointed his staff at a female figure on the path, in whom Goodman Brown recognized a very pious and exemplary dame, who had taught him his catechism in youth, and was still his moral and spiritual adviser, jointly with the minister and Deacon Gookin.

"A marvel, truly, that Goody Cloyse should be so far in the wilderness at nightfall," said he. "But with your leave, friend, I shall take a cut through the woods until we have left this Christian woman behind. Being a stranger to you, she might ask whom I was consorting with and whither I was going."

"Be it so," said his fellow-traveller. "Betake you to the woods, and let me keep the path."

Accordingly the young man turned aside, but took care to watch his companion, who advanced softly along the road until he had come within a staff's length of the old dame. She, meanwhile, was making the best of her way, with singular speed for so aged a woman, and mumbling some indistinct words—a prayer, doubtless—as she went. The traveller put forth his staff and touched her withered neck with what seemed the serpent's tail.

"The devil!" screamed the pious old lady.   30

"Then Goody Cloyse knows her old friend?" observed the traveller, confronting her and leaning on his writhing stick.

"Ah, forsooth, and is it your worship indeed?" cried the good dame. "Yes, truly is it, and in the very image of my old gossip, Goodman Brown, the grandfather of the silly fellow that now is. But—would your worship believe it?—my broomstick hath strangely disappeared, stolen, as I suspect, by that unhanged witch, Goody Cory, and

---

°*Great and General Court*: The colonial legislature of Massachusetts.

that, too, when I was all anointed with the juice of smallage, and cinquefoil, and wolf's bane"—°

"Mingled with fine wheat and the fat of a new-born babe," said the shape of old Goodman Brown.

"Ah, your worship knows the recipe," cried the old lady, cackling aloud. "So, as I was saying, being all ready for the meeting, and no horse to ride on, I made up my mind to foot it, for they tell me there is a nice young man to be taken into communion tonight. But now your good worship will lend me your arm, and we shall be there in a twinkling."

35   "That can hardly be," answered her friend. "I may not spare you my arm, Goody Cloyse; but here is my staff, if you will."

So saying, he threw it down at her feet, where, perhaps, it assumed life, being one of the rods, which its owner had formerly lent to the Egyptian magi:° Of this fact, however, Goodman Brown can not take cognizance. He had cast up his eyes in astonishment, and, looking down again, beheld neither Goody Cloyse nor the serpentine staff, but his fellow-traveller alone, who waited for him as calmly as if nothing had happened.

"That old woman taught me my catechism," said the young man; and there was a world of meaning in this simple comment.

They continued to walk onward, while the elder traveller exhorted his companion to make good speed and persevere in the path, discoursing so aptly that his arguments seemed rather to spring up in the bosom of his auditor than to be suggested by himself. As they went, he plucked a branch of maple to serve for a walking stick, and began to strip it of the twigs and little boughs, which were wet with evening dew. The moment his fingers touched them they became strangely withered and dried up as with a week's sunshine. Thus the pair proceeded, at a good free pace, until suddenly, in a gloomy hollow of the road, Goodman Brown sat himself down on the stump of a tree and refused to go any farther.

"Friend," said he, stubbornly, "my mind is made up. Not another step will I budge on this errand. What if a wretched old woman do choose to go to the devil when I thought she was going to heaven: is that any reason why I should quit my dear Faith and go after her?"

40   "You will think better of this by and by," said his acquaintance, composedly, "Sit here and rest yourself a while; and when you feel like moving again, there is my staff to help you along."

Without words, he threw his companion the maple stick, and was as speedily out of sight as if he had vanished into the deepening gloom. The young man sat a few moments by the roadside, applauding himself greatly, and thinking with how clear a conscience he should meet the minister in his morning walk, nor shrink from the eye of good old Deacon Gookin. And what calm sleep would be his that very night, which was to have been spent so wickedly, but so purely and sweetly now, in the arms of Faith! Amidst these pleasant and praiseworthy meditations, Goodman Brown heard the tramp of horses along the road, and deemed it advisable to conceal himself within the verge of the forest, conscious of the guilty purpose that had brought him thither, though now so happily turned from it.

°*smallage, cinquefoil, wolf's bane*: Plants thought to have powers over evil.
°*Egyptian magi*: See Exodus 7:9–12.

On came the hoof tramps and the voices of the riders, two grave old voices, conversing soberly as they drew near. These mingled sounds appeared to pass along the road, within a few yards of the young man's hiding-place; but, owing doubtless to the depth of the gloom at that particular spot, neither the travellers nor their steeds were visible. Though their figures brushed the small boughs by the wayside, it could not be seen that they intercepted, even for a moment, the faint gleam from the strip of bright sky athwart which they must have passed. Goodman Brown alternately crouched and stood on tiptoe, pulling aside the branches and thrusting forth his head as far as he durst without discerning so much as a shadow. It vexed him the more, because he could have sworn, were such a thing possible, that he recognized the voices of the minister and Deacon Gookin, jogging along quietly, as they were wont to do, when bound to some ordination or ecclesiastical council. While yet within hearing one of the riders stopped to pluck a switch.

"Of the two, reverend sir," said the voice like the deacon's, "I had rather miss an ordination dinner than to-night's meeting. They tell me that some of our community are to be here from Falmouth and beyond, and others from Connecticut and Rhode Island besides several of Indian powwows, who, after their fashion, know almost as much deviltry as the best of us. Moreover, there is a goodly young woman to be taken into communion."

"Mighty well, Deacon Gookin!" replied the solemn old tones of the minister. "Spur up, or we shall be late. Nothing can be done you know until I get on the ground."

The hoofs clattered again; and the voices, talking so strangely in the empty air, passed on through the forest, where no church had ever been gathered or solitary Christian prayed. Whither, then, could these holy men be journeying so deep into the heathen wilderness? Young Goodman Brown caught hold of a tree for support, being ready to sink down on the ground, faint and overburdened with the heavy sickness of his heart. He looked up to the sky, doubting whether there really was a heaven above him. Yet there was the blue arch, and the stars brightening in it. 45

"With heaven above and Faith below, I will yet stand firm against the devil!" cried Goodman Brown.

While he still gazed upward into the deep arch of the firmament and had lifted his hands to pray, a cloud, though no wind was stirring, hurried across the zenith and hid the brightening stars. The blue sky was still visible, except directly overhead, where this black mass of cloud was sweeping swiftly northward. Aloft in the air, as if from the depths of the cloud, came a confused and doubtful sound of voices. Once the listener fancied that he could distinguish the accents of townspeople of his own, men and women, both pious and ungodly, many of whom he had met at the communion table, and had seen others rioting at the tavern. The next moment, so indistinct were the sounds, he doubted whether he had heard aught but the murmur of the old forest, whispering without a wind. Then came a stronger swell of those familiar tones, heard daily in the sunshine at Salem village, but never until now from a cloud of night. There was one voice of a young woman uttering lamentations, yet with an uncertain sorrow, and entreating for some favor, which perhaps, it would grieve her to obtain; and all the unseen multitude, both saints and sinners, seemed to encourage her onward.

"Faith!" shouted Goodman Brown, in a voice of agony and desperation; and the echoes of the forest mocked him, crying, "Faith! Faith!" as if bewildered wretches were seeking her all through the wilderness.

The cry of grief, rage, and terror was yet piercing the night, when the unhappy husband held his breath for a response. There was a scream, drowned immediately in a loud murmur of voices, fading into far-off laughter, as the dark cloud swept away, leaving the clear and silent sky above Goodman Brown. But something fluttered lightly down through the air and caught on the branch of a tree. The young man seized it, and beheld a pink ribbon.

50   "My Faith is gone!" cried he, after one stupefied moment. "There is no good on earth; and sin is but a name. Come, devil; for to thee is this world given."

And, maddened with despair, so that he laughed loud and long, did Goodman Brown grasp his staff and set forth again, at such a rate that he seemed to fly along the forest path rather than to walk or run. The road grew wilder and drearier and more faintly traced, and vanished at length, leaving him in the heart of the dark wilderness, still rushing onward with the instinct that guides mortal man to evil. The whole forest was peopled with frightful sounds—the creaking of the trees, the howling of wild beasts, and the yells of Indians; while sometimes the wind tolled like a distant church bell, and sometimes gave a broad roar around the traveller, as if all Nature were laughing him to scorn. But he was himself the chief horror of the scene, and shrank not from its other horrors.

"Ha! ha! ha!" roared Goodman Brown when the wind laughed at him. "Let us hear which will laugh loudest. Think not to frighten me with your deviltry. Come witch, come wizard, come Indian powwow, come devil himself, and here comes Goodman Brown. You may as well fear him as he fears you."

In truth, all through the haunted forest there could be nothing more frightful than the figure of Goodman Brown. On he flew among the black pines, brandishing his staff with frenzied gestures, now giving vent to an inspiration of horrid blasphemy, and now shouting forth such laughter as set all the echoes of the forest laughing like demons around him. The fiend in his own shape is less hideous than when he rages in the breast of man. Thus sped the demoniac on his course, until, quivering among the trees, he saw a red light before him, as when the felled trunks and branches of a cleaning have been set on fire, and throw up their lurid blaze against the sky, at the hour of midnight. He paused, in a lull of the tempest that had driven him onward, and heard the swell of what seemed a hymn, rolling solemnly from a distance with the weight of many voices. He knew the tune; it was a familiar one in the choir of the village meeting-house. The verse died heavily away, and was lengthened by a chorus, not of human voices, but of all the sounds of the benighted wilderness pealing in awful harmony together. Goodman Brown cried out, and his cry was lost to his own ear by its unison with the cry of the desert.

In the interval of silence he stole forward until the light glared full upon his eyes. At one extremity of an open space, hemmed in by the dark wall of the forest, arose a rock, bearing some rude, natural resemblance either to an altar or a pulpit, and surrounded by four blazing pines, their tops aflame, their stems untouched, like candles at an evening meeting. The mass of foliage that had overgrown the summit of the rock was all on fire, blazing into the night and fitfully illuminating the whole field. Each pendent twig and leafy festoon was in a blaze. As the red light arose and fell, a numerous congregation alternately shone forth, then disappeared in shadow, and again grew, as it were, out of the darkness, peopling the heart of the solitary woods at once.

55   "A grave and dark-clad company," quoth Goodman Brown.

In truth they were such. Among them, quivering to and fro between gloom and splendor, appeared faces that would be seen next day at the council board of the province, and others which, Sabbath after Sabbath, looked devoutly heavenward, and benignantly over the crowded pews, from the holiest pulpits in the land. Some affirm that the lady of the governor was there. At least there were high dames well known to her, and wives of honored husbands, and widows, a great multitude, and ancient maidens, all of excellent repute, and fair young girls, who trembled lest their mothers should espy them. Either the sudden gleams of light flashing over the obscure field bedazzled Goodman Brown, or he recognized a score of the church members of Salem village famous for their special sanctity. Good old Deacon Gookin had arrived, and waited at the skirts of that venerable saint, his revered pastor. But, irreverently consorting with these grave, reputable, and pious people, these elders of the church, these chaste dames and dewy virgins, there were men of dissolute lives and women of spotted fame, wretches given over to all mean and filthy vice, and suspected even of horrid crimes. It was strange to see that the good shrank not from the wicked, nor were the sinners abashed by the saints. Scattered also among their pale-faced enemies were the Indian priests, or powwows, who had often scared their native forest with more hideous incantations than any known to English witchcraft.

"But where is Faith?" thought Goodman Brown; and, as hope came into his heart, he trembled.

Another verse of the hymn arose, a slow and mournful strain, such as the pious love, but joined to words which expressed all that our nature can conceive of sin, and darkly hinted at far more. Unfathomable to mere mortals is the lore of friends. Verse after verse was sung; and still the chorus of the desert swelled between like the deepest tone of a mighty organ; and with the final peal of that dreadful anthem there came a sound, as if the roaring wind, the rushing streams, the howling beasts, and every other voice of the unconverted wilderness were mingling and according with the voice of guilty man in homage to the prince of all. The four blazing pines threw up a loftier flame, and obscurely discovered shapes and visages of horror on the smoke wreaths above the impious assembly. At the same moment the fire on the rock shot redly forth and formed a glowing arch above its base, where now appeared a figure. With reverence be it spoken, the figure bore no slight similitude, both in garb and manner, to some grave divine of the New England churches.

"Bring forth the converts!" cried a voice that echoed through the field and rolled into the forest.

At the word, Goodman Brown stepped forth from the shadow of the trees and approached the congregation, with whom he felt a loathful brotherhood by the sympathy of all that was wicked in his heart. He could have well-nigh sworn that the shape of his own dead father beckoned him to advance, looking downward from a smoke wreath, while a woman, with dim features of despair, threw out her hand to warn him back. Was it his mother? But he had no power to retreat one step, nor to resist, even in thought, when the minister and good old Deacon Gookin seized his arms and led him to the blazing rock. Thither came also the slender form of a veiled female, led between Goody Cloyse, that pious teacher of the catechism, and Martha Carrier, who had received the devil's promise to be queen of hell. A rampant hag was she. And there stood the proselytes beneath the canopy of fire.

"Welcome, my children," said the dark figure, "to the communion of your race. Ye have found thus young your nature and your destiny. My children, look behind you!"

They turned; and flashing forth, as it were, in a sheet of flame, the fiend worshippers were seen; the smile of welcome gleamed darkly on every visage.

"There," resumed the sable form, "are all whom ye have reverenced from youth. Ye deemed them holier than yourself, and shrank from your own sins, contrasting it with their lives of righteousness and prayerful aspirations heavenward. Yet here are they all in my worshipping assembly. This night it shall be granted you to know their secret deeds: how hoary-bearded elders of the church have whispered wanton words to the

60

young maids of their households; how many a woman, eager for widows' weeds, has given her husband a drink at bedtime and let him sleep his last sleep in her bosom; how beardless youths have made haste to inherit their fathers' wealth, and how fair damsels—blush not, sweet ones—have dug little graves in the garden, and bidden me, the sole guest to an infant's funeral. By the sympathy of your human hearts for sin ye shall scent out all the places—whether in church, bed-chamber, street, field, or forest—where crime has been committed, and shall exult to behold the whole earth one stain of guilt, one mighty blood spot. Far more than this. It shall be yours to penetrate, in every bosom, the deep mystery of sin, the fountain of all wicked arts, and which inexhaustibly supplies more evil impulses than human power—than my power at its utmost—can make manifest in deeds. And now, my children, look upon each other."

They did so; and, by the blaze of the hell-kindled torches, the wretched man beheld his Faith, and the wife her husband, trembling before that unhallowed altar.

65   "Lo, there ye stand, my children," said the figure, in a deep and solemn tone, almost sad with its despairing awfulness, as if his once angelic nature could yet mourn for our miserable race. "Depending upon one another's hearts, ye had still hoped that virtue were not all a dream. Now are ye undeceived. Evil is the nature of mankind. Evil must be your only happiness. Welcome again, my children, to the communion of your race."

"Welcome," repeated the fiend worshippers, in one cry of despair and triumph.

And there they stood, the only pair, as it seemed, who were yet hesitating on the verge of wickedness in this dark world. A basin was hollowed, naturally, in the rock. Did it contain water, reddened by the lurid light? or was it blood? or, perchance, a liquid flame? Herein did the shape of evil dip his hand and prepare to lay the mark of baptism upon their foreheads, that they might be partakers of the mystery of sin, more conscious of the secret guilt of others, both in deed and thought, than they could now be of their own. The husband cast one look at his pale wife, and Faith at him. What polluted wretches would the next glance show them to each other, shuddering alike at what they disclosed and what they saw!

"Faith!" Faith!" cried the husband, "look up to heaven, and resist the wicked one."

Whether Faith obeyed he knew not. Hardly had he spoken when he found himself amid calm night and solitude, listening to a roar of the wind which died heavily away through the forest. He staggered against the rock, and felt it chill and damp; while a hanging twig, that had been all on fire, besprinkled his cheek with the coldest dew.

70   The next morning young Goodman Brown came slowly into the street of Salem village, staring around him like a bewildered man. The good old minister was taking a walk along the graveyard to get an appetite for breakfast and meditate his sermon, and bestowed a blessing, as he passed, on Goodman Brown. He shrank from the venerable saint as if to avoid an anathema. Old Deacon Gookin was at domestic worship, and the holy words of his prayer were heard through the open window. "What God does the wizard pray to?" quoth Goodman Brown. Goody Cloyse, that excellent old Christian, stood in the early sunshine at her own lattice, catechizing a little girl who had brought her a pint of morning's milk. Goodman Brown snatched away the child as from the grasp of the fiend himself. Turning the corner by the meeting-house, he spied the head of Faith, with the pink ribbons, gazing anxiously forth, and bursting into such joy at sight of him that she skipped along the street and almost kissed her husband before the whole village. But Goodman Brown looked sternly and sadly into her face, and passed on without a greeting.

Had Goodman Brown fallen asleep in the forest and only dreamed a wild dream of a witch-meeting?

Be it so if you will; but, alas! it was a dream of evil omen for young Goodman Brown. A stern, a sad, a darkly meditative, a distrustful, if not a desperate man did he become from the night of that fearful dream. On the Sabbath day, when the congregation were singing a holy psalm, he could not listen because an anthem of sin rushed loudly upon his ears and drowned all the blessed strain. When the minister spoke from the pulpit with power and fervid eloquence, and, with his hand on the open Bible, of the sacred truths of our religion, and of saint-like lives and triumphant death and of future bliss or misery unutterable, then did Goodman Brown turn pale, dreading lest the roof should thunder down upon the gray blasphemer and his hearers. Often, waking suddenly at midnight, he shrank from the bosom of Faith; and at morning or eventide, when the family knelt down at prayer, he scowled and muttered to himself, and gazed sternly at his wife, and turned away. And when he had lived long, and was borne to his grave a hoary corpse, followed by Faith, an aged woman, and children and grandchildren, a goodly procession, besides neighbors not a few, they carved no hopeful verse upon his tombstone, for his dying hour was gloom.   [1835]

QUESTIONS

1. The modern reader is about as distant from the time that Hawthorne wrote this story as Hawthorne was from his subject. Does this historical distance create problems of interpretation for the modern reader?
2. What is Brown's motive for going into the forest?
3. How does the author evoke the dreamlike atmosphere of the story? What is his purpose?
4. What is the function of Faith's pink ribbons? Why are they pink?
5. How is Brown affected by each of the people he meets in the forest?
6. Is the theme of the story ambiguous? Can an argument be made that ambiguity was the author's intention?

RESPONSES

1. Compare this story to Donald Barthelme's "A City of Churches."
2. Research Hawthorne's life and/or the history of Puritan thought, especially in Salem, Massachusetts. Write an essay explaining what biographical or historical information adds to your understanding.

FOCUS ON FILM

1. View the film *Eyes Wide Shut*. How does that film use basic plot points and thematic ideas that are also part of "Young Goodman Brown?"

BESSIE HEAD

Bessie Head (1937–1986) was born in South Africa, the child of a white mother and black father. After a childhood in foster care and in an orphanage in Durban, she trained as a primary teacher and taught school for several years. In 1962 she married a journalist, Harold Head, and they had a son. In 1964, estranged from her husband, she left South Africa for Botswana where she made her life. Her first novel, *When Rain Clouds Gather*, appeared in 1967. As her writings made her better known, she traveled to the United States and to Australia. Granted Botswanan citizenship in 1979, she died in 1986 of hepatitis.

Looking for a Rain God

It is lonely at the lands where the people go to plough. These lands are vast clearings in the bush, and the wild bush is lonely too. Nearly all the lands are within walking distance from the village. In some parts of the bush where the underground water is very near the surface, people made little rest camps for themselves and dug shallow wells to quench their thirst while on their journey to their own lands. They experienced all kinds of things once they left the village. They could rest at shady watering places full of lush, tangled trees with delicate pale-gold and purple wild flowers springing up between soft green moss and the children could hunt around for wild figs and any berries that might be in season. But from 1958, a seven-year drought fell upon the land and even the watering places began to look as dismal as the dry open thorn-bush country; the leaves of the trees curled up and withered; the moss became dry and hard and, under the shade of the tangled trees, the ground turned a powdery black and white, because there was no rain. People said rather humorously that if you tried to catch the rain in a cup it would only fill a teaspoon. Towards the beginning of the seventh year of drought, the summer had become an anguish to live through. The air was so dry and moisture-free that it burned the skin. No one knew what to do to escape the heat and tragedy was in the air. At the beginning of that summer, a number of men just went out of their homes and hung themselves to death from trees. The majority of the people had lived off crops, but for two years past they had all returned from the lands with only their rolled-up skin blankets and cooking utensils. Only the charlatans, in-canters, and witch-doctors made a pile of money during this time because people were always turning to them in desperation for little talismans and herbs to rub on the plough for the crops to grow and the rain to fall.

The rains were late that year. They came in early November, with a promise of good rain. It wasn't the full, steady downpour of the years of good rain, but thin, scanty, misty rain. It softened the earth and a rich growth of green things sprang up everywhere for the animals to eat. People were called to the village kgotla° to hear the proclamation of the beginning of the ploughing season; they stirred themselves and whole families began to move off to the lands to plough.

The family of the old man, Mokgobja, were among those who left early for the lands. They had a donkey cart and piled everything onto it, Mokgobja—who was over seventy years old; two little girls, Neo and Boseyong; their mother Tiro and an unmarried sister, Nesta; and the father and supporter of the family, Ramadi, who drove the donkey cart. In the rush of the first hope of rain, the man, Ramadi, and the two women, cleared the land of thorn-bush and then hedged their vast ploughing area with this same thorn-bush to protect the future crop from the goats they had brought along for milk. They cleared out and deepened the old well with its pool of muddy water and still in this light, misty rain, Ramadi inspanned two oxen and turned the earth over with a hand plough.

The land was ready and ploughed, waiting for the crops. At night, the earth was alive with insects singing and rustling about in search of food. But suddenly, by mid-November, the rain fled away; the rain-clouds fled away and left the sky bare. The sun danced dizzily in the sky, with a strange cruelty. Each day the land was covered in a haze of mist as the sun sucked up the last drop of moisture out of the earth. The family sat down in despair, waiting and waiting. Their hopes had run so high; the goats had started producing milk, which they had eagerly poured on their porridge, now they ate plain porridge with no milk. It was impossible to plant the corn, maize, pumpkin and water-melon seeds in the dry earth. They sat the whole day in the shadow of the huts and even stopped thinking, for the rain had fled away. Only the children, Neo and Boseyong, were quite happy in their little girl world. They carried on with their game of making house like their mother and chattered to each other in light, soft tones. They made children from sticks around which they tied rags, and scolded them severely in an exact imitation of their own mother. Their voices could be heard scolding the day long: "You stupid thing, when I send you to draw water, why do you spill half of it out of the bucket!" "You stupid thing! Can't you mind the porridge-pot without letting the porridge burn!" And then they would beat the rag-dolls on their bottoms with severe expressions.

The adults paid no attention to this; they did not even hear the funny chatter; they sat waiting for rain; their nerves were stretched to breaking-point willing the rain to fall out of the sky. Nothing was important, beyond that. All their animals had been sold during the bad years to purchase food, and of all their herd only two goats were left. It was the women of the family who finally broke down under the strain of waiting for rain. It was really the two women who caused the death of the little girls. Each night they started a weird, high-pitched wailing that began on a low, mournful note and whipped up to a frenzy. Then they would stamp their feet and shout as though they had lost their heads. The men sat quiet and self-controlled; it was important for men to maintain their self-control at all times but their nerve was breaking too. They knew the women were haunted by the starvation of the coming year.

5

°*kgotla*: Center (Khoisan language of southern Africa).

Finally, an ancient memory stirred in the old man, Mokgobja. When he was very young and the customs of the ancestors still ruled the land, he had been witness to a rain-making ceremony. And he came alive a little, struggling to recall the details which had been buried by years and years of prayer in a Christian church. As soon as the mists cleared a little, he began consulting in whispers with his youngest son, Ramadi. There was, he said, a certain rain god who accepted only the sacrifice of the bodies of children. Then the rain would fall; then the crops would grow, he said. He explained the ritual and as he talked, his memory became a conviction and he began to talk with unshakable authority. Ramadi's nerves were smashed by the nightly wailing of the women and soon the two men began whispering with the two women. The children continued their game: "You stupid thing! How could you have lost the money on the way to the shop! You must have been playing again!"

After it was all over and the bodies of the two little girls had been spread across the land, the rain did not fall. Instead, there was a deathly silence at night and the devouring heat of the sun by day. A terror, extreme and deep, overwhelmed the whole family. They packed, rolling up their skin blankets and pots, and fled back to the village.

People in the village soon noted the absence of the two little girls. They had died at the lands and were buried there, the family said. But people noted their ashen, terror-stricken faces and a murmur arose. What had killed the children, they wanted to know? And the family replied that they had just died. And people said amongst themselves that it was strange that the two deaths had occurred at the same time. And there was a feeling of great unease at the unnatural looks of the family. Soon the police came around. The family told them the same story of death and burial at the lands. They did not know what the children had died of. So the police asked to see the graves. At this, the mother of the children broke down and told everything.

Throughout that terrible summer the story of the children hung like a dark cloud of sorrow over the village, and the sorrow was not assuaged when the old man and Ramadi were sentenced to death for ritual murder. All they had on the statute books was that ritual murder was against the law and must be stamped out with the death penalty. The subtle story of strain and starvation and breakdown was inadmissable evidence at court; but all the people who lived off crops knew in their hearts that only a hair's breadth had saved them from sharing a fate similar to that of the Mokgobja family. They could have killed something to make the rain fall.   [1977]

QUESTIONS

1. How would you describe the tone of this story?
2. How is nature perceived by the narrator?
3. Do you agree with the narrator that the women are responsible for the death of the little girls?
4. The people are looking for a rain god. What do they find?
5. Is this fable of an agricultural people relevant to industrial society?

RESPONSES

1. Research the mythology of rain gods. How does the story use and adapt such myths?
2. Compare Head's story to Shirley Jackson's "The Lottery." In each story, what culture is being implicitly criticized?
3. Write a short story set in the contemporary United States. How do we sacrifice our young for "prosperity"?

ERNEST HEMINGWAY

Ernest Hemingway (1899–1961) was born in Oak Park, Illinois. After high school he got a job as a cub reporter on the *Kansas City Star* and then volunteered for service in World War I as an ambulance driver. Wounded in combat, he returned to civilian life as European correspondent for the *Toronto Star*. Mingling with the expatriate community in Paris, Hemingway began to publish muted, understated stories written in the spare, staccato style that made his reputation. In 1926 he published *The Sun Also Rises*, a novel that became a rallying cry for the lost generation. His popularity soared as book followed book, and in 1954 he was awarded the Nobel Prize. Hemingway dramatized the events of his life with the same intensity with which he dramatized the lives of his fictional characters, and such relentless media exposure took its toll. In 1961 he took his own life. His stories are collected in *In Our Time* (1925), *Men Without Women* (1927), and *Winner Take Nothing* (1933).

Hills Like White Elephants

The hills across the valley of the Ebro° were long and white. On this side there was no shade and no trees and the station was between two lines of rails in the sun. Close against the side of the station there was the warm shadow of the building and a curtain, made of strings of bamboo beads, hung across the open door into the bar, to keep out flies. The American and the girl with him sat at a table in the shade, outside the building. It was very hot and the express from Barcelona would come in forty minutes. It stopped at this junction for two minutes and went on to Madrid.

"What should we drink?" the girl asked. She had taken off her hat and put it on the table.

"It's pretty hot," the man said.

"Let's drink beer."

5   "Dos cervezas," the man said into the curtain.

"Big ones?" a woman asked from the doorway.

"Yes. Two big ones."

°*Ebro*: River in northern Spain.

The woman brought two glasses of beer and two felt pads. She put the felt pads and the beer glasses on the table and looked at the man and the girl. The girl was looking off at the line of hills. They were white in the sun and the country was brown and dry.

"They look like white elephants," she said.

"I've never seen one," the man drank his beer.   10

"No, you wouldn't have."

"I might have," the man said. "Just because you say I wouldn't have doesn't prove anything."

The girl looked at the bead curtain. "They've painted something on it," she said. "What does it say?"

"Anis del Toro. It's a drink."

"Could we try it?"   15

The man called "Listen" through the curtain. The woman came out from the bar.

"Four reales."°

"We want two Anis del Toro."

"With water?"

"Do you want it with water?"   20

"I don't know," the girl said. "Is it good with water?"

"It's all right."

"You want them with water?" asked the woman.

"Yes, with water."

"It tastes like licorice," the girl said and put the glass down.   25

"That's the way with everything."

"Yes," said the girl. "Everything tastes of licorice. Especially all the things you've waited so long for, like absinthe."

"Oh, cut it out."

"You started it," the girl said. "I was being amused. I was having a fine time."

"Well, let's try and have a fine time."   30

"All right. I was trying. I said the mountains looked like white elephants. Wasn't that bright?"

"That was bright."

"I wanted to try this new drink. That's all we do, isn't it—look at things and try new drinks?"

"I guess so."

The girl looked across at the hills.   35

"They're lovely hills," she said. "They don't really look like white elephants. I just meant the coloring of their skin through the trees."

"Should we have another drink?"

"All right."

The warm wind blew the bead curtain against the table.

"The beer's nice and cool," the man said.   40

"It's lovely," the girl said.

"It's really an awfully simple operation, Jig," the man said. "It's not really an operation at all."

The girl looked at the ground the table legs rested on.

"I know you wouldn't mind it, Jig. It's really not anything. It's just to let the air in."

The girl did not say anything.   45

°*reales*: Spanish coins.

"I'll go with you and I'll stay with you all the time. They just let the air in and then it's all perfectly natural."

"Then what will we do afterward?"

"We'll be fine afterward. Just like we were before."

"What makes you think so?"

50   "That's the only thing that bothers us. It's the only thing that's made us unhappy."

The girl looked at the bead curtain, put her hand out and took hold of two of the strings of beads.

"And you think then we'll be all right and be happy."

"I know we will. You don't have to be afraid. I've known lots of people that have done it."

"So have I," said the girl. "And afterward they were all so happy."

55   "Well," the man said, "if you don't want to you don't have to. I wouldn't have you do it if you didn't want to. But I know it's perfectly simple."

"And you really want to?"

"I think it's the best thing to do. But I don't want you to do it if you don't really want to."

"And if I do it you'll be happy and things will be like they were and you'll love me?"

"I love you now. You know I love you."

60   "I know. But if I do it, then it will be nice again if I say things are like white elephants, and you'll like it?"

"I'll love it. I love it now but I just can't think about it. You know how I get when I worry."

"If I do it you won't ever worry?"

"I won't worry about that because it's perfectly simple."

"Then I'll do it. Because I don't care about me."

65   "What do you mean?"

"I don't care about me."

"Well, I care about you."

"Oh, yes. But I don't care about me. And I'll do it and then everything will be fine."

"I don't want you to do it if you feel that way."

70   The girl stood up and walked to the end of the station. Across, on the other side, were fields of grain and trees along the banks of the Ebro. Far away, beyond the river, were mountains. The shadow of a cloud moved across the field of grain and she saw the river through the trees.

"And we could have all this," she said. "And we could have everything and every day we make it more impossible."

"What did you say?"

"I said we could have everything."

"We can have everything."

75   "No, we can't."

"We can have the whole world."

"No, we can't."

"We can go everywhere."

"No, we can't. It isn't ours any more."

80   "It's ours."

"No, it isn't. And once they take it away, you never get it back."

"But they haven't taken it away."

"We'll wait and see."

"Come on back in the shade," he said. "You mustn't feel that way."

"I don't feel any way," the girl said. "I just know things."

"I don't want you to do anything that you don't want to do—"

"Nor that isn't good for me," she said. "I know. Could we have another beer?"

"All right. But you've got to realize—"

"I realize," the girl said. "Can't we maybe stop talking?"

They sat down at the table and the girl looked across at the hills on the dry side of the valley and the man looked at her and at the table.

"You've got to realize," he said, "that I don't want you to do it if you don't want to. I'm perfectly willing to go through with it if it means anything to you."

"Doesn't it mean anything to you? We could get along."

"Of course it does. But I don't want anybody but you. I don't want anyone else. And I know it's perfectly simple."

"Yes, you know it's perfectly simple."

"It's all right for you to say that, but I do know it."

"Would you do something for me now?"

"I'd do anything for you."

"Would you please please please please please please please stop talking?"

He did not say anything but looked at the bags against the wall of the station. There were labels on them from all the hotels where they had spent nights.

"But I don't want you to," he said, "I don't care anything about it."

"I'll scream," the girl said.

The woman came out through the curtains with two glasses of beer and put them down on the damp felt pads. "The train comes in five minutes," she said.

"What did she say?" asked the girl.

"That the train is coming in five minutes."

The girl smiled brightly at the woman, to thank her.

"I'd better take the bags over to the other side of the station," the man said. She smiled at him.

"All right. Then come back and we'll finish the beer."

He picked up the two heavy bags and carried them around the station to the other tracks. He looked up the tracks but could not see the train. Coming back, he walked through the barroom, where people waiting for the train were drinking. He drank an Anis at the bar and looked at the people. They were all waiting reasonably for the train. He went out through the bead curtain. She was sitting at the table and smiled at him.

"Do you feel better?" he asked.

"I feel fine," she said. "There's nothing wrong with me. I feel fine." [1927] 110

QUESTIONS

1. From what point of view is the story told?

2. Since the story offers so little information about the background and appearance of the characters, discuss the implications of such details as are provided.

3. How is the setting at a Spanish railroad crossing appropriate to the theme?

4. What is the significance of the title?

5. As the man drinks his Anis, he thinks to himself, "They were all waiting reasonably for the train." What is the force of the word "reasonably"?

RESPONSE

1. Write an essay from the reader's response perspective. How did you ask questions and discover answers as you "overheard" this conversation? Who do you think the audience of this "performance" was? Who did Hemingway imagine reading the story?

FOCUS ON FILM

1. Research Hemingway's life. How did the writers of the screenplay use Hemingway's life to add "back story" to the man's character?
2. Examine the actor's choice in how to say the lines, "Would you please please please please please please stop talking?" What does such a choice add or detract from the story?

ZORA NEALE HURSTON

Zora Neale Hurston (1901–1960) was born in Eatonville, Florida, one of eight children of a Baptist minister. Her family did not survive intact the death of her mother in 1912, and during her adolescence she was shunted from family to family. She studied at Howard University and later at Columbia with the distinguished anthropologist Franz Boaz. Under his influence she returned to her native Florida to record the oral traditions of African-American culture. Her novels and nonfiction, long in eclipse, have been rediscovered. They include her novel of a black preacher, *Jonah's Gourd Vine* (1934), and *Mules and Men* (1935), an account of black folkways in Florida.

Spunk

I

A giant of a brown-skinned man sauntered up the one street of the village and out into the palmetto thickets with a small pretty woman clinging lovingly to his arm.

"Looka theah, folkses!" cried Elijah Mosley, slapping his leg gleefully. "Theah they go, big as life an' brassy as tacks.

All the loungers in the store tried to walk to the door with an air of nonchalance but with small success.

"Now pee-eople!" Walter Thomas gasped. "Will you look at 'em!"

"But that's one thing Ah likes about Spunk Banks—he ain't skeered of nothin' on God's green footstool—*nothin'!* He rides that log down at saw-mill jus' like he struts 'round wid another man's wife—jus' don't give a kitty. When Tes' Miller got cut to giblets on that circle-saw, Spunk steps right up and starts ridin'. The rest of us was skeered to go near it." 5

A round-shouldered figure in overalls much too large came nervously in the door and the talking ceased. The men looked at each other and winked.

"Gimme some soda-water. Sass'prilla Ah reckon," the newcomer ordered, and stood far down the counter near the open pickled pig-feet tub to drink it.

Elijah nudged Walter and turned with mock gravity to the new-comer.

"Say, Joe, how's everything up yo' way? How's yo' wife?"

Joe started and all but dropped the bottle he was holding. He swallowed several times painfully and his lips trembled.

"Aw 'Lige, you oughtn't do nothin' like that," Walter grumbled. Elijah ignored him.

"She jus' passed heah a few minutes ago goin' thata way," with a wave of his hand in the direction of the woods.

Now Joe knew his wife had passed that way. He knew that the men lounging in the general store had seen her, moreover, he knew that the men knew *he* knew. He stood there silent for a long moment staring blankly, with his Adam's apple twitching nervously up and down his throat. One could actually *see* the pain he was suffering, his eyes, his face, his hands, and even the dejected slump of his shoulders. He set the bottle down upon the counter. He didn't bang it, just eased it out of his hand silently and fiddled with his suspender buckle.

"Well, Ah'm goin' after her to-day. Ah'm goin' an' fetch her back. Spunk's done gone too fur."

He reached deep down into his trouser pocket and drew out a hollow ground razor, large and shiny, and passed his moistened thumb back and forth over the edge.

"Talkin' like a man, Joe. 'Course that's *yo'* fambly affairs, but Ah like to see grit in anybody."

Joe Kanty laid down a nickel and stumbled out into the street.

Dusk crept in from the woods. Ike Clarke lit the swinging oil lamp that was almost immediately surrounded by candle-flies. The men laughed boisterously behind Joe's back as they watched him shamble woodward.

"You oughtn't to said whut you said to him, 'Lige—look how it worked him up," Walter chided.

"And Ah hope it did work him up. Tain't even decent for a man to take and take like he do."

"Spunk will sho' kill him."

"Aw, Ah doan know. You never kin tell. He might turn him up an' spank him fur gettin' in the way, but Spunk wouldn't shoot no unarmed man. Dat razor he carried outa heah ain't gonna run Spunk down an' cut him, an' Joe ain't got the nerve to go to Spunk with it knowing he totes that Army .45. He makes that break outa heah to bluff us. He's gonna hide that razor behind the first palmetto root an' sneak back home to bed. Don't tell me nothin' 'bout that rabbit-foot colored man. Didn't he meet Spunk an' Lena face to face one day las' week an' mumble sumthin' to Spunk 'bout lettin' his wife alone?"

"What did Spunk say?" Walter broke in. "Ah like him fine but tain't right the way he carries on wid Lena Kanty, jus' 'cause Joe's timid 'bout fightin'."

"You wrong theah, Walter. Tain't 'cause Joe's timid at all, it's 'cause Spunk wants Lena. If Joe was a passel of wile cats Spunk would tackle the job just the same. He'd go after *anything* he wanted the same way. As Ah wuz sayin' a minute ago, he tole Joe right to his face that Lena was his. 'Call her and see if she'll come. A woman knows her boss an' she answers when he calls.' 'Lena, ain't I yo' husband?' Joe sorter whines out. Lena looked at him real disgusted but she don't answer and she don't move outa her tracks. Then Spunk reaches out an' takes hold of her arm an' says: 'Lena, youse mine. From now on Ah works for you an' fights for you an' Ah never wants you to look to nobody for a crumb of bread, a stitch of close or a shingle to go over yo' head, but *me* long as Ah live. Ah'll git the lumber foh owah house tomorrow. Go home an' git yo' things together!'

"'Thass mah house,' Lena speaks up. 'Papa gimme that.'"

"'Well,' says Spunk, 'doan give up whut's yours, but when youse inside doan for-git youse mine, an' let no other man git outa his place wid you!"

"Lena looked up at him with her eyes so full of love that they wuz runnin' over, an' Spunk seen it an' Joe seen it too, and his lip started to tremblin' and his Adam's apple was galloping up and down his neck like a race horse. Ah bet he's wore out half a dozen Adam's apples since Spunk's been on the job with Lena. That's all he'll do. He'll be back heah after while swallowin' an' workin' his lips like he wants to say somethin' an' can't."

"But didn't he do *nothin'* to stop 'em?"

"Nope, not a frazzlin' thing—jus' stood there. Spunk took Lena's arm and walked off jus' like nothin' ain't happened and he stood there gazin' after them till they was outa sight. Now you know a woman don't want no man like that. I'm jus' waitin' to see whut he's goin' to say when he gits back."

II

But Joe Kanty never came back, never. The men in the store heard the sharp report of   30
a pistol somewhere distant in the palmetto thicket and soon Spunk came walking leisurely, with his big black Stetson set at the same rakish angle and Lena clinging to his arm, came walking right into the general store. Lena wept in a frightened manner.

"Well," Spunk announced calmly, "Joe came out there wid a meat axe an' made me kill him."

He sent Lena home and led the men back to Joe—crumpled and limp with his right hand still clutching his razor.

"See mah back? Mah close cut clear through. He sneaked up an' tried to kill me from the back, but Ah got him, an' got him good, first shot," Spunk said.

The men glared at Elijah, accusingly.

"Take him up an' plant him in Stony Lonesome," Spunk said in a careless voice. "Ah   35
didn't wanna shoot him but he made me do it. He's a dirty coward, jumpin' on a man from behind."

Spunk turned on his heel and sauntered away to where he knew his love wept in fear for him and no man stopped him. At the general store later on, they all talked of locking him up until the sheriff should come from Orlando, but no one did anything but talk.

A clear case of self-defense, the trial was a short one, and Spunk walked out of the court house to freedom again. He could work again, ride the dangerous log-carriage that fed the singing, snarling, biting circle-saw; he could stroll the soft dark lanes with his guitar. He was free to roam the woods again; he was free to return to Lena. He did all of these things.

III

"Whut you reckon, Walt?" Elijah asked one night later. "Spunk's gittin' ready to marry Lena!"

"Naw! Why, Joe ain't had time to git cold yit. Nohow Ah didn't figger Spunk was the marryin' kind."

"Well, he is," rejoined Elijah. "He done moved most of Lena's things—and her   40
along wid 'em—over to the Bradley house. He's buying it. Jus' like Ah told yo' all

right in heah the night Joe was kilt. Spunk's crazy 'bout Lena. He don't want folks to keep on talkin' 'bout her—thass reason he's rushin' so. Funny thing 'bout that bob-cat, wan't it?"

"What bob-cat, 'Lige? Ah ain't heered 'bout none."

"Ain't cher? Well, night befo' las' as they was goin' to bed, a big black bob-cat, black all over, you hear me, *black*, walked round and round that house and howled like forty, an' when Spunk got his gun an' went to the winder to shoot it, he says it stood right still an' looked him in the eye, an' howled right at him. The thing got Spunk so nervoused up he couldn't shoot. But Spunk says twan't no bob-cat nohow. He says it was Joe done sneaked back from Hell!"

"Hymph!" sniffed Walter, "he oughter be nervous after what he done. Ah reckon Joe come back to dare him to marry Lena, or to come out an' fight. Ah bet he'll be back time and again, too. Know what Ah think? Joe wuz a braver man than Spunk."

There was a general shout of derision from the group.

45 "Thass a fact," went on Walter. "Lookit whut he done; took a razor an' went out to fight a man he knowed toted a gun an' wuz a crack shot, too; 'nother thing Joe wuz skeered of Spunk, skeered plumb stiff! But he went jes' the same. It took him a long time to get his nerve up. Tain't nothin' for Spunk to fight when he ain't skeered of nothin'. Now, Joe's done come back to have it out wid the man that's got all he ever had. Y'all know Joe ain't never had nothin' nor wanted nothin' besides Lena. It musta been a h'ant cause ain't nobody never seen no black bob-cat."

"Nother thing," cut in one of the men, "Spunk was cussin' a blue streak today 'cause he 'lowed dat saw wuz wobblin'—almos' got 'im once. The machinist come, looked it over an said it wuz alright. Spunk musta been leanin' t'wards it some. Den he claimed somebody pushed 'im but twan't nobody close to 'im. Ah wuz glad when knockin' off time came. I'm skeered of dat man when he gits hot. He'd beat you full of button holes as quick as he's look atcher."

IV

The men gathered the next evening in a different mood, no laughter. No badinage this time.

"Look, 'Lige, you goin' to set up wid Spunk?"

"Naw, Ah reckon not, Walter. Tell yuh the truth, Ah'm a li'l bit skittish. Spunk died too wicket—died cussin' he did. You know he thought he was done outa life."

50 "Good Lawd, who'd he think done it?"

"Joe."

"Joe Kanty? How come?"

"Walter, Ah b'leeve Ah will walk up thata way an' set. Lena would like it Ah reckon."

"But whut did he say, 'Lige?"

55 Elijah did not answer until they had left the lighted store and were strolling down the dark street.

"Ah wuz loadin' a wagon wid scantlin' right near the saw when Spunk fell on the carriage but 'fore Ah could git to him the saw got him in the body—awful sight. Me an' Skint Miller got him off but it was too late. Anybody could see that. The fust thing he said wuz: 'He pushed me, 'Lige—the dirty hound pushed me in the back!'—he was spittin' blood at ev'ry breath. We laid him on the sawdust pile with his face to the East so's he could die easy. He helt mah han' till the last, Walter, and said: 'It was Joe, 'Lige . . . the dirty sneak shoved me . . . he didn't dare come to mah face . . . but Ah'll git the son-of-a-wood louse soon's Ah get there an' make hell too hot for him . . . Ah felt him shove me. . . .!' Thass how he died."

"If spirits kin fight, there's a powerful tussle goin' on somewhere ovah Jordan 'cause Ah b'leeve Joe's ready for Spunk an' ain't skeered any more—yas, Ah b'leeve Joe pushed 'im mahself."

They had arrived at the house. Lena's lamentations were deep and loud. She had filled the room with magnolia blossoms that gave off a heavy sweet odor. The keepers of the wake tipped about whispering in frightened tones. Everyone in the village was there, even old Jeff Kanty, Joe's father, who a few hours before would have been afraid to come within ten feet of him, stood leering triumphantly down upon the fallen giant as if his fingers had been the teeth of steel that laid him low.

The cooling board consisted of three sixteen-inch boards on saw horses, a dingy sheet was his shroud.

The women ate heartily of the funeral baked meats and wondered who would be Lena's next. The men whispered coarse conjectures between guzzles of whiskey. [1927] 60

QUESTIONS

1. Do you find elements of the traditional folk tale in this story?
2. Do you have difficulty with the colloquial dialogue? What seems to you to be the advantages and disadvantages of its use?
3. On the evidence, can the reader conclude whether Joe Kanty is a coward? What do you believe the story has to say about heroism?
4. What is your opinion of the author's use of the supernatural to resolve the conflict? Has the author played fair with the reader?
5. The women at the funeral evidently believe that Lena must bear some responsibility for the deaths. Does the story support that interpretation?

RESPONSES

1. In addition to being a fiction writer, Zora Neale Hurston was a folklorist. Locate her works on folklore in a library, read them, and write an essay analyzing how she used her folklore research in her fiction.
2. Compare Hurston's story to Wideman's "Damballah."

SHIRLEY JACKSON

Shirley Jackson (1919–1965) was born in San Francisco. Educated at Syracuse University (A.B. 1940), she married one of her classmates, Stanley
Edgar Hyman, and they settled in Vermont, where he was a college professor. Together they wrote their books and raised a large family. Although
Jackson was remarkably gifted and wrote a number of macabre novels
and witty accounts of child rearing, she seems destined to be remembered
best for one short story, "The Lottery," which is probably the most widely anthologized story in history.

The Lottery

The morning of June 27th was clear and sunny, with the fresh warmth of a full-
summer day; the flowers were blossoming profusely and the grass was richly green.
The people of the village began to gather in the square, between the post office
and the bank, around ten o'clock; in some towns there were so many people that
the lottery took two days and had to be started on June 26th, but in this village,
where there were only about three hundred people, the whole lottery took less
than two hours, so it could begin at ten o'clock in the morning and still be through
in time to allow the villagers to get home for noon dinner.

The children assembled first, of course. School was recently over for the summer, and
the feeling of liberty sat uneasily on most of them; they tended to gather together quietly for a while before they broke into boisterous play, and their talk was still of the classroom and the teacher, of books and reprimands. Bobby Martin had already stuffed his
pockets full of stones, and the other boys soon followed his example, selecting the
smoothest and roundest stones; Bobby and Harry Jones and Dickie Delacroix—the villagers pronounced his name "Delacroy"—eventually made a great pile of stones in one
corner of the square and guarded it against the raids of the other boys. The girls stood
aside, talking among themselves, looking over their shoulders at the boys, and the very
small children rolled in the dust or clung to the hands of their older brothers or sisters.

Soon the men began to gather, surveying their own children, speaking of planting and
rain, tractors and taxes. They stood together, away from the pile of stones in the corner,
and their jokes were quiet and they smiled rather than laughed. The women, wearing
faded house dresses and sweaters, came shortly after their menfolk. They greeted one

another and exchanged bits of gossip as they went to join their husbands. Soon the women, standing by their husbands, began to call to their children, and the children came reluctantly, having to be called four or five times. Bobby Martin ducked under his mother's grasping hand and ran, laughing, back to the pile of stones. His father spoke up sharply, and Bobby came quickly and took his place between his father and his oldest brother.

The lottery was conducted—as were the square dances, the teenage club, the Halloween program—by Mr. Summers, who had time and energy to devote to civic activities. He was a round-faced, jovial man and he ran the coal business, and people were sorry for him, because he had no children and his wife was a scold. When he arrived in the square, carrying the black wooden box, there was a murmur of conversation among the villagers, and he waved and called, "Little late today, folks." The postmaster, Mr. Graves, followed him, carrying a three-legged stool, and the stool was put in the center of the square and Mr. Summers set the black box down on it. The villagers kept their distance, leaving a space between themselves and the stool, and when Mr. Summers said, "Some of you fellows want to give me a hand?" there was a hesitation before two men, Mr. Martin and his oldest son, Baxter, came forward to hold the box steady on the stool while Mr. Summers stirred up the papers inside it.

The original paraphernalia for the lottery had been lost long ago, and the black box now resting on the stool had been put into use even before Old Man Warner, the oldest man in town, was born. Mr. Summers spoke frequently to the villagers about making a new box, but no one liked to upset even as much tradition as was represented by the black box. There was a story that the present box had been made with some pieces of the box that had preceded it, the one that had been constructed when the first people settled down to make a village here. Every year, after the lottery, Mr. Summers began talking again about a new box, but every year the subject was allowed to fade off without anything's being done. The black box grew shabbier each year; by now it was no longer completely black but splintered badly along one side to show the original wood color, and in some places faded or stained.

Mr. Martin and his oldest son, Baxter, held the black box securely on the stool until Mr. Summers had stirred the papers thoroughly with his hand. Because so much of the ritual had been forgotten or discarded, Mr. Summers had been successful in having slips of paper substituted for the chips of wood that had been used for generations. Chips of wood, Mr. Summers had argued, had been all very well when the village was tiny, but now that the population was more than three hundred and likely to keep on growing, it was necessary to use something that would fit more easily into the black box. The night before the lottery, Mr. Summers and Mr. Graves made up the slips of paper and put them in the box, and it was then taken to the safe of Mr. Summers's coal company and locked up until Mr. Summers was ready to take it to the square next morning. The rest of the year, the box was put away, sometimes one place, sometimes another; it had spent one year in Mr. Graves's barn and another year underfoot in the post office, and sometimes it was set on a shelf in the Martin grocery and left there.

There was a great deal of fussing to be done before Mr. Summers declared the lottery open. There were the lists to make up—of heads of families, heads of households in each family, members of each household in each family. There was the proper swearing-in of Mr. Summers by the postmaster, as the official of the lottery; at one time, some people remembered, there had been a recital of some sort, performed by the official of the lottery, a perfunctory, tuneless chant that had been rattled off duly each year; some people believed that the official of the lottery used to stand just so when he said or sang it, others believed that he was supposed to walk among the people, but years and years ago this part of the ritual had been allowed to lapse. There had been, also, a ritual salute, which the official of the lottery had had to use in addressing each person who came up to draw from the box, but this also had changed with time, until now it was felt necessary only for the official to speak to each person approaching. Mr. Summers was very good at all this; in his clean white shirt and blue jeans, with one hand resting carelessly on the black box, he seemed very proper and important as he talked interminably to Mr. Graves and the Martins.

Just as Mr. Summers finally left off talking and turned to the assembled villagers, Mrs. Hutchinson came hurriedly along the path to the square, her sweater thrown over her shoulders, and slid into place in the back of the crowd. "Clean forgot what day it was," she said to Mrs. Delacroix, who stood next to her, and they both laughed softly. "Thought my old man was out back stacking wood," Mrs. Hutchinson went on, "and then I looked out the window and the kids was gone, and then I remembered it was the twenty-seventh and came a-running." She dried her hands on her apron, and Mrs. Delacroix said, "You're in time, though. They're still talking away up there."

Mrs. Hutchinson craned her neck to see through the crowd and found her husband and children standing near the front. She tapped Mrs. Delacroix on the arm as a farewell and began to make her way through the crowd. The people separated good-humoredly to let her through; two or three people said, in voices just loud enough to be heard across the crowd, "Here comes your Missus, Hutchinson," and "Bill, she made it after all." Mrs. Hutchinson reached her husband, and Mr. Summers, who had been waiting, said cheerfully, "Thought we were going to have to get on without you, Tessie." Mrs. Hutchinson said, grinning, "Wouldn't have me leave m' dishes in the sink, now, would you, Joe?" and soft laughter ran through the crowd as the people stirred back into position after Mrs. Hutchinson's arrival.

10   "Well, now," Mr. Summers said soberly, "guess we better get started, get this over with, so's we can go back to work. Anybody ain't here?"

"Dunbar," several people said. "Dunbar, Dunbar."

Mr. Summers consulted his list. "Clyde Dunbar," he said. "That's right. He's broke his leg, hasn't he? Who's drawing for him?"

"Me, I guess," a woman said, and Mr. Summers turned to look at her. "Wife draws for her husband," Mr. Summers said. "Don't you have a grown boy to do it for you, Janey?" Although Mr. Summers and everyone else in the village knew the answer perfectly well, it was the business of the official of the lottery to ask such questions formally. Mr. Summers waited with an expression of polite interest while Mrs. Dunbar answered.

"Horace's not but sixteen yet," Mrs. Dunbar said regretfully. "Guess I gotta fill in for the old man this year."

15   "Right," Mr. Summers said. He made a note on the list he was holding. Then he asked, "Watson boy drawing this year?"

A tall boy in the crowd raised his hand. "Here," he said. "I'm drawing for m' mother and me." He blinked his eyes nervously and ducked his head as several voices in the crowd said things like "Good fellow, Jack," and "Glad to see your mother's got a man to do it."

"Well," Mr. Summers said, "guess that's everyone. Old Man Warner make it?"

"Here," a voice said, and Mr. Summers nodded.

A sudden hush fell on the crowd as Mr. Summers cleared his throat and looked at the list. "All ready?" he called. "Now, I'll read the names—heads of families first—and the men come up and take a paper out of the box. Keep the paper folded in your hand without looking at it until everyone has had a turn. Everything clear?"

The people had done it so many times that they only half-listened to the directions;   20
most of them were quiet, wetting their lips, not looking around. Then Mr. Summers
raised one hand high and said, "Adams." A man disengaged himself from the crowd
and came forward. "Hi, Steve," Mr. Summers said, and Mr. Adams said, "Hi, Joe."
They grinned at one another humorlessly and nervously. Then Mr. Adams reached
into the black box and took out a folded paper. He held it firmly by one corner as he
turned and went hastily back to his place in the crowd, where he stood a little apart
from his family, not looking down at his hand.

"Allen," Mr. Summers said. "Anderson. . . . Bentham."

"Seems like there's no time at all between lotteries any more," Mrs. Delacroix said
to Mrs. Graves in the back row. "Seems like we got through with the last one only last
week."

"Time sure goes fast," Mrs. Graves said.

"Clark. . . . Delacroix."

"There goes my old man," Mrs. Delacroix said. She held her breath while her hus-   25
band went forward.

"Dunbar," Mr. Summers said, and Mrs. Dunbar went steadily to the box while one
of the women said, "Go on, Janey," and another said, "There she goes."

"We're next," Mrs. Graves said. She watched while Mr. Graves came around from
the side of the box, greeted Mr. Summers gravely, and selected a slip of paper from the
box. By now, all through the crowd there were men holding the small folded papers
in their large hands, turning them over and over nervously. Mrs. Dunbar and her two
sons stood together, Mrs. Dunbar holding the slip of paper.

"Harburt. . . . Hutchinson."

"Get up there, Bill," Mrs. Hutchinson said, and the people near her laughed.

"Jones."   30

"They do say," Mr. Adams said to Old Man Warner, who stood next to him, "that
over in the north village they're talking of giving up the lottery."

Old Man Warner snorted. "Pack of crazy fools," he said. "Listening to the young
folks, nothing's good enough for *them*. Next thing you know, they'll be wanting to go
back to living in caves, nobody work any more, live *that* way for a while. Used to be
a saying about 'Lottery in June, corn be heavy soon.' First thing you know, we'd all be
eating stewed chickweed and acorns. There's *always* been a lottery," he added petulantly. "Bad enough to see young Joe Summers up there joking with everybody."

"Some places have already quit lotteries," Mrs. Adams said.

"Nothing but trouble in *that*," Old Man Warner said stoutly. "Pack of young fools."

"Martin." And Bobby Martin watched his father go forward. "Overdyke. . . . Percy."   35

"I wish they'd hurry," Mrs. Dunbar said to her older son. "I wish they'd hurry."

"They're almost through," her son said.

"You get ready to run tell Dad," Mrs. Dunbar said.

Mr. Summers called his own name and then stepped forward precisely and selected a slip from the box. Then he called, "Warner."

"Seventy-seventh year I been in the lottery," Old Man Warner said as he went   40
through the crowd. "Seventy-seventh time."

"Watson." The tall boy came awkwardly through the crowd. Someone said, "Don't
be nervous, Jack," and Mr. Summers said, "Take your time, son."

"Zanini."

After that, there was a long pause, a breathless pause, until Mr. Summers, holding
his slip of paper in the air, said, "All right, fellows." For a minute, no one moved, and
then all the slips of paper were opened. Suddenly, all the women began to speak at

once, saying, "Who is it?," "Who's got it?," "Is it the Dunbars?," "Is it the Watsons?" Then the voices began to say, "It's Hutchinson. It's Bill," "Bill Hutchinson's got it."

"Go tell your father," Mrs. Dunbar said to her older son.

45 People began to look around to see the Hutchinsons. Bill Hutchinson was standing quiet, staring down at the paper in his hand. Suddenly, Tessie Hutchinson shouted to Mr. Summers, "You didn't give him time enough to take any paper he wanted. I saw you. It wasn't fair!"

"Be a good sport, Tessie," Mrs. Delacroix called, and Mrs. Graves said, "All of us took the same chance."

"Shut up, Tessie," Bill Hutchinson said.

"Well, everyone," Mr. Summers said, "that was done pretty fast, and now we've got to be hurrying a little more to get done in time." He consulted his next list. "Bill," he said, "you draw for the Hutchinson family. You got any other households in the Hutchinsons?"

"There's Don and Eva," Mrs. Hutchinson yelled. "Make *them* take their chance!"

50 "Daughters draw with their husbands' families, Tessie," Mr. Summers said gently. "You know that as well as anyone else."

"It wasn't *fair*," Tessie said.

"I guess not, Joe," Bill Hutchinson said regretfully. "My daughter draws with her husband's family, that's only fair. And I've got no other family except the kids."

"Then, as far as drawing for families is concerned, it's you," Mr. Summers said in explanation, "and as far as drawing for households is concerned, that's you, too. Right?"

"Right," Bill Hutchinson said.

55 "How many kids, Bill?" Mr. Summers asked formally.

"Three," Bill Hutchinson said. "There's Bill, Jr., and Nancy, and little Dave. And Tessie and me."

"All right, then," Mr. Summers said. "Harry, you got their tickets back?"

Mr. Graves nodded and held up the slips of paper. "Put them in the box, then," Mr. Summers directed. "Take Bill's and put it in."

"I think we ought to start over," Mrs. Hutchinson said, as quietly as she could. "I tell you it wasn't *fair*. You didn't give him time enough to choose. *Every*body saw that."

60 Mr. Graves had selected the five slips and put them in the box, and he dropped all the papers but those onto the ground, where the breeze caught them and lifted them off.

"Listen, everybody," Mrs. Hutchinson was saying to the people around her.

"Ready, Bill?" Mr. Summers asked, and Bill Hutchinson, with one quick glance around at his wife and children, nodded.

"Remember," Mr. Summers said, "take the slips and keep them folded until each person has taken one. Harry, you help little Dave." Mr. Graves took the hand of the little boy, who came willingly with him up to the box. "Take a paper out of the box, Davy," Mr. Summers said. Davy put his hand into the box and laughed. "Take just *one* paper," Mr. Summers said. "Harry, you hold it for him." Mr. Graves took the child's hand and removed the folded paper from the tight fist and held it while little Dave stood next to him and looked up at him wonderingly.

"Nancy next," Mr. Summers said. Nancy was twelve, and her school friends breathed heavily as she went forward, switching her skirt, and took a slip daintily from the box. "Bill, Jr.," Mr. Summers said, and Billy, his face red and his feet over-large, nearly knocked the box over as he got a paper out. "Tessie," Mr. Summers said.

She hesitated for a minute, looking around defiantly, and then set her lips and went up to the box. She snatched a paper out and held it behind her.

"Bill," Mr. Summers said, and Bill Hutchinson reached into the box and felt around, 65 bringing his hand out at last with the slip of paper in it.

The crowd was quiet. A girl whispered, "I hope it's not Nancy," and the sound of the whisper reached the edges of the crowd.

"It's not the way it used to be," Old Man Warner said clearly. "People ain't the way they used to be."

"All right," Mr. Summers said. "Open the papers. Harry, you open little Dave's."

Mr. Graves opened the slip of paper and there was a general sigh through the crowd as he held it up and everyone could see that it was blank. Nancy and Bill, Jr., opened theirs at the same time, and both beamed and laughed, turning around to the crowd and holding their slips of paper above their heads.

"Tessie," Mr. Summers said. There was a pause, and then Mr. Summers looked at 70 Bill Hutchinson, and Bill unfolded his paper and showed it. It was blank.

"It's Tessie," Mr. Summers said, and his voice was hushed. "Show us her paper, Bill."

Bill Hutchinson went over to his wife and forced the slip of paper out of her hand. It had a black spot on it, the black spot Mr. Summers had made the night before with the heavy pencil in the coal-company office. Bill Hutchinson held it up, and there was a stir in the crowd.

"All right, folks," Mr. Summers said. "Let's finish quickly."

Although the villagers had forgotten the ritual and lost the original black box, they still remembered to use stones. The pile of stones the boys had made earlier was ready; there were stones on the ground with the blowing scraps of paper that had come out of the box. Mrs. Delacroix selected a stone so large she had to pick it up with both hands and turned to Mrs. Dunbar. "Come on," she said. "Hurry up."

Mrs. Dunbar had small stones in both hands, and she said, gasping for breath, "I 75 can't run at all. You'll have to go ahead and I'll catch up with you."

The children had stones already, and someone gave little Davy Hutchinson a few pebbles.

Tessie Hutchinson was in the center of a cleared space by now, and she held her hands out desperately as the villagers moved in on her. "It isn't fair," she said. A stone hit her on the side of the head.

Old Man Warner was saying, "Come on, come on, everyone." Steve Adams was in the front of the crowd of villagers, with Mrs. Graves beside him.

"It isn't fair, it isn't right," Mrs. Hutchinson screamed, and then they were upon her.   [1948]

QUESTIONS

1. How has the stoning of Mrs. Hutchinson been foreshadowed?
2. Why is the setting left purposely vague?
3. How is the point of view of the story related to its tone?
4. What varying attitudes toward tradition and ritual are expressed by characters in the story?
5. This story has been much praised for its unity of effect. How has the author combined and balanced the elements of fiction to achieve this hypnotic power?

RESPONSES

1. Research the mythology of corn gods and sacrifices. How do those myths form the basis for this story?
2. Compare this story to another scapegoat story, such as Bessie Head's "Looking for a Rain God."

FOCUS ON FILM

1. If you can locate a copy of *The Lottery* (1996), a television version of the story, examine and evaluate the plot changes made to the print story.
2. Another televised version of "The Lottery" appeared in 1997, directed by Garry Marshall. Examine and evaluate the plot changes made to the print story.

Henry James

Henry James (1843–1916) was born in New York City into a patrician and intellectual family. Educated privately by tutors and by travel abroad, James committed himself early to the literary life with something like monastic dedication. He began to publish in Boston during the mid-1860s, and from that time until his death a constant stream of stories, novels, reviews, essays, plays, and memoirs issued from his pen. He settled in England in 1875, and in 1915 he became a British subject. He was not only a practitioner of the art of fiction but also a theorist, and it is probably not an exaggeration to say that no author after James can write without taking him into account. The New York edition of his work (1907–1909), with its revisions and prefaces, is a landmark in modern fiction. James's short stories are readily available in a variety of editions.

The Real Thing

1

When the porter's wife, who used to answer the house-bell, announced "A gentleman and a lady, sir" I had, as I often had in those days—the wish being father to the thought—an immediate vision of sitters. Sitters my visitors in this case proved to be; but not in the sense I should have preferred. There was nothing at first however to indicate that they mightn't have come for a portrait. The gentleman, a man of fifty, very high and very straight, with a moustache slightly grizzled and a dark grey walking-coat admirably fitted, both of which I noted professionally—I don't mean as a barber or yet as a tailor—would have struck me as a celebrity if celebrities often were striking. It was a truth of which I had for some time been conscious that a figure with a good deal of frontage was, as one might say, almost a public institution. A glance at the lady helped to remind me of this paradoxical law: she also looked too distinguished to be a "personality." Moreover one would scarcely come across two variations together.

Neither of the pair immediately spoke—they only prolonged the preliminary gaze suggesting that each wished to give the other a chance. They were visibly shy; they stood there letting me take them in—which, as I afterwards perceived, was the most practical thing they could have done. In this way their embarrassment served their cause. I had seen people painfully reluctant to mention that they desired anything so gross as to be represented on canvas; but the scruples of my new friends appeared almost insurmountable. Yet the gentleman might have said "I should like a portrait of my wife," and the lady might have said "I should like a portrait of my husband." Perhaps they weren't husband and wife—this naturally would make the matter more delicate. Perhaps they wished to be done together—in which case they ought to have brought a third person to break the news.

"We come from Mr. Rivet," the lady finally said with a dim smile that had the effect of a moist sponge passed over a "sunk" piece of painting, as well as of a vague allusion to vanished beauty. She was as tall and straight, in her degree, as her companion, and with ten years less to carry. She looked as sad as a woman could look whose face was not charged with expression; that is her tinted oval mask showed waste as an exposed surface shows friction. The hand of time had played over her freely, but to an effect of elimination. She was slim and stiff, and so well-dressed, in dark blue cloth, with lappets and pockets and buttons, that it was clear she employed the same tailor as her husband. The couple had an indefinable air of prosperous thrift—they evidently got a good deal of luxury for their money. If I was to be one of their luxuries it would behoove me to consider my terms.

"Ah Claude Rivet recommended me?" I echoed; and I added that it was very kind of him, though I could reflect that, as he only painted landscape, this wasn't a sacrifice.

5   The lady looked very hard at the gentleman, and the gentleman looked round the room. Then staring at the floor a moment and stroking his moustache, he rested his pleasant eyes on me with the remark: "He said you were the right one."

"I try to be, when people want to sit."

"Yes, we should like to," said the lady anxiously.

"Do you mean together?"

My visitors exchanged a glance. "If you could do anything with *me* I suppose it would be double," the gentleman stammered.

10   "Oh yes, there's naturally a higher charge for two figures than for one."

"We should like to make it pay," the husband confessed.

"That's very good of you," I returned, appreciating so unwonted a sympathy—for I supposed he meant pay the artist.

A sense of strangeness seemed to dawn on the lady.

"We mean for the illustrations—Mr. Rivet said you might put one in."

15   "Put in—an illustration?" I was equally confused.

"Sketch her off, you know," said the gentleman, colouring.

It was only then that I understood the service Claude Rivet had rendered me; he had told them how I worked in black-and-white, for magazines, for storybooks, for sketches of contemporary life, and consequently had copious employment for models. These things were true, but it was not less true—I may confess it now; whether because the aspiration was to lead to everything or to nothing I leave the reader to guess—that I couldn't get the honours, to say nothing of the emoluments, of a great painter of portraits out of my head. My "illustrations" were my pot-boilers; I looked to a different branch of art—far and away the most interesting it had always seemed to me—to perpetuate my fame. There was no shame in looking to it also to make my fortune; but that fortune was by so much further from being made from the moment my visitors wished to be "done" for nothing. I was disappointed; for in the pictorial sense I had immediately *seen* them. I had seized their type—I had already settled what I would do with it. Something that wouldn't absolutely have pleased them, I afterwards reflected.

"Ah you're—you're—a—?" I began as soon as I had mastered my surprise. I couldn't bring out the dingy word "models": it seemed so little to fit the case.

"We haven't had much practice," said the lady.

"We've got to *do* something, and we've thought that an artist in your line might perhaps make something of us," her husband threw off. He further mentioned that they didn't know many artists and that they had gone first, on the off-chance—he painted views of course, but sometimes put in figures; perhaps I remembered—to Mr. Rivet, whom they had met a few years before at a place in Norfolk where he was sketching.

"We used to sketch a little ourselves," the lady hinted.

"It's very awkward, but we absolutely *must* do something," her husband went on.

"Of course we're not so *very* young," she admitted with a wan smile.

With the remark that I might as well know something more about them the husband had handed me a card extracted from a neat new pocket-book—their appurtenances were all of the freshest—and inscribed with the words "Major Monarch." Impressive as these words were they didn't carry my knowledge much further; but my visitor presently added: "I've left the army and we've had the misfortune to lose our money. In fact our means are dreadfully small."

"It's awfully trying—a regular strain," said Mrs. Monarch.

They evidently wished to be discreet—to take care not to swagger because they were gentlefolk. I felt them willing to recognize this as something of a drawback, at the same time that I guessed at an underlying sense—their consolation in adversity—that they *had* their points. They certainly had; but these advantages struck me as preponderantly social; such for instance as would help to make a drawing-room look well. However, a drawing-room was always, or ought to be, a picture.

In consequence of his wife's allusion to their age Major Monarch observed: "Naturally it's more for the figure that we thought of going in. We can still hold ourselves up." On the instant I saw that the figure was indeed their strong point. His "naturally" didn't sound vain, but it lighted up the question. "She has the best one," he continued, nodding at his wife with a pleasant after-dinner absence of circumlocution. I could only reply, as if we were in fact sitting over our wine, that this didn't prevent his own from being very good; which led him in turn to make answer: "We thought that if you ever had to do people like us we might be something like it. *She* particularly—for a lady in a book, you know."

I was so amused by them that, to get more of it, I did my best to take their point of view; and though it was an embarrassment to find myself appraising physically, as if they were animals on hire or useful blacks, a pair whom I should have expected to meet only in one of the relations in which criticism is tacit, I looked at Mrs. Monarch judicially enough to be able to exclaim after a moment with conviction: "Oh yes, a lady in a book!" She was singularly like a bad illustration.

"We'll stand up, if you like," said the Major; and he raised himself before me with a really grand air.

I could take his measure at a glance—he was six feet two and a perfect gentleman. It would have paid any club in process of formation and in want of a stamp to engage him at a salary to stand in the principal window. What struck me at once was that in coming to me they had rather missed their vocation; they could surely have been turned to better account for advertising purposes. I couldn't of course see the thing in detail, but I could see them make somebody's fortune—I don't mean their own. There was something in them for a waistcoat-maker, an hotel-keeper or a soap-vendor. I could imagine "We always use it" pinned on their bosoms with the greatest effect; I had a vision of the brilliancy with which they would launch a table d'hôte.

Mrs. Monarch sat still, not from pride but from shyness, and presently her husband said to her: "Get up, my dear, and show how smart you are." She obeyed, but she had no need to get up to show it. She walked to the end of the studio and then came back blushing, her fluttered eyes on the partner of her appeal. I was reminded of an incident I had accidentally had a glimpse of in Paris being with a friend there, a dramatist about to produce a play, when an actress came to him to ask to be entrusted with a part. She went through her paces before him, walked up and down as Mrs. Monarch was doing. Mrs. Monarch did it quite as well, but I abstained from applauding. It was very odd to see such people apply for such poor pay. She looked as if she had ten thousand a year. Her husband had used the word that described her: she was in the London current jargon essentially and typically "smart." Her figure was, in the same order of ideas, conspicuously and irreproachably "good." For a woman of her age her waist was surprisingly small; her elbow moreover had the orthodox crook. She held her head at the conventional angle, but why did she come to *me*? She ought to have tried on jackets at a big shop. I feared my visitors were not only destitute but "artistic"—which would be a great complication. When she sat down again I thanked her, observing that what a draughtsman most valued in his model was the faculty of keeping quiet.

"Oh *she* can keep quiet," said Major Monarch. Then he added jocosely: "I've always kept her quiet."

"I'm not a nasty fidget, am I?" It was going to wring tears from me, I felt, the way she hid her head, ostrich-like, in the other broad bosom.

The owner of this expanse addressed his answer to me. "Perhaps it isn't out of place to mention—because we ought to be quite business-like, oughtn't we?—that when I married her she was known as the Beautiful Statue."

35 "Oh dear!" said Mrs. Monarch ruefully.

"Of course I should want a certain amount of expression," I rejoined.

"Of *course*!"—and I had never heard such unanimity.

"And then I suppose you know that you'll get awfully tired."

"Oh we *never* get tired!" they eagerly cried.

40 "Have you had any kind of practice?"

They hesitated—they looked at each other. "We've been photographed—*immensely*," said Mrs. Monarch.

"She means the fellows have asked us themselves," added the Major.

"I see—because you're so good-looking."

"I don't know what they thought, but they were always after us."

45 "We always got our photographs for nothing," smiled Mrs. Monarch.

"We might have brought some, my dear," her husband remarked.

"I'm not sure we have any left. We've given quantities away," she explained to me.

"With our autographs and that sort of thing," said the Major.

"Are they to be got in the shops?" I enquired as a harmless pleasantry.

50 "Oh yes, *hers*—they used to be."

"Not now," said Mrs. Monarch with her eyes on the floor.

2

I could fancy the "sort of thing" they put on the presentation copies of their photographs, and I was sure they wrote a beautiful hand. It was odd how quickly I was sure of everything that concerned them. If they were now so poor as to have to earn shillings and pence they could never have had much of a margin. Their good looks had been their capital, and they had good-humouredly made the most of the career that this resource marked out for them. It was in their faces, the blankness, the deep intellectual repose of the twenty years of country-house visiting that had given them pleasant intonations. I could see the sunny drawing-rooms, sprinkled with periodicals she didn't read, in which Mrs. Monarch had continuously sat; I could see the wet shrubberies in which she had walked, equipped to admiration for either exercise. I could see the rich covers the Major had helped to shoot and the wonderful garments in which, late at night, he repaired to the smoking-room to talk about them. I could imagine their leggings and waterproofs, their knowing tweeds and rugs, their rolls of sticks and cases of tackle and neat umbrellas; and I could evoke the exact appearance of their servants and the compact variety of their luggage on the platforms of country stations.

They gave small tips, but they were liked; they didn't do anything themselves, but they were welcome. They looked so well everywhere; they gratified the general relish for stature, complexion and "form." They knew it without fatuity or vulgarity, and they respected themselves in consequence. They weren't superficial; they were thorough and kept themselves up—it had been their line. People with such a taste for activity had to have some line. I could feel how even in a dull house they could have been counted on for the joy of life. At present something had happened—it didn't matter what, their little income had grown less, it had grown least—and they had to do something for pocket-money. Their friends could like them, I made out, without liking to support them. There was something about them that represented credit—their clothes, their manners, their type; but if credit is a large empty pocket in which an occasional chink reverberates, the chink at least must be audible. What they wanted of me was to help to make it so. Fortunately they had no children—I soon divined that. They would also perhaps wish our relations to be kept secret: this was why it was "for the figure"—the reproduction of the face would betray them.

I liked them—I felt, quite as their friends must have done—they were so simple; and I had no objection to them if they would suit. But somehow with all their perfections I didn't easily believe in them. After all they were amateurs, and the ruling passion of my life was the detestation of the amateur. Combined with this was another perversity—an innate preference for the represented subject over the real one: the defect of the real one was so apt to be a lack of representation. I like things that appeared; then one was sure. Whether they *were* or not was a subordinate and almost always a profitless question. There were other considerations, the first of which was that I already had two or three recruits in use, notably a young person with big feet, in alpaca, from Kilburn, who for a couple of years had come to me regularly for my illustrations and with whom I was still—perhaps ignobly—satisfied. I frankly explained to my visitors how the case stood, but they had taken more precautions than I supposed. They had reasoned out their opportunity, for Claude Rivet had told them of the projected *édition de luxe* of one of the writers of our day—the rarest of the novelists—who, long neglected by the multitudinous vulgar and dearly prized by the attentive (need I mention Philip Vincent?) had had the happy fortune of seeing, late in life, the dawn and then the full light of a higher criticism; an estimate in which on the part of the public there was something really of expiation. The edition preparing, planned by a publisher of taste, was practically an act of high reparation; the wood-cuts with which it was to be enriched were the homage of English art to one of the most independent representatives of English letters. Major and Mrs. Monarch con-fessed to me they had hoped I might be able to work *them* into my branch of the en-terprise. They knew I was to do the first of the books, "Rutland Ramsay," but I had to make clear to them that my participation in the rest of the affair—this first book was to be a test—must depend on the satisfaction I should give. If this should be limited my employers would drop me with scarce common forms. It was therefore a crisis for me, and naturally I was making special preparations, looking about for new people, should they be necessary, and securing the best types. I admitted however that I should like to settle down to two or three good models who would do for everything.

55   "Should we have often to—a—put on special clothes?" Mrs. Monarch timidly demanded.

"Dear yes—that's half the business."

"And should we be expected to supply our own costumes?"

"Oh no; I've got a lot of things. A painter's models put on—or put off—anything he likes."

"And you mean—a—the same?"

60   "The same?"

Mrs. Monarch looked at her husband again.

"Oh she was just wondering," he explained, "if the costumes are in *general* use." I had to confess that they were, and I mentioned further that some of them—I had a lot of genuine greasy last-century things—had served their time, a hundred years ago, on living world-stained men and women; on figures not perhaps so far removed, in that vanished world, from *their* type, the Monarchs', *quoi!* of a breeched and bewigged age. "We'll put on anything that *fits*," said the Major.

"Oh I arrange that—they fit in the pictures."

"I'm afraid I should do better for the modern books. I'd come as you like," said Mrs. Monarch.

65   "She has got a lot of clothes at home: they might do for contemporary life," her husband continued.

"Oh I can fancy scenes in which you'd be quite natural." And indeed I could see the slipshod rearrangements of stale properties—the stories I tried to produce pictures for without the exasperation of reading them—whose sandy tracts the good lady might help to people. But I had to return to the fact that for this sort of work—the daily me-chanical grind—I was already equipped: the people I was working with were fully adequate.

"We only thought we might be more like *some* characters," said Mrs. Monarch mild-ly, getting up.

Her husband also rose; he stood looking at me with a dim wistfulness that was touching in so fine a man.

"Wouldn't it be rather a pull sometimes to have—a—to have—?" He hung fire; he wanted me to help him by phrasing what he meant. But I couldn't—I didn't know. So he brought it out awkwardly: "The *real* thing; a gentleman, you know, or a lady." I was quite ready to give a general assent—I admitted that there was a great deal in that. This encouraged Major Monarch to say, following up his appeal with an unact-ed gulp: "It's awfully hard—we've tried everything." The gulp was communicative; it proved too much for his wife. Before I knew it Mrs. Monarch had dropped again upon a divan and burst into tears. Her husband sat down beside her, holding one of her hands; whereupon she quickly dried her eyes with the other, while I felt embarrassed as she looked up at me. "There isn't a confounded job I haven't applied for—waited for—prayed for. You can fancy we'd be pretty bad first. Secretaryships and that sort of thing? You might as well ask for a peerage. I'd be anything—I'm strong; a messenger or a coalheaver. I'd put on a gold-laced cap and open carriage-doors in front of the haberdasher's; I'd hang about a station to carry portmanteaux; I'd be a postman. But they won't *look* at you; there are thousands as good as yourself already on the ground. *Gentlemen,* poor beggars, who've drunk their wine, who've kept their hunters!"

I was as reassuring as I knew how to be, and my visitors were presently on their feet 70 again while, for the experiment, we agreed on an hour. We were discussing it when the door opened and Miss Churm came in with a wet umbrella. Miss Churm had to take the omnibus to Maida Vale and then walk half a mile. She looked a trifle blowsy and slightly splashed. I scarcely ever saw her come in without thinking fresh how odd it was that, being so little in herself, she should yet be so much in others. She was a meagre little Miss Churm, but was such an ample heroine of romance. She was only a freckled cockney, but she could represent everything, from a fine lady to a shepherdess; she had the faculty as she might have had a fine voice or long hair. She couldn't spell and she loved beer, but she had two or three "points," and practice, and a knack, and mother-wit, and a whimsical sensibility, and a love of the theatre, and seven sisters, and not an ounce of respect, especially for the *h.* The first thing my visitors saw was that her umbrella was wet, and in their spotless perfection they visibly winced at it. The rain had come on since their arrival.

"I'm all in a soak; there *was* a mess of people in the 'bus. I wish you lived near a station," said Miss Churm. I requested her to get ready as quickly as possible, and she passed into the room in which she always changed her dress. But before going out she asked me what she was to get into this time.

"It's the Russian princess, don't you know?" I answered; "The one with the 'golden eyes,' in black velvet, for the long thing in the *Cheapside.*"

"Golden eyes? I *say!*" cried Miss Churm, while my companions watched her with intensity as she withdrew. She always arranged herself, when she was late, before I could turn around; and I kept my visitors a little on purpose, so that they might get an idea, from seeing her, what would be expected of themselves. I mentioned that she was quite my notion of an excellent model—she was really very clever.

"Do you think she looks like a Russian princess?" Major Monarch asked with lurking alarm.

"When I make her, yes." 75

"Oh if you have to *make* her—!" he reasoned, not without point.

"That's the most you can ask. There are so many who are not makeable."

"Well now, *here's* a lady"—and with a persuasive smile he passed his arm into his wife's—"who's already made!"

"Oh, I'm not a Russian princess," Mrs. Monarch protested a little coldly. I could see she had known some and didn't like them. There at once was a complication of a kind I never had to fear with Miss Churm.

This young lady came back in black velvet—the gown was rather rusty and very 80 low on her lean shoulders—and with a Japanese fan in her red hands. I reminded her that in the scene I was doing she had to look over some one's head. "I forget whose it is; but it doesn't matter. Just look over a head."

"I'd rather look over a stove," said Miss Churm; and she took her station near the fire. She fell into position, settled herself into a tall attitude, gave a certain backward inclination to her head and a certain forward droop to her fan, and looked, at least to my prejudiced sense, distinguished and charming, foreign and dangerous. We left her looking so while I went downstairs with Major and Mrs. Monarch.

"I believe I could come about as near it as that," said Mrs. Monarch.

"Oh, you think she's shabby, but you must allow for the alchemy of art."

However, they went off with an evident increase of comfort founded on their demonstrable advantage in being the real thing. I could fancy them shuddering over Miss Churm. She was very droll about them when I went back, for I told her what they wanted.

85 "Well, if *she* can sit I'll tyke to bookkeeping," said my model.

"She's very ladylike," I replied as an innocent form of aggravation.

"So much the worse for *you*. That means she can't turn round."

"She'll do for the fashionable novels."

"Oh yes, she'll *do* for them!" my model humorously declared.

90 "Ain't they bad enough without her?" I had often sociably denounced them to Miss Churm.

3

It was for the elucidation of a mystery in one of these works that I first tried Mrs. Monarch. Her husband came with her, to be useful if necessary—it was sufficiently clear that as a general thing he would prefer to come with her. At first I wondered if this were for "propriety's" sake—if he were going to be jealous and meddling. The idea was too tiresome, and if it had been confirmed it would speedily have brought our acquaintance to a close. But I soon saw there was nothing in it and that if he accompanied Mrs. Monarch it was—in addition to the chance of being wanted—simply because he had nothing else to do. When they were separate his occupation was gone and they never *had* been separate. I judged rightly that in their awkward situation their close union was their main comfort and that this union had no weak spot. It was a real marriage, an encouragement to the hesitating, a nut for pessimists to crack. Their address was humble—I remember afterwards thinking it had been the only thing about them that was really professional—and I could fancy the lamentable lodgings in which the Major would have been left alone. He could sit there more or less grimly with his wife—he couldn't sit there anyhow without her.

He had too much tact to try and make himself agreeable when he couldn't be useful; so when I was too absorbed in my work to talk he simply sat and waited. But I liked to hear him talk—it made my work, when not interrupting it, less mechanical, less special. To listen to him was to combine the excitement of going out with the economy of staying at home. There was only one hindrance—that I seemed not to know any of the people this brilliant couple had known. I think he wondered extremely, during the term of our intercourse, whom the deuce I *did* know. He hadn't a stray sixpence of an idea to fumble for, so we didn't spin it very fine; we confined ourselves to questions of leather and even of liquor—saddlers and breeches-makers and how to get excellent claret cheap—and matters like "good trains" and the habits of small game. His lore on these last subjects was astonishing—he managed to interweave the station-master with the ornithologist. When he couldn't talk about greater things he could talk cheerfully about smaller, and since I couldn't accompany him into reminiscences of the fashionable world he could lower the conversation without a visible effort to my level.

So earnest a desire to please was touching in a man who could so easily have knocked one down. He looked after the fire and had an opinion on the draught of the stove without my asking him, and I could see that he thought many of my arrangements not half knowing. I remember telling him that if I were only rich I'd offer him a salary to come and teach me how to live. Sometimes he gave a random sigh of which the essence might have been: "Give me even such a bare old barrack as *this*, and I'd do something with it!" When I wanted to use him he came alone; which was an illustration of the superior courage of women. His wife could bear her solitary second floor, and she was in general more discreet; showing by various small reserves that she was alive to the propriety of keeping our relations markedly professional—not letting them slide into sociability. She wished it to remain clear that she and the Major were employed, not cultivated, and if she approved of me as a superior, who could be kept in his place, she never thought me quite good enough for an equal.

She sat with great intensity, giving the whole of her mind to it, and was capable of remaining for an hour almost as motionless as before a photographer's lens. I could see she had been photographed often, but somehow the very habit that made her good for that purpose unfitted her for mine. At first I was extremely pleased with her ladylike air, and it was a satisfaction, on coming to follow her lines, to see how good they were and how far they could lead the pencil. But after a little skirmishing I began to find her too insurmountably stiff; do what I would with it my drawing looked like a photograph or a copy of a photograph. Her figure had no variety of expression—she herself had no sense of variety. You may say that this was my business and was only a question of placing her. Yet I placed her in every conceivable position and she managed to obliterate their differences. She was always a lady certainly, and into the bargain was always the same lady. She was the real thing, but always the same thing. There were moments when I rather writhed under the serenity of her confidence that she *was* the real thing. All her dealings with me and all her husband's were an implication that this was lucky for *me*. Meanwhile I found myself trying to invent types that approached her own, instead of making her own transform itself—in the clever way that was not impossible for instance to poor Miss Churm. Arrange as I would and take the precautions I would, she always came out, in my pictures, too tall—landing me in the dilemma of having represented a fascinating woman as seven feet high, which (out of respect perhaps to my own very much scantier inches) was far from my idea of such personage.

The case was worse with the Major—nothing I could do would keep *him* down, so 95 that he became useful only for the representation of brawny giants. I adored variety and range, I cherished human accidents, the illustrative note; I wanted to characterise closely, and the thing in the world I most hated was the danger of being ridden by a type. I had quarrelled with some of my friends about it; I had parted company with them for maintaining that one *had* to be, and that if the type was beautiful—witness Raphael and Leonardo—the servitude was only a gain. I was neither Leonardo nor Raphael—I might only be a presumptuous young modern searcher; but I held that everything was to be sacrificed sooner than character. When they claimed that the obsessional form could easily *be* character I retorted, perhaps superficially, "Whose?" It couldn't be everybody's—it might end in being nobody's.

After I had drawn Mrs. Monarch a dozen times I felt surer even than before that the value of such a model as Miss Churm resided precisely in the fact that she had no positive stamp, combined of course with the other fact that what she did have was a curious and inexplicable talent for imitation. Her usual appearance was like a curtain which she could draw up at request for a capital performance. This performance was simply suggestive; but it was a word to the wise—it was vivid and pretty. Sometimes even I thought it, though she was plain herself, too insipidly pretty; I made it a reproach to her that the figures drawn from her were monotonously (*bêtement,*° as we used to say) graceful. Nothing made her more angry: it was so much her pride to feel she could sit for characters that had nothing in common with each other. She would accuse me at such moments of taking away her "reputytion."

It suffered a certain shrinkage, this queer quantity, from the repeated visits of my new friends. Miss Churm was greatly in demand, never in want of employment, so I had no scruple in putting her off occasionally, to try them more at my ease. It was certainly amusing at first to do the real thing—it was amusing to do Major Monarch's trousers. They *were* the real thing, even if he did come out colossal. It was amusing to do his wife's back hair—it was so mathematically neat—and the particular "smart" tension of her tight stays. She lent herself especially to positions in which the face was somewhat averted or blurred; she abounded in ladylike back views and *profils perdus.*° When she stood erect she took naturally one of the attitudes in which court-painters represent queens and princesses; so that I found myself wondering whether, to draw out this accomplishment, I couldn't get the editor of the *Cheapside* to publish a really royal romance, "A Tale of Buckingham Palace." Sometimes however the real thing and the make-believe came into contact; by which I mean that Miss Churm, keeping an appointment or coming to make one on days when I had much work in hand, encountered her invidious rivals. The encounter was not on their part, for they noticed her no more than if she had been the housemaid; not from intentional loftiness, but simply because as yet, professionally, they didn't know how to fraternise, as I could imagine they would have liked—or at least that the Major would. They couldn't talk about the omnibus—they always walked; and they didn't know what else to try—she wasn't interested in good trains or cheap claret. Besides, they must have felt—in the air—that she was amused at them, secretly derisive of their ever knowing how. She wasn't a person to conceal the limits of her faith if she had had a chance to show them. On the other hand Mrs. Monarch didn't think her tidy; for why else did she take pains to say to me—it was going out of the way, for Mrs. Monarch—that she didn't like dirty women?

One day when my young lady happened to be present with my other sitters—she even dropped in, when it was convenient, for a chat—I asked her to be so good as to lend a hand in getting tea, a service with which she was familiar and which was one of a class that, living as I did in a small way, with slender domestic resources, I often appealed to my models to render. They liked to lay hands on my property, to break the sitting, and sometimes the china—it made them feel Bohemian. The next time I saw Miss Churm after this incident she surprised me greatly by making a scene about it—she accused me of having wished to humiliate her. She hadn't resented the outrage at the time, but had seemed obliging and amused, enjoying the comedy of asking Mrs. Monarch, who sat vague and silent, whether she would have cream and sugar, and putting an exaggerated simper into the question. She had tried intonations—as if she too wished to pass for the real thing—till I was afraid my other visitors would take offence.

°*bêtement*: Foolishly.
°*profils perdus*: Oblique angle "losing" the profile.

Oh they were determined not to do this, and their touching patience was the measure of their great need. They would sit by the hour, uncomplaining, till I was ready to use them; they would come back on the chance of being wanted and would walk away cheerfully if it failed. I used to go to the door with them to see in what magnificent order they retreated. I tried to find other employment for them—I introduced them to several artists. But they didn't "take," for reasons I could appreciate, and I became rather anxiously aware that after such disappointments they fell back upon me with a heavier weight. They did me the honor to think me most *their* form. They weren't romantic enough for the painters, and in those days there were few serious workers in black-and-white. Besides, they had an eye to the great job I had mentioned to them—they had secretly set their hearts on supplying the right essence for my pictorial vindication of our fine novelist. They knew that for this undertaking I should want no costume-effects, none of the frippery of past ages—that it was a case in which everything would be contemporary and satirical and presumably genteel. If I could work them into it their future would be assured, for the labour would of course be long and the occupation steady.

One day Mrs. Monarch came without her husband—she explained his absence by his having had to go to the City. While she sat there in her usual relaxed majesty there came at the door a knock which I immediately recognised as the subdued appeal of a model out of work. It was followed by the entrance of a young man whom I at once saw to be a foreigner and who proved in fact an Italian acquainted with no English word but my name, which he uttered in a way that made it seem to include all others. I hadn't then visited his country, nor was I proficient in his tongue; but as he was not so meanly constituted—what Italian is?—as to depend only on that member for expression he conveyed to me, in familiar but graceful mimicry, that he was in search of exactly the employment in which the lady before me was engaged. I was not struck with him at first, and while I continued to draw I dropped few signs of interest or encouragement. He stood his ground however—not importunately, but with a dumb dog-like fidelity in his eyes that amounted to innocent impudence, the manner of a devoted servant—he might have been in the house for years—unjustly suspected. Suddenly it struck me that this very attitude and expression made a picture; whereupon I told him to sit down and wait till I should be free. There was another picture in the way he obeyed me, and I observed as I worked that there were others still in the way he looked wonderingly, with his head thrown back, about the high studio. He might have been crossing himself in Saint Peter's. Before I finished I said to myself "The fellow's a bankrupt orange-monger, but a treasure."

When Mrs. Monarch withdrew he passed across the room like a flash to open the door for her, standing there with the rapt pure gaze of the young Dante spell-bound by the young Beatrice. As I never insisted, in such situations, on the blankness of the British domestic, I reflected that he had the making of a servant—and I needed one, but couldn't pay him to be only that—as well as of a model; in short I resolved to adopt my bright adventurer if he would agree to officiate in the double capacity. He jumped at my offer, and in the event my rashness—for I had really known nothing about him—wasn't brought home to me. He proved a sympathetic though a desultory ministrant, and had in a wonderful degree the *sentiment de la pose.*° It was uncultivated, instinctive, a part of the happy instinct that had guided him to my door and helped him to spell out my name on the card nailed to it. He had had no other introduction to me than

---

°*sentiment de la pose*: A flair for posing.

100

a guess, from the shape of my high north window, seen outside, that my place was a studio and that as a studio it would contain an artist. He had wandered to England in search of fortune, like other itinerants, and had embarked, with a partner and a small green hand-cart, on the sale of penny ices. The ices had melted away and the partner had dissolved in their train. My young man wore tight yellow trousers with reddish stripes and his name was Oronte. He was sallow but fair, and when I put him into some old clothes of my own he looked like an Englishman. He was as good as Miss Churm, who could look, when requested, like an Italian.

4

I thought Mrs. Monarch's face slightly convulsed when, on her coming back with her husband, she found Oronte installed. It was strange to have to recognise in a scrap of a lazzarone° a competitor to her magnificent Major. It was she who scented danger first, for the Major was anecdotically unconscious. But Oronte gave us tea, with a hundred eager confusions—he had never been concerned in so queer a process— and I think she thought better of me for having at last an "establishment." They saw a couple of drawings that I had made of the establishment, and Mrs. Monarch hinted that it never would have struck her he had sat for them. "Now the drawings you make from *us*, they look exactly like us," she reminded me, smiling in triumph; and I recognized that this was indeed just their defect. When I drew the Monarchs I couldn't anyhow get away from them—get into the character I wanted to represent; and I hadn't the least desire my model should be discoverable in my picture. Miss Churm never was, and Mrs. Monarch thought I hid her, very properly, because she was vulgar; whereas if she was lost it was only as the dead who go to heaven are lost—in the gain of an angel the more.

By this time I had got a certain start with "Rutland Ramsay," the first novel in the great projected series; that is, I had produced a dozen drawings, several with the help of the Major and his wife, and I had sent them in for approval. My understanding with the publishers, as I have already hinted, had been that I was to be left to do my work, in this particular case, as I liked, with the whole book committed to me; but my connexion with the rest of the series was only contingent. There were moments when, frankly, it *was* a comfort to have the real thing under one's hand; for there were characters in "Rutland Ramsay" that were very much like it. There were people presumably as erect as the Major and women of as good a fashion as Mrs. Monarch. There was a great deal of country-house life—treated, it is true, in a fine fanciful ironical generalised way—and there was a considerable implication of knickerbockers and kilts. There were certain things I had to settle at the outset; such things for instance as the exact appearance of the hero and the particular bloom and figure of the heroine. The author of course gave me a lead, but there was a margin for interpretation. I took the Monarchs into my confidence, I told them frankly what I was about, I mentioned my embarrassments and alternatives. "Oh take *him*!" Mrs. Monarch murmured sweetly, looking at her husband; and "What could you want better than my wife?" the Major enquired with the comfortable candour that now prevailed between us.

°*lazzarone:* (Italian) lazy bum.

I wasn't obliged to answer these remarks—I was only obliged to place my sitters. I wasn't easy in mind, and I postponed a little timidly perhaps the solving of my question. The book was a large canvas, the other figures were numerous, and I worked off at first some of the episodes in which the hero and the heroine were not concerned. When once I had set *them* up I should have to stick to them—I couldn't make my young man seven feet high in one place and five feet nine in another. I inclined on the whole to the latter measurement, though the Major more than once reminded me that *he* looked about as young as any one. It was indeed quite possible to arrange him, for the figure, so that it would have been difficult to detect his age. After the spontaneous Oronte had been with me a month, and after I had given him to understand several times over that his native exuberance would presently constitute an insurmountable barrier to our further intercourse, I waked to a sense of his heroic capacity. He was only five feet seven, but the remaining inches were latent. I tried him almost secretly at first for I was really rather afraid of the judgment my other models would pass on such a choice. If they regarded Miss Churm as little better than a snare what would they think of the representation by a person so little the real thing as an Italian street-vendor of a protagonist formed by a public school?

If I went a little in fear of them it wasn't because they bullied me, because they had got an oppressive foothold, but because in their really pathetic decorum and mysteriously permanent newness they counted on me so intensely. I was therefore very glad when Jack Hawley came home: he was always of such good counsel. He painted badly himself, but there was no one like him for putting his finger on the place. He had been absent from England for a year; he had been somewhere—I don't remember where— to get a fresh eye. I was in a good deal of dread of any such organ, but we were old friends; he had been away for months and a sense of emptiness was creeping into my life. I hadn't dodged a missile for a year. 105

He came back with a fresh eye, but with the same old black velvet blouse, and the first evening he spent in my studio we smoked cigarettes till the small hours. He had done no work himself, he had only got the eye; so the field was clear for the production of my little things. He wanted to see what I had produced for the *Cheapside*, but he was disappointed in the exhibition. That at least seemed the meaning of two or three comprehensive groans which, as he lounged on my big divan, his leg folded under him, looking at my latest drawings, issued from his lips with the smoke of the cigarette.

"What's the matter with you?" I asked

"What's the matter with *you?*"

"Nothing save that I'm mystified."

"You are indeed. You're quite off the hinge. What's the meaning of this new fad?" 110 And he tossed me, with visible irreverence, a drawing in which I happened to have depicted both my elegant models. I asked if he didn't think it good, and he replied that it struck him as execrable, given the sort of thing I had always represented myself to him as wishing to arrive at; but I let that pass—I was so anxious to see exactly what he meant. The two figures in the picture looked colossal, but I supposed this was *not* what he meant, inasmuch as, for aught he knew to the contrary, I might have been trying for some such effect. I maintained that I was working exactly in the same way as when he last had done me the honour to tell me I might do something some day. "Well, there's a screw loose somewhere," he answered; "wait a bit and I'll discover it." I depended upon him to do so: where else was the fresh eye? But he produced at last nothing more luminous than "I don't know—I don't like your types." This was lame for a critic who had never consented to discuss with me anything but the question of execution, the direction of strokes and the mystery of values.

"In the drawings you've been looking at I think my types are very handsome."

"Oh they won't do!"

"I've been working with new models."

"I see you have. *They* won't do."

115   "Are you very sure of that?"

"Absolutely—they're stupid."

"You mean *I* am—for I ought to get round that."

"You *can't*—with such people. Who are they?"

I told him, so far as was necessary, and he concluded heartlessly:

120   "Ce sont des gens qu'il faut mettre à la porte."°

"You've never seen them; they're awfully good"—I flew to their defence.

"Not seen them? Why all this recent work of yours drops to pieces with them. It's all I want to see of them."

"No one else has said anything against it—the *Cheapside* people are pleased."

"Every one else is an ass, and the *Cheapside* people the biggest asses of all. Come, don't pretend at this time of day to have pretty illusions about the public, especially about publishers and editors. It's not for *such* animals you work—it's for those who know, *coloro che sanno;*° so keep straight for *me* if you can't keep straight for yourself. There was a certain sort of thing you used to try for—and a very good thing it was. But this twaddle isn't *in* it." When I talked with Hawley later about "Rutland Ramsay" and its possible successors he declared that I must get back into my boat again or I should go to the bottom. His voice in short was the voice of warning.

125   I noted the warning, but I didn't turn my friends out of doors. They bored me a good deal; but the very fact that they bored me admonished me not to sacrifice them—if there was anything to be done with them—simply to irritation. As I look back at this phase they seem to me to have pervaded my life not a little. I have a vision of them as most of the time in my studio, seated against the wall on an old velvet bench to be out of the way, and resembling the while a pair of patient courtiers in a royal ante-chamber. I'm convinced that during the coldest weeks of the winter they held their ground because it saved them fire. Their newness was losing its gloss, and it was impossible not to feel them objects of charity. Whenever Miss Churm arrived they went away, and after I was fairly launched in "Rutland Ramsay" Miss Churm arrived pretty often. They managed to express to me tacitly that they supposed I wanted her for the low life of the book, and I let them suppose it, since they had attempted to study the work—it was lying about the studio—without discovering that it dealt only with the highest circles. They had dipped into the most brilliant of our novelists without deciphering many passages. I still took an hour from them, now and again, in spite of Jack Hawley's warning: it would be time enough to dismiss them, if dismissal should be necessary, when the rigour of the season was over. Hawley had made their acquaintance—he had met them at my fireside—and thought them a ridiculous pair. Learning that he was a painter they tried to approach him, to show him too that they were the real thing; but he looked at them, across the big room, as if they were miles away: they were a compendium of everything he most objected to in the social system of his country. Such

---

°*Ce sont . . . à la porte:* They are the sort of people one must show to the door.
°*coloro che sanno:* See Dante, *Inferno,* IV:131.

people as that, all convention and patent-leather, with ejaculations that stopped conversation, had no business in a studio. A studio was a place to learn to see, and how could you see through a pair of feather-beds?

The main inconvenience I suffered at their hands was that at first I was shy of letting it break upon them that my artful little servant had begun to sit to me for "Rutland Ramsay." They knew I had been odd enough—they were prepared by this time to allow oddity to artists—to pick a foreign vagabond out of the streets when I might have had a person with whiskers and credentials; but it was some time before they learned how high I rated his accomplishments. They found him in an attitude more than once, but they never doubted I was doing him as an organ-grinder. There were several things they never guessed, and one of them was that for a striking scene in the novel, in which a footman briefly figured, it occurred to me to make use of Major Monarch as the menial. I kept putting this off, I didn't like to ask him to don the livery—besides the difficulty of finding a livery to fit him. At last, one day late in the winter, when I was at work on the despised Oronte, who caught one's idea on the wing, and was in the glow of feeling myself go very straight, they came in, the Major and his wife, with their society laugh about nothing (there was less and less to laugh at); came on like country-callers—they always reminded me of that—who have walked across the park after church and are presently persuaded to stay to luncheon. Luncheon was over, but they could stay to tea—I knew they wanted it. The fit was on me, however, and I couldn't let my ardour cool and my work wait, with the fading daylight, while my model prepared it. So I asked Mrs. Monarch if she would mind laying it out—a request which for an instant brought all the blood to her face. Her eyes were on her husband's for a second, and some mute telegraphy passed between them. Their folly was over the next instant; his cheerful shrewdness put an end to it. So far from pitying their wounded pride, I must add, I was moved to give it as complete a lesson as I could. They bustled about together and got out the cups and saucers and made the kettle boil. I know they felt as if they were waiting on my servant, and when the tea was prepared I said: "He'll have a cup, please—he's tired." Mrs. Monarch brought him one where he stood, and he took it from her, as if he had been a gentleman at a party squeezing a crush-hat with an elbow.

Then it came over me that she had made a great effort for me—made it with a kind of nobleness—and that I owed her a compensation. Each time I saw her after this I wondered what the compensation could be. I couldn't go on doing the wrong thing to oblige them. Oh it *was* the wrong thing, the stamp of the work for which they sat—Hawley was not the only person to say it now. I sent in a large number of the drawings I had made for "Rutland Ramsay," and I received a warning that was more to the point than Hawley's. The artistic adviser of the house for which I was working was of opinion that many of my illustrations were not what had been looked for. Most of these illustrations were the subjects in which the Monarchs had figured. Without going into the question of what *had* been looked for, I had to face the fact that at this rate I shouldn't get the other books to do. I hurled myself in despair on Miss Churm—I put her through all her paces. I not only adopted Oronte publicly as my hero, but one morning when the Major looked in to see if I didn't require him to finish a *Cheapside* figure for which he had begun to sit the week before, I told him I had changed my mind—I'd do the drawing from my man. At this my visitor turned pale and stood looking at me. "Is *he* your idea of an English gentleman?" he asked.

I was disappointed, I was nervous, I wanted to get on with my work; so I replied with irritation: "Oh my dear Major—I can't be ruined for *you!*"

It was a horrid speech, but he stood another moment—after which, without a word, he quitted the studio. I drew a long breath, for I said to myself that I shouldn't see him again. I hadn't told him definitely that I was in danger of having my work rejected, but I was vexed at his not having felt the catastrophe in the air, read with me the moral of our fruitless collaboration, the lesson that in the deceptive atmosphere of art even the highest respectability may fail of being plastic.

130   I didn't owe my friends money, but I did see them again. They reappeared together three days later, and, given all the other facts, there was something tragic in that one. It was a clear proof they could find nothing else in life to do. They had threshed the matter out in a dismal conference—they had digested the bad news that they were not in for the series. If they weren't useful to me even for the *Cheapside* their function seemed difficult to determine, and I could only judge at first that they had come, forgivingly, decorously, to take a last leave. This made me rejoice in secret that I had little leisure for a scene; for I had placed both my other models in position together and I was pegging away at a drawing from which I hoped to derive glory. It had been suggested by the passage in which Rutland Ramsay, drawing up a chair to Artemisia's piano-stool, says extraordinary things to her while she ostensibly fingers out a difficult piece of music. I had done Miss Churm at the piano before—it was an attitude in which she knew how to take on an absolutely poetic grace. I wished the two figures to "compose" together with intensity, and my little Italian had entered perfectly into my conception. The pair were vividly before me, the piano had been pulled out; it was a charming show of blended youth and murmured love, which I had only to catch and keep. My visitors stood and looked at it, and I was friendly to them over my shoulder.

They made no response, but I was used to silent company and went on with my work, only a little disconcerted—even though exhilarated by the sense that *this* was at least the ideal thing—at not having got rid of them after all. Presently I heard Mrs. Monarch's sweet voice beside or rather above me: "I wish her hair were a little better done." I looked up and she was staring with a strange fixedness at Miss Churm, whose back was turned to her. "Do you mind my just touching it?" she went on—a question which made me spring up for an instant as with the instinctive fear that she might do the young lady a harm. But she quieted me with a glance I shall never forget—I confess I should like to have been able to paint *that*—and went for a moment to my model. She spoke to her softly, laying a hand on her shoulder and bending over her; and as the girl, understanding, gratefully assented, she disposed her rough curls, with a few quick passes, in such a way as to make Miss Churm's head twice as charming. It was one of the most heroic personal services I've ever seen rendered. Then Mrs. Monarch turned away with a low sigh and, looking about her as if for something to do, stooped to the floor with a noble humility and picked up a dirty rag that had dropped out of my paint-box.

The Major meanwhile had also been looking for something to do, and, wandering to the other end of the studio, saw before him my breakfast-things neglected, unremoved. "I say, can't I be useful *here*?" he called out to me with an irrepressible quaver. I assented with a laugh that I fear was awkward, and for the next ten minutes, while I worked, I heard the light clatter of china and the tinkle of spoons and glass. Mrs. Monarch assisted her husband—they washed up my crockery, they put it away. They wandered off into my little scullery, and I afterwards found that they had cleaned my knives and that my slender stock of plate had an unprecedented surface. When it came over me, the latent eloquence of what they were doing, I confess that my drawing was blurred for a moment—the picture swam. They had accepted their failure, but they couldn't accept their fate. They had bowed their heads in bewilderment to the perverse and cruel law in virtue of which the real thing could be so much less precious than the unreal; but they didn't want to starve. If my servants were my models; then my models might be my servants. They would reverse the parts—the others would sit for the ladies and gentlemen and *they* would do the work. They would still be in the studio—it was an intense dumb appeal to me not to turn them out. "Take us on," they wanted to say—"we'll do *anything*."

My pencil dropped from my hand; my sitting was spoiled and I got rid of my sitters, who were also evidently rather mystified and awestruck. Then, alone with the Major and his wife I had a most uncomfortable moment. He put their prayer into a single sentence: "I say, you know—just let *us* do for you, can't you?" I couldn't—it was dreadful to see them emptying my slops; but I pretended I could, to oblige them, for about a week. Then I gave them a sum of money to go away, and I never saw them again. I obtained the remaining books, but my friend Hawley repeats that Major and Mrs. Monarch did me a permanent harm, got me into false ways. If it be true I'm content to have paid the price—for the memory.   [1892]

QUESTIONS

1. What do the misunderstandings of the opening scene reveal about the artist and the Monarchs?
2. What is the function of Jack Hawley in the story? Of Miss Churm? Of Oronte?
3. Why is the narrator "content to have paid the price—for the memory"?
4. To whom does the title refer?
5. What does the story have to say about the relationship of life to art?

RESPONSES

1. Research the life of Henry James. To what extent do you see the artistic values expressed in this story embodied in his life?
2. Approaching this story with the psychological method, what processes and awareness are needed to develop a healthy, secure sense of self and ego?

SARAH ORNE JEWETT

Sarah Orne Jewett (1849–1909) was born in South Berwick, Maine. Although her education seems to have been sporadic because of poor health, she read widely and gained a knowledge of her rural neighborhood by accompanying her doctor father on his calls. By the age of nineteen she had a sketch accepted by *The Atlantic Monthly*, and her first collection of stories, *Deephaven*, appeared in 1877. Then followed a novel inspired by her father, *A Country Doctor* (1884), and her best-known book of tales, *The Country of the Pointed Firs* (1896). Influenced by Flaubert and the American local colorists, she evoked with sympathy the once vigorous and bustling Maine seaports now falling into decay.

A White Heron

1

The woods were already filled with shadows one June evening, just before eight o'-clock, though a bright sunset still glimmered faintly among the trunks of the trees. A little girl was driving home her cow, a plodding, dilatory, provoking creature in her behavior, but a valued companion for all that. They were going away from the western light, and striking deep into the dark woods, but their feet were familiar with the path, and it was no matter whether their eyes could see it or not.

There was hardly a night the summer through when the old cow could be found waiting at the pasture bars; on the contrary, it was her greatest pleasure to hide herself away among the high huckleberry bushes, and though she wore a loud bell she had made the discovery that if one stood perfectly still it would not ring. So Sylvia had to hunt for her until she found her, and call Co'! Co'! with never an answering Moo, until her childish patience was quite spent. If the creature had not given good milk and plenty of it, the case would have seemed very different to her owners. Besides, Sylvia had all the time there was, and very little use to make of it. Sometimes in pleasant weather it was a consolation to look upon the cow's pranks as an intelligent attempt to play hide and seek, and as the child had no playmates she lent herself to this amusement with a good deal of zest. Though this chase had been so long that the wary animal herself had given an unusual signal of her whereabouts, Sylvia had only laughed when she came upon Mistress Moolly at the swamp-side, and urged her affectionate-ly homeward with a twig of birch leaves. The old cow was not inclined to wander far-ther, she even turned in the right direction for once as they left the pasture, and stepped along the road at a good pace. She was quite ready to be milked now, and seldom stopped to browse. Sylvia wondered what her grandmother would say because they were so late. It was a great while since she had left home at half past five o'clock, but everybody knew the difficulty of making this errand a short one. Mrs. Tilley had chased the horned torment too many summer evenings herself to blame any one else for lin-gering, and was only thankful as she waited that she had Sylvia, nowadays, to give such valuable assistance. The good woman suspected that Sylvia loitered occasional-ly on her own account; there never was such a child for straying about out-of-doors since the world was made! Everybody said that it was a good change for a little maid who had tried to grow for eight years in a crowded manufacturing town, but, as for Sylvia herself, it seemed as if she never had been alive at all before she came to live at the farm. She thought often with wistful compassion of a wretched dry geranium that belonged to a town neighbor.

"'Afraid of folks,'" old Mrs. Tilley said to herself, with a smile, after she had made the unlikely choice of Sylvia from her daughter's houseful of children, and was re-turning to the farm. "'Afraid of folks,' they said! I guess she won't be troubled no great with 'em up to the old place!" When they reached the door of the lonely house and stopped to unlock it, and the cat came to purr loudly, and rub against them, a desert-ed pussy, indeed, but fat with young robins, Sylvia whispered that this was a beauti-ful place to live in, and she never should wish to go home.

The companions followed the shady wood-road, the cow taking slow steps, and the child very fast ones. The cow stopped long at the brook to drink, as if the pasture were not half a swamp, and Sylvia stood still and waited, letting her bare feet cool them-selves in the shoal water, while the great twilight moths struck softly against her. She waded on through the brook as the cow moved away, and listened to the thrushes with a heart that beat fast with pleasure. There was a stirring in the great boughs overhead. They were full of little birds and beasts that seemed to be wide-awake, and going about their world, or else saying good-night to each other in sleepy twitters. Sylvia herself felt sleepy as she walked along. However, it was not much farther to the house, and the air was soft and sweet. She was not often in the woods so late as this, and it made her feel as if she were a part of the gray shadows and the moving leaves. She was just thinking how long it seemed since she first came to the farm a year ago, and wondering if every-thing went on in the noisy town just the same as when she was there; the thought of the great red-faced boy who used to chase and frighten her made her hurry along the path to escape from the shadow of the trees.

Suddenly this little woods-girl is horror-stricken to hear a clear whistle not very far away. Not a bird's whistle, which would have a sort of friendliness, but a boy's whis-tle, determined, and somewhat aggressive. Sylvia left the cow to whatever sad fate might await her, and stepped discreetly aside into the bushes, but she was just too late. The enemy had discovered her, and called out in a very cheerful and persuasive tone, "Halloa, little girl, how far is it to the road?" and trembling Sylvia answered almost in-audibly, "A good ways." 5

She did not dare to look boldly at the tall young man, who carried a gun over his shoulder, but she came out of her bush and again followed the cow, while he walked alongside.

"I have been hunting for some birds," the stranger said kindly, "and I have lost my way, and need a friend very much. Don't be afraid," he added gallantly. "Speak up and tell me what your name is, and whether you think I can spend the night at your house, and go out gunning early in the morning."

Sylvia was more alarmed than before. Would not her grandmother consider her much to blame? But who could have foreseen such an accident as this? It did not appear to be her fault, and she hung her head as if the stem of it were broken, but managed to answer, "Sylvy," with much effort when her companion again asked her name.

Mrs. Tilley was standing in the doorway when the trio came into view. The cow gave a loud moo by way of explanation.

10   "Yes, you'd better speak up for yourself, you old trial! Where'd she tucked herself away this time, Sylvy?" Sylvia kept an awed silence; she knew by instinct that her grandmother did not comprehend the gravity of the situation. She must be mistaking the stranger for one of the farmer-lads of the region.

The young man stood his gun beside the door, and dropped a heavy game-bag beside it; then he bade Mrs. Tilley good-evening, and repeated his wayfarer's story, and asked if he could have a night's lodging.

"Put me anywhere you like," he said. "I must be off early in the morning, before day; but I am very hungry, indeed. You can give me some milk at any rate, that's plain."

"Dear sakes, yes," responded the hostess, whose long slumbering hospitality seemed to be easily awakened. "You might fare better if you went out on the main road a mile or so, but you're welcome to what we've got. I'll milk right off, and you make yourself at home. You can sleep on husks or feathers," she proffered graciously. "I raised them all myself. There's good pasturing for geese just below here towards the ma'sh. Now step round and set a plate for the gentleman, Sylvy!" And Sylvia promptly stepped. She was glad to have something to do, and she was hungry herself.

It was a surprise to find so clean and comfortable a little dwelling in this New England wilderness. The young man had known the horrors of its most primitive housekeeping, and the dreary squalor of that level of society which does not rebel at the companionship of hens. This was the best thrift of an old-fashioned farmstead, though on such a small scale that it seemed like a hermitage. He listened eagerly to the old woman's quaint talk, he watched Sylvia's pale face and shining gray eyes with ever growing enthusiasm, and insisted that this was the best supper he had eaten for a month; then, afterward, the new-made friends sat down in the doorway together while the moon came up.

15   Soon it would be berry-time, and Sylvia was a great help at picking. The cow was a good milker, though a plaguy thing to keep track of, the hostess gossiped frankly, adding presently that she had buried four children, so that Sylvia's mother, and a son (who might be dead) in California were all the children she had left. "Dan, my boy, was a great hand to go gunning," she explained sadly. "I never wanted for pa'tridges or gray squer'ls while he was to home. He's been a great wand'rer, I expect, and he's no hand to write letters. There, I don't blame him, I'd ha' seen the world myself if it had been so I could.

"Sylvia takes after him," the grandmother continued affectionately, after a minute's pause. "There ain't a foot o' ground she don't know her way over, and the wild creatur's counts her one o' themselves. Squer'ls she'll tame to come an' feed right out o' her hands, and all sorts o' birds. Last winter she got the jay-birds to bangeing here, and I believe she'd 'a' scanted herself of her own meals to have plenty to throw out amongst 'em, if I hadn't kep' watch. Anything but crows, I tell her, I'm willin' to help support— though Dan he went an' tamed one o' them that did seem to have reason same as folks.

It was round here a good spell after he went away. Dan an' his father they didn't hitch—but he never held up his head ag'in after Dan had dared him an' gone off."

The guest did not notice this hint of family sorrows in his eager interest in something else.

"So Sylvy knows all about birds, does she?" he exclaimed, as he looked round at the little girl who sat, very demure but increasingly sleepy, in the moonlight. "I am making a collection of birds myself. I have been at it ever since I was a boy." (Mrs. Tilley smiled.) "There are two or three very rare ones I have been hunting for these five years. I mean to get them on my own ground if they can be found."

"Do you cage 'em up?" asked Mrs. Tilley doubtfully, in response to this enthusiastic announcement.

"Oh, no, they're stuffed and preserved, dozens and dozens of them," said the ornithologist, "and I have shot or snared every one myself. I caught a glimpse of a white heron three miles from here on Saturday, and I have followed it in this direction. They have never been found in this district at all. The little white heron, it is," and he turned again to look at Sylvia with the hope of discovering that the rare bird was one of her acquaintances.   20

But Sylvia was watching a hop-toad in the narrow footpath.

"You would know the heron if you saw it," the stranger continued eagerly. "A queer tall white bird with soft feathers and long thin legs. And it would have a nest perhaps in the top of a high tree, made of sticks, something like a hawk's nest."

Sylvia's heart gave a wild beat; she knew that strange white bird, and had once stolen softly near where it stood in some bright green swamp grass, away over at the other side of the woods. There was an open place where the sunshine always seemed strangely yellow and hot, where tall, nodding rushes grew, and her grandmother had warned her that she might sink in the soft black mud underneath and never be heard of more. Not far beyond were the salt marshes and beyond those was the sea, the sea which Sylvia wondered and dreamed about, but never had looked upon, though its great voice could often be heard above the noise of the woods on stormy nights.

"I can't think of anything I should like so much as to find that heron's nest," the handsome stranger was saying. "I would give ten dollars to anybody who could show it to me," he added desperately, "and I mean to spend my whole vacation hunting for it if need be. Perhaps it was only migrating, or had been chased out of its own region by some bird of prey."

Mrs. Tilley gave amazed attention to all this, but Sylvia still watched the toad, not   25
divining, as she might have done at some calmer time, that the creature wished to get to its hole under the doorstep, and was much hindered by the unusual spectators at that hour of the evening. No amount of thought, that night, could decide how many wished-for treasures the ten dollars, so lightly spoken of, would buy.

The next day the young sportsman hovered about the woods, and Sylvia kept him company, having lost her first fear of the friendly lad, who proved to be most kind and sympathetic. He told her many things about the birds and what they knew and where they lived and what they did with themselves. And he gave her a jack-knife, which she thought as great a treasure as if she were a desert-islander. All day long he did not once make her troubled or afraid except when he brought down some unsuspecting singing creature from its bough. Sylvia would have liked him vastly better without his gun; she could not understand why he killed the very birds he seemed to like so much. But as the day waned, Sylvia still watched the young man with loving admiration. She had never seen anybody so charming and delightful; the woman's heart, asleep in the child, was vaguely thrilled by a dream of love. Some premonition of that great power stirred and swayed these young foresters who traversed the solemn woodlands with soft-footed silent care. They stopped to listen to a bird's song; they pressed forward again eagerly, parting the branches—speaking to each other rarely and in whispers; the young man going first and Sylvia following, fascinated, a few steps behind, with her gray eyes dark with excitement.

She grieved because the longed-for white heron was elusive, but she did not lead the guest, she only followed, and there was no such thing as speaking first. The sound of her own unquestioned voice would have terrified her—it was hard enough to answer yes or no when there was need of that. At last evening began to fall, and they drove the cow home together, and Sylvia smiled with pleasure when they came to the place where she heard the whistle and was afraid only the night before.

2

Half a mile from home, at the farther edge of the woods, where the land was highest, a great pine-tree stood, the last of its generation. Whether it was left for a boundary mark, or for what reason, no one could say; the woodchoppers who had felled its mates were dead and gone long ago, and a whole forest of sturdy trees, pines and oaks and maples, had grown again. But the stately head of this old pine towered above them all and made a landmark for sea and shore miles and miles away. Sylvia knew it well. She had always believed that whoever climbed to the top of it could see the ocean; and the little girl had often laid her hand on the great rough trunk and looked up wistfully at those dark boughs that the wind always stirred, no matter how hot and still the air might be below. Now she thought of the tree with a new excitement, for why, if one climbed it at break of day, could not one see all the world, and easily discover whence the white heron flew, and mark the place, and find the hidden nest?

What a spirit of adventure, what wild ambition! What fancied triumph and delight and glory for the later morning when she could make known the secret! It was almost too real and too great for the childish heart to bear.

30   All night the door of the little house stood open, and the whippoorwills came and sang upon the very step. The young sportsman and his old hostess were sound asleep, but Sylvia's great design kept her broad awake and watching. She forgot to think of sleep. The short summer night seemed as long as the winter darkness, and at last when the whippoorwills ceased, and she was afraid the morning would after all come too soon, she stole out of the house and followed the pasture path through the woods, hastening toward the open ground beyond, listening with a sense of comfort and companionship to the drowsy twitter of a half-awakened bird, whose perch she had jarred in passing. Alas, if the great wave of human interest which flooded for the first time this dull little life should sweep away the satisfactions of an existence heart to heart with nature and the dumb life of the forest!

There was the huge tree asleep yet in the paling moonlight, and small and hopeful Sylvia began with utmost bravery to mount to the top of it, with tingling, eager blood coursing the channels of her whole frame, with her bare feet and fingers, that pinched and held like bird's claws to the monstrous ladder reaching up, up, almost to the sky itself. First she must mount the white oak tree that grew along side, where she was almost lost among the dark branches and the green leaves heavy and wet with dew; a bird fluttered off its nest, and a red squirrel ran to and fro and scolded pettishly at the harmless housebreaker. Sylvia felt her way easily. She had often climbed there, and knew that higher still one of the oak's upper branches chafed against the pine trunk, just where its lower boughs were set close together. There, when she made the dangerous pass from one tree to the other, the great enterprise would really begin.

She crept out along the swaying oak limb at last, and took the daring step across into the old pine-tree. The way was harder than she thought; she must reach far and hold fast, the sharp dry twigs caught and held her and scratched her like angry talons, the pitch made her thin little fingers clumsy and stiff as she went round and round the tree's great stem, higher and higher upward. The sparrows and robins in the woods below were beginning to wake and twitter to the dawn, yet it seemed much lighter there aloft in the pine-tree, and the child knew that she must hurry if her project were to be of any use.

The tree seemed to lengthen itself out as she went up, and to reach farther and farther upward. It was like a great main-mast to the voyaging earth; it must truly have been amazed that morning through all its ponderous frame as it felt this determined spark of human spirit creeping and climbing from higher branch to branch. Who knows how steadily the least twigs held themselves to advantage this light, weak creature on her way! The old pine must have loved his new dependent. More than all the hawks, and bats, and moths, and even the sweet-voiced thrushes, was the brave, beating heart of the solitary gray-eyed child. And the tree stood still and held away the winds that June morning while the dawn grew bright in the east.

Sylvia's face was like a pale star, if one had seen it from the ground, when the last thorny bough was past, and she stood trembling and tired but wholly triumphant, high in the tree-top. Yes, there was the sea with the dawning sun making a golden dazzle over it, and toward that glorious east flew two hawks with slow-moving pinions. How low they looked in the air from that height when before one had only seen them far up, and dark against the blue sky. Their gray feathers were as soft as moths; they seemed only a little way from the tree, and Sylvia felt as if she too could go flying away among the clouds. Westward, the woodlands and farms reached miles and miles into the distance; here and there were church steeples, and white villages; truly it was a vast and awesome world.

The birds sang louder and louder. At last the sun came up bewilderingly bright. 35 Sylvia could see the white sails of ships out at sea, and the clouds that were purple and rose-colored and yellow at first began to fade away. Where was the white heron's nest in the sea of green branches, and was this wonderful sight and pageant of the world the only reward for having climbed to such a giddy height? Now look down again, Sylvia, where the green marsh is set among the shining birches and dark hemlocks; there where you saw the white heron once you will see him again; look, look! a white spot of him like a single floating feather comes up from the dead hemlock and grows larger, and rises, and comes close at last, and goes by the landmark pine with steady sweep of wing and outstretched slender neck and crested head. And wait! wait! do not move a foot or a finger, little girl, do not send an arrow of light and consciousness from your two eager eyes, for the heron has perched on a pine bough not far beyond yours, and cries back to his mate on the nest, and plumes his feathers for the new day!

The child gives a long sigh a minute later when a company of shouting catbirds comes also to the tree, and vexed by their fluttering and lawlessness the solemn heron goes away. She knows his secret now, the wild, light, slender bird that floats and wavers, and goes back like an arrow presently to his home in the green world beneath. Then Sylvia, well satisfied, makes her perilous way down again, not daring to look far below the branch she stands on, ready to cry sometimes because her fingers ache and her lamed feet slip. Wondering over and over again what the stranger would say to her, and what he would think when she told him how to find his way straight to the heron's nest.

"Sylvy, Sylvy!" called the busy old grandmother again and again, but nobody answered, and the small husk bed was empty, and Sylvia had disappeared.

The guest waked from a dream, and remembering his day's pleasure hurried to dress himself that it might sooner begin. He was sure from the way the shy little girl looked once or twice yesterday that she had at least seen the white heron, and now she must really be persuaded to tell. Here she comes now, paler than ever, and her worn old frock is torn and tattered, and smeared with pine pitch. The grandmother and the sportsman stand in the door together and question her, and the splendid moment has come to speak of the dead hemlock-tree by the green marsh.

But Sylvia does not speak after all, though the old grandmother fretfully rebukes her, and the young man's kind appealing eyes are looking straight in her own. He can make them rich with money; he has promised it, and they are poor now. He is so well worth making happy, and he waits to hear the story she can tell.

40   No, she must keep silence! What is it that suddenly forbids her and makes her dumb? Has she been nine years growing, and now, when the great world for the first time puts out a hand to her, must she thrust it aside for a bird's sake? The murmur of the pine's green branches is in her ears, she remembers how the white heron came flying through the golden air and how they watched the sea and the morning together, and Sylvia cannot speak; she cannot tell the heron's secret and give its life away.

Dear loyalty, that suffered a sharp pang as the guest went away disappointed later in the day, that could have served and followed him and loved him as a dog loves! Many a night Sylvia heard the echo of his whistle haunting the pasture path as she came home with the loitering cow. She forgot even her sorrow at the sharp report of his gun and the piteous sight of thrushes and sparrows dropping silent to the ground, their songs hushed and their pretty feathers stained and wet with blood. Were the birds better friends than their hunter might have been—who can tell? Whatever treasures were lost to her, woodlands and summertime, remember! Bring your gifts and graces and tell your secrets to this lonely country child.   [1886]

QUESTIONS

1. What does the description of the cow in the opening paragraphs contribute to the story?
2. How is the story shaped by its shifting point of view?
3. What is the dilemma that confronts Sylvia? What factors determine her course of action?
4. What does Sylvia have in common with the hunter? With the heron?
5. What is the significance of Sylvia's climb to the top of the pine tree?

DENIS JOHNSON

Denis Johnson (b. 1948) is an American citizen who was born in Munich, West Germany. He is a writer of poetry and novels, as well as short stories, and the winner of the National Poetry Series Award and the Whiting Writers Award. His books include *Fiskadaro* (1983), *Reservation of a Hanged Man* (1991), *Throne of the Third Heaven of the Nations Millennium General Assembly* (1995), and *The Name of the World* (2000). His short stories are collected in *Jesus' Son* (1992), which was adapted for a film of the same name. His recent work includes *Shoppers: Two Plays* (2002).

Car Crash While Hitchhiking

A salesman who shared his liquor and steered while sleeping . . . A Cherokee filled with bourbon . . . A VW no more than a bubble of hashish fumes, captained by a college student . . .

And a family from Marshalltown who head-onned and killed forever a man driving west out of Bethany, Missouri . . .

. . . I rose up sopping wet from sleeping under the pouring rain, and something less than conscious, thanks to the first three of the people I've already named—the salesman and the Indian and the student—all of whom had given me drugs. At the head of the entrance ramp I waited without hope of a ride. What was the point, even, of rolling up my sleeping bag when I was too wet to be let into anybody's car? I draped it around me like a cape. The downpour raked the asphalt and gurgled in the ruts. My thoughts zoomed pitifully. The travelling salesman had fed me pills that made the linings of my veins feel scraped out. My jaw ached. I knew every raindrop by its name. I sensed everything before it happened. I knew a certain Oldsmobile would stop for me even before it slowed, and by the sweet voices of the family inside it I knew we'd have an accident in the storm.

I didn't care. They said they'd take me all the way.

The man and the wife put the little girl up front with them and left the baby in back with me and my dripping bedroll. "I'm not taking you anywhere very fast," the man said. "I've got my wife and babies here, that's why."

You are the ones, I thought. And I piled my sleeping bag against the left-hand door and slept across it, not caring whether I lived or died. The baby slept free on the seat beside me. He was about nine months old.

5

... But before any of this, that afternoon, the salesman and I had swept down into Kansas City in his luxury car. We'd developed a dangerous cynical camaraderie beginning in Texas, where he'd taken me on. We ate up his bottle of amphetamines, and every so often we pulled off the Interstate and bought another pint of Canadian Club and a sack of ice. His car had cylindrical glass holders attached to either door and a white, leathery interior. He said he'd take me home to stay overnight with his family, but first he wanted to stop and see a woman he knew.

Under Midwestern clouds like great grey brains we left the superhighway with a drifting sensation and entered Kansas City's rush hour with a sensation of running aground. As soon as we slowed down, all the magic of travelling together burned away. He went on and on about his girlfriend. "I like this girl, I think I love this girl— but I've got two kids and a wife, and there's certain obligations there. And on top of everything else, I love my wife. I'm gifted with love. I love my kids. I love all my relatives." As he kept on, I felt jilted and sad: "I have a boat, a little sixteen-footer. I have two cars. There's room in the back yard for a swimming pool." He found his girlfriend at work. She ran a furniture store, and I lost him there.

The clouds stayed the same until night. Then, in the dark, I didn't see the storm gathering. The driver of the Volkswagen, a college man, the one who stoked my head with all the hashish, let me out beyond the city limits just as it began to rain. Never mind the speed I'd been taking, I was too overcome to stand up. I lay out in the grass off the exit ramp and woke in the middle of a puddle that had filled up around me.

10   And later, as I've said, I slept in the back seat while the Oldsmobile—the family from Marshalltown—splashed along through the rain. And yet I dreamed I was looking right through my eyelids, and my pulse marked off the seconds of time. The Interstate through western Missouri was, in that era, nothing more than a two-way road, most of it. When a semi truck came toward us and passed going the other way, we were lost in a blinding spray and a warfare of noises such as you get being towed through an automatic car wash. The wipers stood up and lay down across the windshield without much effect. I was exhausted, and after an hour I slept more deeply.

I'd known all along exactly what was going to happen. But the man and his wife woke me up later, denying it viciously.

"Oh—*no!*"

"NO!"

I was thrown against the back of their seat so hard that it broke. I commenced bouncing back and forth. A liquid which I knew right away was human blood flew around the car and rained down on my head. When it was over I was in the back seat again, just as I had been. I rose up and looked around. Our headlights had gone out. The radiator was hissing steadily. Beyond that, I didn't hear a thing. As far as I could tell, I was the only one conscious. As my eyes adjusted I saw that the baby was lying on its back beside me as if nothing had happened. Its eyes were open and it was feeling its cheeks with its little hands.

15   In a minute the driver, who'd been slumped over the wheel, sat up and peered at us. His face was smashed and dark with blood. It made my teeth hurt to look at him— but when he spoke, it didn't sound as if any of his teeth were broken.

"What happened?"

"We had a wreck," he said.

"The baby's okay," I said, although I had no idea how the baby was.

He turned to his wife.

20   "Janice," he said. "Janice, Janice!"

"Is she okay?"

"She's dead!" he said, shaking her angrily.

"No, she's not." I was ready to deny everything myself now.

Their little girl was alive, but knocked out. She whimpered in her sleep. But the man went on shaking his wife.

"Janice!" he hollered. 25

His wife moaned.

"She's not dead," I said, clambering from the car and running away.

"She won't wake up," I heard him say.

I was standing out here in the night, with the baby, for some reason, in my arms. It must have still been raining, but I remember nothing about the weather. We'd collided with another car on what I now perceived was a two-lane bridge. The water beneath us was invisible in the dark.

Moving toward the other car I began to hear rasping, metallic snores. Somebody was 30 flung halfway out the passenger door, which was open, in the posture of one hanging from a trapeze by his ankles. The car had been broadsided, smashed so flat that no room was left inside it even for this person's legs, to say nothing of a driver or any other passengers. I just walked right on past.

Headlights were coming from far off. I made for the head of the bridge, waving them to a stop with one arm and clutching the baby to my shoulder with the other.

It was a big semi, grinding its gears as it decelerated. The driver rolled down his window and I shouted up at him, "There's a wreck. Go for help."

"I can't turn around here," he said.

He let me and the baby up on the passenger side, and we just sat there in the cab, looking at the wreckage in his headlights.

"Is everybody dead?" he asked. 35

"I can't tell who is and who isn't," I admitted.

He poured himself a cup of coffee from a thermos and switched off all but his parking lights.

"What time is it?"

"Oh, it's around quarter after three," he said.

By his manner he seemed to endorse the idea of not doing anything about this. I was 40 relieved and tearful. I'd thought something was required of me, but I hadn't wanted to find out what it was.

When another car showed coming in the opposite direction, I thought I should talk to them. "Can you keep the baby?" I asked the truck driver.

"You'd better hang on to him," the driver said. "It's a boy, isn't it?"

"Well, I think so," I said.

The man hanging out of the wrecked car was still alive as I passed, and I stopped, grown a little more used to the idea now of how really badly broken he was, and made sure there was nothing I could do. He was snoring loudly and rudely. His blood bubbled out of his mouth with every breath. He wouldn't be taking many more. I knew that, but he didn't, and therefore I looked down into the great pity of a person's life on this earth. I don't mean that we all end up dead, that's not the great pity. I mean that he couldn't tell me what he was dreaming, and I couldn't tell him what was real.

Before too long there were cars backed up for a ways at either end of the bridge, and 45 headlights giving a night-game atmosphere to the steaming rubble, and ambulances and cop cars nudging through so that the air pulsed with color. I didn't talk to anyone. My secret was that in this short while I had gone from being the president of this tragedy to being a faceless onlooker at a gory wreck. At some point an officer learned that I was one of the passengers, and took my statement. I don't remember any of this, except that he told me, "Put out your cigarette." We paused in our conversation to watch the dying man being loaded into the ambulance. He was still alive, still dreaming obscenely. The blood ran off him in strings. His knees jerked and his head rattled.

There was nothing wrong with me, and I hadn't seen anything, but the policeman had to question me and take me to the hospital anyway. The word came over his car radio that the man was now dead, just as we came under the awning of the emergency-room entrance.

I stood in a tiled corridor with my wet sleeping bag bunched against the wall beside me, talking to a man from the local funeral home.

The doctor stopped to tell me I'd better have an X-ray.

"No."

50   "Now would be the time. If something turns up later . . ."

"There's nothing wrong with me."

Down the hall came the wife. She was glorious, burning. She didn't know yet that her husband was dead. We knew. That's what gave her such power over us. The doctor took her into a room with a desk at the end of the hall, and from under the closed door a slab of brilliance radiated as if, by some stupendous process, diamonds were being incinerated in there. What a pair of lungs! She shrieked as I imagined an eagle would shriek. It felt wonderful to be alive to hear it! I've gone looking for that feeling everywhere.

"There's nothing wrong with me"—I'm surprised I let those words out. But it's always been my tendency to lie to doctors, as if good health consisted only of the ability to fool them.

Some years later, one time when I was admitted to the Detox at Seattle General Hospital, I took the same tack.

55   "Are you hearing unusual sounds or voices?" the doctor asked.

"Help us, oh God, it hurts," the boxes of cotton screamed.

"Not exactly," I said.

"Not exactly," he said. "Now, what does that mean."

"I'm not ready to go into all that," I said. A yellow bird fluttered close to my face, and my muscles grabbed. Now I was flopping like a fish. When I squeezed shut my eyes, hot tears exploded from the sockets. When I opened them, I was on my stomach.

60   "How did the room get so white?" I asked.

A beautiful nurse was touching my skin. "These are vitamins," she said, and drove the needle in.

It was raining. Gigantic ferns leaned over us. The forest drifted down a hill. I could hear a creek rushing down among rocks. And you, you ridiculous people, you expect me to help you.   [1990]

QUESTIONS

1. Describe the narrator. What kind of person says, "I'd thought something was required of me, but I hadn't wanted to find out what it was"?

2. The setting changes a good deal for a relatively brief story. How are these changes in setting appropriate to the theme of the story?

3. When the woman screamed in the hospital, the narrator says, "I've been looking for that feeling everywhere." Do you believe him? Why?

4. Examine the language in the story. To what extent is it literal or figurative?
5. What is the conflict in the story?

RESPONSES

1. Write an essay analyzing why the narrator seems trustworthy given all the drugs he takes.
2. The end of Johnson's story occurs years after the main events occur. Another story that uses this technique is Porter's "The Grave." Write an essay explaining what effects a writer achieves with this "flash forward" technique.

FOCUS ON FILM

1. This story forms the opening sequence in the film *Jesus' Son*. How well does the film convey Johnson's use of language?
2. Does the film *Jesus' Son*, which is based on the volume of stories by that name, further examine and answer the narrator's question, "And you, you ridiculous people, you expect me to help you?"

JAMES JOYCE

James Joyce (1882–1941) was born in Dublin. Educated at Jesuit schools and at University College, Dublin, he early abandoned the study of medicine to give his life to literature. Feeling stultified by Catholic Ireland, he lived much of his life abroad. His sense of the "paralysis" of his birthplace is reflected in his collection of short stories, *Dubliners* (1914), and in the autobiographical *Portrait of the Artist as a Young Man* (1916). In 1922 he published his masterpiece, *Ulysses,* a work that achieved notoriety not for its extraordinary technical virtuosity but for its sexually explicit passages, which caused it to be banned in the United States until 1933. Joyce continued his experiments in language in *Finnegans Wake* (1939). Joyce reportedly boasted that the reader must spend a lifetime studying his work, and a surprising number of academic critics are prepared to do exactly that.

Araby

North Richmond Street, being blind, was a quiet street except at the hour when the Christian Brothers' School set the boys free. An uninhabited house of two storeys stood at the blind end, detached from its neighbours in a square ground. The other houses of the street, conscious of decent lives within them, gazed at one another with brown imperturbable faces.

The former tenant of our house, a priest, had died in the back drawing-room. Air, musty from having been long enclosed, hung in all the rooms, and the waste room behind the kitchen was littered with old useless papers. Among these I found a few paper-covered books, the pages of which were curled and damp: *The Abbot*, by Walter Scott, *The Devout Communicant* and *The Memoirs of Vidocq*. I liked the last best because its leaves were yellow. The wild garden behind the house contained a central apple-tree and a few straggling bushes under one of which I found the late tenant's rusty bicycle-pump. He had been a very charitable priest; in his will he had left all his money to institutions and the furniture of his house to his sister.

When the short days of winter came dusk fell before we had well eaten our dinners. When we met in the street the houses had grown sombre. The space of sky above us was the colour of ever-changing violet and towards it the lamps of the street lifted their feeble lanterns. The cold air stung us and we played till our bodies glowed. Our shouts echoed in the silent street. The career of our play brought us through the dark muddy lanes behind the houses where we ran the gauntlet of the rough tribes from the cottages, to the back doors of the dark dripping gardens where odours arose from the ashpits, to the dark odorous stables where a coachman smoothed and combed the horse or shook music from the buckled harness. When we returned to the street light from the kitchen windows had filled the areas. If my uncle was seen turning the corner we hid in the shadow until we had seen him safely housed. Or if Mangan's sister came out on the doorstep to call her brother in to his tea we watched her from our shadow peer up and down the street. We waited to see whether she would remain or go in and, if she remained, we left our shadow and walked up to Mangan's steps resignedly. She was waiting for us, her figure defined by the light from the half-opened door. Her brother always teased her before he obeyed and I stood by the railings looking at her. Her dress swung as she moved her body and the soft rope of her hair tossed from side to side.

Every morning I lay on the floor in the front parlour watching her door. The blind was pulled down to within an inch of the sash so that I could not be seen. When she came out on the doorstep my heart leaped. I ran to the hall, seized my books and followed her. I kept her brown figure always in my eye and, when we came near the point at which our ways diverged, I quickened my pace and passed her. This happened morning after morning. I had never spoken to her, except for a few casual words, and yet her name was like a summons to all my foolish blood.

Her image accompanied me even in places the most hostile to romance. On Saturday evenings when my aunt went marketing I had to go to carry some of the parcels. We walked through the flaring streets, jostled by drunken men and bargaining women, amid the curses of labourers, the shrill litanies of shop-boys who stood on guard by the barrels of pigs' cheeks, the nasal chanting of street-singers, who sang a *come-all-you* about O'Donovan Rossa, or a ballad about the troubles in our native land. These noises converged in a single sensation of life for me: I imagined that I bore my chalice safely through a throng of foes. Her name sprang to my lips at moments in strange prayers and praises which I myself did not understand. My eyes were often full of tears (I could not tell why) and at times a flood from my heart seemed to pour itself out into my bosom. I thought little of the future. I did not know whether I would ever speak to her or not or, if I spoke to her, how I could tell her of my confused adoration. But my body was like a harp and her words and gestures were like fingers running upon the wires.

One evening I went into the back drawing-room in which the priest had died. It was a dark rainy evening and there was no sound in the house. Through one of the broken panes I heard the rain impinge upon the earth, the fine incessant needles of water playing in the sodden beds. Some distant lamp or lighted window gleamed below me. I was thankful that I could see so little. All my senses seemed to desire to veil themselves and, feeling that I was about to slip from them, I pressed the palms of my hands together until they trembled, murmuring: *"O love! O love!"* many times.

At last she spoke to me. When she addressed the first words to me I was so confused that I did not know what to answer. She asked me was I going to *Araby*. I forgot whether I answered yes or no. It would be a splendid bazaar, she said she would love to go.

"And why can't you?" I asked.

While she spoke she turned a silver bracelet round and round her wrist. She could not go, she said, because there would be a retreat that week in her convent. Her brother and two other boys were fighting for their caps and I was alone at the railings. She

held one of the spikes, bowing her head towards me. The light from the lamp opposite our door caught the white curve of her neck, lit up her hair that rested there and,
falling, lit up the hand upon the railing. It fell over one side of her dress and caught
the white border of a petticoat, just visible as she stood at ease.

10   "It's well for you," she said.

"If I go," I said, "I will bring you something."

What innumerable follies laid waste my waking and sleeping thoughts after that
evening! I wished to annihilate the tedious intervening days. I chafed against the work
of school. At night in my bedroom and by day in the classroom her image came between me and the page I strove to read. The syllables of the word *Araby* were called
to me through the silence in which my soul luxuriated and cast an Eastern enchantment over me. I asked for leave to go to the bazaar on Saturday night. My aunt was
surprised and hoped it was not some Freemason affair. I answered few questions in
class. I watched my master's face pass from amiability to sternness; he hoped I was not
beginning to idle. I could not call my wandering thoughts together. I had hardly any
patience with the serious work of life which, now that it stood between me and my desire, seemed to me child's play, ugly monotonous child's play.

On Saturday morning I reminded my uncle that I wished to go to the bazaar in the
evening. He was fussing at the hallstand, looking for the hat-brush, and answered me
curtly:

"Yes, boy, I know."

15   As he was in the hall I could not go into the front parlour and lie at the window. I
left the house in bad humour and walked slowly towards the school. The air was pitilessly raw and already my heart misgave me.

When I came home to dinner my uncle had not yet been home. Still it was early. I
sat staring at the clock for some time and, when its ticking began to irritate me, I left
the room. I mounted the staircase and gained the upper part of the house. The high cold
empty gloomy rooms liberated me and I went from room to room singing. From the
front window I saw my companions playing below in the street. Their cries reached
me weakened and indistinct and, leaning my forehead against the cool glass, I looked
over at the dark house where she lived. I may have stood there for an hour, seeing
nothing but the brown-clad figure cast by my imagination, touched discreetly by the
lamplight at the curved neck, at the hand upon the railings and at the border below
the dress.

When I came downstairs again I found Mrs. Mercer sitting at the fire. She was an
old garrulous woman, a pawnbroker's widow, who collected used stamps for some
pious purpose. I had to endure the gossip of the tea-table. The meal was prolonged beyond an hour and still my uncle did not come. Mrs. Mercer stood up to go: she was
sorry she couldn't wait any longer, but it was after eight o'clock and she did not like
to be out late, as the night air was bad for her. When she had gone I began to walk up
and down the room, clenching my fists. My aunt said:

"I'm afraid you may put off your bazaar for this night of Our Lord."

At nine o'clock I heard my uncle's latchkey in the halldoor. I heard him talking to
himself and heard the hallstand rocking when it had received the weight of his overcoat. I could interpret these signs. When he was midway through his dinner I asked
him to give me the money to go to the bazaar. He had forgotten.

20   "The people are in bed and after their first sleep now," he said.

I did not smile. My aunt said to him energetically:

"Can't you give him the money and let him go? You've kept him late enough as it is."

My uncle said he was very sorry he had forgotten. He said he believed in the old saying: "All work and no play makes Jack a dull boy." He asked me where I was going and, when I had told him a second time he asked me did I know *The Arab's Farewell to his Steed*. When I left the kitchen he was about to recite the opening lines of the piece to my aunt.

I held a florin tightly in my hand as I strode down Buckingham Street towards the station. The sight of the streets thronged with buyers and glaring with gas recalled to me the purpose of my journey. I took my seat in a third-class carriage of a deserted train. After an intolerable delay the train moved out of the station slowly. It crept onward among ruinous houses and over the twinkling river. At Westland Row Station a crowd of people pressed to the carriage doors; but the porters moved them back, saying that it was a special train for the bazaar. I remained alone in the bare carriage. In a few minutes the train drew up beside an improvised wooden platform. I passed out on to the road and saw by the lighted dial of a clock that it was ten minutes to ten. In front of me was a large building which displayed the magical name.

I could not find any sixpenny entrance and, fearing that the bazaar would be   25 closed, I passed in quickly through a turnstile, handing a shilling to a weary-looking man. I found myself in a big hall girdled at half its height by a gallery. Nearly all the stalls were closed and the greater part of the hall was in darkness. I recognised a silence like that which pervades a church after a service. I walked into the centre of the bazaar timidly. A few people were gathered about the stalls which were still open. Before a curtain, over which the words *Café Chantant* were written in coloured lamps, two men were counting money on a salver. I listened to the fall of the coins.

Remembering with difficulty why I had come I went over to one of the stalls and examined porcelain vases and flowered tea-sets. At the door of the stall a young lady was talking and laughing with two young gentlemen. I remarked their English accents and listened vaguely to their conversation.

"O, I never said such a thing!"

"O, but you did!"

"O, but I didn't!"

"Didn't she say that?"   30

"Yes. I heard her."

"O, there's a . . . fib!"

Observing me the young lady came over and asked me did I wish to buy anything. The tone of her voice was not encouraging; she seemed to have spoken to me out of a sense of duty. I looked humbly at the great jars that stood like eastern guards at either side of the dark entrance to the stall and murmured:

"No, thank you."

The young lady changed the position of one of the vases and went back to the two   35 young men. They began to talk of the same subject. Once or twice the young lady glanced at me over her shoulder.

I lingered before her stall, though I knew my stay was useless, to make my interest in her wares seem the more real. Then I turned away slowly and walked down the middle of the bazaar. I allowed the two pennies to fall against the sixpence in my pocket. I heard a voice call from one end of the gallery that the light was out. The upper part of the hall was now completely dark.

Gazing up into the darkness I saw myself as a creature driven and derided by vanity; and my eyes burned with anguish and anger.   [1914]

QUESTIONS

1. Approximately how old is the narrator? How does his age affect his reminiscences?

2. What do the two opening paragraphs add to the story?

3. Interpret the sentence: "I had never spoken to her, except for a few casual words, and yet her name was like a summons to all my foolish blood."

4. How does the description of Mangan's sister reveal the narrator's attitude toward romantic love?

5. What does the narrator learn as a consequence of his quest?

JAMES JOYCE

The Dead

Lily, the caretaker's daughter, was literally run off her feet. Hardly had she brought one gentleman into the little pantry behind the office on the ground floor and helped him off with his overcoat than the wheezy hall-door bell clanged again and she had to scamper along the bare hallway to let in another guest. It was well for her she had not to attend to the ladies also. But Miss Kate and Miss Julia had thought of that and had converted the bathroom upstairs into a ladies' dressing-room. Miss Kate and Miss Julia were there, gossiping and laughing and fussing, walking after each other to the head of the stairs, peering down over the banisters and calling down to Lily to ask her who had come.

It was always a great affair, the Misses Morkan's annual dance. Everybody who knew them came to it, members of the family, old friends of the family, the members of Julia's choir, any of Kate's pupils that were grown up enough and even some of Mary Jane's pupils too. Never once had it fallen flat. For years and years it had gone off in splendid style as long as anyone could remember; ever since Kate and Julia, after the death of their brother Pat, had left the house in Stoney Batter and taken Mary Jane, their only niece, to live with them in the dark gaunt house on Usher's Island, the upper part of which they had rented from Mr. Fulham, the cornfactor on the ground floor. That was a good thirty years ago if it was a day. Mary Jane, who was then a little girl in short clothes, was now the main prop of the household for she had the organ in Haddirigton Road. She had been through the Academy and gave a pupils' concert every year in the upper room of the Antient Concert Rooms. Many of her pupils belonged to better-class families on the Kingstown and Dalkey line. Old as they were, her aunts also did their share. Julia, though she was quite grey, was still the leading soprano in Adam and Eve's, and Kate, being too feeble to go about much, gave music lessons to beginners on the old square piano in the back room. Lily, the caretaker's daughter, did housemaid's work for them. Though their life was modest they believed in eating well; the best of everything: diamond-bone sirloins, three-shilling tea and the best bottled stout. But Lily seldom made a mistake in the orders so that she got on well with her three mistresses. They were fussy, that was all. But the only thing they would not stand was back answers.

Of course they had good reason to be fussy on such a night. And then it was long after ten o'clock and yet there was no sign of Gabriel and his wife. Besides they were dreadfully afraid that Freddy Malins might turn up screwed. They would not wish for worlds that any of Mary Jane's pupils should see him under the influence; and when he was like that it was sometimes very hard to manage him. Freddy Malins always came late but they wondered what could be keeping Gabriel: and that was what brought them every two minutes to the banisters to ask Lily had Gabriel or Freddy come.

—O, Mr. Conroy, said Lily to Gabriel when she opened the door for him, Miss Kate and Miss Julia thought you were never coming. Good-night, Mrs. Conroy.

5   —I'll engage they did, said Gabriel, but they forgot that my wife here takes three mortal hours to dress herself.

He stood on the mat, scraping the snow from his goloshes, while Lily led his wife to the foot of the stairs and called out:

—Miss Kate, here's Mrs. Conroy.

Kate and Julia came toddling down the dark stairs at once. Both of them kissed Gabriel's wife, said she must be perished alive and asked was Gabriel with her.

—Here I am as right as the mail, Aunt Kate! Go on up. I'll follow, called out Gabriel from the dark.

10   He continued scraping his feet vigorously while the three women went upstairs, laughing, to the ladies' dressing-room. A light fringe of snow lay like a cape on the shoulders of his overcoat and like toecaps on the toes of his goloshes; and, as the buttons of his overcoat slipped with a squeaking noise through the snow-stiffened frieze, a cold fragrant air from out-of-doors escaped from crevices and folds.

—Is it snowing again, Mr. Conroy? asked Lily.

She had preceded him into the pantry to help him off with his overcoat. Gabriel smiled at the three syllables she had given his surname and glanced at her. She was a slim, growing girl, pale in complexion and with hay-coloured hair. The gas in the pantry made her look still paler. Gabriel had known her when she was a child and used to sit on the lowest step nursing a rag doll.

—Yes, Lily, he answered, and I think we're in for a night of it.

He looked up at the pantry ceiling, which was shaking with the stamping and shuffling of feet on the floor above, listened for a moment to the piano and then glanced at the girl, who was folding his overcoat carefully at the end of a shelf.

15   —Tell me, Lily, he said in a friendly tone, do you still go to school?

—O no, sir, she answered. I'm done schooling this year and more.

—O, then, said Gabriel gaily, I suppose we'll be going to your wedding one of these fine days with your young man, eh?

The girl glanced back at him over her shoulder and said with great bitterness:

—The men that is now is only all palaver and what they can get out of you.

20   Gabriel coloured as if he felt he had made a mistake and, without looking at her, kicked off his goloshes and flicked actively with his muffler at his patent-leather shoes.

He was a stout tallish young man. The high colour of his cheeks pushed upwards even to his forehead where it scattered itself in a few formless patches of pale red; and on his hairless face there scintillated restlessly the polished lenses and the bright gilt rims of the glasses which screened his delicate and restless eyes. His glossy black hair was parted in the middle and brushed in a long curve behind his ears where it curled slightly beneath the groove left by his hat.

When he had flicked lustre into his shoes he stood up and pulled his waistcoat down more tightly on his plump body. Then he took a coin rapidly from his pocket.

—O Lily, he said, thrusting it into her hands, it's Christmastime, isn't it? Just . . . here's a little. . . .

He walked rapidly towards the door.

—O no, sir! cried the girl, following him. Really, sir, I wouldn't take it.   25

—Christmas-time! Christmas-time! said Gabriel, almost trotting to the stairs and waving his hand to her in deprecation.

The girl, seeing that he had gained the stairs, called out after him:

—Well, thank you, sir.

He waited outside the drawing-room door until the waltz should finish, listening to the skirts that swept against it and to the shuffling of feet. He was still discomposed by the girl's bitter and sudden retort. It had cast a gloom over him which he tried to dispel by arranging his cuffs and the bows of his tie. Then he took from his waistcoat pocket a little paper and glanced at the headings he had made for his speech. He was undecided about the lines from Robert Browning for he feared they would be above the heads of his hearers. Some quotation that they could recognise from Shakespeare or from the Melodies would be better. The indelicate clacking of the men's heels and the shuffling of their soles reminded him that their grade of culture differed from his. He would only make himself ridiculous by quoting poetry to them which they could not understand. They would think that he was airing his superior education. He would fail with them just as he had failed with the girl in the pantry. He had taken up a wrong tone. His whole speech was a mistake from first to last, an utter failure.

Just then his aunts and his wife came out of the ladies' dressing-room. His aunts   30
were two small plainly dressed old women. Aunt Julia was an inch or so the taller. Her hair, drawn low over the tops of her ears, was grey; and grey also, with darker shadows, was her large flaccid face. Though she was stout in build and stood erect her slow eyes and parted lips gave her the appearance of a woman who did not know where she was or where she was going. Aunt Kate was more vivacious. Her face, healthier than her sister's, was all puckers and creases, like a shrivelled red apple, and her hair, braided in the same old-fashioned way, had not lost its ripe nut colour.

They both kissed Gabriel frankly. He was their favorite nephew, the son of their dead elder sister, Ellen, who had married T.J. Conroy of the Port and Docks.

—Gretta tells me you're not going to take a cab back to Monkstown to-night, Gabriel, said Aunt Kate.

—No, said Gabriel, turning to his wife, we had quite enough of that last year, hadn't we? Don't you remember, Aunt Kate, what a cold Gretta got out of it? Cab windows rattling all the way, and the east wind blowing in after we passed Merrion. Very jolly it was. Gretta caught a dreadful cold.

Aunt Kate frowned severely and nodded her head at every word.

—Quite right, Gabriel, quite right, she said. You can't be too careful.   35

—But as for Gretta there, said Gabriel, she'd walk home in the snow if she were let.

Mrs. Conroy laughed.

—Don't mind him, Aunt Kate, she said. He's really an awful bother, what with green shades for Tom's eyes at night and making him do the dumb-bells, and forcing Eva to eat the stirabout. The poor child! And she simply hates the sight of it! . . . O, but you'll never guess what he makes me wear now!

She broke out into a peal of laughter and glanced at her husband, whose admiring and happy eyes had been wandering from her dress to her face and hair. The two aunts laughed heartily too, for Gabriel's solicitude was a standing joke with them.

—Goloshes! said Mrs. Conroy. That's the latest. Whenever it's wet underfoot I must   40
put on my goloshes. To-night even he wanted me to put them on, but I wouldn't. The next thing he'll buy me will be a diving suit.

Gabriel laughed nervously and patted his tie reassuringly while Aunt Kate nearly doubled herself, so heartily did she enjoy the joke. The smile soon faded from Aunt Julia's face and her mirthless eyes were directed towards her nephew's face. After a pause she asked:

—And what are goloshes, Gabriel?

—Goloshes, Julia! exclaimed her sister. Goodness me, don't you know what goloshes are? You wear them over your . . . over your boots, Gretta, isn't it?

—Yes, said Mrs. Conroy. Guttapercha things. We both have a pair now. Gabriel says everyone wears them on the continent.

45   —O, on the continent, murmured Aunt Julia, nodding her head slowly.

Gabriel knitted his brows and said, as if he were slightly angered:

—It's nothing very wonderful but Gretta thinks it very funny because she says the word reminds her of Christy Minstrels.°

—But tell me, Gabriel, said Aunt Kate, with brisk tact. Of course, you've seen about the room. Gretta was saying . . .

—O, the room is all right, replied Gabriel. I've taken one in the Gresham.

50   —To be sure, said Aunt Kate, by far the best thing to do. And the children, Gretta, you're not anxious about them?

—O, for one night, said Mrs. Conroy. Besides, Bessie will look after them.

—To be sure, said Aunt Kate again. What a comfort it is to have a girl like that, one you can depend on! There's that Lily, I'm sure I don't know what has come over her lately. She's not the girl she was at all.

Gabriel was about to ask his aunt some questions on this point but she broke off suddenly to gaze after her sister who had wandered down the stairs and was craning her neck over the banisters.

—Now, I ask you, she said, almost testily, where is Julia going? Julia! Julia! Where are you going?

55   Julia, who had gone halfway down one flight, came back and announced blandly:

—Here's Freddy.

At the same moment a clapping of hands and a final flourish of the pianist told that the waltz had ended. The drawing-room door was opened from within and some couples came out. Aunt Kate drew Gabriel aside hurriedly and whispered into his ear:

—Slip down, Gabriel, like a good fellow and see if he's all right, and don't let him up if he's screwed. I'm sure he's screwed. I'm sure he is.

Gabriel went to the stairs and listened over the banisters. He could hear two persons talking in the pantry. Then he recognised Freddy Malins' laugh. He went down the stairs noisily.

60   —It's such a relief, said Aunt Kate to Mrs. Conroy, that Gabriel is here. I always feel easier in my mind when he's here. . . . Julia, there's Miss Daly and Miss Power will take some refreshment. Thanks for your beautiful waltz, Miss Daly. It made lovely time.

A tall wizen-faced man, with a stiff grizzled moustache and swarthy skin, who was passing out with his partner said:

—And may we have some refreshment, too, Miss Morkan?

—Julia, said Aunt Kate summarily, and here's Mr. Browne and Miss Furlong. Take them in, Julia, with Miss Daly and Miss Power.

°*Christy Minstrels*: Widely popular nineteenth-century minstrel company organized by Edward Christy.

—I'm the man for the ladies, said Mr. Browne, pursing his lips until his moustache bristled and smiling in all his wrinkles. You know, Miss Morkan, the reason they are so fond of me is—

He did not finish his sentence, but, seeing that Aunt Kate was out of earshot, at 65
once led the three young ladies into the back room. The middle of the room was oc-cupied by two square tables placed end to end, and on these Aunt Julia and the care-taker were straightening and smoothing a large cloth. On the sideboard were arrayed dishes and plates, and glasses and bundles of knives and forks and spoons. The top of the closed square piano served also as a sideboard for viands and sweets. At a small-er sideboard in one corner two young men were standing, drinking hop-bitters.

Mr. Browne led his charges thither and invited them all, in jest, to some ladies' punch, hot, strong and sweet. As they said they never took anything strong he opened three bottles of lemonade for them. Then he asked one of the young men to move aside, and, taking hold of the decanter, filled out for himself a goodly measure of whisky. The young men eyed him respectfully while he took a trial sip.

—God help me, he said, smiling, it's the doctor's orders.

His wizened face broke into a broader smile, and the three young ladies laughed in musical echo to his pleasantry, swaying their bodies to and fro, with nervous jerks of their shoulders. The boldest said:

—O, now, Mr. Browne, I'm sure the doctor never ordered anything of the kind.

Mr. Browne took another sip of his whiskey and said, with sidling mimicry: 70

—Well, you see, I'm like the famous Mrs. Cassidy, who is reported to have said: *Now, Mary Grimes, if I don't take it, make me take it, for I feel I want it.*

His hot face had leaned forward a little too confidentially and he had assumed a very low Dublin accent so that the young ladies, with one instinct, received his speech in silence. Miss Furlong, who was one of Mary Jane's pupils, asked Miss Daly what was the name of the pretty waltz she had played; and Mr. Browne, seeing that he was ig-nored, turned promptly to the two young men who were more appreciative.

A red-faced young woman, dressed in pansy, came into the room, excitedly clap-ping her hands and crying:

—Quadrilles! Quadrilles!

Close on her heels came Aunt Kate, crying: 75

—Two gentlemen and three ladies, Mary Jane!

—O, here's Mr. Bergin and Mr. Kerrigan, said Mary Jane. Mr. Kerrigan, will you take Miss Power? Miss Furlong, may I get you a partner, Mr. Bergin. O, that'll just do now.

—Three ladies, Mary Jane, said Aunt Kate.

The two young gentlemen asked the ladies if they might have the pleasure, and Mary Jane turned to Miss Daly.

—O, Miss Daly, you're really awfully good, after playing for the last two dances, but 80
really we're so short of ladies to-night.

—I don't mind in the least, Miss Morkan.

—But I've a nice partner for you, Mr. Bartell D' Arcy, the tenor. I'll get him to sing later on. All Dublin is raving about him.

—Lovely voice, lovely voice! said Aunt Kate.

As the piano had twice begun the prelude to the first figure Mary Jane led her re-cruits quickly from the room. They had hardly gone when Aunt Julia wandered slow-ly into the room, looking behind her at something.

—What is the matter, Julia? asked Aunt Kate anxiously. Who is it? 85

Julia, who was carrying in a column of table-napkins turned to her sister and said, simply, as if the question had surprised her:

—It's only Freddy, Kate, and Gabriel with him.

In fact right behind her Gabriel could be seen piloting Freddy Malins across the landing. The latter, a young man of forty, was of Gabriel's size and build, with very round shoulders. His face was fleshy and pallid, touched with colour only at the thick hanging lobes of his ears and at the wide wings of his nose. He had coarse features, a blunt nose, a convex and receding brow, tumid and protruded lips. His heavy-lidded eyes and the disorder of his scanty hair made him look sleepy. He was laughing heartily in a high key at a story which he had been telling Gabriel on the stairs and at the same time rubbing the knuckles of his left fist backwards and forwards into his left eye.

—Good-evening, Freddy, said Aunt Julia.

90   Freddy Malins bade the Misses Morkan good-evening in what seemed an off-hand fashion by reason of the habitual catch in his voice and then, seeing that Mr. Browne was grinning at him from the sideboard, crossed the room on rather shaky legs and began to repeat in an undertone the story he had just told to Gabriel.

—He's not so bad, is he? said Aunt Kate to Gabriel.

Gabriel's brows were dark but he raised them quickly and answered:

—O no, hardly noticeable.

—Now, isn't he a terrible fellow! she said. And his poor mother made him take the pledge on New Year's Eve. But come on, Gabriel, into the drawing-room.

95   Before leaving the room with Gabriel she signalled to Mr. Browne by frowning and shaking her forefinger in warning to and fro. Mr. Browne nodded in answer and, when she had gone, said to Freddy Malins:

—Now, then, Teddy, I'm going to fill you out a good glass of lemonade just to buck you up.

Freddy Malins, who was nearing the climax of his story, waved the offer aside impatiently but Mr. Browne, having first called Freddy Malins' attention to a disarray in his dress, filled out and handed him a full glass of lemonade. Freddy Malins' left hand accepted the glass mechanically, his right hand being engaged in the mechanical readjustment of his dress. Mr. Browne, whose face was once more wrinkling with mirth, poured out for himself a glass of whisky while Freddy Malins exploded, before he had well reached the climax of his story, in a kink of high-pitched bronchitic laughter and, setting down his untasted and overflowing glass, began to rub the knuckles of his left fist backwards and forwards into his left eye, repeating words of his last phrase as well as his fit of laughter would allow him.

Gabriel could not listen while Mary Jane was playing her Academy piece, full of runs and difficult passages, to the hushed drawing-room. He liked music but the piece she was playing had no melody for him and he doubted whether it had any melody for the other listeners, though they had begged Mary Jane to play something. Four young men, who had come from the refreshment-room to stand in the doorway at the sound of the piano, had gone away quietly in couples after a few minutes. The only persons who seemed to follow the music were Mary Jane herself, her hands racing along the key-board or lifted from it at the pauses like those of a priestess in momentary imprecation, and Aunt Kate standing at her elbow to turn the page.

Gabriel's eyes, irritated by the floor, which glittered with beeswax under the heavy chandelier, wandered to the wall above the piano. A picture of the balcony scene in *Romeo and Juliet* hung there and beside it was a picture of the two murdered princes in the Tower which Aunt Julia had worked in red, blue and brown wools when she was a girl. Probably in the school they had gone to as girls that kind of work had been taught, for one year his mother had worked for him as a birthday present a waistcoat of purple tabinet, with little foxes' heads upon it, lined with brown satin and having round mulberry buttons. It was strange that his mother had had no musical talent though Aunt Kate used to call her the brains carrier of the Morkan family. Both she and Julia had always seemed a little proud of their serious and matronly sister. Her photograph stood before the pierglass. She held an open book on her knees and was pointing out something in it to Constantine who, dressed in a man-o'-war suit, lay at her feet. It was she who had chosen the names for her sons for she was very sensible of the dignity of family life. Thanks to her, Constantine was now senior curate in Balbriggan and, thanks to her, Gabriel himself had taken his degree in the Royal University. A shadow passed over his face as he remembered her sullen opposition to his marriage. Some slighting phrases she had used still rankled in his memory; she had once spoken of Gretta as being country cute and that was not true of Gretta at all. It was Gretta who had nursed her during all her last long illness in their house at Monkstown.

He knew that Mary Jane must be near the end of her piece for she was playing   100
again the opening melody with runs of scales after every bar and while he waited for the end the resentment died down in his heart. The piece ended with a trill of octaves in the treble and a final deep octave in the bass. Great applause greeted Mary Jane as, blushing and rolling up her music nervously, she escaped from the room. The most vigorous clapping came from the four young men in the doorway who had gone away to the refreshment-room at the beginning of the piece but had come back when the piano had stopped.

Lancers were arranged. Gabriel found himself partnered with Miss Ivors. She was a frank-mannered talkative young lady, with a freckled face and prominent brown eyes. She did not wear a low-cut bodice and the large brooch which was fixed in the front of her collar bore on it an Irish device.

When they had taken their places she said abruptly:

—I have a crow to pluck with you.

—With me? said Gabriel.

She nodded her head gravely.   105

—What is it? asked Gabriel, smiling at her solemn manner.

—Who is G.C.? answered Miss Ivors, turning her eyes upon him.

Gabriel coloured and was about to knit his brows, as if he did not understand, when she said bluntly:

—O, innocent Amy! I have found out that you write for *The Daily Express*. Now, aren't you ashamed of yourself?

—Why should I be ashamed of myself? asked Gabriel, blinking his eyes and trying   110
to smile.

—Well, I'm ashamed of you, said Miss Ivors frankly. To say you'd write for a rag like that. I didn't think you were a West Briton.

A look of perplexity appeared on Gabriel's face. It was true that he wrote a literary column every Wednesday in *The Daily Express*, for which he was paid fifteen shillings. But that did not make him a West Briton surely. The books he received for review were almost more welcome than the paltry cheque. He loved to feel the covers and turn over the pages of newly printed books. Nearly every day when his teaching in the college was ended he used to wander down the quays to the second-hall booksellers, to Hickey's on Bachelor's Walk, to Webb's or Massey's on Aston's Quay, or to O'Clohissey's in the by-street. He did not know how to meet her charge. He wanted to say that literature was above politics. But they were friends of many years' standing and their careers had been parallel, first at the University and then as teachers: he could not risk a grandiose phrase with her. He continued blinking his eyes and trying to smile and murmured lamely that he saw nothing political in writing reviews of books.

When their turn to cross had come he was still perplexed and inattentive. Miss Ivors promptly took his hand in a warm grasp and said in a soft friendly tone:

—Of course, I was only joking. Come, we cross now.

115 When they were together again she spoke of the University question, and Gabriel felt more at ease. A friend of hers had shown her his review of Browning's poems. That was how she had found out the secret: but she liked the review immensely. Then she said suddenly:

—O, Mr. Conroy, will you come for an excursion to the Aran Isles this summer? We're going to stay there a whole month. It will be splendid out in the Atlantic. You ought to come. Mr. Clancy is coming, and Mr. Kilkelly and Kathleen Kearney. It would be splendid for Gretta too if she'd come. She's from Connacht, isn't she?

—Her people are, said Gabriel shortly.

—But you will come, won't you? said Miss Ivors, laying her warm hand eagerly on his arm.

—The fact is, said Gabriel, I have already arranged to go—

120 —Go where? asked Miss Ivors.

—Well, you know, every year I go for a cycling tour with some fellows and so—

—But where? asked Miss Ivors.

—Well, we usually go to France or Belgium or perhaps Germany, said Gabriel awkwardly.

—And why do you go to France and Belgium, said Miss Ivors, instead of visiting your own land?

125 —Well, said Gabriel, it's partly to keep in touch with the languages and partly for a change.

—And haven't you your own language to keep in touch with—Irish? asked Miss Ivors.

—Well, said Gabriel, if it comes to that, you know, Irish is not my language.

Their neighbours had turned to listen to the cross-examination. Gabriel glanced right and left nervously and tried to keep his good humour under the ordeal which was making a blush invade his forehead.

—And haven't you your own land to visit, continued Miss Ivors, that you know nothing of, your own people, and your own country?

130 —O, to tell you the truth, retorted Gabriel suddenly, I'm sick of my own country, sick of it!

—Why? asked Miss Ivors.

Gabriel did not answer for his retort had heated him.

—Why? repeated Miss Ivors.

They had to go visiting together and, as he had not answered her, Miss Ivors said warmly:

135 —Of course, you've no answer.

Gabriel tried to cover his agitation by taking part in the dance with great energy. He avoided her eyes for he had seen a sour expression on her face. But when they met in the long chain he was surprised to feel his hand firmly pressed. She looked at him from under her brows for a moment quizzically until he smiled. Then, just as the chain was about to start again, she stood on tiptoe and whispered into his ear:

—West Briton!

When the lancers were over Gabriel went away to a remote corner of the room where Freddy Malins' mother was sitting. She was a stout feeble old woman with white hair. Her voice had a catch in it like her son's and she stuttered slightly. She had been told that Freddy had come and that he was nearly all right. Gabriel asked her whether she had had a good crossing. She lived with her married daughter in Glasgow and came to Dublin on a visit once a year. She answered placidly that she had had a beautiful crossing and that the captain had been most attentive to her. She spoke also of the beautiful house her daughter kept in Glasgow, and of all the nice friends they had there. While her tongue rambled on Gabriel tried to banish from his mind all memory of the unpleasant incident with Miss Ivors. Of course the girl or woman, or whatever she was, was an enthusiast but there was a time for all things. Perhaps he ought not to have answered her like that. But she had no right to call him a West Briton before people, even in joke. She had tried to make him ridiculous before people, heckling him and staring at him with her rabbit's eyes.

He saw his wife making her way towards him through the waltzing couples. When she reached him she said into his ear:

—Gabriel, Aunt Kate wants to know won't you carve the goose as usual. Miss Daly   140
will carve the ham and I'll do the pudding.

—All right, said Gabriel.

—She's sending in the younger ones first as soon as this waltz is over so that we'll have the table to ourselves.

—Were you dancing? asked Gabriel.

—Of course I was. Didn't you see me? What words had you with Molly Ivors?

—No words. Why? Did she say so?   145

—Something like that. I'm trying to get that Mr. D'Arcy to sing. He's full of conceit, I think.

—There were no words, said Gabriel moodily, only she wanted me to go for a trip to the west of Ireland and I said I wouldn't.

His wife clasped her hands excitedly and gave a little jump.

—O, do go, Gabriel, she cried. I'd love to see Galway again.

—You can go if you like, said Gabriel coldly.   150

She looked at him for a moment, then turned to Mrs. Malins and said:

—There's a nice husband for you, Mrs. Malins.

While she was threading her way back across the room Mrs. Malins, without adverting to the interruption, went on to tell Gabriel what beautiful places there were in Scotland and beautiful scenery. Her son-in-law brought them every year to the lakes and they used to go fishing. Her son-in-law was a splendid fisher. One day he caught a fish, a beautiful big big fish, and the man in the hotel boiled it for their dinner.

Gabriel hardly heard what she said. Now that supper was coming near he began to think again about his speech and about the quotation. When he saw Freddy Malins coming across the room to visit his mother Gabriel left the chair free for him and retired into the embrasure of the window. The room had already cleared and from the back room came the clatter of plates and knives. Those who still remained in the drawing-room seemed tired of dancing and were conversing quietly in little groups. Gabriel's warm trembling fingers tapped the cold pane of the window. How cool it must be outside! How pleasant it would be to walk out alone, first along by the river and then through the park! The snow would be lying on the branches of the trees and forming a bright cap on the top of the Wellington Monument. How much more pleasant it would be there than at the supper-table!

He ran over the headings of his speech: Irish hospitality, sad memories, the Three   155
Graces, Paris, the quotation from Browning. He repeated to himself a phrase he had written in his review: *One feels that one is listening to a thought-tormented music.* Miss

Ivors had praised the review. Was she sincere? Had she really any life of her own behind all her propagandism? There had never been any ill-feeling between them until
that night. It unnerved him to think that she would be at the supper-table, looking up
at him while he spoke with her critical quizzing eyes. Perhaps she would not be sorry
to see him fail in his speech. An idea came into his mind and gave him courage. He
would say, alluding to Aunt Kate and Aunt Julia: *Ladies and Gentlemen, the generation
which is now on the wane among us may have had its faults but for my part I think it had certain qualities of hospitality, of humour, of humanity, which the new and very serious and hypereducated generation that is growing up around us seems to me to lack.* Very good: that was
one for Miss Ivors. What did he care that his aunts were only two ignorant old women?

A murmur in the room attracted his attention. Mr. Browne was advancing from the
door, gallantly escorting Aunt Julia, who leaned upon his arm, smiling and hanging
her head. An irregular musketry of applause escorted her also as far as the piano and
then, as Mary Jane seated herself on the stool, and Aunt Julia, no longer smiling, half
turned so as to pitch her voice fairly into the room, gradually ceased. Gabriel recognized the prelude. It was that of an old song of Aunt Julia's—*Arrayed for the Bridal*. Her
voice, strong and clear in tone, attacked with great spirit the runs which embellish the
air and though she sang very rapidly she did not miss even the smallest of the grace
notes. To follow the voice, without looking at the singer's face, was to feel and share the
excitement of swift and secure flight. Gabriel applauded loudly with all the others at
the close of the song and loud applause was borne in from the invisible supper-table.
It sounded so genuine that a little colour struggled into Aunt Julia's face as she bent to
replace in the music-stand the old leather-bound song-book that had her initials on the
cover. Freddy Malins, who had listened with his head perched sideways to hear her better, was still applauding when everyone else had ceased and talking animatedly to his
mother who nodded her head gravely and slowly in acquiescence. At last, when he
could clap no more, he stood up suddenly and hurried across the room to Aunt Julia
whose hand he seized and held in both his hands, shaking it when words failed him or
the catch in his voice proved too much for him.

—I was just telling my mother, he said, I never heard you sing so well, never. No,
I never heard your voice so good as it is to-night. Now! Would you believe that now?
That's the truth. Upon my word and honour that's the truth. I never heard your voice
sound so fresh and so . . . so clear and fresh, never.

Aunt Julia smiled broadly and murmured something about compliments as she released her hand from his grasp. Mr. Browne extended his open hand towards her and
said to those who were near in the manner of a showman introducing a prodigy to an
audience:

—Miss Julia Morkan, my latest discovery!

160   He was laughing very heartily at this himself when Freddy Malins turned to him
and said:

—Well, Browne, if you're serious you might make a worse discovery. All I can say
is I never heard her sing half so well as long as I am coming here. And that's the honest truth.

—Neither did I, said Mr. Browne. I think her voice has greatly improved.

Aunt Julia shrugged her shoulders and said with meek pride:

—Thirty years ago I hadn't a bad voice as voices go.

165   —I often told Julia, said Aunt Kate emphatically, that she was simply thrown away
in that choir. But she never would be said by me.

She turned as if to appeal to the good sense of the others against a refractory child while Aunt Julia gazed in front of her, a vague smile of reminiscence playing on her face.

—No, continued Aunt Kate, she wouldn't be said or led by anyone, slaving there in that choir night and day, night and day. Six o'clock on Christmas morning! And all for what?

—Well, isn't it for the honour of God, Aunt Kate? asked Mary Jane, twisting round on the piano-stool and smiling.

Aunt Kate turned fiercely on her niece and said:

—I know all about the honour of God, Mary Jane, but I think it's not at all hon-   170
ourable for the pope to turn out the women out of the choirs that have slaved there all their lives and put little whipper-snappers of boys over their heads. I suppose it is for the good of the Church if the pope does it. But it's not just, Mary Jane, and it's not right.

She had worked herself into a passion and would have continued in defence of her sister for it was a sore subject with her but Mary Jane, seeing that all the dancers had come back, intervened pacifically:

—Now, Aunt Kate, you're giving scandal to Mr. Browne who is of the other persuasion.

Aunt Kate turned to Mr. Browne, who was grinning at this allusion to his religion, and said hastily:

—O, I don't question the pope's being right. I'm only a stupid old woman and I wouldn't presume to do such a thing. But there's such a thing as common everyday politeness and gratitude. And if I were in Julia's place I'd tell that Father Healy straight up to his face . . .

—And besides, Aunt Kate, said Mary Jane, we really are all hungry and when we   175
are hungry we are all very quarrelsome.

—And when we are thirsty we are also quarrelsome, added Mr. Browne.

—So that we had better go to supper, said Mary Jane, and finish the discussion afterwards.

On the landing outside the drawing-room Gabriel found his wife and Mary Jane try-ing to persuade Miss Ivors to stay for supper. But Miss Ivors, who had put on her hat and was buttoning her cloak, would not stay. She did not feel in the least hungry and she had already overstayed her time.

—But only for ten minutes, Molly, said Mrs. Conroy. That won't delay you.

—To take a pick itself, said Mary Jane, after all your dancing.   180

—I really couldn't, said Miss Ivors.

—I am afraid you didn't enjoy yourself at all, said Mary Jane hopelessly.

—Ever so much, I assure you, said Miss Ivors, but you really must let me run off now.

—But how can you get home? asked Mrs. Conroy.

—O, it's only two steps up the quay.   185

Gabriel hesitated a moment and said:

—If you will allow me, Miss Ivors, I'll see you home if you really are obliged to go.

But Miss Ivors broke away from them.

—I won't hear of it, she cried. For goodness sake go in to your suppers and don't mind me. I'm quite well able to take care of myself.

—Well, you're the comical girl, Molly, said Mrs. Conroy frankly.   190

—*Beannacht libh,*° cried Miss Ivors, with a laugh, as she ran down the staircase.

Mary Jane gazed after her, a moody puzzled expression on her face, while Mrs. Conroy leaned over the banisters to listen for the hall-door. Gabriel asked himself was he the cause of her abrupt departure. But she did not seem to be in ill humour: she had gone away laughing. He stared blankly down the staircase.

At that moment Aunt Kate came toddling out of the supper-room, almost wringing her hands in despair.

—Where is Gabriel? she cried. Where on earth is Gabriel? There's everyone waiting in there, stage to let, and nobody to carve the goose!

195 —Here I am, Aunt Kate! cried Gabriel, with sudden animation, ready to carve a flock of geese, if necessary.

A fat brown goose lay at one end of the table and at the other end, on a bed of creased paper strewn with sprigs of parsley, lay a great ham, stripped of its outer skin and peppered over with crust crumbs, a neat paper frill round its shin and beside this was a round of spiced beef. Between these rival ends ran parallel lines of side-dishes: two little minsters of jelly, red and yellow; a shallow dish full of blocks of blancmange and red jam, a large green leaf-shaped dish with a stalk-shaped handle, on which lay bunches of purple raisins and peeled almonds, a companion dish on which lay a solid rectangle of Smyrna figs, a dish of custard topped with grated nutmeg, a small bowl full of chocolates and sweets wrapped in gold and silver papers and a glass vase in which stood some tall celery stalks. In the centre of the table there stood, as sentries to a fruit-stand which upheld a pyramid of oranges and American apples, two squat old-fashioned decanters of cut glass, one containing port and the other dark sherry. On the closed square piano a pudding in a huge yellow dish lay in waiting and behind it were three squads of bottles of stout and ale and minerals, drawn up according to the colours of their uniforms, the first two black, with brown and red labels, the third and smallest squad white, with transverse green sashes.

Gabriel took his seat boldly at the head of the table and, having looked to the edge of the carver, plunged his fork firmly into the goose. He felt quite at ease now for he was an expert carver and liked nothing better than to find himself at the head of a well-laden table.

—Miss Furlong, what shall I send you? he asked. A wing or a slice of the breast?

—Just a small slice of the breast.

200 —Miss Higgins, what for you?

—O, anything at all, Mr. Conroy.

While Gabriel and Miss Daly exchanged plates of goose and plates of ham and spiced beef Lily went from guest to guest with a dish of hot floury potatoes wrapped in a white napkin. This was Mary Jane's idea and she had also suggested apple sauce for the goose but Aunt Kate had said that plain roast goose without apple sauce had always been good enough for her and she hoped she might never eat worse. Mary Jane waited on her pupils and saw that they got the best slices and Aunt Kate and Aunt Julia opened and carried across from the piano bottles of stout and ale for the gentlemen and bottles of minerals for the ladies. There was a great deal of confusion and laughter and noise, the noise of orders and counter-orders, of knives and forks, of corks and glass-stoppers. Gabriel began to carve second helpings as soon as he had finished the first round without serving himself. Everyone protested loudly so that he compromised by taking a long draught of stout for he had found the carving hot work.

°*Beannacht libh*: Gaelic for "blessings on you."

Mary Jane settled down quietly to her supper but Aunt Kate and Aunt Julia were still toddling round the table, walking on each other's heels, getting in each other's way and giving each other unheeded orders. Mr. Browne begged of them to sit down and eat their suppers and so did Gabriel but they said there was time enough so that, at last, Freddy Malins stood up and, capturing Aunt Kate, plumped her down on her chair amid general laughter.

When everyone had been well served Gabriel said, smiling:

—Now, if anyone wants a little more of what vulgar people call stuffing let him or her speak.

A chorus of voices invited him to begin his own supper and Lily came forward   205
with three potatoes which she had reserved for him.

—Very well, said Gabriel amiably, as he took another preparatory draught, kindly forget my existence, ladies and gentlemen, for a few minutes.

He set to his supper and took no part in the conversation with which the table covered Lily's removal of the plates. The subject of talk was the opera company which was then at the Theatre Royal. Mr. Bartell D'Arcy, the tenor, a dark-complexioned young man with a smart moustache, praised very highly the leading contralto of the company but Miss Furlong thought she had a rather vulgar style of production. Freddy Malins said there was a Negro chieftain singing in the second part of the Gaiety pantomime who had one of the finest tenor voices he had ever heard.

—Have you heard him? he asked Mr. Bartell D'Arcy across the table.

—No, answered Mr. Bartell D'Arcy carelessly.

—Because, Freddy Malins explained, now I'd be curious to hear your opinion of   210
him. I think he has a grand voice.

—It takes Teddy to find out the really good things, said Mr. Browne familiarly to the table.

—And why couldn't he have a voice too? asked Freddy Malins sharply. Is it because he's only a black?

Nobody answered this question and Mary Jane led the table back to the legitimate opera. One of her pupils had given her a pass for *Mignon*. Of course it was very fine, she said, but it made her think of poor Georgina Burns. Mr. Browne could go back farther still, to the old Italian companies that used to come to Dublin—Tietjens, Ilma de Murzka, Campanini, the great Trebelli, Giuglini, Ravelli, Aramburo. Those were the days, he said, when there was something like singing to be heard in Dublin. He told too of how the top gallery of the old Royal used to be packed night after night, of how one night an Italian tenor had sung five encores to *Let Me Like a Soldier Fall*, introducing a high C every time, and of how the gallery boys would sometimes in their enthusiasm unyoke the horses from the carriage of some great *prima donna* and pull her themselves through the streets to her hotel. Why did they never play the grand old operas now, he asked, *Dinorah, Lucrezia Borgia?* Because they could not get the voices to sing them: that was why.

—O, well, said Mr. Bartell D'Arcy, I presume there are as good singers to-day as there were then.

—Where are they? asked Mr. Browne defiantly.   215

—In London, Paris, Milan, said Mr. Bartell D'Arcy warmly. I suppose Caruso, for example, is quite as good, if not better than any of the men you have mentioned.

—Maybe so, said Mr. Browne. But I may tell you I doubt it strongly.

—O, I'd give anything to hear Caruso sing, said Mary Jane.

—For me, said Aunt Kate, who had been picking a bone, there was only one tenor. To please me, I mean. But I suppose none of you ever heard of him.

220 —Who was he, Miss Morkan? asked Mr. Bartell D'Arcy politely.

—His name, said Aunt Kate, was Parkinson. I heard him when he was in his prime and I think he had then the purest tenor voice that was ever put into a man's throat.

—Strange, said Mr. Bartell D'Arcy. I never even heard of him.

—Yes, yes, Miss Morkan is right, said Mr. Browne: I remember hearing of old Parkinson but he's too far back for me.

—A beautiful pure sweet mellow English tenor, said Aunt Kate with enthusiasm.

225 Gabriel having finished, the huge pudding was transferred to the table. The clatter of forks and spoons began again. Gabriel's wife served out spoonfuls of the pudding and passed the plates down the table. Midway down they were held up by Mary Jane, who replenished them with raspberry or orange jelly or with blancmange and jam. The pudding was of Aunt Julia's making and she received praises for it from all quarters. She herself said that it was not quite brown enough.

—Well, I hope, Miss Morkan, said Mr. Browne, that I'm brown enough for you because, you know, I'm all brown.

All the gentlemen, except Gabriel, ate some of the pudding out of compliment to Aunt Julia. As Gabriel never ate sweets the celery had been left for him. Freddy Malins also took a stalk of celery and ate it with his pudding. He had been told that celery was a capital thing for the blood and he was just then under doctor's care. Mrs. Malins, who had been silent all through the supper, said that her son was going down to Mount Melleray in a week or so. The table then spoke of Mount Melleray, how bracing the air was down there, how hospitable the monks were and how they never asked for a penny-piece from their guests.

—And do you mean to say, asked Mr. Browne incredulously, that a chap can go down there and put up there as if it were a hotel and live on the fat of the land and then come away without paying a farthing?

—O, most people give some donation to the monastery when they leave, said Mary Jane.

230 —I wish we had an institution like that in our Church, said Mr. Browne candidly.

He was astonished to hear that the monks never spoke, got up at two in the morning and slept in their coffins. He asked what they did it for.

—That's the rule of the order, said Aunt Kate firmly.

—Yes, but why? asked Mr. Browne.

Aunt Kate repeated that it was the rule, that was all. Mr. Browne still seemed not to understand. Freddy Malins explained to him, as best he could, that the monks were trying to make up for the sins committed by all the sinners in the outside world. The explanation was not very clear for Mr. Browne grinned and said:

235 —I like that idea very much but wouldn't a comfortable spring bed do them as well as a coffin?

—The coffin, said Mary Jane, is to remind them of their last end.

As the subject had grown lugubrious it was buried in a silence of the table during which Mrs. Malins could be heard saying to her neighbour in an indistinct undertone:

—They are very good men, the monks, very pious men.

The raisins and almonds and figs and apples and oranges and chocolates and sweets were now passed about the table and Aunt Julia invited all the guests to have either port or sherry. At first Mr. Bartell D'Arcy refused to take either but one of his neighbours nudged him and whispered something to him upon which he allowed his glass to be filled. Gradually as the last glasses were being filled the conversation ceased. A pause followed, broken only by the noise of the wine and by unsettlings of chairs. The Misses Morkan, all three, looked down at the tablecloth. Someone coughed once or twice and then a few gentlemen patted the table gently as a signal for silence. The silence came and Gabriel pushed back his chair and stood up.

The patting at once grew louder in encouragement and then ceased altogether. 240 Gabriel leaned his ten trembling fingers on the tablecloth and smiled nervously at the company. Meeting a row of upturned faces he raised his eyes to the chandelier. The piano was playing a waltz tune and he could hear the skirts sweeping against the drawing-room door. People, perhaps, were standing in the snow on the quay outside, gazing up at the lighted windows and listening to the waltz music. The air was pure there. In the distance lay the park where the trees were weighted with snow. The Wellington Monument wore a gleaming cap of snow that flashed westward over the white field of Fifteen Acres.

He began:

—Ladies and Gentlemen.

—It has fallen to my lot this evening, as in years past, to perform a very pleasing task but a task for which I am afraid my poor powers as a speaker are all too inadequate.

—No, no! said Mr. Browne.

—But, however that may be, I can only ask you to-night to take the will for the 245 deed and to lend me your attention for a few moments while I endeavour to express to you in words what my feelings are on this occasion.

—Ladies and Gentlemen. It is not the first time that we have gathered together under this hospitable roof, around this hospitable board. It is not the first time that we have been the recipients—or perhaps, I had better say, the victims—of the hospitality of certain good ladies.

He made a circle in the air with his arm and paused. Everyone laughed or smiled at Aunt Kate and Aunt Julia and Mary Jane who all turned crimson with pleasure. Gabriel went on more boldly:

—I feel more strongly with every recurring year that our country has no tradition which does it so much honour and which it should guard so jealously as that of its hospitality. It is a tradition that is unique as far as my experience goes (and I have visited not a few places abroad) among the modern nations. Some would say, perhaps, that with us it is rather a failing than anything to be boasted of. But granted even that, it is, to my mind, a princely failing, and one that I trust will long be cultivated among us. Of one thing, at least, I am sure. As long as this one roof shelters the good ladies aforesaid—and I wish from my heart it may do so for many and many a long year to come—the tradition of genuine warm-hearted courteous Irish hospitality, which our forefathers have handed down to us and which we in turn must hand down to our descendants, is still alive among us.

A hearty murmur of assent ran round the table. It shot through Gabriel's mind that Miss Ivors was not there and that she had gone away discourteously: and he said with confidence in himself:

—Ladies and Gentlemen.   250

—A new generation is growing up in our midst, a generation actuated by new ideas and new principles. It is serious and enthusiastic for these new ideas and its enthusiasm, even when it is misdirected, is, I believe, in the main sincere. But we are living in a sceptical and, if I may use the phrase, a thought-tormented age: and sometimes I fear that this new generation, educated or hypereducated as it is, will lack those qualities of humanity, of hospitality, of kindly humour which belonged to an older day. Listening to-night to the names of all those great singers of the past it seemed to me, I must confess, that we were living in a less spacious age. Those days might, without exaggeration, be called spacious days: and if they are gone beyond recall let us hope, at least, that in gatherings such as this we shall still speak of them with pride and affection, still cherish in our hearts the memory of those dead and gone great ones whose fame the world will not willingly let die.

—Hear, hear! said Mr. Browne loudly.

—But yet, continued Gabriel, his voice falling into a softer inflection, there are always in gatherings such as this sadder thoughts that will recur to our minds: thoughts of the past, of youth, of changes, of absent faces that we miss here tonight. Our path through life is strewn with many such sad memories: and were we to brood upon them always we could not find the heart to go on bravely with our work among the living. We have all of us living duties and living affections which claim, and rightly claim, our strenuous endeavours.

—Therefore, I will not linger on the past. I will not let any gloomy moralising intrude upon us here to-night. Here we are gathered together for a brief moment from the bustle and rush of our everyday routine. We are met here as friends, in the spirit of good-fellowship, as colleagues, also to a certain extent, in the true spirit of *camaraderie*, and as the guests of—what shall I call them?—the Three Graces of the Dublin musical world.

255   The table burst into applause and laughter at this sally. Aunt Julia vainly asked each of her neighbours in turn to tell her what Gabriel had said.

—He says we are the Three Graces, Aunt Julia, said Mary Jane.

Aunt Julia did not understand but she looked up, smiling, at Gabriel, who continued in the same vein:

—Ladies and Gentlemen.

—I will not attempt to play to-night the part that Paris played on another occasion. I will not attempt to choose between them. The task would be an invidious one and one beyond my poor powers. For when I view them in turn, whether it be our chief hostess herself, whose good heart, whose too good heart, has become a byword with all who know her, or her sister, who seems to be gifted with perennial youth and whose singing must have been a surprise and a revelation to us all tonight, or, last but not least, when I consider our youngest hostess, talented, cheerful, hard-working and the best of nieces, I confess, Ladies and Gentlemen, that I do not know to which of them I should award the prize.

260   Gabriel glanced down at his aunts and, seeing the large smile on Aunt Julia's face and the tears which had risen to Aunt Kate's eyes, hastened to his close. He raised his glass of port gallantly, while every member of the company fingered a glass expectantly, and said loudly:

—Let us toast them all three together. Let us drink to their health, wealth, long life, happiness and prosperity and may they long continue to hold the proud and self-won position which they hold in their profession and the position of honour and affection which they hold in our hearts.

All the guests stood up, glass in hand, and, turning towards the three seated ladies, sang in unison, with Mr. Browne as leader:

> *For they are jolly gay fellows,*
> *For they are jolly gay fellows,*
265 > *For they are jolly gay fellows,*
> *Which nobody can deny.*

Aunt Kate was making frank use of her handkerchief and even Aunt Julia seemed moved. Freddy Malins beat time with his pudding-fork and the singers turned towards one another, as if in melodious conference, while they sang, with emphasis:

> *Unless he tells a lie,*
> *Unless he tells a lie.*

Then, turning once more towards their hostesses, they sang: 270

> *For they are jolly gay fellows,*
> *For they are jolly gay fellows,*
> *For they are jolly gay fellows,*
> *Which nobody can deny.*

The acclamation which followed was taken up beyond the door of the supper-room   275
by many of the other guests and renewed time after time, Freddy Malins acting as officer with his fork on high.

The piercing morning air came into the hall where they were standing so that Aunt Kate said:

—Close the door, somebody. Mrs. Malins will get her death of cold.

—Browne is out there, Aunt Kate, said Mary Jane.

—Browne is everywhere, said Aunt Kate, lowering her voice.

Mary Jane laughed at her tone.   280

—Really, she said archly, he is very attentive.

—He has been laid on here like the gas, said Aunt Kate in the same tone, all during the Christmas.

She laughed herself this time good-humouredly and then added quickly:

—But tell him to come in, Mary Jane, and close the door. I hope to goodness he didn't hear me.

At that moment the hall-door was opened and Mr. Browne came in from the   285
doorstep, laughing as if his heart would break. He was dressed in a long green overcoat with mock astrakhan cuffs and collar and wore on his head an oval fur cap. He pointed down the snow-covered quay from where the sound of shrill prolonged whistling was borne in.

—Teddy will have all the cabs in Dublin out, he said.

Gabriel advanced from the little pantry behind the office, struggling into his overcoat and, looking round the hall, said:

—Gretta not down yet?

—She's getting on her things, Gabriel, said Aunt Kate.

—Who's playing up there? asked Gabriel.   290

—Nobody. They're all gone.

—O no, Aunt Kate, said Mary Jane. Bartell D'Arcy and Miss O'Callaghan aren't gone yet.

—Someone is strumming at the piano, anyhow, said Gabriel.

Mary Jane glanced at Gabriel and Mr. Browne and said with a shiver:

—It makes me feel cold to look at you two gentlemen muffled up like that. I   295
wouldn't like to face your journey home at this hour.

—I'd like nothing better this minute, said Mr. Browne stoutly, than a rattling fine walk in the country or a fast drive with a good spanking goer between the shafts.

—We used to have a very good horse and trap at home, said Aunt Julia sadly.

—The never-to-be-forgotten Johnny, said Mary Jane, laughing.

Aunt Kate and Gabriel laughed too.

300 —Why, what was wonderful about Johnny? asked Mr. Browne.

—The late lamented Patrick Morkan, our grandfather, that is, explained Gabriel, commonly known in his later years as the old gentleman, was a glue-boiler.

—O, now, Gabriel, said Aunt Kate, laughing, he had a starch mill.

—Well, glue or starch, said Gabriel, the old gentleman had a horse by the name of Johnny. And Johnny used to work in the old gentleman's mill, walking round and round in order to drive the mill. That was all very well; but now comes the tragic part about Johnny. One fine day the old gentleman thought he'd like to drive out with the quality to a military review in the park.

—The Lord have mercy on his soul, said Aunt Kate compassionately.

305 —Amen, said Gabriel. So the old gentleman, as I said, harnessed Johnny and put on his very best tall hat and his very best stock collar and drove out in grand style from his ancestral mansion somewhere near Back Lane, I think.

Everyone laughed, even Mrs. Malins, at Gabriel's manner and Aunt Kate said:

—O now, Gabriel, he didn't live in Back Lane, really. Only the mill was there.

—Out from the mansion of his forefathers, continued Gabriel, he drove with Johnny. And everything went on beautifully until Johnny came in sight of King Billy's statue: and whether he fell in love with the horse King Billy sits on or whether he thought he was back again in the mill, anyhow he began to walk round the statue.

Gabriel paced in a circle round the hall in his goloshes amid the laughter of the others.

310 —Round and round he went, said Gabriel, and the old gentleman, who was a very pompous old gentleman, was highly indignant. *Go on, sir! What do you mean, sir? Johnny! Johnny! Most extraordinary conduct! Can't understand the horse!*

The peals of laughter which followed Gabriel's imitation of the incident were interrupted by a resounding knock at the hall-door. Mary Jane ran to open it and let in Freddy Malins. Freddy Malins, with his hat well back on his head and his shoulders humped with cold, was puffing and steaming after his exertions.

—I could only get one cab, he said.

—O, we'll find another along the quay, said Gabriel.

—Yes, said Aunt Kate. Better not keep Mrs. Malins standing in the draught.

315 Mrs. Malins was helped down the front steps by her son and Mr. Browne and, after many manoeuvres, hoisted into the cab. Freddy Malins clambered in after her and spent a long time settling her on the seat, Mr. Browne helping him with advice. At last she was settled comfortably and Freddy Malins invited Mr. Browne into the cab. There was a good deal of confused talk, and then Mr. Browne got into the cab. The cabman settled his rug over his knees, and bent down for the address. The confusion grew greater and the cabman was directed differently by Freddy Malins and Mr. Browne, each of whom had his head out through a window of the cab. The difficulty was to know where to drop Mr. Browne along the route and Aunt Kate, Aunt Julia and Mary Jane helped the discussion from the doorstep with cross-directions and contradictions and abundance of laughter. As for Freddy Malins he was speechless with laughter. He popped his head in and out of the window every moment, to the great danger of his hat, and told his mother how the discussion was progressing till at last Mr. Browne shouted to the bewildered cabman above the din of everybody's laughter:

—Do you know Trinity College?

—Yes, sir, said the Cabman.

—Well, drive bang up against. Trinity College gates, said Mr. Browne, and then we'll tell you where to go. You understand now?

—Yes, sir, said the cabman.

—Make like a bird for Trinity College.

—Right, sir, cried the cabman.

The horse was whipped up and the cab rattled off along the quay amid a chorus of laughter and adieus.

Gabriel had not gone to the door with the others. He was in a dark part of the hall gazing up the staircase. A woman was standing near the top of the first flight, in the shadow also. He could not see her face but he could see the terracotta and salmonpink panels of her skirt which the shadow made appear black and white. It was his wife. She was leaning on the banisters, listening to something. Gabriel was surprised at her stillness and strained his ear to listen also. But he could hear little save the noise of laughter and dispute on the front steps, a few chords struck on the piano and a few notes of a man's voice singing.

He stood still in the gloom of the hall, trying to catch the air that the voice was singing and gazing up at his wife. There was grace and mystery in her attitude as if she were a symbol of something. He asked himself what is a woman standing on the stairs in the shadow, listening to distant music, a symbol of. If he were a painter he would paint her in that attitude. Her blue felt hat would show off the bronze of her hair against the darkness and the dark panels of her skirt would show off the light ones. *Distant Music* he would call the picture if he were a painter.

The hall-door was closed; and Aunt Kate, Aunt Julia and Mary Jane came down the hall, still laughing.

—Well, isn't Freddy terrible? said Mary Jane. He's really terrible.

Gabriel said nothing but pointed up the stairs towards where his wife was standing. Now that the hall-door was closed the voice and the piano could be heard more clearly. Gabriel held up his hand for them to be silent. The song seemed to be in the old Irish tonality and the singer seemed uncertain both of his words and of his voice. The voice, made plaintive by distance and by the singer's hoarseness, faintly illuminated the cadence of the air with words expressing grief:

> *O, the rain falls on my heavy locks*
> *And the dew wets my skin,*
> *My babe lies cold . . .*

—O, exclaimed Mary Jane. It's Bartell D'Arcy singing and he wouldn't sing all the night. O, I'll get him to sing a song before he goes.

—O do, Mary Jane, said Aunt Kate.

Mary Jane brushed past the others and ran to the staircase but before she reached it the singing stopped and the piano was closed abruptly.

—O, what a pity! she cried. Is he coming down, Gretta?

Gabriel heard his wife answer yes and saw her come down towards them. A few steps behind her were Mr. Bartell D'Arcy and Miss O'Callaghan.

—O, Mr. D'Arcy, cried Mary Jane, it's downright mean of you to break off like that when we were all in raptures listening to you.

—I have been at him all the evening, said Miss O'Callaghan, and Mrs. Conroy too and he told us he had a dreadful cold and couldn't sing.

—O, Mr. D'Arcy, said Aunt Kate, now that was a great fib to tell.

—Can't you see that I'm as hoarse as a crow? said Mr. D'Arcy roughly.

340   He went into the pantry hastily and put on his overcoat. The others, taken aback by his rude speech, could find nothing to say. Aunt Kate wrinkled her brows and made signs to the others to drop the subject. Mr. D'Arcy stood swathing his neck carefully and frowning.

    —It's the weather, said Aunt Julia, after a pause.

    —Yes, everybody has colds, said Aunt Kate readily, everybody.

    —They say, said Mary Jane, we haven't had snow like it for thirty years; and I read this morning in the newspapers that the snow is general all over Ireland.

    —I love the look of snow, said Aunt Julia sadly.

345   —So do I, said Miss O'Callaghan. I think Christmas is never really Christmas unless we have the snow on the ground.

    —But poor Mr. D'Arcy doesn't like the snow, said Aunt Kate, smiling.

    Mr. D'Arcy came from the pantry, fully swathed and buttoned, and in a repentant tone told them the history of his cold. Everyone gave him advice and said it was a great pity and urged him to be very careful of his throat in the night air. Gabriel watched his wife who did not join in the conversation. She was standing right under the dusty fanlight and the flame of the gas lit up the rich bronze of her hair which he had seen her drying at the fire a few days before. She was in the same attitude and seemed unaware of the talk about her. At last she turned towards them and Gabriel saw that there was colour on her cheeks and that her eyes were shining. A sudden tide of joy went leaping out of his heart.

    —Mr. D'Arcy, she said, what is the name of that song you were singing?

    —It's called *The Lass of Aughrim*, said Mr. D'Arcy, but I couldn't remember it properly. Why? Do you know it?

350   —The *Lass of Aughrim*, she repeated. I couldn't think of the name.

    —It's a very nice air, said Mary Jane. I'm sorry you were not in voice to-night.

    —Now, Mary Jane, said Aunt Kate, don't annoy Mr. D'Arcy. I won't have him annoyed.

    Seeing that all were ready to start she shepherded them to the door where good-night was said:

    —Well, good-night, Aunt Kate, and thanks for the pleasant evening.

355   —Good-night, Gabriel. Good-night, Gretta!

    —Good-night, Aunt Kate, and thanks ever so much. Good-night, Aunt Julia.

    —O, good-night, Gretta, I didn't see you.

    —Good-night, Mr. D'Arcy. Good-night, Miss O'Callaghan.

    —Good-night, Miss Morkan.

360   —Good-night, again.

    —Good-night, all. Safe home.

    —Good-night. Good-night.

    The morning was still dark. A dull yellow light brooded over the houses and the river; and the sky seemed to be descending. It was slushy underfoot; and only streaks and patches of snow lay on the roofs, on the parapets of the quay and on the area railings. The lamps were still burning redly in the murky air and, across the river, the palace of the Four Courts stood out menacingly against the heavy sky.

    She was walking on before him with Mr. Bartell D'Arcy, her shoes in a brown parcel tucked under one arm and her hands holding her skirt up from the slush. She had no longer any grace of attitude but Gabriel's eyes were still bright with happiness. The blood went bounding along his veins; and the thoughts went rioting through his brain, proud, joyful, tender, valorous.

She was walking on before him so lightly and so erect that he longed to run after her noiselessly, catch her by the shoulders and say something foolish and affectionate into her ear. She seemed to him so frail that he longed to defend her against something and then to be alone with her. Moments of their secret life together burst like stars upon his memory. A heliotrope envelope was lying beside his breakfast-cup and he was caressing it with his hand. Birds were twittering in the ivy and the sunny web of the curtain was shimmering along the floor: he could not eat for happiness. They were standing on the crowded platform and he was placing a ticket inside the warm palm of her glove. He was standing with her in the cold, looking in through a grated window at a man making bottles in a roaring furnace. It was very cold. Her face, fragrant in the cold air, was quite close to his; and suddenly she called out to the man at the furnace:

—Is the fire hot, sir?

But the man could not hear her with the noise of the furnace. It was just as well. He might have answered rudely.

A wave of yet more tender joy escaped from his heart and went coursing in warm flood along his arteries. Like the tender fires of stars moments of their life together, that no one knew of or would ever know of, broke upon and illumined his memory. He longed to recall to her those moments, to make her forget the years of their dull existence together and remember only their moments of ecstasy. For the years, he felt, had not quenched his soul or hers. Their children, his writing, her household cares had not quenched all their souls' tender fire. In one letter that he had written to her then he had said: *Why is it that words like these seem to me so dull and cold? Is it because there is no word tender enough to be your name?*

Like distant music these words that he had written years before were borne towards him from the past. He longed to be alone with her. When the others had gone away, when he and she were in their room in the hotel, then they would be alone together. He would call her softly:

—Gretta!

Perhaps she would not hear at once: she would be undressing. Then something in his voice would strike her. She would turn and look at him.

At the corner of Winetavern Street they met a cab. He was glad of its rattling noise as it saved him from conversation. She was looking out of the window and seemed tired. The others spoke only a few words, pointing out some building or street. The horse galloped along wearily under the murky morning sky, dragging his old rattling box after his heels, and Gabriel was again in a cab with her, galloping to catch the boat, galloping to their honeymoon.

As the cab drove across O'Connell Bridge Miss O'Callaghan said:

—They say you never cross O'Connell Bridge without seeing a white horse.

—I see a white man this time, said Gabriel.

—Where? asked Mr. Bartell D'Arcy.

Gabriel pointed to the statue, on which lay patches of snow. Then he nodded familiarly to it and waved his hand.

—Good-night, Dan, he said gaily.

When the cab drew up before the hotel Gabriel jumped out and, in spite of Mr. Bartell D'Arcy's protest, paid the driver. He gave the man a shilling over his fare. The man saluted and said:

—A prosperous New Year to you, sir.

—The same to you, said Gabriel cordially.

She leaned for a moment on his arm in getting out of the cab and while standing at the curbstone, bidding the others good-night. She leaned lightly on his arm, as lightly as when she had danced with him a few hours before. He had felt proud and happy then, happy that she was his, proud of her grace and wifely carriage. But now, after the kindling again of so many memories, the first touch of her body, musical and strange and perfumed, sent through him a keen pang of lust. Under cover of her silence he pressed her arm closely to his side; and, as they stood at the hotel door, he felt that they had escaped from their lives and duties, escaped from home and friends and run away together with wild and radiant hearts to a new adventure.

An old man was dozing in a great hooded chair in the hall. He lit a candle in the office and went before them to the stairs. They followed him in silence, their feet falling in soft thuds on the thickly carpeted stairs. She mounted the stairs behind the porter, her head bowed in the ascent, her frail shoulders curved as with a burden, her skirt girt tightly about her. He could have flung his arms about her hips and held her still for his arms were trembling with desire to seize her and only the stress of his nails against the palms of his hands held the wild impulse of his body in check. The porter halted on the stairs to settle his guttering candle. They halted too on the steps below him. In the silence Gabriel could hear the falling of the molten wax into the tray and the thumping of his own heart against his ribs.

The porter led them along a corridor and opened a door. Then he set his unstable candle down on a toilet-table and asked at what hour they were to be called in the morning.

385   —Eight, said Gabriel.

The porter pointed to the tap of the electric-light and began a muttered apology but Gabriel cut him short.

—We don't want any light. We have light enough from the street. And I say, he added, pointing to the candle, you might remove that handsome article, like a good man.

The porter took up his candle again, but slowly for he was surprised by such a novel idea. Then he mumbled good-night and went out. Gabriel shot the lock to.

A ghostly light from the street lamp lay in a long shaft from one window to the door. Gabriel threw his overcoat and hat on a couch and crossed the room towards the window. He looked down into the street in order that his emotion might calm a little. Then he turned and leaned against a chest of drawers with his back to the light. She had taken off her hat and cloak and was standing before a large swinging mirror, unhooking her waist. Gabriel paused for a few moments, watching her, and then said:

390   —Gretta!

She turned away from the mirror slowly and walked along the shaft of light towards him. Her face looked so serious and weary that the words would not pass Gabriel's lips. No, it was not the moment yet.

—You looked tired, he said.

—I am a little, she answered.

—You don't feel ill or weak?

395   —No, tired: that's all.

She went on to the window and stood there, looking out. Gabriel waited again and then, fearing that diffidence was about to conquer him, he said abruptly:

—By the way, Gretta!

—What is it?

—You know that poor fellow Malins? he said quickly.

—Yes. What about him?   400

—Well, poor fellow, he's a decent sort of chap after all, continued Gabriel in a false voice. He gave me back that sovereign I lent him and I didn't expect it really. It's a pity he wouldn't keep away from that Browne, because he's not a bad fellow at heart.

He was trembling now with annoyance. Why did she seem so abstracted? He did not know how he could begin. Was she annoyed, too, about something? If she would only turn to him or come to him of her own accord! To take her as she was would be brutal. No, he must see some ardour in her eyes first. He longed to be master of her strange mood.

—When did you lend him the pound? she asked, after a pause.

Gabriel strove to restrain himself from breaking out into brutal language about the sottish Malins and his pound. He longed to cry to her from his soul, to crush her body against his, to overmaster her. But he said:

—O, at Christmas, when he opened that little Christmas-card shop in Henry Street.   405

He was in such a fever of rage and desire that he did not hear her come from the window. She stood before him for an instant, looking at him strangely. Then, suddenly raising herself on tiptoe and resting her hands lightly on his shoulders, she kissed him.

—You are a very generous person, Gabriel, she said.

Gabriel, trembling with delight at her sudden kiss and at the quaintness of her phrase, put his hands on her hair and began smoothing it back, scarcely touching it with his fingers. The washing had made it fine and brilliant. His heart was brimming over with happiness. Just when he was wishing for it she had come to him of her own accord. Perhaps her thoughts had been running with his. Perhaps she had felt the impetuous desire that was in him and then the yielding mood had come upon her. Now that she had fallen to him so easily he wondered why he had been so diffident.

He stood, holding her head between his hands. Then, slipping one arm swiftly about her body and drawing her towards him, he said softly:

—Gretta dear, what are you thinking about?   410

She did not answer nor yield wholly to his arm. He said again, softly:

—Tell me what it is, Gretta. I think I know what is the matter. Do I know?

She did not answer at once. Then she said in an outburst of tears:

—O, I am thinking about that song, *The Lass of Aughrim*.

She broke loose from him and ran to the bed and, throwing her arms across the   415
bed-rail, hid her face. Gabriel stood stock-still for a moment in astonishment and then followed her. As he passed in the way of the cheval-glass he caught sight of himself in full length, his broad, well-filled shirt-front, the face whose expression always puzzled him when he saw it in a mirror and his glimmering gilt-rimmed eye-glasses. He halted a few paces from her and said:

—What about the song? Why does that make you cry?

She raised her head from her arms and dried her eyes with the back of her hand like a child. A kinder note than he had intended went into his voice.

—Why, Gretta? he asked.

—I am thinking about a person long ago who used to sing that song.

—And who was the person long ago? asked Gabriel, smiling.   420

—It was a person I used to know in Galway when I was living with my grandmother, she said.

The smile passed away from Gabriel's face. A dull anger began to gather again at the back of his mind and the dull fires of his lust began to glow angrily in his veins.

—Someone you were in love with? he asked ironically.

—It was a young boy I used to know, she answered, named Michael Furey. He used to sing that song, *The Lass of Aughrim*. He was very delicate.

425 Gabriel was silent. He did not wish her to think that he was interested in this delicate boy.

—I can see him so plainly, she said after a moment. Such eyes as he had: big dark eyes! And such an expression in them—an expression!

—O then, you were in love with him? said Gabriel.

—I used to go out walking with him, she said, when I was in Galway.

A thought flew across Gabriel's mind.

430 —Perhaps that was why you wanted to go to Galway with that Ivors girl? he said coldly.

She looked at him and asked in surprise:

—What for?

Her eyes made Gabriel feel awkward. He shrugged his shoulders and said:

—How do I know? To see him perhaps.

435 She looked away from him along the shaft of light towards the window in silence.

—He is dead, she said at length. He died when he was only seventeen. Isn't it a terrible thing to die so young as that?

—What was he? asked Gabriel, still ironically.

—He was in the gasworks, she said.

Gabriel felt humiliated by the failure of his irony and by the evocation of this figure from the dead, a boy in the gasworks. While he had been full of memories of their secret life together, full of tenderness and joy and desire, she had been comparing him in her mind with another. A shameful consciousness of his own person assailed him. He saw himself as a ludicrous figure, acting as a pennyboy for his aunts, a nervous well-meaning sentimentalist, orating to vulgarians and idealising his own clownish lusts, the pitiable fatuous fellow he had caught a glimpse of in the mirror. Instinctively he turned his back more to the light lest she might see the shame that burned upon his forehead.

440 He tried to keep up his tone of cold interrogation but his voice when he spoke was humble and indifferent.

—I suppose you were in love with this Michael Furey, Gretta, he said.

—I was great with him at that time, she said.

Her voice was veiled and sad. Gabriel, feeling now how vain it would be to try to lead her whither he had purposed, caressed one of her hands and said, also sadly:

—And what did he die of so young, Gretta? Consumption, was it?

445 —I think he died for me, she answered.

A vague terror seized Gabriel at this answer as if, at that hour when he had hoped to triumph, some impalpable and vindictive being was coming against him, gathering forces against him in its vague world. But he shook himself free of it with an effort of reason and continued to caress her hand. He did not question her again for he felt that she would tell him of herself. Her hand was warm and moist: it did not respond to his touch but he continued to caress it just as he had caressed her first letter to him that spring morning.

—It was in the winter, she said, about the beginning of the winter when I was going to leave my grandmother's and come up here to the convent. And he was ill at the time in his lodgings in Galway and wouldn't be let out and his people in Oughterard were written to. He was in decline, they said, or something like that. I never knew rightly.

She paused for a moment and sighed.

—Poor fellow, she said. He was very fond of me and he was such a gentle boy. We used to go out together, walking, you know, Gabriel, like the way they do in the country. He was going to study singing only for his health. He had a very good voice, poor Michael Furey.

—Well; and then? asked Gabriel.

—And then when it came to the time for me to leave Galway and come up to the convent he was much worse and I wouldn't be let see him so I wrote a letter saying I was going up to Dublin and would be back in the summer and hoping he would be better then.

She paused for a moment to get her voice under control and then went on:

—Then the night before I left I was in my grandmother's house in Nun's Island, packing up, and I heard gravel thrown up against the window. The window was so wet I couldn't see so I ran downstairs as I was and slipped out the back into the garden and there was the poor fellow at the end of the garden, shivering.

—And did you not tell him to go back? asked Gabriel.

—I implored of him to go home at once and told him he would get his death in the rain. But he said he did not want to live. I can see his eyes as well as well! He was standing at the end of the wall where there was a tree.

—And did he go home? asked Gabriel.

—Yes, he went home. And when I was only a week in the convent he died and he was buried in Oughterard where his people came from. O, the day I heard that, that he was dead!

She stopped, choking with sobs, and, overcome by emotion, flung herself face downward on the bed, sobbing in the quilt. Gabriel held her hand for a moment longer, irresolutely, and then, shy of intruding on her grief, let it fall gently and walked quietly to the window.

She was fast asleep.

Gabriel, leaning on his elbow, looked for a few moments unresentfully on her tangled hair and half-open mouth, listening to her deep-drawn breath. So she had had that romance in her life: a man had died for her sake. It hardly pained him now to think how poor a part he, her husband, had played in her life. He watched her while she slept as though he and she had never lived together as man and wife. His curious eyes rested long upon her face and on her hair; and, as he thought of what she must have been then, in that time of her first girlish beauty, a strange friendly pity for her entered his soul. He did not like to say even to himself that her face was no longer beautiful but he knew that it was no longer the face for which Michael Furey had braved death.

Perhaps she had not told him all the story. His eyes moved to the chair over which she had thrown some of her clothes. A petticoat string dangled to the floor. One boot stood upright, its limp upper fallen down: the fellow of it lay upon its side. He wondered at his riot of emotions of an hour before. From what had it proceeded? From his aunt's supper, from his own foolish speech, from the wine and dancing, the merrymaking when saying good-night in the hall, the pleasure of the walk along the river in the snow. Poor Aunt Julia! She, too, would soon be a shade with the shade of Patrick Morkan and his horse. He had caught that haggard look upon her face for a moment when she was singing *Arrayed for the Bridal*. Soon, perhaps, he would be sitting in that same drawing-room, dressed in black, his silk hat on his knees. The blinds would be drawn down and Aunt Kate would be sitting beside him, crying and blowing her nose and telling him how Julia had died. He would cast about in his mind for some words that might console her, and would find only lame and useless ones. Yes, yes: that would happen very soon.

The air of the room chilled his shoulders. He stretched himself cautiously along under the sheets and lay down beside his wife. One by one they were all becoming shades. Better pass boldly into that other world, in the full glory of some passion, than fade and wither dismally with age. He thought of how she who lay beside him had locked in her heart for so many years that image of her lover's eyes when he had told her that he did not wish to live.

Generous tears filled Gabriel's eyes. He had never felt like that himself towards any woman but he knew that such a feeling must be love. The tears gathered more thickly in his eyes and in the partial darkness he imagined he saw the form of a young man standing under a dripping tree. Other forms were near. His soul had approached that region where dwell the vast hosts of the dead. He was conscious of, but could not apprehend, their wayward and flickering existence. His own identity was fading out into a grey impalpable world: the solid world itself which these dead had one time reared and lived in was dissolving and dwindling.

A few light taps upon the pane made him turn to the window. It had begun to snow again. He watched sleepily the flakes, silver and dark, falling obliquely against the lamplight. The time had come for him to set out on his journey westward. Yes, the newspapers were right: snow was general all over Ireland. It was falling on every part of the dark central plain, on the treeless hills, falling softly upon the Bog of Allen and, farther westward, softly falling into the dark mutinous Shannon waves. It was falling, too, upon every part of the lonely churchyard on the hill where Michael Furey lay buried. It lay thickly drifted on the crooked crosses and headstones, on the spears of the little gate, on the barren thorns. His soul swooned slowly as he heard the snow falling faintly through the universe and faintly falling, like the descent of their last end, upon all the living and the dead.   [1914]

QUESTIONS

1. What is the nature of the conflict between Gabriel and Gretta? Is the scene in the hotel room adequately foreshadowed?

2. What is the theme of the story? How do the many minor characters who attend the party contribute to the theme?

3. What does Gabriel's relationship with Miss Ivors reveal about him?

4. List some of the references to snow in the story. How do they enhance the theme?

5. What is the significance of the names "Lily" and "Gabriel"? Why is the story entitled "The Dead"?

6. How does the final paragraph recapitulate much that has occurred earlier in the story?

RESPONSES

1. Research the history of Ireland at the time period of this story. How do the political struggles of Ireland enter into this story?

2. "The Dead" is from Joyce's only volume of short stories. Research Joyce's artistic development. What was he trying to achieve in his short stories as he worked his way toward his novels? How are these efforts apparent in "The Dead?"

FOCUS ON FILM

1. Examine the various mis-en-scenes in John Huston's *The Dead*. Does the décor, clothing, color palette, etc. adequately portray the setting, characters, conflicts, and tone of the prose story?
2. Examine the scene near the end of the film in which Greta listens to the tenor singing. How does the scene evoke religious paintings? Is that portrayal consistent with the prose story?

FRANZ KAFKA

Franz Kafka (1883–1924) was born in Prague. Educated in the law, he did not practice but instead took a position in the civil service until poor health forced his retirement. He wrote steadily throughout his life but published very little. Fortunately, his friend and literary executor Max Brod ignored Kafka's injunction to burn his manuscripts and saw many of them through the press. Kafka's view of the world, in which anxious and isolated characters are buffeted and ultimately destroyed by an oddly distorted and alien world that is yet frighteningly like our own, has struck a responsive chord with many modern readers. Kafka's stories in English translation have been collected in *The Great Wall of China* (1933), *The Penal Colony* (1948), and *The Complete Stories* (1976).

A Country Doctor

I was in a most awkward predicament: I needed to leave at once on an urgent journey; a seriously ill patient was waiting for me in a village ten miles away; a heavy snowstorm filled the wide interval between him and me; I had a carriage, light, with large wheels, perfectly suited to our country roads; wrapped in my fur coat, my instrument bag in my hand, I was already standing in the yard ready to go; but I lacked a horse, a horse. The previous night my own horse had died as a result of overwork in this glacial winter; my maid was now running all over the village trying to borrow a horse; but it was hopeless, I knew, and with more and more snow piling up on me, becoming more and more immobile, I stood there aimlessly. The maid showed up at the gate alone, swinging her lantern; naturally, who would lend his horse for such a ride? I walked across the yard once again; I could see no possibility; distracted, tormented, I kicked at the ramshackle door of the pigpen, which hadn't been used for years. It opened and swung back and forth on its hinges. Warmth and a smell like that of horses came out of it. A murky stable lantern was swinging by a rope inside. A man, crouching in the low shed, showed his candid, blue-eyed face. "Shall I hitch up?" he asked, creeping out on all fours. I could think of nothing to say, and only stooped down to see what else was in the pen. The maid stood next to me. "People don't know what they've got available in their own house," she said, and we both laughed. "Hey there, Brother! Hey there, Sister!"

called the groom, and two horses, powerful animals with strong flanks, their legs drawn up tight to their bodies, lowering their well-formed heads like camels, slid out of the door one after the other solely by twisting their bodies to and fro, and occupied the doorway completely with not an inch to spare. But immediately they stood up on tall legs, their bodies steaming with dense vapor. "Help him," I said, and the willing maid ran to hand the groom the carriage harness. But the moment she has reached him, the groom embraces her and shoves his face against hers. She yells out and escapes over to me; two rows of teeth have left their red marks on the girl's cheek. "You beast," I shout furiously, "would you like to feel my whip?" But I instantly recall that he's a stranger, that I don't know where he has come from, and that he's volunteering to help me when all the rest are failing me. As if he knew my thoughts, he isn't vexed by my threat, but still busy with the horses, merely turns once to face me. "Get in," he then says, and truly: everything is in readiness. I observe that I have never before handled such a beautiful team, and I get in cheerfully. "I'll do the driving, you don't know the way," I say. "Sure," he says, "I'm not going along at all, I'm staying with Rosa." "No!" yells Rosa and with a true foreboding that her fate is inevitable, she runs into the house; I hear the door chain rattle as she draws it tight; I hear the lock snap shut; I watch as, in addition, she turns off all the lights, first in the vestibule and then racing through the rooms, so she won't be found. "You're coming along," I say to the groom, "or I'm giving up the trip, no matter how urgent it is. I have no wish to hand the maid over to you as fare for the ride." "Giddy-up!" he says and claps his hands; the carriage is swept away like a piece of wood in a current; I can still hear the door of my house cracking and splintering as the groom assaults it, then my eyes and ears are filled with a rustling wind that penetrates all my senses uniformly. But even that lasts only a moment, because, as if my patient's farmyard opened up directly in front of the gate of my own yard, I am already there; the horses are standing calmly; the snowfall has ended; moonlight all around; the parents of the patient rush out of the house; his sister after them; they practically lift me out of the carriage; I can't make out any of their confused talk; in the sickroom the air is barely breathable; the stove, which hadn't been tended to, is smoking. I intend to open the window; but first I want to see the patient. Then, with no fever, not cold, not warm, with expressionless eyes, without a shirt, the boy raises himself up under the feather bed, embraces my neck and whispers in my ear: "Doctor, let me die." I look around; no one has heard; his parents are standing in silence, bending forward in expectation of my medical opinion; the sister has brought a chair for my bag. I open the bag and look through my instruments; the boy continues to grope toward me from his bed in order to remind me of his request; I take hold of some tweezers, examine them in the candlelight and put them down again. "Yes," I think blasphemously, "in such cases, the gods come to your aid; they send the missing horse; because of the urgency, they add a second one; and in their bounty they then grant you the groom—" It is only then that I think of Rosa again; what am I to do, how can I rescue her, how can I pull her out from under that groom when I am ten miles away from her and unmanageable horses are harnessed to my carriage? Those horses, which somehow have now loosened the reins and in some unknown way have opened the windows from outside! Each one has thrust its head in through a window and, heedless of the family's outcry, is scrutinizing the patient. "I'll ride right back," I think, as if the horses are inviting me to go, but I allow the sister, who believes I am numb from the heat, to take off my fur coat. A glass of rum is prepared for me, the old man pats me on the shoulder; the surrender of this treasure of his justifies that familiarity. I shake my head; I would grow ill within the old man's circumscribed way of thinking; for that reason alone, I refuse the drink. The mother stands by the bed and entices me over; I obey and, while a horse neighs loudly at the ceiling, I place my head on the chest of the boy, who shivers at the touch of my wet beard. What I know is confirmed: the boy is healthy, with somewhat poor circulation, glutted with coffee by his anxious mother, but healthy, so that the best thing would be to shove him out of bed. But I'm not out to improve the world, and I let him lie there. I'm an employee of the district government and I do my duty to the hilt, to the point where it's almost too much. Though badly paid, I'm generous and helpful to the poor. I still must take care of Rosa, then the boy may be right and I, too, shall die. What am I doing here in this endless winter? My horse is dead, and there's no one in the village who'll lend me his. I have to find my team in the pigpen; if, by chance, they weren't horses, I'd have to drive with sows. That's the way it is. And I nod at the family. They know nothing about it, and if they knew, they wouldn't believe it. Writing prescriptions is easy, but, otherwise, communicating with people is hard. Well, this seems to be the end of my call here, once again I've been annoyed for nothing; I'm used to that, with the help of my night bell the whole district tortures me; but having to give up Rosa, too, this time, that beautiful girl who has lived in my house for years, and whom I scarcely noticed—that sacrifice is too great, and I must somehow square it temporarily in my own mind through sophistries if I'm not to make an all-out attack on this family, because, even with the best will in the world, they can't give me back Rosa. But as I am closing my bag and signaling to have my coat brought over, as the family stands there together, the father sniffing at the glass of rum in his hand, the mother, whom I have most likely disappointed—what do the people expect of me?—biting her lips tearfully, and the sister waving a blood-soaked towel, I am somehow ready to admit on certain conditions that the boy is perhaps ill after all. I go over to him, he smiles at me as I approach as if I were bringing him, say, the most invigorating soup—oh, now both horses are neighing; the noise, ordained by some lofty powers, is probably meant to facilitate my examination—and I find: yes, the boy is ill. On his right side, around the hip, a wound as large as the palm of one's hand has opened up. Pink, in many shades, dark as it gets deeper, becoming light at the edges, softly granular, with irregular accumulations of blood, wide open as the surface entrance to a mine. That's how it looks from some distance. But, close up, a complication can be seen, as well. Who can look at it without giving a low whistle? Worms as long and thick as my little finger, naturally rose-colored and in addition spattered with blood, firmly attached to the inside of the wound, with white heads and many legs, are writhing upward into the light. Poor boy, there's no hope for you. I have discovered your great wound; you will be destroyed by this flower on your side. The family is happy; it sees me active; the sister tells it to the mother, the mother to the father, the father to a few guests who are entering the open door through the moonlight on tiptoe, balancing with outstretched arms. "Will you save me?" the boy whispers with a sob, completely dazzled by the life in his wound. That's how the people are in my area. Always asking the doctor for the impossible. They've lost their old faith; the priests sits home and picks his vestments to pieces, one after another; but the doctor is supposed to accomplish everything with his gentle, surgical hands. Well, have it any way you like: I didn't offer my services; if you misuse me for religious purposes, I'll go along with that, too; what better can I ask for, an old country doctor, robbed of my maid! And they come, the family and the village elders, and they undress me; a school choir led by their teacher is standing in front of the house and singing an extremely simple setting of these words:

> Undress him, then he will cure,
> And if he doesn't cure, then kill him!
> It's only a doctor, it's only a doctor.

Then I'm undressed and, my fingers in my beard, I look at the people calmly with head bowed. I am completely composed and superior to them all, and remain so, too, even though it doesn't help me, because now they take me by the head and feet and carry me into the bed. They lay me against the wall, on the side where the wound is. Then they all leave the room; the door is closed; the singing dies away; clouds pass in front of the moon; the bedclothes lie warmly on top of me, the horses' heads in the window openings waver like shadows. "Do you know," I hear, spoken into my ear, "I don't have much confidence in *you*. You just drifted in here from somewhere, you didn't come on your own two feet. Instead of helping, you're just crowding me out of my deathbed. I'd like most of all to scratch your eyes out." "Right," I say, "it's a disgrace. But I'm a doctor, you see. What should I do? Believe me, it's not easy for me, either." "Am I supposed to be contented with that excuse? Oh, I guess I must, I'm always forced to be contented. I came into the world with a fine wound; that was my entire portion in life." "My young friend," I say, "your mistake is this: you don't have the big picture. I, who have already been in all sickrooms, far and wide, tell you: your wound isn't that bad. Brought on by two hatchet blows at an acute angle. Many people offer their sides and scarcely hear the hatchet in the forest, let alone having it come closer to them." "Is it really so, or are you fooling me in my fever?" "It's really so, take a government doctor's word of honor into the next world with you." And he took it, and fell silent. But now it was time to think about how to save myself. The horses still stood faithfully in their places. Clothing, fur coat and bag were quickly seized and bundled together; I didn't want to waste time getting dressed; if the horses made the same good time as on the way over, I would, so to speak, be jumping out of this bed into mine. Obediently a horse withdrew from the window; I threw the bundle into the carriage; the fur coat flew too far, it just barely caught on to a hook with one sleeve. Good enough. I leaped onto the horse. The reins loosely trailing along, one horse just barely attached to the other, the carriage meandering behind, the fur coat bringing up the rear in the snow. "Giddy-up, and look lively," I said, but the ride wasn't lively; as slowly as old men we proceeded across the snowy waste; for a long time there resounded behind us the new, but incorrect, song of the children:

> Rejoice, O patients,
> The doctor has been put in bed alongside you!

Traveling this way, I'll never arrive home; my flourishing practice is lost; a successor is robbing me, but it will do him no good, because he can't replace me; in my house the loathsome groom is rampaging; Rosa is his victim; I don't want to think of all the consequences. Naked, exposed to the frost of this most unhappy era, with an earthly carriage and unearthly horses, I, an old man, roam about aimlessly. My fur coat is hanging in back of the carriage, but I can't reach it, and no one among the sprightly rabble of my patients lifts a finger to help. Betrayed! Betrayed! Having obeyed the false ringing of the night bell just once—the mistake can never be rectified. [1919]

QUESTIONS

1. How is the story like a fairy tale? How is it not like one?
2. What is the tone of the story? How does Kafka create it? What other elements of fiction contribute to it?
3. Why is the doctor, who had hardly noticed Rose before this night, so concerned about her now?
4. How can one explain the doctor's missing the boy's wound on first inspection? And why does the boy, who has asked to die, now want to live?
5. What does the last line of the story mean?

RESPONSE

1. Compare this story to William Carlos Williams's "The Use of Force."

Franz Kafka

A Hunger Artist

During these last decades the interest in professional fasting has markedly diminished. It used to pay very well to stage such great performances under one's own management, but today that is quite impossible. We live in a different world now. At one time the whole town took a lively interest in the hunger artist; from day to day of his fast the excitement mounted; everybody wanted to see him at least once a day; there were people who bought season tickets for the last few days and sat from morning till night in front of his small barred cage; even in the nighttime there were visiting hours, when the whole effect was heightened by torch flares; on fine days the cage was set out in the open air, and then it was the children's special treat to see the hunger artist; for their elders he was often just a joke that happened to be in fashion, but the children stood open-mouthed, holding each other's hands for greater security, marveling at him as he sat there pallid in black tights, with his ribs sticking out so prominently, not even on a seat but down among straw on the ground, sometimes giving a courteous nod, answering questions with a constrained smile, or perhaps stretching an arm through the bars so that one might feel how thin it was, and then again withdrawing deep into himself, paying no attention to anyone or anything, not even to the all-important striking of the clock that was the only piece of furniture in his cage, but merely staring into vacancy with halfshut eyes, now and then taking a sip from a tiny glass of water to moisten his lips.

Besides casual onlookers there were also relays of permanent watchers selected by the public, usually butchers, strangely enough, and it was their task to watch the hunger artist day and night, three of them at a time, in case he should have some secret recourse to nourishment. This was nothing but a formality, instituted to reassure the masses, for the initiates knew well enough that during his fast the artist would never in any circumstances, not even under forcible compulsion, swallow the smallest morsel of food: the honor of his profession forbade it. Not every watcher, of course, was capable of understanding this, there were often groups of night watchers who were very lax in carrying out their duties and deliberately huddled together in a retired corner to play cards with great absorption, obviously intending to give the hunger artist the chance of a little refreshment, which they supposed he could draw from some private hoard. Nothing annoyed the artist more than such watchers; they made him miserable; they made his fast seem unendurable; sometimes he mastered his feebleness sufficiently to sing during their watch for as long as he could keep going, to show them how unjust their suspicions were. But that was of little use; they only wondered at his cleverness in being able to fill his mouth even while singing. Much more to his taste were the watchers who sat close up to the bars, who were not content with the dim night lighting of the hall but focused him in the full glare of the electric pocket torch given them by the impresario. The harsh light did not trouble him at all, in any case he could never sleep properly, and he could always drowse a little, whatever the light, at any hour, even when the hall was thronged with noisy onlookers. He was quite happy at the prospect of spending a sleepless night with such watchers; he was ready to exchange jokes with them, to tell them stories out of his nomadic life, anything at all to keep them awake and demonstrate to them again that he had no eatables in his cage and that he was fasting as not one of them could fast. But his happiest moment was when the morning came and an enormous breakfast was brought them, at his expense, on which they flung themselves with the keen appetite of healthy men after a weary night of wakefulness. Of course there were people who argued that this breakfast was an unfair attempt to bribe the watchers, but that was going rather too far, and when they were invited to take on a night's vigil without a breakfast, merely for the sake of the cause, they made themselves scarce, although they stuck stubbornly to their suspicions.

Such suspicions, anyhow, were a necessary accompaniment to the profession of fasting. No one could possibly watch the hunger artist continuously, day and night, and so no one could produce first-hand evidence that the fast had really been rigorous and continuous; only the artist himself could know that, he was therefore bound to be the sole completely satisfied spectator of his own fast. Yet for other reasons he was never satisfied; it was not perhaps mere fasting that had brought him to such skeleton thinness that many people had regretfully to keep away from his exhibitions, because the sight of him was too much for them, perhaps it was dissatisfaction with himself that had worn him down. For he alone knew, what no other initiate knew, how easy it was to fast. It was the easiest thing in the world. He made no secret of this, yet people did not believe him, at the best they set him down as modest, most of them, however, thought he was out for publicity or else was some kind of cheat who found it easy to fast because he had discovered a way of making it easy, and then had the impudence to admit the fact, more or less. He had to put up with all that, and in the course of time had got used to it, but his inner dissatisfaction always rankled, and never yet, after any term of fasting—this must be granted to his credit—had he left the cage of his own free will. The longest period of fasting was fixed by his impresario at forty days, beyond that term he was not allowed to go, not even in great cities, and there was good reason for it, too. Experience had proved that for about forty days the interest of the public could be stimulated by a steadily increasing pressure of advertisement, but after that the town began to lose interest, sympathetic support began notably to fall off; there were of course local variations as between one town and another or one country and another, but as a general rule forty days marked the limit. So on the fortieth day the flower-bedecked cage was opened, enthusiastic spectators filled the hall, a military band played, two doctors entered the cage to measure the results of the fast, which were announced through a megaphone, and finally two young ladies appeared, blissful at having been selected for the honor, to help the hunger artist down the few steps leading to a small table on which was spread a carefully chosen invalid repast. And at this very moment the artist always turned stubborn. True, he would entrust his bony arms to the outstretched helping hands of the ladies bending over him, but stand up he would not. Why stop fasting at this particular moment, after forty days of it? He had held out for a long time, an illimitably long time; why stop now, when he was in his best fasting form, or rather, not yet quite in his best fasting form? Why should he be cheated of the fame he would get for fasting longer, for being not only the record hunger artist of all time, which presumably he was already, but for beating his own record by a performance beyond human imagination, since he felt that there were no limits to his capacity for fasting? His public pretended to admire him so much, why should it have so little patience with him; if he could endure fasting longer, why shouldn't the public endure it? Besides, he was tired, he was comfortable sitting in the straw, and now he was supposed to lift himself to his full height and go down to a meal the very thought of which gave him a nausea that only the presence of the ladies kept him from betraying, and even that with an effort. And he looked up into the eyes of the ladies who were apparently so friendly and in reality so cruel, and shook his head, which felt too heavy on its strengthless neck. But then there happened yet again what always happened. The impresario came forward, without a word—for the band made speech impossible—lifted his arms in the air above the artist, as if inviting Heaven to look down upon its creature here in the straw, this suffering martyr, which indeed he was, although in quite another sense; grasped him round the emaciated waist, with exaggerated caution, so that the frail condition he was in might be appreciated; and committed him to the care of the blenching ladies, not without secretly giving him a shaking so that his legs and body tottered and swayed. The artist now submitted completely; his head lolled on his breast as if it had landed there by chance; his body was hollowed out; his legs in a spasm of self-preservation clung close to each other at the knees, yet scraped on the ground as if it were not really solid ground, as if they were only trying to find solid ground; and the whole weight of his body, a feather-weight after all, relapsed onto one of the ladies, who, looking round for help and panting a little—this post of honor was not at all what she had expected it to be—first stretched her neck as far as she could to keep her face at least free from contact with the artist, when finding this impossible, and her more fortunate companion not coming to her aid but merely holding extended on her own trembling hand the little bunch of knucklebones that was the artist's, to the great delight of the spectators burst into tears and had to be replaced by an attendant who had long been stationed in readiness. Then came the food, a little of which the impresario managed to get between the artist's lips, while he sat in a kind of half-fainting trance, to the accompaniment of cheerful patter designed to distract the public's attention from the artist's condition; after that, a toast was drunk to the public, supposedly prompted by a whisper from the artist in the impresario's ear; the band confirmed it with a mighty flourish, the spectators melted away, and no one had any cause to be dissatisfied with the proceedings, no one except the hunger artist himself, he only, as always.

So he lived for many years, with small regular intervals of recuperation, in visible glory, honored by the world, yet in spite of that troubled in spirit, and all the more troubled because no one would take his trouble seriously. What comfort could he possibly need? What more could he possibly wish for? And if some good-natured person, feeling sorry for him, tried to console him by pointing out that his melancholy was probably caused by fasting, it could happen, especially when he had been fasting for some time, that he reacted with an outburst of fury and to the general alarm began to shake the bars of his cage like a wild animal. Yet the impresario had a way of punishing these outbreaks which he rather enjoyed putting into operation. He would apologize publicly for the artist's behavior, which was only to be excused, he admitted, because of the irritability caused by fasting; a condition hardly to be understood by well-fed people; then by natural transition he went on to mention the artist's equally incomprehensible boast that he could fast for much longer than he was doing; he praised the high ambition, the good will, the great self-denial undoubtedly implicit in such a statement; and then quite simply countered it by bringing out photographs, which were also on sale to the public, showing the artist on the fortieth day of a fast lying in bed almost dead from exhaustion. This perversion of the truth, familiar to the artist though it was, always unnerved him afresh and proved too much for him. What was a consequence of the premature ending of his fast was here presented as the cause of it! To fight against this lack of understanding, against a whole world of nonunderstanding, was impossible. Time and again in good faith he stood by the bars listening to the impresario, but as soon as the photographs appeared he always let go and sank with a groan back on to his straw, and the reassured public could once more come close and gaze at him.

5   A few years later when the witnesses of such scenes called them to mind, they often failed to understand themselves at all. For meanwhile the aforementioned change in public interest had set in; it seemed to happen almost overnight; there may have been profound causes for it, but who was going to bother about that; at any rate the pampered hunger artist suddenly found himself deserted one fine day by the amusement seekers, who went streaming past him to other more favored attractions. For the last time the impresario hurried him over half of Europe to discover whether the old interest might still survive here and there; all in vain; everywhere, as if by secret agreement, a positive revulsion from professional fasting was in evidence. Of course it could not really have sprung up so suddenly as all that, and many premonitory symptoms which had not been sufficiently remarked or suppressed during the rush and glitter of success now came retrospectively to mind, but it was now too late to take any countermeasures. Fasting would surely come into fashion again at some future date, yet that was no comfort for those living in the present. What, then, was the hunger artist to do? He had been applauded by thousands in his time and could hardly come down to showing himself in a street booth at village fairs, and as for adopting another profession, he was not only too old for that but fanatically devoted to fasting. So he took leave of the impresario, his partner in an unparalleled career, and hired himself to a large circus; in order to spare his own feelings he avoided reading the conditions of his contract.

A large circus with its enormous traffic in replacing and recruiting men, animals and apparatus can always find a use for people at any time, even for a hunger artist, provided of course that he does not ask too much, and in this particular case anyhow it was not only the artist who was taken on but his famous and long-known name as well, indeed considering the peculiar nature of his performance, which was not impaired by advancing age, it could not be objected that here was an artist past his prime, no longer at the height of his professional skill, seeking a refuge in some quiet corner of a circus; on the contrary, the hunger artist averred that he could fast as well as ever, which was entirely credible, he even alleged that if he were allowed to fast as he liked, and this was at once promised him without more ado, he could astound the world by establishing a record never yet achieved, a statement which certainly provoked a smile among the other professionals, since it left out of account the change in public opinion, which the hunger artist in his zeal conveniently forgot.

He had not, however, actually lost his sense of the real situation and took it as a matter of course that he and his cage should be stationed, not in the middle of the ring as a main attraction, but outside, near the animal cages, on a site that was after all easily accessible. Large and gaily painted placards made a frame for the cage and announced what was to be seen inside it. When the public came thronging out in the intervals to see the animals, they could hardly avoid passing the hunger artist's cage and stopping there for a moment, perhaps they might even have stayed longer had not those pressing behind them in the narrow gangway, who did not understand why they should be held up on their way toward the excitements of the menagerie, made it impossible for anyone to stand gazing quietly for any length of time. And that was the reason why the hunger artist, who had of course been looking forward to these visiting hours as the main achievement of his life, began instead to shrink from them. At first he could hardly wait for the intervals; it was exhilarating to watch the crowds come streaming his way, until only too soon—not even the most obstinate self-deception, clung to almost consciously, could hold out against the fact—the conviction was borne in upon him that these people, most of them, to judge from their actions, again and again, without exception, were all on their way to the menagerie. And the first sight of them from the distance remained the best. For when they reached his cage he was at once deafened by the storm of shouting and abuse that arose from the two contending factions, which renewed themselves continuously, of those who wanted to stop and stare at him—he soon began to dislike them more than the others—not out of real interest but only out of obstinate self-assertiveness, and those who wanted to go straight on to the animals. When the first great rush was past, the stragglers came along, and these, whom nothing could have prevented from stopping to look at him as long as they had breath, raced past with long strides, hardly even glancing at him, in their haste to get to the menagerie in time. And all too rarely did it happen that he had a stroke of luck, when some father of a family fetched up before him with his children, pointed a finger at the hunger artist and explained at length what the phenomenon meant, telling stories of earlier years when he himself had watched similar but much more thrilling performances, and the children, still rather uncomprehending, since neither inside nor outside school had they been sufficiently prepared for this lesson—what did they care about fasting?—yet showed by the brightness of their intent eyes that new and better times might be coming. Perhaps, said the hunger artist to himself many a time, things would be a little better if his cage were set not quite so near the menagerie. That made it too easy for people to make their choice, to say nothing of what he suffered from the stench of the menagerie, the animals' restlessness by night, the carrying past of raw lumps of flesh for the beasts of prey, the roaring at feeding times, which depressed him continually. But he did not dare to lodge a complaint with the management; after all, he had the animals to thank for the troops of people who passed his cage, among whom there might always be one here and there to take an interest in him, and who could tell where they might seclude him if he called attention to his existence and thereby to the fact that, strictly speaking, he was only an impediment on the way to the menagerie.

A small impediment, to be sure, one that grew steadily less. People grew familiar with the strange idea that they could be expected, in times like these, to take an interest in a hunger artist, and with this familiarity the verdict went out against him. He might fast as much as he could, and he did so; but nothing could save him now, people passed him by. Just try to explain to anyone the art of fasting! Anyone who has no feeling for it cannot be made to understand it. The fine placards grew dirty and illegible, they were torn down; the little notice board telling the number of fast days achieved, which at first was changed carefully every day, had long stayed at the same figure, for after the first few weeks even this small task seemed pointless to the staff; and so the artist simply fasted on and on, as he had once dreamed of doing, and it was no trouble to him, just as he had always foretold, but no one counted the days, no one, not even the artist himself, knew what records he was already breaking, and his heart grew heavy. And when once in a time some leisurely passer-by stopped, made merry over the old figure on the board and spoke of swindling, that was in its way the stupidest lie ever invented by indifference and inborn malice, since it was not the hunger artist who was cheating; he was working honestly, but the world was cheating him of his reward.

Many more days went by, however, and that too came to an end. An overseer's eye fell on the cage one day and he asked the attendants why this perfectly good cage should be left standing there unused with dirty straw inside it; nobody knew, until one man, helped out by the notice board, remembered about the hunger artist. The poked into the straw with sticks and found him in it. "Are you still fasting?" asked the overseer. "When on earth do you mean to stop?" "Forgive me, everybody," whispered the hunger artist; only the overseer, who had his ear to the bars, understood him. "Of course," said the overseer, and tapped his forehead with a finger to let the attendants know what state the man was in, "we forgive you." "I always wanted you to admire my fasting," said the hunger artist. "We do admire it," said the overseer, affably. "But you shouldn't admire it," said the hunger artist. "Well, then we don't admire it," said the overseer, "but why shouldn't we admire it?" "Because I have to fast, I can't help it," said the hunger artist. "What a fellow you are," said the overseer, "and why can't you help it?" "Because," said the hunger artist, lifting his head a little and speaking, with his lips pursed, as if for a kiss, right into the overseer's ear, so that no syllable might be lost, "because I couldn't find the food I liked. If I had found it, believe me, I should have made no fuss and stuffed myself like you or anyone else." These were his last words, but in his dimming eyes remained the firm though no longer proud persuasion that he was still continuing to fast.

10   "Well, clear this out now!" said the overseer, and they buried the hunger artist, straw and all. Into the cage they put a young panther. Even the most insensitive felt it refreshing to see this wild creature leaping around the cage that had so long been dreary. The panther was all right. The food he liked was brought him without hesitation by the attendants; he seemed not even to miss his freedom; his noble body, furnished almost to the bursting point with all that it needed, seemed to carry freedom around with it too; somewhere in his jaws it seemed to lurk; and the joy of life streamed with such ardent passion from his throat that for the onlookers it was not easy to stand the shock of it. But they braced themselves, crowded round the cage, and did not want ever to move away.   [1924]

QUESTIONS

1. What associations does the word *fasting* have for you? Are they relevant to the story?
2. Why is the exact setting of the story left purposely vague?
3. What is the central conflict? Is the ambiguity of the title a key to the nature of the conflict?
4. In what sense is the protagonist an artist? How is he defined by his relationship to the impresario?
5. What does the story say about the relation of the artist to society? To himself?

RESPONSES

1. Research Kafka's life and write an essay that illustrates how "A Hunger Artist" illustrates or does not illustrate Kafka's experiences as a writer.
2. From an ecocritical perspective, how does our treatment of wild creatures mirror our treatment of wild elements in human nature? How is this idea explored in "A Hunger Artist"?

Franz Kafka

The Metamorphosis

I

When Gregor Samsa awoke from troubled dreams one morning, he found that he had been transformed in his bed into an enormous bug. He lay on his back, which was hard as armor, and, when he lifted his head a little, he saw his belly—rounded, brown, partitioned by archlike ridges—on top of which the blanket, ready to slip off altogether, was just barely perched. His numerous legs, pitifully thin in comparison to the rest of his girth, flickered helplessly before his eyes.

"What's happened to me?" he thought. It was no dream. His room, a real room meant for human habitation, though a little too small, lay peacefully within its four familiar walls. Above the table, on which an unpacked sampling of fabric swatches was strewn—Samsa was a traveling salesman—hung the picture that he had recently cut out of an illustrated magazine and had placed in a pretty gilt frame. It depicted a lady who, decked out in a fur hat and a fur boa, sat upright, raising toward the viewer a heavy fur muff in which her whole forearm was encased.

Gregor's gaze then turned toward the window, and the dismal weather—you could hear raindrops beating against the window gutter—made him quite melancholy. "What if I went back to sleep for another while and forgot all this foolishness?" he thought; but that was totally out of the question, because he was used to sleeping on his right side, and in his present state he couldn't get into that position. No matter how energetically he threw himself onto his right side, each time he rocked back into the supine position. He must have tried a hundred times, closing his eyes to avoid seeing his squirming legs, not stopping until he began to feel a slight, dull pain in his side that he had never felt before.

"My God," he thought, "what a strenuous profession I've chosen! Traveling day in and day out. The turmoil of business is much greater than in the home office, and on top of that I'm subjected to this torment of traveling, to the worries about train connections, the bad meals at irregular hours, an intercourse with people that constantly changes, never lasts, never becomes cordial. The devil take it all!" He felt a slight itch up on his belly; slowly shoved himself on his back closer to the bedpost, so he could lift his head better, found the itchy place, which was all covered with little white spots that he was unable to diagnose; and wanted to feel the area with one leg, but drew it back immediately, because when he touched it he was invaded by chills.

He slid back into his former position. "Getting up early like this," he thought, "makes you totally idiotic. People must have their sleep. Other traveling salesmen live like harem women. For instance, when during the course of the morning I go back to the hotel to copy out the orders I've received, those fine gentlemen are just having their breakfast. I should try that with my boss; I'd be fired on the spot. Anyway, who knows whether that wouldn't be a good thing for me after all. If I didn't hold myself back because of my parents, I would have quit long ago; I would have walked right up to the boss and let my heart out to him. He would surely have fallen off his desk! That's a peculiar habit of his, too, sitting on his desk and talking down to his employees from up above; and, besides, they have to step way up close because the boss is so hard of hearing. Now, I haven't given up all hope yet; once I have the money together to pay off my parents' debt to him—that should still take five or six years—I'll definitely go through with it. Then I'll make the big break. At the moment, of course, I've got to get up, because my train leaves at five."

And he glanced over toward his alarm clock, which was ticking on the wardrobe. "Father in Heaven!" he thought. It was half past six, and the hands were moving ahead peacefully; in fact, it was later than half past, it was almost a quarter to seven. Could the alarm have failed to ring? From the bed he could see that it was correctly set for four; surely, it had also rung. Yes, but was it possible to sleep peacefully through that furniture-shaking ring? Well, he hadn't slept peacefully, but probably all the more soundly for that. Yet, what should he do now? The next train left at seven; to catch it he would have had to make a mad dash, his sample case wasn't packed yet, and he himself definitely didn't feel particularly fresh and lively. And even if he caught the train, he couldn't escape a bawling out from his boss, because the office messenger had waited at the five-o'clock train and had long since made a report about his negligence. He was a creature of the boss's, spineless and stupid. Now, what if he reported in sick? But that would be extremely distressing and suspicious, because during his five years' employment Gregor had not been ill even once. The boss would surely arrive with the health-insurance doctor, would complain to his parents about their lazy son and would cut short all objections by referring them to the health-insurance doctor, in whose eyes the only people that exist at all are perfectly healthy specimens who are work-shy. And besides, would he be so wrong in this case? Actually, aside from a truly excessive drowsiness after all that sleep, Gregor felt quite well and in fact was particularly hungry.

While he was considering all this in the greatest haste, still unable to decide whether to get out of bed—the clock was just striking six forty-five—there was a cautious knock on the door at the head of his bed. "Gregor," a voice called—it was his mother—"it's six forty-five. Didn't you intend to make a trip?" That gentle voice! Gregor was frightened when he heard his own answering voice, which, to be sure, was unmistakably his accustomed one, but in which there now appeared, as if rising from below, an irrepressible, painful peeping sound, so that his words retained their clarity only at the very outset but became distorted as they faded away, so that you couldn't tell if you had heard them correctly. Gregor had meant to give a detailed answer and explain everything, but under the circumstances he merely said: "Yes, yes; thanks, Mother; I'm getting up now." Because the door was made of wood, the alteration in Gregor's voice was probably not noticeable, since his mother was pacified by that explanation and shuffled away. But as a result of that brief conversation the other members of the family had become aware that, contrary to expectation, Gregor was still at home; and his father was soon knocking at one of the side doors, softly, but with his fist. "Gregor, Gregor," he called, "what's going on?" And before very long he admonished him again, in a deeper voice: "Gregor! Gregor!" But at the other side door his sister was quietly lamenting: "Gregor? Aren't you well? Do you need anything?" Gregor answered in both directions: "Be right there!" He made an effort, by enunciating most carefully and by inserting long pauses between the individual words, to free his voice of anything out of the ordinary. His father then returned to his breakfast, but his sister whispered: "Gregor, open up, I beg you." But Gregor had not the slightest intention of opening the door; in fact, he was now glad he had formed the cautious habit, an offshoot of his business trips, of locking all his doors at night even at home.

First he wanted to get up in peace and unmolested, get dressed and, especially, have breakfast, and only afterwards give the matter further thought, because, as he now realized, in bed he would never arrive at any sensible conclusion to his musings. He recalled that, often in the past, while in bed, he had felt some slight pain or other, perhaps caused by lying in an awkward position, and that, when he got out of bed, the pain had proved to be purely imaginary; and he was eager to find out how his impressions of that morning would gradually be dispelled. That the alteration in his voice was nothing more than the harbinger of a nasty cold, a professional hazard of traveling salesmen, he had not the slightest doubt.

To throw off the blanket was quite easy; all he needed to do was puff himself up a little and it fell down by itself. But after that things became difficult, especially since he was so unusually wide. He would normally have used his arms and hands to hoist himself up; but instead of them he now had only the numerous little legs, which were uninterruptedly moving in the most confused way and which, in addition, he couldn't control. Whenever he intended to bend one of them, at first he extended it; and when he finally succeeded in executing his wishes with that particular leg, all of the others meanwhile would thrash about as if they were completely independent, in an extreme, painful agitation. "But I can't stay in bed doing nothing," Gregor said to himself.

10   First he wanted to leave the bed with the lower part of his body, but this lower part, which, by the way, he hadn't seen yet and of which he couldn't form any clear idea, either, proved to be too difficult to move around; the procedure was so slow; and when finally, having grown almost wild, he gathered all his strength and pushed forward heedlessly, he went in the wrong direction and collided violently with the lower bedpost. The burning pain that he felt taught him that it was precisely the lower part of his body that was perhaps the most sensitive at the moment.

Therefore, he tried to get the upper part of his body out of bed first, and carefully turned his head toward the edge of the bed. He managed to do this easily and, despite its width and weight, finally the bulk of his body slowly followed in the direction his head had turned. But when at last he had moved his head into the open space outside the bed, he became afraid of continuing to edge forward in this manner, because if he finally let himself fall like that, it would take a real miracle to keep his head from being injured. And now of all times he must take every precaution not to lose consciousness; rather than that, he would stay in bed.

But when once again, heaving a sigh after similar efforts, he lay there just as before, and once again saw his little legs battling one another even more pitifully, if that were possible—when he could find no possibility of bringing calm and order into that arbitrary turmoil—he told himself again that he couldn't possibly stay in bed, and that the most sensible thing was to make every sacrifice if there existed even the smallest hope of thereby freeing himself from bed. But at the same time he didn't forget to remind himself occasionally that the calmest possible reflection is far preferable to desperate decisions. At such moments he would direct his eyes as fixedly as possible toward the window, but unfortunately there was not much confidence or cheer to be derived from the sight of the morning fog, which even shrouded the other side of the narrow street. "Seven o'clock already," he said to himself as the clock struck again, "seven o'clock already and still such a fog." And for a little while he lay there calmly, breathing very gently, as if perhaps expecting the total silence to restore him to his real, understandable condition.

But then he said to himself: "Before it strikes seven fifteen, I just have to be all the way out of bed. Besides, by that time someone from the firm will come to ask about me, because the office opens before seven o'clock." And now he prepared to rock his entire body out of bed at its full length in a uniform movement. If he let himself fall out of bed in this manner, he expected that his head, which he intended to lift up high during the fall, would receive no injury. His back seemed to be hard; when falling onto the carpet, surely nothing would happen to it. His greatest fear was the thought of the loud crash which must certainly result, and which would probably cause, if not a scare, then at least concern on the other side of all the doors. But that risk had to be taken.

When Gregor was already projecting halfway out of bed—this new method was more of a game than a hard task, all he needed to do was keep on rocking back and forth in short spurts—it occurred to him how simple everything would be if someone came to help him. Two strong people—he thought of his father and the maid—would have completely sufficed; they would only have had to shove their arms under his rounded back, extract him from bed that way like a nut from its shell, stoop down under his bulk and then merely wait cautiously until he had swung himself entirely over on the floor, where hopefully his little legs would find their use. Now, completely apart from the fact that the doors were locked, should he really have called for help? Despite all his tribulations, he was unable to suppress a smile at that thought.

He had now proceeded so far that, when rocking more vigorously, he could barely still maintain his equilibrium, and would very soon have to reach a definitive decision, because in five minutes it would be seven fifteen—when there was a ring at the apartment door. "That's somebody from the firm," he said to himself and nearly became rigid, while his little legs danced all the more quickly. For a moment everything remained quiet. "They aren't opening," Gregor said to himself, enmeshed in some unreasoning hope. But then, naturally, just as always, the maid went to the door with a firm tread and opened it. Gregor needed only to hear the visitor's first words of greeting and he already knew who it was—the chief clerk himself. Why was only Gregor condemned to work for a firm where people immediately conceived the greatest suspicions at the smallest sign of negligence? Were all employees simply scoundrels, was there among them not one loyal, devoted person who, even though he had merely failed to utilize a couple of morning hours on behalf of the firm, had become crazed by pangs of conscience, to the point of being incapable of getting out of bed? Wouldn't it really have been enough to send an apprentice to ask—if all this questioning was necessary at all—did the chief clerk himself have to come, thereby indicating to the entire innocent family that the investigation into this suspicious incident could only be entrusted to the intelligence of the chief clerk? And, more as a result of the irritation that

15

these reflections caused Gregor, than as a result of a proper decision, he swung himself out of bed with all his might. There was a loud thump, but it wasn't a real crash. The fall was deadened somewhat by the carpet, and in addition Gregor's back was more resilient than he had thought, so that the muffled sound wasn't so noticeable. But he hadn't held his head carefully enough and had bumped it; he turned it and rubbed it against the carpet in vexation and pain.

"Something fell in there," said the chief clerk in the room on the left side. Gregor tried to imagine whether the chief clerk might not some day have an experience similar to his of today: the possibility really had to be conceded. But, as if in brutal response to this question, the chief clerk now took a few determined steps in the adjoining room, which made his patent-leather boots squeak. From the room on the right side Gregor's sister whispered, to inform him: "Gregor, the chief clerk is here." "I know," said Gregor to himself, but he didn't dare to raise his voice so loud that his sister could hear him.

"Gregor," his father now said from the room on the left side, "the chief clerk has come and is inquiring why you didn't leave by the early train. We don't know what to tell him. Besides, he wants to talk with you personally. So please open the door. He will surely be kind enough to forgive the disorder in your room." "Good morning, Mr. Samsa," the chief clerk meanwhile called, in a friendly tone. "He isn't well," Gregor's mother said to the chief clerk while his father was still talking at the door, "he isn't well, believe me, sir. How otherwise would Gregor miss a train! The boy has no head for anything but the business. I'm almost upset, as it is, that he never goes out at night; he's been in town for eight days this time, but has stayed at home every night. He sits with us at the table and reads the paper quietly or studies timetables. It's already a distraction for him when he busies himself with fretsaw work. So, for example, during two or three evenings he carved a small frame; you'll be amazed how pretty it is; it's hanging in his room; you'll see it right away when Gregor opens up. Besides, I'm glad you're here, sir; on our own we couldn't have persuaded Gregor to open the door; he's so obstinate; and I'm sure he's not feeling well, even though he denied it earlier this morning." "I'll be right there," said Gregor slowly and deliberately, but not making a move, so as to lose not a word of the conversation. "I, too, my dear lady, can think of no other explanation," said the chief clerk; "I hope it's nothing serious. Although I am also bound to state that we business people—unfortunately or fortunately, according to how you look at it—very often simply have to overcome a slight indisposition out of regard for the business." "Well, can the gentleman go in to see you now?" asked the impatient father, and knocked on the door again. "No," said Gregor. In the room on the left side a painful silence ensued, in the room on the right side the sister began to sob.

Why didn't the sister go and join the others? She had probably just gotten out of bed and hadn't even begun dressing. And why was she crying? Because he didn't get up and let the chief clerk in? Because he was in danger of losing his job, and because then his boss would once more dun their parents for his old claims? For the time being those were needless worries, after all. Gregor was still here and hadn't the slightest thought of abandoning his family. At the moment he was lying there on the carpet, and no one acquainted with his current state could seriously have asked him to let in the chief clerk. But, after all, Gregor couldn't really be discharged at once on account of this slight discourtesy, for which a suitable excuse would easily be found later on. And it seemed to Gregor that it would be much more sensible to leave him in peace for now instead of disturbing him with tears and exhortations. But it was precisely all the uncertainty that was oppressing the others and that excused their behavior.

"Mr. Samsa," the chief clerk now called in a louder voice, "what's going on? You're barricading yourself in your room, giving just 'yes' and 'no' answers, causing your parents big, needless worries and—to mention this just incidentally—neglecting your business duties in a truly unheard-of fashion. I am speaking here in the name of your parents and of your employer, and I am asking you quite seriously for an immediate, lucid explanation. I'm amazed, I'm amazed. I thought I knew you for a calm, sensible person, and now suddenly you apparently want to begin making an exhibition of peculiar caprices. To be sure, early this morning our employer, when speaking to me, hinted at a possible explanation for your negligence—it concerned the cash receipts that were recently entrusted to you—but, honestly, I all but gave him my word of honor that that explanation couldn't be the true one. Now, however, I see your incomprehensible stubbornness here and I am losing all willingness to say a good word for you in the slightest way. Nor is your position by any means the most solid. I originally had the intention of telling you all this between ourselves, but since you are making me waste my time here pointlessly, I don't know why your parents shouldn't hear it, too. Well, then, your performance recently has been most unsatisfactory; true, this isn't the season for doing especially good business, we acknowledge that; but a season for doing no business at all just doesn't exist, Mr. Samsa, it can't be allowed to exist." "But, sir," Gregor called out in distraction, forgetting everything else in his excitement, "I'm going to open the door immediately, this minute. A slight indisposition, a dizzy spell, has prevented me from getting up. I'm still lying in bed. But now I feel quite lively again. I am just now climbing out of bed. Be patient for just another moment! I'm not quite as well yet as I thought. But I now feel all right. The things that can affect a person! Just last evening I felt perfectly fine, my parents know that; or it might be better to say that even last evening I had a little advance indication. People should have noticed it from the way I looked. Why didn't I report it at the office?! But you always think that you'll be able to fight off an illness without having to stay home. Sir! Spare my parents! There is no basis for all the complaints you're now making against me; and no one has said a word to me about them. Perhaps you haven't read the last orders I sent in. Besides, I'll still make the trip on the eight-o'clock train, the couple of hours of rest have strengthened me. Don't waste your time here, sir; I'll be at the office myself in no time, and please be good enough to tell them that and give my best wishes to our employer!"

And while Gregor was pouring all of this out hastily, scarcely knowing what he was saying, he had approached the wardrobe without difficulty, probably because of the practice he had already had in bed, and was now trying to draw himself up against it. He wanted actually to open the door, actually to show himself and speak with the chief clerk; he was eager to learn what the others, who were now so desirous of his presence, would say when they saw him. If they got frightened, then Gregor would have no further responsibility and could be calm. But if they accepted everything calmly, then he, too, would have no cause to be upset, and, if he hurried, he could really be at the station at eight o'clock. At first, now, he slid back down the smooth wardrobe several times, but finally, giving himself one last thrust, he stood there upright; he paid no more attention to the pains in his abdomen, severe as they were. Now he let himself fall against the backrest of a nearby chair and held tight to its edges with his little legs. By doing so, moreover, he had also gained control over himself and he fell silent, because now he could listen to the chief clerk.

"Did you understand even a single word?" the chief clerk was asking his parents; "he isn't trying to make a fool of us, is he?" "God forbid," called his mother, who was weeping by this time, "he may be seriously ill, and we're torturing him. Grete! Grete!"

20

she then shouted. "Mother?" called his sister from the other side. They were communicating across Gregor's room. "You must go to the doctor's at once. Gregor is sick. Fetch the doctor fast. Did you hear Gregor speaking just now?" "That was an animal's voice," said the chief clerk, noticeably quietly in contrast to the mother's shouting. "Anna! Anna!" called the father through the hallway into the kitchen, clapping his hands, "get a locksmith right away!" And already the two girls were running down the hallway with rustling skirts—how had his sister gotten dressed so quickly?—and tore open the apartment door. There was no sound of the door closing; they had most likely left it open, as is the case in apartments where a great misfortune has occurred.

But Gregor had become much calmer. To be sure, he now realized that his speech was no longer intelligible, even though it had seemed clear enough to him, clearer than before, perhaps because his ears were getting used to it. But anyway they were now believing that there was something wrong with him and they were ready to help him. The confidence and security with which the first measures had been taken, comforted him. He felt that he was once more drawn into the circle of humanity and hoped for magnificent and surprising achievements on the part of both, the doctor and the locksmith, without really differentiating much between them. In order to restore his voice to its maximum clarity for the imminent decisive discussions, he cleared it a little by coughing, but took care to do this in very muffled tones, since possibly even that noise might sound different from human coughing, and he no longer trusted himself to make the distinction. Meanwhile it had become completely quiet in the adjoining room. Perhaps his parents were sitting at the table with the chief clerk and whispering quietly, perhaps they were all leaning against the door and listening.

Gregor shoved himself slowly to the door, using the chair; once there, he let it go and threw himself against the door, holding himself upright against it—the balls of his little feet contained some sticky substance—and rested there from his exertions for the space of a minute. But then he prepared to turn the key in the lock with his mouth. Unfortunately it seemed that he had no real teeth—what was he to grasp the key with?—but, instead, his jaws were actually pretty strong; with their help he did really get the key to move, paying no heed to the fact that he doubtless was doing himself some injury, because a brown fluid issued from his mouth, ran down over the key and dripped onto the floor. "Listen there," said the chief clerk in the adjoining room, "he's turning the key." That was a great encouragement for Gregor; but all of them should have called out to him, even his father and mother; "Go to it, Gregor!" they should have called, "keep at it, work on that lock!" And, imagining that they were all following his efforts in suspense, he bit recklessly into the key with all the strength he could muster. He danced around the lock, now here, now there, following the progress of the key as it turned; now he was keeping himself upright solely with his mouth, and, as the need arose, he either hung from the key or pushed it down again with the full weight of his body. The sharper sound of the lock, as it finally snapped back, woke Gregor up completely. With a sigh of relief he said to himself: "So then, I didn't need the locksmith," and he placed his head on the handle, in order to open the door all the way.

Since he had to open the door in this manner, he was still out of sight after it was already fairly wide open. First he had to turn his body slowly around one leaf of the double door, and very carefully at that, if he didn't want to fall squarely on his back right before entering the room. He was still occupied by that difficult maneuver and had no time to pay attention to anything else, when he heard the chief clerk utter a loud "Oh!"—it sounded like the wind howling—and now he saw him as well. He had been the closest to the door; now, pressing his hand against his open mouth, he stepped slowly backward as if driven away by some invisible force operating with uniform pressure. Gregor's mother—despite the presence of the chief clerk, she stood there with her hair still undone from the previous night and piled in a high, ruffled mass—first looked at his father with folded hands, then took two steps toward Gregor and collapsed in the midst of her petticoats, which billowed out all around her, her face completely lost to view and sunk on her chest. His father clenched his fist with a hostile expression, as if intending to push Gregor back into his room; then he looked around the parlor in uncertainty, shaded his eyes with his hands and wept so hard that it shook his powerful chest.

Gregor now refrained from entering the room; he stayed inside, leaning on the leaf of the door that was firmly latched, so that all that could be seen was half of his body and, above it, his head tilted to the side, with which he peered toward the others. Meanwhile it had become much brighter outside; clearly visible on the other side of the street was a section of the building situated opposite from them, endless, grayblack—it was a hospital—with its regularly placed windows harshly piercing its facade; the rain was still falling, but only in large drops that were individually visible and were literally flung down upon the ground one by one. An excessive number of breakfast dishes and utensils stood on the table, because for Gregor's father breakfast was the most important meal of the day and he would stretch it out for hours while reading a number of newspapers. On the wall precisely opposite hung a photograph of Gregor that dated from his military service, showing him as a lieutenant, hand on sword, with a carefree smile, demanding respect for his bearing and his uniform. The door to the hallway was open and, since the apartment door was open, too, there was a clear view all the way out onto the landing and the beginning of the downward staircase.

"Now," said Gregor, who was perfectly conscious of being the only one who had remained calm, "I'll get dressed right away, pack the sample case and catch the train. Is it all right, is it all right with you if I make the trip? Now, sir, you see that I'm not stubborn and I am glad to do my job; traveling is a nuisance, but without the traveling I couldn't live. Where are you off to, sir? To the office? Yes? Will you make an honest report of everything? There's a moment now and then when a man is incapable of working, but that's precisely the right moment to recall his past performance and to consider that, later on, when the obstacle is cleared away, he will surely work all the more diligently and with greater concentration. I am so deeply obligated to our employer, you know that very well. Besides, I have my parents and sister to worry about. I'm in a jam, but I'll work my way out of it. But don't make it harder for me than it already is. Speak up for me in the firm! A traveling salesman isn't well liked, I know. People think he makes a fortune and lives in clover. They have no particular reason to reflect on it and get over that prejudice. But you, sir, you have a better overview of the true state of affairs than the rest of the staff; in fact, speaking in all confidence, a better overview than our employer himself, who, in his role as entrepreneur, can easily be led to misjudge one of his employees. You are also well aware that a traveling salesman, who is away from the home office almost all year long, can thus easily fall victim to gossip, contingencies and groundless complaints that he's completely unable to defend himself against because he generally hears nothing about them; or else he finds out only when he has just come back from a trip, all worn out, and gets to feel the bad results at home, personally, when it's too late even to fathom the reasons for them. Sir, don't go away without saying a word to me that shows me that you agree with me even a little bit!"

But at Gregor's first words the chief clerk had already turned away, and only looked back at Gregor over his jerking shoulder, his lips pouting. And during Gregor's speech he didn't stand still for a minute, but, never losing sight of Gregor, retreated toward the door, very gradually, as if under a secret prohibition against leaving the room. By now he was in the hallway, and, from the abrupt movement with which he finally withdrew his foot from the parlor, anyone might think he had just burnt the sole of it. But in the hallway he stretched out his right hand as far as it could go in the direction of the stairway, as if a truly superterrestrial deliverance were awaiting him there.

Gregor realized that it simply wouldn't do to let the chief clerk depart in that frame of mind, or else his position in the firm would be seriously endangered. His parents didn't understand things like that so well: in all those long years they had gained the conviction that Gregor was set up for life in this firm, and, besides, they were now so preoccupied by the troubles of the moment that they had lost track of all foresight. But Gregor possessed that foresight. The chief clerk must be retained, pacified, persuaded and finally won over; after all, the future of Gregor and his family depended on it! If only his sister were here! She was clever; she had already started to cry while Gregor was still lying calmly on his back. And surely the chief clerk, who was an admirer of women, would have let her manage him; she would have closed the parlor door and talked him out of his fears in the hallway. But his sister *wasn't* there, Gregor had to act on his own behalf. And without stopping to think that he was still completely unfamiliar with his own present powers of locomotion, without stopping to think that once again his oration had possibly—in fact, probably—not been understood, he let go of the leaf of the door; shoved himself through the opening; tried to reach the chief clerk, who was already clutching the railing on the landing with both hands in a ridiculous manner; but immediately, while seeking a support, fell down onto his numerous legs with a brief cry. Scarcely had that occurred when, for the first time that morning, he felt a sense of bodily comfort; his little legs had solid ground below them; they obeyed perfectly, as he noticed to his joy; in fact, they were eager to carry him wherever he wanted to go; and he now believed that a definitive cure for all his sorrow was immediately due. But at that very instant, rocking back and forth as he contained his forward propulsion for a moment, he had come very close to his mother, directly opposite her on the floor. Suddenly she leaped up into the air, even though she had seemed so totally lost to the world; she stretched out her arms wide, spread her fingers and shouted: "Help, for the love of God, help!" She kept her head lowered as if she wanted to get a better look at Gregor, but in contradiction to that, she ran backwards recklessly. Forgetting that the laid table was behind her, when she reached it she hastily sat down on it, as if absentminded, and seemed not to notice that alongside her the coffee was pouring onto the carpet in a thick stream out of the big overturned pot.

"Mother, Mother," Gregor said softly, looking up at her. For a moment he had completely forgotten about the chief clerk; on the other hand, seeing the flowing coffee, he couldn't resist snapping at the air with his jaws a few times. This made his mother scream again, dash away from the table and fall into the arms of his father, who hastened to receive her. But now Gregor had no time for his parents; the chief clerk was already on the staircase; his chin on the railing, he was still looking back for a last time. Gregor spurted forward, to be as sure as possible of catching up with him; the chief clerk must have had some foreboding, because he made a jump down several steps and disappeared; but he was still shouting "Aaaah!"—the sound filled the whole stairwell. Unfortunately this flight of the chief clerk now also seemed to confuse Gregor's father, who up to that point had been relatively composed: instead of running after the chief clerk himself or at least not obstructing Gregor in *his* pursuit, with his right hand he seized the chief clerk's walking stick, which the latter had left behind on a chair along with his hat and overcoat; with his left hand he gathered up a big newspaper from the table and, stamping his feet, began to drive Gregor back into his room by brandishing the walking stick and the paper. No plea of Gregor's helped; in fact, no plea was understood; no matter how humbly he turned his head, his father only stamped his feet harder. On the other side of the room his mother had torn open a window despite the cool weather, and, leaning out, was pressing her face into her hands far beyond the window frame. Between the street and the stairwell a strong draught was created, the window curtains flew up, the newspapers on the table rustled and a few sheets blew across the floor. Implacably the father urged him back, uttering hisses like a savage. Gregor, however, had no practice in walking backwards, and, to tell the truth, it was very slow going for him. If Gregor had only been able to turn around, he would have been back in his room right away, but he was afraid of making his father impatient by such a time-consuming turn, and at every moment he was threatened by a fatal blow on the back or head from the stick in his father's hand. But finally Gregor had no other choice, because he observed with horror that, when walking backwards, he wasn't even able to keep in one direction; and so, with uninterrupted, anguished sidewise glances at his father, he began to turn around as quickly as he could, but nevertheless very slowly. Perhaps his father noticed his good will, because he didn't disturb him in this procedure but from time to time even conducted the rotary movement from a distance with the tip of his stick. If only his father had stopped that unbearable hissing! It made Gregor lose his head altogether. He was almost completely turned around when, constantly on the alert for that hissing, he made a mistake and turned himself back again a little. But when at last he had happily brought his head around to the opening in the doorway, it turned out that his body was too wide to get through without further difficulty. Naturally, in his present mood it didn't even remotely occur to his father to open the other leaf of the door in order to create an adequate passageway for Gregor. His idée fixe was merely that Gregor was to get into his room as quickly as possible. Nor would he ever have allowed the circumstantial preparations that were necessary for Gregor to hoist himself upright and perhaps get through the door in that way. Instead, as if there were no obstacle, he was now driving Gregor forward and making a lot of noise about it; what Gregor now heard behind him was no longer anything like the voice of merely one father; it was really no longer a joking matter, and Gregor squeezed into the doorway, no matter what the consequences. One side of his body lifted itself up; he was lying obliquely in the opening; one of his sides was completely abraded; ugly stains were left on the white door; now he was stuck tight and wouldn't have been able to stir from the spot; on one side his little legs were hanging up in the air and trembling, those on the other side were painfully crushed on the ground—then his father gave him a strong push from behind that was a truly liberating one, and, bleeding profusely, he sailed far into his room. Next, the door was slammed shut with the stick, then all was finally quiet.

II

It was only at twilight that Gregor awoke from his deep, swoonlike sleep. He would surely have awakened not much later even if there had been no disturbance, because he felt sufficiently rested and refreshed by sleep, but it seemed to him as if he had been aroused by a hasty footfall and a cautious locking of the door that led to the hallway. The light of the electric street lamps lay pallidly here and there on the ceiling and on

30

the upper parts of the furniture, but down where Gregor was, it was dark. Slowly, still feeling his way clumsily with his antennae, which he was just now beginning to appreciate, he heaved himself over to the door to see what had happened there. His left side seemed to be one long scar, with an unpleasant tightness to it, and he actually had to limp on his two rows of legs. In addition, one leg had been severely damaged during the morning's events—it was a almost a miracle that only one had been damaged—and now dragged after him lifelessly.

It was only when he had reached the door that he noticed what had really lured him there; it was the aroma of something edible. For a basin stood there, filled with milk in which little slices of white bread were floating. He could almost have laughed for joy, because he was even hungrier than in the morning, and immediately he plunged his head into the milk almost over his eyes. But soon he pulled it out again in disappointment; it was not only that eating caused him difficulties because of his tender left side—and he could eat only when his whole body participated, puffing away—on top of that, he didn't at all like the milk, which was formerly his favorite beverage and which therefore had surely been placed there by his sister for that very reason; in fact, he turned away from the basin almost with repugnance and crept back to the center of the room.

In the parlor, as Gregor saw through the crack in the door, the gas was lit, but, whereas usually at that time of day his father was accustomed to read his afternoon paper to his mother, and sometimes his sister, in a loud voice, now there was not a sound to be heard. Maybe that practice of reading aloud, which his sister always told and wrote him about, had fallen out of use recently. But it was so quiet all around, too, even though the apartment was surely not empty. "What a quiet life the family leads," Gregor said to himself, and while he stared ahead into the darkness, he felt very proud of himself for having been able to provide his parents and sister with a life like that, in such a beautiful apartment. But what if now all the peace, all the prosperity, all the contentment were to come to a fearful end? In order not to give way to such thoughts, Gregor preferred to start moving, and he crawled back and forth in the room.

Once during the long evening one of the side doors, and once the other one, was opened a tiny crack and swiftly shut again; someone had probably needed to come in but was too disinclined to do so. Now Gregor came to a halt directly in front of the parlor door, determined to bring in the hesitant visitor in some way or another, or else at least find out who it was; but the door wasn't opened again and Gregor waited in vain. That morning, when the doors were locked, they had all wanted to come into his room; now, after he had himself opened one door and the others had obviously been opened during the day, no one came any longer, and, in addition, the keys were now on the outside.

It wasn't until late at night that the light in the parlor was turned off, and now it was easy to ascertain that his parents and sister had been up all that time, because, as could clearly be heard, all three now stole away on tiptoe. Surely no one would come into Gregor's room any more before morning, and so he had plenty of time in which to think without disturbance about how he should now reorganize his life. But the high, open room, in which he was compelled to lie flat on the floor, filled him with anguish, although he couldn't discover the reason for it, because, after all, it was the room he had occupied for five years—and, making a semiconscious turn, not without a slight feeling of shame, he dashed under the couch, where, even though his back was a little squeezed and he could no longer lift his head, he immediately felt quite comfortable, only regretting that his body was too wide to fit under the couch completely.

There he remained the whole night, which he spent partly in a half-slumber, from 35 which he was startled awake time and again by hunger, and partly in worries and ill-defined hopes, all of which led to the conclusion that for the time being he had to stay calm and, by exercising patience and being as considerate as possible to his family, make bearable the unpleasantness that he was absolutely compelled to cause them in his present condition.

By the early morning, when the night had barely passed, Gregor had the opportunity to test the strength of his newly made resolutions, because his sister, almost fully dressed, opened the door from the hallway side and looked in uneasily. She didn't catch sight of him at once, but when she noticed him under the couch—God, he had to be somewhere, he couldn't have flown away—she received such a fright that, unable to control herself, she slammed the door again from outside. But, as if regretting her behavior, she immediately opened the door again and walked in on tiptoe as if she were visiting a seriously ill person or even a stranger. Gregor had moved his head out almost to the edge of the couch, and was observing her. Would she notice that he had left the milk standing, and by no means because he wasn't hungry, and would she bring some other food that suited him better? If she didn't do so of her own accord, he would rather starve to death than call it to her attention, even though in reality he had a tremendous urge to shoot out from under the couch, throw himself at his sister's feet and ask her for something good to eat. But his sister immediately noticed with surprise that the basin was still full, and that only a little milk had been spilled out of it all around; she picked it up at once, not with her bare hands, of course, but with a rag, and carried it out. Gregor was extremely curious to see what she would bring to replace it, and the most varied things came to mind. But he could never have guessed what his sister in her kindness actually did. In order to test his likings, she brought him a big selection, all spread out on an old newspaper. There were old, half-rotten vegetables; bones from their supper, coated with a white gravy that had solidified; a few raisins and almonds; a cheese that two days earlier Gregor would have considered inedible; a dry slice of bread, a slice of bread and butter, and a slice of salted bread and butter. In addition she set down the basin that had probably been designated permanently for Gregor; she had now poured water into it. And from a feeling of delicacy, since she knew Gregor wouldn't eat in her presence, she withdrew hastily and even turned the key in the lock so that Gregor would see he could make himself as comfortable as he wished. Gregor's little legs whirred as he now moved toward the food. Moreover, his wounds must have completely healed by this time; he felt no more hindrance. He was amazed at that, remembering how, more than a month earlier, he had cut his finger slightly with a knife and how that cut had still hurt him considerably even the day before yesterday. "Am I less sensitive now?" he thought, and was already greedily sucking on the cheese, which had attracted him immediately and imperatively more than any of the other foods. Quickly, one after the other, tears of contentment coming to his eyes, he devoured the cheese, the vegetables and the gravy; on the other hand, he didn't like the fresh food, he couldn't even endure its smell, and he went so far as to drag away to a little distance the things he wanted to eat. He was long finished with everything and was just lying lazily on the same spot when, as a sign that he should withdraw, his sister slowly turned the key. That startled him at once, even though he was almost drowsing by that time, and he hastened back under the couch. But it took enormous self-control to stay under the couch for even the brief time his sister was in the room, because the hearty meal had swelled his body to some extent, and he could hardly breathe in that cramped space. In between brief bouts of asphyxia, with slightly protruding eyes he watched his unsuspecting sister sweep together with a broom not only the leftovers of what he had eaten, but even the foods Gregor hadn't touched at all, as if those too were no longer usable; and he saw how she hastily dropped everything into a bucket, which she closed with a wooden cover, and then carried everything out. She had scarcely turned around when Gregor moved out from under the couch, stretched and let himself expand.

In this manner Gregor received his food every day, once in the morning, while his parents and the maid were still asleep, and the second time after everyone's midday meal, because then his parents took a short nap and the maid was sent away by his sister on some errand. Surely *they* didn't want Gregor to starve, either, but perhaps they couldn't have endured the experience of his eating habits except through hearsay; perhaps his sister also wanted to spare them one more sorrow, though possibly only a small one, because they were really suffering enough as it was.

Gregor couldn't find out what excuses had been used on that first morning to get the doctor and the locksmith out of the apartment again, because the others, even his sister, not understanding him, had no idea that *he* could understand *them*; and so, when his sister was in his room, he had to content himself with hearing her occasional sighs and invocations of the saints. Only later, when they had gotten used to it all to some degree—naturally, their ever getting used to it altogether was out of the question—Gregor sometimes seized on a remark that was meant to be friendly or could be so interpreted. "He really liked it today," she said when Gregor had stowed away his food heartily, whereas, when the opposite was the case, which gradually occurred more and more frequently, she used to say almost sadly: "This time he didn't touch anything again."

But even though Gregor couldn't learn any news directly, he overheard many things from the adjoining rooms, and whenever the sound of voices reached him, he would immediately run to the appropriate door and press his whole body against it. Especially in the early days there was no conversation that didn't deal with him in some way, if only in secret. At every mealtime for two days he could hear discussions about how they should now behave; but between meals, as well, they spoke on the same subject, because there were at least two family members at home at any given time, since no one apparently wanted to stay home alone and yet the apartment could in no case be deserted altogether. Besides, on the very first day the servant—it was not quite clear what or how much she knew of the incident—had asked Gregor's mother on her knees to discharge her at once, and when she said good-bye fifteen minutes later, she thanked them tearfully for letting her go, as if that were the greatest benefit they could confer upon her, and, without being asked to do so, swore a fearsome oath that she would never reveal the slightest thing to anyone.

40   Now Gregor's sister had to join their mother in doing the cooking; of course that didn't entail much effort because they ate practically nothing. Time and again Gregor heard them fruitlessly urge one another to eat, receiving no other answer than "Thanks, I've had enough" or the like. Maybe they didn't drink anything, either. Often his sister asked their father whether he wanted any beer, and offered lovingly to fetch it herself; then, as the father remained silent, she said, to overcome any reservations he might have, that she could also send the janitor's wife for it, but finally the father would utter a decided "No" and the matter was discussed no further.

Even in the course of the first day the father already laid their entire financial situation and prospects before both the mother and the sister. From time to time he got up from the table and took some document or some memorandum book out of his small

Wertheim° safe, which he had held onto even after the collapse of his business five years earlier. He could be heard opening the complicated lock and closing it again after removing what he had been looking for. In part, these declarations by his father were the first heartening things Gregor had heard since his captivity. He had believed that his father had nothing at all left from that business—at least, his father had never told him anything to the contrary—and naturally Gregor hadn't asked him about it. Gregor's concern at the time had been to do everything in his power to make his family forget as quickly as possible the commercial disaster that had reduced them all to complete hopelessness. And so, at that time he had begun to work with extreme enthusiasm and almost overnight had changed from a junior clerk into a traveling salesman; as such, he naturally had many more possibilities of earning money, and his successful efforts were immediately transformed into cash in the form of commissions, cash that could be plunked down on the table at home before the eyes of his amazed and delighted family. Those had been good times and had never been repeated later, at least not so gloriously, even though Gregor subsequently earned so much money that he was enabled to shoulder the expenses of the entire family, and did so. They had grown used to it, the family as well as Gregor; they accepted the money gratefully, he handed it over gladly, but no particularly warm feelings were generated any longer. Only his sister had still remained close to Gregor all the same, and it was his secret plan—because, unlike Gregor, she dearly loved music and could play the violin soulfully—to send her to the conservatory the following year, regardless of the great expenses which that had to entail, and which would have to be made up for in some other way. Often during Gregor's brief sojourns in the city the conservatory was referred to in his conversations with his sister, but always merely as a lovely dream, which couldn't possibly come true, and their parents disliked hearing even those innocent references; but Gregor was planning it most resolutely and intended to make a formal announcement on Christmas Eve.

Thoughts like those, completely pointless in his present state, occupied his mind while he stood upright there, pasting his legs to the door and listening. Sometimes, out of total weariness, he could no longer listen and let his head knock carelessly against the door, but immediately held it firm again, because even the slight noise he had caused by doing so had been heard in the next room and had made everyone fall silent. "How he keeps carrying on!" his father would say after a pause, obviously looking toward the door, and only then was the interrupted conversation gradually resumed.

Because his father used to repeat himself frequently in his explanations—partly because he hadn't concerned himself with these things for some time, partly also because the mother didn't understand it all the first time—Gregor had full opportunity to ascertain that, despite all their misfortune, a sum of money, of course very small, was still left over from the old days and had grown somewhat in the interim, since the interest had never been touched. And, besides that, the money Gregor had brought home every month—he had kept only a few *gulden* for himself—had not been completely used up and amounted to a small capital. Gregor, behind his door, nodded vigorously, delighted by this unexpected foresight and thrift. To tell the truth, with that surplus money he could have further reduced his father's debt to his boss, and the day when he could get rid of that job would have been much closer, but now it was without a doubt better the way his father had arranged it.

°Wertheim: An Austrian brand of safe widely used by businessmen at the time.—TRANSLATOR.

Now, this money was by no means sufficient for the family even to think of living off the interest; it might suffice to maintain the family for one or, at the most, two years, no more than that. It was thus merely a sum that should really not be drawn upon, but only kept in reserve for an emergency; money to live on had to be earned. Now, the father was a healthy man, to be sure, but old; he hadn't done any work for five years and in any case couldn't be expected to overexert himself; in those five years, which represented his first free time in a laborious though unsuccessful life, he had put on a lot of fat and had thus become pretty slow-moving. And was Gregor's old mother perhaps supposed to earn money now, a victim of asthma, for whom an excursion across the apartment was already cause for strain, and who spent every other day on the sofa by the open window gasping for breath? And was his sister supposed to earn money, at seventeen still a child whom one could hardly begrudge the way she had always lived up to now: dressing nicely, sleeping late, helping out in the house, enjoying a few modest amusements and, most of all, playing the violin? Whenever the conversation led to this necessity of earning money, Gregor would always first let go of the door and then throw himself onto the cool leather sofa located next to the door, because he was hot all over with shame and sorrow.

45   Often he would lie there all through the long nights, not sleeping for a minute but only scratching on the leather for hours on end. At other times he didn't spare the exertion of shoving a chair over to the window; he would then crawl up the ledge and, supporting himself against the chair, lean against the window, obviously only through some sort of recollection of the liberating feeling he always used to experience when looking out the window. Because, in reality, with each passing day his view of things at only a slight distance was becoming increasingly blurry; the hospital opposite, the all-too-frequent sight of which he used to curse, he now could no longer see at all, and if he hadn't been perfectly well aware that he lived on the tranquil but thoroughly urban Charlottenstrasse, he might have thought that what he saw from his window was a featureless solitude, in which the gray sky and the gray earth blended inseparably. His attentive sister had only needed to notice twice that the chair was standing by the window, and now, each time she had finished cleaning up the room, she shoved the chair right back to the window, and from that time on even left the inner casement open.

If Gregor had only been able to speak with his sister and thank her for all she had to do for him, he would have endured her services more easily; but, as it was, they made him suffer. Of course, his sister tried to soften the painfulness of the situation as much as possible, and as more and more time went by, she was naturally more successful at it, but with time Gregor, too, made a much keener analysis of everything. Her very entrance was terrible for him. The moment she walked in, without taking the time to close the door, even though she was otherwise most careful to spare everyone the sight of Gregor's room, she ran straight to the window and tore it open hastily, as if she were almost suffocating, and then remained a while at the window breathing deeply, no matter how cold it was. She frightened Gregor twice a day with that running and noise; during the whole time, he trembled under the couch, even though he knew perfectly well that she would surely have spared him that gladly if she had been at all capable of staying in a room containing Gregor with the window closed.

Once—probably a month had already elapsed since Gregor's transformation, and his sister should no longer have had any particular reason to be surprised at Gregor's appearance—she came a little earlier than usual and encountered Gregor while he was still looking out the window, motionless and posed there like some hideous scarecrow. It wouldn't have surprised Gregor if she hadn't stepped in, since by his location he was preventing her from opening the window at once; but not only did she not step in, she even jumped back and closed the door; a stranger might even have thought that Gregor had been lying in wait for her, intending to bite her. Naturally, Gregor immediately hid under the couch, but he had to wait until noon before his sister returned, and she seemed much more restless than usual. From this he realized that the sight of him was still unbearable for her and would surely remain unbearable for her in the future, and that she probably had to exercise terrific self-control not to run away at the sight of even the small portion of his body that protruded below the couch. To spare her even that sight, one day—he needed four hours for this task—he carried the bedsheet on his back over to the couch and draped it in such a way that he was now completely covered and his sister couldn't see him even when she bent down. If that sheet, in her opinion, hadn't been necessary, she could have removed it, because it was clear enough that it was no pleasure for Gregor to close himself off so completely; but she left the sheet where it was, and Gregor believed he caught a grateful look when he once cautiously raised the sheet a little with his head to see how his sister reacted to the new arrangement.

In the first two weeks his parents couldn't muster the courage to come into his room, and he often heard them expressing complete satisfaction with the work his sister was now doing, whereas up to that time they had frequently been vexed with his sister because she had seemed a rather good-for-nothing girl to them. But often now, both of them, the father and the mother, waited in front of Gregor's room while his sister was cleaning up in there, and the moment she came out she had to report in detail on how the room looked, what Gregor had eaten, how he had behaved this time, and whether a slight improvement could perhaps be noticed. As it was, the mother wanted to visit Gregor relatively early on, but at first the father and the sister held her back with sensible reasons, which Gregor listened to most attentively, and which he fully concurred with. Later, however, she had to be restrained forcefully, and when she then called: "Let me in to Gregor; after all, he's my poor son! Don't you understand I must go to him?," Gregor thought it might be a good thing after all if his mother came in, not every day of course, but perhaps once a week; after all, she understood everything much better than his sister, who, despite all her spunk, was still only a child and, in the final analysis, had perhaps undertaken such a difficult task only out of childish thoughtlessness.

Gregor's wish to see his mother was soon fulfilled. During the day Gregor didn't want to show himself at the window, if only out of consideration for his parents, but he also couldn't crawl very much on the few square yards of the floor; even at night he found it difficult to lie still. Soon he no longer derived the slightest pleasure from eating, either, and so for amusement he acquired the habit of crawling in all directions across the walls and ceiling. He especially enjoyed hanging up on the ceiling; it was quite different from lying on the floor; one could breathe more easily; a mild vibration passed through his body; and in the almost happy forgetfulness that Gregor experienced up there, it sometimes happened that to his own surprise he let go and crashed onto the floor. But now he naturally had much greater control over his body than before and even such a great fall did him no harm. Now, his sister immediately noticed this new diversion that Gregor had discovered for himself—even when crawling he left behind traces of his sticky substance here and there—and then she got the notion of enabling Gregor to crawl around as freely as possible, by removing the furniture that prevented this, especially the wardrobe and the desk. But she was unable to do this on her own; she didn't dare ask her father to help; the servant surely wouldn't have helped her, because even though this girl of about sixteen was sticking it out bravely since the previous cook had been discharged, she had nevertheless requested permission to keep the kitchen locked at all times and to open it only when specially called; thus the sister had no other choice than to fetch her mother while the father was away one day. And the mother approached with exclamations of excitement and joy, but fell silent at the door to Gregor's room. Naturally, the sister looked in first to see if everything in the room was in order; only then did she allow the mother to enter. Gregor had in extreme haste pulled the sheet even lower down, making more folds in it; the whole thing really looked like a sheet that had been thrown over the couch merely by chance. Also, this time Gregor refrained from peering out from under the sheet; he gave up the opportunity of seeing his mother this first time, in his happiness that she had finally come. "Come on, you can't see him," said the sister, and obviously she was leading the mother by the hand. Gregor now heard how the two weak women moved the old wardrobe, heavy as it was, from its place, and how the sister constantly undertook the greater part of the work, paying no heed to the warnings of the mother, who feared she would overexert herself. It took a very long time. After about a quarter-hour's work the mother said it would be better to leave the wardrobe where it was, because, for one thing, it was too heavy, they wouldn't get through before the father arrived, and, with the wardrobe in the middle of the room, they would leave Gregor no open path; and, secondly, it was not at all certain that Gregor would be pleased by the removal of the furniture. She thought the opposite was the case; the sight of the bare wall actually made her heart ache; and why shouldn't Gregor, too, feel the same way, since after all he was long accustomed to the furniture in his room and would thus feel isolated in the empty room? "And, besides, doesn't it seem," the mother concluded very quietly— throughout her speech she had been almost whispering, as if she wanted to keep Gregor, whose exact whereabouts she didn't know, from hearing even the sound of her voice (she was convinced he didn't understand the words)—"and doesn't it seem as if, by removing the furniture, we were showing that we have given up all hope for an improvement and were inconsiderately leaving him to his own resources? I think it would be best if we tried to keep the room in exactly the same condition as before, so that when Gregor comes back to us again, he'll find everything unchanged and it will be easier for him to forget what happened in between."

50   On hearing these words of his mother's, Gregor realized that the lack of all direct human communication, together with the monotonous life in the midst of the family, must have confused his mind in the course of these two months, because he couldn't explain to himself otherwise how he could seriously have wished for his room to be emptied out. Did he really want to have the warm room, comfortably furnished with heirloom pieces, transformed into a cave, in which he would, of course, be able to crawl about freely in all directions, but at the cost of simultaneously forgetting his human past, quickly and totally? Even now he was close to forgetting it, and only his mother's voice, which he hadn't heard for some time, had awakened him to the fact. Nothing must be removed, everything must stay; he couldn't do without the beneficent effects of the furniture on his well-being, and if the furniture prevented him from going on with that mindless crawling around, that was no disadvantage, but a great asset.

Unfortunately, however, his sister was of a different opinion; not without some justification, true, she had grown accustomed to play herself up to her parents as a special expert whenever matters affecting Gregor were discussed; and so now, too, the mother's advice was cause enough for the sister to insist on the removal of not only the wardrobe and the desk, which were all she had thought of at first, but all the furniture, except for the indispensable couch. Naturally, it was not only childish defiance and the self-confidence she had recently acquired so unexpectedly and with such great efforts, that determined her to make this demand; she had also made the real observation that Gregor needed a lot of space to crawl in, while on the other hand he didn't use the furniture in the least, from all one could see. But perhaps a further element was the romantic spirit of girls of her age, which seeks for satisfaction on every occasion, and by which Grete now let herself be tempted to make Gregor's situation even more frightful, so that she could do even more for him than hitherto—because nobody except Grete would ever dare to enter a space in which Gregor on his own dominated the bare walls.

And so she wouldn't let herself be dissuaded by her mother, who seemed unsure of herself, as well, in that room, out of sheer nervousness, and who soon fell silent, helping the sister move out the wardrobe with all her might. Now, in an emergency Gregor could still do without the wardrobe, but the desk—that had to stay. And no sooner had the women left the room with the wardrobe, which they were pushing while emitting groans, than Gregor thrust out his head from under the couch to see how he could intervene cautiously and with the greatest possible consideration for them. But, as bad luck would have it, it was his mother who came back first, while Grete in the adjoining room had her arms around the wardrobe and was swinging it back and forth unaided, naturally without being able to move it from the spot. But the mother wasn't used to the sight of Gregor, which might make her sick, so in a panic Gregor hastened backwards up to the other end of the couch but could no longer prevent the sheet from stirring a little in front. That was enough to attract his mother's attention. She stopped in her tracks, stood still a moment and then went back to Grete.

Although Gregor told himself over and over that nothing unusual was going on, just a few pieces of furniture being moved around, he soon had to admit to himself that this walking to and fro by the women, their brief calls to each other and the scraping of the furniture on the floor affected him like a tremendous uproar, sustained on all sides; and, no matter how tightly he pulled in his head and legs and pressed his body all the way to the floor, he was irresistibly compelled to tell himself that he wouldn't be able to endure all of this very long. They were emptying out his room, taking away from him everything he was fond of; they had already carried out the wardrobe, which contained his fretsaw and other tools; now they were prying loose the desk, which had long been firmly entrenched in the floor, and at which he had done his homework when he was in business college, in secondary school and even back in primary school. At this point, he really had no more time for testing the good intentions of the two women, whose existence he had almost forgotten, anyway, because in their state of exhaustion they were now working in silence, and only their heavy footfalls could be heard.

And so he broke out—at the moment, the women were leaning on the desk in the adjoining room, to catch their breath a little—he changed direction four times, not really knowing what he should rescue first; and then he saw hanging conspicuously on the now otherwise bare wall the picture of the lady dressed in nothing but furs. He crawled up to it in haste and pressed against the glass, which held him fast and felt good on his hot belly. That picture, at least, which Gregor was now completely covering, surely no one would now take away. He twisted his head around toward the door of the parlor in order to observe the women when they returned.

They hadn't allowed themselves much time to rest, and were now coming back; Grete had put her arm around her mother and was almost carrying her. "Well, what should we take now?" said Grete and looked around. Then her eyes met those of Gregor on the wall. It was probably only because her mother was there that she kept her

55

composure; she lowered her face to her mother to keep her from looking around, and said, although tremblingly and without thinking: "Come, shouldn't we rather go back into the parlor for another minute?" Grete's intention was clear to Gregor; she wanted to lead her mother to safety and then chase him down off the wall. Well, just let her try! He sat there on his picture and wouldn't relinquish it. He would sooner jump onto Grete's face.

But Grete's words had been just what it took to upset her mother, who stepped to one side, caught sight of the gigantic brown spot on the flowered wallpaper, and, before she was actually aware that what she saw there was Gregor, called in a hoarse shout: "Oh, God, oh, God!" She then fell across the couch with outspread arms, as if giving up everything, and lay there perfectly still. "Just wait, Gregor!" called the sister with raised fist and piercing glances. Those were the first words she had addressed to him directly since the transformation. She ran into the adjoining room to fetch some medicine to revive her mother from her faint; Gregor wanted to help, too—there was still time to rescue the picture—but he was stuck tight to the glass and had to tear himself loose by force. Then he, too, ran into the adjoining room, as if he could give his sister some advice, as in the past; but he was forced to stand behind her idly. While she was rummaging among various little bottles, she got a fright when she turned around; a bottle fell on the floor and broke; a splinter wounded Gregor in the face, and some kind of corrosive medicine poured over him. Now, without waiting there any longer, Grete picked up as many bottles as she could hold and ran in to her mother with them, slamming the door shut with her foot. Gregor was now cut off from his mother, who was perhaps close to death, all on his account. He didn't dare open the door for fear of driving away his sister, who had to remain with their mother. Now there was nothing for him to do but wait; and oppressed by self-reproaches and worry, he began to crawl; he crawled all over everything, walls, furniture and ceiling, and finally, in his desperation, when the whole room was starting to spin around him, he fell onto the middle of the big table.

A brief while passed, Gregor lay there limply, it was quiet all around; maybe that was a good sign. Then the bell rang. Naturally, the servant was locked in her kitchen, and so Grete had to go open up. Her father had arrived. "What's happened?" were his first words; Grete's appearance had probably revealed everything to him. Grete answered in a muffled voice, probably pressing her face against her father's chest: "Mother fainted, but she's feeling better now. Gregor has broken loose." "I expected it," said the father, "I always told you so, but you women won't listen." It was clear to Gregor that his father had put a bad interpretation on Grete's excessively brief communication and assumed that Gregor had been guilty of some act of violence. Therefore Gregor now had to try to pacify his father, because he had neither the time nor the means to enlighten him. And so he sped away to the door of his room and pressed himself against it, so that when his father came in from the hallway he could immediately see that Gregor fully intended to return to his room at once, and that it was unnecessary to chase him back; instead, all they needed to do was to open the door, and he would disappear right away.

But his father was in no mood to observe such niceties; as soon as he walked in, he yelled "Ah!" in a tone that suggested he was both furious and happy at the same time. Gregor drew his head back from the door and lifted it toward his father. He hadn't really pictured his father the way he now stood there; recently, to be sure, he had been so occupied by the new sensation of crawling around that he had neglected to pay attention to events in the rest of the apartment, as he had done earlier; and he should really have been prepared to encounter altered circumstances. And yet, and yet, was this still his father? The same man who would lie wearily, buried in his bed, when Gregor used to "move out smartly" on a business trip; who had received him wearing a bathrobe and sitting in an armchair when he returned home in the evening; who hadn't been fully capable of standing up, and had merely raised his arms as a sign of joy; who, during their rare family strolls on a few Sundays of the year and on the major holidays, would walk between Gregor and his mother, who walked slowly even on their own, but would always be a little slower yet, bundled up in his old coat and working his way forward with his crook-handled stick always placed cautiously before him; who, when he wanted to say something, almost always came to a halt and gathered the rest of the group around him? Now, however, he was perfectly erect, dressed in a tight blue uniform with gold buttons, like those worn by messengers in banking houses. Above the high, stiff collar of the jacket his pronounced double chin unfurled; below his bushy eyebrows the gaze of his dark eyes shone brightly and observantly; his usually tousled white hair was combed down flat and gleaming, with a painfully exact part. He threw his hat, which was adorned by a gold monogram, probably that of some bank, in an arc across the whole room onto the couch; and, pushing back the tails of his long uniform jacket, his hands in his trousers pockets, he walked toward Gregor with a morose expression. He most likely had no idea himself of what he intended to do; nevertheless, he raised his feet unusually high, and Gregor was amazed at the gigantic size of his boot soles. But he didn't dwell on that, for he had known ever since the first day of his new life that his father considered nothing but the greatest severity appropriate where he was concerned. And so he ran in front of his father, came to a halt when his father stood still and immediately sprinted forward if his father made any kind of move. In that way they circled the room several times, without anything decisive occurring; in fact, because of the slow tempo the whole thing didn't have the appearance of a pursuit. For that reason, as well, Gregor stayed on the floor for the time being, especially because he was afraid that his father might look upon a scurry onto the walls or ceiling as being particularly malicious. And yet Gregor had to tell himself that even the present activity would soon be too much for him, because for every step his father took he had to execute a huge number of movements. Shortness of breath was already becoming noticeable, and even in his earlier days his lungs hadn't been the most reliable. As he was now staggering along, in order to gather all his strength for running, and could barely keep his eyes open— unable, in his dazed condition, to think of any other refuge than running, and almost forgetting that the walls were open to him (although in this room they were obstructed by painstakingly carved furniture full of prongs and points)—something that had been lightly tossed flew right by him and rolled in front of him on the floor. It was an apple; another flew at him immediately afterward; Gregor stood still in fright; to continue running was pointless, because his father had decided to bombard him. He had filled his pockets from the fruit bowl on the sideboard and now, without aiming carefully for the moment, was throwing one apple after another. A weakly thrown apple grazed Gregor's back, but rolled off harmlessly. One that flew right after it actually penetrated Gregor's back; Gregor wanted to drag himself onward, as if the surprising and unbelievable pain might pass if he changed location; but he felt pinned down and he surrendered, all his senses fully bewildered. It was only with his last glance that he still saw the door of his room being torn open; he saw his mother dash out ahead of his screaming sister (the mother was in her shift, because the sister had undressed her to make it easier for her to breathe when she had fainted); he then saw the mother run over to the father, her untied petticoats slipping to the floor one after the other as she went. Tripping over the petticoats, she rushed upon the father and,

embracing him, in absolute union with him—at this point all went dark for Gregor—
with her hands behind the father's head, she begged him to spare Gregor's life.

III

Gregor's severe injury, from which he suffered for more than a month—since no one
dared to remove the apple, it remained in his flesh as a visible reminder—seemed to
have made even his father recall that, despite his present sad and disgusting shape, Gregor was a member of the family who shouldn't be treated as an enemy, but in whose
case family obligations demanded that one swallow one's repulsion and be patient,
only patient.

And even if Gregor's wound had probably impaired his mobility for good, and he
now, like an old invalid, needed long, long minutes to cross his room—crawling up
high was out of the question—he received in exchange for this worsening of his condition something he considered a perfectly adequate replacement: as every evening approached, the parlor door, which he would begin to watch carefully an hour or two
ahead of time, was opened so that, lying in the dark, invisible from the parlor, he could
see the whole family at the brightly lit table and listen to their conversation, to some
extent with everyone's permission, and thus quite otherwise than before.

Of course, these were no longer the lively discussions of the old days, to which
Gregor's thoughts had always turned with some yearning in his tiny hotel rooms,
when he had had to throw himself wearily into the damp bedclothes. Generally the
talks were very quiet. Right after supper the father fell asleep in his chair; the mother
and sister admonished each other to be quiet; the mother, leaning far forward under
the light, sewed fine linen for a clothing store; the sister, who had taken work as a
salesgirl, was learning stenography and French at night so that she might possibly get
a better job some day. At times the father woke up and, as if he didn't even know he'd
been sleeping, he said to the mother: "How long you've been sewing again today!" and
went right back to sleep, while mother and sister smiled at each other wearily.

With a sort of obstinacy the father refused to take off his messenger's uniform even
at home; and while his bathrobe hung unused on the hook, the father drowsed in his
chair fully dressed, as if he were always ready to do his work and were awaiting his
superior's orders even here. Consequently, despite all the mother and sister's care, the
uniform, which hadn't been brand new at the outset, became less and less clean; and
often for entire evenings Gregor would look at this garment, stained all over, but with
constantly polished and gleaming gold buttons, in which the old man slept in great discomfort and yet peacefully.

The moment the clock struck ten, the mother tried to wake the father by addressing him softly and then tried to convince him to go to bed, because here he couldn't
get any proper sleep, which the father needed very badly, since he had to begin work
at six. But with the obstinacy that had taken hold of him since he had become a messenger, he constantly insisted on remaining longer at the table, although he regularly
fell asleep, and then, on top of that, could only be persuaded with the greatest difficulty to give up his chair for his bed. In this situation mother and sister might urge him
over and over with little reminders, for periods of fifteen minutes at a time he would
shake his head slowly, keep his eyes closed and refuse to stand up. The mother tugged
at his sleeve and said sweet things in his ear, the sister would leave her task to help the
mother, but this had no effect on the father. He merely sank more deeply into his chair.

Only when the women seized him under his arms would he open his eyes, look now at the mother and now at the sister, and say: "This is living! This is the repose of my old age!" And, supported by the two women, he would get up, slowly and fussily, as if he were his own greatest burden, and would allow himself to be led to the door by the women; there he would wave them away and proceed on his own, while the mother hastily flung down her sewing things and the sister her pen in order to run after the father and continue to be of service to him.

In this overworked and overtired family, who had time to be concerned about Gregor beyond what was absolutely necessary? There were constant retrenchments in their way of living; they finally had to let the servant go; a gigantic, bony cleaning woman with white hair fluttering around her head now came in the morning and evening to do the heaviest chores; everything else was attended to by the mother, who also had all that sewing to do. It even came to pass that various pieces of family jewelry, which the mother and sister had formerly worn at parties and on great occasions, were sold, as Gregor learned in the evening from the family's discussion of the prices they had received. But the greatest complaint always was that they couldn't leave this apartment, which was far too big for their present means, since no one could figure out how to move Gregor. But Gregor realized that it was not only the concern for him that prevented a move, because after all he could easily have been shipped in a suitable crate with a few air holes; what principally kept the family from changing apartments was rather the complete hopelessness of the situation and the thought that they had been afflicted with a misfortune unlike any other in their entire circle of relatives and acquaintances. They were performing to the hilt all that the world demands of poor people: the father carried in breakfast for the junior bank clerks, the mother sacrificed herself for the linen of strangers, the sister ran back and forth behind her counter at the customers' command, but by this time the family's strength was taxed to the limit. And the sore on his back began to hurt Gregor all over again when, after putting his father to bed, his mother and sister came back, let their work rest, moved close together and sat cheek to cheek; when the mother, pointing to Gregor's room, now said, "Close the door there, Grete," and Gregor was again in the dark, while in the next room the women wept together or just stared at the table with dry eyes.

Gregor spent the nights and days almost completely without sleep. Sometimes he thought that, the next time the door opened, he would once again take charge of the family's problems just as he used to; in his thoughts there reappeared, after a long interval, his boss and the chief clerk, the clerks and the apprentices, the office messenger who was so dense, two or three friends from other firms, a chambermaid in a provincial hotel (a charming, fleeting recollection), a cashier in a hat shop whom he had courted seriously but too slowly—they all appeared, mingling with strangers or people he'd forgotten, but instead of helping him and his family, they were all inaccessible, and he was glad when they disappeared. But at other times he was no longer at all in the mood to worry about his family; he was filled with nothing but rage over how badly he was looked after; and even though he couldn't imagine anything he might have had an appetite for, he laid plans for getting into the pantry so he could take what was still his by rights, even if he wasn't hungry. No longer reflecting about what might give Gregor some special pleasure, his sister now hastily shoved any old food into Gregor's room with her foot before running off to work in the morning and at noon; in the evening, not caring whether the food had perhaps been just merely tasted or—most frequently—left completely untouched, she would sweep it out with a swing of the broom. The cleaning of the room, which she now always took care of in the evening, was done at breakneck speed. Long trails of dirt lined the walls, here and

65

there lay heaps of dust and filth. At first, when his sister arrived, Gregor would station himself at particularly glaring corners of that sort, thereby intending to reproach her to some degree. But he could have remained there for weeks on end without seeing any improvement in his sister; she saw the dirt just as well as he did, but she had simply made up her mind to leave it there. At the same time, with a touchiness that was quite new to her, and which had come over the whole family, she took care that the cleaning of Gregor's room should be reserved exclusively for her. On one occasion the mother had undertaken a thorough cleaning of Gregor's room, which she had only managed to do by using several buckets of water—the excessive dampness harmed Gregor, too, and he lay stretched out on the couch, embittered and motionless—but the mother didn't escape the penalty: the moment the sister noticed the change in Gregor's room in the evening, she ran into the parlor, highly insulted, and, despite the mother's imploringly uplifted hands, she broke into a crying jag that the parents—the father had naturally been frightened out of his chair—at first watched in amazement and helplessness until they themselves began to stir. To his right, the father reproached the mother for not leaving the cleaning of Gregor's room to the sister; to his left, on the other hand, he yelled at the sister, saying she would never again be permitted to clean Gregor's room, while the mother tried to drag the father, who was beside himself with agitation, into the bedroom; the sister, shaken with sobs, belabored the table with her little fists; and Gregor hissed loudly with rage because it didn't occur to anyone to close the door and spare him that sight and that commotion.

But even if the sister, worn out by her job, had grown tired of caring for Gregor as before, still the mother would not have been compelled to take over for her, and Gregor wouldn't have needed to be neglected. Because the cleaning woman was now there. This elderly widow, who, thanks to her powerful frame, had probably endured the worst during her long life, had no real horror of Gregor. Without being in the least curious, she had once accidentally opened the door to Gregor's room; at the sight of Gregor, who, taken by surprise, began to run back and forth although no one was chasing him, she had stood still in amazement, her hands folded over her stomach. Since then she never failed to open the door a little for just a moment in the morning and evening and to look in at Gregor. At the beginning she even called him over with words she probably thought were friendly, such as "Come on over here, old dung beetle" or "Just look at the old dung beetle!" Gregor never responded to such calls, but remained motionless where he stood, as if the door had never been opened. But if, instead of letting this cleaning woman disturb him needlessly as the fancy took her, they had only given her orders to clean his room every day! Once, early in the morning—a heavy rain, perhaps already foretokening the coming spring, was beating on the window panes—when the cleaning woman began with her series of expressions again, Gregor was so infuriated that he turned in her direction as if to attack, but slowly and feebly. The cleaning woman, however, instead of being frightened, merely lifted high in the air a chair that was near the door, and, as she stood there with her mouth wide open, she clearly intended not to close her mouth again until the chair in her hand crashed down on Gregor's back. "So you're not advancing?" she asked as Gregor turned around again, and placed the chair back calmly in the corner.

By this time Gregor was hardly eating. Only when he accidentally passed by the spread-out food would he take a bit in his mouth playfully, hold it there for hours and then generally spit it out again. At first he thought it was his dejection over the state of his room that kept him from eating, but he was soon more reconciled to the changes in his room than to anything else. They had grown accustomed to put in his room things there was no space for elsewhere, and there were now a lot of such things, because they had rented one room in the apartment to three lodgers. These serious gentlemen—all three had full beards, as Gregor once ascertained through a crack in the door—were sticklers for strict housekeeping, not only in their room, but also, since they were after all paying rent there, all over the apartment, and especially in the kitchen. They wouldn't stand for useless, not to mention dirty, odds and ends. Furthermore, they had for the most part brought along their own furnishings. Therefore many items had become superfluous that couldn't be sold but no one wanted to throw out. All of these were moved into Gregor's room. And so were the ash box and the garbage box from the kitchen. Whatever was unusable at the moment, the cleaning woman, who was always in a hurry, simply flung into Gregor's room; fortunately, Gregor generally saw only the object in question and the hand that held it. Perhaps the cleaning woman intended to retrieve the things when she had the time and opportunity, or to throw them all out at the same time, but in reality they remained wherever they had landed at the first toss, unless Gregor twisted through the rubbish and set it in motion, at first out of necessity, because no other space was open to crawl through, but later with increasing delight, although after such excursions, tired to death and dejected, he would again remain motionless for hours.

Since the lodgers sometimes also took their evening meal at home in the common parlor, the parlor door was closed on many evenings, but Gregor readily made do without the opening of the door, for on many earlier evenings when it was open he hadn't taken advantage of it, but instead, without the family noticing, had lain in the darkest corner of his room. But on one occasion the cleaning woman had left the door to the parlor a little open; and it remained open like that even when the lodgers entered in the evening and the light was turned on. They sat at the head of the table, where in earlier days the father, the mother and Gregor had sat; they unfolded their napkins and picked up their knives and forks. Immediately the mother appeared in the doorway with a platter of meat, and right behind her the sister with a plate piled high with potatoes. The food was steaming copiously. The lodgers bent over the plates that were placed in front of them as if wishing to examine them before eating, and, in fact, the one sitting in the middle, whom the others seemed to look up to as an authority, cut a piece of meat on the plate, obviously to ascertain whether it was tender enough and didn't perhaps need to be sent back to the kitchen. He was satisfied, and the mother and sister, who had watched in suspense, breathed easily and began to smile.

The family themselves ate in the kitchen. Nevertheless, before the father went into the kitchen, he entered the parlor and, with a single protracted bow, walked around the table, cap in hand. The lodgers all stood up and murmured something into their beards. Then, when they were alone, they ate with almost no conversation. It seemed odd to Gregor that, among all the multifarious noises of eating, their chewing teeth stood out again and again, as if to indicate to Gregor that teeth were indispensable for eating and that even with the finest toothless jaws nothing could be accomplished. "I do have an appetite," said Gregor uneasily to himself, "but not for those things. How these lodgers pack it away, and I'm perishing!"

On that very evening—Gregor had no recollection of having heard the violin during that whole time—it was audible from the kitchen. The lodgers had already finished their supper, the one in the middle had pulled out a newspaper, handing one sheet apiece to the two others, and now they were leaning back, reading and smoking. When the violin began to play, they noticed it, stood up and walked on tiptoe to the hallway door, remaining there in a tight group. They must have been heard in the

70

kitchen, because the father called: "Does the playing perhaps bother you? We can stop it at once." "On the contrary," said the gentleman in the middle, "wouldn't the young lady like to come in here with us and play in this room, which is much more comfortable and cozy?" "Of course," called the father, as if *he* were the violinist. The gentlemen stepped back into the room and waited. Soon the father came with the music stand, the mother with the sheet music and the sister with the violin. The sister calmly put everything in readiness for playing; the parents, who had never rented out rooms before and therefore overdid the courtesy due to lodgers, didn't dare to sit on their own chairs; the father leaned on the door, his right hand placed between two buttons of his closed uniform jacket; but the mother was offered a chair by one of the gentlemen and, since she left the chair where the man happened to have placed it, she sat off to one side in a corner.

The sister began to play; the father and mother, each on his side, watched the motions of her hands closely. Gregor, attracted by the playing, had ventured out a little further and already had his head in the parlor. He was scarcely surprised that recently he was so little concerned about the feelings of the others; previously this considerateness had been his pride. As it was, right now he might have had even more cause to hide, because as a result of the dust that had settled all over in his room and blew around at the slightest movement, he was also completely covered with dust; he was dragging threads, hairs and crumbs of food around with him on his back and sides; his indifference to everything was much too great for him to turn over on his back and scour himself on the carpet, as he used to do several times a day. But despite being in this state, he had no qualms about moving a little bit forward on the immaculate floor of the parlor.

To be sure, no one was paying attention to him. The family was completely engrossed in the violin performance; on the other hand, the lodgers, who, hands in trousers pockets, had first of all moved their chairs much too close behind the sister's music stand, so that they could all have looked at the sheet music, which assuredly had to disturb the sister, soon withdrew, with semiaudible remarks and lowered heads, to the window, where they stayed put, watched by the father with concern. It was now abundantly evident that they were disappointed in their assumption that they were going to hear some pretty or entertaining violin music; they were clearly tired of the whole performance and were permitting their peace and quiet to be disturbed merely out of courtesy. It was especially the way they all blew their cigar smoke up into the air through their noses and mouths that indicated a terrific strain on their nerves. And yet the sister was playing beautifully. Her face was inclined to one side, her eyes followed the lines of music searchingly and sorrowfully. Gregor crawled a little bit further forward, keeping his head close to the floor in hopes of making eye contact with her. Was he an animal if music stirred him that way? He felt as if he were being shown the way to the unknown nourishment he longed for. He was resolved to push his way right up to his sister and tug at her skirt, as an indication to her to come into his room with her violin, because nobody here was repaying her for her playing the way he would repay her. He intended never to let her out of his room again, at least not as long as he lived; his horrifying shape was to be beneficial to him for the first time; he would be on guard at all the doors to his room at once, and spit at his assailants like a cat; but his sister would remain with him not under compulsion but voluntarily; she was to sit next to him on the couch and incline her ear toward him, and he would then confide to her that he had had the firm intention of sending her to the conservatory, and that, if the misfortune hadn't intervened, he would have told everyone so last Christmas— Christmas *was* over by now, wasn't it?—without listening to any objections. After this declaration his sister would burst into tears of deep emotion, and Gregor would raise himself to the level of her shoulder and kiss her neck, which, since she had begun her job, she had left bare, without any ribbon or collar.

"Mr. Samsa!" the gentleman in the middle called to the father and, without wasting another word, pointed with his index finger to Gregor, who was moving slowly forward. The violin fell silent, the gentleman in the middle first smiled at his friends, shaking his head, and then looked at Gregor again. The father seemed to think that, to begin with, it was more necessary to placate the lodgers than to chase away Gregor, even though the men were not at all excited and Gregor seemed to entertain them more than the violin playing. He ran over to them and, with arms outspread, he tried to make them withdraw into their room, at the same time blocking their view of Gregor with his body. Now they actually got a little sore; it was no longer possible to tell whether this was due to the father's behavior or to the realization now dawning on them that, without their knowledge, they had had a next-door neighbor like Gregor. They demanded explanations from the father, they themselves now raised their arms, they plucked uneasily at their beards, and only slowly retreated toward their room. Meanwhile the sister had gotten over the state of total absence that had come over her after the abruptly terminated performance; after she had held the violin and the bow for some time in her limply hanging hands and had continued to look at the music as if she were still playing, she had roused herself all at once; she had placed the instrument on the lap of her mother, who was still sitting on her chair gasping for breath, her lungs pumping violently, and had run into the adjoining room, which the lodgers were approaching more quickly now under pressure from the father. One could see the blankets and pillows on the beds fly up and arrange themselves neatly in the sister's skilled hands. Even before the gentlemen had reached their room, she had finished making the beds and slipped out. The father seemed once more so infected by his obstinacy that he forgot all the respect he after all owed his lodgers. All he did was crowd them and crowd them until, already in the doorway to the room, the gentleman in the middle stamped his foot resoundingly, thereby bringing the father to a halt. "I hereby announce," he said, raising his hand and looking around for the mother and sister as well, "that in view of the disgusting conditions prevailing in this apartment and family"— here he spat promptly on the floor—"I am giving up my room as of tomorrow morning. Naturally I won't pay a thing for the days that I've lived here, either; on the contrary, I'm going to think seriously about whether I shouldn't sue you—believe me, the proof wouldn't be hard to come by." He fell silent and looked straight ahead of him, as if he were expecting something. And, indeed, his two friends immediately chimed in with the words: "We're also leaving tomorrow." Thereupon he seized the door handle and slammed the door violently.

The father staggered to his chair with groping hands and let himself fall onto it; it looked as if he were stretching out for his customary evening nap, but the rapid nodding of his seemingly uncontrollable head showed that he was by no means asleep. Gregor had lain still the whole time on the same spot where the lodgers had detected him. The disappointment over the failure of his plan, but perhaps also the weakness caused by so much fasting, made it impossible for him to move. He was afraid that, almost as a certainty, everything would come tumbling down upon him at the very next moment; and he was waiting. Not even the violin startled him when it slipped from the mother's trembling fingers, fell off her lap and emitted a resounding note.

"Dear parents," the sister said, striking the table with her hand by way of preamble, "we can't go on like this. If you perhaps don't realize it, I do. In front of this monstrous creature I refuse to pronounce my brother's name, and therefore I merely say: 75

we have to try to get rid of it. We've tried all that's humanly possible to take care of it and put up with it; I think no one can reproach us in the slightest."

"She's perfectly right," said the father to himself. The mother, who was still too short of breath, began to cough hollowly into the hand she held before her, with a crazed look in her eyes.

The sister ran over to the mother and held her forehead. The sister's words seemed to have helped the father collect his thoughts; he had sat up straight and was playing with his messenger's cap between the dishes that were still left on the table after the lodgers' supper; and from time to time he looked over at the motionless Gregor.

"We have to try to get rid of it," the sister now said to her father only, because the mother, with her coughing, couldn't hear anything; "eventually it'll kill both of you, I can see it coming. When people already have to work as hard as all of us, they can't stand this perpetual torment at home, as well. I can't any more." And she burst into such a violent fit of weeping that her tears rained down onto her mother's face, from which she wiped them away with mechanical movements of the hand.

"My child," said the father sympathetically and with noticeable comprehension, "what are we supposed to do?"

80   The sister merely shrugged her shoulders to indicate the perplexity that had now taken hold of her during her crying fit, in contrast to her earlier self-confidence.

"If he understood us," said the father half-questioningly; in the midst of her tears she shook her hand violently to indicate that that was out of the question.

"If he understood us," repeated the father and, closing his eyes, absorbed in his own mind the sister's conviction of that impossibility, "then perhaps we could reach an agreement with him. But, as it is—"

"It's got to go," called the sister, "that's the only remedy, Father. All you have to do is try to shake off the idea that that's Gregor. Our real misfortune comes from having believed it for so long. But how can it be Gregor? If it were Gregor, he would long since have realized that it's impossible for people to live side by side with an animal like that, and would have gone away of his own free will. Then we would have had no more brother, but we could go on living and honor his memory. But, as it is, this animal persecutes us, drives away our lodgers, and obviously wants to take over the whole apartment and make us sleep in the street. Just look, Father," she suddenly yelled, "he's starting again!" And, in a panic that Gregor couldn't understand at all, the sister even deserted her mother, literally hurling herself from her chair, as if she would rather sacrifice her mother than remain in Gregor's vicinity; she dashed behind her father, who, agitated solely by her behavior, also stood up and, as if protecting the sister, half-raised his arms in front of her.

But Gregor hadn't the slightest wish to frighten anyone, least of all his sister. He had merely started to turn around, in order to regain his room, and that was naturally conspicuous because in his ailing condition he could only execute those difficult turns with the aid of his head, raising it and bumping it on the floor many times. He stopped and looked around. His good intentions seemed to have been recognized; the panic had lasted only for a moment. Now they all looked at him in silent sorrow. The mother was slumped in her chair, her legs outstretched and pressed together; her eyes were almost closing with exhaustion; the father and sister were sitting side by side; the sister had placed her hand around the father's neck.

85   "Now perhaps I can turn around," thought Gregor, and resumed his labors. He was unable to suppress the heavy breathing caused by the exertion, and had to stop to rest from time to time. Otherwise, no one was rushing him, everything was left to him. When he had completed the turn, he immediately began to head back in a straight

line. He was amazed at the great distance that separated him from his room, and couldn't comprehend how, feeling so weak, he had just a while before covered the same ground almost without noticing it. His mind being constantly bent on nothing but fast crawling, he scarcely paid attention to the fact that he was not being disturbed by any word or outcry from his family. Only when already in the doorway did he turn his head, not all the way, because he felt his neck growing stiff, but enough to see that nothing had changed behind him except that his sister had stood up. His last look was at his mother, who had fallen asleep completely.

Scarcely was he inside his room when the door was hastily closed, barred and locked. The sudden noise behind him scared Gregor so badly that his little legs buckled. It was his sister who had been in such a rush. She had already been standing there on her feet and waiting, then she had leaped forward with light steps—Gregor hadn't heard her approaching—and she called "At last!" to her parents as she turned the key in the lock.

"And now?" Gregor asked himself, and looked around in the darkness. He soon made the discovery that he could no longer move at all. This didn't surprise him; in fact, he found it unnatural that up until then he had actually been able to get around on those thin little legs. Besides, he felt relatively comfortable. True, he had pains all over his body, but he felt as if they were getting gradually milder and milder and would finally pass away altogether. By now he hardly felt the rotten apple in his back and the inflamed area around it, which were completely covered with soft dust. He recalled his family with affection and love. His opinion about the necessity for him to disappear was, if possible, even firmer than his sister's. He remained in this state of vacant and peaceful contemplation until the tower clock struck the third morning hour. He was still alive when the world started to become brighter outside the window. Then his head involuntarily sank down altogether, and his last breath issued faintly from his nostrils.

When the cleaning woman arrived early in the morning—in her natural strength and haste, despite frequent requests not to do so, she slammed all the doors so loud that throughout the apartment, from the moment she came, it was impossible to sleep peacefully—she found nothing out of the ordinary at first during her customary brief visit to Gregor. She thought he was lying motionless like that on purpose, acting insulted; she gave him credit for full reasoning powers. Because by chance she was carrying the long broom, she tried to tickle Gregor with it from her position in the doorway. When this proved fruitless, she became annoyed and jabbed Gregor a little, and only when she had moved him from the spot, without any resistance on his part, did she take notice. When she soon recognized the true state of affairs, she opened her eyes wide and gave a whistle, but didn't stay there long; instead, she tore open the bedroom door and shouted into the darkness: "Come take a look, it's croaked; it's lying there, a total goner."

The Samsas sat up in bed and were hard put to overcome the fright that the cleaning woman had given them until they finally grasped her announcement. Then Mr. and Mrs. Samsa got out of bed quickly, each on his side; Mrs. Samsa threw the blanket over his shoulders, Mrs. Samsa came out wearing only her nightgown; in this way they entered Gregor's room. Meanwhile the parlor door had also opened; Grete had been sleeping there since the lodgers moved in; she was fully dressed as if she hadn't slept at all; the pallor of her face seemed to indicate that, too. "Dead?" asked Mrs. Samsa, and looked up questioningly at the cleaning woman, even though she was able to examine everything herself and could recognize it even without any examination. "I'll say!" replied the cleaning woman, and, as a proof, pushed Gregor's corpse another long way to the side with her broom. Mrs. Samsa made a motion as if to restrain the broom, but didn't do so. "Well," said Mr. Samsa, "now we can thank God." He crossed himself, and the three women followed his example. Grete, who didn't take her eyes off the corpse, said: "Just look how thin he was. Yes, he hadn't been eating anything for so long. The food came out of his room just the way it went in." Indeed, Gregor's body was completely flat and dry; actually that could be seen only now, when he was no longer lifted up on his little legs and nothing else diverted their attention.

90 "Come into our room for a while, Grete," said Mrs. Samsa with a melancholy smile, and, not without looking back at the corpse, Grete followed her parents into their bedroom. The cleaning woman shut the door and opened the window all the way. Despite the early morning hour, the fresh air already had a warm feeling to it. For by now it was the end of March.

The three lodgers stepped out of their room and, in amazement, looked around for their breakfast; the family had forgotten it. "Where's breakfast?!" the gentleman in the middle grumpily asked the cleaning woman. But she put her finger to her lips and then hastily and silently beckoned to the gentlemen to come into Gregor's room. They did so, and then, with their hands in the pockets of their somewhat shabby jackets, they stood around Gregor's corpse in the now completely bright room.

Then the bedroom door opened, and Mr. Samsa appeared in his uniform, with his wife on one arm and his daughter on the other. All of them had obviously been weeping; from time to time Grete pressed her face against her father's arm.

"Leave my home at once!" said Mr. Samsa, and pointed to the door, without freeing himself from the women. "What do you mean?" said the gentleman in the middle, somewhat taken aback, and put on a saccharine smile. The two others kept their hands behind their backs, rubbing them together uninterruptedly, as if in joyous anticipation of a major quarrel, which had to come out in their favor. "I mean exactly what I say," Mr. Samsa answered, and, with his two female companions, moved in a direct line toward the lodger. The latter stood still at first, looking at the floor, as if all the ideas in his head were being rearranged. "In that case, we're going," he then said, looking up at Mr. Samsa, as if, with a humility that was suddenly setting in, he were requesting new permission even for that decision. Mr. Samsa merely gave him a few brief nods, his eyes glaring. Thereupon the gentleman did indeed immediately take long strides into the hallway; his two friends, who for a while now had been listening with their hands completely at rest, now practically leaped after him, as if fearing that Mr. Samsa might enter the hall before them and cut off the liaison with their leader. In the hallway, all three took their hats off the hooks, drew their walking sticks out of the walking-stick stand, bowed in silence and left the apartment. With a mistrust that proved to be totally unjustified, Mr. Samsa and the two women stepped out onto the landing; leaning against the railing, they watched the three gentlemen descend the long staircase slowly but steadily, disappear on each floor into the same bend of the stairwell, and emerge again after a few moments; the lower they got, the more the Samsa family lost interest in them, and when a butcher boy, proudly bearing his tray on his head, met up with them and then climbed the stairs far above them, Mr. Samsa and the women left the railing, and they all returned to their apartment as if they were relieved.

They decided to spend that day resting and strolling; they not only deserved that pause from work, they absolutely needed it. And so they sat down at the table and wrote three letters of excuse, Mr. Samsa to the bank directors, Mrs. Samsa to the people who gave her piecework and Grete to her employer. While they were writing, the cleaning woman came in to say she was leaving because her morning chores were done. At first the three writers merely nodded, without looking up; it was only when the cleaning woman made no signs of going that they looked up in annoyance. "Well?" asked Mr. Samsa. The cleaning woman stood in the doorway smiling, as if she had a message that would make the family tremendously happy but would only deliver it if they questioned her thoroughly. The almost vertical little ostrich feather on her hat, which had annoyed Mr. Samsa all the time she'd been working for them, was waving slightly in all directions. "Well, what is it you want?" asked Mrs. Samsa, for whom the cleaning woman still had the most respect. "Yes," answered the cleaning woman, whose friendly laughter prevented her from continuing right away, "you don't have to worry your heads about how to clear out that trash next door. It's all taken care of." Mrs. Samsa and Grete lowered their heads to their letters, as if they wanted to go on writing; Mr. Samsa, who perceived that the cleaning woman now wanted to start describing everything in detail, forbade that decisively with an upheld hand. Now that she wasn't able to deliver a narration, she recalled the big hurry she was in; shouted, obviously peeved, "So long, one and all!"; turned on her heels furiously and left the apartment, slamming every door thunderously.

"We'll discharge her tonight," said Mr. Samsa, but received no reply from either his wife or his daughter, since the cleaning woman seemed to have once more disturbed the peace of mind they had just barely attained. They got up, went over to the window and stayed there, their arms around each other. Mr. Samsa turned around toward them on his chair and watched them silently for a while. Then he called: "Oh, come on over. Let bygones be bygones now. And have a little consideration for me, too." The women obeyed him at once, rushed over to him, caressed him and finished their letters quickly.

Then all three of them left the apartment together, something they hadn't done for months, and took the trolley out to the country on the edge of town. The car, in which they were the only passengers, was brightly lit by the warm sun. Leaning back comfortably on their seats, they discussed their prospects for the future, and it proved that, on closer examination, these were not at all bad, because the jobs that all three had, but which they hadn't really asked one another about before, were thoroughly advantageous and particularly promising for later on. Naturally the greatest immediate improvement in their situation would result easily from a change of apartment; now they would take a smaller and cheaper, but better located and in general more practical, apartment than their present one, which Gregor had found for them. While they were conversing in this way, Mr. and Mrs. Samsa, looking at their daughter, who was becoming more lively all the time, realized at almost the very same moment that recently, in spite of all the cares that had made her cheeks pale, she had blossomed out into a beautiful, well-built girl. Becoming more silent and almost unconsciously communicating with each other by looks, they thought it was now time to find a good husband for her. And they took it as a confirmation of their new dreams and good intentions when, at the end of their ride, their daughter stood up first and stretched her young body. [1915]

95

QUESTIONS

1. Gregor Samsa is the principal wage earner of the family. Does Samsa resent his pre-insect situation?
2. Kafka objected to having any illustration showing Samsa as an insect. What is gained by having no illustration?

3. How does the family first react to Gregor's transformation? Over time do their reactions change?
4. Reread the description of turning the key. How do you think Kafka wants you to feel while you read that scene?
5. What functions do outsiders perform? Consider, especially, Kafka's use of the chief clerk and the lodgers.

RESPONSES

1. Read the materials in the "Context: Writers on Writing" section. How does this material contribute to your understanding of this and other Kafka stories?
2. What elements of Kafka's style and ideas do you see in work by Borges, Cortázar, Kundera, and Sontag?
3. Compare Kafka's approach to the short story to Chekhov's. Which do you prefer? Why?

FOCUS ON FILM

1. Write an essay explaining and evaluating the use that the film *Franz Kafka's It's a Wonderful Life* makes of "The Metamorphosis."
2. While the film *Kafka* is completely fiction, it does make creative use of Kafka's themes and images from several works. How does the film recreate Kafka's themes, images, and ironies that can be seen in the stories included in this text? You might also use Kundera's essay "Somewhere Behind" in the Context section of this anthology.

JAMAICA KINCAID

Jamaica Kincaid (b. 1949) was born in St. Johns, Antigua, and educated there at the Princess Margaret School. She left home to attend college in the United States, was eventually published in *Rolling Stone* and *The Paris Review*, and in 1978 became a staff writer for the *New Yorker*. Her first collection of short fiction, *At the Bottom of the River* (1983), was quickly followed by a second, *Annie John* (1985). Kincaid is an expert on gardening and frequently writes about it. *The Autobiography of My Mother* (1995) is a novel; a memoir, *My Brother* (1997), was nominated for a National Book Award. She recently published *Talk Stories* (2001) and *Mr. Potter* (2002).

Girl

Wash the white clothes on Monday and put them on the stone heap; wash the color clothes on Tuesday and put them on the clothesline to dry; don't walk barehead in the hot sun; cook pumpkin fritters in very hot sweet oil; soak your little clothes right after you take them off; when buying cotton to make yourself a nice blouse, be sure that it doesn't have gum in it, because that way it won't hold up well after a wash; soak salt fish overnight before you cook it; is it true that you sing benna° in Sunday school?; always eat your food in such a way that it won't turn someone else's stomach; on Sundays try to walk like a lady and not like the slut you are so bent on becoming; don't sing benna in Sunday school; you mustn't speak to wharf-rat boys, not even to give directions; don't eat fruits on the street—flies will follow you; *but I don't sing benna on Sundays at all and never in Sunday school;* this is how to sew on a button; this is how to make a buttonhole for the button you have just sewed on; this is how to hem a dress when you see the hem coming down and so to prevent yourself from looking like the slut I know you are so bent on becoming; this is how you iron your father's khaki shirt so that it doesn't have a crease; this is how you iron your father's khaki pants so that they don't have a crease; this is how you grow okra—far from the house, because okra tree harbors red ants; when you are growing dasheen,° make sure it gets plenty of

---

°*benna*: Calypso (music).
°*dasheen*: Starchy edible root (taro).

water or else it makes your throat itch when you are eating it; this is how you sweep a corner; this is how you sweep a whole house; this is how you sweep a yard; this is how you smile to someone you don't like too much; this is how you smile to someone you don't like at all; this is how you smile to someone you like completely; this is how you set a table for tea; this is how you set a table for dinner; this is how you set a table for dinner with an important guest; this is how you set a table for lunch; this is how you set a table for breakfast; this is how to behave in the presence of men who don't know you very well, and this way they won't recognize immediately the slut I have warned you against becoming; be sure to wash every day, even if it is with your own spit; don't squat down to play marbles—you are not a boy, you know; don't pick people's flowers—you might catch something; don't throw stones at blackbirds, because it might not be a blackbird at all; this is how to make a bread pudding; this is how to make doukona;° this is how to make pepper pot; this is how to make a good medicine for a cold; this is how to make a good medicine to throw away a child before it even becomes a child; this is how to catch a fish; this is how to throw back a fish you don't like, and that way something bad won't fall on you; this is how to bully a man; this is how a man bullies you; this is how to love a man, and if this doesn't work there are other ways, and if they don't work don't feel too bad about giving up; this is how to spit up in the air if you feel like it, and this is how to move quick so that it doesn't fall on you; this is how to make ends meet; always squeeze bread to make sure it's fresh; *but what if the baker won't let me feel the bread?*; you mean to say that after all you are really going to be the kind of woman who the baker won't let near the bread?   [1978]

QUESTIONS

1. What are the mother's chief concerns?
2. Are any of her instructions shocking?
3. In this string of comments, are there any two in a row that do not have a perceptible connection?
4. Is the sequence chronological, topical, or random?
5. Is there more attention given to morality, manners, or domestic abilities?

RESPONSES

1. Write an essay arguing whether this long paragraph is or is not a short story.
2. In an essay compare Kincaid's story to Cisneros's "Barbie-Q."

°*doukona*: A pudding.

PERRI KLASS

Perri Klass (b. 1958) was born in Trinidad and grew up in New York City and Leonia, New Jersey. She is a graduate of Radcliffe College and the Harvard Medical School, and she also studied at Berkeley and in Rome. Her stories have twice been chosen for inclusion in *Prize Stories: The O. Henry Awards*, and she is the author of two novels. A practicing pediatrician, she published in 1992 an account of her training, *Baby Doctor*. Recent works include *Love and Modern Medicine* (2001) and *Mystery of Breathing* (2004).

Not a Good Girl

Men nowadays can be very strange, if you ask me. I went to bed with one I had just met when I was up in Boston for two days. This is not something I do ferociously often, jump into bed with men I've just met. In fact, for the last six months or so, I haven't jumped into bed with anyone. Not that I've been celibate on principle, or anything like that. It's just that I've been pretty busy lately.

This man I went to bed with in Boston was a graduate student in biochemistry at Harvard who had come to my seminar, the first of the two I was going to give. (You would never say, would you, "the man with whom I went to bed"? I suppose the whole phrase has its roots in such a cute, euphemistic view of things that it has to be kept schoolgirlish and ungrammatical.) Anyway, he was a graduate student in my field, which is immunology. That, of course, lends itself easily to crude sexual analogies, since it is concerned with the body's defenses against foreign intruders, but never mind all that now. I didn't take any particular notice of him at my seminar, except when he asked a reasonably intelligent question. Then he turned up again that evening, when the people who were "hosting" me took me to an Italian restaurant; there was a big group of junior-faculty types and graduate students, including this one, Eric. After dinner, which was extremely so-so and which seemed to leave everyone feeling a little discouraged, my hosts wanted to take me out drinking, but I said I thought I would just go back to the hotel, and Eric said he had a car and would drop me off. In his car I was conscious of our different clothes, me in my give-a-seminar outfit, blazer and wool skirt and stockings, Eric in very worn corduroy pants and a workshirt frayed at the cuffs. We stopped for a traffic light, he put his hand, ragged cuff and all, on my stockinged knee, and asked perfectly straightforwardly if I wanted "company for the night." As simple as that. I considered for a minute, maybe less, aware that I wanted his hand to travel further up my leg, and said okay, appropriately nonchalant.

I could not possibly have been more than four or five years older than he, though, of course, there was that infinite spiritual distance between still-in-school and out-of-school-and-working. Still, I was inclined to put his lack of romantic finesse down to his callow youth. I don't mean the come-on in the car; that seemed to me very acceptable and even sweet and disarming. And of course I wasn't expecting genuine romantic feeling and wouldn't have welcomed it if it had materialized, but once we were in the hotel room, I was less than thrilled when he kissed me and said, "Well, why don't you take your clothes off?" then started to pull off his own. It would frankly have done more for me if he'd unbuttoned even one or two of the buttons on my shirt. He did switch off the light, which might have indicated a romantic awareness of the full moon coming through the window, but more likely just meant he wanted the conventional darkened room. Anyway, we had sex on the professionally large and accommodating hotel double bed, in the romantic silver splash of the full moon.

It just knocked me out how good he was, which shows that she who doesn't expect much is sometimes richly rewarded. But then, afterward, when we were exchanging bits of information to give our mutual nakedness some small base of intimacy (how we had no boyfriends, girlfriends, husbands, wives, how much he respected my work, that kind of thing), he said to me, "Women nowadays can be very strange, if you ask me." And he went on to tell me that women nowadays expect men to be gentle and tender but still to go on filling all the traditional male roles, by which he meant, for example, expecting the man to get out of bed and investigate noises in the night. I was protesting halfheartedly that I personally could imagine nothing worse than being left alone in bed to listen to night noises, when it occurred to me that this "complaint" was Eric's way of letting me know how sensitive he was, that he took seriously what he thought were feminist expectations of men, at least seriously enough to complain about them. A scientist who truly cared about his human relationships. I felt, with some irritation, that we had omitted all the traditional first-night trappings; there had been no false tenderness, no ersatz romance, and neither had there been any hard-bitten bedpost notching. Eric and I seemed to have skipped emotionally to some point later on in a relationship (and not a very appealing relationship), when sweeping generalizations about "men" and "women" were just another way of attacking each other.

5   But I didn't want to worry about any of this. Isn't the point of a one-night stand that you get off on the novelty and the adventure without having to worry about the person?

In any case, it didn't turn out to be exactly a one-night stand. It turned out to be a two-night stand, though something should be said about the day between the two nights. I was supposed to go visit some labs, but it was a beautiful morning, and as Eric was driving me past the Boston Common, he suggested that we stop and enjoy the sunshine. So we got out of the car and went to the Public Gardens. I sat on Eric's wool lumberjack jacket which he had spread for me in deference to my costume, stockings again, and a different wool skirt and a different shirt, the same blazer. He, of course, was wearing exactly the same clothes he had worn the day before. I was feeling tension about the seminar I had to give that afternoon, and mindless pleasure in the sun and the smell of the earth, and I had half-forgotten the details of Eric's after-sex conversation, except that something about it had been faintly disagreeable. I also retained somewhere, between my legs perhaps, the impression that the preconversation sex had been distinctly agreeable. Overall, though, I was finding Eric, today, rather less attractive than I had the day before.

Mentally, I redesigned him, giving him truly curly hair instead of vaguely wavy tendrils, making him taller and thinner to entitle him to his awkwardness, while knitting his body more carefully so that the awkwardness would be more superficial. Though, in all fairness, I had to admit that he hadn't been the least bit awkward in bed. Just then, he put his arms around me and kissed me. I let him, first amused, then aroused, though I don't really believe in making out in public. Soon, we had gotten each other pretty thoroughly worked up, and then without any apparent reason, certainly nothing as definite as anyone's orgasm, we slacked off and began to relax. I began thinking about my seminar again. Then, three boys, who apparently had been watching us climb all over each other, began to call things out at us, encouraging us to finish what we had started. They couldn't have been more than ten years old, maybe less, and they were all three small and thin and pale and should have been in school. One of them carried an enormous portable radio, a ghetto blaster, as they say, though they were as white as Eric and I. After a moment, when they still hadn't gone away, Eric got to his feet and ran toward them, running with rather surprising grace, for someone engaged in such an awkward and ridiculous bit of behavior. I supposed that his motive was simple irritation and a desire to protect me from the jibes of these children, but he must have realized almost immediately, finding himself running across the grass, that he could only look sillier and sillier. The children retreated, slightly scared but triumphant in having provoked him, and he gave up the chase, veering around in a would-be-casual semicircle, as if he had just been running a little ways to work off his exuberance at the feeling of spring in the air.

Needless to say, I was not fooled. I was annoyed with his silliness and more annoyed because I had just discovered a run in my stocking, which I attributed to our making out. Now, I would have to stop at a drugstore sometime before my seminar and replace the stockings. Again I felt, watching him lope shamefacedly back to me, that we were somewhere deep into a relationship, maybe someone else's relationship, certainly not mine. The man making a fool of himself in public, attempting to defend his woman's honor against the onslaughts of smartass ten-year-olds. Someone else's relationship, someone else's man.

I might not have slept with Eric again if my second seminar had not gone so exceptionally well. I had been much more nervous about this one than the first, since I'd given the first one many times before. The second seminar, though, explained my very recent work, including work still in progress. I felt vulnerable and a little unconvinced about some of the material, but it went almost devastatingly well, the applause at the end was genuine, and the questions had a slightly awestruck air, even the challenging questions, the ones that were meant to suggest major gaps in my thinking. I had no trouble with the questions. And I felt that one reason it had gone so well was Eric's presence; I was showing off particularly for him and also trying to intimidate him and dazzle him and so on. And so then I felt a little in his debt; also I enjoyed the tentativeness of his offer: "Do you want me to come with you tonight?" It was much more tentative than you would expect, considering that I had slept with him the night before. It took us out of the middle of all those other relationships.

Once again, things turned out very well in bed, and we were both satiated and   10
asleep at 2:30 in the morning, when the phone by the bed rang and it turned out to be my friend Eleanora, calling from New York to say she'd broken my big blue platter. Eleanora and her husband lived two floors up from me, and I had given her my key

when I left for Boston and asked her to feed my cat. She had had company that night and had needed a big serving platter and had taken mine and broken it while she was washing it. Then she cried and drank steadily, until she was drunk and miserable enough to call me at the hotel in Boston.

She was crying over the phone. Don't cry, it doesn't matter, I told her, aware that it mattered, that I would not forgive her. I had not told her she could take the platter. Eleanora, I kept saying, why are you carrying on like this, it doesn't matter, I'll buy a new platter. The rhyme was becoming a refrain. Eric was awake and had turned on the bedside lamp. The sight of him was reassuring; he was calm, and we were not emotionally mixed up with each other. I wanted to hang up on Eleanora and see if Eric could get it up again. I was angry about the platter and angry with myself for caring about the platter, and angry with Eleanora for having judged me so correctly that she knew I would be angry about it.

I'm so messy, she was saying. Everything I touch turns out to be a mess. My life is one mess after another. After the platter broke, she had a fight with her husband, a plump and pompous man. He had gone to sleep without forgiving her, she told me, and she was in the living room, with, I assumed, an empty bottle of Southern Comfort in front of her. I know Eleanora's tastes. Why did you have a fight, I asked wearily. Eric was lying back against his pillow, watching me, looking a little surprised. Eleanora said something incoherent, dinner had not gone well, things had not come out right, important guests. For heaven's sake, Eleanora, I said, this is right out of some TV sitcom when the husband's boss comes to dinner. Don't take it so seriously. But then I had to listen to a long speech about how awful her life was and how I couldn't understand. I had no husband, after all. Immunology. Fancy hotels.

Are you alone? she asked suddenly. Well, no, as a matter of fact, I'm not, I said. But it's okay. By which I meant, go ahead and keep me on the phone, we were only sleeping when you called, the sex was over and done with. Immediately, Eleanora's voice took on a giggly quality. She assured me that she hadn't meant to interrupt, that clearly I had more important things to worry about than a broken platter. I'll tell you all about it when I get home, I said. Eric raised his eyebrows; I shrugged. You just bet you will, Eleanora giggled, I'm not going to let you off without a full description. And she said good-bye in high spirits, so I guess I really did manage to do a good turn and cheer up a friend in distress.

I explained a little to Eric, feeling he deserved it. He seemed a bit off balance. It was the sudden awareness of my real, tangled life, which he did not know anything about, in which he had no place. He had asked me all the wrong questions, it seemed—did I have a husband, a boyfriend?—and should have asked, instead, if I had a cat and if I had a friend named Eleanora who broke things.

15 "What's your cat's name?" he asked me, after I explained why Eleanora had the key to my apartment; then, after I told him, he said, "You have a cat named Carmen?" I wondered if he thought that was a ridiculous name, if he would, after all, turn out to be some kind of kindred sensibility, so I said, "Someone else named her," leaving him free to make fun of the name. But he had no particular opinion; he had perhaps begun to wonder who had named my cat—an ex-lover, someone I used to live with—and I thought of telling him that my little sister had chosen the name; giving me one of her own cat's kittens, she had thought to please me, knowing I like music. I didn't say it. Instead, Eric and I investigated and discovered that he could indeed get it up again, though, to be honest, it took him so damn long to reach orgasm that I lost interest. But I kept my eyes wide open; it is very bad manners to fall asleep in such a situation.

As if in return for his unexpected glimpse into my life, he offered me a confidence the next morning as he drove me to the airport to catch the air shuttle to New York. He told me that sometimes he was afraid he wouldn't be able to write his dissertation. All I could say was that I was sure he would be fine. I wondered whether he actually would be fine and whether I would see his name on articles or run into him in the future at scientific meetings. "Can I ask you something?" he said. I nodded. "If we lived near each other, would you have an affair with me?" I was silent too long to make it convincing before saying that we'd certainly give it a try, didn't he think? Fortunately, we got to the airport very soon after that and, instead of letting him park, I just got out in front of the terminal and kissed him good-bye and escaped.

Later, on the plane, I was thinking about all the little pieces of far-advanced and none-too-pleasant relationships that I had sensed between myself and Eric. I was wondering what my two-night stand might have to teach me; in science, of course, you have to learn from your experiments, and one valuable lesson is that you can never control all the variables. It can be scary when an experiment gets out of hand, and back at the airport, I'd had the distinct feeling that Eric was ready for all sorts of complications. I suspected there was something to be learned from this interlude with him about the nature of entanglements that occur between lives, the extremely fine line between no relationship and all relationships. And then suddenly, I began to smile to myself, almost to giggle, because it occurred to me that Eric had wanted to follow this experiment to wherever it might lead us, but that I had prevented it. I'd kept it to something more like a seminar—short, controlled, ending neatly on schedule. But it had been educational, I decided; it's hard to learn major lessons in quick little seminars, but they can serve to expose you to new ideas, to start you thinking. The most important thing about seminars is that they should surprise you a little. You shouldn't know, walking in, exactly how you'll feel walking out. And if, in addition, you enjoy them while they last, then you have to consider them successful, I suppose.   [1983]

QUESTIONS

1. How well does the narrator know herself? Is she in any sense playing a role expected of her?
2. What is the function of Eleanora's interruption?
3. What are the various meanings of "good" in the title?
4. What is the force of the final "I suppose"?
5. The narrator does not expect "major lessons" but does expect at least a "surprise." Has she had either?

RESPONSES

1. Perri Klass is a medical doctor. Read her books about being a medical student and about being a pediatrician: *A Not Entirely Benign Procedure* and *Baby Doctor*. Compare her professional persona to the professional persona of the narrator in "Not a Good Girl."
2. Write an essay about who the audience for this story is. For instance, are there jokes and metaphors that are more poignant for particular audiences?

MILAN KUNDERA

Milan Kundera (b. 1929) was born and educated in Czechoslovakia, and became one of his country's most important intellectuals. Beginning his career as a poet and dramatist, Kundera also taught cinematography at Prague University. His first novel enjoyed great popularity before Russian forces invaded Czechoslovakia, and Kundera was the first from the university to have his books banned. In 1975, he emigrated to France, where he has since been teaching and writing. *Laughable Loves* (1969) is his only volume of short fiction, but among his novels are *The Book of Laughter and Forgetting* (1979), *The Unbearable Lightness of Being* (1984), *Identity* (1998), and *Ignorance* (2002). Two works of nonfiction, originally written in French, are *The Art of the Novel* (1988) and *Testaments Betrayed* (1995).

*Let the Old Dead Make Room
for the Young Dead*

1

He was returning home along the street of a small Bohemian town, where he had been living for several years, reconciled to his not-too-exciting life, his backbiting neighbors, and the monotonous rowdiness that surrounded him at work, and he was walking so totally without seeing (as one walks along a path traversed a hundred times) that he almost passed her by. But she had already recognized him from a distance, and coming toward him she gave him that gentle smile of hers; only at the last moment, when they had almost passed each other, did the smile ring a bell in his memory and snap him out of his drowsy state.

"I wouldn't have recognized you!" he apologized, but it was an awkward apology, because it brought them precipitously to a painful subject, about which it would have been advisable to keep silent; they had not seen each other for fifteen years and during this time they had both aged. "Have I changed so much?" she asked, and he replied that she hadn't, and even if this was a lie it wasn't an out-and-out lie, because that gentle smile (expressing demurely and restrainedly a capacity for some sort of eternal enthusiasm) emerged from the distance of many years quite unchanged, and it confused him: it evoked for him so distinctly the former appearance of this woman that he had to make a definite effort to disregard it and to see her as she was now: she was almost an old woman.

He asked her where she was going and what was on her schedule, and she replied that she had nothing else to do but wait for the train that would take her back to Prague that evening. He evinced pleasure at their unexpected meeting, and because they agreed (with good reason) that the two local cafés were overcrowded and dirty, he invited her to his bachelor apartment, which wasn't very far away; he had both coffee and tea there, and, more important, it was clean and peaceful.

2

Right from the start it had been a bad day. Her husband (twenty-five years ago she had lived here with him for a short time as a new bride, then they had moved to Prague, where he'd died ten years back) was buried, thanks to an eccentric wish in his last will and testament, in the local cemetery. At that time she had paid in advance for a ten-year lease on the grave, but a few days before, she had become afraid that the time limit had expired and that she had forgotten to renew the lease. Her first impulse had been to write the cemetery administration, but then she had realized how futile it was to correspond with the authorities, and she had come out here.

She knew the path to her husband's grave from memory, and yet today she felt as   5
if she was in this cemetery for the first time. She couldn't find the grave, and it seemed to her that she had gone astray. It took her a while to understand. There, where the gray sandstone monument with the name of her husband in gold lettering used to be, precisely on that spot (she confidently recognized the two neighboring graves) now stood a black marble headstone with a quite different name in gilt.

Upset, she went to the cemetery administration. There they told her that upon expiration of the leases, the graves were canceled. She reproached them for not having advised her that she should renew the lease, and they replied that there was little room in the cemetery and that *the old dead must make room for the young dead*. This exasperated her, and she told them, holding back her tears, that they knew absolutely nothing of human dignity or respect for others, but she understood that the conversation was useless. Just as she could not have prevented her husband's death, so also she was defenseless against his second death, this death of an *old dead* who is now forbidden to exist even as dead.

She went off into town, and anxiety quickly began to mingle with her sorrow as she tried to imagine how she would explain to her son the disappearance of his father's grave and how she would justify her neglect. At last fatigue overtook her: she didn't know how to pass the long hours until time for the departure of her train, for she no longer knew anyone here, and nothing encouraged her to take even a sentimental stroll, because over the years the town had changed too much, and the once familiar places looked quite strange to her now. That is why she gratefully accepted the invitation of the (half-forgotten) old acquaintance she'd met by chance: She could wash her hands in his bathroom and then sit in his soft armchair (her legs ached), look around his room, and listen to the boiling water bubbling away behind the screen that separated the kitchen nook from the room.

3

Not long ago he had turned thirty-five, and exactly at that time he had noticed that the hair on top of his head was thinning very visibly. The bald spot wasn't there yet, but its appearance was quite conceivable (the scalp was showing beneath the hair) and, more important, it was certain to appear and in the not-too-distant future. Certainly it was ridiculous to make thinning hair a matter of life or death, but he realized that baldness would change his face and that his hitherto youthful appearance (undeniably his best) was on its way out.

And now these considerations made him think about how the balance sheet of this person (with hair), who was going away bit by bit, actually stood, what he had actually experienced and enjoyed. What astounded him was the knowledge that he had experienced rather little; when he thought about this he felt embarrassed; yes, he was ashamed, because to live here on earth so long and to experience so little was ignominious.

10   What did he actually mean when he said to himself that he had not experienced much? Did he mean by this travel, work, public service, sports, women? Of course he meant all of these things; yet, above all, women; because if his life was deficient in other spheres it certainly upset him, but he didn't have to lay the blame for it on himself; anyhow, not for work that was uninteresting and without prospects; not for curtailing his travels because he didn't have money or reliable party references; finally, not even for the fact that when he was twenty he had injured his knee and had had to give up sports, which he had enjoyed. On the other hand, the realm of women was for him a sphere of relative freedom, and that being so, he couldn't make any excuses about it; here he could have demonstrated his wealth; women became for him the one legitimate criterion of life's *density*.

But no such luck! Things had gone somewhat badly for him with women: Until he was twenty-five (though he was a good-looking guy) shyness would tie him up in knots; then he fell in love, got married, and after seven years had persuaded himself that it was possible to find the infinity of erotic possibilities in one woman: then he got divorced and the one-woman apologetics (and the illusion of infinity) melted away, and in their place came an agreeable taste for and boldness in the pursuit of women (a pursuit of their varied finiteness): unfortunately his bad financial situation frustrated his newfound desires (he had to pay his former wife for the support of a child he was allowed to see once or twice a year), and conditions in the small town were such that the curiosity of the neighbors was as enormous as the choice of women was scant.

And time was already passing very quickly, and all at once he was standing in the bathroom in front of the oval mirror located above the washbasin; in his right hand he held over his head a round mirror and was transfixed examining the bald spot that had begun to appear; this sight suddenly (without preparation) brought home to him the banal truth that what he'd missed couldn't be made good. He found himself in a state of chronic ill humor and was even assailed by thoughts of suicide. Naturally (and it is necessary to emphasize this, in order not to see him as a hysterical or stupid person), he appreciated the comic aspects of these thoughts, and he knew that he would never carry them out (he laughed inwardly at his own suicide note: *I won't put up with my bald spot. Farewell!*), but it is enough that these thoughts, however platonic they may have been, assailed him at all. Let us try to understand: the thoughts made themselves felt within him perhaps as the overwhelming desire to give up the race makes itself felt within a marathon runner, when halfway through he discovers that shamefully (and moreover through his own fault, his own blunders) he is losing. He also considered his race lost, and he didn't feel like running any farther.

And now he bent down over the small table and placed one cup of coffee on it in front of the couch (on which he was going to sit down), the other in front of the arm-chair, in which his visitor was sitting, and said to himself that there was a strange spitefulness in the fact that he had encountered this woman, with whom he had once been madly in love and whom he had allowed to escape him (through his own fault), encountered her precisely when he found himself in this state of mind and at a time when it was no longer possible to recapture anything.

4

She would hardly have guessed that in his eyes she was *the one who had escaped him;* still, she had always remembered the night they had spent together; she remembered how he had looked then (he was twenty, didn't know how to dress, used to blush, and his boyishness amused her); and she remembered what she had been like (she had been almost forty, and a thirst for beauty drove her into the arms of other men, but also drove her away from them; she had always thought that her life should have resembled a *delightful ball,* and she feared that her unfaithfulness to her husband might turn into an ugly habit).

Yes, she had decreed beauty for herself, as people decree moral injunctions for themselves; if she had noticed any ugliness in her own life, she would perhaps have fallen into despair. And because she was now aware that after fifteen years she must seem old to her host (with all the ugliness that this brings with it), she wanted quick-ly to unfold an imaginary fan in front of her face, and to this end she deluged him with questions: she asked him how he had come to this town; she asked him about his job; she complimented him on the coziness of his bachelor apartment, and praised the view from the window over the rooftops of the town (she said that it was of course no special view, but that there was an airiness and freedom about it). She named the painters of several framed reproductions of impressionist pictures (this was not dif-ficult, in the apartments of most Czech intellectuals one was certain to find these cheap prints), then she got up from the table with her unfinished cup of coffee in her hand and bent over a small writing desk, on which were a few photographs in a stand (it didn't escape her that among them there was no photo of a young woman), and she asked whether the face of the old woman in one of them belonged to his mother (he confirmed this).

Then he asked her what she had meant when she had told him earlier that she had come here to take care of some things. She really dreaded speaking about the cemetery (here on the sixth floor she not only felt high above the roofs, but also pleasantly high above her own life); when he insisted, though, she finally confessed (but very briefly, because the immodesty of hasty frankness had always been foreign to her) that she had lived here many years before, that her husband was buried here (she was silent about the cancellation of the grave), and that she and her son had been coming here for the last ten years without fail on All Souls' Day.

15

5

"Every year?" This statement saddened him, and once again he thought of the spite-fulness of fate; if only he'd met her six years ago when he'd moved here, everything could have been possible; she wouldn't have been so marked by age, her appearance wouldn't have been so different from the image he had of the woman he had loved fif-teen years before; it would have been within his power to surmount the difference and perceive both images (the image of the past and that of the present) as one. But now they stood hopelessly far apart.

She drank her coffee and talked. He tried hard to determine precisely the extent of the transformation by means of which she was escaping him *for the second time:* her face was wrinkled (in vain did the layer of powder try to deny this); her neck was withered (in vain did the high collar try to hide this); her cheeks sagged; her hair (but it was al-most beautiful!) had grown gray; however, her hands drew his attention most of all (un-fortunately, it was not possible to touch them up with powder or paint): bunches of blue veins stood out on them, so that all at once they were the hands of a man.

In him pity was mixed with anger, and he felt like drowning their too-long-put-off meeting in alcohol; he asked her if she wanted some cognac (he had an opened bottle in the cabinet behind the screen); she replied that she didn't, and he remembered that even fifteen years before she had drunk almost not at all, perhaps so that alcohol wouldn't make her behave contrary to the demands of good taste and decorum. And when he saw the delicate movement of her hand with which she refused the offer of cognac, he realized that this charm, this magic, this grace, which had enraptured him, was still the same in her, though hidden beneath the mask of old age, and was in it-self still attractive, even though it was behind a grille.

20   When it crossed his mind that this was *the grille of age,* he felt immense pity for her, and this pity brought her nearer to him (this woman who had once been so dazzling, before whom he used to be tongue-tied), and he wanted to have a conversation with her and to talk the way a friend talks with a friend, at length, in a blue atmosphere of melancholy resignation. He started to talk (and it did indeed turn into a long talk) and eventually he got to the pessimistic thoughts that had visited him of late. Naturally he was silent about the bald spot that was beginning to appear (it was just like her si-lence about the canceled grave); on the other hand the vision of the bald spot was tran-substantiated into quasi-philosophical maxims to the effect that time passes more quickly than man is able to live, and that life is terrible, because everything in it is nec-essarily doomed to extinction; he voiced these and similar maxims, to which he wait-ed a sympathetic response; but he didn't get it.

"I don't like that kind of talk," she said almost vehemently. "Everything you've been saying is awfully superficial."

6

She didn't like conversations about growing old or dying, because they contained im-ages of physical ugliness, which went against the grain with her. Several times, almost in a fluster, she repeated to her host that his opinions were *superficial;* after all, she said, a man is more than just a body that wastes away, a man's work is substantial and that is what he leaves behind for others. Her advocacy of this opinion wasn't new: it had first come to her aid when, thirty years earlier, she had fallen in love with her for-mer husband, who was nineteen years older than she. She had never ceased to respect him wholeheartedly (in spite of all her infidelities, about which he either didn't know or didn't want to know), and she took pains to convince herself that her husband's intellect and importance would fully outweigh the heavy load of his years.

"What kind of work, I ask you? What kind of work do we leave behind?" protested her host with a bitter laugh.

She didn't want to refer to her dead husband, though she firmly believed in the lasting value of everything that he had accomplished; she therefore only said that every man accomplishes something, which in itself may be most modest, but that in this and only in this is his value; then she went on to talk about herself, how she worked in a house of culture in a suburb of Prague, how she organized lectures and poetry readings; she spoke (with an excitement that seemed out of proportion to him) about "the grateful faces" of the public; then she expatiated on how beautiful it was to have a son and to see her own features (her son looked like her) changing into the face of a man; how it was beautiful to give him everything that a mother can give a son and then to fade quietly into the background of his life.

It was not by chance that she had begun to talk about her son, because all day her   25
son had been in her thoughts, a reproachful reminder of the morning's failure at the cemetery; it was strange; she had never let any man impose his will on her, but her own son subjugated her, and she didn't understand how. The failure at the cemetery had upset her so much today, above all because she felt guilty before him and feared his reproaches. Of course she had long suspected that her son so jealously watched over the way she honored his father's memory (it was he who insisted every All Souls' Day that they should not fail to visit the cemetery!), not so much out of love for his dead father as from a desire to usurp his mother, to assign her to a widow's proper confines. For that's how it was, even if he never voiced it and she tried hard (without success) not to know it: the idea that his mother could still have a sex life disgusted him: everything in her that remained sexual (at least in the realm of possibility and chance) disgusted him, and because the idea of sex is connected with the idea of youthfulness, he was disgusted by everything that was still youthful in her; he was no longer a child, and his mother's youthfulness (combined with the aggressiveness of her motherly care) disagreeably thwarted his relationship with girls, who had begun to interest him; he wanted to have an old mother; only from such a mother would he tolerate love, and it was only such a mother he was capable of loving. And although at times she realized that in this way he was pushing her toward the grave, she had finally submitted to him, succumbed to his pressure, and even idealized her capitulation, persuading herself that the beauty of her life consisted precisely in quietly fading out in the shadow of another life. In the name of this idealization (without which the wrinkles on her face would have made her far more uneasy), she now conducted with such unexpected warmth this dispute with her host.

But her host suddenly leaned across the low table that stood between them, stroked her hand, and said: "Forgive my chatter. You know that I always was an idiot."

7

Their dispute didn't irritate him; on the contrary his visitor yet again confirmed her identity for him. In her protest against his pessimistic talk (wasn't this above all a protest against ugliness and bad taste?), he recognized her as the person he had once known, so her former appearance and their old adventure filled his thoughts all the more. Now he wished only that nothing destroy the intimate mood, so favorable to their conversation (for that reason he stroked her hand and called himself an idiot), and he wanted to tell her about the thing that seemed most important to him at this moment: their adventure together. For he was convinced that he had experienced something very special with her, which she didn't suspect and which he himself with difficulty would now try to put into precise words.

He no longer even remembered how they had met; apparently she sometimes came in contact with his student friends, but he remembered perfectly the out-of-the-way Prague café where they had been alone together for the first time: he had been sitting opposite her in a plush booth, depressed and silent, but at the same time thoroughly elated by her delicate hints that she was favorably disposed toward him. He had tried hard to visualize (without daring to hope for the fulfillment of these dreams) how she would look if he kissed her, undressed her, and made love to her—but he just couldn't manage it. Yes, there was something odd about it: He had tried a thousand times to imagine her in bed, but in vain. Her face kept on looking at him with its calm, gentle smile and he couldn't (even with the most dogged efforts of his imagination) distort it with the grimace of erotic ecstasy. *She absolutely escaped his imagination.*

And that was the situation, which had never since been repeated in his life. At that time he had stood face-to-face with the *unimaginable.* Obviously he was experiencing that very short period (the *paradisiac* period) when the imagination is not yet satiated by experience, has not become routine, knows little, and knows how to do little, so that the unimaginable still exists; and should the unimaginable become reality (without the mediation of the imaginable, without that narrow bridge of images), a man will be seized by panic and vertigo. Such vertigo did actually overtake him, when after several further meetings, in the course of which he hadn't resolved anything, she began to ask him in detail and with meaningful curiosity about his student room in the dormitory, so that she soon forced him to invite her there.

30   He had shared the little room in the dorm with another student, who for a glass of rum had promised not to return until after midnight; it bore little resemblance to his bachelor apartment of today: two metal cots, two chairs, a cupboard, a glaring, unshaded lightbulb, and frightful disorder. He tidied up the room, and at seven o'clock (it went with her refinement that she was habitually on time) she knocked on the door. It was September, and only gradually did it begin to get dark. They sat down on the edge of a cot and kissed. Then it got even darker, and he didn't want to switch on the light, because he was glad that he couldn't be seen, and hoped that the darkness would relieve the state of embarrassment in which he would find himself having to undress in front of her. (If he knew tolerably well how to unbutton women's blouses, he himself would undress in front of them with bashful haste.) This time, however, he didn't for a long time dare to undo her first button (it seemed to him that in the matter of beginning to undress there must exist some tasteful and elegant procedure, which only men who were experts knew, and he was afraid of betraying his inexperience), so that in the end she herself stood up and, asking with a smile, said: "Shouldn't I take off this armor?" She began to undress. It was dark, however, and he saw only the shadows of her movements. He hastily undressed too and gained some confidence only when they began (thanks to her patience) to make love. He looked into her face, but in the dusk her expression entirely eluded him, and he couldn't even make out her features. He regretted that it was dark, but it seemed impossible for him to get up and move away from her at that moment to turn on the switch by the door, so vainly he went on straining his eyes. But he didn't recognize her. It seemed to him that he was making

love with someone else; with someone spurious or else someone quite unreal and unindividuated.

Then she had got on top of him (he could see only her raised shadow), and moving her hips, she said something in a muffled tone, in a whisper, but it wasn't clear whether she was talking to him or to herself. He couldn't make out the words and asked her what she had said. She went on whispering, and even when he clasped her to him again, he couldn't understand what she was saying.

8

She listened to her host and became increasingly absorbed in details she had long ago forgotten: for instance, in those days she used to wear a pale blue summer suit, in which, they said, she looked like an inviolable angel (yes, she recalled that suit); she used to wear a large ivory comb stuck in her hair, which they said gave her a majestically old-fashioned look; at the café she always used to order tea with rum (her only alcoholic vice), and all this pleasantly carried her away from the cemetery, away from the vanished monument, away from her sore feet, away from the house of culture, and away from the reproachful eyes of her son. Ah, she thought, whatever I am today, if a bit of my youth lives on in this man's memory, I haven't lived in vain. This immediately struck her as a new corroboration of her conviction that the worth of a human being lies in the ability to extend oneself, to go outside oneself, to exist in and for other people.

She listened and didn't resist him when from time to time he stroked her hand; the stroking merged with the soothing tone of the conversation and had a disarming indefiniteness about it (for whom was it intended? for the woman *about whom* he was speaking or for the woman *to whom* he was speaking?); after all, she liked the man who was stroking her; she even said to herself that she liked him better than the young man of fifteen years ago, whose boyishness, if she remembered correctly, had been rather a nuisance.

When he, in his account, got to the moment when her moving shadow had risen above him and he had vainly endeavored to understand her whispering, he fell silent for an instant, and she (foolishly, as if he could know those words and would want to remind her of them after so many years like some forgotten mystery) asked softly: "And what was I saying?"

9

"I don't know," he replied. He didn't know; at that time she had escaped not only his imagination but also his perceptions; she had escaped his sight and hearing. When he had switched on the light in the dormitory room, she was already dressed, everything about her was once again sleek, dazzling, perfect, and he vainly sought a connection between her face in the light and the face that a moment before he had been guessing at in the darkness. They hadn't parted yet, but he was already trying to remember her; he tried to imagine how her (unseen) face and (unseen) body had looked when they'd made love a little while before—but without success. She was still escaping his imagination.

He had made up his mind that next time he would make love to her with the light on. Only there wasn't a next time. From that day on she adroitly and tactfully avoided him. He had failed hopelessly, yet it wasn't clear why. They'd certainly made love beautifully, but he also knew how impossible he had been *beforehand*, and he was ashamed of this; he felt condemned by her avoidance and no longer dared to pursue her.

"Tell me, why did you avoid me then?"

"I beg you," she said in the gentlest of voices. "It was so long ago that I don't know." And when he pressed her further she protested: "You shouldn't always return to the past. It's enough that we have to devote so much time to it against our will." She said this only to ward off his insistence (and perhaps the last sentence, spoken with a light sigh, referred to her morning visit to the cemetery), but he perceived her statement differently: as an intense and purposeful clarification for him of the fact (this obvious thing) that there were not two women (from the past and from the present), but only one and the same woman, and that she, who had escaped him fifteen years earlier, was here now, was within reach of his hand.

"You're right, the present is more important," he said in a meaningful tone, and he looked intently at her face. She was smiling with her mouth half open, and he glimpsed a row of white teeth. At that instant a recollection flashed through his head: that time in his dorm room she had put his fingers into her mouth and bitten them hard until it had hurt. Meanwhile he had been feeling the whole inside of her mouth, and he distinctly remembered that on one side at the back her upper teeth were missing (this had not disgusted him at the time; on the contrary such a trivial imperfection went with her age, which attracted and aroused him). But now, looking into the space between her teeth and the corner of her mouth, he saw that her teeth were too strikingly white and that none were missing, and this made him shudder; once again she split apart into images of two women, but he didn't want to admit it; he wanted to reunite them by force and violence, and so said: "Don't you really feel like having some cognac?" When with a charming smile and a mildly raised eyebrow she shook her head, he went behind the screen, took out the bottle, put it to his lips, and took a swig. Then it occurred to him that she would be able to detect his secret action from his breath, and so he picked up two small glasses and the bottle and carried them into the room. Once more she shook her head. "At least symbolically," he said and filled both glasses. He clinked her glass and made a toast: "This is to talking about you only in the present tense!" He downed his drink, and she moistened her lips. He took a seat on the arm of her chair and seized her hands.

10

40   She hadn't suspected when she had agreed to go to his bachelor apartment that it could come to *such* touching, and at first she had been struck by fright; as if touching had come before she had been able to prepare herself (the *state of permanent preparedness* that is familiar to the mature woman she had lost long ago; we should perhaps find in this fright something akin to the fright of a very young girl who has just been kissed for the first time, for if the young girl is *not yet* and she, the visitor, was *no longer* prepared, then this "no longer" and "not yet" are mysteriously related as the peculiarities of old age and childhood are related). Then he moved her from the armchair to the couch, clasped her to him, and stroked her whole body, and in his arms she felt formlessly soft (yes, soft, because her body had long ago lost the sensuality that had once

ruled it, the sensuality that had endowed her muscles with the rhythm of tensing and relaxation and with the activity of a hundred delicate movements).

But the moment of fright quickly melted in his embrace, and she, very far from the beauty she had once been, now reverted, with dizzying speed, to being that woman, reverted to that woman's feelings and to her consciousness, and retrieved the old self-confidence of an erotically experienced woman, and because this was a self-confidence long unfelt, she felt it now more intensely than ever before; her body, which a short while before had still been surprised, fearful, passive, and soft, revived and respond-ed now with its own caresses, and she felt the distinctness and adeptness of these ca-resses, and it filled her with happiness; these caresses, the way she put her face to his body, the delicate movements with which her torso answered his embrace—she found all this not like something learned, something she knew how to do and was now per-forming with cool satisfaction, but like something essentially *her own*, with which she merged in intoxication and exaltation as she found her own familiar continent (ah, the continent of beauty!), from which she had been banished and to which she now re-turned in celebration.

Her son was now infinitely far away; when her host had clasped her, in a corner of her mind she caught sight of the boy warning her of the danger, but then he quickly disappeared, and there remained only she and the man who was stroking and em-bracing her. But when he placed his lips on her lips and tried to open her mouth with his tongue, everything changed: she woke up. She firmly clenched her teeth (she felt her denture pressed against the roof of her mouth, she felt that her mouth had been filled), and she gently pushed him away, saying: "No. Really, please, I'd rather not."

When he kept on insisting, she held him by the wrists and repeated her refusal; then she said (it was hard for her to speak, but she knew that she must speak if she wanted him to obey her) that it was too late for them to make love; she reminded him of her age, if they did make love he would be disgusted with her and she would feel wretched about it, because what he had told her about the two of them was for her im-mensely beautiful and important. Her body was mortal and wasted, but she now knew that of it there still remained something incorporeal, something like the glow that shines even after a star has burned out; it didn't matter that she was growing old if her youth remained intact, present within another being. "You've erected a monument to me within your memory. We cannot allow it to be destroyed. Please understand me," she said, warding him off. "Don't let it happen. No, don't let it happen!"

11

He assured her that she was still beautiful, that in fact nothing had changed, that a human being always remains the same, but he knew that he was deceiving her and that she was right: he was well aware of his physical supersensitivity, his increasing fas-tidiousness about the external defects of a woman's body, which in recent years had driven him to ever younger and therefore, as he bitterly realized, also ever emptier and stupider women; yes, there was no doubt about it: if he got her to make love it would end in disgust, and this disgust would then splatter with mud not only the pre-sent, but also the image of the beloved woman of long ago, an image cherished like a jewel in his memory.

He knew all this, but only intellectually, and the intellect meant nothing in the face   45
of this desire, which knew only one thing: the woman he had thought of as unattain-able and elusive for fifteen years was here; at last he could see her in broad daylight,

at last he might discern from her body of today what her body had been like then, from her face of today what her face had been like then. Finally he might read the unimaginable expression on her face while making love.

He clasped her shoulders and looked into her eyes: "Don't fight me. It's absurd to fight me."

12

But she shook her head, because she knew that it wasn't absurd for her to refuse him; she knew men and their approach to the female body; she was aware that in love even the most passionate idealism will not rid the body's surface of its terrible, basic importance; it is true that she still had a nice figure, which had preserved its original proportions, and especially in her clothes she looked quite youthful; but she knew that when she undressed she would expose the wrinkles in her neck, the long scar from stomach surgery ten years before.

And just as the consciousness of her present physical appearance, which she had forgotten a short while before, returned to her, so there arose from the street below (until now, this room had seemed to her safely high above her life) the anxieties of the morning; they were filling the room, they were alighting on the prints behind glass, on the armchair, on the table, on the empty coffee cup—and her son's face dominated their procession; when she caught sight of it, she blushed and fled somewhere deep inside herself; foolishly she had been on the point of wishing to escape from the path he had assigned to her and which she had trodden up to now with a smile and words of enthusiasm; she had been on the point of wishing (at least for a moment) to escape, and now she must obediently return and admit that it was the only path suitable for her. Her son's face was so derisive that, in shame, she felt herself growing smaller and smaller before him until, humiliated, she turned into the mere scar on her stomach.

Her host held her by the shoulders and once again repeated: "It's absurd for you to fight me," and she shook her head, but quite mechanically, because what she was seeing was not her host but the face of her son-enemy, whom she hated the more the smaller and the more humiliated she felt. She heard him reproaching her about the canceled grave, and now, from the chaos of her memory, illogically there surged forth the sentence she had shouted at his face with rage: *The old dead must make room for the young dead, my boy!*

13

50   He didn't have the slightest doubt that this would actually end in disgust, for even now the look he fixed on her (a searching and penetrating look) was not free from a certain disgust, but the curious thing was that he didn't mind; on the contrary, it aroused him and goaded him on as if he were wishing for this disgust: the desire for coition approached the desire for disgust; the desire to read on her body what he had for so long been unable to know mingled with the desire immediately to soil the newly deciphered secret.

Where did this passion come from? Whether he realized it or not, a unique opportunity was presenting itself: to him his visitor embodied everything that he had never had, that had escaped him, that he had missed, everything that by its absence made his present age intolerable, with his thinning hair, his dismally meager balance sheet; and he, whether he realized it or only vaguely suspected it, could now strip all these pleasures that had been denied him of their significance and color (for it was precisely their terrific colorfulness that made his life so sadly colorless), he could reveal that they were worthless, that they were only appearances doomed to destruction, that they were only metamorphosed dust; he could take revenge upon them, demean them, destroy them.

"Don't fight me," he repeated as he tried to draw her close.

14

Before her eyes she still saw her son's derisive face, and when now her host drew her to him by force she said. "Please, leave me alone for a minute," and she escaped his embrace; she didn't want to interrupt what was racing through her head: the old dead must make room for the young dead and monuments were useless, even her monument, which this man beside her had honored for fifteen years in his thoughts, was useless, all monuments were useless. That is what she silently said to her son. And with vengeful delight she watched his contorted face and heard him shout: "You never talked like this before, Mother!" Of course she knew that she had never spoken like this, but this moment was filled with a light, under which everything became quite different.

There was no reason why she should give preference to monuments over life; her own monument had a single meaning for her: that at this moment she could abuse it for the sake of her disparaged body; the man who was sitting beside her appealed to her; he was young and very likely (almost certainly) he was the last man who would appeal to her and whom, at the same time, she could have, and that alone was important; if he then became disgusted with her and destroyed her monument in his thoughts, it made no difference because her monument was outside her, just as his thoughts and memory were outside her, and everything that was outside her made no difference. "You never talked like this before, Mother!" She heard her son's cry, but she paid no attention to him. She was smiling.

"You're right, why should I fight you?" she said quietly, and she got up. Then she slowly began to unbutton her dress. Everything was still a long way off. This time the room was filled with light. [1969]

QUESTIONS

1. Neither of these characters have names. What effect did that have on you as you read the story?
2. How has Kundera related the structure of the plot and his use of point of view? What does the technique add to the story?
3. How important is the setting in the story?
4. Does the narrator sympathize with the characters equally, or is one character more sympathetically presented?
5. What changes in the woman at the end of the story?

RESPONSES

1. Read Kundera's comments about Kafka's fiction in "Somewhere Behind." How is this story like a story by Kafka?

2. Read Kate Chopin's "A Respectable Woman" and Peri Klass's "Not a Good Girl." Write an essay explaining what Kundera adds to our understanding, if anything, of women's sexuality.

HANIF KUREISHI

Hanif Kureishi (b. 1954) is of Pakistani and English heritage and was raised in the suburbs of London. He is a playwright, screenwriter, and director. His plays include *Bloodline* (1981); his films include *My Beautiful Laundrette* (1986), *Sammy and Rosie Get Laid* (1988), and *My Son the Fanatic* (1998). Among his novels are *The Buddha of Suburbia* (1990), *The Black Album* (1995), *Intimacy* (1998) and *Body* (2004). His short fiction has been collected in *Love in a Blue Time* (1997) and *Midnight All Day* (1999). He is a winner of the Whiting Award for best first novel. In 2002, he published *Collected Screenplays*.

My Son the Fanatic

Surreptitiously the father began going into his son's bedroom. He would sit there for hours, rousing himself only to seek clues. What bewildered him was that Ali was getting tidier. Instead of the usual tangle of clothes, books, cricket bats, video games, the room was becoming neat and ordered; spaces began appearing where before there had been only mess.

Initially Parvez had been pleased: his son was outgrowing his teenage attitudes. But one day, beside the dustbin, Parvez found a torn bag which contained not only old toys, but computer discs, video tapes, new books and fashionable clothes the boy had bought just a few months before. Also without explanation, Ali had parted from the English girlfriend who used to come often to the house. His old friends had stopped ringing.

For reasons he didn't himself understand, Parvez wasn't able to bring up the subject of Ali's unusual behaviour. He was aware that he had become slightly afraid of his son, who, alongside his silences, was developing a sharp tongue. One remark Parvez did make, 'You don't play your guitar any more,' elicited the mysterious but conclusive reply, 'There are more important things to be done.'

Yet Parvez felt his son's eccentricity as an injustice. He had always been aware of the pitfalls which other men's sons had fallen into in England. And so, for Ali, he had worked long hours and spent a lot of money paying for his education as an accountant. He had bought him good suits, all the books he required and a computer. And now the boy was throwing his possessions out!

5   The TV, video and sound system followed the guitar. Soon the room was practically bare. Even the unhappy walls bore marks where Ali's pictures had been removed.

Parvez couldn't sleep; he went more to the whisky bottle, even when he was at work. He realised it was imperative to discuss the matter with someone sympathetic.

Parvez had been a taxi driver for twenty years. Half that time he'd worked for the same firm. Like him, most of the other drivers were Punjabis. They preferred to work at night, the roads were clearer and the money better. They slept during the day, avoiding their wives. Together they led almost a boy's life in the cabbies' office, playing cards and practical jokes, exchanging lewd stories, eating together and discussing politics and their problems.

But Parvez had been unable to bring this subject up with his friends. He was too ashamed. And he was afraid, too, that they would blame him for the wrong turning his boy had taken, just as he had blamed other fathers whose sons had taken to running around with bad girls, truanting from school and joining gangs.

For years Parvez had boasted to the other men about how Ali excelled at cricket, swimming and football, and how attentive a scholar he was, getting straight 'A's in most subjects. Was it asking too much for Ali to get a good job now, marry the right girl and start a family? Once this happened, Parvez would be happy. His dreams of doing well in England would have come true. Where had he gone wrong?

10   But one night, sitting in the taxi office on busted chairs with his two closest friends watching a Sylvester Stallone film, he broke his silence.

'I can't understand it!' he burst out. 'Everything is going from his room. And I can't talk to him any more. We were not father and son—we were brothers! Where has he gone? Why is he torturing me!'

And Parvez put his head in his heads.

Even as he poured out his account the men shook their heads and gave one another knowing glances. From their grave looks Parvez realised they understood the situation.

'Tell me what is happening!' he demanded.

15   The reply was almost triumphant. They had guessed something was going wrong. Now it was clear. Ali was taking drugs and selling his possessions to pay for them. That was why his bedroom was emptying.

'What must I do then?'

Parvez's friends instructed him to watch Ali scrupulously and then be severe with him, before the boy went mad, overdosed or murdered someone.

Parvez staggered out into the early morning air, terrified they were right. His boy— the drug addict killer!

To his relief he found Bettina sitting in his car.

20   Usually the last customers of the night were local 'brasses' or prostitutes. The taxi drivers knew them well, often driving them to liaisons. At the end of the girls' shifts, the men would ferry them home, though sometimes the women would join them for a drinking session in the office. Occasionally the drivers would go with the girls. 'A ride in exchange for a ride,' it was called.

Bettina had known Parvez for three years. She lived outside the town and on the long drive home, where she sat not in the passenger seat but beside him, Parvez had talked to her about his life and hopes, just as she talked about hers. They saw each other most nights.

He could talk to her about things he'd never be able to discuss with his own wife. Bettina, in turn, always reported on her night's activities. He liked to know where she was and with whom. Once he had rescued her from a violent client, and since then they had come to care for one another.

Though Bettina had never met the boy, she heard about Ali continually. That late night, when he told Bettina that he suspected Ali was on drugs, she judged neither the boy nor his father, but became businesslike and told him what to watch for.

'It's all in the eyes,' she said. They might be bloodshot; the pupils might be dilated; he might look tired. He could be liable to sweats, or sudden mood changes. 'Okay?'

Parvez began his vigil gratefully. Now he knew what the problem might be, he   25
felt better. And surely, he figured, things couldn't have gone too far? With Bettina's help he would soon sort it out.

He watched each mouthful the boy took. He sat beside him at every opportunity and looked into his eyes. When he could he took the boy's hand, checking his temperature. If the boy wasn't at home Parvez was active, looking under the carpet, in his drawers, behind the empty wardrobe, sniffing, inspecting, probing. He knew what to look for: Bettina had drawn pictures of capsules, syringes, pills, powders, rocks. Every night she waited to hear news of what he'd witnessed.

After a few days of constant observation, Parvez was able to report that although the boy had given up sports, he seemed healthy, with clear eyes. He didn't, as his father expected, flinch guiltily from his gaze. In fact the boy's mood was alert and steady in this sense: as well as being sullen, he was very watchful. He returned his father's long looks with more than a hint of criticism, of reproach even, so much so that Parvez began to feel that it was he who was in the wrong, and not the boy!

'And there's nothing else physically different?' Bettina asked.

'No!' Parvez thought for a moment. 'But he is growing a beard.'   30

One night, after sitting with Bettina in an all-night coffee shop, Parvez came home particularly late. Reluctantly he and Bettina had abandoned their only explanation, the drug theory, for Parvez had found nothing resembling any drug in Ali's room. Besides, Ali wasn't selling his belongings. He threw them out, gave them away or donated them to charity shops.

Standing in the hall, Parvez heard his boy's alarm clock go off. Parvez hurried into his bedroom where his wife was still awake, sewing in bed. He ordered her to sit down and keep quiet, though she had neither stood up nor said a word. From this post, and with her watching him curiously, he observed his son through the crack in the door.

The boy went into the bathroom to wash. When he returned to his room Parvez sprang across the hall and set his ear at Ali's door. A muttering sound came from within. Parvez was puzzled but relieved.

Once this clue had been established, Parvez watched him at other times. The boy was praying. Without fail, when he was at home, he prayed five times a day.

Parvez had grown up in Lahore where all the boys had been taught the Koran. To   35
stop him falling asleep when he studied, the Moulvi had attached a piece of string to the ceiling and tied it to Parvez's hair, so that if his head fell forward, he would instantly awake. After this indignity Parvez had avoided all religions. Not that the other taxi drivers had more respect. In fact they made jokes about the local mullahs walking around with their caps and beards, thinking they could tell people how to live, while their eyes roved over the boys and girls in their care.

Parvez described to Bettina what he had discovered. He informed the men in the taxi office. The friends, who had been so curious before, now became oddly silent. They could hardly condemn the boy for his devotions.

Parvez decided to take a night off and go out with the boy. They could talk things over. He wanted to hear how things were going at college; he wanted to tell him stories about their family in Pakistan. More than anything he yearned to understand how Ali had discovered the 'spiritual dimension,' as Bettina described it.

To Parvez's surprise, the boy refused to accompany him. He claimed he had an appointment. Parvez had to insist that no appointment could be more important than that of a son with his father.

The next day, Parvez went immediately to the street where Bettina stood in the rain wearing high heels, a short skirt and a long mac on top, which she would open hopefully at passing cars.

40   'Get in, get in!' he said.

They drove out across the moors and parked at the spot where on better days, with a view unimpeded for many miles by nothing but wild deer and horses, they'd lie back, with their eyes half closed, saying 'This is the life.' This time Parvez was trembling. Bettina put her arms around him.

'What's happened?'

'I've just had the worse experience of my life.'

As Bettina rubbed his head Parvez told her that the previous evening he and Ali had gone to a restaurant. As they studied the menu, the waiter, whom Parvez knew, brought him his usual whisky and water. Parvez had been so nervous he had even prepared a question. He was going to ask Ali if he was worried about his imminent exams. But first, wanting to relax, he loosened his tie, crunched a popadom and took a long drink.

45   Before Parvez could speak, Ali made a face.

'Don't you know it's wrong to drink alcohol?' he said.

'He spoke to me very harshly,' Parvez told Bettina. 'I was about to castigate the boy for being insolent, but managed to control myself.'

He had explained patiently to Ali that for years he had worked more than ten hours a day, that he had few enjoyments or hobbies and never went on holiday. Surely it wasn't a crime to have a drink when he wanted one?

'But it is forbidden,' the boy said.

50   Parvez shrugged, 'I know.'

'And so is gambling, isn't it?'

'Yes. But surely we are only human?'

Each time Parvez took a drink, the boy winced, or made a fastidious face as an accompaniment. This made Parvez drink more quickly. The waiter, wanting to please his friend, brought another glass of whisky. Parvez knew he was getting drunk, but he couldn't stop himself. Ali had a horrible look on his face, full of disgust and censure. It was as if he hated his father.

Halfway through the meal Parvez suddenly lost his temper and threw a plate on the floor. He had felt like ripping the cloth from the table, but the waiters and other customers were staring at him. Yet he wouldn't stand for his own son telling him the difference between right and wrong. He knew he wasn't a bad man. He had a conscience. There were a few things of which he was ashamed, but on the whole he had lived a decent life.

55   'When have I had time to be wicked?' he asked Ali.

In a low monotonous voice the boy explained that Parvez had not, in fact, lived a good life. He had broken countless rules of the Koran.

'For instance?' Parvez demanded.

Ali hadn't needed time to think. As if he had been waiting for this moment, he asked his father if he didn't relish pork pies?

'Well . . .'

Parvez couldn't deny that he loved crispy bacon smothered with mushrooms and 60
mustard and sandwiched between slices of fried bread. In fact he ate this for breakfast
every morning.

Ali then reminded Parvez that he had ordered his own wife to cook pork sausages,
saying to her, 'You're not in the village now, this is England. We have to fit in!'

Parvez was so annoyed and perplexed by this attack that he called for more drink.

'The problem is this,' the boy said. He leaned across the table. For the first time that
night his eyes were alive. 'You are too implicated in Western civilisation.'

Parvez burped; he thought he was going to choke. 'Implicated!' he said. 'But we live
here!'

'The Western materialists hate us,' Ali said. 'Papa, how can you love something 65
which hates you?'

'What is the answer then?' Parvez said miserably. 'According to you.'

Ali addressed his father fluently, as if Parvez were a rowdy crowd that had to be
quelled and convinced. The Law of Islam would rule the world; the skin of the infidel
would burn off again and again; the Jews and Christers would be routed. The West was
a sink of hypocrites, adulterers, homosexuals, drug takers and prostitutes.

As Ali talked, Parvez looked out of the window as if to check that they were still in
London.

'My people have taken enough. If the persecution doesn't stop there will be *jihad*.
I, and millions of others, will gladly give our lives for the cause.'

'But why, why?' Parvez said. 70

'For us the reward will be in paradise.'

'Paradise!'

Finally, as Parvez's eyes filled with tears, the boy urged him to mend his ways.

'How is that possible?' Parvez asked.

'Pray,' Ali aid. 'Pray beside me.' 75

Parvez called for the bill and ushered his boy out of the restaurant as soon as he was
able. He couldn't take any more. Ali sounded as if he'd swallowed someone else's
voice.

On the way home the boy sat in the back of the taxi, as if he were a customer.

'What has made you like this?' Parvez asked him, afraid that somehow he was to
blame for all this. 'Is there a particular event which has influenced you?'

'Living in this country.'

'But I love England,' Parvez said, watching his boy in the mirror. 'They let you do 80
almost anything here.'

'That is the problem,' he replied.

For the first time in years Parvez couldn't see straight. He knocked the side of the
car against a lorry, ripping off the wing mirror. They were lucky not to have been
stopped by the police: Parvez would have lost his license and therefore his job.

Getting out of the car back at the house, Parvez stumbled and fell in the road,
scraping his hands and ripping his trousers. He managed to haul himself up. The boy
didn't even offer him his hand.

Parvez told Bettina he was now willing to pray, if that was what the boy wanted,
if that would dislodge the pitiless look from his eyes.

'But what I object to,' he said, 'is being told by my own son that I am going to hell!' 85

What finished Parvez off was that the boy had said he was giving up accountancy.
When Parvez had asked why, Ali had said sarcastically that it was obvious.

'Western education cultivates an anti-religious attitude.'

And, according to Ali, in the world of accountants it was usual to meet women, drink alcohol and practise usury.

'But it's well-paid work,' Parvez argued. 'For years you've been preparing!'

90   Ali said he was going to begin to work in prisons, with poor Muslims who were struggling to maintain their purity in the face of corruption. Finally, at the end of the evening, as Ali was going to bed, he had asked his father why he didn't have a beard, or at least a moustache.

'I feel as if I've lost my son,' Parvez told Bettina. 'I can't bear to be looked at as if I'm a criminal. I've decided what to do.'

'What is it?'

'I'm going to tell him to pick up his prayer mat and get out of my house. It will be the hardest thing I've ever done, but tonight I'm going to do it.'

'But you mustn't give up on him,' said Bettina. 'Many young people fall into cults and superstitious groups. It doesn't mean they'll always feel the same way.'

95   She said Parvez had to stick by his boy, giving him support, until he came through.

Parvez was persuaded that she was right, even though he didn't feel like giving his son more love when he had hardly been thanked for all he had already given.

Nevertheless, Parvez tried to endure his son's looks and reproaches. He attempted to make conversation about his beliefs. But if Parvez ventured any criticism, Ali always had a brusque reply. On one occasion Ali accused Parvez of 'grovelling' to the whites; in contrast, he explained, he was not 'inferior'; there was more to the world than the West, though the West always thought it was best.

'How is it you know that?' Parvez said, 'seeing as you've never left England?'

Ali replied with a look of contempt.

100   One night, having ensured there was no alcohol on his breath, Parvez sat down at the kitchen table with Ali. He hoped Ali would compliment him on the beard he was growing but Ali didn't appear to notice.

The previous day Parvez had been telling Bettina that he thought people in the West sometimes felt inwardly empty and that people needed a philosophy to live by.

'Yes,' said Bettina. 'That's the answer. You must tell him what your philosophy of life is. Then he will understand that there are other beliefs.'

After some fatiguing consideration, Parvez was ready to begin. The boy watched him as if he expected nothing.

Haltingly Parvez said that people had to treat one another with respect, particularly children their parents. This did seem, for a moment, to affect the boy. Heartened, Parvez continued. In his view this life was all there was and when you died you rotted in the earth. 'Grass and flowers will grow out of me, but something of me will live on—'

105   'How?'

'In other people. I will continue—in you.' At this the boy appeared a little distressed. 'And your grandchildren,' Parvez added for good measure. 'But while I am here on earth I want to make the best of it. And I want you to, as well!'

'What d'you mean by "make the best of it"?' asked the boy.

'Well,' said Parvez. 'For a start . . . you should enjoy yourself. Yes. Enjoy yourself without hurting others.'

Ali said that enjoyment was a '"bottomless pit."'

110   'But I don't mean enjoyment like that!' said Parvez. 'I mean the beauty of living!'

'All over the world our people are oppressed,' was the boy's reply.

'I know,' Parvez replied, not entirely sure who 'our people' were, 'but still—life is for living!'

Ali said, 'Real morality has existed for hundreds of years. Around the world millions and millions of people share my beliefs. Are you saying you are right and they are all wrong?'

Ali looked at his father with such aggressive confidence that Parvez could say no more.

One evening Bettina was sitting in Parvez's car, after visiting a client, when they passed a boy on the street.   115

'That's my son,' Parvez said suddenly. They were on the other side of town, in a poor district, where there were two mosques.

Parvez set his face hard.

Bettina turned to watch him. 'Slow down then, slow down!' She said, 'He's good-looking. Reminds me of you. But with a more determined face. Please, can't we stop?'

'What for?'

'I'd like to talk to him.'   120

Parvez turned the cab round and stopped beside the boy.

'Coming home?' Parvez asked. 'It's quite a way.'

The sullen boy shrugged and got into the back seat. Bettina sat in the front. Parvez became aware of Bettina's short skirt, gaudy rings and ice-blue eyeshadow. He became conscious that the smell of her perfume, which he loved, filled the cab. He opened the window.

While Parvez drove as fast as he could, Bettina said gently to Ali, 'Where have you been?'

'The mosque,' he said.   125

'And how are you getting on at college? Are you working hard?'

'Who are you to ask me these questions?' he said, looking out of the window. Then they hit bad traffic and the car came to a standstill.

By now Bettina had inadvertently laid her hand on Parvez's shoulder. She said, 'Your father, who is a good man, is very worried about you. You know he loves you more than his own life.'

'You say he loves me,' the boy said.

'Yes!' said Bettina.   130

'Then why is he letting a woman like you touch him like that?'

If Bettina looked at the boy in anger, he looked back at her with twice as much cold fury.

She said, 'What kind of woman am I that deserves to be spoken to like that?'

'You know,' he said. 'Now let me out.'

'Never,' Parvez replied.   135

'Don't worry, I'm getting out,' Bettina said.

'No, don't!' said Parvez. But even as the car moved she opened the door, threw herself out and ran away across the road. Parvez shouted after her several times, but she had gone.

Parvez took Ali back to the house, saying nothing more to him. Ali went straight to his room. Parvez was unable to read the paper, watch television or even sit down. He kept pouring himself drinks.

At last he went upstairs and paced up and down outside Ali's room. When, finally, he opened the door, Ali was praying. The boy didn't even glance his way.

Parvez kicked him over. Then he dragged the boy up by his shirt and hit him.   140
The boy fell back. Parvez hit him again. The boy's face was bloody. Parvez was panting. He knew that the boy was unreachable, but he struck him nonetheless. The boy

neither covered himself nor retaliated; there was no fear in his eyes. He only said, through his split lip: 'So who's the fanatic now?'   [1994]

QUESTIONS

1. To what extent has Parvez acculturated? Is he English or Pakistani?
2. Does this story concern a generational conflict or an ideological conflict?
3. What does it mean that Parvez is taking the advice of a prostitute?
4. How does Kureishi expect the typical Western reader to react to the story?
5. In the end, is the son or the father the more sympathetic character?

RESPONSE

1. Write an essay comparing E. M. Forster's description of an Islamic-British encounter to Kureishi's description of the Islamic-British encounter.

FOCUS ON FILM

1. Write an essay examining the thematic changes the film *My Son the Fanatic* makes to the print story.
2. Compare similar scenes from the film and the print story. For instance, the scene of Parviz and Ali's dinner, or the closing scene in the print story.

MARY LAVIN

Mary Lavin (1912–1996) was born in East Walpole, Massachusetts. At the age of nine she was taken to Ireland by her parents, who had emigrated before her birth. She was educated at a convent school and at University College, Dublin. In 1942 she published *Tales from Bective Bridge*, which won the James Tait Black Memorial Prize for the best work of fiction published that year. Many collections of her stories followed. Although her stories have been published and acclaimed in the United States, and she had on several occasions been a writer-in-residence at the University of Connecticut, her work reveals few traces of her stay in this country. In 1964 *The Stories of Mary Lavin* appeared in two volumes.

My Vocation

I'm not married yet, but I'm still in hopes. One thing is certain though: I was never cut out to be a nun in the first place. Anyway, I was only thirteen when I got the Call, and I think if we were living out here in Crumlin at the time, in the new houses that the Government gave us, I'd never have got it at all, because we hardly ever see nuns out here, somehow, and a person wouldn't take so much notice of them out here anyway. It's so airy you know, and they blow along in their big white bonnets and a person wouldn't take any more notice of them than the seagulls that blow in from the sea. And then, too, you'd never get near enough to them out here to get the smell of them.

It was the smell of them I used to love in the Dorset Street days, when they'd stop us in the street to talk to us, when we'd be playing hopscotch on the path. I used to push up as close to them as possible and take big sniffs of them. But that was nothing to when they came up to the room to see Mother. You'd get it terribly strong then.

"What smell are you talking about?" said my father one day when I was going on about them after they went. "That's no way to talk about people in Religious Orders," he said. "There's no smell at all off the like of them."

That was right, of course, and I saw where I was wrong. It was the no-smell that I used to get, but there were so many smells fighting for place in Dorset Street, fried onions, and garbage, and the smell of old rags, that a person with no smell at all stood out a mile from everybody else. Anyone with an eye in their head could see that I didn't mean any disrespect. It vexed me shockingly to have my father think such a thing. I told him so, too, straight out.

5   "And if you want to know," I finished up, "I'm going to be a nun myself when I get big."

But my father only roared laughing.

"Do you hear that?" he said, turning to mother. "Isn't that a good one? She'll be joining the same order as you, I'm thinking." And he roared out laughing again: a very common laugh I thought, even though he was my father.

And he was nothing to my brother Paudeen.

"We'll be all right if it isn't the Order of Mary Magdalen that one joins," he said.

10   What do you make of that for commonness? Is it any wonder I wanted to get away from the lot of them?

He was always at me, that fellow, saying I was cheapening myself, and telling Ma on me if he saw me as much as lift my eye to a fellow passing me in the street.

"She's mad for boys, that one," he used to say. And it wasn't true at all. It wasn't my fault if the boys were always after me, was it? And even if I felt a bit sparky now and then, wasn't that the kind that always became nuns? I never saw a plain-looking one, did you? I never did. Not in those days, I mean. The ones that used to come visiting us in Dorset Street were all gorgeous-looking, with pale faces and not a rotten tooth in their heads. They were twice as good-looking as the Tiller Girls in the Gaiety. And on Holy Thursday, when we were doing the Seven Churches, and we used to cross over the Liffey to the south side to make up the number, I used to go into the Convent of the Reparation just to look at the nuns. You see them inside in a kind of little golden cage, back of the altar in their white habits with blue sashes and their big silver beads dangling down by their side. They were like angels: honest to God. You'd be sure of it if you didn't happen to hear them give an odd cough now and again, or a sneeze.

It was in there with them I'd like to be, but Sis—she's my girlfriend—she told me they were all ladies, titled ladies too, some of them, and I'd have to be a lay sister. I wasn't having any of that, thank you. I could have gone away to domestic service any day if that was only all the ambition I had. It would have broken my mother's heart to see me scrubbing floors and the like. She never sank that low, although there were fourteen of them in the family, and only eleven of us. She was never anything less than a wards' maid in the Mater Hospital, and they're sort of nurses, if you like, and when she met my father she was after getting an offer of a great job as a barmaid in Geary's of Parnell Street. She'd never have held with me being a lay sister.

"I don't hold with there being any such things as lay sisters at all," she said. "They're not allowed a hot jar in their beds, I believe, and they have to sit at the back of the chapel with no red plush on their kneeler. If you ask me, it's a queer thing to see the Church making distinctions."

15   She had a great regard for the Orders that had no lay sisters at all, like the Little Sisters of the Poor, and the Visiting Sisters.

"Oh, they're the grand women!" she said.

You'd think then, wouldn't you, that she'd be glad when I decided to join them. But she was as much against me as any of them.

"Is it you?" she cried. "You'd want to get the impudent look taken off your face if that's the case!" she said, tightly.

I suppose it was the opposition that nearly drove me mad. It made me dead set on going ahead with the thing.

20   You see, they never went against me in any of the things I was going to be before that. The time I said I was going to be a Tiller Girl in the Gaiety, you should have seen the way they went on: all of them. They were dead keen on the idea.

"Are you tall enough though—that's the thing," said Paudeen.

And the tears came into my mother's eyes.

"That's what I always wanted to be when I was a girl," she said, and she dried her eyes and turned to my father. "Do you think there is anyone you could ask to use his influence?" she said. Because she was always sure and certain that influence was the only thing that would get you any job.

But it wasn't influence in the Tiller Girls: it was legs. And I knew that, and my legs were never my strong point, so I gave up that idea.

"Then there was the time I thought I'd like to be a waitress, even though I wasn't   25
a blonde," said Paudeen morosely.

But you should see the way they went on then too.

"A packet of henna would soon settle the hair question," said my mother.

"Although I'm sure some waitresses are good girls," she said. "It all depends on a girl herself, and the kind of a home she comes from."

They were doubtful if I'd get any of these jobs, but they didn't raise any obstacles, and they didn't laugh at me like they did in this case.

"And what will I do for money," said my father, "when they come looking for   30
your dowry? If you haven't an education you have to have money, going into those convents."

But I turned a deaf ear to him.

"The Lord will provide," I said. "If it's His will for me to be a nun He'll find a way out of all difficulties," I said grandly, and in a voice I imagined to be as near as I could make it to the ladylike voices of the Visiting Sisters.

But I hadn't much hope of getting into the Visiting Sisters. To begin with, they always seemed to take it for granted I'd get married.

"I hope you're a good girl," they used to say to me, and you'd know by the way they said it what they meant. "Boys may like a fast girl when it comes to having a good time, but it's the modest girl they pick when it comes to choosing a wife," they said. And such-like things. They were always harping on the one string. Sure they'd never get over it if I told them what I had in mind. I'd never have the face to tell them!

And then one day what did I see but an advertisement in the paper.   35

"Wanted, Postulants," it said, in big letters, and then underneath in small letters, there was the address of the Reverend Mother you were to apply to, and in smaller letters still, at the very bottom, were the words that made me sit up and take notice. "No Dowry," they said.

"That's me," said I, and there and then I up and wrote off to them, without as much as saying a word to anyone only Sis.

Poor Sis: you should have seen how bad she took it.

"I can't believe it," she said over and over again, and she threw her arms around me and burst out crying. She was always a good sort, Sis.

Every time she looked at me she burst out crying. And I must say that was more like   40
the way I expected people to take me. But as a matter of fact Sis started the ball rolling, and it wasn't long after that everyone began to feel bad, because you see, the next thing that happened was a telegram arrived from the Reverend Mother in answer to my letter.

"It can't be for you," said my mother, as she ripped it open. "Who'd be sending you a telegram?"

And I didn't know who could have sent it either until I read the signature. It was Sister Mary Alacoque.

That was the name of the nun in the paper.

"It's for me all right," I said then. "I wrote to her," I said and I felt a bit awkward.

45 My mother grabbed back the telegram.

"Glory be to God!" she said, but I don't think she meant it as a prayer. "Do you see what it says? 'Calling to see you this afternoon, Deo Gratias.' What on earth is the meaning of all this?"

"Well," I said defiantly, "when I told you I was going to be a nun you wouldn't believe me. Maybe you'll believe it when I'm out among the savages!" I added. Because it was a missionary order: that's why they didn't care about the dowry. People are always leaving money in their wills to the Foreign Missions, and you don't need to be too highly educated to teach savages, I suppose.

"Glory be to God!" said my mother again. And then she turned on me. "Get up out of that and we'll try and put some sort of front on things before they get here: there'll be two of them, I'll swear. Nuns never go out alone. Hurry up, will you?"

Never in your life did you see anyone carry on like my mother did that day. For the few hours that remained of the morning she must have worked like a lunatic, running mad around the room, shoving things under the bed, and ramming home the drawers of the chest, and sweeping things off the seats of the chairs.

50 "They'll want to see a chair they can sit on, anyway," she said. "And I suppose we'll have to offer them a bite to eat."

"Oh, a cup of tea," said my father.

But my mother had very grand ideas at times.

"Oh, I always heard you should give monks or nuns a good meal," she said. "They can eat things out in the world that they can't eat in the convent. As long as you don't ask them. Don't say will you or won't you! Just set it in front of them—that's what I always heard."

I will say this for my mother, she has a sense of occasion, because we never heard any of this lore when the Visiting Sisters called, or even the Begging Sisters, although you'd think they could do with a square meal by the look of them sometimes.

55 But no: there was never before seen such a fuss as she made on this occasion.

"Run out to Mrs. Mullins in the front room and ask her for the lend of her brass fender," she cried, giving me a push out the door. "And see if poor Mr. Duffy is home from work—he'll be good enough to let us have a chair, I'm sure, the poor soul, the one with the plush seat," she cried, coming out to the landing after me, and calling across the well of the stairs.

As I disappeared into Mrs. Mullins's I could see her standing in the doorway as if she was trying to make up her mind about something. And sure enough, when I came out lugging the fender with me, she ran across and took it from me.

"Run down to the return room, like a good child," she said, "and ask old Mrs. Dooley for her tablecloth—the one with the lace edging she got from America." And as I showed some reluctance, she caught my arm. "You might give her a wee hint of what's going on. Won't everyone know it as soon as the nuns arrive, and it'll give her the satisfaction of having the news ahead of everyone else."

But it would be hard to say who had the news first because I was only at the foot of the steps leading to the return room when I could hear doors opening in every direction on our own landing, and the next minute you'd swear they were playing a new kind of postman's knock, in which each one carried a piece of furniture round with him, by the way our friends and neighbors were rushing back and forth across the landing; old Ma Dunne with her cuckoo clock, and young Mrs. McBride, that shouldn't be carrying heavy things at all, with our old wicker chair that she was going to exchange for the time with a new one of her own. And I believe she wanted to get her piano rolled in to us too, only there wasn't time!

That was the great thing about Dorset Street: you could meet any and all occasions, you had so many friends at your back. And you could get anything you wanted, all in a few minutes, without anyone outside the landing being any the wiser.

My mother often said it was like one big happy family, that landing—including the return room, of course.

The only thing was everyone wanted to have a look at the room.

"We'll never get shut of them before the nuns arrive," I thought.

"Isn't this the great news entirely," said old Mrs. Dooley, making her way up the stairs as soon as I told her. And she rushed up to my mother and kissed her. "Not but that you deserve it," she said. "I never knew a priest or a nun yet that hadn't a good mother behind them!" And then Mrs. McBride coming out, she drew her into it. "Isn't that so, Mrs. McBride?" she cried. "I suppose you heard the news?"

"I did indeed," said Mrs. McBride. "Not that I was surprised," she said, but I think she only wanted to let on she was greater with us than she was, because as Sis could tell you, there was nothing of the Holy Molly about me—far from it.

What old Mr. Duffy said was more like what you'd expect.

"Well, doesn't that beat all!" he cried, hearing the news as he came up the last step of the stairs. "Ah, well, I always heard it's the biggest divils that make the best saints, and now I can believe it!"

He was a terribly nice old man.

"And is it the Foreign Missions?" he asked, calling me to one side, "because if that's the case I want you to know you can send me raffle tickets for every draw you hold, and I'll sell the lot for you and get the stubs back in good time, with the money along with it in postal orders. And what's more—" he was going on, when Mrs. Mullins let out a scream:

"You didn't tell me it was the Missions," she cried. "Oh, God help you, you poor child!" And she threw up her hands. "How will any of us be saved at all with the like of you going to the ends of the earth where you'll never see a living soul only blacks till the day you die! Oh, glory be to God. And to think we never knew who we had in our midst!"

In some ways it was what I expected, but in another way I'd have liked if they didn't all look at me in such a pitying way.

And old Mrs. Dooley put the lid on it.

"A saint—that's what you are, child," she cried, and she caught my hand and pulled me down close to her—she was a low butt of a little woman. "They tell me it's out to the poor lepers you're going?"

That was the first I heard about lepers, I can tell you. And I partly guessed the poor old thing had picked it up wrong, but all the same I put a knot in my handkerchief to remind me to ask where I was going.

And I may as well admit straight out, that I wasn't having anything to do with any lepers. I hadn't thought of backing out of the thing entirely at that time, but I was backing out of it if it was to be lepers!

The thought of the lepers gave me the creeps, I suppose. Did you ever get the feeling when a thing was mentioned that you *had* it? Well, that was the way I felt. I kept going over to the basin behind the screen (Mrs. McBride's) and washing my hands every minute, and as for spitting out, my throat was raw by the time I heard the cab at the door.

"Here they come," cried my father, raising his hand like the starter at the dog track.

"Out of this, all of you," cried Mrs. Mullins, rushing out and giving an example to everyone.

"Holy God!" said my mother, but I don't think that was meant to be a prayer either. But she had nothing to be uneasy about: the room was gorgeous.

That was another thing: I thought they'd be delighted with the room. We never did it up any way special for the Visiting Sisters, but they were always saying how nice we kept it: maybe that was only to encourage my mother, but all the same it was very nice of them. But when the two Recruiting Officers arrived (it was my father called them that after they went), they didn't seem to notice the room at all in spite of what we'd done to it.

And do you know what I heard one of them say to the other?

"It seems clean, anyway," she said.

Now I didn't like that "seems." And what did she mean by the "anyway" I'd like to know?

It sort of put me off from the start—would you believe that? That, and the look of them. They weren't a bit like the Visiting Sisters—or even the Begging Sisters; who all had lovely figures—like statues. One of them was thin all right, but I didn't like the look of her all the same. She didn't look thin in an ordinary way; she looked worn away, if you know what I mean? And the other one was fat. She was so fat I was afraid if she fell on the stairs she'd start to roll like a ball.

She was the boss: the fat one.

And do you know one of the first things she asked me? You'd never guess. I don't even like to mention it. She caught a hold of my hair.

"I hope you keep it nice and clean," she said.

What do you think of that? I was glad my mother didn't hear her. My mother forgets herself entirely if she's mad about anything. She didn't hear it, though. But I began to think to myself that they must have met some very low-class girls if they had to ask *that* question. And wasn't that what you'd think?

Then the worn-looking one said a queer thing, not to me, but to the other nun.

"She seems strong, anyway," she said. And there again I don't think she meant my health. I couldn't help putting her remark alongside the way she was so worn-looking, and I began to think I'd got myself into a nice pickle.

But I was prepared to go through with it all the same. That's me: I have great determination although you mightn't believe it. Sis often says I'd have been well able for the savages if I'd gone on with the thing.

But I didn't.

I missed it by a hair's breadth, though. I won't tell you all the interview, but at the end of it anyway they gave me the name of the Convent where I was to go for Probation, and they told me the day to go, and they gave me a list of clothes I was to get.

"Will you be able to pay for them?" they said, turning to my father. They hadn't taken much notice of him up to that.

I couldn't help admiring the way he answered.

"Well, I managed to pay for plenty of style for her up to now," he said, "and seeing that this mourning outfit is to be the last I'll be asked to pay for, I think I'll manage it all right. Why?"

I admired the "why?"

"Oh, we have to be ready for all eventualities," said the fat one.

Sis and I nearly died laughing afterwards thinking of those words. But I hardly noticed them at the time, because I was on my way out the door to order a cab. They had asked me to get one and they had given me so many instructions that I was nearly daft.

They didn't want a flighty horse, and they didn't want a cab that was too high up off the ground, and I was to pick a cabby that looked respectable.

Now at this time, although there were still cabs to be hired, you didn't have an almighty great choice, and I knew I had my work cut out for me to meet all their requirements.

But I seemed to be dead in luck in more ways than one, because when I went to the cab stand there, among the shiny black cabs, with big black horses that rolled their eyes at me, there was one old cab and it was all battered and green-mouldy. The cabby too looked about as mouldy as the cab. And as for the horse—well, wouldn't anyone think that he'd be mouldy too. But as a matter of fact the horse wasn't mouldy in any way. Indeed, it was due to the way he bucketed it about that the old cab was so racked-looking: it was newer than the others I believe, and as for the cabby, I believe it was the horse had him so bad-looking. That horse had the heart scalded in him.

But it was only afterwards I heard all this. I thought I'd done great work, and I went up and got the nuns, and put them into it and off they went, with the thin one waving to me.

It was while I was still waving that I saw the horse starting his capers.   105

My first thought was to run, but I thought I'd have to face them again, so I didn't do that. Instead, I ran after the cab and shouted to the driver to stop.

Perhaps that was what did the damage. Maybe I drove the horse clean mad altogether, because the next thing he reared up and let his hind legs fly. There was a dreadful crash and a sound of splintering, and the next thing I knew the bottom of the cab came down on the road with a clatter. I suppose it had got such abuse from that animal from time to time it was on the point of giving way all the time.

It was a miracle for them they weren't let down on the road—the two nuns. It was a miracle for me too in another way because if they did I'd have to go and pick them up and I'd surely be drawn deeper into the whole thing.

But that wasn't what happened. Off went the horse, as mad as ever down the street, rearing and leaping, but the nuns must have got a bit of a warning and held on to the sides, because the next thing I saw, along with the set of four feet under the horse, was four more feet showing out under the body of the cab, and running for dear life.

Honest to God, I started to laugh. Wasn't that awful? They could have been killed,   110 and I knew it, although as a matter of fact someone caught hold of the cab before it got to Parnell Street and they were taken out of it and put into another cab. But once I started to laugh I couldn't stop, and in a way—if you can understand such a thing— I laughed away my vocation. Wasn't that awful?

Not but that I have a great regard for nuns even to this day, although, mind you, I sometimes think the nuns that are going nowadays are not the same as the nuns that were going in our Dorset Street days. I saw a terribly plain-looking one the other day in Cabra Avenue. But all the same, they're grand women! I'm going to make a point of sending all my kids to school with the nuns anyway, when I have them. But of course it takes a fellow with a bit of money to educate his kids nowadays. A girl has to have an eye to the future, as I always tell Sis—she's my girlfriend, you remember.

Well, we're going out to Dollymount this afternoon, Sis and me, and you'd never know who we'd pick up. So long for the present!   [1956]

QUESTIONS

1. Why does the narrator wish to be a nun?
2. What does the scene of furnishing the parlor contribute to the story?
3. How do the minor characters in the story function to reveal the narrator?
4. What are the narrator's special gifts as a raconteur?
5. Some stories have an economy and intensity that causes them to suggest a much larger world than the one described. Is this such a story?

RESPONSES

1. Define the characteristics of a television situation comedy. Which of these qualities does this story possess; which does it not possess?
2. Compare this story to Joyce's "Araby." What do you believe accounts for their differences?
3. Write a similar story set in your childhood neighborhood. Who are the supporting characters? What visitor would cause such a commotion? For instance, what would have happened if as a teen you won a contest and a famous actor or singer came to visit you?

D. H. LAWRENCE

D. H. Lawrence (1885–1930) was born in Eastwood, near Nottingham, England. The son of a coal miner and a former school teacher, Lawrence put much of the struggle of his early years into his novel *Sons and Lovers* (1913). Dissatisfied with what he felt to be the dehumanizing effects of industrial society and suffering from increasingly poor health, he eloped with the wife of a Nottingham university professor. Together they made a restless pilgrimage through Italy, Australia, Mexico, New Mexico, and France, searching for a society in which they could feel at home. Lawrence had a gift for controversy, and his attacks on the status quo drew the fire of the censors and the guardians of public morals. Among his best-known novels are *The Rainbow* (1915), *Women in Love* (1920), and *Lady Chatterley's Lover* (1928).

The Rocking-Horse Winner

There was a woman who was beautiful, who started with all the advantages, yet she had no luck. She married for love, and the love turned to dust. She had bonny children, yet she felt they had been thrust upon her, and she could not love them. They looked at her coldly, as if they were finding fault with her. And hurriedly she felt she must cover up some fault in herself. Yet what it was that she must cover up she never knew. Nevertheless, when her children were present, she always felt the centre of her heart go hard. This troubled her, and in her manner she was all the more gentle and anxious for her children, as if she loved them very much. Only she herself knew that at the centre of her heart was a hard little place that could not feel love, no, not for anybody. Everybody else said of her: "She is such a good mother. She adores her children." Only she herself, and her children themselves, knew it was not so. They read it in each other's eyes.

There were a boy and two little girls. They lived in a pleasant house, with a garden, and they had discreet servants, and felt themselves superior to anyone in the neighbourhood.

Although they lived in style, they felt always an anxiety in the house. There was never enough money. The mother had a small income, and the father had a small income, but not nearly enough for the social position which they had to keep up. The father went into town to some office. But though he had good prospects, these prospects never materialised. There was always the grinding sense of the shortage of money, though the style was always kept up.

At last the mother said: "I will see if *I* can't make something." But she did not know where to begin. She racked her brains, and tried this thing and the other, but could not find anything successful. The failure made deep lines come into her face. Her children were growing up, they would have to go to school. There must be more money, there must be more money. The father, who was always very handsome and expensive in his tastes, seemed as if he never *would* be able to do anything worth doing. And the mother, who had a great belief in herself, did not succeed any better, and her tastes were just as expensive.

5   And so the house came to be haunted by the unspoken phrase: *There must be more money! There must be more money!* The children could hear it all the time, though nobody said it aloud. They heard it at Christmas, when the expensive and splendid toys filled the nursery. Behind the shining modern rocking-horse, behind the smart doll's house, a voice would start whispering: "There *must* be more money! There *must* be more money!" And the children would stop playing, to listen for a moment. They would look into each other's eyes, to see if they had all heard. And each one saw in the eyes of the other two that they too had heard. "There *must* be more money! There *must* be more money!"

It came whispering from the springs of the still-swaying rocking-horse, and even the horse, bending his wooden, champing head, heard it. The big doll, sitting so pink and smirking in her new pram, could hear it quite plainly, and seemed to be smirking all the more self-consciously because of it. The foolish puppy, too, that took the place of the teddy-bear, he was looking so extraordinarily foolish for no other reason but that he heard the secret whisper all over the house: "There *must* be more money!"

Yet nobody ever said it aloud. The whisper was everywhere, and therefore no one spoke it. Just as no one ever says: "We are breathing!" in spite of the fact that breath is coming and going all the time.

"Mother," said the boy Paul one day, "why don't we keep a car of our own? Why do we always use uncle's, or else a taxi?"

"Because we're the poor members of the family," said the mother.

10   "But why *are* we, Mother?"

"Well—I suppose," she said slowly and bitterly, "it's because your father has no luck."

The boy was silent for some time.

"Is luck money, Mother?" he said, rather timidly.

"No, Paul. Not quite. It's what causes you to have money."

15   "Oh!" said Paul vaguely. "I thought when Uncle Oscar said *filthy lucker*, it meant money."

"*Filthy lucre* does mean money," said the mother. "But it's lucre, not luck."

"Oh!" said the boy. "Then what *is* luck, Mother?"

"It's what causes you to have money. If you're lucky you have money. That's why it's better to be born lucky than rich. If you're rich, you may lose your money. But if you're lucky, you will always get more money."

"Oh! Will you? And is Father not lucky?"

20   "Very unlucky, I should say," she said bitterly.

The boy watched her with unsure eyes.

"Why?" he asked.

"I don't know. Nobody ever knows why one person is lucky and another unlucky."

"Don't they? Nobody at all? Does *nobody* know?"

"Perhaps God. But He never tells." 25

"He ought to, then. And aren't you lucky either, Mother?"

"I can't be, if I married an unlucky husband."

"But by yourself, aren't you?"

"I used to think I was, before I married. Now I think I am very unlucky indeed."

"Why?" 30

"Well—never mind! Perhaps I'm not really," she said.

The child looked at her to see if she meant it. But he saw, by the lines of her mouth, that she was only trying to hide something from him.

"Well, anyhow," he said stoutly, "I'm a lucky person."

"Why?" said his mother, with a sudden laugh.

He stared at her. He didn't even know why he had said it. 35

"God told me," he asserted, brazening it out.

"I hope He did, dear!" she said, again with a laugh, but rather bitter.

"He did, Mother!"

"Excellent!" said the mother, using one of her husband's exclamations.

The boy saw she did not believe him; or rather, that she paid no attention to his as- 40 sertion. This angered him somewhere, and made him want to compel her attention.

He went off by himself, vaguely, in a childish way, seeking for the clue to "luck." Absorbed, taking no heed of other people, he went about with a sort of stealth, seeking inwardly for luck. He wanted luck, he wanted it, he wanted it. When the two girls were playing dolls in the nursery, he would sit on his big rocking-horse, charging madly into space, with a frenzy that made the little girls peer at him uneasily. Wildly the horse careered, the waving dark hair of the boy tossed, his eyes had a strange glare in them. The little girls dared not speak to him.

When he had ridden to the end of his mad little journey, he climbed down and stood in front of his rocking-horse, staring fixedly into its lowered face. Its red mouth was slightly open, its big eye was wide and glassy-bright.

"Now!" he would silently command the snorting steed. "Now, take me to where there is luck! Now take me!"

And he would slash the horse on the neck with the little whip he had asked Uncle Oscar for. He *knew* the horse could take him to where there was luck, if only he forced it. So he would mount again and start on his furious ride, hoping at last to get there. He knew he could get there.

"You'll break your horse, Paul!" said the nurse. 45

"He's always riding like that! I wish he'd leave off!" said his elder sister Joan.

But he only glared down on them in silence. Nurse gave him up. She could make nothing of him. Anyhow, he was growing beyond her.

One day his mother and his Uncle Oscar came in when he was on one of his furious rides. He did not speak to them.

"Hallo, you young jockey! Riding a winner?" said his uncle.

"Aren't you growing too big for a rocking-horse? You're not a very little boy any 50 longer, you know," said his mother.

But Paul only gave a blue glare from his big, rather close-set eyes. He would speak to nobody when he was in full tilt. His mother watched him with an anxious expression on her face.

At last he suddenly stopped forcing his horse into the mechanical gallop and slid down.

"Well, I got there!" he announced fiercely, his blue eyes still flaring, and his sturdy long legs straddling apart.

"Where did you get to?" asked his mother.

55 "Where I wanted to go," he flared back at her.

"That's right, son!" said Uncle Oscar. "Don't you stop till you get there. What's the horse's name?"

"He doesn't have a name," said the boy.

"Gets on without all right?" asked the uncle.

"Well, he has different names. He was called Sansovino last week."

60 "Sansovino, eh? Won the Ascot. How did you know this name?"

"He always talks about horse-races with Bassett," said Joan.

The uncle was delighted to find that his small nephew was posted with all the racing news. Bassett, the young gardener, who had been wounded in the left foot in the war and had got his present job through Oscar Cresswell, whose batman° he had been, was a perfect blade of the "turf." He lived in the racing events, and the small boy lived with him.

Oscar Cresswell got it all from Bassett.

"Master Paul comes and asks me, so I can't do more than tell him, sir," said Bassett, his face terribly serious, as if he were speaking of religious matters.

65 "And does he ever put anything on a horse he fancies?"

"Well—I don't want to give him away—he's a young sport, a fine sport, sir. Would you mind asking him himself? He sort of takes a pleasure in it, and perhaps he'd feel I was giving him away, sir, if you don't mind."

Bassett was serious as a church.

The uncle went back to his nephew and took him off for a ride in the car.

"Say, Paul, old man, do you ever put anything on a horse?" the uncle asked.

70 The boy watched the handsome man closely.

"Why, do you think I oughtn't to?" he parried.

"Not a bit of it! I thought perhaps you might give me a tip for the Lincoln."

The car sped on into the country, going down to Uncle Oscar's place in Hampshire.

"Honour bright?" said the nephew.

75 "Honour bright, son!" said the uncle.

"Well, then, Daffodil."

"Daffodil! I doubt it, sonny. What about Mirza?"

"I only know the winner," said the boy. "That's Daffodil."

"Daffodil, eh?"

80 There was a pause. Daffodil was an obscure horse comparatively.

"Uncle!"

"Yes, son?"

"You won't let it go any further, will you? I promised Bassett."

"Bassett be damned, old man! What's he got to do with it?"

85 "We're partners. We've been partners from the first. Uncle, he lent me my first five shillings, which I lost. I promised him, honour bright, it was only between me and him; only you gave me that ten-shilling note I started winning with, so I thought you were lucky. You won't let it go any further, will you?"

The boy gazed at his uncle from those big, hot, blue eyes, set rather close together. The uncle stirred and laughed uneasily.

"Right you are, son! I'll keep your tip private. Daffodil, eh? How much are you putting on him?"

°*batman:* An orderly.

"All except twenty pounds," said the boy. "I keep that in reserve."

The uncle thought it a good joke.

"You keep twenty pounds in reserve, do you, you young romancer? What are you betting, then?"

"I'm betting three hundred," said the boy gravely. "But it's between you and me, Uncle Oscar! Honour bright?"

The uncle burst into a roar of laughter.

"It's between you and me all right, you young Nat Gould,"° he said, laughing. "But where's your three hundred?"

"Bassett keeps it for me. We're partners."

"You are, are you! And what is Bassett putting on Daffodil?"

"He won't go quite as high as I do, I expect. Perhaps he'll go a hundred and fifty."

"What, pennies?" laughed the uncle.

"Pounds," said the child, with a surprised look at his uncle. "Bassett keeps a bigger reserve than I do."

Between wonder and amusement Uncle Oscar was silent. He pursued the matter no further, but he determined to take his nephew with him to the Lincoln races.

"Now, son," he said, "I'm putting twenty on Mirza, and I'll put five on for you on any horse you fancy. What's your pick?"

"Daffodil, Uncle."

"No, not the fiver on Daffodil!"

"I should if it was my own fiver," said the child.

"Good! Good! Right you are! A fiver for me and a fiver for you on Daffodil."

The child had never been to a race-meeting before, and his eyes were blue fire. He pursed his mouth tight and watched. A Frenchman just in front had put his money on Lancelot. Wild with excitement, he flayed his arms up and down, yelling "*Lancelot! Lancelot!*" in his French accent.

Daffodil came in first, Lancelot second, Mirza third. The child, flushed and with eyes blazing, was curiously serene. His uncle brought him four five-pound notes, four to one.

"What am I to do with these?" he cried, waving them before the boy's eyes.

"I suppose we'll talk to Bassett," said the boy. "I expect I have fifteen hundred now; and twenty in reserve; and this twenty."

His uncle studied him for some moments.

"Look here, son!" he said. "You're not serious about Bassett and that fifteen hundred, are you?"

"Yes, I am. But it's between you and me, Uncle. Honour bright?"

"Honour bright all right, son! But I must talk to Bassett."

"If you'd like to be a partner, Uncle, with Bassett and me, we could all be partners. Only, you'd have to promise, honour bright, Uncle, not to let it go beyond us three. Bassett and I are lucky, and you must be lucky, because it was your ten shillings I started winning with. . . ."

Uncle Oscar took both Bassett and Paul into Richmond Park for an afternoon, and there they talked.

"It's like this, you see, sir," Bassett said. "Master Paul would get me talking about racing events, spinning yarns, you know, sir. And he was always keen on knowing if I'd made or if I'd lost. It's about a year since, now, that I put five shillings on Blush of

---

°*Nat Gould*: Author of horse-racing novels.

Dawn for him: and we lost. Then the luck turned, with that ten shillings he had from you: that we put on Singhalese. And since that time, it's been pretty steady, all things considering. What do you say, Master Paul?"

"We're all right when we're sure," said Paul. "It's when we're not quite sure that we go down."

"Oh, but we're careful then," said Bassett.

"But when are you *sure?*" smiled Uncle Oscar.

"It's Master Paul, sir," said Bassett in a secret, religious voice. "It's as if he had it from heaven. Like Daffodil, now, for the Lincoln. That was as sure as eggs."

120　"Did you put anything on Daffodil?" asked Oscar Cresswell.

"Yes, sir. I made my bit."

"And my nephew?"

Bassett was obstinately silent, looking at Paul.

"I made twelve hundred, didn't I, Bassett? I told Uncle I was putting three hundred on Daffodil."

125　"That's right," said Bassett, nodding.

"But where's the money?" asked the uncle.

"I keep it safe locked up, sir. Master Paul he can have it any minute he likes to ask for it."

"What, fifteen hundred pounds?"

"And twenty! And *forty,* that is, with the twenty he made on the course."

130　"It's amazing!" said the uncle.

"If Master Paul offers you to be partners, sir, I would, if I were you: if you'll excuse me," said Bassett.

Oscar Cresswell thought about it.

"I'll see the money," he said.

They drove home again, and, sure enough, Bassett came round to the garden-house with fifteen hundred pounds in notes. The twenty pounds reserve was left with Joe Glee, in the Turf Commission deposit.

135　"You see, it's all right, Uncle, when I'm *sure!* Then we go strong, for all we're worth. Don't we, Bassett?"

"We do that, Master Paul."

"And when are you sure?" said the uncle, laughing.

"Oh, well, sometimes I'm *absolutely* sure, like about Daffodil," said the boy; "and sometimes I have an idea; and sometimes I haven't even an idea, have I, Bassett? Then we're careful, because we mostly go down."

"You do, do you! And when you're sure, like about Daffodil, what makes you sure, sonny?"

140　"Oh, well, I don't know," said the boy uneasily. "I'm sure, you know, Uncle; that's all."

"It's as if he had it from heaven, sir," Bassett reiterated.

"I should say so!" said the uncle.

But he became a partner. And when the Leger was coming on Paul was "sure" about Lively Spark, which was a quite inconsiderable horse. The boy insisted on putting a thousand on the horse, Bassett was for five hundred, and Oscar Cresswell two hundred. Lively Spark came in first, and the betting had been ten to one against him. Paul had made ten thousand.

"You see," he said, "I was absolutely sure of him."

145　Even Oscar Cresswell had cleared two thousand.

"Look here, son," he said, "this sort of thing makes me nervous."

"It needn't, Uncle! Perhaps I shan't be sure again for a long time."

"But what are you going to do with your money?" asked the uncle.

"Of course," said the boy, "I started it for Mother. She said she had no luck, because Father is unlucky, so I thought if *I* was lucky, it might stop whispering."

"What might stop whispering?" 150

"Our house. I *hate* our house for whispering."

"What does it whisper?"

"Why—why"—the boy fidgeted—"why, I don't know. But it's always short of money, you know, Uncle."

"I know it, son, I know it."

"You know people send mother writs, don't you, Uncle?" 155

"I'm afraid I do," said the uncle.

"And then the house whispers, like people laughing at you behind your back. It's awful, that is! I thought if I was lucky—"

"You might stop it," added the uncle.

The boy watched him with big blue eyes, that had an uncanny cold fire in them, and he said never a word.

"Well, then!" said the uncle. "What are we doing?" 160

"I shouldn't like Mother to know I was lucky," said the boy.

"Why not, son?"

"She'd stop me."

"I don't think she would."

"Oh!"—and the boy writhed in an odd way—"I *don't* want her to know, uncle." 165

"All right, son! We'll manage it without her knowing."

They managed it very easily. Paul, at the other's suggestion, handed over five thousand pounds to his uncle, who deposited it with the family lawyer, who was then to inform Paul's mother that a relative had put five thousand pounds into his hands, which sum was to be paid out a thousand pounds at a time, on the mother's birthday, for the next five years.

"So she'll have a birthday present of a thousand pounds for five successive years," said Uncle Oscar. "I hope it won't make it all the harder for her later."

Paul's mother had her birthday in November. The house had been "whispering" worse than ever lately, and, even in spite of his luck, Paul could not bear up against it. He was very anxious to see the effect of the birthday letter, telling his mother about the thousand pounds.

When there were no visitors, Paul now took his meals with his parents, as he was 170 beyond the nursery control. His mother went into town nearly every day. She had discovered that she had an odd knack of sketching furs and dress materials, so she worked secretly in the studio of a friend who was the chief "artist" for the leading drapers. She drew the figures of ladies in furs and ladies in silk and sequins for the newspaper advertisements. This young woman artist earned several thousand pounds a year, but Paul's mother only made several hundreds, and she was again dissatisfied. She so wanted to be first in something, and she did not succeed, even in making sketches for drapery advertisements.

She was down to breakfast on the morning of her birthday. Paul watched her face as she read her letters. He knew the lawyer's letter. As his mother read it, her face hardened and became more expressionless. Then a cold, determined look came on her mouth. She hid the letter under the pile of others, and said not a word about it.

"Didn't you have anything nice in the post for your birthday, Mother?" said Paul.

"Quite moderately nice," she said, her voice cold and absent.

She went away to town without saying more.

175   But in the afternoon Uncle Oscar appeared. He said Paul's mother had had a long interview with the lawyer, asking if the whole five thousand could not be advanced at once, as she was in debt.

"What do you think, Uncle?" said the boy.

"I leave it to you, son."

"Oh, let her have it, then! We can get some more with the other," said the boy.

"A bird in the hand is worth two in the bush, laddie!" said Uncle Oscar.

180   "But I'm sure to *know* for the Grand National; or the Lincolnshire; or else the Derby. I'm sure to know for *one* of them," said Paul.

So Uncle Oscar signed the agreement, and Paul's mother touched the whole five thousand. Then something very curious happened. The voices in the house suddenly went mad, like a chorus of frogs on a spring evening. There were certain new furnishings, and Paul had a tutor. He was *really* going to Eton, his father's school, in the following autumn. There were flowers in the winter, and a blossoming of the luxury Paul's mother had been used to. And yet the voices in the house, behind the sprays of mimosa and almond-blossom, and from under the piles of iridescent cushions, simply trilled and screamed in a sort of ecstasy: "There *must* be more money! Oh-h-h; there *must* be more money. Oh, now now-w! Now-w-w—there *must* be more money!—more than ever! More than ever!"

It frightened Paul terribly. He studied away at his Latin and Greek with his tutor. But his intense hours were spent with Bassett. The Grand National had gone by: he had not "known," and had lost a hundred pounds. Summer was at hand. He was in agony for the Lincoln. But even for the Lincoln he didn't "know," and he lost fifty pounds. He became wild-eyed and strange, as if something were going to explode in him.

"Let it alone, son! Don't you bother about it!" urged Uncle Oscar. But it was as if the boy couldn't really hear what his uncle was saying.

"I've got to know for the Derby! I've got to know for the Derby!" the child reiterated, his big blue eyes blazing with a sort of madness.

185   His mother noticed how overwrought he was.

"You'd better go to the seaside. Wouldn't you like to go now to the seaside, instead of waiting? I think you'd better," she said, looking down at him anxiously, her heart curiously heavy because of him.

But the child lifted his uncanny blue eyes.

"I couldn't possibly go before the Derby, Mother!" he said. "I couldn't possibly!"

"Why not?" she said, her voice becoming heavy when she was opposed. "Why not? You can still go from the seaside to see the Derby with your Uncle Oscar, if that's what you wish. No need for you to wait here. Besides, I think you care too much about these races. It's a bad sign. My family has been a gambling family, and you won't know till you grow up how much damage it has done. But it has done damage. I shall have to send Bassett away, and ask Uncle Oscar not to talk racing to you, unless you promise to be reasonable about it: go away to the seaside and forget it. You're all nerves!"

190   "I'll do what you like, Mother, so long as you don't send me away till after the Derby," the boy said.

"Send you away from where? Just from this house?"

"Yes," he said, gazing at her.

"Why, you curious child, what makes you care about this house so much, suddenly? I never knew you loved it."

He gazed at her without speaking. He had a secret within a secret, something he had not divulged, even to Bassett or to his Uncle Oscar.

But his mother, after standing undecided and a little bit sullen for some moments, said: 195

"Very well, then! Don't go to the seaside till after the Derby, if you don't wish it. But promise me you won't let your nerves go to pieces. Promise you won't think so much about horse-racing and *events,* as you call them!"

"Oh no," said the boy casually. "I won't think much about them, Mother. You needn't worry. I wouldn't worry, Mother, if I were you."

"If you were me and I were you," said his mother, "I wonder what we *should* do!"

"But you know you needn't worry, mother, don't you?" the boy repeated.

"I should be awfully glad to know it," she said wearily. 200

"Oh, well, you *can,* you know. I mean, you *ought* to know you needn't worry," he insisted.

"Ought I? Then I'll see about it," she said.

Paul's secret of secrets was his wooden horse, that which had no name. Since he was emancipated from a nurse and nursery-governess, he had had his rocking-horse removed to his own bedroom at the top of the house.

"Surely you're too big for a rocking-horse!" his mother had remonstrated.

"Well, you see, mother, till I can have a *real* horse, I like to have *some* sort of animal about," had been his quaint answer. 205

"Do you feel he keeps you company?" she laughed.

"Oh yes! He's very good, he always keeps me company, when I'm there," said Paul.

So the horse, rather shabby, stood in an arrested prance in the boy's bedroom.

The Derby was drawing near, and the boy grew more and more tense. He hardly heard what was spoken to him, he was very frail, and his eyes were really uncanny. His mother had sudden strange seizures of uneasiness about him. Sometimes, for half an hour, she would feel a sudden anxiety about him that was almost anguish. She wanted to rush to him at once, and know he was safe.

Two nights before the Derby, she was at a big party in town, when one of her rushes of anxiety about her boy, her first-born, gripped her heart till she could hardly speak. She fought with the feeling, might and main, for she believed in common sense. But it was too strong. She had to leave the dance and go downstairs to telephone to the country. The children's nursery-governess was terribly surprised and startled at being rung up in the night. 210

"Are the children all right, Miss Wilmot?"

"Oh yes, they are quite all right."

"Master Paul? Is he all right?"

"He went to bed as right as a trivet. Shall I run up and look at him?"

"No," said Paul's mother reluctantly. "No! Don't trouble. It's all right. Don't sit up. We shall be home fairly soon." She did not want her son's privacy intruded upon. 215

"Very good," said the governess.

It was about one o'clock when Paul's mother and father drove up to their house. All was still. Paul's mother went to her room and slipped off her white fur cloak. She had told her maid not to wait up for her. She heard her husband downstairs, mixing a whisky and soda.

And then, because of the strange anxiety at her heart, she stole upstairs to her son's room. Noiselessly she went along the upper corridor. Was there a faint noise? What was it?

She stood, with arrested muscles, outside his door, listening. There was a strange, heavy, and yet not loud noise. Her heart stood still. It was a soundless noise, yet rushing and powerful. Something huge, in violent, hushed motion. What was it? What in

God's name was it? She ought to know. She felt that she knew the noise. She knew what it was.

Yet she could not place it. She couldn't say what it was. And on and on it went, like a madness.

Softly, frozen with anxiety and fear, she turned the doorhandle.

The room was dark. Yet in the space near the window, she heard and saw something plunging to and fro. She gazed in fear and amazement.

Then suddenly she switched on the light, and saw her son, in his green pyjamas, madly surging on the rocking-horse. The blaze of light suddenly lit him up, as he urged the wooden horse, and lit her up, as she stood, blonde, in her dress of pale green and crystal, in the doorway.

"Paul!" she cried. "Whatever are you doing?"

"It's Malabar!" he screamed in a powerful, strange voice. "It's Malabar!"

His eyes blazed at her for one strange and senseless second, as he ceased urging his wooden horse. Then he fell with a crash to the ground, and she, all her tormented motherhood flooding upon her, rushed to gather him up.

But he was unconscious, and unconscious he remained, with some brain-fever. He talked and tossed, and his mother sat stonily by his side.

"Malabar! It's Malabar! Bassett, Bassett, I *know*! It's Malabar!"

So the child cried, trying to get up and urge the rocking-horse that gave him his inspiration.

"What does he mean by Malabar?" asked the heart-frozen mother.

"I don't know," said the father stonily.

"What does he mean by Malabar?" she asked her brother Oscar.

"It's one of the horses running for the Derby," was the answer.

And, in spite of himself, Oscar Cresswell spoke to Bassett, and himself put a thousand on Malabar: at fourteen to one.

The third day of the illness was critical: they were waiting for a change. The boy, with his rather long, curly hair, was tossing ceaselessly on the pillow. He neither slept nor regained consciousness, and his eyes were like blue stones. His mother sat, feeling her heart had gone, turned actually into a stone.

In the evening, Oscar Cresswell did not come, but Bassett sent a message, saying could he come up for one moment, just one moment? Paul's mother was very angry at the intrusion, but on second thoughts she agreed. The boy was the same. Perhaps Bassett might bring him to consciousness.

The gardener, a shortish fellow with a little brown moustache and sharp little brown eyes, tiptoed into the room, touched his imaginary cap to Paul's mother, and stole to the bedside, staring with glittering, smallish eyes at the tossing, dying child.

"Master Paul!" he whispered. "Master Paul! Malabar came in first all right, a clean win. I did as you told me. You've made over seventy thousand pounds, you have; you've got over eighty thousand. Malabar came in all right, Master Paul."

"Malabar! Malabar! Did I say Malabar, Mother? Did I say Malabar? Do you think I'm lucky, Mother! I knew Malabar, didn't I? Over eighty thousand pounds! I call that lucky, don't you Mother? Over eighty thousand pounds! I knew, didn't I know I knew? Malabar came in all right. If I ride my horse till I'm sure, then I tell you, Bassett, you can go as high as you like. Did you go for all you were worth, Bassett?"

"I went a thousand on it, Master Paul."

"I never told you, Mother, that if I can ride my horse, and *get there*, then I'm absolutely sure—oh, absolutely! Mother, did I ever tell you? I *am* lucky!"

"No, you never did," said his mother.

But the boy died in the night.

And even as he lay dead, his mother heard her brother's voice saying to her: "My God, Hester, you're eighty-odd thousand to the good, and a poor devil of a son to the bad. But, poor devil, poor devil, he's best gone out of a life where he rides his rocking-horse to find a winner."

[1926]

QUESTIONS

1. Define the relationship between mother and son.
2. What does the rocking horse represent?
3. What are the varying attitudes toward luck expressed in the story?
4. What is the function of Bassett? Why is he "serious as a church"?
5. Who is responsible for Paul's death? What is the meaning of Oscar's final comment?

RESPONSES

1. Approach this story from a feminist perspective. Compare how Lawrence portrays women and men.
2. Approach this story from a sociological/Marxist perspective. What is Lawrence saying about the role of money in our lives?
3. Approach this story from the psychological perspective. What is Lawrence saying about the development of a healthy, secure sense of self and ego?

FOCUS ON FILM

1. Compare the portrayal of the mother and Paul in the film and in the print version of "The Rocking-Horse Winner."
2. Evaluate how well the film conveys the fairy-tale qualities of this story.
3. As you view the film, study the framing and camera angles used. Do they support the tone and themes of the film? Do they reflect the tone and theme of the prose story?

DAVID LEAVITT

David Leavitt (b. 1961) was born in Pittsburgh, Pennsylvania, grew up in Palo Alto, California, and attended Yale University, studying English. At age twenty, while still in college, his first story was published in the *New Yorker* and won the O. Henry Prize. His stories have been published in four collections, *Family Dancing* (1984), *A Place I Have Never Been* (1986), *Marble Quilt* (2001), and *Collected Stories* (2003). His novels are *The Lost Language of Cranes* (1986), *While England Sleeps* (1995), *Arkansas: Three Novellas* (1997), *The Page Turner* (1998), *Martin Bauman; or, a Sure Thing* (2000), and *Body of Jonah Boyd* (2004).

Gravity

Theo had a choice between a drug that would save his sight and a drug that would keep him alive, so he chose not to go blind. He stopped the pills and started the injections—these required the implantation of an unpleasant and painful catheter just above his heart—and within a few days the clouds in his eyes started to clear up; he could see again. He remembered going into New York City to a show with his mother, when he was twelve and didn't want to admit he needed glasses. "Can you read that?" she'd shouted, pointing to a Broadway marquee, and when he'd squinted, making out only one or two letters, she'd taken off her own glasses—harlequins with tiny rhinestones in the corners—and shoved them onto his face. The world came into focus, and he gasped, astonished at the precision around the edges of things, the legibility, the hard, sharp, colorful landscape. Sylvia had to squint through *Fiddler on the Roof* that day, but for Theo, his face masked by his mother's huge glasses, everything was as bright and vivid as a comic book. Even though people stared at him, and muttered things, Sylvia didn't care; he could *see*.

Because he was dying again, Theo moved back to his mother's house in New Jersey. The DHPG injections she took in stride—she'd seen her own mother through *her* dying, after all. Four times a day, with the equanimity of a nurse, she cleaned out the plastic tube implanted in his chest, inserted a sterilized hypodermic and slowly dripped the bag of sight-giving liquid into his veins. They endured this procedure silently, Sylvia sitting on the side of the hospital bed she'd rented for the duration of Theo's stay—his life, he sometimes thought—watching reruns of *I Love Lucy* or the news, while he tried not to think about the hard piece of pipe stuck into him, even though it was a constant reminder of how wide and unswimmable the gulf was becoming between him and the ever-receding shoreline of the well. And Sylvia was intricately cheerful. Each day she urged him to go out with her somewhere—to the library, or the little museum with the dinosaur replicas he'd been fond of as a child—and when his thinness and the cane drew stares, she'd maneuver him around the people who were staring, determined to shield him from whatever they might say or do. It had been the same that afternoon so many years ago, when she'd pushed him through a lobbyful of curious and laughing faces, determined that nothing should interfere with the spectacle of his seeing. What a pair they must have made, a boy in ugly glasses and a mother daring the world to say a word about it!

This warm, breezy afternoon in May they were shopping for revenge. "Your cousin Howard's engagement party is next month," Sylvia explained in the car. "A very nice girl from Livingston. I met her a few weeks ago, and really, she's a superior person."

"I'm glad," Theo said. "Congratulate Howie for me."

"Do you think you'll be up to going to the party?"   5

"I'm not sure. Would it be okay for me just to give him a gift?"

"You already have. A lovely silver tray, if I say so myself. The thank-you note's in the living room."

"Mom," Theo said, "why do you always have to—"

Sylvia honked her horn at a truck making an illegal left turn.

"Better they should get something than no present at all, is what I say," she said.   10
"But now, the problem is, *I* have to give Howie something, to be from me, and it better be good. It better be very, very good."

"Why?"

"Don't you remember that cheap little nothing Bibi gave you for your graduation? It was disgusting."

"I can't remember what she gave me."

"Of course you can't. It was tacky pen-and pencil set. Not even a real leather box. So naturally, it stands to reason that I have to get something truly spectacular for Howard's engagement. Something that will make Bibi blanch. Anyway, I think I've found just the thing, but I need your advice."

"Advice? Well, when my old roommate Nick got married, I gave him a garlic press.   15
It cost five dollars and reflected exactly how much I felt, at the moment, our friendship was worth."

Sylvia laughed. "Clever. But my idea is much more brilliant, because it makes it possible for me to get back at Bibi *and* give Howard the nice gift he and his girl deserve." She smiled, clearly pleased with herself. "Ah, you live and learn."

"You live," Theo said.

Sylvia blinked. "Well, look, here we are." She pulled the car into a handicapped-parking place on Morris Avenue and got out to help Theo, but he was already hoisting himself up out of his seat, using the door handle for leverage. "I can manage myself," he said with some irritation. Sylvia stepped back.

"Clearly one advantage to all this for you," Theo said, balancing on his cane, "is that it's suddenly so much easier to get a parking place."

"Oh Theo, please," Sylvia said. "Look, here's where we're going."   20

She leaned him into a gift shop filled with porcelain statuettes of Snow White and all seven of the dwarves, music boxes which, when you opened them, played "The Shadow of Your Smile," complicated-smelling potpourris in purple wallpapered boxes, and stuffed snakes you were supposed to push up against drafty windows and doors.

"Mrs. Greenman," said an expansive, gray-haired man in a cream-colored cardigan sweater. "Look who's here, Archie, it's Mrs. Greenman."

Another man, this one thinner and balding, but dressed in an identical cardigan, peered out from the back of the shop. "Hello there!" he said, smiling. He looked at Theo, and his expression changed.

"Mr. Sherman, Mr. Baker. This is my son, Theo."

25   "Hello," Mr. Sherman and Mr. Baker said. They didn't offer to shake hands.

"Are you here for that item we discussed last week?" Mr. Sherman asked.

"Yes," Sylvia said. "I want advice from my son here." She walked over to a large ridged crystal bowl, a very fifties sort of bowl, stalwart and square-jawed. "What do you think? Beautiful, isn't it?"

"Mom, to tell the truth, I think it's kind of ugly."

"Four hundred and twenty-five dollars," Sylvia said admiringly.

30   "You have to feel it."

Then she picked up the big bowl and tossed it to Theo, like a football.

The gentlemen in the cardigan sweaters gasped and did not exhale. When Theo caught it, it sank his hands. His cane rattled as it hit the floor.

"That's heavy," Sylvia said, observing with satisfaction how the bowl had weighted Theo's arms down. "And where crystal is concerned, heavy is impressive."

She took the bowl back from him and carried it to the counter.

35   Mr. Sherman was mopping his brow. Theo looked at the floor, still surprised not to see shards of glass around his feet.

Since no one else seemed to be volunteering, he bent over and picked up the cane.

Four hundred and fifty-nine, with tax," Mr. Sherman said, his voice still a bit shaky, and a look of relish came over Sylvia's face as she pulled out her checkbook to pay. Behind the counter, Theo could see Mr. Baker put his hand on his forehead and cast his eyes to the ceiling.

It seemed Sylvia had been looking a long time for something like this, something heavy enough to leave an impression, yet so fragile it could make you sorry.

They headed back out to the car.

40   "Where can we go now?" Sylvia asked, as she got in. "There must be someplace else to go."

"Home," Theo said. "It's almost time for my medicine."

"Really? Oh. All right." She pulled on her seat belt, inserted the car key in the ignition and sat there.

For just a moment, but perceptibly, her face broke. She squeezed her eyes shut so tight the blue shadow on the lids cracked.

Almost as quickly she was back to normal again, and they were driving. "It's getting hotter," Sylvia said. "Shall I put on the air?"

45   "Sure," Theo said. He was thinking about the bowl, or more specifically, about how surprising its weight had been, pulling his hands down. For a while now he'd been worried about his mother, worried about what damage his illness might secretly be doing to her that of course she would never admit. On the surface things seemed all right. She still broiled herself a skinned chicken breast for dinner every night, still swam a mile and a half a day, still kept used teabags wrapped in foil in the refrigerator. Yet she had also, at about three o'clock one morning, woken him up to tell him she was going to the twenty-four-hour supermarket, and was there anything he wanted. Then there was the gift shop: She had literally pitched that bowl toward him, pitched

it like a ball, and as that great gleam of flight and potential regret came sailing his direction, it had occurred to him that she was trusting his two feeble hands, out of the whole world, to keep it from shattering. What was she trying to test? Was it his newly regained vision? Was it the assurance that he was there, alive, that he hadn't yet slipped past all her caring, a little lost boy in rhinestone-studded glasses? There are certain things you've already done before you even think how to do them—a child pulled from in front of a car, for instance, or the bowl, which Theo was holding before he could even begin to calculate its brief trajectory. It had pulled his arms down, and from that apish posture he'd looked at his mother, who smiled broadly as if, in the war between heaviness and shattering, he'd just helped her win some small but sustaining victory.   [1990]

QUESTIONS

1. How many meanings of "gravity" apply to this story?
2. Why does Theo make the decision to see and to die, rather than to go blind and to live? Is it significant that Leavitt chooses to phrase the decision "so he chose not to go blind"?
3. How important is it for the tone of the story that Theo and his mother are financially secure?
4. Compare the scene where Mrs. Greenman gives the young Theo her glasses and the scene where she tosses him the bowl.
5. Many writers and critics advise "show; don't tell." But Leavitt chooses to end his story with a long paragraph about the meaning of the scene where Theo caught the expensive bowl. What has Leavitt gained by ending the story in this manner?

RESPONSES

1. Write an essay about parents of gay children. Use this story and Gaitskill's "Tiny, Smiling Daddy."
2. Research the medical literature on AIDS. How accurate is Leavitt's story? What does he emphasize and what does he not include?

Ursula K. Le Guin

Ursula K. Le Guin (b. 1929) was born in Berkeley, California, was educated at Radcliffe and Columbia, and lives in Portland, Oregon. She has been a prolific and distinguished writer of science fiction and fantasy novels for both adults and children; and, among other honors, she has won the Hugo and the Nebula awards. *The Farthest Shore* (1972) won the National Book Award. *Unlocking the Air* was published in 1996; *The Telling* in 2000; *Searoad* in 2004; and *Fisherman of the Inland Sea: Stories* in 2005.

The Professor's Houses

The professor had two houses, one inside the other. He lived with his wife and child in the outer house, which was comfortable, clean, disorderly, not quite big enough for all his books, her papers, their daughter's bright deciduous treasures. The roof leaked after heavy rains early in the fall before the wood swelled, but a bucket in the attic sufficed. No rain fell upon the inner house, where the professor lived without his wife and child, or so he said jokingly sometimes: "Here's where I live. My house." His daughter often added, without resentment, for the visitor's information, "It started out to be for me, but it's really his." And she might reach in to bring forth an inch-high table lamp with fluted shade, or a blue bowl the size of her little fingernail, marked "Kitty" and half full of eternal milk; but she was sure to replace these, after they had been admired, pretty near exactly where they had been. The little house was very orderly, and just big enough for all it contained, though to some tastes the bric-a-brac in the parlor might seem excessive. The daughter's preference was for the store-bought gimmicks and appliances, the toasters and carpet sweepers of Lilliput, but she knew that most adult visitors would admire the perfection of the furnishings her father himself had so delicately and finely made and finished. He was inclined to be a little shy of showing off his own work, so she would point out the more ravishing elegances: the glass-fronted sideboard, the hardwood parquetry and the dadoes, the widow's walk. No visitor, child or adult, could withstand the fascination of the Venetian blinds, the infinitesimal slats that slanted and slid in perfect order on their cords of double-weight sewing thread. "Do you know how to make a Venetian blind?" the professor would inquire, setting up the visitor for his daughter, who would forestall or answer the hesitant negative with a joyful "Put his eyes out!" Her father, who was entertained by involutions and, like all teachers, willing to repeat a good thing, would then remark that after working for two weeks on those blinds he had established that a Venetian blind can also make an American blind.

"I did that awful rug in the nursery," the professor's wife, Julia, might say, evidencing her participation in the inner house, her approbation, her incompetence. "It's not up to Ian's standard, but he accepted the intent." The crocheted rug was, in fact, coarse-looking and curly-edged; the needlepoint rugs in the other rooms, miniature Orientals and a gaudy floral in the master bedroom, lay flat and flawless.

The inner house stood on a low table in an open alcove, called "the bookshelf end," of the long living room of the outer house. Friends of the family checked the progress of its construction, furnishing, and fitting out as they came to dinner or for a drink from time to time, from year to year. Occasional visitors assumed that it belonged to the daughter and was kept downstairs on display because it was a really fine doll's house, a regular work of art, and miniatures were coming into or recently had been in vogue. To certain rather difficult guests, including the dean of his college, the professor, without affirming or denying his part as architect, cabinetmaker, roofer, glazier, electrician, and *tapissier,* might quote Claude Lévi-Strauss.° "It's in *La Pensée Sauvage,* I think," he would say. "His idea is that the reduced model—the miniature—allows a knowledge of the whole to precede the knowledge of the parts. A reversal of the usual process of knowing. Essentially, all the arts proceed that way, reducing a material dimension in favor of an intellectual dimension." He found that persons entirely incapable of, and averse to, the kind of concrete thought that was his chief pleasure in working on the house went rigid as bird dogs at the name of the father of structuralism, and sometimes continued to gaze at the doll's house for some minutes with the tense and earnest gaze of a pointer at a sitting duck. The professor's wife had to entertain a good many strangers when she became state coordinator of the conservation organization for which she worked, but her guests, with urgent business on their minds, admired the doll's house perfunctorily if they noticed it at all.

As the daughter, Victoria, passed through the Vickie period and, at thirteen, entered upon the Tori period, her friends no longer had to be restrained or distracted from fiddling with the fittings of the little house, wearing out the fragile mechanisms, sometimes handling the furniture carelessly in their story games with its occupants. For there was, or had been, a family living in it. Victoria at eight had requested and received for Christmas a rather expensive European mama, papa, brother, sister, and baby, all cleverly articulated so that they could sit in the armchairs, and reach up to the copper-bottom saucepans hung above the stove, and hit or clasp one another in moments of passion. Family dramas of great intensity were enacted from time to time in the then incompletely furnished house. The brother's left leg came off at the hip and was never properly mended. Papa Bendsky received

---

°*Lévi-Strauss:* Claude Lévi-Strauss (b. 1908), professor of social anthropology in the Collège de France and "the father of structuralism," published *La Pensée Sauvage* in 1962. It was translated as *The Savage Mind* in 1966. For his theory that in the case of miniatures, "knowledge of the whole precedes knowledge of the parts," see *The Savage Mind* (Chicago, 1966), 23–24.

a marking-pen mustache and eyebrows that gave him an evil squint, like the half-breed lascar in an Edwardian thriller. The baby got lost. Victoria no longer played with the survivors; and the professor gratefully put them into the drawer of the table on which the house stood. He had always hated them, invaders, especially the papa, so thin, so flexible, with his nasty little Austrian-looking green jacket and his beady lascar eyes.

5   Victoria had recently bought with her earnings from babysitting a gift to the house and her father: a china cat to drink the eternal milk from the blue bowl marked "Kitty." The professor did not put the cat in the drawer. He believed it to be worthy of the house, as the Bendsky family had never been. It was a finely modelled little figure, glazed tortoiseshell on white. Curled on the hearth rug at twilight in the ruddy glow of the flames (red cellophane and a penlight bulb), it looked very comfortable indeed. But since it lay curled up, it could never go into the kitchen to drink from the blue bowl; and this was evidently a trouble or burden to the professor's unconscious mind, for he had not exactly a dream about it, one night while he was going to sleep after working late on a complex and difficult piece of writing, a response he was to give to a paper to be presented later in the year at the A.A.A.S.; not a dream but a kind of half-waking experience. He was looking into or was in the kitchen of the inner house. That was not unusual, for when fitting the cabinets and wall panelling and building in the sink, he had become deeply familiar with the proportions and aspects of the kitchen from every angle, and had frequently and deliberately visualized it from the perspective of a six-inch person standing by the stove or at the pantry door. But in this case he had no sense of volition; he was merely there; and while standing there, near the big wood-burning stove, he saw the cat come in, look up at him, and settle itself down to drink the milk. The experience included the auditory: he heard the neat and amusing sound a cat makes lapping.

Next day he remembered this little vision clearly. His mind ran upon it, now and then. Walking across campus after a lecture, he thought with some intensity that it would be very pleasant to have an animal in the house, a live animal. Not a cat, of course. Something very small. But his precise visual imagination at once presented him with a gerbil the size of the sofa, a monstrous hamster in the master bedroom, like the dreadful Mrs. Bhoolabhoy in *Staying On,* billowing in the bed, immense, and he laughed inwardly, and winced away from the spectacle.

Once, indeed, when he had been installing the pull-chain toilet—the house and its furnishings were generally Victorian; that was the original eponymous joke—he had glanced up to see that a moth had got into the attic, but only after a moment of shock did he recognize it as a moth, the marvellous, soft-winged, unearthly owl beating there beneath the rafters. Flies, however, which often visited the house, brought only thoughts of horror movies and about professors who tampered with what man was not meant to know and ended up buzzing at the windowpane, crying vainly, "Don't! No!" as the housewife's inexorable swatter fell. And serve them right. Would a ladybug do for a tortoise? The size was right, the colors wrong. The Victorians did not hesitate to paint live tortoises' shells. But tortoises do not raise their shells and fly away home. There was no pet suitable for the house. Lately he had not been working much on the house; weeks and months went by before he got the tiny Landseer framed, and then it was a plain gilt frame fitted up on a Sunday afternoon, not the scrollwork masterpiece he had originally planned. Sketches for a glassed-in sun porch were never, as his dean would have put it, implemented. The personal and professional stresses in his department at the university, which had first driven him to this small escape hatch, were considerably eased under the new chairman; he and Julia had worked out their problems well enough to go on; and anyway the house and all its furnishings were done, in place, complete. Every armchair its antimacassars. Now that the Bendskys were gone, nothing got lost or broken, nothing even got moved. And no rain fell. The outer house was in real need of reroofing; it had required three attic buckets this October, and even so there had been some damage to the study ceiling. But the cedar shingles on the inner house were still blond, virginal. They knew little of sunlight, and nothing of the rain.

I could, the professor thought, pour water on the roof, to weather the shingles a bit. It ought to be sprinkled on, somehow, so it would be more like rain. He saw himself stand with Julia's green plastic half-gallon watering can at the low table in the book-lined alcove of the living room; he saw water falling on the little shingles, pooling on the table, dripping to the ancient but serviceable domestic Oriental rug. He saw a mad professor watering a toy house. Will it grow, Doctor? Will it grow?

That night he dreamed that the inner house, his house, was outside. It stood in a garden patch on a rickety support of some kind. The ground around it had been partly dug up as if for planting. The sky was low and dingy, though it was not raining yet. Some slats had come away from the back of the house, and he was worried about the glue. "I'm worried about the glue," he said to the gardener or whomever it was that was there with a short-handled shovel, but the person did not understand. The house should not be outside, but it was outside, and it was too late to do anything about it.

He woke in great distress from this dream and could not find rest from it until his mind came upon the notion of, as it were, obeying the dream: actually moving the inner house outdoors, into the garden, which would then become the garden of both houses. An inner garden within the outer garden could be designed. Julia's advice would be needed for that. Miniature roses for hawthorn trees, surely. Scotch moss for the lawn? What could you use for hedges? She might know. A fountain? . . . He drifted back to sleep contentedly planning the garden of the house. And for months, even years, after that he amused or consoled himself from time to time, on troubled nights or in boring meetings, by reviving the plans for the miniature garden. But really it was not a practicable idea, given the rainy weather of his part of the world.

He and Julia got their house reroofed eventually, and brought the buckets down from the attic. The inner house was moved upstairs into Victoria's room when she went off to college. Looking into that room toward dusk of a November evening, the professor saw the peaked roofs and widow's walk sharp against the window light. They were still dry. Dust falls here, not rain, he thought. It isn't fair. He opened the front of the house and turned on the fireplace. The little cat lay curled up on the rug before the ruddy glow, the illusion of warmth, the illusion of shelter. And the dry milk in the half-full bowl marked "Kitty" by the kitchen door. And the child gone.   [1982]

10

Questions

1. What does the dollhouse mean to each member of the family?
2. Why does the professor hate the model family?
3. What do the recurring references to rain contribute to the theme?

4. The garden is not a "practicable idea." Are there other reasons why the professor rejects it?

5. What does the story say about the relationship of art to life?

Response

1. Read the excerpt from Le Guin's essay "Where Do You Get Your Ideas From?" Write an essay explaining your role as reader in contributing to the creation of "The Professor's Houses."

DORIS LESSING

Doris Lessing (b. 1919) was born in Persia but grew up on a farm in Rhodesia (now Zimbabwe). She has written more than two dozen novels; her first, *The Grass Is Singing*, was published in 1950, a year after she left Africa for London. Her first collection of stories, *This Was the Old Chief's Country*, was published in 1951. *The Golden Notebook* (1962), a novel, includes an account of her rejection of communism and is renowned for what it reveals about a writer's rich, internal life. *Walking in the Shade* (1997) is Lessing's second volume of autobiography and covers her early years as a writer. *Mara and Darin* is a recent novel (1999), and *Grandmothers: Four Short Novels* appeared in 2003.

A Sunrise on the Veld

Every night that winter he said aloud into the dark of the pillow: Half-past four! Half-past four! till he felt his brain had gripped the words and held them fast. Then he fell asleep at once, as if a shutter had fallen; and lay with his face turned to the clock so that he could see it first thing when he woke.

It was half-past four to the minute, every morning. Triumphantly pressing down the alarm-knob of the clock, which the dark half of his mind had outwitted, remaining vigilant all night and counting the hours as he lay relaxed in sleep, he huddled down for a last warm moment under the clothes, playing with the idea of lying abed for this once only. But he played with it for the fun of knowing that it was a weakness he could defeat without effort; just as he set the alarm each night for the delight of the moment when he woke and stretched his limbs, feeling the muscles tighten, and thought: Even my brain—even that! I can control every part of myself.

Luxury of warm rested body, with the arms and legs and fingers waiting like soldiers for a word of command! Joy of knowing that the precious hours were given to sleep voluntarily!—for he had once stayed awake three nights running, to prove that he could, and then worked all day, refusing even to admit that he was tired; and now sleep seemed to him a servant to be commanded and refused.

The boy stretched his frame full-length, touching the wall at his head with his hands, and the bedfoot with his toes; then he sprung out, like a fish leaping from water. And it was cold, cold.

5   He always dressed rapidly, so as to try and conserve his nightwarmth till the sun rose two hours later; but by the time he had on his clothes his hands were numbed and he could scarcely hold his shoes. These he could not put on for fear of waking his parents, who never came to know how early he rose.

As soon as he stepped over the lintel, the flesh of his soles contracted on the chilled earth, and his legs began to ache with cold. It was night: the stars were glittering, the trees standing black and still. He looked for signs of day, for the greying of the edge of a stone, or a lightening in the sky where the sun would rise, but there was nothing yet. Alert as an animal he crept past the dangerous window, standing poised with his hand on the sill for one proudly fastidious moment, looking in at the stuffy blackness of the room where his parents lay.

Feeling for the grass-edge of the path with his toes, he reached inside another window further along the wall, where his gun had been set in readiness the night before. The steel was icy, and numbed fingers slipped along it, so that he had to hold it in the crook of his arm for safety. Then he tiptoed to the room where the dogs slept, and was fearful that they might have been tempted to go before him; but they were waiting, their haunches crouched in reluctance at the cold, but ears and swinging tails greeting the gun ecstatically. His warning undertone kept them secret and silent till the house was a hundred yards back: then they bolted off into the bush, yelping excitedly. The boy imagined his parents turning in their beds and muttering: Those dogs again! before they were dragged back in sleep; and he smiled scornfully. He always looked back over his shoulder at the house before he passed a wall of trees that shut it from sight. It looked so low and small, crouching there under a tall and brilliant sky. Then he turned his back on it, and on the frowsting sleepers, and forgot them.

He would have to hurry. Before the light grew strong he must be four miles away; and already a tint of green stood in the hollow of a leaf, and the air smelled of morning and the stars were dimming.

He slung the shoes over his shoulder, veld *skoen* that were crinkled and hard with the dews of a hundred mornings. They would be necessary when the ground became too hot to bear. Now he felt the chilled dust push up between his toes, and he let the muscles of his feet spread and settle into the shapes of the earth; and he thought: I could walk a hundred miles on feet like these! I could walk all day, and never tire!

10   He was walking swiftly through the dark tunnel of foliage that in day-time was a road. The dogs were invisibly ranging the lower travelways of the bush, and he heard them panting. Sometimes he felt a cold muzzle on his leg before they were off again, scouting for a trail to follow. They were not trained, but free-running companions of the hunt, who often tired of the long stalk before the final shots, and went off on their own pleasure. Soon he could see them, small and wild-looking in a wild strange light, now that the bush stood trembling on the verge of colour, waiting for the sun to paint earth and grass afresh.

The grass stood to his shoulders; and the trees were showering a faint silvery rain. He was soaked; his whole body was clenched in a steady shiver.

Once he bent to the road that was newly scored with animal trails, and regretfully straightened, reminding himself that the pleasure of tracking must wait till another day.

He began to run along the edge of a field, noting jerkily how it was filmed over with fresh spiderweb, so that the long reaches of great black clods seemed netted in glistening grey. He was using the steady lope he had learned by watching the natives, the run that is a dropping of the weight of the body from one foot to the next in a slow balancing movement that never tires, nor shortens the breath; and he felt the blood pulsing down his legs and along his arms, and the exultation and pride of body mounted in him till he was shutting his teeth hard against a violent desire to shout his triumph.

Soon he had left the cultivated part of the farm. Behind him the bush was low and black. In front was a long vlei, acres of long pale grass that sent back a hollowing gleam of light to a satiny sky. Near him thick swathes of grass were bent with the weight of water, and diamond drops sparkled on each frond.

The first bird woke at his feet and at once a flock of them sprang into the air call-ing shrilly that day had come; and suddenly, behind him, the bush woke into song, and he could hear the guinea fowl calling far ahead of him. That meant they would now be sailing down from their trees into thick grass, and it was for them he had come: he was too late. But he did not mind. He forgot he had come to shoot. He set his legs wide, and balanced from foot to foot, and swung his gun up and down in both hands horizontally, in a kind of improvised exercise, and let his head sink back till it was pil-lowed in his neck muscles, and watched how above him small rosy clouds floated in a lake of gold.

Suddenly it all rose in him: it was unbearable. He leapt up into the air, shouting and yelling wild, unrecognisable noises. Then he began to run, not carefully, as he had be-fore, but madly, like a wild thing. He was clean crazy, yelling mad with the joy of liv-ing and a superfluity of youth. He rushed down the vlei under a tumult of crimson and gold, while all the birds of the world sang about him. He ran in great leaping strides, and shouted as he ran, feeling his body rise into the crisp rushing air and fall back surely onto sure feet; and thought briefly, not believing that such a thing could hap-pen to him, that he could break his ankle any moment, in this thick tangled grass. He cleared bushes like a duiker, leapt over rocks; and finally came to a dead stop at a place where the ground fell abruptly away below him to the river. It had been a two-mile-long dash through waist-high growth, and he was breathing hoarsely and could no longer sing. But he poised on a rock and looked down at stretches of water that gleamed though stopping trees, and thought suddenly, I am fifteen! Fifteen! The words came new to him; so that he kept repeating them wonderingly, with swelling excitement; and he felt the years of his life with his hands, as if he were counting marbles, each one hard and separate and compact, each one a wonderful shining thing. That was what he was: fifteen years of this rich soil, and this slow-moving water, and air that smelt like a challenge whether it was warm and sultry at noon, or as brisk as cold water, like it was now.

There was nothing he couldn't do, nothing! A vision came to him, as he stood there, like when a child hears the word "eternity" and tries to understand it, and time takes possession of the mind. He felt his life ahead of him as a great and wonderful thing, something that was his; and he said aloud, with the blood rising to his head: all the great men of the world have been as I am now, and there is nothing I can't become, nothing I can't do; there is no country in the world I cannot make part of myself, if I choose. I contain the world. I can make of it what I want. If I choose, I can change everything that is going to happen: it depends on me, and what I decide now.

The urgency, and the truth and the courage of what his voice was saying exulted him so that he began to sing again, at the top of his voice, and the sound went echo-ing down the river gorge. He stopped for the echo, and sang again: stopped and shout-ed. That was what he was!—he sang, if he chose; and the world had to answer him.

And for minutes he stood there, shouting and singing and waiting for the lovely ed-dying sound of the echo; so that his own new strong thoughts came back and washed round his head, as if someone were answering him and encouraging him; till the gorge was full of soft voices clashing back and forth from rock to rock over the river. And then it seemed as if there was a new voice. He listened, puzzled, for it was not his own. Soon he was leaning forward, all his nerves alert, quite still: somewhere close to him there was a noise that was no joyful bird, nor tinkle of falling water, nor ponderous movement of cattle.

20   There it was again. In the deep morning hush that held his future and his past, was a sound of pain, and repeated over and over: it was a kind of shortened scream, as if someone, something, had no breath to scream. He came to himself, looked about him, and called for the dogs. They did not appear: they had gone off on their own business, and he was alone. Now he was clean sober, all the madness gone. His heart beating fast, because of that frightened screaming, he stepped carefully off the rock and went towards a belt of trees. He was moving cautiously, for not so long ago he had seen a leopard in just this spot.

At the edge of the trees he stopped and peered, holding his gun ready; he advanced, looking steadily about him, his eyes narrowed. Then, all at once, in the middle of a step, he faltered, and his face was puzzled. He shook his head impatiently, as if he doubted his own sight.

There, between two trees, against a background of gaunt black rocks, was a figure from a dream, a strange beast that was horned and drunken-legged, but like something he had never even imagined. It seemed to be ragged. It looked like a small buck that had black ragged tufts of fur standing up irregularly all over it, with patches of raw flesh beneath . . . but the patches of rawness were disappearing under moving black and came again elsewhere; and all the time the creature screamed, in small gasping screams, and leaped drunkenly from side to side, as if it were blind.

Then the boy understood: it *was* a buck. He ran closer, and again stood still, stopped by a new fear. Around him the grass was whispering and alive. He looked wildly about, and then down. The ground was black with ants, great energetic ants that took no notice of him, but hurried and scurried towards the fighting shape, like glistening black water flowing through the grass.

And, as he drew in his breath and pity and terror seized him, the beast fell and the screaming stopped. Now he could hear nothing but one bird singing, and the sound of the rustling, whispering ants.

25   He peered over at the writhing blackness that jerked convulsively with the jerking nerves. It grew quieter. There were small twitches from the mass that still looked vaguely like the shape of a small animal.

It came into his mind that he should shoot it and end its pain; and he raised the gun. Then he lowered it again. The buck could no longer feel; its fighting was a mechanical protest of the nerves. But it was not that which made him put down the gun. It was a swelling feeling of rage and misery and protest that expressed itself in the thought: if I had not come it would have died like this: so why should I interfere? All over the bush things like this happen; they happen all the time; this is how life goes on, by living things dying in anguish. He gripped the gun between his knees and felt in his own limbs the myriad swarming pain of the twitching animal that could no longer feel, and set his teeth, and said over and over again under his breath: I can't stop it. I can't stop it. There is nothing I can do.

He was glad that the buck was unconscious and had gone past suffering so that he did not have to make a decision to kill it even when he was feeling with his whole body: this is what happens, this is how things work.

It was right—that was what he was feeling. *It was right and nothing could alter it.*

The knowledge of fatality, of what has to be, had gripped him and for the first time in his life; and he was left unable to make any movement of brain or body, except to say: "Yes, yes. That is what living is." It had entered his flesh and his bones and grown in to the furthest corners of his brain and would never leave him. And at that moment he could not have performed the smallest action of mercy, knowing as he did, having lived on it all his life, the vast unalterable, cruel veld, where at any moment one might stumble over a skull or crush the skeleton of some small creature.

Suffering, sick, and angry, but also grimly satisfied with his new stoicism, he stood there leaning on his rifle, and watched the seething black mound grow smaller. At his feet, now, were ants trickling back with pink fragments in their mouths, and there was a fresh acid smell in his nostrils. He sternly controlled the uselessly convulsing muscles of his empty stomach, and reminded himself: the ants must eat too! At the same time he found that the tears were streaming down his face, and his clothes were soaked with the sweat of that other creature's pain. {30}

The shape had grown small. Now it looked like nothing recognisable. He did not know how long it was before he saw the blackness thin, and bits of white showed through, shining in the sun—yes, there was the sun, just up, glowing over the rocks. Why, the whole thing could not have taken longer than a few minutes.

He began to swear, as if the shortness of the time was in itself unbearable, using the words he had heard his father say. He strode forward, crushing ants with each step, and brushing them off his clothes, till he stood above the skeleton, which lay sprawled under a small bush. It was clean-picked. It might have been lying there years, save that on the white bone were pink fragments of gristle. About the bones ants were ebbing away, their pincers full of meat.

The boy looked at them, big black ugly insects. A few were standing and gazing up at him with small glittering eyes.

"Go away!" he said to the ants, very coldly. "I am not for you—not just yet, at any rate. Go away." And he fancied that the ants turned and went away.

He bent over the bones and touched the sockets in the skull; that was where the eyes were, he thought incredulously, remembering the liquid dark eyes of a buck. And then he bent the slim foreleg bone, swinging it horizontally in his palm. {35}

That morning, perhaps an hour ago, this small creature had been stepping proud and free through the brush, feeling the chill on its hide even as he himself had done, exhilarated by it. Proudly stepping the earth, tossing its horns, frisking a pretty white tail, it had sniffed the cold morning air. Walking like kings and conquerors it had moved through this free-held bush, where each blade of grass grew for it alone, and where the river ran pure sparkling water for its slaking.

And then—what had happened? Such a swift surefooted thing could surely not be trapped by a swarm of ants?

The boy bent curiously to the skeleton. Then he saw that the back leg that lay uppermost and strained out in the tension of death, was snapped midway in the thigh, so that broken bones jutted over each other uselessly. So that was it! Limping into the ant-masses it could not escape, once it had sensed the danger. Yes, but how had the leg been broken? Had it fallen, perhaps? Impossible, a buck was too light and graceful. Had some jealous rival horned it?

What could possibly have happened? Perhaps some Africans had thrown stones at it, as they do, trying to kill it for meat, and had broken its leg. Yes, that must be it.

Even as he imagined the crowd of running, shouting natives, and the flying stones, and the leaping buck, another picture came into his mind. He saw himself, on any one of these bright ringing mornings, drunk with excitement, taking a snap shot at some half-seen buck. He saw himself with the gun lowered, wondering whether he had missed or not; and thinking at last that it was late, and he wanted his breakfast, and it {40} was not worthwhile to track miles after an animal that would very likely get away from him in any case.

For a moment he would not face it. He was a small boy again, kicking sulkily at the skeleton, hanging his head, refusing to accept the responsibility.

Then he straightened up, and looked down at the bones with an odd expression of dismay, all the anger gone out of him. His mind went quite empty: all around him he could see trickles of ants disappearing into the grass. The whispering noise was faint and dry, like the rustling of a cast snakeskin.

At last he picked up his gun and walked homewards. He was telling himself half defiantly that he wanted his breakfast. He was telling himself that it was getting very hot, much too hot to be out roaming the brush.

Really, he was tired. He walked heavily, not looking where he put his feet. When he came within sight of his home he stopped, knitting his brows. There was something he had to think out. The death of that small animal was a thing that concerned him, and he was by no means finished with it. It lay at the back of his mind uncomfortably.

Soon, the very next morning, he would get clear of everybody and go to the bush
45 and think about it.   [1951]

QUESTIONS

1. How is the boy's psychological state mirrored in the rich description of the veld?
2. Trace some of the images of sound, touch, and sight. Do they form a pattern?
3. The narrator says of the boy, "the dark half of his mind had outwitted" the clock. Is there a sense in which this comment is ironic?
4. Why is the boy "grimly satisfied"?
5. What precisely has the boy learned from the experience?

RESPONSES

1. In this story, as in Sherwood Anderson's "I Want to Know Why," the narrator ends the story still considering the meaning of story's events. What is gained with that narrative strategy?
2. Compare this story to Porter's "The Grave" and/or Viramontes's "The Moths." Sometimes we learn about death from a death in nature; sometimes we learn about it from a death in our families. How are these experiences and the lessons we take from them similar and different?

JACK LONDON

Jack London (1876–1916) was born in San Francisco. He spent his forma-
tive years as a rancher and sailor and, at the age of nineteen, returned to
graduate from high school and to enroll for a semester at the University
of California at Berkeley. Seeking his fortune, he journeyed to the Alaskan
gold fields. Although he failed as a miner, his stories of that experience,
sold to magazines like *The Overland Monthly* and *The Atlantic Monthly*,
won him a readership that he quickly exploited. His swift climb to fame
is told in his autobiographical novel, *Martin Eden* (1909). Disillusioned
with his celebrity status and losing a battle with alcoholism, he took his
own life at the age of forty.

To Build a Fire

Day had broken cold and grey, exceedingly cold and grey, when the man turned aside
from the main Yukon trail and climbed the high earth-bank, where a dim and little-
travelled trail led eastward through the fat spruce timberland. It was a steep bank,
and he paused for breath at the top, excusing the act to himself by looking at his watch.
It was nine o'clock. There was no sun nor hint of sun, though there was not a cloud in
the sky. It was a clear day, and yet there seemed an intangible pall over the face of
things, a subtle gloom that made the day dark, and that was due to the absence of sun.
This fact did not worry the man. He was used to the lack of sun. It had been days since
he had seen the sun, and he knew that a few more days must pass before that cheerful orb, due south, would just peep above the skyline and dip immediately from view.

The man flung a look back along the way he had come. The Yukon lay a mile wide
and hidden under three feet of ice. On top of this ice were as many feet of snow. It was
all pure white, rolling in gentle undulations where the ice jams of the freeze-up had
formed. North and south, as far as his eye could see, it was unbroken white, save for a
dark hairline that curved and twisted from around the spruce-covered island to the
south, and that curved and twisted away into the north, where it disappeared behind
another spruce-covered island. This dark hairline was the trail—the main trail—that led
south five hundred miles to the Chilcoot Pass, Dyea, and salt water; and that led north
seventy miles to Dawson, and still on to the north a thousand miles to Nulato, and finally to St. Michael, on the Bering Sea, a thousand miles and half a thousand more.

But all this—the mysterious, far-reaching hairline trail, the absence of sun from the sky, the tremendous cold, and the strangeness and weirdness of it all—made no impression on the man. It was not because he was long used to it. He was a newcomer in the land, a *chechaquo,* and this was his first winter. The trouble with him was that he was without imagination. He was quick and alert in the things of life, but only in the things, and not in the significances. Fifty degrees below zero meant eighty-odd degrees of frost. Such fact impressed him as being cold and uncomfortable, and that was all. It did not lead him to mediate upon his frailty as a creature of temperature, and upon man's frailty in general, able only to live within certain narrow limits of heat and cold; and from there on it did not lead him to the conjectural field of immortality and man's place in the universe. Fifty degrees below zero stood for a bite of frost that hurt and that must be guarded against by the use of mittens, ear flaps, warm moccasins, and thick socks. Fifty degrees below zero. That there should be anything more to it than that was a thought that never entered his head.

As he turned to go on, he spat speculatively. There was a sharp explosive crackle that startled him. He spat again. And again, in the air, before it could fall to the snow, the spittle crackled. He knew that at fifty below spittle crackled on the snow, but this spittle had crackled in the air. Undoubtedly it was colder than fifty below—how much colder he did not know. But the temperature did not matter. He was bound for the old claim on the left fork of Henderson Creek, where the boys were already. They had come over across the divide from the Indian Creek country, while he had come the roundabout way to take a look at the possibilities of getting out logs in the spring from the islands in the Yukon. He would be into camp by six o'clock; a bit after dark, it was true, but the boys would be there, a fire would be going, and a hot supper would be ready. As for lunch, he pressed his hand against the protruding bundle under his jacket. It was also under his shirt, wrapped up in a handkerchief and lying against the naked skin. It was the only way to keep the biscuits from freezing. He smiled agreeably to himself as he thought of those biscuits, each cut open and sopped in bacon grease, and each enclosing a generous slice of fried bacon.

5   He plunged in among the big spruce trees. The trail was faint. A foot of snow had fallen since the last sled had passed over, and he was glad he was without a sled, travelling light. In fact, he carried nothing but the lunch wrapped in the handkerchief. He was surprised, however, at the cold. It certainly was cold, he concluded, as he rubbed his numb nose and cheekbones with his mittened hand. He was a warm-whiskered man, but the hair on his face did not protect the high cheekbones and the eager nose that thrust itself aggressively into the frosty air.

At the man's heels trotted a dog, a big native husky, the proper wolf-dog, greycoated and without any visible or temperamental difference from its brother, the wild wolf. The animal was depressed by the tremendous cold. It knew that it was no time for travelling. Its instinct told it a truer tale than was told to the man by the man's judgment. In reality, it was not merely colder than fifty below zero; it was colder than sixty below, than seventy below. It was seventy-five below zero. Since the freezing point is thirty-two above zero, it meant that one hundred and seven degrees of frost obtained. The dog did not know anything about thermometers. Possibly in its brain there was no sharp consciousness of a condition of very cold such as was in the man's brain. But the brute had its instinct. It experienced a vague but menacing apprehension that subdued it and made it slink along at the man's heels, and that made it question eagerly every unwonted movement of the man as if expecting him to go into camp and to seek shelter somewhere and build a fire. The dog had learned fire, and it wanted fire, or else to burrow under the snow and cuddle its warmth away from the air.

The frozen moisture of its breathing had settled on its fur in a fine powder of frost, and especially were its jowls, muzzle, and eyelashes whitened by its crystal breath. The man's red beard and moustache were likewise frosted, but more solidly, the deposit taking the form of ice and increasing with every warm, moist breath he exhaled. Also, the man was chewing tobacco, and the muzzle of ice held his lips so rigidly that he was unable to clear his chin when he expelled the juice. The result was a crystal beard of the colour and solidity of amber was increasing its length on his chin. If he fell down it would shatter itself, like glass, into brittle fragments. But he did not mind the appendage. It was the penalty all tobacco chewers paid in that country, and he had been out before in two cold snaps. They had not been so cold as this, he knew, but by the spirit thermometer at Sixty Mile he knew they had been registered at fifty below and at fifty-five.

He held on through the level stretch of woods for several miles, crossed a wide flat of nigger heads, and dropped down a bank to the frozen bed of a small stream. This was Henderson Creek, and he knew he was ten miles from the forks. He looked at his watch. It was ten o'clock. He was making four miles an hour, and he calculated that he would arrive at the forks at half-past twelve. He decided to celebrate that event by eating his lunch there.

The dog dropped in again at his heels, with a tail drooping discouragement, as the man swung along the creek bed. The furrow of the old sled trail was plainly visible, but a dozen inches of snow covered up the marks of the last runners. In a month no man had come up or down that silent creek. The man held steadily on. He was not much given to thinking, and just then particularly he had nothing to think about save that he would eat lunch at the forks and that at six o'clock he would be in camp with the boys. There was nobody to talk to; and, had there been, speech would have been impossible because of the ice muzzle on his mouth. So he continued monotonously to chew tobacco and to increase the length of his amber beard.

Once in a while the thought reiterated itself that it was very cold and that he had never experienced such cold. As he walked along he rubbed his cheekbones and nose with the back of his mittened hand. He did this automatically, now and again changing hands. But, rub as he would, the instant he stopped his cheekbones went numb, and the following instant the end of his nose went numb. He was sure to frost his cheeks; he knew that, and experienced a pang of regret that he had not devised a nose strap of the sort Bud wore in cold snaps. Such a strap passed across the cheeks, as well, and saved them. But it didn't matter much, after all. What were frosted cheeks? A bit painful, that was all; they were never serious.

Empty as the man's mind was of thoughts, he was keenly observant, and he noticed the changes in the creeks, the curves and bends and timber jams, and always he sharply noted where he placed his feet. Once, coming round a bend, he shied abruptly, like a startled horse, curved away from the place where he had been walking, and retreated several paces back along the trail. The creek he knew was frozen clear to the bottom—no creek could contain water in that arctic winter—but he knew also that there were springs that bubbled out from the hillsides and ran along under the snow and on top of the ice of the creek. He knew that the coldest snaps never froze these springs, and he knew likewise their danger. They were traps. They hid pools of water under the snow that might be three inches deep, or three feet. Sometimes a skin of ice half an inch thick covered them, and in turn was covered by the snow. Sometimes there were alternate layers of water and ice skin, so that when one broke through he kept on breaking through for a while, sometimes wetting himself to the waist.

That was why he had shied in such a panic. He had felt the give under his feet and heard the crackle of a snow-hidden ice skin. And to get his feet wet in such a temperature meant trouble and danger. At the very least it meant delay, for he would be forced to stop and build a fire, and under its protection to bare his feet while he dried his socks and moccasins. He stood and studied the creek bed and its banks, and decided that the flow of water came from the right. He reflected awhile, rubbing his nose and cheeks, then skirted to the left, stepping gingerly and testing the footing for each step. Once clear of the danger, he took a fresh chew of tobacco and swung along at his four-mile gait.

In the course of the next two hours he came upon several similar traps. Usually the snow above the hidden pools had a sunken, candied appearance that advertised the danger. Once again, however, he had a close call; and once, suspecting danger, he compelled the dog to go on in front. The dog did not want to go. It hung back until the man shoved it forward, and then it went quickly across the white, unbroken surface. Suddenly it broke through, floundered to one side, and got away to firmer footing. It had wet its forefeet and legs, and almost immediately the water that clung to it turned to ice. It made quick efforts to lick the ice off its legs, then dropped down in the snow and began to bite out the ice that had formed between the toes. This was a matter of instinct. To permit the ice to remain would mean sore feet. It did not know this. It merely obeyed the mysterious prompting that arose from the deep crypts of its being. But the man knew, having achieved a judgment on the subject, and he removed the mitten from his right hand and helped to tear out the ice particles. He did not expose his fingers more than a minute, and was astonished at the swift numbness that smote them. It certainly was cold. He pulled on the mitten hastily, and beat the hand savagely across his chest.

At twelve o'clock the day was at its brightest. Yet the sun was too far south on its winter journey to clear the horizon. The bulge of the earth intervened between it and Henderson Creek, where the man walked under a clear sky at noon and cast no shadow. At half-past twelve, to the minute, he arrived at the forks of the creek. He was pleased at the speed he had made. If he kept it up, he would certainly be with the boys by six. He unbuttoned his jacket and shirt and drew forth his lunch. The action consumed no more than a quarter of a minute, yet in that brief moment the numbness laid hold of the exposed fingers. He did not put the mitten on, but, instead, struck the fingers a dozen sharp smashes against his leg. Then he sat down on a snow-covered log to eat. The sting that followed upon the striking of his fingers against his leg ceased so quickly that he was startled. He had had no chance to take a bit of biscuit. He struck the fingers repeatedly and returned them to the mitten, baring the other hand for the purpose of eating. He tried to take a mouthful, but the ice muzzle prevented. He had forgotten to build a fire and thaw out. He chuckled at his foolishness, and as he chuckled he noted the numbness creeping into the exposed fingers. Also, he noted that the stinging which had first come to his toes when he sat down was already passing away. He wondered whether the toes were warm or numb. He moved them inside the moccasins and decided that they were numb.

15   He pulled the mitten on hurriedly and stood up. He was a bit frightened. He stamped up and down until the stinging returned into the feet. It certainly was cold, was his thought. That man from Sulphur Creek had spoken the truth when telling how cold it sometimes got in the country. And he had laughed at him at the time! That showed one must not be too sure of things. There was no mistake about it, it *was* cold. He strode up and down, stamping his feet and threshing his arms, until reassured by the returning warmth. Then he got out matches and proceeded to make a fire. From

the undergrowth, where high water of the previous spring had lodged a supply of seasoned twigs, he got his firewood. Working carefully from a small beginning, he soon had a roaring fire, over which he thawed the ice from his face and in the protection of which he ate his biscuits. For the moment the cold of space was outwitted. The dog took satisfaction in the fire, stretching out close enough for warmth and far enough away to escape being singed.

When the man had finished, he filled his pipe and took his comfortable time over a smoke. Then he pulled on his mittens, settled the ear-flaps of his cap firmly about his ears, and took the creek trail up the left fork. The dog was disappointed and yearned back towards the fire. This man did not know cold. Possibly all the generations of his ancestry had been ignorant of cold, of real cold, of cold one hundred and seven degrees below freezing point. But the dog knew; all its ancestry knew, and it had inherited the knowledge. And it knew that it was not good to walk abroad in such fearful cold. It was the time to lie snug in a hole in the snow and wait for a curtain of cloud to be drawn across the face of outer space whence this cold came. On the other hand, there was no keen intimacy between the dog and the man. The one was the toil slave of the other, and the only caresses it had ever received were the caresses of the whip lash and of harsh and menacing throat sounds that threatened the whip lash. So the dog made no effort to communicate its apprehension to the man. It was not concerned in the welfare of the man; it was for its own sake that it yearned back towards the fire. But the man whistled, and spoke to it with the sound of whip lashes, and the dog swung in at the man's heels and followed after.

The man took a chew of tobacco and proceeded to start a new amber beard. Also, his moist breath quickly powdered with white his moustache, eyebrows, and lashes. There did not seem to be so many springs on the left fork of the Henderson, and for half an hour the man saw no signs of any. And then it happened. At a place where there were no signs, where the soft, unbroken snow seemed to advertise solidity beneath, the man broke through. It was not deep. He wet himself half-way to the knees before he floundered out to the firm crust.

He was angry, and cursed his luck aloud. He had hoped to get into camp with the boys at six o'clock, and this would delay him an hour, for he would have to build a fire and dry out his footgear. This was imperative at that low temperature—he knew that much; and he turned aside to the bank, which he climbed. On top, tangled in the underbrush about the trunks of several small spruce trees, was a high-water deposit of dry firewood—sticks and twigs, principally, but also larger portions of seasoned branches and fine, dry, last year's grasses. He threw down several large pieces on top of the snow. This served for a foundation and prevented the young flame from drowning itself in the snow it otherwise would melt. The flame he got by touching a match to a small shred of birch bark that he took from his pocket. This burned even more readily than paper. Placing it on the foundation, he fed the young flame with wisps of dry grass and with the tiniest dry twigs.

He worked slowly and carefully, keenly aware of his danger. Gradually, as the flame grew stronger, he increased the size of the twigs with which he fed it. He squatted in the snow pulling the twigs out from their entanglement in the brush and feeding directly to the flame. He knew there must be no failure. When it is seventy-five below zero, a man must not fail in his first attempt to build a fire—that is, if his feet are wet. If his feet are dry, and he fails, he can run along the trail for half a mile and restore his circulation. But the circulation of wet and freezing feet cannot be restored by running when it is seventy-five below. No matter how fast he runs, the wet feet will freeze the harder.

20   All this the man knew. The old-timer on Sulphur Creek had told him about it the previous fall, and now he was appreciating the advice. Already all sensation had gone out of his feet. To build the fire he had been forced to remove his mittens, and the fingers had quickly gone numb. His pace of four miles an hour had kept his heart pumping blood to the surface of his body and to all the extremities. But the instant he stopped, the action of the pump eased down. The cold of space smote the unprotected tip of the planet, and he, being on that unprotected tip, received the full force of the blow. The blood of his body recoiled before it. The blood was alive, like the dog, and like the dog it wanted to hide away and cover itself up from the fearful cold. So long as he walked four miles an hour, he pumped that blood, willy-nilly, to the surface; but now it ebbed away and sank down into the recesses of his body. The extremities were the first to feel its absence. His wet feet froze the faster, and his exposed fingers numbed the faster, though they had not yet begun to freeze. Nose and cheeks were already freezing, while the skin of all his body chilled as it lost its blood.

But he was safe. Toes and nose and cheeks would be only touched by the frost, for the fire was beginning to burn with strength. He was feeding it with twigs the size of his finger. In another minute he would be able to feed it with branches the size of his wrist, and then he could remove his wet footgear, and, while it dried, he could keep his naked feet warm by the fire, rubbing them at first, of course, with snow. The fire was a success. He was safe. He remembered the advice of the old-timer on Sulphur Creek, and smiled. The old-timer had been very serious in laying down the law that no man must travel alone in the Klondike after fifty below. Well, here he was; he had had the accident; he was alone; and he had saved himself. Those old-timers were rather womanish, some of them, he thought. All a man had to do was to keep his head, and he was all right. Any man who was a man could travel alone. But it was surprising, the rapidity with which his cheeks and nose were freezing. And he had not thought his fingers could go lifeless in so short a time. Lifeless they were, for he could scarcely make them move together to grip a twig, and they seemed remote from his body and from him. When he touched a twig, he had to look and see whether or not he had hold of it. The wires were pretty well down between him and his finger ends.

All of which counted for little. There was the fire, snapping and crackling and promising life with every dancing flame. He started to untie his moccasins. They were coated with ice; the thick German socks were like sheaths of iron halfway to the knees; and the moccasin strings were like rods of steel all twisted and knotted as by some conflagration. For a moment he tugged with his numb fingers, then, realizing the folly of it, he drew his sheath knife.

But before he could cut the strings, it happened. It was his own fault or, rather, his mistake. He should not have built the fire under the spruce tree. He should have built it in the open. But it had been easier to pull the twigs from the brush and drop them directly on the fire. Now the tree under which he had done this carried a weight of snow on its boughs. No wind had blown for weeks, and each bough was fully freighted. Each time he had pulled a twig he had communicated a slight agitation to the tree—an imperceptible agitation, so far as he was concerned, but an agitation sufficient to bring about the disaster. High up in the tree one bough capsized its load of snow. This fell on the boughs beneath, capsizing them. This process continued, spreading out and involving the whole tree. It grew like an avalanche, and it descended without warning upon the man and the fire, and the fire was blotted out! Where it had burned was a mantle of fresh and disordered snow.

The man was shocked. It was as though he had just heard his own sentence of death. For a moment he sat and stared at the spot where the fire had been. Then he grew very calm. Perhaps the old-timer on Sulphur Creek was right. If he had only had a trail mate he would have been in no danger now. The trail mate could have built the fire. Well, it was up to him to build the fire over again, and this second time there must be no failure. Even if he succeeded, he would most likely lose some toes. His feet must be badly frozen by now, and there would be some time before the second fire was ready.

Such were his thoughts, but he did not sit and think them. He was busy all the time they were passing through his mind. He had made a new foundation for a fire, this time in the open, where no treacherous tree could blot it out. Next he gathered dry grasses and tiny twigs from the high-water flotsam. He could not bring his fingers together to pull them out, but he was able to gather them by the handful. In this way he got many rotten twigs and bits of green moss that were undesirable, but it was the best he could do. He worked methodically, even collecting an armful of the larger branches to be used later when the fire gathered strength. And all the while the dog sat and watched him, a certain yearning wistfulness in its eyes, for it looked upon him as the fire provider, and the fire was slow in coming. 25

When all was ready, the man reached in his pocket for a second piece of birch bark. He knew the bark was there, and, though he could not feel it with his fingers, he could hear its crisp rustling as he fumbled for it. Try as he would, he could not clutch hold of it. And all the time, in his consciousness, was the knowledge that each instant his feet were freezing. This thought tended to put him in a panic, but he fought against it and kept calm. He pulled on his mittens with his teeth, and threshed his arms back and forth, beating his hands with all his might against his sides. He did this sitting down, and he stood up to do it; and all the while the dog sat in the snow, its wolf brush of a tail curled around warmly over its forefront, its sharp wolf ears pricked forward intently as it watched the man. And the man, as he beat and threshed with his arms and hands, felt a great surge of envy as he regarded the creature that was warm and secure in its natural covering.

After a time he was aware of the first faraway signals of sensation in his beaten fingers. The faint tingling grew stronger till it evolved into a stinging ache that was excruciating, but which the man hailed with satisfaction. He stripped the mitten from his right hand and fetched forth the birch bark. The exposed fingers were quickly going numb again. Next he brought out his bunch of sulphur matches. But the tremendous cold had already driven the life out of his fingers. In his effort to separate one match from the others, the whole bunch fell in the snow. He tried to pick it out of the snow, but failed. The dead fingers could neither touch nor clutch. He was very careful. He drove the thought of his freezing feet, and nose, and cheeks, out of his mind, devoting his whole soul to the matches. He watched, using the sense of vision in place of that touch, and when he saw his fingers on each side the bunch, he closed them—that is, he willed to close them, for the wires were down, and the fingers did not obey. He pulled the mitten on the right hand, and beat it fiercely against his knee. Then with both mittened hands, he scooped the bunch of matches, along with much snow, into his lap. Yet he was no better off.

After some manipulation he managed to get the bunch between the heels of his mittened hands. In this fashion he carried it to his mouth. The ice crackled and snapped when by a violent effort he opened his mouth. He drew the lower jaw in, curled the upper lip out of the way, and scraped the bunch with his upper teeth in order to separate a match. He succeeded in getting one, which he dropped on his lap. He was no better off. He could not pick it up. Then he devised a way. He picked it up in his teeth and scratched it on his leg. Twenty times he scratched before he succeeded in lighting it. As it flamed he held it with his teeth to the birch bark. But the burning brimstone went up his nostrils and into his lungs, causing him to cough spasmodically. The match fell into the snow and went out.

The old-timer on Sulphur Creek was right, he thought in the moment of controlled despair that ensued: after fifty below, a man should travel with a partner. He beat his hands, but failed in exciting any sensation. Suddenly he bared both hands, removing the mittens with his teeth. He caught the whole bunch between the heels of his hands. His arm muscles not being frozen enabled him to press the hand heels tightly against the matches. Then he scratched the bunch along his leg. It flared into flame, seventy sulphur matches at once! There was no wind to blow them out. He kept his head to one side to escape the strangling fumes, and held the blazing bunch to the birch bark. As he so held it, he became aware of sensation in his hand. His flesh was burning. He could smell it. Deep down below the surface he could feel it. The sensation developed into pain that grew acute. And still he endured it, holding the flame of the matches clumsily to the bark that would not light readily because his own burning hands were in the way, absorbing most of the flame.

30   At last, when he could endure no more, he jerked his hands apart. The blazing matches fell sizzling into the snow, but the birch bark was alight. He began laying dry grasses and the tiniest twigs on the flame. He could not pick and choose, for he had to lift the fuel between the heels of his hands. Small pieces of rotten wood and green moss clung to the twigs, and he bit them off as well as he could with his teeth. He cherished the flame carefully and awkwardly. It meant life, and it must not perish. The withdrawal of blood from the surface of his body now made him begin to shiver, and he grew more awkward. A large piece of green moss fell squarely on the little fire. He tried to poke it out with his fingers, but his shivering frame made him poke too far, and he disrupted the nucleus of the little fire, the burning grasses and tiny twigs separating and scattering. He tried to poke them together again, but in spite of the tenseness of the effort, his shivering got away with him, and the twigs were hopelessly scattered. Each twig gushed a puff of smoke and went out. The fire provider had failed. As he looked apathetically about him, his eyes chanced on the dog, sitting across the ruins of the fire from him, in the snow, making restless, hunching movements, slightly lifting one forefoot and then the other, shifting its weight back and forth on them with wistful eagerness.

The sight of the dog put a wild idea into his head. He remembered the tale of the man, caught in a blizzard, who killed a steer and crawled inside the carcass, and so was saved. He would kill the dog and bury his hands in the warm body until the numbness went out of them. Then he could build another fire. He spoke to the dog, calling it to him; but in his voice was a strange note of fear that frightened the animal, who had never known the man to speak in such a way before. Something was the matter, and its suspicious nature sensed danger—it knew not what danger, but somewhere, somehow, in its brain arose an apprehension of the man. It flattened its ears down at the sound of the man's voice, and its restless, hunching movements and the liftings and shiftings of its forefeet became more pronounced; but it would not come to the man. He got on his hands and knees and crawled towards the dog. This unusual posture again excited suspicion, and the animal sidled mincingly away.

The man sat up in the snow for a moment and struggled for calmness. Then he pulled on his mittens, by means of his teeth, and got upon his feet. He glanced down at first in order to assure himself that he was really standing up, for the absence of sensation in his feet left him unrelated to the earth. His erect position in itself started to drive the webs of suspicion from the dog's mind; and when he spoke peremptorily, with the sound of whip lashes in his voice, the dog rendered its customary allegiance and came to him. As it came within reaching distance, the man lost his control. His arm flashed out to the dog, and he experienced genuine surprise when he discovered that his hands could not clutch, that there was neither bend nor feeling in the fingers. He had forgotten for the moment that they were frozen and that they were freezing more and more. All this happened quickly, and before the animal could get away, he encircled its body with his arms. He sat down in the snow, and in his fashion held the dog, while it snarled and whined and struggled.

But it was all he could do, hold its body encircled in his arms and sit there. He realized he could not kill the dog. There was no way to do it. With his helpless hands he could neither draw nor hold his sheath knife nor throttle the animal. He released it, and it plunged wildly away, with tail between its legs, and still snarling. It halted forty feet away and surveyed him curiously, with ears sharply pricked forward.

The man looked down at his hands in order to locate them, and found them hanging on the ends of his arms. It struck him as curious that one should have to use his eyes in order to find out where his hands were. He began threshing his arms back and forth, beating the mittened hands against his sides. He did this for five minutes, violently, and his heart pumped enough blood up to the surface to put a stop to his shivering. But no sensation was aroused in the hands. He had an impression that they hung like weights on the ends of his arms, but when he tried to run the impression down, he could not find it.

A certain fear of death, dull and oppressive, came to him. This fear quickly became poignant as he realized that it was no longer a mere matter of freezing his fingers and toes, or losing his hands and feet, but that it was a matter of life and death with the chances against him. This threw him into a panic, and he turned and ran up the creek bed along the old, dim trail. The dog joined in behind him and kept up with him. He ran blindly, without intention, in fear such as he had never known in his life. Slowly, as he ploughed and floundered through the snow, he began to see things again—the banks of the creek, the old timber jams, the leafless aspens, and the sky. The running made him feel better. He did not shiver. Maybe, if he ran on, his feet would thaw out; and, anyway, if he ran far enough, he would reach camp and the boys. Without doubt he would lose some fingers and toes and some of his face; but the boys would take care of him, and save the rest of him when he got there. And at the same time there was another thought in his mind that said he would never get to the camp and the boys; that it was too many miles away, that the freezing had too great a start on him, and that he would soon be stiff and dead. This thought he kept in the background and refused to consider. Sometimes it pushed itself forward and demanded to be heard, but he thrust it back and strove to think of other things.

It struck him as curious that he could run at all on feet so frozen that he could not feel them when they struck the earth and took the weight of his body. He seemed to himself to skim along above the surface, and to have no connection with the earth. Somewhere he had once seen a winged Mercury, and he wondered if Mercury felt as he felt when skimming over the earth.

His theory of running until he reached camp and the boys had one flaw in it: he lacked the endurance. Several times he stumbled, and finally he tottered, crumpled up, and fell. When he tried to rise, he failed. He must sit and rest, he decided, and next time he would merely walk and keep on going. As he sat and regained his

35

breath, he noted that he was feeling quite warm and comfortable. He was not shivering, and it even seemed that a warm glow had come to his chest and trunk. And yet, when he touched his nose or cheeks, there was no sensation. Running would not thaw them out. Nor would it thaw out his hands and feet. Then the thought came to him that the frozen portions of his body must be extending. He tried to keep this thought down, to forget it, to think of something else; he was aware of the panicky feeling that it caused, and he was afraid of the panic. But the thought asserted itself, and persisted, until it produced a vision of his body totally frozen. This was too much, and he made another wild run along the trail. Once he slowed down to a walk, but the thought of the freezing extending itself made him run again.

And all the time the dog ran with him, at his heels. When he fell down a second time, it curled its tail over its forefeet and sat in front of him, facing him, curiously eager and intent. The warmth and security of the animal angered him, and he cursed it till it flattened down its ears appeasingly. This time the shivering came more quickly upon the man. He was losing in his battle with the frost. It was creeping into his body from all sides. The thought of it drove him on, but he ran no more than a hundred feet, when he staggered and pitched headlong. It was his last panic. When he had recovered his breath and control, he sat up and entertained in his mind the conception of meeting death with dignity. However, the conception did not come to him in such terms. His idea of it was that he had been making a fool of himself, running around like a chicken with its head cut off—such was the simile that occurred to him. Well, he was bound to freeze anyway, and he might as well take it decently. With this new-found peace of mind came the first glimmerings of drowsiness. A good idea, he thought, to sleep off to death. It was like taking an anaesthetic. Freezing was not so bad as people thought. There were lots worse ways to die.

He pictured the boys finding his body next day. Suddenly he found himself with them, coming along the trail looking for himself. And, still with them, he came around a turn in the trail and found himself lying in the snow. He did not belong with himself any more, for even then he was out of himself, standing with the boys and looking at himself in the snow. It certainly was cold, was his thought. When he got back to the States he could tell the folks what real cold was. He drifted on from this to a vision of the old-timer on Sulphur Creek. He could see him quite clearly, warm and comfortable, and smoking a pipe.

40 'You were right, old hoss; you were right,' the man mumbled to the old-timer of Sulphur Creek.

Then the man drowsed off into what seemed to him the most comfortable and satisfying sleep he had ever known. The dog sat facing him and waiting. The brief day drew to a close in a long, slow twilight. There were no signs of a fire to be made, and, besides, never in the dog's experience had it known a man to sit like that in the snow and make no fire. As the twilight drew on, its eager yearning for the fire mastered it, and with a great lifting and shifting of forefeet, it whined softly, then flattened its ears down in anticipation of being chidden by the man. But the man remained silent. Later the dog whined loudly. And still later it crept close to the man and caught the scent of death. This made the animal bristle and back away. A little longer it delayed, howling under the stars that leaped and danced and shone brightly in the cold sky. Then it turned and trotted up the trail in the direction of the camp it knew, where were the other food providers and fire providers.   [1908]

QUESTIONS

1. What techniques does London use to establish the atmosphere of the story?
2. Why do you think London does not give the traveler a name?
3. How has London evoked a sense of tragic inevitability?
4. Is the man's lack of imagination the cause of his downfall?
5. What is the significance of concluding the story from the dog's point of view?

RESPONSES

1. Using the ecocritical approach, write an essay that describes the story as a fable for mankind's relationship with planet.
2. Write an essay comparing London's story with other stories about extreme cold, such as Silko's "Storyteller," or about extreme heat, such as Rivera's "... And the Earth Did Not Devour Him," or García Márquez's "Tuesday Siesta."
3. Stephen Crane and Jack London wrote at approximately the same time. Do you see similarities in their stories? Differences?

FOCUS ON FILM

1. The film *To Build a Fire* features an extensive voice-over by Orson Welles. What features of the print story make the voice-over a logical and almost necessary decision by the filmmaker?
2. Examine the use of editing and of music in the film. How do these techniques and features help create the conflict, development, and climax of the film?

NAGUIB MAHFOUZ

Naguib Mahfouz (b. 1911) was born in Cairo, Egypt, received a degree in philosophy from Cairo University in 1934, and worked in the Ministry of Islamic Affairs until 1971. He has published dozens of novels: Some are historical fiction, others view contemporary life and have been controversial. *Midaq Alley* (1947, 1966), *The Thief and the Dogs* (1961, 1984), and *Miramar* (1967, 1978) are widely available in the United States. *God's World: An Anthology of Short Stories* was published in 1988, the year Mahfouz was awarded the Nobel Prize for Literature. *Echoes of an Autobiography* was published in 1997. *Khufu's Wisdom* and *Rhapsodies of Nubia* Appeared in 2003.

Half a Day

I proceeded alongside my father, clutching his right hand, running to keep up with the long strides he was taking. All my clothes were new: the black shoes, the green school uniform, and the red tarboosh.° My delight in my new clothes, however, was not altogether unmarred, for this was no feast day but the day on which I was to be cast into school for the first time.

My mother stood at the window watching our progress, and I would turn toward her from time to time, as though appealing for help. We walked along a street lined with gardens; on both sides were extensive fields planted with crops, prickly pears, henna trees, and a few date palms.

"Why school?" I challenged my father openly. "I shall never do anything to annoy you."

"I'm not punishing you," he said laughing. "School's not a punishment. It's the factory that makes useful men out of boys. Don't you want to be like your father and brothers?"

5   I was not convinced. I did not believe there was really any good to be had in tearing me away from the intimacy of my home and throwing me into this building that stood at the end of the road like some huge, high-walled fortress, exceedingly stern and grim.

°*tarboosh*: Hat similar to a fez.

When we arrived at the gate we could see the courtyard, vast and crammed full of boys and girls. "Go in by yourself," said my father, "and join them. Put a smile on your face and be a good example to others."

I hesitated and clung to his hand, but he gently pushed me from him. "Be a man," he said. "Today you truly begin life. You will find me waiting for you when it's time to leave."

I took a few steps, then stopped and looked but saw nothing. Then the faces of boys and girls came into view. I did not know a single one of them, and none of them knew me. I felt I was a stranger who had lost his way. But glances of curiosity were directed toward me, and one boy approached and asked, "Who brought you?"

"My father," I whispered.

"My father's dead," he said quite simply. 10

I did not know what to say. The gate was closed, letting out a pitiable screech. Some of the children burst into tears. The bell rang. A lady came along, followed by a group of men. The men began sorting us into ranks. We were formed into an intricate pattern in the great courtyard surrounded on three sides by high buildings of several floors; from each floor we were overlooked by a long balcony roofed in wood.

"This is your new home," said the woman. "Here too there are mothers and fathers. Here there is everything that is enjoyable and beneficial to knowledge and religion. Dry your tears and face life joyfully."

We submitted to the facts, and this submission brought a sort of contentment. Living beings were drawn to other living beings, and from the first moments my heart made friends with such boys as were to be my friends and fell in love with such girls as I was to be in love with, so that it seemed my misgivings had had no basis. I had never imagined school would have this rich variety. We played all sorts of different games: swings, the vaulting horse, ball games. In the music room we chanted our first songs. We also had our first introduction to language. We saw a globe of the Earth, which revolved and showed the various continents and countries. We started learning the numbers. The story of the Creator of the universe was read to us, we were told of His present world and of His Hereafter, and we heard examples of what He said. We ate delicious food, took a little nap, and woke up to go on with friendship and love, play and learning.

As our path revealed itself to us, however, we did not find it as totally sweet and unclouded as we had presumed. Dust-laden winds and unexpected accidents came about suddenly, so we had to be watchful, at the ready, and very patient. It was not all a matter of playing and fooling around. Rivalries could bring about pain and hatred or give rise to fighting. And while the lady would sometimes smile, she would often scowl and scold. Even more frequently she would resort to physical punishment.

In addition, the time for changing one's mind was over and gone and there was no 15 question of ever returning to the paradise of home. Nothing lay ahead of us but exertion, struggle, and perseverance. Those who were able took advantage of the opportunities for success and happiness that presented themselves amid the worries.

The bell rang announcing the passing of the day and the end of work. The throngs of children rushed toward the gate, which was opened again. I bade farewell to friends and sweethearts and passed through the gate. I peered around but found no trace of my father, who had promised to be there. I stepped aside to wait. When I had waited for a long time without avail, I decided to return home on my own. After I had taken a few steps, a middle-aged man passed by, and I realized at once that I knew him. He came toward me, smiling, and shook me by the hand, saying, "It's a long time since we last met—how are you?"

With a nod of my head, I agreed with him and in turn asked, "And you, how are you?"

"As you can see, not all that good, the Almighty be praised!"

Again he shook me by the hand and went off. I proceeded a few steps, then came to a startled halt. Good Lord! Where was the street lined with gardens? Where had it disappeared to? When did all these vehicles invade it? And when did all these hordes of humanity come to rest upon its surface? How did these hills of refuse come to cover its sides? And where were the fields that bordered it? High buildings had taken over, the street surged with children, and disturbing noises shook the air. At various points stood conjurers showing off their tricks and making snakes appear from baskets. Then there was a band announcing the opening of a circus, with clowns and weight lifters walking in front. A line of trucks carrying central security troops crawled majestically by. The siren of a fire engine shrieked, and it was not clear how the vehicle would cleave its way to reach the blazing fire. A battle raged between a taxi driver and his passenger, while the passenger's wife called out for help and no one answered. Good God! I was in a daze. My head spun. I almost went crazy. How could all this have happened in half a day, between early morning and sunset? I would find the answer at home with my father. But where was my home? I could see only tall buildings and hordes of people. I hastened on to the crossroads between the gardens and Abu Khoda. I had to cross Abu Khoda to reach my house, but the stream of cars would not let up. The fire engine's siren was shrieking at full pitch as it moved at a snail's pace, and I said to myself, "Let the fire take its pleasure in what it consumes." Extremely irritated, I wondered when I would be able to cross. I stood there a long time, until the young lad employed at the ironing shop on the corner came up to me. He stretched out his arm and said gallantly, "Grandpa, let me take you across."   [1989]

QUESTIONS

1. What are some of the indications that the narrator is experiencing more than his first day at school?
2. Could the colors in the first paragraph have any symbolic suggestion?
3. Why would Mahfouz (or any writer) represent most of the narrator's life as having taken place in a single school day?
4. Aside from a few local details, could this story be set in other countries?
5. At the very end of the story, do you think the narrator has died and is being offered help into the next world, or is he simply a very old man?

RESPONSES

1. Mahfouz uses the metaphor of "life is a day"; Welty, in "A Worn Path," employs the metaphor of "life is a path." How do these metaphors merge? How do they remain distinct?
2. Approaching the story from the perspective of gender studies, how is this a "male story," and perhaps less so a "female story?" How is it a nongendered story?

KATHERINE MANSFIELD

Katherine Mansfield (1889–1923) was born in Wellington, New Zealand. For three years (1903–1906) she studied music at Queen's College, London, but upon returning to New Zealand found it unbearably provincial. She moved back to London and began to write, first journalism and then fiction. Her life during those early years was shadowed by poverty, uncertain health, and a brief, unhappy marriage. Recognition came with the publication of her first book of stories, *In a German Pension*, in 1911. That same year she met John Middleton Murry, whom she later married. Often compared with Chekhov, she continued to write beautifully crafted stories that earned her well-deserved recognition. Among the collections of her stories are *Bliss and Other Stories* (1920) and *The Garden Party and Other Stories* (1922).

A Dill Pickle

And then, after six years, she saw him again. He was seated at one of those little bamboo tables decorated with a Japanese vase of paper daffodils. There was a tall plate of fruit in front of him, and very carefully, in a way she recognized immediately as his "special" way, he was peeling an orange.

He must have felt that shock of recognition in her for he looked up and met her eyes. Incredible! He didn't know her! She smiled; he frowned. She came towards him. He closed his eyes an instant, but opening them his face lit up as though he had struck a match in a dark room. He laid down the orange and pushed back his chair, and she took her little warm hand out of her muff and gave it to him.

"Vera!" he exclaimed. "How strange. Really, for a moment I didn't know you. Won't you sit down? You've had lunch? Won't you have some coffee?"

She hesitated, but of course she meant to.

"Yes, I'd like some coffee." And she sat down opposite him.

"You've changed. You've changed very much," he said, staring at her with that eager, lighted look. "You look so well. I've never seen you look so well before." 5

"Really?" She raised her veil and unbuttoned her high fur collar. "I don't feel very well. I can't bear this weather, you know."

"Ah, no. You hate the cold. . . ."

"Loathe it." She shuddered. "And the worst of it is that the older one grows . . ."

10   He interrupted her. "Excuse me," and tapped on the table for the waitress. "Please bring some coffee and cream." To her: "You are sure you won't eat anything? Some fruit, perhaps. The fruit here is very good."

"No, thanks. Nothing."

"Then that's settled." And smiling just a hint too broadly he took up the orange again. "You were saying—the older one grows—"

"The colder," she laughed. But she was thinking how well she remembered that trick of his—the trick of interrupting her—and of how it used to exasperate her six years ago. She used to feel then as though he, quite suddenly, in the middle of what she was saying, put his hand over her lips, turned from her, attended to something different, and then took his hand away, and with just the same slightly too broad smile, gave her his attention again. . . . Now we are ready. That is settled.

"The colder!" He echoed her words, laughing too. "Ah, ah. You still say the same things. And there is another thing about you that is not changed at all—your beautiful voice—your beautiful way of speaking." Now he was very grave; he leaned towards her, and she smelled the warm, stinging scent of the orange peel. "You have only to say one word and I would know your voice among all other voices. I don't know what it is—I've often wondered—that makes your voice such a—haunting memory. . . . Do you remember that first afternoon we spent together at Kew Gardens? You were so surprised because I did not know the names of any flowers. I am still just as ignorant for all your telling me. But whenever it is very fine and warm, and I see some bright colours—it's awfully strange—I hear your voice saying: 'Geranium, marigold and verbena.' And I feel those three words are all I recall of some forgotten, heavenly language. . . . You remember that afternoon?"

15   "Oh, yes, very well." She drew a long, soft breath, as though the paper daffodils between them were almost too sweet to bear. Yet, what had remained in her mind of that particular afternoon was an absurd scene over the tea table. A great many people taking tea in a Chinese pagoda, and he behaving like a maniac about the wasps—waving them away, flapping at them with his straw hat, serious and infuriated out of all proportion to the occasion. How delighted the sniggering tea drinkers had been. And how she had suffered.

But now, as he spoke, that memory faded. His was the truer. Yes, it had been a wonderful afternoon, full of geranium and marigold and verbena, and—warm sunshine. Her thoughts lingered over the last two words as though she sang them.

In the warmth, as it were, another memory unfolded. She saw herself sitting on a lawn. He lay beside her, and suddenly, after a long silence, he rolled over and put his head in her lap.

"I wish," he said, in a low, troubled voice, "I wish that I had taken poison and were about to die—here now!"

At that moment a little girl in a white dress, holding a long, dripping water lily, dodged from behind a bush, stared at them, and dodged back again. But he did not see. She leaned over him.

20   "Ah, why do you say that? I could not say that."

But he gave a kind of soft moan, and taking her hand he held it to his cheek.

"Because I know I am going to love you too much—far too much. And I shall suffer so terribly, Vera, because you never, never will love me."

He was certainly far better looking now than he had been then. He had lost all that dreamy vagueness and indecision. Now he had the air of a man who has found his place in life, and fills it with a confidence and an assurance which was, to say the least, impressive. He must have made money, too. His clothes were admirable, and at that moment he pulled a Russian cigarette case out of his pocket.

"Won't you smoke?"

"Yes, I will." She hovered over them. "They look very good." 25

"I think they are. I get them made for me by a little man in St. James's Street. I don't smoke very much. I'm not like you—but when I do, they must be delicious, very fresh cigarettes. Smoking isn't a habit with me; it's a luxury—like perfume. Are you still so fond of perfumes? Ah, when I was in Russia . . ."

She broke in: "You've really been to Russia?"

"Oh, yes. I was there for over a year. Have you forgotten how we used to talk of going there?"

"No, I've not forgotten."

He gave a strange half laugh and leaned back in his chair. "Isn't it curious. I have 30 really carried out all those journeys that we planned. Yes, I have been to all those places that we talked of, and stayed in them long enough to—as you used to say, 'air oneself' in them. In fact, I have spent the last three years of my life travelling all the time. Spain, Corsica, Siberia, Russia, Egypt. The only country left is China, and I mean to go there, too, when the war is over."

As he spoke, so lightly, tapping the end of his cigarette against the ash-tray, she felt the strange beast that had slumbered so long within her bosom stir, stretch itself, yawn, prick up its ears, and suddenly bound to its feet, and fix its longing, hungry stare upon those far away places. But all she said was, smiling gently: "How I envy you."

He accepted that. "It has been," he said, "very wonderful—especially Russia. Russia was all that we had imagined, and far, far more. I even spent some days on a river boat on the Volga. Do you remember that boatman's song that you used to play?"

"Yes." It began to play in her mind as she spoke.

"Do you ever play it now?"

"No, I've no piano." 35

He was amazed at that. "But what has become of your beautiful piano?"

She made a little grimace. "Sold. Ages ago."

"But you were so fond of music," he wondered.

"I've no time for it now," said she.

He let it go at that. "That river life," he went on, "is something quite special. After 40 a day or two you cannot realize that you have ever known another. And it is not necessary to know the language—the life of the boat creates a bond between you and the people that's more than sufficient. You eat with them, pass the day with them, and in the evening there is that endless singing."

She shivered, hearing the boatman's song break out again loud and tragic, and seeing the boat floating on the darkening river with melancholy trees on either side. . . . "Yes, I should like that," said she, stroking her muff.

"You'd like almost everything about Russian life," he said warmly. "It's so informal, so impulsive, so free without question. And then the peasants are so splendid. They are such human beings—yes, that is it. Even the man who drives your carriage has—has some real part in what is happening. I remember the evening a party of us, two friends of mine and the wife of one of them, went for a picnic by the Black Sea. We took supper and champagne and ate and drank on the grass. And while we were eating the coachman came up. 'Have a dill pickle,' he said. He wanted to share with us. That seemed to me so right, so—you know what I mean?"

And she seemed at that moment to be sitting on the grass beside the mysteriously Black Sea, black as velvet, and rippling against the banks in silent, velvet waves. She saw the carriage drawn up to one side of the road, and the little group on the grass, their faces and hands white in the moonlight. She saw the pale dress of the woman outspread and her folded parasol, lying on the grass like a huge pearl crochet hook. Apart from them, with his supper in a cloth on his knees, sat the coachman. "Have a dill pickle," said he, and although she was not certain what a dill pickle was, she saw the greenish glass jar with a red chili like a parrot's beak glimmering through. She sucked in her cheeks; the dill pickle was terribly sour. . . .

"Yes, I know perfectly what you mean," she said.

45   In the pause that followed they looked at each other. In the past when they had looked at each other like that they had felt such a boundless understanding between them that their souls had, as it were, put their arms round each other and dropped into the same sea, content to be drowned, like mournful lovers. But now, the surprising thing was that it was he who held back. He who said:

"What a marvellous listener you are. When you look at me with those wild eyes I feel that I could tell you things that I would never breathe to another human being."

Was there just a hint of mockery in his voice or was it her fancy? She could not be sure.

"Before I met you," he said, "I had never spoken of myself to anybody. How well I remember one night, the night that I brought you the little Christmas tree, telling you all about my childhood. And of how I was so miserable that I ran away and lived under a cart in our yard for two days without being discovered. And you listened, and your eyes shone, and I felt that you had even made the little Christmas tree listen too, as in a fairy story."

But of that evening she had remembered a little pot of caviare. It had cost seven and sixpence. He could not get over it. Think of it—a tiny jar like that costing seven and sixpence. While she ate it he watched her, delighted and shocked.

50   "No, really, that is eating money. You could not get seven shillings into a little pot that size. Only think of the profit they must make. . . ." And he had begun some immensely complicated calculations. . . . But now good-bye to the caviare. The Christmas tree was on the table, and the little boy lay under the cart with his head pillowed on the yard dog.

"The dog was called Bosun," she cried delightedly.

But he did not follow. "Which dog? Had you a dog? I don't remember a dog at all."

"No, no. I mean the yard dog when you were a little boy." He laughed and snapped the cigarette case to.

"Was he? Do you know I had forgotten that. It seems such ages ago. I cannot believe that it is only six years. After I had recognized you to-day—I had to take such a leap—I had to take a leap over my whole life to get back to that time. I was such a kid then." He drummed on the table. "I've often thought how I must have bored you. And now I understand so perfectly why you wrote to me as you did—although at the time that letter nearly finished my life. I found it again the other day, and I couldn't help laughing as I read it. It was so clever—such a true picture of me." He glanced up. "You're not going?"

55   She had buttoned her collar again and drawn down her veil.

"Yes, I am afraid I must," she said, and managed a smile. Now she knew that he had been mocking.

"Ah, no, please," he pleaded. "Don't go just for a moment," and he caught up one of her gloves from the table and clutched at it as if that would hold her. "I see so few people to talk to nowadays, that I have turned into a sort of barbarian," he said. "Have I said something to hurt you?"

"Not a bit," she lied. But as she watched him draw her glove through his fingers, gently, gently, her anger really did die down, and besides, at the moment he looked more like himself of six years ago. . . .

"What I really wanted then," he said softly, "was to be a sort of carpet—to make myself into a sort of carpet for you to walk on so that you need not be hurt by the sharp stones and the mud that you hated so. It was nothing more positive than that— nothing more selfish. Only I did desire, eventually, to turn into a magic carpet and carry you away to all those lands you longed to see."

As he spoke she lifted her head as though she drank something; the strange beast in her bosom began to purr. . . .   60

"I felt that you were more lonely than anybody else in the world," he went on, "and yet, perhaps, that you were the only person in the world who was really, truly alive. Born out of your time," he murmured, stroking the glove, "fated."

Ah, God! What had she done! How had she dared to throw away her happiness like this. This was the only man who had ever understood her. Was it too late? Could it be too late? *She* was that glove that he held in his fingers. . . .

"And then the fact that you had no friends and never had made friends with people. How I understood that, for neither had I. Is it just the same now?"

"Yes," she breathed. "Just the same. I am as alone as ever."

"So am I," he laughed gently, "just the same."   65

Suddenly with a quick gesture he handed her back the glove and scraped his chair on the floor. "But what seemed to me so mysterious then is perfectly plain to me now. And to you, too, of course. . . . It simply was that we were such egoists, so self-engrossed, so wrapped up in ourselves that we hadn't a corner in our hearts for anybody else. Do you know," he cried, naïve and hearty, and dreadfully like another side of that old self again, "I began studying a Mind System when I was in Russia, and I found that we were not peculiar at all. It's quite a well known form of . . ."

She had gone. He sat there, thunder-struck, astounded beyond words. . . . And then he asked the waitress for his bill.

"But the cream has not been touched," he said. "Please do not charge me for it."   [1920]

QUESTIONS

1. What is the meaning of the title?
2. What do the references to travel reveal about the two characters?
3. What is the significance of the flowers like "some forgotten, heavenly language"? Why "paper" daffodils between them?
4. How clearly did the lovers understand one another six years ago? How clearly do they understand one another now?
5. Does the revelation of the last paragraph depend on a shift in the point of view?

RESPONSE

1. Write an essay analyzing how Colette's "The Other Wife," Hemingway's "Hills Like White Elephants," and Mansfield's "A Dill Pickle" use setting and point of view to explore their characters' inner lives.

FOCUS ON FILM

1. In the film *High Fidelity*, available on video, a character calls up his old girlfriends in an attempt to understand his life. View the film and compare how clarity comes or doesn't come to Vera in "A Dill Pickle" and the character in the film as they talk with old companions.

Miss Brill

Although it was so brilliantly fine—the blue sky powdered with gold and great spots of light like white wine splashed over the Jardins Publiques—Miss Brill was glad that she had decided on her fur. The air was motionless, but when you opened your mouth there was just a faint chill, like a chill from a glass of iced water before you sip, and now and again a leaf came drifting—from nowhere, from the sky. Miss Brill put up her hand and touched her fur. Dear little thing! It was nice to feel it again. She had taken it out of its box that afternoon, shaken out the mothpowder, given it a good brush, and rubbed the life back into the dim little eyes. "What has been happening to me?" said the sad little eyes. Oh, how sweet it was to see them snap at her again from the red eiderdown! . . . But the nose, which was of some black composition, wasn't at all firm. It must have had a knock, somehow. Never mind—a little dab of black sealing-wax when the time came—when it was absolutely necessary. . . . Little rogue! Yes, she really felt like that about it. Little rogue biting its tail just by her left ear. She could have taken it off and laid it on her lap and stroked it. She felt a tingling in her hands and arms, but that came from walking, she supposed. And when she breathed, something light and sad—no, not sad, exactly—something gentle seemed to move in her bosom.

There were a number of people out this afternoon, far more than last Sunday. And the band sounded louder and gayer. That was because the Season had begun. For although the band played all the year round on Sundays, out of season it was never the same. It was like some one playing with only the family to listen; it didn't care how it played if there weren't any strangers present. Wasn't the conductor wearing a new coat, too? She was sure it was new. He scraped with his foot and flapped his arms like a rooster about to crow, and the bandsmen sitting in the green rotunda blew out their cheeks and glared at the music. Now there came a little "flutey" bit—very pretty!—a little chain of bright drops. She was sure it would be repeated. It was; she lifted her head and smiled.

Only two people shared her "special" seat: a fine old man in a velvet coat, his hands clasped over a huge carved walking-stick, and a big old woman, sitting upright, with a roll of knitting on her embroidered apron. They did not speak. This was disappointing, for Miss Brill always looked forward to the conversation. She had become really quite expert, she thought, at listening as though she didn't listen, at sitting in other people's lives just for a minute while they talked round her.

She glanced, sideways, at the old couple. Perhaps they would go soon. Last Sunday, too, hadn't been as interesting as usual. An Englishman and his wife, he wearing a dreadful Panama hat and she button boots. And she'd gone on the whole time about how she ought to wear spectacles; she knew she needed them; but that it was no good getting any; they'd be sure to break and they'd never keep on. And he'd been so patient. He'd suggested everything—gold rims, the kind that curved round your ears, little pads inside the bridge. No, nothing would please her. "They'll always be sliding down my nose!" Miss Brill had wanted to shake her.

5   The old people sat on the bench, still as statues. Never mind, there was always the crowd to watch. To and fro, in front of the flower-beds and the band rotunda, the couples and groups paraded, stopped to talk, to greet, to buy a handful of flowers from the old beggar who had his tray fixed to the railings. Little children ran among them, swooping and laughing; little boys with big white silk bows under their chins, little girls, little French dolls, dressed up in velvet and lace. And sometimes a tiny stagger-er came suddenly rocking into the open from under the trees, stopped, stared, as suddenly sat down "flop," until its small high-stepping mother, like a young hen, rushed scolding to its rescue. Other people sat on the benches and green chairs, but they were nearly always the same, Sunday after Sunday, and—Miss Brill had often noticed—there was something funny about nearly all of them. They were odd, silent, nearly all old, and from the way they stared they looked as though they'd just come from dark little rooms or even—even cupboards!

Behind the rotunda the slender trees with yellow leaves down drooping, and through them just a line of sea, and beyond the blue sky with gold-veined clouds.

Tum-tum-tum tiddle-um! tiddle-um! tum tiddley-um tum ta! blew the band.

Two young girls in red came by and two young soldiers in blue met them, and they laughed and paired and went off arm-in-arm. Two peasant women with funny straw hats passed, gravely, leading beautiful smoke-coloured donkeys. A cold, pale nun hurried by. A beautiful woman came along and dropped her bunch of violets, and a little boy ran after to hand them to her, and she took them and threw them away as if they'd been poisoned. Dear me! Miss Brill didn't know whether to admire that or not! And now an ermine toque and a gentleman in grey met just in front of her. He was tall, stiff, dignified, and she was wearing the ermine toque she'd bought when her hair was yellow. Now everything, her hair, her face, even her eyes, was the same colour as the shabby ermine, and her hand, in its cleaned glove, lifted to dab her lips, was a tiny yellowish paw. Oh, she was so pleased to see him—delighted! She rather thought they were going to meet that afternoon. She described where she'd been—everywhere, here, there, along by the sea. The day was so charming—didn't he agree? And wouldn't he, perhaps? . . . But he shook his head, lighted a cigarette, slowly breathed a great deep puff into her face, and, even while she was still talking and laughing, flicked the match away and walked on. The ermine toque was alone; she smiled more brightly than ever. But even the band seemed to know what she was feeling and played more softly, played tenderly, and the drum beat, "The Brute! The Brute!" over and over. What would she do? What was going to happen now? But as Miss Brill wondered, the ermine toque turned, raised her hand as though she'd seen some one else, much nicer, just over there, and pattered away. And the band changed again and played more quickly, more gaily than ever, and the old couple on Miss Brill's seat got up and marched away, and such a funny old man with long whiskers hobbled along in time to the music and was nearly knocked over by four girls walking abreast.

Oh, how fascinating it was! How she enjoyed it! How she loved sitting here, watching it all! It was like a play. It was exactly like a play. Who could believe the sky at the back wasn't painted? But it wasn't till a little brown dog trotted on solemn and then slowly trotted off, like a little "theatre" dog, a little dog that had been drugged, that Miss Brill discovered what it was that made it so exciting. They were all on the stage. They weren't only the audience, not only looking on; they were acting. Even she had a part and came every Sunday. No doubt somebody would have noticed if she hadn't been there; she was part of the performance after all. How strange she'd never thought of it like that before! And yet it explained why she made such a point of starting from home at just the same time each week—so as not to be late for the performance—and it also explained why she had quite a queer, shy feeling at telling her English pupils how she spent her Sunday afternoons. No wonder! Miss Brill nearly laughed out loud. She was on the stage. She thought of the old invalid gentleman to whom she read the newspaper four afternoons a week while he slept in the garden. She had got quite used to the frail head on the cotton pillow, the hollowed eyes, the open mouth and the high pinched nose. If he'd been dead she mightn't have noticed for weeks; she wouldn't have minded. But suddenly he knew he was having the paper read to him by an actress! "An actress!" The old head lifted; two points of light quivered in the old eyes. "An actress—are ye?" And Miss Brill smoothed the newspaper as though it were the manuscript of her part and said gently: "Yes, I have been an actress for a long time."

The band had been having a rest. Now they started again. And what they played   10 was warm, sunny, yet there was just a faint chill—a something, what was it?—not sadness—no, not sadness—a something that made you want to sing. The tune lifted, lifted, the light shone; and it seemed to Miss Brill that in another moment all of them, all the whole company, would begin singing. The young ones, the laughing ones who were moving together, they would begin, and the men's voices, very resolute and brave, would join them. And then she too, she too, and the others on the benches—they would come in with a kind of accompaniment—something low, that scarcely rose or fell, something so beautiful—moving. . . . And Miss Brill's eyes filled with tears and she looked smiling at all the other members of the company. Yes, we understand, we understand, she thought—though what they understood she didn't know.

Just at that moment a boy and a girl came and sat down where the old couple had been. They were beautifully dressed; they were in love. The hero and heroine, of course, just arrived from his father's yacht. And still soundlessly singing, still with that trembling smile, Miss Brill prepared to listen.

"No, not now," said the girl. "Not here, I can't."

"But why? Because of that stupid old thing at the end there?" asked the boy. "Why does she come here at all—who wants her? Why doesn't she keep her silly old mug at home?"

"It's her fu-fur which is so funny," giggled the girl. "It's exactly like a fried whiting."

"Ah, be off with you!" said the boy in an angry whisper. Then: "Tell me, ma petite   15 chère—"

"No, not here," said the girl. "Not *yet*."

On her way home she usually bought a slice of honey-cake at the baker's. It was her Sunday treat. Sometimes there was an almond in her slice, sometimes not. It made a great difference. If there was an almond it was like carrying home a tiny present— a surprise—something that might very well not have been there. She hurried on the almond Sundays and struck the match for the kettle in quite a dashing way.

But to-day she passed the baker's by, climbed the stairs, went into the little dark room—her room like a cupboard—and sat down on the red eiderdown. She sat there for a long time. The box that the fur came out of was on the bed. She unclasped the necklet quickly; quickly, without looking, laid it inside. But when she put the lid on she thought she heard something crying.   [1922]

QUESTIONS

1. What aspect of the story is emphasized by placing Miss Brill, a teacher of English, in France?
2. List the references to eyes and seeing. How do they enhance the theme?
3. How does the author's language create the sense of a fantasy life?
4. In what sense has Miss Brill "been an actress for a long time"?
5. What is the significance of the fox fur? The honey-cake with its almond?

RESPONSES

1. From a New Historicist perspective, explore either the importance of public places, like parks, in early twentieth-century urban life or the place in society of unmarried women in this time period. Explain how the story "Miss Brill" is or is not a record of these ideas.
2. Compare the actual and fantasy lives of Miss Brill and Mrs. Mallard (in Chopin's "The Story of an Hour.")

Bobbie Ann Mason

Bobbie Ann Mason (b. 1940) was born on a Kentucky farm, did her undergraduate work at the University of Kentucky, and earned a Ph.D. from the University of Connecticut. She wrote for popular magazines, taught at Mansfield State College in Pennsylvania, and wrote several critical works, including *Nabokov's Garden* (1974) and *The Girl Sleuth: A Feminist Guide to the Bobbsey Twins, Nancy Drew, and Their Sisters* (1975). Major magazines began to publish her short fiction, and *Shiloh and Other Stories* (1982) was followed by *Love Stories* (1989) and three novels; the most recent is *Feather Crowns* (1993). *Clear Springs: A Memoir* appeared in 1999. *Zigzagging down a Wild Trail & Stories* was published in 2001.

Shiloh°

Leroy Moffitt's wife, Norma Jean, is working on her pectorals. She lifts three-pound dumbbells to warm up, then progresses to a twenty-pound barbell. Standing with her legs apart, she reminds Leroy of Wonder Woman.

"I'd give anything if I could just get these muscles to where they're real hard," says Norma Jean. "Feel this arm. It's not as hard as the other one."

"That's 'cause you're right-handed," says Leroy, dodging as she swings the barbell in an arc.

"Do you think so?"

"Sure." 5

Leroy is a truckdriver. He injured his leg in a highway accident four months ago, and his physical therapy, which involves weights and a pulley, prompted Norma Jean to try building herself up. Now she is attending a body-building class. Leroy has been collecting temporary disability since his tractor-trailer jackknifed in Missouri, badly twisting his left leg in its socket. He has a steel pin in his hip. He will probably not be able to drive his rig again. It sits in the backyard, like a gigantic bird that has flown home to roost. Leroy has been home in Kentucky for three months, and his leg is almost healed, but the accident frightened him and he does not want to drive any more long hauls. He is not sure what to do next. In the meantime, he makes things from

---

°The Battle of Shiloh, in April 1862, was a bloody affair. There was no clear victory, but Southern casualties, though less than the North's, were more difficult to replace.

craft kits. He started by building a miniature log cabin from notched Popsicle sticks. He varnished it and placed it on the TV set, where it remains. It reminds him of a rustic Nativity scene. Then he tried string art (sailing ships on black velvet), a macramé owl kit, a snap-together B-17 Flying Fortress, and a lamp made out of a model truck, with a light fixture screwed in the top of the cab. At first the kits were diversions, something to kill time, but now he is thinking about building a full-scale log house from a kit. It would be considerably cheaper than building a regular house, and besides, Leroy has grown to appreciate how things are put together. He has begun to realize that in all the years he was on the road he never took time to examine anything. He was always flying past scenery.

"They won't let you build a log cabin in any of the new subdivisions," Norma Jean tells him.

"They will if I tell them it's for you," he says, teasing her. Ever since they were married, he has promised Norma Jean he would build her a new home one day. They have always rented, and the house they live in is small and nondescript. It does not even feel like a home, Leroy realizes now.

Norma Jean works at the Rexall drugstore, and she has acquired an amazing amount of information about cosmetics. When she explains to Leroy the three stages of complexion care, involving creams, toners, and moisturizers, he thinks happily of other petroleum products—axle grease, diesel fuel. This is a connection between him and Norma Jean. Since he has been home, he has felt unusually tender about his wife and guilty over his long absences. But he can't tell what she feels about him. Norma Jean has never complained about his traveling; she has never made hurt remarks, like calling his truck a "widow-maker." He is reasonably certain she has been faithful to him, but he wishes she would celebrate his permanent homecoming more happily. Norma Jean is often startled to find Leroy at home, and he thinks she seems a little disappointed about it. Perhaps he reminds her too much of the early days of their marriage, before he went on the road. They had a child who died as an infant, years ago. They never speak about their memories of Randy, which have almost faded, but now that Leroy is home all the time, they sometimes feel awkward around each other, and Leroy wonders if one of them should mention the child. He has the feeling that they are waking up out of a dream together—that they must create a new marriage, start afresh. They are lucky they are still married. Leroy has read that for most people losing a child destroys the marriage—or else he heard this on *Donahue.* He can't always remember where he learns things anymore.

10   At Christmas, Leroy bought an electric organ for Norma Jean. She used to play the piano when she was in high school. "It don't leave you," she told him once. "It's like riding a bicycle."

The new instrument had so many keys and buttons that she was bewildered by it at first. She touched the keys tentatively, pushed some buttons, then pecked out "Chopsticks." It came out in an amplified fox-trot rhythm, with marimba sounds.

"It's an orchestra!" she cried.

The organ had a pecan-look finish and eighteen preset chords, with optional flute, violin, trumpet, clarinet, and banjo accompaniments. Norma Jean mastered the organ almost immediately. At first she played Christmas songs. Then she bought *The Sixties Songbook* and learned every tune in it, adding variations to each with the rows of brightly colored buttons.

"I didn't like these old songs back then," she said. "But I have this crazy feeling I missed something."

15   "You didn't miss a thing," said Leroy.

Leroy likes to lie on the couch and smoke a joint and listen to Norma Jean play "Can't Take My Eyes Off You" and "I'll Be Back." He is back again. After fifteen years on the road, he is finally settling down with the woman he loves. She is still pretty. Her skin is flawless. Her frosted curls resemble pencil trimmings.

Now that Leroy has come home to stay, he notices how much the town has changed. Subdivisions are spreading across western Kentucky like an oil slick. The sign at the edge of town says "Pop: 11,500"—only seven hundred more than it said twenty years before. Leroy can't figure out who is living in all the new houses. The farmers who used to gather around the courthouse square on Saturday afternoons to play checkers and spit tobacco juice have gone. It has been years since Leroy has thought about the farmers, and they have disappeared without his noticing.

Leroy meets a kid named Stevie Hamilton in the parking lot at the new shopping center. While they pretend to be strangers meeting over a stalled car, Stevie tosses an ounce of marijuana under the front seat of Leroy's car. Stevie is wearing orange jogging shoes and a T-shirt that says CHATTAHOOCHEE SUPER-RAT. His father is a prominent doctor who lives in one of the expensive subdivisions in a new white-columned brick house that looks like a funeral parlor. In the phone book under his name there is a separate number, with the listing "Teenagers."

"Where do you get this stuff?" asks Leroy. "From your pappy?"

"That's for me to know and you to find out," Stevie says. He is slit-eyed and   20
skinny.

"What else you got?"

"What you interested in?"

"Nothing special. Just wondered."

Leroy used to take speed on the road. Now he has to go slowly. He needs to be mellow. He leans back against the car and says, "I'm aiming to build me a log house, soon as I get time. My wife, though, I don't think she likes the idea."

"Well, let me know when you want me again," Stevie says. He has a cigarette in his   25
cupped palm, as though sheltering it from the wind. He takes a long drag, then stomps it on the asphalt and slouches away.

Stevie's father was two years ahead of Leroy in high school. Leroy is thirty-four. He married Norma Jean when they were both eighteen, and their child Randy was born a few months later, but he died at the age of four months and three days. He would be about Stevie's age now. Norma Jean and Leroy were at the drive-in, watching a double feature (*Dr. Strangelove* and *Lover Come Back*), and the baby was sleeping in the back seat. When the first movie ended, the baby was dead. It was the sudden infant death syndrome. Leroy remembers handing Randy to a nurse at the emergency room, as though he were offering her a large doll as a present. A dead baby feels like a sack of flour. "It just happens sometimes," said the doctor, in what Leroy always recalls as a nonchalant tone. Leroy can hardly remember the child anymore, but he still sees vividly a scene from *Dr. Strangelove* in which the President of the United States was talking in a folksy voice on the hot line to the Soviet premier about the bomber accidentally headed toward Russia. He was in the War Room, and the world map was lit up. Leroy remembers Norma Jean standing catatonically beside him in the hospital and himself thinking: Who is this strange girl? He had forgotten who she was. Now scientists are saying that crib death is caused by a virus. Nobody knows anything, Leroy thinks. The answers are always changing.

When Leroy gets home from the shopping center, Norma Jean's mother, Mabel Beasley, is there. Until this year, Leroy has not realized how much time she spends with Norma Jean. When she visits, she inspects the closets and then the plants, informing Norma Jean when a plant is droopy or yellow. Mabel calls the plants "flowers," although there are never any blooms. She always notices if Norma Jean's laundry is piling up. Mabel is a short, overweight woman whose tight, brown-dyed curls look more like a wig than the actual wig she sometimes wears. Today she has brought Norma Jean an off-white dust ruffle she made for the bed; Mabel works in a custom-upholstery shop.

"This is the tenth one I made this year," Mabel says. "I got started and couldn't stop."

"It's real pretty," says Norma Jean.

30   "Now we can hide things under the bed," says Leroy, who gets along with his mother-in-law primarily by joking with her. Mabel has never really forgiven him for disgracing her by getting Norma Jean pregnant. When the baby died, she said that fate was mocking her.

"What's that thing?" Mabel says to Leroy in a loud voice, pointing to a tangle of yarn on a piece of canvas.

Leroy holds it up for Mabel to see. "It's my needlepoint," he explains. "This is a *Star Trek* pillow cover."

"That's what a woman would do," says Mabel. "Great day in the morning!"

"All the big football players on TV do it," he says.

35   "Why, Leroy, you're always trying to fool me. I don't believe you for one minute. You don't know what to do with yourself—that's the whole trouble. Sewing!"

"I'm aiming to build us a log house," says Leroy. "Soon as my plans come."

"Like *heck* you are," says Norma Jean. She takes Leroy's needlepoint and shoves it into a drawer. "You have to find a job first. Nobody can afford to build now anyway."

Mabel straightens her girdle and says, "I still think before you get tied down y'all ought to take a little run to Shiloh."

"One of these days, mama," Norma Jean says impatiently.

40   Mabel is talking about Shiloh, Tennessee. For the past few years, she has been urging Leroy and Norma Jean to visit the Civil War battleground there. Mabel went there on her honeymoon—the only real trip she ever took. Her husband died of a perforated ulcer when Norma Jean was ten, but Mabel, who was accepted into the United Daughters of the Confederacy in 1975, is still preoccupied with going back to Shiloh.

"I've been to kingdom come and back in that truck out yonder," Leroy says to Mabel, "but we never yet set foot in that battleground. Ain't that something? How did I miss it?"

"It's not even that far," Mabel says.

After Mabel leaves, Norma Jean reads to Leroy from a list she has made. "Things you could do," she announces. "You could get a job as a guard at Union Carbide, where they'd let you set on a stool. You could get on at the lumberyard. You could do a little carpenter work, if you want to build so bad. You could—"

"I can't do something where I'd have to stand up all day."

45   "You ought to try standing up all day behind a cosmetics counter. It's amazing that I have strong feet, coming from two parents that never had strong feet at all." At the moment Norma Jean is holding on to the kitchen counter, raising her knees one at a time as she talks. She is wearing two-pound ankle weights.

"Don't worry," says Leroy. "I'll do something."

"You could truck calves to slaughter for somebody. You wouldn't have to drive any big old truck for that."

"I'm going to build you this house," says Leroy. "I want to make you a real home."

"I don't want to live in any log cabin."

"It's not a cabin. It's a house." 50

"I don't care. It looks like a cabin."

"You and me together could lift those logs. It's just like lifting weights."

Norma Jean doesn't answer. Under her breath, she is counting. Now she is marching through the kitchen. She is doing goose steps.

Before his accident, when Leroy came home he used to stay in the house with Norma Jean, watching TV in bed and playing cards. She would cook fried chicken, picnic ham, chocolate pie—all his favorites. Now he is home alone much of the time. In the mornings, Norma Jean disappears, leaving a cooling place in the bed. She eats a cereal called Body Buddies, and she leaves the bowl on the table, with the soggy tan balls floating in a milk puddle. He sees things about Norma Jean that he never realized before. When she chops onions, she stares off into a corner, as if she can't bear to look. She puts on her house slippers almost precisely at nine o'clock every evening and nudges her jogging shoes under the couch. She saves bread heels for the birds. Leroy watches the birds at the feeder. He notices the peculiar way goldfinches fly past the window. They close their wings, then fall, then spread their wings to catch and lift themselves. He wonders if they close their eyes when they fall. Norma Jean closes her eyes when they are in bed. She wants the lights turned out. Even then, he is sure she closes her eyes.

He goes for long drives around town. He tends to drive a car rather carelessly. 55 Power steering and an automatic shift make a car feel so small and inconsequential that his body is hardly involved in the driving process. His injured leg stretches out comfortably. Once or twice he has almost hit something, but even the prospect of an accident seems minor in a car. He cruises the new subdivisions, feeling like a criminal rehearsing for a robbery. Norma Jean is probably right about a log house being inappropriate here in the new subdivisions. All the houses look grand and complicated. They depress him.

One day when Leroy comes home from a drive he finds Norma Jean in tears. She is in the kitchen making a potato and mushroom-soup casserole, with grated-cheese topping. She is crying because her mother caught her smoking.

"I didn't hear her coming. I was standing here puffing away pretty as you please," Norma Jean says, wiping her eyes.

"I knew it would happen sooner or later," says Leroy, putting his arm around her.

"She doesn't know the meaning of the word 'knock,'" says Norma Jean. "It's a wonder she hadn't caught me years ago."

"Think of it this way," Leroy says. "What if she caught me with a joint?" 60

"You better not let her!" Norma Jean shrieks. "I'm warning you, Leroy Moffitt!"

"I'm just kidding. Here, play me a tune. That'll help you relax."

Norma Jean puts the casserole in the oven and sets the timer. Then she plays a ragtime tune, with horns and banjo, as Leroy lights up a joint and lies on the couch, laughing to himself about Mabel's catching him at it. He thinks of Stevie Hamilton— a doctor's son pushing grass. Everything is funny. The whole town seems crazy and small. He is reminded of Virgil Mathis, a boastful policeman Leroy used to shoot pool with. Virgil recently led a drug bust in a back room at a bowling alley, where he seized ten thousand dollars' worth of marijuana. The newspaper had a picture of him holding up the bags of grass and grinning widely. Right now, Leroy can imagine Virgil breaking down the door and arresting him with a lungful of smoke. Virgil would probably have been alerted to the scene because of all the racket Norma Jean is making. Now she sounds like a hard-rock band. Norma Jean is terrific. When she switches to a Latin-rhythm version of "Sunshine Superman," Leroy hums along. Norma Jean's foot goes up and down, up and down.

"Well, what do you think?" Leroy says, when Norma Jean pauses to search through her music.

65   "What do I think about what?"

His mind has gone blank. Then he says, "I'll sell my rig and build us a house." That wasn't what he wanted to say. He wanted to know what she thought—what she *really* thought—about them.

"Don't start in on that again," says Norma Jean. She begins playing "Who'll Be the Next in Line?"

Leroy used to tell hitchhikers his whole life story—about his travels, his hometown, the baby. He would end with a question: "Well, what do you think?" It was just a rhetorical question. In time, he had the feeling that he'd been telling the same story over and over to the same hitchhikers. He quit talking to hitchhikers when he realized how his voice sounded—whining and self-pitying, like some teenage-tragedy song. Now Leroy has the sudden impulse to tell Norma Jean about himself, as if he had just met her. They have known each other so long they have forgotten a lot about each other. They could become reacquainted. But when the oven timer goes off and she runs to the kitchen, he forgets why he wants to do this.

The next day, Mabel drops by. It is Saturday and Norma Jean is cleaning. Leroy is studying the plans of his log house, which have finally come in the mail. He has them spread out on the table—big sheets of stiff blue paper, with diagrams and numbers printed in white. While Norma Jean runs the vacuum, Mabel drinks coffee. She sets her coffee cup on a blueprint.

70   "I'm just waiting for time to pass," she says to Leroy, drumming her fingers on the table.

As soon as Norma Jean switches off the vacuum, Mabel says in a loud voice, "Did you hear about the datsun dog that killed the baby?"

Norma Jean says, "The word is 'dachshund.'"

"They put the dog on trial. It chewed the baby's legs off. The mother was in the next room all the time." She raises her voice. "They thought it was neglect."

Norma Jean is holding her ears. Leroy manages to open the refrigerator and get some Diet Pepsi to offer Mabel. Mabel still has some coffee and she waves away the Pepsi.

75   "Datsuns are like that," Mabel says. "They're jealous dogs. They'll tear a place to pieces if you don't keep an eye on them."

"You better watch out what you're saying, Mabel," says Leroy.

"Well, facts is facts."

Leroy looks out the window at his rig. It is like a huge piece of furniture gathering dust in the backyard. Pretty soon it will be an antique. He hears the vacuum cleaner. Norma Jean seems to be cleaning the living room rug again.

Later, she says to Leroy, "She just said that about the baby because she caught me smoking. She's trying to pay me back."

80   "What are you talking about?" Leroy says, nervously shuffling blueprints.

"You know good and well," Norma Jean says. She is sitting in a kitchen chair with her feet up and her arms wrapped around her knees. She looks small and helpless. She says, "The very idea, her bringing up a subject like that! Saying it was neglect."

"She didn't mean that," Leroy says.

"She might not have *thought* she meant it. She always says things like that. You don't know how she goes on."

"But she didn't really mean it. She was just talking."

Leroy opens a king-sized bottle of beer and pours it into two glasses, dividing it carefully. He hands a glass to Norma Jean and she takes it from him mechanically. For a long time, they sit by the kitchen window watching the birds at the feeder.

Something is happening. Norma Jean is going to night school. She has graduated from her six-week body-building course and now she is taking an adult-education course in composition at Paducah Community College. She spends her evenings outlining paragraphs.

"First you have a topic sentence," she explains to Leroy. "Then you divide it up. Your secondary topic has to be connected to your primary topic."

To Leroy, this sounds intimidating. "I never was any good in English," he says.

"It makes a lot of sense."

"What are you doing this for, anyhow?"

She shrugs. "It's something to do." She stands up and lifts her dumbbells a few times.

"Driving a rig, nobody cared about my English."

"I'm not criticizing your English."

Norma Jean used to say, "If I lose ten minutes' sleep, I just drag all day." Now she stays up late, writing compositions. She got a B on her first paper—a how-to theme on soup-based casseroles. Recently Norma Jean has been cooking unusual foods—tacos, lasagna, Bombay chicken. She doesn't play the organ anymore, though her second paper was called "Why Music Is Important to Me." She sits at the kitchen table, concentrating on her outlines, while Leroy plays with his log house plans, practicing with a set of Lincoln Logs. The thought of getting a truckload of notched, numbered logs scares him, and he wants to be prepared. As he and Norma Jean work together at the kitchen table, Leroy has the hopeful thought that they are sharing something, but he knows he is a fool to think this. Norma Jean is miles away. He knows he is going to lose her. Like Mabel, he is just waiting for time to pass.

One day, Mabel is there before Norma Jean gets home from work, and Leroy finds himself confiding in her. Mabel, he realizes, must know Norma Jean better than he does.

"I don't know what's got into that girl," Mabel says. "She used to go to bed with the chickens. Now you say she's up all hours. Plus her a-smoking. I like to died."

"I want to make her this beautiful home," Leroy says, indicating the Lincoln Logs. "I don't think she even wants it. Maybe she was happier with me gone."

"She don't know what to make of you, coming home like this."

"Is that it?"

Mabel takes the roof off his Lincoln Log cabin. "You couldn't get *me* in a log cabin," she says. "I was raised in one. It's no picnic, let me tell you."

"They're different now," says Leroy.

"I tell you what," Mabel says, smiling oddly at Leroy.

"What?"

"Take her on down to Shiloh. Y'all need to get out together, stir a little. Her brain's all balled up over them books."

Leroy can see traces of Norma Jean's features in her mother's face. Mabel's worn face has the texture of crinkled cotton, but suddenly she looks pretty. It occurs to Leroy that Mabel has been hinting all along that she wants them to take her with them to Shiloh.

"Let's all go to Shiloh," he says. "You and me and her. Come Sunday."

Mabel throws up her hands in protest. "Oh, no, not me. Young folks want to be by theirselves."

When Norma Jean comes in with groceries, Leroy says excitedly, "Your mama here's been dying to go to Shiloh for thirty-five years. It's about time we went, don't you think?"

"I'm not going to butt in on anybody's second honeymoon," Mabel says.

"Who's going on a honeymoon, for Christ's sake?" Norma Jean says loudly.

"I never raised no daughter of mine to talk that-a-way," Mabel says.

"You ain't seen nothing yet," says Norma Jean. She starts putting away boxes and cans, slamming cabinet doors.

"There's a log cabin at Shiloh," Mabel says. "It was there during the battle. There's bullet holes in it."

"When are you going to *shut up* about Shiloh, Mama?" asks Norma Jean.

"I always thought Shiloh was the prettiest place, so full of history," Mabel goes on. "I just hoped y'all could see it once before I die, so you could tell me about it." Later, she whispers to Leroy, "You do what I said. A little change is what she needs."

"Your name means 'the king,'" Norma Jean says to Leroy that evening. He is trying to get her to go to Shiloh, and she is reading a book about another century.

"Well, I reckon I ought to be right proud."

"I guess so."

"Am I still king around here?"

Norma Jean flexes her biceps and feels them for hardness. "I'm not fooling around with anybody, if that's what you mean," she says.

"Would you tell me if you were?"

"I don't know."

"What does *your* name mean?"

"It was Marilyn Monroe's real name."

"No kidding!"

"Norma comes from the Normans. They were invaders," she says. She closes her book and looks hard at Leroy. "I'll go to Shiloh with you if you'll stop staring at me."

On Sunday, Norma Jean packs a picnic and they go to Shiloh. To Leroy's relief, Mabel says she does not want to come with them. Norma Jean drives, and Leroy, sitting beside her, feels like some boring hitchhiker she has picked up. He tries some conversation, but she answers him in monosyllables. At Shiloh, she drives aimlessly through the park, past bluffs and trails and steep ravines. Shiloh is an immense place, and Leroy cannot see it as a battleground. It is not what he expected. He thought it would look like a golf course. Monuments are everywhere, showing through the thick clusters of trees. Norma Jean passes the log cabin Mabel mentioned. It is surrounded by tourists looking for bullet holes.

"That's not the kind of log house I've got in mind," says Leroy apologetically.

"I know *that*."

"This is a pretty place. Your mama was right."

"It's O.K.," says Norma Jean. "Well, we've seen it. I hope she's satisfied."

They burst out laughing together.

At the park museum, a movie on Shiloh is shown every half hour, but they decide that they don't want to see it. They buy a souvenir Confederate flag for Mabel, and then they find a picnic spot near the cemetery. Norma Jean has brought a picnic cooler, with pimiento sandwiches, soft drinks, and Yodels. Leroy eats a sandwich and then smokes a joint, hiding it behind the picnic cooler. Norma Jean has quit smoking altogether. She is picking cake crumbs from the cellophane wrapper, like a fussy bird.

Leroy says, "So the boys in gray ended up in Corinth. The Union soldiers zapped 'em finally. April 7, 1862."

They both know that he doesn't know any history. He is just talking about some of the historical plaques they have read. He feels awkward, like a boy on a date with an older girl. They are still just making conversation. 135

"Corinth is where Mama eloped to," says Norma Jean.

They sit in silence and stare at the cemetery for the Union dead and, beyond, at a tall cluster of trees. Campers are parked nearby, bumper to bumper, and small children in bright clothing are cavorting and squealing. Norma Jean wads up the cake wrapper and squeezes it tightly in her hand. Without looking at Leroy, she says, "I want to leave you."

Leroy takes a bottle of Coke out of the cooler and flips off the cap. He holds the bottle poised near his mouth but cannot remember to take a drink. Finally he says, "No, you don't."

"Yes, I do."

"I won't let you." 140

"You can't stop me."

"Don't do me that way."

Leroy knows Norma Jean will have her own way. "Didn't I promise to be home from now on?" he says.

"In some ways, a woman prefers a man who wanders," says Norma Jean. "That sounds crazy, I know."

"You're not crazy." 145

Leroy remembers to drink from his Coke. Then he says, "Yes, you *are* crazy. You and me could start all over again. Right back at the beginning."

"We *have* started all over again," says Norma Jean. "And this is how it turned out."

"What did I do wrong?"

"Nothing."

"Is this one of those women's lib things?" Leroy asks. 150

"Don't be funny."

The cemetery, a green slope dotted with white markers, looks like a subdivision site. Leroy is trying to comprehend that his marriage is breaking up, but for some reason he is wondering about white slabs in a graveyard.

"Everything was fine till Mama caught me smoking," says Norma Jean, standing up. "That set something off."

"What are you talking about?"

"She won't leave me alone—*you* won't leave me alone." Norma Jean seems to be crying, but she is looking away from him. "I feel eighteen again. I can't face that all over again." She starts walking away. "No, it *wasn't* fine. I don't know what I'm saying. Forget it." 155

Leroy takes a lungful of smoke and closes his eyes as Norma Jean's words sink in. He tries to focus on the fact that thirty-five hundred soldiers died on the grounds around him. He can only think of that war as a board game with plastic soldiers. Leroy almost smiles, as he compares the Confederates' daring attack on the Union camps and Virgil Mathis's raid on the bowling alley. General Grant, drunk and furious, shoved the Southerners back to Corinth, where Mabel and Jet Beasley were married years later, when Mabel was still thin and good-looking. The next day, Mabel and Jet visited the battleground, and then Norma Jean was born, and then she married Leroy and they had a baby, which they lost, and now Leroy and Norma Jean are here at the same battleground. Leroy knows he is leaving out a lot. He is leaving out the insides of history. History was always just names and dates to him. It occurs to him that building a house out of logs is similarly empty—too simple. And the real inner workings of a marriage, like most of history, have escaped him. Now he sees that building a log house is the dumbest idea he could have had. It was clumsy of him to think Norma Jean would want a log house. It was a crazy idea. He'll have to think of something else, quickly. He will wad the blueprints into tight balls and fling them into the lake. Then he'll get moving again. He opens his eyes. Norma Jean has moved away and is walking through the cemetery, following a serpentine brick path.

Leroy gets up to follow his wife, but his good leg is asleep and his bad leg still hurts him. Norma Jean is far away, walking rapidly toward the bluff by the river, and he tries to hobble toward her. Some children run past him, screaming noisily. Norma Jean has reached the bluff, and she is looking out over the Tennessee River. Now she turns toward Leroy and waves her arms. Is she beckoning to him? She seems to be doing an exercise for her chest muscles. The sky is unusually pale—the color of the dust ruffle Mabel made for their bed.   [1982]

QUESTIONS

1. Is Leroy anything at all like his rig?
2. In what ways are Leroy and Norma Jean fundamentally different?
3. Does the story need Mabel, Norma Jean's mother?
4. Why would Mason choose the battle of Shiloh for the scene of the breakup of Norma Jean and Leroy's marriage?
5. What function does the log cabin serve?

RESPONSES

1. Research the history and importance of the Battle of Shiloh. How does the conflict and resolution between these characters reflect the forces in that battle?
2. Compare this story of marital disharmony to Gilb's "Hollywood!"

W. Somerset Maugham

W. Somerset Maugham (1874–1965) was born in Paris of English parents. Having trained to be a physician, he abandoned his profession in favor of a career as a writer. His first great success came as a playwright for the London stage, after which in middle life he turned to the writing of novels and stories. His semi-autobiographical novels *Of Human Bondage* (1915) and *Cakes and Ale* (1930) continue to attract readers, as does his remarkable intellectual autobiography, *The Summing Up* (1938). An excellent selection of his short stories may be found in *The Collected Stories* (1951).

The Outstation

The new assistant arrived in the afternoon. When the Resident, Mr. Warburton, was told that the prahu was in sight he put on his solar topee and went down to the landing-stage. The guard, eight little Dyak soldiers, stood to attention as he passed. He noted with satisfaction that their bearing was martial, their uniforms neat and clean, and their guns shining. They were a credit to him. From the landing-stage he watched the bend of the river round which in a moment the boat would sweep. He looked very smart in his spotless ducks and white shoes. He held under his arm a gold-headed Malacca cane which had been given him by the Sultan of Perak. He awaited the newcomer with mingled feelings. There was more work in the district than one man could properly do, and during his periodical tours of the country under his charge it had been inconvenient to leave the station in the hands of a native clerk, but he had been so long the only white man there that he could not face the arrival of another without misgiving. He was accustomed to loneliness. During the war he had not seen an English face for three years; and once when he was instructed to put up an afforestation officer he was seized with panic, so that when the stranger was due to arrive, having arranged everything for his reception, he wrote a note telling him he was obliged to go up-river, and fled; he remained away till he was informed by a messenger that his guest had left.

Now the prahu appeared in the broad reach. It was manned by prisoners, Dyaks under various sentences, and a couple of warders were waiting on the landing-stage to take them back to jail. They were sturdy fellows, used to the river, and they rowed with a powerful stroke. As the boat reached the side a man got out from under the attap awning and stepped on shore. The guard presented arms.

769

"Here we are at last. By God, I'm as cramped as the devil. I've brought you your mail."

He spoke with exuberant joviality. Mr. Warburton politely held out his hand.

5   "Mr. Cooper, I presume?"

"That's right. Were you expecting any one else?"

The question had a facetious intent, but the Resident did not smile.

"My name is Warburton. I'll show you your quarters. They'll bring your kit along."

He preceded Cooper along the narrow pathway and they entered a compound in which stood a small bungalow.

10   "I've had it made as habitable as I could, but of course no one has lived in it for a good many years."

It was built on piles. It consisted of a long living-room which opened on to a broad verandah, and behind, on each side of a passage, were two bedrooms.

"This'll do me all right," said Cooper.

"I daresay you want to have a bath and a change. I shall be very much pleased if you'll dine with me to-night. Will eight o'clock suit you?"

"Any old time will do for me."

15   The Resident gave a polite, but slightly disconcerted, smile and withdrew. He returned to the Fort where his own residence was. The impression which Allen Cooper had given him was not very favourable, but he was a fair man, and he knew that it was unjust to form an opinion on so brief a glimpse. Cooper seemed to be about thirty. He was a tall, thin fellow, with a sallow face in which there was not a spot of colour. It was a face all in one tone. He had a large, hooked nose and blue eyes. When, entering the bungalow, he had taken off his topee and flung it to a waiting boy, Mr. Warburton noticed that his large skull, covered with short, brown hair, contrasted somewhat oddly with a weak, small chin. He was dressed in khaki shorts and a khaki shirt, but they were shabby and soiled; and his battered topee had not been cleaned for days. Mr. Warburton reflected that the young man had spent a week on a coasting steamer and had passed the last forty-eight hours lying in the bottom of a prahu.

"We'll see what he looks like when he comes in to dinner."

He went into his room where his things were as neatly laid out as if he had an English valet, undressed, and, walking down the stairs to the bath-house, sluiced himself with cool water. The only concession he made to the climate was to wear a white dinner-jacket; but otherwise, in a boiled shirt and a high collar, silk socks and patent-leather shoes, he dressed as formally as though he were dining at his club in Pall Mall. A careful host, he went into the dining-room to see that the table was properly laid. It was gay with orchids and the silver shone brightly. The napkins were folded into elaborate shapes. Shaded candles in silver candlesticks shed a soft light. Mr. Warburton smiled his approval and returned to the sitting-room to await his guest. Presently he appeared. Cooper was wearing the khaki shorts, the khaki shirt, and the ragged jacket in which he had landed. Mr. Warburton's smile of greeting froze on his face.

"Hulloa, you're all dressed up," said Cooper. "I didn't know you were going to do that. I very nearly put on a sarong."

"It doesn't matter at all. I daresay your boys were busy."

20   "You needn't have bothered to dress on my account, you know."

"I didn't. I always dress for dinner."

"Even when you're alone?"

"Especially when I'm alone," replied Mr. Warburton, with a frigid stare.

He saw a twinkle of amusement in Cooper's eyes, and he flushed an angry red. Mr. Warburton was a hot-tempered man; you might have guessed that from his red face with its pugnacious features and from his red hair, now growing white; his blue eyes, cold as a rule and observing, could flush with sudden wrath; but he was a man of the world and he hoped a just one. He must do his best to get on with this fellow.

"When I lived in London I moved in circles in which it would have been just as ec- 25 centric not to dress for dinner every night as not to have a bath every morning. When I came to Borneo I saw no reason to discontinue so good a habit. For three years, during the war, I never saw a white man. I never omitted to dress on a single occasion on which I was well enough to come in to dinner. You have not been very long in this country; believe me, there is no better way to maintain the proper pride which you should have in yourself. When a white man surrenders in the slightest degree to the influences that surround him he very soon loses his self-respect, and when he loses his self-respect you may be quite sure that the natives will soon cease to respect him."

"Well, if you expect me to put on a boiled shirt and a stiff collar in this heat I'm afraid you'll be disappointed."

"When you are dining in your own bungalow you will, of course, dress as you think fit, but when you do me the pleasure of dining with me, perhaps you will come to the conclusion that it is only polite to wear the costume usual in civilized society."

Two Malay boys, in sarongs and songkoks, with smart white coats and brass buttons, came in, one bearing gin pahits, and the other a tray on which were olives and anchovies. Then they went in to dinner. Mr. Warburton flattered himself that he had the best cook, a Chinese, in Borneo, and he took great trouble to have as good food as in the difficult circumstances was possible. He exercised much ingenuity in making the best of his materials.

"Would you care to look at the menu?" he said, handing it to Cooper.

It was written in French and the dishes had resounding names. They were waited 30 on by the two boys. In opposite corners of the room two more waved immense fans, and so gave movement to the sultry air. The fare was sumptuous and the champagne excellent.

"Do you do yourself like this every day?" said Cooper.

Mr. Warburton gave the menu a careless glance.

"I have not noticed that the dinner is any different from usual," he said. "I eat very little myself, but I make a point of having a proper dinner served to me every night. It keeps the cook in practice and it's good discipline for the boys."

The conversation proceeded with effort. Mr. Warburton was elaborately courteous, and it may be that he found a slightly malicious amusement in the embarrassment which he thereby occasioned in his companion. Cooper had not been more than a few months in Sembulu, and Mr. Warburton's enquiries about friends of his in Kuala Solor were soon exhausted.

"By the way," he said presently, "did you meet a lad called Hennerley? He's come 35 out recently, I believe."

"Oh, yes, he's in the police. A rotten bounder."

"I should hardly have expected him to be that. His uncle is my friend Lord Barraclough. I had a letter from Lady Barraclough only the other day asking me to look out for him."

"I heard he was related to somebody or other. I suppose that's how he got the job. He's been to Eton and Oxford and he doesn't forget to let you know it."

"You surprise me," said Mr. Warburton. "All his family have been at Eton and Oxford for a couple of hundred years. I should have expected him to take it as a matter of course."

"I thought him a damned prig." 40

"To what school did you go?"

"I was born in Barbadoes. I was educated there."

"Oh, I see."

Mr. Warburton managed to put so much offensiveness into his brief reply that Cooper flushed. For a moment he was silent.

"I've had two or three letters from Kuala Solor," continued Mr. Warburton, "and my impression was that young Hennerley was a great success. They say he's a first-rate sportsman."

"Oh, yes, he's very popular. He's just the sort of fellow they would like in K.S. I haven't got much use for the first-rate sportsman myself. What does it amount to in the long run that a man can play golf and tennis better than other people? And who cares if he can make a break of seventy-five at billiards? They attach a damned sight too much importance to that sort of thing in England."

"Do you think so? I was under the impression that the first-rate sportsman had come out of the war certainly no worse than any one else."

"Oh, if you're going to talk of the war then I do know what I'm talking about. I was in the same regiment as Hennerley and I can tell you that the men couldn't stick him at any price."

"How do you know?"

"Because I was one of the men."

"Oh, you hadn't got a commission."

"A fat chance I had of getting a commission. I was what was called a Colonial. I hadn't been to a public school and I had no influence. I was in the ranks the whole damned time."

Cooper frowned. He seemed to have difficulty in preventing himself from breaking into violent invective. Mr. Warburton watched him, his little blue eyes narrowed, watched him and formed his opinion. Changing the conversation, he began to speak to Cooper about the work that would be required of him, and as the clock struck ten he rose.

"Well, I won't keep you any more. I daresay you're tired by your journey."

They shook hands.

"Oh, I say, look here," said Cooper, "I wonder if you can find me a boy. The boy I had before never turned up when I was starting from K.S. He took my kit on board and all that and then disappeared. I didn't know he wasn't there till we were out of the river."

"I'll ask my head-boy. I have no doubt he can find you some one."

"All right. Just tell him to send the boy along and if I like the look of him I'll take him."

There was a moon, so that no lantern was needed. Cooper walked across from the Fort to his bungalow.

"I wonder why on earth they've sent me a fellow like that?" reflected Mr. Warburton. "If that's the kind of man they're going to get out now I don't think much of it."

He strolled down his garden. The Fort was built on the top of a little hill and the garden ran down to the river's edge; on the bank was an arbour, and hither it was his habit to come after dinner to smoke a cheroot. And often from the river that flowed below him a voice was heard, the voice of some Malay too timorous to venture into the light of day, and a complaint or an accusation was softly wafted to his ears, a piece of information was whispered to him or a useful hint, which otherwise would never have come into his official ken. He threw himself heavily into a long rattan chair. Cooper! An envious, ill-bred fellow, bumptious, self-assertive and vain. But Mr. Warburton's irritation could not withstand the silent beauty of the night. The air was scented with the sweet-smelling flowers of a tree that grew at the entrance to the arbour, and the fire-flies, sparkling dimly, flew with their slow and silvery flight. The moon made a path-way on the broad river for the light feet of Siva's bride, and on the further bank a row of palm trees was delicately silhouetted against the sky. Peace stole into the soul of Mr. Warburton.

He was a queer creature and he had had a singular career. At the age of twenty-one he had inherited a considerable fortune, a hundred thousand pounds, and when he left Oxford he threw himself into the gay life which in those days (now Mr. Warburton was a man of four and fifty) offered itself to the young man of good family. He had his flat in Mount Street, his private hansom, and his hunting-box in Warwickshire. He went to all the places where the fashionable congregate. He was handsome, amusing and generous. He was a figure in the society of London in the early nineties, and so-ciety then had not lost its exclusiveness nor its brilliance. The Boer War which shook it was unthought of; the Great War which destroyed it was prophesied only by the pessimists. It was no unpleasant thing to be a rich young man in those days, and Mr. Warburton's chimney-piece during the season was packed with cards for one great function after another. Mr. Warburton displayed them with complacency. For Mr. War-burton was a snob. He was not a timid snob, a little ashamed of being impressed by his betters, nor a snob who sought the intimacy of persons who had acquired celebri-ty in politics or notoriety in the arts, not the snob who was dazzled by riches; he was the naked, unadulterated common snob who dearly loved a lord. He was touchy and quick-tempered, but he would much rather have been snubbed by a person of quali-ty than flattered by a commoner. His name figured insignificantly in Burke's Peerage, and it was marvellous to watch the ingenuity he used to mention his distant relation-ship to the noble family he belonged to; but never a word did he say of the honest Liv-erpool manufacturer from whom, through his mother, a Miss Gubbins, he had come by his fortune. It was the terror of his fashionable life that at Cowes, maybe, or at Ascot, when he was with a duchess or even with a prince of the blood, one of these relatives would claim acquaintance with him.

His failing was too obvious not soon to become notorious, but its extravagance saved it from being merely despicable. The great whom he adored laughed at him, but in their hearts felt his adoration was not unnatural. Poor Warburton was a dread-ful snob, of course, but after all he was a good fellow. He was always ready to back a bill for an impecunious nobleman, and if you were in a tight corner you could safely count on him for a hundred pounds. He gave good dinners. He played whist badly, but never minded how much he lost if the company was select. He happened to be a gambler, an unlucky one, but he was a good loser, and it was impossible not to admire the coolness with which he lost five hundred pounds at a sitting. His passion for cards, almost as strong as his passion for titles, was the cause of his undoing. The life he led was expensive and his gambling losses were formidable. He began to plunge more heavily, first on horses, and then on the Stock Exchange. He had a certain simplicity of character and the unscrupulous found him an ingenuous prey. I do not know if he ever realized that his smart friends laughed at him behind his back, but I think he had an obscure instinct that he could not afford to appear other than careless of his money. He got into the hands of money-lenders. At the age of thirty-four he was ruined.

He was too much imbued with the spirit of his class to hesitate in the choice of his next step. When a man in his set had run through his money he went out to the colonies. No one heard Mr. Warburton repine. He made no complaint because a noble friend had advised a disastrous speculation, he pressed nobody to whom he had lent money to repay it, he paid his debts (if he had only known it, the despised blood of the Liverpool manufacturer came out in him there), sought help from no one, and, never having done a stroke of work in his life, looked for a means of livelihood. He remained cheerful, unconcerned and full of humour. He had no wish to make any one with whom he happened to be uncomfortable by the recital of his misfortune. Mr. Warburton was a snob, but he was also a gentleman.

65   The only favour he asked of any of the great friends in whose daily company he had lived for years was a recommendation. The able man who was at that time Sultan of Sembulu took him into his service. The night before he sailed he dined for the last time at his club.

"I hear you're going away, Warburton," the old Duke of Hereford said to him.

"Yes, I'm going to Borneo."

"Good God, what are you going there for?"

"Oh, I'm broke."

70   "Are you? I'm sorry. Well, let us know when you come back. I hope you have a good time."

"Oh, yes. Lots of shooting, you know."

The Duke nodded and passed on. A few hours later Mr. Warburton watched the coast of England recede into the mist, and he left behind everything which to him made life worth living.

Twenty years had passed since then. He kept up a busy correspondence with various great ladies and his letters were amusing and chatty. He never lost his love for titled persons and paid careful attention to the announcements in The Times (which reached him six weeks after publication) of their comings and goings. He perused the column which records births, deaths, and marriages, and he was always ready with his letter of congratulation or condolence. The illustrated papers told him how people looked and on his periodical visits to England, able to take up the threads as though they had never been broken, he knew all about any new person who might have appeared on the social surface. His interest in the world of fashion was as vivid as when himself had been a figure in it. It still seemed to him the only thing that mattered.

But insensibly another interest had entered into his life. The position he found himself in flattered his vanity; he was no longer the sycophant craving the smiles of the great, he was the master whose word was law. He was gratified by the guard of Dyak soldiers who presented arms as he passed. He liked to sit in judgment on his fellow men. It pleased him to compose quarrels between rival chiefs. When the head-hunters were troublesome in the old days he set out to chastise them with a thrill of pride in his own behaviour. He was too vain not to be of dauntless courage, and a pretty story was told of his coolness in adventuring single-handed into a stockaded village and demanding the surrender of a bloodthirsty pirate. He became a skillful administrator. He was strict, just and honest.

75   And little by little he conceived a deep love for the Malays. He interested himself in their habits and customs. He was never tired of listening to their talk. He admired their virtues, and with a smile and a shrug of the shoulders condoned their vices.

"In my day," he would say, "I have been on intimate terms with some of the greatest gentlemen in England, but I have never known finer gentlemen than some well-born Malays whom I am proud to call my friends."

He liked their courtesy and their distinguished manners, their gentleness and their sudden passions. He knew by instinct exactly how to treat them. He had a genuine tenderness for them. But he never forgot that he was an English gentleman and he had no patience with the white men who yielded to native customs. He made no surrenders. And he did not imitate so many of the white men in taking a native woman to wife, for an intrigue of this nature, however sanctified by custom, seemed to him not only shocking but undignified. A man who had been called George by Albert Edward, Prince of Wales, could hardly be expected to have any connection with a native. And when he returned to Borneo from his visits to England it was now with something like relief. His friends, like himself, were no longer young, and there was a new generation which looked upon him as a tiresome old man. It seemed to him that the England of to-day had lost a good deal of what he had loved in the England of his youth. But Borneo remained the same. It was home to him now. He meant to remain in the service as long as was possible, and the hope in his heart was that he would die before at last he was forced to retire. He had stated in his will that wherever he died he wished his body to be brought back to Sembulu and buried among the people he loved within sound of the softly flowing river.

But these emotions he kept hidden from the eyes of men; and no one, seeing this spruce, stout, well-set-up man, with his clean-shaven strong face and his whitening hair, would have dreamed that he cherished so profound a sentiment.

He knew how the work of the station should be done, and during the next few days he kept a suspicious eye on his assistant. He saw very soon that he was painstaking and competent. The only fault he had to find with him was that he was brusque with the natives.

"The Malays are shy and very sensitive," he said to him. "I think you will find   80
that you will get much better results if you take care always to be polite, patient and kindly."

Cooper gave a short, grating laugh.

"I was born in Barbadoes and I was in Africa in the war. I don't think there's much about niggers that I don't know."

"I know nothing," said Mr. Warburton acidly. "But we were not talking of them. We were talking of Malays."

"Aren't they niggers?"

"You are very ignorant," replied Mr. Warburton.   85

He said no more.

On the first Sunday after Cooper's arrival he asked him to dinner. He did everything ceremoniously, and though they had met on the previous day in the office and later, on the Fort verandah where they drank a gin and bitters together at six o'clock, he sent a polite note across to the bungalow by a boy. Cooper, however unwillingly, came in evening dress and Mr. Warburton, though gratified that his wish was respected, noticed with disdain that the young man's clothes were badly cut and his shirt ill-fitting. But Mr. Warburton was in a good temper that evening.

"By the way," he said to him, as he shook hands, "I've talked to my head-boy about finding you some one and he recommends his nephew. I've seen him and he seems a bright and willing lad. Would you like to see him?"

"I don't mind."

"He's waiting now."   90

Mr. Warburton called his boy and told him to send for his nephew. In a moment a tall, slender youth of twenty appeared. He had large dark eyes and a good profile. He was very neat in his sarong, a little white coat, and a fez, without a tassel, of plum-coloured velvet. He answered to the name of Abas. Mr. Warburton looked on him with approval, and his manner insensibly softened as he spoke to him in fluent and idiomatic Malay. He was inclined to be sarcastic with white people, but with the Malays he had a happy mixture of condescension and kindliness. He stood in the place of the

Sultan. He knew perfectly how to preserve his own dignity, and at the same time put a native at his ease.

"Will he do?" said Mr. Warburton, turning to Cooper.

"Yes, I daresay he's no more of a scoundrel than any of the rest of them."

Mr. Warburton informed the boy that he was engaged and dismissed him.

95   "You're very lucky to get a boy like that," he told Cooper. "He belongs to a very good family. They came over from Malacca nearly a hundred years ago."

"I don't much mind if the boy who cleans my shoes and brings me a drink when I want it has blue blood in his veins or not. All I ask is that he should do what I tell him and look sharp about it."

Mr. Warburton pursed his lips, but made no reply.

They went in to dinner. It was excellent, and the wine was good. Its influence presently had its effect on them and they talked not only without acrimony, but even with friendliness. Mr. Warburton liked to do himself well, and on Sunday night he made it a habit to do himself even a little better than usual. He began to think he was unfair to Cooper. Of course he was not a gentleman, but that was not his fault, and when you got to know him it might be that he would turn out a very good fellow. His faults, perhaps, were faults of manner. And he was certainly good at his work, quick, conscientious and thorough. When they reached the dessert Mr. Warburton was feeling kindly disposed towards all mankind.

"This is your first Sunday and I'm going to give you a very special glass of port. I've only got about two dozen of it left and I keep it for special occasions."

100   He gave his boy instructions and presently the bottle was brought. Mr. Warburton watched the boy open it.

"I got this port from my old friend Charles Hollington. He'd had it for forty years and I've had it for a good many. He was well known to have the best cellar in England."

"Is he a wine merchant?"

"Not exactly," smiled Mr. Warburton. "I was speaking of Lord Hollington of Castle Reagh. He's one of the richest peers in England. A very old friend of mine. I was at Eton with his brother."

This was an opportunity that Mr. Warburton could never resist and he told a little anecdote of which the only point seemed to be that he knew an earl. The port was certainly very good; he drank a glass and then a second. He lost all caution. He had not talked to a white man for months. He began to tell stories. He showed himself in the company of the great. Hearing him you would have thought that at one time ministries were formed and policies decided on his suggestion whispered into the ear of a duchess or thrown over the dinner-table to be gratefully acted on by the confidential adviser of the sovereign. The old days at Ascot, Goodwood and Cowes lived again for him. Another glass of port. There were the great house-parties in Yorkshire and in Scotland to which he went every year.

105   "I had a man called Foreman then, the best valet I ever had, and why do you think he gave me notice? You know in the Housekeeper's Room the ladies' maids and the gentlemen's gentlemen sit according to the precedence of their masters. He told me he was sick of going to party after party at which I was the only commoner. It meant that he always had to sit at the bottom of the table and all the best bits were taken before a dish reached him. I told the story to the old Duke of Hereford and he roared. 'By God, sir,' he said, 'if I were King of England I'd make you a viscount just to give your man a chance.' 'Take him yourself, Duke,' I said. 'He's the best valet I've ever had.' 'Well, Warburton,' he said, 'if he's good enough for you he's good enough for me. Send him along.'"

Then there was Monte Carlo where Mr. Warburton and the Grand Duke Fyodor, playing in partnership, had broken the bank one evening; and there was Marienbad. At Marienbad Mr. Warburton had played baccarat with Edward VII.

"He was only Prince of Wales then, of course. I remember him saying to me, 'George, if you draw on a five you'll lose your shirt.' He was right; I don't think he ever said a truer word in his life. He was a wonderful man. I always said he was the greatest diplomatist in Europe. But I was a young fool in those days, I hadn't the sense to take his advice. If I had, if I'd never drawn on a five, I daresay I shouldn't be here to-day."

Cooper was watching him. His blue eyes, deep in their sockets, were hard and supercilious, and on his lips was a mocking smile. He had heard a good deal about Mr. Warburton in Kuala Solor. Not a bad sort, and he ran his district like clockwork, they said, but by heaven, what a snob! They laughed at him good-naturedly, for it was impossible to dislike a man who was so generous and so kindly, and Cooper had already heard the story of the Prince of Wales and the game of baccarat. But Cooper listened without indulgence. From the beginning he had resented the Resident's manner. He was very sensitive and he writhed under Mr. Warburton's polite sarcasms. Mr. Warburton had a knack of receiving a remark of which he disapproved with a devastating silence. Cooper had lived little in England and he had a peculiar dislike of the English. He resented especially the public-school boy since he always feared that he was going to patronize him. He was so much afraid of others putting on airs with him that, in order as it were to get in first, he put on such airs as to make every one think him insufferably conceited.

"Well, at all events the war has done one good thing for us," he said at last. "It's smashed up the power of the aristocracy. The Boer War started it, and 1914 put the lid on."

"The great families of England are doomed," said Mr. Warburton with the complacent melancholy of an *émigré* who remembered the court of Louis XV. "They cannot afford any longer to live in their splendid palaces and their princely hospitality will soon be nothing but a memory."   110

"And a damned good job too in my opinion."

"My poor Cooper, what can you know of the glory that was Greece and the grandeur that was Rome?"

Mr. Warburton made an ample gesture. His eyes for an instant grew dreamy with a vision of the past.

"Well, believe me, we're fed up with all that rot. What we want is a business government by business men. I was born in a Crown Colony and I've lived practically all my life in the colonies. I don't give a row of pins for a lord. What's wrong with England is snobbishness. And if there's anything that gets my goat it's a snob."

A snob! Mr. Warburton's face grew purple and his eyes blazed with anger. That   115
was a word that had pursued him all his life. The great ladies whose society he had enjoyed in his youth were not inclined to look upon his appreciation of themselves as unworthy, but even great ladies are sometimes out of temper and more than once Mr. Warburton had had the dreadful word flung in his teeth. He knew, he could not help knowing, that there were odious people who called him a snob. How unfair it was! Why, there was no vice he found so detestable as snobbishness. After all, he liked to mix with people of his own class, he was only at home in their company, and how in heaven's name could any one say that was snobbish? Birds of a feather.

"I quite agree with you," he answered. "A snob is a man who admires or despises another because he is of a higher social rank than his own. It is the most vulgar failing of our English middle class."

He saw a flicker of amusement in Cooper's eyes. Cooper put up his hand to hide the broad smile that rose to his lips, and so made it more noticeable. Mr. Warburton's hands trembled a little.

Probably Cooper never knew how greatly he had offended his chief. A sensitive man himself he was strangely insensitive to the feelings of others.

Their work forced them to see one another for a few minutes now and then during the day, and they met at six to have a drink on Mr. Warburton's verandah. This was an old-established custom of the country which Mr. Warburton would not for the world have broken. But they ate their meals separately, Cooper in his bungalow and Mr. Warburton at the Fort. After the office work was over they walked till dusk fell, but they walked apart. There were but few paths in this country, where the jungle pressed close upon the plantations of the village, and when Mr. Warburton caught sight of his assistant passing along with his loose stride, he would make a circuit in order to avoid him. Cooper, with his bad manners, his conceit in his own judgment and his intolerance, had already got on his nerves; but it was not till Cooper had been on the station for a couple of months that an incident happened which turned the Resident's dislike into bitter hatred.

120   Mr. Warburton was obliged to go up-country on a tour of inspection, and he left the station in Cooper's charge with more confidence, since he had definitely come to the conclusion that he was a capable fellow. The only thing he did not like was that he had no indulgence. He was honest, just and painstaking, but he had no sympathy for the natives. It bitterly amused Mr. Warburton to observe that this man, who looked upon himself as every man's equal, should look upon so many men as his own inferiors. He was hard, he had no patience with the native mind, and he was a bully. Mr. Warburton very quickly realized that the Malays disliked and feared him. He was not altogether displeased. He would not have liked it very much if his assistant had enjoyed a popularity which might rival his own. Mr. Warburton made his elaborate preparations, set out on his expedition, and in three weeks returned. Meanwhile the mail had arrived. The first thing that struck his eyes when he entered his sitting-room was a great pile of open newspapers. Cooper had met him, and they went into the room together. Mr. Warburton turned to one of the servants who had been left behind and sternly asked him what was the meaning of those open papers. Cooper hastened to explain.

"I wanted to read all about the Wolverhampton murder and so I borrowed your Times. I brought them back again. I knew you wouldn't mind."

Mr. Warburton turned on him, white with anger.

"But I do mind. I mind very much."

"I'm sorry," said Cooper, with composure. "The fact is, I simply couldn't wait till you came back."

125   "I wonder you didn't open my letters as well."

Cooper, unmoved, smiled at his chief's exasperation.

"Oh, that's not quite the same thing. After all, I couldn't imagine you'd mind my looking at your newspapers. There's nothing private in them."

"I very much object to any one reading my paper before me." He went up to the pile. There were nearly thirty numbers there. "I think it extremely impertinent of you. They're all mixed up."

"We can easily put them in order," said Cooper, joining him at the table.

130   "Don't touch them," cried Mr. Warburton.

"I say, it's childish to make a scene about a little thing like that."

"How dare you speak to me like that!"

"Oh, go to hell," said Cooper, and he flung out of the room.

Mr. Warburton, trembling with passion, was left contemplating his papers. His greatest pleasure in life had been destroyed by those callous, brutal hands. Most people living in out-of-the-way places when the mail comes tear open impatiently their papers and taking the last ones first glance at the latest news from home. Not so Mr. Warburton. His newsagent had instructions to write on the outside of the wrapper the date of each paper he despatched and when the great bundle arrived Mr. Warburton looked at these dates and with his blue pencil numbered them. His head-boy's orders were to place one on the table every morning in the verandah with the early cup of tea, and it was Mr. Warburton's especial delight to break the wrapper as he sipped his tea, and read the morning paper. It gave him the illusion of living at home. Every Monday morning he read the Monday Times of six weeks back and so went through the week. On Sunday he read the Observer. Like his habit of dressing for dinner it was a tie to civilization. And it was his pride that no matter how exciting the news was he had never yielded to the temptation of opening a paper before its allotted time. During the war the suspense sometimes had been intolerable, and when he read one day that a push was begun he had undergone agonies of suspense which he might have saved himself by the simple expedient of opening a later paper which lay waiting for him on a shelf. It had been the severest trial to which he had ever exposed himself, but he victoriously surmounted it. And that clumsy fool had broken open those neat tight packages because he wanted to know whether some horrid woman had murdered her odious husband.

Mr. Warburton sent for his boy and told him to bring wrappers. He folded up the papers as neatly as he could, placed a wrapper round each and numbered it. But it was a melancholy task.

"I shall never forgive him," he said. "Never."

Of course his boy had been with him on his expedition; he never travelled without him, for his boy knew exactly how he liked things, and Mr. Warburton was not the kind of jungle traveller who was prepared to dispense with his comforts; but in the interval since their arrival he had been gossiping in the servants' quarters. He had learnt that Cooper had had trouble with his boys. All but the youth Abas had left him. Abas had desired to go too, but his uncle had placed him there on the instructions of the Resident, and he was afraid to leave without his uncle's permission.

"I told him he had done well, Tuan," said the boy. "But he is unhappy. He says it is not a good house and he wishes to know if he may go as the others have gone."

"No, he must stay. The tuan must have servants. Have those who went been replaced?"

"No, Tuan, no one will go."

Mr. Warburton frowned. Cooper was an insolent fool, but he had an official position and must be suitably provided with servants. It was not seemly that his house should be improperly conducted.

"Where are the boys who ran away?"

"They are in the kampong, Tuan."

"Go and see them to-night and tell them that I expect them to be back at Tuan Cooper's house at dawn tomorrow."

"They say they will not go, Tuan."

"On my order?"

The boy had been with Mr. Warburton for fifteen years, and he knew every intonation of his master's voice. He was not afraid of him, they had gone through too much together, once in the jungle the Resident had saved his life and once, upset in

135

140

145

some rapids, but for him the Resident would have been drowned; but he knew when the Resident must be obeyed without question.

"I will go to the kampong," he said.

Mr. Warburton expected that his subordinate would take the first opportunity to apologize for his rudeness, but Cooper had the ill-bred man's inability to express regret; and when they met next morning in the office he ignored the incident. Since Mr. Warburton had been away for three weeks it was necessary for them to have a somewhat prolonged interview. At the end of it Mr. Warburton dismissed him.

150 "I don't think there's anything else, thank you." Cooper turned to go, but Mr. Warburton stopped him. "I understand you've been having some trouble with your boys."

Cooper gave a harsh laugh.

"They tried to blackmail me. They had the damned cheek to run away, all except that incompetent fellow Abas—he knew when he was well off—but I just sat tight. They've all come to heel again."

"What do you mean by that?"

"This morning they were all back on their jobs, the Chinese cook and all. There they were, as cool as cucumbers; you would have thought they owned the place. I suppose they'd come to the conclusion that I wasn't such a fool as I looked."

155 "By no means. They came back on my express order."

Cooper flushed slightly.

"I should be obliged if you wouldn't interfere with my private concerns."

"They're not your private concerns. When your servants run away it makes you ridiculous. You are perfectly free to make a fool of yourself, but I cannot allow you to be made a fool of. It is unseemly that your house should not be properly staffed. As soon as I heard that your boys had left you, I had them told to be back in their place at dawn. That'll do."

Mr. Warburton nodded to signify that the interview was at an end. Cooper took no notice.

160 "Shall I tell you what I did? I called them and gave the wholy bally lot the sack. I gave them ten minutes to get out of the compound."

Mr. Warburton shrugged his shoulders.

"What makes you think you can get others?"

"I've told my own clerk to see about it."

Mr. Warburton reflected for a moment.

165 "I think you behaved very foolishly. You will do well to remember in future that good masters make good servants."

"Is there anything else you want to teach me?"

"I should like to teach you manners, but it would be an arduous task, and I have not the time to waste. I will see that you get boys."

"Please don't put yourself to any trouble on my account. I'm quite capable of getting them for myself."

Mr. Warburton smiled acidly. He had an inkling that Cooper disliked him as much as he disliked Cooper, and he knew that nothing is more galling than to be forced to accept the favours of a man you detest.

170 "Allow me to tell you that you have no more chance of getting Malay or Chinese servants here now than you have of getting an English butler or a French chef. No one will come to you except on an order from me. Would you like me to give it?"

"No."

"As you please. Good morning."

Mr. Warburton watched the development of the situation with acrid humour. Cooper's clerk was unable to persuade Malay, Dyak or Chinese to enter the house of such a master. Abas, the boy who remained faithful to him, knew how to cook only native food, and Cooper, a coarse feeder, found his gorge rise against the everlasting rice. There was no water-carrier, and in that great heat he needed several baths a day. He cursed Abas, but Abas opposed him with sullen resistance and would not do more than he chose. It was galling to know that the lad stayed with him only because the Resident insisted. This went on for a fortnight and then, one morning, he found in his house the very servants whom he had previously dismissed. He fell into a violent rage, but he had learnt a little sense, and this time, without a word, he let them stay. He swallowed his humiliation, but the impatient contempt he had felt for Mr. Warburton's idiosyncrasies changed into a sullen hatred; the Resident with this malicious stroke had made him the laughing-stock of all the natives.

The two men now held no communication with one another. They broke the time-honoured custom of sharing, notwithstanding personal dislike, a drink at six o'clock with any white man who happened to be at the station. Each lived in his own house as though the other did not exist. Now that Cooper had fallen into the work, it was necessary for them to have little to do with one another in the office. Mr. Warburton used his orderly to send any message he had to give his assistant, and his instructions he sent by formal letter. They saw one another constantly, that was inevitable, but did not exchange half a dozen words in a week. The fact that they could not avoid catching sight of one another got on their nerves. They brooded over their antagonism and Mr. Warburton, taking his daily walk, could think of nothing but how much he detested his assistant.

And the dreadful thing was that in all probability they would remain thus, facing 175 each other in deadly enmity, till Mr. Warburton went on leave. It might be three years. He had no reason to send in a complaint to headquarters: Cooper did his work very well, and at that time men were hard to get. True, vague complaints reached him and hints that the natives found Cooper harsh. There was certainly a feeling of dissatisfaction among them. But when Mr. Warburton looked into specific cases, all he could say was that Cooper had shown severity where mildness would not have been misplaced and had been unfeeling when himself would have been sympathetic. He had done nothing for which he could be taken to task. But Mr. Warburton watched him. Hatred will often make a man clear-sighted, and he had a suspicion that Cooper was using the natives without consideration, yet keeping within the law, because he felt that thus he could exasperate his chief. One day perhaps he would go too far. None knew better than Mr. Warburton how irritable the incessant heat could make a man and how difficult it was to keep one's self-control after a sleepless night. He smiled softly to himself. Sooner or later Cooper would deliver himself into his hand.

When at last the opportunity came Mr. Warburton laughed aloud. Cooper had charge of the prisoners; they made roads, built sheds, rowed when it was necessary to send the prahu up- or downstream, kept the town clean and otherwise usefully employed themselves. If well-behaved they even on occasion served as house-boys. Cooper kept them hard at it. He liked to see them work. He took pleasure in devising tasks for them; and seeing quickly enough that they were being made to do useless things the prisoners worked badly. He punished them by lengthening their hours. This was contrary to the regulations, and as soon as it was brought to the attention of Mr. Warburton, without referring the matter back to his subordinate, he gave instructions that the old hours should be kept; Cooper, going out for his walk, was astounded to see the prisoners strolling back to the jail; he had given instructions that they were not to knock off till dusk. When he asked the warder in charge why they had left off work he was told that it was the Resident's bidding.

White with rage he strode to the Fort. Mr. Warburton, in his spotless white ducks and his neat topee, with a walking-stick in his hand, followed by his dogs, was on the point of starting out on his afternoon stroll. He had watched Cooper go and knew that he had taken the road by the river. Cooper jumped up the steps and went straight up to the Resident.

"I want to know what the hell you mean by countermanding my order that the prisoners were to work till six," he burst out, beside himself with fury.

Mr. Warburton opened his cold blue eyes very wide and assumed an expression of great surprise.

180   "Are you out of your mind? Are you so ignorant that you do not know that that is not the way to speak to your official superior?"

"Oh go to hell. The prisoners are my pidgin and you've got no right to interfere. You mind your business and I'll mind mine. I want to know what the devil you mean by making a damned fool of me. Every one in the place will know that you've countermanded my order."

Mr. Warburton kept very cool.

"You had no power to give the order you did. I countermanded it because it was harsh and tyrannical. Believe me, I have not made half such a damned fool of you as you have made of yourself."

"You disliked me from the first moment I came here. You've done everything you could to make the place impossible for me because I wouldn't lick your boots for you. You got your knife into me because I wouldn't flatter you."

185   Cooper, spluttering with rage, was nearing dangerous ground, and Mr. Warburton's eyes grew on a sudden colder and more piercing.

"You are wrong. I thought you were a cad, but I was perfectly satisfied with the way you did your work."

"You snob. You damned snob. You thought me a cad because I hadn't been to Eton. Oh, they told me in K.S. what to expect. Why, don't you know that you're the laughing-stock of the whole country? I could hardly help bursting into a roar of laughter when you told your celebrated story about the Prince of Wales. My God, how they shouted at the club when they told it. By God, I'd rather be the cad I am than the snob you are."

He got Mr. Warburton on the raw.

"If you don't get out of my house this minute I shall knock you down," he cried.

190   The other came a little closer to him and put his face in his.

"Touch me, touch me," he said. "By God, I'd like to see you hit me. Do you want me to say it again? Snob. Snob."

Cooper was three inches taller than Mr. Warburton, a strong, muscular young man. Mr. Warburton was fat and fifty-four. His clenched fist shot out. Cooper caught him by the arm and pushed him back.

"Don't be a damned fool. Remember I'm not a gentleman, I know how to use my hands."

He gave a sort of hoot, and, grinning all over his pale, sharp face jumped down the verandah steps. Mr. Warburton, his heart in his anger pounding against his ribs, sank exhausted into a chair. His body tingled as though he had prickly heat. For one horrible moment he thought he was going to cry. But suddenly he was conscious that his head-boy was on the verandah and instinctively regained control of himself. The boy came forward and filled him a glass of whisky and soda. Without a word Mr. Warburton took it and drank it to the dregs.

"What do you want to say to me?" asked Mr. Warburton, trying to force a smile on to his strained lips.

"Tuan, the assistant tuan is a bad man. Abas wishes again to leave him."

"Let him wait a little. I shall write to Kuala Solor and ask that Tuan Cooper should go elsewhere."

"Tuan Cooper is not good with the Malays."

"Leave me."

The boy silently withdrew. Mr. Warburton was left alone with his thoughts. He saw the club at Kuala Solor, the men sitting round the table in the window in their flannels, when the night had driven them in from golf and tennis, drinking whiskies and gin pahits and laughing when they told the celebrated story of the Prince of Wales and himself at Marienbad. He was hot with shame and misery. A snob! They all thought him a snob. And he had always thought them very good fellows, he had always been gentleman enough to let it make no difference to him that they were of very second-rate position. He hated them now. But his hatred for them was nothing compared with his hatred for Cooper. And if it had come to blows Cooper could have thrashed him. Tears of mortification ran down his red, fat face. He sat there for a couple of hours smoking cigarette after cigarette, and he wished he were dead.

At last the boy came back and asked him if he would dress for dinner. Of course! He always dressed for dinner. He rose wearily from his chair and put on his stiff shirt and the high collar. He sat down at the prettily decorated table and was waited on as usual by the two boys while two others waved their great fans. Over there in the bungalow, two hundred yards away, Cooper was eating a filthy meal clad only in a sarong and a baju. His feet were bare and while he ate he probably read a detective story. After dinner Mr. Warburton sat down to write a letter. The Sultan was away, but he wrote, privately and confidentially, to his representative. Cooper did his work very well, he said, but the fact was that he couldn't get on with him. They were getting dreadfully on each other's nerves and he would look upon it as a very great favour if Cooper could be transferred to another post.

He despatched the letter next morning by special messenger. The answer came a fortnight later with the month's mail. It was a private note and ran as follows:

My dear Warburton:

I do not want to answer your letter officially and so I am writing you a few lines myself. Of course if you insist I will put the matter up to the Sultan, but I think you would be much wiser to drop it. I know Cooper is a rough diamond, but he is capable, and he had a pretty thin time in the war, and I think he should be given every chance. I think you are a little too much inclined to attach importance to a man's social position. You must remember that times have changed. Of course it's a very good thing for a man to be a gentleman, but it's better that he should be competent and hardworking. I think if you'll exercise a little tolerance you'll get on very well with Cooper.

Yours very sincerely
Richard Temple

The letter dropped from Mr. Warburton's hand. It was easy to read between the lines. Dick Temple, whom he had known for twenty years, Dick Temple, who came from quite a good country family, thought him a snob and for that reason had no patience with his request. Mr. Warburton felt on a sudden discouraged with life. The world of which he was a part had passed away, and the future belonged to a meaner generation. Cooper represented it and Cooper he hated with all his heart. He stretched out his hand to fill his glass and at the gesture his head-boy stepped forward.

"I didn't know you were there."

The boy picked up the official letter. Ah, that was why he was waiting.

210   "Does Tuan Cooper go, Tuan?"

"No."

"There will be a misfortune."

For a moment the words conveyed nothing to his lassitude. But only for a moment. He sat up in his chair and looked at the boy. He was all attention.

"What do you mean by that?"

215   "Tuan Cooper is not behaving rightly with Abas."

Mr. Warburton shrugged his shoulders. How should a man like Cooper know how to treat servants? Mr. Warburton knew the type: he would be grossly familiar with them at one moment and rude and inconsiderate the next.

"Let Abas go back to his family."

"Tuan Cooper holds back his wages so that he may not run away. He has paid him nothing for three months. I tell him to be patient. But he is angry, he will not listen to reason. If the tuan continues to use him ill there will be a misfortune."

"You were right to tell me."

220   The fool! Did he know so little of the Malays as to think he could safely injure them? It would serve him damned well right if he got a kris in his back. A kris. Mr. Warburton's heart seemed on a sudden to miss a beat. He had only to let things take their course and one fine day he would be rid of Cooper. He smiled faintly as the phrase, a masterly inactivity, crossed his mind. And now his heart beat a little quicker, for he saw the man he hated lying on his face in a pathway of the jungle with a knife in his back. A fit end for the cad and the bully, Mr. Warburton sighed. It was his duty to warn him and of course he must do it. He wrote a brief and formal note to Cooper asking him to come to the Fort at once.

In ten minutes Cooper stood before him. They had not spoken to one another since the day when Mr. Warburton had nearly struck him. He did not now ask him to sit down.

"Did you wish to see me?" Cooper asked.

He was untidy and none too clean. His face and hands were covered with little red blotches where mosquitoes had bitten him and he had scratched himself till the blood came. His long, thin face bore a sullen look.

"I understand that you are again having trouble with your servants. Abas, my head-boy's nephew, complains that you have held back his wages for three months. I consider it a most arbitrary proceeding. The lad wishes to leave you, and I certainly do not blame him. I must insist on your paying what is due to him."

225   "I don't choose that he should leave me. I am holding back his wages as a pledge of his good behaviour."

"You do not know the Malay character. The Malays are very sensitive to injury and ridicule. They are passionate and revengeful. It is my duty to warn you that if you drive this boy beyond a certain point you run a great risk."

Cooper gave a contemptuous chuckle.

"What do you think he'll do?"

"I think he'll kill you."

230   "Why should you mind?"

"Oh, I wouldn't," replied Mr. Warburton, with a faint laugh. "I should bear it with the utmost fortitude. But I feel the official obligation to give you a proper warning."

"Do you think I'm afraid of a damned nigger?"

"It's a matter of entire indifference to me."

"Well, let me tell you this, I know how to take care of myself; that boy Abas is a dirty, thieving rascal, and if he tries any monkey tricks on me, by God, I'll wring his bloody neck."

"That was all I wished to say to you," said Mr. Warburton. "Good evening."

235

Mr. Warburton gave him a little nod of dismissal. Cooper flushed, did not for a moment know what to say or do, turned on his heel and stumbled out of the room. Mr. Warburton watched him go with an icy smile on his lips. He had done his duty. But what would he have thought had he known that when Cooper got back to his bungalow, so silent and cheerless, he threw himself down on his bed and in his bitter loneliness on a sudden lost all control of himself? Painful sobs tore his chest and heavy tears rolled down his thin cheeks.

After this Mr. Warburton seldom saw Cooper, and never spoke to him. He read his Times every morning, did his work at the office, took his exercise, dressed for dinner, dined and sat by the river smoking his cheroot. If by chance he ran across Cooper he cut him dead. Each, though never for a moment unconscious of the propinquity, acted as though the other did not exist. Time did nothing to assuage their animosity. They watched one another's actions and each knew what the other did. Though Mr. Warburton had been a keen shot in his youth, with age he had acquired a distaste for killing the wild things of the jungle, but on Sundays and holidays Cooper went out with his gun: if he got something it was a triumph over Mr. Warburton; if not, Mr. Warburton shrugged his shoulders and chuckled. These counterjumpers trying to be sportsmen! Christmas was a bad time for both of them: they ate their dinners alone, each in his own quarters, and they got deliberately drunk. They were the only white men within two hundred miles and they lived within shouting distance of each other. At the beginning of the year Cooper went down with fever, and when Mr. Warburton caught sight of him again he was surprised to see how thin he had grown. He looked ill and worn. The solitude, so much more unnatural because it was due to no necessity, was getting on his nerves. It was getting on Mr. Warburton's too, and often he could not sleep at night. He lay awake brooding. Cooper was drinking heavily and surely the breaking point was near; but in his dealings with the natives he took care to do nothing that might expose him to his chief's rebuke. They fought a grim and silent battle with one another. It was a test of endurance. The months passed, and neither gave sign of weakening. They were like men dwelling in regions of eternal night, and their souls were oppressed with the knowledge that never would the day dawn for them. It looked as though their lives would continue for ever in this dull and hideous monotony of hatred.

And when at last the inevitable happened it came upon Mr. Warburton with all the shock of the unexpected. Cooper accused the boy Abas of stealing some of his clothes, and when the boy denied the theft took him by the scruff of the neck and kicked him down the steps of the bungalow. The boy demanded his wages, and Cooper flung at his head every word of abuse he knew. If he saw him in the compound in an hour he would hand him over to the police. Next morning the boy waylaid him outside the Fort when he was walking over to his office, and again demanded his wages. Cooper struck him the face with his clenched fist. The boy fell to the ground and got up with blood streaming from his nose.

Cooper walked on and set about his work. But he could not attend it. The blow had calmed his irritation, and he knew that he had gone too far. He was worried. He felt ill, miserable and discouraged. In the adjoining office sat Mr. Warburton, and his impulse was to go and tell him what he had done; he made a movement in his chair, but he knew with what icy scorn he would listen to the story. He could see his patronizing smile. For a moment he had an uneasy fear of what Abas might do. Warburton had warned him all right. He sighed. What a fool he had been! But he shrugged his shoulders impatiently. He did not care; a fat lot he had to live for. It was all Warburton's fault; if he hadn't put his back up nothing like this would have happened. Warburton had made life a hell for him from the start. The snob. But they were all like that: it was because he was a Colonial. It was a damned shame that he had never got his commission in the war; he was as good as any one else. They were a lot of dirty snobs. He was damned if he was going to knuckle under now. Of course Warburton would hear of what had happened; the old devil knew everything. He wasn't afraid. He wasn't afraid of any Malay in Borneo, and Warburton could go to blazes.

240   He was right in thinking that Mr. Warburton would know what had happened. His head-boy told him when he went in to tiffin.

"Where is your nephew now?"

"I do not know, Tuan. He has gone."

Mr. Warburton remained silent. After luncheon as a rule he slept a little, but to-day he found himself very wide awake. His eyes involuntarily sought the bungalow where Cooper was now resting.

The idiot! Hesitation for a little was in Mr. Warburton's mind. Did the man know in what peril he was? He supposed he ought to send for him. But each time he had tried to reason with Cooper, Cooper had insulted him. Anger, furious anger welled up suddenly in Mr. Warburton's heart, so that the veins on his temples stood out and he clenched his fists. The cad had had his warning. Now let him take what was coming to him. It was no business of his and if anything happened it was not his fault. But perhaps they would wish in Kuala Solor that they had taken his advice and transferred Cooper to another station.

245   He was strangely restless that night. After dinner he walked up and down the verandah. When the boy went away to his own quarters, Mr. Warburton asked him whether anything had been seen of Abas.

"No, Tuan, I think maybe he has gone to the village of his mother's brother."

Mr. Warburton gave him a sharp glance, but the boy was looking down and their eyes did not meet. Mr. Warburton went down to the river and sat in his arbour. But peace was denied him. The river flowed ominously silent. It was like a great serpent gliding with sluggish movement towards the sea. And the trees of the jungle over the water were heavy with a breathless menace. No bird sang. No breeze ruffled the leaves of the cassias. All around him it seemed as though something waited.

He walked across the garden to the road. He had Cooper's bungalow in full view from there. There was a light in his sitting-room and across the road floated the sound of ragtime. Cooper was playing his gramophone. Mr. Warburton shuddered; he had never got over his instinctive dislike of that instrument. But for that he would have gone over and spoken to Cooper. He turned and went back to his own house. He read late into the night, and at last he slept. But he did not sleep very long, he had terrible dreams, and he seemed to be awakened by a cry. Of course that was a dream too, for no cry—from the bungalow for instance—could be heard in his room. He lay awake till dawn. Then he heard hurried steps and the sound of voices, his head-boy burst suddenly into the room without his fez, and Mr. Warburton's heart stood still.

"Tuan, Tuan."

Mr. Warburton jumped out of bed.   250

"I'll come at once."

He put on his slippers; and in his sarong and pyjama-jacket walked across his compound and into Cooper's. Cooper was lying in bed, with his mouth open, and a kris sticking in his heart. He had been killed in his sleep. Mr. Warburton started, but not because he had not expected to see just such a sight, he started because he felt in himself a sudden glow of exultation. A great burden had been lifted from his shoulders.

Cooper was quite cold. Mr. Warburton took the kris out of the wound, it had been thrust in with such force that he had to use an effort to get it out, and looked at it. He recognized it. It was a kris that a dealer had offered him some weeks before and which he knew Cooper had bought.

"Where is Abas?" he asked sternly.

"Abas is at the village of his mother's brother."   255

The sergeant of the native police was standing at the foot of the bed.

"Take two men and go to the village and arrest him."

Mr. Warburton did what was immediately necessary. With set face he gave orders. His words were short and peremptory. Then he went back to the Fort. He shaved and had his bath, dressed and went into the dining-room. By the side of his plate The Times in its wrapper lay waiting for him. He helped himself to some fruit. The head-boy poured out his tea while the second handed him a dish of eggs. Mr. Warburton ate with a good appetite. The head-boy waited.

"What is it?" asked Mr. Warburton.

"Tuan, Abas, my nephew, was in the house of his mother's brother all night. It can   260
be proved. His uncle will swear that he did not leave the kampong."

Mr. Warburton turned upon him with a frown.

"Tuan Cooper was killed by Abas. You know it as well as I know. Justice must be done."

"Tuan, you would not hang him?"

Mr. Warburton hesitated an instant, and though his voice remained set and stern a change came into his eyes. It was a flicker which the Malay was quick to notice and across his own eyes flashed an answering look of understanding.

"The provocation was very great. Abas will be sentenced to a term of imprison-   265
ment." There was a pause while Mr. Warburton helped himself to marmalade. "When he has served a part of his sentence in prison I will take him into this house as a boy. You can train him in his duties. I have no doubt that in the house of Tuan Cooper he got into bad habits."

"Shall Abas give himself up, Tuan?"

"It would be wise of him."

The boy withdrew. Mr. Warburton took his Times and neatly slit the wrapper. He loved to unfold the heavy, rustling pages. The morning, so fresh and cool, was delicious and for a moment his eyes wandered out over his garden with a friendly glance. A great weight had been lifted from his mind. He turned to the columns in which were announced the births, deaths, and marriages. That was what he always looked at first. A name he knew caught his attention. Lady Ormskirk had had a son at last. By George, how pleased the old dowager must be! He would write her a note of congratulation by the next mail.

Abas would make a very good house-boy.

That fool Cooper!   [1926]   270

Questions

1. How is the theme of the story shaped by the jungle setting?
2. From what point of view is the story told? Is it maintained consistently throughout the story?
3. In telling the story, does Maugham betray a bias toward either Mr. Warburton or Cooper?
4. Are Mr. Warburton's motives altruistic in warning Cooper that he may be in danger?
5. How does the author use specific details to characterize Mr. Warburton and Cooper by class and generation?

Responses

1. Compare the imperialist immigrant experience to its opposite as shown in Kureishi's "My Son the Fanatic." Or compare the conflict of cultures as shown in Maugham's story and Achebe's "Dead Men's Path" and Ahmad's "A Bicycle."
2. Approaching the story from a sociological/Marxist perspective, what does the story say about money and class?

GUY DE MAUPASSANT

Guy de Maupassant (1850–1893) was born near Dieppe, France. After his parents separated, he was raised by his mother, a highly cultivated woman. He saw service in the French Army during the Franco-Prussian War and then entered upon a long literary apprenticeship to Gustave Flaubert. Maupassant's first published story, "Boule de Suif" (Ball of Fat), won him instant fame, and over the next decade he wrote about three hundred stories, six novels, plays, poems, and articles. In 1889 his mind began to be affected by syphilis, and, after an unsuccessful suicide attempt, he was committed to an asylum in Paris, where he died insane. Selections of his short stories are available in many editions.

The Necklace

She was one of those pretty and charming women born, as though fate had blundered, into a family of junior clerks. She had no dowry, no expectations, no means of getting known, understood, loved, wedded by a man of wealth and distinction; and she let herself be married off to a minor clerk in the Ministry of Education.

Her tastes were simple because she had never been able to afford otherwise, but she was as unhappy as though she had married beneath her; for women have neither caste nor class—their beauty, grace, and charm serving them for birth or family. Their natural delicacy, their instinctive elegance, their nimbleness of wit are their only mark of rank, and put the working-class woman on a level with the highest lady in the land.

She suffered endlessly, feeling herself born for every delicacy and luxury. She suffered from the poorness of her house, from its mean walls, worn chairs, and ugly curtains. All those things, of which other women of her class would not even have been aware, tormented and insulted her. The sight of the little Breton girl who came to do the work in her little house aroused heart-broken regrets and hopeless dreams in her mind. She imagined silent antechambers, heavy with Oriental tapestries, lit by torches in lofty bronze candelabras, with two tall footmen in knee breeches asleep in large armchairs, overcome by the heavy warmth of the heating stove. She imagined vast drawing rooms hung with antique skills, exquisite pieces of furniture supporting priceless ornaments, and small, charming, perfumed rooms, created just for little parties of intimate friends, men who were famous and sought after, whose homage roused every other woman's envious longings.

When she sat down for dinner at the round table covered with a tablecloth that had not been changed in three days, opposite her husband, who uncovered the stew pot, exclaiming delightedly: "Ah, good old *pot-au-feu!*° What could be better?" she imagined delicate meals, gleaming silver, wall hangings with people of long ago and strange birds in enchanted forests; she imagined delicate food served in marvelous dishes, whispered gallantries, listened to with an inscrutable smile as one trifled with the pink flesh of a trout or the wings of a quail.

5   She had no fine clothes, no jewels, nothing. And these were the only things she loved; she felt that she was made for them. She had longed so eagerly to charm, to be desired, to be wildly attractive and sought after.

She had a rich friend, a former convent schoolmate whom she would no longer visit, because she suffered so keenly when she returned home. She would weep all day with grief, regret, despair, and misery.

One evening her husband came home with an exultant air, holding a large envelope in his hand.

"Here's something for you," he said.

Swiftly she tore open the envelope and drew out a printed card on which were these words:

10   The Minister of Education and Madame Georges Ramponneau would be honored by the presence of Monsieur and Madame Loisel at the Ministry on Monday evening, January eighth.

Instead of being delighted, as her husband had expected, she flung the invitation petulantly across the table, muttering:

"What do you want me to do with this?"

"Why, darling, I thought you'd be pleased. You never go out, and this is a special occasion. I went to great pains to get an invitation. Everyone wants one; it's very select, and very few are given to the clerks. You'll see all the really big people there."

She eyed him furiously and said impatiently:

15   "And what do you suppose I am to wear to such an affair?"

He had not thought about it; he stammered:

"Why, the gown you wear to the theater. It looks very nice to me. . . ."

He stopped, stupefied and utterly at a loss when he saw that his wife was beginning to cry. Two large tears ran slowly down from the corners of her eyes towards the corners of her mouth.

"What's the matter? What's the matter?" he faltered.

20   With a violent effort she composed herself and replied in a calm voice, wiping her wet cheeks:

"Nothing. Only I have no evening gown and so I can't go to this ball. Give your invitation to one of your friends whose wife will be turned out better than I shall."

He was heart-broken.

"Look here, Mathilde," he persisted. "How much would it cost for a suitable gown, one you could use on other occasions as well, something very simple?"

She thought for several seconds, figuring amounts and also wondering how large a sum she could ask for without obtaining an immediate refusal and a horrified outcry from the frugal clerk.

25   At last she replied with some hesitation:

°*pot-au-feu*: A stew of beef and vegetables.

"I don't know exactly, but I think I could do it on four hundred francs."

He blanched, for this was exactly the amount he had been saving up for a gun, intending to do a little shooting the following summer on the plain of Nanterre, with some friends who went lark-shooting there on Sundays.

Nevertheless he said: "Very well. I'll give you four hundred francs. But try and get a really nice gown with the money."

The day of the ball drew near, and Madame Loisel seemed sad, uneasy, and anxious. Her gown was ready, however. One evening her husband said to her:

"What's the matter with you? You've been very strange the last three days."   30

"I'm utterly miserable because I have no jewels to wear, not a single stone," she replied. "I shall look like a nobody. I would almost rather not go to the ball."

"You can wear a corsage," he said. "Flowers are in style right now. For ten francs you can get two or three gorgeous roses."

She was not convinced.

"No . . . there's nothing so humiliating as looking poor in the company of rich women."

"How stupid you are!" exclaimed her husband. "Go and see Madame Forestier and   35
ask her to lend you some jewels. You know her quite well enough for that."

She uttered a cry of delight.

"That's true. I never thought of it."

Next day she went to see her friend and told her her trouble.

Madame Forestier went to her mirrored wardrobe, took out a large jewelry box, brought it to Madame Loisel, opened it, and said:

"Choose, my dear."   40

First she saw some bracelets, then a pearl necklace, then a Venetian cross in gold and gems of exquisite workmanship. She tried on the jewels before the mirror, hesitating, unable to make up her mind which to take, which to leave. She kept asking:

"Haven't you anything else?"

"Yes. Look for yourself. I don't know what you would like best."

Suddenly she discovered, in a black satin case, a superb diamond necklace; her heart began to beat with longing. Her hands trembled as she picked it up. She fastened it around her throat over her high-necked dress, and stood there in ecstasy at sight of herself.

Then, hesitating, she asked in anguish: 45

"Could you lend me this, just this alone?"

"Yes, of course."

She flung herself on her friend's neck, kissed her fervently, and took off with her treasure.

The day of the ball arrived. Madame Loisel was a success. She was the prettiest woman there, elegant, graceful, smiling, and beside herself with joy. All the men stared at her, asked her name, and tried to be introduced. All the administrative officers were eager to waltz with her. The Minister noticed her.

She danced ecstatically, drunk with pleasure, unmindful of all else in the triumph   50
of her beauty, in the pride of her success, in a cloud of happiness made up of this universal homage and admiration, of the desires she had aroused, of the completeness of a victory so dear to her feminine heart.

She left about four o'clock in the morning. Since midnight her husband had been dozing in an empty waiting room, with three other men whose wives were having a good time.

He threw over her shoulders the cloak he had brought for her to wear on the way home, a modest everyday garment whose poverty contrasted with her elegant ball-gown. She was conscious of this and was anxious to hurry away so as not to be noticed by the other women who were donning their costly furs.

Loisel restrained her.

"Wait a bit. You'll catch cold outside. I'll go find a cab."

But she did not listen to him and rapidly descended the staircase. When they were in the street they could not find a cab; they began to look for one, shouting at the drivers they saw passing in the distance.

They walked down towards the Seine, desperate and shivering. At last they found on the quay one of those old night-running carriages that appear in Paris only after dark, as though they were ashamed to show their shabbiness in the daylight.

It brought them to their door in the Rue des Martyrs, and sadly they walked up to their apartment. It was the end, for her. As for him, he was thinking that he must be at the office at ten o'clock.

She took off the cloak wrapped around her shoulders in front of the mirror so as to see herself once more in all her glory. But suddenly she uttered a cry. The necklace was no longer around her throat!

"What's the matter with you?" asked her husband, already half undressed.

She turned towards him in the utmost distress.

"I . . . I . . . I've lost Madame Forestier's necklace. . . ."

He started with astonishment.

"What! . . . Impossible!"

They searched in the folds of her gown, in the folds of the cloak, in the pockets, everywhere. They could not find it.

"Are you sure you still had it on when you left the ball?" he asked.

"Yes, I touched it in the vestibule at the Ministry."

"But if you had lost it in the street, we should have heard it fall. It must be in the cab."

"Yes. Probably. Did you take the number?"

"No. You didn't notice it, did you?"

"No."

They stared at one another, dumbfounded. At last Loisel put on his clothes again.

"I'll go over all the ground we walked," he said, "and see if I can't find it."

And he went out. She remained in her ballgown, lacking the strength to go to bed, huddled on a chair, unable to think or act.

Her husband returned about seven. He had found nothing.

He went to the police station, to the newspaper office to offer a reward, to the cab companies—everywhere that a ray of hope impelled him.

She waited all day long, in the same state of bewilderment at this fearful catastrophe.

Loisel came home at night, his face lined and pale; he had discovered nothing.

"You must write to your friend," he said, "and tell her that you've broken the clasp of her necklace and are getting it mended. That will give us time to look around."

She wrote at his dictation.

By the end of a week they had lost all hope.

Loisel, who had aged five years, declared:

"We must see about replacing the diamonds."

Next day they took the box that had held the necklace and went to the jeweler whose name was inside. He consulted his books.

"It was not I who sold this necklace, Madame; I must have merely supplied the box."

Then they went from jeweler to jeweler, searching for another necklace like the first, consulting their memories, both ill with remorse and anguish.

In a shop at the Palais-Royal they found a diamond necklace that seemed to them exactly like the one they were looking for. It cost forty thousand francs. They could have it for thirty-six thousand.

They begged the jeweler not to sell it for three days, and they got him to agree to take it back for thirty-four thousand francs if the first one was recovered before the end of February.

Loisel had eighteen thousand francs that were left to him by his father. He intended to borrow the rest.

And borrow he did—a thousand from one man, five hundred from another, five louis° here, three louis there. He wrote promissary notes, entered into ruinous agreements, did business with usurers and the whole tribe of money-lenders. He mortgaged all the remaining years of his life, risked his signature without knowing if he could honor it and, appalled at the agonizing face of the future, at the black misery about to befall him, at the prospect of every possible physical privation and moral torture, he went to get the new necklace and put down on the jeweler's counter thirty-six thousand francs.

When Madame Loisel returned the necklace, Madame Forestier said to her in a chilly voice:

"You ought to have brought it back sooner; I might have needed it."

She did not open the box, as her friend had feared. If she had noticed the substitution, what would she have thought? What would she have said? Would she not have taken her for a thief?

Madame Loisel came to know the horrible life of abject poverty. From the very first she played her part heroically. That dreadful debt had to be paid. She would pay it. They dismissed the maid; they moved to a garret apartment.

She came to know what heavy housework meant, the hateful duties of the kitchen. She washed the dishes, wearing out her pink nails on greasy pots and pans. She washed the dirty linen, the shirts, and dish towels, and hung them out on a line to dry; every morning she took the garbage pail down to the street and carried up water, stopping on each landing to catch her breath. And, clad like a poor woman, she went to the fruiterer, to the grocer, to the butcher, a basket on her arm, haggling, insulting, fighting over every measly cent.

Every month notes had to be paid off, others renewed, time gained.

Her husband worked in the evenings at putting straight a merchant's accounts, and often at night he did copying at five cents a page.

And this life lasted for ten years.

At the end of ten years everything was paid off, everything, the finance charges and the compound interest on the loans.

Madame Loisel looked old now. She had become like all the other strong, hard, coarse women of poor households. Her hair was unkempt, her skirts were awry, her

---

°*louis*: A gold coin worth twenty francs.

hands were red. She spoke in a shrill voice and slopped water all over the floor when she scrubbed it. But sometimes, when her husband was at the office, she sat down by the window and thought of that evening long ago, of the ball at which she had been so beautiful and so much admired.

100   What would have happened if she had never lost that necklace? Who knows? Who knows? How strange life is, how fickle! How little it takes to ruin you or to save you!

One Sunday, as she was taking a walk along the Champs-Élysées to relax from the toils of the week, she caught sight suddenly of a woman who was walking with a child. It was Madame Forestier, still young, still beautiful, still attractive.

Madame Loisel felt moved. Should she speak to her? Yes, certainly. And now that she had paid, she would tell her all. Why not?

She went up to her.

"Good morning, Jeanne."

105   The other did not recognize her, and was surprised at being so familiarly addressed by a poor woman.

"But . . . Madame . . ." she stammered. "I don't know . . . you must be making a mistake."

"No . . . I am Mathilde Loisel."

Her friend uttered a cry.

"Oh! . . . my poor Mathilde, how you have changed! . . ."

110   "Yes, I've had some hard times since I saw you last; and many sorrows . . . and all because of you."

"Because of me! . . . How was that?"

"You remember the diamond necklace you lent me for the ball at the Ministry?"

"Yes. Well?"

"Well, I lost it."

115   "How so? Why, you brought it back."

"I brought you another one just like it. And for the last ten years we have been paying for it. You realize it wasn't easy for us; we had no money. . . . Well, it's paid for at last, and I'm glad indeed."

Madame Forestier had halted.

"You say you bought a diamond necklace to replace mine?"

"Yes. You didn't notice it? They were very much alike."

120   And she smiled with a proud and innocent joy.

Madame Forestier, deeply moved, took her two hands.

"Oh, my poor Mathilde! But mine was imitation. It was worth at the very most five hundred francs! . . ."   [1884]

Questions

1. Is the ending a complete surprise, or has it been in part foreshadowed?
2. Is the characterization of Madame Loisel consistent?
3. Why does Madame Loisel choose to tell Madame Forestier the truth?
4. What is the role of Madame Loisel's husband?
5. How is Madame Loisel's life symbolized by the necklace?

HERMAN MELVILLE

Herman Melville (1819–1891) was born in New York City. He was thrown on his own resources by the death of his father in 1832, and having tried life as a farmer, a bank messenger, and a schoolteacher, Melville went to sea. The fruits of that experience were incorporated into six novels: *Typee* (1846), *Omoo* (1847), *Mardi* (1849), *Redburn* (1849), *White-Jacket* (1850), and, finally, his masterpiece, *Moby Dick* (1851). These works, unfortunately, followed a declining curve of commercial success, and with the total failure of his next book, *Pierre* (1852), Melville turned to the writing of short stories. Although they did not revive his literary fortunes, posterity has treated them kindly, and some discerning readers consider them to be his best work. Melville spent his last years as an obscure customs inspector, and he owes his high critical standing to a revival that began in the 1920s and continues to this day.

Bartleby the Scrivener

A Story of Wall Street

I am a rather elderly man. The nature of my avocations, for the last thirty years, has brought me into more than ordinary contact with what would seem an interesting and somewhat singular set of men, of whom, as yet, nothing, that I know of, has ever been written—I mean, the law-copyists, or scriveners.° I have known very many of them, professionally and privately, and, if I pleased, could relate divers histories, at which good-natured gentlemen might smile, and sentimental souls might weep. But I waive the biographies of all other scriveners, for a few passages in the life of Bartleby, who was a scrivener, the strangest I ever saw, or heard of. While, of other law-copyists, I might write the complete life, of Bartleby nothing of that sort can be done. I believe that no materials exist for a full and satisfactory biography of this man. It is an irreparable loss to literature. Bartleby was one of those beings of whom nothing is ascertainable,

---

°*scriveners*: Clerks who copy legal documents by hand.

except from the original sources, and, in his case, those are very small. What my own astonished eyes saw of Bartleby, *that* is all I know of him, except, indeed, one vague report, which will appear in the sequel.

Ere introducing the scrivener, as he first appeared to me, it is fit I make some mention of myself, my *employés*, my business, my chambers, and general surroundings; because some such description is indispensable to an adequate understanding of the chief character about to be presented. Imprimis:° I am a man who, from his youth upwards, has been filled with a profound conviction that the easiest way of life is the best. Hence, though I belong to a profession proverbially energetic and nervous, even to turbulence, at times, yet nothing of that sort have I ever suffered to invade my peace. I am one of those unambitious lawyers who never addresses a jury, or in any way draws down public applause; but, in the cool tranquillity of a snug retreat, do a snug business among rich men's bonds, and mortgages, and title-deeds. All who know me, consider me an eminently *safe* man. The late John Jacob Astor, a personage little given to poetic enthusiasm, had no hesitation in pronouncing my first grand point to be prudence; my next, method. I do not speak it in vanity, but simply record the fact, that I was not unemployed in my profession by the late John Jacob Astor; a name which, I admit, I love to repeat; for it hath a rounded and orbicular sound to it, and rings like unto bullion. I will freely add, that I was not insensible to the late John Jacob Astor's good opinion.

Some time prior to the period at which this little history begins, my avocations had been largely increased. The good old office, now extinct in the State of New York, of a Master in Chancery, had been conferred upon me. It was not a very arduous office, but very pleasantly remunerative. I seldom lose my temper; much more seldom indulge in dangerous indignation at wrongs and outrages; but, I must be permitted to be rash here, and declare that I consider the sudden and violent abrogation of the office of Master of Chancery, by the new Constitution, as a——premature act; inasmuch as I had counted upon a life-lease of the profits, whereas I only received those of a few short years. But this is by the way.

My chambers were up stairs, at No.——Wall Street. At one end, they looked upon the white wall of the interior of a spacious sky-light shaft, penetrating the building from top to bottom.

5   This view might have been considered rather tame than otherwise, deficient in what landscape painters call "life." But, if so, the view from the other end of my chambers offered, at least, a contrast, if nothing more. In that direction, my windows commanded an unobstructed view of a lofty brick wall, black by age and everlasting shade; which wall required no spyglass to bring out its lurking beauties, but, for the benefit of all near-sighted spectators, was pushed up to within ten feet of my window panes. Owing to the great height of the surrounding buildings, and my chambers being on the second floor, the interval between this wall and mine not a little resembled a huge square cistern.

At the period just preceding the advent of Bartleby, I had two persons as copyists in my employment, and a promising lad as an office-boy. First, Turkey; second, Nippers; third, Ginger Nut. These may seem names, the like of which are not usually found in the Directory. In truth, they were nicknames, mutually conferred upon each other by my three clerks, and were deemed expressive of their respective persons or

---

°*Imprimis:* "In the first place"; legal jargon.

characters. Turkey was a short, pursy Englishman, of about my own age—that is, somewhere not far from sixty. In the morning, one might say, his face was of a fine florid hue, but after twelve o'clock, meridian—his dinner hour—it blazed like a grate full of Christmas coals; and continued blazing—but, as it were, with a gradual wane—till six o'clock P.M., or thereabouts; after which, I saw no more of the proprietor of the face, which, gaining its meridian with the sun, seemed to set with it, to rise, culminate, and decline the following day, with the like regularity and undiminished glory. There are many singular coincidences I have known in the course of my life, not the least among which was the fact, that, exactly when Turkey displayed his fullest beams from his red and radiant countenance, just then, too, at that critical moment, began the daily period when I considered his business capacities as seriously disturbed for the remainder of the twenty-four hours. Not that he was absolutely idle, or averse to business, then; far from it. The difficulty was, he was apt to be altogether too energetic. There was a strange, inflamed, flurried, flighty recklessness of activity about him. He would be incautious in dipping his pen into his inkstand. All his blots upon my documents were dropped there after twelve o'clock meridian. Indeed, not only would he be reckless, and sadly given to making blots in the afternoon, but, some days, he went further, and was rather noisy. At such times, too, his face flamed with augmented blazonry, as if cannel coal had been heaped on anthracite. He made an unpleasant racket with his chair; spilled his sandbox; in mending his pens, impatiently split them all to pieces, and threw them on the floor in a sudden passion; stood up, and leaned over his table, boxing his papers about in a most indecorous manner, very sad to behold in an elderly man like him. Nevertheless, as he was in many ways a most valuable person to me, and all the time before twelve o'clock meridian, was the quickest, steadiest creature, too, accomplishing a great deal of work in a style not easily to be matched—for these reasons, I was willing to overlook his eccentricities, though, indeed, occasionally, I remonstrated with him. I did this very gently, however, because, though the civilest, nay, the blandest and most reverential of men in the morning, yet, in the afternoon, he was disposed, upon provocation, to be slightly rash with his tongue—in fact, insolent. Now, valuing his morning services as I did, and resolved not to lose them—yet, at the same time, made uncomfortable by his inflamed ways after twelve o'clock—and being a man of peace, unwilling by my admonitions to call forth unseemly retorts from him, I took upon me, one Saturday noon (he was always worse on Saturdays) to hint to him, very kindly, that, perhaps, now that he was growing old, it might be well to abridge his labors; in short, he need not come to my chambers after twelve o'clock, but, dinner over, had best go home to his lodgings, and rest himself till tea-time. But no; he insisted upon his afternoon devotions. His countenance became intolerably fervid, as he oratorically assured me—gesticulating with a long ruler at the other end of the room—that if his services in the morning were useful, how indispensable, then, in the afternoon?

"With submission, sir," said Turkey, on this occasion, "I consider myself your right-hand man. In the morning I but marshal and deploy my columns; but in the afternoon I put myself at their head, and gallantly charge the fore, thus"—and he made a violent thrust with the ruler.

"But the blots, Turkey," intimated I.

"True; but, with submission, sir, behold these hairs! I am getting old. Surely, sir, a blot or two of a warm afternoon is not to be severely urged against gray hairs. Old age—even if it blot the page—is honorable. With submission, sir, we *both* are getting old."

10   This appeal to my fellow-feeling was hardly to be resisted. At all events, I saw that go he would not. So, I made up my mind to let him stay, resolving, nevertheless, to see to it that, during the afternoon, he had to do with my less important papers.

Nippers, the second on my list, was a whiskered, sallow, and upon the whole, rather piratical-looking young man, of about five and twenty. I always deemed him the victim of two evil powers—ambition and indigestion. The ambition was evinced by a certain impatience of the duties of a mere copyist, an unwarrantable usurpation of strictly professional affairs, such as the original drawing up of legal documents. The indigestion seemed betokened in an occasional nervous testiness and grinning irritability, causing the teeth to audibly grind together over mistakes committed in copying; unnecessary maledictions, hissed, rather than spoken, in the heat of business; and especially by a continual discontent with the height of the table where he worked. Though of a very ingenious, mechanical turn, Nippers could never get this table to suit him. He put chips under it, blocks of various sorts, bits of pasteboard, and at last went so far as to attempt an exquisite adjustment, by final pieces of folded blotting-paper. But no invention would answer. If, for the sake of easing his back, he brought the table lid at a sharp angle well up towards his chin, and wrote there like a man using the steep roof of a Dutch house for his desk, then he declared that it stopped the circulation in his arms. If now he lowered the table to his waistbands, and stooped over it in writing, then there was a sore aching in his back. In short, the truth of the matter was, Nippers knew not what he wanted. Or, if he wanted anything, it was to be rid of a Scrivener's table altogether. Among the manifestations of his diseased ambition was a fondness he had for receiving visits from certain ambiguous-looking fellows in seedy coats, whom he called his clients. Indeed, I was aware that not only was he, at times, considerable of a ward-politician, but he occasionally did a little business at the Justices' courts, and was not unknown on the steps of the Tombs.° I have good reason to believe, however, that one individual who called upon him at my chambers, and who, with a grand air, he insisted was his client, was no other than a dun, and the alleged title-deed, a bill. But, with all his failings, and the annoyances he caused me, Nippers, like his compatriot Turkey, was a very useful man to me; wrote a neat, swift hand; and, when he chose, was not deficient in a gentlemanly sort of deportment. Added to this, he always dressed in a gentlemanly sort of way; and so, incidentally, reflected credit upon my chambers. Whereas, with respect to Turkey, I had much ado to keep him from being a reproach to me. His clothes were apt to look oily, and smell of eating-houses. He wore his pantaloons very loose and baggy in summer. His coats were execrable; his hat not to be handled. But while the hat was a thing of indifference to me, inasmuch as his natural civility and deference, as a dependent Englishman, always led him to doff it the moment he entered the room, yet his coat was another matter. Concerning his coats, I reasoned with him; but with no effect. The truth was, I suppose, that a man with so small an income could not afford to sport such a lustrous face and a lustrous coat at one and the same time. As Nippers once observed, Turkey's money went chiefly for red ink. One winter day, I presented Turkey with a highly respectable-looking coat of my own—a padded gray coat, of a most comfortable warmth, and which buttoned straight up from the knee to the neck. I thought Turkey would appreciate the favor, and abate his rashness and obstreperousness of afternoons. But no; I verily believe that buttoning himself up in so

---

°*Tombs*: Halls of Justice.

downy and blanket-like a coat had a pernicious effect upon him—upon the same principle that too much oats are bad for horses. In fact, precisely as a rash, restive horse is said to feel his oats, so Turkey felt his coat. It made him insolent. He was a man whom prosperity harmed.

Though, concerning the self-indulgent habits of Turkey, I had my own private surmises, yet, touching Nippers, I was well persuaded that, whatever might be his faults in other respects, he was, at least, a temperate young man. But, indeed, nature herself seemed to have been his vintner, and, at his birth, charged him so thoroughly with an irritable, brandy-like disposition, that all subsequent potations were needless. When I consider how, amid the stillness of my chambers, Nippers would sometimes impatiently rise from his seat, and stopping over his table, spread his arms wide apart, seize the whole desk, and move it, and jerk it, with a grim, grinding motion on the floor, as if the table were a perverse voluntary agent and vexing him, I plainly perceive that, for Nippers, brandy-and-water were altogether superfluous.

It was fortunate for me that, owing to its peculiar cause—indigestion—the irritability and consequent nervousness of Nippers were mainly observable in the morning, while in the afternoon he was comparatively mild. So that, Turkey's paroxysms only coming on about twelve o'clock, I never had to do with their eccentricities at one time. Their fits relieved each other, like guards. When Nippers's was on, Turkey's was off; and *vice versa.* This was a good natural arrangement, under the circumstances.

Ginger Nut, the third on my list, was a lad, some twelve years old. His father was a car-man, ambitious of seeing his son on the bench instead of a cart, before he died. So he sent him to my office, as student at law, errand-boy, cleaner and sweeper, at the rate of one dollar a week. He had a little desk to himself; but he did not use it much. Upon inspection, the drawer exhibited a great array of shells of various sorts of nuts. Indeed, to this quick-witted youth, the whole noble science of the law was contained in a nutshell. Not the least among the employments of Ginger Nut, as well as one which he discharged with the most alacrity, was his duty as cake and apple purveyor for Turkey and Nippers. Copying law-papers being proverbially a dry, husky sort of business, my two scriveners were fain to moisten their mouths very often with Spitzenbergs,° to be had at the numerous stalls nigh the Custom House and Post Office. Also, they sent Ginger Nut very frequently for that peculiar cake—small, flat, round, and very spicy—after which he had been named by them. Of a cold morning, when business was but dull, Turkey would gobble up scores of these cakes, as if they were mere wafers—indeed, they sell them at the rate of six or eight for a penny—the scrape of his pen blending with the crunching of the crisp particles in his mouth. Rashest of all the fiery afternoon blunders and flurried rashnesses of Turkey, was his once moistening a ginger-cake between his lips, and clapping it on to a mortgage, for a seal. I came within an ace of dismissing him then. But he mollified me by making an oriental bow, and saying—

"With submission, sir, it was generous of me to find you in stationery on my own account."

15

Now my original business—that of a conveyancer and title hunter, and drawer-up of recondite documents of all sorts—was considerably increased by receiving the master's office. There was now great work for scriveners. Not only must I push the clerks already with me, but I must have additional help.

°*Spitzenbergs*: Apples.

In answer to my advertisement, a motionless young man one morning stood upon my office threshold, the door being open, for it was summer. I can see that figure now— pallidly neat, pitiably respectable, incurably forlorn! It was Bartleby.

After a few words touching his qualifications, I engaged him, glad to have among my corps of copyists a man of so singularly sedate an aspect, which I thought might operate beneficially upon the flighty temper of Turkey, and the fiery one of Nippers.

I should have stated before that ground glass folding-doors divided my premises into two parts, one of which was occupied by my scriveners, the other by myself. According to my humor, I threw open these doors, or closed them. I resolved to assign Bartleby a corner by the folding-doors, but on my side of them, so as to have this quiet man within easy call, in case any trifling thing was to be done. I placed his desk close up to a small side-window in that part of the room, a window which originally had afforded a lateral view of certain grimy backyards and bricks, but which, owing to subsequent erections, commanded at present no view at all, though it gave some light. Within three feet of the panes was a wall, and the light came down from far above, between two lofty buildings, as from a very small opening in a dome. Still further to a satisfactory arrangement, I procured a high green folding screen, which might entirely isolate Bartleby from my sight, though not remove him from my voice. And thus, in a manner, privacy and society were conjoined.

20   At first, Bartleby did an extraordinary quantity of writing. As if long famishing for something to copy, he seemed to gorge himself on my documents. There was no pause for digestion. He ran a day and night line, copying by sun-light and by candle-light. I should have been quite delighted with his application, had he been cheerfully industrious. But he wrote on silently, palely, mechanically.

It is, of course, an indispensable part of a scrivener's business to verify the accuracy of his copy, word by word. Where there are two or more scriveners in an office, they assist each other in this examination, one reading from the copy, the other holding the original. It is a very dull, wearisome, and lethargic affair. I can readily imagine that, to some sanguine temperaments, it would be altogether intolerable. For example, I cannot credit that the mettlesome poet, Byron, would have contentedly sat down with Bartleby to examine a law document of, say five hundred pages, closely written in a crimpy hand.

Now and then, in the haste of business, it had been my habit to assist in comparing some brief document myself, calling Turkey or Nippers for this purpose. One object I had, in placing Bartleby so handy to me behind the screen, was to avail myself of his services on such trivial occasions. It was on the third day, I think, of his being with me, and before any necessity had arisen for having his own writing examined, that, being much hurried to complete a small affair I had in hand, I abruptly called to Bartleby. In my haste and natural expectancy of instant compliance, I sat with my head bent over the original on my desk, and my right hand sideways, and somewhat nervously extended with the copy, so that, immediately upon emerging from his retreat, Bartleby might snatch it and proceed to business without the least delay.

In this very attitude did I sit when I called to him, rapidly stating what it was I wanted him to do—namely, to examine a small paper with me. Imagine my surprise, nay, my consternation, when, without moving from his privacy, Bartleby, in a singularly mild, firm voice, replied, "I would prefer not to."

I sat awhile in perfect silence, rallying my stunned faculties. Immediately it occurred to me that my ears had deceived me, or Bartleby had entirely misunderstood my meaning. I repeated my request in the clearest tone I could assume; but in quite as clear a one came the previous reply, "I would prefer not to."

"Prefer not to," echoed I, rising in high excitement, and crossing the room with a   25
stride. "What do you mean? Are you moon-struck? I want you to help me compare this
sheet here—take it," and I thrust it towards him.

"I would prefer not to," said he.

I looked at him steadfastly. His face was leanly composed; his gray eye dimly calm.
Not a wrinkle of agitation rippled him. Had there been the least uneasiness, anger,
impatience, or impertinence in his manner; in other words, had there been any thing
ordinarily human about him, doubtless I should have violently dismissed him from the
premises. But as it was, I should have as soon thought of turning my pale plaster-of-
paris bust of Cicero out of doors. I stood gazing at him awhile, as he went on with his
own writing, and then reseated myself at my desk. This is very strange, thought I.
What had one best do? But my business hurried me. I concluded to forget the matter
for the present, reserving it for my future leisure. So calling Nippers from the other
room, the paper was speedily examined.

A few days after this, Bartleby concluded four lengthy documents, being quadru-
plicates of a week's testimony taken before me in my High Court of Chancery. It became necessary to examine them. It was an important suit, and great accuracy was
imperative. Having all things arranged, I called Turkey, Nippers, and Ginger Nut from
the next room, meaning to place the four copies in the hands of my four clerks, while
I should read from the original. Accordingly, Turkey, Nippers, and Ginger Nut had
taken their seats in a row, each with his document in his hand, when I called to Bartleby to join this interesting group.

"Bartleby! quick, I am waiting."

I heard a slow scrape of his chair legs on the uncarpeted floor, and soon he ap-   30
peared standing at the entrance of his hermitage.

"What is wanted?" said he, mildly.

"The copies, the copies," said I, hurriedly. "We are going to examine them. There—
" and I held towards him the fourth quadruplicate.

"I would prefer not to," he said, and gently disappeared behind the screen.

For a few moments I was turned into a pillar of salt,° standing at the head of my seated column of clerks. Recovering myself, I advanced towards the screen, and demanded
the reason for such extraordinary conduct.

"*Why* do you refuse?"   35

"I would prefer not to."

With any other man I should have flown outright into a dreadful passion, scorned
all further words, and thrust him ignominiously from my presence. But there was
something about Bartleby that not only strangely disarmed me, but in a wonderful
manner, touched and disconcerted me. I began to reason with him.

"These are your own copies we are about to examine. It is labor saving to you, because one examination will answer for your four papers. It is common usage. Every
copyist is bound to help examine his copy. Is it not so? Will you not speak? Answer!"

"I prefer not to," he replied in a flutelike tone. It seemed to me that, while I had been
addressing him, he carefully revolved every statement that I made; fully comprehended the meaning; could not gainsay the irresistible conclusion; but, at the same
time, some paramount consideration prevailed with him to reply as he did.

"You are decided, then, not to comply with my request—a request made according   40
to common usage and common sense?"

°*pillar of salt*: See Genesis 19:26.

He briefly gave me to understand, that on that point my judgment was sound. Yes: his decision was irreversible.

It is not seldom the case that, when a man is browbeaten in some unprecedented and violently unreasonable way, he begins to stagger in his own plainest faith. He begins, as it were, vaguely to surmise that, wonderful as it may be, all the justice and all the reason is on the other side. Accordingly, if any disinterested persons are present, he turns to them for some reinforcement of his own faltering mind.

"Turkey," said I, "what do you think of this? Am I not right?"

"With submission, sir," said Turkey, in his blandest tone, "I think that you are."

45   "Nippers," said I, "what do *you* think of it?"

"I think I should kick him out of the office."

(The reader, of nice perceptions, will here perceive that, it being morning, Turkey's answer is couched in polite and tranquil terms, but Nippers replies in ill-tempered ones. Or, to repeat a previous sentence, Nippers's ugly mood was on duty, and Turkey's off.)

"Ginger Nut," said I, willing to enlist the smallest suffrage in my behalf, "what do *you* think of it?"

"I think, sir, he's a little *luny*," replied Ginger Nut, with a grin.

50   "You hear what they say," said I, turning towards the screen, "come forth and do your duty."

But he vouchsafed no reply. I pondered a moment in sore perplexity. But once more business hurried me. I determined again to postpone the consideration of this dilemma to my future leisure. With a little trouble we made out to examine the papers without Bartleby, though at every page or two Turkey deferentially dropped his opinion, that this proceeding was quite out of the common; while Nippers, twitching in his chair with a dyspeptic nervousness, ground out, between his set teeth, occasional hissing maledictions against the stubborn oaf behind the screen. And for his (Nippers's) part, this was the first and the last time he would do another man's business without pay.

Meanwhile Bartleby sat in his hermitage, oblivious to everything but his own peculiar business there.

Some days passed, the scrivener being employed upon another lengthy work. His late remarkable conduct led me to regard his ways narrowly. I observed that he never went to dinner; indeed, that he never went anywhere. As yet I had never, of my personal knowledge, known him to be outside of my office. He was a perpetual sentry in the corner. At about eleven o'clock though, in the morning, I noticed that Ginger Nut would advance toward the opening in Bartleby's screen, as if silently beckoned thither by a gesture invisible to me where I sat. The boy would then leave the office, jingling a few pence, and reappear with a handful of ginger-nuts, which he delivered in the hermitage, receiving two of the cakes for his trouble.

He lives, then, on ginger-nuts, thought I; never eats a dinner, properly speaking; he must be a vegetarian, then; but no; he never eats even vegetables; he eats nothing but ginger-nuts. My mind then ran on in reveries concerning the probable effects upon the human constitution of living entirely on ginger-nuts. Ginger-nuts are so called, because they contain ginger as one of their peculiar constituents, and the final flavoring one. Now, what was ginger? A hot, spicy thing. Was Bartleby hot and spicy? Not at all. Ginger, then, had no effect upon Bartleby. Probably he preferred it should have none.

55   Nothing so aggravates an earnest person as a passive resistance. If the individual so resisted be of a not inhumane temper, and the resisting one perfectly harmless in his

passitivity, then, in the better moods of the former, he will endeavor charitably to con-
strue to his imagination what proves impossible to be solved by his judgment. Even
so, for the most part, I regarded Bartleby and his ways. Poor fellow! thought I, he
means no mischief; it is plain he intends no insolence; his aspect sufficiently evinces
that his eccentricities are involuntary. He is useful to me. I can get along with him. If
I turn him away, the chances are he will fall in with some less-indulgent employer,
and then he will be rudely treated, and perhaps driven forth miserably to starve. Yes.
Here I can cheaply purchase a delicious self-approval. To befriend Bartleby; to humor
him in his strange willfulness, will cost me little or nothing, while I lay up in my soul
what will eventually prove a sweet morsel for my conscience. But this mood was not
invariable with me. The passiveness of Bartleby sometimes irritated me. I felt strangely goaded on to encounter him in new opposition—to elicit some angry spark from him
answerable to my own. But, indeed, I might as well have essayed to strike fire with my
knuckles against a bit of Windsor soap. But one afternoon the evil impulse in me mastered me, and the following little scene ensued:

"Bartleby," said I, "when those papers are all copied, I will compare them with
you."

"I would prefer not to."

"How? Surely you do not mean to persist in that mulish vagary?"

No answer.

I threw open the folding-doors near by, and, turning upon Turkey and Nippers,   60
exclaimed:

"Bartleby a second time says, he won't examine his papers. What do you think of
it, Turkey?"

It was afternoon, be it remembered. Turkey sat glowing like a brass boiler; his bald
head steaming; his hands reeling among his blotted papers.

"Think of it?" roared Turkey; "I think I'll just step behind his screen, and black his
eyes for him!"

So saying, Turkey rose to his feet and threw his arms into a pugilistic position. He
was hurrying away to make good his promise, when I detained him, alarmed at the
effect of incautiously rousing Turkey's combativeness after dinner.

"Sit down, Turkey," said I, "and hear what Nippers has to say. What do you think   65
of it, Nippers? Would I not be justified in immediately dismissing Bartleby?"

"Excuse me, that is for you to decide, sir. I think his conduct quite unusual, and, indeed, unjust, as regards Turkey and myself. But it may only be a passing whim."

"Ah," exclaimed I, "you have strangely changed your mind, then—you speak very
gently of him now."

"All beer," cried Turkey: "gentleness is effects of beer—Nippers and I dined together to-day. You see how gentle I am, sir. Shall I go and black his eyes?"

"You refer to Bartleby, I suppose. No, not to-day, Turkey," I replied; "pray, put up
your fists."

I closed the doors, and again advanced towards Bartleby. I felt additional incen-   70
tives tempting me to my fate. I burned to be rebelled against again. I remembered that
Bartleby never left the office.

"Bartleby," said I, "Ginger Nut is away; just step around to the Post Office, won't
you? (it was but a three minutes' walk), and see if there is anything for me."

"I would prefer not to."

"You *will* not?"

"I *prefer* not."

75   I staggered to my desk, and sat there in a deep study. My blind inveteracy returned. Was there any other thing in which I could procure myself to be ignominiously repulsed by this lean, penniless wight?—my hired clerk? What added thing is there, perfectly reasonable, that he will be sure to refuse to do? "Bartleby!"

No answer.

"Bartleby," in a louder tone.

No answer.

"Bartleby," I roared.

80   Like a very ghost, agreeably to the laws of magical invocation, at the third summons, he appeared at the entrance of his hermitage.

"Go the next room, and tell Nippers to come to me."

"I prefer not to," he respectfully and slowly said and mildly disappeared.

"Very good, Bartleby," said I, in a quiet sort of serenely-severe, self-possessed tone, intimating the unalterable purpose of some terrible retribution very close at hand. At the moment I half intended something of the kind. But upon the whole, as it was drawing towards my dinner-hour, I thought it best to put on my hat and walk home for the day, suffering much from perplexity and distress of mind.

Shall I acknowledge it? The conclusion of this whole business was, that it soon became a fixed fact of my chambers, that a pale young scrivener, by the name of Bartleby, had a desk there; that he copied for me at the usual rate of four cents a folio (one hundred words); but he was permanently exempt from examining the work done by him, that duty being transferred to Turkey and Nippers, out of compliment, doubtless, to their superior acuteness; moreover, said Bartleby was never, on any account, to be dispatched on the most trivial errand of any sort; and that even if entreated to take upon him such a matter, it was generally understood that he would "prefer not to"—in other words, he would refuse point blank.

85   As days passed on, I became considerably reconciled to Bartleby. His steadiness, his freedom from all dissipation, his incessant industry (except when he chose to throw himself into a standing revery behind his screen), his great stillness, his unalterableness of demeanor under all circumstances, made him a valuable acquisition. One prime thing was this—*he was always there*—first in the morning, continually through the day, and the last at night. I had a singular confidence in his honesty. I felt my most precious papers perfectly safe in his hands. Sometimes, to be sure, I could not, for the very soul of me, avoid falling into sudden spasmodic passions with him. For it was exceeding difficult to bear in mind all the time those strange peculiarities, privileges, and unheard of exemptions, forming the tacit stipulations on Bartleby's part under which he remained in my office. Now and then, in the eagerness of dispatching pressing business, I would inadvertently summon Bartleby, in a short, rapid tone, to put his finger, say, on the incipient tie of a bit of red tape with which I was about compressing some papers. Of course, from behind the screen the usual answer, "I prefer not to," was sure to come; and then, how could a human creature, with the common infirmities of our nature, refrain from bitterly exclaiming upon such perverseness—such unreasonableness. However, every added repulse of this sort which I received only tended to lessen the probability of my repeating the inadvertence.

Here it must be said, that according to the custom of most legal gentlemen occupying chambers in densely-populated law buildings, there were several keys to my door. One was kept by a woman residing in the attic, which person weekly scrubbed and daily swept and dusted my apartments. Another was kept by Turkey for convenience sake. The third I sometimes carried in my own pocket. The fourth I knew not who had.

Now, one Sunday morning I happened to go to Trinity Church, to hear a celebrated preacher, and finding myself rather early on the ground I thought I would walk around to my chambers for a while. Luckily I had my key with me; but upon applying it to the lock, I found it resisted by something inserted from the inside. Quite surprised, I called out; when to my consternation a key was turned from within; and thrusting his lean visage at me, and holding the door ajar, the apparition of Bartleby appeared, in his shirt sleeves, and otherwise in a strangely tattered *déshabillé*, saying quietly that he was sorry, but he was deeply engaged just then, and—preferred not admitting me at present. In a brief word or two, he moreover added, that perhaps I had better walk around the block two or three times, and by that time he would probably have concluded his affairs.

Now, the utterly unsurmised appearance of Bartleby, tenanting my law-chambers of a Sunday morning, with his cadaverously gentlemanly *nonchalance*, yet withal firm and self-possessed, had such a strange effect upon me, that incontinently I slunk away from my own door, and did as desired. But not without sundry twinges of impotent rebellion against the mild effrontery of this unaccountable scrivener. Indeed, it was his wonderful mildness chiefly, which not only disarmed me, but unmanned me as it were. For I consider that one, for the time, is somehow unmanned when he tranquilly permits his hired clerk to dictate to him, and order him away from his own premises. Furthermore, I was full of uneasiness as to what Bartleby could possibly be doing in my office in his shirt sleeves, and in an otherwise dismantled condition of a Sunday morning. Was anything amiss going on? Nay, that was out of the question. It was not to be thought of for a moment that Bartleby was an immoral person. But what could he be doing there?—copying? Nay again, whatever might be his eccentricities, Bartleby was an eminently decorous person. He would be the last man to sit down to his desk in any state approaching to nudity. Besides, it was Sunday; and there was something about Bartleby that forbade the supposition that he would by any secular occupation violate the proprieties of the day.

Nevertheless, my mind was not pacified; and full of a restless curiosity, at last I returned to the door. Without hindrance I inserted my key, opened it, and entered. Bartleby was not to be seen. I looked round anxiously, peeped behind his screen; but it was very plain that he was gone. Upon more closely examining the place, I surmised that for an indefinite period Bartleby must have eaten, dressed, and slept in my office, and that, too, without plate, mirror, or bed. The cushioned seat of a rickety old sofa in one corner bore the faint impress of a lean, reclining form. Rolled away under his desk, I found a blanket; under the empty grate, a blacking box and brush; on a chair, a tin basin, with soap and a ragged towel; in a newspaper a few crumbs of ginger-nuts and a morsel of cheese. Yes, thought I, it is evident enough that Bartleby has been making his home here, keeping bachelor's hall all by himself. Immediately then the thought came sweeping across me, what miserable friendlessness and loneliness are here revealed! His poverty is great; but his solitude, how horrible! Think of it. Of a Sunday, Wall Street is deserted as Petra; and every night of every day it is an emptiness. This building, too, which of week-days hums with industry and life, at nightfall echoes with sheer vacancy, and all through Sunday is forlorn. And here Bartleby makes his home; sole spectator of a solitude which he has seen all populous—a sort of innocent and transformed Marius brooding among the ruins of Carthage!

For the first time in my life a feeling of over-powering stinging melancholy seized me. Before, I had never experienced aught but a not unpleasing sadness. The bond of a common humanity now drew me irresistibly to gloom. A fraternal melancholy! for both I and Bartleby were sons of Adam. I remembered the bright silks and sparkling

90

faces I had seen that day, in gala trim, swan-like sailing down the Mississippi of Broadway; and I contrasted them with the pallid copyist, and thought to myself, Ah, happiness courts the light, so we deem the world is gay; but misery hides aloof, so we deem that misery there is none. These sad fancyings—chimeras, doubtless, of a sick and silly brain—led on to other and more special thoughts, concerning the eccentricities of Bartleby. Presentiments of strange discoveries hovered round me. The scrivener's pale form appeared to me laid out, among uncaring strangers, in its shivering winding sheet.

Suddenly I was attracted by Bartleby's closed desk, the key in open sight left in the lock.

I mean no mischief, seek the gratification of no heartless curiosity, thought I; besides, the desk is mine, and its contents, too, so I will make bold to look within. Everything was methodically arranged, the papers smoothly placed. The pigeon holes were deep, and removing the files of documents, I groped into their recesses. Presently I felt something there, and dragged it out. It was an old bandanna handkerchief, heavy and knotted. I opened it, and saw it was a savings bank.

I now recalled all the quiet mysteries which I had noted in the man. I remembered that he never spoke but to answer; that, though at intervals he had considerable time to himself, yet I had never seen him reading—no, not even a newspaper; that for long periods he would stand looking out, at his pale window behind the screen, upon the dead brick wall; I was quite sure he never visited any refectory or eating house; while his pale face clearly indicated that he never drank beer like Turkey, or tea and coffee even, like other men; that he never went anywhere in particular that I could learn; never went out for a walk, unless, indeed, that was the case at present; that he had declined telling who he was, or whence he came, or whether he had any relatives in the world; that though so thin and pale, he never complained of ill health. And more than all, I remember a certain unconscious air of pallid—how shall I call it?—of pallid haughtiness, say, or rather an austere reserve about him, which had positively awed me into my tame compliance with his eccentricities, when I had feared to ask him to do the slightest incidental thing for me, even though I might know, from his long-continued motionlessness, that behind his screen he must be standing in one of those dead-wall reveries of his.

Revolving all these things, and coupling them with the recently discovered fact, that he made my office his constant abiding place and home, and not forgetful of his morbid moodiness; revolving all these things, a prudential feeling began to steal over me. My first emotions had been those of pure melancholy and sincerest pity; but just in proportion as the forlornness of Bartleby grew and grew to my imagination, did that same melancholy merge into fear, that pity into repulsion. So true it is, and so terrible, too, that up to a certain point the thought or sight of misery enlists our best affections; but, in certain special cases, beyond that point it does not. They err who would assert that invariably this is owing to the inherent selfishness of the human heart. It rather proceeds from a certain hopelessness of remedying excessive and organic ill. To a sensitive being, pity is not seldom pain. And when at last it is perceived that such pity cannot lead to effectual succor, common sense bids the soul be rid of it. What I saw that morning persuaded me that the scrivener was the victim of innate and incurable disorder. I might give alms to his body; but his body did not pain him; it was his soul that suffered, and his soul I could not reach.

95   I did not accomplish the purpose of going to Trinity Church that morning. Somehow, the things I had seen disqualified me for the time from churchgoing. I walked homeward, thinking what I would do with Bartleby. Finally, I resolved upon this—I

would put certain calm questions to him the next morning, touching his history, etc., and if he declined to answer them openly and unreservedly (and I supposed he would prefer not), then to give him a twenty dollar bill over and above whatever I might owe him, and tell him his services were no longer required; but that if in any other way I could assist him, I would be happy to do so, especially if he desired to return to his native place, wherever that might be, I would willingly help to defray the expenses. Moreover, if, after reaching home, he found himself at any time in want of aid, a letter from him would be sure of a reply.

The next morning came.

"Bartleby," said I, gently calling to him behind his screen.

No reply.

"Bartleby," said I, in a still gentler tone, "come here; I am not going to ask you to do anything you would prefer not to do—I simply wish to speak to you."

Upon this he noiselessly slid into view. 100

"Will you tell me, Bartleby, where you were born?"

"I would prefer not to."

"Will you tell me *anything* about yourself?"

"I would prefer not to."

"But what reasonable objection can you have to speak to me? I feel friendly towards 105 you."

He did not look at me while I spoke, but kept his glance fixed upon my bust of Cicero, which, as I then sat, was directly behind me, some six inches above my head.

"What is your answer, Bartleby," said I, after waiting a considerable time for a reply, during which his countenance remained immovable, only there was the faintest conceivable tremor of the white attenuated mouth.

"At present I prefer to give no answer," he said, and retired into his hermitage.

It was rather weak in me I confess, but his manner, on this occasion, nettled me. Not only did there seem to lurk in it a certain calm disdain, but his perverseness seemed ungrateful, considering the undeniable good usage and indulgence he had received from me.

Again I sat ruminating what I should do. Mortified as I was at his behaviour, and 110 resolved as I had been to dismiss him when I entered my office, nevertheless I strangely felt something superstitious knocking at my heart, and forbidding me to carry out my purpose, and denouncing me for a villain if I dared to breathe one bitter word against this forlornest of mankind. At last, familiarly drawing my chair behind his screen, I sat down and said: "Bartleby, never mind, then, about revealing your history; but let me entreat you, as a friend, to comply as far as may be with the usages of this office. Say now, you will help to examine papers to-morrow or next day: in short, say now, that in a day or two you will begin to be a little reasonable:— say so, Bartleby."

"At present I would prefer not to be a little reasonable," was his mildly cadaverous reply.

Just then the folding-doors opened, and Nippers approached. He seemed suffering from an unusually bad night's rest, induced by severer indigestion than common. He overheard those final words of Bartleby.

"*Prefer not*, eh?" gritted Nippers—"I'd *prefer* him, if I were you, sir," addressing me—"I'd *prefer* him; I'd give him preferences, the stubborn mule! What is it, sir, pray, that he *prefers* not to do now?"

Bartleby moved not a limb.

"Mr. Nippers," said I, "I'd prefer that you would withdraw for the present." 115

Somehow, of late, I had got into the way of involuntarily using this word "prefer" upon all sorts of not exactly suitable occasions. And I trembled to think that my contact with the scrivener had already and seriously affected me in a mental way. And what further and deeper aberration might it not yet produce? This apprehension had not been without efficacy in determining me to summary measures.

As Nippers, looking very sour and sulky, was departing, Turkey blandly and deferentially approached.

"With submission, sir," said he, "yesterday I was thinking about Bartleby here, and I think that if he would but prefer to take a quart of good ale every day, it would do much towards mending him, and enabling him to assist in examining his papers."

"So you have got the word, too," said I, slightly excited.

120 "With submission, what word, sir," asked Turkey, respectfully crowding himself into the contracted space behind the screen, and by so doing, making me jostle the scrivener. "What word, sir?"

"I would prefer to be left alone here," said Bartleby, as if offended at being mobbed in his privacy.

"*That's* the word, Turkey," said I—"*that's* it."

"Oh, *prefer?* oh yes—queer word. I never use it myself. But, sir, as I was saying, if he would but prefer—"

"Turkey," interrupted I, "you will please withdraw."

125 "Oh certainly, sir, if you prefer that I should."

As he opened the folding-door to retire, Nippers at his desk caught a glimpse of me, and asked whether I would prefer to have a certain paper copied on blue paper or white. He did not in the least roguishly accent the word prefer. It was plain that it involuntarily rolled from his tongue. I thought to myself, surely I must get rid of a demented man, who already has in some degree turned the tongues, if not the heads of myself and clerks. But I thought it prudent not to break the dismission at once.

The next day I noticed that Bartleby did nothing but stand at his window in his dead-wall revery. Upon asking him why he did not write, he said that he had decided upon doing no more writing.

"Why, how now? What next?" exclaimed I, "do no more writing?"

"No more."

130 "And what is the reason?"

"Do you not see the reason for yourself?" he indifferently replied.

I looked steadfastly at him, and perceived that his eyes looked dull and glazed. Instantly it occurred to me, that his unexampled diligence in copying by his dim window for the first few weeks of his stay with me might have temporarily impaired his vision.

I was touched. I said something in condolence with him. I hinted that of course he did wisely in abstaining from writing for a while; and urged him to embrace that opportunity of taking wholesome exercise in the open air. This, however, he did not do. A few days after this, my other clerks being absent, and being in a great hurry to dispatch certain letters by the mail, I thought that, having nothing else earthly to do, Bartleby would surely be less inflexible than usual, and carry these letters to the post-office. But he blankly declined. So, much to my inconvenience, I went myself.

Still added days went by. Whether Bartleby's eyes improved or not, I could not say. To all appearance I thought they did. But when I asked him if they did, he vouchsafed no answer. At all events, he would do no copying. At last, in reply to my urgings, he informed me that he had permanently given up copying.

135 "What!" exclaimed I; "suppose your eyes should get entirely well—better than ever before—would you not copy then?"

"I have given up copying," he answered, and slid aside.

He remained as ever, a fixture in my chamber. Nay—if that were possible—he became still more of a fixture than before. What was to be done? He would do nothing in the office; why should he stay there? In plain fact, he had now become a millstone° to me, not only useless as a necklace, but afflictive to bear. Yet I was sorry for him. I speak less than truth when I say that, on his own account, he occasioned me uneasiness. If he would but have named a single relative or friend, I would instantly have written, and urged their taking the poor fellow away to some convenient retreat. But he seemed alone, absolutely alone in the universe. A bit of wreck in the mid Atlantic. At length, necessities connected with my business tyrannized over all other considerations. Decently as I could, I told Bartleby that in six days time he must unconditionally leave the office. I warned him to take measures, in the interval, for procuring some other abode. I offered to assist him in his endeavor, if he himself would but take the first step towards a removal. "And when you finally quit me, Bartleby," added I, "I shall see that you go not away entirely unprovided. Six days from this hour, remember."

At the expiration of that period, I peeped behind the screen, and lo! Bartleby was there.

I buttoned up my coat, balanced myself; advanced slowly towards him, touched his shoulder, and said, "The time has come; you must quit this place; I am sorry for you; here is money; but you must go."

"I would prefer not" he replied, with his back still towards me.   140

"You *must*."

He remained silent.

Now I had an unbounded confidence in this man's common honesty. He had frequently restored to me sixpences and shillings carelessly dropped upon the floor, for I am apt to be very reckless in such shirt-button affairs. The proceeding, then, which followed will not be deemed extraordinary.

"Bartleby," said I, "I owe you twelve dollars on account; here are thirty-two; the odd twenty are yours—Will you take it?" and I handed the bills towards him.

But he made no motion.   145

"I will leave them here, then," putting them under a weight on the table. Then taking my hat and cane and going to the door, I tranquilly turned and added—"After you have removed your things from these offices, Bartleby, you will of course lock the door—since every one is now gone for the day but you—and if you please, slip your key underneath the mat, so that I may have it in the morning. I shall not see you again; so good-by to you. If, hereafter, in your new place of abode, I can be of any service to you, do not fail to advise me by letter. Good-by, Bartleby, and fare you well."

But he answered not a word; like the last column of some ruined temple, he remained standing mute and solitary in the middle of the otherwise deserted room.

As I walked home in a pensive mood, my vanity got the better of my pity. I could not but highly plume myself on my masterly management in getting rid of Bartleby. Masterly I call it, and such it must appear to any dispassionate thinker. The beauty of my procedure seemed to consist in its perfect quietness. There was no vulgar bullying, no bravado of any sort, no choleric hectoring, and striding to and fro across the apartment, jerking out vehement commands for Bartleby to bundle himself off with his beggarly traps. Nothing of the kind. Without loudly bidding Bartleby depart—as an inferior genius might have done—I *assumed* the ground that depart he must; and upon

---

°*millstone*: See Matthew 18:4–6.

that assumption built all I had to say. The more I thought over my procedure, the more I was charmed with it. Nevertheless, next morning, upon awakening, I had my doubts—I had somehow slept off the fumes of vanity. One of the coolest and wisest hours a man has, is just after he awakes in the morning. My procedure seemed as sagacious as ever—but only in theory. How it would prove in practice—there was the rub. It was truly a beautiful thought to have assumed Bartleby's departure; but, after all, that assumption was simply my own, and none of Bartleby's. The great point was, not whether I had assumed that he would quit me, but whether he would prefer so to do. He was more a man of preferences than assumptions.

After breakfast, I walked down town, arguing the probabilities *pro* and *con*. One moment I thought it would prove a miserable failure, and Bartleby would be found all alive at my office as usual; the next moment it seemed certain that I should find his chair empty. And so I kept veering about. At the corner of Broadway and Canal Street, I saw quite an excited group of people standing in earnest conversation.

150   "I'll take odds he doesn't," said a voice as I passed.

"Doesn't go?—done!" said I; "put up your money."

I was instinctively putting my hand in my pocket to produce my own, when I remembered that this was an election day. The words I had overheard bore no reference to Bartleby, but to the success or non-success of some candidate for the mayoralty. In my intent frame of mind, I had, as it were, imagined that all Broadway shared in my excitement, and were debating the same question with me. I passed on, very thankful that the uproar of the street screened my momentary absent-mindedness.

As I had intended, I was earlier than usual at my office door. I stood listening for a moment. All was still. He must be gone. I tried the knob. The door was locked. Yes, my procedure had worked to a charm; he indeed must be vanished. Yet a certain melancholy mixed with this: I was almost sorry for my brilliant success. I was fumbling under the door mat for the key, which Bartleby was to have left there for me, when accidentally my knee knocked against a panel, producing a summoning sound, and in response a voice came to me from within—"Not yet; I am occupied."

It was Bartleby.

155   I was thunderstruck. For an instant I stood like the man who, pipe in mouth, was killed one cloudless afternoon long ago in Virginia, by summer lightning; at his own warm open window he was killed, and remained leaning out there upon the dreamy afternoon, till some one touched him, when he fell.

"Not gone!" I murmured at last. But again obeying that wondrous ascendancy which the inscrutable scrivener had over me, and from which ascendancy, for all my chafing, I could not completely escape, I slowly went down stairs and out into the street, and while walking round the block, considered what I should next do in this unheard-of perplexity. Turn the man out by an actual thrusting I could not; to drive him away by calling him hard names would not do; calling in the police was an unpleasant idea; and yet, permit him to enjoy his cadaverous triumph over me—this, too, I could not think of. What was to be done? or, if nothing could be done, was there anything further that I could *assume* in the matter? Yes, as before I had prospectively assumed that Bartleby would depart, so now I might retrospectively assume that departed he was. In the legitimate carrying out of this assumption, I might enter my office in a great hurry, and pretending not to see Bartleby at all, walk straight against him as if he were air. Such a proceeding would in a singular degree have the appearance of a home-thrust. It was hardly possible that Bartleby could withstand such an application of the doctrine of assumptions. But upon second thoughts the success of the plan seemed rather dubious. I resolved to argue the matter over with him again.

"Bartleby," said I, entering the office, with a quietly severe expression, "I am seriously displeased. I am pained, Bartleby. I had thought better of you. I had imagined you of such a gentlemanly organization, that in any delicate dilemma a slight hint would suffice—in short, an assumption. But it appears I am deceived. Why," I added, unaffectedly starting, "you have not even touched that money yet," pointing to it, just where I had left it the evening previous.

He answered nothing.

"Will you, or will you not, quit me?" I now demanded in a sudden passion, advancing close to him.

"I would prefer *not* to quit you," he replied, gently emphasizing the *not*.   160

"What earthly right have you to stay here? Do you pay any rent? Do you pay my taxes? Or is this property yours?"

He answered nothing.

"Are you ready to go on and write now? Are your eyes recovered? Could you copy a small paper for me this morning? or help examine a few lines? or step round to the post-office? In a word, will you do anything at all, to give a coloring to your refusal to depart the premises?"

He silently retired into his hermitage.

I was now in such a state of nervous resentment that I thought it but prudent to   165
check myself at present from further demonstrations. Bartleby and I were alone. I remembered the tragedy of the unfortunate Adams and the still more unfortunate Colt° in the solitary office of the latter; and how poor Colt, being dreadfully incensed by Adams, and imprudently permitting himself to get wildly excited, was at unawares hurried into his fatal act—an act which certainly no man could possibly deplore more than the actor himself. Often it had occurred to me in my ponderings upon the subject, that had that altercation taken place in the public street, or at a private residence, it would not have terminated as it did. It was the circumstance of being alone in a solitary office, up stairs, of a building entirely unhallowed by humanizing domestic associations—an uncarpeted office, doubtless, of a dusty, haggard sort of appearance—this it must have been, which greatly helped to enhance the irritable desperation of the hapless Colt.

But when this old Adam of resentment rose in me and tempted me concerning Bartleby, I grappled him and threw him. How? Why, simply by recalling the divine injunction: "A new commandment give I unto you, that ye love one another."° Yes, this it was that saved me. Aside from higher considerations, charity often operates as a vastly wise and prudent principle—a great safeguard to its possessor. Men have committed murder for jealousy's sake, and anger's sake, and hatred's sake, and selfishness' sake, and spiritual pride's sake; but no man that ever I heard of, ever committed a diabolical murder for sweet charity's sake. Mere self-interest, then, if no better motive can be enlisted, should, especially with high-tempered men, prompt all beings to charity and philanthropy. At any rate, upon the occasion in question, I strove to drown my exasperated feelings towards the scrivener by benevolently construing his conduct. Poor fellow, poor fellow! thought I, he don't mean anything; and besides, he has seen hard times, and ought to be indulged.

I endeavored, also, immediately to occupy myself, and at the same time to comfort my despondency. I tried to fancy, that in the course of the morning, at such time as might prove agreeable to him, Bartleby, of his own free accord, would emerge from his

---

°*Colt:* The reference is to a famous nineteenth-century murder trial.
°*". . . love one another.":* See John 15:12–13.

hermitage and take up some decided line of march in the direction of the door. But no. Half-past twelve o'clock came; Turkey began to glow in the face, overturn his ink-stand, and become generally obstreperous; Nippers abated down into quietude and courtesy; Ginger Nut munched his noon apple; and Bartleby remained standing at his window in one of his profoundest dead-wall reveries. Will it be credited? Ought I to acknowledge it? That afternoon I left the office without saying one further word to him.

Some days now passed, during which, at leisure intervals I looked a little into "Edwards on the Will," and "Priestley on Necessity." Under the circumstances, those books induced a salutary feeling. Gradually I slid into the persuasion that these troubles of mine, touching the scrivener, had been all predestinated from eternity, and Bartleby was billeted upon me for some mysterious purpose of an all-wise Providence, which it was not for a mere mortal like me to fathom. Yes, Bartleby, stay there behind your screen, thought I; I shall persecute you no more; you are harmless and noiseless as any of these old chairs; in short, I never feel so private as when I know you are here. At last I see it, I feel it; I penetrate to the predestinated purpose of my life. I am content. Others may have loftier parts to enact; but my mission in this world, Bartleby, is to furnish you with office-room for such period as you may see fit to remain.

I believe that this wise and blessed frame of mind would have continued with me, had it not been for the unsolicited and uncharitable remarks obtruded upon me by my professional friends who visited the rooms. But thus it often is, that the constant friction of illiberal minds wears out at last the best resolves of the more generous. Though to be sure, when I reflected upon it, it was not strange that people entering my office should be struck by the peculiar aspect of the unaccountable Bartleby, and so be tempted to throw out some sinister observations concerning him. Sometimes an attorney, having business with me, and calling at my office, and finding no one but the scrivener there, would undertake to obtain some sort of precise information from him touching my whereabouts; but without heeding his idle talk, Bartleby would remain standing immovable in the middle of the room. So after contemplating him in that position for a time, the attorney would depart, no wiser than he came.

170   Also, when a reference° was going on, and the room full of lawyers and witnesses, and business driving fast, some deeply-occupied legal gentlemen present, seeing Bartleby wholly unemployed, would request him to run round to his (the legal gentleman's) office and fetch some papers for him. Thereupon, Bartleby would tranquilly decline, and yet remain idle as before. Then the lawyer would give a great start, and turn to me. And what could I say? At last I was made aware that all through the circle of my professional acquaintance, a whisper of wonder was running round, having reference to the strange creature I kept at my office. This worried me very much. And as the idea came upon me of his possibly turning out a long-lived man, and keep occupying my chambers, and denying my authority; and perplexing my visitors; and scandalizing my professional reputation; and casting a general gloom over the premises; keeping soul and body together to the last upon his savings (for doubtless he spent but half a dime a day), and in the end perhaps outlive me, and claim possession of my office by right of his perpetual occupancy: as all these dark anticipations crowded upon me more and more, and my friends continually intruded their relentless remarks upon the apparition in my room; a great change was wrought in me. I resolved to gather all my faculties together, and forever rid me of this intolerable incubus.

°*reference*: The act of referring a case to the Court of Chancery.

Ere revolving any complicated project, however, adapted to this end, I first simply suggested to Bartleby the propriety of his permanent departure. In a calm and serious tone, I commended the idea to his careful and mature consideration. But, having taken three days to mediate upon it, he apprised me, that his original determination remained the same; in short, that he still preferred to abide with me.

What shall I do? I now said to myself, buttoning up my coat to the last button. What shall I do? what ought I to do? what does conscience say I *should* do with this man, or, rather, ghost. Rid myself of him, I must; go, he shall. But how? You will not thrust him, the poor, pale, passive mortal—you will not thrust such a helpless creature out of your door? you will not dishonour yourself by such cruelty? No, I will not, I cannot do that. Rather would I let him live and die here, and then mason up his remains in the wall. What, then, will you do? For all your coaxing, he will not budge. Bribes he leaves under your own paper-weight on your table; in short, it is quite plain that he prefers to cling to you.

Then something severe, something unusual must be done, What! surely you will not have him collared by a constable, and commit his innocent pallor to the common jail? And upon what ground could you procure such a thing to be done?—a vagrant, is he? What! he a vagrant, a wanderer, who refuses to budge? It is because he will *not* be a vagrant, then, that you seek to count him *as* a vagrant. This is too absurd. No visible means of support: there I have him. Wrong again: for indubitably he *does* support himself, and that is the only unanswerable proof that any man can show of his possessing the means so to do. No more, then. Since he will not quit me, I must quit him. I will change my offices; I will move elsewhere, and give him fair notice, that if I find him on my new premises I will then proceed against him as a common trespasser.

Acting accordingly, next day I thus addressed him: "I find these chambers too far from the City Hall; the air is unwholesome. In a word, I propose to remove my offices next week, and shall no longer require your services. I tell you this now, in order that you may seek another place."

He made no reply; and nothing more was said. 175

On the appointed day I engaged carts and men, proceeded to my chambers, and, having but little furniture, everything was removed in a few hours. Throughout, the scrivener remained standing behind the screen, which I directed to be removed the last thing. It was withdrawn; and, being folded up like a huge folio, left him the motionless occupant of a naked room. I stood in the entry watching him a moment, while something from within me upbraided me.

I re-entered, with my hand in my pocket—and—and my heart in my mouth.

"Good-by, Bartleby; I am going—good-by, and God some way bless you; and take that," slipping something in his hand. But it dropped upon the floor, and then—strange to say—I tore myself from him whom I had so longed to be rid of.

Established in my new quarters, for a day or two I kept the door locked, and started at every footfall in the passages. When I returned to my rooms, after any little absence, I would pause at the threshold for an instant, and attentively listen, ere applying my key. But these fears were needless. Bartleby never came nigh me.

I thought all was going well, when a perturbed-looking stranger visited me, inquiring whether I was the person who had recently occupied rooms at No.——Wall Street. 180

Full of forebodings, I replied that I was.

"Then, sir," said the stranger, who proved a lawyer, "you are responsible for the man you left there. He refuses to do any copying; he refuses to do anything; he says he prefers not to; and he refuses to quit the premises."

"I am very sorry, sir," said I, with assumed tranquillity, but an inward tremor, "but, really, the man you allude to is nothing to me—he is no relation or apprentice of mine, that you should hold me responsible for him."

"In mercy's name, who is he?"

185   "I certainly cannot inform you. I know nothing about him. Formerly I employed him as a copyist; but he has done nothing for me now for some time past."

"I shall settle him, then—good morning, sir."

Several days passed, and I heard nothing more; and, though I often felt a charitable prompting to call at the place and see poor Bartleby, yet a certain squeamishness, of I know not what, withheld me.

All is over with him, by this time, thought I, at last, when, through another week, no further intelligence reached me. But, coming to my room the day after, I found several persons waiting at my door in a high state of nervous excitement.

"That's the man—here he comes," cried the foremost one, whom I recognized as the lawyer who had previously called upon me alone.

190   "You must take him away, sir, at once," cried a portly person among them, advancing upon me, and whom I knew to be the landlord of No.——Wall Street. "These gentlemen, my tenants, cannot stand it any longer; Mr. B——," pointing to the lawyer, "has turned him out of his room, and he now persists in haunting the building generally, sitting upon the banisters of the stairs by day, and sleeping in the entry by night. Everybody is concerned; clients are leaving the offices; some fears are entertained of a mob; something you must do, and that without delay."

Aghast at this torrent, I fell back before it, and would fain have locked myself in my new quarters. In vain I persisted that Bartleby was nothing to me—no more than to any one else. In vain—I was the last person known to have anything to do with him, and they held me to the terrible account. Fearful, then, of being exposed in the papers (as one person present obscurely threatened), I considered the matter, and, at length, said, that if the lawyer would give me a confidential interview with the scrivener, in his (the lawyer's) own room, I would, that afternoon, strive my best to rid them of the nuisance they complained of.

Going up stairs to my old haunt, there was Bartleby silently sitting upon the banister at the landing.

"What are you doing here, Bartleby?" said I.

"Sitting upon the bannister," he mildly replied.

195   I motioned him into the lawyer's room, who then left us.

"Bartleby," said I, "are you aware that you are the cause of great tribulation to me, by persisting in occupying the entry after being dismissed from the office?"

No answer.

"Now one of two things must take place. Either you must do something, or something must be done to you. Now what sort of business would you like to engage in? Would you like to re-engage in copying for some one?"

"No; I would prefer not to make any change."

200   "Would you like a clerkship in a dry-goods store?"

"There is too much confinement about that. No, I would not like a clerkship; but I am not particular."

"Too much confinement," I cried, "why you keep yourself confined all the time!"

"I would prefer not to take a clerkship," he rejoined, as if to settle that little item at once.

"How would a bar-tender's business suit you? There is no trying of the eyesight in that."

"I would not like it at all; though, as I said before, I am not particular." 205
His unwonted wordiness inspirited me. I returned to the charge.

"Well, then, would you like to travel through the country collecting bills for the merchants? That would improve your health."

"No, I would prefer to be doing something else."

"How, then, would going as a companion to Europe, to entertain some young gentleman with your conversation—how would that suit you?"

"Not at all. It does not strike me that there is anything definite about that. I like to 210
be stationary. But I am not particular."

"Stationary you shall be, then," I cried, now losing all patience, and, for the first time in all my exasperating connection with him, fairly flying into a passion. "If you do not go away from these premises before night, I shall feel bound—indeed, I *am* bound—to—to—to quit the premises myself!" I rather absurdly concluded, knowing not with what possible threat to try to frighten his immobility into compliance. Despairing of all further efforts, I was precipitately leaving him, when a final thought occurred to me—one which had not been wholly unindulged before.

"Bartleby," said I, in the kindest tone I could assume under such exciting circumstances, "will you go home with me now—not to my office, but my dwelling—and remain there till we can conclude upon some convenient arrangement for you at our leisure? Come, let us start now, right away."

"No: at present I would prefer not to make any change at all."

I answered nothing; but, effectually dodging every one by the suddenness and rapidity of my flight, rushed from the building, ran up Wall Street towards Broadway, and, jumping into the first omnibus, was soon removed from pursuit. As soon as tranquillity returned, I distinctly perceived that I had now done all that I possibly could, both in respect to the demands of the landlord and his tenants, and with regard to my own desire and sense of duty, to benefit Bartleby, and shield him from rude persecution. I now strove to be entirely care-free and quiescent; and my conscience justified me in the attempt; though, indeed, it was not so successful as I could have wished. So fearful was I of being again hunted out by the incensed landlord and his exasperated tenants, that, surrendering my business to Nippers, for a few days, I drove about the upper part of the town and through the suburbs, in my rockaway; crossed over to Jersey City and Hoboken, and paid fugitive visits to Manhattanville and Astoria. In fact, I almost lived in my rockaway for the time.

When again I entered my office, lo, a note from the landlord lay upon the desk. I 215
opened it with trembling hands. It informed me that the writer had sent to the police, and had Bartleby removed to the Tombs as a vagrant. Moreover, since I knew more about him than any one else, he wished me to appear at that place, and make a suitable statement of the facts. These tidings had a conflicting effect upon me. At first I was indignant; but, at last, almost approved. The landlord's energetic, summary disposition, had led him to adopt a procedure which I do not think I would have decided upon myself; and yet, as a last resort, under such peculiar circumstances, it seemed the only plan.

As I afterwards learned, the poor scrivener, when told that he must be conducted to the Tombs, offered not the slightest obstacle, but, in his pale, unmoving way, silently acquiesced.

Some of the compassionate and curious bystanders joined the party; and headed by one of the constables arm in arm with Bartleby, the silent procession filed its way through all the noise, and heat, and joy of the roaring thoroughfares at noon.

The same day I received the note, I went to the Tombs, or, to speak more properly, the Halls of Justice. Seeking the right officer, I stated the purpose of my call, and was informed that the individual I described was, indeed, within. I then assured the functionary that Bartleby was a perfectly honest man, and greatly to be compassionated, however unaccountably eccentric. I narrated all I knew, and closed by suggesting the idea of letting him remain in as indulgent confinement as possible, till something less harsh might be done—though, indeed, I hardly knew what. At all events, if nothing else could be decided upon, the alms-house must receive him. I then begged to have an interview.

Being under no disgraceful charge, and quite serene and harmless in all his ways, they had permitted him freely to wander about the prison, and, especially, in the inclosed grass-platted yards thereof. And so I found him there, standing all alone in the quietest of the yards, his face towards a high wall, while all around, from the narrow slits of the jail windows, I thought I saw peering out upon him the eyes of murderers and thieves.

220   "Bartleby!"

"I know you," he said, without looking round—"and I want nothing to say to you."

"It was not I that brought you here, Bartleby," said I, keenly pained at his implied suspicion. "And to you, this should not be so vile a place. Nothing reproachful attaches to you by being here. And see, it is not so sad a place as one might think. Look, there is the sky, and here is the grass."

"I know where I am," he replied, but would say nothing more, and so I left him.

As I entered the corridor again, a broad meat-like man, in an apron, accosted me, and, jerking his thumb over his shoulder, said—"Is that your friend?"

225   "Yes."

"Does he want to starve? If he does, let him live on the prison fare, that's all."

"Who are you?" asked I, not knowing what to make of such an unofficially speaking person in such a place.

"I am the grub-man. Such gentlemen as have friends here, hire me to provide them with something good to eat."

"Is this so?" said I, turning to the turnkey.

230   He said it was.

"Well, then," said I, slipping some silver into the grub-man's hands (for so they called him), "I want you to give particular attention to my friend there; let him have the best dinner you can get. And you must be as polite to him as possible."

"Introduce me, will you?" said the grub-man, looking at me with an expression which seemed to say he was all impatience for an opportunity to give a specimen of his breeding.

Thinking it would prove of benefit to the scrivener, I acquiesced; and, asking the grub-man his name, went up with him to Bartleby.

"Bartleby, this is a friend; you will find him very useful to you."

235   "Your sarvant, sir, your sarvant," said the grub-man, making a low salutation behind his apron. "Hope you find it pleasant here, sir; nice grounds—cool apartments—hope you'll stay with us sometime—try to make it agreeable. What will you have for dinner to-day?"

"I prefer not to dine to-day," said Bartleby, turning away. "It would disagree with me; I am unused to dinners." So saying, he slowly moved to the other side of the inclosure, and took up a position fronting the dead-wall.

"How's this?" said the grub-man, addressing me with a stare of astonishment. "He's odd, ain't he?"

"I think he is a little deranged," said I, sadly.

"Deranged? deranged is it? Well, now, upon my word, I thought that friend of yourn was a gentleman forger; they are always pale and genteel-like, them forgers. I can't help pity 'em—can't help it, sir. Did you know Monroe Edwards?"° he added, touchingly, and paused. Then, laying his hand piteously on my shoulder, sighed, "He died of consumption at Sing-Sing. So you weren't acquainted with Monroe?"

"No, I was never socially acquainted with any forgers. But I cannot stop longer. Look to my friend yonder. You will not lose by it. I will see you again."   240

Some few days after this, I again obtained admission to the Tombs, and went through the corridors in quest of Bartleby; but without finding him.

"I saw him coming from his cell not long ago," said a turnkey, "may be he's gone to loiter in the yards."

So I went in that direction.

"Are you looking for the silent man?" said another turnkey, passing me. "Yonder he lies—sleeping in the yard there. 'Tis not twenty minutes since I saw him lie down."

The yard was entirely quiet. It was not accessible to the common prisoners. The   245
surrounding walls of amazing thickness, kept off all sounds behind them. The Egyptian character of the masonry weighed upon me with its gloom. But a soft imprisoned turf grew under foot. The heart of the eternal pyramids, it seemed, wherein, by some strange magic, through the clefts, grass-seed, dropped by birds, had sprung.

Strangely huddled at the base of the wall, his knees drawn up, and lying on his side, his head touching the cold stones, I saw the wasted Bartleby. But nothing stirred. I paused; then went close up to him; stooped over, and saw that his dim eyes were open; otherwise he seemed profoundly sleeping. Something prompted me to touch him. I felt his hand, when a tingling shiver ran up my arm and down my spine to my feet.

The round face of the grub-man peered upon me now. "His dinner is ready. Won't he dine to-day, either? Or does he live without dining?"

"Lives without dining," said I, and closed the eyes.

"Eh!—He's asleep, ain't he?"

"With kings and counselors,"° murmured I.   250

There would seem little need for proceeding further in this history. Imagination will readily supply the meagre recital of poor Bartleby's interment. But, ere parting with the reader, let me say, that if this little narrative has sufficiently interested him, to awaken curiosity as to who Bartleby was, and what manner of life he led prior to the present narrator's making his acquaintance, I can only reply, that in such curiosity I fully share, but am wholly unable to gratify it. Yet here I hardly know whether I should divulge one little item of rumor, which came to my ear a few months after the scrivener's decease. Upon what basis it rested, I could never ascertain; and hence, how true it is I cannot now tell. But, inasmuch as this vague report had not been without a certain suggestive interest to me, however said, it may prove the same with some others; and so I will briefly mention it. The report was this: that Bartleby had been a subordinate clerk in the Dead Letter Office at Washington, from which he had been suddenly removed by a change in the administration. When I think over this rumor, hardly can I express the emotions which seize me. Dead letters! does it not sound like dead

---

°*Monroe Edwards*: Allusion to the 1842 trial of a notorious swindler.
°*kings and counselors*: See Job 3:11–16.

men? Conceive a man by nature and misfortune prone to a pallid hopelessness, can any business seem more fitted to heighten it than that of continually handling these dead letters, and assorting them for the flames? For by the cart-load they are annually burned. Some times from out of the folded paper the pale clerk takes a ring—the finger it was meant for, perhaps, moulders in the grave; a bank-note sent in swiftest charity—he whom it would relieve, nor eats nor hungers any more; pardon for those who died despairing; hope for those who died unhoping; good tidings for those who died stifled by unrelieved calamities. On errands of life, these letters speed to death.

Ah, Bartleby! Ah, humanity!   [1853]

QUESTIONS

1. Characterize the narrator. How is he affected by his relationship with Bartleby?
2. What is the narrator's tone? How is it appropriate to the theme?
3. What do Nippers, Turkey, and Ginger Nut contribute to the narrative?
4. What is the significance of Bartleby's connection with the Dead Letter Office?
5. Interpret the concluding words, "Ah, Bartleby! Ah, humanity!"

RESPONSES

1. Write an essay answering this question: "Is Bartleby illiterate?"
2. Approach the story from a psychological perspective. What does Bartleby represent as a psychological force?
3. Write an essay arguing that "Bartleby the Scrivener" is an example of The Romance or an example of realist fiction. For example, is the technique of the story closer to Hawthorne's or to Henry James's?

FOCUS ON FILM

1. View the film *Bartleby* (2000). What elements of the print story do the filmmakers highlight in setting the story in a garish office park? How does the portrayal of the characters in the office support this emphasis in theme?
2. *Bartleby* (2000) begins with a shot of Bartleby holding on to and looking through a chain-linked fence. What thematic motif is created with this shot and how is it continued throughout the film?
3. Paul Scofield, who plays the narrator in *Bartleby* (1972), is an actor noted for playing dignified characters (Sir Thomas More in *A Man for All Seasons*, Mark Van Doren in *Quiz Show*). What features of the narrator does he emphasize? Where do we see these features developed in the film? Where do we see them created in the print story?

4. In the print version, Bartleby dies in a city pauper's prison. In setting the story in contemporary times, how do the filmmakers of both versions translate that feature of the narrative?

5. Study the looks and performance of the two actors who play Bartleby in the two films. How are these actors and their portrayals similar? What choices do the actors and the filmmakers make that differentiate them from each other and from Melville's character?

YUKIO MISHIMA

Yukio Mishima (Kimitake Hiraoka) (1925–1970) was born in Tokyo and educated at Tokyo University. He was a man of remarkable gifts and prodigious energy, and his production of plays, poems, stories, and essays brought him early to prominence in the Japanese literary world. At the same time, Mishima was deeply involved in politics. In 1968, dissatisfied with the direction his nation was taking in world affairs, he founded the Shield Society, a group of men dedicated to bringing Japan back to the *samurai* tradition. Discouraged by lack of support, Mishima committed *hara-kiri*. His best-known novels in America are *The Temple of the Golden Pavilion* (1959) and *The Sailor Who Fell from Grace with the Sea* (1965).

Patriotism

1

On the twenty-eighth of February, 1936 (on the third day, that is, of the February 26 Incident), Lieutenant Shinji Takeyama of the Konoe Transport Battalion—profoundly disturbed by the knowledge that his closest colleagues had been with the mutineers from the beginning, and indignant at the imminent prospect of Imperial troops attacking Imperial troops—took his officer's sword and ceremonially disemboweled himself in the eight-mat room of his private residence in the sixth block of Aoba-chō, in Yotsuya Ward. His wife, Reiko, followed him, stabbing herself to death. The lieutenant's farewell note consisted of one sentence: "Long live the Imperial Forces." His wife's, after apologies for her unfilial conduct in thus preceding her parents to the grave, concluded: "The day which, for a soldier's wife, had to come, has come. . . ." The last moments of this heroic and dedicated couple were such as to make the gods themselves weep. The lieutenant's age, it should be noted, was thirty-one, his wife's twenty-three; and it was not half a year since the celebration of their marriage.

2

Those who saw the bride and bridegroom in the commemorative photograph—perhaps no less than those actually present at the lieutenant's wedding—had exclaimed in wonder at the bearing of this handsome couple. The lieutenant, majestic in military uniform, stood protectively beside his bride, his right hand resting upon his sword, his officer's cap held at his left side. His expression was severe, and his dark brows and wide-gazing eyes well conveyed the clear integrity of youth. For the beauty of the bride in her white over-robe no comparisons were adequate. In the eyes, round beneath soft brows, in the slender, finely shaped nose, and in the full lips, there was both sensuousness and refinement. One hand, emerging shyly from a sleeve of the over-robe, held a fan, and the tips of the fingers, clustering delicately, were like the bud of a moonflower.

After the suicide, people would take out this photograph and examine it, and sadly reflect that too often there was a curse on these seemingly flawless unions. Perhaps it was no more than imagination, but looking at the picture after the tragedy it almost seemed as if the two young people before the gold-lacquered screen were gazing, each with equal clarity, at the deaths which lay before them.

Thanks to the good offices of their go-between, Lieutenant General Ozeki, they had been able to set themselves up in a new home at Aoba-chō in Yotsuya. "New home" is perhaps misleading. It was an old three-room rented house backing onto a small garden. As neither the six- nor the four-and-a-half-mat room downstairs was favored by the sun, they used the upstairs eight-mat room as both bedroom and guest room. There was no maid, so Reiko was left alone to guard the house in her husband's absence.

The honeymoon trip was dispensed with on the grounds that these were times of national emergency. The two of them had spent the first night of their marriage at this house. Before going to bed, Shinji, sitting erect on the floor with his sword laid before him, had bestowed upon his wife a soldierly lecture. A woman who had become the wife of a soldier should know and resolutely accept that her husband's death might come at any moment. It could be tomorrow. It could be the day after. But, no matter when it came—he asked—was she steadfast in her resolve to accept it? Reiko rose to her feet, pulled open a drawer of the cabinet, and took out what was the most prized of her new possessions, the dagger her mother had given her. Returning to her place, she laid the dagger without a word on the mat before her, just as her husband had laid his sword. A silent understanding was achieved at once, and the lieutenant never again sought to test his wife's resolve. 5

In the first few months of her marriage Reiko's beauty grew daily more radiant, shining serene like the moon after rain.

As both were possessed of young, vigorous bodies, their relationship was passionate. Nor was this merely a matter of the night. On more than one occasion, returning home straight from maneuvers, and begrudging even the time it took to remove his mud-splashed uniform, the lieutenant had pushed his wife to the floor almost as soon as he had entered the house. Reiko was equally ardent in her response. For a little more or a little less than a month, from the first night of their marriage Reiko knew happiness, and the lieutenant, seeing this, was happy too.

Reiko's body was white and pure, and her swelling breasts conveyed a firm and chaste refusal; but, upon consent, those breasts were lavish with their intimate, welcoming warmth. Even in bed these two were frighteningly and awesomely serious. In the very midst of wild, intoxicating passion, their hearts were sober and serious.

By day the lieutenant would think of his wife in the brief rest periods between training; and all day long, at home, Reiko would recall the image of her husband. Even when apart, however, they had only to look at the wedding photograph for their happiness to be once more confirmed. Reiko felt not the slightest surprise that a man who had been a complete stranger until a few months ago should now have become the sun about which her whole world revolved.

10   All these things had a moral basis, and were in accordance with the Education Rescript's injunction that "husband and wife should be harmonious." Not once did Reiko contradict her husband, nor did the lieutenant ever find reason to scold his wife. On the god shelf below the stairway, alongside the tablet from the Great Ise Shrine, were set photographs of their Imperial Majesties, and regularly every morning, before leaving for duty, the lieutenant would stand with his wife at this hallowed place and together they would bow their heads low. The offering water was renewed each morning, and the sacred sprig of *sasaki*° was always green and fresh. Their lives were lived beneath the solemn protection of the gods and were filled with an intense happiness which set every fiber in their bodies trembling.

3

Although Lord Privy Seal Saitō's house was in their neighborhood, neither of them heard any noise of gunfire on the morning of February 26. It was a bugle, sounding muster in the dim, snowy dawn, when the ten-minute tragedy had already ended, which first disrupted the lieutenant's slumbers. Leaping at once from his bed, and without speaking a word, the lieutenant donned his uniform, buckled on the sword held ready for him by his wife, and hurried swiftly out into the snow-covered streets of the still darkened morning. He did not return until the evening of the twenty-eighth.

Later, from the radio news, Reiko learned the full extent of this sudden eruption of violence. Her life throughout the subsequent two days was lived alone, in complete tranquility and behind locked doors.

In the lieutenant's face, as he hurried silently out into the snowy morning, Reiko had read the determination to die. If her husband did not return, her own decision was made: she too would die. Quietly she attended to the disposition of her personal possessions. She chose her sets of visiting kimonos as keepsakes for friends of her schooldays, and she wrote a name and address on the stiff paper wrapping in which each was folded. Constantly admonished by her husband never to think of the morrow, Reiko had not even kept a diary and was now denied the pleasure of assiduously rereading her record of the happiness of the past few months and consigning each page to the fire as she did so. Ranged across the top of the radio were a small china dog, a rabbit, a squirrel, a bear, a fox. There were also a small vase and a water pitcher. These comprised Reiko's one and only collection. But it would hardly do, she imagined, to give such things as keepsakes. Nor again would it be quite proper to ask specifically for them to be included in the coffin. It seemed to Reiko, as these thoughts passed through her mind, that the expressions on the small animals' faces grew even more lost and forlorn.

°*sasaki*: Ceremonial evergreen plant.

Reiko took the squirrel in her hand and looked at it. And then, her thoughts turning to a realm far beyond these childlike affections, she gazed up into the distance at the great sunlike principle which her husband embodied. She was ready, and happy, to be hurtled along to her destruction in that gleaming sun chariot—but now, for these few moments of solitude, she allowed herself to luxuriate in this innocent attachment to trifles. The time when she had genuinely loved these things, however, was long past. Now she merely loved the memory of having once loved them, and their place in her heart had been filled by more intense passions, by a more frenzied happiness. . . . For Reiko had never, even to herself, thought of those soaring joys of the flesh as a mere pleasure. The February cold, and the icy touch of the china squirrel, had numbed Reiko's slender fingers; yet, even so, in her lower limbs, beneath the ordered repetition of the pattern which crossed the skirt of her trim *meisen* kimono, she could feel now, as she thought of the lieutenant's powerful arms reaching out toward her, a hot moistness of the flesh which defied the snows.

She was not in the least afraid of the death hovering in her mind. Waiting alone   15
at home, Reiko firmly believed that everything her husband was feeling or thinking now, his anguish and distress, was leading her—just as surely as the power in his flesh—to a welcome death. She felt as if her body could melt away with ease and be transformed to the merest fraction of her husband's thought.

Listening to the frequent announcements on the radio, she heard the names of several of her husband's colleagues mentioned among those of the insurgents. This was news of death. She followed the developments closely, wondering anxiously, as the situation became daily more irrevocable, why no Imperial ordinance was sent down, and watching what had at first been taken as a movement to restore the nation's honor come gradually to be branded with the infamous name of mutiny. There was no communication from the regiment. At any moment, it seemed, fighting might commence in the city streets, where the remains of the snow still lay.

Toward sundown on the twenty-eighth Reiko was startled by a furious pounding on the front door. She hurried downstairs. As she pulled with fumbling fingers at the bolt, the shape dimly outlined beyond the frosted-glass panel made no sound, but she knew it was her husband. Reiko had never known the bolt on the sliding door to be so stiff. Still it resisted. The door just would not open.

In a moment, almost before she knew she had succeeded, the lieutenant was standing before her on the cement floor inside the porch, muffled in a khaki greatcoat, his top boots heavy with slush from the street. Closing the door behind him, he returned the bolt once more to its socket. With what significance, Reiko did not understand.

"Welcome home."

Reiko bowed deeply, but her husband made no response. As he had already un-   20
fastened his sword and was about to remove his greatcoat, Reiko moved around behind to assist. The coat, which was cold and damp and had lost the odor of horse dung it normally exuded when exposed to the sun, weighed heavily upon her arm. Draping it across a hanger, and cradling the sword and leather belt in her sleeves, she waited while her husband removed his top boots and then followed behind him into the "living room." This was the six-mat room downstairs.

Seen in the clear light from the lamp, her husband's face, covered with a heavy growth of bristle, was almost unrecognizably wasted and thin. The cheeks were hollow, their luster and resilience gone. In his normal good spirits he would have changed into old clothes as soon as he was home and have pressed her to get supper at once, but now he sat before the table still in his uniform, his head dropping dejectedly. Reiko refrained from asking whether she should prepare the supper.

After an interval the lieutenant spoke.

"I knew nothing. They hadn't asked me to join. Perhaps out of consideration, because I was newly married. Kanō, and Homma too, Yamaguchi."

Reiko recalled momentarily the faces of high-spirited young officers, friends of her husband, who had come to the house occasionally as guests.

25   "There may be an Imperial ordinance sent down tomorrow. They'll be posted as rebels, I imagine. I shall be in command of a unit with orders to attack them. . . . I can't do it. It's impossible to do a thing like that."

He spoke again.

"They've taken me off guard duty, and I have permission to return home for one night. Tomorrow morning, without question, I must leave to join the attack. I can't do it, Reiko."

Reiko sat erect with lowered eyes. She understood clearly that her husband had spoken of his death. The lieutenant was resolved. Each word, being rooted in death, emerged sharply and with powerful significance against this dark, unmovable background. Although the lieutenant was speaking of his dilemma, already there was no room in his mind for vacillation.

However, there was a clarity, like the clarity of a stream fed from melting snows, in the silence which rested between them. Sitting in his own home after the long two-day ordeal, and looking across at the face of his beautiful wife, the lieutenant was for the first time experiencing true peace of mind. For he had at once known, though she said nothing, that his wife divined the resolve which lay beneath his words.

30   "Well, then . . ." The lieutenant's eyes opened wide. Despite his exhaustion they were strong and clear, and now for the first time they looked straight into the eyes of his wife. "Tonight I shall cut my stomach."

Reiko did not flinch.

Her round eyes showed tension, as taut as the clang of a bell.

"I am ready," she said. "I ask permission to accompany you."

The lieutenant felt almost mesmerized by the strength in those eyes. His words flowed swiftly and easily, like the utterances of a man in delirium, and it was beyond his understanding how permission in a matter of such weight could be expressed so casually.

35   "Good. We'll go together. But I want you as a witness, first, for my own suicide. Agreed?"

When this was said a sudden release of abundant happiness welled up in both their hearts. Reiko was deeply affected by the greatness of her husband's trust in her. It was vital for the lieutenant, whatever else might happen, that there should be no irregularity in his death. For that reason there had to be a witness. The fact that he had chosen his wife for this was the first mark of his trust. The second, and even greater mark, was that though he had pledged that they should die together he did not intend to kill his wife first—he had deferred her death to a time when he would no longer be there to verify it. If the lieutenant had been a suspicious husband, he would doubtless, as in the usual suicide pact, have chosen to kill his wife first.

When Reiko said, "I ask permission to accompany you," the lieutenant felt these words to be the final fruit of the education which he had himself given his wife, starting on the first night of their marriage, and which had schooled her, when the moment came, to say what had to be said without a shadow of hesitation. This flattered the lieutenant's opinion of himself as a self-reliant man. He was not so romantic or conceited as to imagine that the words were spoken spontaneously, out of love for her husband.

With happiness welling almost too abundantly in their hearts, they could not help smiling at each other. Reiko felt as if she had returned to her wedding night.

Before her eyes was neither pain nor death. She seemed to see only a free and limitless expanse opening out into vast distances.

"The water is hot. Will you take your bath now?" 40

"Ah yes, of course."

"And supper . . .?"

The words were delivered in such level, domestic tones that the lieutenant came near to thinking, for the fraction of a second, that everything had been a hallucination.

"I don't think we'll need supper. But perhaps you could warm some sake?"

"As you wish." 45

As Reiko rose and took a *tanzen* gown from the cabinet for after the bath, she purposely directed her husband's attention to the open drawer. The lieutenant rose, crossed to the cabinet, and looked inside. From the ordered array of paper wrappings he read, one by one, the addresses of the keepsakes. There was no grief in the lieutenant's response to this demonstration of heroic resolve. His heart was filled with tenderness. Like a husband who is proudly shown the childish purchases of a young wife, the lieutenant, overwhelmed by affection, lovingly embraced his wife from behind and implanted a kiss upon her neck.

Reiko felt the roughness of the lieutenant's unshaven skin against her neck. This sensation, more than being just a thing of this world, was for Reiko almost the world itself, but now—with the feeling that it was soon to be lost forever—it had freshness beyond all her experience. Each moment had its own vital strength, and the senses in every corner of her body were reawakened. Accepting her husband's caresses from behind, Reiko raised herself on the tips of her toes, letting the vitality seep through her entire body.

"First the bath, and then, after some sake . . . lay out the bedding upstairs, will you?"

The lieutenant whispered the words into his wife's ear. Reiko silently nodded.

Flinging off his uniform, the lieutenant went to the bath. To faint background nois- 50 es of slopping water Reiko tended the charcoal brazier in the living room and began the preparations for warming the sake.

Taking the *tanzen*, a sash, and some underclothes, she went to the bathroom to ask how the water was. In the midst of a coiling cloud of steam the lieutenant was sitting cross-legged on the floor, shaving, and she could dimly discern the rippling movements of the muscles on his damp, powerful back as they responded to the movement of his arms.

There was nothing to suggest a time of any special significance. Reiko, going busily about her tasks, was preparing side dishes from odds and ends in stock. Her hands did not tremble. If anything, she managed even more efficiently and smoothly than usually. From time to time, it is true, there was a strange throbbing deep within her breast. Like distant lightning, it had a moment of sharp intensity and then vanished without trace. Apart from that, nothing was in any way out of the ordinary.

The lieutenant, shaving in the bathroom, felt his warmed body miraculously healed at last of the desperate tiredness of the days of indecision and filled—in spite of the death which lay ahead—with pleasurable anticipation. The sound of his wife going about her work came to him faintly. A healthy physical craving, submerged for two days, reasserted itself.

The lieutenant was confident there had been no impurity in that joy they had experienced when resolving upon death. They had both sensed at that moment—though not, of course, in any clear and conscious way—that those permissible pleasures which they shared in private were once more beneath the protection of Righteousness and Divine Power, and of a complete and unassailable morality. On looking into each other's eyes and discovering there an honorable death, they had felt themselves safe once more behind steel walls which none could destroy, encased in an impenetrable armor of Beauty and Truth. Thus, so far from seeing any inconsistency or conflict between the urges of his flesh and the sincerity of his patriotism, the lieutenant was even able to regard the two as parts of the same thing.

55   Thrusting his face close to the dark, cracked, misted wall mirror, the lieutenant shaved himself with great care. This would be his death face. There must be no unsightly blemishes. The clean-shaven face gleamed once more with a youthful luster, seeming to brighten the darkness of the mirror. There was a certain elegance, he even felt, in the association of death with this radiantly healthy face.

Just as it looked now, this would become his death face! Already, in fact, it had half departed from the lieutenant's personal possession and had become the bust above a dead soldier's memorial. As an experiment he closed his eyes tight. Everything was wrapped in blackness, and he was no longer a living, seeing creature.

Returning from the bath, the traces of the shave glowing faintly blue beneath his smooth cheeks, he seated himself beside the now well-kindled charcoal brazier. Busy though Reiko was, he noticed, she had found time lightly to touch up her face. Her cheeks were gay and her lips moist. There was no shadow of sadness to be seen. Truly, the lieutenant felt, as he saw this mark of his young wife's passionate nature, he had chosen the wife he ought to have chosen.

As soon as the lieutenant had drained his sake cup he offered it to Reiko. Reiko had never before tasted sake, but she accepted without hesitation and sipped timidly.

"Come here," the lieutenant said.

60   Reiko moved to her husband's side and was embraced as she leaned backward across his lap. Her breast was in violent commotion, as if sadness, joy, and the potent sake were mingling and reacting within her. The lieutenant looked down into his wife's face. It was the last face he would see in this world, the last face he would see of his wife. The lieutenant scrutinized the face minutely, with the eyes of a traveler bidding farewell to splendid vistas which he will never revisit. It was a face he could not tire of looking at—the features regular yet not cold, the lips lightly closed with a soft strength. The lieutenant kissed those lips, unthinkingly. And suddenly, though there was not the slightest distortion of the face into the unsightliness of sobbing, he noticed that tears were welling slowly from beneath the long lashes of the closed eyes and brimming over into a glistening stream.

When, a little later, the lieutenant urged that they should move to the upstairs bedroom, his wife replied that she would follow after taking a bath. Climbing the stairs alone to the bedroom, where the air was already warmed by the gas heater, the lieutenant lay down on the bedding with arms outstretched and legs apart. Even the time at which he lay waiting for his wife to join him was no later and no earlier than usual.

He folded his hands beneath his head and gazed at the dark boards of the ceiling in the dimness beyond the range of the standard lamp. Was it death he was now waiting for? Or a wild ecstasy of the senses? The two seemed to overlap, almost as if the object of this bodily desire was death itself. But, however that might be, it was certain that never before had the lieutenant tasted such total freedom.

There was the sound of a car outside the window. He could hear the screech of its tires skidding in the snow piled at the side of the street. The sound of its horn reechoed from near-by walls. . . . Listening to these noises he had the feeling that this house rose like a solitary island in the ocean of a society going as restlessly about its business as ever. All around, vastly and untidily, stretched the country for which he grieved. He was to give his life for it. But would that great country, with which he was prepared to remonstrate to the extent of destroying himself, take the slightest heed of his death? He did not know; and it did not matter. His was a battlefield without glory, a battle-field where none could display deeds of valor: it was the front line of the spirit.

Reiko's footsteps sounded on the stairway. The steep stairs in this old house creaked badly. There were fond memories in that creaking, and many a time, while waiting in bed, the lieutenant had listened to its welcome sound. At the thought that he would hear it no more he listened with intense concentration, striving for every corner of every moment of this precious time to be filled with the sound of those soft footfalls on the creaking stairway. The moments seemed transformed to jewels, sparkling with inner light.

Reiko wore a Nagoya sash about the waist of her *yukata,* but as the lieutenant   65
reached toward it, its redness sobered by the dimness of the light, Reiko's hand moved to his assistance and the sash fell away, slithering swiftly to the floor. As she stood be-fore him, still in her *yukata,* the lieutenant inserted his hands through the side slits be-neath each sleeve, intending to embrace her as she was; but at the touch of his finger tips upon the warm naked flesh, and as the armpits closed gently about his hands, his whole body was suddenly aflame.

In a few moments the two lay naked before the glowing gas heater.

Neither spoke the thought, but their hearts, their bodies, and their pounding breasts blazed with the knowledge that this was the very last time. It was as if the words "The Last Time" were spelled out, in invisible brushstrokes, across every inch of their bodies.

The lieutenant drew his wife close and kissed her vehemently. As their tongues ex-plored each other's mouths, reaching out into the smooth, moist interior, they felt as if the still-unknown agonies of death had tempered their senses to the keenness of red-hot steel. The agonies they could not yet feel, the distant pains of death, had refined their awareness of pleasure.

"This is the last time I shall see your body," said the lieutenant. "Let me look at it closely." And, tilting the shade on the lampstand to one side, he directed the rays along the full length of Reiko's outstretched form.

Reiko lay still with her eyes closed. The light from the low lamp clearly revealed the   70
majestic sweep of her white flesh. The lieutenant, not without a touch of egocentrici-ty, rejoiced that he would never see this beauty crumble in death.

At his leisure, the lieutenant allowed the unforgettable spectacle to engrave itself upon his mind. With one hand he fondled the hair, with the other he softly stroked the magnificent face, implanting kisses here and there where his eyes lingered. The quiet coldness of the high, tapering forehead, the closed eyes with their long lashes beneath faintly etched brows, the set of the finely shaped nose, the gleam of teeth glimpsed be-tween full, regular lips, the soft cheeks and the small, wise chin . . . these things con-jured up in the lieutenant's mind the vision of a truly radiant death face, and again and again he pressed his lips tight against the white throat—where Reiko's own hand was soon to strike—and the throat reddened faintly beneath his kisses. Returning to the mouth he laid his lips against it with the gentlest of pressures, and moved them rhythmically over Reiko's with the light rolling motion of a small boat. If he closed his eyes, the world became a rocking cradle.

Wherever the lieutenant's eyes moved his lips faithfully followed. The high, swelling breasts, surmounted by nipples like the buds of a wild cherry, hardened as the lieutenant's lips closed about them. The arms followed smoothly downward from each side of the breast, tapering toward the wrists, yet losing nothing of their roundness or symmetry, and at their tips were those delicate fingers which had held the fan at the wedding ceremony. One by one, as the lieutenant kissed them, the fingers withdrew behind their neighbor as if in shame. . . . The natural hollow curving between the bosom and the stomach carried in its lines a suggestion not only of softness but of resilient strength, and while it gave forewarning of the rich curves spreading outward from here to the hips it had, in itself, an appearance only of restraint and proper discipline. The whiteness and richness of the stomach and hips was like milk brimming in a great bowl, and the sharply shadowed dip of the navel could have been the fresh impress of a raindrop, fallen there that very moment. Where the shadows gathered more thickly, hair clustered, gentle and sensitive, and as the agitation mounted in the now no longer passive body there hung over this region a scent like the smoldering of fragrant blossoms, growing steadily more pervasive.

At length, in a tremulous voice, Reiko spoke.

"Show me. . . . Let me look too, for the last time."

75　　Never before had he heard from his wife's lips so strong and unequivocal a request. It was as if something which her modesty had wished to keep hidden to the end had suddenly burst its bonds of constraint. The lieutenant obediently lay back and surrendered himself to his wife. Lithely she raised her white, trembling body, and—burning with an innocent desire to return to her husband what he had done for her—placed two white fingers on the lieutenant's eyes, which gazed fixedly up at her, and gently stroked them shut.

Suddenly overwhelmed by tenderness, her cheeks flushed by a dizzying uprush of emotion, Reiko threw her arms about the lieutenant's close-cropped head. The bristly hairs rubbed painfully against her breast, the prominent nose was cold as it dug into her flesh, and his breath was hot. Relaxing her embrace, she gazed down at her husband's masculine face. The severe brows, the closed eyes, the splendid bridge of the nose, the shapely lips drawn firmly together . . . the blue, clean-shaven cheeks reflecting the light and gleaming smoothly. Reiko kissed each of these. She kissed the broad nape of the neck, the strong, erect shoulders, the powerful chest with its twin circles like shields and its russet nipples. In the armpits, deeply shadowed by the ample flesh of the shoulders and chest, a sweet and melancholy odor emanated from the growth of hair, and in the sweetness of this odor was contained, somehow, the essence of young death. The lieutenant's naked skin glowed like a field of barley, and everywhere the muscles showed in sharp relief, converging on the lower abdomen about the small, unassuming navel. Gazing at the youthful, firm stomach, modestly covered by a vigorous growth of hair, Reiko thought of it as it was soon to be, cruelly cut by the sword, and she laid her head upon it, sobbing in pity, and bathed it with kisses.

At the touch of his wife's tears upon his stomach the lieutenant felt ready to endure with courage the cruelest agonies of his suicide.

What ecstasies they experienced after these tender exchanges may well be imagined. The lieutenant raised himself and enfolded his wife in a powerful embrace, her body now limp with exhaustion after her grief and tears. Passionately they held their faces close, rubbing cheek against cheek. Reiko's body was trembling. Their breasts, moist with sweat, were tightly joined, and every inch of the young and beautiful bodies had become so much one with the other that it seemed impossible there should ever again be a separation. Reiko cried out. From the heights they plunged into the abyss, and from the abyss they took wing and soared once more to dizzying heights. The lieutenant panted like the regimental standard-bearer on a route march. . . . As one cycle ended, almost immediately a new wave of passion would be generated, and together—with no trace of fatigue—they would climb again in a single breathless movement to the very summit.

4

When the lieutenant at last turned away, it was not from weariness. For one thing, he was anxious not to undermine the considerable strength he would need in carrying out his suicide. For another, he would have been sorry to mar the sweetness of these last memories by overindulgence.

Since the lieutenant had clearly desisted, Reiko too, with her usual compliance, followed his example. The two lay naked on their backs, with fingers interlaced, staring fixedly at the dark ceiling. The room was warm from the heater, and even when the sweat had ceased to pour from their bodies they felt no cold. Outside, in the hushed night, the sounds of passing traffic had ceased. Even the noise of the trains and streetcars around Yotsuya station did not penetrate this far. After echoing through the region bounded by the moat, they were lost in the heavily wooded park fronting the broad driveway before Akasaka Palace. It was hard to believe in the tension gripping this whole quarter, where the two factions of the bitterly divided Imperial Army now confronted each other, poised for battle. 80

Savoring the warmth glowing within themselves, they lay still and recalled the ecstasies they had just known. Each moment of the experience was relived. They remembered the taste of kisses which had never wearied, the touch of naked flesh, episode after episode of dizzying bliss. But already, from the dark boards of the ceiling, the face of death was peering down. These joys had been final, and their bodies would never know them again. Not that joy of this intensity—and the same thought had occurred to them both—was ever likely to be re-experienced, even if they should live on to old age.

The feel of their fingers intertwined—this too would soon be lost. Even the woodgrain patterns they now gazed at on the dark ceiling boards would be taken from them. They could feel death edging in, nearer and nearer. There could be no hesitation now. They must have the courage to reach out to death themselves, and to seize it.

"Well, let's make our preparations," said the lieutenant. The note of determination in the words was unmistakable, but at the same time Reiko had never heard her husband's voice so warm and tender.

After they had risen, a variety of tasks awaited them.

The lieutenant, who had never once before helped with the bedding, now cheerfully slid back the door of the closet, lifted the mattress across the room by himself, and stowed it away inside. 85

Reiko turned off the gas heater and put away the lamp standard. During the lieutenant's absence she had arranged this room carefully, sweeping and dusting it to a fresh cleanness, and now—if one overlooked the rosewood table drawn into one corner—the eight-mat room gave all the appearance of a reception room ready to welcome an important guest.

"We've seen some drinking here, haven't we? With Kanō and Homma and Noguchi . . ."

"Yes, they were great drinkers, all of them."

"We'll be meeting them before long, in the other world. They'll tease us, I imagine, when they find I've brought you with me."

Descending the stairs, the lieutenant turned to look back into this calm, clean room, now brightly illuminated by the ceiling lamp. There floated across his mind the faces of the young officers who had drunk there, and laughed, and innocently bragged. He had never dreamed then that he would one day cut open his stomach in this room.

In the two rooms downstairs husband and wife busied themselves smoothly and serenely with their respective preparations. The lieutenant went to the toilet, and then to the bathroom to wash. Meanwhile Reiko folded away her husband's padded robe, placed his uniform tunic, his trousers, and a newly cut bleached loincloth in the bathroom, and set out sheets of paper on the living-room table for the farewell notes. Then she removed the lid from the writing box and began rubbing ink from the ink tablet. She had already decided upon the wording of her own note.

Reiko's fingers pressed hard upon the cold gilt letters of the ink tablet, and the water in the shallow well at once darkened, as if a black cloud had spread across it. She stopped thinking that this repeated action, the pressure from her fingers, this rise and fall of faint sound, was all and solely for death. It was a routine domestic task, a simple paring away of time until death should finally stand before her. But somehow, in the increasingly smooth motion of the tablet rubbing on the stone, and in the scent from the thickening ink, there was unspeakable darkness.

Neat in his uniform, which he now wore next to his skin, the lieutenant emerged from the bathroom. Without a word he seated himself at the table, bolt upright, took a brush in his hand, and stared undecidedly at the paper before him.

Reiko took a white silk kimono with her and entered the bathroom. When she reappeared in the living room, clad in the white kimono and with her face lightly made up, the farewell note lay completed on the table beneath the lamp. The thick black brushstrokes said simply:

"Long Live the Imperial Forces—Army Lieutenant Takeyama Shinji."

While Reiko sat opposite him writing her own note, the lieutenant gazed in silence, intensely serious, at the controlled movement of his wife's pale fingers as they manipulated the brush.

With their respective notes in their hands—the lieutenant's sword strapped to his side, Reiko's small dagger thrust into the sash of her white kimono—the two of them stood before the god shelf and silently prayed. Then they put out all the downstairs lights. As he mounted the stairs the lieutenant turned his head and gazed back at the striking, white-clad figure of his wife, climbing behind him, with lowered eyes, from the darkness beneath.

The farewell notes were laid side by side in the alcove of the upstairs room. They wondered whether they ought not to remove the hanging scroll, but since it had been written by their go-between, Lieutenant General Ozeki, and consisted, moreover, of two Chinese characters signifying "Sincerity," they left it where it was. Even if it were to become stained with splashes of blood, they felt that the lieutenant general would understand.

The lieutenant, sitting erect with his back to the alcove, laid his sword on the floor before him.

Reiko sat facing him, a mat's width away. With the rest of her so severely white the touch of rouge on her lips seemed remarkably seductive.

Across the dividing mat they gazed intently into each other's eyes. The lieutenant's sword lay before his knees. Seeing it, Reiko recalled their first night and was overwhelmed with sadness. The lieutenant spoke, in a hoarse voice:

"As I have no second to help me I shall cut deep. It may look unpleasant, but please do not panic. Death of any sort is a fearful thing to watch. You must not be discouraged by what you see. Is that all right?"

"Yes."

Reiko nodded deeply.

Looking at the slender white figure of his wife the lieutenant experienced a bizarre   105
excitement. What he was about to perform was an act in his public capacity as a soldier, something he had never previously shown his wife. It called for a resolution equal to the courage to enter battle; it was a death of no less degree and quality than death in the front line. It was his conduct on the battlefield that he was now to display.

Momentarily the thought led the lieutenant to a strange fantasy. A lonely death on the battlefield, a death beneath the eyes of his beautiful wife . . . in the sensation that he was now to die in these two dimensions, realizing an impossible union of them both, there was sweetness beyond words. This must be the very pinnacle of good fortune, he thought. To have every moment of his death observed by those beautiful eyes—it was like being borne to death on a gentle, fragrant breeze. There was some special favor here. He did not understand precisely what it was, but it was a domain unknown to others: a dispensation granted to no one else had been permitted to himself. In the radiant, bridelike figure of his white-robed wife the lieutenant seemed to see a vision of all those things he had loved and for which he was to lay down his life—the Imperial Household, the Nation, the Army Flag. All these, no less than the wife who sat before him, were presences observing him closely with clear and never-faltering eyes.

Reiko too was gazing intently at her husband, so soon to die, and she thought that never in this world had she seen anything so beautiful. The lieutenant always looked well in uniform, but now, as he contemplated death with severe brows and firmly closed lips, revealed what was perhaps masculine beauty at its most superb.

"It's time to go," the lieutenant said at last.

Reiko bent her body low to the mat in a deep bow. She could not raise her face. She did not wish to spoil her make-up with tears, but the tears could not be held back.

When at length she looked up she saw hazily through the tears that her husband   110
had wound a white bandage around the blade of his now unsheathed sword, leaving five or six inches of naked steel showing at the point.

Resting the sword in its cloth wrapping on the mat before him, the lieutenant rose from his knees, resettled himself cross-legged, and unfastened the hooks of his uniform collar. His eyes no longer saw his wife. Slowly, one by one, he undid the flat brass buttons. The dusky brown chest was revealed, and then the stomach. He unclasped his belt and undid the buttons of his trousers. The pure whiteness of the thickly coiled loincloth showed itself. The lieutenant pushed the cloth down with both hands, further to ease his stomach, and then reached for the white-bandaged blade of his sword. With his left hand he massaged his abdomen, glancing downward as he did so.

To reassure himself on the sharpness of his sword's cutting edge the lieutenant folded back the left trouser flap, exposing a little of his thigh, and lightly drew the blade across the skin. Blood welled up in the wound at once, and several streaks of red trickled downward, glistening in the strong light.

It was the first time Reiko had ever seen her husband's blood, and she felt a violent throbbing in her chest. She looked at her husband's face. The lieutenant was looking at the blood with calm appraisal. For a moment—though thinking at the same time that it was hollow comfort—Reiko experienced a sense of relief.

The lieutenant's eyes fixed his wife with an intense, hawk-life stare. Moving the sword around to his front, he raised himself slightly on his hips and let the upper half of his body lean over the sword point. That he was mustering his whole strength was apparent from the angry tension of the uniform at his shoulders. The lieutenant aimed to strike deep into the left of his stomach. His sharp cry pierced the silence of the room.

115   Despite the effort he had himself put into the blow, the lieutenant had the impression that someone else had struck the side of his stomach agonizingly with a thick rod of iron. For a second or so his head reeled and he had no idea what had happened. The five or six inches of naked point had vanished completely into his flesh, and the white bandage, gripped in his clenched fist, pressed directly against his stomach.

He returned to consciousness. The blade had certainly pierced the wall of the stomach, he thought. His breathing was difficult, his chest thumped violently, and in some far deep region, which he could hardly believe was a part of himself, a fearful and excruciating pain came welling up as if the ground had split open to disgorge a boiling stream of molten rock. The pain came suddenly nearer, with terrifying speed. The lieutenant bit his lower lip and stifled an instinctive moan.

Was this *seppuku*°—he was thinking. It was a sensation of utter chaos, as if the sky had fallen on his head and the world was reeling drunkenly. His willpower and courage, which had seemed so robust before he made the incision, had now dwindled to something like a single hairlike thread of steel, and he was assailed by the uneasy feeling that he must advance along this thread, clinging to it with desperation. His clenched fist had grown moist. Looking down, he saw that both his hand and the cloth about the blade were drenched in blood. His loincloth too was dyed a deep red. It struck him as incredible that, amidst this terrible agony, things which could be seen could still be seen, and existing things existed still.

The moment the lieutenant thrust the sword into his left side and she saw the deathly pallor fall across his face, like an abruptly lowered curtain, Reiko had to struggle to prevent herself from rushing to his side. That was the duty her husband had laid upon her. Opposite her, a mat's space away, she could clearly see her husband biting his lip to stifle the pain. The pain was there, with absolute certainty, before her eyes. And Reiko had no means of rescuing him from it.

The sweat glistened on her husband's forehead. The lieutenant closed his eyes, and then opened them again, as if experimenting. The eyes had lost their luster, and seemed innocent and empty like the eyes of a small animal.

120   The agony before Reiko's eyes burned as strong as the summer sun, utterly remote from the grief which seemed to be tearing herself apart within. The pain grew steadily in stature, stretching upward. Reiko felt that her husband had already become a man in a separate world, a man whose whole being had been resolved into pain, a prisoner in a cage of pain where no hand could reach out to him. But Reiko felt no pain at all. Her grief was not pain. As she thought about this, Reiko began to feel as if someone had raised a cruel wall of glass high between herself and her husband.

Ever since her marriage her husband's existence had been her own existence, and every breath of his had been a breath drawn by herself. But now, while her husband's existence in pain was a vivid reality, Reiko could find in this grief of hers no certain proof at all of her own existence.

°*seppuku*: Traditional suicide of soldiers.

With only his right hand on the sword the lieutenant began to cut sideways across his stomach. But as the blade became entangled with the entrails it was pushed constantly outward by their soft resilience; and the lieutenant realized that it would be necessary, as he cut, to use both hands to keep the point pressed deep into his stomach. He pulled the blade across. It did not cut as easily as he had expected. He directed the strength of his whole body into his right hand and pulled again. There was a cut of three or four inches.

The pain spread slowly outward from the inner depths until the whole stomach reverberated. It was like the wild clanging of a bell. Or like a thousand bells which jangled simultaneously at every breath he breathed and every throb of his pulse, rocking his whole being. The lieutenant could no longer stop himself from moaning. But by now the blade had cut its way through to below the navel, and when he noticed this he felt a sense of satisfaction, and a renewal of courage.

The volume of blood had steadily increased, and now it spurted from the wound as if propelled by the beat of the pulse. The mat before the lieutenant was drenched red with splattered blood, and more blood overflowed onto it from pools which gathered in the folds of the lieutenant's khaki trousers. A spot, like a bird, came flying across to Reiko and settled on the lap of her white silk kimono.

By the time the lieutenant had at last drawn the sword across to the right side of his stomach, the blade was already cutting shallow and had revealed its naked tip, slippery with blood and grease. But, suddenly stricken by a fit of vomiting, the lieutenant cried out hoarsely. The vomiting made the fierce pain fiercer still, and the stomach, which had thus far remained firm and compact, now abruptly heaved, opening wide its wound, and the entrails burst through, as if the wound too were vomiting. Seemingly ignorant of their master's suffering, the entrails gave an impression of robust health and almost disagreeable vitality as they slipped smoothly out and spilled over into the crotch. The lieutenant's head dropped, his shoulders heaved, his eyes opened to narrow slits, and a thin trickle of saliva dribbled from his mouth. The gold markings on his epaulettes caught the light and glinted.

Blood was scattered everywhere. The lieutenant was soaked in it to his knees, and he sat now in a crumpled and listless posture, one hand on the floor. A raw smell filled the room. The lieutenant, his head drooping, retched repeatedly, and the movement showed vividly in his shoulders. The blade of the sword, now pushed back by the entrails and exposed to its tip, was still in the lieutenant's right hand.

It would be difficult to imagine a more heroic sight than that of the lieutenant at this moment, as he mustered his strength and flung back his head. The movement was performed with sudden violence, and the back of his head struck with a sharp crack against the alcove pillar. Reiko had been sitting until now with her face lowered, gazing in fascination at the tide of blood advancing toward her knees, but the sound took her by surprise and she looked up.

The lieutenant's face was not the face of a living man. The eyes were hollow, the skin parched, the once so lustrous cheeks and lips the color of dried mud. The right hand alone was moving. Laboriously gripping the sword, it hovered shakily in the air like the hand of a marionette and strove to direct the point at the base of the lieutenant's throat. Reiko watched her husband make this last, most heart-rending, futile exertion. Glistening with blood and grease, the point was thrust at the throat again and again. And each time it missed its aim. The strength to guide it was no longer there. The straying point struck the collar and the collar badges. Although its hooks had been unfastened, the stiff military collar had closed together again and was protecting the throat.

Reiko could bear the sight no longer. She tried to go to her husband's help, but she could not stand. She moved through the blood on her knees, and her white skirts grew deep red. Moving to the rear of her husband, she helped no more than by loosening the collar. The quivering blade at last contacted the naked flesh of the throat. At that moment Reiko's impression was that she herself had propelled her husband forward; but that was not the case. It was a movement planned by the lieutenant himself, his last exertion of strength. Abruptly he threw his body at the blade, and the blade pierced his neck, emerging at the nape. There was a tremendous spurt of blood and the lieutenant lay still, cold blue-tinged steel protruding from his neck at the back.

5

130   Slowly, her socks slippery with blood, Reiko descended the stairway. The upstairs room was now completely still.

Switching on the ground-floor lights, she checked the gas jet and the main gas plug and poured water over the smoldering, half-buried charcoal in the brazier. She stood before the upright mirror in the four-and-a-half-mat room and held up her skirts. The bloodstains made it seem as if a bold, vivid pattern was printed across the lower half of her white kimono. When she sat down before the mirror, she was conscious of the dampness and coldness of her husband's blood in the region of her thighs, and she shivered. Then, for a long while, she lingered over her toilet preparations. She applied the rouge generously to her cheeks, and her lips too she painted heavily. This was no longer make-up to please her husband. It was make-up for the world which she would leave behind, and there was a touch of the magnificent and the spectacular in her brushwork. When she rose, the mat before the mirror was wet with blood. Reiko was not concerned about this.

Returning from the toilet, Reiko stood finally on the cement floor of the porchway. When her husband had bolted the door here last night it had been in preparation for death. For a while she stood immersed in the consideration of a simple problem. Should she now leave the bolt drawn? If she were to lock the door, it could be that the neighbors might not notice their suicide for several days. Reiko did not relish the thought of their two corpses putrifying before discovery. After all, it seemed, it would be best to leave it open. . . . She released the bolt, and also drew open the frosted-glass door a fraction. . . . At once a chill wind blew in. There was no sign of anyone in the midnight streets, and stars glittered ice-cold through the trees in the large house opposite.

Leaving the door as it was, Reiko mounted the stairs. She had walked here and there for some time and her socks were no longer slippery. About halfway up, her nostrils were already assailed by a peculiar smell.

The lieutenant was lying on his face in a sea of blood. The point protruding from his neck seemed to have grown even more prominent than before. Reiko walked heedlessly across the blood. Sitting beside the lieutenant's corpse, she stared intently at the face, which lay on one cheek on the mat. The eyes were opened wide, as if the lieutenant's attention had been attracted by something. She raised the head, folding it in her sleeve, wiped the blood from the lips, and bestowed a last kiss.

135   Then she rose and took from the closet a new white blanket and a waist cord. To prevent any derangement of her skirts, she wrapped the blanket about her waist and bound it there firmly with the cord.

Reiko sat herself on a spot about one foot distant from the lieutenant's body. Drawing the dagger from her sash, she examined its dully gleaming blade intently, and held it to her tongue. The taste of the polished steel was slightly sweet.

Reiko did not linger. When she thought how the pain which had previously opened such a gulf between herself and her dying husband was now to become a part of her own experience, she saw before her only the joy of herself entering a realm her husband had already made his own. In her husband's agonized face there had been something inexplicable which she was seeing for the first time. Now she would solve the riddle. Reiko sensed that at last she too would be able to taste the true bitterness and sweetness of that great moral principle in which her husband believed. What had until now been tasted only faintly through her husband's example she was about to savor directly with her own tongue.

Reiko rested the point of the blade against the base of her throat. She thrust hard. The wound was only shallow. Her head blazed, and her hands shook uncontrollably. She gave the blade a strong pull sideways. A warm substance flooded into her mouth, and everything before her reddened, in a vision of spouting blood. She gathered her strength and plunged the point of the blade deep into her throat.   [1966]

QUESTIONS

1. What function is served by the capsule summary of the plot at the opening of the story?

2. How does the author structure his story by its shifting point of view?

3. Is there a connection in the story between its plot and its concern with tradition and ritual?

4. What does the story have to say about the relationship between love and death? Between husband and wife?

5. What is the nature of the "patriotism" displayed by the "heroic and dedicated" couple?

RESPONSES

1. Research the history of the Ni Ni Roku Incident and the tradition of *seppuku*. Write an essay placing the story in historical and cultural context.

2. In this story, in Ellison's "A Party down at the Square," in Head's "Looking for a Rain God," and in Jackson's "The Lottery," we have examples of death/murder/sacrifice performed within a cultural context. How do we, as readers, react differently if we believe the writer shares our values and reading of the story's events?

3. From a feminist perspective, analyze the relationship between Takeyama and Reiko.

FOCUS ON FILM

1. View the film *Mishima*. Discuss the moments of beauty and of pain in the film and how such moments also appear in "Patriotism."

2. Discuss ritual suicide as presented in the film and in the story.

BHARATI MUKHERJEE

Bharati Mukherjee (b. 1940), born in Calcutta, attended the universities of Calcutta (B.A.) and Baroda (M.A.), then earned an M.F.A. from the University of Iowa (1963) and later a Ph.D. (1969). She taught at Marquette, the University of Wisconsin, and McGill University, Montréal. Her second novel, *Wife* (1975), was a finalist for the Governor General's Award. She has published two collections of short stories and several novels, including *The Holder of the World* (1993), *Leave It to Me* (1997), *Desirable Daughters* (2002), and *Tree Bride* (2004), and currently teaches English at Berkeley.

A Father

One Wednesday morning in mid-May Mr. Bhowmick woke up as he usually did at 5:43 A.M., checked his Rolex against the alarm clock's digital readout, punched down the alarm (set for 5:45), then nudged his wife awake. She worked as a claims investigator for an insurance company that had an office in a nearby shopping mall. She didn't really have to leave the house until 8:30, but she liked to get up early and cook him a big breakfast. Mr. Bhowmick had to drive a long way to work. He was a naturally dutiful, cautious man, and he sat the alarm clock early enough to accommodate a margin for accidents.

While his wife, in a pink nylon negligee she had paid for with her own MasterCard card, made him a new version of French toast from a clipping ("Eggs-cellent Recipes!") Scotchtaped to the inside of a kitchen cupboard, Mr. Bhowmick brushed his teeth. He brushed, he gurgled with the loud, hawking noises that he and his brother had been taught as children to make in order to flush clean not merely teeth but also tongue and palate.

After that he showered, then, back in the bedroom again, he recited prayers in Sanskrit to Kali, the patron goddess of his family, the goddess of wrath and vengeance. In the pokey flat of his childhood in Ranchi, Bihar, his mother had given over a whole bedroom to her collection of gods and goddesses. Mr. Bhowmick couldn't be that extravagant in Detroit. His daughter, twenty-six and an electrical engineer, slept in the other of the two bedrooms in his apartment. But he had done his best. He had taken Woodworking I and II at a nearby recreation center and built a grotto for the goddess. Kali-Mata was eight inches tall, made of metal and painted a glistening black so that the metal glowed like the oiled, black skin of a peasant woman. And though Kali-Mata was totally nude except for a tiny gilt crown and a garland strung together from sinners' chopped off heads, she looked warm, cozy, *pleased*, in her makeshift wooden shrine in Detroit. Mr. Bhowmick had gathered quite a crowd of admiring, fellow woodworkers in those final weeks of decoration.

"Hurry it up with the prayers," his wife shouted from the kitchen. She was an agnostic, a believer in ambition, not grace. She frequently complained that his prayers had gotten so long that soon he wouldn't have time to go to work, play duplicate bridge with the Ghosals, or play the tabla in the Bengali Association's one Sunday per month musical soirees. Lately she'd begun to drain him in a wholly new way. He wasn't praying, she nagged; he was shutting her out of his life. There'd be no peace in the house until she hid Kali-Mata in a suitcase.

5   She nagged, and he threatened to beat her with his shoe as his father had threatened his mother: it was the thrust and volley of marriage. There was no question of actually taking off a shoe and applying it to his wife's body. She was bigger than he was. And, secretly, he admired her for having the nerve, the agnosticism, which as a college boy in backward Bihar he too had claimed.

"I have time," he shot at her. He was still wrapped in a damp terry towel.

"You have time for everything but domestic life."

It was the fault of the shopping mall that his wife had started to buy pop psychology paperbacks. These paperbacks preached that for couples who could sit down and talk about their "relationship," life would be sweet again. His engineer daughter was on his wife's side. She accused him of holding things in.

"Face it, Dad," she said. "You have an affect deficit."

10   But surely everyone had feelings they didn't want to talk about or talk over. He definitely did not want to blurt out anything about the sick-in-the-guts sensations that came over him most mornings and that he couldn't bubble down with Alka-Seltzer or smother with Gas-X. The women in his family were smarter than him. They were cheerful, outgoing, more American somehow.

How could he tell these bright, mocking women that in the 5:43 A.M. darkness, he sensed invisible presences: gods and snakes frolicked in the master bedroom, little white sparks of cosmic static crackled up the legs of his pajamas. Something was out there in the dark, something that could invent accidents and coincidences to remind mortals that even in Detroit they were no more than mortal. His wife would label this paranoia and dismiss it. Paranoia, premonition: whatever it was, it had begun to undermine his composure.

Take this morning. Mr. Bhowmick had woken up from a pleasant dream about a man taking a Club Med vacation, and the postdream satisfaction had lasted through the shower, but when he'd come back to the shrine in the bedroom, he'd noticed all at once how scarlet and saucy was the tongue that Kali-Mata stuck out at the world. Surely he had not lavished such alarming detail, such admonitory colors on that flap of flesh.

Watch out, ambulatory sinners. Be careful out there, the goddess warned him, and not with the affection of Sergeant Esterhaus, either.

"French toast must be eaten hot-hot," his wife nagged.

15   "Otherwise they'll taste like rubber."

Mr. Bhowmick laid the trousers of a two-trouser suit he had bought on sale that winter against his favorite tweed jacket. The navy stripes in the trousers and the small, navy tweed flecks in the jacket looked quite good together. So what if the Chief Engineer had already started wearing summer cottons?

"I am coming, I am coming," he shouted back. "You want me to eat hot-hot, you start the frying only when I am sitting down. You didn't learn anything from Mother in Ranchi?"

"Mother cooked French toast from fancy recipes? I mean French Sandwich Toast with complicated filling?"

He came into the room to give her his testiest look. "You don't know the meaning of complicated cookery. And mother had to get the coal fire of the *chula*° going first."

His daughter was already at the table. "Why don't you break down and buy her a   20
microwave oven? That's what I mean about sitting down and talking things out." She had finished her orange juice. She took a plastic measure of Slim-Fast out of its can and poured the powder into a glass of skim milk. "It's ridiculous."

Babli was not the child he would have chosen as his only heir. She was brighter certainly than the sons and daughters of the other Bengalis he knew in Detroit, and she had been the only female student in most of her classes at Georgia Tech, but as she sat there in her beige linen business suit, her thick chin dropping into a polka-dotted cravat, he regretted again that she was not the child of his dreams. Babli would be able to help him out moneywise if something happened to him, something so bad that even his pension plans and his insurance policies and his money market schemes wouldn't be enough. But Babli could never comfort him. She wasn't womanly or tender the way that unmarried girls had been in the wistful days of his adolescence. She could sing Hindi film songs, mimicking exactly the high, artificial voice of Lata Mungeshkar, and she had taken two years of dance lessons at Sona Devi's Dance Academy in Southfield, but these accomplishments didn't add up to real femininity. Not the kind that had given him palpitations in Ranchi.

Mr. Bhowmick did his best with his wife's French toast. In spite of its filling of marshmallows, apricot jam and maple syrup, it tasted rubbery. He drank two cups of Darjeeling tea, said, "Well, I'm off," and took off.

All might have gone well if Mr. Bhowmick hadn't fussed longer than usual about putting his briefcase and his trenchcoat in the backseat. He got in behind the wheel of his Oldsmobile, fixed his seatbelt and was just about to turn the key in the ignition when his neighbor, Al Stazniak, who was starting up his Buick Skylark, sneezed. A sneeze at the start of a journey brings bad luck. Al Stazniak's sneeze was fierce, made up of five short bursts, too loud to be ignored.

Be careful out there! Mr. Bhowmick could see the goddess's scarlet little tongue tip wagging at him.

He was a modern man, an intelligent man. Otherwise he couldn't have had the op-   25
tions in life that he did have. He couldn't have given up a good job with perks in Bombay and found a better job with General Motors in Detroit. But Mr. Bhowmick was also a prudent enough man to know that some abiding truth lies bunkered within each wanton Hindu superstition. A sneeze was more than a sneeze. The heedless are carried off in ambulances. He had choices to make. He could ignore the sneeze, and so challenge the world unseen by men. Perhaps Al Stazniak had hayfever. For a sneeze to be a potent omen, surely it had to be unprovoked and terrifying, a thunderclap

---

°*chula*: Stove.

cleaving the summer skies. Or he could admit the smallness of mortals, undo the fate of the universe by starting over, and go back inside the apartment, sit for a second on the sofa, then re-start his trip.

Al Stazniak rolled down his window. "Everything okay?"

Mr. Bhowmick nodded shyly. They weren't really friends in the way neighbors can sometimes be. They talked as they parked or pulled out of their adjacent parking stalls. For all Mr. Bhowmick knew, Al Stazniak had no legs. He had never seen the man out of his Skylark.

He let the Buick back out first. Everything was okay, yes, please. All the same he undid his seatbelt. Compromise, adaptability, call it what you will. A dozen times a day he made these small trade-offs between new-world reasonableness and old-world beliefs.

While he was sitting in his parked car, his wife's ride came by. For fifty dollars a month, she was picked up and dropped off by a hard up, newly divorced woman who worked at a florist's shop in the same mall. His wife came out the front door in brown K-Mart pants and a burgundy windbreaker. She waved to him, then slipped into the passenger seat of the florist's rusty Japanese car.

30 He was a metallurgist. He knew about rust and ways of preventing it, secret ways, thus far unknown to the Japanese.

Babli's fiery red Mitsubishi was still in the lot. She wouldn't leave for work for another eight minutes. He didn't want her to know he'd been undone by a sneeze. Babli wasn't tolerant of superstitions. She played New Wave music in her tapedeck. If asked about Hinduism, all she'd ever said to her American friends was that "it's neat." Mr. Bhowmick had heard her on the phone years before. The cosmos balanced on the head of a snake was like a beachball balanced on the snout of a circus seal. "This Hindu myth stuff," he'd heard her say, "is like a series of super graphics."

He'd forgiven her. He could probably forgive her anything. It was her way of surviving high school in a city that was both native to her, and alien.

There was no question of going back where he'd come from. He hated Ranchi. Ranchi was no place for dreamers. All through his teenage years, Mr. Bhowmick had dreamed of success abroad. What form that success would take he had left vague. Success had meant to him escape from the constant plotting and bitterness that wore out India's middle class.

Babli should have come out of the apartment and driven off to work by now. Mr. Bhowmick decided to take a risk, to dash inside and pretend he'd left his briefcase on the coffee table.

35 When he entered the living room, he noticed Babli's spring coat and large vinyl pocketbook on the sofa. She was probably sorting through the junk jewelry on her dresser to give her business suit a lift. She read hints about dressing in women's magazines and applied them to her person with seriousness. If his luck held, he could sit on the sofa, say a quick prayer and get back to the car without her catching on.

It surprised him that she didn't shout out from her bedroom, "Who's there?" What if he had been a rapist?

Then he heard Babli in the bathroom. He heard unladylike squawking noises. She was throwing up. A squawk, a spitting, then the horrible gurgle of a waterfall.

A revelation came to Mr. Bhowmick. A woman vomiting in the privacy of the bathroom could mean many things. She was coming down with the flu. She was nervous about a meeting. But Mr. Bhowmick knew at once that his daughter, his untender, unloving daughter whom he couldn't love and hadn't tried to love, was not, in the larger world of Detroit, unloved. Sinners are everywhere, even in the bosom of an upright, unambitious family like the Bhowmicks. It was the goddess sticking out her tongue at him.

The father sat heavily on the sofa, shrinking from contact with her coat and pocketbook. His brisk, bright engineer daughter was pregnant. Someone had taken time to make love to her. Someone had thought her tender, feminine. Someone even now was perhaps mooning over her. The idea excited him. It was so grotesque and wondrous. At twenty-six Babli had found the man of her dreams; whereas at twenty-six Mr. Bhowmick had given up on truth, beauty and poetry and exchanged them for two years at Carnegie Tech.

Mr. Bhowmick's tweed-jacketed body sagged against the sofa cushions. Babli would abort, of course. He knew his Babli. It was the only possible option if she didn't want to bring shame to the Bhowmick family. All the same, he could see a chubby baby boy on the rug, crawling to his granddaddy. Shame like that was easier to hide in Ranchi. There was always a barren womb sanctified by marriage that could claim sudden fructifying by the goddess Parvati. Babli would do what she wanted. She was headstrong and independent and he was afraid of her. 40

Babli staggered out of the bathroom. Damp stains ruined her linen suit. It was the first time he had seen his daughter look ridiculous, quite unprofessional. She didn't come into the living room to investigate the noises he'd made. He glimpsed her shoeless stockinged feet flip-flop on collapsed arches down the hall to her bedroom.

"Are you all right?" Mr. Bhowmick asked, standing in the hall. "Do you need Sinutab?"

She wheeled around. "What're you doing here?"

He was the one who should be angry. "I'm feeling poorly too," he said. "I'm taking the day off."

"I feel fine," Babli said. 45

Within fifteen minutes Babli had changed her clothes and left. Mr. Bhowmick had the apartment to himself all day. All day for praising or cursing the life that had brought him along with its other surprises an illegitimate grandchild.

It was his wife that he blamed. Coming to America to live had been his wife's idea. After the wedding, the young Bhowmicks had spent two years in Pittsburgh on his student visa, then gone back home to Ranchi for nine years. Nine crushing years. Then the job in Bombay had come through. All during those nine years his wife had screamed and wept. She was a woman of wild, progressive ideas—she'd called them her "American" ideas—and she'd been martyred by her neighbors for them. American *memsahib. Markin mem, Markin mem.* In bazaars the beggar boys had trailed her and hooted. She'd done provocative things. She'd hired a *chamar*° woman who by caste rules was forbidden to cook for higher caste families, especially for widowed mothers of decent men. This had caused a blowup in the neighborhood. She'd made other, lesser errors. While other wives shopped and cooked every day, his wife had cooked the whole week's menu on weekends.

"What's the point of having a refrigerator, then?" She'd been scornful of the Ranchi women.

His mother, an old-fasioned widow, had accused her of trying to kill her by poisoning. "You are in such a hurry? You want to get rid of me quick-quick so you can go back to the States?"

Family life had been turbulent. 50

°*chamar*: Leather-worker (member of a Hindu caste).

He had kept aloof, inwardly siding with his mother. He did not love his wife now, and he had not loved her then. In any case, he had not defended her. He felt some affection, and he felt guilty for having shunned her during those unhappy years. But he had thought of it then as revenge. He had wanted to marry a beautiful woman. Not being a young man of means, only a young man with prospects, he had had no right to yearn for pure beauty. He cursed his fate and after a while, settled for a barrister's daughter, a plain girl with a wide, flat plank of a body and myopic eyes. The barrister had sweetened the deal by throwing in an all-expenses-paid two years' study at Carnegie Tech to which Mr. Bhowmick had been admitted. Those two years had changed his wife from pliant girl to ambitious woman. She wanted America, nothing less.

It was his wife who had forced him to apply for permanent resident status in the U.S. even though he had a good job in Ranchi as a government engineer. The putting together of documents for the immigrant visa had been a long and humbling process. He had had to explain to a chilly clerk in the Embassy that, like most Indians of his generation, he had no birth certificate. He had to swear out affidavits, suffer through police checks, bribe orderlies whose job it was to move his dossier from desk to desk. The decision, the clerk had advised him, would take months, maybe years. He hadn't dared hope that merit might be rewarded. Merit could collapse under bad luck. It was for grace that he prayed.

While the immigration papers were being processed, he had found the job in Bombay. So he'd moved his mother in with his younger brother's family, and left his hometown for good. Life in Bombay had been lighthearted, almost fulfilling. His wife had thrown herself into charity work with the same energy that had offended the Ranchi women. He was happy to be in a big city at last. Bombay was the Rio de Janeiro of the East; he'd read that in a travel brochure. He drove out to Nariman Point at least once a week to admire the necklace of municipal lights, toss coconut shells into the dark ocean, drink beer at the Oberoi-Sheraton where overseas Indian girls in designer jeans beckoned him in sly ways. His nights were full. He played duplicate bridge, went to the movies, took his wife to Bingo nights at his club. In Detroit he was a lonelier man.

Then the green card had come through. For him, for his wife, and for the daughter who had been born to them in Bombay. He sold what he could sell, and put in his brother's informal trust what he couldn't to save on taxes. Then he had left for America, and one more start.

55   All through the week, Mr. Bhowmick watched his daughter. He kept furtive notes on how many times she rushed to the bathroom and made hawking, wrenching noises, how many times she stayed late at the office, calling her mother to say she'd be taking in a movie and pizza afterwards with friends.

He had to tell her that he knew. And he probably didn't have much time. She shouldn't be on Slim-Fast in her condition. He had to talk things over with her. But what would he say to her? What position could he take? He had to choose between public shame for the family, and murder.

For three more weeks he watched her and kept his silence. Babli wore shifts to the office instead of business suits, and he liked her better in those garments. Perhaps she was dressing for her young man, not from necessity. Her skin was pale and blotchy by turn. At breakfast her fingers looked stiff, and she had trouble with silverware.

Two Saturdays running, he lost badly at duplicate bridge. His wife scolded him. He had made silly mistakes. When was Babli meeting this man? Where? He must be American; Mr. Bhowmick prayed only that he was white. He pictured his grandson crawling to him, and the grandson was always fat and brown and buttery-skinned, like the infant Krishna. An American son-in-law was a terrifying notion. Why was she not mentioning men, at least, preparing the way for the major announcement? He listened sharply for men's names, rehearsed little lines like, "Hello, Bob, I'm Babli's old man," with a cracked little laugh. Bob, Jack, Jimmy, Tom. But no names surfaced. When she went out for pizza and a movie it was with the familiar set of Indian girls and their strange, unpopular, American friends, all without men. Mr. Bhowmick tried to be reasonable. Maybe she had already gotten married and was keeping it secret. "Well, Bob, you and Babli sure had Mrs. Bhowmick and me going there, heh-heh," he mumbled one night with the Sahas and Ghosals, over cards. "Pardon?" asked Pronob Saha. Mr. Bhowmick dropped two tricks, and his wife glared. "Such stupid blunders," she fumed on the drive back. A new truth was dawning; there would be no marriage for Babli. Her young man probably was not so young and not so available. He must be already married. She must have yielded to passion or been raped in the office. His wife seemed to have noticed nothing. Was he a murderer, or a conspirator? He kept his secret from his wife; his daughter kept her decision to herself.

Nights, Mr. Bhowmick pretended to sleep, but as soon as his wife began her snoring—not real snores so much as loud, gaspy gulpings for breath—he turned on his side and prayed to Kali-Mata.

In July, when Babli's belly had begun to push up against the waistless dresses she'd bought herself, Mr. Bhowmick came out of the shower one weekday morning and found the two women screaming at each other. His wife had a rolling pin in one hand. His daughter held up a *National Geographic* as a shield for her head. The crazy look that had been in his wife's eyes when she'd shooed away beggar kids was in her eyes again.

"Stop it!" His own boldness overwhelmed him. "Shut up! Babli's pregnant, so what? It's your fault, you made us come to the States."

Girls like Babli were caught between rules, that's the point he wished to make. They were too smart, too impulsive for a backward place like Ranchi, but not tough nor smart enough for sex-crazy places like Detroit.

"My fault?" his wife cried. "I told her to do hanky-panky with boys? I told her to shame us like this?"

She got in one blow with the rolling pin. The second glanced off Babli's shoulder and fell on his arm which he had stuck out for his grandson's sake.

"I'm calling the police," Babli shouted. She was out of the rolling pin's range. "This is brutality. You can't do this to me."

"Shut up! Shut your mouth, foolish woman." He wrenched the weapon from his wife's fist. He made a show of taking off his shoe to beat his wife on the face.

"What do you know? You don't know anything." She let herself down slowly on a dining chair. Her hair, curled overnight, stood in wild whorls around her head. "Nothing."

"And you do!" He laughed. He remembered her tormentors, and laughed again. He had begun to enjoy himself. Now *he* was the one with the crazy, progressive ideas.

"Your daughter is pregnant, yes," she said, "any fool knows that. But ask her the name of the father. Go, ask."

He stared at his daughter who gazed straight ahead, eyes burning with hate, jaw clenched with fury.

"Babli?"

"Who needs a man?" she hissed. "The father of my baby is a bottle and a syringe. Men louse up your lives. I just want a baby. Oh, don't worry—he's a certified fit donor.

No diseases, college graduate, above average, and he made the easiest twenty-five dollars of his life—"

"Like animals," his wife said. For the first time he heard horror in her voice. His daughter grinned at him. He saw her tongue, thick and red, squirming behind her row of perfect teeth.

"Yes, yes, yes," she screamed, "like livestock. Just like animals. You should be happy—that's what marriage is all about, isn't it? Matching bloodlines, matching horoscopes, matching castes, matching, matching, matching . . ." and it was difficult to know if she was laughing or singing, or mocking and like a madwoman.

75   Mr. Bhowmick lifted the rolling pin high above his head and brought it down hard on the dome of Babli's stomach. In the end, it was his wife who called the police.   [1985]

QUESTIONS

1. What has "A Father" shown you about the everyday difficulties of living in a new country and culture?
2. How useful are Mukherjee's explanations of Hindu deities?
3. How does Mr. Bhowmick feel about the fact that his wife and daughter are "more American" than he is?
4. Is there internal evidence that setting the story in Detroit has a specific purpose?
5. The reality of Babli's pregnancy is beyond anything Mr. Bhowmick has imagined. Has he tried to be a good husband and father?

RESPONSES

1. Write an essay about the effect of using brand names in fiction. You can use this story, Oates's "Shopping," and, to a certain degree, Barthelme's "A City of Churches."
2. Compare this story to Kureishi's "My Son the Fanatic."

VLADIMIR NABOKOV

Vladimir Nabokov (1899–1977) was born in St. Petersburg. He went into exile after the Revolution, finished his education at Cambridge University, and for the next two decades lived in Berlin and Paris while writing novels in Russian, German, French, and English. He emigrated to the United States in 1940, became a citizen five years later, and taught at various colleges while writing novels in English. The best known is *Lolita* (1958). Its success enabled Nabokov and his wife to move to Switzerland, where he spent his last years continuing to write while living on the shores of Lake Geneva in a hotel. *Speak Memory* (1967) is a collection of autobiographical essays.

The Passenger

"Yes, Life is more talented than we," sighed the writer, tapping the cardboard mouthpiece of his Russian cigarette against the lid of his case. "The plots Life thinks up now and then! How can we compete with that goddess? Her works are untranslatable, undescribable."

"Copyright by the author," suggested the critic, smiling; he was a modest, myopic man with slim, restless fingers.

"Our last recourse, then, is to cheat," continued the writer, absentmindedly throwing a match into the critic's empty wineglass. "All that's left to us is to treat her creations as a film producer does a famous novel. The producer needs to prevent servant maids from being bored on Saturday nights; therefore he alters the novel beyond recognition; minces it, turns it inside out, throws out hundreds of episodes, introduces new characters and incidents he has invented himself—and all this for the sole purpose of having an entertaining film unfold without a hitch, punishing virtue in the beginning and vice at the end, a film perfectly natural in terms of its own conventions, and, above all, furnished with an unexpected but all-resolving outcome. Exactly thus do we, writers, alter the themes of Life to suit us in our drive toward some kind of conventional harmony, some kind of artistic conciseness. We spice our savorless plagiarisms with our own devices. We think that Life's performance is too sweeping, too uneven, that her genius is too untidy. To indulge our readers we cut out of Life's untrammeled novels our neat little tales for the use of schoolchildren. Allow me, in this connection, to impart to you the following experience.

"I happened to be traveling in the sleeping car of an express. I love the process of settling into viatic quarters—the cool linen of the berth, the slow passage of the station's departing lights as they start moving behind the black windowpane. I remember how pleased I was that there was nobody in the bunk above me. I undressed, I lay down supine with my hands clasped under my head, and the lightness of the scant regulation blanket was a treat in comparison to the puffiness of hotel featherbeds. After some private musings—at the time I was anxious to write a story about the life of railway-car cleaning women—I put out the light and was soon asleep. And here let me use a device cropping up with dreary frequency in the sort of story to which mine promises to belong. Here it is—that old device which you must know so well: 'In the middle of the night I woke up suddenly.' What follows, however, is something less stale. I woke up and saw a foot."

5   "Excuse me, a what?" interrupted the modest critic, leaning forward and lifting his finger.

"I saw a foot," repeated the writer. "The compartment was now lighted. The train stood at a station. It was a man's foot, a foot of considerable size, in a coarse sock, through which the bluish toenail had worked a hole. It was planted solidly on a step of the bed ladder close to my face, and its owner, concealed from my sight by the upper bunk roofing me, was just on the point of making a last effort to hoist himself onto his ledge. I had ample time to inspect that foot in its gray, black-checkered sock and also part of the leg: the violet vee of the garter on the side of the stout calf and its little hairs nastily sticking out through the mesh of the long underwear. It was altogether a most repellent limb. While I looked, it tensed, the tenacious big toe moved once or twice; then, finally, the whole extremity vigorously pushed off and soared out of sight. From above, came grunting and snuffling sounds leading one to conclude that the man was preparing to sleep. The light went out, and a few moments later the train jerked into motion.

"I don't know how to explain it to you, but that limb anguished me most oppressively. A resilient varicolored reptile. I found it disturbing that all I knew of the man was that evil-looking leg. His figure, his face, I never saw. His berth, which formed a low, dark ceiling over me, now seemed to have come lower; I almost felt its weight. No matter how hard I tried to imagine the aspect of my nocturnal fellow traveler all I could visualize was that conspicuous toenail which showed its bluish mother-of-pearl sheen through a hole in the wool of the sock. It may seem strange, in a general way, that such trifles should bother me but, per contra,° is not every writer precisely a person who bothers about trifles? Anyhow, sleep did not come. I kept listening—had my unknown companion started to snore? Apparently he was not snoring but moaning. Of course, the knocking of train wheels at night is known to encourage aural hallucinations; yet I could not get over the impression that from up there, above me, came sounds of an unusual nature. I raised myself on one elbow. The sounds grew more distinct. The man on the upper berth was sobbing."

"What's that?" interrupted the critic. "Sobbing? I see. Sorry—didn't quite catch what you said." And, again dropping his hands in his lap and inclining his head to one side, the critic went on listening to the narrator.

"Yes, he was sobbing, and his sobs were atrocious. They choked him; he would noisily let his breath out as if having drunk at one gulp a quart of water, whereupon

---

°*per contra*: On the contrary.

there followed rapid spasms of weeping with the mouth shut—the frightful parody of a cackle—and again he would draw in air and again let it out in short expirations of sobbing, with his mouth now open—to judge by the hahhah-ing note. And all this against the shaky background of hammering wheels, which by this token became something like a moving stairway along which his sobs went up and came down. I lay motionless and listened—and felt, incidentally, that my face in the dark looked awfully silly, for it is always embarrassing to hear a stranger sobbing. And mind you, I was helplessly shackled to him by the fact of our sharing the same two-berth compartment, in the same unconcernedly rushing train. And he did not stop weeping; those dreadful arduous sobs kept up with me: we both—I below, the listener, and he overhead, the weeping one—sped sideways into night's remoteness at eighty kilometers an hour, and only a railway crash could have cleft our involuntary link.

"After a while he seemed to stop crying, but no sooner was I about to drop off than his sobs started to swell again and I even seemed to hear unintelligible words which he uttered in a kind of sepulchral, belly-deep voice between convulsive sighs. He was silent again, only snuffling a bit, and I lay with my eyes closed and saw in fancy his disgusting foot in its checkered sock. Somehow or other I managed to fall asleep; and at half past five the conductor wrenched the door open to call me. Sitting on my bed—and knocking my head every minute against the edge of the upper berth—I hurried to dress. Before going out with my bags into the corridor, I turned to look up at the upper berth, but the man was lying with his back to me, and had covered his head with his blanket. It was morning in the corridor, the sun had just risen, the fresh, blue shadow of the train ran over the grass, over the shrubs, swept sinuously up the slopes, rippled across the trunks of flickering birches—and an oblong pondlet shone dazzlingly in the middle of a field, then narrowed, dwindled to a silvery slit, and with a rapid clatter a cottage scuttled by, the tail of a road whisked under a crossing gate—and once more the numberless birches dizzied one with their flickering, sun-flecked palisade.

"The only other people in the corridor were two women with sleepy, sloppily made-up faces, and a little old man wearing suede gloves and a traveling cap. I detest rising early: for me the most ravishing dawn in the world cannot replace the hours of delicious morning sleep; and therefore I limited myself to a grumpy nod when the old gentleman asked me if I, too, was getting off at . . . he mentioned a big town where we were due in ten or fifteen minutes.

"The birches suddenly dispersed, half-a-dozen small houses poured down a hill, some of them, in their haste, barely missing being run over by the train; then a huge purple-red factory strode by flashing its windowpanes; somebody's chocolate hailed us from a ten-yard poster; another factory followed with its bright glass and chimneys; in short, there happened what usually happens when one is nearing a city. But all at once, to our surprise, the train braked convulsively and pulled up at a desolate whistle-stop, where an express had seemingly no business to dawdle. I also found it surprising that several policemen stood out there on the platform. I lowered a window and leaned out. 'Shut it, please,' said one of the men politely. The passengers in the corridor displayed some agitation. A conductor passed and I asked what was the matter. 'There's a criminal on the train,' he replied and briefly explained that in the town at which we had stopped in the middle of the night, a murder had occurred on the eve: a betrayed husband had shot his wife and her lover. The ladies exclaimed '*ach!*', the old gentleman shook his head. Two policemen and a rosy-cheeked, plump, bowler-hatted detective who looked like a bookmaker entered the corridor. I was asked to go back to my berth. The policemen remained in the corridor, while the detective visited one

10

compartment after another. I showed him my passport. His reddish-brown eyes glided over my face; he returned my passport. We stood, he and I, in that narrow coupé on the upper bunk of which slept a dark-cocooned figure. 'You may leave,' said the detective and stretched his arm toward that upper darkness: 'Papers, please.' The blanketed man kept on snoring. As I lingered in the doorway, I still heard that snoring and seemed to make out through it the sibilant echoes of his nocturnal sobs. 'Please, wake up,' said the detective, raising his voice; and with a kind of professional jerk he pulled at the edge of the blanket at the sleeper's nape. The latter stirred but continued to snore. The detective shook him by the shoulder. This was rather sickening. I turned away and stared at the window across the corridor, but did not really see it, while listening with my whole being to what was happening in the compartment.

"And imagine, I heard absolutely nothing out of the ordinary. The man on the upper berth sleepily mumbled something, the detective distinctly demanded his passport, distinctly thanked him, then went out and entered another compartment. That is all. But think only how nice it would have seemed—from the writer's viewpoint, naturally— if the evil-footed, weeping passenger had turned out to be a murderer, how nicely his tears in the night could have been explained, and, what is more, how nicely all that would have fitted into the frame of my night journey, the frame of a short story. Yet, it would appear that the plan of the Author, the plan of Life, was in this case, as in all others, a hundred times nicer."

The writer sighed and fell silent, as he sucked his cigarette, which had gone out long ago and was now all chewed up and damp with saliva. The critic was gazing at him with kindly eyes.

15   "Confess," spoke the writer again, "that beginning with the moment when I mentioned the police and the unscheduled stop, you were sure my sobbing passenger was a criminal?"

"I know your manner," said the critic, touching his interlocutor's shoulder with the tips of his fingers and in a gesture peculiar to him, instantly snatching back his hand. "If you were writing a detective story, your villain would have turned out to be not the person whom none of the characters suspect but the person whom everybody in the story suspects from the very beginning, thus fooling the experienced reader who is used to solutions proving to be *not* the obvious ones. I am well aware that you like to produce an impression of inexpectancy by means of the most natural denouement; but don't get carried away by your own method. There is much in life that is casual, and there is also much that is unusual. The Word is given the sublime right to enhance chance and to make of the transcendental something that is not accidental. Out of the present case, out of the dance of chance, you could have created a well-rounded story if you had transformed your fellow traveler into a murderer."

The writer sighed again.

"Yes, yes, that did occur to me. I might have added several details. I would have alluded to the passionate love he had for his wife. All kinds of inventions are possible. The trouble is that we are in the dark—maybe Life had in mind something totally different, something much more subtle and deep. The trouble is that I did not learn, and shall never learn, why the passenger cried."

"I intercede for the Word," gently said the critic. "You, as a writer of fiction, would have at least thought up some brilliant solution: your character was crying, perhaps, because he had lost his wallet at the station. I once knew someone, a grown-up man of martial appearance, who would weep or rather bawl when he had a toothache. No, thanks, no—don't pour me any more. That's sufficient, that's quite sufficient."   [1976]

QUESTIONS

1. What views of art are represented by the writer and the critic?
2. What do the descriptions of the railway car and the landscape rushing by add to the story?
3. Why does the author consider the plan of Life "a hundred times nicer"? Is the writer altogether serious?
4. To whom does the title refer?
5. If you responded to the story in the way the writer intended you to respond, what does that prove?

RESPONSE

1. Read Harold Bloom's Context essay "Summary Observations on the Short Story" and Nabokov's Context comments on Chekhov and Kafka. Write an essay explaining whether Nabokov follows the "Chekhov school" or "Kafka school" of story telling.

Jonathan Nolan

Jonathan Nolan (b. 1976) was born in London, England. His story, "Memento Mori" was first published in *Esquire* magazine and was later reprinted in *The O'Henry Prize Stories* 2002. His brother, Christopher Nolan, and he adapted the short story into the film *Memento* before the story had been printed, and their screenplay was nominated for an academy award for Achievement in Writing directly for the screen. It has been announced that Jonathan Nolan is working on screenplays, including one titled *The Exec.*

Memento Mori

"What like a bullet can undeceive!"

—Herman Melville

Your wife always used to say you'd be late for your own funeral. Remember that? Her little joke because you were such a slob—always late, always forgetting stuff, even before the incident.

Right about now you're probably wondering if you were late for hers.

You were there, you can be sure of that. That's what the picture's for—the one tacked to the wall by the door. It's not customary to take pictures at a funeral, but somebody, your doctors, I guess, knew you wouldn't remember. They had it blown up nice and big and stuck it right there, next to the door, so you couldn't help but see it every time you got up to find out where she was.

The guy in the picture, the one with the flowers? That's you. And what are you doing? You're reading the headstone, trying to figure out whose funeral you're at, same as you're reading it now, trying to figure why someone stuck that picture next to your door. But why bother reading something that you won't remember?

5   *She's gone, gone for good, and you must be hurting right now, hearing the news. Believe me, I know how you feel. You're probably a wreck. But give it five minutes, maybe ten. Maybe you can even go a whole half hour before you forget.*

But you will forget—I guarantee it. A few more minutes and you'll be heading for the door, looking for her all over again, breaking down when you find the picture. How many times do you have to hear the news before some other part of your body, other than that busted brain of yours, starts to remember?

Never-ending grief, never-ending anger. Useless without direction. Maybe you can't understand what's happened. Can't say I really understand, either. Backwards amnesia. That's what the sign says. CRS disease. Your guess is as good as mine. Maybe you can't understand what happened to you. But you do remember what happened to HER, don't you? The doctors don't want to talk about it. They won't answer my questions. They don't think it's right for a man in your condition to hear about those things. But you remember enough, don't you? You remember his face.

This is why I'm writing to you. Futile, maybe. I don't know how many times you'll have to read this before you listen to me. I don't even know how long you've been locked up in this room already. Neither do you. But your advantage in forgetting is that you'll forget to write yourself off as a lost cause.

Sooner or later you'll want to do something about it. And when you do, you'll just have to trust me, because I'm the only one who can help you.

Earl opens one eye after another to a stretch of white ceiling tiles interrupted by a   10
hand-printed sign taped right above his head, large enough for him to read from the
bed. An alarm clock is ringing somewhere. He reads the sign, blinks, reads it again, then
takes a look at the room.

It's a white room, overwhelmingly white, from the walls and the curtains to the institutional furniture and the bedspread. The alarm clock is ringing from the white
desk under the window with the white curtains. At this point Earl probably notices
that he is lying on top of his white comforter. He is already wearing a dressing gown
and slippers.

He lies back and reads the sign taped to the ceiling again. It says, in crude block capitals, THIS IS YOUR ROOM. THIS IS A ROOM IN A HOSPITAL. THIS IS WHERE
YOU LIVE NOW.

Earl rises and takes a look around. The room is large for a hospital—empty linoleum
stretches out from the bed in three directions. Two doors and a window. The view isn't
very helpful, either—a close of trees in the center of a carefully manicured piece of
turf that terminates in a sliver of two-lane blacktop. The trees, except for the evergreens, are bare—early spring or late fall, one or the other.

Every inch of the desk is covered with Post-it notes, legal pads, neatly printed lists,
psychological textbooks, framed pictures. On top of the mess is a half-completed crossword puzzle. The alarm clock is riding a pile of folded newspapers. Earl slaps the
snooze button and takes a cigarette from the pack taped to the sleeve of his dressing
gown. He pats the empty pockets of his pajamas for a light. He rifles the papers on the
desk, looks quickly through the drawers. Eventually he finds a box of kitchen matches taped to the wall next to the window. Another sign is taped just above the box. It
says in loud yellow letters, CIGARETTE? CHECK FOR LIT ONES FIRST, STUPID.

Earl laughs at the sign, lights his cigarette, and takes a long draw. Taped to the win-   15
dow in front of him is another piece of looseleaf paper headed YOUR SCHEDULE.

It charts off the hours, every hour, in blocks: 10:00 P.M. to 8:00 A.M. is labeled go
BACK TO SLEEP. Earl consults the alarm clock: 8:15. Given the light outside, it must
be morning. He checks his watch: 10:30. He presses the watch to his ear and listens. He
gives the watch a wind or two and sets it to match the alarm clock.

According to the schedule, the entire block from 8:00 to 8:30 has been labeled
BRUSH YOUR TEETH. Earl laughs again and walks over to the bathroom.

The bathroom window is open. As he flaps his arms to keep warm, he notices the
ashtray on the windowsill. A cigarette is perched on the ashtray, burning steadily

through a long finger of ash. He frowns, extinguishes the old butt, and replaces it with the new one.

The toothbrush has already been treated to a smudge of white paste. The tap is of the push-button variety—a dose of water with each nudge. Earl pushes the brush into his cheek and fiddles it back and forth while he opens the medicine cabinet. The shelves are stocked with single-serving packages of vitamins, aspirin, antidiuretics. The mouthwash is also single-serving, about a shot-glass-worth of blue liquid in a sealed plastic bottle. Only the toothpaste is regular-sized. Earl spits the paste out of his mouth and replaces it with the mouthwash. As he lays the toothbrush next to the toothpaste, he notices a tiny wedge of paper pinched between the glass shelf and the steel backing of the medicine cabinet. He spits the frothy blue fluid into the sink and nudges for some more water to rinse it down. He closes the medicine cabinet and smiles at his reflection in the mirror.

20   "Who needs half an hour to brush their teeth?"

The paper has been folded down to a minuscule size with all the precision of a sixth-grader's love note. Earl unfolds it and smooths it against the mirror. It reads—

IF YOU CAN STILL READ THIS, THEN YOU'RE A FUCKING COWARD.

Earl stares blankly at the paper, then reads it again. He turns it over. On the back it reads—

P.S.: AFTER YOU'VE READ THIS, HIDE IT AGAIN.

25   Earl reads both sides again, then folds the note back down to its original size and tucks it underneath the toothpaste.

Maybe then he notices the scar. It begins just beneath the ear, jagged and thick, and disappears abruptly into his hairline. Earl turns his head and stares out of the corner of his eye to follow the scar's progress. He traces it with a fingertip, then looks back down at the cigarette burning in the ashtray. A thought seizes him and he spins out of the bathroom.

He is caught at the door to his room, one hand on the knob. Two pictures are taped to the wall by the door. Earl's attention is caught first by the MRI, a shiny black frame for four windows into someone's skull. In marker, the picture is labeled YOUR BRAIN. Earl stares at it. Concentric circles in different colors. He can make out the big orbs of his eyes and, behind these, the twin lobes of his brain. Smooth wrinkles, circles, semicircles. But right there in the middle of his head, circled in marker, tunneled in from the back of his neck like a maggot into an apricot, is something different. Deformed, broken, but unmistakable. A dark smudge, the shape of a flower, right there in the middle of his brain.

He bends to look at the other picture. It is a photograph of a man holding flowers, standing over a fresh grave. The man is bent over, reading the headstone. For a moment this looks like a hall of mirrors or the beginnings of a sketch of infinity: the one man bent over, looking at the smaller man, bent over, reading the headstone. Earl looks at the picture for a long time. Maybe he begins to cry. Maybe he just stares silently at the picture. Eventually, he makes his way back to the bed, flops down, seals his eyes shut, tries to sleep.

The cigarette burns steadily away in the bathroom. A circuit in the alarm clock counts down from ten, and it starts ringing again.

30   Earl opens one eye after another to a stretch of white ceiling tiles, interrupted by a hand-printed sign taped right above his head, large enough for him to read from the bed.

You can't have a normal life anymore. You must know that. How can you have a girl-friend if you can't remember her name? Can't have kids, not unless you want them to grow up with a dad who doesn't recognize them. Sure as hell can't hold down a job. Not too many professions out there that value forgetfulness. Prostitution, maybe. Politics, of course.

No. Your life is over. You're a dead man. The only thing the doctors are hoping to do is teach you to be less of a burden to the orderlies. And they'll probably never let you go home, wherever that would be.

So the question is not "to be or not to be," because you aren't. The question is whether you want to do something about it. Whether revenge matters to you.

It does to most people. For a few weeks, they plot, they scheme, they take measures to get even. But the passage of time is all it takes to erode that initial impulse. Time is theft, isn't that what they say? And time eventually convinces most of us that forgiveness is a virtue. Conveniently, cowardice and forgiveness look identical at a certain distance. Time steals your nerve.

If time and fear aren't enough to dissuade people from their revenge, then there's al- 35 *ways authority, softly shaking its head and saying, We understand, but you're the better man for letting it go. For rising above it. For not sinking to their level. And besides, says authority, if you try anything stupid, we'll lock you up in a little room.*

But they already put you in a little room, didn't they? Only they don't really lock it or even guard it too carefully because you're a cripple. A corpse. A vegetable who probably wouldn't remember to eat or take a shit if someone wasn't there to remind you.

And as for the passage of time, well, that doesn't really apply to you anymore, does it? Just the same ten minutes, over and over again. So how can you forgive if you can't re-member to forget?

You probably were the type to let it go, weren't you? Before. But you're not the man you used to be. Not even half. You're a fraction; you're the ten-minute man.

Of course, weakness is strong. It's the primary impulse. You'd probably prefer to sit in your little room and cry. Live in your finite collection of memories, carefully polishing each one. Half a life set behind glass and pinned to cardboard like a collection of exotic in-sects. You'd like to live behind that glass, wouldn't you? Preserved in aspic.

You'd like to but you can't, can you? You can't because of the last addition to your col- 40 *lection. The last thing you remember. His face. His face and your wife, looking to you for help.*

And maybe this is where you can retire to when it's over. Your little collection. They can lock you back up in another little room and you can live the rest of your life in the past. But only if you've got a little piece of paper in your hand that says you got him.

You know I'm right. You know there's a lot of work to do. It may seem impossible, but I'm sure if we all do our part, we'll figure something out. But you don't have much time. You've only got about ten minutes, in fact. Then it starts all over again. So do something with the time you've got.

Earl opens his eyes and blinks into the darkness. The alarm clock is ringing. It says 3:20, and the moonlight streaming through the window means it must be the early morning. Earl fumbles for the lamp, almost knocking it over in the process. In-candescent light fills the room, painting the metal furniture yellow, the walls yel-low, the bedspread, too. He lies back and looks up at the stretch of yellow ceiling tiles above him, interrupted by a handwritten sign taped to the ceiling. He reads the sign two, maybe three times, then blinks at the room around him.

It is a bare room. Institutional, maybe. There is a desk over by the window. The desk is bare except for the blaring alarm clock. Earl probably notices, at this point, that he is fully clothed. He even has his shoes on under the sheets. He extracts himself from the bed and crosses to the desk. Nothing in the room would suggest that anyone lived there, or ever had, except for the odd scrap of tape stuck here and there to the wall. No pictures, no books, nothing. Through the window, he can see a full moon shining on carefully manicured grass.

45   Earl slaps the snooze button on the alarm clock and stares a moment at the two keys taped to the back of his hand. He picks at the tape while he searches through the empty drawers. In the left pocket of his jacket, he finds a roll of hundred-dollar bills and a letter sealed in an envelope. He checks the rest of the main room and the bathroom. Bits of tape, cigarette butts. Nothing else.

Earl absentmindedly plays with the lump of scar tissue on his neck and moves back toward the bed. He lies back down and stares up at the ceiling and the sign taped to it. The sign reads, GET UP, GET OUT RIGHT NOW. THESE PEOPLE ARE TRYING TO KILL YOU.

Earl closes his eyes.

They tried to teach you to make lists in grade school, remember? Back when your day planner was the back of your hand. And if your assignments came off in the shower, well, then they didn't get done. No direction, they said. No discipline. So they tried to get you to write it all down somewhere more permanent.

Of course, your grade-school teachers would be laughing their pants wet if they could see you now. Because you've become the exact product of their organizational lessons. Because you can't even take a piss without consulting one of your lists.

50   *They were right. Lists are the only way out of this mess.*

Here's the truth: People, even regular people, are never just any one person with one set of attributes. It's not that simple. We're all at the mercy of the limbic system, clouds of electricity drifting through the brain. Every man is broken into twenty-four-hour fractions, and then again within those twenty-four hours. It's a daily pantomime, one man yielding control to the next: a backstage crowded with old hacks clamoring for their turn in the spotlight. Every week, every day. The angry man hands the baton over to the sulking man, and in turn to the sex addict, the introvert, the conversationalist. Every man is a mob, a chain gang of idiots.

This is the tragedy of life. Because for a few minutes of every day, every man becomes a genius. Moments of clarity, insight, whatever you want to call them. The clouds part, the planets get in a neat little line, and everything becomes obvious. I should quit smoking, maybe, or here's how I could make a fast million, or such and such is the key to eternal happiness. That's the miserable truth. For a few moments, the secrets of the universe are opened to us. Life is a cheap parlor trick.

But then the genius, the savant, has to hand over the controls to the next guy down the pike, most likely the guy who just wants to eat potato chips, and insight and brilliance and salvation are all entrusted to a moron or a hedonist or a narcoleptic.

The only way out of this mess, of course, is to take steps to ensure that you control the idiots that you become. To take your chain gang, hand in hand, and lead them. The best way to do this is with a list.

55   *It's like a letter you write to yourself. A master plan, drafted by the guy who can see the light, made with steps simple enough for the rest of the idiots to understand. Follow steps one through one hundred. Repeat as necessary.*

Your problem is a little more acute, maybe, but fundamentally the same thing.

It's like that computer thing, the Chinese room. You remember that? One guy sits in a lit-
tle room, laying down cards with letters written on them in a language he doesn't understand,
laying them down one letter at a time in a sequence according to someone else's instructions.
The cards are supposed to spell out a joke in Chinese. The guy doesn't speak Chinese, of course.
He just follows his instructions.

There are some obvious differences in your situation, of course: You broke out of the room
they had you in, so the whole enterprise has to be portable. And the guy giving the instructions—
that's you, too, just an earlier version of you. And the joke you're telling, well, it's got a punch
line. I just don't think anyone's going to find it very funny.

So that's the idea. All you have to do is follow your instructions. Like climbing a ladder or
descending a staircase. One step at a time. Right down the list. Simple.

And the secret, of course, to any list is to keep it in a place where you're bound to see it.   60

He can hear the buzzing through his eyelids. Insistent. He reaches out for the alarm
clock, but he can't move his arm.

Earl opens his eyes to see a large man bent double over him. The man looks up at
him, annoyed, then resumes his work. Earl looks around him. Too dark for a doctor's
office.

Then the pain floods his brain, blocking out the other questions. He squirms again,
trying to yank his forearm away, the one that feels like it's burning. The arm doesn't
move, but the man shoots him another scowl. Earl adjusts himself in the chair to see
over the top of the man's head.

The noise and the pain are both coming from a gun in the man's hand—a gun with
a needle where the barrel should be. The needle is digging into the fleshy underside
of Earl's forearm, leaving a trail of puffy letters behind it.

Earl tries to rearrange himself to get a better view, to read the letters on his arm, but   65
he can't. He lies back and stares at the ceiling.

Eventually the tattoo artist turns off the noise, wipes Earl's forearm with a piece of
gauze, and wanders over to the back to dig up a pamphlet describing how to deal
with a possible infection. Maybe later he'll tell his wife about this guy and his little note.
Maybe his wife will convince him to call the police.

Earl looks down at the arm. The letters are rising up from the skin, weeping a little. They run from just behind the strap of Earl's watch all the way to the inside of his
elbow. Earl blinks at the message and reads it again. It says, in careful little capitals, I
RAPED AND KILLED YOUR WIFE.

It's your birthday today, so I got you a little present. I would have just bought you a beer,
but who knows where that would have ended?

So instead, I got you a bell. I think I may have had to pawn your watch to buy it, but what
the hell did you need a watch for, anyway?

You're probably asking yourself, Why a bell? In fact, I'm guessing you're going to be   70
asking yourself that question every time you find it in your pocket. Too many of these let-
ters now. Too many for you to dig back into every time you want to know the answer to some
little question.

It's a joke, actually. A practical joke. But think of it this way: I'm not really laughing at
you so much as with you.

I'd like to think that every time you take it out of your pocket and wonder, Why do I have
this bell? a little part of you, a little piece of your broken brain, will remember and laugh, like
I'm laughing now.

Besides, you do know the answer. It was something you learned before. So if you think about it, you'll know.

Back in the old days, people were obsessed with the fear of being buried alive. You remember now? Medical science not being quite what it is today, it wasn't uncommon for people to suddenly wake up in a casket. So rich folks had their coffins outfitted with breathing tubes. Little tubes running up to the mud above so that if someone woke up when they weren't supposed to, they wouldn't run out of oxygen. Now, they must have tested this out and realized that you could shout yourself hoarse through the tube, but it was too narrow to carry much noise. Not enough to attract attention, at least. So a string was run up the tube to a little bell attached to the headstone. If a dead person came back to life, all he had to do was ring his little bell till someone came and dug him up again.

75   *I'm laughing now, picturing you on a bus or maybe in a fast-food restaurant, reaching into your pocket and finding your little bell and wondering to yourself where it came from, why you have it. Maybe you'll even ring it.*

Happy birthday, buddy.

I don't know who figured out the solution to our mutual problem, so I don't know whether to congratulate you or me. A bit of a lifestyle change, admittedly, but an elegant solution, nonetheless.

Look to yourself for the answer.

That sounds like something out of a Hallmark card. I don't know when you thought it up, but my hat's off to you. Not that you know what the hell I'm talking about. But, honestly, a real brainstorm. After all, everybody else needs mirrors to remind themselves who they are. You're no different.

80   The little mechanical voice pauses, then repeats itself. It says, "The time is 8:00 A.M. This is a courtesy call." Earl opens his eyes and replaces the receiver. The phone is perched on a cheap veneer headboard that stretches behind the bed, curves to meet the corner, and ends at the minibar. The TV is still on, blobs of flesh color nattering away at each other. Earl lies back down and is surprised to see himself, older now, tanned, the hair pulling away from his head like solar flares. The mirror on the ceiling is cracked, the silver fading in creases. Earl continues to stare at himself, astonished by what he sees. He is fully dressed, but the clothes are old, threadbare in places.

Earl feels the familiar spot on his left wrist for his watch, but it's gone. He looks down from the mirror to his arm. It is bare and the skin has changed to an even tan, as if he never owned a watch in the first place. The skin is even in color except for the solid black arrow on the inside of Earl's wrist, pointing up his shirtsleeve. He stares at the arrow for a moment. Perhaps he doesn't try to rub it off anymore. He rolls up his sleeve.

The arrow points to a sentence tattooed along Earl's inner arm. Earl reads the sentence once, maybe twice. Another arrow picks up at the beginning of the sentence, points farther up Earl's arm, disappearing under the rolled-up shirtsleeve. He unbuttons his shirt.

Looking down on his chest, he can make out the shapes but cannot bring them into focus, so he looks up at the mirror above him.

The arrow leads up Earl's arm, crosses at the shoulder, and descends onto his upper torso, terminating at a picture of a man's face that occupies most of his chest. The face is that of a large man, balding, with a mustache and a goatee. It is a particular face, but like a police sketch it has a certain unreal quality.

The rest of his upper torso is covered in words, phrases, bits of information, and in- 85
structions, all of them written backward on Earl, forward in the mirror.

Eventually Earl sits up, buttons his shirt, and crosses to the desk. He takes out a pen
and a piece of notepaper from the desk drawer, sits, and begins to write.

*I don't know where you'll be when you read this. I'm not even sure if you'll bother to read
this. I guess you don't need to.*

*It's a shame, really, that you and I will never meet. But, like the song says, "By the time you
read this note, I'll be gone."*

*We're so close now. That's the way it feels. So many pieces put together, spelled out. I guess
it's just a matter of time until you find him.*

Who knows what we've done to get here? Must be a hell of a story, if only you could re- 90
member any of it. I guess it's better that you can't.

I had a thought just now. Maybe you'll find it useful.

*Everybody is waiting for the end to come, but what if it already passed us by? What if the
final joke of Judgment Day was that it had already come and gone and we were none the wiser?
Apocalypse arrives quietly; the chosen are herded off to heaven, and the rest of us, the ones who
failed the test, just keep on going, oblivious. Dead already, wandering around long after the gods
have stopped keeping score, still optimistic about the future.*

*I guess if that's true, then it doesn't matter what you do. No expectations. If you can't find
him, then it doesn't matter, because nothing matters. And if you do find him, then you can kill
him without worrying about the consequences. Because there are no consequences.*

*That's what I'm thinking about right now, in this scrappy little room. Framed pictures of
ships on the wall. I don't know, obviously, but if I had to guess, I'd say we're somewhere up the
coast. If you're wondering why your left arm is five shades browner than your right, I don't know
what to tell you. I guess we must have been driving for a while. And, no, I don't know what
happened to your watch.*

And all these keys: I have no idea. Not a one that I recognize. Car keys and house keys and 95
the little fiddly keys for padlocks. What have we been up to?

*I wonder if he'll feel stupid when you find him. Tracked down by the ten-minute man. As-
sassinated by a vegetable.*

*I'll be gone in a moment. I'll put down the pen, close my eyes, and then you can read this
through if you want.*

*I just wanted you to know that I'm proud of you. No one who matters is left to say it. No
one left is going to want to.*

Earl's eyes are wide open, staring through the window of the car. Smiling eyes.
Smiling through the window at the crowd gathering across the street. The crowd gathering around the body in the doorway. The body emptying slowly across the sidewalk
and into the storm drain.

A stocky guy, facedown, eyes open. Balding head, goatee. In death, as in police 100
sketches, faces tend to look the same. This is definitely somebody in particular. But
really, it could be anybody.

Earl is still smiling at the body as the car pulls away from the curb. The car? Who's
to say? Maybe it's a police cruiser. Maybe it's just a taxi.

As the car is swallowed into traffic, Earl's eyes continue to shine out into the
night, watching the body until it disappears into a circle of concerned pedestrians.

He chuckles to himself as the car continues to make distance between him and the growing crowd.

Earl's smile fades a little. Something has occurred to him. He begins to pat down his pockets; leisurely at first, like a man looking for his keys, then a little more desperately. Maybe his progress is impeded by a set of handcuffs. He begins to empty the contents of his pockets out onto the seat next to him. Some money. A bunch of keys. Scraps of paper.

A round metal lump rolls out of his pocket and slides across the vinyl seat. Earl is frantic now. He hammers at the plastic divider between him and the driver, begging the man for a pen. Perhaps the cabbie doesn't speak much English. Perhaps the cop isn't in the habit of talking to suspects. Either way, the divider between the man in front and the man behind remains closed. A pen is not forthcoming.

105   The car hits a pothole, and Earl blinks at his reflection in the rearview mirror. He is calm now. The driver makes another corner, and the metal lump slides back over to rest against Earl's leg with a little jingle. He picks it up and looks at it, curious now. It is a little bell. A little metal bell. Inscribed on it are his name and a set of dates. He recognizes the first one: the year in which he was born. But the second date means nothing to him. Nothing at all.

As he turns the bell over in his hands, he notices the empty space on his wrist where his watch used to sit. There is a little arrow there, pointing up his arm. Earl looks at the arrow, then begins to roll up his sleeve.

"You'd be late for your own funeral," she'd say. Remember? The more I think about it, the more trite that seems. What kind of idiot, after all, is in any kind of rush to get to the end of his own story?

And how would I know if I were late, anyway? I don't have a watch anymore. I don't know what we did with it.

What the hell do you need a watch for, anyway? It was an antique. Deadweight tugging at your wrist. Symbol of the old you. The you that believed in time.

110   *No. Scratch that. It's not so much that you've lost your faith in time as that time has lost its faith in you. And who needs it, anyway? Who wants to be one of those saps living in the safety of the future, in the safety of the moment after the moment in which they felt something powerful? Living in the next moment, in which they feel nothing. Crawling down the hands of the clock, away from the people who did unspeakable things to them. Believing the lie that time will heal all wounds—which is just a nice way of saying that time deadens us.*

But you're different. You're more perfect. Time is three things for most people, but for you, for us, just one. A singularity. One moment. This moment. Like you're the center of the clock, the axis on which the hands turn. Time moves about you but never moves you. It has lost its ability to affect you. What is it they say? That time is theft? But not for you. Close your eyes and you can start all over again. Conjure up that necessary emotion, fresh as roses.

Time is an absurdity. An abstraction. The only thing that matters is this moment. This moment a million times over. You have to trust me. If this moment is repeated enough, if you keep trying—and you have to keep trying—eventually you will come across the next item on your list.   [2001]

QUESTIONS

1. Identify the two points of view in the story. What are the different kinds of information that the two points of view provide?
2. Identify and describe the various settings in the story? How do these settings help develop the story's themes?
3. Discuss the relationship between point of view and conflict in this story.
4. Does the writer create a character that the reader can understand and sympathize with? How? How not?
5. The story has no secondary characters. What is the effect of that choice by the writer?

RESPONSES

1. Compare the story to Gilman's "The Yellow Wallpaper." How do the stories confront illness, institutions, and attempts at freedom? What similarities are there in the use of the elements of fiction?
2. Discuss this story as a contemporary treatment of themes and approaches toward fiction pioneered by Poe and by Kafka.

FOCUS ON FILM

1. Jonathan Nolan's brother wrote and directed the film *Memento*. Compare the two works in the use of point of view and plot.
2. What is the effect of the film's presentation of plot in reverse chronological order? Using the DVD's "chapter selection" capabilities, view the film in chronological order. How does the film's theme and effect differ from those created by the original reverse chronological order?
3. The film adds several characters and incidents to the story. How do these additions change the overall effect of the story?

JOYCE CAROL OATES

Joyce Carol Oates (b. 1938), born in Lockport, New York (the setting for some of her early work), did her undergraduate work at Syracuse and received an M.A. from the University of Wisconsin. Oates has published an enormous amount of work, most of it fiction, and is an acknowledged expert on professional boxing. Her novels include *A Garden of Earthly Delights* (1967), *Bellefleur* (1980), *Black Water* (1992), and *Foxfire* (1993). Her more recent collections of short fiction are *Heat and Other Stories* (1991), *Haunted: Tales of the Grotesque* (1994), and *Will You Always Love Me?* (1996). She has received an O. Henry and a National Book Award and teaches creative writing at Princeton University. *Blonde*, a novel, was published in 2000, followed by *Freaky Green Eyes* (2003), *Falls* (2004), and *Sexy* (2005).

Shopping

An old ritual, Saturday morning shopping. Mother and daughter. Mrs. Dietrich and Nola. Shops in the village, stores and boutiques at the splendid Livingstone Mall on Route 12: Bloomingdale's, Saks, Lord & Taylor, Bonwit's, Neiman-Marcus, and the rest. Mrs. Dietrich would know her way around the stores blindfolded but there is always the surprise of lavish seasonal displays, extraordinary holiday sales, the openings of new stores at the mall like Laura Ashley, Paraphernalia. On one of their mall days Mrs. Dietrich and Nola would try to get there at midmorning, have lunch around 1 P.M. at one or another of their favorite restaurants, shop for perhaps an hour after lunch, then come home. Sometimes the shopping trips were more successful than at other times, but you have to have faith, Mrs. Dietrich tells herself. Her interior voice is calm, neutral, free of irony. Even since her divorce her interior voice has been free of irony. You have to have faith.

Tomorrow morning Nola returns to school in Maine; today will be spent at the mall. Mrs. Dietrich has planned it for days—there are numerous things Nola needs, mainly clothes, a pair of good shoes; Mrs. Dietrich must buy a birthday present for one of her aunts; mother and daughter need the time together. At the mall, in such crowds of shoppers, moments of intimacy are possible as they rarely are at home. (Seventeen-year-old Nola, home on spring break for a brief eight days, seems always to be *busy*, always out with her *friends*, the trip to the mall has been postponed twice.)

But Saturday, 10:30 A.M., they are in the car at last headed south on Route 12, a bleak March morning following a night of freezing rain; there's a metallic cast to the air and no sun anywhere in the sky but the light hurts Mrs. Dietrich's eyes just the same. "Does it seem as if spring will ever come? It must be twenty degrees colder up in Maine," she says. Driving in heavy traffic always makes Mrs. Dietrich nervous and she is overly sensitive to her daughter's silence, which seems deliberate, perverse, when they have so little time remaining together—not even a full day.

Nola asks politely if Mrs. Dietrich would like her to drive and Mrs. Dietrich says no, of course not, she's fine, it's only a few more miles and maybe traffic will lighten. Nola seems about to say something more, then thinks better of it. So much between them is precarious, chancy—but they've been kind to each other these past seven days. Nola's secrets remain her own and Mrs. Dietrich isn't going to pry; she's beyond that. She loves Nola with a fierce unreasoned passion stronger than any she felt for the man who had been her husband for thirteen years, certainly far stronger than any she ever felt for her own mother. Sometimes in weak despondent moods, alone, lonely, self-pitying, when she has had too much to drink, Mrs. Dietrich thinks she is in love with her daughter, but this is a thought she can't contemplate for long. And how Nola would snort in amused contempt, incredulous, mocking—"Oh, *Mother!*"—if she were told.

("Why do you make so much of things? Of people who don't seem to care about you?" Mr. Dietrich once asked. He had been speaking of one or another of their Livingstone friends, a woman in Mrs. Dietrich's circle; he hadn't meant to be insulting but Mrs. Dietrich was stung as if he'd slapped her.)

Mrs. Dietrich tries to engage her daughter in conversation of a harmless sort but Nola answers in monosyllables; Nola is rather tired from so many nights of partying with her friends, some of whom attend the local high school, some of whom are home for spring break from prep schools—Exeter, Lawrenceville, Concord, Andover, Portland. Late nights, but Mrs. Dietrich doesn't consciously lie awake waiting for Nola to come home; they've been through all that before. Now Nola sits beside her mother looking wan, subdued, rather melancholy. Thinking her private thoughts. She is wearing a bulky quilted jacket Mrs. Dietrich has never liked, the usual blue jeans, black calfskin boots zippered tightly to mid-calf. Her delicate profile, thick-lashed eyes. Mrs. Dietrich must resist the temptation to ask, Why are you so quiet, Nola? What are you thinking? They've been through all that before.

Route 12 has become a jumble of small industrial parks, high-rise office and apartment buildings, torn-up landscapes: mountains of raw earth, uprooted trees, ruts and ditches filled with muddy water. Everywhere are yellow bulldozers, earthmovers, construction workers operating cranes, ACREAGE FOR SALE signs. When Mr. and Mrs. Dietrich first moved out to Livingstone from the city sixteen years ago this stretch along Route 12 was quite attractive, mainly farmland, woods, a scattering of small suburban houses; now it has nearly all been developed. There is no natural sequence to what you see—buildings, construction work, leveled woods, the lavish grounds owned by Squibb. Though she has driven this route countless times, Mrs. Dietrich is never quite certain where the mall is and must be prepared for a sudden exit. She remembers getting lost the first several times, remembers the excitement she and her friends felt about the grand opening of the mall, stores worthy of serious shopping at last. Today is much the same. No, today is worse. Like Christmas when she was a small child, Mrs. Dietrich thinks. She'd hoped so badly to be happy she'd felt actual pain, a constriction in her throat like crying.

5

"*Are* you all right, Nola? You've been so quiet all morning," Mrs. Dietrich asks, half scolding. Nola stirs from her reverie, says she's fine, a just perceptible edge to her reply, and for the remainder of the drive there's some stiffness between them. Mrs. Dietrich chooses to ignore it. In any case she is fully absorbed in driving—negotiating a tricky exit across two lanes of traffic, then the hairpin curve of the ramp, the numerous looping drives of the mall. Then the enormous parking lot, daunting to the inexperienced, but Mrs. Dietrich always heads for the area behind Lord & Taylor on the far side of the mall, Lot D; her luck holds and she finds a space close in. "Well, we made it," she says, smiling happily at Nola. Nola laughs in reply—what does a seventeen-year-old's laughter *mean?*—but she remembers, getting out, to lock both doors on her side of the car. Even here at the Livingstone Mall unattended cars are no longer safe. The smile Nola gives Mrs. Dietrich across the car's roof is careless and beautiful and takes Mrs. Dietrich's breath away.

The March morning tastes of grit with an undercurrent of something acrid, chemical; inside the mall, beneath the first of the elegant brass-buttressed glass domes, the air is fresh and tonic, circulating from invisible vents. The mall is crowded, rather noisy—it *is* Saturday morning—but a feast for the eyes after that long trip on Route 12. Tall slender trees grow out of the mosaic-tiled pavement; there are beds of Easter lilies, daffodils, jonquils, tulips of all colors. There are cobblestone walkways, fountains illuminated from within, wide promenades as in an Old World setting. Mrs. Dietrich smiles with relief. She senses that Nola too is relieved, cheered. It's like coming home.

The shopping excursions began when Nola was a small child but did not acquire their special significance until she was twelve or thirteen years old and capable of serious, sustained shopping with her mother. Sometimes Mrs. Dietrich and Nola would shop with friends, another mother and daughter perhaps, sometimes Mrs. Dietrich invited one or two of Nola's school friends to join them, but she preferred to be alone with Nola and she believed Nola preferred to be alone with her. This was about the time when Mr. Dietrich moved out of the house and back into their old apartment building in the city—a separation, he'd called it initially, to give them perspective, though Mrs. Dietrich had no illusions about what "perspective" would turn out to entail—so the shopping trips were all the more significant. Not that Mrs. Dietrich and Nola spent very much money; they really didn't, *really* they didn't, when compared to friends and neighbors. And Mr. Dietrich rarely objected: the financial arrangement he made with Mrs. Dietrich was surprisingly generous.

10   At seventeen Nola is shrewd and discerning as a shopper, not easy to please, knowledgeable as a mature woman about certain aspects of fashion, quality merchandise, good stores. She studies advertisements, she shops for bargains. Her closets, like Mrs. Dietrich's, are crammed, but she rarely buys anything that Mrs. Dietrich thinks shoddy or merely faddish. Up in Portland, at the academy, she hasn't as much time to shop, but when she is home in Livingstone it isn't unusual for her and her girlfriends to shop nearly every day. Sometimes she shops at the mall with a boyfriend—but she prefers girls. Like all her friends she has charge accounts at the better stores, her own credit cards, a reasonable allowance. At the time of their settlement Mr. Dietrich said guiltily that it was the least he could do for them: if Mrs. Dietrich wanted to work part-time, she could (she was trained, more or less, in public relations of a small-scale sort); if not, not. Mrs. Dietrich thought, It's the most you can do for us too.

Near Baumgarten's entrance mother and daughter see a disheveled woman sitting by herself on one of the benches. Without seeming to look at her, shoppers are making a discreet berth around her, a stream following a natural course. Nola, taken by surprise, stares. Mrs. Dietrich has seen the woman from time to time at the mall, always alone, smirking and talking to herself, frizzed gray hair in a tangle, puckered mouth. Always wearing the same black wool coat, a garment of fairly good quality but shapeless, rumpled, stained, as if she sleeps in it. She might be anywhere from forty to sixty years of age. Once Mrs. Dietrich saw her make menacing gestures at children who were teasing her, another time she'd seen the woman staring belligerently at *her.* A white paste had gathered in the corners of her mouth.

"My God, that poor woman," Nola says. "I didn't think there were people like her here—I mean, I didn't think they would allow it."

"She doesn't seem to cause any disturbance," Mrs. Dietrich says. "She just sits. Don't stare, Nola, she'll see you."

"You've seen her here before? Here?"

"A few times this winter."   15

"Is she always like that?"

"I'm sure she's harmless, Nola. She just *sits.*"

Nola is incensed, her pale blue eyes like washed glass. "I'm sure *she's* harmless, Mother. It's the harm the poor woman has to endure that is the tragedy."

Mrs. Dietrich is surprised and a little offended by her daughter's passionate tone but she knows enough not to argue. They enter Baumgarten's, taking their habitual route. So many shoppers! So much merchandise! Dazzling displays of tulips, chrome, neon, winking lights, enormous painted Easter eggs in wicker baskets. Nola speaks of the tragedy of women like that woman—the tragedy of the homeless, the mentally disturbed: bag ladies out on the street, outcasts of an affluent society—but she's soon distracted by the busyness on all sides, the attractive items for sale. They take the escalator up to the third floor, to the Clubhouse Juniors department, where Nola often buys things. From there they will move on to Young Collector, then to Act IV, then to Petite Corner, then one or another boutique and designer—Liz Claiborne, Christian Dior, Calvin Klein, Carlos Falchi, and the rest. And after Baumgarten's the other stores await, to be visited each in turn. Mrs. Dietrich checks her watch and sees with satisfaction that there's just enough time before lunch but not *too* much time. She gets ravenously hungry, shopping at the mall.

Nola is efficient and matter-of-fact about shopping, though she acts solely upon instinct. Mrs. Dietrich likes to watch her at a short distance, holding items of clothing up to herself in the three-way mirrors, modeling things she thinks especially promising. A twill blazer, a dress with rounded shoulders and blouson jacket, a funky zippered jumpsuit in white sailcloth, a pair of straight-leg Evan Picone pants, a green leather vest: Mrs. Dietrich watches her covertly. At such times Nola is perfectly content, fully absorbed in the task at hand; Mrs. Dietrich knows she isn't thinking about anything that would distress her. (Like Mr. Dietrich's betrayal. Like Nola's difficulties with her friends. Like her difficulties at school—as much as Mrs. Dietrich knows of them.) When Nola glances in her mother's direction Mrs. Dietrich pretends to be examining clothes for her own purposes. As if she's hardly aware of Nola. Once, at the mall, perhaps in this very store in this very department, Nola saw Mrs. Dietrich watching her and walked away angrily, and when Mrs. Dietrich caught up with her she said, "I can't stand it, Mother." Her voice was choked and harsh, a vein prominent in her forehead. "Let me go. For Christ's sake will you let me go." Mrs. Dietrich didn't dare touch her though she could see Nola was trembling. For a long terrible moment mother and daughter stood side by side near a display of bright brash Catalina beachwear while

20

Nola whispered, "Let me go. *Let me go.*" How the scene ended Mrs. Dietrich can't recall—it erupts in an explosion of light, like a bad dream—but she knows better than to risk it again.

Difficult to believe that girl standing so poised and self-assured in front of the three-way mirror was once a plain, rather chunky, unhappy child. She'd been unpopular at school. Overly serious. Anxious. Quick to tears. Aged eleven she hid herself away in her room for hours at a time, reading, drawing pictures, writing little stories she could sometimes be prevailed upon to read aloud to her mother, sometimes even to her father, though she dreaded his judgment. She went through a "scientific" phase a little later; Mrs. Dietrich remembers an ambitious bas-relief map of North America, meticulous illustrations for "photosynthesis," a pastel drawing of an eerie ball of fire labeled RED GIANT (a dying star?), which won a prize in a state competition for junior high students. Then for a season it was stray facts Nola confronted them with, often at the dinner table. Interrupting her parents' conversation to say brightly, "Did you know that Nero's favorite color was green? He carried a giant emerald and held it up to his eye to watch Christians being devoured by lions." And, "Did you ever hear of the raving ghosts of Siberia, with their mouths always open, starving for food, screaming?" And once at a large family gathering, "Did you all know that last week downtown a little baby's nose was chewed off by rats in his crib—a little *black* baby?" Nola meant only to call attention to herself, but you couldn't blame her listeners for being offended. They stared at her, not knowing what to say. What a strange child! What queer glassy-pale eyes! Mr. Dietrich told her curtly to leave the table; he'd had enough of the game she was playing and so had everyone else.

Nola stared at him, her eyes filling with tears. Game?

When they were alone Mr. Dietrich said angrily to Mrs. Dietrich, "Can't you control her in front of other people, at least?" Mrs. Dietrich was angry, too, and frightened. She said, "I *try*."

They sent her off aged fourteen to the Portland Academy up in Maine, and without their help she matured into a girl of considerable beauty. A heart-shaped face, delicate features, glossy red-brown hair scissor-cut to her shoulders. Five feet seven inches tall weighing less than one hundred pounds, the result of constant savage dieting. (Mrs. Dietrich, who has weight problems herself, doesn't dare inquire as to details. They've been through that already.) All the girls sport flat bellies, flat buttocks, jutting pelvic bones. Many, like Nola, are wound tight, high-strung as pedigreed dogs, whippets for instance, the breed that lives for running. Thirty days after they'd left her at the Portland Academy, Nola telephoned home at 11 P.M. one Sunday giggly and high, telling Mrs. Dietrich she adored the school she adored her suitemates she adored most of her teachers particularly her riding instructor Terri, Terri the Terrier they called the woman because she was so fierce, such a character, eyes that bore right through your skull, wore belts with the most amazing silver buckles! Nola loved Terri but she wasn't *in* love—there's a difference!

25   Mrs. Dietrich broke down weeping, *that* time.

Now of course Nola has boyfriends. Mrs. Dietrich has long since given up trying to keep track of their names. And, in any case, the Paul of this spring isn't necessarily the Paul of last November, nor are all the boys necessarily students at the academy. There is even one "boy"—or young man—who seems to be married: who seems to be, in fact, one of the junior instructors at the school. (Mrs. Dietrich does not eavesdrop on her daughter's telephone conversations but there are things she cannot help over-hearing.) Is your daughter on the pill? the women in Mrs. Dietrich's circle asked one another for a while, guiltily, surreptitiously. Now they no longer ask.

But Nola has announced recently that she loathes boys—she's fed up.

She's never going to get married. She'll study languages in college, French, Italian, something exotic like Arabic, go to work for the American foreign service. Unless she drops out of school altogether to become a model.

"Do you think I'm too fat, Mother?" she asks frequently, worriedly, standing in front of the mirror, twisted at the waist to reveal her small round belly which, it seems, can't help being round: she bloats herself on diet Cokes all day long. "Do you think it *shows?*"

When Mrs. Dietrich was pregnant with Nola she'd been twenty-nine years old and   30
she and Mr. Dietrich had tried to have a baby for nearly five years. She'd lost hope, begun to despise herself; then suddenly it happened: like grace. Like happiness swelling so powerfully it can barely be contained. I can hear its heartbeat! her husband exclaimed. He'd been her lover then, young, vigorous, dreamy. Caressing the rock-hard belly, splendid white tight-stretched skin, that roundness like a warm puls-ing melon. Never before so happy, and never since. Husband and wife. One flesh. Mr. Dietrich gave Mrs. Dietrich a reproduction on stiff glossy paper of Dante Gabriel Ros-setti's° *Beata Beatrix,*° embarrassed, apologetic, knowing it was sentimental and per-haps a little silly but that was how he thought of her—so beautiful, rapturous, pregnant with their child. Her features were ordinarily pretty, her wavy brown hair cut short; Mrs. Dietrich looked nothing like the extraordinary woman in Rossetti's painting in her transport of ecstasy but she was immensely flattered and moved by her husband's gift, knowing herself adored, worthy of adoration. She told no one, but she knew the baby was to be a girl. It would be herself again, reborn and this time perfect.

Not until years later did she learn by chance that the woman in Rossetti's painting was in fact his dead wife Lizzy Siddal, who had killed herself with an overdose of lau-danum after the stillbirth of their only child.

"Oh, Mother, isn't it *beautiful!*" Nola exclaims.

It is past noon. Past twelve-thirty. Mrs. Dietrich and Nola have made the rounds of a half dozen stores, traveled countless escalators, one clothing department has blend-ed into the next and the chic smiling saleswomen have become indistinguishable, and Mrs. Dietrich is beginning to feel the urgent need for a glass of white wine. Just a glass. "Isn't it beautiful? It's *perfect,*" Nola says. Her eyes glow with pleasure, her smooth skin is radiant. Modeling in the three-way mirror a queer little yellow-and-black striped sweater with a ribbed waist, punk style, mock cheap (though the sweater by Sergio Va-lente, even "drastically reduced," is certainly not cheap), Mrs. Dietrich feels the moth-erly obligation to register a mild protest, knowing Nola will not hear. She must have it and will have it. She'll wear it a few times, then retire it to the bottom of a drawer with so many other novelty sweaters, accumulated since sixth grade. (She's like her mother in that regard—can't bear to throw anything away. Clothes, shoes, cosmetics, records; once bought by Nola Dietrich they are hers forever, crammed in drawers and closets.)

"*Isn't* it beautiful?" Nola demands, studying her reflection in the mirror.

°*Dante Gabriel Rossetti* (1828–1882): English poet and painter.
°*Beata Beatrix*: Rossetti's painting of the poet Dante's beloved Beatrice.

35   Mrs. Dietrich pays for the sweater on her charge account.

Next they buy Nola a good pair of shoes. And a handbag to go with them. In Paraphernalia where rock music blasts overhead and Mrs. Dietrich stands to one side, rather miserable, Nola chats companionably with two girls—tall, pretty, cutely made up—she'd gone to public school in Livingstone with, says afterward with an upward rolling of her eyes, "God, I was afraid they'd latch onto us!" Mrs. Dietrich has seen women friends and acquaintances of her own in the mall this morning but has shrunk from being noticed, not wanting to share her daughter with anyone. She has a sense of time passing ever more swiftly, cruelly.

Nola wants to try on an outfit in Paraphernalia, just for fun, a boxy khaki-colored jacket with matching pants, fly front, zippers, oversized buttons, so aggressively ugly it must be chic, yes of course it *is* chic, "drastically reduced" from $245 to $219. An import by Julio Vicente and Mrs. Dietrich can't reasonably disapprove of Julio Vicente, can she. She watches Nola preening in the mirror, watches other shoppers watching her. My daughter. Mine. But of course there is no connection between them, they don't even resemble each other. A seventeen-year-old, a forty-seven-year-old. When Nola is away she seems to forget her mother entirely—doesn't telephone, certainly doesn't write. It's the way all their daughters are, Mrs. Dietrich's friends tell her. It doesn't *mean* anything. Mrs. Dietrich thinks how when she was carrying Nola, those nine long months, they'd been completely happy—not an instant's doubt or hesitation. The singular weight of the body. A state like trance you are tempted to mistake for happiness because the body is incapable of thinking, therefore incapable of anticipating change. Hot rhythmic blood, organs packed tight and moist, the baby upside down in her sac in her mother's belly, always present tense, always *now*. It was a shock when the end came so abruptly, but everyone told Mrs. Dietrich she was a natural mother, praised and pampered her. For a while. Then of course she'd had her baby, her Nola. Even now Mrs. Dietrich can't really comprehend the experience. *Giving birth. Had a baby. Was born.* Mere words, absurdly inadequate. She knows no more of how love ends than she knew as a child, she knows only of how love begins—in the belly, in the womb, where it is always present tense.

The morning's shopping has been quite successful, but lunch at La Crêperie doesn't go well. For some reason—surely there can be no reason?—lunch doesn't go well at all.

La Crêperie is Nola's favorite mall restaurant, always amiably crowded, bustling, a simulated sidewalk café with red-striped umbrellas, wrought-iron tables and chairs, menus in French, music piped in overhead. Mrs. Dietrich's nerves are chafed by the pretense of gaiety, the noise, the openness onto one of the mall's busy promenades where at any minute a familiar face might emerge, but she is grateful for her glass of chilled white wine—isn't it red wine that gives you headaches, hangovers?—white wine is safe. She orders a small tossed salad and a creamed chicken crêpe and devours it hungrily—she *is* hungry—while Nola picks at her seafood crêpe with a disdainful look. A familiar scene: mother watching while daughter pushes food around on her plate. Suddenly Nola is tense, moody, corners of her mouth downturned. Mrs. Dietrich wants to ask, What's wrong? She wants to ask, Why are you unhappy? She wants to smooth Nola's hair back from her forehead, check to see if her forehead is overly warm, wants to hug her close, hard. Why, why? What did I do wrong? Why do you hate me?

40   Calling the Portland Academy a few weeks ago Mrs. Dietrich suddenly lost control, began crying. She hadn't been drinking and she hadn't known she was upset. A girl

unknown to her, one of Nola's suitemates, was saying, "Please, Mrs. Dietrich, it's all right, I'm sure Nola will call you back later tonight—or tomorrow, Mrs. Dietrich? I'll tell her you called, all right, Mrs. Dietrich?" as embarrassed as if Mrs. Dietrich had been her own mother.

How love begins. How love ends.

Mrs. Dietrich orders a third glass of wine. This is a celebration of sorts, isn't it? Their last shopping trip for a long time. But Nola resists, Nola isn't sentimental. In casual defiance of Mrs. Dietrich she lights up a cigarette—yes, Mother, Nola has said ironically, since *you* stopped smoking *everybody* is supposed to stop—and sits with her arms crossed, watching streams of shoppers pass. Mrs. Dietrich speaks lightly of practical matters, tomorrow morning's drive to the airport and will Nola telephone when she gets to Portland to let Mrs. Dietrich know she has arrived safely? La Crêperie opens onto an atrium three stories high, vast, airy, lit with artificial sunlight, tastefully decorated with trees, potted spring flowers, a fountain, a gigantic white Easter bunny, cleverly mechanized, atop a nest of brightly painted wooden eggs. The bunny has an animated tail, an animated nose; paws, ears, eyes that move. Children stand watching it, screaming with excitement, delight. Mrs. Dietrich notes that Nola's expression is one of faint contempt and says, "It *is* noisy here, isn't it?"

"Little kids have all the fun," Nola says.

Then with no warning—though of course she'd been planning this all along—Nola brings up the subject of a semester in France, in Paris and Rouen, the fall semester of her senior year it would be; she has put in her application, she says, and is waiting to hear if she's been accepted. She smokes her cigarette calmly, expelling smoke from her nostrils in a way Mrs. Dietrich thinks particularly coarse. Mrs. Dietrich, who believed that particular topic was finished, takes care to speak without emotion. "I just don't think it's a very practical idea right now, Nola," she says. "We've been through it, haven't we? I—"

"I'm going," Nola says. 45

"The extra expense, for one thing. Your father—"

"If I get accepted, I'm going."

"Your father—"

"The hell with him too."

Mrs. Dietrich would like to slap her daughter's face. Bring tears to those steely 50 eyes. But she sits stiff, turning her wineglass between her fingers, patient, calm; she's heard all this before; she says, "Surely this isn't the best time to discuss it, Nola."

Mrs. Dietrich is afraid her daughter will leave the restaurant, simply walk away; that has happened before and if it happens today she doesn't know what she will do. But Nola sits unmoving, her face closed, impassive. Mrs. Dietrich feels her quickened heartbeat. It's like seeing your own life whirling in a sink, in a drain, one of those terrible dreams in which you're paralyzed—the terror of losing her daughter. Once after one of their quarrels Mrs. Dietrich told a friend of hers, the mother too of a teenaged daughter, "I just don't know her any longer; how can you keep living with someone you don't know?" and the woman said, "Eventually you can't."

Nola says, not looking at Mrs. Dietrich, "Why don't we talk about it, Mother."

"Talk about what?" Mrs. Dietrich asks.

"You know."

"The semester in France? Again?" 55

"No."

"What, then?"

"You *know*."

"I don't know, really. Really!" Mrs. Dietrich smiles, baffled. She feels the corners of her eyes pucker white with strain.

60 Nola says, sighing, "How exhausting it is."

"How *what*?"

"How exhausting it is."

"What is?"

"You and me."

65 "What?"

"Being together."

"Being together how?"

"The two of us, like this—"

"But we're hardly ever together, Nola," Mrs. Dietrich says.

70 Her expression is calm but her voice is shaking. Nola turns away, covering her face with a hand; for a moment she looks years older than her age—in fact exhausted. Mrs. Dietrich sees with pity that her daughter's skin is fair and thin and dry—unlike her own, which tends to be oily—it will wear out before she's forty. Mrs. Dietrich reaches over to squeeze her hand. The fingers are limp, ungiving. "You're going back to school tomorrow, Nola," she says. "You won't come home again until June twelfth. And you probably will go to France—if your father consents."

Nola gets to her feet, drops her cigarette to the flagstone terrace, and grinds it out beneath her boot. A dirty thing to do, Mrs. Dietrich thinks, considering there's an ashtray right on the table, but she says nothing. She dislikes La Crêperie anyway.

Nola laughs, showing her lovely white teeth. "Oh, the hell with him," she says. "Fuck Daddy, right?"

They separate for an hour, Mrs. Dietrich to Neiman-Marcus to buy a birthday gift for her elderly aunt, Nola to the trendy new boutique Pour Vous. By the time Mrs. Dietrich rejoins her daughter she's quite angry, blood beating hot and hard and measured in resentment; she has had time to relive old quarrels between them, old exchanges, stray humiliating memories of her marriage as well; these last-hour disagreements are the cruelest and they are Nola's specialty. She locates Nola in the rear of the boutique amid blaring rock music, flashing neon lights, chrome-edged mirrors, her face still hard, closed, prim, pale. She stands beside another teenaged girl, looking in a desultory way through a rack of blouses, shoving the hangers roughly along, taking no care when a blouse falls to the floor. Mrs. Dietrich remembers seeing Nola slip a pair of panty hose into her purse in a village shop because, she said afterward, the saleswoman was so damned slow coming to wait on her; fortunately Mrs. Dietrich was there, took the panty hose right out, and replaced it on the counter. No big deal, Mother, Nola said, don't have a stroke or something. Seeing Nola now, Mrs. Dietrich is charged with hurt, rage; the injustice of it, she thinks, the cruelty of it, and why, and why? And as Nola glances up, startled, not prepared to see her mother in front of her, their eyes lock for an instant and Mrs. Dietrich stares at her with hatred. Cold calm clear unmistakable hatred. She is thinking, Who are *you*? What have I to do with *you*? I don't know *you*, I don't love *you*, why should I?

Has Nola seen, heard? She turns aside as if wincing, gives the blouses a final dismissive shove. Her eyes look tired, the corners of her mouth downturned. Anxious, immediately repentant, Mrs. Dietrich asks if she has found anything worth trying on. Nola says with a shrug, "Not a thing, Mother."

On their way out of the mall Mrs. Dietrich and Nola see the disheveled woman in the black coat again, this time sitting prominently on a concrete ledge in front of Lord & Taylor's busy main entrance, shopping bag at her feet, shabby purse on the ledge beside her. She is shaking her head in a series of annoyed twitches as if arguing with someone but her hands are loose, palms up, in her lap. Her posture is unfortunate— she sits with her knees parted, inner thighs revealed, fatty, dead white, the tops of cotton stockings rolled tight cutting into the flesh. Again, streams of shoppers are making a careful berth around her. Alone among them Nola hesitates, seems about to approach the woman—Please don't, Nola, please! Mrs. Dietrich thinks—then changes her mind and keeps on walking. Mrs. Dietrich murmurs, "Isn't it a pity, poor thing, don't you wonder where she lives, who her family is?" but Nola doesn't reply. Her pace through the first floor of Lord & Taylor is so rapid that Mrs. Dietrich can barely keep up.

But she's upset. Strangely upset. As soon as they are in the car, packages and bags in the back seat, she begins crying.

It's childish helpless crying, as though her heart is broken. But Mrs. Dietrich knows it isn't broken; she's heard these very sobs before. Many times before. Still she comforts her daughter, embraces her, hugs her hard, hard. A sudden fierce passion. Vehemence. "Nola honey, Nola dear, what's wrong, dear? everything will be all right, dear," she says, close to weeping herself. She would embrace Nola even more tightly except for the girl's quilted jacket, that bulky L. L. Bean thing she has never liked, and Nola's stubborn lowered head. Nola has always been ashamed, crying, frantic to hide her face. Strangers are passing close by the car, curious, staring. Mrs. Dietrich wishes she had a cloak to draw over her daughter and herself, so that no one would see. [1991]

QUESTIONS

1. What is the effect of so many real brands and real stores being mentioned?
2. What is the purpose of the "disheveled woman sitting by herself on one of the benches"?
3. How well does Mrs. Dietrich know Nola?
4. What does Oates mean by comparing mother and daughter: Neither can "bear to throw anything away"?
5. Is there any purpose to setting the story in the spring, at Easter time?

RESPONSES

1. Compare this story to Mukherjee's "A Father."
2. From a sociological/Marxist perspective, what role does money and class play in this story?

Joyce Carol Oates

Where Are You Going,
Where Have You Been?

To Bob Dylan

Her name was Connie. She was fifteen and she had a quick nervous giggling habit of craning her neck to glance into mirrors or checking other people's faces to make sure her own was all right. Her mother, who noticed everything and knew everything and who hadn't much reason any longer to look at her own face, always scolded Connie about it. "Stop gawking at yourself, who are you? You think you're so pretty?" she would say. Connie would raise her eyebrows at these familiar complaints and look right through her mother, into a shadowy vision of herself as she was right at that moment: she knew she was pretty and that was everything. Her mother had been pretty once too, if you could believe those old snapshots in the album, but now her looks were gone and that was why she was always after Connie.

"Why don't you keep your room clean like your sister? How've you got your hair fixed—what the hell stinks? Hair spray? You don't see your sister using that junk."

Her sister June was twenty-four and still lived at home. She was a secretary in the high school Connie attended, and if that wasn't bad enough—with her in the same building— she was so plain and chunky and steady that Connie had to hear her praised all the time by her mother and her mother's sisters. June did this, June did that, she saved money and helped clean the house and cooked and Connie couldn't do a thing, her mind was all filled with trashy daydreams. Their father was away at work most of the time and when he came home he wanted supper and he read the newspaper at supper and after supper he went to bed. He didn't bother talking much to them, but around his bent head Connie's mother kept picking at her until Connie wished her mother were dead and she herself were dead and it were all over. "She makes me want to throw up sometimes," she complained to her friends. She had a high, breathless, amused voice which made everything she said sound a little forced, whether it was sincere or not.

There was one good thing: June went places with girlfriends of hers, girls who were just as plain and steady as she, and so when Connie wanted to do that her mother had no objections. The father of Connie's best girlfriend drove the girls the three miles to town and left them off at a shopping plaza, so that they could walk through the stores or go to a movie, and when he came to pick them up again at eleven he never bothered to ask what they had done.

They must have been familiar sights, walking around that shopping plaza in their shorts and flat ballerina slippers that always scuffed the sidewalk, with charm bracelets jingling on their thin wrists; they would lean together to whisper and laugh secretly if someone passed by who amused or interested them. Connie had long dark blond hair that drew anyone's eye to it, and she wore part of it pulled up on her head and puffed out and the rest of it she let fall down her back. She wore a pullover jersey blouse that looked one way when she was at home and another way when she was away from home. Everything about her had two sides to it, one for home and one for anywhere that was not home: her walk that could be childlike and bobbing, or languid enough to make anyone think she was hearing music in her head, her mouth which was pale and smirking most of the time, but bright and pink on these evenings out, her laugh which was cynical and drawling at home—"Ha, ha, very funny"—but high-pitched and nervous anywhere else, like the jingling of the charms on her bracelet.

Sometimes they did go shopping or to a movie, but sometimes they went across the highway, ducking fast across the busy road, to a drive-in restaurant where older kids hung out. The restaurant was shaped like a big bottle, though squatter than a real bottle, and on its cap was a revolving figure of a grinning boy who held a hamburger aloft. One night in midsummer they ran across, breathless with daring, and right away someone leaned out a car window and invited them over, but it was just a boy from high school they didn't like. It made them feel good to be able to ignore him. They went up through the maze of parked and cruising cars to the bright-lit, fly-infested restaurant, their faces pleased and expectant as if they were entering a sacred building that loomed out of the night to give them what haven and what blessing they yearned for. They sat at the counter and crossed their legs at the ankles, their thin shoulders rigid with excitement, and listened to the music that made everything so good: the music was always in the background like music at a church service, it was something to depend upon.

A boy named Eddie came in to talk with them. He sat backward on his stool, turning himself jerkily around in semicircles and then stopping and turning again, and after a while he asked Connie if she would like something to eat. She said she did and so she tapped her friend's arm on her way out—her friend pulled her face up into a brave droll look—and Connie said she would meet her at eleven, across the way. "I just hate to leave her like that," Connie said earnestly, but the boy said that she wouldn't be alone for long. So they went out to his car and on the way Connie couldn't help but let her eyes wander over the windshields and faces all around her, her face gleaming with a joy that had nothing to do with Eddie or even this place; it might have been the music. She drew her shoulders up and sucked in her breath with the pure pleasure of being alive, and just at that moment she happened to glance at a face just a few feet from hers. It was a boy with shaggy black hair, in a convertible jalopy painted gold. He stared at her and then his lips widened into a grin. Connie slit her eyes at him and turned away, but she couldn't help glancing back and there he was still watching her. He wagged a finger and laughed and said, "Gonna get you, baby," and Connie turned away again without Eddie noticing anything.

She spent three hours with him, at the restaurant where they ate hamburgers and drank Cokes in wax cups that were always sweating, and then down an alley a mile or so away, and when he left her off at five to eleven only the movie house was still open at the plaza. Her girlfriend was there, talking with a boy. When Connie came up the two girls smiled at each other and Connie said, "How was the movie?" and the girl said, "*You* should know." They rode off with the girl's father, sleepy and pleased, and Connie couldn't help but look at the darkened shopping plaza with its big empty parking lot and its signs that were faded and ghostly now, and over at the drive-in restaurant where cars were still circling tirelessly. She couldn't hear the music at this distance.

Next morning June asked her how the movie was and Connie said, "So-so."

10   She and that girl and occasionally another girl went out several times a week that way, and the rest of the time Connie spent around the house—it was summer vacation—getting in her mother's way and thinking, dreaming, about the boys she met. But all the boys fell back and dissolved into a single face that was not even a face, but an idea, a feeling, mixed up with the urgent insistent pounding of the music and the humid night air of July. Connie's mother kept dragging her back to the daylight by finding things for her to do or saying, suddenly, "What's this about the Pettinger girl?"

And Connie would say nervously, "Oh, her. That dope." She always drew thick clear lines between herself and such girls, and her mother was simple and kindly enough to believe her. Her mother was so simple, Connie thought, that it was maybe cruel to fool her so much. Her mother went scuffling around the house in old bedroom slippers and complained over the telephone to one sister about the other, then the other called up and the two of them complained about the third one. If June's name was mentioned her mother's tone was approving, and if Connie's name was mentioned it was disapproving. This did not really mean she disliked Connie and actually Connie thought that her mother preferred her to June because she was prettier, but the two of them kept up a pretense of exasperation, a sense that they were tugging and struggling over something of little value to either of them. Sometimes, over coffee, they were almost friends, but something would come up—some vexation that was like a fly buzzing suddenly around their heads—and their faces went hard with contempt.

One Sunday Connie got up at eleven—none of them bothered with church—and washed her hair so that it could dry all day long, in the sun. Her parents and sisters were going to a barbecue at an aunt's house and Connie said no, she wasn't interested, rolling her eyes to let her mother know just what she thought of it. "Stay home alone then," her mother said sharply. Connie sat out back in a lawn chair and watched them drive away, her father quiet and bald, hunched around so that he could back the car out, her mother with a look that was still angry and not at all softened through the windshield, and in the back seat poor old June all dressed up as if she didn't know what a barbecue was, with all the running yelling kids and the flies. Connie sat with her eyes closed in the sun, dreaming and dazed with the warmth about her as if this were a kind of love, the caresses of love, and her mind slipped over onto thoughts of the boy she had been with the night before and how nice he had been, how sweet it always was, not the way someone like June would suppose but sweet, gentle, the way it was in movies and promised in songs; and when she opened her eyes she hardly knew where she was, the back yard ran off into weeds and a fence line of trees and behind it the sky was perfectly blue and still. The asbestos "ranch house" that was now three years old startled her—it looked small. She shook her head as if to get awake.

It was too hot. She went inside the house and turned on the radio to drown out the quiet. She sat on the edge of her bed, barefoot, and listened for an hour and a half to a program called XYZ Sunday Jamboree, record after record of hard, fast, shrieking songs she sang along with, interspersed by exclamations from "Bobby King": "An' look here you girls at Napoleon's—Son and Charley want you to pay real close attention to this song coming up!"

And Connie paid close attention herself, bathed in a glow of slow-pulsed joy that seemed to rise mysteriously out of the music itself and lay languidly about the airless little room, breathed in and breathed out with each gentle rise and fall of her chest.

After a while she heard a car coming up the drive. She sat up at once, startled, because it couldn't be her father so soon. The gravel kept crunching all the way in from the road—the driveway was long—and Connie ran to the window. It was a car she didn't know. It was an open jalopy, painted a bright gold that caught the sunlight opaquely. Her heart began to pound and her fingers snatched at her hair, checking it, and she whispered "Christ, Christ," wondering how bad she looked. The car came to a stop at the side door and the horn sounded four short taps as if this were a signal Connie knew.

She went into the kitchen and approached the door slowly, then hung out the screen door, her bare toes curling down off the step. There were two boys in the car and now she recognized the driver: he had shaggy, shabby black hair that looked crazy as a wig and he was grinning at her.

"I ain't late, am I?" he said.

"Who the hell do you think you are?" Connie said.

"Toldja I'd be out, didn't I?"

"I don't even know who you are."

She spoke sullenly, careful to show no interest or pleasure, and he spoke in a fast bright monotone. Connie looked past him to the other boy, taking her time. He had fair brown hair, with a lock that fell onto his forehead. His sideburns gave him a fierce, embarrassed look, but so far he hadn't even bothered to glance at her. Both boys wore sunglasses. The driver's glasses were metallic and mirrored everything in miniature.

"You wanta come for a ride?" he said.

Connie smirked and let her hair fall loose over one shoulder.

"Don'tcha like my car? New paint job," he said. "Hey."

"What?"

"You're cute."

She pretended to fidget, chasing flies away from the door.

"Don'tcha believe me, or what?" he said.

"Look, I don't even know who you are," Connie said in disgust.

"Hey, Ellie's got a radio, see. Mine's broke down." He lifted his friend's arm and showed her the little transistor the boy was holding, and now Connie began to hear the music. It was the same program that was playing inside the house.

"Bobby King?" she said.

"I listen to him all the time. I think he's great."

"He's kind of great," Connie said reluctantly.

"Listen, that guy's *great*. He knows where the action is."

Connie blushed a little, because the glasses made it impossible for her to see just what this boy was looking at. She couldn't decide if she liked him or if he was just a jerk, and so she dawdled in the doorway and wouldn't come down or go back inside. She said, "What's all that stuff painted on your car?"

"Can'tcha read it?" He opened the door very carefully, as if he was afraid it might fall off. He slid out just as carefully, planting his feet firmly on the ground, the tiny metallic world in his glasses slowing down like gelatine hardening and in the midst of it Connie's bright green blouse. "This here is my name, to begin with," he said. ARNOLD FRIEND was written in tarlike black letters on the side, with a drawing of a round grinning face that reminded Connie of a pumpkin, except it wore sunglasses. "I wanta introduce myself, I'm Arnold Friend and that's my real name and I'm gonna be your friend, honey, and inside the car's Ellie Oscar, he's kinda shy." Ellie brought his transistor radio up to his shoulder and balanced it there. "Now these numbers are a secret code, honey," Arnold Friend explained. He read off the numbers 33, 19, 17 and raised his eyebrows at her to see what she thought of that, but she didn't think much of it. The left rear fender had been smashed and around it was written, on the gleaming gold background: DONE BY CRAZY WOMAN DRIVER. Connie had to laugh at that. Arnold Friend was pleased at her laughter and looked up at her. "Around the other side's a lot more—you wanta come and see them?"

"No."

"Why not?"

"Why should I?"

40   "Don'tcha wanta see what's on the car? Don'tcha wanta go for a ride?"

"I don't know."

"Why not?"

"I got things to do."

"Like what?"

45   "Things."

He laughed as if she had said something funny. He slapped his thighs. He was standing in a strange way, leaning back against the car as if he were balancing himself. He wasn't tall, only an inch or so taller than she would be if she came down to him. Connie liked the way he was dressed, which was the way all of them dressed: tight faded jeans stuffed into black, scuffed boots, a belt that pulled his waist in and showed how lean he was, and a white pullover shirt that was a little soiled and showed the hard small muscles of his arms and shoulders. He looked as if he probably did hard work, lifting and carrying things. Even his neck looked muscular. And his face was a familiar face, somehow: the jaw and chin and cheeks slightly darkened, because he hadn't shaved for a day or two, and the nose long and hawklike, sniffing as if she were a treat he was going to gobble up and it was all a joke.

"Connie, you ain't telling the truth. This is your day set aside for a ride with me and you know it," he said, still laughing. The way he straightened and recovered from his fit of laughing showed that it had been all fake.

"How do you know what my name is?" she said suspiciously.

"It's Connie."

50   "Maybe and maybe not."

"I know my Connie," he said, wagging his finger. Now she remembered him even better, back at the restaurant, and her cheeks warmed at the thought of how she sucked in her breath just at the moment she passed him—how she must have looked at him. And he had remembered her. "Ellie and I come out here especially for you," he said. "Ellie can sit in back. How about it?"

"Where?"

"Where what?"

"Where're we going?"

55   He looked at her. He took off the sunglasses and she saw how pale the skin around his eyes was, like holes that were not in shadow but instead in light. His eyes were like chips of broken glass that catch the light in an amiable way. He smiled. It was as if the idea of going for a ride somewhere, to some place, was a new idea to him.

"Just for a ride, Connie sweetheart."

"I never said my name was Connie," she said.

"But I know what it is. I know your name and all about you, lots of things," Arnold Friend said. He had not moved yet but stood still leaning back against the side of his jalopy. "I took a special interest in you, such a pretty girl, and found out all about you like I know your parents and sister are gone somewheres and I know where and how long they're going to be gone, and I know who you were with last night, and your best girlfriend's name is Betty. Right?"

He spoke in a simple lilting voice, exactly as if he were reciting the words to a song. His smile assured her that everything was fine. In the car Ellie turned up the volume on his radio and did not bother to look around at them.

"Ellie can sit in the back seat," Arnold Friend said. He indicated his friend with a casual jerk of his chin, as if Ellie did not count and she should not bother with him.

"How'd you find out all that stuff?" Connie said.

"Listen: Betty Schultz and Tony Fitch and Jimmy Pettinger and Nancy Pettinger," he said, in a chant. "Raymond Stanley and Bob Hutter—"

"Do you know all those kids?"

"I know everybody."

"Look, you're kidding. You're not from around here."

"Sure."

"But—how come we never saw you before?"

"Sure you saw me before," he said. He looked down at his boots, as if he were a little offended. "You just don't remember."

"I guess I'd remember you," Connie said.

"Yeah?" He looked up at this, beaming. He was pleased. He began to mark time with the music from Ellie's radio, tapping his fists lightly together. Connie looked away from his smile to the car, which was painted so bright it almost hurt her eyes to look at it. She looked at that name, ARNOLD FRIEND. And up at the front fender was an expression that was familiar—MAN THE FLYING SAUCERS. It was an expression kids had used the year before, but didn't use this year. She looked at it for a while as if the words meant something to her that she did not yet know.

"What're you thinking about? Huh?" Arnold Friend demanded. "Not worried about your hair blowing around in the car, are you?"

"No."

"Think I maybe can't drive good?"

"How do I know?"

"You're a hard girl to handle. How come?" he said. "Don't you know I'm your friend? Didn't you see me put my sign in the air when you walked by?"

"What sign?"

"My sign." And he drew an X in the air, leaning out toward her. They were maybe ten feet apart. After his hand fell back to his side the X was still in the air, almost visible. Connie let the screen door close and stood perfectly still inside it, listening to the music from her radio and the boy's blend together. She stared at Arnold Friend. He stood there so stiffly relaxed, pretending to be relaxed, with one hand idly on the door handle as if he were keeping himself up that way and had no intention of ever moving again. She recognized most things about him, the tight jeans that showed his thighs and buttocks and the greasy leather boots and the tight shirt, and even that slippery friendly smile of his, that sleepy dreamy smile that all the boys used to get across ideas they didn't want to put into words. She recognized all this and also the singsong way he talked, slightly mocking, kidding, but serious and a little melancholy, and she recognized the way he tapped one fist against the other in homage of the perpetual music behind him. But all these things did not come together.

She said suddenly, "Hey, how old are you?"

His smile faded. She could see then that he wasn't a kid, he was much older—thirty, maybe more. At this knowledge her heart began to pound faster.

80   "That's a crazy thing to ask. Can'tcha see I'm your own age?"

"Like hell you are."

"Or maybe a coupla years older, I'm eighteen."

"Eighteen?" she said doubtfully.

He grinned to reassure her and lines appeared at the corners of his mouth. His teeth were big and white. He grinned so broadly his eyes became slits and she saw how thick the lashes were, thick and black as if painted with a black tarlike material. Then he seemed to become embarrassed, abruptly, and looked over his shoulder at Ellie. "*Him*, he's crazy," he said. "Ain't he a riot, he's a nut, a real character." Ellie was still listening to the music. His sunglasses told nothing about what he was thinking. He wore a bright orange shirt unbuttoned halfway to show his chest, which was a pale, bluish chest and not muscular like Arnold Friend's. His shirt collar was turned up all around and the very tips of the collar pointed out past his chin as if they were protecting him. He was pressing the transistor radio up against his ear and sat there in a kind of daze, right in the sun.

85   "He's kinda strange," Connie said.

"Hey, she says you're kinda strange! Kinda strange!" Arnold Friend cried. He pounded on the car to get Ellie's attention. Ellie turned for the first time and Connie saw with shock that he wasn't a kid either—he had a fair, hairless face, cheeks reddened slightly as if the veins grew too close to the surface of his skin, the face of a forty-year-old baby. Connie felt a wave of dizziness rise in her at this sight and she stared at him as if waiting for something to change the shock of the moment, make it all right again. Ellie's lips kept shaping words, mumbling along with the words blasting in his ear.

"Maybe you two better go away," Connie said faintly.

"What? How come?" Arnold Friend cried. "We come out here to take you for a ride. It's Sunday." He had the voice of the man on the radio now. It was the same voice, Connie thought. "Don'tcha know it's Sunday all day and honey, no matter who you were with last night today you're with Arnold Friend and don't you forget it!—Maybe you better step out here," he said, and this last was in a different voice. It was a little flatter, as if the heat was finally getting to him.

"No. I got things to do."

90   "Hey."

"You two better leave."

"We ain't leaving until you come with us."

"Like hell I am—"

"Connie, don't fool around with me. I mean, I mean, don't fool *around*," he said, shaking his head. He laughed incredulously. He placed his sunglasses on top of his head, carefully, as if he were indeed wearing a wig, and brought the stems down behind his ears. Connie stared at him, another wave of dizziness and fear rising in her so that for a moment he wasn't even in focus but was just a blur, standing there against his gold car, and she had the idea that he had driven up the driveway all right but had come from nowhere before that and belonged nowhere and that everything about him and even about the music that was so familiar to her was only half real.

95   "If my father comes and sees you—"

"He ain't coming. He's at a barbecue."

"How do you know that?"

"Aunt Tillie's. Right now they're—uh—they're drinking. Sitting around," he said vaguely, squinting as if he were staring all the way to town and over to Aunt Tillie's back yard. Then the vision seemed to get clear and he nodded energetically. "Yeah. Sitting around. There's your sister in a blue dress, huh? And high heels, the poor sad bitch—nothing like you, sweetheart! And your mother's helping some fat woman with the corn, they're cleaning the corn—husking the corn—"

"What fat woman?" Connie cried.

"How do I know what fat woman, I don't know every goddam fat woman in the world!" Arnold laughed. 100

"Oh, that's Mrs. Hornby . . . Who invited her?" Connie said. She felt a little light-headed. Her breath was coming quickly.

"She's too fat. I don't like them fat. I like them the way you are, honey," he said, smiling sleepily at her. They stared at each other for a while, through the screen door. He said softly, "Now what you're going to do is this: you're going to come out that door. You're going to sit up front with me and Ellie's going to sit in the back, the hell with Ellie, right? This isn't Ellie's date. You're my date. I'm your lover, honey."

"What? You're crazy—"

"Yes, I'm your lover. You don't know what that is, but you will," he said. "I know that too. I know all about you. But look: it's real nice and you couldn't ask for nobody better than me, or more polite. I always keep my word. I'll tell you how it is, I'm always nice at first, the first time. I'll hold you so tight you won't think you have to try to get away or pretend anything because you'll know you can't. And I'll come inside you where it's all secret and you'll give in to me and you'll love me—"

"Shut up! You're crazy!" Connie said. She backed away from the door. She put her hands against her ears as if she'd heard something terrible, something not meant for her. "People don't talk like that, you're crazy," she muttered. Her heart was almost too big now for her chest and its pumping made sweat break out all over her. She looked out to see Arnold Friend pause and then take a step toward the porch lurching. He almost fell. But, like a clever drunken man, he managed to catch his balance. He wobbled in his high boots and grabbed hold of one of the porch posts. 105

"Honey?" he said. "You still listening?"

"Get the hell out of here!"

"Be nice, honey. Listen."

"I'm going to call the police—"

He wobbled again and out of the side of his mouth came a fast spat curse, an aside not meant for her to hear. But even this "Christ!" sounded forced. Then he began to smile again. She watched this smile come, awkward as if he were smiling from inside a mask. His whole face was a mask, she thought wildly, tanned down onto his throat but then running out as if he had plastered makeup on his face but had forgotten about his throat. 110

"Honey—? Listen, here's how it is. I always tell the truth and I promise you this: I ain't coming in that house after you."

"You better not! I'm going to call the police if you—if you don't—"

"Honey," he said, talking right through her voice, "honey, I'm not coming in there but you are coming out here. You know why?"

She was panting. The kitchen looked like a place she had never seen before, some room she had run inside but which wasn't good enough, wasn't going to help her. The kitchen window had never had a curtain, after three years, and there were dishes in the sink for her to do—probably—and if you ran your hand across the table you'd probably feel something sticky there.

"You listening, honey? Hey?" 115

"—going to call the police—"

"Soon as you touch the phone I don't need to keep my promise and can come inside. You won't want that."

She rushed forward and tried to lock the door. Her fingers were shaking. "But why lock it," Arnold Friend said gently, talking right into her face. "It's just a screen door. It's just nothing." One of his boots was at a strange angle, as if his foot wasn't in it. It pointed out to the left, bent at the ankle. "I mean, anybody can break through a screen door and glass and wood and iron or anything else if he needs to, anybody at all and specially Arnold Friend. If the place got lit up with a fire honey you'd come runnin' out into my arms, right into my arms an' safe at home—like you knew I was your lover and'd stopped fooling around. I don't mind a nice shy girl but I don't like no fooling around." Part of those words were spoken with a slight rhythmic lilt, and Connie somehow recognized them—the echo of a song from last year, about a girl rushing into her boyfriend's arms and coming home again—

Connie stood barefoot on the linoleum floor, staring at him. "What do you want?" she whispered.

120   "I want you," he said.

"What?"

"Seen you that night and thought, that's the one, yes sir. I never needed to look any more."

"But my father's coming back. He's coming to get me. I had to wash my hair first—" She spoke in a dry, rapid voice, hardly raising it for him to hear.

"No, your Daddy is not coming and yes, you had to wash your hair and you washed it for me. It's nice and shining and all for me, I thank you, sweetheart," he said, with a mock bow, but again he almost lost his balance. He had to bend and adjust his boots. Evidently his feet did not go all the way down; the boots must have been stuffed with something so that he would seem taller. Connie stared out at him and behind him Ellie in the car, who seemed to be looking off toward Connie's right into nothing. This Ellie said, pulling the words out of the air one after another as if he were just discovering them, "You want me to pull out the phone?"

125   "Shut your mouth and keep it shut," Arnold Friend said, his face red from bending over or maybe from embarrassment because Connie had seen his boots. "This ain't none of your business."

"What—what are you doing? What do you want?" Connie said. "If I call the police they'll get you, they'll arrest you—"

"Promise was not to come in unless you touch that phone, and I'll keep that promise," he said. He resumed his erect position and tried to force his shoulders back. He sounded like a hero in a movie, declaring something important. He spoke too loudly and it was as if he were speaking to someone behind Connie. "I ain't made plans for coming in that house where I don't belong but just for you to come out to me, the way you should. Don't you know who I am?"

"You're crazy," she whispered. She backed away from the door but did not want to go into another part of the house, as if this would give him permission to come through the door. "What do you . . . You're crazy, you . . ."

"Huh? What're you saying, honey?"

130   Her eyes darted everywhere in the kitchen. She could not remember what it was, this room.

"This is how it is, honey; you come out and we'll drive away, have a nice ride. But if you don't come out we're gonna wait till your people come home and then they're all going to get it."

"You want that telephone pulled out?" Ellie said. He held the radio away from his ear and grimaced, as if without the radio the air was too much for him.

"I toldja shut up, Ellie," Arnold Friend said, "you're deaf, get a hearing aid, right? Fix yourself up. This little girl's no trouble and's gonna be nice to me, so Ellie keep to yourself, this ain't your date—right? Don't hem in on me. Don't hog. Don't crush. Don't bird dog. Don't trail me," he said in a rapid meaningless voice, as if he were running through all the expressions he'd learned but was no longer sure which one of them was in style, then rushing on to new ones, making them up with his eyes closed, "Don't crawl under my fence, don't squeeze in my chipmunk hole, don't sniff my glue, suck my popsicle, keep your own greasy fingers on yourself!" He shaded his eyes and peered in at Connie, who was backed against the kitchen table. "Don't mind him honey he's just a creep. He's a dope. Right! I'm the boy for you and like I said you come out here nice like a lady and give me your hand, and nobody else gets hurt, I mean, your nice old bald-headed daddy and your mummy and your sister in her high heels. Because listen: why bring them in this?"

"Leave me alone," Connie whispered.

"Hey, you know that old woman down the road, the one with the chickens and   135
stuff—you know her?"

"She's dead!"

"Dead? What? You know her?" Arnold Friend said.

"She's dead—"

"Don't you like her?"

"She dead—she's—she isn't there any more—"   140

"But don't you like her, I mean, you got something against her? Some grudge or something?" Then his voice dipped as if he were conscious of a rudeness. He touched the sunglasses perched on top of his head as if to make sure they were still there. "Now you be a good girl."

"What are you going to do?"

"Just two things, or maybe three," Arnold Friend said. "But I promise it won't last long and you'll like me the way you get to like people you're close to. You will. It's all over for you here, so come on out. You don't want your people in any trouble, do you?"

She turned and bumped against a chair or something, hurting her leg, but she ran into the back room and picked up the telephone. Something roared in her ear, a tiny roaring, and she was so sick with fear that she could do nothing but listen to it—the telephone was clammy and very heavy and her fingers groped down to the dial but were too weak to touch it. She began to scream into the phone, into the roaring. She cried out, she cried for her mother, she felt her breath start jerking back and forth in her lungs as if it were something Arnold Friend were stabbing her with again and again with no tenderness. A noisy sorrowful wailing rose all about her and she was locked inside it the way she was locked inside this house.

After a while she could hear again. She was sitting on the floor with her wet   145
back against the wall.

Arnold Friend was saying from the door, "That's a good girl. Put the phone back."

She kicked the phone away from her.

"No, honey. Pick it up. Put it back right."

She picked it up and put it back. The dial tone stopped.

"That's a good girl. Now you come outside."   150

She was hollow with what had been fear, but what was now just an emptiness. All that screaming had blasted it out of her. She sat, one leg cramped under her, and deep inside her brain was something like a pinpoint of light that kept going and would not let her relax. She thought, I'm not going to see my mother again. She thought, I'm not going to sleep in my bed again. Her bright green blouse was all wet.

Arnold Friend said, in a gentle-loud voice that was like a stage voice. "The place where you came from ain't there any more, and where you had in mind to go is canceled out. This place you are now—inside your daddy's house—is nothing but a cardboard box I can knock down any time. You know that and always did know it. You hear me?"

She thought, I have got to think. I have to know what to do.

"We'll go out to a nice field, out in the country here where it smells so nice and it's sunny," Arnold Friend said. "I'll have my arms tight around you so you won't need to try to get away and I'll show you what love is like, what it does. The hell with this house! It looks solid all right," he said. He ran a fingernail down the screen and the noise did not make Connie shiver, as it would have the day before. "Now put your hand on your heart, honey. Feel that? That feels solid too, but we know better, be nice to me, be sweet like you can because what else is there for a girl like you but to be sweet and pretty and give in?—and get away before her people come back?"

She felt her pounding heart. Her hand seemed to enclose it. She thought for the first time in her life that it was nothing that was hers, that belonged to her, but just a pounding, living thing inside this body that wasn't really hers either.

"You don't want them to get hurt," Arnold Friend went on. "Now get up, honey. Get up all by yourself."

She stood.

"Now turn this way. That's right. Come over here to me—Ellie, put that away, didn't I tell you? You dope. You miserable creepy dope," Arnold Friend said. His words were not angry but only part of an incantation. The incantation was kindly. "Now come out through the kitchen to me honey, and let's see a smile, try it, you're a brave sweet little girl and now they're eating corn and hot dogs cooked to bursting over an outdoor fire, and they don't know one thing about you and never did and honey you're better than them because not a one of them would have done this for you."

Connie felt the linoleum under her feet; it was cool. She brushed her hair back out of her eyes. Arnold Friend let go of the post tentatively and opened his arms for her, his elbows pointing in toward each other and his wrists limp, to show that this was an embarrassed embrace and a little mocking, he didn't want to make her self-conscious.

She put out her hand against the screen. She watched herself push the door slowly open as if she were safe back somewhere in the other doorway, watching this body and this head of long hair moving out into the sunlight where Arnold Friend waited.

"My sweet little blue-eyed girl," he said, in a half-sung sigh that had nothing to do with her brown eyes but was taken up just the same by the vast sunlit reaches of the land behind him and on all sides of him, so much land that Connie had never seen before and did not recognize except to know that she was going to it.   [1966]

QUESTIONS

1. What does the narrator mean when she says of Connie that "everything about her had two sides to it"?
2. How do Arnold's clothes and car reflect his character?

3. What is the significance of Eddie in the story? Of Ellie?
4. How does the author create an increasing sense of terror in Connie?
5. What do the references to popular music and popular religion contribute to the story?

RESPONSES

1. Compare this story to Flannery O'Connor's "A Good Man Is Hard to Find."
2. Write an essay exploring your emotional reactions as you read the story. Can you read the story as someone might have when the story was first published?

FOCUS ON FILM

1. View the film *Smooth Talk*. Evaluate the filmmakers choices of actors for this film? Do they seem appropriate in age, looks, and skill for their roles?
2. Examine the filmmakers' use of outdoor and indoor spaces. Are they consistent? What do they contribute to the film? Are such uses based upon similar uses in the print story?
3. The endings to the film and the print story are different. Are the changes that the film makes consistent with other changes in the story? Explain the changes in theme that the changes in the endings create.

Joyce Carol Oates

Why Don't You Come
Live with Me It's Time

The other day, it was a sunswept windy March morning, I saw my grandmother staring at me, those deep-socketed eyes, that translucent skin, a youngish woman with very dark hair as I hadn't quite remembered her who had died while I was in college, years ago, in 1966. Then I saw, of course it was virtually in the same instant I saw the face was my own, my own eyes in that face floating there not in a mirror but in a metallic mirrored surface, teeth bared in a startled smile and seeing my face that was not my face I laughed, I think that was the sound.

You're an insomniac, you tell yourself: there are profound truths revealed only to the insomniac by night like those phosphorescent minerals veined and glimmering in the dark but coarse and ordinary otherwise, you have to examine such minerals in the absence of light to discover their beauty: you tell yourself.

Maybe because I was having so much trouble sleeping at the time, twelve or thirteen years old, no one would have called the problem insomnia, that sounds too clinical, too adult and anyway they'd said "You can sleep if you try" and I'd overheard "She just wants attention—you know what she's like" and I was hurt and angry but hopeful too wanting to ask, But what am I like, are you the ones to tell me?

In fact, Grandmother had insomnia too—"suffered from insomnia" was the somber expression—but no one made the connection between her and me. Our family was that way: worrying that one weakness might find justification in another and things would slip out of containment and control.

5 In fact, I'd had trouble sleeping since early childhood but I had not understood that anything was wrong. Not secrecy nor even a desire to please my parents made me pretend to sleep, I thought it was what you do, I thought when Mother put me to bed I had to shut my eyes so she could leave and that was the way of releasing her though immediately afterward when I was alone my eyes opened wide and sleepless. Sometimes it was day, sometimes night. Often by night I could see, I could discern the murky shapes of objects, familiar objects that had lost their names by night as by night lying motionless with no one to observe me it seemed I had no name and my body was shapeless and undefined. The crucial thing was to lie motionless, scarcely breathing,

until at last—it might be minutes or it might be hours, if there were noises in the house or out on the street (we lived on a busy street for most of my childhood in Hammond) it would be hours—a dark pool of warm water would begin to lap gently over my feet, eventually it would cover my legs, my chest, my face . . . what adults called "sleep" this most elusive and strange and mysterious of experiences, a cloudy transparency of ever-shifting hues and textures surrounding tense islands of wakefulness so during the course of a night I would sleep, and wake, and sleep, and wake, a dozen times, as the water lapped over my face and retreated from it, this seemed altogether natural it was altogether desirable, for when I slept another kind of sleep, heavily, deeply, plunged into a substance not water and not a transparency but an oozy lightless muck, when I plunged down into that sleep and managed to wake from it shivering and sweating with a pounding heart and a pounding head as if my brain trapped inside my skull (but "brain" and "skull" were not concepts I would have known, at that time) had been racing feverishly like a small machine gone berserk it was to a sense of total helplessness and an exhaustion so profound it felt like death: sheer nonexistence, oblivion: and I did not know, nor do I know now, decades later, which sleep is preferable, which sleep is normal, how is one defined by sleep, from where in fact does "sleep" arise.

When I was older, a teenager, with a room at a little distance from my parents' bedroom, I would often, those sleepless nights, simply turn on my bedside lamp and read, I'd read until dawn and day and the resumption of daytime routine in a state of complete concentration, or sometimes I'd switch on the radio close beside my bed, I was cautious of course to keep the volume low, low and secret and I'd listen fascinated to stations as far away as Pittsburgh, Toronto, Cleveland, there was a hillbilly station broadcasting out of Cleveland, country-and-western music I would never have listened to by day. One by one I got to know intimately the announcers' voices along the continuum of the glowing dial, hard to believe those strangers didn't know *me*. But sometimes my room left me short of breath, it was fresh air I craved, hurriedly I'd dress pulling on clothes over my pajamas, and even in rainy or cold weather I went outside leaving the house by the kitchen door so quietly in such stealth no one ever heard, not once did one of them hear *I will do it: because I want to do it* sleeping their heavy sleep that was like the sleep of molluscs, eyeless. And outside: in the night: the surprise of the street transformed by the lateness of the hour, the emptiness, the silence: I'd walk to the end of our driveway staring, listening, my heart beating hard. *So this is—what it is!* The ordinary sights were made strange, the sidewalks, the street lights, the neighboring houses. Yet the fact had no consciousness of itself except through *me.*

For that has been one of the principles of my life.

And if here and there along the block a window glowed from within (another insomniac?), or if a lone car passed in the street casting its headlights before it, or a train sounded in the distance, or, high overhead, an airplane passed winking and glittering with lights, what happiness swelled my lungs, what gratitude, what conviction, I was utterly alone for the moment, and invisible, which is identical with being alone.

Come by anytime dear, no need to call first my grandmother said often, *Come by after school, anytime, please!* I tried not to hear the pleading in her voice, tried not to see the soft hurt in her eyes, and the hope.

Grandmother was a "widow": her husband, my step-grandfather had died of cancer of the liver when I was five years old.   10

Grandmother had beautiful eyes. Deep-set, dark, intelligent, alert. And her hair was a lovely silvery-gray, not coarse like others' hair but fine-spun, silky.

Mother said, "In your grandmother's eyes you can do no wrong." She spoke as if amused but I understood the accusation.

Because Grandmother loved me best of the grandchildren, yes and she loved me best of all the family, I basked in her love as in the warmth of a private sun. Grandmother loved me without qualification and without criticism which angered my parents since they understood that so fierce a love made me impervious to their more modulated love, not only impervious but indifferent to the threat of its being withdrawn . . . which is the only true power parents have over their children. Isn't it?

We visited Grandmother often, especially now she was alone. She visited us. Sundays, holidays, birthdays. And I would bicycle across the river to her house once or twice a week, or drop in after school, Grandmother encouraged me to bring my friends but I was too shy, I never stayed long, her happiness in my presence made me uneasy. Always she would prepare one of my favorite dishes, hot oatmeal with cream and brown sugar, apple cobbler, brownies, fudge, lemon custard tarts. . . and I sat and ate as she watched, and, eating, I felt hunger, the hunger was in my mouth. To remember those foods brings the hunger back now, the sudden rush of it, the pain. In my mouth.

15   At home Mother would ask, "Did you spoil your appetite again?"

The river that separated us was the Cassadaga, flowing from east to west, to Lake Ontario, through the small city of Hammond, New York.

After I left, aged eighteen, I only returned to Hammond as a visitor. Now everyone is dead, I never go back.

The bridge that connected us was the Ferry Street bridge, the bridge we crossed hundreds of times. Grandmother lived south of the river (six blocks south, two blocks west), we lived north of the river (three blocks north, one and a half blocks east), we were about three miles apart. The Ferry Street bridge, built in 1919, was one of those long narrow spiky nightmare bridges, my childhood was filled with such bridges, this one thirty feet above the Cassadaga, with high arches, steep ramps on both sides, six concrete supports, rusted iron grillwork, and neoclassical ornamentation of the kind associated with Chicago Commercial architecture, which was the architectural style of Hammond generally.

The Ferry Street bridge. Sometimes in high winds you could feel the bridge sway, I lowered my eyes when my father drove us over, he'd joke as the plank floor rattled and beneath the rattling sound there came something deeper and more sinister, the vibrating hum of the river itself, a murmur, a secret caress against the soles of our feet, our buttocks, and between our legs so it was an enormous relief when the car had passed safely over the bridge and descended the ramp to land. The Ferry Street bridge was almost too narrow for two ordinary-sized automobiles to pass but only once was my father forced to stop about a quarter of the way out, a gravel truck was bearing down upon us and the driver gave no sign of slowing down so my father braked the car, threw it hurriedly into reverse and backed up red-faced the way we'd come and after that the Ferry Street bridge was no joke to him, any more than it was to his passengers.

20   The other day, that sunny gusty day when I saw Grandmother's face in the mirror, I mean the metallic mirrored surface downtown, I mean the face that had seemed to be Grandmother's face but was not, I began to think of the Ferry Street bridge and since then I haven't slept well seeing the bridge in my mind's eye the way you do when you're insomniac, the images that should be in dreams are loosed and set careening through the day like lethal bubbles in the blood. I had not known how I'd memorized that bridge, and I'd forgotten why.

The time I am thinking of, I was twelve or thirteen years old, I know I was that age because the Ferry Street bridge was closed for repairs then and it was over the Ferry Street bridge I went, to see Grandmother. I don't remember if it was a conscious decision or if I'd just started walking, not knowing where I was going, or why. It was three o'clock in the morning. No one knew where I was. Beyond the barricade and the DETOUR—BRIDGE OUT signs, the moon so bright it lit my way like a manic face.

A number of times I'd watched with trepidation certain of the neighborhood boys inch their way out across the steel beams of the skeletal bridge, walking with arms extended for balance, so I knew it could be done without mishap, I knew I could do it if only I had the courage, and it seemed to me I had sufficient courage, now was the time to prove it. Below the river rushed past slightly higher than usual, it was October, there had been a good deal of rain, but tonight the sky was clear, stars like icy pinpricks, and that bright glaring moon illuminating my way for me so I thought *I will do it* already climbing up onto what would be the new floor of the bridge when at last it was completed: not planks but a more modern sort of iron mesh, not yet laid into place. But the steel beams were about ten inches wide and there was a grid of them, four beams spanning the river and (I would count them as I crossed, I would never forget that count) fourteen narrower beams at perpendicular angles with the others, and about three feet below these beams there was a complex crisscrossing of cables you might define as a net of sorts if you wanted to think in such terms, a safety net, there was no danger really *I will do it because I want to do it, because there is no one to stop me.*

And on the other side, Grandmother's house. And even if its windows were darkened, even if I did no more than stand looking quietly at it, and then come back home, never telling anyone what I'd done, even so I would have proved something *Because there is no one to stop me* which has been one of the principles of my life. To regret that principle is to regret my entire life.

I climbed up onto one of the beams, trembling with excitement. But how cold it was!—I'd come out without my gloves.

And how loud the river below, the roaring like a kind of jeering applause; and it smelled too, of something brackish and metallic. I knew not to glance down at it, steadying myself as a quick wind picked up, teasing tears into my eyes, I was thinking *There is no turning back: never* but instructing myself too that the beam was perfectly safe if I was careful for had I not seen boys walking across without slipping? didn't the workmen walk across too, many times a day? I decided not to stand, though—I was afraid to stand—I remained squatting on my haunches, gripping the edge of the beam with both hands, inching forward in this awkward way, hunched over, right foot, and then left foot, and then right foot, and then left foot: passing the first of the perpendicular beams, and the second, and the third, and the fourth: and so in this clumsy and painful fashion forcing myself to continue until my thigh muscles ached so badly I had to stop and I made the mistake which even in that instant I knew was a mistake of glancing down: seeing the river thirty feet below: the way it was flowing so swiftly and with such power, and seeming rage, ropy sinuous coils of churning water, foam-flecked, terrible, and its flow exactly perpendicular to the direction in which I was moving.

"Oh no. Oh no. Oh no."

A wave of sharp cold terror shot up into me as if into my very bowels, piercing me between the legs rising from the river itself and I could not move, I squatted there on the beam unable to move, all the strength drained out of my muscles and I

25

was paralyzed knowing *You're going to die: of course, die* even as with another part of my mind (there is always this other part of my mind) I was thinking with an almost teacherly logic that the beam *was* safe, it was wide enough, and flat enough, and not damp or icy or greasy yes certainly it *was* safe: if this were land, for instance in our backyard, if for instance my father had set down a plank flat in the grass, a plank no more than half the width of the beam couldn't I, Claire, have walked that plank without the slightest tremor of fear? boldly? even gracefully? even blindfolded? without a moment's hesitation? not the flicker of an eyelid, not the most minute leap of a pulse?—*You know you aren't going to die: don't be silly* but it must have been five minutes before I could force myself to move again, my numbed right leg easing forward, my aching foot, I forced my eyes upward too and fixed them resolutely on the opposite shore, or what I took on faith to be the opposite shore, a confusion of sawhorses and barrels and equipment now only fitfully illuminated by the moon.

But I got there, I got to where I meant to go without for a moment exactly remembering why.

Now the worst of it's done: for now.

30   Grandmother's house, what's called a bungalow, plain stucco, one-story, built close to the curb, seemed closer to the river than I'd expected, maybe I was running, desperate to get there, hearing the sound of the angry rushing water that was like many hundreds of murmurous voices, and the streets surprised me with their emptiness—so many vacant lots, murky transparencies of space where buildings had once stood—and a city bus passed silently, lit gaily from within, yet nearly empty too, only the driver and a single (male) passenger sitting erect and motionless as mannequins, and I shrank panicked into the shadows so they would not see me: maybe I would be arrested: a girl of my age on the street at such an hour, alone, with deep-set frightened eyes, a pale face, guilty mouth, zip-up corduroy jacket and jeans over her pajamas, disheveled as a runaway. But the bus passed, turned a corner, and vanished. And there was Grandmother's house, not darkened as I'd expected but lighted, and from the sidewalk staring I could see Grandmother inside, or a figure I took to be Grandmother, but why was she awake at such an hour, how remarkable that she should be awake as if awaiting me, and I remembered then—how instantaneously these thoughts came to me, eerie as tiny bubbles that, bursting, yielded riches of a sort that would require a considerable expenditure of time to relate though their duration was in fact hardly more than an instant!—I remembered having heard the family speak of Grandmother's sometimes strange behavior, worrisome behavior in a woman of her age, or of any age, the problem was her insomnia unless insomnia was not cause but consequence of a malady of the soul, so it would be reported to my father, her son, that she'd been seen walking at night in neighborhoods unsafe for solitary women, she'd been seen at a midnight showing of a film in downtown Hammond, and even when my step-grandfather was alive (he worked on a lake freighter, he was often gone) she might spend time in local taverns, not drinking heavily, but drinking, and this was behavior that might lead to trouble, or so the family worried, though there was never any specific trouble so far as anyone knew, and Grandmother smoked too, smoked on the street which "looks cheap," my mother said, my mother too smoked but never on the street, the family liked to tell and retell the story of a cousin of my father's coming to Hammond on a Greyhound bus, arriving at the station at about six in the morning, and there in the waiting room was my grandmother in her old fox-fur coat sitting there with a book in her lap, a cigarette in one hand, just sitting there placidly and with no mind for the two or three others, distinctly odd near-derelict men, in the room with her,

just sitting there reading her book (Grandmother was always reading, poetry, bi-ographies of great men like Lincoln, Mozart, Julius Caesar, Jesus of Nazareth) and my father's cousin came in, saw her, said, "Aunt Tina, what on earth are you doing here?" and Grandmother had looked up calmly, and said, "Why not?—it's for wait-ing isn't it?"

Another strange thing Grandmother had done, it had nothing to do with her in-somnia that I could see unless all our strangenesses, as they are judged in other's eyes, are morbidly related, was arranging for her husband's body to be cremated: not buried in a cemetery plot, but cremated: which means burnt to mere ash: which means anni-hilation: and though cremation had evidently been my step-grandfather's wish it had seemed to the family that Grandmother had complied with it too readily, and so im-mediately following her husband's death that no one had a chance to dissuade her. "What a thing," my mother said, shivering, "to do to your own husband!"

I was thinking of this now seeing through one of the windows a man's figure, a man talking with Grandmother in her kitchen, it seemed to me that perhaps my step-grandfather had not yet died, thus was not yet cremated, and some of the disagreement might be resolved, but I must have already knocked at the door since Grandmother was there opening it, at first she stared at me as if scarcely recognizing me then she laughed, she said, "What are *you* doing here?" and I tried to explain but could not: the words failed to come: my teeth were chattering with cold and fright and the words failed to come but Grandmother led me inside, she was taller than I remembered, and younger, her hair dark, wavy, falling to her shoulders, and her mouth red with lipstick, she laughed leading me into the kitchen where a man, a stranger, was waiting, "Harry this is my granddaughter Claire," Grandmother said, and the man stepped forward re-garding me with interest, yet speaking of me as if I were somehow not present, "She's your granddaughter?" "She is." "I didn't know you had a granddaughter." "You don't know lots of things."

And Grandmother laughed at us both, who gazed in perplexity and doubt at each other. Laughing, she threw her head back like a young girl or a man, and bared her strong white teeth.

I was then led to sit at the kitchen table, in my usual place, Grandmother went to the stove to prepare something for me and I sat quietly, not frightened now, yet not quite at ease though I understood I was safe now, Grandmother would take care of me now and nothing could happen, I saw that the familiar kitchen had been altered, it was very brightly lit, almost blindingly lit, yet deeply shadowed in the corners, the rear wall where the sink should have been dissolved into what would have been the back-yard but I had a quick flash of the backyard where there were flower and vegetable beds, Grandmother loved to work in the yard, she brought flowers and vegetables in the summer wherever she visited, the most beautiful of her flowers were peonies, big gorgeous crimson peonies, and the thought of the peonies was confused with the smell of the oatmeal Grandmother was stirring on the stove for me to eat, oatmeal was the first food of my childhood: the first food I can remember: but Grandmother made it her own way, her special way stirring in brown sugar, cream, a spoonful of dark honey, so just thinking of it I felt my mouth water violently, almost it hurt, the saliva flooded so and I was embarrassed that a trickle ran down my chin and I couldn't seem to wipe it off and Grandmother's friend Harry was watching me: but finally I managed to wipe it off on my fingers: and Harry smiled.

The thought came to me, not a new thought but one I'd had for years, but now it 35 came with unusual force, like the saliva flooding my mouth, that when my parents died I would come live with Grandmother—of course: I would come live with

Grandmother: and Grandmother at the stove stirring my oatmeal in a pan must have heard my thoughts for she said, "—Claire why don't you come live with me it's time isn't it?" and I said, "Oh yes," and Grandmother didn't seem to have heard for she repeated her question, turning now to look at me, to smile, her eyes shining and her mouth so amazingly red, two delicate spots of rouge on her cheeks so my heart caught seeing how beautiful she was, as young as my mother, or younger, and she laughed saying, "—Claire why don't you come live with me it's time isn't it?" and again I said, "Oh yes Grandmother," nodding and blinking tears from my eyes, they were tears of infinite happiness, and relief, "—oh Grandmother, *yes*."

Grandmother's friend Harry was a navy radio operator, he said, or had been, he wore no uniform and he was no age I could have guessed, with silvery-glinting hair in a crewcut, muscular shoulders and arms, but maybe his voice was familiar? maybe I'd heard him over the radio? Grandmother was urging him to tell me about the universe, distinctly she said those odd words "Why don't you tell Claire about the universe," and Harry stared at me frowning and said, "Tell Claire what about the universe?" and Grandmother laughed and said, "Oh—anything!" and Harry said, shrugging, "Hell—I don't know," then raising his voice, regarding me with a look of compassion, "—the universe goes back a long way, I guess. Ten billion years? Twenty billion? Is there a difference? They say it got started with an explosion and in a second, well really a fraction of a second a tiny bit of tightness got flung out, it's flying out right now, expanding"—he drew his hands, broad stubby hands, dramatically apart— "and most of it is emptiness I guess, whatever 'emptiness' is. It's still expanding, all the pieces flying out, there's a billion galaxies like ours, or maybe a billion billion galaxies like ours, but don't worry it goes on forever even when we die—" but at this Grandmother turned sharply, sensing my reaction, she said, "Oh dear don't tell the child *that*, don't frighten poor little Claire with *that*."

"You told me to tell her about the—"

"Oh just *stop*."

Quickly Grandmother came to hug me, settled me into my chair as if I were a much smaller child sitting there at the kitchen table, my feet not touching the floor; and there was my special bowl, the bowl Grandmother kept for me, sparkling yellow with lambs running around the rim, yes and my special spoon too, a beautiful silver spoon with the initial C engraved on it which Grandmother kept polished so I understood I was safe, nothing could harm me, Grandmother would not let anything happen to me so long as I was there. She poured my oatmeal into my dish, she was saying, "—It's true we must all die one day, darling, but not just yet, you know, not tonight, you've just come to visit haven't you dear? and maybe you'll stay? maybe you won't ever leave? *now it's time?*"

40   The words *it's time* rang with a faint echo.

I can hear them now: *it's time: time.*

Grandmother's arms were shapely and attractive, her skin pale and smooth and delicately translucent as a candled egg, and I saw that she was wearing several rings, the wedding band that I knew but others, sparkling with light, and there so thin were my arms beside hers, my hands that seemed so small, sparrow-sized, and my wrists so bony, and it came over me, the horror of it, that meat and bone should define my presence in the universe: the point of entry in the universe that was *me* that was *me* that was *me*: and no other: yet of a fragile materiality that any fire could consume. "Oh Grandmother—I'm so afraid!" I whimpered, seeing how I would be burned to ash, and Grandmother comforted me, and settled me more securely into the chair, pressed my pretty little spoon between my fingers and said, "Darling don't think of such things, just *eat*. Grandmother made this for *you*."

I was eating the hot oatmeal which was a little too hot, but creamy as I loved it, I was terribly hungry eating like an infant at the breast so blindly my head bowed and eyes nearly shut brimming with tears and Grandmother asked *is it good? is it good?* she'd spooned in some dark honey too *is it good?* and I nodded mutely, I could taste grains of brown sugar that hadn't melted into the oatmeal, stark as bits of glass, and I realized they were in fact bits of glass, some of them large as grape pits, and I didn't want to hurt Grandmother's feelings but I was fearful of swallowing the glass so as I ate I managed to sift the bits through the chewed oatmeal until I could maneuver it into the side of my mouth into a little space between my lower right gum and the inside of my cheek and Grandmother was watching asking *is it good?* and I said, "Oh yes," half choking and swallowing "—oh *yes*."

A while later when neither Grandmother nor Harry was watching I spat out the glass fragments into my hand but I never knew absolutely, I don't know even now: if they were glass and not for instance grains of sand or fragments of eggshell or even bits of brown sugar crystallized into such a form not even boiling oatmeal could dissolve it.

I was leaving Grandmother's house, it was later, time to leave, Grandmother said,   45
"But aren't you going to stay?" and I said, "No Grandmother I can't," and Grandmother said, "I thought you were going to stay dear," and I said, "No Grandmother I can't," and Grandmother said, "But why?" and I said, "I just can't," and Grandmother said, laughing so her laughter was edged with annoyance, "Yes but *why*?" Grandmother's friend Harry had disappeared from the kitchen, there was no one in the kitchen but Grandmother and me, but we were in the street too, and the roaring of the river was close by, so Grandmother hugged me a final time and gave me a little push saying, "Well—goodnight Claire," and I said apologetically, "Goodnight, Grandmother," wondering if I should ask her not to say anything to my parents about this visit in the middle of the night, and she was backing away, her dark somber gaze fixed upon me half in reproach, "Next time you visit Grandmother you'll stay—won't you? Forever?" and I said, "Yes Grandmother," though I was very frightened and as soon as I was out of Grandmother's sight I began to run.

At first I had a hard time finding the Ferry Street bridge. Though I could hear the river close by—I can always hear the river close by.

Eventually, I found the bridge again. I know I found the bridge, otherwise how did I get home? That night?   [1990]

QUESTIONS

1. Looking at the first paragraph, what can we learn about the narrator, her values and the way her mind works?

2. Discuss the significance of the road and the bridge between the grandmother's and the narrator's parents' houses.

3. What do the various images of water contribute to the story? What do the images of empty spaces contribute? What do the images of metal and glass contribute?

4. What importance does Harry play in the story?
5. Explain the importance of the oatmeal. Explain the importance of the bits of glass.

RESPONSES

1. After reading the three stories in this anthology by Joyce Carol Oates, discuss the relationships that children have with their parents. Or discuss the importance that Oates places on danger and its role in our lives.
2. Research insomnia. How accurate is Oates's description of it and the way that people react to it? What did you learn that helps interpret and understand the story better?
3. Compare this story to "Little Red Riding Hood" and to Carter's "The Werewolf."

TIM O'BRIEN

Tim O'Brien (b. 1946) was born in Austin, Minnesota, and educated at Macalester College and Harvard. He served as a sergeant in the Vietnam War and was awarded a Purple Heart. *If I Die in a Combat Zone* (1973) is a fictionalized account of his combat experience. His short fiction is collected in *The Things They Carried* (1990). O'Brien's novels include *Northern Lights* (1974), *Going After Cacciato* (1978), which won a National Book Award, *The Nuclear Age* (1985), *In the Lake of the Woods* (1994), *Tomcat in Love* (1998), and *July, July* (2002).

The Things They Carried

First Lieutenant Jimmy Cross carried letters from a girl named Martha, a junior at Mount Sebastian College in New Jersey. They were not love letters, but Lieutenant Cross was hoping, so he kept them folded in plastic at the bottom of his rucksack. In the late afternoon, after a day's march, he would dig his foxhole, wash his hands under a canteen, unwrap the letters, hold them with the tips of his fingers, and spend the last hour of light pretending. He would imagine romantic camping trips into the White Mountains in New Hampshire. He would sometimes taste the envelope flaps, knowing her tongue had been there. More than anything, he wanted Martha to love him as he loved her, but the letters were mostly chatty, elusive on the matter of love. She was a virgin, he was almost sure. She was an English major at Mount Sebastian, and she wrote beautifully about her professors and roommates and midterm exams, about her respect for Chaucer and her great affection for Virginia Woolf. She often quoted lines of poetry; she never mentioned the war, except to say, Jimmy, take care of yourself. The letters weighed ten ounces. They were signed "Love, Martha," but Lieutenant Cross understood that "Love" was only a way of signing and did not mean what he sometimes pretended it meant. At dusk, he would carefully return the letters to his rucksack. Slowly, a bit distracted, he would get up and move among his men, checking the perimeter, then at full dark he would return to his hole and watch the night and wonder if Martha was a virgin.

The things they carried were largely determined by necessity. Among the necessities or near necessities were P-38 can openers, pocket knives, heat tabs, wrist watches, dog tags, mosquito repellant, chewing gum, candy, cigarettes, salt tablets, packets of Kool-Aid, lighters, matches, sewing kits, Military Payment Certificates, C rations, and two or three canteens of water. Together, these items weighed between fifteen and twenty pounds, depending upon a man's habits or rate of metabolism. Henry Dobbins, who was a big man, carried extra rations; he was especially fond of canned peaches in heavy syrup over pound cake. Dave Jensen, who practiced field hygiene, carried a toothbrush, dental floss, and several hotel-size bars of soap he'd stolen on R&R in Sydney, Australia. Ted Lavender, who was scared, carried tranquilizers until he was shot in the head outside the village of Than Khe in mid-April. By necessity, and because it was SOP,° they all carried steel helmets that weighed five pounds including the liner and camouflage cover. They carried the standard fatigue jackets and trousers. Very few carried underwear. On their feet they carried jungle boots—2.1 pounds—and Dave Jensen carried three pairs of socks and a can of Dr. Scholl's foot powder as a precaution against trench foot. Until he was shot, Ted Lavender carried six or seven ounces of premium dope, which for him was a necessity. Mitchell Sanders, the RTO,° carried condoms. Norman Bowker carried a diary. Rat Kiley carried comic books. Kiowa, a devout Baptist, carried an illustrated New Testament that had been presented to him by his father, who taught Sunday school in Oklahoma City, Oklahoma. As a hedge against bad times, however, Kiowa also carried his grandmother's distrust of the white man, his grandfather's old hunting hatchet. Necessity dictated. Because the land was mined and booby-trapped, it was SOP for each man to carry a steel-centered, nylon-covered flak jacket, which weighed 6.7 pounds, but which on hot days seemed much heavier. Because you could die so quickly, each man carried at least one large compress bandage, usually in the helmet band for easy access. Because the nights were cold, and because the monsoons were wet, each carried a green plastic poncho that could be used as a raincoat or ground sheet or makeshift tent. With its quilted liner, the poncho weighed almost two pounds, but it was worth every ounce. In April, for instance, when Ted Lavender was shot, they used his poncho to wrap him up, then to carry him across the paddy, then to lift him into the chopper that took him away.

They were called legs or grunts.

To carry something was to "hump" it, as when Lieutenant Jimmy Cross humped his love for Martha up the hills and through the swamps. In its intransitive form, "to hump" meant "to walk," or "to march," but it implied burdens far beyond the intransitive.

5   Almost everyone humped photographs. In his wallet, Lieutenant Cross carried two photographs of Martha. The first was a Kodachrome snapshot signed "Love," though he knew better. She stood against a brick wall. Her eyes were gray and neutral, her lips slightly open as she stared straight-on at the camera. At night, sometimes, Lieutenant Cross wondered who had taken the picture, because he knew she had boyfriends, because he loved her so much, and because he could see the shadow of the picture taker spreading out against the brick wall. The second photograph had been clipped from the 1968 Mount Sebastian yearbook. It was an action shot—women's volleyball—and Martha was bent horizontal to the floor, reaching, the palms of her hands in sharp focus, the tongue taut, the expression frank and competitive. There was no visible sweat. She wore white gym shorts. Her legs, he thought, were almost certainly the legs of a virgin, dry and without hair, the left knee cocked and carrying her entire weight, which was just over one hundred pounds. Lieutenant Cross remembered

---

°*SOP*: Standard Operating Procedure.
°*RTO*: Radio telephone operator.

touching that left knee. A dark theater, he remembered, and the movie was *Bonnie and Clyde,* and Martha wore a tweed skirt, and during the final scene, when he touched her knee, she turned and looked at him in a sad, sober way that made him pull his hand back, but he would always remember the feel of the tweed skirt and the knee beneath it and the sound of the gunfire that killed Bonnie and Clyde, how embarrassing it was, how slow and oppressive. He remembered kissing her good night at the dorm door. Right then, he thought, he should've done something brave. He should've carried her up the stairs to her room and tied her to the bed and touched that left knee all night long. He should've risked it. Whenever he looked at the photographs, he thought of new things he should've done.

What they carried was partly a function of rank, partly of field specialty.

As a first lieutenant and platoon leader, Jimmy Cross carried a compass, maps, code books, binoculars, and a .45-caliber pistol that weighed 2.9 pounds fully loaded. He carried a strobe light and the responsibility for the lives of his men.

As an RTO, Mitchell Sanders carried the PRC-25 radio, a killer, twenty-six pounds with its battery.

As a medic, Rat Kiley carried a canvas satchel filled with morphine and plasma and malaria tablets and surgical tape and comic books and all the things a medic must carry, including M&M's for especially bad wounds, for a total weight of nearly twenty pounds.

As a big man, therefore a machine gunner, Henry Dobbins carried the M-60, which weighed twenty-three pounds unloaded, but which was almost always loaded. In addition, Dobbins carried between ten and fifteen pounds of ammunition draped in belts across his chest and shoulders.

As PFCs or Spec 4s, most of them were common grunts and carried the standard M-16 gas-operated assault rifle. The weapon weighed 7.5 pounds unloaded, 8.2 pounds with its full twenty-round magazine. Depending on numerous factors, such as topography and psychology, the riflemen carried anywhere from twelve to twenty magazines, usually in cloth bandoliers, adding on another 8.4 pounds at minimum, fourteen pounds at maximum. When it was available, they also carried M-16 maintenance gear—rods and steel brushes and swabs and tubes of LSA oil—all of which weighed about a pound. Among the grunts, some carried the M-79 grenade launcher, 5.9 pounds unloaded, a reasonably light weapon except for the ammunition, which was heavy. A single round weighed ten ounces. The typical load was twenty-five rounds. But Ted Lavender, who was scared, carried thirty-four rounds when he was shot and killed outside Than Khe, and he went down under an exceptional burden, more than twenty pounds of ammunition, plus the flak jacket and helmet and rations and water and toilet paper and tranquilizers and all the rest, plus the unweighed fear. He was dead weight. There was no twitching or flopping. Kiowa, who saw it happen, said it was like watching a rock fall, or a big sandbag or something—just boom, then down—not like the movies where the dead guy rolls around and does fancy spins and goes ass over teakettle—not like that, Kiowa said, the poor bastard just flatfuck fell. Boom. Down. Nothing else. It was a bright morning in mid-April. Lieutenant Cross felt the pain. He blamed himself. They stripped off Lavender's canteens and ammo, all the heavy things, and Rat Kiley said the obvious, the guy's dead, and Mitchell Sanders used his radio to report one U.S. KIA° and to request a chopper. Then they wrapped Lavender in his

10

°*KIA*: Killed in action.

poncho. They carried him out to a dry paddy, established security, and sat smoking the dead man's dope until the chopper came. Lieutenant Cross kept to himself. He pictured Martha's smooth young face, thinking he loved her more than anything, more than his men, and now Ted Lavender was dead because he loved her so much and could not stop thinking about her. When the dust-off arrived, they carried Lavender aboard. Afterward they burned Than Khe. They marched until dusk, then dug their holes, and that night Kiowa kept explaining how you had to be there, how fast it was, how the poor guy just dropped like so much concrete. Boom-down, he said. Like cement.

In addition to the three standard weapons—the M-60, M-16, and M-79—they carried whatever presented itself, or whatever seemed appropriate as a means of killing or staying alive. They carried catch-as-catch-can. At various times, in various situations, they carried M-14s and CAR-15s and Swedish Ks and grease guns and captured AK-47s and Chi-Coms and RPGs and Simonov carbines and black-market Uzis and .38-caliber Smith & Wesson handguns and 66 mm LAWs and shotguns and silencers and blackjacks and bayonets and C-4 plastic explosives. Lee Strunk carried a slingshot; a weapon of last resort, he called it. Mitchell Sanders carried brass knuckles. Kiowa carried his grandfather's feathered hatchet. Every third or fourth man carried a Claymore antipersonnel mine—3.5 pounds with its firing device. They all carried fragmentation grenades—fourteen ounces each. They all carried at least one M-18 colored smoke grenade—twenty-four ounces. Some carried CS or tear-gas grenades. Some carried white-phosphorus grenades. They carried all they could bear, and then some, including a silent awe for the terrible power of the things they carried.

In the first week of April, before Lavender died, Lieutenant Jimmy Cross received a good-luck charm from Martha. It was a simple pebble, an ounce at most. Smooth to the touch, it was a milky-white color with flecks of orange and violet, oval-shaped, like a miniature egg. In the accompanying letter, Martha wrote that she had found the pebble on the Jersey shoreline, precisely where the land touched water at high tide, where things came together but also separated. It was this separate-but-together quality, she wrote, that had inspired her to pick up the pebble and to carry it in her breast pocket for several days, where it seemed weightless, and then to send it through the mail, by air, as a token of her truest feelings for him. Lieutenant Cross found this romantic. But he wondered what her truest feelings were, exactly, and what she meant by separate-but-together. He wondered how the tides and waves had come into play on that afternoon along the Jersey shoreline when Martha saw the pebble and bent down to rescue it from geology. He imagined bare feet. Martha was a poet, with the poet's sensibilities, and her feet would be brown and bare, the toenails unpainted, the eyes chilly and somber like the ocean in March, and though it was painful, he wondered who had been with her that afternoon. He imagined a pair of shadows moving along the strip of sand where things came together but also separated. It was phantom jealousy, he knew, but he couldn't help himself. He loved her so much. On the march, through the hot days of early April, he carried the pebble in his mouth, turning it with his tongue, tasting sea salts and moisture. His mind wandered. He had difficulty keeping his attention on the war. On occasion he would yell at his men to spread out the column, to keep their eyes open, but then he would slip away into daydreams, just pretending, walking barefoot along the Jersey shore, with Martha, carrying nothing. He would feel himself rising. Sun and waves and gentle winds, all love and lightness.

What they carried varied by mission.

When a mission took them to the mountains, they carried mosquito netting, ma- 15
chetes, canvas tarps, and extra bug juice.

If a mission seemed especially hazardous, or if it involved a place they knew to be
bad, they carried everything they could. In certain heavily mined AOs,° where the
land was dense with Toe Poppers and Bouncing Betties, they took turns humping a
twenty-eight-pound mine detector. With its headphones and big sensing plate, the
equipment was a stress on the lower back and shoulders, awkward to handle, often useless because of the shrapnel in the earth, but they carried it anyway, partly for safety,
partly for the illusion of safety.

On ambush, or other night missions, they carried peculiar little odds and ends.
Kiowa always took along his New Testament and a pair of moccasins for silence. Dave
Jensen carried night-sight vitamins high in carotin. Lee Strunk carried his slingshot;
ammo, he claimed, would never be a problem. Rat Kiley carried brandy and M&M's.
Until he was shot, Ted Lavender carried the starlight scope, which weighed 6.3 pounds
with its aluminum carrying case. Henry Dobbins carried his girlfriend's pantyhose
wrapped around his neck as a comforter. They all carried ghosts. When dark came, they
would move out single file across the meadows and paddies to their ambush coordi-
nates, where they would quietly set up the Claymores and lie down and spend the
night waiting.

Other missions were more complicated and required special equipment. In mid-
April, it was their mission to search out and destroy the elaborate tunnel complexes
in the Than Khe area south of Chu Lai. To blow the tunnels, they carried one-pound
blocks of pentrite high explosives, four blocks to a man, sixty-eight pounds in all. They
carried wiring, detonators, and battery-powered clackers. Dave Jensen carried earplugs.
Most often, before blowing the tunnels, they were ordered by higher command to
search them, which was considered bad news, but by and large they just shrugged
and carried out orders. Because he was a big man, Henry Dobbins was excused from
tunnel duty. The others would draw numbers. Before Lavender died there were seventeen men in the platoon, and whoever drew the number seventeen would strip off
his gear and crawl in head first with a flashlight and Lieutenant Cross's .45-caliber
pistol. The rest of them would fan out as security. They would sit down or kneel, not
facing the hole, listening to the ground beneath them, imagining cobwebs and ghosts,
whatever was down there—the tunnel walls squeezing in—how the flashlight seemed
impossibly heavy in the hand and how it was tunnel vision in the very strictest sense,
compression in all ways, even time, and how you had to wiggle in—ass and elbows—
a swallowed-up feeling—and how you found yourself worrying about odd things—
will your flashlight go dead? Do rats carry rabies? If you screamed, how far would
the sound carry? Would your buddies hear it? Would they have the courage to drag
you out? In some respects, though not many, the waiting was worse than the tunnel
itself. Imagination was a killer.

On April 16, when Lee Strunk drew the number seventeen, he laughed and muttered something and went down quickly. The morning was hot and very still. Not
good, Kiowa said. He looked at the tunnel opening, then out across a dry paddy toward the village of Than Khe. Nothing moved. No clouds or birds or people. As they
waited, the men smoked and drank Kool-Aid, not talking much, feeling sympathy for
Lee Strunk but also feeling the luck of the draw. You win some, you lose some, said

---

°*AOs:* Areas of operation.

Mitchell Sanders, and sometimes you settle for a rain check. It was a tired line and no one laughed.

20   Henry Dobbins ate a tropical chocolate bar. Ted Lavender popped a tranquilizer and went off to pee.

After five minutes, Lieutenant Jimmy Cross moved to the tunnel, leaned down, and examined the darkness. Trouble, he thought—a cave-in maybe. And then suddenly, without willing it, he was thinking about Martha. The stresses and fractures, the quick collapse, the two of them buried alive under all that weight. Dense, crushing love. Kneeling, watching the hole, he tried to concentrate on Lee Strunk and the war, all the dangers, but his love was too much for him, he felt paralyzed, he wanted to sleep inside her lungs and breathe her blood and be smothered. He wanted her to be a virgin and not a virgin, all at once. He wanted to know her. Intimate secrets—why poetry? Why so sad? Why the grayness in her eyes? Why so alone? Not lonely, just alone—riding her bike across campus or sitting off by herself in the cafeteria. Even dancing, she danced alone—and it was the aloneness that filled him with love. He remembered telling her that one evening. How she nodded and looked away. And how, later, when he kissed her, she received the kiss without returning it, her eyes wide open, not afraid, not a virgin's eyes, just flat and uninvolved.

Lieutenant Cross gazed at the tunnel. But he was not there. He was buried with Martha under the white sand at the Jersey shore. They were pressed together, and the pebble in his mouth was her tongue. He was smiling. Vaguely, he was aware of how quiet the day was, the sullen paddies, yet he could not bring himself to worry about matters of security. He was beyond that. He was just a kid at war, in love. He was twenty-two years old. He couldn't help it.

A few moments later Lee Strunk crawled out of the tunnel. He came up grinning, filthy but alive. Lieutenant Cross nodded and closed his eyes while the others clapped Strunk on the back and made jokes about rising from the dead.

Worms, Rat Kiley said. Right out of the grave. Fuckin' zombie.

25   The men laughed. They all felt great relief.

Spook City, said Mitchell Sanders.

Lee Strunk made a funny ghost sound, a kind of moaning, yet very happy, and right then, when Strunk made that high happy moaning sound, when he went *Ahhooooo*, right then Ted Lavender was shot in the head on his way back from peeing. He lay with his mouth open. The teeth were broken. There was a swollen black bruise under his left eye. The cheekbone was gone. Oh shit, Rat Kiley said, the guy's dead. The guy's dead, he kept saying, which seemed profound—the guy's dead. I mean really.

The things they carried were determined to some extent by superstition. Lieutenant Cross carried his good-luck pebble. Dave Jensen carried a rabbit's foot. Norman Bowker, otherwise a very gentle person, carried a thumb that had been presented to him as a gift by Mitchell Sanders. The thumb was dark brown, rubbery to the touch, and weighed four ounces at most. It had been cut from a VC corpse, a boy of fifteen or sixteen. They'd found him at the bottom of an irrigation ditch, badly burned, flies in his mouth and eyes. The boy wore black shorts and sandals. At the time of his death he had been carrying a pouch of rice, a rifle, and three magazines of ammunition.

You want my opinion, Mitchell Sanders said, there's a definite moral here.

30   He put his hand on the dead boy's wrist. He was quiet for a time, as if counting a pulse, then he patted the stomach, almost affectionately, and used Kiowa's hunting hatchet to remove the thumb.

Henry Dobbins asked what the moral was.

Moral?

You know. *Moral.*

Sanders wrapped the thumb in toilet paper and handed it across to Norman Bowker. There was no blood. Smiling, he kicked the boy's head, watched the flies scatter, and said, It's like with that old TV show—Paladin. Have gun, will travel.

Henry Dobbins thought about it.

Yeah, well, he finally said. I don't see no moral.

There it *is,* man.

Fuck off.

They carried USO stationery and pencils and pens. They carried Sterno, safety pins, trip flares, signal flares, spools of wire, razor blades, chewing tobacco, liberated joss sticks and statuettes of the smiling Buddha, candles, grease pencils, *The Stars and Stripes,* fingernail clippers, Psy Ops° leaflets, bush hats, bolos, and much more. Twice a week, when the resupply choppers came in, they carried hot chow in green Mermite cans and large canvas bags filled with iced beer and soda pop. They carried plastic water containers, each with a two-gallon capacity. Mitchell Sanders carried a set of starched tiger fatigues for special occasions. Henry Dobbins carried Black Flag insecticide. Dave Jensen carried empty sandbags that could be filled at night for added protection. Lee Strunk carried tanning lotion. Some things they carried in common. Taking turns, they carried the big PRC-77 scrambler radio, which weighed thirty pounds with its battery. They shared the weight of memory. They took up what others could no longer bear. Often, they carried each other, the wounded or weak. They carried infections. They carried chess sets, basketballs, Vietnamese-English dictionaries, insignia of rank, Bronze Stars and Purple Hearts, plastic cards imprinted with the Code of Conduct. They carried diseases, among them malaria and dysentery. They carried lice and ringworm and leeches and paddy algae and various rots and molds. They carried the land itself—Vietnam, the place, the soil—a powdery orange-red dust that covered their boots and fatigues and faces. They carried the sky. The whole atmosphere, they carried it, the humidity, the monsoons, the stink of fungus and decay, all of it, they carried gravity. They moved like mules. By daylight they took sniper fire, at night they were mortared, but it was not battle, it was just the endless march, village to village, without purpose, nothing won or lost. They marched for the sake of the march. They plodded along slowly, dumbly, leaning forward against the heat, unthinking, all blood and bone, simple grunts, soldiering with their legs, toiling up the hills and down into the paddies and across the rivers and up again and down, just humping, one step and then the next and then another, but no volition, no will, because it was automatic, it was anatomy, and the war was entirely a matter of posture and carriage, the hump was everything, a kind of inertia, a kind of emptiness, a dullness of desire and intellect and conscience and hope and human sensibility. Their principles were in their feet. Their calculations were biological. They had no sense of strategy or mission. They searched the villages without knowing what to look for, not caring, kicking over jars of rice, frisking children and old men, blowing tunnels, sometimes setting fires and sometimes not, then forming up and moving on to the next village, then other villages, where it would always be the same. They carried their own lives. The pressures were enormous. In the heat of early afternoon, they would remove their helmets and flak jackets, walking

---

°*Psy Ops*: Psychological operations.

bare, which was dangerous but which helped ease the strain. They would often discard things along the route of march. Purely for comfort, they would throw away rations, blow their Claymores and grenades, no matter, because by nightfall the resupply choppers would arrive with more of the same, then a day or two later still more, fresh watermelons and crates of ammunition and sunglasses and woolen sweaters—the resources were stunning—sparklers for the Fourth of July, colored eggs for Easter. It was the great American war chest—the fruits of science, the smokestacks, the canneries, the arsenals at Hartford, the Minnesota forests, the machine shops, the vast fields of corn and wheat—they carried like freight trains; they carried it on their backs and shoulders—and for all the ambiguities of Vietnam, all the mysteries and unknowns, there was at least the single abiding certainty that they would never be at a loss for things to carry.

40   After the chopper took Lavender away, Lieutenant Jimmy Cross led his men into the village of Than Khe. They burned everything. They shot chickens and dogs, they trashed the village well, they called in artillery and watched the wreckage, then they marched for several hours through the hot afternoon, and then at dusk, while Kiowa explained how Lavender died, Lieutenant Cross found himself trembling.

He tried not to cry. With his entrenching tool, which weighed five pounds, he began digging a hole in the earth.

He felt shame. He hated himself. He had loved Martha more than his men, and as a consequence Lavender was now dead, and this was something he would have to carry like a stone in his stomach for the rest of the war.

All he could do was dig. He used his entrenching tool like an ax, slashing, feeling both love and hate, and then later, when it was full dark, he sat at the bottom of his foxhole and wept. It went on for a long while. In part, he was grieving for Ted Lavender, but mostly it was for Martha, and for himself, because she belonged to another world, which was not quite real, and because she was a junior at Mount Sebastian College in New Jersey, a poet and a virgin and uninvolved, and because he realized she did not love him and never would.

Like cement, Kiowa whispered in the dark. I swear to God—boomdown. Not a word.

45   I've heard this, said Norman Bowker.

A pisser, you know? Still zipping himself up. Zapped while zipping.

All right, fine. That's enough.

Yeah, but you had to see it, the guy just—

I *heard,* man. Cement. So why not shut the fuck *up?*

50   Kiowa shook his head sadly and glanced over at the hole where Lieutenant Jimmy Cross sat watching the night. The air was thick and wet. A warm, dense fog had settled over the paddies and there was the stillness that precedes rain.

After a time Kiowa sighed.

One thing for sure, he said. The Lieutenant's in some deep hurt. I mean that crying jag—the way he was carrying on—it wasn't fake or anything, it was real heavy-duty hurt. The man cares.

Sure, Norman Bowker said.

Say what you want, the man does care.

55   We all got problems.

Not Lavender.

No, I guess not, Bowker said. Do me a favor, though.

Shut up?

That's a smart Indian. Shut up.

Shrugging, Kiowa pulled off his boots. He wanted to say more, just to lighten up 60 his sleep, but instead he opened his New Testament and arranged it beneath his head as a pillow. The fog made things seem hollow and unattached. He tried not to think about Ted Lavender, but then he was thinking how fast it was, no drama, down and dead, and how it was hard to feel anything except surprise. It seemed unChristian. He wished he could find some great sadness, or even anger, but the emotion wasn't there and he couldn't make it happen. Mostly he felt pleased to be alive. He liked the smell of the New Testament under his cheek, the leather and ink and paper and glue, whatever the chemicals were. He liked hearing the sounds of night. Even his fatigue, it felt fine, the stiff muscles and the prickly awareness of his own body, a floating feeling. He enjoyed not being dead. Lying there, Kiowa admired Lieutenant Jimmy Cross's capacity for grief. He wanted to share the man's pain, he wanted to care as Jimmy Cross cared. And yet when he closed his eyes, all he could think was Boomdown, and all he could feel was the pleasure of having his boots off and the fog curling in around him and the damp soil and the Bible smells and the plush comfort of night.

After a moment Norman Bowker sat up in the dark.

What the hell, he said. You want to talk, *talk*. Tell it to me.

Forget it.

No, man, go on. One thing I hate, it's a silent Indian.

For the most part they carried themselves with poise, a kind of dignity. Now and 65 then, however, there were times of panic, when they squealed or wanted to squeal but couldn't, when they twitched and made moaning sounds and covered their heads and said Dear Jesus and flopped around on the earth and fired their weapons blindly and cringed and sobbed and begged for the noise to stop and went wild and made stupid promises to themselves and to God and to their mothers and fathers, hoping not to die. In different ways, it happened to all of them. Afterward, when the firing ended, they would blink and peek up. They would touch their bodies, feeling shame, then quickly hiding it. They would force themselves to stand. As if in slow motion, frame by frame, the world would take on the old logic—absolute silence, then the wind, then sunlight, then voices. It was the burden of being alive. Awkwardly, the men would reassemble themselves, first in private, then in groups, becoming soldiers again. They would repair the leaks in their eyes. They would check for casualties, call in dust-offs, light cigarettes, try to smile, clear their throats and spit and begin cleaning their weapons. After a time someone would shake his head and say, No lie, I almost shit my pants, and someone else would laugh, which meant it was bad, yes, but the guy had obviously not shit his pants, it wasn't that bad, and in any case nobody would ever do such a thing and then go ahead and talk about it. They would squint into the dense, oppressive sunlight. For a few moments, perhaps, they would fall silent, lighting a joint and tracking its passage from man to man, inhaling, holding in the humiliation. Scary stuff, one of them might say. But then someone else would grin or flick his eyebrows and say, Roger-dodger, almost cut me a new asshole, *almost*.

There were numerous such poses. Some carried themselves with a sort of wistful resignation, others with pride or stiff soldierly discipline or good humor or macho zeal. They were afraid of dying but they were even more afraid to show it.

They found jokes to tell.

They used a hard vocabulary to contain the terrible softness. *Greased,* they'd say. *Offed, lit up, zapped while zipping.* It wasn't cruelty, just stage presence. They were actors and the war came at them in 3-D. When someone died, it wasn't quite dying, because in a curious way it seemed scripted, and because they had their lines mostly memorized, irony mixed with tragedy, and because they called it by other names, as if to encyst and destroy the reality of death itself. They kicked corpses. They cut off thumbs. They talked grunt lingo. They told stories about Ted Lavender's supply of tranquilizers, how the poor guy didn't feel a thing, how incredibly tranquil he was.

There's a moral here, said Mitchell Sanders.

70   They were waiting for Lavender's chopper, smoking the dead man's dope.

The moral's pretty obvious, Sanders said, and winked. Stay away from drugs. No joke, they'll ruin your day every time.

Cute, said Henry Dobbins.

Mind-blower, get it? Talk about wiggy—nothing left, just blood and brains.

They made themselves laugh.

75   There it is, they'd say, over and over, as if the repetition itself were an act of poise, a balance between crazy and almost crazy, knowing without going. There it is, which meant be cool, let it ride, because oh yeah, man, you can't change what can't be changed, there it is, there it absolutely and positively and fucking well *is.*

They were tough.

They carried all the emotional baggage of men who might die. Grief, terror, love, longing—these were intangibles, but the intangibles had their own mass and specific gravity, they had tangible weight. They carried shameful memories. They carried the common secret of cowardice barely restrained, the instinct to run or freeze or hide, and in many respects this was the heaviest burden of all, for it could never be put down, it required perfect balance and perfect posture. They carried their reputations. They carried the soldier's greatest fear, which was the fear of blushing. Men killed, and died, because they were embarrassed not to. It was what had brought them to the war in the first place, nothing positive, no dreams of glory or honor, just to avoid the blush of dishonor. They died so as not to die of embarrassment. They crawled into tunnels and walked point and advanced under fire. Each morning, despite the unknowns, they made their legs move. They endured. They kept humping. They did not submit to the obvious alternative, which was simply to close the eyes and fall. So easy, really. Go limp and tumble to the ground and let the muscles unwind and not speak and not budge until your buddies picked you up and lifted you into the chopper that would roar and dip its nose and carry you off to the world. A mere matter of falling, yet no one ever fell. It was not courage, exactly; the object was not valor. Rather, they were too frightened to be cowards.

By and large they carried these things inside, maintaining the masks of composure. They sneered at sick call. They spoke bitterly about guys who had found release by shooting off their own toes or fingers. Pussies, they'd say. Candyasses. It was fierce, mocking talk, with only a trace of envy or awe, but even so, the image played itself out behind their eyes.

They imagined the muzzle against flesh. They imagined the quick, sweet pain, then the evacuation to Japan, then a hospital with warm beds and cute geisha nurses.

80   They dreamed of freedom birds.

At night, on guard, staring into the dark, they were carried away by jumbo jets. They felt the rush of takeoff. *Gone!* they yelled. And then velocity, wings and engines, a smiling stewardess—but it was more than a plane, it was a real bird, a big sleek silver bird with feathers and talons and high screeching. They were flying. The weights fell off, there was nothing to bear. They laughed and held on tight, feeling the cold slap of wind and altitude, soaring, thinking *It's over, I'm gone!*—they were naked, they were light and free—it was all lightness, bright and fast and buoyant, light as light, a helium buzz in the brain, a giddy bubbling in the lungs as they were taken up over the clouds and the war, beyond duty, beyond gravity and mortification and global entanglements—*Sin loi!°* they yelled, *I'm sorry, motherfuckers, but I'm out of it, I'm goofed, I'm on a space cruise, I'm gone!*—and it was a restful, disencumbered sensation, just riding the light waves, sailing that big silver freedom bird over the mountains and oceans, over America, over the farms and great sleeping cities and cemeteries and highways and the golden arches of McDonald's. It was flight, a kind of fleeing, a kind of falling, falling higher and higher, spinning off the edge of the earth and beyond the sun and through the vast, silent vacuum where there were no burdens and where everything weighed exactly nothing. *Gone!* they screamed, *I'm sorry but I'm gone!* And so at night, not quite dreaming, they gave themselves over to lightness, they were carried, they were purely borne.

On the morning after Ted Lavender died, First Lieutenant Jimmy Cross crouched at the bottom of his foxhole and burned Martha's letters. Then he burned the two photographs. There was a steady rain falling, which made it difficult, but he used heat tabs and Sterno to build a small fire, screening it with his body, holding the photographs over the tight blue flame with the tips of his fingers.

He realized it was only a gesture. Stupid, he thought. Sentimental, too, but mostly just stupid.

Lavender was dead. You couldn't burn the blame.

Besides, the letters were in his head. And even now, without photographs, Lieutenant Cross could see Martha playing volleyball in her white gym shorts and yellow T-shirt. He could see her moving in the rain. 85

When the fire died out, Lieutenant Cross pulled his poncho over his shoulders and ate breakfast from a can.

There was no great mystery, he decided.

In those burned letters Martha had never mentioned the war, except to say, Jimmy, take care of yourself. She wasn't involved. She signed the letters "Love," but it wasn't love, and all the fine lines and technicalities did not matter.

The morning came up wet and blurry. Everything seemed part of everything else, the fog and Martha and the deepening rain.

It was a war, after all. 90

Half smiling, Lieutenant Jimmy Cross took out his maps. He shook his head hard, as if to clear it, then bent forward and began planning the day's march. In ten minutes, or maybe twenty, he would rouse the men and they would pack up and head west, where the maps showed the country to be green and inviting. They would do what they had always done. The rain might add some weight, but otherwise it would be one more day layered upon all the other days.

He was realistic about it. There was that new hardness in his stomach.

No more fantasies, he told himself.

Henceforth, when he thought about Martha, it would be only to think that she belonged elsewhere. He would shut down the daydreams. This was not Mount Sebastian, it was another world, where there were no pretty poems or midterm exams, a

---

°*Sin loi!*: Sorry about that!

place where men died because of carelessness and gross stupidity. Kiowa was right. Boomdown, and you were dead, never partly dead.

95   Briefly, in the rain, Lieutenant Cross saw Martha's gray eyes gazing back at him. He understood.

It was very sad, he thought. The things men carried inside. The things men did or felt they had to do.

He almost nodded at her, but didn't.

Instead he went back to his maps. He was now determined to perform his duties firmly and without negligence. It wouldn't help Lavender, he knew that, but from this point on he would comport himself as a soldier. He would dispose of his good-luck pebble. Swallow it, maybe, or use Lee Strunk's slingshot, or just drop it along the trail. On the march he would impose strict field discipline. He would be careful to send out flank security, to prevent straggling or bunching up, to keep his troops moving at the proper pace and at the proper interval. He would insist on clean weapons. He would confiscate the remainder of Lavender's dope. Later in the day, perhaps, he would call the men together and speak to them plainly. He would accept the blame for what had happened to Ted Lavender. He would be a man about it. He would look them in the eyes, keeping his chin level, and he would issue the new SOPs in a calm, impersonal tone of voice, an officer's voice, leaving no room for argument or discussion. Commencing immediately, he'd tell them, they would no longer abandon equipment along the route of march. They would police up their acts. They would get their shit together, and keep it together, and maintain it neatly and in good working order.

100   He would not tolerate laxity. He would show strength, distancing himself.

Among the men there would be grumbling, of course, and maybe worse, because their days would seem longer and their loads heavier, but Lieutenant Cross reminded himself that his obligation was not to be loved but to lead. He would dispense with love; it was not now a factor. And if anyone quarreled or complained, he would simply tighten his lips and arrange his shoulders in the correct command posture. He might give a curt little nod. Or he might not. He might just shrug and say Carry on, then they would saddle up and form into a column and move out toward the villages of Than Khe.   [1985]

QUESTIONS

1. How is the reader to assess the "weight" of the "things" of the title?
2. Because of the nature of combat, Army training attempts to subordinate the individual to the unit. Has the training succeeded in the squad of this story?
3. What is the effect on the soldiers of Ted Lavender's death?
4. How is Jimmy Cross's character defined by his evolving attitude toward Martha?
5. Tim O'Brien has said of war stories: "If at the end of a war story you feel uplifted, or if you feel that some small bit of rectitude has been salvaged from the larger waste, then you have been made the victim of a very old and terrible lie. There is no rectitude whatsoever. There is no virtue. As a first rule of thumb, therefore, you can tell a true war story by its absolute and uncompromising allegiance to obscenity and evil." Does "The Things They Carried" illustrate this generalization?

Response

1. Examine this story and compare its focus on things to the focus on things in stories such as Oates's "Shopping" and Cisneros's "Barbie-Q." What importance do the writers place on these material objects? What role do these objects play in propelling the plot and conflict, in establishing character and setting?

Focus on Film

1. View the film *Platoon*. Focus on the early scenes of the film, and other scenes such as the ending with the final voice-over. Discuss how both film and story emphasize the material burdens and emotional "baggage." How do the works convey the lessons of traveling light?
2. Choose characters from the film and compare them to characters in the story.
3. Discuss the narrative voice and point of view in the print story. Examine how Chris's voice-over in the film reflects and/or differs from that narrative voice.

FLANNERY O'CONNOR

Flannery O'Connor (1925–1964) was born in Savannah, Georgia, and educated at Georgia State College for Women and the University of Iowa. She published her first stories while living in and about New York City, but a debilitating disease diagnosed as lupus forced her to return to her ancestral home in Milledgeville, Georgia. For the remaining fourteen years of her life she fought the disease, meanwhile writing her powerful and haunting stories and venturing forth during periods of remission to lecture to college students. Her *Complete Stories*, published in 1972, won the National Book Award for Fiction.

A Good Man Is Hard to Find

The grandmother didn't want to go to Florida. She wanted to visit some of her connections in east Tennessee and she was seizing at every chance to change Bailey's mind. Bailey was the son she lived with, her only boy. He was sitting on the edge of his chair at the table, bent over the orange sports section of the *Journal*. "Now look here, Bailey," she said, "see here, and read this," and she stood with one hand on her thin hip and the other rattling the newspaper at his bald head. "Here this fellow that calls himself The Misfit is aloose from the Federal Pen and headed toward Florida and you read here what it says he did to these people. Just you read it. I wouldn't take my children in any direction with a criminal like that aloose in it. I couldn't answer to my conscience if I did."

Bailey didn't look up from his reading so she wheeled around then and faced the children's mother, a young woman in slacks, whose face was as broad and innocent as a cabbage and was tied around with a green head-kerchief that had two points on the top like a rabbit's ears. She was sitting on the sofa, feeding the baby his apricots out of a jar. "The children have been to Florida before," the old lady said. "You all ought to take them somewhere else for a change so they would see different parts of the world and be broad. They never have been to east Tennessee."

The children's mother didn't seem to hear her but the eight-year-old boy, John Wesley, a stocky child with glasses, said, "If you don't want to go to Florida, why dontcha stay at home?" He and the little girl, June Star, were reading the funny papers on the floor.

"She wouldn't stay at home to be queen for a day," June Star said without raising her yellow head.

"Yes and what would you do if this fellow, The Misfit, caught you?" the grand-   5
mother asked.

"I'd smack his face," John Wesley said.

"She wouldn't stay at home for a million bucks," June Star said. "Afraid she'd miss something. She has to go everywhere we go."

"All right, Miss," the grandmother said. "Just remember that the next time you want me to curl your hair."

June Star said her hair was naturally curly.

The next morning the grandmother was the first one in the car, ready to go. She   10
had her big black valise that looked like the head of a hippopotamus in one corner, and underneath it she was hiding a basket with Pitty Sing, the cat, in it. She didn't intend for the cat to be left alone in the house for three days because he would miss her too much and she was afraid he might brush against one of the gas burners and acciden-tally asphyxiate himself. Her son, Bailey, didn't like to arrive at a motel with a cat.

She sat in the middle of the back seat with John Wesley and June Star on either side of her. Bailey and the children's mother and the baby sat in front and they left At-lanta at eight forty-five with the mileage on the car at 55890. The grandmother wrote this down because she thought it would be interesting to say how many miles they had been when they got back. It took them twenty minutes to reach the outskirts of the city.

The old lady settled herself comfortably, removing her white cotton gloves and putting them up with her purse on the shelf in front of the back window. The chil-dren's mother still had on slacks and still had her head tied up in a green kerchief, but the grandmother had on a navy blue straw sailor hat with a bunch of white violets on the brim and a navy blue dress with a small white dot in the print. Her collars and cuffs were white organdy trimmed with lace and at her neckline she had pinned a purple spray of cloth violets containing a sachet. In case of an accident, anyone seeing her dead on the highway would know at once that she was a lady.

She said she thought it was going to be a good day for driving, neither too hot nor too cold, and she cautioned Bailey that the speed limit was fifty-five miles an hour and that the patrolmen hid themselves behind billboards and small clumps of trees and sped out after you before you had a chance to slow down. She pointed out interesting details of the scenery: Stone Mountain; the blue granite that in some places came up to both sides of the highway; the brilliant red clay banks slightly streaked with pur-ple; and the various crops that made rows of green lace-work on the ground. The trees were full of silver-white sunlight and the meanest of them sparkled. The children were reading comic magazines and their mother had gone back to sleep.

"Let's go through Georgia fast so we won't have to look at it much," John Wesley said.

"If I were a little boy," said the grandmother, "I wouldn't talk about my native state   15
that way. Tennessee has the mountains and Georgia has the hills."

"Tennessee is just a hillbilly dumping ground," John Wesley said, "and Georgia is a lousy state too."

"You said it," June Star said.

"In my time," said the grandmother, folding her thin veined fingers, "children were more respectful of their native states and their parents and everything else. People did right then. Oh look at the cute little pickaninny!" she said and pointed to a Negro child standing in the door of a shack. "Wouldn't that make a picture, now?" she asked and they all turned and looked at the little Negro out of the back window. He waved.

"He didn't have any britches on," June Star said.

20   "He probably didn't have any," the grandmother explained. "Little niggers in the country don't have things like we do. If I could paint, I'd paint that picture," she said.

The children exchanged comic books.

The grandmother offered to hold the baby and the children's mother passed him over the front seat to her. She set him on her knee and bounced him and told him about the things they were passing. She rolled her eyes and screwed up her mouth and stuck her leathery thin face into his smooth bland one. Occasionally he gave her a faraway smile. They passed a large cotton field with five or six graves fenced in the middle of it, like a small island. "Look at the graveyard!" the grandmother said, pointing it out. "That was the old family burying ground. That belonged to the plantation."

"Where's the plantation?" John Wesley asked.

"Gone With the Wind," said the grandmother. "Ha. Ha."

25   When the children finished all the comic books they had brought, they opened the lunch and ate it. The grandmother ate a peanut butter sandwich and an olive and would not let the children throw the box and the paper napkins out the window. When there was nothing else to do they played a game by choosing a cloud and making the other two guess what shape it suggested. John Wesley took one the shape of a cow and June Star guessed a cow and John Wesley said, no, an automobile, and June Star said he didn't play fair, and they began to slap each other over the grandmother.

The grandmother said she would tell them a story if they would keep quiet. When she told a story, she rolled her eyes and waved her head and was very dramatic. She said once when she was a maiden lady she had been courted by a Mr. Edgar Atkins Teagarden from Jasper, Georgia. She said he was a very good-looking man and a gentleman and that he brought her a watermelon every Saturday afternoon with his initials cut in it, E. A. T. Well, one Saturday, she said, Mr. Teagarden brought the watermelon and there was nobody at home and he left it on the front porch and returned in his buggy to Jasper, but she never got the watermelon, she said, because a nigger boy ate it when he saw the initials, E. A. T.! This story tickled John Wesley's funny bone and he giggled and giggled but June Star didn't think it was any good. She said she wouldn't marry a man that just brought her a watermelon on Saturday. The grandmother said she would have done well to marry Mr. Teagarden because he was a gentleman and had bought Coca-Cola stock when it first came out and that he had died only a few years ago, a very wealthy man.

They stopped at The Tower for barbecued sandwiches. The Tower was a part stucco and part wood filling station and dance hall set in a clearing outside of Timothy. A fat man named Red Sammy Butts ran it and there were signs stuck here and there on the building and for miles up and down the highway saying, TRY RED SAMMY'S FAMOUS BARBECUE. NONE LIKE FAMOUS RED SAMMY'S! RED SAM! THE FAT BOY WITH THE HAPPY LAUGH! A VETERAN! RED SAMMY'S YOUR MAN!

Red Sammy was lying on the bare ground outside The Tower with his head under a truck while a gray monkey about a foot high, chained to a small chinaberry tree, chattered nearby. The monkey sprang back into the tree and got on the highest limb as soon as he saw the children jump out of the car and run toward him.

Inside, The Tower was a long dark room with a counter at one end and tables at the other and dancing space in the middle. They sat down at a board table next to the nickelodeon and Red Sam's wife, a tall burnt-brown woman with hair and eyes lighter than her skin, came and took their order. The children's mother put a dime in the machine and played "The Tennessee Waltz," and the grandmother said that tune always made her want to dance. She asked Bailey if he would like to dance but he only glared at her. He didn't have a naturally sunny disposition like she did and trips made him nervous. The grandmother's brown eyes were very bright. She swayed her head from side to side and pretended she was dancing in her chair. June Star said play something she could tap to so the children's mother put in another dime and played a fast number and June Star stepped out onto the dance floor and did her tap routine.

"Ain't she cute?" Red Sam's wife said, leaning over the counter. "Would you like   30
to come be my little girl?"

"No I certainly wouldn't," June Star said. "I wouldn't live in a broken-down place like this for a million bucks!" and she ran back to the table.

"Ain't she cute?" the woman repeated, stretching her mouth politely.

"Aren't you ashamed?" hissed the grandmother.

Red Sam came in and told his wife to quit lounging on the counter and hurry up with these people's order. His khaki trousers reached just to his hip bones and his stomach hung over them like a sack of meal swaying under his shirt. He came over and sat down at a table nearby and let out a combination sigh and yodel. "You can't win," he said. "You can't win," and he wiped his sweating red face off with a gray handkerchief. "These days you don't know who to trust," he said. "Ain't that the truth?"

"People are certainly not nice like they used to be," said the grandmother.   35

"Two fellers come in here last week," Red Sammy said, "driving a Chrysler. It was a old beat-up car but it was a good one and these boys looked all right to me. Said they worked at the mill and you know I let them fellers charge the gas they bought? Now why did I do that?"

"Because you're a good man!" the grandmother said at once.

"Yes'm, I suppose so," Red Sam said as if he were struck with this answer.

His wife brought the orders, carrying the five plates all at once without a tray, two in each hand and one balanced on her arm. "It isn't a soul in this green world of God's that you can trust," she said. "And I don't count nobody out of that, not nobody," she repeated, looking at Red Sammy.

"Did you read about that criminal, The Misfit, that's escaped?" asked the grand-   40
mother.

"I wouldn't be a bit surprised if he didn't attack this place right here," said the woman. "If he hears about it being here, I wouldn't be none surprised to see him. If he hears it's two cent in the cash register, I wouldn't be a tall surprised if he . . ."

"That'll do," Red Sam said. "Go bring these people their Co'-Colas," and the woman went off to get the rest of the order.

"A good man is hard to find," Red Sammy said. "Everything is getting terrible. I remember the day you could go off and leave your screen door unlatched. Not no more."

He and the grandmother discussed better times. The old lady said that in her opinion Europe was entirely to blame for the way things were now. She said the way Europe acted you would think we were made of money and Red Sam said it was no use talking about it, she was exactly right. The children ran outside into the white sunlight and looked at the monkey in the lacy chinaberry tree. He was busy catching fleas on himself and biting each one carefully between his teeth as if it were a delicacy.

They drove off again into the hot afternoon. The grandmother took cat naps and   45
woke up every few minutes with her own snoring. Outside of Toombsboro she woke up and recalled an old plantation that she had visited in this neighborhood once when

she was a young lady. She said the house had six white columns across the front and that there was an avenue of oaks leading up to it and two little wooden trellis arbors on either side in front where you sat down with your suitor after a stroll in the garden. She recalled exactly which road to turn off to get to it. She knew that Bailey would not be willing to lose any time looking at an old house, but the more she talked about it, the more she wanted to see it once again and find out if the little twin arbors were still standing. "There was a secret panel in this house," she said craftily, not telling the truth but wishing that she were, "and the story went that all the family silver was hidden in it when Sherman came through but it was never found . . ."

"Hey!" John Wesley said. "Let's go see it! We'll find it! We'll poke all the woodwork and find it! Who lives there? Where do you turn off at? Hey Pop, can't we turn off there?"

"We never have seen a house with a secret panel!" June Star shrieked. "Let's go to the house with the secret panel! Hey Pop, can't we go see the house with the secret panel!"

"It's not far from here, I know," the grandmother said. "It wouldn't take over twenty minutes."

Bailey was looking straight ahead. His jaw was as rigid as a horseshoe. "No," he said.

50   The children began to yell and scream that they wanted to see the house with the secret panel. John Wesley kicked the back of the front seat and June Star hung over her mother's shoulder and whined desperately into her ear that they never had any fun even on their vacation, that they could never do what THEY wanted to do. The baby began to scream and John Wesley kicked the back of the seat so hard that his father could feel the blows in his kidney.

"All right!" he shouted and drew the car to a stop at the side of the road. "Will you all shut up? Will you all just shut up for one second? If you don't shut up, we won't go anywhere."

"It would be very educational for them," the grandmother murmured.

"All right," Bailey said, "but get this: this is the only time we're going to stop for anything like this. This is the one and only time."

"The dirt road that you have to turn down is about a mile back," the grandmother directed. "I marked it when we passed."

55   "A dirt road," Bailey groaned.

After they had turned around and were headed toward the dirt road, the grandmother recalled other points about the house, the beautiful glass over the front doorway and the candle-lamp in the hall. John Wesley said that the secret panel was probably in the fireplace.

"You can't go inside this house," Bailey said. "You don't know who lives there."

"While you all talk to the people in front, I'll run around behind and get in a window," John Wesley suggested.

"We'll all stay in the car," his mother said.

60   They turned onto the dirt road and the car raced roughly along in a swirl of pink dust. The grandmother recalled the times when there were no paved roads and thirty miles was a day's journey. The dirt road was hilly and there were sudden washes in it and sharp curves on dangerous embankments. All at once they would be on a hill, looking down over the blue tops of trees for miles around, then the next minute, they would be in a red depression with the dust-coated trees looking down on them.

"This place had better turn up in a minute," Bailey said, "or I'm going to turn around."

The road looked as if no one had traveled on it in months.

"It's not much farther," the grandmother said and just as she said it, a horrible thought came to her. The thought was so embarrassing that she turned red in the face and her eyes dilated and her feet jumped up, upsetting her valise in the corner. The instant the valise moved, the newspaper top she had over the basket under it rose with a snarl and Pitty Sing, the cat, sprang onto Bailey's shoulder.

The children were thrown to the floor and their mother, clutching the baby, was thrown out the door onto the ground; the old lady was thrown into the front seat. The car turned over once and landed right-side-up in a gulch off the side of the road. Bailey remained in the driver's seat with the cat—gray-striped with a broad white face and an orange nose—clinging to his neck like a caterpillar.

As soon as the children saw they could move their arms and legs, they scrambled out of the car, shouting, "We've had an ACCIDENT!" The grandmother was curled up under the dashboard, hoping she was injured so that Bailey's wrath would not come down on her all at once. The horrible thought she had had before the accident was that the house she had remembered so vividly was not in Georgia but in Tennessee. 65

Bailey removed the cat from his neck with both hands and flung it out the window against the side of a pine tree. Then he got out of the car and started looking for the children's mother. She was sitting against the side of the red gutted ditch, holding the screaming baby, but she only had a cut down her face and a broken shoulder. "We've had an ACCIDENT!" the children screamed in a frenzy of delight.

"But nobody's killed," June Star said with disappointment as the grandmother limped out of the car, her hat still pinned to her head but the broken front brim standing up at a jaunty angle and the violet spray hanging off the side. They all sat down in the ditch, except the children, to recover from the shock. They were all shaking.

"Maybe a car will come along," said the children's mother hoarsely.

"I believe I have injured an organ," said the grandmother, pressing her side, but no one answered her. Bailey's teeth were clattering. He had on a yellow sport shirt with bright blue parrots designed in it and his face was as yellow as the shirt. The grandmother decided that she would not mention that the house was in Tennessee.

The road was about ten feet above and they could see only the tops of the trees on the other side of it. Behind the ditch they were sitting in there were more woods, tall and dark and deep. In a few minutes they saw a car some distance away on top of a hill, coming slowly as if the occupants were watching them. The grandmother stood up and waved both arms dramatically to attract their attention. The car continued to come on slowly, disappeared around a bend and appeared again, moving even slower, on top of the hill they had gone over. It was a big black battered hearse-like automobile. There were three men in it. 70

It came to a stop just over them and for some minutes, the driver looked down with a steady expressionless gaze to where they were sitting, and didn't speak. Then he turned his head and muttered something to the other two and they got out. One was a fat boy in black trousers and a red sweat shirt with a silver stallion embossed on the front of it. He moved around on the right side of them and stood staring, his mouth partly open in a kind of loose grin. The other had on khaki pants and a blue striped coat and a gray hat pulled down very low, hiding most of his face. He came around slowly on the left side. Neither spoke.

The driver got out of the car and stood by the side of it, looking down at them. He was an older man than the other two. His hair was just beginning to gray and he wore silver-rimmed spectacles that gave him a scholarly look. He had a long creased face and didn't have on any shirt or undershirt. He had on blue jeans that were too tight for him and was holding a black hat and a gun. The two boys also had guns.

"We've had an ACCIDENT!" the children screamed.

The grandmother had the peculiar feeling that the bespectacled man was someone she knew. His face was as familiar to her as if she had known him all her life but she could not recall who he was. He moved away from the car and began to come down the embankment, placing his feet carefully so that he wouldn't slip. He had on tan and white shoes and no socks, and his ankles were red and thin. "Good afternoon," he said. "I see you all had you a little spill."

75   "We turned over twice!" said the grandmother.

"Oncet," he corrected. "We seen it happen. Try their car and see will it run, Hiram," he said quietly to the boy with the gray hat.

"What you got that gun for?" John Wesley asked. "Whatcha gonna do with that gun?"

"Lady," the man said to the children's mother, "would you mind calling them children to sit down by you? Children make me nervous. I want all you all to sit down right together there where you're at."

"What are you telling US what to do for?" June Star asked.

80   Behind them the line of woods gaped like a dark open mouth. "Come here," said their mother.

"Look here now," Bailey began suddenly, "we're in a predicament! We're in . . ."

The grandmother shrieked. She scrambled to her feet and stood staring. "You're The Misfit!" she said. "I recognized you at once!"

"Yes'm," the man said, smiling slightly as if he were pleased in spite of himself to be known, "but it would have been better for all of you, lady, if you hadn't of reckernized me."

Bailey turned his head sharply and said something to his mother that shocked even the children. The old lady began to cry and The Misfit reddened.

85   "Lady," he said, "don't you get upset. Sometimes a man says things he don't mean. I don't reckon he meant to talk to you thataway."

"You wouldn't shoot a lady, would you?" the grandmother said and removed a clean handkerchief from her cuff and began to slap at her eyes with it.

The Misfit pointed the toe of his shoe into the ground and made a little hole and then covered it up again. "I would hate to have to," he said.

"Listen," the grandmother almost screamed, "I know you're a good man. You don't look a bit like you have common blood. I know you must come from nice people!"

"Yes mam," he said, "finest people in the world." When he smiled he showed a row of strong white teeth. "God never made a finer woman than my mother and my daddy's heart was pure gold," he said. The boy with the red sweat shirt had come around behind them and was standing with his gun at his hip. The Misfit squatted down on the ground. "Watch them children, Bobby Lee," he said. "You know they make me nervous." He looked at the six of them huddled together in front of him and he seemed to be embarrassed as if he couldn't think of anything to say. "Ain't a cloud in the sky," he remarked, looking up at it. "Don't see no sun but don't see no cloud neither."

90   "Yes, it's a beautiful day," said the grandmother. "Listen," she said, "you shouldn't call yourself The Misfit because I know you're a good man at heart. I can just look at you and tell."

"Hush!" Bailey yelled. "Hush! Everybody shut up and let me handle this!" He was squatting in the position of a runner about to sprint forward but he didn't move.

"I pre-chate that, lady," The Misfit said and drew a little circle in the ground with the butt of his gun.

"It'll take a half a hour to fix this here car," Hiram called, looking over the raised hood of it.

"Well, first you and Bobby Lee get him and that little boy to step over yonder with you," The Misfit said, pointing to Bailey and John Wesley. "The boys want to ask you something," he said to Bailey. "Would you mind stepping back in them woods there with them?"

"Listen," Bailey began, "we're in a terrible predicament! Nobody realizes what 95 this is," his voice cracked. His eyes were as blue and intense as the parrots in his shirt and he remained perfectly still.

The grandmother reached up to adjust her hat brim as if she were going to the woods with him but it came off in her hand. She stood staring at it and after a second she let it fall on the ground. Hiram pulled Bailey up by the arm as if he were assisting an old man. John Wesley caught hold of his father's hand and Bobby Lee followed. They went off toward the woods and just as they reached the dark edge, Bailey turned and supporting himself against a gray naked pine trunk, he shouted, "I'll be back in a minute, Mamma, wait on me!"

"Come back this instant!" his mother shrilled but they all disappeared into the woods.

"Bailey Boy!" the grandmother called in a tragic voice but she found she was looking at The Misfit squatting on the ground in front of her. "I just know you're a good man," she said desperately. "You're not a bit common!"

"Nome, I ain't a good man," The Misfit said after a second as if he had considered her statement carefully, "but I ain't the worst in the world neither. My daddy said I was a different breed of dog from my brothers and sisters. 'You know,' Daddy said, 'it's some that can live their whole life out without asking about it and it's others has to know why it is, and this boy is one of the latters. He's going to be into everything!'" He put on his black hat and looked up suddenly and then away deep into the woods as if he were embarrassed again. "I'm sorry I don't have on a shirt before you ladies," he said, hunching his shoulders slightly. "We buried our clothes that we had on when we escaped and we're just making do until we can get better. We borrowed these from some folks we met," he explained.

"That's perfectly all right," the grandmother said. "Maybe Bailey has an extra 100 shirt in his suitcase."

"I'll look and see terrectly," The Misfit said.

"Where are they taking him?" the children's mother screamed.

"Daddy was a card himself," The Misfit said. "You couldn't put anything over on him. He never got in trouble with the Authorities though. Just had the knack of handling them."

"You could be honest too if you'd only try," said the grandmother. "Think how wonderful it would be to settle down and live a comfortable life and not have to think about somebody chasing you all the time."

The Misfit kept scratching in the ground with the butt of his gun as if he were 105 thinking about it. "Yes'm, somebody is always after you," he murmured.

The grandmother noticed how thin his shoulder blades were just behind his hat because she was standing up looking down on him. "Do you ever pray?" she asked.

He shook his head. All she saw was the black hat wiggle between his shoulder blades. "Nome," he said.

There was a pistol shot from the woods, followed closely by another. Then silence. The old lady's head jerked around. She could hear the wind move through the tree tops like a long satisfied insuck of breath. "Bailey Boy!" she called.

"I was a gospel singer for a while," The Misfit said. "I been most everything. Been in the arm service, both land and sea, at home and abroad, been twice married, been an undertaker, been with the railroads, plowed Mother Earth, been in a tornado, seen a man burnt alive oncet," and looked up at the children's mother and the little girl who were sitting close together, their faces white and their eyes glassy; "I even seen a woman flogged," he said.

110   "Pray, pray," the grandmother began, "pray, pray . . ."

"I never was a bad boy that I remember of," The Misfit said in an almost dreamy voice, "but somewheres along the line I done something wrong and got sent to the penitentiary. I was buried alive," and he looked up and held her attention to him by a steady stare.

"That's when you should have started to pray," she said. "What did you do to get sent to the penitentiary that first time?"

"Turn to the right, it was a wall," The Misfit said, looking up again at the cloudless sky. "Turn to the left, it was a wall. Look up it was a ceiling, look down it was a floor. I forget what I done, lady. I set there and set there, trying to remember what it was I done and I ain't recalled it to this day. Oncet in a while, I would think it was coming to me, but it never come."

"Maybe they put you in by mistake," the old lady said vaguely.

115   "Nome," he said. "It wasn't no mistake. They had the papers on me."

"You must have stolen something," she said.

The Misfit sneered slightly. "Nobody had nothing I wanted," he said. "It was a head-doctor at the penitentiary said what I had done was kill my daddy but I know that for a lie. My daddy died in nineteen ought nineteen of the epidemic flu and I never had a thing to do with it. He was buried in the Mount Hopewell Baptist churchyard and you can go there and see for yourself."

"If you would pray," the old lady said, "Jesus would help you."

"That's right," The Misfit said.

120   "Well then, why don't you pray?" she asked trembling with delight suddenly.

"I don't want no hep," he said. "I'm doing all right by myself."

Bobby Lee and Hiram came ambling back from the woods. Bobby Lee was dragging a yellow shirt with bright blue parrots in it.

"Throw me that shirt, Bobby Lee," The Misfit said. The shirt came flying at him and landed on his shoulder and he put it on. The grandmother couldn't name what the shirt reminded her of. "No, lady," The Misfit said while he was buttoning it up, "I found out the crime don't matter. You can do one thing or you can do another, kill a man or take a tire off his car, because sooner or later you're going to forget what it was you done and just be punished for it."

The children's mother had begun to make heaving noises as if she couldn't get her breath. "Lady," he asked, "would you and that little girl like to step off yonder with Bobby Lee and Hiram and join your husband?"

125   "Yes, thank you," the mother said faintly. Her left arm dangled helplessly and she was holding the baby, who had gone to sleep, in the other. "Hep that lady up, Hiram," The Misfit said as she struggled to climb out of the ditch, "and Bobby Lee, you hold onto that little girl's hand."

"I don't want to hold hands with him," June Star said. "He reminds me of a pig."

The fat boy blushed and laughed and caught her by the arm and pulled her off into the woods after Hiram and her mother.

Alone with the Misfit, the grandmother found that she had lost her voice. There was not a cloud in the sky nor any sun. There was nothing around her but woods. She wanted to tell him that he must pray. She opened and closed her mouth several times before anything came out. Finally she found herself saying, "Jesus, Jesus," meaning, Jesus will help you, but the way she was saying it, it sounded as if she might be cursing.

"Yes'm" The Misfit said as if he agreed. "Jesus thrown everything off balance. It was the same case with Him as with me except He hadn't committed any crime and they could prove I had committed one because they had the papers on me. Of course," he said, "they never shown me my papers. That's why I sign myself now. I said long ago, you get you a signature and sign everything you do and keep a copy of it. Then you'll know what you done and you can hold up the crime to the punishment and see do they match and in the end you'll have something to prove you ain't been treated right. I call myself The Misfit," he said, "because I can't make what all I done wrong fit what all I gone through in punishment."

There was a piercing scream from the woods, followed closely by a pistol report. 130 "Does it seem right to you, lady, that one is punished a heap and another ain't punished at all?"

"Jesus!" the old lady cried. "You've got good blood! I know you wouldn't shoot a lady! I know you come from nice people! Pray! Jesus, you ought not to shoot a lady. I'll give you all the money I've got!"

"Lady," The Misfit said, looking beyond her far into the woods, "there never was a body that give the undertaker a tip."

There were two more pistol reports and the grandmother raised her head like a parched old turkey hen crying for water and called, "Bailey Boy, Bailey Boy!" as if her heart would break.

"Jesus was the only One that ever raised the dead." The Misfit continued, "and He shouldn't have done it. He thrown everything off balance. If He did what He said, then it's nothing for you to do but throw away everything and follow him, and if He didn't, then it's nothing for you to do but enjoy the few minutes you got left the best way you can—by killing somebody or burning down his house or doing some other meanness to him. No pleasure but meanness," he said and his voice had become almost a snarl.

"Maybe He didn't raise the dead," the old lady mumbled, not knowing what she 135 was saying and feeling so dizzy that she sank down in the ditch with her legs twisted under her.

"I wasn't there so I can't say He didn't," The Misfit said. "I wisht I had of been there," he said, hitting the ground with his fist. "It ain't right I wasn't there because if I had of been there I would of known. Listen lady," he said in a high voice, "if I had of been there I would of known and I wouldn't be like I am now." His voice seemed about to crack and the grandmother's head cleared for an instant. She saw the man's face twisted close to her own as if he were going to cry and she murmured, "Why you're one of my babies. You're one of my own children!" She reached out and touched him on the shoulder. The Misfit sprang back as if a snake had bitten him and shot her three times through the chest. Then he put his gun down on the ground and took off his glasses and began to clean them.

Hiram and Bobby Lee returned from the woods and stood over the ditch, looking down at the grandmother who half sat and half lay in a puddle of blood with her legs crossed under her like a child's and her face smiling up at the cloudless sky.

Without his glasses, The Misfit's eyes were red-rimmed and pale and defenseless-looking. "Take her off and throw her where you thrown the others," he said, picking up the cat that was rubbing itself against his leg.

"She was a talker, wasn't she?" Bobby Lee said, sliding down the ditch with a yodel.

140 "She would have been a good woman," The Misfit said, "if it had been somebody there to shoot her every minute of her life."

"Some fun!" Bobby Lee said.

"Shut up, Bobby Lee," The Misfit said. "It's no real pleasure in life." [1955]

QUESTIONS

1. Discuss the role of coincidence in the story. Are the later events adequately foreshadowed?
2. What is the effect of juxtaposing realistic and grotesque elements in the story?
3. What is the function of the scene at the Tower?
4. Since the story turns on the confrontation between the grandmother and The Misfit, what are the roles of the other family members?
5. Paraphrase The Misfit's philosophy. In what sense could Jesus be said to throw "everything off balance"?

RESPONSES

1. Read Flannery O'Connor's "A Reasonable Use of the Unreasonable" in the "Context: Writers on Writing" section of this book. What do her comments add to your understanding of this story?
2. Using a gender studies approach to the story, write an essay that explores how O'Connor portrays men and women.
3. Compare this story to Joyce Carol Oates's "Where Are You Going, Where Have You Been?"

FRANK O'CONNOR

Frank O'Connor (Michael O'Donovan) (1903–1966) was born in Cork, Ireland, to a family too poor to give him more than the rudiments of an education. While still in his teens he joined the Irish Republican Army, was captured fighting the British, and was imprisoned until 1924. Working as a librarian, he began to write the stories that were collected in 1931 in his first volume, *Guests of the Nation*. From that time he regularly published stories, occasionally revising them for republication. In addition to writing fiction, he worked as an editor, literary critic, translator, travel writer, and memoirist. Later in life he taught at several American universities. His *Collected Stories* appeared in 1981.

Guests of the Nation

1

At dusk the big Englishman, Belcher, would shift his long legs out of the ashes and say "Well, chums, what about it?" and Noble or me would say "All right, chum" (for we had picked up some of their curious expressions), and the little Englishman, Hawkins, would light the lamp and bring out the cards. Sometimes Jeremiah Donovan would come up and supervise the game and get excited over Hawkins's cards, which he always played badly, and shout at him as if he was one of our own, "Ah, you divil, you, why didn't you play the tray?"

But ordinarily Jeremiah was a sober and contented poor devil like the big Englishman, Belcher, and was looked up to only because he was a fair hand at documents, though he was slow enough even with them. He wore a small cloth hat and big gaiters over his long pants, and you seldom saw him with his hands out of his pockets. He reddened when you talked to him, tilting from toe to heel and back, and looking down all the time at his big farmer's feet. Noble and me used to make fun of his broad accent, because we were from the town.

I couldn't at the time see the point of me and Noble guarding Belcher and Hawkins at all, for it was my belief that you could have planted that pair down anywhere from this to Claregalway and they'd have taken root there like a native weed. I never in my short experience seen two men to take to the country as they did.

They were handed on to us by the Second Battalion when the search for them became too hot, and Noble and myself, being young, took over with a natural feeling of responsibility, but Hawkins made us look like fools when he showed that he knew the country better than we did.

5 "You're the bloke they calls Bonaparte," he says to me. "Mary Brigid O'Connell told me to ask you what you done with the pair of her brother's socks you borrowed."

For it seemed, as they explained it, that the Second used to have little evenings, and some of the girls of the neighborhood turned in, and, seeing they were such decent chaps, our fellows couldn't leave the two Englishmen out of them. Hawkins learned to dance "The Walls of Limerick," "The Siege of Ennis," and "The Waves of Tory" as well as any of them, though, naturally, we couldn't return the compliment, because our lads at that time did not dance foreign dances on principle.

So whatever privileges Belcher and Hawkins had with the Second they just naturally took with us, and after the first day or two we gave up all pretense of keeping a close eye on them. Not that they could have got far, for they had accents you could cut with a knife and wore khaki tunics and overcoats with civilian pants and boots. But it's my belief that they never had any idea of escaping and were quite content to be where they were.

It was a treat to see how Belcher got off with the old woman of the house where we were staying. She was a great warrant to scold, and cranky even with us, but before ever she had a chance of giving our guests, as I may call them, a lick of her tongue, Belcher had made her his friend for life. She was breaking sticks, and Belcher, who hadn't been more than ten minutes in the house, jumped up from his seat and went over to her.

"Allow me, madam," he says, smiling his queer little smile, "please allow me"; and he takes the bloody hatchet. She was struck too paralytic to speak, and after that, Belcher would be at her heels, carrying a bucket, a basket, or a load of turf, as the case might be. As Noble said, he got into looking before she leapt, and hot water, or any little thing she wanted, Belcher would have it ready for her. For such a huge man (and though I am five foot ten myself I had to look up at him) he had an uncommon shortness—or should I say lack?—of speech. It took us some time to get used to him, walking in and out, like a ghost, without a word. Especially because Hawkins talked enough for a platoon, it was strange to hear big Belcher with his toes in the ashes come out with a solitary "Excuse me, chum," or "That's right, chum." His one and only passion was cards, and I will say for him that he was a good cardplayer. He could have fleeced myself and Noble, but whatever we lost to him Hawkins lost to us, and Hawkins played with the money Belcher gave him.

10 Hawkins lost to us because he had too much old gab, and we probably lost to Belcher for the same reason. Hawkins and Noble would spit at one another about religion into the early hours of the morning, and Hawkins worried the soul out of Noble, whose brother was a priest, with a string of questions that would puzzle a cardinal. To make it worse, even in treating of holy subjects, Hawkins had a deplorable tongue. I never in all my career met a man who could mix such a variety of cursing and bad language into an argument. He was a terrible man, and a fright to argue. He never did a stroke of work, and when he had no one else to talk to, he got stuck in the old woman.

He met his match in her, for one day when he tried to get her to complain profanely of the drought, she gave him a great come-down by blaming it entirely on Jupiter Pluvius (a deity neither Hawkins nor I had ever heard of, though Noble said that among the pagans it was believed that he had something to do with the rain). Another day he was swearing at the capitalists for starting the German war° when the old lady laid down her iron, puckered up her little crab's mouth, and said: "Mr. Hawkins, you can say what you like about the war, and think you'll deceive me because I'm only a simple poor countrywoman, but I know what started the war. It was the Italian Count that stole the heathen divinity out of the temple in Japan. Believe me, Mr. Hawkins, nothing but sorrow and want can follow the people that disturb the hidden powers."

A queer old girl, all right.

2

We had our tea one evening, and Hawkins lit the lamp and we all sat into cards. Jeremiah Donovan came in too, and sat down and watched us for a while, and it suddenly struck me that he had no great love for the two Englishmen. It came as a great surprise to me, because I hadn't noticed anything about him before.

Late in the evening a really terrible argument blew up between Hawkins and Noble, about capitalists and priests and love of your country.

"The capitalists," says Hawkins with an angry gulp, "pays the priests to tell you   15
about the next world so as you won't notice what the bastards are up to in this."

"Nonsense, man!" says Noble, losing his temper. "Before ever a capitalist was thought of, people believed in the next world."

Hawkins stood up as though he was preaching a sermon.

"Oh, they did, did they?" he says with a sneer. "They believed all the things you believe, isn't that what you mean? And you believe that God created Adam, and Adam created Shem, and Shem created Jehoshaphat. You believe all that silly old fairytale about Eve and Eden and the apple. Well, listen to me, chum. If you're entitled to hold a silly belief like that, I'm entitled to hold my silly belief—which is that the first thing your God created was a bleeding capitalist, with morality and Rolls-Royce complete. Am I right, chum?" he says to Belcher.

"You're right, chum," says Belcher with his amused smile, and got up from the table to stretch his long legs into the fire and stroke his moustache. So, seeing that Jeremiah Donovan was going, and that there was no knowing when the argument about religion would be over, I went out with him. We strolled down to the village together, and then he stopped and started blushing and mumbling and saying I ought to be behind, keeping guard on the prisoners. I didn't like the tone he took with me, and anyway I was bored with life in the cottage, so I replied by asking him what the hell we wanted guarding them at all for. I told him I'd talked it over with Noble, and that we'd both rather be out with a fighting column.

"What use are those fellows to us?" says I.   20

He looked at me in surprise and said: "I thought you knew we were keeping them as hostages."

"Hostages?" I said.

"The enemy have prisoners belonging to us," he says, "and now they're talking of shooting them. If they shoot our prisoners, we'll shoot theirs."

"Shoot them?" I said.

°*German War*: World War I.

25   "What else did you think we were keeping them for?" he says.

"Wasn't it very unforeseen of you not to warn Noble and myself of that in the beginning?" I said.

"How was it?" says he. "You might have known it."

"We couldn't know it, Jeremiah Donovan," says I. "How could we when they were on our hands so long?"

"The enemy have our prisoners as long and longer," says he.

30   "That's not the same thing at all," says I.

"What difference is there?" says he.

I couldn't tell him, because I knew he wouldn't understand. If it was only an old dog that was going to the vet's, you'd try and not get too fond of him, but Jeremiah Donovan wasn't a man that would ever be in danger of that.

"And when is this thing going to be decided?" says I.

"We might hear tonight," he says. "Or tomorrow or the next day at latest. So if it's only hanging round here that's a trouble to you, you'll be free soon enough."

35   It wasn't the hanging round that was a trouble to me at all by this time. I had worse things to worry about. When I got back to the cottage the argument was still on. Hawkins was holding forth in his best style, maintaining that there was no next world, and Noble was maintaining that there was; but I could see that Hawkins had had the best of it.

"Do you know what, chum?" he was saying with a saucy smile. "I think you're just as big a bleeding unbeliever as I am. You say you believe in the next world, and you know just as much about the next world as I do, which is sweet damn-all. What's heaven? You don't know. Where's heaven? You don't know. You know sweet damn-all! I ask you again, do they wear wings?"

"Very well, then," says Noble, "they do. Is that enough for you? They do wear wings."

"Where do they get them, then? Who makes them? Have they a factory for wings? Have they a sort of store where you hands in your chit and takes your bleeding wings?"

"You're an impossible man to argue with," says Noble. "Now, listen to me—" And they were off again.

40   It was long after midnight when we locked up and went to bed. As I blew out the candle I told Noble what Jeremiah Donovan was after telling me. Noble took it very quietly. When we'd been in bed about an hour he asked me did I think we ought to tell the Englishmen. I didn't think we should, because it was more than likely that the English wouldn't shoot our men, and even if they did, the brigade officers, who were always up and down with the Second Battalion and knew the Englishmen well, wouldn't be likely to want them plugged. "I think so too," says Noble. "It would be great cruelty to put the wind up them now."

"It was very unforeseen of Jeremiah Donovan anyhow," says I.

It was next morning that we found it so hard to face Belcher and Hawkins. We went about the house all day scarcely saying a word. Belcher didn't seem to notice; he was stretched into the ashes as usual, with his usual look of waiting in quietness for something unforeseen to happen, but Hawkins noticed and put it down to Noble's being beaten in the argument of the night before.

"Why can't you take a discussion in the proper spirit?" he says severely. "You and your Adam and Eve! I'm a Communist, that's what I am. Communist or anarchist, it all comes to much the same thing." And for hours he went round the house, muttering when the fit took him. "Adam and Eve! Adam and Eve! Nothing better to do with their time than picking bleeding apples!"

3

I don't know how we got through that day, but I was very glad when it was over, the tea things were cleared away, and Belcher said in his peaceable way: "Well, chums, what about it?" We sat round the table and Hawkins took out the cards, and just then I heard Jeremiah Donovan's footstep on the path and a dark presentiment crossed my mind. I rose from the table and caught him before he reached the door.

"What do you want?" I asked.   45

"I want those two soldier friends of yours," he says, getting red.

"Is that the way, Jeremiah Donovan?" I asked.

"That's the way. There were four of our lads shot this morning, one of them a boy of sixteen."

"That's bad," I said.

At that moment Noble followed me out, and the three of us walked down the path   50
together, talking in whispers. Feeney, the local intelligence officer, was standing by the gate.

"What are you going to do about it?" I asked Jeremiah Donovan.

"I want you and Noble to get them out; tell them they're being shifted again; that'll be the quietest way."

"Leave me out of that," says Noble under his breath.

Jeremiah Donovan looks at him hard.

"All right," he says. "You and Feeney get a few tools from the shed and dig a hole   55
by the far end of the bog. Bonaparte and myself will be after you. Don't let anyone see you with the tools. I wouldn't like it to go beyond ourselves."

We saw Feeney and Noble go round to the shed and went in ourselves. I left Jeremiah Donovan to do the explanations. He told them that he had orders to send them back to the Second Battalion. Hawkins let out a mouthful of curses, and you could see that though Belcher didn't say anything, he was a bit upset too. The old woman was for having them stay in spite of us, and she didn't stop advising them until Jeremiah Donovan lost his temper and turned on her. He had a nasty temper, I noticed. It was pitch-dark in the cottage by this time, but no one thought of lighting the lamp, and in the darkness the two Englishmen fetched their topcoats and said good-bye to the old woman.

"Just as a man makes a home of a bleeding place, some bastard at headquarters thinks you're too cushy and shunts you off," says Hawkins, shaking her hand.

"A thousand thanks, madam," says Belcher. "A thousand thanks for everything"— as though he'd made it up.

We went round to the back of the house and down towards the bog. It was only then that Jeremiah Donovan told them. He was shaking with excitement.

"There were four of our fellows shot in Cork this morning and now you're to be shot 60
as a reprisal."

"What are you talking about?" snaps Hawkins. "It's bad enough being mucked about as we are without having to put up with your funny jokes."

"It isn't a joke," says Donovan. "I'm sorry, Hawkins, but it's true," and begins on the usual rigmarole about duty and how unpleasant it is.

I never noticed that people who talk a lot about duty find it much of a trouble to them.

"Oh, cut it out!" says Hawkins.

"Ask Bonaparte," says Donovan, seeing that Hawkins isn't taking him seriously.   65
"Isn't it true, Bonaparte?"

"It is," I say, and Hawkins stops.

"Ah, for Christ's sake, chum."

"I mean it, chum," I say.

"You don't sound as if you meant it."

70 "If he doesn't mean it, I do," says Donovan, working himself up.

"What have you against me, Jeremiah Donovan?"

"I never said I had anything against you. But why did your people take out four of our prisoners and shoot them in cold blood?"

He took Hawkins by the arm and dragged him on, but it was impossible to make him understand that we were in earnest. I had the Smith and Wesson° in my pocket and I kept fingering it and wondering what I'd do if they put up a fight for it or ran, and wishing to God they'd do one or the other. I knew if they did run for it, that I'd never fire on them. Hawkins wanted to know was Noble in it, and when we said yes, he asked why Noble wanted to plug him. Why did any of us want to plug him? What had he done to us? Weren't we all chums? Didn't we understand him and didn't he understand us? Did we imagine for an instant that he'd shoot us for all the so-and-so officers in the so-and-so British Army?

By this time we'd reached the bog, and I was so sick I couldn't even answer him. We walked along the edge of it in the darkness, and every now and then Hawkins would call a halt and begin all over again, as if he was wound up, about our being chums, and I knew that nothing but the sight of the grave would convince him that we had to do it. And all the time I was hoping that something would happen; that they'd run for it or that Noble would take over the responsibility from me. I had the feeling that it was worse on Noble than on me.

4

75 At last we saw the lantern in the distance and made towards it. Noble was carrying it, and Feeney was standing somewhere in the darkness behind him, and the picture of them so still and silent in the bogland brought it home to me that we were in earnest, and banished the last bit of hope I had.

Belcher, on recognizing Noble, said: "Hallo, chum," in his quiet way, but Hawkins flew at him at once, and the argument began all over again, only this time Noble had nothing to say for himself and stood with his head down, holding the lantern between his legs.

It was Jeremiah Donovan who did the answering. For the twentieth time, as though it was haunting his mind, Hawkins asked if anybody thought he'd shoot Noble.

"Yes, you would," says Jeremiah Donovan.

"No, I wouldn't, damn you!"

80 "You would, because you'd know you'd be shot for not doing it."

"I wouldn't, not if I was to be shot twenty times over. I wouldn't shoot a pal. And Belcher wouldn't—isn't that right, Belcher?"

"That's right, chum," Belcher said, but more by way of answering the question than of joining in the argument. Belcher sounded as though whatever unforeseen thing he'd always been waiting for had come at last.

°*Smith and Wesson*: American-made revolver.

"Anyway, who says Noble would be shot if I wasn't? What do you think I'd do if I was in his place, out in the middle of a blasted bog?"

"What would you do?" asks Donovan.

"I'd go with him wherever he was going, of course. Share my last bob° with him and stick by him through thick and thin. No one can ever say of me that I let down a pal."

"We had enough of this," says Jeremiah Donovan, cocking his revolver. "Is there any message you want to send?"

"No, there isn't."

"Do you want to say your prayers?"

Hawkins came out with a cold-blooded remark that even shocked me and turned on Noble again.

"Listen to me, Noble," he says. "You and me are chums. You can't come over to my side, so I'll come over to your side. That show you I mean what I say? Give me a rifle and I'll go along with you and the other lads."

Nobody answered him. We knew that was no way out.

"Hear what I'm saying?" he says. "I'm through with it. I'm a deserter or anything else you like. I don't believe in your stuff, but it's no worse than mine. That satisfy you?"

Noble raised his head, but Donovan began to speak and he lowered it again without replying.

"For the last time, have you any messages to send?" says Donovan in a cold, excited sort of voice.

"Shut up, Donovan! You don't understand me, but these lads do. They're not the sort to make a pal and kill a pal. They're not the tools of any capitalist."

I alone of the crowd saw Donovan raise his Webley° to the back of Hawkins's neck, and as he did so I shut my eyes and tried to pray. Hawkins had begun to say something else when Donovan fired, and as I opened my eyes at the bang, I saw Hawkins stagger at the knees and lie out flat at Noble's feet, slowly and as quiet as a kid falling asleep, with the lantern-light on his lean legs and bright farmer's boots. We all stood very still, watching him settle out in the last agony.

Then Belcher took out a handkerchief and began to tie it about his own eyes (in our excitement we'd forgotten to do the same for Hawkins), and, seeing it wasn't big enough, turned and asked for the loan of mine. I gave it to him and he knotted the two together and pointed with his foot at Hawkins.

"He's not quite dead," he says. "Better give him another."

Sure enough, Hawkins's left knee is beginning to rise. I bend down and put my gun to his head; then, recollecting myself, I get up again. Belcher understands what's in my mind.

"Give him his first," he says. "I don't mind. Poor bastard, we don't know what's happening to him now."

I knelt and fired. By this time I didn't seem to know what I was doing. Belcher, who was fumbling a bit awkwardly with the handkerchiefs, came out with a laugh as he heard the shot. It was the first time I heard him laugh and it sent a shudder down my back; it sounded so unnatural.

°*bob*: Shilling.

°*Webley*: British-made revolver.

"Poor bugger!" he said quietly. "And last night he was so curious about it all. It's very queer, chums, I always think. Now he knows as much about it as they'll ever let him know, and last night he was all in the dark."

Donovan helped him to tie the handkerchiefs about his eyes. "Thanks, chum," he said. Donovan asked if there were any messages he wanted sent.

"No, chum," he says. "Not for me. If any of you would like to write to Hawkins's mother, you'll find a letter from her in his pocket. He and his mother were great chums. But my missus left me eight years ago. Went away with another fellow and took the kid with her. I like the feeling of a home, as you may have noticed, but I couldn't start again after that."

105   It was an extraordinary thing, but in those few minutes Belcher said more than in all the weeks before. It was just as if the sound of the shot had started a flood of talk in him and he could go on the whole night like that, quite happily, talking about himself. We stood round like fools now that he couldn't see us any longer. Donovan looked at Noble, and Noble shook his head. Then Donovan raised his Webley, and at that moment Belcher gives his queer laugh again. He may have thought we were talking about him, or perhaps he noticed the same thing I'd noticed and couldn't understand it.

"Excuse me, chums," he says. "I feel I'm talking the hell of a lot, and so silly, about my being so handy about a house and things like that. But this thing came on me suddenly. You'll forgive me, I'm sure."

"You don't want to say a prayer?" asked Donovan.

"No, chum," he says. "I don't think it would help. I'm ready, and you boys want to get it over."

"You understand that we're only doing our duty?" says Donovan.

110   Belcher's head was raised like a blind man's, so that you could only see his chin and the tip of his nose in the lantern-light.

"I never could make out what duty was myself," he said. "I think you're all good lads, if that's what you mean. I'm not complaining."

Noble, just as if he couldn't bear any more of it, raised his fist at Donovan, and in a flash Donovan raised his gun and fired. The big man went over like a sack of meal, and this time there was no need of a second shot.

I don't remember much about the burying, but that it was worse than all the rest because we had to carry them to the grave. It was all mad lonely with nothing but a patch of lantern-light between ourselves and the dark, and birds hooting and screeching all round, disturbed by the guns. Noble went through Hawkins's belongings to find the letter from his mother, and then joined his hands together. He did the same with Belcher. Then, when we'd filled in the grave, we separated from Jeremiah Donovan and Feeney and took our tools back to the shed. All the way we didn't speak a word. The kitchen was dark and cold as we'd left it, and the old woman was sitting over the hearth, saying her beads. We walked past her into the room, and Noble struck a match to light the lamp. She rose quietly and came to the doorway with all her cantankerousness gone.

"What did ye do with them?" she asked in a whisper, and Noble started so that the match went out in his hand.

115   "What's that?" he asked without turning round.

"I heard ye," she said.

"What did you hear?" asked Noble.

"I heard ye. Do ye think I didn't hear ye, putting the spade back in the houseen?"

Noble struck another match and this time the lamp lit for him.

120   "Was that what ye did to them?" she asked.

Then, by God, in the very doorway, she fell on her knees and began praying, and after looking at her for a minute or two Noble did the same by the fireplace. I pushed my way out past her and left them at it. I stood at the door, watching the stars and listening to the shrieking of the birds dying out over the bogs. It is so strange what you feel at times like that you can't describe it. Noble says he saw everything ten times the size, as though there were nothing in the whole world but that little patch of bog with the two Englishmen stiffening into it, but with me it was as if the patch of bog where the Englishmen were was a million miles away, and even Noble and the old woman, mumbling behind me, and the birds and the bloody stars were all far away, and I was somehow very small and very lost and lonely like a child astray in the snow. And anything that happened to me afterwards, I never felt the same about again.   [1931]

QUESTIONS

1. Describe the atmosphere of the story and explain how it is related to the theme.
2. List the contrasting elements in the characters of Belcher and Hawkins. Do they in any way parallel the characters of Bonaparte and Donovan?
3. How do the arguments about politics and religion serve as foreshadowing?
4. What function does the old woman have in the story?
5. At the conclusion of the story, what is the significance of the contrasting visions of Noble and Bonaparte?

RESPONSES

1. Read O'Connor's Context essay "The Legacy of Gogol's 'Overcoat.'" Comment on how it relates to "Guests of the Nation."
2. Write an essay that explores the pairs of opposites, such as light and dark, used throughout the story.

FOCUS ON FILM

1. View the film *The Crying Game*, which also deals with political struggles in Ireland. Discuss how the film explores the human connections that transcend political division between Britain and Ireland.
2. Compare the rise in tension and plot development in "The Guests of the Nation" and in the first half of *The Crying Game*. Discuss how conversation is used to develop this tension. Or discuss how setting is used to develop this tension.

TILLIE OLSEN

Tillie Olsen (b. 1913) was born in Omaha, Nebraska. During the Great Depression she was active in the labor movement and wrote a novel, *Yonnondio: From the Thirties,* an account of a blue-collar family, but it was not published until 1974. She married and raised four children, not returning to writing until the 1950s. *Tell Me a Riddle* (1956), short fiction, won an O. Henry award. Olsen's growing reputation led to appointments as writer-in-residence at several universities. She has written a biography, *Rebecca Harding Davis* (1972), a collection of essays, *Silences* (1978), and another collection of short stories, *Life in the Iron Mills* (1985). Recent work includes *Silences* (2003).

I Stand Here Ironing

I stand here ironing, and what you asked me moves tormented back and forth with the iron.

"I wish you would manage the time to come in and talk with me about your daughter. I'm sure you can help me understand her. She's a youngster who needs help and whom I'm deeply interested in helping."

"Who needs help." . . . Even if I came, what good would it do? You think because I am her mother I have a key, or that in some way you could use me as a key? She has lived for nineteen years. There is all that life that has happened outside of me, beyond me.

And when is there time to remember, to sift, to weigh, to estimate, to total? I will start and there will be an interruption and I will have to gather it all together again. Or I will become engulfed with all I did or did not do, with what should have been and what cannot be helped.

5   She was a beautiful baby. The first and only one of our five that was beautiful at birth. You do not guess how new and uneasy her tenancy in her now-loveliness. You did not know her all those years she was thought homely, or see her poring over her baby pictures, making me tell her over and over how beautiful she had been—and would be, I would tell her—and was now, to the seeing eye. But the seeing eyes were few or nonexistent. Including mine.

I nursed her. They feel that's important nowadays. I nursed all the children, but with her, with all the fierce rigidity of first motherhood, I did like the books then said.

Though her cries battered me to trembling and my breasts ached with swollenness, I waited till the clock decreed.

Why do I put that first? I do not even know if it matters, or if it explains anything.

She was a beautiful baby. She blew shining bubbles of sound. She loved motion, loved light, loved color and music and textures. She would lie on the floor in her blue overalls patting the surface so hard in ecstasy her hands and feet would blur. She was a miracle to me, but when she was eight months old I had to leave her daytimes with the woman downstairs to whom she was no miracle at all, for I worked or looked for work and for Emily's father, who "could no longer endure" (he wrote in his good-bye note) "sharing want with us."

I was nineteen. It was the pre-relief, pre-WPA world of the depression. I would start running as soon as I got off the streetcar, running up the stairs, the place smelling sour, and awake or asleep to startle awake, when she saw me she would break into a clogged weeping that could not be comforted, a weeping I can hear yet.

After a while I found a job hashing at night so I could be with her days, and it was better. But it came to where I had to bring her to his family and leave her. 10

It took a long time to raise the money for her fare back. Then she got chicken pox and I had to wait longer. When she finally came, I hardly knew her, walking quick and nervous like her father, looking like her father, thin, and dressed in a shoddy red that yellowed her skin and glared at the pockmarks. All the baby loveliness gone.

She was two. Old enough for nursery school they said, and I did not know then what I know now—the fatigue of the long day, and the lacerations of group life in the kinds of nurseries that are only parking places for children.

Except that it would have made no difference if I had known. It was the only place there was. It was the only way we could be together, the only way I could hold a job.

And even without knowing, I knew. I knew the teacher that was evil because all these years it has curdled into my memory, the little boy hunched in the corner, her rasp, "why aren't you outside, because Alvin hits you? that's no reason, go out, scaredy." I knew Emily hated it even if she did not clutch and implore "don't go Mommy" like the other children, mornings.

She always had a reason why we should stay home. Momma, you look sick. Momma, 15 I feel sick. Momma, the teachers aren't there today, they're sick. Momma, we can't go, there was a fire there last night. Momma, it's a holiday today, no school, they told me.

But never a direct protest, never rebellion. I think of our others in their three-four-year-oldness—the explosions, the tempers, the denunciations, the demands—and I feel suddenly ill. I put the iron down. What in me demanded that goodness in her? And what was the cost, the cost to her of such goodness?

The old man living in the back once said in his gentle way: "You should smile at Emily more when you look at her." What *was* in my face when I looked at her? I loved her. There were all the acts of love.

It was only with the others I remembered what he said, and it was the face of joy, and not of care or tightness or worry I turned to them—too late for Emily. She does not smile easily, let alone almost always as her brothers and sisters do. Her face is closed and sombre, but when she wants, how fluid. You must have seen it in her pantomimes, you spoke of her rare gift for comedy on the stage that rouses a laughter out of the audience so dear they applaud and applaud and do not want to let her go.

Where does it come from, that comedy? There was none of it in her when she came back to me that second time, after I had had to send her away again. She had a new daddy now to learn to love, and I think perhaps it was a better time.

20   Except when we left her alone nights, telling ourselves she was old enough.

"Can't you go some other time, Mommy, like tomorrow?" she would ask. "Will it be just a little while you'll be gone? Do you promise?"

The time we came back, the front door open, the clock on the floor in the hall. She rigid awake. "It wasn't just a little while. I didn't cry. Three times I called you, just three times, and then I ran downstairs to open the door so you could come faster. The clock talked loud. I threw it away, it scared me what it talked."

She said the clock talked loud again that night I went to the hospital to have Susan. She was delirious with the fever that comes before red measles, but she was fully conscious all the week I was gone and the week after we were home when she could not come near the new baby or me.

She did not get well. She stayed skeleton thin, not wanting to eat, and night after night she had nightmares. She would call for me, and I would rouse from exhaustion to sleepily call back: "You're all right, darling, go to sleep, it's just a dream," and if she still called, in a sterner voice, "now go to sleep, Emily, there's nothing to hurt you." Twice, only twice, when I had to get up for Susan anyhow, I went in to sit with her.

25   Now when it is too late (as if she would let me hold and comfort her like I do the others) I get up and go to her at once at her moan or restless stirring. "Are you awake, Emily? Can I get you something?" And the answer is always the same: "No, I'm all right, go back to sleep, Mother."

They persuaded me at the clinic to send her away to a convalescent home in the country where "she can have the kind of food and care you can't manage for her, and you'll be free to concentrate on the new baby." They still send children to that place. I see pictures on the society page of sleek young women planning affairs to raise money for it, or dancing at the affairs, or decorating Easter eggs or filling Christmas stockings for the children.

They never have a picture of the children so I do not know if the girls still wear those gigantic red bows and the ravaged looks on the every other Sunday when parents can come to visit "unless otherwise notified"—as we were notified the first six weeks.

Oh it is a handsome place, green lawns and tall trees and fluted flower beds. High up on the balconies of each cottage the children stand, the girls in their red bows and white dresses, the boys in white suits and giant red ties. The parents stand below shrieking up to be heard and the children shriek down to be heard, and between them the invisible wall "Not To Be Contaminated by Parental Germs or Physical Affection."

There was a tiny girl who always stood hand in hand with Emily. Her parents never came. One visit she was gone. "They moved her to Rose Cottage" Emily shouted in explanation. "They don't like you to love anybody here."

30   She wrote once a week, the labored writing of a seven-year-old. "I am fine. How is the baby. If I write my leter nicly I will have a star. Love." There never was a star. We wrote every other day, letters she could never hold or keep but only hear read—once. "We simply do not have room for children to keep any personal possessions," they patiently explained when we pieced one Sunday's shrieking together to plead how much it would mean to Emily, who loved so to keep things, to be allowed to keep her letters and cards.

Each visit she looked frailer. "She isn't eating," they told us.

(They had runny eggs for breakfast or mush with lumps, Emily said later, I'd hold it in my mouth and not swallow. Nothing ever tasted good, just when they had chicken.)

It took us eight months to get her released home, and only the fact that she gained back so little of her seven lost pounds convinced the social worker.

I used to try to hold and love her after she came back, but her body would stay stiff, and after a while she'd push away. She ate little. Food sickened her, and I think much of life too. Oh she had physical lightness and brightness, twinkling by on skates, bouncing like a ball up and down up and down over the jump rope, skimming over the hill; but these were momentary.

She fretted about her appearance, thin and dark and foreign-looking at a time when 35 every little girl was supposed to look or thought she should look a chubby blonde replica of Shirley Temple. The doorbell sometimes rang for her, but no one seemed to come and play in the house or be a best friend. Maybe because we moved so much.

There was a boy she loved painfully through two school semesters. Months later she told me how she had taken pennies from my purse to buy him candy. "Licorice was his favorite and I brought him some every day, but he still liked Jennifer better 'n me. Why, Mommy?" The kind of question for which there is no answer.

School was a worry to her. She was not glib or quick in a world where glibness and quickness were easily confused with ability to learn. To her overworked and exasperated teachers she was an overconscientious "slow learner" who kept trying to catch up and was absent entirely too often.

I let her be absent, though sometimes the illness was imaginary. How different from my now-strictness about attendance with the others. I wasn't working. We had a new baby, I was home anyhow. Sometimes, after Susan grew old enough, I would keep her home from school, too, to have them all together.

Mostly Emily had asthma, and her breathing, harsh and labored, would fill the house with a curiously tranquil sound. I would bring the two old dresser mirrors and her boxes of collections to her bed. She would select beads and single earrings, bottle tops and shells, dried flowers and pebbles, old postcards and scraps, all sorts of oddments; then she and Susan would play Kingdom, setting up landscapes and furniture, peopling them with action.

Those were the only times of peaceful companionship between her and Susan. I 40 have edged away from it, that poisonous feeling between them, that terrible balancing of hurts and needs I had to do between the two, and did so badly, those earlier years.

Oh there are conflicts between the others too, each one human, needing, demanding, hurting, taking—but only between Emily and Susan, no, Emily toward Susan that corroding resentment. It seems so obvious on the surface, yet it is not obvious. Susan, the second child, Susan, golden- and curly-haired and chubby, quick and articulate and assured, everything in appearance and manner Emily was not; Susan, not able to resist Emily's precious things, losing or sometimes clumsily breaking them; Susan telling jokes and riddles to company for applause while Emily sat silent (to say to me later: that was *my* riddle, Mother, I told it to Susan); Susan, who for all the five years' difference in age was just a year behind Emily in developing physically.

I am glad for that slow physical development that widened the difference between her and her contemporaries, though she suffered over it. She was too vulnerable for that terrible world of youthful competition, of preening and parading, of constant measuring of yourself against every other, of envy, "If I had that copper hair," "If I had that skin. . . ." She tormented herself enough about not looking like the others, there was enough of the unsureness, the having to be conscious of words before you speak, the constant caring—what are they thinking of me? without having it all magnified by the merciless physical drives.

Ronnie is calling. He is wet and I change him. It is rare there is such a cry now. That time of motherhood is almost behind me when the ear is not one's own but must always be racked and listening for the child cry, the child call. We sit for a while and I hold him, looking out over the city spread in charcoal with its soft aisles of light. "*Shoogily*," he breathes and curls closer. I carry him back to bed, asleep. *Shoogily*. A funny word, a family word, inherited from Emily, invented by her to say: *comfort*.

In this and other ways she leaves her seal, I say aloud. And startle at my saying it. What do I mean? What did I start to gather together, to try and make coherent? I was at the terrible, growing years. War years. I do not remember them well. I was working, there were four smaller ones now, there was not time for her. She had to help be a mother, and housekeeper, and shopper. She had to set her seal. Mornings of crisis and near hysteria trying to get lunches packed, hair combed, coats and shoes found, everyone to school or Child Care on time, the baby ready for transportation. And always the paper scribbled on by a smaller one, the book looked at by Susan then mislaid, the homework not done. Running out to that huge school where she was one, she was lost, she was a drop; suffering over the unpreparedness, stammering and unsure in her classes.

45   There was so little time left at night after the kids were bedded down. She would struggle over books, always eating (it was in those years she developed her enormous appetite that is legendary in our family) and I would be ironing, or preparing food for the next day, or writing V-mail to Bill, or tending the baby. Sometimes, to make me laugh, or out of her despair, she would imitate happenings or types at school.

I think I said once: "Why don't you do something like this in the school amateur show?" One morning she phoned me at work, hardly understandable through the weeping: "Mother, I did it. I won, I won; they gave me first prize; they clapped and clapped and wouldn't let me go."

Now suddenly she was Somebody, and as imprisoned in her difference as she had been in anonymity.

She began to be asked to perform at other high schools, even in colleges, then at city and statewide affairs. The first one we went to, I only recognized her that first moment when thin, shy, she almost drowned herself into the curtains. Then: Was this Emily? The control, the command, the convulsing and deadly clowning, the spell, then the roaring, stamping audience, unwilling to let this rare and precious laughter out of their lives.

Afterwards: You ought to do something about her with a gift like that—but without money or knowing how, what does one do? We have left it all to her, and the gift has as often eddied inside, clogged and clotted, as been used and growing.

50   She is coming. She runs up the stairs two at a time with her light graceful step, and I know she is happy tonight. Whatever it was that occasioned your call did not happen today.

"Aren't you ever going to finish the ironing, Mother? Whistler painted his mother in a rocker. I'd have to paint mine standing over an ironing board." This is one of her communicative nights and she tells me everything and nothing as she fixes herself a plate of food out of the icebox.

She is so lovely. Why did you want me to come in at all? Why were you concerned? She will find her way.

She starts up the stairs to bed. "Don't get me up with the rest in the morning." "But I thought you were having midterms." "Oh, those," she comes back in, kisses me, and says quite lightly, "in a couple of years when we'll all be atom-dead they won't matter a bit."

She has said it before. She *believes* it. But because I have been dredging the past, and all that compounds a human being is so heavy and meaningful in me, I cannot endure it tonight.

I will never total it all. I will never come in to say: She was a child seldom smiled at. Her father left me before she was a year old. I had to work her first six years when there was work, or I sent her home and to his relatives. There were years she had care she hated. She was dark and thin and foreign-looking in a world where the prestige went to blondeness and curly hair and dimples, she was slow where glibness was prized. She was a child of anxious, not proud, love. We were poor and could not afford for her the soil of easy growth. I was a young mother, I was a distracted mother. There were the other children pushing up, demanding. Her younger sister seemed all that she was not. There were years she did not want me to touch her. She kept too much in herself, her life was such she had to keep too much in herself. My wisdom came too late. She has much to her and probably little will come of it. She is a child of her age, of depression, of war, of fear.

Let her be. So all that is in her will not bloom—but in how many does it? There is still enough left to live by. Only help her to know—help make it so there is cause for her to know—that she is more than this dress on the ironing board, helpless before the iron.   [1953]

QUESTIONS

1. To whom is the narrator talking?
2. Is the narrator rationalizing her conduct, or is she generally clearsighted about the past?
3. How are the iron and the clock used symbolically in the story?
4. Why is Emily's "gift" particularly appropriate for this story?
5. Who is responsible for the situation in which the mother and daughter find themselves?

RESPONSES

1. Compare "I Stand Here Ironing" to Oates's "Shopping" or to Silko's "Lullaby."
2. Using the feminist approach, explain how the values of U.S. society make possible such stories as the one the narrator tells.
3. Write a story that uses another domestic activity, such as cleaning, as a metaphor for women's or men's lives.

GRACE PALEY

Grace Paley (b. 1922), born in New York City, attended Hunter College and New York University and has taught at Syracuse, Columbia, and Sarah Lawrence. Although she has published relatively little, her vision and her vital and expressive style have won a loyal and enthusiastic readership; in 1988 an act of the state legislature named her the first New York State Author. Her short story collections are *The Little Disturbances of Man* (1959), *Enormous Changes at the Last Minute* (1974), and *Later the Same Day* (1985). *The Collected Stories* was published in 1994 and *Begin Again: Collected Poems* in 2000.

A Conversation with My Father

My father is eighty-six years old and in bed. His heart, that bloody motor, is equally old and will not do certain jobs any more. It still floods his head with brainy light. But it won't let his legs carry the weight of his body around the house. Despite my metaphors, this muscle failure is not due to his old heart, he says, but to a potassium shortage. Sitting on one pillow, leaning on three, he offers last-minute advice and makes a request.

"I would like you to write a simple story just once more," he says, "the kind de Maupassant wrote, or Chekhov, the kind you used to write. Just recognizable people and then write down what happened to them next."

I say, "Yes, why not? That's possible." I want to please him, though I don't remember writing that way. I *would* like to try to tell such a story, if he means the kind that begins: "There was a woman . . ." followed by plot, the absolute line between two points which I've always despised. Not for literary reasons, but because it takes all hope away. Everyone, real or invented, deserves the open destiny of life.

Finally I thought of a story that had been happening for a couple of years right across the street. I wrote it down, then read it aloud. "Pa," I said, "how about this? Do you mean something like this?"

5   Once in my time there was a woman and she had a son. They lived nicely, in a small apartment in Manhattan. This boy at about fifteen became a junkie, which is not unusual in our neighborhood. In order to maintain her close friendship

with him, she became a junkie too. She said it was part of the youth culture, with which she felt very much at home. After a while, for a number of reasons, the boy gave it all up and left the city and his mother in disgust. Hopeless and alone, she grieved. We all visit her.

"O.K., Pa, that's it," I said, "an unadorned and miserable tale."

"But that's not what I mean," my father said. "You misunderstood me on purpose. You know there's a lot more to it. You know that. You left everything out. Turgenev wouldn't do that. Chekhov wouldn't do that. There are in fact Russian writers you never heard of, you don't have an inkling of, as good as anyone, who can write a plain ordinary story, who would not leave out what you have left out. I object not to facts but to people sitting in trees talking senselessly, voices from who knows where . . ."

"Forget that one, Pa, what have I left out now? In this one?"

"Her looks, for instance."

"Oh. Quite handsome, I think. Yes."   10

"Her hair?"

"Dark, with heavy braids, as though she were a girl or a foreigner."

"What were her parents like, her stock? That she became such a person. It's interesting, you know."

"From out of town. Professional people. The first to be divorced in their county. How's that? Enough?" I asked.

"With you, it's all a joke," he said. "What about the boy's father? Why didn't you   15
mention him? Who was he? Or was the boy born out of wedlock?"

"Yes," I said. "He was born out of wedlock."

"For Godsakes, doesn't anyone in your stories get married? Doesn't anyone have the time to run down to City Hall before they jump into bed?"

"No," I said. "In real life, yes. But in my stories, no."

"Why do you answer me like that?"

"Oh, Pa, this is a simple story about a smart woman who came to N.Y.C. full of in-   20
terest love trust excitement very up to date, and about her son, what a hard time she had in this world. Married or not, it's of small consequence."

"It is of great consequence," he said.

"O.K.," I said.

"O.K. O.K. yourself," he said, "but listen. I believe you that she's good-looking, but I don't think she was so smart."

"That's true," I said. "Actually that's the trouble with stories. People start out fantastic. You think they're extraordinary, but it turns out as the work goes along, they're just average with a good education. Sometimes the other way around, the person's a kind of dumb innocent, but he outwits you and you can't even think of an ending good enough."

"What do you do then?" he asked. He had been a doctor for a couple of decades   25
and then an artist for a couple of decades and he's still interested in details, craft, technique.

"Well, you just have to let the story lie around till some agreement can be reached between you and the stubborn hero."

"Aren't you talking silly, now?" he asked. "Start again," he said. "It so happens I'm not going out this evening. Tell the story again. See what you can do this time."

"O.K.," I said. "But it's not a five-minute job." Second attempt:

Once, across the street from us, there was a fine handsome woman, our neighbor. She had a son whom she loved because she'd known him since birth (in helpless chubby infancy, and in the wrestling, hugging ages, seven to ten, as well as earlier and later). This boy, when he fell into the fist of adolescence, became a junkie. He was not a hopeless one. He was in fact hopeful, an ideologue and successful converter. With his busy brilliance, he wrote persuasive articles for his high-school newspaper. Seeking a wider audience, using important connections, he drummed into Lower Manhattan newsstand distribution a periodical called *Oh! Golden Horse!*

30   In order to keep him from feeling guilty (because guilt is the stony heart of nine tenths of all clinically diagnosed cancers in America today, she said), and because she had always believed in giving bad habits room at home where one could keep an eye on them, she too became a junkie. Her kitchen was famous for a while—a center for intellectual addicts who knew what they were doing. A few felt artistic like Coleridge and others were scientific and revolutionary like Leary.° Although she was often high herself, certain good mothering reflexes remained, and she saw to it that there was lots of orange juice around and honey and milk and vitamin pills. However, she never cooked anything but chili, and that no more than once a week. She explained, when we talked to her, seriously, with neighborly concern, that it was her part in the youth culture and she would rather be with the young, it was an honor, than with her own generation.

One week, nodding through an Antonioni° film, this boy was severely jabbed by the elbow of a stern and proselytizing girl, sitting beside him. She offered immediate apricots and nuts for his sugar level, spoke to him sharply, and took him home.

She had heard of him and his work and she herself published, edited, and wrote a competitive journal called *Man Does Live By Bread Alone*. In the organic heat of her continuous presence he could not help but become interested once more in his muscles, his arteries, and nerve connections. In fact he began to love them, treasure them, praise them with funny little songs in *Man Does Live* . . . .

> the fingers of my flesh transcend
> my transcendental soul
35 > the tightness in my shoulders end
> my teeth have made me whole

To the mouth of his head (that glory of will and determination) he brought hard apples, nuts, wheat germ, and soybean oil. He said to his old friends, From now on, I guess I'll keep my wits about me. I'm going on the natch. He said he was about to begin a spiritual deep-breathing journey. How about you too, Mom? he asked kindly.

His conversion was so radiant, splendid, that neighborhood kids his age began to say that he had never been a real addict at all, only a journalist along for the

---

°*Leary*: Timothy Leary (1920–1996), psychologist and exponent of psychedelic drug-induced experiences.
°*Antonioni*: Michelangelo Antonioni (1912), Italian film director.

smell of the story. The mother tried several times to give up what had become without her son and his friends a lonely habit. This effort only brought it to supportable levels. The boy and his girl took their electronic mimeograph and moved to the bushy edge of another borough. They were very strict. They said they would not see her again until she had been off drugs for sixty days.

At home alone in the evening, weeping, the mother read and reread the seven issues of *Oh! Golden Horse!* They seemed to her as truthful as ever. We often crossed the street to visit and console. But if we mentioned any of our children who were at college or in the hospital or dropouts at home, she would cry out, My baby! My baby! and burst into terrible, face-scarring, time-consuming tears. The End.

First my father was silent, then he said, "Number One: You have a nice sense of humor. Number Two: I see you can't tell a plain story. So don't waste time." Then he said sadly, "Number Three: I suppose that means she was alone, she was left like that, his mother. Alone. Probably sick?"

I said, "Yes."

"Poor woman. Poor girl, to be born in a time of fools, to live among fools. The end. The end. You were right to put that down. The end."

I didn't want to argue, but I had to say, "Well, it is not necessarily the end, Pa."

"Yes," he said, "what a tragedy. The end of a person."

"No, Pa," I begged him. "It doesn't have to be. She's only about forty. She could be a hundred different things in this world as time goes on. A teacher or a social worker. An ex-junkie! Sometimes it's better than having a master's in education."

"Jokes," he said. "As a writer that's your main trouble. You don't want to recognize it. Tragedy! Plain tragedy! Historical tragedy! No hope. The end."

"Oh, Pa," I said. "She could change."

"In your own life, too, you have to look it in the face." He took a couple of nitroglycerin. "Turn to five," he said, pointing to the dial on the oxygen tank. He inserted the tubes into his nostrils and breathed deep. He closed his eyes and said, "No."

I had promised the family to always let him have the last word when arguing, but in this case I had a different responsibility. That woman lives across the street. She's my knowledge and my invention. I'm sorry for her. I'm not going to leave her there in that house crying. (Actually neither would Life, which unlike me has no pity.)

Therefore: She did change. Of course her son never came home again. But right now, she's the receptionist in a storefront community clinic in the East Village. Most of the customers are young people, some old friends. The head doctor has said to her, "If we only had three people in this clinic with your experiences . . ."

"The doctor said that?" My father took the oxygen tubes out of his nostrils and said, "Jokes. Jokes again."

"No, Pa, it could really happen that way, it's a funny world nowadays."

"No," he said. "Truth first. She will slide back. A person must have character. She does not."

"No, Pa," I said. "That's it. She's got a job. Forget it. She's in that storefront working."

"How long will it be?" he asked. "Tragedy! You too. When will you look it in the face?"   [1971]

QUESTIONS

1. What is the fundamental conflict between father and daughter?
2. What does the setting—the neighborhood and the sick room—contribute to the narration?
3. What are the differing relationships between art and life explored in the story?
4. What is the significance of the two titles *Oh! Golden Horse* and *Man Does Live By Bread Alone?*
5. What does the narrator discover about her writing and herself?

EDGAR ALLAN POE

Edgar Allan Poe (1809–1849) was born in Boston, the child of traveling actors. Orphaned at the age of three, he was raised by John Allan of Richmond, Virginia. Educated in England and for a brief period at the University of Virginia, Poe enlisted in the U.S. Army in 1827, meanwhile publishing *Tamerlane and Other Poems* (1827). Poe received an appointment to West Point in 1830, but, unsuited to academy life, he provoked his discharge. Poe embarked on a career in literary journalism, editing a series of periodicals and writing the poems, stories, and criticism on which his reputation rests. That reputation is secure. In a career of barely seventeen years, lived out in an atmosphere hostile to his aims, Poe created a body of work that has had an international impact. His critical writings defined the short story at its birth, and he was one critic who could practice what he preached. He invented the detective story. His poetry has been admired and is influential around the world, especially in France, and detractors can generally recite it from memory—of what other poet can that be said? And detractors of his prose are cheerfully ignored by the common reader, who keeps Poe's work alive in numerous anthologies and editions.

The Cask of Amontillado

The thousand injuries of Fortunato I had borne as I best could, but when he ventured upon insult I vowed revenge. You, who so well know the nature of my soul, will not suppose, however, that I gave utterance to a threat. *At length* I would be avenged; this was a point definitely settled—but the very definitiveness with which it was resolved precluded the idea of risk. I must not only punish but punish with impunity. A wrong is unredressed when retribution overtakes its redresser. It is equally unredressed when the avenger fails to make himself felt as such to him who has done the wrong.

It must be understood that neither by word nor deed had I given Fortunato cause to doubt my good will. I continued, as was my wont, to smile in his face, and he did not perceive that my smile *now* was at the thought of his immolation.

He had a weak point—this Fortunato—although in other regards he was a man to be respected and even feared. He prided himself on his connoisseurship in wine. Few Italians have the true virtuoso spirit. For the most part their enthusiasm is adopted to suit the time and opportunity, to practice imposture upon the British and Austrian millionaires. In painting and gemmary, Fortunato, like his countrymen, was quack, but in the matter of old wines he was sincere. In this respect I did not differ from him materially;—I was skilful in the Italian vintages myself, and bought largely whenever I could.

It was about dusk, one evening during the supreme madness of the carnival season, that I encountered my friend. He accosted me with excessive warmth, for he had been drinking much. The man wore motley. He had on a tight-fitting parti-striped dress, and his head was surmounted by the conical cap and bells. I was so pleased to see him that I thought I should never have done wringing his hand.

5   I said to him—"My dear Fortunato, you are luckily met. How remarkably well you are looking to-day. But I have received a pipe of what passes for Amontillado, and I have my doubts."

"How?" said he. "Amontillado? A pipe? Impossible! And in the middle of the carnival!"

"I have my doubts," I replied; "and I was silly enough to pay the full Amontillado price without consulting you in the matter. You were not to be found, and I was fearful of losing a bargain."

"Amontillado!"

"I have my doubts."

10   "Amontillado!"

"And I must satisfy them."

"Amontillado!"

"As you are engaged, I am on my way to Luchresi. If any one has a critical turn, it is he. He will tell me—"

"Luchresi cannot tell Amontillado from Sherry."

15   "And yet some fools will have it that his taste is a match for your own."

"Come, let us go."

"Whither?"

"To your vaults."

"My friend, no; I will not impose upon your good nature. I perceive you have an engagement. Luchresi—"

20   "I have no engagement;—come."

"My friend, no. It is not the engagement, but the severe cold with which I perceive you are afflicted. The vaults are insufferably damp. They are encrusted with niter."

"Let us go, nevertheless. The cold is merely nothing. Amontillado! You have been imposed upon. And as for Luchresi, he cannot distinguish Sherry from Amontillado."

Thus speaking, Fortunato possessed himself of my arm; and putting on a mask of black silk and drawing a *roquelaire*° closely about my person, I suffered him to hurry me to my palazzo.

There were no attendants at home; they had absconded to make merry in honor of the time. I had told them that I should not return until the morning, and had given them explicit orders not to stir from the house. These orders were sufficient, I well knew, to insure their immediate disappearance, one and all, as soon as my back was turned.

25   I took from their sconces two flambeaux, and giving one to Fortunato, bowed him through several suites of rooms to the archway that led into the vaults. I passed down a long and winding staircase, requesting him to be cautious as he followed. We came at length to the foot of the descent, and stood together on the damp ground of the catacombs of the Montresors.

___
°*roquelaire*: A heavy cloak.

The gait of my friend was unsteady, and the bells upon his cap jingled as he strode.

"The pipe?" said he.

"It is farther on," said I; "but observe the white web-work which gleams from these cavern walls."

He turned towards me, and looked into my eyes with two filmy orbs that distilled the rheum of intoxication.

"Niter?" he asked at length.   30

"Niter," I replied. "How long have you had that cough?"

"Ugh! ugh! ugh!—ugh! ugh! ugh!—ugh! ugh! ugh! ugh! ugh! ugh!—ugh! ugh! ugh!"

My poor friend found it impossible to reply for many minutes.

"It is nothing," he said, at last.

"Come," I said, with decision, "we will go back; your health is precious. You are rich,   35
respected, admired, beloved; you are happy, as once I was. You are a man to be missed. For me it is no matter. We will go back; you will be ill, and I cannot be responsible. Besides, there is Luchresi—"

"Enough," he said; "the cough is a mere nothing; it will not kill me. I shall not die of a cough."

"True—true," I replied; "and, indeed, I had no intention of alarming you unnecessarily—but you should use all proper caution. A draft of this Medoc will defend us from the damps."

Here I knocked off the neck of a bottle which I drew from a long row of its fellows that lay upon the mold.

"Drink," I said, presenting him the wine.

He raised it to his lips with a leer. He paused and nodded to me familiarly, while   40
his bells jingled.

"I drink," he said, "to the buried that repose around us."

"And I to your long life."

He again took my arm, and we proceeded.

"These vaults," he said, "are extensive."

"The Montresors," I replied, "were a great and numerous family."   45

"I forget your arms."

"A huge human foot d'or, in a field azure; the foot crushes a serpent rampant whose fangs are imbedded in the heel."

"And the motto?"

"*Nemo me impune lacessit.*"°

"Good!" he said.   50

The wind sparkled in his eyes and the bells jingled. My own fancy grew warm with the Medoc. We had passed through long walls of piled skeletons, with casks and puncheons intermingling, into the inmost recesses of the catacombs. I paused again, and this time I made bold to seize Fortunato by an arm above the elbow.

"The niter!" I said; "see, it increases. It hangs like moss upon the vaults. We are below the river's bed. The drops of moisture trickle among the bones. Come, we will go back ere it is too late. Your cough—"

"It is nothing," he said; "let us go on. But first, another draft of the Medoc."

I broke and reached him a flagon of De Grâve. He emptied it at a breath. His eyes flashed with a fierce light. He laughed and threw the bottle upward with a gesticulation I did not understand.

I looked at him in surprise. He repeated the movement—a grotesque one.   55

°*Nemo me impune lacessit*: "No one harms me unpunished."

"You do not comprehend?" he said.

"Not I," I replied.

"Then you are not of the brotherhood."

"How?"

60   "You are not of the masons."

"Yes, yes," I said; "yes, yes."

"You? Impossible! A mason?"

"A mason," I replied.

"A sign," he said, "a sign."

65   "It is this," I answered, producing from beneath the folds of my *roquelaire* a trowel.

"You jest," he exclaimed, recoiling a few paces. "But let us proceed to the Amontillado."

"Be it so," I said, replacing the tool beneath the cloak and again offering him my arm. He leaned upon it heavily. We continued our route in search of the Amontillado. We passed through a range of low arches, descended, passed on, and descending again, arrived at a deep crypt, in which the foulness of the air caused our flambeaux rather to glow than flame.

At the most remote end of the crypt there appeared another less spacious. Its walls had been lined with human remains, piled to the vault overhead, in the fashion of the great catacombs of Paris. Three sides of this interior crypt were still ornamented in this manner. From the fourth the bones had been thrown down, and lay promiscuously upon the earth, forming at one point a mound of some size. Within the wall thus exposed by the displacing of the bones, we perceived a still interior crypt or recess, in depth about four feet, in width three, in height six or seven. It seemed to have been constructed from no especial use within itself, but formed merely the interval between two of the colossal supports of the roof of the catacombs, and was backed by one of their circumscribing walls of solid granite.

It was in vain that Fortunato, uplifting his dull torch, endeavored to pry into the depth of the recess. Its termination the feeble light did not enable us to see.

70   "Proceed," I said; "herein is the Amontillado. As for Luchresi—"

"He is an ignoramus," interrupted my friend, as he stepped unsteadily forward, while I followed immediately at his heels. In an instant he had reached the extremity of the niche, and finding his progress arrested by the rock, stood stupidly bewildered. A moment more and I had fettered him to the granite. In its surface were two iron staples, distant from each other about two feet, horizontally. From one of these depended a short chain, from the other a padlock. Throwing the links about his waist, it was but the work of a few seconds to secure it. He was too much astounded to resist. Withdrawing the key I stepped back from the recess.

"Pass your hand," I said, "over the wall; you cannot help feeling the niter. Indeed it is *very* damp. Once more let me *implore* you to return. No? Then I must positively leave you. But I must first render you all the little attentions in my power."

"The Amontillado!" ejaculated my friend, not yet recovered from his astonishment.

"True," I replied; "the Amontillado."

75   As I said these words I busied myself among the pile of bones of which I have before spoken. Throwing them aside, I soon uncovered a quantity of building stone and mortar. With these materials and with the aid of my trowel, I began vigorously to wall up the entrance of the niche.

I had scarcely laid the first tier of the masonry when I discovered that the intoxication of Fortunato had in a great measure worn off. The earliest indication I had of this was a low moaning cry from the depth of the recess. It was *not* the cry of a drunken man. There was then a long and obstinate silence. I laid the second tier, and the third, and the fourth; and then I heard the furious vibrations of the chain. The noise lasted for several minutes, during which, that I might hearken to it with the more satisfaction, I ceased my labors and sat down upon the bones. When at last the clanking subsided, I resumed the trowel, and finished without interruption the fifth, the sixth, and the seventh tier. The wall was now nearly upon a level with my breast. I again paused, and holding the flambeaux over the masonwork, threw a few feeble rays upon the figure within.

A succession of loud and shrill screams, bursting suddenly from the throat of the chained form, seemed to thrust me violently back. For a brief moment I hesitated, I trembled. Unsheathing my rapier, I began to grope with it about the recess; but the thought of an instant reassured me. I placed my hand upon the solid fabric of the catacombs, and felt satisfied. I reapproached the wall. I replied to the yells of him who clamored. I reechoed, I aided, I surpassed them in volume and in strength. I did this, and the clamorer grew still.

It was now midnight, and my task was drawing to a close. I had completed the eighth, the ninth and the tenth tier. I had finished a portion of the last and the eleventh; there remained but a single stone to be fitted and plastered in. I struggled with its weight; I placed it partially in its destined position. But now there came from out the niche a low laugh that erected the hairs upon my head. It was succeeded by a sad voice, which I had difficulty in recognizing as that of the noble Fortunato. The voice said—

"Ha! ha! ha!—he! he! he!—a very good joke, indeed—an excellent jest. We will have many a rich laugh about it at the palazzo—he! he! he!—over our wine—he! he! he!"

"The Amontillado!" I said.   80

"He! he! he!—he! he! he!—yes, the Amontillado. But is it not getting late? Will not they be awaiting us at the palazzo, the Lady Fortunato and the rest? Let us be gone."

"Yes," I said, "let us be gone."

"For the love of God, Montresor!"

"Yes," I said, "for the love of God!"

But to these words I hearkened in vain for a reply. I grew impatient. I called aloud—   85
"Fortunato!"

No answer. I called again—
"Fortunato!"

No answer still. I thrust a torch through the remaining aperture and let it fall within. There came forth in return only a jingling of the bells. My heart grew sick; it was the dampness of the catacombs that made it so. I hastened to make an end of my labor. I forced the last stone into its position; I plastered it up. Against the new masonry I reelected the old rampart of bones. For the half of a century no mortal has disturbed them. *In pace requiescat!*°   [1846]

°*In pace requiescat!*: Rest in peace!

QUESTIONS

1. How is the setting expressive of the theme?
2. What is the significance of Montresor's name, dress, coat of arms, and family motto?
3. What are the aspects of Fortunato's character that victimize him?
4. What is the tone of Fortunato's *"For the love of God, Montresor!"* and of Montresor's reply? What is the significance in the story of this exchange?
5. Is the final *"In pace requiescat!"* ironic?

EDGAR ALLAN POE

The Fall of the House of Usher

Son coeur est un luth suspendu;
Sitôt qu'on le touche il résonne.°
—de Béranger

During the whole of a dull, dark, and soundless day in the autumn of the year, when the clouds hung oppressively low in the heavens, I had been passing alone, on horseback, through a singularly dreary tract of country, and at length found myself, as the shades of the evening drew on, within view of the melancholy House of Usher. I know not how it was—but, with the first glimpse of the building, a sense of insufferable gloom pervaded my spirit. I say insufferable; for the feeling was unrelieved by any of that half-pleasurable, because poetic, sentiment with which the mind usually receives even the sternest natural images of the desolate or terrible. I looked upon the scene before me—upon the mere house, and the simple landscape features of the domain—upon the bleak walls—upon the vacant eye-like windows—upon a few rank sedges—and upon a few white trunks of decayed trees—with an utter depression of soul which I can compare to no earthly sensation more properly than to the afterdream of the reveller upon opium—the bitter lapse into everyday life—the hideous dropping off of the veil. There was an iciness, a sinking, a sickening of the heart—an unredeemed dreariness of thought which no goading of the imagination could torture into aught of the sublime. What was it—I paused to think—what was it that so unnerved me in the contemplation of the House of Usher? It was a mystery all insoluble; nor could I grapple with the shadowy fancies that crowded upon me as I pondered. I was forced to fall back upon the unsatisfactory conclusion, that while, beyond doubt, there *are* combinations of very simple natural objects which have the power of thus affecting us, still the analysis of this power lies among considerations beyond our depth. It was possible, I reflected, that a mere different arrangement of the particulars of the scene, of the details of the picture, would be sufficient to modify, or perhaps to annihilate its capacity for sorrowful impression; and, acting upon this idea, I reined my horse to the

---

°. . . *il résonne*: "His heart is a suspended lute / Whenever one touches it, it resounds." From a poem, "Le Refus," by Pierre-Jean de Béranger (1780–1857).

precipitous brink of a black and lurid tarn that lay in unruffled lustre by the dwelling, and gazed down—but with a shudder even more thrilling than before—upon the re-modelled and inverted images of the gray sedge, and the ghastly tree-stems, and the vacant and eye-like windows.

Nevertheless, in this mansion of gloom I now proposed to myself a sojourn of some weeks. Its proprietor, Roderick Usher, had been one of my boon companions in boy-hood; but many years had elapsed since our last meeting. A letter, however, had late-ly reached me in a distant part of the country—a letter from him—which, in its wildly importunate nature, had admitted of no other than a personal reply. The MS. gave ev-idence of nervous agitation. The writer spoke of acute bodily illness—of a mental dis-order which oppressed him—and of an earnest desire to see me, as his best and, indeed, his only personal friend, with a view of attempting, by the cheerfulness of my society, some alleviation of his malady. It was the manner in which all this, and much more, was said—it was the apparent heart that went with his request—which allowed me no room for hesitation; and I accordingly obeyed forthwith what I still considered a very singular summons.

Although as boys, we had been even intimate associates, yet I really knew little of my friend. His reserve had been always excessive and habitual. I was aware, howev-er, that his very ancient family had been noted, time out of mind, for a peculiar sensi-bility of temperament, displaying itself, through long ages, in many works of exalted art, and manifested, of late, in repeated deeds of munificent yet unobtrusive charity, as well as in a passionate devotion to the intricacies, perhaps even more than to the or-thodox and easily recognizable beauties, of musical science. I had heard, too, the very remarkable fact, that the stem of the Usher race, all time-honored as it was, had put forth, at no period, any enduring branch; in other words, that the entire family lay in the direct line of descent, and had always, with very trifling and very temporary vari-ations, so lain. It was this deficiency, I considered, while running over in thought the perfect keeping of the character of the premises with the accredited character of the peo-ple, and while speculating upon the possible influence which the one, in the long lapse of centuries, might have exercised upon the other—it was this deficiency, perhaps, of collateral issue, and the consequent undeviating transmission, from sire to son, of the patrimony with the name, which had, at length, so identified the two as to merge the original title of the estate in the quaint and equivocal appellation of the "House of Usher"—an appellation which seemed to include, in the minds of the peasantry who used it, both the family and the family mansion.

I have said that the sole effect of my somewhat childish experiment—that of look-ing down within the tarn—had been to deepen the first singular impression. There can be no doubt that the consciousness of the rapid increase of my superstition—for why should I not so term it?—served mainly to accelerate the increase itself. Such, I have long known, is the paradoxical law of all sentiments having terror as a basis. And it might have been for this reason only, that, when I again uplifted my eyes to the house itself, from its image in the pool, there grew in my mind a strange fancy—a fancy so ridiculous, indeed, that I but mention it to show the vivid force of the sensations which oppressed me. I had so worked upon my imagination as really to believe that about the whole mansion and domain there hung an atmosphere peculiar to them-selves and their immediate vicinity—an atmosphere which had no affinity with the air of heaven, but which had reeked up from the decayed trees, and the gray wall, and the silent tarn—a pestilent and mystic vapor, dull, sluggish, faintly discernible and leaden-hued.

Shaking off from my spirit what *must* have been a dream, I scanned more narrow- 5
ly the real aspect of the building. Its principal feature seemed to be that of an excessive antiquity. The discoloration of ages had been great. Minute fungi overspread the
whole exterior, hanging in a fine tangled web-work from the eaves. Yet all this was
apart from any extraordinary dilapidation. No portion of the masonry had fallen; and
there appeared to be a wild inconsistency between its still perfect adaptation of parts,
and the crumbling condition of the individual stones. In this there was much that reminded me of the specious totality of old woodwork which has rotted for long years
in some neglected vault, with no disturbance from the breath of the external air. Beyond
this indication of extensive decay, however, the fabric gave little token of instability. Perhaps the eye of a scrutinizing observer might have discovered a barely perceptible fissure, which extending from the roof of the building in front, made its way down the
wall in a zigzag direction, until it became lost in the sullen waters of the tarn.

Noticing these things, I rode over a short causeway to the house. A servant in waiting took my horse, and I entered the Gothic archway of the hall. A valet, of stealthy step,
thence conducted me, in silence, through many dark and intricate passages in my
progress to the *studio* of his master. Much that I encountered on the way contributed,
I know not how, to heighten the vague sentiments of which I have already spoken.
While the objects around me—while the carvings of the ceilings, the sombre tapestries of the walls, the ebon blackness of the floors, and the phantasmagoric armorial
trophies which rattled as I strode, were but matters to which, or to such as which, I had
been accustomed from my infancy—while I hesitated not to acknowledge how familiar was all this—I still wondered to find how unfamiliar were the fancies which ordinary images were stirring up. On one of the staircases, I met the physician of the family.
His countenance, I thought, wore a mingled expression of low cunning and perplexity. He accosted me with trepidation and passed on. The valet now threw open a door
and ushered me into the presence of his master.

The room in which I found myself was very large and lofty. The windows were
long, narrow, and pointed, and at so vast a distance from the black oaken floor as to
be altogether inaccessible from within. Feeble gleams of encrimsoned light made their
way through the trellised panes, and served to render sufficiently distinct the more
prominent objects around; the eye, however, struggled in vain to reach the remoter
angles of the chamber, or the recesses of the vaulted and fretted ceiling. Dark draperies
hung upon the walls. The general furniture was profuse, comfortless, antique, and tattered. Many books and musical instruments lay scattered about, but failed to give any
vitality to the scene. I felt that I breathed an atmosphere of sorrow. An air of stern,
deep, and irredeemable gloom hung over and pervaded all.

Upon my entrance, Usher arose from a sofa on which he had been lying at full length,
and greeted me with a vivacious warmth which had much in it, I at first thought, of an
overdone cordiality—of the constrained effort of the *ennuyé* man of the world. A glance,
however, at his countenance convinced me of his perfect sincerity. We sat down; and for
some moments, while he spoke not, I gazed upon him with a feeling half of pity, half
of awe. Surely, man had never before so terribly altered, in so brief a period, as had
Roderick Usher! It was with difficulty that I could bring myself to admit the identity of
the wan being before me with the companion of my early boyhood. Yet the character
of his face had been at all times remarkable. A cadaverousness of complexion; an eye
large, liquid, and luminous beyond comparison; lips somewhat thin and very pallid, but
of a surpassingly beautiful curve; a nose of a delicate Hebrew model, but with a breadth
of nostril unusual in similar formations; a finely molded chin, speaking, in its want of

prominence, of a want of moral energy; hair of a more than web-like softness and tenuity;—these features, with an inordinate expansion above the regions of the temple, made up altogether a countenance not easily to be forgotten. And now in the mere exaggeration of the prevailing character of these features, and of the expression they were wont to convey, lay so much of change that I doubted to whom I spoke. The now ghastly pallor of the skin, and the now miraculous lustre of the eye, above all things startled and even awed me. The silken hair, too, had been suffered to grow all unheeded, and as, in its wild gossamer texture, it floated rather than fell about the face, I could not, even with effort, connect its Arabesque expression with any idea of simple humanity.

In the manner of my friend I was at once struck with an incoherence—an inconsistency; and I soon found this to arise from a series of feeble and futile struggles to overcome an habitual trepidancy—an excessive nervous agitation. For something of this nature I had indeed been prepared, no less by his letter, than by reminiscences of certain boyish traits, and by conclusions deduced from his peculiar physical conformation and temperament. His action was alternately vivacious and sullen. His voice varied rapidly from a tremulous indecision (when the animal spirits seemed utterly in abeyance) to that species of energetic concision—that abrupt, weighty, unhurried, and hollow-sounding enunciation—that leaden, self-balanced, and perfectly modulated guttural utterance, which may be observed in the lost drunkard, or the irreclaimable eater of opium, during the periods of his most intense excitement.

10   It was thus that he spoke of the object of my visit, of his earnest desire to see me, and of the solace he expected me to afford him. He entered, at some length, into what he conceived to be the nature of his malady. It was, he said, a constitutional and a family evil and one for which he despaired to find a remedy—a mere nervous affection, he immediately added, which would undoubtedly soon pass off. It displayed itself in a host of unnatural sensations. Some of these, as he detailed them, interested and bewildered me; although, perhaps, the terms and the general manner of their narration had their weight. He suffered much from a morbid acuteness of the senses; the most insipid food was alone endurable; he could wear only garments of certain texture; the odors of all flowers were oppressive; his eyes were tortured by even a faint light; and there were but peculiar sounds, and these from stringed instruments, which did not inspire him with horror.

To an anomalous species of terror, I found him a bounden slave. "I shall perish," said he, "I *must* perish in this deplorable folly. Thus, thus, and not otherwise, shall I be lost. I dread the events of the future, not in themselves, but in their results. I shudder at the thought of any, even the most trivial, incident, which may operate upon this intolerable agitation of soul. I have, indeed, no abhorrence of danger, except in its absolute effect—in terror. In this unnerved, in this pitiable condition I feel that the period will sooner or later arrive when I must abandon life and reason together, in some struggle with the grim phantasm, Fear."

I learned, moreover, at intervals, and through broken and equivocal hints, another singular feature of his mental condition. He was enchained by certain superstitious impressions in regard to the dwelling which he tenanted, and whence, for many years, he had never ventured forth—in regard to an influence whose suppositious force was conveyed in terms too shadowy here to be re-stated—an influence which some peculiarities in the mere form and substance of his family mansion had, by dint of long sufferance, he said, obtained over his spirit—an effect which the *physique* of the gray walls and turrets, and of the dim tarn into which they all looked down, had, at length, brought about upon the *morale* of his existence.

He admitted, however, although with hesitation, that much of the peculiar gloom which thus afflicted him could be traced to a more natural and far more palpable origin—to the severe and long-continued illness—indeed to the evidently approaching dissolution—of a tenderly beloved sister, his sole companion for long years, his last and only relative on earth. "Her decease," he said, with a bitterness which I can never forget, "would leave him (him, the hopeless and the frail) the last of the ancient race of the Ushers." While he spoke, the lady Madeline (for so was she called) passed through a remote portion of the apartment, and, without having noticed my presence, disappeared. I regarded her with an utter astonishment not unmingled with dread and yet I found it impossible to account for such feelings. A sensation of stupor oppressed me as my eyes followed her retreating steps. When a door, at length, closed upon her, my glance sought instinctively and eagerly the countenance of the brother; but he had buried his face in his hands, and I could only perceive that a far more than ordinary wanness had overspread the emaciated fingers through which trickled many passionate tears.

The disease of the lady Madeline had long baffled the skill of her physicians. A settled apathy, a gradual wasting away of the person, and frequent although transient affections of a partially cataleptical-character were the usual diagnosis. Hitherto she had steadily borne up against the pressure of her malady, and had not betaken herself finally to bed; but on the closing in of the evening of my arrival at the house, she succumbed (as her brother told me at night with inexpressible agitation) to the prostrating power of the destroyer; and I learned that the glimpse I had obtained of her person would thus probably be the last I should obtain—that the lady, at least while living, would be seen by me no more.

For several days ensuing, her name was unmentioned by either Usher or myself; and during this period I was busied in earnest endeavors to alleviate the melancholy of my friend. We painted and read together, or I listened, as if in a dream, to the wild improvisations of his speaking guitar. And thus, as a closer and still closer intimacy admitted me more unreservedly into the recesses of his spirit, the more bitterly did I perceive the futility of all attempts at cheering a mind from which darkness, as if an inherent positive quality, poured forth upon all objects of the moral and physical universe in one unceasing radiation of gloom.

I shall ever bear about me a memory of the many solemn hours I thus spent alone with the master of the House of Usher. Yet I should fail in any attempt to convey an idea of the exact character of the studies, or of the occupations, in which he involved me, or led me the way. An excited and highly distempered ideality threw a sulphureous lustre over all. His long improvised dirges will ring forever in my ears. Among other things, I hold painfully in mind a certain singular perversion and amplification of the wild air of the last waltz of Von Weber.° From the painting over which his elaborate fancy brooded, and which grew, touch by touch, into vaguenesses at which I shuddered the more thrillingly, because I shuddered knowing not why—from these paintings (vivid as their images now are before me) I would in vain endeavor to educe more than a small portion which should lie within the compass of merely written words. By the utter simplicity, by the nakedness of his designs, he arrested and overawed attention. If ever mortal painted an idea, that mortal was Roderick Usher. For me at least, in the circumstances then surrounding me, there arose out of the pure abstractions which the hypochondriac contrived to throw upon his canvas, an intensity

15

°*Von Weber*: Karl Maria von Weber (1786–1826), composer of German operas.

of intolerable awe, no shadow of which felt I ever yet in the contemplation of the certainly glowing yet too concrete reveries of Fuseli.°

One of the phantasmagoric conceptions of my friend, partaking not so rigidly of the spirit of abstraction, may be shadowed forth, although feebly, in words. A small picture presented the interior of an immensely long and rectangular vault or tunnel, with low walls, smooth, white and without interruption or device. Certain accessory points of the design served well to convey the idea that this excavation lay at an exceeding depth below the surface of the earth. No outlet was observed in any portion of its vast extent, and no torch or other artificial source of light was discernible; yet a flood of intense rays rolled throughout, and bathed the whole in a ghastly and inappropriate splendor.

I have just spoken of that morbid condition of the auditory nerve which rendered all music intolerable to the sufferer, with the exception of certain effects of stringed instruments. It was, perhaps, the narrow limits to which he thus confined himself upon the guitar which gave birth, in great measure, to the fantastic character of his performances. But the fervid *facility* of his *impromptus* could not be so accounted for. They must have been, and were, in the notes, as well as in the words of his wild fantasias (for he not unfrequently accompanied himself with rhymed verbal improvisations), the result of that intense mental collectedness and concentration to which I have previously alluded as observable only in particular moments of the highest artificial excitement. The words of one of these rhapsodies I have easily remembered. I was, perhaps, the more forcibly impressed with it as he gave it, because, in the under or mystic current of its meaning, I fancied that I perceived, and for the first time, a full consciousness on the part of Usher of the tottering of his lofty reason upon her throne. The verses, which were entitled "The Haunted Palace," ran very nearly, if not accurately, thus:

I

In the greenest of our valleys,
    By good angels tenanted,
Once a fair and stately palace—
    Radiant palace—reared its head.
In the monarch Thought's dominion—
    It stood there!
Never seraph spread a pinion
    Over fabric half so fair.

II

Banners yellow, glorious, golden,
    On its roof did float and flow
(This—all this—was in the olden
    Time long ago);
And every gentle air that dallied,
    In that sweet day,

20

25

30

°*Fuseli*: Henry Fuseli (1741–1825), English romantic painter.

> Along the ramparts plumed and pallid,
>   A winged odor went away.

III

> Wanderers in that happy valley 35
>   Through two luminous windows saw
> Spirits moving musically
>   To a lute's well-tuned law;
> Round about a throne, where sitting
>   (Porphyrogene!) 40
> In state his glory well befitting,
>   The ruler of the realm was seen.

IV

> And all with pearl and ruby glowing
>   Was the fair palace door,
> Through which came flowing, flowing, flowing 45
>   And sparkling evermore,
> A troop of Echoes whose sweet duty
>   Was but to sing,
> In voices of surpassing beauty,
>   The wit and wisdom of their king. 50

V

> But evil things, in robes of sorrow,
>   Assailed the monarch's high estate;
> (Ah, let us mourn, for never morrow
>   Shall dawn upon him, desolate!)
> And, round about his home, the glory 55
>   That blushed and bloomed
> Is but a dim-remembered story
>   Of the old time entombed.

VI

> And travellers now within that valley,
>   Through the red-litten windows see 60
> Vast forms that move fantastically
>   To a discordant melody;
> While, like a rapid ghastly river,
>   Through the pale door,
> A hideous throng rush out forever, 65
>   And laugh—but smile no more.

I well remember that suggestions arising from this ballad led us into a train of thought wherein there became manifest an opinion of Usher's, which I mention not so much on account of its novelty (for other men have thought thus), as on account of the pertinacity with which he maintained it. This opinion, in its general form, was that of the sentience of all vegetable things. But, in his disordered fancy, the idea had assumed a more daring character, and trespassed, under certain conditions, upon the kingdom of inorganization. I lack words to express the full extent, or the earnest *abandon* of his persuasion. The belief, however, was connected (as I have previously hinted) with the gray stones of the home of his forefathers. The conditions of the sentience had been here, he imagined, fulfilled in the method of collocation of these stones—in the order of their arrangement, as well as in that of the many *fungi* which overspread them, and of the decayed trees which stood around—above all, in the long undisturbed endurance of this arrangement, and in its reduplication in the still waters of the tarn. Its evidence—the evidence of the sentience—was to be seen, he said (and I here started as he spoke), in the gradual yet certain condensation of an atmosphere of their own about their waters and the walls. The result was discoverable, he added, in that silent yet importunate and terrible influence which for centuries had molded the destinies of his family, and which made *him* what I now saw him—what he was. Such opinions need no comment, and I will make none.

Our books—the books which, for years, had formed no small portion of the mental existence of the invalid—were, as might be supposed, in strict keeping with this character of phantasm. We pored together over such works as the "Ververt et Chartreuse" of Gresset; the "Belphegor" of Machiavelli; the "Heaven and Hell" of Swedenborg; the "Subterranean Voyage of Nicholas Klimm" by Holberg; the "Chiromancy" of Robert Flud, of Jean D'Indaginé and of de la Chambre; the "Journey into the Blue Distance" of Tieck; and the "City of the Sun" of Campanella. One favorite volume was a small octavo edition of the "Directorium Inquisitorium," by the Dominican Eymeric de Gironne; and there were passages in Pomponius Mela, about the old African Satyrs and Oegipans, over which Usher would sit dreaming for hours. His chief delight, however, was found in the perusal of an exceedingly rare and curious book in quarto Gothic—the manual of a forgotten church—the *Vigiliae Mortuorum secundum Chorum Ecclesiae Maguntinae.*°

I could not help thinking of the wild ritual of this work, and of its probable influence upon the hypochondriac, when, one evening, having informed me abruptly that the lady Madeline was no more, he stated his intention of preserving her corpse for a fortnight (previously to its final interment), in one of the numerous vaults within the main walls of the building. The worldly reason, however, assigned for this singular proceeding, was one which I did not feel at liberty to dispute. The brother had been led to his resolution (so he told me) by consideration of the unusual character of the malady of the deceased, of certain obtrusive and eager inquiries on the part of her

---

°. . . *Ecclesiae Maguntinae: Vairvert* and *Chartreuse* are antireligious satires by Jean-Baptiste-Louis Gresset (1709–1777); *Belphegor* by Niccolò Machiavelli (1469–1527) describes a demon who visits earth to show that women are man's damnation; in *Heaven and Hell* Emanuel Swedenborg (1688–1772) is concerned with the continuity of spiritual identity; *Subterranean Voyage* by Ludwig Holberg (1684–1754) describes a trip to the land of the dead; chiromancy, or palmreading, is the subject of Robert Flud (1574–1637), Jean D'Indaginé (*Chiromantia*, 1522), and Marin Cireau de la Chambre (1594–1669); *Journey into the Blue Distance* by Johann Ludwig Tieck (1773–1853) and *City of the Sun* by Tommaso Campanella (1568–1639) both describe trips to other worlds; the work by Nicolas Eymeric de Gironne (1320–1399) concerns procedures for tortures; the first-century Roman, Pomponius Mela, described "Aegipans," allegedly goatmen, of Africa in his *Geography; The Vigils of the Dead according to the Choir of the Church of Mayence*, printed at Basel in 1500.

medical men, and of the remote and exposed situation of the burial-ground of the family. I will not deny that when I called to mind the sinister countenance of the person whom I met upon the staircase, on the day of my arrival at the house, I had no desire to oppose what I regarded as at best but a harmless, and by no means an unnatural, precaution.

At the request of Usher, I personally aided him in the arrangements for the temporary entombment. The body having been encoffined, we two alone bore it to its rest. The vault in which we placed it (and which had been so long unopened that our torches, half smothered in its oppressive atmosphere, gave us little opportunity for investigation) was small, damp, and entirely without means of admission for light; lying, at great depth, immediately beneath that portion of the building in which was my own sleeping apartment. It had been used, apparently, in remote feudal times, for the worst purposes of a donjon-keep, and, in later days, as a place of deposit for powder, or some other highly combustible substance, as a portion of its floor, and the whole interior of a long archway through which we reached it, were carefully sheathed with copper. The door, of massive iron, had been, also, similarly protected. Its immense weight caused an unusually sharp, grating sound, as it moved upon its hinges.

Having deposited our mournful burden upon tressels within this region of horror, we partially turned aside the yet unscrewed lid of the coffin, and looked upon the face of the tenant. A striking similitude between the brother and sister now first arrested my attention; and Usher, divining, perhaps, my thoughts, murmured out some few words from which I learned that the deceased and himself had been twins, and that sympathies of a scarcely intelligible nature had always existed between them. Our glances, however, rested not long upon the dead—for we could not regard her unawed. The disease which had thus entombed the lady in the maturity of youth, had left, as usual in all maladies of a strictly cataleptical character, the mockery of a faint blush upon the bosom and the face, and that suspiciously lingering smile upon the lip which is so terrible in death. We replaced and screwed down the lid, and, having secured the door of iron, made our way, with toil, into the scarcely less gloomy apartments of the upper portion of the house.

And now, some days of bitter grief having elapsed, an observable change came over the features of the mental disorder of my friend. His ordinary manner had vanished. His ordinary occupations were neglected or forgotten. He roamed from chamber to chamber with hurried, unequal, and objectless step. The pallor of his countenance had assumed, if possible, a more ghastly hue—but the luminousness of his eye had utterly gone out. The once occasional huskiness of his tone was heard no more; and a tremulous quaver, as if of extreme terror, habitually characterized his utterance. There were times, indeed, when I thought his unceasingly agitated mind was laboring with some oppressive secret, to divulge which he struggled for the necessary courage. At times, again, I was obliged to resolve all into the mere inexplicable vagaries of madness, for I beheld him gazing upon vacancy for long hours, in an attitude of the profoundest attention, as if listening to some imaginary sound. It was no wonder that his condition terrified—that it infected me. I felt creeping upon me, by slow yet certain degrees, the wild influences of his own fantastic yet impressive superstitions.

It was, especially, upon retiring to bed late in the night of the seventh or eighth day after the placing of the lady Madeline within the donjon, that I experienced the full power of such feelings. Sleep came not near my couch—while the hours waned and waned away. I struggled to reason off the nervousness which had dominion over me. I endeavored to believe that much, if not all of what I felt, was due to the bewildering influence of the gloomy furniture of the room—of the dark and tattered draperies, which, tortured into motion by the breath of a rising tempest, swayed fitfully to and fro upon the walls, and rustled uneasily about the decorations of the bed. But my efforts were fruitless. An irrepressible tremor gradually pervaded my frame; and, at length, there sat upon my very heart an incubus of utterly causeless alarm. Shaking this off with a gasp and a struggle, I uplifted myself upon the pillows, and, peering earnestly within the intense darkness of the chamber, hearkened—I know not why, except that an instinctive spirit prompted me—to certain low and indefinite sounds which came, through the pauses of the storm, at long intervals, I knew not whence. Overpowered by an intense sentiment of horror, unaccountable yet unendurable, I threw on my clothes with haste (for I felt that I should sleep no more during the night), and endeavored to arouse myself from the pitiable condition into which I had fallen by pacing rapidly to and fro through the apartment.

I had taken but few turns in this manner, when a light step on an adjoining staircase arrested my attention. I presently recognized it as that of Usher. In an instant afterward he rapped, with a gentle touch, at my door, and entered, bearing a lamp. His countenance was, as usual, cadaverously wan—but, moreover, there was a species of mad hilarity in his eyes—an evidently restrained *hysteria* in his whole demeanor. His air appalled me—but anything was preferable to the solitude which I had so long endured, and I even welcomed his presence as a relief.

75 "And you have not seen it?" he said abruptly, after having stared about him for some moments in silence—"you have not then seen it?—but, stay! you shall." Thus speaking, and having carefully shaded his lamp, he hurried to one of the casements, and threw it freely open to the storm.

The impetuous fury of the entering gust nearly lifted us from our feet. It was, indeed, a tempestuous yet sternly beautiful night, and one wildly singular in its terror and its beauty. A whirlwind had apparently collected its force in our vicinity; for there were frequent and violent alterations in the direction of the wind; and the exceeding density of the clouds (which hung so low as to press upon the turrets of the house) did not prevent our perceiving the lifelike velocity with which they flew careening from all points against each other, without passing away into the distance. I say that even their exceeding density did not prevent our perceiving this—yet we had no glimpse of the moon or stars, nor was there any flashing forth of the lightning. But the under surfaces of the huge masses of agitated vapor, as well as all terrestrial objects immediately around us, were glowing in the unnatural light of a faintly luminous and distinctly visible gaseous exhalation which hung about and enshrouded the mansion.

"You must not—you shall not behold this!" said I, shuddering, to Usher, as I led him, with a gentle violence, from the window to a seat. "These appearances, which bewilder you, are merely electrical phenomena not uncommon—or it may be that they have their ghastly origin in the rank miasma of the tarn. Let us close this casement;—the air is chilling and dangerous to your frame. Here is one of your favorite romances. I will read, and you shall listen:—and so we will pass away this terrible night together."

The antique volume which I had taken up was the "Mad Trist" of Sir Launcelot Canning but I had called it a favorite of Usher's more in sad jest than in earnest; for, in truth, there is little in its uncouth and unimaginative prolixity which could have had interest for the lofty and spiritual ideality of my friend. It was, however, the only book immediately at hand; and I indulged a vague hope that the excitement which now agitated the hypochondriac, might find relief (for the history of mental disorder is full of similar anomalies) even in the extremeness of the folly which I should read. Could I have judged, indeed, by the wild overstrained air of vivacity with which he hearkened, or apparently hearkened, to the words of the tale, I might well have congratulated myself upon the success of my design.

I had arrived at the well-known portion of the story where Ethelred, the hero of the Trist, having sought in vain for peaceable admission to the dwelling of the hermit, proceeds to make good an entrance by force. Here, it will be remembered, the words of the narrative run thus:

"And Ethelred, who was by nature of a doughty heart, and who was now mighty withal, on account of the powerfulness of the wine which he had drunken, waited no longer to hold parley with the hermit, who, in sooth, as of an obstinate and maliceful turn, but feeling the rain upon his shoulders, and fearing the rising of the tempest, uplifted his mace outright, and, with blows, made quickly room in the plankings of the door for his gauntleted hand; and now pulling therewith sturdily, he so cracked, and ripped, and tore all asunder, that the noise of the dry and hollow-sounding wood alarmed and reverberated throughout the forest." 80

At the termination of this sentence I started and, for a moment, paused; for it appeared to me (although I at once concluded that my excited fancy had deceived me)— it appeared to me that, from some very remote portion of the mansion, there came, indistinctly to my ears, what might have been, in its exact similarity of character, the echo (but a stifled and dull one certainly) of the very cracking and ripping sound which Sir Launcelot had so particularly described. It was, beyond doubt, the coincidence alone which had arrested my attention; for, amid the rattling of the sashes of the casements, and the ordinary commingled noises of the still increasing storm, the sound, in itself, had nothing, surely, which should have interested or disturbed me. I continued the story:

"But the good champion Ethelred, now entering within the door, was sore enraged and amazed to perceive no signal of the maliceful hermit; but, in the stead thereof, a dragon of a scaly and prodigious demeanor, and of a fiery tongue, which sate in guard before a palace of gold, with a floor of silver; and upon the wall there hung a shield of shining brass with this legend enwritten—

> *Who entereth herein, a conqueror hath bin;*
> *Who slayeth the dragon, the shield he shall win.*

And Ethelred uplifted his mace, and struck upon the head of the dragon, which fell before him, and gave up his pesty breath, with a shriek so horrid and harsh, and withal so piercing, that Ethelred had fain to close his ears with his hands against the dreadful noise of it, the like whereof was never before heard."

Here again I paused abruptly, and now with a feeling of wild amazement—for there could be no doubt whatever that, in this instance, I did actually hear (although from what direction it proceeded I found it impossible to say) a low and apparently distant, but harsh, protracted, and most unusual screaming or grating sound—the exact counterpart of what my fancy had already conjured up for the dragons' unnatural shriek as described by the romancer.

Oppressed, as I certainly was, upon the extraordinary coincidence, by a thousand conflicting sensations, in which wonder and extreme terror were predominant, I still retained sufficient presence of mind to avoid exciting, by an observation, the sensitive nervousness of my companion. I was by no means certain that he had noticed the sounds in question; although, assuredly, a strange alteration had, during the last few minutes, taken place in his demeanor. From a position fronting my own, he had gradually brought round his chair, so as to sit with his face to the door of the chamber; and thus I could but partially perceive his features, although I saw that his lips trembled as if he were murmuring inaudibly. His head had dropped upon his breast—yet I knew that he was not asleep, from the wide and rigid opening of the eye as I caught a glance of it in profile. The motion of his body, too, was at variance with this idea—for he rocked from side to side with a gentle yet constant and uniform sway. Having rapidly taken notice of all this, I resumed the narrative of Sir Launcelot, which thus proceeded:

85   "And now, the champion, having escaped from the terrible fury of the dragon, bethinking himself of the brazen shield, and of the breaking up of the enchantment which was upon it, removed the carcass from out of the way before him, and approached valorously over the silver pavement of the castle to where the shield was upon the wall; which in sooth tarried not for his full coming, but fell down at his feet upon the silver floor, with a mighty great and terrible ringing sound."

No sooner had these syllables passed my lips, than—as if a shield of brass had indeed, at the moment, fallen heavily upon a floor of silver—I became aware of a distinct, hollow, metallic, and clangorous, yet apparently muffled, reverberation. Completely unnerved, I leaped to my feet but the measured rocking movement of Usher was undisturbed. I rushed to the chair in which he sat. His eyes were bent fixedly before him, and throughout his whole countenance there reigned a stony rigidity. But, as I placed my hand upon his shoulder, there came a stronger shudder over his whole person; a sickly smile quivered about his lips; and I saw that he spoke in a low, hurried, and glibbering murmur, as if unconscious of my presence. Bending closely over him I at length drank in the hideous import of his words.

"Not hear it?—yes, I hear it, and *have* heard it. Long—long—long—many minutes, many hours, many days, have I heard it—yet I dared not—oh, pity me, miserable wretch that I am!—I dared not—I *dared* not speak! *We have put her living in the tomb!* Said I not that my senses were acute? I *now* tell you that I heard her first feeble movements in the hollow coffin. I heard them—many, many days ago—yet I dared not—*I dared not speak!* And now—to-night—Ethelred—ha! ha!—the breaking of the hermit's door, and the death-cry of the dragon, and the clangor of the shield—say, rather, the rending of her coffin, and the grating of the iron hinges of her prison, and her struggles within the coppered archway of the vault! Oh! whither shall I fly? Will she not be here anon? Is she not hurrying to upbraid me for my haste? Have I not heard her footsteps on the stair? Do I not distinguish that heavy and horrible beating of her heart? Madman!"—here he sprang furiously to his feet, and shrieked out his syllables, as if in the effort he were giving up his soul—"*Madman! I tell you that she now stands without the door!*"

As if in the superhuman energy of his utterance there had been found the potency of a spell, the huge antique panels to which the speaker pointed threw slowly back, upon the instant, their ponderous and ebony jaws. It was the work of the rushing gust—but then without those doors there *did* stand the lofty and enshrouded figure of the lady Madeline of Usher. There was blood upon her white robes, and the evidence of some bitter struggle upon every portion of her emaciated frame. For a moment she remained trembling and reeling to and fro upon the threshold—then, with a low moaning cry, fell heavily inward upon the person of her brother, and in her violent and now final death-agonies, bore him to the floor a corpse, and a victim of the terrors he had anticipated.

From that chamber, and from that mansion, I fled aghast. The storm was still abroad in all its wrath as I found myself crossing the old causeway. Suddenly there shot along the path a wild light, and I turned to see whence a gleam so unusual could have issued, for the vast house and its shadows were alone behind me. The radiance was that of the full, setting, and blood-red moon, which now shone vividly through that once barely discernible fissure, of which I have before spoken as extending from the roof of the building, in a zigzag direction, to the base. While I gazed, this fissure rapidly widened—there came a fierce breath of the whirlwind—the entire orb of the satellite burst at once upon my sight—my brain reeled as I saw the mighty walls rushing asunder—there was a long tumultuous shouting sound like the voice of a thousand waters—and the deep and dank tarn at my feet closed sullenly and silently over the fragments of the *"House of Usher."* [1840]

QUESTIONS

1. What devices does Poe use to create the atmosphere of the story?
2. What is the relation of Usher's song to the theme?
3. How does Poe foreshadow the final collapse of the House of Usher?
4. Characterize the narrator. Could it be argued that he, and not Usher, is the protagonist?
5. Is this story a tale of the supernatural, or is it an analysis of mental illness and the dissolution of the self? How is either interpretation dependent on an explanation of the final events of the story?

RESPONSES

1. From the psychological perspective, explore Poe's presentation of mental unity and stability.
2. From a feminist perspective, write an essay about the role of Lady Madeline in the story.
3. Compare Poe's view of aristocracy with Maugham's in "The Outstation."

FOCUS ON FILM

1. The film, *The Fall of the House of Usher* (1960), changes the relationships between the narrator and the Ushers. Were these changes necessary to make a unified film? What other justification for the changes can you imagine?
2. Examine the use of camera lens, camera angles, and framing. What importance do they play in the film? What parallel might they have in the print story?

EDGAR ALLAN POE

The Purloined Letter

Nil sapientae odiosius acumine nimio.°
—Seneca

At Paris, just after dark one gusty evening in the autumn of 18——, I was enjoying the twofold luxury of meditation and a meerschaum, in company with my friend C. Auguste Dupin, in his little back library, or book-closet, *au troisième, No. 33, Rue Dunôt, Faubourg St. Germain*. For one hour at least we had maintained a profound silence; while each, to any casual observer, might have seemed intently and exclusively occupied with the curling eddies of smoke that oppressed the atmosphere of the chamber. For myself, however, I was mentally discussing certain topics which had formed matter for conversation between us at an earlier period of the evening; I mean the affair of the Rue Morgue, and the mystery attending the murder of Marie Rogêt. I looked upon it, therefore, as something of a coincidence, when the door of our apartment was thrown open and admitted our old acquaintance, Monsieur G——, the Prefect of the Parisian police.

We gave him a hearty welcome; for there was nearly half as much of the entertaining as of the contemptible about the man, and we had not seen him for several years. We had been sitting in the dark, and Dupin now arose for the purpose of lighting a lamp, but sat down again, without doing so, upon G.'s saying that he had called to consult us, or rather to ask the opinion of my friend, about some official business which had occasioned a great deal of trouble.

"If it is any point requiring reflection," observed Dupin, as he forbore to enkindle the wick, "we shall examine it to better purpose in the dark."

"That is another of your odd notions," said the Prefect, who had a fashion of calling every thing "odd" that was beyond his comprehension, and thus lived amid an absolute legion of "oddities."

5   "Very true," said Dupin, as he supplied his visitor with a pipe, and rolled towards him a comfortable chair.

"And what is the difficulty now?" I asked. "Nothing more in the assassination way, I hope?"

° . . . *nimio*: "Nothing is more hateful to wisdom than too much cunning."

"Oh no; nothing of that nature. The fact is, the business is *very* simple indeed, and I make no doubt that we can manage it sufficiently well ourselves; but then I thought Dupin would like to hear the details of it, because it is so excessively *odd*."

"Simple and odd," said Dupin.

"Why, yes; and not exactly that either. The fact is, we have all been a good deal puzzled because the affair *is* so simple, and yet baffles us altogether."

"Perhaps it is the very simplicity of the thing which puts you at fault," said my friend.

"What nonsense you *do* talk!" replied the Prefect, laughing heartily.

"Perhaps the mystery is a little *too* plain," said Dupin.

"Oh, good heavens! who ever heard of such an idea?"

"A little *too* self-evident."

"Ha! ha! ha!—ha! ha! ha!—ho! ho! ho!"—roared our visitor, profoundly amused, "oh, Dupin, you will be the death of me yet!"

"And what, after all, *is* the matter on hand?" I asked.

"Why, I will tell you," replied the Prefect, as he gave a long, steady, and contemplative puff, and settled himself in his chair. "I will tell you in a few words; but, before I begin, let me caution you that this is an affair demanding the greatest secrecy, and that I should most probably lose the position I now hold, were it known that I confided it to any one."

"Proceed," said I.

"Or not," said Dupin.

"Well, then; I have received personal information, from a very high quarter, that a certain document of the last importance has been purloined from the royal apartments. The individual who purloined it is known; this beyond a doubt; he was seen to take it. It is known, also, that it still remains in his possession."

"How is this known?" asked Dupin.

"It is clearly inferred," replied the Prefect, "from the nature of the document, and from the non-appearance of certain results which would at once arise from its passing *out* of the robber's possession;—that is to say, from his employing it as he must design in the end to employ it."

"Be a little more explicit," I said.

"Well, I may venture so far as to say that the paper gives its holder a certain power in a certain quarter where such power is immensely valuable." The Prefect was fond of the cant of diplomacy.

"Still I do not quite understand," said Dupin.

"No? Well; the disclosure of the document to a third person, who shall be nameless, would bring in question the honour of a personage of most exalted station; and this fact gives the holder of the document an ascendancy over the illustrious personage whose honour and peace are so jeopardized."

"But this ascendancy," I interposed, "would depend upon the robber's knowledge of the loser's knowledge of the robber. Who would dare—"

"The thief," said G——, "is the Minister D——, who dares all things, those unbecoming as well as those becoming a man. The method of the theft was not less ingenious than bold. The document in question—a letter, to be frank—had been received by the personage robbed while alone in the royal *boudoir*. During its perusal she was suddenly interrupted by the entrance of the other exalted personage from whom especially it was her wish to conceal it. After a hurried and vain endeavour to thrust it in a drawer, she was forced to place it, open it was, upon a table. The address, however, was uppermost, and, the contents thus unexposed, the letter escaped notice. At this juncture enters the Minister D——. His lynx eye immediately perceives the paper, recognizes the handwriting of the address, observes the confusion of the personage addressed, and fathoms her secret. After some business transactions, hurried through in his ordinary manner, he produces a letter somewhat similar to the one in question, opens it, pretends to read it, and then places it in close juxtaposition to the other. Again he converses, for some fifteen minutes, upon the public affairs. At length, in taking leave, he takes also from the table the letter to which he had no claim. Its rightful owner saw, but, of course, dared not call attention to the act, in the presence of the third personage who stood at her elbow. The minister decamped; leaving his own letter—one of no importance—upon the table."

"Here, then," said Dupin to me, "you have precisely what you demand to make the ascendancy complete—the robber's knowledge of the loser's knowledge of the robber."

30   "Yes," replied the Prefect; "and the power thus attained has, for some months past, been wielded, for political purposes, to a very dangerous extent. The personage robbed is more thoroughly convinced, every day, of the necessity of reclaiming her letter. But this, of course, cannot be done openly. In fine, driven to despair, she has committed the matter to me."

"Than whom," said Dupin, amid a perfect whirlwind of smoke, "no more sagacious agent could, I suppose, be desired, or even imagined."

"You flatter me," replied the Prefect; "but it is possible that some such opinion may have been entertained."

"It is clear," said I, "as you observe, that the letter is still in the possession of the minister; since it is this possession, and not any employment of the letter, which bestows the power. With the employment the power departs."

"True," said G.; "and upon this conviction I proceeded. My first care was to make thorough search of the minister's hotel, and here my chief embarrassment lay in the necessity of searching without his knowledge. Beyond all things, I have been warned of the danger which would result from giving him reason to suspect our design."

35   "But," said I, "you are quite *au fait*° in these investigations. The Parisian police have done this thing often before."

"O yes; and for this reason I did not despair. The habits of the minister gave me, too, a great advantage. He is frequently absent from home all night. His servants are by no means numerous. They sleep at a distance from their master's apartment, and being chiefly Neapolitans, are readily made drunk. I have keys, as you know, with which I can open any chamber or cabinet in Paris. For three months a night has not passed, during the greater part of which I have not been engaged, personally, in ransacking the D——Hôtel. My honour is interested, and, to mention a great secret, the reward is enormous. So I did not abandon the search until I had become fully satisfied that the thief is a more astute man than myself. I fancy that I have investigated every nook and corner of the premises in which it is possible that the paper can be concealed."

"But is it not possible," I suggested, "that although the letter may be in the possession of the minister, as it unquestionably is, he may have concealed it elsewhere than upon his own premises?"

"This is barely possible," said Dupin. "The present peculiar condition of affairs at court, and especially of those intrigues in which D——is known to be involved, would render the instant availability of the document—its susceptibility of being produced at a moment's notice—a point of nearly equal importance with its possession."

°*au fait*: Adept.

"Its susceptibility of being produced?" said I.

"That is to say, of being *destroyed*," said Dupin.   40

"True," I observed; "the paper is clearly then upon the premises. As for its being upon the person of the minister, we may consider that as out of the question."

"Entirely," said the Prefect. "He had been twice waylaid, as if by footpads, and his person rigorously searched under my own inspection."

"You might have spared yourself this trouble," said Dupin. "D——, I presume, is not altogether a fool, and, if not, must have anticipated these waylayings, as a matter of course."

"Not *altogether* a fool," said G., "but then he is a poet, which I take to be only one remove from a fool."

"True," said Dupin, after a long and thoughtful whiff from his meerschaum, "al-   45
though I have been guilty of certain doggerel myself."

"Suppose you detail," said I, "the particulars of your search."

"Why the fact is, we took our time, and we searched *every where*. I have had long experience in these affairs. I took the entire building, room by room; devoting the nights of a whole week to each. We examined, first, the furniture of each apartment. We opened every possible drawer; and I presume you know that, to a properly trained police agent, such a thing as a *secret* drawer is impossible. Any man is a dolt who permits a 'secret' drawer to escape him in a search of this kind. The thing is *so* plain. There is a certain amount of bulk—of space—to be accounted for in every cabinet. Then we have accurate rules. The fiftieth part of a line could not escape us. After the cabinets we took the chairs. The cushions we probed with the fine long needles you have seen me employ. From the tables we removed the tops."

"Why so?"

"Sometimes the top of a table, or other similarly arranged piece of furniture, is removed by the person wishing to conceal an article; then the leg is excavated, the article deposited within the cavity, and the top replaced. The bottoms and tops of bedposts are employed in the same way."

"But could not the cavity be defected by sounding?" I asked.   50

"By no means, if, when the article is deposited, a sufficient wadding of cotton be placed around it. Besides, in our case, we were obliged to proceed without noise."

"But you could not have removed—you could not have taken to pieces *all* articles of furniture in which it would have been possible to make a deposit in the manner you mention. A letter may be compressed into a thin spiral roll, not differing much in shape or bulk from a large knitting-needle, and in this form it might be inserted into the rung of a chair, for example. You did not take to pieces all the chairs?"

"Certainly not; but we did better—we examined the rungs of every chair in the hotel, and indeed the jointings of every description of furniture, by the aid of a most powerful microscope.° Had there been any traces of recent disturbance we should not have failed to detect it instantly. A single grain of gimlet-dust, for example, would have been as obvious as an apple. Any disorder in the glueing—any unusual gaping in the joints—would have sufficed to insure detection."

"I presume you looked to the mirrors, between the boards and the plates, and you probed the beds and the bed-clothes, as well as the curtains and carpets."

"That of course; and when we had absolutely completed every particle of the fur-   55
niture in this way, then we examined the house itself. We divided its entire surface

---

°*microscope*: Magnifying glass.

into compartments, which we numbered, so that none might be missed; then we scrutinized each individual square inch throughout the premises, including the two houses immediately adjoining, with the microscope as before."

"The two houses adjoining!" I exclaimed; "you must have had a great deal of trouble."

"We had; but the reward offered is prodigious."

"You include the *grounds* about the houses?"

"All the grounds are paved with brick. They gave us comparatively little trouble. We examined the moss between the bricks, and found it undisturbed."

60 "You looked among D——'s papers, of course, and into the books of the library?"

"Certainly; we opened every package and parcel; we not only opened every book, but we turned over every leaf in each volume, not contenting ourselves with a mere shake, according to the fashion of some of our police officers. We also measured the thickness of every book-*cover*, with the most accurate admeasurement, and applied to each the most jealous scrutiny of the microscope. Had any of the bindings been recently meddled with, it would have been utterly impossible that the fact should have escaped observation. Some five or six volumes, just from the hands of the binder, we carefully probed, longitudinally, with the needles."

"You explored the floors beneath the carpets?"

"Beyond doubt. We removed every carpet, and examined the boards with the microscope."

"And the paper on the walls?"

65 "Yes."

"You looked into the cellars?"

"We did."

"Then," I said, "you have been making a miscalculation, and the letter is *not* upon the premises as you suppose."

"I fear you are right there," said the Prefect. "And now, Dupin, what would you advise me to do?"

70 "To make a thorough re-search of the premises."

"That is absolutely needless," replied G——. "I am not more sure that I breathe than I am that the letter is not at the Hôtel."

"I have no better advice to give you," said Dupin. "You have, of course, an accurate description of the letter?"

"Oh, yes!"—And here the Prefect, producing a memorandum-book, proceeded to read aloud a minute account of the internal, and especially of the external, appearance of the missing document. Soon after finishing the perusal of this description, he took his departure, more entirely depressed in spirits than I had ever known the good gentleman before.

In about a month afterward he paid us another visit, and found us occupied very nearly as before. He took a pipe and a chair and entered into some ordinary conversation. At length I said;—

75 "Well, but G——, what of the purloined letter? I presume you have at last made up your mind that there is no such thing as overreaching the Minister?"

"Confound him, say I—yes; I made the re-examination, however, as Dupin suggested—but it was all labour lost, as I knew it would be."

"How much was the reward offered, did you say?" asked Dupin.

"Why, a very great deal—a *very* liberal reward—I don't like to say how much, precisely; but one thing I *will* say, that I wouldn't mind giving my individual check for fifty thousand francs to any one who could obtain me that letter. The fact is, it is becoming of more and more importance every day; and the reward has been lately doubled. If it were trebled, however, I could do no more than I have done."

"Why, yes," said Dupin, drawlingly, between the whiffs of his meeschaum, "I really—think, G——, you have not exerted yourself—to the utmost in this matter. You might—do a little more, I think, eh?"

"How?—in what way?"

"Why—puff, puff,—you might—puff, puff—employ counsel in the matter, eh?— puff, puff, puff. Do you remember the story they tell of Abernethy?"°

"No; hang Abernethy!"

"To be sure! hang him and welcome. But, once upon a time, a certain rich miser conceived the design of spunging upon this Abernethy for a medical opinion. Getting up, for this purpose, an ordinary conversation in a private company, he insinuated his case to the physician, as that of an imaginary individual.

"'We will suppose,' said the miser, 'that his symptoms are such and such; now, doctor, what would *you* have directed him to take?'"

"'Take!' said Abernethy, 'why, take *advice*, to be sure.'"

"But," said the Prefect, a little discomposed, "I am *perfectly* willing to take advice, and to pay for it. I would *really* give fifty thousand francs to any one who would aid me in the matter."

"In that case," replied Dupin, opening a drawer, and producing a check-book, "you may as well fill me up a check for the amount you mentioned. When you have signed it, I will hand you the letter."

I was astounded. The Prefect appeared absolutely thunderstricken. For some minutes he remained speechless and motionless, looking incredulously at my friend with open mouth, and eyes that seemed starting from their sockets; then, apparently recovering himself in some measure, he seized a pen, and after several pauses and vacant stares, finally filled up and signed a check for fifty thousand francs, and handed it across the table to Dupin. The latter examined it carefully and deposited it in his pocket-book; then, unlocking an *escritoire*, took thence a letter and gave it to the Prefect. This functionary grasped it in a perfect agony of joy, opened it with a trembling hand, cast a rapid glance at its contents, and then, scrambling and struggling to the door, rushed at length unceremoniously from the room and from the house, without having uttered a syllable since Dupin had requested him to fill up the check.

When he had gone, my friend entered into some explanations.

"The Parisian police," he said, "are exceedingly able in their way. They are persevering, ingenious, cunning, and thoroughly versed in the knowledge which their duties seem chiefly to demand. Thus, when G——detailed to us his mode of searching the premises at the Hôtel D——, I felt entire confidence in his having made a satisfactory investigation—so far as his labours extended."

"So far as his labours extended?" said I.

"Yes," said Dupin. "The measures adopted were not only the best of their kind, but carried out to absolute perfection. Had the letter been deposited within the range of their search, these fellows would, beyond a question, have found it."

I merely laughed—but he seemed quite serious in all that he said.

"The measures, then," he continued, "were good in their kind, and well executed; their defect lay in their being inapplicable to the case, and to the man. A certain set of highly ingenious resources are, with the Prefect, a sort of Procrustean bed, to which he

---

°*Abernethy*: John Abernethy (1764–1831), English physician.

forcibly adapts his designs. But he perpetually errs by being too deep or too shallow, for the matter in hand; and many a schoolboy is a better reasoner than he. I knew one about eight years of age, whose success at guessing in the game of 'even and odd' attracted universal admiration. This game is simple, and is played with marbles. One player holds in his hand a number of these toys, and demands of another whether that number is even or odd. If the guess is right, the guesser wins one; if wrong, he loses one. The boy to whom I allude won all the marbles of the school. Of course he had some principle of guessing; and this lay in mere observation and admeasurement of the astuteness of his opponents. For example, an arrant simpleton is his opponent, and, holding up his closed hand, asks: 'Are they even or odd?' Our schoolboy replies, 'Odd,' and loses; but upon the second trial he wins, for he then says to himself, 'The simpleton had them even upon the first trial, and his amount of cunning is just sufficient to make him have them odd upon the second; I will therefore guess odd;'—he guesses odd, and wins. Now, with a simpleton a degree above the first, he would have reasoned thus: 'This fellow finds that in the first instance I guessed odd, and, in the second, he will propose to himself upon the first impulse, a simple variation from even to odd, as did the first simpleton; but then a second thought will suggest that this is too simple a variation, and finally he will decide upon putting it even as before. I will therefore guess even;'—he guesses even, and wins. Now this mode of reasoning in the schoolboy, whom his fellows termed 'lucky,'—what, in its last analysis, is it?"

95   "It is merely," I said, "an identification of the reasoner's intellect with that of his opponent."

"It is," said Dupin; "and, upon inquiring of the boy by what means he effected the *thorough* identification in which his success consisted, I received answer as follows: 'When I wish to find out how wise, or how stupid, or how good, or how wicked is any one, or what are his thoughts at the moment, I fashion the expression on my face, as accurately as possible, in accordance with the expression of his, and then wait to see what thoughts or sentiments arise in my mind or heart, as if to match or correspond with the expression.' This response of the schoolboy lies at the bottom of all the spurious profundity which has been attributed to Rochefoucault, to La Bougive, to Machiavelli, and to Campanella."°

"And the identification," I said, "of the reasoner's intellect with that of his opponent, depends, if I understand you aright, upon the accuracy with which the opponent's intellect is admeasured."

"For its practical value it depends upon this," replied Dupin; "and the Prefect and his cohort fail so frequently, first, by default of this identification, and secondly, by ill-admeasurement, or rather through non-admeasurement, of the intellect with which they are engaged. They consider only their *own* ideas of ingenuity; and, in searching for anything hidden, advert only to the modes in which *they* would have hidden it. They are right in this much—that their own ingenuity is a faithful representative of that of *the mass*; but when the cunning of the individual felon is diverse in character from their own, the felon foils them, of course. This always happens when it is above their own, and very usually when it is below. They have no variation of principle in their investigations; at best, when urged by some unusual emergency—by some extraordinary reward—they extend or exaggerate their old modes of *practice*, without touching their principles. What, for example, in this case of D——, has been done to vary the

---

°. . . *to Campanella*: Francois de La Rochefoucauld (1613–1680), Niccolò Machiavelli (1469–1597), and Tommaso Campanella (1568–1639) all saw self-interest as the mainspring of human motivation. In "La Bougive," Poe probably intended a reference to Jean de la Bruyère (1645–1696).

principle of action? What is all this boring, and probing, and sounding, and scrutinizing with the microscope, and dividing the surface of the building into registered square inches—what is it all but an exaggeration *of the application* of one principle or set of principles of search, which are based upon the one set of notions regarding human ingenuity, to which the Prefect, in the long routine of his duty, has been accustomed? Do you not see he has taken it for granted that *all* men proceed to conceal a letter,—not exactly in a gimlet-hole bored in a chair-leg—but, at least, in *some* out-of-the-way hole or corner suggested by the same tenor or thought which would urge a man to secrete a letter in a gimlet-hole bored in a chair-leg? As do you not see also, that such *recherchés*° nooks for concealment are adapted only for ordinary occasions, and would be adopted only by ordinary intellects; for, in all cases of concealment, a disposal of the article concealed—a disposal of it in this *recherché* manner—is, in the very first instance, presumable and presumed; and thus its discovery depends, not at all upon the acumen, but altogether upon the mere care, patience, and determination of the seekers; and where the case is of importance—or, what amounts to the same thing in the political eyes, when the reward is of magnitude,—the qualities in question have *never* been known to fail. You will now understand what I meant in suggesting that, had the purloined letter been hidden anywhere within the limits of the Prefect's examination—in other words, had the principle of its concealment been comprehended within the principles of the Prefect—its discovery would have been a matter altogether beyond question. This functionary, however, has been thoroughly mystified; and the remote source of his defeat lies in the supposition that the Minister is a fool, because he has acquired renown as a poet. All fools are poets; this the Prefect *feels*; and he is merely guilty of a *non distributio medii*° in thence inferring that all poets are fools.

"But is this really the poet?" I asked. "There are two brothers, I know; and both have attained reputation in letters. The Minister I believe has written learnedly on the Differential Calculus. He is a mathematician, and no poet."

"You are mistaken; I know him well: he is both. As poet *and* mathematician, he would reason well; as mere mathematician, he could not have reasoned at all, and thus would have been at the mercy of the Prefect." 100

"You surprise me," I said, "by these opinions, which have been contradicted by the voice of the world. You do not mean to set at naught the well-digested idea of centuries. The mathematical reason has long been regarded as *the* reason *par excellence*."

"'*Il y a à parier*,'" replied Dupin, quoting from Chamfort, "'*que toute idée publique, toute convention reçue, est une sottise, car elle a convenu au plus grand nombre.*'"° The mathematicians, I grant you, have done their best to promulgate the popular error to which you allude, and which is none the less an error for its promulgation as truth. With an art worthy a better cause, for example, they have insinuated the term 'analysis' into application to algebra. The French are the originators of this particular deception; but if a term is of any importance—if words derive any value from applicability—then 'analysis' conveys 'algebra' about as much as, in Latin, '*ambitus*' implies 'ambition,' '*religio*' 'religion,' or '*homines honesti*,' a set of *honourable* men."

"You have a quarrel on hand, I see," said I, "with some of the algebraists of Paris; but proceed."

°*recherchés*: Excessively clever.
°*non distributio medii*: The undistributed middle, an error in deductive reasoning.
°"*. . . plus grand nombre.*": "The chances are that every popular idea, every accepted convention, is nonsense, because it is acceptable to the majority." *Maximes et Pensées* by Sébastien Chamfort (1741–1794).

"I dispute the availability, and thus the value, of that reason which is cultivated in any especial form other than the abstractly logical. I dispute, in particular, the reason educed by mathematical study. The mathematics are the science of form and quantity; mathematical reasoning is merely logic applied to observation upon form and quantity. The great error lies in supposing that even the truths of what is called *pure* algebra, are abstract or general truths. And this error is so egregious that I am confounded at the universality with which it has been received. Mathematical axioms are *not* axioms of general truth. What is true of *relation*—of form and quantity—is often grossly false in regard to morals, for example. In this latter science it is very usually *un*true that the aggregated parts are equal to the whole. In chemistry also the axiom fails. In the consideration of motive it fails; for two motives, each of a given value, have not, necessarily, a value when united, equal to the sum of their values apart. There are numerous other mathematical truths which are only truths within the limits of *relation*. But the mathematician argues from his *finite truths*, through habit, as if they were of an absolutely general applicability—as the world indeed imagines them to be. Bryant, in his very learned 'Mythology,'° mentions an analogous source of error, when he says that 'although the Pagan fables are not believed, yet we forget ourselves continually, and make inferences from them as existing realities.' With the algebraists, however, who are Pagans themselves, the 'Pagan fables' *are* believed, and the inferences are made, not so much through lapse of memory as through an unaccountable addling of the brains. In short, I never yet encountered the mere mathematician who could be trusted out of equal roots, or one who did not clandestinely hold it as a point of his faith that $x^2 - px$ was absolutely and unconditionally equal to q. Say to one of these gentlemen, by way of experiment, if you please, that you believe occasions may occur where $x^2 + px$ is not altogether equal to q, and having made him understand what you mean, get out of his reach as speedily as convenient, for, beyond doubt, he will endeavour to knock you down.

105   "I mean to say," continued Dupin, while I merely laughed at his last observations, "that if the Minister had been no more than a mathematician, the Prefect would have been under no necessity of giving me this check. I knew him, however, as both mathematician and poet, and my measures were adapted to his capacity, with reference to the circumstances by which he was surrounded. I knew him as a courtier, too, and as a bold *intriguant*. Such a man, I considered, could not fail to be aware of the ordinary political modes of action. He could not have failed to anticipate—and events have proved that he did not fail to anticipate—the waylayings to which he was subjected. He must have foreseen, I reflected, the secret investigations of his premises. His frequent absences from home at night, which were hailed by the Prefect as certain aids to his success, I regarded only as *ruses*, to afford opportunity for thorough search to the police, and thus the sooner to impress them with the conviction to which G——, in fact, did finally arrive—the conviction that the letter was not upon the premises. I felt, also, that the whole train of thought, which I was at some pains in detailing to you just now, concerning the invariable principle of political action in searches for articles concealed—I felt that this whole train of thought would necessarily pass through the mind of the Minister. It would imperatively lead him to despise all the ordinary *nooks* of concealment. *He* could not, I reflected, be so weak as not to see that the most intricate and remote recess of his hotel would be as open as his commonest closets to the eyes, to the probes, to the gimlets, and to the microscopes of the Prefect. I saw, in fine, that he

---

°*Mythology*: *Antient Mythology* by Jacob Bryant (1715–1804).

would be driven, as a matter of course, to simplicity, if not deliberately induced to it as a matter of choice. You will remember, perhaps, how desperately the Prefect laughed when I suggested, upon our first interview, that it was just possible this mystery troubled him so much on account of its being so *very* self-evident."

"Yes," said I, "I remember his merriment well. I really thought he would have fallen into convulsions."

"The material world," continued Dupin, "abounds with very strict analogies to the immaterial; and thus some color of truth has been given to the rhetorical dogma, that metaphor, or simile, may be made to strengthen an argument as well as to embellish a description. The principle of the *vis inertiae*,° for example, seems to be identical in physics and metaphysics. It is not more true in the former, that a large body is with more difficulty set in motion than a smaller one, and that its subsequent *momentum* is commensurate with this difficulty, than it is, in the latter, that intellects of the vaster capacity, while more forcible, more constant, and more eventful in their movements than those of inferior grade, are yet the less readily moved, and more embarrassed and full of hesitation in the first few steps of their progress. Again: have you ever noticed which of the street signs, over the shop doors, are the most attractive of attention?"

"I have never given the matter a thought," I said.

"There is a game of puzzles," he resumed, "which is played upon a map. One party playing requires another to find a given word—the name of town, river, state, or empire—any word, in short, upon the motley and perplexed surface of the chart. A novice in the game generally seeks to embarrass his opponents by giving them the most minutely lettered names; but the adept selects such words as stretch, in large characters, from one end of the chart to the other. These, like the over-largely lettered signs and placards of the street, escape observation by the dint of being excessively obvious; and here the physical oversight is precisely analogous with the moral inapprehension by which the intellect suffers to pass unnoticed those considerations which are too obtrusively and too palpably self-evident. But this is a point, it appears, somewhat above or beneath the understanding of the Prefect. He never once thought it probable, or possible, that the Minister had deposited the letter immediately beneath the nose of the whole world, by way of best preventing any portion of that world from perceiving it.

"But the more I reflected upon the daring, dashing, and discriminating ingenuity   110 of D——; upon the fact that the document must always have been *at hand*, if he intended to use it to good purpose; and upon the decisive evidence, obtained by the Prefect, that it was not hidden within the limits of that dignitary's ordinary search—the more satisfied I became that, to conceal this letter, the Minister had resorted to the comprehensive and sagacious expedient of not attempting to conceal it at all.

"Full of these ideas, I prepared myself with a pair of green spectacles, and called one fine morning, quite by accident, at the Ministerial hotel. I found D——at home, yawning, lounging, and dawdling, as usual, and pretending to be in the last extremity of *ennui*. He is, perhaps, the most really energetic human being now alive—but that is only when nobody sees him.

"To be even with him, I complained of my weak eyes, and lamented the necessity of the spectacles, under cover of which I cautiously and thoroughly surveyed the whole apartment, while seemingly intent only upon the conversation of my host.

"I paid especial attention to a large writing-table near which he sat, and upon which lay confusedly, some miscellaneous letters and other papers, with one or two musical

---

°*vis inertiae*: The power of inertia.

instruments and a few books. Here, however, after a long and very deliberate scrutiny, I saw nothing to excite particular suspicion.

"At length my eyes, in going the circuit of the room, fell upon a trumpery filigree
card-rack of pasteboard, that hung dangling by a dirty blue ribbon, from a little brass
knob just beneath the middle of the mantel-piece. In this rack, which had three or four
compartments, were five or six visiting cards and a solitary letter. This last was much
soiled and crumpled. It was torn nearly in two, across the middle—as if a design, in
the first instance, to tear it entirely up as worthless, had been altered, or stayed, in the
second. It has a large black seal, bearing the D——cipher *very* conspicuously, and was
addressed, in a diminutive female hand, to D——, the minister, himself. It was thrust
carelessly, and even, as it seemed, contemptuously, into one of the upper divisions of
the rack.

115   "No sooner had I glanced at this letter then I concluded it to be that of which I was
in search. To be sure, it was, to all appearance, radically different from the one of which
the Prefect had read us so minute a description. Here the seal was large and black,
with the D——cipher; there it was small and red, with the ducal arms of the S——
family. Here, the address, to the Minister, was diminutive and feminine; there the su-
perscription, to a certain royal personage, was markedly bold and decided; the size
alone formed a point of correspondence. But, then, the *radicalness* of these differences,
which was excessive; the dirt; the soiled and torn condition of the paper, so inconsis-
tent with the *true* methodical habits of D——, and so suggestive of a design to delude
the beholder into an idea of the worthlessness of the document; these things, together with the hyperobtrusive situation of this document, full in the view of every visitor, and thus exactly in accordance with the conclusions to which I had previously
arrived; these things, I say, were strongly corroborative of suspicion, in one who came
with the intention to suspect.

"I protracted my visit as long as possible, and, while I maintained a most animated discussion with the Minister, upon a topic which I knew well had never failed to
interest and excite him, I kept my attention really riveted upon the letter. In this examination, I committed to memory its external appearance and arrangement in the
rack; and also fell, at length, upon a discovery which set at rest whatever trivial doubt
I might have entertained. In scrutinizing the edges of the paper, I observed them to be
more *chafed* than seemed necessary. They presented the *broken* appearance which is
manifested when a stiff paper, having been once folded and pressed with a folder, is
refolded in a reversed direction, in the same creases or edges which had formed the
original fold. This discovery was sufficient. It was clear to me that the letter had been
turned, as a glove, inside out, re-directed, and resealed. I bade the Minister good morning, and took my departure at once, leaving a gold snuff-box upon the table.

"The next morning I called for the snuff-box, when we resumed, quite eagerly, the
conversation of the preceding day. While thus engaged, however, a loud report, as if
of a pistol, was heard immediately beneath the windows of the hotel, and was succeeded by a series of fearful screams, and the shoutings of a mob. D——rushed to a
casement, threw it open, and looked out. In the meantime I stepped to the cardrack,
took the letter, put it in my pocket, and replaced it by a *fac-simile,* (so far as regards externals) which I had carefully prepared at my lodgings; imitating the D——cipher,
very readily, by means of a seal formed of bread.

"The disturbance in the street had been occasioned by the frantic behaviour of a man
with a musket. He had fired it among a crowd of women and children. It proved, however, to have been without ball, and the fellow was suffered to go his way as a lunatic

or a drunkard. When he had gone, D——came from the window, whither I had followed him immediately upon securing the object in view. Soon afterward I bade him farewell. The pretended lunatic was a man in my own pay."

"But what purpose had you," I asked, "in replacing the letter by a *fac-simile?* Would it not have been better, at the first visit, to have seized it openly, and departed?"

"D——," replied Dupin, "is a desperate man, and a man of nerve. His hotel, too, is   120
not without attendants devoted to his interests. Had I made the wild attempt you suggest, I might never have left the Ministerial presence alive. The good people of Paris might have heard of me no more. But I had an object apart from these considerations. You know my political prepossessions. In this matter, I act as a partisan of the lady concerned. For eighteen months the Minister has had her in his power. She has now him in hers; since, being unaware that the letter is not in his possession, he will proceed with his exactions as if it was. Thus will he inevitably commit himself, at once, to his political destruction. His downfall, too, will not be more precipitate than awkward. It is all very well to talk about the *facilis descensus Averni;*° but in all kinds of climbing, as Catalani° said of singing, it is far more easy to get up than to come down. In the present instance I have no sympathy—at least no pity—for him who descends. He is that *monstrum horrendum*, an unprincipled man of genius. I confess, however, that I should like very well to know the precise character of his thoughts, when, being defied by her whom the Prefect terms 'a certain personage,' he is reduced to opening the letter which I left for him in the card-rack."

"How? did you put any thing particular in it?"

"Why—it did not seem altogether right to leave the interior blank—that would have been insulting. D——, at Vienna once, did me an evil turn, which I told him, quite good-humouredly, that I should remember. So, as I knew he would feel some curiosity in regard to the identity of the person who had outwitted him, I thought it a pity not to give him a clue. He is well acquainted with my MS., and I just copied into the middle of the blank sheet the words—

> ——*Un dessein si funeste,*
> *S'il n'est digne d' Atrée, est digne*
> *de Thyeste.*   125

They are to be found in Crébillon's 'Atrée.'"°   [1845]

QUESTIONS

1. How are the opening epigraph and the closing quotation appropriate to the story?
2. What do the Parisian setting and atmosphere contribute to the plot?
3. How do the narrator and Dupin complement one another?

°*facilis descensus Averni*: "Easy is the descent into hell." Vergil's *Aeneid.*
°*Catalini*: Angelica Catalini (1780–1849), Italian singer.
°*Crébillon's Atrée*: "A design so deadly, if not worthy of Atreus, is worthy of Thyestes." *Atrée et Thyeste* by Prosper Jolyot de Crebillon (1674–1762).

4. What does the story have to say about the scientific and poetic character?
5. How is the focus of the story changed by revealing the thief at the beginning?

RESPONSES

1. Write an essay exploring the division between scientific thought and poetic thought as presented in this story. Also consider these ideas as explored by Hawthorne in "The Birthmark."
2. Compare Poe's detective story to Nolan's story "Memento Mori" and to the movie *Memento*. What qualities of Poe's technique are preserved in the contemporary narratives?

KATHERINE ANNE PORTER

Katherine Anne Porter (1890–1980) was born in Indian Creek, Texas. By the time she was twenty-one she had been married for five years, divorced, and was working as a journalist in the Midwest. After World War I she went to Mexico, an experience that provided subject matter for several of her finest stories. Her first collection of stories, *Flowering Judas and Other Stories*, appeared in 1930 and was followed by her critically acclaimed novellas *Noon Wine* (1937) and *Pale Horse, Pale Rider* (1939). Though few, her stories are superbly crafted. After World War II she taught in several universities while working on her long-awaited novel *Ship of Fools*, which appeared in 1962. *The Collected Stories of Katherine Anne Porter* (1965) was awarded both the Pulitzer Prize and the National Book Award.

Flowering Judas

Braggioni sits heaped upon the edge of a straight-backed chair much too small for him, and sings to Laura in a furry, mournful voice. Laura has begun to find reasons for avoiding her own house until the latest possible moment, for Braggioni is there almost every night. No matter how late she is, he will be sitting there with a surly, waiting expression, pulling at his kinky yellow hair, thumbing the strings of his guitar, snarling a tune under his breath. Lupe the Indian maid meets Laura at the door, and says with a flicker of a glance towards the upper room, "He waits."

Laura wishes to lie down, she is tired of her hairpins and the feel of her long tight sleeves, but she says to him, "Have you a new song for me this evening?" If he says yes, she asks him to sing it. If he says no, she remembers his favorite one, and asks him to sing it again. Lupe brings her a cup of chocolate and a plate of rice, and Laura eats at the small table under the lamp, first inviting Braggioni, whose answer is always the same: "I have eaten, and besides, chocolate thickens the voice."

Laura says, "Sing, then," and Braggioni heaves himself into song. He scratches the guitar familiarly as though it were a pet animal, and sings passionately off key, taking the high notes in a prolonged painful squeal. Laura, who haunts the markets listening to the ballad singers, and stops every day to hear the blind boy playing his reed-flute in Sixteenth of September Street, listens to Braggioni with pitiless courtesy, because she dares not smile at his miserable performance. Nobody dares to smile at

967

him. Braggioni is cruel to everyone, with a kind of specialized insolence, but he is so vain of his talents, and so sensitive to slights, it would require a cruelty and vanity greater than his own to lay a finger on the vast cureless wound of his self-esteem. It would require courage, too, for it is dangerous to offend him, and nobody has this courage.

Braggioni loves himself with such tenderness and amplitude and eternal charity that his followers—for he is a leader of men, a skilled revolutionist, and his skin has been punctured in honorable warfare—warm themselves in the reflected glow, and say to each other: "He has a real nobility, a love of humanity raised above mere personal affections." The excess of this self-love has flowed out, inconveniently for her, over Laura, who, with so many others, owes her comfortable situation and her salary to him. When he is in a very good humor, he tells her, "I am tempted to forgive you for being a *gringa. Gringita!*"° and Laura, burning, imagines herself leaning forward suddenly, and with a sound back-handed slap wiping the suety smile from his face. If he notices her eyes at these moments he gives no sign.

5   She knows what Braggioni would offer her, and she must resist tenaciously without appearing to resist, and if she could avoid it she would not admit even to herself the slow drift of his intention. During these long evenings which have spoiled a long month for her, she sits in her deep chair with an open book on her knees, resting her eyes on the consoling rigidity of the printed page when the sight and sound of Braggioni singing threaten to identify themselves with all her remembered afflictions and to add their weight to her uneasy premonitions of the future. The gluttonous bulk of Braggioni has become a symbol of her many disillusions, for a revolutionist should be lean, animated by heroic fath, a vessel of abstract virtues. This is nonsense, she knows it now and is ashamed of it. Revolution must have leaders, and leadership is a career for energetic men. She is, her comrades tell her, full of romantic error, for what she defines as cynicism in them is merely "a developed sense of reality." She is almost too willing to say, "I am wrong, I suppose I don't really understand the principles," and afterward she makes a secret truce with herself, determined not to surrender her will to such expedient logic. But she cannot help feeling that she has been betrayed irreparably by the disunion between her way of living and her feeling of what life should be, and at times she is almost contented to rest in this sense of grievance as a private store of consolation. Sometimes she wishes to run away, but she stays. Now she longs to fly out of this room, down the narrow stairs, and into the street where the houses lean together like conspirators under a single mottled lamp, and leave Braggioni singing to himself.

Instead she looks at Braggioni, frankly and clearly, like a good child who understands the rules of behavior. Her knees cling together under sound blue serge, and her round white collar is not purposely nun-like. She wears the uniform of an idea, and has renounced vanities. She was born Roman Catholic, and in spite of her fear of being seen by someone who might make a scandal of it, she slips now and again into some crumbling little church, kneels on the chilly stone, and says a Hail Mary on the gold rosary she bought in Tehuantepec. It is no good and she ends by examining the altar with its tinsel flowers and ragged brocades, and feels tender about the battered doll-shape of some male saint whose white, lace-trimmed drawers hang limply around his ankles below the hieratic dignity of his velvet robe. She has encased herself in a set of principles derived from her early training, leaving no detail of gesture or of personal taste untouched, and for this reason she will not wear lace made on machines. This is

---

°*Gringita*: Female diminutive of *gringa*, pejorative term for foreigners.

her private heresy, for in her special group the machine is sacred, and will be the salvation of the workers. She loves fine lace, and there is a tiny edge of fluted cobweb on this collar, which is one of twenty precisely alike, folded in blue tissue paper in the upper drawer of her clothes chest.

Braggioni catches her glance solidly as if he had been waiting for it, leans forward, balancing his paunch between his spread knees, and sings with tremendous emphasis, weighing his words. He has, the song relates, no father and no mother, nor even a friend to console him; lonely as a wave of the sea he comes and goes, lonely as a wave. His mouth opens round and yearns sideways, his balloon cheeks grow oily with the labor of song. He bulges marvelously in his expensive garments. Over his lavender collar, crushed upon a purple necktie, held by a diamond hoop: over his ammunition belt of tooled leather worked in silver, buckled cruelly around his gasping middle: over the tops of his glossy yellow shoes Braggioni swells with ominous ripeness, his mauve silk hose stretched taut, his ankles bound with the stout leather thongs of his shoes.

When he stretches his eyelids at Laura she notes again that his eyes are the true tawny yellow cat's eyes. He is rich, not in money, he tells her, but in power, and this power brings with it the blameless ownership of things, and the right to indulge his love of small luxuries. "I have a taste for the elegant refinements," he said once, flourishing a yellow silk handkerchief before her nose. "Smell that? It is Jockey Club, imported from New York." Nonetheless he is wounded by life. He will say so presently. "It is true everything turns to dust in the hand, to gall on the tongue." He sighs and his leather belt creaks like a saddle girth. "I am disappointed in everything as it comes. Everything." He shakes his head. "You, poor thing, you will be disappointed too. You are born for it. We are more alike than you realize in some things. Wait and see. Some day you will remember what I have told you, you will know that Braggioni was your friend."

Laura feels a slow chill, a purely physical sense of danger, a warning in her blood that violence, mutilation, a shocking death, wait for her with lessening patience. She has translated this fear into something homely, immediate, and sometimes hesitates before crossing the street. "My personal fate is nothing, except as the testimony of a mental attitude," she reminds herself, quoting from some forgotten philosophic primer, and is sensible enough to add, "Anyhow, I shall not be killed by an automobile if I can help it."

"It may be true I am as corrupt, in another way, as Braggioni," she thinks in spite of herself, "as callous, as incomplete," and if this is so, any kind of death seems preferable. Still she sits quietly, she does not run. Where could she go? Uninvited she has promised herself to this place; she can no longer imagine herself as living in another country, and there is no pleasure in remembering her life before she came here.

Precisely what is the nature of this devotion, its true motives, and what are its obligations? Laura cannot say. She spends part of her days in Xochimilco, near by, teaching Indian children to say in English, "The cat is on the mat." When she appears in the classroom they crowd about her with smiles on their wise, innocent, clay-colored faces, crying, "Good morning, my titcher!" in immaculate voices, and they make of her desk a fresh garden of flowers every day.

During her leisure she goes to union meetings and listens to busy important voices quarreling over tactics, methods, internal politics. She visits the prisoners of her own political faith in their cells, where they entertain themselves with counting cockroaches, repenting of their indiscretions, composing their memoirs, writing out manifestos and plans for their comrades who are still walking about free, hands in pockets,

10

sniffing fresh air. Laura brings them food and cigarettes and a little money, and she brings messages disguised in equivocal phrases from the men outside who dare not set foot in the prison for fear of disappearing into the cells kept empty for them. If the prisoners confuse night and day, and complain, "Dear little Laura, time doesn't pass in this infernal hole, and I won't know when it is time to sleep unless I have a reminder," she brings them their favorite narcotics, and says in a tone that does not wound them with pity, "Tonight will really be night for you," and though her Spanish amuses them, they find her comforting, useful. If they lose patience and all faith, and curse the slowness of their friends in coming to their rescue with money and influence, they trust her not to repeat everything, and if she inquires, "Where do you think we can find money, or influence?" they are certain to answer, "Well, there is Braggioni, why doesn't he do something?"

She smuggles letters from headquarters to men hiding from firing squads in back streets in mildewed houses, where they sit in tumbled beds and talk bitterly as if all Mexico were at their heels, when Laura knows positively they might appear at the band concert in the Alameda on Sunday morning, and no one would notice them. But Braggioni says, "Let them sweat a little. The next time they may be careful. It is very restful to have them out of the way for a while." She is not afraid to knock on any door in any street after midnight, and enter in the darkness, and say to one of these men who is really in danger: "They will be looking for you—seriously—tomorrow morning after six. Here is some money from Vicente. Go to Vera Cruz and wait."

She borrows money from the Roumanian agitator to give to his bitter enemy the Polish agitator. The favor of Braggioni is their disputed territory, and Braggioni holds the balance nicely, for he can use them both. The Polish agitator talks love to her over café tables, hoping to exploit what he believes is her secret sentimental preference for him, and he gives her misinformation which he begs her to repeat as the solemn truth to certain persons. The Roumanian is more adroit. He is generous with his money in all good causes, and lies to her with an air of ingenuous candor, as if he were her good friend and confidant. She never repeats anything they may say. Braggioni never asks questions. He has other ways to discover all that he wishes to know about them.

15   Nobody touches her, but all praise her gray eyes, and the soft, round under lip which promises gayety, yet is always grave, nearly always firmly closed: and they cannot understand why she is in Mexico. She walks back and forth on her errands, with puzzled eyebrows, carrying her little folder of drawings and music and school papers. No dancer dances more beautifully than Laura walks, and she inspires some amusing, unexpected ardors, which cause little gossip, because nothing comes of them. A young captain who had been a soldier in Zapata's° army attempted, during a horseback ride near Cuernavaca, to express his desire for her with the noble simplicity befitting a rude folk-hero: but gently, because he was gentle. This gentleness was his defeat, for when he alighted, and removed her foot from the stirrup, and essayed to draw her down into his arms, her horse, ordinarily a tame one, shied fiercely, reared and plunged away. The young hero's horse careered blindly after his stable-mate, and the hero did not return to the hotel until rather late that evening. At breakfast he came to her table in full charro° dress, gray buckskin jacket and trousers with strings of silver buttons down the leg, and he was in a humorous, careless mood. "May I sit with you?" and "You are a wonderful rider. I was terrified that you might be thrown and dragged. I should never have forgiven myself. But I cannot admire you enough for your riding!"

°*Zapata*: Emiliano Zapata (1879–1919), a leader of the Mexican revolution.
°*Charro*: Cowboy.

"I learned to ride in Arizona," said Laura.

"If you will ride with me again this morning, I promise you a horse that will not shy with you," he said. But Laura remembered that she must return to Mexico City at noon.

Next morning the children made a celebration and spent their playtime writing on the blackboard. "We lov ar ticher," and with tinted chalks they drew wreaths of flowers around the words. The young hero wrote her a letter: "I am a very foolish, wasteful, impulsive man. I should have first said I love you, and then you would not have run away. But you shall see me again." Laura thought, "I must send him a box of colored crayons," but she was trying to forgive herself for having spurred her horse at the wrong moment.

A brown, shock-haired youth came and stood in her patio one night and sang like a lost soul for two hours, but Laura could think of nothing to do about it. The moonlight spread a wash of gauzy silver over the clear spaces of the garden, and the shadows were cobalt blue. The scarlet blossoms of the Judas trees° were dull purple, and the names of the colors repeated themselves automatically in her mind, while she watched not the boy, but his shadow, fallen like a dark garment across the fountain rim, trailing in the water. Lupe came silently and whispered expert counsel in her ear: "If you will throw him one little flower, he will sing another song or two and go away!" Laura threw the flower, and he sang a last song and went away with the flower tucked in the band of his hat. Lupe said, "He is one of the organizers of the Typographers Union, and before that he sold corridos° in the Merced market, and before that, he came from Guanajuato, where I was born. I would not trust any man, but I trust least those from Guanajuato."

She did not tell Laura that he would be back again the next night, and the next, nor that he would follow her at a certain fixed distance around the Merced market, through the Zócolo, up Francisco I. Madero Avenue, and so along the Paseo de la Reforma to Chapultepec Park, and into the Philospher's Footpath, still with that flower withering in his hat, and an indivisible attention in his eyes.   20

Now Laura is accustomed to him, it means nothing except that he is nineteen years old and is observing a convention with all propriety, as though it were founded on a law of nature, which in the end it might well prove to be. He is beginning to write poems which he prints on a wooden press, and he leaves them stuck like handbills in her door. She is pleasantly disturbed by the abstract, unhurried watchfulness of his black eyes which will in time turn easily towards another object. She tells herself that throwing the flower was a mistake, for she is twenty-two years old and knows better; but she refuses to regret it, and persuades herself that her negation of all external events as they occur is a sign that she is gradually perfecting herself in the stoicism she strives to cultivate against that disaster she fears, though she cannot name it.

She is not at home in the world. Every day she teaches children who remain strangers to her, though she loves their tender round hands and their charming opportunist savagery. She knocks at unfamiliar doors not knowing whether a friend or a stranger shall answer, and even if a known face emerges from the sour gloom of that unknown interior, still it is the face of a stranger. No matter what this stranger says to her, nor what her message to him, the very cells of that flesh reject knowledge and kinship in one monotonous word. No. No. No. She draws her strength from this one

---

°*Judas trees*: According to legend, Judas Iscariot hanged himself on a tree of this kind.
°*corridos*: Ballads.

holy talismanic word which does not suffer her to be led into evil. Denying every-thing, she may walk anywhere in safety, she looks at everything without amazement.

No, repeats this firm unchanging voice of her blood; and she looks at Braggioni without amazement. He is a great man, he wishes to impress this simple girl who cov-ers her great round breasts with thick dark cloth, and who hides long, invaluably beau-tiful legs under a heavy skirt. She is almost thin except for the incomprehensible fullness of her breasts, like a nursing mother's, and Braggioni, who considers himself a judge of women, speculates again on the puzzle of her notorious virginity, and takes the liberty of speech which she permits without a sign of modesty, indeed, without any sort of sign, which is disconcerting.

"You think you are so cold, *gringita!* Wait and see. You will surprise yourself some day! May I be there to advise you!" He stretches his eyelids at her, and his ill-humored cat's eyes waver in a separate glance for the two points of light marking the opposite ends of a smoothly drawn path between the swollen curve of her breasts. He is not put off by that blue serge, nor by her resolutely fixed gaze. There is all the time in the world. His cheeks are bellying with the wind of song. "O girl with the dark eyes," he sings, and reconsiders. "But yours are not dark. I can change all that. O girl with the green eyes, you have stolen my heart away!" then his mind wanders to the song, and Laura feels the weight of his attention being shifted elsewhere. Singing thus, he seems harmless, he is quite harmless, there is nothing to do but sit patiently and say "No," when the moment comes. She draws a full breath, and her mind wanders also, but not far. She dares not wander too far.

25   Not for nothing has Braggioni taken pains to be a good revolutionist and a profes-sional lover of humanity. He will never die of it. He has the malice, the cleverness, the wickedness, the sharpness of wit, the hardness of heart, stipulated for loving the world profitably. *He will never die of it.* He will live to see himself kicked out from his feeding trough by other hungry world-saviors. Traditionally he must sing in spite of his life which drives him to bloodshed, he tells Laura, for his father was a Tuscany peasant who drifted to Yucatan and married a Maya woman: a woman of race, an aristocrat. They gave him the love and knowledge of music, thus: and under the tip of his thumbnail, the strings of the instrument complain like exposed nerves.

Once he was called Delgadito by all the girls and married women who ran after him; he was so scrawny all his bones showed under his thin cotton clothing, and he could squeeze his emptiness to the very backbone with his two hands. He was a poet and the revolution was only a dream then; too many women loved him and sapped away his youth, and he could never find enough to eat anywhere, anywhere! Now he is a leader of men, crafty men who whisper in his ear, hungry men who wait for hours outside his office for a word with him, emaciated men with wild faces who waylay him at the street gate with a timid, "Comrade, let me tell you . . ." and they blow the foul breath from their empty stomachs in his face.

He is always sympathetic. He gives them handfuls of small coins from his own pocket, he promises them work, there will be demonstrations, they must join the unions and attend the meetings, above all they must be on the watch for spies. They are clos-er to him than his own brothers, without them he can do nothing—until tomorrow, comrade!

Until tomorrow. "They are stupid, they are lazy, they are treacherous, they would cut my throat for nothing," he says to Laura. He has good food and abundant drink, he hires an automobile and drives in the Paseo on Sunday morning, and enjoys plen-ty of sleep in a soft bed beside a wife who dares not disturb him; and he sits pamper-ing his bones in easy billows of fat, singing to Laura, who knows and thinks these things about him. When he was fifteen, he tried to drown himself because he loved a girl, his first love, and she laughed at him. "A thousand women have paid for that," and his tight little mouth turns down at the corners. Now he perfumes his hair with Jockey Club, and confides to Laura: "One woman is really as good as another for me, in the dark. I prefer them all."

His wife organizes unions among the girls in the cigarette factories, and walks in picket lines, and even speaks at meetings in the evening. But she cannot be brought to acknowledge the benefits of true liberty. "I tell her I must have my freedom, net. She does not understand my point of view." Laura has heard this many times. Braggioni scratches the guitar and meditates. "She is an instinctively virtuous woman, pure gold, no doubt of that. If she were not, I should lock her up, and she knows it."

His wife, who works so hard for the good of the factory girls, employs part of her leisure lying on the floor weeping because there are so many women in the world, and only one husband for her, and she never knows where nor when to look for him. He told her: "Unless you can learn to cry when I am not here, I must go away for good." That day he went away and took a room at the Hotel Madrid. 30

It is this month of separation for the sake of higher principles that has been spoiled not only for Mrs. Braggioni, whose sense of reality is beyond criticism, but for Laura, who feels herself bogged in a nightmare. Tonight Laura envies Mrs. Braggioni, who is alone, and free to weep as much as she pleases about a concrete wrong. Laura has just come from a visit to the prison, and she is waiting for tomorrow with a bitter anxiety as if tomorrow may not come, but time may be caught immovably in this hour, with herself transfixed, Braggioni singing on forever, and Eugenio's body not yet discovered by the guard.

Braggioni says: "Are you going to sleep?" Almost before she can shake her head, he begins telling her about the May-day disturbances coming on in Morelia, for the Catholics hold a festival in honor of the Blessed Virgin, and the Socialists celebrate their martyrs on that day. "There will be two independent processions, starting from either end of town, and they will march until they meet, and the rest depends . . ." He asks her to oil and load his pistols. Standing up, he unbuckles his ammunition belt, and spreads it laden across her knees. Laura sits with the shells slipping through the cleaning cloth dipped in oil, and he says again he cannot understand why she works so hard for the revolutionary idea unless she loves some man who is in it. "Are you not in love with someone?" "No," says Laura. "And no one is in love with you?" "No." "Then it is your own fault. No woman need go begging. Why, what is the matter with you? The legless beggar woman in the Alameda has a perfectly faithful lover. Did you know that?"

Laura peers down the pistol barrel and says nothing, but a long, slow faintness rises and subsides in her; Braggioni curves his swollen fingers around the throat of the guitar and softly smothers the music out of it, and when she hears him again he seems to have forgotten her, and is speaking in the hypnotic voice he uses when talking in small rooms to a listening, close-gathered crowd. Some day this world, now seemingly so composed and eternal, to the edges of every sea shall be merely a tangle of gaping trenches, of crashing walls and broken bodies. Everything must be torn from its accustomed place where it has rotted for centuries, hurled skyward and distributed, cast down again clean as rain, without separate identity. Nothing shall survive that the stiffened hands of poverty have created for the rich and no one shall be left alive except the elect spirits destined to procreate a new world cleansed of cruelty and injustice, ruled by benevolent anarchy: "Pistols are good, I love them, cannon are even better, but in the end I pin my faith to good dynamite," he concludes, and strokes the pistol lying in her hands. "Once I dreamed of destroying this city, in case it offered resistance to General Ortíz,° but it fell into his hands like an overripe pear."

He is made restless by his own words, rises and stands waiting. Laura holds up the belt to him: "Put that on, and go kill somebody in Morelia, and you will be happier," she says softly. The presence of death in the room makes her bold. "Today, I found Eugenio going into a stupor. He refused to allow me to call the prison doctor. He had taken all the tablets I brought him yesterday. He said he took them because he was bored."

35   "He is a fool, and his death is his own business," says Braggioni, fastening his belt carefully.

"I told him if he had waited only a little while longer, you would have got him set free," says Laura. "He said he did not want to wait."

"He is a fool and we are well rid of him," says Braggioni, reaching for his hat.

He goes away. Laura knows his mood has changed, she will not see him any more for a while. He will send word when he needs her to go on errands into strange streets, to speak to the strange faces that will appear, like clay masks with the power of human speech, to mutter their thanks to Braggioni for his help. Now she is free, and she thinks, I must run while there is time. But she does not go.

Braggioni enters his own house where for a month his wife has spent many hours every night weeping and tangling her hair upon her pillow. She is weeping now, and she weeps more at the sight of him, the cause of all her sorrows. He looks about the room. Nothing is changed, the smells are good and familiar, he is well acquainted with the woman who comes toward him with no reproach except grief on her face. He says to her tenderly: "You are so good, please don't cry any more, you dear good creature." She says, "Are you tired, my angel? Sit here and I will wash your feet." She brings a bowl of water, and kneeling, unlaces his shoes, and when from her knees she raises her sad eyes under her blackened lids, he is sorry for everything, and bursts into tears. "Ah, yes, I am hungry, I am tired, let us eat something together," he says, between sobs. His wife leans her head on his arm and says, "Forgive me!" and this time he is refreshed by the solemn, endless rain of her tears.

40   Laura takes off her serge dress and puts on a white linen nightgown and goes to bed. She turns her head a little to one side, and lying still, reminds herself that it is time to sleep. Numbers tick in her brain like little clocks, soundless doors close of themselves around her. If you would sleep, you must not remember anything, the children will say tomorrow, good morning, my teacher, the poor prisoners who come every day bringing flowers to their jailer. 1–2–3–4–5—it is monstrous to confuse love with revolution, night with day, life with death—ah, Eugenio!

The tolling of the midnight bell is a signal, but what does it mean? Get up, Laura, and follow me: come out of your sleep, out of your bed, out of this strange house. What are you doing in this house? Without a word, without fear she rose and reached for Eugenio's hand, but he eluded her with a sharp, sly smile and drifted away. This is not all, you shall see—Murderer, he said, follow me. I will show you a new country, but it is far away and we must hurry. No, said Laura, not unless you take my hand, no; and she clung first to the stair rail, and then to the topmost branch of the Judas tree that bent down slowly and set her upon the earth, and then to the rocky ledge of a cliff, then to the jagged wave of a sea that was not water but a desert of crumbling stone. Where are you taking me, she asked in wonder but without fear. To death, and it is a long way

---

°*General Ortíz*: Pascual Ortiz Rubio (1877–1963), general who became president of Mexico.

off, and we must hurry, said Eugenio. No, said Laura, not unless you take my hand. Then eat these flowers, poor prisoner, said Eugenio in a voice of pity, take and eat: and from the Judas tree he stripped the warm bleeding flowers, and held them to her lips. She saw that his hand was fleshless, a cluster of small white petrified branches, and his eye sockets were without light, but she ate the flowers greedily for they satisfied both hunger and thirst. Murderer! said Eugenio, and Cannibal! This is my body and my blood. Laura cried No! And at the sound of her own voice, she awoke trembling, and was afraid to sleep again.   [1930]

Questions

1. How is Laura defined by her three suitors?
2. What does the Mexican setting contribute to the theme?
3. Why is Laura an isolated figure in her world?
4. What does the story have to say about the relation between orthodox religion and political revolution?
5. How effective is the dream at the end of the story in resolving Laura's conflicts?

Responses

1. For a time, Katherine Anne Porter did live in Mexico. Research this period of her life and this period in Mexico's history. What insights does that biographical and historical information bring to the story?
2. Review Porter's "The Writing of 'Flowering Judas,'" included in the "Context: Writers on Writing" section. To what extent can Porter and her character Laura be seen as imperialists?

The Grave

The grandfather, dead for more than thirty years, had been twice disturbed in his long repose by the constancy and possessiveness of his widow. She removed his bones first to Louisiana and then to Texas as if she had set out to find her own burial place, knowing well she would never return to the places she had left. In Texas she set up a small cemetery in a corner of her first farm, and as the family connection grew, and oddments of relations came over from Kentucky to settle, it contained at last about twenty graves. After the grandmother's death, part of her land was to be sold for the benefit of certain of her children, and the cemetery happened to lie in the part set aside for sale. It was necessary to take up the bodies and bury them again in the family plot in the big new public cemetery, where the grandmother had been buried. At last her husband was to lie beside her for eternity, as she had planned.

The family cemetery had been a pleasant small neglected garden of tangled rose bushes and ragged cedar trees and cypress, the simple flat stones rising out of uncropped sweet-smelling wild grass. The graves were lying open and empty one burning day when Miranda and her brother Paul, who often went together to hunt rabbits and doves, propped their twenty-two Winchester rifles carefully against the rail fence, climbed over and explored among the graves. She was nine years old and he was twelve.

They peered into the pits all shaped alike with such purposeful accuracy, and looking at each other with pleased adventurous eyes, they said in solemn tones: "These were graves!" trying by words to shape a special, suitable emotion in their minds, but they felt nothing except an agreeable thrill of wonder: they were seeing a new sight, doing something they had not done before. In them both there was also a small disappointment at the entire commonplaceness of the actual spectacle. Even if it had once contained a coffin for years upon years, when the coffin was gone a grave was just a hole in the ground. Miranda leaped into the pit that had held her grandfather's bones. Scratching around aimlessly and pleasurably as any young animal, she scooped up a lump of earth and weighted it in her palm. It had a pleasantly sweet, corrupt smell, being mixed with cedar needles and small leaves, and as the crumbs fell apart, she saw a silver dove no larger than a hazel nut, with spread wings and a neat fan-shaped tail. The breast had a deep round hollow in it. Turning it up to the fierce sunlight, she saw that the inside of the hollow was cut in little whorls. She scrambled out, over the pile of loose earth that had fallen back into one end of the grave, calling to Paul that she had found something, he must guess what . . . His head appeared smiling over the rim of another grave. He waved a closed hand at her. "I've got something too!" They ran to compare treasures, making a game of it, so many guesses each, all wrong, and a final showdown with opened palms. Paul had found a thin wide gold ring carved with intricate flowers and leaves. Miranda was smitten at sight of the ring and wished to have it. Paul seemed more impressed by the dove. They made a trade, with some little bickering. After he had got the dove in his hand, Paul said, "Don't you know what this is? This is a screw head for a *coffin!* . . . I'll bet nobody else in the world has one like this!"

Miranda glanced at it without covetousness. She had the gold ring on her thumb; it fitted perfectly. "Maybe we ought to go now," she said, "maybe one of the niggers'll see us and tell somebody." They knew the land had been sold, the cemetery was no longer theirs, and they felt like trespassers. They climbed back over the fence, slung their rifles loosely under their arms—they had been shooting at targets with various kinds of firearms since they were seven years old—and set out to look for the rabbits and doves or whatever small game might happen along. On these expeditions Miranda always followed at Paul's heels along the path, obeying instructions about handling her gun when going through fences; learning how to stand it up properly so it would not slip and fire unexpectedly; how to wait her time for a shot and not just bang away in the air without looking, spoiling shots for Paul, who really could hit things if given a chance. Now and then, in her excitement at seeing birds whizz up suddenly before her face, or a rabbit leap across her very toes, she lost her head, and almost without sighting she flung her rifle up and pulled the trigger. She hardly ever hit any sort of mark. She had no proper sense of hunting at all. Her brother would be often completely disgusted with her. "You don't care whether you get your bird or not," he said. "That's no way to hunt." Miranda could not understand his indignation. She had seen him smash his hat and yell with fury when he had missed his aim. "What I like about shooting," said Miranda, with exasperating inconsequence, "is pulling the trigger and hearing the noise."

"Then, by golly," said Paul, "whyn't you go back to the range and shoot at bullseyes?"

"I'd just as soon," said Miranda, "only like this, we walk around more."

"Well, you just stay behind and stop spoiling my shots," said Paul, who, when he made a kill, wanted to be certain he had made it. Miranda, who alone brought down a bird once in twenty rounds, always claimed as her own any game they got when they fired at the same moment. It was tiresome and unfair and her brother was sick of it.

"Now, the first dove we see, or the first rabbit, is mine," he told her. "And the next will be yours. Remember that and don't get smarty."

"What about snakes?" asked Miranda idly. "Can I have the first snake?"

Waving her thumb gently and watching her gold ring glitter, Miranda lost interest in shooting. She was wearing her summer roughing outfit: dark blue overalls, a light blue shirt, a hired-man's straw hat, and thick brown sandals. Her brother had the same outfit except his was a sober hickory-nut color. Ordinarily Miranda preferred her overalls to any other dress, though it was making rather a scandal in the countryside, for the year was 1903, and in the back country the law of female decorum had teeth in it. Her father had been criticized for letting his girls dress like boys and go careering around astride barebacked horses. Big sister Maria, the really independent and fearless one, in spite of her rather affected ways, rode at a dead run with only a rope knotted around her horse's nose. It was said the motherless family was running down, with the Grandmother no longer there to hold it together. It was known that she had discriminated against her son Harry in her will, and that he was in straits about money. Some of his old neighbors reflected with vicious satisfaction that now he would probably not be so stiff-necked, nor have any more high-stepping horses either. Miranda knew this, though she could not say how. She had met along the road old women of the kind who smoked corn-cob pipes, who had treated her grandmother with most sincere respect. They slanted their gummy old eyes side-ways at the granddaughter and said, "Ain't you ashamed of yoself, Missy? It's aginst the Scriptures to dress like that. Whut yo Pappy thinkin about?" Miranda, with her powerful social sense, which was like a fine set of antennae radiating from every pore of her skin, would feel ashamed because she knew well it was rude and ill-bred to shock anybody, even bad-tempered old crones, though she had faith in her father's judgment and was perfectly comfortable in the clothes. Her father had said, "They're just what you need, and they'll save your dresses for school . . ." This sounded quite simple and natural to her. She had been brought up in rigorous economy. Wastefulness was vulgar. It was also a sin. These were truths; she had heard them repeated many times and never once disputed.

Now the ring, shining with the serene purity of fine gold on her rather grubby thumb, turned her feelings against her overalls and sockless feet, toes sticking through the thick brown leather straps. She wanted to go back to the farmhouse, take a good cold bath, dust herself with plenty of Maria's violet talcum powder—provided Maria was not present to object, of course—put on the thinnest, most becoming dress she owned, with a big sash, and sit in a wicker chair under the trees . . . These things were not all she wanted, of course; she had vague stirrings of desire for luxury and a grand way of living which could not take precise form in her imagination but were founded on family legend of past wealth and leisure. These immediate comforts were what she could have, and she wanted them at once. She lagged rather far behind Paul, and once she thought of just turning back without a word and going home. She stopped, thinking that Paul would never do that to her, and so she would have to tell him. When a rabbit leaped, she let Paul have it without dispute. He killed it with one shot.

When she came up with him, he was already kneeling, examining the wound, the rabbit trailing from his hands. "Right through the head," he said complacently, as if he had aimed for it. He took out his sharp, competent bowie knife and started to skin the body. He did it very cleanly and quickly. Uncle Jimbilly knew how to prepare the skins so that Miranda always had fur coats for her dolls, for though she never cared much for her dolls she liked seeing them in fur coats. The children knelt facing each other over the dead animal. Miranda watched admiringly while her brother stripped the skin away as if he were taking off a glove. The flayed flesh emerged dark scarlet, sleek, firm; Miranda with thumb and finger felt the long fine muscles with the silvery flat strips binding them to the joints. Brother lifted the oddly bloated belly. "Look," he said, in a low amazed voice. "It was going to have young ones."

Very carefully he slit the thin flesh from the center ribs to the flanks, and a scarlet bag appeared. He slit again and pulled the bag open, and there lay a bundle of tiny rabbits, each wrapped in a thin scarlet veil. The brother pulled these off and there they were, dark gray, their sleek wet down lying in minute even ripples, like a baby's head just washed, their unbelievably small delicate ears folded close, their little blind faces almost featureless.

Miranda said, "Oh, I want to *see*," under her breath. She looked and looked—excited but not frightened, for she was accustomed to the sight of animals killed in hunting—filled with pity and astonishment and a kind of shocked delight in the wonderful little creatures for their own sakes, they were so pretty. She touched one of them ever so carefully, "Ah, there's blood running over them," she said and began to tremble without knowing why. Yet she wanted most deeply to see and to know. Having seen, she felt at once as if she had known all along. The very memory of her former ignorance faded, she had always known just this. No one had ever told her anything outright, she had been rather unobservant of the animal life around her because she was so accustomed to animals. They seemed simply disorderly and unaccountably rude in their habits, but altogether natural and not very interesting. Her brother had spoken as if he had known about everything all along. He may have seen all this before. He had never said a word to her, but she knew now a part at least of what he knew. She understood a little of the secret, formless intuitions in her own mind and body, which had been clearing up, taking form, so gradually and so steadily she had not realized that she was learning what she had to know. Paul said cautiously, as if he were talking about something forbidden: "They were just about ready to be born." His voice dropped on the last word. "I know," said Miranda, "like kittens. I know, like babies." She was quietly and terribly agitated, standing again with her rifle under her arm, looking down at the bloody heap. "I don't want the skin," she said, "I won't have it." Paul buried the young rabbits again in their mother's body, wrapped the skin around her, carried her to a clump of sage bushes, and hid her away. He came out again at once and said to Miranda, with an eager friendliness, a confidential tone quite unusual in him, as if he were taking her into an important secret on equal terms: "Listen now. Now you listen to me, and don't ever forget. Don't you ever tell a living soul that you saw this. Don't tell a soul. Don't tell Dad because I'll get into trouble. He'll say I'm leading you into things you ought not to do. He's always saying that. So now don't you go and forget and blab out sometime the way you're always doing . . . Now, that's a secret. Don't you tell."

Miranda never told, she did not even wish to tell anybody. She thought about the whole worrisome affair with confused unhappiness for a few days. Then it sank quietly into her mind and was heaped over by accumulated thousands of impressions, for nearly twenty years. One day she was picking her path among the puddles and crushed refuse of a market street in a strange city of a strange country, when without warning, plain and clear in its true colors as if she looked through a frame upon a scene that had not stirred nor changed since the moment it happened, the episode of that far-off day leaped from its burial place before her mind's eye. She was so reasonlessly horrified she halted suddenly staring, the scene before her eyes dimmed by the vision back of them. An Indian vendor had held up before her a tray of dyed sugar sweets, in the shapes of all kinds of small creatures: birds, baby chicks, baby rabbits, lambs, baby pigs. They were in gay colors and smelled of vanilla, maybe. . . . It was a very hot day and the smell in the market, with its piles of raw flesh and wilting flowers, was like the mingled sweetness and corruption she had smelled that other day in the empty cemetery at home: the day she had remembered always until now vaguely as the time she and her brother had found treasure in the opened graves. Instantly upon this thought the dreadful vision faded, and she saw clearly her brother, whose childhood face she had forgotten, standing again in the blazing sunshine, again twelve years old, a pleased sober smile in his eyes, turning the silver dove over and over in his hands. [1944]

QUESTIONS

1. What is the significance of the ring and the silver dove that the children find in the grave? Why do they trade?
2. Why does the episode of the rabbits strike Miranda so forcibly?

3. How does the final scene in the market connect with the opening scene in the cemetery and the death of the rabbit?

4. What does Miranda learn as a result of the experience?

5. By the conclusion of the story, what has the grave come to signify?

RESPONSES

1. Compare this story to other coming-of-age stories, such as Viramontes's "The Moths" or Mary Lavin's "My Vocation."

2. Miranda is a character that Katherine Anne Porter returned to in several stories. Look up those stories and write an essay about Miranda's growth as a character.

REYNOLDS PRICE

Reynolds Price (b. 1933) was born in Macon, North Carolina. He attended university at Duke and as a Rhodes Scholar at Oxford. His first novel,
A Long and Happy Life (1962), was published to critical acclaim, and he has
since published more than ten novels, including *The Surface of the Earth*
(1975), *Kate Viaden* (1986), *Tongues of Angels* (1990), *Blue Cahoun* (1992), and
Perfect Friend (2000). He is also the author of three volumes of short stories,
The Names and Faces of Heroes (1962), *Permanent Errors* (1970), and *The Collected Stories* (1993). Though confined to a wheelchair for several years,
Price has served on the faculty at Duke University, while publishing
poems, plays, and essays, in addition to his fiction.

An Evening Meal

Sam Traynor had got the reprieve two days ago—the five-year cure of his stomach cancer—
and he'd spent both days in quiet pleasure, not unstrung but high on a joy he'd hardly
known since boyhood. Because his parents were long dead though, and he'd lived alone
since chemotherapy made him reckless for weeks on end, he had no close friend to tell
the news. A woman who worked at the next desk over and the doorman in his apartment
building seemed at least to notice a change. The doorman remarked on the tie Sam spent
thirty dollars for, in celebration; the woman said "Sam, are you wearing blush?" (it was
healthy color). And that was all, for human response. Sam wouldn't phone his aunt or
her sons; they'd offered so little when it would have counted.

So after work that pleasant Friday, he walked ten blocks to eat at a diner he'd last
visited the week before surgery, not even sensing a near ambush. It was not his favorite restaurant, then or now; but he'd planned this evening in further celebration—
or the risk of one. That last visit he was also alone; but a new waiter was working the
counter, a boy just off the plane from Amalfi and as good to see as any face that rushed
toward Sam too fast to use, in his early days. The boy had accepted his invitation,
turned up after the diner closed and—through a whole night—lent Sam his stunning
body and smile, free as air.

And never again. When he left at dawn, he thanked Sam, saying "I liked you, sir."
Sam stopped him there with a silent hand and fixed the moment in his mind where he
knew it was safe as long as he lived. Five years later though, the boy wouldn't be

there—surely not. His name was Giulio, called Giuli; and still his memory seemed worth the risk.

But there he was after all at the grill end when Sam took a stool up near the cash register. A few pounds thicker but lit with a heat that spread from inside him, the generous fearless eyes of a creature better than humankind anyhow. He was talking intently with an ancient woman in a genuine cloche hat, stained pink velvet. The one other worker in sight was a girl who served the counter and the booths by the street wall. Final daylight was strong at the windows, colored green by water-oak leaves.

5   Right off, Sam knew he'd give no sign. If Giuli glanced his way or walked by, Sam would look right at him but not speak first. That would test many things—how much the wait had changed Sam's looks, how deep his face had registered on Giuli that one dark night, what Sam's whole life might hold from here out: a whole new life. He was calmer than he'd expected to be and was halfway through a bowl of good soup before Giuli passed to ring the woman's check.

No look Sam's way; and once the woman passed back of Sam, blowing a dry old kiss at Giuli—and Giuli had actually turned to Sam and asked if the crackers were fresh enough—still no door swung open between them. Giuli grinned but in a general direction.

Sam knew it was strange, but he wasn't disappointed. The most he'd hoped for was some shared memory and the chance of Giuli's pleasure in the news. It was plain anyhow that Giuli's forgetfulness was real when their hands touched to exchange the crackers. The skin was warm as before and tougher. On the right ring finger, Italian-style, was a wedding band.

By the time his turkey sandwich was ready, Sam had agreed they'd touched near enough. They'd silently proved they were still alive and had asked for no more; but then Sam's mind set off on its own, watching a clear line of pictures that came from the night they'd shared nearly all they had. The same pictures had been a main help through the six hard months after surgery and X-ray—Sam's old skill as a home projectionist of well-kept memories. In lucky hours he could shut his eyes and play through a useful number of scenes, from minutes to days, in keener detail than when they were new, tasting individual pleasures and thanks strong as ever. There were twenty-some scenes from his adult years, eight of which were masterworks of time and light; and the scene that centered on the early Giuli contended for best. In the next half-hour, through his sandwich and tapioca pudding, Sam had again everything Giuli gave him and needed no more.

He believed that at least till he asked for his check and Giuli brought it, clearing the dishes in graceful ease—not a clink or scrape. But one more time their hands brushed; and Sam was startled by the wash of gratitude poured out in him—an unexpected need to say his own name, then allude to their meeting and tell Giuli what that memory had meant to a man condemned by a ring of doctors to die in a month. *It hauled me back*; Sam knew that much. At first a cold-scared hunkered patience of constant pain; then slowly an easier slog through time, dense at first as hip-deep seaweed.

10   Terrified and then edgy as the wait was, it came to feel better than what went before; and the new years turned out, of all things, celibate. In eighteen hundred ominous nights, however often Sam ran the scenes, he'd never once felt compelled to reach for another man near him. A bigger surprise by far than his cure; and he sometimes wondered if the X-ray had done it, burning out some nerve for longing. Or was it simply fear of more sickness? Whatever, Sam took the world through his eyes now. With no

real blame and no regret, though he'd sometimes wonder *Am I dead and punished? Or maybe it's Heaven.* Alone on his stool he actually laughed.

Giuli turned from cutting a blueberry pie and seemed to nod toward a table beyond them—a nod and a frown to hush the air, then a dark-eyed sadness.

Sam hushed and tried to see a reflection in the glass pie-cabinet; it curved too sharply. So when he'd sat another two minutes, dawdling through the last of his coffee, he laid a small stack of bills on the check, caught Giuli's eye and said "Keep the change," then turned on his stool.

Four yards ahead—close to the door in a four-seat booth with the low light on him—a single man was huddled inward on himself as tight as if a blunt pole had pierced him, threaded his chest and bolted him shut. He might just weigh a hundred pounds; his rusty hair was parched and limp. His eyes hit Sam's a moment, then skittered.

It's Richard Boileau, already dead. Sam guessed it that fast; but since the man's eyes wandered to the window and watched the street, Sam stayed in place and tested his hunch. He'd last seen Richard in '78, the November morning after they'd proved through a long bleak night how well they'd learned each other's least weakness and how they could each flay the other with words. Then as daylight had streaked the roof, Sam suddenly found the one path out. He stood from the bed they'd shared for three years, picked up a few good things from the bureau—his father's gold watch, a comb of his mother's, his wallet and knife—and said "All right, the rest is yours."

The rest had literally been the rest—Sam's clothes, books, records, two years of a   15
diary, a few nice pieces of furniture he'd more than half paid for. All well lost and Richard with it, the dazzling tramp hungry as any moray eel, cored-out by a set of monster parents. Through the years Sam heard second-hand of his whereabouts, always in town at a new address; but the two had never collided till now, if this was Richard.

For whatever reason, of Sam's old loves—vanished or lost—it was only Richard he'd thought of as dying, purple-splotched with Kaposi's sarcoma or drowning in lung and nerve parasites. Each day he'd read the obituaries, crouched against the name on the page; and while he chalked off friend after friend, Richard stayed inexplicably free. Even in Sam's own worst days though, when radiation seared his gut in third-degree lesions, he somehow knew he'd outlast the havoc inside his skin while Richard Boileau would certainly die in this new plague. And not from an endless hunger for bodies—scrupulous Sam could have picked a killer any calm night—but from some cold rage in Richard's mind to leave a string of his riders appalled.

But is this helpless scarecrow Richard? In two more seconds Sam all but knew. The worn blue shirt that swallowed the long neck was one Sam had left—a red *S.T.* still edged the pocket, sewed by Sam's mother. Had a stranger bought it at the Salvation Army? Sam turned away to steady himself.

By now Giuli was back by the grill, laughing with a cook that had just turned up, a rangy boy with a knife-blade profile.

Sam thought of quietly walking their way and asking if they knew the man in the booth—was he a regular; what was his problem?

But the young cook met Sam's eyes, gave a wave with his spatula, then kissed   20
Giuli's jaw—their eyes were identical; they had to be brothers. Giuli called out *"Grazie,"* smiled at the whole room, took a short bow and scrubbed at his neck.

Sam stood up and faced the booth. The man was still pressed close to the window, though Sam could see there was nothing to notice, nothing Richard would have spent ten seconds on. The fact freed Sam; he stepped across, took the opposite bench two feet from the man's head and said "See anything good out there?"

The man turned gradually and, at close range, the skin of his upper face was transparent—that thin and taut on the beautiful skull.

Sam thought he could see a whole brain through it, a raddled mind, whatever it knew or had lost for good. But Sam stayed still till he'd drawn a direct look from the eyes—they'd kept their color, an arctic blue. Then he said "Is it Richard?"

No move or sign from the frozen face.

25   Sam tried a new way. "Bertrand? Remember?" In the early days he'd sometimes called Richard "Bertrand Le Beau" when nothing yet had dulled the shine.

At first the name seemed to penetrate. The eyes widened and the dry lips cracked.

But then a quiet voice said "You know him?" The waitress was there with a dry slice of toast and a cup of milk that gave off smoke. She set it by the man's right hand and spoke to him gently, "This'll warm you fast."

Sam took the risk and looked to the girl. "You know his name?"

The man might have been on the moon, engrossed.

30   The waitress smiled. "I know he's been bad off a long time. I know this is what he eats every night. But he's gaining strength now—aren't you, friend?" She touched the wrist that was nearly all bone.

The man faced her, his smile a ruin. He managed to lift the cup of milk though and drink a short swallow.

The waitress tapped Sam's shoulder lightly. "Sit with him some. He never sees people; make him drink his milk." As she left, she asked Sam if he was still hungry.

He shook his head No; but when she was gone, he saw she'd left an idle fork and spoon on the table, bound in a napkin. He took out the clean spoon, stirred the milk, drank a spoonful himself; then slowly over the next ten minutes, he fed Richard Boileau the whole cup.   [1994]

QUESTIONS

1. What does the narrator mean in the observation that Sam Traynor was "not sensing a near ambush"?

2. What conflict does Sam Traynor have? What is he looking for in seeing Giuli again?

3. What do we know about Sam Traynor when we learn about his "skill as a home projectionist of well-kept memories"?

4. What is the tone of the story?

5. Compare Sam Traynor's memories of Guili and of Richard Boileau. Why is it important that Traynor sit with Boileau?

RESPONSE

1. Compare the themes of love, compassion, and forgiveness in this story with those themes in James Baldwin's "Sonny's Blues."

TOMÁS RIVERA

Tomás Rivera (1935–1985) was born in Crystal City, Texas, in a family that earned its living as migrant workers. He earned degrees from Southwest Texas State University (B.S. in 1958 and M.Ed. in 1964) and the University of Oklahoma (Ph.D. 1969). Serving at several universities as professor and as an administrator, Rivera became Chancellor of the University of California, Riverside in 1979. He is the author of a seminal work in Chicano fiction. . . *y no se lo trago la tierra* (1971). The novel has been translated and filmed under various titles. His short fiction was collected in *The Harvest* (1989). *Tomás Rivera: The Complete Works* was published in 1998.

. . . And the Earth Did Not Devour Him

The first time he felt hate and anger was when he saw his mother crying for his uncle and his aunt. They both had caught tuberculosis and had been sent to different sanitariums. So, between the brothers and sisters, they had split up the children among themselves and had taken care of them as best they could. Then the aunt died, and soon thereafter they brought the uncle back from the sanitarium, but he was already spitting blood. That was when he saw his mother crying every little while. He became angry because he was unable to do anything against anyone. Today he felt the same. Only today it was for his father.

"You all should've come home right away, m'ijo. Couldn't you see that your Daddy was sick? You should have known that he'd suffered a sunstroke. Why didn't you come home?"

"I don't know. Us being so soaked with sweat, we didn't feel so hot, but I guess that when you're sunstruck it's different. But I did tell him to sit down under the tree that's at the edge of the rows, but he didn't want to. And that was when he started throwing up. Then we saw he couldn't hoe anymore and we dragged him and put him under a tree. He didn't put up a fuss at that point. He just let us take him. He didn't even say a word."

"Poor viejo, my poor viejo. Last night he hardly slept. Didn't you hear him outside the house. He squirmed in bed all night with cramps. God willing, he'll get well. I've been giving him cool lemonade all day, but his eyes still look glassy.

If I'd gone to the fields yesterday, I tell you, he wouldn't have gotten sick. My poor viejo, he's going to have cramps all over his body for three days and three nights at the least. Now, you all take care of yourselves. Don't overwork yourselves so much. Don't pay any mind to that boss if he tries to rush you. Just don't do it. He thinks its so easy since he's not the one who's out there stooped."

5   He became even angrier when he heard his father moan outside the chicken coop. He wouldn't stay inside because he said it made him feel very anxious. Outside where he could feel the fresh air was where he got some relief. And also when the cramps came he could roll over on the grass. Then he thought about whether his father might die from the sunstroke. At times he heard his father start to pray and ask for God's help. At first he had faith that he would get well soon but by the next day he felt the anger growing inside of him. And all the more when he heard his mother and his father clamoring for God's mercy. That night, well past midnight, he had been awakened by his father's groans. His mother got up and removed the scapularies from around his neck and washed them. Then she lit some candles. But nothing happened. It was like his aunt and uncle all over again.

"What's to be gained from doing all that, Mother? Don't tell me you think it helped my aunt and uncle any. How come we're like this, like we're buried alive? Either the germs eat us alive or the sun burns us up. Always some kind of sickness. And every day we work and work. For what? Poor Dad, always working so hard. I think he was born working. Like he says, barely five years old and already helping his father plant corn. All the time feeding the earth and the sun, only to one day, just like that, get struck down by the sun. And there you are, helpless. And them, begging for God's help . . . why, God doesn't care about us . . . I don't think there even is . . . No, better not say it, what if Dad gets worse. Poor Dad, I guess that at least gives him some hope."

His mother noticed how furious he was, and that morning she told him to calm down, that everything was in God's hands and that with God's help his father was going to get well.

"Oh, Mother, do you really believe that? I am certain that God has no concern for us. Now you tell me, is Dad evil or mean-hearted? You tell me if he has ever done any harm to anyone."

"Of course not."

10   "So there you have it. You see? And my aunt and uncle? You explain. And the poor kids, now orphans, never having known their parents. Why did God have to take them away? I tell you, God could care less about the poor. Tell me, why must we live here like this? What have we done to deserve this? You're so good and yet you have to suffer so much."

"Oh, please, m'ijo, don't talk that way. Don't speak against the will of God. Don't talk that way, please, m'ijo. You scare me. It's as if already the blood of Satan runs through your veins."

"Well, maybe. That way at least, I could get rid of this anger. I'm so tired of thinking about it. Why? Why you? Why Dad? Why my uncle? Why my aunt? Why their kids? Tell me, Mother, why? Why us, burrowed in the dirt like animals with no hope for anything? You know the only hope we have is coming out here every year. And like you yourself say, only death brings rest. I think that's the way my aunt and uncle felt and that's how Dad must feel too."

"That's how it is, m'ijo. Only death brings us rest."
"But why us?"
"Well, they say that . . ."
"Don't say it. I know what you're going to tell—that the poor go to heaven."

That day started out cloudy and he could feel the morning coolness brushing his eyelashes as he and his brothers and sisters began the day's labor. Their mother had to stay home to care for her husband. Thus, he felt responsible for hurrying on his brothers and sisters. During the morning, at least for the first few hours, they endured the heat but by ten-thirty the sun had suddenly cleared the skies and pressed down against the world. They began working more slowly because of the weakness, dizziness and suffocation they felt when they worked too fast. Then they had to wipe the sweat from their eyes every little while because their vision would get blurred.

"If you start blacking out, stop working, you hear me? Or go a little slower. When we reach the edge we'll rest a bit to get our strength back. It's gonna be hot today. If only it'd stay just a bit cloudy like this morning, then nobody would complain. But no, once the sun bears down like this not even one little cloud dares to appear out of fear. And the worst of it is we'll finish up here by two and then we have to go over to that other field that's nothing but hills. It's okay at the top of the hill but down in the lower part of the slopes it gets to be real suffocating. There's no breeze there. Hardly any air goes through. Remember?"
"Yeah."
"That's where the hottest part of the day will catch us. Just drink plenty of water every little while. It don't matter if the boss gets mad. Just don't get sick. And if you can't go on, tell me right away, all right? We'll go home. Y'all saw what happened to Dad when he pushed himself too hard. The sun has no mercy, it can eat you alive."

Just as they had figured, they had moved on to the other field by early afternoon. By three o'clock they were all soaked with sweat. Not one part of their clothing was dry. Every little while they would stop. At times they could barely breathe, then they would black out and they would become fearful of getting sunstruck, but they kept on working.

"How do y'all feel?"
"Man, it's so hot! But we've got to keep on. 'Til six, at least. Except this water don't help our thirst any. Sure wish I had a bottle of cool water, real cool, fresh from the well, or a coke ice-cold."
"Are you crazy? That'd sure make you sunsick right now. Just don't work so fast. Let's see if we can make it until six. What do you think?"

At four o'clock the youngest became ill. He was only nine years old, but since he was paid the same as a grown up he tried to keep up with the rest. He began vomiting. He sat down, then he laid down. Terrified, the other children ran to where he lay and looked at him. It appeared that he had fainted and when they opened his eyelids they saw his eyes were rolled back. The next youngest child started crying but right away he told him to stop and help him carry his brother home. It seemed he was having cramps all over his little body. He lifted him and carried him by himself and, again, he began asking himself *why?*

"Why Dad and then my little brother? He's only nine years old. Why? He has to work like a mule buried in the earth. Dad, Mom, and my little brother here, what are they guilty of?"

Each step that he took towards the house resounded with the question, *why?* About halfway to the house he began to get furious. Then he started crying out of rage. His little brothers and sisters did not know what to do, and they, too, started crying, but out of fear. Then he started cursing. And without even realizing it, he said what he had been wanting to say for a long time. He cursed God. Upon doing this he felt that fear instilled in him by the years and by his parents. For a second he saw the earth opening up to devour him. Then he felt his footsteps against the earth, compact, more solid then ever. Then his anger swelled up again and he vented it by cursing God. He looked at his brother, he no longer looked sick. He didn't know whether his brothers and sisters had understood the graveness of his curse.

That night he did not fall asleep until very late. He felt at peace as never before. He felt as though he had become detached from everything. He no longer worried about his father nor his brother. All that he awaited was the new day, the freshness of the morning. By daybreak his father was doing better. He was on his way to recovery. And his little brother, too; the cramps had almost completely subsided. Frequently he felt a sense of surprise upon recalling what he had done the previous afternoon. He thought of telling his mother, but he decided to keep it secret. All he told her was that the earth did not devour anyone, nor did the sun.

He left for work and encountered a very cool morning. There were clouds in the sky and for the first time he felt capable of doing and undoing anything that he pleased. He looked down at the earth and kicked it hard and said.

30   "Not yet, you can't swallow me up yet. Someday, yes. But I'll never know it."

[1971]

QUESTIONS

1. Why do the characters continue to go to work, especially since they know how dangerous work is?
2. Is there a difference between the characters' attitudes toward their bosses and the narrator's attitude toward the bosses?
3. What effect does Rivera's word choice and sentence structure have on the story?
4. After cursing God, why does the boy feel better?
5. What is Rivera's commentary about the role of religion in the lives of the poor?

RESPONSES

1. Using the ecocritical approach, how do Rivera's setting and theme compare to the setting and theme of García Márquez's "Tuesday Siesta"?
2. Write an essay explaining why you think Rivera is a realist, a modernist, or a postmodernist writer.

Focus on Film

1. The print story is one of many stories that make up the book ... *And the Earth Did Not Devour Him,* and the film by the same name is an adaptation of the entire book. Looking at the part of the film devoted to this story, examine how the film creates the sense of dangerous and unbearable heat that is so much part of the lives and conflicts in the print story.
2. Describe how the filmmakers adapted the print story's first person subjective point of view into the objective point of view of the film.

SALMAN RUSHDIE

Salman Rushdie (b. 1947) was born in Bombay, India, and graduated with an M.A. from King's College at Cambridge. His novels include *Midnight's Children* (1981), *Satanic Verses* (1989), *Ground Beneath Her Feet* (2000), and *Fury* (2001). He also publishes essays, some of which are included in *Imaginary Homeland: Essays and Criticism 1981–1991* (1991) and *Step Across This Line*: *Collected Non-Fiction 1992–2002* (2003). *East, West* (1994) is a volume of short fiction.

Good Advice Is Rarer Than Rubies

On the last Tuesday of the month, the dawn bus, its headlamps still shining, brought Miss Rehana to the gates of the British Consulate. It arrived pushing a cloud of dust, veiling her beauty from the eyes of strangers until she descended. The bus was brightly painted in multicoloured arabesques, and on the front it said 'MOVE OVER DARLING' in green and gold letters; on the back it added 'TATA-BATA' and also 'O.K. GOOD-LIFE.' Miss Rehana told the driver it was a beautiful bus, and he jumped down and held the door open for her, bowing theatrically as she descended.

Miss Rehana's eyes were large and black and bright enough not to need the help of antimony, and when the advice expert Muhammad Ali saw them he felt himself becoming young again. He watched her approaching the Consulate gates as the light strengthened, and asking the bearded lala who guarded them in a gold-buttoned khaki uniform with a cockaded turban when they would open. The lala, usually so rude to the Consulate's Tuesday women, answered Miss Rehana with something like courtesy.

'Half an hour,' he said gruffly. 'Maybe two hours. Who knows? The sahibs are eating their breakfast.'

The dusty compound between the bus stop and the Consulate was already full of Tuesday women, some veiled, a few barefaced like Miss Rehana. They all looked frightened, and leaned heavily on the arms of uncles or brothers, who were trying to look confident. But Miss Rehana had come on her own, and did not seem at all alarmed.

5   Muhammad Ali, who specialized in advising the most vulnerable-looking of these weekly supplicants, found his feet leading him towards the strange, big-eyed, independent girl.

'Miss,' he began. 'You have come for permit to London, I think so?'

She was standing at a hot-snack stall in the little shanty-town by the edge of the compound, munching chilli-pakoras contentedly. She turned to look at him, and at close range those eyes did bad things to his digestive tract.

'Yes, I have.'

'Then, please, you allow me to give some advice? Small cost only.'

Miss Rehana smiled. 'Good advice is rarer than rubies,' she said. 'But alas, I cannot   10
pay. I am an orphan, not one of your wealthy ladies.'

'Trust my grey hairs,' Muhammad Ali urged her. 'My advice is well tempered by experience. You will certainly find it good.'

She shook her head. 'I tell you I am a poor potato. There are women here with male family members, all earning good wages. Go to them. Good advice should find good money.'

I am going crazy, Muhammad Ali thought, because he heard his voice telling her of its own volition, 'Miss, I have been drawn to you by Fate. What to do? Our meeting was written. I also am a poor man only, but for you my advice comes free.'

She smiled again. 'Then I must surely listen. When Fate sends a gift, one receives good fortune.'

He led her to the low wooden desk in his own special corner of the shanty-town.   15
She followed, continuing to eat pakoras from a little newspaper packet. She did not offer him any.

Muhammad Ali put a cushion on the dusty ground. 'Please to sit.' She did as he asked. He sat cross-legged across the desk from her, conscious that two or three dozen pairs of male eyes were watching him enviously, that all the other shanty-town men were ogling the latest young lovely to be charmed by the old grey-hair fraud. He took a deep breath to settle himself.

'Name, please.'

'Miss Rehana,' she told him. 'Fiancée of Mustafa Dar of Bradford, London.'

'Bradford, England,' he corrected her gently. 'London is a town only, like Multan or Bahawalpur. England is a great nation full of the coldest fish in the world.'

'I see. Thank you,' she responded gravely, so that he was unsure if she was mak-   20
ing fun of him.

'You have filled application form? Then let me see, please.'

She passed him a neatly folded document in a brown envelope.

'Is it OK?' For the first time there was a note of anxiety in her voice.

He patted the desk quite near the place where her hand rested. 'I am certain,' he said. 'Wait on and I will check.'

She finished the pakoras while he scanned her papers.   25

'Tip-top,' he pronounced at length. 'All in order.'

'Thank you for your advice,' she said, making as if to rise. 'I'll go now and wait by the gate.'

'What are you thinking?' he cried loudly, smiting his forehead. 'You consider this is easy business? Just give the form and poof, with a big smile they hand over the permit? Miss Rehana, I tell you, you are entering a worse place than any police station.'

'Is it so, truly?' His oratory had done the trick. She was a captive audience now, and he would be able to look at her for a few moments longer.

Drawing another calming breath, he launched into his set speech. He told her   30
that the sahibs thought that all the women who came on Tuesdays, claiming to be

dependents of bus drivers in Luton or chartered accountants in Manchester, were crooks and liars and cheats.

She protested, 'But then I will simply tell them that I, for one, am no such thing!'

Her innocence made him shiver with fear for her. She was a sparrow, he told her, and they were men with hooded eyes, like hawks. He explained that they would ask her questions, personal questions, questions such as a lady's own brother would be too shy to ask. They would ask if she was virgin, and, if not, what her fiancé's love-making habits were, and what secret nicknames they had invented for one another.

Muhammad Ali spoke brutally, on purpose, to lessen the shock she would feel when it, or something like it, actually happened. Her eyes remained steady, but her hands began to flutter at the edges of the desk.

He went on:

35   'They will ask you how many rooms are in your family home, and what colour are the walls, and what days do you empty the rubbish. They will ask your man's moth-er's third cousin's aunt's step-daughter's middle name. And all these things they have already asked your Mustafa Dar in his Bradford. And if you make one mistake, you are finished.'

'Yes,' she said, and he could hear her disciplining her voice. 'And what is your ad-vice, old man?'

It was at this point that Muhammad Ali usually began to whisper urgently, to men-tion that he knew a man, a very good type, who worked in the Consulate, and through him, for a fee, the necessary papers could be delivered, with all the proper authenti-cating seals. Business was good, because the women would often pay him five hun-dred rupees or give him a gold bracelet for his pains, and go away happy.

They came from hundreds of miles away—he normally made sure of this before be-ginning to trick them—so even when they discovered they had been swindled they were unlikely to return. They went away to Sargodha or Lalukhet and began to pack, and who knows at what point they found out they had been gulled, but it was at a too-late point, anyway.

Life is hard, and an old man must live by his wits. It was not up to Muhammad Ali to have compassion for these Tuesday women.

40   But once again his voice betrayed him, and instead of starting his customary speech it began to reveal to her his greatest secret.

'Miss Rehana,' his voice said, and he listened to it in amazement, 'you are a rare per-son, a jewel, and for you I will do what I would not do for my own daughter, perhaps. One document has come into my possession that can solve all your worries at one stroke.'

'And what is this sorcerer's paper?' she asked, her eyes unquestionably laughing at him now.

His voice fell low-as-low.

'Miss Rehana, it is a British passport. Completely genuine and pukka goods. I have a good friend who will put your name and photo, and then, hey-presto, England there you come!'

45   He had said it!

Anything was possible now, on this day of his insanity. Probably he would give her the thing free-gratis, and then kick himself for a year afterwards.

Old fool, he berated himself. *The oldest fools are bewitched by the youngest girls.*

'Let me understand you,' she was saying. 'You are proposing I should commit a crime . . .'

'Not crime,' he interposed. 'Facilitation.'

'. . . and go to Bradford, London, illegally, and therefore justify the low opinion the 50 Consulate sahibs have of us all. Old babuji, this is not good advice.'

'Bradford, *England*,' he corrected her mournfully. 'You should not take my gift in such a spirit.'

'Then how?'

'Bibi, I am a poor fellow, and I have offered this prize because you are so beautiful. Do not spit on my generosity. Take the thing. Or else don't take, go home, forget England, only do not go into that building and lose your dignity.'

But she was on her feet, turning away from him, walking towards the gates, where the women had begun to cluster and the lala was swearing at them to be patient or none of them would be admitted at all.

'So be a fool,' Muhammad Ali shouted after her. 'What goes of my father's if you 55 are?' (Meaning, what was it to him.)

She did not turn.

'It is the curse of our people,' he yelled. 'We are poor, we are ignorant, and we completely refuse to learn.'

'Hey, Muhammad Ali,' the woman at the betel-nut stall called across to him. 'Too bad, she likes them young.'

That day Muhammad Ali did nothing but stand around near the Consulate gates. Many times he scolded himself, *Go from here, old goof, lady does not desire to speak with you any further.* But when she came out, she found him waiting.

'Salaam, advice wallah,' she greeted him. 60

She seemed calm, and at peace with him again, and he thought, *My God, ya Allah, she has pulled it off. The British sahibs also have been drowning in her eyes and she has got her passage to England.*

He smiled at her hopefully. She smiled back with no trouble at all.

'Miss Rehana Begum,' he said, 'felicitations, daughter, on what is obviously your hour of triumph.'

Impulsively, she took his forearm in her hand.

'Come,' she said. 'Let me buy you a pakora to thank you for your advice and to 65 apologise for my rudeness, too.'

They stood in the dust of the afternoon compound near the bus, which was getting ready to leave. Coolies were tying bedding rolls to the roof. A hawker shouted at the passengers, trying to sell them love stories and green medicines, both of which cured unhappiness. Miss Rehana and a happy Muhammad Ali ate their pakoras sitting on the bus's 'front mud-guard,' that is, the bumper. The old advice expert began softly to hum a tune from a movie soundtrack. The day's heat was gone.

'It was an arranged engagement,' Miss Rehana said all at once. 'I was nine years old when my parents fixed it. Mustafa Dar was already thirty at that time, but my father wanted someone who could look after me as he had done himself and Mustafa was a man known to Daddyji as a solid type. Then my parents died and Mustafa Dar went to England and said he would send for me. That was many years ago. I have his photo, but he is like a stranger to me. Even his voice, I do not recognise it on the phone.'

The confession took Muhammad Ali by surprise, but he nodded with what he hoped looked like wisdom.

'Still and after all,' he said, 'one's parents act in one's best interests. They found you a good and honest man who has kept his word and sent for you. And now you have a lifetime to get to know him, and to love.' He was puzzled, now, by the bitterness that had infected her smile.

70   'But, old man,' she asked him, 'why have you already packed me and posted me off to England?'

He stood up, shocked.

'You looked happy—so I just assumed . . . excuse me, but they turned you down or what?'

'I got all their questions wrong,' she replied. 'Distinguishing marks I put on the wrong cheeks, bathroom decor I completely redecorated, all absolutely topsy-turvy, you see.'

'But what to do? How will you go?'

75   'Now I will go back to Lahore and my job. I work in a great house, as ayah to three good boys. They would have been sad to see me leave.'

'But this is tragedy!' Muhammad Ali lamented. 'Oh, how I pray that you had taken up my offer! Now, but, it is not possible, I regret to inform. Now they have your form on file, cross-check can be made, even the passport will not suffice.

'It is spoilt, all spoilt, and it could have been so easy if advice had been accepted in good time.'

'I do not think,' she told him, 'I truly do not think you should be sad.'

Her last smile, which he watched from the compound until the bus concealed it in a dust-cloud, was the happiest thing he had ever seen in his long, hot, hard, unloving life.   [1994]

QUESTIONS

1. In what way did the old man give Miss Rehana good advice?
2. Did the old man learn anything in his encounter with the young woman?
3. Does the line "When Fate sends a gift, one receives good fortune" become true? In what way?
4. How does the first paragraph establish the tone of the story?
5. In what ways are the characters in the story stereotypes? In what ways are they not?

RESPONSE

1. Compare this story to Mukherjee's "A Father." What is being said in these stories about women and tradition?

DONATIEN ALPHONSE FRANCOIS COMPTE DE SADE

Donatien Alphonse Francois Compte de Sade (1740–1814) was born in France to a wealthy, aristocratic family. He attended a Jesuit college and served in the calvary in the Seven Years War. After marriage, he was imprisoned many times for criminal sexual misconduct. In 1790, he served as judge for the revolution in France, but was back in jail by 1793. Finally, he was incarcerated in an asylum until his death. His books, notorious in their day, have gained greater fame in the twentieth century. Among his titles are *Justine* (1791), *Philosophy in the Bedroom* (1795) and *The 120 Days of Sodom* (1804). His short stories are currently collected in *The Misfortunes of Virtue and Other Early Tales*.

The Lady of the Manor of Longeville, or a Woman's Revenge

In the days when the aristocracy ruled their lands like despots—those glorious days when France contained within her boundaries countless sovereign lords and not thirty thousand cowed slaves bending the knee to a single man—the Lord of Longeville, master of a fief near Fimes in Champagne, resided on his not inconsiderable estates. With him lived his wife who was small, dark of hair and pert of face, vivacious, not very pretty but brazen, and passionately fond of her pleasures. The Lady of the Manor was perhaps 25 or 26 and her Lord and Master 30 at most. They had been married for ten years and being both of an age to relish whatever might relieve the tedium of wedded bliss, they each set about satisfying their needs as well as could be managed out of what the locality could furnish. The town, or rather the hamlet of Longeville had little to offer. However, a pretty little farmer's wife, pleasing to the eye and with the bloom of her 18 years still on her, had succeeded in catching his Lordship's fancy and for two years past she had fitted his bill most satisfactorily. Louison, as his darling turtle-dove was called, came each evening to her master's bed by a secret staircase built into one of the towers which housed his Lordship's apartments, and decamped each morning before Madame, as was her custom, arrived to breakfast with her husband.

Madame de Longeville was fully aware of her husband's unseemly little *amour* but being herself nothing loath to enjoy similar sport, made no comment. There is nothing sweeter-tempered than faithless wives: having such good reason to hide their own dealings, they do not look into other people's lives as keenly as do the prudes. A local miller named Colas, a young dog of 18 or 20, as pure as his own flour, as muscular as his mule, and as pretty as the roses which grew in his little garden, came each night just as Louison did and let himself into a room adjoining Madame's apartments and thence, when all was quiet in the château, into her bed. There was no more tranquil sight to behold than these twin *ménages*. If the Devil had not taken a hand in the business, I am convinced that they would have been trumpeted loud throughout the province of Champagne as examples to be followed.

Do not smile, reader, no, you should not scoff at the word *example*. When there is a want of virtue, vice suitably garbed and discreetly hidden may properly serve as a model: is it not a thing as worthy as it is deft to sin without scandalizing one's fellows? And when the offence is not made public, where can be the harm in it? Come, decide for yourselves: are not such trifling irregularities preferable to the spectacles furnished by the manners of the present time? Would you not prefer the Lord of Longeville duly and tranquilly settled in the arms of his pretty farmer's wife, and his respectable Lady installed by the side of a handsome miller whose good fortune is known to no one, to some Paris Duchess or other who publicly changes gallants once a month or takes her pleasure with the servants while her lord and master works his way through 200,000 écus a year with one of those despicable creatures who are gilded by wealth, base by birth, and cankered by the pox? I say again: had it not been for the discord distilled by life's poisons over these four favoured children of Love, nothing could have been sweeter and more exemplary than their charming little arrangements.

But the Lord of Longeville, cruelly believing like many unjust husbands that while he had a right to be happy his wife did not, and imagining, like the partridge, that he was invisible because he kept his head buried, discovered his wife's little intrigue and was not amused, as though his own behaviour did not fully justify the conduct which he now took it into his head to censure.

5   From discovery to revenge is but a small step for a jealous mind. Monsieur de Longeville decided to say nothing but to rid himself of the knave who had caused horns to sprout on his forehead: 'It is one thing for a man of my rank to be deceived by a gentleman,' said he to himself, 'but quite another to be cuckolded by a miller! Monsieur Colas, you will please be good enough to do your grinding in someone else's mill, for from this day forth it shall never more be said that my wife's took in your seed.' Now seeing that the hatred of the little sovereign despots of those times was ever cruel to a degree, and since they regularly abused the power of life and death which feudal law granted them over their vassals, Monsieur de Longeville determined upon no less a course than to have poor Colas thrown into the waters of the moat which surrounded his château.

'Clodomir,' said he one day to his head cook, 'I want you and the rest of the kitchen staff to rid me of a vassal who is fouling Madame's bed.'

'At once, your Lordship,' replied Clodomir. 'We'll slit his throat if you like and serve him up trussed like a sucking pig.'

'No, nothing like that,' said Monsieur de Longeville. 'It will suffice to put him in a sack with some stones and drop the sack and him with it into the moat.'

'It shall be done.'

10   'Yes, but first we'll have to catch him and we haven't got him yet.'

'We will, your Lordship. He'll have to be pretty smart to get away from us. We'll have him. I guarantee it.'

'He will be here tonight at nine,' said the injured husband. 'He'll come through the garden and proceed directly to the rooms on the ground floor. He'll hide in the little room just off the chapel and stay there until Madame thinks I've gone to sleep. Then she will come, let him out, and take him off to her apartment. You must let him go through all the preliminaries—we will merely keep watch—but the moment he thinks he is safely hidden, we'll seize him and give him a long drink that will put out his fire.'

This scheme was excellently contrived and poor Colas would certainly have been food for the fishes if everyone had kept their mouths shut. But his Lordship had told his plans to too many people and he was betrayed. A kitchen lad who was very fond of his mistress and perhaps hoped one day to share her favours with the miller, surrendering more to the feelings which his mistress stirred in him than to the jealousy which should by rights have made him rejoice at his rival's imminent downfall, hurried away to tell her of the plot that was hatching and was rewarded by a kiss and by two shiny gold écus which he valued less than the kiss.

'His Lordship,' said Madame de Longeville when she was alone with the maid who assisted her in her intrigues, 'is most assuredly a very unjust man. Why, he does whatever he likes and I never say a word; yet he takes exception to my making up for the quantity of abstinence he requires me to observe. I won't have it! I simply won't put up with it! Listen, Jeannette, are you prepared to help me carry out a plan I have thought of which will not only save Colas but also put his Lordship in his place?'

'O yes, Madame. I'll do anything: Madame has only to say the word. Poor Colas is   15
such a nice boy. I never saw a boy with so strong a back on him nor with such colour in his cheek. O yes, Madame, of course I'll help. What must I do?'

'I want you to go this very minute,' the Lady said, 'and warn Colas that he is not to come to the château unless I first send to him. You will also ask him to lend me the complete suit of clothes he usually wears when he . . . visits. When you have them, I want you to go and find Louison, my false husband's love-pet, and tell her that his Lordship sent you. Say she is to wear the clothes you have in your apron pocket. She mustn't come her usual way but through the garden, across the courtyard, and into the ground-floor rooms. Once she's in the house, she must go to the little room next to the chapel° and hide there until his Lordship comes to fetch her. She will probably question you about this new arrangement, and you will say the reason is that Madame is jealous, that she knows everything, and that she has ordered the route she normally follows to be watched. If she is frightened, reassure her, give her some present or other and above all tell her that she must not fail to come because tonight his Lordship has matters of the greatest consequence to impart about what happened after Madame's jealous outburst.'

Jeannette left, discharged both errands to the letter, and at nine that evening the unfortunate Louison, wearing Colas's clothes, was hiding in the little room where, according to the plan, Madame's lover was to be apprehended.

'Forward!' said Monsieur de Longeville to his men who, like him, had been keeping a sharp look out. 'Go to it! You all saw him as plain as I did, did you not?'

'O yes, your Lordship, and by God he's a fine-looking lad.'

'Now open the door quickly, throw these clouts over his head to stop him from cry-   20
ing out, then stuff him into the sack and drown him without further ado.'

All this was done to perfection. The mouth of the unfortunate captive was so tightly gagged that she found it impossible to identify herself. She was put into the sack, at the bottom of which large stones had been carefully placed. Then from the window

---

°The physical disposition of the Château de Longeville is unchanged to this day. [*Author's note*]

of the same room where her capture had taken place, she was thrown into the middle of the moat. Once their work was done, all the men withdrew and Monsieur de Longeville returned to his apartment, being most eager to welcome the wench who he knew would not be long in coming and who he never imagined for a moment to be lying in so chill a bed. Half the night went by and no one came. As there was a large, bright moon, the anxious lover thought he would venture as far as her house and see for himself what motive there could be for her not appearing. He went out and in his absence Madame de Longeville, who was aware of his every move, got into her husband's bed. On reaching Louison's house, Monsieur de Longeville learned that she had left as usual and that she must certainly be at the château. No one said anything about her disguise because Louison had taken no one into her confidence and had slipped away unobserved. His Lordship returned home and the candle he had left in his room having gone out, went over to his bedside to fetch the tinder-box to relight it. As he did so, he heard breathing, assumed that his dearest Louison had come while he had been out looking for her and that, growing impatient on not finding him in his apartment, she had gone to bed. He did not hesitate. In a trice he was between the sheets caressing his wife with the words of love and the expressions of tenderness he normally used with his darling Louison.

'Why did you make me wait, my pretty? Where were you, dearest Louison?'

'So, you hypocrite!' exclaimed Madame de Longeville at this juncture, exposing the flame of a dark-lantern which she had kept hidden, 'I can no longer entertain any doubts about your behaviour. Behold your wife and not the whore to whom you give what rightfully belongs to me!'

'Madame,' said the husband without losing his calm, 'I believe I may be allowed to be master of my own actions since you yourself play me false in so essential a matter?'

25   'Play you false, sir? And in what manner of wise, pray?'

'Am I not aware of your intrigue with Colas, one of the sorriest peasants to disgrace my estate?'

'I, sir?' his Lady replied haughtily, 'I? You think I would stoop so low? You are imagining things. There has never been a word of truth in what you say and I challenge you to produce your evidence.'

'In truth, Madame, the evidence would indeed be difficult to furnish at this moment seeing that I have ordered the knave who dishonoured me to be thrown into the moat. You shall never see him again.'

'Sir,' said his Lady, rising to an even higher pitch of effrontery, 'if you have indeed ordered the unfortunate man to be thrown into the moat on the strength of your suspicions, then you are certainly guilty of a great injustice. But if, as you say, he was punished simply because he came to the château, then I am greatly afraid that you have made a grave mistake, for he never set foot here in his life.'

30   'Truly, Madame, you make me fear for my wits!'

'Let us look into the matter, sir. Let us cast light on it. Nothing could be simpler. Give the order yourself and send Jeannette here to fetch this peasant fellow of whom you are so mistakenly and ridiculously jealous, and we shall see who is right.'

His Lordship agreed, Jeannette set off and brought back Colas who had been told how to behave. When he saw him, Monsieur de Longeville rubbed his eyes and immediately summoned all the servants out of bed, commanding them to waste not a moment in finding out who it was, then, he had ordered to be thrown into the moat. They rushed off but all they brought back was a body, the corpse of the unhappy Louison, which they set down for her lover to see.

'O just Heaven!' cried his Lordship, 'an unknown hand has been at work in this business. And yet that hand was guided by Providence and I shall not complain of the blows it has struck. Whether it was you or another, Madame, who was the cause of this unfortunate occurrence, I shall not inquire. You are now free of a woman who made your mind uneasy. Do as much to rid me of the man who troubles mine and see to it that Colas goes away and does not come back. Will you agree to this, Madame?'

'I shall do more, sir. I join with you in ordering him to go. Let peace be restored between us. Let love and mutual respect come into their own once more and let nothing dislodge them ever again from their rightful place.'

Colas left the district and was never seen again, Louison was given a decent burial,   35
and never since that time was there a more devoted couple in the whole of the province of Champagne than the Lord and Lady of Longeville.   [1926]

QUESTIONS

1. What is the narrator's view of the expectations of conventional society?
2. In what way is class a part of the story's structure and theme?
3. Who is the protagonist of the story? Is that person admirable? Why or why not?
4. Why do the Lord and Lady seem to grieve so little over the fates of their lovers?
5. Is there a moral to this story?

RESPONSES

1. The Marquis de Sade has a scandalous personal and literary reputation. Do you see anything scandalous in this story?
2. This story was written in the era of the French Revolution. How is that reflected in the politics inherent in the story?
3. Compare this story to Perri Klass's "Not a Good Girl." Does the knowledge that a man wrote this story and a woman wrote the other story change your view of the stories?

FOCUS ON FILM

1. View the film *Quills*, which concerns, fictionally, the life of the Marquis de Sade. Discuss the ways that the film explores the subversion of traditional modes of morality and compare that subversion to the themes in the short story "The Lady of the Manor of Longeville."
2. The film *Swimming Pool* makes brief reference to the Marquis de Sade. How can the themes of the film be seen as "a woman's revenge"? What other connections can you make between de Sade's work and the film?

Jean-Paul Sartre

Jean-Paul Sartre (1905–1980) was one of the great philosophical minds of the twentieth century. With Albert Camus and Martin Hiedegger, he was a leading proponent of existentialism. He won the Nobel Prize in Literature in 1964. A writer of many genres, his works include short fiction in *The Wall and Other Stories* (1939), plays in *No Exit* (1943), novels in *Nausea* (1938) and *Age of Reason* (1945), philosophy in *Being and Nothingness* (1943), criticism in *What Is Literature?* (1948), and biographies of Baudelaire, Genet, and Flaubert.

Erostratus

You really have to see men from above. I put out the light and went to the window: they never suspected for a moment you could watch them from up there. They're careful of their fronts, sometimes of their backs, but their whole effect is calculated for spectators of about five feet eight. Who ever thought about the shape of a derby hat seen from the seventh floor? They neglect protecting their heads and shoulders with bright colors and garish clothes, they don't know how to fight this great enemy of Humanity, the downward perspective. I leaned on the window sill and began to laugh: where was this wonderful upright stance they're so proud of: they were crushed against the sidewalk and two long legs jumped out from under their shoulders.

On a seventh floor balcony: that's where I should have spent my whole life. You have to prop up moral superiorities with material symbols or else they'll tumble. But exactly what is my superiority over men? Superiority of position, nothing more: I have placed myself above the human within me and I study it. That's why I always liked the towers of Notre-Dame, the platforms of the Eiffel Tower, the Sacré-Coeur, my seventh floor on the Rue Delambre. These are excellent symbols.

Sometimes I had to go down into the street. To the office, for example. I stifled. It's much harder to consider people as ants when you're on the same plane as they are: they *touch* you. Once I saw a dead man in the street. He had fallen on his face. They turned him over, he was bleeding. I saw his open eyes and his cockeyed look and all the blood. I said to myself, "It's nothing, it's no more touching than wet paint. They painted his nose red, that's all." But I felt a nasty softness in my legs and neck and I fainted. They took me into a drugstore, gave me a few slaps on the face and a drink. I could have killed them.

I knew they were my enemies but they didn't know it. They liked each other, they rubbed elbows; they would even have given me a hand, here and there, because they thought I was like them. But if they could have guessed the least bit of the truth, they would have beaten me. They did later, anyhow. When they got me and knew *who* I was, they gave me the works; they beat me up for two hours in the station house, they slapped me and punched me and twisted my arms, they ripped off my pants and to finish they threw my glasses on the floor and while I looked for them, on all fours, they laughed and kicked me. I always knew they'd end up beating me; I'm not strong and I can't defend myself. Some of them had been on the lookout for me for a long time: the big ones. In the street they'd bump into me to see what I'd do. I said nothing. I acted as if I didn't understand. But they still got me. I was afraid of them: it was a foreboding. But don't think I didn't have more serious reasons for hating them.

As far as that was concerned, everything went along much better starting from the day I bought a revolver. You feel strong when you assiduously carry on your person something that can explode and make a noise. I took it every Sunday, I simply put it in my pants pocket and then went out for a walk—generally along the boulevards. I felt it pulling at my pants like a crab, I felt it cold against my thigh. But little by little it got warmer with the contact of my body. I walked with a certain stiffness, I looked like a man with a hard-on, with his thing sticking out at every step. I slipped my hand in my pocket and felt the *object*. From time to time I went into a *urinoir*—even in there I had to be careful because I often had neighbors—took out my revolver, I felt the weight of it, I looked at its black checkered butt and its trigger that looked like a half-closed eyelid. The others, the ones who saw me from the outside, thought I was pissing. But I never piss in the *urinoirs*.

One night I got the idea of shooting people. It was a Saturday evening, I had gone out to pick up Lea, a blonde who works out in front of a hotel on the Rue Montparnasse. I never had intercourse with a woman: I would have felt robbed. You get on top of them, of course, but they eat you up with their big hairy mouth and, from what I hear, they're the ones—by a long shot—who gain on the deal. I don't ask anybody for anything, but I don't give anything, either. Or else I'd have to have a cold, pious woman who would give in to me with disgust. The first Saturday of every month I went to one of the rooms in the Hotel Duquesne with Lea. She undressed and I watched her without touching her. Sometimes I went off in my pants all by myself, other times I had time to get home and finish it. That night I didn't find her. I waited for a little while and, as I didn't see her coming, I supposed she had a cold. It was the beginning of January and it was very cold. I was desolated: I'm the imaginative kind and I had pictured to myself all the pleasure I would have gotten from the evening. On the Rue Odessa there was a brunette I had often noticed, a little ripe but firm and plump: I don't exactly despise ripe women: when they're undressed they look more naked than the others. But she didn't know anything of my wants and I was a little scared to ask her right off the bat. And then I don't care too much for new acquaintances: these women can be hiding some thug behind a door, and after, the man suddenly jumps out and takes your money. You're lucky if you get off without a beating. Still, that evening I had nerve, I decided to go back to my place, pick up the revolver and try my luck.

So when I went up to this woman, fifteen minutes later, my gun was in my pocket and I wasn't afraid of anything. Looking at her closely, she seemed rather miserable. She looked like my neighbor across the way, the wife of the police sergeant, and I was very pleased because I'd been wanting to see her naked for a long time. She dressed with the window open when the sergeant wasn't there, and I often stayed behind my curtain to catch a glimpse of her. But she always dressed in the back of the room.

There was only one free room in the Hotel Stella, on the fifth floor. We went up. The woman was fairly heavy and stopped to catch her breath after each step. I felt good: I have a wiry body, in spite of my belly, and it takes more than five floors to wind me. On the fifth floor landing, she stopped and put her right hand to her heart and breathed heavily. She had the key to the room in her left hand.

"It's a long way up," she said, trying to smile at me. Without answering, I took the key from her and opened the door. I held my revolver in my left hand, pointing straight ahead through the pocket and I didn't let go of it until I switched the light on. The room was empty. They had put a little square of green soap on the washbasin, for a one-shot. I smiled: I don't have much to do with bidets and little squares of soap. The woman was still breathing heavily behind me and that excited me. I turned; she put out her lips towards me. I pushed her away.

10   "Undress," I told her.

There was an upholstered armchair; I sat down and made myself comfortable. It's at times like this I wish I smoked. The woman took off her dress and stopped, looking at me distrustfully.

"What's your name," I asked, leaning back.

"Renée."

"All right, Renée, hurry up. I'm waiting."

15   "You aren't going to undress?"

"Go on," I said, "don't worry about me."

She dropped her panties, then picked them up and put them carefully on top of her dress along with her brassiere.

"So you're a little lazybones, honey?" she asked me. "You want your little girl to do all the work?"

At the same time she took a step towards me, and, leaning her hands on the arm of the chair, tried heavily to kneel between my legs. I got up brusquely.

20   "None of that," I told her.

She looked at me with surprise.

"Well, what do you want me to do?"

"Nothing. Just walk. Walk around. I don't want any more from you."

She began to walk back and forth awkwardly. Nothing annoys women more than walking when they're naked. They don't have the habit of putting their heels down flat. The whore arched her back and let her arms hang. I was in heaven: there I was, calmly sitting in an armchair, dressed up to my neck, I had even kept my gloves on and this ripe woman had stripped herself naked at my command and was turning back and forth in front of me. She turned her head towards me, and, for appearance, smile coquettishly.

25   "You think I'm pretty? You're getting an eyeful?"

"Don't worry about that."

"Say," she asked with sudden indignation, "do you think you're going to make me walk up and down like this very long?"

"Sit down."

She sat down on the bed and we watched each other in silence. She had gooseflesh. I could hear the ticking of an alarm clock from the other side of the wall. Suddenly I told her:

30   "Spread your legs."

She hesitated a fraction of a second then obeyed. I looked between her legs and turned up my nose. Then I began to laugh so hard that tears came to my eyes. I said, simply, "Look at that!"

And I started laughing again.

She looked at me, stupefied, then blushed violently and clapped her legs shut.

"Bastard," she said between her teeth.

But I laughed louder, then she jumped up and took her brassiere from the chair. 35

"Hey!" I said, "it isn't over. I'm going to give you fifty francs after a while, but I want my money's worth."

She picked up her panties nervously.

"I've had enough, get it? I don't know what you want. And if you had me come up here to make a fool out of me . . ."

Then I took out my revolver and showed it to her. She looked at me seriously and dropped the panties without a word.

"Walk," I told her, "walk around." 40

She walked around for another five minutes. Then I gave her my cane and made her do exercises. When I felt my drawers were wet I got up and gave her a fifty-franc note. She took it.

"So long," I added. "I don't think I tired you out very much for the money."

I went out, I left her naked in the middle of the room, the brassiere in one hand and the fifty-franc note in the other. I didn't regret the money I spent; I had dumbfounded her and it isn't easy to surprise a whore. Going down the stairs I thought, "That's what I want. To surprise them all." I was happy as a child. I had brought along the green soap and after I reached home I rubbed it under the hot water for a long time until there was nothing left of it but a thin film between my fingers and it looked like a mint candy someone had sucked on for a long time.

But that night I woke up with a start and I saw her face again, her eyes when I showed her my gun, and her fat belly that bounced up and down at every step.

What a fool, I thought. And I felt bitter remorse: I should have shot her while I was 45 at it, shot that belly full of holes. That night and three nights afterward, I dreamed of six little red holes grouped in a circle about the navel.

As a result, I never went out without my revolver. I looked at people's backs, and I imagined, from their walk, the way they would fall if I shot them. I was in the habit of hanging around the Châtelet every Sunday when the classical concerts let out. About six o'clock I heard a bell ring and the ushers came to fasten back the plate glass doors with hooks. This was the beginning: the crowd came out slowly; the people walked with floating steps, their eyes still full of dreams, their hearts still full of pretty sentiments. There were a lot of them who looked around in amazement: the street must have seemed quite strange to them. Then they smiled mysteriously: they were passing from one world to another. I was waiting for them in this other world. I slid my right hand into my pocket and gripped the gun butt with all my strength. After a while, I *saw* myself shooting them. I knocked them off like clay pipes, they fell, one after the other and the panic-stricken survivors streamed back into the theatre, breaking the glass in the doors. It was an exciting game: when it was over, my hands were trembling and I had to go to Dreher's and drink a cognac to get myself in shape.

I wouldn't have killed the women. I would have shot them in the kidneys. Or in the calves, to make them dance.

I still hadn't decided anything. But I did everything just as though my power of decision had stopped. I began with minor details. I went to practice in a shooting gallery at Denfert-Rochereau. My scores weren't tremendous, but men are bigger targets, especially when you shoot point blank. Then I arranged my publicity. I chose a day when all my colleagues would be together in the office. On Monday morning. I was always very friendly with them, even though I had a horror of shaking their hands. They took off their gloves to greet you; they had an obscene way of undressing their hand, pulling the glove back and sliding it slowly along the fingers, unveiling the fat, wrinkled nakedness of the palm. I always kept my gloves on.

We never did much on Mondays. The typist from the commercial service came to bring us receipts. Lemercier joked pleasantly with her and when she had gone, they described her charms with a blasé competence. Then they talked about Lindbergh. They liked Lindbergh. I told them:

50 "I like the black heroes."

"Negroes?" Masse asked.

"No, black as in Black Magic. Lindbergh is a white hero. He doesn't interest me."

"Go see if it's easy to cross the Atlantic," Bouxin said sourly.

I told them my conception of the black hero.

55 "An anarchist," Lemercier said.

"No," I said quietly, "the anarchists like their own kind of men."

"Then it must be a crazy man."

But Masse, who had some education, intervened just then.

"I know your character," he said to me. "His name is Erostratus. He wanted to become famous and he couldn't find anything better to do than to burn down the temple of Ephesus, one of the seven wonders of the world."

60 "And what was the name of the man who built the temple?"

"I don't remember," he confessed, "I don't believe anybody knows his name."

"Really? But you remember the name of Erostratus? You see, he didn't figure things out too badly."

The conversation ended on these words, but I was quite calm. They would remember it when the time came. For myself, who, until then, had never heard of Erostratus, his story was encouraging. He had been dead for more than two thousand years and his act was still shining like a black diamond. I began to think that my destiny would be short and tragic. First it frightened me but I got used to it. If you look at it a certain way, it's terrible but, on the other hand, it gives the passing moment considerable force and beauty. I felt a strange power in my body when I went down into the street. I had my revolver on me, the thing that explodes and makes noise. But I no longer drew my assurance from that, it was from myself: I was a being like a revolver, a torpedo or a bomb. I too, one day at the end of my somber life, would explode and light the world with a flash as short and violent as magnesium. At that time I had the same dream several nights in a row. I was an anarchist. I had put myself in the path of the Tsar and I carried an infernal machine on me. At the appointed hour, the cortège passed, the bomb exploded and we were thrown into the air, myself, the Tsar, and three gold-braided officers, before the eyes of the crowd.

I now went for weeks on end without showing up at the office. I walked the boulevards in the midst of my future victims or locked myself in my room and made my plans. They fired me at the beginning of October. Then I spent my leisure working on the following letter, of which I made 102 copies.

65 Monsieur:

You are a famous man and your works sell by the thousands. I am going to tell you why: because you love men. You have humanism in your blood: you are lucky. You expand when you are with people; as soon as you see one of your fellows, even without knowing him, you feel sympathy for him. You have a taste for his body, for the way he is jointed, for his legs which open and close at will, and above all for his hands: it pleases you because he has five fingers on each hand and he can set his thumb against the other fingers. You are delighted when your neighbor takes a cup from the table because there is a way of taking it which is strictly human and which you have often described in your works; less supple, less rapid than that of a monkey, but is it not so much more intelligent? You also love the flesh of man, his look of being heavily wounded with re-education, seeming to reinvent walking at every step, and his famous look which even wild beasts cannot bear. So it has been easy for you to find the proper accent for speaking to man about himself: a modest, yet frenzied accent. People throw themselves greedily upon your books, they read them in a good armchair, they think of a great love, discreet and unhappy, which you bring them and that makes up for many things, for being ugly, for being cowardly, for being cuckolded, for not getting a raise on the first of January. And they say willingly of your latest book: it's a good deed.

I suppose you might be curious to know what a man can be like who does not love men. Very well, I am such a man, and I love them so little that soon I am going out and kill half a dozen of them: perhaps you might wonder why *only*, half a dozen? Because my revolver has only six cartridges. A monstrosity, isn't it? And moreover, an act strictly impolitic? But I tell you I *cannot* love them. I understand very well the way you feel. But what attracts you to them disgusts me. I have seen, as you, men chewing slowly, all the while keeping an eye on everything, the left hand leafing through an economic review. Is it my fault I prefer to watch the sea-lions feeding? Man can do nothing with his face without its turning into a game of physiognomy. When he chews, keeping his mouth shut, the corners of his mouth go up and down, he looks as though he were passing incessantly from serenity to tearful surprise. You love this, I know, you call it the watchfulness of the Spirit. But it makes me sick; I don't know why; I was born like that.

If there were only a difference of taste between us I would not trouble you. But everything happens as if you had grace and I had none. I am free to like or dislike lobster newburg, but if I do not like men I am a wretch and can find no place in the sun. They have monopolized the sense of life. I hope you will understand what I mean. For the past 33 years I have been beating against closed doors above which is written "No entrance if not a humanist." I have had to abandon all I have undertaken; I had to choose: either it was an absurd and ill-fated attempt, or sooner or later it had to turn to their profit. I could not succeed in detaching from myself thoughts I did not expressly destine for them, in formulating them: they remained in me as slight organic movements. Even the tools I used I felt belonged to them; words, for example: I wanted *my own* words. But the ones I use have dragged through I don't know how many consciences; they arrange themselves in my head by virtue of the habits I have picked up from the others and it is not without repugnance that I use them in writing to you. But this is the last time. I say to you: love men or it is only right for them to let you sneak out of it. Well, I do not want to sneak out. Soon I am going to take my revolver, I am going down into the street and see if anybody can do anything to *them*. Goodbye, perhaps it will be you I shall meet. You will never know then with what pleasure I shall blow your brains out. If not—and this is more likely—read tomorrow's papers. There you will see that an individual named Paul Hilbert has killed, in a moment of fury, six passers-by on the Boulevard Edgar-Quinet. You know better than anyone the value of newspaper prose.

You understand then that I am not "furious." I am, on the contrary, quite calm and I pray you to accept, Monsieur, the assurance of my distinguished sentiments.

Paul Hilbert

70   I slipped the 102 letters in 102 envelopes and on the envelopes I wrote the addresses of 102 French writers. Then I put the whole business in my table drawer along with six books of stamps.

I went out very little during the two weeks that followed. I let myself become slowly occupied by my crime. In the mirror, to which I often went to look at myself, I noticed the changes in my face with pleasure. The eyes had grown larger, they seemed to be eating up the whole face. They were black and tender behind the glasses and I rolled them like planets. The fine eyes of an artist or assassin. But I counted on changing even more profoundly after the massacre. I have seen photographs of two beautiful girls—those servants who killed and plundered their mistress. I saw their photos *before* and *after*. *Before*, their faces poised like sky flowers above piqué collars. They smelled of hygiene and appetizing honesty. A discreet curling iron had waved their hair exactly alike. And, even more reassuring than their curled hair, their collars and their look of being at the photographer's, there was their resemblance as sisters, their well considered resemblance which immediately put the bonds of blood and natural roots of the family circle to the fore. *After*, their faces were resplendent as fire. They had the bare neck of prisoners about to be beheaded. Everywhere wrinkles, horrible wrinkles of fear and hatred, folds, holes in the flesh as though a beast with claws had walked over their faces. And those eyes, always those black, depthless eyes—like mine. Yet they did not resemble one another. Each one, in her own way, bore the memory of the common crime. "If it is enough," I told myself, "for a crime which was mostly chance, to transform these orphans' faces, what can I not hope for from a crime entirely conceived and organized by myself." It would possess me, overturning my all-too-human ugliness . . . a crime, cutting the life of him who commits it in two. There must be times when one would like to turn back, but this shining object is there behind you, barring the way. I asked only an hour to enjoy mine, to feel its crushing weight. This time, I would arrange to have everything my way: I decided to carry out the execution at the top of the Rue Odessa. I would profit by the confusion to escape, leaving them to pick up their dead. I would run, I would cross the Boulevard Edgar-Quinet and turn quickly into the Rue Delambre. I would need only 30 seconds to reach the door of my building. My pursuers would still be on the Boulevard Edgar-Quinet, they would lose my trail and it would surely take them more than an hour to find it again. I would wait for them in my room, and when I would hear the beating on the door I would re-load my revolver and shoot myself in the mouth.

I began to live more expensively; I made an arrangement with the proprietor of a restaurant on the Rue Vavin who had a tray sent up every morning and evening. The boy rang, but I didn't open, I waited a few minutes then opened the door halfway and saw full plates steaming in a long basket set on the floor.

On October 27, at six in the evening, I had only 17 and a half francs left. I took my revolver and the packet of letters and went downstairs. I took care not to close the door, so as to re-enter more rapidly once I had finished. I didn't feel well, my hands were cold and blood was rushing to my head, my eyes tickled me. I looked at the stores, the Hotel de l'Ecole, the stationer's where I buy my pencils and I didn't recognize them. I wondered, "What street is this?" The Boulevard Montparnasse was full of people. They jostled me, pushed me, bumped me with their elbows or shoulders. I let myself be shoved around, I didn't have the strength to slip in between them.

Suddenly I saw myself in the heart of this mob, horribly alone and little. How they could have hurt me if they wanted! I was afraid because of the gun in my pocket. It seemed to me they could guess it was there. They would look at me with their hard eyes and would say: "Hey there . . . hey . . .!" with happy indignation, harpooning me with their men's paws. Lynched! They would throw me above their heads and I would fall back in their arms like a marionette. I thought it wiser to put off the execution of my plan until the next day. I went to eat at the *Cupole* for 16 francs 80. I had 70 centimes left and I threw them in the gutter.

I stayed three days in my room, without eating, without sleeping. I had drawn the blinds and I didn't dare go near the window or make a light. On Monday, someone rang at my door. I held my breath and waited. After a minute they rang again. I went on tiptoe and glued my eye to the keyhole. I could only see a piece of black cloth and a button. The man rang again and then went away. I don't know who it was. At night I had refreshing visions, palm trees, running water, a purple sky above a dome. I wasn't thirsty because hour after hour I went and drank at the spigot. But I was hungry. I saw the whore again. It was in a castle I had built in Causses Noires, about 60 miles from any town. She was naked and alone with me. Threatening her with my revolver I forced her to kneel and then run on all fours; then I tied her to a pillar and after I explained at great length what I was going to do, I riddled her with bullets. These images troubled me so much that I had to satisfy myself. Afterwards, I lay motionless in the darkness, my head absolutely empty. The furniture began to creak. It was five in the morning. I would have given anything to leave the room, but I couldn't go out because of the people walking in the street.

Day came, I didn't feel hungry any more, but I began to sweat: my shirt was soaked. 75
Outside there was sunlight. Then I thought "He is crouched in blackness, in a closed room, for three days. He has neither eaten nor slept. They rang and He didn't open. Soon, He is going into the street and He will kill."

I frightened myself. At six o'clock in the evening hunger struck me again. I was mad with rage. I bumped into the furniture, then I turned lights on in the rooms, the kitchen, the bathroom. I began to sing at the top of my voice. I washed my hands and I went out. It took me a good two minutes to put all the letters in the box. I shoved them in by tens. I must have crumpled a few envelopes. Then I followed the Boulevard Montparnasse as far as the Rue Odessa. I stopped in front of a haberdasher's window and when I saw my face I thought, "Tonight."

I posted myself at the top of the Rue Odessa, not far from the street lamp, and waited. Two women passed, arm in arm.

I was cold but I was sweating freely. After a while I saw three men come up; I let them by: I needed six. The one on the left looked at me and clicked his tongue. I turned my eyes away.

At seven-five, two groups, following each other closely, came out onto the Boulevard Edgar-Quinet. There was a man and a woman with two children. Behind them came three old women. I took a step forward. The woman looked angry and was shaking the little boy's arm. The man drawled,

"What a little bastard he is." 80

My heart was beating so hard it hurt my arms. I advanced and stood in front of them, motionless. My fingers, in my pocket, were all soft around the trigger.

"Pardon," the man said, bumping into me.

I remembered I had closed the door of the apartment and that provoked me. I would have to lose precious time opening it. The people were getting further away. I turned around and followed them mechanically. But I didn't feel like shooting them any more.

They were lost in the crowd on the boulevard. I leaned against the wall. I heard eight and nine o'clock strike. I repeated to myself, "Why must I kill all these people who are dead *already?*" and I wanted to laugh. A dog came and sniffed at my foot.

When the big man passed me, I jumped and followed him. I could see the fold of his red neck between his derby and the collar of his overcoat. He bounced a little in walking and breathed heavily, he looked husky. I took out my revolver: it was cold and bright, it disgusted me, I couldn't remember very well what I was supposed to do with it. Sometimes I looked at it and sometimes I looked at his neck. The fold in his neck smiled at me like a smiling, bitter mouth. I wondered if I wasn't going to throw my revolver into the sewer.

85 Suddenly, the man turned around and looked at me, irritated. I stepped back.

"I wanted to ask you . . ."

He didn't seem to be listening, he was looking at my hands.

"Can you tell me how to get to the Rue de la Gaité?"

His face was thick and his lips trembled. He said nothing. He stretched out his hand. I drew back further and said:

90 "I'd like . . ."

Then I *knew* I was going to start screaming. I didn't want to: I shot him three times in the belly. He fell with an idiotic look on his face, dropped to his knees and his head rolled on his left shoulder.

"Bastard," I said, "rotten bastard!"

I ran. I heard him coughing. I also heard shouts and feet clattering behind me. Somebody asked, "Is it a fight?" then right after that someone shouted "Murder! Murder!" I didn't think these shouts concerned me. But they seemed sinister, like the sirens of the fire engines when I was a child. Sinister and slightly ridiculous. I ran as fast as my legs could carry me.

Only I had committed an unpardonable error: instead of going up the Rue Odessa to the Boulevard Edgar-Quinet, *I was running down it toward the Boulevard Montparnasse.* When I realized it, it was too late: I was already in the midst of the crowd, astonished faces turned toward me (I remember the face of a heavily rouged woman wearing a green hat with an aigrette) and I heard the fools in the Rue Odessa shouting "murder" after me. A hand took me by the shoulder. I lost my head then: I didn't want to die stifled by this mob. I shot twice. People began to scream and scatter. I ran into a café. The drinkers jumped up as I ran through but made no attempt to stop me, I crossed the whole length of the café and locked myself in the lavatory. There was still one bullet in my revolver.

95 A moment went by. I was out of breath and gasping. Everything was extraordinarily silent, as though the people were keeping quiet on purpose. I raised the gun to my eyes and I saw its small hole, round and black: the bullet would come out there; the powder would burn my face. I dropped my arm and waited. After a while they came; there must have been a crowd of them, judging by the scuffling of feet on the floor. They whispered a little and then were quiet. I was still breathing heavily and I thought they must hear me breathing from the other side of the partition. Someone advanced quietly and rattled the door knob. He must have been flattened beside the door to avoid my bullets. I still wanted to shoot—but the last bullet was for me.

"What are they waiting for," I wondered. "If they pushed against the door and broke it down *right away* I wouldn't have time to kill myself and they would take me alive." But they were in no hurry; they gave me all the time in the world to die. The bastards, they were afraid.

After a while, a voice said, "All right, open up. We won't hurt you."

There was silence and the same voice went on, "You know you can't get away."

I didn't answer, I was still gasping for breath. To encourage myself to shoot, I told myself, "If they get me, they're going to beat me, break my teeth, maybe put an eye out." I wanted to know if the big man was dead. Maybe I only wounded him . . . They were getting something ready, they were dragging something heavy across the floor. I hurriedly put the barrel of the gun in my mouth, and I bit hard on it. But I couldn't shoot, I couldn't even put my finger on the trigger. Everything was dead silent.

I threw away the revolver and opened the door. [1939]

QUESTIONS

1. What is the narrator's conflict with humanity?
2. Does the narrator's life and experience live up to the story of Erostratus?
3. In what ways does the gun become a psychosexual symbol?
4. What does the letter tell us about the narrator? Why did he address the letter to writers?
5. Should we feel any sympathy for this man? Does Sartre have sympathy for him?

RESPONSES

1. Read Sartre's description of the role of writers in the Context essay "For Whom Does One Write?" Does this excerpt provide any context for how the protagonist views writers in the story?
2. Compare the manner in which this protagonist deals with his place in society with the protagonists of Gogol's "The Overcoat," Kafka's "The Metamorphosis," and Sontag's "The Dummy." Write an essay on how Sartre's character is similar to and different from these other characters.

Leslie Marmon Silko

Leslie Marmon Silko (b. 1948) was born in Albuquerque, New Mexico. A Laguna Pueblo, Silko attended Bureau of Indian Affairs schools and the University of New Mexico. She has taught in community colleges in Arizona, at the University of Arizona, and at the University of New Mexico. As a poet, short story writer, novelist, and essayist, Silko has published several books to great critical acclaim. Her novels are *Ceremony* (1977) and *Almanac of the Dead* (1991). *Storyteller* (1981) and *Sacred Water* (1993) include short fiction. Her essays are included in *Yellow Woman and a Beauty of the Spirit* (1996). She has won several awards including the MacArthur Foundation Grant.

Lullaby

The sun had gone down but the snow in the wind gave off its own light. It came in thick tufts like new wool—washed before the weaver spins it. Ayah reached out for it like her own babies had, and she smiled when she remembered how she had laughed at them. She was an old woman now, and her life had become memories. She sat down with her back against the wide cottonwood tree, feeling the rough bark on her back bones; she faced east and listened to the wind and snow sing a high-pitched Yeibechei song. Out of the wind she felt warmer, and she could watch the wide fluffy snow fill in her tracks, steadily, until the direction she had come from was gone. By the light of the snow she could see the dark outline of the big arroyo a few feet away. She was sitting on the edge of Cebolleta Creek, where in the springtime the thin cows would graze on grass already chewed flat to the ground. In the wide deep creek bed where only a trickle of water flowed in the summer, the skinny cows would wander, looking for new grass along winding paths splashed with manure.

Ayah pulled the old Army blanket over her head like a shawl. Jimmie's blanket—the one he had sent to her. That was a long time ago and the green wool was faded, and it was unraveling on the edges. She did not want to think about Jimmie. So she thought about the weaving and the way her mother had done it. On the tall wooden loom set into the sand under a tamarack tree for shade. She could see it clearly. She had been only a little girl when her grandma gave her the wooden combs to pull the twigs and burrs from the raw, freshly washed wool. And while she combed the wool, her grandma sat beside her, spinning a silvery strand of yarn around the smooth cedar spindle. Her mother worked at the loom with yarns dyed bright yellow and red and gold. She watched them dye the yarn in boiling black pots full of beeweed petals, juniper berries, and sage. The blankets her mother made were soft and woven so tight that rain rolled off them like birds' feathers. Ayah remembered sleeping warm on cold windy nights, wrapped in her mother's blankets on the hogan's sandy floor.

The snow drifted now, with the northwest wind hurling it in gusts. It drifted up around her black overshoes—old ones with little metal buckles. She smiled at the snow which was trying to cover her little by little. She could remember when they had no black rubber overshoes; only the high buckskin leggings that they wrapped over their elkhide moccasins. If the snow was dry or frozen, a person could walk all day and not get wet; and in the evenings the beams of the ceiling would hang with lengths of pale buckskin leggings, drying out slowly.

She felt peaceful remembering. She didn't feel cold any more. Jimmie's blanket seemed warmer than it had ever been. And she could remember the morning he was born. She could remember whispering to her mother, who was sleeping on the other side of the hogan, to tell her it was time now. She did not want to wake the others. The second time she called to her, her mother stood up and pulled on her shoes; she knew. They walked to the old stone hogan together, Ayah walking a step behind her mother. She waited alone, learning the rhythms of the pains while her mother went to call the old woman to help them. The morning was already warm even before dawn and Ayah smelled the bee flowers blooming and the young willow growing at the springs. She could remember that so clearly, but his birth merged into the births of the other children and to her it became all the same birth. They named him for the summer morning and in English they called him Jimmie.

It wasn't like Jimmie died. He just never came back, and one day a dark blue sedan with white writing on its doors pulled up in front of the boxcar shack where the rancher let the Indians live. A man in a khaki uniform trimmed in gold gave them a yellow piece of paper and told them that Jimmie was dead. He said the Army would try to get the body back and then it would be shipped to them; but it wasn't likely because the helicopter had burned after it crashed. All of this was told to Chato because he could understand English. She stood inside the doorway holding the baby while Chato listened. Chato spoke English like a white man and he spoke Spanish too. He was taller than the white man and he stood straighter too. Chato didn't explain why; he just told the military man they could keep the body if they found it. The white man looked bewildered; he nodded his head and he left. Then Chato looked at her and shook his head, and then he told her, "Jimmie isn't coming home anymore," and when he spoke, he used the words to speak of the dead. She didn't cry then, but she hurt inside with anger. And she mourned him as the years passed, when a horse fell with Chato and broke his leg, and the white rancher told them he wouldn't pay Chato until he could work again. She mourned Jimmie because he would have worked for his father then; he would have saddled the big bay horse and ridden the fence lines each day, with wire cutters and heavy gloves, fixing the breaks in the barbed wire and putting the stray cattle back inside again.

She mourned him after the white doctors came to take Danny and Ella away. She was at the shack alone that day they came. It was back in the days before they hired Navajo women to go with them as interpreters. She recognized one of the doctors. She had seem him at the children's clinic at Cañoncito about a month ago. They were wearing khaki uniforms and they waved papers at her and a black ball-point pen, trying to make her understand their English words. She was frightened by the way they looked at the children, like the lizard watches the fly. Danny was swinging on the tire

5

swing on the elm tree behind the rancher's house, the Ella was toddling around the front door, dragging the broomstick horse Chato made for her. Ayah could see they wanted her to sign the papers, and Chato had taught her to sign her name. It was something she was proud of. She only wanted them to go, and to take their eyes away from her children.

She took the pen from the man without looking at his face and she signed the papers in three different places he pointed to. She stared at the ground by their feet and waited for them to leave. But they stood there and began to point and gesture at the children. Danny stopped swinging. Ayah could see his fear. She moved suddenly and grabbed Ella into her arms; the child squirmed, trying to get back to her toys. Ayah ran with the baby toward Danny; she screamed for him to run and then she grabbed him around his chest and carried him too. She ran south into the foothills of juniper trees and black lava rock. Behind her she heard the doctors running, but they had been taken by surprise, and as the hills became steeper and the cholla cactus were thicker, they stopped. When she reached the top of the hill, she stopped to listen in case they were circling around her. But in a few minutes she heard a car engine start and they drove away. The children had been too surprised to cry while she ran with them. Danny was shaking and Ella's little fingers were gripping Ayah's blouse.

She stayed up in the hills for the rest of the day, sitting on a black lava boulder in the sunshine where she could see for miles all around her. The sky was light blue and cloudless, and it was warm for late April. The sun warmth relaxed her and took the fear and anger away. She lay back on the rock and watched the sky. It seemed to her that she could walk into the sky, stepping through clouds endlessly. Danny played with little pebbles and stones, pretending they were birds eggs and then little rabbits. Ella sat at her feet and dropped fistfuls of dirt into the breeze, watching the dust and particles of sand intently. Ayah watched a hawk soar high above them, dark wings gliding; hunting or only watching, she did not know. The hawk was patient and he circled all afternoon before he disappeared around the high volcanic peak the Mexicans called Guadalupe.

Late in the afternoon, Ayah looked down at the gray boxcar shack with the paint all peeled from the wood; the stove pipe on the roof was rusted and crooked. The fire she had built that morning in the oil drum stove had burned out. Ella was asleep in her lap now and Danny sat close to her, complaining that he was hungry; he asked when they would go to the house. "We will stay up here until your father comes," she told him, "because those white men were chasing us." The boy remembered then and he nodded at her silently.

10   If Jimmie had been there he could have read those papers and explained to her what they said. Ayah would have known then, never to sign them. The doctors came back the next day and they brought a BIA policeman with them. They told Chato they had her signature and that was all they needed. Except for the kids. She listened to Chato sullenly; she hated him when he told her it was the old woman who died in the winter, spitting blood; it was her old grandma who had given the children this disease. "They don't spit blood," she said coldly. "The whites lie." She held Ella and Danny close to her, ready to run to the hills again. "I want a medicine man first," she said to Chato, not looking at him. He shook his head. "It's too late now. The policeman is with them. You signed the paper." His voice was gentle.

It was worse than if they had died: to lose the children and to know that somewhere, in a place called Colorado, in a place full of sick and dying strangers, her children were without her. There had been babies that died soon after they were born, and one that died before he could walk. She had carried them herself, up to the boulders and great pieces of the cliff that long ago crashed down from Long Mesa; she laid them in the crevices of sandstone and buried them in the fine brown sand with round quartz pebbles that washed down the hills in the rain. She had endured it because they had been with her. But she could not bear this pain. She did not sleep for a long time after they took her children. She stayed on the hill where they had fled the first time, and she slept rolled up in the blanket Jimmie had sent her. She carried the pain in her belly and it was fed by everything she saw: the blue sky of their last day together and the dust and pebbles they played with; the swing in the elm tree and broomstick horse choked life from her. The pain filled her stomach and there was no room for food or for her lungs to fill with air. The air and the food would have been theirs.

She hated Chato, not because he let the policeman and doctors put the screaming children in the government car, but because he had taught her to sign her name. Because it was like the old ones always told her about learning their language or any of their ways: it endangered you. She slept alone on the hill until the middle of November when the first snow came. Then she made a bed for herself where the children had slept. She did not lie down beside Chato again until many years later, when he was sick and shivering and only her body could keep him warm. The illness came after the white rancher told Chato he was too old to work for him anymore, and Chato and his old woman should be out of the shack by the next afternoon because the rancher had hired new people to work there. That had satisfied her. To see how the white man repaid Chato's years of loyalty and work. All of Chato's fine-sounding English talk didn't change things.

It snowed steadily and the luminous light from the snow gradually diminished into the darkness. Somewhere in Cebolleta a dog barked and other village dogs joined with it. Ayah looked in the direction she had come, from the bar where Chato was buying the wine. Sometimes he told her to go on ahead and wait; and then he never came. And when she finally went back looking for him, she would find him passed out at the bottom of the wooden steps to Azzie's Bar. All the wine would be gone and most of the money too, from the pale blue check that came to them once a month in a government envelope. It was then that she would look at his face and his hands, scarred by ropes and the barbed wire of all those years, and she would think, this man is a stranger; for forty years she had smiled at him and cooked his food, but he remained a stranger. She stood up again, with the snow almost to her knees, and she walked back to find Chato.

It was hard to walk in the deep snow and she felt the air burn in her lungs. She stopped a short distance from the bar to rest and readjust the blanket. But this time he wasn't waiting for her on the bottom step with his old Stetson hat pulled down and his shoulders hunched up in his long wool overcoat.

She was careful not to slip on the wooden steps. When she pushed the door open, warm air and cigarette smoke hit her face. She looked around slowly and deliberately, in every corner, in every dark place that the old man might find to sleep. The bar owner didn't like Indians in there, especially Navajos, but he let Chato come in because he could talk Spanish like he was one of them. The men at the bar stared at her, and the bartender saw that she left the door open wide. Snowflakes were flying inside like moths and melting into a puddle on the oiled wood floor. He motioned to her to close the door, but she did not see him. She held herself straight and walked across the room slowly, searching the room with every step. The snow in her hair melted and she could feel it on her forehead. At the far corner of the room, she saw red flames at the mica window of the old stove door; she looked behind the stove just to make sure. The bar got quiet except for the Spanish polka music playing on the jukebox. She stood by the stove and shook the snow from her blanket and held it near the stove to dry. The wet wool smell reminded her of new-born goats in early March, brought inside to warm near the fire. She felt calm.

In past years they would have told her to get out. But her hair was white now and her face was wrinkled. They looked at her like she was a spider crawling slowly across the room. They were afraid; she could feel the fear. She looked at their faces steadily. They reminded her of the first time the white people brought her children back to her that winter. Danny had been shy and hid behind the thin white woman who brought them. And the baby had not known her until Ayah took her into her arms, and then Ella had nuzzled close to her as she had when she was nursing. The blonde woman was nervous and kept looking at a dainty gold watch on her wrist. She sat on the bench near the small window and watched the dark snow clouds gather around the mountains; she was worrying about the unpaved road. She was frightened by what she saw inside too: the strips of venison drying on a rope across the ceiling and the children jabbering excitedly in a language she did not know. So they stayed for only a few hours. Ayah watched the government car disappear down the road and she knew they were already being weaned from these lava hills and from this sky. The last time they came was in early June, and Ella stared at her the way the men in the bar were now staring. Ayah did not try to pick her up; she smiled at her instead and spoke cheerfully to Danny. When he tried to answer her, he could not seem to remember and he spoke English words with the Navajo. But he gave her a scrap of paper that he had found somewhere and carried in his pocket; it was folded in half, and he shyly looked up at her and said it was a bird. She asked Chato if they were home for good this time. He spoke to the white woman and she shook her head. "How much longer?" he asked, and she said she didn't know; but Chato saw how she stared at the boxcar shack. Ayah turned away then. She did not say good-bye.

She felt satisfied that the men in the bar feared her. Maybe it was her face and the way she held her mouth with teeth clenched tight, like there was nothing anyone could do to her now. She walked north down the road, searching for the old man. She did this because she had the blanket, and there would be no place for him except with her and the blanket in the old adobe barn near the arroyo. They always slept there when they came to Cebolleta. If the money and the wine were gone, she would be relieved because then they could go home again; back to the old hogan with a dirt roof and rock walls where she herself had been born. And the next day the old man could go back to the few sheep they still had, to follow along behind them, guiding them, into dry sandy arroyos where sparse grass grew. She knew he did not like walking behind old ewes when for so many years he rode big quarter horses and worked with cattle. But she wasn't sorry for him; he should have known all along what would happen.

There had not been enough rain for their garden in five years; and that was when Chato finally hitched a ride into the town and brought back brown boxes of rice and sugar and big tin cans of welfare peaches. After that, at the first of the month they went to Cebolleta to ask the postmaster for the check; and then Chato would go to the bar and cash it. They did this as they planted the garden every May, not because anything would survive the summer dust, but because it was time to do this. The journey passed the days that smelled silent and dry like the caves above the canyon with yellow painted buffaloes on their walls.

He was walking along the pavement when she found him. He did not stop or turn around when he heard her behind him. She walked beside him and she noticed how slowly he moved now. He smelled strong of woodsmoke and urine. Lately he had been forgetting. Sometimes he called her by his sister's name and she had been gone for a long time. Once she had found him wandering on the road to the white man's ranch, and she asked him why he was going that way; he laughed at her and said, "You know they can't run that ranch without me," and he walked on determined, limping on the leg that had been crushed many years before. Now he looked at her curiously, as if for the first time, but he kept shuffling along, moving slowly along the side of the highway. His gray hair had grown long and spread out on the shoulders of the long overcoat. He wore the old felt hat pulled down over his ears. His boots were worn out at the toes and he had stuffed pieces of an old red shirt in the holes. The rags made his feet look like little animals up to their ears in snow. She laughed at his feet; the snow muffled the sound of her laugh. He stopped and looked at her again. The wind had quit blowing and the snow was falling straight down; the southeast sky was beginning to clear and Ayah could see a star.

"Let's rest awhile," she said to him. They walked away from the road and up the   20
slope to the giant boulders that had tumbled down from the red sandrock mesa throughout the centuries of rainstorms and earth tremors. In a place where the boulders shut out the wind, they sat down with their backs against the rock. She offered half of the blanket to him and they sat wrapped together.

The storm passed swiftly. The clouds moved east. They were massive and full, crowding together across the sky. She watched them with the feeling of horses—steely blue-gray horses startled across the sky. The powerful haunches pushed into the distances and the tail hairs streamed white mist behind them. The sky cleared. Ayah saw that there was nothing between her and the stars. The light was crystalline. There was no shimmer, no distortion through earth haze. She breathed the clarity of the night sky; she smelled the purity of the half moon and the stars. He was lying on his side with his knees pulled up near his belly for warmth. His eyes were closed now, and in the light from the stars and the moon, he looked young again.

She could see it descend out of the night sky: an icy stillness from the edge of the moon. She recognized the freezing. It came gradually, sinking snowflake by snowflake until the crust was heavy and deep. It had the strength of the stars in Orion, and its journey was endless. Ayah knew that with the wine he would sleep. He would not feel it. She tucked the blanket around him, remembering how it was when Ella had been with her; and she felt the rush so big inside her heart for the babies. And she sang the only song she knew to sing for babies. She could not remember if she had ever sung it to her children, but she knew that her grandmother had sung it and her mother had sung it:

> The earth is your mother,
>   she holds you.
> The sky is your father,   25
>   he protects you.
> Sleep,
>   sleep.
> Rainbow is your sister,
>   she loves you.   30

> *The winds are your brothers,*
>   *they sing to you.*
>   *Sleep,*
>   *sleep.*
> *We are together always*
> *We are together always*
> *There never was a time*
>   *when this*
>   *was not so.*

[1974]

Questions

1. What is the tone of this story? Why should we sympathize with Ayah?
2. How would you describe Ayah's conflict in the story?
3. Explain the significance of the closing story.
4. Explore how Silko mixes images of despair and beauty throughout the story.
5. Compare the impact of oral and written language in the story.

Responses

1. Using a sociological/Marxist approach, write an essay examining the effects of capitalism on this family.
2. Compare this story to Rivera's ". . . And the Earth Did Not Devour Him." What features explain the authors' different themes?
3. Read the supporting materials in the "Context: Writers on Writing" section of this book and write an essay that uses that material to interpret this story.

Storyteller

Every day the sun came up a little lower on the horizon, moving more slowly until one day she got excited and started calling the jailer. She realized she had been sitting there for many hours, yet the sun had not moved from the center of the sky. The color of the sky had not been good lately; it had been pale blue, almost white, even when there were no clouds. She told herself it wasn't a good sign for the sky to be indistinguishable from the river ice, frozen solid and white against the earth. The tundra rose up behind the river but all the boundaries between the river and hills and sky were lost in the density of the pale ice.

She yelled again, this time some English words which came randomly into her mouth, probably swear words she'd heard from the oil drilling crews last winter. The jailer was an Eskimo, but he would not speak Yupik to her. She had watched people in other cells, when they spoke to him in Yupik he ignored them until they spoke English.

He came and stared at her. She didn't know if he understood what she was telling him until he glanced behind her at the small high window. He looked at the sun, and turned and walked away. She could hear the buckles on his heavy snowmobile boots jingle as he walked to the front of the building.

It was like the other buildings that white people, the Gussucks, brought with them: BIA and school buildings, portable buildings that arrived sliced in halves, on barges coming up the river. Squares of metal paneling bulged out with the layers of insulation stuffed inside. She had asked once what it was and someone told her it was to keep out the cold. She had not laughed then, but she did now. She walked over to the small double-pane window and she laughed out loud. They thought they could keep out the cold with stringy yellow wadding. Look at the sun. It wasn't moving: it was frozen, caught in the middle of the sky. Look at the sky, solid as the river with ice which had trapped the sun. It had not moved for a long time; in a few more hours it would be weak, and heavy frost would begin to appear on the edges and spread across the face of the sun like a mask. Its light was pale yellow, worn thin by the winter.

She could see people walking down the snow-packed roads, their breath steaming out from their parka hoods, faces hidden and protected by deep ruffs of fur. There were no cars or snowmobiles that day; the cold had silenced their machines. The metal froze; it split and shattered. Oil hardened and moving parts jammed solidly. She had seen it happen to their big yellow machines and the giant drill last 5 winter when they came to drill their test holes. The cold stopped them, and they were helpless against it.

Her village was many miles upriver from this town, but in her mind she could see it clearly. Their house was not near the village houses. It stood alone on the bank upriver from the village. Snow had drifted to the eaves of the roof on the north side, but on the west side, by the door, the path was almost clear. She had nailed scraps of red tin over the logs last summer. She had done it for the bright red color, not for added warmth the way the village people had done. This final winter had been coming even then; there had been signs of its approach for many years.

She went because she was curious about the big school where the Government sent all the other girls and boys. She had not played much with the village children while she was growing up because they were afraid of the old man, and they ran when her grandmother came. She went because she was tired of being alone with the old woman whose body had been stiffening for as long as the girl could remember. Her knees and knuckles were swollen grotesquely, and the pain had squeezed the brown skin of her face tight against the bones; it left her eyes hard like river stone. The girl asked once what it was that did this to her body, and the old woman had raised up from sewing a sealskin boot, and stared at her.

"The joints," the old woman said in a low voice, whispering like wind across the roof, "the joints are swollen with anger."

Sometimes she did not answer and only stared at the girl. Each year she spoke less and less, but the old man talked more—all night sometimes, not to anyone but himself; in a soft deliberate voice, he told stories, moving his smooth brown hands above the blankets. He had not fished or hunted with the other men for many years, although he was not crippled or sick. He stayed in his bed, smelling like dry fish and urine, telling stories all winter; and when warm weather came, he went to his place on the river bank. He sat with a long willow stick, poking at the smoldering moss he burned against the insects while he continued with the stories.

10   The trouble was that she had not recognized the warnings in time. She did not see what the Gussuck school would do to her until she walked into the dormitory and realized that the old man had not been lying about the place. She thought he had been trying to scare her as he used to when she was very small and her grandmother was outside cutting up fish. She hadn't believed what he told her about the school because she knew he wanted to keep her there in the log house with him. She knew what he wanted.

The dormitory matron pulled down her underpants and whipped her with a leather belt because she refused to speak English.

"Those backwards village people," the matron said, because she was an Eskimo who had worked for the BIA a long time, "they kept this one until she was too big to learn." The other girls whispered in English. They knew how to work the showers, and they washed and curled their hair at night. They ate Gussuck food. She lay on her bed and imagined what her grandmother might be sewing, and what the old man was eating in his bed. When summer came, they sent her home.

The way her grandmother had hugged her before she left for school had been a warning too, because the old woman had not hugged or touched her for many years. Not like the old man, whose hands were always hunting, like ravens circling lazily in the sky, ready to touch her. She was not surprised when the priest and the old man met her at the landing strip, to say that the old lady was gone. The priest asked her where she would like to stay. He referred to the old man as her grandfather, but she did not bother to correct him. She had already been thinking about it; if she went with the priest, he would send her away to a school. But the old man was different. She knew he wouldn't send her back to school. She knew he wanted to keep her.

He told her one time, that she would get too old for him faster than he got too old for her; but again she had not believed him because sometimes he lied. He had lied about what he would do with her if she came into his bed. But as the years passed, she realized what he said was true. She was restless and strong. She had no patience with the old man who had never changed his slow smooth motions under the blankets.

The old man was in his bed for the winter; he did not leave it except to use the slop   15
bucket in the corner. He was dozing with his mouth open slightly; his lips quivered and sometimes they moved like he was telling a story even while he dreamed. She pulled on the sealskin boots, the mukluks with the bright red flannel linings her grandmother had sewn for her, and she tied the braided red yarn tassels around her ankles over the gray wool pants. She zipped the wolfskin parka. Her grandmother had worn it for many years, but the old man said that before she died, she instructed him to bury her in an old black sweater, and to give the parka to the girl. The wolf pelts were creamy colored and silver, almost white in some places, and when the old lady had walked across the tundra in the winter, she was invisible in the snow.

She walked toward the village, breaking her own path through the deep snow. A team of sled dogs tied outside a house at the edge of the village leaped against their chains to bark at her. She kept walking, watching the dusky sky for the first evening stars. It was warm and the dogs were alert. When it got cold again, the dogs would lie curled and still, too drowsy from the cold to bark or pull at the chains. She laughed loudly because it made them howl and snarl. Once the old man had seen her tease the dogs and he shook his head. "So that's the kind of woman you are," he said, "in the wintertime the two of us are no different from those dogs. We wait in the cold for someone to bring us a few dry fish."

She laughed out loud again, and kept walking. She was thinking about the Gussuck oil drillers. They were strange; they watched her when she walked near their machines. She wondered what they looked like underneath their quilted goose-down trousers; she wanted to know how they moved. They would be something different from the old man.

The old man screamed at her. He shook her shoulders so violently that her head bumped against the log wall. "I smelled it!" he yelled, "as soon as I woke up! I am sure of it now. You can't fool me!" His thin legs were shaking inside the baggy wool trousers; he stumbled over her boots in his bare feet. His toenails were long and yellow like bird claws; she had seen a gray crane last summer fighting another in the shallow water on the edge of the river. She laughed out loud and pulled her shoulder out of his grip. He stood in front of her. He was breathing hard and shaking; he looked weak. He would probably die next winter.

"I'm warning you," he said, "I'm warning you." He crawled back into his bunk then, and reached under the old soiled feather pillow for a piece of dry fish. He lay back on the pillow, staring at the ceiling and chewed dry strips of salmon. "I don't know what the old woman told you," he said, "but there will be trouble." He looked over to see if she was listening. His face suddenly relaxed into a smile, his dark slanty eyes were lost in wrinkles of brown skin. "I could tell you, but you are too good for warnings now. I can smell what you did all night with the Gussucks."

20   She did not understand why they came there, because the village was small and so far upriver that even some Eskimos who had been away to school did not want to come back. They stayed downriver in the town. They said the village was too quiet. They were used to the town where the boarding school was located, with electric lights and running water. After all those years away at school, they had forgotten how to set nets in the river and where to hunt seals in the fall. When she asked the old man why the Gussucks bothered to come to the village, his narrow eyes got bright with excitement.

"They only come when there is something to steal. The fur animals are too difficult for them to get now, and the seals and fish are hard to find. Now they come for oil deep in the earth. But this is the last time for them." His breathing was wheezy and fast; his hands gestured at the sky. "It is approaching. As it comes, ice will push across the sky." His eyes were open wide and he stared at the low ceiling rafters for hours without blinking. She remembered all this clearly because he began the story that day, the story he told from that time on. It began with a giant bear which he described muscle by muscle, from the curve of the ivory claws to the whorls of hair at the top of the massive skull. And for eight days he did not sleep, but talked continuously of the giant bear whose color was pale blue glacier ice.

The snow was dirty and worn down in a path to the door. On either side of the path, the snow was higher than her head. In front of the door there were jagged yellow stains melted into the snow where men had urinated. She stopped in the entry way and kicked the snow off her boots. The room was dim; a kerosene lantern by the cash register was burning low. The long wooden shelves were jammed with cans of beans and potted meats. On the bottom shelf a jar of mayonnaise was broken open, leaking oily white clots on the floor. There was no one in the room except the yellowish dog sleeping in the front of the long glass display case. A reflection made it appear to be lying on the knives and ammunition inside the case. Gussucks kept dogs inside their houses with them; they did not seem to mind the odors which seeped out of the dogs. "They tell us we are dirty for the food we eat—raw fish and fermented meat. But we do not live with dogs," the old man once said. She heard voices in the back room, and the sound of bottles set down hard on tables.

They were always confident. The first year they waited for the ice to break up on the river, and then they brought their big yellow machines up river on barges. They planned to drill their test holes during the summer to avoid the freezing. But the imprints and graves of their machines were still there, on the edge of the tundra above the river, where the summer mud had swallowed them before they ever left sight of the river. The village people had gathered to watch the white men, and to laugh as they drove the giant machines, one by one, off the steel ramp into the bogs; as if sheer numbers of vehicles would somehow make the tundra solid. But the old man said they behaved like desperate people, and they would come back again. When the tundra was frozen solid, they returned.

Village women did not even look through the door to the back room. The priest had warned them. The storeman was watching her because he didn't let Eskimos or Indians sit down at the tables in the back room. But she knew he couldn't throw her out if one of his Gussuck customers invited her to sit with him. She walked across the room. They stared at her, but she had the feeling she was walking for someone else, not herself, so their eyes did not matter. The red-haired man pulled out a chair and motioned for her to sit down. She looked back at the storeman while the red-haired man poured her a glass of red sweet wine. She wanted to laugh at the storeman the way she laughed at the dogs, straining against the chains, howling at her.

The red-haired man kept talking to the other Gussucks sitting around the table, but he slid one hand off the top of the table to her thigh. She looked over at the storeman to see if he was still watching her. She laughed out loud at him and the red-haired man stopped talking and turned to her. He asked if she wanted to go. She nodded and stood up. 25

Someone in the village had been telling him things about her, he said as they walked down the road to his trailer. She understood that much of what he was saying, but the rest she did not hear. The whine of the big generators at the construction camp sucked away the sound of his words. But English was of no concern to her anymore, and neither was anything the Christians in the village might say about her or the old man. She smiled at the effect of the subzero air on the electric lights around the trailers; they did not shine. They left only flat yellow holes in the darkness.

It took him a long time to get ready, even after she had undressed for him. She waited in the bed with the blankets pulled close, watching him. He adjusted the thermostat and lit candles in the room, turning out the electric lights. He searched through a stack of record albums until he found the right one. She was not sure about the last thing he did: he taped something on the wall behind the bed where he could see it while he lay on top of her. He was shriveled and white from the cold; he pushed against her body for warmth. He guided her hands to his thighs; he was shivering.

She had returned a last time because she wanted to know what it was he stuck on the wall above the bed. After he finished each time, he reached up and pulled it loose, folding it carefully so that she could not see it. But this time she was ready; she waited for his fast breathing and sudden collapse on top of her. She slid out from under him and stood up beside the bed. She looked at the picture while she got dressed. He did not raise his face from the pillow, and she thought she heard teeth rattling together as she left the room.

She heard the old man move when she came in. After the Gussuck's trailer, the log house felt cool. It smelled like dry fish and cured meat. The room was dark except for the blinking yellow flame in the mica window of the oil stove. She squatted in front of the stove and watched the flames for a long time before she walked to the bed where her grandmother had slept. The bed was covered with a mound of rags and fur scraps the old woman had saved. She reached into the mound until she felt something cold and solid wrapped in a wool blanket. She pushed her fingers around it until she felt smooth stone. Long ago, before the Gussucks came, they had burned whale oil in the big stone lamp which made light and heat as well. The old woman had saved everything they would need when the time came.

In the morning, the old man pulled a piece of dry caribou meat from under the blankets and offered it to her. While she was gone, men from the village had brought a bundle of dry meat. She chewed it slowly, thinking about the way they still came from the village to take care of the old man and his stories. But she had a story now, about the red-haired Gussuck. The old man knew what she was thinking, and his smile made his face seem more round than it was. 30

"Well," he said, "what was it?"

"A woman with a big dog on top of her."

He laughed softly to himself and walked over to the water barrel. He dipped his cup into the water.

"It doesn't surprise me," he said.

35 "Grandma," she said, "there was something red in the grass that morning. I remember." She had not asked about her parents before. The old woman stopped splitting the fish bellies open for the willow drying racks. Her jaw muscles pulled so tightly against her skull, the girl thought the old woman would not be able to speak.

"They bought a tin can full of it from the storeman. Late at night. He told them it was alcohol safe to drink. They traded a rifle for it." The old woman's voice sounded like each word stole strength from her. "It made no difference about the rifle. That year the Gussuck boats had come, firing big guns at the walrus and seals. There was nothing left to hunt after that anyway. So," the old lady said, in a low soft voice the girl had not heard for a long time, "I didn't say anything to them when they left that night."

"Right over there," she said, pointing at the fallen poles, half buried in the river sand and tall grass, "in the summer shelter. The sun was high half the night then. Early in the morning when it was still low, the policeman came around. I told the interpreter to tell him that the storeman had poisoned them." She made outlines in the air in front of her, showing how their bodies lay twisted on the sand; telling the story was like laboring to walk through deep snow; sweat shone in the white hair around her forehead. "I told the priest too, after he came. I told him the storeman lied." She turned away from the girl. She held her mouth even tighter, set solidly, not in sorrow or anger, but against the pain, which was all that remained. "I never believed," she said, "not much anyway. I wasn't surprised when the priest did nothing."

The wind came off the river and folded the tall grass into itself like river waves. She could feel the silence the story left, and she wanted to have the old woman go on.

"I heard sounds that night, grandma. Sounds like someone was singing. It was light outside. I could see something red on the ground." The old woman did not answer her; she moved to the tub full of fish on the ground beside the workbench. She stabbed her knife into the belly of a whitefish and lifted it onto the bench. "The Gussuck storeman left the village right after that," the old woman said as she pulled the entrails from the fish, "otherwise, I could tell you more." The old woman's voice flowed with the wind blowing off the river; they never spoke of it again.

40 When the willows got their leaves and the grass grew tall along the river banks and around the sloughs, she walked early in the morning. While the sun was still low on the horizon, she listened to the wind off the river; its sound was like the voice that day long ago. In the distance, she could hear the engines of the machinery the oil drillers had left the winter before, but she did not go near the village or the store. The sun never left the sky and the summer became the same long day, with only the winds to fan the sun into brightness or allow it to slip into twilight.

She sat beside the old man at his place on the river bank. She poked the smoky fire for him, and felt herself growing wide and thin in the sun as if she had been split from belly to throat and strung on the willow pole in preparation for the winter to come. The old man did not speak anymore. When men from the village brought him fresh fish he hid them deep in the river grass where it was cool. After he went inside, she split the fish open and spread them to dry on the willow frame the way the old woman had done. Inside, he dozed and talked to himself. He had talked all winter, softly and incessantly, about the giant polar bear stalking a lone hunter across Bering Sea ice. After all the months the old man had been telling the story, the bear was within a hundred feet of the man; but the ice fog had closed in on them now and the man could only smell the sharp ammonia odor of the bear, and hear the edge of the snow crust crack under the giant paws.

One night she listened to the old man tell the story all night in his sleep, describing each crystal of ice and the slightly different sounds they made under each paw; first the left and then the right paw, then the hind feet. Her grandmother was there suddenly, a shadow around the stove. She spoke in her low wind voice and the girl was afraid to sit up to hear more clearly. Maybe what she said had been to the old man because he stopped telling the story and began to snore softly the way he had long ago when the old woman had scolded him for telling his stories while others in the house were trying to sleep. But the last words she heard clearly: "It will take a long time, but the story must be told. There must not be any lies." She pulled the blankets up around her chin, slowly, so that her movements would not be seen. She thought her grandmother was talking about the old man's bear story; she did not know about the other story then.

She left the old man wheezing and snoring in his bed. She walked through the river grass glistening with frost; the bright green summer color was already fading. She watched the sun move across the sky, already lower on the horizon, already moving away from the village. She stopped by the fallen poles of the summer shelter where her parents had died. Frost glittered on the river sand too; in a few more weeks there would be snow. The predawn light would be the color of an old woman. An old woman full of snow. There had been something red lying on the ground the morning they died. She looked for it again, pushing aside the grass with her foot. She knelt in the sand and looked under the fallen structure for some trace of it. When she found it, she would know what the old woman had never told her. She squatted down close to the gray poles and leaned her back against them. The wind made her shiver.

The summer rain had washed the mud from between the logs; the sod blocks stacked as high as her belly next to the log walls had lost their square-cut shape and had grown into soft mounds of tundra moss and stiff-bladed grass bending with clusters of seed bristles. She looked at the northwest, in the direction of the Bering Sea. The cold would come down from there to find narrow slits in the mud, rainwater holes in the outer layer of sod which protected the log house. The dark green tundra stretched away flat and continuous. Somewhere the sea and the land met; she knew by their dark green colors there were no boundaries between them. That was how the cold would come: when the boundaries were gone the polar ice would range across the land into the sky. She watched the horizon for a long time. She would stand in that place on the north side of the house and she would keep watch on the northwest horizon, and eventually she would see it come. She would watch for its approach in the stars, and hear it come with the wind. These preparations were unfamiliar, but gradually she recognized them as she did her own footprints in the snow.

She emptied the slop jar beside his bed twice a day and kept the barrel full of water   45
melted from river ice. He did not recognize her anymore, and when he spoke to her, he called her by her grandmother's name and talked about people and events from long ago, before he went back to telling the story. The giant bear was creeping across the new snow on its belly, close enough now that the man could hear the rasp of its breathing. On and on in a soft singing voice, the old man caressed the story, repeating the words again and again like gentle strokes.

The sky was gray like a river crane's egg; its density curved into the thin crust of frost already covering the land. She looked at the bright red color of the tin against the ground and the sky and she told the village men to bring the pieces for the old man and her. To drill the test holes in the tundra, the Gussucks had used hundreds of barrels of fuel. The village people split open the empty barrels that were abandoned on the river bank, and pounded the red tin into flat sheets. The village people were using the strips of tin to mend walls and roofs for winter. But she nailed it on the log walls for its color. When she finished, she walked away with the hammer in her hand, not turning around until she was far away, on the ridge above the river banks, and then she looked back. She felt a chill when she saw how the sky and the land were already losing their boundaries, already becoming lost in each other. But the red tin penetrated the thick white color of earth and sky; it defined the boundaries like a wound revealing the ribs and heart of a great caribou about to bolt and be lost to the hunter forever. That night the wind howled and when she scratched a hole through the heavy frost on the inside of the window, she could see nothing but the impenetrable white; whether it was blowing snow or snow that had drifted as high as the house, she did not know.

It had come down suddenly, and she stood with her back to the wind looking at the river, its smoky water clotted with ice. The wind had blown the snow over the frozen river, hiding thin blue streaks where fast water ran under ice translucent and fragile as memory. But she could see shadows of boundaries, outlines of paths which were slender branches of solidity reaching out from the earth. She spent days walking on the river, watching the colors of ice that would safely hold her, kicking the heel of her boot into the snow crust, listening for a solid sound. When she could feel the paths through the soles of her feet, she went to the middle of the river where the fast gray water churned under a thin pane of ice. She looked back. On the river bank in the distance she could see the red tin nailed to the log house, something not swallowed up by the heavy white belly of the sky or caught in the folds of the frozen earth. It was time.

The wolverine fur around the hood of her parka was white with the frost from her breathing. The warmth inside the store melted it, and she felt tiny drops of water on her face. The storeman came in from the back room. She unzipped the parka and stood by the oil stove. She didn't look at him, but stared instead at the yellowish dog, covered with scabs of matted hair, sleeping in front of the stove. She thought of the Gussuck's picture, taped on the wall above the bed and she laughed out loud. The sound of her laughter was piercing; the yellow dog jumped to its feet and the hair bristled down its back. The storeman was watching her. She wanted to laugh again because he didn't know about the ice. He did not know that it was prowling the earth, or that it had already pushed its way into the sky to seize the sun. She sat down in the chair by the stove and shook her long hair loose. He was like a dog tied up all winter, watching while the others got fed. He remembered how she had gone with the oil drillers, and his blue eyes moved like flies crawling over her body. He held his thin pale lips like he wanted to spit on her. He hated the people because they had something of value, the old man said, something which the Gussucks could never have. They thought they could take it, suck it out of the earth or cut it from the mountains; but they were fools.

There was a matted hunk of dog hair on the floor by her foot. She thought of the yellow insulation coming unstuffed: their defense against the freezing going to pieces as it advanced on them. The ice was crouching on the northwest horizon like the old man's bear. She laughed out loud again. The sun would be down now; it was time.

The first time he spoke to her, she did not hear what he said, so she did not answer or even look up at him. He spoke to her again but his words were only noises coming from his pale mouth, trembling now as his anger began to unravel. He jerked her up and the chair fell over behind her. His arms were shaking and she could feel his hands tense up, pulling the edges of the parka tighter. He raised his fist to hit her, his thin body quivering with rage; but the fist collapsed with the desire he had for the valuable things, which, the old man had rightly said, was the only reason they came. She could hear his heart pounding as he held her close and arched his hips against her, groaning and breathing in spasms. She twisted away from him and ducked under his arms.

She ran with a mitten over her mouth, breathing through the fur to protect her lungs from the freezing air. She could hear him running behind her, his heavy breathing, the occasional sound of metal jingling against metal. But he ran without his parka or mittens, breathing the frozen air; its fire squeezed the lungs against the ribs and it was enough that he could not catch her near his store. On the river bank he realized how far he was from his stove, and the wads of yellow stuffing that held off the cold. But the girl was not able to run very fast through the deep drifts at the edge of the river. The twilight was luminous and he could still see clearly for a long distance; he knew he could catch her so he kept running.

When she neared the middle of the river she looked over her shoulder. He was not following her tracks; he went straight across the ice, running the shortest distance to reach her. He was close then; his face was twisted and scarlet from the exertion and the cold. There was satisfaction in his eyes; he was sure he could outrun her.

She was familiar with the river, down to the instant ice flexed into hairline fractures, and the cracking bone-sliver sounds gathered momentum with the opening ice until the churning gray water was set free. She stopped and turned to the sound of the river and the rattle of swirling ice fragments where he fell through. She pulled off a mitten and zipped the parka to her throat. She was conscious then of her own rapid breathing.

She moved slowly, kicking the ice ahead with the heel of her boot, feeling for sinews of ice to hold her. She looked ahead and all around herself; in the twilight, the dense white sky had merged into the flat snow-covered tundra. In the frantic running she had lost her place on the river. She stood still. The east bank of the river was lost in the sky; the boundaries had been swallowed by the freezing white. But then, in the distance, she saw something red, and suddenly it was as she had remembered it all those years.

She sat on her bed and while she waited, she listened to the old man. The hunter had found a small jagged knoll on the ice. He pulled his beaver fur cap off his head; the fur inside it steamed with his body heat and sweat. He left it upside down on the ice for the great bear to stalk, and he waited downwind on top of the ice knoll; he was holding the jade knife. 55

She thought she could see the end of his story in the way he wheezed out the words; but still he reached into his cache of dry fish and dribbled water into his mouth from the tin cup. All night she listened to him describe each breath the man took, each motion of the bear's head as it tried to catch the sound of the man's breathing, and tested the wind for his scent.

The state trooper asked her questions, and the woman who cleaned house for the priest translated them in to Yupik. They wanted to know what happened to the storeman, the Gussuck who had been seen running after her down the road onto the river late last evening. He had not come back, and the Gussuck boss in Anchorage was concerned about him. She did not answer for a long time because the old man suddenly sat up in his bed and began to talk excitedly, looking at all of them—the trooper in his dark glasses and the housekeeper in her corduroy parka. He kept saying, "The story! The story! Eh-ya! The great bear! The hunter!"

They asked her again, what happened to the man from the Northern Commercial store. "He lied to them. He told them it was safe to drink. But I will not lie." She stood up and put on the gray wolfskin parka. "I killed him," she said, "but I don't lie."

The attorney came back again, and the jailer slid open the steel doors and opened the cell to let him in. He motioned for the jailer to stay to translate for him. She laughed when she saw how the jailer would be forced by this Gussuck to speak Yupik to her. She liked the Gussuck attorney for that, and for the thinning hair on his head. He was very tall, and she liked to think about the exposure of his head to the freezing; she wondered if he would feel the ice descending from the sky before the others did. He wanted to know why she told the state trooper she had killed the storeman. Some village children had seen it happen, he said, and it was an accident. "That's all you have to say to the judge: it was an accident." He kept repeating it over and over again to her, slowly in a loud but gentle voice: "It was an accident. He was running after you and he fell through the ice. That's all you have to say in court. That's all. And they will let you go home. Back to your village." The jailer translated the words sullenly, staring down at the floor. She shook her head. "I will not change the story, not even to escape this place and go home. I intended that he die. The story must be told as it is." The attorney exhaled loudly; his eyes looked tired. "Tell her that she could not have killed him that way. He is a white man. He ran after her without a parka or mittens. She could not have planned that." He paused and turned toward the cell door. "Tell her I will do all I can for her. I will explain to the judge that her mind is confused." She laughed out loud when the jailer translated what the attorney said. The Gussucks did not understand the story; they could not see the way it must be told, year after year as the old man had done, without lapse or silence.

60   She looked out the window at the frozen white sky. The sun had finally broken loose from the ice but it moved like a wounded caribou running on strength which only dying animals find, leaping and running on bullet-shattered lungs. Its light was weak and pale; it pushed dimly through the clouds. She turned and faced the Gussuck attorney.

"It began a long time ago," she intoned steadily, "in the summertime. Early in the morning, I remember, something red in the tall river grass. . . ."

The day after the old man died, men from the village came. She was sitting on the edge of her bed, across from the woman the trooper hired to watch her. They came into the room slowly and listened to her. At the foot of her bed they left a king salmon that had been split open wide and dried last summer. But she did not pause or hesitate; she went on with the story, and she never stopped, not even when the woman got up to close the door behind the village men.

The old man would not change the story even when he knew the end was approaching. Lies could not stop what was coming. He thrashed around on the bed, pulling the blankets loose, knocking bundles of dried fish and meat on the floor. The hunter had been on the ice for many hours. The freezing winds on the ice knoll had numbed his hands in the mittens, and the cold had exhausted him. He felt a single muscle tremor in his hand that he could not stop, and the jade knife fell; it shattered on the ice, and the blue glacier bear turned slowly to face him.   [1974]

Questions

1. Who is the storyteller in the title?
2. Why does Silko devote so much description to the setting of the story?
3. What role does the old man play? What does he contribute?
4. Does the strip of red tin become a symbol? If so, of what?
5. Is this a story about revenge? Is revenge achieved?

Responses

1. Compare the effect of setting in this story and in Jack London's "To Build a Fire."
2. Can you read this story from an ecocritical perspective? If so, what solutions to the ecological crises does Silko recommend?

LESLIE MARMON SILKO

Yellow Woman

My thigh clung to his with dampness, and I watched the sun rising up through the tamaracks and willows. The small brown water birds came to the river and hopped across the mud, leaving brown scratches in the alkali-white crust. They bathed in the river silently. I could hear the water, almost at our feet where the narrow fast channel bubbled and washed green ragged moss and fern leaves. I looked at him beside me, rolled in the red blanket on the white river sand. I cleaned the sand out of the cracks between my toes, squinting because the sun was above the willow trees. I looked at him for the last time, sleeping on the white river sand.

I felt hungry and followed the river south the way we had come the afternoon before, following our footprints that were already blurred by lizard tracks and bug trails. The horses were still lying down, and the black one whinnied when he saw me but he did not get up—maybe it was because the corral was made out of thick cedar branches and the horses had not yet felt the sun like I had. I tried to look beyond the pale red mesas to the pueblo. I knew it was there, even if I could not see it, on the sandrock hill above the river, the same river that moved past me now and had reflected the moon last night.

The horse felt warm underneath me. He shook his head and pawed the sand. The bay whinnied and leaned against the gate trying to follow, and I remembered him asleep in the red blanket beside the river. I slid off the horse and tied him close to the other horse, I walked north with the river again, and the white sand broke loose in footprints over footprints.

"Wake up."

5   He moved in the blanket and turned his face to me with his eyes still closed. I knelt down to touch him.

"I'm leaving."

He smiled now, eyes still closed. "You are coming with me, remember?" He sat up now with his bare dark chest and belly in the sun.

"Where?"

"To my place."

10   "And will I come back?"

He pulled his pants on. I walked away from him, feeling him behind me and smelling the willows.

"Yellow Woman," he said.

1028

I turned to face him. "Who are you?" I asked.

He laughed and knelt on the low, sandy bank, washing his face in the river. "Last night you guessed my name, and you knew why I had come."

I stared past him at the shallow moving water and tried to remember the night, but I could only see the moon in the water and remember his warmth around me.

"But I only said that you were him and that I was Yellow Woman—I'm not really her—I have my own name and I come from the pueblo on the other side of the mesa. Your name is Silva and you are a stranger I met by the river yesterday afternoon."

He laughed softly. "What happened yesterday has nothing to do with what you will do today, Yellow Woman."

"I know—that's what I'm saying—the old stories about the ka'tsina spirit and Yellow Woman can't mean us."

My old grandpa liked to tell those stories best. There is one about Badger and Coyote who went hunting and were gone all day, and when the sun was going down they found a house. There was a girl living there alone, and she had light hair and eyes and she told them that they could sleep with her. Coyote wanted to be with her all night so he sent Badger into a prairie-dog hole, telling him he thought he saw something in it. As soon as Badger crawled in, Coyote blocked up the entrance with rocks and hurried back to Yellow Woman.

"Come here," he said gently.

He touched my neck and I moved close to him to feel his breathing and to hear his heart. I was wondering if Yellow Woman had known who she was—if she knew that she would become part of the stories. Maybe she'd had another name that her husband and relatives called her so that only the ka'tsina from the north and the storytellers would know her as Yellow Woman. But I didn't go on; I felt him all around me, pushing me down into the white river sand.

Yellow Woman went away with the spirit from the north and lived with him and his relatives. She was gone for a long time, but then one day she came back and she brought twin boys.

"Do you know the story?"

"What story?" He smiled and pulled me close to him as he said this. I was afraid lying there on the red blanket. All I could know was the way he felt, warm, damp, his body beside me. This is the way it happens in the stories, I was thinking, with no thought beyond the moment she meets the ka'tsina spirit and they go.

"I don't have to go. What they tell in stories was real only then, back in time immemorial, like they say."

He stood up and pointed at my clothes tangled in the blanket. "Let's go," he said.

I walked beside him, breathing hard because he walked fast, his hand around my wrist. I had stopped trying to pull away from him, because his hand felt cool and the sun was high, drying the river bed into alkali. I will see someone, eventually I will see someone, and then I will be certain that he is only a man—some man from nearby— and I will be sure that I am not Yellow Woman. Because she is from out of time past and I live now and I've been to school and there are highways and pickup trucks that Yellow Woman never saw.

It was an easy ride north on horseback. I watched the change from the cottonwood trees along the river to the junipers that brushed past us in the foothills, and finally there were only piñons, and when I looked up at the rim of the mountain plateau I could see pine trees growing on the edge. Once I stopped to look down, but the pale sandstone had disappeared and the river was gone and the dark lava hills were all around. He touched my hand, not speaking, but always singing softly a mountain song and looking into my eyes.

I felt hungry and wondered what they were doing at home now—my mother, my grandmother, my husband, and the baby. Cooking breakfast, saying, "Where did she go?—maybe kidnapped." And Al going to the tribal police with the details: "She went walking along the river."

30   The house was made with black lava rock and red mud. It was high above the spreading miles of arroyos and long mesas. I smelled a mountain smell of pitch and buck brush. I stood there beside the black horse, looking down on the small, dim country we had passed, and I shivered.

"Yellow Woman, come inside where it's warm." He lit a fire in the stove. It was an old stove with a round belly and an enamel coffeepot on top. There was only the stove, some faded Navajo blankets, and a bedroll and cardboard box. The floor was made of smooth adobe plaster, and there was one small window facing east. He pointed at the box.

"There's some potatoes and the frying pan." He sat on the floor with his arms around his knees pulling them close to his chest and he watched me fry the potatoes. I didn't mind him watching me because he was always watching me—he had been watching me since I came upon him sitting on the river bank trimming leaves from a willow twig with his knife. We ate from the pan and he wiped the grease from his fingers on his Levi's.

"Have you brought women here before?" He smiled and kept chewing, so I said, "Do you always use the same tricks?"

"What tricks?" He looked at me like he didn't understand.

35   "The story about being a ka'tsina from the mountains. The story about Yellow Woman."

Silva was silent; his face was calm.

"I don't believe it. Those stories couldn't happen now," I said.

He shook his head and said softly, "But someday they will talk about us, and they will say, 'Those two lived long ago when things like that happened.'"

He stood up and went out. I ate the rest of the potatoes and thought about things—about the noise the stove was making and the sound of the mountain wind outside. I remembered yesterday and the day before, and then I went outside.

40   I walked past the corral to the edge where the narrow trail cut through the black rim rock. I was standing in the sky with nothing around me but the wind that came down from the blue mountain peak behind me. I could see faint mountain images in the distance miles across the vast spread of mesas and valleys and plains. I wondered who was over there to feel the mountain wind on those sheer blue edges—who walks on the pine needles in those blue mountains.

"Can you see the pueblo?" Silva was standing behind me.

I shook my head. "We're too far away."

"From here I can see the world." He stepped out on the edge. "The Navajo reservation begins over there." He pointed to the east. "The Pueblo boundaries are over here." He looked below us to the south, where the narrow trail seemed to come from. "The Texans have their ranches over there, starting with that valley, the Concho Valley. The Mexicans run some cattle over there too."

"Do you ever work for them?"

45   "I steal from them," Silva answered. The sun was dropping behind us and the shadows were filling the land below. I turned away from the edge that dropped forever into the valleys below.

"I'm cold," I said, "I'm going inside." I started wondering about this man who could speak the Pueblo language so well but who lived on a mountain and rustled cattle. I decided that this man Silva must be Navajo, because Pueblo men didn't do things like that.

"You must be a Navajo."

Silva shook his head gently. "Little Yellow Woman," he said, "you never give up, do you? I have told you who I am. The Navajo people know me, too." He knelt down and unrolled the bedroll and spread the extra blankets out on a piece of canvas. The sun was down, and the only light in the house came from outside—the dim orange light from sundown.

I stood there and waited for him to crawl under the blankets.

"What are you waiting for?" he said, and I lay down beside him. He undressed me   50
slowly like the night before beside the river—kissing my face gently and running his hands up and down my belly and legs. He took off my pants and then he laughed.

"Why are you laughing?"

"You are breathing so hard."

I pulled away from him and turned my back to him.

He pulled me around and pinned me down with his arms and chest. "You don't understand, do you, little Yellow Woman? You will do what I want."

And again he was all around me with his skin slippery against mine, and I was   55
afraid because I understood that his strength could hurt me. I lay underneath him and I knew that he could destroy me. But later, while he slept beside me, I touched his face and I had a feeling—the kind of feeling for him that overcame me that morning along the river. I kissed him on the forehead and he reached out for me.

When I woke up in the morning he was gone. It gave me a strange feeling because for a long time I sat there on the blankets and looked around the little house for some object of his—some proof that he had been there or maybe that he was coming back. Only the blankets and the cardboard box remained. The .30-30 that had been leaning in the corner was gone, and so was the knife I had used the night before. He was gone, and I had my chance to go now. But first I had to eat, because I knew it would be a long walk home.

I found some dried apricots in the cardboard box, and I sat down on a rock at the edge of the plateau rim. There was no wind and the sun warmed me. I was surrounded by silence. I drowsed with apricots in my mouth, and I didn't believe that there were highways or railroads or cattle to steal.

When I woke up, I stared down at my feet in the black mountain dirt. Little black ants were swarming over the pine needles around my foot. They must have smelled the apricots. I thought about my family far below me. They would be wondering about me, because this had never happened to me before. The tribal police would file a report. But if old Grandpa weren't dead he would tell them what happened—he would laugh and say, "Stolen by a ka'tsina, a mountain spirit. She'll come home—they usually do." There are enough of them to handle things. My mother and grandmother will raise the baby like they raised me. Al will find someone else, and they will go on like before, except that there will be a story about the day I disappeared while I was walking along the river. Silva had come for me; he said he had. I did not decide to go. I just went. Moonflowers blossom in the sand hills before dawn, just as I followed him. That's what I was thinking as I wandered along the trail through the pine trees.

It was noon when I got back. When I saw the stone house I remembered that I had meant to go home. But that didn't seem important any more, maybe because there were little blue flowers growing in the meadow behind the stone house and the gray squirrels were playing in the pines next to the house. The horses were standing in the corral, and there was a beef carcass hanging on the shady side of a big pine in front of the house. Flies buzzed around the clotted blood that hung from the carcass. Silva was washing his hands in a bucket full of water. He must have heard me coming because he spoke to me without turning to face me.

60   "I've been waiting for you."

"I went walking in the big pine trees."

I looked into the bucket full of bloody water with brown-and-white animal hairs floating in it. Silva stood there letting his hand drip, examining me intently.

"Are you coming with me?"

"Where?" I asked him.

65   "To sell the meat in Marquez."

"If you're sure it's O.K."

"I wouldn't ask you if it wasn't," he answered.

He sloshed the water around in the bucket before he dumped it out and set the bucket upside down near the door. I followed him to the corral and watched him saddle the horses. Even beside the horses he looked tall, and I asked him again if he wasn't Navajo. He didn't say anything; he just shook his head and kept cinching up the saddle.

"But Navajos are tall."

70   "Get on the horse," he said, "and let's go."

The last thing he did before we started down the steep trail was to grab the .30-30 from the corner. He slid the rifle into the scabbard that hung from his saddle.

"Do they ever try to catch you?" I asked.

"They don't know who I am."

"Then why did you bring the rifle?"

75   "Because we are going to Marquez where the Mexicans live."

The trail leveled out on a narrow ridge that was steep on both sides like an animal spine. On one side I could see where the trail went around the rocky gray hills and disappeared into the southeast where the pale sandrock mesas stood in the distance near my home. On the other side was a trail that went west, and as I looked far into the distance I thought I saw the little town. But Silva said no, that I was looking in the wrong place, that I just thought I saw houses. After that I quit looking off into the distance; it was hot and the wildflowers were closing up their deep-yellow petals. Only the waxy cactus flowers bloomed in the bright sun, and I saw every color that a cactus blossom can be; the white ones and the red ones were still buds, but the purple and the yellow were blossoms, open full and the most beautiful of all.

Silva saw him before I did. The white man was riding a big gray horse, coming up the trail towards us. He was traveling fast and the gray horse's feet sent rocks rolling off the trail into the dry tumbleweeds. Silva motioned for me to stop and we watched the white man. He didn't see us right away, but finally his horse whinnied at our horses and he stopped. He looked at us briefly before he lapped the gray horse across the three hundred yards that separated us. He stopped his horse in front of Silva, and his young fat face was shadowed by the brim of his hat. He didn't look mad, but his small, pale eyes moved from the blood-soaked gunny sacks hanging from my saddle to Silva's face and then back to my face.

"Where did you get the fresh meat?" the white man asked.

"I've been hunting," Silva said, and when he shifted his weight in the saddle the leather creaked.

"The hell you have, Indian. You've been rustling cattle. We've been looking for the   80
thief for a long time."

The rancher was fat, and sweat began to soak through his white cowboy shirt and
the wet cloth stuck to the thick rolls of belly fat. He almost seemed to be panting from
the exertion of talking, and he smelled rancid, maybe because Silva scared him.

Silva turned to me and smiled. "Go back up the mountain, Yellow Woman."

The white man got angry when he heard Silva speak in a language he couldn't understand. "Don't try anything, Indian. Just keep riding to Marquez. We'll call the state
police from there."

The rancher must have been unarmed because he was very frightened and if he
had a gun he would have pulled it out then. I turned my horse around and the rancher yelled, "Stop!" I looked at Silva for an instant and there was something ancient and
dark—something I could feel in my stomach—in his eyes, and when I glanced at his
hand I saw his finger on the trigger of the .30-30 that was still in the saddle scabbard.
I slapped my horse across the flank and the sacks of raw meat swung against my knees
as the horse leaped up the trail. It was hard to keep my balance, and once I thought I
felt the saddle slipping backward; it was because of this that I could not look back.

I didn't stop until I reached the ridge where the trail forked. The horse was breath-   85
ing deep gasps and there was a dark film of sweat on its neck. I looked down in the
direction I had come from, but I couldn't see the place. I waited. The wind came up and
pushed warm air past me. I looked up at the sky, pale blue and full of thin clouds and
fading vapor trails left by jets.

I think four shots were fired—I remember hearing four hollow explosions that
reminded me of deer hunting. There could have been more shots after that, but I
couldn't have heard them because my horse was running again and the loose rocks
were making too much noise as they scattered around his feet.

Horses have a hard time running downhill, but I went that way instead of uphill
to the mountain because I thought it was safer. I felt better with the horse running
southeast past the round gray hills that were covered with cedar trees and black lava
rock. When I got to the plain in the distance I could see the dark green patches of tamaracks that grew along the river; and beyond the river I could see the beginning of the
pale sandrock mesas. I stopped the horse and looked back to see if anyone was coming; then I got off the horse and turned the horse around, wondering if it would go back
to its corral under the pines in the mountain. It looked back at me for a moment and
then plucked a mouthful of green tumbleweeds before it trotted back up the trail with
its ears pointed forward, carrying its head daintily to one side to avoid stepping on the
dragging reins. When the horse disappeared over the last hill, the gunny sacks full of
meat were still swinging and bouncing.

I walked toward the river on a wood-hauler's road that I knew would eventually
lead to the paved road. I was thinking about waiting beside the road for someone to
drive by, but by the time I got to the pavement I had decided it wasn't very far to walk
if I followed the river back the way Silva and I had come.

The river water tasted good, and I sat in the shade under a cluster of silvery willows.
I thought about Silva, and I felt sad at leaving him; still, there was something strange
about him, and I tried to figure it out all the way back home.

I came back to the place on the river bank where he had been sitting the first time   90
I saw him. The green willow leaves that he had trimmed from the branch were still
lying there, wilted in the sand. I saw the leaves and I wanted to go back to him—
to kiss him and to touch him—but the mountains were too far away now. And I told

myself, because I believe it, he will come back sometime and be waiting again by the river.

I followed the path up from the river into the village. The sun was getting low, and I could smell supper cooking when I got to the screen door of my house. I could hear their voices inside—my mother was telling my grandmother how to fix the Jell-O and my husband, Al, was playing with the baby. I decided to tell them that some Navajo had kidnapped me, but I was sorry that old Grandpa wasn't alive to hear my story because it was the Yellow Woman stories he liked to tell best.   [1974]

Questions

1. Why do you think Silko chooses to tell this story in first person?
2. Discuss the ways that Silko incorporates both myth and contemporary life in the story.
3. What effect do the four shots have on our understanding of Silva and of Yellow Woman's attraction to him?
4. What elements of a contemporary Romance or a Western does this story contain?
5. Why do you think grandpa liked to tell Yellow Woman stories?

Responses

1. Write an essay exploring all of Silko's stories for elements of myth and elements of contemporary verisimilitude.
2. Compare this story with Chopin's "The Story of an Hour," especially examining the implications of the downstairs/valley and upstairs/mountain structural device.

ISAAC BASHEVIS SINGER

Isaac Bashevis Singer (1904–1991) was born in Radzymin, Poland. The son of a rabbi, he left seminary after a year to follow a career in journalism and literature. He emigrated to New York City in 1935 and worked as a journalist for the *Jewish Daily Forward*, publishing his stories and sketches in Yiddish. His novel *The Family Moskat* was published in English translation in 1950. From that time his novels and collections have followed in a steady stream. *A Crown of Feathers* (1973) won the National Book Award. *The Collected Stories* (1981) won the Pulitzer Prize, and in 1978 Singer was awarded the Nobel Prize for Literature. He said he preferred young readers because "children read books, not reviews." Not only that, "they still believe in God, the family, angels, devils, witches, goblins, logic, clarity, punctuation and other such obsolete stuff."

Gimpel the Fool

1

I am Gimpel the fool. I don't think myself a fool. On the contrary. But that's what folks call me. They gave me the name while I was still in school. I had seven names in all: imbecile, donkey, flax-head, dope, glump, ninny, and fool. The last name stuck. What did my foolishness consist of? I was easy to take in. They said, "Gimpel, you know the rabbi's wife has been brought to childbed?" So I skipped school. Well, it turned out to be a lie. How was I supposed to know? She hadn't had a big belly. But I never looked at her belly. Was that really so foolish? The gang laughed and hee-hawed, stomped and danced and chanted a good-night prayer. And instead of the raisins they give when a woman's lying in, they stuffed my hand full of goat turds. I was no weakling. If I slapped someone he'd see all the way to Cracow. But I'm really not a slugger by nature. I think to myself: Let it pass. So they take advantage of me.

I was coming home from school and heard a dog barking. I'm not afraid of dogs, but of course I never want to start up with them. One of them may be mad, and if he bites there's not a Tartar in the world who can help you. So I made tracks. Then I looked around and saw the whole market place wild with laughter. It was no dog at all but Wolf-Leib the Thief. How was I supposed to know it was he? It sounded like a howling bitch.

When the pranksters and leg-pullers found that I was easy to fool, every one of them tried his luck with me. "Gimpel, the Czar is coming to Frampol; Gimpel, the moon fell down in Turbeen; Gimpel, little Hodel Furpiece found a treasure behind the bathhouse." And I like a golem° believed everyone. In the first place, everything is possible, as it is written in the Wisdom of the Fathers, I've forgotten just how. Second, I had to believe when the whole town came down on me! If I ever dared to say, "Ah, you're kidding!" there was trouble. People got angry. "What do you mean! You want to call everyone a liar?" What was I to do? I believed them, and I hope at least that did them some good.

I was an orphan. My grandfather who brought me up was already bent toward the grave. So they turned me over to a baker, and what a time they gave me there! Every woman or girl who came to bake a batch of noodles had to fool me at least once. "Gimpel, there's a fair in heaven; Gimpel, the rabbi gave birth to a calf in the seventh month; Gimpel, a cow flew over the roof and laid brass eggs." A student from the yeshiva came once to buy a roll, and he said, "You, Gimpel, while you stand here scraping with your baker's shovel the Messiah has come. The dead have arisen." "What do you mean?" I said. "I heard no one blowing the ram's horn!" He said, "Are you deaf?" And all began to cry, "We heard it, we heard!" Then in came Rietze the Candle-dipper and called out in her hoarse voice, "Gimpel, your father and mother have stood up from the grave. They're looking for you."

5   To tell the truth, I knew very well that nothing of the sort had happened, but all the same, as folks were talking, I threw on my wool vest and went out. Maybe something had happened. What did I stand to lose by looking? Well, what a cat music went up! And then I took a vow to believe nothing more. But that was no go either. They confused me so that I didn't know the big end from the small.

I went to the rabbi to get some advice. He said, "It is written, better to be a fool all your days than for one hour to be evil. You are not a fool. They are the fools. For he who causes his neighbor to feel shame loses Paradise himself." Nevertheless the rabbi's daughter took me in. As I left the rabbinical court she said, "Have you kissed the wall yet?" I said, "No; what for?" She answered, "It's the law; you've got to do it after every visit." Well, there didn't seem to be any harm in it. And she burst out laughing. It was a fine trick. She put one over on me, all right.

I wanted to go off to another town, but then everyone got busy matchmaking, and they were after me so they nearly tore my coat tails off. They talked at me and talked until I got water on the ear. She was no chaste maiden, but they told me she was virgin pure. She had a limp, and they said it was deliberate, from coyness. She had a bastard, and they told me the child was her little brother. I cried, "You're wasting your time. I'll never marry that whore." But they said indignantly, "What a way to talk! Aren't you ashamed of yourself? We can take you to the rabbi and have you fined for giving her a bad name." I saw then that I wouldn't escape them so easily and I thought: They're set on making me their butt. But when you're married the husband's the master, and if that's all right with her it's agreeable to me too. Besides, you can't pass through life unscathed, nor expect to.

I went to her clay house, which was built on the sand, and the whole gang hollering and chorusing, came after me. They acted like bear-baiters. When we came to the

---

°*golem:* Stupid person; automaton.

well they stopped all the same. They were afraid to start anything with Elka. Her mouth would open as if it were on a hinge, and she had a fierce tongue. I entered the house. Lines were strung from wall to wall and clothes were drying. Barefoot she stood by the tub, doing the wash. She was dressed in a worn hand-me-down gown of plush. She had her hair put up in braids and pinned across her head. It took my breath away, almost, the reek of it all.

Evidently she knew who I was. She took a look at me and said, "Look who's here! He's come, the drip. Grab a seat."

I told her all; I denied nothing. "Tell me the truth," I said, "are you really a virgin; and is that mischievous Yechiel actually your little brother? Don't be deceitful with me, for I'm an orphan." 10

"I'm an orphan myself," she answered, "and whoever tries to twist you up, may the end of his nose take a twist. But don't let them think they can take advantage of me. I want a dowry of fifty guilders, and let them take up a collection besides. Otherwise they can kiss my you-know-what." She was very plainspoken. I said, "It's the bride and not the groom who gives a dowry." Then she said, "Don't bargain with me. Either a flat 'yes' or a flat 'no'—Go back where you came from."

I thought: No bread will ever be baked from *this* dough. But ours is not a poor town. They consented to everything and proceeded with the wedding. It so happened that there was a dysentery epidemic at the time. The ceremony was held at the cemetery gates, near the little corpse-washing hut. The fellows got drunk. While the marriage contract was being drawn up I heard the most pious high rabbi ask, "Is the bride a widow or a divorced woman?" And the sexton's wife answered for her, "Both a widow and divorced." It was a black moment for me. But what was I to do, run away from under the marriage canopy?

There was singing and dancing. An old granny danced opposite me, hugging a braided white *chalah*.° The master of revels made a "God 'a mercy' in memory of the bride's parents. The schoolboys threw burrs, as on Tishe b'Av fast day.° There were a lot of gifts after the sermon: a noodle board, a kneading trough, a bucket, brooms, ladles, household articles galore. Then I took a look and saw two strapping young men carrying a crib. "What do we need this for?" I asked. So they said, "Don't rack your brains about it. It's all right, it'll come in handy." I realized I was going to be rooked. Take it another way though, what did I stand to lose? I reflected: I'll see what comes of it. A whole town can't go altogether crazy.

2

At night I came where my wife lay, but she wouldn't let me in. "Say, look here, is this what they married us for?" I said. And she said, "My monthly has come." "But yesterday they took you to the ritual bath, and that's afterward, isn't it supposed to be?" "Today isn't yesterday," said she, "and yesterday's not today. You can beat it if you don't like it." In short, I waited.

Not four months later she was in childbed. The townsfolk hid their laughter with their knuckles. But what could I do? She suffered intolerable pains and clawed at the 15

°*chalah*: Sabbath bread.
°*Tishe b'Av fast day*: Day of mourning commemorating the destruction of the Temple in Jerusalem.

walls. "Gimpel," she cried, "I'm going. Forgive me!" The house filled with women. They were boiling pans of water. The screams rose to the welkin.

The thing to do was to go the House of Prayer to repeat Psalms, and that was what I did.

The townsfolk liked that, all right. I stood in a corner saying Psalms and prayers, and they shook their heads at me. "Pray, pray!" they told me. "Prayer never made any woman pregnant." One of the congregation put a straw to my mouth and said, "Hay for the cows." There was something to that too, by God!

She gave birth to a boy. Friday at the synagogue the sexton stood up before the Ark, pounded on the reading table, and announced, "The wealthy Reb Gimpel invites the congregation to a feast in honor of the birth of a son." The whole House of Prayer rang with laughter. My face was flaming. But there was nothing I could do. After all, I *was* the one responsible for the circumcision honors and rituals.

Half the town came running. You couldn't wedge another soul in. Women brought peppered chick-peas, and there was a keg of beer from the tavern. I ate and drank as much as anyone, and they all congratulated me. Then there was a circumcision, and I named the boy after my father, may he rest in peace. When all were gone and I was left with my wife alone, she thrust her head through the bed-curtain and called me to her.

20   "Gimpel," said she, "why are you silent? Has your ship gone and sunk?"

"What shall I say?" I answered. "A fine thing you've done to me! If my mother had known of it she'd have died a second time."

She said, "Are you crazy, or what?"

"How can you make such a fool," I said, "of one who should be the lord and master?"

"What's the matter with you?" she said. "What have you taken it into your head to imagine?"

25   I saw that I must speak bluntly and openly. "Do you think this is the way to use an orphan?" I said. "You have borne a bastard."

She answered, "Drive this foolishness out of your head. The child is yours."

"How can he be mine?" I argued. "He was born seventeen weeks after the wedding."

She told me then that he was premature. I said, "Isn't he a little too premature?" She said, she had had a grandmother who carried just as short a time and she resembled this grandmother of hers as one drop of water does another. She swore to it with such oaths that you would have believed a peasant at the fair if he had used them. To tell the plain truth, I didn't believe her; but when I talked it over next day with the schoolmaster he told me that the very same thing had happened to Adam and Eve. Two they went up to bed, and four they descended.

"There isn't a woman in the world who is not the granddaughter of Eve," he said.

30   That was how it was; they argued me dumb. But then, who really knows how such things are?

I began to forget my sorrow. I loved the child madly, and he loved me too. As soon as he saw me he'd wave his little hands and want me to pick him up, and when he was colicky I was the only one who could pacify him. I bought him a little bone teething ring and a little gilded cap. He was forever catching the evil eye from someone, and then I had to run to get one of those abracadabras for him that would get him out of it. I worked like an ox. You know how expenses go up when there's an infant in the house. I don't want to lie about it; I didn't dislike Elka either, for that matter. She swore at me and cursed, and I couldn't get enough of her. What strength she had! One of her looks could rob you of the power of speech. And her orations! Pitch and sulphur, that's what they were full of, and yet somehow also full of charm. I adored her every word. She gave me bloody wounds though.

In the evening I brought her a white loaf as well as a dark one, and also poppyseed rolls I baked myself. I thieved because of her and swiped everything I could lay hands on: macaroons, raisins, almonds, cakes. I hope I may be forgiven for stealing from the Saturday pots the women left to warm in the baker's oven. I would take out scraps of meat, a chunk of pudding, a chicken leg or head, a piece of tripe, whatever I could nip quickly. She ate and became fat and handsome.

I had to sleep away from home all during the week, at the bakery. On Friday nights when I got home she always made an excuse of some sort. Either she had heartburn, or a stitch in the side, or hiccups, or headaches. You know what women's excuses are. I had a bitter time of it. It was rough. To add to it, this little brother of hers, the bastard, was growing bigger. He'd put lumps on me, and when I wanted to hit back she'd open her mouth and curse so powerfully I saw a green haze floating before my eyes. Ten times a day she threatened to divorce me. Another man in my place would have taken French leave and disappeared. But I'm the type that bears it and says nothing. What's one to do? Shoulders are from God, and burdens too.

One night there was a calamity in the bakery; the oven burst, and we almost had a fire. There was nothing to do but go home, so I went home. Let me, I thought, also taste the joy of sleeping in bed in mid-week. I didn't want to wake the sleeping mite and tiptoed into the house. Coming in, it seemed to me that I heard not the snoring of one but, as it were, a double snore, one a thin enough snore and the other like the snoring of a slaughtered ox. Oh, I didn't like that! I didn't like it at all. I went up to the bed, and things suddenly turned black. Next to Elka lay a man's form. Another in my place would have made an uproar, and enough noise to rouse the whole town, but the thought occurred to me that I might wake the child. A little thing like that—why frighten a little swallow, I thought. All right then, I went back to the bakery and stretched out on a sack of flour and till morning I never shut an eye. I shivered as if I had had malaria. "Enough of being a donkey," I said to myself. "Gimpel isn't going to be a sucker all his life. There's a limit even to the foolishness of a fool like Gimpel."

In the morning I went to the rabbi to get advice, and it made a great commotion in the town. They sent the beadle for Elka right away. She came, carrying the child. And what do you think she did? She denied it, denied everything, bone and stone! "He's out of his head," she said. "I know nothing of dreams or divinations." They yelled at her, warned her, hammered on the table, but she stuck to her guns: it was a false accusation, she said.

The butchers and the horse-traders took her part. One of the lads from the slaughterhouse came by and said to me, "We've got our eye on you, you're a marked man." Meanwhile the child started to bear down and soiled itself. In the rabbinical court there was an Ark of the Covenant, and they couldn't allow that, so they sent Elka away.

I said to the rabbi, "What shall I do?"

"You must divorce her at once," said he.

"And what if she refuses?" I asked.

He said, "You must serve the divorce. That's all you'll have to do."

I said, "Well, all right, Rabbi. Let me think about it."

"There's nothing to think about," said he. "You mustn't remain under the same roof with her."

"And if I want to see the child?" I asked.

35

40

"Let her go, the harlot," said he, "and her brood of bastards with her."

The verdict he gave was that I mustn't even cross her threshold—never again, as long as I should live.

During the day it didn't bother me so much. I thought: It was bound to happen, the abscess had to burst. But at night when I stretched out upon the sacks I felt it all very bitterly. A longing took me, for her and for the child. I wanted to be angry, but that's my misfortune exactly, I don't have it in me to be really angry. In the first place—this was how my thoughts went—there's bound to be a slip sometimes. You can't live without errors. Probably that lad who was with her led her on and gave her presents and what not, and women are often long on hair and short on sense, and so he got around her. And then since she denies it so, maybe I was only seeing things? Hallucinations do happen. You see a figure or a mannikin or something, but when you come up closer it's nothing, there's not a thing there. And if that's so, I'm doing her an injustice. And when I got so far in my thoughts I started to weep. I sobbed so that I wet the flour where I lay. In the morning I went to the rabbi and told him that I had made a mistake. The rabbi wrote on with his quill, and he said that if that were so he would have to reconsider the whole case. Until he had finished I wasn't to go near my wife, but I might send her bread and money by messenger.

3

Nine months passed before all the rabbis could come to an agreement. Letters went back and forth. I hadn't realized that there could be so much erudition about a matter like this.

Meanwhile Elka gave birth to still another child, a girl this time. On the Sabbath I went to the synagogue and invoked a blessing on her. They called me up to the Torah, and I named the child for my mother-in-law—may she rest in peace. The louts and loudmouths of the town who came into the bakery gave me a going over. All Frampol refreshed its spirits because of my trouble and grief. However, I resolved that I would always believe what I was told. What's the good of *not* believing? Today it's your wife you don't believe; tomorrow it's God Himself you won't take stock in.

By an apprentice who was her neighbor I sent her daily a corn or a wheat loaf, or a piece of pastry, rolls or bagels, or, when I got the chance, a slab of pudding, a slice of honeycake, or wedding strudel—whatever came my way. The apprentice was a good-hearted lad, and more than once he added something on his own. He had formerly annoyed me a lot, plucking my nose and digging me in the ribs, but when he started to be a visitor to my house he became kind of friendly. "Hey, you, Gimpel," he said to me, "you have a very decent little wife and two fine kids. You don't deserve them."

"But the things people say about her," I said.

"Well, they have long tongues," he said, "and nothing to do with them but babble. Ignore it as you ignore the cold of last winter."

One day the rabbi sent for me and said, "Are you certain, Gimpel, that you were wrong about your wife?"

I said, "I'm certain."

"Why, but look here! You yourself saw it."

"It must have been a shadow," I said.

"The shadow of what?"

"Just one of the beams, I think."

"You can go home then. You owe thanks to the Yanover rabbi. He found an obscure reference in Maimonides that favored you."

I seized the rabbi's hand and kissed it.

I wanted to run home immediately. It's no small thing to be separated for so long a time from wife and child. Then I reflected: I'd better go back to work now, and go home in the evening. I said nothing to anyone, although as far as my heart was concerned it was like one of the Holy Days. The women teased and twitted me as they did every day, but my thought was: Go on, with your loose talk. The truth is out, like the oil upon the water. Maimonides says it's right, and therefore it is right!

At night, when I had covered the dough to let it rise, I took my share of bread and a little sack of flour and started homeward. The moon was full and the stars were glistening, something to terrify the soul. I hurried onward, and before me darted a long shadow. It was winter, and a fresh snow had fallen. I had a mind to sing, but it was growing late and I didn't want to wake the householders. Then I felt like whistling, but I remembered that you don't whistle at night because it brings the demons out. So I was silent and walked as fast as I could.

Dogs in the Christian yards barked at me when I passed, but I thought: Bark your teeth out! What are you but mere dogs? Whereas I am a man, the husband of a fine wife, the father of promising children.

As I approached the house my heart started to pound as though it were the heart of a criminal. I felt no fear, but my heart went thump! thump! Well, no drawing back. I quietly lifted the latch and went in. Elka was asleep. I looked at the infant's cradle. The shutter was closed, but the moon forced its way through the cracks. I saw the newborn child's face and loved it as soon as I saw it—immediately—each tiny bone.

Then I came nearer to the bed. And what did I see but the apprentice lying there beside Elka. The moon went out all at once. It was utterly black, and I trembled. My teeth chattered. The bread fell from my hands, and my wife waked and said, "Who is that, ah?"

I muttered, "It's me."

"Gimpel?" she asked. "How come you're here? I thought it was forbidden."

"The rabbi said," I answered and shook as with a fever.

"Listen to me, Gimpel," she said, "go out to the shed and see if the goat's all right. It seems she's been sick." I have forgotten to say that we had a goat. When I heard she was unwell I went into the yard. The nanny goat was a good little creature. I had a nearly human feeling for her.

With hesitant steps I went up to the shed and opened the door. The goat stood there on her four feet. I felt her everywhere, drew her by the horns, examined her udders, and found nothing wrong. She had probably eaten too much bark. "Good night, little goat," I said. "Keep well." And the little beast answered with a "Maa" as though to thank me for the good will.

I went back. The apprentice had vanished.

"Where," I asked, "is the lad?"

"What lad?" my wife answered.

"What do you mean?" I said. "The apprentice. You were sleeping with him."

"The things I have dreamed this night and the night before," she said, "may they come true and lay you low, body and soul! An evil spirit has taken root in you and dazzles your sight." She screamed out, "You hateful creature! You moon calf! You spook! You uncouth man! Get out, or I'll scream all Frampol out of bed!"

Before I could move, her brother sprang out from behind the oven and struck me a blow on the back of the head. I thought he had broken my neck. I felt that something about me was deeply wrong, and I said, "Don't make a scandal. All that's needed now is that people should accuse me of raising spooks and *dybbuks.*"° For that was what she had meant. "No one will touch bread of my baking."

In short, I somehow calmed her.

"Well," she said, "that's enough. Lie down, and be shattered by wheels."

Next morning I called the apprentice aside. "Listen here, brother!" I said. And so on and so forth. "What do you say?" He stared at me as though I had dropped from the roof or something.

"I swear," he said, "you'd better go to an herb doctor or some healer. I'm afraid you have a screw loose, but I'll hush it up for you." And that's how the thing stood.

80   To make a long story short, I lived twenty years with my wife. She bore me six children, four daughters and two sons. All kinds of things happened, but I neither saw nor heard. I believed, and that's all. The rabbi recently said to me, "Belief in itself is beneficial. It is written that a good man lives by his faith."

Suddenly my wife took sick. It began with a trifle, a little growth upon the breast. But she evidently was not destined to live long; she had no years. I spent a fortune on her. I have forgotten to say that by this time I had a bakery of my own and in Frampol was considered to be something of a rich man. Daily the healer came, and every witch doctor in the neighborhood was brought. They decided to use leeches, and after that to try cupping. They even called a doctor from Lublin, but it was too late. Before she died she called me to her bed and said, "Forgive me, Gimpel."

I said, "What is there to forgive? You have been a good and faithful wife."

"Woe, Gimpel!" she said. "It was ugly how I deceived you all these years. I want to go clean to my Maker, and so I have to tell you that the children are not yours."

If I had been clouted on the head with a piece of wood it couldn't have bewildered me more.

85   "Whose are they?" I asked.

"I don't know," she said. "There were a lot . . . but they're not yours." And as she spoke she tossed her head to the side, her eyes turned glassy, and it was all up with Elka. On her whitened lips there remained a smile.

I imagined that, dead as she was, she was saying, "I deceived Gimpel. That was the meaning of my brief life."

4

One night, when the period of mourning was done, as I lay dreaming on the flour sacks, there came the Spirit of Evil himself and said to me, "Gimpel, why do you sleep?"

I said, "What should I be doing? Eating *kreplach?*"°

90   "The whole world deceives you," he said, "and you ought to deceive the world in your turn."

"How can I deceive the world?" I asked him.

He answered, "You might accumulate a bucket of urine every day and at night pour it into the dough. Let the sages of Frampol eat filth."

"What about the judgment in the world to come?" I said.

°*dybbuks*: Condemned souls capable of possessing human bodies.
°*kreplach*: Dumplings containing chopped meats.

"There is no world to come," he said. "They've sold you a bill of goods and talked you into believing you carried a cat in your belly. What nonsense!"

"Well then," I said, "and is there a God?"

He answered, "There is no God either."

"What," I said, "*is* there, then?"

"A thick mire."

He stood before my eyes with a goatish beard and horn, long-toothed, and with a tail. Hearing such words, I wanted to snatch him by the tail, but I tumbled for the flour sacks and nearly broke a rib. Then it happened that I had to answer the call of nature, and, passing, I saw the risen dough, which seemed to say to me, "Do it!" In brief, I let myself be persuaded.

At dawn the apprentice came. We kneaded the bread, scattered caraway seeds on it, and set it to bake. Then the apprentice went away, and I was left sitting in the little trench by the oven, on a pile of rags. Well, Gimpel, I thought, you've revenged yourself on them for all the shame they've put on you. Outside the frost glittered, but it was warm beside the oven. The flames heated my face. I bent my head and fell into a doze.

I saw in a dream, at once, Elka in her shroud. She called to me, "What have you done, Gimpel?"

I said to her, "It's all your fault," and started to cry.

"You fool!" she said. "You fool! Because I was false is everything false too? I never deceived anyone but myself. I'm paying for it all, Gimpel. They spare you nothing here."

I looked at her face. It was black; I was startled and waked, and remained sitting dumb. I sensed that everything hung in the balance. A false step now and I'd lose Eternal Life. But God gave me His help. I seized the long shovel and took out the loaves, carried them into the yard, and started to dig a hole in the frozen earth.

My apprentice came back as I was doing it. "What are you doing, boss?" he said, and grew pale as a corpse.

"I know what I'm doing," I said, and I buried it all before his very eyes.

Then I went home, took my hoard from its hiding place, and divided it among the children. "I saw your mother tonight," I said. "She's turning black, poor thing."

They were so astounded they couldn't speak a word.

"Be well," I said, "and forget that such a one as Gimpel ever existed." I put on my short coat, a pair of boots, took the bag that held my prayer shawl in one hand, my stock in the other, and kissed the *mezzuzah.°* When people saw me in the street they were greatly surprised.

"Where are you going?" they said.

I answered, "Into the world." And so I departed from Frampol.

I wandered over the land, and good people did not neglect me. After many years I became old and white; I heard a great deal, many lies and falsehoods, but the longer I lived the more I understood that there were really no lies. Whatever doesn't really happen is dreamed at night. It happens to one if it doesn't happen to another, tomorrow if not today, or a century hence if not next year. What difference can it make? Often I heard tales of which I said, "Now this is a thing that cannot happen." But before a year had elapsed I heard that it actually had come to pass somewhere.

°*mezzuzah:* A parchment scroll inscribed with the basic creed of Judaism and enclosed in a case that is fastened to one's doorpost to ward off evil.

Going from place to place, eating at strange tables, it often happens that I spin yarns—improbable things that could never have happened—about devils, magicians, windmills, and the like. The children run after me, calling, "Grandfather, tell us a story." Sometimes they ask for particular stories, and I try to please them. A fat young boy once said to me, "Grandfather, it's the same story you told us before." The little rogue, he was right.

So it is with dreams too. It is many years since I left Frampol, but as soon as I shut my eyes I am there again. And whom do you think I see? Elka. She is standing by the washtub, as at our first encounter, but her face is shining and her eyes are as radiant as the eyes of a saint, and she speaks outlandish words to me, strange things. When I wake I have forgotten it all. But while the dream lasts I am comforted. She answers all my queries, and what comes out is that all is right. I weep and implore, "Let me be with you." And she consoles me and tells me to be patient. The time is nearer than it is far. Sometimes she strokes and kisses me and weeps upon my face. When I awaken I feel her lips and taste the salt of her tears.

115   No doubt the world is entirely an imaginary world, but it is only once removed from the true world. At the door of the hovel where I lie, there stands the plank on which the dead are taken away. The gravedigger Jew has his spade ready. The grave waits and the worms are hungry; the shrouds are prepared—I carry them in my beggar's sack. Another *shnorrer*° is waiting to inherit my bed of straw. When the time comes I will go joyfully. Whatever may be there, it will be real, without complication, without ridicule, without deception. God be praised: there even Gimpel cannot be deceived.   [1953]

QUESTIONS

1. How is the effect of the story dependent upon first-person narration?
2. What elements of the folk tale has the author incorporated into the story?
3. How does Gimpel's employment as a baker function in the story?
4. Has the author managed to make the character of Gimpel credible?
5. What does Gimpel mean when he says that "the longer I lived the more I understood that there were really no lies"?

RESPONSES

1. Compare "Gimpel the Fool" to Tolstoy's "The Death of Ivan Ilych."
2. View the film *Forest Gump* and compare the protagonists of the movie and this story. How are they portrayed as foolish? How are they portrayed as wise?

°*shnorrer*: Beggar.

SUSAN SONTAG

Susan Sontag (1933–2004) was born in New York City and spent her youth in Tucson and Los Angeles. She attended the University of California at Berkeley, University of Chicago, and Harvard, earning a Ph.D. in philosophy. She completed further study at Oxford and the University of Paris. In addition to being the writer and director of several films, Sontag published many books. Her nonfiction is collected in *Against Interpretation* (1966), *Styles of Radical Will* (1969), *Illness as a Metaphor* (1978), and *AIDS and Its Metaphors* (1989). Her novels include *Death Kit* (1967), *The Volcano Lover* (1992), and *In America* (2000), for which she won the National Book Award. Her short stories are published in *I, etcetera* (1978).

The Dummy

Since my situation is intolerable, I have decided to take steps to resolve it. So I have constructed a lifelike dummy made of various brands of Japanese plastic simulating flesh, hair, nails, and so forth. An electronics engineer of my acquaintance, for a sizable fee, built the interior mechanism of the dummy: it will be able to talk, eat, work, walk, and copulate. I hired an important artist of the old realistic school to paint the features; it took twelve sittings to make a face that perfectly resembles mine. My broad nose is there, my brown hair, the lines on each side of my mouth. Even I could not tell the dummy and myself apart, were it not that from my peculiar vantage point it is quite obvious that he is he and that I am I.

What remains is to install the dummy in the center of my life. He will go to work instead of me, and receive the approval and censure of my boss. He will bow and scrape and be diligent. All I require of him is that he bring me the check every other Wednesday; I will give him carfare and money for his lunches, but no more. I'll make out the checks for the rent and the utilities, and pocket the rest myself. The dummy will also be the one who is married to my wife. He will make love to her on Tuesday and Saturday night, watch television with her every evening, eat her wholesome dinners, quarrel with her about how to bring up the children. (My wife, who also works, pays the grocery bills out of her salary.) I will also assign the dummy Monday night bowling with the team from the office, the visit to my mother on Friday night, reading the newspaper each morning, and perhaps buying my clothes (two sets—one for him, one for me). Other tasks I will assign as they come up, as I wish to divest myself of them. I want to keep for myself only what gives me pleasure.

An ambitious enterprise, you say? But why not? The problems of this world are only truly solved in two ways: by extinction or by duplication. Former ages had only the first choice. But I see no reason not to take advantage of the marvels of modern technology for personal liberation. I have a choice. And, not being the suicidal type, I have decided to duplicate myself.

On a fine Monday morning I wind the dummy up and set him loose, after making sure he knows what to do—that is, he knows just how I would behave in any familiar situation. The alarm goes off. He rolls over and pokes my wife, who wearily gets out of the double bed and turns off the alarm. She puts on her slippers and robe, then limps, stiff-ankled, into the bathroom. When she comes out and heads for the kitchen, he gets up and takes her place in the bathroom. He urinates, gargles, shaves, comes back into the bedroom and takes his clothes out of the dresser and closet, returns to the bathroom, dresses, then joins my wife in the kitchen. My children are already at the table. The younger girl didn't finish her homework last night, and my wife is writing a note of excuse to the teacher. The older girl sits haughtily munching the cold toast. "Morning, Daddy," they say to the dummy. The dummy pecks them on the cheek in return. Breakfast passes without incident, I observe with relief. The children leave. They haven't noticed a thing. I begin to feel sure my plan is going to work and realize, by my excitement, that I had greatly feared it would not—that there would be some mechanical failure, that the dummy would not recognize his cues. But no, everything is going right, even the way he folds the *New York Times* is correct; he reproduces exactly the amount of time I spent on the foreign news, and it takes him just as long to read the sports pages as it took me.

5   The dummy kisses my wife, he steps out the door, he enters the elevator. (Do machines recognize each other, I wonder.) Into the lobby, out the door, on the street walking at a moderate pace—the dummy has left on time, he doesn't have to worry—into the subway he goes. Steady, calm, clean (I cleaned him myself Sunday night), untroubled, he goes about his appointed tasks. He will be happy as long as I am satisfied with him. And so I will be, whatever he does, as long as others are satisfied with him.

Nobody notices anything different in the office, either. The secretary says hello, he smiles back as I always do; then he walks to my cubicle, hangs up his coat, and sits at my desk. The secretary brings him my mail. After reading it, he calls for some dictation. Next, there is a pile of my unfinished business from last Friday to attend to. Phone calls are made, an appointment is set up for lunch with a client from out of town. There is only one irregularity that I notice: the dummy smokes seven cigarettes during the morning; I usually smoke between ten and fifteen. But I set this down to the fact that he is new at his work and has not had time to accumulate the tensions that I feel after working six years in this office. It occurs to me that he will probably not have two martinis—as I always do—during the lunch, but only one, and I am right. But these are mere details, and will be to the dummy's credit if anyone notices them, which I doubt. His behavior with the out-of-town client is correct—perhaps a shade too deferential, but this, too, I put down to inexperience. Thank God, no simple matter trips him up. His table manners are as they should be. He doesn't pick at his food, but eats with appetite. And he knows he should sign the check rather than pay with a credit card; the firm has an account at this restaurant.

In the afternoon there is a sales conference. The vice president explains a new promotional campaign for the Midwest. The dummy makes suggestions. The boss nods.

The dummy taps his pencil on the long mahogany table and looks thoughtful. I notice he is chain-smoking. Could he be feeling the pressure so soon? What a hard life I led! After less than a day of it, even a dummy shows some wear and tear. The rest of the afternoon passes without incident. The dummy makes his way home to my wife and children, eats my dinner appreciatively, plays Monopoly with the children for an hour, watches a Western on TV with my wife, bathes, makes himself a ham sandwich, and then retires. I don't know what dreams he has, but I hope they are restful and pleasant. If my approval can give him an untroubled sleep, he has it. I am entirely pleased with my creation.

The dummy has been on the job for several months. What can I report? A greater degree of proficiency? But that's impossible. He was fine the first day. He couldn't be any more like me than he was at the very beginning. He does not have to get better at his job but only stick at it contentedly, unrebelliously, without mechanical failure. My wife is happy with him—at least, no more unhappy than she was with me. My children call him Daddy and ask him for their allowance. My fellow workers and my boss continue to entrust him with my job.

Lately, though—just the past week, really—I have noticed something that worries me. It is the attention that the dummy pays to the new secretary, Miss Love. (I hope it isn't her name that arouses him somewhere in the depths of that complex machinery; I imagine that machines can be literal-minded.) A slight lingering at her desk when he comes in in the morning, a second's pause, no more, when she says hello; whereas I— and he until recently—used to walk by that desk without breaking stride. And he does seem to be dictating more letters. Could it be from increased zeal on behalf of the firm? I remember how, the very first day, he spoke up at the sales conference. Or could it be the desire to detain Miss Love? Are those letters necessary? I could swear he thinks so. But then you never know what goes on behind that imperturbable dummy's face of his. I'm afraid to ask him. Is it because I don't want to know the worst? Or because I'm afraid he'll be angry at my violation of his privacy? In any case, I have decided to wait until he tells me.

Then one day it comes—the news I had dreaded. At eight in the morning the dummy corners me in the shower, where I have been spying on him while he shaves, marveling how he remembers to cut himself every once in a while, as I do. He unburdens himself to me. I am astonished at how much he is moved—astonished and a little envious. I never dreamed a dummy could have so much feeling, that I would see a dummy weep. I try to quiet him. I admonish him, then I reprimand him. It's no use. His tears become sobs. He, or rather his passion, whose mechanism I cannot fathom, begins to revolt me. I'm also terrified my wife and children will hear him, rush to the bathroom, and there find this berserk creature who would be incapable of normal responses. (Might they find both of us here in the bathroom? That, too, is possible.) I run the shower, open both the sink faucets, and flush the toilet to drown out the painful noises he is making. All this for love! All this for the love of Miss Love! He has barely spoken to her, except in the way of business. Certainly, he hasn't slept with her, of that I am sure. And yet he is madly, desperately in love. He wants to leave my wife. I explain to him how impossible that is. First of all, he has duties and responsibilities. He is the husband and father to my wife and children. They depend on him; their lives would be smashed by his selfish act. And second, what does he know about Miss Love? She's at least ten years younger than he is, has given no particular sign of noticing him at all, and probably has a nice boyfriend her own age whom she's planning to marry.

10

The dummy refuses to listen. He is inconsolable. He will have Miss Love or—here he makes a threatening gesture—he will destroy himself. He will bang his head against the wall, or jump out of a window, disassembling irrevocably his delicate machinery. I become really alarmed. I see my marvelous scheme, which has left me so beautifully at my leisure and in peace the last months, ruined. I see myself back at the job, making love again to my wife, fighting for space in the subway during the rush hour, watching television, spanking the children. If my life was intolerable to me before, you can imagine how unthinkable it has become. Why, if only you knew how I have spent these last months, while the dummy was administering my life. Without a care in the world, except for occasional curiosity as to the fate of my dummy. I have slid to the bottom of the world. I sleep anywhere now: in flophouses, on the subway (which I only board very late at night), in alleys and doorways. I don't bother to collect my paycheck from the dummy any more, because there is nothing I want to buy. Only rarely do I shave. My clothes are torn and stained.

Does this sound very dreary to you? It is not, it is not. Of course, when the dummy first relieved me of my own life, I had grandiose plans for living the lives of others. I wanted to be an Arctic explorer, a concert pianist, a great courtesan, a world statesman. I tried being Alexander the Great, then Mozart, then Bismarck, then Greta Garbo, then Elvis Presley—in my imagination, of course. I imagined that, being none of these people for long, I could have only their pleasure, none of their pain; for I could escape, transform myself, whenever I wanted. But the experiment failed, for lack of interest, from exhaustion, call it what you will. I discovered that I am tired of being a person. Not just tired of being the person I was, but any person at all. I like watching people, but I don't like talking to them, dealing with them, pleasing them, or offending them. I don't even like talking to the dummy. I am tired. I would like to be a mountain, a tree, a stone. If I am to continue as a person, the life of the solitary derelict is the only one tolerable. So you will see that it is quite out of the question that I should allow the dummy to destroy himself, and have to take his place and live my old life again.

I continue my efforts of persuasion. I get him to dry his tears and go out and face the family breakfast, promising him that we will continue our conversation in the office, after he dictates his morning batch of letters to Miss Love. He agrees to try, and makes his red-eyed, somewhat belated appearance at the table. "A cold, dear?" says my wife. The dummy blushes and mumbles something. I pray that he will hurry up. I am afraid he will break down again. I notice with alarm that he can hardly eat, and leaves his coffee cup two-thirds full.

The dummy makes his way sadly out of the apartment, leaving my wife perplexed and apprehensive. I see him hail a cab instead of heading for the subway. In the office, I eavesdrop as he dictates his letters, sighing between every sentence. Miss Love notices, too. "Why, what's the matter?" she asks cheerfully. There is a long pause. I peep out of the closet, and what do I see! The dummy and Miss Love in a hot embrace. He is stroking her breasts, her eyes are closed, with their mouths they wound each other. The dummy catches sight of me staring from behind the closet door. I signal wildly, trying to make him understand that we must talk, that I'm on his side, that I'll help him. "Tonight?" whispers the dummy, slowly releasing the ecstatic Miss Love. "I adore you," she whispers. "I adore you," says the dummy in a voice above a whisper, "and I must see you." "Tonight," she whispers back. "My place. Here's the address."

15   One more kiss and Miss Love goes out. I emerge from the closet and lock the door of the little office. "Well," says the dummy. "It's Love or death." "All right," I say sadly. "I won't try to talk you out of it any more. She seems like a nice girl. And quite attractive. Who knows, if she had been working here when I was here . . ." I see the

dummy frowning angrily, and don't finish the sentence. "But you'll have to give me a little time," I say. "What are you going to do? As far as I can see, there's nothing you can do," says the dummy. "If you think I'm going home to your wife and kids any more, after I've found Love—" I plead with him for time.

What do I have in mind? Simply this. The dummy is now in my original position. His present arrangements for life are intolerable to him. But having more appetite for a real, individual life than I ever had, he doesn't want to vanish from the world. He just wants to replace my admittedly second-hand wife and two noisy daughters with the delightful, childless Miss Love. Well then, why shouldn't my solution—duplication—work for him as it did for me? Anything is better than suicide. The time I need is time to make another dummy, one to stay with my wife and children and go to my job while this dummy (the true dummy, I must now call him) elopes with Miss Love.

Later that morning, I borrow some money from him to go to a Turkish bath and get cleaned up, to get a haircut and shave at the barber's, and to buy myself a suit like the one he is wearing. On his suggestion, we meet for lunch at a small restaurant in Greenwich Village, where it is impossible that he meet anyone who might recognize him. I'm not sure what he is afraid of. Of having lunch alone, and being seen talking to himself? Of being seen with me? But I am perfectly presentable now. And if we are seen as two, what could be more normal than a pair of identical adult male twins, dressed alike, having lunch together and engaged in earnest conversation? We both order spaghetti *al burro* and baked clams. After three drinks, he comes around to my point of view. In consideration of my wife's feelings, he says—not mine, he insists several times in a rather harsh tone of voice—he will wait. But only a few months, no more. I point out that in this interim I will not ask that he not sleep with Miss Love but only that he be discreet in his adultery.

Making the second dummy is harder than making the first. My entire savings are wiped out. The prices of humanoid plastic and the other material, the fees of the engineer and the artist, have all gone up within just a year's time. The dummy's salary, I might add, hasn't gone up at all, despite the boss's increased appreciation of his value to the firm. The dummy is annoyed that I insist that he, rather than I, sit for the artist when the facial features are being molded and painted. But I point out to him that if the second dummy is modeled on me again, there is a chance that it would be a blurred or faded copy. Undoubtedly, some disparities have developed between the appearance of the first dummy and my own, even though I cannot detect them. I want the second dummy to be like him, wherever there is the slightest difference between him and me. I shall have to take the risk that in the second dummy might also be reproduced the unforeseen human passion that robbed the first dummy of his value to me.

Finally, the second dummy is ready. The first dummy, at my insistence (and reluctantly, since he wanted to spend his spare time with Miss Love), takes charge of his training and indoctrination period, lasting several weeks. Then the great day arrives. The second dummy is installed in the first dummy's life in the midst of a Saturday afternoon baseball game, during the seventh-inning stretch. It has been arranged that the first dummy will go out to buy hot dogs and Cokes for my wife and children. It is the first dummy who goes out, the second who returns laden with the food and drinks. The first dummy then leaps into a cab, off to the waiting arms of Miss Love.

That was nine years ago. The second dummy is living with my wife in no more exalted or depressed a fashion than I had managed. The older girl is in college, the second in high school; and there is a new child, a boy, now six years old. They have moved to a co-op apartment in Forest Hills; my wife has quit her job; and the second dummy

20

is assistant vice president of the firm. The first dummy went back to college nights while working as a waiter during the day; Miss Love also went back to college and got her teacher's license. He is now an architect with a growing practice; she teaches English at Julia Richman High School. They have two children, a boy and a girl, and are remarkably happy. From time to time, I visit both my dummies—never without sprucing myself up first, you understand. I consider myself a relative and the godfather, sometimes the uncle, of all their children. They are not very happy to see me, perhaps because of my shabby appearance, but they haven't the courage to turn me out. I never stay long, but I wish them well, and congratulate myself for having solved in so equitable and responsible a manner the problems of this one poor short life that was allotted me.   [1963]

QUESTIONS

1. Examine the verb tense in the story. What effects does Sontag achieve by telling the story in such a manner?
2. The narrator begins his story "Since my situation is intolerable." Do you believe he has evaluated his life accurately?
3. Why does the narrator say, "If I am to continue as a person, the life of the solitary derelict is the only one tolerable."
4. How can one explain that the second dummy's new life is satisfying for him and Miss Love?
5. Why does the narrator keep checking in on the lives of the two dummies?

RESPONSES

1. Compare how this character reacts to the tedium of everyday life to the characters in either Franz Kafka's "The Metamorphosis" or Julio Cortázar's "Axolotl."
2. Read Cheever's "The Swimmer" and Jackson's "The Lottery." Write an essay detailing how Cheever, Jackson, and Sontag viewed conformity to middle-class American life in the 1950s and 1960s.

FOCUS ON FILM

1. Although the film *Multiplicity* is not adapted from Sontag's story, the film and the story examine a character's inability to find emotional fulfillment in his life. How do the two works resolve that conflict?
2. Sontag wrote "The Dummy" in the 1960s and the film *Multiplicity* was made in the 1990s. Discuss how the two works reflect the societal and political climate of their days.
3. Examine the comic tone of both the film and print story. How does the humor of the two works differ? What features of the print story and of the film help create their humor?

John Steinbeck

John Steinbeck (1902–1968) was born in Salinas, California. An indifferent student, he left Stanford University in 1925 without taking a Degree. He saw the Depression from the underside, and his experience of the life of ordinary people during hard times informs his novels *In Dubious Battle* (1936), *Of Mice and Men* (1937), and *The Grapes of Wrath* (1939), which won the Pulitzer Prize. During World War II Steinbeck served as a war correspondent in Italy, and in 1952 he published *East of Eden*, a bestseller that drew on his family history. Perhaps his best-known collection of short stories is *The Long Valley* (1938). In 1962, Steinbeck won the Nobel Prize for Literature.

Chrysanthemums

The high grey-flannel fog of winter closed off the Salinas Valley from the sky and from all the rest of the world. On every side it sat like a lid on the mountains and made of the great valley a closed pot. On the broad, level land floor the gang plows bit deep and left the black earth shining like metal where the shares had cut. On the foothill ranches across the Salinas River, the yellow stubble fields seemed to be bathed in pale cold sunshine, but there was no sunshine in the valley now in December. The thick willow scrub along the river flamed with sharp and positive yellow leaves.

It was a time of quiet and of waiting. The air was cold and tender. A light wind blew up from the southwest so that the farmers were mildly hopeful of a good rain before long; but fog and rain do not go together.

Across the river, on Henry Allen's foothill ranch there was little work to be done, for the hay was cut and stored and the orchards were plowed up to receive the rain deeply when it should come. The cattle on the higher slopes were becoming shaggy and rough-coated.

Elisa Allen, working in her flower garden, looked down across the yard and saw Henry, her husband, talking to two men in business suits. The three of them stood by the tractor shed, each man with one foot on the side of the little Fordson. They smoked cigarettes and studied the machine as they talked.

Elisa watched them for a moment and then went back to her work. She was thirty-five. Her face was lean and strong and her eyes were as clear as water. Her figure looked blocked and heavy in her gardening costume, a man's black hat pulled low   5 down over her eyes, clod-hopper shoes, a figured print dress almost completely covered by a big corduroy apron with four big pockets to hold the snips, the trowel and scratcher, the seeds and the knife she worked with. She wore heavy leather gloves to protect her hands while she worked.

She was cutting down the old year's chrysanthemum stalks with a pair of short and powerful scissors. She looked down toward the men by the tractor shed now and then. Her face was eager and mature and handsome; even her work with the scissors was over-eager, over-powerful. The chrysanthemum stems seemed too small and easy for her energy.

She brushed a cloud of hair out of her eyes with the back of her glove, and left a smudge of earth on her cheek in doing it. Behind her stood the neat white farm house with red geraniums close-banked around it as high as the windows. It was a hard-swept looking little house with hard-polished windows, and a clean mud-mat on the front steps.

Elisa cast another glance toward the tractor shed. The strangers were getting into their Ford coupe. She took off a glove and put her strong fingers down into the forest of new green chrysanthemum sprouts that were growing around the old roots. She spread the leaves and looked down among the close-growing stems. No aphids were there, no sowbugs or snails or cutworms. Her terrier fingers destroyed such pests before they could get started.

Elisa started at the sound of her husband's voice. He had come near quietly, and he leaned over the wire fence that protected her flower garden from cattle and dogs and chickens.

10   "At it again," he said. "You've got a strong new crop coming."

Elisa straightened her back and pulled on the gardening glove again. "Yes. They'll be strong this coming year." In her tone and on her face there was a little smugness.

"You've got a gift with things," Henry observed. "Some of those yellow chrysanthemums you had this year were ten inches across. I wish you'd work out in the orchard and raise some apples that big."

Her eyes sharpened. "Maybe I could do it, too. I've a gift with things, all right. My mother had it. She could stick anything in the ground and make it grow. She said it was having planters' hands that knew how to do it."

"Well, it sure works with flowers," he said.

15   "Henry, who were those men you were talking to?"

"Why, sure, that's what I came to tell you. They were from the Western Meat Company. I sold those thirty head of three-year-old steers. Got nearly my own price, too."

"Good," she said. "Good for you."

"And I thought," he continued, "I thought how it's Saturday afternoon, and we might go into Salinas for dinner at a restaurant, and then to a picture show—to celebrate, you see."

"Good," she repeated. "Oh, yes. That will be good."

20   Henry put on his joking tone. "There's fights tonight. How's you like to go to the fights?"

"Oh, no," she said breathlessly. "No, I wouldn't like fights."

"Just fooling, Elisa. We'll go to a movie. Let's see. It's two now. I'm going to take Scotty and bring down those steers from the hill. It'll take us maybe two hours. We'll go in town about five and have dinner at the Cominos Hotel. Like that?"

"Of course I'll like it. It's good to eat away from home."

"All right, then. I'll go get up a couple of horses."

She said, "I'll have plenty of time to transplant some of these sets, I guess." 25

She heard her husband calling Scotty down by the barn. And a little later she saw the two men ride up the pale yellow hillside in search of the steers.

There was a little square sandy bed kept for rooting the chrysanthemums. With her trowel she turned the soil over and over, and smoothed it and patted it firm. Then she dug ten parallel trenches to receive the sets. Back at the chrysanthemum bed she pulled out the little crisp shoots, trimmed off the leaves of each one with her scissors and laid it on a small orderly pile.

A squeak of wheels and plod of hoofs came from the road. Elisa looked up. The country road ran along the dense bank of willows and cottonwoods that bordered the river, and up this road came a curious vehicle, curiously drawn. It was an old spring-wagon, with a round canvas top on it like the cover of a prairie schooner. It was drawn by an old bay horse and a little grey-and-white burro. A big stubble-bearded man sat between the cover flaps and drove the crawling team. Underneath the wagon, between the hind wheels, a lean and rangy mongrel dog walked sedately. Words were painted on the canvas, in clumsy, crooked letters. "Pots, pans, knives, sisors, lawn mores, Fixed." Two rows of articles, and the triumphantly definitive "Fixed" below. The black paint had run down in little sharp points beneath each letter.

Elisa, squatting on the ground, watched to see the crazy, loose-jointed wagon pass by. But it didn't pass. It turned into the farm road in front of her house, crooked old wheels skirling and squeaking. The rangy dog darted from between the wheels and ran ahead. Instantly the two ranch shepherds flew out at him. Then all three stopped, and with stiff and quivering tails, with taut straight legs, with ambassadorial dignity, they slowly circled, sniffing daintily. The caravan pulled up to Elisa's wire fence and stopped. Now the newcomer dog, feeling outnumbered, lowered his tail and retired under the wagon with raised hackles and bared teeth.

The man on the wagon seat called out, "That's a bad dog in a fight when he gets 30 started."

Elisa laughed. "I see he is. How soon does he generally get started?"

The man caught up her laughter and echoed it heartily. "Sometimes not for weeks and weeks," he said. He climbed stiffly down, over the wheel. The horse and the donkey drooped like unwatered flowers.

Elisa saw that he was a very big man. Although his hair and beard were greying, he did not look old. His worn black suit was wrinkled and spotted with grease. The laughter had disappeared from his face and eyes the moment his laughing voice ceased. His eyes were dark, and they were full of the brooding that gets in the eyes of teamsters and of sailors. The calloused hands he rested on the wire fence were cracked, and every crack was a black line. He took off his battered hat.

"I'm off my general road, ma'am," he said. "Does this dirt road cut over across the river to the Los Angeles highway?"

Elisa stood up and shoved the thick scissors in her apron pocket. "Well, yes, it does, 35 but it winds around and then fords the river. I don't think your team could pull through the sand."

He replied with some asperity, "It might surprise you what them beasts can pull through."

"When they get started?" she asked.

He smiled for a second. "Yes. When they get started."

"Well," said Elisa, "I think you'll save time if you go back to the Salinas road and pick up the highway there."

40   He drew a big finger down the chicken wire and made it sing. "I ain't in any hurry, ma'am. I go from Seattle to San Diego and back every year. Takes all my time. About six months each way. I aim to follow nice weather."

Elisa took off her gloves and stuffed them in the apron pocket with the scissors. She touched the under edge of her man's hat, searching for fugitive hairs. "That sounds like a nice kind of a way to live," she said.

He leaned confidentially over the fence. "Maybe you noticed the writing on my wagon. I mend pots and sharpen knives and scissors. You got any of them things to do?"

"Oh, no," she said, quickly. "Nothing like that." Her eyes hardened with resistance.

"Scissors is the worst thing," he explained. "Most people just ruin scissors trying to sharpen 'em, but I know how. I got a special tool. It's a little bobbit kind of thing, and patented. But it sure does the trick."

45   "No. My scissors are all sharp."

"All right, then. Take a pot," he continued earnestly, "a bent pot, or a pot with a hole. I can make it like new so you don't have to buy no new ones. That's a saving for you."

"No," she said shortly. "I tell you I have nothing like that for you to do."

His face fell to an exaggerated sadness. His voice took on a whining undertone. "I ain't had a thing to do today. Maybe I won't have no supper tonight. You see I'm off my regular road. I know folks on the highway clear from Seattle to San Diego. They save their things for me to sharpen up because they know I do it so good and save them money."

"I'm sorry," Elisa said irritably. "I haven't anything for you to do."

50   His eyes left her face and fell to searching the ground. They roamed about until they came to the chrysanthemum bed where she had been working. "What's them plants, ma'am?"

The irritation and resistance melted from Elisa's face. "Oh, those are chrysanthemums, giant whites and yellows. I raise them every year, bigger than anybody around here."

"Kind of a long-stemmed flower? Looks like a quick puff of colored smoke?" he asked.

"That's it. What a nice way to describe them."

"They smell kind of nasty till you get used to them," he said.

55   "It's a good bitter smell," she retorted, "not nasty at all."

He changed his tone quickly. "I like the smell myself."

"I had ten-inch blooms this year," she said.

The man leaned farther over the fence. "Look. I know a lady down the road a piece, has got the nicest garden you ever seen. Got nearly every kind of flower but no chrysanthemums. Last time I was mending a copper-bottom washtub for her (that's a hard job but I do it good), she said to me, "If you ever run acrost some nice chrysanthemums I wish you'd try to get me a few seeds.' That's what she told me."

Elisa's eyes grew alert and eager. "She couldn't have known much about chrysanthemums. You *can* raise them from seed, but it's much easier to root the little sprouts you see there."

60   "Oh," he said. "I s'pose I can't take none to her, then."

"Why yes you can," Elisa cried. "I can put some in damp sand, and you can carry them right along with you. They'll take root in the pot if you keep them damp. And then she can transplant them."

"She'd sure like to have some, ma'am. You say they're nice ones?"

"Beautiful," she said. "Oh, beautiful." Her eyes shone. She tore off the battered hat and shook out her dark pretty hair. "I'll put them in a flower pot, and you can take them right with you. Come into the yard."

While the man came through the picket gate Elisa ran excitedly along the geranium-bordered path to the back of the house. And she returned carrying a big red flower pot. The gloves were forgotten now. She kneeled on the ground by the starting bed and dug up the sandy soil with her fingers and scooped it into the bright new flower pot. Then she picked up the little pile of shoots she had prepared. With her strong fingers she pressed them into the sand and tamped around them with her knuckles. The man stood over her. "I'll tell you what to do," she said. "You remember so you can tell the lady."

"Yes, I'll try to remember." 65

"Well, look. These will take root in about a month. Then she must set them out, about a foot apart in good rich earth like this, see?" She lifted a handful of dark soil for him to look at. "They'll grow fast and tall. Now remember this: In July tell her to cut them down, about eight inches from the ground."

"Before they bloom?" he asked.

"Yes, before they bloom." Her face was tight with eagerness. "They'll grow right up again. About the last of September the buds will start."

She stopped and seemed perplexed. "It's the budding that takes the most care," she said hesitantly. "I don't know how to tell you." She looked deep into his eyes, searchingly. Her mouth opened a little, and she seemed to be listening. "I'll try to tell you," she said. "Did you ever hear of planting hands?"

"Can't say I have, ma'am." 70

"Well, I can only tell you what it feels like. It's when you're picking off the buds you don't want. Everything goes right down into your fingertips. You watch your fingers work. They do it themselves. You can feel how it is. They pick and pick the buds. They never make a mistake. They're with the plant. Do you see? Your fingers and the plant. You can feel that, right up your arm. They know. They never make a mistake. You can feel it. When you're like that you can't do anything wrong. Do you see that? Can you understand that?"

She was kneeling on the ground looking up at him. Her breast swelled passionately.

The man's eyes narrowed. He looked away self-consciously. "Maybe I know," he said. "Sometimes in the night in the wagon there—"

Elisa's voice grew husky. She broke in on him, "I've never lived as you do, but I know what you mean. When the night is dark—why, the stars are sharp-pointed, and there's quiet. Why, you rise up and up! Every pointed star gets driven into your body. It's like that. Hot and sharp and—lovely."

Kneeling there, her hand went out toward his legs in the greasy black trousers. Her 75 hesitant fingers almost touched the cloth. Then her hand dropped to the ground. She crouched low like a fawning dog.

He said, "It's nice, just like you say. Only when you don't have no dinner, it ain't."

She stood up then, very straight, and her face was ashamed. She held the flower pot out to him and placed it gently in his arms. "Here. Put it in your wagon, on the seat, where you can watch it. Maybe I can find something for you to do."

At the back of the house she dug in the can pile and found two old and battered aluminum saucepans. She carried them back and gave them to him. "Here, maybe you can fix these."

His manner changed. He became professional. "Good as new I can fix them." At the back of his wagon he set a little anvil, and out of an oily tool box dug a small machine hammer. Elisa came through the gate to watch him while he pounded out the dents in the kettles. His mouth grew sure and knowing. At a difficult part of the work he sucked his under-lip.

80   "You sleep right in the wagon?" Elisa asked.

"Right in the wagon, ma'm. Rain or shine I'm dry as a cow in there."

"It must be nice," she said. "It must be very nice. I wish women could do such things."

"It ain't the right kind of a life for a woman."

Her upper lip raised a little, showing her teeth. "How do you know? How can you tell?" she said.

85   "I don't know, ma'am," he protested. "Of course I don't know. Now here's your kettles, done. You don't have to buy no new ones."

"How much?"

"Oh, fifty cents'll do. I keep my prices down and my work good. That's why I have all them satisfied customers up and down the highway."

Elisa brought him a fifty-cent piece from the house and dropped it in his hand. "You might be surprised to have a rival some time. I can sharpen scissors, too. And I can beat the dents out of the little pots. I could show you what a woman might do."

He put his hammer back in the oily box and shoved the little anvil out of sight. "It would be a lonely life for a woman, ma'am, and a scarey life, too, with animals creeping under the wagon all night." He climbed over the singletree, steadying himself with a hand on the burro's white rump. He settled himself in the seat, picked up the lines. "Thank you kindly, ma'am," he said. "I'll do like you told me; I'll go back and catch the Salinas road."

90   "Mind," she called, "if you're long in getting there, keep the sand damp."

"Sand, ma'am? . . . Sand? Oh, sure. You mean around the chrysanthemums. Sure I will." He clucked his tongue. The beasts leaned luxuriously into their collars. The mongrel dog took his place between the back wheels. The wagon turned and crawled out the entrance road and back the way it had come, along the river.

Elisa stood in front of her wire fence watching the slow progress of the caravan. Her shoulders were straight, her head thrown back, her eyes half-closed, so that the scene came vaguely into them. Her lips moved silently, forming the words "Good-bye—good-bye." Then she whispered. "That's a bright direction. There's a glowing there." The sound of her whisper startled her. She shook herself free and looked about to see whether anyone had been listening. Only the dogs had heard. They lifted their heads toward her from their sleeping in the dust, and then stretched out their chins and settled asleep again. Elisa turned and ran hurriedly into the house.

In the kitchen she reached behind the stove and felt the water tank. It was full of hot water from the noonday cooking. In the bathroom she tore off her soiled clothes and flung them into the corner. And then she scrubbed herself with a little block of pumice, legs and thighs, loins and chest and arms, until her skin was scratched and red. When she had dried herself she stood in front of a mirror in her bedroom and looked at her body. She tightened her stomach and threw out her chest. She turned and looked over her shoulder at her back.

After a while she began to dress, slowly. She put on her newest underclothing and her nicest stockings and the dress which was the symbol of her prettiness. She worked carefully on her hair, penciled her eyebrows and rouged her lips.

Before she was finished she heard the little thunder of hoofs and the shouts of Henry 95
and his helper as they drove the red steers into the corral. She heard the gate bang
shut and set herself for Henry's arrival.

His step sounded on the porch. He entered the house calling, "Elisa, where are
you?"

"In my room, dressing. I'm not ready. There's hot water for your bath. Hurry up.
It's getting late."

When she heard him splashing in the tub, Elisa laid his dark suit on the bed, and
shirt and socks and tie beside it. She stood his polished shoes on the floor beside the
bed. Then she went to the porch and sat primly and stiffly down. She looked toward
the river road where the willow-line was still yellow with frosted leaves so that under
the high grey fog they seemed a thin band of sunshine. This was the only color in the
grey afternoon. She sat unmoving for a long time. Her eyes blinked rarely.

Henry came banging out of the door, shoving his tie inside his vest as he came.
Elisa stiffened and her face grew tight. Henry stopped short and looked at her. "Why—
why, Elisa. You look so nice!"

"Nice? You think I look nice? What do you mean by 'nice'?" 100

Henry blundered on. "I don't know. I mean you look different, strong and happy."

"I am strong? Yes, strong. What do you mean 'strong'?"

He looked bewildered. "You're playing some kind of a game," he said helplessly.
"It's a kind of a play. You look strong enough to break a calf over your knee, happy
enough to eat it like a watermelon."

For a second she lost her rigidity. "Henry! Don't talk like that. You didn't know
what you said." She grew complete again. "I'm strong," she boasted. "I never knew before how strong."

Henry looked down toward the tractor shed, and when he brought his eyes back 105
to her, they were his own again. "I'll get out the car. You can put on your coat while
I'm starting."

Elisa went into the house. She heard him drive to the gate and idle down his motor,
and then she took a long time to put on her hat. She pulled it here and pressed it there.
When Henry turned the motor off she slipped into her coat and went out.

The little roadster bounced along on the dirt road by the river, raising the birds and
driving the rabbits into the brush. Two cranes flapped heavily over the willow-line
and dropped into the river-bed.

Far ahead on the road Elisa saw a dark speck. She knew.

She tried not to look as they passed it, but her eyes would not obey. She whispered
to herself sadly, "He might have thrown them off the road. That wouldn't have been
much trouble, not very much. But he kept the pot," she explained, "He had to keep the
pot. That's why he couldn't get them off the road."

The roadster turned a bend and she saw the caravan ahead. She swung full around 110
toward her husband so she could not see the little covered wagon and the mismatched
team as the car passed them.

In a moment it was over. The thing was done. She did not look back.

She said loudly, to be heard above the motor, "It will be good, tonight, a good
dinner."

"Now you're changed again." Henry complained. He took one hand from the wheel
and patted her knee. "I ought to take you in to dinner oftener. It would be good for both
of us. We get so heavy out on the ranch."

"Henry," she asked, "could we have wine at dinner?"

115   "Sure we could. Say! That will be fine."

She was silent for a while; then she said, "Henry, at those prize fights, do the men hurt each other very much?"

"Sometimes a little, not often. Why?"

"Well, I've read how they break noses, and blood runs down their chests. I've read how the fighting gloves get heavy and soggy with blood."

He looked around at her. "What's the matter, Elisa? I didn't know you read things like that." He brought the car to a stop, then turned to the right over the Salinas River bridge.

120   "Do any women ever go to the fights?" she asked.

"Oh, sure, some. What's the matter, Elisa? Do you want to go? I don't think you'd like it, but I'll take you if you really want to go."

She relaxed limply in the seat. "Oh, no. No. I don't want to go. I'm sure I don't." Her face was turned away from him. "It will be enough if we can have wine. It will be plenty." She turned up her coat collar so he could not see that she was crying weakly—like an old woman.   [1937]

QUESTIONS

1. How does the opening paragraph of natural description establish the setting and atmosphere of the story and foreshadow the theme?
2. How are Elisa's age and the fact that she has no children important to the reader's understanding of her character?
3. What is Elisa's relationship to her husband and to the tinker? How do these relationships help to define the conflict?
4. How does Elisa's curiosity about boxing reveal her state of mind?
5. How does the symbolic value of the chrysanthemums change in the course of the action?

RESPONSES

1. Compare Elisa Allen's life to that of the narrator's in Sontag's "The Dummy."
2. From a mythological approach, research the story of the Southwestern character Kokopelli. How is the myth of this "traveling salesman" dramatized in Steinbeck's story?

AMY TAN

Amy Tan (b. 1952) was born in Oakland, California. Her father, an engineer, and her mother, a nurse, had emigrated from China. Tan was educated at Linfield College in Oregon and California State College in San Jose. *The Joy Luck Club* (1989), her first novel, was nominated for the National Book Award. Since then she has published three more novels, *The Kitchen God's Wife* (1991), *The Hundred Secret Senses* (1995), and *The Bonesetter's Daughter* in 2001. *Opposite of Fate: A Book of Musings* appeared in 2003.

A Pair of Tickets

The minute our train leaves the Hong Kong border and enters Shenzhen, China, I feel different. I can feel the skin on my forehead tingling, my blood rushing through a new course, my bones aching with a familiar old pain. And I think, My mother was right. I am becoming Chinese.

"Cannot be helped," my mother said when I was fifteen and had vigorously denied that I had any Chinese whatsoever below my skin. I was a sophomore at Galileo High in San Francisco, and all my Caucasian friends agreed: I was about as Chinese as they were. But my mother had studied at a famous nursing school in Shanghai, and she said she knew all about genetics. So there was no doubt in her mind, whether I agreed or not: Once you are born Chinese, you cannot help but feel and think Chinese.

"Someday you will see," said my mother. "It is in your blood, waiting to be let go."

And when she said this, I saw myself transforming like a werewolf, a mutant tag of DNA suddenly triggered, replicating itself insidiously into a *syndrome,* a cluster of telltale Chinese behaviors, all those things my mother did to embarrass me—haggling with store owners, pecking her mouth with a toothpick in public, being color-blind to the fact that lemon yellow and pale pink are not good combinations for winter clothes.

But today I realize I've never really known what it means to be Chinese. I am thirty-six years old. My mother is dead and I am on a train, carrying with me her dreams of coming home. I am going to China. 5

We are first going to Guangzhou, my seventy-two-year-old father, Canning Woo, and I, where we will visit his aunt, whom he has not seen since he was ten years old. And I don't know whether it's the prospect of seeing his aunt or if it's because he's back in China, but now he looks like he's a young boy, so innocent and happy I want to button his sweater and pat his head. We are sitting across from each other, separated by a little table with two cold cups of tea. For the first time I can ever remember, my father has tears in his eyes, and all he is seeing out the train window is a sectioned field of yellow, green, and brown, a narrow canal flanking the tracks, low rising hills, and three people in blue jackets riding an ox-driven cart on this early October morning. And I can't help myself. I also have misty eyes, as if I had seen this a long, long time ago, and had almost forgotten.

In less than three hours, we will be in Guangzhou, which my guidebook tells me is how one properly refers to Canton these days. It seems all the cities I have heard of, except Shanghai, have changed their spellings. I think they are saying China has changed in other ways as well. Chungking is Chongqing. And Kweilin is Guilin. I have looked these names up, because after we see my father's aunt in Guangzhou, we will catch a plane to Shanghai, where I will meet my two half-sisters for the first time.

They are my mother's twin daughters from her first marriage, little babies she was forced to abandon on a road as she was fleeing Kweilin for Chungking in 1944. That was all my mother had told me about these daughters, so they had remained babies in my mind, all these years, sitting on the side of a road, listening to bombs whistling in the distance while sucking their patient red thumbs.

And it was only this year that someone found them and wrote with this joyful news. A letter came from Shanghai, addressed to my mother. When I first heard about this, that they were alive, I imagined my identical sisters transforming from little babies into six-year-old girls. In my mind, they were seated next to each other at a table, taking turns with the fountain pen. One would write a neat row of characters: *Dearest Mama. We are alive.* She would brush back her wispy bangs and hand the other sister the pen, and she would write: *Come get us. Please hurry.*

10   Of course they could not know that my mother had died three months before, suddenly, when a blood vessel in her brain burst. One minute she was talking to my father, complaining about the tenants upstairs, scheming how to evict them under the pretense that relatives from China were moving in. The next minute she was holding her head, her eyes squeezed shut, groping for the sofa, and then crumpling softly to the floor with fluttering hands.

So my father had been the first one to open the letter, a long letter it turned out. And they did call her Mama. They said they always revered her as their true mother. They kept a framed picture of her. They told her about their life, from the time my mother last saw them on the road leaving Kweilin to when they were finally found.

And the letter had broken my father's heart so much—these daughters calling my mother from another life he never knew—that he gave the letter to my mother's old friend Auntie Lindo and asked her to write back and tell my sisters, in the gentlest way possible, that my mother was dead.

But instead Auntie Lindo took the letter to the Joy Luck Club and discussed with Auntie Ying and Auntie An-mei what should be done, because they had known for many years about my mother's search for her twin daughters, her endless hope. Auntie Lindo and the others cried over this double tragedy, of losing my mother three months before, and now again. And so they couldn't help but think of some miracle, some possible way of reviving her from the dead, so my mother could fulfill her dream.

So this is what they wrote to my sisters in Shanghai: "Dearest Daughters, I too have never forgotten you in my memory or in my heart. I never gave up hope that we would see each other again in a joyous reunion. I am only sorry it has been too long. I want to tell you everything about my life since I last saw you. I want to tell you this when our family comes to see you in China. . . ." They signed it with my mother's name.

It wasn't until all this had been done that they first told me about my sisters, the letter they received, the one they wrote back.

"They'll think she's coming, then," I murmured. And I had imagined my sisters now being ten or eleven, jumping up and down, holding hands, their pigtails bouncing, excited that their mother—*their* mother—was coming, whereas my mother was dead.

"How can you say she is not coming in a letter?" said Auntie Lindo. "She is their mother. She is your mother. You must be the one to tell them. All these years, they have been dreaming of her." And I thought she was right.

But then I started dreaming, too, of my mother and my sisters and how it would be if I arrived in Shanghai. All these years, while they waited to be found, I had lived with my mother and then had lost her. I imagined seeing my sisters at the airport. They would be standing on their tiptoes, looking anxiously, scanning from one dark head to another as we got off the plane. And I would recognize them instantly, their faces with the identical worried look.

"*Jyejye, Jyejye.* Sister, Sister. We are here." I saw myself saying in my poor version of Chinese.

"Where is Mama?" they would say, and look around, still smiling, two flushed and eager faces. "Is she hiding?" And this would have been like my mother, to stand behind just a bit, to tease a little and make people's patience pull a little on their hearts. I would shake my head and tell my sisters she was not hiding.

"Oh, that must be Mama, no?" one of my sisters would whisper excitedly, pointing to another small woman completely engulfed in a tower of presents. And that, too, would have been like my mother, to bring mountains of gifts, food, and toys for children—all bought on sale—shunning thanks, saying the gifts were nothing, and later turning the labels over to show my sisters, "Calvin Klein, 100% wool."

I imagined myself starting to say, "Sisters, I am sorry, I have come alone . . ." and before I could tell them—they could see it in my face—they were wailing, pulling their hair, their lips twisted in pain, as they ran away from me. And then I saw myself getting back on the plane and coming home.

After I had dreamed this scene many times—watching their despair turn from horror into anger—I begged Auntie Lindo to write another letter. And at first she refused.

"How can I say she is dead? I cannot write this," said Auntie Lindo with a stubborn look.

"But it's cruel to have them believe she's coming on the plane," I said. "When they see it's just me, they'll hate me."

"Hate you? Cannot be." She was scowling. "You are their own sister, their only family."

"You don't understand," I protested.

"What I don't understand?" she said.

And I whispered, "They'll think I'm responsible, that she died because I didn't appreciate her."

And Auntie Lindo looked satisfied and sad at the same time, as if this were true and I had finally realized it. She sat down for an hour, and when she stood up she handed me a two-page letter. She had tears in her eyes. I realized that the very thing I had feared, she had done. So even if she had written the news of my mother's death in English, I wouldn't have had the heart to read it.

"Thank you," I whispered.

The landscape has become gray, filled with low flat cement buildings, old factories, and then tracks and more tracks filled with trains like ours passing by in the opposite direction. I see platforms crowded with people wearing drab Western clothes, with spots of bright colors: little children wearing pink and yellow, red and peach. And there are soldiers in olive green and red, and old ladies in gray tops and pants that stop mid-calf. We are in Guangzhou.

Before the train even comes to a stop, people are bringing down their belongings from above their seats. For a moment there is a dangerous shower of heavy suitcases laden with gifts to relatives, half-broken boxes wrapped in miles of string to keep the contents from spilling out, plastic bags filled with yarn and vegetables and packages of dried mushrooms, and camera cases. And then we are caught in a stream of people rushing, shoving, pushing us along, until we find ourselves in one of a dozen lines waiting to go through customs. I feel as if I were getting on the number 30 Stockton bus in San Francisco. I am in China, I remind myself. And somehow the crowds don't bother me. It feels right. I start pushing too.

I take out the declaration forms and my passport. "Woo," it says at the top, and below that, "June May," who was born in "California, U.S.A.," in 1951. I wonder if the customs people will question whether I'm the same person as in the passport photo. In this picture, my chin-length hair is swept back and artfully styled. I am wearing false eyelashes, eye shadow, and lip liner. My cheeks are hollowed out by bronze blusher. But I had not expected the heat in October. And now my hair hangs limp with the humidity. I wear no makeup; in Hong Kong my mascara had melted into dark circles and everything else had felt like layers of grease. So today my face is plain, unadorned except for a thin mist of shiny sweat on my forehead and nose.

35　　　Even without makeup, I could never pass for true Chinese. I stand five-foot-six, and my head pokes above the crowd so that I am eye level only with other tourists. My mother once told me my height came from my grandfather, who was a northerner, and may have even had some Mongol blood. "This is what your grandmother once told me," explained my mother. "But now it is too late to ask her. They are all dead, your grandparents, your uncles, and their wives and children, all killed in the war, when a bomb fell on our house. So many generations in one instant."

She had said this so matter-of-factly that I thought she had long since gotten over any grief she had. And then I wondered how she knew they were all dead.

"Maybe they left the house before the bomb fell," I suggested.

"No," said my mother. "Our whole family is gone. It is just you and I."

"But how do you know? Some of them could have escaped."

40　　　"Cannot be," said my mother, this time almost angrily. And then her frown was washed over by a puzzled blank look, and she began to talk as if she were trying to remember where she had misplaced something. "I went back to that house. I kept looking up to where the house used to be. And it wasn't a house, just the sky. And below, underneath my feet, were four stories of burnt bricks and wood, all the life of our house. Then off to the side I saw things blown into the yard, nothing valuable. There was a bed someone used to sleep in, really just a metal frame twisted up at one corner. And a book, I don't know what kind, because every page had turned black. And I saw a teacup which was unbroken but filled with ashes. And then I found my doll, with her hands and legs broken, her hair burned off. . . . When I was a little girl, I had cried for that doll, seeing it all alone in the store window, and my mother had bought it for me. It was an American doll with yellow hair. It could turn its legs and arms. The eyes moved up and down. And when I married and left my family home, I gave the doll to my youngest niece, because she was like me. She cried if that doll was not with her always. Do you see? If she was in the house with that doll, her parents were there, and so everybody was there, waiting together, because that's how our family was."

The woman in the customs booth stares at my documents, then glances at me briefly, and with two quick movements stamps everything and sternly nods me along. And soon my father and I find ourselves in a large area filled with thousands of people and suitcases. I feel lost and my father looks helpless.

"Excuse me," I say to a man who looks like an American. "Can you tell me where I can get a taxi?" He mumbles something that sounds Swedish or Dutch.

"Syau Yen! Syau Yen!" I hear a piercing voice shout from behind me. An old woman in a yellow knit beret is holding up a pink plastic bag filled with wrapped trinkets. I guess she is trying to sell us something. But my father is staring down at this tiny sparrow of a woman, squinting into her eyes. And then his eyes widen, his face opens up and he smiles like a pleased little boy.

"*Aiyi! Aiyi!*"—Auntie Auntie!—he says softly.

"Syau Yen!" coos my great-aunt. I think it's funny she has just called my father "Little Wild Goose." It must be his baby milk name, the name used to discourage ghosts from stealing children. 45

They clasp each other's hands—they do not hug—and hold on like this, taking turns saying, "Look at you! You are so old. Look how old you've become!" They are both crying openly, laughing at the same time, and I bite my lip, trying not to cry. I'm afraid to feel their joy. Because I am thinking how different our arrival in Shanghai will be tomorrow, how awkward it will feel.

Now Aiyi beams and points to a Polaroid picture of my father. My father had wisely sent pictures when he wrote and said we were coming. See how smart she was, she seems to intone as she compares the picture to my father. In the letter, my father had said we would call her from the hotel once we arrived, so this is a surprise, that they've come to meet us. I wonder if my sisters will be at the airport.

It is only then that I remember the camera. I had meant to take a picture of my father and his aunt the moment they met. It's not too late.

"Here, stand together over here," I say, holding up the Polaroid. The camera flashes and I hand them the snapshot. Aiyi and my father still stand close together, each of them holding a corner of the picture, watching as their images begin to form. They are almost reverentially quiet. Aiyi is only five years older than my father, which makes her around seventy-seven. But she looks ancient, shrunken, a mummified relic. Her thin hair is pure white, her teeth are brown with decay. So much for stories of Chinese women looking young forever, I think to myself.

Now Aiyi is crooning to me: "*Jandale.*" So big already. She looks up at me, at my full height, and then peers into her pink plastic bag—her gifts to us, I have figured out— as if she is wondering what she will give to me, now that I am so old and big. And then she grabs my elbow with her sharp pincerlike grasp and turns me around. A man and woman in their fifties are shaking hands with my father, everybody smiling and saying, "Ah! Ah!" They are Aiyi's oldest son and his wife, and standing next to them are four other people, around my age, and a little girl who's around ten. The introductions go by so fast, all I know is that one of them is Aiyi's grandson, with his wife, and the other is her granddaughter, with her husband. And the little girl is Lili, Aiyi's great-granddaughter. 50

Aiyi and my father speak the Mandarin dialect from their childhood, but the rest of the family speaks only the Cantonese of their village. I understand only Mandarin but can't speak it that well. So Aiyi and my father gossip unrestrained in Mandarin, exchanging news about people from their old village. And they stop only occasionally to talk to the rest of us, sometimes in Cantonese, sometimes in English.

"Oh, it is as I suspected," says my father, turning to me. "He died last summer." And I already understood this. I just don't know who this person, Li Gong, is. I feel as if I were in the United Nations and the translators had run amok.

"Hello," I say to the little girl. "My name is Jing-mei." But the little girl squirms to look away, causing her parents to laugh with embarrassment. I try to think of Cantonese words I can say to her, stuff I learned from friends in Chinatown, but all I can think of are swear words, terms for bodily functions, and short phrases like "tastes good," "tastes like garbage," and "she's really ugly." And then I have another plan: I hold up the Polaroid camera, beckoning Lili with my finger. She immediately jumps forward, places one hand on her hip in the manner of a fashion model, juts out her chest, and flashes me a toothy smile. As soon as I take the picture she is standing next to me, jumping and giggling every few seconds as she watches herself appear on the greenish film.

By the time we hail taxis for the ride to the hotel, Lili is holding tight onto my hand, pulling me along.

55   In the taxi, Aiyi talks nonstop, so I have no chance to ask her about the different sights we are passing by.

"You wrote and said you would come only for one day," says Aiyi to my father in an agitated tone. "One day! How can you see your family in one day! Toishan is many hours' drive from Guangzhou. And this idea to call us when you arrive. This is nonsense. We have no telephone."

My heart races a little. I wonder if Auntie Lindo told my sisters we would call from the hotel in Shanghai?

Aiyi continues to scold my father. "I was so beside myself, ask my son, almost turned heaven and earth upside down trying to think of a way! So we decided the best was for us to take the bus from Toishan and come into Guangzhou—meet you right from the start."

And now I am holding my breath as the taxi driver dodges between trucks and buses, honking his horn constantly. We seem to be on some sort of long freeway overpass, like a bridge above the city. I can see row after row of apartments, each floor cluttered with laundry hanging out to dry on the balcony. We pass a public bus, with people jammed in so tight their faces are nearly wedged against the window. Then I see the skyline of what must be downtown Guangzhou. From a distance, it looks like a major American city, with highrises and construction going on everywhere. As we slow down in the more congested part of the city, I see scores of little shops, dark inside, lined with counters and shelves. And then there is a building, its front laced with scaffolding made of bamboo poles held together with plastic strips. Men and women are standing on narrow platforms, scraping the sides, working without safety straps or helmets. Oh, would OSHA° have a field day here, I think.

60   Aiyi's shrill voice rises up again: "So it is a shame you can't see our village, our house. My sons have been quite successful, selling our vegetables in the free market. We had enough these last few years to build a big house, three stories, all of new brick,

---

°*OSHA*: Occupational Safety and Health Administration.

big enough for our whole family and then some. And every year, the money is even better. You Americans aren't the only ones who know how to get rich!"

The taxi stops and I assume we've arrived, but then I peer out at what looks like a grander version of the Hyatt Regency. "This is communist China?" I wonder out loud. And then I shake my head toward my father. "This must be the wrong hotel." I quickly pull out our itinerary, travel tickets, and reservations. I had explicitly instructed my travel agent to choose something inexpensive, in the thirty-to-forty-dollar range. I'm sure of this. And there it says on our itinerary: Garden Hotel, Huanshi Dong Lu. Well, our travel agent had better be prepared to eat the extra, that's all I have to say.

The hotel is magnificent. A bellboy complete with uniform and sharp-creased cap jumps forward and begins to carry our bags into the lobby. Inside, the hotel looks like an orgy of shopping arcades and restaurants all encased in granite and glass. And rather than be impressed, I am worried about the expense, as well as the appearance it must give Aiyi, that we rich Americans cannot be without our luxuries even for one night.

But when I step up to the reservation desk, ready to haggle over this booking mistake, it is confirmed. Our rooms are prepaid, thirty-four dollars each. I feel sheepish, and Aiyi and the others seem delighted by our temporary surroundings. Lili is looking wide-eyed at an arcade filled with video games.

Our whole family crowds into one elevator, and the bellboy waves, saying he will meet us on the eighteenth floor. As soon as the elevator door shuts, everybody becomes very quiet, and when the door finally opens again, everybody talks at once in what sounds like relieved voices. I have the feeling Aiyi and the others have never been on such a long elevator ride.

Our rooms are next to each other and are identical. The rugs, drapes, bedspreads are all in shades of taupe. There's a color television with remote-control panels built into the lamp table between the two twin beds. The bathroom has marble walls and floors. I find a built-in wet bar with a small refrigerator stocked with Heineken beer, Coke Classic, and Seven-Up, mini-bottles of Johnnie Walker Red, Bacardi rum, and Smirnoff vodka, and packets of M & M's, honey-roasted cashews, and Cadbury chocolate bars. And again I say out loud, "This is communist China?"

My father comes into my room. "They decided we should just stay here and visit," he says, shrugging his shoulders. "They say, Less trouble that way. More time to talk."

"What about dinner?" I ask. I have been envisioning my first real Chinese feast for many days already, a big banquet with one of those soups steaming out of a carved winter melon, chicken wrapped in clay, Peking duck, the works.

My father walks over and picks up a room service book next to a *Travel & Leisure* magazine. He flips through the pages quickly and then points to the menu. "This is what they want," says my father.

So it's decided. We are going to dine tonight in our rooms, with our family, sharing hamburgers, french fries, and apple pie à la mode.

Aiyi and her family are browsing the shops while we clean up. After a hot ride on the train, I'm eager for a shower and cooler clothes.

The hotel has provided little packets of shampoo which, upon opening, I discover is the consistency and color of hoisin sauce.° This is more like it, I think. This is China. And I rub some in my damp hair.

65

70

°*hoisin sauce*: A thick, dark-brown condiment that is the consistency of apple butter.

Standing in the shower, I realize this is the first time I've been by myself in what seems like days. But instead of feeling relieved, I feel forlorn. I think about what my mother said, about activating my genes and becoming Chinese. And I wonder what she meant.

Right after my mother died, I asked myself a lot of things, things that couldn't be answered, to force myself to grieve more. It seemed as if I wanted to sustain my grief, to assure myself that I had cared deeply enough.

But now I ask the questions mostly because I want to know the answers. What was that pork stuff she used to make that had the texture of sawdust? What were the names of the uncles who died in Shanghai? What had she dreamt all these years about her other daughters? All the times when she got mad at me, was she really thinking about them? Did she wish I were they? Did she regret that I wasn't?

75   At one o'clock in the morning, I awake to tapping sounds on the window. I must have dozed off and now I feel my body uncramping itself. I'm sitting on the floor, leaning against one of the twin beds. Lili is lying next to me. The others are asleep, too, sprawled out on the beds and floor. Aiyi is seated at a little table, looking very sleepy. And my father is staring out the window, tapping his fingers on the glass. The last time I listened my father was telling Aiyi about his life since he last saw her. How he had gone to Yenching University, later got a post with a newspaper in Chungking, met my mother there, a young widow. How they later fled together to Shanghai to try to find my mother's family house, but there was nothing there. And then they traveled eventually to Canton and then to Hong Kong, then Haiphong and finally to San Francisco. . . .

"Suyuan didn't tell me she was trying all these years to find her daughters," he is now saying in a quiet voice. "Naturally, I did not discuss her daughters with her. I thought she was ashamed she had left them behind."

"Where did she leave them?" asks Aiyi. "How were they found?"

I am wide awake now. Although I have heard parts of this story from my mother's friends.

"It happened when the Japanese took over Kweilin," says my father.

80   "Japanese in Kweilin?" says Aiyi. "That was never the case. Couldn't be. The Japanese never came to Kweilin."

"Yes, that is what the newspapers reported. I know this because I was working for the news bureau at the time. The Kuomintang often told us what we could say and could not say. But we knew the Japanese had come into Kwangsi Province. We had sources who told us how they had captured the Wuchang-Canton railway. How they were coming overland, making very fast progress, marching toward the provincial capital."

Aiyi looks astonished. "If people did not know this, how could Suyuan know the Japanese were coming?"

"An officer of the Kuomintang° secretly warned her," explains my father. "Suyuan's husband also was an officer and everybody knew that officers and their families would be the first to be killed. So she gathered a few possessions and, in the middle of the night, she picked up her daughters and fled on foot. The babies were not even one year old."

°*Kuomintang*: The National People's Party led by Chiang Kai-shek (1887–1975).

"How could she give up those babies!" sighs Aiyi. "Twin girls. We have never had such luck in our family." And then she yawns again.

"What were they named?" she asks. I listen carefully. I had been planning on using just the familiar "Sister" to address them both. But now I want to know how to pronounce their names.

"They have their father's surname, Wang," says my father. "And their given names are Chwun Yu and Chwun Hwa."

"What do the names mean?" I ask.

"Ah." My father draws imaginary characters on the window. "One means 'Spring Rain,' the other 'Spring Flower,'" he explains in English, "because they born in the spring, and of course rain come before flower, same order these girls are born. Your mother like a poet, don't you think?"

I nod my head. I see Aiyi nod her head forward, too. But it falls forward and stays there. She is breathing deeply, noisily. She is asleep.

"And what does Ma's name mean?" I whisper.

"'Suyuan,'" he says, writing more invisible characters on the glass. "The way she write it in Chinese, it mean 'Long-Cherished Wish.' Quite a fancy name, not so ordinary like flower name. See this first character, it mean something like 'Forever Never Forgotten.' But there is another way to write 'Suyuan.' Sound exactly the same, but the meaning is opposite." His finger creates the brushstrokes of another character. "The first part look the same: 'Never Forgotten.' But the last part add to first part make the whole word mean 'Long-Held Grudge.' Your mother get angry with me, I tell her her name should be Grudge."

My father is looking at me, moist-eyed. "See, I pretty clever, too, hah?"

I nod, wishing I could find some way to comfort him. "And what about my name," I ask, "what does 'Jing-mei' mean?"

"Your name also special," he says. I wonder if any name in Chinese is not something special. "'Jing' like excellent *jing*. Not just good, it's something pure, essential, the best quality. *Jing* is good leftover stuff when you take impurities out of something like gold, or rice, or salt. So what is left—just pure essence. And 'Mei,' this is common *mei*, as in *meimei*, 'younger sister.'"

I think about this. My mother's long-cherished wish. Me, the younger sister who was supposed to be the essence of the others. I feed myself with the old grief, wondering how disappointed my mother must have been. Tiny Aiyi stirs suddenly, her head rolls and then falls back, her mouth opens as if to answer my question. She grunts in her sleep, tucking her body more closely into the chair.

"So why did she abandon those babies on the road?" I need to know, because now I feel abandoned too.

"Long time I wondered this myself," says my father. "But then I read that letter from her daughters in Shanghai now, and I talk to Auntie Lindo, all the others. And then I knew. No shame in what she done. None."

"What happened?"

"Your mother running away—" begins my father.

"No, tell me in Chinese," I interrupt. "Really, I can understand."

He begins to talk, still standing at the window, looking into the night.

After fleeing Kweilin, your mother walked for several days trying to find a main road. Her thought was to catch a ride on a truck or wagon, to catch enough rides until she reached Chungking, where her husband was stationed.

She had sewn money and jewelry into the lining of her dress, enough, she thought, to barter rides all the way. If I am lucky, she thought, I will not have to trade the heavy gold bracelet and jade ring. These were things from her mother, your grandmother.

By the third day, she had traded nothing. The roads were filled with people, everybody running and begging for rides from passing trucks. The trucks rushed by, afraid to stop. So your mother found no rides, only the start of dysentery pains in her stomach.

105   Her shoulders ached from the two babies swinging from scarf slings. Blisters grew on her palms from holding two leather suitcases. And then the blisters burst and began to bleed. After a while, she left the suitcases behind, keeping only the food and a few clothes. And later she also dropped the bags of wheat flour and rice and kept walking like this for many miles, singing songs to her little girls, until she was delirious with pain and fever.

Finally, there was not one more step left in her body. She didn't have the strength to carry those babies any farther. She slumped to the ground. She knew she would die of her sickness, or perhaps from thirst, from starvation, or from the Japanese, who she was sure were marching right behind her.

She took the babies out of the slings and sat them on the side of the road, then lay down next to them. You babies are so good, she said, so quiet. They smiled back, reaching their chubby hands for her, wanting to be picked up again. And then she knew she could not bear to watch her babies die with her.

She saw a family with three young children in a cart going by. "Take my babies, I beg you," she cried to them. But they stared back with empty eyes and never stopped.

She saw another person pass and called out again. This time a man turned around, and he had such a terrible expression—your mother said it looked like death itself—she shivered and looked away.

110   When the road grew quiet, she tore open the lining of her dress, and stuffed jewelry under the shirt of one baby and money under the other. She reached into her pocket and drew out the photos of her family, the picture of her father and mother, the picture of herself and her husband on their wedding day. And she wrote on the back of each the names of the babies and this same message: "Please care for these babies with the money and valuables provided. When it is safe to come, if you bring them to Shanghai, 9 Weichang Lu, the Li family will be glad to give you a generous reward. Li Suyuan and Wang Fuchi."

And then she touched each baby's cheek and told her not to cry. She would go down the road to find them some food and would be back. And without looking back, she walked down the road, stumbling and crying, thinking only of this one last hope, that her daughters would be found by a kindhearted person who would care for them. She would not allow herself to imagine anything else.

She did not remember how far she walked, which direction she went, when she fainted, or how she was found. When she awoke, she was in the back of a bouncing truck with several other sick people, all moaning. And she began to scream, thinking she was now on a journey to Buddhist hell. But the face of an American missionary lady bent over her and smiled, talking to her in a soothing language she did not understand. And yet she could somehow understand. She had been saved for no good reason, and it was now too late to go back and save her babies.

When she arrived in Chungking, she learned her husband had died two weeks before. She told me later she laughed when the officers told her this news, she was so delirious with madness and disease. To come so far, to lose so much and to find nothing.

I met her in a hospital. She was lying on a cot, hardly able to move, her dysentery had drained her so thin. I had come in for my foot, my missing toe, which was cut off by a piece of falling rubble. She was talking to herself, mumbling.

"Look at these clothes," she said, and I saw she had on a rather unusual dress for wartime. It was silk satin, quite dirty, but there was no doubt it was a beautiful dress.

"Look at this face," she said, and I saw her dusty face and hollow cheeks, her eyes shining back. "Do you see my foolish hope?"

"I thought I had lost everything, except these two things," she murmured. "And I wondered which I would lose next. Clothes or hope? Hope or clothes?"

"But now, see here, look what is happening," she said, laughing, as if all her prayers had been answered. And she was pulling hair out of her head as easily as one lifts new wheat from wet soil.

It was an old peasant woman who found them. "How could I resist?" the peasant woman later told your sisters when they were older. They were still sitting obediently near where your mother had left them, looking like little fairy queens waiting for their sedan to arrive.

The woman, Mei Ching, and her husband, Mei Han, lived in a stone cave. There were thousands of hidden caves like that in and around Kweilin so secret that the people remained hidden even after the war ended. The Meis would come out of their cave every few days and forage for food supplies left on the road, and sometimes they would see something that they both agreed was a tragedy to leave behind. So one day they took back to their cave a delicately painted set of rice bowls, another day a little footstool with a velvet cushion and two new wedding blankets. And once, it was your sisters.

They were pious people. Muslims, who believed the twin babies were a sign of double luck, and they were sure of this when, later in the evening, they discovered how valuable the babies were. She and her husband had never seen rings and bracelets like those. And while they admired the pictures, knowing the babies came from a good family, neither of them could read or write. It was not until many months later that Mei Ching found someone who could read the writing on the back. By then, she loved these baby girls like her own.

In 1952 Mei Han, the husband, died. The twins were already eight years old, and Mei Ching now decided it was time to find your sisters' true family.

She showed the girls the picture of their mother and told them they had been born into a great family and she would take them back to see their true mother and grandparents. Mei Ching told them about the reward, but she swore she would refuse it. She loved these girls so much, she only wanted them to have what they were entitled to—a better life, a fine house, educated ways. Maybe the family would let her stay on as the girls' amah. Yes, she was certain they would insist.

Of course, when she found the place at 9 Weichang Lu, in the old French Concession, it was something completely different. It was the site of a factory building, recently constructed, and none of the workers knew what had become of the family whose house had burned down on that spot.

Mei Ching could not have known, of course, that your mother and I, her new husband, had already returned to that same place in 1945 in hopes of finding both her family and her daughters.

Your mother and I stayed in China until 1947. We went to many different cities—back to Kweilin, to Changsha, as far south as Kunming. She was always looking out of one corner of her eye for twin babies, then little girls. Later we went to Hong Kong, and when we finally left in 1949 for the United States, I think she was even looking for them on the boat. But when we arrived, she no longer talked about them. I thought, At last, they have died in her heart.

When letters could be openly exchanged between China and the United States, she wrote immediately to old friends in Shanghai and Kweilin. I did not know she did this. Auntie Lindo told me. But of course, by then, all the street names had changed. Some people had died, others had moved away. So it took many years to find a contact. And when she did find an old schoolmate's address and wrote asking her to look for her daughters, her friend wrote back and said this was impossible, like looking for a needle on the bottom of the ocean. How did she know her daughters were in Shanghai and not somewhere else in China? The friend, of course, did not ask, How do you know your daughters are still alive?

So her schoolmate did not look. Finding babies lost during the war was a matter of foolish imagination, and she had no time for that.

But every year, your mother wrote to different people. And this last year, I think she got a big idea in her head, to go to China and find them herself. I remember she told me, "Canning, we should go, before it is too late, before we are too old." And I told her we were already too old, it was already too late.

130   I just thought she wanted to be a tourist! I didn't know she wanted to go and look for her daughters. So when I said it was too late, that must have put a terrible thought in her head that her daughters might be dead. And I think this possibility grew bigger and bigger in her head, until it killed her.

Maybe it was your mother's dead spirit who guided her Shanghai schoolmate to find her daughters. Because after your mother died, the schoolmate saw your sisters, by chance, while shopping for shoes at the Number One Department Store on Nanjing Dong Road. She said it was like a dream, seeing these two women who looked so much alike, moving down the stairs together. There was something about their facial expressions that reminded the schoolmate of your mother.

She quickly walked over to them and called their names, which of course, they did not recognize at first, because Mei Ching had changed their names. But your mother's friend was so sure, she persisted. "Are you not Wang Chwun Yu and Wang Chwun Hwa?" she asked them. And then these double-image women became very excited, because they remembered the names written on the back of an old photo, a photo of a young man and woman they still honored, as their much-loved first parents, who had died and become spirit ghosts still roaming the earth looking for them.

At the airport, I am exhausted. I could not sleep last night. Aiyi had followed me into my room at three in the morning, and she instantly fell asleep on one of the twin beds, snoring with the might of a lumberjack. I lay awake thinking about my mother's story, realizing how much I have never known about her, grieving that my sisters and I had both lost her.

And now at the airport, after shaking hands with everybody, waving good-bye, I think about all the different ways we leave people in this world. Cheerily waving good-bye to some at airports, knowing we'll never see each other again. Leaving others on the side of the road, hoping that we will. Finding my mother in my father's story and saying good-bye before I have a chance to know her better.

135   Aiyi smiles at me as we wait for our gate to be called. She is so old. I put one arm around her and one arm around Lili. They are the same size, it seems. And then it's time. As we wave good-bye one more time and enter the waiting area, I get the sense

I am going from one funeral to another. In my hand I'm clutching a pair of tickets to Shanghai. In two hours we'll be there.

The plane takes off. I close my eyes. How can I describe to them in my broken Chinese about our mother's life? Where should I begin?

"Wake up, we're here," says my father. And I awake with my heart pounding in my throat. I look out the window and we're already on the runway. It's gray outside.

And now I'm walking down the steps of the plane, onto the tarmac and toward the building. If only, I think, if only my mother had lived long enough to be the one walking toward them. I am so nervous I cannot even feel my feet. I am just moving somehow.

Somebody shouts, "She's arrived!" And then I see her. Her short hair. Her small body. And that same look on her face. She has the back of her hand pressed hard against her mouth. She is crying as though she had gone through a terrible ordeal and were happy it is over.

And I know it's not my mother, yet it is the same look she had when I was five and   140
had disappeared all afternoon, for such a long time, that she was convinced I was dead. And when I miraculously appeared, sleepy-eyed, crawling from underneath my bed, she wept and laughed, biting the back of her hand to make sure it was true.

And now I see her again, two of her, waving, and in one hand there is a photo, the Polaroid I sent them. As soon as I get beyond the gate, we run toward each other, all three of us embracing, all hesitations and expectations forgotten.

"Mama, Mama," we all murmur, as if she is among us.

My sisters look at me, proudly. "*Meimei jandale,*" says one sister proudly to the other. "Little Sister has grown up." I look at their faces again and I see no trace of my mother in them. Yet they still look familiar. And now I also see what part of me is Chinese. It is so obvious. It is my family. It is in our blood. After all these years, it can finally be let go.

My sisters and I stand, arms around each other, laughing and wiping the tears from each other's eyes. The flash of the Polaroid goes off and my father hands me the snapshot. My sisters and I watch quietly together, eager to see what develops.

The gray-green surface changes to the bright colors of our three images, sharpen-   145
ing and deepening all at once. And although we don't speak, I know we all see it: Together we look like our mother. Her same eyes, her same mouth, open in surprise to see, at last, her long-cherished wish.

[1989]

QUESTIONS

1. Why does the narrator go to China?
2. How does the author use setting to delineate character?
3. Naming, usually important in stories, is crucial to this one. Why?
4. Why do you think the author switches point of view to have Canning Woo tell his wife's story?
5. How does the China of the narrator's imagination differ from the China she visits? What does that difference tell about her?

RESPONSES

1. Read the novel *The Joy Luck Club*. Explain how this story from that novel presents and develops themes that occur throughout the novel.

2. Research critical literature about the relationships between mothers and daughters. Explain what it is that the narrator needs from her mother. How does she find it in one of her half-sisters?

FOCUS ON FILM

1. View the film *The Joy Luck Club*. In the "present day" United States, to what economic class do the daughters and mothers belong? How is that indicated in the film? In the print story, are the same signs of status and success included?

2. Explain how the film has changed portions of the story and omitted other portions. What overall effect do the changes have on the theme and effect of the story?

LEO TOLSTOY

Leo Tolstoy (1828–1910) was born at Yasnaya Polyana, the family estate near Tula, Russia. Orphaned at an early age, he lived for a few years the profligate life of a bachelor noble and then joined the army, where he served with distinction. In 1857 he returned to his country estate, married in 1862, and entered upon the life of a wealthy landowner. During this period he wrote the two novels that brought him worldwide fame, *War and Peace* (1869) and *Anna Karenina* (1877). In later life he underwent a religious conversion, renounced his earlier life and work, and devoted himself to his version of the spiritual life. His writings on moral themes won him enormous prestige as an ethical teacher, but tragically he never found the peace that he was seeking.

The Death of Ivan Ilych

1

During an interval in the Melvinski trial in the large building of the Law Courts the members and public prosecutor met in Ivan Egorovich Shebek's private room, where the conversation turned on the celebrated Krasovski case. Fedor Vasilievich warmly maintained that it was not subject to their jurisdiction, Ivan Egorovich maintained the contrary, while Peter Ivanovich, not having entered into the discussion at the start, took no part in it but looked through the *Gazette* which had just been handed in.

"Gentlemen," he said, "Ivan Ilych has died!"

"You don't say so!"

"Here, read it yourself," replied Peter Ivanovich, handing Fedor Vasilievich the paper still damp from the press. Surrounded by a black border were the words "Praskovya Fedorovna Golovina, with profound sorrow, informs relatives and friends of the demise of her beloved husband Ivan Ilych Golovin, Member of the Court of Justice, which occurred on February the 4th of this year 1882. The funeral will take place on Friday at one o'clock in the afternoon."

Ivan Ilych had been a colleague of the gentlemen present and was liked by them all. He had been ill for some weeks with an illness said to be incurable. His post had been

⁵

kept open for him, but there had been conjectures that in case of his death Alexeev might receive his appointment, and that either Vinnikov or Shtabel would succeed Alexeev. So on receiving the news of Ivan Ilych's death the first thought of each of the gentlemen in that private room was of the changes and promotions it might occasion among themselves or their acquaintances.

"I shall be sure to get Shtabel's place or Vinnikov's," thought Fedor Vasilievich. "I was promised that long ago, and the promotion means an extra eight hundred rubles a year for me besides the allowance."

"Now I must apply for my brother-in-law's transfer from Kaluga," thought Peter Ivanovich. "My wife will be very glad, and then she won't be able to say that I never do anything for her relations."

"I thought he would never leave his bed again," said Peter Ivanovich aloud. "It's very sad."

"But what really was the matter with him?"

"The doctors couldn't say—at least they could, but each of them said something different. When last I saw him I thought he was getting better."

"And I haven't been to see him since the holidays. I always meant to go."

"Had he any property?"

"I think his wife had a little—but something quite trifling."

"We shall have to go to see her, but they live so terribly far away."

"Far away from you, you mean. Everything's far away from your place."

"You see, he never can forgive my living on the other side of the river," said Peter Ivanovich, smiling at Shebek. Then, still talking of the distances between different parts of the city, they returned to the Court.

Besides considerations as to the possible transfers and promotions likely to result from Ivan Ilych's death, the mere fact of the death of a near acquaintance aroused, as usual, in all who heard of it the complacent feeling that "it is he who is dead and not I."

Each one thought or felt, "Well, he's dead but I'm alive!" But the more intimate of Ivan Ilych's acquaintances, his so-called friends, could not help thinking also that they would now have to fulfill the very tiresome demands of propriety by attending the funeral service and paying a visit of condolence to the widow.

Fedor Vasilievich and Peter Ivanovich had been his nearest acquaintances. Peter Ivanovich had studied law with Ivan Ilych and had considered himself to be under obligations to him.

Having told his wife at dinner-time of Ivan Ilych's death, and of his conjecture that it might be possible to get her brother transferred to their circuit, Peter Ivanovich sacrificed his usual nap, put on his evening clothes, and drove to Ivan Ilych's house.

At the entrance stood a carriage and two cabs. Leaning against the wall in the hall downstairs near the cloak-stand was a coffin-lid covered with cloth of gold, ornamented with gold cord and tassels, that had been polished up with metal powder. Two ladies in black were taking off their fur cloaks. Peter Ivanovich recognized one of them as Ivan Ilych's sister, but the other was a stranger to him. His colleague Schwartz was just coming downstairs, but on seeing Peter Ivanovich enter he stopped and winked at him, as if to say: "Ivan Ilych has made a mess of things—not like you and me."

Schwartz's face with his Piccadilly whiskers, and his slim figure in evening dress, had as usual an air of elegant solemnity which contrasted with the playfulness of his character and had a special piquancy here, or so it seemed to Peter Ivanovich.

Peter Ivanovich allowed the ladies to precede him and slowly followed them upstairs. Schwartz did not come down but remained where he was, and Peter Ivanovich understood that he wanted to arrange where they should play bridge that evening. The ladies went upstairs to the widow's room, and Schwartz with seriously compressed lips but a playful look in his eyes, indicated by a twist of his eyebrows the room to the right where the body lay.

Peter Ivanovich, like everyone else on such occasions, entered feeling uncertain what he would have to do. All he knew was that at such times it is always safe to cross oneself. But he was not quite sure whether one should make obeisances while doing so. He therefore adopted a middle course. On entering the room he began crossing himself and made a slight movement resembling a bow. At the same time, as far as the motion of his head and arm allowed, he surveyed the room. Two young men—apparently nephews, one of whom was a high school pupil—were leaving the room, crossing themselves as they did so. An old woman was standing motionless, and a lady with strangely arched eyebrows was saying something to her in a whisper. A vigorous, resolute Church Reader, in a frock-coat, was reading something in a loud voice with an expression that precluded any contradiction. The butler's assistant, Gerasim, stepping lightly in front of Peter Ivanovich, was strewing something on the floor. Noticing this, Peter Ivanovich was immediately aware of a faint odour of a decomposing body.

The last time he had called on Ivan Ilych, Peter Ivanovich had seen Gerasim in the study. Ivan Ilych had been particularly fond of him and he was performing the duty of a sick nurse.

25

Peter Ivanovich continued to make the sign of the cross slightly inclining his head in an intermediate direction between the coffin, the Reader, and the icons on the table in a corner of the room. Afterwards, when it seemed to him that this movement of his arm in crossing himself had gone on too long, he stopped and began to look at the corpse.

The dead man lay, as dead men always lie, in a specially heavy way, his rigid limbs sunk in the soft cushions of the coffin, with the head forever bowed on the pillow. His yellow waxen brow with bald patches over his sunken temples was thrust up in the way peculiar to the dead, the protruding nose seeming to press on the upper lip. He was much changed and had grown even thinner since Peter Ivanovich had last seen him, but, as is always the case with the dead, his face was handsomer and above all more dignified than when he was alive. The expression on the face said that what was necessary had been accomplished, and accomplished rightly. Besides this there was in that expression a reproach and a warning to the living. This warning seemed to Peter Ivanovich out of place, or at least not applicable to him. He felt a certain discomfort and so he hurriedly crossed himself once more and turned and went out of the door—too hurriedly and too regardless of propriety, as he himself was aware.

Schwartz was waiting for him in the adjoining room with legs spread wide apart and both hands toying with his top-hat behind his back. The mere sight of that playful, well-groomed, and elegant figure refreshed Peter Ivanovich. He felt that Schwartz was above all these happenings and would not surrender to any depressing influences. His very look said that this incident of a church service for Ivan Ilych could not be a sufficient reason for infringing the order of the session—in other words, that it would certainly not prevent his unwrapping a new pack of cards and shuffling them that evening while a footman placed four fresh candles on the table: in fact, there was no reason for supposing that this incident would hinder their spending the evening agreeably. Indeed he said this in a whisper as Peter Ivanovich passed him, proposing that they should meet for a game at Fedor Vasilievich's. But apparently Peter Ivanovich was not destined to play bridge that evening. Praskovya Fedorovna (a short, fat woman who despite all efforts to the contrary had continued to broaden steadily from her shoulders downwards and who had the same extraordinarily arched eyebrows as the lady who had been standing by the coffin), dressed all in black, her head covered with lace, came out of her own room with some other ladies, conducted them to the room where the dead body lay, and said: "The service will begin immediately. Please go in."

Schwartz, making an indefinite bow, stood still, evidently neither accepting nor declining this invitation. Praskovya Fedorovna recognizing Peter Ivanovich, sighed, went close up to him, took his hand, and said: "I know you were a true friend to Ivan Ilych . . ." and looked at him awaiting some suitable response. And Peter Ivanovich knew that, just as it had been the right thing to cross himself in that room, so what he had to do here was to press her hand, sigh, and say, "Believe me . . ." So he did all this and as he did it felt that the desired result had been achieved: that both he and she were touched.

30   "Come with me. I want to speak to you before it begins," said the widow. "Give me your arm."

Peter Ivanovich gave her his arm and they went to the inner rooms, passing Schwartz who winked at Peter Ivanovich compassionately.

"That does for our bridge! Don't object if we find another player. Perhaps you can cut in when you do escape," said his playful look.

Peter Ivanovich sighed still more deeply and despondently, and Praskovya Fedorovna pressed his arm gratefully. When they reached the drawing-room, upholstered in pink cretonne and lighted by a dim lamp, they sat down at the table—she on a sofa and Peter Ivanovich on a low pouffe, the springs of which yielded spasmodically under his weight. Praskovya Fedorovna had been on the point of warning him to take another seat, but felt that such a warning was out of keeping with her present condition and so changed her mind. As he sat down on the pouffe Peter Ivanovich recalled how Ivan Ilych had arranged this room and had consulted him regarding this pink cretonne with green leaves. The whole room was full of furniture and knick-knacks, and on her way to the sofa the lace of the widow's black shawl caught on the carved edge of the table. Peter Ivanovich rose to detach it, and the springs of the pouffe, relieved of his weight, rose also and gave him a push. The widow began detaching her shawl herself, and Peter Ivanovich again sat down, suppressing the rebellious springs of the pouffe under him. But the widow had not quite freed herself and Peter Ivanovich got up again, and again the pouffe rebelled and even creaked. When this was all over she took out a clean cambric handkerchief and began to weep. The episode with the shawl and the struggle with the pouffe had cooled Peter Ivanovich's emotions and he sat there with a sullen look on his face. This awkward situation was interrupted by Sokolov, Ivan Ilych's butler, who came to report that the plot in the cemetery that Praskovya Fedorovna had chosen would cost two hundred rubles. She stopped weeping and, looking at Peter Ivanovich with the air of a victim, remarked in French that it was very hard for her. Peter Ivanovich made a silent gesture signifying his full conviction that it must indeed be so.

"Please smoke," she said in a magnanimous yet crushed voice, and turned to discuss with Sokolov the price of the plot for the grave.

35   Peter Ivanovich while lighting his cigarette heard her inquiring very circumstantially into the price of different plots in the cemetery and finally decide which she would take.

When that was done she gave instructions about engaging the choir. Sokolov then left the room.

"I look after everything myself," she told Peter Ivanovich, shifting the albums that lay on the table; and noticing that the table was endangered by his cigarette-ash, she immediately passed him an ashtray, saying as she did so: "I consider it an affectation to say that my grief prevents my attending to practical affairs. On the contrary, if anything can—I won't say console me, but—distract me, it is seeing to everything concerning him." She again took out her handkerchief as if preparing to cry, but suddenly, as if mastering her feeling, she shook herself and began to speak calmly. "But there is something I want to talk to you about."

Peter Ivanovich bowed, keeping control of the springs of the pouffe, which immediately began quivering under him.

"He suffered terribly the last few days."

"Did he?" said Peter Ivanovich.

"Oh, terribly! He screamed unceasingly, not for minutes but for hours. For the last   40
three days he screamed incessantly. It was unendurable. I cannot understand how I bore it; you could hear him three rooms off. Oh, what I have suffered!"

"Is it possible that he was conscious all that time?" asked Peter Ivanovich.

"Yes," she whispered. "To the last moment. He took leave of us a quarter of an hour before he died, and asked us to take Volodya away."

The thought of the sufferings of this man he had known so intimately, first as a merry little boy, then as a school-mate, and later as a grown-up colleague, suddenly struck Peter Ivanovich with horror, despite an unpleasant consciousness of his own and this woman's dissimulation. He again saw that brow, and that nose pressing down on the lip, and felt afraid for himself.

"Three days of frightful suffering and then death! Why, that might suddenly, at any time, happen to me," he thought, and for a moment felt terrified. But—he did not himself know how—the customary reflection at once occurred to him that this had happened to Ivan Ilych and not to him, and that it should not and could not happen to him, and that to think that it could would be yielding to depression which he ought not to do, as Schwartz's expression plainly showed. After which reflection Peter Ivanovich felt reassured, and began to ask with interest about the details of Ivan Ilych's death, as though death was an accident natural to Ivan Ilych but certainly not to himself.

After many details of the really dreadful physical sufferings Ivan Ilych had endured   45
(which details he learnt only from the effect those sufferings had produced on Praskovya Fedorovna's nerves) the widow apparently found it necessary to get to business.

"Oh, Peter Ivanovich, how hard it is! How terribly, terribly hard!" and she again began to weep.

Peter Ivanovich sighed and waited for her to finish blowing her nose. When she had done so he said, "Believe me . . ." and she again began talking and brought out what was evidently her chief concern with him—namely, to question him as to how she could obtain a grant of money from the government on the occasion of her husband's death. She made it appear that she was asking Peter Ivanovich's advice about her pension, but he soon saw that she already knew about that to the minutest detail, more even than he did himself. She knew how much could be got out of the government in consequence of her husband's death, but wanted to find out whether she could not possibly extract something more. Peter Ivanovich tried to think of some means of doing so, but after reflecting for a while and, out of propriety, condemning the government for its niggardliness, he said he thought that nothing more could be got. Then she sighed and evidently began to devise means of getting rid of her visitor. Noticing this, he put out his cigarette, rose, pressed her hand, and went out into the anteroom.

In the dining-room where the clock stood that Ivan Ilych had liked so much and had bought at an antique shop, Peter Ivanovich met a priest and a few acquaintances who had come to attend the service, and he recognized Ivan Ilych's daughter, a handsome young woman. She was in black and her slim figure appeared slimmer than ever. She had a gloomy, determined, almost angry expression, and bowed to Peter Ivanovich as though he were in some way to blame. Behind her, with the same offended look, stood a wealthy young man, an examining magistrate, whom Peter Ivanovich also knew and who was her fiancé, as he had heard. He bowed mournfully to them and was about to pass into the death-chamber, when from under the stairs appeared the figure of Ivan Ilych's schoolboy son, who was extremely like his father. He seemed a little Ivan Ilych, such as Peter Ivanovich remembered when they studied law together. His tear-stained eyes had in them the look that is seen in the eyes of boys of thirteen or fourteen who are not pure-minded. When he saw Peter Ivanovich he scowled morosely and shame-facedly. Peter Ivanovich nodded to him and entered the death-chamber. The service began: candles, groans, incense, tears, and sobs. Peter Ivanovich stood looking gloomily down at his feet. He did not look once at the dead man, did not yield to any depressing influence, and was one of the first to leave the room. There was no one in the anteroom, but Gerasim darted out of the dead man's room, rummaged with his strong hands among the fur coats to find Peter Ivanovich's and helped him on with it.

"Well, friend Gerasim," said Peter Ivanovich, so as to say something. "It's a sad affair, isn't it?"

50   "It's God's will. We shall all come to it some day," said Gerasim, displaying his teeth—the even, white teeth of a healthy peasant—and, like a man in the thick of urgent work, he briskly opened the front door, called the coachman, helped Peter Ivanovich into the sledge, and sprang back to the porch as if in readiness for what he had to do next.

Peter Ivanovich found the fresh air particularly pleasant after the smell of incense, the dead body, and carbolic acid.

"Where to, sir?" asked the coachman.

"It's not too late even now. . . . I'll call around on Fedor Vasilievich."

He accordingly drove there and found them just finishing the first rubber, so that it was quite convenient for him to cut in.

2

55   Ivan Ilych's life had been most simple and most ordinary and therefore most terrible.

He had been a member of the Court of Justice, and died at the age of forty-five. His father had been an official who after serving in various ministries and departments of Petersburg had made the sort of career which brings men to positions from which by reason of their long service they cannot be dismissed, though they are obviously unfit to hold any responsible position, and for whom therefore posts are specially created, which though fictitious carry salaries of from six to ten thousand rubles that are not fictitious, and in receipt of which they live on to a great age.

Such was the Privy Councillor and superfluous member of various superfluous institutions, Ilva Epimovich Golovin.

He had three sons, of whom Ivan Ilych was the second. The eldest son was following in his father's footsteps only in another department, and was already approaching that stage in the service at which a similar sinecure would be reached. The third son was a failure. He had ruined his prospects in a number of positions and was now serving in the railway department. His father and brothers, and still more their wives, not merely disliked meeting him, but avoided remembering his existence unless compelled to do so. His sister had married Baron Greff, a Petersburg official of her father's type. Ivan Ilych was *le phénix de la famille* as people said. He was neither as cold and formal as his elder brother nor as wild as the younger, but was a happy mean between them—an intelligent, polished, lively and agreeable man. He had studied with his younger brother at the School of Law, but the latter had failed to complete the course and was expelled when he was in the fifth class. Ivan Ilych finished the course well. Even when he was at the School of Law he was just what he remained for the rest of his life: a capable, cheerful, good-natured, and sociable man, though strict in the fulfilment of what he considered to be his duty: and he considered his duty to be what was so considered by those in authority. Neither as a boy nor as a man was he a toady, but from early youth was by nature attracted to people of high station as a fly is drawn to the light, assimilating their ways and views of life and establishing friendly relations with them. All the enthusiasms of childhood and youth passed without leaving much trace on him; he succumbed to sensuality, to vanity, and latterly among the highest classes to liberalism, but always within limits which his instinct unfailingly indicated to him as correct.

At school he had done things which had formerly seemed to him very horrid and made him feel disgusted with himself when he did them; but when later on he saw that such actions were done by people of good position and that they did not regard them as wrong, he was able not exactly to regard them as right, but to forget about them entirely or not be at all troubled at remembering them.

Having graduated from the School of Law and qualified for the tenth rank of civil service, and having received money from his father for his equipment, Ivan Ilych ordered himself clothes at Scharmer's, the fashionable tailor, hung a medallion inscribed *respice finem*° on his watch-chain, took leave of his professor and the prince who was patron of the school, had a farewell dinner with his comrades at Donon's first-class restaurant, and with his new and fashionable portmanteau, linen, clothes, shaving and other toilet appliances, and a travelling rug, all purchased at the best shops, he set off for one of the provinces where, through his father's influence, he had been attached to the Governor as an official for special service.

In the province Ivan Ilych soon arranged as easy and agreeable a position for himself as he had had at the School of Law. He performed his official tasks, made his career, and at the same time amused himself pleasantly and decorously. Occasionally he paid official visits to country districts, where he behaved with dignity both to his superiors and inferiors, and performed the duties entrusted to him, which related chiefly to the sectarians, with an exactness and incorruptible honesty of which he could not but feel proud.

In official matters, despite his youth and taste for frivolous gaiety, he was exceedingly reserved, punctilious, and even severe; but in society he was often amusing and witty, and always good-natured, correct in his manner, and *bon enfant*, as the governor and his wife—with whom he was like one of the family—used to say of him.

°*respice finem*: "Take heed of the end"; that is, look before you leap.

In the provinces he had an affair with a lady who made advances to the elegant young lawyer, and there was also a milliner; and there were carousals with aides-de-camp who visited the district, and after-supper visits to a certain outlying street of doubtful reputation; and there was too some obsequiousness to his chief and even to his chief's wife, but all this was done with such a tone of good breeding that no hard names could be applied to it. It all came under the heading of the French saying: "Il faut que jeunesse se passe."° It was all done with clean hands, in clean linen, with French phrases, and above all among people of the best society and consequently with the approval of people of rank.

So Ivan Ilych served for five years and then came a change in his official life. The new and reformed judicial institutions were introduced, and new men were needed. Ivan Ilych became such a new man. He was offered the post of Examining Magistrate, and he accepted it though the post was in another province and obliged him to give up the connexions he had formed and to make new ones. His friends met to give him a send-off; they had a group-photograph taken and presented him with a silver cigarette-case, and he set off to his new post.

65   As examining magistrate Ivan Ilych was just as *comme il faut*° and decorous a man, inspiring general respect and capable of separating his official duties from his private life, as he had been when acting as an official on special service. His duties now as examining magistrate were far more interesting and attractive than before. In his former position it had been pleasant to wear an undress uniform made by Scharmer, and to pass through the crowd of petitioners and officials who were timorously awaiting an audience with the governor, and who envied him as with free and easy gait he went straight into his chief's private room to have a cup of tea and a cigarette with him. But not many people had then been directly dependent on him—only police officials and the sectarians when he went on special missions—and he liked to treat them politely, almost as comrades, as if he were letting them feel that he who had the power to crush them was treating them in this simple, friendly way. There were then but few such people. But now, as an examining magistrate, Ivan Ilych felt that everyone without exception, even the most important and self-satisfied, was in his power, and that he need only write a few words on a sheet of paper with a certain heading, and this or that important, self-satisfied person would be brought before him in the role of an accused person or a witness, and if he did not choose to allow him to sit down, would have to stand before him and answer his questions. Ivan Ilych never abused his power; he tried on the contrary to soften its expression, but the consciousness of it and of the possibility of softening its effect, supplied the chief interest and attraction of his office. In his work itself, especially in his examinations, he very soon acquired a method of eliminating all considerations irrelevant to the legal aspect of the case, and reducing even the most complicated case to a form in which it would be presented on paper only in its externals, completely excluding his personal opinion of the matter, while above all observing every prescribed formality. The work was new and Ivan Ilych was one of the first men to apply the new Code of 1864.°

On taking up the post of examining magistrate in a new town, he made new acquaintances and connexions, placed himself on a new footing, and assumed a somewhat different tone. He took up an attitude of rather dignified aloofness towards the

---

°*Il faut que jeunesse se passe*: "Youth must have its fling."

°*comme il faut*: Proper.

°*Code of 1864*: The emancipation of the serfs in 1861 was followed by a thorough all-around reform of judicial proceedings.

provincial authorities, but picked out the best circle of legal gentlemen and wealthy gentry living in the town and assumed a tone of slight dissatisfaction with the government, of moderate liberalism, and of enlightened citizenship. At the same time, without at all altering the elegance of his toilet, he ceased shaving his chin and allowed his beard to grow as it pleased.

Ivan Ilych settled down very pleasantly in this new town. The society there, which inclined towards opposition to the Governor, was friendly, his salary was larger, and he began to play *vint*, which he found added not a little to the pleasure of life, for he had a capacity for cards, played good-humouredly, and calculated rapidly and astutely, so that he usually won.

After living there for two years he met his future wife, Praskovya Fedorovna Mikhel, who was the most attractive, clever, and brilliant girl of the set in which he moved, and among other amusements and relaxations from his labours as examining magistrate, Ivan Ilych established light and playful relations with her.

While he had been an official on special service he had been accustomed to dance, but now as an examining magistrate it was exceptional for him to do so. If he danced now, he did it as if to show that though he served under the reformed order of things, and had reached the fifth official rank, yet when it came to dancing he could do it better than most people. So at the end of an evening he sometimes danced with Praskovya Fedorovna, and it was chiefly during these dances that he captivated her. She fell in love with him. Ivan Ilych had at first no definite intention of marrying, but when the girl fell in love with him he said to himself: "Really, why shouldn't I marry?"

Praskovya Fedorovna came of a good family, was not bad looking and had some little property. Ivan Ilych might have aspired to a more brilliant match, but even this was good. He had his salary, and she, he hoped, would have an equal income. She was well connected, and was a sweet, pretty, and thoroughly correct young woman. To say that Ivan Ilych married because he fell in love with Praskovya Fedorovna and found that she sympathized with his views of life would be as incorrect as to say that he married because his social circle approved of the match. He was swayed by both these considerations: the marriage gave him personal satisfaction, and at the same time it was considered the right thing by the most highly placed of his associates.

So Ivan Ilych got married.

The preparations for marriage and the beginning of married life, with its conjugal caresses, the new furniture, new crockery, and new linen, were very pleasant until his wife became pregnant—so that Ivan Ilych had begun to think that marriage would not impair the easy, agreeable, gay and always decorous character of his life, approved of by society and regarded by himself as natural, but would even improve it. But from the first months of his wife's pregnancy, something new, unpleasant, depressing, and unseemly, and from which there was no way of escape, unexpectedly showed itself.

His wife, without any reason—*de gaieté de coeur°* as Ivan Ilych expressed it to himself—began to disturb the pleasure and propriety of their life. She began to be jealous without any cause, expected him to devote his whole attention to her, found fault with everything, and made coarse and ill-mannered scenes.

At first Ivan Ilych hoped to escape from the unpleasantness of this state of affairs by the same easy and decorous relation to life that had served him heretofore: he tried to ignore his wife's disagreeable moods, continued to live in his usual easy and pleasant way, invited friends to his house for a game of cards, and also tried going out to

---

°*de gaieté de coeur*: Lightheartedness.

his club or spending his evenings with friends. But one day his wife began upbraiding him so vigorously, using such coarse words, and continued to abuse him every time he did not fulfil her demands, so resolutely and with such evident determination not to give way till he submitted—that is, till he stayed at home and was bored just as she was—that he became alarmed. He now realized that matrimony—at any rate with Praskovya Fedorovna—was not always conducive to the pleasures and amenities of life but on the contrary often infringed both comfort and propriety, and that he must therefore entrench himself against such infringement. And Ivan Ilych began to seek for means of doing so. His official duties were the one thing that imposed upon Praskovya Fedorovna, and by means of his official work and the duties attached to it he began struggling with his wife to secure his own independence.

75   With the birth of their child, the attempts to feed it and the various failures in doing so, and with the real and imaginary illnesses of mother and child, in which Ivan Ilych's sympathy was demanded but about which he understood nothing, the need of securing for himself an existence outside his family life became still more imperative.

As his wife grew more irritable and exacting and Ivan Ilych transferred the centre of gravity of his life more and more to his official work, so did he grow to like his work better and became more ambitious than before.

Very soon, within a year of his wedding, Ivan Ilych had realized that marriage, though it may add some comforts to life, is in fact a very intricate and difficult affair towards which in order to perform one's duty, that is, to lead a decorous life approved of by society, one must adopt a definite attitude just as towards one's official duties.

And Ivan Ilych evolved such an attitude towards married life. He only required of it those conveniences—dinner at home, housewife, and bed—which it could give him, and above all that propriety of external forms required by public opinion. For the rest he looked for light-hearted pleasure and propriety, and was very thankful when he found them, but if he met with antagonism and querulousness he at once retired into his separate fenced-off world of official duties, where he found satisfaction.

Ivan Ilych was esteemed a good official, and after three years was made Assistant Public Prosecutor. His new duties, their importance, the possibility of indicting and imprisoning anyone he chose, the publicity his speeches received, and the success he had in all these things, made his work still more attractive.

80   More children came. His wife became more and more querulous and ill-tempered, but the attitude Ivan Ilych had adopted towards his home life rendered him almost impervious to her grumbling.

After seven years' service in that town he was transferred to another province as Public Prosecutor. They moved, but were short of money and his wife did not like the place they moved to. Though the salary was higher the cost of living was greater, besides which two of their children died and family life became still more unpleasant for him.

Praskovya Fedorovna blamed her husband for every inconvenience they encountered in their new home. Most of the conversations between husband and wife, especially as to the children's education, led to topics which recalled former disputes, and those disputes were apt to flare up again at any moment. There remained only those rare periods of amorousness which still came to them at times but did not last long. These were islets at which they anchored for a while and then again set out upon that ocean of veiled hostility which showed itself in their aloofness from one another. This aloofness might have grieved Ivan Ilych had he considered that it ought not to exist, but he now regarded the position as normal, and even made it the goal at which he

aimed in family life. His aim was to free himself more and more from those unpleas-
antnesses and to give them a semblance of harmlessness and propriety. He attained this
by spending less and less time with his family, and when obliged to be at home he
tried to safeguard his position by the presence of outsiders. The chief thing however
was that he had his official duties. The whole interest of his life now centered in the
official world and that interest absorbed him. The consciousness of his power, being
able to ruin anybody he wished to ruin, the importance, even the external dignity of
his entry into court, or meetings with his subordinates, his success with superiors and
inferiors, and above all his masterly handling of cases, of which he was conscious—
all this gave him pleasure and filled his life, together with chats with his colleagues,
dinners, and bridge. So that on the whole Ivan Ilych's life continued to flow as he considered it should do—pleasantly and properly.

So things continued for another seven years. His eldest daughter was already sixteen, another child had died, and only one son was left, a schoolboy and a subject of
dissension. Ivan Ilych wanted to put him in the School of Law, but to spite him
Praskovya Fedorovna entered him at the High School. The daughter had been educated
at home and had turned out well: the boy did not learn badly either.

3

So Ivan Ilych lived for seventeen years after his marriage. He was already a Public
Prosecutor of long standing, and had declined several proposed transfers while awaiting a more desirable post, when an unanticipated and unpleasant occurrence quite
upset the peaceful course of his life. He was expecting to be offered the post of presiding
judge in a University town, but Happe somehow came to the front and obtained the
appointment instead. Ivan Ilych became irritable, reproached Happe, and quarrelled
both with him and with his immediate superiors—who became colder to him and
again passed him over when other appointments were made.

This was in 1880, the hardest year of Ivan Ilych's life. It was then that it became ev- 85
ident on the one hand that his salary was insufficient for them to live on, and on the
other that he had been forgotten, and not only this, but that what was for him the
greatest and most cruel injustice appeared to others a quite ordinary occurrence. Even
his father did not consider it his duty to help him. Ivan Ilych felt himself abandoned
by everyone, and that they regarded his position with a salary of 3,500 rubles as quite
normal and even fortunate. He alone knew that with the consciousness of the injustices
done him, with his wife's incessant nagging, and with the debts he had contracted by
living beyond his means, his position was far from normal.

In order to save money that summer he obtained leave of absence and went with
his wife to live in the country at her brother's place.

In the country, without his work, he experienced *ennui* for the first time in his life,
and not only *ennui* but intolerable depression, and he decided that it was impossible
to go on living like that, and that it was necessary to take energetic measures.

Having passed a sleepless night pacing up and down the veranda, he decided to go
to Petersburg and bestir himself, in order to punish those who had failed to appreciate him and to get transferred to another ministry.

Next day, despite many protests from his wife and her brother, he started for Petersburg with the sole object of obtaining a post with a salary of five thousand rubles

a year. He was no longer bent on any particular department, or tendency, or kind of activity. All he now wanted was an appointment to another post with a salary of five thousand rubles, either in the administration, in the banks, with the railways, in one of the Empress Marya's Institutions,° or even in the customs—but it had to carry with it a salary of five thousand rubles and be in a ministry other than that in which they had failed to appreciate him.

90 And this quest of Ivan Ilych's was crowned with remarkable and unexpected success. At Kursk an acquaintance of his, F. I. Ilyin, got into the first-class carriage, sat down beside Ivan Ilych, and told him of a telegram just received by the Governor of Kursk announcing that a change was about to take place in the ministry: Peter Ivanovich was to be superseded by Ivan Semenovich.

The proposed change, apart from its significance for Russia, had a special significance for Ivan Ilych, because by bringing forward a new man, Peter Petrovich, and consequently his friend Zachar Ivanovich, it was highly favourable for Ivan Ilych, since Zachar Ivanovich was a friend and colleague of his.

In Moscow this news was confirmed, and on reaching Petersburg Ivan Ilych found Zachar Ivanovich and received a definite promise of an appointment in his former Department of Justice.

A week later he telegraphed to his wife: "Zachar in Miller's place. I shall receive appointment on presentation of report."

Thanks to this change of personnel, Ivan Ilych had unexpectedly obtained an appointment in his former ministry which placed him two stages above his former colleagues besides giving him five thousand rubles salary and three thousand five hundred rubles for expenses connected with his removal. All his ill humour towards his former enemies and the whole department vanished, and Ivan Ilych was completely happy.

95 He returned to the country more cheerful and contented than he had been for a long time. Praskovya Fedorovna also cheered up and a truce was arranged between them. Ivan Ilych told of how he had been feted by everybody in Petersburg, how all those who had been his enemies were put to shame and now fawned on him, how envious they were of his appointment, and how much everybody in Petersburg had liked him.

Praskovya Fedorovna listened to all this and appeared to believe it. She did not contradict anything, but only made plans for their life in the town to which they were going. Ivan Ilych saw with delight that these plans were his plans, that he and his wife agreed, and that, after a stumble, his life was regaining its due and natural character of pleasant lightheartedness and decorum.

Ivan Ilych had come back for a short time only, for he had to take up his new duties on the 10th of September. Moreover, he needed time to settle into the new place, to move all his belongings from the province, and to buy and order many additional things: in a word, to make such arrangements as he had resolved on, which were almost exactly what Praskovya Fedorovna too had decided on.

Now that everything had happened so fortunately, and that he and his wife were at one in their aims and moreover saw so little of one another, they got on together better than they had done since the first years of marriage. Ivan Ilych had thought of taking his family away with him at once, but the insistence of his wife's brother and her

---

°*Empress Marya's Institutions*: Charitable agencies.

sister-in-law, who had suddenly become particularly amiable and friendly to him and his family, induced him to depart alone.

So he departed, and the cheerful state of mind induced by his success and by the harmony between his wife and himself, the one intensifying the other, did not leave him. He found a delightful house, just the thing both he and his wife had dreamt of. Spacious, lofty reception rooms in the old style, a convenient and dignified study, rooms for his wife and daughter, a study for his son—it might have been specially built for them. Ivan Ilych himself superintended the arrangement, chose the wallpapers, supplemented the furniture (preferably with antiques which he considered particularly *comme il faut*), and supervised the upholstering. Everything progressed and progressed and approached the ideal he had set himself: even when things were only half completed they exceeded his expectations. He saw what a refined and elegant character, free from vulgarity, it would all have when it was ready. On falling asleep he pictured to himself how the reception-room would look. Looking at the yet unfinished drawing-room he could see the fireplace, the screen, the what-not, the little chairs dotted here and there, the dishes and plates on the walls, and the bronzes, as they would be when everything was in place. He was pleased by the thought of how his wife and daughter, who shared his taste in this matter, would be impressed by it. They were certainly not expecting as much. He had been particularly successful in finding, and buying cheaply, antiques which gave a particularly aristocratic character to the whole place. But in his letters he intentionally understated everything in order to be able to surprise them. All this so absorbed him that his new duties—though he liked his official work—interested him less than he had expected. Sometimes he even had moments of absentmindedness during the Court Sessions, and would consider whether he should have straight or curved cornices for his curtains. He was so interested in it all that he often did things himself, rearranging the furniture, or rehanging the curtains. Once when mounting a step-ladder to show the upholsterer, who did not understand, how he wanted the hangings draped, he made a false step and slipped, but being a strong and agile man he clung on and only knocked his side against the knob of the window frame. The bruised place was painful but the pain soon passed, and he felt particularly bright and well just then. He wrote: "I feel fifteen years younger." He thought he would have everything ready by September, but it dragged on till mid-October. But the result was charming not only in his eyes but to everyone who saw it.

In reality it was just what is usually seen in the houses of people of moderate means who want to appear rich, and therefore succeed only in resembling others like themselves: there were damasks, dark wood, plants, rugs, and dull and polished bronzes—all the things people of a certain class have in order to resemble other people of that class. His house was so like the others that it would never have been noticed, but to him it all seemed to be quite exceptional. He was very happy when he met his family at the station and brought them to the newly furnished house all lit up, where a footman in a white tie opened the door into the hall decorated with plants, and when they went on into the drawing-room and the study uttering exclamations of delight. He conducted them everywhere, drank in their praises eagerly, and beamed with pleasure. At tea that evening, when Praskovya Fedorovna among other things asked him about his fall, he laughed, and showed them how he had gone flying and had frightened the upholsterer.

"It's a good thing I'm a bit of an athlete. Another man might have been killed, but I merely knocked myself, just here; it hurts when it's touched, but it's passing off already—it's only a bruise."

So they began living in their new home—in which, as always happens, when they got thoroughly settled in they found they were just one room short—and with the increased income, which as always was just a little (some five hundred rubles) too little, but it was all very nice.

Things went particularly well at first, before everything was finally arranged and while something had still to be done: this thing bought, that thing ordered, another thing moved, and something else adjusted. Though there were some disputes between husband and wife, they were both so well satisfied and had so much to do that it all passed off without any serious quarrels. When nothing was left to arrange it became rather dull and something seemed to be lacking, but they were then making acquaintances, forming habits, and life was growing fuller.

Ivan Ilych spent his mornings at the law court and came home to dinner, and at first he was generally in a good humour, though he occasionally became irritable just on account of his house. (Every spot on the tablecloth or the upholstery, and every broken window-blind string, irritated him. He had devoted so much trouble to arranging it all that every disturbance of it distressed him.) But on the whole his life ran its course as he believed life should do: easily, pleasantly, and decorously.

He got up at nine, drank his coffee, read the paper, and then put on his undress uniform and went to the law courts. There the harness in which he worked had already been stretched to fit him and he donned it without a hitch: petitioners, inquiries at the chancery, the chancery itself, and the sittings public and administrative. In all this the thing was to exclude everything fresh and vital, which always disturbs the regular course of official business, and to admit only official relations with people, and then only on official grounds. A man would come, for instance, wanting some information. Ivan Ilych, as one in whose sphere the matter did not lie, would have nothing to do with him: but if the man had some business with him in his official capacity, something that could be expressed on officially stamped paper, he would do everything, positively everything he could within the limits of such relations, and in doing so would maintain the semblance of friendly human relations, that is, would observe the courtesies of life. As soon as the official relations ended, so did everything else. Ivan Ilych possessed this capacity to separate his real life from the official side of affairs and not mix the two, in the highest degree, and by long practice and natural aptitude had brought it to such a pitch that sometimes, in the manner of a virtuoso, he would even allow himself to let the human and official relations mingle. He let himself do this just because he felt that he could at any time he chose resume the strictly official attitude again and drop the human relation. And he did it all easily, pleasantly, correctly, and even artistically. In the intervals between the sessions he smoked, drank tea, chatted a little about politics, a little about general topics, a little about cards, but most of all about official appointments. Tired, but with the feelings of a virtuoso—one of the first violins who has played his part in an orchestra with precision—he would return home to find that his wife and daughter had been out paying calls, or had a visitor, and that his son had been to school, had done his homework with his tutor, and was duly learning what is taught at High Schools. Everything was as it should be. After dinner, if they had no visitors, Ivan Ilych sometimes read a book that was being much discussed at the time, and in the evening settled down to work, that is, read official papers, compared the depositions of witnesses, and noted paragraphs of the Code applying to them. This was neither dull nor amusing. It was dull when he might have been playing bridge, but if no bridge was available it was at any rate better than doing nothing or sitting with his wife. Ivan Ilych's chief pleasure was giving little dinners to which he invited men and women of good social position, and just as his drawing-room resembled all other drawing-rooms so did his enjoyable little parties resemble all other such parties.

Once they even gave a dance. Ivan Ilych enjoyed it and everything went off well, except that it led to a violent quarrel with his wife about the cakes and sweets. Praskovya Fedorovna had made her own plans, but Ivan Ilych insisted on getting everything from an expensive confectioner and ordered too many cakes, and the quarrel occurred because some of those cakes were left over and the confectioner's bill came to forty-five rubles. It was a great and disagreeable quarrel. Praskovya Fedorovna called him "a fool and an imbecile," and he clutched at his head and made angry allusions to divorce.

But the dance itself had been enjoyable. The best people were there, and Ivan Ilych had danced with Princess Trufonova, a sister of the distinguished founder of the Society "Bear my Burden."

The pleasures connected with his work were pleasures of ambition; his social pleasures were those of vanity; but Ivan Ilych's greatest pleasure was playing bridge. He acknowledged that whatever disagreeable incident happened in his life, the pleasure that beamed like a ray of light above everything else was to sit down to bridge with good players, not noisy partners, and of course to four-handed bridge (with five players it was annoying to have to stand out, though one pretended not to mind), to play a clever and serious game (when the cards allowed it) and then to have supper and drink a glass of wine. After a game of bridge, especially if he had won a little (to win a large sum was unpleasant), Ivan Ilych went to bed in specially good humour.

So they lived. They formed a circle of acquaintances among the best people and were visited by people of importance and by young folk. In their views as to their acquaintances, husband, wife and daughter were entirely agreed, and tacitly and unanimously kept at arm's length and shook off the various shabby friends and relations who, with much show of affection, gushed into the drawing-room with its Japanese plates on the walls. Soon these shabby friends ceased to obtrude themselves and only the best people remained in the Golovins' set.

Young men made up to Lisa, and Petrishchev, an examining magistrate and Dmitri Ivanovich Petrishchev's son and sole heir, began to be so attentive to her that Ivan Ilych had already spoken to Praskovya Fedorovna about it, and considered whether they should not arrange a party for them or get up some private theatricals.

So they lived, and all went well, without change, and life flowed pleasantly.

110

4

They were all in good health. It could not be called ill health if Ivan Ilych sometimes said that he had a queer taste in his mouth and felt some discomfort in his left side.

But this discomfort increased and, though not exactly painful, grew into a sense of pressure in his side accompanied by ill humour. And his irritability became worse and worse and began to mar the agreeable, easy, and correct life that had established itself in the Golovin family. Quarrels between husband and wife became more and more frequent, and soon the ease and amenity disappeared and even the decorum was barely maintained. Scenes again became frequent, and very few of those islets remained on which husband and wife could meet without an explosion. Praskovya Fedorovna now had good reason to say that her husband's temper was trying. With characteristic exaggeration she said he had always had a dreadful temper, and that it had needed all her good nature to put up with it for twenty years. It was true that now the quarrels were started by him. His bursts of temper always came just before dinner, often just as he began to eat his soup. Sometimes he noticed that a plate or dish was chipped, or the food was not right, or his son put his elbow on the table, or his daughter's hair was not done as he liked it, and for all this he blamed Praskovya Fedorovna. At first she retorted and said disagreeable things to him, but once or twice he fell into such a rage at the beginning of dinner that she realized it was due to some physical derangement brought on by taking food, and so she restrained herself and did not answer, but only hurried to get the dinner over. She regarded this self-restraint as highly praiseworthy. Having come to the conclusion that her husband had a dreadful temper and made her life miserable, she began to feel sorry for herself, and the more she pitied herself the more she hated her husband. She began to wish he would die; yet she did not want him to die because then his salary would cease. And this irritated her against him still more. She considered herself dreadfully unhappy just because not even his death could save her, and though she concealed her exasperation, that hidden exasperation of hers increased his irritation also.

After one scene in which Ivan Ilych had been particularly unfair and after which he had said in explanation that he certainly was irritable but that it was due to his not being well, she said that if he was ill it should be attended to, and insisted on his going to see a celebrated doctor.

115   He went. Everything took place as he had expected and as it always does. There was the usual waiting and the important air assumed by the doctor, with which he was so familiar (resembling that which he himself assumed in court), and the sounding and listening, and the questions which called for answers that were forgone conclusions and were evidently unnecessary, and the look of importance which implied that "if only you put yourself in our hands we will arrange everything—we know indubitably how it has to be done, always in the same way for everybody alike." It was all just as it was in the law courts. The doctor put on just the same air towards him as he himself put on towards an accused person.

The doctor said that so-and-so indicated that there was so-and-so inside the patient, but if the investigation of so-and-so did not confirm this, then he must assume that and that. If he assumed that and that, then . . . and so on. To Ivan Ilych only one question was important: was his case serious or not? But the doctor ignored that inappropriate question. From his point of view it was not the one under consideration, the real question was to decide between a floating kidney, chronic catarrh, or appendicitis. It was not a question of Ivan Ilych's life or death, but one between a floating kidney and appendicitis. And that question the doctor solved brilliantly, as it seemed to Ivan Ilych, in favour of the appendix, with the reservation that should an examination of the urine give fresh indications the matter would be reconsidered. All this was just what Ivan Ilych had himself brilliantly accomplished a thousand times in dealing with men on trial. The doctor summed up just as brilliantly, looking over his spectacles triumphantly and even gaily at the accused. From the doctor's summing up Ivan Ilych concluded that things were bad, but that for the doctor, and perhaps for everybody else, it was a matter of indifference, though for him it was bad. And this conclusion struck him painfully, arousing in him a great feeling of pity for himself and of bitterness towards the doctor's indifference to a matter of such importance.

He said nothing of this, but rose, placed the doctor's fee on the table, and remarked with a sigh: "We sick people probably often put inappropriate questions. But tell me, in general, is this complaint dangerous, or not? . . ."

The doctor looked at him sternly over his spectacles with one eye, as if to say: "Prisoner, if you will not keep to the questions put to you, I shall be obliged to have you removed from the court."

"I have already told you what I consider necessary and proper. The analysis may show something more." And the doctor bowed.

Ivan Ilych went out slowly, seated himself disconsolately in his sledge, and drove home. All the way home he was going over what the doctor had said, trying to translate those complicated, obscure, scientific phrases into plain language and find in them an answer to the question: "Is my condition bad? Is it very bad? Or is there as yet nothing much wrong?" And it seemed to him that the meaning of what the doctor had said was that it was very bad. Everything in the streets seemed depressing. The cabmen, the houses, the passers-by, and the shops, were dismal. His ache, this dull gnawing ache that never ceased for a moment, seemed to have acquired a new and more serious significance from the doctor's dubious remarks. Ivan Ilych now watched it with a new and oppressive feeling.

He reached home and began to tell his wife about it. She listened, but in the middle of his account his daughter came in with her hat on, ready to go out with her mother. She sat down reluctantly to listen to this tedious story, but could not stand it long, and her mother too did not hear him to the end.

"Well, I am very glad," she said. "Mind now to take your medicine regularly. Give me the prescription and I'll send Gerasim to the chemist's." And she went to get ready to go out.

While she was in the room Ivan Ilych had hardly taken time to breathe, but he sighed deeply when she left it.

"Well," he thought, "perhaps it isn't so bad after all."

He began taking his medicine and following the doctor's directions, which had been altered after the examination of the urine. But then it happened that there was a contradiction between the indications drawn from the examination of the urine and the symptoms that showed themselves. It turned out that what was happening differed from what the doctor had told him, and that he had either forgotten, or blundered, or hidden something from him. He could not, however, be blamed for that, and Ivan Ilych still obeyed his orders implicitly and at first derived some comfort from doing so.

From the time of his visit to the doctor, Ivan Ilych's chief occupation was the exact fulfilment of the doctor's instructions regarding hygiene and the taking of medicine, and the observation of his pain and his excretions. His chief interests came to be people's ailments and people's health. When sickness, deaths, or recoveries were mentioned in his presence, especially when the illness resembled his own, he listened with agitation which he tried to hide, asked questions, and applied what he heard to his own case.

The pain did not grow less, but Ivan Ilych made efforts to force himself to think that he was better. And he could do this so long as nothing agitated him. But as soon as he had any unpleasantness with his wife, any lack of success in his official work, or held bad cards at bridge, he was at once acutely sensible of his disease. He had formerly borne such mischances, hoping soon to adjust what was wrong, to master it and attain success, or make a grand slam. But now every mischance upset him and plunged him into despair. He would say to himself: "There now, just as I was beginning to get better and the medicine had begun to take effect, comes this accursed misfortune, or unpleasantness . . ." And he was furious with the mishap, or with the people who were

120

125

causing the unpleasantness and killing him, for he felt that this fury was killing him but could not restrain it. One would have thought that it should have been clear to him that this exasperation with circumstances and people aggravated his illness, and that he ought therefore to ignore unpleasant occurrences. But he drew the very opposite conclusion: he said that he needed peace, and he watched for everything that might disturb it and became irritable at the slightest infringement of it. His condition was rendered worse by the fact that he read medical books and consulted doctors. The progress of his disease was so gradual that he could deceive himself when comparing one day with another—the difference was so slight. But when he consulted the doctors it seemed to him that he was getting worse, and even very rapidly. Yet despite this he was continually consulting them.

That month he went to see another celebrity, who told him almost the same as the first had done but put his questions rather differently, and the interview with this celebrity only increased Ivan Ilych's doubts and fears. A friend of a friend of his, a very good doctor, diagnosed his illness again quite differently from the others, and though he predicted recovery, his questions and suppositions bewildered Ivan Ilych still more and increased his doubts. A homoeopathist diagnosed the disease in yet another way, and prescribed medicine which Ivan Ilych took secretly for a week. But after a week, not feeling any improvement and having lost confidence both in the former doctor's treatment and in this one's, he became still more despondent. One day a lady acquaintance mentioned a cure effected by a wonder-working icon. Ivan Ilych caught himself listening attentively and beginning to believe that it had occurred. This incident alarmed him. "Has my mind really weakened to such an extent?" he asked himself. "Nonsense! It's all rubbish. I mustn't give way to nervous fears but having chosen a doctor must keep strictly to his treatment. That is what I will do. Now it's all settled. I won't think about it, but will follow the treatment seriously till summer, and then we shall see. From now there must be no more of this wavering!" This was easy to say but impossible to carry out. The pain in his side oppressed him and seemed to grow worse and more incessant, while the taste in his mouth grew stranger and stranger. It seemed to him that his breath had a disgusting smell, and he was conscious of a loss of appetite and strength. There was no deceiving himself: something terrible, new, and more important than anything before in his life, was taking place within him of which he alone was aware. Those about him did not understand or would not understand it, but thought everything in the world was going on as usual. That tormented Ivan Ilych more than anything. He saw that his household, especially his wife and daughter who were in a perfect whirl of visiting, did not understand anything of it and were annoyed that he was so depressed and so exacting, as if he were to blame for it. Though they tried to disguise it he saw that he was an obstacle in their path, and that his wife had adopted a definite line in regard to his illness and kept to it regardless of anything he said or did. Her attitude was this: "You know," she would say to her friends, "Ivan Ilych can't do as other people do, and keep to the treatment prescribed for him. One day he'll take his drops and keep strictly to his diet and go to bed in good time, but the next day unless I watch him he'll suddenly forget his medicine, eat sturgeon—which is forbidden—and sit up playing cards till one o'clock in the morning."

"Oh, come, when was that?" Ivan Ilych would ask in vexation. "Only once at Peter Ivanovich's."

"And yesterday with Shebek."

"Well, even if I hadn't stayed up, this pain would have kept me awake."

"Be that as it may you'll never get well like that, but will always make us wretched."

Praskovya Fedorovna's attitude to Ivan Ilych's illness, as she expressed it both to others and to him, was that it was his own fault and was another of the annoyances he caused her. Ivan Ilych felt that this opinion escaped her involuntarily—but that did not make it easier for him.

At the law courts too, Ivan Ilych noticed, or thought he noticed, a strange attitude towards himself. It sometimes seemed to him that people were watching him inquisitively as a man whose place might soon be vacant. Then again, his friends would suddenly begin to chaff him in a friendly way about his low spirits, as if the awful, horrible, and unheard-of thing that was going on within him, incessantly gnawing at him and irresistibly drawing him away, was a very agreeable subject for jests. Schwartz in particular irritated him by his jocularity, vivacity, and *savoir-faire*, which reminded him of what he himself had been ten years ago.

Friends came to make up a set and they sat down to cards. They dealt, bending the new cards to soften them, and he sorted the diamonds in his hand and found he had seven. His partner said "No trumps" and supported him with two diamonds. What more could be wished for? It ought to be jolly and lively. They would make a grand slam. But suddenly Ivan Ilych was conscious of that gnawing pain, that taste in his mouth, and it seemed ridiculous that in such circumstances he should be pleased to make a grand slam.

He looked at his partner Mikhail Mikhaylovich, who rapped the table with his strong hand and instead of snatching up the tricks pushed the cards courteously and indulgently towards Ivan Ilych that he might have the pleasure of gathering them up without the trouble of stretching out his hand for them. "Does he think I am too weak to stretch out my arm?" thought Ivan Ilych, and forgetting what he was doing he overtrumped his partner, missing the grand slam by three tricks. And what was most awful of all was that he saw how upset Mikhail Mikhaylovich was about it but did not himself care. And it was dreadful to realize why he did not care.

They all saw that he was suffering, and said: "We can stop if you are tired. Take a rest." Lie down? No, he was not at all tired, and he finished the rubber. All were gloomy and silent. Ivan Ilych felt that he diffused this gloom over them and could not dispel it. They had supper and went away, and Ivan Ilych was left alone with the consciousness that his life was poisoned and was poisoning the lives of others, and that this poison did not weaken but penetrated more and more deeply into his whole being.

With this consciousness, and with physical pain besides the terror, he must go to bed, often to lie awake the greater part of the night. Next morning he had to get up again, dress, go to the law courts, speak, and write; or if he did not go out, spend at home those twenty-four hours a day each of which was a torture. And he had to live thus all alone on the brink of an abyss, with no one who understood or pitied him.

135

5

So one month passed and then another. Just before the New Year his brother-in-law came to town and stayed at their house. Ivan Ilych was at the law courts and Praskovya Fedorovna had gone shopping. When Ivan Ilych came home and entered his study he found his brother-in-law there—a healthy, florid man—unpacking his portmanteau himself. He raised his head on hearing Ivan Ilych's footsteps and looked up at him for a moment without a word. That stare told Ivan Ilych everything. His brother-in-law opened his mouth to utter an exclamation of surprise but checked himself, and that action confirmed it all.

140 "I have changed, eh?"

"Yes, there is a change."

And after that, try as he would to get his brother-in-law to return to the subject of his looks, the latter would say nothing about it. Praskovya Fedorovna came home and her brother went out to her. Ivan Ilych locked the door and began to examine himself in the glass, first full face, then in profile. He took up a portrait of himself taken with his wife, and compared it with what he saw in the glass. The change in him was immense. Then he bared his arms to the elbow, looked at them, drew the sleeves down again, sat down on an ottoman, and grew blacker than night.

"No, no, this won't do!" he said to himself, and jumped up, went to the table, took up some law papers and began to read them, but could not continue. He unlocked the door and went into the reception-room. The door leading to the drawing-room was shut. He approached it on tiptoe and listened.

"No, you are exaggerating!" Praskovya Fedorovna was saying.

145 "Exaggerating! Don't you see it? Why, he's a dead man! Look at his eyes—there's no light in them. But what is it that is wrong with him?"

"No one knows. Nikolaevich (that was another doctor) said something, but I don't know what. And Leshchetitsky (this was the celebrated specialist) said quite the contrary . . ."

Ivan Ilych walked away, went to his own room, lay down, and began musing: "The kidney, a floating kidney." He recalled all the doctors had told him of how it detached itself and swayed about. And by an effort of imagination he tried to catch that kidney and arrest it and support it. So little was needed for this, it seemed to him. "No, I'll go to see Peter Ivanovich again." (That was the friend whose friend was a doctor.) He rang, ordered the carriage, and got ready to go.

"Where are you going, Jean?" asked his wife, with a specially sad and exceptionally kind look.

This exceptionally kind look irritated him. He looked morosely at her.

150 "I must go to see Peter Ivanovich."

He went to see Peter Ivanovich, and together they went to see his friend, the doctor. He was in, and Ivan Ilych had a long talk with him.

Reviewing the anatomical and physiological details of what in the doctor's opinion was going on inside him, he understood it all.

There was something, a small thing, in the vermiform appendix. It might all come right. Only stimulate the energy of one organ and check the activity of another, then absorption would take place and everything would come right. He got home rather late for dinner, ate his dinner, and conversed cheerfully, but could not for a long time bring himself to go back to work in his room. At last, however, he went to his study and did what was necessary, but the consciousness that he had put something aside—an important, intimate matter which he would revert to when his work was done—never left him. When he had finished his work he remembered that this intimate matter was the thought of his vermiform appendix. But he did not give himself up to it, and went to the drawing-room for tea. There were callers there, including the examining magistrate who was a desirable match for his daughter, and they were conversing, playing the piano and singing. Ivan Ilych, as Praskovya Fedorovna remarked, spent that evening more cheerfully than usual, but he never for a moment forgot that he had postponed the important matter of the appendix. At eleven o'clock he said good-night and went to his bedroom. Since his illness he had slept alone in a small room next to his study.

He undressed and took up a novel by Zola,° but instead of reading it he fell into thought, and in his imagination that desired improvement in the vermiform appendix occurred. There was the absorption and evacuation and the reestablishment of normal activity. "Yes, that's it!" he said to himself. "One need only assist nature, that's all." He remembered his medicine, rose, took it, and lay down on his back watching for the beneficent action of the medicine and for it to lessen the pain. "I need only take it regularly and avoid all injurious influences. I am already feeling better, much better." He began touching his side: it was not painful to the touch. "There, I really don't feel it. It's much better already." He put out the light and turned on his side. . . ." The appendix is getting better, absorption is occurring." Suddenly he felt the old, familiar, dull, gnawing pain, stubborn and serious. There was the same familiar loathsome taste in his mouth. His heart sank and he felt dazed. "My God! My God!" he muttered. "Again, again! And it will never cease." And suddenly the matter presented itself in a quite different aspect. "Vermiform appendix! Kidney!" he said to himself. "It's not a question of appendix or kidney, but of life and . . . death. Yes, life was there and now it is going, going and I cannot stop it. Yes. Why deceive myself? Isn't it obvious to everyone but me that I'm dying, and that it's only a question of weeks, days . . . it may happen this moment. There was light and now there is darkness. I was here and now I'm going there! Where?" A chill came over him, his breathing ceased, and he felt only the throbbing of his heart.

"When I am not, what will there be? There will be nothing. Then where shall I be when I am no more? Can this be dying? No, I don't want to!" He jumped up and tried to light the candle, felt for it with trembling hands, dropped candle and candlestick on the floor, and fell back on his pillow.

"What's the use? It makes no difference," he said to himself, staring with wide-open eyes into the darkness. "Death. Yes, death. And none of them know or wish to know it, and they have no pity for me. Now they are playing." (He heard through the door the distant sound of a song and its accompaniment.) "It's all the same to them, but they will die too! Fools! I first, and they later, but it will be the same for them. And now they are merry . . . the beasts!"

Anger choked him and he was agonizingly, unbearably miserable. "It is impossible that all men have been doomed to suffer this awful horror!" He raised himself.

"Something must be wrong. I must calm myself—must think it all over from the beginning." And he again began thinking. "Yes, the beginning of my illness: I knocked my side, but I was still quite well that day and the next. It hurt a little, then rather more. I saw the doctors, then followed despondency and anguish, more doctors, and I drew nearer to the abyss. My strength grew less and I kept coming nearer and nearer, and now I have wasted away and there is no light in my eyes. I think of the appendix—but this is death! I think of mending the appendix, and all the while here is death! Can it really be death?" Again terror seized him and he gasped for breath. He leant down and began feeling for the matches, pressing with his elbow on the stand beside the bed. It was in his way and hurt him, he grew furious with it, pressed on it still harder, and upset it. Breathless and in despair he fell on his back, expecting death to come immediately.

Meanwhile the visitors were leaving. Praskovya Fedorovna was seeing them off. She heard something fall and came in.

"What has happened?"

°*Zola:* Emile Zola (1840–1902), a French novelist concerned with social reforms.

160　　"Nothing. I knocked it over accidentally."

She went out and returned with a candle. He lay there panting heavily, like a man who has run a thousand yards, and stared upwards at her with a fixed look.

"What is it, Jean?"°

"No . . . o . . . thing. I upset it." ("Why speak of it? She won't understand," he thought.)

And in truth she did not understand. She picked up the stand, lit his candle, and hurried away to see another visitor off. When she came back he still lay on his back, looking upwards.

165　　"What is it? Do you feel worse?"

"Yes."

She shook her head and sat down.

"Do you know, Jean, I think we must ask Leshchetitsky to come and see you here."

This meant calling in the famous specialist, regardless of expense. He smiled malignantly and said "No." She remained a little longer and then went up to him and kissed his forehead.

170　　While she was kissing him he hated her from the bottom of his soul and with difficulty refrained from pushing her away.

"Good-night. Please God you'll sleep."

"Yes."

6

Ivan Ilych saw that he was dying, and he was in continual despair.

In the depth of his heart he knew he was dying, but not only was he not accustomed to the thought, he simply did not and could not grasp it.

175　　The syllogism he had learnt from Kiezewetter's Logic:° "Caius is a man, men are mortal, therefore Caius is mortal," had always seemed to him correct as applied to Caius, but certainly not as applied to himself. That Caius—man in the abstract—was mortal, was perfectly correct, but he was not Caius, not an abstract man, but a creature quite, quite separate from all others. He had been little Vanya, with a mamma and a papa; with Mitya and Volodya, and the toys, a coachman and a nurse, afterwards with Katenka and with all the joys, griefs, and delights of childhood, boyhood, and youth. What did Caius know of the smell of that striped leather ball Vanya had been so fond of? Had Caius kissed his mother's hand like that, and did the silk of her dress rustle so for Caius? Had he rioted like that at school when the pastry was bad? Had Caius been in love like that? Could Caius preside at a session as he did? "Caius really was mortal, and it was right for him to die; but for me, little Vanya, Ivan Ilych, with all my thoughts and emotions, it's altogether a different matter. It cannot be that I ought to die. That would be too terrible."

Such was his feeling.

"If I had to die like Caius I should have known it was so. An inner voice would have told me so, but there was nothing of the sort in me and I and all my friends felt

---

°*Jean*: French form of Ivan.
°*Kiezewetter's Logic*: *An Outline of Logic* (1796) by Klaus Kiezewetter (1760–1819).

that our case was quite different from that of Caius. And now here it is!" he said to himself. "It can't be. It's impossible! But here it is. How is this? How is one to understand it?"

He could not understand it, and tried to drive this false, incorrect, morbid thought away and to replace it by other proper and healthy thoughts. But that thought and not the thought only but the reality itself, seemed to come and confront him.

And to replace that thought he called up a succession of others, hoping to find in them some support. He tried to get back into the former current of thoughts that had once screened the thought of death from him. But strange to say, all that had formerly shut off, hidden, and destroyed, his consciousness of death, no longer had that effect. Ivan Ilych now spent most of his time in attempting to re-establish that old current. He would say to himself: "I will take up my duties again—after all I used to live by them." And banishing all doubts he would go to the law courts, enter into conversation with his colleagues, and sit carelessly as was his wont, scanning the crowd with a thoughtful look and leaning both his emaciated arms on the arms of his oak chair; bending over as usual to a colleague and drawing his papers nearer he would interchange whispers with him, and then suddenly raising his eyes and sitting erect would pronounce certain words and open the proceedings. But suddenly in the midst of those proceedings the pain in his side, regardless of the stage the proceedings had reached, would begin its own gnawing work. Ivan Ilych would turn his attention to it and try to drive the thought of it away, but without success. *It* would come and stand before him and look at him, and he would be petrified and the light would die out of his eyes, and he would again begin asking himself whether *It* alone was true. And his colleagues and subordinates would see with surprise and distress that he, the brilliant and subtle judge, was becoming confused and making mistakes. He would shake himself, try to pull himself together, manage somehow to bring the sitting to a close, and return home with the sorrowful consciousness that his judicial labours could not as formerly hide from him what he wanted them to hide, and could not deliver him from *It*. And what was worst of all was that *It* drew his attention to itself not in order to make him take some action but only that he should look at *It*, look it straight in the face: look at it and without doing anything, suffer inexpressibly.

And to save himself from this condition Ivan Ilych looked for consolations—new screens—and new screens were found and for a while seemed to save him, but then they immediately fell to pieces or rather became transparent, as if *It* penetrated them and nothing could veil *It*. 180

In these latter days he would go into the drawing-room he had arranged—that drawing-room where he had fallen and for the sake of which (how bitterly ridiculous it seemed) he had sacrificed his life—for he knew that his illness originated with that knock. He would enter and see that something had scratched the polished table. He would look for the cause of this and find that it was the bronze ornamentation of an album, that had got bent. He would take up the expensive album which he had lovingly arranged, and feel vexed with his daughter and her friends for their untidiness—for the album was torn here and there and some of the photographs turned upside down. He would put it carefully in order and bend the ornamentation back into position. Then it would occur to him to place all those things in another corner of the room, near the plants. He could call the footman, but his daughter or wife would come to help him. They would not agree, and his wife would contradict him, and he would dispute and grow angry. But that was all right, for then he did not think about *It*. It was invisible.

But then, when he was moving something himself, his wife would say: "Let the servants do it. You will hurt yourself again." And suddenly *It* would flash through the screen and he would see it. It was just a flash, and he hoped it would disappear, but he would involuntarily pay attention to his side. "It sits there as before, gnawing just the same!" And he could no longer forget *It*, but could distinctly see it looking at him from behind the flowers. "What is it all for?"

"It really is so! I lost my life over that curtain as I might have done when storming a fort. Is that possible? How terrible and how stupid. It can't be true! It can't, but it is!"

He would go to his study, lie down, and again be alone with *It*: face to face with *It*. And nothing could be done with *It* except to look at it and shudder.

7

185 How it happened it is impossible to say because it came about step by step, unnoticed, but in the third month of Ivan Ilych's illness, his wife, his daughter, his son, his acquaintances, the doctors, the servants, and above all he himself, were aware that the whole interest he had for other people was whether he would soon vacate his place, and at last release the living from the discomfort caused by his presence and be himself released from his sufferings.

He slept less and less. He was given opium and hypodermic injections of morphine, but this did not relieve him. The dull depression he experienced in a somnolent condition at first gave him a little relief, but only as something new, afterwards it became as distressing as the pain itself or even more so.

Special foods were prepared for him by the doctors' orders, but all those foods became increasingly distasteful and disgusting to him.

For his excretions also special arrangements had to be made, and this was a torment to him every time—a torment from the uncleanliness, the unseemliness, and the smell, and from knowing that another person had to take part in it.

But just through this most unpleasant matter Ivan Ilych obtained comfort. Gerasim, the butler's young assistant, always came in to carry the things out. Gerasim was a clean, fresh peasant lad, grown stout on town food and always cheerful and bright. At first the sight of him, in his clean Russian peasant costume, engaged on that disgusting task embarrassed Ivan Ilych.

190 Once when he got up from the commode too weak to draw up his trousers, he dropped into a soft armchair and looked with horror at his bare, enfeebled thighs with the muscles so sharply marked on them.

Gerasim with a firm light tread, his heavy boots emitting a pleasant smell of tar and fresh winter air, came in wearing a clean Hessian apron, the sleeves of his print shirt tucked up over his strong bare young arms; and refraining from looking at his sick master out of consideration for his feelings, and restraining the joy of life that beamed from his face, went up to the commode.

"Gerasim!" said Ivan Ilych in a weak voice.

Gerasim started, evidently afraid he might have committed some blunder, and with a rapid movement turned his fresh, kind, simple young face which just showed the first downy signs of a beard.

"Yes, sir?"

195 "That must be very unpleasant for you. You must forgive me. I am helpless."

"Oh, why, sir," and Gerasim's eyes beamed and he showed his glistening white teeth, "what's a little trouble? It's a case of illness with you, sir."

And his deft strong hands did their accustomed task, and he went out of the room stepping lightly. Five minutes later he as lightly returned.

Ivan Ilych was still sitting in the same position in the armchair.

"Gerasim," he said when the latter had replaced the freshly-washed utensil. "Please come here and help me." Gerasim went up to him. "Lift me up. It is hard for me to get up, and I have sent Dmitri away."

Gerasim went up to him, grasped his master with his strong arms deftly but gently, in the same way that he stepped—lifted him, supported him with one hand, and with the other drew up his trousers and would have set him down again, but Ivan Ilych asked to be led to the sofa. Gerasim, without an effort and without apparent pressure, led him, almost lifting him, to the sofa and placed him on it. 200

"Thank you. How easily and well you do it all!"

Gerasim smiled again and turned to leave the room. But Ivan Ilych felt his presence such a comfort that he did not want to let him go.

"One thing more, please move up that chair. No, the other one—under my feet. It is easier for me when my feet are raised."

Gerasim brought the chair, set it down gently in place, and raised Ivan Ilych's legs on to it. It seemed to Ivan Ilych that he felt better while Gerasim was holding up his legs.

"It's better when my legs are higher," he said. "Place that cushion under them." 205

Gerasim did so. He again lifted the legs and placed them, and again Ivan Ilych felt better while Gerasim held his legs. When he set them down Ivan Ilych fancied he felt worse.

"Gerasim," he said. "Are you busy now?"

"Not at all, sir," said Gerasim, who had learnt from the townsfolk how to speak to gentlefolk.

"What have you still to do?"

"What have I to do? I've done everything except chopping the logs for tomorrow." 210

"Then hold my legs up a bit higher, can you?"

"Of course I can. Why not?" And Gerasim raised his master's legs higher and Ivan Ilych thought that in that position he did not feel any pain at all.

"And how about the logs?"

"Don't trouble about that, sir. There's plenty of time."

Ivan Ilych told Gerasim to sit down and hold his legs, and began to talk to him. 215
And strange to say it seemed to him that he felt better while Gerasim held his legs up.

After that Ivan Ilych would sometimes call Gerasim and get him to hold his legs on his shoulders, and he liked talking to him. Gerasim did it all easily, willingly, simply, and with a good nature that touched Ivan Ilych. Health, strength, and vitality in other people were offensive to him, but Gerasim's strength and vitality did not mortify but soothed him.

What tormented Ivan Ilych most was the deception, the lie, which for some reason they all accepted, that he was not dying but was simply ill, and that he only need keep quiet and undergo a treatment and then something very good would result. He however knew that do what they would nothing would come of it, only still more agonizing suffering and death. This deception tortured him—their not wishing to admit what they all knew and what he knew, but wanting to lie to him concerning his terrible condition, and wishing and forcing him to participate in that lie. Those lies—lies enacted over him on the eve of his death and destined to degrade this awful, solemn act to the level of their visitings, their curtains, their sturgeon for dinner—were a terrible agony for Ivan Ilych. And strangely enough, many times when they were going through their antics over him he had been within a hair-breadth of calling out to them: "Stop lying! You know and I know that I am dying. Then at least stop lying about it!" But he had never had the spirit to do it. The awful, terrible act of his dying was, he could see, reduced by those about him to the level of a casual, unpleasant, and almost indecorous incident (as if someone entered a drawing-room diffusing an unpleasant odour) and this was done by that very decorum which he had served all his life long. He saw that no one felt for him, because no one even wished to grasp his position. Only Gerasim recognized it and pitied him. And so Ivan Ilych felt at ease only with him. He felt comforted when Gerasim supported his legs (sometimes all night long) and refused to go to bed, saying: "Don't you worry, Ivan Ilych. I'll get sleep enough later on," or when he suddenly became familiar and exclaimed: "If you weren't sick it would be another matter, but as it is, why should I grudge a little trouble?" Gerasim alone did not lie; everything showed that he alone understood the facts of the case and did not consider it necessary to disguise them, but simply felt sorry for his emaciated and enfeebled master. Once when Ivan Ilych was sending him away he even said straight out: "We shall all of us die, so why should I grudge a little trouble?"—expressing the fact that he did not think his work burdensome, because he was doing it for a dying man and hoped someone would do the same for him when his time came.

Apart from this lying, or because of it, what most tormented Ivan Ilych was that no one pitied him as he wished to be pitied. At certain moments after prolonged suffering he wished most of all (though he would have been ashamed to confess it) for someone to pity him as a sick child is pitied. He longed to be petted and comforted. He knew he was an important functionary, that he had a beard turning grey, and that therefore what he longed for was impossible, but still he longed for it. And in Gerasim's attitude towards him there was something akin to what he wished for, and so that attitude comforted him. Ivan Ilych wanted to weep, wanted to be petted and cried over, and then his colleague Shebek would come, and instead of weeping and being petted, Ivan Ilych would assume a serious, severe, and profound air, and by force of habit would express his opinion on a decision of the Court of Cessation and would stubbornly insist on that view. This falsity around him and within him did more than anything else to poison his last days.

8

It was morning. He knew it was morning because Gerasim had gone, and Peter the footman had come and put out the candles, drawn back one of the curtains, and begun quietly to tidy up. Whether it was morning or evening, Friday or Sunday, made no difference, it was all just the same: the gnawing, unmitigated, agonizing pain, never ceasing for an instant, the consciousness of life inexorably waning but not yet extinguished, that approach of that ever dreaded and hateful Death which was the only reality, and always the same falsity. What were days, weeks, hours, in such a case?

220   "Will you have some tea, sir?"

"He wants things to be regular, and wishes the gentlefolk to drink tea in the morning," thought Ivan Ilych, and only said "No."

"Wouldn't you like to move onto the sofa, sir?"

"He wants to tidy up the room, and I'm in the way. I am uncleanliness and disorder," he thought, and said only:

"No, leave me alone."

The man went on bustling about. Ivan Ilych stretched out his hand. Peter came up, ready to help.   225

"What is it, sir?"

"My watch."

Peter took the watch which was close at hand and gave it to his master.

"Half-past eight. Are they up?"

"No sir, except Vladimir Ivanich" (the son) "who has gone to school. Praskovya   230
Fedorovna ordered me to wake her if you asked for her. Shall I do so?"

"No, there's no need to." "Perhaps I'd better have some tea," he thought, and added aloud: "Yes, bring me some tea."

Peter went to the door but Ivan Ilych dreaded being left alone. "How can I keep him here? Oh yes, my medicine." "Peter, give me my medicine." "Why not? Perhaps it may still do me some good." He took a spoonful and swallowed it. "No, it won't help. It's all tomfoolery, all deception," he decided as soon as he became aware of the familiar, sickly, hopeless taste. "No, I can't believe in it any longer. But the pain, why this pain? If it would only cease just for a moment!" And he moaned. Peter turned towards him. "It's all right. Go and fetch me some tea."

Peter went out. Left alone Ivan Ilych groaned not so much with pain, terrible though that was, as from mental anguish. Always and for ever the same, always these endless days and nights. If only it would come quicker! If only *what* would come quicker? Death, darkness? . . . No, no! Anything rather than death!

When Peter returned with the tea on a tray, Ivan Ilych stared at him for a time in perplexity, not realizing who and what he was. Peter was disconcerted by that look and his embarrassment brought Ivan Ilych to himself.

"Oh, tea! All right, put it down. Only help me to wash and put on a clean shirt."   235

And Ivan Ilych began to wash. With pauses for rest, he washed his hands and then his face, cleaned his teeth, brushed his hair, and looked in the glass. He was terrified by what he saw, especially by the limp way in which his hair clung to his pallid forehead.

While his shirt was being changed he knew that he would be still more frightened at the sight of his body, so he avoided looking at it. Finally he was ready. He drew on a dressing-gown, wrapped himself in a plaid, and sat down in the armchair to take his tea. For a moment he felt refreshed, but as soon as he began to drink the tea he was again aware of the same taste, and the pain also returned. He finished it with an effort, and then lay down stretching out his legs, and dismissed Peter.

Always the same. Now a spark of hope flashes up, then a sea of despair rages, and always pain; always pain, always despair, and always the same. When alone he had a dreadful and distressing desire to call someone, but he knew beforehand that with others present it would be still worse. "Another dose of morphine—to lose consciousness. I will tell him, the doctor, that he must think of something else. It's impossible, impossible, to go on like this."

An hour and another pass like that. But now there is a ring at the door bell. Perhaps it's the doctor? It is. He comes in fresh, hearty, plump, and cheerful, with that look on his face that seems to say: "There now, you're in a panic about something, but we'll arrange it all for you directly!" The doctor knows this expression is out of place here, but he has put it on once for all and can't take it off—like a man who has put on a frock-coat in the morning to pay a round of calls.

The doctor rubs his hands vigorously and reassuringly.   240

"Brr! How cold it is! There's such a sharp frost; just let me warm myself!" he says, as if it were only a matter of waiting till he was warm, and then he would put everything right.

"Well now, how are you?"

Ivan Ilych feels that the doctor would like to say: "Well, how are our affairs?" but that even he feels that this would not do, and says instead; "What sort of a night have you had?"

Ivan Ilych looks at him as much as to say: "Are you really never ashamed of lying?" But the doctor does not wish to understand this question, and Ivan Ilych says: "Just as terrible as ever. The pain never leaves me and never subsides. If only something . . ."

245   "Yes, you sick people are always like that. . . . There, now I think I am warm enough. Even Praskovya Fedorovna, who is so particular, could find no fault with my temperature. Well, now I can say good-morning," and the doctor presses his patient's hand.

Then, dropping his former playfulness, he begins with a most serious face to examine the patient, feeling his pulse and taking his temperature, and then begins the sounding and auscultation.

Ivan Ilych knows quite well and definitely that all this is nonsense and pure deception, but when the doctor, getting down on his knee, leans over him, putting his ear first higher then lower, and performs various gymnastic movements over him with a significant expression on his face, Ivan Ilych submits to it all as he used to submit to the speeches of the lawyers, though he knew very well that they were all lying and why they were lying.

The doctor, kneeling on the sofa, is still sounding him when Praskovya Fedorovna's silk dress rustles at the door and she is heard scolding Peter for not having let her know of the doctor's arrival.

She comes in, kisses her husband, and at once proceeds to prove that she has been up a long time already, and only owing to a misunderstanding failed to be there when the doctor arrived.

250   Ivan Ilych looks at her, scans her all over, sets against her the whiteness and plumpness and cleanness of her hands and neck, the gloss of her hair, and the sparkle of her vivacious eyes. He hates her with his whole soul. And the thrill of hatred he feels for her makes him suffer from her touch.

Her attitude towards him and his disease is still the same. Just as the doctor had adopted a certain relation to his patient which he could not abandon, so had she formed one towards him—that he was not doing something he ought to do and was himself to blame, and that she reproached him lovingly for this—and she could not now change that attitude.

"You see he doesn't listen to me and doesn't take his medicine at the proper time. And above all he lies in a position that is no doubt bad for him—with his legs up."

She described how he made Gerasim hold his legs up.

The doctor smiled with a contemptuous affability that said: "What's to be done? These sick people do have foolish fancies of that kind, but we must forgive them."

255   When the examination was over the doctor looked at his watch, and then Praskovya Fedorovna announced to Ivan Ilych that it was of course as he pleased, but she had sent to-day for a celebrated specialist who would examine him and have a consultation with Michael Danilovich (their regular doctor).

"Please don't raise any objections. I am doing this for my own sake," she said ironically, letting it be felt that she was doing it all for his sake and only said that to leave him no right to refuse. He remained silent, knitting his brows. He felt that he was so surrounded and involved in a mesh of falsity that it was hard to unravel anything.

Everything she did for him was entirely for her own sake, and she told him she was doing for herself what she actually was doing for herself, as if that was so incredible that he must understand the opposite.

At half-past eleven the celebrated specialist arrived. Again the sounding began and the significant conversations in his presence and in another room, but the kidneys and the appendix, and the questions and answers, with such an air of importance that again, instead of the real question of life and death which now alone confronted him, the question arose of the kidney and appendix which were not behaving as they ought to and would now be attacked by Michael Danilovich and the specialist and forced to amend their ways.

The celebrated specialist took leave of him with a serious though not hopeless look, and in reply to the timid question Ivan Ilych, with eyes glistening with fear and hope, put to him as to whether there was a chance of recovery, said that he could not vouch for it but there was a possibility. The look of hope with which Ivan Ilych watched the doctor out was so pathetic that Praskovya Fedorovna, seeing it, even wept as she left the room to hand the doctor his fee.

The gleam of hope kindled by the doctor's encouragement did not last long. The same room, the same pictures, curtains, wallpaper, medicine bottles, were all there, and the same aching suffering body, and Ivan Ilych began to moan. They gave him a subcutaneous injection and he sank into oblivion. 260

It was twilight when he came to. They brought him his dinner and he swallowed some beef tea with difficulty, and then everything was the same again and night was coming on.

After dinner, at seven o'clock, Praskovya Fedorovna came into the room in evening dress, her full bosom pushed up by her corset, and with traces of powder on her face. She had reminded him in the morning that they were going to the theatre. Sarah Bernhardt was visiting the town and they had a box, which he had insisted on their taking. Now he had forgotten about it and her toilet offended him, but he concealed his vexation when he remembered that he had himself insisted on their securing a box and going because it would be an instructive and aesthetic pleasure for the children.

Praskovya Fedorovna came in, self-satisfied but yet with a rather guilty air. She sat down and asked how he was but, as he saw, only for the sake of asking and not in order to learn about it, knowing that there was nothing to learn—and then went on to what she really wanted to say: that she would not on any account have gone but that the box had been taken and Helen and their daughter were going, as well as Petrishchev (the examining magistrate, their daughter's fiancé) and that it was out of the question to let them go alone; but that she would have much preferred to sit with him for a while; and he must be sure to follow the doctor's orders while she was away.

"Oh, and Fedor Petrovich" (the fiancé) "would like to come in. May he? And Lisa?"

"All right." 265

Their daughter came in in full evening dress, her fresh young flesh exposed (making a show of that very flesh which in his own case caused so much suffering), strong, healthy, evidently in love, and impatient with illness, suffering, and death, because they interfered with her happiness.

Fedor Petrovich came in too, in evening dress, his hair curled *á la Capoul*, a tight stiff collar round his long sinewy neck, an enormous white shirt-front and narrow black trousers tightly stretched over his strong thighs. He had one white glove tightly drawn on, and was holding his opera hat in his hand.

Following him the schoolboy crept in unnoticed, in a new uniform, poor little fellow, and wearing gloves. Terribly dark shadows showed under his eyes, the meaning of which Ivan Ilych knew well.

His son had always seemed pathetic to him, and now it was dreadful to see the boy's frightened look of pity. It seemed to Ivan Ilych that Vasya was the only one besides Gerasim who understood and pitied him.

270   They all sat down and again asked how he was. A silence followed. Lisa asked her mother about the opera-glasses, and there was an altercation between mother and daughter as to who had taken them and where they had been put. This occasioned some unpleasantness.

Fedor Petrovich inquired of Ivan Ilych whether he had ever seen Sarah Bernhardt. Ivan Ilych did not at first catch the question, but then replied: "No, have you seen her before?"

"Yes, in *Adrienne Lecouvreur*."°

Praskovya Fedorovna mentioned some roles in which Sarah Bernhardt was particularly good. Her daughter, disagreed. Conversation sprang up as to the elegance and realism of her acting—the sort of conversation that is always repeated and is always the same.

In the midst of the conversation Fedor Petrovich glanced at Ivan Ilych and became silent. The others also looked at him and grew silent. Ivan Ilych was staring with glittering eyes straight before him, evidently indignant with them. This had to be rectified, but it was impossible to do so. The silence had to be broken, but for a time no one dared to break it and they all became afraid that the conventional deception would suddenly become obvious and the truth become plain to all. Lisa was the first to pluck up courage and break that silence, but by trying to hide what everybody was feeling, she betrayed it.

275   "Well, if we are going it's time to start," she said, looking at her watch, a present from her father, and with a faint and significant smile at Fedor Petrovich relating to something known only to them. She got up with a rustle of her dress.

They all rose, said good-night, and went away.

When they had gone it seemed to Ivan Ilych that he felt better; the falsity had gone with them. But the pain remained—that same pain and that same fear that made everything monotonously alike, nothing harder and nothing easier. Everything was worse.

Again minute followed minute and hour followed hour. Everything remained the same and there was no cessation. And the inevitable end of it all became more and more terrible.

"Yes, send Gerasim here," he replied to a question Peter asked.

9

280   His wife returned late at night. She came in on tiptoe, but he heard her, opened his eyes, and made haste to close them again. She wished to send Gerasim away and to sit with him herself, but he opened his eyes and said: "No, go away."

"Are you in great pain?"

"Always the same."

"Take some opium."

° *Adrienne Lecouvreur*: Written in 1849 by the French playwrights Eugéne Scribe (1791–1861) and Gabriel Legouvé (1807–1903).

He agreed and took some. She went away.

Till about three in the morning he was in a state of stupefied misery. It seemed to him that he and pain were being thrust into a narrow, deep black sack, but though they were pushed further and further in they could not be pushed to the bottom. And this, terrible enough in itself, was accompanied by suffering. He was frightened yet wanted to fall through the sack, he struggled but yet co-operated. And suddenly he broke through, fell, and regained consciousness. Gerasim was sitting at the foot of the bed dozing quietly and patiently, while he himself lay with his emaciated stockinged legs resting on Gerasim's shoulders; the same shaded candle was there and the same unceasing pain.

"Go away, Gerasim," he whispered.

"It's all right, sir. I'll stay a while."

"No. Go away."

He removed his legs from Gerasim's shoulders, turned sideways onto his arm, and felt sorry for himself. He only waited till Gerasim had gone into the next room and then restrained himself no longer but wept like a child. He wept on account of his helplessness, his terrible loneliness, the cruelty of man, the cruelty of God, and the absence of God.

"Why hast Thou done all this? Why hast Thou brought me here? Why, why dost Thou torment me so terribly?"

He did not expect an answer and yet wept because there was no answer and could be none. The pain again grew more acute, but he did not stir and did not call. He said to himself: "Go on! Strike me! But what is it for? What have I done to Thee? What is it for?"

Then he grew quiet and not only ceased weeping but even held his breath and became all attention. It was as though he were listening not to an audible voice but to the voice of his soul, to the current of thoughts arising within him.

"What is it you want?" was the first clear conception capable of expression in words, that he heard.

"What do you want? What do you want?" he repeated to himself.

"What do I want? To live and not to suffer," he answered.

And again he listened with such concentrated attention that even his pain did not distract him.

"To live? How?" asked his inner voice.

"Why, to live as I used to—well and pleasantly."

"As you lived before, well and pleasantly?" the voice repeated.

And in imagination he began to recall the best moments of his pleasant life. But strange to say none of these best moments of his pleasant life now seemed at all what they had then seemed—none of them except the first recollections of childhood. There, in childhood, there had been something really pleasant with which it would be possible to live if it could return. But the child who had experienced that happiness existed no longer, it was like a reminiscence of somebody else.

As soon as the period began which had produced the present Ivan Ilych, all that had then seemed joys now melted before his sight and turned into something trivial and often nasty.

And the further he departed from childhood and the nearer he came to the present the more worthless and doubtful were the joys. This began with the School of Law. A little that was really good was still found there—there was light-heartedness, friendship, and hope. But in the upper classes there had already been fewer of such good moments. Then during the first years of his official career, when he was in the service of the Governor, some pleasant moments again occurred: They were the memories of love for a woman. Then all became confused and there was still less of what was good; later on again there was still less that was good, and the further he went the less there was. His marriage, a mere accident, then the disenchantment that followed it, his wife's bad breath and the sensuality and hypocrisy: then that deadly official life and those preoccupations about money, a year of it, and two, and ten, and twenty, and always the same thing. And the longer it lasted the more deadly it became. "It is as if I had been going downhill while I imagined I was going up. And that is really what it was. I was going up in public opinion, but to the same extent life was ebbing away from me. And now it is all done and there is only death."

"Then what does it mean? Why? It can't be that life is so senseless and horrible. But if it really has been so horrible and senseless, why must I die and die in agony? There is something wrong!"

"Maybe I did not live as I ought to have done," it suddenly occurred to him. "But how could that be, when I did everything properly?" he replied, and immediately dismissed from his mind this, the sole solution of all the riddles of life and death, as something quite impossible.

305   "Then what do you want now? To live? Live how? Live as you lived in the law courts when the usher proclaimed 'The judge is coming!'" "The judge is coming, the judge!" he repeated to himself. "Here he is, the judge. But I am not guilty!" he exclaimed angrily. "What is it for?" And he ceased crying, but turning his face to the wall continued to ponder on the same question: Why, and for what purpose, is there all this horror? But however much he pondered he found no answer. And whenever the thought occurred to him, as it often did, that it all resulted from his not having lived as he ought to have done, he at once recalled the correctness of his whole life and dismissed so strange an idea.

10

Another fortnight passed. Ivan Ilych now no longer left his sofa. He would not lie in bed but lay on the sofa, facing the wall nearly all the time. He suffered ever the same unceasing agonies and in his loneliness pondered always on the same insoluble question: "What is this? Can it be that it is Death?" And the inner voice answered: "Yes, it is Death."

"Why these sufferings?" And the voice answered, "For no reason—they just are so." Beyond and besides this there was nothing.

From the very beginning of his illness, ever since he had first been to see the doctor, Ivan Ilych's life had been divided between two contrary and alternating moods: now it was despair and the expectation of this uncomprehended and terrible death, and now hope and an intently interested observation of the functioning of his organs. Now before his eyes there was only a kidney or an intestine that temporarily evaded its duty, and now only that incomprehensible and dreadful death from which it was impossible to escape.

These two states of mind had alternated from the very beginning of his illness, but the further it progressed the more doubtful and fantastic became the conception of the kidney, and the more real the sense of impending death.

310   He had but to call to mind what he had been three months before and what he was now, to call to mind with what regularity he had been going downhill, for every possibility of hope to be shattered.

Latterly during that loneliness in which he found himself as he lay facing the back of the sofa, a loneliness in the midst of a populous town and surrounded by numerous acquaintances and relations but that yet could not have been more complete anywhere—either at the bottom of the sea or under the earth—during that terrible loneliness Ivan Ilych had lived only in memories of the past. Pictures of his past rose before him one after another. They always began with what was nearest in time and then went back to what was more remote—to his childhood—and rested there. If he thought of the stewed prunes that had been offered him that day, his mind went back to the raw shrivelled French plums of his childhood, their peculiar flavour and the flow of saliva when he sucked their stones, and along with the memory of that taste came a whole series of memories of those days: his nurse, his brother, and their toys. "No, I mustn't think of that. . . . It is too painful," Ivan Ilych said to himself, and brought himself back to the present—to the bottom of the back of the sofa and the creases in its morocco. "Morocco is expensive, but it does not wear well: There had been a quarrel about it. It was a different kind of quarrel and a different kind of morocco that time when we tore father's portfolio and were punished, and mamma brought us some tarts. . . ." And again his thoughts dwelt on his childhood, and again it was painful and he tried to banish them and fix his mind on something else.

Then again together with that chain of memories another series passed through his mind—of how his illness had progressed and grown worse. There also the further back he looked the more life there had been. There had been more of what was good in life and more of life itself. The two merged together. "Just as the pain went on getting worse and worse so my life grew worse and worse," he thought. "There is one bright spot there at the back, at the beginning of life, and afterwards all becomes blacker and blacker and proceeds more and more rapidly—in inverse ratio to the square of the distance from death," thought Ivan Ilych. And the example of a stone falling downwards with increasing velocity entered his mind. Life, a series of increasing sufferings, flies, further and further towards its end—the most terrible suffering. "I am flying. . . ." He shuddered, shifted himself, and tried to resist, but was already aware that resistance was impossible, and again with eyes weary of gazing but unable to cease seeing what was before them, he stared at the back of the sofa and waited—awaiting the dreadful fall and shock and destruction.

"Resistance is impossible!" he said to himself. "If I could only understand what it is all for! But that too is impossible. An explanation would be possible if it could be said that I have not lived as I ought to. But it is impossible to say that," and he remembered all the legality, correctitude, and propriety of his life. "That at any rate can certainly not be admitted," he thought, and his lips smiled ironically as if someone could see that smile and be taken in by it. "There is no explanation! Agony, death. . . . What for?"

<h2 style="text-align:center">11</h2>

Another two weeks went by in this way and during that fortnight an event occurred that Ivan Ilych and his wife had desired. Petrishchev formally proposed. It happened in the evening. The next day Praskovya Fedorovna came into her husband's room considering how best to inform him of it, but that very night there had been a fresh change for the worse in his condition. She found him still lying on the sofa but in a different position. He lay on his back, groaning and staring fixedly straight in front of him.

315　　She began to remind him of his medicines, but he turned his eyes towards her with such a look that she did not finish what she was saying; so great an animosity, to her in particular, did that look express.

"For Christ's sake, let me die in peace!" he said.

She would have gone away, but just then their daughter came in and went up to say good morning. He looked at her as he had done at his wife, and in reply to her inquiry about his health said dryly that he would soon free them all of himself. They were both silent and after sitting with him for a while went away.

"Is it our fault?" Lisa said to her mother. "It's as if we were to blame! I am sorry for papa, but why should we be tortured?"

The doctor came at his usual time. Ivan Ilych answered "Yes" and "No," never taking his angry eyes from him, and at last said: "You know you can do nothing for me, so leave me alone."

320　　"We can ease your sufferings."

"You can't even do that. Let me be."

The doctor went into the drawing-room and told Praskovya Fedorovna that the case was very serious and that the only resource left was opium to allay her husband's sufferings, which must be terrible.

It was true, as the doctor said, that Ivan Ilych's physical sufferings were terrible, but worse than the physical sufferings were his mental sufferings which were his chief torture.

His mental sufferings were due to the fact that that night, as he looked at Gerasim's sleepy, good-natured face with its prominent cheek-bones, the question suddenly occurred to him: "What if my whole life has really been wrong?"

325　　It occurred to him that what had appeared perfectly impossible before, namely that he had not spent his life as he could have done, might after all be true. It occurred to him that his scarcely perceptible attempts to struggle against what was considered good by the most highly placed people, those scarcely noticeable impulses which he had immediately suppressed, might have been the real thing, and all the rest false. And his professional duties and the whole arrangement of his life and of his family, and all his social and official interests, might all have been false. He tried to defend all those things to himself and suddenly felt the weakness of what he was defending. There was nothing to defend.

"But if that is so," he said to himself, "and I am leaving this life with the consciousness that I have lost all that was given me and it is impossible to rectify it—what then?"

He lay on his back and began to pass his life in review in quite a new way. In the morning when he saw first his footman, then his wife, then his daughter, and then the doctor, their every word and movement confirmed to him the awful truth that had been revealed to him during the night. In them he saw himself—all that for which he had lived—and saw clearly that it was not real at all, but a terrible and huge deception which had hidden both life and death. This consciousness intensified his physical suffering tenfold. He groaned and tossed about, and pulled at his clothing which choked and stifled him. And he hated them on that account.

He was given a large dose of opium and became unconscious, but at noon his sufferings began again. He drove everybody away and tossed from side to side.

His wife came to him and said:

330　　"Jean, my dear, do this for me. It can't do any harm and often helps. Healthy people often do it."

He opened his eyes wide.

"What? Take communion? Why? It's unnecessary! However. . . ."

She began to cry.

"Yes, do, my dear. I'll send for our priest. He is such a nice man."

"All right. Very well," he muttered. 335

When the priest came and heard his confession, Ivan Ilych was softened and seemed to feel a relief from his doubts and consequently from his sufferings, and for a moment there came a ray of hope. He again began to think of the vermiform appendix and the possibility of correcting it. He received the sacrament with tears in his eyes.

When they laid him down again afterwards he felt a moment's ease, and the hope that he might live awoke in him again. He began to think of the operation that had been suggested to him. "To live! I want to live!" he said to himself.

His wife came in to congratulate him after his communion, and when uttering the usual conventional words she added:

"You feel better, don't you?"

Without looking at her he said "Yes." 340

Her dress, her figure, the expression of her face, the tone of her voice, all revealed the same thing. "This is wrong, it is not as it should be. All you have lived for and still live for is falsehood and deception, hiding life and death from you." And as soon as he admitted that thought, his hatred and his agonizing physical suffering again sprang up, and with that suffering a consciousness of the unavoidable, approaching end. And to this was added a new sensation of grinding shooting pain and a feeling of suffocation.

The expression of his face when he uttered that "yes" was dreadful. Having uttered it, he looked her straight in the eyes, turned on his face with a rapidity extraordinary in his weak state and shouted:

"Go away! Go away and leave me alone!"

12

From that moment the screaming began that continued for three days, and was so terrible that one could not hear it through two closed doors without horror. At the moment he answered his wife he realized that he was lost, that there was no return, that the end had come, the very end, and his doubts were still unsolved and remained doubts.

"Oh! Oh! Oh!" he cried in various intonations. He had begun by screaming "I 345 won't!" and continued screaming on the letter "o."

For three whole days, during which time did not exist for him, he struggled in that black sack into which he was being thrust by an invisible, resistless force. He struggled as a man condemned to death struggles in the hands of the executioner, knowing that he cannot save himself. And every moment he felt that despite all his efforts he was drawing nearer and nearer to what terrified him. He felt that his agony was due to his being thrust into that black hole and still more to his not being able to get right into it. He was hindered from getting into it by his conviction that his life had been a good one. That very justification of his life held him fast and prevented his moving forward, and it caused him most torment of all.

Suddenly some force struck him in the chest and side, making it still harder to breathe, and he fell through the hole and there at the bottom was a light. What had happened to him was like the sensation one sometimes experiences in a railway carriage when one thinks one is going backwards while one is really going forwards and suddenly becomes aware of the real direction.

"Yes, it was all not the right thing," he said to himself, "but that's no matter. It can be done. But what is the right thing?" he asked himself, and suddenly grew quiet.

This occurred at the end of the third day, two hours before his death. Just then his schoolboy son had crept softly in and gone up to the bedside. The dying man was still screaming desperately and waving his arms. His hand fell on the boy's head, and the boy caught it, pressed it to his lips, and began to cry.

350   At that very moment Ivan Ilych fell through and caught sight of the light, and it was revealed to him that though his life had not been what it should have been, this could still be rectified. He asked himself, "What *is* the right thing?" and grew still, listening. Then he felt that someone was kissing his hand. He opened his eyes, looked at his son, and felt sorry for him. His wife came up to him and he glanced at her. She was gazing at him open-mouthed, with undried tears on her nose and cheek and a despairing look on her face. He felt sorry for her too.

"Yes, I am making them wretched," he thought. "They are sorry, but it will be better for them when I die." He wished to say this but had not the strength to utter it. "Besides, why speak? I must act," he thought. With a look at his wife he indicated his son and said: "Take him away . . . sorry for him . . . sorry for you too. . . ." He tried to add, "forgive me," but said "forego" and waved his hand, knowing that He whose understanding mattered would understand.

And suddenly it grew clear to him that what had been oppressing him and would not leave him was all dropping away at once from two sides, from ten sides, and from all sides. He was sorry for them, he must act so as not to hurt them: release them and free himself from these sufferings. "How good and how simple!" he thought. "And the pain?" he asked himself. "What has become of it? Where are you, pain?"

He turned his attention to it.

"Yes, here it is. Well, what of it? Let the pain be."

355   "And death . . . where is it?"

He sought his former accustomed fear of death and did not find it. "Where is it? What death?" There was no fear because there was no death.

In place of death there was light.

"So that's what it is!" he suddenly exclaimed aloud. "What joy!"

To him all this happened in a single instant, and the meaning of that instant did not change. For those present his agony continued for another two hours. Something rattled in his throat, his emaciated body twitched, then the gasping and rattle became less and less frequent.

360   "It is finished!" said someone near him.

He heard these words and repeated them in his soul.

"Death is finished," he said to himself. "It is no more!"

He drew in a breath, stopped in the midst of a sigh, stretched out, and died.   [1886]

QUESTIONS

1. Why do you think Tolstoy elected to sacrifice suspense in favor of opening the story with the death of the hero?

2. What is the tone of the narrator, and how does it qualify the reader's view of Ivan's character?

3. Interpret the sentence, "Ivan Ilych's life had been most simple and most ordinary and therefore most terrible."
4. How does Gerasim serve as a foil to Ivan Ilych?
5. What does Ivan Ilych come to understand about the meaning of his life? Is he consoled? Redeemed?

RESPONSES

1. Research the life, philosophy, and influence of Leo Tolstoy. Write an essay exploring how this story could have influenced the politics and practices of Gandhi and Martin Luther King, Jr.
2. The Russian Revolution occurred only a few decades after this story was written. What ideas do you see dramatized in the story that may predict the coming revolution?

FOCUS ON FILM

1. *Ivan's XTC* adapts Tolstoy's story and sets the action in contemporary Hollywood. If you can acquire a copy of the film, which currently is not easily available in the United States, explain which features of the print story are emphasized in shifting the setting.
2. How does the film *Ivan's XTC* accommodate itself to the slow and deliberate pacing of Tolstoy's story?

JOHN UPDIKE

John Updike (b. 1932) was born in Shillington, Pennsylvania. Following graduation from Harvard, he studied for a year in London. Upon his return, he was employed by *The New Yorker* from 1955 to 1957. A prolific and versatile author, Updike writes novels, stories, poems, essays, and literary criticism. *The Centaur* (1963), his third novel, was awarded the National Book Award; *Rabbit Is Rich*, part of his "Rabbit" tetralogy, received the 1981 Pulitzer Prize; *Hugging the Shore* won the 1983 National Critics Circle Award for literary criticism. Updike published a new collection of criticism, *Odd Jobs*, in 1991, and *Afterlife and Other Stories* in 1994. Recent novels are *In the Beauty of the Lilies* (1996) and *Gertrude and Claudius* (2000).

A & P

In walks these three girls in nothing but bathing suits. I'm in the third checkout slot, with my back to the door, so I don't see them until they're over by the bread. The one that caught my eye first was the one in the plaid green two-piece. She was a chunky kid, with a good tan and a sweet broad soft-looking can with those two crescents of white just under it, where the sun never seems to hit, at the top of the backs of her legs. I stood there with my hand on a box of HiHo crackers trying to remember if I rang it up or not. I ring it up again and the customer starts giving me hell. She's one of these cash-register-watchers, a witch about fifty with rouge on her cheekbones and no eyebrows, and I know it made her day to trip me up. She'd been watching cash registers for fifty years and probably never seen a mistake before.

By the time I got her feathers smoothed and her goodies into a bag—she gives me a little snort in passing, if she'd been born at the right time they would have burned her over in Salem—by the time I get her on her way the girls had circled around the bread and were coming back, without a pushcart, back my way along the counters, in the aisle between the checkouts and the Special bins. They didn't even have shoes on. There was this chunky one, with the two-piece—it was bright green and the seams on the bra were still sharp and her belly was still pretty pale so I guessed she just got it (the suit)—there was this one, with one of those chubby berry-faces, the lips all bunched together under her nose, this one, and a tall one, with black hair that hadn't quite frizzed right, and one of these sunburns right across under the eyes, and a chin that

1110

was too long—you know, the kind of girl other girls think is very "striking" and "attractive" but never quite makes it, as they very well know, which is why they like her so much—and then the third one, that wasn't quite so tall. She was the queen. She kind of led them, the other two peeking around and making their shoulders round. She didn't look around, not this queen, she just walked straight on slowly, on these long white prima-donna legs. She came down a little hard on her heels, as if she didn't walk in her bare feet that much, putting down her heels and then letting the weight move along to her toes as if she was testing the floor with every step, putting a little deliberate extra action into it. You never know for sure how girls' minds work (do you really think it's a mind in there or just a little buzz like a bee in a glass jar?) but you got the idea she had talked the other two into coming in here with her, and now she was showing them how to do it, walk slow and hold yourself straight.

She had on a kind of dirty-pink—beige maybe, I don't know—bathing suit with a little nubble all over it and, what got me, the straps were down. They were off her shoulders looped loose around the cool tops of her arms, and I guess as a result the suit had slipped a little on her, so all around the top of the cloth there was this shining rim. If it hadn't been there you wouldn't have known there could have been anything whiter than those shoulders. With the straps pushed off, there was nothing between the top of the suit and the top of her head except just *her*, this clean bare plane of the top of her chest down from the shoulder bones like a dented sheet of metal tilted in the light. I mean, it was more than pretty.

She had sort of oaky hair that the sun and salt had bleached, done up in a bun that was unravelling, and a kind of prim face. Walking into the A & P with your straps down, I suppose it's the only kind of face you *can* have. She held her head so high her neck, coming up out of those white shoulders, looked kind of stretched, but I didn't mind. The longer her neck was, the more of her there was.

She must have felt in the corner of her eye me and over my shoulder Stokesie in the second slot watching, but she didn't tip. Not this queen. She kept her eyes moving across the racks, and stopped, and turned so slow it made my stomach rub the inside of my apron, and buzzed to the other two, who kind of huddled against her for relief, and then they all three of them went up the cat-and-dog-food-breakfast-cereal-macaroni-rice-raisins-seasonings-spreads-spaghetti-soft-drinks-crackers-and-cookies aisle. From the third slot I look straight up this aisle to the meat counter, and I watched them all the way. The fat one with the tan sort of fumbled with the cookies, but on second thought she put the package back. The sheep pushing their carts down the aisle—the girls were walking against the usual traffic (not that we have one-way signs or anything)—were pretty hilarious. You could see them, when Queenie's white shoulders dawned on them, kind of jerk, or hop, or hiccup, but their eyes snapped back to their own baskets and on they pushed. I bet you could set off dynamite in an A & P and the people would by and large keep reaching and checking oatmeal off their lists and muttering "Let me see, there was a third thing, began with A, asparagus, no, ah, yes, applesauce!" or whatever it is they do mutter. But there was no doubt, this jiggled them. A few houseslaves in pin curlers even looked around after pushing their carts past to make sure what they had seen was correct.

You know, it's one thing to have a girl in a bathing suit down on the beach, where what with the glare nobody can look at each other much anyway, and another thing in the cool of the A & P, under the fluorescent lights, against all those stacked packages, with her feet paddling along naked over our checkerboard green-and-cream rubber-tile floor.

"Oh Daddy," Stokesie said beside me. "I feel so faint."

5

"Darling," I said. "Hold me tight." Stokesie's married, with two babies chalked up on his fuselage already, but as far as I can tell that's the only difference. He's twenty-two, and I was nineteen this April.

"Is it done?" he asks, the responsible married man finding his voice. I forgot to say he thinks he's going to be manager some sunny day, maybe in 1990 when it's called the Great Alexandrov and Petrooshki Tea Company or something.

10   What he meant was, our town is five miles from a beach, with a big summer colony out on the Point, but we're right in the middle of town, and the women generally put on a shirt or shorts or something before they get out of the car into the street. And anyway these are usually women with six children and varicose veins mapping their legs and nobody, including them, could care less. As I say, we're right in the middle of town, and if you stand at our front doors you can see two banks and the Congregational church and the newspaper store and three real-estate offices and about twenty-seven old freeloaders tearing up Central Street because the sewer broke again. It's not as if we're on the Cape, we're north of Boston and there's people in this town haven't seen the ocean for twenty years.

The girls had reached the meat counter and were asking McMahon something. He pointed, they pointed, and they shuffled out of sight behind a pyramid of Diet Delight peaches. All that was left for us to see was old McMahon patting his mouth and looking after them sizing up their joints. Poor kids, I began to feel sorry for them, they couldn't help it.

Now here comes the sad part of the story, at least my family says it's sad, but I don't think it's so sad myself. The store's pretty empty, it being Thursday afternoon, so there was nothing much to do except lean on the register and wait for the girls to show up again. The whole store was like a pinball machine and I didn't know which tunnel they'd come out of. After a while they come around out of the far aisle, around the light bulbs, records at discount of the Caribbean Six or Tony Martin Sings or some such gunk you wonder they waste the wax on, sixpacks of candy bars, and plastic toys done up in cellophane that fall apart when a kid looks at them anyway. Around they come, Queenie still leading the way, and holding a little gray jar in her hand. Slots Three through Seven are unmanned and I could see her wondering between Stokes and me, but Stokesie with his usual luck draws an old party in baggy gray pants who stumbles up with four giant cans of pineapple juice (what do these bums *do* with all that pineapple juice? I've often asked myself). So the girls come to me. Queenie puts down the jar and I take it into my fingers icy cold. Kingfish Fancy Herring Snacks in Pure Sour Cream: 49¢. Now her hands are empty, not a ring or a bracelet, bare as God made them, and I wonder where the money's coming from. Still with that prim look she lifts a folded dollar bill out of the hollow at the center of her nubbled pink top. The jar went heavy in my hand. Really, I thought that was so cute.

Then everybody's luck begins to run out. Lengel comes in from haggling with a truck full of cabbages on the lot and is about to scuttle into that door marked MANAGER behind which he hides all day when the girls touch his eye. Lengel's pretty dreary, teaches Sunday school and the rest, but he doesn't miss that much. He comes over and says, "Girls, this isn't the beach."

Queenie blushes, though maybe it's just a brush of sunburn I was noticing for the first time, now that she was so close. "My mother asked me to pick up a jar of herring snacks." Her voice kind of startled me, the way voices do when you see the people first, coming out so flat and dumb yet kind of tony, too, the way it ticked over "pick up" and "snacks." All of a sudden I slid right down her voice into her living room. Her father and the other men were standing around in ice-cream coats and bow ties and the women were in sandals picking up herring snacks on toothpicks off a big glass plate and they were all holding drinks the color of water with olives and sprigs of mint in them. When my parents have somebody over they get lemonade and if it's a real racy affair Schlitz in tall glasses with "They'll Do It Every Time" cartoons stencilled on.

"That's all right," Lengel said. "But this isn't the beach." His repeating this struck me as funny, as if it had just occurred to him, and he had been thinking all these years the A & P was a great big dune and he was the head lifeguard. He didn't like my smiling—as I say he doesn't miss much—but he concentrates on giving the girls that sad Sunday-school-superintendent stare.

Queenie's blush is no sunburn now, and the plump one in plaid, that I liked better from the back—a really sweet can—pipes up, "We weren't doing any shopping. We just came in for the one thing."

"That makes no difference," Lengel tells her, and I could see from the way his eyes went that he hadn't noticed she was wearing a two-piece before. "We want you decently dressed when you come in here."

"We *are* decent," Queenie says suddenly, her lower lip pushing, getting sore now that she remembers her place, a place from which the crowd that runs the A & P must look pretty crummy. Fancy Herring Snacks flashed in her very blue eyes.

"Girls, I don't want to argue with you. After this come in here with your shoulders covered. It's our policy." He turns his back. That's policy for you. Policy is what the kingpins want. What the others want is juvenile delinquency.

All this while, the customers had been showing up with their carts but, you know, sheep, seeing a scene, they had all bunched up on Stokesie, who shook open a paper bag as gently as peeling a peach, not wanting to miss a word. I could feel in the silence everybody getting nervous, most of all Lengel, who asks me, "Sammy, have you rung up their purchase?"

I thought and said "No" but it wasn't about that I was thinking. I go through the punches, 4, 9, GROC, TOT—it's more complicated than you think, and after you do it often enough, it begins to make a little song, that you hear words to, in my case "Hello (*bing*) there, you (*gung*) hap-py *pee*-pul (*splat*)!"—the *splat* being the drawer flying out. I uncrease the bill, tenderly as you may imagine, it just having come from between the two smoothest scoops of vanilla I had ever known were there, and pass a half and a penny into her narrow pink palm, and nestle the herrings in a bag and twist its neck and hand it over, all the time thinking.

The girls, and who'd blame them, are in a hurry to get out, so I say "I quit" to Lengel quick enough for them to hear, hoping they'll stop and watch me, their unsuspected hero. They keep right on going, into the electric eye; the door flies open and they flicker across the lot to their car, Queenie and Plaid and Big Tall Goony-Goony (not that as raw material she was so bad), leaving me with Lengel and a kink in his eyebrow.

"Did you say something, Sammy?"

"I said I quit."

"I thought you did."

"You didn't have to embarrass them."

"It was they who were embarrassing us."

I started to say something that came out "Fiddle-de-doo." It's a saying of my grandmother's, and I know she would have been pleased.

"I don't think you know what you're saying," Lengel said.

"I know you don't," I said. "But I do." I pull the bow at the back of my apron and start shrugging it off my shoulders. A couple customers that had been heading for my slot begin to knock against each other, like scared pigs in a chute.

Lengel sighs and begins to look very patient and old and gray. He's been a friend of my parents for years. "Sammy, you don't want to do this to your Mom and Dad," he tells me. It's true, I don't. But it seems to me that once you begin a gesture it's fatal not to go through with it. I fold the apron, "Sammy" stitched in red on the pocket, and put it on the counter, and drop the bow tie on top of it. The bow tie is theirs, if you've ever wondered. "You'll feel this for the rest of your life," Lengel says, and I know that's true, too, but remembering how he made the pretty girl blush makes me so scrunchy inside I punch the No Sale tab and the machine whirs "pee-pul" and the drawer splats out. One advantage to this scene taking place in summer, I can follow this up with a clean exit, there's no fumbling around getting your coat and galoshes, I just saunter into the electric eye in my white shirt that my mother ironed the night before, and the door heaves itself open, and outside the sunshine is skating around on the asphalt.

I look around for my girls, but they're gone, of course. There wasn't anybody but some young married screaming with her children about some candy they didn't get by the door of a powder-blue Falcon station wagon. Looking back in the big windows, over the bags of peat moss and aluminum lawn furniture stacked on the pavement, I could see Lengel in my place in the slot, checking the sheep through. His face was dark gray and his back stiff, as if he'd just had an injection of iron, and my stomach kind of fell as I felt how hard the world was going to be to me hereafter.   [1962]

QUESTIONS

1. How aware is Sammy of his motives for quitting?
2. In any sense can the three girls be said to have provoked Sammy's gesture?
3. What might be the theme of this story if it were told from Lengel's point of view? From Stokesie's?
4. How is the title of the story related to the theme?
5. What do the figures of speech that Sammy uses tell about his attitude toward the A & P?

RESPONSES

1. Using the sociological/Marxist approach, explain what Updike's presentation says about money and middle-class values.
2. Is there any evidence that Sammy is male? Write an essay comparing two readings of the story, one with Sammy as male, the other with Sammy as female.
3. Over the past three decades, "A & P" has been a popular story in college classrooms. Can you make an argument, however, that "A & P" is too innocent a story for contemporary young adult audiences?

LUISA VALENZUELA

Luisa Valenzuela (b. 1938) was born in Buenos Aires, Argentina, and educated at the University of Buenos Aires. Her mother wrote short fiction, and Valenzuela grew up in a house where Argentina's most distinguished authors were frequent visitors. She wrote her first novel at twenty-one, and much of her work is political and controversial (e.g., *The Lizard's Tail*, 1983). Valenzuela has lived for extended periods in France, Mexico, and the United States, and has taught creative writing at New York University. *Bedside Manners* was published in English in 1995 (Spanish, 1990).

The Verb to Kill

He kills—he killed—he will kill—he has killed—he had killed—he will have killed—he would have killed—he is killing—he was killing—he has been killing—he would have been killing—he will have been killing—he will be killing—he would be killing—he may kill.

We decided that none of these tenses or moods suited him. Did he kill, will he kill, will he have killed? We think he *is* killing, with every step, with every breath, with every . . . We don't like him to get close to us but we come across him when we go clam-digging on the beach. We walk from north to south, and he comes from south to north, closer to the dunes, as if looking for pebbles. He looks at us and we look at him—did he kill, will he kill, would he have killed, is he killing? We put down the sack with the clams and hold each other's hand till he passes. He doesn't throw so much as one little pebble at us, he doesn't even look at us, but afterward we're too weak in the knees to go on digging clams.

The other day he walked by us and right afterward we found an injured sea gull on the beach. We took the poor thing home and on the way we told it that we were good, not like him, that it didn't have to be afraid of us, and we even covered it up with my jacket so the cold wind wouldn't hurt its broken wing. Later we ate it in a stew. A little tough, but tasty.

The next day we went back to run on the beach. We didn't see him and we didn't find a single injured sea gull. He may be bad, but he's got something that attracts animals. For example, when we were fishing: hours without a bite until he suddenly showed up and then we caught a splendid sea bass. He didn't look at our catch or smile, and it's good he didn't because he looked more like a murderer than ever with his long bushy hair and gleaming eyes. He just went on gathering his pebbles as though nothing were wrong, thinking about the girls that he has killed, will kill, kills.

5   When he passes by we're petrified—will it be our turn someday? In school we conjugate the verb *to kill* and the shiver that goes up our spine isn't the same as when we see him passing on the beach, all puffed up with pride and gathering his pebbles. The shiver on the beach is lower down in our bodies and more stimulating, like sea air. He gathers all those pebbles to cover up the graves of his victims— very small, transparent pebbles that he holds up to the sun and looks through from time to time so as to make certain that the sun exists. Mama says that if he spends all day looking for pebbles, it's because he *eats* them. Mama can't think about anything but food, but I'm sure he eats something else. The last breath of his victims, for example. There's nothing more nourishing than the last sigh, the one that brings with it everything that a person has gathered over the years. He must have some secret for trapping this essence that escapes his victims, and that's why he doesn't need vitamins. My sister and I are afraid he'll catch us some night and kill us to absorb everything that we've been eating over the last few years. We're terribly afraid because we're well nourished, Mama has always seen to it that we eat balanced meals and we've never lacked for fruit or vegetables even though they're very expensive in this part of the country. And clams have lots of iodine, Mama says, and fish are the healthiest food there is even though the taste of it bores us but why should he be bored because while he kills his victims (always girls, of course) he must do those terrible things to them that my sister and I keep imagining, just for fun. We spend hours talking about the things that he does to his victims before killing them just for fun. The papers often talk about degenerates like him but he's one of the worst because that's all he eats. The other day we spied on him while he was talking to the lettuce he has growing in his garden (he's crazy as well as degenerate). He was saying affectionate things to it and we were certain it was poisoned lettuce. For our part we don't say anything to lettuce, we have to eat it with oil and lemon even though it's disgusting, all because Mama says it has lots of vitamins. And now we have to swallow vitamins for him, what a bother, because the better fed we are the happier we'll make him and the more he'll like doing those terrible things the papers talk about and we imagine, just before killing us so as to gulp down our last breath full of vitamins in one big mouthful. He's going to do a whole bunch of things so repulsive we'll be ashamed to tell anybody, and we only say them in a whisper when we're on the beach and there's nobody within miles. He's going to take our last breath and then he'll be as strong as a bull to go kill other little girls like us. I hope he catches Pocha. But I hope he doesn't do any of those repulsive things to her before killing her because she might like it, the dirty thing. I hope he kills her straight away by plunging a knife in her belly. But he'll have his fun with us for a long time because we're pretty and he'll like our bodies and our voices when we scream. And we will scream and scream but nobody will hear us because he's going to take us to a place very far away and then he will put in our mouths that terrible thing we know he has. Pocha already told us about it—he must have an enormous thing that he uses to kill his victims.

An enormous one, even though we've never seen it. To show how brave we are, we tried to watch him while he made peepee, but he saw us and chased us away. I wonder why he didn't want to show it to us. Maybe it's because he wants to surprise us on our last day here and catch us while we're pure so's to get more pleasure. That must be it. He's saving himself for our last day and that's why he doesn't try to get close to us.

Not anymore.

Papa finally lent us the rifle after we asked and asked for it to hunt rabbits. He told us we were big girls now, that we can go out alone with the rifle if we want to, but to be careful, and he said it was a reward for doing so well in school. It's true we're doing well in school. It isn't hard at all to learn to conjugate verbs:

He will be killed—he is killed—he has been killed.   [1979]

QUESTIONS

1. What is achieved by having the story told by "we"?
2. Why do you think the author did not use dialogue?
3. What does it tell about these sisters that they link their action to conjugating a verb?
4. The author has succeeded in writing a story of intense atmosphere without the usual details of setting. How is this effect achieved?
5. Try to imagine the story from the victim's point of view.

RESPONSES

1. Compare this story to Cisneros's "Barbie-Q" or Kincaid's "Girl."
2. Write an essay arguing that this story is or is not a horror story.

HELENA MARÍA VIRAMONTES

Helena María Viramontes (b. 1954) was born in East Los Angeles. In 1988 she coedited *Chicana Creativity and Criticism: New Frontiers in American Literature* (revised edition, 1996). She published *The Moths and Other Stories* (1985) and novels, *Under the Feet of Jesus* (1995) and *Their Dogs Came with Them* (2000). She currently teaches at Cornell.

The Moths

I was fourteen years old when Abuelita° requested my help. And it seemed only fair. Abuelita had pulled me through the rages of scarlet fever by placing, removing and replacing potato slices on the temples of my forehead; she had seen me through several whippings, an arm broken by a dare jump off Tío Enrique's° toolshed, puberty, and my first lie. Really, I told Amá,° it was only fair.

Not that I was her favorite granddaughter or anything special. I wasn't even pretty or nice like my older sisters and I just couldn't do the girl things they could do. My hands were too big to handle the fineries of crocheting or embroidery and I always pricked my fingers or knotted my colored threads time and time again while my sisters laughed and called me bull hands with their cute waterlike voices. So I began keeping a piece of jagged brick in my sock to bash my sisters or anyone who called me bull hands. Once, while we all sat in the bedroom, I hit Teresa on the forehead, right above her eyebrow and she ran to Amá with her mouth open, her hand over her eye while blood seeped between her fingers. I was used to the whippings by then.

I wasn't respectful either. I even went so far as to doubt the power of Abuelita's slices, the slices she said absorbed my fever. "You're still alive, aren't you?" Abuelita snapped back, her pasty gray eye beaming at me and burning holes in my suspicions. Regretful that I had let secret questions drop out of my mouth, I couldn't look into her eyes. My hands began to fan out, grow like a liar's nose until they hung by my side like low weights. Abuelita made a balm out of dried moth wings and Vicks and rubbed my hands, shaped them back to size and it was the strangest feeling. Like

---

°*Abuelita*: Grandmother.
°*Tío Enrique*: Uncle Henry.
°*Amá*: Mama.

1118

bones melting. Like sun shining through the darkness of your eyelids. I didn't mind helping Abuelita after that, so Amá would always send me over to her.

In the early afternoon Amá would push her hair back, hand me my sweater and shoes, and tell me to go to Mama Luna's. This was to avoid another fight and another whipping, I knew. I would deliver one last direct shot on Marisela's arm and jump out of our house, the slam of the screen door burying her cries of anger, and I'd gladly go help Abuelita plant her wild lilies or jasmine or heliotrope or cilantro or hierbabuena in red Hills Brothers coffee cans. Abuelita would wait for me at the top step of her porch holding a hammer and nail and empty coffee cans. And although we hardly spoke, hardly looked at each other as we worked over root transplants, I always felt her gray eye on me. It made me feel, in a strange sort of way, safe and guarded and not alone. Like God was supposed to make you feel.

On Abuelita's porch, I would puncture holes in the bottom of the coffee cans with a nail and a precise hit of a hammer. This completed, my job was to fill them with red clay mud from beneath her rose bushes, packing it softly, then making a perfect hole, four fingers round, to nest a sprouting avocado pit, or the spidery sweet potatoes that Abuelita rooted in mayonnaise jars with toothpicks and daily water, or prickly chayotes that produced vines that twisted and wound all over her porch pillars, crawling to the roof, up and over the roof, and down the other side, making her small brick house look like it was cradled within the vines that grew pear-shaped squashes ready for the pick, ready to be steamed with onions and cheese and butter. The roots would burst out of the rusted coffee cans and search for a place to connect. I would then feed the seedlings with water. 5

But this was a different kind of help, Amá said, because Abuelita was dying. Looking into her gray eye, then into her brown one, the doctor said it was just a matter of days. And so it seemed only fair that these hands she had melted and formed found use in rubbing her caving body with alcohol and marihuana, rubbing her arms and legs, turning her face to the window so that she could watch the Bird of Paradise blooming or smell the scent of clove in the air. I toweled her face frequently and held her hand for hours. Her gray wiry hair hung over the mattress. Since I could remember, she'd kept her long hair in braids. Her mouth was vacant and when she slept, her eyelids never closed all the way. Up close, you could see her gray eye beaming out the window, staring hard as if to remember everything. I never kissed her. I left the window open when I went to the market.

Across the street from Jay's Market there was a chapel. I never knew its denomination, but I went in just the same to search for candles. I sat down on one of the pews because there were none. After I cleaned my fingernails, I looked up at the high ceiling. I had forgotten the vastness of these places, the coolness of the marble pillars and the frozen statues with blank eyes. I was alone. I knew why I had never returned.

That was one of Apá's° biggest complaints. He would pound his hands on the table, rocking the sugar dish or spilling a cup of coffee and scream that if I didn't go to mass every Sunday to save my god-damn sinning soul, then I had no reason to go out of the house, period. Punto final. He would grab my arm and dig his nails into me to make sure I understood the importance of catechism. Did he make himself clear? Then he strategically directed his anger at Amá for her lousy ways of bringing up daughters, being disrespectful and unbelieving, and my older sisters would pull me aside and tell

---

°*Apá*: Papa, Daddy (baby's word for father).

me if I didn't get to mass right this minute, they were all going to kick the holy shit out
of me. Why am I so selfish? Can't you see what it's doing to Amá, you idiot? So I would
wash my feet and stuff them in my black Easter shoes that shone with Vaseline, grab
a missal and veil, and wave good-bye to Amá.

I would walk slowly down Lorena to First to Evergreen, counting the cracks on the
cement. On Evergreen I would turn left and walk to Abuelita's. I liked her porch because it was shielded by the vines of the chayotes and I could get a good look at the
people and car traffic on Evergreen without them knowing. I would jump up the porch
steps, knock on the screen door as I wiped my feet and call Abuelita? mi Abuelita? As
I opened the door and stuck my head in, I would catch the gagging scent of toasting
chile on the placa. When I entered the sala, she would greet me from the kitchen, wringing her hands in her apron. I'd sit at the corner of the table to keep from being in her
way. The chiles made my eyes water. Am I crying? No, Mama Luna, I'm sure not crying. I don't like going to mass, but my eyes watered anyway, the tears dropping on the
tablecloth like candle wax. Abuelita lifted the burnt chiles from the fire and sprinkled
water on them until the skins began to separate. Placing them in front of me, she turned
to check the menudo. I peeled the skins off and put the flimsy, limp looking green and
yellow chiles in the molcajete and began to crush and crush and twist and crush the
heart out of the tomato, the clove of garlic, the stupid chiles that made me cry, crushed
them until they turned into liquid under my bull hand. With a wooden spoon, I scraped
hard to destroy the guilt, and my tears were gone. I put the bowl of chile next to a vase
filled with freshly cut roses. Abuelita touched my hand and pointed to the bowl of
menudo that steamed in front of me. I spooned some chile into the menudo and rolled
a corn tortilla thin with the palms of my hands. As I ate, a fine Sunday breeze entered
the kitchen and a rose petal calmly feathered down to the table.

10   I left the chapel without blessing myself and walked to Jay's. Most of the time Jay
didn't have much of anything. The tomatoes were always soft and the cans of Campbell soups had rusted spots on them. There was dust on the tops of cereal boxes. I
picked up what I needed: rubbing alcohol, five cans of chicken broth, a big bottle of
Pine Sol. At first Jay got mad because I thought I had forgotten the money. But it was
there all the time, in my back pocket.

When I returned from the market, I heard Amá crying in Abuelita's kitchen. She
looked up at me with puffy eyes. I placed the bags of groceries on the table and began
putting the cans of soup away. Amá sobbed quietly. I never kissed her. After a while,
I patted her on the back for comfort. Finally: "¿Y mi Amá?" she asked in a whisper, then
choked again and cried into her apron.

Abuelita fell off the bed twice yesterday, I said, knowing that I shouldn't have said
it and wondering why I wanted to say it because it only made Amá cry harder. I guess
I became angry and just so tired of the quarrels and beatings and unanswered prayers
and my hands just there hanging helplessly by my side. Amá looked at me again, confused, angry, and her eyes were filled with sorrow. I went outside and sat on the porch
swing and watched the people pass. I sat there until she left. I dozed off repeating the
words to myself like rosary prayers: when do you stop giving when do you start giving when do you . . . and when my hands fell from my lap, I awoke to catch them. The
sun was setting, an orange glow, and I knew Abuelita was hungry.

There comes a time when the sun is defiant. Just about the time when moods
change, inevitable seasons of a day, transitions from one color to another, that hour
or minute or second when the sun is finally defeated, finally sinks into the realization that it cannot with all its power to heal or burn, exist forever, there comes an illumination where the sun and earth meet, a final burst of burning red orange fury

reminding us that although endings are inevitable, they are necessary for rebirths, and when that time came, just when I switched on the light in the kitchen to open Abuelita's can of soup, it was probably then that she died.

The room smelled of Pine Sol and vomit and Abuelita had defecated the remains of her cancerous stomach. She had turned to the window and tried to speak, but her mouth remained open and speechless. I heard you, Abuelita, I said, stroking her cheek, I heard you. I opened the windows of the house and let the soup simmer and overboil on the stove. I turned the stove off and poured the soup down the sink. From the cabinet I got a tin basin, filled it with lukewarm water and carried it carefully to the room. I went to the linen closet and took out some modest bleached white towels. With the sacredness of a priest preparing his vestments, I unfolded the towels one by one on my shoulders. I removed the sheets and blankets from her bed and peeled off her thick flannel night-gown. I toweled her puzzled face, stretching out the wrinkles, removing the coils of her neck, toweled her shoulders and breasts. Then I changed the water. I returned to towel the creases of her stretch-marked stomach, her sporadic vaginal hairs, and her sag-ging thighs. I removed the lint from between her toes and noticed a mapped birthmark on the fold of her buttock. The scars on her back which were as thin as the life lines on the palms of her hands made me realize how little I really knew of Abuelita. I covered her with a thin blanket and went into the bathroom. I washed my hands, and turned on the tub faucets and watched the water pour into the tub with vitality and steam. When it was full, I turned off the water and undressed. Then, I went to get Abuelita.

She was not as heavy as I thought and when I carried her in my arms, her body fell   15
into a V, and yet my legs were tired, shaky, and I felt as if the distance between the bed-room and bathroom was miles and years away. Amá, where are you?

I stepped into the bathtub one leg first, then the other. I bent my knees slowly to de-scend into the water slowly so I wouldn't scald her skin. There, there, Abuelita, I said, cradling her, smoothing her as we descended, I heard you. Her hair fell back and spread across the water like eagle's wings. The water in the tub overflowed and poured onto the tile of the floor. Then the moths came. Small, gray ones that came from her soul and out through her mouth fluttering to light, circling the single dull light bulb of the bath-room. Dying is lonely and I wanted to go to where the moths were, stay with her and plant chayotes whose vines would crawl up her fingers and into the clouds; I wanted to rest my head on her chest with her stroking my hair, telling me about the moths that lay within the soul and slowly eat the spirit up; I wanted to return to the waters of the womb with her so that we would never be alone again. I wanted. I wanted my Amá. I removed a few strands of hair from Abuelita's face and held her small light head with-in the hollow of my neck. The bathroom was filled with moths, and for the first time in a long time I cried, rocking us, crying for her, for me, for Amá, the sobs emerging from the depths of anguish, the misery of feeling half born, sobbing until finally the sobs rip-pled into circles and circles of sadness and relief. There, there, I said to Abuelita, rock-ing us gently, there, there.   [c. 1985]

QUESTIONS

1. Does the narrator's bad behavior make her a more or a less interesting char-acter? Why?

2. If you do not already know them, look at pictures of the plants and food men-tioned in this story; read descriptions of their smells, tastes, and uses. Does having this knowledge make Mama Luna's house and garden easier to see?

3. What denomination does the chapel seem to be? What explanation in the text reveals why the narrator "never returned"?

4. Viramontes does not have her narrator tell the story in a straight and unbending line. What is the effect of her shifts in chronology? Can you see a purpose in telling a story this way?

5. Is this a love story or a coming-of-age story? Of course, a story can be both, but which theme is the stronger?

RESPONSES

1. Write an essay comparing Helena María Viramontes's story either to "Barbie-Q" by Sandra Cisneros or to "To Hell with Dying" by Alice Walker.

2. Compare how Viramontes handles the perspective of a young girl with how Mary Lavin does so in "My Vocation."

ALICE WALKER

Alice Walker (b. 1944) was born in Eatonton, Georgia, the eighth child of sharecroppers. She attended Spelman College, Atlanta, but received her degree from Sarah Lawrence (1965). She worked with the civil rights movement and taught at Jackson State University, Mississippi. Walker has written novels, poetry, short stories, essays, and a children's biography of Langston Hughes (1974). *The Color Purple*, one of her novels, won the American Book Award and the Pulitzer Prize (1982). An eclectic group of her essays, *In Search of Our Mothers' Gardens*, appeared in 1983. She co-authored *Warrior Marks: Female Genital Mutilation* (1993); her novel *Possessing the Secret of Joy* (1992) is on the same subject. *The Complete Stories* was published in 1994. *The Way Forward Is with a Broken Heart* appeared in 2000, and *Now Is the Time to Open Your Heart* appeared in 2004.

Roselily

Dearly Beloved,

She dreams; dragging herself across the world. A small girl in her mother's white robe and veil, knee raised waist high through a bowl of quicksand soup. The man who stands beside her is against this standing on the front porch of her house, being married to the sound of cars whizzing by on highway 61.

we are gathered here

Like cotton to be weighed. Her fingers at the last minute busily removing dry leaves and twigs. Aware it is a superficial sweep. She knows he blames Mississippi for the respectful way the men turn their heads up in the yard, the women stand waiting and knowledgeable, their children held from mischief by teachings from the wrong God. He glares beyond them to the occupants of the cars, white faces glued to promises beyond a country wedding, noses thrust forward like dogs on a track. For him they usurp the wedding.

in the sight of God

Yes, open house. That is what country black folks like. She dreams she does not already have three children. A squeeze around the flowers in her hands chokes off three and four and five years of breath. Instantly she is ashamed and frightened in her superstition. She looks for the first time at the preacher, forces humility into her eyes, as if she believes he is, in fact, a man of God. She can imagine God, a small black boy, timidly pulling the preacher's coattail.

to join this man and this woman

She thinks of ropes, chains, handcuffs, his religion. His place of worship. Where she will be required to sit apart with covered head. In Chicago, a word she hears when thinking of smoke, from his description of what a cinder was, which they never had in Panther Burn. She sees hovering over the heads of the clean neighbors in her front yard black specks falling, clinging, from the sky. But in Chicago. Respect, a chance to build. Her children at last from underneath the detrimental wheel. A chance to be on top. What a relief, she thinks. What a vision, a view, from up so high.

in holy matrimony.

10   Her fourth child she gave away to the child's father who had some money. Certainly a good job. Had gone to Harvard. Was a good man but weak because good language meant so much to him he could not live with Roselily. Could not abide TV in the living room, five beds in three rooms, no Bach except from four to six on Sunday afternoons. No chess at all. She does not forget to worry about her son among his father's people. She wonders if the New England climate will agree with him. If he will ever come down to Mississippi, as his father did, to try to right the country's wrongs. She wonders if he will be stronger than his father. His father cried off and on throughout her pregnancy. Went to skin and bones. Suffered nightmares, retching and falling out of bed. Tried to kill himself. Later told his wife he found the right baby through friends. Vouched for, the sterling qualities that would make up his character.

It is not her nature to blame. Still, she is not entirely thankful. She supposes New England, the North, to be quite different from what she knows. It seems right somehow to her that people who move there to live return home completely changed. She thinks of the air, the smoke, the cinders. Imagines cinders big as hailstones; heavy, weighing on the people. Wonders how this pressure finds its way into the veins, roping the springs of laughter.

If there's anybody here that knows a reason why

But of course they know no reason why beyond what they daily have come to know. She thinks of the man who will be her husband, feels shut away from him because of the stiff severity of his plain black suit. His religion. A lifetime of black and white. Of veils. Covered head. It is as if her children are already gone from her. Not dead, but exalted on a pedestal, a stalk that has no roots. She wonders how to make new roots. It is beyond her. She wonders what one does with memories in a brand-new life. This had seemed easy, until she thought of it. "The reasons why . . . the people who" . . . she thinks, and does not wonder where the thought is from.

these two should not be joined

She thinks of her mother, who is dead. Dead, but still her mother. Joined. This is con- 15
fusing. Of her father. A gray old man who sold wild mink, rabbit, fox skins to Sears,
Roebuck. He stands in the yard, like a man waiting for a train. Her young sisters stand
behind her in smooth green dresses, with flowers in their hands and hair. They giggle,
she feels, at the absurdity of the wedding. They are ready for something new. She
thinks the man beside her should marry one of them. She feels old. Yoked. An arm
seems to reach out from behind her and snatch her backward. She thinks of cemeteries and the long sleep of grandparents mingling in the dirt. She believes that she believes in ghosts. In the soil giving back what it takes.

together,

In the city. He sees her in a new way. This she knows, and is grateful. But is it new
enough? She cannot always be a bride and virgin, wearing robes and veil. Even now
her body itches to be free of satin and voile, organdy and lily of the valley. Memories
crash against her. Memories of being bare to the sun. She wonders what it will be like.
Not to have to go to a job. Not to work in a sewing plant. Not to worry about learning
to sew straight seams in workingmen's overalls, jeans, and dress pants. Her place will
be in the home, he has said, repeatedly, promising her rest she had prayed for. But
now she wonders. When she is rested, what will she do? They will make babies—she
thinks practically about her fine brown body, his strong black one. They will be inevitable. Her hands will be full. Full of what? Babies. She is not comforted.

let him speak

She wishes she had asked him to explain more of what he meant. But she was impatient. Impatient to be done with sewing. With doing everything for three children,
alone. Impatient to leave the girls she had known since childhood, their children growing up, their husbands hanging around her, already old, seedy. Nothing about them
that she wanted, or needed. The fathers of her children driving by, waving, not waving; reminders of times she would just as soon forget. Impatient to see the South Side,
where they would live and build and be respectable and respected and free. Her husband would free her. A romantic hush. Proposal. Promises. A new life! Respectable, reclaimed, renewed. Free! In robe and veil.

or forever hold 20

She does not even know if she loves him. She loves his sobriety. His refusal to sing
just because he knows the tune. She loves his pride. His blackness and his gray car. She
loves his understanding of her *condition*. She thinks she loves the effort he will make
to redo her into what he truly wants. His love of her makes her completely conscious
of how unloved she was before. This is something; though it makes her unbearably sad.
Melancholy. She blinks her eyes. Remembers she is finally being married, like other
girls. Like other girls, women? Something strains upward behind her eyes. She thinks
of the something as a rat trapped, cornered, scurrying to and fro in her head, peering
through the windows of her eyes. She wants to live for once. But doesn't know quite
what that means. Wonders if she has ever done it. If she ever will. The preacher is odious to her. She wants to strike him out of the way, out of her light, with the back of her
hand. It seems to her he has always been standing in front of her, barring her way.

his peace.

The rest she does not hear. She feels a kiss, passionate, rousing, within the general pandemonium. Cars drive up blowing their horns. Firecrackers go off. Dogs come from under the house and begin to yelp and bark. Her husband's hand is like the clasp of an iron gate. People congratulate. Her children press against her. They look with awe and distaste mixed with hope at their new father. He stands curiously apart, in spite of the people crowding about to grasp his free hand. He smiles at them all but his eyes are as if turned inward. He knows they cannot understand that he is not a Christian. He will not explain himself. He feels different, he looks it. The old women thought he was like one of their sons except that he had somehow got away from them. Still a son, not a son. Changed.

She thinks how it will be later in the night in the silvery gray car. How they will spin through the darkness of Mississippi and in the morning be in Chicago, Illinois. She thinks of Lincoln, the president. That is all she knows about the place. She feels ignorant, *wrong*, backward. She presses her worried fingers into his palm. He is standing in front of her. In the crush of well-wishing people, he does not look back.   [1972]

QUESTIONS

1. Is there special significance in the name of the eponymous character?
2. How does the story both employ and challenge the conventions of prose fiction?
3. How does Roselily's language, especially her use of simile and metaphor, reveal her character?
4. What does Chicago symbolize to Roselily?
5. Interpret the last sentence.

RESPONSES

1. Compare Walker's use of point of view to Virginia Woolf's in "Kew Gardens."
2. Compare the protagonist's experiences and concerns to those of the protagonist in Silko's "Lullaby."

ALICE WALKER

To Hell with Dying

"To hell with dying," my father would say. "These children want Mr. Sweet!"

Mr. Sweet was a diabetic and an alcoholic and a guitar player and lived down the road from us on a neglected cotton farm. My older brothers and sisters got the most benefit from Mr. Sweet, for when they were growing up he had quite a few years ahead of him and so was capable of being called back from the brink of death any number of times—whenever the voice of my father reached him as he lay expiring. "To hell with dying, man," my father would say, pushing the wife away from the bedside (in tears although she knew the death was not necessarily the last one unless Mr. Sweet really wanted it to be). "These children want Mr. Sweet!" And they did want him, for at a signal from Father they would come crowding around the bed and throw themselves on the covers, and whoever was the smallest at the time would kiss him all over his wrinkled brown face and tickle him so that he would laugh all down in his stomach, and his mustache, which was long and sort of straggly, would shake like Spanish moss and was also that color.

Mr. Sweet had been ambitious as a boy, wanted to be a doctor or lawyer or sailor, only to find that black men fare better if they are not. Since he could become none of these things he turned to fishing as his only earnest career and playing the guitar as his only claim to doing anything extraordinarily well. His son, the only one that he and his wife, Miss Mary, had, was shiftless as the day is long and spent money as if he were trying to see the bottom of the mint, which Mr. Sweet would tell him was the clean brown palm of his hand. Miss Mary loved her "baby," however, and worked hard to get him the "li'l necessaries" of life, which turned out mostly to be women.

Mr. Sweet was a tall, thinnish man with thick kinky hair going dead white. He was dark brown, his eyes were squinty and sort of bluish, and he chewed Brown Mule tobacco. He was constantly on the verge of being blind drunk, for he brewed his own liquor and was not in the least a stingy sort of man, and was always very melancholy and sad, though frequently when he was "feelin' good" he'd dance around the yard with us, usually keeling over just as my mother came to see what the commotion was.

Toward all of us children he was very kind, and had the grace to be shy with us, which is unusual in grown-ups. He had great respect for my mother for she never held his drunkenness against him and would let us play with him even when he was about to fall in the fireplace from drink. Although Mr. Sweet would sometimes lose complete or nearly complete control of his head and neck so that he would loll in his chair,

5

his mind remained strangely acute and his speech not too affected. His ability to be drunk and sober at the same time made him an ideal playmate, for he was as weak as we were and we could usually best him in wrestling, all the while keeping a fairly coherent conversation going.

We never felt anything of Mr. Sweet's age when we played with him. We loved his wrinkles and would draw some on our brows to be like him, and his white hair was my special treasure and he knew it and would never come to visit us just after he had had his hair cut off at the barbershop. Once he came to our house for something, probably to see my father about fertilizer for his crops because, although he never paid the slightest attention to his crops, he liked to know what things would be best to use on them if he ever did. Anyhow, he had not come with his hair since he had just had it shaved off at the barbershop. He wore a huge straw hat to keep off the sun and also to keep his head away from me. But as soon as I saw him I ran up and demanded that he take me up and kiss me with his funny beard which smelled so strongly of tobacco. Looking forward to burying my small fingers into his woolly hair I threw away his hat only to find he had done something to his hair, that it was no longer there! I let out a squall which made my mother think that Mr. Sweet had finally dropped me in the well or something and from that day I've been wary of men in hats. However, not long after, Mr. Sweet showed up with his hair grown out and just as white and kinky and impenetrable as it ever was.

Mr. Sweet used to call me his princess, and I believed it. He made me feel pretty at five and six, and simply outrageously devastating at the blazing age of eight and a half. When he came to our house with his guitar the whole family would stop whatever they were doing to sit around him and listen to him play. He liked to play "Sweet Georgia Brown," that was what he called me sometimes, and also he liked to play "Caldonia" and all sorts of sweet, sad, wonderful songs which he sometimes made up. It was from one of these songs that I heard that he had had to marry Miss Mary when he had in fact loved somebody else (now living in Chi-ca-go, or De-stroy, Michigan). He was not sure that Joe Lee, her "baby," was also his baby. Sometimes he would cry and that was an indication that he was about to die again. And so we would all get prepared, for we were sure to be called upon.

I was seven the first time I remember actually participating in one of Mr. Sweet's "revivals"—my parents told me I had participated before, I had been the one chosen to kiss him and tickle him long before I knew the rite of Mr. Sweet's rehabilitation. He had come to our house, it was a few years after his wife's death, and was very sad, and also, typically, very drunk. He sat on the floor next to me and my older brother, the rest of the children were grown up and lived elsewhere, and began to play his guitar and cry. I held his woolly head in my arms and wished I could have been old enough to have been the woman he loved so much and that I had not been lost years and years ago.

When he was leaving, my mother said to us that we'd better sleep light that night for we'd probably have to go over to Mr. Sweet's before daylight. And we did. For soon after we had gone to bed one of the neighbors knocked on our door and called my father and said that Mr. Sweet was sinking fast and if he wanted to get in a word before the crossover he'd better shake a leg and get over to Mr. Sweet's house. All the neighbors knew to come to our house if something was wrong with Mr. Sweet, but they did not know how we always managed to make him well, or at least stop him from dying, when he was so often near death. As soon as we heard the cry we got up, my brother and I and my mother and father, and put on our clothes. We hurried out of the house and down the road for we were always afraid that we might someday be too late and Mr. Sweet would get tired of dallying.

When we got to the house, a very poor shack really, we found the front room full of neighbors and relatives and someone met us at the door and said it was all very sad that old Mr. Sweet Little (for Little was his family name, although we mostly ignored it) was about to kick the bucket. My parents were advised not to take my brother and me into the "death room," seeing we were so young and all, but we were so much more accustomed to the death room than he that we ignored him and dashed in without giving his warning a second thought. I was almost in tears, for these deaths upset me fearfully, and the thought of how much depended on me and my brother (who was such a ham most of the time) made me very nervous.

The doctor was bending over the bed and turned back to tell us for at least the tenth time in the history of my family that, alas, old Mr. Sweet Little was dying and that the children had best not see the face of implacable death (I didn't know what "implacable" was, but whatever it was, Mr. Sweet was not!). My father pushed him rather abruptly out of the way saying, as he always did and very loudly for he was saying it to Mr. Sweet, "To hell with dying, man, these children want Mr. Sweet"—which was my cue to throw myself upon the bed and kiss Mr. Sweet all around the whiskers and under the eyes and around the collar of his nightshirt where he smelled so strongly of all sorts of things, mostly liniment.

I was very good at bringing him around, for as soon as I saw that he was struggling to open his eyes I knew he was going to be all right, and so could finish my revival sure of success. As soon as his eyes were open he would begin to smile and that way I knew that I had surely won. Once, though, I got a tremendous scare, for he could not open his eyes and later I learned that he had had a stroke and that one side of his face was stiff and hard to get into motion. When he began to smile I could tickle him in earnest because I was sure that nothing would get in the way of his laughter, although once he began to cough so hard that he almost threw me off his stomach, but that was when I was very small, little more than a baby, and my bushy hair had gotten in his nose.

When we were sure he would listen to us we would ask him why he was in bed and when he was coming to see us again and could we play his guitar, which more than likely would be leaning against the bed. His eyes would get all misty and he would sometimes cry out loud, but we never let it embarrass us, for he knew that we loved him and that we sometimes cried too for no reason. My parents would leave the room to just the three of us; Mr. Sweet, by that time, would be propped up in bed with a number of pillows behind his head and with me sitting and lying on his shoulder and along his chest. Even when he had trouble breathing he would not ask me to get down. Looking into my eyes he would shake his white head and run a scratchy old finger all around my hairline, which was rather low down, nearly to my eyebrows, and made some people say I looked like a baby monkey.

My brother was very generous in all this, he let me do all the revivaling—he had done it for years before I was born and so was glad to be able to pass it on to someone new. What he would do while I talked to Mr. Sweet was pretend to play the guitar, in fact pretend that he was a young version of Mr. Sweet, and it always made Mr. Sweet glad to think that someone wanted to be like him—of course, we did not know this then, we played the thing by ear, and whatever he seemed to like, we did. We were desperately afraid that he was just going to take off one day and leave us.

It did not occur to us that we were doing anything special; we had not learned that death was final when it did come. We thought nothing of triumphing over it so many times, and in fact became a trifle contemptuous of people who let themselves be carried away. It did not occur to us that if our father had been dying we could not have stopped it, that Mr. Sweet was the only person over whom we had power.

When Mr. Sweet was in his eighties I was studying in the university many miles from home. I saw him whenever I went home, but he was never on the verge of dying that I could tell and I began to feel that my anxiety for his health and psychological well-being was unnecessary. By this time he not only had a mustache but a long flowing snow-white beard, which I loved and combed and braided for hours. He was very peaceful, fragile, gentle, and the only jarring note about him was his old steel guitar, which he still played in the old sad, sweet, down-home blues way.

On Mr. Sweet's ninetieth birthday I was finishing my doctorate in Massachusetts and had been making arrangements to go home for several weeks' rest. That morning I got a telegram telling me that Mr. Sweet was dying again and could I please drop everything and come home. Of course I could. My dissertation could wait and my teachers would understand when I explained to them when I got back. I ran to the phone, called the airport, and within four hours I was speeding along the dusty road to Mr. Sweet's.

The house was more dilapidated than when I was last there, barely a shack, but it was overgrown with yellow roses which my family had planted many years ago. The air was heavy and sweet and very peaceful. I felt strange walking through the gate and up the old rickety steps. But the strangeness left me as I caught sight of the long white beard I loved so well flowing down the thin body over the familiar quilt coverlet. Mr. Sweet!

His eyes were closed tight and his hands, crossed over his stomach, were thin and delicate, no longer scratchy. I remembered how always before I had run and jumped up on him just anywhere; now I knew he would not be able to support my weight. I looked around at my parents, and was surprised to see that my father and mother also looked old and frail. My father, his own hair very gray, leaned over the quietly sleeping old man, who, incidentally, smelled still of wine and tobacco, and said, as he'd done so many times, "To hell with dying, man! My daughter is home to see Mr. Sweet!" My brother had not been able to come as he was in the war in Asia. I bent down and gently stroked the closed eyes and gradually they began to open. The closed, wine-stained lips twitched a little, then parted in a warm, slightly embarrassed smile. Mr. Sweet could see me and he recognized me and his eyes looked very spry and twinkly for a moment. I put my head down on the pillow next to his and we just looked at each other for a long time. Then he began to trace my peculiar hairline with a thin, smooth finger. I closed my eyes when his finger halted above my ear (he used to rejoice at the dirt in my ears when I was little), his hand stayed cupped around my cheek. When I opened my eyes, sure that I had reached him in time, his were closed.

20   Even at twenty-four how could I believe that I had failed? that Mr. Sweet was really gone? He had never gone before. But when I looked at my parents I saw that they were holding back tears. They had loved him dearly. He was like a piece of rare and delicate china which was always being saved from breaking and which finally fell. I looked long at the old face, the wrinkled forehead, the red lips, the hands that still reached out to me. Soon I felt my father pushing something cool into my hands. It was Mr. Sweet's guitar. He had asked them months before to give it to me; he had known that even if I came next time he would not be able to respond in the old way. He did not want me to feel that my trip had been for nothing.

The old guitar! I plucked the strings, hummed "Sweet Georgia Brown." The magic of Mr. Sweet lingered still in the cool steel box. Through the window I could catch the fragrant delicate scent of tender yellow roses. The man on the high old-fashioned bed with the quilt coverlet and the flowing white beard had been my first love.   [1967]

QUESTIONS

1. Trace the changes in the narrator during the course of the story. Does the point of view change? Does the language?
2. In what sense did the narrator's brothers and sisters get the most "benefit" from Mr. Sweet? Is the observation ironical?
3. What are the implications of characterizing Mr. Sweet as a "diabetic and an alcoholic and a guitar player . . ."? Why is he so appealing to children?
4. How do the minor characters function in the story?
5. How does her relationship to Mr. Sweet help the narrator to clarify her attitudes toward both life and death? In what sense is Mr. Sweet her "first love"?

RESPONSES

1. Read Walker's account of writing this story, "The Old Artist: Notes on Mr. Sweet," included in the "Context: Writers on Writing" section. What does that account add to your understanding of the story?
2. Look at several stories set in or related to the South; for instance, look at works by Dorothy Allison, William Faulkner, Flannery O'Connor, Eudora Welty, or Richard Wright. What kind of place is Walker's South and how does it compare to the South of other writers?

ALICE WALKER

The Welcome Table

FOR SISTER CLARA WARD

> *I'm going to sit at the Welcome table*
> *Shout my troubles over*
> *Walk and talk with Jesus*
> *Tell God how you treat me*
> *One of these days!*
>
> —*Spiritual*

The old woman stood with eyes uplifted in her Sunday-go-to-meeting clothes: high shoes polished about the tops and toes, a long rusty dress adorned with an old corsage, long withered, and the remnants of an elegant silk scarf as headrag stained with grease from the many oily pigtails underneath. Perhaps she had known suffering. There was a dazed and sleepy look in her aged blue-brown eyes. But for those who searched hastily for "reasons" in that old tight face, shut now like an ancient door, there was nothing to be read. And so they gazed nakedly upon their own fear transferred; a fear of the black and the old, a terror of the unknown as well as of the deeply known. Some of those who saw her there on the church steps spoke words about her that were hardly fit to be heard, others held their pious peace; and some felt vague stirrings of pity, small and persistent and hazy, as if she were an old collie turned out to die.

She was angular and lean and the color of poor gray Georgia earth, beaten by king cotton and the extreme weather. Her elbows were wrinkled and thick, the skin ashen but durable, like the bark of old pines. On her face centuries were folded into the circles around one eye, while around the other, etched and mapped as if for print, ages more threatened again to live. Some of them there at the church saw the age, the dotage, the missing buttons down the front of her mildewed black dress. Others saw cooks, chauffeurs, maids, mistresses, children denied or smothered in the deferential way she held her cheek to the side, toward the ground. Many of them saw jungle orgies in an evil place, while others were reminded of riotous anarchists looting and raping in the streets. Those who knew the hesitant creeping up on them of the law, saw the beginning of the end of the sanctuary of Christian worship, saw the desecration of Holy Church, and saw an invasion of privacy, which they struggled to believe they still kept.

Still she had come down the road toward the big white church alone. Just herself, an old forgetful woman, nearly blind with age. Just her and her eyes raised dully to the glittering cross that crowned the sheer silver steeple. She had walked along the road in a stagger from her house a half mile away. Perspiration, cold and clammy, stood on her brow and along the creases by her thin wasted nose. She stopped to calm herself on the wide front steps, not looking about her as they might have expected her to do, but simply standing quite still, except for a slight quivering of her throat and tremors that shook her cotton-stockinged legs.

The reverend of the church stopped her pleasantly as she stepped into the vestibule. Did he say, as they thought he did, kindly, "Auntie, you know this is not your church?" As if one could choose the wrong one. But no one remembers, for they never spoke of it afterward, and she brushed past him anyway, as if she had been brushing past him all her life, except this time she was in a hurry. Inside the church she sat on the very first bench from the back, gazing with concentration at the stained-glass window over her head. It was cold, even inside the church, and she was shivering. Everybody could see. They stared at her as they came in and sat down near the front. It was cold, very cold to them, too; outside the church it was below freezing and not much above inside. But the sight of her, sitting there somehow passionately ignoring them, brought them up short, burning.

The young usher, never having turned anyone out of his church before, but not   5
even considering this job as *that* (after all, she had no right to be there, certainly), went up to her and whispered that she should leave. Did he call her "Grandma," as later he seemed to recall he had? But for those who actually hear such traditional pleasantries and to whom they actually mean something, "Grandma" was not one, for she did not pay him any attention, just muttered, "Go 'way," in a weak sharp *bothered* voice, waving his frozen blond hair and eyes from near her face.

It was the ladies who finally did what to them had to be done. Daring their burly indecisive husbands to throw the old colored woman out they made their point. God, mother, country, earth, church. It involved all that, and well they knew it. Leather bagged and shoed, with good calfskin gloves to keep out the cold, they looked with contempt at the bloodless gray arthritic hands of the old woman, clenched loosely, restlessly in her lap. Could their husbands expect them to sit up in church with *that*? No, no, the husbands were quick to answer and even quicker to do their duty.

Under the old woman's arms they placed their hard fists (which afterward smelled of decay and musk—the fermenting scent of onionskins and rotting greens). Under the old woman's arms they raised their fists, flexed their muscular shoulders, and out she flew through the door, back under the cold blue sky. This done, the wives folded their healthy arms across their trim middles and felt at once justified and scornful. But none of them said so, for none of them ever spoke of the incident again. Inside the church it was warmer. They sang, they prayed. The protection and promise of God's impartial love grew more not less desirable as the sermon gathered fury and lashed itself out above their penitent heads.

The old woman stood at the top of the steps looking about in bewilderment. She had been singing in her head. They had interrupted her. Promptly she began to sing again, though this time a sad song. Suddenly, however, she looked down the long gray highway and saw something interesting and delightful coming. She started to grin, toothlessly, with short giggles of joy, jumping about and slapping her hands on her knees. And soon it became apparent why she was so happy. For coming down the highway at a firm though leisurely pace was Jesus. He was wearing an immaculate white, long dress trimmed in gold around the neck and hem, and a red, a bright red, cape. Over his left arm he carried a brilliant blue blanket. He was wearing sandals and a beard and he had long brown hair parted on the right side. His eyes, brown, had wrinkles around them as if he smiled or looked at the sun a lot. She would have known him, recognized him, anywhere. There was a sad but joyful look to his face, like a candle was glowing behind it, and he walked with sure even steps in her direction, as if he were walking on the sea. Except that he was not carrying in his arms a baby sheep, he looked exactly like the picture of him that she had hanging over her bed at home. She had taken it out of a white lady's Bible while she was working for her. She had looked at that picture for more years than she could remember, but never once had she really expected to see him. She squinted her eyes to be sure he wasn't carrying a little sheep in one arm, but he was not. Ecstatically she began to wave her arms for fear he would miss seeing her, for he walked looking straight ahead on the shoulder of the highway, and from time to time looking upward at the sky.

All he said when he got up close to her was "Follow me," and she bounded down to his side with all the bob and speed of one so old. For every one of his long determined steps she made two quick ones. They walked along in deep silence for a long time. Finally she started telling him about how many years she had cooked for them, cleaned for them, nursed them. He looked at her kindly but in silence. She told him indignantly about how they had grabbed her when she was singing in her head and not looking, and how they had tossed her out of his church. A old heifer like me, she said, straightening up next to Jesus, breathing hard. But he smiled down at her and she felt better instantly and time just seemed to fly by. When they passed her house, forlorn and sagging, weatherbeaten and patched, by the side of the road, she did not even notice it, she was so happy to be out walking along the highway with Jesus.

10   She broke the silence once more to tell Jesus how glad she was that he had come, how she had often looked at his picture hanging on her wall (she hoped he didn't know she had stolen it) over her bed, and how she had never expected to see him down here in person. Jesus gave her one of his beautiful smiles and they walked on. She did not know where they were going; someplace wonderful, she suspected. The ground was like clouds under their feet, and she felt she could walk forever without becoming the least bit tired. She even began to sing out loud some of the old spirituals she loved, but she didn't want to annoy Jesus, who looked so thoughtful, so she quieted down. They walked on, looking straight over the treetops into the sky, and the smiles that played over her dry wind-cracked face were like first clean ripples across a stagnant pond. On they walked without stopping.

The people in church never knew what happened to the old woman; they never mentioned her to one another or to anybody else. Most of them heard sometime later that an old colored woman fell dead along the highway. Silly as it seemed, it appeared she had walked herself to death. Many of the black families along the road said they had seen the old lady high-stepping down the highway; sometimes jabbering in a low insistent voice, sometimes singing, sometimes merely gesturing excitedly with her hands. Other times silent and smiling, looking at the sky. She had been alone, they said. Some of them wondered aloud where the old woman had been going so stoutly that it had worn her heart out. They guessed maybe she had relatives across the river, some miles away, but none of them really knew.   [1973]

Questions

1. The old woman has stolen a picture of Jesus. Does this act make her a bad person?
2. Discuss Walker's use of colors.
3. What function does the occasional use of authorial comment have?
4. What use does Walker make of situational irony?
5. Are we meant to believe that Jesus really does appear to the old woman?

Responses

1. Write an essay detailing how you would have reacted to the old woman who visited the church.
2. Write an essay examining Walker's attitude toward and relationship with her characters in this and other stories.

DAVID FOSTER WALLACE

David Foster Wallace (b. 1962) was born in Ithaca, New York. He has graduated from Amherst (A.B.) and the University of Arizona (M.F.A.). He published his first novel, *The Broom in the System* (1986), while still a graduate student. His second novel is *Infinite Jest* (1996). His short fiction is collected in *Girl with the Curious Hair* (1989), *Brief Interviews with Hideous Men* (1999), and *Oblivion* (2004). His nonfiction is included in the volumes *Signifying Rappers* (1990), *A Supposedly Funny Thing That I'll Never Do Again* (1997), and *Everything and More: A Complete History of Infinity* (2003). He is the winner of several awards, including the MacArthur Fellowship, and is considered one of the best writers of his generation following the line of American fiction developed by Nabokov and Barth.

Suicide as a Sort of Present

There was once a mother who had a very hard time indeed, emotionally, inside.

As she remembered it, she had always had a hard time, even as a child. She remembered few of her childhood's specifics, but what she could remember were feelings of self-loathing, terror, and despair that seemed to have been with her always.

From an objective perspective, it would not be inaccurate to say that this mother-to-be had had some very heavy psychic shit laid on her as a little girl, and that some of this shit qualified as parental abuse. Her childhood had not been as bad as some, but it had been no picnic. All this, while accurate, would not be to the point.

The point is that, from as early an age as she could recall, this mother-to-be loathed herself. She viewed everything in life with apprehension, as if every occasion or opportunity were some sort of dreadfully important exam for which she had been too lazy or stupid to prepare properly. It felt as if a perfect score on each such exam was necessary in order to avert some shattering punishment.° She was terrified of everything, and terrified to show it.

5   The mother-to-be knew perfectly well, from an early age, that this constant horrible pressure she felt was an internal pressure. That it was not anyone else's fault. Thus

---

°Her parents, by the way, did not beat her or ever even really discipline her, nor did they pressure her. [The footnotes are Wallace's.]

she loathed herself even more. Her expectations of herself were of utter perfection, and each time she fell short of perfection she was filled with an unbearable plunging despair that threatened to shatter her like a cheap mirror.° These very high expectations applied to every department of the future mother's life, particularly those departments which involved other's approval or disapproval. She was thus, in childhood and adolescence, viewed as bright, attractive, popular, impressive; she was commended and approved. Peers appeared to envy her energy, drive, appearance, intelligence, disposition, and unfailing consideration for the needs and feelings of others°; she had few close friends. Throughout her adolescence, authorities such as teachers, employers, troop leaders, pastors, and F.S.A. Faculty Advisers commented that the young mother-in-waiting 'seem[ed] to have very, very high expectations of [her]self,' and while these comments were often delivered in a spirit of gentle concern or reproof, there was no failing to discern in them that slight unmistakable note of approval—of an authority's detached, objective judgment and decision to approve—and at any rate the future mother felt (for the moment) approved. And felt seen: her standards *were* high. She took a sort of abject pride in her mercilessness toward herself.°

By the time she was grown up, it would be accurate to say that the mother-to-be was having a very hard interior time of it indeed.

When she became a mother, things became even harder. The mother's expectations of her small child were also, it turned out, impossibly high. And every time the child fell short, her natural inclination was to loathe it. In other words, every time it (the child) threatened to compromise the high standards that were all the mother felt she really had, inside, the mother's instinctive self-loathing tended to project itself outward and downward onto the child itself. This tendency was compounded by the fact that there existed only a very tiny and indistinct separation in the mother's mind between her own identity and that of her small child. The child appeared in a sense to be the mother's own reflection in a diminishing and deeply flawed mirror. Thus every time the child was rude, greedy, foul, dense, selfish, cruel, disobedient, lazy, foolish, willful, or childish, the mother's deepest and most natural inclination was to loathe it.

But she could not loathe it. No good mother can loathe her child or judge it or abuse it or wish it harm in any way. The mother knew this. And her standards for herself as a mother were, as one would expect, extremely high. It was thus that whenever she 'slipped,' 'snapped,' 'lost her patience' and expressed (or even felt) loathing (however brief) for the child, the mother was instantly plunged into such a chasm of self-recrimination and despair that she felt it just could not be borne. Hence the mother was at war. Her expectations were in fundamental conflict. It was a conflict in which she felt her very life was at stake: to fail to overcome her instinctive dissatisfaction with her child would result in a terrible, shattering punishment which she knew she herself would administer, inside. She was determined—desperate—to succeed, to satisfy her expectations of herself as a mother, no matter what it cost.

From an objective perspective, the mother was wildly successful in her efforts at self-control. In her outward conduct toward the child, the mother was indefatigably

---

°Her parents had been low-income, physically imperfect, and not very bright—features which the child disliked herself for noting.

°The phrases *lighten up* and *chill out* had not at this time come into currency (nor, in fact, had *psychic shit*: nor had *parental abuse* or even *objective perspective*).

°In fact, one explanation the soon-to-be mother's own parents gave for their disciplining her so little was that their daughter had seemed so mercilessly to upbraid herself for any shortcoming or transgression that disciplining her would have felt 'a little bit like kicking a dog.'

loving, compassionate, empathetic, patient, warm, effusive, unconditional, and devoid of any apparent capacity to judge or disapprove or withhold love in any form. The more loathsome the child was, the more loving the mother required herself to be. Her conduct was, by any standard of what an outstanding mother might be expected to be, impeccable.

10   In return, the small child, as it grew, loved the mother more than all other things in the world put together. If it had had the capacity to speak of itself truly somehow, the child would have said that it felt itself to be a very wicked, loathsome child who through some undeserved stroke of good fortune got to have the very best, most loving and patient and beautiful mother in the whole world.

Inside, as the child grew, the mother was filled with self-loathing and despair. Surely, she felt, the fact that the child lied and cheated and terrorized neighborhood pets was her fault; surely the child was simply expressing for all the world to see her own grotesque and pathetic deficiencies as a mother. Thus, when the child stole his class's UNICEF money or swung a cat by its tail and struck it repeatedly against the sharp corner of a brick home next door, she took the child's grotesque deficiencies upon herself, rewarding the child's tears and self-recriminations with an unconditionally loving forgiveness that made her seem to the child to be his lone refuge in a world of impossible expectations and merciless judgment and unending psychic shit. As he (the child) grew, the mother took all that was imperfect in him deep into herself and bore it all and thus absolved him, redeemed and renewed him, even as she added to her own inner fund of loathing.

So it went, throughout his childhood and adolescence, such that, by the time the child was old enough to apply for various licenses and permits, the mother was almost entirely filled, deep inside, with loathing: loathing for herself, for the delinquent and unhappy child, for a world of impossible expectations and merciless judgment. She could not, of course, express any of this. And so the son—desperate, as are all children, to repay the perfect love we may expect only of mothers—expressed it all for her.   [1999]

QUESTIONS

1. Look at the instances where the narrator lists adjectives. What effect does this create?
2. Describe the tone of the story.
3. In spite of how much the narrator tells us about the mother, is she a character in any traditional way?
4. What is the setting? When and where does the story take place?
5. What does the phrase "objective perspective" come to mean in the story?

RESPONSES

1. Examine the effects of a mother's love in this story, in D. H. Lawrence's "The Rocking-Horse Winner," and/or in Joyce Carol Oates's "Shopping."
2. Read Wallace's description of the fiction writer as voyeur in the Context essay "Act Natural." Write an essay on the voyeuristic qualities of this story.

EUDORA WELTY

Eudora Welty (1909–2001) was born in Jackson, Mississippi. After graduation from the University of Wisconsin (B.A. 1929), she studied and worked briefly in New York City. She returned to Jackson in 1932 and, while holding a number of jobs, began to write the stories that she collected in her first book, *A Curtain of Green* (1941). Many readers have noted the contrast between the quiet life she led in Jackson and the wide range of subject matter and the technical variety of her stories and novels. Her achievement in fiction has been recognized with a long list of prizes, awards, fellowships, and memberships in honorary societies. *The Collected Stories* appeared in 1980. Of great interest is her series of autobiographical essays, *One Writer's Beginnings* (1984).

Petrified Man

"Reach in my purse and git me a cigarette without no powder in it if you kin, Mrs. Fletcher, honey," said Leota to her ten o'clock shampoo-and-set customer. "I don't like no perfumed cigarettes."

Mrs. Fletcher gladly reached over to the lavender shelf under the lavender-framed mirror, shook a hair net loose from the clasp of the patent-leather bag, and slapped her hand down quickly on a powder puff which burst out when the purse was opened.

"Why, look at the peanuts, Leota!" said Mrs. Fletcher in her marvelling voice.

"Honey, them goobers has been in my purse a week if they's been in it a day. Mrs. Pike bought them peanuts."

"Who's Mrs. Pike?" asked Mrs. Fletcher, settling back. Hidden in this den of curling fluid and henna packs, separated by a lavender swing-door from the other customers, who were being gratified in other booths, she could give her curiosity its freedom. She looked expectantly at the black part in Leota's yellow curls as she bent to light the cigarette. [5]

"Mrs. Pike is this lady from New Orleans," said Leota, puffing, and pressing into Mrs. Fletcher's scalp with strong red-nailed fingers. "A friend, not a customer. You see, like maybe I told you last time, me and Fred and Sal and Joe all had us a fuss, so Sal and Joe up and moved out, so we didn't do a thing but rent out their room. So we rented it to Mrs. Pike. And Mr. Pike." She flicked an ash into the basket of dirty towels. "Mrs. Pike is a very decided blonde. *She* bought me the peanuts."

1139

"She must be cute," said Mrs. Fletcher.

"Honey, 'cute' ain't the word for what she is. I'm tellin' you, Mrs. Pike is attractive. She has her a good time. She's got a sharp eye out, Mrs. Pike has."

She dashed the comb through the air, and paused dramatically as a cloud of Mrs. Fletcher's hennaed hair floated out of the lavender teeth like a small storm-cloud.

10   "Hair fallin'."

"Aw, Leota."

"Uh-huh, commencin' to fall out," said Leota, combing again, and letting fall another cloud.

"Is it any dandruff in it?" Mrs. Fletcher was frowning, her hair-lined eyebrows diving down toward her nose, and her wrinkled, beady-lashed eyelids batting with concentration.

"Nope." She combed again. "Just fallin' out."

15   "Bet it was that last perm'nent you gave me that did it," Mrs. Fletcher said cruelly. "Remember you cooked me fourteen minutes."

"You had fourteen minutes comin' to you," said Leota with finality.

"Bound to be somethin'," persisted Mrs. Fletcher. "Dandruff, dandruff. I couldn't of caught a thing like that from Mr. Fletcher, could I?"

"Well," Leota answered at last, "you know what I heard in here yestiddy, one of Thelma's ladies was settin' over yonder in Thelma's booth gittin' a machineless, and I don't mean to insist or insinuate or anything, Mrs. Fletcher, but Thelma's lady just happ'med to throw out—I forgotten what she was talkin' about at the time—that you was p-r-e-g., and lots of times that'll make your hair do awful funny, fall out and God knows what all. It just ain't our fault, is the way I look at it."

There was a pause. The women stared at each other in the mirror.

20   "Who was it?" demanded Mrs. Fletcher.

"Honey, I really couldn't say," said Leota. "Not that you look it."

"Where's Thelma? I'll get it out of her," said Mrs. Fletcher.

"Now, honey, I wouldn't go and git mad over a little thing like that," Leota said, combing hastily, as though to hold Mrs. Fletcher down by the hair. "I'm sure it was somebody didn't mean no harm in the world. How far gone are you?"

"Just wait," said Mrs. Fletcher, and shrieked for Thelma, who came in and took a drag from Leota's cigarette.

25   "Thelma, honey, throw your mind back to yestiddy if you kin," said Leota, drenching Mrs. Fletcher's hair with a thick fluid and catching the overflow in a cold wet towel at her neck.

"Well, I got my lady half wound for a spiral," said Thelma doubtfully.

"This won't take but a minute," said Leota. "Who is it you got in there, old Horse Face? Just cast your mind back and try to remember who your lady was yestiddy who happ'm to mention that my customer was pregnant, that's all. She's dead to know."

Thelma drooped her blood-red lips and looked over Mrs. Fletcher's head into the mirror. "Why, honey, I ain't got the faintest," she breathed. "I really don't recollect the faintest. But I'm sure she meant no harm. I declare, I forgot my hair finally got combed and thought it was a stranger behind me."

"Was it that Mrs. Hutchinson?" Mrs. Fletcher was tensely polite.

30   "Mrs. Hutchinson? Oh, Mrs. Hutchinson." Thelma batted her eyes. "Naw, precious, she come on Thursday and didn't ev'm mention your name. I doubt if she ev'm knows you're on the way."

"Thelma!" cried Leota staunchly.

"All I know is, whoever it is 'll be sorry some day. Why, I just barely knew it myself!" cried Mrs. Fletcher. "Just let her wait!"

"Why? What're you gonna do to her?"

It was a child's voice, and the women looked down. A little boy was making tents with aluminum wave pinchers on the floor under the sink.

"Billy Boy, hon, mustn't bother nice ladies," Leota smiled. She slapped him bright- 35 ly and behind her back waved Thelma out of the booth. "Ain't Billy Boy a sight? Only three years old and already just nuts about the beauty-parlor business."

"I never saw him here before," said Mrs. Fletcher, still unmollified.

"He ain't been here before, that's how come," said Leota. "He belongs to Mrs. Pike. She got her a job but it was Fay's Millinery. He oughtn't to try on those ladies' hats, they come down over his eyes like I don't know what. They just git to look ridiculous, that's what, an' of course he's gonna put 'em on: hats. They tole Mrs. Pike they didn't appreciate him hangin' around there. Here, he couldn't hurt a thing."

"Well! I don't like children that much," said Mrs. Fletcher.

"Well!" said Leota moodily.

"Well! I'm almost tempted not to have this one," said Mrs. Fletcher. "That Mrs. 40 Hutchinson! Just looks straight through you when she sees you on the street and then spits at you behind your back."

"Mr. Fletcher would beat you on the head if you didn't have it now," said Leota reasonably. "After going this far."

Mrs. Fletcher sat up straight. "Mr. Fletcher can't do a thing with me."

"He can't!" Leota winked at herself in the mirror.

"No, siree, he can't. If he so much as raises his voice against me, he knows good and well I'll have one of my sick headaches, and then I'm just not fit to live with. And if I really look that pregnant already—"

"Well, now, honey, I just want you to know—I habm't told any of my ladies and I 45 ain't goin' to tell 'em—even that you're losin' your hair. You just get you one of those Stork-a-Lure dresses and stop worryin'. What people don't know don't hurt nobody, as Mrs. Pike says."

"Did you tell Mrs. Pike?" asked Mrs. Fletcher sulkily.

"Well, Mrs. Fletcher, look, you ain't ever goin' to lay eyes on Mrs. Pike or her lay eyes on you, so what diffunce does it make in the long run?"

"I knew it!" Mrs. Fletcher deliberately nodded her head so as to destroy a ringlet Leota was working on behind her ear. "Mrs. Pike!"

Leota sighed. "I reckon I might as well tell you. It wasn't any more Thelma's lady tole me you was pregnant than a bat."

"Not Mrs. Hutchinson?" 50

"Naw, Lord! It was Mrs. Pike."

"Mrs. Pike!" Mrs. Fletcher could only sputter and let curling fluid roll into her ear. "How could Mrs. Pike possibly know I was pregnant or otherwise, when she doesn't even know me? The nerve of some people!"

"Well, here's how it was. Remember Sunday?"

"Yes," said Mrs. Fletcher.

"Sunday, Mrs. Pike an' me was all by ourself. Mr. Pike and Fred had gone over to 55 Eagle Lake, sayin' they was goin' to catch 'em some fish, but they didn't a course. So we was settin' in Mrs. Pike's car, it's a 1939 Dodge—"

"1939, eh," said Mrs. Fletcher.

"—An' we was gettin' us a Jax beer apiece—that's the beer that Mrs. Pike says is made right in N.O., so she won't drink no other kind. So I seen you drive up to the drugstore an' run in for just a secont, leavin' I reckon Mr. Fletcher in the car, an' come runnin' out with looked like a perscription. So I says to Mrs. Pike, just to be makin' talk,

'Right yonder's Mrs. Fletcher, and I reckon that's Mr. Fletcher—she's one of my regular customers,' I says."

"I had on a figured print," said Mrs. Fletcher tentatively.

"You sure did," agreed Leota. "So Mrs. Pike, she give you a good look—she's very observant, a good judge of character, cute as a minute, you know—and she says, 'I bet you another Jax that lady's three months on the way.'"

60   "What gall!" said Mrs. Fletcher. "Mrs. Pike!"

"Mrs. Pike ain't goin' to bite you," said Leota. "Mrs. Pike is a lovely girl, you'd be crazy about her, Mrs. Fletcher. But she can't sit still a minute. We went to the travellin' freak show yestidday after work. I got through early—nine o'clock. In the vacant store next door. What, you ain't been?"

"No, I despise freaks," declared Mrs. Fletcher.

"Aw. Well, honey, talkin' about bein' pregnant an' all, you ought to see those twins in a bottle, you really owe it to yourself."

"What twins?" asked Mrs. Fletcher out of the side of her mouth.

65   "Well, honey, they got these two twins in a bottle, see? Born joined plumb together—dead a course." Leota dropped her voice into a soft lyrical hum. "They was about this long—pardon—must have been full time, all right, wouldn't you say?—an' they had these two heads an' two faces an' four arms an' four legs, all kind of joined *here*. See, this face looked this-a-way, and the other face looked that-a-way, over their shoulder, see. Kinda pathetic."

"Glah!" said Mrs. Fletcher disapprovingly.

"Well, ugly? Honey, I mean to tell you—their parents was first cousins and all like that. Bill Boy, git me a fresh towel from off Teeny's stack—this 'n's wringin' wet—an' quit ticklin' my ankles with that curler. I declare! He don't miss nothin'."

"Me and Mr. Fletcher aren't one speck of kin, or he could never of had me," said Mrs. Fletcher placidly.

"Of course not!" protested Leota. "Neither is me an' Fred, not that we know of. Well, honey, what Mrs. Pike liked was the pygmies. They've got these pygmies down there, too, an' Mrs. Pike was just wild about 'em. You know, the teeniest men in the universe? Well, honey, they can just rest back on their little bohunkus an' roll around an' you can't hardly tell if they're sittin' or standin'. That'll give you some idea. They're about forty-two years old. Just suppose it was your husband!"

70   "Well, Mr. Fletcher is five foot nine and one half," said Mrs. Fletcher quickly.

"Fred's five foot ten," said Leota, "but I tell him he's still a shrimp, account of I'm so tall." She made a deep wave over Mrs. Fletcher's other temple with the comb. "Well, these pygmies are a kind of a dark brown, Mrs. Fletcher. Not bad-lookin' for what they are, you know."

"I wouldn't care for them," said Mrs. Fletcher. "What does that Mrs. Pike see in them?"

"Aw, I don't know," said Leota. "She's just cute, that's all. But they got this man, this petrified man, that ever'thing ever since he was nine years old, when it goes through his digestion, see, somehow Mrs. Pike says it goes to his joints and has been turning to stone."

"How awful!" said Mrs. Fletcher.

75   "He's forty-two too. That looks like a bad age."

"Who said so, that Mrs. Pike? I bet she's forty-two," said Mrs. Fletcher.

"Naw," said Leota, "Mrs. Pike's thirty-three, born in January, an Aquarian. He could move his head—like this. A course his head and mind ain't a joint, so to speak, and I guess his stomach ain't, either—not yet, anyways. But see—his food, he eats it, and it goes down, see, and then he digests it"—Leota rose on her toes for an instant—"and it goes out to his joints and before you can say 'Jack Robinson,' it's stone—pure stone. He's turning to stone. How'd you like to be married to a guy like that? All he can do, he can move his head just a quarter of an inch. A course he *looks* just *terrible*."

"I should think he would," said Mrs. Fletcher frostily. "Mr. Fletcher takes bending exercises every night of the world. I make him."

"All Fred does is lay around the house like a rug. I wouldn't be surprised if he woke up some day and couldn't move. The petrified man just sat there moving his quarter of an inch though," said Leota reminiscently.

"Did Mrs. Pike like the petrified man?" asked Mrs. Fletcher.   80

"Not as much as she did the others," said Leota deprecatingly. "And then she likes a man to be a good dresser, and all that."

"Is Mr. Pike a good dresser?" asked Mrs. Fletcher skeptically.

"Oh, well, yeah," said Leota, "but he's twelve or fourteen years older'n her. She ast Lady Evangeline about him."

"Who's Lady Evangeline?" asked Mrs. Fletcher.

"Well, it's this mind reader they got in the freak show," said Leota. "Was real good.   85
Lady Evangeline is her name, and if I had another dollar I wouldn't do a thing but have my other palm read. She had what Mrs. Pike said was the 'sixth mind' but she had the worst manicure I ever saw on a living person."

"What did she tell Mrs. Pike?" asked Mrs. Fletcher.

"She told her Mr. Pike was as true to her as he could be and besides, would come into some money."

"Humph!" said Mrs. Fletcher. "What does he do?"

"I can't tell," said Leota, "because he don't work. Lady Evangeline didn't tell me enough about my nature or anything. And I would like to go back and find out some more about this boy. Used to go with this boy until he got married to this girl. Oh, shoot, that was about three and a half years ago, when you was still goin' to the Robert E. Lee Beauty Shop in Jackson. He married her for her money. Another fortune-teller told me that at the time. So I'm not in love with him any more, anyway, besides being married to Fred, but Mrs. Pike thought, just for the hell of it, see, to ask Lady Evange-line was he happy."

"Does Mrs. Pike know everything about you already?" asked Mrs. Fletcher unbe-   90
lievingly. "Mercy!"

"Oh, yeah, I tole her ever'thing about ever'thing, from now on back to I don't know when—to when I first started goin' out," said Leota. "So I ast Lady Evangeline for one of my questions, was he happily married, and she says, just like she was glad I ask her, 'Honey,' she says, 'naw, he idn't. You write down this day, March 8, 1941,' she says, 'and mock it down: three years from today him and her won't be occupyin' the same bed.' There it is, up on the wall with them other dates—see, Mrs. Fletcher? And she says, 'Child, you ought to be glad you didn't git him, because he's so mercenary.' So I'm glad I married Fred. He sure ain't mercenary, money don't mean a thing to him. But I sure would like to go back and have my other palm read."

"Did Mrs. Pike believe in what the fortune-teller said?" asked Mrs. Fletcher in a superior tone of voice.

"Lord, yes, she's from New Orleans. Ever'body in New Orleans believes ever'thing spooky. One of 'em in New Orleans before it was raided says to Mrs. Pike one sum-mer she was goin' to go from State to State and meet some grey-headed men, and, sure enough, she says she went on a beautician convention up to Chicago. . . ."

"Oh!" said Mrs. Fletcher. "Oh, is Mrs. Pike a beautician too?"

95   "Sure she is," protested Leota. "She's a beautician. I'm going to git her in here if I can. Before she married. But it don't leave you. She says sure enough, there was three men who was a very large part of making her trip what it was, and they all three had grey in their hair and they went in six States. Got Christmas cards from 'em. Billy Boy, go see if Thelma's got any dry cotton. Look how Mrs. Fletcher's a-drippin'."

"Where did Mrs. Pike meet Mr. Pike?" asked Mrs. Fletcher primly.

"On another train," said Leota.

"I met Mr. Fletcher, or rather he met me, in a rental library," said Mrs. Fletcher with dignity, as she watched the net come down over her head.

"Honey, me an' Fred, we met in a rumble seat eight months ago and we was practically on what you might call the way to the altar inside of half an hour," said Leota in a guttural voice, and bit a bobby pin open. "Course it don't last. Mrs. Pike says nothin' like that ever lasts."

100   "Mr. Fletcher and myself are as much in love as the day we married," said Mrs. Fletcher belligerently as Leota stuffed cotton into her ears.

"Mrs. Pike says it don't last," repeated Leota in a louder voice. "Now go git under the dryer. You can turn yourself on, can't you? I'll be back to comb you out. Durin' lunch I promised to give Mrs. Pike a facial. You know—free. Her bein' in the business, so to speak."

"I bet she needs one," said Mrs. Fletcher, letting the swing-door fly back against Leota. "Oh, pardon me."

A week later, on time for her appointment, Mrs. Fletcher sank heavily into Leota's chair after first removing a drug-store rental book, called *Life Is Like That*, from the seat. She stared in a discouraged way into the mirror.

"You can tell it when I'm sitting down, all right," she said.

105   Leota seemed preoccupied and stood shaking out a lavender cloth. She began to pin it around Mrs. Fletcher's neck in silence.

"I said you sure can tell it when I'm sitting straight on and coming at you this way," Mrs. Fletcher said.

"Why, honey, naw you can't," said Leota gloomily. "Why, I'd never know. If somebody was to come up to me on the street and say, 'Mrs. Fletcher is pregnant!' I'd say, 'Heck, she don't look it to me.'"

"If a certain party hadn't found it out and spread it around, it wouldn't be too late even now," said Mrs. Fletcher frostily, but Leota was almost choking her with the cloth, pinning it so tight, and she couldn't speak clearly. She paddled her hands in the air until Leota wearily loosened her.

"Listen, honey, you're just a virgin compared to Mrs. Montjoy," Leota was going on, still absent-minded. She bent Mrs. Fletcher back in the chair and, sighing, tossed liquid from a teacup on to her head and dug both hands into her scalp. "You know Mrs. Montjoy—her husband's that premature-grey-headed fella?"

110   "She's in the Trojan Garden Club, is all I know," said Mrs. Fletcher.

"Well, honey," said Leota, but in a weary voice, "she come in here not the week before and not the day before she had her baby—she come in here the very self-same day, I mean to tell you. Child, we was all plumb scared to death. There she was! Come for her shampoo an' set. Why, Mrs. Fletcher, in an hour an' twenty minuets she was layin' up there in the Babtist Hospital with a seb'm-pound son. It was that close a shave. I declare, if I hadn't been so tired I would of drank up a bottle of gin that night."

"What gall," said Mrs. Fletcher. "I never knew her at all well."

"See, her husband was waitin' outside in the car, and her bags was all packed an' in the back seat, an' she was all ready, 'cept she wanted her shampoo an' set. An' havin' one pain right after another. Her husband kep' comin' in here, scared-like, but couldn't do nothin' with her a course. She yelled bloody murder, too, but she always yelled her head off when I give her a perm'nent."

"She must of been crazy," said Mrs. Fletcher. "How did she look?"

"Shoot!" said Leota.

"Well, I can guess," said Mrs. Fletcher. "Awful."

"Just wanted to look pretty while she was havin' her baby, is all," said Leota airily. "Course, we was glad to give the lady what she was after—that's our motto—but I bet a hour later she wasn't payin' no mind to them little end curls. I bet she wasn't thinkin' about she ought to have on a net. It wouldn't of done her no good if she had."

"No, I don't suppose it would," said Mrs. Fletcher.

"Yeah man! She was a-yellin'. Just like when I give her perm'nent."

"Her husband ought to make her behave. Don't it seem that way to you?" asked Mrs. Fletcher. "He ought to put his foot down."

"Ha," said Leota. "A lot he could do. Maybe some women is soft."

"Oh, you mistake me, I don't mean for her to get soft—far from it! Women have to stand up for themselves, or there's just no telling. But now you take me—I ask Mr. Fletcher's advice now and then, and he appreciates it, especially on something important, like is it time for a permanent—not that I've told him about the baby. He says, 'Why, dear, go ahead!' Just ask their *advice*."

"Huh! If I ever ast Fred's advice we'd be floatin' down the Yazoo River on a houseboat or somethin' by this time," said Leota. "I'm sick of Fred. I told him go over to Vicksburg."

"Is he going?" demanded Mrs. Fletcher.

"Sure. See, the fortune-teller—I went back and had my other palm read, since we've got to rent the room again—said my lover was goin' to work in Vicksburg, so I don't know who she could mean, unless she meant Fred. And Fred ain't workin' here—that much is so."

"Is he going to work in Vicksburg?" asked Mrs. Fletcher. "And—"

"Sure. Lady Evangeline said so. Said the future is going to be brighter than the present. He don't want to go, but I ain't gonna put up with nothin' like that. Lays around the house an' bulls—did bull—with that good-for-nothin' Mr. Pike. He says if he goes who'll cook, but I says I never get to eat anyway—not meals. Billy Boy, take Mrs. Grover that *Screen Secrets* and leg it."

Mrs. Fletcher heard stamping feet go out the door.

"Is that that Mrs. Pike's little boy here again?" she asked, sitting up gingerly.

"Yeah, that's still him." Leota stuck out her tongue.

Mrs. Fletcher could hardly believe her eyes. "Well! How's Mrs. Pike, your attractive new friend with the sharp eyes who spreads it around town that perfect strangers are pregnant?" she asked in a sweetened tone.

"Oh, Mizziz Pike." Leota combed Mrs. Fletcher's hair with heavy strokes.

"You act like you're tired," said Mrs. Fletcher.

"Tired? Feel like it's four o'clock in the afternoon, already," said Leota. "I ain't told you the awful luck we had, me and Fred? It's the worst thing you ever heard of. Maybe *you* think Mrs. Pike's got sharp eyes. Shoot, there's a limit! Well, you know, we rented out our room to this Mr. and Mrs. Pike from New Orleans when Sal an' Joe Fentress got mad at us 'cause they drank up some home-brew we had in the closet—Sal an'

Joe did. So, a week ago Sat'day Mr. and Mrs. Pike moved in. Well, I kinda fixed up the room, you know—put a sofa pillow on the couch and picked some ragged rob-bins and put in a vase, but they never did say they appreciated it. Anyway, then I put some old magazines on the table."

135   "I think that was lovely," said Mrs. Fletcher.

"Wait. So, come night 'fore last, Fred and this Mr. Pike, who Fred just took up with, was back from they said they was fishin', bein' as neither one of 'em has got a job to his name, and we was all settin' around in their room. So Mrs. Pike was settin' there readin' a old *Startling G-Men Tales* that was mine, mind you, I'd bought it myself, and all of a sudden she jumps!—into the air—you'd'a'thought she'd set on a spider—an' says, 'Canfield'—ain't that silly, that's Mr. Pike—'Canfield, my God A'mighty,' she says, 'honey,' she says, 'we're rich, and you won't have to work.' Not that he turned one hand anyway. Well, me and Fred rushes over to her, and Mr. Pike, too, and there she sets, pointin' her finger at a photo in my copy of *Startling G Man*. 'See that man?' yells Mrs. Pike. 'Remember him, Canfield?' 'Never forget a face,' says Mr. Pike. 'It's Mr. Petrie, that we stayed with him in the apartment next to ours in Toulouse Street in N.O. for six weeks. Mr. Petrie.' 'Well,' says Mrs. Pike, like she can't hold out one secont longer, 'Mr. Petrie is want-ed for five hundred dollars cash, for rapin' four women in California, and I know where he is.'"

"Mercy!" said Mrs. Fletcher. "Where was he?"

At some time Leota had washed her hair and now she yanked her up by the back locks and sat her up.

"Know where he was?"

140   "I certainly don't," Mrs. Fletcher said. Her scalp hurt all over.

Leota flung a towel around the top of her customer's head. "Nowhere else but in that freak show! I saw him just as plain as Mrs. Pike. *He* was the petrified man!"

"Who would ever have thought that!" cried Mrs. Fletcher sympathetically.

"So Mr. Pike says, 'Well whatta you know about that,' an' he looks real hard at the photo and whistles. And she starts dancin' and singin' about their good luck. She meant our bad luck! I made a point of tellin' that fortune-teller the next time I saw her. I said, 'Listen, that magazine was layin' around the house for a month, and there was the freak show runnin' night an' day, not two steps away from my own beauty parlor, with Mr. Petrie just settin' there waitin'. An' it had to be Mr. and Mrs. Pike, almost perfect strangers.'"

"What gall," said Mrs. Fletcher. She was only sitting there, wrapped in a turban, but she did not mind.

145   "Fortune-tellers don't care. And Mrs. Pike, she goes around actin' like she thinks she was Mrs. God," said Leota. "So they're goin' to leave tomorrow, Mr. and Mrs. Pike. And in the meantime I got to keep that mean, bad little ole kid here, getting' under my feet ever' minute of the day an' talkin' back too."

"Have they gotten the five hundred dollars' reward already?" asked Mrs. Fletcher.

"Well," said Leota, "at first Mr. Pike didn't want to do anything about it. Can you feature that? Said he kinda liked that ole bird and said he was real nice to 'em, lent 'em money or somethin'. But Mrs. Pike simply tole him he could just go to hell, and I can see her point. She says, 'You ain't worked a lick in six months, and here I make five hundred dollars in two seconts, and what thanks do I get for it? You go to hell, Canfield,' she say. So," Leota went on in a despondent voice, "they called up the cops and they caught the ole bird, all right, right there in the freak show where I saw him with my own eyes, thinkin' he was petrified. He's the one. Did it under his real name—Mr. Petrie. Four women in California, all in the month of August. So Mrs. Pike gits five hundred dollars. And my magazine, and right next door to my beauty parlor. I cried all night, but Fred said it wasn't a bit of use and to go to sleep, because the whole thing was just a sort of coincidence—you know: can't do nothin' about it. He says it put him clean out of the notion of goin' to Vicksburg for a few days till we rent out the room again—no tellin' who we'll git this time."

"But can you imagine anybody knowing this old man, that's raped four women?" persisted Mrs. Fletcher, and she shuddered audibly. "Did Mrs. Pike *speak* to him when she met him in the freak show?"

Leota had begun to comb Mrs. Fletcher's hair. "I says to her, I says, 'I didn't notice you fallin' on his neck when he was the petrified man—don't tell me you didn't recognize your fine friend?' And she says, 'I didn't recognize him with that white powder all over his face. He just looked familiar.' Mrs. Pike says, 'and lots of people look familiar.' But she says that ole petrified man did put her in mind of somebody. She wondered who it was! Kep' her awake, which man she'd ever knew it reminded her of. So when she seen the photo, it all come to her. Like a flash. Mr. Petrie. The way he'd turn his head and look at her when she took him in his breakfast."

"Took him in his breakfast!" shrieked Mrs. Fletcher. "Listen—don't tell me. I'd   150
a' felt something."

"Four women. I guess those women didn't have the faintest notion at the time they'd be worth a hundred an' twenty-five bucks a piece some day to Mrs. Pike. We ast her how old the fella was then, an' she says he musta had one foot in the grave, at least. Can you beat it?"

"Not really petrified at all, of course," said Mrs. Fletcher meditatively. She drew herself up. "I'd a' felt something," she said proudly.

"Shoot! I did feel somethin'," said Leota. "I tole Fred when I got home I felt so funny. I said, 'Fred, that ole petrified man sure did leave me with a funny feelin'.' He says, 'Funny-haha or funny-peculiar?' and I says, 'Funny-peculiar.'" She pointed her comb into the air emphatically.

"I'll bet you did," said Mrs. Fletcher.

They both heard a crackling noise.   155

Leota screamed, "Billy Boy! What you doin' in my purse?"

"Aw, I'm just eatin' these ole stale peanuts up," said Billy Boy.

"You come here to me!" screamed Leota, recklessly flinging down the comb, which scattered a whole ashtray full of bobby pins and knocked down a row of Coca-Cola bottles. "This is the last straw!"

"I caught him! I caught him!" giggled Mrs. Fletcher. "I'll hold him on my lap. You bad, bad boy, you! I guess I better learn how to spank little old bad boys," she said.

Leota's eleven o'clock customer pushed open the swing-door upon Leota paddling   160
him heartily with the brush, while he gave angry but belittling screams which penetrated beyond the booth and filled the whole curious beauty parlor. From everywhere ladies began to gather round to watch the paddling. Billy Boy kicked both Leota and Mrs. Fletcher as hard as he could, Mrs. Fletcher with her new fixed smile.

Billy Boy stomped through the group of wildhaired ladies and went out the door, but flung back the words, "If you're so smart, why ain't you rich?"   [1941]

QUESTIONS

1. What is at issue between Leota and Mrs. Fletcher?
2. How is dialogue used in this story to reveal character?
3. Although this is a story of "petrified" men and women, do any of the characters grow or change in the course of the action?
4. How is the two-part organization of the story expressive of its theme?
5. What is the role of Billy Boy in the story? Why is he given the last word?

EUDORA WELTY

A Worn Path

It was December—a bright frozen day in the early morning. Far out in the country there was an old Negro woman with her head tied in a red rag, coming along a path through the pinewoods. Her name was Phoenix Jackson. She was very old and small and she walked slowly in the dark pine shadows, moving a little from side to side in her steps, with the balanced heaviness and lightness of a pendulum in a grandfather clock. She carried a thin, small cane made from an umbrella, and with this she kept tapping the frozen earth in front of her. This made a grave and persistent noise in the still air, that seemed meditative like the chirping of a solitary little bird.

She wore a dark striped dress reaching down to her shoe tops, and an equally long apron of bleached sugar sacks, with a full pocket: all neat and tidy, but every time she took a step she might have fallen over her shoelaces, which dragged from her unlaced shoes. She looked straight ahead. Her eyes were blue with age. Her skin had a pattern all its own of numberless branching wrinkles and as though a whole little tree stood in the middle of her forehead, but a golden color ran underneath, and the two knobs of her cheeks were illuminated by a yellow burning under the dark. Under the red rag her hair came down on her neck in the frailest of ringlets, still black, and with an odor like copper.

Now and then there was a quivering in the thicket. Old Phoenix said, "Out of my way, all you foxes, owls, beetles, jack rabbits, coons and wild animals! . . . Keep out from under these feet, little bob-whites. . . . Keep the big wild hogs out of my path. Don't let none of those come running my direction. I got a long way." Under her small black-freckled hand her cane, limber as a buggy whip, would switch at the brush as if to rouse up any hiding things.

On she went. The woods were deep and still. The sun made the pine needles almost too bright to look at, up where the wind rocked. The cones dropped as light as feathers. Down in the hollow was the mourning dove—it was not too late for him.

The path ran up a hill. "Seem like there is chains about my feet, time I get this far," she said, in the voice of argument old people keep to use with themselves. "Something always take a hold of me on this hill—pleads I should stay."   5

After she got to the top she turned and gave a full, severe look behind her where she had come. "Up through pines," she said at length. "Now down through oaks."

Her eyes opened their widest, and she started down gently. But before she got to the bottom of the hill a bush caught her dress.

1149

Her fingers were busy and intent, but her skirts were full and long, so that before she could pull them free in one place they were caught in another. It was not possible to allow the dress to tear. "I in the thorny bush," she said. "Thorns, you doing your appointed work. Never want to let folks pass, no sir. Old eyes thought you was a pretty little *green* bush."

Finally, trembling all over, she stood free, and after a moment dared to stoop for her cane.

"Sun so high!" she cried, leaning back and looking, while the thick tears went over her eyes. "The time getting all gone here."

At the foot of this hill was a place where a log was laid across the creek.

"Now comes the trial," said Phoenix.

Putting her right foot out, she mounted the log and shut her eyes. Lifting her skirt, leveling her cane fiercely before her, like a festival figure in some parade, she began to march across. Then she opened her eyes and she was safe on the other side.

"I wasn't as old as I thought," she said.

But she sat down to rest. She spread her skirts on the bank around her and folded her hands over her knees. Up above her was a tree in a pearly cloud of mistletoe. She did not dare to close her eyes, and when a little boy brought her a plate with a slice of marble-cake on it she spoke to him. "That would be acceptable," she said. But when she went to take it there was just her own hand in the air.

So she left that tree, and had to go through a barbed-wire fence. There she had to creep and crawl, spreading her knees and stretching her fingers like a baby trying to climb the steps. But she talked loudly to herself: she could not let her dress be torn now, so late in the day, and she could not pay for having her arm or her leg sawed off if she got caught fast where she was.

At last she was safe through the fence and risen up out in the clearing. Big dead trees, like black men with one arm, were standing in the purple stalks of the withered cotton field. There sat a buzzard.

"Who you watching?"

In the furrow she made her way along.

"Glad this not the season for bulls," she said, looking sideways, "and the good Lord made his snakes to curl up and sleep in the winter. A pleasure I don't see no two-headed snake coming around that tree, where it come once. It took a while to get by him, back in the summer."

She passed through the old cotton and went into a field of dead corn. It whispered and shook and was taller than her head. "Through the maze now," she said, for there was no path.

Then there was something tall, black, and skinny there, moving before her.

At first she took it for a man. It could have been a man dancing in the field. But she stood still and listened, and it did not make a sound. It was as silent as a ghost.

"Ghost," she said sharply, "who be you the ghost of? For I have heard of nary death close by."

But there was no answer—only the ragged dancing in the wind.

She shut her eyes, reached out her hand, and touched a sleeve. She found a coat and inside that an emptiness, cold as ice.

"You scarecrow," she said. Her face lighted. "I ought to be shut up for good," she said with laughter. "My senses is gone. I too old. I the oldest people I ever know. Dance, old scarecrow," she said, "while I dancing with you."

She kicked her foot over the furrow, and with mouth drawn down, shook her head once or twice in a little strutting way. Some husks blew down and whirled in streamers about her skirts.

Then she went on, parting her way from side to side with the cane, through the whispering field. At last she came to the end, to a wagon track where the silver grass blew between the red ruts. The quail were walking around like pullets, seeming all dainty and unseen.

"Walk pretty," she said. "This the easy place. This the easy going." 30

She followed the track, swaying through the quiet bare fields, through the little strings of trees silver in their dead leaves, past cabins silver from weather, with the doors and windows boarded shut, all like old women under a spell sitting there. "I walking in their sleep," she said, nodding her head vigorously.

In a ravine she went where a spring was silent flowing through a hollow log. Old Phoenix bent and drank. "Sweet-gum makes the water sweet," she said, and drank more. "Nobody know who made this well, for it was here when I was born."

The track crossed a swampy part where the moss hung as white as lace from every limb. "Sleep on, alligators, and blow your bubbles." Then the track went into the road.

Deep, deep the road went down between the high green-colored banks. Overhead the live-oaks met, and it was as dark as a cave.

A black dog with a lolling tongue came up out of the weeds by the ditch. She was 35 meditating, and not ready, and when he came at her she only hit him a little with her cane. Over she went in the ditch, like a little puff of milkweed.

Down there, her senses drifted away. A dream visited her, and she reached her hand up, but nothing reached down and gave her a pull. So she lay there and presently went to talking. "Old woman," she said to herself, "that black dog come up out of the weeds to stall you off, and now there he sitting on his fine tail, smiling at you."

A white man finally came along and found her—a hunter, a young man, with his dog on a chain.

"Well, Granny!" he laughed. "What are you doing there?"

"Lying on my back like a June-bug waiting to be turned over, mister," she said, reaching up her hand.

He lifted her up, gave her a swing in the air, and set her down. "Anything bro- 40 ken, Granny?"

"No, sir, them old dead weeds is springy enough," said Phoenix, when she had got her breath. "I thank you for your trouble."

"Where do you live, Granny?" he asked, while the two dogs were growling at each other.

"Away back yonder, sir, behind the ridge. You can't even see it from here."

"On your way home?"

"No sir, I going to town." 45

"Why, that's too far! That's as far as I walk when I come out myself, and I get something for my trouble." He patted the stuffed bag he carried, and there hung down a little closed claw. It was one of the bob-whites, and its beak hooked bitterly to show it was dead. "Now you go home, Granny!"

"I bound to go to town, mister," said Phoenix. "The time come around."

He gave another laugh, filling the whole landscape. "I know you old colored people! Wouldn't miss going to town to see Santa Claus!"

But something held old Phoenix very still. The deep lines in her face went into a fierce and different radiation. Without warning, she had seen with her own eyes a flashing nickel fall out of the man's pocket onto the ground.

"How old are you, Granny?" he was saying.

"There is no telling, mister," she said, "no telling."

Then she gave a little cry and clapped her hands and said, "Git on away from here, dog! Look! Look at that dog!" She laughed as if in admiration. "He ain't scared of nobody. He a big black dog." She whispered, "Sic him!"

"Watch me get rid of that cur," said the man. "Sic him, Pete! Sic him!"

Phoenix heard the dogs fighting, and heard the man running and throwing sticks. She even heard a gunshot. But she was slowly bending forward by that time, further and further forward, the lids stretched down over her eyes, as if she were doing this in her sleep. Her chin was lowered almost to her knees. The yellow palm of her hand came out from the fold of her apron. Her fingers slid down and along the ground under the piece of money with the grace and care they would have in lifting an egg from under a setting hen. Then she slowly straightened up, she stood erect, and the nickel was in her apron pocket. A bird flew by. Her lips moved. "God watching me the whole time. I come to stealing."

The man came back, and his own dog panted about them. "Well, I scared him off that time," he said, and then he laughed and lifted his gun and pointed it at Phoenix.

She stood straight and faced him.

"Doesn't the gun scare you?" he said, still pointing it.

"No, sir, I seen plenty go off closer by, in my day, and for less than what I done," she said, holding utterly still.

He smiled, and shouldered the gun. "Well, Granny," he said, "you must be a hundred years old, and scared of nothing. I'd give you a dime if I had any money with me. But you take my advice and stay home, and nothing will happen to you."

"I bound to go on my way, mister," said Phoenix. She inclined her head in the red rag. Then they went in different directions, but she could hear the gun shooting again and again over the hill.

She walked on. The shadows hung from the oak trees to the road like curtains. Then she smelled wood-smoke, and smelled the river, and she saw a steeple and the cabins on their steep steps. Dozens of little black children whirled around her. There ahead was Natchez shining. Bells were ringing. She walked on.

In the paved city it was Christmas time. There were red and green electric lights strung and criss-crossed everywhere, and all turned on in the daytime. Old Phoenix would have been lost if she had not distrusted her eyesight and depended on her feet to know where to take her.

She paused quietly on the sidewalk where people were passing by. A lady came along in the crowd, carrying an armful of red-, green- and silver-wrapped presents; she gave off perfume like the red roses in hot summer, and Phoenix stopped her.

"Please, missy, will you lace up my shoe?" She held up her foot.

"What do you want, Grandma?"

"See my shoe," said Phoenix. "Do all right for out in the country, but wouldn't look right to go in a big building."

"Stand still then, Grandma," said the lady. She put her packages down on the sidewalk beside her and laced and tied both shoes tightly.

"Can't lace 'em with a cane," said Phoenix. "Thank you, missy. I doesn't mind asking a nice lady to tie up my shoe, when I gets out on the street."

Moving slowly and from side to side, she went into the big building, and into a tower of steps, where she walked up and around and around until her feet knew to stop.

She entered a door, and there she saw nailed up on the wall the document that had been stamped with the gold seal and framed in the gold frame, which matched the dream that was hung up in her head.

"Here I be," she said. There was a fixed and ceremonial stiffness over her body.

"A charity case, I suppose," said an attendant who sat at the desk before her.

But Phoenix only looked above her head. There was sweat on her face, the wrinkles in her skin shone like a bright net.

"Speak up, Grandma," the woman said. "What's your name? We must have your history, you know. Have you been here before? What seems to be the trouble with you?"

Old Phoenix only gave a twitch to her face as if a fly were bothering her.

"Are you deaf?" cried the attendant.

But then the nurse came in.

"Oh, that's just old Aunt Phoenix," she said. "She doesn't come for herself—she has a little grandson. She makes these trips just as regular as clockwork. She lives away back off the Old Natchez Trace." She bent down. "Well, Aunt Phoenix, why don't you just take a seat? We won't keep you standing after your long trip." She pointed.

The old woman sat down, bolt upright in the chair.

"Now, how is the boy?" asked the nurse.

Old Phoenix did not speak.

"I said, how is the boy?"

But Phoenix only waited and stared straight ahead, her face very solemn and withdrawn into rigidity.

"Is his throat any better?" asked the nurse. "Aunt Phoenix, don't you hear me? Is your grandson's throat any better since the last time you came for the medicine?"

With her hands on her knees, the old woman waited, silent, erect and motionless, just as if she were in armor.

"You mustn't take up our time this way, Aunt Phoenix," the nurse said. "Tell us quickly about your grandson, and get it over. He isn't dead, is he?"

At last there came a flicker and then a flame of comprehension across her face, and she spoke.

"My grandson. It was my memory had left me. There I sat and forgot why I made my long trip."

"Forgot?" The nurse frowned. "After you came so far?"

Then Phoenix was like an old woman begging a dignified forgiveness for waking up frightened in the night. "I never did go to school, I was too old at the Surrender," she said in a soft voice. "I'm an old woman without an education. It was my memory fail me. My little grandson, he is just the same, and I forgot it in the coming."

"Throat never heals, does it?" said the nurse, speaking in a loud, sure voice to old Phoenix. By now she had a card with something written on it, a little list. "Yes. Swallowed lye. When was it?—January—two-three years ago—"

Phoenix spoke unasked now. "No, missy, he not dead, he just the same. Every little while his throat begin to close up again, and he not able to swallow. He not get his breath. He not able to help himself. So the time come around, and I go on another trip for the soothing medicine."

"All right. The doctor said as long as you came to get it, you could have it," said the nurse. "But it's an obstinate case."

"My little grandson, he sit up there in the house all wrapped up, waiting by himself," Phoenix went on. "We is the only two left in the world. He suffer and it don't seem to put him back at all. He got a sweet look. He going to last. He wear a little patch quilt and peep out holding his mouth open like a little bird. I remembers so plain now. I not going to forget him again, no, the whole enduring time. I could tell him from all the others in creation."

95   "All right." The nurse was trying to hush her now. She brought her a bottle of medicine. "Charity," she said, making a check mark in a book.

Old Phoenix held the bottle close to her eyes, and then carefully put it into her pocket. "I thank you," she said.

"It's Christmas time, Grandma," said the attendant. "Could I give you a few pennies out of my purse?"

"Five pennies is a nickel," said Phoenix stiffly.

100   "Here's a nickel," said the attendant.

Phoenix rose carefully and held out her hand. She received the nickel and then fished the other nickel out of her pocket and laid it beside the new one. She stared at her palm closely, with her head on one side.

Then she gave a tap with her cane on the floor.

"This is what come to me to do," she said. "I going to the store and buy my child a little windmill they sells, made out of paper. He going to find it hard to believe there such a thing in the world. I'll march myself back where he waiting, holding it straight up in this hand."

She lifted her free hand, gave a little nod, turned around, and walked out of the doctor's office. Then her slow step began on the stairs, going down.   [1941]

QUESTIONS

1. To what extent is the effectiveness of this story dependent on setting and atmosphere?
2. What is the significance of Phoenix's name? How is she defined by conversations with herself?
3. What does the episode with the hunter contribute to the story?
4. Why is it appropriate that the nurse check off Phoenix as "charity"?
5. How do the references to birds underscore the theme?

RESPONSES

1. Write an essay analyzing "A Worn Path," beginning by examining Welty's Context essay "Is Phoenix Jackson's Grandson Really Dead?"
2. Using this story, Wideman's "Damballah," Silko's "Yellow Woman," and others, write an essay that examines how myth is used in contemporary fiction.
3. Using stories by Flannery O'Connor and William Faulkner for comparison, explore this story as a Southern story.
4. Approach this story through ecocriticism. What does it mean that Phoenix Jackson's journey was from a natural to a city setting?

Edith Wharton

Edith Wharton (1862–1937) was born in New York City. The daughter of a wealthy family, she was educated privately by tutors. The moneyed, genteel society into which she was born looked with embarrassment if not disdain on a woman ambitious for authorship, and Wharton spent her life struggling against indifference and, on occasion, hostility. She won, very dramatically, her victory; and her reputation, which declined during the Depression when her subject matter seemed to be irrelevant to many politically oriented critics, is now deservedly high. Selections from her eleven volumes of short stories are available in a variety of editions. Among her novels are *The House of Mirth* (1905), *Ethan Frome* (1911), and *The Age of Innocence* (1920).

Mrs. Manstey's View

The view from Mrs. Manstey's window was not a striking one, but to her at least it was full of interest and beauty. Mrs. Manstey occupied the back room on the third floor of a New York boarding-house, in a street where the ash-barrels lingered late on the side-walk and the gaps in the pavement would have staggered a Quintus Curtius. She was the widow of a clerk in a large wholesale house, and his death had left her alone, for her only daughter had married in California, and could not afford the long journey to New York to see her mother. Mrs. Manstey, perhaps, might have joined her daughter in the West, but they had now been so many years apart that they had ceased to feel any need of each other's society, and their intercourse had long been limited to the exchange of a few perfunctory letters, written with indifference by the daughter, and with difficulty by Mrs. Manstey, whose right hand was growing stiff with gout. Even had she felt a stronger desire for her daughter's companionship, Mrs. Manstey's increasing infirmity, which caused her to dread the three flights of stairs between her room and the street, would have given her pause on the eve of undertaking so long a journey; and without, perhaps, formulating these reasons she had long since accepted as a matter of course her solitary life in New York.

She was, indeed, not quite lonely, for a few friends still toiled up now and then to her room; but their visits grew rare as the years went by. Mrs. Manstey had never been a sociable woman, and during her husband's lifetime his companionship had been all-sufficient to her. For many years she had cherished a desire to live in the country, to have a hen-house and a garden; but this longing had faded with age, leaving only in the breast of the uncommunicative old woman a vague tenderness for plants and animals. It was, perhaps, this tenderness which made her cling so fervently to her view from her window, a view in which the most optimistic eye would at first have failed to discover anything admirable.

Mrs. Manstey, from her coign of vantage (a slightly projecting bow-window where she nursed an ivy and a succession of unwholesome-looking bulbs), looked out first upon the yard of her own dwelling, of which, however, she could get but a restricted glimpse. Still, her gaze took in the topmost boughs of the ailanthus below her window, and she knew how early each year the clump of dicentra strung its bending stalk with hearts of pink.

But of greater interest were the yards beyond. Being for the most part attached to boarding-houses they were in a state of chronic untidiness and fluttering, on certain days of the week, with miscellaneous garments and frayed table-cloths. In spite of this Mrs. Manstey found much to admire in the long vista which she commanded. Some of the yards were, indeed, but stony wastes, with grass in the cracks of the pavement and no shade in spring save that afforded by the intermittent leafage of the clothes-lines. These yards Mrs. Manstey disapproved of, but the others, the green ones, she loved. She had grown used to their disorder; the broken barrels, the empty bottles and paths unswept no longer annoyed her; hers was the happy faculty of dwelling on the pleasanter side of the prospect before her.

5   In the very next enclosure did not a magnolia open its hard white flowers against the watery blue of April? And was there not, a little way down the line, a fence foamed over every May by lilac waves of wistaria? Farther still, a horse-chestnut lifted its candelabra of buff and pink blossoms above broad fans of foliage; while in the opposite yard June was sweet with the breath of a neglected syringa, which persisted in growing in spite of the countless obstacles opposed to its welfare.

But if nature occupied the front rank in Mrs. Manstey's view, there was much of a more personal character to interest her in the aspect of the houses and their inmates. She deeply disapproved of the mustard-colored curtains which had lately been hung in the doctor's window opposite; but she glowed with pleasure when the house farther down had its old bricks washed with a coat of paint. The occupants of the houses did not often show themselves at the back windows, but the servants were always in sight. Noisy slatterns, Mrs. Manstey pronounced the greater number; she knew their ways and hated them. But to the quiet cook in the newly painted house, whose mistress bullied her, and who secretly fed the stray cats at nightfall, Mrs. Manstey's warmest sympathies were given. On one occasion her feelings were racked by the neglect of a housemaid, who for two days forgot to feed the parrot committed to her care. On the third day, Mrs. Manstey, in spite of her gouty hand, had just penned a letter, beginning: "Madam, it is now three days since your parrot has been fed," when the forgetful maid appeared at the window with a cup of seed in her hand.

But in Mrs. Manstey's more meditative moods it was the narrowing perspective of far-off yards which pleased her best. She loved, at twilight, when the distant brownstone spire seemed melting in the fluid yellow of the west, to lose herself in vague memories of a trip to Europe, made years ago, and now reduced in her mind's eye to a pale phantasmagoria of indistinct steeples and dreamy skies. Perhaps at heart Mrs. Manstey was an artist; at all events she was sensible of many changes of color unnoticed by the average eye, and dear to her as the green of early spring was the black lattice of branches against a cold sulphur sky at the close of a snowy day. She enjoyed, also, the sunny thaws of March, when patches of earth showed through the snow, like ink-spots spreading on a sheet of white blotting-paper; and, better still, the haze of boughs, leafless but swollen, which replaced the clear-cut tracery of winter. She even watched with a certain interest the trail of smoke from a far-off factory chimney, and missed a detail in the landscape when the factory was closed and the smoke disappeared.

Mrs. Manstey, in the long hours which she spent at her window, was not idle. She read a little, and knitted numberless stockings; but the view surrounded and shaped her life as the sea does a lonely island. When her rare callers came it was difficult for her to detach herself from the contemplation of the opposite window-washing, or the scrutiny of certain green points in a neighboring flower-bed which might, or might not, turn into hyacinths, while she feigned an interest in her visitor's anecdotes about some unknown grandchild. Mrs. Manstey's real friends were the denizens of the yards, the hyacinths, the magnolia, the green parrot, the maid who fed the cats, the doctor who studied late behind his mustard-colored curtains; and the confidant of her tenderer musings was the churchspire floating in the sunset.

One April day, as she sat in her usual place, with knitting cast aside and eyes fixed on the blue sky mottled with round clouds, a knock at the door announced the entrance of her landlady. Mrs. Manstey did not care for her landlady, but she submitted to her visits with ladylike resignation. To-day, however, it seemed harder than usual to turn from the blue sky and the blossoming magnolia to Mrs. Sampson's unsuggestive face, and Mrs. Manstey was conscious of a distinct effort as she did so.

"The magnolia is out earlier than usual this year, Mrs. Sampson," she remarked, yielding to a rare impulse, for she seldom alluded to the absorbing interest of her life. In the first place it was a topic not likely to appeal to her visitors and, besides, she lacked the power of expression and could not have given utterance to her feelings had she wished to.

"The what, Mrs. Manstey?" inquired the landlady, glancing about the room as if to find there the explanation of Mrs. Manstey's statement.

"The magnolia in the next yard—in Mrs. Black's yard," Mrs. Manstey repeated.

"Is it, indeed? I didn't know there was a magnolia there," said Mrs. Sampson, carelessly. Mrs. Manstey looked at her; she did not know that there was a magnolia in the next yard!

"By the way," Mrs. Sampson continued, "speaking of Mrs. Black reminds me that the work on the extension is to begin next week."

"The what?" it was Mrs. Manstey's turn to ask.

"The extension," said Mrs. Sampson, nodding her head in the direction of the ignored magnolia. "You knew, of course, that Mrs. Black was going to build an extension to her house? Yes, ma'am. I hear it is to run right back to the end of the yard. How she can afford to build an extension in these hard times I don't see; but she always was crazy about building. She used to keep a boarding-house in Seventeenth Street, and she nearly ruined herself then by sticking out bow-windows and what not; I should have thought that would have cured her of building, but I guess it's a disease, like drink. Anyhow, the work is to begin on Monday."

Mrs. Manstey had grown pale. She always spoke slowly, so the landlady did not heed the long pause which followed. At last Mrs. Manstey said: "Do you know how high the extension will be?"

"That's the most absurd part of it. The extension is to be built right up to the roof of the main building; now, did you ever?"

Mrs. Manstey paused again. "Won't it be a great annoyance to you, Mrs. Sampson?" she asked.

10

15

20   "I should say it would. But there's no help for it; if people have got a mind to build extensions there's no law to prevent 'em, that I'm aware of." Mrs. Manstey, knowing this, was silent. "There is no help for it," Mrs. Sampson repeated, "but if I *am* a church member, I wouldn't be so sorry if it ruined Eliza Black. Well, good-day, Mrs. Manstey; I'm glad to find you so comfortable."

So comfortable—so comfortable! Left to herself the old woman turned once more to the window. How lovely the view was that day! The blue sky with its round clouds shed a brightness over everything; the ailanthus had put on a tinge of yellow-green, the hyacinths were budding, the magnolia flowers looked more than ever like rosettes carved in alabaster. Soon the wistaria would bloom, then the horse-chestnut; but not for her. Between her eyes and them a barrier of brick and mortar would swiftly rise; presently even the spire would disappear, and all her radiant world be blotted out. Mrs. Manstey sent away untouched the dinner-tray brought to her that evening. She lingered in the window until the windy sunset died in bat-colored dusk; then, going to bed, she lay sleepless all night.

Early the next day she was up and at the window. It was raining, but even through the slanting gray gauze the scene had its charm—and then the rain was so good for the trees. She had noticed the day before that the ailanthus was growing dusty.

"Of course I might move," said Mrs. Manstey aloud, and turning from the window she looked about her room. She might move, of course; so might she be flayed alive; but she was not likely to survive either operation. The room, though far less important to her happiness than the view, was as much a part of her existence. She had lived in it seventeen years. She knew every stain on the wall-paper, every rent in the carpet; the light fell in a certain way on her engravings, her books had grown shabby on their shelves, her bulbs and ivy were used to their window and knew which way to lean to the sun. "We are all too old to move," she said.

That afternoon it cleared. Wet and radiant the blue reappeared through torn rags of cloud; the ailanthus sparkled; the earth in the flower-borders looked rich and warm. It was Thursday, and on Monday the building of the extension was to begin.

25   On Sunday afternoon a card was brought to Mrs. Black, as she was engaged in gathering up the fragments of the boarders' dinner in the basement. The card, black-edged, bore Mrs. Manstey's name.

"One of Mrs. Sampson's boarders; wants to move, I suppose. Well, I can give her a room next year in the extension. Dinah," said Mrs. Black, "tell the lady I'll be upstairs in a minute."

Mrs. Black found Mrs. Manstey standing in the long parlor garnished with statuettes and antimacassars; in that house she could not sit down.

Stooping hurriedly to open the register, which let out a cloud of dust, Mrs. Black advanced on her visitor.

"I'm happy to meet you, Mrs. Manstey; take a seat, please," the landlady remarked in her prosperous voice, the voice of a woman who can afford to build extensions. There was no help for it; Mrs. Manstey sat down.

30   "Is there anything I can do for you, ma'am?" Mrs. Black continued. "My house is full at present, but I am going to build an extension, and—"

"It is about the extension that I wish to speak," said Mrs. Manstey, suddenly. "I am a poor woman, Mrs. Black, and I have never been a happy one. I shall have to talk about myself first to—to make you understand."

Mrs. Black, astonished but imperturbable, bowed at this parenthesis.

"I never had what I wanted," Mrs. Manstey continued. "It was always one disappointment after another. For years I wanted to live in the country. I dreamed and dreamed about it; but we never could manage it. There was no sunny window in our house, and so all my plants died. My daughter married years ago and went away—besides, she never cared for the same things. Then my husband died and I was left alone. That was seventeen years ago. I went to live at Mrs. Sampson's, and I have been there ever since. I have grown a little infirm, as you see, and I don't get out often; only on fine days, if I am feeling very well. So you can understand my sitting a great deal in my window—the back window on the third floor—"

"Well, Mrs. Manstey," said Mrs. Black, liberally, "I could give you a back room, I dare say; one of the new rooms in the ex—"

"But I don't want to move; I can't move," said Mrs. Manstey, almost with a scream. 35 "And I came to tell you that if you build that extension I shall have no view from my window—no view! Do you understand?"

Mrs. Black thought herself face to face with a lunatic, and she had always heard that lunatics must be humored.

"Dear me, dear me," she remarked, pushing her chair back a little way, "that is too bad, isn't it? Why, I never thought of that. To be sure, the extension *will* interfere with your view, Mrs. Manstey."

"You do understand?" Mrs. Manstey gasped.

"Of course I do. And I'm real sorry about it, too. But there, don't you worry, Mrs. Manstey. I guess we can fix that all right."

Mrs. Manstey rose from her seat, and Mrs. Black slipped toward the door. 40

"What do you mean by fixing it? Do you mean that I can induce you to change your mind about the extension? Oh, Mrs. Black, listen to me. I have two thousand dollars in the bank and I could manage, I know I could manage, to give you a thousand if—" Mrs. Manstey paused; the tears were rolling down her cheeks.

"There, there, Mrs. Manstey, don't you worry," repeated Mrs. Black, soothingly. "I am sure we can settle it. I am sorry that I can't stay and talk about it any longer, but this is such a busy time of day, with supper to get—"

Her hand was on the door-knob, but with sudden vigor Mrs. Manstey seized her wrist.

"You are not giving me a definite answer. Do you mean to say that you accept my proposition?"

"Why, I'll think it over, Mrs. Manstey, certainly I will. I wouldn't annoy you for the 45 world—"

"But the work is to begin to-morrow, I am told," Mrs. Manstey persisted.

Mrs. Black hesitated. "It shan't begin, I promise you that; I'll send word to the builder this very night." Mrs. Manstey tightened her hold.

"You are not deceiving me, are you?" she said.

"No—no," stammered Mrs. Black. "How can you think such a thing of me, Mrs. Manstey?"

Slowly Mrs. Manstey's clutch relaxed, and she passed through the open door. "One 50 thousand dollars," she repeated, pausing in the hall; then she let herself out of the house and hobbled down the steps, supporting herself on the cast-iron railing.

"My goodness," exclaimed Mrs. Black, shutting and bolting the hall-door, "I never knew the old woman was crazy! And she looks so quiet and ladylike, too."

Mrs. Manstey slept well that night, but early the next morning she was awakened by a sound of hammering. She got to her window with what haste she might and looking out saw that Mrs. Black's yard was full of workmen. Some were carrying loads of brick from the kitchen to the yard, others beginning to demolish the old-fashioned wooden balcony which adorned each story of Mrs. Black's house. Mrs. Manstey saw that she had been deceived. At first she thought of confiding her trouble to Mrs. Sampson, but a settled discouragement soon took possession of her and she went back to bed, not caring to see what was going on.

Toward afternoon, however, feeling that she must know the worst, she rose and dressed herself. It was a laborious task, for her hands were stiffer than usual, and the hooks and buttons seemed to evade her.

When she seated herself in the window, she saw that the workmen had removed the upper part of the balcony, and that the bricks had multiplied since morning. One of the men, a coarse fellow with a bloated face, picked a magnolia blossom and, after smelling it, threw it to the ground; the next man, carrying a load of bricks, trod on the flower in passing.

55 "Look out, Jim," called one of the men to another who was smoking a pipe, "if you throw matches around near those barrels of paper you'll have the old tinder-box burning down before you know it." And Mrs. Manstey, leaning forward, perceived that there were several barrels of paper and rubbish under the wooden balcony.

At length the work ceased and twilight fell. The sunset was perfect and a roseate light, transfiguring the distant spire, lingered late in the west. When it grew dark Mrs. Manstey drew down the shades and proceeded, in her usual methodical manner, to light her lamp. She always filled and lit it with her own hands, keeping a kettle of kerosene on a zinc-covered shelf in a closet. As the lamp-light filled the room it assumed its usual peaceful aspect. The books and pictures and plants seemed, like their mistress, to settle themselves down for another quiet evening, and Mrs. Manstey, as was her wont, drew up her armchair to the table and began to knit.

That night she could not sleep. The weather had changed and a wild wind was abroad, blotting the stars with close-driven clouds. Mrs. Manstey rose once or twice and looked out of the window; but of the view nothing was discernible save a tardy light or two in the opposite windows. These lights at last went out, and Mrs. Manstey, who had watched for their extinction, began to dress herself. She was in evident haste, for she merely flung a thin dressing-gown over her night-dress and wrapped her head in a scarf; then she opened her closet and cautiously took out the kettle of kerosene. Having slipped a bundle of wooden matches into her pocket she proceeded, with increasing precautions, to unlock her door, and a few moments later she was feeling her way down the dark staircase, led by a glimmer of gas from the lower hall. At length she reached the bottom of the stairs and began the more difficult descent into the utter darkness of the basement. Here, however, she could move more freely, as there was less danger of being overheard; and without much delay she contrived to unlock the iron door leading into the yard. A gust of cold wind smote her as she stepped out and groped shiveringly under the clothes-lines.

That morning at three o'clock an alarm of fire brought the engines to Mrs. Black's door, and also brought Mrs. Sampson's startled boarders to their windows. The wooden balcony at the back of Mrs. Black's house was ablaze, and among those who watched the progress of the flames was Mrs. Manstey, leaning in her thin dressing-gown from the open window.

The fire, however, was soon put out, and the frightened occupants of the house, who had fled in scant attire, reassembled at dawn to find that little mischief had been done beyond the cracking of window panes and smoking of ceilings. In fact, the chief sufferer by the fire was Mrs. Manstey, who was found in the morning gasping with pneumonia, a not unnatural result, as everyone remarked, of her having hung out of an open window at her age in a dressing-gown. It was easy to see that she was very ill, but no one had guessed how grave the doctor's verdict would be, and the faces gathered that evening about Mrs. Sampson's table were awestruck and disturbed. Not that any of the boarders knew Mrs. Manstey well; she "kept to herself," as they said, and seemed to fancy herself too good for them; but then it is always disagreeable to have anyone dying in the house and, as one lady observed to another: "It might just as well have been you or me, my dear."

But it was only Mrs. Manstey; and she was dying, as she had lived, lonely if not   60
alone. The doctor had sent a trained nurse, and Mrs. Sampson, with muffled step, came in from time to time; but both, to Mrs. Manstey, seemed remote and unsubstantial as the figures in a dream. All day she said nothing; but when she was asked for her daughter's address she shook her head. At times the nurse noticed that she seemed to be listening attentively for some sound which did not come; then again she dozed.

The next morning at daylight she was very low. The nurse called Mrs. Sampson and as the two bent over the old woman they saw her lips move.

"Lift me up—out of bed," she whispered.

They raised her in their arms, and with her stiff hand she pointed to the window.

"Oh, the window—she wants to sit in the window. She used to sit there all day," Mrs. Sampson explained. "It can do her no harm, I suppose?"

"Nothing matters now," said the nurse.   65

They carried Mrs. Manstey to the window and placed her in her chair. The dawn was abroad, a jubilant spring dawn; the spire had already caught a golden ray, though the magnolia and horse-chestnut still slumbered in shadow. In Mrs. Black's yard all was quiet. The charred timbers of the balcony lay where they had fallen. It was evident that since the fire the builders had not returned to their work. The magnolia had unfolded a few more sculptural flowers; the view was undisturbed.

It was hard for Mrs. Manstey to breathe; each moment it grew more difficult. She tried to make them open the window, but they would not understand. If she could have tasted the air, sweet with the penetrating ailanthus savor, it would have eased her; but the view at least was there—the spire was golden now, the heavens had warmed from pearl to blue, day was alight from east to west, even the magnolia had caught the sun.

Mrs. Manstey's head fell back and smiling she died.

That day the building of the extension was resumed.   [1890]

QUESTIONS

1. Is Mrs. Manstey a sympathetic character? How does Wharton create a picture of Mrs. Manstey that makes the reader want to know more about her?

2. Compare the descriptions of Mrs. Manstey's room with the descriptions of the world outside her window? What does it say about Mrs. Manstey that she does not view her close surroundings with the precision with which she sees the world further away?

3. Discuss the various levels of conflict that Mrs. Manstey suffers from. Are any of her conflicts resolved?

4. The author, Edith Wharton, was wealthy. Are descriptions of the life of an impoverished woman convincing?

5. What do you think Wharton wants her readers to feel at the end of the story? Are we supposed to feel good about Mrs. Manstey's act? Sad about her death? Anger that her neighbors ignored her? Satisfied that her death was punishment for her act?

RESPONSES

1. Compare this story to Guy de Maupassant's "The Necklace." How are the plot devices and conflict resolutions similar?
2. Compare this story to Anzia Yezierska's "Hunger."

JOHN EDGAR WIDEMAN

John Edgar Wideman (b. 1941) was born in Washington, D.C., but grew up in Pittsburgh; much of his fiction is set in that city's Homewood section. He earned a degree from the University of Pennsylvania and went to Oxford as a Rhodes scholar. *Philadelphia Fire* (1990), one of his more recent novels, won the PEN/Faulkner Prize. In addition to novels and short story collections, he published *Fatheralong: A Meditation on Fathers and Sons, Race and Society* (1995) and edited *The Best American Stories: 1996*. Most of Wideman's fiction has been contemporary, but his most recent novel, *The Cattle Killing* (1996), is partially set in Philadelphia in the eighteenth century. *Twin Cities* was published in 1998. *God's Gym: Stories* appeared in 2005.

Damballah°

Orion let the dead, gray cloth slide down his legs and stepped into the river. He picked his way over slippery stones till he stood calf deep. Dropping to one knee he splashed his groin, then scooped river to his chest, both hands scrubbing with quick, kneading spirals. When he stood again, he stared at the distant gray clouds. A hint of rain in the chill morning air, a faint, clean presence rising from the far side of the hills. The promise of rain coming to him as all things seemed to come these past few months, not through eyes or ears or nose but entering his black skin as if each pore had learned to feel and speak.

He watched the clear water race and ripple and pucker. Where the sun cut through the pine trees and slanted into the water he could see the bottom, see black stones, speckled stones, shining stones whose light came from within. Above a stump at the far edge of the river, clouds of insects hovered. The water was darker there, slower, appeared to stand in deep pools where tangles of root, bush and weed hung over the bank. Orion thought of the eldest priest chalking a design on the floor of the sacred *obi*.° Drawing the watery door no living hands could push open, the crossroads where the spirits passed between worlds. His skin was becoming like that in-between place the priest scratched in the dust. When he walked the cane rows and dirt paths of the plantation he could feel the air of this strange land wearing out his skin, rubbing it thinner and thinner until one day his skin would not be thick enough to separate what

---

°*Damballah*: Paternal god, who lives in rivers and lakes, and may appear in the form of a snake.
°*obi*: House (particularly that of an important person or a king).

was inside from everything outside. Some days his skin whispered he was dying. But he was not afraid. The voices and faces of his fathers bursting through would not drown him. They would sweep him away, carry him home again.

In his village across the sea were men who hunted and fished with their voices. Men who could talk the fish up from their shadowy dwellings and into the woven baskets slung over the fishermen's shoulders. Orion knew the fish in this cold river had forgotten him, that they were darting in and out of his legs. If the whites had not stolen him, he would have learned the fishing magic. The proper words, the proper tones to please the fish. But here in this blood-soaked land everything was different. Though he felt their slick bodies and saw the sudden dimples in the water where they were feeding, he understood that he would never speak the language of these fish. No more than he would ever speak again the words of the white people who had decided to kill him.

The boy was there again hiding behind the trees. He could be the one. This boy born so far from home. This boy who knew nothing but what the whites told him. This boy could learn the story and tell it again. Time was short but he could be the one.

5 "That Ryan, he a crazy nigger. One them wild African niggers act like he fresh off the boat. Kind you stay away from less you lookin for trouble." Aunt Lissy had stopped popping string beans and frowned into the boy's face. The pause in the steady drumming of beans into the iron pot, the way she scrunched up her face to look mean like one of the Master's pit bulls told him she had finished speaking on the subject and wished to hear no more about it from him. When the long green pods began to shuttle through her fingers again, it sounded like she was cracking her knuckles, and he expected something black to drop into the huge pot.

"Fixin to rain good. Heard them frogs last night just a singing at the clouds. Frog and all his brothers calling down the thunder. Don't rain soon them fields dry up and blow away." The boy thought of the men trudging each morning to the fields. Some were brown, some yellow, some had red in their skins and some white as the Master. Ryan black, but Aunt Lissy blacker. Fat, shiny blue-black like a crow's wing.

"Sure nuff crazy." Old woman always talking. Talking and telling silly stories. The boy wanted to hear something besides an old woman's mouth. He had heard about frogs and bears and rabbits too many times. He was almost grown now, almost ready to leave in the mornings with the men. What would they talk about? Would Orion's voice be like the hollers the boy heard early in the mornings when the men still sleepy and the sky still dark and you couldn't really see nobody but knew they were there when them cries and hollers came rising through the mist.

Pine needles crackled with each step he took, and the boy knew old Ryan knew somebody spying on him. Old nigger guess who it was, too. But if Ryan knew, Ryan didn't care. Just waded out in the water like he the only man in the world. Like maybe wasn't no world. Just him and that quiet place in the middle of the river. Must be fishing out there, some funny old African kind of fishing. Nobody never saw him touch victuals Master set out and he had to be eating something, even if he was half crazy, so the nigger must be fishing for his breakfast. Standing there like a stick in the water till the fish forgot him and he could snatch one from the water with his beaky fingers.

A skinny-legged, black waterbird in the purring river. The boy stopped chewing his stick of cane, let the sweet juice blend with his spit, a warm syrup then whose taste he prolonged by not swallowing, but letting it coat his tongue and the insides of his mouth, waiting patiently like the figure in the water waited, as the sweet taste seeped away. All the cane juice had trickled down his throat before he saw Orion move. After the stillness, the illusion that the man was a tree rooted in the rocks at the riverbed, when motion came, it was too swift to follow. Not so much a matter of seeing Orion move as it was feeling the man's eyes inside him, hooking him before he could crouch lower in the weeds. Orion's eyes on him and through him boring a hole in his chest and thrusting into that space one word *Damballah.* Then the hooded eyes were gone.

On a spoon you see the shape of a face is an egg. Or two eggs because you can change the shape from long oval to moons pinched together at the middle seam or any shape egg if you tilt and push the spoon closer or farther away. Nothing to think about. You go with Mistress to the chest in the root cellar. She guides you with a candle and you make a pouch of soft cloth and carefully lay in each spoon and careful it don't jangle as up and out of the darkness following her rustling dresses and petticoats up the earthen steps each one topped by a plank which squirms as you mount it. You are following the taper she holds and the strange smell she trails and leaves in rooms. Then shut up in a room all day with nothing to think about. With rags and pieces of silver. Slowly you rub away the tarnished spots; it is like finding something which surprises you though you knew all the time it was there. Spoons lying on the strip of indigo: perfect, gleaming fish you have coaxed from the black water.

Damballah was the word. Said it to Aunt Lissy and she went upside his head, harder than she had ever slapped him. Felt like crumpling right there in the dust of the yard it hurt so bad but he bit his lip and didn't cry out, held his ground and said the word again and again silently to himself, pretending nothing but a bug on his burning cheek and twitched and sent it flying. Damballah. Be strong as he needed to be. Nothing touch him if he don't want. Before long they'd cut him from the herd of pickaninnies. No more chasing flies from the table, no more silver spoons to get shiny, no fat, old woman telling him what to do. He'd go to the fields each morning with the men. Holler like they did before the sun rose to burn off the mist. Work like they did from can to caint. From first crack of light to dusk when the puddles of shadow deepened and spread so you couldn't see your hands or feet or the sharp tools hacking at the cane.

He was already taller than the others, a stork among the chicks scurrying behind Aunt Lissy. Soon he'd rise with the conch horn and do a man's share so he had let the fire rage on half his face and thought of the nothing always there to think of. In the spoon, his face long and thin as a finger. He looked for the print of Lissy's black hand on his cheek, but the image would not stay still. Dancing like his face reflected in the river. Damballah. "Don't you ever, you hear me, ever let me hear that heathen talk no more. You hear me, boy? You talk Merican, boy." Lissy's voice like chicken cackle. And his head a barn packed with animal noise and animal smell. His own head but he had to sneak round in it. Too many others crowded in there with him. His head so crowded and noisy lots of time don't hear his own voice with all them braying and cackling.

Orion squatted the way the boy had seen the other old men collapse on their haunches and go still as a stump. Their bony knees poking up and their backsides resting on their ankles. Looked like they could sit that way all day, legs folded under them like wings. Orion drew a cross in the dust. Damballah. When Orion passed his hands over the cross the air seemed to shimmer like it does above a flame or like it does when the sun so hot you can see waves of heat rising off the fields. Orion talked to the emptiness he shaped with his long black fingers. His eyes were closed. Orion wasn't speaking but sounds came from inside him the boy had never heard before, strange words, clicks, whistles and grunts. A singsong moan that rose and fell and floated like the old man's busy hands above the cross. Damballah like a drum beat in the chant. Damballah a place the boy could enter, a familiar sound he began to anticipate, a sound outside of him which slowly forced its way inside, a sound measuring his heartbeat then one with the pumping surge of his blood.

The boy heard part of what Lissy saying to Primus in the cooking shed: "Ryan he yell that heathen word right in the middle of Jim talking bout Sweet Jesus the Son of God. Jump up like he snake bit and scream that word so everybody hushed, even the white folks what came to hear Jim preach. Simple Ryan standing there at the back of the chapel like a knot poked out on somebody's forehead. Lookin like a nigger caught wid his hand in the chicken coop. Screeching like some crazy hoot owl while Preacher Jim praying the word of the Lord. They gon kill that simple nigger one day."

15   Dear Sir:

The nigger Orion which I purchased of you in good faith sight unseen on your promise that he was of sound constitution "a full grown and able-bodied house servant who can read, write, do sums and cipher" to recite the exact words of your letter dated April 17, 1852, has proved to be a burden, a deficit to the economy of my plantation rather than the asset I fully believed I was receiving when I agreed to pay the price you asked. Of the vaunted intelligence so rare in his kind, I have seen nothing. Not an English word has passed through his mouth since he arrived. Of his docility and tractability I have seen only the willingness with which he bares his leatherish back to receive the stripes constant misconduct earn him. He is a creature whose brutish habits would shame me were he quartered in my kennels. I find it odd that I should write at such length about any nigger, but seldom have I been so struck by the disparity between promise and performance. As I have accrued nothing but expense and inconvenience as a result of his presence, I think it only just that you return the full amount I paid for this *flawed piece of the Indies.*°

You know me as an honest and fair man and my regard for those same qualities in you prompts me to write this letter. I am not a harsh master, I concern myself with the spiritual as well as the temporal needs of my slaves. My nigger Jim is renowned in this county as a preacher. Many say I am foolish, that the words of scripture are wasted on these savage blacks. I fear you have sent me a living argument to support the critics of my Christianizing project. Among other absences of truly human qualities I have observed in this Orion is the utter lack of a soul.

She said it time for Orion to die. Broke half the overseer's bones knocking him off his horse this morning and everybody thought Ryan done run away sure but Mistress come upon the crazy nigger at suppertime on the big house porch naked as the day he born and he just sat there staring into her eyes till Mistress screamed and run away. Aunt Lissy said Ryan ain't studying no women, ain't gone near to woman since he been here and she say his ain't the first black butt Mistress done seen all them nearly grown boys walkin round summer in the onliest shirt Master give em barely come down to they knees and niggers man nor woman don't get drawers the first. Mistress and Master both seen plenty. Wasn't what she saw scared her less she see the ghost leaving out Ryan's body.

° *"flawed piece of the Indies"*: Slaves were taken by ship first to islands in the West Indies and then to North and South America.

The ghost wouldn't steam out the top of Orion's head. The boy remembered the sweaty men come in from the fields at dusk when the nights start to cool early, remembered them with the drinking gourds in they hands scooping up water from the wooden barrel he filled, how they throw they heads back and the water trickles from the sides of they mouth and down they chin and they let it roll on down they chests, and the smoky steam curling off they shoulders. Orion's spirit would not rise up like that but wiggle out his skin and swim off up the river.

The boy knew many kinds of ghosts and learned the ways you get round their 20
tricks. Some spirits almost good company and he filled the nothing with jingles and whistles and took roundabout paths and sang to them when he walked up on a crossroads and yoo-hooed at doors. No way you fool the haunts° if a spell conjured strong on you, no way to miss a beating if it your day to get beat, but the ghosts had everything in they hands, even the white folks in they hands. You know they there, you know they floating up in the air watching and counting and remembering them strokes Ole Master laying cross your back.

They dragged Orion across the yard. He didn't buck or kick but it seemed as if the four men carrying him were struggling with a giant stone rather than a black bag of bones. His ashy nigger weight swung between the two pairs of white men like a lazy hammock but the faces of the men all red and twisted. They huffed and puffed and sweated through they clothes carrying Ryan's bones to the barn. The dry spell had layered the yard with a coat of dust. Little squalls of yellow spurted from under the men's boots. Trudging steps heavy as if each man carried seven Orions on his shoulders. Four grown men struggling with one string of black flesh. The boy had never seen so many white folks dealing with one nigger. Aunt Lissy had said it time to die and the boy wondered what Ryan's ghost would think dropping onto the dust surrounded by the scowling faces of the Master and his overseers.

One scream that night. Like a bull when they cut off his maleness. Couldn't tell who it was. A bull screaming once that night and torches burning in the barn and Master and the men coming out and no Ryan.

Mistress crying behind a locked door and Master messing with Patty down the quarters.

In the morning light the barn swelling and rising and teetering in the yellow dust, moving the way you could catch the ghost of something in a spoon and play with it, bending it, twisting it. That goldish ash on everybody's bare shins. Nobody talking. No cries nor hollers from the fields. The boy watched till his eyes hurt, waiting for a moment when he could slip unseen into the shivering barn. On his hands and knees hiding under a wagon, then edging sideways through the loose boards and wedge of space where the weathered door hung crooked on its hinge.

The interior of the barn lay in shadows. Once beyond the sliver of light coming 25
in at the cracked door the boy stood still till his eyes adjusted to the darkness. First he could pick out the stacks of hay, the rough partitions dividing the animals. The smells, the choking heat there like always, but rising above these familiar sensations the buzz of flies, unnaturally loud, as if the barn breathing and each breath

---

°*haunts*: Ghosts, spirits.

shook the wooden walls. Then the boy's eyes followed the sound to an open space at the center of the far wall. A black shape there. Orion there, floating in his own blood. The boy ran at the blanket of flies. When he stomped, some of the flies buzzed up from the carcass. Others too drunk on the shimmering blood ignored him except to join the ones hovering above the body in a sudden droning peal of annoyance. He could keep the flies stirring but they always returned from the recesses of the high ceiling, the dark corners of the building, to gather in a cloud above the body. The boy looked for something to throw. Heard his breath, heavy and threatening like the sound of the flies. He sank to the dirt floor, sitting cross-legged where he had stood. He moved only once, ten slow paces away from Orion and back again, near enough to be sure, to see again how the head had been cleaved from the rest of the body, to see how the ax and tongs, branding iron and other tools were scattered around the corpse, to see how one man's hat and another's shirt, a letter that must have come from someone's pocket lay about in a helter-skelter way as if the men had suddenly bolted before they had finished with Orion.

Forgive him, Father. I tried to the end of my patience to restore his lost soul. I made a mighty effort to bring him to the Ark of Salvation but he had walked in darkness too long. He mocked Your Grace. He denied Your Word. Have mercy on him and forgive his heathen ways as you forgive the soulless beasts of the fields and birds of the air.

She say Master still down slave row. She say everybody fraid to go down and get him. Everybody fraid to open the barn door. Overseer half dead and the Mistress still crying in her locked room and that barn starting to stink already with crazy Ryan and nobody gon get him.

And the boy knew his legs were moving and he knew they would carry him where they needed to go and he knew the legs belonged to him but he could not feel them, he had been sitting too long thinking on nothing for too long and he felt the sweat running on his body but his mind off somewhere cool and quiet and hard and he knew the space between his body and mind could not be crossed by anything, knew you mize well try to stick the head back on Ryan as try to cross that space. So he took what he needed out of the barn, unfolding, getting his gangly crane's legs together under him and shouldered open the creaking double doors and walked through the flame in the center where he had to go.

Damballah said it be a long way a ghost be going and Jordan chilly and wide and a new ghost take his time getting his wings together. Long way to go so you can sit and listen till the ghost ready to go on home. The boy wiped his wet hands on his knees and drew the cross and said the word and settled down and listened to Orion tell the stories again. Orion talked and he listened and couldn't stop listening till he saw Orion's eyes rise up through the back of the severed skull and lips rise up through the skull and the wings of the ghost measure out the rhythm of one last word.

30   Late afternoon and the river slept dark at its edges like it did in the mornings. The boy threw the head as far as he could and he knew the fish would hear it and swim to it and welcome it. He knew they had been waiting. He knew the ripples would touch him when he entered.   [1981]

QUESTIONS

1. Does Wideman's picture of life on a plantation seem believable?
2. Wideman moves from one character's mind to another's. What practical problem of storytelling does this omniscient point of view solve?
3. Why does Aunt Lissy slap the boy over the word "Damballah"?
4. What is the effect of Wideman's use of "perfect, gleaming fish" as a metaphor for "spoons"?
5. Does the use of the word "him" in the story's last sentence refer solely to Orion?

WILLIAM CARLOS WILLIAMS

William Carlos Williams (1883–1963) was born in Rutherford, New Jersey. He graduated from the medical school of the University of Pennsylvania and, amazingly, balanced the successful practice of pediatrics with a prolific and distinguished literary career. He published novels, stories, plays, essays, poems, and his epic chronicle *Paterson* (1946–1958). Williams's dedication to the idea of America and his technical innovations have been a source of inspiration to many later writers.

The Use of Force

They were new patients to me, all I had was the name, Olson. Please come down as soon as you can, my daughter is very sick.

When I arrived I was met by the mother, a big startled looking woman, very clean and apologetic who merely said, Is this the doctor? And let me in. In the back, she added. You must excuse us, doctor, we have her in the kitchen where it is warm. It is very damp here sometimes.

The child was fully dressed and sitting on her father's lap near the kitchen table. He tried to get up, but I motioned for him not to bother, took off my overcoat and started to look things over. I could see that they were all very nervous, eyeing me up and down distrustfully. As often, in such cases, they weren't telling me more than they had to, it was up to me to tell them; that's why they were spending three dollars on me.

The child was fairly eating me up with her cold, steady eyes, and no expression to her face whatever. She did not move and seemed, inwardly, quiet; an unusually attractive little thing, and as strong as a heifer in appearance. But her face was flushed, she was breathing rapidly, and I realized that she had a high fever. She had magnificent blonde hair, in profusion. One of those picture children often reproduced in advertising leaflets and the photogravure sections of the Sunday papers.

5   She's had a fever for three days, began the father and we don't know what it comes from. My wife has given her things, you know, like people do, but it don't do no good. And there's been a lot of sickness around. So we tho't you'd better look her over and tell us what is the matter.

As doctors often do I took a trial shot at it as a point of departure. Has she had a sore throat?

Both parents answered me together, No . . . No, she says her throat don't hurt her.

Does your throat hurt you? added the mother to the child. But the little girl's expression didn't change nor did she move her eyes from my face.

Have you looked?

I tried to, said the mother, but I couldn't see.

As it happens we had been having a number of cases of diphtheria in the school to which this child went during that month and we were all, quite apparently, thinking of that, though no one had as yet spoken of the thing.

Well, I said, suppose we take a look at the throat first. I smiled in my best professional manner and asking for the child's first name I said, come on, Mathilda, open your mouth and let's take a look at your throat.

Nothing doing.

Aw, come on, I coaxed, just open your mouth wide and let me take a look. Look, I said opening both hands wide, I haven't anything in my hands. Just open up and let me see.

Such a nice man, put in the mother. Look how kind he is to you. Come on, do what he tells you to. He won't hurt you.

At that I ground my teeth in disgust. If only they wouldn't use the word "hurt" I might be able to get somewhere. But I did not allow myself to be hurried or disturbed but speaking quietly and slowly I approached the child again.

As I moved my chair a little nearer suddenly with one catlike movement both her hands clawed instinctively for my eyes and she almost reached them too. In fact she knocked my glasses flying and they fell, though unbroken, several feet away from me on the kitchen floor.

Both the mother and father almost turned themselves inside out in embarrassment and apology. You bad girl, said the mother, taking her and shaking her by one arm. Look what you've done. The nice man . . .

For heaven's sake, I broke in. Don't call me a nice man to her. I'm here to look at her throat on the chance that she might have diphtheria and possibly die of it. But that's nothing to her. Look here, I said to the child, we're going to look at your throat. You're old enough to understand what I'm saying. Will you open it now by yourself or shall we have to open it for you?

Not a move. Even her expression hadn't changed. Her breaths however were coming faster and faster. Then the battle began. I had to do it. I had to have a throat culture for her own protection. But first I told the parents that it was entirely up to them. I explained the danger but said that I would not insist on a throat examination so long as they would take the responsibility.

If you don't do what the doctor says you'll have to go the hospital, the mother admonished her severely.

Oh yeah? I had to smile to myself. After all, I had already fallen in love with the savage brat, the parents were contemptible to me. In the ensuing struggle they grew more and more abject, crushed, exhausted while she surely rose to magnificent heights of insane fury of effort bred of her terror of me.

The father tried his best, and he was a big man but the fact that she was his daughter, his shame at her behavior and his dread of hurting her made him release her just at the critical times when I had almost achieved success, till I wanted to kill him. But his dread also that she might have diphtheria made him tell me to go on, go on though he himself was almost fainting, while the mother moved back and forth behind us raising and lowering her hands in an agony of apprehension.

Put her in front of you on your lap, I ordered, and hold both her wrists.

25   But as soon as he did the child let out a scream. Don't, you're hurting me. Let go of
my hands. Let them go I tell you. Then she shrieked terrifyingly, hysterically. Stop it!
You're killing me!

Do you think she can stand it, doctor! said the mother.

You get out, said the husband to his wife. Do you want her to die of diphtheria?

Come on now, hold her, I said.

Then I grasped the child's head with my left hand and tried to get the wooden
tongue depressor between her teeth. She fought, with clenched teeth, desperately! But
now I also had grown furious—at a child. I tried to hold myself down but I couldn't.
I know how to expose a throat for inspection. And I did my best. When finally I got
the wooden spatula behind the last teeth and just the point of it into the mouth cavity, she opened up for an instant but before I could see anything she came down again
and gripping the wooden blade between her molars she reduced it to splinters before
I could get it out again.

30   Aren't you ashamed, the mother yelled at her. Aren't you ashamed to act like that
in front of the doctor?

Get me a smooth-handled spoon of some sort, I told the mother. We're going
through with this. The child's mouth was already bleeding. Her tongue was cut and
she was screaming in wild hysterical shrieks. Perhaps I should have desisted and come
back in an hour or more. No doubt it would have been better. But I have seen at least
two children lying dead in bed of neglect in such cases, and feeling that I must get a
diagnosis now or never I went at it again. But the worst of it was that I too had got beyond reason. I could have torn the child apart in my own fury and enjoyed it. It was
a pleasure to attack her. My face was burning with it.

The damned little brat must be protected against her own idiocy, one says to one's
self at such times. Others must be protected against her. It is a social necessity. And all
these things are true. But a blind fury, a feeling of adult shame, bred of a longing for
muscular release are the operatives. One goes on to the end.

In the final unreasoning assault I overpowered the child's neck and jaws. I forced
the heavy silver spoon back of her teeth and down her throat till she gagged. And
there it was—both tonsils covered with membrane. She had fought valiantly to keep
me from knowing her secret. She had been hiding that sore throat for three days at
least and lying to her parents in order to escape just such an outcome as this.

Now truly she was furious. She had been on the defensive before but now she attacked. Tried to get off her father's lap and fly at me while tears of defeat blinded her
eyes.   [1950]

QUESTIONS

1. What part do differences in social class play in the development of the conflict?

2. For such a short story do the characters seem adequately developed?

3. What reasons might be advanced for the disregard of some of the conventions
   of English grammar in the story?

4. Would the author have achieved the same effect if he had chosen the student-
   teacher relationship rather than the doctor-patient?

5. Did the doctor have to resort to the use of force? What does his conduct have
   to say about the values of civilization?

JEANETTE WINTERSON

Jeanette Winterson (b. 1959) was adopted by a Pentecostal family in Lancashire, England. An avid reader in a family that restricted reading and a lesbian in a fundamentalist family, Winterson left home early, working in mental hospitals and funeral parlors. She was accepted to and graduated from Oxford University, studying English. Her first novel, *Oranges Are Not the Only Fruit* (1985), won the Whitbread First Novel Award. Often compared to the work of Jorge Luis Borges and Angela Carter, Winterson's further fiction includes *Boating for Beginners* (1985), *The Passion* (1987), *Sexing the Cherry* (1989), *Cut Symmetries* (1994), *Art and Lies* (1995), *The Powerbook* (2000) and *Lighthouse Keeping* (2003). Her short stories can be found in *The World and Other Places* (1988). Her nonfiction is collected in *Art Objects: Essays on Ecstasy and Effrontery* (1995).

Newton

This is the story of Tom.
   This is the story of Tom and his neighbours.
   This is the story of Tom and his neighbours and his neighbour's garden.
   This is the story of Tom.

"All of my neighbours are Classical Physicists," said Tom. "Their laws of motion are   5
determined. They rise at 7 A.M. and leave for work at 8 A.M. The women take coffee at 10 A.M. If you see a body on the street between 1 and 2 P.M. lunchtime, it can only be the doctor, it can only be the undertaker, it can only be the stranger.
   "I am the stranger," said Tom.

"What is the First Law of Thermodynamics?" said Tom.
   "You can't transfer heat from a colder to a hotter. I've never known any warmth from my neighbours so I would reckon this is true. Here in Newton we don't talk much. That is, my neighbours talk all the time, they swap gossip, but I never have any, although sometimes I am some."

"What is the Second Law of Thermodynamics?" said Tom.

10   "Everything tends towards the condition of entropy. That is, the energy is still there somewhere but for all useful purposes it is lost. Take a look at my neighbours here in Newton and you'll see what it means."

My neighbour has a garden full of plastic flowers. "It's easy," she says, "and so nice." When her husband died she had him laminated, and he stands outside now, hands on his hips, carefully watching the sky.

"What's the matter Tom?" she says, her head bobbing along the fence like a duck in a shooting parlour.

"Why don't you get married? In my day nobody had any trouble finding someone. We just did it and made the best of it. There were no screwballs then."

"What none?"

15   She bobbed faster and faster, gathering a bosom-load of underwear from the washing line. I knew she wanted me to stare at it, she wants to prove that I am a screwball. After all, if it's me, it's not her, it's not the others. You can't have more than one per block.

She wheeled round, ready to bob back up the other way, knickers popping from every pore.

"Tom, we were glad to be normal. In those days it was something good, something to be proud of."

Tom the screwball. Here I am with my paperback foreign editions and my corduroy trousers ("You got something against Levi's?" he asked me, before he was laminated). All the men round here wear Levi's, denims or chinos. The only stylistic difference is whether they pack their stomach inside or outside the waistband.

They suspect me of being a homosexual. I wouldn't care. I wouldn't care what I was if only I were something.

20   "What do you want to be when you grow up?" said my mother, a long time ago, many times a long time ago.

"A fireman, an astronaut, a spy, a train driver, a hard hat, an inventor, a deep sea diver, a doctor and a nurse."

"What do you want to be when you grow up?" I ask myself in the mirror most days.

"Myself. I want to be myself."

And who is that, Tom?

25   Into the clockwork universe the quantum child. Why doesn't every mother believe her child can change the world? The child can. This is the joke. Here we are still looking for a saviour and hundreds are being born every second. Look at it, this tiny capsule of new life, indifferent to your prejudices, your miseries, unmindful of the world already made. Make it again? They could if we let them, but we make sure they grow up just like us, fearful like us. Don't let them know the potential that they are. Don't let them hear the grass singing. Let them live and die in Newton, tick-tock, the last breath.

There was a knock at my door, I hid my Camus in the fridge and peered through the frosted glass. Of course I can't see anything. They never remind you of that when you fit frosted glass.

"Tom? Tom?" RAP RAP.

It's my neighbour. I shuffled to the door, feet bare, shirt loose. There she is, her hair coiled on her head like a wreath on a war memorial. She was dressed solely in pink.

"I'm not interrupting am I Tom?" she said, her eyes shoving past me into the kitchen.

"I was reading." 30

"That's what I thought. I said to myself, poor Tom will be reading. He won't be busy. I'll ask him to help me out. You know how difficult it is for a woman to manage alone. Since my husband was laminated, I haven't had it easy, Tom."

She smelled of woman; warm, perfumed, slightly threatening. I had to be careful not to act like a screwball. I offered her coffee. She seemed pleased, although she kept glancing at my bare feet and loose shirt. Never mind, she needs me to help her with something in the house. That's normal, that's nice, I want to be normal and nice.

"My mother's here. Will you help me get her into the house."

"Now? Shall we go now?"

"She's had a long journey. She can rest in the truck a while. Shall we have that cof- 35
fee you offered me first?"

I don't love my neighbour but still my hand trembled over the sugar spoon. They've made me feel odd and outside for so long, that now even the simplest things feel strange.

How does a normal person make coffee? What is it about me that worries them so much? I'm clean. I have a job.

"Tom, tell me, is it the modern thing to keep books in the refrigerator?"

In cheap crime novels, you often read the line, "He spun round." It makes me laugh to imagine a human being so animated, but when she asked me that question, I spun. One second I was facing the sink, the next second I was facing her, and she was facing me, holding my copy of Camus.

"I was just fetching out the milk Tom. Who is Albert K Mew?" She pronounced it 40
like an enraged cat.

"He's a Frenchman. A French writer. I don't know how he came to be in the fridge."

She repeated my words slowly as though I had just offered her a universal truth.

"You don't know how he came to be in the fridge?" I shrugged and smiled and tried to disarm her.

"It's a big fridge. Don't you ever find things in the fridge you had forgotten about?"

"No Tom. Never. I store cheese at the top, and then beer and bacon underneath, 45
and underneath those I keep my weekend chicken, and at the bottom I have salad things and eggs. Those are the rules. It was the same when my husband was alive and it is the same now."

I was beginning to regard her with a new respect. The Grim Reaper came to call. He took her husband from the bed but left the weekend chicken on the shelf.

O Death, where is thy sting?

My neighbour, still holding my Camus, leaned forward confidentially, her arms resting on the table. She looked intimate, soft, I could see the beginning of her breasts.

"Tom, have you ever wondered whether you need help?" She said HELP with four capital letters, like a doorstep evangelist.

"If you mean the fridge, anyone can make a mistake." She leaned forward a little 50
further. More breast.

"Tom, I'm going to be tough with you. You know what your problem is? You read too many geniuses. I don't know if Mr K Mew is a genius but the other day you were seen in the main square reading Picasso's notebooks. Children were coming out of school and you were reading Picasso. Miss Fin at the library tells me that all you ever borrow are works of genius. She has no record of you ever ordering a sea story. Now that's unhealthy. Why is it unhealthy? You yourself are not a genius, if you were we would have found out by now. You are ordinary like the rest of us and ordinary people should lead ordinary lives. Like the rest of us, here in Tranquil Gardens."

She leaned back, her bosom with her.

"Shall we go and help your mother?" I said.

Outside, my neighbour walked towards a closed van parked in front of her house. I'd seen her mother a couple of years previously but I couldn't see her now.

55   "She's in the back Tom. Go round the back."

My neighbour flung open the back doors of the hired van and certainly there was her mother, sitting upright in the wheel-chair that had been her home and her car. She was smiling a fearful plasticy smile, her teeth as perfect as a cheetah's.

"Haven't they done a wonderful job Tom? She's even better than Doug, and he was pretty advanced at the time. I wish she could see herself. She never guessed I'd laminate her. She'd be so proud."

"Are those her own teeth?"

"They are now Tom."

60   "Where will you put her?"

"In the garden with the flowers. She loved flowers."

Slowly, slowly, we heaved down mother. We wheeled her over the swept pavement to the whitewashed house. It was afternoon coffee time and a lot of neighbours had been invited to pay their respects. They were so respectful that we were outside talking plastic until the men came home. My neighbour gets an incentive voucher for every successful lamination she introduces. She reckons that if Newton will only do it her way, she'll have 75 percent of her own lamination costs paid by the time she dies.

"I've seen you hanging around the cemetery Tom. It's not hygienic."

What does she think I am? A ghoul? I've told her before that my mother is buried there but she just shakes her head and tells me that young couples need the land.

65   "Until we learn to stop dying Tom, we have to live with the consequences. There's no room for the dead unless you treat them as ornamental."

I have tried to tell her that if we stop dying, all the cemeteries in the world can never release enough land for the bulging, ageing population. She doesn't listen, she just looks dreamy and thinks about the married couples.

Newton is jammed with married couples. We need one-way streets to let the singles through. I hate going shopping in Newton. I hate clubbing my way through the crocodile files, two by two in Main street, as though the ark has landed. Complacent shoulder blades, battered baby buggys. DIY stores crammed with HIM and shopping malls heaving with HER. Don't they know that too much role playing is bad for the health? Imagine being a wife and saying 'Honey, have you got time to fix the toilet?' Imagine being a husband and figuring out how to clean the toilet when she's left you.

Why are they married? It's normal, it's nice. They do it the way they do everything else in Newton. Tick-tock says the clock.

"Tom, thank you Tom," she cooed at me when her mother was safely settled beside the duck pond. The ducks are bath time yellow with chirpy red beaks and their pond has real water with a bit of chlorine in it just in case. I had never been in my neighbour's garden before. It was quiet. No rustling in the undergrowth. No undergrowth to rustle in. No birds yammering. She tells me that peace is what the countryside is all about.

"If you were a genius Tom you could work here. The silence. The air. I have a unit 70
you know, filters the air as it enters the garden."

It was autumn and there were a few plastic leaves scattered about on the AstroTurf. At the bottom of the garden, my neighbour has a shed, made of imitation wood, where she keeps her stocks for the changing of the seasons. She has told me many times that a garden must have variety and in her ventilated Aladdin's cave are the reassuring copies of nature. Tulips, red and white, hang meekly upside down by their stems. Daffodils in bright bunches are jumbled with loose camellia blooms, waiting to be slotted into the everlasting tree. She even has a row of squirrels clutching identical nuts.

"Those are going out soon, along with the autumn creeper." She has Virginia Creeper cascading down the house. It's still green. This is the burnt and blazing version.

"Mine's turning already," I said.

"Too early," she said. "You can't depend on nature. I don't like leaves falling. They don't fall where they should. If you don't regulate nature, why, she'll just go ahead and do what she likes. We have to regulate her. If we don't, it's volcanoes and forest fires and floods and death and bodies scattered everywhere, just like leaves."

Like leaves. Just like leaves. Don't you like them just a little where they fall? Don't 75
you turn them over to see what is written on the other side? I like that. I like the simple text that can be read or not, that lies beneath your feet and mine, read or not. That falls, rain and wind, though nobody scoops it up to take it home. Life fell at your feet and you kicked her away and she bled on your shoes and when you came home, your mother said, "Look at you, covered in leaves."

You were covered in leaves. You peeled them off one by one, exposing the raw skin beneath. All those leavings. And when what had to fall was fallen, you picked it up and read what was written on the other side. It made no sense to you. You screwed it up in your pocket where it burned like a live coal. Tell me why they left you, one by one, the ones you loved? Didn't they like you? Didn't they, like you, need a heart that was a book with no last page? Turn the leaves.

"The leaves are turning," said Tom.

She asked me back to supper as a thank you, and I thought I should go because that's what normal people do; eat with their neighbours, even though it is boring and the food is horrible. I searched for a tie and wore it.

"Tom, come in, what a lovely surprise!"

She must mean what a lovely surprise for me. It can hardly be a surprise for her, 80
she's been cooking all afternoon.

Once inside the dining room, I know she means me. I know that because the entire population of Newton is already seated at the dinner table, a table that begins crammed up against the display cabinet of Capodimonte and extends . . . and extends . . . through a jagged hole blown in the side of the house, out and on towards the bus station.

"I think you know everyone Tom," says my neighbour. "Sit here, by me, in Doug's place. You're about his height." Do I know everyone? It's hard to say, since beyond the hole, all is lost.

"Tom, take a plate. We're having chicken cooked in bacon strips and stuffed with hard-boiled eggs. There's a salad I made and plenty of cheese and beer in the fridge if you want it."

She drifted away from me, her dress clinging to her like a drowned man. Nobody looked up from their plates. They were eating chicken, denims and chinos all, eating the three or four hundred fowl laid on the table, half a dozen eggs per ass. I was still trying to work out the roasting details, the oven size, when BAM, one of the chickens exploded, pelting my neighbour with eggs like hand-grenades. One of her arms flew off but luckily for her, not the one she needed for her fork. Nobody noticed. I wanted to speak, I wanted to act, I began to speak, to act, just as my neighbour herself returned carrying a covered silver dish.

85   "It's for you Tom," she says, as the table falls silent. Already on my feet I was able to lift the huge lid with some dignity. Underneath was a chicken.

"It's your chicken Tom."

She's telling the truth. Poking out of the ass of the chicken, I can see my copy of *L'Etranger* by Albert Camus. It hasn't been shredded, so I can take it out. When I open it I see that there are no words left on any of the pages. The pages are blank.

"We wanted to help you Tom." Her eyes are full of tears. "Not just me. All of us. A helping hand for Tom."

Slowly the table starts to clap, faster and louder. The table shakes, the dishes roll from side to side like the drunken tableware in a sea story. This is a sea story. The captain and the crew have gone mad and I am the only passenger. Reeling, I ran from the dining room into the kitchen and slammed the door behind me. Here was peace. Hygienic enamelled peace.

90   Tom slid to the floor and cried.

Time passed. In Newton it always does and everyone knows how long it takes for time to pass and so nobody gets confused. Tom didn't know how much time had passed. He woke from an aching sleep and put his fist through the frosted glass kitchen door. He went home and took his big coat and filled the pockets with books and the books seemed like live coals to him. He walked away from Newton, but he did look back once, and what he saw was a table stretching out past the bend in the road and on through the streets and houses joining them together in an orgy of matching cutlery. World without end.

"But now," says Tom, "the hills are ripe and the water leaps at my throat when I shave."

Tick-tock says the clock in Newton.   [1998]

QUESTIONS

1. Look at how Winterson varies the point of view in the story. How does the story change because of this technique?
2. Why does the neighbor believe it's bad for Tom to read the works only of geniuses?
3. What is the neighbor trying to accomplish in laminating her family?
4. Explain the significance of the dinner party.
5. What does Tom mean by "All of my neighbors are Classical Physicists"? How does physics relate to the title?

RESPONSES

1. Compare Jeanette Winterson's "Newton" to Donald Barthelme's "A City of Churches."
2. Research the twentieth century's response to Newtonian physics. Write an essay explicating Winterson's story in the light of that response.
3. Write an ecocritical interpretation of the landscape of Newton.

VIRGINIA WOOLF

Virginia Woolf (1882–1941) was born in London. The daughter of Sir Leslie Stephen, a Victorian critic and biographer, Woolf educated herself by using her father's extensive library. In 1912, she married Leonard Woolf and with him founded the Hogarth Press, which published works by E. M. Forster, Gertrude Stein, and Woolf herself. Her most famous novels include *Mrs. Dalloway* (1925), *To the Lighthouse* (1927), and *The Waves* (1931). Woolf suffered a nervous breakdown in 1916. She suffered from fits of acute depression and, in 1941, convinced that she was about to have an incurable relapse into an earlier state of mental illness, took her own life by drowning.

Kew Gardens

From the oval-shaped flower-bed there rose perhaps a hundred stalks spreading into heart-shaped or tongue-shaped leaves halfway up and unfurling at the tip red or blue or yellow petals marked with spots of colour raised upon the surface; and from the red, blue or yellow gloom of the throat emerged a straight bar, rough with gold dust and slightly clubbed at the end. The petals were voluminous enough to be stirred by the summer breeze, and when they moved, the red, blue and yellow lights passed one over the other, staining an inch of the brown earth beneath with a spot of the most intricate colour. The light fell either upon the smooth, grey back of a pebble, or, the shell of a snail with its brown, circular veins, or falling into a raindrop, it expanded with such intensity of red, blue and yellow the thin walls of water that one expected them to burst and disappear. Instead, the drop was left in a second silver grey once more, and the light now settled upon the flesh of a leaf, revealing the branching thread of fibre beneath the surface, and again it moved on and spread its illumination in the vast green spaces beneath the dome of the heart-shaped and tongue-shaped leaves. Then the breeze stirred rather more briskly overhead and the colour was flashed into the air above, into the eyes of the men and women who walk in Kew Gardens° in July.

    The figures of these men and women straggled past the flower-bed with a curiously irregular movement not unlike that of the white and blue butterflies who crossed

---

°*Kew Gardens*: London suburb, site of the Royal Botanic Gardens.

the turf in zig-zag flights from bed to bed. The man was about six inches in front of the woman, strolling carelessly, while she bore on with greater purpose, only turning her head now and then to see that the children were not too far behind. The man kept this distance in front of the woman purposely, though perhaps unconsciously, for he wished to go on with his thoughts.

"Fifteen years ago I came here with Lily," he thought. "We sat somewhere over there by a lake and I begged her to marry me all through the hot afternoon. How the dragonfly kept circling round us: how clearly I see the dragonfly and her shoe with the square silver buckle at the toe. All the time I spoke I saw her shoe and when it moved impatiently I knew without looking up what she was going to say: the whole of her seemed to be in her shoe. And my love, my desire, were in the dragonfly; for some reason I thought that if it settled there, on that leaf, the broad one with the red flower in the middle of it, if the dragonfly settled on the leaf she would say 'Yes' at once. But the dragonfly went round and round: it never settled anywhere—of course not, happily not, or I shouldn't be walking here with Eleanor and the children. Tell me, Eleanor. D'you ever think of the past?"

"Why do you ask, Simon?"

"Because I've been thinking of the past. I've been thinking of Lily, the woman I   5
might have married. . . . Well, why are you silent? Do you mind my thinking of the past?"

"Why should I mind, Simon? Doesn't one always think of the past, in a garden with men and women lying under the trees. Aren't they one's past, all that remains of it, those men and women, those ghosts lying under the trees,. . . one's happiness, one's reality?"

"For me, a square silver shoe buckle and a dragonfly—"

"For me, a kiss. Imagine six little girls sitting before their easels twenty years ago, down by the side of a lake, painting the water-lilies, the first red water-lilies I'd ever seen. And suddenly a kiss, there on the back of my neck. And my hand shook all the afternoon so that I couldn't paint. I took out my watch and marked the hour when I would allow myself to think of the kiss for five minutes only—it was so precious—the kiss of an old grey-haired woman with a wart on her nose, the mother of all my kisses all my life. Come, Caroline, come, Hubert."

They walked on past the flower-bed, now walking four abreast, and soon diminished in size among the trees and looked half transparent as the sunlight and shade swam over their backs in large trembling irregular patches.

In the oval flower-bed the snail, whose shell had been stained red, blue and yellow   10
for the space of two minutes or so, now appeared to be moving very slightly in its shell, and next began to labour over the crumbs of loose earth which broke away and rolled down as it passed over them. It appeared to have a definite goal in front of it, differing in this respect from the singular high stepping angular green insect who attempted to cross in front of it, and waited for a second with its antennae trembling as if in deliberation, and then stepped off as rapidly and strangely in the opposite direction. Brown cliffs with deep green lakes in the hollows, flat, blade-like trees that waved from root to tip, round boulders of grey stone, vast crumpled surfaces of a thin crackling texture—all these objects lay across the snail's progress between one stalk and another to his goal. Before he had decided whether to circumvent the arched tent of a dead leaf or to breast it there came past the bed the feet of other human beings.

This time they were both men. The younger of the two wore an expression of perhaps unnatural calm; he raised his eyes and fixed them very steadily in front of him while his companion spoke, and directly his companion had done speaking he looked on the ground again and sometimes opened his lips only after a long pause and sometimes did not open them at all. The elder man had a curiously uneven and shaky method of walking, jerking his hand forward and throwing up his head abruptly, rather in the manner of an impatient carriage horse tired of waiting outside a house; but in the man these gestures were irresolute and pointless. He talked almost incessantly; he smiled to himself and again began to talk, as if the smile had been an answer. He was talking about spirits—the spirits of the dead, who, according to him, were even now telling him all sorts of odd things about their experiences in Heaven.

"Heaven was known to the ancients as Thessaly, William, and now, with this war, the spirit matter is rolling between the hills like thunder." He paused, seemed to listen, smiled, jerked his head and continued:

"You have a small electric battery and a piece of rubber to insulate the wire—isolate?—insulate?—well, we'll skip the details, no good going into details that wouldn't be understood—and in short the little machine stands in any convenient position by the head of the bed, we will say, on a neat mahogany stand. All arrangements being properly fixed by workmen under my direction, the widow applies her ear and summons the spirit by sign as agreed. Women! Widows! Women in black—"

Here he seemed to have caught sight of a woman's dress in the distance, which in the shade looked a purple black. He took off his hat, placed his hand upon his heart, and hurried towards her muttering and gesticulating feverishly. But William caught him by the sleeve and touched a flower with the tip of his walking-stick in order to divert the old man's attention. After looking at it for a moment in some confusion the old man bent his ear to it and seemed to answer a voice speaking from it, for he began talking about the forests of Uruguay which he had visited hundreds of years ago in company with the most beautiful young woman in Europe. He could be heard murmuring about forests of Uruguay blanketed with the wax petals of tropical roses, nightingales, sea beaches, mermaids, and women drowned at sea, as he suffered himself to be moved on by William, upon whose face the look of stoical patience grew slowly deeper and deeper.

15   Following his steps so closely as to be slightly puzzled by his gestures came two elderly women of the lower middle class, one stout and ponderous, the other rosy cheeked and nimble. Like most people of their station they were frankly fascinated by other signs of eccentricity betokening a disordered brain, especially in the well-to-do; but they were too far off to be certain whether the gestures were merely eccentric or genuinely mad. After they had scrutinized the old man's back in silence for a moment and given each other a queer, sly look, they went on energetically piecing together their very complicated dialogue:

"Nell, Bert, Lot, Cess, Phil, Pa, he says, I says, she says, I says, I says—"

"My Bert, Sis, Bill, Grandad, the old man, sugar,

Sugar, flour, kippers, greens,
Sugar, sugar, sugar."

20   The ponderous woman looked through the pattern of falling words at the flowers standing cool, firm, and upright in the earth, with a curious expression. She saw them as a sleeper waking from a heavy sleep sees a brass candlestick reflecting the light in an unfamiliar way, and closes his eyes and opens them, and seeing the brass candlestick again, finally starts broad awake and stares at the candlestick with all his powers. So the heavy woman came to a standstill opposite the oval-shaped flower-bed,

and ceased even to pretend to listen to what the other woman was saying. She stood there letting the words fall over her, swaying the top part of her body slowly backwards and forwards, looking at the flowers. Then she suggested that they should find a seat and have their tea.

The snail had now considered every possible method of reaching his goal without going round the dead leaf or climbing over it. Let alone the effort needed for climbing a leaf, he was doubtful whether the thin texture which vibrated with such an alarming crackle when touched even by the tips of his horns would bear his weight; and this determined him finally to creep beneath it, for there was a point where the leaf curved high enough from the ground to admit him. He had just inserted his head in the opening and was taking stock of the high brown roof and was getting used to the cool brown light when two other people came past outside on the turf. This time they were both young, a young man and a young woman. They were both in the prime of youth, the season before the smooth pink folds of the flower have burst their gummy case, when the wings of the butterfly, though fully grown, are motionless in the sun.

"Lucky it isn't Friday," he observed.

"Why? D'you believe in luck?"

"They make you pay sixpence on Friday."

"What's a sixpence anyway? Isn't it worth sixpence?" 25

"What's 'it'—what do you mean by 'it'?"

"O, anything—I mean—you know what I mean."

Long pauses came between each of these remarks; they were uttered in toneless and monotonous voices. The couple stood still on the edge of the flower-bed, and together pressed the end of her parasol deep down into the soft earth. The action and the fact that his hand rested on the top of hers expressed their feelings in a strange way, as these short insignificant words also expressed something, words with short wings for their heavy body of meaning, inadequate to carry them far and thus alighting awkwardly upon the very common objects that surrounded them, and were to their inexperienced touch so massive; but who knows (so they thought as they pressed the parasol into the earth) what precipices aren't concealed in them, or what slopes of ice don't shine in the sun on the other side? Who knows? Who has ever seen this before? Even when she wondered what sort of tea they gave you at Kew, he felt that something loomed up behind her words, and stood vast and solid behind them; and the mist very slowly rose and uncovered—O, Heavens, what were those shapes?—little white tables, and waitresses who looked first at her and then at him; and there was a bill that he would pay with a real two-shilling piece, and it was real, all real, he assured himself, fingering the coin in his pocket, real to everyone except to him and to her; even to him it began to seem real; and then—but it was too exciting to stand and think any longer, and he pulled the parasol out of the earth with a jerk and was impatient to find the place where one had tea with other people, like other people.

"Come along, Trissie; it's time we had our tea."

"Wherever *does* one have one's tea?" she asked with the oddest thrill of excitement in her voice, looking vaguely round and letting herself be drawn on down the grass path, trailing her parasol; turning her head this way and that way forgetting her tea, wishing to go down there and then down there, remembering orchids and cranes among wild flowers, a Chinese pagoda and a crimson crested bird; but he bore her on. 30

Thus one couple after another with much the same irregular and aimless movement passed the flower-bed and were enveloped in layer after layer of green-blue vapour, in which at first their bodies had substance and a dash of colour, but later both substance and colour dissolved in the green-blue atmosphere. How hot it was! So hot that even the thrush chose to hop, like a mechanical bird, in the shadow of the flowers, with long pauses between one movement and the next; instead of rambling vaguely the white butterflies danced one above another, making with their white shifting flakes the outline of a shattered marble column above the tallest flowers; the glass roofs of the palm house shone as if a whole market full of shiny green umbrellas had opened in the sun; and in the drone of the aeroplane the voice of the summer sky murmured its fierce soul. Yellow and black, pink and snow white, shapes of all these colours, men, women, and children were spotted for a second upon the horizon, and then, seeing the breadth of yellow that lay upon the grass, they wavered and sought shade beneath the trees, dissolving like drops of water in the yellow and green atmosphere, staining it faintly with red and blue. It seemed as if all gross and heavy bodies had sunk down in the heat motionless and lay huddled upon the ground, but their voices went wavering from them as if they were flames lolling from the thick waxen bodies of candles. Voices. Yes, voices. Wordless voices, breaking the silence suddenly with such depth of contentment, such passion of desire, or, in the voices of children, such freshness of surprise; breaking the silence? But there was no silence; all the time the motor omnibuses were turning their wheels and changing their gear; like a vast nest of Chinese boxes all of wrought steel turning ceaselessly one within another the city murmured; on the top of which the voices cried aloud and the petals of myriads of flowers flashed their colours into the air.   [1919]

QUESTIONS

1. From what point of view is the story told? Given the subject matter, is any other point of view possible?
2. Does the reader learn enough about the characters to visualize them? Do the groups of characters have anything in common?
3. Why does the author devote as much—or more—attention to the garden as she does to the people in it? What can the reader infer about her attitude toward her subject?
4. What is the significance of personifying the snail?
5. Describe the imagery of the story. Are there ways in which the images are interrelated? What is the relation of the imagery to the theme?

RESPONSES

1. Research the technical experimentations that modernist writers were making in the early years of twentieth century. How does Virginia Woolf's story reflect those experimentations?
2. Compare "Kew Gardens" with Cortázar's "Axolotl" as experiments in point of view.
3. Write an essay speculating on the influence Virginia Woolf had on such writers as Jeanette Winterson.
4. Read Woolf's Context essay "Craftsmanship." What insights does the essay provide in understanding the story?

Focus on Film

1. The film *The Hours* was adapted from a novel of the same title, which is based, in part, on the life and work of Virginia Woolf. After viewing the film and reading "Kew Gardens," examine how concepts such as point of view and perspective, nature, and society and societal expectations are developed in the two works.

RICHARD WRIGHT

Richard Wright (1908–1960) was born on a plantation near Natchez, Mississippi. His childhood, told powerfully in his memoir *Black Boy* (1945), was a nightmare of poverty, domestic turmoil, and bigotry. He made his way north to Chicago, survived the Depression, and in 1940 published his brutal naturalistic novel *Native Son*. After World War II, Wright moved to Paris, where he continued to write novels, stories, and his account of his travels in Africa, *Black Power* (1954). During his lifetime he was indisputably America's foremost black writer, and his career has served as both a model and an inspiration for a later generation.

The Man Who Was Almost a Man

Dave struck out across the fields, looking homeward through paling light. Whut's the use talkin wid em niggers in the field? Anyhow, his mother was putting supper on the table. Them niggers can't understan nothing. One of these days he was going to get a gun and practice shooting, then they couldn't talk to him as though he were a little boy. He slowed, looking at the ground. Shucks, Ah ain scareda them even ef they are biggern me! Aw, Ah know whut Ahma do. Ahm going by ol Joe's sto n git that Sears Roebuck catlog n look at them guns. Mebbe Ma will lemme buy one when she gits mah pay from ol man Hawkins. Ahma beg her t gimme some money. Ahm ol ernough to hava gun. Ahm seventeen. Almost a man. He strode, feeling his long loose-jointed limbs. Shucks, a man oughta hava little gun aftah he done worked hard all day.

He came in sight of Joe's store. A yellow lantern glowed on the front porch. He mounted steps and went through the screen door, hearing it bang behind him. There was a strong smell of coal oil and mackerel fish. He felt very confident until he saw fat Joe walk in through the rear door, then his courage began to ooze.

"Howdy, Dave! Whutcha want?"

"How yuh, Mistah Joe? Aw, Ah don wanna buy nothing. Ah jus wanted t see ef yuhd lemme look at tha catlog erwhile."

5   "Sure! You wanna see it here?"

"Nawsuh. Ah wants t take it home wid me. Ah'll bring it back termorrow when Ah come in from the fiels."

"You plannin on buying something?"

"Yessuh."

"Your ma lettin you have your own money now?"

"Shucks. Mistah Joe, Ahm gittin t be a man like anybody else!"   10

Joe laughed and wiped his greasy white face with a red bandanna.

"What you plannin on buyin?"

Dave looked at the floor, scratched his head, scratched his thigh, and smiled. Then he looked up shyly.

"Ah'll tell yuh, Mistah Joe, ef yuh promise yuh won't tell."

"I promise."   15

"Waal, Ahma buy a gun."

"A gun? What you want with a gun?"

"Ah wanna keep it."

"You ain't nothing but a boy. You don't need a gun."

"Aw, lemme have the catlog, Mistah Joe. Ah'll bring it back."   20

Joe walked through the rear door. Dave was elated. He looked around at barrels of sugar and flour. He heard Joe coming back. He craned his neck to see if he were bringing the book. Yeah, he's got it. Gawddog, he's got it!

"Here, but be sure you bring it back. It's the only one I got."

"Sho, Mistah Joe."

"Say, if you wanna buy a gun, why don't you buy one from me? I gotta gun to sell."

"Will it shoot?"   25

"Sure it'll shoot."

"Whut kind is it?"

"Oh, it's kinda old . . . a left-hand Wheeler. A pistol. A big one."

"Is it got bullets in it?"

"It's loaded."   30

"Kin Ah see it?"

"Where's your money?"

"What yuh wan fer it?"

"I'll let you have it for two dollars."

"Just two dollahs? Shucks, Ah could buy tha when Ah git mah pay."   35

"I'll have it here when you want it."

"Awright, suh. Ah be in fer it."

He went through the door, hearing it slam again behind him. Ahma git some money from Ma n buy me a gun! Only two dollahs! He tucked the thick catalogue under his arm and hurried.

"Where yuh been, boy?" His mother held a steaming dish of black-eyed peas.

"Aw, Ma, Ah just stopped down the road t talk wid the boys."   40

"Yuh know bettah t keep suppah waiting."

He sat down, resting the catalogue on the edge of the table.

"Yuh git up from there and git to the well n wash yosef! Ah ain feedin no hogs in mah house!"

She grabbed his shoulder and pushed him. He stumbled out of the room, then came back to get the catalogue.

"Whut this?"   45

"Aw, Ma, it's jusa catlog."

"Who yuh git it from?"

"From Joe, down at the sto."

"Waal, thas good. We kin use it in the outhouse."

50   "Naw, Ma." He grabbed for it. "Gimme ma catlog, Ma."

She held onto it and glared at him.

"Quit hollerin at me! Whut's wrong wid yuh? Yuh crazy?"

"But Ma, please. It ain mine! It's Joe's! He tol me t bring it back t im termorrow."

She gave up the book. He stumbled down the back steps, hugging the thick book under his arm. When he had splashed water on his face and hands, he groped back to the kitchen and fumbled in a corner for the towel. He bumped into a chair; it clattered to the floor. The catalogue sprawled at his feet. When he had dried his eyes he snatched up the book and held it again under his arms. His mother stood watching him.

55   "Now, ef yuh gonna act a fool over that ol book, Ah'll take it n burn it up."

"Naw, Ma, please."

"Waal, set down n be still!"

He sat down and drew the oil lamp close. He thumbed page after page, unaware of the food his mother set on the table. His father came in. Then his small brother.

"Whutcha got there, Dave?" his father asked.

60   "Jusa catlog," he answered, not looking up.

"Yeah, here they is!" His eyes glowed at blue-and-black revolvers. He glanced up, feeling sudden guilt. His father was watching him. He eased the book under the table and rested it on his knees. After the blessing was asked, he ate. He scooped up peas and swallowed fat meat without chewing. Buttermilk helped to wash it down. He did not want to mention money before his father. He would do much better by cornering his mother when she was alone. He looked at his father uneasily out of the edge of his eye.

"Boy, how come yuh don quit foolin wid tha book n eat yo suppah?"

"Yessuh."

"How you n ol man Hawkins gitten erlong?"

65   "Suh?"

"Can't yuh hear? Why don yuh listen? Ah ast yu how wuz yuh n ol man Hawkins gittin erlong?"

"Oh, swell, Pa. Ah plows mo lan than anybody over there."

"Waal, yuh oughta keep you mind on whut yuh doin."

"Yessuh."

70   He poured his plate full of molasses and sopped it up slowly with a chunk of corn-bread. When his father and brother had left the kitchen, he still sat and looked again at the guns in the catalogue, longing to muster courage enough to present his case to his mother. Lawd, ef Ah only had tha pretty one! He could almost feel the slickness of the weapon with his fingers. If he had a gun like that he would polish it and keep it shining so it would never rust. N Ah'd keep it loaded, by Gawd!

"Ma?" His voice was hesitant.

"Hunh?"

"Ol man Hawkins give yuh mah money yit?"

"Yeah, but ain no usa yuh thinking about throwin nona it erway. Ahm keepin tha money sos yuh kin have cloes t go to school this winter."

75   He rose and went to her side with the open catalogue in his palms. She was washing dishes, her head bent low over a pan. Shyly he raised the book. When he spoke, his voice was husky, faint.

"Ma, Gawd knows Ah wans one of these."

"One of whut?" she asked, not raising her eyes.

"One of these," he said again, not daring even to point. She glanced up at the page, then at him with wide eyes.

"Nigger, is yuh gone plumb crazy?"

"Aw Ma—"   80

"Git outta here! Don yuh talk t me bout no gun! Yuh a fool!"

"Ma, Ah kin buy one fer two dollahs."

"Not ef Ah knows it, yuh ain!"

"But yuh promised me one—"

"Ah don care what Ah promised! Yuh ain nothing but a boy yit!"   85

"Ma ef yuh lemme buy one Ah'll *never* ast yuh fer nothing no mo."

"Ah tol yuh t git outta here! Yuh ain gonna toucha penny of tha money fer no gun! Thas how come Ah has Mistah Hawkins t pay yu wages t me, cause Ah knows yuh ain got no sense."

"But, Ma, we needa gun. Pa ain got no gun. We needa gun in the house. Yuh kin never tell whut might happen."

"Now don yuh try to maka fool outta me, boy! Ef we did hava gun, yuh wouldn't have it!"

He laid the catalogue down and slipped his arm around her waist.   90

"Aw, Ma, Ah done worked hard alla summer n ain ast yuh fer nothing, is Ah, now?"

"Thas whut yuh spose t do!"

"But Ma, Ah wans a gun. Yuh kin lemme have two dollahs outta mah money. Please, Ma. I kin give it to Pa . . . Please, Ma! Ah loves yuh, Ma."

When she spoke her voice came soft and low.

"What yu wan wida gun, Dave? Yuh don need no gun. Yuh'll git in trouble. N ef   95
yo pa jus thought Ah let yuh have money t buy a gun he'd hava fit."

"Ah'll hide it, Ma. It ain but two dollahs."

"Lawd, chil, whut's wrong wid yuh?"

"Ain nothin wrong, Ma. Ahm almos a man now. Ah wans a gun."

"Who gonna sell yuh a gun?"

"Ol Joe at the sto."   100

"N it don cos but two dollahs?"

"Thas all, Ma. Jus two dollahs. Please, Ma."

She was stacking the plates away; her hands moved slowly, reflectively. Dave kept an anxious silence. Finally, she turned to him.

"Ah'll let yuh git tha gun ef yuh promise me one thing."

"Whut's tha, Ma?"   105

"Yuh bring it straight back t me, yuh hear? It be fer Pa."

"Yessum! Lemme go now, Ma."

She stooped, turned slightly to one side, raised the hem of her dress, rolled down the top of her stocking, and came up with a slender wad of bills.

"Here," she said. "Lawd knows yuh don need no gun. But yer pa does. Yuh bring it right back t me, yuh hear? Ahma put it up. Now ef yuh don, Ahma have yuh pa lick yuh so hard yuh won fergit it."

"Yessum."   110

He took the money, ran down the steps, and across the yard.

"Dave! Yuuuuu Daaaaave!"

He heard, but he was not going to stop now. "Naw, Lawd!"

The first movement he made the following morning was to reach under his pillow for the gun. In the gray light of dawn he held it loosely, feeling a sense of power. Could kill a man with a gun like this. Kill anybody, black or white. And if he were holding his gun in his hand, nobody could run over him; they would have to respect him. It was a big gun, with a long barrel and a heavy handle. He raised and lowered it in his hand, marveling at its weight.

115   He had not come straight home with it as his mother had asked; instead he had stayed out in the fields, holding the weapon in his hand, aiming it now and then at some imaginary foe. But he had not fired it; he had been afraid that his father might hear. Also he was not sure he knew how to fire it.

To avoid surrendering the pistol he had not come into the house until he knew that they were all asleep. When his mother had tiptoed to his bedside late that night and demanded the gun, he had first played possum; then he had told her that the gun was hidden outdoors, that he would bring it to her in the morning. Now he lay turning it slowly in his hands. He broke it, took out the cartridges, felt them, and then put them back.

He slid out of bed, got a long strip of old flannel from a trunk, wrapped the gun in it, and tied it to his naked thigh while it was still loaded. He did not go in to breakfast. Even though it was not yet daylight, he started for Jim Hawkins' plantation. Just as the sun was rising he reached the barns where the mules and plows were kept.

"Hey! That you, Dave?"

He turned. Jim Hawkins stood eyeing him suspiciously.

120   "What're yuh doing here so early?"

"Ah didn't know Ah wuz gittin up so early, Mistah Hawkins. Ah was fixin t hitch up ol Jenny n take her t the fiels."

"Good. Since you're so early, how about plowing that stretch down by the woods?"

"Suits me, Mistah Hawkins."

"O.K. Go to it!"

125   He hitched Jenny to a plow and started across the fields. Hot dog! This was just what he wanted. If he could get down by the woods, he could shoot his gun and nobody would hear. He walked behind the plow, hearing the traces creaking, feeling the gun tied tight to his thigh.

When he reached the woods, he plowed two whole rows before he decided to take out the gun. Finally, he stopped, looked in all directions, then untied the gun and held it in his hand. He turned to the mule and smiled.

"Know whut this is, Jenny? Naw, yuh wouldn know! Yuhs jusa ol mule! Anyhow, this is a gun, n it kin shoot, by Gawd!"

He held the gun at arm's length. Whut t hell, Ahma shoot this thing! He looked at Jenny again.

"Lissen here, Jenny! When Ah pull this ol trigger, Ah don wan yuh to run n acka fool now?"

130   Jenny stood with head down, her short ears pricked straight. Dave walked off about twenty feet, held the gun far out from him at arm's length, and turned his head. Hell, he told himself, Ah ain afraid. The gun felt loose in his fingers; he waved it wildly for a moment. Then he shut his eyes and tightened his forefinger. *Bloom!* A report half deafened him and he thought his right hand was torn from his arm. He heard Jenny whinnying and galloping over the field, and he found himself on his knees, squeezing his fingers hard between his legs. His hand was numb; he jammed it into his mouth, trying to warm it, trying to stop the pain. The gun lay at his feet. He did not quite know what had happened. He stood up and stared at the gun as though it were a living thing. He gritted his teeth and kicked the gun. Yuh almos broke mah arm! He turned to look for Jenny; she was far over the fields, tossing her head and kicking wildly.

"Hol on there, ol mule!"

When he caught up with her she stood trembling, walling her big white eyes at him. The plow was far away; the traces had broken. Then Dave stopped short, looking, not believing. Jenny was bleeding. Her left side was red and wet with blood. He went closer. Lawd, have mercy! Wondah did Ah shoot this mule? He grabbed for Jenny's mane. She flinched, snorted, whirled, tossing her head.

"Hol on now! Hol on."

Then he saw the hole in Jenny's side, right between the ribs. It was round, wet, red. A crimson stream streaked down the front leg, flowing fast. Good Gawd! Ah wuzn't shootin at tha mule. He felt panic. He knew he had to stop that blood, or Jenny would bleed to death. He had never seen so much blood in all his life. He chased the mule for half a mile, trying to catch her. Finally she stopped, breathing hard, stumpy tail half arched. He caught her mane and led her back to where the plow and gun lay. Then he stooped and grabbed handfuls of damp black earth and tried to plug the bullet hole. Jenny shuddered, whinnied, and broke from him.

"Hol on! Hol on now!"

He tried to plug it again, but blood came anyhow. His fingers were hot and sticky. He rubbed dirt into his palms, trying to dry them. Then again he attempted to plug the bullet hole, but Jenny shied away, kicking her heels high. He stood helpless. He had to do something. He ran at Jenny; she dodged him. He watched a red stream of blood flow down Jenny's leg and form a bright pool at her feet.

"Jenny . . . Jenny," he called weakly.

His lips trembled. She's bleeding t death! He looked in the direction of home, wanting to go back, wanting to get help. But he saw the pistol lying in the damp black clay. He had a queer feeling that if he only did something, this would not be; Jenny would not be there bleeding to death.

When he went to her this time, she did not move. She stood with sleepy, dreamy eyes; and when he touched her she gave a low-pitched whinny and knelt to the ground, her front knees slopping in blood.

"Jenny . . . Jenny . . ." he whispered.

For a long time she held her neck erect; then her head sank, slowly. Her ribs swelled with a mighty heave and she went over.

Dave's stomach felt empty, very empty. He picked up the gun and held it gingerly between his thumb and forefinger. He buried it at the foot of a tree. He took a stick and tried to cover the pool of blood with dirt—but what was the use? There was Jenny lying with her mouth open and her eyes walled and glassy. He could not tell Jim Hawkins he had shot his mule. But he had to tell something. Yeah, Ah'll tell em Jenny started gittin ill n fell on the joint of the plow. . . . But that would hardly happen to a mule. He walked across the field slowly, head down.

It was sunset. Two of Jim Hawkins' men were over near the edge of the woods digging a hole in which to bury Jenny. Dave was surrounded by a knot of people, all of whom were looking down at the dead mule.

"I don't see how in the world it happened," said Jim Hawkins for the tenth time.

The crowd parted and Dave's mother, father, and small brother pushed into the center.

"Where Dave?" his mother called.

"There he is," said Jim Hawkins.

His mother grabbed him.

"Whut happened, Dave? Whut yuh done?"

135

140

145

150 "Nothin."

"C'mon, boy, talk," his father said.

Dave took a deep breath and told the story he knew nobody believed.

"Waal," he drawled. "Ah brung ol Jenny down here sos Ah could do mah plowin. Ah plowed bout two rows, just like yuh see." He stopped and pointed at the long rows of upturned earth. "Then somethin musta been wrong wid ol Jenny. She wouldn ack right a-tall. She started snortin n kickin her heels. Ah tried t hol her, but she pulled erway, rearin n goin in. Then when the point of the plow was stickin up in the air, she swung erroun n twisted herself back on it. . . . She stuck herself n started t bleed. N fo Ah could do anything, she wuz dead."

"Did you ever hear of anything like that in all your life?" asked Jim Hawkins.

155 There were white and black standing in the crowd. They murmured. Dave's mother came close to him and looked hard into his face. "Tell the truth, Dave," she said.

"Looks like a bullet hole to me," said one man.

"Dave, whut yuh do wid tha gun?" his mother asked.

The crowd surged in, looking at him. He jammed his hands into his pockets, shook his head slowly from left to right, and backed away. His eyes were wide and painful.

"Did he hava gun?" asked Jim Hawkins.

160 "By Gawd, Ah tol yuh tha wuz a gun wound," said a man, slapping his thigh.

His father caught his shoulders and shook him till his teeth rattled.

"Tell whut happened, yuh rascal! Tell whut . . ."

Dave looked at Jenny's stiff legs and began to cry.

"Whut yuh do wid tha gun?" his mother asked.

165 "Whut wuz he doin wida gun?" his father asked.

"Come on and tell the truth," said Hawkins. "Ain't nobody going to hurt you . . ."

His mother crowded close to him.

"Did yuh shoot tha mule, Dave?"

Dave cried, seeing blurred white and black faces.

170 "Ahh ddinn gggo tt sshooot hher . . . Ah sswear tt Gawd Ahh ddin. . . . Ah wuz a-tryin t sssee ef the gggun would sshoot—"

"Where yuh git the gun from?" his father asked.

"Ah got it from Joe, at the sto."

"Where yuh git the money?"

"Ma give it t me."

175 "He kept worryin me, Bob. Ah had t. Ah tol im t bring the gun right back t me . . . It was fer yuh, the gun."

"But how yuh happen to shoot that mule?" asked Jim Hawkins.

"Ah wuzn shootin at the mule, Mistah Hawkins! The gun jumped when Ah pulled the trigger . . . N fo Ah knowed anythin Jenny was there a-bleedin."

Somebody in the crowd laughed. Jim Hawkins walked close to Dave and looked into his face.

"Well, looks like you have bought you a mule, Dave."

180 "Ah swear fo Gawd. Ah didn go t kill the mule, Mistah Hawkins!"

"But you killed her!"

All the crowd was laughing now. They stood on tiptoe and poked heads over one another's shoulders.

"Well, boy, looks like yuh done bought a dead mule! Hahaha!"

"Ain tha ershame."

185 "Hohohohoho."

Dave stood, head down, twisting his feet in the dirt.

"Well, you needn't worry about it, Bob," said Jim Hawkins to Dave's father. "Just let the boy keep on working and pay me two dollars a month."

"Whut yuh wan fer yo mule, Mistah Hawkins?"

Jim Hawkins screwed up his eyes.

"Fifty dollars." 190

"Whut yuh do wid tha gun?" Dave's father demanded.

Dave said nothing.

"Yuh wan me t take a tree n beat yuh till yuh talk!"

"Nawsuh!"

"Whut yuh do wid it?" 195

"Ah throwed it erway."

"Where?"

"Ah . . . Ah throwed it in the creek."

"Waal, c mon home. N firs thing in the mawnin git to tha creek n fin tha gun."

"Yessuh." 200

"Whut yuh pay fer it?"

"Two dollahs."

"Take tha gun n git yo money back n carry it t Mistah Hawkins, yuh hear? N don fergit Ahma lam you black bottom good fer this! Now march yoself on home, suh!"

Dave turned and walked slowly. He heard people laughing. Dave glared, his eyes welling with tears. Hot anger bubbled in him. Then he swallowed and stumbled on.

That night Dave did not sleep. He was glad that he had gotten out of killing the mule 205 so easily, but he was hurt. Something hot seemed to turn over inside him each time he remembered how they had laughed. He tossed on his bed, feeling his hard pillow. N Pa says he's gonna beat me . . . He remembered other beatings, and his back quivered. Naw, naw, Ah sho don wan im t beat me tha way no mo. Dam em all! Nobody ever gave him anything. All he did was work. They treat me like a mule, n then they beat me. He gritted his teeth. N Ma had t tell on me.

Well, if he had to, he would take old man Hawkins that two dollars. But that meant selling the gun. And he wanted to keep that gun. Fifty dollars for a dead mule.

He turned over, thinking how he had fired the gun. He had an itch to fire it again. Ef other men kin shoota gun, by Gawd, Ah kin! He was still, listening. Mebbe they all sleepin now. The house was still. He heard the soft breathing of his brother. Yes, now! He would go down and get that gun and see if he could fire it! He eased out of bed and slipped into overalls.

The moon was bright. He ran almost all the way to the edge of the woods. He stumbled over the ground, looking for the spot where he had buried the gun. Yeah, here it is. Like a hungry dog scratching for a bone, he pawed it up. He puffed his black cheeks and blew dirt from the trigger and barrel. He broke it and found four cartridges unshot. He looked around; the fields were filled with silence and moonlight. He clutched the gun stiff and hard in his fingers. But, as soon as he wanted to pull the trigger, he shut his eyes and turned his head. Naw, Ah can't shoot wid mah eyes closed n mah head turned. With effort he held his eyes open; then he squeezed. *Blooooom!* He was stiff, not breathing. The gun was still in his hands. Dammit, he'd done it! He fired again. *Blooooom!* He smiled. *Blooooom! Blooooom! Click, click.* There! It was empty. If anybody could shoot a gun, he could. He put the gun into his hip pocket and started across the fields.

When he reached the top of a ridge he stood straight and proud in the moonlight, looking at Jim Hawkins' big white house, feeling the gun sagging in his pocket. Lawd, ef Ah had just one mo bullet Ah'd taka shot at tha house. Ah'd like t scare ol man Hawkins jusa little . . . Jusa enough t let im know Dave Saunders is a man.

210   To his left the road curved, running to the tracks of the Illinois Central. He jerked his head, listening. From far off came a faint *hoooof-hoooof; hoooof-hoooof* . . . He stood rigid. Two dollahs a mont. Les see now . . . Tha means it'll take bout two years. Shucks! Ah'll be dam!

He started down the road, toward the tracks. Yeah, here she comes! He stood beside the track and held himself stiffly. Here she comes, erroun the ben . . . C mon, yuh slow poke! C mon! He had his hand on his gun; something quivered in his stomach. Then the train thundered past, the gray and brown box cars rumbling and clinking. He gripped the gun tightly; then he jerked his hand out of his pocket. Ah betcha Bill wouldn't do it! Ah betcha . . . The cars slid past, steel grinding upon steel. Ahm ridin yuh ternight, so hep me Gawd! He was hot all over. He hesitated just a moment; then he grabbed, pulled atop of a car, and lay flat. He felt his pocket; the gun still there. Ahead the long rails were glinting in the moonlight, stretching away, away to somewhere, somewhere where he could be a man . . .   [1940]

QUESTIONS

1. From what point of view is the story told? Is it consistent throughout the story?
2. How is Dave's character shaped by the rural setting?
3. What is the function of the minor characters?
4. What is the significance of Dave's identification with the mule?
5. What does Dave's interest in guns reveal about his needs and aspirations?

RESPONSES

1. Like many people during the Great Depression, for a period Richard Wright considered himself a communist. Research this period in Wright's life. Do you see any influence of this philosophy in this story?
2. Compare this story to stories by Anglo writers on related themes. For instance, how does Dave's life compare to Elisa's in Steinbeck's "Chrysanthemums"? Or how do Dave's difficulties growing up compare to Sammy's in Updike's "A & P"?
3. Read Sartre's description of Richard Wright's work in the Context essay "For Whom Does One Write?" Based on your reading of "The Man Who Was Almost a Man," write an essay supporting or disagreeing with Sartre's thesis.

ANZIA YEZIERSKA

Anzia Yezierska (c. 1885–1970) was born near Warsaw, Poland, and immigrated as a child to the United States. She grew up in New York City. Living in deep poverty, she worked in menial jobs while studying English in night school. In early adulthood, she was befriended by feminist Henrietta Rodman and by John Dewey, both of whom encouraged her desire to write. In 1920, she published her first volume of short stories, *Hungry Hearts*, which was made into a film. After a period in Hollywood, she returned to New York and continued writing novels and short stories. Her works include *Hungry Hearts* (1920), *Salome of the Tenements* (1922), *Children of Loneliness* (1923), *Bread Givers* (1925), and *All I Could Ever Be* (1932). Her autobiography is *Red Ribbon on a White Horse* (1950).

Hunger

Shenah Pessah paused in the midst of scrubbing the stairs of the tenement. "Ach!" she sighed. "How can his face still burn so in me when he is so long gone? How the deadness in me flames up with life at the thought of him!"

The dark hallway seemed flooded with white radiance. She closed her eyes that she might see more vividly the beloved features. The glowing smile that healed all ills of life and changed her from the weary drudge into the vibrant creature of joy.

It was all a miracle—his coming, this young professor from one of the big colleges. He had rented a room in the very house where she was janitress so as to be near the people he was writing about. But more wonderful than all was the way he stopped to talk to her, to question her about herself as though she were his equal. What warm friendliness had prompted him to take her out of her dark basement to the library where there were books to read!

And then—that unforgettable night on the way home, when the air was poignant with spring! Only a moment—a kiss—a pressure of hands! And the world shone with light—the empty, unlived years filled with love!

She was lost in dreams of her one hour of romance when a woman elbowed her way through the dim passage, leaving behind her the smell of herring and onions.

Shenah Pessah gripped the scrubbing-brush with suppressed fury. "Meshugeneh! Did you not swear to yourself that you would tear his memory out from your heart?

If he would have been only a man I could have forgotten him. But he was not a man! He was God Himself! On whatever I look shines his face!"

The white radiance again suffused her. The brush dropped from her hand. "he—he is the beating in my heart! He is the life in me—the hope in me—the breath of prayer in me! If not for him in me, then what am I? Deadness—emptiness—nothingness! You are going out of your head. You are living only on rainbows. He is no more real—

"What is real? These rags I wear? This pail? This black hole? Or him and the dreams of him?" She flung her challenge to the murky darkness.

"Shenah Pessah! A black year on you!" came the answer from the cellar below. It was the voice of her uncle, Moisheh Rifkin.

10   "Oi weh!" she shrugged young shoulders, wearied by joyless toil. "He's beginning with his hollering already." And she hurried down.

"You piece of earth! Worms should eat you! How long does it take you to wash up the stairs?" he stormed. "Yesterday, the eating was burned to coal; and to-day you forget the salt."

"What a fuss over a little less salt!"

"In the Talmud it stands a man has a right to divorce his wife for only forgetting him the salt in his soup."

"Maybe that's why Aunt Gittel went to the grave before her time—worrying how to please your taste in the mouth."

15   The old man's yellow, shriveled face stared up at her out of the gloom. "What has he from life? Only his pleasure in eating and going to the synagogue. How long will he live yet?" And moved by a surge of pity, "Why can't I be a little kind to him?"

"Did you chop me some herring and onions?" he interrupted harshly.

She flushed with conscious guilt. Again she wondered why ugly things and ugly smells so sickened her.

"What don't you forget?" His voice hammered upon her ears. "No care lays in your head. You're only dreaming in the air."

Her compassion was swept away in a wave of revolt that left her trembling. "I can't no more stand it from you! Get yourself somebody else!" She was surprised at her sudden spirit.

20   "You big mouth, you! That's your thanks for saving you from hunger."

"Two years already I'm working the nails off my fingers and you didn't give me a cent."

"Beggerin! Money yet, you want? The minute you get enough to eat you turn up your head with freshness. Are you used to anything from home? What were you out there in Savel? The dirt under people's feet. You're already forgetting how you came off from the ship—a bundle of rags full of holes. If you lived in Russia a hundred years would you have lived to wear a pair of new shoes on your feet?"

"Other girls come naked and with nothing to America and they work themselves up. Everybody gets wages in America—"

"Americanerin! Didn't I spend out enough money on your ship-ticket to have a little use from you? A thunder should strike you!"

25   Shenah Pessah's eyes flamed. Her broken finger-nails pierced the callous flesh of her hands. So this was the end—the awakening of her dreams of America! Her memory went back to the time her ship-ticket came. In her simple faith she had really believed that they wanted her—her father's brother and his wife who had come to the new world before ever she was born. She thought they wanted to give her a chance for happiness, for life and love. And then she came—to find the paralytic aunt—

housework—janitor's drudgery. Even after her aunt's death, she had gone on un-complainingly, till her uncle's nagging had worn down her last shred of self-control.

"It's the last time you'll holler on me!" she cried. "You'll never see my face again if I got to go begging in the street." Seizing her shawl, she rushed out. "Woe is me! Bit-ter is me! For what is my life? Why didn't the ship go under and drown me before I came to America?"

Through the streets, like a maddened thing, she raced, not knowing where she was going, not caring. "For what should I keep on suffering? Who needs me? Who wants me? I got nobody—nobody!"

And then the vision of the face she worshiped flashed before her. His beautiful kindness that had once warmed her into new life breathed over her again. "Why did he ever come but to lift me out of my darkness into his light?"

Instinctively her eyes sought the rift of blue above the tenement roofs and were caught by a boldly printed placard: "HANDS WANTED." It was as though the sign swung open on its hinges like a door and arms stretched out inviting her to enter. From the sign she looked to her own hands—vigorous, young hands—made strong through toil.

Hope leaped within her. "Maybe I got yet luck to have it good in this world. Ach! God from the sky! I'm so burning to live—to work myself up for a somebody! And why not?" With clenched fist she smote her bosom. "Ain't everything possible in the new world? Why is America but to give me the chance to lift up my head with everybody alike?"

Her feet scarcely touched the steps as she ran up. But when she reached the huge, iron door of Cohen Brothers, a terror seized her. "Oi weh! They'll give a look on my greenhorn rags, and down I go—For what are you afraid, you fool?" she command-ed herself. "You come not to beg. They need hands. Don't the sign say so? And you got good, strong hands that can turn over the earth with their strength. America is before you. You'll begin to earn money. You'll dress yourself up like a person and men will fall on their knees to make love to you—even him—himself!"

All fear had left her. She flung open the door and beheld the wonder of a factory—people—people—seas of bent heads and busy hands of people—the whirr of ma-chinery—flying belts—the clicking clatter of whirling wheels—all seemed to blend and fuse into one surging song of hope—of new life—a new world—America!

A man, his arms heaped with a bundle of shirts, paused at sight of the radiant face. Her ruddy cheeks, the film of innocence shining out of eyes that knew no guile, car-ried him back to the green fields and open plains of his native Russia.

"Her mother's milk is still fresh on her lips," he murmured, as his gaze enveloped her.

The bundle slipped and fell to her feet. Their eyes met in spontaneous recognition of common race. With an embarrassed laugh they stooped to gather up the shirts.

"I seen downstairs hands wanted," came in a faltering voice.

"Then you're looking for work?" he questioned with keen interest. She was so dif-ferent from the others he had known in his five years in this country. He was seized with curiosity to know more.

"You ain't been long in America?" His tone was an unconscious caress.

"Two years already," she confessed. "But I ain't so green like I look," she added quickly, overcome by the old anxiety.

"Trust yourself on me," Sam Arkin assured her. "I'm a feller that knows himself on a person first off. I'll take you to the office myself. Wait only till I put away these things."

Grinning with eagerness, he returned and together they sought the foreman.

"Good luck to you! I hope you'll be pushed up soon to my floor," Sam Arkin encouraged, as he hurried back to his machine.

Because of the rush of work and the scarcity of help, Shenah Pessah was hired without delay. Atremble with excitement, she tiptoed after the foreman as he led the way into the workroom.

"Here, Sadie Kranz, is another learner for you." He addressed a big-bosomed girl, the most skillful worker in the place.

45   "Another greenhorn with a wooden head!" she whispered to her neighbor as Shenah Pessah removed her shawl. "Gevalt! All these greenhorn hands tear the bread from our mouths by begging to work so cheap."

But the dumb appeal of the immigrant stirred vague memories in Sadie Kranz. As she watched her run her first seam, she marveled at her speed. "I got to give it to you, you have a quick head." There was conscious condescension in her praise.

Shenah Pessah lifted a beaming face. "How kind it was from you to learn me! You good heart!"

No one had ever before called Sadie Kranz "good heart." The words lingered pleasantly.

"Ut! I like to help anybody, so long it don't cost me nothing. I get paid by the week anyhow," she half apologized.

50   Shenah Pessah was so thrilled with the novelty of the work, the excitement of mastering the intricacies of her machine, that she did not realize that the day was passed until the bell rang, the machines came to a halt, and the "hands" made a wild rush for the cloak-room.

"Oi weh! Is it a fire?" Shenah Pessah blanched with dread.

Loud laughter quelled her fears. "Greenie! It's six o'clock. Time to go home," chorused the voices.

"Home?" The cry broke from her. "Where will I go? I got no home." She stood bewildered, in the fast-dwindling crowd of workers. Each jostling by her had a place to go. Of them all, she alone was friendless, shelterless!

"Help me find a place to sleep!" she implored, seizing Sadie Kranz by the sleeve of her velvet coat. "I got no people. I ran away."

55   Sadie Kranz narrowed her eyes at the girl. A feeling of pity crept over her at sight of the outstretched, hungry hands.

"I'll fix you by me for the while." And taking the shawl off the shelf, she tossed it to the forlorn bundle of rags. "Come along. You must be starved for some eating."

As Shenah Pessah entered the dingy hallroom which Sadie Kranz called home, its chill and squalor carried her back to the janitor's basement she had left that morning. In silence she watched her companion prepare the hot dogs and potatoes on the oil-stove atop the trunk. Such pressing sadness weighed upon her that she turned from even the smell of food.

"My heart pulls me so to go back to my uncle." She swallowed hard her crust of black bread. "He's so used to have me help him. What'll he do—alone?"

"You got to look out for yourself in this world." Sadie Kranz gesticulated with a hot potato. "With your quickness, you got a chance to make money and buy clothes. You can go to shows—dances. And who knows—maybe meet a man to get married."

60   "Married? You know how it burns in every girl to get herself married—that's how it burns in me to work myself up for a person."

"Ut! For what need you to work yourself up. Better marry yourself up to a rich feller and you're fixed for life."

"But him I want—he ain't just a man. He is—" She paused seeking for words and a mist of longing softened the heavy peasant features. "He is the golden hills on the sky. I'm as far from him as the earth is from the stars."

"Yok! Why wills itself in you the stars?" her companion ridiculed between swallows.

Shenah Pessah flung out her hands with Jewish fervor. "Can I help it what's in my heart? It always longs in me for the higher. Maybe he has long ago forgotten me, but only one hope drives in me like madness—to make myself alike to him."

"I'll tell you the truth," laughed Sadie Kranz, fishing in the pot for the last frank- 65
furter. "You are a little out of your head—plain mehsugeh."

"Mehsugeh?" Shenah Pessah rose to her feet vibrant with new resolve. "Mehsug-eh?" she challenged, her peasant youth afire with ambition. "I'll yet show the world what's in me. I'll not go back to my uncle—till it rings with my name in America."

She entered the factory, the next day, with a light in her face, a sureness in her step that made all pause in wonder. "Look only! How high she holds herself her head! Has the matchmaker promised her a man?"

Then came her first real triumph. Shenah Pessah was raised above old hands who had been in the shop for years and made assistant to Sam Arkin, the man who had welcomed her that first day in the factory. As she was shown to the bench be-side him, she waited expectantly for a word of welcome. None came. Instead, he bent the closer to his machine and the hand that held the shirt trembled as though he were cold, though the hot color flooded his face.

Resolutely, she turned to her work. She would show him how skillful she had become in those few weeks. The seams sped under her lightning touch when a sudden clatter startled her. She jumped up terror-stricken.

"The belt! The belt slipped! But it's nothing, little bird," Sam Arkin hastened to 70
assure her. "I'll fix it." And then the quick warning, "Sh-h! The foreman is coming!"

Accustomed to her uncle's harsh bickering, this man's gentleness overwhelmed her. There was something she longed to say that trembled on her lips, but her voice refused to come.

Sam Arkin, too, was inarticulate. He felt he must talk to her, must know more of her. Timidly he touched her sleeve. "Lunch-time—here—wait for me," he whis-pered, as the foreman approached.

A shrill whistle—the switch thrown—the slowing-down of the machines, then the deafening hush proclaiming noon. Followed the scraping of chairs, raucous voices, laughter, and the rush on the line to reach the steaming cauldron. One by one, as their cups of tea were filled, the hungry workers dispersed into groups. Seated on window-sills, table-tops, machines, and bales of shirts, they munched black bread and herring and sipped tea from saucers. And over all rioted the acrid odor of garlic and onions.

Rebecca Feist, the belle of the shop, pulled up the sleeve of her Georgette waist and glanced down at her fifty-nine-cent silk stocking. "A lot it pays for a girl to kill herself to dress stylish. Give only a look on Sam Arkin, how stuck he is on that new hand."

There followed a chorus of voices. "Such freshness! We been in the shop so long 75
and she just gives a come-in and grabs the cream as if it's coming to her."

"It's her innocent-looking baby eyes that fools him in—"

"Innocent! Pfui! These make-believe innocent girls! Leave it to them! They know how to shine themselves up to a feller!"

Bleemah Levine, a stoop-shouldered, old hand, grown gray with the grayness of unrelieved drudgery, cast a furtive look in the direction of the couple. "Ach! The little bit of luck! Not looks, not smartness, but only luck, and the world falls to your feet." Her lips tightened with envy. "It's her greenhorn, red cheeks—"

Rebecca Feist glanced at herself in the mirror of her vanity bag. It was a pretty, young face, but pale and thin from undernourishment. Adroitly applying a lip-stick, she cried indignantly: "I wish I could be such a false thing like her. But only, I'm too natural—the hypocrite!"

80   Sadie Kranz rose to her friend's defense. "What are you falling on her like a pack of wild dogs, just because Sam Arkin gives a smile on her? He ain't marrying her yet, is he?"

"We don't say nothing against her," retorted Rebecca Feist, tapping her diamond-buckled foot, "only, she pushes herself too much. Give her a finger and she'll grab your whole hand. Is there a limit to the pushings of such a green animal? Only a while ago, she was a learner, a nobody, and soon she'll jump over all our heads and make herself for a forelady."

Sam Arkin, seated beside Shenah Pessah on the window-sill, had forgotten that it was lunch-hour and that he was savagely hungry. "It shines so from your eyes," he beamed. "What happy thoughts lay in your head?"

"Ach! When I give myself a look around on all the people laughing and talking, it makes me so happy I'm one of them."

"Ut! These Americanerins! Their heads is only on ice-cream soda and style."

85   "But it makes me feel so grand to be with all these hands alike. It's as if I just got out from the choking prison into the open air of my own people."

She paused for breath—a host of memories overpowering her. "I can't give it out in words," she went on. "But just as there ain't no bottom to being poor, there ain't no bottom to being lonely. Before, everything I done was alone, by myself. My heart hurt so with hunger for people. But here, in the factory, I feel I'm with everybody together. Just the sight of people lifts me on wings in the air."

Opening her bag of lunch which had lain unheeded in her lap, she turned to him with a queer, little laugh, "I don't know why I'm so talking myself out to you—"

"Only talk more. I want to know everything about yourself." An aching tenderness rushed out of his heart to her, and in his grave simplicity he told her how he had overheard one of the girls say that she, Shenah Pessah, looked like a "greeneh yenteh," just landed from the ship, so that he cried out, "Gottuniu! If only the doves from the sky were as beautiful!"

They looked at each other solemnly—the girl's lips parted, her eyes wide and serious.

90   "That first day I came to the shop, the minute I gave a look on you, I felt right away, here's somebody from home. I used to tremble so to talk to a man, but you—you—I could talk myself out to you like thinking in myself."

"You're all soft silk and fine velvet," he breathed reverently. "In this hard world, how could such fineness be?"

An embarrassed silence fell between them as she knotted and unknotted her colored kerchief.

"I'll take you home? Yes?" he found voice at last.

Under lowered lashes she smiled her consent.

95   "I'll wait for you downstairs, closing time." And he was gone.

The noon hour was not yet over, but Shenah Pessah returned to her machine. "Shall I tell him?" she mused. "Sam Arkin understands so much, shall I tell him of this man that burns in me? If I could only give out to some one about him in my heart—it would make me a little clear in the head." She glanced at Sam Arkin furtively. "He's kind, but could he understand? I only made a fool from myself trying to tell Sadie Kranz." All at once she began to sob without reason. She ran to the cloak-room and hid from prying eyes, behind the shawls and wraps. The emptiness of all for which she struggled pressed upon her like a dead weight, dragging her down, down—the reaction of her ecstasy.

As the gong sounded, she made a desperate effort to pull herself together and returned to her work.

The six o'clock whistles still reverberated when Sam Arkin hurried down the factory stairs and out to the corner where he was to meet Shenah Pessah. He cleared his throat to greet her as she came, but all he managed was a bashful grin. She was so near, so real, and he had so much to say—if he only knew how to begin.

He cracked his knuckles and bit his fingertips, but no words came. "Ach! You yok! Why ain't you saying something?" He wrestled with his shyness in vain. The tense silence remained unbroken till they reached her house.

"I'm sorry"—Shenah Pessah colored apologetically—"But I got no place to invite you. My room is hardly big enough for a push-in of one person." 100

"What say you to a bite of eating with me?" he blurted.

She thought of her scant supper upstairs and would have responded eagerly, but glancing down at her clothes, she hesitated. "Could I go dressed like this in a restaurant?"

"You look grander plain, like you are, than those twisted up with style. I'll take you to the swellest restaurant on Grand Street and be proud with you!"

She flushed with pleasure. "Nu, come on, then. It's good to have a friend that knows himself on what's in you and not what's on you, but still, when I go to a place, I like to be dressed like a person so I can feel like a person."

"You'll yet live to wear diamonds that will shine up the street when you pass!" he cried. 105

Through streets growing black with swarming crowds of toil-released workers they made their way. Sam Arkin's thick hand rested with a lightness new to him upon the little arm tucked under his. The haggling pushcart peddlers, the newsboys screaming, "Tageblatt, Abendblatt, Herold," the roaring noises of the elevated trains resounded the pæan of joy swelling his heart.

"America was good to me, but I never guessed how good till now." The words were out before he knew it. "Tell me only, what pulled you to this country?"

"What pulls anybody here? The hope for the better. People who got it good in the old world don't hunger for the new."

A mist filled her eyes at memory of her native village. "How I suffered in Savel. I never had enough to eat. I never had shoes on my feet. I had to go barefoot even in the freezing winter. But still I love it. I was born there. I love the houses and the straw roofs, the mud streets, the cows, the chickens and the goats. My heart always hurts me for what is no more."

The brilliant lights of Levy's Café brought her back to Grand Street. 110

"Here is it." He led her in and over to a corner table. "Chopped herring and onions for two," he ordered with a flourish.

"Ain't there some American eating on the card?" interposed Shenah Pessah.

He laughed indulgently. "If I lived in America for a hundred years I couldn't get used to the American eating. What can make the mouth so water like the taste and the smell from herring and onions?"

"There's something in me—I can't help—that so quickly takes on to the American taste. It's as if my outside skin only was Russian; the heart in me is for everything of the new world—even the eating."

115 "Nu, I got nothing to complain against America. I don't like the American eating, but I like the American dollar. Look only on me!" He expanded his chest. "I came to America a ragged nothing—and—see—" He exhibited a bank-book in four figures, gesticulating grandly, "And I learned in America how to sign my name!"

"Did it come hard to learn?" she asked under her breath.

"Hard?" His face purpled with excitement. "It would be easier for me to lift up this whole house on my shoulders than to make one little dot of a letter. When I took my pencil—Oi weh! The sweat would break out on my face! 'I can't, I can't!' I cried, but something in me jumped up. 'You can—you yok—you must!'—Six months, night after night, I stuck to it—and I learned to twist around the little black hooks till it means—me—Sam Arkin."

He had the rough-hewn features of the common people, but he lifted his head with the pride of a king. "Since I can write out my name, I feel I can do anything. I can sign checks, put money in the bank, or take it out without nobody to help me."

As Shenah Pessah listened, unconsciously she compared Sam Arkin, glowing with the frank conceit of the self-made man, his neglected teeth, thick, red lips, with that of the Other One—made ever more beautiful with longings and dreams.

120 "But in all these black years, I was always hoping to get to the golden country," Sam Arkin's voice went on, but she heard it as from afar. "Before my eyes was always the shine of the high wages and the easy money and I kept pushing myself from one city to another, and saving and saving till I saved up enough for my ship-ticket to the new world. And then when I landed here, I fell into the hands of a cockroach boss."

"A cockroach boss?" she questioned absently and reproached herself for her inattention.

"A black year on him! He was a landsman, that's how he fooled me in. He used to come to the ship with a smiling face of welcome to all the greenhorns what had nobody to go to. And then he'd put them to work in his sweatshop and sweat them into their grave."

"Don't I know it?" she cried with quickened understanding. "Just like my uncle, Moisheh Rifkin."

"The blood-sucker!" he gasped. "When I think how I slaved for him sixteen hours a day—for what? Nothing!"

125 She gently stroked his hand as one might a child in pain. He looked up and smiled gratefully.

"I want to forget what's already over. I got enough money now to start for myself—maybe a tailor-shop—and soon—I—I want to marry myself—but none of those crazy chickens for me." And he seemed to draw her unto himself by the intensity of his gaze.

Growing bolder, he exclaimed: "I got a grand idea. It's Monday and the bank is open yet till nine o'clock. I'll write over my bankbook on your name? Yes?"

"My name?" She fell back, dumbstruck.

"Yes—you—everything I only got—you—" he mumbled. "I'll give you dove's milk to drink—silks and diamonds to wear—you'll hold all my money."

130 She was shaken by this supreme proof of his devotion.

"But I—I can't—I got to work myself up for a person. I got a head. I got ideas. I can catch on to the Americans quicker'n lightning."

"My money can buy you everything. I'll buy you teachers. I'll buy you a piano. I'll make you for a lady. Right away you can stop from work." He leaned toward her, his eyes welling with tears of earnestness.

"Take your hard-earned money? Could I be such a beggerin?"

"God from the world! You are dearer to me than the eyes from my head! I'd give the blood from under my nails for you! I want only to work for you—to live for you—to die for you—" He was spent with the surge of his emotion.

Ach! To be loved as Sam Arkin loved! She covered her eyes, but it only pressed   135
upon her the more. Home, husband, babies, a bread-giver for life!

And the Other—a dream—a madness that burns you up alive. "You might as well want to marry yourself to the President of America as to want him. But I can't help it. *Him and him only* I want."

She looked up again. "No—no!" she cried, cruel in the self-absorption of youth and ambition. "You can't make me for a person. It's not only that I got to go up higher, but I got to push myself up by myself, by my own strength—"

"Nu, nu," he sobbed. "I'll not bother you with me—only give you my everything. My bank-book is more than my flesh and blood—only take it, to do what you want with it."

Her eyes deepened with humility. "I know your goodness—but there's something like a wall around me—him in my heart."

"Him?" The word hurled itself at him like a bomb-shell. He went white with pain.   140
And even she, immersed in her own thoughts, lowered her head before the dumb suffering on his face. She felt she owed it to him to tell him.

"I wanted to talk myself out to you about him yet before.—He ain't just a man. He is all that I want to be and am not yet. He is the hunger of me for the life that ain't just eating and sleeping and slaving for bread."

She pushed back her chair and rose abruptly. "I can't be inside walls when I talk of him. I need the earth, the whole free sky to breathe when I think of him. Come out in the air."

They walked for a time before either spoke. Sam Arkin followed where she led through the crooked labyrinth of streets. The sight of the young mothers with their nursing infants pressed to their bared bosoms stabbed anew his hurt.

Shenah Pessah, blind to all but the vision that obsessed her, talked on. "All that my mother and father and my mother's mother and father ever wanted to be is in him. This fire in me, it's not just the hunger of a woman for a man—it's the hunger of all my people back of me, from all ages, for light, for the life higher!"

A veil of silence fell between them. She felt almost as if it were a sacrilege to have   145
spoken of that which was so deeply centered within her.

Sam Arkin's face became lifeless as clay. Bowed like an old man, he dragged his leaden feet after him. The world was dead—cold—meaningless. Bank-book, money—of what use were they now? All his years of saving couldn't win her. He was suffocated in emptiness.

On they walked till they reached a deserted spot in the park. So spent was he by his sorrow that he lost the sense of time or place or that she was near.

Leaning against a tree, he stood, dumb, motionless, unutterable bewilderment in his sunken eyes.

"I lived over the hunger for bread—but this—" He clutched at his aching bosom. "Highest One, help me!" With his face to the ground he sank, prostrate.

"Sam Arkin!" She bent over him tenderly. "I feel the emptiness of words—but I got   150
to get it out. All that you suffer I have suffered, and must yet go on suffering. I see no end. But only—there is a something—a hope—a help out—it lifts me on top of my hungry body—the hunger to make from myself a person that can't be crushed by nothing nor nobody—the life higher!"

Slowly, he rose to his feet, drawn from his weakness by the spell of her. "With one hand you throw me down and with the other you lift me up to life again. Say to me only again, your words," he pleaded, helplessly.

"Sam Arkin! Give yourself your own strength!" She shook him roughly. "I got no pity on you, no more than I got pity on me."

He saw her eyes fill with light as though she were seeing something far beyond them both. "This," she breathed, "is only the beginning of the hunger that will make from you a person who'll yet ring in America."   [1920]

QUESTIONS

1. What is Pessah's most dominate character trait?
2. Explain the many meanings that "hunger" takes on in this story.
3. Why doesn't Pessah accept Arkin's money?
4. Explain the meaning of Pessah's statement "Give yourself your own strength." Explain its importance in the story.
5. In what ways is the story realistic? In what ways does the story lose verisimilitude?

RESPONSES

1. Research the history of Jewish immigration to the United States. Explain how this story captures that historical reality.
2. Explore the binaries expressed in this story—wealth/poverty, male/female, literacy/illiteracy, American/Eastern European—and explain how Yezierska attempts to use them to develop a theme. Do the binaries begin to contradict themselves, to deconstruct thematically?
3. Compare this story of immigration to others such as "Hollywood!" "A Father," or "My Son the Fanatic," or compare this story to ". . . And the Earth Did Not Devour Him."

FOCUS ON FILM

1. Yezierska's story "Hunger," along with several other of her stories, was adapted into the Hollywood silent film *Hungry Hearts*. Acquire the film if you can, and discuss the methods by which melodrama is emphasized in this early Hollywood silent film. How is melodrama created in the print story?
2. Since the film *Hungry Hearts* is not easily available, rent other films of the period, such as Charlie Chaplin's *Modern Times*. After watching Chaplin's *Modern Times*, for instance, discuss the ways that Chaplin and Yezierska portray the poor and their role within the newly industrialized nation. In addition, what similarities does Chaplin's character bear to Yezierska's Shenah Pessah?

Banana Yoshimoto

Banana Yoshimoto (b. 1964), the pen name for Yoshimoto Mahoko, was born in Tokyo, Japan. Her father was an influential poet during the 1960s. Yoshimoto graduated from Nihon University in 1987, and soon published her first novel, *Kitchen* (1987), which won several awards and sold over six million copies worldwide. She has since published over a dozen books, including novels, short fiction, and essays. These include *N. D.: A Novel* (1994), *Lizard* (1996), *Amrita* (1997), *Honeymoon* (1997), and *SLY* (2002). The story "Love Songs" is included in the volume *Asleep* (2001).

Love Songs

Late at night the trees in my garden seemed to shine.

Awash in light from the street, the quiet glittering green of the leaves and the deep brown of the trunk seemed startlingly vivid.

I'd noticed this for the first time just recently, after I'd started drinking more heavily. Each time I looked out on that scenery with drunken eyes I'd be overwhelmed by the unbelievable purity of those colors, and I'd start feeling as if nothing really mattered, like I wouldn't really care at all even if I were to lose everything I had.

This wasn't resignation, or desperation. It was a much more natural form of acceptance, a feeling that arose from a sweep of emotion that was quiet and cool and crystal-clear.

Every night I fell asleep thinking about these things. 5

Of course I realized that I was drinking too much and that it would be a good idea for me to start drinking less, and during the daytime I always swore that I'd drink only the tiniest amount that night. But then night would come and the first glass of beer would lead to the next and soon I'd be flying along. I'd start thinking about how well I'd sleep if I just drank a little bit more, and I'd find myself fixing yet another gin and tonic. As the night deepened I'd start increasing the amount of gin, and the drinks would get stronger. And as I munched my way through a bag of the greatest snack this century has produced—Butter Soy Sauce Popcorn—I'd think, *Damn, I've done it again.* . . . *Here I am drinking.* I never drank enough to make me feel that I'd done something wrong, but I sometimes got a bit of a shock when I discovered that there was an empty bottle standing on the table in front of me.

It was only after my head started reeling and my body started weaving and I tumbled into bed that I'd hear that soothing voice singing.

At first I thought it was my pillow. Because it seemed to me that the pillow that always cradled my cheek so gently—no matter what was happening, however bad things were—would have a voice just like the one I was hearing, just that clear. I only heard the voice when my eyes were closed, so I figured it was a comfy sort of dream. At times like these I was never lucid enough to think very deeply about anything.

The reverberations of that voice wandered sweetly, softly, working like a massage on the area of my heart that was the most tightly clenched, helping those knots to loosen. It was like the rush of waves, and like the laughter of people I'd met in all kinds of places, people I'd become friendly with and then separated from, and like the kind words all those people had said to me, and like the mewing of a cat I had lost, and like the mixture of noises that rang in the background in a place that was dear to me, a place far away, a place that no longer existed, and like the rushing of trees that whisked past my ears as I breathed in the scent of fresh greenery on a trip someplace . . . the voice was like a combination of all this.

10   That night I heard it again.

A faint song that felt more sensual than an angel's, and also more real. I tried to catch the melody, fixed the little that remained of my consciousness on it, listened desperately. Sleep trickled down around me, and the happy tune dissolved away into my dreams.

Long ago I'd fallen in love with a strange man and ended up acting out one of the parts in a bizarre triangular relationship. He'd been a friend of the guy I was going out with now, and he'd had the aura of a man whom women love fleetingly but with explosive force. Actually, he was a slightly peculiar and rather boisterous sort of guy, something of a thug, I could see that now, but I'd been young at the time and of course I'd fallen for him. I didn't remember much about him anymore. We'd slept together any number of times, done it again and again, but we'd never gone out on the sort of dates where you get to spend time looking at each other, so I could hardly even remember his face.

For some reason I remembered only the nasty woman, Haru.

Apparently Haru and I had both fallen for the man at the same time. As time passed and the two of us kept running into each other at his house, we began little by little to get acquainted, and then toward the end things got so bad that it was almost as if the three of us were living together. Haru was three years older than me, and she worked part-time. I was in college.

15   Naturally we despised each other, cursed each other, and sometimes we'd even whip out our fists and get tangled up in all-out fights. Never in my life had I come so vividly close to another person, and never in my life had I resented anyone so much. Haru was all that stood in my way. I must have wished for her death a hundred times, and wished in earnest. Of course Haru probably wished for my death too.

Our two loves finally came to an abrupt end one day when the man, exhausted by the life we'd been living, ran off to some faraway place and didn't come back. My relationship with Haru ended then too. I went on living in the same town, but from what I'd heard through the grapevine, Haru had run off to Paris or someplace like that.

That was the last I'd heard of her.

I had no idea why all of a sudden I'd started remembering her, thinking of her almost fondly. I didn't particularly want to see her again, and I wasn't interested in knowing what she was doing. That period in my life had been so filled with passionate emotion that it had ended up spinning around and becoming nothing but a string of blank memories. Ultimately it hadn't made any profound impression on me at all.

Knowing her, it seemed likely that she'd have ended up as some kind of two-bit hustler, sponging off some artist in Paris, or maybe if she was lucky she'd have found some elderly patron and she'd be living off of him, very elegantly. That's the sort of woman she was. She was skinny as a bone, and her manner of talking was irritatingly frigid; her voice was deep, and she always wore black. She had thin lips, and there were always wrinkles carved into the space between her eyebrows, and she complained constantly. Yet when she smiled, she looked sort of like a child.

It kind of hurt to remember her smile.   20

Of course when you go to sleep having drunk as much as I had, waking up is total hell. It felt like the alcohol had pounded me flat, like my entire body—both inside and out—had been soaking in a bath of hot sake. My mouth was like a desert, and it was a while before I could even roll over.

I couldn't even begin to consider getting up and brushing my teeth, or taking a shower. I found it impossible to believe that in the past I'd done those things quite casually, as if they were nothing at all.

Arrowlike rays of sun bit into my head.

I couldn't even stand to tally up all my symptoms, there were so many, and it was all so terrible that I just wanted to burst into tears. I didn't see how I could ever be saved.

Lately every morning was like this.   25

Finally I gave up and dragged myself limply out of bed. If I just left my aching head on its own it would start swaying from side to side, so I held it in my hands. Still holding it, I fixed myself a cup of tea and drank it.

For some reason my nights tended to stretch out to surprising lengths, like rubber, and they were endlessly sweet. And my mornings were unforgivingly sharp. The light seemed to stab at me with some sort of pointy object. It was hard and translucent and stubborn. It was wretched.

Every thought I had just made me unhappy. And then, like an army in pursuit of an already thoroughly pummeled foe, the phone started to shriek. It was an awful sound. The insistent clangor got on my nerves so much that I answered with intentionally exaggerated vitality.

"Hello!"

"Wow, you sure sound lively," said Mizuo cheerfully.   30

Mizuo was my boyfriend. He'd known both Haru and the man. When the two of them made their exits, he and I were left alone.

"I'm not. I've got a hangover and my head's throbbing."

"Not again?"

"You're off today, right? Are you coming over?"

"Yeah, I'll be over soon," Mizuo said.   35

He hung up.

He owned a store that sold various little household goods, so weekdays were his days off. I'd been working in the same kind of store until recently, but the place had gone out of business. It had been decided that I'd go to work at a new branch Mizuo was about to open in the next town, and I was waiting for it to open, which would be in about six months.

Every once in a while Mizuo looked at me with the same eyes he used to look at objects. Like he was thinking, *It'd really be better without this floral pattern here . . . it might get a good price if it didn't have this chip . . . this stripe here might look tacky but it captures people's hearts.*

At times like these the look in his eyes was so coldly penetrating it was shocking, and when I noticed it I'd give a little gasp. But it seemed he was also inspecting the changes that took place within my heart, regarding even those as just another pattern.

40   He brought flowers that afternoon.

We ate sandwiches and a salad, feeling peaceful. I was still stretched out in bed, and every time we kissed he'd chuckle and say things like, "You stink so terribly of alcohol it's amazing. I wouldn't be surprised if your hangover made its way through your mucus membranes into me!" It seemed as if his smile ought to give off a perfume like a flower—maybe something along the lines of a white lily.

Winter was almost over. Though inside the room everything felt incredibly happy, I had the feeling that outside the window things were frighteningly dry. It seemed like the wind blowing past was hitting up against the sky, scraping noisily across its surface.

I figured it was just too sweet inside, too warm.

"I just remembered something," I said. The sweetness and the warmth had reminded me. "I've been having something like a dream every night as I'm about to fall asleep, you know, it's always the same, and so I'm kind of worried that I might be starting to have hallucinations. Except hallucinations aren't supposed to feel very good, are they? Do you think with the amount I'm drinking I could be an alcoholic? Could I be that far gone?"

45   "Don't be ridiculous," Mizuo said. "Even if you do have something of a tendency toward dependence, the real problem is just that you have time on your hands, so you end up drinking too much—that's all. Things will go back to normal as soon as you start working again, and of course it's totally fine for you to be living the sort of slowed-down life you're living now. But the dream you mentioned . . . what sort of dream is it?"

"I'm not sure I'd actually call it a dream." The pain and the nausea I'd felt were finally starting to soften. In this new mood I tried desperately to trace my way back to that happiness. "It's like . . . I get drunk and tumble into bed, right? And then I start to feel like I'm being sucked up into something, you know, it's like I'm walking in this place that used to be really important to me, a place that's precious to me, but with my eyes closed—that's the sort of feeling I have. There's this nice smell, and I feel so safe and relaxed, and then I start to hear this song, always the same song, ever so faintly. The voice singing it is so sweet I almost start to cry . . . maybe it's not even a song. But it's something like a melody, and it's ever so faint, and it's far away, and it's singing of absolutely perfect joy. Yeah, and it's always the same melody."

"Sounds bad. You must be an alcoholic."

"Huh?" I squinted at him, startled.

Mizuo burst out laughing. "Just kidding. Actually I've heard a story like that before. In fact it was just like yours. They say it means someone wants to speak to you."

50   "What do you mean someone? Who?"

"Someone who's died. Has anyone you know died?"

I puzzled for a bit, but no one came to mind. I shook my head.

"They say that when a dead person wants to say something to someone it was close to in life, that's how it gets the message across. And when you get drunk or when you're just about to fall asleep, at times like that it's easier to get synchronized, you know, so that's when it happens. Anyway that's what I heard somewhere."

Suddenly I felt icy cold. I pulled the blanket up over my shoulders.

55   "Is it always someone you know?" I asked.

No matter how happy the song made me feel, the idea of having some dead stranger singing into my ear was not something I liked.

"So they say. Maybe . . . could it be Haru?" he said.

Mizuo is very quick to sense these things. And it's true—I gave a little start and felt almost immediately that he was probably right. In fact what I felt was almost a certainty. I hadn't heard a word from her, and then lately all these memories of her drifting through my mind. . . .

"You should see what you can find out."

"Yeah, I'll ask some friends," I said.   60

Mizuo nodded.

No matter what people said to him, Mizuo never butted in with stories of his own or ignored what they were saying. His parents must have raised him well. And yet you can't deny that his name—Mizuo, written with characters meaning "water" and "man"—is fairly weird, and it's certainly not easy to try and figure out how his parents came up with it. The extraordinary truth is that when his mother was young, conditions made it necessary for her to have an abortion, even though she didn't want one. When she had Mizuo she named him "water-man," hoping that he'd be happy enough for two—the fetus that had been lost, the "waterbaby" as they're called in Japanese, and himself.

Is that the sort of name you give a child?

The whole interior of the room was flooded with the sweet scent of the white roses he'd brought. It occurred to me that if the scent lasted until night, I might be able to fall asleep without drinking so much. We kissed once again and embraced.

"Yeah, Haru died."   65

This half-expected answer came so smoothly it was shocking.

Mizuo had told me that a guy whom Haru and the man and I had all known was working at a certain all-night coffee shop now, and so I'd jumped in a taxi and rushed straight there, hoping he might be able to tell me something—I'd made a special trip, in fact—and this was the answer I got. If that was all he was going to say, I might as well just have called. I spent a few moments peering at his eyes and understood that he wasn't joking. He was standing behind the crowded shop's counter, dressed in his waiter's uniform, drying dishes. His eyes were grim.

"You mean overseas? How? Did she have AIDS?" I asked.

"It was drinking. She died from drinking," he said quietly.

Icy chills, like a double shock, jittered down my spine. For an instant I felt sure I   70
must be cursed, just as she'd been.

"She got to where she was drunk all the time, and then one day in the apartment her patron kept for her she just . . . she'd been in and out of some specialist rehab center for alcoholics, and from what I hear it sounds like she just totally collapsed toward the end. This friend of mine who just got back from Paris told me about it—said he'd heard it all from some guy who was close to her."

"Oh."

I took a gulp of coffee and nodded slightly, as if appreciating the flavor.

"I thought you two hated each other's guts. What's up?"

"'Even travelers who brush sleeves on the road are bound by ties from a former life'   75
. . . isn't exactly what I mean, but I hadn't heard a word from her since she left, you know, so I started wondering what she was doing. After all, I'm with Mizuo now, and I'm happy—you know what I mean?"

"Yeah, stuff like that happens sometimes, doesn't it?"

Back during the days when Haru and the man and I were pretty much living together, this guy was working as a bartender, and I was always going to the bar where
he worked, to get drunk and blow off steam. He'd always been completely indifferent
to things that were happening in other people's lives, so it was easy to talk to him,
and you could talk to him about anything. I sat looking at him now, his form hovering in the dim light of the shop, feeling paralyzed, and found myself remembering
the feeling that had hung in the air in those days—felt it all coming back. Weary, to-
morrowless, smoldering. I certainly had no desire to put myself back there, to feel the
sensations whose memory I was now reliving, and yet they called up an odd sentimentality.

"Well, so Haru's no longer in this world," I said.

Across the counter my old friend nodded.

80   I went back to my apartment and drank all alone in memory of Haru. For some
reason I felt that it was okay for me to drink a lot that night, so I was able to pour in
as much as I wanted and still feel good. In the past, whenever my mind had begun to
circle vaguely around thoughts of Haru, an image of the Eiffel Tower had drifted up
before me, like a shot of it on television, but tonight the image didn't appear. Instead
I saw the world that had opened up inside Haru after she lost the only outlet she'd had
for her overabundance of energy, and quickly lost herself in drink. I completely understood what Haru had gone through when the man left, and why she hadn't been
able to pull herself together and move on again. Because that's how totally involved
our love for him was—both of us had given it everything we could. The man was extremely attractive to begin with, of course, but to tell the truth, Haru and I couldn't have
put so much effort into that love if we hadn't been competing. I don't know if he found
all this amusing or if it made him feel like he needed some space to breathe or what,
but for some reason the man always used to do stuff like invite one of us over to his
house and then go out on a date with the other. Toward the end he frequently left Haru
and me at his house together and didn't come back all night.

I'm naturally clumsy, and it takes everything I have just to cook a meal or mend
some little tear in a piece of clothing, to tie the strings on little packages or put together a cardboard box. Haru was particularly good at that kind of thing, so whenever she found me struggling over something she'd shout out, "God, are you clumsy!"
and "I sure would love to see what kind of parents you've got!" and all sorts of stuff,
jeering at me without mercy. In return I'd coolly point out that she had no breasts, and
that her taste in clothes was absolutely atrocious. The man was the sort of person who
praised what was good and told you honestly that what was bad was bad, and that just
spurred the two of us on, making us even more paranoid.

"You really are a foul cook, aren't you? It's unbelievable! It's not as if you're using
a microwave. Ugghh, this looks repulsive!" Haru said.

I was making Chinese-style mixed vegetables that night. The man had gone out
with her that afternoon, keeping it a secret from me, so I was in no mood to put up with
her.

"There's no reason why I should have to listen to such rude things from someone
dressed in clothes as laughable as yours. I think you need to have slightly larger breasts
to wear black knitwear like that."

85   Haru jabbed me very sharply in the back with her elbow. I was sautéing vegetables,
and my hand very nearly went into the wok.

"What the hell are you doing?" I shouted.

The fierce sizzling of the vegetables and the waves of heat washed over my voice and made it sound achingly sad.

"You have no right to say that," Haru said.

"Maybe not," I replied, and turned off the heat.

Now that the room was suddenly quiet, our silence drifted up into the foreground. By that point neither of us could figure out whether it was okay for us to be sharing the body of a single man—a slightly eccentric man, a man who seemed to be laughing at the world, living life in his own way—and whether it was normal or abnormal. The same was true of the fact that even though he never demanded that we stay, we were spending all our time cooped up in his house, and of the fact that the two of us were always there together. All I knew was that Haru's gloomy voice and her crazy thinness were getting on my nerves. She was always weaving around in front of me, making me want to wring her neck like a chicken's.

"Why are we doing this?" Haru said then, her tone peculiarly absent. "There are other women who like him, you know, but you and I are the only ones doing this stuff. And he's not even here."

"That's how it goes."

"I feel like I'm going crazy, you get on my nerves so much."

"Those ought to be my lines. Anyway, it's too late to complain now."

I found Haru's hackneyed way of thinking about things and her darkly cheerless point of view sickening. I hated it.

"What's with you, anyway? Do you even really want him?" Haru said this as if she were scolding me.

"Yes, I want him!" I said. "That's why I'm stuck here with you, isn't it? With a moron like you—"

Wham!

Apparently I'd said too much. Before I'd even finished speaking Haru slapped me across the cheek with the flat of her hand, producing a loud smack. I was stunned for a moment, unable to grasp what had happened. Then, as the seconds passed, I felt my right cheek getting hotter.

"You've really pissed me off now, so I'm leaving," I said, and stood up. "You can have him tonight. If he comes back."

Haru went on staring at me as I picked up my bag, and then as I walked out the front door. She had her eyes open so wide, and they shone with such an earnest light, that I seriously thought she might call out for me to stop. That's the kind of gleam she had in her eyes. A look that says *Don't go*, not a look that says *I'm sorry*. I suspect that she only remained silent because it would have seemed weird if she'd actually spoken those words.

Her small, fair, tackily made-up face was half hidden by her long hair. I noticed how lovely and insubstantial she looked when you saw her from a distance. Without saying a word I closed the door.

Just thinking about other women I knew sleeping with the man gave me heartburn and left me fuming, and yet where Haru was concerned I no longer minded. In fact there were times, when the three of us were all sleeping together, when he and Haru would start going at it, and I hardly gave it a second thought. If it had been any other woman I probably would have killed her on the spot.

As long as we were together I could sort of understand how the man felt toward her.

105   I'm not talking about who she was inside.

Inside she was probably just a strange, high-strung, unpleasant woman. But there was something truly special in her appearance. The soft shadow you saw in her panties, slender shoulders flickering in and out of the blackness of her long hair, odd little valleys over her collarbone, the curves under her breasts that seemed so impossibly, untouchably distant . . . she could have been the embodiment of the diaphanous image of Woman herself, come shakily to life, stumbling around. That's certainly what you felt.

I saw the glimmering uproar of the trees in my garden again that night, outside the window. It was a beautiful scene, one that seemed to break off in bizarre angles, coming to points, just as I'd remembered. In the wash of light I had the feeling that these points were gentle, not pitilessly hard.

No doubt this was because I was drunk.

I turned out the lights. The various objects in the room were even more sharply visible now.

110   I could hear my breath, and my heartbeat.

I pulled the covers up over myself and sank my head deep down into the pillow. And then I heard it again.

The reverberations of a voice as pure as an angel's, the light tenderness, the melody—all this made my heart begin to flutter, to dance achingly. Like waves, distant and close, full of nostalgia, rolling on . . . .

Haru, is there something you want to say?

My heart felt like it was spinning, like something that goes on spinning even when it's hidden from view—I tried to lock the spinning on that sound. But there was no sign of Haru, nothing at all but the beautiful stream of sound stabbing through my chest. Perhaps on the other side of this beautiful melody I'd find Haru's smile. Or maybe— maybe she was screaming in a voice filled with hatred that my happiness and her death were two sides of a single sheet of paper. I didn't care, either way I wanted terribly to hear.

115   I needed to know what she was trying to say. I concentrated so intensely that the space between my eyebrows started to ache, and before long exhaustion rolled out on waves of sleep from the far side of the song. Deep down inside I gave up, murmured words expressing my decision to give up. As if they were the words of a prayer.

I feel bad, Haru. But I can't hear you. I'm sorry.

Good night.

"You were right, Haru's dead," I said.

Mizuo just opened his eyes a little wider; that was it.

120   "So she really is?" he said, and shifted his gaze to the window.

The glittering nighttime town was stunning.

We were only fourteen stories up, but the view was quite good. I'd suggested that we go eat someplace sky-high for a change, and Mizuo had asked if I meant sky-high in cost or elevation. I'd laughed and said I meant both, and that's how we'd ended up here.

The world beyond the window was awash with shining beads of night, these beads were everywhere—I was overwhelmed. The lines of cars were a necklace circling the rim of night.

"What makes you think it's Haru?" I asked.

"The two of you were so close to each other." 125

He said this in a perfectly ordinary tone, then cut himself a bit of meat and lifted it to his mouth. For a moment my hands stopped moving. Because all of a sudden I was on the verge of tears.

"Does Haru want to say something to me?"

"Afraid I wouldn't know that."

"No, I guess not."

I looked back down at my dinner. Maybe it wasn't such a big deal after all. Maybe 130 the various lingering regrets that kept drifting up to the surface now that my alcohol-spattered life was getting ready to enter a new stage had simply taken form as an image of Haru. We'd already emptied two bottles of wine tonight—I'd had help from Mizuo—and the world before me was starting to get fuzzy around the edges.

I felt like I wouldn't mind even if those inescapable regrets that we're all left with, that lie buried deep inside every one of us, ended up being nothing more than a bit of color added to the night—as long as I could enjoy the incredible beauty of this quietly blurring, infinitely reflected scenery until morning, when everything would return once again to zero.

"Would you like to go see Haru now?" Mizuo asked suddenly.

"Excuse me?" I said this in a rather jarring tone. I was so taken aback that the other people in the restaurant glanced over at me.

"I know a guy who can do that sort of stuff," Mizuo said, grinning.

"This sounds extre-e-emely suspect," I replied, and grinned back. 135

"Actually, it's pretty impressive. The guy's a midget—I got to know him way back when I was doing a kind of work much more unsavory than what I'm doing now. He lets you talk to dead people. It's kind of like hypnotism, you know, except it's totally real," Mizuo said.

"And you've tried this?" I asked.

"Yeah. I once killed someone, see, by mistake."

These words just slipped off his tongue. His casualness indicated how unfathomably deep his remorse was.

"What, in a fight or something?" 140

"Nope. I lent him my car when it was broken."

Mizuo seemed unwilling to say more. He changed the topic. "It left a really bad aftertaste, you know, so I went to this midget . . . and then I met the guy and talked things over with him, and even if it was bogus it made me feel better—it totally cleared the air. And I meant it when I said that I think you and Haru were close to each other. If there hadn't been a man standing between you, I'm sure you would have hit it off really well. That guy has turned into a real loser now, and he's living a sleazy life, but back then he had this super-cheery kind of air about him, right? I always thought that since the two of you reacted in the same way to that sort of radiance, you must be pretty similar."

It occurred to me once again that the coldness of Mizuo's personality was like that of water, just as his name suggested. I realized that the trees and all kinds of other things scattered throughout the gorgeous scene spread beneath the window—a scene that ought to have been perfectly still—were shaking. There must be a strong wind blowing. The headlights of cars kept flowing on, quietly burying the streets.

"Of course you're much more my type. Flat nose, klutzy . . ."

He said this in the same tone he'd use to say that a chipped vase had a certain appeal, and I liked that way of speaking, so I thought again how much I liked Mizuo. 145

"Okay, let's go see the midget," I said. "It sounds neat."

"You bet it is," Mizuo replied, sipping his wine. "Even if it's a lie, even if it's who knows what, if it clears the air, you know, if it's fun, you might as well try it. As long as it makes you feel better, it's all right."

The shop Mizuo took me to was an ordinary snack bar, the sort of place you come across all over, down below street level, with nothing in it but a counter. There was no denying that the man in charge was a midget. But apart from the badly proportioned arrangement of his body, he seemed like a regular enough person, and there was nothing about him that made you feel uncomfortable. He gazed at me with steady eyes.

"Your girlfriend?" the midget asked Mizuo suddenly.

150 "Yeah—her name's Fumi."

I nodded slightly and said it was nice to meet him.

"This here's my buddy, Tanaka the midget."

Tanaka laughed when Mizuo said this.

"If I were an American I'd be Mr. John Doe," he said. "That's me."

155 He was about as sketchy as you can get, but the intelligence behind his words made me feel that I could trust him. He pushed open the small gate and stepped out from behind the counter, then walked over to the heavy front door and turned the lock.

"You're here to see someone dead?" he said.

"Right. Got to keep you working!" Mizuo said, grinning.

"I haven't been doing this at all lately. Takes strength. I have to charge a lot," Tanaka said, and looked at me. "When did this person die?"

"Just recently. She's a young woman—I hadn't seen her in about two years. We were battling each other over a man." My heart was pounding fast and hard. "I wonder if I could have something to drink?"

160 "Yeah, I could use something too. Break out a bottle," Mizuo said.

"Well then, tonight the bar is yours," Tanaka said.

He climbed a ladder and took a bottle down from one of the shelves up near the top, then started mixing two whiskeys and soda, moving his hands quickly and deftly.

"This one here's been overdoing it lately," Mizuo said, with a smile. "You better make it super strong."

"Gotcha."

165 Tanaka laughed, and I laughed along with him. There was something I kept noticing. Mizuo trusted me, he treated me just like he would any adult. And that called forth an incomparable feeling of relief and security. I really believe that no matter how old people get, they tend to change in certain ways depending on how people treat them—they change their colors. Mizuo was always very skilled at using people. We said cheers and drank.

"I don't get it," said Tanaka, tilting his head slightly to the side. "Why would you want to see a woman you fought with over a man?"

My mouth felt numb from the strong whiskey and soda.

I answered him honestly. "It seems we may really have liked each other. In fact we might have had a little lesbian dynamic going on."

Tanaka exploded into laughter. "You're honest, good for you."

170 I kept gazing vaguely at his small shoes, inspecting the shape of his tiny hands, thinking about what I'd say to Haru if I actually connected with her. But as hard as I tried, I couldn't think of anything.

"Shall we start?" Tanaka said. We'd finished our drinks.

Mizuo had become very quiet. No doubt he was thinking of the things that had happened when he'd come here himself, long ago.

"What do you mean? How do we start?" I asked.

"It's simple. You don't have to take any drugs, and there's no counting involved. All you've got to do is close your eyes and keep quiet and you'll go to this room. That's the room where the meetings take place. There's just one thing I ought to warn you about, and that's that even if she invites you to leave, you can't step outside that door. You remember what happened to Earless Hôichi in the old ghost story when he went along with the ghost. That's how he became earless. And there have been plenty of people like that—people who leave the room and then realize that they can't get back. A few of them never returned. So you've got to be careful, see?"

I was now so scared I couldn't even speak. 175

Mizuo saw this and laughed. "Don't worry, you'll be fine," he said. "You're strong."

I nodded and closed my eyes. I sensed that Tanaka had come out from behind the counter again. Almost immediately I felt a smooth coolness spread quietly through my body.

Suddenly I found myself in the room.

It was a strange, cramped room, with one small frosted glass window. I was sitting on a worn red sofa. There was a second small sofa shaped just like mine directly across from me—there wasn't even a table in the middle. It was a lot like the House of Surprises that they used to have way back when, in amusement parks, that thing where the walls rotate, and even though you're not moving you have the illusion that the whole house is spinning. The lights were dim, and I felt sort of melancholy.

And then there was the wooden door. 180

I figured it would probably be okay if I just touched it, so I stretched my hand out toward the doorknob. It was narrow and soothingly cool, a dull gold in color. The moment I closed my hand around it, I felt a sweep of vibrations come throbbing up into my arm. If I had to describe the feeling, I'd say it was as if the door were holding something back, as if this were the only quiet place in an incredible whirl of energy that was spiraling around outside, someplace like the eye of a hurricane, or like walled-off sacred ground. Every cell in my body started to quake and gibber. I realized that I had an instinctive fear of the world beyond that door.

Yet at the same time I could understand that certain people might be tempted to open this door. I understood that Mizuo must have felt that urge. And that several people had stepped outside, and that it was true—those people had probably never come back.

Yeah, it makes sense.

I stepped away from the door and sat back down on the couch. My head had cleared. I stamped my feet on the wooden floor and slid my hands across the sandpapery beige wall. Everything felt extremely real. Like the deserted waiting room of a train station way out in the country, the room had a certain unnatural feeling about it, a certain oppressive air.

And then it happened. All of a sudden the door crashed open and Haru came 185 bounding into the room.

I was so surprised I couldn't speak.

For just a moment, over the top of Haru's shoulders, I caught a glimpse of a tremendous expanse of heavy ash-colored gray, and heard a wild moaning, like the noise of some kind of storm. That scenery was any number of times more frightening for me than the fact that Haru had actually come.

"It's been a while," Haru said.

She gave me a small smile, tightening her lips.

190 You had the feeling that smile would be sucked up by the room and by the frightening grayness outside almost before you knew it. It seemed like a terribly lonely smile.

"It's great that we're able to meet like this," I said.

The words came out as smooth as oil.

"I'm glad I figured out that you wanted to see me. Because to tell the truth, I liked you a lot, Haru, you know? The days we spent together had this special feeling of tension—it was a lot of fun. And that's only because it was you. You mean a lot to me. And just being with you taught me so much. There were all these things that I wanted to talk to you about, but we never had the chance. I really regret that."

I couldn't say that this was all the truth. It was like a confession. It was like shouting love at a boat as it glides off into the distance.

195 But Haru—thin as ever, still dressed in black—nodded.

"Me too," she said. Then, "But take a look at this!"

She stood up. And as she did, a bit of her long hair brushed lightly across my hand. It was an amazingly swishy, ticklish feeling.

I focused on the sensation to make sure it was real.

It was then that she yanked the door open.

200 I stiffened, readying myself.

Even if she invites you to leave, you can't step outside.

Haru giggled, gently brushing aside my ungenerous impulses. "Boy, are you suspicious! It's okay, I'm just showing you. Here, watch this, I'll put my head out. Okay?"

Haru thrust her head back into that ash-gray world. And the instant she did so her hair began to flap and tangle with awesome energy, but without making any sound at all. She kept her head thrust back as she spoke.

"You remember that day when there was a huge storm like this and you and I were in his house alone? It felt just like it does here. You know, I made my way through this storm with my eyes shut, that's how I got here. I did that because I wanted to see you. I mean, I wouldn't have come for that man we were both so crazy about, you know, seriously. Because it's rough getting here, it really is rough."

205 "Same for me," I said. "It seemed like I should see you."

"Because I was calling you, kiddo. I'd been hanging around for a while, you know, down where you were," Haru said.

She seemed much more grown up than the Haru I'd known.

"Why did you call me?" I asked.

"I don't really know. Maybe because I never felt lonely when we were together. I mean I wasn't ever truly lonely, but whenever I think about you I get this feeling that I was least lonely when I was with you. And I get the feeling that on the day of that storm, you know, I wanted to kiss you."

210 There was no expression on Haru's face.

"I'm happy to hear that," I said.

But I felt unbearably sad. The ashy gray outside was so heavy that I felt how great a distance separates us from the past when I looked at Haru's tangled hair whipping in the wind. It was a distance greater than that between life and death, wider than the unfillable chasm that separates us all from one another.

I called her name. "Haru!"

Haru gave a little smile and fixed her hair, took hold of the door with a movement that seemed perfectly natural, said good-bye and touched my hand, then vanished into the space beyond the door. I was thinking: *Yeah, come to think of it, I guess the only time we ever talked to each other like this was that day, that was the only time. . . .*

The bang of the door and the coldness of her hand lingered on. 215

"Welcome back!" shouted Tanaka.

Glancing quickly around, I realized that I was back in the shop.

"Wow! That was awesome! What's the trick?" I said.

I was trying to hide my confusion, but I was also genuinely impressed.

"That's a nice thing to say! It's the real thing, kid." Tanaka sounded slightly pissed 220 off.

"Basically, Tanaka here is like that animal the Chinese thought up that eats people's bad dreams, see? Think of it that way," Mizuo said.

"Right, that's a good way to put it," Tanaka said.

"Yeah, I guess so. It made me really happy to see her. I don't know, it's like some poison has been sucked out of my chest," I said.

I felt myself gradually returning to reality—I checked to make sure that my mind and body were still as they should be. My breath, and everything I saw, was so sharp and clear it seemed like some mist dissolving.

"You feel like you do after you get a lot of exercise, right?" Tanaka said, plonking 225 a glass of ice water down on the counter in front of me. "That's because you've just been someplace very far away."

Yes—that stormy day.

Early autumn and a typhoon had blown up.

The situation between Haru and me had been steadily getting more and more dangerous, and we'd been quarreling the entire week. Our love for the man was starting to wear thin, and there was nothing we could do to turn things around, so we were constantly irritated and always anxious. The man almost never came by the house anymore, but neither of us cared much about that.

"It's thundering like crazy outside," I said.

I wanted to go home but I couldn't go home, so I had no choice but to say some- 230 thing to Haru; I'd unthinkingly made the mistake of speaking. But she responded in a surprisingly ordinary tone.

"I wish it would stop. I hate thunder."

She drew her eyebrows together. It was an extremely erotic, sorrowful expression, and every time I saw it I felt charmed—if only for an instant.

"Fumi! Help me, I'm scared!"

There'd been a bright flash of lightning, and then almost immediately a growl of thunder so fierce it was like getting hit on the head. It was the first time Haru had ever said anything like that to me, and so I looked over at her, stunned, and found that she was sitting facing me, grinning like a little girl. Suddenly I understood. *Haru knows too. This love affair is moving through its final stage, and after that the two of us will never see each other again. She knows it as well as I do.*

"It's pretty close," I said. 235

"I really wish it'd stop," Haru repeated.

She moved away from the window and circled around behind my back, pretending that she was trying to hide.

No doubt the coming of the storm had made her feel lonely.

"Don't give me that. You're not scared," I said, my voice incredulous. I turned around to look at her.

240 "Actually, I am a little scared."

Haru laughed. I smiled back.

And then her face filled with surprise.

"Hey, aren't we kind of getting along? Just a bit?"

I nodded. "You know, I think maybe we are."

245 The room was shut off from the rest of the world, and the thunder kept crashing over us, again and again, coming from ever so far away. The air that filled the room had turned thick and hard, and it felt as if even our silenced breathing was disturbing that small perfection. Nothing but a certain sense of preciousness glittered there, steeped in stillness and quiet. Soon it would all be over. All of this would wither away, it would all disappear. We'd go our separate ways. Again and again this conviction crashed over us.

"I wonder how he's doing in all this."

Haru's profile looked small and beautiful in the flashes of light.

"It certainly is stormy out."

I wanted us to be still now. Together, quiet and still.

250 "Do you think he's got an umbrella?"

"It wouldn't help in this weather. You'd get hit by lightning."

"It'd suit him, wouldn't it? A death like that."

"I wish he'd hurry up and come home."

"Yeah."

255 We sat alongside each other, leaning up against the wall, hugging our knees and talking. This was the only time I ever spoke with Haru like that—it had never happened before and it would never happen again. The flowing roar of the rain never stopped getting in the way of our thoughts. It felt like the whole time we'd been in this room we'd been friends, as close to each other as we were right now. Like all along we'd just been pretending not to like each other.

"It sounds like a flash flood."

"Yeah. It hasn't rained like this in a while."

"I wonder where he could be."

"Anywhere's okay as long as he's safe."

260 "Don't worry, he's fine."

"Yeah, he's probably fine."

Haru was hugging her knees, resting her narrow chin on her kneecaps.

She nodded elegantly and strongly.

It was close to dawn when Mizuo and I left Tanaka's shop.

265 I questioned him as we walked. "So how long was I actually unconscious?"

"About two hours. We drank as we waited—and boy, am I drunk!"

Mizuo's voice echoed loudly in the deserted alley.

"Really? Was it that long?"

I'd only been with Haru for a few moments, so I was surprised to hear this. All the same, I was feeling cool and relaxed. The light of the moon and stars was incredibly vivid, so brilliant it seemed as if they'd been washed, and it felt like I hadn't seen them so bright in years. It made me feel happy just to walk, and my pace sped up all on its own. *Haru, an angel's song, the midget medium, Haru. . . .*

270 "But that's fine. As long as you feel better," Mizuo said suddenly, and then put his arm around my shoulder. "For now, don't think."

I nodded without saying anything.

Did I just happen to get drunk every night?

Was Haru always somewhere close by?

Was that beautiful song Haru trying to call me?

Where did I go just now at the shop?   275

Who was that midget? Why is he able to do that?

Was that really Haru? Even though she's dead?

Or was it just a one-person play acted out inside me?

And then Haru made her exit, and I was left alone.

Greater than all the mysteries, a calm evening breeze slid through me, cleansing   280
me.

"I kind of feel like, starting tomorrow, I won't be drinking that much. I wonder if
I've been doing it on purpose," I said. "But I don't know . . . it really seems like I'll be
able to stop."

"I'm sure you've just reached that stage." Mizuo smiled.

Is everything just a "stage" for Mizuo? All these things inside me, and his being with
me?

Isn't he excessively gentle because he's excessively cold?

I have no idea what's coming, and if I love him any more than I do now, I'll prob-   285
ably become completely transparent.

What will happen to us as we begin our new life together?

And yet . . .

Mizuo's smile still seemed to pierce straight through to my heart, and I had the
feeling that this smile was the spitting image of the cold and beautiful night. Even if
this night we were spending together and everything else was just going to disappear
into the past, that was all right—and it seemed to me that I held this allrightness pre-
ciously in my hands, and that it was glittering there. Just like the time I'd spent with
Haru.

At any rate, I'd probably never hear that singing voice again, that voice so lovely
it made you shudder: suddenly I understood this. And that alone made me feel terribly sad.

That feeling of security, that sweetness, that pain, that gentleness. I felt sure that   290
every time I saw the green of the trees in my garden awash in light from the street, I'd
be struck by a sudden flicker of remembrance—the tail of that soft melody—and I'd
chase along behind it, as if sniffing my way forward in pursuit of a pleasant scent.

And then I'd stop wanting to remember, and I'd forget.

Walking with Mizuo's hand on my shoulder, I realized this.   [1989]

QUESTIONS

1. Fumi has experienced three love stories—with the unnamed man, with Haru,
   and with Mizuo. How are these love stories similar? How are they different?

2. How is this story a typical ghost story? How is it different?

3. How does Fumi's experiences at Tanaka's place affect the conflict she has
   been having?

4. How is the description of Mizuo as a "water man" meaningful in the story?

5. Examine the setting of the story. How are its symbolic meanings similar to
   western meanings? How are they different?

Responses

1. Examine this story from a psychological/archetypal approach. How is the story about a fractured sense of self and the healing of that self? How is Haru an archetype of a part of ourselves that we contend with?
2. Compare this story to Fuentes's "Chac-Mool" or to Cortázar's "Axolotl."

Context: Writers on Writing

"What really knocks me out," Holden Caulfield observes in J. D. Salinger's *The Catcher in the Rye*, "is a book that, when you're all done reading it, you wish the author that wrote it was a terrific friend of yours and you could call him up on the phone whenever you felt like it."

Readers of fiction will understand at once what Holden is talking about. If we enjoy a work of fiction, we get quickly on terms of intimacy with the author and respond to the story as if we were listening to an old and trusted friend. But our response is not passive. When we listen to a story told aloud, we actively participate, nodding in agreement, groaning in sympathy, laughing aloud, asking questions for clarification. Similarly, when we read a story—and especially when we reread it—we bring into play all our resources of intellect and feeling so that we can enter fully into the experience. And when we put the book down we may wish, as does Holden Caulfield, that we could pick up the telephone and talk the whole thing over with the author.

Yet even if we succeeded in placing the call, the author's interpretation of the story would not be the last word. As D. H. Lawrence said, "Never trust the teller. Trust the tale." The author's view is authoritative but not definitive. Once the story is published, it belongs to the world.

The following section includes a wide variety of interviews, letters, and essays by the writers of the stories in this anthology. Several writers provide useful ways of approaching their own stories, while others look at broader approaches to reading and writing fiction.

Context

One summer, almost ten years ago, I brought my lover down to Greenville to visit my aunt Dot and the rest of my mama's family. We took our time getting there, spending one day in D.C. and another in Durham. I even thought about suggesting a side trip over to the Smoky Mountains, until I realized the reason I was thinking about that was that I was afraid. It was not my family I feared. It was my lover. I was afraid to take my lover home with me because of what I might see in her face once she had spent some time with my aunt, met a few of my uncles, and tried to talk to any of my cousins. I was afraid of the distance, the fear, or the contempt that I imagined could suddenly appear between us. I was afraid that she might see me through new eyes, hateful eyes, the eyes of someone who suddenly knew fully how different we were. My aunts' distance, my cousins' fear, or my uncles' contempt seemed much less threatening.

I was right to worry. My lover did indeed see me with new eyes, though it turned out that she was more afraid of my distancing myself from her than of her fear and discomfort coming between us. What I saw in her face after the first day in South Carolina was nothing I had expected. Her features were marked with a kind of tenuous awe, confusion, uncertainty, and shame. All she could say was that she hadn't been prepared. My aunt Dot had welcomed her, served ice tea in a tall glass, and made her sit in the best seat at the kitchen table, the one near the window where my uncle's cigarette smoke wouldn't bother her. But my lover had barely spoken.

"It's a kind of a dialect, isn't it," she said to me in the motel that night. "I couldn't understand one word in four of anything your aunt said." I looked at her. Aunt Dot's accent was pronounced, but I had never thought of it as a dialect. It was just that she hadn't ever been out of Greenville County. She had a television, but it was for the kids in the living room. My aunt lived her life at that kitchen table.

My lover leaned into my shoulder so that her cheek rested against my collar bone. "I thought I knew what it would be like—your family, Greenville. You told me so many stories. But the words . . ." She lifted her hand palm up into the air and flexed the fingers as if she were reaching for an idea.

5   "I don't know," she said. "I thought I understood what you meant when you said 'working class' but I just didn't have a context."

I lay still. Although the motel air conditioner was working hard, I could smell the steamy moist heat from outside. It was slipping in around the edges of the door and windows, a swampy earth-rich smell that reminded me of being ten years old and climbing down to sleep on the floor with my sisters, hoping it would be a little cooler there. We had never owned an air conditioner, never stayed in a motel, never eaten in a restaurant where my mother did not work. Context. I breathed in the damp metallic air-conditioner smell and remembered Folly Beach.

When I was about eight my stepfather drove us there, down the road from Charleston, and all five of us stayed in one room that had been arranged for us by a friend of his at work. It wasn't a motel. It was a guesthouse, and the lady who managed it didn't seem too happy that we showed up for a room someone else had already paid for. I slept in a fold-up cot that kept threatening to collapse in the night. My sisters slept together in the bed across from the one my parents shared. My mama cooked on a two-burner stove to save us the cost of eating out, and our greatest treat was take-out food—fried fish my stepfather swore was bad and hamburgers from the same place that sold the fish. We were in awe of the outdoor shower under the stairs where we were expected to rinse off the sand we picked up on the beach. We longed to be able to rent one of the rafts, umbrellas, and bicycles you could get on the beach. But my stepfather insisted all that stuff was listed at robbery rates and cursed the men who tried to tempt us with it. That didn't matter to us. We were overcome with the sheer freedom of being on a real vacation in a semi-public place all the time where my stepfather had to watch his temper, and of running everywhere in bathing suits and flip-flops.

We were there a week. Twice my stepfather sent us to the beach while he and Mama stayed in the room. We took the opportunity to follow other families around, to listen to fathers praising their sons and watch mothers blushing with pride at how people looked at their girls. We listened to accents and studied picnic menus. Everyone was strange and wonderful, on vacation.

My stepfather lost his temper only once on that trip. He was horrified at the prices in the souvenir shops and made us keep our hands in our pockets.

"Jew bastards will charge me if you break anything," he cursed.   10

I flinched at his words and then realized that the man behind the counter heard him. I saw his blush and outrage as his eyes followed my stepfather's movement toward the door. Then I saw his eyes flicker over to me and my sisters, registering the same contempt with which he had looked at my stepfather. Heat flamed in my neck and I wanted to apologize—to tell him we were not like our stepfather—but I could do nothing. I couldn't speak a word to him in front of my stepfather, and if I had, why would he have believed me? Remember this, I thought. Don't go deaf and blind to what this feels like, remember it. I gritted my teeth and kept my head up, looked that man in the face and mouthed, "I'm sorry," but I could not tell if he understood me.

What context did he have for people like us?

WALTER BENJAMIN

FROM *The Storyteller*

Reflections on the Works of Nikolai Leskov

I

Familiar though his name may be to us, the storyteller in his living immediacy is by no means a present force. He has already become something remote from us and something that is getting even more distant. To present someone like Leskov as a storyteller does not mean bringing him closer to us but, rather, increasing our distance from him. Viewed from a certain distance, the great, simple outlines which define the storyteller stand out in him, or rather, they become visible in him, just as in a rock a human head or an animal's body may appear to an observer at the proper distance and angle of vision. This distance and this angle of vision are prescribed for us by an experience which we may have almost every day. It teaches us that the art of storytelling is coming to an end. Less and less frequently do we encounter people with the ability to tell a tale properly. More and more often there is embarrassment all around when the wish to hear a story is expressed. It is as if something that seemed inalienable to us, the securest among our possessions, were taken from us: the ability to exchange experiences.

One reason for this phenomenon is obvious: experience has fallen in value. And it looks as if it is continuing to fall into bottomlessness. Every glance at a newspaper demonstrates that it has reached a new low, that our picture, not only of the external world but of the moral world as well, overnight has undergone changes which were never thought possible. With the [First] World War a process began to become apparent which has not halted since then. Was it not noticeable at the end of the war that men returned from the battlefield grown silent—not richer, but poorer in communicable experience? What ten years later was poured out in the flood of war books was anything but experience that goes from mouth to mouth. And there was nothing remarkable about that. For never has experience been contradicted more thoroughly than strategic experience by tactical warfare, economic experience by inflation, bodily experience by mechanical warfare, moral experience by those in power. A generation that had gone to school on a horse-drawn streetcar now stood under the open sky in a countryside in which nothing remained unchanged but the clouds, and beneath these clouds, in a field of force of destructive torrents and explosions, was the tiny, fragile human body.

II

Experience which is passed on from mouth to mouth is the source from which all storytellers have drawn. And among those who have written down the tales, it is the great ones whose written version differs least from the speech of the many nameless storytellers. Incidentally, among the last named there are two groups which, to be sure, overlap in many ways. And the figure of the storyteller gets its full corporeality only for the one who can picture them both. "When someone goes on a trip, he has something to tell about," goes the German saying, and people imagine the storyteller as someone who has come from afar. But they enjoy no less listening to the man who has stayed at home, making an honest living, and who knows the local tales and traditions. If one wants to picture these two groups through their archaic representatives, one is embodied in the resident tiller of the soil, and the other in the trading seaman. Indeed, each sphere of life has, as it were, produced its own tribe of storytellers. Each of these tribes preserves some of its characteristics centuries later. Thus, among nineteenth-century German storytellers, writers like Hebel and Gotthelf stem from the first tribe, writers like Sealsfield and Gerstäcker from the second. With these tribes, however, as stated above, it is only a matter of basic types. The actual extension of the realm of storytelling in its full historical breadth is inconceivable without the most intimate interpenetration of these two archaic types. Such an interpenetration was achieved particularly by the Middle Ages in their trade structure. The resident master craftsman and the traveling journeymen worked together in the same rooms; and every master had been a traveling journeyman before he settled down in his home town or somewhere else. If peasants and seamen were past masters of storytelling, the artisan class was its university. In it was combined the lore of faraway places, such as a much-traveled man brings home, with the lore of the past, as it best reveals itself to natives of a place.

III

Leskov was at home in distant places as well as distant times. He was a member of the Greek Orthodox Church, a man with genuine religious interests. But he was a no less sincere opponent of ecclesiastic bureaucracy. Since he was not able to get along any better with secular officialdom, the official positions he held were not of long duration. Of all his posts, the one he held for a long time as Russian representative of a big English firm was presumably the most useful one for his writing. For this firm he traveled through Russia, and these trips advanced his worldly wisdom as much as they did his knowledge of conditions in Russia. In this way he had an opportunity of becoming acquainted with the organization of the sects in the country. This left its mark on his works of fiction. In the Russian legends Leskov saw allies in his fight against Orthodox bureaucracy. There are a number of his legendary tales whose focus is a righteous man, seldom an ascetic, usually a simple, active man who becomes a saint apparently in the most natural way in the world. Mystical exaltation is not Leskov's

forte. Even though he occasionally liked to indulge in the miraculous, even in pious-
ness he prefers to stick with a sturdy nature. He sees the prototype in the man who
finds his way about the world without getting too deeply involved with it.

5   He displayed a corresponding attitude in worldly matters. It is in keeping with this
that be began to write late, at the age of twenty-nine. That was after his commercial
travels. His first printed work was entitled "Why Are Books Expensive in Kiev?" A
number of other writings about the working class, alcoholism, police doctors, and unemployed salesmen are precursors of his works of fiction.

VI

One must imagine the transformation of epic forms occurring in rhythms comparable
to those of the change that has come over the earth's surface in the course of thousands of centuries. Hardly any other forms of human communication have taken shape
more slowly, been lost more slowly. It took the novel, whose beginnings go back to
antiquity, hundreds of years before it encountered in the evolving middle class those
elements which were favorable to its flowering. With the appearance of these elements,
storytelling began quite slowly to recede into the archaic; in many ways, it is true, it
took hold of the new material, but it was not really determined by it. On the other
hand, we recognize that with the full control of the middle class, which has the press
as one of its most important instruments in fully developed capitalism, there emerges
a form of communication which, no matter how far back its origin may lie, never before influenced the epic form in a decisive way. But now it does exert such an influence.
And it turns out that it confronts storytelling as no less of a stranger than did the novel,
but in a more menacing way, and that it also brings about a crisis in the novel. This new
form of communication is information.

Villemessant, the founder of *Le Figaro*, characterized the nature of information in
a famous formulation. "To my readers," he used to say, "an attic fire in the Latin Quarter is more important than a revolution in Madrid." This makes strikingly clear that
it is no longer intelligence coming from afar, but the information which supplies a
handle for what is nearest that gets the readiest hearing. The intelligence that came
from afar—whether the spatial kind from foreign countries or the temporal kind of
tradition—possessed an authority which gave it validity, even when it was not subject to verification. Information, however, lays claim to prompt verifiability. The prime
requirement is that it appear "understandable in itself." Often it is no more exact than
the intelligence of earlier centuries was. But while the latter was inclined to borrow
from the miraculous, it is indispensable for information to sound plausible. Because
of this it proves incompatible with the spirit of storytelling. If the art of storytelling
has become rare, the dissemination of information has had a decisive share in this
state of affairs.

Every morning brings us the news of the globe, and yet we are poor in noteworthy
stories. This is because no event any longer comes to us without already being shot
through with explanation. In other words, by now almost nothing that happens benefits storytelling; almost everything benefits information. Actually, it is half the art of
storytelling to keep a story free from explanation as one reproduces it. Leskov is a
master at this (compare pieces like "The Deception" and "The White Eagle"). The most
extraordinary things, marvelous things, are related with the greatest accuracy, but the
psychological connection of the events is not forced on the reader. It is left up to him

to interpret things the way he understands them, and thus the narrative achieves an amplitude that information lacks.

VII

Leskov was grounded in the classics. The first storyteller of the Greeks was Herodotus. In the fourteenth chapter of the third book of his *Histories* there is a story from which much can be learned. It deals with Psammenitus.

When the Egyptian king Psammenitus had been beaten and captured by the Persian king Cambyses, Cambyses was bent on humbling his prisoner. He gave orders to place Psammenitus on the road along which the Persian triumphal procession was to pass. And he further arranged that the prisoner should see his daughter pass by as a maid going to the well with her pitcher. While all the Egyptians were lamenting and bewailing this spectacle, Psammenitus stood alone, mute and motionless, his eyes fixed on the ground; and when presently he saw his son, who was being taken along in the procession to be executed, he likewise remained unmoved. But when afterwards he recognized one of his servants, an old, impoverished man, in the ranks of the prisoners, he beat his fists against his head and gave all the signs of deepest mourning.

From this story it may be seen what the nature of true storytelling is. The value of information does not survive the moment in which it was new. It lives only at that moment; it has to surrender to it completely and explain itself to it without losing any time. A story is different. It does not expend itself. It preserves and concentrates its strength and is capable of releasing it even after a long time. Thus Montaigne referred to this Egyptian king and asked himself why he mourned only when he caught sight of his servant. Montaigne answers: "Since he was already overfull of grief, it took only the smallest increase for it to burst through its dams." Thus Montaigne. But one could also say: The king is not moved by the fate of those of royal blood, for it is his own fate. Or: We are moved by much on the stage that does not move us in real life; to the king, this servant is only an actor. Or: Great grief is pent up and breaks forth only with relaxation. Seeing this servant was the relaxation. Herodotus offers no explanations. His report is the driest. That is why this story from ancient Egypt is still capable after thousands of years of arousing astonishment and thoughtfulness. It resembles the seeds of grain which have lain for centuries in the chambers of the pyramids shut up air-tight and have retained their germinative power to this day.

VIII

There is nothing that commends a story to memory more effectively than that chaste compactness which precludes psychological analysis. And the more natural the process by which the storyteller forgoes psychological shading, the greater becomes the story's claim to a place in the memory of the listener, the more completely is it integrated into his own experience, the greater will be his inclination to repeat it to someone else someday, sooner or later. This process of assimilation, which takes place in depth, requires a state of relaxation which is becoming rarer and rarer. If sleep is the apogee of physical relaxation, boredom is the apogee of mental relaxation. Boredom is the dream bird that hatches the egg of experience. A rustling in the leaves drives him away. His nesting places—the activities that are intimately associated with boredom—are already extinct in the cities and are declining in the country as well. With this the gift for listening is lost and the community of listeners disappears. For storytelling is always the art of repeating stories, and this art is lost when the stories are no longer retained. It is lost because there is no more weaving and spinning to go on while they are being listened to. The more self-forgetful the listener is, the more deeply is what he listens to impressed upon his memory. When the rhythm of work has seized him, he listens to the tales in such a way that the gift of retelling them comes to him all by itself. This, then, is the nature of the web in which the gift of storytelling is cradled. This is how today it is becoming unraveled at all its ends after being woven thousands of years ago in the ambience of the oldest forms of craftsmanship.

XIII

It has seldom been realized that the listener's naïve relationship to the storyteller is controlled by his interest in retaining what he is told. The cardinal point for the unaffected listener is to assure himself of the possibility of reproducing the story. Memory is the epic faculty *par excellence*. Only by virtue of a comprehensive memory can epic writing absorb the course of events on the one hand and, with the passing of these, make its peace with the power of death on the other. It is not surprising that to a simple man of the people, such as Leskov once invented, the Czar, the head of the sphere in which his stories take place, has the most encyclopedic memory at his command. "Our Emperor," he says, "and his entire family have indeed a most astonishing memory."

Mnemosyne, the rememberer, was the Muse of the epic art among the Greeks. This name takes the observer back to a parting of the ways in world history. For if the record kept by memory—historiography—constitutes the creative matrix of the various epic forms (as great prose is the creative matrix of the various metrical forms), its oldest form, the epic, by virtue of being a kind of common denominator includes the story and the novel. When in the course of centuries the novel began to emerge from the womb of the epic, it turned out that in the novel the element of the epic mind that is derived from the Muse—that is, memory—manifests itself in a form quite different from the way it manifests itself in the story.

15   *Memory* creates the chain of tradition which passes a happening on from generation to generation. It is the Muse-derived element of the epic art in a broader sense and encompasses its varieties. In the first place among these is the one practiced by the storyteller. It starts the web which all stories together form in the end. One ties on to the next, as the great storytellers, particularly the Oriental ones, have always readily shown. In each of them there is a Scheherazade who thinks of a fresh story whenever her tale comes to a stop. This is epic remembrance and the Muse-inspired element of the narrative. But this should be set against another principle, also a Muse-derived element in a narrower sense, which as an element of the novel in its earliest form—that is, in the epic—lies concealed, still undifferentiated from the similarly derived element of the story. It can, at any rate, occasionally be divined in the epics, particularly at moments of solemnity in the Homeric epics, as in the invocations to the Muse at their beginning. What announces itself in these passages is the perpetuating remembrance of the novelist as contrasted with the short-lived reminiscences of the storyteller. The first is dedicated to *one* hero, *one* odyssey, *one* battle; the second, to *many* diffuse occurrences. It is, in other words, *remembrance* which, as the Muse-derived element of the novel, is

added to reminiscence, the corresponding element of the story, the unity of their origin in memory having disappeared with the decline of the epic.

XVII

Few storytellers have displayed so profound a kinship with the spirit of the fairy tale as did Leskov. This involves tendencies that were promoted by the dogmas of the Greek Orthodox Church. As is well known, Origen's speculation about *apokatastasis*—the entry of all souls into Paradise—which was rejected by the Roman Church plays a significant part in these dogmas. Leskov was very much influenced by Origen and planned to translate his work *On First Principles*. In keeping with Russian folk belief he interpreted the Resurrection less as a transfiguration than as a disenchantment, in a sense akin to the fairy tale. Such an interpretation of Origen is at the bottom of "The Enchanted Pilgrim." In this, as in many other tales by Leskov, a hybrid between fairy tale and legend is involved, not unlike that hybrid which Ernst Bloch mentions in a connection in which he utilizes our distinction between myth and fairy tale in his fashion.

"A hybrid between fairy tale and legend," he says, "contains figuratively mythical elements, mythical elements whose effect is certainly captivating and static, and yet not outside man. In the legend there are Taoist figures, especially very old ones, which are 'mythical' in this sense. For instance, the couple Philemon and Baucis: magically escaped though in natural repose. And surely there is a similar relationship between fairy tale and legend in the Taoist climate of Gotthelf, which, to be sure, is on a much lower level. At certain points it divorces the legend from the locality of the spell, rescues the flame of life, the specifically human flame of life, calmly burning, within as without."

"Magically escaped" are the beings that lead the procession of Leskov's creations: the righteous ones. Pavlin, Figura, the toupee artiste, the bear keeper, the helpful sentry—all of them embodiments of wisdom, kindness, comfort the world, crowd about the storyteller. They are unmistakably suffused with the *imago* of his mother.

This is how Leskov describes her: "She was so thoroughly good that she was not capable of harming any man, nor even an animal. She ate neither meat nor fish, because she had such pity for living creatures. Sometimes my father used to reproach her with this. But she answered: 'I have raised the little animals myself, they are like my children to me. I can't eat my own children, can I?' She would not eat meat at a neighbor's house either. 'I have seen them alive,' she would say; 'they are my acquaintances. I can't eat my acquaintances, can I?'"

The righteous man is the advocate for created things and at the same time he is their highest embodiment. In Leskov he has a maternal touch which is occasionally intensified into the mythical (and thus, to be sure, endangers the purity of the fairy tale). Typical of this is the protagonist of his story "Kotin the Provider and Platonida." This figure, a peasant named Pisonski, is a hermaphrodite. For twelve years his mother raised him as a girl. His male and female organs mature simultaneously, and his bisexuality "becomes the symbol of God incarnate."

In Leskov's view, the pinnacle of creation has been attained with this, and at the same time he presumably sees it as a bridge established between this world and the other. For these earthily powerful, maternal male figures which again and again claim Leskov's skill as a storyteller have been removed from obedience to the sexual drive in the bloom of their strength. They do not, however, really embody an ascetic ideal;

rather, the continence of these righteous men has so little privative character that it becomes the elemental counterpoise to uncontrolled lust which the storyteller has personified in *Lady Macbeth of Mzensk*. If the range between a Pavlin and this merchant's wife covers the breadth of the world of created beings, in the hierarchy of his characters Leskov has no less plumbed its depth.

XIX

The lower Leskov descends on the scale of created things the more obviously does his way of viewing things approach the mystical. Actually, as will be shown, there is much evidence that in this, too, a characteristic is revealed which is inherent in the nature of the storyteller. To be sure, only a few have ventured into the depths of inanimate nature, and in modern narrative literature there is not much in which the voice of the anonymous storyteller, who was prior to all literature, resounds so clearly as it does in Leskov's story "The Alexandrite." It deals with a semiprecious stone, the chrysoberyl. The mineral is the lowest stratum of created things. For the storyteller, however, it is directly joined to the highest. To him it is granted to see in this chrysoberyl a natural prophecy of petrified, lifeless nature concerning the historical world in which he himself lives. This world is the world of Alexander II. The storyteller—or rather, the man to whom he attributes his own knowledge—is a gem engraver named Wenzel who has achieved the greatest conceivable skill in his art. One can juxtapose him with the silversmiths of Tula and say that—in the spirit of Leskov—the perfect artisan has access to the innermost chamber of the realm of created things. He is an incarnation of the devout. We are told of this gem cutter: "He suddenly squeezed my hand on which was the ring with the alexandrite, which is known to sparkle red in artificial light, and cried: 'Look, here it is, the prophetic Russian stone! O crafty Siberian. It was always green as hope and only toward evening was it suffused with blood. It was that way from the beginning of the world, but it concealed itself for a long time, lay hidden in the earth, and permitted itself to be found only on the day when Czar Alexander was declared of age, when a great sorcerer had come to Siberia to find the stone, a magician. . . .' 'What nonsense are you talking,' I interrupted him; 'this stone wasn't found by a magician at all, it was a scholar named Nordenskjöld!' 'A magician! I tell you, a magician!' screamed Wenzel in a loud voice. 'Just look; what a stone! A green morning is in it and a bloody evening . . . This is fate, the fate of noble Czar Alexander!' With these words old Wenzel turned to the wall, propped his head on his elbows, and . . . began to sob."

One can hardly come any closer to the meaning of this significant story than by some words which Paul Valéry wrote in a very remote context. "Artistic observation," he says in reflections on a woman artist whose work consisted in the silk embroidery of figures, "can attain an almost mystical depth. The objects on which it falls lose their names. Light and shade form very particular systems, present very individual questions which depend upon no knowledge and are derived from no practice, but get their existence and value exclusively from a certain accord of the soul, the eye, and the hand of someone who was born to perceive them and evoke them in his own inner self."

With these words, soul, eye, and hand are brought into connection. Interacting with one another, they determine a practice. We are no longer familiar with this practice. The role of the hand in production has become more modest, and the place it filled in storytelling lies waste. (After all, storytelling, in its sensory aspect, is by no means a job for the voice alone. Rather, in genuine storytelling the hand plays a part which supports what is expressed in a hundred ways with its gestures trained by work.) That old co-ordination of the soul, the eye, and the hand which emerges in Valéry's words is that of the artisan which we encounter wherever the art of storytelling is at home. In fact, one can go on and ask oneself whether the relationship of the storyteller to his material, human life, is not in itself a craftsman's relationship, whether it is not his very task to fashion the raw material of experience, his own and that of others, in a solid, useful, and unique way. It is a kind of procedure which may perhaps most adequately be exemplified by the proverb if one thinks of it as an ideogram of a story. A proverb, one might say, is a ruin which stands on the site of an old story and in which a moral twines about a happening like ivy around a wall.

Seen in this way, the storyteller joins the ranks of the teachers and sages. He has counsel—not for a few situations, as the proverb does, but for many, like the sage. For it is granted to him to reach back to a whole lifetime (a life, incidentally, that comprises not only his own experience but no little of the experience of others; what the storyteller knows from hearsay is added to his own). His gift is the ability to relate his life; his distinction, to be able to tell his entire life. The storyteller: he is the man who could let the wick of his life be consumed completely by the gentle flame of his story. This is the basis of the incomparable aura about the storyteller, in Leskov as in Hauff, in Poe as in Stevenson. The storyteller is the figure in which the righteous man encounters himself.

Summary Observations
on the Short Story

It is useful to consider modern short stories as dividing themselves into rival traditions, Chekhovian and Borgesian.

Flannery O'Connor, despite surface appearances, is as much in Chekhov's tradition as Italo Calvino is in the rival line of Kafka and Borges. The Chekhovian short story is *not* fantasy, however outrageous it turns in the work of Flannery O'Connor. Hemingway, who wanted to be Tolstoy, is very Chekhovian, as was Joyce's *Dubliners*, though Joyce denied he had read Chekhov. Chekhovian stories start off suddenly, end elliptically, and do not bother to fill in the gaps that we would expect to find closed up in the stories (particularly the longer ones) of Henry James. Still, Chekhov expects you to believe in his realism, his faithfulness to our ordinary existence. Kafka, and Borges after him, invest themselves in phantasmagoria. Kafka and Borges do not give you dirges for the unlived life.

It is not always easy to distinguish the Chekhovian-Hemingwayesque mode from the Kafkan-Borgesian, because neither style of narration is necessarily interested in telling you a story, as Tolstoy so thoroughly and completely tells you of the life and death of Hadji Murad, the Chechen hero in the short novel named after him. Chekhov and Kafka create from an abyss or void; Tolstoy's superb sense of reality persuades you as only Shakespeare and Cervantes can. But short stories, whether of the Chekhovian or Borgesian kind, constitute an essential form, as Borges remarked. The best of them demand and reward many rereadings. Henry James observed that short stories are placed "at that exquisite point where poetry ends and reality begins." That puts them between poems and novels, and their characters, as James again said, must be "so strangely, fascinatingly particular and yet so recognizably general."

Plays traditionally imitate actions; short stories frequently do not. Eudora Welty, probably our best living American storyteller, remarked that D. H. Lawrence's characters "don't really speak their words—not conversationally, not to one another—they are *not* speaking on the street, but are playing like fountains or radiating like the moon or storming like the sea, or their silence is the silence of wicked rocks." Lawrence is a visionary extremist, but Welty's eloquent point is well taken for all great stories, which must find their own form, whether Chekhovian or Kafkan. In major short stories, reality becomes fantastic and phantasmagoria becomes disconcertingly mundane. That may be why so many readers, these days, shy away from volumes of stories, and purchase novels instead, even when the stories are of much higher quality.

Short stories favor the tacit; they compel the reader to be active, and to discern explanations that the writer avoids. The reader, as I have said before, must slow down, quite deliberately, and start listening with the *inner* ear. Such listening overhears the characters, as well as hearing them; think of them as *your* characters, and wonder at what is implied, rather than told about them. Unlike most figures in novels, their foregrounding and postgrounding are largely up to you, utilizing the hints subtly provided by the writer.

From Turgenev through Eudora Welty and beyond, short story writers refrain from moral judgments. George Eliot was one of the finest of novelists, and *Middlemarch* (her masterpiece) abounds in fascinating moral judgments. But the most skilled short story writers are as elliptical in regard to moral judgments as they are in regard to continuities of action or the details of a character's past life. You, as reader, are to decide if moral judgment is relevant, and then the judgment will be yours to make.

The reader derives immense benefits from the significant blanks provided both by the Chekhovian and the Borgesian mode. At the same time one has to be wary of supposed symbolism, which is more often absent than present in a masterful short story. Even the great horror story "The Horla" of Maupassant does not overtly render the Horla symbolic, though I have suggested above that there may be some relation between Maupassant's syphilitic madness and his nameless protagonist's obsession with the Horla. To a certain degree, symbolism is as foreign to the good short story as literary allusion should be: Nabokov is a superbly outrageous exception to my attempt to formulate a Bloom's Law for short fiction. Nabokov is frequently allusive, though rarely symbolic. Symbolism is dangerous for short stories, since novels can have world enough and time to mask emblems naturalistically, but stories, necessarily more abrupt, have difficulty in rendering them unobtrusive.

I conclude this epilogue to the how and why of reading the short story by offering the double judgment that the Chekhovian-Hemingwayesque and Borgesian modes need never be preferred one to the other. We want them for different needs; if the first gratifies our hunger for reality, the second teaches us how ravenous we still are for what is beyond supposed reality. Clearly, we read the two schools differently, questing for truth with Chekhov, or for the turning-inside-out of truth with the Kafkan-Borgesians. Landolfi's Gogol destroys his rubber doll of a wife, and we are as strongly affected as we are when Chekhov's student stops by the campfire of the two bereft women and tells them the tale of St. Peter. Our energies of response are different in quality, but they are equally intense.

About the Story "Errand"

In early 1987 an editor at E. P. Dutton sent me a copy of the newly published Henri Troyat biography, *Chekhov*. Immediately upon the book's arrival, I put aside what I was doing and started reading. I seem to recall reading the book pretty much straight through, able, at the time, to devote entire afternoons and evenings to it.

On the third or fourth day, nearing the end of the book, I came to the little passage where Chekhov's doctor—a Badenweiler physician by the name of Dr Schwöhrer, who attended Chekhov during his last days—is summoned by Olga Knipper Chekhov to the dying writer's bedside in the early morning hours of July 2, 1904. It is clear that Chekhov has only a little while to live. Without any comment on the matter, Troyat tells his readers that this Dr Schwöhrer ordered up a bottle of champagne. Nobody had asked for champagne, of course; he just took it upon himself to do it. But this little piece of human business struck me as an extraordinary action. Before I really knew what I was going to do with it, or how I was going to proceed, I felt I had been launched into a short story of my own then and there. I wrote a few lines and then a page or two more. How did Dr Schwöhrer go about ordering champagne and at that late hour at this hotel in Germany? How was it delivered to the room and by whom, etc.? What was the protocol involved when the champagne arrived? Then I stopped and went ahead to finish reading the biography.

But just as soon as I'd finished the book I once again turned my attention back to Dr Schwöhrer and that business of the champagne. I was seriously interested in what I was doing. But what *was* I doing? The only thing that was clear to me was that I thought I saw an opportunity to pay homage—if I could bring it off, do it rightly and honorably—to Chekhov, the writer who has meant so much to me for such a long time.

I tried out ten or twelve openings to the piece, first one beginning and then another, but nothing felt right. Gradually I began to move the story away from those final moments back to the occasion of Chekhov's first public hemorrhage from tuberculosis, something that occurred in a restaurant in Moscow in the company of his friend and publisher, Suvorin. Then came the hospitalization and the scene with Tolstoy, the trip with Olga to Badenweiler, the brief period of time there in the hotel together before the end, the young bellman who makes two important appearances in the Chekhov suite and, at the end, the mortician who, like the bellman, isn't to be found in the biographical account.

The story was a hard one to write, given the factual basis of the material. I couldn't   5
stray from what had happened, nor did I want to. As much as anything, I needed to
figure out how to breathe life into actions that were merely suggested or not given
moment in the biographical telling. And, finally, I saw that I needed to set my imagination free and simply invent within the confines of the story. I knew as I was writing
this story that it was a good deal different from anything I'd ever done before. I'm
pleased, and grateful, that it seems to have come together.

Anton Chekhov

From His Letters

In Anton Chekhov's letters to his friends, he gave, when asked, opinions about their work and his own.

From a letter to A. S. Suvorin, a publisher and close friend:

October 27, 1888

. . . you are confusing two concepts: the solution of a problem and the correct formulation of a problem. Only the second is required of an artist. Not a single problem is resolved in *Anna Karenina* or *[Eugene] Onegin,*° but they satisfy you completely only because all the problems in them are formulated correctly.

From a letter to Lidia Avilova, a writer and friend:

April 29, 1892

5   I wrote to you before that you have to be cold when you write touching stories. But you didn't understand me. You can cry over your stories and groan, and suffer together with your characters, but I think it must be done in such a way that the reader never notices it. The more objective you are, the stronger will be the impression you make.

From a letter to the younger writer Maxim Gorky:

September 3, 1899

Another piece of advice: when you read proof cross out as many adjectives and adverbs as you can. You have so many modifiers that the reader has trouble understanding and gets worn out. It is comprehensible when I write: "The man sat on the grass," because it is clear and does not detain one's attention. On the other hand, it is difficult to figure out and hard on the brain if I write: "The tall, narrow-chested man of medium height and with a red beard sat down on the green grass that had already been trampled down by the pedestrians, sat down silently, looking around timidly and fearfully." The brain can't grasp all that at once, and art must be grasped at once, instantaneously.

°*Anna Karenina* or *[Eugene] Onegin*: Major nineteenth-century Russian works by Leo Tolstoy and Alexander Pushkin, respectively.

KATE CHOPIN

On Certain Brisk, Bright Days

On certain brisk, bright days I like to walk from my home, near Thirty-fourth street, down to the shopping district. After a few such experiments I begin to fancy that I have the walking habit. Doubtless I convey the same impression to acquaintances who see me from the car window "hot-footing" it down Olive street or Washington avenue. But in my sub-consciousness, as my friend Mrs. R—would say, I know that I have not the walking habit.

Eight or nine years ago I began to write stories—short stories which appeared in the magazines, and I forthwith began to suspect I had the writing habit. The public shared this impression, and called me an author. Since then, though I have written many short stories and a novel or two, I am forced to admit that I have not the writing habit. But it is hard to make people with the questioning habit believe this.

"Now, where, when, why, what do you write?" are some of the questions that I remember. How do I write? On a lapboard with a block of paper, a stub pen and a bottle of ink bought at the corner grocery, which keeps the best in town.

Where do I write? In a Morris chair beside the window, where I can see a few trees and a patch of sky, more or less blue.

When do I write? I am greatly tempted here to use slang and reply "any old time," 5 but that would lend a tone of levity to this bit of confidence, whose seriousness I want to keep intact if possible. So I shall say I write in the morning, when not too strongly drawn to struggle with the intricacies of a pattern, and in the afternoon, if the temptation to try a new furniture polish on an old table leg is not too powerful to be denied; sometimes at night, though as I grow older I am more and more inclined to believe that night was made for sleep.

"Why do I write?" is a question which I have often asked myself and never very satisfactorily answered. Story-writing—at least with me—is the spontaneous expression of impressions gathered goodness knows where. To seek the source, the impulse of a story is like tearing a flower to pieces for wantonness.

What do I write? Well, not everything that comes into my head, but much of what I have written lies between the covers of my books.

There are stories that seem to write themselves, and others which positively refuse to be written—which no amount of coaxing can bring to anything. I do not believe any writer has ever made a "portrait" in fiction. A trick, a mannerism, a physical trait or mental characteristic go a very short way towards portraying the complete individual in real life who suggests the individual in the writer's imagination. The "material" of a writer is to the last degree uncertain, and I fear not marketable. I have been told stories which were looked upon as veritable gold mines by the generous narrators who placed them at my disposal. I have been taken to spots supposed to be alive with local color. I have been introduced to excruciating characters with frank permission to use them as I liked, but never, in any single instance, has such material been of the slightest service. I am completely at the mercy of unconscious selection. To such an extent is this true, that what is called the polishing up process has always proved disastrous to my work, and I avoid it, preferring the integrity of crudities to artificialities.

How hard it is for one's acquaintances and friends to realize that one's books are to be taken seriously, and that they are subject to the same laws which govern the existence of others' books! I have a son who is growing wroth over the question: "Where can I find your mother's books, or latest book?"

10   "The very next time any one asks me that question," he exclaimed excitedly, "I am going to tell them to try the stock yards!"

I hope he won't. He might thus offend a possible buyer. Politeness, besides being a virtue, is sometimes an art. I am often met with the same question, and I always try to be polite. "My latest book? Why, you will find it, no doubt, at the bookseller's or the libraries."

"The libraries! Oh, no, they don't keep it." She hadn't thought of the bookseller's. It's real hard to think of everything! Sometimes I feel as if I should like to get a good, remunerative job to do the thinking for some people. This may sound conceited, but it isn't. If I had space (I have plenty of time; time is my own, but space belongs to the *Post-Dispatch*), I should like to demonstrate satisfactorily that it is not conceited.

I trust it will not be giving away professional secrets to say that many readers would be surprised, perhaps shocked, at the questions which some newspaper editors will put to a defenseless woman under the guise of flattery.

For instance: "How many children have you?" This form is subtle and greatly to be commended in dealing with women of shy and retiring propensities. A woman's reluctance to speak of her children has not yet been chronicled. I have a good many, but they'd be simply wild if I dragged them into this. I might say something of those who are at a safe distance—the idol of my soul in Kentucky; the light of my eye off in Colorado; the treasure of his mother's heart in Louisiana—but I mistrust the form of their displeasure, with poisoned candy going through the mails.

15   "Do you smoke cigarettes?" is a question which I consider impertinent, and I think most women will agree with me. Suppose I do smoke cigarettes? Am I going to tell it out in meeting? Suppose I don't smoke cigarettes. Am I going to admit such a reflection upon my artistic integrity, and thereby bring upon myself the contempt of the guild?

In answering questions in which an editor believes his readers to be interested, the victim cannot take herself too seriously.

STEPHEN CRANE

Stephen Crane's Own Story

By late 1896 the rebellion in Cuba against Spanish rule had reached a critical stage. To weaken the rebels, Spain had attempted to seal off the island by a naval blockade. On New Year's Day 1897, Stephen Crane, a war correspondent for the New York Press, *sailed from Jacksonville, Florida, on the steamer* Commodore, *which was running arms to the Cuban insurgents. Possibly as a result of sabotage, the* Commodore *went down, and Crane, with three or four members of the crew, among them the captain, Edward Murphy, and the oiler, Billy Higgins, were cast adrift in a ten-foot dinghy. After thirty hours at sea, the open boat was swamped in the Florida surf and the oiler was drowned. Crane's dispatch to the* Press *appeared on January 7, 1897. Readers interested in the way life is transmuted into fiction can profit by comparing Crane's newspaper account with the story that evolved from it, "The Open Boat."*

JACKSONVILLE, FLA., Jan. 6—It was the afternoon of New Year's. The *Commodore* lay at her dock in Jacksonville and negro stevedores processioned steadily toward her with box after box of ammunition and bundle after bundle of rifles. Her hatch, like the mouth of a monster, engulfed them. It might have been the feeding time of some legendary creature of the sea. It was in broad daylight and the crowd of gleeful Cubans on the pier did not forbear to sing the strange patriotic ballads of their island.

Everything was perfectly open. The *Commodore* was cleared with a cargo of arms and munitions for Cuba. There was none of that extreme modesty about the proceeding which had marked previous departures of the famous tug. She loaded up as placidly as if she were going to carry oranges to New York, instead of Remingtons to Cuba. Down the river, furthermore, the revenue cutter *Boutwell*, the old isosceles triangle that protects United States interests in the St. Johns, lay at anchor, with no sign of excitement aboard her.

On the decks of the *Commodore* there were exchanges of farewells in two languages. Many of the men who were to sail upon her had many intimates in the old Southern town, and we who had left our friends in the remote North received our first touch of melancholy on witnessing these strenuous and earnest good-bys.

It seems, however, that there was more difficulty at the custom house. The officers of the ship and the Cuban leaders were detained there until a mournful twilight settled upon the St. Johns, and through a heavy fog the lights of Jacksonville blinked dimly.

5   Then at last the *Commodore* swung clear of the dock, amid a tumult of good-bys. As she turned her bow toward the distant sea the Cubans ashore cheered and cheered. In response the *Commodore* gave three long blasts of her whistle, which even to this time impressed me with their sadness. Somehow they sounded as wails.

Then at last we began to feel like filibusters. I don't suppose that the most stolid brain could contrive to believe that there is not a mere trifle of danger in filibustering, and so as we watched the lights of Jacksonville swing past us and heard the regular thump, thump, thump of the engines we did considerable reflecting.

But I am sure that there was no hifalutin emotions visible upon any of the faces which fronted the speeding shore. In fact, from cook's boy to captain, we were all enveloped in a gentle satisfaction and cheerfulness.

But less than two miles from Jacksonville this atrocious fog caused the pilot to ram the bow of the *Commodore* hard upon the mud, and in this ignominious position we were compelled to stay until daybreak.

It was to all of us more than a physical calamity. We were now no longer filibusters. We were men on a ship stuck in the mud. A certain mental somersault was made once more necessary. But word had been sent to Jacksonville to the captain of the revenue cutter *Boutwell*, and Captain Kilgore turned out promptly and generously fired up his old triangle and came at full speed to our assistance. She dragged us out of the mud and again we headed for the mouth of the river. The revenue cutter pounded along a half mile astern of us, to make sure that we did not take on board at some place along the river men for the Cuban army.

10   This was the early morning of New Year's Day, and the fine golden Southern sunlight fell full upon the river. It flashed over the ancient *Boutwell* until her white sides gleamed like pearl and her rigging was spun into little threads of gold. Cheers greeted the old *Commodore* from passing ships and from the shore. It was a cheerful, almost merry, beginning to our voyage.

At Mayport, however, we changed our river pilot for a man who could take her to open sea, and again the *Commodore* was beached. The *Boutwell* was fussing around us in her venerable way, and, upon seeing our predicament, she came again to assist us, but this time with engines reversed the *Commodore* dragged herself away from the grip of the sand and again the *Commodore* headed for the open sea.

The captain of the revenue cutter grew curious. He hailed the *Commodore*: "Are you fellows going to sea to-day?"

Captain Murphy of the *Commodore* called back: "Yes, sir." And then as the whistle of the *Commodore* saluted him Captain Kilgore doffed his cap and said: "Well, gentlemen, I hope you have a pleasant cruise," and this was our last words from shore.

When the *Commodore* came to the enormous rollers that flee over the bar, a certain light-heartedness departed from the throats of the ship's company. The *Commodore* began to turn handsprings, and by the time she had gotten fairly to sea and turned into the eye of the roaring breeze that was blowing from the southeast there was an almost general opinion on board the vessel that a life on the rolling wave was not the finest thing in the world. On deck amidships lay five or six Cubans, limp, forlorn and infinitely depressed. In the bunks below lay more Cubans, also limp, forlorn and infinitely depressed. In the captain's quarters, back of the pilot house, the Cuban leaders were stretched out in postures of complete contentment to this terrestrial realm of their stomachs.

15   The *Commodore* was heavily laden and in this strong sea she rolled like a rubber ball. She appeared to be a gallant sea boat and bravely flung off the waves that swarmed over her bow. At this time the first mate was at the wheel, and I remember

how proud he was of the ship as she dashed the white foaming waters aside and arose to the swells like a duck.

"Ain't she a daisy?" said he. But she certainly did do a remarkable lot of pitching and presently even some American seamen were made ill by the long wallowing motion of the ship. A squall confronted us dead ahead and in the impressive twilight of this New Year's Day the *Commodore* steamed sturdily toward a darkened part of the horizon. The State of Florida is very large when you look at it from an airship, but it is as narrow as a sheet of paper when you look at it sideways. The coast was merely a faint streak.

As darkness came upon the waters the *Commodore's* wake was a broad, flaming path of blue and silver phosphorescence, and as her stout bow lunged at the great black waves she threw flashing, roaring cascades to either side. And all that was to be heard was the rhythmical and mighty pounding of the engines.

Being an inexperienced filibuster, the writer had undergone considerable mental excitement since the starting of the ship, and consequently he had not yet been to sleep, and so I went to the first mate's bunk to indulge myself in all the physical delights of holding one's self in bed. Every time the ship lurched I expected to be fired through a bulkhead, and it was neither amusing nor instructive to see in the dim light a certain accursed valise aiming itself at the top of my stomach with every lurch of the ship.

The cook was asleep on a bench in the galley. He was of a portly and noble exterior, and by means of a checker board he had himself wedged on this bench in such a manner that the motion of the ship would be unable to dislodge him. He awoke as I entered the galley, and, feeling moved, he delivered himself of some dolorous sentiments. "God," he said, in the course of his observations, "I don't feel right about this ship somehow. It strikes me that something is going to happen to us. I don't know what it is, but the old ship is going to get it in the neck, I think."

"Well, how about the men on board of her?" said I. "Are any of us going to get out, prophet?" 20

"Yes," said the cook, "sometimes I have these damned feelings come over me, and they are always right, and it seems to me somehow that you and I will both get out and meet again somewhere, down at Coney Island, perhaps, or some place like that."

Finding it impossible to sleep, I went back to the pilot house. An old seaman named Tom Smith, from Charleston, was then at the wheel. In the darkness I could not see Tom's face, except at those times when he leaned forward to scan the compass and the dim light from the box came upon his weather-beaten features.

"Well, Tom," said I, "how do you like filibustering?"

He said: "I think I am about through with it. I've been in a number of these expeditions, and the pay is good, but I think if I ever get back safe this time I will cut it."

I sat down in the corner of the pilot house and went almost to sleep. In the meantime the captain came on duty and he was standing near me when the chief engineer rushed up the stairs and cried hurriedly to the captain that there was something wrong in the engine room. He and the captain departed swiftly. I was drowsing there in my corner when the captain returned, and, going to the door of the little room directly back of the pilot house, cried to the Cuban leader: 25

"Say, can't you get those fellows to work? I can't talk their language and I can't get them started. Come on and get them going."

The Cuban leader turned to me then and said: "Go help in the fire-room. They are going to bail with buckets."

The engine room, by the way, represented a scene at this time taken from the middle kitchen of hades. In the first place, it was insufferably warm, and the lights burned faintly in a way to cause mystic and grewsome shadows. There was a quantity of soapish sea water swirling and sweeping and swishing among machinery that roared and banged and clattered and steamed, and in the second place, it was a devil of a ways down below.

Here I first came to know a certain young oiler named Billy Higgins. He was sloshing around this inferno filling buckets with water and passing them to a chain of men that extended up to the ship's side. Afterward we got orders to change our point of attack on the water and to operate through a little door on the windward side of the ship that led into the engine room.

30   During this time there was much talk of pumps out of order and many other statements of a mechanical kind, which I did not altogether comprehend, but understood to mean that there was a general and sudden ruin in the engine room.

There was no particular agitation at this time, and even later there was never a panic on board the *Commodore*. The party of men who worked with Higgins and me at this time were all Cubans, and we were under the direction of the Cuban leaders. Presently we were ordered again to the afterhold, and there was some hesitation about going into the abominable fire-room again, but Higgins dashed down the companionway with a bucket.

The heat and hard work in the fire-room affected me and I was obliged to come on deck again. Going forward I heard as I went talk of lowering the boats. Near the corner of the galley the mate was talking with a man.

"Why don't you send up a rocket?" said this unknown person. And the mate replied: "What the hell do we want to send up a rocket for? The ship is all right."

Returning with a little rubber and cloth overcoat, I saw the first boat about to be lowered. A certain man was the first person in this first boat, and they were handing him in a valise about as large as a hotel. I had not entirely recovered from my astonishment and pleasure in witnessing this noble deed, when I saw another valise go to him. This valise was not perhaps so large as a hotel, but it was a big valise anyhow. Afterward there went to him something which looked to me like an overcoat.

35   Seeing the chief engineer leaning out of his little window, I remarked to him: "What do you think of that blank, blank, blank?"

"Oh, he's a bird," said the old chief.

It was now that was heard the order to get away the lifeboat, which was stowed on top of the deckhouse. The deckhouse was a mighty slippery place, and with each roll of the ship the men there thought themselves likely to take headers into the deadly black sea. Higgins was on top of the deckhouse, and, with the first mate and two colored stokers, we wrestled with that boat, which I am willing to swear weighed as much as a Broadway cable car. She might have been spiked to the deck. We could have pushed a little brick schoolhouse along a corduroy road as easily as we could have moved this boat. But the first mate got a tackle to her from a leaward davit, and on the deck below the captain corralled enough men to make an impression upon the boat. We were ordered to cease hauling then, and in this lull the cook of the ship came to me and said: "What are you going to do?"

I told him of my plans, and he said: "Well, my God, that's what I am going to do."

Now the whistle of the *Commodore* had been turned loose, and if there ever was a voice of despair and death it was in the voice of this whistle. It had gained a new tone. It was as if its throat was already choked by the water, and this cry on the sea at night, with a wind blowing the spray over the ship, and the waves roaring over the bow, and swirling white along the decks, was to each of us probably a song of man's end.

It was now that the first mate showed a sign of losing his grip. To us who were try-   40
ing in all stages of competence and experience to launch the lifeboat he raged in all
terms of fiery satire and hammer-like abuse. But the boat moved at last and swung
down toward the water.

Afterward when I went aft I saw the captain standing with his arm in a sling, holding on to a stay with his one good hand and directing the launching of the boat. He gave
me a five-gallon jug of water to hold, and asked me what I was going to do. I told him
what I thought was about the proper thing, and he told me then that the cook had the
same idea, and ordered me to go forward and be ready to launch the ten-foot dingy. I
remember very well that he turned then to swear at a colored stoker who was prowling around, done up in life preservers until he looked like a feather bed.

I went forward with my five-gallon jug of water, and when the captain came we
launched the dingy, and they put me over the side to fend her off from the ship with
an oar.

They handed me down the water jug, and then the cook came into the boat, and we
sat there in the darkness, wondering why, by all our hopes of future happiness, the captain was so long in coming over the side and ordering us away from the doomed ship.

The captain was waiting for the other boat to go. Finally he hailed in the darkness:
"Are you all right, Mr. Graines?"

The first mate answered: "All right, sir."   45

"Shove off then," cried the captain. The captain was just about to swing over the rail
when a dark form came forward and a voice said: "Captain, I go with you."

The captain answered: "Yes, Billy; get in."

It was Billy Higgins, the oiler. Billy dropped into the boat and a moment later the
captain followed, bringing with him an end of about forty yards of lead line. The other
end was attached to the rail of the ship. As we swung back to leeward the captain said:
"Boys, we will stay right near the ship till she goes down."

This cheerful information, of course, filled us all with glee. The line kept us headed properly into the wind and as we rode over the monstrous roarers we saw upon each
rise the swaying lights of the dying *Commodore*.

When came the gray shade of dawn, the form of the *Commodore* grew slowly clear   50
to us as our little ten-foot boat rose over each swell. She was floating with such an air
of buoyancy that we laughed when we had time, and said: "What a guy it would be
on those other fellows if she didn't sink at all."

But later we saw men aboard of her, and later still they began to hail us. I had forgotten to mention that previously we had loosened the end of the lead line dropped
much further to leeward. The men on board were a mystery to us, of course, as we had
seen all the boats leave the ship. We rowed back to the ship, but did not approach too
near, because we were four men in a ten-foot boat, and we knew that the touch of a
hand on our gunwale would assuredly swamp us.

The first mate cried out from the ship that the third boat had foundered alongside. He
cried that they had made rafts and wished us to tow them. The captain said: "All right."

Their rafts were floating astern.

"Jump in," cried the captain, but here was a singular and most harrowing hesitation. There were five white men and two negroes. This scene in the gray light of morning impressed one as would a view into some place where ghosts move slowly. These
seven men on the stern of the sinking *Commodore* were silent. Save the words of the
mate to the captain there was no talk. Here was death, but here also was a most singular and indefinable kind of fortitude.

55   Four men, I remember, clambered over the railing and stood there watching the cold, steely sheen of the sweeping waves.

"Jump," cried the captain again. The old chief engineer first obeyed the order. He landed on the outside raft and the captain told him how to grip the raft, and he obeyed as promptly and as docilely as a scholar in riding school.

A stoker followed him, and then the first mate threw his hands over his head and plunged into the sea. He had no life belt, and for my part, even when he did this horrible thing, I somehow felt that I could see in the expression of his hands, and in the very toss of his head, as he leaped thus to death, that it was rage, rage, rage unspeakable that was in his heart at the time.

And then I saw Tom Smith, the man who was going to quit filibustering after this expedition, jump to a raft and turn his face toward us. On board the *Commodore* three men strode, still in silence and with their faces turned toward us. One man had his arms folded and was leaning against the deckhouse. His feet were crossed, so that the toe of his left foot pointed downward. There they stood gazing at us, and neither from the deck nor from the rafts was a voice raised. Still was there this silence.

The colored stoker on the first raft threw us a line and we began to tow. Of course, we perfectly understood the absolute impossibility of any such thing; our dingy was within six inches of the water's edge, there was an enormous sea running, and I knew that under the circumstances a tugboat would have no light task in moving these rafts. But we tried it, and would have continued to try it indefinitely, but that something critical came to pass. I was at an oar and so faced the rafts. The cook controlled the line. Suddenly the boat began to go backward, and then we saw this negro on the first raft pulling on the line hand over hand and drawing us to him.

60   He had turned into a demon. He was wild, wild as a tiger. He was crouched on this raft and ready to spring. Every muscle of him seemed to be turned into an elastic spring. His eyes were almost white. His face was the face of a lost man reaching upward, and we knew that the weight of his hand on our gunwale doomed us. The cook let go of the line.

We rowed around to see if we could not get a line from the chief engineer, and all this time, mind you, there were no shrieks, no groans, but silence, silence and silence, and then the *Commodore* sank. She lurched to windward, then swung afar back, righted and dove into the sea, and the rafts were suddenly swallowed by this frightful maw of the ocean. And then by the men on the ten-foot dingy were words said that were still not words, something far beyond words.

The lighthouse of Mosquito Inlet stuck up above the horizon like the point of a pin. We turned our dingy toward the shore. The history of life in an open boat for thirty hours would no doubt be very instructive for the young, but none is to be told here now. For my part I would prefer to tell the story at once, because from it would shine the splendid manhood of Captain Edward Murphy and of William Higgins, the oiler, but let it suffice at this time to say that when we were swamped in the surf and making the best of our way toward the shore the captain gave orders amid the wildness of the breakers as clearly as if he had been on the quarterdeck of a battleship.

John Kitchell of Daytona came running down the beach, and as he ran the air was filled with clothes. If he had pulled a single lever and undressed, even as the fire horses harness, he could not to me seem to have stripped with more speed. He dashed into the water and grabbed the cook. Then he went after the captain, but the captain sent him to me, and then it was that we saw Billy Higgins lying with his forehead on sand that was clear of the water, and he was dead.

RALPH ELLISON

What America Would Be Like Without Blacks

The fantasy of an America free of blacks is at least as old as the dream of creating a truly democratic society. While we are aware that there is something inescapably tragic about the cost of achieving our democratic ideals, we keep such tragic awareness segregated in the rear of our minds. We allow it to come to the fore only during moments of great national crisis.

On the other hand, there is something so embarrassingly absurd about the notion of purging the nation of blacks that it seems hardly a product of thought at all. It is more like a primitive reflex, a throwback to the dim past of tribal experience, which we rationalize and try to make respectable by dressing it up in the gaudy and highly questionable trappings of what we call the "concept of race." Yet despite its absurdity, the fantasy of a blackless America continues to turn up. It is a fantasy born not merely of racism but of petulance, exasperation and moral fatigue. It is like a boil bursting forth from impurities in the bloodstream of democracy.

In its benign manifestations, it can be outrageously comic, as in the picaresque adventures of Percival Brownlee, who appears in William Faulkner's story "The Bear." Exasperating to his white masters because his aspirations and talents are for preaching and conducting choirs rather than for farming, Brownlee is "freed" after much resistance and ends up as the prosperous proprietor of a New Orleans brothel. In Faulkner's hands the uncomprehending drive of Brownlee's owners to "get shut" of him is comically instructive. Indeed, the story resonates certain abiding, tragic themes of American history with which it is interwoven, and which are causing great turbulence in the social atmosphere today. I refer to the exasperation and bemusement of the white American with the black, the black American's ceaseless (and swiftly accelerating) struggle to escape the misconceptions of whites, and the continual confusing of the black American's racial background with his individual culture. Most of all, I refer to the recurring fantasy of solving one basic problem of American democracy by "getting shut" of the blacks through various wishful schemes that would banish them from the nation's bloodstream, from its social structure, and from its conscience and historical consciousness.

This fantastic vision of a lily-white America appeared as early as 1713, with the suggestion of a white "native American," thought to be from New Jersey, that all the

Negroes be given their freedom and returned to Africa. In 1777, Thomas Jefferson, while serving in the Virginia legislature, began drafting a plan for the gradual emancipation and exportation of the slaves. Nor were Negroes themselves immune to the fantasy. In 1815 Paul Cuffe, a wealthy merchant, shipbuilder and landowner from the New Bedford area, shipped and settled at his own expense thirty-eight of his fellow Negroes in Africa. It was perhaps his example that led in the following year to the creation of the American Colonization Society, which was to establish in 1821 the colony of Liberia. Great amounts of cash and a perplexing mixture of motives went into the venture. The slave-owners and many Border-state politicians wanted to use it as a scheme to rid the country not of slaves but of the militant free Negroes who were agitating against the "peculiar institution." The abolitionists, until they took a lead from free Negro leaders and began attacking the scheme, also participated as a means of righting a great historical injustice. Many blacks went along with it simply because they were sick of the black-and-white American mess and hoped to prosper in the quiet peace of the old ancestral home.

5   Such conflicting motives doomed the Colonization Society to failure, but what amazes one even more than the notion that anyone could have believed in its success is the fact that it was attempted during a period when blacks, slave and free, made up eighteen percent of the total population. When we consider how long blacks had been in the New World and had been transforming it and being Americanized by it, the scheme appears not only fantastic, but the product of a free-floating irrationality—indeed, a national pathology.

Nevertheless, some of the noblest of Americans were bemused. Not only Jefferson but later Abraham Lincoln was to give the scheme credence. According to historian John Hope Franklin, Negro colonization seemed as important to Lincoln as emancipation. In 1862, Franklin notes, Lincoln called a group of prominent free Negroes to the White House and urged them to support colonization, telling them, "Your race suffers greatly, many of them by living among us, while ours suffers from your presence. If this is admitted, it affords a reason why we should be separated."

In spite of his unquestioned greatness, Abraham Lincoln was a man of his times and limited by some of the less worthy thinking of his times. This is demonstrated both by his reliance upon the concept of race in his analysis of the American dilemma and by his involvement in a plan of purging the nation of blacks as a means of healing the badly shattered ideals of democratic federalism. Although benign, his motive was no less a product of fantasy. It envisaged an attempt to relieve an inevitable suffering that marked the growing pains of the youthful body politic by an operation which would have amounted to the severing of a healthy and indispensable member.

Yet like its twin, the illusion of secession, the fantasy of a benign amputation that would rid the country of black men to the benefit of a nation's health not only persists; today, in the form of neo-Garveyism, it fascinates black men no less than it once hypnotized whites. Both fantasies become operative whenever the nation grows weary of the struggle toward the ideal of American democratic equality. Both would use the black man as a scapegoat to achieve a national catharsis, and both would, by way of curing the patient, destroy him.

What is ultimately intriguing about the fantasy of "getting shut" of the Negro American is the fact that no one who entertains it seems ever to have considered what the nation would have become had Africans *not* been brought to the New World, and had their descendants not played such a complex and confounding role in the creation of American history and culture. Nor do they appear to have considered with any seriousness the effect upon the nation of having any of the schemes for exporting blacks succeed beyond settling some fifteen thousand or so in Liberia.

We are reminded that Daniel Patrick Moynihan, who has recently aggravated our social confusion over the racial issue while allegedly attempting to clarify it, is co-author of a work which insists that the American melting pot didn't melt because our white ethnic groups have resisted all assimilative forces that appear to threaten their identities. The problem here is that few Americans know who and what they really are. That is why few of these groups—or at least few of the children of these groups—have been able to resist the movies, television, baseball, jazz, football, drum-majoretting, rock, comic strips, radio commercials, soap operas, book clubs, slang, or any of a thousand other expressions and carriers of our pluralistic and easily available popular culture. It is here precisely that ethnic resistance is least effective. On this level the melting pot did indeed melt, creating such deceptive metamorphoses and blending of identities, values and lifestyles that most American whites are culturally part Negro American without even realizing it.

If we can resist for a moment the temptation to view everything having to do with Negro Americans in terms of their racially imposed status, we become aware of the fact that for all the harsh reality of the social and economic injustices visited upon them, these injustices have failed to keep Negroes clear of the cultural mainstream; Negro Americans are, in fact, one of its major tributaries. If we can cease approaching American social reality in terms of such false concepts as white and nonwhite, black culture and white culture, and think of these apparently unthinkable matters in the realistic manner of Western pioneers confronting the unknown prairie, perhaps we can begin to imagine what the United States would have been, or not been, had there been no blacks to give it—if I may be so bold as to say—color.

For one thing, the American nation is in a sense the product of the American language, a colloquial speech that began emerging long before the British colonials and Africans were transformed into Americans. It is a language that evolved from the King's English but, basing itself upon the realities of the American land and colonial institutions—or lack of institutions—began quite early as a vernacular revolt against the signs, symbols, manners and authority of the mother country. It is a language that began by merging the sounds of many tongues, brought together in the struggle of diverse regions. And whether it is admitted or not, much of the sound of that language is derived from the timbre of the African voice and the listening habits of the African ear. So there is a *de'z* and *do'z* of slave speech sounding beneath our most polished Harvard accents, and if there is such a thing as a Yale accent, there is a Negro wail in it—doubtless introduced there by Old Yalie John C. Calhoun, who probably got it from his mammy.

Whitman viewed the spoken idiom of Negro Americans as a source for a native grand opera. Its flexibility, its musicality, its rhythms, freewheeling diction and metaphors, as projected in Negro American folklore, were absorbed by the creators of our great nineteenth-century literature even when the majority of blacks were still enslaved. Mark Twain celebrated it in the prose of *Huckleberry Finn;* without the presence of blacks, the book could not have been written. No Huck and Jim, no American novel as we know it. For not only is the black man a co-creator of the language that Mark Twain raised to the level of literary eloquence, but Jim's condition as American and Huck's commitment to freedom are at the moral center of the novel.

In other words, had there been no blacks, certain creative tensions arising from the cross-purposes of whites and blacks would also not have existed. Not only would there have been no Faulkner; there would have been no Stephen Crane, who found certain basic themes of his writing in the Civil War. Thus also there would have been no Hemingway, who took Crane as a source and guide. Without the presence of Negro American style, our jokes, tall tales, even our sports would be lacking in the sudden turns, shocks and swift changes of pace (all jazz-shaped) that serve to remind us that the world is ever unexplored, and that while a complete mastery of life is mere illusion, the real secret of the game is to make life swing. It is its ability to articulate this tragic-comic attitude toward life that explains much of the mysterious power and attractiveness of that quality of Negro American style known as "soul." An expression of American diversity within unity, of blackness with whiteness, soul announces the presence of a creative struggle against the realities of existence.

15   Without the presence of blacks, our political history would have been otherwise. No slave economy, no Civil War, no violent destruction of the Reconstruction, no K.K.K. and no Jim Crow system. And without the disenfranchisement of black Americans and the manipulation of racial fears and prejudices, the disproportionate impact of white Southern politicians upon our domestic and foreign policies would have been impossible. Indeed, it is almost impossible to conceive of what our political system would have become without the snarl of forces—cultural, racial, religious—that make our nation what it is today.

Absent, too, would be the need for that tragic knowledge which we try ceaselessly to evade: that the true subject of democracy is not simply material well-being, but the extension of the democratic process in the direction of perfecting itself. And that the most obvious test and clue to that perfection is the inclusion, *not* assimilation, of the black man.

Since the beginning of the nation, white Americans have suffered from a deep inner uncertainty as to who they really are. One of the ways that has been used to simplify the answer has been to seize upon the presence of black Americans and use them as a marker, a symbol of limits, a metaphor for the "outsider." Many whites could look at the social position of blacks and feel that color formed an easy and reliable gauge for determining to what extent one was or was not American. Perhaps that is why one of the first epithets that many European immigrants learned when they got off the boat was the term "nigger"; it made them feel instantly American. But this is tricky magic. Despite his racial difference and social status, something indisputably American about Negroes not only raised doubts about the white man's value system, but aroused the troubling suspicion that whatever else the true American is, he is also somehow black.

Materially, psychologically and culturally, part of the nation's heritage is Negro American, and whatever it becomes will be shaped in part by the Negro's presence. Which is fortunate, for today it is the black American who puts pressure upon the nation to live up to its ideals. It is he who gives creative tension to our struggle for justice and for the elimination of those factors, social and psychological, which make for slums and shaky suburban communities. It is he who insists that we purify the American language by demanding that there be a closer correlation between the meaning of words and reality, between ideal and conduct, between our assertions and our actions. Without the black American, something irrepressibly hopeful and creative would go out of the American spirit, and the nation might well succumb to the moral slobbism that has always threatened its existence from within.

When we look objectively at how the dry bones of the nation were hung together, it seems obvious that some one of the many groups that compose the United States had to suffer the fate of being allowed no easy escape from experiencing the harsh realities of the human condition as they were to exist under even so fortunate a democracy as ours. It would seem that some one group had to be stripped of the possibility of escaping such tragic knowledge by taking sanctuary in moral equivocation, racial chauvinism or the advantage of superior social status. There is no point in complaining over the past or apologizing for one's fate. But for blacks there are no hiding places down here, not in suburbia or in penthouse, neither in country nor in city. They are an American people who are geared to what *is*, and who yet are driven by a sense of what it is possible for human life to be in this society. The nation could not survive being deprived of their presence because, by the irony implicit in the dynamics of American democracy, they symbolize both its most stringent testing and the possibility of its greatest human freedom.

E. M. FORSTER

FROM *Plot*

Let us define a plot. We have defined a story as a narrative of events arranged in their time-sequence. A plot is also a narrative of events, the emphasis falling on causality. "The king died and then the queen died" is a story. "The king died, and then the queen died of grief" is a plot. The time-sequence is preserved, but the sense of causality over-shadows it. Or again: "The queen died, no one knew why, until it was discovered that it was through grief at the death of the king." This is a plot with a mystery in it, a form capable of high development. It suspends the time-sequence, it moves as far away from the story as its limitations will allow. Consider the death of the queen. If it is in a story we say "and then?" If it is in a plot we ask "why?" That is the fundamental difference between these two aspects of the novel. A plot cannot be told to a gaping audience of cave-men or to a tyrannical sultan or to their modern descendant the movie-public. They can only be kept awake by "and then—and then—" They can only supply curiosity. But a plot demands intelligence and memory also.

Curiosity is one of the lowest of the human faculties. You will have noticed in daily life that when people are inquisitive they nearly always have bad memories and are usually stupid at bottom. The man who begins by asking you how many brothers and sisters you have is never a sympathetic character, and if you meet him in a year's time he will probably ask you how many brothers and sisters you have, his mouth again sag-ging open, his eyes still bulging from his head. It is difficult to be friends with such a man, and for two inquisitive people to be friends must be impossible. Curiosity by it-self takes us a very little way, nor does it take us far into the novel—only as far as the story. If we would grasp the plot we must add intelligence and memory.

Intelligence first. The intelligent novel-reader, unlike the inquisitive one who just runs his eye over a new fact, mentally picks it up. He sees it from two points of view: isolated, and related to the other facts that he has read on previous pages. Probably he does not understand it, but he does not expect to do so yet awhile. The facts in a high-ly organized novel (like *The Egoist*) are often of the nature of cross-correspondences and the ideal spectator cannot expect to view them properly until he is sitting up on a hill at the end. This element of surprise or mystery—the detective element as it is some-times rather emptily called—is of great importance in a plot. It occurs through a sus-pension of the time-sequence; a mystery is a pocket in time, and it occurs crudely, as in "Why did the queen die?" and more subtly in half-explained gestures and words, the true meaning of which only dawns pages ahead. Mystery is essential to a plot, and cannot be appreciated without intelligence. To the curious it is just another "and then—" To appreciate a mystery, part of the mind must be left behind, brooding, while the other part goes marching on.

That brings us to our second qualification: memory.

Memory and intelligence are closely connected, for unless we remember we cannot understand. If by the time the queen dies we have forgotten the existence of the king we shall never make out what killed her. The plot-maker expects us to remember, we expect him to leave no loose ends. Every action or word ought to count; it ought to be economical and spare; even when complicated it should be organic and free from dead-matter. It may be difficult or easy, it may and should contain mysteries, but it ought not to mislead. And over it, as it unfolds, will hover the memory of the reader (that dull glow of the mind of which intelligence is the bright advancing edge) and will constantly rearrange and reconsider, seeing new clues, new chains of cause and effect, and the final sense (if the plot has been a fine one) will not be of clues or chains, but of something aesthetically compact, something which might have been shown by the novelist straight away, only if he had shown it straight away it would never have become beautiful. We come up against beauty here—for the first time in our inquiry: beauty at which a novelist should never aim, though he fails if he does not achieve it. I will conduct beauty to her proper place later on. Meanwhile please accept her as part of a completed plot. She looks a little surprised at being there, but beauty ought to look a little surprised: it is the emotion that best suits her face, as Botticelli knew when he painted her risen from the waves, between the winds and the flowers. The beauty who does not look surprised, who accepts her position as her due—she reminds us too much of a prima donna.

BESSIE HEAD

Let Me Tell a Story Now . . .

I don't know why this is so but the first thing a person you've just been introduced to will ask you is: "What work do you do?" I don't mean that he or she will ask it bluntly, just like that. They will hedge around a bit but eventually they will get down to the point and drag it out of you. As I say, I don't know why you dare to ask such a personal question but the reason that I do is because each person that I meet is a complete mystery to me. I have to find a quick and superficial way of piecing him together so that I know where I stand. I mean, I don't like to behave like a fool and some people instantly give you the feeling that you are behaving like a fool. I'm specifically referring to a hard case lawyer I once knew. I struggled quite unsuccessfully to explain a delicate matter to him that needed just a bit of understanding and humane feeling and couldn't understand why he kept pulling me to shreds. Only later I learnt that the man's mind worked this way: "Let's consider it on a judicial basis." The poor man had completely identified himself with his work. He was all one-sided. A very dangerous type that because they can bust your ego to bits and you won't know what's happening to you, especially if your enemies are around and watching the terrific beating you are taking from one who knows all the answers.

In a broad sense then I would say a person's character type makes him gravitate to a certain type of work. The fussy-fussy, jumpy sort of woman becomes a typist where she can mess around all day minding other people's businesses. The rather heartless, dominating you-actually-deserve-all-you-get type becomes a social worker. The tough guy with sadistic tendencies becomes a jail warder or a policeman. The dull, drab and toiling type a waitress, shop-girl or nurse. And so on.

I'm sorry but it has taken me quite a long time to get down to what I actually wanted to say. When anyone asked me this question, namely: "What work do you do?" I used to answer: "Oh, I'm a writer." Which is quite a lie because I've hardly written a thing, and I've tried but I know I just wouldn't be able to earn a living by writing. Working people are earning a living. I won't truthfully be a writer until I'm *earning* something from the business.

When they said: "Oh, that's interesting and what have you written?" I would say: "Well . . . I have two unpublished manuscripts. One got lost in the post. The other got lost among the papers and rubble on a publisher's desk." Nobody believed me, of course, and funnily enough I was telling the truth. I didn't have the guts to defend myself because I wouldn't have liked them to read what I had written. It was a hotch-potch of under-done ideas, and monotonous in the extreme. There was always a Coloured man here, an African man there and a white somewhere around the corner. Always the same old pattern. I tried to be poetic but even that didn't help. I just bored myself to death and I assumed that I would bore others too so I shut my mouth pretty quick about what I had written. If I had to write one day I would just like to say *people is people* and not damn white, damn black. Perhaps if I was a good enough writer I could still write damn white, damn black and still make people *live*. Make them real. Make you love them, not because of the colour of their skin but because they are important as human beings.

For instance, I would like to write the story about a man who is a packing hand at the railways and lives in one of the tumbling down, leaky houses in District Six. One year for his annual leave he decided to make use of the railway concession and take a free train ride with his wife to Durban. All the neighbours knew about it because they are a popular and sociable couple, as are most people in District Six. No one has much of a private life in District Six. The neighbours make it their business to know all about you and they don't mind what your sins are. In fact, if it comes to the push they'll defend even if the law considers you in the wrong. The only suspicious man in District Six is the man who doesn't show his face and keeps a closed door. We are the real good and jolly neighbours, minding each other's business the way neighbours should. We can't help it because we're all piled up on each other. 5

Well, to get back to the story. This man and his wife had a crowd of friends tagging along as they went to catch the train to Durban. Ticket and booking all arranged. Bags stacked with food for the journey. Things like roast fowl, fish cakes, meat balls and plenty of sandwiches and some booze. The wife, a huge, adventurous, generous, loud-talking, happy and care-free woman climbed on the train first. The husband remained on the platform with the friends. He was sort of glum with a I'm-figuring-this-thing-out look on his face. He always gets that look on his face when he's not too pleased about something. Just as the first warning bell rang he shouted with real terror in his voice: "Ma, get off. Let's go home." And that was that. He didn't even have to explain. Everyone understood. To leave Cape Town and go gallivanting around like some fool in a foreign place like Durban would be an act of the most vile treachery. Cape Town is his home. He was born here. He will die here. Besides, nobody in Durban would understand him. He has a very special kind of language. His very own. He has a special kind of face that is comfortingly reflected in the faces around him. Those faces swear with the exact same nuance that he does. They eat the exact same food. They have the exact same humour. Why go to that fool of a place called Durban? What is there in it for him? To leave Cape Town would be like dying. It would be the destruction of all that he is as a man. He just doesn't have the kind of pretentiousness that makes an American tourist come and gape at the Zulu dances.

Well there it is. I would like to write the story of the man and his wife who never took the train journey, but I can't. When I think of writing any single thing I panic and go dead inside. Perhaps it's because I have my ear too keenly attuned to the political lumberjacks who are busy making capital on human lives. Perhaps I'm just having nightmares. Whatever my manifold disorders are, I hope to get them sorted out pretty soon, because *I've just got to tell a story.*

SHIRLEY JACKSON

Biography of a Story

On the morning of June 28, 1948, I walked down to the post office in our little Vermont town to pick up the mail. I was quite casual about it, as I recall—I opened the box, took out a couple of bills and a letter or two, talked to the postmaster for a few minutes, and left, never supposing that it was the last time for months that I was to pick up the mail without an active feeling of panic. By the next week I had had to change my mailbox to the largest one in the post office, and casual conversation with the postmaster was out of the question, because he wasn't speaking to me. June 28, 1948, was the day *The New Yorker* came out with a story of mine in it. It was not my first published story, nor my last, but I have been assured over and over that if it had been the only story I ever wrote or published, there would be people who would not forget my name.

I had written the story three weeks before, on a bright June morning when summer seemed to have come at last, with blue skies and warm sun and no heavenly signs to warn me that my morning's work was anything but just another story. The idea had come to me while I was pushing my daughter up the hill in her stroller—it was, as I say, a warm morning, and the hill was steep, and beside my daughter the stroller held the day's groceries—and perhaps the effort of that last fifty yards up the hill put an edge to the story; at any rate, I had the idea fairly clearly in my mind when I put my daughter in her playpen and the frozen vegetables in the refrigerator, and, writing the story, I found that it went quickly and easily, moving from beginning to end without pause. As a matter of fact, when I read it over later I decided that except for one or two minor corrections, it needed no changes, and the story I finally typed up and sent off to my agent the next day was almost word for word the original draft. This, as any writer of stories can tell you, is not a usual thing. All I know is that when I came to read the story over I felt strongly that I didn't want to fuss with it. I didn't think it was perfect, but I didn't want to fuss with it. It was, I thought, a serious, straightforward story, and I was pleased and a little surprised at the ease with which it had been written; I was reasonably proud of it, and hoped that my agent would sell it to some magazine and I would have the gratification of seeing it in print.

My agent did not care for the story, but—as she said in her note at the time—her job was to sell it, not to like it. She sent it at once to *The New Yorker*, and about a week after the story had been written I received a telephone call from the fiction editor of *The New Yorker*; it was quite clear that he did not really care for the story, either, but *The New*

Yorker was going to buy it. He asked for one change—that the date mentioned in the story be changed to coincide with the date of the issue of the magazine in which the story would appear, and I said of course. He then asked, hesitantly, if I had any particular interpretation of my own for the story; Mr. Harold Ross, then the editor of *The New Yorker*, was not altogether sure that he understood the story, and wondered if I cared to enlarge upon its meaning. I said no. Mr. Ross, he said, thought that the story might be puzzling to some people, and in case anyone telephoned the magazine, as sometimes happened, or wrote in asking about the story, was there anything in particular I wanted them to say? No, I said, nothing in particular; it was just a story I wrote.

I had no more preparation than that. I went on picking up the mail every morning, pushing my daughter up and down the hill in her stroller, anticipating pleasurably the check from *The New Yorker*, and shopping for groceries. The weather stayed nice and it looked as though it was going to be a good summer. Then, on June 28, *The New Yorker* came out with my story.

Things began mildly enough with a note from a friend at *The New Yorker:* "Your 5
story has kicked up quite a fuss around the office," he wrote. I was flattered; it's nice to think that your friends notice what you write. Later that day there was a call from one of the magazine's editors; they had had a couple of people phone in about my story, he said, and was there anything I particularly wanted him to say if there were any more calls? No, I said, nothing particular; anything he chose to say was perfectly all right with me; it was just a story.

I was further puzzled by a cryptic note from another friend: "Heard a man talking about a story of yours on the bus this morning," she wrote. "Very exciting. I wanted to tell him I knew the author, but after I heard what he was saying I decided I'd better not."

One of the most terrifying aspects of publishing stories and books is the realization that they are going to be read, and read by strangers. I had never fully realized this before, although I had of course in my imagination dwelt lovingly upon the thought of the millions and millions of people who were going to be uplifted and enriched and delighted by the stories I wrote. It had simply never occurred to me that these millions and millions of people might be so far from being uplifted that they would sit down and write me letters I was downright scared to open; of the three-hundred-odd letters that I received that summer I can count only thirteen that spoke kindly to me, and they were mostly from friends. Even my mother scolded me: "Dad and I did not care at all for your story in *The New Yorker*," she wrote sternly; "it does seem, dear, that this gloomy kind of story is what all you young people think about these days. Why don't you write something to cheer people up?"

By mid-July I had begun to perceive that I was very lucky indeed to be safely in Vermont, where no one in our small town had ever heard of *The New Yorker*, much less read my story. Millions of people, and my mother, had taken a pronounced dislike to me.

The magazine kept no track of telephone calls, but all letters addressed to me care of the magazine were forwarded directly to me for answering, and all letters addressed to the magazine—some of them addressed to Harold Ross personally; these were the most vehement—were answered at the magazine and then the letters were sent me in great batches, along with carbons of the answers written at the magazine. I have all the letters still, and if they could be considered to give any accurate cross section of the reading public, or the reading public of *The New Yorker*, or even the reading public of one issue of *The New Yorker*, I would stop writing now.

Judging from these letters, people who read stories are gullible, rude, frequently illiterate, and horribly afraid of being laughed at. Many of the writers were positive 10 that *The New Yorker* was going to ridicule them in print, and the most cautious letters were headed, in capital letters: NOT FOR PUBLICATION or PLEASE DO NOT PRINT THIS LETTER, or, at best, THIS LETTER MAY BE PUBLISHED AT YOUR USUAL RATES OF PAYMENT. Anonymous letters, of which there were a few, were destroyed. *The New Yorker* never published any comment of any kind about the story in the magazine, but did issue one publicity release saying that the story had received more mail than any piece of fiction they had ever published; this was after the newspapers had gotten into the act, in midsummer, with a front-page story in the San Francisco *Chronicle* begging to know what the story meant, and a series of columns in New York and Chicago papers pointing out that *New Yorker* subscriptions were being canceled right and left.

Curiously, there are three main themes which dominate the letters of that first summer—three themes which might be identified as bewilderment, speculation, and plain old-fashioned abuse. In the years since then, during which the story has been anthologized, dramatized, televised, and even—in one completely mystifying transformation—made into a ballet, the tenor of letters I receive has changed. I am addressed more politely, as a rule, and the letters largely confine themselves to questions like what does this story mean? The general tone of the early letters, however, was a kind of wide-eyed, shocked innocence. People at first were not so much concerned with what the story meant; what they wanted to know was where these lotteries were held, and whether they could go there and watch.

MICHAEL JOYCE

FROM *Hypertext Fiction*

Hypertext is, of course, young by almost any measure—at the time of this writing (1992) 47 years since Vannevar Bush's Memex, 29 since Englebart's Augment, 27 since Nelson's hypertext, and 5 years since a number of us gathered for the first of the ACM hypertext meetings in 1987.

Narrative is old. Historically, in the Sumer narrative poems joined warehouse inventories as the first texts known. This is quite fitting since, as Ezra Pound has argued, "the artist is one of the few producers": "He, the farmer, and the artisan create wealth; the rest shift and consume it" (1954).

Narrative creates wealth. Yet hypertext, thus far at least, mimics most computational systems in shifting and consuming rather than creating wealth. This is because hypertext thinks itself to be structural rather than serial thought—thought in space rather than thought for space. "Serial thought," says Umberto Eco, "aims at the production of history and not at the rediscovery—beneath history—of the atemporal abscissae of all possible communication" (1989, 221).

Hypertext, at least when it is seen as constructive rather than exploratory, is serial thought. Its "mode of spatialization," Deleuze and Guattari's term, is being *for* space, what I call the constructive, a form for what does not yet exist, rather than being *in* space, or the exploratory and colonizing. Like AI, its elder sister in this science, hypertext would like to claim its creative powers but to do so must become the art it claims it is.

"Look," we want to say of the hypertext, "see this traversal, this web, this trail, this graph. . . . No one has ever thought this before. Look how, like pearls on a string, these nodes glitter on their path . . . ." 5

But always some emperor-baiting child within us will out. "Pardon," she says, "But why, if this is new, is it there already? Surely you mean no one has gotten to this point in this way before; surely that is what is new."

"No, child," we say, "You don't understand. This substance is an object of value unto itself . . . ."

Then she asks the terrifying questions: "Who is the author of this new thing? What will you call it? And where will you put it?"

For the reader of a *technical* communication, theoretically at least, there *is* some nethermost node, a gleaming target that represents the meaning of a text. (In reality, of course, this node likely encompasses the span of a series of nodes.) This theoretical

1257

terminal node can be systematically described by both its location and its links. Even if the meaning is potentiated, as an inference or discovery, e.g., the node is thought to be present and reachable. I.e., every reading by every reader is thought to be anticipated by the system of the exploratory text. We might call this belief the myth of emerging order (Figure 1).

Within the mythic system of emerging order the reader's task is to make meaning by perceiving order in space. This characteristic Eco identifies with structural thought: "The aim of structural thought is to discover, whereas that of serial thought is to produce" (1989, 221). In the exploratory hypertext interaction is recognition; the system of the text is the author of its additions.

Should the reader wish to add her perceived meaning to the document, there is theoretically no impediment, only a question of privilege and location. We determine the reader's privilege and judge the utility of the addition according to the match we perceive between the reader's order and what we take to be inherent order. We ask *if* a reader can add to the document: Is the summary unique? the inference supported? the discovery consonant? I.e., is this addition authorized?

We likewise determine *where* a reader can add to the document. Once you are privileged you can write into a technical document if its structure accounts for what you add. The document is seen as the atomic shell within which the valency of each addition finds its weighted place. The addition is a terminal node; the text may be seen as leading to it. Yet the addition is perpetually marginal. Interaction does not reorder the text but, rather, conserves authority. Reordering requires a new text, new authority.

The myth of emerging order seems especially instrumental in maintaining technical hypertexts. Because technical hypertexts are thus far treated like centralized rather than distributed knowledge (manuscripts rather than books), individuated meaning must be marginalized and inherent order privileged. Authority, because it is given, is ungained. Interaction remains a utility for the individual reader, i.e., annotation. Hypertext programming—in the double sense of instructed machine behavior and information content: the thing that, like situation comedy, weather map, or docudrama, is shown on the screen—is privileged, centralized, and self-sufficient.

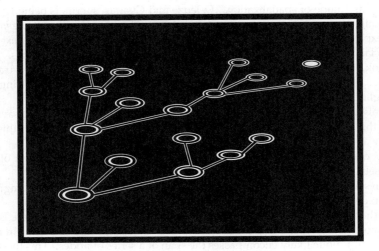

Figure 1   "... The addition is perpetually marginal."

Hypertext narrative transposes this mythic system. If a technical reading is marginal to its text, the text of a narrative is marginal to its reading. Technical communication is governed by the myth of emergent order, i.e., a belief that the structure of meaning emerges from the text. Hypertext narrative produces the present-tense contour of meaningful structures. Meaning in narrative is an orderly but continual replacement of meaningful structures throughout the text. "Although conventional reading habits apply within each lexia," says George P. Landow—borrowing this term for the "nodes and links" from Barthes—"once one leaves the shadowy bounds of any text unit, new rules and new experiences apply" (1992, 4). We judge an addition to narrative by asking if the story continues to "read right," a reader's question, instead of how in technical communication one asks if it fits.

Self-sufficient meaning is not generally characteristic of nontrivial narratives. Only riddles or games, and few of those, offer a target node that truly holds their meaning. In most cases meaning literally has no place in narrative; the meaning of narrative is not in its space but, rather, exists for the space of its unfolding. The moral of a story that has one is part of its story, not its meaning. Meaning in narrative is always strictly potentiated— outside and in some sense prior to the text. It is unreachable and thus not yet linked.

"The fable unwinds from sentence to sentence, and where is it leading?" writes Italo Calvino, "To the point at which something not yet said, something as yet only darkly felt by presentiment, suddenly appears and seizes us and tears us to pieces" (1982, 18). Every reading by every reader becomes privileged and authorized. Reading becomes (and therefore alters) the system of the text.

The reader cannot avoid adding her own meaning to the document. Addition is not merely privileged but is, in fact, required in order to span to the nethermost target node outside the text. Interaction is perception of the principles of ordering. Because hypertexts are read where they are written and written as they are read, interaction is the assumption of authority over the replacement of one writing by another. The reader's orderly perception leads to the placement of an apparent meaning.

Under such circumstances each addition is an initial node to the replaced story she tells in her reading. The target node becomes, instead, a source node; the text may be seen as leading from it. To accommodate the location of the addition, the text itself becomes marginal; meaning reorders the text (Figure 2). The meaning of a story that had

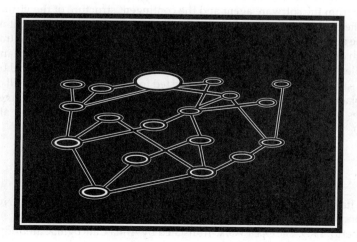

Figure 2   "... **The text itself becomes marginal; meaning reorders the text.**"

none becomes part of its story. Reordering requires a new text; every reading thus becomes a new text.

Despite these heroic claims, readers are thus far not particularly apt to participate in maintaining, i.e., coauthoring, narrative hypertexts. Coauthorship, rather than the Disneyite laurels of perceived first-personhood, is the true index of interaction. It is not the case that a reader can only interact if she is convinced she is in her own idea space or story world. Millennia of human experiences of empathy—not to mention the most recent one hundred years of psychobiology—not only suggest that I can be lost in your story or your idea but also that I am lost if I do not make it my own. It is in this sense that the four principles of the TINAC Dryden Statement (1988) suggested a future text:

20

1. No interruptions: Reading should be a seamless and uninterrupted experience. Its choices proceed from the expression of possibilities as a narrative medium and depend upon the complicity of the reader in the creation of a narrative. Reading is design enacted.

2. Any person: Interaction manifests itself through recognition, sympathy, and witness as much as through impersonation, perception, and exploration. Apprehension of character is participatory design.

3. Every ending: Closure, as it has been described by Andrew Sussman, is "the completion of self by the reader." It is, in this sense, design determined.

4. A read-write revolution: Interactive narratives are "evolving narratives," written, whether by reader or writer. Authorship is an invitation to active design.

Hypertext narratives become virtual storytellers, and narrative is no longer disseminated irreversibly from singer to listener or writer to reader. It exists, instead, as a cycle in which readers become coauthors and artificially intelligent systems "read" their responses. At the moment most interest centers on the machine side of this cycle, focusing on hypertext or virtual reality systems and intelligent agent/navigators who can structure or generate narratives. Even in a system that generates narrative, however, interaction is the assumption of authority over the replacement of one writing by another. Thus, the human side of the cycle demands primary attention.

25

To do so, the primacy of the text must be marginalized. The reader declares independence from the software agent and the contingent structure of the virtual reality alike. If the reader is programming, the reader is programmed. Hypertext narrative asserts the authority of the individual reader, no longer privileged and centralized by the system of the text but, rather, by her reading itself. "Once we have dismantled and reassembled the process of literary composition, the decisive moment will be that of reading" says Calvino, "even though entrusted to machines, literature will continue to be a 'place' of privilege within human consciousness, a way of exercising the potentialities contained in the system of signs belonging to all societies at all times" (1982, 16).

Works Cited

Calvino. Italo. 1982. *The Uses of Literature*. Translated by Patrick Creigh. New York: Harcourt Brace Jovanovich.

Eco, Umberto. 1989. *The Open Work*. Translated by Anna Cancogni. Cambridge, Mass: Harvard University Press.

Landow. George P. 1992. *Hypertext: the Convergence of Contemporary Critical Theory and Technology*. Baltimore: Johns Hopkins University Press.

Pound. Ezra. 1954. *Literary Essays of Ezra Pound*. New York: New Directions.

Various authors. The Dryden Statement., Broadsheet and electronic minifesto. TINAC Report, Dryden, New York and elsewhere 1988 and after.

Milan Kundera

FROM *Somewhere Behind*

Poets don't invent poems
The poem is somewhere behind
It's been there for a long long time
The poet merely discovers it.

—Jan Skacel

1

In one of his books, my friend Josef Skvorecky tells this true story:

An engineer from Prague is invited to a professional conference in London. So he goes, takes part in the proceedings, and returns to Prague. Some hours after his return, sitting in his office, he picks up *Rude Pravo*—the official daily paper of the Party—and reads: A Czech engineer, attending a conference in London, has made a slanderous statement about his socialist homeland to the Western press and has decided to stay in the West.

Illegal emigration combined with a statement of that kind is no trifle. It would be worth twenty years in prison. Our engineer can't believe his eyes. But there's no doubt about it, the article refers to him. His secretary, coming into his office, is shocked to see him: My God, she says, you're back! I don't understand—did you see what they wrote about you?

The engineer sees fear in his secretary's eyes. What can he do? He rushes to the *Rude Pravo* office. He finds the editor responsible for the story. The editor apologizes; yes, it really is an awkward business, but he, the editor, has nothing to do with it, he got the text of the article direct from the Ministry of the Interior.

So the engineer goes off to the Ministry. There they say yes, of course, it's all a mistake, but they, the Ministry, have nothing to do with it, they got the report on the engineer from the intelligence people at the London embassy. The engineer asks for a retraction. No, he's told, they never retract, but nothing can happen to him, he has nothing to worry about.

But the engineer does worry. He soon realizes that all of a sudden he's being close-ly watched, that his telephone is tapped, and that he's being followed in the street. He sleeps poorly and has nightmares until, unable to bear the pressure any longer, he takes a lot of real risks to leave the country illegally. And so he actually becomes an émigré.

2

The story I've just told is one that we would immediately call *Kafkan*. This term, drawn from an artist's work, determined solely by a novelist's images, stands as the only common denominator in situations (literary or real) that no other word allows us to grasp and to which neither political nor social nor psychological theory gives us any key.

But what is the *Kafkan?*

Let's try to describe some of its aspects:

One:

The engineer is confronted by a power that has the character of a *boundless labyrinth*. He can never get to the end of its interminable corridors and will never succeed in finding out who issued the fateful verdict. He is therefore in the same situation as Joseph K. before the Court, or the Land-Surveyor K. before the Castle. All three are in a world that is nothing but a single, huge labyrinthine institution they cannot escape and cannot understand.

Novelists before Kafka often exposed institutions as arenas where conflicts between different personal and public interests were played out. In Kafka the institution is a mechanism that obeys its own laws; no one knows now who programmed those laws or when; they have nothing to do with human concerns and are thus unintelligible.

Two:

In Chapter Five of *The Castle*, the village Mayor explains in detail to K. the long his-tory of his file. Briefly: Years earlier, a proposal to engage a land-surveyor came down to the village from the Castle. The Mayor wrote a negative response (there was no need for any land-surveyor), but his reply went astray to the wrong office, and so after an intricate series of bureaucratic misunderstandings, stretching over many years, the job offer was inadvertently sent to K., at the very moment when all the offices involved were in the process of canceling the old obsolete proposal. After a long journey, K. thus arrived in the village by mistake. Still more: Given that for him there is no possi-ble world other than the Castle and its village, his *entire* existence is a mistake.

In the Kafkan world, the file takes on the role of a Platonic idea. It represents true reality, whereas man's physical existence is only a shadow cast on the screen of illu-sion. Indeed, both the Land-Surveyor K. and the Prague engineer are but the shad-ows of their file cards; and they are even much less than that: they are the shadows of a *mistake* in the file, shadows without even the right to exist as shadows.

But if man's life is only a shadow and true reality lies elsewhere, in the inaccessi-ble, in the inhuman or the suprahuman, then we suddenly enter the domain of theol-ogy. Indeed, Kafka's first commentators explained his novels as religious parables.

Such an interpretation seems to me wrong (because it sees allegory where Kafka grasped concrete situations of human life) but also revealing: wherever power deifies itself, it automatically produces its own theology; wherever it behaves like God, it awakens religious feelings toward itself; such a world can be described in theological terms.

Kafka did not write religious allegories, but the *Kafkan* (both in reality and in fiction) is inseparable from its theological (or rather: *pseudotheological*) dimension.

Three:

20 Raskolnikov cannot bear the weight of his guilt, and to find peace he consents to his punishment of his own free will. It's the well-known situation where *the offense seeks the punishment.*

In Kafka the logic is reversed. The person punished does not know the reason for the punishment. The absurdity of the punishment is so unbearable that to find peace the accused needs to find a justification for his penalty: the *punishment seeks the offense.*

The Prague engineer is punished by intensive police surveillance. This punishment demands the crime that was not committed, and the engineer accused of emigrating ends up emigrating in fact. *The punishment has finally found the offense.*

Not knowing what the charges against him are, K. decides, in Chapter Seven of *The Trial*, to examine his whole life, his entire past "down to the smallest details." The "autoculpabilization" machine goes into motion. *The accused seeks his offense.*

One day, Amalia receives an obscene letter from a Castle official. Outraged, she tears it up. The Castle doesn't even need to criticize Amalia's rash behavior. Fear (the same fear our engineer saw in his secretary's eyes) acts all by itself. With no order, no perceptible sign from the Castle, everyone avoids Amalia's family like the plague.

25 Amalia's father tries to defend his family. But there is a problem: Not only is the source of the verdict impossible to find, but the verdict itself does not exist! To appeal, to request a pardon, you have to be convicted first! The father begs the Castle to proclaim the crime. So it's not enough to say that the punishment seeks the offense. In this pseudotheological world, *the punished beg for recognition of their guilt!*

It often happens in Prague nowadays that someone fallen into disgrace cannot find even the most menial job. In vain he asks for certification of the fact that he has committed an offense and that his employment is forbidden. The verdict is nowhere to be found. And since in Prague work is a duty laid down by law, he ends up being charged with parasitism; that means he is guilty of avoiding work. *The punishment finds the offense.*

Four:

The tale of the Prague engineer is in the nature of a funny story, a joke: it provokes laughter.

Two gentlemen, perfectly ordinary fellows (not "inspectors," as in the French translation), surprise Joseph K. in bed one morning, tell him he is under arrest, and eat up his breakfast. K. is a well-disciplined civil servant: instead of throwing the men out of his flat, he stands in his nightshirt and gives a lengthy self-defense. When Kafka read the first chapter of *The Trial* to his friends, everyone laughed, including the author.

30 Philip Roth's imagined film version of *The Castle*: Groucho Marx plays the Land-Surveyor K., with Chico and Harpo as the two assistants. Yes, Roth is quite right: The comic is inseparable from the very essence of the *Kafkan.*

But it's small comfort to the engineer to know that his story is comic. He is trapped in the joke of his own life like a fish in a bowl; he doesn't find it funny. Indeed, a joke is a joke only if you're outside the bowl; by contrast, the *Kafkan* takes us inside, into the guts of a joke, into the *horror of the comic.*

In the world of the *Kafkan*, the comic is not a counterpoint to the tragic (the tragiccomic) as in Shakespeare; it's not there to make the tragic more bearable by lightening the tone; it doesn't *accompany* the tragic, not at all, it *destroys it in the egg* and thus deprives the victims of the only consolation they could hope for: the consolation to be found in the (real or supposed) grandeur of tragedy. The engineer loses his homeland, and everyone laughs.

6

In speaking of the microsocial practices that generate the *Kafkan*, I mean not only the family but also the organization in which Kafka spent all his adult life: the office.

Kafka's heroes are often seen as allegorical projections of the intellectual, but there's nothing intellectual about Gregor Samsa. When he wakes up metamorphosed into a beetle, he has only one concern: in this new state, how to get to the office on time. In his head he has nothing but the obedience and discipline to which his profession has accustomed him: he's an employee, a *functionary*, as are all Kafka's characters; a functionary not in the sense of a sociological type (as in Zola) but as one human possibility, as one of the elementary ways of being.

In the bureaucratic world of the functionary, first, there is no initiative, no invention, no freedom of action; there are only orders and rules: *it is the world of obedience.* 35

Second, the functionary performs a small part of a large administrative activity whose aim and horizons he cannot see: *it is the world where actions have become mechanical* and people do not know the meaning of what they do.

Third, the functionary deals only with unknown persons and with files: *it is the world of the abstract.*

To place a novel in this world of obedience, of the mechanical, and of the abstract, where the only human adventure is to move from one office to another, seems to run counter to the very essence of epic poetry. Thus the question: How has Kafka managed to transform such gray, antipoetical material into fascinating novels?

The answer can be found in a letter he wrote to Milena: "The office is not a stupid institution; it belongs more to the realm of the fantastic than of the stupid." The sentence contains one of Kafka's greatest secrets. He saw what no one else could see: not only the enormous importance of the bureaucratic phenomenon for man, for his condition and for his future, but also (even more surprisingly) the poetic potential contained in the phantasmic nature of offices.

But what does it mean to say the office belongs to the realm of the fantastic? 40

The Prague engineer would understand: a mistake in his file projected him to London; so he wandered around Prague, a veritable *phantom*, seeking his *lost body*, while the offices he visited seemed to him a *boundless labyrinth* from some unknown *mythology*.

The quality of the fantastic that he perceived in the bureaucratic world allowed Kafka to do what had seemed unimaginable before: he transformed the profoundly antipoetic material of a highly bureaucratized society into the great poetry of the novel; he transformed a very ordinary story of a man who cannot obtain a promised job (which is actually the story of *The Castle*) into myth, into epic, into a kind of beauty never before seen.

By expanding a bureaucratic setting to the gigantic dimensions of a universe, Kafka unwittingly succeeded in creating an image that fascinates us by its resemblance to a society he never knew, that of today's Prague.

A totalitarian state is in fact a single, immense administration: since all work in it is for the state, everyone of every occupation has become an *employee*. A worker is no longer a worker, a judge no longer a judge, a shopkeeper no longer a shopkeeper, a priest no longer a priest; they are all functionaries of the State. "I belong to the Court," the priest says to Joseph K. in the Cathedral. In Kafka, the lawyers, too, work for the Court. A citizen in today's Prague does not find that surprising. He would get no better legal defense than K. did. His lawyers don't work for the defendants either, but for the Court.

7

In a cycle of one hundred quatrains that sound the gravest and most complex depths with an almost childlike simplicity, the great Czech poet writes:

> *Poets don't invent poems*
> *The poem is somewhere behind*
> *It's been there for a long long time*
> *The poet merely discovers it.*

For the poet, then, writing means breaking through a wall behind which something immutable ("the poem") lies hidden in darkness. That's why (because of this surprising and sudden unveiling) "the poem" strikes us first as a *dazzlement*.

I read *The Castle* for the first time when I was fourteen, and the book will never enchant me so thoroughly again, even though all the vast understanding it contains (all the real import of the *Kafkan*) was incomprehensible to me then: I was dazzled.

Later on my eyes adjusted to the light of "the poem" and I began to see my own lived experience in what had dazzled me; yet the light was still there.

"The poem," says Jan Skacel, has been waiting for us, immutable, "for a long long time." However, in a world of perpetual change, is the immutable not a mere illusion?

No. Every situation is of man's making and can only contain what man contains; thus one can imagine that the situation (and all its metaphysical implications) has existed as a human possibility "for a long long time."

But in that case, what does History (the nonimmutable) represent for the poet?

In the eyes of the poet, strange as it may seem, History is in a position similar to the poet's own: History does not *invent*, it *discovers*. Through new situations, History reveals what man is, what has been in him "for a long long time," what his possibilities are.

If "the poem" is already there, then it would be illogical to impute to the poet the gift of *foresight*; no, he "only discovers" a human possibility ("the poem" that has been there "a long long time") that History will in its turn discover one day.

Kafka made no prophecies. All he did was see what was "behind." He did not know that his seeing was also a fore-seeing. He did not intend to unmask a social system. He shed light on the mechanisms he knew from private and microsocial human practice, not suspecting that later developments would put those mechanisms into action on the great stage of History.

The hypnotic eye of power, the desperate search for one's own offense, exclusion and the anguish of being excluded, the condemnation to conformism, the phantasmic nature of reality and the magical reality of the file, the perpetual rape of private life, etc.—all these experiments that History has performed on man in its immense test tubes, Kafka performed (some years earlier) in his novels.

The convergence of the real world of totalitarian states with Kafka's "poem" will   60
always be somewhat uncanny, and it will always bear witness that the poet's act, in its
very essence, is incalculable; and paradoxical: the enormous social, political, and
"prophetic" import of Kafka's novels lies precisely in their "nonengagement," that is
to say, in their total autonomy from all political programs, ideological concepts, and
futurological prognoses.

Indeed, if instead of seeking "the poem" hidden "somewhere behind" the poet "engages" himself to the service of a truth known from the outset (which comes forward
on its own and is "out in front"), he has renounced the mission of poetry. And it matters little whether the preconceived truth is called revolution or dissidence, Christian
faith or atheism, whether it is more justified or less justified; a poet who serves any truth
other than the truth *to be discovered* (which is *dazzlement*) is a false poet.

If I hold so ardently to the legacy of Kafka, if I defend it as my personal heritage, it
is not because I think it worthwhile to imitate the inimitable (and rediscover the *Kafkan*)
but because it is such a tremendous example of the *radical autonomy* of the novel (of the
poetry that is the novel). This autonomy allowed Franz Kafka to say things about our
human condition (as it reveals itself in our century) that no social or political thought
could ever tell us.

URSULA K. LE GUIN

FROM *Where Do You Get Your Ideas From?*

This brings me to the relationship of the writer to the reader: a matter I again find easiest to approach through explainable failure. The shared imaginative world of fiction cannot be taken for granted, even by a writer telling a story set right here and now in the suburbs among people supposed to be familiar to everybody. The fictional world has to be created by the author, whether by the slightest hints and suggestions, which will do for the suburbs, or by very careful guidance and telling detail, if the reader is being taken to the planet Gzorx. When the writer fails to imagine, to *image,* the world of the narrative, the work fails. The usual result is abstract, didactic fiction. Plots that make points. Characters who don't talk or act like people, and who are in fact not imaginary people at all but mere bits of the writer's ego got loose, glibly emitting messages. The intellect cannot do the work of the imagination; the emotions cannot do the work of the imagination; and neither of them can do anything much in fiction without the imagination.

Where the writer and the reader collaborate to make the work of fiction is perhaps, above all, in the imagination. In the joint creation of the fictive world.

Now, writers are egoists. All artists are. They can't be altruists and get their work done. And writers love to whine about the Solitude of the Author's Life, and lock themselves into cork-lined rooms or droop around in bars in order to whine better. But although most writing is done in solitude, I believe that it is done, like all the arts, for an audience. That is to say, with an audience. All the arts are performance arts, only some of them are sneakier about it than others.

I beg you please to attend carefully now to what I am not saying. I am not saying that you should think about your audience when you write. I am not saying that the writing writer should have in mind, "Who will read this? Who will buy it? Who am I aiming this at?"—as if it were a gun. No.

5   While *planning* a work, the writer may and often must think about readers; particularly if it's something like a story for children, where you need to know whether your reader is likely to be a five-year-old or a ten-year-old. Considerations of who will or might read the piece are appropriate and sometimes actively useful in planning it, thinking about it, thinking it out, inviting images. But once you start writing, it is fatal to think about anything but the writing. True work is done for the sake of doing it.

What is to be done with it afterwards is another matter, another job. A story rises from the springs of creation, from the pure will to be; it tells itself; it takes its own course, finds its own way, its own words; and the writer's job is to be its medium. What a teacher or editor or market or critic or Alice will think of it has to be as far from the writing writer's mind as what breakfast was last Tuesday. Farther. The breakfast might be useful to the story.

Once the story is written, however, the writer must forgo that divine privacy and accept the fact that the whole thing has been a performance, and it had better be a good one.

When I, the writer, reread my work and settle down to reconsider it, reshape it, revise it, then my consciousness of the reader, of collaborating with the reader, is appropriate and, I think, necessary. Indeed I may have to make an act of faith and declare that they will exist, those unknown, perhaps unborn people, my dear readers. The blind, beautiful arrogance of the creative moment must grow subtle, self-conscious, clear-sighted. It must ask questions, such as: Does this say what I thought it said? Does it say all I thought it did? It is at this stage that I, the writer, may have to question the nature of my relationship to my readers, as manifested in my work. Am I shoving them around, manipulating them, patronizing them, showing off to them? Am I punishing them? Am I using them as a dump site for my accumulated psychic toxins? Am I telling them what they better damn well believe or else? Am I running circles around them, and will they enjoy it? Am I scaring them, and did I intend to? Am I interesting them, and if not, hadn't I better see to it that I am? Am I amusing, teasing, alluring them? Flirting with them? Hypnotizing them? Am I giving to them, tempting them, inviting them, drawing them into the work *to work with me*—to be the one, the Reader, who completes my vision?

Because the writer cannot do it alone. The unread story is not a story; it is little black marks on wood pulp. The reader, reading it, makes it live: a live thing, a story.

A special note to the above: If the writer is a socially privileged person—particularly a White or a male or both—his imagination may have to make an intense and conscious effort to realize that people who don't share his privileged status may read his work and will not share with him many attitudes and opinions that he has been allowed to believe or to pretend are shared by "everybody." Since the belief in a privileged view of reality is no longer tenable outside privileged circles, and often not even within them, fiction written from such an assumption will make sense only to a decreasing, and increasingly reactionary, audience. Many women writing today, however, still choose the male viewpoint, finding it easier to do so than to write from the knowledge that feminine experience of reality is flatly denied by many potential readers, including the majority of critics and professors of literature, and may rouse defensive hostility and contempt. The choice, then, would seem to be between collusion and subversion; but there's no use pretending that you can get away without making the choice. Not to choose, these days, is a choice made. All fiction has ethical, political, and social weight, and sometimes the works that weigh the heaviest are those apparently fluffy or escapist fictions whose authors declare themselves "above politics," "just entertainers," and so on.

The writer writing, then, is trying to get all the patterns of sounds, syntax, imagery, ideas, emotions, working together in one process, in which the reader will be drawn to participate. This implies that writers do one hell of a lot of controlling. They control all their material as closely as they can, and in doing so they are trying to control the reader, too. They are trying to get the reader to go along helplessly, putty in their hands, 10 seeing, hearing, feeling, believing the story, laughing at it, crying at it. They are trying to make innocent little children cry.

But though control is a risky business, it need not be conceived in confrontational terms as a battle with and a victory over the material or the reader. Again, I think it comes down to collaboration, or sharing the gift: the writer tries to get the reader working with the text in the effort to keep the whole story all going along in one piece in the right direction (which is my general notion of a good piece of fiction).

In this effort, writers need all the help they can get. Even under the most skilled control, the words will never fully embody the vision. Even with the most sympathetic reader, the truth will falter and grow partial. Writers have to get used to launching something beautiful and watching it crash and burn. They also have to learn when to let go control, when the work takes off on its own and flies, farther than they ever planned or imagined, to places they didn't know they knew. All makers must leave room for the acts of the spirit. But they have to work hard and carefully, and wait patiently, to deserve them.

A Letter to Richard Murray

This letter, to the younger brother of her husband (John Murray), is printed pretty much as it was written, mistakes included. Mansfield was living near Nice, in the south of France, dying of tuberculosis and trying, despite her precarious financial position, to stay away from England's cold and wet winters.

VILLA ISOLA BELLA / GARAVAN / MENTON
A/M. 17.I.1921.

My dear Richard,

If you knew how I love hearing from you and how honoured I am by your confidence! I want you to feel I am a *real* sister to you. Will you? Remember that here is your sister Katherine who is not only interested in everything that you do but who wants to be made use of. Treat me as a person you have the right to ask things of. Look here—if you want anything & you haven't the dibs—come to me *bang* off and if I have the money you're welcome to it—without a single hesitation. Ill always be truthful with you, that's a promise. Ill be dead straight with you in everything.

Why I am saying all this is (I see your eyes rolling and your hair rising in festoons of amazement and I dont care!) Well, why I am saying it is that we 'artists' are not like ordinary people and there are times when to know we have a fellow workman who's ready to do all in his power, because he loves you and believes in you, is a nice comfortable feeling. I adore *Life* but my experience of the world is that its pretty terrible. I hope yours will be a very different one dear old boy, but just in case . . . [if] you'd like to shout Katherine at any moment here she is. See?

Having got that off my ches' (which is at this moment more like a chest of super-sharp-edged cutlery) let me say how I appreciate all you feel about *craft*. Yes, I think youre absolutely right. I see your *approach* to painting as very individual. Emotion for you seems to grow out of deliberation—looking long at a thing. Am I getting at anything right? In the way a thing is made—it may be a tree or a woman or a gazelle or a dish of fruit—you get your inspiration. This sounds a bit too simple when it is written down & rather like 'Professor Leonard The Indian Palmist.' I mean something though. Its a very queer thing how *craft*

5

comes into writing. I mean down to details. Par exemple. In Miss Brill I chose not only the length of every sentence, but even the sound of every sentence—I chose the rise and fall of every paragraph to fit her—and to fit her on that day at that very moment. After Id written it I read it aloud numbers of times just as one would *play over* a musical composition, trying to get it nearer and nearer to the expression of Miss Brill—until it fitted her.

Don't think Im vain about the little sketch. Its only the method I wanted to explain. I often wonder whether other writers do the same. If a thing has really come off it seems to me there mustn't be one single word out of place or one word that could be taken out. Thats how I AIM at writing. It will take some time to get anywhere near there.

But you know Richard, I was only thinking last night people have hardly begun to write yet. Put poetry out of it for a moment & leave out Shakespeare— now I mean prose. Take the very best of it. Aren't they still cutting up sections rather than tackling the whole of a mind? I had a moment of absolute terror in the night. I suddenly thought of a *living mind*—a whole mind—with absolutely nothing left out. With *all* that one knows how much does one *not* know? I used to fancy one knew all but some kind of mysterious core (or one could). But now I believe just the opposite. The unknown is far far greater than the known. The known is only a mere shadow. This is a fearful thing and terribly hard to face. But it must be faced.

Well, thats enough at a time for you. I hope you're not bored. I long to see the landscape. Am I to be allowed to hang it on my walls to bear me company?

With my love to you
Ever
Katherine.

10

VLADIMIR NABOKOV

FROM *Anton Chekhov:*
"The Lady with the Little Dog"

Chekhov comes into the story "The Lady with the Little Dog" without knocking. There is no dilly-dallying. The very first paragraph reveals the main character, the young fair-haired lady followed by her white Spitz dog on the waterfront of a Crimean resort, Yalta, on the Black Sea. And immediately after, the male character Gurov appears. His wife, whom he has left with the children in Moscow, is vividly depicted: her solid frame, her thick black eyebrows, and the way she had of calling herself "a woman who thinks." One notes the magic of the trifles the author collects—the wife's manner of dropping a certain mute letter in spelling and her calling her husband by the longest and fullest form of his name, both traits in combination with the impressive dignity of her beetle-browed face and rigid poise forming exactly the necessary impression. A hard woman with the strong feminist and social ideas of her time, but one whom her husband finds in his heart of hearts to be narrow, dull-minded, and devoid of grace. The natural transition is to Gurov's constant unfaithfulness to her, to his general attitude toward women—"that inferior race" is what he calls them, but without that inferior race he could not exist. It is hinted that these Russian romances were not altogether as light-winged as in the Paris of Maupassant. Complications and problems are unavoidable with those decent hesitating people of Moscow who are slow heavy starters but plunge into tedious difficulties when once they start going.

Then with the same neat and direct method of attack, with the bridging formula "and so . . .," we slide back to the lady with the dog. Everything about her, even the way her hair was done, told him that she was bored. The spirit of adventure—though he realized perfectly well that his attitude toward a lone woman in a fashionable sea town was based on vulgar stories, generally false—this spirit of adventure prompts him to call the little dog, which thus becomes a link between her and him. They are both in a public restaurant.

"He beckoned invitingly to the Spitz, and when the dog approached him, shook his finger at it. The Spitz growled; Gurov threatened it again.

"The lady glanced at him and at once dropped her eyes.

"'He doesn't bite,' she said and blushed.

"'May I give him a bone?' he asked; and when she nodded he inquired affably, 'Have you been in Yalta long?'

5

1273

"'About five days.'"

They talk. The author has hinted already that Gurov was witty in the company of women; and instead of having the reader take it for granted (you know the old method of describing the talk as "brilliant" but giving no samples of the conversation), Chekhov makes him joke in a really attractive, winning way. "Bored, are you? An average citizen lives in . . . (here Chekhov lists the names of beautifully chosen, super-provincial towns) and is not bored, but when he arrives here on his vacation it is all boredom and dust. One could think he came from Grenada" (a name particularly appealing to the Russian imagination). The rest of their talk, for which this sidelight is richly sufficient, is conveyed indirectly. Now comes a first glimpse of Chekhov's own system of suggesting atmosphere by the most concise details of nature, "the sea was of a warm lilac hue with a golden path for the moon"; whoever has lived in Yalta knows how exactly this conveys the impression of a summer evening there. This first movement of the story ends with Gurov alone in his hotel room thinking of her as he goes to sleep and imagining her delicate weak-looking neck and her pretty gray eyes. It is to be noted that only now, through the medium of the hero's imagination, does Chekhov give a visible and definite form to the lady, features that fit in perfectly with her listless manner and expression of boredom already known to us.

"Getting into bed he recalled that she had been a schoolgirl only recently, doing lessons like his own daughter; he thought how much timidity and angularity there was still in her laugh and her manner of talking with a stranger. It must have been the first time in her life that she was alone in a setting in which she was followed, looked at, and spoken to for one secret purpose alone, which she could hardly fail to guess. He thought of her slim, delicate throat, her lovely gray eyes.

10   "'There's something pathetic about her, though,' he thought, and dropped off."

The next movement (each of the four diminutive chapters or movements of which the story is composed is not more than four or five pages long), the next movement starts a week later with Gurov going to the pavilion and bringing the lady iced lemonade on a hot windy day, with the dust flying; and then in the evening when the sirocco subsides, they go on the pier to watch the incoming steamer. "The lady lost her lorgnette in the crowd," Chekhov notes shortly, and this being so casually worded, without any direct influence on the story—just a passing statement—somehow fits in with that helpless pathos already alluded to.

Then in her hotel room her awkwardness and tender angularity are delicately conveyed. They have become lovers. She was now sitting with her long hair hanging down on both sides of her face in the dejected pose of a sinner in some old picture. There was a watermelon on the table. Gurov cut himself a piece and began to eat unhurriedly. This realistic touch is again a typical Chekhov device.

She tells him about her existence in the remote town she comes from and Gurov is slightly bored by her naiveté, confusion, and tears. It is only now that we learn her husband's name: von Dideritz—probably of German descent.

They roam about Yalta in the early morning mist. "At Oreanda they sat on a bench not far from the church, looked down at the sea, and were silent. Yalta was barely visible through the morning mist; white clouds rested motionlessly on the mountaintops. The leaves did not stir on the trees, the crickets chirped, and the monotonous muffled sound of the sea that rose from below spoke of the peace, the eternal sleep awaiting us. So it rumbled below when there was no Yalta, no Oreanda here; so it rumbles now, and it will rumble as indifferently and hollowly when we are no more. . . . Sitting beside a young woman who in the dawn seemed so lovely, Gurov, soothed and spellbound by these magical surroundings—the sea, the mountains, the clouds, the wide sky—thought how everything is really beautiful in this world when one reflects: everything except what we think or do ourselves when we forget the higher aims of life and our own human dignity.

"A man strolled up to them—probably a watchman—looked at them and walked away. And this detail, too, seemed so mysterious and beautiful. They saw a steamer arrive from Feodosia, its lights extinguished in the glow of dawn.

"'There is dew on the grass,' said Anna Sergeievna, after a silence.

"'Yes, it's time to go home.'"

Then several days pass and then she has to go back to her home town.

"'Time for me, too, to go North,' thought Gurov as he returned after seeing her off." And there the chapter ends.

The third movement plunges us straight into Gurov's life in Moscow. The richness of a gay Russian winter, his family affairs, the dinners at clubs and restaurants, all this is swiftly and vividly suggested. Then a page is devoted to a queer thing that has happened to him: he cannot forget the lady with the little dog. He has many friends, but the curious longing he has for talking about his adventure finds no outlet. When he happens to speak in a very general way of love and women, nobody guesses what he means, and only his wife moves her dark eyebrows and says: "Stop that fatuous posing; it does not suit you."

And now comes what in Chekhov's quiet stories may be called the climax. There is something that your average citizen calls romance and something he calls prose—though both are the meat of poetry for the artist. Such a contrast has already been hinted at by the slice of watermelon which Gurov crunched in a Yalta hotel room at a most romantic moment, sitting heavily and munching away. This contrast is beautifully followed up when at last Gurov blurts out to a friend late at night as they come out of the club: If you knew what a delightful woman I met in Yalta! His friend, a bureaucratic civil servant, got into his sleigh, the horses moved, but suddenly he turned and called back to Gurov. Yes? asked Gurov, evidently expecting some reaction to what he had just mentioned. By the way, said the man, you were quite right. That fish at the club was decidedly smelly.

This is a natural transition to the description of Gurov's new mood, his feeling that he lives among savages where cards and food are life. His family, his bank, the whole trend of his existence, everything seems futile, dull, and senseless. About Christmas he tells his wife he is going on a business trip to St. Petersburg, instead of which he travels to the remote Volga town where the lady lives.

Critics of Chekhov in the good old days when the mania for the civic problem flourished in Russia were incensed with his way of describing what they considered to be trivial unnecessary matters instead of thoroughly examining and solving the problems of bourgeois marriage. For as soon as Gurov arrives in the early hours to that town and takes the best room at the local hotel, Chekhov, instead of describing his mood or intensifying his difficult moral position, gives what is artistic in the highest sense of the word: he notes the gray carpet, made of military cloth, and the inkstand, also gray with dust, with a horseman whose hand waves a hat and whose head is gone. That is all: it is nothing but it is everything in authentic literature. A feature in the same line is the phonetic transformation which the hotel porter imposes on the German name von Dideritz. Having learned the address Gurov goes there and looks at the house. Opposite was a long gray fence with nails sticking out. An unescapable fence, Gurov says to himself, and here we get the concluding note in the rhythm of drabness and grayness already suggested by the carpet, the inkstand, the illiterate accent of the porter. The unexpected little turns and the lightness of the touches are what places Chekhov, above all Russian writers of fiction, on the level of Gogol and Tolstoy.

Presently he saw an old servant coming out with the familiar little white dog. He wanted to call it (by a kind of conditional reflex), but suddenly his heart began beating fast and in his excitement he could not remember the dog's name—another delightful touch. Later on he decides to go to the local theatre, where for the first time the operetta *The Geisha* is being given. In sixty words Chekhov paints a complete picture of a provincial theatre, not forgetting the town-governor who modestly hid in his box behind a plush curtain so that only his hands were visible. Then the lady appeared. And he realized quite clearly that now in the whole world there was none nearer and dearer and more important to him than this slight woman, lost in a small-town crowd, a woman perfectly unremarkable, with a vulgar lorgnette in her hand. He saw her husband and remembered her qualifying him as a flunkey—he distinctly resembled one.

25   A remarkably fine scene follows when Gurov manages to talk to her, and then their mad swift walk up all kinds of staircases and corridors, and down again, and up again, amid people in the various uniforms of provincial officials. Neither does Chekhov forget "two schoolboys who smoked on the stairs and looked down at him and her."

" 'You must leave,' Anna Sergeievna went on in a whisper. 'Do you hear, Dmitri Dmitrich? I will come and see you in Moscow. I have never been happy; I am unhappy now, and I never, never shall be happy, never! So don't make me suffer still more! I swear I'll come to Moscow. But now let us part. My dear, good, precious one, let us part!'

"She pressed his hand and walked rapidly downstairs, turning to look around at him, and from her eyes he could see that she really was unhappy. Gurov stood for a while, listening, then when all grew quiet, he found his coat and left the theatre."

The fourth and last little chapter gives the atmosphere of their secret meetings in Moscow. As soon as she would arrive she used to send a redcapped messenger to Gurov. One day he was on his way to her and his daughter was with him. She was going to school, in the same direction as he. Big damp snowflakes were slowly coming down.

The thermometer, Gurov was saying to his daughter, shows a few degrees above freezing point (actually 37° above, fahrenheit), but nevertheless snow is falling. The explanation is that this warmth applies only to the surface of the earth, while in the higher layers of the atmosphere the temperature is quite different.

30   And as he spoke and walked, he kept thinking that not a soul knew or would ever know about these secret meetings.

What puzzled him was that all the false part of his life, his bank, his club, his conversations, his social obligations—all this happened openly, while the real and interesting part was hidden.

"He had two lives: an open one, seen and known by all who needed to know it, full of conventional truth and conventional falsehood, exactly like the lives of his friends and acquaintances; and another life that went on in secret. And through some strange, perhaps accidental, combination of circumstances, everything that was of interest and importance to him, everything that was essential to him, everything about which he felt sincerely and did not deceive himself, everything that constituted the core of his life, was going on concealed from others; while all that was false, the shell in which he hid to cover the truth—his work at the bank for instance, his discussions at the club, his references to the 'inferior race,' his appearances at anniversary celebrations with his wife—all that went on in the open. Judging others by himself, he did not believe what he saw, and always fancied that every man led his real, most interesting life under cover of secrecy as under cover of night. The personal life of every individual is based on secrecy, and perhaps it is partly for that reason that civilized man is so nervously anxious that personal privacy should be respected."

The final scene is full of that pathos which has been suggested in the very beginning. They meet, she sobs, they feel that they are the closest of couples, the tenderest of friends, and he sees that his hair is getting a little gray and knows that only death will end their love.

"The shoulders on which his hands rested were warm and quivering. He felt compassion for this life, still so warm and lovely, but probably already about to begin to fade and wither like his own. Why did she love him so much? He always seemed to women different from what he was, and they loved in him not himself, but the man whom their imagination had created and whom they had been eagerly seeking all their lives; and afterwards, when they saw their mistake, they loved him nevertheless. And not one of them had been happy with him. In the past he had met women, come together with them, parted from them, but he had never once loved; it was anything you please, but not love. And only now when his head was gray he had fallen in love, really, truly—for the first time in his life."

They talk, they discuss their position, how to get rid of the necessity of this sordid   35 secrecy, how to be together always. They find no solution and in the typical Chekhov way the tale fades out with no definite full-stop but with the natural motion of life.

"And it seemed as though in a little while the solution would be found, and then a new and glorious life would begin; and it was clear to both of them that the end was still far off, and that what was to be most complicated and difficult for them was only just beginning."

All the traditional rules of story telling have been broken in this wonderful short story of twenty pages or so. There is no problem, no regular climax, no point at the end. And it is one of the greatest stories ever written.

We will now repeat the different features that are typical for this and other Chekhov tales.

First: The story is told in the most natural way possible, not beside the afterdinner fireplace as with Turgenev or Maupassant but in the way one person relates to another the most important things in his life, slowly and yet without a break, in a slightly subdued voice.

Second: Exact and rich characterization is attained by a careful selection and care-   40 ful distribution of minute but striking features, with perfect contempt for the sustained description, repetition, and strong emphasis of ordinary authors. In this or that description one detail is chosen to illume the whole setting.

Third: There is no special moral to be drawn and no special message to be received. Compare this to the special delivery stories of Gorki or Thomas Mann.

Fourth: The story is based on a system of waves, on the shades of this or that mood. If in Gorki's world the molecules forming it are matter, here, in Chekhov, we get a world of waves instead of particles of matter, which, incidentally, is a nearer approach to the modern scientific understanding of the universe.

Fifth: The contrast of poetry and prose stressed here and there with such insight and humor is, in the long run, a contrast only for the heroes; in reality we feel, and this is again typical of authentic genius, that for Chekhov the lofty and the base are *not* different, that the slice of watermelon and the violet sea, and the hands of the town-governor, are essential points of the "beauty plus pity" of the world.

Sixth: The story does not really end, for as long as people are alive, there is no possible and definite conclusion to their troubles or hopes or dreams.

45   Seventh: The storyteller seems to keep going out of his way to allude to trifles, every one of which in another type of story would mean a signpost denoting a turn in the action—for instance, the two boys at the theatre would be eavesdroppers, and rumors would spread, or the inkstand would mean a letter changing the course of the story; but just because these trifles are meaningless, they are all-important in giving the real atmosphere of this particular story.

VLADIMIR NABOKOV

FROM *Franz Kafka: "The Metamorphosis"*

Born in 1883, Franz Kafka came from a German-speaking Jewish family in Prague, Czechoslovakia. He is the greatest German writer of our time. Such poets as Rilke or such novelists as Thomas Mann are dwarfs or plaster saints in comparison to him. He read for law at the German university in Prague and from 1908 on he worked as a petty clerk, a small employee, in a very Gogolian office for an insurance company. Hardly any of his now famous works, such as his novels *The Trial* (1925) and *The Castle* (1926), were published in his lifetime. His greatest short story "The Metamorphosis," in German "Die Verwandlung," was written in the fall of 1912 and published in Leipzig in October 1915. In 1917 he coughed blood, and the rest of his life, a period of seven years, was punctuated by sojourns in Central European sanatoriums. In those last years of his short life (he died at the age of forty-one), he had a happy love affair and lived with his mistress in Berlin, in 1923, not far from me. In the spring of 1924 he went to a sanatorium near Vienna where he died on 3 June, of tuberculosis of the larynx. He was buried in the Jewish cemetery in Prague. He asked his friend Max Brod to burn everything he had written, even published material. Fortunately Brod did not comply with his friend's wish.

Before starting to talk of "The Metamorphosis," I want to dismiss two points of view. I want to dismiss completely Max Brod's opinion that the category of sainthood, not that of literature, is the only one that can be applied to the understanding of Kafka's writings. Kafka was first of all an artist, and although it may be maintained that every artist is a manner of saint (I feel that very clearly myself), I do not think that any religious implications can be read into Kafka's genius. The other matter that I want to dismiss is the Freudian point of view. His Freudian biographers, like Neider in *The Frozen Sea* (1948), contend, for example, that "The Metamorphosis" has a basis in Kafka's complex relationship with his father and his lifelong sense of guilt; they contend further that in mythical symbolism children are represented by vermin—which I doubt—and then go on to say that Kafka uses the symbol of the bug to represent the son according to these Freudian postulates. The bug, they say, aptly characterizes his sense of worthlessness before his father. I am interested here in bugs, not in humbugs, and I reject this nonsense. Kafka himself was extremely critical of Freudian ideas. He considered psychoanalysis (I quote) "a helpless error," and he regarded Freud's theories as very approximate, very rough pictures, which did not do justice to details or, what is more, to the essence of the matter. This is another reason why I should like to dismiss the Freudian approach and concentrate, instead, upon the artistic moment.

The greatest literary influence upon Kafka was Flaubert's. Flaubert who loathed pretty-pretty prose would have applauded Kafka's attitude towards his tool. Kafka liked to draw his terms from the language of law and science, giving them a kind of ironic precision, with no intrusion of the author's private sentiments; this was exactly Flaubert's method through which he achieved a singular poetic effect.

The hero of "The Metamorphosis" is Gregor Samsa (pronounced *Zamza*), who is the son of middle-class parents in Prague, Flaubertian philistines, people interested only in the material side of life and vulgarians in their tastes. Some five years before, old Samsa lost most of his money, whereupon his son Gregor took a job with one of his father's creditors and became a traveling salesman in cloth. His father then stopped working altogether, his sister Grete was too young to work, his mother was ill with asthma; thus young Gregor not only supported the whole family but also found for them the apartment they are now living in. This apartment, a flat in an apartment house, in Charlotte Street to be exact, is divided into segments as he will be divided himself. We are in Prague, central Europe, in the year 1912; servants are cheap so that the Samsas can afford a servant maid, Anna, aged sixteen (one year younger than Grete), and a cook. Gregor is mostly away traveling, but when the story starts he is spending a night at home between two business trips, and it is then that the dreadful thing happened. "As Gregor Samsa awoke one morning from a troubled dream he found himself transformed in his bed into a monstrous insect. He was lying on his hard, as it were armor-plated, back and when he lifted his head a little he could see his dome-like brown belly divided into corrugated segments on top of which the bed quilt could hardly keep in position and was about to slide off completely. His numerous legs, which were pitifully thin compared to the rest of his bulk, flimmered [*flicker + shimmer*] helplessly before his eyes.

5   "What has happened to me? he thought. It was no dream. . . .

"Gregor's eyes turned next to the window—one could hear rain drops beating on the tin of the windowsill's outer edge and the dull weather made him quite melancholy. What about sleeping a little longer and forgetting all this nonsense, he thought, but it could not be done, for he was accustomed to sleep on his right side and in his present condition he could not turn himself over. However violently he tried to hurl himself on his right side he always swung back to the supine position. He tried it at least a hundred times, shutting his eyes° to keep from seeing his wriggly legs, and only desisted when he began to feel in his side a faint dull ache he had never experienced before.

"Ach Gott, he thought, what an exhausting job I've picked on! Traveling about day in, day out. Many more anxieties on the road than in the office, the plague of worrying about train connections, the bad and irregular meals, casual acquaintances never to be seen again, never to become intimate friends. The hell with it all! He felt a slight itching on the skin of his belly; slowly pushed himself on his back nearer the top of the bed so that he could lift his head more easily; identified the itching place which was covered with small white dots the nature of which he could not understand and tried to touch it with a leg, but drew the leg back immediately, for the contact made a cold shiver run through him."

°"A regular beetle has no eyelids and cannot close its eyes—a beetle with human eyes." About the passage in general he has the note: "In the original German there is a wonderful flowing rhythm here in this dreamy sequence of sentences. He is half-awake—he realizes his plight without surprise, with a childish acceptance of it, and at the same time he still clings to human memories, human experience. The metamorphosis is not quite complete as yet. [Nabokov's Note. Ed.]

Now what exactly is the "vermin" into which poor Gregor, the seedy commercial traveler, is so suddenly transformed? It obviously belongs to the branch of "jointed leggers" (*Arthropoda*), to which insects, and spiders, and centipedes, and crustaceans belong. If the "numerous little legs" mentioned in the beginning mean more than six legs, then Gregor would not be an insect from a zoological point of view. But I suggest that a man awakening on his back and finding he has as many as six legs vibrating in the air might feel that six was sufficient to be called numerous. We shall therefore assume that Gregor has six legs, that he is an insect.

Next question: what insect? Commentators say *cockroach*, which of course does not make sense. A cockroach is an insect that is flat in shape with large legs, and Gregor is anything but flat: he is convex on both sides, belly and back, and his legs are small. He approaches a cockroach in only one respect: his coloration is brown. That is all. Apart from this he has a tremendous convex belly divided into segments and a hard rounded back suggestive of wing cases. In beetles these cases conceal flimsy little wings that can be expanded and then may carry the beetle for miles and miles in a blundering flight. Curiously enough, Gregor the beetle never found out that he had wings under the hard covering of his back. (This is a very nice observation on my part to be treasured all your lives. Some Gregors, some Joes and Janes, do not know that they have wings.) Further, he has strong mandibles. He uses these organs to turn the key in a lock while standing erect on his hind legs, on his third pair of legs (a strong little pair), and this gives us the length of his body, which is about three feet long. In the course of the story he gets gradually accustomed to using his new appendages—his feet, his feelers. This brown, convex, dog-sized beetle is very broad. . . .

In the original German text the old charwoman calls him *Mistkäfer*, a "dung beetle." 10 It is obvious that the good woman is adding the epithet only to be friendly. He is not, technically, a dung beetle. He is merely a big beetle. (I must add that neither Gregor nor Kafka saw that beetle any too clearly.)

Let us look closer at the transformation. The change, though shocking and striking, is not quite so odd as might be assumed at first glance. A commonsensical commentator (Paul L. Landsberg in *The Kafka Problem* [1946], ed. Angel Flores) notes that "When we go to bed in unfamiliar surroundings, we are apt to have a moment of bewilderment upon awakening, a sudden sense of unreality, and this experience must occur over and over again in the life of a commercial traveller, a manner of living that renders impossible any sense of continuity." The sense of reality depends upon continuity, upon duration. After all, awakening as an insect is not much different from awakening as Napoleon or George Washington. (I knew a man who awoke as the Emperor of Brazil.) On the other hand, the isolation, and the strangeness, of so-called reality—this is, after all, something which constantly characterizes the artist, the genius, the discoverer. The Samsa family around the fantastic insect is nothing else than mediocrity surrounding genius.

JOYCE CAROL OATES

The Making of a Writer

Telling stories, I discovered at the age of three or four, is a way of being told stories. One picture yields another: one set of words, another set of words. Like our dreams, the stories we tell are also the stories we are told. If I say that I write with the enormous hope of altering the world—and why write without that hope?—I should first say that I write to discover what it is *I will have written*. A love of reading stimulates the wish to write—so that one can read, as a reader, the words one has written. Storytellers may be finite in number but stories appear to be inexhaustible.

For many days—in fact for weeks—I have been tormented by the proposition that if I could set down, in reasonably lucid prose, the story of "the making of the writer Joyce Carol Oates," I might in some rudimentary way be defined, at least to myself. Stretched upon a grammatical framework, who among us does not appear to make sense? But the story will not cohere. The necessary words will not arrange themselves. Of the forty-odd pages I have written (each, I should confess, with the rapt, naïve certainty, *At last I have it*) very little strikes me as useful. The miniature stories I have told myself, by way of analyzing "myself," are not precisely lies; but, since each contains so small a fraction of the truth, it is untrue. Each angle of vision, each voice, yields (by way of that process of fictional abiogenesis all storytellers know) a separate writer-self, an alternative Joyce Carol Oates. Each miniature story exerts so powerful an appeal (to the author, that is) that it could, in time, evolve into a novel—for me the divine form, the ultimate artwork, toward which all the arts aspire. Consequently this "story" you are reading is an admission of failure, or, at the very most, a record of failed attempts. If knowing oneself is an alphabet, I seem to be stuck at *A*, and take solace from the elderly Yeats's° remark in a letter: "Man can embody truth but he cannot know it."

One of the stories I tell myself has to do with the dream of a "sacred text."

Perhaps it is a dream, an actual dream: to set down words with such talismanic precision, such painstaking love, that they cannot be altered—that they constitute a reality of their own, and are not merely referential. It is one of the enigmas of our craft (so my writer friends agree) that, with the passage of time, *how* becomes an obsession,

---

°*Yeats*: William Butler Yeats (1865–1939), Irish poet and dramatist.

rather than *what*: It becomes increasingly more difficult to say the simplest things. Content yields to form, theme to "voice." But we don't know what voice is.

The story of the elusive sacred text has something to do with a childlike notion of   5
omnipotent thoughts, a wish for immortality through language, a command that time stand still. What is curious is that writing, the act of writing, often satisfies these demands. We throw ourselves into it with such absorption, writing eight or ten hours at a time, writing in our daydreams, composing in our sleep; we enter that fictional world so deeply that time seems to warp or to fold back in upon itself. Where do you find the time, people ask, to write so much? But the time I inhabit is protracted; my interior clock moves with frustrating slowness.

The melancholy secret at the heart of all creative activity (we are not talking here of quality, that ambiguous term) has something to do with our desire to complete a work and to perfect it—this very desire bringing with it our exclusion from that phase of our lives. Though a novel must be begun, often with extraordinary effort, it eventually acquires its own rhythm, its own voice, and begins to write itself; and when it is completed, the writer is expelled—the door closes slowly upon him or her, but it does close. A work of prose may be many things to many people, but to the author it is a monument to a certain chunk of time: so many pulsebeats, so much effort.

Joyce Carol Oates

"Where Are You Going, Where Have You Been?" and Smooth Talk: Short Story into Film

Some years ago in the American Southwest there surfaced a tabloid psychopath known as "The Pied Piper of Tucson." I have forgotten his name, but his specialty was the seduction and occasional murder of teen-aged girls. He may or may not have had actual accomplices, but his bizarre activities were known among a circle of teenagers in the Tucson area, for some reason they kept his secret, deliberately did not inform parents or police. It was this fact, not the fact of the mass murderer himself, that struck me at the time. And this was a pre-Manson time, early or mid-1960s.

The Pied Piper mimicked teenagers in talk, dress, and behavior, but he was not a teenager—he was a man in his early thirties. Rather short, he stuffed rags in his leather boots to give himself height. (And sometimes walked unsteadily as a consequence: did none among his admiring constituency notice?) He charmed his victims as charismatic psychopaths have always charmed their victims, to the bewilderment of others who fancy themselves free of all lunatic attractions. The Pied Piper of Tucson: a trashy dream, a tabloid archetype, sheer artifice, comedy, cartoon—surrounded, however improbably, and finally tragically, by real people. You think that, if you look twice, he won't be there. But there he is.

I don't remember any longer where I first read about this Pied Piper—very likely in *Life* Magazine. I do recall deliberately not reading the full article because I didn't want to be distracted by too much detail. It was not after all the mass murderer himself who intrigued me, but the disturbing fact that a number of teenagers—from "good" families—aided and abetted his crimes. This is the sort of thing authorities and responsible citizens invariably call "inexplicable" because they can't find explanations for it. They would not have fallen under this maniac's spell, after all.

An early draft of my short story "Where Are You Going, Where Have You Been?"— from which the film *Smooth Talk* was adapted by Joyce Chopra and Tom Cole—had the rather too explicit title "Death and the Maiden." It was cast in a mode of fiction to which I am still partial—indeed, every third or fourth story of mine is probably in this mode—"realistic allegory," it might be called. It is Hawthornean, romantic, shading into

1284

parable. Like the medieval German engraving from which my title was taken, the story was minutely detailed yet clearly an allegory of the fatal attractions of death (or the devil). An innocent young girl is seduced by way of her own vanity; she mistakes death for erotic romance of a particularly American/trashy sort.

In subsequent drafts the story changed its tone, its focus, its language, its title. It became "Where Are You Going, Where Have You Been?" Written at a time when the author was intrigued by the music of Bob Dylan, particularly the hauntingly elegiac song "It's All Over Now, Baby Blue," it was dedicated to Bob Dylan. The charismatic mass murderer drops into the background and his innocent victim, a fifteen-year-old, moves into the foreground. She becomes the true protagonist of the tale, courting and being courted by her fate, a self-styled 1950s pop figure, alternately absurd and winning. There is no suggestion in the published story that "Arnold Friend" has seduced and murdered other young girls, or even that he necessarily intends to murder Connie. Is his interest "merely" sexual? (Nor is there anything about the complicity of other teenagers. I saved that yet more provocative note for a current story, "Testimony.") Connie is shallow, vain, silly, hopeful, doomed—but capable nonetheless of an unexpected gesture of heroism at the story's end. Her smooth-talking seducer. who cannot lie, promises her that her family will be unharmed if she gives herself to him; and so she does. The story ends abruptly at the point of her "crossing over." We don't know the nature of her sacrifice, only that she is generous enough to make it.

In adapting a narrative so spare and thematically foreshortened as "Where Are You Going, Where Have You Been?" film director Joyce Chopra and screenwriter Tom Cole were required to do a good deal of filling in, expanding, inventing. Connie's story becomes lavishly, and lovingly, textured; she is not an allegorical figure so much as a "typical" teenaged girl (if Laura Dern, spectacularly good-looking, can be so defined). Joyce Chopra, who has done documentary films on contemporary teenage culture and, yet more authoritatively, has an adolescent daughter of her own, creates in *Smooth Talk* a vivid and absolutely believable world for Connie to inhabit. Or worlds: as in the original story there is Connie-at-home, and there is Connie-with-her-friends. Two fifteen-year-old girls, two finely honed styles, two voices, sometimes but not often overlapping. It is one of the marvelous visual features of the film that we see Connie and her friends transform themselves, once they are safely free of parental observation. The girls claim their true identities in the neighborhood shopping mall. What freedom, what joy!

Smooth Talk is, in a way, as much Connie's mother's story as it is Connie's; its center of gravity, its emotional nexus, is frequently with the mother—warmly and convincingly played by Mary Kay Place. (Though the mother's sexual jealousy of her daughter is slighted in the film.) Connie's ambiguous relationship with her affable, somewhat mysterious father (well played by Levon Helm) is an excellent touch: I had thought, subsequent to the story's publication, that I should have built up the father, suggesting, as subtly as I could, an attraction there paralleling the attraction Connie feels for her seducer, Arnold Friend. And Arnold Friend himself—"A. Friend" as he says—is played with appropriately overdone sexual swagger by Treat Williams, who is perfect for the part; and just the right age. We see that Arnold Friend isn't a teenager even as Connie, mesmerized by his presumed charm, does not seem to *see* him at all. What is so difficult to accomplish in prose—nudging the reader to look over the protagonist's shoulder, so to speak—is accomplished with enviable ease in film.

Treat Williams as Arnold Friend is supreme in his very awfulness, as, surely, the original Pied Piper of Tucson must have been. (Though no one involved in the film knew about the original source.) Mr. Williams flawlessly impersonates Arnold Friend as Arnold Friend impersonates—is it James Dean? James Dean regarding himself in mirrors, doing James Dean impersonations? That Connie's fate is so trashy is in fact her fate.

What is outstanding in Joyce Chopra's *Smooth Talk* is its visual freshness, its sense of motion and life; the attentive intelligence the director has brought to the semi-secret world of the American adolescent—shopping mall flirtations, drive-in restaurant romances, highway hitchhiking, the fascination of rock music played very, very loud. (James Taylor's music for the film is wonderfully appropriate. We hear it as Connie hears it; it is the music of her spiritual being.) Also outstanding, as I have indicated, and numerous critics have noted, are the acting performances. Laura Dern is so dazzlingly right as "my" Connie that I may come to think I modeled the fictitious girl on her, in the way that writers frequently delude themselves about motions of causality.

10   My difficulties with *Smooth Talk* have primarily to do with my chronic hesitation—about seeing/hearing work of mine abstracted from its contexture of language. All writers know that Language is their subject; quirky word choices, patterns of rhythm, enigmatic pauses, punctuation marks. Where the quick scanner sees "quick" writing, the writer conceals nine tenths of the iceberg. Of course we all have "real" subjects, and we will fight to the death to defend those subjects, but beneath the tale-telling it is the tale-telling that grips us so very fiercely. The writer works in a single dimension, the director works in three. I assume they are professionals to their fingertips; authorities in their medium as I am an authority (if I am) in mine. I would fiercely defend the placement of a semicolon in one of my novels but I would probably have deferred in the end to Joyce Chopra's decision to reverse the story's conclusion, turn it upside down, in a sense, so that the film ends not with death, not with a sleepwalker's crossing over to her fate, but upon a scene of reconciliation, rejuvenation.

A girl's loss of virginity, bittersweet but not necessarily tragic. Not today. A girl's coming-of-age that involves her succumbing to, but then rejecting, the "trashy dreams" of her pop teenage culture. "Where Are You Going, Where Have You Been?" defines itself as allegorical in its conclusion: Death and Death's chariot (a funky souped-up convertible) have come for the Maiden. Awakening is, in the story's final lines, moving out into the sunlight where Arnold Friend waits:

> "My sweet little blue-eyed girl," he said in a half-sung sigh that had nothing to do with [Connie's] brown eyes but was taken up just the same by the vast sunlit reaches of the land behind him and on all sides of him—so much land that Connie had never seen before and did not recognize except to know that she was going to it.

—a conclusion impossible to transfigure into film.

FLANNERY O'CONNOR

A Reasonable Use
of the Unreasonable

Last fall° I received a letter from a student who said she would be "graciously appreciative" if I would tell her "just what enlightenment" I expected her to get from each of my stories. I suspect she had a paper to write. I wrote her back to forget about the enlightenment and just try to enjoy them. I knew that was the most unsatisfactory answer I could have given because, of course, she didn't want to enjoy them, she just wanted to figure them out.

In most English classes the short story has become a kind of literary specimen to be dissected. Every time a story of mine appears in a Freshman anthology, I have a vision of it, with its little organs laid open, like a frog in a bottle.

I realize that a certain amount of this what-is-the-significance has to go on, but I think something has gone wrong in the process when, for so many students, the story becomes simply a problem to be solved, something which you evaporate to get Instant Enlightenment.

A story really isn't any good unless it successfully resists paraphrase, unless it hangs on and expands in the mind. Properly, you analyze to enjoy, but it's equally true that to analyze with any discrimination, you have to have enjoyed already, and I think that the best reason to hear a story read is that it should stimulate that primary enjoyment.

I don't have any pretensions to being an Aeschylus or Sophocles and providing you in this story with a cathartic experience out of your mythic background, though this story I'm going to read certainly calls up a good deal of the South's mythic background, and it should elicit from you a degree of pity and terror, even though its way of being serious is a comic one. I do think, though, that like the Greeks you should know what is going to happen in this story so that any element of suspense in it will be transferred from its surface to its interior. 5

I would be most happy if you had already read it, happier still if you knew it well, but since experience has taught me to keep my expectations along these lines modest,

---

°*Last fall:* In 1962.

I'll tell you that this is the story of a family of six which, on its way driving to Florida, gets wiped out by an escaped convict who calls himself the Misfit. The family is made up of the Grandmother and her son, Bailey, and his children, John Wesley and June Star and the baby, and there is also the cat and the children's mother. The cat is named Pitty Sing, and the Grandmother is taking him with them, hidden in a basket.

Now I think it behooves me to try to establish with you the basis on which reason operates in this story. Much of my fiction takes its character from a reasonable use of the unreasonable, though the reasonableness of my use of it may not always be apparent. The assumptions that underlie this use of it, however, are those of the central Christian mysteries. These are assumptions to which a large part of the modern audience takes exception. About this I can only say that there are perhaps other ways than my own in which this story could be read, but none other by which it could have been written. Belief, in my own case anyway, is the engine that makes perception operate.

The heroine of this story, the Grandmother, is in the most significant position life offers the Christian. She is facing death. And to all appearances she, like the rest of us, is not too well prepared for it. She would like to see the event postponed. Indefinitely.

I've talked to a number of teachers who use this story in class and who tell their students that the Grandmother is evil, that in fact, she's a witch, even down to the cat. One of these teachers told me that his students, and particularly his Southern students, resisted this interpretation with a certain bemused vigor, and he didn't understand why. I had to tell him that they resisted it because they all had grandmothers or great-aunts just like her at home, and they knew, from personal experience, that the old lady lacked comprehension, but that she had a good heart. The Southerner is usually tolerant of those weaknesses that proceed from innocence, and he knows that a taste for self-preservation can be readily combined with the missionary spirit.

10   This same teacher was telling his students that morally the Misfit was several cuts above the Grandmother. He had a really sentimental attachment to the Misfit. But then a prophet gone wrong is almost always more interesting than your grandmother, and you have to let people take their pleasures where they find them.

It is true that the old lady is a hypocritical old soul; her wits are no match for the Misfit's, nor is her capacity for grace equal to his; yet I think the unprejudiced reader will feel that the Grandmother has a special kind of triumph in this story which instinctively we do not allow to someone altogether bad.

I often ask myself what makes a story work, and what makes it hold up as a story, and I have decided that it is probably some action, some gesture of a character that is unlike any other in the story, one which indicates where the real heart of the story lies. This would have to be an action or a gesture which was both totally right and totally unexpected; it would have to be one that was both in character and beyond character; it would have to suggest both the world and eternity. The action or gesture I'm talking about would have to be on the anagogical level, that is, the level which has to do with the Divine life and our participation in it. It would be a gesture that transcended any neat allegory that might have been intended or any pat moral categories a reader could make. It would be a gesture which somehow made contact with mystery.

There is a point in this story where such a gesture occurs. The Grandmother is at last alone, facing the Misfit. Her head clears for an instant and she realizes, even in her limited way, that she is responsible for the man before her and joined to him by ties of kinship which have their roots deep in the mystery she has been merely prattling about so far. And at this point, she does the right thing, she makes the right gesture.

I find that students are often puzzled by what she says and does here, but I think myself that if I took out this gesture and what she says with it, I would have no story. What was left would not be worth your attention. Our age not only does not have a very sharp eye for the almost imperceptible intrusions of grace, it no longer has much feeling for the nature of the violences which precede and follow them. The devil's greatest wile, Baudelaire has said, is to convince us that he does not exist.

I suppose the reasons for the use of so much violence in modern fiction will differ with each writer who uses it, but in my own stories I have found that violence is strangely capable of returning my characters to reality and preparing them to accept their moment of grace. Their heads are so hard that almost nothing else will do the work. This idea, that reality is something to which we must be returned at considerable cost, is one which is seldom understood by the casual reader, but it is one which is implicit in the Christian view of the world.

I don't want to equate the Misfit with the devil. I prefer to think that, however unlikely this may seem, the old lady's gesture, like the mustard-seed, will grow to be a great crow-filled tree in the Misfit's heart, and will be enough of a pain to him there to turn him into the prophet he was meant to become. But that's another story.

This story has been called grotesque, but I prefer to call it literal. A good story is literal in the same sense that a child's drawing is literal. When a child draws, he doesn't intend to distort but to set down exactly what he sees, and as his gaze is direct, he sees the lines that create motion. Now the lines of motion that interest the writer are usually invisible. They are lines of spiritual motion. And in this story you should be on the lookout for such things as the action of grace in the Grandmother's soul, and not for the dead bodies.

We hear many complaints about the prevalence of violence in modern fiction, and it is always assumed that this violence is a bad thing and meant to be an end in itself. With the serious writer, violence is never an end in itself. It is the extreme situation that best reveals what we are essentially, and I believe these are times when writers are more interested in what we are essentially than in the tenor of our daily lives. Violence is a force which can be used for good or evil, and among other things taken by it is the kingdom of heaven. But regardless of what can be taken by it, the man in the violent situation reveals those qualities least dispensable in his personality, those qualities which are all he will have to take into eternity with him; and since the characters in this story are all on the verge of eternity, it is appropriate to think of what they take with them. In any case, I hope that if you consider these points in connection with the story, you will come to see it as something more than an account of a family murdered on the way to Florida.

FRANK O'CONNOR

The Legacy of Gogol's "Overcoat"

Yet, even from its beginnings, the short story has functioned in a quite different way from the novel, and, however difficult it may be to describe the difference, describing it is the critic's principal business.

"We all came out from under Gogol's 'Overcoat'" is a familiar saying of Turgenev, and though it applies to Russian rather than European fiction, it has also a general truth.

Read now, and by itself, "The Overcoat" does not appear so very impressive. All the things Gogol has done in it have been done frequently since his day, and sometimes done better. But if we read it again in its historical context, closing our minds so far as we can to all the short stories it gave rise to, we can see that Turgenev was not exaggerating. We have all come out from under Gogol's "Overcoat."

It is the story of a poor copying clerk, a nonentity mocked by his colleagues. His old overcoat has become so threadbare that even his drunken tailor refuses to patch it further since there is no longer any place in it where a patch would hold. Akakey Akakeivitch, the copying clerk, is terrified at the prospect of such unprecedented expenditure. As a result of a few minor fortunate circumstances, he finds himself able to buy a new coat, and for a day or two this makes a new man of him, for after all, in real life he is not much more than an overcoat.

5   Then he is robbed of it. He goes to the Chief of Police, a bribe-taker who gives him no satisfaction, and to an Important Personage who merely abuses and threatens him. Insult piled on injury is too much for him and he goes home and dies. The story ends with a whimsical description of his ghost's search for justice, which, once more, to a poor copying clerk has never meant much more than a warm overcoat.

There the story ends, and when one forgets all that came after it, like Chekhov's "Death of a Civil Servant," one realizes that it is like nothing in the world of literature before it. It uses the old rhetorical device of the mock-heroic, but uses it to create a new form that is neither satiric nor heroic, but something in between—something that perhaps finally transcends both. So far as I know, it is the first appearance in fiction of the Little Man, which may define what I mean by the short story better than any terms I may later use about it. Everything about Akakey Akakeivitch, from his absurd name to his absurd job, is on the same level of mediocrity, and yet his absurdity is somehow transfigured by Gogol.

1290

Only when the jokes were too unbearable, when they jolted his arm and prevented him from going on with his work, he would bring out: "Leave me alone! Why do you insult me?" and there was something strange in the words and in the voice in which they were uttered. There was a note in it of something that roused compassion, so that one young man, new to the office, who, following the example of the rest, had allowed himself to mock at him, suddenly stopped as though cut to the heart, and from that day forth, everything was as it were changed and appeared in a different light to him. Some unnatural force seemed to thrust him away from the companions with whom he had become acquainted, accepting them as well-bred, polished people. And long afterwards, at moments of the greatest gaiety, the figure of the humble little clerk with a bald patch on his head rose before him with his heart-rending words "Leave me alone! Why do you insult me?" and in those heart-rending words he heard others: "I am your brother." And the poor young man hid his face in his hands, and many times afterwards in his life he shuddered, seeing how much inhumanity there is in man, how much savage brutality lies hidden under refined, cultured politeness, and my God! even in a man whom the world accepts as a gentleman and a man of honour.

One has only to read that passage carefully to see that without it scores of stories by Turgenev, by Maupassant, by Chekhov, by Sherwood Anderson and James Joyce could never have been written. If one wanted an alternative description of what the short story means, one could hardly find better than that single half-sentence, "and from that day forth, everything was as it were changed and appeared in a different light to him." If one wanted an alternative title for this work, one might choose "I Am Your Brother." What Gogol has done so boldly and brilliantly is to take the mock-heroic character, the absurd little copying clerk, and imposed his image over that of the crucified Jesus, so that even while we laugh we are filled with horror at the resemblance.

Now, this is something that the novel cannot do. For some reason that I can only guess at, the novel is bound to be a process of identification between the reader and the character. One could not make a novel out of a copying clerk with a name like Akakey Akakeivitch who merely needed a new overcoat any more than one could make one out of a child called Tommy Tompkins whose penny had gone down a drain. One character at least in any novel must represent the reader in some aspect of his own conception of himself—as the Wild Boy, the Rebel, the Dreamer, the Misunderstood Idealist—and this process of identification invariably leads to some concept of normality and to some relationship—hostile or friendly—with society as a whole. People are abnormal insofar as they frustrate the efforts of such a character to exist in what he regards as a normal universe, normal insofar as they support him. There is not only the Hero, there is also the Semi-Hero and the Demi-Semi-Hero. I should almost go so far as to say that without the concept of a normal society the novel is impossible. I know there are examples of the novel that seem to contradict this, but in general I should say that it is perfectly true. The President of the Immortals is called in only when society has made a thorough mess of the job.

But in "The Overcoat" this is not true, nor is it true of most of the stories I shall have to consider. There is no character here with whom the reader can identify himself, unless it is that nameless horrified figure who represents the author. There is no form of society to which any character in it could possibly attach himself and regard

10

as normal. In discussions of the modern novel we have come to talk of it as the novel without a hero. In fact, the short story has never had a hero.

What it has instead is a submerged population group—a bad phrase which I have had to use for want of a better. That submerged population changes its character from writer to writer, from generation to generation. It may be Gogol's officials, Turgenev's serfs, Maupassant's prostitutes, Chekhov's doctors and teachers, Sherwood Anderson's provincials, always dreaming of escape.

Edgar Allan Poe

The Brief Prose Tale

The following excerpt is taken from Poe's famous review of Nathaniel Hawthorne's Twice-Told Tales, *published in* Graham's Magazine *in May 1842. Beginning at the fourth paragraph, Poe undertakes to define the short story as a literary genre. He was the first to formulate such a definition. Since Poe was both an author of short stories and a critic of them, readers may judge for themselves how closely his practice conforms to his theory.*

. . . But it is of [Hawthorne's] tales that we desire principally to speak. The tale proper, in our opinion, affords unquestionably the fairest field for the exercise of the loftiest talent, which can be afforded by the wide domains of mere prose. Were we bidden to say how the highest genius could be most advantageously employed for the best display of its own powers, we should answer, without hesitation—in the composition of a rhymed poem, not to exceed in length what might be perused in an hour. Within this limit alone can the highest order of true poetry exist. We need only here say, upon this topic, that, in almost all classes of composition, the unity of effect or impression is a point of the greatest importance. It is clear moreover, that this unity cannot be thoroughly preserved in productions whose perusal cannot be completed at one sitting. We may continue the reading of a prose composition, from the very nature of prose itself, much longer than we can persevere, to any good purpose, in the perusal of a poem. This latter, if truly fulfilling the demands of the poetic sentiment, induces an exaltation of the soul which cannot be long sustained. All high excitements are necessarily transient. Thus a long poem is a paradox. And, without unity of impression, the deepest effects cannot be brought about. Epics were the offspring of an imperfect sense of Art, and their reign is no more. A poem too brief may produce a vivid, but never an intense or enduring impression. Without a certain continuity of effort—without a certain duration or repetition of purpose—the soul is never deeply moved. There must be the dropping of the water upon the rock. De Béranger° has wrought brilliant things—pungent and spirit-stirring—but, like all immassive bodies, they lack *momentum,* and thus fail to satisfy the Poetic Sentiment. They sparkle and excite, but, from want of continuity, fail deeply to impress. Extreme brevity will degenerate into

---

°*De Béranger*: Pierre-Jean de Béranger (1780–1857), French political poet widely translated into English during the nineteenth century. Note the epigraph to "The Fall of the House of Usher."

epigrammatism; but the sin of extreme length is even more unpardonable. *In medio tutissimus ibis.*°

Were we called upon however to designate that class of composition which, next to such a poem as we have suggested, should best fulfil the demands of high genius—should offer it the most advantageous field of exertion—we should unhesitatingly speak of the prose tale, as Mr. Hawthorne has here exemplified it. We allude to the short prose narrative, requiring from a half-hour to one or two hours in its perusal. The ordinary novel is objectionable, from its length, for reasons already stated in substance. As it cannot be read at one sitting, it deprives itself, of course, of the immense force derivable from *totality*. Worldly interests intervening during the pauses of perusal, modify, annul, or counteract, in a greater or less degree, the impressions of the book. But simple cessation in reading would, of itself, be sufficient to destroy the true unity. In the brief tale, however, the author is enabled to carry out the fulness of his intention, be it what it may. During the hour of perusal the soul of the reader is at the writer's control. There are no external or extrinsic influences—resulting from weariness or interruption.

A skillful literary artist has constructed a tale. If wise, he has not fashioned his thoughts to accommodate his incidents; but having conceived, with deliberate care, a certain unique or single *effect* to be wrought out, he then invents such incidents—he then combines such events as may best aid him in establishing this preconceived effect. If his very initial sentence tend not to the outbringing of this effect, then he has failed in his first step. In the whole composition there should be no word written, of which the tendency, direct or indirect, is not to the one pre-established design. And by such means, with such care and skill, a picture is at length painted which leaves in the mind of him who contemplates it with a kindred art, a sense of the fullest satisfaction. The idea of the tale has been presented unblemished, because undisturbed; and this is an end unattainable by the novel. Undue brevity is just as exceptionable here as in the poem; but undue length is yet more to be avoided.

We have said that the tale has a point of superiority even over the poem. In fact, while the *rhythm* of this latter is an essential aid in the development of the poem's highest idea—the idea of the Beautiful—the artificialities of this rhythm are an inseparable bar to the development of all points of thought or expression which have their basis in *Truth*. But Truth is often, and in very great degree, the aim of the tale. Some of the finest tales are tales of ratiocination. Thus the field of this species of composition, if not in so elevated a region on the mountain of Mind, is a table-land of far vaster extent than the domain of the mere poem. Its products are never so rich, but infinitely more numerous, and more appreciable by the mass of mankind. The writer of the prose tale, in short, may bring to his theme a vast variety of modes or inflections of thought and expression—(the ratiocinative, for example, the sarcastic or the humorous) which are not only antagonistical to the nature of the poem, but absolutely forbidden by one of its most peculiar and indispensable adjuncts; we allude of course, to rhythm. It may be added, here *par parenthése*, that the author who aims at the purely beautiful in a prose tale is laboring at great disadvantage. For Beauty can be better treated in the poem. Not so with terror, or passion, or horror, or a multitude of such other points. And here it will be seen how full of prejudice are the usual animadversions against those *tales of effect* many fine examples of which were found in the earlier numbers of Blackwood.° The impressions produced were wrought in a legitimate

---

°*In medio . . .:* Latin, "You're safer in the middle ground."
°*Blackwood: Blackwood's Edinburgh Monthly Magazine*, founded in 1817, published much romantic fiction.

sphere of action, and constituted a legitimate although sometimes an exaggerated interest. They were relished by every man of genius: although there were found many men of genius who condemned them without just ground. The true critic will but demand that the design intended be accomplished, to the fullest extent, by the means most advantageously applicable.

We have very few American tales of real merit—we may say, indeed, none, with the exception of "The Tales of a Traveller" of Washington Irving, and these "Twice-Told Tales" of Mr. Hawthorne. Some of the pieces of Mr. John Neal° abound in vigor and originality; but in general, his compositions of this class are excessively diffuse, extravagant, and indicative of an imperfect sentiment of Art. Articles at random are, now and then, met with in our periodicals which might be advantageously compared with the best effusions of the British Magazines; but, upon the whole,'we are far behind our progenitors in this department of literature.

Of Mr. Hawthorne's Tales we would say, emphatically, that they belong to the highest region of Art—an Art subservient to genius of a very lofty order. We had supposed, with good reason for so supposing, that he had been thrust into his present position by one of the impudent *cliques* which beset our literature, and whose pretensions it is our full purpose to expose at the earliest opportunity; but we have been most agreeably mistaken. We know of few compositions which the critic can more honestly commend then these "Twice-Told Tales." As Americans, we feel proud of the book.

Mr. Hawthorne's distinctive trait is invention, creation, imagination, originality—a trait which, in the literature of fiction, is positively worth all the rest. But the nature of originality, so far as regards its manifestation in letter, is but imperfectly understood. The inventive or original mind as frequently displays itself in novelty of *tone* as in novelty of matter. Mr. Hawthorne is original at *all* points. . . .

°*John Neal*: American author (1793–1876) of melodramatic novels.

KATHERINE ANNE PORTER

The Writing of "Flowering Judas"

In 1917 Katherine Anne Porter, who was then twenty-seven years old, survived a serious attack of influenza and, intent on redirecting her life, left for Mexico, determined to become an artist. That trip led to some of her best work, including the story reprinted in this anthology, "Flowering Judas." In an interview in the magazine Paris Review, *Porter discussed the genesis of that story. In the excerpt printed here, she has just been asked by the interviewer if some particular event crystallized her dream to become an artist.*

PORTER: Yes, that was the plague of influenza, at the end of the First World War, in which I almost died. It just simply divided my life, cut across it like that. So that everything before that was just getting ready, and after that I was in some strange way altered, ready. It took me a long time to go out and live in the world again. I was really "alienated," in the pure sense. It was, I think, the fact that I really had participated in death, that I knew what death was, and had almost experienced it. I had what the Christians call the "beatific vision," and the Greeks called the "happy day," the happy vision just before death. Now if you have had that, and survived it, come back from it, you are no longer like other people, and there's no use deceiving yourself that you are. But you see, I did: I made the mistake of thinking I was quite like anybody else, of trying to live like other people. It took me a long time to realize that that simply wasn't true, that I had my own needs and that I had to live like me.

INTERVIEWER: And that freed you?

PORTER: I just got up and bolted. I went running off on that wild escapade to Mexico, where I attended, you might say, and assisted at, in my own modest way, a revolution.

INTERVIEWER: That was the Obregón Revolution of 1921?

5   PORTER: Yes—though actually I went to Mexico to study the Aztec and Mayan art designs. I had been in New York, and was getting ready to go to Europe. Now, New York was full of Mexican artists at that time, all talking about the renaissance, as they called it, in Mexico. And they said, "Don't go to Europe, go to Mexico. That's where the exciting things are going to happen." And they were right! I ran smack into the Obregón Revolution, and had, in the midst of it, the most marvelous, natural, spontaneous experience of my life. It was a terribly exciting time. It was alive, but death was in it. But nobody seemed to think of that: life was in it, too.

1296

INTERVIEWER: What do you think are the best conditions for a writer, then? Something like your Mexican experience, or—

PORTER: Oh, I can't say what they are. It would be such an individual matter. Everyone needs something different. . . . I went to Mexico because I felt I had business there. And there I found friends and ideas that were sympathetic to me. That was my entire milieu. I don't think anyone even knew I was a writer. I didn't show my work to anybody or talk about it, because—well, no one was particularly interested in that. It was a time of revolution, and I was running with almost pure revolutionaries!

INTERVIEWER: Has a story never surprised you in the writing? A character suddenly taken a different turn?

PORTER: Well, in the vision of death at the end of "Flowering Judas" I knew the real ending—that she was not going to be able to face her life, what she'd done. And I knew that the vengeful spirit was going to come in a dream to tow her away into death, but I didn't know until I'd written it that she was going to wake up saying, "No!" and be afraid to go to sleep again.

INTERVIEWER: That was, in a fairly literal sense, a "true" story, wasn't it?   10

PORTER: The truth is, I have never written a story in my life that didn't have a very firm foundation in actual human experience—somebody else's experience quite often, but an experience that became my own by hearing the story, by witnessing the thing, by hearing just a word perhaps. It doesn't matter, it just takes a little—tiny seed. Then it takes root, and it grows. It's an organic thing. That story had been on my mind for years, growing out of this one little thing that happened in Mexico. It was forming and forming in my mind, until one night I was quite desperate. People are always so sociable, and I'm sociable too, and if I live around friends. . . . Well, they were insisting that I come and play bridge. But I was very firm, because I knew the time had come to write that story, and I had to write it.

INTERVIEWER: What was that "little thing" from which the story grew?

PORTER: Something I saw as I passed a window one evening. A girl I knew had asked me to come and sit with her, because a man was coming to see her, and she was a little afraid of him. And as I went through the courtyard, past the flowering judas tree, I glanced in the window and there she was sitting with an open book on her lap, and there was this great big fat man sitting beside her. Now Mary and I were friends, both American girls living in this revolutionary situation. She was teaching at an Indian school, and I was teaching dancing at a girls' technical school in Mexico City. And we were having a very strange time of it. I was more skeptical, and so I had already begun to look with a skeptical eye on a great many of the revolutionary leaders. Oh, the idea was all right, but a lot of men were misapplying it.

And when I looked through that window that evening, I saw something in Mary's face, something in her pose, something in the whole situation, that set up a commotion in my mind. Because until that moment I hadn't really understood that she was not able to take care of herself, because she was not able to face her own nature and was afraid of everything. I don't know why I saw it. I don't believe in intuition. When you get sudden flashes of perception, it is just the brain working faster than usual. But you've been getting ready to know it for a long time, and when it comes, you feel you've known it always.

INTERVIEWER: You speak of a story "forming" in your mind. Does it begin as a visual impression, growing to a narrative? Or how?   15

PORTER: All my senses were very keen; things came to me through my eyes, through all my pores. Everything hit me at once, you know. That makes it very difficult to describe just exactly what is happening. And then, I think the mind works in such a variety of ways. Sometimes an idea starts completely inarticulately. You're not thinking in images or words or—well, it's exactly like a dark cloud moving in your head. You keep wondering what will come out of this, and then it will dissolve itself into a set of—well, not images exactly, but really thoughts. You begin to think directly in words. Abstractly. Then the words transform themselves into images. By the time I write the story my people are up and alive and walking around and taking things into their own hands. They exist as independently inside my head as you do before me now. I have been criticized for not enough detail in describing my characters, and not enough furniture in the house. And the odd thing is that I see it all so clearly.

INTERVIEWER: What about the technical problems a story presents—its formal structure? How deliberate are you in matters of technique? For example, the use of the historical present in "Flowering Judas"?

PORTER: The first time someone said to me, "Why did you write 'Flowering Judas' in the historical present?" I thought for a moment and said, "Did I?" I'd never noticed it. Because I didn't *plan* to write it any way. A story forms in my mind and forms and forms, and when it's ready to go, I strike it down—it takes just the time I sit at the typewriter. I never think about form at all. In fact, I would say that I've never been interested in anything about writing after having learned, I hope, to write. That is, I mastered my craft as well as I could.

Jean-Paul Sartre

FROM *For Whom Does One Write?*

I shall say that a writer is committed when he tries to achieve the most lucid and the most complete consciousness of being embarked, that is, when he causes the commitment of immediate spontaneity to advance, for himself and others, to the reflective. The writer is, *par excellence*, a mediator and his commitment is to mediation. But, if it is true that we must account for his work on the basis of his condition, it must also be borne in mind that his condition is not only that of a man in general but precisely that of a writer as well. Perhaps he is a Jew, and a Czech, and of peasant family, but he is a Jewish *writer*, a Czech *writer* and of rural stock. When, in another article, I tried to define the situation of the Jew, the best I could do was this: 'The Jew is a man whom other men consider as a Jew and who is obliged to choose himself on the basis of the situation which is made for him.' For there are qualities which come to us solely by means of the judgement of others. In the case of the writer, the case is more complex, for no one is obliged to choose himself as a writer. Hence, freedom is at the origin. I am an author, first of all, by my free intention to write. But at once it follows that I become a man whom other men consider as a writer, that is, who has to respond to a certain demand and who has been invested, whether he likes it or not, with a certain social function. Whatever game he may want to play, he must play it on the basis of the representation which others have of him. He may want to modify the character that one attributes to the man of letters in a given society; but in order to change it, he must first slip into it. Hence, the public intervenes, with its customs, its vision of the world, and its conception of society and of literature within that society. It surrounds the writer, it hems him in, and its imperious or sly demands, its refusals and its flights, are the given facts on whose basis a work can be constructed.

Let us take the case of the great negro writer, Richard Wright. If we consider only his condition as a *man*, that is, as a Southern 'nigger' transported to the North, we shall at once imagine that he can only write about Negroes or Whites *seen through the eyes of Negroes*. Can one imagine for a moment that he would agree to pass his life in the contemplation of the eternal True, Good, and Beautiful when ninety per cent of the negroes in the South are practically deprived of the right to vote? And if anyone speaks here about the treason of the clerks, I answer that there are no clerks among the oppressed. Clerks are necessarily the parasites of oppressing classes or races. Thus, if an American negro finds that he has a vocation as a writer, he discovers his subject at the same time. He is the man who sees the whites from the outside, who assimilates the white culture from the outside, and each of whose books will show the alienation of the black race within American society. Not objectively, like the realists, but passionately, and in a way that will compromise his reader. But this examination leaves the nature of his work undetermined; he might be a pamphleteer, a blues-writer, or the Jeremiah of the Southern negroes.

If we want to go further, we must consider his public. To whom does Richard Wright address himself? Certainly not to the universal man. The essential characteristic of the notion of the universal man is that he is not involved in any particular age, and that he is no more and no less moved by the lot of the negroes of Louisiana than by that of the Roman slaves in the time of Spartacus. The universal man can think of nothing but universal values. He is a pure and abstract affirmation of the inalienable right of man. But neither can Wright think of intending his books for the white racialists of Virginia or South Carolina whose minds are made up in advance and who will not open them. Nor to the black peasants of the bayous who cannot read. And if he seems to be happy about the reception his books have had in Europe, still it is obvious that at the beginning he had not the slightest idea of writing for the European public. Europe is far away. Its indignation is ineffectual and hypocritical. Not much is to be expected from the nations which have enslaved the Indies, IndoChina, and negro Africa. These considerations are enough to define his readers. He is addressing himself to the cultivated negroes of the North and the white Americans of goodwill (intellectuals, democrats of the left, radicals, C.I.O. workers).

It is not that he is not aiming through them at all men but it is *through them* that he is thus aiming. Just as one can catch a glimpse of eternal freedom at the horizon of the historical and concrete freedom which it pursues, so the human race is at the horizon of the concrete and historical group of its readers. The illiterate negro peasants and the Southern planters represent a margin of abstract possibilities around its real public. After all, an illiterate may learn to read. *Black Boy* may fall into the hands of the most stubborn of negrophobes and may open his eyes. This merely means that every human project exceeds its actual limits and extends itself step by step to the infinite.

5   Now, it is to be noted that there is a fracture at the very heart of this *actual public*. For Wright, the negro readers represent the subjective. The same childhood, the same difficulties, the same complexes: a mere hint is enough for them; they understand with their hearts. In trying to become clear about his own personal situation, he clarifies theirs for them. He mediates, names, and shows them the life they lead from day to day in its immediacy, the life they suffer without finding words to formulate their sufferings. He is their conscience, and the movement by which he raises himself from the immediate to the reflective recapturing of his condition is that of his whole race. But whatever the goodwill of the white readers may be, for a negro author they represent the *Other*. They have not lived through what he has lived through. They can understand the negro's condition only by an extreme stretch of the imagination and by relying upon analogies which at any moment may deceive them. On the other hand, Wright does not completely know them. It is only from without that he conceives their proud security and that tranquil certainty, common to all white Aryans, that the world is white and that they own it. The words he puts down on paper have not the same context for whites as for negroes. They must be chosen by guesswork, since he does not know what resonances they will set up in those strange minds. And when he speaks to them, their very aim is changed. It is a matter of implicating them and making them take stock of their responsibilities. He must make them indignant and ashamed.

Thus, each of Wright's works contains what Baudelaire would have called 'a double simultaneous postulation'; each word refers to two contexts; two forces are applied simultaneously to each phrase and determine the incomparable tension of his tale. Had he spoken to the whites alone, he might have turned out to be more prolix, more didactic, and more abusive; to the negroes alone, still more elliptical, more of a confederate, and more elegiac. In the first case, his work might have come close to satire; in the second, to prophetic lamentations. Jeremiah spoke only to the Jews. But Wright, a writer for a split public, has been able both to maintain and go beyond this split. He has made it the pretext for a work of art.

Leslie Marmon Silko

Through the Stories
We Hear Who We Are

All summer the people watch the west horizon, scanning the sky from south to north for rain clouds. Corn must have moisture at the time the tassels form. Otherwise pollination will be incomplete, and the ears will be stunted and shriveled. An inadequate harvest may bring disaster. Stories told at Hopi, Zuni, and at Acoma and Laguna describe drought and starvation as recently as 1900. Precipitation in west-central New Mexico averages fourteen inches annually. The western pueblos are located at altitudes over 5,600 feet above sea level, where winter temperatures at night fall below freezing. Yet evidence of their presence in the high desert plateau country goes back ten thousand years. The ancient Pueblo people not only survived in this environment, but many years they thrived. In A.D. 1100 the people at Chaco Canyon had built cities with apartment buildings of stone five stories high. Their sophistication as sky-watchers was surpassed only by Mayan and Inca astronomers. Yet this vast complex of knowledge and belief, amassed for thousands of years, was never recorded in writing.

Instead, the ancient Pueblo people depended upon collective memory through successive generations to maintain and transmit an entire culture, a world view complete with proven strategies for survival. The oral narrative, or "story," became the medium in which the complex of Pueblo knowledge and belief was maintained. Whatever the event or the subject, the ancient people perceived the world and themselves within that world as part of an ancient continuous story composed of innumerable bundles of other stories.

The ancient Pueblo vision of the world was inclusive. The impulse was to leave nothing out. Pueblo oral tradition necessarily embraced all levels of human experience. Otherwise, the collective knowledge and beliefs comprising ancient Pueblo culture would have been incomplete. Thus stories about the Creation and Emergence of human beings and animals into this World continue to be retold each year for four days and four nights during the winter solstice. The "humma-hah" stories related events from the time long ago when human beings were still able to communicate with animals and other living things. But, beyond these two preceding categories, the Pueblo oral tradition knew no boundaries. Accounts of the appearance of the first Europeans in Pueblo country or of the tragic encounters between Pueblo people and

Apache raiders were no more and no less important than stories about the biggest mule deer ever taken or adulterous couples surprised in cornfields and chicken coops. Whatever happened, the ancient people instinctively sorted events and details into a loose narrative structure. Everything became a story.

Traditionally everyone, from the youngest child to the oldest person, was expected to listen and to be able to recall or tell a portion, if only a small detail, from a narrative account or story. Thus the remembering and retelling were a communal process. Even if a key figure, an elder who knew much more than others, were to die unexpectedly, the system would remain intact. Through the efforts of a great many people, the community was able to piece together valuable accounts and crucial information that might otherwise have died with an individual.

Communal storytelling was a self-correcting process in which listeners were encouraged to speak up if they noted an important fact or detail omitted. The people were happy to listen to two or three different versions of the same event or the same humma-hah story. Even conflicting versions of an incident were welcomed for the entertainment they provided. Defenders of each version might joke and tease one another, but seldom were there any direct confrontations. Implicit in the Pueblo oral tradition was the awareness that loyalties, grudges, and kinship must always influence the narrator's choices as she emphasizes to listeners this is the way *she* has always heard the story told. The ancient Pueblo people sought a communal truth, not an absolute. For them this truth lived somewhere within the web of differing versions, disputes over minor points, outright contradictions tangling with old feuds and village rivalries. 5

A dinner-table conversation, recalling a deer hunt forty years ago when the largest mule deer ever was taken, inevitably stimulates similar memories in listeners. But hunting stories were not merely after-dinner entertainment. These accounts contained information of critical importance about behavior and migration patterns of mule deer. Hunting stories carefully described key landmarks and locations of fresh water. Thus a deer-hunt story might also serve as a "map." Lost travelers, and lost piñon-nut gatherers, have been saved by sighting a rock formation they recognize only because they once heard a hunting story describing this rock formation.

The importance of cliff formations and water holes does not end with hunting stories. As offspring of the Mother Earth, the ancient Pueblo people could not conceive of themselves without a specific landscape. Location, or "place," nearly always plays a central role in the Pueblo oral narratives. Indeed, stories are most frequently recalled as people are passing by a specific geographical feature or the exact place where a story takes place. The precise date of the incident often is less important than the place or location of the happening. "Long, long ago," "a long time ago," "not too long ago," and "recently" are usually how stories are classified in terms of time. But the places where the stories occur are precisely located, and prominent geographical details recalled, even if the landscape is well-known to listeners. Often because the turning point in the narrative involved a peculiarity or special quality of a rock or tree or plant found only at that place. Thus, in the case of many of the Pueblo narratives, it is impossible to determine which came first: the incident or the geographical feature which begs to be brought alive in a story that features some unusual aspect of this location.

There is a giant sandstone boulder about a mile north of Old Laguna, on the road to Paguate. It is ten feet tall and twenty feet in circumference. When I was a child, and we would pass this boulder driving to Paguate village, someone usually made reference to the story about Kochininako, Yellow Woman, and the Estrucuyo, a monstrous giant who nearly ate her. The Twin Hero Brothers saved Kochininako, who had been out hunting rabbits to take home to feed her mother and sisters. The Hero Brothers had heard her cries just in time. The Estrucuyo had cornered her in a cave too small to fit its monstrous head. Kochininako had already thrown to the Estrucuyo all her rabbits, as well as her moccasins and most of her clothing. Still the creature had not been satisfied. After killing the Estrucuyo with their bows and arrows, the Twin Hero Brothers slit open the Estrucuyo and cut out its heart. They threw the heart as far as they could. The monster's heart landed there, beside the old trail to Paguate village, where the sandstone boulder rests now.

It may be argued that the existence of the boulder precipitated the creation of a story to explain it. But sandstone boulders and sandstone formations of strange shapes abound in the Laguna Pueblo area. Yet most of them do not have stories. Often the crucial element in a narrative is the terrain—some specific detail of the setting.

10   A high dark mesa rises dramatically from a grassy plain fifteen miles southeast of Laguna, in an area known as Swanee. On the grassy plain one hundred and forty years ago, my great-grandmother's uncle and his brother-in-law were grazing their herd of sheep. Because visibility on the plain extends for over twenty miles, it wasn't until the two sheepherders came near the high dark mesa that the Apaches were able to stalk them. Using the mesa to obscure their approach, the raiders swept around from both ends of the mesa. My great-grandmother's relatives were killed, and the herd lost. The high dark mesa played a critical role: the mesa had compromised the safety which the openness of the plains had seemed to assure. Pueblo and Apache alike relied upon the terrain, the very earth herself, to give them protection and aid. Human activities or needs were maneuvered to fit the existing surroundings and conditions. I imagine the last afternoon of my distant ancestors as warm and sunny for late September. They might have been traveling slowly, bringing the sheep closer to Laguna in preparation for the approach of colder weather. The grass was tall and only beginning to change from green to a yellow which matched the late-afternoon sun shining off it. There might have been comfort in the warmth and the sight of the sheep fattening on good pasture which lulled my ancestors into their fatal inattention. They might have had a rifle whereas the Apaches had only bows and arrows. But there would have been four or five Apache raiders, and the surprise attack would have canceled any advantage the rifles gave them.

Survival in any landscape comes down to making the best use of all available resources. On that particular September afternoon, the raiders made better use of the Swanee terrain than my poor ancestors did. Thus the high dark mesa and the story of the two lost Laguna herders became inextricably linked. The memory of them and their story resides in part with the high black mesa. For as long as the mesa stands, people within the family and clan will be reminded of the story of that afternoon long ago. Thus the continuity and accuracy of the oral narratives are reinforced by the landscape—and the Pueblo interpretation of that landscape is *maintained.*

SUSAN SONTAG

FROM *Against Interpretation*

Content is a glimpse of something, an encounter like a flash. It's very tiny—very tiny, content.

Willem de Kooning, *in an interview*

It is only shallow people who do not judge by appearances. The mystery of the world is the visible, not the invisible.

Oscar Wilde, *in a letter*

The earliest *experience* of art must have been that it was incantatory, magical; art was an instrument of ritual. (Cf. the paintings in the caves at Lascaux, Altamira, Niaux, La Pasiega, etc.) The earliest *theory* of art, that of the Greek philosophers, proposed that art was mimesis, imitation of reality.

It is at this point that the peculiar question of the *value* of art arose. For the mimetic theory, by its very terms, challenges art to justify itself.

Plato, who proposed the theory, seems to have done so in order to rule that the value of art is dubious. Since he considered ordinary material things as themselves mimetic objects, imitations of transcendent forms or structures, even the best painting of a bed would be only an "imitation of an imitation." For Plato, art is neither particularly useful (the painting of a bed is no good to sleep on), nor, in the strict sense, true. And Aristotle's arguments in defense of art do not really challenge Plato's view that all art is an elaborate *trompe l'oeil,* and therefore a lie. But he does dispute Plato's idea that art is useless. Lie or no, art has a certain value according to Aristotle because it is a form of therapy. Art is useful, after all, Aristotle counters, medicinally useful in that it arouses and purges dangerous emotions.

In Plato and Aristotle, the mimetic theory of art goes hand in hand with the assumption that art is always figurative. But advocates of the mimetic theory need not close their eyes to decorative and abstract art. The fallacy that art is necessarily a "realism" can be modified or scrapped without ever moving outside the problems delimited by the mimetic theory.

The fact is, all Western consciousness of and reflection upon art have remained within the confines staked out by the Greek theory of art as mimesis or representation. It is through this theory that art as such—above and beyond given works of

5

1305

art—becomes problematic, in need of defense. And it is the defense of art which gives birth to the odd vision by which something we have learned to call "form" is separated off from something we have learned to call "content," and to the well-intentioned move which makes content essential and form accessory.

Even in modern times, when most artists and critics have discarded the theory of art as representation of an outer reality in favor of the theory of art as subjective expression, the main feature of the mimetic theory persists. Whether we conceive of the work of art on the model of a picture (art as a picture of reality) or on the model of a statement (art as the statement of the artist), content still comes first. The content may have changed. It may now be less figurative, less lucidly realistic. But it is still assumed that a work of art *is* its content. Or, as it's usually put today, that a work of art by definition says something. ("What X is saying is . . .," "What X is trying to say is . . .," "What X said is . . ." etc., etc.)

2

None of us can ever retrieve that innocence before all theory when art knew no need to justify itself, when one did not ask of a work of art what it *said* because one knew (or thought one knew) what it *did*. From now to the end of consciousness, we are stuck with the task of defending art. We can only quarrel with one or another means of defense. Indeed, we have an obligation to overthrow any means of defending and justifying art which becomes particularly obtuse or onerous or insensitive to contemporary needs and practice.

This is the case, today, with the very idea of content itself. Whatever it may have been in the past, the idea of content is today mainly a hindrance, a nuisance, a subtle or not so subtle philistinism.

Though the actual developments in many arts may seem to be leading us away from the idea that a work of art is primarily its content, the idea still exerts an extraordinary hegemony. I want to suggest that this is because the idea is now perpetuated in the guise of a certain way of encountering works of art thoroughly ingrained among most people who take any of the arts seriously. What the overemphasis on the idea of content entails is the perennial, never consummated project of *interpretation*. And, conversely, it is the habit of approaching works of art in order to *interpret* them that sustains the fancy that there really is such a thing as the content of a work of art.

5

10　　In most modern instances, interpretation amounts to the philistine refusal to leave the work of art alone. Real art has the capacity to make us nervous. By reducing the work of art to its content and then interpreting *that*, one tames the work of art. Interpretation makes art manageable, conformable.

This philistinism of interpretation is more rife in literature than in any other art. For decades now, literary critics have understood it to be their task to translate the elements of the poem or play or novel or story into something else. Sometimes a writer will be so uneasy before the naked power of his art that he will install within the work itself—albeit with a little shyness, a touch of the good taste of irony—the clear and explicit interpretation of it. Thomas Mann is an example of such an overcooperative author. In the case of more stubborn authors, the critic is only too happy to perform the job.

The work of Kafka, for example, has been subjected to a mass ravishment by no less than three armies of interpreters. Those who read Kafka as a social allegory see case studies of the frustrations and insanity of modern bureaucracy and its ultimate issuance in the totalitarian state. Those who read Kafka as a psychoanalytic allegory see desperate revelations of Kafka's fear of his father, his castration anxieties, his sense of his own impotence, his thralldom to his dreams. Those who read Kafka as a religious allegory explain that K. in *The Castle* is trying to gain access to heaven, that Joseph K. in *The Trial* is being judged by the inexorable and mysterious justice of God. . . . Another *oeuvre* that has attracted interpreters like leeches is that of Samuel Beckett. Beckett's delicate dramas of the withdrawn consciousness—pared down to essentials, cut off, often represented as physically immobilized—are read as a statement about modern man's alienation from meaning or from God, or as an allegory of psychopathology.

Proust, Joyce, Faulkner, Rilke, Lawrence, Gide . . . one could go on citing author after author; the list is endless of those around whom thick encrustations of interpretation have taken hold. But it should be noted that interpretation is not simply the compliment that mediocrity pays to genius. It is, indeed, *the* modern way of understanding something, and is applied to works of every quality. Thus, in the notes that Elia Kazan published on his production of *A Streetcar Named Desire,* it becomes clear that, in order to direct the play, Kazan had to discover that Stanley Kowalski represented the sensual and vengeful barbarism that was engulfing our culture, while Blanche Du Bois was Western civilization, poetry, delicate apparel, dim lighting, refined feelings and all, though a little the worse for wear to be sure. Tennessee Williams' forceful psychological melodrama now became intelligible: it was *about* something, about the decline of Western civilization. Apparently, were it to go on being a play about a handsome brute named Stanley Kowalski and a faded mangy belle named Blanche Du Bois, it would not be manageable.

ALICE WALKER

Interview with Eudora Welty

Alice Walker interviewed Eudora Welty in the summer of 1973, nearly nine years before The Color Purple *was published. Welty's short fiction had made her a legend; Walker's voice was largely unknown. The interview took place in Welty's home in Jackson, Mississippi.*

How many books have you written?

Well, I believe I've written eleven, counting the collections of short stories.

Do you write mostly short stories? Novels? Which do you like to write best?

I think I'm more of a natural short story writer. I've written many more short stories. In fact, the novels I've written usually began as short stories. And I then realized they were developing beyond the bounds of a story . . .

5   *Do you feel that all short stories are potential novels?*

No, they are two different things. I think that one of my faults as a novelist is that I don't think as a novelist does. I think the short story is a sustained thing, all in one piece, and compact. You don't have any of the expansion and scope that the novel can have. So any time I've made the mistake of writing a short story that became a novel I've had to go back and start at the beginning again. It's like starting for the long jump or the short hop. You don't have the same impulse.

Do you ever write poems?

No.

Never? Not any? Not even one or two?

10 Oh, maybe one. I don't think I count as a poet. I think poetry takes a very special gift. I do think the lyric impulse, which is in poetry, is also in the short story. I mean I can see the affinity, but I've never been led to try the other form.

Do you like any poets?

Oh yes, I do. I'm not too up on the new ones, although I've read a good many of the new ones. But I mostly turn to poets I've liked all my life, such as Yeats, John Donne . . . I tend to go back to them, no matter what else I read.

How long did you live in New York City, and when was that?

Well, I went to school there for a year, at Columbia, which was the longest I've ever been there. And I have gone up and stayed many times for several weeks. Then one summer I worked on the *New York Times Book Review* for about three months; that was the longest time I've been there since I began working for my living.

You know Langston Hughes spent a year at Columbia too, in the twenties; one year. He hated 15
it. He said the teachers were dull and the buildings looked like factories. Did you like it?

Oh, I enjoyed it. What I really went for was to learn my way around New York. I was taking a business course which took up almost no time and so I could go to the theatre every night!

A business course! I don't understand. Why did you take a business course?

Well, I'm glad I did. My father, when he learned I wanted to be a writer, very wisely said that I could never hope to earn a living at it, which turned out to be absolutely true. He said I should learn a business or profession that would keep me going. When I came home during the Depression I got a job at the radio broadcasting station and I also worked for the WPA.

And you took the pictures you collected in One Time, One Place *while working for the WPA?*

Yes. My father died that same year. I was thankful to get a job. Of course I was writ- 20
ing, at the same time. But although my stories from the first were given an encouraging welcome in college quarterlies and the so-called "little" magazines, they took six years of trying to find a place in a magazine of national circulation. It wasn't until the *Atlantic* took two and published them that the charm was broken. After that, some of the same stories that had been rejected by magazines before were accepted by those same magazines. Over all, I've always been lucky in publishing—in the people I've worked with. I mean, especially.

What did your parents think about you going to New York?

They knew it was what I wanted to do. They'd always believed in the value of gaining new experience. They were extraordinarily sympathetic parents both of them.

Did you think there was anything wrong with Mississippi [in terms of race] in those days,
when you were young? Did you see a way in which things might change?

Well, I could tell when things were wrong with *people,* and when things happened to individual people, people that we knew or knew of, they were very real to me. It was the same with my parents. I felt their sympathy, I guess it guided mine, when they responded to these things in the same way. And I think this is the way real sympathy *has* to start—from direct feeling for something present and known. People are first and last individuals, and I don't think of them in the mass when I feel for them most.

How does living in Jackson affect your writing? 25

It's where I live and look around me—it's my piece of the world—it teaches me. Also as a domestic scene it's completely familiar and self-explanatory. It's not everything, though—it's just a piece of everything, that happens to be my sample. It lets me alone to work as I like. It's full of old friends with whom I'm happy to be. And I'm not stuck, either, not compelled to stay here—I'm free to leave when I feel like it, which makes me love it more, I suppose.

What do your friends think of your writing? Do they read it? Do any of them ever creep into your fiction?

Oh yes. They do read it. But they don't creep in. I never write about people that I know. I don't want to, and couldn't if I did want to. I work entirely in terms of the imagination— using, of course, bits and pieces of the real world along with the rest.

Do you write every day?

30   No, I don't write every day—I write only when I'm in actual work on a particular story. I'm not a notebook keeper. Sustained time is what I fight for, would probably sell my soul for—it's so hard to manage that. I'd like to write a story from beginning to end right through without having to stop. Where I write is upstairs in my bedroom.

In bed?

Oh no, I write at a desk. I have a long room with six big windows in it, and a desk and typewriter at one end.

What does it overlook? A garden? Trees?

It overlooks the street. I like to be aware of the world going on while I'm working. I think I'd get claustrophobic sitting in front of a blank wall with life cut off from view.

35   *Do you have a "Philosophy of Life"? Some pithy saying that you quote to yourself when you seem inundated with troubles?*

No. I have work in place of it, I suppose. My "philosophy" is like the rest of my thinking— it comes out best in the translation of fiction. I put what I think about people and their acts in my stories. Of course back of it all there would have to be honesty.

Many modern writers don't seem overly concerned with it.

It's noticeable. Truth doesn't seem to be the thing they're getting at, a good deal of the time.

In fact, much popular poetry, some of it black, engages in clever half-truths, designed to shock only. Or to entertain.

40   Some of the black poets I've read I have not been able to understand. It hasn't so far as I know anything to do with race. I don't quite understand the virtue of the idiom they strain so over, the language—I don't see the good of it. I feel *tactics* are being used on me, the reader—not the easiest way to persuade *this* reader. It's hard to see the pas- sion behind it.

Oh, I understand the idiom and the language; I can see the passion behind it and admire the rage. My question is whether witty half-truths are good for us in the long run, after we've stopped laughing. And whether poetry shouldn't stick to more difficult if less funny ground, the truth.

That's its real business. I don't believe any writing that has falsity in it can endure for very long. Its end will take care of itself.

Let's hope. What are your thoughts on the Women's Movement?

Well, equal pay for equal work, and so on, fine. But some of the other stuff is hilarious.

45   *Hilarious? Oh, you mean "the lunatic fringe," the flamboyant stances used to attract attention.*

Some of the effervescences. Of course, I haven't any bones to pick, myself. A writer never has the problem to face. Being a woman has never kept me from writing or from finding publication for my work.

That's interesting. In the course I teach on black women writers I find that in critical stud-ies black women writers are always given scant attention and sometimes none. They may have published with ease, as Zora Hurston did, but later they were forgotten. Until quite recent-ly, of course. Of course to many women your life would seem ideal, you have your work, which is substantial, both in what it gives you and what it gives others. You have a house of your own—a lovely one—and all the freedom you want. You are rare, a successful writer who is a woman!

Well, I do have freedom. The successful part is not so much to the point. I think that any artist has it over other people.

Well, some women artists feel that when they marry they must share too much of their time with their husbands and children. They feel they lose single-mindedness, energy they need to put into their own work.

That of course I couldn't say—about husbands and children, I mean. But my ten-dency is to believe that all experience is an enrichment instead of an impoverish-ment. My own relationships with people are the things that mean the most to me. I couldn't say what marriage and childbearing would do, of course.

But have you regretted not having been married and not having children?

Oh, I would have been glad if it had come along. Yes I would have. Of course. It wasn't a matter of choosing one thing in place of the other. I think the more things the better.

Over the years have you known any black women? Really known them?

I think I have. Better in Jackson than anywhere, though only, as you'd expect, with-in the framework of the home. That's the only way I'd have had a chance, in the Jackson up until now. Which doesn't take away from the reality of the knowledge, or its depth of affection—on the contrary. A schoolteacher who helped me on week-ends to nurse my mother through a long illness—she was beyond a nurse, she was a friend and still is, we keep in regular touch. A very bright young woman, who's now in a very different field of work, began in her teens as a maid in our house. She was with us for ten years or more. Then she went on to better things—her story is a very fine one. She's a friend, and we are in regular touch too. Of course I've met black people professionally, in my experience along the fringes of teaching. Lectur-ing introduced us. The first college anywhere, by the way, that ever invited me to speak was Jackson State—years ago. I read them a story in chapel, as I remember. Now I don't count meeting people at cocktail parties in New York—black or any other kind—to answer the rest of your question. But I do know at least a few black people that mean a good deal to me, and I think they like me too.

Have any of them ever crept into your fiction?

No. As I said before, I never write about real people. You know, human beings are incapable of being made into characters, as is. They are so much more fluid, and so opaque in places where they need to be transparent and so transparent in places where they need to be opaque. But I think that what I put into a short story in the form of characters might be called certain *qualities* of people in certain situations—no, pin it down more—some quality that makes them unique. I try to dramatize something like this in a way that can show it better than life shows it. Better picked out.

Has it ever been assumed that because you were born and raised in Mississippi your black characters would necessarily suffer from a racist perspective?

I hardly see how anyone could claim that. Indeed to my knowledge no one ever has. I see all my characters as individuals, not as colors, but as people, alive—unique.

Have you ever been called a Gothic Writer?

60 They better not call me that!

No?

Yes, I have been, though. Inevitably, because I'm a Southerner. I've never had anybody call me that to my face. I've read that I'm Gothic, or I get asked by students to explain why I am.

Why do they try to put all Southern writers in that mold?

I don't know. It's just easy.

65 *I was never even sure of what it meant, exactly.*

I'm not sure either. When I hear the word I see in my mind a Gustave Dore illustration for "The Fall of the House of Usher." Anyway it sounds as if it has nothing to do with real life, and I feel that my work has something to do with real life. At least I hope it has.

ALICE WALKER

The Old Artist: Notes on Mr. Sweet

There was in my rural, farming, middle-Georgia childhood, in the late 40s and early 50s, an old guitar player called Mr. Sweet. If people had used his family name, he would have been called Mr. Little; obviously nobody agreed that this was accurate. Sweet was. The only distinct memory I have is of him playing his guitar while sitting in an ancient, homemade (by my grandfather) oak-bottomed chair in my grandmother's cozy kitchen while she baked biscuits and a smothered chicken. He called the guitar his "box." I must have been eight or nine at the time.

He was an extremely soulful player and singer, and his position there by the warm stove in the good-smelling kitchen, "picking his box" and singing his own blues, while we sat around him silent and entranced, seemed inevitable and right. Although this is the only memory I have, and it is hazy, I know that Mr. Sweet was a fixture, a rare and honored presence in our family, and we were taught to respect him—no matter that he drank, loved to gamble and shoot off his gun, and went "crazy" several times a year. He was an artist. He went deep into his own pain and brought out words and music that made us happy, made us feel empathy for anyone in trouble, made us think. We were taught to be thankful that anyone would assume this risk. That he was offered the platter of chicken and biscuits first (as if he were the preacher and even if he was tipsy) seemed only just.

Mr. Sweet died in the 60s, while I was a student at Sarah Lawrence College in Westchester, in an environment so different from the one in which he and my parents lived, and in which I had been brought up, that it might have existed on another planet. There were only three or four other black people there, and no poor people at all as far as the eye could see. For reasons not perhaps unrelated to this discrepancy, I was thinking of dying myself at the very time I got the news of his death. But something of my memory of Mr. Sweet stopped me: I remembered the magnitude of his problems—problems I was just beginning to truly understand—as a black man and as an artist, growing up poor, forced to endure the racist terrorism of the American South. He was unlucky in love, and no prince as a parent. *Irregardless,* as the old people said, and Mr. Sweet himself liked to say, not only had he lived to a ripe old age (I don't doubt that killing himself never entered his head, however, since I think alcoholism was, in his case, a slow method of suicide), but he had continued to share all his troubles and his insights with anyone who would listen, taking special care to craft them for the necessary effect. *He continued to sing.*

This was obviously my legacy, as someone who also wanted to be an artist and who was not only black and poor, but a woman besides, if only I had the guts to accept it.

5   Turning my back on the razor blade, I went to a friend's house for the Christmas holidays (I was too poor even to consider making the trip home, a distance of about a thousand miles), and on the day of Mr. Sweet's burial I wrote "To Hell With Dying." If in my poverty I had no other freedom—not even to say goodbye to him in death— I still had the freedom to love him and the means to express it, if only to myself. I wrote the story with tears pouring down my cheeks. I was grief-stricken, I was crazed, I was fighting for my own life. I was twenty-one.

It was the first short story I ever published, though it was not the first one I wrote. The first one I wrote, before my memory of Mr. Sweet saved me, was entitled "The Suicide of an American Girl."

The poet Muriel Rukeyser was my don (primary teacher) and friend at Sarah Lawrence. So was Jane Cooper, in whose writing course I wrote the story. Between them they warmly affirmed the life of Mr. Sweet and the vitality of my art, which, I was beginning to see, merged in unexpected ways, very healing and effective ways, with my life. I was still hanging by a thread, so their enthusiasm was important. Without my knowledge, Muriel sent the story to the greatest of the old black singer poets, Langston Hughes, who was able to publish it two years after he read it.

When I met Langston Hughes I was amazed. He was another Mr. Sweet! Aging and battered, full of pain, but writing poetry, and laughing, too, and always making other people feel better. It was as if my love for one great old man down in the poor and beautiful and simple South had magically, in the new world of college and literature and poets and publishing and New York, led me to another.

DAVID FOSTER WALLACE

Act Natural

Fiction writers as a species tend to be oglers. They tend to lurk and to stare. They are born watchers. They are viewers. They are the ones on the subway about whose nonchalant stare there is something creepy, somehow. Almost predatory. This is because human situations are writers' food. Fiction writers watch other humans sort of the way gapers slow down for car wrecks: they covet a vision of themselves as *witnesses*.

But fiction writers tend at the same time to be terribly self-conscious. Devoting lots of productive time to studying closely how people come across to them, fiction writers also spend lots of less productive time wondering nervously how they come across to other people. How they appear, how they seem, whether their shirttail might be hanging out of their fly, whether there's maybe lipstick on their teeth, whether the people they're ogling can maybe size them up as somehow creepy, as lurkers and starers.

The result is that a majority of fiction writers, born watchers, tend to dislike being objects of people's attention, dislike being watched. The exceptions to this rule—Mailer, McInerney—sometimes create the impression that most belletristic types covet people's attention Most don't. The few who like attention just naturally get more attention. The rest of us watch.

Most of the fiction writers I know are Americans under 40. I don't know whether fiction writers under 40 watch more television than other American species. Statisticians report that television is watched over six hours a day in the average American household. I don't know any fiction writers who live in average American households. I suspect Louise Erdrich might. Actually I have never seen an average American household. Except on TV.

Right away you can see a couple of things that look potentially great, for U.S. fiction writers, about U.S. television. First, television does a lot of our predatory human research for us. American human beings are a slippery and protean bunch in real life, hard as hell to get any kind of universal handle on. But television comes equipped with just such a handle. It's an incredible gauge of the generic. If we want to know what American normality is—i.e., what Americans want to regard as normal—we can trust television. For television's whole raison is reflecting what people want to see. It's a mirror. Not the Stendhalian mirror that reflects the blue sky and mudpuddle. More like the overlit bathroom mirror before which the teenager monitors his biceps and determines his better profile. This kind of window on nervous American self-perception is simply invaluable in terms of writing fiction. And writers can have faith in television. There is a lot of money at stake, after all; and television owns the best demographers applied social science has to offer, and these researchers can determine precisely what Americans in the 1990s are, want, see—what we as Audience want to see ourselves as. Television, from the surface on down, is about desire. And, fiction-wise, desire is the sugar in human food.

The second great-seeming thing is that television looks to be an absolute godsend for a human subspecies that loves to watch people but hates to be watched itself. For the television screen affords access only one-way. A psychic ball-check valve. We can see Them; They can't see Us. We can relax, unobserved, as we ogle. I happen to believe this is why television also appeals so much to lonely people. To voluntary shut-ins. Every lonely human I know watches way more than the average U.S. six hours a day. The lonely, like the fictive, love one-way watching. For lonely people are usually lonely not because of hideous deformity or odor or obnoxiousness—in fact there exist today support- and social groups for persons with precisely these attributes. Lonely people tend, rather, to be lonely because they decline to bear the psychic costs of being around other humans. They are allergic to people. People affect them too strongly. Let's call the average U.S. lonely person Joe Briefcase. Joe Briefcase fears and loathes the strain of the special self-consciousness which seems to afflict him only when other real human beings are around, staring, their human sense-antennae abristle. Joe B. fears how he might appear, come across, to watchers. He chooses to sit out the enormously stressful U.S. game of appearance poker.

But lonely people, at home, alone, still crave sights and scenes, company. Hence television. Joe can stare at Them on the screen; They remain blind to Joe. It's almost like voyeurism. I happen to know lonely people who regard television as a veritable deus ex machina for voyeurs. And a lot of the criticism, the really rabid criticism less leveled than sprayed at networks, advertisers, and audiences alike, has to do with the charge that television has turned us into a nation of sweaty, slack-jawed voyeurs. This charge turns out to be untrue, but it's untrue for interesting reasons.

What classic voyeurism is is espial, i.e., watching people who don't know you're there as those people go about the mundane but erotically charged little businesses of private life. It's interesting that so much classic voyeurism involves media of framed glass—windows, telescopes, etc. Maybe the framed glass is why the analogy to television is so tempting. But TV-watching is different from genuine Peeping-Tomism. Because the people we're watching through TV's framed-glass screen are not really ignorant of the fact that somebody is watching them. In fact a whole *lot* of somebodies. In fact the people on television know that it is by virtue of this truly huge crowd of ogling somebodies that they are on the screen engaging in broad non-mundane gestures at all. Television does not afford true espial because television is performance, spectacle, which by definition requires watchers. We're not voyeurs here at all. We're just viewers. We are the Audience, megametrically many, though most often we watch alone: E Unibus Pluram.°

One reason fiction writers seem creepy in person is that by vocation they really *are* voyeurs. They need that straightforward visual theft of watching somebody who hasn't prepared a special watchable self. The only illusion in true espial is suffered by the voyee, who doesn't know he's giving off images and impressions. A problem with so many of us fiction writers under 40 using television as a substitute for true espial,

---

°This, and thus part of this essay's title, is from a marvelous toss-off in Michael Sorkin's "Faking It," published in Todd Gitlin, ed., *Watching Television*, Random House/Pantheon, 1987. [Wallace's footnotes, ED.]

however, is that TV "voyeurism" involves a whole gorgeous orgy of illusions for the pseudo-spy, when we watch. Illusion (1) is that we're voyeurs here at all: the "voyees" behind the screen's glass are only pretending ignorance. They know perfectly well we're out there. And that we're there is also very much on the minds of those behind the second layer of glass, viz. the lenses and monitors via which technicians and arrangers apply enormous ingenuity to hurl the visible images at us. What we see is far from stolen; it's proffered—illusion (2). And, illusion (3), what we're seeing through the framed panes isn't people in real situations that do or even could go on without consciousness of Audience. I.e., what young writers are scanning for data on some reality to fictionalize is *already* composed of fictional characters in highly formalized narratives. And (4), we're not really even seeing "characters" at all: it's not Major Frank Burns, pathetic self-important putz from Fort Wayne, Indiana; it's Larry Linville of Ojai, California, actor stoic enough to endure thousands of letters (still coming in, even in syndication) from pseudo-voyeurs berating him for being a putz from Indiana. And then (5) it's ultimately of course not even actors we're espying, not even people: it's EM-propelled analog waves and ion streams and rear-screen chemical reactions throwing off phosphenes in grids of dots not much more lifelike than Seurat's own Impressionist commentaries on perceptual illusion. Good Lord and (6) the dots are coming out of our *furniture*, all we're really spying on is our own *furniture*, and our very own chairs and lamps and bookspines sit visible but unseen at our gaze's frame as we contemplate "Korea" or are taken "live to Jerusalem" or regard the plusher chairs and classier spines of the Huxtable "home" as illusory cues that this is some domestic interior whose membrane we have (slyly, unnoticed) violated—(7) and (8) and illusions ad inf.

Not that these realities about actors and phosphenes and furniture are unknown to us. We choose to ignore them. They are part of the disbelief we suspend. But it's an awfully heavy load to hoist aloft for six hours a day; illusions of voyeurism and privileged access require serious complicity from the viewer. How can we be made so willingly to acquiesce to the delusion that the people on the TV don't know they're being watched, to the fantasy that we're somehow transcending privacy and feeding on unself-conscious human activity? There might be lots of reasons why these unrealities are so swallowable, but a big one is that the performers behind the glass are—varying degrees of thespian talent notwithstanding—absolute *geniuses* at seeming unwatched. Make no mistake—seeming unwatched in front of a TV camera is an art. Take a look at how non-professionals act when a TV camera is pointed at them: they often spaz out, or else they go all stiff, frozen with self-consciousness. Even PR people and politicians are, in terms of being on camera, rank amateurs. And we love to laugh at how stiff and fake non-pros appear on television. How unnatural.

But if you've ever once been the object of that terrible blank round glass stare, you know all too well how paralyzingly self-conscious it makes you feel. A harried guy with earphones and a clipboard tells you to "act natural" as your face begins to leap around on your skull, struggling for a seeming-unwatched expression that feels so impossible because "seeming unwatched" is, like "acting natural," oxymoronic. Try hitting a golfball right after someone asks you whether you in- or exhale on your backswing, or getting promised lavish rewards if you can avoid thinking of a green rhinoceros for ten seconds, and you'll get some idea of the truly heroic contortions of body and mind that must be required for a David Duchovny or Don Johnson to act unwatched as he's watched by a lens that's an overwhelming emblem of what Emerson, years before TV, called "the gaze of millions."°

10

°Quoted by Stanley Cavell in *Pursuits of Happiness*, Harvard U. Press, 1981; subsequent Emerson quotes ibid.

For Emerson, only a certain very rare species of person is fit to stand this gaze of millions. It is not your normal, hardworking, quietly desperate species of American. The man who can stand the megagaze is a walking imago, a certain type of transcendent semihuman who, in Emerson's phrase, "carries the holiday in his eye." The Emersonian holiday that television actors' eyes carry is the promise of a vacation from human self-consciousness. Not worrying about how you come across. A total unallergy to gazes. It is contemporarily heroic. It is frightening and strong. It is also, of course, an act, for you have to be just abnormally self-conscious and self-controlled to appear unwatched before cameras and lenses and men with clipboards. This self-conscious appearance of unself-consciousness is the real door to TV's whole mirror-hall of illusions, and for us, the Audience, it is both medicine and poison.

For we gaze at these rare, highly-trained, unwatched-seeming people for six hours daily. And we love these people. In terms of attributing to them true supernatural assets and desiring to emulate them, it's fair to say we sort of worship them. In a real Joe Briefcase-world that shifts ever more starkly from some community of relationships to networks of strangers connected by self-interest and technology, the people we espy on TV offer us familiarity, community. Intimate friendship. But we split what we see. The characters may be our "close friends," but the *performers* are beyond strangers: they're imagos, demigods, and they move in a different sphere, hang out with and marry only each other, seem even as actors accessible to Audience only via the mediation of tabloid, talk show, EM signal. And yet both actors and characters, so terribly removed and filtered, seem so terribly, gloriously *natural* when we watch.

Given how much we watch and what watching means, it's inevitable, for those of us fictionists or Joe Briefcases who fancy ourselves voyeurs, to get the idea that these persons behind the glass—persons who are often the most colorful, attractive, animated, *alive* people in our daily experience—are also people who are oblivious to the fact that they are watched. This illusion is toxic. It's toxic for lonely people because it sets up an alienating cycle (viz. "Why can't *I* be like that?" etc.), and it's toxic for writers because it leads us to confuse actual fiction-research with a weird kind of fiction-*consumption*. Self-conscious people's oversensitivity to real humans tends to put us before the television and its one-way window in an attitude of relaxed and total reception, rapt. We watch various actors play various characters, etc. For 360 minutes per diem, we receive unconscious reinforcement of the deep thesis that the most significant quality of truly alive persons is watchableness, and that genuine human worth is not just identical with but *rooted in* the phenomenon of watching. Plus the idea that the single biggest part of real watchableness is seeming to be unaware that there's any watching going on. Acting natural. The persons we young fiction writers and assorted shut-ins study, feel for, feel through most intently are, by virtue of a genius for feigned unself-consciousness, fit to stand people's gazes. And we, trying desperately to be nonchalant, perspire creepily on the subway.

EUDORA WELTY

Is Phoenix Jackson's Grandson Really Dead?

A story writer is more than happy to be read by students; the fact that these serious readers think and feel something in response to his work he finds life-giving. At the same time he may not always be able to reply to their specific questions in kind. I wondered if it might clarify something, for both the questioners and myself, if I set down a general reply to the question that comes to me most often in the mail, from both students and their teachers, after some classroom discussion. The unrivaled favorite is this: "Is Phoenix Jackson's grandson really *dead?*"

It refers to a short story I wrote years ago called "A Worn Path," which tells of a day's journey an old woman makes on foot from deep in the country into town and into a doctor's office on behalf of her little grandson; he is at home, periodically ill, and periodically she comes for his medicine; they give it to her as usual, she receives it and starts the journey back.

I had not meant to mystify readers by withholding any fact; it is not a writer's business to tease. The story is told through Phoenix's mind as she undertakes her errand. As the author at one with the character as I tell it, I must assume that the boy is alive. As the reader, you are free to think as you like, of course: the story invites you to believe that no matter what happens, Phoenix for as long as she is able to walk and can hold to her purpose will make her journey. The *possibility* that she would keep on even if he were dead is there in her devotion and its single-minded, single-track errand. Certainly the *artistic* truth, which should be good enough for the fact, lies in Phoenix's own answer to that question. When the nurse asks, "He isn't dead, is he?" she speaks for herself: "He still the same. He going to last."

The grandchild is the incentive. But it is the journey, the going of the errand, that is the story, and the question is not whether the grandchild is in reality alive or dead. It doesn't affect the outcome of the story or its meaning from start to finish. But it is not the question itself that has struck me as much as the idea, almost without exception implied in the asking, that for Phoenix's grandson to be dead would somehow make the story "better."

It's *all right*, I want to say to the students who write to me, for things to be what they appear to be, and for words to mean what they say. It's all right, too, for words   5 and appearances to mean more than one thing—ambiguity is a fact of life. A fiction writer's responsibility covers not only what he presents as the facts of a given story but what he chooses to stir up as their implications; in the end, these implications, too, become facts, in the larger, fictional sense. But it is not all right, not in good faith, for things *not* to mean what they say.

The grandson's plight was real and it made the truth of the story, which is the story of an errand of love carried out. If the child no longer lived, the truth would persist in the "wornness" of the path. But his being dead can't increase the truth of the story, can't affect it one way or the other. I think I signal this, because the end of the story has been reached before old Phoenix gets home again: she simply starts back. To the question "Is the grandson really dead?" I could reply that it doesn't make any difference. I could also say that I did not make him up in order to let him play a trick on Phoenix. But my best answer would be: *"Phoenix is alive."*

The origin of a story is sometimes a trustworthy clue to the author—or can provide him with the clue—to its key image; maybe in this case it will do the same for the reader. One day I saw a solitary old woman like Phoenix. She was walking; I saw her, at middle distance, in a winter country landscape, and watched her slowly make her way across my line of vision. That sight of her made me write the story. I invented an errand for her, but that only seemed a living part of the figure she was herself: what errand other than for someone else could be making her go? And her going was the first thing, her persisting in her landscape was the real thing, and the first and the real were what I wanted and worked to keep. I brought her up close enough, by imagination, to describe her face, make her present to the eyes, but the full-length figure moving across the winter fields was the indelible one and the image to keep, and the perspective extending into the vanishing distance the true one to hold in mind.

I invented for my character, as I wrote, some passing adventures—some dreams and harassments and a small triumph or two, some jolts to her pride, some flights of fancy to console her, one or two encounters to scare her, a moment that gave her cause to feel ashamed, a moment to dance and preen—for it had to be a *journey,* and all these things belonged to that, parts of life's uncertainty.

A narrative line is in its deeper sense, of course, the tracing out of a meaning, and the real continuity of a story lies in this probing forward. The real dramatic force of a story depends on the strength of the emotion that has set it going. The emotional value is the measure of the reach of the story. What gives any such content to "A Worn Path" is not its circumstances but its *subject:* the deep-grained habit of love.

10   What I hoped would come clear was that in the whole surround of this story, the world it threads through, the only certain thing at all is the worn path.

Jeanette Winterson

FROM *A Work of My Own*

In my own fiction I try to drive together lyric intensity and breadth of ideas. It is not possible, not desirable, I think, to maintain lyrical intensity over very long stretches and this is something every poet working with size has had to think about. It is to poets that I turn for the lesson I need and the lesson seems to be to use variety of mood and tone to make way for those intenser moments where the writer and the word are working at maximum tautness. To pay a little slack around those places makes it possible for the reader to bear them. I do not mean that any part of the work should be less than the best it needs to be, but the writer's critical judgement is in deciding where the weights and measures should be placed. There is no system for working this out in advance and there is no trick to be learned. There is only constant experiment and a very definite idea of what it is one wants to achieve. I have said before that a writer does not work in an inspirational daze but in a fully conscious compact with words. This state of fully-consciousness allows for penetration into states of super-consciousness and every true writer finds a gift of wings. To assume that the wings can be ready bought and fitted is a problem for modern Daedaluses everywhere.

Variety of tone and mood, which longer work needs, is not got simply by displaying a selection of goods and gadgets. There is much more to be done than adding character or plot interest or philosophical digressions. The fabric of a book is more than its material; it is the weave of the words, and the lighter textures will have to show their own colour and style as obviously if not as sublimely as the richer cuts. Tennyson and Wordsworth are particularly good at this, which is why it is so terrible when they are particularly bad at it, and most readers will remember ploughing through dreadful bogs of *Maud* or *The Excursion* where there is no poetry and no relief. Dickens runs into the same kind of trouble and I think that the reason for those failures is no more arcane than this: Exhaustion.

Huge pieces of work are particularly difficult to sustain and it seems inevitable that the lighter measures within them sometimes become so light that they evaporate, or so weighed down with their author's sweat that they weigh us down with them. When I read poetry or prose of any kind from the nineteenth century what often strikes me is a sense of *toil*. I do not find it in the Romantics and their predecessors. The nineteenth century was a toilsome century, and no writer can escape their period, although it is interesting the Yeats and Graves, whom we think of as Modern, but who are Victorian-reared both chose the lyric form as a means of escape.

Graves argues for the lyric, choosing jewel-like intensity over breadth of ideas, a poetic philosophy shared by the Imagists but undermined by T. S. Eliot who succeeded in his search for new vigour in a poem of length. In any case, Graves, unlike the Imagist poets, has achieved in his lifetime of lyric, an organic continuity, so that the individual poems flow together, a river of writing unstopped by dates and collections and themes. This organic continuity brings Graves, as a poet, close to George Herbert (1593–1633) whose meditative religious lyrics form a pattern outside of their pattern, so that when read together, they seem to the reader to be some great arc made up of many colours and perfectly broken into one another.

5   This river of writing, this rainbow of writing is not what the reader finds in say, Keats, or Marianne Moore. It is peculiar to those writers who were obsessed by a single all-consuming idea; in Herbert's case, God, and for Graves, the goddess as lover and Muse.

It is perhaps unsurprising that I should be in sympathy with poets of obsession, and in particular with those two very different poets of religious and romantic ecstasy. As a reader I am drawn to them, but it is as a writer that I owe them the greater debt.

I want for my own work those talismans of intensity that I find in their work, and if I look to more expansive writers for breadth, I look to Herbert and to Graves for perfect expressions of taut emotion.

When a writer has learned how to use rhythm and pace and accent and design to move her matter along she is still left with the question of poetry and it is not a question she can ignore if she hopes to do more than tell a story.

If prose-fiction is to survive it will have to do more than to tell a story. Fiction that is printed television is redundant fiction. Fiction that is a modern copy of a nineteenth-century novel is no better than any other kind of reproduction furniture. What literature can offer, it should be unembarrassed about offering, there is no need for art to strive to be like everything else. In so much as television and film have largely occupied the narrative function of the novel, just as the novel annexed the narrative function of epic poetry, fiction will have to move on, and find new territory of its own.

10   We have to admit that with one or two surprising exceptions, fiction is not being developed by writers who understand the nature of the problem. This is partly because too many academics, critics and reviewers tout a system in which Modernism is a kind of cul-de-sac, a literary bywater which produced a few brilliant names but which was errant to the true current of literature, deemed to flow, fiction-wise, from George Eliot to Anita Brookner. Writers who we are applauding and encouraging are not writers who are doing new work. They are writers who are plodding on with methods and forms worked out by their ancestors. And not their Modernist ancestors.

To assume that Modernism has no real relevance to the way that we need to be developing fiction now, is to condemn writers and readers to dingy Victorian twilight. To say that the experimental novel is dead is to say that literature is dead. Literature is experimental. Once the novel was *novel*; if we cannot continue to alter it, to expand its boundaries without dropping it into even greater formlessness than the shape tempts, then we can only museum it. Literature is not a museum it is a living thing.

Modernism has happened and it was the mainstream. It is no use looking for the new George Eliot, and if she were to appear, what a ghastly creature she would be. We cannot look for the new Virginia Woolf either. We can only look for writers who know what tradition is, who understand Modernism within that tradition, and who are committed to a fresh development of language and to new forms of writing.

VIRGINIA WOOLF

FROM *Craftsmanship*

The title of this series is 'Words Fail Me,' and this particular talk is called 'Craftsmanship.' We must suppose, therefore, that the talker is meant to discuss the craft of words—the craftsmanship of the writer. But there is something incongruous, unfitting, about the term 'craftsmanship' when applied to words. The English dictionary, to which we always turn in moments of dilemma, confirms us in our doubts. It says that the word 'craft' has two meanings; it means in the first place making useful objects out of solid matter—for example, a pot, a chair, a table. In the second place, the word 'craft' means cajolery, cunning, deceit. Now we know little that is certain about words, but this we do know—words never make anything that is useful; and words are the only things that tell the truth and nothing but the truth. Therefore, to talk of craft in connexion with words is to bring together two incongruous ideas, which if they mate can only give birth to some monster fit for a glass case in a museum. Instantly, therefore, the title of the talk must be changed, and for it substituted another—A Ramble round Words, perhaps. For when you cut off the head of a talk it behaves like a hen that has been decapitated. It runs round in a circle till it drops dead—so people say who have killed hens. And that must be the course, or circle, of this decapitated talk. Let us then take for our starting point the statement that words are not useful. This happily needs little proving, for we are all aware of it. When we travel on the Tube, for example, when we wait on the platform for a train, there, hung up in front of us, on an illuminated signboard, are the word 'Passing Russell Square.' We look at those words; we repeat them; we try to impress that useful fact upon our minds; the next train will pass Russell Square. We say over and over again as we pace, 'Passing Russell Square, passing Russell Square.' And then as we say them, the words shuffle and change, and we find ourselves saying 'Passing away saith the world, passing away . . . The leaves decay and fall, the vapours weep their burthen to the ground. Man comes . . .' And then we wake up and find ourselves at King's Cross.

Take another example. Written up opposite us in the railway carriage are the words: 'Do not lean out of the window.' At the first reading the useful meaning, the surface meaning, is conveyed; but soon, as we sit looking at the words, they shuffle, they change; and we begin saying, 'Windows, yes windows—casements opening on the foam of perilous seas in faery lands forlorn.' And before we know what we are doing, we have leant out of the window; we are looking for Ruth in tears amid the alien corn. The penalty for that is twenty pounds or a broken neck.

This proves, if it needs proving, how very little natural gift words have for being useful. If we insist on forcing them against their nature to be useful, we see to our cost how they mislead us, how they fool us, how they land us a crack on the head. We have been so often fooled in this way by words, they have so often proved that they hate being useful, that it is their nature not to express one simple statement but a thousand possibilities—they have done this so often that at last, happily, we are beginning to face the fact. We are beginning to invent another language—a language perfectly and beautifully adapted to express useful statements, a language of signs. There is one great living master of this language to whom we are all indebted, that anonymous writer—whether man, woman or disembodied spirit nobody knows—who describes hotels in the Michelin Guide. He wants to tell us that one hotel is moderate, another good, and a third the best in the place. How does he do it? Not with words; words would at once bring into being shrubberies and billiard tables, men and women, the moon rising and the long splash of the summer sea—all good things, but all here beside the point. He sticks to signs; one gable; two gables; three gables. That is all he says and all he needs to say. Baedeker carries the sign language still further into the sublime realms of art. When he wishes to say that a picture is good, he uses one star; if very good, two stars; when, in his opinion, it is a work of transcendent genius, three black stars shine on the page, and that is all. So with a handful of stars and daggers the whole of art criticism, the whole of literary criticism could be reduced to the size of a sixpenny bit—there are moments when one could wish it. But this suggests that in time to come writers will have two languages at their service; one for fact, one for fiction. When the biographer has to convey a useful and necessary fact, as, for example, that Oliver Smith went to college and took a third in the year 1892, he will say so with a hollow O on top of the figure five. When the novelist is forced to inform us that John rang the bell; after a pause the door was opened by a parlourmaid who said, 'Mrs. Jones is not at home,' he will to our great gain and his own comfort convey that repulsive statement not in words, but in signs—say, a capital H on top of the figure three. Thus we may look forward to the day when our biographies and novels will be slim and muscular; and a railway company that says: 'Do not lean out of the window' in words will be fined a penalty not exceeding five pounds for the improper use of language.

Words, then, are not useful. Let us now inquire into their other quality, their positive quality, that is, their power to tell the truth. According once more to the dictionary there are at least three kinds of truth: God's or gospel truth; literary truth; and home truth (generally unflattering). But to consider each separately would take too long. Let us then simplify and assert that since the only test of truth is length of life, and since words survive the chops and changes of time longer than any other substance, therefore they are the truest. Buildings fall; even the earth perishes. What was yesterday a cornfield is today a bungalow. But words, if properly used, seem able to live for ever. What, then, we may ask next, is the proper use of words? Not, so we have said, to make a useful statement; for a useful statement is a statement that can mean only one thing. And it is the nature of words to mean many things. Take the simple sentence 'Passing Russell Square.' That proved useless because besides the surface meaning it contained so many sunken meanings. The word 'passing' suggested the transiency of things, the passing of time and the changes of human life. Then the word 'Russell' suggested the rustling of leaves and the skirt on a polished floor; also the ducal house of Bedford and half the history of England. Finally the word 'Square' brings in the sight, the shape of an actual square combined with some visual suggestion of the stark angularity of stucco. Thus one sentence of the simplest kind rouses the imagination, the memory, the eye and the ear—all combine in reading it.

But they combine—they combine unconsciously together. The moment we single out and emphasize the suggestions as we have done here they become unreal; and we, too, become unreal—specialists, word mongers, phrase finders, not readers. In reading we have to allow the sunken meanings to remain sunken, suggested, not stated; lapsing and flowing into each other like reeds on the bed of a river. But the words in that sentence—Passing Russell Square—are of course very rudimentary words. They show no trace of the strange, of the diabolical power which words possess when they are not tapped out by a typewriter but come fresh from a human brain—the power that is to suggest the writer; his character, his appearance, his wife, his family, his house—even the cat on the hearthrug. Why words do this, how they do it, how to prevent them from doing it nobody knows. They do it without the writer's will; often against his will. No writer presumably wishes to impose his own miserable character, his own private secrets and vices upon the reader. But has any writer, who is not a typewriter, succeeded in being wholly impersonal? Always, inevitably, we know them as well as their books. Such is the suggestive power of words that they will often make a bad book into a very lovable human being, and a good book into a man whom we can hardly tolerate in the room. Even words that are hundreds of years old have this power; when they are new they have it so strongly that they deafen us to the writer's meaning—it is them we see, them we hear. That is one reason why our judgments of living writers are so wildly erratic. Only after the writer is dead do his words to some extent become disinfected, purified of the accidents of the living body.

Approaching Short Fiction Critically

Many people want to keep their experience of reading a story or any work of literature personal and private. If they loved the work and if they read it for a course in college, they may even dread going to class and being forced to talk about it or to listen to their professor and fellow students discuss it. They don't want to see their favorite work placed in the middle of the classroom and cut open like a dead reptile, its insides poked, prodded, and removed by everyone's sharp scalpels. There are even teachers—you may know one—who will not teach certain works for fear that discussing them too often in class will dull the joy they felt in first reading them. One very important aspect of reading literature is the personal emotional response that we have to it. It is this deeply felt connection to the work that most writers are striving to help us experience.

Still, at some point in our reading experience, all of us shift from being readers of literature to interpreters of literature. We answer to our own satisfaction the question "What happened?" and begin to ask the question "What does it mean?" This shift may occur privately as we continue to think about the story, or it may occur publicly as we share our response to the work with our friends. Very often we will say to our friends, "You've got to read this story," and instead of giving them a plot summary—this happened; then that happened—we say, "It's about the kinds of choices we make in our careers and how those choices affect our families." At this moment, we have become interpreters of the story. Whether we make this statement privately, never sharing it with others, or publicly, discussing our thoughts with ten friends at a coffee shop, we have made an important step in our development as readers.

Some of us made this step years before we came to this anthology and now do not even notice when we begin to construct interpretations of a story as we read it. Others of us are just beginning to realize that we are able to make this jump from knowing what happens in a story to understanding what it means that it did happen. Furthermore, we begin to learn that throughout the three to four thousand year history of reading, people have been interpreting what they read, discussing it and writing about it, leaving more words to be read and interpreted and so on. The history of law, religious studies, medicine, nature studies, as well as literature is essentially the history of interpreting the meaning of what came before and responding to it—accepting it or discarding it and developing new ideas.

Because the history of reading and interpreting literature is so long and varied, we contemporary readers have at our disposal many critical tools to help us understand and interpret literature. "Tools" is probably an accurate word. Just as nowadays the specialized tools developed in the past centuries make it easier to build a sturdy, comfortable house, certain critical theories, or approaches to literature, help us understand and interpret what we read in ways unavailable before.

Becoming proficient with these critical tools can take many years of study and practice, just as learning to use routers and drill presses does. This general difficulty need not deter us, however, as even a light familiarity with them is beneficial in several ways. First, becoming familiar with various ways of interpreting literature simply gives us more tools. Certain pieces of literature make more sense when approached with particular critical theories. Often a screwdriver cannot do what pliers can. Second, using more than one critical approach sometimes provides several layers of interpretation, thus making the reading experience richer and deeper. Third, we are able to understand better the other writers who are interpreting stories we read. Almost all critics and scholars of literature use these same critical tools. In knowing the tools they use, you can better make use of their ideas. Fourth, these approaches to literature are applicable to our lives outside of literature. In very real ways, many of these approaches to literature are smaller, specialized versions of larger political and social concerns. If you learn to read literature with these tools, you will better be equipped to "read" personal, social, and historical events. Finally, these approaches to literature help us think. They are similar to algebra, geometry, and calculus—abstract methods for looking at reality, for thinking about reality. Just practicing algebra can make us better logical thinkers; similarly, just practicing a critical approach focuses our thoughts, requires us to ask certain questions, and mandates that we search for and evaluate answers. Besides, these critical approaches can also be just plain fun.

THE FORMALIST, NEW CRITICAL APPROACH

For most of the twentieth century, the approach alternatively called **Formalist** and **New Critical** dominated the ways literature was discussed by critics and even by the general reading public. It is probably the method that most of us learned in school. "The Elements of Fiction" section at the beginning of this anthology provides the essentials for the New Critical approach. In its simplest form, the New Critical approach asserts that the only thing one needs to do in interpreting a story is to read the text, what New Critics call "a close reading." We do not need to know who the author is, what the author intended, where or when the story was written, or any other information that exists outside of the text of the story. In performing a close reading of a story, New Critics assume that a story is a unified presentation of an idea or theme, and that all the formal elements of fiction—plot, character, conflict, point-of-view, setting, language, and tone—substantiate and support that theme.

New Criticism found its greatest expression as a critical tool in the 1940s and 1950s in the work of several writers in the United States. In 1941 John Crowe Ransom, a writer originally associated with a group of Southern writers who called themselves The Fugitives, published the book *The New Criticism*, in which he discussed the work of contemporary new critics. The name caught on and stuck. Ransom, a poet still included in anthologies of American literature, was an influential teacher at various universities and editor of the important journal *The Kenyon Review*. Other books soon appeared, however, that solidified the New Critical approach. Cleanth Brooks wrote *The Well-Wrought Urn* (1947), which demonstrated close readings of many often-read poems. Later, he joined with Robert Penn Warren, a former associate of Ransom's, to produce the very influential anthology *Understanding Fiction*. In 1949 Rene Welleck and Austin Warren published *Theory of Literature*, and in 1954, W. K. Wimsatt's *The*

Verbal Icon: Studies in the Meaning of Poetry appeared, containing the essays he wrote with Monroe Beardsley—"The Intentional Fallacy" and "The Affective Fallacy." These two essays provide support for two important premises for New Criticism: that the author's intention is unknowable and unimportant and that the emotional effects of the work of art on the reader is unimportant in interpreting its meaning.

Two points are extremely helpful in understanding the assumptions and foundations of the New Critical approach. First, the critics who practiced the formal approach to literature emphasized that a work of literature should be viewed and understood as an object separate from any context, including the circumstances of its creation. They wanted to apply to a work of art the same rigorous analysis that objects existing in nature receive from scientists. In this way, they believed that no matter who the reader was, if the reader were skilled, he or she would come to the same understanding about the meaning of the work of art. To repeat, everything that is needed to understand the work is included in the work. Readers do not bring anything to the work; they simply read and interpret the codes. A major implication of this assumption about the nature of the critical act is the belief that the work of literature is essentially amoral and apolitical. While readers may be offended by particular features of the story (subject matter, characters, language) and while readers may disagree with the moral or political stance of the work of art, these are not concerns that should enter into the interpretation of the work. Just as a scientist would not make a moral judgment about the behavior of an atom, a literary critic would not make a moral judgment about the subject of a story.

Second, a careful analysis of the work examines the tensions and ambiguities of the text. This premise points to an assumption many New Critics made about the nature of works of art. The best works of art are not simple, but are complicated and sophisticated; the best writers, therefore, use the elements of their genre to set up a system of conflicts and contradictions that eventually are resolved in the work thus providing its unity. One example of a work in this anthology is F. Scott Fitzgerald's "Babylon Revisited." One conflict set up in that story is between Charlie Wales and his sister-in-law. Both want to be the custodian to Wales's daughter, Honoria. There are many reasons for the tension between these two characters, dealing with money, personal values, and responsibility. The tension in the story is illustrated near the end of the story when Wales's brother-in-law, aptly named Lincoln, holds Honoria, as if in the scales of justice. The tension is resolved when Lincoln gives the girl to his wife. New Critics would emphasize that any interpretation of this story must include the meaning derived from this resolution of the tension. New Critics examine patterns of conflict, tension, ambiguity, and their development and resolution in all the elements of fiction.

THE BIOGRAPHICAL APPROACH

One group of writers popular today is the group called "The Beats." This group includes American writers from the 1950s and 1960s such as Jack Kerouac, Allen Ginsberg, William Burroughs, Diane DiPrima, Charles Bukowski, and many others. One of the major reasons for their popularity lies in the lives that these writers portrayed in their fiction and poetry and often themselves lived. Some readers find these writers' lives provocative and romantic—with their use of alcohol and other drugs, their focus on sexual and intellectual freedom, their criticism of mainstream middle-class lives, and their interest in spiritual experiences of various kinds. Often readers of The Beats supplement their enjoyment of these works by reading biographies of and autobiographical writings by these writers.

These readers are practicing an elemental form of the **Biographical approach.** Many critics in the past have believed that the facts from writers' lives provide information that is important and even essential to understanding their work. Similarly, critics have felt that writers' stories and poems provided insight into what kinds of people the writers were. Some critics, primarily in the nineteenth century, believed that writers were examples of superior beings, and that by reading their works and by understanding their lives we were able to somehow tap into their individual genius. You may be familiar with the work of Thomas Carlyle or Ralph Waldo Emerson, who wrote about heroes and representative people, many of them writers. The relationship between writers' lives, on the one hand, and their works, on the other, provides the basis for two separate approaches: biography and the biographical approach to criticism. If we use writers' artistic production to illuminate the writers' lives, we are engaged in biography. If we use writers' lives to illuminate the writers' work, we are engaged in biographical criticism.

Biographical criticism can provide us with important information. First, we might learn that particular characters, places, events have their sources in a writer's life, and thus we can understand the work better by understanding how the writer adapted these sources. One approach that critics use is to examine the manuscript drafts of a writer's works, which may reveal how a writer diminished or enlarged real life events for artistic effect. Second, by knowing various events in a writer's life and other works by the writer, we might be able (1) to trace the development and permutations of those events as they were retold in stories and poems (If a writer were alcoholic, how did the writer treat alcohol in his or her works?) and (2) to isolate the particular use of the event in one isolated work (If the writer's early work included a lot of drinking but the later work did not, how does this one story fit into that progression?). Third, we might be able to learn something of writers' audience and intentions in writing a particular work that helps us interpret it. In researching, we might find letters in which writers actually declare what they wanted to achieve in a particular work. This information may not define absolutely what a particular work says, but it may provide information that aids our own interpretation. In the same way, many writers publish statements about what fiction ought to strive for. Edgar Allan Poe is just one example.

THE HISTORICAL AND NEW HISTORICIST APPROACHES

Closely related to the biographical approach is the historical approach. Once we begin using information about the writers' lives to help us interpret works, we are not far from using the information about the time period when the work was written and/or the time period that the work concerns. The **Historical approach** is an obvious choice when dealing with works written centuries before our own time. The work may have been written in a time long past that was very different in the way society was organized, the way religious institutions related to the rest of society, or the kinds of scientific information known to the writer and to society at large. The entire scope of economic, cultural, intellectual, and religious events, beliefs, and assumptions are useful in understanding what occurs in a work of art. All you have to do is imagine yourself reading the literature from a country about which you know very little, which includes names of historical figures and events, and you see the importance.

One thing that the practitioners of the Historical approach do is to divide the history of literature into periods and then to look at particular works in the context of those periods. Therefore, we could explore how a story by Stephen Crane might exemplify characteristics of the naturalist period or how a story by Katherine Anne Porter exemplifies the characteristics of modernist literature. Related to this is the author's use of language that is no longer current. Here we conduct some historical research into language to make sure we know what all the words mean.

In the previous twenty years, a new kind of historical criticism has emerged called the **New Historicist approach.** This approach is a reaction to previous historical criticism and employs ideas developed by the structuralists and post-structuralists (see those sections below). Whereas previous historical approaches to literature focused on explaining the cultural, social, and intellectual contexts of a work of literature, New Historicism might instead look at how the particular work was received by its audience and perhaps how the reception of the work has changed over time. In other words, instead of using history to explain what a work means, New Historicists use the work to explain the meaning of the historical period. One of the major ways New Historicists do this is to place the work of art beside other kinds of writing that may be associated—diaries, advertisements, newspapers, institutional histories. What this approach assumes is that history does not exist in ways that we might have habitually thought of it. For all practical purposes, history does not exist—we cannot go back "there" in the same way we can go to Dallas today, but history is made of text, of words. All we can know of history is what has been recorded about it or what was recorded at the time. In this way, a short story then can be viewed as artifact that is both made by its historical period and makes its historical period.

Perhaps the most important practitioner of the New Historicist approach was Michael Focault, who demonstrated his method in various works. One of his achievements was to show how a concept like "mentally ill," which we today may accept without thinking, developed and changed over time. What this means, therefore, is that such concepts as marriage, education, spirituality, freedom, and progress are products of the time periods in which they exist. They are part of a network of ideas that are at work in all aspects of a social, cultural, historical world. Therefore, another concept becomes clear—any particular historical period and all those ideas and texts that are a part of it reflect a particular concept of power. Some ideas dominate and some are subordinated.

THE PSYCHOLOGICAL APPROACH

The last half of the nineteenth century saw the rise of several ideas that have influenced us ever since. Three of these ideas—evolution, socialism, and psychology—were developed by Charles Darwin, Karl Marx, and Sigmund Freud, respectively. Two of these ideas, socialism and psychology, have become the basis for two important approaches to reading and interpreting literature. The theory of evolution, with its simplification as "survival of the fittest," even had its influence on literature at the turn of the century as an idea called Naturalism. In the section "The Sociological/Marxist Approach," we will look at Karl Marx's influence in literary studies; here we will look at Sigmund Freud's.

Psychology is the science or study of the mind and of behavior. At the risk of simplifying too much, it can be said that psychology is the examination of motivation, asking the basic question "why has this behavior occurred?" This question can be asked in literary studies on several levels. First, we can ask why a particular character or group of characters is behaving in a certain way. In asking this question, we are trying to get at the root conflict or confusion that a character may have. We are not necessarily looking for values or beliefs that the character is aware of; we are trying to delve into parts of the character that the character is not aware of. Second, we can ask the question to discover how a particular writer continues to return to basic ideas, images, characters, and settings. Third, we can ask the question hoping to understand the creative process in one writer, or generally in all writers: "What goes on inside the mind of someone who creates?" The second and third of these questions are important approaches to biographical criticism and biography. Here we will focus on the first implication of the question.

A little background on Freud's ideas may be helpful. Freud was interested in explaining why humans behave in certain ways, without being aware of the causes of those behaviors: Someone is afraid of going outside; someone falls in love over and over with alcoholics; someone keeps getting into fights. In working with his patients, Freud developed the idea that the human psyche is made of three forces: id, ego, and superego. The id is a name for our very basic desires, drives, and instincts, both of sexual and violent nature. The superego is that part of us that has been created by our contact with authorities, such as our parents, family, schools, and churches. The ego is that portion of us that negotiates between the drives of the id and the rules of the superego. The mark of a healthy ego is that the negotiation has occurred without too much being suppressed into the unconscious.

Experiences that have been suppressed to the unconscious, Freud theorizes, return to the surface as neurotic behaviors, compulsions, fixations, and the like. Dreams are another place where the contents of the unconscious make themselves known, in this case in symbols, visual puns, and images. One of Freud's most important ideas is that of the Oedipal complex, which examines a child's desire to merge with the mother and kill the father and avoid castration. Freud postulated that since, of course, the child is not able to kill the father and become one with the mother, the idea is suppressed and is the cause for the creation of the unconscious.

The relationship between psychology and literature is long and complex. Much of what Freud developed as theory, he discovered by reading literature—for instance, the Oedipal complex is related to Sophocles's play "Oedipus the King." But many writers from the early twentieth century forward have read Freud's many works; some even entered in psychological analysis with Freud himself. Many of these writers consciously applied his ideas or variations of his ideas in their own stories. Katherine Anne Porter demonstrates the power of repression and the unconscious in "The Grave." Other writers, from D. H. Lawrence, James Joyce, and William Faulkner to Tillie Olsen and Grace Paley, can be profitably read with a psychological perspective.

Finally, though Freud was the founder of the field of psychology, he is not the only writer whose work can aid us. Carl Jung, whom we will look at as an influence on the mythological approach, developed the idea of the collective unconscious and explored fruitfully the world of myth and dream. Maslow developed a hierarchy of human needs; Erikson theorized about the process of adult development. Harold Bloom has postulated that poems and stories are written in an "anxiety of influence" as a way to kill the elder writers, and to understand a work we can look at the previous work it is a response to. Even such widespread notions as co-dependency, battered wife syndrome, and post-traumatic stress disorders can be used to analyze works of fiction.

THE MYTHOLOGICAL APPROACH

The **Mythological approach** is related to the psychological approach to literary analysis because, as some people would point out, the patterns and behaviors that occur on a personal level or in an individual's dreams are often the same patterns and behaviors that occur in the world's myths and religions. We can, therefore, apply our knowledge of the world's myths to analyzing stories in at least three ways. First, because writers often know the world's myths and use them, we can understand their work as repetitions or elaborations on the basic framework of myths. Second, we can examine a story for use of individual archetypes. Some of these archetypes include the king and queen, warrior, lover, magician, orphan, wounded one, innocent, trickster, fool, and tempter. And third, we can examine one writer's work for repetitions in particular archetypal narrative patterns, characters, or symbols.

The Mythological approach in the twentieth century is based in the work of Carl Jung. Jung was an associate of Sigmund Freud, but he broke away from Freud and his approach to psychology to explore the concept of the collective unconscious. The collective unconscious can be thought of as a reservoir of images and their meanings that somehow all humanity has some contact with. This was Jung's way of explaining how cultures that never had contact with each other still used images in their stories and myths that were similar to each other and seemed to have similar meanings. In many cultures, for instance, circles mean completeness, snakes are agents of transformation, and mountains are where one goes for wisdom.

In this way, Jung developed the idea of archetypes. Archetypes are symbols or images, characters, or even narrative patterns that are not necessarily bound to only one culture. As a psychologist, Jung might say that an individual was not merely expressing his or her neurosis due to personal experiences, but that his or her behavior was an reenactment of a particular mythic, or archetypal pattern. A strong, tough-minded woman who wants to become educated can see herself as trying to get her father's attention, or she can understand herself as a person similar to the goddess Athena.

Although Jung is the most important proponent of mythological thought, there have been several others. Joseph Campbell's *The Hero with a Thousand Faces* is an exploration of the hero archetype. Northrop Frye studied the archetypal patterns of certain genres of literature and wrote several influential works. In addition, the structuralists, discussed below, influenced by anthropological studies have contributed to our understanding of archetypal relationships between such images as sun/moon, land/sea, male/female, mountains/valleys, and the like.

One source for those critics looking at archetypal patterns in literature is fairy tales. There we can see many of the basic characters and patterns. The story of Cinderella is repeated often in movies, such as in *Pretty Woman*. The archetype of the foolish son who is really wise shows up in *Forest Gump*, and also in Singer's "Gimpel the Fool." Little Red Riding Hood shows up in any number of stories in which an innocent girl is victimized by someone older. For instance, "Little Red Riding Hood" is obviously important to Angela Carter's "The Werewolf." It might also be perceived in the background of Margaret Atwood's "Rape Fantasies."

THE SOCIOLOGICAL/MARXIST APPROACH

As the Psychological approach has its roots in the nineteenth century and early twentieth century ideas of Sigmund Freud, the Sociological approach grew from ideas and theories of the nineteenth century. The **Sociological approach,** like the Biographical and Historical approaches, recognizes that a literary text is a document written by a person in a particular time and place and in a particular society. Time, place, and society exerted their influence upon the story in various ways. The writer was of a particular class, economically, educationally, and politically. Thus it occurred either consciously or unconsciously to the writer to say only particular things in his or her stories. In a basic way, then, the story was written either in support of or in reaction against the society that read it.

A reader who approaches a work of fiction sociologically examines these forces as they display themselves in the work. We can then look at how the ideas of education, literacy, race, ethnicity, gender, money, work, industrialization, science, and many other ideas are either examined by the writer as part of the theme of the work, or are assumptions the writer makes almost without comment.

Various critics have looked at literature's relationship to society. In the nineteenth century the French writer Hippolyte Taine, for instance, declared that literature is a product of a particular time, race, and society. However, the sociological ideas that have attracted the most critical interest in the past hundred years have been Marxism and Feminism. We will save Feminism for its own separate comments and focus here on how the ideas of Karl Marx and Friedrich Engels are useful in interpreting a story.

The basic lesson that critics have applied to reading stories is that stories reflect the sociological structures that produce them. And just as a society will contain certain conflicts of power, especially, in the Marxist view, conflict of economic class, so will the literature. Therefore, much can be learned from a story by looking at how the writer has presented money, class, and power. Certainly, a writer like F. Scott Fitzgerald, who came from a middle-class family and who in his twenties earned, spent, and lost large sums of money, presents rich material in a story like "Babylon Revisited." Just as fascinating, from the perspective of class and money, are the stories of migrant workers by Tomás Rivera. In addition, it can be important to look at what class the writer belongs to. For instance, how important to "Mrs. Manstey's View" is it that Edith Wharton came from a very wealthy family? How does that story compare to "Spunk" by Zora Neale Hurston, who sometimes earned her living as a maid?

Although literature always reflects its relationship with its society, Marxist concern for the working class and the power of capital found itself expressed in the literature of the United States in important ways during the Depression and in the decades following. Writers such as John Steinbeck, William Faulkner, Zora Neale Hurston, Richard Wright, and many others explored the lives of the poor and powerless. During the 1940s and 1950s, as the government of the United States began openly to combat these political and economic expressions (as in the McCarthy hearings), writers continued to express their concern, but perhaps in more carefully veiled ways.

One final point should be made. As anti-Communists would judge the quality and morality of works of fiction based on their political and social themes, often critics of a Marxist sympathy would do the same (as would certain feminists and antifeminists). This is a question we all must face in our evaluation of literature: To what extent do we judge the quality of a work based on the political and social ideas expressed in it? Do we negatively judge a work, otherwise written with verve, style, and power, because we disagree with the way the rich, poor, whites, blacks, Hispanics, Jews, men, or women are presented? These are difficult and important questions.

THE FEMINIST APPROACH AND GENDER STUDIES

The Feminist approach to interpreting literature has its basis in the Sociological approach. The Sociological approach, as discussed in the section above, focuses on the ways that the social structures of a culture both create a literature and are reflected in it. Therefore, just as societal components such as race and class are part of literature, so are the issues of gender. The **Feminist approach** to literary studies raises such issues as how women are portrayed in various works of literature, how their roles compare to those of men, and how their roles in literature reflect the roles they play in society. In other words, feminist literary criticism helps us to reflect on questions of power and how power is held and portrayed by both men and women. The approach can enable us to ask questions such as the following: Are there male and female literary sensibilities? Are women attracted to different kinds or genres of literature? If so, what are they and how do those genres differ from genres men seem to prefer?

Although the role of women in society has been, to some degree or another, a part of most western literature for thousands of years, it was not until the late 1940s that the place of women in literature became the force that it is today in literary criticism. The approach developed in the years since the 1960s, when more women entered universities and other professions. One of the first writers to reflect on the role of women in literature and the status of women as writers was Virginia Woolf, a British novelist and essayist. In *A Room of One's Own*, she examines how the kinds of lives that society traditionally allowed women to live—caretakers, mothers, helpers of various kinds— did not allow time or place for the creation of literature, which, in addition to needing societal approval, above all requires a certain amount of otherwise unoccupied time and solitude. In the 1940s, the French writer Simon De Beauvoir in the book *The Second Sex* developed the idea that women were treated by men essentially as "The Other," as outsiders to the main work of literature and of society. More works followed, and by the time Kate Millet's *Sexual Politics* appeared in 1970, the feminist critical approach to society and literature was on strong footing.

As the Feminist approach was developed, it seemed to have gone through several stages. Elaine Showalter has postulated that feminism began by examining the distorted image of women in literature written by men. This is certainly one area that is still important as we read both classic and contemporary literature. Second, another interest developed as feminist critics concentrated on works by women writers. Over the years they have brought to the public's attention many writers from the past who seemed to have been forgotten by both the general reading public and by academics. Long is the list of writers in this anthology and in others who for one reason or another had been neglected. One of the outgrowths of this reexamination of women writers of the past, in addition to the development of New Historicism, has been the reconsideration of how genres of literature are developed, practiced, and received. To what extent, it has been asked, is it important that many women, as well as minority writers, wrote nonfiction and short fiction, but that it is novels that have received the greatest attention from traditionally male critics and scholars? Finally, the undeniable importance of the Feminist finally has led to a total reconsideration of how gender identities— for males and females and for heterosexuals, homosexuals, and bisexuals—are created by our society and writers, by our literature, and even by readers as they read works of literature. A relatively new field, **Gender Studies,** opens new avenues for understanding how literature creates and reflects traditional and nontraditional gender roles.

THE ECOCRITICAL APPROACH

Just as Marxist and Feminist literary theory have their roots in political moments outside the sphere of literary studies, the **Ecocritical approach,** also called ecocriticism, can trace its roots first to the environmental movement and second to a long history of nature writing. Proponents of this approach might say that as the history of criticism has focused on the wealthy, ruling class and on men, so has criticism focused the human element of artistic creations. Why not, they might say, explore the natural element to these works? Why not seek to understand literature as it displays human's relationship with the natural world? Why not explore the role of human technology? Why not ask how does one writer, one time period, or one culture treat nature in its literature? For example, Richard Wright's short story "The Man Who Was Almost a Man" can be understood as a sociological statement about racism, a historical statement about the American South, a biographical statement, a gender statement about men and guns. In addition, it might also be understood as a statement about our relationship to nature and the land. After all, Dave does kill an animal with a piece of technology and his decision is to hop on a train and move to the city. With such an approach, "The Man Who Was Almost a Man" becomes a story about the long history of humans abdicating their place in the natural system.

Because the Ecological approach was developed after other approaches to interpreting literature, ecocritics are often conscious of parallel concerns. For instance, Cheryll Glotfelty, in her introduction to *The Ecocriticism Reader*, describes how Elaine Showalter's history of the development of feminist criticism might be useful to ecocritics. For instance, the first stage of ecocriticism might be the discovery of how nature has been portrayed in literature. The second stage might be to rediscover forgotten, but classic, works that explore and define a nature-centered literature. A third stage might be to theorize about how humans have constructed an understanding of themselves as a species. Another approach might explore how the body—after all, a part of nature—has influenced and perhaps even determines the development of language, consciousness, and thought, those elements that we often believe separates us from animals and nature.

On a basic level, we can employ the ecological approach simply by looking at the role of setting in a story. For instance, John Steinbeck is very clear in "Chrysanthemums" that a difficult part of Elisa Allen's life is her isolation, the distance from her home to the city. Leslie Marmon Silko is equally clear in "Storyteller" that the Anglos have lost any natural wisdom they might have had, that their relationship with nature is perverse, and that there is a terrible cost for that loss and perversion. We can also employ the ecological approach simply by looking at the metaphors used in a story. In "Sonny's Blues," for example, Baldwin describes Sonny's attempts to find himself as he plays the piano. The story takes place in one of the largest cities of the world, but when Sonny plays, the bandleader "wanted Sonny to leave the shoreline and strike out for the deep water. He was Sonny's witness that deep water and drowning were not the same thing." The ecocritic might ask what wisdom is Baldwin alluding to that cannot be understood without metaphors from nature.

THE READER-RESPONSE APPROACH

The **Reader-Response approach** to interpreting literature, like others developed in the last half of the twentieth century, is, in part, a response to New Criticism. Reader-Response critics confront the assumption made by New Critics that the text of the story is the one and only place where meaning resides. One common sense observation is that New Critics disagree among themselves about the meaning of particular stories. How could that be, someone may ask, if a close reading of the story provides all the information that one needs to understand the story? Something else must be happening when readers interact with a text. That something else, certain Reader-Response critics would argue, is that the reader, in reading the story, creates meaning also. Different people, even different, educated people, read in different ways. For instance, when the word "cross" appears in a story, a Muslim will interpret its meaning and importance differently from a Christian. Both of them will interpret it differently from an atheist. A New Critic cannot respond by pointing out what the writer meant by "cross," because, to a New Critic, the author's intention is unimportant.

Another example often used to explain the concerns of the Reader-Response approach is that when we read a story at different times in our lives the story means something different to us. For instance, a story read as a child might change meaning when we read it again as a parent.

Although the roots of Reader-Response approach go back to the work of Louise Rosenblatt, who published *Literature as Exploration* in 1939, it has made its greatest impact since the mid to late 1970s. The approach has at least two major strands of thought. One, developed by Wolfgang Iser, examines, as his book title indicates, *The Act of Reading*. Reading is a continuous act of responding to the text being read, so what a critic like Iser might emphasize is how readers make meaning while reading. Are we surprised, affected, changed by the words we read? Iser argues that each text contained gaps in meaning that the reader continually fills in. How the reader fills in these gaps alters the meaning. A second strand focuses on how who the reader is—the reader's knowledge, values, and concerns—influences his or her interpretation. Many women read the works of Ernest Hemingway in ways very different from men.

Thus, one technique for analyzing a short story using the Reader-Response approach is to note how we as readers change as we read a story. In this instance, our interpretation of a short story can be based not only on close reading of the text, but also a "close reading" of ourselves. In this sense, the importance of a work of literature is not what it is, but what it does. Therefore, an interpretation of a text need not be a "spatial" interpretation; rather, it can be a temporal one. In other words, meaning is not made merely on a static page—say, making a connection between words at the top of page one and in the middle of page three. But we create meaning dynamically, making connections between what we thought and felt at the beginning of the story with what we thought and felt in the middle or after we read the last word.

Another avenue for exploration using the reader response approach is to look at a story to discover a multiplicity of meanings. For instance, Leslie Marmon Silko's story "Lullaby" can be read, one supposes, by a Native American as an indictment of Anglo-American culture. If this is the case, how then should or can an Anglo-American read this story? With shame? With defensiveness? And do all Native Americans read the story in the same way? How would someone experience the story if he or she had been taken from impoverished parents, enculturated into middle-class urban U.S. lifestyle, and prospered? How would the daughter of an alcoholic read the story?

The Reader-Response approach is sometimes criticized for legitimizing loose, emotional responses to literature. Advocates of the approach would argue that instead the approach forces the reader to become conscious of how he or she creates the meaning of the story. In addition, the approach forces the reader to imagine, explore, and understand how alternate meanings might be created.

THE STRUCTURALIST AND POST-STRUCTURALIST APPROACHES

It is probably no exaggeration to say that the Structuralist and Post-Structuralist approaches to interpreting and criticizing literature have dominated the highest levels of American literary studies for the past twenty to thirty years. In some ways, proponents of these approaches have actively tried to push approaches like Biographical, Historical, and New Criticism out of classrooms. In other ways, contemporary literary criticism might be described as a large smorgasbord with many methods coexisting peacefully in their own steam tables. Some approaches, like New Criticism, seem to appear more in undergraduate classes, especially in freshman and sophomore classes; while others, like Post-Structuralism are important tools in graduate-level classes.

While New Criticism was primarily an Anglo-American invention, Structuralism and Post-Structuralism were developed in Europe. Although the approaches are different in some very important ways—ways that almost make them seem contradictory approaches—they share one important feature. All three emphasize close and almost exclusive reading of the text.

Structuralism, as its name implies, focuses on the structures that are inherent in the story. This attention to structure distinguishes two kinds. One is the large units of a work, things like chapters, sections, units in plot. The second is the smaller units that are usually examined as binary opposites—that is, two ideas, images, structures, and so on—that have a contradictory or conflictual relationship. In many ways these binary opposites are obvious structures—light/dark, before/after, up/down, inside/outside. They can also be less obvious, such as helpful/hurtful, sickness/health, nature/city. And in some cases they can be very small or particular relationships, like long sentences/short sentences, i-sound/o-sound. What the structuralist critic does with the concepts is to look for their patterns in a story. In essence, the story becomes simply a relationship of patterns. Are the patterns repeated in the same ways? Are they changed? Inverted? If, at the beginning of a story, the character who is wild is standing below the character who is civilized, does that pattern change at the end of the story with the wild character standing above? In its purest form, this is all the structuralist will do: explore the patterns. Themes become unimportant, specifics become unimportant. One character's descent into Hell is the same as another's going into the basement.

Structuralism has its roots in the linguistic theories developed by Ferdinand de Saussure (1857–1913). He defined a language as made of a system of signs that contains a signifier (the word that we speak or write) and the signified (the thing the word refers to). An example of a signifier is the word "book"; an example of the signified is the object you are holding in your hand. In other words, the thing and its name are separate entities in the language. He went further saying that the relationship between signifier and signified is arbitrary; it could be named anything, as different languages attest. Saussure also explained that a language was a self-contained system, meaning that French functions as French and English functions as English. We do not understand an English word by referring to the French language; the English word refers to what it refers to as understood by English speakers. But it also implies that meanings of words are composed of other words. Anyone who looks a word up in a dictionary experiences this. A word is defined by other words that are themselves defined by other words. This means that it is the differences between words that makes meaning possible. Book, boot, booze, look, loot, loose—each is a different signifier randomly agreed upon by English speakers to represent a different signified, all because of their differences.

But we are not finished yet. The next step in the development of this linguistic theory as it becomes a literary theory is the work of anthropologist Claude Levi-Strauss. Levi-Strauss adapted Saussure's idea of a closed system of signs and applied it to cultures, their religions, eating habits, technology, and so on. Practitioners of structuralism then say that cultures unconsciously develop structures that reflect the culture's values, and these are often expressed in binary oppositions. One of Levi-Strauss's important works, for example, was named *The Raw and the Cooked.*

So like New Criticism, the Structural approach emphasizes the language of a story and disregards any biographical and historical background. However, in most cases the language is explored not for its literal meanings but for its structural relationships that lie beneath the surface meanings of the words. "Light bulb" has no significance as a light bulb, but does have significance in so far as it leads to relationships of brightness, size, colors, location, and so forth.

The **Post-Structuralist approach,** sometimes referred to as deconstruction, adapts the work of Saussure and the Structuralists in new ways. Instead of accepting that the relationship between the signifier and the signified is fixed and stable, Post-Structuralists insist that language is unstable. In a commonsense way, we all know that in almost any statement, confusion and even contradiction can occur. Post-Structuralists take this observation a few steps further, saying that, in final analysis, authors have no control over their language, that they are users of language that is itself unstable, and that meaning is finally and always deferred because of contradictions contained in the author's language.

For some, these principles are frightening and become a kind of intellectual nihilism, where the final purpose of reading and interpreting is to point out that the story has no unity, contradicts itself, and is meaningless. But this appears not to be the purpose of those who developed this approach to literature. Their purpose, instead, was to open up texts that often seemed difficult to penetrate and understand because of some cultural or political exclusivity they seemed to have. In important ways, the Post-Structuralists begin reading and understanding a story in the same ways a New Critic might, by looking at its tensions, conflicts, and ambiguities. Like the Structuralists, they might express these tensions as binary opposites. Next, they will look at how, on the surface, these tensions appear to be resolved; this resolution, they will note, is the favored or privileged interpretation. It is here they begin to depart from the New Critics, for it is at this point they will begin to look for the remaining contradictions in the story, its images, metaphors, connotations, and so on.

Post-Structuralism then becomes, like its related approach, New Historicism, a critique of a story as a product of a particular value system, usually the dominant value system in the culture. The goal then seems not to be to interpret the isolated story, but to comment upon it as an artifact of a particular time and place. It seems to assert that we need not accept blindly any interpretation just because someone in power asserts it.

Approaching Short Fiction Through Film

If you had your choice, would you rather watch a movie or read a short story or novel? For a large majority, the answer is more likely "watch a film." But why? Is it cost? Time? Ease?

Cost may be a reason that some people prefer movies. The price of one book of short stories, even in paperback form, is about twice that of a ticket to a movie. Cable, which per month is as expensive as three or four books, is still quite the deal, given that in one month one can watch dozens of films and scores of television dramas.

Time may be a second factor. Reading takes time in ways that viewing a film does not. Even the most accomplished readers, those who can read novels in an evening or in a day, cannot read the typical novel more quickly than they can watch the typical film. This is especially true if we consider reading fiction a leisure activity, and so few of us believe we have time that we can allot to leisure activities. Also, more often than not reading is a solitary activity. Many of us lead lives that, for one reason or another, reduce the time in our day in which we can be alone.

Ease, or as some would say, laziness, may be another reason. For many people, it is just plain easier to lie on a couch, popcorn by their side, and "escape" for a couple of hours than it is to read for the same time period. The reasons for this "ease" are complicated and are the subject of many scientific studies on the physiology of eye movements and brain wave patterns, and the subject of literary and cultural criticism in genre studies, the teaching of reading, and economics of cultural production. Behind all our statements that "I just like watching movies," resides a set of very complicated reactions—physical, psychological, cultural, and philosophical in nature. As fascinating as these reactions are—and as important as they are to our conceptions of ourselves as intelligent and productive members of our culture—we cannot explore them here. But in considering how we "consume" narratives, we need to note that we develop our concepts of "cost," "time," and "ease," not in isolation, but within our particular culture and the values that it promotes.

Just as important to us, as readers of fiction in a college classroom, is the fact that most of us have more experience in "reading" narrative presented as films and television programs than we do reading narratives in print format. For some social critics, this fact causes great concern. However, rather than damning our personal and cultural situations and shaming ourselves and others for watching more films than we read books, we can examine and understand how we "read" narrative films and let that understanding guide and aid us in reading and understanding printed narratives. By doing so, we might also grow to appreciate what a printed story can do that a filmed story cannot.

LISTENING TO, READING, AND VIEWING STORIES

The stories in this anthology derive from a specific time period: the late eighteenth century to the present day, a period of slightly over two hundred years. As has been stated in other places in the anthology, the stories collected here, for all their differences, represent a singular development in the art of telling a story. In the eyes of nineteenth-century writer Edgar Allan Poe, the short story is a great human achievement. Poe writes, "Were we called upon however to designate that class of composition which, next to such a poem as we have suggested, should best fulfill the demands of genius—should offer it the most advantageous field of exertion—we should unhesitatingly speak of the prose tale. . . ."

In the eyes of twentieth-century writer Walter Benjamin, though, the prose tale of his day was in decline from a greater moment—a longer moment—the period of oral storytelling. Benjamin writes, "The storyteller in his living immediacy is by no means a present force. He has already become something remote from us and something that is getting even more distant." In the Context essay in this anthology titled "Through the Stories We Hear Who We Are," Leslie Marmon Silko writes about the great tradition of storytelling among the Pueblos in North America. "The oral narrative, or 'story,' became the medium in which the complex of Pueblo knowledge and belief was maintained." In her story "Storyteller," a dying man speaks a wondrous story in the days before his death, and she says about him, "The old man would not change the story even when he knew the end was approaching." That end can be interpreted as the end of his life, the end of the lives of Native Americans separate from Anglos, and the end of the tradition of oral story telling. Benjamin made the same point almost a century earlier, "The art of storytelling is reaching its end because the epic side of truth, wisdom, is dying out."

However, during the twentieth century, as Benjamin wrote in the early part of the century and Silko writes in the latter part, another form of fiction, of storytelling, neither oral nor written, captured the imagination of the greater part of the "literate" reading public. This form is, of course, film—stories told visually. This form, beginning in the late nineteenth century, was appropriately called "moving pictures." It could be pointed out that moving pictures—be they Hollywood blockbusters, independent films, television films—follow Edgar Allan Poe's requirements for art: "In all classes of composition, the unity of effect or impression is a point of greatest importance. It is clear, moreover, that this unity cannot be thoroughly preserved in productions whose perusal cannot be completed at one sitting." What does "one sitting" mean? Poe says it is one-half hour to two hours—the length of television programs and movies.

A scene in the movie *Smoke Signals*, which was written by Sherman Alexie and which includes as part of its plot Alexie's story in this anthology, "Because My Father Always Said He Was the Only Indian Who Saw Jimi Hendrix Play 'The Star-Spangled Banner' at Woodstock," illustrates the tensions inherent in the changes storytelling has experienced in the recent centuries. In this scene, a young Native American, Thomas, tells the story about his friend's father. He is bartering this story for a ride in an automobile (one that moves only backwards) that will take Thomas and his friend, Victor, to a bus station where they will journey from the reservation and into the modern Anglo United States. Much might be said of this situation. Victor is traveling to pick up the ashes of his father, who had journeyed previously into modern Anglo territory and died. But Victor's father, as Thomas tells the incident in the movie and as Victor tells the incident in the short story, had already traveled literally and figuratively into the Anglo culture by going to Woodstock, by protesting the Vietnam War, and by going to an Anglo jail.

The film makes important points about storytelling, though. After all, Thomas tells the oral tale in a moving picture. Therefore, all three developments of storytelling—the oral, the written, and the visual are represented here. In this scene, and several others in which Thomas tells stories, Alexie presents, with no lack of irony, the complicated nature of storytelling in the twentieth century, in the age of moving pictures. One feature of this storytelling is the expanding audience and expanded complications of presentation of these stories. The audience of a spoken story is small. In the fiction of this film, the audience is three people, and requires only one person with a memory. The printed story has a larger audience of literary journal readers and book readers, and getting the story into the hands of those readers requires a few editors, printers, binders, truck drivers, and bookstore personnel. In another essay, "The Work of Art in the Age of Mechanical Reproduction," Walter Benjamin calls attention to the machinery required to produce and distribute works of art. So in addition to the people who help create and distribute a journal or book of stories, we need to remember the machinery, typewriters, printing presses, telephones, trucks, computers, and so on. Lastly, the film requires a much greater number of people and many more machines. The audience for the film *Smoke Signals*, though small by Hollywood blockbuster standards, is quite large compared to the audience for a literary journal or book in the contemporary United States.

Many of the stories included in this anthology have been adapted for the screen. Because many of the adaptations are available in videotape and digital formats, many of us will "view" these stories as films as well as read them as short stories. There are people who will lament this fact, much as, say, others lament the fact that learning to read means that some people first meet fairy tales or Native-American myths in written, not oral, form. The original form of oral stories, if they can be experienced in literate societies, no doubt provides an experience very different from reading the same stories. Similarly, there are those who will lament the fact that students and other viewers of film may first experience "The Heart of Darkness," "Bartleby the Scrivener," "The Fall of the House of Usher," or "My Son the Fanatic" as films. Certainly much is lost but much is gained when a person first meets a story on a screen rather than on the page.

The fact remains, however, that the experience of reading a short story is still available to the general educated public in a way that the experience of oral stories is not. More important is the fact that, just as the literate public brings something to the experience of listening to an oral story, movie viewers bring something to the reading of a short story that the movie-less reader does not bring.

In the creation and in the viewing of a short story as a film, at least two types of adaptation occur. Adaptation occurs when a story becomes a film, but adaptation also occurs when a film viewer reads a story. People who watch film know a great deal about plot, character, conflict, point of view, language, and tone. They know a great deal about the unity of effect, as a twentieth-century Poe might define it. Film viewers know what to expect in terms of narrative pacing. They know how to read transitions between scenes, and many know how to connect repeated images and film motifs. When they read printed fiction, they bring all these skills to their reading.

LANGUAGE AND THE LANGUAGE OF FILM

As a reader of stories in this anthology, you are familiar with the process of transforming the words on the page into the experience of fiction. In a very basic kind of reading, you read a sentence that conveys information, and you decipher that information and log it into your memory, perhaps for future reconsideration. For instance, take the sentence from "My Son the Fanatic": "Initially, Parvez had been pleased: his son was outgrowing his teenage attitudes." You note bits of information, such as the fact that Parvez is a father of a son, and that Parvez thinks about this son and his development as a man. There is information that you cannot do much with except to hold it in suspension. The word "Initially" tells you that something will probably change about Parvez's pleasure and his interpretation of his son's actions.

In a slightly less basic kind of reading, you convert words into pictures in your imagination. For instance, in "My Son the Fanatic," the sentence following the one quoted above provides information in a description. "But one day, beside the dust bin, Parvez found a torn bag which contained not only old toys, but computer disks, video tapes, new books and fashionable clothes the boy had bought just a few months before." This sentence offers a different way to process words. You can see this information depicted in pictures. To some degree, the pictures are specific—a bag, a tear, toys, computer disks, clothing. In your mind's eye, you can see a man looking at the bag and at these items. Yet, you must add details to the picture in your brain. You create specific toys—teddy bear, *Star Trek* figures, checkers? And you have to consider what the fashionable clothes look like. What are their colors? The brand names? The style and cut? All this the writer leaves for the reader to imagine.

Then in other places in the story, such as in conversations, you will visualize scenes even more directly. In a scene such as this,

> "But it's forbidden," the boy said.
> Parvez shrugged, "I know."
> "And so is gambling, isn't it?"
> "Yes. But surely we are only human?"

by the end of the third line, you do not need the tag lines identifying the speaker. You simply see and hear the characters speaking.

All of this kind of reading is fairly simple. We process the language of the story either by imagining that we see and hear the scenes that are depicted or by cataloging information the narrator provides into a kind of understanding.

Compared to reading a story, watching a film, on the simplest levels, is much more direct. Most films provide both information and scene without a narrator's language. In the most obvious distinctions, no narrator ever says, "The boy said" or "Parvez shrugged." No narrator ever says, "Initially, Parvez had been pleased." The information is depicted when the boy speaks and Parvez actually shrugs. The information may be depicted as Parvez looks at his son, and we interpret his expression as pleasure.

Similarly, when viewing a film, you do not convert the words "torn bag" or "computer disks" into a picture of a torn bag or computer disks. Nor do you imagine the size and color of the bag, the extent of the tear, the number and type of computer disks. You do not have to covert the concept "old toys" into any specific example of old toys. In a film it is impossible to *portray* "old toys." Rather the picture on the screen will include a teddy bear with stains and tears, a mess of black and red checkers, and it is up to the viewer to create generalities from the specifics. Still, not every picture must be specific. It is possible to show *generic* video tapes and new books—as opposed to specific titles—by the arrangement of objects and by camera movement so that titles are unreadable.

The processes of reading a story and of viewing a film, obviously, are much more complicated than the description above; however, we can see the basic point that how readers process language and how viewers process the "language of film" is very different. In many ways the language of film is much more direct and requires less "conversion" of linguistic information into visualized information.

This is not to say that a film does not convey basic information linguistically. In some films, there is a voice over. In *Memento*, for example, we hear the thoughts of the main character, essentially telling the viewer what action is occurring and the character's reaction to the action. Also, often a film communicates basic information either at the bottom of the screen ("Three weeks later") or places information in and on certain objects within the frame of the scene, the name of the city on a street sign, dates and headlines on newspapers, handwriting on the back of a photo that a character is looking at, or, as in *Memento*, on tattoos on a body. Still, most films convey most of their information with photographic images and speech, not expository or descriptive language.

Therefore, it can be argued that the experience of reading is much more personal and internal. In a print story, everything occurs in the reader's mind. In a film, everything first occurs on a screen that is then perceived by the viewer. That is, a character appears on the screen. He has a very particular color of hair, is a specific height, has teeth of particular size and shape. With a print story, readers create their own visualizations of "brown hair," "tall," "bright smile." With a film, viewers see what the director of the film creates for them to see, only one visualization—the director's—of "brown hair," "tall," and "bright smile."

Viewing a film, however, is not so mindlessly passive as some would make it. At some point in the viewing of a scene in a film, the viewer converts the object seen on a screen into "linguistic knowledge," an understanding that is constructed of language. At a certain point with certain objects and actions, viewers turn the sight of a teddy bear, torn and ragged, into a concept somewhat like "old toy." That concept may very well be expressed within the mind as language: "Wow—he has thrown away his childhood toys." Indeed, for users of language, which is virtually every human of a certain age, it is impossible to conceive of viewing a film without at some point converting the sights and actions into language.

In both media, the experience of the readers/viewers depends a great deal upon their mental activities. It depends on how carefully perceptive they are, how carefully they read the words, how carefully they "read" the objects and actions. It also depends upon how knowledgeable the receivers of the language and images are. It is this knowledge that allows the receiver to interpret the story or film. For instance, with "My Son the Fanatic," the readers' experience of the story is greatly enhanced if they have some knowledge of Islam, of the history of English imperialism, of the values of militant Muslims. With *Smoke Signals* and the stories by Sherman Alexie, the viewers'/readers' understanding depends a good deal upon a knowledge of the history of Native Americans in the United States. With the film *The Swimmer* and the story "The Swimmer," the viewers'/readers' understanding is enhanced by knowledge of Cold War politics, American class consciousness, the rise of the corporate class, and the changing attitudes toward alcoholism.

It is, then, at this point that readers and viewers begin performing more or less similar acts of interpretation, as distinguished from simple decoding and understanding. But these acts also occur in slightly different ways. For instance, in "My Son the Fanatic," when the narrator says that Ali is disposing of his "fashionable clothes," the reader does not necessarily have to envision particular clothes that were in fashion at the time the story was set. It may help to know this kind of thing, but the author has provided here a different kind of information to interpret. The adjective "fashionable" tells us something about the kind of boy Ali was before he began discarding his old possessions. It tells us that before his conversion, he participated fully, perhaps enthusiastically, in all the English cultural definitions of success and happiness. The very word "fashionable" provides a linguistic short cut that films cannot use in the exact same way. With a film, the viewer must look at the clothing of the character, categorize it as either fashionable or not, and then interpret its meaning in relationship to the character's development and the theme of the film. In this way, the language of short stories can do things that the "language of film" cannot.

"The Elements of Fiction" section at the beginning of this anthology outlined the importance and kinds of language in fiction. Since film is a visual medium, the phrase "the language of film" serves as an analogy alluding to those features of film presentation that help create meaning for the viewer. Texts in film studies can provide full discussions of these elements of film making, but a brief list of aspects of a film that viewers *read* includes actors, sets, lighting, sound effects and sound tracks, film stock, camera lenses, camera placement and angle, framing and placement of characters and objects in the frame, and editing techniques.

NARRATIVE STRUCTURE, NARRATIVE RHYTHM—PLOT

In viewing films, perhaps more so than in reading stories, we become highly attuned to the fact that the plot of the film is constructed as a series of scenes. In film the plot is propelled through the sequence of conversations and actions, one leading to the other, without passages of pure exposition. The film *The Fall of the House of Usher* illustrates this principal early as the character approaches the house, knocks on the front door, talks with the butler, enters the house, looks around, rejoins with the butler, and goes to meet Roderick. Missing from this sequence of scenes are the expository passages in the short story. In the story, Poe writes "The room in which I found myself was very large and lofty. The windows were long, narrow, and pointed." The paragraph continues for another hundred or so words, none of which would we think of as a scene. In the film, all these words are converted into a scene in which the visitor examines the house and reacts with puzzlement to the objects he discovers.

Additionally, in film a scene is constructed in a more visually complex manner than, say, a scene in a short story or play. The experienced film viewer knows how to read the techniques used to create film scenes and plots, including editing for plot rhythms, transitions, and interruptions such as flashbacks and dreams.

EDITING AND PLOT RHYTHMS

In a film, a scene is constructed from a series of shots, that is, individually filmed performances. Very rarely is a scene in a movie filmed in one continuous shot from the same camera in the same position. Rather, there are a variety of shots, each taken from different positions with different focal ranges. Some shots will show large portions of a landscape, some will be mid-range shots of the set, and some will be close-ups of the actors' faces or of objects on the set. One of the effects that editing has on the viewer is that of creating a rhythm to the plot. A scene that is created from a single take may feel leisurely, whereas scenes constructed from many shots from several angles and lasting only briefly may feel more quickly paced.

In this way, directors and editors control how viewers react to segments of the film and to the film overall. As you view a film, notice in particular scenes how many times the film cuts from one shot to another and how quickly. One interesting directorial choice occurs in *Smooth Talk*, the film adaptation of Joyce Carol Oates's "Where Are You Going, Where Have You Been?" A late scene that does not occur in the printed story features Arnold Friend's car parked in a field, golden and brightly lit. The camera moves slowly with no cuts, always focused on the car. The lack of editing forces the viewer's attention on the fact that, off screen, Friend is raping Connie. The pace of the cutting supports the fact that the rape was not quick and violent, but slow and deliberate.

In prose fiction, the writer can manipulate the reader's experience of time in several ways. In "Kew Gardens," Virginia Woolf writes very closely and in detail about the movement of a snail. Other writers may lengthen or shorten their sentences to alter the pace of reading. Charlotte Perkins Gilman constructs the mental landscape of her narrator, and thus that of her reader, in "The Yellow Wallpaper" by writing very short paragraphs and shifting the focus of those paragraphs. On the other hand, Stephen Crane writes at length about the slow passages of time in "The Open Boat."

EDITING AND TRANSITIONS

Writers of short stories often have to develop techniques for transitioning from one scene to another. This is often accomplished with basic verbal cues: "Later that night," "On the third day," and "When they arrived at the park." Sometimes writers will divide stories into sections by leaving spaces between scenes or by numbering them. In films, editors have developed several techniques for accomplishing this plot necessity, and viewers of films have accommodated themselves to these techniques and read them easily. Viewers understand what is occurring when one scene fades out and the screen goes blank momentarily, then another scene fades in. Another technique, called a "form cut," makes visual and thus conceptual connections for the viewer. In this case, a shot of a burning light bulb in a dark room may fade out to reveal a sunrise, the sun superimposed where the bulb previously burned. The viewer understands, of course, that a night has passed and a new day has begun.

FLASHBACKS, DREAM SEQUENCES, AND INTERNAL THOUGHTS

Two plot features often introduced into the plot by transitional devices are flashbacks and dream sequences. The film *Smoke Signals* is constructed upon a simple forward-moving plot of a young man learning that his father has died and going to retrieve his ashes in a distant state. Yet the father appears in many scenes, detailing the relationship between the father and the young son. The editor of *Smoke Signals* transitions back and forth between these two time periods through repetition of similar actions. In one sequence, the film moves from the present time action of the young man leaving the inside of a store to a boy (the young man at a younger age) stepping out of the store. Several scenes follow showing the boy riding home with his father and having a quarrel with him. The boy opens the door to enter his house, and then from inside the house we see the young man entering. Viewers of this film have no difficulties shifting between the two time periods of present day action and past action.

It is a film cliché to transition from a character falling asleep into a dream by making the screen fade out or go wavy, indicating those moments of semi-consciousness before the character is fully asleep. In the film version of "The Fall of the House of Usher," a dream sequence, which does not occur in the print story, is introduced in this manner. The dream sequence, which depicts the visitor searching for Madeline, reveals the growing fear and frustration and guilt that he has concerning Madeline's death.

Similarly, the internal thoughts or fantasies of characters are often depicted in films. In prose stories, writers often introduce these thoughts through simple transitional phrases such as, "He began to think about." In films, these transitions will be executed by showing the character quietly thinking and cutting to a depiction of the action the character is thinking about. Then after the character's thoughts have been depicted, the shot of the character thinking returns. We know that the actions between these two shots of the character thinking are what the character was thinking about.

All film viewers are familiar with moments in the film in which the narrative is compressed or summarized in a sequence of brief, quickly sequenced scenes. In popular love stories, these sequences compress the events of the day in which the couple realizes they are in love. In heist movies, the sequences might show the various preparations being made and completed: clothing and equipment purchased, charts studied, locations cased. In police dramas, the sequence could collapse the officers collecting evidence, evaluating the evidence, suspects interviewed, and so forth. Often these sequences are accompanied by a unifying soundtrack.

The purpose of these sequences is to summarize a series of events, without which the story would be unclear, but which, if portrayed completely, would disrupt the rhythm of the film. In addition, they also help create and maintain the tone of the film—the breezy sweetness of a love story, the hurried worry of a detective film, the care and precision of an intelligent robbery, all of which may set up the future sadness of the breakup, the confusion and frustration of future setbacks.

In short prose fictions, which are already very condensed, there may not be a similar technique, or a need for one. Certainly all prose fictions include brief summaries of events. The writer simply summarizes the events in a paragraph or two. In "Bartleby the Scrivener," Melville does this in passages like "As days passed on, I became considerably reconciled to Bartleby. His steadfastness, his freedom from all dissipations, his incessant industry . . ., his great stillness, his unalterable demeanor under all circumstances, made him a valuable acquisition." Through such description, Melville makes the reader imagine Bartleby doing a variety of chores and tasks. Still, such passages are relatively rare in short fiction, which more often depicts an emblematic action, a scene that represents many similar scenes, rather than summarizing a series of scenes.

MISE-EN-SCENE—CHARACTER, CONFLICT, SETTING

One of the great pleasures of reading a story and in watching a film is seeing characters behaving in a setting. In other parts of this "Approaching Short Fiction Through Film" section, we have emphasized the different experiences of a reader's converting words into pictures in the mind, and in a viewer receiving pictures on the screen. Here we will discuss the physical design of scenes for the camera, for the viewer. Works in the field of film studies often emphasize the concept of *mise-en-scene*—that is, the arrangement and design of characters, sets, and lighting in the frame of the film.

In most cases, especially in films produced for large audiences, very little that is shown on the screen is left to chance. What we see on the screen often has been designed and choreographed to the smallest details. The opening scene of the film *My Son the Fanatic* is a case in point. This scene does not appear in the printed version of the story. The scene depicts the meeting of the Pakistani family of Parvez, his wife and son, at the home of his son's fiancée, a traditional Anglo family.

The mise-en-scene includes a living room. We notice furniture, walls, colors. We see clothing—one woman (we learn later she is Parvez's wife) wears a bright red sari; another woman, an Anglo woman of about the same age, wears beige matching top and slacks. Every feature in the scene is a code for the viewer to decipher. This code tells the viewer that the house belongs to an upper-middle class, traditional, Anglo-English family—decorated to be tasteful and calm. Parvez's wife's clothing tells us that she is a foreigner here. Parvez, dressed in a navy blazer and tie, and his son, dressed in slacks and a collared shirt, indicate a certain dissonance in the Pakistani family.

In the midst of this setting, Parvez talks quickly and nervously in English, but in an accent different from that of the English woman. He moves about quickly and loudly. He is behaving inappropriately for the setting, and much is made of that inappropriate behavior in the facial and body expressions of the English family—frowns, looks of astonishment. We viewers "read" all this as a culture clash between the established and establishment English family and the immigrant working-class foreigners.

In viewing and interpreting the components of mise-en-scene in a film, we utilize the skills that we have learned through our day to day living, combined with the skills we have learned studying cultural signs. We know that someone wearing a studded leather collar and black leather jacket is different or trying to be different from someone wearing a red tie and dark gray suit. We suspect that different things might well occur in a trailer filled with empty beer cans than in the West Wing of the White House. In adapting these "reading" and interpretive skills to reading fiction, we simply have to remember that what we *see* in viewing a film is what is very often *described* by writers in print fiction, for us to imagine and visualize. The qualities of mise-en-scene—actors and acting, sets and wardrobes, lighting effects, and sounds and soundtracks—are, for the most part, equivalent to the elements of fiction discussed earlier—character, conflict, and setting.

ACTORS AND ACTING

Most print fiction primarily concerns the lives and conflicts of the characters in the story. It is through the characters and how they face their obstacles that we participate in, enjoy, and learn from the work of fiction. Similarly, most films are "character driven." Of course, exceptions exist, both in print and film narratives. Virginia Woolf's story "Kew Gardens" is a clear example of a story focused on the idea of point of view rather than on any one character.

In viewing a scene in a film, one of our most important observations is that of the characters as portrayed by the actors. We immediately notice their age, gender, race and ethnicity, height, weight, general looks, clothing, accents, and language use. From this information, we begin to place the character into various value-laden categories: frat boy, rich woman, doctor, migrant worker, and so on.

Then we begin to read the characters in the film through the behaviors and skills of the actors as they portray and create those characters. These skills include the use of their faces and bodies, their expressions and postures. The skills also include the ways in which the actors speak to convey emotion. In studying their craft, actors sometimes practice a basic exercise of repeating one simple line—like, "Here comes your mother"—but repeating it conveying different emotions, such as happiness, relief, panic, guilt, anger, or boredom. When we watch a film, we see and hear actors making these kinds of choices, the total of which helps create their overall portrayal of the characters and our overall understanding of the characters. In reading, we are forced to provide these kinds of interpretations ourselves as we proceed through the story. Occasionally a writer may include a tag like, "she screams happily," but this is rare because modern and contemporary writers generally wish the reader to provide such information themselves.

To experiment with analyzing the different ways that actors create information and interpretations, view the two filmed versions of "Bartleby the Scrivener" and notice the way the two actors say the famous line "Ah, Bartleby. Ah, Humanity!" Or view the adaptation of "Hills Like White Elephants" and examine how Melanie Griffith says the lines "Would you please, please, please. . . ." Did she say the lines the way you read them? Do you bring something to the lines that she does not? What does her reading of the lines contribute to your understanding of the story?

In addition to how the actors speak, how the actors behave tells us much about the characters they portray. This is nowhere more true than in the way they depict conflicts within their characters and between other characters. Popular films, the "blockbusters," often focus more on the external conflicts of characters, and most often do so with violence. As a medium, film seems particularly well suited for car crashes, knife fights, bullets, and bombs. Serious mainstream fiction, perhaps especially short fiction, relies less on these kinds of conflicts, and most often employs verbal conflicts and inner conflicts. As we watch a film, we can notice how an actor portrays the various shifts and permutation of the character's conflict, slightly developing the expression of these conflicts from scene to scene. As you view a film, note these shifts in facial expressions and physical gestures, the speed of the delivery of lines, and the emotions expressed in the lines. As an example, in the film *Smooth Talk* examine Laura Dern's body movements and postures as she changes from a happy-go-lucky teenager to one confronting sexual danger. Then go back to the story "Where Are You Going, Where Have You Been?" and determine if Joyce Carol Oates described or alluded to these shifts.

One factor in "reading" actors on the screen is the history and career of the actor. For instance, when we see Dennis Leary and Jack Black in *Jesus' Son*, we cannot help but remember other performances by them and somehow superimpose those characters upon our reading of their characters in *Jesus' Son*. Filmmakers know that viewers will do this and try to use the viewers' memories to help build the characters in the new film—either by casting the actor in a similar role or by casting the actor against type. Sometimes, non-actors are cast in roles for these reasons. *Round Midnight*, an original film, though one with many concerns similar to Baldwin's "Sonny's Blues," features the great jazz saxophonist Dexter Gordon in the lead role. He gave the role a depth and credibility that a professional actor may not have given. And he won an Academy Award nomination! Writers of serious print fiction do not have recourse to such techniques in creating characters for readers, except by describing characters as similar to actors or other living people or perhaps to characters from other fiction.

SETS AND WARDROBES

The actors and their portrayal of the characters are one part of the mise-en-scene. A second part is the setting and what the actors are wearing. These two facets of a scene are developed by set designers and wardrobe coordinators in collaboration with directors and cinematographers. Two important aspects of sets and wardrobes are (1) their verisimilitude and their iconographic qualities and (2) their color schemes and their emotional resonance.

The verisimilitude of the setting and wardrobes is determined by how realistic they appear to the viewer; how "true" they are to the time period and location of the story. In looking at this aspect of the mise-en-scene of a film, we effortlessly take in many pieces of information. The houses and trailers depicted in *Smoke Signals* present us with a very different world from the middle-class comfort pictured in the contemporary homes of *The Joy Luck Club*. Similarly, the jeans and the flannel shirts of the Native Americans in *Smoke Signals* tell us that the characters are very different from *The Joy Luck Club*'s prosperous Chinese Americans, who wear fashionable and expensive clothes. We view these settings—the furniture, dishes, pictures on the wall, and so on—and accept them as realistic and begin to assemble a context for the actions of the characters. Reading a story— especially contemporary stories—we may find that we have to provide a good deal of this information ourselves. Rarely are rooms described in any detail; rarely is a person's complete wardrobe described. Instead, a prose story may mention one or two details that the writer wants to highlight—and to which the reader will need to give focused attention—

and then leave it to the reader to imagine the rest. For instance, after reading Sherman Alexie's short story "Because My Father Always Said He Was the Only Indian Who Saw Jimi Hendrix Play 'The Star-Spangled Banner' at Woodstock," describe the house that Victor grows up in. Can you? Can you describe it in the detail that you can after seeing *Smoke Signals*? Probably not. This fact is, perhaps, one reason that some people find reading modern and contemporary fiction, which requires the reader to provide many omitted details, less pleasant than seeing films, which by necessity provides all details.

In addition to creating the realism of the sets and wardrobes, filmmakers also choose to add more specific details, communicating various kinds of information through iconographic selections. In this regard, filmmakers repeat the work of writers of prose fiction. The fact that certain scenes take place in bedrooms, bathrooms, or kitchens tells us something different in each case. The fact that in *My Son the Fanatic* Parvez's private room, where he listens to jazz and drinks scotch, is behind closed doors downstairs indicates something about his role and his habits within the context of his family. In *Smooth Talk*, there is a scene between Connie and Arnold Friend where he is pressuring her to come with him and the only thing standing between them is a screen door. That screen door indicates just how fragile Connie's defenses are. Clothing can take on the same iconic meanings. For instance, again in *Smooth Talk*, when Connie goes to the mall and later when she goes to the hamburger joint, she changes clothing, indicating clearly that she is changing her personality from who she is with her family.

Certainly films don't always depend upon the verisimilitude of their setting and wardrobes. Two films that concern writers' lives and depict moments from their stories— *Mishima* and *Kafka*—both include settings and sequences that rely upon creative blendings of verisimilitude and imagination. In *Kafka*, many aspects of street and café life appear to be realistic for Prague in the early twentieth century, but the castle/factory that Kafka sneaks into is an iconographic depiction of a society enslaving its citizens. Similarly, *Bartleby* (2000) pictures a landscape mountain horror unlike anything in real urban life, but uses recent tacky décor for the claustrophobic offices.

Another important feature of the settings and wardrobes of films is the pallet of colors chosen for the film. In part, this pallet is determined by the verisimilitude of the film. A suburban house in the 1970s will contain different colors from a city flat in the late 1990s. But the filmmakers also choose specific pallets for a film based on the emotional feel they wish to communicate. A location dominated by bright reds and oranges will convey very different emotions from one containing muted browns and beiges. For comparison, examine the offices and wardrobes in the two versions of *Bartleby*. One, set in a kind of surreal present, contains many bright clashing colors; the other is set in a drab present and features grays, blacks, and dark browns and blues. The color pallet is one way that filmmakers create the atmosphere of the film, that emotional quality of the setting.

In noticing these aspects in a film, we can begin to see the emotions and themes that the filmmakers wish to communicate. In printed fiction, all of these qualities are created by the writers through direct description of scenes and characters, and by the reader through filling in details. For instance, in "Bartleby the Scrivener," Melville does not use a great number of words describing the actual looks and layout of the law offices. Instead, he tells the reader about the most important aspects of the offices, things that have particular symbolic or iconographic meaning, such as the close proximity of Bartleby to the narrator and the wall outside the window. Melville leaves it up to the reader to determine the height of the ceilings, the composition of the floor, the size of the rooms, and the color of paint. A film requires the filmmakers to specify these aspects that stories leave open, and thus films can teach readers how to imagine details that prose writers by necessity must leave out or else bore the readers with too lengthy descriptions.

LIGHTING EFFECTS

Another aspect of the mise-en-scene is how the filmmakers choose to light the scene. In some obvious ways, lighting develops the atmospheric qualities of setting. A scene that is crisply lighted so that the characters and sets are clear and well-defined has a very different atmosphere from a scene that is dimly lighted so that the characters pass in and out of darkness. The lighting of Roger Corman's film of *The Fall of the House of Usher* is predictably muted and dark to enhance the frightening feelings and themes of the story. Similarly, the lighting of the scenes featuring the assassination of Col. Kurtz in *Apocalypse Now* are very dark, dramatizing the night time light sources of moonlight and torches, and enhancing the themes about the confrontation with evil. Conversely, the lighting of Arnold Friend's automobile during Connie's rape in *Smooth Talk* is exceptionally bright and defining. Here, the filmmakers decided not to depict the rape but slowly to pan the camera around Arnold's car in a field. Arnold's car, which has become a symbol of his power and cruel persuasiveness, shines brightly in a field, without guilt or shame.

But lighting is more complicated than its qualities of lightness and darkness. While lighting can be discussed with many technical terms—"fore lighting," "back lighting," "fill," and so on—for the average viewers of film, a basic understanding of lighting need only focus on the effects of lighting. Everyone notices how a beautiful female actor is made even more beautiful when her hair is shining and has a kind of halo around it. Everyone can see the one object on a desk that is highlighted more than others. Everyone is aware how, when a character is deciding between right and wrong, his face is filmed half in light and half in a dark shadow. In these ways, lighting can recreate what the narrator or a character feels about another character ("Boy, is she beautiful") or what the narrator is saying about characters ("For a moment, he debated whether he should retaliate.")

Lighting can thus be used as a factor in developing the viewer's perceptions and understanding of the characters. It is not too unusual for filmmakers to design different kinds of lighting for different characters or for characters in different places in a film. For instance, if a character's story moves him from being tired and desperate at the beginning of the story to being happy and satisfied at the end of the film, the lighting of that character may shift (along with make-up and wardrobe) from exaggerating his tiredness to highlighting his happiness.

Finally, lighting can parallel larger stylistic factors in a work of prose, or the tone of a work. If lighting effects are extreme, such as an emphasis on lighting from below the actors, distorting their bodies and faces, viewers will experience a general unease. Examine, for instance, the use of lighting in *Kafka*, a film emphasizing a kind of paranoiac relationship with society. Or consider the symbolic use of lighting at the end of *My Son the Fanatic*, a film that is relatively darkly lit throughout. At the end, Parvez walks through his dark house turning on the lights in each room. As a closing scene, the filmmakers must have consciously been making some statement about Parvez's life from that moment on.

SOUNDS AND SOUNDTRACKS

While many scholars do not consider sounds and soundtracks to be aspects of mise-en-scene, we will consider them here, because many sounds in a film do grow from the scene itself. In "reading" a scene in a film, we listen as much as we watch. In almost every scene, the director, sound director, sound editor, and soundtrack composer enhance the scene's emotional and thematic power. In considering mise-en-scene, two kinds of sound are paramount: dialogue and noises. Along with the voices of the actors, the auditory portion of the film contains various noises from the sound of tea cups clinking in saucers to car crashes.

The sounds of actors' voices communicate a great deal. What is the pitch and timber and pace of an actor's speaking? What do these tell us about the character and her situation? Sometimes the director includes voices from actors who are not within the frame at the moments we hear the voice. One technique directors use is to cut to the actor who is listening to the speaking actor. This way the director presents both the words being spoken and their effect on the listener. Do they provoke anger? Shame? Grief? In another technique, the director might speed the plot rhythms of a film by cutting the visual scene of a character speaking, but continue the speaking over the new scene. At the beginning of *Smoke Signals*, consider how much "description" of the reservation is accomplished while the radio announcer speaks and we view different places on the reservation.

A similar technique turns the voice of a character into a narrator of a scene shown in flashback or flash forward or in a fiction within the fiction of the film. Again, *Smoke Signals* contains several dramatized scenes of stories that the character Thomas tells. In one, Thomas describes how Victor's mother is famous for her fry bread, and as he tells this story, a moment in his story when she tears a piece of fry bread in two is shown on the screen.

Another voice often heard in films is the "voice-over," which is the voice of an omniscient narrator or of a character within the film speaking directly to the audience. Generally films are constructed in omniscient point of view, allowing the viewers to see events from many perspectives. But certain stories are told from first person by a character within the story. The film *Jesus' Son*, adapted from the stories of Denis Johnson, includes a voice-over in several moments of the story. Johnson's story in this book, "Car Crash While Hitchhiking," a first-person narrative, provides the opening sequence in the film with various scenes depicted as the character talks about them, using language directly from the story.

Besides the voices of the actors, films include many sounds that are the noises that accompany the actions of people and objects in the film. These sounds can be small and precise like a dripping faucet, percussive like a pounding basketball, or frightening like car crashes or dogs growling. In most cases, in print stories these sounds are either assumed or mentioned. But in films they become literal. Like wardrobes and sets, they are not represented: They are actualized. As such, the filmmakers make the choice whether to be realistic—to record an actual dog barking—or to enhance it in some way. They can make it louder, change its pitch, or alter it in other ways. It is not unusual for filmmakers to include enhanced sounds to scenes, such as altered animal sounds to a fight between two people. We can consider moments like these as equivalents to metaphorical statements in prose stories. A sentence such as "She yelled like a wounded bear" can become literal in a film if a sound of a bear is placed subtly in the background as the character screams.

Finally, films include music. Nowadays soundtracks seem to come in two types. One is the type that sounds like classical music or jazz, that is, music composed precisely for the individual scenes within the film and meant to add to the emotional texture of the film by building tension, expressing sadness or joy, and the like. There is no real equivalent to this effect in prose fiction, unless we consider the prose style of the writer. Some assert that a writer's pace of sentences and the vowel and consonant sounds are a kind of music in reading a work of fiction. Most films include this kind of composed soundtrack. One adaptation of a short story seems to rely on a soundtrack more than most. Examine the use of music in the film adaptation of "To Build a Fire." This story by Jack London focuses on a man's travels, alone, through the quiet landscape of the snow-covered Yukon. There are very few occasions for ambient or natural sound and few ways to depict the man's inner conflicts. The filmmakers must, therefore, rely heavily on the soundtrack to enhance the conflicts and provide a sound texture for the film.

The other kind of soundtrack is composed of popular songs, whether contemporary or not. Sometimes these songs are actually part of the mise-en-scene; that is, they are songs on a radio or songs being sung by a band at a party, and so forth. At other times, a song is placed on top of the action in the film. One example is Francis Ford Coppola's use of the song "The End" by The Doors in the opening scenes of *Apocalypse Now*. In viewing a film, we have to decide if the filmmakers are using the piece of music to develop thematic threads in the film—as in *Apocalypse Now*—or as part of the verisimilitude of the scene, including the piece of music because it is the kind of thing the characters would listen to. In a piece of prose fiction, these kinds of references to songs and song lyrics occur only by direct inclusion of the song within the story in some way. Joyce Carol Oates provides a kind of soundtrack to "Where Are You Going, Where Have You Been?" by placing lines from a Bob Dylan song at the beginning of the story. T. C. Boyle does the same thing in "Greasy Lake" with lyrics by Bruce Springstein. Similarly, but even more directly, Sherman Alexie places Jimi Hendrix's music as a central facet of the relationship between father and son in "Because My Father Always Said He Was the Only Indian Who Saw Jimi Hendrix Play 'The Star-Spangled Banner' at Woodstock."

Mise-en-Shot—Point of View, Language, and Tone

Another concept of film studies is the mise-en-shot, the manner in which the mise-en-scene is filmed and to a degree how the film itself is perceived. The concept of mise-en-shot provides a means to consider what kinds of lens and film are used, where the camera is placed, how the camera moves, and how long the shot continues. (Many film scholars do not use the term "mise-en-shot," referring instead to the individual components of the shot. But the term "mise-en-shot" is used by Warren Buckland in his little book *Film Studies* and is a useful distinction.)

If the mise-en-scene represents the "what" of the film—who is doing what and where—the shot is a means for considering the "how" of the film. While it is true that content and form should not be separated too decisively, we can think of characters and setting as the content of the film, and the elements of the filmed shot as the form.

While watching a film, we are greatly affected, often without our knowing, by how the shot or sequence of shots is filmed. But we can begin to understand better how we react to parts of a film by understanding more about how the individual properties of a shot are put to film. Several aspects of the shot deserve our notice—the photographic qualities, film speed, perspectives of the image, framing, camera movement, and duration of shot. For instance, the opening scenes of *My Son the Fanatic* are shot to emphasize the discord between the British and Pakistani family, as was discussed in previous sections. After two outdoor shots that establish wealth and status symbolically with a home on a hill above a waterway, there is a series of shots that comprise an indoor scene where the Pakistani family and English family meet. One thing that is noticeable in these shots is that, except for two occasions, the camera is very still. Another thing to notice is that the height of the camera varies in subtle ways, at times standing over Parvez's wife and at others looking up at the British father, who is an Inspector General and in uniform. A third thing to notice is how depth of field is manipulated so that people and objects in the background are out of focus: In this scene things are very much on the surface. The scene ends with a series of six "snapshots" that Parvez, the Pakistani father, takes to commemorate the day. If we examine these snapshots closely—looking at objects in the distance, a credenza with a clock, closed doors, and a staircase behind the family members—we can see how different lenses have been used to highlight and distort the people and objects in the shots. Again, very little of this is noticeable on the first viewing of a film, just as few of the ways that a writer manipulates language, point of view, and tone are noticeable on a first reading of a story. But looking closely at films has its rewards. We can begin to see and appreciate the art of filmmaking that is beyond plot and character, and in considering these aspects of telling stories on film, we can become more aware of the limitations and the possibilities of prose storytelling.

PHOTOGRAPHIC QUALITIES

The most obvious fact about a film is that it is a film, a photographed set of images or, recently, a digitally recorded set of images. This is not the place for an extensive discussion of film stock and various methods of developing film. Instead, as viewers of films we need mostly to be sensitive to what we actually see on the screen. Are the images presented in high contrast or low? Are the images crisp or grainy? Are colors particularly rich and startling? Are particular color tones emphasized, blues or greens, for instance? Do these properties shift over the course of the film?

The film *Mishima*, a kind of biography of the Japanese writer Yukio Mishima by Paul Schrader, uses at least three different kinds of film and/or film processing. First, there are the crisp, but realistic sequences that tell the story of Mishima's last day of life. The shots detailing this part of the film seem to reflect the military precision with which Mishima approaches this final day of his life. Second, Mishima's early life and development as a person and writer are photographed in high contrast black and white, with areas of stark light and deep shadow within the frame. Third, the movie adapts and blends within the narrative of the film several of Mishima's literary works. These works are photographed in shots saturated with color in ways that match the highly stylized sets. There is nothing realistic about these sequences.

While the filmmakers of *Mishima* are more obvious and extreme in the ways that they manipulate photographic qualities of their shots, they do provide a quick lesson in the many possibilities open to filmmakers. Comparable techniques are open to writers in the ways that they can change and manipulate their writing style, but writers rarely make such drastic shifts in style, at least not in short fictions. But one can imagine a work of fiction in which one portion is told in Hemingway's terse style, another portion told with Faulkner's rich style, and yet another in the magical realism of García Márquez or Cortázar.

FILM SPEED

Films run through projectors at standard rates of speed, but filmmakers can manipulate our perceptions of the filmed scenes by speeding up or slowing down the number of frames they shoot per second. We are all familiar with the effects of these techniques. If the bud of a flower is filmed with fewer frames per second, we can watch the flower open (time-lapse photography). If a car crash is filmed with more frames per second, we can see the car crash more clearly with more details of the crash (slow motion photography). Many fictional films will employ these techniques at important moments in the film's development. One interesting instance of slow motion occurs early in *Bartleby* (2000). The character who we will later learn is Bartleby is walking in slow motion toward the camera. He is walking in a caged pedestrian crosswalk that looks like a chain-link tunnel. Interestingly, as Bartleby strides toward the camera, the camera recedes so that Bartleby, despite his walking, never gets any closer. Finally, he stops and turns away from the camera. The question for the viewer is, why is the technique employed at that moment in the film? What effects are the filmmakers striving for by manipulating our perceptions? Parallel instances in prose fiction may be a writer's description, within a story, of a moment in precise detail over a lengthy paragraph, thus slowing down time so an event can be examined more closely. Or there may be places in a story where long actions are condensed into a sentence or two.

PERSPECTIVE OF THE IMAGE

Filmmakers are usually very conscious of what they want the viewers to focus on and how they want the viewers to react to what they see; thus, their choice of camera lens is of, great importance. In viewing a filmed image, as in viewing paintings and other images, we can consider three major planes of depth: the foreground (what is up close), the middle ground (what is in the middle distance within the image), and the background (what appears to be furthest away within the image). A long practiced technique called "deep focus" allows the filmmakers to make people and objects on all three planes clear. Through the use of various lenses, filmmakers can control what the viewer focuses on by making clear or distorted what appears in the various planes. Early scenes from *My Son the Fanatic* provide examples of shots where only the middle ground or foreground are in focus. In one particular scene, the filmmakers shoot Parvez and the Inspector General inside the house talking, in a medium shot from the chest up. Parvez and the Inspector General, however, are placed at the sides of the screen, so that we can see behind them where, in the distance, a double doorway opens, leading to another room. (In the far distance is a blurry traditional British hunting painting.) While their parents talk, Parvez's son and his girlfriend step beneath that double doorway, listen to their fathers, and make faces. All the time, though, the son and the girl are out of focus. Our attention is always placed on the parents, but since the young people are set in the center of the shot, our attention also strays to them. One of the things that this shot and others in the scene begin to tell us is that all of the characters are reacting to the day in their own different ways, and that what we see may not be what really is true.

A technique used by some filmmakers called "racking" allows the camera to focus, say, on one person talking in the foreground leaving a person in the background out of focus, then shift focus to the person in the background, thus putting the person in the foreground out of focus. This technique is used in *My Son the Fanatic* as Parvez drives his taxi. First, the camera focuses on the sights that are occurring outside of the car; then the camera brings the rear view mirror inside the car into focus, and we see Parvez's eyes as he looks out. In most cases, the viewer can probably assume that the filmmakers are guiding the viewers' eyes to the most important person, thing, or action in the frame. However, it is possible that the filmmakers (like magicians) will deliberately misguide the viewers' eyes.

By using various lenses, filmmakers can also distort images. The typical 35mm lens creates the images that most of us are used to seeing in films. Shorter lenses (wide-angle lenses) tend to make the outside portion of a shot curve; thus when something is shot close-up with this lens, the image will distort at the edges, making people's faces, for instance, look bug-eyed or making things that are close together appear further apart. Longer lenses (telephoto lenses) will flatten the planes of an image, so that objects in the background appear to be closer to the foreground than they really are.

While we can spend a good amount of time learning the technical intricacies of cameras and lenses, the average viewer will profit simply by asking what is in focus in the image; are there distortions in the image; do objects seem closer together or further apart than they probably are; do these patterns repeat in the film; do they change during the film?

FRAMING

In looking at an image, the first thing we notice, of course, is what is included in the image. But the image also contains a frame, that is, the image ends and has a *de facto* border around it where the image ceases. How the image is framed greatly determines how we view the image itself. Framing is a large and complicated subject, ranging from the size and shape of the image (e.g., wide screen vs. television screen) to the relationship of on-screen spaces to off-screen spaces (e.g., a fist that suddenly appears from the foreground of the frame to hit a face in the middle ground). Here we will examine the point of view of the camera as it creates the viewer's perspective in seeing the image on the screen.

It is important to know where the camera is in relation to the images within the frame. The first variable is distance. Is the frame a close-up shot of a person's face or of an important object? Is it shot from a medium distance, showing people or objects relatively full-sized? Or is the image shown from a distance, for instance, a single ship seen as a speck on a vast stretch of water? In viewing an image in a film, we are always aware of the distances from which the filmmakers film their scenes. *Bartleby* (2000) is full of interesting shots. One is a close-up of an air vent on a ceiling. Bartleby complains that he needs a little air, and the secretary points up. We then see a close-up of the vent and the large amount of dust collected on it. It is both fascinatingly dirty and repulsive. It is as if a writer had devoted a dozen sentences to describing the air vent.

In prose fiction, we may be less aware of the distance from which a narrator views a scene. In the first couple of paragraphs of the short story "To Build a Fire," Jack London describes the Yukon and a man walking through it from a seemingly far distance.

> The Yukon lay a mile wide and hidden under three feet of ice. On top of this ice were as many feet of snow. . . . North and South, as far as his eye could see, it was unbroken white, save from a dark hairline that curved and twisted around the spruce-covered island to the south, and that curved and twisted away into the north, where it disappeared behind spruce-covered island. This dark hairline was the trail—the main trail—that led south five hundred miles to . . .; and that led north seventy miles north . . ., and still on to the north a thousand miles. . . .

London's description is an exception in that most descriptions in fiction do not attempt to cover such vast distances.

In the first eight shots of adaptation of this story, the filmmakers attempt to convey both the sense of distance and the reality of a single man with a dog in this space. An initial shot establishing daybreak is followed by four shots of a wide swath of white snow beneath small plateaus of trees. These four shots are photographed from on top of the plateaus or seemingly higher. In each of these shots, we see a thin, grayish line through the snow. In one we see clearly two dots moving along the trail. Then, interestingly, the filmmakers include something not included in the early paragraphs of the story: a close-up of a little spring of water running through some rocks surrounded by snow. Suddenly, something moves into the screen. It is the hips and legs of the man stepping carefully over the little stream. Here the filmmakers shock us, breaking the borders of the frame, by having something move into the frame so quickly and closely.

The angle from which the camera frames the scene is also important. Most shots are filmed level with the people or sets in the scene, as if the camera were more or less at the height of the eyes of an average-sized person. And most films include adjustments to the normal perspective. Sometimes the camera may stand above the action of a scene. This could be an attempt to show a character's perspective, say, of looking down upon a street from the top of a building. It could also be a filmmaker's attempt to offer an "objective" or distant perspective, a perspective that is omniscient and unbiased. Similarly, the camera can be placed below the object being filmed. A typical instance of this practice is the image of people descending from the top of a staircase viewed from the bottom of the stairs, duplicating the perspective of someone looking up. The early scenes of *The Company of Wolves* include many shots of this nature: shots of a young woman running up stairs, from different angles; shots of a dog approaching from down the hall, filmed at the dog's height; shots of a girl in bed, seen from above; shots of scary dolls on shelves, but framed even at the dolls' level.

Related to angle is the concept of height. Just as filmmakers may photograph an airplane parallel to the plane as it flies high above the earth, so they may also place a camera on the ground to duplicate what a character lying down would see, someone else's feet, for instance. *Memento* uses this technique portraying Leonard's perspective, lying on the bathroom floor, watching his wife die beside him. Conversely, *Memento* occasionally includes a shot of Leonard in his motel room, filmed, unrealistically, from a upper corner of the room.

Finally, objects can be photographed so that they appear to be tilted in some way. Level floors cut diagonally across the frame, or tall buildings look as if they were leaning, as in early scenes of *Bartleby* (1970). Often the effect of such framing is to create a sense that things are unbalanced and confused.

As one can imagine, framing is one of the most important ways that filmmakers provide perspective and point of view to their individual shots and to the film as a whole. Usually, a film is shot to reflect an omniscient point of view toward the characters and events. In print stories, a hallmark of the omniscient point of view is the revelation of what characters feel or think. Films rarely find ways to show viewers what a character is thinking in any direct way, the way a prose story writer can. But filmmakers can show us what characters see and then show us the characters' body and facial reactions to what they see. In the early scenes of *My Son the Fanatic*, the Inspector General and his wife offer paragraphs of internal thoughts through their facial reactions to Parvez's constant chattering. A tight smile here and a raised eyebrow there and we know clearly that the parents in this traditional English family want nothing to do with these immigrants. With this mixture of subjective shots and objective shots, the film finds a way to do what a print story does with ease.

MOVEMENT

A film is, as noted before, "a moving picture." The camera can move, and thus what we see within the frame moves and changes. Over the last century, filmmakers have developed various kinds of machines and devices that allow them to move the camera in different ways to accomplish an array of shots. Each of these kind of shots have names:

pan—a shot in which the camera turns horizontally. It is as if the viewers were turning their heads, left and right.

tilt—a shot in which the camera turns vertically. It is as if the viewers were raising or lowering their heads.

tracking shot—a shot in which the camera moves, sometimes on tracks, toward, away from, beside, around the people and objects being filmed.

crane shot—a shot in which the camera moves, on a crane—in the air toward, away from, beside, around the people and object being filmed.

Steadicam shot—a shot from a held camera equipped to remain balanced and steady.

hand-held shot—a shot from a held camera that is not equipped to remain balanced and steady.

While the effects of many of these shots can overlap to some degree, they each can provide visual information in unique ways that vary in substance and in the responses they provoke. In the opening sequences of *To Build a Fire*, the filmmakers set up a camera on a plateau and film the wide swaths of snow below; then they pan to the right showing the swath to be long and vast, indicating just how large and desolate the Yukon is and how long the traveler's journey is. In *The Company of Wolves*, the camera pans around the sleeping girl's room, beginning at the closed door, behind which, in the hall, the girl's sister is yelling. The camera pans to the left showing various objects on the wall, but we also see, as the camera appears to tilt down slightly, reflected in a mirror, a partial view of the girl in her bed. The camera continues to pan left until we see the girl sleeping feverishly in her bed.

While the pan and the tilt seem to allow the camera to perform in ways similar to viewers turning and tilting their heads, the tracking shot both duplicates and extends the range of what humans can see and experience. In basic ways, the tracking shot duplicates the effect of a person walking toward or away from or beside the people and objects being observed. Often, however, the camera appears to travel along without the necessary fiction of a viewer in motion. Instead, the tracking shot can create a moving image that humans would not ordinarily be able to see. For example, in an early shot in *The Company of Wolves*, the camera tracks beside a dog running in the woods—running at a high rate of speed for a long distance. As a depiction of a realistic human activity, the shot is ridiculous. No human could run that fast for that long beside the dog, and certainly not so smoothly. But the filmmakers are not attempting to duplicate a typical human viewing experience. Already, this early in a film about dreams and fantasy, the filmmakers are dislodging any semblance to normal human reality. They are telling viewers that there is something unreal about these canines and that in this movie we will experience new things. In print stories, especially those told with the omniscient point of view, writers are bound less by the expectation that every description will in some way be grounded in typical human perception. We expect a writer, even in so-called realistic fiction, to transgress the boundaries of typical human knowledge, to tell us about, to imagine for us, things we do not normally see and consider. For instance, consider the closing scenes in "The Open Boat," where the narrator tells us about how four shipwrecked men struggle to get ashore. Or consider Virginia Woolf's description of the movements of a snail in "Kew Gardens."

Another shot that replicates, in some ways, the omniscient narrator is the crane shot, sometimes also called a "dolly shot." The crane shot is basically created by shooting from a camera attached to a crane that can lift the camera above the set and actors and "float" the viewer into and out of the action. On several occasions, the filmmakers of *Mishima* begin the presentation of scenes from Mishima's writings high above what appears to be a theater stage or a film soundstage. The camera glides down into the set, as if saying that now the viewers are leaving the biographical portions of Mishima's life and entering into the fictional portions. In these cases, the crane shot is used as a kind of transitional device. The crane shot is also used to provide kinds of information and perspectives that are more objective and "distant." In these cases, the crane shot, perhaps, helps establish tone in the film. It can be as if the author were pulling back emotionally from the characters' lives and conflicts and offering a more objective view of them.

The Steadicam and hand-held shots allow the filmmakers to create a more intimate and close up feel to their shots. Both allow the camera operators to get into the middle of a moving group of people in the way that a tracking shot would not. In the latter half of *My Son the Fanatic* appear two scenes that most likely were filmed with this technology. In the first, Parvez wakes up in his house to find it crowded with his son's religious friends and their leaders. Parvez moves within this crowd, pausing and turning within the crowd. All the while the camera follows Parvez and shows what he is seeing and experiencing, tilting a bit, panning a bit. Soon after that scene, Parvez drives upon a riot, gets out of his taxi, and soon has to separate his son from fighting Parvez's woman friend. Much of this scene, though not all, appears to be shot with a hand-held camera, which emphasizes the bumps and jostling that occur in the fight and in making his way through the crowd. Hand-cameras are a relatively recent addition to the kinds of shots that filmmakers have available, and they add a strong sense of realism and/or participation in the actions being filmed. In prose fiction, only the best writers, through powerful description, seem to be able to place readers right in the middle of the action in any comparable way.

DURATION

One final facet of the mise-en-shot is the length or duration of the shot itself. In the history of film, the average duration of shots has varied with styles prevalent in certain decades and with the style of various filmmakers. In the nineteen forties, the average duration of a shot was nine seconds. This means that the average 90 minute film contains something like 600 individual shots. Alfred Hitchcock, on the other hand, constructed the film *Rope* from only eight shots. The manner with which the filmmakers edit these pieces together is an important facet of film editing and thus of narrative pacing, as was discussed previously. The length of the shot might be considered something akin to writing style. It is probably not a totally accurate analogy, but it can be useful to think about the information contained in a short take (a second or two) to be comparable to a sentence in prose storytelling. A longer take (a minute or more) is perhaps analogous to a paragraph.

The long take makes demands upon the film viewer in much the same ways that long passages in a prose work do. They force the viewers to fix their attention continuously upon the screen, perhaps roaming their eyes to different parts of the screen gathering information, remembering information, all the while they feel a subtle rise in tension, waiting for the shot to change and return the film to a more normal pacing. The final scene in *My Son the Fanatic* is a case in point. This scene, which merely shows Parvez returning home, turning on lights, and getting a bottle of scotch for a drink, lasts over two and a half minutes without a cut. It is probably the longest shot in the entire film. While the narrative within the shot is very simple, the shot itself forces us to reconsider the entire film. He travels the entire film, all over again, in this one scene, going down stairs to his room, going into the living room and kitchen, going upstairs to his son's room. Is Parvez happy? Sad? Is this empty house the result of moving his family to England? Is this why he adopted Western values? Is this life larger or smaller because of his friendship with the prostitute? The long take allows all of these questions to arise.

ADAPTING SHORT FICTION INTO FILM

Whenever we think of film adaptations of works of literature, we most often think of adaptations of novels. The list of films adapted from novels is, indeed, very long, *Gone with the Wind* being perhaps the most famous. Recently films based on novels by Jane Austen have been popular. Yet the long list also includes current popular novels by John Grisham, Steven King, and Elmore Leonard. Even powerful cult films such as *One*

Flew over the Cuckoo's Nest, A Clockwork Orange, Blade Runner, and *Crash* are adaptations of important novels.

Certainly films adapted from plays have also become enjoyable movies. Shakespeare's works continue to inspire new generations of film makers, as do Chekhov's, Eugene O'Neill's, Arthur Miller's, and Neal Simon's. Contemporary plays have become the basis for film adaptations, such as *A Few Good Men, M. Butterfly,* and more.

As the selections in this anthology attest, classic and contemporary works of short fiction also often inspire screenwriters and directors to create film adaptations. This anthology contains about thirty stories that have been adapted. And there are other works of short fiction not in this anthology that have been adapted into film—Cortázar's "Blow Up," Hemingway's "The Snows of Kilimanjaro," Gaitskill's "Secretary," and Larry Brown's stories in *Big Bad Love* come quickly to mind.

While novels and plays appear to be the literary forms most compatible to film adaptation—and poetry appears to be the least, though Sherman Alexie did a very credible job adapting his poetry in the film *Fancy Dancing*—they do pose difficulties. For novels, the greatest difficulty is length and complexity. A two-hour film, which by contemporary standards is somewhat long already, cannot portray all the minor characters and subplots that a typical novel includes. Plays bring their own set of difficulties. First, a play, set on a single stage, is a static viewing experience. The actors stand a relatively constant distance from the audience and the members of the audience can see the entire set and choose to look at whatever character they wish to observe. In addition, a play is a genre most often based on dialogue. Neither of these facets are the strengths of film, where action, variety of visual distances, and variety of settings are commonplace and expected.

Short fiction poses its own difficulties in adaptation to film. Like a play, a short story may have only one or two settings and, if it is a modern story, it may be constructed primarily of dialogue, such as "Hills Like White Elephants." Unlike the novel, a single short story with its close attention on one or two characters in a conflict that is relatively focused provides too little material for a full-length film. The story "My Son the Fanatic" is a good example. It is a contemporary story of average length, focused on a father, his son, and the father's friend, who is a prostitute. Its setting is limited to the father's taxi, his home, and a restaurant. The filmed version, which was written by the author of the story, adds several settings—a hotel, bar, the friend's home, a mosque, and more. Similarly, new characters are added, a German business man, other prostitutes, and a Muslim leader and his followers.

Several things, therefore, occur in the adaptations of short fiction into film. First, settings will be added. Second, characters will be added. Third, characters' back stories, their personal histories, may be created or expanded. Fourth, scenes may be added or cut. Fifth, themes may be adapted. Sixth, linear plots may be collapsed through flashbacks and non-linear plots made chronological. If stories are well-known and considered classics, like a Shakespearian play, they may be updated and put into modern dress. Two filmed adaptations of "Bartleby the Scrivener" have changed the setting of Melville's 1850s New York story to a 1970s London and to a strange contemporary distopia.

In *Adventures in the Screen Trade: A Personal View of Hollywood and Screenwriting,* William Goldman discusses the craft and dangers of adapting a literary work into film. Goldman is a writer with strong credentials. Not only is he a novelist—*The Princess Bride* and *Marathon Man*—he is a successful screenwriter of such films as *Butch Cassidy and the Sundance Kid* and *All the King's Men.* In a hundred-page section of *Adventures in the Screen Trade,* Goldman takes the reader on the journey of adapting a ten-page short story into a forty-page screenplay, a work that would play, with commercials, for about an hour.

Goldman also provides a list of questions he asks when adapting a literary work into a screenplay:

1. What's the story about?
2. What's the story really about?
3. What about time?
4. Who tells the story?
5. Where does the story take place?
6. What about characters?
7. What must we cling to?

Goldman's questions highlight certain qualities of narratives. The first are thematic qualities ("What's the story about?" and "What's the story really about?") In "My Son the Fanatic," the answer to the first questions could be, it's about the conflict between a father and a son. The answer to the second points toward broader issues: It's about the hidden fanatical nature of Western secular culture. Another answer to the second question could be that it's about the reasons that people become fundamentalists.

Goldman's questions "Who tells the story?" "Where does the story take place?" and "What about characters?" are questions readers of fiction habitually ask about point of view, setting, characters and conflict. In adapting a story for a screenplay, the writer will ask these questions from the perspective of their practicality in a film adaptation. How must the film change the perspective from which the story is told? How does one depict the setting, what changes occur, and can one depict those changes? How do we know these characters, through their thoughts or their actions? How must the film depict the development of the characters and what troubles them?

Goldman's question "What about time" examines the two times of film story telling, "the time *of* the story (time period) and the time *in* the story (duration)." In "My Son the Fanatic," the time period *of* the original story is contemporary, within the previous decade or so. The time *in* the story is the amount of time certain events take individually and collectively on screen. If the writer wants to affect the film viewer in certain ways, scenes may have to be compressed or expanded.

Goldman's final question—"What must we cling to?"—forces the screenwriter to evaluate various scenes, motifs, metaphors, for their value to the narrative. Is a character's age really important? In "The Rocking-Horse Winner," one, presumably, would believe that Paul must remain very young. The effect of a teenager or young adult riding a rocking horse would be unsettling in ways that would destroy the effect of the story. However, the filmmakers of "The Fall of the House of Usher" felt that the narrator and Roderick need not be school friends and turned the narrator into a love interest for Madeline. Two adaptations of "Bartleby the Scrivener" reflect a belief that the setting of New York City in the 1850s was not essential, but both adaptations did cling to Bartleby's refrain "I prefer not to."

In looking at the film adaptations of stories included in this anthology, two distinctions can be noted about the art of adaptations. These include the markets or the audiences that the films are created for and the faithfulness of the adaptations.

THE MARKET

Film adaptations of works of short fiction are aimed at two distinct audiences. One is the educational market. The primary goal of these films appears to be to reproduce the story as faithfully as possible. This often means that the viewing time of these films is short, around or under thirty minutes. Thirty minutes is a workable time for classroom presentations, and with most short stories it is an accurate reproduction of the time *in* the story, for the duration of the telling of the story. Filmed adaptations for the educational market often feature stories that are not controversial in their presentations of such matters as sexual content, language, and violence. The primary reason for adapting these stories to film appears to be pedagogical—to introduce good literature to students—and cultural—to preserve and make available stories that are or should be in "the canon," that list of works that should be known by all educated, literate persons.

A second market for filmed adaptations of works of short fiction is the same as that of most films—the general movie-going public. However, currently there seem to be at least two, perhaps three, different kinds of films produced for the general public. The first is the "Hollywood blockbuster." The stories these films are based on generally fit neatly into the pre-existing genres of large scale movies—science fiction, westerns, mysteries, and love stories. They provide relatively safe "vehicles" for established Hollywood stars. Recently, Keanu Reeves starred in *Johnny Mnemonic*, and previously Michael Caine and Sean Connery starred in *The Man Who Would Be King*, and in the fifties Gregory Peck and Ava Gardner starred in *The Snows of Kilimanjaro*.

Most filmed adaptations of short stories are productions of what are now called independent films. These films call for smaller casts, tighter budgets, and are created for a more discerning movie viewer. They often deal with those areas of artistic creation that do not easily fall into mass genres—the stories of real people facing real human problems. While some of these films, such as Robert Altman's *Short Cuts* or Chris Eyre's *Smoke Signals* attract a surprisingly large number of viewers, most become popular with a smaller, more dedicated population of film viewers—those who watch movies, not to escape, but to consider life and art in new ways.

A third kind of general popular market for film adaptation is what used to be called "the art film." The recent rise of "independent" filmmaking appears to have grown from the legacies of the art film, films by the great innovative directors. Perhaps the most famous example of an art house film based on a work of short fiction is Antonioni's *Blow Up*, loosely based on Julio Cortázar's story. Although director John Huston was certainly an important Hollywood director of such films as *The African Queen*, *The Treasure of the Sierra Madre*, and *The Man Who Would Be King*, some of his late films, such as *Wise Blood*, based on Flannery O'Connor's novella, and *The Dead*, based on James Joyce's long story, could be considered films that were neither typically mass market genre nor typically independent film fare.

FAITHFULNESS OF ADAPTATION

Another distinction that can be made among films made from short fiction is the faithfulness of adaptation. Several factors can affect the adaptation of a film. One of the most important of these is the nature and length of the source short story. Faithful adaptation does not necessarily mean that all the characters are depicted in exactly the ways they are described in the source story, but rather that what occurs in the film is more or less contained, in spirit, in the source story.

Long Stories Adapted into Average-Length Movies   It appears that the form of fiction most suitable for film adaptation is the long story or the novella. While adaptations of novels often require the screenwriter to excise large portions of the novel's plotlines, the long story, with its close focus on one or two plots, seems to inspire the most faithful adaptations. In this anthology, long stories that have been adapted into films include Conrad's "The Heart of Darkness," Joyce's "The Dead," and Melville's "Bartleby the

Scrivener." All of these stories provide sufficient plot lines and a sufficient number of characters and conflicts to occupy the typical-length film.

Short Films Made from Average-Length Short Stories   As has been noted, the average-length short story occupies something like thirty minutes of screen time. Many films that faithfully adapt one short story, therefore, are not films created for the movie-going public, but rather for educational and cultural purposes, as in the case of the American Short Story series, first produced for the Public Broadcasting Service and then purchased by many libraries. In one case, Home Box Office combined productions of three short stories in a kind of anthology called *Women and Men: Stories of Seduction.* One of the stories included—Hemingway's "Hills Like White Elephants"—is included in this anthology.

Films Made from Several Stories   In a number of cases, filmmakers have adapted several stories in combination to produce a typical-length film. Often the stories are already combined in a single volume. This is the case with *Smoke Signals,* based on Sherman Alexie stories; *Jesus' Son,* based on a volume of related stories by Denis Johnson; *Short Cuts,* based on several unrelated stories by Raymond Carver; *The Joy Luck Club,* based on a novel in stories by Amy Tan; and *And the Earth Did Not Swallow Him,* based on a novel in short works by Tomás Rivera. Stories by all these writers are included in this anthology.

Films Based on One Short Story That Has Been Changed and Expanded   In other cases, filmmakers may like the general idea in a short story and then change the story in any number of ways for any number of reasons. The outcome is a typical-length film that owes its genesis to the original story. Angela Carter expanded and adapted her own short stories based on The Little Red Riding Hood stories into *In the Company of Wolves,* directed by Neal Jordan. Hanif Kureishi expanded his short story "My Son the Fanatic," adding several characters and plot lines. F. Scott Fitzgerald's story "Babylon Revisited" underwent many changes in setting, characters, and conflict to become a movie for Elizabeth Taylor.

Films Tangentially Related to Short Stories   There are films that are related to short stories in a number of slight ways. Sometimes the film may simply contain a reference to the short story. This is the case with *Franz Kafka's It's a Wonderful Life,* which one might say was inspired by Kafka's "The Metamorphosis," but one would also have to say that the film was inspired just as powerfully by the popular Christmas film *It's a Wonderful Life.* Francis Ford Coppola's *Apocalypse Now* is famous for its loose adaptation of plot elements from Conrad's "The Heart of Darkness," though the movie is so independent of the story that the movie can be enjoyed and appreciated without knowing the source plot.

Films Thematically Related to Short Stories   Finally, there are a number of films that can be examined profitably in light of previously published short works. Although the film *Multiplicity,* which concerns cloning, credits another short story as the source story, Susan Sontag's story "The Dummy" predates both by several decades. Similarly, recent films like *Eyes Wide Shut* and *Round Midnight* repeat plot lines and themes of "Young Goodman Brown" and "Sonny's Blues," respectively. Additionally, the many Hollywood films concerned with infidelity—*Unfaithful* and *The Bridges of Madison County*—might profitably bear comparison with Chekhov's classic "The Lady with the Dog."

We might also include in this group films that are based on writers' lives. Some of these films, such as *Mishima* and *Kafka,* bear very directly upon the writer's work. In these films, it seems that the writer's works of fiction were used as part of the screenplay. Other films, such as *Mrs. Parker and Her Vicious Circle,* a recent film about Dorothy Parker, or *Beloved Infidel,* an older film about F. Scott Fitzgerald, give us important and interesting interpretations of a writer's life.

THE ART OF FICTIONAL NARRATION

Over the past few decades, films and film studies have found fairly secure places in English departments and in the literature classroom. While many, and maybe most, instructors worry that for the general public watching films is replacing the reading of quality fiction, it is still not at all unusual for people to say after watching a film, "Oh, but you must read the book. The book is so much better." People realize, no matter how many movies they see, that one writer at full command of his or her powers is still a potent force in storytelling. Just as there is a romance of turning out the lights and giving oneself to a movie, there is still also a romance to sitting in a comfortable chair and giving oneself to a good book or short story.

The truth is that filmed fiction and written fiction, while similar in many ways, provide two very different narrative experiences. To experience either at its best, each requires a knowledge of the elements of storytelling—character, conflict, setting, point of view, language, and tone. Each requires attention and perception and analysis. In both media, we can find a lot of "mind candy," whether it be genre mysteries, simple science fiction, or predictable love stories. And in both, we can find art practiced at high levels.

Finally, one question seems inevitable—should we read the novel or story before seeing the film? Traditionally, there have been plenty of opinions saying that one should read the story first. But perhaps answering that question can be avoided by recognizing and accepting that the two media are just that, two media. One is not a replacement for the other. Both works, if approached seriously by the writers and by the audiences, are separate works of art. After all, no one suggests that seeing Mendelssohn's ballet *A Mid-Summer Night's Dream* is a substitute for seeing Shakespeare's play. No one says—do they?—that we should watch the play before the seeing the ballet. It is up to us readers and viewers to be intelligent about how we approach narratives in various media. In the long run, won't we become more intelligent and perceptive readers of fiction if we remember what we know from watching films? And similarly, won't we become more intelligent and perceptive movie goers if we remember what we know from reading fiction?

A LIST OF SHORT FICTIONS AND FILMED ADAPTATIONS

Alexie, Sherman. "Because My Father Always Said He Was the Only Indian Who Saw Jimi Hendrix Play 'The Star-Spangled Banner' at Woodstock." *Smoke Signals*. Dir. Chris Eye. Perf. Adam Beach, Evan Adams. Miramax, 1998. 89 min. PG-13.

Balzac, Honoré de. "A Passion in the Desert." *Passion in the Desert*. Dir. by Lavinia Currier. Perf. Ben Daniels, Michel Piccoli. Fine Line, 1998. 91 min. PG-13.

Carter, Angela. "The Werewolf." *The Company of Wolves* Dir. Neil Jordan. Perf. Angela Lansbury, David Warner, Micha Bergese. ITC Entertainment, 1984. R.

Chekhov, Anton. "The Lady with the Dog." *The Lady with a Dog*. Dir. Josef Heifit. Perf. Iya Savvina, Alexei Batalov, Ala Chostakova. Corinth Films, 1960. Russian with subtitles. 89 min. NR.

Bierce, Ambrose. "An Occurrence at Owl Creek Bridge." *An Occurrence at Owl Creek Bridge*. Dir. Robert Enrico. Perf. Roger Jacquet, Ann Cornaly, Anker Larsen. 1962. 28 mins.

Carver, Raymond. "Cathedral."
Cathedral. Dir. Bruce Schwartz. Perf. James Eckhouse, Mark Rolston. Bruce R.
Schwartz. 35 mins. NR.

Carver, Raymond. "A Small, Good Thing."
Short Cuts. Dir. Robert Altman. Perf. Tim Robbins, Julianne Moore, Anne Archer.
New Line. 1993. 187 mins. R.

Cather, Willa. "Paul's Case."
Paul's Case. Dir. Lamont Johnson. Perf. Lindsay Crouse, Eric Roberts. The American Short Story Series, 1978. 52 min. NR.

Cheever, John. "The Swimmer."
The Swimmer. Dir. Frank Perry. Perf. Burt Lancaster, Janet Landgard, Janice Rule.
Sony Pictures, 1968. 94 min. PG.

Chopin, Kate. "The Story of an Hour."
The Joy that Kills. Dir. Tina Rathborne. Perf. Barbara Shapiro. Cypress Films,
1984. 56 min. NR.

Conrad, Joseph. "The Heart of Darkness."
Heart of Darkness. Dir. Nicolas Roeg. Perf. John Malkovich, Tim Roth, James Fox,
Issach de Bankole. Turner Home Entertainment, 1993. 105 min. NR.
Apocalypse Now. Dir. Francis Ford Coppola. Perf. Marlon Brando, Martin Sheen.
Paramount Pictures, 1979. 153 min. R

Dick, Philip K. "We Can Remember It for You Wholesale."
Total Recall. Dir. Paul Verhoeven. Perf. Arnold Schwarzenegger, Sharon Stone.
Aritsan. 1990. 113 mins. R.

Fitzgerald, F. Scott. "Babylon Revisited."
The Last Time I Saw Paris. Dir. Richard Brooks. Perf. Elizabeth Taylor, Van Johnson, Donna Reed. 1954. NR.

Gibson, William. "Johnny Mnemonic."
Johnny Mnemonic. Dir. Robert Blongo. Perf. Keanu Reeves, Dolph Lundgren. Co-
lumbia/Tri Star. 1995. 96 mins. R.

Gilman, Charlotte Perkins. "The Yellow Wallpaper."
The Yellow Wallpaper. Dir. John Clive. Perf. Stephen Dellane, Julia Watson. PBS.
Masterpiece Theater. 1989. 31 mins. R.
The Yellow Wallpaper. Dir. Tony Romain. Perf. Rachael Lillis, Michael Slayton.
1996. 16 mm. 25 minutes. NR.

Gogol, Nikolai. "The Overcoat."
Il Cappotto. Dir. Alberto Lattuada. Perf. Renato Rascel, Yvonne Sanson. Faro
Film/Titanus. 1952. 95 mins. Black and White. NR.
The Overcoat. Dir. Morris Panych. Perf. Dean Paul Gibson. Radio-Canada/Cana-
dian Broadcasting Corp. 2001.
Shinel. Dir. Aleksei Batalov. Perf. Rolan Bykov. 1959. 75 minutes. Black and
White. With English subtitles as *The Overcoat.* Hens Tooth Video 1991. NR.

Hemingway, Ernest. "Hills Like White Elephants."
Hills Like White Elephants. Dir. Tony Richardson. Perf. Melanie Griffith, James
Woods. In *Men and Women: Stories of Seduction.* Edde Entertainment, 1995 NR.

Jackson, Shirley. "The Lottery."
The Lottery. Dir. Garry Marshall. Perf. Bette Midler. 1987.

The Lottery. Dir. Daniel Sackheim. Perf. Dan Cortese, Keri Russell, Platinium Disc Corp. 1996. 94 mins. PG-13.

Johnson, Denis. "Car Crash While Hitchhiking."
Jesus' Son. Dir. Alison Maclean. Perf. Billy Crudup, Samantha Morton, Holly Hunter. Lionsgate, 1999. 107 min. R.

Joyce, James. "The Dead."
The Dead. Dir. John Huston. Perf. Angelica Huston, Donal McCann. Zenith Productions, 1987. 82 min. PG.

London, Jack. "To Build a Fire."
To Build a Fire. Dir. David Cobham. Perf. Ian Hogg. VCI Home Video, 1969, 56 min. NR.

Kureishi, Hanif. "My Son the Fanatic."
My Son the Fanatic. Dir. Udayan Prasad. Perf. Rachel Griffiths, Om Puri, Stellan Skarsgaard. Miramax. 87 min. R.

Lawrence, D. H. "The Rocking-Horse Winner."
The Rocking Horse Winner. Dir. Anthony Pelissier. Perf. John Howard Davis, Valerie Hobson. 1950. B&W. 91 min.

Melville, Herman. "Bartleby the Scrivener."
Bartleby. Dir. Jonathan Parker. Perf. Crispin Glover, David Paymer. Outrider Pictures, 2000. 83 min. Color. PG13.
Bartleby. Dir. Anthony Friedman. Perf. Paul Scofield, John McEnery. Corinth Films, 1972. 79 min. Color. PG13.

Nolan, Jonathan. "Memento Mori."
Memento. Dir. Christopher Nolan. Perf. Guy Pearce, Carrie-Anne Moss, Joe Pantoliano. Columbia Tri-Star, 2001. 113 min. B&W and Color. R.

Oates, Joyce Carol. "Where Are You Going, Where Have You Been?"
Smooth Talk. Dir. Joyce Chopra. Perf. Laura Dern, Treat Williams. Lionsgate/Fox. 1985. 92 mins. PG13.

Poe, Edgar Allan. "The Fall of the House of Usher."
The Fall of the House of Usher. Dir. Roger Corman. Perf. Vincent Price, Mark Damon, Myrna Fahey. MGM, 1960. 89 min. Color. NR.

Rivera, Tomás, ". . . And the Earth Did Not Devour Him."
And the Earth Did Not Swallow Him. Dir. Severo Perez. Perf. Jose Alcala, Rose Portillo. Kino Video. 1995. NR.

Steinbeck, John. "Chrysanthemums."
The Chrysanthemums. Dir. Steve Rosen. Perf. Nina Capriola, Paul Henri. Pyramid Film. 1990. 22 min. NR.

Tan, Amy. "A Pair of Tickets."
The Joy Luck Club. Dir. Wayne Wang. Perf. Rosalind Chao, Joan Chen, France Nuyen. Hollywood Pictures. 1993. 139 min. Color. R.

Tolstoy, Leo. "The Death of Ivan Ilych."
Ivan's XTC. Dir. Bernard Rose. Perf. Danny Huston, Peter Weller. Enos, 2002.

Updike, John. "A & P."
A & P. Dir. Bruce Schwartz. Perf. Sean Hayes, Amy Smart. Bruce R. Schwartz. 18 mins. NR.

Welty, Eudora. "A Worn Path."
A Worn Path. Dir. Bruce Schwartz. Perf. Cora Lee Day, Brad Dourif. Bruce R. Schwartz. 20 mins. NR.

Richard Wright. "The Man Who Was Almost a Man."
Almost' a Man. Perf. LaVar Burton, Henry Fonda. The American Short Story Series, 1977. 51 min. Color. NR.

Anzia Yezierska. "Hunger."
Hungry Hearts. Dir. E. Mason Hooper. Perf. Rosa Rosanova, Sara Levin. Goldwyn Pictures. 1922. 80 mins. NR.

SHORT FICTIONS AND FILMS ON RELATED TOPICS OR THEMES

Baldwin, James. "Sonny's Blues."
'Round Midnight. Dir. Bertrand Tavernier. Perf. Dexter Gordon, François Cluzet, Lonette McKee. Warner Bros, 1986. 131 min. Color. R.

Chekhov, Anton. "The Lady with the Dog."
The Bridges of Madison County. Dir. Clint Eastwood. Perf. Meryl Streep, Clint Eastwood, Victor Slezak. Warner Bros. 1995. 135 min. PG-13.
Unfaithful. Dir. Adrian Lyne. Per. Diane Lane, Richard Gere, Olivier Martinez. Fox. 2002. 124 mins. R.

Hawthorne, Nathaniel. "Young Goodman Brown."
Eyes Wide Shut. Dir. Stanley Kubrick. Perf. Tom Cruise, Nicole Kidman. Warner Bros. 1999. 159 mins. R.

Kafka, Franz. "The Metamorphosis."
Kafka. Dir. Steven Soderbergh. Perf. Jeremy Irons, Theresa Russell, Joel Grey. Miramax, 1991. 98 min. B&W. NR.
Franz Kafka's It's a Wonderful Life. Dir. Peter Capaldi. Perf. Richard E. Grant, Phyllis Logan. 1995. 25 min. B&W. NR.

Mishima, Yukio. "Patriotism."
Mishima. Dir. Paul Schrader. Perf. Ken Ogata, Kenji Sawara, Yasosuke Bando. Warner Bros., 1985. 120 min. Color. R.
Afraid to Die. Dir. Yasuzo Masumura. Perf. Yukio Mishima. 1960. 94 min. NR.

O'Brien,Tim. "The Things They Carried."
Platoon. Dir. Oliver Stone. Perf. Tom Beringer, Willem Defoe, Charlie Sheen. MGM/United Artists. 1986. 120 mins. R.

O'Connor, Frank. "Guests of the Nation."
The Crying Game. Dir. Neil Jordan. Perf. Stephen Rea, Miranda Richardson, Stephen Rea. Artisan. 1992. 112 mins. R.

Susan Sontag. "The Dummy."
Multiplicity. Dir. Harold Ramis. Perf. Michael Keaton, Andie MacDowell. Columbia Tri-Star, 1996. 117 min. Color. PG13.

Writing About Short Fiction

You are not able to relax. Something bothers you—it has been bothering you longer than you can remember. Sooner than you like you must hand in your first essay—your first writing assignment of the new term—and you can't get started. You flick on the computer: It boots up right away; there is plenty of paper in the printer; next to the printer is this text. If anything had been missing, you could convince yourself that you couldn't begin.

Maybe a cup of coffee would help. You decide it's too much trouble to make it yourself, so you walk to Java Java. You could have gone to the convenience store; it's closer; but no matter how busy or frustrated you are, there are some things you will not stoop to, like drinking bad coffee. Sitting under the trees on the patio of Java Java, you sip from your coffee cup, trying not to think about your essay. Since you are already outside, you try to picture yourself smoking a cigarette—maybe that would help. Then you remember that you don't smoke.

But relaxing in the shade of the trees, you begin to think about stories you have read so far during the semester. Some stories troubled you: Ida Fink's "A Scrap of Time" was about the genocide of Jews in Europe; Ralph Ellison's "A Party down at the Square" portrayed lynching in the American South. Some stories were humorous, like Mary Lavin's "My Vocation" and Donald Barthelme's "A City of Churches." And there were a few that left you feeling flat, so you decide you don't want to think about them. Then you remember all of those stories about adultery. You wonder why there are so many stories on that subject: "The Lady with the Dog," "A Respectable Woman," "Let the Old Dead Make Room for the Young Dead." You wonder what it is about these writers that makes them so fixated on this. And then there are those stories about creepy, obsessive mothers—D. H. Lawrence's "The Rocking-Horse Winner," David Foster Wallace's "Suicide as a Sort of Present," Joyce Carol Oates's "Shopping."

Suddenly, you realize there are many stories you could write about. Well, the coffee certainly helped, you think. It's time to return home and get the essay started.

THINK ABOUT YOUR PURPOSE

No matter what kind of writing project you have—whether it is a school assignment, a personal interest, or a work project—you want to be clear about your purpose. In college essays, the purpose usually is to inform the reader about some topic or to persuade the reader to think or act in a particular way. In college English classes, these two purposes are often combined into what instructors call argumentative writing. In argumentative writing, you propose a way to understand a story, and then, with whatever facts, logic, and creativity you have, you argue its validity.

One of the first things to do as you start to write an assigned essay is to look at the language of the instructor's assignment. It helps to understand fully the meaning of four words: summarize, analyze, explicate, and evaluate. If your instructor uses one of these words in the assignment, the purpose of your essay is determined for you. If your instructor has left the purpose of the essay to you to determine, consider one of these four.

SUMMARIZE

One straightforward assignment your instructor may make at the beginning of the semester is to write a summary of a short story. Even if your instructor does not assign a summary essay, it may be a kind of writing you want to practice on your own. The skill of writing a brief, accurate summary of any piece of writing is useful in many walks of life. Lawyers write briefs of previous cases; Hollywood screenwriters produce "treatments" as part of the process of developing and marketing scripts; business people write executive summaries of business plans. In other writing assignments in an English class, you will need to summarize a plot or a scene as you argue a particular interpretation of the work.

The goal in writing a summary is to retell the story in a condensed form, but to do so accurately. Accuracy is maintained in several ways. First, you insure that your summary is factually correct by verifying the names of people and places. Second, you make your summary comprehensive—you include everything needed for a complete understanding. Third, your summary will maintain the focus of the original story. The writer of the short story stresses and emphasizes certain aspects of the story; one group of scenes, therefore, may be more important than another group. Your summary will reflect the original writer's sense of weight and balance.

Another goal in writing a summary is objectivity. The better you are at leaving out interpretations and evaluations, the better the summary will be. Jack Webb, a police officer on the television program *Dragnet*, said as he interviewed victims and suspects, "Just the facts, please." His goal, of course, was to write a police report that was objective. In a summary, strive to leave out your opinions and judgments. Avoid telling what things mean; just tell what happens.

You can write summaries in any length. A typical short story of about 5,000 words can be condensed to 100 words or 500. Short summaries can be kept to one paragraph, but if you need more than one paragraph, your paragraph breaks should reflect the structure of the story. See page 1381 for an example of a summary.

ANALYZE

An analysis of a work of literature is one step beyond a summary. The purpose of summarizing a story is to retell it accurately and objectively, in essence to answer such questions as *who*, *what*, *when*, and *where*. The purpose of analyzing a story is to answer *how*, especially how the parts of the story relate to the whole of the story. Writing an analysis can be a natural development of the attentive reading of a story, because when we read we begin analyzing. We ask such questions as "Who is this character, really?" "Why is he behaving in this way?" "How will the character resolve the conflict?" "What does it mean that the character is new to this town?" "Why are there so many images of ice in one section and of water in another?" By asking such questions of ourselves and of the story, we begin to divide the whole of the story into parts, which we have called the elements of fiction. One way to analyze a story, then, is to study how each element—theme, character, conflict, setting, point of view, language, tone—is related to the other elements.

A thorough understanding of a story requires that we analyze how it is put together, and an effective analytical essay requires that we communicate the fruits of this labor. How thorough an essay is depends on several factors, including how long the essay is, how much time we have to write the essay, and who is reading the essay and why. Most analytical essays, especially those not requiring research, are about 500 to 1500 words, and therefore require us to narrow greatly the focus of the essay. An analytical essay does not have to answer every question a reader might have about a story, but it must define the parameters of the analysis. You can do this in several ways. You can limit discussion to one theme of the work, or to one element of fiction. You might also limit your analysis to one section of the work, an approach called explication (which is discussed separately below).

If your instructor has asked you to write an analysis, you can begin by asking yourself what aspect of the story most interests you and which element of fiction best helps you understand that aspect. See page 1384 for an example of an analytical essay.

EXPLICATE

Explication and analysis are closely related methods of interpreting a work of literature. An analysis of a story will often consider one aspect of that story, such as setting, and how that aspect relates to the rest of the story. An explication will examine, in close detail, one passage in the story and how that passage relates to the story as a whole. In explicating a passage from a story, you might focus on any or all of the elements of fiction, but you do so by examining the passage sentence by sentence, and sometimes word by word. This method has the advantage of telescoping the thematic material of a story, thus opening interpretations that might have been missed by looking at larger issues. Some stories contain passages that serve as generative seeds for the rest of the story; they are almost small holographic images of story. Some stories, on the other hand, contain passages that serve almost as thematic counterpoints, bass chords for the main melody of the story. Explicating these passages often provides rich material for interpretation. If your instructor has asked you to write an explication, you can begin by noting the passages in the story that most interest you, either intellectually or emotionally. The structure of your essay will grow as you explore the relationship that the passage has with the whole story.

EVALUATE

Occasionally, we are asked to evaluate a work of literature. We may be uncomfortable publicly evaluating a story, foisting our judgments onto others, and dealing with their possible defenses. However, we have probably already evaluated the work privately, sometimes without even realizing it. Anytime we say that a story is "boring" or "exciting," "offensive" or "predictable," we have evaluated it. The problem with writing an essay that evaluates is that we have to justify and explain ourselves. For some of us, this means we have to explore why we have made such a judgment. This exploration makes us become aware of the criteria we use to judge the quality of a work of literature. To become more aware of our criteria means we have to understand what we expect from a story; it also means we have to understand what a story expects from us.

In evaluating the quality of a short story, you can use any of the qualities below. You probably also have others of your own.

- Is the work unified? Do all the elements of the story work together to provide a coherent theme?
- Does the work provide new and different experiences and meanings in repeated readings?
- Is the work believable?
- Is the work mature and serious?

- Does the work provide meaning for more than one kind of reader?
- Does the work provide meaning for readers of different time periods?

If your instructor asks you to write an evaluation of a story, you don't need to be afraid of the assignment. If you can seriously examine what you expect from a story and determine if the story lives up to those expectations, you can write a clear and reasonable evaluation. See page 1395 for an example of an evaluative essay.

THINK ABOUT YOUR READER

One aspect of writing that we easily forget is that an essay isn't a one-way communication that ends when we turn it in. Writing is part of a process of communication, part of the ongoing process of creating meaning. Just as the creation of a short story doesn't end until you, or someone else, reads it, your writing of an essay doesn't end when you hit the print command on your computer. It ends when your instructor has read what you've written *and* responded to it. Because readers are so important in the process, you have to think about them as you write.

In most cases in college, your reader will be your instructor. You say, "Of course! Everybody knows that. What's the difference?" Well, since he or she obviously has read the story, you know that you won't have to retell the plot—that is, unless your instructor has specifically asked you to write for an audience who hasn't read the story. And because you probably use more formal language in talking to your instructor, you'll be reminded that you need to use more formal language in your essay than you would, say, in a letter to a friend.

In your writing, you should take advantage of everything you know about your reader. In class, does your instructor seem impatient with details and want to get to the main point right away? Or does he or she like to work through a problem, to be persuaded step by step? Does your instructor prefer one critical approach over others, or does he or she use an eclectic approach that employs many methods? Your answers to these questions will affect the way you organize and present your information.

However, it is also helpful to think of your reader as part of a general audience. Doing so focuses your work in several ways. First, thinking of a general audience, not a college instructor, may remind you to explain in detail any generalities and observations you make about a story. If you are writing only to your instructor, you may think, "Oh, Dr. Jones already knows this." But your instructor, you may forget, is hoping for essays that make strong points and illustrate those points. Most instructors, especially those in undergraduate classes, know that many, if not most, of their students are not English majors. So one of the benefits of the class, they probably believe, is that it helps all students to practice thinking clearly and presenting that thinking intelligently. Second, writing to a general audience may remind you to write interestingly. Sometimes, sadly, we begin to think that writing in a college classroom has little to do with writing in the world outside a classroom. "It's just some old teacher that's going to read it; what does it matter, right?" By thinking about a general audience—an audience like you, like the people you see in libraries or bookstores, like you see on the airplane with paperbacks in their laps—you will try to say things that are interesting to know and to think about and you will try to say them with verve and respect. Even if you don't know your instructor well, he or she is probably very much like you, a person who hopes that reading is a pleasure not a chore, a creative activity, an informative activity.

Think About Your Critical Approach

An important step in writing about a work of fiction is deciding what your critical approach is. These critical approaches include New Criticism, Biographical and Historical criticism, Marxist, Feminist, Post-Structuralist, among others. Several critical approaches are discussed in Part V, "Approaching Short Fiction Critically."

Sometimes in an English class the method of criticism may actually be part of the assignment. For instance, if your instructor asks you to write an essay about "*Luck* and *Lucre* in 'The Rocking-Horse Winner,'" then you may very well approach the essay with a Marxist viewpoint, as you will be looking at questions of class and capital. On the other hand, if your instructor assigns an essay "The Mother-and-Son Relationship in 'The Rocking-Horse Winner,'" then you will find yourself approaching the story from a Psychological perspective.

Other times, you may be asked to decide which critical approach to use. The best way is to look at both the story and at how you read the story. Many stories provide clues about which critical method may actually be fruitful. The examples above concerning "The Rocking-Horse Winner" illustrate this point. Any story that makes money an important part of the theme can probably be approached using the Marxist approach. For instance, the stories "Shopping," "Babylon Revisited," "The Death of Ivan Ilych," "A & P," and "The Man Who Was Almost a Man," just to name a few from this volume, can profitably be explored using the Marxist approach.

You can also decide which critical method to use simply by watching how you personally react to a story. If you are particularly attuned to how women are treated in a story, then you are probably already reading in a manner related to feminism. If you read a story with an attention to how it repeats basic images and plots from older literature and myth, then you are reading with mythological approach. If you get wrapped up in the characters of a story or in the historical background, then you may want to use the Biographical or Historical approach. Some of us find ourselves reading literature habitually, using the same approaches, either because of previous classes we have had or from our personal pasts with reading and our experiences with life. Psychology majors may have their own personal approach, as may majors in economics, history, political science, and religion.

One final word is that sometimes it is very profitable to use multiple approaches when studying a story in preparation for writing an essay. Even if you choose not to write your essay from one of the approaches, the exercise of exploring a work from multiple approaches can help you see the story from other perspectives. Each method tends to highlight different kinds of information and responses. For instance, exploring the gender issues in D. H. Lawrence's "The Rocking-Horse Winner" might raise interesting questions about the role of money in families. Why is it the mother who wants more money? Why do the father and the uncle play such unimportant roles? These might not be questions a purely Marxist approach would provoke.

Develop a Thesis

At some point in the writing process, you will determine the central idea or theme that will hold all the parts of your essay together. The central idea often becomes the thesis for your essay and grows from knowledge of your purpose, your reader, your critical approach, and the story you are writing about. For instance, a thesis for an evaluative essay of "A & P" from a Marxist perspective may sound something like "Although Updike is clearly critical of middle-class values, Sammy's comically immature tone undermines that criticism, rendering the story an entertaining failure." A thesis for an explication of "A Party down at the Square" from a mythological perspective might be "In the storm scene, God's witnessing eye descends upon this evil town." Similarly, a thesis for an analysis of character in "Gooseberries" from a New Critical approach could be "Through the characters of Nikolay, Alyohim, and Ivan, Chekhov shows us that we must accept both our physical and mental selves."

Developing a thesis for an essay can be an easy or difficult part of the writing process. Sometimes a wonderful idea comes along during a first reading. At other times, it comes to you at the end of a fourth draft. Often the writing of a thesis—explaining the purpose of your essay in a single sentence—is the result of writing and rewriting, challenging your idea, challenging the way you have expressed your idea, and exchanging one word for another (over and over again). The more you write, the easier you will find organizing ideas and developing a clear sense of purpose.

But it will help if you are prepared to change your focus and your thesis. There are many good ideas, and you might have several ideas worth developing for each essay you write. But sooner or later, as you write your essay, you will decide that one idea is the best. Trying to fit too many ideas into a single essay often results in confusion for your reader or inadequate support or both. Abandoning one idea in favor of another is simply one of those practical decisions we all must make. No matter if your thesis comes to you easily or if you can't quite get one into focus, at some point you will need to return to the story. You may return to the story to review it, trying to remember enough to develop your thesis. You will certainly return to the story to rediscover information to support your thesis.

RETURN TO THE STORY

The process of writing an essay is so personal and individualistic that no one can tell you exactly what steps you should go through and in what order. But a moment comes in the process—it may be the first thing you do or follow after you have already outlined an organization—when you need to sit down and once again look at the text of the story. If you made any notes when you read the story, you will want to look at those notes also.

The purpose of returning to the story as you write about it should be multifaceted. First, you want to make sure that anything you present as a fact or an interpretation is valid and justifiable. Second, you want to double-and triple-check that your thesis represents a thorough and precise interpretation of the entire story. Third, you want to make note of the specific presentation of the story, to record for use in your essay the writer's exact words and phrases. Not only do these quoted passages ensure the accuracy of your essay, but they also make your essay more specific and, therefore, clearer and livelier.

REVIEW YOUR ANNOTATIONS AND QUESTIONS

In Part II of this text, we looked at some of the tools that you can use as an active reader. There we emphasized that you would use those tools to help you enjoy, understand, and interpret the story. If you never write an essay, those tools and techniques are worth learning and practicing. But if you are writing an essay, your immediate reactions to the story as you record them in your annotations can provide the basis for many kinds of essays. An essay employing the Reader-Response approach is founded on your personal reactions as you read the story. Examine your annotations for assumptions you made, for places of frustrations, for moments of understanding. However, in all writing situations, your comments and annotations help lead you back to passages that struck you as important.

REVIEW THE ELEMENTS OF FICTION

One technique suggested by many instructors is reviewing the elements of fiction. This process entails an orderly examination of the story you are writing about, making notes of any details that concern character, conflict, setting, point-of-view, language, and tone. In the discussions of the elements of fiction in Part I of this anthology, passages from stories are examined fairly closely to reveal how writers develop characters and other elements. One approach sometimes suggested is devoting the front and back of an index card to notes about each element.

MAKE LISTS

You probably know how helpful lists are and already make a few yourself: what to pick up at the grocery store, chores to do tomorrow, people you have dated, beers you have tasted. So it should not surprise you that making lists can be very helpful in writing an essay about a short story. Of course, you can make a list about anything you want dealing with a story: names of characters, their characteristics, places a particular word is used, books that characters have mentioned, aspects of a myth that is used, the times a character lied or cheated, products that are mentioned, and so on.

Not only do lists become the details that you might use in your essay, but they can also help you rethink how you understand a story. For instance, reviewing a list with the names of the products mentioned in "A & P" might make you look more closely at the tone of the story. Seeing the number of times that the word "deep" is used in "The Birthmark" might force you to examine Hawthorne's attitudes toward the intellect and toward beauty. In other words, lists are very useful throughout the writing process.

FREEWRITE

For some writers tackling a college essay, the most productive activity is writing freely and quickly. The point of freewriting is to get words on the page as rapidly as possible, without heavy concentration and strain. Very often, after we have outlined our essay and organized our notes, our writing becomes serious, focused, and sometimes narrow and fearful. So freewriting is a great tool to loosen our writing and our thinking. In reviewing a story, read a passage and then just write whatever comes to your mind as quickly as you can. Try not to censor yourself; no one will read this piece of writing. Ask yourself questions: What do I think of this character's action? What could this image mean? Why is the narrator trying to be funny here? What is the writer's attitude toward women here? Ask any question you are curious about. You may find that when it comes time to write the first draft of the essay, you have already written a few sentences or a paragraph or two that can be included. At the very worst, freewriting helps you work through ideas that later you will abandon. At best, you will have discovered gems of understanding that might not have come to you by studiously listing and outlining. One element you can freewrite about is the "Questions" that follow each story.

Review Biographical, Historical, and Critical Sources

Depending on your purpose in writing, you may want to research what previous writers and critics have said about your topic. In college classrooms, very often you will be assigned to write a researched essay. On other occasions, you may believe you do not yet fully understand or appreciate a story. Your goals in research, therefore, can vary. You may need biographical information on Franz Kafka because you do not understand how a person can imagine the stories that he writes. Another time, you may decide to research the history of migrant workers in the United States because, while reading Tomás Rivera's work you cannot believe people had to work under the conditions he describes. In reading Margaret Atwood's "Rape Fantasies," you become curious about what magazines in the 1970s actually said about rape. Or you begin noticing connections between the topics and styles of various writers and wonder if other readers had noticed these connections also. For instance, you may feel that Sandra Cisneros and Helena María Viramontes seem to be reacting similarly to their family and personal backgrounds. And after a trip to the library, you discover that professors across the nation have noticed many of the same similarities, but the writings of these professors also point out many ways these writers are unique.

LOCATE SOURCES

Research can be time consuming, but it can also be very rewarding. Nothing quite compares to the feeling of locating, after a prolonged search, the book or journal article that clearly documents that one of your hunches is supported by an esteemed critic. Since research is so time consuming, you want to become as efficient as possible. The best way to become efficient is to become proficient in using resources in the library and on the Web.

Most college, university, and public libraries today are fully automated with on-line catalogues for books and journals and with on-line databases. Locating books and journals in a library can be done using at least three criteria: author, title, and subject. Once you've located the catalog search page for your library, search for information using all three of the criteria. An author search will locate all the works in your library by your writer's last name. Sometimes this search will lead you to titles you had no idea your author had written: memoirs, autobiographies, children's books, volumes of letters, essays, privately printed works, and the like. In researching short fiction, you may not find information using the title search, but if you know the name of the book or journal the story appeared in you will be able to locate that title. Finally, a subject search can take you in several directions. By typing in your writer's name, you will find works about that writer, biographies, works of criticism, and sometimes theses and dissertations by graduate students at your university. In addition, you may discover interesting resources by typing in various related terms. For instance, in searching for information concerning Leslie Marmon Silko, you might look under such subjects as Native Americans, Indians, Pueblos, Yellow Woman, Bureau of Indian Affairs, Myth, New Mexico, women writers, and many others you might think of yourself.

Since most college students have access to computers, either at home, at the library, or in college computer centers, many students now use the World Wide Web as an important tool in researching. Through any computer connected to the internet, you can access such search engines as Yahoo.com, InfoSeek.com, and Altavista.com. In using these search engines, it is best to narrow your search as much as possible. You can do this by putting quotation marks around names, titles, and subjects made of several words (i.e., "Leslie Marmon Silko" or "Native-American fiction"). Otherwise, your search will include "hits" for each word: "Leslie," "Marmon," and "Silko" or "Native," "American," and "fiction." Another method to narrow searches is to use Boolian commands: "and," "or," and "not." For instance, searching for "'Leslie Marmon Silko' NOT 'poetry'" will lead you to sources that discuss Silko's work, excluding those that discuss her poetry. The Companion Website for this book (www.prenhall.com/bohner) includes between three and five World Wide Web sites for each writer in the anthology. These sites should not be the end of your research, but they can provide information that you are able to use.

An excellent guide to literary research is James L. Harner's *Literary Research Guide: A Guide to Reference Sources for the Study of Literatures in English and Related Topics*. Listed below are some of the most important sources: books, journals, databases, and World Wide Web sources. Most of the sources listed below are discussed in Dr. Harner's work.

Books and Academic Journals

American Literary Scholarship: An Annual [1963–]. Durham: Duke UP, 1965– .

Blain, Virginia, Patricia Clements, and Isobel Grundy, eds. *The Feminist Companion to Literature in English: Woman Writers from the Middle Ages to the Present*. New Haven: Yale UP, 1990.

Brady, Anne M., and Brian Cleeve. *A Biographical Dictionary of Irish Writers*. New York: St. Martin's, 1985.

Columbia Literary History of the United States. Gen. ed. Emory Elliot. New York: Columbia UP, 1988.

Contemporary Authors: A Bio-bibliographical Guide to Current Writers in Fiction, General Nonfiction, Poetry, Journalism, Drama, Motion Pictures, Television, and Other Fields. Detroit: Gale, 1962– .

Dictionary of Literary Biography. Detroit: Gale, 1978– .

Egar, Ernestina N. *A Bibliography of Criticism of Contemporary Chicano Literature*. Berkeley: Chicano Library Publications, U of California, 1982.

European Writers. George Stade and William T. Jackson. 7 vols. New York: Macmillan, 1983–1985.

Facts on File Bibliography of American Fiction through 1865. Ed. Kent P. Ljungquist. 1994.

Facts on File Bibliography of American Fiction, 1866–1918. Ed. James Nagel and Gwen L. Nagel. 1993.

Facts on File Bibliography of American Fiction, 1919–1988. Ed. Matthew J. Bruccoli and Judith S. Baughman. 2 vols. 1991.

Fairbank, Carol, and Eugene A. Engeldinger. *Black American Fiction: A Bibliography*. Metuchen: Scarecrow, 1978.

Harris, Wendell V. *British Short Fiction in the Nineteenth Century: A Literary and Bibliographic Guide*. Detroit: Wayne State UP, 1979.

MLA International Bibliography. New York: MLA, 1921– .

McPheron, William, and Jocelyn Sheppard. *The Bibliography of Contemporary American Fiction, 1945–1988: An Annotated Checklist*. Westport: Meckler, 1989.

Nadel, Ira Bruce. *Jewish Writers of North America: A Guide to Information Sources*. American Studies Information Guide Series. Detroit: Gale, 1981.

The New Guide to Modern World Literature. Ed. Martin Seymour-Smith. 4 vols. New York: Peter Bedrick Books, 1985.

The Oxford History of English Literature. 13 vols. Oxford: Oxford UP, 1945– .

Rice, Thomas Jackson. *English Fiction, 1900–1950: A Guide to Information Sources*. 2 vols. Detroit: Gale, 1979–1983.

Ruoff, A. LaVonne Brown. *American Indian Literatures: An Introduction. Bibliographic Review, and Selected Bibliography*. New York: MLA, 1990.

Short Story Index: An Index to Stories in Collections and Periodicals. New York: Wilson, 1953– Annual, with quinquennial and other cumulations extending coverage to 1900.

Thurston, Jarvis, et al. *Short Fiction Criticism: A Checklist of Interpretation since 1925 of Stories and Novelettes (American, British, Continental). 1800–1958*. Swallow Checklists of Criticism and Explication. Denver: Swallow, 1960.

Twentieth-Century Short Story Explications: Interpretations 1900–1975 of Short Fiction since 1800, 3rd ed. Comp. Warren S. Walker. Hamden: Shoe String, 1977. *Supplement I*, 1980. *Supplement II*, 1984. *Supplement III*, 1987. *Supplement IV*, 1989. *Supplement V*, 1991.

Twentieth-Century Short Story Explication New Series [1989–]. 1989–1990. Ed. Walker. 1993. 1991–1992. Ed. Wendell M. Aycock, 1995. 1993–1994, 1997.

Weiner, Alan R. *Literary Criticism Index*. 2nd ed. Metuchen: Scarecrow, 1994.

Weixlmann, Joe. *American Short-Fiction Criticism and Scholarship, 1959–1977: A Checklist.*
    Chicago: Swallow-Ohio UP, 1982.

Journals

African American Review
American Short Fiction
American Literary Realism
American Literature: A Journal of Literary History, Criticism, and Bibliography
Callaloo: A Journal of Afro-American and African Arts and Letters
Critique: Studies in Modern Fiction
Explicator
International Fiction Review
Irish University Review: A Journal of Irish Studies
Journal of the Short Story
Modern Fiction Studies
Publications of the Modern Language Association
SAIL: Studies in American Indian Literatures
Studies in Short Fiction
University of Texas Studies in Contemporary Spanish-American Fiction

Databases

American Fiction Database. Accessible through the Ohio State University Libraries OPAC
    (OSCAR) telnet://oscar.us.ohio-state.edu
Arts and Humanities Search
Book Review Index (1969–present)
Book Review Digest (1983–present)
Essay and General Literature Index
DiscLit
Humanities Index
The MLA International Bibliography (1964–present)
National Newspaper Index (1979–present)
Reader's Guide to Periodical Literature (1983–present)

The World Wide Web

First, look at the Web page for this book:
http://www.prenhall.com/bohner
Canadian Literature Archive
http://canlit.st-john.umanitoba.ca/Canlitx/Canlit_hompage.html
The Columbia University Bartleby Library
http://www.columbia.edu/acis/bartleby/index.html
Crossroads Project
http://georgetown.edu/crossroads
Literary Research on the Net
http://english.upenn.edu~jlynch/Lit
Literature Resources for the High School and College Student
http://www.teleport.com/~mgroves
Native Web
http://web.maxwell.syr.edu/nativeweb/
Ozlit
www.vicnet.net.au/~ozlit/index.html
Project Gutenberg
http://promo.net/pg

EVALUATE SOURCES

Locating sources is not the end of research. Perhaps even more important is evaluating them. In evaluating books, you will look at who the writer is, who the publisher is, the date of the information, the sources used, and the primary audience. Is the writer from a major university and trained in literary research? Was the writer of the criticism a friend or enemy of the writer you are researching? Is the writer objective? Does the writer have an agenda? Does the writer have a narrow critical perspective or critical approach? Is the work from a major literary publisher or a university press? If the book is a biography, was the book written during the subject's life, early in the subject's career, or late in the subject's career? Did the writer use trustworthy sources? What kind of sources: interviews, letters and memoirs, criticism from other scholars? Who is the audience? Fellow scholars? The general public? College-educated readers or elementary school children? No particular answer to any of these questions disqualifies the source, but it may determine how you use the source. For instance, a work by Ernest Hemingway's son may not be a good source for evaluating the quality of Hemingway's stories, but it may very well provide important information about Hemingway's view toward violence.

Evaluating Web sites is even more important. Anybody can say almost anything on the Web. Just because something is on the Web does not mean you can use it as a source for a college essay. As in evaluating books, examine the Web site for who the critic is, what sources the critic uses, and who the audience is. Also note the kind of site the information appears on: edu, org, or com. In most cases, you can trust material on educational Web sites (edu). As an example, reviews of books that amazon.com includes on its site are useful for deciding whether you want to read the book, but they are virtually useless as sources of critical comment in a researched essay.

DECIDE ON ORGANIZATION

So far you have completed an extraordinary amount of preparatory work. Probably you have already even begun writing the essay, having made lists, done some freewriting, written out your thesis, and, if the assignment called for it, collected information from secondary sources. Many times, by this point, an organization for your essay has already suggested itself. For instance, if you are writing a summary, you know that your essay will be organized by the narrative of the story. If you are writing about the three characters in "Gooseberries," you know that after the introduction you will devote a paragraph or two to each of the characters then conclude the essay.

However, there are times when you might not think of an organization as quickly as you hope. One helpful process is to review the basic organizational schemes and choose one that seems relevant. Those that are often used include the following:

- **Compare and contrast** works well in differentiating two or more characters, conflicts, settings, themes, and tones; also is used to examine two or more full stories; effective for Biographical and Historical approaches.
- **Cause and effect** works well in exploring conflicts and their resolutions, changes in characters, the effects of point-of-view; effective for Psychological, Sociological, and Reader-Response approaches.
- **Classification** works well in examining uses of language, such as syntax, diction, images, symbolism; also works well when looking at several elements of fiction in one essay; effective for Structuralist and Post-Structuralist approaches.

Some writers consider analysis and evaluation to be methods of organization. While you can use compare and contrast, cause and effect, and classification to organize your analysis or evaluation, you can also use the organization called enumeration, which basically means to list. For instance, an analysis of a character in a story may be organized by devoting separate paragraphs to several aspects of the character. An evaluation may be organized by examining three or four criteria you have for judging the quality of the story.

WRITE A DRAFT

Because you have done the preliminary work, the actual writing of the essay will be much easier. You now have something specific to say, you have a plan, and you can concentrate on writing clear sentences that will convey the meaning you want.

Essays normally contain three parts: an introductory paragraph that contains the thesis, body paragraphs to develop and support the thesis, and a concluding paragraph. When you start writing, it may be easier to postpone the introductory paragraph and begin with the body paragraphs. Rereading these paragraphs might help you to state both your thesis and your conclusion more effectively. On the other hand, your thesis or conclusion might be so clear to you that you will want to write it down first.

Your opening paragraph (no matter when you actually write it) will normally contain a thesis sentence that lets the reader know what to expect in the rest of the essay. The opening paragraph is to the essay as a topic sentence is to a paragraph. In other words, in many cases the opening paragraph gives a clear statement of the main idea of the essay. The opening paragraph may also hint at the organization of the rest of the essay; for example, if you plan to discuss three characters, you will mention them in the order that you plan to discuss them in the essay.

In writing the concluding paragraph, you draw together the various points that you have made. Therefore, you will not introduce any new ideas. In a short essay, you do not need to mention everything that you have previously said, but you want to restate, in an altered form, the main point, or thesis, of the essay. The reader should finish reading your essay with a sense that your point has been focused and clear and that you have discussed everything important to your thesis in the body of the essay.

REVISE AND EDIT

All good writing is the result of rewriting. Good writing is the product of diligence and care, which usually means that the writer has found time to work on the essay on several occasions with some amount of time—a few hours or a few days—between those occasions. However you accomplish it, learning to look at your own writing like a stranger is an invaluable aid to good, clear, thoughtful writing. As writers, we can become like parents who believe their children can do no wrong. But we best resist that parental urge and find ways to look at our own work with an objective, critical eye.

As you look over your drafts, ask yourself the following questions:

- Am I dealing with a single major idea?
- Are my sentences coherent?
- Do my sentences move smoothly from point to point?

- Do I have sentences that need revision? Are introductory phrases clearly punctuated? Are subjects and verbs clear?
- Do I need to add any important information?
- Do I need to omit any unneeded information?
- Is my vocabulary appropriate? Do I know what all my words mean?
- Have I supported my points with material from the story?
- Do I have a balance between paraphrase and quotation? Have I quoted when the exact words are powerful and suggestive?
- Can I add connecting words and phrases to smooth out transitions, especially transitions between my ideas and quotations from the story or from other authorities?

FILL IN DETAILS

The most effective writing is precise and shows readers, rather than telling them, what you want them to know and think. Writing that shows does two things: It helps readers understand what is being said and holds the readers' interest more than vague, abstract writing does. In revising your writing, then, look for places where you have been general and abstract and then find ways to make your information as specific as possible.

One of the best ways to do this is to return to the story and to your notes for instances of specific language. If you make a general statement, follow it with, or substitute, a specific statement. For instance, if you are writing about the boy Paul in "The Rocking-Horse Winner," you might write "Paul rides his rocking horse to learn the names of winning horses in local horse races." But you could substitute, "Paul mounts his rocking horse and whips it fiercely, violently riding it with close-set, glaring eyes, until, exhausted, he dismounts, the name of the winning horse upon his lips." The above description is derived from various descriptions of Paul as he rides the rocking horse. Of course, direct quotations from the story are always helpful, that is, if they include instances of specific language and if you have not already relied too heavily on quotations. Probably one or two direct quotations per paragraph is sufficient.

SAVE REVISIONS

Nowadays computers and word processors are the most important tools for writers. Obviously, this wasn't always the case. Computers have made writing a much easier process. Errors are corrected at the touch of a button; paragraphs that were composed using freewriting can, at the touch of a couple of buttons, be incorporated into an essay. However, one problem with computers as writing tools is that because our essay is preserved in a form we can almost effortlessly amend, we are losing the concept of drafts. We "open" our "file," do some "cutting" and "pasting," then save the file. And nothing remains of the earlier version of the "file."

You might want to consider saving your earlier drafts, either under different file names or pasted at the end of the file. Then you will be able to compare your different approaches to your subject. You never know if you might remember that an earlier version of a sentence or paragraph was better than the one currently in the essay.

Some writers periodically print hard copies of the essay, even when they know the version is incomplete. That way they are protected against disasters like a disk being stolen or a computer being infected by a virus. In addition, there is still something to be said for old-fashioned editing by pencil. Sometimes reading a printed essay allows you to see things you missed while reading it on the computer screen. Last, printing a copy allows you to share it with friends, who can write on the essay and return it to you with their comments, without having to deal with word processing conversion questions and still somewhat unwieldy comment functions in their word processing programs.

PREPARE THE FINAL DRAFT

Finally, you have almost completed your essay. The last step is to make certain that the essay is formatted in the manner your readers, probably your instructors, desire. You probably need a title. Has your instructor given you any instructions about titles? Some instructors want titles that are straightforward and serious; others want titles to be creative and evocative. Of the two below, which would your instructor prefer?

A Comparison of Three Characters in Chekhov's "Gooseberries"

or

Upstairs/Downstairs

Next you will want to know if your instructor prefers a particular format for the first page or cover pages. Many English instructors prefer the format prescribed by the Modern Language Association, referred to as the MLA format. The MLA format suggests that you place your name, course title, date, and instructor's name double-spaced in the upper left-hand corner of the first page; the title is centered; then the essay begins, double-spaced with indented paragraphs. If your essay includes internal documentation of sources and a Works Cited page, you will definitely want to learn which style your instructor prefers. The essays printed in the section "Sample Student Essays," including the researched essay, follow MLA format.

If you have any questions about the MLA style, there are many English handbooks on the market. One published by Prentice Hall/Pearson Education, the publisher of this book, is *CommonSense: A Handbook and Guide for Writers* by Lennis Polnac, Lyman Grant, and Tom Cameron.

Once you have printed the essay, examine once more how it looks. Have you forgotten page numbers? Is your typeface readable? In most cases, a 10- or 12-point typeface is appropriate. And most often a serif typeface is the best choice for formal essays. One small but important matter to look at is if you have a last page with only a line or two on it. Probably you can make some minor changes in the essay, shortening a sentence or two, that will eliminate the need for running over to that last page.

Last, if all the last-minute editing and formatting starts to frustrate you, try to remember your reader, not necessarily your instructor, but that general reader, the one just like you have been as you have read the many stories in this book and in others. All the work the writers and editors have done on these stories, they hope, has made your reading experience enjoyable and profitable. And now it's your turn to provide other readers with pleasure and interest. Just take a deep breath; spend five more minutes to correct that one last problem; and then turn in your essay with a sigh of relief . . . and of pride.

Sample Student Essays

A SUMMARY

A. Williams
English 1302
Prof. Grant
Assignment 1
July 8, 2001

Driven to Murder:
A Summary of "Looking for a Rain God"

In her short story "Looking for a Rain God," Bessie Head describes a hell on earth created by a severe seven-year drought in a rural African village. Under "normal" water conditions, this agricultural society plows crop clearings in the forest area near the village. By the seventh year, only trees remain alive on barren earth. For a few weeks, a misty rain finally falls, and some families head for the forest lands to plow their fields. One farmer named Ramadi moves his entire family outside the village to camp and plow their plot. When the rain stops, they experience horrible anguish and psychological dysfunction, and they begin to face the likelihood of starvation. In their terror, Ramadi's old father is able to convince the other adults that they must sacrifice their two young daughters to appease an ancient rain god. After the murders are committed and still no rain falls, the family, wrought with guilt and anguish, returns to their home and the suspicions of fellow villagers. Eventually the family faces criminal convictions and death sentences. Bessie Head ends her story with the other villagers reflecting on what has happened and admitting this same capacity for horror within themselves, writing "[A]ll the people who lived off crops knew in their hearts that only a hair's breadth had saved them from sharing a similar fate" ("Looking" 550). While it might be tempting to assert that Head is criticizing the beliefs of native Africans, this is a dangerous assumption. Head herself warned against such approaches to literature, saying "*people* is *people* and not damn white, damn black" ("Let Me" 1253). Therefore, it is much more likely that Bessie Head is telling us that all humans have great capacity for insanity and violence.

Works Cited

Head, Bessie. "Let Me Tell a Story Now . . ." *Short Fiction: Classic and Contemporary.* 6th ed. Ed. Charles Bohner and Lyman Grant. Upper Saddle River, NJ: Prentice Hall, 2006. 1252–1253.

———. "Looking for a Rain God." *Short Fiction: Classic and Contemporary.* 6th ed. Ed. Charles Bohner and Lyman Grant. Upper Saddle River, NJ: Prentice Hall, 2006. 548–551.

AN ANALYSIS OF SEVEN ELEMENTS OF FICTION

A. Sulvaran
English 1302
Prof. Grant
July 15, 2001
Assignment 2

I Really Do Not Want to Be Raped, But . . .:
An Analysis of the Elements of Fiction in "Rape Fantasies"

Margaret Atwood's "Rape Fantasies" is a story of a woman describing her co-workers' and her own "rape fantasies," which turn out upon closer examination to be romantic, sexual fantasies. Estelle, the main character, is in a bar with a man whom she barely knows. She tells him how the media presents rape as though it were something superficial and common. She tells him that while she and her fellow female co-workers were eating lunch and playing bridge, one of them, having read a magazine article about women's rape fantasies, asked the group what their fantasies were. Her co-workers' fantasies usually involve a handsome man appearing out of nowhere and seducing them. On the other hand, Estelle's fantasies, which comprise the bulk of the story, usually involve a threatening, but eventually bungling, character who is eventually repulsed or dissuaded by Estelle. In one fantasy, she asks the attacker if he is going to rape her, and when he answers "yes," she enlists his help in searching through the chaotic contents of her purse to find a plastic lemon to squeeze into his eyes (79). In this story, Margaret Atwood's central theme points out that, contrary to what popular media may present, women are unable to fantasize about being raped because of the physical and emotional pain that such an act causes.

Estelle is the protagonist of the story. She is a round and static character who presents herself with brash humor. She probably has little formal education and, perhaps, from smaller towns or rural areas. Her most distinguishing characteristic is her sense of humor. She makes jokes about her co-workers. She allows the man she is talking to to know her and her co-workers' fantasies, thoughts, and attitudes. She is very sociable. Her job as a filer reveals her to belong to the working class. In addition, she fears rape and violence. When she discusses her co-workers—Sondra, Darlene, Chrissy, and Greta—she makes them appear static also in their lives, but more important, she makes it clear her co-workers cannot imagine being raped. "'. . . those aren't *rape* fantasies,'" she says. "'I mean, you aren't getting *raped*, it's just some guy you haven't met formally who happens to be more attractive than Derek Cummins [their homely assistant manager]'" (79). Estelle, on the other hand, instead of imagining scenarios of seduction, as her co-workers do, can imagine scenes where rape is intended, but still cannot fantasize a rape completed.

Several conflicts appear in "Rape Fantasies," but the one that is least obvious is the most important. Underneath Estelle's humor is her fear of rape. Although she devotes great thought to the scene, dialogue, and circumstances of each of her fantasies, Estelle always has a strategy to escape from being raped. The strategy consists of beginning a conversation with the aggressor as a way of creating some sense of connection with him. She imagines the motive of each rapist, disarms him with sympathy, and even tries to help him in some way. In other words, her "rape fantasies" never get to a point where she is harmed. She attempts to understand how a man—"once you let them know you're human"—could hurt her (83). Another conflict that Estelle has is with the idea that life is precarious. She does not want to deprive herself from doing enjoyable things like going out for drinks and meeting men. Both of these conflicts come together in the conflict that becomes apparent at the end of the story. Estelle is worried over whether she can trust the man she is speaking to. As she says, "how could a fellow do that to a person he's just had a long conversation with" (83).

The setting of the story is not obvious at first. However, by the end of the story the reader realizes that the story takes place in a bar in a big city and that Estelle is talking with a man she has just met. She says, "it is harder to meet people in a big city" and "like here for instance, the waiters all know me" (81, 82). In looking at Estelle's life, we realize that bars are not places where people are able to find the nicest people with manners and culture.

The point of view in "Rape Fantasies" is first person. Estelle is the narrator, in addition to being the protagonist. She is talking with a man at a bar. On two occasions she says, "maybe it is different for a guy" (82). That this story is a monologue occurring as Estelle speaks is seen when she describes how Darlene wrinkles her nose when saying she feels disgusted by "rape fantasies." Estelle then wrinkles her own nose "like this" to show the man the way Darlene did it (78). Atwood's use of first person point of view is very effective. First, readers may believe that Estelle is speaking directly to them. Then readers discover that they are overhearing a monologue spoken by Estelle to a man in a bar. After overhearing all Estelle's fantasies about disengaging men with conversation, readers realize that this is exactly what Estelle is doing with the man with whom she is speaking. Estelle knows everything that magazines say about rape, but unable to imagine rape, she still believes that talking can prevent it.

Atwood's use of language, especially diction and imagery, plays a vital role in this story. Although each rape fantasy is short, each is painted with colorful adjectives and told with specific detail, from Kleenex and cigarettes in a purse to a puffy nothing face covered in pimples. In the first paragraph of the story, Estelle uses a couple of metaphors, comparing the article in the magazine, "RAPE, TEN THINGS TO DO ABOUT IT" to a vaccine for cancer or ten new hairdos (77). This use of imagery helps the reader see clearly Estelle's humorous, yet troubled view of the subject. Another example of Estelle's uneasy humor is calling Greta's imaginary rapist "Tarzan," when he climbs up and down the apartment building (79). Estelle also says that Chrissy might get bubbles up her nose if she screams while she is in the bathtub (79). Perhaps the most important aspect of language in "Rape Fantasies" is the irony that Estelle is using the same technique in "real life" that she uses in her "fantasies." In her fantasies, she uses humor and conversation to disarm her rapists: In the bar she is doing the same thing—talking with a man, who is not attempting to rape her, but who at some future time might attempt it.

The author's tone in this story is a combination of subtle sadness, disappointment, and humor. At the beginning of the story, the narrator is very cheerful and funny while she makes jokes and teases her co-workers. Neither she nor her co-workers seem to have any major conflicts. It is when Estelle narrates her rape fantasies that the readers notice that underneath the humor of her silly fantasies, she is really afraid to face the fact that it does not matter how well she knows a man—he may still attempt to rape her. Atwood appears both to love and pity Estelle, who is admirable in her spunk and bravery, and pitiable in her desperation to meet men she can date. It is the fact that none of Estelle's fantasies nor her co-workers' are really "rape fantasies" that permits readers to understand Atwood's point that rape is violent and hurtful, and that this kind of violation is something no one wants to fantasize about. Even Atwood, as the writer, refuses to "fantasize" about her likeable character being raped.

Work Cited

Atwood, Margaret. "Rape Fantasies." *Short Fiction: Classic and Contemporary*. 6th ed. Ed. Charles Bohner and Lyman Grant. Upper Saddle River, NJ: Prentice Hall, 2006. 77–83.

AN ANALYSIS OF ONE ELEMENT OF FICTION

A. Williams
English 1302
Prof. Grant
July 18, 2001
Assignment 3

Blueprints of a Family

Franz Kafka's short story "The Metamorphosis" takes place in an apartment flat, the home of the Samsa family. Except for a few climatic moments, most of the action of the story occurs in a central bedroom. The occupant of that bedroom is Gregor Samsa. The story begins as Gregor wakes up and discovers that not only has he overslept, but also he has become a giant dung beetle with a hard armored back and many "pitifully thin" legs that wave helplessly in the air. Gregor is concerned about being late for work. He has a lucrative job as a cloth salesman, earning the sole income of his family. He has come to despise this stressful and boring job, which he took five years ago after some "catastrophe" had "overwhelmed" his father's business, leaving Gregor's parents in debt to the man who is Gregor's boss. Despite his condition, Gregor intends to get out of bed and go to work to fulfill his obligation to this family. He tries to talk to his family from inside his locked bedroom, but his squeaky voice only horrifies them. When the chief clerk arrives to inquire about why Gregor is late for work, Gregor becomes so agitated that he falls out of bed, struggles to his feet, and goes to great lengths to unlock his bedroom door. Upon seeing Gregor, the chief runs away in disgust, the mother collapses in shock, and the father convulses in tears and with a stick herds Gregor back into his room.

In the days that follow, Gregor lives alone in his one room listening to the activities of his family, who do not realize that he can understand their words. He notes their transformation also as they all become very busy earning money. Working constantly, they wish to move to a smaller, more economical apartment, and finally rent out the sister's apartment to three demanding strangers. When the lodgers finally see Gregor, they threaten to sue the family for the dirty conditions of the apartment. That night Gregor limps back into his room where he dies alone in the darkness. The family grieves his death, but are also empowered, kicking out the lodgers. The story ends with the father, mother, and sister spending the day together in thoughtful reflection in the country side, hopeful of their future lives. This last scene is the only one that takes place outside the apartment. Gregor's death seems to have liberated all of them. The change in the setting in the very last scene symbolizes this transformation.

The setting of a family home is very appropriate for this story about how people are often imprisoned by family dynamics. The structure and state of the apartment reflect the emotional interplay of this family. Gregor's strange bedroom in the middle of this apartment seems to have false boundaries. When Gregor doesn't get up for work that first morning, his family becomes immediately alarmed. They begin knocking on doors and talking at him from all directions. First his mother "knocks at the door behind the head of his bed" imploring Gregor to get up. Seconds later, "at one of the side doors, his father was already knocking. . . . At the other side door his sister asks him if he is all right. Gregor seems glad for the small amount of privacy he has created by locking his doors: He "felt thankful for the prudent habit he had acquired in travelling of locking all doors during the night, even at home." As a dung beetle, Gregor no longer locks his own doors, but he is trapped in his bedroom because his family doesn't want to see him or have anything to do with him. They don't talk to him, and only his sister enters to leave food or sweep the floor. Only once does his sister knock before entering, not out of respect for him, only to spare herself the horror of catching Gregor looking out the window, as once before Gregor had been lost in a daydream and forgot to hide under the sofa.

Gregor's entrapment in his bedroom mirrors the entrapment he felt in working at a job that he hated, only to please his family, who seem incapable of earning money for themselves. As Gregor once was trapped by family expectation, he is now imprisoned by family revulsion. Ironically, when he cannot work, his family does quite well at earning an income. Gregor overhears that his father had been putting away extra money leftover from Gregor's monthly earnings, and Gregor thinks:

> True, he could have paid off some more of his father's debts to the chief with this extra money, and so brought nearer the day on which he could quit his job, but doubtless it was better the way his father had arranged it.

It appears that this family has neglected to concern themselves with Gregor's feelings about his job: They assume he will work there for life. No one knows that Gregor finds his job so "irritating" and "exhausting" that he thinks, as expressed on the first page of the story, "The devil take it all!" Gregor has also contributed to his own loss of power by never speaking his mind and assuming that his father knows best. It appears that the doors to Gregor's room have metaphorical locks on both sides. It is difficult to know if Gregor is locked inside in himself or if his family locked him there.

Kafka continues to portray these family dynamics in the setting of the story as the state of Gregor's room begins to deteriorate with neglect. "Streaks of dirt stretched along the walls, here and there lay balls of dust and filth." Later his room becomes a dumping ground for "things there was no room for elsewhere . . . anything that was not needed was simply flung into Gregor's room." Although the state of the room bothers Gregor, he remains powerless over his family's neglect. As time passes, Gregor's family seems to be able to totally ignore his bedroom in the middle of their apartment.

The three times in the story when Gregor does leave his bedroom are the times when peak conflict occurs. These confrontations always leave him wounded. One time "his flank was quite bruised" and after a kick from his father "flew far into the room, bleeding freely." The second time his father throws apples at him, landing one in his back.

> The serious injury done to Gregor, which disabled him for more than a month—the apple went on sticking in his body as a visible reminder since no one ventured to remove it—seemed to have made even his father recollect that Gregor was a member of the family.

Gregor leaves his room one final time when his family is arguing about him. He is already so weak that he can barely move "except by lifting his head and then bracing it against the floor over and over again." Gregor's family would rather he hide away, powerless in his room, than upset the state of things with his grotesque appearances in the living room. After this last appearance, they lock the door behind Gregor; he dies later that night.

After Gregor's death the family suddenly stops acting like poor victims entrapped in this high-maintenance apartment. They had claimed before that they could not move to a new apartment because of Gregor, but as Gregor states, what really kept them from moving was "their own complete hopelessness and the belief that they had been singled out for a misfortune." They had claimed that the apartment was too big and yet they had to displace the daughter from her room to let in lodgers. They claimed to be so poor, yet they still had a housekeeper. After Gregor dies they let go of all of these attachments, taking the day off work and leaving the apartment. As they reflect positively on their future, the text reads. "The greatest immediate improvement in their condition would of course arise from moving to another house." Kafka's emphasis on the locations of significant conflicts and description of Gregor's bedroom and the apartment exemplify the importance of the setting of this story.

AN EXPLICATION

R. Dennis
English 1302
Prof. Grant
November 4, 2003
Assignment 4

The Drifter's Conscience

Denis Johnson's "Car Crash While Hitchhiking" begins with a drug-addled drifter standing in the rain on the side of a road trying to hitch a ride from the passing cars. When an Oldsmobile stops and he hears "the sweet voices of the family inside," he knows there will be an accident in the storm, but he doesn't care because they say they will take him "all the way" (593). While the drifter sleeps in the back seat of the Oldsmobile next to a baby, he feels the drugs in his veins. The husband and wife wake him up an instant before the crash "denying it viciously" (594). Despite his knowing all along of the impending accident, the drifter still asks the driver "What happened?" (594) after the accident. He gets out of the car into the rain, holding the baby, and walks across the bridge to a speak with a trucker who has stopped for the wreck. He walks back across the wreckage toward another stopped car, passing the dying man hanging out of the side of his car and choking on his own blood. When the police and ambulance arrive, the drifter thinks of how he has "gone from being the president of this tragedy to being a faceless onlooker at a gory wreck" (595). He is taken to the hospital after giving his statement to the police. There he hears the wife scream when she learns of her husband's death, and he envies the feeling she has. Then the story shifts to a scene in another hospital a few years later, the drifter is asked if he hears unusual sounds or voices, and he hears a box of cotton speak to him. He sees a yellow bird flutter near his face and feels his muscles jerk just before he falls to the floor. As the nurse inserts a needle into his arm, he imagines that they are in a forest and it is raining. He hears the water from a creek and thinks, "And you, you ridiculous people, you expect me to help you?" pointing to one of the story's main themes that one cannot help others without first saving oneself (596).

The story is centered on the car wreck with supporting information before and after it. In first-person point of view, the drifter explains his state of mind during the rides he had encountered earlier that day and the drugs he was given, and the feeling he is addicted to. He ends the story with the final effects of those drugs later in his life during his downfall.

As the story progresses, the reader is dragged through the narrator's feelings, thoughts, and conscience. The drifter's state of mind is unclear, intangible and filled with supernatural experiences all of which are perceived and communicated by him clearly and precisely. This is particularly so when he walks through the scene of the wreck with the baby in his arms and passes the dying man hanging out of his car. The drifter assures himself that there is nothing he can do for the man and thinks,

> He was snoring loudly and rudely. His blood bubbled out of his mouth with every breath. He wouldn't be taking many more. I knew that, but he didn't, and therefore I looked down into the great pity of a person's life on this earth. I don't mean that we all end up dead, that's not the great pity. I mean that he couldn't tell me what he was dreaming, and I couldn't tell him what was real. (595)

Through the narrator's thoughts in this passage, the reader can understand the drifter's psyche and the overall theme of the story. It is apparent that the drifter looks further into things than an average person would. He understands things on a level different from an average person, but he is so hyped up on drugs that he has difficulty distinguishing what is real and what is imagined. He is a man with the potential to help others and is gifted enough to know that there is a deeper meaning to life than the obvious, but he is unable to use those talents for the greater good because he is addicted to the drugs that help him forget about his responsibilities and fog his mind.

As the drifter thinks, "He was snoring loudly and rudely," the reader receives a shock through the language applied to the scene (595). There is a man hanging out of his car, choking on his blood, dying, and the drifter thinks *he is loud and rude*. He cares nothing that this man has a life or a family, only how the situation affects him, specifically, at that particular time. The story goes on to describe the blood bubbling out of the man's mouth with each breath. The language the author uses here is strong and descriptive imagery. The reader can clearly see the violent scene that is described and the severity of the accident. As the drifter goes on to think, "He wouldn't be taking many more," the reader is able to see that he is able to foretell things that an average person could not possibly know (595). The drifter is not an average person. He is someone who is unlucky enough to have a car crash while he is hitchhiking, and he has the gift to know about it before it even happens. The author gives the reader this information through foreshadowing, allowing the reader to see first hand that the drifter has unnatural knowledge and abilities, yet he does nothing to prevent terrible things he knows will happen. This is the reason that he thinks of himself as the president of the accident. The language in the story is specifically worded to give readers the knowledge they need to understand the story. They know that the drifter has the ability to know things that will happen, but they watch as he does nothing to prevent harm to others, so long as they take him "all the way" (593). He is so focused on the drugs and the feelings they give him that he does not have the time or the concern to help anyone else.

The drifter moves on from the gory scene to think, "I knew that, but he didn't, and therefore I looked down into the great pity of a person's life on this earth. I don't mean that we all end up dead, that's not the great pity" (595). The drifter's character is one who looks further into things than someone else. He is gifted enough to see a situation for more than what it is. Although the setting of this passage is a car wreck with a dying man hanging out of his car, blood bubbling from his mouth, the drifter sees more than that. He looks beyond the obvious for a deeper meaning. An average person would compare the great pity to death and destruction, but the drifter actually makes it a point to say that it is not death that is the great pity. He is not afraid of death as others are, so he does not look at life in terms of life or death. This is reinforced in the scene when he sleeps in the Oldsmobile, "not caring whether I lived or died" (593). Although the drifter does not care whether he dies, he still never thinks of other people. He is a selfish person who uses other people for drugs and transportation. He is so concerned with himself that he is blinded to the fact that other people have lives as well. And in his blindness, he does not consider their needs.

The last section of the passage explains the great pity in the drifter's point of view. "I don't mean that we all end up dead, that's not the great pity. I mean that he couldn't tell me what he was dreaming, and I couldn't tell him what was real" (595). Throughout the entire story, the point of view is first-person narrative through the drifter's eyes. Therefore, the reader clearly sees the narrator's state of mind and his thoughts and feelings. The reader knows exactly how the drugs affect: "The traveling salesman had fed me pills that made the lining of my veins feel scraped out" (593). As he sleeps in the back of the Oldsmobile, he explains that "I dreamed I was looking right through my eyelids, and my pulse marked off the seconds of time" (594). The drifter is clearly not in a stable state of mind. When he says that he can not tell the dying man what is real, he is referring to his mental state of not knowing himself what was real or not. And this inability to distinguish reality from dream continues for the drifter. In some later time in another hospital, he again hears voices and sees visions, and in this addled state, he continues to find excuse not to help others.

Therefore, we can see that when the two conflicts are put together—that of the dying man being physically unable to tell the drifter what he was dreaming and the drifter being mentally unable to tell the dying man what was real—there resides the great pity. Without the physical and mental, there is nothing. Despite how much thought he gives to understanding the great pity, he never regrets the fact that as the president of the tragedy, he does not prevent it. He stands by as a faceless onlooker, as though he had nothing to do with it. His selfishness and dependency on the feeling he craves so much blind him to the fact that he has the power to help others and end the voices in his head.

Work Cited

Denis Johnson. "Car Crash While Hitchhiking." *Short Fiction: Classic and Contemporary*, 6th ed. Ed. Charles Bohner and Lyman Grant. Upper Saddle River, NJ: Prentice Hall, 2006. 593–597.

Abrahamson
English Comp II
Prof. Lyman Grant
April 4, 2003
Assignment 5

Imperfection
This Reader's Response to Hawthorne's "The Birthmark"

Nathanial Hawthorne's story "The Birthmark" is about a "man of science," Aylmer, and his nearly perfect wife, Georgiana (528). Aylmer is a man who is in love with science, so when he finds a woman, Georgiana, whom he loves more than science, he decides to marry her. Soon after their wedlock, he finds an imperfection on his perfect wife, a tiny red hand-shaped birthmark on her left cheek. Since Georgiana has been living with it her whole life, it does not seem to bother her and in fact she considers it to be a charm. Other people say that "some fairy at her birth hour laid her tiny hand upon the infant's cheek, and left this impress there in token of the magic endowments that were to give her such sway over all hearts" (592). Aylmer, however, believes the birthmark to be a "symbol of imperfection" (530). Eventually, Georgiana begins to hate the birthmark as much as Aylmer does. It bothers Aylmer to the point where he cannot look at it without disgust and he even dreams about its removal. In his dream he operates on Georgiana to remove the birthmark, but during the operation he finds that the red birthmark is attached to her heart so when he removes it she dies. After the dream, Aylmer believes that he can use science to remove the birthmark and make his wife perfect, so he goes to his laboratory to invent a concoction to remove the imperfection.

Aylmer and his Igor-like assistant, Aminadab, start to work on the experiment. Aminadab is against the experiment and says that "if she were my wife, I'd never part with that birthmark," but he continues to assist Aylmer anyway (592). They try several lotions and potions, but nothing seems to work because the mark is deeper than it appears. After spending much time in the laboratory trying new concoctions, Aylmer finally brings her a dangerous potion that he believes will rid her face of the birthmark. He advises her that there is risk with this potion because of its strength, but because she is so desperate to remove the mark, she does not care about the risk. She drinks the potion and falls asleep. As she sleeps, Aylmer watches the birthmark fade away until it is almost completely invisible. When she awakes she sees that the potion is working and congratulates him on his success, but also tells him that she is dying. "As the last crimson tint of the birthmark . . . faded from her cheek, the parting breath of the now perfect woman passed into the atmosphere, and her soul, lingering a moment near her husband, took its heavenward flight" (538). When I read the story, I interpret it to mean that all people have imperfections—they are what make us all unique—and people should not dwell on the imperfections or drastically try to change them.

After reading the story for the first time, there was only one thing that came to my mind: my ugly toe. When I was about ten or eleven years old I dropped a large glass bowl on my right foot causing the toenail on my longest toe, the second one from the big toe, to fall off.

Luckily, the toenail grew back; unfortunately, it was deformed and very ugly. Growing up, I always hated my toe, but it was easy to cover up with nail polish or close-toed shoes. It was hardly ever noticeable unless I pointed it out, which I never did.

While reading the story, I began to find similarities between Georgiana, with her birthmark, and me. Her little imperfection is not as easy to hide as mine is, but she does not feel the need, at first, to hide it because it is a charm to her. When Aylmer notices the birthmark it shocks him as he feels that it is a "visible mark of earthly imperfection" (529). This is where the story really starts to take meaning for me because when I uncovered my toe to my current boyfriend, Will, he was pretty surprised as well. He thought, and still thinks, that it is really ugly, and he always tells me that I am perfect except for that one toe. Aylmer thinks the same about Georgiana and her birthmark, and he says that she "came so nearly perfect from the hand of Nature that this slightest possible defect . . . shocks [him]" (529). The difference between Georgiana and me is that I am not as desperate to remove my imperfection as she is. She is willing to die to remove it, but I will not go that far. After reading the story, I told my boyfriend what it is about and he shrugged it off and mumbled some comments about it. I am not sure, but I think in guy talk he was saying that he would rather me have an ugly toe than be dead. From reading the story once, this is what I get out of it: Do not kill yourself trying to be perfect—it is not worth it.

As I read the story for the second time, I realized how much control Aylmer has over Georgiana and tries to have over Nature. For example, I think Aylmer really does possess a "degree of faith in man's ultimate control over Nature" (528). He feels that he has the right and the power to create potions and poisons to kill any person that he wants. He can even decide how fast they are to die by determining "the strength of the dose . . . [that will cause the death] to linger out years, or drop dead in the midst of a breath" (534). Aylmer is a power hungry man that wants to control everything, including who lives and dies. "'It is terrible to possess such power, or even to dream of possessing it'" (533). Once he realizes that Georgiana's birthmark is, in his eyes, an imperfection he wants to remove it and he dwells on it until he convinces her that he must remove it for her.

Something that she once considered to be a charm, turns into something that she can no longer live with because of the pressure that he puts on her to be his perfect wife. Throughout the story I see him pulling her closer to his insanity until she reaches her ultimate demise. As I think about the end of the story I wonder what she really dies for. She obviously dies to be perfect, but who is the real person to blame? Being a woman, I will have to say that Aylmer is at fault for her death because he causes her to be so insecure with herself that he drives her to this point of desperation. I see young impressionable women all of the time, especially now, who strive to be perfect at any cost: surgery, starvation, etc. Some women get to the same point of desperation that Georgiana does and either come close to death or actually die. There are stories all over the media and in movies about young ladies like this. We should all celebrate people's differences and imperfections, not destroy them.

During the class discussion, I picked up on something else on a more personal level. This time when analyzing the story, with the help of several other minds, I realized more how much I relate to this story. People always tell me that I am too hard on myself, that I try too hard to be perfect. Georgiana tries to be perfect for her husband, where I try to be perfect for myself. I know that I am not perfect and as I reflect on some things in my own life I realize how much the theme of this story is true. I am on a constant quest to be the best at work, to always make the A at school, to look like all of the pretty girls, and to stay on top of the game of life. I think that it is time for me to really think about what winning really means.

Georgiana's mind has been manipulated so that she feels it is necessary to go to any extreme to remove the birthmark. In Georgiana's mind winning means making her husband happy, and to do that she has to make herself perfect in his eyes. For me, I have to remember that if I gain five pounds, or make a B in a class, I will still be alright. I tell myself that all the time, but it has not really set in yet. My mom says that I will not realize how good I have it until I am forty and it is all gone. I hope it does not get to that point, so I am trying to reevaluate some things in my life so that I do not end up like Georgiana.

On top of all of this, I am in a relationship that holds more meaning to this story than I originally thought. Take a look at my email address: willsbabydoll. This makes me look like someone's property, like someone controls me. I did not realize how others would interpret this, but once it was brought to my attention it does sound pretty demeaning. In my search to find a better me, I have forgotten to be my own person. I learned from this story that perfection is not what it seems and that I should appreciate what I have. I think that everyone should look at him- or herself with this idea in mind. Whatever each person has, it is better than the alternative solution in this story.

Work Cited

Hawthorne, Nathaniel. "The Birthmark." *Short Fiction: Classic and Contemporary.* 6th ed. Ed. Charles Bohner and Lyman Grant. Upper Saddle River, NJ: Prentice Hall, 2006. 528–538.

AN ESSAY USING A CRITICAL APPROACH

P. Thompson
English 1302
Prof. Lyman Grant
August 9, 2001
Assignment 6

A Story of Wall Street:
A Psychological Approach to Melville's "Bartleby the Scrivener"

Herman Melville's "Bartleby the Scrivener" contains several unique characters, each of whom behaves in his own strange ways. As readers confront each character, they soon are asking why does this character behave as he does? Thus, psychology—the science of the mind and mental states and processes—can be an essential tool in helping readers understand the minds of Melville's peculiar characters. Sigmund Freud's concept of the id, ego, and superego can be especially helpful in mapping the relationships these characters have with each other. Briefly, Freud's concept postulates that individuals develop a healthy sense of self (the healthy ego) by successfully balancing or negotiating the demands of the id (passions and appetites) with those of the superego (the values of parents or society). Neuroses develop when the individual has not successfully negotiated these demands and has repressed the demands of the id. In "Bartleby the Scrivener," we see several individuals with unique and entertaining neuroses, but only in the narrator does Melville give us a character who comes close to a healthy balance of id and superego.

The first character that the narrator describes at length is Turkey. Melville tells us that "In the morning, one might say, his face was of a fine florid hue, but after twelve o'clock, the meridian—his dinner hour—it blazed like a grate full of Christmas coals" (797). Thus, as this character exhibits unusual behavior, Freud might say that Turkey's ego is perhaps an unbalanced or unhealthy one. It would appear that Turkey has suppressed various experiences into his subconscious, and that as the day progresses matters from his subconscious begin to reappear. As the narrator puts it, "There was a strange, inflamed, flurried, flighty recklessness of activity about him" (797). He is so energetic that he becomes reckless in dipping his pen into his inkstand. Consequently, he would leave many blots on the narrator's documents. When Turkey is confronted about the issue, he simply blames it on his age. Therefore, it seems that Turkey is not fully aware of his change of mood in the afternoons. We can certainly assume that Turkey has experiences that he has repressed to his subconscious that are now resurfacing in neurotic behavior, as blots on the documents of his character.

The second eccentric character is Nippers, who has behavior problems similar to that of Turkey. However, Nippers has his bad moods first thing in the morning and seems to overcome them by afternoon. For example, the narrator reveals that "indigestion—the irritability and consequent nervousness of Nippers were mainly observable in the morning, while in the afternoon he was comparatively mild" (799). Nippers is constantly fidgeting around and always experimenting with his desk to suit his comfort. As the narrator takes note,

> The indigestion seemed betokened in an occasional nervous testiness and grinning irritability, causing the teeth to audibly grind together over mistakes committed in copying; unnecessary maledictions, hissed, rather than spoken, in the heat of business; and especially by a continual discontent with the height of the table where he worked. (798)

The narrator finds this disturbing, as Nippers displays a mood imbalance much like Turkey's. Psychologically, Nippers is in the same situation as Turkey, because his ego appears to be abnormal. Since his ego doesn't create balance between the drives of the id and the rules of the superego, it allows expressions of the suppressed id to take control. Hence, he has an unruly drive that pushes him to behave as he does in the mornings. In other words, he involuntarily chooses to be extra-energetic and fidgety, adjusting to his workspace.

The third and oddest character is Bartleby. Bartleby definitely suffers from a neurotic behavior of some sort. He is a hermit who stays cooped up in his cube throughout the story. If it were up to him, he would never speak a word to anyone. When he does speak, his five-word response is "I would prefer not to" (800). This leaves the narrator inquiring about Bartleby. He recalls that he

> never spoke but to answer: that, though at intervals he had considerable time to himself, yet I had never seen him reading-no, not even a newspaper: that for long periods he would stand looking out, at his pale window behind the screen, upon the dead brick wall. (806)

The other characters do not exhibit such drastic behavior. They, at least, are sociable half of each day; whereas Bartleby faces more serious issues. Bartleby's ego must be extremely weak, as it appears not to be negotiating at all between the id and the super-ego. Whereas Bartleby's passions and appetites appear to be completely quelled, his only response to the superego of business authority is complete and total resistance, if only passive resistance. Bartleby resembles a beaten puppy. Once he may have had instincts to play, interact, and express himself, but somewhere, sometime, he appears to have been so mistreated by those with greater power that he has neither the strength of id based drives nor the guilt of superego authority.

The narrator proves to have the strongest and most well-balanced ego. He is aware of all his drives. For instance, he is conscious of the strong desires he has to fire Bartleby. However, as his ego negotiates between the superego and id, he is reminded, for instance, of how he is connected to the church. When he discovers that Bartleby has not left the office upon his numerous requests, the narrator, who once felt pity for Bartleby, now feels revulsion for the character: "I was now in such a state of nervous resentment that I thought it but prudent to check myself at present from further demonstrations" (811). During a moment when he struggles to compose himself, his mind wanders off recalling a famous murder trial. He plots out where such a crime could have taken place. However, as the resentful thoughts lurk in his mind, he begins to think of his religious beliefs. Thus the passions of the id are kept in check by the rules of the superego. The narrator returns to himself and able to distinguish between the moral and immoral.

But the church is not the only institutional authority in this story. After all, it is subtitled, "A Story of Wall Street." Throughout the story, the narrator is conscious of the expectations of his clients. Turkey and Nippers are allowed to continue to work in the law office because, regardless of their idiosyncrasies, they perform the job required of them. Bartleby is troublesome for many reasons, but one in particular is that he will not proofread his documents to insure their accuracy, surely a superego activity. Even when the narrator abandons one set of law offices for another, he returns, responsibly, to help the new tenants reason with Bartleby.

Even the ending of the story illustrates the narrator negotiating with the superego of law enforcement agencies, which has almost literally buried Bartleby in the subconscious with obviously instinctual grub-man. It is not surprising then when we come to the last lines of the story, and the narrator, thinking of all humans communicating, sending letters, our beings negotiating in this world of drives and authority, says "Ah, Bartleby! Ah, humanity!" (818).

Work Cited

Melville, Herman. "Bartleby the Scrivener." *Short Fiction: Classic and Contemporary.* 6th ed. Ed. Charles Bohner and Lyman Grant. Upper Saddle River, NJ: Prentice Hall, 2006. 795–819.

AN EVALUATION

M. Garcia
English 1302
Prof. Lyman Grant
August 18, 2001
Assignment 7

A Suggestive Little Story

Kate Chopin's "A Respectable Woman" explores a woman's thoughts and emotions about infidelity. The main character of the story is Mrs. Baroda. She lives with her husband, Gaston, in their Louisiana plantation. Gouvernail, Gaston's college friend, arrives for a two-week visit. Mrs. Baroda "rather liked him when he first presented himself." Soon she begins to feel confused about her feelings, so she tells her husband that she does not like Gouvernail's company and that she wishes for him to leave. But her husband remains unaware of her true feelings for Gouvernail. One night, Gouvernail finds her sitting alone on a bench and joins her. At this moment she fears her passions will take the best of her, so she leaves the garden. The next morning she escapes to the city, and does not return until Gouvernail has left. The story ends with Mrs. Baroda's resolution for Gouvernail to come for another stay in their plantation the following summer. "A Respectable Woman" is a pleasantly coy story that opens to various methods of interpretation, simultaneously remains timeless and universal, and maintains a complex, ambiguous texture.

Kate Chopin was a late-nineteenth century writer who attempted to write the truth about women's lives. Daring to discuss women's passions and desires, she was controversial in her time. Some critics considered her book *The Awakening* to be immoral. "A Respectable Woman," which was published in 1897, deals with many of the issues that were important in Chopin's works. In this story, Mrs. Baroda is forced to deal with her attraction to her husband's friend. She struggles with herself because her desires contradict what is expected of a "respectable woman." As Chopin writes, "she wanted to draw close to him and whisper against his cheek—she did not care what—as she might have done if she had not been a respectable woman."

One quality of excellent fiction is how well it opens up to analysis. Not surprisingly, "A Respectable Woman" provides for a rich feminist interpretation. It illustrates the entrapment that the expectations of society impose on women. The story appeals to women because many women feel the same way Mrs. Baroda does. They might not be attracted to their husband's best friend specifically, but they are very conscious of the limitations that their sex suffers. In this story, we know all of the men by their first name. However, even though Mrs. Baroda is the protagonist, we know her by only her husband's name, as if she did not have an identity of her own. Even one hundred years after this story was first published, women still feel these subtle limitations on their lives.

However, this story responds not only to a feminist interpretation: Other types of analysis also provide interesting interpretations. When looked at with a psychological focus, this story allows us to enter the mind of Mrs. Baroda, and we discover her fears, her desires, and her thoughts, and so arrive at a rich interpretation of her character. Sociologically, we can debate whether these issues are tied to the superficial desires of a bored wealthy plantation wife, who goes "to the city in the morning to have [her] spring gowns fitted." This story also allows us to consider what society was like in the nineteenth century, and why it reacted as it did to such controversial issues as they were presented in popular magazines.

"A Respectable Woman" is also a timeless and universal story. Even though it was published more than a century ago, the story could still be used to describe the situation of women today. In fact, if we were to simply change their residence to a home in Beverly Hills and revise her trips to the city to have gowns fitted to be a visit to a local mall, this story could well have been written last year. Nor has the value system by which women are judged changed considerably, and what makes a "respectable woman" today is more or less the same as it was in Chopin's day. This story also applies to most women in the world. Infidelity is not condoned by many cultures of the world.

Another quality of excellent fiction is a certain level of ambiguity, situations that the writer has presented but not completely or simply defined. One place where ambiguity occurs in this story is in the motivations of the two men. For instance, what is Gaston Baroda's relationship with his wife? Does he patronize her? Or, is he a loving and trusting husband who does not deserve to be betrayed by his wife? There appears to be evidence to support both of these arguments. "Gaston took his wife's pretty face between his hands and looked tenderly and laughingly into her troubled eyes." However, Mrs. Baroda does admit that her husband "was also her friend." Gaston appears to be a nice man who shows a "frank and wordy hospitality." If Gaston is truly kind, is his wife to receive blame alone? And how can we remain sympathetic to her?

Second, what do we know of Gouvernail's motivations? When Chopin uses the phrase "but her white gown revealed her to him" at the beginning of the scene in which Mrs. Baroda is most tempted by her passions, it seems to lead us to believe that Gouvernail was not ignorant of Mrs. Baroda's feelings. He did not do anything when she "imposed her society upon him." As Chopin writes, "He talked [to her] freely and intimately in a low, hesitating drawl that was not unpleasant to hear." Maybe, Gouvernail was unconsciously leading her on, and was thus betraying Gaston's friendship. If this was the case, then the author is trying to tell us that it is easy to point the finger at the unfaithful wife, but that such accusations often fail to consider the other participant in the affair.

One of the things that makes this story so great is the ending. As the story concludes, Mrs. Baroda insists that she and her husband invite Gouvernail over for another stay next summer, and she says, "I have overcome everything! You will see. This time I shall be very nice to him." This is an open ending. We do not know exactly what she means by this. Does she mean that she has freed herself from the temptation and overcome her attraction for Gouvernail? Or, does she mean that she has overcome her inhibitions, that she no longer cares if she is not a respectable woman, and will take a chance with Gouvernail? Just how "nice" is she going to be with him? Or, is Chopin telling us even more, something about the desires and behaviors of other "respectable women"?

"A Respectable Woman" is an excellent story that can be enjoyed by both men and women and interpreted in a variety of ways. Even though it was written more than a century ago, it still applies to society today. It deals with topics that are still controversial, and it leaves the ending open for the reader to interpret. However we see it, this is an enjoyable story to read.

AN ANALYSIS OF A FILMED ADAPTATION

A. Curtis
English 1302
Prof. Grant
April 12, 2003
Assignment 8

Bunnies Squashed in Otherwise Healing Hands

Jesus' Son, the film directed by Alison MacLean, is a beautiful adaptation of the collection of short stories under the same name written by Denis Johnson. The stories chronicle the adventures of Fuckhead (played by Billy Crudup in the film), aptly nicknamed by his friends for his uncanny ability to "turn everything to shit" (84). The book opens with a story that ties the whole set of stories together, the car crash that enables him to capture the feeling of compassion that he would seek for years. In this first story, "Car Crash while Hitchhiking," the unnamed narrator and main character (we'll call him FH) catches a ride with a family who he knows will have an accident while he sleeps in the back seat with their baby. He doesn't care, and takes the ride anyway. After the accident, he is able to save the baby, to save a soul for the first time in a life full of overdoses, lost love, and self-destruction.

Arriving at the hospital with the baby he saves, FH witnesses the doctor telling the woman that her husband did not make it through the wreckage, and he feels her pain, another person's pain, for the first time in his life, "What a pair of lungs! She shrieked as I imagined an eagle would shriek. It felt wonderful to be alive to hear it! I've gone looking for that feeling everywhere" (11). It is through this epiphany that FH, the narrator of his own stories, offers the reader a glimpse down the highway that brings him to another hospital and onto the steps toward becoming a whole soul again. In looking for this feeling, the main character narrates his way back through a dreamlike collection of drughazed vignettes in which time seems to pause then rewind, causing moments to stretch out like hours. In one segment, he attempts to save a litter of unborn bunnies, but ends up sitting on them while riding with a fellow multi-drugged co-worker (played by Jack Black). In another, he drives his friend McInnis (played by John Ventimiglia) to the hospital after he has been shot accidentally, but McInnis dies while the narrator drives through Iowa farmland. At other points, entire years go by without mention. Then he has a baby he is afraid of, and he marries his girlfriend Michelle (played by Samantha Morton) without ceremony. In both the movie and the book, these stories are full of incredible imagery, so fantastical that they cannot be defined as pure reality or pure dreamscape. Throughout most of the book and movie, the main character is high, but doesn't seem to notice that drugs cause him to fail in his attempts to find the meaning and compassion that he seeks in life. He consumes pills, shoots heroin and drinks down to his last dollar, but he lacks the desire to do battle with his demons. Instead his demons take him for a cheap county fair amusement park ride.

When FH finally ends up in the hospital himself after overdosing—a scene that occurs late in the movie, but is depicted in the opening story in the book—he still seems to be floating through his ride, not caring that the box of cotton balls calls out to him as he shoos a yellow bird out of his face. It is through sobriety in Arizona that he finally finds his place, his love, his meaning—his compassion. He ends up, reluctantly at first, with a job writing a newsletter for the Beverly Home, a place for those unable to take care of themselves. He begins to understand these sad people and is able to feel their pain. He learns to understand them and offers his newfound healing compassion, having a relationship with the oft-widowed Mira (played by Holly Hunter). Redeemed, he is able to feel good about himself, finally. Though both the book and movie touch on love and loneliness, death and religion, it is this concept of human compassion where both genres of book and film come together.

Jesus' Son, the book and the movie, explores several underlying ideas and motifs that support the main theme that we must have compassion to be fully human. The first of these underlying ideas is that of love and loneliness. As the narrator of book and movie, FH is clearly a very lonely man. He wanders from story to story, seeking companionship and affirmation of life. In Johnson's version, the main character seems to show a desperation that is not as evident in the movie. The book portrays him seeking out love and affection not only from his girlfriend, but also from anyone else that will give it to him. He befriends a salesman who later makes a pass at him; he spends a night kissing a woman at a bar while dancing to the jukebox; and he sleeps with several other women along the way. The movie portrays a much more romantic picture of this lost soul. Maclean's adaptation chooses the Hollywood path by casting Crudup and Morton as a pair of renegade lovers seeking solace in each other from the evils of the world. Maclean develops a cute affectionate sense of blossoming love that comes to life on the screen. Johnson, on the other hand, touches on their passion matter-of-factly, as if it were a thing of the past. Though Johnson's narrator spends a great part of the book searching for Michelle, he could be just as well searching for anyone who would give him the love that he craves. The movie, as Hollywood dictates, casts the characters as lovers torn apart by passion and drugs.

The second idea of death plays itself out in many ways throughout both the book and movie, and both seem to treat the concept with the same relevance in respect to the theme. The powerful, crucial scene of the grieving woman in the beginning is significant in both book and movie. Johnson writes that the doctor takes the wife into an office and closes the door, and "from under the closed door a slab of brilliance radiated as if, by some stupendous process, diamonds were being incinerated in there" (11). Maclean creates the visual counterpart by showing the door close and then creating a fantastic white light seen through the translucent glass window of the door. Maclean also films Crudup as if he were being pulled toward the door and the light.

In another story in the book and another scene from the movie, the narrator and a friend, Wayne (played by Dennis Leary), split a bag of heroin, and go their separate ways. The movie beautifully illustrates the moment using a split screen to show the two men arriving at their respective apartments, shooting up, and overdosing. Michelle, who comes home in time to resuscitate him, saves FH, but his friend has no one to save him, and dies alone. In split screen, both stories are told simultaneously, emphasizing the importance of luck, companionship, and compassion. "His breath failed without anybody's noticing. He simply went under. He died. I am still alive" (42).

Though this theme of death is comparable in both genres, it contrasts when it comes to the details of Michelle's death, as again Hollywood has its hand in remaking the stories into a more romantic, marketable, movie. Johnson writes Michelle's death as a suicide, and the movie follows. But in the book, the suicide occurs during the time she has run off with John Smith. The narrator never reconciles with Michelle after she leaves him, and he never sees her alive again. In Johnson's book, John Smith is haunted by her ghost and dies soon thereafter. In the Hollywood version, the main character follows Michelle and finds her in a hotel in Iowa City. They make love, talk, shoot up, puke, and fight. In a scene that is almost reminiscent of *Romeo and Juliet*, when he comes back late one night, high, he doesn't notice her dying on the bed next to him until it is too late. In this way the film creates a tragic irony by juxtaposing Michelle's overdose, in which the narrator does nothing, and the narrator's overdose, in which she saves him.

Given the name *Jesus' Son*, obviously religion is an idea that is carried throughout the book and the movie. The book touches on several obvious points of religious symbolism and imagery, including the man at the laundry-mat who looks like Jesus, and a recitation of the Lord's Prayer over the intercom at the hospital. The name of the book, however, comes from a Lou Reed lyric and appears to be more concerned with the feeling of taking heroin than merely a reference to the Son of God. However, the movie treats this point quite differently, and takes the theme of Jesus and runs with it. The Christ-like imagery and representations in the movie are frequent and recurring. In contrast to the book, the movie portrays the main character as the possible son of Jesus, complete with healing powers. In one instance, the viewer sees him looking out the window of a diner

where the paint on the window forms a crown of thorns on his head, and the waitress exclaims, "You're the one!" Later, an old drive-in looks like a graveyard full of crosses, whereas
the book illustrates them as tombstones. The book and movie both depict the man in the
laundry-mat as Christ-like. In the movie version, he has a throbbing, glowing *corazon
sagrado* coming from his chest. Various cross images appear in the movie that are not evident in the book, including the scene of Michelle's death, in which the camera angle on her
naked body and his head combine to make a cross. During the opening scene before the
car crash, Crudup waits for his ride in a Christ-like pose, arms outstretched, crucified. At the
end of the novel, the narrator finds a place in his heart for compassion for other humans;
Johnson leaves it at that. The movie, however, seems to give him a "laying of hands" healing power, as he touches the patients at the Beverly Home, healing them, and reaches like
Christ through a window to touch the head of the Mennonite woman.

The place where Johnson's version and Maclean's version meet eye to eye is the main
theme of the movie, the importance of human compassion. Both the movie and the book
weave their way from place to place chronicling the main character's search for a meaning in
life, a purpose that he later finds to be compassion. The movie seems to stay truest to the
book in all of the scenes revolving around this concept and his quest for it. In both pieces, he
has an overwhelming desire to help people around him, often finding himself at or near hospitals, but he stumbles every time. When he tries to save the baby bunnies, he ends up
squashing them. When he attempts to comfort Michelle at the abortion clinic, it comes out all
wrong, and he begs to start over. Instead he is escorted out by security. His friend is shot
and the narrator tries to take him to the hospital, but the friend dies on the way.

As shown in the movie and book, it is not until he arrives at the Beverly Home that
he understands that he can do it right, that he can help others with what he has inside.
Without the haze of drugs, he realizes he is not FH anymore; he has found his home
among the freaks. "All these weirdos, and me getting a little better every day right in
front of them. I had never known, never even imagined for a heartbeat, that there might
be a place for people like us" (160).

Though the movie takes liberties in the Christ-like representation of the main character, and in the relationship between him and Michelle, overall it remains true to the book.
In fact, though Johnson's book is able to stand on its own without the differences in plot,
without changes, as a movie it lacks the money making formula necessary for a major
motion picture deal. Maclean's liberties in playing up the love life and reconciliation of the
star-crossed lovers are likely all in the interest of money; Hollywood knows better than
anyone, sex sells. Overall, however, Maclean's adaptation takes into account all of Johnson's themes of love, loneliness, death, religion and most of all compassion. She weaves
his stories together to create a rich picture full of incredible, fantastic imagery, but sadly,
none that can touch those painted by the imagination of a reader of *Jesus' Son.*

Works Cited

Jesus' Son. Dir. Alison Maclean. Perf. Billy Crudup, Samantha Morton, Dennis Leary,
    Jack Black, and Holly Hunter. Lions Gate, 1999.
Johnson, Denis. *Jesus' Son: Stories.* New York: Harper Collins, 1992.

E. Gray
English 1302
Prof. Lyman Grant
August 21, 2001
Assignment 9

Without Regret

In St. Louis, Missouri, on July 12, 1850, Catherine O'Flaherty, later known as Kate Chopin, was born to a prominent businessman, Thomas O'Flaherty, and his wife, Catherine. Chopin's father died when she was only five years old, and her mother assumed the dominant role she would play for the rest of Chopin's life. Chopin graduated from high school when she was seventeen from the St. Louis Academy of the Sacred Heart (Toth 15). On June 9, 1870, Chopin married Oscar Chopin, who was a Creole cotton broker. Then moving to Southern Louisiana, she bore five sons and a daughter. Only three years after the daughter was born, Oscar suddenly died and Kate Chopin not only became a widow but also was forced to become a businesswoman. Later Chopin moved her children back to St. Louis to live near her mother, where she began to support her family with her writing. By all accounts Chopin was an intelligent woman of great independence and strength. Skaggs observes, "The early loss of her father, grandfather, and great grandfather prevented her as she matured from experiencing in her own family the traditional submissiveness of women to men" (2). And Charlotte McClure speculates, "Her great grandmother educated her, teaching her through story telling, so that at an early age Chopin learned the contradictions, restrictions, and hypocrisies of society" (234). In her stories "The Story of an Hour," "A Respectable Woman," and "Regret," we see central female characters living submissive or restricted lives, women who choose one life but who later realize that they should have lived differently. Chopin's life reflects no such resemblance to her characters' lives.

In the short story "Regret," Mamzelle Aurelie represents a strong independent woman who never thought of marrying and received a proposal when she was twenty, which she "promptly had declined, and at the age of fifty she had not yet lived to regret it" (Chopin, "Regret" 259). Aurelie takes care of her neighbor's four children for a short while and at first is "very inept in her management of Odelie's children" and tells her cook that she "would rather manage a dozen plantation' than fo' chil'ren" (261). Toward the end of the story, Aurelie grows quite fond of these four children and enjoys the "laughing, the crying, and the chattering that echoed through the house all day long" (261). This transition in the character of Aurelie shows that even though Kate Chopin writes about strong, independent, and self-sufficient women, there is still a sentimental and emotional side to her characters. In this particular story, the character has a change of heart through the middle of the story and lives to regret the choice she made some thirty years earlier, which was not to marry and bear children. Chopin, of course, did not face such a regret in her life, and appears to have been both an indulgent and protective parent. One facet of her love of her own children can be seen in her autobiographical essay "On Certain Brisk, Bright Days," in which she says "A woman's reluctance to speak of her children has not yet been chronicled. . . . [But] I might say something of those that are at a safe distance—the idol of my soul is in Kentucky; the light of my eye off in Colorado; the treasure of his mother's heart in Louisiana" (1238). Here is a woman who has no regrets for the choices she has made.

The story "The Story of an Hour" represents the majority of women who lived during the nineteenth and twentieth century. This story is "itself in large part about what Mrs. Mallard sees, about what the story's narrator sees that Mrs. Mallard sees" (Koloski 4). Mrs. Mallard is a housewife who learns that her husband has been killed in a train wreck. At first, Mrs. Mallard "wept at once, with sudden, 'wild abandonment' in her sister's arms. When the storm of grief had spent itself she went away to her room alone" (Chopin, "Story" 267). This tragic news brings Mrs. Mallard freedom because divorce was not an option during that period. Mrs. Mallard was repressed by her husband and now "there would be no one to live for during those coming years: she would live for herself" (268). Kate Chopin writes of a woman who desperately wants to be free from marriage, which she feels controls her every move, and the reader completely understands this by the explicit feelings that Mrs. Mallard expresses, "Free! Body and soul free!" (268). Although this short story has an eerie twist at the very end when Mrs. Mallard comes down the stairs to find her husband walk in the front door and she dies, the freedom that Mrs. Mallard so desperately yearns for all these years only lasts for one short hour. Ross Moss observes, "*Free* has not been a word forbidden in polite society. No one would call it unladylike" (195). However, for Mrs. Mallard the word had been unspeakable, unthinkable. "Everything involved in being a dutiful wife forbade it" (Moss 195). "The Story of an Hour" expresses a central theme of a woman who yearns to break free of her husband and experience life as an independent woman even though she is still too insecure to drop everything and leave for a better life.

"A Respectable Woman" is a story that is rather humorous and representative of the women in the world today. Mrs. Baroda's husband has a young, attractive friend from college who comes to visit and stay with them at their plantation. At first, Mrs. Baroda does not like her husband's friend, Gouvernail, although, toward the end of his visit, she realizes that she is sexually attracted to him and chooses not to tell her husband. I think it is interesting that she does not share her feelings with her husband because back in the 1800s to have feeling or to be attracted to another man other than your husband was quite scandalous. Chopin pays close attention to this because when she writes of the conflict that Mrs. Baroda experiences because of her sexual desire Chopin writes, "beside being a respectable woman" and "a very sensible one . . . there are some battles in life which a human being must fight alone" ("Respectable" 265). All three of these stories represent protagonists who seem to be searching for self-understanding (Skaggs 3).

Much of Kate Chopin's work was published during the later years of her life. Many things contributed to her writing: "One, she had always been a voracious reader; second, she needed to provide for her large family; third, many friends and family encouraged her; and finally she had through almost thirty-nine years of living learned some things she wanted to say" (Skaggs 4). She wrote many short stories and a world-renowned novel, *The Awakening*. "The Story of an Hour," like many other short stories, was turned down by many editors because many of "her women became more passionate and emancipated" (Seyersted 60). Emphasizing character and much more rather than plot, she "centers on a small event, takes us right into the story, and develops it logically toward an inevitable conclusion (Seyersted 62). Chopin achieves "her effects through her insight into character, her sense of form, her lucid and precise language and her light touch (Seyersted 62). In the story "Regret" is a perfect example of how Chopin uses these qualities and packs all kinds of drama into a short story. It also shows her simplicity and economy of means, her unobtrusive humor, and the sympathy and intensity she hid behind her restraint and objectivity (Seyersted 62). In "A Respectable Woman," Chopin writes of sexual passions and realizes the threat in security of a career or a happy marriage and the need to be controlled. Chopin is "an ironist and leaves her stories open-ended, thus giving the reader the sense that carefully adjusted solutions can never be free of future intimidations. Marriage without love or mutual respect is, to her, clearly immoral" (Rocks 70).

That Chopin was an independent woman who lived life on her own terms can be illustrated from a few events in her life. Emily Toth's biography of Chopin portrays several incidents from the writer's life that indicate her independence. During her years of marriage, Chopin often lived in New Orleans, becoming part of the fashionable life there. Acquaintances have described Chopin with affection. "She was an individual in the style of her clothes as in everything else . . . and the children were allowed to enjoy themselves" (Toth 72). However, Toth notes, "But we can read between the lines to suspect that Chopin never truly fit in, that Oscar was too kind and fun-loving to be good at business, and that the children were loud, undisciplined creatures" (72). Similarly, the independent, cigarette smoking writer, who rode horses bare-back, was never accepted by the citizens of Cloutierville, where Chopin and her family settled when Oscar's business in New Orleans turned sour. It is even suspected that the widow Chopin had an affair with a married man (Toth 97).

Another piece of biographical information, told by a descendent illustrates that Chopin acted upon her beliefs, without regard for public pressure, even as a teenager.

> The story goes that during the time of the Civil War the sympathies were for the South and she went out one time and tore down an American flag that was on the porch. I don't know if she was going to replace it with a Confederate flag or not, but she got into a lot of hot water because of that. Well, she was that kind of a person, you know, she had a strong feeling and she acted on it, and a lot of people would have been afraid to do it. But she was . . . I guess you might call her either impetuous or concerned or dedicated and so forth, so she went ahead and did it, and it almost landed her in jail. ("Interviews")

Throughout her life, Chopin did as her conscience spoke, as her inner being demanded. As she wrote in an essay for the St. Louis *Post Dispatch* in 1899, explaining why she writes, "Short story writing—at least for me—is the spontaneous expression of impressions gathered goodness knows where. To seek the source, the impulse of a story is like tearing a flower to pieces for wantonness ("On Certain Brisk" 1217). And though she admitted that she did not write everything that came into her head, what she did write usually was sent out for publication.

Chopin is an author who represented all of the women during the 1800s and the 1900s who wanted to live free lives but did not know how to achieve them. To each of those women, Chopin was the voice and bravery that they so desperately needed. Fortunately for her, she experienced a marriage that was filled mutually with love, respect and freedom. She lived her life as a woman fully, respectably—with marriage and children and career—and freely without regret.

Works Cited

Chopin, Kate. "On Certain Brisk, Bright Days." *Short Fiction: Classic and Contemporary*. 6th ed. Ed. Charles Bohner and Lyman Grant. Upper Saddle River, NJ: Prentice Hall, 2006. 1237–1238.

———. "Regret." *Short Fiction: Classic and Contemporary*. 6th ed. Ed. Charles Bohner and Lyman Grant. Upper Saddle River, NJ: Prentice Hall, 2006. 259–262.

———. "A Respectable Woman." *Short Fiction: Classic and Contemporary*. 6th ed. Ed. Charles Bohner and Lyman Grant. Upper Saddle River, NJ: Prentice Hall, 2006. 263–266.

———. "The Story of an Hour." *Short Fiction: Classic and Contemporary*. 6th ed. Ed. Charles Bohner and Lyman Grant. Upper Saddle River, NJ: Prentice Hall, 2006. 267–269.

"Interviews." *Kate Chopin: A Re-Awakening*. Public Broadcasting System. 18 August 2000. http://www.pbs.orq/katechooin/interviews.html

Koloski, Bernard. *Kate Chopin: A Study of the Short Fiction*. New York: Twayne Publishers, 1966.

McClure, Charlotte S. "From Impersonators to Persons: Breaking Patterns, Finding Voices." *Private Voices, Public Lives*. Ed. Nancy Owens Nelson, Denton: University of North Texas Press, 1995. 225–237.

Moss, Ross. "Barriers of Reticence and Reserve." *Still the Frame Holds: Essays of Women Poets and Writers*. Ed. Sheila Roberts. San Bernadino: The Bargo Press, 1993. 191–200.

Rocks, James E. "Kate Chopin's Ironic Vision." *Revue de Louisiane* 1.2 (1972): 110–120. Rpt. In *Twentieth Century Literary Criticism*. Vol. 14. Detroit: Gale, 1984. 67–70.

Seyersted, Per. Introduction. *The Complete Works of Kate Chopin*. Vol. 1. By Kate Chopin. Baton Rouge: Louisiana State UP, 1969. 21–33. Rpt. In *Twentieth Century Literary Criticism*. Vol. 14. Detroit: Gale, 1984. 59–63.

Skaggs, Peggy. *Kate Chopin*. Boston: Twayne Publishers, 1985.

Toth, Emily. *Unveiling Kate Chopin*. Jackson: University Press of Mississippi, 1999.

Glossary of Terms for Short Fiction

Terms in italics are defined in this glossary.

Action Events that take place in a story. *Actions* form the story's *plot*. *Action* is also one part of *characterization*.

Activating circumstance An event that sets the *plot* in motion.

Allegory A story in which characters, places, and events represent abstract ideas or qualities. An allegory is often designed to teach a lesson (i.e., *didactic*). Modern stories are rarely allegories, but they often use allegorical elements. *Example:* Achebe's "Dead Men's Path" and Lawrence's "The Rocking-Horse Winner."

Allusion A reference to a well-known person, place, time, or event that enriches meaning by suggesting specific and relevant associations.

Ambiguity A word, a phrase, an event, or a situation that allows more than one possible interpretation. Deliberate ambiguity can contribute to the effectiveness and richness of a work; unintentional ambiguity can obscure meaning and confuse the reader.

Antagonist The character who opposes the *protagonist*.

Anticlimax An event that, in itself, seems unimportant. An anticlimax can seem trivial, ludicrous, humorous, or misleading, but often it makes some comment about the story's theme. In Mansfield's "A Dill Pickle," the last, brief paragraph is an anticlimax. It seems trivial, but its real importance lies not so much in what the man says but in that he chooses, at that moment, to say it.

Atmosphere The spirit or *mood* pervading any work of art. In fiction, atmosphere is largely evoked by *setting* and *imagery*. *Example:* the first paragraph of Faulkner's "Dry September."

Authorial comment An explanatory remark obviously put into the narration by the author. Authorial commentary tells us what to think instead of showing us. *Example:* The fourth paragraph of Chekhov's "The Lady with the Dog."

Character Anyone in a story. There are two main types: *round characters* and *flat characters*. *Round characters* are complex and show the inconsistencies and complexities found in real people (Charlie Wales in Fitzgerald's "Babylon Revisited"). *Flat characters* usually display a single trait and serve a limited purpose (Duncan Schaeffer in the same story).

Characterization The means by which a writer creates characters: *action*, spoken words (*dialogue*) or thoughts, and *authorial comment*.

Climax The point of highest tension in a story: the turning point, the place where things begin to change.

Coherence Consistency in the selection and arrangement of the various elements in a piece of writing. A lack of coherence can confuse the reader. Modern writers of fiction may want some degree of short-term confusion, but writers of nonfiction, as intermediaries between their readers and some event or issue, want their arrangement of words and ideas to be clear.

Coming of age   A story in which an event changes a young person's life.

Complication   Events, words, or thoughts that increase tension. One or more complications occur during the story's *rising action* (between the *activating circumstance* and the *climax).*

Conflict   The struggle that grows out of opposing forces in a story. Generally there are considered to be four types of conflict: character versus character; character versus society; character versus self; and character versus nature (the forces of nature: storms, floods, fires, etc., not human nature). Most works of fiction include more than one type of conflict. In serious short fiction, character versus nature is the rarest type of conflict (see Crane's "The Open Boat" for an example of this type).

Connotation   The cluster of meanings suggested by a word or associated with that word. The specific thing indicated by a word is called *Denotation.* The word "Mother" denotes a woman who has borne a child; however, the word "Mother" may connote or suggest ideas of female guidance, love, sex, nourishment, protection, and selflessness.

Convention   See *literary convention* and *social convention.*

Credibility   That quality in a narrative that persuades a reader that the story is plausible.

Crisis   The incident that is decisive for a *protagonist.* After the crisis, the *protagonist's* fortunes either rise or fall. *Example:* in Joyce's "Araby," see the *narrator's* arrival at the fair.

Critical analysis   A detailed examination of a story (or part of a story) for the purpose of interpretation; see also *explication.*

Denotation   See *connotation.*

Denouement   A French word literally meaning "the unraveling of a knot"; in fiction, it denotes the resolution of a conflict, the outcome of the story.

Dialogue   Speech between characters. See *literary convention.*

Didactic   Intended to teach a moral lesson. Examples in fiction include the *allegory,* the *fable,* and the *parable.*

Distance   The degree of passion or concern with which the author seems to regard events and characters; the degree of distance with which the reader is meant to regard them.

Dramatic irony   See *irony.*

Epigraph   A quotation at the beginning of a story. Often it contains a clue to the writer's intentions. It is more common in novels than short stories, but see Walker's "The Welcome Table" for an example.

Epiphany   A character's sudden realization of the true and essential nature of something very important. *Example:* the last sentence of Joyce's "Araby."

Episode   An incident, complete in itself, that forms part of the continuing action of a story.

Explication   A type of detailed *critical analysis* that minutely examines the variety of relationships and meanings in a story's parts.

Exposition   The part of a story, often at the beginning, that provides essential background information about characters and their situations. See also *flashback.* Exposition may be used as *foreshadowing.*

Fable   A *didactic* story often employing animals who behave like human beings. George Orwell's novel *Animal Farm* is a twentieth-century example.

Fantasy   A *narrative* that has for its subject an imaginary world rather than everyday reality. *Example:* Barthelme's "A City of Churches."

Figure of speech   The use of language in a way that is not strictly *literal;* see *metaphor* and *simile.*

First-person narration   See *point of view.*

Flashback   A break in the development of a story to introduce an earlier episode or memory. See several examples in Mansfield's "A Dill Pickle."

Flat character   See *character.*

Foreshadowing   One of the most important elements in serious fiction. Foreshadowing suggests or anticipates later events. *Example:* the first paragraph in Richard Wright's story is an oasis of foreshadowing.

Image   A word or phrase that represents something that can be understood by one of the senses, usually something that can be seen. Some, certainly not all, images can be interpreted as *symbols.*

Imagery   The use of associated words, phrases, or *figures of speech* to present or suggest ideas.

Interior monologue   See *monologue.*

Irony   The gap between what is anticipated and what is revealed. Near the bottom of the second page of Hemingway's "Hills Like White Elephants," Jig says, "And afterward they were all so happy." This is an example of *verbal irony.* Sometimes writers tell their readers things that the characters do not know. At other times, writers want readers to know a thing before a specific character realizes it. When writers do this, they are using *dramatic irony.* Many events are different from what we expect them to be. This condition is the most common form of irony, *situational irony.* The element of irony is a major element in serious fiction, but we should not believe that every single instance of irony is of great importance.

Literary convention   The way we normally write. This is a huge element that includes areas as basic as spelling, punctuation, and grammar. For example, Americans use the spelling "theater," whereas the British use "theatre." The American and British methods of punctuation are very similar, but there are differences, particularly with regard to the placement of quotation marks and the comma and period. If you consult a dictionary and a standard grammar book, you will have few problems with the basics of *literary convention.*

Literature as art, however, has its own conventions. For example, stories generally begin at one point in time and move forward chronologically. Stories are normally consistent in their use of a single *point of view* (for an exception, see the last large paragraph of Hemingway's "Hills Like White Elephants"). Short stories are usually set in one place, so we ought to pay special attention to a major shift in location.

A break with a literary convention should be intentional, but not all breaks with literary convention are of equal importance.

Metaphor   A nonliteral comparison without the use of the words "like" or "as"; see *simile.* At the beginning of Part 2 of Crane's "The Open Boat," we are told that "The crest of each of these waves was a hill...." The "crest" of a wave is not a "hill"; hills are made of earth and rock, not water, but Crane makes the comparison to stress one important way in which the "crest" of water is like a "hill"; however, Crane does not use the words "like" or "as"; the result is a forceful, direct comparison, but one that we know is not literally true.

Monologue   A speech of some length by one person. A monologue does not need to be spoken aloud. Any first-person story is likely to make use of the *interior monologue,* a monologue that is not spoken but thought, revealing the narrator's opinions and state of mind. Even though Gilman's "The Yellow Wallpaper" occasionally reports Jane's husband's dialogue, the story is essentially a series of *interior monologues.*

Mood   See *atmosphere.*

Moral   The lesson a story teaches. See *didactic* and *allegory.*

Motif   A recurring element—image, phrase, idea, situation—whose reappearance unifies a work and is thematically (see *theme*) important. *Examples:* the use of time in Faulkner's "A Rose for Emily"; the young boy's eyes in Lawrence's "The Rocking-Horse Winner"; circular imagery in Ellison's "King of the Bingo Game."

Motivation   Internal and external causes that make a character act a certain way. These are usually revealed through *characterization.*

Narrative   A prose account of an event or a series of events.

Narrator   The person who tells the story. This person (or character) should not be confused with the author. See *point of view* and *unreliable narrator*.

Pace   The speed and rhythm with which a story appears to move.

Parable   A story that illustrates a moral truth. See *didactic*.

Paradox   A statement that appears to be contradictory or unbelievable but may actually be true. See the reference to Dmitri's being in love in the last section of Chekhov's "The Lady with the Dog."

Parody   An imitation with an intent to ridicule. A writer who has a very recognizable *style* will eventually be the subject of parody. Crane, Hemingway, Joyce, Lawrence, and Poe have all been parodied. Parody is similar to what comedians do when they imitate famous people.

Pathetic fallacy   Human traits given to things that are not human. There are many examples in the works of Poe and Crane. For example, in Crane's "The Open Boat," waves are described as "nervously anxious."

Plot   The pattern of events in a work of fiction. While a story often begins with some *exposition*, the plot begins with a situation in which there is *conflict*. An *activating circumstance* provokes a *complication*. This complication begins the *rising action* (a series of events that increase the story's tension). The *crisis*, at the height of the *action*, is followed by a shorter series of events called *falling action*. The conclusion is the *denouement* or *resolution*.

Point of view   The view or vantage point that a reader has of the events in a story. Very often a character who is in the story tells that story. This method is called first-person point of view, and the narrator will refer to himself or herself as "I."

The third-person point of view is the second major way in which stories are told, and three types of this point of view are normally considered. In the third-person objective point of view we enter into no character's mind. Since the story has an objective point of view (rather than a subjective or personal one), the story is not shaped by the thoughts of one or more characters.

A more common point of view (especially in novels but in some short stories, too) is the third-person omniscient point of view. Since "omniscient" means "all-knowing," readers may know what any of the characters is thinking. In a short story, however, it is more likely (and more practical) for writers to allow readers to know the thoughts of only a few characters.

The most frequently used third-person point of view in short fiction is called third-person limited omniscient. The writer limits our knowledge to what one character thinks. We may see others acting and may read what they say, but we are in the mind of only one character.

Protagonist   Usually the central character of a story. When this word is used, there is generally someone in conflict with the *protagonist*, an *antagonist*. *Examples:* Maugham's "The Outstation"—Warburton and Cooper; Hurston's "Spunk"—Joe Kanty and Spunk Banks; Updike's "A & P"—Sammy and Lengel.

Reversal   A sudden change in the fortunes of a character, usually the *protagonist*. *Example:* Michael Obi in Chinua Achebe's "Dead Men's Path."

Rising action   See *plot*.

Round character   See *character*.

Satire   A work of art that aims to improve society by treating human behavior with ridicule or contempt.

Sentimentality   The effort by an author to induce an emotional response in the reader in excess of the situation being described.

Setting   When and where a story takes place.

Simile   A nonliteral comparison that uses "like" or "as"; a *figure of speech*. In Crane's "The Open Boat": "The craft pranced and reared and plunged like an animal." A "craft" (or boat) is clearly not an animal, but the writer makes the comparison to emphasize the small crew's lack of control. As readers we understand that in many other ways, the "craft" is not "like an animal." See *metaphor*.

Situational irony   See *irony*.

Social convention   Customs and behavior that are usual for a society during a certain time period. When a story has a *setting* (time and place) that is different from the reader's, characters often think, say, or do things in ways that the reader would not. Examples are found in Faulkner's "A Rose for Emily" and Jackson's "The Lottery."

Stream of consciousness   A literary convention in which a writer tries to represent the flow of thought and the impact of internal and external stimuli on a character's mind. Joyce's *Ulysses* and *Finnegan's Wake* remain the most admired examples of stream of consciousness in the English language. *Example:* The *interior monologues* of Dave Saunders in Wright's "The Man Who Was Almost a Man."

Style   An author's characteristic manner of expression, including diction, *syntax*, sentence rhythms, and *imagery*.

Symbol   Something that stands for something else. In art there are two types of symbols. The first type has a specific meaning that many people will recognize: a Canadian flag has meaning; a swastika has meaning; a cross, a crescent, the Star of David, our favorite team's logo or mascot, all suggest specific things.

There is a second type of symbol whose meaning depends upon its context, that is, the way it is used. Darth Vader's mask in the *Star Wars* trilogy had no meaning until the movie was made. The fox fur in Mansfield's "Miss Brill" has no meaning until we read the story. When we do, we can see its meaning in the context of the writer's work.

Syntax   The order in which words are arranged to convey meaning.

Theme   The controlling idea or ideas in a work of art.

Tone   The author's or narrator's attitude toward his or her subject.

Unity   The pattern and coherence of a story.

Unreliable narrator   This is hardly a new idea, but in the twentieth century the unreliable narrator has become a more important part of serious fiction. We might expect a very young *narrator* to be deceived by the complexities of an adult world; characters suffering from some mental disorder (see Poe's "The Cask of Amontillado") are not new; but the unreliable *narrator* may seem quite sensible, sophisticated, and intelligent, and may, at the same time, give a view of events that the author wants readers to see as inaccurate. There are, understandably, degrees of unreliability; for two very different examples, read the stories by Klass and Updike.

Verbal irony   See *irony*.

Voice   The characteristic *tone* of a narrator.

Chronological List of Authors and Titles

Donatien Alphonse Francois Compte de Sade (1740–1814)
  The Lady of the Manor of Longeville, or a Woman's Revenge (1926)
Honoré de Balzac (1799–1850)
  A Passion in the Desert (1830)
Nathaniel Hawthorne (1804–1864)
  Young Goodman Brown (1835)
  The Birthmark (1846)
Nikolai Gogol (1809–1852)
  The Overcoat (1842)
Edgar Allan Poe (1809–1849)
  The Fall of the House of Usher (1840)
  The Purloined Letter (1845)
  The Cask of Amontillado (1846)
Herman Melville (1819–1891)
  Bartelby the Scrivener (1853)
Alice Carey (1820–1871)
  The Pride of Sarah Worthington (1852)
Leo Tolstoy (1828–1910)
  The Death of Ivan Ilych (1886)
Samuel Clemens (1835–1910)
  The Celebrated Jumping Frog of Calaveras County (1865)
Ambrose Bierce (1842–1914?)
  An Occurrence at Owl Creek Bridge (1891)
Henry James (1843–1916)
  The Real Thing (1892)
Sarah Orne Jewett (1849–1909)
  A White Heron (1886)
Guy de Maupassant (1850–1893)
  The Necklace (1884)
Kate Chopin (1851–1904)
  Regret (1894)
  A Respectable Woman (1894)
  The Story of an Hour (1894)
Mary Wilkins Freeman (1852–1930)
  Old Woman Magoun (1905)

Joseph Conrad (1857–1924)
  The Heart of Darkness (1902)
Charles W. Chesnutt (1858–1932)
  The Doll (1912)
Anton Chekhov (1860–1904)
  Gooseberries (1898)
  The Darling (1899)
  The Lady with the Dog (1899)
Charlotte Perkins Gilman (1860–1935)
  The Yellow Wallpaper (1892)
Edith Wharton (1862–1937)
  Mrs. Manstey's View (1890)
Stephen Crane (1871–1900)
  The Open Boat (1897)
Willa Cather (1873–1947)
  Paul's Case (1905)
Colette (1873–1954)
  The Other Wife (1926)
W. Somerset Maugham (1874–1965)
  The Outstation (1926)
Sherwood Anderson (1876–1941)
  I Want to Know Why (1921)
Jack London (1876–1916)
  To Build a Fire (1908)
E. M. Forster (1879–1970)
  Mr. Andrews (1928)
James Joyce (1882–1941)
  Araby (1914)
  The Dead (1914)
Virginia Woolf (1882–1941)
  Kew Gardens (1919)
Franz Kafka (1883–1924)
  The Metamorphosis (1915)
  A Country Doctor (1919)
  A Hunger Artist (1924)
William Carlos Williams (1883–1963)
  The Use of Force (1950)
Isak Dinesen (1885–1962)
  The Blue Jar (1942)

Acknowledgments

CHINUA ACHEBE, "Dead Men's Path," from *Girls at War and Other Stories*. Copyright © 1972, 1973 by Chinua Achebe. Used by permission of Doubleday, a division of Random House, Inc., and reprinted by permission of Harold Ober Associates Incorporated.

IQBAL AHMAD, "A Bicycle," from *The Opium Eater and Other Stories*. Copyright © 1992 by Iqbal Ahmad. Reprinted with the permission of Cormorant Books, Inc.

SHERMAN ALEXIE, "Because My Father Always Said He Was the Only Indian Who Saw Jimi Hendrix Play 'The Star-Spangled Banner' at Woodstock," from *The Lone Ranger and Tonto Fistfight in Heaven*. Copyright © 1993 by Sherman Alexie. Used by permission of Grove/Atlantic, Inc.

ISABEL ALLENDE, "And of Clay Are We Created," from *The Stories of Eva Luna*. Copyright © 1989 by Isabel Allende. English Translation Copyright © 1991 by Macmillan Publishing Company. Reprinted with the permission of Scribner, an imprint of Simon & Schuster Adult Publishing Group.

DOROTHY ALLISON, "I'm Working on My Charm," from *Trash*. Copyright © 1988 by Dorothy Allison. Reprinted by permission of Frances Goldin Literary Agency. "Context," from *Skin*. Copyright © by Dorothy Allison. Reprinted by permission of Firebrand Books.

MARGARET ATWOOD, "Rape Fantasies," from *Dancing Girls and Other Stories*. Copyright © 1977, 1982 by O.W. Toad, Ltd. Reprinted by permission of McClelland & Stewart, Inc. and the author.

JAMES BALDWIN, "Sonny's Blues," © 1957 by James Baldwin, originally published in *Partisan Review*. Copyright renewed. Collected in *Going to Meet the Man*, published by Vintage Books. Reprinted by arrangement with the James Baldwin Estate.

TONI CADE BAMBARA, "The Lesson," from *Gorilla, My Love*. Copyright © 1972 by Toni Cade Bambara. Used by permission of Random House, Inc.

DONALD BARTHELME, "A City of Churches," from *Sadness*. Copyright © 1972 by Donald Barthelme. Reprinted with the permission of the Wylie Agency, Inc.

ANN BEATTIE, "What Was Mine," from *What Was Mine*. Copyright © 1991 by Irony & Pity, Inc. Used by permission of Random House, Inc.

WALTER BENJAMIN, "The Storyteller: Reflections on the Works of Nikolai Leskov," from *Illuminations*. Copyright © 1955 by SuhrkampVerlag, Frankfurt A.M. English translation by Harry Zohn. Copyright © 1968 and renewed 1996 by Harcourt, Inc. Reprinted by permission of Harcourt, Inc.

HAROLD BLOOM, "Summary Observations," from *How to Read and Why*. Copyright © 2000 by Harold Bloom. Reprinted with the permission of Scribner, an imprint of Simon & Schuster Adult Publishing Group.

JORGE LUIS BORGES, "The Other Duel," from *Collected Fictions*, translated by Andrew Hurley. Copyright © 1998 by Maria Kodama; translation copyright © 1998 by

IDA FINK, "A Scrap of Time," from *A Scrap of Time and Other Stories*, translated by Madeline Levine and Francine Prose. Originally published in the Polish language as *Skrawek Czasu* by Aneks Publishers, London. Copyright © 1983 by Ida Fink. English translation first published by Pantheon Books, a division of Random House, Inc. in 1987; copyright © 1987 by Random House, Inc. Northwestern University Press edition published 1995 by arrangement with Ida Fink. Used by permission of Northwestern University Press. All rights reserved.

F. SCOTT FITZGERALD, "Babylon Revisited," from *The Short Stories of F. Scott Fitzgerald*, edited by Matthew J. Bruccoli. Copyright 1931 by The Curtis Publishing Company. Copyright renewed 1959 by Francis Scott Fitzgerald Lanahan. Reprinted with the permission of Scribner, a Division of Simon & Schuster Adult Publishing Group.

E. M. FORSTER, extract from "Plot," from *Aspects of the Novel*. Copyright 1927 by Harcourt, Inc. and renewed 1954 by E.M. Forster. Reprinted by permission of the publisher, and The Provost and Scholars of King's College, Cambridge, and The Society of Authors as the Literary Representatives of the Estate of E.M. Forster.

CARLOS FUENTES, "Chac-Mool," from *Burnt Water*, translated by Margaret Sayers Peden. Translation copyright © 1980 by Farrar, Straus and Giroux, LLC. Reprinted by permission of Farrar, Straus & Giroux, LLC.

MARY GAITSKILL, "Tiny, Smiling Daddy," from *Because They Wanted To: Stories*. Copyright © 1997 by Mary Gaitskill. Reprinted with the permission of Simon & Schuster Adult Publishing Group. All rights reserved.

GABRIEL GARCÍA MÁRQUEZ, "Tuesday Siesta," from *No One Writes to the Colonel and Other Stories*, translated by J. S. Bernstein. Copyright © 1968 in the English translation by Harper & Row Publishers, Inc. Reprinted by permission of HarperCollins Publishers Inc.

WILLIAM GIBSON, "Johnny Mnemonic," from *Burning Chrome*. Copyright © 1986 by William Gibson. Reprinted by permission of HarperCollins Publishers Inc.

DAGOBERTO GILB, "Hollywood!" from *The Magic of Blood*. Copyright © 1993 by Dagoberto Gilb. Reprinted by permission of University of New Mexico Press.

NADINE GORDIMER, "The Life of the Imagination," from *Livingstone's Companions*. Copyright © 1965, 1966, 1967, 1968, 1969, 1971 by Nadine Gordimer. Used by permission of Viking Penguin, a division of Penguin Group (USA) Inc.

BESSIE HEAD, "Looking for a Rain God," from *The Collector of Treasures and Other Botswana Village Tales*. Copyright © 1977 by the Estate of Bessie Head. Reprinted with the permission of John Johnson, Authors' Agent, Ltd. and William Heinemann Ltd. "Let Me Tell a Story Now . . .," from *Woman Alone: Autobiographical Writings*. Originally published in *The New African*, 1962. Reprinted with the permission of John Johnson, Authors' Agent, Ltd. and William Heinemann Ltd.

ERNEST HEMINGWAY, "Hills Like White Elephants," from *The Short Stories of Ernest Hemingway*. Copyright © 1927 by Charles Scribner's Sons. Copyright renewed © 1955 by Ernest Hemingway. Reprinted with the permission of Scribner, a Division of Simon & Schuster Adult Publishing Group. All rights reserved.

ZORA NEALE HURSTON, "Spunk," from *The Complete Stories*. Introduction copyright © 1995 by Henry Louis Gates, Jr. and Sieglinde Lemke. Compilation copyright © 1995 by Vivian Bowden, Lois J. Hurston Gaston, Clifford Hurston, Lucy Ann Hurston, Winifred Hurston Clark, Zora Mack Goins, Edgar Hurston, Sr., and Barbara Hurston Lewis. Afterword and Bibliography copyright © 1995 by Henry Louis Gates. Reprinted by permission of HarperCollins Publishers Inc.

SHIRLEY JACKSON, "The Lottery," from *The Lottery*. Copyright 1948, 1949 by Shirley Jackson. Renewed 1976, 1977 by Laurence Hyman, Barry Hyman, Mrs. Sarah Webster, and Mrs. Joanne Schnurer. Reprinted by permission of Farrar, Straus and Giroux, LLC. "Biography of a Story," from *Come Along with Me*. Copyright © 1948, 1952, 1960 by Shirley Jackson. Used by permission of Viking Penguin, a division of Penguin Group (USA) Inc.

DENIS JOHNSON, "Car Crash While Hitchhiking," from *Jesus' Son*. Copyright © 1992 by Denis Johnson. Reprinted by permission of Farrar, Straus and Giroux, LLC.

JAMES JOYCE, "Araby," "The Dead," from *Dubliners*. Copyright 1916 by B.W. Heubsch. Definitive text Copyright © 1967 by the Estate of James Joyce. Used by permission of Viking Penguin, a division of Penguin Group (USA) Inc.

MICHAEL JOYCE, excerpt from *Of Two Minds: Hypertext Pedagogy and Poetics*. Copyright © 1995 by Michael Joyce. Reprinted by permission of the University of Michigan Press.

FRANZ KAFKA, "A Hunger Artist," from *Franz Kafka: The Complete Stories*, edited by Nahum N. Glatzer, translated by Willa & Edwin Muir. Copyright 1946, 1947, 1948, 1949, 1954, © 1958, 1971 by Schocken Books. Used by permission of Schocken Books, a division of Random House, Inc.

JAMAICA KINCAID, "Girl," from *At the Bottom of the River*. Copyright © 1983 by Jamaica Kincaid. Reprinted by permission of Farrar, Straus and Giroux, LLC.

PERRI KLASS, "Not a Good Girl," from *Mademoiselle* (1983). Copyright © 1983 by Perri Klass. Reprinted with the permission of the author, c/o the Maxine Groffsky Literary Agency.

MILAN KUNDERA, "Let the Old Dead Make Room for the Young Dead," from *Laughable Loves*, translated by Suzanne Rappaport. Copyright © 1974 by Alfred A. Knopf, a division of Random House, Inc. Used by permission of Alfred A. Knopf, a division of Random House, Inc. Extract from "Somewhere Behind," from *The Art of the Novel*, translated by Linda Asher. Copyright © 1988 by Grove Press. Used by permission of Grove/Atlantic, Inc.

HANIF KUREISHI, "My Son the Fanatic," from *Love in a Blue Time*. Copyright © 1997 by Hanif Kureishi. Reprinted with the permission of Scribner, an imprint of Simon & Schuster Adult Publishing Group.

MARY LAVIN, "My Vocation," from *Collected Stories*, Volume 2. Copyright © 1964 by Mary Lavin. Reprinted with the permission of the author.

D. H. LAWRENCE, "The Rocking-Horse Winner," from *Complete Short Stories of D. H. Lawrence*. Copyright 1933 by the Estate of D. H. Lawrence, renewed © 1961 by Angelo Ravagli and C.M. Weekley, Executors of the Estate of Frieda Lawrence. Used by permission of Viking Penguin, a division of Penguin Group (USA) Inc.

DAVID LEAVITT, "Gravity," from *A Place I've Never Been*. Copyright © 1990 by David Leavitt. Reprinted with the permission of the Wylie Agency, Inc.

URSULA K. LE GUIN, "The Professor's Houses," from *Unlocking the Air and Other Stories*. Copyright © 1982 by Ursula K. Le Guin. First appeared in *The New Yorker*. Reprinted by permission of the author and the author's agents, the Virginia Kidd Literary Agency, Inc. Portion of "Where Do You Get Your Ideas From?" from *Dancing at the Edge of the World*. Copyright © 1987 by Ursula K. Le Guin. Used by permission of Grove/Atlantic, Inc.

DORIS LESSING, "A Sunrise on the Veld," from *African Stories*. Copyright 1951 by Doris Lessing. Reprinted by kind permission of Jonathan Clowes Ltd., London, on behalf of Doris Lessing.

NAGUIB MAHFOUZ, "Half a Day," translated by Denys Johnson-Davis, from *The Time and the Place and Other Stories*. Copyright © 1991 by American University in Cairo Press. Used by permission of Doubleday, a division of Random House, Inc.

BOBBIE ANN MASON, "Shiloh," from *Shiloh and Other Stories*. Copyright © 1982 by Bobbie Ann Mason. Reprinted by permission of International Creative Management, Inc.

W. SOMERSET MAUGHAM, "The Outstation," from *Collected Short Stories*, published by Heinemann. Used by permission of The Random House Group Limited and the Estate of W. Somerset Maugham.

YUKIO MISHIMA, "Patriotism," translated by Geoffrey W. Sargent, from *Death in Midsummer*. Copyright © 1966 by New Directions Publishing Corp. Reprinted by permission of New Directions.

BHARATI MUKHERJEE, "A Father," from *Darkness*. Copyright © 1985 by Bharati Mukherjee. Reprinted by permission of the author.

VLADIMIR NABOKOV, "The Passenger," from *The Stories of Vladimir Nabokov*. Copyright © 1995 by Dmitri Nabokov. Used by permission of Alfred A. Knopf, a division of Random House, Inc. Excerpts from commentary by Vladimir Nabokov in "Anton Chekhov: 'The Lady with the Little Dog,'" from *Lectures on Russian Literature*. Copyright © 1981 by the Estate of Vladimir Nabokov. Reprinted by permission of Harcourt, Inc. Excerpts from commentary by Vladimir Nabokov in "Franz Kafka (1882–1924): The Metamorphosis," from *Lectures on Literature*. Copyright © 1980 by the Estate of Vladimir Nabokov. Reprinted by permission of Harcourt, Inc.

JONATHAN NOLAN, "Memento Mori," from *Esquire*, March 2001. Used by permission of *Esquire* magazine. © The Hearst Corporation. Esquire is a trademark of The Hearst Corporation. All Rights Reserved.

JOYCE CAROL OATES, "Shopping," from *Heat and Other Stories*, published by Dutton, 1991. Copyright © 1991 by Ontario Review, Inc. Reprinted by permission of John Hawkins & Associates, Inc. "Where Are You Going, Where Have You Been?" from *The Wheel of Love and Other Stories*, published by Vanguard. Copyright © 1970 by Ontario Review, Inc. Reprinted by permission of John Hawkins & Associates, Inc. "Why Don't You Come Live with Me It's Time," from *Tikkun: A Bimonthly Jewish Critique of Politics, Culture, and Society*. © 1990 by Ontario Review Press. Reprinted with the permission of John Hawkins and Associates, Inc. "The Making of a Writer," published in *New York Times Book Review*, 1982. Copyright © 1982 by Ontario Review, Inc. Reprinted by permission of John Hawkins & Associates, Inc. "Smooth Talk," from *Woman Writer: Occasions and Opportunities*. Copyright © 1970 The Ontario Press. Reprinted with the permission of John Hawkins and Associates, Inc.

TIM O'BRIEN, "The Things They Carried," from *The Things They Carried*. Copyright © 1990 by Tim O'Brien. Reprinted by permission of Houghton Mifflin Company. All rights reserved.

FLANNERY O'CONNOR, "A Good Man Is Hard to Find," from *A Good Man Is Hard to Find and Other Stories*. Copyright 1953 by Flannery O'Connor and renewed 1981 by Regina O'Connor. Reprinted by permission of Harcourt, Inc. "A Reasonable Use of the Unreasonable," from "On Her Own Work," from *Mystery and Manners*. Copyright © 1969 by the Estate of Mary Flannery O'Connor. Reprinted by permission of Farrar, Straus and Giroux, LLC.

FRANK O'CONNOR, "Guests of the Nation," from *The Collected Stories of Frank O'Connor*. Copyright © 1981 by Harriet O'Donovan Sheehy, Executrix of the Estate of Frank O'Connor. Used by permission of Alfred A. Knopf, a division of Random House, Inc. and The Estate of Frank O'Connor c/o Writer's House, Inc., New York. "The Legacy of Gogol's 'Overcoat,'" from *The Lonely Voice: A Study of the Short Story*. Copyright © 1963 by Frank O'Connor. Reprinted with permission of The Estate of Frank O'Connor c/o Writer's House, Inc., New York.

TILLIE OLSEN, "I Stand Here Ironing," from *Tell Me a Riddle*, Introduction by John Leonard. Copyright © 1956, 1957, 1960, 1961 by Tillie Olsen. Used by permission of Dell Publishing, a division of Random House, Inc.

GRACE PALEY, "A Conversation with My Father," from *Enormous Changes at the Last Minute*. Copyright © 1971, 1974 by Grace Paley. Reprinted by permission of Farrar, Straus and Giroux, LLC.

KATHERINE ANNE PORTER, "Flowering Judas," from *Flowering Judas and Other Stories*. Copyright 1930 and renewed 1958 by Katherine Anne Porter. Reprinted by permission of Harcourt, Inc. "The Grave," from *The Leaning Tower and Other Stories*. Copyright 1944 and renewed 1972 by Katherine Anne Porter. Reprinted by permission of Harcourt, Inc. Excerpt from "The Writing of 'Flowering Judas,'" from *Writers at Work*, Second Series by George A. Plimpton. Copyright © 1963 by the Paris Review. Reprinted by permission of Barbara Thompson.

Index of Authors and Titles